2003

WRITER'S MARKET®

3,100+ BOOK AND MAGAZINE EDITORS WHO BUY WHAT YOU WRITE

EDITOR
KATHRYN STRUCKEL BROGAN

ASSISTANT EDITOR
ROBERT LEE BREWER

WRITER'S DIGEST BOOKS
CINCINNATI, OH

Praise for *Writer's Market*

"No writer should be without the *Writer's Market* . . . This is the biggest and best book in the industry for American markets." ***—American Markets Newsletter***

"The *Writer's Market* is by far and away the premier source for [finding a publication or publisher] for writers in all stages in ther career(s)." ***—John Austin, Book of the Month***

"The *Writer's Market* is another must-have book for writers seeking to profit from their writing endeavors." ***—Writer's Write, The Internet Writing Journal***

"An invaluable resource that lays out the nuts and bolts of getting published." ***—Library Journal***

"The writer's bible and best friend. If you're serious about selling what you write and submit material regularly, you need a new copy every year." ***—Freelance Writer's Report***

"This volume is a freelancer's working tool, as important as the basic computer or typewriter." ***—The Bloomsbury Review***

If your company or contest would like to be considered for a listing in the next edition of *Writer's Market* or on WritersMarket.com, send a message specifying which section of the book you wish to be in by e-mail to writersmarket@fwpubs.com or by mail to Writer's Market—Questionnaire, 4700 East Galbraith Rd., Cincinnati OH 45236.

All listings in *Writer's Market* are paying markets.

Supervisory Editor, Annuals Department: Alice Pope
Editorial Director, Annuals Department: Barbara Kuroff
Cover photo by Al Parrish

Writer's Market Website: www.writersmarket.com

Writer's Digest Website: www.writersdigest.com

Library of Congress Catalog Number 31-20772
International Standard Serial Number 0084-2729
International Standard Book Number 1-58297-120-X
International Standard Book Number 1-58297-125-0 (Writer's Market Online)

Attention Booksellers: This is an annual directory of F&W Publications. Return deadline for this edition is December 31, 2003.

contents at a glance

Contents

THE BUSINESS OF WRITING

LITERARY AGENTS

LITERARY AGENTS SUBJECT INDEX

THE MARKETS

RESOURCES

COMPLAINT PROCEDURE

If you feel you have not been treated fairly by a listing in ***Writer's Market***, we advise you to take the following steps:

- First try to contact the listing. Sometimes one phone call or a letter can quickly clear up the matter.
- Document all your correspondence with the listing. When you write to us with a complaint, provide the details of your submission, the date of your first contact with the listing, and the nature of your subsequent correspondence.
- We will enter your letter into our files and attempt to contact the listing.
- The number and severity of complaints will be considered in our decision whether to delete the listing from the next edition.

From the Editor

When I was 17 years old, a high school English teacher told me that I would never make it as a writer. My prose was weak, my grammar poor, my ideas stale. What did she know? Absolutely nothing.

Upon entering college and still wanting to become a published writer, I took as many writing and editing courses as I could. One of those classes was a freelance writing class, and the only way you could earn an "A" in the class was to query a magazine and land a paying assignment. That was when I was introduced to "the writer's bible." That introduction to *Writer's Market* was the first day of the rest of my life as a published writer.

Since 1921, the editors of *Writer's Market* have been bringing you the most comprehensive guide to getting your work published. As the years have passed, many things have changed—the number of paying markets, who owns what in the publishing world—and *Writer's Market* has adjusted accordingly to these changes. The result? *Writer's Market* and now WritersMarket.com, too, continue the tradition of being "the writer's bible."

In the *2003 Writer's Market* we continue to offer content for both the yet-to-be-published writer and the already-published writer. For both types of writer, we've included more than **3,800 markets, over 350 of them new to this edition**. For our **WritersMarket.com users, you'll find an additional 1,350+ listings** for agents, book publishers, magazines, and contests & awards. **New this year on WritersMarket.com are listings for newspapers and online publications**—two sections you asked for through e-mail, letters, and phone calls. These markets will provide you with the same listing information as the traditional market listings and, as with all the market listings, are updated daily. We've even taken the best advice from WritersMarket.com and put select articles in the book under a new section, **Expert Advice**.

Beyond the listings that will land you a lucrative assignment or book deal, we've also covered all of the bases with **new articles** geared toward the beginning writer as well as the already-published writer. For those new to publishing we've given you articles on the magazines most open to new writers (page 16) as well as ten tips to refocus, rework, rewrite, and recycle your articles (page 32). For the published writer we've shown you how to sell serial rights from your book and make money from them (page 67), as well as how to land more writing gigs by pitching sidebars, shorts, and quizzes (page 69).

And you thought that was it! Wrong! In addition to the ever-popular Query Letter Clinic, which now contains a critique of e-mail queries, **we've also brought back an old favorite—Publishers and Their Imprints**. You can use this family tree to find out who owns whom in the ever-evolving world of book publishing. We have, however, removed the annual How Much Should I Charge? feature so that we may better serve you with up-to-date pay ranges for typical freelance jobs. Once this article is updated it will be accessible through WritersMarket.com and will appear in the *2004 Writer's Market*.

I hope you find the information in the *2003 Writer's Market* helpful, and that you can apply the information provided in "the writer's bible" to your writing.

I leave you with this: Never let anyone dissuade you from your passion to write. The intense drive and talent that lie within you will help make you a published writer.

Hey teach, look at me now!

Kathryn Struckel Brogan

Katie Struckel Brogan, Editor, *Writer's Market*
writersmarket@fwpubs.com

Writer's Market
Feedback Form

If you have a suggestion for improving *Writer's Market*, or would like to take part in a reader survey we conduct from time to time, please make a photocopy of this form (or cut it out of the book), fill it out, and return it to:

Writer's Market Feedback
4700 E. Galbraith Rd.
Cincinnati OH 45236
Fax: (513)531-2686

☐ Yes! I'm willing to fill out a short survey by mail or online to provide feedback on *Writer's Market* or other books on writing.

☐ Yes! I have a suggestion to improve *Writer's Market* (attach a second sheet if more room is necessary):

____

____

____

____

____

____

____

____

____

Name: ______________________________

Address: ______________________________

City: ______________ State: ______________ Zip: ______________

Phone: ______________________ Fax: ______________________

E-mail: ______________________ Website: ______________________

I am
☐ a beginning writer (not-yet published)
☐ a published writer

I write
☐ fiction
☐ nonfiction
☐ both

Using Your *Writer's Market* to Sell Your Writing

Writer's Market is here to help you decide where and how to submit your writing to appropriate markets. Each listing contains information about the editorial focus of the market, how it prefers material to be submitted, payment information, and other helpful tips.

WHAT'S INSIDE?

Since 1921, *Writer's Market* has been giving you the important information you need to know in order to approach a market knowledgeably. We've continued to search out improvements to help you access that information more efficiently.

Symbols. There are a variety of symbols that appear before each listing. A key to all of the symbols appears on the front and back inside covers. However, there are a few symbols we'd like to point out. In book publishers, the ⊶ quickly sums up a publisher's interests, along with information on what subjects are currently being emphasized or phased out. In Consumer Magazines the ⊶ zeroes in on what areas of that market are particularly open to freelancers to help you break in to that market. Other symbols let you know whether a listing is new to the book (N), a book publisher accepts only agented writers (A), comparative pay rates for a magazine (**$-$$$$**), and more.

Literary agents. Recognizing the role of literary agents in the book publishing field, we've researched and included 75 agents (50 literary and 25 script agents) at the beginning of the listings on page 77. All of these agents have indicated a willingness to work with new, previously unpublished writers as well as more established authors. All of the agents listed are members of the Association of Authors' Representatives (AAR), or the Writers Guild of America (WGA).

Acquisition names, royalty rates, and advances. In the Book Publishers section we identify acquisition editors with the boldface word **Acquisitions** to help you get your manuscript to the right person. Royalty rates and advances are highlighted in boldface, as well as other important information on the percentage of first-time writers and unagented writers the company publishes, the number of books published and manuscripts received each year.

Editors, pay rates, and percentage of material written by freelance writers. In Consumer Magazines and Trade, Technical & Professional Journal sections, we identify who to send your query or article to by the boldface word **Contact**. The amount (percentage) of material accepted from freelance writers, and the pay rates for features, columns and departments, and fillers are also highlighted in boldface to help you quickly identify the information you need to know when considering whether to submit your work.

Query formats. We asked editors how they prefer to receive queries and have indicated in the listings whether they prefer queries by mail, e-mail, fax, or phone. Be sure to check an editor's individual preference before sending your query.

New articles. Be sure to check out the new articles geared to more experienced writers in Minding the Details. In Sell Serial Rights, Make Money, an excerpt from *Guerrilla Marketing for Writers* (Writer's Digest Books), Jay Conrad Levinson, Rick Frishman, and Michael Larsen tell you how selling serial rights to your book can help you make money and create a name for yourself in the marketplace. Freelancer Jennifer Nelson explains how sidebars, shorts, and quizzes can land you feature-writing gigs in Pitching Sidebars, Shorts, & Quizzes.

The "family tree" of publishers is back! Back by popular demand is Publishers and Their

Imprints. This feature will show you who owns what in the ever-changing world of book publishing.

IF *WRITER'S MARKET* IS NEW TO YOU . . .

A quick look at the Table of Contents will familiarize you with the arrangement of *Writer's Market*. The three largest sections of the book are the market listings of Book Publishers; Consumer Magazines; and Trade, Technical & Professional Journals. You will also find other sections of market listings for Scriptwriting, Syndicates, Greeting Cards, and Contests & Awards. The section introductions contain specific information about trends, submission methods, and other helpful resources for the material included in that section (which are indicated by the For More Information boxes).

The articles in the first section, Getting Published, are included with newer, unpublished writers in mind. In The Magazines Most Open to New Writers, Greg Daugherty gives you the inside edge on how to find magazines that use and rely on new freelancers. Query Letter Clinic shows you eight real-life examples of letters that hit the mark and those that missed it. In The Four R's of Freelancing, Gloria Burke offers you ten tips to refocus, rework, rewrite, and recycle.

Narrowing your search

After you've identified the market categories you're interested in, you can begin researching specific markets within each section.

Book Publishers are categorized, in the Book Publishers Subject Index, according to types of books they are interested in. If, for example, you plan to write a book on a religious topic, simply turn to the Book Publishers Subject Index and look under the Religion subhead in Nonfiction for the names and page numbers of companies that publish such books.

Consumer Magazines and Trade, Technical & Professional Journals are categorized by subject to make it easier for you to identify markets for your work. If you want to publish an article dealing with some aspect of retirement, you could look under the Retirement category of Consumer Magazines to find an appropriate market. You would want to keep in mind, however, that magazines in other categories might also be interested in your article (for example, women's magazines publish such material as well). Keep your antennae up while studying the markets: Less obvious markets often offer the best opportunities.

Interpreting the markets

Once you've identified companies or publications that cover the subjects you're interested in, you can begin evaluating specific listings to pinpoint the markets most receptive to your work and most beneficial to you.

In evaluating an individual listing, first check the location of the company, the types of material it is interested in seeing, submission requirements, and rights and payment policies. Depending upon your personal concerns, any of these items could be a deciding factor as you determine which markets you plan to approach. Many listings also include a reporting time, which lets you know how long it will typically take for the publisher to respond to your initial query or submission. (We suggest that you allow an additional two months for a response, just in case your submission is under further review or the publisher is backlogged.)

Check the Glossary at the back of the book for unfamiliar words. Specific symbols and abbreviations are explained in the key appearing on the front and back inside covers. The most important abbreviation is SASE—self-addressed, stamped envelope. Always enclose one when you send unsolicited queries, proposals, or manuscripts. This requirement is not included in most of the individual market listings because it is a "given" that you must follow if you expect to receive a reply.

Important Listing Information

- Listings are based on editorial questionnaires and interviews. They are not advertisements; publishers do not pay for their listings. The markets are not endorsed by *Writer's Market* editors. F&W Publications, Inc., Writer's Digest Books, and its employees go to great effort to ascertain the validity of information in this book. However, transactions between users of the information and individuals and/or companies are strictly between those parties.
- All listings have been verified before publication of this book. If a listing has not changed from last year, then the editor told us the market's needs have not changed and the previous listing continues to accurately reflect its policies.
- *Writer's Market* reserves the right to exclude any listing.
- When looking for a specific market, check the index. A market may not be listed for one of these reasons:
    1. It doesn't solicit freelance material.
    2. It doesn't pay for material.
    3. It has gone out of business.
    4. It has failed to verify or update its listing for this edition.
    5. It was in the middle of being sold at press time, and rather than disclose premature details, we chose not to list it.
    6. It hasn't answered *Writer's Market* inquiries satisfactorily. (To the best of our ability, and with our readers' help, we try to screen out fraudulent listings.)
    7. It buys few manuscripts, constituting a very small market for freelancers.
- Individual markets that appeared in last year's edition but are not listed in this edition are included in the General Index, with a notation giving the reason for their exclusion.

A careful reading of the listings will reveal that many editors are very specific about their needs. Your chances of success increase if you follow directions to the letter. Often companies do not accept unsolicited manuscripts and return them unread. If a company does not accept unsolicited manuscripts, it is indicated in the listing. Read each listing closely, heed the tips given, and follow the instructions. Work presented professionally will normally be given more serious consideration.

Whenever possible, obtain writer's guidelines before submitting material. You can usually obtain the guidelines by sending a SASE to the address in the listing. Magazines often post their guidelines on their website as well. Most of the listings indicate how writer's guidelines are made available. You should also familiarize yourself with the company's publications. Many of the listings contain instructions on how to obtain sample copies, catalogs, or market lists. The more research you do upfront, the better your chances of acceptance, publication, and payment.

Additional help

The book contains many articles on a variety of helpful topics. Some of the articles contain For More Information boxes to provide you with additional information about the topic covered in the article. Some listings contain editorial comments, indicated by a bullet (●), that provide additional information discovered during our compilation of this year's *Writer's Market*. E-mail addresses and websites have been included for many markets. The Resources section includes some, but by no means all, trade magazines, directories, and sources of information on writing-related topics. The Websites section points you to writing-related material on the Web.

Newer or unpublished writers should be sure to read Before Your First Sale. Minding the Details offers valuable information about rights, taxes, and other practical matters.

Guide to Listing Features

Below is an example of the market listings you'll find in each of the listing sections in *Writer's Market*. Note the callouts that identify various format features of the listing. The front and back covers of the book contain a key to the symbols used at the beginning of all listings.

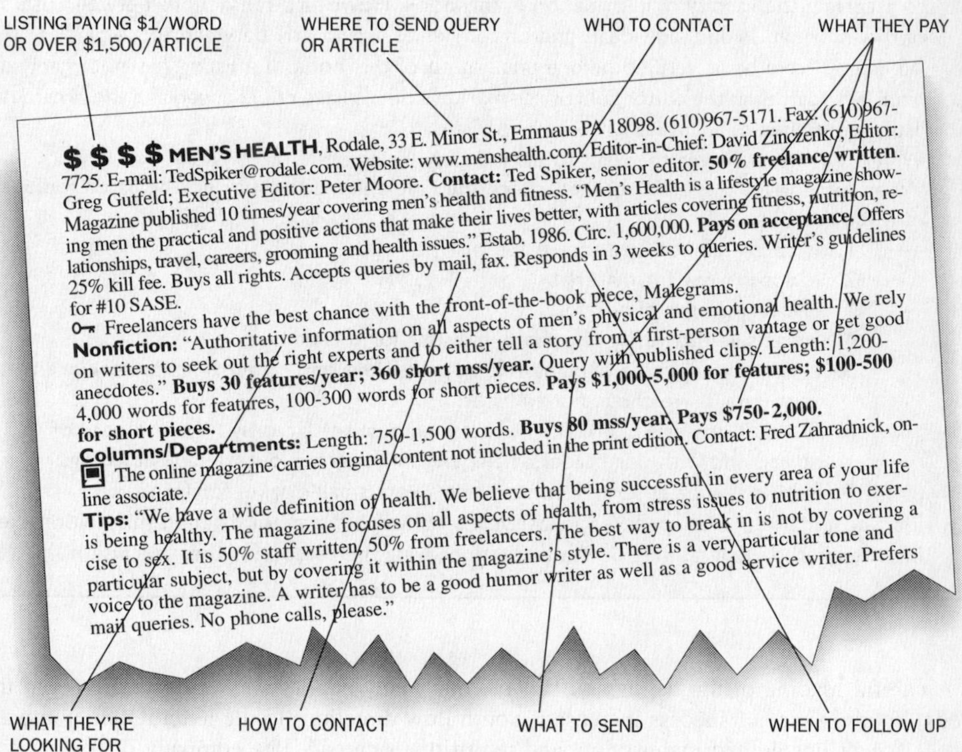

$ $ $ $ **MEN'S HEALTH**, Rodale, 33 E. Minor St., Emmaus PA 18098. (610)967-5171. Fax: (610)967-7725. E-mail: TedSpiker@rodale.com. Website: www.menshealth.com. Editor-in-Chief: David Zinczenko; Editor: Greg Gutfeld; Executive Editor: Peter Moore. **Contact:** Ted Spiker, senior editor. **50% freelance written.** Magazine published 10 times/year covering men's health and fitness. "Men's Health is a lifestyle magazine showing men the practical and positive actions that make their lives better, with articles covering fitness, nutrition, relationships, travel, careers, grooming and health issues." Estab. 1986. Circ. 1,600,000. **Pays on acceptance.** Offers 25% kill fee. Buys all rights. Accepts queries by mail, fax. Responds in 3 weeks to queries. Writer's guidelines for #10 SASE.

Freelancers have the best chance with the front-of-the-book piece, Malegrams.

Nonfiction: "Authoritative information on all aspects of men's physical and emotional health. We rely on writers to seek out the right experts and to either tell a story from a first-person vantage or get good anecdotes." **Buys 30 features/year; 360 short mss/year.** Query with published clips. Length: 1,200-4,000 words for features, 100-300 words for short pieces. **Pays $1,000-5,000 for features; $100-500 for short pieces.**

Columns/Departments: Length: 750-1,500 words. **Buys 80 mss/year. Pays $750-2,000.**

The online magazine carries original content not included in the print edition. Contact: Fred Zahradnick, online associate.

Tips: "We have a wide definition of health. We believe that being successful in every area of your life is being healthy. The magazine focuses on all aspects of health, from stress issues to nutrition to exercise to sex. It is 50% staff written, 50% from freelancers. The best way to break in is not by covering a particular subject, but by covering it within the magazine's style. There is a very particular tone and voice to the magazine. A writer has to be a good humor writer as well as a good service writer. Prefers mail queries. No phone calls, please."

Getting Published

Before Your First Sale

Everything in life has to start somewhere and that somewhere is always at the beginning. The same is true for writers. Stephen King, J.K. Rowling, John Grisham, Nora Roberts—they all had to start at the beginning. It would be great to say that becoming a writer is as easy as waving a magic wand over your manuscript and "Poof!" you're a published writer, but that's not how it happens. There's no magic potion or one true "key" to a successful writing career. However, a long, successful, well-paid writing career *can* happen when you combine four elements:

- Good writing
- Knowledge of writing markets (magazines and book publishers)
- Professionalism
- Persistence

Good writing is useless if you don't know which markets will buy your work or how to pitch and sell your writing. If you aren't professional and persistent in your contact with editors, your writing is just that—your writing. But if you are a writer who possesses, and can manipulate, the above four elements, then you have a good chance at becoming a paid, published writer who will reap the benefits of a long and successful career.

Many writers assume that if you are unpublished then you don't stand a chance of being published—but that's not true. As with any business profession, experience is valued, but not essential. What truly matters is the idea behind your writing and what you do to sell that idea. While it is true that many magazine editors prefer to work with established writers, they also realize that their readers like variety when it comes to content, style, and voice. These are the same editors that value professional writing and good, new ideas—the same editors that want you.

The same situation applies to nonfiction book publishers. While they publish many experienced, well-known writers, they also value new writers who possess experience and knowledge in a particular subject. Your knowledge of a given topic shows the publisher your ability and expertise in an area that may be previously untouched. Again, as with magazines, the idea is key.

As you become more involved with writing, you may read new articles or talk with editors and writers with conflicting opinions about the right way to submit your work. The truth is there are many different routes a writer can follow to get published, but no matter which route you choose, the end is always the same—becoming a published writer.

The following information on submissions has worked for many writers, but it is by no means the be-all-end-all of proper submission guidelines. It's very easy to get wrapped up in the specifics of submitting (should I put my last name on every page of my manuscript?) and ignore the more important issues (will this idea on ice fishing in Alaska be appropriate for a regional magazine in Seattle?). Don't allow yourself to become so blinded by submission procedures that you forget the basic principle that guides everyone in life—common sense. If you use your common sense and employ professional, courteous relations with editors, you will eventually find and develop your own submission methods.

DEVELOP YOUR IDEAS, THEN TARGET THE MARKETS

Writers often think of an interesting story, complete the manuscript, and then begin the search for a suitable publisher or magazine. While this approach is common for fiction, poetry, and screenwriting, it reduces your chances of success in many nonfiction writing areas. Instead, try choosing categories that interest you and study those sections in *Writer's Market*. Select several listings that you consider good prospects for your type of writing. Sometimes the individual listings will even help you generate ideas.

Next, make a list of the potential markets for each idea. Make the initial contact with markets using the method stated in the market listings. If you exhaust your list of possibilities, don't give up. Instead, reevaluate the idea or try another angle. Continue developing ideas and approaching markets with the ideas. Identify and rank potential markets for an idea and continue the process.

As you submit to the various publications listed in *Writer's Market*, it's important to remember that every magazine is published with a particular audience and slant in mind. Probably the number one complaint we receive from editors is that the submissions they receive are completely wrong for their magazines. The first mark of professionalism is to know your market well. That knowledge starts in *Writer's Market*, but you should also do your own detective work. Search out back issues of the magazines you wish to write for, pick up recent issues at your local newsstand, or visit magazines' websites—anything that will help you figure out what subjects specific magazines publish. This research is also helpful in learning what topics have been covered ad nauseum—the topics that you should stay away from or approach in a fresh, new way. Magazine's websites are invaluable as most websites post the current issue of the magazine as well as back issues of the magazine, and most offer writer's guidelines.

Prepare for rejection and the sometimes lengthy wait. When a submission is returned, check your file folder of potential markets for that idea. Cross off the market that rejected the idea. If the editor has given you suggestions or reasons why the manuscript was not accepted, you might want to incorporate these suggestions when revising your manuscript. After revising your manuscript mail it to the next market on your list.

About rejection. Rejection is a way of life in the publishing world. It's inevitable in a business that deals with such an overwhelming number of applicants for such a limited number of positions. Anyone who has published has lived through many rejections, and writers with thin skin are at a distinct disadvantage. A rejection letter is not a personal attack. It simply indicates that your submission is not appropriate for that one specific market. Writers who let rejection dissuade them from pursuing their dream or who react to an editor's "No" with indignation or fury do themselves a disservice. Writers who let rejection stop them do not publish. Resign yourself to facing rejection now. You will live through it, and you'll eventually overcome it.

QUERY AND COVER LETTERS

A query letter is a brief, one-page letter used as a tool to hook an editor and get him interested in your idea. When you send a query letter to a magazine, you are trying to get an editor to buy your idea or article. When you query a book publisher, you are attempting to get an editor interested enough in your idea to request your book proposal or your entire manuscript. (*Note:* Some book editors prefer to receive book proposals on first contact. Check individual listings for which method editors prefer.)

While there are no set-in-stone rules for writing query letters, there are some basic guidelines to help you write a polished, well-organized query:

- Limit it to one page, single-spaced, and address the editor by name (Mr. or Ms. and the surname). *Note:* Do not assume that a person is a Mr. or Ms. unless it is obvious from the name listed. For example, if you are contacting a D.J. Smith, do not assume that D.J. should be preceded by Mr. or Ms. Instead, address the letter to D.J. Smith.
- Grab the editor's interest with a strong opening. Some magazine queries begin with a paragraph meant to approximate the lead of the intended article.

- Indicate how you intend to develop the article or book. Give the editor some idea of the work's structure and content.
- Let the editor know if you have photos or illustrations available to accompany your magazine article.
- Mention any expertise or training that qualifies you to write the article or book. If you've been published before, mention it; if not, don't.
- End with a direct request to write the article (or, if you're pitching a book, ask for the go-ahead to send in a full proposal or the entire manuscript). Give the editor an idea of the expected length and delivery date of your manuscript.

Another question that arises is: If I don't hear from an editor in the reported response time, how do I know when I can safely send the query to another market? Many writers find it helpful to indicate in their query that if they don't receive a response from the editor (slightly after the listed reporting time), they will assume the editor is not interested. It's best to take this approach, particularly if your topic is timely.

A brief, single-spaced cover letter is helpful when sending a manuscript as it helps personalize the submission. However, if you have previously queried the editor, use the cover letter to politely and briefly remind the editor of that query—when it was sent, what it contained, etc. "Here is the piece on low-fat cooking that I queried you about on December 12. I look forward to hearing from you at your earliest convenience." Do not use the cover letter as a sales pitch.

If you are submitting to a market that accepts unsolicited manuscripts, a cover letter is useful in that it personalizes your submission. You can, and should, include information about the manuscript, yourself, your publishing history, and your qualifications.

Once an editor has accepted your manuscript, it is then appropriate to offer to get involved in the editing process. Editing processes vary from magazine to magazine, but should an editor want you involved, he will send you galleys. At that point, you should read the galleys and return them to the editor immediately. Some magazines, however, do not send galleys. Book publishers generally involve you in rewrites, whether you like it or not.

The Query Letter Clinic on page 21 offers eight different query letters, some that work and some that don't, as well as editors' comments on why the letters were either successful or failed to garner an assignment.

Write Great Query Letters, Cover Letters, and Book Proposals

Books on the following list provide you with more detailed information on writing query letters, cover letters, and book proposals. All titles are published by Writer's Digest Books.

- *How to Write Irresistible Query Letters*, by Lisa Collier Cool.
- *How to Write Attention-Grabbing Query & Cover Letters*, by John Wood.
- *The Marshall Plan for Novel Writing*, by Evan Marshall.
- *Your Novel Proposal From Creation to Contract*, by Blythe Camenson and Marshall J. Cook.
- *How to Write a Book Proposal*, by Michael Larsen.
- *Formatting & Submitting Your Manuscript*, by Jack and Glenda Neff and Don Prues.

Querying for fiction

Fiction is sometimes queried, but more often not. Many fiction editors won't decide on a submission until they have seen the complete manuscript. When submitting a fiction book idea, most editors prefer to see at least a synopsis and sample chapters (usually the first three). For fiction that is published in magazines, most editors want to see the complete short story manuscript. If an editor does request a query for fiction, it should include a description of the main theme and story line, including the conflict and resolution. Take a look at individual listings to see what editors prefer to receive.

NONFICTION BOOK PROPOSALS

Most nonfiction books are sold by a book proposal, a package of materials that details what your book is about, who its intended audience is, and how you intend to write the book. It includes some combination of a cover or query letter, an overview, an outline, author's information sheet, and sample chapters. Editors also want to see information about the audience for your book and about titles that compete with your proposed book.

If a listing does not specify what a publisher would like to see, send as much of the above information as you can. Below is a brief description of the items you should include.

- The cover or query letter should be a short introduction to the material you include in the proposal.
- An overview is a brief summary of your book. For nonfiction, it should detail your book's subject and give an idea of how that subject will be developed. If you're sending a synopsis of a novel, cover the basic plot.
- An outline covers your book chapter by chapter. The outline should include all major points covered in each chapter. Some outlines are done in traditional outline form, but most are written in paragraph form.
- An author's information sheet should—as succinctly and clearly as possible—acquaint the editor with your writing background and convince her of your qualifications to write about the subject of your book.
- Many editors like to see sample chapters, especially for a first book. Sample chapters show the editor how well you write and develop the ideas from your outline.
- Marketing information—i.e., facts about how and to whom your book can be successfully marketed—is now expected to accompany every book proposal. If you can provide information about the audience for your book and suggest ways the book publisher can reach those people, you will increase your chances of acceptance.
- Competitive title analysis is an integral part of the marketing information. Check the *Subject Guide* to *Books in Print* for other titles on your topic. Write a one- or two-sentence synopsis of each. Point out how your book differs and improves upon existing topics.

A WORD ABOUT AGENTS

Recognizing the importance of literary agents in publishing today, we've included a section of 75 agents, 50 that represent books and 25 that represent scripts, beginning on page 77. We've selected agents who describe themselves as open to both previously published and newer writers, and who do not charge a fee to look at work. The literary agents we have included belong to the Association of Authors' Representatives (AAR), a voluntary professional organization. The script agents are all signatory agencies of The Writers Guild of America (WGA).

An agent represents a writer's work to buyers, negotiates contracts, follows up to see that contracts are fulfilled, and generally handles a writer's business affairs, leaving the writer free to write. Effective agents are valued for their contacts in the publishing industry, their savvy about which publishers and editors to approach with which ideas, their ability to guide an author's career, and their business sense.

While most book publishers listed in *Writer's Market* publish books by unagented writers, some of the larger houses are reluctant to consider submissions that have not reached them through a literary agent. Companies with such a policy are noted by a symbol (A) at the beginning of the listing, as well as in the submission information within the listing.

For more information about finding and working with a literary agent, as well as over 500 listings of literary and script agents, see *Guide to Literary Agents* (Writer's Digest Books). The annual *Guide* offers listings similar to those presented here, as well as a wealth of informational articles on the author-agent relationship and publishing process.

PROFESSIONALISM AND COURTESY

An editor's time is precious. Between struggling to meet deadlines, maintain budgets, and deal with hundreds of submissions on a daily basis, it's only natural that an editor's communication with writers is limited. Therefore, an editor must strike a professional balance between efficiency and bluntness.

But what about me, you ask. I am just as busy as an editor is, and writing is a business for me. I am the one taking the time to write queries and manuscripts, establish contact with editors, spend money on photocopying and postage. Don't I deserve to be treated with respect? An editor owes it to me to read my query or manuscript and give me helpful feedback while still pointing out the strong points in my submissions, right? Well, yes and no.

Editors are editors. Editors are not counselors, therapists, or coaches. They are not there to stroke a writer's ego; that's not their job. An editor's job is to find and publish writing that works for a given publication. That's not to say, though, that an editor should not follow common business courtesy. You will find that most good editors are professional in their communication with writers.

To help advance your communication with editors and receive professional communication in return, there are a few things you can do. Keep all correspondence, whether written or spoken, short and to the point. Don't hound an editor with follow up e-mails, letters, or phone calls to find out the status of your submission. Honor all agreements that you make with an editor. This includes deadlines, payment, and rewrites. Give all of your efforts 100 percent. As with all things in life, try to remain pleasant, keep your sense of humor, and be honest and reliable. If you keep these things in mind when dealing with an editor, your communication with most editors will be a pleasant and rewarding experience.

MANUSCRIPT FORMAT

You can increase your chances of publication by following a few standard guidelines regarding the physical format of your manuscript. Most writers who, like yourself, want to display their manuscript in the best possible light use the guidelines listed below. It should be your goal to make your manuscript readable. Use these suggestions as you would any other suggestions: Use what works for you and discard what doesn't. If anything, by following these suggestions (again, there are no hard-and-fast rules here), you will be displaying your work in the best possible light, thus proving to the editor that you are a professional who is serious about your writing.

Most manuscripts do not use a cover sheet or title page. Use a paper clip to hold pages together, not staples. This allows editors to separate the pages easily for editing. Scripts should be submitted with plain cardstock covers front and back, held together by Chicago or Revere screws.

The upper corners of the first page of an article manuscript contain important information about you and your manuscript. This information should be single-spaced. In the upper *left* corner, list your name, address, phone number, and e-mail address. If you are using a pseudonym for your byline, your legal name should still appear in this space. In the upper *right* corner, indicate the approximate word count of the manuscript, the rights you are offering for sale, and your copyright notice (©Susan Smith). A handwritten copyright symbol is acceptable. (For more information about rights and copyright, see Minding the Details on page 61.) For a book manuscript include the same information with the exception of rights. Do not number the first page of your manuscript.

Center the title in capital letters one-third of the way down the page. Set the spacing to double-space. Type "by" and your name or pseudonym centered one double-space beneath the title.

After the title and byline, drop down two double-spaces, use the standard paragraph indent (five spaces), and begin the body of your manuscript. Always double-space the body of your manuscript. Margins should be about 1¼ inches on all sides of each full page of the manuscript.

On every page after the first page of your manuscript, type your last name, a dash, and the page number in either the upper left or right corner. The title of your manuscript may, but need not, be typed on this line or beneath it. For example, page number two would read: Smith—2.

If you are submitting novel chapters, leave the top one-third of the first page of each chapter blank before typing the chapter title. Subsequent pages should include the author's last name, the page number, and a shortened form of the book's title: Smith—2—Running. (In a variation on this, some authors place the title before the name on the left side and put the page number in the right-hand margin.)

When submitting poetry, the poems should be typed single-spaced (double-space between stanzas), one poem per page. For a long poem requiring more than one page, paper clip the pages together. You may want to write "continued" at the bottom of the page, so if the pages are separated, editors, typesetters, and proofreaders won't assume your poem ends at the bottom of the first page.

ESTIMATING WORD COUNT

Many computers will provide you with a word count of your manuscript. Your editor will count again after editing the manuscript. Although your computer is counting characters, an editor or production editor is more concerned about the amount of space the text will occupy on a page. Several small headlines or subheads, for instance, will be counted the same by your computer as any other word of text. However, headlines and subheads usually employ a different font size than the body text, so an editor may count them differently to be sure enough space has been estimated for larger type.

For short manuscripts, it's often quickest to count each word on a representative page and multiply by the number of pages. You can get a very rough count by multiplying the number of pages in your manuscript by 250 (the average number of words on a double-spaced typewritten page). Do not count words for a poetry manuscript or put the word count at the top of the manuscript because most poems are "counted" by lines, not words.

PHOTOGRAPHS AND SLIDES

In some cases, the availability of photographs and slides can be the deciding factor as to whether an editor will accept your submission. This is especially true when querying a publication that relies heavily on photographs, illustrations, or artwork to enhance the article (i.e., craft magazines, hobby magazines, etc.). In some instances, the publication may offer additional payment for photographs or illustrations.

Check the individual listings for photograph submission guidelines and to find out which magazines review photographs. Most publications prefer that you do not send photographs with your submission. However, if photographs or illustrations are available, you should indicate as such in your query. As with manuscripts, never send the originals of your photographs or illustrations. Instead, send prints or duplicates of slides and transparencies.

On all your photographs and slides, you should stamp or print your copyright notice and "Return to:" followed by your name, address, phone number, and e-mail address. Rubber stamps (which can be ordered from stationery or office supply stores) are preferred for labeling photos since they are less likely to cause damage. If you use a pen to write this information on the back of your photos, be careful not to damage the print by pressing too hard or by allowing ink to bleed through the paper. A felt tip pen is best, but you should take care not to put photos or copy together before the ink dries.

Captions can be typed on adhesive labels and affixed to the back of the prints. Some writers, when submitting several transparencies or photos, number the photos and type captions (numbered accordingly) on a separate 8½ × 11 sheet of paper.

PHOTOCOPIES

If there is one hard-and-fast rule in publishing, it's this: *Never* send the original (or only) copy of your manuscript. Most editors cringe when they find out that a writer has sent the only copy of their manuscript. You should always send photocopies of your manuscript for any one of the following reasons:

- Mail can get lost.
- Businesses can fold at a moment's notice.
- Time can expire on forwarding addresses.
- Editors may not accept unsolicited manuscripts, and if that's the case, they will pitch your manuscript.

Some writers choose to send a self-addressed, stamped postcard with a photocopied submission. In their cover letter they suggest that if the editor is not interested in their manuscript, it may be tossed out and a reply sent on the postcard. This method is particularly helpful when sending your submissions to international markets.

MAILING SUBMISSIONS

No matter what size manuscript you're mailing, always include a self-addressed, stamped envelope (SASE) with sufficient return postage. The website for the U.S. Postal Service, www.usps.gov, and the website for the Canadian Postal Service, www.canadapost.ca, both have handy postage calculators if you are unsure of how much postage you'll need to affix.

A manuscript of fewer than six pages may be folded into thirds and mailed as if it were a letter using a #10 (business-size) envelope. The enclosed SASE can be a #10 folded in thirds or a #9 envelope, which will slip into the mailing envelope without being folded. Some editors also appreciate the convenience of having a manuscript folded into halves in a 6 × 9 envelope. For manuscripts of six pages or longer, use 9 × 12 envelopes for both mailing and return. The return SASE may be folded in half.

A book manuscript should be mailed in a sturdy, well-wrapped box. Enclose a self-addressed mailing label and paper clip your return postage to the label. However, be aware that some book publishers do not return unsolicited manuscripts, so make sure that you know the practice of the publisher before sending any unsolicited material.

Always mail photos and slides First Class. The rougher handling received by Standard Mail could damage the photos and slides. If you are concerned about losing prints or slides, send them Certified or Registered Mail. For any photo submission that is mailed separately from a manuscript, enclose a short cover letter of explanation, separate self-addressed label, adequate return postage, and an envelope. Never submit photos or slides in mounted glass.

To mail up to 20 prints, you can buy photo mailers that are stamped "Photos—Do Not Bend" and contain two cardboard inserts to sandwich your prints. If you do not want to buy a ready-made photo mailer, you can also send the prints in a 9 × 12 manila envelope, write, "Photos—Do Not Bend" on the envelope, and make your own cardboard inserts to sandwich the prints. Some photography supply stores also carry heavy cardboard envelopes that are reusable.

When mailing a number of prints, say 25-250 for a book with illustrations, pack the prints in a sturdy cardboard box. A box for typing paper or photo paper is an adequate mailer. If, after packing both the manuscript and photos, there's empty space in the box, slip in enough cardboard inserts or packing paper to fill the box. Wrap the box securely. However, when wrapping the box, use only enough tape to securely close the box. Don't tape the box over and over just to make it more secure. A package like this may look suspicious to a publisher, especially if they are not expecting the package.

To mail transparencies, first slip them into protective vinyl sleeves, then mail as you would prints. If you're mailing a number of sheets, use a cardboard box.

Types of mail service

There are many different mailing service options available to you whether you are sending a query letter, complete manuscript, or photos. You can work with the U.S. Postal Service, United Parcel Service, Federal Express, or any number of private mailing companies. The following are the five most common types of mailing services offered by the U.S. Postal Service.

- **First Class** is an expensive way to mail a manuscript, but many writers prefer it. First-Class Mail generally receives better handling and is delivered more quickly than Standard Mail. First Class is only available for packages that weigh 13 ounces or less. Mail sent First Class is also forwarded for one year if the addressee has moved, and is returned if it is undeliverable. First Class also offers two confirmation options (both with retail and electronic options): delivery confirmation and signature confirmation. Delivery confirmation can be purchased for $.55 (retail) and $.13 (electronic); electronic confirmation for $1.80 (retail) and $1.30 (electronic).
- **Priority Mail** reaches its destination within two or three days. To mail a package of up to 2 pounds costs $3.85, less than either United Parcel Service or Federal Express. First-Class Mail over 13 ounces is classified Priority. Confirmation of delivery is an additional $.40.
- **Standard Mail** rates are available for packages, but be sure to pack your materials carefully because they will be handled roughly. To make sure your package will be returned to you if it is undeliverable, print "Return Postage Guaranteed" under your address.
- **Certified Mail** must be signed for when it reaches its destination. If requested, a signed receipt is returned to the sender. There is a $2.10 charge for this service, in addition to the required postage, and a $2.35 charge for a return receipt.
- **Registered Mail** is a high-security method of mailing where the contents are insured. The package is signed in and out of every office it passes through, and a receipt is returned to the sender when the package reaches its destination. The cost depends on the weight, destination, and whether you obtain insurance.

If you're in a hurry to get your material to your editor, you have a lot of choices including overnight and two-day mail services as provided by the U.S. Postal Service and several private firms. More information on next-day service is available from the U.S. Post Office or check the Yellow Pages under "Delivery Services."

Other correspondence details

Never send cash through the mail if you are ordering sample copies or supplies. Use money orders if you do not have checking services. Money orders provide you with a receipt and they are traceable. Money orders for up to $700 can be purchased from the U.S. Postal Service for a $.90 service charge. International money orders are also available from the post office for a charge of $1.58 or $3.80. Banks, savings and loans, and some commercial businesses also carry money orders; their fees vary.

Insurance is available for items handled by the U.S. Postal Service but is payable only on typing fees or the tangible value of the item in the package—such as typing paper—so your best insurance when mailing manuscripts is to keep a copy of what you send. Insurance is $1.10 for $50 or less and goes up to a $50-plus postage maximum charge for $5,000. *Never* send the only copy of your manuscript.

When corresponding with publishers in other countries, International Reply Coupons (IRCs) must be used for return postage. Surface rates in other countries differ from those in the U.S., and U.S. postage stamps are of use only in the U.S.

U.S. stamps can be purchased online with a credit card at www.usps.gov, by calling 1-800-

STAMP24, or through the mail by filling out Form 3227 (available at the post office or from your local letter carrier). NonU.S. residents can call 1-800-782-6724 to order stamps. Canadian postage can be purchased online at www.canadapost.ca.

Because some post offices don't carry IRCs (or because of the added expense), many writers dealing with international mail send photocopies and tell the publisher to dispose of them if the manuscript is not appropriate. When you use this method, it's best to set a deadline for withdrawing your manuscript from consideration, so you can market it elsewhere.

RECORDING SUBMISSIONS

Once you begin sending out queries and manuscripts you will find that it becomes a business. As with any business, organization and management are essential. You should always keep records of any correspondence you have with editors as well as the dates relating to the correspondence.

Many writers find it helpful to set up spreadsheets for queries and manuscripts. You can easily set up two types of tracking systems for your work: one for materials sent and one for materials received. When setting up a system for materials sent, it is best to include dates, materials sent, enclosures, editors' names, titles of manuscripts, etc. The system for materials received should log dates of responses, rejection letters, whether the material was accepted, and if it was accepted, any rewrites completed, deadlines, publication dates, and pay rates.

Some writers find it helpful to keep a separate calendar just for dates. You can use the calendar to mark the dates material is sent, when you plan on following up, when you plan on sending to new markets, etc. The Query Letter Clinic on page 21 includes important information about how and when you should follow up on queries.

WritersMarket.com, the online edition of *Writer's Market*, has taken recording submissions to another level. The site contains a special feature called the Submission Tracker. This feature has been set up to allow you to record all of the above mentioned information in an easy-to-understand electronic format—all you have to do is enter your personal submission information.

The Magazines Most Open to New Writers

BY GREG DAUGHERTY

Some magazines are more receptive to new writers than others. Here are five types of publications that are almost always looking for fresh talent.

1. New magazines.

Some 800 to 900 new magazines are launched each year, according to Samir A. Husni, a University of Mississippi journalism professor who compiles an annual guide to new magazines.

New magazines are especially receptive to new writers for a couple of reasons. One, obviously, is that they don't have a vast network of writers in place yet. Another is that new magazines usually don't have the editorial budgets of larger ones, so they're often willing to take a chance on less-experienced (in other words, cheaper) writers.

How do you find out about new magazines before they're old magazines? The easiest way is to keep checking both your local newsstand and the supermarket magazine racks for titles you've never seen before, and trade magazines that people in the publishing business read. Among the most useful are *Advertising Age*, *Adweek*, and *Folio: The Magazine for Magazine Management.*

And never underestimate the value of your own mailbox. What may be mere junk mail to your neighbors could be valuable information to you. Years ago I received a mailing from *Yankee* magazine, announcing a new spin-off called *Collectibles Illustrated*. I wrote to the editor of the new magazine, enclosed some clippings of articles I'd done, and offered my services in case he ever needed a correspondent where I lived. Within weeks I had an assignment.

2. Old magazines with new owners.

When a magazine gets a new owner, things tend to change. A new owner almost inevitably means a new team of editors and, sometimes, a new approach to whatever the magazine covers. Any change of that sort means an opportunity for writers.

The best way to keep track of ownership changes is to read the trade magazines mentioned above. Another is to take note when a magazine alters its logo or overall design. A new design may mean a new art director, another near inevitability after an ownership change.

3. Magazines that are changing frequency.

A magazine expanding from six issues a year to 12 may need twice as much editorial material to fill its pages. Even a magazine going from ten issues a year to 12 may need 20 percent more. Any frequency boost is likely to mean the magazine is more open to new writers.

---

4. Magazines that are changing focus.

Sometimes magazines take a new direction even without changing owners. That, too, may spell opportunity, since not all of the magazine's current writers will be right for the new and improved model.

5. Small magazines.

Whether they're under new management or have been run by the same family since the War of 1812, small-circulation magazines tend to be more open to new writers than their giant competitors. Small magazines also tend to have smaller budgets, which means they often have to take talent where they find it. You may never make a living by writing for small magazines, but they can be a terrific place to gain some experience and accumulate a few good clips.

Strategies for Starting Your Online-Writing Career

BY ANTHONY TEDESCO

Novice writers, be still your hearts. Online writing markets are particularly winsome for you right now; sort of the sweet, bright-eyed siblings of stodgy old print markets. They're fetchingly easy and affordable to approach, forsaking paper, envelopes, and postage for short e-mails with electronic clips attached. And once queried, online markets don't act aloof, gracing you with a response in a few months. They're considerate/enabled enough to get right back to you within a week or two, often within only a few days. The best part? Despite their empowering allure, most online markets are sheepishly more receptive than print markets. Internet publishing is still so new that there's simply less competition, fewer writing suitors vying for their attention. Endearing, isn't it? Online markets don't even know how attractive they are.

If you've been flirting with the idea of writing for online publications—or if my wannabe-cupid routine has recently sparked your interest—it's time to make your move. With such a multitude of markets already online (e.g., consumer magazines, corporate sites seeking customer-entertaining content, e-mail newsletters, etc.) and with so many dot-coms trimming costs by paying freelancers instead of staff salaries and benefits, your chances are better than ever to launch your writing career or to bolster your budding print-writing income. Like many of my fellow print writers, I started writing for online markets as an explorative foray, but soon found that what I thought might be a novel supplement to my print income soon surpassed my print income altogether.

Here are few insights and strategies for getting started. Couple these offerings with the advice generously provided by your very own panel of guardian mentors (see Insider Tips for Tapping Online Markets on page 34), and you'll be well on your way.

GETTING STARTED

We all get cold feet sometimes, so let me begin by debunking some online myths that may have been daunting your transition into the Internet-writing world.

1. Attention Luddites: If you write for online markets, the printed word will not end. Online writers like the printed word, too. We intend to keep it around.

2. You won't have to converse in 12-letter acronyms or those geek-speak emoticon hieroglyphic winkey-smiley code symbols. Sure, some Net users communicate almost exclusively in that cryptic high-tech vernacular, but they're a minority. An astute little space-alien minority. Most online writers aren't techies writing for techies about techie things. We're just opportunists who've tapped into hundreds of new markets.

FINDING MARKETS THAT PAY

One difficulty writers often face is finding out which of those hundreds of new markets actually pay writers for freelance work. Usually, if the magazine features advertising or a recog-

---

ANTHONY TEDESCO *(anthony@marketsforwriters.com) is co-author of* Online Markets for Writers: How to Make Money By Selling Your Writing on the Internet (Holt) *and publisher of MarketsForWriters .com, a free Web resource to help writers live off of the writing they love.*

nizable parent company, it has a content budget. But the only way to be sure is to request each publication's pay information and writer's guidelines.

A few books and online resources provide some of these online-market listings, including *Writer's Online Marketplace: How and Where to Get Published Online*, by Debbie Ridpath Ohi (Writer's Digest Books); *Online Markets for Writers: How to Make Money by Selling Your Writing On The Internet*, by Anthony Tedesco and Paul Tedesco (Holt); WritersMarket.com (www.writersmarket.com); and The Writer's Place (www.awoc.com).

Other Ways to Locate Online Magazines

Another way to locate online magazines are directories and electronic newsstands, including:

- Etext Archives (www.etext.org) which is home to electronic texts of all kinds.
- Ezine Newsgroup (alt.ezines) which is a good place to query the e-zine community about any genre of magazine.
- Chip Rowe's Zine Resource Start Page (www.zinebook.com) which is a clearinghouse for all things zine and e-zine.
- Zinos (www.zinos.com/) which is a digest of some of the top e-zines on the Web.
- The Well's Publications Area (gopher://gopher.well.com/11/) offers information on the full gamut of online magazines.

With a little online foraging, however, you can customize your very own list of potential online publications. A good place to start is on the pages of the very same markets you've targeted in traditional print media. Check the masthead page for the publication's corresponding online address or simply type the publication's title into the Internet browser (e.g., www.thetitle.com). Finally, try entering the title into one of the Internet's many search engines.

DON'T WRITE FOR FREE

OK, you've found the online market that makes your heart go "pitter-patter," and you've honed the piece you consider your Pulitzer Prize winner. Now what? Before you start the query process, resolve yourself not to write for free. Professional writers know not to provide their services for free, but I need to stress this here because the Internet is so conducive to personal experience and community that it's enabled new writers of all ages and experience to publish their work—stay-at-home dads sharing their time-management tricks, teenagers sharing their personal journal entries, grandmothers sharing their secret recipes—and these new writers are often eager to publish regardless of payment. The bottom line is that even new writers don't have to write for free.

Print and online writer, Christina Tourigny, further explains: "It's your work, and if you want to make writing your livelihood, you need to be paid. If you're trying to build up your credit list then start out with online markets that pay very little and work up—even if it's only a penny or two a word the first few times or maybe $15-20 for your whole piece. If you build up your credit list with free markets, editors will take notice and offer you a fraction of what you could have gotten or offer you only a credit line like the others. New writers need to be aware that there are plenty of paying online markets out there for them to break into. Don't just shoot for the big guns. Go after the smaller ones too—they're almost always your bread-and-butter makers. All nonpaying markets have survived this long because new writers are misguided and don't realize they can negotiate with magazines. Don't sell yourself short."

There are only a few instances, I believe, when you may rightly consider contributing your work for free. If you believe in a cause and want to contribute to the nonprofit efforts of that cause, or if you want to market yourself for promotion, not for clips, in which case you would pick one of your columns that you've already sold (and have retained at least nonexclusive reprint rights) and let that column be your calling card. Make sure it's evergreen so it can promote you for eternity because that's how long each market's online archives can promote your work.

QUERYING ONLINE EDITORS

At the risk of sounding obvious: Remember to read through the online market that made your heart go "pitter-patter" before sending your article. You'd be surprised at how many writers apparently don't. Online editors, like print editors, don't want a 12,000-word fiction book excerpt if all they publish is breaking news.

Obviously it's best to send your e-mail directly to the appropriate editor. Sometimes, however, his or her e-mail isn't listed on the masthead of the magazine. Fret not. You still have a few options.

You can rummage through the site until you find a general editorial e-mail address (e.g., editorial@thetitle.com or feedback@thetitle.com) or even the ubiquitous e-mail address of the site's webmaster (technical overseer) who will probably do you the favor of forwarding your query—unless he is particularly busy doing [insert obscure technical task] or he just doesn't feel like it. Let's face it, with a title like webmaster and the perceived power to crash your computer and then charge a celebratory bottle of Dom to your credit card, he can do whatever he wants, whenever he wants.

Option two shows a little resourcefulness of your own, though don't tell anyone I showed you. Even though an editor's e-mail address might not be listed in the magazine's masthead, it doesn't mean it doesn't exist, and it doesn't mean you can't find it. Sites such as WhoWhere? (www.whowhere.lycos.com) and Yahoo People Search (http://people.yahoo.com) have gathered millions of e-mail addresses from the Internet so you can get in touch with your long-lost best high school pal or fave celebrity. As well as, of course, the editor who's going to jump for joy after reading your revolutionary query.

Yes, the non-joy-jumping editor in me says you shouldn't send e-mails directly (I'm busy), you shouldn't risk simultaneous submissions, and you shouldn't pitch to me over the phone. But then I'm also a freelance writer doing all of those things for the advantages they provide.

Make your own decision. And mum's the word.

SENDING YOUR QUERY

When you do finally send the article, don't send those 12,000 words as an e-mail attachment unless it's been requested. You could be that one writer with one jumbled photo attachment that crashes the editor's computer and all the files that hadn't been backed up, a.k.a., all the files.

Your best bet with editors is to send your query without clips (more computer crashing). Just offer to send them, and the editors will let you know their—greatly varying and often vehement—preferred method of receiving clips (as attachments, as e-mail text, or as URLs pointing to clips on the Web). If you don't have online clips yet, offer to mail or fax hard-copy clips.

And don't forget to send all e-mails to yourself first to make sure they're formatted how you want them. A little extra effort understanding the Internet and the Internet's readers (and editors) will go a long way to tapping this promising new market.

Query Letter Clinic

BY KATHRYN STRUCKEL BROGAN AND CYNTHIA LAUFENBERG

The query letter is the catalyst in the chemical reaction of publishing. Overall, writing a query letter is a fairly simple process that serves one purpose—selling an article.

There are two types of queries, a query for a finished manuscript, and a query for an idea that has yet to be developed into an article. Either way, a query letter is the tool that sells an idea using brief, attention-getting prose.

WHAT SHOULD I INCLUDE IN A QUERY LETTER?

A query should tell an editor how you plan to handle and develop the proposed article. Many writers even include the lead of the article as the first sentence of their query as a sales pitch to the editor. A query letter should also show that you are familiar with the publication and tell the editor why you are the most qualified person to write the article.

Beyond the information mentioned above, a query letter is also the appropriate place to state the availability of photographs or artwork. Do not send photographs with your query. You can also include a working title and a projected word count. Some writers also indicate whether a sidebar or other accompanying short would be appropriate, and the type of research they plan to conduct. It is also appropriate to include a tentative deadline and to indicate if the query is being simultaneously submitted.

WHAT SHOULD I *NOT* INCLUDE IN A QUERY LETTER?

The query letter is not the place to discuss pay rates. By mentioning what you would like to be paid, you are prematurely assuming that the editor is going to buy your article. Plus, if you are really just looking to get published and get paid some amount of money, you could be doing yourself a disservice. If you offer a rate that is higher than what the editor is willing to pay, you could lose the assignment. And, if you offer a figure that's too low, you are short-changing yourself on what could possibly be a lucrative assignment.

Another thing you should avoid is requesting writer's guidelines or a sample copy of the publication. This is a red flag to the editor because it indicates that you are not familiar with the magazine or its content. Don't use the query letter to list pages of qualifications. Only list those qualifications that you feel would best help you land the gig. If you have too many qualifications that you still feel would convince the editor to give you the assignment, include them as a separate page. Finally, never admit if five other editors rejected the query. This is your chance to shine and sell the best article ever written.

HOW DO I FORMAT A QUERY LETTER?

There are no hard-and-fast rules when it comes to formatting your query letter. But there are some general, widely accepted guidelines like those listed below from *Formatting & Submitting Your Manuscript*, by Jack and Glenda Neff, and Don Prues (Writer's Digest Books).

KATHRYN STRUCKEL BROGAN *is the editor of* Writer's Market *and* Writer's Market Online.

CYNTHIA LAUFENBERG *is editor-in-chief of* HealthyPet *magazine and former managing editor of Writer's Digest Books. She lives in Princeton, New Jersey.*

Fourteen Things Not to Do In Your Query Letter

1. Don't try any cute attention-getting devices, like marking the envelope "Personal." This also includes fancy stationery that lists every publication you've ever sold to, or "clever" slogans.
2. Don't talk about fees.
3. Keep your opinions to yourself.
4. Don't tell the editors what others you've shown the idea to think of it. ("Several of my friends have read this and think it's marvelous . . ." is a certain sign of the amateur writer.) The same goes for comments from other editors.
5. Don't name drop. However, if you do know somebody who works for that magazine, or writes for it, or if you know an editor on another magazine who has bought your work and likes it, say so.
6. Don't try to soft soap the editor by telling him or her how great the magazine is, but definitely make it clear that you read it.
7. Don't send in any unnecessary enclosures, such as a picture of yourself (or your prize-winning Labrador Retriever).
8. Don't offer irrelevant information about yourself. Simply tell the editor what there might be in your background that qualifies you to write this story.
9. Don't offer such comments as, "I never read your magazine, but this seems to be a natural . . ." or "I know you don't usually publish articles about mountain-climbing, but . . ." Know the magazine, and send only those ideas that fit the format.
10. Don't ask for a meeting to discuss your idea further. If the editor feels this is necessary, he or she will suggest it.
11. Don't ask for advice, such as, "If you don't think you can use this, could you suggest another magazine that could?"
12. Don't offer to rewrite, as this implies you know it's not good enough as you've submitted it. Again, editors will ask for rewrites, if necessary, and they usually are.
13. Don't make such threats as, "If I don't hear from you within four weeks I'll submit it elsewhere."
14. Don't include a multiple-choice reply card, letting the editor check a box to indicate whether he likes it.

From Magazine Writing That Sells, *by Don McKinney (Writer's Digest Books).*

- Use a standard font or typeface (avoid bold, script, or italics, except for publication titles).
- Your name, address, and phone number (plus e-mail and fax, if possible) should appear in the top right corner or on your letterhead.
- Use a 1-inch margin on all sides.
- Address the query to a specific editor, preferably the editor assigned to handle freelance submissions or who handles the section you're writing for. Note: The listings in *Writer's Market* provide a contact name for all submissions.
- Keep it to one page. If necessary, use a résumé or list of credits attached separately to provide additional information.
- Include a SASE or postcard for reply; state you have done so, either in the body of the letter or in a listing of enclosures.
- Use block format (no indentations).
- Single-space the body of the letter and double-space between paragraphs.
- When possible, mention that you can send the manuscript on disk or via e-mail.
- Thank the editor for considering your proposal.

How to Include Clips with E-Mailed Queries

When you send an e-mail query, you can provide clips five ways. There are no generally accepted standards yet for which is best, but the pros and cons of each method are described below:

1. Include a line telling the editor that clips are available on request. Then, mail, fax, or e-mail clips according to the editor's preference. This is a convenient solution for the writer, but not necessarily for the editor. The clips aren't available immediately, so you potentially slow the decision process by adding an additional step, and you lose any speed you've gained by e-mailing the query in the first place.
2. Include electronic versions of the clips in the body of the e-mail message. This can make for an awfully long e-mail, and it doesn't look as presentable as other alternatives, but it may be better than making the editor wait to download attachments or log on to a website.
3. Include electronic versions of the articles as attachments. The disadvantage here is the editor has to download the clips, which can take several minutes. Also, if there's a format disparity, the editor may not be able to read the attachment. The safest bet is to attach the documents as ".rtf" or ".txt" files, which should be readable with any word processing software, although you will lose formatting.
4. Send the clips as a separate e-mail message. This cuts the download time and eliminates software-related glitches, but it clutters the editor's e-mail queue.
5. Set up a personal web page and include your clips as hypertext links in or at the end of the e-mail (e.g., http://www.aolmembers.com/jackneff/smallbusinessclips). Setting up and maintaining the page takes a considerable amount of effort, but it may be the most convenient and reliable way for editors to access your clips electronically.

From Formatting & Submitting Your Manuscript, *by Jack and Glenda Neff, and Don Prues (Writer's Digest Books).*

WHEN SHOULD I FOLLOW UP?

Sometimes things happen to your query and it never reaches the editor's hands. Problems can arise with the mail delivery, the query may have been sent to a different department, or the editor may have inadvertently thrown the query away. Whatever the reason, there are a few simple guidelines you should use when you send a follow-up letter.

You should wait to follow up on your query at least until after the reported response time in the *Writer's Market* listing for that publication. If, after two months, you have not received a response to your query, you should compose a brief follow-up letter. The letter should describe the original query sent, the date the query was sent, and a reply postcard or SASE. Some writers find it helpful to include a photocopy of the original query to help jog the editor's memory.

Above all, though, be polite and businesslike when following up. Don't take the lack of response personal. Editors are only human—situations can arise that are beyond their control.

WHAT THE CLINIC SHOWS YOU

Unpublished writers wonder how published writers break into print. It's not a matter of luck. Published writers know how to craft a well-written, hard-hitting query. What follows are eight actual queries (two are e-mail queries) submitted to editors (names and addresses have been altered). Four queries are strong; four are not. Detailed comments from the editors show what the writer did and did not do to secure a sale. As you'll see, there is not a cut-and-dry "good" query format; every strong query works because of its own merit.

Good

Jane Goodquery
7 Rosewood Lane
Washington, DC 20226

Trey Hall
Absey & Co.
23011 Northcrest Drive
Spring, Texas 77389

RE: FICTION BOOK PROPOSAL: FIFTY DAYS TO LEAVE YOUR LOVER

Dear Mr. Trey Hall,

For single women in Washington, DC, there's more to life than those extra ten pounds or the perfect orgasm—there's heartbreak, revenge, and the brilliant realizations that can come out of a good bottle of Chianti. After spending six years in our nation's capitol, I feel qualified to tell the tale.

Shows me that she can manipulate words and sentences. It may not be 100% original, but she has my attention. Notice how she never tells me what to think or what I should do. Instead, she keeps focused on her work and her abilities.

I graduated from the American University with a double major in English and Psychology and have since held internships at *Psychology Today* and *Newsweek*. I am currently attending graduate school for my doctorate in Psychology.

The novel that I am currently seeking publication for, *Fifty Days to Leave Your Lover*, tells the story of what life in the nation's capitol has to offer. SUZANNE gets her heart broken by her ambitious boyfriend, TRICIA has an affair with a politician and is forced to deal with an unwanted pregnancy, and MEGAN looks to anything from alternative medicine to seeking advice from the dead in order to help her deal with the trials of being a single young woman in Washington, DC. The novel is set during the months before the attack on the World Trade Center and lightly touches on the effects that this declaration of war has on the young women in the political center.

She gives a quick bio then immediately follows with three well-written sentences about the work she wants me to consider. She gets in and gets out without getting bogged down with minutia or trying to impress me with her brilliance. Rather, I see clear, progressive prose.

I believe that just as Helen Fielding's *Bridget Jones's Diary* appealed to the single, working thirty-something and the way that Christopher Buckley's *Little Green Men* appealed to Washington pundits and politicians, this book will appeal to urban women in the 18-34 year old age group who need to laugh at themselves before they admit defeat. Each city has its own identity and its own rules that beg to be followed in order to succeed in the dating scene. In Los Angeles, looks are everything, and in New York City, money and the right address can do wonders for a girl's dating life. But, in Washington, DC, the rules are largely based on perception and public relations because everyone is a politician at heart.

She lets me in on where she sees her work fitting in terms of the market.

It strikes me that she is writing about something she knows. She is writing from experience and the human condition.

Thank you for taking the time to review my material. I can be reached via e-mail at diane@writer.com, or via telephone at (222) 555-3737.

Sincerely,

Jane Goodquery

The letter is coherent and shows a certain amount of intelligence. She is neither informal nor mechanical. The letter strikes a nice enough tone; I'm not insulted or pummeled. While this may be the writer's first attempt at getting published, I am intrigued enough to want to see if she can write a tale, weave words into something magical, and has something to say.

Comments provided by Edward Wilson, publisher of Absey & Co.

Notgood, Montana, March 6, 2002

ABSEY & Co.
5706 Root Rd., Suite #5
Spring TX 77389

"Since we are a small, new press, we are looking for. . . ."

Our descriptor in Writer's Market. I am well aware of that and do not need the author of this letter to remind me of what was written.

Dear Editor-in-Chief:]—Salutation is general

The Lord knows, so do you and I, this is not the first book that has been written about BILL AND MONICA. Lately so many writers have been pretty busy expressing in varied literary forms what happened to them that you would think the subject has been almost exhausted. There seems to be no reason to add a new book to the mile-long shelf of books that recount BILL AND MONICA's affair unless this new book offers something fresh, capable of attracting new as well as old readers of the story.

Lets me know I can stop here. Any writer using the "Lord" in any query should reconsider this tactic. The informal tone, like I would pretend to know that this writer's Lord knows, is presumptuous.

Gives me a good reason not to consider another book on his chosen topic.

The facts about BILL AND MONICA's story are fascinating and the characters are unique, that's true. But these are the facts and almost everybody knows them. The temptation to write is there, too, for any writer to try again. Temptation is a strong word. ADAM AND EVE were tempted, so were BILL AND MONICA.

The lack of logical coherence leaves me with a big question mark instead of any real understanding. If this letter is illogical, then the manuscript will certainly be.

As a writer of fantasy I gave up to temptation and wrote the same story from a different angle, from a Fairy's point of view. In this fairy tale BILLY is a clown and MONIK is a cow. The tale doesn't entirely stick to the facts as you can already see. Very often the tale digresses to explore different angles of the real story. From this fantastic point of view the reader will explore new and fantastic venues, and will wonder when he finds out why BILLY AND MONIK fell in love with each other and the extraordinary consequences of their romance.

Finally, what the book is about. There isn't a reader alive who would find Bill as a clown or Monica as a cow a fresh and new idea. It's so trite, it's sophomoric. The author admits to not sticking to the facts. So is this an allegory or isn't it? Be true to something.

Let me introduce you to the first page of this fairy tale:

"Once upon a time in a town named Chikitown which was inhabited by mischievous clowns, there lived, among those wonderful people, a loving couple. He was a clown and she was a cow. Everybody in this town was happy, very happy, until one day, one ominous day . . ."

The author does one of the things a query should never do. He quotes from the manuscript.

If you are the kind of editor who believes in fairy tales, upon your request, I will send you a copy of BILLY AND MONIK's script. And if after reading it (only 100 pages, double space) you decide, after carefully weighing the odds, that BILLY AND MONIK, as a story, stands by itself and deserves to be considered a work of modern fantasy capable of standing side by side with THE WIZARD OF OZ, then it is up to you to call the shots.

If I wasn't confused before, this clinches it. Does he want to send a book manuscript or a script? Again, I find the imprecision of language offensive. If the query is this sloppy, I'm expecting the manuscript to be also.

According to the Chinese calendar this is the year of the Horse. It may also turn out to be the year of the Cow and the Clown, editorially speaking that is.

The writer's attempt at what he thinks is humor falls flat.

Sincerely yours,

Adam Amateur
558 Unknown Lane
Notgood, MT 55684

It is so obvious that the writer has no first-hand knowledge of the topic he is trying to write about. I would never spend any time seriously considering this query.

Comments provided by Edward Wilson, publisher of Absey & Co.

Good

LISA JUSTRIGHT
93A 24th Street
Prosperity, PA 19653
215-555-8696
lisajustright@goodmail.com

June 8, 2002

Although the letter is addressed to our former editor, I'm not offended because the change has been recent.

Susanne Kass, Executive Editor
Antietam Review
41 South Potomac Street
Hagerstown, MD 21740

Dear Ms. Kass,

The writer makes a personal connection to our publication. She references her work by title, hoping we will remember her previous submissions and shows a pride of ownership of her work.

Thank you for your continued encouragement of my short stories, including my most recent submission, "The Bench-Warmers." At your suggestion, I've enclosed a new story, "Adultery," for your review.

Her experience and publishing credits are impressive and presented professionally with the publications listed in italics. She positions herself as a well-established writer.

Since last submitting to the *Antietam Review*, I have had stories accepted by *The Hudson Review* and *Harvard Review* (both forthcoming), stories published in *Berkeley Fiction Review* and *ByLine Magazine*, and I recently secured representation for my first novel. My fiction has also appeared in *Salmagundi*, *The Seattle Review*, *Black Warrior Review* and *Room of One's Own*.

I am originally from the Philadelphia area, and returned here last fall after completing the Creative Writing Program at the University of Iowa. I now teach writing at Philadelphia's University of the Arts.

Thank you for considering "Adultery."

Sincerely,

Lisa Justright

Enc.
Ms
SASE

This paragraph is important to our publication and the writer lets us know she has read our guidelines. Until very recently, we only accepted manuscripts from residents of six states—including her state. Adding to her credentials and her commitment to the craft is that she teaches writing.

Overall, this is a good query. I like the look of the letter. It is clean, neat, and easy to read. The writer knows us and has done her homework. The only thing missing (which would make my job easier) is the word count of the submission.

Comments provided by Winnie Wagaman, managing editor of *Antietam Review.*

Bad

I would rather the query be addressed to me personally as managing editor.

Dear Antietam Review,

Enclosed in this envelope are some of my writings. Thirty-one years old. Poor. Pist. Ready to unleash some malcontented words upon paper and society. Not having a degree in english leaves me at a disadvantage. Writing was once just a hobby. Now I feel that it could be more. My dream is to someday have something, anything published. Whether it be a short story, prose, or novel. This is what I will work for. Working long taxing hours. Late hours as a waiter adds to the white noise that I call my meager existence. Okay, maybe it's not that bad. Actually every night is like a Saturday night. Women, alcohol, and fun. Words come with ease but I feel that they are unnoticed. Prose is the great escape. Shorts are, well like the silent fart of a mongoloid. All writing is enjoyable to me. My true passion is the working of a novel. Last week I embarked upon Blowjobs, Whiskey, and Steak. This is my arena. Believe me when I say that I will send you the work. You will not be able to ignore the way the words will speak to you. Safe to say that you have not heard the last of me. Yes I am in love with the word; it has never let me down. With this in mind I am ready for failure. I believe that a man or women can only be measured by their reaction to failure. So any words of encouragement, or even if you feel the need to rip me apart. It would be greatly appreciated. I would even settle for a list of other publishers in your area that might offer some advice. My expectations are low, but my writing is different. Thank you for your time. Hope to hear from you in the near future.

Not that "Pist" is a word—but I believe the conjugation would be "pissed."

English.

Don't offer information that you've never been published unless the publication specializes in unpublished writers or amateurs.

If the words in his story are anything like the query, count me out.

Michael Dismal

He didn't sign the letter.

Michael Dismal
14 Third Ave. #5
Greenhorn, R.I.
41251

E-mail me please
M_dis ail.com

Cell 204-555-5423
Home 204-555-7896

There was no SASE included. Our magazine is a 20-year-old award-winning literary magazine and his style would never fit in or be accepted. The writer did not read our guidelines. This is, by far, the most offensive and profane letter I have ever received. If the goal was to capture my attention and make me want to read the manuscript, the writer failed miserably. The query disgusted me. Period.

Comments provided by Winnie Wagaman, managing editor of *Antietam Review.*

Good

From: pampro@mail.com
To: pbennett@entrepreneur.com
Sent: April 5, 2002
Subject: Query

I like getting email queries, but many I receive are informal, with a simple "Hi" or similarly casual greeting. This greeting shows professionalism.

Pamela Professional
555-494-9338
123 Main Street, Success, NY 11234
pampro@email.com

Peggy Reeves Bennett
Entrepreneur Magazine
2445 McCabe Way
Irvine, CA 92614

Dear Ms. Reeves Bennett:

Compelling beginning that relates directly to our readers. Also, the query is based on recent important news events, which makes it more topical and relevant than typical queries.

Just when small business owners thought things couldn't get any worse, two planes crashed into New York City's World Trade Center, sending the economy into a tailspin and bringing many businesses to a screeching halt. The September 11 terrorist attack has displaced many small companies. Some expect to return to their offices soon. Others can only hope to piece back together a business that was largely destroyed by fire and debris. Some lost employees when the two towers collapsed.

She's obviously done some research on the topic, a big plus. I like specifics.

Although the U.S. Small Business Administration is still struggling to determine how many small companies have been affected by the attacks, it is clear that many were. The agency has already approved 134 disaster loans in New York, for a total of $13 million.

Well-written, intriguing profiles that would be inspiring to our readers. This gives me a good idea of her writing style, which fits well with our magazine's style.

Amidst the devastation, however, there are inspiring stories of entrepreneurs building their companies anew. More than two weeks after the attack, Michael Stevens was still locked out of his small law practice, just two blocks from where the World Trade Center once stood. He eventually "scammed" his way back into the building to recover backup tapes and other vital information. He forwarded his phones, recovered his files and setup temporary shop in a client's offices.

Christopher Keenan wasn't as lucky. His software company, ABC Designs, was located directly across from 7 World Trade Center. That building caught fire and collapsed—on top of Keenan's building, which was severely damaged and will likely be demolished. "We lost everything," he says. But even as he bemoaned the loss of equipment and data, Keenan pieced together source codes, new equipment and temporary office space. ABC Designs was up and running less than two weeks after the attack.

Widens the scope of the article for more impact. The sources she proposes are well thought-out and strong.

Would you be interested in a story about these business owners? I propose to profile Stevens, Keenan and one entrepreneur whose business was located in the World Trade Center. In addition to chronicling the challenges they faced and the solutions they implemented, I will provide general information about the breadth of the tragedy and the resources that city, state and federal agencies have made available to companies affected by the attack. I will also detail the help that has come from the small business community itself.

Includes an expert quote from a relevant source, further showing the depth of research she's put into the story. Very impressive.

"Business owners are a resilient bunch," says Kevin Ray, chief economist of the Small Business Agency, a small business advocacy group. "This is just an unthinkable, horrendous tragedy. But certainly folks that start up and build businesses are the types that can come back and do it again."

Adds her credentials, which I like to see, especially since it shows she's written specifically for our market in the past.

I have extensive experience writing about entrepreneurs. I am a former senior editor from *Opportunities* magazine, and my work has appeared in *The Wall Street Journal Interactive Edition*, *BusinessWeek Online*, *Monster.com* and other publications. I now write regularly for *Small Business Computing* magazine and work as an adjunct journalism professor at Long Island University. I am attaching a resume and several clips.

I believe this would be a compelling story; I hope you agree.

Sincerely,
Pamela Professional

Comments provided by Peggy Reeves Bennett, articles editor of *Entrepreneur* magazine.

Bad

Greeting shows she's put no time into finding out to whom she should send this query. This makes me think straight off that she hasn't made much effort to learn about *Entrepreneur* before sending the query.

From: AnnAwkward@email.com
Sent: Saturday, February 09, 2002
To: entmag@entrepreneur.com
Subject: Article Query

Dear Editor,
I am a published freelance writer working on an article for small business entitled: Ethical Conduct for Small Companies. The Enron debacle has caused a trickle down effect to small business and the concern for reevaluating business ethics and practices. I have solid background information including quotes from Business Information Services regarding common misconduct and first step initiatives to evaluating and developing a program, influences of ethical conduct from a source at New York School of Business Ethics, and recommendations for promoting good employee conduct. This article is being prepared for a small business newspaper in which I own all rights to my material. Therefore, I am wondering if you would be interested in pursing the piece as well. I will be glad to furnish other clips of my work too. I look forward to your reply.

The misspelling gives me doubts about her attention to detail. First-time query letters, in particular, should be letter perfect.

Ann Awkward

What does she mean by "I'm working on an article . . .?" Is it for someone else? Is it just an article she's writing which she then plans to throw out there for whoever will pick it up? These questions are answered at the end of the query, but it's a confusing start.

Awkwardly worded pitch makes me wonder whether the article will be as convoluted.

If she'd taken a minute to look at our Writer Guidelines (which are available online), she'd know we accept original submissions only. Again shows a lack of effort.

Comments provided by Peggy Reeves Bennett, articles editor of *Entrepreneur* magazine.

Good

Ms. Holly Taines White
Senior Editor
Ten Speed Press
P.O. Box 7123
Berkeley, CA 94707-2665

Has all the correct info.

Dear Holly:

RE: **Feng Shui Gourmet: A Guide to Entertaining that Awakens the Spirit** by Shelly Author and Mary Author

We had talked on the phone, but she still reminds me of the title and provides a good, succinct description of the book.

I'm delighted to send you *Feng Shui Gourmet* by Shelly Author and Mary Author per your recent request. This unique and sumptuous book is a guide to entertaining with seasonal theme dinners designed to ensure health and good fortune for friends and family. The table settings and gracious mealtime rituals are inspired by Feng Shui, the Chinese art of placement, while the delectable dinner party menus with recipes incorporate a gourmet whole foods cooking approach.

Excellent background info on authors. Includes only relevant credentials.

Shelly Author is one of the few Americans who has mastered multiple Feng Shui traditions, and clients include IKEA, Smith & Hawken, Whole Foods Market as well as other national corporations. Mary Author, formerly of *Natural Cooking* magazine, has authored three cookbooks. Her most recent book, *Natural Vegetarian*, won the London World Cookbook Fair Award for Best Vegetarian Cookbook in English for 2001.

Good to know up front that these are publicity-inclined authors.

Good to know they have a thought-through vision of a completed book.

With their exceptional connections in the healing arts and cuisine markets, the authors are committed to actively participating in publicizing and marketing this book. They envision an illustrated volume, but are open to a discussion of the visual component of the book.

There is nothing else like this book on the market; I hope you will consider publishing *Feng Shui Gourmet*. I look forward to hearing from you.

Best regards,

Polite closing.

Andrea Agent
andreaagent@aol.com
(999) 555-1212

Great to have quick contact info included for easy follow-up.

Overall, a well-organized, effective letter that tells you what the book is and who the authors are. No extraneous info, and includes everything necessary.

Comments provided by Holly Taines White, senior editor with Ten Speed Press.

Ms. Holly Taines White
Senior Editor
Ten Speed Press
P.O. Box 7123
Berkeley, CA 94707

Just about the most offensive salutation to send a female editor.

Dear Sirs:

The Orion Foundation is a not-for-profit charity and research foundation in Virginia focusing on holistic health care. The therapeutic interest is the negative effect of the facial-oracular system on the mastication system.

Appears he's proposing a medical book, which we don't do—he didn't do his research.

The relationship of these two systems can be compromised as a result of disturbances in the connective tissue medium within which the nerves are imbedded. The mode of assessing and treating this compromise is accomplished with a system called Orapathy.

Medical speak. Not written for a lay audience.

Orapathy is not as widely known as are other expressions of health care but this is changing. Orapathy is well known in Asia, especially China. There are schools in Beijing, Tokyo, and in Los Angeles.

Why would we publish a book on an unknown subject? No audience.

Orapathy was first put into use in 1938. I have been in active practice since 1984. Along with maintaining communication with orapaths ~~and other~~ health care practitioners throughout the world, I ~~have been~~ a former dean of academics and instructor at the Los Angeles school. I have also written a series of articles and a book on the subject. This is the reason for my contact with you.

Does the school have a name?

First mention of why he's writing. Too deep into letter, and he doesn't explain what the book is. Plus, Ten Speed Press doesn't publish articles.

I am interested in publication of the book and articles. I think if the public had some awareness of the clinical benefit of this great profession, there would be an intense desire to know as much as they could.

Please let me know if I may offer further information.

Thank you for your consideration.

No, the public won't buy a book on something they've never heard of. Need an audience, then a book.

Yours sincerely,

Dr. John Smith, D.O.
Doctor of Orapathy

Overall odd writing style and totally inappropriate subject for Ten Speed Press. Never describes the book and hasn't defined his audience.

Comments provided by Holly Taines White, senior editor with Ten Speed Press.

The Four R's of Freelancing: Refocus, Rework, Rewrite, and Recycle

BY GLORIA BURKE

Freelance success is a very personal matter. Learning the little quirks and nuances that lead to bylines requires practice, but practice can help get your writing off the computer page and where you want it to be—in an editor's hands. Freelancing depends on you; no one else can do it for you. Here are ten tips to help you refocus, rework, rewrite, and recycle—the four "R's" of freelancing.

1. If you don't have it already, you need to develop a strong sense of curiosity.

You want to know "just because." There doesn't have to be any other reason. The payoff is when this curiosity leads to a publishable piece. The freelancer digs deep, always looking for that fresh, new approach that will make his work stand out among all the rest.

2. Write "flexible" on your forehead, keeping an open mind about your writing.

Regularly scan the pages of magazines and newspapers for which you'd like to write. Keep clippings of articles that strike a particular chord for future idea reference.

3. Tailor-write to fit the needs of the publication you have in mind.

Be sensitive to audience and style, constantly aware that following the publication's lead enhances your chances of getting published. Recognize that the way articles are written is often a dead giveaway of reader age range, education, and socioeconomic status. For example, the regular *Atlantic Monthly* or *Smithsonian* reader may have a different background from someone who regularly reads *Cosmopolitan* and *Redbook*. Study the markets just as you would study to pass an exam.

4. Be write smart. Refocus. Rework. Rewrite. Recycle.

Once you've made a sale, however small, refocus the article by giving it a different angle and targeting a different audience. If you aimed it at the senior reader in its original form, try rewriting it for the 30-somethings. Rework it by editing and re-editing over and over again. Recycle it by earmarking it for another market. Rewrite it again to try for resale in a different geographical area.

5. Keep a small spiral notebook with you at all times.

Keeping a notebook by your side allows you to jot down a few key words and phrases as soon as that creative idea hits. Keep the notebook at your bedside to record inspiration that often

---

GLORIA BURKE *has been published in* Mature Living, Bend of the River, Sylvania Advantage, Woman's World, *and the* Toledo Blade. *She has been teaching "Writing Your Memories" for over ten years as well as other courses related to freelance writing.*

awakens us in the wee small hours. Ideas can be so elusive; if you let them get away, they may never be remembered.

6. Don't overlook your lifetime memories as a source for ideas.

Go back and think about the people who have crossed your path, the places you've been, and the events you've experienced. Keep a written memory bank in the form of notes, even stories, articles, or anecdotes, about those people, places, and events. Make regular "deposits" in your memory bank so you can withdraw new ideas.

7. If you can't think of anything to write about, write anyhow.

Get into detective mode. Put on your trench coat, dark glasses, and get out the magnifying glass. Go to your clipping file or memory bank to find fresh ideas. Writing requires practice. You never know when a "practice" session with your yellow legal pad or computer keyboard will develop into a publishable article.

8. Don't let your computer be the only tool in your house to say, "You've got mail!"

Keep a minimum of three queries in your outgoing snail mail at all times. Then, if a rejection slip does come, you've got at least two other queries to fall back on.

9. Teach yourself how to self-critique, how to stand back from your own work and look at it objectively.

Read your writing out loud to hear the sounds of the words as they're strung together, listening for repetitive words and phrases. Be ruthless if a sentence doesn't seem to fit. No matter how creative your words may sound, don't clutch them to your bosom. If they don't belong, get rid of them. Put the piece away for a few days, then take it out and psyche yourself up by saying, "I'm going to look at this with fresh eyes."

10. If you get a rejection slip, regroup.

You're not the first one to receive a rejection slip, and you won't be the last. Go back to the four "R's"—refocus, rework, rewrite, and recycle. Improve. Change. Do whatever you need to do, but get the piece out there again. Be write smart.

Insider Tips for Tapping Online Markets

BY ANTHONY TEDESCO

Yes, the Internet often seems to be all hype and hopes, continually projected to deliver infinite everything—eventually. But I hereby do solemnly swear: There's nothing virtual or pending about online writing markets. They're here now and they're real, featuring real editors with real checks, which can really be cashed for money. (Real money.) You just need to know how to adapt your print-writing skills to the online-publishing world. The following online writers and editors are here to help.

ELLEN ULLMAN

Former Editorial Director, Online Services of *Princeton Review Online*

"Online writing needs to be snappy and exciting because it's harder to read on computer screens, and I think much harder to retain the information you read. So you need to write in a very conversational, friendly, and upbeat way. Use provocative leads, short paragraphs, and lots of subheads to break up the text and make it easier on the eyes."

DEBBIE RIDPATH OHI

Online writer

"The Internet has enormous networking and research potential; invest the time to explore the possibilities. Check out newsgroups, discussion mailing lists, online writing groups, and live chats. Learn proper 'netiquette' and always read guidelines before posting a message that will be read by many people. If you're surfing the Web for research information, be efficient. Take the time to learn how to properly use several good search engines. Also, don't assume that all information you find online is accurate: Always verify the source. If you're using URLs or specific Internet information in your article (e.g., names of mailing lists, newsgroups), be sure to double-check spellings before submitting the final copy. Websites and other Internet-based sources frequently move and disappear, and editors are likely to be unimpressed if they receive an article in which half the URLs prove to be defunct. They're bound to wonder how much other information in your article is also outdated."

ALICE BRADLEY

Former Editor of *Charged.com*

"You should have a general sense of what the design for the story will be. Think of how the text will look on the site. What should be hyperlinked? Should it have simultaneous narratives?

ANTHONY TEDESCO *(anthony@marketsforwriters.com) is co-author of* Online Markets for Writers: How to Make Money By Selling Your Writing on the Internet (Holt) *and publisher of MarketsForWriters .com, a free Web resource to help writers live off of the writing they love.*

Should it have a left-side frame with links to specific paragraphs? Could it be a choose-your-own-adventure piece? It obviously depends on what piece you're talking about, but the format should direct your story to some extent. Ideally, you and a producer would determine together what kind of format fits the story, and you would write it accordingly. Long, linear stories will make for a boring design—or a story that has been totally rewritten by an editor."

KIMBERLY HILL

Online writer

"Spend the time to keep up with technology. Put the time it takes into learning about the online world and the software tools you'll need to be competent as an online writer."

GARY WELZ

Online writer

"Although writers need to be compensated accordingly, it can be quite beneficial to have your online articles archived by the publication and available to readers forever. It's even worth setting up your own web page with your clips and credentials—whether or not you've ever been published online. Print articles run for their month and then that's usually it—they're out of the public eye. But I've received so many opportunities from editors and companies who came across a past online article of mine, or who did an Internet search on a certain subject and my name and article came up—even for articles that I wrote a long time ago. With archived articles, I'm also able to query new online markets with URLs pointing to my previous clips. Get out and meet editors. Sure, you could conduct business entirely through e-mail, but meeting people face-to-face is still extremely important. Build some rapport. Go to events and conferences, and introduce yourself to people. It's a huge advantage to have an editor put a face with your name."

MELISSA WEINER

Former Editor of *Swoon.com*

"The Web's interactivity is what distinguishes it from print. For example, you can search for inexpensive airline fares in seconds or check out your investments at a glance. While you are not going to produce a database of inexpensive airline fares or stock market feeds, you can come up with short, interactive, and easy-to-implement features. Depending on the site, quizzes, games, forums, links, or interactive polls might be the way to go. Each content site has its own idea of interactivity and user experience. Keep the value of the Web's immediate return in mind when you are developing your pitches, and determine the focus of the site you are pitching so your stories fit accordingly. Since a good website is not simply an electronic version of your favorite print magazine, coming up with pieces for an online publication requires a different thought process. Take a step back and think about what you would go online to read."

BRUCE MIRKEN

Online writer

"In my experience, good writing is good writing, and good editors—online or print—will appreciate it. All of the things that print editors appreciate—timeliness, queries that are appropriate for the market you're approaching, etc.—apply here as well."

Columnist Adair Lara Stresses Honesty, Humor

BY WILL ALLISON

Readers might be surprised to learn that columnist and memoirist Adair Lara considers herself to be shy. After all, twice a week, she opens her life to half a million readers in her award-winning personal column on the back page of the *San Francisco Chronicle*.

In the tradition of personal essayists, Lara's columns frequently seek truth through the small details and events of daily living. "A woman once told me that I have made her think that ordinary life has a lot of meaning in it," says Lara. "I loved that."

Photo by Deborah Feingold

Adair Lara

Lara was born in San Francisco and raised in Marin County, one of seven children. She's married to Bill LeBlond, a cookbook editor for Chronicle Books, and has two children, Patrick, 22, and Morgan, 23. She became a staff columnist for the *Chronicle* in 1989 and one year later was named best California columnist by the Associated Press. Since then, she has won numerous awards in the categories of humor, general interest, and commentary.

Lara is also the author of five books, including three collections of columns—*Welcome to Earth, Mom* (Chronicle Books, 1992), *At Adair's House: More Columns from America's Favorite Former Single Mom* (Chronicle Books, 1995), and *The Best of Adair Lara: Prize Winning Columns from the San Francisco Chronicle* (Scottwall Associates, 1999)—and *Slowing Down in a Speeded Up World* (Conari Press, 1994), which has been translated into five languages. Her latest book, *Hold Me Close, Let Me Go* (Broadway Books, 2001), is a memoir of raising a teenaged daughter.

Her work has appeared in many newspapers and magazines including *Cosmopolitan*, *Reader's Digest*, *Working Mother*, *Child*, *Parenting*, *Glamour*, *Redbook*, *Ladies' Home Journal*, *American Woman*, *Departures*, *Health*, *Westways*, *American Way*, *Via*, *Fitness*, and *Good Housekeeping*. She teaches first-person writing workshops at UC Berkeley Extension, at Book Passage, a bookstore in Corte Madera, California, at conferences, and in private seminars.

How did you become a columnist?

I started by freelancing for the Sunday paper, selling short humor pieces, mainly about my kids. After three years of that, they hired me on staff. I had to write ten sample columns for them.

What makes a good personal column?

The writing charms and diverts you, the story interests you, and the point the writer is making gives you a moment of tenderness toward your own struggles. The writing has to be good. As columnist Mark Patinkin said, "Write a mediocre third-person feature and people will turn the page. Write a mediocre first-person column and people will say, 'What an imbecile.'"

WILL ALLISON *(willalliso@aol.com) is former editor at large of* Zoetrope: All-Story, *former executive editor of* Story, *and former editor of* Novel & Short Story Writer's Market.

It has to be honest. If you're writing about teenage smoking, then you talk about your own 16-year-old nicotine addict. No soapboxes—just one ordinary person saying, "This is what happened to me, and this is what I think it means." When you write from your private store of images and associations, no one can argue with you. When you write about how it felt when you had an abortion yourself at 17, no one can say you didn't have the experience you say you had and that you don't feel about it the way you say you do. You learn to offer the reader the evidence of your own mistakes, regrets, and weirdnesses.

You write about the time your friend called saying she had cancer, and you waited until the next day to call her back. And humor—you gotta have that. Humor is defined as the difference between the way things are and the way things ought to be.

How long does it typically take you to finish a column, and how do you know when it's done?

I don't write one at a sitting, but over a period of days or weeks or even months, revisiting it the way a painter revisits a canvas, to add a stroke here or there. I suppose if I added up all the time I spent on a given column, it would be five or six hours. I've been at this 12 years, so I don't go down as many wrong roads as I used to. My fastest column (about the bombing in Omagh) took 20 minutes, and the slowest (about my high school reunion) took two years. I can be very stubborn, a quality I think is essential for a writer, given all the ego discouragement of the trade. The fastest ones are the best ones. I know a column is done when I notice myself changing things back to the way they were a draft or so ago.

Does the often autobiographical nature of your column pose particular challenges?

I have learned through painful experience to be careful when mentioning other people, relatives and such. I show people what I'm saying before it goes in and routinely change names. When my kids were little I'd give them $20 for a column if it was all about them. Nothing for incidental mentions. Then my parents started clamoring to be paid.

What for you is the most difficult aspect of writing?

Going out, making telephone calls to strangers. Since it's a personal column, I don't have to do it much, but when I do, I have to whip myself to pick up the phone. Also, writing a column can be like feeding a fire—I toss a column in, it's instantly devoured, and the fire must be fed again, by 4 p.m. every Tuesday and every Friday. I always feel the heat of that fire on my back, so I am never truly not working.

And what's the easiest part?

Sitting at a desk. I can do that all day, no problem. Also I have a nice workday—a five-second commute to my office at home, lots of time to fiddle, take the dog for a walk. I am never not working, but I'm also seldom truly at work.

Any tips on writing humor?

Unlikely comparisons can make great humorous angles. I once compared having a boyfriend to having a fern. "If you leave town for a day or two, the fern will simply use the time to put out new fronds, or to see how many leaves it can drop on the rug, or experiment with leaning over in arresting new postures. It will not call up an old girlfriend and get itself invited to dinner." Or take a statement literally: When I asked my 9-year-old where his homework was, he said, "Somebody stole it. It was right in my pocket." In the piece, I say that his statement made me shiver. "We live in the Duboce Triangle in San Francisco. With several schools nearby, it's a favorite turf of the dread spelling-homework gangs. . . ."

Humor comes from a good angle, from word choice, and from tone. (Phillip Lopate refers to this as "the need to assert a quite specific temperament.") When Laura Blumfeld begins a piece by saying, "I was speaking with two female friends recently, and in an instant came face-to-face with the odious beast that is my soul," the words "odious beast" establish a humorous, self-deprecating tone that draws the reader in. Humor also comes from exaggeration, not of circumstances, but of your own emotions. If you have the flu, you are not merely feeling unwell: You are near death and in fact have become anxious that whoever handles your funeral will get everything wrong. Lots of very specific detail—brands, names, all that—also adds to humor.

Do you ever find the length limitations of a newspaper column restrictive?

I've learned to have 700-word ideas. Longer themes seem to get worked out in successive columns, so there's no problem with not getting everything said.

With two columns a week (and after all these years) do you ever worry about running out of material?

Indeed. Yes. I'm not so much worried about repeating stories, as life delivers new stories every day—but I worry about repeating my take on them. Everybody knows I am nuts about San Francisco, that Bill is a neatnik, Morgan used to be wild, Dad was charming but no good. I have gotten halfway through a column before realizing I wrote it already, years ago. The solution to this problem is to expand what I do, get out more. But I'm shy.

Do you receive much feedback from readers?

Yes, quite a bit, especially since it became policy to put e-mail addresses at the end of every piece. My mail is mostly positive, as I don't write much on controversial topics, but I still find I have to throw out the top and bottom 20 percent of responses on the assumption they're probably triggered by something entirely different than what I wrote. You mention a Suzy Homemaker oven and they love you. You say "awoke" instead of "awakened," and they worry about your education.

And how would you characterize your relationship with your readers?

I would call it a deep and abiding friendship. I have told them so much, and they have told me so much. They know my weirdnesses, my little collection of quirks and complaints and passions, and I know theirs. A young reader pointed out the other day that it works the way an AA meeting does. You confess your drinking sins, and no one comments—they just tell their own stories.

What books or authors would you recommend to writers of personal narrative?

I just discovered a wonderful book called *Writing Fiction* by Janet Burroway. It's a college textbook and is excellent. Phillip Lopate's *The Art of the Personal Essay.* Anne Lamott's *Bird by Bird.*

What's your best piece of advice for budding personal columnists?

Take lots of classes. The teachers give interesting assignments and can help you improve your skills. The class itself fosters a sense of a writing community and allows you to find good writing partners (I'm a big believer in writing partners). And don't wait for editors to break into your living room and demand to see some of your work. Start sending work out to local publications, not overlooking the free ones, the neighborhood shopping guides, anything. When you're ready, put together ten sample columns, and send them around to newspapers, asking if they'd like to run your stuff regularly. Pay no attention at first to whether you get paid or how much—that all comes later.

Adair Lara can be reached in care of Scottwall Associates (publisher of *The Best of Adair Lara*) at scotwall@pacbell.net or online through the *San Francisco Chronicle* (www.sfgate.com).

Novelist Karen Joy Fowler Blurs the Lines Between Genre and Literary Writing

BY WILL ALLISON

Is a background in genre writing a liability for a mainstream novelist, or is it an asset? For Karen Joy Fowler, whose body of work encompasses everything from science fiction and fantasy to literary historical fiction, it's both.

Photo by Kelly Link

Karen Joy Fowler

"On a bad day, I feel I've chosen to be second string in two fields when I could have been first string in one," she says. "On a good day I feel my work has benefitted from the cross-pollination, and nothing matters as much as the quality of the work itself."

First-rate writing is the characteristic that links Fowler's otherwise far-ranging books, which resist the tidy classifications of the publishing industry. Her books include *Artificial Things* (Bantam, 1986) and *Black Glass* (Henry Holt, 1998), two story collections that blend elements of realism, fantasy, and science fiction. Fowler is also the author of three critically acclaimed novels, all with historical settings: the fantastical *Sarah Canary* (Henry Holt, 1991), the somewhat less fantastical romantic comedy *The Sweetheart Season* (Henry Holt, 1996), and the literary urban novel, *Sister Noon* (Putnam, 2001), which was nominated for the 2002 Pen/Faulkner Award for Fiction.

You've said that your childhood move from Bloomington, Indiana, to Palo Alto, California, left you "devastated." Has that move influenced you as a writer?

Without question. I was 11 years old, which I now understand is the usual age at which things go bad anyway, but since I moved I associate all my adolescent troubles with that [moving] instead. I have, I imagine, an unrealistically rosy nostalgia about Bloomington as a place of fireflies, unfenced yards, sudden thunderstorms, huge neighborhood games of capture the flag, backyard baseball, sledding and snowballs, school fairs, iced lemonade. In Palo Alto, life was more confined, more of an indoor affair. I lived there seven years, and I never got comfortable. My dad had left IU for a corporate job, but he was a scientist, and there was pressure to produce experimental results pleasing to the corporate underwriters. He was unwilling to do this, and it all ended very badly. So it wasn't merely the schoolyard situation that changed; within my family things became tense and unhappy. Much of the impetus for my writing, I think, is a response to the losses of this period. I find myself particularly moved by stories in which children (or their animal stand-ins, I confess it, I'm an enormous sap) are taken from their happy homes. Such stories, of course, abound. I've recently finished a lot of Joan Aiken's books for children, very satisfying in this and every other regard.

WILL ALLISON *(willalliso@aol.com) is former editor at large for* Zoetrope: All-Story. *His latest short story appeared in* Shenandoah.

You decided to become a writer on your thirtieth birthday. Do you feel like you got a late start?

I feel this was a very late start; I often look at writers who are my same age as calculated in writer years, and they're all so young; I can't help but find this rude. On the other hand I don't think I was capable of starting any earlier. I was so terrified of failure and exposure. Until I was 30 I wasn't nearly tough or interesting enough. And I put those years to good use. I raised two children. They turned out swell, so I have no regrets. They could be more punctual. So could my books.

Who are some of the writers whose work you admire?

I admire so many writers. You haven't given me nearly enough space to list them. I admire Dr. Seuss. I feel he's the one writer of our times certain to still be read a hundred years from now. In response to his death, I wrote a scene at a dinner party where, in his honor, all conversation had to rhyme. Unfortunately, I've no context into which this scene fits.

Unlike many authors who write year-round, you used to write in the fall and winter, and teach in the spring and summer. What's your writing schedule these days?

I am trying to cut back on my teaching this year to see if I can do as so many others, and finish the first draft of a novel in about 12 months. It's an experiment. So many of the people I love in my life and so many opportunities have come through my teaching, I don't really want to give it up. And I always need the steadier paycheck.

But I want to write faster. I have a novel idea I really feel eager about (suggested by my daughter, one of those two great kids referred to above). My usual progress is snail paced, and I feel this novel deserves better.

In his book *Writing Life Stories*, Bill Roorbach refers to research as "a creative process." Is this true for you? In what ways does research shape your books?

I love research. I love dusty books and mind-numbing microfiche. I love to take cramped notes in thin-lined spiral notebooks and tell the people at Bogey's, my local used bookstore, what I'm after so they'll be on the lookout for me. Generally my research has been into historical periods, so what I'm trying to do is see the world of my novel vividly through newspaper accounts and photographs and maps (I love maps—someday I want maps on the frontis pages of all my books. Is that so much to ask?) and diaries.

Then I draw on the energy of the surprises I've found while researching to keep me interested in the parts of the piece I'm actually inventing. As a general rule, the more outlandish and unlikely something in my books appears to be, the greater the odds are that I didn't make it up.

What's the most rewarding aspect of writing historical fiction?

Time travel.

Do you think in terms of genre as you're writing?

Not as part of the creative process. More as an interested observer, noting whatever is happening in the particular piece with which I'm engaged.

You've referred to *Sister Noon* as "relentlessly mainstream." Were you making a conscious decision to move away from elements of science fiction and fantasy?

I have not made a conscious decision, but it has been happening to me a little bit at a time. *The Sweetheart Season* has fewer genre elements than *Sarah Canary*, and *Sister Noon* none at all. *Sister Noon* is my first urban novel, and I discovered while writing it that my usual source of the fantastic is in the natural world. There was less scope for this sort of magic in the city, even when the city was San Francisco. I was also hampered by the steady stream of occultists in *Sister Noon*. There are palm and tea-leaf readers, mediums, and doomsayers, and to introduce an actual element of the fantastic seemed to me to credit these characters more than I wished to.

Finally, the historical data was muddied enough; I didn't think the novel could survive more mystery from any source whatever.

But perhaps the next will require magic again. Too early to tell.

Do you think the multiple-genre range of your books has helped or hurt your career?

Helped and hurt. My first audience was in science fiction, and many of those readers have been gratifyingly loyal. My closest friends include many of the writers in that field, and I try to keep up with what is being written there.

But many readers specialize absolutely. They never stray out of, or they never stray into, the science fiction/fantasy aisle of the bookstore. I'm likely to lose on both sides, therefore—by readers who won't touch science fiction and hear rumors that I've been tainted by it, and by readers who won't touch anything else and hear I'm not writing it anymore. Certainly it's been an issue that's followed me throughout my career.

You once told an interviewer, "I think I'm hilarious as a writer, not difficult and brooding as critics say." How important is it to be hilarious?

I need be no funnier than Jane Austen. I mean, I don't have to be show-offy about it. Just devastatingly witty.

Over the years and books, how have you changed as a writer?

When I was a child, I would read books and forget who and where I was. It would actually surprise me to be called to dinner. It's harder for me to become so absolutely involved as an adult reader, and I doubt I have the skill to pull it off as a writer, but it's what I want, so why not aim for it? As a result, I've become obsessed with setting. I used to think of telling a story—something happens to someone. Now I think first of creating a world.

And I want the world to be greater than the story I'm telling inside it. I want always to acknowledge the fact of the bigger world, the natural world, going about its business, oblivious to the story I'm telling. Having its own story.

Joy Johannessen Offers Tips on Working with Freelance Editors

BY WILL ALLISON

If you've ever considered hiring a freelance editor to help you turn your manuscript into a bestseller, don't. No editor can promise such results. However, there are times when the help of a good freelancer can pay big dividends. In the following interview, freelance editor Joy Johannessen provides insights into her work and offers tips that will help you determine whether you might benefit from a freelance editor's help.

Like most of the best freelance editors, Johannessen is a publishing veteran. She's been a senior editor at Chelsea House, Grove Press, and HarperCollins Publishers, and a development editor at Oxford University Press. Most recently she was editor of Delphinium Books, a small press primarily devoted to new writers and literary fiction. She has edited hundreds of writers, including Dorothy Allison, Amy Bloom, Harold Bloom, Rebecca Brown, Christopher Browning, Susan Brownmiller, Nien Cheng, Ellis Cose, Vicki Hearne, Anita Hill, Ursula Le Guin, Bia Lowe, Arthur Miller, Larry Rivers, Clancy Sigal, and Anthony Storr.

How did you become a freelance editor?

I began freelancing after I moved to a part of Connecticut largely populated by cows and too remote for commuting. What I've always liked best about being an editor is working closely with writers on their manuscripts—something I had less and less time to do at my various jobs in New York publishing—so in that respect freelancing suits me. What I miss, of course, is being able to publish a manuscript I've fallen in love with.

What kinds of projects do you handle?

Early in my career I worked almost exclusively on nonfiction of all kinds, from cookbooks to memoirs to scholarly treatises, but for the last decade I've mainly been editing fiction, and that's my preference these days. I used to take on a lot of projects from publishing houses, but most of my current clients are writers whom I've met at conferences, or who've come to me through recommendations from agents or other writers.

How do you typically charge for your work?

My strong preference is to charge by the hour, and to give an estimate of the minimum and maximum times the job will take. Occasionally I'll quote a flat fee if the demands and scope of the job are very clear both to me and to the client.

What can your clients expect when they hire you for a project?

I'm sometimes asked to evaluate a manuscript or proposal and write an editorial letter, and in that case the client can expect my most thoughtful assessment of the strengths and weaknesses of the manuscript as a piece of writing. Most often I'm hired to edit a completed manuscript,

---

WILL ALLISON *(willalliso@aol.com) is former editor at large for* Zoetrope: All-Story, *a staff member of the Squaw Valley Community of Writers, and former executive editor of* Story.

and in that case the client can expect meticulous line editing, along with my best advice about every aspect of the work: structure, organization, pace, narrative continuity, character development, dialogue—whatever elements may be involved.

What my clients cannot expect is a marketing strategy. I'm not in the business of telling writers what to do to make their work more "publishable," since I don't presume to know. In my view, a piece of writing becomes more publishable by becoming the best piece of writing it can be, on its own terms, not by being tailored to some editor's idea, or even the writer's own idea, of what will sell.

When is a freelance editor worth the money?

A good editor is a good investment whenever you want a trusted second eye on your work, for any reason. Here are some particularly good reasons.

1. You have an agent who believes that your manuscript can be placed if it's tighter, cleaner, better paced, better organized, or if it has a stronger opening or a stronger ending or a stronger middle, or whatever the case may be, but you haven't been able to do the necessary work yourself.
2. An agent or editor has expressed strong interest in representing you or publishing you but thinks your manuscript needs to be tighter, cleaner, better paced, etc. By "strong interest" I don't mean the kind of vague praise often encountered in rejection letters. I mean clear and specific indications that the agent or editor is very likely to take you on if you improve your manuscript.
3. You're trying your hand at a particular genre—mystery, science fiction, historical fiction—and you want the guidance of an editor versed in the requirements of that genre.
4. You want to work on your manuscript for its own sake, to make it the best piece of writing it can be, but you've done all the revising you can do on your own. Perhaps you already have a book under contract, and you want editorial attention that your publishing house isn't providing. Or perhaps you simply want to experience the give-and-take of the editorial process and see what an editor might suggest. I've heard writers say that they've learned more from working with a good editor than from courses, workshops, or even M.F.A. programs.

. . . And when is a freelance editor not worth the money?

In my opinion, you're wasting your money if you expect the editor's work to guarantee you an agent or a contract. No editor, no matter how skilled, can make that kind of guarantee. Nor are you likely to get your money's worth if you find yourself resisting the editor's suggestions or hooting with laughter at the marginal notes or wincing at the line editing. Not that you have to agree with everything the editor recommends, but you do have to trust the editor's overall judgment and ear for language. Some writers tell me that a good rule of thumb is this: When the editor thinks there's something wrong, you can see that there is something wrong, even if you disagree with the editor about the exact nature of the problem or the solution.

When you approach a freelance editor, it makes sense to ask if he or she will do a sample chapter or story or section (for which you'll pay the editor's going rate) before undertaking the entire project. That way both of you can get a good idea of what the working relationship will be like, and how long the project will actually take.

How do you go about finding a good freelance editor?

Talk to other writers. As in much of life, word of mouth is often your best bet.

What advice can you offer to writers who'd like to become freelance editors themselves?

Don't, unless you have very good reason to believe that you're a very good editor of other people's writing and that the work won't interfere with your own writing. Freelance editing isn't something to undertake simply as a way of supplementing your income, since it isn't particularly lucrative, especially when you're starting out. If you feel drawn to try it despite these caveats, pull every string you've got, and try to land a job editing a published or about-to-be-published writer, which is probably the quickest way to establish your credentials.

Joy Johannessen's e-mail address is Norskjoy@aol.com.

The Best Expert Advice from WritersMarket.com

WritersMarket.com has thousands of extra market listings that the print edition of *Writer's Market* just can't fit between the front and back covers. However, you probably didn't know there are hundreds of extra articles and insider advice located online. Besides the monthly Agent Q&A feature, WritersMarket.com also features a new marketing tip each week.

Many of these tips have been linked and/or reprinted in various websites, electronic magazines, and newsletters. They've garnered a lot of praise in the past year from writers, agents, publishers, and editors. In fact, the highly respected Preditors & Editors website awarded WritersMarket.com an Editor's Choice award based solely on the articles.

Here are five of the best pieces from the site during the past year. All of the articles in this section were posted on WritersMarket.com between August 2001 and January 2002. The styles of the articles range from a feature piece to Q&A to how-to. Each of the articles are informative and intended to help you get writing, get published, and get paid.

Writing for TV: Sandy Siegel Tells Her Own Tales from the Script

BY VANESSA LYMAN

Hollywood. Tinseltown. Land of the Stars. Factory of Dreams. And that inexhaustible supply of cash. How does a writer break in, steal his portion of the silver screen, and make a mad dash for it?

Hollywood survivor Sandy Siegel has been a scriptwriter for over 20 years. She's written for *Laverne and Shirley, Facts of Life, The Love Boat,* a short-lived soap opera called *Sunset Beach,* as well as writing the "Tales from Tinseltown" column on the now defunct Themestream.com. Scriptwriting is very difficult to break into, and Siegel is willing to tell this to aspiring writers.

For example, the average scriptwriter in Hollywood is between the ages of 21 and 35. Siegel addresses this fact frankly. "I hate to say this, but if you're over 30 and just trying to get started, it's really tough. And if you don't have a hit series or a good movie before you're 40, your chances of having that happen are next to nil," she says. "Hollywood is very ageist. There is a pending lawsuit right now, a class action lawsuit, against a lot of studios and agencies. It'll be interesting to see what's going to happen with this, but I don't think [the industry] is going to change."

Why do studios give preference to younger writers? "The audience they're going after is very young. [The studios] don't feel that older people can understand those problems or get the language or the attitude right. They gear TV shows to younger people, but who really buys the product?" Siegel picks a car company as an example of the typical advertising sponsor. The younger audience, she says, isn't buying Buicks. "The whole thing doesn't make a lot of sense."

Still, if you've only begun to develop an interest in TV scriptwriting in your teens or 20s, that might not be good enough. Childhood TV viewing, and lots of it, is the true path to a future in scriptwriting, and Siegel's training was top rate. "I'm part of that first generation of TV viewers. I grew up on a steady diet of *Leave It to Beaver, The Donna Reed Show, Father Knows Best*, and *My Three Sons*, and later things like *Laugh-in.* I just loved it," Siegel says. "Also, living in Los Angeles, everywhere you go, you see stars. You're kind of immersed in that. I think I was just a star-struck little kid." When she was a teenager, Siegel began to write. At first, it was little things like funny poems or jokes for a particular program. "I just thought, 'Well, I'm gonna be a writer!' It didn't strike me that I couldn't be."

After graduating from college, Siegel took secretarial positions in the industry and kept writing, but by then she was writing spec scripts to show studios. "When you're young, nothing stops you. If I was 21 or 22 and someone like me was saying what I'm saying now, I would have laughed and said, 'Leave me alone. *I'm* going to do it, *I'm* going to make it.' Which is how it should be."

A childhood diet of sitcoms and a determined postgraduate attitude will get a writer far in Hollywood, but there's nothing like plain old-fashioned persistence. "And thick skin. You have to be able to take rejection because you're going to get a lot of it. If you read this interview and think, 'Oh, this is negative, maybe I shouldn't go into the business,' you shouldn't. You have

---

VANESSA LYMAN *is assistant editor of* Poet's Market *and* Novel & Short Story Writer's Market.

to say, 'You know what? I'm gonna defy the odds.'" After a moment, Siegel adds, "Talent helps, too. And connections. That's a real big one."

BREAKING INTO THE MARKET

There are two basic ways to operate as a scriptwriter in Los Angeles. You can be a staff writer on a show, or you can freelance. Even though there are more outlets for scripts, there are far fewer freelance opportunities than when Siegel began writing 20 years ago. The cable and pay channels may have added a slew of hit series, but these shows are very difficult to write for. Siegel mentions that several shows are, in essence, written and produced by one person.

As a way to break in, Siegel recommends writing movie scripts rather than writing spec scripts for TV episodes. That, and living in Los Angeles. "Every other person in L.A. is a screenwriter, and every other one is an actor," Siegel says. "Even though a lot of production is in Canada, the hub is still here. It's hard to miss [the industry] here."

Siegel admits that it's become easier for a scriptwriter to live outside California because of the Internet; online "scriptbrokers" allow you to post a script synopsis, and if a producer or director or maybe an agent wants to read it, you can be contacted. This brings us back to writing spec scripts for movies. "You can't really do that with an episode. They're not going onto the Internet to look for someone who can write an episode. But they're always looking for a good movie idea."

Siegel explains that it's easier for a writer to break into movies and, from there, into TV. TV producers look for youthful yet experienced writers, a tricky combination to find. "In movies, if a screenplay is good and it's castable and can make a lot of money, they don't really care what your credits are."

Whereas TV is a tight market. "There are tons of [movie] production companies out there, there are independent production companies out there, there are people with money who want to get into the business . . . There are just more outlets for a screenplay. Plus, there are contests you can enter. Several writers in town got started by winning contests."

If writing for the big screen so that one day you can aspire to the small screen seems backward, who ever said Hollywood isn't convoluted? "It used to be that a lot of movie writers didn't want to write for television," but they were attracted by steady paychecks (a hit series always is able to earn more than a hit movie) and the immediacy of TV (a matter of months to produce a show, a matter of years to produce a film).

There's also the allure of more creative control. Siegel explains that writers have little say in movies; "that's the director's medium. Television is a producer's medium, and most producers started as writers."

FREELANCING VS. STAFF WRITING

Being a staff writer on a hit series is an enviable position, but freelance work, if you can find it, has its attractions. The pay for either is, quite honestly, very good. One half-hour episode—"45 pages, double-spaced"—can continue to earn money farther down the line. "If you're on a hit series, you will get about 70 percent [of the original fee] for a prime time repeat. We also get residuals in perpetuity, which means that wherever it plays, whenever it plays, you will get something."

Writers also receive clip fees if another show (an A&E Biography, for example) uses a brief part of your episode. "I think each 30 seconds [the fee] goes up. I actually see more money from those than from an entire [re-aired] episode."

Freelancing can be lucrative, if unstable. Writing on a hit series, if you're lucky enough to get on staff, can be lucrative *and* stable. Writing for a soap opera, well . . . "If you can get on a show, then it's 52 weeks a year. You get two weeks vacation," Siegel says and then, as if this is a bad thing, "It's like having a real job."

Since soap operas aren't rerun in the United States, there are no domestic residual fees, but a writer might receive a second check from a European airing. It's not one of the most financially rewarding positions in the Writer's Guild, and it's probably one of the most demanding of an individual writer as well. "You have to turn out a script a week. There's no excuse short of death. And even then, I envisioned people coming into my apartment and getting into my computer to see how far I'd gotten in that week's script. Sickness, personal problems, it didn't matter—you had to turn in that script."

Fewer soap operas are being produced than previously, making it even more difficult to join a show. Siegel believes the only reasons she wrote for the short-lived soap opera *Sunset Beach* were because she had a connection, she had the prime time experience they were looking for, and she was available. She was required to write a sample script from an outline, a step peculiar to soap opera writing that Siegel hadn't been asked to do before, but the producers liked her script. After that, she was on staff but went through over a year's worth of 13-week deals. When she finally left, Siegel was relieved. "It afforded a nice living. And you had money paid into the Writer's Guild pension and health plans, so there are definite benefits," Siegel says. "But it's not easy."

Being a Hollywood writer has its share of glitz and glamour. "In the beginning, it was wonderful. It was like Cinderella time. Obviously, as time goes on, you find it's work." Siegel laughs and says, "Yet it beats doing a lot of things, I can tell you that."

The Effects of Anthrax on Writers' Submissions

BY ROBERT LEE BREWER

"I think we would all be willing to get our mail a day or two later if we didn't have to worry about infection," remarks Chris Miller, editor of *Outlaw Biker* and *Skin Art* magazines about the new mail-borne menace, anthrax. Even before you know how it works, anthrax just sounds creepy. As a result of all the coverage in the media, it's probably common knowledge now that anthrax is a bacterial disease typical in farm animals, such as cattle and sheep, which can also be spread to humans. Though easy to cure, if it goes long enough without detection, it can be fatal. The spread of this disease through the mail has people in all professions on the alert.

Recently, many writers have contacted WritersMarket.com to report return-to-sender mail from magazines, book publishers, and agents. These leads often mean a certain company has changed address. Usually, we follow up on such leads and make the appropriate contact changes in our online databases. However, most of these markets have not moved; they're just changing submission policies, at least for awhile.

Since September 11, 2001, it seems almost every piece of information regarding terrorism has been playing up the negative possibilities, often looking at just how bad things could get at any minute. Some theorize that many media outlets have been promoting terror to increase ratings, often by running stories before all the facts are reported and verified.

For this article, more than 150 magazine editors, book publishers, and literary agents completed a survey to assess the current state of the publishing industry in relation to the anthrax scares. Here are the results.

MAGAZINE EDITORS

"There's been so much contradictory information and lack of comment (about how to deal with anthrax) that it creates a vacuum, and that causes more fear than is probably necessary," observes Gretchen Lee, editor of *Curve* magazine.

Lee, like most of the surveyed magazine editors, has not changed her policies regarding writers' submissions. Though many editors expressed an interest in receiving story pitches via e-mail, only a small fraction feel receiving snail mail is too dangerous to handle. Many agree that it will just take some common sense to decide if a potential query or submission looks suspicious.

"Our submission policies have not changed," responds Lori Blachford, managing editor of *Country Home* magazine. "However, we are being more careful when opening mail. Our company is continuously communicating to employees tips for recognizing suspicious mail so we are well prepared to act."

Most magazine editors seem to feel the same as Blachford; they're ready to act, but only if there is an appropriate reason to do so. "I think the best thing we can do is not overreact," says Marcia Preston of *ByLine*. "This is made more difficult because of the constant media coverage, which may actually be out of proportion to the dangers."

ROBERT LEE BREWER *is the assistant editor of* Writer's Market *and editor of WritersMarket.com.*

Indeed, it may seem the world is coming to an end when really, it's just changing. It makes sense that magazine editors, for their own safety, are open to changing how they view submissions. As Hope Daniels, editor of *American Style* and *Niche*, remarks, "Things are changing so quickly from day to day that the best policy, it seems to me, is to be flexible: No hard-and-fast rules; a willingness to change rules and procedures depending on new and accurate information from informed sources; and the ability to stay calm, not jump to conclusions or to spread faulty or outrageous information just to have something to say.

"At our publications, we're concerned, and we're vigilant, but we're not scared. We're doing everything we can to proceed normally with our work and our lives."

BOOK PUBLISHERS

Perhaps because they deal with bulkier packages, a higher percentage of book publishers (compared to magazine editors) have recently changed their submission guidelines in response to the anthrax scares. Many of the publishers that have not changed their policies mentioned they're still considering a change from the norm a possibility.

Quite a few literary agents, who deal with publishing houses frequently, mentioned they've heard the days of slush piles at major publishers are officially over. Whether this rumor pans out remains to be seen. However, book publishers are still accepting manuscripts, and for the most part, the rules are still the same.

"Nothing yet suggests to me that publishers need to take extraordinary precautions in the post-9/11 world," states Sharon Woodhouse of Lake Claremont Press. "I think overreacting, misplaced fears, and the erosion of common sense in times such as these, though understandable, can interfere with recognizing and responding to real dangers should they occur, while reducing our sanity, security, freedoms, and quality of life along the way."

Whether book publishers have changed policies or not, the decisions seem to be made rationally and not in a frenzy or panic. In some cases, the full conversion to e-mail submissions was only pushed forward by the recent anthrax scares. In fact, many of the book publishers have been accepting e-mail and snail mail submissions simultaneously for years.

"Most of our unsolicited submissions come in regular mail, but an increasing number are coming over e-mail. I personally prefer e-mail," explains Mary Lou Bertucci, senior editor for Swedenborg Foundation Publishers/Chrysalis Books. She adds, "I don't feel any sense of panic, but I do wonder about mailed submissions. However, I still tear them open as I always have—no gloves or face mask or anything like that."

Just like Bertucci, most publishing houses have kept relatively calm and separated the media-portrayed threat from the real threat. Most have acted appropriately by preparing their employees for action without letting it stop their businesses altogether. In fact, many of those surveyed expressed that e-mail-spread computer viruses concerned them more than the threat of anthrax.

As Laurence Jacobs of the Craftsman Book Company says, "You're much more likely to die in a car accident on the way to work than from an anthrax attack. And we all drive to work every day without a trace of fear."

LITERARY AGENTS

Literary agents deal with many of the same packages that book publishers do. It then comes as no surprise that agents responded to the survey pretty much in line with the publishing houses. There have been some changes in submission guidelines. There is some fear. But for the most part, agents are trying to get on with their work in a cautious but productive manner.

"No," responds Justin E. Fernandez, literary agent/attorney, in response to whether or not he feels threatened by the recent anthrax scares. "But I would never open a package with no return address, or with wires sticking out, or with oil stains, a funny smell, or an odd shape. There are plenty of nonterrorist lunatics out there. So anything suspicious would be tossed unopened—after a call to the bomb squad or other authorities."

Many of the agents surveyed seemed to have a good handle on what the real threats of anthrax are and the chances of getting infected. In fact, the major scare is not that they'll be targeted but that they may receive a piece of cross-contaminated mail, something many feel is highly unlikely.

"One can't grow so paranoid as to not live one's life, but in light of recent events one needs to be alert and aware," says Agent Felicia Eth. "I see this as a trial balloon of some sort. Which is to say, I don't feel any particular immediate threat at the moment. I don't anticipate receiving a letter with anthrax spores, mostly because as a one-person agency who is not 'well-known,' I don't see myself as the symbol (of American capitalism) these individuals are looking to attack."

But at the same time, Eth says she feels threatened by the attack (as several agents and book publishers have expressed). "I received two queries last week in small envelopes and addressed by hand, with a writing similar to the envelopes containing anthrax," explains Janet Kobobel Grant from Books & Such Literary Agency. "I paused, checked the postmarks to see if they were from New Jersey or Florida, and opened them carefully. I'd say I've become a bit more cautious and nervous."

The consensus seems to be that people in publishing do feel threatened. But these same professionals are moving on with business. As literary agent Alison Picard believes, "We should not allow terrorists to create an atmosphere of fear and paranoia. I'm conducting business as usual, and I encourage all writers and publishing professionals to do the same."

THE EFFECT ON WRITERS

At the moment, the publishing industry does not seem to be a direct target of whichever group is sending terror in the mail (with the exception of American Media, which unfortunately has a misleading name). It makes no sense to quit everything you're working on to prepare for a threat that may never present itself. However, because the threat is present, writers can expect magazine editors, book publishers, and literary agents to take certain precautions to avoid being infected. As a result, the need for professionalism from writers is perhaps at its highest level ever.

This professionalism means that writers need to make sure their package is clean and presented professionally. They may also need to be more patient with response time. The possibility of a slower postal service is real. Also, many of the people surveyed mentioned that their mailing service departments are moving a little slower to check postmarks against return addresses.

Many submission policies have changed rather quickly. The speed of change should not be interpreted as anything other than what it is though. The publishing industry is not under attack, and writers are still encouraged to submit good content on all subjects and in all genres. The way writers submit work will always be in a state of revolution.

So, the effect on writers? The effect on writers is that they need to be even more professional with their submissions than usual. Period. Get back to your writing; the world can't go on without some form of positive creative energy.

Handling Rejection Plays an Important Role in the Writing Process

BY TRAVIS ADKINS

Many how-to writing books tell writers how to get published, but very few tell them how to deal with rejection, other than the standard "keep a stiff upper lip" advice.

Catherine Wald, "President and Chief Rejective Officer" of rejectioncollection.com, a website which offers writers and artists a forum to share their rejection experiences, has plenty of firsthand knowledge about this painful subject, having had a writing career "unmistakably marked by rejection." But it has also been marked by quite a bit of success.

Over two dozen of Wald's articles on women's issues and family life have appeared in *Woman's Day* and *Reader's Digest*. Her other publishing credits include essays in *Newsday* and *Writer's Digest*, among others. We asked Wald if she would be willing to share some of what she has learned about rejection with our readers. She graciously agreed.

How crucial a role do you think learning to deal with rejection plays in the overall formation of a writer? Would you say that rejection is a necessity in the maturation process?

Learning to deal with rejection is absolutely crucial for writers because it's part of the territory. The trick is to see rejection as part of the process rather than an insurmountable obstacle. I've interviewed dozens of famous writers, as well as many other successful professional writers, and they all have rejection stories. More importantly, they all keep writing and submitting in spite of the rejections. I've also spoken with many people who have given up on their dream of writing because of a few rejections, or even because of one rejection. I find that incredibly sad, not to mention unnecessary. If you love to write, enjoy writing, need to write, or care in any way about writing, don't let the rejections stop you!

To answer your second question—yes, learning to deal with rejection is a part of the maturation process, the same as learning to handle criticism, critiques, suggestions, and editing. All of these are hallmarks of the committed, professional writer.

Rejection engenders highly personal feelings.

It sure does—that is, if you consider rage, impotence, vitriolic fury, despair, and hopelessness to be highly personal feelings. (Believe me, I've been there!)

What strategies do you think a writer should develop in order to transform the experience of rejection from a personal one to a creative one?

I could write a book! In fact, I am writing a book about rejection that includes lots of information about how to overcome it. Here's a short answer: The strategies that have worked for me include

---

TRAVIS ADKINS *was an editorial assistant for* Songwriter's Market *and* Writer's Market. *Recently, he began work as a copy editor for an advertising company in Cincinnati, Ohio.*

acknowledging my feelings and venting them in a safe way (preferably in a dark, soundproof closet or on my website) and then taking a little time to get some distance and perspective. Once I've calmed down and reminded myself that a rejection of my work is not a rejection of me personally, I can go back and look at the letter and see if it contains any information I can use to improve my work or my chances of publication.

By the way, the same thing holds true if you ever have your work critiqued in a workshop. My strategy is to maintain a mature facade (i.e., nod and smile politely and refrain from bursting into tears until I leave the room). Then, a few days later, I'm often surprised to find that some of the criticism actually makes sense and is quite helpful.

Any suggestions for a writer lucky enough to receive a personalized rejection note with specific suggestions about how to improve the piece? Would they be better advised to simply try another market, or take these suggestions to heart and try to tailor their work to fit the publication's needs?

It's really important to consider suggestions very, very carefully and also to feel free to disregard them when they don't resonate with you in some way. Better yet, before you decide, send the piece out a few more times and see if you get a similar response. If five people tell you your lead is convoluted, for example, or your main character is unsympathetic, that carries a lot more weight than if only one person says it.

A writer who recently posted a rejection letter from a literary agent on my site comments that "since (the agent) was so detailed about why he didn't like it, I was ready to shelve everything—especially the voice and the pacing." She adds, "I'm glad I didn't. The next agent accepted the query. She said she'd be delighted to read my novel!"

One suggestion that editors often make is, "This piece is not for us, but do try us again." Amazingly, many writers either get offended by this statement or don't take it seriously. They don't get that "try us again" is a sincere offer as well as a compliment. No overworked editor in his or her right mind (and they're all overworked) would ever invite an author to resubmit if they didn't see some promise in the work. In fact, I broke into a major women's magazine by submitting new ideas to an editor who wrote the exact same words to me.

The standard advice for any unpublished writer is "know your market." In your opinion, what does this mean and how does a writer come by this knowledge?

All it basically means is reading—a lot. Oh, and also thinking about what you're reading. For example, if you want to write articles for a particular magazine, don't just read the latest issue. Read two years of back issues. Visit their website. Then go to their competitors and read some of their back issues and websites. As you do, ask yourself questions like: What kind of piece does this magazine always/often/sometimes/never run? Who is the audience? What makes it different from its competitors? Whose point of view are the articles written from? How long or short are they? Really get to know the thing inside and out. The same thing goes for nonfiction books and fiction, especially genre fiction. Read a lot; get to know what's expected in terms of structure, writing style, and characterization. It's well worth the trouble—and it's fun, too!

What differences have you noticed in the responses between large markets and small markets?

I have found that small markets such as literary magazines are sometimes more generous with critiques and sometimes more brutal and unnecessarily cruel. It's a strange dichotomy. As for attempting small vs. large markets: I think it often works really well to try small markets first, and then use those clips to go after the larger markets. It's extremely rare for a large publication to accept a query from someone without clips. Then again, it never hurts to shoot [for] the moon, especially with fiction or personal essays, where the quality of the piece can speak for itself.

What's the worst rejection letter you ever received, and were you able to turn that into a positive experience?

It's funny, when I reread the rejection letter that sent me over the edge, it really doesn't look so bad. At the time, though, I went into total despair because it was the last of a long string of rejections sent to me, via my then-agent, for my first novel. One phrase, which I still find irksome, goes like this: "The plot was almost too familiar and predictable to be all that exciting." Ouch! How did I turn this into a positive experience? You mean, after I broke the lamp and yelled at my kids? Well, I sat down and did a lot of writing about rejection, in which I let myself rant and rave as much as I wanted. Out of that came my idea for the rejectioncollection.com website and a book about rejection. I've been having fun with it ever since.

What's the most helpful rejection letter you ever received?

Three years ago, an agent named Christina Ward sent me a letter rejecting my first novel that read: "Thanks for the chance to read this portion of your novel. You've got a great idea here, a wonderful blend of woman in action and a spiritual quest as well. For all its attractions, though, I can't persuade myself that I'm the right advocate for this novel. The fiction I represent is generally "literary" (for want of a better description) rather than action-driven, and I'm concerned that I don't know the right editors for the novel. I do wish you well with it. Again, thanks so much for letting me consider your work."

I found that letter to be so considerate and thoughtful that I maintained the utmost respect for the agent, even though she rejected my novel. So much so that, last year, I submitted a nonfiction proposal to her, and she's now my agent.

What's worse—a rejection letter that stings at first but is ultimately helpful, or a form letter that doesn't bruise your feelings but also doesn't help your growth?

That depends on where the writer is in his or her career. Beginning writers bruise so easily! For them, a nonhurtful letter is usually best. More experienced writers tend to value criticism more, even if it stings. Personally, I'd rather know the truth about why someone hates my work because I understand that I have the choice to either use that information to improve my work or to ignore it.

What is the most common complaint about rejection letters?

That they are impersonal. People hate form letters, especially form letters that don't address the writer by name. Form letters that consist of a low-quality reproduction on a quarter of a page (presumably to save money on paper) drive writers absolutely nuts!

People also hate slow turnarounds—several months to up to two years in some cases. One contributor to my website received a rejection letter for her manuscript after her book had been accepted and published by another company. At least she had the last laugh!

Ask the Editor: How Do I Get My Fiction Published?

BY ANNE BOWLING

Storytelling is communication, and communication requires an audience. So as a fiction writer, how do you find the best venue for your novel or short story? It would be an exaggeration to say there are as many paths to publication as there are writers, but not by much. As editor of *Novel & Short Story Writer's Market*, the majority of questions I hear pertain to the submission process. Here's a sampling of the questions I am most often asked. For more information on submitting your fiction for publication—whether you've got a science fiction short story, mainstream novel, or literary short short—see the 2003 edition of *Novel & Short Story Writer's Market* (available in bookstores November 2002).

What's the single most important thing I need to know to get my work published?

Always remember: When submitting your fiction for publication, you are your own business manager. You distance yourself from the passion of your writing, and approach the submission process as completely different from the creative. Assuming you're not using an agent, you'll need to precisely meet the submission specifications of each publication you're sending your work to. This will accomplish the first and most important goal—it will increase your odds of getting your manuscript read. Editors are far outnumbered by writers looking for publication, and they need a method of thinning the slush piles. One of the first methods they use to reject manuscripts is by pitching out those which do not follow submission guidelines. Ultimately (and in spite of the fact that it's often not profitable), publishing fiction is a business—a business of passion, yes, but still a business. Don't make the novice's mistake of believing that an editor will overlook a hand-scrawled stack of loose-leaf paper to find that the author is actually the creative heir to James Joyce. Doesn't happen. For some very fine instruction on this subject, see "Perfecting Your Submission Process," by I.J. Schecter, and "The Big Challenges of Publishing in Little Magazines," by Will Allison, in the 2002 edition of *Novel & Short Story Writer's Market*.

Is it better to use an agent, or to handle submissions myself?

It depends. If you're writing short stories, you'll probably manage your own submissions. Not many short stories are agented. If you've written a novel, on the other hand, it's really up to you. Some writers, such as *Breathing Room* author Patricia Elam, prefer to rely on the expertise of a professional to find the right editor for their novel, and to help them negotiate contracts, rights, and royalties. Others, such as best-selling author Janet Fitch (*White Oleander*) choose to go it alone. Fitch sold her novel to the first editor she approached. So it certainly can—and does—happen either way. An agent will give you a leg up on finding the right editor for your manuscript. They are industry insiders who know the needs and tastes of editors at both independent publishers and imprints of the big houses. But of course it's a service you'll pay for—the

---

ANNE BOWLING *is the editor of* Novel & Short Story Writer's Market.

average contract stipulates the agent earns 15 percent of your book's domestic sales, and the foreign sales percentage may be higher.

Is it important to have a novel completed before you submit it?

First-time and newer authors will need to have a completed novel to shop for publication. An agent or editor is unlikely to sign a contract for a manuscript when the author has no proven track record. (As many, many writers can attest, starting a novel is a lot easier than finishing it.) More established writers can—and do—work on contracts which sign them to two, three, or more books.

What's "hot" in fiction publishing today?

It doesn't matter! The only "hot" property is that which tells a good story to its audience, and editors are always looking for that. The popularity of legal thrillers shot up with the publication of Scott Turow's *Presumed Innocent*—they've since peaked and fallen. Those novels now called "women's fiction" (think the Oprah Book Club) are at a peak right now, but it's impossible to "predict how long" that will be sustained. Category and mainstream romance are always strong as markets; Westerns have been struggling for years; horror changes fashion fairly regularly. You could scout bookstores and publishers' catalogues looking for trends to follow, but chances are once you've completed your "hot" manuscript, there will be another trend taking off. Someone once said, "A good book will find its audience," and I believe that's true. First and foremost, write what you love, and worry about the market later.

I've been unsuccessful in getting my novel/short story published through a traditional print market. Should I consider electronic publishing?

First, be sure you've given your manuscript every possible shot through print publication. There may be a reason—other than a crowded market—that your story hasn't been published. But if you're confident you've written and revised your work into the best possible story you can tell, and that you've followed submission guidelines for specifications and response times and still no luck, certainly electronic publishing is an option. Electronic publishing for novels and short stories has the advantage of being a fresh field. Editors are not as swamped with submissions as in print venues, and the speed of electronic submissions can cut back on response times.

That said, there's a great deal of difference between publishing your short story in an e-magazine (literary or genre) and selling your novel to an e-book publisher. Online magazines that publish short fiction have exploded in number over the past three years and show no sign of waning. And as the field continues to grow and diversify, so grow opportunities for writers. Many literary journals, finding the cost of print publishing too high and subscriber numbers dropping off, are turning to online-only publication. There are many fine genre sites as well, and in terms of industry legitimacy, they're picking up.

E-book publishing is not sharing quite the same renaissance, perhaps because it is easier to read a short story electronically than it is a novel. Regardless of the reasons, e-book publishing is not quite what the industry expected when the form first came out, and Stephen King tried his publication-in-installments experiment with *Riding the Bullet*. In a *Publishers Weekly* roundtable interview last January, one industry insider predicted: "When the hubbub has died down and the opportunists on the business side have milked it for all it's worth, (e-books) will subside into about 5 percent of the book market, somewhat akin to audio books." And not a year later, that prediction seems to be coming true. If you are seriously considering publishing your novel electronically, be aware that e-book publishers are not gaining legitimacy among print publishers as quickly as their electronic magazine counterparts. Two titles which might be worth researching before you make your decision are: *Writer's Online Marketplace*, by Debbie Ridpath Ohi (Writer's Digest Books), and *Electronic Publishing: The Definitive Guide (2002 Edition)*, by Karen S. Wiesner (Avid Press).

I'm thinking of joining a writer's group, but I'm not sure whether it would be valuable. What do you recommend?

If you can find a good one, writer's groups can be enormously helpful, both through the advice and critiques you receive from other writers and the external discipline they impose to keep writing. For that matter, workshops and conferences can provide the same benefits and synergy. Author Elizabeth Graver (*The Honey Thief*) was a member of a writer's group which included Pagan Kennedy and a handful of other emerging women writers whose work all began to get published at about the same time. Workshops and conferences can connect you with industry players you would not have been able to reach otherwise—Patricia Elam, who I mentioned earlier, connected with powerhouse agent Molly Friedrich through a friend in a writer's workshop, and Friedrich was able to negotiate an auction for Elam's first novel. So getting out into the writing community in one way or another is usually a good idea.

On the other hand, it's a good idea not to choose a group indiscriminately. Terry McMillan (*Waiting to Exhale*) has cautioned that bad writer's groups can be downright dangerous to the writer, trapping them in a cycle of writing and rewriting that becomes self-perpetuating.

To find a writer's group that may meet your needs, contact your local bookstore, library, or writer's organization (you'll find a listing of those in *Novel & Short Story Writer's Market*, or ask your librarian for other resources). Connecting with the right group of writers has helped many an author through the process of mastering craft and on to publication.

10 Ways to Effectively Promote Your Writing Through Your Website

BY ROBERT LEE BREWER

If there is one rule that shakes up writers more than any other in the publishing business, it may well be that the marketing of a book is usually more important than the actual book. While word of mouth is the best advertising a writer can hope for, the trick is how to initiate that sought-after promotional buzz. Perhaps one of the cheapest and most effective ways to do this is through your own website.

It may seem bizarre to think about promoting your book online. However, it shouldn't. More than 90 percent of Americans have online access, and a healthy percentage of these people are ready to know about your book. The only catch is that you must figure out not only how to present yourself online but also how to attract attention to your website.

You don't have to be a cyber-recluse typing codes in the basement of an abandoned warehouse to be able to accomplish your goals. Often, you need only have a friend that does such things. Or you can pick up a "Dummies" guide. You might even be able to cajole your book publisher into having a web designer create a site for you.

Here I've presented some specific points to keep in mind when you're ready to promote yourself online. By following these tips, you should increase your name recognition and your book's sales.

1. Make sure your home page is user-friendly.

Before anyone gets to your website, you need to make sure it's easy to use. After all, there are plenty of destinations for users online. If your site is not easy to use, then the reader will move on to some other website, never giving your site a second thought. A user-friendly home page is a home page that makes sense. Don't come up with catchy lingo that you think sounds cool or funny to describe something simple. For instance, if you offer reprints of your articles on your site, call the link "Reprinted Articles" as opposed to "The Same Old Stuff," which says nothing about where the link will lead a user.

2. Make your books easy to find.

There are many ways you can do this, all of them located on your home page. You can play it cool and just have a link like "Books By Me," or you can go for the gold and display the cover of your most recent book in the top-middle or top-left of your website. Of course, you'll still want to have that "Books By Me" link for your other books. Remember: Potential customers can't be impressed by your books unless they know the books exist in the first place.

3. Link to selling points.

If you do impress visitors, you need to make the most of the moment and offer a way for them to order your book online. This may mean having a link from which people can order directly from your website, or it may mean linking up to Amazon, Barnes & Noble, or your

---

ROBERT LEE BREWER *is the assistant editor of* Writer's Market *and editor of WritersMarket.com.*

book publisher's website. The answer isn't in the how, it's in the where. The ordering information needs to be easy to find and accessible from your site, even if it's a link to another site. This will make the link from your website to profit more directly felt.

4. Offer a newsletter.

Getting traffic to your website is one way to promote yourself. An even more effective form of promotion is to keep the traffic that hits your website. One way to stay in touch with these potential readers is by offering a free newsletter. Newsletters require some original material of interest to your readers. There is an investment of time required to do a newsletter, but it may be a small sacrifice to keep in touch with the people who could possibly make your next book a *New York Times* bestseller.

5. Add new material regularly.

Whether or not you offer the free online newsletter, you will need to offer new material on a regular basis. This material, which can be original or reprinted writing, must contain enough punch to keep drawing back first-time visitors for future visits. Sometimes the draw is as simple as having a weekly journal that describes the progress of a novel or a book tour. Such material should be added on at least a weekly basis, if not daily.

6. Offer article links to newsletters and websites.

This may be one of the most cost-effective online marketing maneuvers. Your website should have some of your articles, even if they're reprints or excerpts from a longer manuscript. The trick to marketing here is that you need to have top quality writing online that you can link up to other websites and/or online newsletters that have readers in your field. For instance, if you wrote a great piece on how to raise your children after September 11, 2001, you'll want to link to the scores of parenting websites and online newsletters available. Often, you just need to describe the piece to the editor and add the URL where the article can be found. Everyone that clicks on the link will then be transported to your user-friendly website of self-promotional greatness.

7. Offer a press release.

There is a great need for new material online. As a result, editors and freelancers are constantly scouring the Internet for useful and/or interesting information. By offering a press release, you can give prospective interviewers a glimpse of why you are worth interviewing.

8. Provide a "Contact Me" function.

You want contact with your prospective readers and media. The least successful form of self-promotion is adopting the attitude of a hermit. So make sure to go out of your way to let people know how to contact you. This includes posting your e-mail, since this is the fastest way for people to make contact. No need to worry about phone tag, and you can print up the message for an easy access hard copy of your correspondence. (Note: I do recommend keeping your online correspondence in a folder filed under "just in case," because you never know when you might need to contact someone yourself.)

9. Try to get an easy-to-remember URL.

Word of mouth is the most effective form of advertising. As such, it makes sense that you make your URL easy to remember. This can be as simple as making your site a "YourName.com" or just inventing a cool phrase and adding .com to the end of it. Also, remember there are other options like .net, .cc, and coming soon—.info and .biz. Keep in mind: Numbers are not easy to remember but words and catchy phrases are.

10. Provide links to other online sources.

The more you offer, the better you look. If you offer lots of information that is easy to find, people will love your site. As a result, they will love you, and eventually this love will translate into book sales. It is easy to provide information online. There are a lot of articles that you can link to your site. Often, all you need to do is zip an e-mail over to an editor who can then provide you with a specific URL. After all, it's often promoting the site you wish to link to. Online promotion is a reciprocal business. This is good for you because it translates into word of mouth, which often translates into money.

The Business of Writing

Minding the Details

Writers who have been successful in getting their work published know that publishing requires two different mind-sets. The first is the actual act of writing the manuscript. The second is the business of writing—the marketing and selling of the manuscript. This shift in perspective is necessary if you want to become a successful career writer. That said, you need to keep the business side of writing in mind as you continually develop your writing.

Each of the following sections and accompanying sidebars discusses a writing business topic that affects anyone selling a manuscript. We'll take a look at contracts and agreements—the documents that license a publisher to use your work. We'll consider your rights as a writer and sort out some potentially confusing terminology. We'll cover the basics of copyright protection—a topic of perennial concern for writers. And, for those of you who are already making money with your writing, we'll offer some tips for keeping track of financial matters and staying on top of your tax liabilities.

Our treatment of the business topics that follow is necessarily limited, so look for short blocks of information and resources throughout this section to help you further research the content mentioned.

For More Information

RESOURCES

- *The Writer's Guide to Contract Negotiations*, by Richard Balkin (Writer's Digest Books, 1985)—this book is out of print, but should be available in libraries.
- *From Printout to Published*, by Michael Seidman (Carroll & Graf, 1992).
- *The Copyright Handbook: How to Protect and Use Written Works*, by Stephen Fishman (Nolo Press, 1994).
- *Every Writer's Guide to Copyright & Publishing Law*, by Ellen M. Kozak (Henry Holt, 1990).
- *Your Federal Income Tax* (Publication 17); *Tax Guide for Small Business* (Publication 334); *Business Use of Your Home* (Publication 587); and *Self-Employment Tax* (Publication 533), all available from the IRS.

CONTRACTS AND AGREEMENTS

If you've been freelancing, you know that contracts and agreements vary from publisher to publisher. Very rarely will you find two contracts that are exactly the same. Some magazine editors work only by verbal agreement, as do many agents; others have elaborate documents you must sign in duplicate and return to the editor before you even begin the assignment. It is essential that you consider all of the elements involved in a contract, whether verbal or written, and know what you stand to gain and lose by agreeing to the contract. Maybe you want to repurpose the article and resell it to a market that is different from the first publication to which you sold the article. If that's the case, then you need to know what rights you want to sell. (For more information on various rights see Rights and the Writer below.)

In contract negotiations, the writer is usually interested in licensing the work for a particular use but limiting the publisher's ability to make other uses of the work in the future. It's in the publisher's best interest, however, to secure as many rights as possible, both now and later on. Those are the basic positions of both parties. The negotiation is a process of compromise on questions relating to those basic points—and the amount of compensation to be given the writer for his work. If at any time you are unsure about any portion of the contract, it is best to consult a lawyer who specializes in media law and contract negotiation.

A contract is rarely a take-it-or-leave-it proposition. If an editor tells you that his company will allow no changes to the contract, you will then have to decide how important the assignment is to you. However, most editors are open to negotiations, so you need to learn how to compromise on points that don't matter to you, and stand your ground on those that do matter.

For More Information

CONTRACTS AND CONTRACT NEGOTIATION

- **The Authors Guild** (www.authorsguild.org), 31 E. 28th St., 10th Floor, New York NY 10016. (212)563-5904. E-mail: staff@authorsguild.org.
- **The National Writers Union** (www.nwu.org), 113 University Place, 6th Floor, New York NY 10003. (212)254-0279. E-mail: nwu@wu.org.

RIGHTS AND THE WRITER

A creative work can be used in many different ways. As the author of the work, you hold all rights to the work in question. When you agree to have your work published, you are granting a publisher the right to use your work in any number of ways. Whether that right is to publish the manuscript for the first time in a publication or to publish it as many times and in many different ways as a publisher wishes is up to you—it all depends on the agreed upon terms. As a general rule, the more rights you license away, the less control you have over your work and the money you're paid. You should strive to keep as many rights to your work as you can from the outset; otherwise, your attempts to resell your work may be seriously hampered.

Writers and editors sometimes define rights in a number of different ways. Below you will find a classification of terms as they relate to rights.

- **First Serial Rights**—Rights that the writer offers a newspaper or magazine to publish the manuscript for the first time in any periodical. All other rights remain with the writer. Sometimes the qualifier "North American" is added to these rights to specify a geographical limitation to the license.

  When content is excerpted from a book scheduled to be published, and it appears in a magazine or newspaper prior to book publication, this is also called first serial rights.
- **One-Time Rights**—Nonexclusive rights (rights that can be licensed to more than one market) purchased by a periodical to publish the work once (also known as simultaneous rights). That is, there is nothing to stop the author from selling the work to other publications at the same time.
- **Second Serial (Reprint) Rights**—Nonexclusive rights given to a newspaper or magazine to publish a manuscript after it has already appeared in another newspaper or magazine.

- **All Rights**—This is exactly what it sounds like. All rights mean that an author is selling every right they have to a work. If you license all rights to your work, you forfeit the right to ever use the work again. If you think you may want to use the article again, you should avoid submitting to such markets or refuse payment and withdraw your material.
- **Electronic Rights**—Rights that cover a broad range of electronic media, from online magazines and databases to CD-ROM magazine anthologies and interactive games. The contract should specify if—and which—electronic rights are included. The presumption is that unspecified rights remain with the writer.
- **Subsidiary Rights**—Rights, other than book publication rights, that should be covered in a book contract. These may include various serial rights; movie, TV, audiotape, and other electronic rights; translation rights, etc. The book contract should specify who controls the rights (author or publisher) and what percentage of sales from the licensing of these rights goes to the author.
- **Dramatic, TV, and Motion Picture Rights**—Rights for use of material on the stage, in TV, or in the movies. Often a one-year option to buy such rights is offered (generally for 10 percent of the total price). The party interested in the rights then tries to sell the idea to other people—actors, directors, studios, or TV networks. Some properties are optioned numerous times, but most fail to become full productions. In those cases, the writer can sell the rights again and again.

Sometimes editors don't take the time to specify the rights they are buying. If you sense that an editor is interested in getting stories, but doesn't seem to know what his and the writer's responsibilities are, be wary. In such a case, you'll want to explain what rights you're offering (preferably one-time or first serial rights only) and that you expect additional payment for subsequent use of your work.

The Copyright Law that went into effect January 1, 1978, states that writers are primarily selling one-time rights to their work unless they—and the publisher—agree otherwise in writing. Book rights are covered fully by contract between the writer and the book publisher.

SELLING SUBSIDIARY RIGHTS

The primary right in book publishing is the right to publish the book itself. All other rights (movie rights, audio rights, book club rights, etc.) are considered secondary, or subsidiary, to the right to print publication. In contract negotiations, authors and their agents traditionally try to avoid granting the publisher subsidiary rights that they feel comfortable marketing themselves. Publishers, on the other hand, want to obtain as many of the subsidiary rights as they can.

Larger agencies have experience selling subsidiary rights, and many authors represented by such agents prefer to retain those rights and let their agents do the selling. On the other hand, book publishers have subsidiary rights departments whose sole job is to exploit the subsidiary rights the publisher was able to retain during the contract negotiation. That job might begin with a push to sell foreign rights, which normally bring in advance money that is divided among the author, agent, and publisher. Further efforts might then be made to publish the book as a paperback and so forth.

The marketing of electronic rights can be tricky. With the proliferation of electronic and multimedia formats, publishers, agents, and authors are going to great lengths to make sure contracts specify exactly which electronic rights are being conveyed (or retained). Compensation for these rights is a major source of conflict because many book publishers seek control of them, and many magazines routinely include electronic rights in the purchase of all rights, often with no additional payment.

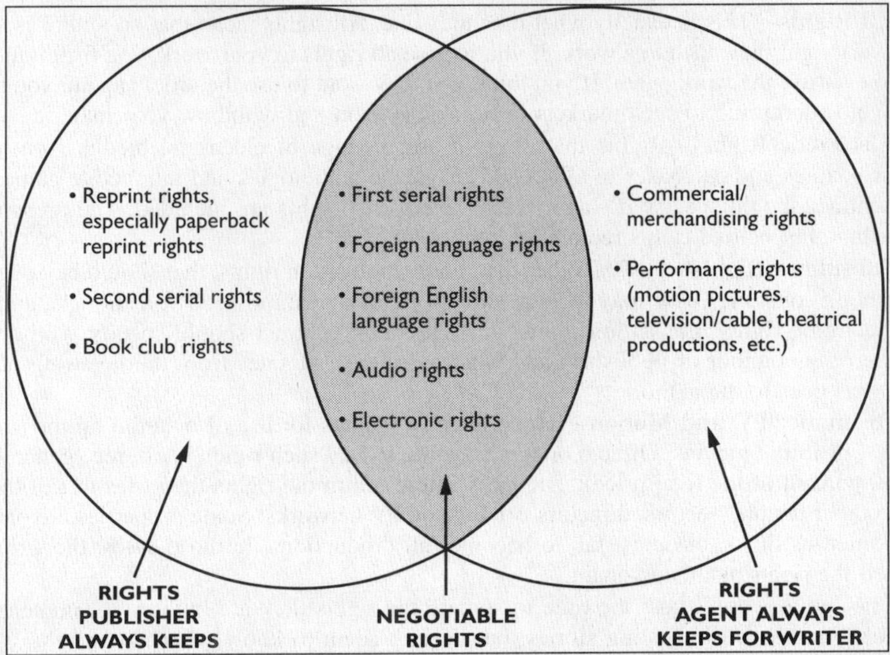

Some subsidiary rights are always granted to the publisher. Some should always be retained by the author. The remainder are negotiable, and require knowledgeable advice from a literary agent or attorney in deciding whether it is more advantageous to grant the rights to the publisher or to reserve them.

COPYRIGHT

Copyright law exists to protect creators of original works. Copyright law is designed to encourage the production of creative works by ensuring that artists and writers hold the rights by which they can profit from their hard work.

The moment you finish a piece of writing—or in fact, the second you begin to pen the manuscript—the law recognizes that only you can decide how the work is used. Copyright protects your writing, recognizes you (its sole creator) as its owner, and grants you all the rights and benefits that accompany ownership. With very few exceptions, anything you write today will enjoy copyright protection for your lifetime, plus 70 years. Copyright protects "original

For More Information

COPYRIGHT

- To learn more about general copyright information, filling out copyright forms, and links to other websites related to copyright issues, contact the Copyright Office (http://lcweb.loc.gov.), Library of Congress, Washington DC 20559. (202)707-3000 (weekdays between 8:30 a.m. and 5 p.m.).

- If you want to register your work with the U.S. Copyright Office you need to fill out an application form (Form TX) which is available by calling (202)707-9100 or by downloading from http://lcweb.loc.gov/copyright. Send the completed form, a nonreturnable copy of the work in question, and a check for $30 to the Library of Congress, Copyright Office, Register of Copyrights, 101 Independence Ave. SE, Washington DC 20559-6000.

What is Copyright Law?

Copyright law gives you the right to:

- make and distribute copies of your written work,
- prepare derivative works (dramatizations, translations, musical arrangements, etc.—any work based on the original), and
- to perform or publicly display your work.

works of authorship" that are fixed in a tangible form of expression. *Copyright law cannot protect titles, ideas, and facts.*

Some writers are under the mistaken impression that a registered copyright with the Library of Congress Copyright Office is necessary to protect their work, and that their work is not protected until they "receive" their copyright paperwork from the government. *This is not true.* You don't have to register your work with the Copyright Office for it to be protected. Registration for your work does, however, offer some additional protection (specifically, the possibility of recovering punitive damages in an infringement suit) as well as legal proof of the date of copyright.

Most magazines are registered with the Copyright Office as single collective entities themselves; that is, the individual works that make up the magazine are *not* copyrighted individually in the names of the authors. You'll need to register your article yourself if you wish to have the additional protection of copyright (your name, the year of first publication, and the copyright symbol ©) appended to any published version of your work. You may use the copyright notice regardless of whether your work has been registered with the Copyright Office.

One thing you need to pay particular attention to is work-for-hire arrangements. If you sign a work-for-hire agreement, you are agreeing that your writing will be done as a work for hire, you will not control the copyright of the completed work—the person or organization who hired you will be the copyright owner. These agreements and transfers of exclusive rights must appear in writing to be legal. However, it's a good idea to get every publishing agreement you negotiate in writing before the sale.

FINANCES AND TAXES

You will find that as your writing business expands, so will your need to keep track of all writing-related expenses and incomes. Keeping a close eye on these details will prove very helpful when it comes time to report your income to the IRS. It will also help you pay as little tax as possible and keep you aware of the state of your freelance writing as a business. It's essential that you maintain your writing business as any other business. This means that you need to set up a detailed tracking and organizing system to log all expenses and income. Without such a system, your writing as a business will eventually fold. If you dislike handling finance-related tasks, you can always hire a professional to oversee these duties for you. However, even if you do hire a professional, you still need to keep all original records with an eye to providing the professional with the appropriate information.

The following tips will help you keep track of the finance-related tasks associated with your freelance business.

- Keep accurate records.
- Separate your writing income and expenses from your personal income and expenses.
- Maintain a separate bank account and credit card for business-related expenses.
- Record every transaction (expenses and earnings) related to your writing.
- Begin keeping records when you make your first writing-related purchase.
- Establish a working, detailed system of tracking expenses and income. Include the date;

Important Tax Information

While we cannot offer you tax advice or interpretations, we can suggest several sources for the most current information.

- Check the IRS website (www.irs.ustreas.gov) which offers helpful tips, information, and important IRS forms and publications.
- Call your local IRS office. Look in the White Pages of the telephone directory under U.S. Government—Internal Revenue Service.
- Obtain the basic IRS publications. You can order the publications by phone or by mail from any IRS office; most are available at libraries and some post offices.
- Consider other information sources. Many public libraries have detailed tax instructions available on tape. Some colleges and universities offer free assistance in preparing tax returns. If you decide to consult a professional tax preparer, know that the fee is a deductible business expense on your tax return.

the source of income (or the vendor of your purchase); a description of what was sold or bought; how the payment was rendered (cash, check, credit card); and the amount of the transaction.

- Keep all check stubs and receipts (cash purchases and credit cards).
- Set up a record-keeping system, such as a file folder system, to store all receipts.

Beyond managing and organizing their writing business, many freelance writers, artists, and photographers are concerned about taxes. These concerns—deductions, self-employment tax, and home office credits—go beyond those of a regular employee. Many freelance expenses can be deducted in the year in which they are incurred (rather than having to be capitalized, or depreciated, over a period of years).

There also is a home office deduction that can be claimed if the area in your home is used *exclusively* and *regularly* for business, and you have no other fixed location from where you conduct business. Contact the IRS for information on requirements and limitations for this deduction. If your freelance income exceeds your expenses, regardless of the amount, you must declare that profit.

Sell Serial Rights, Make Money

BY JAY CONRAD LEVINSON, RICK FRISHMAN, AND MICHAEL LARSEN

Selling first serial rights—slices of your book that run before publication—offers you the opportunity to get paid to publicize your book. If you have been writing articles about your subject for trade or consumer newspapers, magazines, newsletters, or websites, you may already have the connections you need to sell excerpts.

The best time for first-serial excerpts to appear is on publication, when your book is in stores. This is especially true if your book has newsworthy revelations that you don't want to leak out before publication.

However, there are two reasons to steal your own thunder by selling serial rights before publication:

- You need money to sustain yourself while you write your proposal, or you will need more money to write your book than you can expect in an advance. Selling one or more excerpts from your book, or even serializing the whole book as you write it, may make the difference in whether you can survive while you write it. In this case, the money you earn will be the meat, and the publicity you generate will be gravy.
- You want to use an article to attract agents and editors. The right article in the right publication at the right time will sell a book. If your idea and your article about it are impressive enough:

— Editors and agents will find you. (If you have a novel in progress, your short story may enable you to sell it with only a partial manuscript and a synopsis.)

— You may be able to use the article as a sample chapter in a nonfiction proposal. (Your idea and your ability as a writer will have greater credibility if a magazine pays you to write about your topic.)

Can someone else who sees your article write a book based on your idea? You betcha. You can't protect an idea. However, stating in the brief bio that appears with your article that the piece is from "a forthcoming book" or "a book in progress" will signal agents and editors that a book is in the works and will help deflect potential competitors.

Unless they sell articles or first-serial rights on a regular basis, agents won't have the connections, the time, or the interest to sell them for you. And unless excerpts from your books will have strong commercial potential or your publisher is giving your book a big push, their subsidiary rights department won't do much, if anything, to sell them.

You want whoever has the most skill and commitment to sell serial rights. Unless you are convinced that someone else will devote more time and energy to selling them than you will, you're better off trying to serialize your book yourself, even if you have to learn how to do it as you go along.

Use your networks, agent, editor, and your publisher's subsidiary rights department to advise you on how to go about it. Your goals are to generate as much exposure as you can for your book and pocket as much money as you can.

Serial rights are worth more if:

- you are well known
- your previous books were successful
- your excerpts contain newsworthy revelations or juicy dish on a celebrity
- your excerpts appear before rather than after publication when people have access to your book
- you sell them on an exclusive basis
- you sell as many excerpts as you can (or even the same excerpt) to noncompeting newspapers or magazines
- you serialize the whole book

The 7,500 trade magazines and newsletters in the U.S. directed to business usually don't pay a lot (medical magazines are an exception), but every industry has at least one magazine. *Publishers Weekly* is the trade magazine for publishing. Trade media can make up in well-targeted exposure what they lack in pay. They may be willing to trade an excerpt for ad space that may be worth far more than what the magazine pays for excerpts. Another upside: Trade media may attract other media.

Your publisher will keep second-serial rights, the right to sell excerpts after publication. The contract usually calls for a 50/50 split of resulting profits. Even though excerpts rarely command a significant sum, they are still worth selling because they help publicize your books. So if magazine editors express interest in second-serial rights, pass the word on to your editor.

Two caveats about excerpting books:

- It's far more likely to happen for nonfiction books than novels. A novel may not lend itself to excerpting as a short story, and few magazines use short stories.
- As we mentioned above, you can't protect your ideas. Magazine editors have been known to take ideas submitted by freelance writers and assign them to a staff writer. This may be cheaper, and they know they'll get an article tailored to their magazine.

Pitching Sidebars, Shorts, & Quizzes

BY JENNIFER NELSON

When it comes to writing for magazines, some writers think longer equals better. Their minds capture a stellar idea and they can't wait to pitch an editor a 2,500-word feature on the subject. That's just the nature of the freelance beast. The more words writers are asked to squeeze into an article, generally the more cash flow that follows. But many magazines don't have that kind of space, or they reserve these large features for well-established writers they've worked with previously. Where does this leave the less-experienced writer, or even a veteran word crafter, trying to break into a new publication? The short, sidebar, or quiz, that's where.

Generally, shorts, sidebars, and quizzes run 200-400 words, are straightforward, compact, don't usually require an extensive amount of research or interviews, and often pay a dollar or more per word on the national level. Shorts are common in many types of magazines. Most publications even state in their guidelines that the short is the best way to break in. Perhaps writers haven't given this idea its due. I've broken into my share of major magazines this way. So before you dismiss the short, know that it's a surefire way to show an editor what you can do.

LIVING IN THE REAL WRITING WORLD

Why are shorts the standard for writers who are new to a magazine? Simple. In a perfect world, every Joe and Jess Writer who pitches a decent feature idea at a new magazine will snag an assignment (and a fat fee). They'll all turn in clean, tight copy that sparkles with brilliance. Their articles will be delivered on time—heck, let's even say early. Their prose will twinkle. Each sentence will move the article forward with rapt mastery, and the words will roll from the page in monolithic splendor like Shakespeare's iambic pentameter.

The reality, however, is that many Jess and Joe Writers won't turn in suitable work. They may not submit anything at all. These writers won't beat their deadline; their pieces won't remotely resemble the articles they pitched in the first place. Some will even fall off the face of cyberspace without so much as a farewell e-mail back to the editor who took a chance on them. Can you imagine? They are the Adam and Eve of the Writing Garden. Why did they ever have to eat that forbidden feature article and ruin it for the rest of us?

But don't despair. It's true that since Jess and Joe's work fell into the writing abyss, editors are a cautious bunch when it comes to offering feature assignments to writers they don't know. Can we really blame them? Post Jess and Joe, magazine editors hand over smaller assignments first and take a good gander at how well writers handle them. If a writer doesn't deliver, the editor has but a wee void to fill where that byline should have appeared—and a minor kill fee to fork over.

But when writers turn in a dazzling short, sidebar, or quiz, they join the exalted ranks of wordsmiths editors can depend on. These writers have proven themselves. They've plowed the writing garden and are ripe for more short assignments as well as the much-coveted feature articles to come.

JENNIFER NELSON *is a full-time freelancer in Jacksonville, Florida. Her work has appeared in* Writer's Digest, Parenting, Woman's Day, Fitness, Shape, Health, Self, The Christian Science Monitor, *and many other publications.*

GETTING STARTED

Check out the magazines where you'd like to break in. Read their guidelines. Do they run shorts? Telltale signs are the presence of front- and back-of-the-book newsy pieces or departments like health, technology, medicine, and fitness—often found in the first third of the magazine. Are these departments freelanced? A quick crosscheck of the bylines against the editors in the masthead will let you know whether staff writers or freelancers pen this content. Next, check the word length. Do the majority of articles run 200, 300, 400, or more words? Scout a few back issues to see if the publication runs quizzes. Many do. Tally the length so you can propose something in the same ballpark. Establish whether the quiz is multiple choice, true/false, or a combination, and how the scoring details are conveyed. Is the quiz riddled with humor or seriously structured?

Lastly, check out some of the feature articles. Do they include sidebars? If so, notice if an author other than the feature writer or an editor has scribed this side box. Some magazines offer writers sidebar opportunities. Say a writer pitches an idea for a feature article similar to something another writer is already covering, or an author provides a newfound spin on a subject the magazine has planned. In these cases, the editor may assign the sidebar—a snippet of some uncovered information present in the proposal. If the magazine works within an editorial calendar, familiarize yourself with forthcoming feature topics and propose related sidebars. Sidebars are a snap. They are often comprised of a table, chart, or listing of pertinent information, details on where to go for additional data, or information to test the reader's knowledge. Do a bang up job and the editor will happily consider you for future (read longer) assignments.

FINDING IDEAS FOR SHORTS

Where will the creative juice for these shorts turn up? And are they just feature ideas whittled down in length? Not by a long shot. For the best possible odds of landing a short, read the ones published in magazines for which you want to write. They're frequently driven by the latest information: technological advances, health updates, academic studies, medical breakthroughs, celebrity happenings, and more. The only way to know what kind of content the editor will fancy is to have a thorough grasp of the shorts they're already running.

Once you know the type of shorts a publication prefers, look for ideas in newspapers, gossip columns, entertainment news, and health and technology developments, on websites and TV shows. Subscribe to mailing lists and press releases. Watch TV for tidbits that can turn into short ideas. Hone in on the current watercooler topic making the rounds in the workplace. Get a grasp on the latest pop culture phenomena.

Stay on top of categories that interest you, and look for ways to spin them into shorts. Ditto for writing quizzes. Stick to subjects that make suitable quiz material. Health, finance, beauty, trivia, and technology are biggies. Quizzes are generally format pieces. Once you look over a few, it's not difficult to devise one. Usually quizzes open with a brief introduction. Then they segue into a handful of questions, depending on word count. Strike a balance between tough and easy questions, striving for a middle ground.

Next, create scoring details so the reader can tally their answers. Quizzes are all about service. Readers must take away information for the quiz to succeed.

A word of caution on shorts: If the topic is saturated in the media, or other magazines are already running with it, it's probably too late. Editors won't touch ideas that have been done ad nauseam—overexposure can kill a short.

PITCHING TO EDITORS

To pitch successful shorts and quizzes, draft a one-page query letter just like you would for a feature article. Hook the editor with your opener, reel her in with the meat of your idea, and give examples and statistics when needed. Tell her about the news; cite the recent study or the latest health innovation. Be sure to spell out why the short will make a good piece for the editor's readers or how the quiz will help them. Yes, your query's word count might come in at, or even longer than, the short you're pitching, but that's OK. Don't forget to mention what department your short fits in by name, and propose a word length similar to the shorts that already appear in that section. This shows you're familiar with the publication. Enclose some clips—other shorts or quizzes if you have them. Then hit the send button or slap the stamp on.

NAILING SHORT ASSIGNMENTS

Once you get the go-ahead for a short, quiz, or sidebar, treat it like any other writing gig. Research, interview, and compile information just like you would for a feature article. Penning shorts is similar to writing features—just on a smaller scale. You'll need a to-the-point lead, the meat in the middle, and a closing, wrapped up tighter than ever. Mimic the magazine's style. Does the prose drip with wit or sarcasm? Are the shorts hard-nosed? Look back over your editor's notes to verify you've done the job that was requested.

Keeping to a short, limited word count can be challenging. It calls for taut, clean copy minus extraneous thoughts and excess verbiage. If you've put together a quiz, have a few friendly readers give it a dry run, and ask them for feedback. You won't want to send it off to the editor if the scoring doesn't compute or the questions aren't clear. Treat your short with the respect of a feature article—maybe even more. Proofread, double and triple check; run a grammar and spelling program; turn it in on time, early if possible. Remember, this work shows the editor what you can do.

Publishers and Their Imprints

The publishing world is constantly changing and evolving. With all of the buying, selling, reorganizing, consolidating, and dissolving, it's hard to keep publishers and their imprints straight. To help you make sense of these changes, we offer this breakdown of major publishers (and their divisions)—who owns whom and which imprints are under each company umbrella. Keep in mind that this information is constantly changing. We have provided the websites to each of the publishers so you can continue to keep an eye on this ever-evolving business.

SIMON & SCHUSTER
(Viacom, Inc.)
www.simonsays.com

Simon & Schuster Audio
Pimsleur
Simon & Schuster Audioworks
Simon & Schuster Sound Ideas

Simon & Schuster Adult Publishing
Atria Books
The Free Press
Kaplan
PB Press
Pocket Books
Scribner
Simon & Schuster
Simon & Schuster Trade Paperback

Simon & Schuster Children's Publishing
Aladdin Paperbacks
Atheneum Books for Young Readers
Little Simon(®)
Margaret K. McElderry Books
Simon & Schuster Books for Young Readers
Simon Pulse
Simon Spotlight(®)

Simon & Schuster Interactive

Simon & Schuster International
Distican
Simon & Schuster Australia
Simon & Schuster UK

HARPERCOLLINS
www.harpercollins.com

HarperCollins General Books Group
Access Press
Amistad Press
Avon
Ecco
Eos
HarperAudio
HarperBusiness
HarperCollins
HarperEntertainment
HarperLargePrint
HarperResource
HarperSanFrancisco
HarperTorch
Perennial
PerfectBound
Quill
Rayo
ReganBooks
William Morrow

HarperCollins Children's Books Group
Avon
Greenwillow Books
HarperCollins Children's Books
HarperFestival
HarperTrophy
Joanna Cotler Books
Laura Geringer Books
Tempest

HarperCollins Australia

HarperCollins Canada

HarperCollins New Zealand

HarperCollins UK

Zondervan

RANDOM HOUSE, INC.
(Bertelsmann Book Group)
www.randomhouse.com

The Ballantine Publishing Group
Ballantine Books
Ballantine Reader's Circle
Del Rey
Del Rey/Lucas Books
Fawcett
Ivy
One World
Wellspring

Bantam Dell Publishing Group
Bantam Hardcover
Bantam Trade Paperback
Bantam Mass Market
Crimeline
Delacorte Press
Dell
Delta
The Dial Press
Domain
DTP
Fanfare
Island
Spectra

The Crown Publishing Group
Bell Tower
Clarkson Potter
Crown Business
Crown Publishers, Inc.
Harmony Books
Shaye Areheart Books
Three Rivers Press

The Doubleday Broadway Publishing Group
Broadway Books
Currency
Doubleday
Doubleday Religious Publishing
Doubleday/Image
Main Street Books
Nan A. Talese

The Knopf Publishing Group
Alfred A. Knopf
Everyman's Library
Pantheon Books
Schocken Books
Vintage Anchor Publishing

Random House Audio Publishing Group
Random House Audible
Random House Audio
Random House Audio Assets
Random House Audio Dimensions
Random House Audio Price-less
Random House Audio Road
Random House Listening Library

Random House Children's Books
Knopf Delacorte Dell Young Readers Group
Alfred A. Knopf
Bantam
Crown
David Fickling Books
Delacorte Press
Dell Dragonfly
Dell Laurel-Leaf
Dell Yearling Books
Doubleday
Wendy Lamb Books

Random House Young Readers Group
Beginner Books
Disney
First Time Books
Landmark Books
LucasBooks
Picturebacks
Sesame Workshop
Step into Reading
Stepping Stones

The Random House Information Group
Fodor's Travel Publications

Living Language
Princeton Review
Random House Espanol
Random House Puzzles & Games
Random House Reference Publishing

The Random House Trade Publishing Group
AtRandom
The Modern Library
Random House Trade Books
Random House Trade Paperbacks
Villard Books

Random House Ventures
ebrary
Random House Audible
Xlibris

Random House Diversified Publishing Group
Random House Large Print Publishing
Random House Value Publishing

Random House Worldwide
Random House Australia
Random House of Canada Ltd.
Random House UK
Transworld UK

PENGUIN PUTNAM, INC.
(Pearson plc)
www.penguinputnam.com

Penguin Putnam, Inc.
Avery
BlueHen Books
Dutton
G.P. Putnam's Sons
Jeremy P. Tarcher
New American Library
Penguin
Plume
Viking

Berkley Publishing Group
Ace Books
Berkley Books
Boulevard
Diamond Books
HPBooks
Jam
Jove
Perigee
Prime Crime
Riverhead Books (paperback)

Penguin Putnam Books for Young Readers
AlloyBooks
Dial Books for Young Readers
Dutton Children's Books
Frederick Warne
G.P. Putnam's Sons
Grosset & Dunlap
Philomel
Phyllis Fogelman Books
Paperstar
Planet Dexter
Platt & Munk
Playskool
Price Stern Sloan
PSS
Puffin Books
Viking Children's Books

AOL TIME WARNER BOOK GROUP
www.twbookmark.com

Time Warner Book Group
Aspect
Mysterious Press
Walk Worthy Press
Warner Books
Warner Faith
Warner Vision

Little, Brown and Company Adult Trade Books
Arcade Books
Back Bay Books
Bulfinch Press

Little, Brown and Company
Children's Publishing
Megan Tingley Books

HOLTZBRINCK PUBLISHERS (Germany)
www.vhpsva.com/bookseller/HBGenInfo.html

St. Martin's Press
LA Weekly Books
St. Martin's Griffin
St. Martin's Minotaur
St. Martin's Paperbacks
St. Martin's Press
St. Martin's Reference
St. Martin's Scholarly & Reference
Thomas Dunne Books
Truman Talley Books
Whitman

Picador USA
Picador USA

Tor/Forge
Forge
Orb
Tor
Tor Classics

Henry Holt
Edge Books
John Macrae Books
Metropolitan Books
Owl Books
Owlets
Redfeather Books

Farrar, Straus & Giroux
Aerial
Faber and Faber
Hill and Wang
Mirasol
Noonday
North Point Press
Sunburst

Literary Agents

The publishing world is never static. There's the quiet ebb and flow of imprints expanding and editors moving, and then there's the cataclysmic explosion when publishing giants collide. Through it all, the literary agent has become an increasingly important mediator, connecting writers, ideas, and publishers to form books.

With an increasing emphasis on profit margins, many of the larger publishers have eliminated the entry level editorial assistants primarily responsible for reading manuscripts sent in by writers—"over the transom" to the "slush pile," in the jargon. As a result, agents have taken over some of this task, separating the literary wheat from the chaff and forwarding the promising manuscripts on to possible publishers. Most publishers remain open to receiving at least query letters directly from authors, but some of the largest publishers accept agented submissions only.

As you look through the Book Publishers section of *Writer's Market*, you will see the symbol [A] at the beginning of some listings. This symbol denotes publishers that accept submissions only from agents. If you find a book publisher that is a perfect market for your work but only reads agented manuscripts, contacting an agent is your next logical step.

Finding an agent is *not* easier than finding a publisher. It may even be harder, since there are far fewer agents than publishing companies. However, if you do secure representation, your "reach" into the publishing world has extended to include everyone that agent knows.

CHOOSING AND USING AN AGENT

Literary agents, like authors, come in all shapes and sizes, with different areas of interest and expertise. It's to your advantage to take the time and choose an agent who is most closely aligned to your interests and your manuscript's subject.

The agents listed in this section have all indicated that they are open to working with new, previously unpublished writers as well as published writers. None of the agents listed here charge a reading fee, which is money paid to an agent to cover the time and effort in reading a manuscript or a few sample chapters. While there is nothing wrong with charging a reading fee (after all, agents have to make a living too), we encourage writers to first try agents that do not.

All of the agents listed here are members of AAR, the Association of Authors' Representatives. The AAR is a voluntary professional organization, whose members agree to abide by a strict code of ethics that prohibits charging fees for reading a manuscript, editorial services, or receiving "consideration fees" for successful referrals to third parties.

We also present a small section of script agents (25), all members of the Writers' Guild of America (WGA). WGA signatory agencies are prohibited from charging fees from WGA members; most do not charge fees of nonmembers.

The listings that follow contain the information you need to determine if an agent is suitable for your work. Read each listing carefully to see if an agency specializes in your subject areas, or go straight to the Literary Agent Subject Index found after the listings to compile a list of agencies specifically interested in the subjects you write. We've broken the Subject Index into three main categories: Nonfiction, Fiction, and Scripts.

Literary & Script Agents: The Listings

This section consists of 75 individual agency listings, followed by a Subject Index of nonfiction and fiction book and script categories which list the names of agencies that have expressed an interest in manuscripts on that subject. We've included listings for both literary and script agents. Literary agents are interested in nonfiction and fiction book manuscripts while script agents read only TV and movie scripts.

You can approach the information listed here in two ways. You can skim through the listings and see if an agent stands out, or you can check the Subject Indexes that follow these listings to focus your search more narrowly. Cross-referencing categories and concentrating on those agents interested in two or more aspects of your manuscript might increase your chances of success.

Either way, it is important to carefully read the information contained in the listing. Each agency has different interests, submission requirements, and response times. They'll tell you what they want, what they don't want, and how they want to receive it. Try to follow their directions as closely as possible. For these agents in particular, time is extremely important and wasting theirs won't help your case.

There are several sections to each listing. The first paragraph lists the agency's name, address, and contact information. It also includes when the agency was established, how many clients it represents, and what percentage of those clients are new/previously unpublished writers. It offers the agency's self-described areas of specialization and a breakdown of the different types of manuscripts it handles (nonfiction, fiction, movie scripts, etc.).

The first subsection is **Members Agents**, which lists the individuals who work at the agency. The next is **Represents**, which outlines the different nonfiction and fiction categories an agency will look at. **How to Contact** specifies how agents want to receive material and how long you should wait for their response. **Needs** identifies subjects the agents are particularly interested in seeing, as well as what they do not handle and will not look at. **Recent Sales** is self-explanatory. **Terms** offers information on the commission an agent takes (domestic and foreign), if a written contract is offered, and whether and what miscellaneous expenses are charged to an author's account. **Writers' Conferences** identifies conferences that agents attend, and **Tips** presents words of advice an agent might want to give prospective authors.

FOR MORE ON THE SUBJECT . . .

The annual *Guide to Literary Agents* (Writer's Digest Books) offers 550 agent listings and a wealth of informational articles on the author/agent relationship and other related topics.

LITERARY AGENTS

ALTAIR LITERARY AGENCY, 141 Fifth Ave., Suite 8N, New York NY 10010. (212)505-3320. **Contact:** Nicholas Smith, partner. Estab. 1996. Member of AAR. Represents 75 clients. Currently handles: 90% nonfiction books; 5% novels; 5% juvenile books.

Member Agents: Andrea Pedolsky, partner; Nicholas Smith, partner.

Represents: Nonfiction books. **Considers these nonfiction areas:** Anthropology/archaeology; art/architecture/design; business/economics; health/medicine; history; money/finance; music/dance; nature/environment; photography; popular culture; psychology; science/technology; sports; women's issues/studies; illustrated books. **Considers these fiction areas:** Historical.

O→ This agency specializes in nonfiction with an emphasis on authors who have a direct connection to their topic, and a high level of public exposure. Actively seeking solid, well-informed authors who have a public platform for the subject specialty. Interested in book to museum exhibition.

How to Contact: Query with SASE. Considers simultaneous queries. Responds in 3 weeks to queries; 1 month to mss. Obtains most new clients through recommendations from others, solicitations, author queries.

Recent Sales: *First You Shave Your Head*, by Geri Larkin (Ten Speed Press/Celestial Arts); *Being an Introvert in an Extrovert World*, by Marti Laney (Workman); *Facing the Fifties*, by Gordon Ehlers, M.D. and Jeffrey Miller (M. Evans & Co.); *Making Her Mark*, by Ernestine Miller (Contemporary Books).

Terms: Agent receives 15% commission on domestic sales; 20% commission on foreign sales. Offers written contract, binding for 1 year; 60-day notice must be given to terminate contract. Charges clients for photocopying (proposal for submission), postage (correspondence to author, proposals for submission), and marketing book for translation rights. May refer writers to outside editor but receives no compensation for referral.

Tips: "Beyond being able to write a compelling book, have an understanding of the market issues that are driving publishing today."

MIRIAM ALTSHULER LITERARY AGENCY, 53 Old Post Rd. N., Red Hook NY 12571. (845)758-9408. Fax: (845)758-3118. E-mail: malalit@ulster.net. **Contact:** Miriam Altshuler. Estab. 1994. Member of AAR. Represents 40 clients. Currently handles: 45% nonfiction books; 45% novels; 5% story collections; 5% juvenile books.

- Ms. Altshuler has been an agent since 1982.

Represents: Nonfiction books, novels, short story collections, juvenile books. **Considers these nonfiction areas:** Biography/autobiography; ethnic/cultural interests; history; language/literature/criticism; memoirs; multicultural; music/dance; nature/environment; popular culture; psychology; sociology; theater/film; women's issues/studies. **Considers these fiction areas:** Literary; mainstream/contemporary; multicultural; thriller.

How to Contact: Query with SASE. Prefers to read materials exclusively. No e-mail or fax queries. Considers simultaneous queries. Responds in 2 weeks to queries; 3 weeks to mss. Returns materials only with SASE. Obtains most new clients through recommendations from others.

Terms: Agent receives 15% commission on domestic sales; 20% commission on foreign sales. No written contract. Charges clients for overseas mailing, photocopies, overnight mail when requested by author.

Writers' Conferences: Bread Loaf Writers' Conference (Middlebury VT, August); Washington Independent Writers Spring Conference (Washington DC, May).

BETSY AMSTER LITERARY ENTERPRISES, P.O. Box 27788, Los Angeles CA 90027-0788. **Contact:** Betsy Amster. Estab. 1992. Member of AAR. Represents over 65 clients. 35% of clients are new/unpublished writers. Currently handles: 65% nonfiction books; 35% novels.

- Prior to opening her agency, Ms. Amster was an editor at Pantheon and Vintage for 10 years and served as editorial director for the Globe Pequot Press for 2 years. "This experience gives me a wider perspective on the business and the ability to give focused editorial feedback to my clients."

Represents: Nonfiction books, novels. **Considers these nonfiction areas:** Biography/autobiography; business/economics; child guidance/parenting; ethnic/cultural interests; gardening; health/medicine; history; money/finance; psychology; sociology; women's issues/studies; Native. **Considers these fiction areas:** Ethnic; literary.

O→ Actively seeking "strong narrative nonfiction, particularly by journalists; outstanding literary fiction (the next Michael Chabon or Jhumpa Lahiri); and high profile self-help and psychology, preferably research-based." Does not want to receive poetry, children's books, romances, westerns, science fiction.

How to Contact: For fiction send query, first 3 pages and SASE. For nonfiction send query or proposal with SASE. No e-mail or fax queries. Considers simultaneous queries. Responds in 1 month to queries; 2 months to mss. Obtains most new clients through recommendations from others, solicitations, conferences.

Recent Sales: *God in the Garden*, by Diana Wells (Algonquin); *Coping with the Sudden Death of a Loved One*, by Dr. Therese A. Rando (Bantam); *The Backbone of the World*, by Frank Clifford (Broadway); *The Memory Room*, by Mary Rakow (Counterpoint). Other clients include Robin Chotzinoff, Mariá Amparo Escandón, Joy Nicholson, Jan DeBlieu, Katie Singer, Mommy & Me Enterprises.

Terms: Agent receives 15% commission on domestic sales; 20% commission on foreign sales. Offers written contract, binding for 1-2 years; 60 days notice must be given to terminate contract. Charges for photocopying, postage, long distance phone calls, messengers and galleys and books used in submissions to foreign and film agents and to magazines for first serial rights.

Writers' Conferences: Squaw Valley; Maui Writers Conference; Pacific Northwest Conference; San Diego Writers Conference; UCLA Writers Conference

DAVID BLACK LITERARY AGENCY, 156 Fifth Ave., New York NY 10010. (212)242-5080. Fax: (212)924-6609. **Contact:** David Black, owner. Estab. 1990. Member of AAR. Represents 150 clients. Currently handles: 90% nonfiction books; 10% novels.

Member Agents: Susan Raihofer (general nonfiction to literary fiction); Gary Morris (commercial fiction to psychology); Joy E. Tutela (general nonfiction to literary fiction); Laureen Rowland (business, health).

Represents: Nonfiction books, novels. **Considers these nonfiction areas:** Biography/autobiography; business/economics; government/politics/law; history; memoirs; military/war; money/finance; multicultural; sports. **Considers these fiction areas:** Literary; mainstream/contemporary; Commercial.

O→ This agency specializes in business, sports, politics, and novels.

How to Contact: Query with SASE, outline. No e-mail or fax queries. Considers simultaneous queries. Responds in 2 months to queries. Returns materials only with SASE.
Recent Sales: *Body for Life*, by Bill Phillips with Mike D'Orso (HarperCollins); *Walking with the Wind*, by John Lewis with Micke D'Orso (Simon & Schuster).
Terms: Agent receives 15% commission on domestic sales. Charges clients for photocopying and books purchased for sale of foreign rights.

BOOK DEALS, INC., 244 Fifth Ave., Suite 216, New York NY 10001-7604. (212)252-2701. Fax: (212)591-6211. E-mail: bookdeals@aol.com. Website: www.bookdealsinc.com. **Contact:** Caroline Francis Carney. Estab. 1996. Member of AAR. Represents 40 clients. 30% of clients are new/unpublished writers. Currently handles: 75% nonfiction books; 25% novels.

- Prior to opening her agency, Ms. Carney was editorial director for a consumer book imprint within Times Mirror and held senior editorial positions in McGraw-Hill and Simon & Schuster.

Represents: Nonfiction books, novels (commercial and literary). **Considers these nonfiction areas:** Business/economics; child guidance/parenting; cooking/foods/nutrition; ethnic/cultural interests; health/medicine (nutrition); history; how-to; money/finance; multicultural; popular culture; psychology (popular); religious/inspirational; science/technology; self-help/personal improvement; spirituality. **Considers these fiction areas:** Ethnic; literary; mainstream/contemporary; women's (contemporary); Urban literature.

O━ This agency specializes in highly commercial nonfiction and books for African-American readers. Actively seeking well-crafted fiction and nonfiction from authors with engaging voices and impeccable credentials.

How to Contact: For nonfiction, send synopsis, outline/proposal with SASE. For fiction, send query and SASE. Considers simultaneous queries. Responds in 1 month to queries.
Recent Sales: Sold 20 titles in the last year. *Stony the Road We Trod*, by Janet Cheatham Bell (Pocket Books); *Sole Sisters*, by Deborah Mathis (Warner Books); *Eat Right for Your Personality Type*, by Dr. Robert Kushner & Nancy Kushner (St. Martin's Press).
Terms: Agent receives 15% commission on domestic sales; 20% commission on foreign sales. Offers written contract. Charges clients for photocopying and postage.
Tips: "Writers should keep on writing; agents should keep on agenting and publishers should keep on publishing. Books are the backbone of our culture. We each need to do our part to keep it strong."

BRANDT & HOCHMAN LITERARY AGENTS INC., 1501 Broadway, New York NY 10036. (212)840-5760. Fax: (212)840-5776. **Contact:** Carl Brandt; Gail Hochman; Marianne Merola; Charles Schlessiger; Meg Giles. Estab. 1913. Member of AAR. Represents 200 clients.
Represents: Nonfiction books, novels, short story collections, novellas, juvenile books, journalism. **Considers these nonfiction areas:** Biography/autobiography; current affairs; ethnic/cultural interests; government/politics/law; health/medicine; history; nature/environment; psychology; science/technology; theater/film; true crime/investigative; women's issues/studies. **Considers these fiction areas:** Action/adventure; contemporary issues; ethnic; family saga; historical; literary; mainstream/contemporary; mystery/suspense; romance; thriller; young adult.
How to Contact: Query with SASE. No submissions by fax. No fax queries. Considers simultaneous queries. Responds in 1 month to queries. Returns materials only with SASE. Obtains most new clients through recommendations from others.
Recent Sales: Sold 50 titles in the last year. This agency prefers not to share information on specific sales. Other clients include Scott Turow, Carlos Fuentes, Ursula Hegi, Michael Cunningham, Mary Pope Osborne, Avi.
Terms: Agent receives 15% commission on domestic sales; 20% commission on foreign sales. Charges clients for "manuscript duplication or other special expenses agreed to in advance."
Tips: "Write a letter which will give the agent a sense of you as a professional writer, your long-term interests as well as a short description of the work at hand."

SHEREE BYKOFSKY ASSOCIATES, INC., 16 W. 36th St., 13th Floor, New York NY 10018. Website: www.shereebee.com. **Contact:** Sheree Bykofsky. Estab. 1984, incorporated 1991. Member of AAR, ASJA, WNBA. Currently handles: 80% nonfiction books; 20% novels.

- Prior to opening her agency, Ms. Bykofsky served as executive editor of The Stonesong Press and managing editor of Chiron Press. She is also the author or co-author of more than 17 books. Ms. Bykofsky teaches publishing at NYU and The Learning Anex.

Represents: Nonfiction books, novels. **Considers these nonfiction areas:** Americana; animals; anthropology/archaeology; art/architecture/design; biography/autobiography; business/economics; child guidance/parenting; computers/electronic; cooking/foods/nutrition; crafts/hobbies; creative nonfiction (1); current affairs; education; ethnic/cultural interests; gardening; gay/lesbian issues; government/politics/law; health/medicine; history; how-to; humor/satire; interior design/decorating; language/literature/criticism; memoirs; military/war; money/finance; multicultural; music/dance; nature/environment; New Age/metaphysics; philosophy; photography; popular culture; psychology; recreation; regional; religious/inspirational; science/technology; self-help/personal improvement; sex; sociology; software; spirituality; sports; theater/film; translation; travel; true crime/investigative; women's issues/studies; **Considers these fiction areas:** Literary; mainstream/contemporary.

O━ This agency specializes in popular reference nonfiction. "I have wide-ranging interests, but it really depends on quality of writing, originality, and how a particular project appeals to me (or not). I take on very little fiction unless I completely love it—it doesn't matter what area or genre." Does not want to receive poetry, material for children, screenplays.

How to Contact: Query with SASE. No unsolicited mss or phone calls. Considers simultaneous queries. Responds in 1 week to queries; 1 month to mss. Returns materials only with SASE. Obtains most new clients through recommendations from others.
Recent Sales: Sold 100 titles in the last year. *How to Make Someone Love You in 30 Minutes or Less*, by Nicholas Boothman (Workman); *A Witness Above*, by Andy Straka (Signet); *Open Your Mind, Open Your Life*, by Taroa Gold (Andrews & McMeel).
Terms: Agent receives 15% commission on domestic sales; 15% commission on foreign sales. Offers written contract, binding for 1 year. Charges for postage, photocopying and fax.
Writers' Conferences: ASJA (New York City); Asilomar (Pacific Grove CA); Kent State; Southwestern Writers; Willamette (Portland); Dorothy Canfield Fisher (San Diego); Writers Union (Maui); Pacific NW; IWWG; and many others.
Tips: "Read the agent listing carefully, and comply with guidelines."

CARLISLE & COMPANY, 24 E. 64th St., New York NY 10021. (212)813-1881. Fax: (212)813-9567. E-mail: mtessler@carlisleco.com. Website: www.carlisleco.com. **Contact:** Michelle Tessler. Estab. 1998. Member of AAR. Represents 100 clients. Currently handles: 60% nonfiction books; 35% novels; 5% story collections.

- Prior to opening his agency, Mr. Carlisle was the Vice President of William Morris for 18 years.

Member Agents: Michael Carlisle; Christy Fletcher; Emma Parry; Michelle Tessler. Affiliates: Donald S. Lamm, Robert Bernstein, Paul Bresnick.
Represents: Considers these nonfiction areas: Biography/autobiography; business/economics; cooking/foods/nutrition; health/medicine; history; memoirs; popular culture; psychology; science/technology; lifestyle. **Considers these fiction areas:** Literary; mainstream/contemporary.

O→ This agency has "expertise in nonfiction. We have a strong focus on editorial input on fiction before submission." Does not want to receive science fiction, fantasy, or romance.

How to Contact: Query with SASE. Responds in 10 days to queries; 3 weeks to mss. Obtains most new clients through recommendations from others.
Recent Sales: Sold 80 titles in the last year. *The Founding*, by Jay Winik (HarperCollins); *The Piano Turner*, by Daniel Philippe Mason (Knopf); *The Americans*, by David M. Kennedy (Viking).
Terms: Agent receives 15% commission on domestic sales; 20% commission on foreign sales. Offers written contract, binding for 1 book only.
Writers' Conferences: Squaw Valley Community Conference (California).
Tips: "Be sure to write as original a story as possible. Remember, you're asking the public to pay $25 for your book."

MARIA CARVAINIS AGENCY, INC., 1350 Avenue of the Americas, Suite 2905, New York NY 10019. (212)245-6365. Fax: (212)245-7196. E-mail: mca@mariacarvainisagency.com. **Contact:** Maria Carvainis, president; Frances Kuffel, executive vice president. Estab. 1977. Member of AAR, Authors Guild, ABA, MWA, RWA; signatory of WGA. Represents 70 clients. 10% of clients are new/unpublished writers. Currently handles: 34% nonfiction books; 65% novels; 1% poetry.

- Prior to opening her agency, Ms. Carvainis spent more than 10 years in the publishing industry as a senior editor with Macmillan Publishing, Basic Books, Avon Books, and Crown Publishers. Ms. Carvainis has served as a member of the AAR Board of Directors and AAR Treasurer, as well as serving as chair of the AAR Contracts Committee. She presently serves on the AAR Royalty Committee.

Member Agents: Maria Carvainis, Frances Kuffel, Anna Del Veccio, Moira Sullivan.
Represents: Nonfiction books, novels. **Considers these nonfiction areas:** Biography/autobiography; business/economics; history; memoirs; science/technology (pop science); women's issues/studies. **Considers these fiction areas:** Historical; literary; mainstream/contemporary; mystery/suspense; thriller; women's fiction; young adult.

O→ Does not want to receive science fiction or children's.

How to Contact: Query with SASE. Responds in 1 week to queries; 3 months to mss. Obtains most new clients through recommendations from others, conferences, 60% from conferences/referrals; 40% from query letters.
Recent Sales: *The Guru Guide to the Knowledge Economy*, by Joseph H. Boyett and Jimmie T. Boyett (John Wiley and Sonts); *Last Breath*, by Peter Stark (Ballantine); *The Devil's Hearth*, by Phillip DePoy (St. Martin's Press). Other clients include Robert Kolb, David Bottoms, Pam Conrad, Cindy Gerard, Hugo Mager, Samantha James, Kristine Rolofson, Charlie Smith, Janet Soares, Jose Yglesias, Fred Haefele, D. Anna Love, Fred Willard.
Terms: Agent receives 15% commission on domestic sales; 20% commission on foreign sales. Offers written contract, binding for 2 years. Charges clients for foreign postage, bulk copying.
Writers' Conferences: BEA; Frankfurt Book Fair.

CASTIGLIA LITERARY AGENCY, 1155 Camino Del Mar, Suite 510, Del Mar CA 92014. (858)755-8761. Fax: (858)755-7063. **Contact:** Julie Castiglia. Estab. 1993. Member of AAR, PEN. Represents 50 clients. Currently handles: 55% nonfiction books; 45% novels.
Member Agents: Winifred Golden; Julie Castiglia.
Represents: Nonfiction books, novels. **Considers these nonfiction areas:** Animals; anthropology/archaeology; biography/autobiography; business/economics; child guidance/parenting; cooking/foods/nutrition; current affairs; ethnic/cultural interests; health/medicine; history; language/literature/criticism; money/finance; nature/environment; New Age/metaphysics; psychology; religious/inspirational; science/technology; self-help/personal improvement; sociology; women's issues/studies. **Considers these fiction areas:** Contemporary issues; ethnic; glitz; literary; mainstream/contemporary; mystery/suspense; women's (especially).

Does not want to receive horror, screenplays or academic nonfiction.

How to Contact: Query with SASE. No fax queries. Responds in 2 months to mss. Returns materials only with SASE. Obtains most new clients through recommendations from others, solicitations, conferences.

Recent Sales: Sold 25 titles in the last year. *Harlem Redux*, by Persia Walker (Simon & Schuster); *Oracle of Love*, by Leeann Richards (Three Rivers/Crown); *West of Kabul, East of New York*, by Tamim Ansary (Farrar, Straus & Giroux).

Terms: Agent receives 15% commission on domestic sales; 25% commission on foreign sales. Offers written contract; 6-week notice must be given to terminate contract. Charges clients for excessive postage and copying.

Writers' Conferences: Southwestern Writers Conference (Albuquerque NM, August); National Writers Conference; Willamette Writers Conference (Oregon); San Diego State University (California); Writers at Work (Utah).

Tips: "Be professional with submissions. Attend workshops and conferences before you approach an agent."

WM CLARK ASSOCIATES, 355 W. 22nd St., New York NY 10011. (212)675-2784. Fax: (646)349-1658. E-mail: query@wmclark.com. Website: www.wmclark.com. **Contact:** William Clark. Estab. 1999. Member of AAR. 4.25% of clients are new/unpublished writers. Currently handles: 50% nonfiction books; 50% novels.

- Prior to opening WCA, Mr. Clark was an agent at the Virginia Barber Literary Agency and William Morris Agency.

Represents: Nonfiction books, novels, short story collections. **Considers these nonfiction areas:** Art/architecture/design; biography/autobiography; current affairs; ethnic/cultural interests; history; memoirs; music/dance; popular culture; religious/inspirational (Eastern religion philosophy only); science/technology; sociology; theater/film; translation. **Considers these fiction areas:** Contemporary issues; ethnic; historical; literary; mainstream/contemporary; Southern fiction.

"As one of the new breed of media agents recognizing their expanded roles in today's ever-changing media landscape, William Clark represents a diverse range of commercial and literary fiction and quality nonfiction to the book publishing, motion picture, television, and new media fields."

How to Contact: Prefers to read materials exclusively. E-mail queries only. Responds in 2-4 weeks to queries. Obtains most new clients through recommendations from others.

Recent Sales: Sold 25 titles in the last year. *Bjork*, by Bjork (Bloomsbury); *Dante's Path*, by Bonney and Richard Schaub (Penguin/Bill Shinker); *Boogie Woogie*, by Danny Moynihan (St. Martin's Press); *Housebroken*, by David Eddie (Riverhead); *Savvy in the City Guides*, (St. Martin's Press); *Stardust Melodies*, by Will Friedwald (Alfred A. Knopf); *Mark Hampton: The Art of Friendship*, by Duane Hampton (HarperCollins). Other clients include Molly Jong-Fast, William Monahan, Cornelia Bailey, James St. James, Jonathan Stone, Dr. Doreen Virtue, Mian Mian.

Terms: Agent receives 15% commission on domestic sales; 20% commission on foreign sales. Offers written contract.

Tips: "E-mail queries should include a general description of the work, a synopsis/outline if available, biographical information, and publishing history, if any."

LIZA DAWSON ASSOCIATES, 240 W. 35th St., Suite 500, New York NY 10001. (212)465-9071 or (212)629-9212. **Contact:** Liza Dawson, Rebecca Kurson, Caitlin Blasdell. Member of AAR, MWA, Women's Media Group. Represents 50 clients. 10% of clients are new/unpublished writers. Currently handles: 60% nonfiction books; 40% novels.

- Prior to becoming an agent, Ms. Dawson was an editor for 20 years, spending 11 years at William Morrow as vice president and 2 at Putnam as executive editor. Ms. Kurson was an associate editor at Farrar Straus; Ms. Blasdell was a senior editor at HarperCollins and Avon.

Member Agents: Liza Dawson; Rebecca Kurson (science, women's issues, narrative nonfiction, literary fiction); Caitlin Blasdell (science fiction, business books, commercial fiction).

Represents: Nonfiction books, novels, scholarly books. **Considers these nonfiction areas:** Biography/autobiography; business/economics; child guidance/parenting; health/medicine; history; memoirs; psychology; sociology; women's issues/studies. **Considers these fiction areas:** Ethnic; family saga; historical; literary; mystery/suspense; regional; thriller.

This agency specializes in readable literary fiction, thrillers, mainstream historicals and women's fiction, academics, historians, business, journalists and psychology. "My specialty is shaping books and ideas so that a publisher will respond quickly." Actively seeking talented professionals. Does not want to receive westerns, sports, computers, juvenile.

How to Contact: Query with SASE. Responds in 3 weeks to queries; 6 weeks to mss. Obtains most new clients through recommendations from others, conferences.

Recent Sales: Sold 40 titles in the last year. *Darjeeling*, by Bharti Kirchner (St. Martin's); *Wild Mothers*, (Algonquin); *My Mother's Island*, by Marnie Mueller (Curbstone); *Life or Debt*, by Stacy Johnson (Ballantine); *The Summer of My Greek Taverna*, by Tom Stone (Simon & Schuster); *Poker Nation*, by Andy Bellin (HarperCollins).

Terms: Agent receives 15% commission on domestic sales; 20% commission on foreign sales. Offers written contract. Charges clients for photocopying and overseas postage.

Writers' Conferences: Pacific Northwest Book Conference (Seattle, July).

Reading List: Reads *The Sun*, *New York Review of Books*, *The New York Observer*, *Utne Reader*, and *The Wall Street Journal* to find new clients.

Tips: "Please include a detailed bio with any query letter, let me know somehow that you've done a little research, that you're not just interested in any agent but someone who is right for you."

DH LITERARY, INC., P.O. Box 990, Nyack NY 10960-0990. (212)753-7942. E-mail: dhendin@aol.com. **Contact:** David Hendin. Estab. 1993. Member of AAR. Represents 30 clients. 20% of clients are new/unpublished writers. Currently handles: 60% nonfiction books; 20% novels; 10% scholarly books; 20% syndicated material.

• Prior to opening his agency, Mr. Hendin served as president and publisher for Pharos Books/World Almanac as well as senior VP and COO at sister company United Feature Syndicate.

Represents: Nonfiction books, novels, syndicated material. **Considers these nonfiction areas:** Animals; anthropology/archaeology; child guidance/parenting; ethnic/cultural interests; government/politics/law; health/medicine; history; language/literature/criticism; money/finance; nature/environment; psychology; science/technology; women's issues/studies. **Considers these fiction areas:** Literary; mainstream/contemporary; mystery/suspense; thriller.

O→ This agency specializes in trade nonfiction and newspaper syndication of columns or comic strips.

How to Contact: Query with SASE. Considers simultaneous queries. Responds in 6 weeks to queries. Returns materials only with SASE. Obtains most new clients through recommendations from others.

Recent Sales: Sold 18-20 titles in the last year. *Pink Flamingo Murders*, by Elaine Viets (Dell); *Age of Anxious Anxiety*, by Tom Tiede (Grove Atlantic); *History of American Etiquette*, by Judith Martin (Norton).

Terms: Agent receives 15% commission on domestic sales; 20% commission on foreign sales. Offers written contract, binding for 1 year. Charges for out of pocket expenses for postage, photocopying ms, and overseas phone calls specifically related to a book.

Tips: "Have your project in mind and on paper before you submit. Too many writers/cartoonists say 'I'm good...get me a project.' Publishers want writers with their own great ideas and their own unique voice. No faxed submissions."

JANIS A. DONNAUD & ASSOCIATES, INC., 525 Broadway, 2nd Floor, New York NY 10012. (212)431-2664. Fax: (212)431-2667. E-mail: jdonnaud@aol.com. **Contact:** Janis A. Donnaud. Member of AAR; signatory of WGA. Represents 40 clients. 10% of clients are new/unpublished writers. Currently handles: 100% nonfiction books.

• Prior to opening her agency, Ms. Donnaud was Vice President, Associate Publisher, Random House Adult Trade group.

Represents: Nonfiction books. **Considers these nonfiction areas:** Art/architecture/design; biography/autobiography; child guidance/parenting; cooking/foods/nutrition; creative nonfiction; current affairs; health/medicine; humor/satire; psychology (pop).

O→ This agency specializes in health, medical, cooking, humor, pop psychology, narrative nonfiction, photography, art, literary fiction, biography, parenting, current affairs. "We give a lot of service and attention to clients." Actively seeking serious narrative nonfiction; literary fiction; cookbooks; health and medical by authors with an established reputation in their area of specialty. Does not want to receive fiction, poetry, mysteries, juvenile books, romances, science fiction, young adult, religious fantasy.

How to Contact: Query with SASE, description of book and 2-3 pages of sample material. Prefers to read materials exclusively. Accepts e-mail and fax queries. Responds in 1 month to queries; 1 month to mss. Obtains most new clients through recommendations from others.

Recent Sales: Sold 25 titles in the last year. *The Flambaya Tree: A Memoir of WWII*, by Clara Kelly (Random House); *Nancy Silverton's Sandwiches from the LaBrea Bakery*, by Nancy Silverton (Knopf).

Terms: Agent receives 15% commission on domestic sales; 20% commission on foreign sales. Offers written contract; 30-day notice must be given to terminate contract. Charges clients for messengers, photocopying, purchase of books.

DUNHAM LITERARY, 156 Fifth Avenue, Suite 625, New York NY 10010-7002. (212)929-0994. Fax: (212)929-0904. **Contact:** Jennie Dunham. Estab. 2000. Member of AAR. Represents 50 clients. 15% of clients are new/unpublished writers. Currently handles: 25% nonfiction books; 25% novels; 50% juvenile books.

• Prior to opening her agency, Ms. Dunham worked as a literary agent for Russell & Volkening.

Member Agents: Donna Lieberman (mainstream fiction and nonfiction, mysteries, suspense, thrillers).

Represents: Nonfiction books, novels, short story collections, juvenile books. **Considers these nonfiction areas:** Anthropology/archaeology; art/architecture/design; biography/autobiography; business/economics; current affairs; education; ethnic/cultural interests; gay/lesbian issues; government/politics/law; health/medicine; history; juvenile nonfiction; language/literature/criticism; music/dance; nature/environment; photography; popular culture; psychology; science/technology; sociology; sports; women's issues/studies. **Considers these fiction areas:** Ethnic; juvenile; literary; mainstream/contemporary; mystery/suspense; picture books; thriller; young adult.

How to Contact: Query with SASE. No fax queries. Responds in 1 week to queries; 2 months to mss. Obtains most new clients through recommendations from others, solicitations.

Recent Sales: *Living Dead Girl*, by Tod Goldberg; *Native New Yorkers*, by Evan Pritchard; *Molly*, by Nancy Jones; *Hidden Witness*, by Jackie Napolean Wilson; *Letters of Intent*, by Anna Bondoc and Meg Daly; *And Baby Makes Four*, by Hilory Wanger; *A Positive Life*, by River Huston and photographed by Mary Berridge; *Everything Motorcycles* and *WICCA for Couples*, by A.J. Drew; *Ezmereld Chronicles: Initiation At Beltane*, by Tamarin Laurel; *Reflexology Sox*, by Michelle Kluck; *Devoted to Deity*, by Judy Harrow; *Magick Made Easy* and *Goddess In My Pocket*, by Trish Telesco; *Clever Beatrice*, illustrated by Heather Solomon; *Lincoln*, illustrated by David A. Johnson; *Who Will Tell My Brother?*, by Marlene Carvell; *Pirates*, by C. Drew Lamm; *Young Naturalist's Handbook of Butterflies/Beetles*, by Robert Sabuda and Matthew Reinhart; *Animal Popposites*, by Matthew Reinhart; *The Tale of Tricky Fox*, illustrated by Barbara McClintock; *Molly and the Magic Wishbone*, by Barbara McClintock; *Dancing Mathilda*, by Sarah Hager.

Terms: Agent receives 15% commission on domestic sales; 20% commission on foreign sales. Writers reimbursed for office fees after the sale of ms.

ANN ELMO AGENCY INC., 60 E. 42nd St., New York NY 10165. (212)661-2880, 2881. Fax: (212)661-2883. **Contact:** Lettie Lee. Estab. 1961. Member of AAR, MWA, Authors Guild.

Member Agents: Lettie Lee; Mari Cronin (plays); A.L. Abecassis (nonfiction).

Represents: Nonfiction books, novels. **Considers these nonfiction areas:** Biography/autobiography; business/economics; child guidance/parenting; cooking/foods/nutrition; current affairs; education; health/medicine; history; how-to; juvenile nonfiction; money/finance; music/dance; popular culture; psychology; science/technology; self-help/personal improvement; theater/film; true crime/investigative; women's issues/studies. **Considers these fiction areas:** Contemporary issues; detective/police/crime; ethnic; family saga; historical; juvenile; literary; mainstream/contemporary; mystery/suspense; regional; romance (contemporary, gothic, historical, regency); thriller; young adult.
How to Contact: Letter queries *only* with SASE. No fax queries. Responds in 3 months to queries. Obtains most new clients through recommendations from others.
Recent Sales: This agency prefers not to share information on specific sales.
Terms: Agent receives 15% commission on domestic sales; 20% commission on foreign sales. Offers written contract, binding for standard AAR contract. Charges clients for "special mailings or shipping considerations or multiple international calls. No charge for usual cost of doing business."
Tips: "Query first, and when asked only please send properly prepared manuscript. A double-spaced, readable manuscript is the best recommendation. Include SASE, of course."

FELICIA ETH LITERARY REPRESENTATION, 555 Bryant St., Suite 350, Palo Alto CA 94301-1700. (650)375-1276. Fax: (650)375-1277. E-mail: feliciaeth@aol.com. **Contact:** Felicia Eth. Estab. 1988. Member of AAR. Represents 25-35 clients. Works with established and new writers. Currently handles: 85% nonfiction books; 15% adult novels.
Represents: Nonfiction books, novels. **Considers these nonfiction areas:** Animals; anthropology/archaeology; biography/autobiography; business/economics; child guidance/parenting; current affairs; ethnic/cultural interests; gay/lesbian issues; government/politics/law; health/medicine; history; nature/environment; popular culture; psychology; science/technology; sociology; true crime/investigative; women's issues/studies. **Considers these fiction areas:** Ethnic; feminist; gay/lesbian; literary; mainstream/contemporary; thriller.

O⊸ This agency specializes in "provocative, intelligent, thoughtful nonfiction on a wide array of subjects which are commercial and high-quality fiction; preferably mainstream and contemporary."

How to Contact: Query with SASE, outline. Considers simultaneous queries. Responds in 3 weeks to queries; 1 month to mss.
Recent Sales: Sold 7-10 titles in the last year. *Recovering the Power of the Ancestral Mind*, by Dr. Gregg Jacobs (Viking); *The Ulster Path*, by Will Ferguson (Grove/Atlantic); *Socrates Cafe*, by Chris Phillips (W.W. Norton); *Imperfect Harmony*, by Joshua Coleman (St. Martin's); *Baby Catcher: Chronicles of a Modern Midwife*, by Peggy Vincent (Charles Scribner's); *The Devil's Cup*, by Stewart Allen (Soho Press).
Terms: Agent receives 15% commission on domestic sales; 20% commission on foreign sales; 20% commission on dramatic rights sales. Charges clients for photocopying, express mail service—extraordinary expenses.
Writers' Conferences: Independent Writers of LA (Los Angeles); Conference of National Coalition of Independent Scholars (Berkley CA); Writers Guild.
Tips: "For nonfiction, established expertise is certainly a plus, as is magazine publication—though not a prerequisite. I am highly dedicated to those projects I represent."

JEANNE FREDERICKS LITERARY AGENCY, INC., 221 Benedict Hill Rd., New Canaan CT 06840. (203)972-3011. Fax: (203)972-3011. E-mail: jfredrks@optonline.net. **Contact:** Jeanne Fredericks. Estab. 1997. Member of AAR, Authors Guild. Represents 90 clients. 10% of clients are new/unpublished writers. Currently handles: 98% nonfiction books; 2% novels.

• Prior to opening her agency, Ms. Fredericks was an agent and acting director with the Susan P. Urstadt Inc. Agency. In an earlier career, she held editorial positions in trade publishing, most recently as editorial director of Ziff-Davis Books.

Represents: Nonfiction books. **Considers these nonfiction areas:** Animals; anthropology/archaeology; biography/autobiography; business/economics; child guidance/parenting; cooking/foods/nutrition; crafts/hobbies; gardening; health/medicine (and alternative health); history; how-to; interior design/decorating; money/finance; nature/environment; photography; psychology; science/technology; self-help/personal improvement; sports; women's issues/studies.

O⊸ This agency specializes in quality adult nonfiction by authorities in their fields.

How to Contact: Query first with SASE. Then send outline/proposal, 1-2 sample chapters and SASE. No fax queries. Accepts e-mail queries if short; no attachments. Considers simultaneous queries. Responds in 3 weeks to queries; 2 months to mss. Returns materials only with SASE. Obtains most new clients through recommendations from others, solicitations, conferences.
Recent Sales: Sold 20 titles in the last year. *From Storebought to Homemade*, by Emyl Jenkins; *The Internet Legal Guide*, by Dennis Powers; *Getting Ready for Baby*, by Hélène Stelian (Chronicle).
Terms: Agent receives 15% commission on domestic sales; 25% commission on foreign sales with co-agent; without co-agent receives 20% commission on foreign sales. Offers written contract, binding for 9 months; 2 months notice must be given to terminate contract. Charges client for photocopying of whole proposals and mss, overseas postage, priority mail and express mail services.
Writers' Conferences: PEN Women Conference (Williamsburg VA, February); Connecticut Press Club Biennial Writer's Conference (Stamford CT, April); ASJA Annual Writers' Conference East (New York NY, May); BEA (New York, May).
Tips: "Be sure to research the competition for your work and be able to justify why there's a need for it. I enjoy building an author's career, particularly if s(he) is professional, hardworking, and courteous. Aside from eight years of

agenting experience, I've had ten years of editorial experience in adult trade book publishing that enables me to help an author polish a proposal so that it's more appealing to prospective editors. My MBA in marketing also distinguishes me from other agents."

SANFORD J. GREENBURGER ASSOCIATES, INC., 55 Fifth Ave., New York NY 10003. (212)206-5600. Fax: (212)463-8718. Website: www.greenburger.com. **Contact:** Heide Lange. Estab. 1945. Member of AAR. Represents 500 clients.

Member Agents: Heide Lange; Faith Hamlin; Beth Vesel; Theresa Park; Elyse Cheney; Dan Mandel; Julie Barer.

Represents: Nonfiction books, novels. **Considers these nonfiction areas:** Agriculture/horticulture; americana; animals; anthropology/archaeology; art/architecture/design; biography/autobiography; business/economics; child guidance/parenting; computers/electronic; cooking/foods/nutrition; crafts/hobbies; creative nonfiction (1); current affairs; education; ethnic/cultural interests; gardening; gay/lesbian issues; government/politics/law; health/medicine; history; how-to; humor/satire; interior design/decorating; juvenile nonfiction; language/literature/criticism; memoirs; military/war; money/finance; multicultural; music/dance; nature/environment; New Age/metaphysics; philosophy; photography; popular culture; psychology; recreation; regional; religious/inspirational; science/technology; self-help/personal improvement; sex; sociology; software; spirituality; sports; theater/film; translation; travel; true crime/investigative; women's issues/studies; young adult. **Considers these fiction areas:** Action/adventure; contemporary issues; detective/police/crime; ethnic; family saga; feminist; gay/lesbian; glitz; historical; humor/satire; literary; mainstream/contemporary; mystery/suspense; psychic/supernatural; regional; sports; thriller.

O→ Does not want to receive romances or westerns.

How to Contact: Query with SASE. Considers simultaneous queries. Responds in 3 weeks to queries; 2 months to mss.

Recent Sales: Sold 200 titles in the last year. This agency prefers not to share information on specific sales. Other clients include Andrew Ross, Margaret Cuthbert, Nicholas Sparks, Mary Kurcinka, Linda Nichols, Edy Clarke and Peggy Claude Pierre, Brad Thor, Dan Brown, Sallie Bissell.

Terms: Agent receives 15% commission on domestic sales; 20% commission on foreign sales. Charges for photocopying, books for foreign and subsidiary rights submissions.

REECE HALSEY NORTH, 98 Main St., #704, Tiburon CA 94920. (415)789-9191. E-mail: info@reecehalseynorth.com. Website: www.reecehalseynorth.com or kimberleycameron.com. **Contact:** Kimberley Cameron. Estab. 1995. Member of AAR. Represents 40 clients. 30% of clients are new/unpublished writers. Currently handles: 30% nonfiction books; 70% fiction.

Member Agents: Kimberley Cameron (Reece Halsey North); Dorris Halsey (by referral only, LA office).

Represents: Nonfiction books, novels. **Considers these nonfiction areas:** Biography/autobiography; current affairs; history; language/literature/criticism; memoirs; popular culture; spirituality; true crime/investigative; women's issues/studies. **Considers these fiction areas:** Action/adventure; ethnic; historical; literary; mainstream/contemporary; mystery/suspense; science fiction. **Considers these script subject areas:** Thriller.

O→ This agency specializes in mystery, literary and mainstream fiction, excellent writing. The Reece Halsey Agency has an illustrious client list largely of established writers, including the estate of Aldous Huxley and has represented Upton Sinclair, William Faulkner and Henry Miller. Ms. Cameron has a Northern California office and all queries should be addressed to her at the Tiburon office.

How to Contact: Query with SASE. No e-mail or fax queries. Considers simultaneous queries. Responds in 6 weeks to queries; 3 months to mss. Obtains most new clients through recommendations from others, solicitations.

Recent Sales: *Jinn*, by Matthew Delaney (St. Martin's Press); *Flu Season*, by Earl Merkel (Dutton-NAL).

Terms: Agent receives 15% commission on domestic sales. Offers written contract, binding for 1 year. Requests 6 copies of ms if representing an author.

Writers' Conferences: BEA; Maui Writers Conference.

Reading List: Reads *Glimmer Train*, *The Sun* and *The New Yorker* to find new clients. Looks for "writing that touches the heart."

Tips: "Please send a polite, well-written query and include a SASE with it!"

THE JOY HARRIS LITERARY AGENCY, INC., 156 Fifth Ave., Suite 617, New York NY 10010. (212)924-6269. Fax: (212)924-6609. E-mail: gen.office@jhlitagent.com. **Contact:** Joy Harris. Member of AAR. Represents 100 clients. Currently handles: 50% nonfiction books; 50% novels.

Member Agents: Leslie Daniels; Stéphanie Abou; Alexia Paul (associate member).

Represents: Nonfiction books, novels. **Considers these fiction areas:** Action/adventure; comic books/cartoon; confession; contemporary issues; detective/police/crime; ethnic; experimental; family saga; feminist; gay/lesbian; glitz; hi-lo; historical; humor/satire; literary; mainstream/contemporary; military/war; multicultural; multimedia; mystery/suspense; New Age; picture books; poetry; poetry in translation; regional; religious/inspirational; short story collections; spiritual; sports; thriller; translation; women's.

O→ Does not want to receive screenplays.

How to Contact: Query with outline/proposal, SASE. Considers simultaneous queries. Responds in 2 months to queries. Obtains most new clients through recommendations from clients and editors.

Recent Sales: Sold 15 titles in the last year. This agency prefers not to share information on specific sales.

Terms: Agent receives 15% commission on domestic sales; 20% commission on foreign sales. Charges clients for some office expenses.

HARVEY KLINGER, INC., 301 W. 53rd St., New York NY 10019. (212)581-7068. Fax: (212)315-3823. E-mail: klingerinc@aol.com. **Contact:** Harvey Klinger. Estab. 1977. Member of AAR. Represents 100 clients. 25% of clients are new/unpublished writers. Currently handles: 50% nonfiction books; 50% novels.

Member Agents: David Dunton (popular culture, parenting, home improvement, thrillers/crime); Lisa Dicker (literary fiction, general nonfiction, sports); Jenny Bent (general nonfiction and women's fiction).

Represents: Nonfiction books, novels. **Considers these nonfiction areas:** Biography/autobiography; cooking/foods/nutrition; health/medicine; psychology; science/technology; self-help/personal improvement; spirituality; sports; true crime/investigative; women's issues/studies. **Considers these fiction areas:** Action/adventure; detective/police/crime; family saga; glitz; literary; mainstream/contemporary; mystery/suspense; thriller.

O→ This agency specializes in "big, mainstream contemporary fiction and nonfiction."

How to Contact: Query with SASE. Accepts e-mail queries. No fax queries. Responds in 1 month to queries; 2 months to mss. Obtains most new clients through recommendations from others.

Recent Sales: Sold 30 titles in the last year. *The Music of the Spheres*, by Elizabeth Redfern (Putnam); *The Carousel*, by Richard Paul Evans (Simon & Schuster); *Sacred Ground*, by Barbara Wood (St. Martin's Press). Other clients include Clare Ansberry, Mac Randall, Barbara De Angelis, Julie Stav, Jill Conner Browne, Terry Kay.

Terms: Agent receives 15% commission on domestic sales; 25% commission on foreign sales. Offers written contract. Charges for photocopying mss, overseas postage for mss.

THE KNIGHT AGENCY, P.O. Box 550648, Atlanta GA 30355. (404)816-9620. E-mail: knightagency@msn.com. Website: www.knightagency.net. Also: 2407 Matthews St., Atlanta GA 30319. **Contact:** Deidre Knight, Pamela Harty, Lisa Payne. Estab. 1996. Member of AAR, RWA, Authors Guild. Represents 65 clients. 25% of clients are new/unpublished writers. Currently handles: 50% nonfiction books; 50% novels.

Member Agents: Deidre Knight (president, agent); Pamela Harty (agent); Lisa Wessling Payne (agency associate).

Represents: Nonfiction books, novels. **Considers these nonfiction areas:** Business/economics; child guidance/parenting; current affairs; ethnic/cultural interests; health/medicine; history; how-to; money/finance; music/dance; popular culture; psychology; religious/inspirational; self-help/personal improvement; theater/film. **Considers these fiction areas:** Ethnic; literary; mainstream/contemporary (commercial); romance (contemporary, historical, inspirational); science fiction; women's; paranormal.

O→ "We are looking for a wide variety of fiction and nonfiction. In the nonfiction area, we're particularly eager to find personal finance, business investment, pop culture, self-help/motivational and popular reference books. In fiction, we're always looking for romance; women's fiction; commercial fiction."

How to Contact: Query with SASE or by e-mail. Considers simultaneous queries. Responds in 2 weeks to queries; 2-3 months to mss.

Recent Sales: Sold approximately 65 titles in the last year. *Kiss of the Highlander*, by Karen Marie Moning (Bantam Dell); *The Friendship Quilt*, by Lauraine Snelling (WaterBrook Press).

Terms: Agent receives 15% commission on domestic sales; 25% commission on foreign sales. Offers written contract, binding for 1 year; 30 days notice must be given to terminate contract. Charges clients for photocopying, postage, overnight courier expenses. "These are deducted from the sale of the work, not billed upfront."

Tips: "At the Knight Agency, a client usually ends up becoming a friend."

ELAINE KOSTER LITERARY AGENCY, LLC, 55 Central Park West, Suite 6, New York NY 10023. (212)362-9488. Fax: (212)712-0164. **Contact:** Elaine Koster. Member of AAR, MWA. Represents 40 clients. 10% of clients are new/unpublished writers. Currently handles: 30% nonfiction books; 70% novels.

- Prior to opening her agency, Ms. Koster was president and publisher of Dutton NAL.

Represents: Nonfiction books, novels. **Considers these nonfiction areas:** Biography/autobiography; business/economics; child guidance/parenting; cooking/foods/nutrition; current affairs; ethnic/cultural interests; health/medicine; history; how-to; money/finance; nature/environment; New Age/metaphysics; popular culture; psychology; self-help/personal improvement; spirituality; women's issues/studies. **Considers these fiction areas:** Action/adventure; contemporary issues; detective/police/crime; ethnic; family saga; feminist; historical; literary; mainstream/contemporary; mystery/suspense (amateur sleuth, cozy, culinary, malice domestic); regional; thriller.

O→ This agency specializes in quality fiction and nonfiction. Does not want to receive juvenile, screenplays, or science fiction.

How to Contact: Query with SASE, outline, 3 sample chapter(s). Prefers to read materials exclusively. No e-mail or fax queries. Responds in 3 weeks to queries; 1 month to mss. Returns materials only with SASE. Obtains most new clients through recommendations from others.

Recent Sales: *Wandering Warrior*, by Da Chen (Random House); *A Taste of Reality*, by Kimberla Lawson Roby (HarperCollins); *Getting Out*, by Gwendolen Gross (Holt).

Terms: Agent receives 15% commission on domestic sales; 20% commission on foreign sales. Offers written contract. Charges clients for photocopying, messengers, express mail, books and book galley, ordered from publisher to exploit other rights, overseas shipment of mss and books.

Tips: "We prefer exclusive submissions. Don't e-mail or fax submissions."

MICHAEL LARSEN/ELIZABETH POMADA LITERARY AGENTS, 1029 Jones St., San Francisco CA 94109-5023. (415)673-0939. E-mail: larsenpoma@aol.com. Website: www.Larsen-Pomada.com. **Contact:** Mike Larsen or Elizabeth Pomada. Estab. 1972. Member of AAR, Authors Guild, ASJA, NWA, PEN, WNBA, California Writers Club. Represents 100 clients. 40-45% of clients are new/unpublished writers. Currently handles: 70% nonfiction books; 30% novels.

● Prior to opening their agency, both Mr. Larsen and Ms. Pomada were promotion executives for major publishing houses. Mr. Larsen worked for Morrow, Bantam and Pyramid (now part of Berkley), Ms. Pomada worked at Holt, David McKay, and The Dial Press.

Member Agents: Michael Larsen (nonfiction); Elizabeth Pomada (fiction, books of interest to women).

Represents: Nonfiction books (adult), novels. **Considers these nonfiction areas:** Anthropology/archaeology; art/architecture/design; biography/autobiography; business/economics; cooking/foods/nutrition; current affairs; ethnic/cultural interests; gay/lesbian issues; government/politics/law; health/medicine; history; how-to; humor/satire; interior design/decorating; memoirs; money/finance; music/dance; nature/environment; New Age/metaphysics; photography; popular culture; psychology; religious/inspirational; science/technology; self-help/personal improvement; sociology; sports; theater/film; travel; true crime/investigative; women's issues/studies; Futurism. **Considers these fiction areas:** Action/adventure; contemporary issues; detective/police/crime; ethnic; experimental; family saga; fantasy; feminist; gay/lesbian; glitz; historical; humor/satire; literary; mainstream/contemporary; mystery/suspense; religious/inspirational; romance (contemporary, gothic, historical).

O╕ "We have very diverse tastes. We look for fresh voices and new ideas. We handle literary, commercial and genre fiction, and the full range of nonfiction books." Actively seeking commercial and literary fiction. Does not want to receive children's books, plays, short stories, screenplays, pornography, poetry.

How to Contact: Query with SASE, first 10 pages of completed novel and 2-page synopsis, SASE. For nonfiction, send title, promotion plan and proposal done according to our plan (See website.) No e-mail or fax queries. Responds in 2 months to queries.

Recent Sales: Sold 25 titles in the last year. *The Money Dragon*, by Pam Chun (Sourcebooks); *Guerilla Creativity*, by Jay C. Levinson (Houghton Mifflin).

Terms: Agent receives 15% commission on domestic sales; 20-30% commission on foreign sales. May charge for printing, postage for multiple submissions, foreign mail, foreign phone calls, galleys, books, and legal fees.

Writers' Conferences: Book Expo America; Santa Barbara Writers Conference (Santa Barbara); Maui Writers Conference (Maui); ASJA.

Tips: "We will not open mail that does not have a return address on it."

ELLEN LEVINE LITERARY AGENCY, INC., 15 E. 26th St., Suite 1801, New York NY 10010. (212)889-0620. Fax: (212)725-4501. **Contact:** Ellen Levine, Diana Finch, Elizabeth Kaplan, Louise Quayle. Estab. 1980. Member of AAR. Represents 200 clients. 20% of clients are new/unpublished writers. Currently handles: 50% nonfiction books; 5% juvenile books; 45% fiction.

Member Agents: Ellen Levine; Elizabeth Kaplan; Diana Finch; Louise Quayle.

Represents: Nonfiction books, novels, short story collections, juvenile books. **Considers these nonfiction areas:** Anthropology/archaeology; biography/autobiography; creative nonfiction (1); current affairs; health/medicine; history; memoirs; popular culture; psychology; religious/inspirational; science/technology; women's issues/studies; Adventure; Books by journalists in all areas. **Considers these fiction areas:** Literary; mystery/suspense; thriller; women's.

How to Contact: Query with SASE. Responds in 6 weeks to mss. Responds in 2 weeks to queries if SASE provided Obtains most new clients through recommendations from others.

Recent Sales: *Diana's Boys*, by Christopher Andersen (William Morrow); *Lake Wobegon Summer 1956*, by Garrison Keillor; *Anil's Ghost* , by Michael Ondaatje; *The Frailty Myth*, by Colette Dowling (Random House). Other clients include Russell Banks, Cristina Garcia, Jane Heller, Michael Gross, Todd Gitlin.

Terms: Agent receives 15% commission on domestic sales; 20% commission on foreign sales. Charges clients for overseas postage, photocopying, messenger fees, overseas telephone and fax, books ordered for use in rights submissions.

Tips: "My three younger colleagues at the agency (Quayle, Finch and Kaplan) are seeking both new and established writers. I prefer to work with established writers, mostly through referrals."

NANCY LOVE LITERARY AGENCY, 250 E. 65th St., New York NY 10021-6614. (212)980-3499. Fax: (212)308-6405. **Contact:** Nancy Love. Estab. 1984. Member of AAR. Represents 60-80 clients. Currently handles: 90% nonfiction books; 10% novels.

Member Agents: Nancy Love.

Represents: Nonfiction books, novels (mysteries and thrillers only). **Considers these nonfiction areas:** Biography/autobiography; child guidance/parenting; cooking/foods/nutrition; current affairs; ethnic/cultural interests; government/politics/law; health/medicine; history; how-to; memoirs; nature/environment; New Age/metaphysics; popular culture; psychology; religious/inspirational; science/technology; self-help/personal improvement; sociology; spirituality; travel (armchair only, no how-to travel); true crime/investigative; women's issues/studies. **Considers these fiction areas:** Mystery/suspense; thriller.

O╕ This agency specializes in adult nonfiction and mysteries. Actively seeking health and medicine (including alternative medicine), parenting, spiritual and inspirational. Does not want to receive novels other than mysteries and thrillers.

How to Contact: Prefers to read materials exclusively. For nonfiction, send a proposal, chapter summary and sample chapter. For fiction, query first. No e-mail or fax queries. Considers simultaneous queries. Responds in 3 weeks to queries; 6 weeks to mss. Returns materials only with SASE. Obtains most new clients through recommendations from others, solicitations.

Recent Sales: Sold 16 titles in the last year. *Buck Fever*, by Ben Rider (St. Martin's Press); *The Philadelphia Sound*, by John Jackson (Oxford University Press); *Menopause: Bridgeing the Gap Between Natural and Conventional Medicine*, by Lorilee Schoenbeck, DNM and Cheryl Gibson, M.D. (Kensington).

Terms: Agent receives 15% commission on domestic sales; 20% commission on foreign sales. Offers written contract. Charges clients for photocopying "if it runs over $20."

Tips: "Nonfiction author and/or collaborator must be an authority in subject area and have a platform."

LOWENSTEIN ASSOCIATES, 121 W. 27th St., Suite 601, New York NY 10001. (212)206-1630. Fax: (212)727-0280. **Contact:** President: Barbara Lowenstein. Estab. 1976. Member of AAR. Represents 150 clients. 20% of clients are new/unpublished writers. Currently handles: 60% nonfiction books; 40% novels.

Member Agents: Barbara Lowenstein (president); Nancy Yost (agent); Eileen Cope (agent); Norman Kurz (business affairs); Dorian Karchmar (associate member).

Represents: Nonfiction books, novels. **Considers these nonfiction areas:** Animals; anthropology/archaeology; biography/autobiography; business/economics; child guidance/parenting; crafts/hobbies; creative nonfiction (1); current affairs; education; ethnic/cultural interests; gay/lesbian issues; government/politics/law; health/medicine; history; how-to; humor/satire; language/literature/criticism; memoirs; money/finance; music/dance; nature/environment; New Age/metaphysics; popular culture; psychology; religious/inspirational; science/technology; self-help/personal improvement; sociology; spirituality; sports; theater/film; travel; women's issues/studies. **Considers these fiction areas:** Contemporary issues; detective/police/crime; erotica; ethnic; feminist; gay/lesbian; historical; literary; mainstream/contemporary; mystery/suspense; romance (contemporary, historical, regency); thriller (medical).

O→ This agency specializes in health, business, spirituality, creative nonfiction, literary fiction, commercial fiction, especially suspense, crime and women's issues. "We are a full-service agency, handling domestic and foreign rights, film rights, and audio rights to all of our books."

How to Contact: Query with SASE. Prefers to read materials exclusively. For fiction, send outline and first chapter. No unsolicited mss. Responds in 6 weeks to queries. Returns materials only with SASE. Obtains most new clients through recommendations from others, solicitations, conferences.

Recent Sales: Sold 75 titles in the last year. *Secrets of the Baby Whisperer*, by Tracy Hogg and Melinda Blau (Ballantine); *Insect Dreams*, by Marc Estrin (Putnam/Blue Hen); *Murad Magic!*, by Dr. Howard Murad (St. Martin's). Other clients include Ishmael Reed, Deborah Crombie, Leslie Glass, Stephanie Laurens, Dr. Grace Cornish, Stephen Raleigh Byler, Harriet Scott Chessman, Camron Wright, Tim Cahill, Gina Nahai, Kevin Young.

Terms: Agent receives 15% commission on domestic sales; 20% commission on foreign sales. Offers written contract, binding for book by book basis. Charges for large photocopy batches and international postage.

Writers' Conferences: Malice Domestic; Bouchercon.

Tips: "Know the genre you are working in and READ!"

DONALD MAASS LITERARY AGENCY, 160 W. 95th St., Suite 1B, New York NY 10025. (212)866-8200. **Contact:** Donald Maass, Jennifer Jackson or Michelle Brummer. Estab. 1980. Member of AAR, SFWA, MWA, RWA. Represents over 100 clients. 5% of clients are new/unpublished writers. Currently handles: 100% novels.

- Prior to opening his agency, Mr. Maass served as an editor at Dell Publishing (NY) and as a reader at Gollancz (London). He is the current president of AAR.

Member Agents: Donald Maass (mainstream, literary, mystery/suspense, science fiction); Jennifer Jackson (commercial fiction, especially romance, science fiction, fantasy, mystery/suspense); Michelle Brummer (fiction: literary, contemporary, feminist, science fiction, fantasy, romance).

Represents: Novels. **Considers these fiction areas:** Detective/police/crime; fantasy; historical; horror; literary; mainstream/contemporary; mystery/suspense; psychic/supernatural; romance (historical, paranormal, time travel); science fiction; thriller; women's.

O→ This agency specializes in commercial fiction, especially science fiction, fantasy, mystery, romance, suspense. Actively seeking "to expand the literary portion of our list and expand in romance and women's fiction." Does not want to receive nonfiction, children's or poetry.

How to Contact: Query with SASE. Returns material only with SASE. Considers simultaneous queries. Responds in 2 weeks to queries; 3 months to mss.

Recent Sales: Sold over 100 titles in the last year. *Funeral in Blue*, by Anne Perry (Ballantine); *The Lightstone*, by David Zendell (Warner Aspect); *Skin Folk*, by Nalo Hopkinson (Warner Aspect); *Brothers of Cain*, by Miriam Monfredo (Penguin Putnam); *The Pillars of the World*, by Anne Bishop (ROC).

Terms: Agent receives 15% commission on domestic sales; 20% commission on foreign sales.

Writers' Conferences: *Donald Maass*: World Science Fiction Convention; Frankfurt Book Fair; Pacific Northwest Writers Conference; Bouchercon and others; *Jennifer Jackson*: World Science Fiction and Fantasy Convention; RWA National and others; *Michelle Brummer*: ReaderCon; Luna Con; Frankfurt.

Tips: "We are fiction specialists, also noted for our innovative approach to career planning. Few new clients are accepted, but interested authors should query with SASE. Subagents in all principle foreign countries and Hollywood. No nonfiction or juvenile works considered."

CAROL MANN AGENCY, 55 Fifth Ave., New York NY 10003. (212)206-5635. Fax: (212)675-4809. E-mail: kim@carolmannagency.com. **Contact:** Kim Goldstein. Estab. 1977. Member of AAR. Represents 100 clients. 25% of clients are new/unpublished writers. Currently handles: 70% nonfiction books; 30% novels.

Member Agents: Ms. Gareth Esersky (health, psychology, spirituality, parenting); Jim Fitzgerald (fiction, popular culture, biography); Carol Mann (literary fiction, nonfiction).

Represents: Nonfiction books, novels. **Considers these nonfiction areas:** Anthropology/archaeology; art/architecture/design; biography/autobiography; business/economics; child guidance/parenting; current affairs; ethnic/cultural interests; government/politics/law; health/medicine; history; money/finance; psychology; self-help/personal improvement; sociology; women's issues/studies. **Considers these fiction areas:** Literary.

O╥ This agency specializes in current affairs; self-help; popular culture; psychology; parenting; history. Actively seeking "nonfiction: pop culture, business and health; fiction: literary fiction." Does not want to receive "genre fiction (romance, mystery, etc.)."

How to Contact: Query with outline/proposal and SASE. Responds in 3 weeks to queries.

Recent Sales: *Dash Diet*, by Dr. Thomas Moore (Free Press); *Hell's Angel*, by Sonny Barger (Harper); *I Thought My Father Was God*, by Paul Auster (Henry Holt); *The Unexpected Legacy of Divorce*, by Judith Wallerstein (Hyperion); *Small Miracles*, by Yitta Halberstam (Adams Media). Other clients include Novelist Marita Golden, Journalists Fox Butterfield and James Tobin, ACLU President Nadine Strossen, Drs. Mary Dan and Michael Eades, authors of *Protein Power*.

Terms: Agent receives 15% commission on domestic sales; 20% commission on foreign sales. Offers written contract.

MANUS & ASSOCIATES LITERARY AGENCY, INC., 375 Forest Ave., Palo Alto CA 94301. (650)470-5151. Fax: (650)470-5159. E-mail: manuslit@manuslit.com. Website: www.manuslit.com. **Contact:** Jillian Manus. Also: 445 Park Ave., New York NY 10022. (212)644-8020. Fax (212)644-3374. **Contact**: Janet Manus. Estab. 1985. Member of AAR. Represents 75 clients. 30% of clients are new/unpublished writers. Currently handles: 55% nonfiction books; 40% novels; 5% juvenile books.

- Prior to becoming agents, Jillian Manus was associate publisher of two national magazines and director of development at Warner Bros. and Universal Studios; Janet Manus has been a literary agent for 20 years.

Member Agents: Jandy Nelson (self-help, health, memoirs, narrative nonfiction, literary fiction, multicultural fiction, thrillers); Stephanie Lee (self-help, memoirs, dramatic nonfiction, commercial literary fiction, multicultural fiction, quirky/edgy fiction).

Represents: Nonfiction books, novels. **Considers these nonfiction areas:** Biography/autobiography; business/economics; child guidance/parenting; creative nonfiction (1); current affairs; ethnic/cultural interests; health/medicine; how-to; memoirs; money/finance; nature/environment; popular culture; psychology; science/technology; self-help/personal improvement; women's issues/studies; Gen X and Gen Y issues. **Considers these fiction areas:** Literary; mainstream/contemporary; multicultural; mystery/suspense; romance; thriller; women's; Southern fiction; quirky/edgy fiction.

O╥ This agency specializes in commercial literary fiction, narrative nonfiction, thrillers, health, pop psychology, women's empowerment. "Our agency is unique in the way that we not only sell the material, but we edit, develop concepts and participate in the marketing effort. We specialize in large, conceptual fiction and nonfiction, and always value a project that can be sold in the TV/feature film market." Actively seeking high-concept thrillers, commercial literary fiction, women's fiction, celebrity biographies, memoirs, multicultural fiction, popular health, women's empowerment, mysteries. Does not want to receive horror, romance, science fiction/fantasy, westerns, young adult, children's, poetry, cookbooks, magazine articles. Usually obtains new clients through recommendations from editors, clients and others; conferences; and unsolicited materials.

How to Contact: Query with SASE. If requested, submit outline, 2-3 sample chapter(s). Accepts e-mail and fax queries. Considers simultaneous queries. Responds in 2 months to queries; 6 weeks to mss. Returns materials only with SASE. Obtains most new clients through recommendations from others, solicitations, conferences.

Recent Sales: *Power Trips: The Untold Story of Airforce One*, by Kenneth T. Walsh (Hyperion); *One Minute Millionaire*, by Mark Victor Hansen and Robert Allen (Three Rivers/Harmony); *Jake & Mimi*, by Frank Baldwin (Little, Brown); *All the Presidents' Children*, by Doug Wead (Pocket Books); *Life is an Open Book: Bibliotherapy, A Novel Approach to Living*, by Jackie Stanley (Riverhead); *Breast Cancer: Beyond Convention*, edited by Mary Tagliaferri, Isaac Dohen and Debu Tripathy (Pocket Books). Other clients include Dr. Lorraine Zappart, Marcus Allen, Carlton Stowers, Alan Jacobson, Ann Brandt, Dr. Richard Marrs, Mary Loverde, Lisa Huang Fleishman, Judy Carter, Daryl Ott Underhill, Glen Kleier, Andrew X. Pham, Lalita Tademy.

Terms: Agent receives 15% commission on domestic sales; 20-25% commission on foreign sales. Offers written contract, binding for 2 years; 60 days notice must be given to terminate contract. Charges for photocopying and postage.

Writers' Conferences: Maui Writers Conference (Maui HI, Labor Day); San Diego Writer's Conference (San Diego CA, January); Willamette Writers Conference (Willamette OR, July).

Tips: "Research agents using a variety of sources, including *LMP*, guides, *Publishers Weekly*, conferences and even acknowledgements in books similar in tone to yours."

CLAUDIA MENZA LITERARY AGENCY, 1170 Broadway, Suite 807, New York NY 10001. (212)889-6850. **Contact:** Claudia Menza. Estab. 1983. Member of AAR. Represents 111 clients. 50% of clients are new/unpublished writers.

- Prior to becoming an agent, Ms. Menza was an editor/managing editor at a publishing company.

Represents: Nonfiction books, novels. **Considers these nonfiction areas:** Current affairs; education; ethnic/cultural interests (especially African-American); health/medicine; history; multicultural; music/dance; photography; psychology; self-help/personal improvement; theater/film.

O╥ This agency specializes in African-American fiction and nonfiction, and editorial assistance.

How to Contact: Submit outline, 1 sample chapter(s). Prefers to read materials exclusively. Responds in 2 weeks to queries; 2-4 months to mss. Returns materials only with SASE. Obtains most new clients through recommendations from others.

Recent Sales: This agency prefers not to share information on specific sales.

Terms: Agent receives 15% commission on domestic sales; 20% (if co-agent is used) commission on foreign sales; 20% commission on dramatic rights sales. Offers written contract.

JEAN V. NAGGAR LITERARY AGENCY, 216 E. 75th St., Suite 1E, New York NY 10021. (212)794-1082. **Contact:** Jean Naggar. Estab. 1978. Member of AAR, Women's Media Group and Women's Forum. Represents 100 clients. 20% of clients are new/unpublished writers. Currently handles: 35% nonfiction books; 45% novels; 15% juvenile books; 5% scholarly books.

- Ms. Naggar served as president of AAR.

Member Agents: Alice Tasman (narrative nonfiction, commercial/literary fiction, thrillers); Anne Engel (academic-based nonfiction for general readership) ; Jennifer Weltz (associate member).

Represents: Nonfiction books, novels. **Considers these nonfiction areas:** Biography/autobiography; child guidance/parenting; current affairs; government/politics/law; health/medicine; history; juvenile nonfiction; memoirs; New Age/metaphysics; psychology; religious/inspirational; self-help/personal improvement; sociology; travel; women's issues/studies. **Considers these fiction areas:** Action/adventure; contemporary issues; detective/police/crime; ethnic; family saga; feminist; historical; literary; mainstream/contemporary; mystery/suspense; psychic/supernatural; thriller.

O→ This agency specializes in mainstream fiction and nonfiction, literary fiction with commercial potential.

How to Contact: Query with SASE. Prefers to read materials exclusively. Responds in 1 day to queries; 2 months to mss. Returns materials only with SASE. Obtains most new clients through recommendations from others, solicitations, conferences.

Recent Sales: *Gracelin O'Malley*, by Ann Moore (NAL); *China Run*, by David Ball (Bantam); *The Associate*, by Phillip Margolin (HarperCollins); *The Shape of Things to Come*, by Maud Casey (William Morrow); *The Eye of the Albatross*, by Carl Safina (Holt); *Nectar*, by Lily Prior (HarperCollins). Other clients include Jean M. Auel, Robert Pollack, Mary McGarry Morris, Lily Prior, Susan Franberg Schaeffer.

Terms: Agent receives 15% commission on domestic sales; 20% commission on foreign sales. Offers written contract. Charges for overseas mailing; messenger services; book purchases; long-distance telephone; photocopying. "These are deductible from royalties received."

Writers' Conferences: Willamette Writers Conference; Pacific Northwest Writers Conference; Breadloaf Writers Conference; Virginia Women's Press Conference (Richmond VA); Marymount Manhattan Writers Conference.

Tips: "Use a professional presentation. Because of the avalanche of unsolicited queries that flood the agency every week, we have had to modify our policy. We will now only guarantee to read and respond to queries from writers who come recommended by someone we know. Our areas are general fiction and nonfiction, no children's books by unpublished writers, no multimedia, no screenplays, no formula fiction, no mysteries by unpublished writers."

NEW ENGLAND PUBLISHING ASSOCIATES, INC., P.O. Box 5, Chester CT 06412-0645. (860)345-READ and (860)345-4976. Fax: (860)345-3660. E-mail: nepa@nepa.com. Website: www.nepa.com. **Contact:** Elizabeth Frost-Knappman, Edward W. Knappman, Kristine Schiavi, Ron Formica, or Victoria Harlow. Estab. 1983. Member of AAR, ASJA, Authors Guild, Connecticut Press Club. Represents 125-150 clients. 15% of clients are new/unpublished writers.

Member Agents: Elizabeth Frost-Knappman; Edward W. Knappman; Kristine Schiavi; Ron Formica; Victoria Harlow.

Represents: Nonfiction books. **Considers these nonfiction areas:** Biography/autobiography; business/economics; child guidance/parenting; government/politics/law; health/medicine; history; language/literature/criticism; military/war; money/finance; nature/environment; psychology; science/technology; self-help/personal improvement; sociology; true crime/investigative; women's issues/studies; reference.

O→ This agency specializes in adult nonfiction of serious purpose.

How to Contact: Send outline/proposal, SASE. Accepts e-mail and fax queries. Considers simultaneous queries. Responds in 1 month to queries; 5 weeks to mss. Returns materials only with SASE.

Recent Sales: Sold 70 titles in the last year. *Mutiny: The Strange Affair of the Warship Somers*, by Buckner Melton, Jr. (Free Press); *Natural Stomach Care: How to Tap Eastern & Western Medical Wisdon to Heal & Prevent Gut Problems*, by Anil Minocha, M.D. and David Carroll (Putnam Avery); *Chronology of American Literature*, by Dan Burt (Houghton Mifflin); *Contrary Winds: Bering, Stellar and the Russian Discovery of America*, by Wallace Kaufman (Morrow).

Terms: Agent receives 15% commission on domestic sales; 20% commission on foreign sales. Offers written contract, binding for 6 months.

Writers' Conferences: BEA (Chicago, June); ALA (San Antonio, January); ALA (New York, July); ASJA (May); Frankfurt (October).

Tips: "Send us a well-written proposal that clearly identifies your audience—who will buy this book and why. Check our website for tips on proposals and advice on how to market your books."

FIFI OSCARD AGENCY INC., 110 W. 40th St., New York NY 10018. (212)764-1100. **Contact:** Literary Department. Estab. 1956. Member of AAR; signatory of WGA. Represents 108 clients. 5% of clients are new/unpublished writers. Currently handles: 60% nonfiction books; 10% novels; 30% stage plays.

Member Agents: Fifi Oscard; Peter Sawyer; Carmen Lavia; Kevin McShane; Ivy Fischer Stone; Carolyn French; Lindley Kirksey; Jerry Rudes.

Represents: Nonfiction books, novels (by referral only), stage plays.

O→ This agency specializes in history, celebrity biography and autobiography, pop culture, travel/adventure, performing arts, fine arts/design.

How to Contact: Query with outline. No unsolicited mss. Returns materials only with SASE.

Recent Sales: *Dances With Demons* (biography of Jerome Robbins), by Greg Lawrence (Putnam); *All Elevations Unknown*, by Sam Lightner, Jr. (Broadway); *Indiscretion*, by Elizabeth Nunez (One World Books); *King of Rock*, by Darryl McDaniels (St. Martin's Press); *Three Roosevelts*, by James Macgregor Burns and Susan Dunn (Atlantic Monthly Press); *Wit* (Faber & Faber); *True Hope*, by Frank Manley.
Terms: Agent receives 15% commission on domestic sales; 20% commission on foreign sales; 10% commission on dramatic rights sales. Charges clients for photocopying expenses.
Tips: "Writer must have published articles or books in major markets or have screen credits if movie scripts, etc."

THE RICHARD PARKS AGENCY, 138 E. 16th St., 5th Floor, New York NY 10003. (212)254-9067. **Contact:** Richard Parks. Estab. 1988. Member of AAR. Currently handles: 50% nonfiction books; 40% novels; 5% story collections; 5% young adult juvenile books.

• Prior to opening his agency, Mr. Parks served as an agent with Curtis Brown, Ltd.

Represents: Nonfiction books, novels. **Considers these nonfiction areas:** Animals; anthropology/archaeology; art/architecture/design; biography/autobiography; business/economics; child guidance/parenting; cooking/foods/nutrition; crafts/hobbies; current affairs; ethnic/cultural interests; gardening; gay/lesbian issues; government/politics/law; health/medicine; history; how-to; humor/satire; language/literature/criticism; memoirs; military/war; money/finance; music/dance; nature/environment; popular culture; psychology; science/technology; self-help/personal improvement; sociology; theater/film; travel; women's issues/studies. **Considers these fiction areas:** Considers fiction by referral only.

O→ Actively seeking nonfiction. Does not want to receive unsolicited material.

How to Contact: Query by mail only with SASE. No e-mail or fax queries. Considers simultaneous queries. Responds in 2 weeks to queries. Returns materials only with SASE. Obtains most new clients through recommendations and referrals.
Recent Sales: This agency prefers not to share information on sales.
Terms: Agent receives 15% commission on domestic sales; 20% commission on foreign sales. Charges clients for photocopying or any unusual expense incurred at the writer's request.

HELEN REES LITERARY AGENCY, 123 N. Washington St., 2nd Floor, Boston MA 02114. (617)723-5232, ext. 233 or 222. **Contact:** Joan Mazmanian, Ann Collette, Barbara Rifkind. Estab. 1981. Member of AAR. Represents 50 clients. 50% of clients are new/unpublished writers. Currently handles: 60% nonfiction books; 40% novels.
Member Agents: Joan Mazmanian; Ann Collette (literary fiction, women's studies, health, biography, history); Barbara Rifkind (business, money/finance/economics, government/politics/law, contemporary issues).
Represents: Nonfiction books, novels. **Considers these nonfiction areas:** Biography/autobiography; business/economics; current affairs; government/politics/law; health/medicine; history; money/finance; women's issues/studies. **Considers these fiction areas:** Contemporary issues; historical; literary; mainstream/contemporary; mystery/suspense; thriller.

O→ This agency specializes in general nonfiction, health, business, world politics, autobiographies, psychology, women's issues.

How to Contact: Query with SASE, outline, 2 sample chapter(s). No e-mail or fax queries. Responds in 2 weeks to queries; 3 weeks to mss. Obtains most new clients through recommendations from others, solicitations, conferences.
Recent Sales: Sold 26 titles in the last year. *Interpreting the Declaration of Independence*, by Alan Dershowitz (Wiley); *Why Should Anyone Be Led By You*, by Rob Goffee and Gareth Jones (Harvard Business School Press); *Killing Time*, by Elise Title (St. Martin's Press).
Terms: Agent receives 15% commission on domestic sales; 20% commission on foreign sales.

JODY REIN BOOKS, INC., 7741 S. Ash Court, Littleton CO 80122. (303)694-4430. Fax: (303)694-0687. Website: jodyreinbooks.com. **Contact:** Winnefred Dollar. Estab. 1994. Member of AAR, Authors Guild. Currently handles: 80% nonfiction books; 20% novels.

• Prior to opening her agency, Jody Rein worked for 13 years as an acquisitions editor for Contemporary Books, Bantam/Doubleday/Dell and Morrow/Avon.

Member Agents: Jody Rein; Alexandre Philippe (screenwriting); Jennie Shortridge; Kristin Nelson.
Represents: Nonfiction books (primarily narrative and commercial nonfiction), novels (select literary novels), movie scripts (some). **Considers these nonfiction areas:** Business/economics; child guidance/parenting; creative nonfiction; current affairs; ethnic/cultural interests; government/politics/law; health/medicine; history; how-to; humor/satire; music/dance; nature/environment; popular culture; psychology; religious/inspirational; science/technology; self-help/personal improvement; sociology; theater/film; women's issues/studies. **Considers these fiction areas:** Literary; mainstream/contemporary.

O→ This agency specializes in commercial and narrative nonfiction.

How to Contact: Query with SASE. No e-mail or fax queries. Considers simultaneous queries. Responds in 6 weeks to queries; 2 months to mss. Obtains most new clients through recommendations from others.
Recent Sales: *8 Simple Rules for Dating My Daughters*, by Bruce Cameron (Workman); *Think Like a Genius*, by Todd Siler (Bantam); *The ADDed Dimension*, by Kate Kelly (Scribner); *Beethoven's Hair*, by Russell Martin (Broadway Books); *The Lakota Way*, by Joseph Marshall III (Viking Penguin); *Skeletons on the Zaharah* by Dean King (Little, Brown).
Terms: Agent receives 15% commission on domestic sales; 25% commission on foreign sales. Offers written contract. Charges clients for express mail, overseas expenses, photocopying ms.
Tips: "Do your homework before submitting. Make sure you have a marketable topic and the credentials to write about it. Well-written books on exciting nonfiction topics that have broad appeal. Authors must be well established in their fields and have strong media experience."

JODIE RHODES LITERARY AGENCY, 8840 Villa La Jolla Dr., Suite 315, La Jolla CA 92037-1957. (858)625-0544. Fax: (858)625-0544. Website: www.writers.net and www.literaryagent.com. **Contact:** Jodie Rhodes, president. Estab. 1998. Member of AAR. Represents 50 clients. 50% of clients are new/unpublished writers. Currently handles: 60% nonfiction books; 35% novels; 5% middle to young adult books.

- Prior to opening her agency, Ms. Rhodes was a university level creative writing teacher, workshop director, published novelist and Vice President Media Director at the N.W. Ayer Advertising Agency.

Member Agents: Jodie Rhodes, president; Clark McCutcheon (fiction); Bob McCarter (nonfiction).
Represents: Nonfiction books, novels, juvenile books. **Considers these nonfiction areas:** Biography/autobiography; child guidance/parenting; ethnic/cultural interests; government/politics/law; health/medicine; history; memoirs; military/war; science/technology; women's issues/studies. **Considers these fiction areas:** Contemporary issues; ethnic; family saga; historical; juvenile; literary; mainstream/contemporary; mystery/suspense; thriller; young adult; women's.

O⁻ Actively seeking "writers passionate about their books with a talent for richly textured narrative, an eye for details, and a nose for research." Nonfiction writers must have recognized credentials and expert knowledge of their subject matter. Does not want to receive erotica, horror, fantasy, romance, science fiction.

How to Contact: Query with brief synopsis, first 50 pages and SASE. No e-mail or fax queries. Considers simultaneous queries. Responds in 10 days to queries. Returns materials only with SASE. Obtains most new clients through recommendations from others, agent sourcebooks.
Recent Sales: *Taming of the Chew*, by Denise Lamothe (Penguin); *Ghostly Encounters*, by Frances Kermeen (Time Warner Books); *Cast Out*, by Jan Murra (New Horizon Press).
Terms: Agent receives 15% commission on domestic sales; 20% commission on foreign sales. Offers written contract; 30-day notice must be given to terminate contract. Charges clients for fax, photocopying, phone calls and postage. "Charges are itemized and approved by writers upfront."
Writers' Conferences: Southern California Writers Conference (San Diego, mid-February); SDSU Writers Conference (San Diego, mid-January); La Jolla Writers' Conference (La Jolla, mid-October).
Tips: "Think your book out before you write it. Do your research, know your subject matter intimately, write vivid specifics, not bland generalities. Care deeply about your book. Don't imitate other writers. Find your own voice. We never take on a book we don't believe in, and we go the extra mile for our writers. We welcome talented new writers."

ANGELA RINALDI LITERARY AGENCY, P.O. Box 7877, Beverly Hills CA 90212-7877. (310)842-7665. Fax: (310)837-8143. E-mail: ARinaldilitagcy@aol.com. **Contact:** Angela Rinaldi. Estab. 1994. Member of AAR. Represents 50 clients. Currently handles: 50% nonfiction books; 50% novels.

- Prior to opening her agency, Ms. Rinaldi was an editor at New American Library, Pocket Books and Bantam, and the Manager of Book Development for *The Los Angeles Times*.

Represents: Nonfiction books, novels, TV and motion picture rights for clients only. **Considers these nonfiction areas:** Biography/autobiography; business/economics; child guidance/parenting; current affairs; health/medicine; money/finance; popular culture; psychology; self-help/personal improvement; sociology; true crime/investigative; women's issues/studies. **Considers these fiction areas:** Literary; mainstream/contemporary.

O⁻ Actively seeking commercial and literary fiction. Does not want to receive scripts, category romances, children's books, westerns, science fiction/fantasy and cookbooks.

How to Contact: For fiction: Send the first 3 chapters, brief synopsis, SASE. For nonfiction: Query with SASE first or send outline/proposal, SASE. Do not send metered mail as SASE. Considers simultaneous queries. Please advise if this is a multiple submission. Responds in 6 weeks to queries. Returns materials only with SASE.
Recent Sales: *Breach of Confidence*, by Eben Paul Perison (NAL/Signet); *Quiet Time*, by Stephanie Kane (Bantam); *Stepwives*, by Lynne Oxhorn, Louise Oxhorn, and Marjorie Krausz (Simon & Schuster); *Who Moved My Cheese?*, by Dr. Spencer Johnson (Putnam).
Terms: Agent receives 15% commission on domestic sales; 20% commission on foreign sales. Offers written contract. Charges clients for photocopying if client doesn't supply copies for submission.

THE PETER RUBIE LITERARY AGENCY, 240 W. 35th St., Suite 500, New York NY 10001. (212)279-1776. Fax: (212)279-0927. Website: www.prlit.com. **Contact:** Peter Rubie or June Clark. Estab. 2000. Member of AAR. Represents 130 clients. 30% of clients are new/unpublished writers.

- Prior to opening his agency, Mr. Rubie was a founding partner at Perkins, Rubie & Associates.

Member Agents: June Clark (New Age, pop culture, gay issues); Peter Rubie (crime, science fiction, fantasy, literary fiction, thrillers, narrative nonfiction, history, commercial science, music).
Represents: Nonfiction books, novels. **Considers these nonfiction areas:** Cooking/foods/nutrition; creative nonfiction (1); current affairs; ethnic/cultural interests; music/dance; popular culture; science/technology; theater/film; Commercial academic material; TV. **Considers these fiction areas:** Action/adventure; detective/police/crime; ethnic; fantasy; gay/lesbian; historical; literary; science fiction; thriller.
How to Contact: Query with SASE. Responds in 2 months to queries; 3 months to mss. Returns materials only with SASE. Obtains most new clients through recommendations from others.
Recent Sales: *The Glass Harmonica*, by Louise Marley (Berkley); *Shooting at Midnight*, by Gregory Rucka (Bantam); *Violence Proof Your Kids*, (Conari Press); *Toward Rational Exuberance* (Farrar, Straus & Giroux); *On Night's Shore*, by Randall Silvis (St. Martin's Press); *Jewboy*, by Allan Kauffman (Fromm); *Einstein's Refrigerator*, by Steve Silverman (Andrews McMeel); *Hope's End*, by Stephen Chambers (TOR).
Terms: Agent receives 15% commission on domestic sales; 20% commission on foreign sales. Offers written contract. Charges clients for photocopying.

Tips: "We look for writers who are experts and outstanding prose style. Be professional. Read *Publishers Weekly* and genre-related magazines. Join writers' organizations. Go to conferences. Know your market, and learn your craft. Read Rubie's book *The Writer's Market FAQs* (Writer's Digest Books)."

RUSSELL & VOLKENING, 50 W. 29th St., #7E, New York NY 10001. (212)684-6050. Fax: (212)889-3026. **Contact:** Joseph Regal. Estab. 1940. Member of AAR. Represents 140 clients. 20% of clients are new/unpublished writers. Currently handles: 45% nonfiction books; 50% novels; 3% story collections; 2% novellas.
Member Agents: Timothy Seldes (nonfiction, literary fiction); Joseph Regal (literary fiction, thrillers, nonfiction); Lauren A. Schott (associate member).
Represents: Nonfiction books, novels, short story collections, novellas. **Considers these nonfiction areas:** Anthropology/archaeology; art/architecture/design; biography/autobiography; business/economics; cooking/foods/nutrition; creative nonfiction (1); current affairs; education; ethnic/cultural interests; gay/lesbian issues; government/politics/law; health/medicine; history; language/literature/criticism; military/war; money/finance; music/dance; nature/environment; photography; popular culture; psychology; science/technology; sociology; sports; theater/film; true crime/investigative; women's issues/studies. **Considers these fiction areas:** Action/adventure; detective/police/crime; ethnic; literary; mainstream/contemporary; mystery/suspense; picture books; sports; thriller.

O╤ This agency specializes in literary fiction and narrative nonfiction.

How to Contact: Query with SASE. Responds in 2 weeks to queries; 2 months to mss. Obtains most new clients through recommendations from others, occasionally through query letters.
Recent Sales: *Back when We Were Grownups*, by Anne Tyler (Knopf); *Warriors of God*, by James Reston Jr. (Doubleday); *No Certain Rest*, by Jim Lehrer (Random House).
Terms: Agent receives 15% commission on domestic sales; 20% commission on foreign sales. Charges clients for "standard office expenses relating to the submission of materials of an author we represent, e.g., photocopying, postage."
Tips: "If the query is cogent, well written, well presented and is the type of book we'd represent, we'll ask to see the manuscript. From there, it depends purely on the quality of the work."

SCOVIL CHICHAK GALEN LITERARY AGENCY, 381 Park Ave. South, Suite 1020, New York NY 10016. (212)679-8686. Fax: (212)679-6710. E-mail: mailroom@scglit.com. **Contact:** Russell Galen. Estab. 1993. Member of AAR. Represents 300 clients. Currently handles: 70% nonfiction books; 30% novels.
Member Agents: Russell Galen; Jack Scovil; Anna Ghosh.
How to Contact: Accepts e-mail and fax queries. Considers simultaneous queries.
Recent Sales: Sold 100 titles in the last year. *Across the Black Waters*, by Minai Hajratwala (Houghton Mifflin); *The Secret*, by Walter Anderson (HarperCollins); *The Pillars of Creation*, by Terry Goodkind (Tor); *In The Hand of Dante*, by Nick Tosches (Little, Brown).
Terms: Charges clients for photocopying and postage.

SEBASTIAN LITERARY AGENCY, The Towers, 172 E. Sixth St., #2005, St. Paul MN 55101. (651)224-6670. Fax: (651)224-6895. E-mail: harperlb@aol.com (query only—no attachments). **Contact:** Laurie Harper. Estab. 1985. Member of AAR, Authors Guild. Represents 50 clients.

- Prior to becoming an agent, Laurie Harper was owner of a small regional publishing company selling mainly to retail bookstores, including B. Dalton and Waldenbooks. She was thus involved in editing, production, distribution, marketing and promotion. She came to publishing with a business and finance background, including eight years in banking.

Represents: Trade nonfiction, select literary fiction. **Considers these nonfiction areas:** Business/economics; creative nonfiction; current affairs; health/medicine; history (popular); money/finance; psychology; science/technology (popular); self-help/personal improvement; sociology; women's issues/studies; Consumer reference.

O╤ Ms. Harper is known for working closely with her authors to plan and execute individual short-term and long-term goals. "A successful publishing experience is dependent upon closely coordinated efforts between the writer, the agent, the editor, the publisher's marketing group and sales force, and the booksellers. I give my authors as much advance information as possible so they can work most efrectively with the publisher. An author needs every advantage he or she can have, and working closely with the agent can be one of those advantages." Does not want to receive scholarly work, screenplays, children's or young adult work.

How to Contact: Taking new clients selectively; mainly by referral. Considers simultaneous queries. Responds in 3 weeks to queries; 6 weeks to mss. Obtains most new clients through "referrals from authors and editors, but some at conferences and some from unsolicited queries from around the country."
Recent Sales: Sold 25 titles in the last year. *Bald in the Land of Big Hair*, by Joni Rodgers (HarperCollins); *Short Cycle Selling*, by James Kasper (McGraw-Hill); *Two in the Field*, by Darryl Brock (NAL/Dutton); *For All We Know*, by Peter S. Beagle (Simon & Schuster); *Latticework: The New Investing*, by Robert Hagstrom (Texere Pub).
Terms: Agent receives 15% commission on domestic sales; 20% commission on foreign sales. Offers written contract. Charges clients a one-time $100 administration fee and charges for photocopies of ms for submission to publisher.
Writers' Conferences: ASJA; various independent conferences throughout the country.

PHILIP G. SPITZER LITERARY AGENCY, 50 Talmage Farm Lane, East Hampton NY 11937. (631)329-3650. Fax: (631)329-3651. E-mail: spitzer516@aol.com. **Contact:** Philip Spitzer. Estab. 1969. Member of AAR. Represents 60 clients. 10% of clients are new/unpublished writers. Currently handles: 50% nonfiction books; 50% novels.

- Prior to opening his agency, Mr. Spitzer served at New York University Press, McGraw-Hill and the John Cushman Associates literary agency.

Represents: Nonfiction books, novels. **Considers these nonfiction areas:** Biography/autobiography; business/economics; current affairs; ethnic/cultural interests; government/politics/law; health/medicine; history; language/literature/criticism; military/war; music/dance; nature/environment; popular culture; psychology; sociology; sports; theater/film; true crime/investigative. **Considers these fiction areas:** Contemporary issues; detective/police/crime; literary; mainstream/contemporary; mystery/suspense; sports; thriller.

O→ This agency specializes in mystery/suspense, literary fiction, sports, general nonfiction (no how-to).

How to Contact: Query with SASE, outline, 1 sample chapter(s). Responds in 1 week to queries; 6 weeks to mss. Obtains most new clients through recommendations from others.

Recent Sales: *Angels Flight*, by Michael Connelly (Little, Brown); *Heartwood*, by James Lee Burke (Hyperion); *Eva Le Gallienne*, by Helen Sheehy (Knopf); *House of Sand and Fog*, by Andre Dubus III (Norton).

Terms: Agent receives 15% commission on domestic sales; 20% commission on foreign sales. Charges clients for photocopying.

Writers' Conferences: BEA (Chicago).

ROBIN STRAUS AGENCY, INC., 229 E. 79th St., New York NY 10021. (212)472-3282. Fax: (212)472-3833. E-mail: springbird@aol.com. **Contact:** Ms. Robin Straus. Estab. 1983. Member of AAR. Currently handles: 65% nonfiction books; 35% novels.

- Prior to becoming an agent, Robin Straus served as a subsidary rights manager at Random House and Doubleday and worked in editorial at Little, Brown.

Represents: Nonfiction books, novels. **Considers these nonfiction areas:** Animals; anthropology/archaeology; art/architecture/design; biography/autobiography; child guidance/parenting; cooking/foods/nutrition; current affairs; ethnic/cultural interests; government/politics/law; health/medicine; history; language/literature/criticism; music/dance; nature/environment; popular culture; psychology; sociology; theater/film; women's issues/studies. **Considers these fiction areas:** Contemporary issues; family saga; historical; literary; mainstream/contemporary.

O→ This agency specializes in high quality fiction and nonfiction for adults (no genre fiction; no screenplays; no books for children). Takes on very few new clients.

How to Contact: For nonfiction: Query with proposal and sample pages. For fiction: Query with brief synopsis and opening chapter or 2. Responds and returns materials only with SASE. We do not download **any** submissions. Responds in 1 month to queries; 1 month to mss. Obtains most new clients through recommendations from others.

Recent Sales: This agency prefers not to share information on specific sales.

Terms: Agent receives 15% commission on domestic sales; 20% commission on foreign sales. Offers written contract. Charges for "photocopying, express mail services, messenger and foreign postage, etc. as incurred."

PATRICIA TEAL LITERARY AGENCY, 2036 Vista Del Rosa, Fullerton CA 92831-1336. Phone/fax: (714)738-8333. **Contact:** Patricia Teal. Estab. 1978. Member of AAR. Represents 60 clients. Currently handles: 10% nonfiction books; 90% novels.

Represents: Nonfiction books, novels. **Considers these nonfiction areas:** Animals; biography/autobiography; child guidance/parenting; health/medicine; how-to; psychology; self-help/personal improvement; true crime/investigative; women's issues/studies. **Considers these fiction areas:** Glitz; mainstream/contemporary; mystery/suspense; romance (contemporary, historical).

O→ This agency specializes in women's fiction and commercial how-to and self-help nonfiction. Does not want to receive poetry, short stories, articles, science fiction, fantasy, regency romance.

How to Contact: *Published authors only.* Query with SASE. No e-mail or fax queries. Considers simultaneous queries. Responds in 10 days to queries; 6 weeks to mss. Returns materials only with SASE. Obtains most new clients through conferences, recommendations from authors and editors.

Recent Sales: Sold 30 titles in the last year. *Billionaire Cinderella School*, by Myrna McKenzie (Silhouette); *Working Overtime*, by Helen Conrad (Silhouette).

Terms: Agent receives 10-15% commission on domestic sales; 20% commission on foreign sales. Offers written contract, binding for 1 year. Charges clients for photocopying.

Writers' Conferences: Romance Writers of America conferences; California State University (San Diego, January); Asilomar (California Writers Club); BEA (Chicago June); Bouchercon; Hawaii Writers Conference (Maui).

Reading List: Reads *Publishers Weekly*, *Romance Report* and *Romantic Times* to find new clients. "I read the reviews of books and excerpts from authors' books."

Tips: "Include SASE with all correspondence."

WALES, LITERARY AGENCY, INC., P.O. Box 9428, Seattle WA 98109-0428. (206)284-7114. E-mail: waleslit@aol.com. **Contact:** Elizabeth Wales, Meg Lemkie or Adrienne Reed. Estab. 1988. Member of AAR, Book Publishers' Northwest. Represents 65 clients. 10% of clients are new/unpublished writers. Currently handles: 60% nonfiction books; 35% novels; 5% story collections.

- Prior to becoming an agent, Ms. Wales worked at Oxford University Press and Viking Penguin.

Member Agents: Elizabeth Wales; Adrienne Reed; Meg Lemke.

Represents: Nonfiction books, novels, short story collections, novellas. **Considers these nonfiction areas:** Animals; biography/autobiography; current affairs; ethnic/cultural interests; gay/lesbian issues; history; memoirs; multicultural; nature/environment; popular culture; science/technology; travel; women's issues/studies; Open to creative or serious treatments of almost any nonfiction subject. **Considers these fiction areas:** Contemporary issues; ethnic; feminist; gay/lesbian; literary; mainstream/contemporary; multicultural; regional.

O→ This agency specializes in mainstream nonfiction and fiction, as well as narrative and literary fiction.

How to Contact: Query with cover letter, writing sample (no more than 30 pages) and SASE. No phone or fax queries. Prefers regular mail queries, but accepts one page only email queries with no attachments. Accepts e-mail queries. No fax queries. Considers simultaneous queries. Responds in 3 weeks to queries; 6 weeks to mss. Returns materials only with SASE.
Recent Sales: Sold 15 titles in the last year. *Fateful Harvest*, by Duff Wilson (HarperCollins); *Midnight to the North*, by Sheila Nickerson (Tarcher Penguin Putnam); *Fifth Life of the Catwoman*, by Kathleen Dexter (Berkley Penguin Putnam); *Rides: An AutoBiography*, by K. Lake (Algonquin).
Terms: Agent receives 15% commission on domestic sales; 20% commission on foreign sales. Offers written contract, binding for book-by-book basis. "We make all our income from commissions. We offer editorial help for some of our clients and help some clients with the development of a proposal, but we do not charge for these services. We do charge clients, after a sale, for express mail, manuscript photocopying costs, foreign postage."
Writers' Conferences: Pacific NW Writers Conference (Seattle, July); Writers at Work (Salt Lake City); Writing Rendezvous (Anchorage).
Tips: "We are interested in published and non-yet-published writers. Especially encourages writers living in the Pacific Northwest, West Coast, Alaska and Pacific Rim countries to submit work."

LYNN WHITTAKER, LITERARY AGENT, Graybill & English, LLC, 1920 N St. NW, Suite 620, Washington DC 20036-1619. (202)861-0106, ext. 37. Fax: (202)457-0662. E-mail: lynnwhittaker@aol.com. Website: www.graybillandenglish.com. Estab. 1998. Member of AAR. Represents 24 clients. 10% of clients are new/unpublished writers. Currently handles: 85% nonfiction books; 15% novels.

- Prior to becoming an agent, Ms. Whittaker was an editor, owner of a small press, and taught at the college level.

Represents: Nonfiction books, novels, short story collections. **Considers these nonfiction areas:** Animals; biography/autobiography; current affairs; ethnic/cultural interests; gay/lesbian issues; history; language/literature/criticism; memoirs; money/finance; multicultural; nature/environment; popular culture; science/technology; sports; travel; women's issues/studies. **Considers these fiction areas:** Detective/police/crime; ethnic; experimental; feminist; historical; literary; multicultural; mystery/suspense; sports.

O→ "As a former editor, I especially enjoy working closely with writers to develop and polish their proposal and manuscripts." Actively seeking literary fiction, sports, history, creative nonfiction of all kinds, nature and science, ethnic/multicultural, women's stories & issues. Does not want to receive romance/women's commercial fiction, children's/young adult, religious, fantasy/horror.

How to Contact: Query with SASE, submit proposal package, outline, 2 sample chapter(s). Responds in 2 weeks to queries; 1 month to mss. Returns materials only with SASE. Obtains most new clients through recommendations from others.
Recent Sales: *Never Say Never: When Others Say You Can't and You Know You Can*, by Phyllis George (McGraw-Hill); *The Art of Death*, by Sarah Stewart Taylor (St. Martin's); *20 Seasons in the Sun: My Baseball Life in Pictures*, by Carl Ripken Jr. and Jerry Wachter (Morrow). Other clients include Leonard Shapiro, John Tallmadge, Dorothy Sucher, James McGregor Burns, American Women in Radio and Television(AWRT), Maniza Naqui, Chris Palmer.
Terms: Agent receives 15% commission on domestic sales; 20% commission on foreign sales. Offers written contract; 30 days notice must be given to terminate contract. Direct expenses for photocopying of proposals and mss, UPS/FedEx.
Writers' Conferences: Creative Nonfiction Conference, (Goucher College MD, August); Washington Independent Writers, (Washington DC, May); Hariette Austin Writers Conference, (Athens GA, July).

WRITERS HOUSE, 21 W. 26th St., New York NY 10010. (212)685-2400. Fax: (212)685-1781. Estab. 1974. Member of AAR. Represents 440 clients. 50% of clients are new/unpublished writers. Currently handles: 25% nonfiction books; 40% novels; 35% juvenile books.
Member Agents: Albert Zuckerman (major novels, thrillers, women's fiction, important nonfiction); Amy Berkower (major juvenile authors, women's fiction, art and decorating, psychology); Merrilee Heifetz (quality children's fiction, science fiction and fantasy, popular culture, literary fiction); Susan Cohen (juvenile and young adult fiction and nonfiction, Judaism, women's issues); Susan Ginsburg (serious and popular fiction, true crime, narrative nonfiction, personality books, cookbooks); Michele Rubin (serious nonfiction); Robin Rue (commercial fiction and nonfiction, YA fiction); Jennifer Lyons (literary, commercial fiction, international fiction, nonfiction and illustrated); Jodi Reamer (juvenile and young adult fiction and nonfiction, adult commercial fiction, popular culture); Simon Lipskar (literary and commercial fiction, narrative nonfiction); Nicole Pitesa (juvenile and young adult fiction, literary fiction).
Represents: Nonfiction books, novels, juvenile books. **Considers these nonfiction areas:** Animals; art/architecture/design; biography/autobiography; business/economics; child guidance/parenting; cooking/foods/nutrition; health/medicine; history; interior design/decorating; juvenile nonfiction; military/war; money/finance; music/dance; nature/environment; psychology; science/technology; self-help/personal improvement; theater/film; true crime/investigative; women's issues/studies. **Considers these fiction areas:** Action/adventure; comic books/cartoon; confession; contemporary issues; detective/police/crime; erotica; ethnic; experimental; family saga; fantasy; feminist; gay/lesbian; glitz; gothic; hi-lo; historical; horror; humor/satire; juvenile; literary; mainstream/contemporary; military/war; multicultural; multimedia; mystery/suspense; New Age; occult; picture books; plays; poetry; poetry in translation; psychic/supernatural; regional; religious/inspirational; romance; science fiction; short story collections; spiritual; sports; thriller; translation; westerns/frontier; young adult; women's.

O→ This agency specializes in all types of popular fiction and nonfiction. Does not want to receive scholarly, professional, poetry, plays or screenplays.

How to Contact: Query with SASE. Responds in 1 month to queries. Obtains most new clients through recommendations from others.

Recent Sales: *Next*, by Michael Lewis (Norton); *Art of Deception*, by Ridley Pearson (Hyperion); *Into the Garden*, by V.C. Andrews (Pocket); *Midnight Bayou*, by Nora Roberts (Penguin/Putnam); *Love That Dog*, by Sharon Creech (HarperCollins). Other clients include Francine Pascal, Ken Follett, Stephen Hawking, Linda Howard, F. Paul Wilson.
Terms: Agent receives 15% commission on domestic sales; 20% commission on foreign sales. Offers written contract, binding for 1 year.
Tips: "Do not send mss. Write a compelling letter. If you do, we'll ask to see your work."

SCRIPT AGENTS

KELVIN C. BULGER AND ASSOCIATES, 11 E. Adams St., Suite 604, Chicago IL 60603. (312)692-1002. Fax: (312)692-1002. E-mail: kcbwoi@aol.com. **Contact:** Kelvin C. Bulger. Estab. 1992. Signatory of WGA. Represents 25 clients. 90% of clients are new/unpublished writers. Currently handles: 75% movie scripts; 25% TV scripts.
Member Agents: Kevin C. Bulger, Melanie Barnes Zeleke, Baku Talbert.
Represents: Feature film, TV movie of the week, documentary, syndicated material. **Considers these script subject areas:** Action/adventure; cartoon/animation; comedy; contemporary issues; ethnic; family saga; religious/inspirational.
How to Contact: Query with SASE. Accepts e-mail and fax queries. Considers simultaneous queries. Responds in 3 weeks to queries; 2 months to mss. Returns materials only with SASE. Obtains most new clients through recommendations from others, solicitations.
Recent Sales: This agency prefers not to share information on specific sales.
Terms: Agent receives 10% commission on domestic sales; 10% commission on foreign sales. Offers written contract, binding for 6-12 months.
Tips: "Proofread before submitting to agent. We only reply to letters of inquiry if SASE is enclosed."

CLIENT FIRST-A/K/A LEO P. HAFFEY AGENCY, P.O.Box 128049, Nashville TN 37212-8049. (615)463-2388. E-mail: c1st@nashville.net. Website: www.c-1st.com or www.nashville.net/~cl. **Contact:** Robin Swensen. Estab. 1990. Signatory of WGA. Represents 21 clients. 25% of clients are new/unpublished writers. Currently handles: 40% novels; 60% movie scripts.
Member Agents: Leo Haffey (attorney/agent in the motion picture industry).
Represents: Nonfiction books (self-help), novels, short story collections, novellas, feature film, animation. **Considers these script subject areas:** Action/adventure; cartoon/animation; comedy; contemporary issues; detective/police/crime; family saga; historical; mystery/suspense; romantic drama (contemporary, historical); science fiction; sports; thriller; western/frontier.

O- This agency specializes in movie scripts and novels for sale to motion picture industry.

How to Contact: Query with SASE, synopsis, treatment or summary. Do not send scripts/screenplays unless requested. Considers simultaneous queries. Responds in 1 week to queries; 2 months to mss. Returns materials only with SASE. Obtains most new clients through recommendations from others.
Recent Sales: This agency prefers not to share information on specific sales.
Terms: Offers written contract, binding for negotiable length of time.
Tips: "The motion picture business is a numbers game like any other. The more you write the better your chances are of success. Please send a SASE along with your query letter."

ROBERT A. FREEDMAN DRAMATIC AGENCY, INC., 1501 Broadway, Suite 2310, New York NY 10036. (212)840-5760. **Contact:** Robert A. Freedman, president; Selma Luttinger, vice president; Marta Praeger and Robin Kaver, associates. Estab. 1928. Member of AAR; signatory of WGA.

- Mr. Freedman has served as vice president of the dramatic division of AAR.

Represents: Movie scripts, TV scripts, stage plays.

O- This agency works with both established and new authors. Specializes in plays, movie scripts and TV scripts.

How to Contact: Query with SASE. All unsolicited mss returned unopened. Responds in 2 weeks to queries; 3 months to mss.
Recent Sales: "We will speak directly with any prospective client concerning sales that are relevant to his/her specific script."
Terms: Agent receives 10% commission on domestic sales. Charges clients for photocopying.

THE LAYA GELFF LITERARY AND TALENT AGENCY, 16133 Ventura Blvd., Suite 700, Encino CA 91436. (818)996-3100. Estab. 1985. Signatory of WGA. Represents many clients. Currently handles: 50% movie scripts; 45% TV scripts; 5% book mss.
Represents: Feature film, TV scripts.

O- This agency specializes in TV and film scripts; WGA members preferred. "Also represents writers to publishers." Does not represent sitcoms for TV.

How to Contact: Query with SASE. Must include SASE for reply. Responds in 3 weeks to queries; 1 month to mss. Obtains most new clients through recommendations from others.
Recent Sales: This agency prefers not to share information on specific sales.
Terms: Agent receives 10% commission on domestic sales; 10% commission on foreign sales. Offers written contract. Charges reading fee for book representation only.
Tips: WGA members preferred.

THE SUSAN GURMAN AGENCY, 865 West End Ave., #15A, New York NY 10025-8403. (212)749-4618. Fax: (212)864-5055. **Contact:** Susan Gurman. Estab. 1993. Signatory of WGA. 28% of clients are new/unpublished writers. Currently handles: 70% movie scripts; 30% stage plays.

Member Agents: Gail Eisenberg (associate agent); Susan Gurman.

Represents: Feature film, TV movie of the week, theatrical stage play. **Considers these nonfiction areas:** Biography/autobiography; true crime/investigative. **Considers these fiction areas:** Action/adventure (adventure); detective/police/crime; family saga; fantasy; horror; literary; mainstream/contemporary; mystery/suspense; picture books; thriller. **Considers these script subject areas:** Comedy; detective/police/crime; family saga; horror; mainstream; mystery/suspense; romantic comedy; romantic drama; thriller; true stories.

O→ This agency specializes in referred screenwriters and playwrights.

How to Contact: Responds in 2 weeks to queries; 2 months to mss. Obtains most new clients through recommendations from others.

Recent Sales: This agency prefers not to share information on specific sales.

Terms: Agent receives 10% commission on domestic sales; 10% commission on foreign sales.

HART LITERARY MANAGEMENT, 3541 Olive St., Santa Ynez CA 93460. (805)686-7912. Fax: (805)686-7912. E-mail: hartliteraryagency@hotmail.com. Website: hartliterary.com. **Contact:** Susan Hart. Estab. 1997. Signatory of WGA. Represents 35 clients. 95% of clients are new/unpublished writers. Currently handles: 2% nonfiction books; 98% movie scripts.

- Prior to opening the agency, Ms. Hart was a screenwriter.

Represents: Movie scripts, feature film, TV movie of the week. **Considers these script subject areas:** Biography/autobiography; family saga; horror; juvenile; mainstream; science fiction; teen.

How to Contact: Query with SASE. Accepts e-mail and fax queries. Considers simultaneous queries. Responds in 2 weeks to queries. Returns materials only with SASE. Obtains most new clients through solicitations.

Recent Sales: *Annus Horribilis (My Horrible Year)*, by J. McIluaine (Millbrook Farm Productions/Showtime).

Terms: Agent receives 10% domestic or worldwide sales on gross income written any source from the screenplays commission on domestic sales. Offers written contract, binding for 1 year but may be cancelled at any time by both parties in writing. Charges clients for photocopies and postage; $6.50 domestic, $10 Canadian and $12 international. This is the same as WGA requirement that screenwriters send copies of all screenplays to their agents and is cheaper than that in most cases.

Tips: "I want a great story spell-checked, formatted, and "typed" in industry standard 12 point Courier or Courier New only, between 95-120 pages maximum. No overt gore, sex, violence. See website for updated genres I may look at."

BARBARA HOGENSON AGENCY, 165 West End Ave., Suite 19-C, New York NY 10023. (212)874-8084. Fax: (212)362-3011. **Contact:** Barbara Hogenson. Estab. 1994. Member of AAR; signatory of WGA. Represents 60 clients. 5% of clients are new/unpublished writers. Currently handles: 35% nonfiction books; 15% novels; 15% movie scripts; 35% stage plays.

- Prior to opening her agency, Ms. Hogenson was with the prestigious Lucy Kroll Agency for 10 years.

Represents: Nonfiction books, novels, feature film, TV movie of the week, sitcom, soap opera, theatrical stage play. **Considers these nonfiction areas:** Biography/autobiography; history; interior design/decorating; music/dance; popular culture; theater/film. **Considers these fiction areas:** Action/adventure; detective/police/crime; ethnic; historical; humor/satire; literary; mainstream/contemporary; mystery/suspense; romance (contemporary); thriller.

How to Contact: Query with SASE, outline. No unsolicited mss. Responds in 1 month to queries. Obtains most new clients through recommendations from others.

Recent Sales: *The Flock*, by Joan Frances Casey Wilder. **Book Sales:** *Peter Loon*, by Van Reid; *Life Lessons*, by Elisabeth Kubler-Ross; *If Winter Comes*, by Hesper Anderson (USA).

Terms: Agent receives 15% commission on domestic sales; 20% commission on foreign sales; 10% commission on dramatic rights sales. Offers written contract.

HUDSON AGENCY, 3 Travis Lane, Montrose NY 10548. (914)737-1475. Fax: (914)736-3064. E-mail: hudagency@juno.com. Website: www.hudsonagency.net. **Contact:** Susan Giordano. Estab. 1994. Signatory of WGA. Represents 30 clients. 50% of clients are new/unpublished writers. Currently handles: 50% movie scripts; 50% TV scripts.

Member Agents: Sue Giordano (features, live action); Cheri Santone (features and animation); Sunny Bik (Canada contact).

Represents: Feature film, TV movie of the week, sitcom, animation, documentary, miniseries. **Considers these script subject areas:** Action/adventure; cartoon/animation; comedy; contemporary issues; detective/police/crime; family saga; fantasy; juvenile; mystery/suspense; romantic comedy; romantic drama; teen; western/frontier.

O→ This agency specializes in feature film and TV. Also specializes in animation writers. Actively seeking "writers with television and screenwriting education or workshops under their belts." Does not want to receive "R-rated material, no occult, no one that hasn't taken at least one screenwriting workshop."

How to Contact: Query by email only. Considers simultaneous queries. Responds in 1 week to queries; 3 weeks to mss. Returns materials only with SASE. Obtains most new clients through recommendations from others.

Recent Sales: Sold 1 scripts in the last year. *Becoming Dick*, by Rick Gitelson (E! TV).

Terms: Agent receives 10% commission on domestic sales; 10% commission on foreign sales.

Tips: "Yes, we may be small, but we work very hard for our clients. Any script we are representing gets excellent exposure to producers. Our network has over 1,000 contacts in the business and growing rapidly. We are GOOD salespeople. Ultimately it all depends on the quality of the writing and the market for the subject matter. Do not query unless you have taken at least one screenwriting course and read all of Syd Field's books."

PAUL KOHNER, INC., 9300 Wilshire Blvd., Suite 555, Beverly Hills CA 90212-3211. (310)550-1060. **Contact:** Stephen Moore. Estab. 1938. Member of ATA; signatory of WGA. Represents 150 clients. 10% of clients are new/ unpublished writers.

Represents: Feature film, TV movie of the week, episodic drama, sitcom, animation, documentary, miniseries, soap opera, variety show, stage plays, Film/TV rights to published books. **Considers these script subject areas:** Action/ adventure; comedy; family saga; historical; mainstream; mystery/suspense; romantic comedy; romantic drama.

O→ This agency specializes in film and TV rights sales and representation of film and TV writers.

Recent Sales: This agency prefers not to share information on specific sales.

Terms: Agent receives 10% commission on domestic sales; 10% commission on foreign sales. Offers written contract, binding for 1-3 years. "We charge clients for copying manuscripts or scripts for submission unless a sufficient quantity is supplied by the author."

LEGACIES, 501 Woodstork Circle, Bradenton FL 34209-7393. (941)792-9159. Fax: (941)795-0552. **Contact:** Marcy Ann Amato, executive director. Estab. 1993. Member of Florida Motion Picture & Television Association, Board of Talent Agents, Dept. of Professional Regulations License No. TA 0000404; signatory of WGA. 50% of clients are new/ unpublished writers. Currently handles: 10% novels; 80% movie scripts; 10% stage plays.

Represents: Feature film. **Considers these script subject areas:** Comedy; contemporary issues; family saga; feminist; historical.

O→ This agency specializes in screenplays.

How to Contact: Query with SASE. Considers simultaneous queries. Responds in 2 weeks to queries; 6 weeks to mss.

Recent Sales: *Death's Parallel*, by Dr. Oakley Jordan (Rainbow Books). ***Movie/TV MOW script(s) optioned/sold:*** *A Bench On Which To Rest*, by Maria Phillips; *Progress of the Sun*, by Patricia Friedberg; *Elsie Venner*, by Raleigh Marcell.

Terms: Agent receives 10% commission on domestic sales; 15% commission on foreign sales. Offers written contract for WGA members.

Tips: "New writers should purchase script writing computer programs, or read and apply screenplay format before submitting."

THE LUEDTKE AGENCY, 1674 Broadway, Suite 7A, New York NY 10019. (212)765-9564. Fax: (212)765-9582. **Contact:** Elaine Devlin. Estab. 1997. Signatory of WGA. Represents 35 clients. 20% of clients are new/unpublished writers. Currently handles: 70% movie scripts; 10% TV scripts; 20% stage plays.

- Prior to becoming an agent, Penny Luedtke was in classical music management; Elain Devlin was in film development, story editing; Marcia Weiss was an attorney, owner of a music agency.

Member Agents: Penny Luedtke (primarily represents talent-some special project writers); Elaine Devlin (screenwriters, playwrights); Marcia Weiss (screenwriters, television writers).

Represents: Movie scripts, feature film, TV scripts, TV movie of the week, sitcom, miniseries, soap opera, theatrical stage play, stage plays. **Considers these script subject areas:** Action/adventure; biography/autobiography; cartoon/ animation; comedy; contemporary issues; detective/police/crime; ethnic; family saga; fantasy; feminist; gay/lesbian; historical; horror; juvenile; mainstream; multicultural; multimedia; mystery/suspense; psychic/supernatural; regional; religious/inspirational; romantic comedy; romantic drama; science fiction; sports; teen; thriller; western/frontier.

O→ "We are a small shop and like it that way. We work closely with our writers developing projets and offer extensive editorial assistance." Actively seeking well-written material. Does not want any project with graphic or explicit violence against women or children.

How to Contact: Query with SASE. No e-mail or fax queries. Considers simultaneous queries. Responds in 1 month to queries; 3 months to mss. Returns materials only with SASE. Obtains most new clients through recommendations from others.

Recent Sales: This agency prefers not to share information on specific sales.

Terms: Agent receives 10% commission on domestic sales; 15% commission on foreign sales. Offers written contract, binding for WGA standard terms. Charges clients for reimbursement of expenses for couriers, messengers, international telephone and photocopying.

THE STUART M. MILLER CO., 11684 Ventura Blvd., #225, Studio City CA 91604-2699. (818)506-6067. Fax: (818)506-4079. E-mail: smmco@aol.com. **Contact:** Stuart Miller. Estab. 1977. Signatory of WGA, DGA. Currently handles: 50% movie scripts; 40% multimedia; 10% books.

Represents: Nonfiction books, novels, movie scripts. **Considers these nonfiction areas:** Biography/autobiography; computers/electronic; current affairs; government/politics/law; health/medicine; history; how-to; memoirs; military/war; self-help/personal improvement; true crime/investigative. **Considers these fiction areas:** Action/adventure; detective/ police/crime; historical; literary; mainstream/contemporary; mystery/suspense; science fiction; sports; thriller. **Considers these script subject areas:** Action/adventure; biography/autobiography; cartoon/animation; comedy; contemporary issues; detective/police/crime; family saga; historical; mainstream; multimedia; mystery/suspense; romantic comedy; romantic drama; science fiction; sports; teen; thriller.

How to Contact: Query with SASE, 2-3 page narrative and outline/proposal. Accepts e-mail and fax queries. Considers simultaneous queries. Responds in 3 days to queries; 6 weeks to mss. Returns materials only with SASE.

Recent Sales: This agency prefers not to share information on specific sales.
Terms: Agent receives 10% for movie/TV commission on domestic sales; 15-25% for books commission on foreign sales. Offers written contract, binding for 2 years; WGA standard notice must be given to terminate contract.
Tips: "Always include SASE, e-mail address, or fax number with query letters. Make it easy to respond."

DOROTHY PALMER, 235 W. 56 St., New York NY 10019. (212)765-4280. Fax: (212)977-9801. Estab. 1990. Signatory of WGA. Represents 12 clients. 0% of clients are new/unpublished writers. Currently handles: 70% movie scripts; 30% TV scripts.

- In addition to being a literary agent, Ms. Palmer has worked as a talent agent for 30 years.

Represents: Feature film, TV movie of the week, episodic drama, sitcom, miniseries. **Considers these script subject areas:** Action/adventure; comedy; contemporary issues; detective/police/crime; family saga; feminist; mainstream; mystery/suspense; romantic comedy; romantic drama; thriller.

O‑ This agency specializes in screenplays, TV. Actively seeking successful, published writers (screenplays only). Does not want to receive work from new or unpublished writers.

How to Contact: Query with SASE. Prefers to read materials exclusively. Published writers *only.* Returns materials only with SASE. Obtains most new clients through recommendations from others.
Recent Sales: This agency prefers not to share information on specific sales.
Terms: Agent receives 10% commission on domestic sales; 10% commission on foreign sales. Offers written contract, binding for 1 year. Charges clients for postage, photocopies.
Tips: "Do *not* telephone. When I find a script that interests me, I call the writer. Calls to me are a turn-off because they cut into my reading time."

BARRY PERELMAN AGENCY, 1155 N. Laceniga, #508, W. Hollywood CA 90069. (310)659-1122. Fax: (310)659-1122. Estab. 1982. Member of DGA; signatory of WGA. Represents 40 clients. 15% of clients are new/unpublished writers. Currently handles: 100% movie scripts.
Member Agents: Barry Perelman (motion picture/packaging).
Represents: Movie scripts. **Considers these script subject areas:** Action/adventure; biography/autobiography; contemporary issues; detective/police/crime; historical; horror; mystery/suspense; romantic comedy; romantic drama; science fiction; thriller.

O‑ This agency specializes in motion pictures/packaging.

How to Contact: Query with SASE, proposal package, outline. Responds in 1 month to queries. Obtains most new clients through recommendations from others, solicitations.
Recent Sales: This agency prefers not to share information on specific sales.
Terms: Agent receives 10% commission on domestic sales; 10% commission on foreign sales. Offers written contract, binding for 1-2 years. Charges clients for postage and photocopying.

A PICTURE OF YOU, 1176 Elizabeth Dr., Hamilton OH 45013-3507. Phone/Fax: (513)863-1108. E-mail: apoy1@aol.com. **Contact:** Lenny Minelli. Estab. 1993. Signatory of WGA. Represents 45 clients. 50% of clients are new/unpublished writers. Currently handles: 80% movie scripts; 10% TV scripts; 10% syndicated material.

- Prior to opening his agency, Mr. Minelli was an actor/producer for 10 years. Also owned and directed a talent agency and represented actors and actresses from around the world.

Member Agents: Michelle Chang (fiction/nonfiction books).
Represents: Nonfiction books, novels, short story collections, novellas, feature film, TV movie of the week, episodic drama, sitcom, animation, documentary, miniseries, syndicated material. **Considers these nonfiction areas:** Gay/lesbian issues; history; juvenile nonfiction; music/dance; religious/inspirational; self-help/personal improvement; theater/film. **Considers these fiction areas:** Action/adventure; detective/police/crime; erotica; ethnic; family saga; fantasy; gay/lesbian; glitz; historical; horror; literary; mainstream/contemporary; mystery/suspense; religious/inspirational; romance (contemporary, gothic, historical); thriller; westerns/frontier; young adult. **Considers these script subject areas:** Action/adventure; biography/autobiography; cartoon/animation; comedy; contemporary issues; detective/police/crime; erotica; ethnic; experimental; family saga; fantasy; feminist; gay/lesbian; glitz; historical; horror; juvenile; mainstream; multicultural; multimedia; mystery/suspense; psychic/supernatural; regional; religious/inspirational; romantic comedy; romantic drama; science fiction; sports; teen; thriller; western/frontier.

O‑ This agency specializes in screenplays and TV scripts.

How to Contact: Query with SASE. Accepts e-mail and fax queries. Considers simultaneous queries. Responds in 3 weeks to queries; 1 month to mss. Obtains most new clients through recommendations from others, solicitations.
Recent Sales: *Lost and Found*, by J.P. Brice; *So Long*, by Patrick Cappella. ***Scripting Assignment(s): The Governor***, by Gary M. Cappetta.
Terms: Agent receives 10% commission on domestic sales; 15% commission on foreign sales. Offers written contract, binding for 1 year; 90-day notice must be given to terminate contract. Charges clients for postage/express mail and long distance calls.
Tips: "Make sure that the script is the best it can be before seeking an agent."

JACK SCAGNETTI TALENT & LITERARY AGENCY, 5118 Vineland Ave., #102, North Hollywood CA 91601. (818)762-3871. Fax: (818)761-6629. **Contact:** Jack Scagnetti. Estab. 1974. Member of Academy of Television Arts and Sciences; signatory of WGA. Represents 50 clients. 50% of clients are new/unpublished writers. Currently handles: 20% nonfiction books; 70% movie scripts; 10% TV scripts.

- Prior to becoming an agent, Mr. Scagnetti wrote nonfiction books and magazine articles on movie stars, sports and health subjects and was a magazine and newspaper editor.

Member Agents: Steven Buchjsbaum (books); Sean Wright (books); David Goldman (script analyst).

Represents: Nonfiction books, novels, feature film, TV movie of the week, episodic drama, sitcom, animation (movie), miniseries. **Considers these nonfiction areas:** Biography/autobiography; cooking/foods/nutrition; current affairs; health/medicine; how-to; military/war; music/dance; self-help/personal improvement; sports; true crime/investigative; women's issues/studies. **Considers these fiction areas:** Action/adventure; contemporary issues; detective/police/crime; family saga; historical; mainstream/contemporary; mystery/suspense; picture books; romance (contemporary); sports; thriller; westerns/frontier. **Considers these script subject areas:** Action/adventure; comedy; detective/police/crime; family saga; historical; horror; mainstream; mystery/suspense; romantic comedy; romantic drama; sports; thriller.

O→ This agency specializes in film books with photographs. Actively seeking books and screenplays. Does not want to receive TV scripts for existing shows.

How to Contact: Query with SASE, outline/proposal. No fax queries. Responds in 1 month to queries; 2 months to mss. Returns materials only with SASE. Obtains most new clients through recommendations from others, solicitations.

Recent Sales: *Kastner's Cutthroats*, (44 Blue Prod.). ***Movie/TV MOW scripts in development***: *Pain*, by Charles Pickett (Concorde-New Horizons); *Club Video*, TV series, Actuality Productions (Hearst Entertainment).

Terms: Agent receives 15% commission on domestic sales; 15% commission on foreign sales; 10% commission on dramatic rights sales. Offers written contract, binding for 6 months-1 year. Offers criticism service (books only). "Fee depends upon condition of original copy and number of pages." Charges clients for postage and photocopies.

Tips: "Write a good synopsis, short and to the point and include marketing data for the book."

SHAPIRO-LICHTMAN, Shapiro-Lichtman Building, 8827 Beverly Blvd., Los Angeles CA 90048. (310)859-8877. Fax: (310)859-7153. **Contact:** Maritn Shapiro. Estab. 1969. Signatory of WGA. 10% of clients are new/unpublished writers.

Represents: Nonfiction books, novels, novellas, feature film, TV movie of the week, episodic drama, sitcom, animation (movie, TV), miniseries, soap opera, variety show. **Considers these nonfiction areas:** Agriculture/horticulture; americana; animals; anthropology/archaeology; art/architecture/design; biography/autobiography; business/economics; child guidance/parenting; computers/electronic; cooking/foods/nutrition; crafts/hobbies; creative nonfiction; current affairs; education; ethnic/cultural interests; gardening; gay/lesbian issues; government/politics/law; health/medicine; history; how-to; humor/satire; interior design/decorating; juvenile nonfiction; language/literature/criticism; memoirs; military/war; money/finance; multicultural; music/dance; nature/environment; New Age/metaphysics; philosophy; photography; popular culture; psychology; recreation; regional; religious/inspirational; science/technology; self-help/personal improvement; sex; sociology; software; spirituality; sports; theater/film; translation; travel; true crime/investigative; women's issues/studies; young adult. **Considers these fiction areas:** Action/adventure; comic books/cartoon; confession; contemporary issues; detective/police/crime; erotica; ethnic; experimental; family saga; fantasy; feminist; gay/lesbian; glitz; gothic; hi-lo; historical; horror; humor/satire; juvenile; literary; mainstream/contemporary; military/war; multicultural; multimedia; mystery/suspense; New Age; occult; picture books; plays; poetry; poetry in translation; psychic/supernatural; regional; religious/inspirational; romance; science fiction; short story collections; spiritual; sports; thriller; translation; westerns/frontier; young adult. **Considers these script subject areas:** Action/adventure; cartoon/animation; comedy; contemporary issues; detective/police/crime; ethnic; family saga; historical; horror; mainstream; mystery/suspense; romantic comedy; romantic drama; science fiction; teen; thriller; western/frontier.

How to Contact: Query with SASE. Responds in 10 days to queries. Returns materials only with SASE. Obtains most new clients through recommendations from others.

Recent Sales: This agency prefers not to share information on specific sales.

Terms: Agent receives 10% commission on domestic sales; 20% commission on foreign sales. Offers written contract, binding for 2 years.

KEN SHERMAN & ASSOCIATES, 9507 Santa Monica Blvd., Beverly Hills CA 90210. (310)273-3840. Fax: (310)271-2875. **Contact:** Ken Sherman. Estab. 1989. Member of BAFTA, PEN Int'l; signatory of WGA, DGA. Represents 50 clients. 10% of clients are new/unpublished writers. Currently handles: nonfiction books; juvenile books; movie scripts; TV scripts; video games/fiction.

- Prior to opening his agency, Mr. Sherman was with the William Morris Agency, The Lantz Office, and Paul Kohner, Inc.

Represents: Nonfiction books, novels, movie scripts, TV scripts, film and television rights to books. **Considers these nonfiction areas:** Agriculture/horticulture; americana; animals; anthropology/archaeology; art/architecture/design; biography/autobiography; business/economics; child guidance/parenting; computers/electronic; cooking/foods/nutrition; crafts/hobbies; creative nonfiction; current affairs; education; ethnic/cultural interests; gardening; gay/lesbian issues; government/politics/law; health/medicine; history; how-to; humor/satire; interior design/decorating; juvenile nonfiction; language/literature/criticism; memoirs; military/war; money/finance; multicultural; music/dance; nature/environment; New Age/metaphysics; philosophy; photography; popular culture; psychology; recreation; regional; religious/inspirational; science/technology; self-help/personal improvement; sex; sociology; software; spirituality; sports; theater/film; translation; travel; true crime/investigative; women's issues/studies; young adult. **Considers these fiction areas:** Action/adventure; comic books/cartoon; confession; contemporary issues; detective/police/crime; erotica; ethnic; experimental; family saga; fantasy; feminist; gay/lesbian; glitz; gothic; hi-lo; historical; horror; humor/satire; juvenile; literary; mainstream/contemporary; military/war; multicultural; multimedia; mystery/suspense; New Age; occult; picture books; plays; poetry; poetry in translation; psychic/supernatural; regional; religious/inspirational; romance; science fiction; short story collections; spiritual; sports; thriller; translation; westerns/frontier; young adult. **Considers these script subject areas:** Action/adventure; biography/autobiography; cartoon/animation; comedy; contemporary issues; detective/police/crime;

erotica; ethnic; experimental; family saga; fantasy; feminist; gay/lesbian; glitz; historical; horror; juvenile; mainstream; multicultural; multimedia; mystery/suspense; psychic/supernatural; regional; religious/inspirational; romantic comedy; romantic drama; science fiction; sports; teen; thriller; western/frontier.

O-ᴿ This agency specializes in solid writers for film TV, books and rights to books for film and TV.

How to Contact: Contact by referral only please. Responds in 1 month to mss.

Recent Sales: Sold 25 scripts in the last year. *Priscilla Salyers Story*, by Andrea Baynes (ABC); *Toys of Glass*, by Martin Booth (ABC/Saban Ent.); *Brazil*, by John Updike (film rights to Glaucia Carmagos); *Fifth Sacred Thing*, by Starhawk (Bantam); *Questions From Dad*, by Dwight Twilly (Tuttle); *Snow Falling on Cedars*, by David Guterson (Universal Pictures); *The Witches of Eastwick-The Musical*, by John Updike (Cameron Macintosh, Ltd.).

Terms: Agent receives 15% commission on domestic sales; 15% commission on foreign sales; 10% commission on dramatic rights sales. Offers written contract. Charges clients for reasonable office expenses, postage, photocopying, and other negotiable expenses.

Writers' Conferences: Maui; Squaw Valley; Santa Barbara; Santa Fe; Aspen Institute; Aspen Writers Foundation.

CAMILLE SORICE AGENCY, 13412 Moorpark St., #C, Sherman Oaks CA 91423. (818)995-1775. **Contact:** Camille Sorice. Estab. 1988. Signatory of WGA.

Represents: Novels, feature film. **Considers these script subject areas:** Action/adventure; comedy; detective/police/crime; family saga; historical; mystery/suspense; romantic comedy; romantic drama; western/frontier.

How to Contact: Query with SASE, synopsis. Prefers to read materials exclusively. No e-mail or fax queries. Responds in 6 weeks to mss.

Recent Sales: This agency prefers not to share information on specific sales.

Tips: "No calls. Query letters accepted."

STONE MANNERS AGENCY, 8436 W. Third St., Suite 740, Los Angeles CA 90048. (323)655-1313. **Contact:** Tim Stone. Estab. 1982. Signatory of WGA. Represents 25 clients.

Represents: Movie scripts, TV scripts. **Considers these script subject areas:** Action/adventure; biography/autobiography; cartoon/animation; comedy; contemporary issues; detective/police/crime; erotica; ethnic; experimental; family saga; fantasy; feminist; gay/lesbian; glitz; historical; horror; juvenile; mainstream; multicultural; multimedia; mystery/suspense; psychic/supernatural; regional; religious/inspirational; romantic comedy; romantic drama; science fiction; sports; teen; thriller; western/frontier.

How to Contact: Not considering scripts at this time.

Recent Sales: This agency prefers not to share information on specific sales.

Terms: Agent receives 10% commission on domestic sales; 10% commission on foreign sales.

SUITE A MANAGEMENT TALENT & LITERARY AGENCY, (formerly Robinson Talent and Literary Management), 1101 S. Robertson Blvd., Suite 210, Los Angeles CA 90035. (310)278-0801. Fax: (310)278-0807. **Contact:** Lloyd Robinson. Estab. 1996. Member of DGA; signatory of WGA. Represents 76 clients. 10% of clients are new/unpublished writers. Currently handles: 15% novels; 40% movie scripts; 40% TV scripts; 5% stage plays.

- Prior to becoming an agent, Mr. Robinson worked as a manager.

Member Agents: Lloyd Robinson (adaptation of books and plays for development as features or TV MOW); Kevin Douglas (scripts for film and TV); Judy Jacobs (feature development).

Represents: Feature film, TV movie of the week, episodic drama, documentary, miniseries, variety show, stage plays, CD-ROM. **Considers these script subject areas:** Action/adventure; cartoon/animation; comedy; contemporary issues; detective/police/crime; erotica; ethnic; experimental; family saga; fantasy; mainstream; mystery/suspense; psychic/supernatural; religious/inspirational; romantic comedy; romantic drama; science fiction; sports; teen; thriller; western/frontier.

O-ᴿ "We represent screenwriters, playwrights, novelists and producers, directors."

How to Contact: Submit synopsis, outline/proposal, log line. Obtains most new clients through recommendations from others.

Recent Sales: This agency prefers not to share information on specific sales or client names.

Terms: Agent receives 10% commission on domestic sales; 10% commission on foreign sales. Offers written contract, binding for 1 year minimum. Charges clients for photocopying, messenger, FedEx, and postage when required.

Tips: "We are a talent agency specializing in the copyright business. Fifty percent of our clients generate copyright-screenwriters, playrights and novelists. Fifty percent of our clients service copyright—producers and directors. We represent produced, published and/or WGA writers who are eligible for staff TV positions as well as novelists and playwrights whose works may be adapted for film on television."

TALENT SOURCE, 107 E. Hall St., P.O. Box 14120, Savannah GA 31416-1120. (912)232-9390. Fax: (912)232-8213. E-mail: mshortt@ix.netcom.com. Website: www.talentsource.com. **Contact:** Michael L. Shortt. Estab. 1991. Signatory of WGA. 35% of clients are new/unpublished writers. Currently handles: 85% movie scripts; 15% TV scripts.

- Prior to becoming an agent, Mr. Shortt was a television program producer/director.

Represents: Feature film, TV movie of the week, episodic drama, sitcom. **Considers these script subject areas:** Comedy; contemporary issues; detective/police/crime; erotica; family saga; juvenile; mainstream; mystery/suspense; romantic comedy; romantic drama; teen.

O-ᴿ Actively seeking "character-driven stories (e.g., *Sling Blade, Sex, Lies & Videotape*)." Does not want to receive "big budget special effects science fiction."

How to Contact: Query with SASE. Include a proper synopsis, please see the literary button on our website for complete submission details. Responds in 10 weeks to queries. Obtains most new clients through recommendations from others.
Recent Sales: This agency prefers not to share information on specific sales.
Terms: Agent receives 10% commission on domestic sales; 15% commission on foreign sales. Offers written contract.

TALESMYTH ENTERTAINMENT, INC., 312 St. John St., Suite #69, Portland ME 04102. (207)879-0307. Fax: (207)775-1067. E-mail: talesmyth@hotmail.com. **Contact:** Thomas Burgess. Estab. 2000. Signatory of WGA. Represents 6 clients. 100% of clients are new/unpublished writers. Currently handles: 10% novels; 10% story collections; 80% movie scripts.

- Prior to becoming an agent, Mr. Burgess produced short films and managed a restaurant.

Member Agents: Thomas "TJ" Burgess (screenplays/book-length fiction).
Represents: Novels, short story collections, movie scripts, feature film. **Considers these fiction areas:** Action/adventure; detective/police/crime; fantasy; historical; horror; humor/satire; mainstream/contemporary; mystery/suspense; New Age; psychic/supernatural; thriller; westerns/frontier. **Considers these script subject areas:** Action/adventure; comedy; detective/police/crime; fantasy; historical; horror; mystery/suspense; psychic/supernatural; romantic comedy; romantic drama; science fiction; thriller; western/frontier.

O→ "As a writer and producer myself I have a keen eye for industry trends and an amazing way to have the right ear hear the right pitch. I work to develop writers to marketable levels as well as represent authors that are ready for publication." Does not want romance, juvenile, children or young adult-oriented stories.

How to Contact: Query with SASE. Talesmyth Entertainment accepts new submissions from July 1-December 31 only. Responds in 20 days to queries; 2 months to mss. Obtains most new clients through recommendations from others.
Recent Sales: Clients include Gary Hauger, Kevin Brown, F. Allen Farnham, Christopher Cairnduff, Michael Lewin, Lawrence Climo, MD.
Terms: Agent receives 10% commission on domestic sales; 15% commission on foreign sales. Offers written contract, binding for 1 year; 60 days notice must be given to terminate contract. "Submissions of appropriate genre, received during our acceptance period, whether accepted or rejected, will receive a one-page critique penned by the agent that reviewed the material. At this time all reviews are completed by T.J. Burgess, president of Talesmyth Entertainment. No fee is charged for this critique."
Tips: "Be sure to submit only your best work for consideration. I don't want to see something you just want to get rid of, because I will probably respond in kind. Be certain that your query does a good job of selling me the story and characters and is not just a playful enticement with a "quirky twist." A solid query should summarize the plot and character development in an interesting fashion in one page or less as well as briefly address your expertise in the area or other relevant facts about the market for the story presented, anything else is a waste of your and my time."

WARDLOW AND ASSOCIATES, 1501 Main St., Suite 204, Venice CA 90291. (310)452-1292. Fax: (310)452-9002. E-mail: wardlowaso@aol.com. **Contact:** Jeff Ordway. Estab. 1980. Signatory of WGA. Represents 30 clients. 5% of clients are new/unpublished writers. Currently handles: 50% movie scripts; 50% TV scripts.
Member Agents: David Wardlow (literary, packaging); Jeff Ordway (literary).
Represents: Feature film, TV movie of the week, episodic drama, sitcom, miniseries. **Considers these script subject areas:** Action/adventure; biography/autobiography; cartoon/animation; comedy; contemporary issues; detective/police/crime; erotica; ethnic; experimental; family saga; fantasy; feminist; gay/lesbian; glitz; historical; horror; juvenile; mainstream; multicultural; multimedia; mystery/suspense; psychic/supernatural; regional; religious/inspirational; romantic comedy; romantic drama; science fiction; sports; teen; thriller; western/frontier.

O→ Does not want to receive "new sitcom/drama series ideas from beginning writers."

How to Contact: Query with SASE. Will not read unsolicited screenplays/mss. Accepts e-mail and fax queries. Considers simultaneous queries. Returns materials only with SASE. Obtains most new clients through recommendations from others, solicitations.
Recent Sales: This agency prefers not to share information on specific sales.
Terms: Agent receives 10% commission on domestic sales; 10% commission on foreign sales. Offers written contract, binding for 1 year.

WRITERS & ARTISTS AGENCY, 19 W. 44th St., Suite 1000, New York NY 10036. (212)391-1112. Fax: (212)575-6397. West Coast location: 8383 Wilshire Blvd., Suite 550, Beverly Hills CA 90211. (323)866-0900. Fax: (323)866-1899 **Contact:** William Craver, Nicole Graham, Christopher Till. Estab. 1970. Member of AAR; signatory of WGA. Represents 100 clients.
Represents: Movie scripts, feature film, TV scripts, TV movie of the week, episodic drama, miniseries, stage plays, stage musicals. **Considers these script subject areas:** Action/adventure; biography/autobiography; cartoon/animation; comedy; contemporary issues; detective/police/crime; erotica; ethnic; experimental; family saga; fantasy; feminist; gay/lesbian; glitz; historical; horror; juvenile; mainstream; multicultural; multimedia; mystery/suspense; psychic/supernatural; regional; romantic comedy; romantic drama; sports; teen; thriller; western/frontier.
How to Contact: Query with SASE, author bio, brief description of the project. No unsolicited mss. Responds in 1 month to queries only when accompanied by SASE. Obtains most new clients through professional recommendation preferred.
Recent Sales: This agency prefers not to share information on specific sales.

Subject Index

LITERARY AGENTS SUBJECT INDEX/FICTION

LITERARY AGENTS SUBJECT INDEX/NONFICTION

Inc., Jody; Rhodes Literary Agency, Jodie; Rubie Literary Agency, The Peter; Russell and Volkening; Shapiro-Lichtman; Sherman & Associates, Ken; Spitzer Literary Agency, Philip G.; Straus Agency, Inc., Robin; Wales, Literary Agency, Inc.; Whittaker, Literary Agent, Lynn

Gardening: Amster Literary Enterprises, Betsy; Bykofsky Associates, Inc. Sheree; Fredericks Literary Agency, Jeanne; Greenburger Associates, Inc., Sanford J.; Parks Agency, The Richard; Shapiro-Lichtman; Sherman & Associates, Ken

Gay/Lesbian: Bykofsky Associates, Inc. Sheree; Dunham Literary; Eth Literary Agency, Felicia; Greenburger Associates, Inc., Sanford J.; Larsen/Elizabeth Pomada Literary Agents, Michael; Lowenstein Associates; Parks Agency, The Richard; Picture of You, A; Russell and Volkening; Shapiro-Lichtman; Sherman & Associates, Ken; Wales, Literary Agency, Inc.; Whittaker, Literary Agent, Lynn

Government/Politics/Law: Black Literary Agency, David; Brandt & Hochman Literary Agents Inc.; Bykofsky Associates, Inc. Sheree; DH Literary, Inc.; Dunham Literary; Eth Literary Agency, Felicia; Greenburger Associates, Inc., Sanford J.; Larsen/Elizabeth Pomada Literary Agents, Michael; Love Literary Agency, Nancy; Lowenstein Associates; Mann Agency, Carol; Miller Co., The Stuart M.; Naggar Literary Agency, Jean V.; New England Publishing Associates Inc.; Parks Agency, The Richard; Rees Literary Agency, Helen; Rein Books, Inc., Jody; Rhodes Literary Agency, Jodie; Russell and Volkening; Shapiro-Lichtman; Sherman & Associates, Ken; Spitzer Literary Agency, Philip G.; Straus Agency, Inc., Robin

Health/Medicine: Altair Literary Agency; Amster Literary Enterprises, Betsy; Book Deals, Inc.; Brandt & Hochman Literary Agents Inc.; Bykofsky Associates, Inc. Sheree; Carlisle & Company; Castiglia Literary Agency; Dawson Associates, Liza; DH Literary, Inc.; Donnaud & Associates, Inc., Janis A.; Dunham Literary; Elmo Agency Inc., Ann; Eth Literary Agency, Felicia; Fredericks Literary Agency, Jeanne; Greenburger Associates, Inc., Sanford J.; Klinger, Inc., Harvey; Knight Agency, The; Koster Literary Agency, LLC, Elaine; Larsen/Elizabeth Pomada Literary Agents, Michael; Levine Literary Agency, Inc., Ellen; Love Literary Agency, Nancy; Lowenstein Associates; Mann Agency, Carol; Manus & Associates Literary Agency, Inc.; Menza Literary Agency, Claudia; Miller Co., The Stuart M.; Naggar Literary Agency, Jean V.; New England Publishing Associates Inc.; Parks Agency, The Richard; Rees Literary Agency, Helen; Rein Books, Inc., Jody; Rhodes Literary Agency, Jodie; Rinaldi Literary Agency, Angela; Russell and Volkening; Scagnetti Talent & Literary Agency, Jack; Sebastian Literary Agency; Shapiro-Lichtman; Sherman & Associates, Ken; Spitzer Literary Agency, Philip G.; Straus Agency, Inc., Robin; Teal Literary Agency, Patricia; Writers House

History: Altair Literary Agency; Altshuler Literary Agency, Miriam; Amster Literary Enterprises, Betsy; Black Literary Agency, David; Book Deals, Inc.; Brandt & Hochman Literary Agents Inc.; Bykofsky Associates, Inc. Sheree; Carlisle & Company; Carvainis Agency, Inc., Maria; Castiglia Literary Agency; Clark Associates, William; Dawson Associates, Liza; DH Literary, Inc.; Dunham Literary; Elmo Agency Inc., Ann; Eth Literary Agency, Felicia; Fredericks Literary Agency, Jeanne; Greenburger Associates, Inc., Sanford J.; Halsey North, Reece; Hogenson Agency, Barbara; Knight Agency, The; Koster Literary Agency, LLC, Elaine; Larsen/Elizabeth Pomada Literary Agents, Michael; Levine Literary Agency, Inc., Ellen; Love Literary Agency, Nancy; Lowenstein Associates; Mann Agency, Carol; Menza Literary Agency, Claudia; Miller Co., The Stuart M.; Naggar Literary Agency, Jean V.; New England Publishing Associates Inc.; Parks Agency, The Richard; Picture of You, A; Rees Literary Agency, Helen; Rein Books, Inc., Jody; Rhodes Literary Agency, Jodie; Russell and Volkening; Sebastian Literary Agency; Shapiro-Lichtman; Sherman & Associates, Ken; Spitzer Literary Agency, Philip G.; Straus Agency, Inc., Robin; Wales, Literary Agency, Inc.; Whittaker, Literary Agent, Lynn; Writers House

How-To: Book Deals, Inc.; Bykofsky Associates, Inc. Sheree; Elmo Agency Inc., Ann; Fredericks Literary Agency, Jeanne; Greenburger Associates, Inc., Sanford J.; Knight Agency, The; Koster Literary Agency, LLC, Elaine; Larsen/Elizabeth Pomada Literary Agents, Michael; Love Literary Agency, Nancy; Lowenstein Associates; Manus & Associates Literary Agency, Inc.; Miller Co., The Stuart M.; Parks Agency, The Richard; Rein Books, Inc., Jody; Scagnetti Talent & Literary Agency, Jack; Shapiro-Lichtman; Sherman & Associates, Ken; Teal Literary Agency, Patricia

Humor/Satire: Bykofsky Associates, Inc. Sheree; Donnaud & Associates, Inc., Janis A.; Greenburger Associates, Inc., Sanford J.; Larsen/Elizabeth Pomada Literary Agents, Michael; Lowenstein Associates; Parks Agency, The Richard; Rein Books, Inc., Jody; Shapiro-Lichtman; Sherman & Associates, Ken

Interior Design/Decorating: Bykofsky Associates, Inc. Sheree; Fredericks Literary Agency, Jeanne; Greenburger Associates, Inc., Sanford J.; Hogenson Agency, Barbara; Larsen/Elizabeth Pomada Literary Agents, Michael; Shapiro-Lichtman; Sherman & Associates, Ken; Writers House

Juvenile Nonfiction: Dunham Literary; Elmo Agency Inc., Ann; Greenburger Associates, Inc., Sanford J.; Naggar Literary Agency, Jean V.; Picture of You, A; Shapiro-Lichtman; Sherman & Associates, Ken; Writers House

Language/Literature/Criticism: Altshuler Literary Agency, Miriam; Bykofsky Associates, Inc. Sheree; Castiglia Literary Agency; DH Literary, Inc.; Dunham Literary; Greenburger Associates, Inc., Sanford J.; Halsey North, Reece; Lowenstein Associates; New England Publishing Associates Inc.; Parks Agency, The Richard; Russell and Volkening; Shapiro-Lichtman; Sherman & Associates, Ken; Spitzer Literary Agency, Philip G.; Straus Agency, Inc., Robin; Whittaker, Literary Agent, Lynn

Memoirs: Altshuler Literary Agency, Miriam; Black Literary Agency, David; Bykofsky Associates, Inc. Sheree; Carlisle & Company; Carvainis Agency, Inc., Maria; Clark Associates, William; Dawson Associates, Liza; Greenburger Associates, Inc., Sanford J.; Halsey North, Reece; Larsen/Elizabeth Pomada Literary Agents, Michael; Levine Literary Agency, Inc., Ellen; Love Literary Agency, Nancy; Lowenstein Associates; Manus & Associates Literary Agency, Inc.; Miller Co., The Stuart M.; Naggar Literary Agency, Jean V.; Parks Agency, The Richard; Rhodes Literary Agency, Jodie; Shapiro-Lichtman; Sherman & Associates, Ken; Wales, Literary Agency, Inc.; Whittaker, Literary Agent, Lynn

Military/War: Black Literary Agency, David; Bykofsky Associates, Inc. Sheree; Greenburger Associates, Inc., Sanford J.; Miller Co., The Stuart M.; New England Publishing Associates Inc.; Parks Agency, The Richard; Rhodes Literary Agency, Jodie; Russell and Volkening; Scagnetti Talent & Literary Agency, Jack; Shapiro-Lichtman; Sherman & Associates, Ken; Spitzer Literary Agency, Philip G.; Writers House

Money/Finance: Altair Literary Agency; Amster Literary Enterprises, Betsy; Black Literary Agency, David; Book Deals, Inc.; Bykofsky Associates, Inc. Sheree; Castiglia Literary Agency; DH Literary, Inc.; Elmo Agency Inc., Ann; Fredericks Literary Agency, Jeanne; Greenburger Associates, Inc., Sanford J.; Knight Agency, The; Koster Literary Agency, LLC, Elaine; Larsen/Elizabeth Pomada Literary Agents, Michael; Lowenstein Associates; Mann Agency, Carol; Manus & Associates Literary Agency, Inc.; New England Publishing Associates Inc.; Parks Agency, The Richard; Rees Literary Agency, Helen; Rinaldi Literary Agency, Angela; Russell and Volkening; Sebastian Literary Agency; Shapiro-Lichtman; Sherman & Associates, Ken; Whittaker, Literary Agent, Lynn; Writers House

Music/Dance: Altair Literary Agency; Altshuler Literary Agency, Miriam; Bykofsky Associates, Inc. Sheree; Clark Associates, William; Dunham Literary; Elmo Agency Inc., Ann; Greenburger Associates, Inc., Sanford J.; Hogenson Agency, Barbara; Knight Agency, The; Larsen/Elizabeth Pomada Literary Agents, Michael; Lowenstein Associates; Menza Literary Agency, Claudia; Parks Agency, The

SCRIPT AGENTS SUBJECT INDEX

The Markets

Book Publishers

The book business, for the most part, runs on hunches. Whether the idea for a book comes from a writer, an agent, or the imagination of an acquiring editor, it is generally expressed in these terms: "This is a book that I *think* people will like. People will *probably* want to buy it." The decision to publish is mainly a matter of the right person, or persons, agreeing that those hunches are sound.

THE PATH TO PUBLICATION

Ideas reach editors in a variety of ways. They arrive unsolicited every day through the mail. They come by phone, sometimes from writers but most often from agents. They arise in the editor's mind because of his daily traffic with the culture in which he lives. The acquisitions editor, so named because he is responsible for securing manuscripts for his company to publish, sifts through the deluge of possibilities, waiting for a book idea to strike him as extraordinary, inevitable or profitable.

In some companies, acquisitions editors possess the authority required to say, "Yes, we will publish this book." In most publishing houses, though, the acquisitions editor must prepare and present the idea to a proposal committee made up of marketing and administrative personnel. Proposal committees are usually less interested in questions of extraordinariness and inevitability than they are in profitability. The editor has to convince the committees that it makes good business sense to publish this book.

Once a contract is signed, several different wheels are set in motion. The author, of course, writes the book if he hasn't done so already. While the editor is helping to assure that the author is making the book the best it can be, promotion and publicity people are planning mailings of review copies to influential newspapers and review periodicals, writing catalog copy that will help sales representatives push the book to bookstores, and plotting a multitude of other promotional efforts (including interview tours and book signings by the author) designed to dangle the book attractively before the reading public's eye.

When the book is published, it usually receives a concerted promotional push for a month or two. After that, the fate of the book—whether it will "grow legs" and set sales records, or sit untouched on bookstore shelves—rests in the hands of the public. Publishers have to compete with all of the other entertainment industries vying for the consumer's money and limited leisure time.

THE STATE OF THE BUSINESS

Publishers sell their products to bookstores on a returnable basis, which means the stores usually have 120 days to either pay the bill or return the order. With independent bookstores continuing to close and superstores experiencing setbacks as well, many publishers were hit with staggering returns. This has slowed somewhat but continues to be a concern. While there are many more outlets to *buy* books, including online bookstores such as Amazon.com, Borders.com, and Barnesandnoble.com, this doesn't necessarily translate into more books being *bought*.

Some feel the superstore phenomenon has proved a mixed blessing. The greater shelf area means there are more materials available, but also drives a need for books as "wallpaper" that is continually refreshed by returning older books and restocking with newer ones.

But that's not to say publishers are rushing to bring esoteric or highly experimental material to the marketplace. The blockbuster mentality—publishing's penchant for sticking with "name brand" novelists—still drives most large publishers. It's simply a less risky venture to continue publishing authors whom they know readers like. On the other hand, the prospects for nonfiction authors are perhaps better than they have been for years. The boom in available shelf space has provided entry to the marketplace for books on niche topics that heretofore would not have seen the light of day in most bookstores. The superstores position themselves as one-stop shopping centers for readers of every stripe. As such, they must carry books on a wide range of subjects.

HOW TO PUBLISH YOUR BOOK

The markets in this year's Book Publishers section offer opportunities in nearly every area of publishing. Large, commercial houses are here as are their smaller counterparts; large and small "literary" houses are represented as well. In addition, you'll find university presses, industry-related publishers, textbook houses, and more.

The Book Publishers Subject Index is the place to start. You'll find it in the back of the book, before the General Index. Subject areas for both fiction and nonfiction are broken out for the over 1,000 total book publisher listings. Not all of them buy the kind of book you've written, but this Index will tell you which ones do.

When you have compiled a list of publishers interested in books in your subject area, read the detailed listings. Pare down your list by cross-referencing two or three subject areas and eliminating the listings only marginally suited to your book. When you have a good list, send for those publishers' catalogs and any manuscript guidelines available, or check publishers' websites, which often contain catalog listings, manuscript preparation guidelines, current contact names, and other information helpful to prospective authors. You want to make sure your book idea is in line with a publisher's list but is not a duplicate of something already published. Visit bookstores and libraries to see if the publisher's books are well represented. When you find a couple of books the house has published that are similar to yours, write or call the company to find out who edited those books. This last, extra bit of research could be the key to getting your proposal to precisely the right editor.

Publishers prefer different kinds of submissions on first contact. Most like to see a one-page query with SASE, especially for nonfiction. Others will accept a brief proposal package that might include an outline and/or a sample chapter. Some publishers will accept submissions from agents only. Virtually no publisher wants to see a complete manuscript on initial contact, and sending one when they prefer another method will signal to the publisher, "this is an amateur's submission." Editors do not have the time to read an entire manuscript, even editors at small presses who receive fewer submissions.

For More Information

RESOURCES

- *Guide to Literary Agents* (Writer's Digest Books).
- Association of Authors' Representatives (www.aar-online.org), P.O. Box 237201, Astonia Station, New York NY 10003.
- Volunteer Lawyers for the Arts, One E. 53rd St., New York NY 10022. (212)319-2787.

In your one-page query, give an overview of your book, mention the intended audience, the competition (check *Books in Print* and local bookstore shelves), and what sets your book apart. Detail any previous publishing experience or special training relevant to the subject of your book. All of this information will help your cause; it is the professional approach.

Only one in a thousand writers will sell a book to the first publisher they query, especially if the book is the writer's first effort. Make a list of a dozen or so publishers that might be interested in your book. Try to learn as much about the books they publish and their editors as you can. Research, knowing the specifics of your subject area, and a professional approach are often the difference between acceptance and rejection.

Personalize your queries by addressing them individually and mentioning what you know about a company from its catalog or books you've seen. Never send a form letter as a query. Envelopes addressed to "Editor" or "Editorial Department" end up in the dreaded slush pile.

If a publisher offers you a contract, you may want to seek advice from either a lawyer or an agent before signing and returning it. An author's agent will very likely take 15 percent if you employ one, but you could be making 85 percent of a larger amount. Some literary agents are available on an hourly basis for contract negotiations only.

AUTHOR-SUBSIDY PUBLISHER'S LISTINGS NOT INCLUDED

Writer's Market is a reference tool to help you sell your writing, and we encourage you to work with publishers that pay a royalty. Subsidy publishing involves paying money to a publishing house to publish a book. The source of the money could be a government, foundation, or university grant, or it could be the author of the book. Publishers offering nonauthor-subsidized arrangements have been included in the appropriate section. If one of the publishers listed here offers you an author-subsidy arrangement (sometimes called "cooperative publishing," "co-publishing," or "joint venture"), asks you to pay for part or all of the cost of any aspect of publishing (editing services, manuscript critiques, printing, advertising, etc.) or to guarantee the purchase of any number of the books yourself, we would like you to let us know about that company immediately.

Sometimes newer publishers will offer author-subsidy contracts to get a leg up in the business and plan to become royalty-only publishers once they've reached a firm financial footing. Some publishers feel they must offer subsidy contracts to expand their lists beyond the capabilities of their limited resources. This may be true, and you may be willing to agree to it, but we choose to list only those publishers paying a royalty without requiring a financial investment from the author.

INFORMATION AT-A-GLANCE

There are a number of symbols at the beginning of each listing to quickly convey certain information at a glance. In the Book Publisher sections, these symbols identify new listings (N), "opportunity" markets that buy at least 50 percent from unagented or first-time writers (★), and publishers that accept agented submissions only (A). Different sections of *Writer's Market* include other symbols; check the front and back inside covers for an explanation of all the symbols used throughout the book.

How much money? What are my odds?

We've also highlighted important information in boldface, the "quick facts" you won't find in any other market guide but should know before you submit your work. This includes: how many manuscripts a publisher buys per year; how many from first-time authors; how many from unagented writers; the royalty rate a publisher pays; and how large an advance is offered.

Publishers, their imprints, and how they are related

In this era of big publishing—and big mergers—the world of publishing has grown even more intertwined. A "family tree" on page 72 lists the imprints and often confusing relationships of the largest conglomerate publishers.

In the listings, "umbrella" listings for these larger houses list the imprints under the company name. Imprint names in boldface indicate a separate, individual listing, easily located alphabetically, which provides much more detailed information about that imprint's specific focus, needs, and contacts.

Most listings include a summary of the editorial mission of the house, an overarching principle that ties together what they publish. Under the heading **Acquisitions:** we list many more editors, often with their specific areas of expertise. We have included the royalty rates for those publishers willing to disclose them, but contract details are closely guarded and a number of larger publishers are reluctant to publicly state these terms. Standard royalty rates for paperbacks generally range from 7½ to 12½ percent, for hardcovers from 10 to 15 percent. Royalty rates for children's books are often lower, generally ranging from 5 to 10 percent.

For a list of publishers according to their subjects of interest, see the nonfiction and fiction sections of the Book Publishers Subject Index. Information on book publishers and producers listed in the previous edition of *Writer's Market* but not included in this edition can be found in the General Index.

A CAPPELLA, Chicago Review Press, 814 N. Franklin St., Chicago IL 60610. (312)337-0747. Fax: (312)640-0342. Website: www.ipgbook.com. **Acquisitions:** Yuval Taylor, editor (music, film). Publishes hardcover originals, trade paperback originals and reprints. **Publishes 3-12 titles/year. 30-40% of books from first-time authors; 50% from unagented writers. Pays 7½-12½% royalty on retail price. Offers $1,500-7,500 advance.** Publishes book 11 months after acceptance of ms. Accepts simultaneous submissions. Responds in 1 month to queries; 1 month to proposals; 1 month to mss. Book catalog free.

Nonfiction: Biography, illustrated book, reference. Subjects include music/dance, film. Submit 2 sample chapter(s), SASE.

Recent Title(s): *Bossa Nova*, by Ruy Castro; *Movie Wars*, by Jonathan Rosenbaum.

Tips: "A Cappella caters to an audience of music fans and film buffs."

A&B PUBLISHERS GROUP, 1000 Atlantic Ave., Brooklyn NY 11238. (718)783-7808. Fax: (718)783-7267. E-mail: maxtay@webspan.net. **Acquisitions:** Maxwell Taylor, production manager (children's, adult nonfiction); Wendy Gift, editor (fiction). Estab. 1992. Publishes hardcover originals, trade paperback originals and reprints. **Publishes 12 titles/year. Receives 120 queries and 150 mss/year. 30% of books from first-time authors; 30% from unagented writers. Pays 5-12% royalty on net receipts. Offers $500-2,500 advance.** Publishes book 18 months after acceptance of ms. Accepts simultaneous submissions. Responds in 2 months to queries; 2 months to proposals; 5 months to mss. Book catalog free.

O→ The audience for A&B Publishers Group is African-Americans. Currently emphasizing children's books.

Nonfiction: Children's/juvenile, coffee table book, cookbook, illustrated book. Subjects include cooking/foods/nutrition, history. Query with SASE. Reviews artwork/photos as part of ms package. Send photocopies.

Fiction: Query with SASE.

Recent Title(s): *Baggage Check* (fiction).

Tips: "Read, read, read. The best writers are developed from good reading. There is not enough attention to quality. Read, write and revise until you get it almost right."

A-R EDITIONS, INC., 8551 Research Way, Suite 180, Middleton WI 53562. (608)836-9000. Fax: (608)831-8200. Website: www.areditions.com. **Acquisitions:** Paul L. Ranzini, managing editor (Recent Researches music editions); James L. Zychowicz, managing editor (Computer Music and Digital Audio Series). Estab. 1962. **Publishes 30 titles/year. Receives 40 queries and 30 mss/year. 75% of books from first-time authors; 100% from unagented writers. Pays royalty or honoraria.** Does not accept simultaneous submissions. Responds in 1 month to queries; 3 months to proposals; 6 months to mss. Book catalog and ms guidelines online.

O→ A-R Editions publishes modern critical editions of music based on current musicological research. Each edition is devoted to works by a single composer or to a single genre of composition. The contents are chosen for their potential interest to scholars and performers, then prepared for publication according to the standards that govern the making of all reliable, historical editions.

Nonfiction: Subjects include computers/electronic, music/dance, software, historical music editions. Computer Music and Digital Audio titles deal with issues tied to digital and electronic media, and include both textbooks and handbooks in this area. Query with SASE or submit outline.

Recent Title(s): *Audio Recording Handbook*, by Alan P. Kefauver; *Orlando di Lasso: The Complete Motets 19*, edited by Peter Bergquist.

ABDO PUBLISHING COMPANY, 4940 Viking Dr., Edina MN 55435. (952)831-1317. Fax: (952)831-1632. E-mail: info@abdopub.com. Website: www.abdopub.com. **Acquisitions:** Paul Abdo, editor-in-chief (nonfiction, sports, history); Bob Italia, senior editor (science, history). Publishes hardcover originals. **Publishes 120 titles/year; imprint publishes 40 titles/year. Receives 300 queries and 100 mss/year. 10% of books from first-time authors; 90% from unagented writers. Makes outright purchase of $500-1,200.** Publishes book 6 months after acceptance of ms. Accepts simultaneous submissions. Responds in 2 months to queries; 4 months to proposals; 6 months to mss. Book catalog can be ordered online.

Imprints: ABDO & Daughters, Buddy Books, Checkerboard Library, SandCastle

O⇀ ABDO publishes nonfiction children's books (pre-kindergarten to 6th grade) for school and public libraries—mainly history, sports and biography.

Nonfiction: Biography, children's/juvenile, how-to. Subjects include animals, history, sports. Query with SASE.

Recent Title(s): *Civil War*, by Ann Guines (children's nonfiction); *Ricky Martin*, by Paul Joseph (children's biography).

ABI PROFESSIONAL PUBLICATIONS, P.O. Box 17446, Clearwater FL 33762. (727)556-0950. Fax: (727)556-2560. E-mail: abipropub@vandamere.com. Website: www.abipropub.com. **Acquisitions:** Art Brown, publisher/editor-in-chief (prosthetics, rehabilitation, dental/medical research). Publishes hardcover and trade paperback originals. **Publishes 10 titles/year. Receives 20-30 queries and 5-10 mss/year. 25% of books from first-time authors; 100% from unagented writers. Pays royalty on revenues generated. Offers small advance.** Publishes book 1+ years after acceptance of ms. Accepts simultaneous submissions. Responds in 3 months to queries. Book catalog and ms guidelines online.

Nonfiction: Reference, technical, textbook. Subjects include health/medicine. Submit proposal package including outline, representative sample chapter(s), author bio or submit complete ms. Reviews artwork/photos as part of ms package. Send photocopies.

Recent Title(s): *Cleft Palate Dentistry*, by Robert McKinstry (dental text); *Managing Stroke*, by Paul R. Rao and John E. Toerge (rehabilitation).

Tips: Audience is allied health professionals, dentists, researchers, patients undergoing physical rehabilitation. "We will not review electronic submissions."

ABINGDON PRESS, The United Methodist Publishing House, 201 Eighth Ave. S., Nashville TN 37203. (615)749-6000. Fax: (615)749-6512. Website: www.abingdon.org. President/Publisher: Neil M. Alexander. Senior Vice President/Publishing: Harriett Jane Olson. **Acquisitions:** Gregory Glover, senior editor (academic); Robert Ratcliff, senior editor (professional clergy); Peg Augustine, editor (children's); Joseph A. Crowe, editor (general interest). Estab. 1789. Publishes hardcover and paperback originals; church supplies. **Publishes 120 titles/year. Receives 3,000 queries and 250 mss/year. Small% of books from first-time authors; 85% from unagented writers. Pays 7½% royalty on retail price.** Publishes book 2 years after acceptance of ms. Does not accept simultaneous submissions. Responds in 2 months to queries. Book catalog free; ms guidelines online.

Imprints: Dimensions for Living, Cokesbury, Abingdon Press.

O⇀ Abingdon Press, America's oldest theological publisher, provides an ecumenical publishing program dedicated to serving the Christian community—clergy, scholars, church leaders, musicians and general readers—with quality resources in the areas of Bible study, the practice of ministry, theology, devotion, spirituality, inspiration, prayer, music and worship, reference, Christian education and church supplies.

Nonfiction: Children's/juvenile, gift book, reference, textbook, religious-lay and professional; scholarly. Subjects include education, music/dance, religion. Query with outline and samples only.

Recent Title(s): *Celtic Praise*, by Van de Weyer (gift).

HARRY N. ABRAMS, INC., La Martiniere Groupe, 100 Fifth Ave., New York NY 10011. (212)206-7715. Fax: (212)645-8437. Website: www.abramsbooks.com. President: Steven Parr. **Acquisitions:** Eric Himmel, editor-in-chief. Estab. 1949. Publishes hardcover and "a few" paperback originals. **Publishes 150 titles/year. Pays royalty. Offers variable advance.** Publishes book 2 years after acceptance of ms. Does not accept simultaneous submissions. Responds in 3 months to queries. Book catalog for $5.

O⇀ "We publish *only* high-quality illustrated art books, i.e., art, art history, museum exhibition catalogs, written by specialists and scholars in the field."

Nonfiction: Illustrated book. Subjects include art/architecture, nature/environment, recreation (outdoor). Requires illustrated material for art and art history, museums. Submit outline, sample chapter(s), illustrations. Reviews artwork/photos as part of ms package.

Tips: "We are one of the few publishers who publish almost exclusively illustrated books. We consider ourselves the leading publishers of art books and high-quality artwork in the U.S. Once the author has signed a contract to write a book for our firm the author must finish the manuscript to agreed-upon high standards within the schedule agreed upon in the contract."

☒ **ABSEY & CO.**, 23011 Northcrest Dr., Spring TX 77389. (281)257-2340. E-mail: abseyandco@aol.com. Website: www.absey.com. **Acquisitions:** Edward Wilson, editor-in-chief. Publishes hardcover, trade paperback and mass market paperback originals. **Publishes 6-10 titles/year. 50% of books from first-time authors; 50% from unagented writers. Royalty and advance vary.** Publishes book 1 year after acceptance of ms. Does not accept simultaneous submissions. Responds in 3 months to queries; 9 months to mss. Ms guidelines online.

O‑ "Our goal is to publish original, creative works of literary merit." Currently emphasizing educational, young adult literature. De-emphasizing self-help.

Nonfiction: Subjects include education, language/literature (language arts), general nonfiction. "We will not open anything without a return address. All submissions sent without return or insufficient postage are discarded." Query with SASE.

Fiction: "Since we are a small, new press, we are looking for book-length manuscripts with a firm intended audience." Query with SASE.

Poetry: Publishes the "Writers and Young Writers Series." Interested in thematic poetry collections of literary merit. Query.

Recent Title(s): *Dragonfly*, by Alice McLerran (fiction); *Where I'm From*, by George Ella Lyon (poetry).

Tips: "We work closely and attentively with authors and their work." Does not accept e-mail submissions.

ACADEMY CHICAGO PUBLISHERS, 363 W. Erie St., Chicago IL 60610-3125. (312)751-7300. Fax: (312)751-7306. E-mail: academy363@aol.com. Website: www.academychicago.com. **Acquisitions:** Anita Miller, editorial director/senior editor. Estab. 1975. Publishes hardcover originals and trade paperback reprints. **Publishes 15 titles/year. Receives 2,000 submissions/year. Pays 7-10% royalty on wholesale price. Offers modest advance.** Publishes book 18 months after acceptance of ms. Responds in 2 months to queries. Book catalog online; ms guidelines online.

O‑ "We publish quality fiction and nonfiction. Our audience is literate and discriminating. No novelized biography, history or science fiction."

Nonfiction: Biography. Subjects include history, travel. No religion or self-help. Submit proposal package including outline, 3 sample chapter(s), author bio.

Fiction: Historical, mainstream/contemporary, military/war, mystery. "We look for quality work, but we do not publish experimental, avant garde novels." Submit proposal package including 3 sample chapter(s), synopsis.

Recent Title(s): *Food & Drink in Britain*, by C. Ann Nelson; *Cutters' Island*, by Vincent Panella.

Tips: "At the moment, we are looking for good nonfiction; we certainly want excellent original fiction, but we are swamped. No fax queries, no disks. No electronic submissions. We are always interested in reprinting good out-of-print books."

[A] **ACE SCIENCE FICTION AND FANTASY**, The Berkley Publishing Group, Penguin Putnam Inc., 375 Hudson St., New York NY 10014. (212)366-2000. Website: www.penguinputnam.com. **Acquisitions:** Anne Sowards, editor. Estab. 1953. Publishes hardcover, paperback and trade paperback originals and reprints. **Publishes 75 titles/year. Pays royalty. Offers advance.** Does not accept simultaneous submissions. Responds in 6 months to queries. Ms guidelines for #10 SASE.

O‑ Ace publishes science fiction and fantasy exclusively.

Fiction: Fantasy, science fiction. *Agented submissions only.* Query first with SASE.

Recent Title(s): *King Kelsori Bride*, by Katherine Kurtz; *All Tomorrow's Parties*, by William Gibson.

[N] **ACEN PRESS**, DNA Press, 730 Daniel Dr., Collegeville PA 19426. (610)489-8404. Fax: (208)692-2855. E-mail: dnapress@yahoo.com. **Acquisitions:** Alexander Kuklin, Ph.D., managing editor (children scientific books); Xela Schenk, operations manager (New Age). Estab. 1998. Publishes trade paperback originals. **Publishes 10 titles/year; imprint publishes 5 titles/year. Receives 75 queries and 20 mss/year. 90% of books from first-time authors; 100% from unagented writers. Pays 10-20% royalty.** Publishes book 4 months after acceptance of ms. Accepts simultaneous submissions. Responds in 2 weeks to queries; 1 month to proposals; 6 weeks to mss. Book catalog free; ms guidelines free.

O‑ Book publisher for young adults, children and adults.

Nonfiction: Children's/juvenile (explaining science), how-to. Subjects include education, New Age, science. "We publish books for children or how-to for adults which carry scientific knowledge and contribute to learning." Submit complete ms. Reviews artwork/photos as part of ms package. Send photocopies.

Fiction: Juvenile, science fiction, young adult. "All books should be oriented to explaining science even if they do not fall 100% under the category of science fiction." Submit complete ms.

Recent Title(s): *How to DNA Test our Family Relationships?*, by Terrence Carmichael and Alexander Kuklin; *How Do Witches Fly?*, by Alexander Kuklin.

Tips: "Quick response, great relationships, high commission/royalty."

[★] **ACTA PUBLICATIONS**, 4848 N. Clark St., Chicago IL 60640-4711. Fax: (773)271-7399. E-mail: actapublications@aol.com. **Acquisitions:** Gregory F. Augustine Pierce. Estab. 1958. Publishes trade paperback originals. **Publishes 12 titles/year. Receives 100 queries and 25 mss/year. 50% of books from first-time authors; 90% from unagented writers. Pays 10-12% royalty on wholesale price.** Publishes book 1 year after acceptance of ms. Does not accept simultaneous submissions. Responds in 1 month to proposals. Book catalog and ms guidelines for #10 SASE.

O‑ ACTA publishes non-academic, practical books aimed at the mainline religious market.

Nonfiction: Self-help. Subjects include religion, spirituality. Submit outline, 1 sample chapter(s). Reviews artwork/photos as part of ms package. Send photocopies.

Recent Title(s): *Invitation to Catholicism*, by Alice Camille (religious education); *Protect Us from All Anxiety: Meditations for the Depressed*, by William Burke (self-help).

Tips: "Don't send a submission unless you have read our catalog or one of our books."

ADAMS-BLAKE PUBLISHING, 8041 Sierra St., Fair Oaks CA 95628. (916)962-9296. Website: www.adams-blake.com. Vice President: Paul Raymond. **Acquisitions:** Monica Blane, senior editor. Estab. 1992. Publishes trade paperback originals and reprints. **Publishes 10-15 titles/year. Receives 150 queries and 90 mss/year. 90% of books from first-time authors; 90% from unagented writers. Pays 15% royalty on wholesale price.** Publishes book 6 months after acceptance of ms. Accepts simultaneous submissions. Responds in 3 months to mss.

Adams-Blake Publishing is looking for business, technology and finance titles as well as data that can be bound/packaged and sold to specific industry groups at high margins. "We publish technical and training material we can sell to the corporate market. We are especially looking for 'high ticket' items that sell to the corporate market for prices between $100-300." Currently emphasizing technical, computers, technology. De-emphasizing business, management.

Nonfiction: How-to, technical. Subjects include business/economics, computers/electronic, health/medicine, money/finance, software. Query with sample chapters or complete ms. Reviews artwork/photos as part of ms package. Send photocopies.

Recent Title(s): *Success From Home*, by Alan Canton.

Tips: "We will take a chance on material the big houses reject. Since we sell the majority of our material directly, we can publish material for a very select market. This year we seek niche market material that we can Docutech and sell direct to the corporate sector. Author should include a marketing plan. Sell us on the project!"

ADDICUS BOOKS, INC., P.O. Box 45327, Omaha NE 68145. (402)330-7493. Website: www.addicusbooks.com. **Acquisitions:** Rod Colvin, president. Estab. 1994. Publishes trade paperback originals. **Publishes 8-10 titles/year. 70% of books from first-time authors; 60% from unagented writers. Pays royalty on retail price. Offers advance.** Publishes book 9 months after acceptance of ms. Accepts simultaneous submissions. Responds in 1 month to proposals. Ms guidelines for #10 SASE.

Addicus Books, Inc. seeks mss with strong national or regional appeal.

Nonfiction: How-to, self-help. Subjects include Americana, business/economics, health/medicine, psychology, regional, true crime, true crime. "We are developing a line of consumer health titles." Query with SASE. Do not send entire ms unless requested. No electronic submissions.

Recent Title(s): *Coronary Heart Disease—A Guide to Diagnosis and Treatment*, by Barry Cohen, M.D., Bobbie Hasselbring; *LASIK—A Guide to Laser Vision Correction*, by Ernest Kornmehl, M.D., et al.

Tips: "We are looking for quick-reference books on health topics. Do some market research to make sure the market is not already flooded with similar books. We're also looking for good true-crime manuscripts, with an interesting story, with twists and turns, behind the crime."

ADIRONDACK MOUNTAIN CLUB, INC., 814 Goggins Rd., Lake George NY 12845-4117. (518)668-4447. Fax: (518)668-3746. E-mail: pubs@adk.org. Website: www.adk.org. **Acquisitions:** John Kettlewell, editor (all titles); Neal Burdick, editor (*Adirondac* magazine, published bimonthly). Publishes hardcover and trade paperback originals and reprints. **Publishes 34 titles/year. Receives 36 queries and 12 mss/year. 95% of books from first-time authors; 95% from unagented writers. Pays 6-10% royalty on retail price. Offers $250-1,000 advance.** Publishes book 1 year after acceptance of ms. Does not accept simultaneous submissions. Responds in 3 months to queries; 4 months to proposals; 4 months to mss. Book catalog free and online; ms guidelines free.

"Our main focus is recreational guides to the Adirondack and Catskill Parks; however, our titles continue to include natural, cultural and literary histories of these regions. Our main interest is in protecting the resource through environmental education. This is the focus of our magazine, *Adirondac*, as well."

Nonfiction: Reference. Subjects include nature/environment, recreation, regional, sports, travel, trail maps. Query with SASE or submit proposal package including outline, 1-2 sample chapter(s), with proposed illustrations and visuals. Reviews artwork/photos as part of ms package. Send photocopies.

Recent Title(s): *Views from on High: Five Tower Trails in the Adirondacks and Catskills*; *Kids on the Trail! Hiking with Children in the Adirondacks*, by Rose Rivezzi and David Trithart.

Tips: "Our audience consists of outdoors people interested in muscle-powered recreation, natural history, and 'armchair traveling' in the Adirondacks and Catskills. Bear in mind the educational mandate implicit in our organization's mission. Note range of current ADK titles."

ADVOCACY PRESS, Box 236, Santa Barbara CA 93102-0236. (805)962-2728. Fax: (805)963-3508. E-mail: advpress@impulse.net. Website: www.advocacypress.com. **Acquisitions:** Curriculum Specialist. Estab. 1983. Publishes hardcover and paperback originals. **Publishes 3-5 titles/year. Pays 5-10% royalty.** Accepts simultaneous submissions. Responds in 3 months to queries. Book catalog for #10 SASE.

"We promote gender equity and positive self-esteem through our programs and publications."

Fiction: Juvenile, picture books (only gender equity/positive esteem messages to boys and girls). Query with SASE or submit SASE or submit complete ms.

Recent Title(s): *Minou*, by Mindy Bingham (picture book); *Kylie's Song*, Patty Sheehan (picture book); *Nature's Wonderful World in Rhyme*, by William Sheehan.

Tips: Wants "stories for children that give messages of self-sufficiency/self-esteem. Please review some of our publications before you submit to us. For layout and writing guidelines, we recommend that you read *The Children's Book: How to Write It, How to Sell It* by Ellen Roberts, Writer's Digest Books. Because of our limited focus, most of our titles have been written inhouse."

AEGIS PUBLISHING GROUP, 796 Aquidneck Ave., Newport RI 02842-7246. (401)849-4200. Fax: (401)849-4231. E-mail: aegis@aegisbooks.com. Website: www.aegisbooks.com. **Acquisitions:** Robert Mastin, publisher. Estab. 1992. Publishes trade paperback originals and reprints. **Publishes 6 titles/year. Pays 12% royalty on net receipts. Offers $1,000-4,000 advance.** Does not accept simultaneous submissions. Responds in 2 months to queries.

O→ "Our specialty is telecommunications books targeted to small businesses, entrepreneurs and telecommuters—how they can benefit from the latest telecom products and services. Our goal is to become the primary publisher of nontechnical telecommunications books for small organizations, end users, new entrants to the industry and telecom managers." Currently emphasizing data networks and the Internet.

Nonfiction: Reference, business. Subjects include telecommunications, data networking. "Author must be an experienced authority in the subject, and the material must be very specific with helpful step-by-step advice." Query with SASE.

Recent Title(s): *Digital Convergence*, by Andy Covell; *Office Emails That Really Click*, by Maureen Chase and Sandy Trupp.

[N] **AFRIMAX, INC.**, 703 Shannon Lane, Kirksville MO 63501. (660)665-0757. **Acquisitions:** Emmanuel Nnadozie, president. Publishes trade paperback originals. **Publishes 4 titles/year. Pays 8% royalty.** Responds in 5 months to queries; 1 month to proposals; 3 months to mss. Ms guidelines free.

Nonfiction: How-to, textbook. Subjects include business/economics, ethnic, money/finance, regional, travel. "International business and African business related interests." Query.

Recent Title(s): *African Culture & American Business in Africa*, by Emmanuel Nnadozie (business/how-to).

Tips: Audience includes business managers, busines educations, students.

AKTRIN FURNITURE INFORMATION CENTER, 164 S. Main St., P.O. Box 898, High Point NC 27261. (336)841-8535. Fax: (336)841-5435. E-mail: aktrin@aktrin.com. Website: www.furniture-info.com. **Acquisitions:** Donna Fincher, director of operations. Estab. 1985. Publishes trade paperback originals. **Publishes 8 titles/year. Receives 5 queries/year. 20% of books from first-time authors; 20% from unagented writers. Makes outright purchase of $1,500 minimum. Offers $300-600 advance.** Publishes book 2 months after acceptance of ms. Accepts simultaneous submissions. Responds in 1 month. *Writer's Market* recommends allowing 2 months for reply to queries. Book catalog free.

Imprints: AKTRIN Furniture Information Center-Canada (151 Randall St., Oakville, Ontario L6J 1P5 Canada. (905)845-3474. Contact: Stefan Wille).

O→ AKTRIN is a full-service organization dedicated to the furniture industry. "Our focus is on determining trends, challenges and opportunities, while also identifying problems and weak spots." Currently emphasizing the wood industry.

Nonfiction: Reference. Subjects include business/economics. "We are writing only about the furniture industry. Have an understanding of business/economics." Query.

Recent Title(s): *The American Demand for Household Furniture and Trends*, by Thomas McCormick (in-depth analysis of American household furniture market).

Tips: Audience is executives of furniture companies (manufacturers and retailers) and suppliers and consultants to the furniture industry.

ALASKA NORTHWEST BOOKS, Graphic Arts Center Publishing, P.O. Box 10306, Portland OR 97296-0306. (503)226-2402. Fax: (503)223-1410. Website: www.gacpc.com. **Acquisitions:** Tricia Brown. Estab. 1959. Publishes hardcover and trade paperback originals and reprints. **Publishes 12 titles/year. Receives hundreds of submissions/year. 10% of books from first-time authors; 90% from unagented writers. Pays 10-14% royalty on net revenues. Buys mss outright (rarely). Offers advance.** Publishes book an average of 2 years after acceptance of ms. Accepts simultaneous submissions. Responds in 6 months to queries. Book catalog for 9×12 SAE with 6 first-class stamps; ms guidelines online.

Nonfiction: Children's/juvenile, cookbook. Subjects include nature/environment, recreation, sports, travel, Native American culture, adventure, the arts. "All written for a general readership, not for experts in the subject." Submit outline, sample chapter(s).

Recent Title(s): *One Wing's Gift: Rescuing Alaska's Wild Birds*; *Kumak's House: A Tale of the Far North.*

Tips: "Book proposals that are professionally written and polished with a clear market receive our most careful consideration. We are looking for originality. We publish a wide range of books for a wide audience. Some of our books are clearly for travelers, others for those interested in outdoor recreation or various regional subjects. If I were a writer trying to market a book today, I would research the competition (existing books) for what I have in mind, and clearly (and concisely) express why my idea is different and better. I would describe the book buyers (and readers)—where they are, how many of them are there, how they can be reached (organizations, publications), why they would want or need my book."

[N] **ALBION PRESS**, 4532 W. Kennedy Blvd., Suite 233, Tampa FL 33609. (813)805-2665 or (888)405-2665. Fax: (813)832-6777. E-mail: abionpr@aol.com. **Acquisitions:** Lonnie Herman, managing editor. Publishes hardcover and trade paperback orginals. **Publishes 20-25 titles/year. Receives 200 queries and 40 mss/year. 50% of books from first-time authors; 80% from unagented writers. 10% royalty on retail price for hardcover and 8% royalty on retail price for trade paperback. Advance varies.** Publishes book 16 months after acceptance of ms. Accepts simultaneous submissions. Responds in 2 months to queries; 2 months to proposals; 3 months to mss. Book catalog free; ms guidelines free.

Nonfiction: "We're always looking for regional nonfiction titles, and especially for sports, biographies, true crime and how-to books." Biography, how-to. Subjects include business/economics, ethnic, history, regional, sports, true crime. "We specialize in nonfiction books that 'tell the story behind the story'." Query with SASE or submit outline, 2 sample chapter(s).

Recent Title(s): *Nightmare on 33rd Street: A Long Season With the New York Rangers*, by Rick Carpiniello.

Tips: "We pride ourselves on working closely with an author and producing a quality product with strong promotional campaigns. Best to have a strong point of view."

N **ALEF DESIGN GROUP**, 4423 Fruitland Ave., Los Angeles CA 90058. (213)585-7312. Website: www.alefdesign.com. **Acquisitions:** Jane Golub. Estab. 1990. Publishes hardcover and trade paperback originals. **Publishes 25 titles/year; imprint publishes 10 titles/year. Receives 30 queries and 30 mss/year. 80% of books from first-time authors; 100% from unagented writers. Pays 10% royalty. Offers advance.** Publishes book 3 years after acceptance of ms. Accepts simultaneous submissions. Responds in 6 months to mss. Ms guidelines for 9×12 SAE with 10 first-class stamps.

O→ The Alef Design Group publishes books of Judaic interest only. Currently de-emphasizing picture books.

Nonfiction: Children's/juvenile, textbook. Subjects include language/literature (Hebrew), religion (Jewish). Query with SASE. Reviews artwork/photos as part of ms package. Send photocopies.

Fiction: Juvenile, religious, young adult. "We publish books of Judaic interest only." Query with SASE.

Recent Title(s): *Scripture Windows*, by Peter Pitzele (nonfiction); *The Road to Exile*, by Didier Nebot (fiction).

ALEXANDER BOOKS, Creativity, Inc., 65 Macedonia Rd., Alexander NC 28701. (828)252-9515. Fax: (828)255-8719. E-mail: sales@abooks.com. Website: abooks.com. **Acquisitions:** Pat Roberts, acquisitions editor. Publishes hardcover originals and trade and mass market paperback originals and reprints. **Publishes 15-20 titles/year. Receives 200 queries and 100 mss/year. 10% of books from first-time authors; 75% from unagented writers. Pays 12-15% royalty on wholesale price. Offers rare (minimum $100) advance.** Publishes book 18 months after acceptance of ms. Does not accept simultaneous submissions. Book catalog for 9×12 SASE with 5 ounces postage; ms guidelines for #10 SASE.

Imprints: Farthest Star (classic science fiction, very few new titles), Mountain Church (mainline Protestant material).

O→ Alexander Books publishes mostly nonfiction national titles, both new and reprints.

Nonfiction: Biography, how-to, reference, self-help. Subjects include computers/electronic, government/politics, history, regional, religion, travel, collectibles. "We are interested in large niche markets." Query or submit 3 sample chapters and proposal package, including marketing plans with SASE. Reviews artwork/photos as part of ms package. Send photocopies.

Fiction: Historical, mainstream/contemporary, mystery, science fiction, western. "We prefer local or well-known authors or local interest settings." Query with SASE or submit 3 sample chapter(s), synopsis.

Recent Title(s): *Sanders Price Guide to Autographs, 5th ed*, by Sanders and Roberts; *Birthright*, by Mike Resnick.

Tips: "Send well-proofed manuscripts in final form. We will not read first rough drafts. Know your market."

ALGONQUIN BOOKS OF CHAPEL HILL, Workman Publishing, P.O. Box 2225, Chapel Hill NC 27515-2225. (919)967-0108. Website: www.algonquin.com. **Acquisitions:** Editorial Department. Publishes hardcover originals, trade paperback originals and reprints of own titles. **Publishes 24 titles/year.** Query by mail before submitting work. No phone, e-mail or fax queries or submissions. Visit our website for full submission policy to queries.

O→ Algonquin Books publishes quality literary fiction and nonfiction.

ALGORA PUBLISHING, 222 Riverside Dr., 16th Floor, New York NY 10025-6809. (212)678-0232. Fax: (212)663-9805. E-mail: editors@algora.com. Website: www.algora.com. **Acquisitions:** Martin DeMers, editor (sociology/philosophy/economics); Claudiu A. Secara, publisher (philosophy/international affairs). Publishes trade paperback originals and reprints. **Publishes 25 titles/year. Receives 500 queries and 200 mss/year. 20% of books from first-time authors; 85% from unagented writers. Pays 7½-12% royalty on net receipts. Offers $0-1,000 advance.** Publishes book 10 months after acceptance of ms. Accepts simultaneous submissions. Responds in 1 month to queries; 1 month to proposals; 2 months to mss. Book catalog and ms guidelines online.

O→ Algora Publishing is an academic-type press, focusing on works by mostly (but not exclusively) American and European authors for the educated general reader.

Nonfiction: General nonfiction for the educated reader. Subjects include anthropology/archeology, business/economics, creative nonfiction, education, government/politics, health/medicine, history, language/literature, military/war, money/finance, music/dance, nature/environment, philosophy, psychology, religion, science, sociology, translation, women's issues/studies. Query by e-mail (preferred) or submit proposal package including outline, 3 sample chapers or complete ms.

Recent Title(s): *Soul Snatchers—The Mechanics of Cults*, by Jean-Marie Abgrall (sociology); *Russian Intelligence Services*, by Vladimir Plougin (history).

Tips: "We welcome first-time writers; we help them outline their project, crafting an author's raw manuscript into a literary work."

ALL WILD-UP PRODUCTIONS, P.O. Box 1354, Puyallup WA 98371. Phone/fax: (206)457-1949. E-mail: mail@allwildup.com. Website: www.allwildup.com. **Acquisitions:** Chris Ihrig, publisher (amusement park industry creativity, innovation). Publishes hardcover originals and reprints, trade paperback originals and reprints, electronic originals and reprints. **Publishes 3-10 titles/year. Receives 175 queries and 75 mss/year. 80% of books from first-time authors; 90% from unagented writers. Pays 12-20% royalty on wholesale price or makes outright purchase.** Publishes book 3 months after acceptance of ms. Accepts simultaneous submissions. Responds in 1 month to queries; 1 month to proposals; 1 month to mss. Book catalog and ms guidelines online.
Nonfiction: Coffee table book, cookbook, gift book, how-to, illustrated book, multimedia (CD/e-book), reference, self-help, technical. Subjects include Americana, art/architecture, business/economics, cooking/foods/nutrition, creative nonfiction, money/finance, photography, recreation, travel. "Our specialty is the amusement and theme park industry. Our subject matter addresses the needs of both the professional and enthusiast."
Tips: "All our publications utilize creativity and innovation to make our world a better place."

ALLEGRO PRESS, Rt. 6, Box 385S, Lake City FL 32025. (386)755-5747. E-mail: publisher@allegro-press.com. Website: www.allegro-press.com. **Acquisitions:** Mike Payne. Publishes trade paperback originals. **Publishes 6 titles/year. 80% of books from first-time authors; 100% from unagented writers. Pays 10% royalty on net sales after direct expenses met.** Publishes book 6 months after acceptance of ms. Does not accept simultaneous submissions. Responds in 1 month to mss. Book catalog online. "Please submit by e-mail only."

O━ Allegro Press works almost exclusively with solicited authors.

Nonfiction: Children's/juvenile, technical. Subjects include government/politics, military/war, philosophy, religion, science. Submit complete ms. Reviews artwork/photos as part of ms package. Send photocopies.
Recent Title(s): *Shall We Clone a Man?*, by Alonso (religion/philosophy); *Melisande* (allegory).
Tips: "A non-majority viewpoint will be treated with serious consideration."

ALLIGATOR PRESS, INC., P.O. Box 81509, Austin TX 78708. (915)585-3426. Fax: (915)585-7576. E-mail: kkimball@alligatorpress.com. Website: www.alligatorpress.com.

O━ Publisher of books in Spanish and their translations.

Nonfiction: Query with SASE.
Recent Title(s): *When Alligators Sing*, by Miguel Santana (historical romance); *Cloven*, by Chae Waters (mystery/suspense).

ALLWORTH PRESS, 10 E. 23rd St., Suite 510, New York NY 10010-4402. Fax: (212)777-8261. E-mail: pub@allworth.com. Website: www.allworth.com. Tad Crawford, publisher. **Acquisitions:** Nicole Potter, senior editor. Estab. 1989. Publishes hardcover and trade paperback originals. **Publishes 36-40 titles/year. Offers advance.** Does not accept simultaneous submissions. Responds in 1 month to queries; 1 month to proposals. Book catalog and ms guidelines free.

O━ Allworth Press publishes business and self-help information for artists, designers, photographers, authors and film and performing artists, as well as books about business, money and the law for the general public. The press also publishes the best of classic and contemporary writing in art and graphic design. Currently emphasizing photography, film, video, music and theater.

Nonfiction: How-to, reference. Subjects include art/architecture, business/economics, film/cinema/stage, music/dance, photography, film, television, graphic design, performing arts, writing, as well as business and legal guides for the public. Query.
Recent Title(s): *Citizen Brand*, by Marc Gobé; *Talking Photography*, by Frank Van Riper; *Hollywood Dealmaking*, by Dina Appleton and Daniel Yankelevits.
Tips: "We are trying to give ordinary people advice to better themselves in practical ways—as well as helping creative people in the fine and commercial arts."

ALYSON PUBLICATIONS, INC., 6922 Hollywood Blvd., Suite 1000, Los Angeles CA 90028. (323)860-6065. Fax: (323)467-0152. E-mail: mail@alyson.com. Website: www.alyson.com. **Acquisitions:** Attn. Editorial Dept.; Scott Brassart, associate publisher (fiction, science); Angela Brown, associate editor (women's fiction, arts). Estab. 1979. Publishes trade paperback originals and reprints. **Publishes 40 titles/year. Receives 1,500 submissions/year. 40% of books from first-time authors; 70% from unagented writers. Pays 8-15% royalty on net receipts. Offers $1,500-15,000 advance.** Publishes book 18 months after acceptance of ms. Does not accept simultaneous submissions. Responds in 2 months to queries. Book catalog and ms guidelines for 6×9 SAE with 3 first-class stamps.
Imprints: Alyson Wonderland, Alyson Classics Library.

O━ Alyson Publications publishes books for and about gay men and lesbians from all economic and social segments of society, and explores the political, legal, financial, medical, spiritual, social and sexual aspects of gay and lesbian life, and contributions to society. They also consider bisexual and transgender material. Emphasizing medical, legal and financial nonfiction titles. Books for children of GLBT parents with illustrations only.

Nonfiction: Subjects include gay/lesbian. "We are especially interested in nonfiction providing a positive approach to gay/lesbian/bisexual issues." Accepts nonfiction translations. No dissertations. Submit 2-page outline with SASE. Reviews artwork/photos as part of ms package.
Fiction: Gay novels. Accepts fiction translations. No short stories or poetry. Submit 1-2 page synopsis with SASE.
Recent Title(s): *The Greatest Taboo*, by Delroy Constantine-Simms; *Under the Mink*, by Lisa Davis.

Tips: "We publish many books by new authors. The writer has the best chance of selling to our firm well-researched, popularly written nonfiction on a subject (e.g., some aspect of gay history) that has not yet been written about much. With fiction, create a strong storyline that makes the reader want to find out what happens. With nonfiction, write in a popular style for a nonacademic audience."

AMACOM BOOKS, American Management Association, 1601 Broadway, New York NY 10019-7406. (212)903-8417. Fax: (212)903-8083. Website: www.amanet.org. President and Publisher: Hank Kennedy. **Acquisitions:** Adrienne Hickey, executive editor (management, human resources development, organizational effectiveness, strategic planning); Ellen Kadin, senior acquisitions editor (marketing, sales, customer service, personal development); Ray O'Connell, senior acquisitions editor (finance, project management); Jacquie Flynn, senior acquisitions editor (information technology, training); Neil Levine, senior acquisitions editor (manufacturing, supply chain management operations and facilities management). Estab. 1923. Publishes hardcover and trade paperback originals, professional books in various formats. **Publishes 80-90 titles/year. Receives 800 submissions/year. 50% of books from first-time authors; 70% from unagented writers. Pays 10-15% royalty on net receipts. Offers advance.** Publishes book 6-9 months after acceptance of ms. Responds in 2 months to queries. Book catalog and ms guidelines free.

Amacom is the publishing arm of the American Management Association, the world's largest training organization for managers and executives. Amacom publishes books on business issues, strategies and tasks to enhance organizational and individual effectiveness. Currently emphasizing leadership/management skills, professional development, technology applications. De-emphasizing small-business management, job-finding.

Nonfiction: Publishes business books of all types, including management, business strategy, organizational effectiveness, sales, marketing, training, technology applications, finance, career, professional skills for retail, direct mail, college and corporate markets. Query or submit outline/synopsis, sample chapters, résumé.

Recent Title(s): *Focal Point*, by Brian Tracy; *The Oracle of Oracle*, by Florence M. Stone; *The Hiring and Firing Question and Answers Book*, by Paul Falcone.

AMBASSADOR BOOKS, INC., 71 Elm St., Worcester MA 01609. (508)756-2893. Fax: (508)757-7055. Website: www.ambassadorbooks.com. **Acquisitions:** Kathryn Conlan, acquisitions editor. Publishes hardcover and trade paperback originals. **Publishes 7 titles/year. Receives 2,000 queries and 100 mss/year. 50% of books from first-time authors; 90% from unagented writers. Pays 8-10% royalty on retail price.** Publishes book 1 year after acceptance of ms. Accepts simultaneous submissions. Responds in 3 months to queries. Book catalog free or online at website.

"We are a Christian publishing company looking for books of intellectual and/or spiritual excellence."

Nonfiction: Books with a spiritual/religious theme. Biography, children's/juvenile, illustrated book, self-help. Subjects include creative nonfiction, regional, religion, spirituality, sports, Catholic and Christian books. Query with SASE or submit complete ms. Reviews artwork/photos as part of ms package. Send photocopies.

Fiction: Books with a spiritual/religious theme. Juvenile, literary, picture books, religious, spiritual, sports, young adult. Query with SASE or submit complete ms.

Recent Title(s): *Emmanuel McClue and the Mystery of the Shroud*, by Tony McCaffrey; *The Lion Who Couldn't Roar*, by John Powers.

AMBER BOOKS PUBLISHING, 1334 E. Chandler Blvd., Suite 5-D67, Phoenix AZ 85048. (480)460-1660. Fax: (480)283-0991. E-mail: amberbks@aol.com. Website: www.amberbooks.com. **Acquisitions:** Tony Rose, publisher (self-help, career books for African-Americans); Tenny Iuony, editor (African-American fashion, style). Estab. 1998. Publishes trade paperback and mass market paperback originals. **Publishes 5-10 titles/year. Receives 150 queries. 90% of books from first-time authors; 90% from unagented writers. Pays 10-15% royalty on wholesale price.** Publishes books 1 year after acceptance of ms. Accepts simultaneous submissions. Responds in 1 month to queries. Book catalog online.

Imprints: Busta Books; Colossus Books.

Nonfiction: Nonfiction only. Submit query with synopsis. Full mss not required. Reviews artwork/photos as part of ms package. Send photocopies.

Recent Title(s): *Beautiful Black Hair—Real Solutions for Real Problems*; *How to Get Rich When You Ain't Got Nothing—The African-American Guide to Gaining and Maintaining Wealth*; *Aaliyah: An R&B Princess in Words and Pictures*.

Tips: "The goal of Amber Books is to build a strong catalog comprised of self-help books and celebrity bio books in print. Topics pertain to, about and for the African-American population."

AMERICA WEST PUBLISHERS, P.O. Box 2208, Carson City NV 89702-2208. (775)885-0700. Fax: (877)726-2632. E-mail: global@nohoax.com. Website: www.nohoax.com. **Acquisitions:** George Green, president. Estab. 1985. Publishes hardcover and trade paperback originals and reprints. **Publishes 20 titles/year. Receives 150 submissions/year. 90% of books from first-time authors; 90% from unagented writers. Pays 10% royalty on wholesale price. Offers $300 average advance.** Publishes book 6 months after acceptance of ms. Accepts simultaneous submissions. Responds in 1 month to queries. Book catalog and ms guidelines free.

Imprints: Bridger House Publishers, Inc.

America West seeks the "other side of the picture," political cover-ups and new health alternatives.

Nonfiction: Subjects include business/economics, government/politics, health/medicine (holistic self-help), New Age, UFO-metaphysical. Submit outline, sample chapter(s). Reviews artwork/photos as part of ms package.

Recent Title(s): *Psychokinesiology*, by Dr. Alec Halub.

Tips: "We currently have materials in all bookstores that have areas of UFOs; also political and economic nonfiction."

N **AMERICAN ATHEIST PRESS**, P.O. Box 5733, Parsippany NJ 07054-6733. (908)276-7300. Fax: (908)276-7402. E-mail: editor@atheists.org. Website: www.atheists.org. **Acquisitions:** Frank Zindler, editor. Estab. 1959. Publishes trade paperback originals and reprints. Publishes quarterly journal, *American Atheist*, for which are needed articles of interest to atheists. **Publishes 12 titles/year. Receives 200 submissions/year. 40-50% of books from first-time authors; 100% from unagented writers. Pays 5-10% royalty on retail price. Offers advance.** Publishes book within 2 years after acceptance of ms. Accepts simultaneous submissions. Responds in 4 months to queries. Book catalog for 6½×9 ½ SAE; ms guidelines for 9×12 SAE.
Imprints: Gustav Broukal Press.

"We are interested in books that will help Atheists gain a deeper understanding of Atheism, improve their ability to critique religious propaganda, and assist them in fighting to maintain the 'wall of separation between state and church.' " Currently emphasizing the politics of religion, science and religion. De-emphasizing biblical criticism (but still doing some).

Nonfiction: Biography, reference, general. Subjects include general nonfiction, government/politics, history (of religion and atheism, of the effects of religion historically), philosophy (from an atheist perspective, particularly criticism of religion), religion, atheism (particularly the lifestyle of atheism; the history of atheism; applications of atheism. "We would like to see more submissions dealing with the histories of specific religious sects, such as the L.D.S., the Worldwide Church of God, etc." Submit outline, sample chapter(s). Reviews artwork/photos as part of ms package.
Fiction: Humor (satire of religion or of current religious leaders), anything of particular interest to atheists. "We rarely publish any fiction. But we have occasionally released a humorous book. No mainstream. For our press to consider fiction, it would have to tie in with the general focus of our press, which is the promotion of atheism and free thought." Submit outline, sample chapter(s).
Recent Title(s): *Living in the Light: Freeing Your Child from the Dark Ages*, by Anne Stone (rearing atheist children).
Tips: "We will need more how-to types of material—how to argue with creationists, how to fight for state/church separation, etc. We have an urgent need for literature for young atheists."

AMERICAN BAR ASSOCIATION BOOK PUBLISHING, 750 N. Lake Shore Dr., Chicago IL 60611. (312)988-5000. Fax: (312)988-6030. E-mail: kayb@staff.abanet.org. Website: www.ababooks.org. **Acquisitions:** Bryan Kay, Esq., publisher/director; Adrienne Cook, Esq., director of new product development. Estab. 1878. Publishes hardcover and trade paperback originals. **Publishes 100 titles/year. Receives 50 queries/year. 20% of books from first-time authors; 95% from unagented writers. Pays 5-15% royalty on net receipts.** Publishes book 18 months after acceptance of ms. Accepts simultaneous submissions. Responds in 1 month to queries; 1 month to proposals; 3 months to mss. Book catalog and ms guidelines on website.

"We are interested in books that will help lawyers practice law more effectively whether it's help in handling clients, structuring a real estate deal or taking an antitrust case to court."

Nonfiction: All areas of legal practice. How-to (in the legal market), reference, technical. Subjects include business/economics, computers/electronic, money/finance, software, legal practice. "Our market is not, generally, the public. Books need to be targeted to lawyers who are seeking solutions to their practice problems. We rarely publish scholarly treatises." Query with SASE.
Recent Title(s): *The Effective Estate Planning Practice*; *The Supreme Çourt and Its Justices (2nd ed.)*; *Sexual Harassment in the Public Workplace*.
Tips: "ABA books are written for busy, practicing lawyers. The most successful books have a practical, reader-friendly voice. If you can build in features like checklists, exhibits, sample contracts, flow charts, and tables of cases, please do so." The Association also publishes over 50 major national periodicals in a variety of legal areas. Contact Susan Yessne, executive editor, at the above address for guidelines.

AMERICAN CATHOLIC PRESS, 16565 S. State St., South Holland IL 60473. (312)331-5845. Fax: (708)331-5484. E-mail: acp@acpress.org. Website: www.acpress.org. **Acquisitions:** Rev. Michael Gilligan, Ph.D., editorial director. Estab. 1967. Publishes hardcover originals and hardcover and paperback reprints. **Publishes 4 titles/year. Makes outright purchase of $25-100.** Does not accept simultaneous submissions.
Nonfiction: Subjects include education, music/dance, religion, spirituality. "We publish books on the Roman Catholic liturgy—for the most part, books on religious music and educational books and pamphlets. We also publish religious songs for church use, including Psalms, as well as choral and instrumental arrangements. We are interested in new music, meant for use in church services. Books, or even pamphlets, on the Roman Catholic Mass are especially welcome. We have no interest in secular topics and are not interested in religious poetry of any kind."
Tips: "Most of our sales are by direct mail, although we do work through retail outlets."

AMERICAN COLLEGE OF PHYSICIAN EXECUTIVES, (ACPE PUBLICATIONS), 4890 W. Kennedy Blvd., Suite 200, Tampa FL 33609. (813)287-2000. E-mail: wcurry@acpe.org. Website: www.acpe.org. **Acquisitions:** Wesley Curry, managing editor. Estab. 1975. Publishes hardcover and trade paperback originals. **Publishes 6-8 titles/year. Receives 12-15 queries and 4-5 mss/year. 80% of books from first-time authors; 100% from unagented writers. Pays 10-15% royalty on wholesale price or makes outright purchase of $1,000-4,000. Offers advance.** Publishes book 8 months after acceptance of ms. Does not accept simultaneous submissions. Responds in 1 month to queries; 2 months to proposals; 1 month to mss. Book catalog and ms guidelines free.

"Our books are aimed at the professional information needs of physicians in management roles."

Nonfiction: Technical, textbook. Subjects include business/economics, health/medicine. Query and submit outline. Reviews artwork/photos as part of ms package. Send photocopies.
Recent Title(s): *The Last Sick Generation*, by Joanne Magda Polenz; *Practicing Medicine Profitably*, by Barry Verkauf; *Leading Physicians through Change*, by Jack Silversin and Mary Jane Kornacki.

AMERICAN CORRECTIONAL ASSOCIATION, 4380 Forbes Blvd., Lanham MD 20706. (301)918-1800. Fax: (301)918-1896. E-mail: afins@aca.org. Website: www.corrections.com/aca. **Acquisitions:** Alice Fins, managing editor. Estab. 1870. Publishes hardcover and trade paperback originals. **Publishes 18 titles/year. Receives 40 submissions/year. 90% of books from first-time authors; 100% from unagented writers. Pays 10% royalty on net receipts.** Publishes book 1 year after acceptance of ms. Responds in 4 months to queries. Book catalog and ms guidelines free.

O⌐ American Correctional Association provides practical information on jails, prisons, boot camps, probation, parole, community corrections, juvenile facilities and rehabilitation programs, substance abuse programs and other areas of corrections.

Nonfiction: "We are looking for practical, how-to texts or training materials written for the corrections profession." How-to, reference, technical, textbook, correspondence courses. Subjects include corrections and criminal justice. No autobiographies or true-life accounts by current or former inmates or correctional officers, theses, or dissertations. No fiction or poetry. Query with SASE. Reviews artwork/photos as part of ms package.
Recent Title(s): *Recess Is Over: Managing Youthful Offenders in Adult Correctional Systems*, by Barry Glick, Ph.D., William Sturgeon; *Arresting Addictions: Drug Education and Relapse Prevention in Corrections*, by Robert Alexander, Ph.D., George J. Pratsinak, Ph.D.
Tips: Authors are professionals in the field and corrections. "Our audience is made up of corrections professionals and criminal justice students. No books by inmates or former inmates." This publisher advises out-of-town freelance editors, indexers and proofreaders to refrain from requesting work from them.

AMERICAN COUNSELING ASSOCIATION, 5999 Stevenson Ave., Alexandria VA 22304-3300. (703)823-9800. **Acquisitions:** Carolyn C. Baker, director of publications. Estab. 1952. Publishes paperback originals. **Publishes 10-15 titles/year. Receives 200 queries and 125 mss/year. 5% of books from first-time authors; 90% from unagented writers. Pays 10-15% royalty on net receipts.** Publishes book 7 months after acceptance of ms. Accepts simultaneous submissions. Responds in 2 months to queries; 2 months to proposals; 4 months to mss. Ms guidelines free.

O⌐ The American Counseling Association is dedicated to promoting public confidence and trust in the counseling profession. "We publish scholarly texts for graduate level students and mental health professionals. We do not publish books for the general public."

Nonfiction: Reference, scholarly, textbook (for professional counselors). Subjects include education, gay/lesbian, health/medicine, multicultural, psychology, religion, sociology, spirituality, women's issues/studies. ACA does not publish self-help books or autobiographies. Query with SASE or submit proposal package including outline, 2 sample chapter(s), vitae.
Recent Title(s): *Using Music in Children of Divorce Groups*, by Janice DeLucia-Waack; *Adventures in Guidance*, by Terry Kottman, Jeffrey Ashby, Don DeGaaf.
Tips: "Target your market. Your books will not be appropriate for everyone across all disciplines."

AMERICAN FEDERATION OF ASTROLOGERS, P.O. Box 22040, Tempe AZ 85285. (480)838-1751. Fax: (480)838-8293. E-mail: afa@msn.com. Website: www.astrologers.com. **Acquisitions:** Kris Brandt Riske, publications manager. Estab. 1938. Publishes trade paperback originals and reprints. **Publishes 10-15 titles/year. Receives 10 queries and 20 mss/year. 50% of books from first-time authors; 100% from unagented writers. Pays 10% royalty. Offers advance.** Publishes book 10 months after acceptance of ms. Accepts simultaneous submissions. Responds in 6 months to mss. Book catalog for $2; ms guidelines free.

O⌐ American Federation of Astrologers publishes astrology books, calendars, charts and related aids.

Nonfiction: Subjects include astrology. Submit complete ms.
Recent Title(s): *Road Map to Your Future*, by Bernie Ashman.

AMERICAN NURSES PUBLISHING, American Nurses Foundation, an affiliate of the American Nurses Association, 600 Maryland Ave. SW, #100 West, Washington DC 20024-2571. (202)651-7212. Fax: (202)651-7003. **Acquisitions:** Rosanne O'Connor, publisher; Eric Wurzbacher, editor/project manager. Publishes professional paperback originals and reprints. **Publishes 12-15 titles/year. Receives 300 queries and 8-10 mss/year. 75% of books from first-time authors; 100% from unagented writers. Pays 10% royalty on retail price. Offers negotiable advance.** Publishes book 4 months after acceptance of ms. Does not accept simultaneous submissions. Responds in 4 months to proposals; 4 months to mss. Book catalog online; ms guidelines free.

O⌐ American Nurses publishes books designed to help professional nurses in their work and careers. Through the publishing program, the Foundation fulfills one of its core missions—to provide nurses in all practice settings with publications that address cutting-edge issues and form a basis for debate and exploration of this century's most critical health care trends.

Nonfiction: Reference, technical, textbook, handbooks, resource guides. Subjects include health/medicine. Subjects include advanced practice, computers, continuing education, ethics, human rights, health care policy, managed care, nursing administration, psychiatric and mental health, quality, research, workplace issues, key clinical topics. Submit outline, 1 sample chapter, cv. Reviews artwork/photos as part of ms package. Send photocopies.

Recent Title(s): *Nursing and the Law*; *Nursing the Spirit*; *Grant Writing Tips for Nurses and Other Health Professionals.*

AMERICAN PRESS, 28 State St., Suite 1100, Boston MA 02109. (617)247-0022. Fax: (617)247-0022. **Acquisitions:** Jana Kirk, editor. Estab. 1911. Publishes college textbooks. **Publishes 25 titles/year. Receives 350 queries and 100 mss/year. 50% of books from first-time authors; 90% from unagented writers. Pays 5-15% royalty on wholesale price.** Publishes book 9 months after acceptance of ms. Does not accept simultaneous submissions. Responds in 3 months to queries. Book catalog free.

Nonfiction: Technical, textbook. Subjects include agriculture/horticulture, anthropology/archeology, art/architecture, business/economics, education, government/politics, health/medicine, history, music/dance, psychology, science, sociology, sports. "We prefer that our authors actually teach courses for which the manuscripts are designed." Query or submit outline with tentative table of contents. No complete mss.

Recent Title(s): *Sexuality Counseling*, by Weinstein.

AMERICAN QUILTER'S SOCIETY, Schroeder Publishing, P.O. Box 3290, Paducah KY 42002-3290. (270)898-7903. Fax: (270)898-8890. E-mail: meredith@aqsquilt.com; editor@aqsquilt.com. Website: www.aqsquilt.com. **Acquisitions:** Barbara Smith, executive book editor (primarily how-to and patterns, but other quilting books sometimes published). Estab. 1984. Publishes hardcover and trade paperback originals. **Publishes 18 titles/year. Receives 300 queries/year. 60% of books from first-time authors; 100% from unagented writers. Pays 5% royalty on retail price.** Publishes book 11 months after acceptance of ms. Accepts simultaneous submissions. Responds in same day to queries to queries; 2 months to proposals. Book catalog and ms guidelines free.

American Quilter's Society publishes how-to and pattern books for quilters (beginners through intermediate skill level).

Nonfiction: Coffee table book, how-to, reference, technical (about quilting). Subjects include creative nonfiction, hobbies (about quilting). Query with SASE or submit proposal package including outline, 2 sample chapter(s), photos and patterns (if available). Reviews artwork/photos as part of ms package. Send photocopies; slides and drawings are also acceptable for a proposal.

Recent Title(s): *Favorite Redwork Designs*, by Betty Alderman (embroidery and applique patterns).

AMERICAN SOCIETY FOR TRAINING AND DEVELOPMENT, 1640 King St., Alexandria VA 22313. (800)628-2783. Fax: (703)683-9591. E-mail: mmorrow@astd.org. Website: www.astd.org. **Acquisitions:** Mark Morrow, senior acquistions editor. Estab. 1944. Publishes trade paperback originals. **Publishes 15-20 titles/year. Receives 50-100 queries and 25-50 mss/year. 50% of books from first-time authors; 95% from unagented writers. Pays 10% royalty on net receipts. Offers $500-1,000 advance.** Publishes book 6-9 months after acceptance of ms. Accepts simultaneous submissions. Responds in 1 month to queries; 1 month to proposals; 1 month to mss. Book catalog free; ms guidelines free.

Nonfiction: Trade Books for training and performance improvement professionals. Subjects include training and development. Submit proposal package including outline, 1 sample chapter(s). Reviews artwork/photos as part of ms package.

Recent Title(s): *Leading E-Learning*, by William Horton; *Training on the Job*, by Diane Walter; *Return on Investment, Vol. 3*, by Jack Phillips.

Tips: Audience includes training professionals including frontline trainers, training managers and executives; performance professionals, including performance consultants; organizational development and human resource development professionals. "Send a good proposal targeted to our audience providing how-to advice that readers can apply now!"

AMHERST MEDIA, INC., 155 Rano St., Suite 300, Buffalo NY 14207. (716)874-4450. Fax: (716)874-4508. E-mail: amherstmed@aol.com. Website: www.AmherstMedia.com. **Acquisitions:** Craig Alesse, publisher. Estab. 1974. Publishes trade paperback originals and reprints. **Publishes 30 titles/year. Receives 100 submissions/year. 60% of books from first-time authors; 90% from unagented writers. Pays 6-8% royalty on retail price. Offers advance.** Publishes book 1 year after acceptance of ms. Accepts simultaneous submissions. Responds in 2 months to queries. Book catalog and ms guidelines free.

Amherst Media publishes how-to photography books.

Nonfiction: How-to. Subjects include photography. "Looking for well-written and illustrated photo books." Query with outline, 2 sample chapters and SASE. Reviews artwork/photos as part of ms package.

Recent Title(s): *Portrait Photographer's Handbook*, by Bill Hurter.

Tips: "Our audience is made up of beginning to advanced photographers. If I were a writer trying to market a book today, I would fill the need of a specific audience and self-edit in a tight manner."

THE AMWELL PRESS, P.O. Box 5385, Clinton NJ 08809-0385. (908)638-9033. Fax: (908)638-4728. President: James Rikhoff. Corporate Secretary: Genevieve Symonds. **Acquisitions:** Monica Sullivan, vice president. Estab. 1976. Publishes hardcover originals. **Publishes 4 titles/year.** Publishes book 18 months after acceptance of ms. Does not accept simultaneous submissions. Responds in 2 months to queries.

The Amwell Press publishes hunting and fishing nonfiction, but not how-to books on these subjects.

Nonfiction: Subjects include hunting and fishing stories/literature (not how-to). Mostly limited editions. No fiction. Query with SASE.

Recent Title(s): *Handy to Home*, by Tom Hennessey; *Beyond Hill Country*, by Rikhoff and Sullivan; *Timber and Tide*, by Bob Elman.

ANCESTRY PUBLISHING, imprint of MyFamily.com, 360 W. 4800 North, Provo UT 84064. (801)705-7000. Fax: (801)705-7120. E-mail: mwright@ancestry.com. Loretto Szucs, executive editor. **Acquisitions:** Matthew Wright, book editor; Jennifer Utley, *Ancestry* magazine editor. Estab. 1983. Publishes hardcover, trade and paperback originals and *Ancestry* magazine. **Publishes 12-20 titles/year. Receives over 100 submissions/year. 70% of books from first-time authors; 100% from unagented writers. Pays 8-12% royalty or makes outright purchase.** Accepts simultaneous submissions. Responds in 2 months to queries. Book catalog for 9×12 SAE with 2 first-class stamps.

O→ "Our publications are aimed exclusively at the genealogist. We consider everything from short monographs to book length works on topics such as immigration, migration, record collections and heraldic topics, among others."

Nonfiction: How-to, reference, genealogy. Subjects include Americana, hobbies, historcial methodology and genealogical research techniques. No mss that are not genealogical or historical. Query with SASE or submit outline, sample chapter(s). Reviews artwork/photos as part of ms package.

Recent Title(s): *Finding Your African-American Ancestors.*

Tips: "Genealogical and historical reference, how-to, and descriptions of source collections have the best chance of selling to our firm. Be precise in your description. Please, no family histories or genealogies."

ANCHORAGE PRESS PLAYS, INC., P.O. Box 2901, Louisville KY 40201. (502)583-2288. Fax: (502)583-2281. E-mail: applays@bellsouth.net. Website: www.applays.com. **Acquisitions:** Marilee Miller, publisher. Estab. 1935. Publishes hardcover and trade paperback originals. **Receives 45-90 submissions/year. 50% of books from first-time authors; 80% from unagented writers. Pays 10-15% royalty. Playwrights also receive 50-75% royalties.** Publishes book 1-2 years after acceptance of ms. Does not accept simultaneous submissions. Responds in 1 month to queries; 6 months to mss. Book catalog online; ms guidelines online.

O→ "We are an international agency for plays for young people. First in the field since 1935."

Nonfiction: Textbook, plays. Subjects include education, theatre, child drama, plays. "We are looking for play anthologies; and texts for teachers of drama/theater." Query. Reviews artwork/photos as part of ms package.

Recent Title(s): *Eziqbo the Spirit Child*, by Max Bush; *Amy Crockett: M.V.P.*, by Frumi Cohen; *Paper Lanterns, Paper Cranes*, by Brian Kral.

[A] **ANDREWS McMEEL UNIVERSAL**, 4520 Main St., Kansas City MO 64111-7701. (816)932-6700. **Acquisitions:** Christine Schillig, vice president/editorial director. Estab. 1973. Publishes hardcover and paperback originals. **Publishes 200 titles/year. Pays royalty on retail price or net receipts. Offers advance.**

O→ Andrews McMeel publishes general trade books, humor books, miniature gift books, calendars, and stationery products.

Nonfiction: How-to, humor, inspirational. Subjects include contemporary culture, general trade, relationships. Also produces gift books. *Agented submissions only.*

Recent Title(s): *The Blue Day Book*, by Bradley Trevor Greive.

ANKER PUBLISHING CO., INC., 176 Ballville Rd., P.O. Box 249, Bolton MA 01740-0249. (978)779-6190. E-mail: ankerpub@aol.com. Website: www.ankerpub.com. **Acquisitions:** James D. Anker, president and publisher. Publishes hardcover and paperback professional books. **Publishes 6 titles/year. Pays royalty. Offers advance.** Publishes book 4 months after acceptance of ms. Accepts simultaneous submissions.

O→ Publishes professional development books for higher education faculty and administrators.

Nonfiction: Professional development. Subjects include education. Query with SASE or submit proposal package including outline, 3 sample chapter(s).

[N] **THE ANONYMOUS PRESS**, P.O. Box 307540, Columbus OH 43230. Fax: (614)322-9893. **Acquisitions:** Gil Bonner, editor (the underground). Publishes trade paperback originals. **Publishes 3 titles/year. Receives 1,000 queries and 100 mss/year. 50% of books from first-time authors; 90% from unagented writers. Pays 10-20% royalty on wholesale price. Offers $5,000 advance.** Publishes book 6 months after acceptance of ms. Accepts simultaneous submissions. Responds in 3 months to queries; 3 months to proposals; 3 months to mss.

O→ The Anonymous Press is for "people who want the truth."

Nonfiction: Biography, how-to, humor, reference, self-help. Subjects include business/economics, government/politics, health/medicine, history, memoirs, military/war, money/finance, philosophy, religion, sex, spirituality. Query with SASE.

Recent Title(s): *Sleeping With the President: My Intimate Years With Bill Clinton*, by Gennifer Flowers (nonfiction).

Tips: "Expect nothing from us."

ANVIL PUBLISHERS, INC., 3852 Allsborough Dr., Tucker GA 30084. (770)938-0289. Fax: (770)493-7232. E-mail: anvilpub@aol.com. **Acquisitions:** Lee Xavier, editor-in-chief. Publishes hardcover and paperback originals, CD-ROMs. **Publishes 3-5 titles/year. Pays royalty.** Responds in 3 months to mss.

Nonfiction: Biography. Subjects include history (American), military/war. Query with SASE or submit outline.

Recent Title(s): *Arthur W. Page: Publisher, Public Relations Pioneer, Patriot*, by Noel L. Griese (biography); *How to Work with Angry People and Outraged Publics*; *How to Manage Organizational Communication During Crisis.*

APDG PUBLISHING, INC., 202 Main St., Fuguay-Varina NC 27526-1936. (919)557-2260. Fax: (919)557-2261. E-mail: info@apdg-inc.com. Website: www.apdg-inc.com. Publisher: Lawrence Harte. **Acquisitions:** Karen Bunn. Publishes hardcover and trade paperback originals. **Publishes 20 titles/year. Receives 50 queries/year. Pays 5-15% royalty on sales.** Publishes book 3-6 months after acceptance of ms. Responds in 3 months to proposals; 6 months to mss. Book catalog online; ms guidelines free.

O→ APDG supplies expertise and services to telecommunications and consumer electronics companies not only through publishing but consulting, research, training and techno-media as well.

Nonfiction: Textbook. Subjects include telecommunications. Query with SASE. Reviews artwork/photos as part of ms package. Send photocopies.

APPALACHIAN MOUNTAIN CLUB BOOKS, 5 Joy St., Boston MA 02108. Fax: (617)523-0722. Website: www.outdoors.org. **Acquisitions:** Beth Krusi, publisher/editor. Estab. 1897. Publishes hardcover and trade paperback originals. **Publishes 10-15 titles/year. Receives 200 queries and 20 mss/year. 30% of books from first-time authors; 90% from unagented writers. Pays 7-10% royalty on retail price. Offers modest advance.** Publishes book 1 year after acceptance of ms. Accepts simultaneous submissions. Responds in 3 months to proposals. Ms guidelines online.

O→ Appalachian Mountain Club publishes hiking guides, water-recreation guides (non-motorized), nature, conservation and mountain-subject guides for America's Northeast. "We connect recreation to conservation and education."

Nonfiction: How-to, guidebooks. Subjects include history (mountains, Northeast), nature/environment, recreation, regional (Northeast outdoor recreation). "Writers should avoid submitting: proposals on Appalachia (rural southern mountains); not enough market research; too much personal experience—autobiography." Query. Reviews artwork/photos as part of ms package. Send photocopies or transparencies.

Recent Title(s): *Not Without Peril*; *Journey North.*

Tips: "Our audience is outdoor recreationalists, conservation-minded hikers and canoeists, family outdoor lovers, armchair enthusiasts. Our guidebooks have a strong conservation message. Visit our website for proposal submission guidelines and more information."

ARCADIA PUBLISHING, Tempus Publishing, 2-A Cumberland St., Charleston SC 29401. (843)853-2070. Fax: (843)853-0044. E-mail: sales@arcadiapublishing.com. Website: www.arcadiapublishing.com. **Acquisitions:** John Pearson, publisher (Midwest); Amy Sutton, publisher (North); Katie White, publisher (South); Mark Berry, publisher (narrative local history). Publishes mass market paperback originals. **Publishes 800 titles/year; imprint publishes 350 titles/year. Receives 100 queries and 20 mss/year. 80% of books from first-time authors; 95% from unagented writers. Pays 10% royalty.** Accepts simultaneous submissions. Responds in 1 month to queries. Book catalog online; ms guidelines for #10 SASE.

O→ Arcadia publishes photographic regional histories. "We have more than 1,000 in print in our 'Images of America' series. We have expanded our program to include Midwest and West Coast locations." Currently emphasizing local history, oral history, Civil War history, college histories, African-American history.

Nonfiction: Coffee table book, gift book. Subjects include history, military/war, regional, sports, pictorial history, local history, African-American history, postcard history, sports history, college history, oral history, Civil War history, local, national and regional publications. Query with SASE. Reviews artwork/photos as part of ms package. Send photocopies.

Recent Title(s): *Charleston: Alone Among the Cities*, by The South Carolina Historical Society.

Tips: "Writers should know that we only publish history titles. The majority of our books are on a city or region, and are pictorial in nature. We are beginning new series, including oral histories, sports histories, black histories and college histories."

ARDEN PRESS INC., P.O. Box 418, Denver CO 80201-0418. (303)697-6766. Fax: (303)697-3443. **Acquisitions:** Susan Conley, publisher. Estab. 1980. Publishes hardcover and trade paperback originals and reprints. **Publishes 4-6 titles/year. Receives 600 submissions/year. 20% of books from first-time authors; 80% from unagented writers. Pays 8-15% royalty on wholesale price. Offers $2,000 average advance.** Publishes book 6 months after acceptance of ms. Accepts simultaneous submissions. Responds in 2 months to queries. Ms guidelines free.

O→ Arden Press publishes nonfiction on women's history and women's issues. "We sell to general and women's bookstores as well as public and academic libraries. Many of our titles are adopted as texts for use in college courses."

Nonfiction: Subjects include women's issues/studies. No personal memoirs or autobiographies. Query with outline/synopsis and sample chapters.

Recent Title(s): *Whatever Happened to the Year of the Woman?*, by Amy Handlin.

Tips: "Writers have the best chance selling us nonfiction on women's subjects. If I were a writer trying to market a book today, I would learn as much as I could about publishers' profiles *then* contact those who publish similar works."

ARDSLEY HOUSE PUBLISHERS, INC., Rowman & Littlefield, 4720 Boston Way, Lanham MD 20706. (301)459-3366. Fax: (301)429-5748. Website: www.rowmanlittlefield.com. **Acquisitions:** Jon Sisk. Estab. 1982. Publishes hardcover and trade paperback originals and reprints. **Publishes 5-8 titles/year. 25% of books from first-time authors; 100% from unagented writers. Pays generally by royalty. Offers advance.** Publishes book 1 year after acceptance of ms. Does not accept simultaneous submissions. Responds in 1 month to queries; 2 months to proposals; 3 months to mss.

O→ Ardsley House publishes only college-level textbooks in mathematics and economics.

Nonfiction: Textbook (college). Subjects include business/economics, mathematics. "We don't accept any other type of manuscript." Query with SASE or submit proposal package including outline, 2-3 sample chapter(s), résumé, author bio, prospectus. Send photocopies.
Recent Title(s): *A Mathemataics Sampler*; *Invention and the Rise of Techno-Capitalism*, by Suarez-Villa.

ARJUNA LIBRARY PRESS, Journal of Regional Criticism, 1025 Garner St., D, Space 18, Colorado Springs CO 80905-1774. **Acquisitions:** Count Joseph A. Uphoff, Jr. Publishes trade paperback originals. **Publishes 3-6 titles/year. Receives 10 queries and 50 mss/year. 10% of books from first-time authors; 90% from unagented writers.** Publishes book 6 months after acceptance of ms. Accepts simultaneous submissions. Book catalog for $2; ms guidelines for #10 SASE.

O— *The Journal of Regional Criticism* has now expressed the mission of studying distinguishments within the context of general surrealism as special surrealism to generate complex movement. This ideology presents such compounds as cultural surrealism, ethnic surrealism or surrealist abstraction.

Nonfiction: Reference, technical, experimental. Subjects include anthropology/archeology, art/architecture, creative nonfiction, philosophy, photography, science, surrealism. "The most appropriate work to send is short; 20 pages is a good size. The work should be adapted to maximize the potential of Xerox reproduction including diagrams, equations and typography. Preferred subjects are literary, aesthetic and relevant science." Currently emphasizing universal and historical surrealism; de-emphasizing traditional and eclectic delimitation of surrealism. Submit complete ms. Reviews artwork/photos as part of ms package. Send photocopies or transparencies or artcards.
Fiction: Adventure, experimental, fantasy, historical, horror, literary, occult, poetry, poetry in translation, science fiction, surrealism. "The work should be short, 20 pages is a good size. The focus being surrealism, the composition should embody principles of the theory in a spirit of experimental inquiry." Submit complete ms.
Poetry: "Poetry is published as single page photocopy. It is most appropriate to send three or four poems with a résumé. A sample will be returned in any SASE. The poetry will be filed."
Recent Title(s): *The Creative Personality*, by Professor S. Giora Shoham; *Thoughtful Fragments*, by Ryan Jackson.
Tips: "These compositions are presented to help writers envision the scope of theoretical attainments and to postulate a reasonable belief that popularity begins with the work itself, not with its distribution. Many irrational agglomerations of words and images are forced into nonrepresentation while others are forced into psychological modes of intrusion. The proper formula for indefinite constructions is a balance in contradictions that will steer ambiguity between severe meaning and dissipation. There should be a shadow for speculation to resolve as the satisfaction of decent curiosity. This shadow transforms art into literature."

ARKANSAS RESEARCH, INC., P.O. Box 303, Conway AR 72033. (501)470-1120. Fax: (501)470-1120. E-mail: desmond@ipa.net. **Acquisitions:** Desmond Walls Allen, owner. Estab. 1985. Publishes hardcover originals and trade paperback originals and reprints. **Publishes 20 titles/year. 90% of books from first-time authors; 100% from unagented writers. Pays 5-10% royalty on retail price.** Publishes book 6 months after acceptance of ms. Does not accept simultaneous submissions. Responds in 1 month to queries. Book catalog for $1; ms guidelines free.
Imprints: Research Associates.

O— "Our company opens a world of information to researchers interested in the history of Arkansas."

Nonfiction: All Arkansas-related subjects. How-to (genealogy), reference, self-help. Subjects include Americana, ethnic, history, hobbies (genealogy), military/war, regional. "We don't print autobiographies or genealogies about one family." Query with SASE. Reviews artwork/photos as part of ms package. Send photocopies.
Recent Title(s): *Life & Times from The Clay County Courier Newspaper Published at Corning, Arkansas, 1893-1900.*

JASON ARONSON, INC., 230 Livingston St., Northvale NJ 07647-1726. (201)767-4093. Fax: (201)767-4330. Website: www.aronson.com. **Acquisitions:** Jason Aronson, editor-in-chief. Estab. 1967. Publishes hardcover and trade paperback originals and reprints. **Publishes 100 titles/year. 50% of books from first-time authors; 95% from unagented writers. Pays 10-15% royalty on retail price.** Publishes book an average of 2 years after acceptance of ms. Does not accept simultaneous submissions. Responds in 1 month to queries. Book catalog and ms guidelines free.

O— "We are looking for high quality, serious, scholarly books in two fields: psychotherapy and Judaica."

Nonfiction: Subjects include history, philosophy, psychology, religion, translation. Query or submit outline and sample chapters. Reviews artwork/photos as part of ms package. Send photocopies.
Recent Title(s): *Parent Therapy: A Relational Alternative to Working With Children*, by Linda Jacobs and Carol Wachs; *Play Therapy Techniques, 2nd Edition*, by Charles E. Schaefer and Donna Cangelosi, Eds.; *Understanding the Borderline Mother*, by Christine Lawson.

ART DIRECTION BOOK COMPANY, INC., 456 Glenbrook Rd., Glenbrook CT 06096-1800. (203)353-1441. Fax: (203)353-1371. **Acquisitions:** Don Barron, editorial director. Estab. 1959. Publishes hardcover and paperback originals. **Publishes 8 titles/year. Pays 10% royalty on retail price. Offers average $1,000 advance.** Publishes book 1 year after acceptance of ms. Does not accept simultaneous submissions. Responds in 3 months to queries. Book catalog for 6×9 SAE.
Imprints: Infosource Publications.

O— Art Direction Book Company is interested in books for the professional advertising art field—books for art directors, designers, etc.; also entry level books for commercial and advertising art students in such fields as typography, photography, paste-up, illustration, clip-art, design, layout and graphic arts.

Nonfiction: Textbook, commercial art; ad art how-to. Subjects include art/architecture. Query with outline and 1 sample chapter. Reviews artwork/photos as part of ms package.
Recent Title(s): *How to Fold, Vol. 4.*

ARTE PUBLICO PRESS, University of Houston, Houston TX 77204-2174. (713)743-2841. Fax: (713)743-2847. Website: www.arte.uh.edu. **Acquisitions:** Nicolas Kanellos, editor. Estab. 1979. Publishes hardcover originals, trade paperback originals and reprints. **Publishes 36 titles/year. Receives 1,000 queries and 500 mss/year. 50% of books from first-time authors; 80% from unagented writers. Pays 10% royalty on wholesale price. Offers $1,000-3,000 advance.** Publishes book 2 years after acceptance of ms. Accepts simultaneous submissions. Responds in 1 month to queries; 1 month to proposals; 4 months to mss. Book catalog free; ms guidelines for #10 SASE.
Imprints: Piñata Books

"We are a showcase for Hispanic literary creativity, arts and culture. Our endeavor is to provide a national forum for Hispanic literature."

Nonfiction: Children's/juvenile, reference. Subjects include ethnic, language/literature, regional, translation, women's issues/studies. Hispanic civil rights issues for new series: "The Hispanic Civil Rights Series." Query with SASE or submit outline, 2 sample chapter(s).
Fiction: Ethnic, literary, mainstream/contemporary. Query with SASE or submit 2 sample chapter(s), synopsis.
Poetry: Submit 10 sample poems.
Recent Title(s): *Shadows and Supposes*, by Gloria Vando (poetry); *Home Killings*, by Marcos McPeek Villatoro (mystery); *Message to Aztlán*, by Rodolfo "Corky" Gonzales (Hispanic Civil Rights Series book).

ARTEMIS CREATIONS PUBLISHING, 3395 Nostrand Ave., 2-J, Brooklyn NY 11229. **Acquisitions:** President: Shirley Oliveira. Publishes trade paperback and mass market paperback originals. **Publishes 4 titles/year. Pays 5-10% royalty on retail price or makes outright purchase of $300 minimum (30,000 words).**
Imprints: FemSuprem, Matriach's Way

"Our publications explore femme supremacy, matriarchy, sex, gender, relationships, etc., masochism (male only)."

Nonfiction: Subjects include language/literature, religion (pagan), science, sex, women's issues/studies. "Strong feminine archetypes, subjects only." Query with SASE or submit outline, 3 sample chapter(s). author bio; marketing plan.
Fiction: Erotica, experimental, fantasy, feminist, gothic, horror, mystery, occult, religious, science fiction. Submit synopsis, SASE.
Recent Title(s): *Lady Killer: Tale of Horror and the Erotic*, by Tony Malo.; *Gospel of Goddess*, by Bond and Suffield (metaphysical).
Tips: "Our readers are looking for strong, powerful feminine archetypes in fiction and nonfiction. Graphic sex and language are OK."

ASA, AVIATION SUPPLIES & ACADEMICS, 7005 132nd Pl. SE, Newcastle WA 98059. (425)235-1500. Fax: (425)235-0128. Website: www.asa2fly.com. Director of Operations: Mike Lorden. Editor: Jennifer Trerise. **Acquisitions:** Fred Boyns, controller; Jacqueline Spanitz, curriculum director and technical advisor (pilot and aviation educator). **Publishes 25-40 titles/year. 100% from unagented writers.** Publishes book 9 months or more after acceptance of ms. Does not accept simultaneous submissions. Book catalog free.

ASA is an industry leader in the development and sales of aviation supplies, publications, and software for pilots, flight instructors, flight engineers and aviation technicians. All ASA products are developed by a team of researchers, authors and editors.

Nonfiction: All subjects must be related to aviation education and training. How-to, technical. Subjects include education. "We are primarily an aviation publisher. Educational books in this area are our specialty; other aviation books will be considered." Query with outline. Send photocopies.
Recent Title(s): *The Savvy Flight Instructor: Secrets of the Successful CFI*, by Greg Brown.
Tips: "Two of our specialty series include ASA's *Focus Series*, and ASA *Aviator's Library*. Books in our *Focus Series* concentrate on single-subject areas of aviation knowledge, curriculum and practice. The *Aviator's Library* is comprised of titles of known and/or classic aviation authors or established instructor/authors in the industry, and other aviation specialty titles."

ASIAN HUMANITIES PRESS, Jain Publishing Co., P.O. Box 3523, Fremont CA 94539. (510)659-8272. Fax: (510)659-0501. E-mail: mail@jainpub.com. Website: www.jainpub.com. **Acquisitions:** M.K. Jain, editor-in-chief. Estab. 1989. Publishes hardcover and trade paperback originals and reprints. **Publishes 6 titles/year. Receives 200 submissions/year. 100% from unagented writers. Pays up to 15% royalty on net receipts.** Publishes book 1-2 years after acceptance of ms. Does not return proposal material. Responds in 3 months to mss. Book catalog and ms guidelines online.

Asian Humanities Press publishes in the areas of humanities and social practices pertaining to Asia, commonly categorized as "Asian Studies." Currently emphasizing undergraduate-level textbooks.

Nonfiction: Reference, textbook, general trade books. Subjects include language/literature, philosophy, psychology, religion, spirituality, Asian classics, social sciences, art/culture. Submit proposal package including vita, list of prior publications. Reviews artwork/photos as part of ms package. Send photocopies.
Recent Title(s): *The Upanishads*, by Shyam N. Shukla.

ASLAN PUBLISHING, 2490 Black Rock Turnpike, #342, Fairfield CT 06432. (203)372-0300. Fax: (203)374-4766. E-mail: info@aslanpublishing.com. Website: www.aslanpublishing.com. **Acquisitions:** Barbara H. Levine, creative director. **Publishes 3-6 titles/year. Receives 75 queries and 50 mss/year. 75% of books from first-time authors; 90% from unagented writers. Pays 8-10% royalty on wholesale price.** Publishes book 18-24 months after acceptance of ms. Accepts simultaneous submissions. Responds in 2 months to queries; 5 months to proposals. Book catalog and ms guidelines online.

O━ "Aslan Publishing offers readers a window to the soul via well-crafted and practical self-help books, inspirational books and modern day parables. Our mission is to publish books that uplift one's mind, body and spirit."

Nonfiction: Biography, how-to, humor, self-help. Subjects include business/economics, child guidance/parenting, education (non-textbook), ethnic, gay/lesbian, health/medicine, memoirs, multicultural, music/dance, psychology, religion, sex, spirituality, women's issues/studies, adoption, relationships, open to unusual ideas. "We want authors who will do their own promotion in addition to our own. Self-help books must include personal examples." No fiction. Query with SASE or submit proposal package including outline, 3 sample chapter(s), author bio, 1-2 page synopsis, brief chapter outlines, table of contents, author's e-mail address.

Recent Title(s): *Workout for the Soul*; *Lion Taming: The Courage to Deal with Difficult People*.

Tips: Audience is general mainstream America, plus New Age, religious, spiritual seekers. "No agent necessary. Include SASE, e-mail address phone number, word count. Be patient. Show me your passion. Use large type and short paragraphs. If possible, have the manuscript professionally edited before submitting."

ASM INTERNATIONAL, 9639 Kinsman Rd., Materials Park OH 44073-0002. (440)338-5151. Fax: (440)338-4634. E-mail: cust-srv@asminternational.org. Website: www.asminternational.org. **Acquisitions:** Scott D. Henry, assistant director of reference publications (metallurgy/materials). Publishes hardcover originals. **Publishes 15-20 titles/year. Receives 50 queries and 10 mss/year. 50% of books from first-time authors; 100% from unagented writers. Pays royalty on wholesale price or makes outright purchase.** Does not accept simultaneous submissions. Responds in 1 month to queries; 4 months to proposals; 2 months to mss. Book catalog free or online at website; ms guidelines free.

O━ "We focus on practical information related to materials selection and processing."

Nonfiction: Reference, technical, textbook. Subjects include engineering reference. Submit proposal package including outline, 1 sample chapter(s), author credentials. Reviews artwork/photos as part of ms package. Send photocopies.

Recent Title(s): *Introduction to Aluminum Alloys and Tempers*, by J.G. Kaufman; *Titanium: A Technical Guide, 2nd edition*, by M.J. Donachie, Jr.

Tips: "Our audience consists of technically trained people seeking practical information on metals and materials to help them solve problems on the job."

ASSOCIATION FOR SUPERVISION AND CURRICULUM DEVELOPMENT, 1703 N. Beauregard St., Alexandria VA 22311. (703)578-9600. Fax: (703)575-5400. Website: www.ascd.org. **Acquisitions:** Scott Willis, acquisitions director. Estab. 1943. Publishes trade paperback originals. **Publishes 24-30 titles/year. Receives 100 queries and 100 mss/year. 50% of books from first-time authors; 100% from unagented writers. Pays negotiable royalty on actual monies received.** Publishes book 1 year after acceptance of ms. Accepts simultaneous submissions. Responds in 3 months to proposals. Book catalog and ms guidelines free or online.

O━ ASCD publishes high-quality professional books for educators.

Nonfiction: Subjects include education (for professional educators). Submit outline, 2 sample chapter(s). Reviews artwork/photos as part of ms package. Send photocopies.

Recent Title(s): *Leadership for the Learning: How to Help Students Succeed*, by Carl Glickman.

ASTRAGAL PRESS, P.O. Box 239, Mendham NJ 07945. (973)543-3045. Fax: (973)543-3044. E-mail: astragalpress@attglobal.net. Website: www.astragalpress.com. **Acquisitions:** Lisa Pollak, president. Estab. 1983. Publishes hardcover and trade paperback originals and reprints. **Publishes 4-6 titles/year. Receives 50 queries/year. Pays 10% royalty on net receipts.** Publishes book 1 year after acceptance of ms. Does not accept simultaneous submissions. Responds in 1 month to queries. Book catalog and ms guidelines free.

O━ "Our primary audience includes those interested in collecting and working with old tools (hand tools especially) and working in traditional early trades (metalworking especially)."

Nonfiction: Books on early tools, trades or technology. Query. Send photocopies.

Recent Title(s): *A Price Guide to Antique Tools, 3rd ed*, by Herbert P. Kean.

Tips: "We sell to niche markets. We are happy to work with knowledgeable amateur authors in developing titles."

ew **Acquisitions:** Michael A. Markowski, editor-in-chief. Ms guidelines for #10 SAE with 2 first-class stamps.

O━ Aviation Publishers publishes books to help people learn more about aviation and model aviation through the written word.

Nonfiction: How-to, technical. Subjects include history, hobbies, recreation, radio control, free flight, indoor models, electric flight, rubber powered flying models, micro radio control, aviation history, homebuilt aircraft, ultralights and hang gliders. Prefers submissions by e-mail.

Recent Title(s): *Birdflight as the Basis of Aviation*, by Otto Lilrenthal.

Tips: "Our focus is on books of short to medium length that will serve the emerging needs of the hobby. We want to help youth get started and enhance everyone's enjoyment of the hobby."

AUGSBURG BOOKS, Augsburg Fortress Publishers, P.O. Box 1209, Minneapolis MN 55440-1209. (612)330-3300. Website: www.augsburgfortress.org. Director of Publications: Roy Harrisville. **Acquisitions:** Robert Klausmeier and

Michael Witt, acquisitions editors. Publishes trade and mass market paperback originals and reprints, hardcover picture books. **Publishes 40 titles/year. 2-3% of books from first-time authors. Pays royalty.** Publishes book 18 months after acceptance of ms. Responds in 3 months to queries. Book catalog for 9×12 SAE with 3 first-class stamps; ms guidelines for #10 SASE.

O→ Augsburg Books publishes for the mainline Christian market.

Nonfiction: Children's/juvenile, self-help. Subjects include religion, spirituality (adult), grief/healing/wholeness, parenting, interactive books for children and families, seasonal and picture books. Submit outline, 1-2 sample chapters (if requested).

Recent Title(s): *Remembering Mama*, by Dara Dokas; *The Bible Guide: An All-in-One Introduction to the Book of Books*, by Andrew Knowles.

AUTONOMEDIA, P.O. Box 568, Williamsburgh Station, Brooklyn NY 11211. (718)963-2603. Fax: (718)963-2603. E-mail: info@autonomedia.org. Website: www.autonomedia.org. **Acquisitions:** Jim Fleming, acquisitions editor. Estab. 1984. Publishes trade paperback originals and reprints. **Publishes 25 titles/year. Receives 350 queries/year. 30% of books from first-time authors; 90% from unagented writers. Pays variable royalty. Offers $100 advance.** Publishes book 6 months after acceptance of ms. Accepts simultaneous submissions. Responds in 2 months to queries. Book catalog for $1; ms guidelines online.

O→ Autonomedia publishes radical and marginal books on culture, media and politics.

Nonfiction: Subjects include anthropology/archeology, art/architecture, business/economics, computers/electronic, gay/lesbian, government/politics, history, multicultural, nature/environment, philosophy, religion, sex, translation, women's issues/studies, world affairs, general nonfiction. Submit outline, SASE. Reviews artwork/photos as part of ms package. Send photocopies.

Fiction: Erotica, experimental, feminist, gay/lesbian, literary, mainstream/contemporary, occult, science fiction, short story collections. Submit synopsis, SASE.

Recent Title(s): *The Anarchists*, by John Henry MacKay.

AVALON TRAVEL PUBLISHING, Avalon Publishing Group, 5855 Beaudry St., Emeryville CA 94608. (510)595-3664. E-mail: acquisitions@avalonpub.com. Website: www.travelmatters.com. Publisher: Bill Newlin. **Acquisitions:** Sarah Coglianse, acquisitions coordinator. Estab. 1973. Publishes trade paperback originals. **Publishes 100 titles/year. Receives 100-200 submissions/year. 50% of books from first-time authors; 95% from unagented writers. Pays royalty on net receipts. Offers up to $10,000 advance.** Publishes book an average of 9 months after acceptance of ms. Accepts simultaneous submissions. Responds in 2 months to queries. Book catalog and ms guidelines for 7½×10 ½ SAE with 2 first-class stamps.

Imprints: *Series*: Adapter Kit; City Smart; Dog Lover's Companion; Moon Handbooks; Rick Steves; Road Trip USA; Travel Smart.

O→ "Avalon Travel Publishing publishes comprehensive, articulate travel information to North and South America, Asia and the Pacific. We have an interest in niche markets such as families, older travelers, Afro-American, disabled, outdoor recreation including camping/hiking/biking."

Nonfiction: Subjects include regional, travel. "We specialize in travel guides to Asia and the Pacific Basin, the United States, Canada, the Caribbean, Latin America and South America, but are open to new ideas." Query with SASE or submit proposal package including outline, table of contents, writing sample. Reviews artwork/photos as part of ms package.

Tips: "Avalon Travel Publishing produces books that are designed by and for independent travelers seeking the most rewarding travel experience possible. Check our website."

AVANYU PUBLISHING INC., P.O. Box 27134, Albuquerque NM 87125. (505)341-1280. Fax: (505)341-1281. E-mail: brentric@aol.com. Website: www.avanyu-publishing.com. **Acquisitions:** J. Brent Ricks, president. Estab. 1984. Publishes hardcover and trade paperback originals and reprints. **Publishes 4 titles/year. Receives 40 submissions/year. 30% of books from first-time authors; 90% from unagented writers. Pays 8% maximum royalty on wholesale price. Offers advance.** Publishes book 1 year after acceptance of ms. Does not accept simultaneous submissions. Responds in 2 months to queries. Book catalog for #10 SASE.

O→ Avanyu publishes highly-illustrated, history-oriented books on American Indians and adventures in the Southwest.

Nonfiction: Biography, children's/juvenile, coffee table book, illustrated book, reference, scholarly. Subjects include Americana (Southwest), anthropology/archeology, art/architecture, ethnic, history, multicultural, photography, regional, sociology, spirituality. Query with SASE. Reviews artwork/photos as part of ms package.

Recent Title(s): *Kachinas Spirit Beings of the Hopi*; *Mesa Verde Ancient Architecture*; *Hopi Snake Ceremonies*.

Tips: "Our audience consists of libraries, art collectors and history students. We publish subjects dealing with modern and historic American Indian matters of all kinds."

AVERY, Penguin Putnam, 375 Hudson St., New York NY 10014. (212)366-2000. Fax: (212)366-2365. Website: www.penguinputnam.com. John Duff, publisher. Estab. 1976. Publishes trade paperback originals. **Publishes 25 titles/year. Receives 3,000 queries and 1,000 mss/year. 70% of books from first-time authors; 50% from unagented writers. Pays royalty. Offers advance.** Publishes book 1 year after acceptance of ms. Accepts simultaneous submissions. Responds in 2 weeks to queries; 1 month to proposals; 6 weeks to mss. Book catalog free; ms guidelines free.

O-ᴿ Avery specializes in health, nutrition, alternative medicine, and fitness.

Nonfiction: "We generally do not publish personal accounts of health topics unless they outline a specific plan that covers all areas of the topic." Submit proposal package including outline, author bio, cover letter, table of contents, preface, SASE.

Recent Title(s): *Natural Highs*, by Hyla Cass, M.D. and Patrick Holford; *Dare to Lose*, by Shari Lieberman, Ph.D.; *Prescription for Nutritional Healing*, by Phyllis A. Balch, CNC.

Tips: "Our mission is to enable people to improve their health through clear and up-to-date information."

AVIATION PUBLISHERS, 1 Oakglade Circle, Hummelstown PA 17036-9525. (717)566-0468. Fax: (717)566-6423. E-mail: avipub@excite.com. **Acquisitions:** Michael A. Markowski, editor-in-chief. Ms guidelines for #10 SAE with 2 first-class stamps.

O-ᴿ Aviation Publishers publishes books to help people learn more about aviation and model aviation through the written word.

Nonfiction: How-to, technical. Subjects include history, hobbies, recreation, radio control, free flight, indoor models, electric flight, rubber powered flying models, micro radio control, aviation history, homebuilt aircraft, ultralights and hang gliders. Prefers submissions by e-mail.

Recent Title(s): *Birdflight as the Basis of Aviation*, by Otto Lilrenthal.

Tips: "Our focus is on books of short to medium length that will serve the emerging needs of the hobby. We want to help youth get started and enhance everyone's enjoyment of the hobby."

AVISSON PRESS, INC., 3007 Taliaferro Rd., Greensboro NC 27408. Fax: (336)288-6989. **Acquisitions:** M.L. Hester, editor. Estab. 1994. Publishes hardcover originals and trade paperback originals and reprints. **Publishes 5-6 titles/year. Receives 600 queries and 400 mss/year. 5% of books from first-time authors; 90% from unagented writers. Pays 8-10% royalty on wholesale price. Offers occasional small advance.** Publishes book 15 months after acceptance of ms. Accepts simultaneous submissions. Responds in 1 week to queries; 1 week to proposals; 3 months to mss. Book catalog for #10 SASE.

O-ᴿ Currently emphasizing young-adult biography only. No fiction or poetry.

Nonfiction: Biography. Subjects include ethnic, sports, women's issues/studies. Query with SASE or submit outline, 1-3 sample chapter(s).

Recent Title(s): *Go, Girl!: Young Women Superstars of Pop Music*, by Jacqueline Robb; *The Experimenters: Eleven Great Chemists*, by Margery Everden.

Tips: Audience is primarily public and school libraries.

AZTEX CORP., P.O. 50046, Tucson AZ 85703-1046. (520)882-4656. Website: www.aztexcorp.com. **Acquisitions:** Elaine Jordan, editor. Estab. 1976. Publishes hardcover and paperback originals. **Publishes 5 titles/year. Receives 250 submissions/year. 100% from unagented writers. Pays 10% royalty.** Publishes book 18 months after acceptance of ms. Responds in 3 months to queries.

Nonfiction: How-to. Subjects include history, transportation, motor sports, automobiles. "We specialize in transportation subjects (how-to and history)." Biographies and autobiographies are of less interest. Accepts nonfiction translations. Submit outline, 2 sample chapter(s). Reviews artwork/photos as part of ms package.

Tips: "We look for accuracy, thoroughness and interesting presentation."

BACKCOUNTRY GUIDES, The Countryman Press, P. O. Box 748, Woodstock VT 05091-0748. (802)457-4826. Fax: (802)457-1678. E-mail: countrymanpress@wwnorton.com. Website: www.countrymanpress.com. **Acquisitions:** Kermit Hummell, editorial director; Ann Kraybill, managing editor. Publishes trade paperback originals. **Publishes 20 titles/year. Receives 1,000 queries and a few mss/year. 25% of books from first-time authors; 75% from unagented writers. Pays 7-10% royalty on retail price. Offers $1,500-2,500 advance.** Publishes book 18 after acceptance of ms. Accepts simultaneous submissions. Responds in 2 months to proposals. Book catalog free; ms guidelines for #10 SASE.

O-ᴿ Backcountry Guides publishes guidebooks that encourage physical fitness and appreciation for and understanding of the natural world, self-sufficiency and adventure. "We publish several series of regional destination guidebooks to outdoor recreation. They include: the 50 Hikes series; Backroad Bicycling series; Trout Streams series; Bicycling America's National Parks series; and a paddling (canoeing and kayaking) series."

Nonfiction: Subjects include nature/environment, recreation (bicycling, hiking, canoeing, kayaking, fly fishing, walking, guidebooks and series), sports. Query with SASE or submit proposal package including outline, market analysis, 50 sample pages.

Recent Title(s): *Bicycling America's National Parks: California*, by David Story; *Kayaking the Maine Coast*, by Dorcas Miller.

Tips: "Look at our existing series of guidebooks to see how your proposal fits in."

BAEN PUBLISHING ENTERPRISES, P.O. Box 1403, Riverdale NY 10471-0671. (718)548-3100. Website: baen.com. **Acquisitions:** Jim Baen, editor-in-chief; Toni Weisskopf, executive editor. Estab. 1983. Publishes hardcover, trade paperback and mass market paperback originals and reprints. **Publishes 120 titles/year. Receives 5,000 submissions/year. 5% of books from first-time authors; 50% from unagented writers. Pays royalty on retail price. Offers advance.** Does not accept simultaneous submissions. Responds in 8 months to queries; 8 months to proposals; 1 year to mss. Book catalog free; ms guidelines for #10 SASE.

O-ᴿ "We publish books at the heart of science fiction and fantasy."

Fiction: Fantasy, science fiction. Submit outline, sample chapter(s), synopsis or submit complete ms.
Recent Title(s): *Ashes of Victory*, by David Weber.
Tips: "See our books before submitting. Send for our writers' guidelines."

BAKER BOOK HOUSE COMPANY, P.O. Box 6287, Grand Rapids MI 49516-6287. (616)676-9185. Fax: (616)676-2315. Website: www.bakerbooks.com.
Imprints: Baker Academic, Baker Books, Baker Bytes, Brazos Press, Chosen, Fleming H. Revell, Spire, Wynwood.

BAKER BOOKS, Baker Book House Company, P.O. Box 6287, Grand Rapids MI 49516-6287. (616)676-9185. Fax: (616)676-9573. Website: www.bakerbooks.com. Director of Publications: Don Stephenson. Estab. 1939. Publishes hardcover and trade paperback originals and trade paperback reprints. **Publishes 80 titles/year. 10% of books from first-time authors; 85% from unagented writers.** Publishes book within 1 year after acceptance of ms.
Imprints: Hamewith, Hourglass, Labyrinth, Raven's Ridge, Spire Books.

O╤ "Baker Books publishes popular religious nonfiction and fiction, children's books, academic and reference books, and professional books for church leaders. Most of our authors and readers are evangelical Christians, and our books are purchased from Christian bookstores, mail-order retailers, and school bookstores." Does not accept unsolicited proposals.

Nonfiction: Biography, children's/juvenile, gift book, illustrated book, multimedia, reference, self-help, textbook, CD-ROM. Subjects include anthropology/archeology, child guidance/parenting, psychology, religion, women's issues/studies, Christian doctrine, books for pastors and church leaders, seniors' concerns, singleness, contemporary issues.
Fiction: Juvenile, literary, mainstream/contemporary, mystery, picture books, religious, young adult.
Recent Title(s): *The Last Days According to Jesus*, by R.C. Sproul (theology); *Resting in the Bosom of the Lamb*, by Augusta Trobaugh (southern fiction).

BALCONY PRESS, 512 E. Wilson, Suite 306, Glendale CA 91206. (818)956-5313. E-mail: ann@balconypress.com. **Acquisitions:** Ann Gray, publisher. Publishes hardcover and trade paperback originals. **Publishes 6-8 titles/year. Pays 10% royalty on wholesale price.** Does not accept simultaneous submissions. Responds in 1 month to queries; 1 month to proposals; 3 months to mss. Book catalog free.

- "We also now publish *LA Architect* magazine focusing on contemporary architecture and design in Southern California. Editor: Laura Hull."

Nonfiction: Coffee table book, illustrated book. Subjects include art/architecture, ethnic, gardening, history (relative to design, art and architecture), regional. "We are interested in the human side of design as opposed to technical or how-to. We like to think our books will be interesting to the general public who might not otherwise select an architecture or design book." Query by telephone or letter. Submit outline and 2 sample chapters with introduction if applicable.
Recent Title(s): *Photographing Architecture & Interiors*, by Julius Shulman.
Tips: Audience consists of architects, designers and the general public who enjoy those fields. "Our books typically cover California subjects but that is not a restriction. It's always nice when an author has strong ideas about how the book can be effectively marketed. We are not afraid of small niches if a good sales plan can be devised."

BALE BOOKS, Bale Publications, 5121 St. Charles Ave., Suite #13, New Orleans LA 70115. **Acquisitions:** Don Bale, Jr, editor-in-chief. Estab. 1963. Publishes hardcover and paperback originals and reprints. **Publishes 10 titles/year. Receives 25 submissions/year. 50% of books from first-time authors; 90% from unagented writers. Offers standard 10-12½% royalty contract on wholesale or retail price; sometimes makes outright purchases of $500.** Publishes book 3 years after acceptance of ms. Does not accept simultaneous submissions. Responds in 3 months to queries. Book catalog for #10 SAE with 2 first-class stamps.

O╤ "Our mission is to educate numismatists about coins, coin collecting and investing opportunities."

Nonfiction: Numismatics. Subjects include hobbies, money/finance. "Our specialties are coin and stock market investment books; especially coin investment books and coin price guides." Submit outline, 3 sample chapter(s).
Recent Title(s): *How to Find Valuable Old & Scarce Coins*, by Jules Penn.
Tips: "Most of our books are sold through publicity and ads in the coin newspapers. We are open to any new ideas in the area of numismatics. Write for a teenage through adult level. Lead the reader by the hand like a teacher, building chapter by chapter. Our books sometimes have a light, humorous treatment, but not necessarily. We look for good English, construction and content, and sales potential."

BALL PUBLISHING, 335 N. River St., Batavia IL 60510. (630)208-9080. Fax: (630)208-9350. E-mail: info@ballpublishing.com. Website: www.ballpublishing.com. **Acquisitions:** Rick Blanchette, managing editor (floriculture, horticulture, agriculture). Publishes hardcover and trade paperback originals. **Publishes 4-6 titles/year. Receives 15 queries and 3 mss/year. 20% of books from first-time authors; 95% from unagented writers. Pays 10-15% royalty on wholesale price, makes outright purchase of $500. Offers up to $3,000 advance.** Publishes book 8 months after acceptance of ms. Accepts simultaneous submissions. Responds in 2 months to queries. Book catalog for 8½×11 SAE with 3 first-class stamps.

O╤ "Our books have been primarily published for professionals in the floriculture and horticulture fields. We are open to books on gardening for the consumer, but that is not our primary focus."

Nonfiction: How-to, reference, technical, textbook. Subjects include agriculture/horticulture, gardening, floriculture. Query with SASE or submit proposal package including outline, 2 sample chapter(s). Reviews artwork/photos as part of ms package. Send photocopies.

Recent Title(s): *The Complete Guide to Garden Center Management*, by John Stanley; *Anyone Can Landscape*, by Joel Lerner; *The Euroamerican Container Garden Cookbook*.

Tips: "Professional growers and retailers in floriculture and horticulture make up the majority of our audience. Serious gardeners are a secondary audience. Make sure you know your subject well and present the material in a way that will be of interest to professionals. We do not publish for the inexperienced gardener. Include photos if they are critical to your proposal."

BALLANTINE BOOKS, Random House, Inc., 1540 Broadway, New York NY 10036. (212)782-9000. Website: www.randomhouse.com/BB. Publisher: Gina Centrello. Senior VP/Editor-in-Chief: Nancy Miller. VP/Editorial Director: Linda Marrow. **Acquisitions:** Joe Blades, vice president/executive editor (*fiction*: suspense, mystery, *nonfiction*: pop culture, film history and criticism, travel); Tracy Brown, senior editor (*fiction*: literary, quality commerical, paperback reprint; *nonfiction*: history, travel, issue-oriented, nature, narrative, biography, paperback reprint); Allison Dickens, associate editor (*fiction*: literary, women's, commercial; *nonfiction*: biography, narrative, history art, culinary, travel); Tracy Bernstein, senior editor (*nonfiction*: health, parenting, self-help, popular culture, women's issues); Elisabeth Dyssegaard, executive editor (*nonfiction*: women's issues, biography, narrative, African-American and Asian-American culture, memoir, parenting; *fiction*: literary); Charlotte Herscher, associate editor (*fiction*: historical and contemporary romance); Linda Marrow, vice president/editorial director (*fiction*: suspense, women's, crime); Nancy Miller, senior vice president/editor-in-chief (*nonfiction*: serious commercial, narrative, memoirs, issue-oriented health, parenting); Maureen O'Neal, vice president/editorial director (*nonfiction*: health, childcare, parenting, narrative, diet; *fiction*: women's, quality commercial, Southern fictiom); Patricia Peters, assistant editor (*nonfiction*: biography, history, travel, narrative; *fiction*: commercial, literary, mysteries); Shauna Summers, senior editor (*fiction*: historical and contemporary romance, general women's fiction, thrillers, suspense). Estab. 1952. Publishes hardcover, trade paperback, mass market paperback originals. **Pays 8-15% royalty. Offers variable advance.**

Ballantine Books publishes a wide variety of nonfiction and fiction.

Nonfiction: Biography, how-to, narrative nonfiction, self-help. Subjects include animals, child guidance/parenting, community, cooking/foods/nutrition, creative nonfiction, education, gay/lesbian, general nonfiction, health/medicine, history, language/literature, memoirs, military/war, recreation, religion, sex, spirituality, travel, true crime, women's issues/studies. *Agented submissions only.* Reviews artwork/photos as part of ms package. Send photocopies.

Fiction: Ethnic, fantasy, historical, humor, literary, mainstream/contemporary (women's), military/war, multicultural, mystery, romance, short story collections, spiritual, suspense, general fiction. *Agented submissions only.*

BANCROFT PRESS, P.O. Box 65360, Baltimore MD 21209-9945. (410)358-0658. Fax: (410)764-1967. E-mail: bruceb@bancroftpress.com. Website: www.bancroftpress.com. **Acquisitions:** Bruce Bortz, publisher (health, investments, politics, history, humor); Fiction Editor (literary novels, mystery/thrillers). Publishes hardcover and trade paperback originals. Also packages books for other publishers (no fee to authors). **Publishes 4 titles/year. Pays various royalties on retail price.** Publishes book up to 3 years after acceptance of ms. Accepts simultaneous submissions. Responds in 4-8 months to proposals.

Bancroft Press is a general trade publisher. Currently emphasizing young adult nonfiction and fiction (single titles and series) and humorous mysteries. De-emphasizing celebrity fiction.

Nonfiction: Biography, how-to, humor, self-help. Subjects include business/economics, government/politics, health/medicine, money/finance, regional, sports, women's issues/studies, popular culture, essays. "We advise writers to visit the website." Submit proposal package including outline, 2 sample chapter(s), competition/market survey.

Fiction: Literary, mystery, thrillers. Query with SASE or submit outline, 2 sample chapter(s), by mail or e-mail.

Recent Title(s): *Finn: A Novel*, by Matthew Olshan; *The Reappearance of Sam Webber*, by Jonathon Scott Fuqua; *For Whom the Minivan Rolls: An Aaron Tucker Suburban Mystery*, by Jeffrey Cohen.

BANTAM DELL PUBLISHING GROUP, Random House, Inc., 1540 Broadway, New York NY 10036. (212)782-9000. Website: www.bantamdell.com. Senior Vice President/Deputy Publisher: Nita Taublib. **Acquisitions:** Toni Burbank (nonfiction: self-help, health/medicine, nature, spirituality, philosophy); Jackie Cantor (fiction: general commercial, literary, women's fiction, memoir); Tracy Devine (fiction and nonfiction: narrative nonfiction, history, adventure, military, science, women's fiction, general upscale commercial fiction, suspense); Anne Groell (fiction: fantasy, science fiction); Susan Kamil (The Dial Press, literary fiction and nonfiction); Robin Michaelson (nonfiction: self-help, child care/parenting, psychology); Kate Miciak (fiction: mystery, suspense, historical fiction); Wendy McCurdy (fiction: romance, women's fiction); Daniel Perez (nonfiction: Americana, self-help, health/medicine); Beth Rashbaum (nonfiction: health, psychology, self-help, women's issues, Judaica, history, memoir); Ann Harris (fiction and nonfiction: general commercial, literary, science, medicine, politics); Bill Massey (fiction and nonfiction: thrillers, suspense, historical, military, nature/outdoors, adventure, popular science). Estab. 1945. Publishes hardcover, trade paperback and mass market paperback originals; mass market paperback reprints. **Publishes 350 titles/year. Offers advance.** Publishes book 1 year after acceptance of ms. Accepts simultaneous submissions.

Imprints: Bantam, Delacorte Press, Dell, Delta, Island, The Dial Press.

Bantam Dell is a division of Random House, publishing both fiction and nonfiction. No unsolicited mss. Agented submissions only.

Nonfiction: Biography, how-to, humor, self-help. Subjects include Americana, business/economics, child guidance/parenting, cooking/foods/nutrition, government/politics, health/medicine, history, humor, language/literature, military/

war, nature/environment, New Age, philosophy, psychology, religion, science, sociology, spirituality, sports, true crime, women's issues/studies, Diet fitness, Mysticism/astrology, True crime. Agent submissions or single-page query letter briefly describing the work (including category and subject matter) and author biography. SASE a must.

Fiction: Adventure, fantasy, horror, mystery, science fiction, women's.

Recent Title(s): *The Cottage*, by Danielle Steel (Delacorte, fiction); *A Painted House*, by John Grisham (Dell, fiction); *The Plutonium Files*, by Eileen Welsom (The Dial Press, nonfiction).

BARBOUR PUBLISHING, INC., P.O. Box 719, Uhrichsville OH 44683. (740)922-6045. Website: www.barbourbooks.com. **Acquisitions:** Paul Muckley, senior editor (all areas); Rebecca Germany, managing editor (fiction). Estab. 1981. Publishes hardcover, trade paperback and mass market paperback originals and reprints. **Publishes 200 titles/year. Receives 500 queries and 1,000 mss/year. 40% of books from first-time authors; 95% from unagented writers. Pays 0-12% royalty on net price or makes outright purchase of $500-5,000. Offers $500-2,500 advance.** Publishes book 2 years after acceptance of ms. Accepts simultaneous submissions. Responds in 1 month to queries; 3 months to proposals; 3 months to mss. Book catalog online or for 9×12 SAE with 2 first-class stamps; ms guidelines for #10 SASE or online.

Imprints: Heartsong Presents (contact Rebecca Germany, managing editor), Barbour Books and Promise Press (contact Paul Muckley, senior editor).

Barbour Books publishes mostly devotional material that is non-denominational and evangelical in nature; Heartsong Presents publishes Christian romance. "We're a Christian evangelical publisher."

Nonfiction: Biography, gift book, humor, reference, devotional, Bible Trivia. Subjects include child guidance/parenting, cooking/foods/nutrition, money/finance, religion (evangelical Christian), women's issues/studies. "We look for book ideas with mass appeal - nothing in narrowly-defined niches. If you can appeal to a wide audience with an important message, creatively presented, we'd be interested to see your proposal." Submit outline, 3 sample chapter(s), SASE. Reviews artwork/photos as part of ms package. Send photocopies.

Fiction: Historical, mainstream/contemporary, religious, romance, short story collections, western. "All of our fiction is 'sweet' romance. No sex, no bad language, etc. Audience is evangelical/Christian, and we're looking for wholesome material for young as well as old. Common writer's mistakes are a sketchy proposal, an unbelievable story and a story that doesn't fit our guidelines for inspirational romances." Submit 3 sample chapter(s), synopsis, SASE.

Recent Title(s): *Simple Matters*, by Bruce Bickel and Stan Jantz (nonfiction); *When I Hear His Call*, by Anita Corrine Donihue (devotional); *Betrayed*, by Rosey Dow and Andrew Snaden (fiction).

Tips: "Audience is evangelical/Christian conservative, non-denominational, young and old. We're looking for *great concepts*, not necessarily a big name author or agent. We want to publish books that will sell millions, not just 'flash in the pan' releases. Send us your ideas!"

BAREFOOT BOOKS, 3 Bow St., 3rd Floor, Cambridge MA 02138. (617)576-0660. Fax: (617)576-0049. E-mail: alisonkeehn@barefootbooks.com. Website: www.barefootbooks.com. **Acquisitions:** Alison Keehn, associate editor (picture books and anthologies of folktales). Publishes hardcover and trade paperback originals. **Publishes 30 titles/year. Receives 500 queries and 8,000 mss/year. 35% of books from first-time authors; 60% from unagented writers. Pays 2.5-5% royalty on retail price or makes outright purchase of $5.99-19.99. Offers advance.** Publishes book 2 years after acceptance of ms. Accepts simultaneous submissions. Responds in 2 months to queries; 2 months to proposals; 3 months to mss. Book catalog for #10 SASE.

Fiction: Juvenile. Barefoot Books only publishes children's picture books and anthologies of folktales and poetry. "We do not publish novels. We are no longer accepting unsolicited manuscripts as we were before because the response has been overwhelming. We do accept query letters, and we encourage authors to send the first page of their manuscript with the query letter." Query with SASE or submit First page of ms.

Poetry: Query or submit 1 sample poems.

Recent Title(s): *Daddy Island*, by Philip Wells (picture book); *Fiesta Femenina: Celebrating Women in Mexican Folktale*, by Mary-Joan Gerson (illustrated anthology); *First Morning: Poems About Time*, by Nikki Siegen-Smith (children's poetry).

Tips: "Our audience is made up of children and parents, teachers and students, of many different ages and cultures." "Since we are a small publisher, and we definitely publish for a 'niche' market, it is helpful to look at our books and our website before submitting, to see if your book would fit into our list."

BARNEGAT LIGHT PRESS, Pine Barrens Press, P.O. Box 607, 3959 Rt. 563, Chatsworth NJ 08019-0607. (609)894-4415. Fax: (609)894-2350. **Acquisitions:** R. Marilyn Schmidt, publisher. Publishes trade paperback originals. **Publishes 4 titles/year. Receives 50 queries and 30 mss/year. 0% of books from first-time authors; 100% from unagented writers. Makes outright purchase.** Publishes book 6 months after acceptance of ms. Responds in 1 month to queries. Book catalog free or online at website.

Imprints: Pine Barrens Press.

"We are a regional publisher emphasizing the mid-Atlantic region. Areas concerned are gardening, cooking and travel."

Nonfiction: Cookbook, how-to, illustrated book. Subjects include agriculture/horticulture, cooking/foods/nutrition, gardening, regional, travel. Query with SASE. Reviews artwork/photos as part of ms package. Send photocopies.

Recent Title(s): *Churches and Graveyards of the Pine Gardens*, R. Marilyn Schmidt.

BARRICADE BOOKS INC., 185 Bridge Plaza N., Suite 308A, Fort Lee NJ 07024-5900. (201)944-7600. Fax: (201)944-6363. **Acquisitions:** Carole Stuart, publisher. Estab. 1991. Publishes hardcover and trade paperback originals, trade paperback reprints. **Publishes 30 titles/year. Receives 200 queries and 100 mss/year. 80% of books from first-time authors; 50% from unagented writers. Pays 10-12% royalty on retail price for hardcover. Offers advance.** Publishes book 18 months after acceptance of ms. Responds in 1 month to queries. Book catalog for $3.

O-ᵣ Barricade Books publishes nonfiction, "mostly of the controversial type, and books we can promote with authors who can talk about their topics on radio and television and to the press."

Nonfiction: Biography, how-to, reference, self-help. Subjects include business/economics, ethnic, gay/lesbian, government/politics, health/medicine, history, nature/environment, psychology, sociology, women's issues/studies. Query with SASE or submit outline, 1-2 sample chapter(s). Material will not be returned without SASE. Reviews artwork/photos as part of ms package. Send photocopies.

Recent Title(s): *Murder at the Conspiracy Convention*, by Paul Riessner; *A German Tale*, by Erika Rarres.

Tips: "Do your homework. Visit bookshops to find publishers who are doing the kinds of books you want to write. Always submit to a *person*—not just 'Editor.' Always enclose SASE or you may not get a response."

BARRON'S EDUCATIONAL SERIES, INC., 250 Wireless Blvd., Hauppauge NY 11788. (631)434-3311. Fax: (631)434-3217. Website: barronseduc.com. **Acquisitions:** Wayne Barr, managing editor/director of acquisitions. Estab. 1941. Publishes hardcover, paperback and mass market originals and software. **Publishes 400 titles/year. Receives 2,000 queries and 1,000 submissions/year. 40% of books from first-time authors; 75% from unagented writers. Pays 12-14% royalty on net receipts. Offers $3-4,000 advance.** Publishes book 18 months after acceptance of ms. Accepts simultaneous submissions. Responds in 3 months to queries; 8 months to mss. Book catalog free.

O-ᵣ Barron's tends to publish series of books, both for adults and children. "We are always on the lookout for creative nonfiction ideas for children and adults."

Nonfiction: Children's/juvenile, cookbook, textbook, student test prep guides. Subjects include art/architecture, business/economics, child guidance/parenting, cooking/foods/nutrition, education, health/medicine, hobbies, language/literature, New Age, sports, translation, travel, adult education, foreign language, review books, guidance, pets, literary guides. Query with SASE or submit outline, 2-3 sample chapter(s). Reviews artwork/photos as part of ms package.

Fiction: Juvenile. Submit sample chapter(s), synopsis.

Recent Title(s): *A Book of Magical Herbs*, by Margaret Picton; *Family Gardener*, by Lucy Peel.

Tips: "Audience is mostly educated self-learners and hobbyists. The writer has the best chance of selling us a book that will fit into one of our series. Children's books have less chance for acceptance because of the glut of submissions. SASE must be included for the return of all materials. Please be patient for replies."

N BASIC BOOKS, Perseus Books, 10 E. 53rd St., 23rd Floor, New York NY 10022. (212)207-7000. Fax: (212)207-7703. Website: www.basicbooks.com. **Acquisitions:** Elizabeth Maguire, VP, associate editor, editorial directory; Jo Ann Miller, executive editor; Don Fehr, executive editor; Bill Frucht, senior editor. Publishes hardcover originals and reprints, trade paperback originals and reprints. **Publishes 100 titles/year. Receives 500 queries and 300 mss/year. 5% of books from first-time authors; 10% from unagented writers. Pays 10-15% royalty on retail price. Offers less than $10,000 advance.** Publishes book 1 year after acceptance of ms. Accepts simultaneous submissions. Responds in 3 months to queries; 3 months to proposals; 6 months to mss. Book catalog free; ms guidelines free.

Nonfiction: Biography, serious adult trade. Subjects include Americana, anthropology/archeology, business/economics, child guidance/parenting, computers/electronic, creative nonfiction, education, ethnic, gay/lesbian, government/politics, health/medicine, history, language/literature, memoirs, military/war, money/finance, multicultural, music/dance, nature/environment, philosophy, psychology, regional, religion, science, sex, sociology, spirituality, translation, women's issues/studies. "Because of the current post 9/11 situation, we are not currently accepting any unsolicited submissions. This is subject to change without notice." Query with SASE or submit proposal package including outline, 3 sample chapter(s), author bio, TOC. **All unsolicited mss returned unopened.** Reviews artwork/photos as part of ms package. Send photocopies.

Recent Title(s): *The Mystery of Capital*, by Hernando de Soto (economics); *The Hidden Hitler*, by Lothar Machton (history/biography); *The Truth Will Set You Free*, by Alice Miller (psychology).

BATTELLE PRESS, Battelle Memorial Institute, 505 King Ave., Columbus OH 43201. (614)424-6393. Fax: (614)424-3819. E-mail: press@battelle.org. Website: www.battelle.org/bookstore. **Acquisitions:** Joe Sheldrick. Estab. 1980. Publishes hardcover and paperback originals and markets primarily by direct mail. **Publishes 15 titles/year. Pays 10% royalty on wholesale price.** Publishes book 6 months after acceptance of ms. Accepts simultaneous submissions. Responds in 1 month to queries. Book catalog free.

O-ᵣ Battelle Press strives to be a primary source of books and software on science and technology management.

Nonfiction: Subjects include science. "We are looking for management, leadership, project management and communication books specifically targeted to engineers and scientists." Query with SASE. Returns submissions with SASE only by writer's request. Reviews artwork/photos as part of ms package. Send photocopies.

Recent Title(s): *Managing the Industry/University Cooperative Research Center*; *Project Manager's Survival Guide*.

Tips: Audience consists of engineers, researchers, scientists and corporate researchers and developers.

N BAY SOMA PUBLISHING, INC., 555 DeHaro St., Suite 220, San Francisco CA 94107. (415)252-4363. Fax: (415)252-4352. E-mail: info@baybooks.com. Website: www.baybooks.com. **Acquisitions:** Floyd Yemont, editorial director. Publishes hardcover originals, trade paperback originals and reprints. **Publishes 15 titles/year. Receives 30**

queries/year. 50% of books from first-time authors. Royalties vary substantially. Offers $0-25,000 advance. Publishes book 6 months-1 year after acceptance of ms. Accepts simultaneous submissions. Responds in 3 months to queries. Book catalog for 9×12 SAE with 3 first-class stamps or see website.

Nonfiction: Coffee table book, cookbook, gift book, how-to, humor, illustrated book. Subjects include cooking/foods/nutrition, gardening, health/medicine, hobbies, nature/environment, travel (armchair travel), cable/PBS series companions. Query with SASE.

Recent Title(s): *Savor the Southwest*, by Barbara Fenzl (cooking); *Low-Carb Meals in Minutes*, by Linda Gassenheimer; *Styleona Shoestring*, by Anne McKevitt.

BAYLOR UNIVERSITY PRESS, P.O. Box 97363, Waco TX 76798. (254)710-3164. Fax: (254)710-3440. E-mail: David-Holcomb@baylor.edu. Website: www.baylor.edu/~BUPress. **Acquisitions:** J. David Holcomb, editor. Publishes hardcover and trade paperback originals. **Publishes 5 titles/year. Pays 10% royalty on wholesale price.** Publishes book 6 months after acceptance of ms. Does not accept simultaneous submissions. Responds in 2 months to proposals.

Imprints: Markham Press Fund.

- "We publish contemporary and historical scholarly works on religion, ethics, church-state studies, and oral history, particularly as these relate to Texas and the Southwest." Currently emphasizing religious studies, history. De-emphasizing art, archaeology.

Nonfiction: Subjects include anthropology/archeology, history, regional, religion, women's issues/studies. Submit outline, 1-3 sample chapter(s).

Recent Title(s): *A Year at the Catholic Worker: A Spiritual Journey Among the Poor*, by Marc H. Ellis (Literature and the Religious Spirit Series).

Tips: "We publish contemporary and historical scholarly works on religion, ethics, church-state studies, and oral history, particularly as these relate to Texas and the Southwest." Currently emphasizing religious studies, history. De-emphasizing art, archaeology.

BAYWOOD PUBLISHING CO., INC., 26 Austin Ave., Amityville NY 11701. (631)691-1270. Fax: (631)691-1770. E-mail: baywood@baywood.com. Website: www.baywood.com. **Acquisitions:** Stuart Cohen, managing editor. Estab. 1964. **Publishes 25 titles/year. Pays 7-15% royalty on retail price. Offers advance.** Publishes book within 1 year after acceptance of ms. Does not accept simultaneous submissions. Book catalog and ms guidelines free.

- Baywood Publishing publishes original and innovative books in the humanities and social sciences, including areas such as health sciences, gerontology, death and bereavement, psychology, technical communications and archaeology.

Nonfiction: Scholarly, technical, scholarly. Subjects include anthropology/archeology, computers/electronic, education, health/medicine, nature/environment, psychology, sociology, women's issues/studies, gerontology, imagery, labor relations, death/dying, drugs. Submit outline, sample chapter(s).

Recent Title(s): *Common Threads: Nine Widows' Journeys Through Love, Loss and Healing*, by Diane S. Kaimann; *Invitation to the Life Course: Toward New Understandings of Later Life*, edited by Richard A. Settersten, Jr.; *Exploding Steamboats, Senate Debates and Technical Reports: The Convergence of Technology, Politics and Rhetoric in the Steamboat Bill of 1838*, by R. John Brockmann.

BEACON HILL PRESS OF KANSAS CITY, Nazarene Publishing House, P.O. Box 419527, Kansas City KS 64141. (816)931-1900. Fax: (816)753-4071. **Acquisitions:** Bonnie Perry, editorial director. Estab. 1912. Publishes hardcover and paperback originals. **Publishes 30 titles/year. Pays 12% royalty on net sales for first 10,000 copies and 14% on subsequent copies. Sometimes makes flat rate purchase.** Publishes book 1 year after acceptance of ms. Responds in 3 months to queries.

Imprints: Crystal Sea Books, Lillenas Publishing

- "Beacon Hill Press is a Christ-centered publisher that provides authentically Christian resources that are faithful to God's word and relevant to life."

Nonfiction: Doctrinally must conform to the evangelical, Wesleyan tradition. Accent on holy living; encouragement in daily Christian life. Subjects include applied Christianity, spiritual formation, leadership resources, contemporary issues. No fiction, autobiography, poetry, short stories or children's picture books. Query with SASE or submit proposal package. Average ms length: 30,000-60,000.

Recent Title(s): *Leading with Vision*, by Dale Galloway.

BEACON PRESS, 25 Beacon St., Boston MA 02108-2892. (617)742-2110. Fax: (617)723-3097. E-mail: cvyce@beacon.org. Website: www.beacon.org. Director: Helene Atwan. **Acquisitions:** Deborah Chasman, editorial director (African-American, Asian-American, Latino, Native American, Jewish and gay and lesbian studies, anthropology); Joanne Wyckoff, executive editor (child and family issues, environmental concerns); Amy Caldwell, associate editor (poetry, gender studies, gay/lesbian studies and Cuban studies); Julie Hassel, assistant editor; Christopher Vyce, assistant editor. Estab. 1854. Publishes hardcover originals and paperback reprints. **Publishes 60 titles/year. Receives 4,000 submissions/year. 10% of books from first-time authors. Pays royalty. Offers advance.** Accepts simultaneous submissions. Responds in 3 months to queries.

Imprints: Bluestreak Series (contact Deb Chasman, editor, innovative literary writing by women of color).

- Beacon Press publishes general interest books that promote the following values: the inherent worth and dignity of every person; justice, equity, and compassion in human relations; acceptance of one another; a free and responsible search for truth and meaning; the goal of world community with peace, liberty and justice for all; respect for the interdependent web of all existence. Currently emphasizing innovative nonfiction writing by people of all colors. De-emphasizing poetry, children's stories, art books, self-help.

Nonfiction: Scholarly. Subjects include anthropology/archeology, child guidance/parenting, education, ethnic, gay/lesbian, nature/environment, philosophy, religion, women's issues/studies, world affairs. General nonfiction including works of original scholarship, religion, women's studies, philosophy, current affairs, anthropology, environmental concerns, African-American, Asian-American, Native American, Latino and Jewish studies, gay and lesbian studies, education, legal studies, child and family issues, Irish studies. *Strongly prefers agented submissions.* Query with SASE or submit outline, sample chapter(s), résumé, CV. *Strongly prefers referred submissions, on exclusive.*

Recent Title(s): *Radical Equation*, by Robert Moses and Charles Cobb; *All Souls*, by Michael Patrick McDonald; *Speak to Me*, by Marcie Hershman.

Tips: "We probably accept only one or two manuscripts from an unpublished pool of 4,000 submissions per year. No fiction, children's book, or poetry submissions invited. An academic affiliation is helpful."

BEEMAN JORGENSEN, INC., 7510 Allisonville Rd., Indianapolis IN 46250. (317)841-7677. Fax: (317)849-2001. **Acquisitions:** Brett Johnson, president (automotive/auto racing). Publishes hardcover and trade paperback originals and hardcover reprints. **Publishes 4 titles/year. Receives 10 queries/year. 50% of books from first-time authors; 100% from unagented writers. Pays 15-30% royalty on wholesale price. Offers up to $1,000 advance.** Publishes book 8 months after acceptance of ms. Responds in 1 month to queries; 2 months to proposals. Book catalog free.

Nonfiction: Publishes books on automobiles and auto racing. Coffee table book, illustrated book, reference. Subjects include sports (auto racing). Query with SASE or submit proposal package including outline, 1 sample chapter(s).

Recent Title(s): *Porsche Speedster*, by Michel Thiriar (coffee table); *Road America*, by Tom Schultz (illustrated book); *Volkswagon KdF, 1934-1945*, by Terry Shuler (illustrated book).

Tips: Audience is automotive enthusiasts, specific marque owners/enthusiasts, auto racing fans and participants.

BEHRMAN HOUSE INC., 11 Edison Place, Springfield NJ 07081. (973)379-7200. Fax: (973)379-7280. E-mail: webmaster@behrmanhouse.com. Website: www.behrmanhouse.com. **Acquisitions:** David Behrman. Estab. 1921. **Publishes 20 titles/year. Receives 200 submissions/year. 20% of books from first-time authors; 95% from unagented writers. Pays 2-10% on wholesale price or retail price or makes outright purchase of $500-10,000. Offers $1,000 average advance.** Publishes book 18 months after acceptance of ms. Accepts simultaneous submissions. Responds in 2 months to queries. Book catalog free.

O┳ "Behrman House publishes quality books of Jewish content—history, Bible, philosophy, holidays, ethics, Israel, Hebrew—for children and adults."

Nonfiction: Children's/juvenile (ages 1-18), reference, textbook. Subjects include ethnic, philosophy, religion. "We want Jewish textbooks for the el-hi market." Query with SASE.

Recent Title(s): *Living As Partners with God*, by Gila Gevirtz (theology).

FREDERIC C. BEIL, PUBLISHER, INC., 609 Whitaker St., Savannah GA 31401. (912)233-2446. Fax: (912)233-6456. E-mail: beilbook@beil.com. Website: www.beil.com. **Acquisitions:** Mary Ann Bowman, editor. Estab. 1982. Publishes hardcover originals and reprints. **Publishes 13 titles/year. Receives 1,800 queries and 13 mss/year. 80% of books from first-time authors; 100% from unagented writers. Pays 7½% royalty on retail price.** Publishes book 20 months after acceptance of ms. Accepts simultaneous submissions. Responds in 2 weeks to queries. Book catalog free.

Imprints: The Sandstone Press, Hypermedia, Inc.

O┳ Frederic C. Beil publishes in the fields of history, literature, biography, books about books, and the book arts.

Nonfiction: Biography, children's/juvenile, illustrated book, reference, general trade. Subjects include art/architecture, general nonfiction, history, language/literature, book arts. Query with SASE. Reviews artwork/photos as part of ms package. Send photocopies.

Fiction: Historical, literary. Query with SASE.

Recent Title(s): *Joseph Jefferson: Dean of the American Theatre*, by Arthur Bloom; *Goya, Are You With Me Now?*, by H.E. Francis.

Tips: "Our objectives are (1) to offer to the reading public carefully selected texts of lasting value; (2) to adhere to high standards in the choice of materials and in bookmaking craftsmanship; (3) to produce books that exemplify good taste in format and design; and (4) to maintain the lowest cost consistent with quality."

BELLWETHER-CROSS PUBLISHING, 18319 Highway 20 W., East Dubuque IL 61025. (815)747-6255 or (888)516-5096. Fax: (815)747-3770. E-mail: jwhite@bellwethercross.com. **Acquisitions:** Janet White, senior developmental editor. Publishes college textbooks. **Publishes 18 titles/year. Receives 100 mss/year. 80% of books from first-time authors; 100% from unagented writers. Pays 10% royalty on wholesale price.** Publishes book 6 months after acceptance of ms. Does not accept simultaneous submissions. Responds in 1 month to queries. Ms guidelines available.

O┳ Bellwether-Cross concentrates on college environmental books and nontraditional textbooks with mainstream possibilities.

Nonfiction: Textbook. Submit cover letter and complete ms with SASE. Reviews artwork/photos as part of ms package. Send photocopies.

Recent Title(s): *Transitional Science*, by H. Sue Way and Gaines B. Jackson; *Daring to Be Different: A Manager's Ascent to Leadership*, by James A. Hatherley.

BENTLEY PUBLISHERS, Automotive Publishers, 1734 Massachusetts Ave., Cambridge MA 02138-1804. (617)547-4170. **Acquisitions:** Janet Barnes, senior editor; Jonathan Stein, editor. Estab. 1949. Publishes hardcover and trade paperback originals and reprints. **Publishes 15-20 titles/year. 20% of books from first-time authors; 95% from unagented writers. Pays 10-15% royalty on net price or makes outright purchase. Offers negotiable advance.** Publishes book 1 year after acceptance of ms. Does not accept simultaneous submissions. Responds in 6 weeks to queries. Book catalog and ms guidelines for 9×12 SAE with 4 first-class stamps.

O━ Bentley Publishers publishes books for automotive enthusiasts.

Nonfiction: Automotive subjects only. Coffee table book, how-to, technical, theory of operation. Subjects include sports (motor sports). Query with SASE or submit outline, sample chapter(s). Reviews artwork/photos as part of ms package.

Recent Title(s): *Road and Track Illustrated Dictionary*, by John Dinkel (reference).

Tips: "Our audience is composed of serious, intelligent automobile, sports car, and racing enthusiasts, automotive technicians and high-performance tuners."

BERKSHIRE HOUSE PUBLISHERS, INC., 480 Pleasant St., Suite #5, Lee MA 01238. (413)243-0303. Fax: (413)243-4737. E-mail: info@berkshirehouse.com. Website: www.berkshirehouse.com. President: Jean J. Rousseau. **Acquisitions:** Philip Rich, editorial director. Estab. 1966. **Publishes 10-15 titles/year. Receives 100 queries and 6 mss/year. 50% of books from first-time authors; 80% from unagented writers. Pays 5-10% royalty on retail price. Offers $500-5,000 advance.** Publishes book 18 months after acceptance of ms. Accepts simultaneous submissions. Responds in 1 month to proposals. Book catalog free.

O━ "We publish a series of travel guides, the Great Destinations Series, about specific U.S. destinations, guides to appeal to discerning travelers. We also specialize in books about our own region (the Berkshires and New England), especially recreational activities such as outdoor exploration. We publish cookbooks related to New England, country living and the northeast. We offer books of historical interest in our American Classics Series." Currently emphasizing Great Destinations series, outdoor recreation, cookbooks related to our region/country living. Please refer to website for more information.

Nonfiction: Cookbook (relating to country inns, travel, especially in New England). Subjects include Americana, history, nature/environment, recreation, regional, travel. "To a great extent, we choose our topics then commission the authors, but we don't discourage speculative submissions. We just don't accept many. Don't overdo it; a well-written outline/proposal is more useful than a full manuscript. Also, include a c.v. with writing credits."

Recent Title(s): *The Finger Lakes Book: A Complete Guide*, by Katherine Delavan Dyson; *New England Cooking*; *Adirondack Cuisine*.

Tips: "Our readers are literate, active and interested in travel, especially in selected 'Great Destinations' areas and outdoor activities and cooking."

BETHANY HOUSE PUBLISHERS, 11400 Hampshire Ave. S., Minneapolis MN 55438. (952)829-2500. Fax: (952)829-2768. Website: www.bethanyhouse.com. Publisher: Gary Johnson. **Acquisitions:** Sharon Madison, ms review editor; Steve Laube, senior editor (nonfiction); David Horton, senior editor (adult fiction); Barbara Lilland, senior editor (adult fiction); Rochelle Gloege, senior editor (children and youth). Estab. 1956. Publishes hardcover and trade paperback originals, mass market paperback reprints. **Publishes 120-150 titles/year. 2% of books from first-time authors; 93% from unagented writers. Pays negotiable royalty on net price. Offers negotiable advance.** Publishes book 1 year after acceptance of ms. Accepts simultaneous submissions. Responds in 3 months to queries. Ms guidelines for 9×12 SAE with 5 first-class stamps.

O━ Bethany House Publishers specializes in books that communicate Biblical truth and assist people in both spiritual and practical areas of life. New interest in contemporary fiction.

Nonfiction: Biography, gift book, how-to, reference, self-help. Subjects include child guidance/parenting, ethnic, psychology, religion, sociology, women's issues/studies, personal growth, devotional, contemporary issues, marriage and family, applied theology, inspirational. "While we do not accept unsolicited queries or proposals via telephone or e-mail, we will consider one-page queries sent by facsimile to (952)996-1304 and directed to Adult Nonfiction, Adult Fiction or Young Adult/Children. Queries of interest to us should receive a reply in four to six weeks." **All unsolicited mss returned unopened.** Reviews artwork/photos as part of ms package. Send photocopies.

Fiction: Adventure, historical, juvenile, young adult, children's fiction series (ages 8-12) and Bethany Backyard (ages 6-12). Send SASE for guidelines.

Recent Title(s): *Unshakable Foundations*, by Dr. Norman Geisler & Peter Bocchino (Christian living); *Serenity Bay*, by Bette Nordberg (fiction); *God's Will, God's Best—for Your Life*, by Josh McDowell and Kevin Johnson (teen Christian living).

Tips: "Bethany House Publishers' publishing program relates Biblical truth to all areas of life—whether in the framework of a well-told story, of a challenging book for spiritual growth, or of a Bible reference work. We are seeking high quality fiction and nonfiction that will inspire and challenge our audience."

BETTERWAY BOOKS, F&W Publications, 4700 E. Galbraith Rd., Cincinnati OH 45236. Fax: (513)531-7107. **Acquisitions:** Brad Crawford (small business; home organization, time management); Sharon Carmack (genealogy) P.O. Box 338, Simla CO 80835. Estab. 1982. Publishes hardcover and trade paperback originals, trade paperback reprints. **Publishes 10 titles/year. Pays 10-20% royalty on net receipts. Offers $3,000-5,000 advance.** Publishes book an average of 18 months after acceptance of ms. Accepts simultaneous submissions. Responds in 6 weeks to queries. Book catalog for 9×12 SAE with 6 first-class stamps.

O→ Betterway books are practical instructional books that are to be *used*. "We like specific step-by-step advice, charts, illustrations, and clear explanations of the activities and projects the books describe."

Nonfiction: How-to, illustrated book, reference. Subjects include business/economics, money/finance, family history, time management/home organization. "We publish 6 how-to family history/genealogy books per year. We are interested mostly in original material, but we will consider republishing self-published nonfiction books and good instructional or reference books that have gone out of print before their time. Send a sample copy, sales information, and reviews, if available. If you have a good idea for a reference book that can be updated annually, try us. We're willing to consider freelance compilers of such works." No cookbooks, diet/exercise, psychology self-help, health or parenting books. Submit outline, sample chapter(s). Reviews artwork/photos as part of ms package.

Recent Title(s): *Jump Start Your Business Brain*, by Doug Hall (business); *The Genealogist's Question & Answer Book*, by Marcia Yannizze Melnyk.

Tips: "Keep the imprint name well in mind when submitting ideas to us. What is the 'better way' you're proposing? How will readers benefit *immediately* from the instruction and information you're giving them?"

BEYOND WORDS PUBLISHING INC., 20827 NW Cornell Rd., Suite 500, Hillsboro OR 97124. (503)531-8700. Fax: (503)531-8773. E-mail: info@beyondword.com. Website: www.beyondword.com. **Acquisitions:** Cynthia Black, editor-in-chief (adult books); Barbara Mann, acquisitions editor (children's books). Publishes hardcover and trade paperback originals. **Publishes 20-25 titles/year. Receives 4,000 queries and 2,000 mss/year. 65% of books from first-time authors; 50% from unagented writers. Pays 10-15% royalty on publishers proceeds. Offers advance.** Publishes book 12-18 months after acceptance of ms. Accepts simultaneous submissions. Responds in 4 months to queries; 4 months to proposals; 4 months to mss. Book catalog and ms guidelines for #10 SASE or online.

Nonfiction: Children's/juvenile, coffee table book, gift book, how-to, self-help. Subjects include animals, child guidance/parenting, health/medicine, photography (selectively), psychology, spirituality, women's issues/studies. Query with SASE or submit proposal package including outline, 3 sample chapter(s). Reviews artwork/photos as part of ms package. Send photocopies.

Tips: "*Beyond Words* markets to cultural, creative people, mostly women ages 30-60. Study our list before you submit and check out our website to make sure your book is a good fit for our list."

BICK PUBLISHING HOUSE, 307 Neck Rd., Madison CT 06443. (203)245-0073. Fax: (203)245-5990. E-mail: bickpubhse@aol.com. Website: www.bickpubhouse.com. **Acquisitions:** Dale Carlson, president (psychology); Hannah Carlson (special needs, disabilities); Irene Ruth (wildlife). Estab. 1994. Publishes trade paperback originals. **Publishes 4 titles/year. Receives 4-6 queries and 4-6 mss/year. 55% of books from first-time authors; 55% from unagented writers. Pays 10% royalty on net receipts. Offers $500-1,000 advance.** Publishes book 1 year after acceptance of ms. Responds in 1 month to queries; 2 months to proposals; 3 months to mss. Book catalog free; ms guidelines for #10 SASE.

O→ Bick Publishing House publishes step-by-step, easy-to-read professional information for the general adult public about physical, psychological and emotional disabilities or special needs. Currently emphasizing teen psychology for teens.

Nonfiction: Subjects include animals (wildlife rehabilitation), health/medicine (disability/special needs), psychology. Query with SASE or submit proposal package including outline, 3 sample chapter(s), résumé. Reviews artwork/photos as part of ms package. Send photocopies.

Recent Title(s): *Stop the Pain: Teen Meditations*; *Stop the Pain: Adult Meditation*, both by Dale Carlson.

[N] **BIOMED BOOKS**, 2352 Stanwell Dr., Concord CA 94520-4822. (925)602-6140. Fax: (925)363-7798. E-mail: info@biomedgeneral.com; publishing@biocorp.com. Website: www.biomedbooks.com. **Acquisitions:** Latoia McFarland, managing editor (health, medicine). Publishes trade paperback originals. **Publishes 5 titles/year. Receives 30 queries/year. 20% of books from first-time authors. Pays 5-10% royalty on retail price. Offers $2,000-5,000 advance.** Publishes book 3 months after acceptance of ms. Accepts simultaneous submissions. Responds in 1 month to queries.

O→ "We publish continuing education courses for health care professionals." Currently emphasizing nutrition, brain science, alternative medicine.

Nonfiction: Subjects include education, health/medicine. Books for continuing health education. Submit proposal package including outline, 2 sample chapter(s). Curriculum vitae. Reviews artwork/photos as part of ms package. Send photocopies.

Recent Title(s): *Sports Nutrition*, by Donal P. O'Mathuna, PhD.

Tips: "We sell primarily to health professionals. Books must be suitable for continuing education credits. We may expand into mass market sales by the year 2000."

BKMK PRESS, University of Missouri-Kansas City, 5101 Rockhill Rd., Kansas City MO 64110-2499. (816)235-2558. Fax: (816)235-2611. E-mail: bkmk@umkc.edu. Website: www.umkc.edu/bkmk. **Acquisitions:** James McKinley, executive editor (fiction/nonfiction); Michelle Boisseau, associate editor (poetry); Ben Furnish, managing editor. Estab. 1971. Publishes trade paperback originals. **Publishes 5-6 titles/year. Receives 450-500 queries and 250 mss/year. 20% of books from first-time authors; 70% from unagented writers. Pays 10% royalty on wholesale price.** Publishes book 1 year after acceptance of ms. Accepts simultaneous submissions. Responds in 4 months to queries; 8 months to mss. Ms guidelines for #10 SASE.

O→ BkMk Press publishes fine literature.

Nonfiction: Subjects include creative nonfiction. Query with SASE.
Fiction: Literary, short story collections. Query with SASE or submit proposal package including 50 pages and cover letter.
Poetry: Submit 10 sample poems.
Recent Title(s): *Father's Mechanical Universe*, by Steve Heller (fiction); *Almanac for Desire*, by Gary Fincke (poetry).
Tips: "We skew toward readers of literature, particularly contemporary writing. Because of our limited number of titles published per year, we discourage apprentice writers or 'scattershot' submissions."

BLACK DOG & LEVENTHAL PUBLISHERS INC., 151 W. 19th St., 12th Floor, New York NY 10011. (212)647-9336. Fax: (212)647-9332. Publishes hardcover and paperback originals and reprints. **Publishes 30-40 titles/year. Receives 12 queries and 12 mss/year. Pays royalty on retail price or on net receipts or makes outright purchase. Offers $1,500-20,000 advance.** Publishes book 6 months after acceptance of ms. Accepts simultaneous submissions. Responds in 6 months to queries.

O‑‑ "We look for very commercial books that will appeal to a broad-based audience."

Nonfiction: Coffee table book, cookbook, gift book, how-to, humor, illustrated book, reference. Subjects include art/architecture, cooking/foods/nutrition, history, music/dance (popular), sports, humor. Query with SASE only. (No ms or artwork; nothing will be returned.)
Recent Title(s): *Moments: The Pulitzer Prize Photographs*, by Hal Buell (photo journalism); *Skyscrapers*, by Judith Dupre (architecture).
Tips: "We look for books that are information-packed and visual."

BLACK HERON PRESS, P.O. Box 95676, Seattle WA 98145. **Acquisitions:** Jerry Gold, publisher. Publishes hardcover and trade paperback originals. **Publishes 4 titles/year. Pays 8-9% royalty on retail price.** Responds in 3 months to queries; 6 months to proposals; 6 months to mss.

O‑‑ "Black Heron Press publishes literary fiction—lately we've tended toward surrealism/science fiction (not fantasy) and social fiction; writers should look at some of our titles. We're especially interested in books on the social or historical significances of independent publishing. We've already done 2 titles."

Fiction: High quality, innovative fiction. Literary, science fiction (surrealism). Query with SASE.
Recent Title(s): *Obscure in the Shade of the Giants*, by Jerome Gold; *The Bathhouse*, by Farnoosh Moshiri.
Tips: "Readers should look at some of our books before submitting—they are easily available. Most submissions we see are done competently but have been sent to the wrong place. We do not publish self-help books or romances."

JOHN F. BLAIR, PUBLISHER, 1406 Plaza Dr., Winston-Salem NC 27103-1470. (336)768-1374. Fax: (336)768-9194. Website: www.blairpub.com. President: Carolyn Sakowski. **Acquisitions:** Acquisitions Committee. Estab. 1954. Publishes hardcover originals and trade paperbacks. **Publishes 20 titles/year. Receives 2,000 submissions/year. 20-30% of books from first-time authors; 90% from unagented writers. Royalty negotiable. Offers advance.** Publishes book 18 months after acceptance of ms. Accepts simultaneous submissions. Responds in 3 months to queries. Book catalog for 9×12 SAE with 5 first-class stamps; ms guidelines online.

O‑‑ John F. Blair publishes in the areas of travel, history, folklore and the outdoors for a general trade audience, most of whom live or travel in the Southeastern U.S.

Nonfiction: Subjects include Americana, history, nature/environment, regional, travel, women's issues/studies. Especially interested in travel guides dealing with the Southeastern U.S. Also interested in Civil War, outdoors, travel and Americana; query on other nonfiction topics. Looks for utility and significance. Submit outline, 3 sample chapter(s). Reviews artwork/photos as part of ms package.
Fiction: "We publish one work of fiction per season relating to the Southeastern U.S." No category fiction, juvenile fiction, picture books, short story collections or poetry. Query with SASE.

BLOOMBERG PRESS, Bloomberg L.P., 100 Business Park Dr., P.O. Box 888, Princeton NJ 08542-0888. Website: www.bloomberg.com/books. **Acquisitions:** Kathleen Peterson, senior acquisitions editor. Estab. 1995. Publishes hardcover and trade paperback originals. **Publishes 18-22 titles/year. Receives 90 queries and 17 mss/year. 45% from unagented writers. Pays negotiable, competitive royalty. Offers negotiable advance.** Publishes book 9 months after acceptance of ms. Accepts simultaneous submissions. Responds in 1 month to queries. Book catalog for 10×13 SAE with 5 first-class stamps.
Imprints: Bloomberg Personal Bookshelf, Bloomberg Professional Library.

O‑‑ Bloomberg Press publishes professional books for practitioners in the financial markets, and finance and investing books for informed personal investors, entrepreneurs, and consumers. "We publish commercially successful, very high-quality books that stand out clearly from the competition by their brevity, ease of use, sophistication, and abundance of practical tips and strategies; books readers need, will use and appreciate."

Nonfiction: How-to, reference, technical. Subjects include business/economics, money/finance, small business, current affairs, personal finance and investing for consumers, professional books on finance, investment and financial services. "We are looking for authorities and experienced service journalists. We are looking for original solutions to widespread problems and books offering fresh investment opportunities. Do not send us management books or unfocused books containing general information already covered by one or more well-established backlist books in the marketplace." Submit outline, sample chapter(s), SAE with sufficient postage or submit complete ms.
Tips: "*Bloomberg Professional Library*: Audience is upscale financial professionals—traders, dealers, brokers, planners and advisors, financial managers, money managers, company executives, sophisticated investors. *Bloomberg Personal*

Bookshelf: audience is upscale consumers and individual investors. Authors are experienced business and financial journalists and/or financial professionals nationally prominent in their specialty for some time who have proven an ability to write a successful book. Research Bloomberg and look at our books in a library or bookstore, read *Bloomberg Personal Finance* magazine and peruse our website."

N **BLUE MOON BOOKS, INC.**, Avalon Publishing Group, 161 William St., New York NY 10038. (646)375-2570. Fax: (646)375-2571. E-mail: tmpress@aol.com. Website: www.avalonpub.com. **Acquisitions:** Gayle Watkins, editor. Estab. 1987. Publishes trade paperback and mass market paperback originals. **Publishes 50-60 titles/year. Receives 1,000 queries and 500 mss/year. Pays 7½-10% royalty on retail price. Offers $500 and up advance.** Publishes book 1 year after acceptance of ms. Responds in 2 months to queries. Book catalog free.

"Blue Moon Books is strictly an erotic press; largely fetish-oriented material, B&D, S&M, etc."

Nonfiction: Subjects include sex. Trade erotic and sexual nonfiction. *No unsolicited mss.*

Fiction: Erotica. *No unsolicited mss.*

Recent Title(s): *Sex Practice*, by Ray Gordon; *66 Chapters About 33 Women*, by Michael Hemmingson.

BLUE POPPY PRESS, Blue Poppy Enterprises, Inc., 5441 Western Ave., #2, Boulder CO 80301-2733. (303)447-8372. Fax: (303)245-8362. E-mail: info@bluepoppy.com. Website: www.bluepoppy.com. **Acquisitions:** Bob Flaws, editor-in-chief. Estab. 1981. Publishes hardcover and trade paperback originals. **Publishes 3-4 titles/year. Receives 50-100 queries and 20 mss/year. 40-50% of books from first-time authors; 100% from unagented writers. Pays 10-15% royalty. Offers advance.** Publishes book 1 year after acceptance of ms. Does not accept simultaneous submissions. Responds in 1 month to queries. Book catalog and ms guidelines free.

Blue Poppy Press is dedicated to expanding and improving the English language literature on acupuncture and Asian medicine for both professional practitioners and lay readers.

Nonfiction: Self-help, technical, textbook (related to acupuncture and Oriental medicine). Subjects include ethnic, health/medicine. "We only publish books on acupuncture and Oriental medicine by authors who can read Chinese and have a minimum of five years clinical experience. We also require all our authors to use Wiseman's *Glossary of Chinese Medical Terminology* as their standard for technical terms." Query with SASE or submit outline, 1 sample chapter(s).

Recent Title(s): *Chinese Medical Psychiatry*, by Bob Flaws & James Lake, MD.

Tips: Audience is "practicing acupuncturists, interested in alternatives in healthcare, preventive medicine, Chinese philosophy and medicine."

BLUE/GRAY BOOKS, Creativity, Inc., 65 Macedonia Rd., Alexander NC 28701. (828)252-9515. Fax: (828)255-8719. Website: blue-gray.com. **Acquisitions:** Pat Roberts, acquisitions editor. Publishes trade paperback originals and reprints. **Publishes 4 titles/year. Pays negotiable royalty on wholesale price. Offers advance.** Publishes book 18 months after acceptance of ms. Book catalog for 9×12 SASE with 5 ounces postage.

Blue/Gray Books specializes in Civil War history.

Nonfiction: Biography. Subjects include military/war (Civil War). Query with SASE or submit proposal package including 3 sample chapter(s), original book if wanting reprint. Reviews artwork/photos as part of ms package. Send photocopies.

Recent Title(s): *Deo Vindice: Heroes in Gray Forever*, by Lee Jacobs.

BLUEWOOD BOOKS, The Siyeh Group, Inc., P.O. Box 689, San Mateo CA 94401. (650)548-0754. Fax: (650)548-0654. E-mail: bluewoodb@aol.com. **Acquisitions:** Richard Michaels, director. Publishes trade paperback originals. **Publishes 8 titles/year. 20% of books from first-time authors; 100% from unagented writers. Makes work for hire assignments—fee depends upon book and writer's expertise. Offers ⅓ fee advance.** Does not accept simultaneous submissions.

"We are looking for qualified writers for nonfiction series—history and biography oriented."

Nonfiction: Biography, illustrated book. Subjects include Americana, anthropology/archeology, art/architecture, business/economics, government/politics, health/medicine, history, military/war, multicultural, science, sports, women's issues/studies. Query with SASE.

Recent Title(s): *American Politics in the 20th Century*, by J. Bonasia (political history); *100 Families Who Shaped World History*, by Samuel Crompton (world history).

Tips: "Our audience consists of adults and young adults. Our books are written on a newspaper level—clear, concise, well organized and easy to understand. We encourage potential writers to send us a résumé, providing background, qualifications and references."

BNA BOOKS, The Bureau of National Affairs, Inc., 1231 25th St. NW, Washington DC 20037-1165. (202)452-4343. Fax: (202)452-4997. E-mail: books@bna.com. Website: www.bnabooks.com. **Acquisitions:** Jim Fattibene, acquisitions manager. Estab. 1929. Publishes hardcover and softcover originals. **Publishes 35 titles/year. Receives 50 submissions/year. 20% of books from first-time authors; 95% from unagented writers. Pays 10-15% royalty on net receipts. Offers $500 average advance.** Publishes book 1 year after acceptance of ms. Accepts simultaneous submissions. Responds in 3 months to queries. Book catalog and ms guidelines online.

BNA Books publishes professional reference books written by lawyers, for lawyers. Currently emphasizing employment, intellectual property, and health law.

Nonfiction: Reference, scholarly. Subjects include labor and employment law, health law, legal practice, labor relations law, intellectual property law. No fiction, biographies, bibliographies, cookbooks, religion books, humor or trade books. Submit detailed table of contents or outline.

Recent Title(s): *Fair Labor Standards Act; Intellectual Property Law in Cyberspace*; *Health Care Fraud and Abuse.*
Tips: "Our audience is made up of practicing lawyers and law librarians. We look for authoritative and comprehensive works that can be supplemented or revised every year or two on subjects of interest to those audiences."

BOA EDITIONS, LTD., 260 East Ave., Rochester NY 14604. (585)546-3410. Fax: (585)546-3913. E-mail: boaedit@frontiernet.net. Website: www.boaeditions.org. **Acquisitions:** Steven Huff, publisher/managing editor; Thom Ward, editor. Estab. 1976. Publishes hardcover and trade paperback originals. **Publishes 10 titles/year. Receives 1,000 queries and 700 mss/year. 15% of books from first-time authors; 90% from unagented writers. Pays 8-10% royalty on retail price. Offers variable advance.** Publishes book 18 months after acceptance of ms. Accepts simultaneous submissions. Responds in 1 week to queries; 4 months to mss. Ms guidelines free.

O‑ BOA Editions publishes distinguished collections of poetry and poetry in translation. "Our goal is to publish the finest American contemporary poetry and poetry in translation."

Poetry: Accepting mss for publication in 2004 and beyond. Query first.
Recent Title(s): *Tell Me*, by Kim Addonizio; *Blessing the Boats*, by Lucille Clifton.
Tips: "Readers who, like Whitman, expect of the poet to 'indicate more than the beauty and dignity which always attach to dumb real objects... They expect him to indicate the path between reality and their souls,' are the audience of BOA's books."

[A] **BOOK PEDDLERS**, 15245 Minnetonka Blvd., Minnetonka MN 55345. (952)912-0036. Fax: (952)912-0105. E-mail: vlansky@bookpeddlers.com. Website: www.bookpeddlers.com. **Acquisitions:** Vicki Lansky, publisher/editor. Publishes hardcover and trade paperback originals. **Publishes 3 titles/year. Receives 50 queries and 10 mss/year. 0% of books from first-time authors; 0% from unagented writers. Pays 10% royalty on wholesale price. Offers $500 advance.** Publishes book 1 year after acceptance of ms. Accepts simultaneous submissions. Responds in 1 week to queries; 1 week to proposals. Book catalog for #10 SASE; ms guidelines online.
Nonfiction: Children's/juvenile, gift book, how-to, self-help. "We accept no fiction and practically nothing that is sent to us. A writer must be *very on target* for our consideration." Query with SASE.
Recent Title(s): *Coming Clean*, by Schar War (dirty little secrets from a professional housecleaner); *Blessings for Hearth and Home*, by Mary I. Farr (gift book).
Tips: "See submission guidelines on website."

BOTTOM DOG PRESS, c/o Firelands College of BGSU, Huron OH 44839. (419)433-5560. **Acquisitions:** Larry Smith, director. Publishes hardcover, trade paperback and mass market paperback originals, hardcover and trade paperback reprints. **Publishes 4 titles/year. Receives 300 queries and 250 mss/year. 30% of books from first-time authors; 90% from unagented writers. Pays 7-15% royalty on wholesale price. Offers $100-300 advance.** Publishes book 1 year after acceptance of ms. Accepts simultaneous submissions. Responds in 1 month to queries; 1 month to proposals; 4 months to mss. Book catalog and ms guidelines free.

O‑ Bottom Dog Press is "Midwest-focused and somewhat literary. We emphasize working-class life in the post-industrial age."

Nonfiction: Biography. Subjects include language/literature, nature/environment, photography, regional (Midwest), women's issues/studies, working class issues. Query with SASE or submit outline, 2 sample chapter(s). Reviews artwork/photos as part of ms package. Send photocopies.
Fiction: Ethnic, literary, mainstream/contemporary, working class. "We do one fiction book/year, Midwest-based with author on locale." Query with SASE or submit 2 sample chapter(s), synopsis.
Poetry: Midwest, working class focus. "Read our books before submitting." Query or submit 10 sample poems.
Recent Title(s): *Kenneth Patchen: Rebel Poet in America*, by Larry Smith (nonfiction); *The Marcy Starcies*, by Fran Zell (fiction); *The Neighborhood Years*, by David Kheridian (poetry).
Tips: "We publish for a broad yet literate public. Do not get an agent—try the small presses first."

[A] **BOULEVARD**, Penguin Putnam Inc., 375 Hudson St., New York NY 10014. (212)366-2000. Website: www.penguinputnam.com. **Acquisitions:** Acquisitions Editor. Estab. 1995. Publishes trade paperback and mass market paperback originals and reprints. **Publishes 85 titles/year. Offers advance.** Does not accept simultaneous submissions. *Agented submissions only.*

BOYDS MILLS PRESS, *Highlights for Children*, 815 Church St., Honesdale PA 18431-1895. (570)253-1164. Website: www.boydsmillspress.com. Publisher: Kent L. Brown. **Acquisitions:** Larry Rosler, editorial director; Kathryn Yerkes, ms coordinator. Estab. 1990. Publishes hardcover originals and trade paperback reprints. **Publishes 50 titles/year. Receives 10,000 queries and 7,500 mss/year. 40% of books from first-time authors; 60% from unagented writers. Pays 4-12% royalty on retail price. Offers varying advance.** Accepts simultaneous submissions. Responds in 1 month to queries; 1 month to mss. Book catalog on request; ms guidelines for #10 SASE.
Imprints: Wordsong (poetry).

O‑ Boyds Mill Press, the book publishing arm of *Highlights for Children*, publishes a wide range of children's books of literary merit, from preschool to young adult. Currently emphasizing picture books and novels (but no fantasy, romance or horror).

Nonfiction: Children's/juvenile. Subjects include agriculture/horticulture, animals, ethnic, history, nature/environment, sports, travel. "Nonfiction should be accurate, tailored to young audience. Prefer simple, narrative style, but in compelling, evocative language. Too many authors overwrite for the young audience and get bogged down in minutiae. Boyds

Mills Press is not interested in mss depicting violence, explicit sexuality, racism of any kind or which promote hatred. We also are not the right market for self-help books." Query with SASE or submit proposal package including outline, 1 sample chapter(s). Reviews artwork/photos as part of ms package.

Fiction: Adventure, ethnic, historical, humor, juvenile, mystery, picture books, young adult. "Don't let a personal agenda dominate to the detriment of plot. In short, tell a good story. Too many writers miss the essence of a good story: beginning, middle, end; conflict and resolution because they're more interested in making a sociological statement." Submit outline/synopsis and 3 sample chapters for novel or complete ms.

Poetry: "Poetry should be appropriate for young audiences, clever, fun language, with easily understood meaning. Too much poetry is either too simple and static in meaning or too obscure." Collections should have a unifying theme.

Recent Title(s): *Black-Eyed Suzie*, by Susan Shaw; *Wild Wings: Poems for Young People*, by Jane Yolen.

Tips: "Our audience is pre-school to young adult. Concentrate first on your writing. Polish it. Then—and only then—select a market. We need primarily picture books with fresh ideas and characters—avoid worn themes of 'coming-of-age,' 'new sibling,' and self-help ideas. We are always interested in multicultural settings. Please—no anthropomorphic characters."

BRANDEN PUBLISHING CO., INC., P.O. Box 812094, Wellesley MA 02482. Fax: (781)790-1056. Website: www.branden.com. **Acquisitions:** Adolph Caso, editor. Estab. 1965. Publishes hardcover and trade paperback originals, reprints and software. **Publishes 15 titles/year. Receives 1,000 submissions/year. 80% of books from first-time authors; 90% from unagented writers. Pays 5-10% royalty on net receipts. Offers $1,000 maximum advance.** Publishes book 10 months after acceptance of ms. Responds in 1 month to queries.

Imprints: International Pocket Library and Popular Technology, Four Seas and Brashear.

Branden publishes books by or about women, children, military, Italian-American or African-American themes.

Nonfiction: Biography, children's/juvenile, illustrated book, reference, technical, textbook. Subjects include Americana, art/architecture, computers/electronic, contemporary culture, education, ethnic, general nonfiction, government/politics, health/medicine, history, military/war, music/dance, photography, sociology, software, classics. Especially looking for "about 10 manuscripts on national and international subjects, including biographies of well-known individuals. Currently specializing in Americana, Italian-American, African-American." No religion or philosophy. *No unsolicited mss.* Paragraph query only with author's vita and SASE. No telephone inquiries, e-mail or fax inquiries. Reviews artwork/photos as part of ms package.

Fiction: Ethnic (histories, integration), religious (historical-reconstructive). No science, mystery or pornography. *No unsolicited mss.* Paragraph query only with author's vita and SASE. No telephone inquiries, e-mail or fax inquiries.

Recent Title(s): *Quilt of America*, by Carole Gariepy; *The Wisdom of Angels*, by Martha Cummings; *Water and Life*, by Adolph Caso.

BRASSEY'S INC., 22841 Quicksilver Dr., Dulles VA 20166. (703)661-1548. Fax: (703)661-1547. E-mail: djacobs@booksintl.com. Website: www.brasseysinc.com. **Acquisitions:** Don McKeon, vice president/publisher; Don Jacobs, senior assistant editor (general inquiries). Estab. 1984. Publishes hardcover and trade paperback originals and reprints. **Publishes 100 titles/year. Receives 900 queries/year. 30% of books from first-time authors; 80% from unagented writers. Pays 6-12% royalty on wholesale price. Offers $20,000 maximum advance.** Publishes book 1 year after acceptance of ms. Accepts simultaneous submissions. Responds in 2 months to queries. Book catalog free; ms guidelines for 9×12 SAE with 4 first-class stamps.

Imprints: Brassey's Sports

Brassey's specializes in national and international affairs, military history, biography, intelligence, foreign policy, defense, transportation, reference and sports. "We are seeking to build our history and international affairs college textbook lists."

Nonfiction: Biography, coffee table book, reference, textbook. Subjects include government/politics, history, military/war, sports, world affairs, national and international affairs, intelligence studies. When submitting nonfiction, be sure to include sufficient biographical information (e.g., track records of previous publications), and "make clear in the proposal how your work might differ from other such works already published and with which yours might compete." Query with SASE or submit proposal package including outline, 2 sample chapter(s), author bio, analysis of book's competition. Reviews artwork/photos as part of ms package. Send photocopies.

Recent Title(s): *Silent Knights: Blowing the Whistle on Military Accidents and Their Cover-ups*, by Alan E. Diehl; *Sacred Secrets: How Soviet Intelligence Operations Changed American History*, by Jerrold and Leona Schecter.

Tips: "Our audience consists of military personnel, government policymakers, undergraduate and graduate students, and general readers with an interest in military history, biography, national/international affairs, defense issues, intelligence studies and sports."

BRASSEY'S SPORTS, Brassey's Inc., 22841 Quicksilver Dr., Dulles VA 20166. (703)996-1004. Fax: (703)661-1547. E-mail: chris@booksintl.com. Website: www.brasseysinc.com. **Acquisitions:** Chris Kahrl, sports editor. Publishes hardcover and trade paperback originals and reprints. **Publishes 20 titles/year. Receives 900 queries/year. 30% of books from first-time authors; 80% from unagented writers. Pays 6-12% royalty on wholesale price. Offers maximum $20,000 advance.** Publishes book 1 year after acceptance of ms. Accepts simultaneous submissions. Responds in 2 months to queries. Book catalog free; ms guidelines for 9×12 SAE with 4 first-class stamps.

Nonfiction: Subjects include sports. Query with SASE. Reviews artwork/photos as part of ms package. Send photocopies.

Recent Title(s): *Baseball Prospectus 2002 Edition*, by Joseph Sheehan, Chris Kahrl, et al. (annual reference); *Mickey Mantle: America's Prodigal Son*, by Tony Castro.

BREAKOUT PRODUCTIONS, P.O. Box 1643, Port Townsend WA 98368. (360)379-1965. Fax: (360)379-3794. **Acquisitions:** Gia Cosindas, editor. Publishes trade paperback originals and reprints. **Publishes 6 titles/year. Pays 10-15% royalty on wholesale price. Offers $500-1,500 advance.** Publishes book 6 months after acceptance of ms. Accepts simultaneous submissions. Responds in 1 month to queries; 3 months to proposals; 3 months to mss. Book catalog and ms guidelines free.
Nonfiction: How-to, self-help, technical. Subjects include agriculture/horticulture, Americana, anthropology/archeology, computers/electronic, creative nonfiction, education, gardening, health/medicine, history, hobbies, military/war, philosophy, psychology, religion, science, sex, travel, unusual jobs, privacy. No electronic submissions. Query with SASE or submit proposal package including outline, sample chapter(s) or submit complete ms. Reviews artwork/photos as part of ms package. Send photocopies.
Recent Title(s): *Be Your Own Dick—Private Investigation Made Easy*, by John Newman (how-to); *Think Free to Be Free*, by Claire Wolfe (self help).
Tips: "We like the unusual 'take' on things. The author who presents his ideas from an unusual 'road less taken' viewpoint has a better chance than someone who recycles old ideas. We never publish fiction or poetry."

BRIGHT MOUNTAIN BOOKS, INC., 138 Springside Rd., Asheville NC 28803. (828)684-8840. Fax: (828)681-1790. E-mail: booksbmb@aol.com. **Acquisitions:** Cynthia F. Bright, editor. Publishes hardcover originals and trade paperback originals and reprints. **Publishes 6 titles/year. Pays 5-10% royalty on retail price.** Responds in 1 month to queries; 3 months to mss.
Imprints: Historical Images.
Nonfiction: Biography. Subjects include history, regional. "Our current emphasis is on regional titles set in the Southern Appalachians and Carolinas, which can include nonfiction by local writers." Query with SASE.
Recent Title(s): *Your Affectionate Daughter, Isabella*, by Ann Williams; *Edge of Heaven*, by Eva McCall; *Children of the Mountain*, by Eva McCall.

BRISTOL FASHION PUBLICATIONS, INC., P.O. Box 4676, Harrisburg PA 17111-4676. Website: www.BFPBOOKS.com. **Acquisitions:** John Kaufman, publisher. Publishes trade paperback originals. **Publishes 25 titles/year. Receives 250 queries and 200 mss/year. 50% of books from first-time authors; 100% from unagented writers. Pays 7-11% royalty on retail price.** Publishes book 3 months after acceptance of ms. Responds in 1 month to queries. Ms guidelines for #10 SASE.

O→ Bristol Fashion publishes books on boats and boating.

Nonfiction: General interest relating to boats and boating. How-to, reference. Subjects include history. "We are interested in any title which relates to these fields. Query with a list of ideas. Include phone number. This is a fast changing market. Our title plans rarely extend past 6 months, although we know the type and quantity of books we will publish over the next 2 years. We prefer good knowledge with simple to understand writing style containing a well-rounded vocabulary." Query with SASE. Reviews artwork/photos as part of ms package. Send photocopies or JPEG files on CD.
Recent Title(s): *Cruising South*; *Electronics Aboard*; *Practical Seamanship*.
Tips: "All of our staff and editors are boaters. As such, we publish what we would want to read relating to boats. Our audience is generally boat owners or expected owners who are interested in learning about boats, boat repair and boating. Keep it easy and simple to follow. Use nautical terms where appropriate. Do not use complicated technical jargon, terms or formulas without a detailed explanation of same. Use experienced craftsmen as a resource for knowledge."

BRISTOL PUBLISHING ENTERPRISES, 14692 Wicks Blvd., San Leandro CA 94577. Fax: (510)895-4459. Website: bristolcookbooks.com. Managing Editor: Aidan Wylde. **Acquisitions:** Pat Hall. Estab. 1988. Publishes trade paperback originals. **Publishes 10-20 titles/year. Receives 100-200 queries/year. 25% of books from first-time authors; 100% from unagented writers. Pays 6% royalty on net proceeds or makes outright purchase. Offers small advance.** Publishes book 1 year after acceptance of ms. Accepts simultaneous submissions. Responds in 4 months to queries. Book catalog online.
Imprints: Nitty Gritty cookbooks, The Best 50 Recipe Series, Pet Care Series
Nonfiction: Cookbook, craft books, pet care books. Subjects include cooking/foods/nutrition. Send a proposal or query with possible outline, brief note about author's background, sample of writing or chapter from ms.
Recent Title(s): *Cooking on the Indoor Grill*, by Catherine Fulde; *Vegetarian Slow Cooker*, by Joanna White; *Best 50 Bar Drinks*, by Dona Z. Mellach.
Tips: Readers of cookbooks are novice cooks. "Our books educate without intimidating. We require our authors to have some form of background in the food industry."

BROADCAST INTERVIEW SOURCE, INC., Free Library, 2233 Wisconsin Ave., NW 301, Washington DC 20007. (202)333-4904. Fax: (202)342-5411. E-mail: davis@yearbooknews.com. Website: www.freelibrary.com. **Acquisitions:** Greg Daly, information-oriented titles. Estab. 1984. Publishes trade paperback originals and reprints. **Publishes 6-10 titles/year. Receives 750 queries and 110 mss/year. 20% of books from first-time authors; 40% from unagented writers. Pays 5-15% royalty on wholesale price or makes outright purchase of $2,000-10,000.** Accepts simultaneous submissions.

O→ Broadcast Interview Source develops and publishes resources for publicists and journalists. Currently emphasizing information/reference. Does not want fiction.

Nonfiction: Biography, gift book, how-to, humor, multimedia, reference, self-help, textbook, catalogs; almanacs. Subjects include agriculture/horticulture, Americana, business/economics, computers/electronic, education, history, hobbies, military/war, money/finance, psychology, recreation, religion, translation. Submit proposal package including outline, 3 sample chapter(s).

Recent Title(s): *Baseball Goes to War.*

Tips: "We expect authors to be available for radio interviews at www.radiotour.com."

BROADMAN & HOLMAN, 127 Ninth Ave. N., Nashville TN 37234. (615)251-2392. Fax: (615)251-3752. Publisher: David Shepherd. **Acquisitions:** Leonard G. Goss, editorial director. Estab. 1934. Publishes hardcover and paperback originals. **Publishes 90 titles/year. Pays negotiable royalty.** Responds in 3 months to queries.

O→ Broadman & Holman publishes books that provide biblical solutions that spiritually transform individuals and cultures. Currently emphasizing inspirational/gift books, general Christian living and books on Christianity and society.

Nonfiction: Children's/juvenile, gift book, illustrated book, reference, textbook, devotional journals. Subjects include religion, spirituality. Christian living, devotionals, prayer, women, youth, spiritual growth, Christian history, parenting, home school, biblical studies, science and faith, current events, marriage and family concerns, church life, pastoral helps, preaching, evangelism. "We are open to freelance submissions in all areas. Materials in these areas must be suited for an evangelical Christian readership." No poetry, biography or sermons. Query with SASE.

Fiction: Religious. "We publish fiction in all the main genres. We want not only a very good story, but also one that sets forth Christian values. Nothing that lacks a positive Christian emphasis (but do NOT preach, however); nothing that fails to sustain reader interest." Query with SASE.

Recent Title(s): *Payne Stewart: The Authorized Biography*, by Tracey Stewart (nonfiction); *To Live is Christ*, by Beth Moore; *In the Shadow of the Cross*, by Ray Pritchard.

[A] **BROADWAY BOOKS**, Doubleday Broadway Publishing Group, Random House, Inc., 1540 Broadway, New York NY 10036. (212)782-9000. Fax: (212)782-8338. Website: www.broadwaybooks.com. **Acquisitions:** Charles Conrad, vice president/executive editor (general nonfiction); Gerald Howard, vice president/editorial director (fiction/nonfiction); Jennifer Josephy, executive editor (cookbooks); Kristine Puopola (self-help, psychology, personal finance, health, wellness); Patricia Medved, senior editor (parenting); Becky Cole, editor (cultural criticism, humor); Ann Campbell, editor (psychology/self-help). Estab. 1995. Publishes hardcover and trade paperback originals and reprints.

O→ Broadway publishes general interest nonfiction and fiction for adults.

Nonfiction: Biography, cookbook, illustrated book, reference, General interest adult books. Subjects include business/economics, child guidance/parenting, contemporary culture, cooking/foods/nutrition, gay/lesbian, general nonfiction, government/politics, health/medicine, history, memoirs, money/finance, multicultural, New Age, psychology, sex, spirituality, sports, travel (narrative), women's issues/studies, current affairs, motivational/inspirational, popular culture, consumer reference, golf. *Agented submissions only.*

Fiction: Publishes a limited list of commercial literary fiction.

Recent Title(s): *The No Spin Zone*, by Bill O'Reilly; *A Long Strange Trip: The Inside History of the Grateful Dead*, by Dennis McNally.

[N] **BROOKS BOOKS**, 3720 N. Woodbridge Dr., Decatur IL 62526. (217)877-2966. E-mail: brooksbooks@q-com.com. Website: www.family-net.net/~brooksbooks. **Acquisitions:** Randy Brooks, editor (haiku poetry, tanka poetry). Publishes hardcover and trade paperback originals. **Publishes 3-5 titles/year. Receives 100 queries and 25 mss/year. 10% of books from first-time authors; 100% from unagented writers. Pays 10-15% royalty on retail price or makes outright purchase of $100-500.** Publishes book 16 months after acceptance of ms. Responds in 1 month to queries; 3 months to proposals; 6 months to mss. Book catalog for #10 SASE or online at website; ms guidelines for #10 SASE.

Imprints: High/Coo Press, Brooks Books.

O→ Brooks Books, formerly High/Coo Press, publishes English-language haiku books, chapbooks, magazines and bibliographies.

Poetry: Submit 10 sample poems.

Recent Title(s): *Amost Unseen: Selected Haiku of George Swede*, by George Swede; *Fresh Scent*, by Lee Gurga (both haiku).

Tips: "Our readers enjoy contemporary haiku based on the literary tradition of Japanese aesthetics (not 5-7-5 Internet jokes)."

BRYANT & DILLON PUBLISHERS, INC., 100 N. Wyoming Ave., S., Orange NJ 07079. (973)763-1470. Fax: (973)763-2533. E-mail: tatajb@aol.com. **Acquisitions:** James Bryant, editor (women's issues, film, photography). Estab. 1993. Publishes hardcover and trade paperback originals. **Publishes 8-10 titles/year. Receives 500 queries and 700 mss/year. 100% of books from first-time authors; 90% from unagented writers. Pays 6-10% royalty on retail price. Offers advance.** Publishes book 1 year after acceptance of ms. Accepts simultaneous submissions. Responds in 3 months to proposals.

O→ Bryant & Dillon publishes books that speak to an African-American audience and others interested in the African-American experience.

Nonfiction: Biography, how-to, self-help. Subjects include business/economics, education, ethnic, film/cinema/stage, government/politics, history, language/literature, money/finance, women's issues/studies, Black studies, film. "Must be on subjects of interest to African-Americans." No poetry or children's books. Submit cover letter, author's information sheet, marketing information, outline and 3 sample chapters with SASE (envelope large enough for contents sent).

BUCKNELL UNIVERSITY PRESS, Lewisburg PA 17837. (570)577-3674. Fax: (570)577-3797. E-mail: clingham@bucknell.edu. Website: www.departments.bucknell.edu/univ_press. **Acquisitions:** Greg Clingham, director. Estab. 1969. Publishes hardcover originals. **Publishes 35-40 titles/year. Receives 400 submissions/year. 20% of books from first-time authors; 99% from unagented writers. Pays royalty.** Publishes book 12-18 months after acceptance of ms. Does not accept simultaneous submissions. Responds in 1 month to queries. Book catalog free.

- "In all fields, our criteria are scholarly excellence, critical originality, and interdisciplinary and theoretical expertise and sensitivity."

Nonfiction: Scholarly. Subjects include art/architecture, history, language/literature, philosophy, religion, sociology, English and American literary criticism, literary theory and cultural studies, historiography (including the history of law, medicine and science), art history, modern languages, classics, anthropology, ethnology, cultural and political geography. Series: Bucknell Studies in Eighteenth-Century Literature and Culture, Bucknell Studies in Latin American Literature and Theory, Eighteenth-Century Scotland. Biannual Journal: *The Bucknell Review: A Scholarly Journal of Letters, Arts, and Science.* Query with SASE.
Recent Title(s): *Presenting Gender: Changing Sex in Early-Modern Culture*, edited by Chris Mounsey; *Poetic Exhibitions: Poetry, Aesthetics, and the Pleasures of the British Museum*, by Eric Gidal; *Encounters Across Borders: The Changing Visions of Spanish Modernism, 1890-1930*, by Mary Lee Bretz.
Tips: "An original work of high-quality scholarship has the best chance. We publish for the scholarly community."

BULFINCH PRESS, AOL Time Warner Book Group, Time Life Building, 1271 Avenue of the Americas, 11th Floor, New York NY 10020. (212)522-8700. Website: www.bulfinchpress.com. Publisher: Jill Cohen. **Acquisitions:** Emily Martin, department assistant. Publishes hardcover and trade paperback originals. **Publishes 60-70 titles/year. Receives 500 queries/year. Pays variable royalty on wholesale price. Offers variable advance.** Publishes book 18 months after acceptance of ms. Accepts simultaneous submissions. Responds in 2 months to proposals.

- Bulfinch Press publishes large format art books.

Nonfiction: Coffee table book, gift book, illustrated book. Subjects include art/architecture, gardening, photography, interior design, lifestyle. Query with SASE or submit outline, sample artwork. Reviews artwork/photos as part of ms package. Send color photocopies or laser prints.
Recent Title(s): *Portraits*, by Mario Testino; *Earthly Bodies*, by Iving Penn; *Wise Women*, by Joyce Tenneson.

THE BUREAU FOR AT-RISK YOUTH, P.O. Box 760, Plainview NY 11803-0760. (516)349-5520. Fax: (516)349-5521. E-mail: info@at-risk.com. Website: www.at-risk.com. **Acquisitions:** Sally Germain, editor-in-chief. Estab. 1988. **Publishes 25-50 titles/year. Receives hundreds submissions/year. 100% from unagented writers. Pays 10% maximum royalty on selling price. Offers variable advance.** Publishes book 1 year after acceptance of ms. Accepts simultaneous submissions. Responds in 8 months to queries. Book catalog free if appropriate after communication with author.

- Publishes materials on youth guidance topics, such as drugs and violence prevention, character education and life skills for young people in grades K-12, and the educators, parents, mental health and juvenile justice professionals who work with them. "We prefer a workbook/activity book, curriculum, or book/booklet series format."

Nonfiction: Educational materials for parents, educators and other professionals who work with youth. Booklets. Subjects include child guidance/parenting, education. "The materials we publish are curriculum, book series, workbook/activity books or how-to-oriented pieces tailored to our audience. They are generally not single book titles and our series are rarely book length." Query with SASE.
Recent Title(s): *Youthlink: Developing Effective Mentoring Programs Curriculum*, by Dr. Nathan Avani.
Tips: "Publications are sold through direct mail catalogs and Internet. Writers whose expertise is a fit with our customers' interests should send query or proposals since we tailor everything very specifically to meet our audience's needs."

BURFORD BOOKS, P.O. Box 388, Short Hills NJ 07078. (973)258-0960. Fax: (973)258-0113. **Acquisitions:** Peter Burford, publisher. Estab. 1997. Publishes hardcover originals, trade paperback originals and reprints. **Publishes 25 titles/year. Receives 300 queries and 200 mss/year. 30% of books from first-time authors; 60% from unagented writers. Pays royalty on wholesale price.** Publishes book 18 months after acceptance of ms. Accepts simultaneous submissions. Responds in 1 month to queries; 1 month to proposals; 2 months to mss. Book catalog and ms guidelines free.

- Burford Books publishes books on all aspects of the outdoors, from gardening to sports, practical and literary.

Nonfiction: How-to, illustrated book. Subjects include agriculture/horticulture, animals, cooking/foods/nutrition, gardening, hobbies, military/war, nature/environment, recreation, sports, travel. Query with SASE or submit outline. Reviews artwork/photos as part of ms package. Send photocopies.
Recent Title(s): *Crossing the Saver: A Memoir of World War II*, by Charles Felix; *Saltwater Fly Fishing*, by Mike Starke.

BUTTE PUBLICATIONS, INC., P.O. Box 1328, Hillsboro OR 97123-1328. (503)648-9791. Fax: (503)693-9526. Website: www.buttepublications.com. **Acquisitions:** M. Brink, president. Estab. 1992. **Publishes 6-8 titles/year. Re-**

ceives 30 queries and 20 mss/year. 50% of books from first-time authors; 100% from unagented writers. Pays 8-12% royalty on net receipts.** Publishes book 1 year after acceptance of ms. Accepts simultaneous submissions. Responds in (usually) 1 month to queries; 4 months to proposals; 6 months to mss. Book catalog and ms guidelines for #10 SASE or online.

O→ Butte publishes classroom books related to deafness and language.

Nonfiction: Children's/juvenile, textbook. Subjects include education (all related to field of deafness and education). Submit proposal package, including author bio, synopsis, market survey and complete ms, if completed. Reviews artwork/photos as part of ms package. Send photocopies.

Recent Title(s): *Myths*, by Paris and Tracy; *Lessons in Syntax*, by McCarr; *El Jardin Silencioso*, by Ogden.

Tips: "Audience is students, teachers, parents and professionals in the arena dealing with deafness and hearing loss. We are not seeking autobiographies or novels."

BUTTERWORTH-HEINEMANN, Reed-Elsevier (USA) Inc., 225 Wildwood Ave., Woburn MA 01801-2041. (800)470-1199. Fax: (781)904-2640. Website: www.bh.com. **Acquisitions:** Jim DeWolf, vice president of technical publishing (engineering, electronics, computing, media and visual, security); Tricia Tyler, publisher (Focal Press); Theron Shreve, publisher (Digital Press); Susan Pioli, publishing director (Medical); Mark Listewnik, associate acquisitions editor (Security). Estab. 1975. Publishes hardcover and trade paperback originals. **Publishes 150 titles/year; imprint publishes 25-30 titles/year. 25% of books from first-time authors; 95% from unagented writers. Pays 10-12% royalty on wholesale price. Offers modest advance.** Publishes book 9 months after acceptance of ms. Responds in 1 month to proposals. Book catalog free; ms guidelines free.

Imprints: Butterworth-Heinemann (engineering, medical, security and criminal justice, business), Medical, Digital Press (computing), Focal Press (media and visual technology), Newnes (electronics), Security & Criminal Justice.

O→ Butterworth-Heinemann publishes technical professional and academic books in technology, medicine and business; no fiction.

Nonfiction: How-to (in our selected areas), reference, technical, textbook. Subjects include business/economics, computers/electronic, health/medicine, photography, science, Security/criminal justice, Audio-video broadcast, Communication technology. Query with SASE or submit outline, 1-2 sample chapter(s), Competing books and how yours is different/better. Reviews artwork/photos as part of ms package. Send photocopies.

Tips: Butterworth-Heinemann has been serving professionals and students for over five decades. "We remain committed to publishing materials that forge ahead of rapidly changing technology and reinforce the highest professional standards. Our goal is to give you the competitive advantage in this rapidly changing digital age."

C&T PUBLISHING, 1651 Challenge Dr., Concord CA 94520. (925)677-0377. Fax: (925)677-0374. E-mail: ctinfo@ctpub.com. Website: www.ctpub.com. **Acquisitions:** Jan Grigsby, editor. Estab. 1983. Publishes hardcover and trade paperback originals. **Publishes 32 titles/year. Receives 120 submissions/year. 20% of books from first-time authors; 100% from unagented writers. Pays 5-10% royalty on retail price.** Accepts simultaneous submissions. Responds in 3 months to queries. Book catalog and proposal guidelines free.

O→ "C&T publishes well-written, beautifully designed books on quilting, dollmaking, fiber arts and ribbonwork."

Nonfiction: How-to (quilting), illustrated book. Subjects include art/architecture, hobbies, quilting books, primarily how-to, occasional quilt picture books, quilt-related crafts, wearable art, needlework, fiber and surface embellishments, other books relating to fabric crafting. "Please call or write for proposal guidelines." Extensive proposal guidelines are also available on their website.

Recent Title(s): *Laurel Burch Quilts*, by Laurel Burch; *Machine Embroidery and More*, by Kristen Dibbs.

Tips: "In our industry, we find that how-to books have the longest selling life. Quiltmakers, sewing enthusiasts, needle artists and fiber artists are our audience. We like to see new concepts or techniques. Include some great examples and you'll get our attention quickly. Dynamic design is hard to resist, and if that's your forte, show us what you've done."

CADENCE JAZZ BOOKS, Cadence Building, Redwood NY 13679. (315)287-2852. Fax: (315)287-2860. E-mail: cjb@cadencebuilding.com. Website: www.cadencebuilding.com. **Acquisitions:** Bob Rusch, Carl Ericson. Estab. 1992. Publishes trade paperback and mass market paperback originals. **Publishes 5-10 titles/year. 90% of books from first-time authors; 100% from unagented writers. Pays royalty or makes outright purchase. Offers advance.** Publishes book 6 months after acceptance of ms. Responds in 1 month to queries.

O→ Cadence publishes jazz histories and discographies.

Nonfiction: Biography, reference. Subjects include music/dance, jazz music biographies, discographies and reference works. Submit outline, sample chapter(s), SASE. Reviews artwork/photos as part of ms package. Send photocopies.

Recent Title(s): *The Earthly Recordings of Sun Ra*, by Robert L. Campbell (discography).

CAMINO BOOKS, INC., P.O. Box 59026, Philadelphia PA 19102. (215)413-1917. Fax: (215)413-3255. Website: www.caminobooks.com. **Acquisitions:** E. Jutkowitz, publisher. Estab. 1987. Publishes hardcover and trade paperback originals. **Publishes 8 titles/year. Receives 500 submissions/year. 20% of books from first-time authors. Pays 6-12% royalty on net receipts. Offers $1,000 average advance.** Publishes book 1 year after acceptance of ms. Responds in 2 weeks to queries.

O→ Camino publishes nonfiction of regional interest to the Mid-Atlantic states.

Nonfiction: Biography, children's/juvenile, cookbook, how-to. Subjects include agriculture/horticulture, Americana, art/architecture, child guidance/parenting, cooking/foods/nutrition, ethnic, gardening, government/politics, history, regional, travel. Query with SASE or submit outline, sample chapter(s).

Tips: "The books must be of interest to readers in the Middle Atlantic states, or they should have a clearly defined niche, such as cookbooks."

CANDLEWICK PRESS, 2067 Massachusetts Ave., Cambridge MA 02140. (617)661-3330. Fax: (617)661-0565. Website: www.candlewick.com. President/Publisher: Karen Lotz. **Acquisitions:** Yolanda Leroy, editor (picture books, nonfiction); Jamie Michalak, associate editor; Joan Powers, editorial director (novelty); Liz Bicknell, editorial director/associate publisher (poetry, picture books, fiction); Mary Lee Donovan, executive editor (picture books, fiction); Kara LaReau, editor; Cynthia Platt, editor (nonfiction). Estab. 1991. Publishes hardcover originals, trade paperback originals and reprints. **Publishes 200 titles/year. Receives 12,000-15,000 submissions/year. 5% of books from first-time authors; 40% from unagented writers. Pays 10% royalty on retail price. Offers varying advance.** Publishes book 1-3 years after acceptance of ms. Accepts simultaneous submissions. Responds in 10 weeks to mss.

O→ Candlewick Press publishes high-quality, illustrated children's books for ages infant through young adult. "We are a truly child-centered publisher."

Nonfiction: Children's/juvenile. "Good writing is essential; specific topics are less important than strong, clear writing."

Fiction: Juvenile, picture books.

Recent Title(s): *It's So Amazing*, by Robie Harris, illustrated by Michael Emberley (nonfiction); *Because of Winn-Dixie*, by Kate DiCamillo (Newberry Honor Winner); *A Poke in the I*, selected by Paul B. Janeczko, illustrated by Chris Raschko (collection of concrete poems).

Tips: "We no longer accept unsolicited mss. See our website for further information about us."

[N] **CAPITAL BOOKS**, 22841 Quicksilver Dr., Dulles VA 20166. (703)661-1533. Fax: (703)661-1547. E-mail: jennifer@booksintl.com. Website: www.capital-books.com. **Acquisitions:** Kathleen Hughes, publisher (self-help, memoirs); Noemi Taylor, acquisitions editor (travel, pets, cooking); Judy Karpinski, senior acquisitions editor (business, health). Estab. 1998. Publishes hardcover, trade paperback, mass market paperback and electronic originals, and trade paperback and mass market paperback reprints. **Publishes 50 titles/year. Receives 200 queries and 200 mss/year. 80% of books from first-time authors; 65% from unagented writers. Pays 1-10% royalty on retail price. Offers $1,000-5,000 advance.** Publishes book 9 months after acceptance of ms. Accepts simultaneous submissions. Responds in 1 month to queries; 2 months to proposals; 3 months to mss. Book catalog and ms guidelines free.

Nonfiction: Autobiography, biography, cookbook, gift book, how-to, reference, self-help. Subjects include animals, art/architecture, business/economics, child guidance/parenting, computers/electronic, contemporary culture, cooking/foods/nutrition, gardening, general nonfiction, health/medicine, memoirs, money/finance, multicultural, nature/environment, psychology, regional, social sciences, software, travel, women's issues/studies. "Capital appreciates good self-help, memoirs and lifestyle books." No religious titles. Submit proposal package including outline, 3 sample chapter(s), Query Letter. Reviews artwork/photos as part of ms package. Send photocopies.

Recent Title(s): *Pardon Me*, by Denise Rich (memoir); *Rivers of a Wounded Heart*, by Michael Wilbur (self-help).

Tips: "Our audience is comprised of enthusiastic readers who look to books for answers and information. Do not send fiction or religious titles. Please tell us how you, the author, can help market and sell the book."

CAPSTONE PRESS, P.O. Box 669, Mankato MN 56002. (507)388-6650. Fax: (507)625-4662. Website: www.capstone-press.com. **Acquisitions:** Helen Moore, product planning editor (nonfiction for students grades K-12). Publishes hardcover originals. **Publishes 300-350 titles/year. Receives 100 queries/year. 5% of books from first-time authors. Makes outright purchase; payment varies by imprint. Offers advance.** Responds in 3 months to queries. Book catalog online.

Imprints: Capstone Books, Blue Earth Books, Bridgestone Books, Pebble Books, A+ Books, LifeMatters.

O→ Capstone publishes nonfiction children's books for schools and libraries.

Nonfiction: Children's/juvenile. Subjects include Americana, animals, child guidance/parenting, cooking/foods/nutrition, health/medicine, history, military/war, multicultural, nature/environment, recreation, science, sports. "We do not accept proposals or manuscripts. Authors interested in writing for Capstone Press can request an author's brochure." Query with SASE.

Recent Title(s): *Extreme Bicycle Stunt Riding Moves*, by Danny Parr; *Sacagawea*, by Barbara Witteman.

Tips: Audience is made up of elementary, middle school, and high school students who are just learning how to read, who are experiencing reading difficulties, or who are learning English. Capstone Press does not publish unsolicited mss submitted by authors, and it rarely entertains proposals. Instead, Capstone hires freelance authors to write on nonfiction topics selected by the company. Authors may send an SASE to request a brochure.

THE CAREER PRESS, INC., Box 687, 3 Tice Rd., Franklin Lakes NJ 07417. (201)848-0310. Fax: (201)848-1727. Website: www.careerpress.com. President: Ronald Fry. **Acquisitions:** Michael Lewis, senior acquisitions editor. Estab. 1985. Publishes hardcover and paperback originals. **Publishes 70 titles/year. Receives 300 queries and 1,000 mss/year. 10% of books from first-time authors; 10% from unagented writers. Offers advance.** Publishes book up to 6 months after acceptance of ms. Accepts simultaneous submissions.

Imprints: New Page Books (www.newpagebooks.com).

O→ Career Press publishes books for adult readers seeking practical information to improve themselves in careers, college, finance, parenting, retirement, motivation and other related topics, as well as management philosophy titles for a small business and management audience. New Page Books publishes practical books in the areas of New Age, health, self-help, reference, and weddings/entertaining. Currently de-emphasizing Judaica.

Nonfiction: How-to, reference, self-help. Subjects include business/economics, money/finance, recreation, nutrition. "Look through our catalog; become familiar with our publications. We like to select authors who are specialists on their topic." Query with SASE or submit outline, 1-2 sample chapter(s), intro, author bio.
Recent Title(s): *Inc. Yourself, 10th Ed.*, by Judith H. McQuown; *Wicca Spellcraft for Men*, by A.J. Drew.

CAROLRHODA BOOKS, INC., Lerner Publishing Group, 241 First Ave. N., Minneapolis MN 55401. (612)332-3344. *No phone calls*. Fax: (612)332-7615. Website: www.lernerbooks.com. **Acquisitions:** Rebecca Poole, submissions editor. Estab. 1969. **Publishes 50-60 titles/year. Receives 2,000 submissions/year. 10% of books from first-time authors; 90% from unagented writers. Offers varied advance.** Does not accept simultaneous submissions. Book catalog for 9×12 SAE with $3.50 postage; ms guidelines for #10 SASE.

- Accepts submissions from March 1-31 and October 1-31 only. Submission received at other times of the year will be returned to sender.

O→ Carolrhoda Books is a children's publisher focused on producing high-quality, socially conscious nonfiction and fiction books with unique and well-developed ideas and angles for young readers that help them learn about and explore the world around them.

Nonfiction: Carolrhoda Books seeks creative children's nonfiction. Biography. Subjects include ethnic, nature/environment, science. "We are always interested in adding to our biography series. Books on the natural and hard sciences are also of interest." Query with SASE. Reviews artwork/photos as part of ms package. Send photocopies.
Fiction: Historical, juvenile, picture books, young reader fiction. Query with SASE, send complete ms for picture books.
Recent Title(s): *The War*, by Anais Vaugelade; *Little Wolf's Haunted Hall for Small Horrors*, by Ian Whybrow.
Tips: Carolrhoda does not publish alphabet books, puzzle books, songbooks, textbooks, workbooks, religious subject matter or plays.

[A] **CARROLL & GRAF PUBLISHERS INC.**, Avalon Publishing Group, 161 William St., New York NY 10038. (646)375-2570. Fax: (646)375-2571. Website: www.avalonpub.com. **Acquisitions:** Herman Graf, publisher; Phillip Turner, executive editor; Tina Pohlman, senior editor. Estab. 1982. Publishes hardcover and trade paperback originals. **Publishes 120 titles/year. 10% of books from first-time authors. Pays 10-15% royalty on retail price for hardcover, 6-7½% for paperback. Offers advance commensurate with the work.** Publishes book 9-18 months after acceptance of ms. Responds in a timely fashion to queries. Book catalog free.

O→ Carroll and Graf Publishers offers quality fiction and nonfiction for a general readership.

Nonfiction: Publish general trade books; interested in developing long term relations with authors. Biography, reference, self-help. Subjects include business/economics, contemporary culture, health/medicine, history, memoirs, military/war, psychology, sports, true crime, adventure/exploration. *Agented submissions only.*
Fiction: Literary, mystery, suspense, thriller. *Agented submissions only.*
Recent Title(s): *The Last Battle: The Mayaguez Incident and the End of the Vietnam War*, by Ralph Wetterhahn; *According to Queeney*, by Beryl Bainbridge; *Places to Look for a Mother*, by Nicole Stansbury.

[★] **CARSON-DELLOSA PUBLISHING CO., INC.**, P.O. Box 35665, Greensboro NC 27425-5665. (336)632-0084. Fax: (336)632-0087. Website: www.carson-dellosa.com. **Acquisitions:** Wolfgang D. Hoelscher, senior editor. **Publishes 20-30 titles/year. Receives 100 submissions/year. 50% of books from first-time authors; 95% from unagented writers. Makes outright purchase.** Accepts simultaneous submissions. Responds in 2 months to proposals. Book catalog online; ms guidelines free.
Nonfiction: We publish supplementary educational materials, such as teacher resource books, workbooks, and activity books. Subjects include education. No textbooks or trade children's books, please. Submit proposal package including sample chapters or pages, SASE. Reviews artwork/photos as part of ms package. Send photocopies.
Tips: "Our audience consists of pre-K through 8 educators, parents and students. Ask for our submission guidelines and a catalog before you send us your materials. We do not publish fiction or nonfiction storybooks."

CARSTENS PUBLICATIONS, INC., Hobby Book Division, P.O. Box 700, Newton NJ 07860-0700. (973)383-3355. Fax: (973)383-4064. Website: www.carstens-publications.com. **Acquisitions:** Harold H. Carstens, publisher. Estab. 1933. Publishes paperback originals. **Publishes 8 titles/year. 100% from unagented writers. Pays 10% royalty on retail price. Offers advance.** Publishes book 1 year after acceptance of ms. Responds in 2 months to queries. Book catalog for #10 SASE.

O→ Carstens specializes in books about railroads, model railroads and airplanes for hobbyists.

Nonfiction: Subjects include hobbies, model railroading, toy trains, model aviation, railroads and model hobbies. "Authors must know their field intimately because our readers are active modelers. Writers cannot write about somebody else's hobby with authority. If they do, we can't use them. Our railroad books presently are primarily photographic essays on specific railroads." Query with SASE. Reviews artwork/photos as part of ms package.
Recent Title(s): *150 Years of Train Models*, by Harold H. Carstens; *B&O Thunder on the Alleghenies*, by Dean Mellander.
Tips: "We need lots of good photos. Material must be in model, hobby, railroad and transportation field only."

[A] **CARTWHEEL BOOKS**, Scholastic, Inc., 557 Broadway, New York NY 10012. (212)343-6200. Website: www.scholastic.com. Vice President/Editorial Director: Ken Geist. **Acquisitions:** Grace Maccarone, executive editor; Sonia Black, senior editor; Jane Gerver, executive editor. Estab. 1991. Publishes novelty books, easy readers, board books, hardcover and trade paperback originals. **Publishes 85-100 titles/year. Receives 250 queries and 1,200 mss/year. Pays royalty on retail price or flat fee. Offers advance.** Publishes book 2 years after acceptance of ms. Accepts simultaneous submissions. Responds in 1-4 months to queries; 6 months to mss.

O→ Cartwheel Books publishes innovative books for children, up to age 8. "We are looking for 'novelties' that are books first, play objects second. Even without its gimmick, a Cartwheel Book should stand alone as a valid piece of children's literature."

Nonfiction: Children's/juvenile. Subjects include animals, history, music/dance, nature/environment, recreation, science, sports. "Cartwheel Books publishes for the very young, therefore nonfiction should be written in a manner that is accessible to preschoolers through 2nd grade. Often writers choose topics that are too narrow or 'special' and do not appeal to the mass market. Also, the text and vocabulary are frequently too difficult for our young audience." *Agented submissions only.* Reviews artwork/photos as part of ms package. Please do not send original artwork.

Fiction: Humor, juvenile, mystery, picture books. "Again, the subject should have mass market appeal for very young children. Humor can be helpful, but not necessary. Mistakes writers make are a reading level that is too difficult, a topic of no interest or too narrow, or manuscripts that are too long." *Agented submissions only.*

Tips: Audience is young children, ages 3-9. "Know what types of books the publisher does. Some manuscripts that don't work for one house may be perfect for another. Check out bookstores or catalogs to see where your writing would 'fit' best."

CATBIRD PRESS, 16 Windsor Rd., North Haven CT 06473-3015. Website: www.catbirdpress.com. **Acquisitions:** Robert Wechsler, publisher. Estab. 1987. Publishes hardcover and trade paperback originals and trade paperback reprints. **Publishes 4-5 titles/year. Receives 1,000 submissions/year. 5% of books from first-time authors; 80% from unagented writers. Pays 10% royalty on retail price. Offers $2,000 average advance.** Publishes book 1 year after acceptance of ms. Accepts simultaneous submissions. Responds in 1 month to queries. Ms guidelines for #10 SASE or online at website.

Imprints: Garrigue Books (Czech works in translation).

O→ Catbird publishes sophisticated, humorous, literary fiction and nonfiction with fresh styles and approaches.

Nonfiction: Humor. Subjects include general nonfiction. "We are looking for up-market prose humorists. No joke, idea, anectdotes or small gift books. We are also interested in very well-written general nonfiction that takes fresh, sophisticated approaches." Submit outline, sample chapter(s), SASE.

Fiction: "We are looking for writers of well-written literature who have a comic vision, take a fresh approach, and have a non-naturalistic style." Humor, literary. No genre, wacky, or slice-of-life fiction. Submit outline, sample chapter(s), SASE.

Recent Title(s): *Labor Day*, by Floyd Kemske (fiction); *All His Sons*, by Frederic Raphael (fiction).

Tips: "First of all, we want writers, not books. Second, we are only interested in writing that is not like what is out there already. The writing should be highly sophisticated, but not obscure; the approach or, better, approaches should be fresh and surprising. Writers more interested in content than in style should look elsewhere."

CATHOLIC UNIVERSITY OF AMERICA PRESS, 620 Michigan Ave. NE, Washington DC 20064. (202)319-5052. Fax: (202)319-4985. E-mail: cua-press@cua.edu. Website: cuapress.cua.edu. **Acquisitions:** Dr. David J. McGonagle, director. Estab. 1939. **Publishes 20-25 titles/year. Receives 100 submissions/year. 50% of books from first-time authors; 100% from unagented writers. Pays variable royalty on net receipts.** Publishes book 2 years after acceptance of ms. Responds in 6 months to queries. Book catalog for #10 SASE.

O→ The Catholic University of America Press publishes in the fields of history (ecclesiastical and secular), literature and languages, philosophy, political theory, social studies, and theology. "We have interdisciplinary emphasis on patristics, medieval studies and Irish studies. Our principal interest is in works of original scholarship intended for scholars and other professionals and for academic libraries, but we will also consider manuscripts whose chief contribution is to offer a synthesis of knowledge of the subject which may be of interest to a wider audience or suitable for use as supplementary reading material in courses."

Nonfiction: Scholarly. Subjects include government/politics, history, language/literature, philosophy, religion, Church-state relations. No unrevised doctoral dissertations. Length: 80,000-200,000 words. Query with outline, sample chapter, cv and list of previous publications.

Recent Title(s): *Mediapolitik: How the Mass Media Have Transformed World Politics*, by Lee Edwards.

Tips: "Scholarly monographs and works suitable for adoption as supplementary reading material in courses have the best chance."

CATO INSTITUTE, 1000 Massachusetts Ave. NW, Washington DC 20001. (202)842-0200. Website: www.cato.org. **Acquisitions:** Gene Healy, senior editor. Estab. 1977. Publishes hardcover originals, trade paperback originals and reprints. **Publishes 12 titles/year. Receives 50 submissions/year. 25% of books from first-time authors; 90% from unagented writers. Makes outright purchase of $1,000-10,000. Offers advance.** Publishes book 9 months after acceptance of ms. Accepts simultaneous submissions. Responds in 3 months to queries. Book catalog free.

O→ Cato Institute publishes books on public policy issues from a free-market or libertarian perspective.

Nonfiction: Scholarly. Subjects include business/economics, education, government/politics, health/medicine, money/finance, sociology, public policy, foreign policy, monetary policy. Query with SASE.

Recent Title(s): *After Prohibition: An Adult Approach to Drug Policies*, by Lynch; *Global Fortune: The Stumble & Rise of World Capitalism*, by Vasquez.

CAVE BOOKS, 756 Harvard Ave,, St. Louis MO 63130-3134. (314)862-7646. **Acquisitions:** Richard Watson, editor. Estab. 1980. Publishes hardcover and trade paperback originals and reprints. **Publishes 2 titles/year. Receives 20 queries and 10 mss/year. 75% of books from first-time authors; 100% from unagented writers. Pays 10% royalty on retail price.** Publishes book 18 months after acceptance of ms. Accepts simultaneous submissions. Responds in 3 months to mss.

O→ Cave Books publishes books only on caves, karst and speleology.

Nonfiction: Biography, technical (science), adventure. Subjects include Americana, animals, anthropology/archeology, history, nature/environment, photography, recreation, regional, science, sports (cave exploration), travel. Submit complete ms. Reviews artwork/photos as part of ms package. Send photocopies.

Fiction: "Must be realistic and centrally concerned with cave exploration. The cave and action in the cave must be central, authentic, and realistic." Adventure, historical, literary. No gothic, science fiction, fantasy, romance, mystery or poetry. No novels that are not entirely about caves. Submit complete ms.

Recent Title(s): *The Life and Death of Floyd Collins*, by Homer Collins.

Tips: "Our readers are interested only in caves, karst and speleology. Please do not send manuscripts on other subjects."

CAXTON PRESS, 312 Main St., Caldwell ID 83605-3299. (208)459-7421. Fax: (208)459-7450. Website: caxtonpress.com. President: Scott Gipson. **Acquisitions:** Wayne Cornell, managing acquisitions editor (Western Americana, regional nonfiction). Estab. 1907. Publishes hardcover and trade paperback originals. **Publishes 6-10 titles/year. Receives 250/year submissions/year. 50% of books from first-time authors; 60% from unagented writers. Pays royalty. Offers advance.** Publishes book 18 months after acceptance of ms. Accepts simultaneous submissions. Responds in 3 months to queries. Book catalog for 9×12 SAE.

O→ "Western Americana nonfiction remains our focus. We define Western Americana as almost any topic that deals with the people or culture of the west, past and present." Currently emphasizing regional issues—primarily Pacific Northwest. De-emphasizing "coffee table" or photographic intensive books.

Nonfiction: Biography, children's/juvenile, cookbook, scholarly. Subjects include Americana, history, regional. "We need good Western Americana, especially the Northwest, emphasis on serious, narrative nonfiction." Query. Reviews artwork/photos as part of ms package.

Recent Title(s): *Rotting Face: Smallpox & the American Indian*, by R.G. Robertson; *Colorado Treasure Tales*, by W.C. Jameson; *Our Native American Legacy*, by Sandra Nestor.

Tips: "Books to us never can or will be primarily articles of merchandise to be produced as cheaply as possible and to be sold like slabs of bacon or packages of cereal over the counter. If there is anything that is really worthwhile in this mad jumble we call the twenty-first century, it should be books."

CCC PUBLICATIONS, LLC, 9725 Lurline Ave., Chatsworth CA 91311. (818)718-0507. **Acquisitions:** Cliff Carle, editorial director. Estab. 1983. Publishes trade paperback originals. **Publishes 40 titles/year. Receives 1,000 mss/year. 30% of books from first-time authors; 50% from unagented writers. Pays 8-12% royalty on wholesale price. Offers variable advance.** Publishes book 6 months after acceptance of ms. Accepts simultaneous submissions. Responds in 3 months to queries. Book catalog for 10×13 SAE with 2 first-class stamps.

O→ CCC publishes humor that is "today" and will appeal to a wide demographic. Currently emphasizing "short, punchy pieces with *lots* of cartoon illustrations, or very well-written text if long form."

Nonfiction: How-to, humor, self-help. "We are looking for *original*, *clever* and *current* humor that is not too limited in audience appeal or that will have a limited shelf life. All of our titles are as marketable five years from now as they are today. No rip-offs of previously published books, or too special interest manuscripts." Query with SASE or submit complete ms. Reviews artwork/photos as part of ms package.

Recent Title(s): *If Men Had Babies. . .*, by Karen Rostoker-Gruber.

Tips: "Humor—we specialize in the subject and have a good reputation with retailers and wholesalers for publishing super-impulse titles. SASE is a must!"

CELESTIAL ARTS, Ten Speed Press, P.O. Box 7123, Berkeley CA 94707. (510)559-1600. Fax: (510)524-1052. **Acquisitions:** Jo Ann Deck, publisher; Veronica Randall, managing editor/interim publisher. Estab. 1966. Publishes hardcover and trade paperback originals, trade paperback reprints. **Publishes 40 titles/year. Receives 500 queries and 200 mss/year. 30% of books from first-time authors; 10% from unagented writers. Pays 15% royalty on wholesale price. Offers modest advance.** Accepts simultaneous submissions. Responds in 6 weeks to queries. Book catalog and ms guidelines free.

O→ Celestial Arts publishes nonfiction for a forward-thinking, open-minded audience interested in psychology, self-help, spirituality, health and parenting.

Nonfiction: Cookbook, how-to, reference, self-help. Subjects include child guidance/parenting, cooking/foods/nutrition, education, gay/lesbian, health/medicine, New Age, psychology, women's issues/studies. "We specialize in parenting, women's issues and health. On gay/lesbian topics, we publish nonfiction only. And please, no poetry!" Submit proposal package including outline, 1-2 sample chapter(s), author bio, SASE. Reviews artwork/photos as part of ms package. Send photocopies.

Recent Title(s): *Uncommon Sense for Parents with Teenagers*, by Mike Riera.

Tips: Audience is fairly well-informed, interested in psychology and sociology-related topics, open-minded, innovative, forward-thinking. "The most completely thought-out (developed) proposals earn the most consideration."

CHALICE PRESS, P.O. Box 179, St. Louis MO 63166. (314)231-8500. Fax: (314)231-8524. E-mail: chalice@cbp21.com. **Acquisitions:** Dr. David P. Polk, editor-in-chief (religion: general); Dr. Jon L. Berquist, senior academic editor (religion: academic); Ulrike Guthrie, academic editor (religion: academic). Publishes hardcover and trade paperback originals. **Publishes 50 titles/year. Receives 500 queries and 400 mss/year. 15% of books from first-time authors; 100% from unagented writers. Pays 14-18% royalty on wholesale price.** Publishes book 1 year after acceptance of ms. Accepts simultaneous submissions. Responds in 1 month to queries; 2 months to proposals; 3 months to mss. Book catalog and ms guidelines free or online.

Nonfiction: Textbook. Subjects include religion, spirituality. Submit proposal package including outline, 1-2 sample chapter(s).

Recent Title(s): *Sacred Acts, Holy Change*, by Eric H. F. Law.

Tips: "We publish for both professional and lay Christian readers."

CHARISMA HOUSE, Strang Communications, 600 Rinehart Rd., Lake Mary FL 32746. (407)333-0600. **Acquisitions:** Sandra Danielson, acquisitions assistant. Publishes hardcover and trade paperback originals. **Publishes 40-50 titles/year. Receives 600 mss/year. 2% of books from first-time authors; 95% from unagented writers. Pays 4-18% royalty on retail price. Offers $1,500-5,000 advance.** Publishes book 9 months after acceptance of ms. Accepts simultaneous submissions. Allow 6-8 months for review to proposals. Ms guidelines for #10 SASE.

Imprints: Siloam Press (emphasizing healthy living in mind, body and spirit)

> O→ "Charisma House publishes books for the Pentecostal/Charismatic Christian market to inspire and equip people to live a Spirit-led life and to walk in the divine purpose for which they were created. We are interested in fiction but have not yet begun a fiction line."

Nonfiction: Biography, cookbook, gift book, self-help. Subjects include child guidance/parenting, cooking/foods/nutrition, health/medicine, religion (Christian), sex, spirituality (charismatic), women's issues/studies, spirit-filled interest. Request guidelines to receive Project Appraisal Form Questionnaire.

Recent Title(s): *Gatekeeper*, by Terry Craig (fiction); *Bible Cure*, by Don Colbert (nonfiction booklets).

Tips: "For all book submission requests, we send a Project Appraisal Questionnaire Form to all who want to submit a manuscript. They must complete and return the form. This allows a thorough review without weeding through excess information."

THE CHARLES PRESS, PUBLISHERS, 117 S. 17th St., Suite 310, Philadelphia PA 19103. (215)496-9616. Fax: (215)496-9637. E-mail: mailbox@charlespresspub.com. Website: www.charlespresspub.com. **Acquisitions:** Lauren Meltzer, publisher. Estab. 1982. Publishes hardcover and trade paperback originals. **Publishes 10-16 titles/year. Receives 1,500 queries and 500 mss/year. Pays 7½-12% royalty. Advances commensurate with first year sales potential.** Publishes book 4-12 months after acceptance of ms. Accepts simultaneous submissions. Responds in 1 month to queries; 2 months to proposals; 3 months to mss. Book catalog online; ms guidelines online.

> O→ Currently emphasizing true crime, criminology, psychology (including suicide, anger and violence).

Nonfiction: Subjects include child guidance/parenting, health/medicine (allied), psychology, counseling, criminology, true crime. No fiction or poetry. Query or submit proposal package, including description of book, intended audience, reasons people will buy it and SASE. Reviews artwork/photos as part of ms package. Send photocopies or transparencies.

Recent Title(s): *The Golden Age of Medical Science and the Dark Age of Healthcare Delivery*, by Sylvan Weinberg, M.D.

CHARLES RIVER MEDIA, 20 Downer Ave., Suite 3, Hingham MA 02043-1132. (781)740-0400. Fax: (781)740-8816. E-mail: info@charlesriver.com. Website: www.charlesriver.com. **Acquisitions:** David Pallai, president (networking, Internet related); Jennifer Niles, publisher (computer graphics, animation, game programming). Publishes hardcover and trade paperback originals. **Publishes 50 titles/year. Receives 1,000 queries and 250 mss/year. 20% of books from first-time authors; 90% from unagented writers. Pays 5-30% royalty on wholesale price. Offers $3,000-20,000 advance.** Publishes book 4 months after acceptance of ms. Accepts simultaneous submissions. Responds in 1 month to queries. Book catalog for #10 SASE; ms guidelines online.

> O→ "Our publishing program concentrates on 3 major areas: Internet, networking, and graphics. The majority of our titles are considered intermediate, not high level research monographs, and not for lowest-level general users."

Nonfiction: Multimedia (Win/Mac format), reference, technical. Subjects include computers/electronic. Query with SASE or submit proposal package including outline, 2 sample chapter(s), résumé. Reviews artwork/photos as part of ms package. Send photocopies or GIF, TIFF or PDF files.

Recent Title(s): *Game Programming Gems*, by Mark DeLoura; *Web Design and Development*, by Kelly Valqui.

Tips: "We are very receptive to detailed proposals by first-time or non-agented authors. Consult our website for proposal outlines. Manuscripts must be completed within 6 months of contract signing."

CHARLESBRIDGE PUBLISHING, School Division, 85 Main St., Watertown MA 02472. (617)926-0329. Fax: (617)926-5720. E-mail: schooleditorial@charlesbridge.com. Website: www.charlesbridge.com/school. **Acquisitions:** Elena Dworkin Wright, vice president school division. Estab. 1980. Publishes hardcover and trade paperback nonfiction children's picture books (80%) and fiction picture books for school programs and supplementary materials, trade bookstores, clubs and mass market. **Publishes 20 titles/year. Receives 2,500 submissions/year. 10-20% of books from first-time authors; 80% from unagented writers. Royalty and advance vary.** Publishes book 2 years after acceptance of ms.

O→ "We're looking for fiction and nonfiction with literary quality for children grades K-6 (ages 3-12)."

Nonfiction: Children's/juvenile, textbook. Subjects include education, multicultural, nature/environment, science. School or craft books that involve problem solving, building, projects, books written with humor and expertise in the field. Submit complete ms.

Fiction: Non-rhyming stories.

Recent Title(s): *The Ugly Vegetables*, written and illustrated by Grace Lin.; *Sir Cumference and the Great Knight of Angleland*, by Cindy Neuschwander.

CHARLESBRIDGE PUBLISHING, Trade Division, 85 Main St., Watertown MA 02472. (617)926-0329. Fax: (617)926-5720. E-mail: tradeeditorial@charlesbridge.com. Website: www.charlesbridge.com. **Acquisitions:** Submission Editor. Estab. 1980. Publishes hardcover and trade paperback nonfiction children's picture picture books (80%) and fiction picture books for the trade and library markets. **Publishes 30 titles/year. Receives 2,500 submissions/year. 10-20% of books from first-time authors; 80% from unagented writers. Pays royalty. Offers advance.** Publishes book 2-4 years after acceptance of ms.

Imprints: Charlesbridge (8 nonfiction titles/season); Talewinds (2 fiction titles/season); Whispering Coyote (3 fiction titles/season)

O→ "We're always interested in innovative approaches to a difficult genre, the nonfiction picture book. No novels or books for older children." Currently emphasizing nature, science, multiculturalism.

Nonfiction: Children's/juvenile. Subjects include animals, creative nonfiction, history, multicultural, nature/environment, science, social science. Strong interest in nature, environment, social studies and other topics for trade and library markets. *Exclusive submissions only.*

Fiction: "Strong, realistic stories with enduring themes." *Exclusive submissions only.*

Recent Title(s): *Ice Cream*, by Jules Order, illustrated by Lyn Severance; *Billy's Big-Boy Bed*, by Phyllis Limbacher Tildes; *Too Young for Yiddish*, by Rich Michelson, illustrated by Neil Waldman.

CHATHAM PRESS, Box A, Greenwich CT 06870. **Acquisitions:** Jane Andrassi. Estab. 1971. Publishes hardcover and paperback originals, reprints and anthologies. **Publishes 10 titles/year. Receives 50 submissions/year. 25% of books from first-time authors; 75% from unagented writers.** Publishes book 6 months after acceptance of ms. Responds in 2 months to queries. Book catalog and ms guidelines for 6×9 SAE with 6 first-class stamps.

O→ Chatham Press publishes "books that relate to the U.S. coastline from Maine to the Carolinas and which bring a new insight, visual or verbal, to the nonfiction topic."

Nonfiction: Illustrated book. Subjects include history, nature/environment, regional (Northeast seaboard), translation (from French and German), natural history. Query with SASE. Reviews artwork/photos as part of ms package.

Recent Title(s): *Exploring Old Martha's Vineyard.*

Tips: "Illustrated New England-relevant titles have the best chance of being sold to our firm. We have a slightly greater (15%) skew towards cooking and travel titles."

CHELSEA GREEN PUBLISHING COMPANY, P.O. Box 428, #205 Gates-Briggs Bldg., White River Junction VT 05001-0428. (802)295-6300. Fax: (802)295-6444. Website: www.chelseagreen.com. **Acquisitions:** Alan Berolzheimer, acquisitions editor. Estab. 1984. Publishes hardcover and trade paperback originals and reprints. **Publishes 16-20 titles/year; imprint publishes 3-4 titles/year. Receives 300-400 queries and 200-300 mss/year. 30% of books from first-time authors; 80% from unagented writers. Pays royalty on publisher's net. Offers $2,500-10,000 advance.** Publishes book 18 months after acceptance of ms. Does not accept simultaneous submissions. Responds in 1 week to queries; 1 month to proposals; 1 month to mss. Book catalog and ms guidelines free or online.

Imprints: Real Goods Solar Living Book series.

O→ Chelsea Green publishes and distributes books relating to issues of sustainability with a special concentration on books about nature, the environment, independent living and enterprise, organic gardening, renewable energy and alternative or natural building techniques. The books reflect positive options in a world of environmental turmoil. Emphasizing food/agriculture/gardening, innovative shelter and natural building, renewable energy, sustainable business and enterprise. De-emphasizing nature/natural history.

Nonfiction: Biography, cookbook, how-to, reference, self-help, technical. Subjects include agriculture/horticulture, art/architecture, cooking/foods/nutrition, gardening, health/medicine, memoirs, money/finance, nature/environment, regional, forestry. Query with SASE or submit proposal package including outline, 1-2 sample chapter(s). Reviews artwork/photos as part of ms package.

Recent Title(s): *The Village Herbalist*, by Nancy and Michael Phillips; *This Organic Life*, by Joan Dye Gussow; *Gaia's Garden*, by Toby Henerway.

Tips: "Our readers are passionately enthusiastic about ecological solutions for contemporary challenges in construction, energy harvesting, agriculture and forestry. Our books are also carefully and handsomely produced to give pleasure to bibliophiles of a practical bent. It would be very helpful for prospective authors to have a look at several of our current books, as well as our catalog and website. For certain types of book, we are the perfect publisher, but we are exceedingly focused on particular areas."

CHELSEA HOUSE PUBLISHERS, Haights Cross Communications, 1974 Sproul Rd., Suite 400, Broomall PA 19008-0914. (610)353-5166. Fax: (610)353-5191. E-mail: editorial@chelseahouse.com. Website: www.chelseahouse.com. **Acquisitions:** Editorial Assistant. Publishes hardcover originals and reprints. **Publishes 350 titles/year. Receives 1,000 queries and 500 mss/year. 25% of books from first-time authors; 98% from unagented writers. Makes**

outright purchase of $1,500-3,500. Publishes book 16 months after acceptance of ms. Accepts simultaneous submissions. Responds in 1 month to queries; 2 months to proposals; 2 months to mss. Book catalog online; ms guidelines for #10 SASE.

O→ "We publish education series primarily for the library market/schools."

Nonfiction: Biography (must be common format, fitting under a series umbrealla), children's/juvenile. Subjects include Americana, animals, anthropology/archeology, ethnic, gay/lesbian, government/politics, health/medicine, history, hobbies, language/literature, military/war, multicultural, music/dance, nature/environment, recreation, regional, religion, science, sociology, sports, travel, women's issues/studies. "We are interested in expanding our topics to include more on the physical, life and environmental sciences." Query with SASE or submit proposal package including outline, 2-3 sample chapter(s), résumé. Reviews artwork/photos as part of ms package. Send photocopies.

Recent Title(s): *The History of Motown*, by Virginia Aronson (African American Achievers series); *Cameron Diaz*, by Anne E. Hill (Galaxy of Superstars series); *Catch-22*, edited by Harold Bloom (literary criticism).

Tips: "Know our product. Do not waste your time or ours by sending something that does not fit our market. Be professional. Send clean, clear submissions that show you read the preferred submission format."

CHEMICAL PUBLISHING COMPANY, INC., 527 Third Ave., #427, New York NY 10016-4168. (212)779-0090. Fax: (212)889-1537. E-mail: chempub@aol.com. Website: www.chemicalpublishing.com. **Acquisitions:** Ms. S. Soto-Galicia, publisher. Estab. 1934. Publishes hardcover originals. **Publishes 8 titles/year. Receives 20 queries/year. 50% of books from first-time authors; 100% from unagented writers. Pays 10% royalty on retail price or makes negotiable outright purchase. Offers negotiable advance.** Publishes book 8 months after acceptance of ms. Does not accept simultaneous submissions. Responds in 3 weeks to queries; 5 weeks to proposals; 2 months to mss. Book catalog and ms guidelines free.

O→ Chemical publishes professional chemistry-technical titles aimed at people employed in the chemical industry, libraries and graduate courses.

Nonfiction: "We request a fax letter with an introduction of the author and the kind of book written. Afterwards, we will reply. If the title is of interest, then we will request samples of the ms." How-to, reference, applied chemical technology (cosmetics, cement, textiles). Subjects include agriculture/horticulture, cooking/foods/nutrition, health/medicine, nature/environment, science, analytical methods, chemical technology, cosmetics, dictionaries, engineering, environmental science, food technology, formularies, industrial technology, medical, metallurgy, textiles. Submit outline, few pages of 3 sample chapter(s), SASE. Reviews artwork/photos as part of ms package.

Recent Title(s): *Cooling Water Treatment, Principles and Practice*; *Harry's Cosmeticology, 8th Edition*; *Library Handbook for Organic Chemists*.

Tips: Audience is professionals in various fields of chemistry, corporate and public libraries, college libraries. "We request a fax letter with an introduction of the author and the kind of book written. Afterwards, we will reply. If the title is of interest, then we will request samples of the ms."

CHICAGO REVIEW PRESS, 814 N. Franklin, Chicago IL 60610-3109. (312)337-0747. Fax: (312)337-5985. E-mail: csherry@ipgbook.com; yuval@ipgbook.com. Website: www.ipgbook.com. **Acquisitions:** Cynthia Sherry, executive editor (general nonfiction, children's); Yuval Taylor, editor (African, African-American and performing arts). Estab. 1973. Publishes hardcover and trade paperback originals and trade paperback reprints. **Publishes 30-35 titles/year. Receives 200 queries and 600 mss/year. 50% of books from first-time authors; 50% from unagented writers. Pays 7-12½% royalty. Offers $1,500-5,000 average advance.** Publishes book 18 months after acceptance of ms. Accepts simultaneous submissions. Responds in 3 months to queries. Book catalog for $3.50; ms guidelines for #10 SASE or online at website.

Imprints: Lawrence Hill Books, A Capella Books (contact Yuval Taylor).

O→ Chicago Review Press publishes intelligent nonfiction on timely subjects for educated readers with special interests.

Nonfiction: Children's/juvenile (activity books only), cookbook (specialty only), how-to. Subjects include art/architecture, child guidance/parenting, cooking/foods/nutrition, creative nonfiction, education, ethnic, gardening (regional), health/medicine, history, hobbies, memoirs, multicultural, music/dance, nature/environment, recreation, regional. Query with outline, toc and 1-2 sample chapters. Reviews artwork/photos as part of ms package.

Recent Title(s): *The Civil War for Kids*, by Janis Herbert.

Tips: "Along with a table of contents and 1-2 sample chapters, also send a cover letter and a list of credentials with your proposal. Also, provide the following information in your cover letter: audience, market and competition—who is the book written for and what sets it apart from what's already out there."

CHILD WELFARE LEAGUE OF AMERICA, 440 First St. NW, 3rd Floor, Washington DC 20001. (202)638-2952. Fax: (202)638-4004. E-mail: books@cwla.org. Website: www.cwla.org. **Acquisitions:** Acquisitions Editor. Publishes hardcover and trade paperback originals. **Publishes 30-50 titles/year. Receives 300 submissions/year. 95% from unagented writers. Pays 0-10% royalty on net domestic sales.** Publishes book 1 year after acceptance of ms. Responds in 3 months to queries. Book catalog and ms guidelines free.

Imprints: CWLA Press (child welfare professional publications), Child & Family Press (children's books and parenting books for the general public).

O→ CWLA is a privately supported, nonprofit, membership-based organization committed to preserving, protecting and promoting the well-being of all children and their families.

Nonfiction: Children's/juvenile. Subjects include child guidance/parenting, sociology. Submit complete ms.

Recent Title(s): *An American Face* (children's book); *Seven Sensible Strategies for Drug Free Kids.*
Tips: "We are looking for positive, kid friendly books for ages 3-9. We are looking for books that have a positive message... a feel-good book."

CHILDSWORK/CHILDSPLAY, LLC, The Guidance Channel, 135 Dupont St., P.O. Box 760, Plainview NY 11803-0760. (516)349-5520. Website: www.childswork.com. **Acquisitions:** Karen Schader, editor (psychological books and games for use with children). Publishes trade paperback originals and reprints. **Publishes 10-12 titles/year. Receives 250 queries and 50 mss/year. 5% of books from first-time authors; 100% from unagented writers. Makes outright purchase of $500-3,000.** Publishes book 9 months after acceptance of ms. Accepts simultaneous submissions. Responds in 1 month to queries; 1 month to proposals; 3 months to mss. Book catalog and ms guidelines for 9×12 SAE with 4 first-class stamps.

- Our target market includes therapists, counselors and teachers working with children who are experiencing behavioral, emotional and social difficulties.

Nonfiction: Psychological storybooks and workbooks, psychological games. Subjects include child guidance/parenting, education, health/medicine, psychology. All books and games are psychologically based and well researched. Query with SASE.
Fiction: Children's storybooks must deal with some aspect of psychological development or difficulty (e.g., ADHD, anger management, social skills, OCD, etc.). "Be in our files (résumé, writing samples) and we will contact you when we develop new projects." Submit complete ms.
Recent Title(s): *Sometimes I Don't Like to Talk*, by Jessica Lamb-Shapiro.
Tips: "Our market is comprised of mental health and education professionals who are primarily therapists, guidance counselors and teachers. A majority of our projects are assignments rather than submissions. Impress us with your writing ability and your background in psychology and education. If submitting rather seeking work on assignment, demonstrate that your work is marketable and profitable."

CHINA BOOKS & PERIODICALS, INC., 2929 24th St., San Francisco CA 94110-4126. (415)282-2994. Fax: (415)282-0994. Website: www.chinabooks.com. **Acquisitions:** Greg Jones, editor (language study, health, history); Baolin Ma, senior editor (music, language study). Estab. 1960. Publishes hardcover and trade paperback originals. **Publishes 5 titles/year. Receives 300 submissions/year. 10% of books from first-time authors; 95% from unagented writers. Pays 6-8% royalty on net receipts. Offers negotiable advance.** Publishes book 1 year after acceptance of ms. Accepts simultaneous submissions. Responds in 3 months to queries. Book catalog free; ms guidelines online.

- China Books is the main importer and distributor of books and magazines from China, providing an ever-changing variety of useful tools for travelers, scholars and others interested in China and Chinese culture. "We are looking for original book ideas, especially in the areas of language study, children's books, history and culture, all relating to China." Currently emphasizing language study. De-emphasizing art, fiction, poetry.

Nonfiction: "*Important*: *All* books *must* be on topics related to China or Chinese-Americans. Books on China's history, politics, environment, women, art/architecture; language textbooks, acupuncture and folklore." Biography, children's/juvenile, coffee table book, how-to, self-help, textbook. Subjects include agriculture/horticulture, art/architecture, business/economics, cooking/foods/nutrition, education, ethnic, gardening, government/politics, health/medicine, history, language/literature, music/dance, nature/environment, religion, sociology, translation, travel, women's issues/studies. Reviews artwork/photos as part of ms package.
Recent Title(s): *Rise of Digital China*, by Lid Wong; *Healing Energy*, by Virginia Newton.
Tips: "We are looking for original ideas, especially in language study, children's education, adoption of Chinese babies, or health issues relating to traditional Chinese medicine."

CHITRA PUBLICATIONS, 2 Public Ave., Montrose PA 18801. (570)278-1984. Fax: (570)278-2223. E-mail: chitra@epix.net. Website: www.Quilttownusa.com. **Acquisitions:** Joyce Libal, senior editor (articles, how-to); Connie Ellsworth, production (patterns, articles); Shalane Weidow, editorial assistant (shows, exhibits, articles). Publishes trade paperback originals. **Publishes 6 titles/year. Receives 70-80 queries and 10-20 mss/year. Pays royalty.** Publishes book 6-12 months after acceptance of ms. Does not accept simultaneous submissions. Responds in 2 weeks to queries; 3 weeks to proposals; 1 month to mss. Book catalog and ms quidelines for #10 SASE.

- "We publish quality quilting magazines and pattern books that recognize, promote, and inspire self expression."

Nonfiction: How-to. Subjects include quilting. Query with SASE. Reviews artwork/photos as part of ms package. Send transparencies.

CHOSEN BOOKS PUBLISHING CO., LTD., 3985 Bradwater St., Fairfax VA 22031-3702. (703)764-8250. Fax: (703)764-3995. E-mail: jecampbell@aol.com. Website: www.bakerbooks.com. **Acquisitions:** Jane Campbell, editorial director. Estab. 1971. Publishes hardcover and trade paperback originals. **Publishes 16 titles/year. Receives 500 submissions/year. 15% of books from first-time authors; 99% from unagented writers. Offers small advance.** Publishes book 12-18 months after acceptance of ms. Accepts simultaneous submissions. Responds in 3 months to queries. Ms guidelines for #10 SASE.

- "We publish well-crafted books that recognize the gifts and ministry of the Holy Spirit, and help the reader live a more empowered and effective life for Jesus Christ."

Nonfiction: Subjects include religion. "We publish books reflecting the current acts of the Holy Spirit in the world, books with a charismatic Christian orientation." No New Age, poetry, fiction, autobiographies, biographies, compilations, Bible studies, booklets, academic or children's books. Submit synopsis, chapter outline, résumé, 2 chapters and SASE. No computer disks or e-mail submissions; brief query only by e-mail.

Recent Title(s): *Healing the Nations: A Call to Global Intercession*, by John Sandford.
Tips: "We look for solid, practical advice for the growing and maturing Christian from authors with professional or personal experience platforms. No conversion accounts or chronicling of life events, please. State the topic or theme of your book clearly in your cover letter."

CHRISTIAN ED. PUBLISHERS, P.O. Box 26639, San Diego CA 92196. (858)578-4700. Fax: (858)578-2431. E-mail: lackelson@aol.com. Website: www.christianedwarehouse.com. **Acquisitions:** Dr. Lon Ackelson, senior editor. **Publishes 64 titles/year. Makes outright purchase of 3¢/word.** Responds in 3 months on assigned material to mss. Book catalog for 9×12 SAE with 4 first-class stamps; ms guidelines for #10 SASE.

O→ Christian Ed. Publishers is an independent, non-denominational, evangelical company founded nearly 50 years ago to produce Christ-centered curriculum materials based on the Word of God for thousands of churches of different denominations throughout the world. "Our mission is to introduce children, teens, and adults to a personal faith in Jesus Christ and to help them grow in their faith and service to the Lord. We publish materials that teach moral and spiritual values while training individuals for a lifetime of Christian service." Currently emphasizing Bible curriculum for preschool through preteen ages.

Nonfiction: Children's/juvenile. Subjects include education, religion. "All subjects are on assignment." Query with SASE.
Fiction: "All writing is done on assignment." Query with SASE.
Recent Title(s): *All-Stars for Jesus: Bible Curriculum for Preteens*.
Tips: "Read our guidelines carefully before sending us a manuscript. All writing is done on assignment only and must be age appropriate (preschool-6th grade)."

CHRISTIAN PUBLICATIONS, INC./HORIZON BOOKS, 3825 Hartzdale Dr., Camp Hill PA 17011. (717)761-7044. Fax: (717)761-7273. E-mail: dfessenden@christianpublications.com. Website: www.christianpublications.com. **Acquisitions:** David E. Fessenden, managing editor. Estab. 1883. Publishes hardcover, mass market and trade paperback originals. **Publishes 35 titles/year. Receives 300 queries and 600 mss/year. 25% of books from first-time authors; 90% from unagented writers. Pays 5-10% royalty on retail price or makes outright purchase. Offers varying advance.** Publishes book 18 months after acceptance of ms. Accepts simultaneous submissions. Responds in 1 month to queries; 3 months to proposals; 3 months to mss. Book catalog for 9×12 SAE with 7 first-class stamps; ms guidelines for #10 SASE or on website.
Imprints: Horizon Books.

O→ "Our purpose is to propagate the gospel of Jesus Christ through evangelistic, deeper life and other publishing, serving our denomination and the wider Christian community. All topics must be from an evangelical Christian viewpoint."

Nonfiction: Biography, gift book, how-to, humor, reference (reprints only), self-help, textbook, teen/young adult. Subjects include Americana, child guidance/parenting, religion (Evangelical Christian perspective), spirituality. Full proposal must accompany ms. Does not want fiction, poetry. Query with SASE or submit proposal package, including chapter synopsis, 2 sample chapters (including chapter 1), audience and market ideas, author bio. Reviews artwork/photos as part of ms package. Send photocopies.
Recent Title(s): *Connecting: 52 Guidelines for Making Your Marriage Work*, by Harold Sala (marriage/family); *A Heart of Excellence*, by Laurie Ellsworth (women/Christian living).
Tips: "Please do not send manuscripts without a complete proposal. We do *not* reprint other publishers' material. We are owned by The Christian and Missionary Alliance denomination; while we welcome and publish authors from various denominations, their theological perspective must be compatible with The Christian and Missionary Alliance. We are especially interested in fresh, practical approaches to deeper life—sanctification with running shoes on. Readers are evangelical, regular church-goers, mostly female, usually leaders in their church. Your book should grow out of a thorough and faithful study of Scripture. You need not be a 'Bible scholar,' but you should be a devoted student of the Bible."

CHRONICLE BOOKS FOR CHILDREN, 85 Second St., 6th Floor, San Francisco CA 94105. (415)537-3730. Fax: (415)537-4420. E-mail: frontdesk@chroniclebooks.com. Website: www.chroniclekids.com. **Acquisitions:** Victoria Rock, director of Children's Books; Beth Weber, managing editor; Jennifer Vetter, editor; Susan Pearson, editor-at-large; Samantha McFerrin, editorial assistant. Publishes hardcover and trade paperback originals. **Publishes 40-50 titles/year. Receives 20,000 submissions/year. 5% of books from first-time authors; 25% from unagented writers. Pays 8% royalty. Offers variable advance.** Publishes book 18 months after acceptance of ms. Accepts simultaneous submissions. Responds in 2-18 weeks to queries; 5 months to mss. Book catalog for 9×12 SAE with 3 first-class stamps; ms guidelines for #10 SASE.

O→ Chronicle Books for Children publishes an eclectic mixture of traditional and innovative children's books. "Our aim is to publish books that inspire young readers to learn and grow creatively while helping them discover the joy of reading. We're looking for quirky, bold artwork and subject matter." Currently emphasizing picture books. De-emphasizing young adult.

Nonfiction: Biography, children's/juvenile (for ages 8-12), illustrated book, picture books (for ages up to 8 years). Subjects include animals, art/architecture, multicultural, nature/environment, science. Query with synopsis and SASE. Reviews artwork/photos as part of ms package.
Fiction: Mainstream/contemporary, multicultural, young adult, picture books; middle grade fiction; young adult projects. "We do not accept proposals by fax, via e-mail, or on disk. When submitting artwork, either as a part of a project or

as samples for review, do not send original art. Please be sure to include an SASE large enough to hold your materials. Projects submitted without an appropriate SASE will be recycled." Query with synopsis and SASE. Send complete ms for picture books.

Recent Title(s): *Ghost Wings*; *Dream Carver*; *Star in the Darkness*.

Tips: "We are interested in projects that have a unique bent to them—be it in subject matter, writing style, or illustrative technique. As a small list, we are looking for books that will lend our list a distinctive flavor. Primarily we are interested in fiction and nonfiction picture books for children ages up to eight years, and nonfiction books for children ages up to twelve years. We publish board, pop-up, and other novelty formats as well as picture books. We are also interested in early chapter books, middle grade fiction, and young adult projects."

CHRONICLE BOOKS, 85 Second St., San Francisco CA 94105. (415)537-3730. Fax: (415)537-4440. E-mail: frontdesk@chroniclebooks.com. Website: www.chroniclebooks.com. President: Jack Jensen. **Acquisitions:** Bill LeBlond (cookbooks); Leslie Jonath (lifestyle); Alan Rapp (art and design); Sarah Malarky (licensing and popular culture); Mikyla Bruder (lifestyle); Steve Mockus (popular culture); Debra Lande (gift books); Children's Book Editor (children's). Estab. 1966. Publishes hardcover and trade paperback originals. **Publishes 200 titles/year.** Publishes book 18 months after acceptance of ms. Accepts simultaneous submissions. Responds in 3 months to queries. Book catalog for 11x14 SAE with 5 first-class stamps; ms guidelines online.

Imprints: Chronicle Books for Children, GiftWorks (ancillary products, such as stationery, gift books).

- "Inspired by the enduring magic and importance of books, our objective is to create and distribute exceptional publishing that is instantly recognizable for its spirit, creativity and value. This objective informs our business relationships and endeavors, be they with customers, authors, suppliers or colleagues."

Nonfiction: Coffee table book, cookbook, gift book. Subjects include art/architecture, cooking/foods/nutrition, gardening, nature/environment, photography, recreation, regional, design, pop culture, interior design. Query or submit outline/synopsis with artwork and sample chapters.

Recent Title(s): *The Beatles Anthology*, by The Beatles; *Worst-Case Scenario Survival Handbook*, by David Borgenicht and Joshua Piven.

CHURCH GROWTH INSTITUTE, P.O. Box 7, Elkton MD 21922-0007. (434)525-0022. Fax: (434)525-0608. E-mail: cgimail@churchgrowth.org. Website: www.churchgrowth.org. **Acquisitions:** Cindy Spear, administrator/resource development director. Estab. 1978. Publishes trade paperback originals, 3-ring-bound manuals, mixed media resource packets. **Publishes 4 titles/year. Pays 6% royalty on retail price.** Publishes book 1 year after acceptance of ms. Accepts simultaneous submissions. Responds in 3 months to queries. Book catalog for 9×12 SAE with 4 first-class stamps; ms guidelines given after query and outline is received.

- "Our mission is to provide practical resources to help pastors, churches and individuals reach their potential for Christ; to promote spiritual and numerical growth in churches, thereby leading Christians to maturity and lost people to Christ; and to equip pastors so they can equip their church members to do the work of the ministry."

Nonfiction: "Material should originate from a conservative Christian view and cover topics that will help churches grow, through leadership training, self-evaluation, and new or unique ministries, or enhancing existing ministries. Self-discovery inventories regarding spiritual growth, relationship improvement, etc., are hot items." How-to. Subjects include education, religion (church-growth related). "Accepted manuscripts will be adapted to our resource packet, manual or inventory format. All material must be practical and easy for the *average* Christian to understand." Query or submit outline and brief explanation of what the packet will accomplish in the local church and whether it is leadership or lay-oriented. Queries accepted by mail or e-mail. No phone queries. Reviews artwork/photos as part of ms package. Send photocopies or transparencies.

Recent Title(s): *Ministry Descriptions: Identifying Opportunities and Clarifying Expectations*; *Sunday School Growth for Rookies*.

Tips: "We are not publishing many *textbooks*. Concentrate on how-to manuals and ministry evaluation and diagnostic tools and spiritual or relationship-oriented 'inventories' for individual Christians."

CIRCLET PRESS INC., 1770 Massachusetts Ave., #278, Cambridge MA 02140. (617)864-0492. Fax: (617)864-0663. E-mail: circlet-info@circlet.com. Website: www.circlet.com. **Acquisitions:** Cecilia Tan, publisher/editor. Estab. 1992. Publishes hardcover and trade paperback originals. **Publishes 4-6 titles/year. Receives 50-100 queries and 500 mss/year. 90% from unagented writers. Pays 4-12% royalty on retail price or makes outright purchase. Also pays in books, if author prefers.** Publishes book 18 months after acceptance of ms. Accepts simultaneous submissions. Responds in 1 months to queries; 6-18 months to mss. Book catalog and ms guidelines on website.

Imprints: The Ultra Violet Library (gay and lesbian science fiction and fantasy "these books will not be as erotic as our others"); Circumflex (erotic and sexual nonfiction titles, how-to and essays).

- "Circlet Press publishes science fiction/fantasy short stories which are too erotic for the mainstream and to promote literature with a positive view of sex and sexuality, which celebrates pleasure and diversity. We also publish other books celebrating sexuality and imagination with our imprints: The Ultra Violet Library and Circumflex."

Fiction: Erotica, fantasy, gay/lesbian, science fiction, short story collections. "Fiction must combine both the erotic and the fantastic. The erotic content needs to be an integral part of a science fiction story, and vice versa. Writers should not assume that any sex is the same as erotica." Submit full short stories up to 10,000 words between April 15 and August 31. Manuscripts received outside this reading period are discarded. Queries only via e-mail.

Recent Title(s): *Nymph*, by Francesca Lia Block; *The Darker Passions: Dracula*, by Amarantha Knight.
Tips: "Our audience is adults who enjoy science fiction and fantasy, especially the works of Anne Rice, Storm Constantine, Samuel Delany, who enjoy vivid storytelling and erotic content. Seize your most vivid fantasy, your deepest dream and set it free onto paper. That is at the heart of all good speculative fiction. Then if it has an erotic theme as well as a science fiction one, send it to me. No horror, rape, death or mutilation! I want to see stories that *celebrate* sex and sexuality in a positive manner. Please write for our guidelines as each year we have a specific list of topics we seek. Short stories only, *no* novels."

CLARION BOOKS, 215 Park Ave. S., New York NY 10003. **Acquisitions:** Dinah Stevenson, editorial director; Michele Coppola, editor (fiction, young science books, picture books); Jennifer B. Greene, editor (contemporary fiction, picture books for all ages, biography); Julie Strauss-Gabel, associate editor (fiction, nonfiction, picture books, Jewish interest). Estab. 1965. Publishes hardcover originals for children. **Publishes 50 titles/year. Pays 5-10% royalty on retail price. Offers minimum of $4,000 advance.** Publishes book 2 years after acceptance of ms. Responds in 2 months to queries Prefers no multiple submissions to mss. Ms guidelines for #10 SASE.

O-ᴿ Clarion Books publishes picture books, nonfiction, and fiction for infants through grade 12. Avoid telling your stories in verse unless you are a professional poet.

Nonfiction: Biography, children's/juvenile, photo essay. Subjects include Americana, history, language/literature, nature/environment, photography, holiday. No unsolicited mss. Query with SASE or submit proposal package including sample chapter(s), SASE. Reviews artwork/photos as part of ms package. Send photocopies.
Fiction: Adventure, historical, humor, mystery, suspense, strong character studies. Clarion is highly selective in the areas of historical fiction, fantasy, and science fiction. A novel must be superlatively written in order to find a place on the list. Mss that arrive without an SASE of adequate size will *not* be responded to or returned. Accepts fiction translations. No unsolicited mss. Submit complete ms.
Recent Title(s): *Sigmund Freud: Pioneer of the Mind*, by Catherine Reef; *Zazoo*, by Richard Mosher; *Pocket Full of Poems*, by Nikki Grimes, illustrated by Javaka Steptoe.
Tips: Looks for "freshness, enthusiasm—in short, life."

CLARITY PRESS INC., 3277 Roswell Rd. NE, #469, Atlanta GA 30305. (877)613-1495. Fax: (404)231-3899 and (877)613-7868. E-mail: claritypress@usa.net. Website: www.claritypress.com. **Acquisitions:** Diana G. Collier, editorial director (contemporary justice issues). Estab. 1984. Publishes hardcover and trade paperback originals. **Publishes 4 titles/year.** Does not accept simultaneous submissions. Responds in 3 months to queries.
Nonfiction: Publishes books on contemporary issues in US, Middle East and Africa. Subjects include ethnic, world affairs, human rights/socio-economic and minority issues. No fiction. Query with synopsis, annotated outline, résumé, publishing history.
Recent Title(s): *In Pursuit of the Right to Self-Determination*, edited by Y.N. Kly and D. Kly.

CLEAR LIGHT PUBLISHERS, 823 Don Diego, Santa Fe NM 87501-4224. (505)989-9590. E-mail: clpublish@aol.com. **Acquisitions:** Harmon Houghton, publisher. Estab. 1981. Publishes hardcover and trade paperback originals. **Publishes 20-24 titles/year. Receives 100 queries/year. 10% of books from first-time authors; 50% from unagented writers. Pays 10% royalty on wholesale price. Offers advance, a percent of gross potential.** Publishes book 1 year after acceptance of ms. Accepts simultaneous submissions. Responds in 3 months to queries. Book catalog free.

O-ᴿ Clear Light publishes books that "accurately depict the positive side of human experience and inspire the spirit."

Nonfiction: Biography, coffee table book, cookbook. Subjects include Americana, anthropology/archeology, art/architecture, cooking/foods/nutrition, ethnic, history, nature/environment, philosophy, photography, regional (Southwest). Query with SASE. Reviews artwork/photos as part of ms package. Send photocopies.
Recent Title(s): *Fourteen Dalai Lamas*, by Glenn H. Mullin; *When Technology Fails*, by Matthew Stein; *Cape Cod Wampanoag Cook Book*, by Chief Earl Mills & Betty Breen.

CLEIS PRESS, P.O. Box 14684, San Francisco CA 94114-0684. (415)575-4700. Fax: (415)575-4705. Website: www.cleispress.com. **Acquisitions:** Frederique Delacoste. Estab. 1980. Publishes trade paperback originals and reprints. **Publishes 20 titles/year. 10% of books from first-time authors; 90% from unagented writers. Pays variable royalty on retail price.** Publishes book 2 years after acceptance of ms. Responds in 1 month to queries. Book catalog for #10 SAE with 2 first-class stamps.

O-ᴿ Cleis Press specializes in feminist and gay/lesbian fiction and nonfiction.

Nonfiction: Subjects include gay/lesbian, women's issues/studies, sexual politics, erotica, human rights, African-American studies. "We are interested in books on topics of sexuality, human rights and women's and gay and lesbian literature. Please consult our website first to be certain that your book fits our list." Query or submit outline and sample chapters.
Fiction: Feminist, gay/lesbian, literary. "We are looking for high quality fiction by women and men." No romances. Submit complete ms. *Writer's Market* recommends sending a query with SASE first.
Recent Title(s): *Black Like Us* (fiction); *Whole Lesbian Sex Book* (nonfiction); *No Place Like Home: Echoes from Kosovo* (nonfiction).
Tips: "Be familiar with publishers' catalogs; be absolutely aware of your audience; research potential markets; present fresh new ways of looking at your topic; avoid 'PR' language and include publishing history in query letter."

N CLEVELAND STATE UNIVERSITY POETRY CENTER, 2121 Euclid Ave., Cleveland OH 44115-2214. (216)687-3986. Fax: (216)687-6943. E-mail: poetrycenter@csuohio.edu. Website: www.csuohio.edu/poetrycenter. Coordinator: Rita M. Grabowski. **Acquisitions:** Dr. Ted Lardner, director. Estab. 1962. Publishes trade paperback and hardcover originals. **Publishes 4 titles/year. Receives 500 queries and 1,000 mss/year. 60% of books from first-time authors; 100% from unagented writers. CSU Poetry Series pays one-time, lump-sum royalty of $200-400, plus 50 copies; Cleveland Poets Series (Ohio poets only) pays 100 copies. $1,000 prize for best full-length ms each year.** Accepts simultaneous submissions. Responds in 1 month to queries; 8 months to mss. Manuscript guidelines for SASE. Manuscripts are not returned.

Poetry: Query; ask for guidelines. Submit only November-January. Postmark deadline: February 1. Charges $20 reading fee. Reviews artwork/photos only if applicable (e.g., concrete poetry). No light verse, inspirational, or greeting card verse. ("This does not mean that we do not consider poetry with humor or philosophical/religious import.").

Recent Title(s): *The Largest Possible Life*, by Alison Luterman; *Before the Blue Hour*, by Deidre O'Connor; *Willow from the Willow*, by Margaret H. Young.

Tips: "Our books are for serious readers of poetry, i.e. poets, critics, academics, students, people who read *Poetry, Field, American Poetry Review*, etc. Trends include movement away from 'confessional' poetry; greater attention to form and craftsmanship. Project an interesting, coherent personality; link poems so as to make coherent unity, not just a miscellaneous collection. Especially need poems with *mystery*, i.e., poems that suggest much, but do not tell all."

CLOUD PEAK, 730 W. 51st St., Casper WY 82601. E-mail: pharwitz@wyoming.com. **Acquisitions:** Paul Harwitz. Publishes hardcover, trade paperback and mass market paperback originals and reprints. **Publishes 36 titles/year. Receives 200 queries and 80 mss/year. 10% of books from first-time authors; 50% from unagented writers. Pays 10% royalty for nonfiction; percentage for fiction varies.** Publishes book 1-2 years after acceptance of ms. Accepts simultaneous submissions. Responds in 2 months to queries; 3 months to proposals; 2 months to mss. Book catalog and ms guidelines for #10 SASE or on website.

- Cloud Peak is currently emphasizing nonfiction books about Indians, African-Americans, Asians, Hispanics and other "minorities" in the West.

Nonfiction: Biography, children's/juvenile, how-to, humor. Subjects include Americana (Western), education, history, humor, military/war, multicultural, sports, women's issues/studies. "Submissions to our 'Women of the West' line of nonfiction will receive special consideration." Query with SASE. **All unsolicited mss returned unopened.** Reviews artwork/photos as part of ms package. Send photocopies, transparencies or computer files on 3.5-inch disk.

Fiction: Adventure, fantasy, historical, horror, humor, juvenile, military/war, multicultural, multimedia, mystery, poetry, science fiction, suspense, western, Native American. "Do everything you can to make the book a real 'page-turner,' Plots and sub-plots must be plausible and suited to the locale(s). Main and secondary characters must speak dialog which matches their respective personality traits. Blacks, Spanish-speaking people and other 'minorities' must *not* be portrayed stereotypically. Historical accuracy is important." Query with SASE. **All unsolicited mss returned unopened.**

Poetry: "We publish Western/cowboy/Indian poetry in single-author collections and multi-author anthologies." Query or submit 3 sample poems or submit complete ms.

Recent Title(s): *Soldiers Falling Into Camp: The Battles at the Rosebud and Little Bighorn*, by Robert Kammen, Frederick Lefthand and Joe Marshall (military history); *The Watcher*, by Robert Kammen (Western/supernatural/ecological); *Riders of the Leafy Spurge*, by Bill Lowman (cowboy poetry).

Tips: "Buy, read and study the *Writer's Market* each year. Writing must flow. Imagine you are a reader visiting a bookstore. Write the first page of the book in such a way that the reader feels *compelled* to buy it. It helps a writer to work from an outline. When we solicit a manuscript for consideration, we like to receive a floppy disk, in order to conserve trees."

COASTAL CAROLINA PRESS, 2231 Wrightsville Ave., Wilmington NC 28403. Website: www.coastalcarolinapress.org. Hardcover, trade paperback and mass market paperback originals and trade paperback reprints. **Publishes 6-8 titles/year. 70% of books from first-time authors; 100% from unagented writers. Pays royalty.** Publishes book 1 year after acceptance of ms. Book catalog and submission guidelines on website.

- "We are a non-profit corporation dedicated to publishing materials about the history, culture and activities of coastal North & South Carolina. We do not publish poetry or religious titles."

Nonfiction: Coffee table book, cookbook, how-to, humor. Subjects include agriculture/horticulture, art/architecture, cooking/foods/nutrition, creative nonfiction, education, ethnic, gardening, history, language/literature, memoirs, military/war, multicultural, music/dance, nature/environment, photography, recreation, regional, sociology, travel, women's issues/studies. Publishes books with regional niche. Query with SASE.

Fiction: Adventure, ethnic, historical, humor, juvenile, literary, mainstream/contemporary, military/war, multicultural, mystery, regional, short story collections, suspense, young adult. Publishes books with regional niche. Query with SASE.

Recent Title(s): *Searching for Virginia Dave: A Fool's Errand*, by Marjorie Hudson (historical nonfiction/memoir); *Island Murders*, by Wanda Campbell (fiction).

COLLECTORS PRESS, INC., P.O. Box 230986, Portland OR 97281-0986. (503)684-3030. Fax: (503)684-3777. Website: www.collectorspress.com. **Acquisitions:** Richard Perry, publisher. Estab. 1992. Publishes hardcover and trade paperback originals. **Publishes 20 titles/year. Receives 500 queries and 200 mss/year. 75% of books from first-time authors; 75% from unagented writers. Pays royalty.** Publishes book 1 year after acceptance of ms. Responds in 1 month to queries. Book catalog and ms guidelines free.

O→ Collectors Press Inc. publishes award-winning popular-culture coffee table and gift books on 20th century and modern collections and interests.

Nonfiction: Illustrated book, reference. Subjects include art/architecture, photography, science-fiction art, fantasy art, graphic design, comic art, magazine art, historical art, poster art, genre specific art. Submit proposal package, including market research, outline, 2 sample chapters and SASE. Reviews artwork/photos as part of ms package. Send transparencies or *very* clear photos.

Recent Title(s): *Science Fiction of the 20th Century: An Illustrated History.*

Tips: "Your professional package must be typed. No computer disks accepted."

THE COLLEGE BOARD, College Entrance Examination Board, 45 Columbus Ave., New York NY 10023-6992. (212)713-8000. Website: www.collegeboard.com. **Acquisitions:** Thomas Vanderberg, director of publications. Publishes trade paperback originals. **Publishes 30 titles/year. Receives 60 submissions/year. 25% of books from first-time authors; 50% from unagented writers. Pays royalty on retail price. Offers advance.** Publishes book 9 months after acceptance of ms. Responds in 2 months to queries. Book catalog free.

O→ The College Board publishes guidance information for college-bound students.

Nonfiction: "We want books to help students make a successful transition from high school to college." Humor, reference. Subjects include education, college guidance. Query with SASE or submit outline, sample chapter(s), SASE.

Recent Title(s): *The College Application Essay*, by Sara McGinty.

COLLEGE PRESS PUBLISHING COMPANY, P.O. Box 1132, Joplin MO 64802. (417)623-6280. Website: www.collegepress.com. **Acquisitions:** Acquisitions Editor. Estab. 1959. Publishes hardcover and trade paperback originals and reprints. **Publishes 15-20 titles/year. Receives 400 queries and 300 mss/year. 25% of books from first-time authors; 90% from unagented writers. Pays 5-15% royalty on wholesale price.** Publishes book 6 months after acceptance of ms. Accepts simultaneous submissions. Responds in 3 months to proposals. Book catalog for 9×12 SAE with 5 first-class stamps; ms guidelines for #10 SASE.

O→ "College Press is an evangelical Christian publishing house primarily associated with the Christian churches/Church of Christ."

Nonfiction: "We seek textbooks used in Christian colleges and universities—leaning toward an Arminian and an amillennial mindset." Textbook (Christian textbooks and small group studies). Subjects include religion, Christian apologetics. Query with SASE or submit proposal package including 3 sample chapter(s), author bio, synopsis.

Recent Title(s): *Encounters with Christ*, by Mark E. Moore.

Tips: "Our core market is Christian Churches/Churches of Christ and conservative evangelical Christians. Have your material critically reviewed prior to sending it. Make sure that it is non-Calvinistic and that it leans more amillennial (if it is apocalyptic writing)."

COMMON COURAGE PRESS, One Red Barn Rd. Box 702, Monroe ME 04951. (207)525-0900 or (800)497-3207. Fax: (207)525-3068. E-mail: orders-info@commoncouragepress.com. Website: www.commoncouragepress.com. **Acquisitions:** Ms. Flic Shooter, publisher (leftist political literature). Publishes hardcover and trade paperback originals and trade paperback reprints. **Publishes 12 titles/year. Receives 50 queries and 200 mss/year. 50% of books from first-time authors; 100% from unagented writers. Pays 10% royalty on wholesale price.** Publishes book 9 months after acceptance of ms. Accepts simultaneous submissions. Responds in 1 month to queries. Book catalog online; ms guidelines online.

O→ "Nonfiction leftist, activist, political, history, feminist, media issues are our niche."

Nonfiction: Reference, textbook. Subjects include anthropology/archeology, creative nonfiction, ethnic, gay/lesbian, government/politics, health/medicine, history, military/war, multicultural, nature/environment, science. Query with SASE or submit proposal package, including outline or submit completed ms. Reviews artwork/photos as part of ms package.

Recent Title(s): *New Military Humanism*, by Noam Chomsky (leftist political); *Rogue State*, by William Blum (leftist political).

Tips: Audience consists of left-wing activists, college audiences.

COMPANION PRESS, P.O. Box 2575, Laguna Hills CA 92654. Fax: (949)362-4489. E-mail: sstewart@companionpress.com. Website: www.companionpress.com. **Acquisitions:** Steve Stewart, publisher. Publishes trade paperback originals. **Publishes 6 titles/year. Receives 50 queries and 25 mss/year. 50% of books from first-time authors; 100% from unagented writers. Pays 6-8% royalty on retail price.** Publishes book 9 months after acceptance of ms. Responds in 1 month. *Writer's Market* recommends allowing 2 months for reply to queries. Book catalog and ms guidelines online.

O→ "We publish gay, lesbian, bisexual, transgender and other sexuality books." Currently emphasizing targeted genre books.

Nonfiction: Subjects include leather, cross-dressing, erotic wrestling, fetishes and other sexuality books from the educational to the erotic. Query with SASE. Reviews artwork/photos as part of ms package. Send photocopies.

Fiction: Gay/lesbian (bisexual, transgender), novels. Query with SASE.

Recent Title(s): *The Gay Adult Video Star Directory* (nonfiction); *Rent Boys, Hustlers & Escorts* (erotic anthology).

CONARI PRESS, 2550 Ninth St., Suite 101, Berkeley CA 94710. (510)649-7175. Fax: (510)649-7190. E-mail: conari@conari.com. Website: www.conari.com. **Acquisitions:** Julie Kessler, editorial assistant (spirituality, personal growth relationships, women's issues, family, inspiration). Publishes hardcover and trade paperback originals and trade paper-

back reprints. **Publishes 35 titles/year. Receives 600 queries and 500 mss/year. Pays royalty.** Publishes book 6-12 months after acceptance of ms. Accepts simultaneous submissions. Responds in 3 months to queries; 3 months to proposals; 3 months to mss. Book catalog and ms guidelines free.
Nonfiction: Cookbook, gift book, self-help. Subjects include animals, child guidance/parenting, cooking/foods/nutrition, education, ethnic, gardening, gay/lesbian, health/medicine, history, hobbies, memoirs, money/finance, multicultural, nature/environment, psychology, religion, science, sex, sociology, spirituality, travel, women's issues/studies. Submit proposal package including outline, 2-3 sample chapter(s), SASE.
Recent Title(s): *The Food Revolution*, by John Robbins; *Life Can Be This Good*, by Jan Goldstein.

CONCORDIA PUBLISHING HOUSE, 3558 S. Jefferson Ave., St. Louis MO 63118-3968. (314)268-1187. Fax: (314)268-1329. E-mail: Brandy.overton@cph.org. Website: www.cph.org. **Acquisitions:** Jane Wilke, acquisitions editor (children's product, adult devotional, teaching resources); Ken Wagener, acquistions editor (adult nonfiction on Christian spirituality and culture, academic works of interest in Lutheran markets). Estab. 1869. Publishes hardcover and trade paperback originals. **Publishes 45 titles/year.**

O→ Concordia publishes Protestant, inspirational, theological, family and juvenile material. All manuscripts must conform to the doctrinal tenets of The Lutheran Church—Missouri Synod. No longer publishes fiction.

Nonfiction: Children's/juvenile, adult. Subjects include child guidance/parenting (in Christian context), religion, inspirational.
Recent Title(s): *Seasons Under the Son*, by Tim Wesemann (inspirational); *Right from the Start*, by Shirley Morgentha (parenting).
Tips: "We are no longer accepting freelance submissions."

CONFLUENCE PRESS, INC., Lewis-Clark State College 500 Eighth Ave., Lewiston ID 83501-1698. (208)792-2336. Fax: (208)792-2324. **Acquisitions:** James R. Hepworth, publisher. Estab. 1975. Publishes hardcover originals and trade paperback originals and reprints. **Publishes 4-5 titles/year. Receives 500 queries and 150 mss/year. 50% of books from first-time authors; 50% from unagented writers. Pays 10-15% royalty on net receipts. Offers $100-2,000 advance.** Publishes book 18 months after acceptance of ms. Accepts simultaneous submissions. Responds in 2 months to queries; 1 month to proposals; 3 months to mss. Book catalog and ms guidelines free.

O→ "We are increasingly moving toward strictly regional books by regional authors and rarely publish writers from outside the western United States." Currently emphasizing essay collections, biography, autobiography. De-emphasizing short stories.

Nonfiction: Subjects include Americana, ethnic, history, language/literature, nature/environment, regional, translation. Query with SASE.
Fiction: Ethnic, literary, mainstream/contemporary, short story collections. Query with SASE.
Poetry: Submit 6 sample poems.
Recent Title(s): *A Little Bit of Wisdom: Conversations with a Nez Perce Elder* (nonfiction); *The Names of Time*, by Mary Ann Waters (poetry).

CONSORTIUM PUBLISHING, 640 Weaver Hill Rd., West Greenwich RI 02817-2261. (401)397-9838. Fax: (401)392-1926. John M. Carlevale, chief of publications. Estab. 1990. Publishes trade paperback originals and reprints. **Publishes 12 titles/year. Receives 150 queries and 50 mss/year. 50% of books from first-time authors; 95% from unagented writers. Pays 10-15% royalty.** Publishes book 3 months after acceptance of ms. Responds in 2 months to queries. Book catalog and ms guidelines for #10 SASE.

O→ Consortium publishes books for all levels of the education market.

Nonfiction: Autobiography, how-to, humor, illustrated book, reference, self-help, technical, textbook. Subjects include business/economics, child guidance/parenting, education, government/politics, health/medicine, history, music/dance, nature/environment, psychology, science, sociology, women's issues/studies. Query or submit proposal package, including table of contents, outline, 1 sample chapter and SASE. Reviews artwork/photos as part of ms package. Send photocopies.
Recent Title(s): *Teaching the Child Under Six, 4th edition*, by James L. Hymes, Jr. (education).
Tips: Audience is college and high school students and instructors, elementary school teachers and other trainers.

CONTEMPORARY BOOKS, McGraw-Hill Company, 130 E. Randolph St., Suite 900, Chicago IL 60601. (312)233-7500. Fax: (312)233-7570. Website: www.mcgraw-hill.com. Vice President: Philip Ruppel. **Acquisitions:** Rob Taylor, associate editor; Denise Betts, assistant editor; Betsy Lane, senior editor. Estab. 1947. Publishes hardcover originals and trade paperback originals and reprints. **Publishes 300 titles/year. Receives 5,000 submissions/year. 10% of books from first-time authors; 25% from unagented writers. Pays 6-15% royalty on retail price. Offers advance.** Publishes book 1 year after acceptance of ms. Accepts simultaneous submissions. Responds in 2 months to queries. Ms guidelines for #10 SASE.
Imprints: Contemporary Books, VGM Career Books, McGraw-Hill.

O→ "We are a midsize, niche-oriented, backlist-oriented publisher. We publish exclusively nonfiction in general interest trade categories."

Nonfiction: How-to, reference, self-help. Subjects include cooking/foods/nutrition, health/medicine, psychology, sports, careers. Query with SASE or submit outline, sample chapter(s). Reviews artwork/photos as part of ms package.
Recent Title(s): *Raising Resilient Children*, by Robert Brooks and Sam Goldstein; *Bob Feller's Little Black Book of Baseball Wisdom.*

N CONTINUUM INTERNATIONAL PUBLISHING GROUP, LTD., The Tower Building, 11 York Rd., London SE1 7NX England. (0) 20-7922-0880. **Acquisitions:** Janet Joyce, editorial director (journals programme and humanities); Robin Baird-Smith, publishing director (religious books); Anthony Haynes, editorial director (philosophy and professional). Publishes hardcover originals and paperback textbooks. **Publishes 350-400 titles/year. Receives 1,000 queries and 400 mss/year. 10% of books from first-time authors; 99% from unagented writers. Pays 0-15% royalty. Offers advance.** Publishes book 9 months after acceptance of ms. Does not accept simultaneous submissions. Responds in 1 month to proposals. Book catalog free; ms guidelines free.

Imprints: Continuum, Pinter, Leicester University Press, Geoffrey Chapman, Mowbray, Mansell, Athlone Press, T&T Clark, Burns & Oates, Sheffield Academic Press.

- Continuum publishes textbooks, monographs and reference works in the humanities, arts and social sciences for students, teachers and professionals worldwide.

Nonfiction: Reference, technical, textbook. Subjects include anthropology/archeology, business/economics, education, film/cinema/stage (performance), government/politics, history, language/literature, music/dance (popular), philosophy, religion, sociology, travel (tourism), therapy culture studies, linguistics. Submit outline.

Recent Title(s): *New History of Jazz*, by Alyn Shipton; *The Continuum Companion to Twentieth Century Theatre*, edited by Colin Chambers.

COOK COMMUNICATIONS MINISTRIES, (formerly Cook Communications), 4050 Lee Vance View, Colorado Springs CO 80918. (719)536-3271. Fax: (719)536-3265. **Acquisitions:** Editorial Assistant. Estab. 1875. Publishes hardcover and trade paperback originals. **Publishes 130 titles/year. 10% of books from first-time authors; 50% from unagented writers. Pays variable royalty on net price. Offers varied advance.** Publishes book 1-2 years after acceptance of ms. Accepts simultaneous submissions. Responds in 3-4 months to queries.

Imprints: Faith Kids Books (children), Faith Kids Toys (toys, media, games), Victor, Faith Parenting, Faith Marriage and Faithful Woman

- Cook Communications publishes children's and family spiritual growth books. Books "must have strong underlying Christian themes or clearly stated biblical value."

Nonfiction: Biography, children's/juvenile, reference (Bible). Subjects include child guidance/parenting, history, religion. Submit proposal package including outline, 1 sample chapter(s), cover letter, SASE.

Fiction: Juvenile, some adult.

Recent Title(s): *Taking the High Ground*, by Col. Jeff O'Leary, USAF (nonfiction); *Understanding the Heartbeat of Jesus*, by Jill Briscoe (women/spiritual growth); *Tale of Three Trees*, by Angela Elwell Hunt (children's picture book).

Tips: "All books must in some way be Bible-related and written by authors who themselves are evangelical Christians with a platform. Only a small fraction of the manuscripts received can be seriously considered for publication. Most books result from contacts that acquisitions editors make with qualified authors, though from time to time an unsolicited proposal triggers enough excitement to result in a contract. A writer has the best chance of selling Cook a well-conceived and imaginative manuscript that helps the reader apply Christianity to her life in practical ways. Christians active in the local church and their children are our audience."

COOPER SQUARE PRESS, (formerly Madison Books), Rowman and Littlefield Publishing Group, 4720 Boston Way, Lanham MD 20706. (212)529-3888. Fax: (212)529-4223. **Acquisitions:** Michael Dorr, acquisitions editor. Estab. 1984. Publishes hardcover originals, trade paperback originals and reprints. **Publishes 40 titles/year. Receives 1,200 submissions/year. 15% of books from first-time authors; 65% from unagented writers. Pays 10-15% royalty on net receipts.** Publishes book 1 year after acceptance of ms. Responds in 2 months to queries. Book catalog and ms guidelines for 9×12 SAE with 4 first-class stamps.

Nonfiction: Biography, reference (trade). Subjects include contemporary culture, history, contemporary affairs. No unsolicited mss. Query with SASE or submit outline, sample chapter(s).

COPPER CANYON PRESS, P.O. Box 271, Port Townsend WA 98368. (360)385-4925. E-mail: poetry@coppercanyonpress.org. Website: www.coppercanyonpress.org. **Acquisitions:** Sam Hamill, editor. Estab. 1972. Publishes trade paperback originals and occasional clothbound editions. **Publishes 18 titles/year. Receives 1,500 queries and 500 mss/year. 10% of books from first-time authors; 95% from unagented writers. Pays royalty.** Publishes book 2 years after acceptance of ms. Responds in 2 months to queries. Book catalog free.

- Copper Canyon Press is dedicated to publishing poetry in a wide range of styles and from a full range of the world's many cultures.

Poetry: "First and second book manuscripts are considered only for our Hayden Carruth Awards, presented annually." Send SASE for entry form in September of each year. *No unsolicited mss.*

Recent Title(s): *Spring Essence*, trans. by John Balaban; *Cool, Calm & Collected*, by Carolyn Kizer; *Orpheus & Eurydice*, by Gregory Orr.

CORNELL MARITIME PRESS, INC., P.O. Box 456, Centreville MD 21617-0456. (410)758-1075. Fax: (410)758-6849. E-mail: cornell@crosslink.net. **Acquisitions:** Charlotte Kurst, managing editor. Estab. 1938. Publishes hardcover originals and quality paperbacks. **Publishes 7-9 titles/year. Receives 150 submissions/year. 80% of books from first-time authors; 99% from unagented writers.** Publishes book 1 year after acceptance of ms. Responds in 2 months to queries. Book catalog for 10×13 SAE with 5 first-class stamps.

Imprints: Tidewater (regional history, folklore and wildlife of the Chesapeake Bay and the Delmarva Peninsula).

O→ Cornell Maritime Press publishes books for the merchant marine and a few recreational boating books for professional mariners and yachtsmen.

Nonfiction: How-to (on maritime subjects), technical, manuals. Subjects include marine subjects (highly technical). Query first, with writing samples and outlines of book ideas.

Recent Title(s): *Master's Handbook on Ship's Business*, by Tuuli Anna Messer.

CORNELL UNIVERSITY PRESS, Sage House, 512 E. State St., Ithaca NY 14850. (607)277-2338. Fax: (607)277-2374. Website: www.cornellpress.cornell.edu. **Acquisitions:** Frances Benson, editor-in-chief. Estab. 1869. Publishes hardcover and paperback originals. **Publishes 150 titles/year. Pays royalty. Offers $0-5,000 advance.** Publishes book 1 year after acceptance of ms. Accepts simultaneous submissions. Book catalog and ms guidelines online.

Imprints: Comstock (contact Peter J. Prescott, science editor), ILR Press (contact Frances Benson).

O→ Cornell Press is an academic publisher of nonfiction with particular strengths in anthropology, Asian studies, biological sciences, classics, history, labor and business, literary criticism, politics and international relations, psychology, women's studies, Slavic studies, philosophy. Currently emphasizing sound scholarship that appeals beyond the academic community.

Nonfiction: Biography, reference, scholarly, textbook. Subjects include agriculture/horticulture, anthropology/archeology, art/architecture, business/economics, education, ethnic, gay/lesbian, government/politics, history, language/literature, military/war, music/dance, philosophy, psychology, regional, religion, science, sociology, translation, women's issues/studies. Submit résumé, cover letter and prospectus.

Recent Title(s): *Ermengard of Narbonne and the World of the Troubadours*, by Fredric L. Cheyette; *Russia's Unfinished Revolution*, by Michael McFaul; *The Birds of Ecuador*, by Robert S. Ridgely and Paul J. Greenfield.

CORWIN PRESS, INC., 2455 Teller Rd., Thousand Oaks CA 91320. (805)499-9734. Fax: (805)499-2692. E-mail: faye.zucker@corwinpress.com. **Acquisitions:** Faye Zucker, executive editor (teaching, learning, curriculum); Robb Clouse, acquisitions editor (administration, special education, technology); Rachel Livsey, acquisitions editor (staff development, assessment, diversity, education issues); Mark Goldberg, editor-at-large. Estab. 1990. Publishes hardcover and paperback originals. **Publishes 90 titles/year.** Publishes book 7 months after acceptance of ms. Responds in 1 month to queries. Ms guidelines for #10 SASE.

O→ Corwin Press, Inc. publishes leading-edge, user-friendly publications for education professionals.

Nonfiction: Professional-level publications for administrators, teachers, school specialists, policymakers, researchers and others involved with K-12 education. Subjects include education. Seeking fresh insights, conclusions, and recommendations for action. Prefers theory or research based books that provide real-world examples and practical, hands-on strategies to help busy educators be successful. No textbooks that simply summarize existing knowledge or mass-market books. Query with SASE.

Recent Title(s): *How the Brain Learns*, by David Sousa; *Keys to the Classroom*, by Carol Moran; *Beginning the Principalship*, by John Daresh.

COTTONWOOD PRESS, INC., 107 Cameron Drive, Fort Collins CO 80525. (800)864-4297. Fax: (970)204-0761. E-mail: cottonwood@cottonwoodpress.com. Website: www.cottonwoodpress.com. **Acquisitions:** Cheryl Thurston, editor. Estab. 1986. Publishes trade paperback originals. **Publishes 2-8 titles/year. Receives 50 queries and 40 mss/year. 50% of books from first-time authors; 100% from unagented writers. Pays 10-12% royalty on net receipts.** Publishes book 1 year after acceptance of ms. Accepts simultaneous submissions. Responds in 1 month to queries; 1 month to proposals; 3 months to mss. Book catalog for 10×12 SAE with 2 first-class stamps; ms guidelines for #10 SASE or see website.

O→ Cottonwood Press publishes creative and practical materials for English and language arts teachers, grades 5-12. "We believe English should be everyone's favorite subject." Currently emphasizing anything helping teachers address improving test scores.

Nonfiction: Textbook. Subjects include education, language/literature. "We are always looking for truly original, creative materials for teachers." Query with SASE or submit outline, 1-3 sample chapter(s).

Recent Title(s): *A to Z: Novel Ideas for Reading Teachers*; *Timewarped: Five Read-Aloud Plays that S-T-R-E-T-C-H the Truth About History.*

Tips: "We publish *only* supplemental textbooks for English/language arts teachers, grades 5-12, with an emphasis upon middle school and junior high materials. Don't assume we publish educational materials for all subject areas. We do not. Never submit anything to us before looking at our catalog. We have a very narrow focus and a distinctive style. Writers who don't understand that are wasting their time. On the plus side, we are eager to work with new authors who show a sense of humor and a familiarity with young adolescents."

COUNCIL OAK BOOKS, 1290 Chestnut St. #2, San Francisco CA 94109. (415)931-6868. Fax: (415)931-5353. E-mail: kevincob@pacbell.net. **Acquisitions:** Kevin Bentley, editor-in-chief (Native American history and spirituality; memoir; small, inspirational gift books; Americana). Estab. 1984. Publishes hardcover originals, trade paperback originals and reprints. **Publishes 10-12 titles/year. Receives 1,000 queries/year. 35% of books from first-time authors; 75% from unagented writers. Pays 10-20% royalty on net receipts.** Publishes book 9-12 months after acceptance of ms. Accepts simultaneous submissions. Responds in 1 month to queries; 1 month to proposals. Book catalog for #10 SASE; ms guidelines for #10 SASE.

Nonfiction: Autobiography, gift book, illustrated book. Subjects include Americana, memoirs, Native American studies. Query with SASE. Reviews artwork/photos as part of ms package. Send photocopies.

Recent Title(s): *Native New Yorkers*, by Evan Pritchard.
Tips: Audience is interested in Native American wisdom.

COUNCIL ON SOCIAL WORK EDUCATION, 1725 Duke St., Suite 500, Alexandria VA 22314-3457. (703)683-8080. Fax: (703)683-8099. E-mail: publications@cswe.org. Website: www.cswe.org. **Acquisitions:** Michael J. Monti, director of publications. Estab. 1952. Publishes trade paperback originals. **Publishes 4 titles/year. Receives 12 queries and 8 mss/year. 25% of books from first-time authors; 100% from unagented writers. Pays sliding royalty scale, starting at 10%.** Publishes book 1 year after acceptance of ms. Responds in 2 months to queries; 3 months to proposals; 3 months to mss. Book catalog and ms guidelines free via website or with SASE.

- Council on Social Work Education produces books and resources for social work educators, students and practitioners.

Nonfiction: Subjects include education, sociology, social work. Books for social work and other educators. Query with proposal package, including cv, outline, 2 sample chapters and SASE. Reviews artwork/photos as part of ms package. Send photocopies.
Recent Title(s): *Group Work Education in the Field*, by Julianne Wayne and Carol S. Cohen; *Ethics Education in Social Work*, by Frederic G. Reamer.
Tips: Audience is "Social work educators and students and others in the helping professions. Check areas of publication interest on website."

COUNTRY MUSIC FOUNDATION PRESS, 222 Fifth Ave. S., Nashville TN 37203. (615)416-2001. Fax: (615)255-2245. Website: www.countrymusichalloffame.com. **Acquisitions:** Paul Kingsbury, deputy director (country music history, biography); Chris Dickinson, associate editor (current country performers, criticism); John Rumble, associate editor (music business, history, bluegrass, Nashville music history); Ronnie Pugh, associate editor (honky-tonk country, old-time country, country gospel music). Publishes hardcover originals and trade paperback originals and reprints. **Publishes 2-4 titles/year. Receives 12 queries/year. Pays 10% royalty on wholesale price. Offers $1,000-5,000 advance.** Publishes book 1 year after acceptance of ms. Accepts simultaneous submissions. Responds in 2 months to queries; 3 months to proposals; 4 months to mss. Book catalog online; ms guidelines free.

- "We publish historical, biographical and reference books about country music, many in a joint imprint with Vanderbilt University Press. We require strict factual accuracy and strive to engage an educated general audience." Currently emphasizes "histories, biographies, and memoirs with a strong narrative and accessible to an educated general audience." De-emphasizing "heavily academic studies."

Nonfiction: All must emphasize country music. Biography, illustrated book, reference, scholarly. Subjects include Americana, history, memoirs, music/dance, photography, regional. Query with SASE or submit proposal package, including outline, 1 sample chapter and introduction. Reviews artwork/photos as part of ms package. Send photocopies.
Recent Title(s): *A Good-Natured Riot: The Birth of the Grand Ole Opry*, by Charles Wolfe (history).
Tips: "Our audience is a balance between educated country music fans and scholars. Submit queries or proposals only if you are very knowledgeable about your subject. Our books are in-depth studies written by experts or by music insiders. We aren't especially receptive to inexperienced beginners."

THE COUNTRYMAN PRESS, P.O. Box 748, Woodstock VT 05091-0748. (802)457-4826. Fax: (802)457-1678. E-mail: countrymanpress@wwnorton.com. Website: www.countrymanpress.com. Editorial Director: Kermit Hummel. **Acquisitions:** Ann Kraybill, managing editor. Estab. 1973. Publishes hardcover originals, trade paperback originals and reprints. **Publishes 35 titles/year. Receives 1,000 queries/year. 30% of books from first-time authors; 70% from unagented writers. Pays 5-15% royalty on retail price. Offers $1,000-5,000 advance.** Publishes book 18 months after acceptance of ms. Accepts simultaneous submissions. Responds in 2 months to proposals. Book catalog free; ms guidelines for #10 SASE.
Imprints: Backcountry Guides

- Countryman Press publishes books that encourage physical fitness and appreciation for and understanding of the natural world, self-sufficiency and adventure.

Nonfiction: "We publish several series of regional recreation guidebooks—hiking, bicycling, walking, fly-fishing, canoeing, kayaking—and are looking to expand them. We're also looking for books of national interest on travel, gardening, rural living, nature and fly-fishing." How-to, guidebooks; general nonfiction. Subjects include cooking/foods/nutrition, gardening, general nonfiction, history (New England), nature/environment, recreation, regional (New England), travel, country living. Submit proposal package including outline, 3 sample chapter(s), author bio, market information, SASE. Reviews artwork/photos as part of ms package. Send photocopies.
Recent Title(s): *The Granite Landscape: A Natural History of America's Mountain Domes, from Arcadia to Yosemite*, by Tom Wessles, illustrated by Brian D. Cohen.

COVENANT COMMUNICATIONS, INC., Box 416, American Fork UT 84003-0416. (801)756-1041. Website: www.covenant-lds.com. **Publishes 50+ titles/year. 35% of books from first-time authors; 100% from unagented writers. Pays 6½-15% royalty on retail price.** Publishes book 6-12 months after acceptance of ms. Responds in 4 months to mss. Ms guidelines online.

- Currently emphasizing inspirational, devotional, historical, biography. Our fiction is also expanding, and we are looking for new approaches to LDS literature and storytelling.

Nonfiction: Biography, children's/juvenile, coffee table book, gift book, humor, illustrated book, multimedia (CD-ROM), reference, scholarly. Subjects include child guidance/parenting, creative nonfiction, history, memoirs, religion (LDS or Mormon), spirituality. Submit completed manuscript with synopsis and one-page cover letter.
Fiction: "We publish exclusively to the 'Mormon' (The Church of Jesus Christ of Latter-Day Saints) market. All work must appeal to that audience." Adventure, fantasy, historical, humor, juvenile, literary, mainstream/contemporary, mystery, picture books, regional, religious, romance, science fiction, spiritual, suspense, young adult. Submit completed manuscript with synopsis and one-page cover letter.
Recent Title(s): *Between Husband and Wife*, by Brinley and Lamb (marriage/self-help); *On Holy Ground: Old Testament Lands*, by S. Michael Wilcox; *Saints at War*, by Robert Freeman and Dennis Wright.
Tips: Our audience is exclusively LDS (Latter-Day Saints, "Mormon").

CQ PRESS, 1255 22nd St. NW, Suite 400, Washington DC 20037. (202)729-1800. Fax: (202)729-1806. E-mail: ksuarez@cqpress.com. Website: www.cqpress.com. **Acquisitions:** David Tarr; Chris Anzalone, Shana Wagger (library/reference); Brenda Carter, Clarisse Kiino (college/political science), acquisitions editors. Estab. 1945. Publishes hardcover and paperback titles. **Publishes 50-70 titles/year. 95% from unagented writers. Pays college or reference royalties or fees. Offers occasional advance.** Publishes book an average of 1 year after acceptance of ms. Accepts simultaneous submissions. Responds in 3 months to queries. Book catalog free.
Imprints: CQ Press; College/Political Science, Library/Reference, Directory.

O→ CQ seeks "to educate the public by publishing authoritative works on American and international government and politics."

Nonfiction: "We are interested in American government, public administration, comparative government, and international relations." Reference, textbook (all levels of college political science texts), information directories (on federal and state governments, national elections, international/state politics and governmental issues). Subjects include government/politics, history (American, reference only). Submit proposal package including outline.
Recent Title(s): *Guide to Congress*.
Tips: "Our books present important information on American government and politics, and related issues, with careful attention to accuracy, thoroughness and readability."

CRAFTSMAN BOOK COMPANY, 6058 Corte Del Cedro, Carlsbad CA 92009-9974. (760)438-7828 or (800)829-8123. Fax: (760)438-0398. E-mail: jacobs@costbook.com. Website: www.craftsman-book.com. **Acquisitions:** Laurence D. Jacobs, editorial manager. Estab. 1957. Publishes paperback originals. **Publishes 12 titles/year. Receives 50 submissions/year. 85% of books from first-time authors; 98% from unagented writers. Pays 7½-12½% royalty on wholesale price or retail price.** Publishes book 2 years after acceptance of ms. Accepts simultaneous submissions. Responds in 2 months to queries. Book catalog and ms guidelines free.

O→ Publishes how-to manuals for professional builders. Currently emphasizing construction software.

Nonfiction: All titles are related to construction for professional builders. How-to, technical. Subjects include building, construction. Query with SASE. Reviews artwork/photos as part of ms package.
Recent Title(s): *Steel-Frame House Construction*, by Tim Waite.
Tips: "The book should be loaded with step-by-step instructions, illustrations, charts, reference data, forms, samples, cost estimates, rules of thumb, and examples that solve actual problems in the builder's office and in the field. The book must cover the subject completely, become the owner's primary reference on the subject, have a high utility-to-cost ratio, and help the owner make a better living in his chosen field."

CREATIVE HOMEOWNER, 24 Park Way, Upper Saddle River NJ 07458. (201)934-7100. Fax: (201)934-7541. E-mail: sharon.ranftle@creativehomeowner.com. Website: www.creativehomeowner.com. **Acquisitions:** Tim Bakke, editorial director; Fran Donegan, editor (home improvement/repair); Kathie Robitz, senior editor (home decorating/design). Estab. 1978. Publishes trade paperback originals. **Publishes 12-16 titles/year. Receives dozens of queries mss/year. 50% of books from first-time authors; 98% from unagented writers. Makes outright purchase of $8,000-35,000.** Publishes book 16 months after acceptance of ms. Responds in 6 months to queries. Book catalog free.

O→ Creative Homeowner is the one source for the largest selection of quality how-to books, booklets and project plans.

Nonfiction: How-to, illustrated book. Subjects include gardening, hobbies, home remodeling/building, home repairs, home decorating/design. Query or submit proposal package, including competitive books (short analysis) and outline and SASE. Reviews artwork/photos as part of ms package.
Recent Title(s): *The Smart Approach to Country Decorating*, by Margaret Sabo Wills; *Decorating with Architectural Trimwork*, by Jay Silber; *Plumbing*, by Merle Henkenius.

CRICKET BOOKS, 332 S. Michigan Ave., #1100, Chicago IL 60604. (312)939-1500. Website: www.cricketbooks.net. **Acquisitions:** Carol Saller, editor (picture books, chapter books, middle-grade and young adult fiction); Marc Aronson, editorial director (fiction and nonfiction primarily for teenagers). Estab. 1999. Publishes hardcover originals. **Publishes 20 titles/year. Receives 500 queries and 1,500 mss/year. Open to first-time and unagented authors. Pays up to 10% royalty on retail price. Offers $1,500 and up advance.** Publishes book 18 months after acceptance of ms. Accepts simultaneous submissions. Responds in 3 months to queries; 3 months to proposals; 4 months to mss. Ms guidelines for #10 SASE.

O→ Cricket Books publishes picture books, chapter books and middle-grade novels and young adult fiction and nonfiction.

Nonfiction: Children's/juvenile, Young Adult. Send proposal, including sample chapters, table of contents, and description of competition.
Fiction: Juvenile, young adult. Submit complete ms.
Recent Title(s): *Seek*, by Paul Fleischman; *Robert and the Weird & Wacky Facts*, by Barbar Seuling; *The Power of Un*, by Nancy Etchemendy.
Tips: "Take a look at the recent titles to see what sort of materials we're interested in, especially for nonfiction. Please note that we aren't doing the sort of strictly educational nonfiction that other publishers specialize in."

CROSSQUARTER PUBLISHING GROUP, P.O. Box 8756, Santa Fe NM 87504. (505)438-9846. Website: www.crossquarter.com. **Acquisitions:** Anthony Ravenscroft. Publishes case and trade paperback originals and reprints. **Publishes 5-10 titles/year. Receives 250 queries/year. 90% of books from first-time authors. Pays 8-10% royalty on wholesale or retail price.** Publishes book 1 year after acceptance of ms. Accepts simultaneous submissions. Responds in 3 months to queries. Book catalog for $1.75; ms guidelines online.

O→ "We emphasize personal sovereignty, self responsibility and growth with pagan or pagan-friendly emphasis for young adults and adults."

Nonfiction: Biography, how-to, self-help. Subjects include health/medicine, nature/environment, New Age, philosophy, psychology, religion (pagan only), spirituality, autobiography. Query with SASE. Reviews artwork/photos as part of ms package. Send photocopies.
Fiction: Science fiction, visionary fiction. Query with SASE.
Recent Title(s): *Dead as I'll Ever Be: Psychic Adventures that Changed My Life*, by Pamela Evans; *Beyond One's Own*, by Gabriel Constans; *My Heart and I*, by Jerry Darenberg.
Tips: "Audience is earth-conscious people looking to grow into balance of body, mind, heart and spirit."

CROSSWAY BOOKS, 1300 Crescent St., Wheaton IL 60187-5800. Fax: (630)682-4785. Editorial Director: Marvin Padgett. **Acquisitions:** Jill Carter. Estab. 1938. Publishes hardcover and trade paperback originals. **Publishes 95 titles/year. Receives 2,500 submissions/year. 2% of books from first-time authors; 75% from unagented writers. Pays negotiable royalty. Offers negotiable advance.** Publishes book 18 months after acceptance of ms. Responds in up to 2 months to queries. Book catalog for 9×12 SAE with 7 first-class stamps; ms guidelines for #10 SASE.

O→ "With 'making a difference in people's lives for Christ' as its maxim, Crossway Books lists titles written from an evangelical Christian worldview."

Nonfiction: Subjects include religion, spirituality. "Books that provide fresh understanding and a distinctively Christian examination of questions confronting Christians and non-Christians in their personal lives, families, churches, communities and the wider culture. The main types include: (1) Issues books that typically address critical issues facing Christians today; (2) Books on the deeper Christian life that provide a deeper understanding of Christianity and its application to daily life; and, (3) Christian academic and professional books directed at an audience of religious professionals. Be sure the books are from an evangelical Christian worldview. Writers often give sketchy information on their book's content." Query with SASE. No phone queries.
Fiction: "We publish fiction that falls into these categories: (1) Christian realism, or novels set in modern, true-to-life settings as a means of telling stories about Christians today in an increasingly post-Christian era; (2) Supernatural fiction, or stories typically set in the 'real world' but that bring supernatural reality into it in a way that heightens our spiritual dimension; (3) Historical fiction, using historical characters, times and places of interest as a mirror for our own times; (4) Some genre-technique fiction (mystery, western); and (5) Children's fiction. We are not interested in romance novels, horror novels, biblical novels (i.e., stories set in Bible times that fictionalize events in the lives of prominent biblical characters), issues novels (i.e., fictionalized treatments of contemporary issues), and end times/prophecy novels. We do not accept full manuscripts or electronic submissions." Submit synopsis with 2 sample chapters and SASE.
Recent Title(s): *The Hidden Smile of God*, by John Piper (nonfiction); *Cry Freedom*, by Marlo Schalesky (fiction).
Tips: "All of our fiction must have 'Christian' content—combine the Truth of God's Word with a passion to live it out. Writers often submit without thinking about what a publisher actually publishes. They also send full manuscripts without a synopsis. Without a synopsis, the manuscript does not get read."

CSLI PUBLICATIONS, Ventura Hall, Stanford University, Stanford CA 94305-4115. (650)723-1839. Fax: (650)725-2166. E-mail: pubs@csli.stanford.edu. Website: cslipublications.stanford.edu. **Acquisitions:** Dikran Karagueuzian, director (linguistics, philosophy, logic, computer science). Publishes hardcover and scholarly paperback originals. **Publishes 40 titles/year. Receives 200 queries and 50 mss/year. Pays 3-10% royalty; honorarium.** Publishes book 1 year after acceptance of ms. Does not accept simultaneous submissions. Responds in 1 month to queries; 4 months to proposals; 6 months to mss. Book catalog free.

O→ "CSLI Publications, part of the Center for the Studies of Language and Information, specializes in books in the areas of formal linguistics, logic, philosophy, computer science and human-computer interaction." Currently emphasizing human-computer interaction, computers and media, voice technology. De-emphasizing pragmatic linguistics.

Nonfiction: Reference, technical, textbook, scholarly. Subjects include anthropology/archeology, computers/electronic, language/literature (linguistics), science, logic, cognitive science. Query with SASE or by email.
Recent Title(s): *Coherence, Reference, and the Theory of Grammar*, by Andrew Kehler.

CUMBERLAND HOUSE PUBLISHING, 431 Harding Industrial Dr., Nashville TN 37211. (615)832-1171. Fax: (615)832-0633. E-mail: cumbhouse@aol.com. Website: www.cumberlandhouse.com. **Acquisitions:** Tilly Katz, acquisitions editor. Estab. 1996. Publishes hardcover, trade paperback and mass market originals and reprints. **Publishes 60 titles/year; imprint publishes 5 titles/year. Receives 3,000 queries and 500 mss/year. 30% of books from first-time authors; 80% from unagented writers. Pays 10-20% royalty on wholesale price. Offers $1,000-10,000 advance.** Publishes book an average of 12 months after acceptance of ms. Accepts simultaneous submissions. Responds in 3 months to queries; 3 months to proposals; 1 year to mss. Book catalog for 8×10 SAE with 4 first-class stamps; ms guidelines online.

Imprints: Cumberland House Hearthside, Highland Books

O‑ Cumberland House publishes "market specific books. We evaluate in terms of how sure we are that we can publish the book successfully and then the quality or uniqueness of a project." Currently emphasizing mystery (exceptional only), history, and sports celebrities. De-emphasizing humor.

Nonfiction: Cookbook, gift book, how-to, humor, reference. Subjects include Americana, cooking/foods/nutrition, government/politics, history, military/war, recreation, regional, sports, travel, popular culture, civil war. Query or submit outline. Reviews artwork/photos as part of ms package. Send photocopies only; not original copies.

Fiction: Mystery. Writers should know "the odds are really stacked against them." Query with SASE.

Recent Title(s): *Smokehouse Ham, Spoon Bread and Scuppernong Wine*, by Joe Dabney (winner of 1999 James Beard Cookbook of the Year Award); *The Encyclopedia of Civil War Usage*, by Webb Garrison; *I Remember Dale Earnhardt*, by Thomas Gillespie.

Tips: Audience is "adventuresome people who like a fresh approach to things. Writers should tell what their idea is, why it's unique and why somebody would want to buy it—but don't pester us."

N CURRENT CLINICAL STRATEGIES PUBLISHING, 27071 Cabot Rd., Suite 126, Laguna Hills CA 92653. (949)348-8404. Fax: (949)348-8405. E-mail: info@ccspublishing.com. Website: www.ccspublishing.com. **Acquisitions:** Camille deTonnancour, editor. Estab. 1988. Publishes trade paperback originals. **Publishes 20 titles/year. Receives 10 queries and 10 mss/year. 50% of books from first-time authors; 50% from unagented writers. Pays royalty.** Publishes book 6 months after acceptance of ms.

O‑ Current Clinical Strategies is a medical publisher for healthcare professionals.

Nonfiction: Technical. Subjects include health/medicine. *Physician authors only.* Submit 6 sample chapter(s). Reviews artwork/photos as part of ms package. Send file by e-mail only.

Recent Title(s): *Family Medicine 2000*, by Paul D. Chan, M.D.; *Pediatrics Five Minute Reviews 2001*, by Karen Scruggs, M.D.

CYPRESS PUBLISHING GROUP, 11835 ROE #187, Leawood KS 66211. (913)681-9875. Fax: (913)498-1524. E-mail: cypressbook@hotmail.com. Website: www.cypresspublishing.com. Vice President Marketing: Carl Heintz. **Acquisitions:** William S. Noblitt, JoAnn Heinz. Publishes hardcover and trade paperback originals. **Publishes 10 titles/year. 80% of books from first-time authors; 90% from unagented writers. Pays 10-15% royalty on wholesale price.** Publishes book 8 months after acceptance of ms. Responds in 1 month to queries; 1 month to proposals; 1 month to mss. Book catalog free.

O‑ "We are an innovative niche publisher of business and finance books, including training materials." Currently emphasizing business, finance, investing.

Nonfiction: How-to, illustrated book, self-help, technical, textbook. Subjects include business/economics, computers/electronic (business related), money/finance (small business, personal finance, investing, accounting), psychology (business related), software (business related). Query with proposal package, including outline, 1-3 sample chapters, overview of book. Send photocopies.

Recent Title(s): *Money*, by Alex Grant; *Number Sense*, by Carl Heintz.

Tips: "Our editorial plans change—we are always looking for outstanding submissions. Many writers fail to consider what other books on the topics are available. The writer must think about the fundamental book marketing question: Why will a customer *buy* the book?"

THE DANA PRESS, 900 15th St., NW, Washington DC 20005. (202)737-9200. Fax: (202)737-9204. Website: www.dana.org/books/press. **Acquisitions:** Jane Nevins, editor-in-chief; Andrew Cocke, editor. Publishes hardcover and trade paperback originals. **Publishes 4 titles/year. Receives 10 queries and 3 mss/year. 50% of books from first-time authors; 90% from unagented writers. Pays 14-20% royalty on wholesale price. Offers $10,000-35,000 advance.** Publishes book 1 year after acceptance of ms. Accepts simultaneous submissions. Responds in 2 weeks to queries; 1 month to proposals; 2 months to mss. Book catalog and ms guidelines online.

Nonfiction: Biography, coffee table book, brain-related health books. Subjects include health/medicine, memoirs, psychology, popular science. "We focus almost exclusively on the brain." Reviews artwork/photos as part of ms package. Send photocopies.

Recent Title(s): *Secret Life of the Brain*, by Richard Restak, M.D.; *Keeping Your Brain Young*, by Guy McKhann, M.D. and Marilyn Albert, Ph.D.; *Understanding Depression*, by Raymond DePaulo, M.D. and Leslie Horvitz.

Tips: "Coherent, thought-out proposals are key. What is the scope of the book? Who is the reader? It's important to have an angle."

JOHN DANIEL AND COMPANY, Daniel & Daniel, Publishers, Inc., P.O. Box 21922, Santa Barbara CA 93121-1922. (805)962-1780. Fax: (805)962-8835. E-mail: jd@danielpublishing.com. Website: www.danielpublishing.com. **Acquisitions:** John Daniel, publisher. Publishes hardcover originals and trade paperback originals. **Publishes 4 titles/year.**

Pays 10% royalty on wholesale price. Offers $0-500 advance. Publishes book 1 year after acceptance of ms. Responds in 1 month to queries; 1 month to proposals; 2 months to mss. Book catalog free or online; ms guidelines for #10 SASE or online.

Nonfiction: Biography, essay. Subjects include creative nonfiction, memoirs. "We seldom publish books over 70,000 words. Other than that, we're looking for books that are important and well-written." Query with SASE or submit proposal package including outline, 50 pages.

Fiction: Literary, poetry, short story collections. Query with SASE or submit proposal package including synopsis, 50 pages.

Poetry: "We publish very little poetry, I'm sorry to say." Query or submit complete ms.

Recent Title(s): *Home Is Where the Bus Is*, by Anne Beck with Johnson (travel memoir); *Seas Outside the Reef*, by Rosalind Brackenbury (novel); *Still Waters*, by Thelma Shaw (poetry).

Tips: "Literate, intelligent general readers. We are very small and very cautious, so any submission to us is a long shot. But we welcome your submissions. By mail only, please. We don't want submissions by phone, fax, disk, or e-mail."

DANTE UNIVERSITY OF AMERICA PRESS, INC., P.O. Box 812158, Wellesley MA 02482. Fax: (781)790-1056. E-mail: danteu@danteuniversity.org. Website: www.danteuniversity.org/dpress.html. **Acquisitions:** Adolph Caso, president. Estab. 1975. Publishes hardcover and trade paperback originals and reprints. **Publishes 5 titles/year. Receives 50 submissions/year. 50% of books from first-time authors; 50% from unagented writers. Pays royalty. Offers negotiable advance.** Publishes book 10 months after acceptance of ms. Responds in 2 months to queries.

O→ "The Dante University Press exists to bring quality, educational books pertaining to our Italian heritage as well as the historical and political studies of America. Profits from the sale of these publications benefit the Foundation, bringing Dante University closer to a reality."

Nonfiction: Biography, reference, scholarly, reprints. Subjects include history (Italian-American), humanities, translation (from Italian and latin), general scholarly nonfiction, Renaissance thought and letter, Italian language and linguistics, Italian-American culture, bilingual education. Query with SASE. Reviews artwork/photos as part of ms package.

Fiction: Translations from Italian and Latin. Query with SASE.

Poetry: "There is a chance that we would use Renaissance poetry translations."

Recent Title(s): *Trapped in Tuscany*, by Tullio Bertini (World War II nonfiction); *Rogue Angel*, by Carol Damioli (mystery).

MAY DAVENPORT, PUBLISHERS, 26313 Purissima Rd., Los Altos Hills CA 94022. (650)947-1275. Fax: (650)947-1373. E-mail: mdbooks@earthlink.net. Website: www.maydavenportpublishers.com. **Acquisitions:** May Davenport, editor/publisher. Estab. 1976. Publishes hardcover and paperback originals. **Publishes 4 titles/year. Receives 1,500 submissions/year. 95% of books from first-time authors; 100% from unagented writers. Pays 15% royalty on retail price. Offers no advance.** Publishes book 1 year after acceptance of ms. Responds in 1 month to queries. Book catalog and ms guidelines for #10 SASE.

Imprints: md Books (nonfiction and fiction).

O→ May Davenport publishes "literature for teenagers (before they graduate from high schools) as supplementary literary material in English courses nationwide." Looking particularly for authors able to write for the "teen Internet" generation who don't like to read in-depth. Currently emphasizing more upper-level subjects for teens.

Nonfiction: Subjects include Americana, language/literature, humorous memoirs for chldren/young adults. "For children ages 6-8: stories to read with pictures to color in 500 words. For preteens and young adults: exhibit your writing skills and entertain them with your literary tools." Query with SASE.

Fiction: Humor, literary. "We want to focus on novels junior and senior high school teachers can share with their reluctant readers in their classrooms."

Recent Title(s): *The Runaway Game*, by Kevin Casey (nonfiction); *Significant Footsteps*, by Ashleigh E. Gramge (fiction); *The Lesson Plan*, by Irvin Gay (fiction).

Tips: "If you have to write only about the ills of today's society of incest, murders, homelessness, divorce, one-parent families, just write your fictional novel humorously. If you can't write that way, create youthful characters so teachers, as well as 15-18 year-old high school readers, will laugh at your descriptive passages and contemporary dialogue. Avoid one-sentence paragraphs. The audience we want to reach is past Nancy Drew and Hardy Boy readers."

JONATHAN DAVID PUBLISHERS, INC., 68-22 Eliot Ave., Middle Village NY 11379-1194. (718)456-8611. Fax: (718)894-2818. E-mail: info@jdbooks.com. Website: www.jdbooks.com. **Acquisitions:** Alfred J. Kolatch, editor-in-chief. Estab. 1948. Publishes hardcover and trade paperback originals and reprints. **Publishes 20-25 titles/year. 50% of books from first-time authors; 90% from unagented writers. Pays royalty or makes outright purchase.** Publishes book 18 months after acceptance of ms. Responds in 1 month to queries; 1 month to proposals; 2 months to mss. Book catalog online; ms guidelines for #10 SASE or on website.

O→ Jonathan David publishes "popular Judaica." Currently emphasizing projects geared toward children.

Nonfiction: Biography, children's/juvenile, coffee table book, cookbook, gift book, how-to, humor, illustrated book, reference, self-help. Subjects include cooking/foods/nutrition, creative nonfiction, ethnic, humor, multicultural, religion, sex, sports. Query with SASE or submit proposal package including outline, 3 sample chapter(s), résumé. Reviews artwork/photos as part of ms package. Send photocopies.

Recent Title(s): *Drawing a Crowd*, by Bill Gallo (sports cartoons/memoir).

DAVIS PUBLICATIONS, INC., 50 Portland St., Worcester MA 01608. (508)754-7201. Fax: (508)753-3834. **Acquisitions:** Helen Ronan, editor-in-chief. Estab. 1901. **Publishes 5-10 titles/year. Pays 10-12% royalty. Offers advance.** Publishes book 1 year after acceptance of ms. Does not accept simultaneous submissions. Book catalog for 9×12 SAE with $2 U.S. postage; ms guidelines for #10 SASE.

O→ Davis publishes art, design and craft books for the elementary through high school art education markets. Our mission is to produce materials that help art teachers do their job better.

Nonfiction: Illustrated book. Subjects include art/architecture, education, history. Submit outline, sample chapter(s). Reviews artwork/photos as part of ms package.

Recent Title(s): *From Ordinary to Extraordinary, Art and Design Problem-Solving*, by Ken Vietn; *Creative Coloring*, by Art Sherwyn; *You Can Weave!*, by Kathleen Monaghan.

Tips: "Keep in mind the intended audience. Our readers are visually oriented. Photos should be good quality transparencies and black and white photographs. Well-selected illustrations should explain, amplify, and enhance the text. We average 2-4 photos/page. We like to see technique photos as well as illustrations of finished artwork, by a variety of artists, including students. Recent books have been on using technology in art teaching, printmaking, art education profession, history through art timeline. We do not publish fiction or poetry in any form!"

DAW BOOKS, INC., Penguin Putnam, Inc., 375 Hudson St., 3rd Floor, New York NY 10014-3658. (212)366-2096. Fax: (212)366-2090. E-mail: daw@penguinputnam.com. Website: www.dawbooks.com. Publishers: Elizabeth Wollheim and Sheila Gilbert. **Acquisitions:** Peter Stampfel, submissions editor. Estab. 1971. Publishes hardcover and paperback originals and reprints. **Publishes 60-80 titles/year. Pays in royalties with an advance negotiable on a book-by-book basis.** Sends galleys to author to proposals. Book catalog free.

- Simultaneous submissions "returned unread at once, unless prior arrangements are made by agent."

O→ DAW Books publishes science fiction and fantasy.

Fiction: Fantasy, science fiction. "We are interested in science fiction and fantasy novels. We need science fiction more than fantasy right now, but we're still looking for both. We like character-driven books with attractive characters. We're not looking for horror novels, but we are looking for mainstream suspense thrillers. We accept both agented and unagented manuscripts. Long books are absolutely not a problem. We are not seeking collections of short stories or ideas for anthologies. We do not want any nonfiction manuscripts." Query with SASE.

Recent Title(s): *The Gates of Sleep*, by Mercedes Lacky (fantasy); *The Eyes of God*, by John Marco (fantasy).

DAWN PUBLICATIONS, P.O. Box 2010, Nevada City CA 95959. (530)478-0111. Fax: (530)478-0112. E-mail: nature@dawnpub.com. Website: www.dawnpub.com. **Acquisitions:** Glenn Hovemann, editor. Estab. 1979. Publishes hardcover and trade paperback originals. **Publishes 6 titles/year. Receives 550 queries and 2,500 mss/year. 15% of books from first-time authors; 90% from unagented writers. Pays royalty on net receipts. Offers advance.** Publishes book 1 to 2 years after acceptance of ms. Accepts simultaneous submissions. Responds in 2 months to queries. Book catalog and ms guidelines online.

O→ Dawn Publications' mission is to assist parents and educators to open the minds and hearts of children to the transforming influence of nature. Dawn Publications is dedicated to inspiring in children a sense of appreciation for all life on earth. Dawn looks for nature awareness and appreciation titles that promote a relationship with the natural world and specific habitats, usually through inspiring treatment and nonfiction.

Nonfiction: Children's/juvenile. Subjects include animals, nature/environment. Query with SASE.

Recent Title(s): *Salmon Stream*, by Carol Reed-Jones.

Tips: Publishes mostly nonfiction with lightness and inspiration.

DEARBORN, Trade Publishing, 155 N. Wacker Dr., Chicago IL 60606-1719. (312)836-4400. Fax: (312)836-1021. E-mail: hull@dearborn.com. Website: www.dearborntrade.com. **Acquisitions:** Donald Hull, editorial director (finance); Jean Iversen, senior acquisitions editor (general business/management); Mary B. Good, acquisitions editor (consumer real estate, sales & marketing). Estab. 1959. Publishes hardcover and paperback originals. **Publishes 50 titles/year. Receives 400 submissions/year. 30% of books from first-time authors; 50% from unagented writers. Pays 10-15% royalty on wholesale price. Offers advance.** Publishes book 6 months after acceptance of ms. Accepts simultaneous submissions. Responds in 1 month to queries. Book catalog and ms guidelines free.

O→ The trade division of Dearborn publishes practical, solutions-oriented books for individuals and corporations on the subjects of finance, consumer real estate, business and entrepreneurship. Currently emphasizing finance, general business/management, consumer real estate. De-emphasizing small business.

Nonfiction: How-to, reference, textbook. Subjects include business/economics, money/finance. Query with SASE.

Recent Title(s): *The Power of Six Sigma*, by Subir Chowdhury; *The New Retirementality*, by Mitch Anthony; *Real Estate a la Carte*, by Julie Garton-Good.

IVAN R. DEE, PUBLISHER, The Rowman & Littlefield Publishing Group, 1332 N. Halsted St., Chicago IL 60622-2694. (312)787-6262. Fax: (312)787-6269. E-mail: elephant@ivanrdee.com. Website: www.ivanrdee.com. **Acquisitions:** Ivan R. Dee, president; Hilary Schaefer, associate editor. Estab. 1988. Publishes hardcover originals and trade paperback originals and reprints. **Publishes 60 titles/year. 10% of books from first-time authors; 80% from unagented writers. Pays royalty. Offers advance.** Publishes book 8 months after acceptance of ms. Accepts simultaneous submissions. Responds in 1 month to queries; 1 month to proposals; 1 month to mss. Book catalog free.

Imprints: Elephant Paperbacks, New Amsterdam Books, J.S. Sanders Books.

O→ Ivan R. Dee publishes serious nonfiction for general informed readers.

Nonfiction: Biography. Subjects include art/architecture, film/cinema/stage, government/politics, history, language/literature, world affairs, contemporary culture, film/cinema/stage, baseball. Submit outline, sample chapter(s). Reviews artwork/photos as part of ms package.
Recent Title(s): *The Search for Roots*, by Primo Levi; *A Short History of the World*, by Geoffrey Blainey; *America Confronts Terrorism*, edited by John Prados.
Tips: "We publish for an intelligent lay audience and college course adoptions."

DEL REY BOOKS, Ballantine Publishing Group, Random House, Inc., 1540 Broadway, 11th Floor-J, New York NY 10036. (212)782-8393. E-mail: delrey@randomhouse.com. Website: www.randomhouse.com/delrey. **Acquisitions:** Betsy Mitchell, editor-in-chief (science fiction, fantasy); Shelly Shapiro, editorial director (science fiction, fantasy); Steve Saffel, senior editor (fantasy, alternate history); Chris Schluep, assistant editor (science fiction); Christopher Evans (military science fiction and fantasy). Estab. 1977. Publishes hardcover, trade paperback, and mass market originals and mass market paperback reprints. **Publishes 70 titles/year. Receives 1,900 submissions/year. 10% of books from first-time authors; 0% from unagented writers. Pays royalty on retail price. Offers competitive advance.** Publishes book 1 year after acceptance of ms. Does not accept simultaneous submissions. Responds in 6 months to queries. Ms guidelines for #10 SASE.

Del Rey publishes top level fantasy, alternate history, and science fiction.

Fiction: Fantasy (should have the practice of magic as an essential element of the plot), science fiction (well-plotted novels with good characterizations, exotic locales and detailed alien creatures), alternate history ("novels that take major historical events, such as the Civil War, and bend history in a new direction sometimes through science fiction and fantasy devices"). *Agented submissions only.*
Recent Title(s): *Vitals*, by Greg Bear; *Morgawr*, by Terry Brooks; *The Scar*, by China Miéville.
Tips: "Del Rey is a reader's house. Pay particular attention to plotting, strong characters, and dramatic, satisfactory conclusions. It must be/feel believable. That's what the readers like. In terms of mass market, we basically created the field of fantasy bestsellers. Not that it didn't exist before, but we put the mass into mass market."

DELACORTE PRESS, Bantam Dell Publishing Group, Random House, Inc., 1540 Broadway, New York NY 10036. (212)782-9000. Fax: (212)782-9523. Website: www.randomhouse.com/kids. Editor-in-Chief: Leslie Schnur. **Acquisitions:** (Ms.) Jackie Cantor (women's fiction and general fiction). Publishes hardcover and trade paperback originals. **Publishes 36 titles/year. Offers advance.** Does not accept simultaneous submissions.
Nonfiction: *Agented submissions only.*
Fiction: *Agented submissions only.*
Recent Title(s): *Why Not Me?*, Al Franken (nonfiction); *Be Cool*, Elmore Leonard (fiction).

THE DENALI PRESS, P.O. Box 021535, Juneau AK 99802-1535. (907)586-6014. Fax: (907)463-6780. E-mail: denalipress@alaska.com. Website: www.denalipress.com. **Acquisitions:** Alan Schorr, editorial director; Sally Silvas-Ottumwa, editorial associate. Estab. 1986. Publishes trade paperback originals. **Publishes 5 titles/year. Receives 120 submissions/year. 50% of books from first-time authors; 80% from unagented writers. Pays 10% royalty on wholesale price or makes outright purchase. Offers advance.** Publishes book 1 year after acceptance of ms. Accepts simultaneous submissions. Responds in 1 month to queries.

The Denali Press looks for reference works suitable for the educational, professional and library market. "Though we publish books on a variety of topics, our focus is most broadly centered on multiculturalism, public policy, Alaskana, and general reference works."

Nonfiction: Reference. Subjects include Americana, anthropology/archeology, ethnic, government/politics, history, multicultural, recreation, regional. "We need reference books—ethnic, refugee and minority concerns." Query with SASE or submit outline, sample chapter(s). **All unsolicited mss returned unopened.**
Recent Title(s): *Winning Political Campaigns: A Comprehensive Guide to Electoral Success*, by William S. Bike.

DESCANT PUBLISHING, P.O. Box 12973, Mill Creek WA 98082. (206)235-3357. Fax: (646)365-7513. E-mail: bret@descantpub.com. Website: www.descantpub.com. **Acquisitions:** Bret Sable, senior editor (nonfiction); Alex Royal, editor (fiction). Estab. 2001. Publishes hardcover, trade paperback, mass market paperback, and electronic originals. **Publishes 10-12 titles/year. Receives 1,200 queries/year. 50% of books from first-time authors; 50% from unagented writers. Pays 6-15% royalty.** Publishes book 18 months after acceptance of ms. Accepts simultaneous submissions. Responds in 3 months to queries; 3 months to proposals; 3 months to mss. Ms guidelines for #10 SASE.

FOR EXPLANATIONS OF THESE SYMBOLS,
SEE THE INSIDE FRONT AND BACK COVERS OF THIS BOOK.

Nonfiction: Children's/juvenile, how-to, self-help. Subjects include community, contemporary culture, creative nonfiction, education, general nonfiction, humanities, memoirs, music/dance, religion, spirituality. Submissions should be original and timely. "Our nonfiction must capture a known audience." Query with SASE.

Fiction: Fantasy, horror, mainstream/contemporary, mystery, religious, science fiction, suspense. Fresh storylines are critical. Query with SASE.

Recent Title(s): *From White House to Crack House*, by Nancy Dudley (current affairs); *At the Manger: The Stories of Those Who Were There*, by Peter Orullian (historical fiction).

THE DESIGN IMAGE GROUP INC., 231 S. Frontage Rd., Suite 17, Burr Ridge IL 60521. (630)789-8991. Fax: (630)789-9013. E-mail: dig@designimagegroup.com. Website: www.designimagegroup.com. **Acquisitions:** Editorial Committee. Estab. 1984. Publishes trade paperback originals and reprints. **Publishes 5-7 titles/year. Receives 1,500+ queries and 500+ mss/year. 60% of books from first-time authors; 80% from unagented writers. Pays 12-20% royalty on wholesale price. Some books done as advance against royalty, some as straight royalty. Offers $3,000-3,500 advance.** Publishes book 6-8 months after acceptance of ms. Accepts simultaneous submissions. Responds in 1 month to queries; 1 month to mss. Book catalog for 9×12 SAE with 2 first-class stamps; ms guidelines for #10 SASE.

The Design Image Group publishes "traditional supernatural, human form, monster-based horror fiction and neo-noir and retro-pulp flavored dark mysteries."

Fiction: Horror, mystery. Query with SASE or submit proposal package including 3 sample chapter(s), synopsis.

Recent Title(s): *The Big Switch*, by Jack Bludis (hard-boiled mystery); *Night Players*, by P.D. Cacek (vampire novel); *Doomed To Repeat It*, by D.G.K. Goldberg (ghost novel).

Tips: Fans of literate, sophisticated dark mysteries (neo-noir, hard-boiled) and sophisticated supernatural horror, both of which enjoy seeing traditional genre icons revitalized in fresh ways. "Small presses are no more interested in work that's not ready for publication than the NYC majors. Revise, edit and proof, then check out our other titles on the website to see if your novel is a good fit for our lines."

DIAL BOOKS FOR YOUNG READERS, Penguin Putnam Inc., 345 Hudson St., 3rd Floor, New York NY 10014. (212)366-2800. President/Publisher: Nancy Paulsen. Editorial Director: Lauri Hornik. **Acquisitions:** Submissions Editor. Publishes hardcover originals. **Publishes 50 titles/year. Receives 5,000 queries/year. 20% of books from first-time authors. Pays royalty. Offers varies advance.** Does not accept simultaneous submissions. Responds in 3 months to queries.

Imprints: Phyllis Fogelman Books.

Dial Books for Young Readers publishes quality picture books for ages 18 months-8 years, lively, believable novels for middle readers and young adults, and occasional nonfiction for middle readers and young adults.

Nonfiction: Children's/juvenile, illustrated book. *Agented submissions only.*

Fiction: Adventure, fantasy, juvenile, picture books, young adult. Especially looking for "lively and well-written novels for middle grade and young adult children involving a convincing plot and believable characters. The subject matter or theme should not already be overworked in previously published books. The approach must not be demeaning to any minority group, nor should the roles of female characters (or others) be stereotyped, though we don't think books should be didactic, or in any way message-y. No topics inappropriate for the juvenile, young adult, and middle grade audiences. No plays." *Agented submissions only. No unsolicited mss.*

Recent Title(s): *Asteroid Impact*, by Doug Henderson; *A Year Down Yonder*, by Richard Parl; *The Missing Mitten Mystery*, by Steven Kellogg.

Tips: "Our readers are anywhere from preschool age to teenage. Picture books must have strong plots, lots of action, unusual premises, or universal themes treated with freshness and originality. Humor works well in these books. A very well thought out and intelligently presented book has the best chance of being taken on. Genre isn't as much of a factor as presentation."

DIAL PRESS, Bantam Dell Publishing Group, Random House, Inc., 1540 Broadway, New York NY 10036. (212)782-9000. Fax: (212)782-8414. Website: www.bbd.com. **Acquisitions:** Susan Kamil, vice president, editorial director. Estab. 1924. **Publishes 6-12 titles/year. Receives 200 queries and 450 mss/year. 75% of books from first-time authors. Pays royalty on retail price. Offers advance.** Publishes book 18 months after acceptance of ms. Accepts simultaneous submissions.

Dial Press publishes quality fiction and nonfiction. *Agented submissions only.*

Nonfiction: Biography. Subjects include contemporary culture, history, memoirs. *Agented submissions only.*

Fiction: Literary (general). *Agented submissions only.*

Recent Title(s): *American Chica* (nonfiction); *Mary and O'Neil* (stories); *Niagara Falls All Over Again* (novel).

DIOGENES PUBLISHING, SAN #253-1615, 965 Alamo Dr., Unit 336, Vacaville CA 95687. (707)447-6482. Fax: (707)447-6482. E-mail: sales@diogenespublishing.com. Website: www.diogenespublishing.com. Marketing Director: Chris Primi. **Acquisitions:** Mary Gillissie, president. Publishes trade paperback originals. **Publishes 6 titles/year. Receives 50 queries and 25 mss/year. 75% of books from first-time authors; 75% from unagented writers. Pays 10% royalty on wholesale price.** Publishes book 1 year after acceptance of ms. Does not accept simultaneous submissions. Responds in 2 months to queries; 2 months to proposals; 4 months to mss. Book catalog online.

Diogenes is a nonfiction publisher seeking "honest and truthful writing that evaluates any facet of contemporary society, including its values, beliefs, families, media, and celebrities. We are not interested in self-help, spiritual, or inspirational material. Instead, we promote independent thinking and represent writers who offer alternative and unpopular points of view. We are more concerned with the quality than the quantity of our publications, thus we opt for works that appeal to a thoughtful and critical—if small—audience."

Nonfiction: Subjects include humor, philosophy, psychology, satire, social commentary. Query with SASE. Reviews artwork/photos as part of ms package. Send photocopies.

Recent Title(s): *Happiness & Other Lies*, by Mary Massaro.

DISCOVERY ENTERPRISES, LTD., 31 Laurelwood Dr., Carlisle MA 07141. (978)287-5401. Fax: (978)287-5402. E-mail: ushistorydocs@aol.com. **Acquisitions:** JoAnne W. Deitch, president (plays for Readers Theatre, on American history). Publishes trade paperback originals. **Publishes 10 titles/year. Receives 50 queries and 20 mss/year. 5% of books from first-time authors; 90% from unagented writers. Pays 20-20% royalty.** Publishes book 3 months after acceptance of ms. Accepts simultaneous submissions. Responds in 1 month to queries. Book catalog for 6×9 SAE with 3 first-class stamps.

Fiction: "We're interested in 40-minute plays (reading time) for students in grades 4-10 on topics in U.S. history." Historical, plays. Query with SASE or submit complete ms.

Recent Title(s): *Life on the Road: Sojourner Truth*, by Sharon Fennessey; *Salem Witch Hunt*, by Hilary Weisman; *Lewis and Clark: Across a Vast Land*, by Harold Torrance.

Tips: "Call or send query letter on topic prior to sending ms for plays."

DO-IT-YOURSELF LEGAL PUBLISHERS, 60 Park Place, Suite 103, Newark NJ 07102. (973)639-0400. Fax: (973)639-1801. **Acquisitions:** Dan Benjamin, associate editor; Anne Torrey, editorial director. Estab. 1978. Publishes trade paperback originals. **Publishes 6 titles/year; imprint publishes 2 titles/year. Receives 25 queries/year. Pays 15-20% royalty on wholesale price.** Publishes book 1 year after acceptance of ms. Accepts simultaneous submissions. Responds in 1 month to queries; 1 month to proposals; 3 months to mss.

Imprints: Selfhelper Law Press of America.

O→ "The fundamental premise underlying our works is that the simplest problems can be effectively handled by anyone with average common sense and a competent guidebook."

Nonfiction: Subject matter should deal with self-help law topics that instruct the lay person on how to undertake legal tasks without the use of attorney or other high cost experts. How-to, self-help. Subjects include law. Query with SASE.

Recent Title(s): *The National Mortgage Qualification Kit*, by Benji O. Anosike, Ph.D.

DORAL PUBLISHING, INC., 10451 W. Palmeras Dr., Suite 225, Sun City AZ 85373-2072. (623)875-2057. Fax: (623)875-2059. E-mail: doralpub@mindspring.com. Website: www.doralpubl.com. **Acquisitions:** Alvin Grossman, publisher; Luana Luther, editor-in-chief (purebred dogs). Estab. 1986. Publishes hardcover and trade paperback originals. **Publishes 7 titles/year. Receives 30 queries and 15 mss/year. 85% from unagented writers. Pays 10% royalty on wholesale price.** Publishes book 6 months after acceptance of ms. Does not accept simultaneous submissions. Responds in 2 months to queries. Book catalog free; ms guidelines for #10 SASE.

O→ Doral Publishing publishes only books about dogs and dog-related topics, mostly geared for pure-bred dog owners and showing. Currently emphasizing breed books. De-emphasizing children's work.

Nonfiction: Children's/juvenile, how-to, reference. Subjects include animals, health/medicine. "We are looking for new ideas. No flowery prose. Manuscripts should be literate, intelligent, but easy to read." Subjects must be dog-related. Query with SASE or submit outline, 2 sample chapter(s). Reviews artwork/photos as part of ms package. Send photocopies.

Fiction: Juvenile. Subjects must center around dogs. Either the main character should be a dog or a dog should play an integral role. Query with SASE.

Recent Title(s): *The Mastiff*; *The Welsh Terrier.*

Tips: "We are currently expanding and are looking for new topics and fresh ideas while staying true to our niche. While we will steadfastly maintain that market—we are always looking for excellent breed books—we also want to explore more 'mainstream' topics."

DORCHESTER PUBLISHING CO., INC., 276 Fifth Ave., Suite 1008, New York NY 10001-0112. (212)725-8811. Fax: (212)532-1054. E-mail: dorchedit@dorchesterpub.com. **Offers advance.** Does not accept simultaneous submissions.

Imprints: Love Spell (romance), Leisure Books.

[A] **DOUBLEDAY**, Doubleday Broadway Publishing Group, Random House, Inc., 1540 Broadway, New York NY 10036. (212)782-9000. Fax: (212)782-9700. Website: www.randomhouse.com. Vice President/Editor-in-Chief: William Thomas. Estab. 1897. Publishes hardcover and trade paperback originals and reprints. **Publishes 200 titles/year. Receives thousands of queries and thousands of mss/year. 30% of books from first-time authors. Pays royalty on retail price. Offers advance.** Publishes book 1 year after acceptance of ms. Does not accept simultaneous submissions.

Imprints: Anchor Books; Currency; Doubleday Religious Division; Image Books; Nan A. Talese.

- Does not accept any unagented submissions. No exceptions.

O→ Doubleday publishes high-quality fiction and nonfiction.

Nonfiction: Biography. Subjects include Americana, anthropology/archeology, business/economics, computers/electronic, education, ethnic, government/politics, health/medicine, history, language/literature, money/finance, nature/environment, philosophy, religion, science, sociology, software, sports, translation, women's issues/studies. *Agented submissions only.*

Fiction: Adventure, confession, ethnic, experimental, feminist, gay/lesbian, historical, humor, literary, mainstream/contemporary, religious, short story collections. *Agented submissions only.*
Recent Title(s): *The Street Lawyer*, by John Grisham (fiction).

🄰 **DOUBLEDAY RELIGIOUS PUBLISHING**, Doubleday Broadway Publishing Group, Random House, Inc., 1540 Broadway, New York NY 10036. (212)354-6500. Fax: (212)782-3735. Website: www.randomhouse.com. **Acquisitions:** Eric Major, vice president, religious division; Trace Murphy, executive editor; Andrew Corbin, editor. Estab. 1897. Publishes hardcover and trade paperback originals and reprints. **Publishes 45-50 titles/year; imprint publishes 12 titles/year. Receives 1,000 queries and 500 mss/year. 3% from unagented writers. Pays 7½-15% royalty. Offers advance.** Publishes book 1 year after acceptance of ms. Accepts simultaneous submissions. Responds in 3 months to proposals. Book catalog for SAE with 3 first-class stamps.
Imprints: Image Books, Anchor Bible Commentary, Anchor Bible Reference, Galilee, New Jerusalem Bible.
Nonfiction: Biography, cookbook, gift book, reference, self-help. Subjects include child guidance/parenting, cooking/foods/nutrition, money/finance, religion, sex, spirituality. *Agented submissions only.*
Fiction: Religious. *Agented submissions only.*
Recent Title(s): *First Comes Love*, by Scott Hahn; *Religions for Peace*, by Cardinal Arinze.

DOUBLEDAY/IMAGE, Doubleday Broadway Publishing Group, Random House, Inc., 1540 Broadway, New York NY 10036. (212)782-9000. Fax: (212)782-9735. Website: www.randomhouse.com. **Acquisitions:** Trace Murphy, executive editor. Estab. 1956. Publishes hardcover, trade and mass market paperback originals and reprints. **Publishes 12 titles/year. Receives 500 queries and 300 mss/year. 10% of books from first-time authors. Pays royalty on retail price. Offers varied advance.** Publishes book 18 months after acceptance of ms. Accepts simultaneous submissions. Responds in 3 months to proposals.

> O‑ъ Image Books has grown from a classic Catholic list to include a variety of current and future classics, maintaining a high standard of quality as the finest in religious paperbacks. Also publishes Doubleday paperbacks/hardcovers for general religion, spirituality, including works based in Buddhism, Islam, Judaism.

Nonfiction: Biography, cookbook, gift book, how-to, humor, illustrated book, reference, self-help. Subjects include cooking/foods/nutrition, humor, philosophy, psychology, religion, women's issues/studies. Query with SASE. Reviews artwork/photos as part of ms package. Send photocopies.
Recent Title(s): *Papal Sin*, by Garry Wills; *Soul Survivor*, by Philip Yancey; *The Lamb's Supper*, by Scott Hahn.

DOVER PUBLICATIONS, INC., 31 E. 2nd St., Mineola NY 11501. (516)294-7000. Fax: (516)873-1401. E-mail: dover@inch.com. Website: www.doverpublications.com. **Acquisitions:** Paul Negri, editor-in-chief; John Grafton (math/science reprints). Estab. 1941. Publishes trade paperback originals and reprints. **Publishes 500 titles/year. Makes outright purchase. Offers advance.** Does not accept simultaneous submissions. Book catalog online.
Nonfiction: Biography, children's/juvenile, coffee table book, cookbook, how-to, humor, illustrated book, textbook. Subjects include agriculture/horticulture, Americana, animals, anthropology/archeology, art/architecture, cooking/foods/nutrition, health/medicine, history, hobbies, humor, language/literature, music/dance, nature/environment, philosophy, photography, religion, science, sports, translation, travel. Publishes mostly reprints. Accepts original paper doll collections, game books, coloring books (juvenile). Query with SASE. Reviews artwork/photos as part of ms package.
Recent Title(s): *The Waning of the Middle Ages*, by John Huizenga.

DOWN EAST BOOKS, Down East Enterprise, Inc., P.O. Box 679, Camden ME 04843-0679. Fax: (207)594-7215. **Acquisitions:** Chris Cornell, editor (Countrysport); Michael Steere, associate editor (general). Estab. 1967. Publishes hardcover and trade paperback originals, trade paperback reprints. **Publishes 20-24 titles/year. Receives 1,000 submissions/year. 50% of books from first-time authors; 90% from unagented writers. Pays 10-15% royalty on net receipts. Offers $200 average advance.** Publishes book 1 year after acceptance of ms. Accepts simultaneous submissions. Responds in 3 months to queries. Ms guidelines for 9×12 SAE with 3 first-class stamps.
Imprints: Countrysport Press (fly fishing and wing-shooting market; Chris Cornell, editor, e-mail: ccornell@downeast.com).

> O‑ъ Down East Books publishes books that capture and illuminate the unique beauty and character of New England's history, culture, and wild places.

Nonfiction: Children's/juvenile. Subjects include Americana, history, nature/environment, recreation, regional, sports. Books about the New England region, Maine in particular. "All of our regional books must have a Maine or New England emphasis." Query with SASE. Reviews artwork/photos as part of ms package.
Fiction: Juvenile, mainstream/contemporary. "We publish 1-2 juvenile titles/year (fiction and nonfiction), and 1-2 adult fiction titles/year." Query with SASE.
Recent Title(s): *The Watercolors of Chet Reneson*, by Robert Abbett; *Gardens Maine Style*, by Rebecca Fay and Lynn Karlin; *Northwest Passage*, by Kenneth Roberts.

DOWN THE SHORE PUBLISHING, Box 3100, Harvey Cedars NJ 08008. (609)978-1233. Website: www.down-the-shore.com. **Acquisitions:** Leslee Ganss, associate editor. Publishes hardcover and trade paperback originals and reprints. **Publishes 5-8 titles/year. Receives 200 queries and 20 mss/year. 80% of books from first-time authors; 100% from unagented writers. Pays royalty on wholesale price or retail price, or makes outright purchase. Offers occasional advance.** Publishes book 1-2 years after acceptance of ms. Accepts simultaneous submissions. Responds in 3 months to queries. Book catalog for 8×10 SAE with 2 first-class stamps or on website; ms guidelines for #10 SASE or on website.

O→ "Bear in mind that our market is regional—New Jersey, the Jersey Shore, the mid-Atlantic, and seashore and coastal subjects."

Nonfiction: Children's/juvenile, coffee table book, gift book, illustrated book. Subjects include Americana, art/architecture, history, nature/environment, regional. Query with SASE or submit proposal package including outline, 1 sample chapter(s). Reviews artwork/photos as part of ms package. Send photocopies.

Fiction: Regional. Query with SASE or submit proposal package including 1 sample chapter(s), synopsis.

Poetry: "We do not publish poetry, unless it is to be included as part of an anthology."

Recent Title(s): *Shore Chronicles: Diaries and Travelers' Tales from the Jersey Shore 1764-1955*, by Margaret Thomas Buchholz, editor (nonfiction); *Shore Stories: An Anthology of the Jersey Shore*, edited by Rich Youmans (fiction).

Tips: "Carefully consider whether your proposal is a good fit for our established market."

[A] **LISA DREW BOOKS**, Scribner, 1230 Avenue of the Americas, New York NY 10020. (212)698-7000. Website: www.simonsays.com. **Acquisitions:** Lisa Drew, publisher. Publishes hardcover originals. **Publishes 10-14 titles/year. Receives 600 queries/year. 10% of books from first-time authors. Pays royalty on retail price. Offers variable advance.** Publishes book 1 year after acceptance of ms. Accepts simultaneous submissions. Responds in 1 month to queries. Book catalog free.

O→ "We publish *reading* books; nonfiction that tells a story, not 'Fourteen Ways to Improve Your Marriage.'"

Nonfiction: Subjects include government/politics, history, women's issues/studies. No unsolicited material. *Agented submissions only.*

DUFOUR EDITIONS, P.O. Box 7, Chester Springs PA 19425. (610)458-5005. Fax: (610)458-5005. E-mail: info@dufoureditions.com. Website: www.dufoureditions.com. **Acquisitions:** Thomas Lavoie, associate publisher. Estab. 1948. Publishes hardcover originals, trade paperback originals and reprints. **Publishes 5-6 titles/year. Receives 100 queries and 15 mss/year. 20-30% of books from first-time authors; 80% from unagented writers. Pays 6-10% royalty on net receipts. Offers $500-1,000 advance.** Publishes book 18 months after acceptance of ms. Accepts simultaneous submissions. Responds in 3 months to queries; 3 months to proposals; 6 months to mss. Book catalog free.

O→ "We publish literary fiction by good writers which is well received and achieves modest sales." De-emphsazing poetry and nonfiction.

Nonfiction: Biography. Subjects include history, translation. Query with SASE. Reviews artwork/photos as part of ms package. Send photocopies.

Fiction: Ethnic, historical, literary, short story collections. Query with SASE.

Poetry: Query.

Recent Title(s): *The Case of the Pederast's Wife*, by Clare Elfman; *Tideland*, by Mitch Cullin; *Night Sounds and Other Stories*, by Karen Gettert Shoemaker.

Tips: "Audience is sophisticated, literate readers especially interested in foreign literature and translations, and a strong Irish-Celtic focus, as well as work from U.S. writers. Check to see if the publisher is really a good match for your subject matter."

[A] **THOMAS DUNNE BOOKS**, St. Martin's Press, 175 Fifth Ave., New York NY 10010. (212)674-5151. **Acquisitions:** Tom Dunne, publisher; Peter J. Wolverton, associate publisher; Ruth Cavin, associate publisher (mysteries). Publishes hardcover originals, trade paperback originals and reprints. **Publishes 210 titles/year. Receives 1,000 queries/year. 20% of books from first-time authors. Pays royalty. Pays 10-15% royalty on retail price for hardcover, 7½% for paperback. Offers varying advance.** Publishes book 1 year after acceptance of ms. Accepts simultaneous submissions. Responds in 2 months to queries.

O→ Thomas Dunne publishes a wide range of fiction and nonfiction. Accepts submissions from agents only.

Nonfiction: Biography. Subjects include government/politics, history, political commentary. "Author's attention to detail is important. We get a lot of manuscripts that are poorly proofread and just can't be considered." Agents submit query or an outline and 100 sample pages. Reviews artwork/photos as part of ms package. Send photocopies.

Fiction: Mainstream/contemporary, suspense, thrillers; women's. Agents submit query or submit synopsis and 100 sample pages.

Recent Title(s): *Knight: My Story*, by Bob Knight; *Death of the West*, by Patrick J. Buchanan.

DUQUESNE UNIVERSITY PRESS, 600 Forbes Ave., Pittsburgh PA 15282-0101. (412)396-6610. Fax: (412)396-5984. Website: www.dupress.duq.edu. **Acquisitions:** Susan Wadsworth-Booth, director. Estab. 1927. Publishes hardcover and trade paperback originals. **Publishes 8-12 titles/year. Receives 500 queries and 75 mss/year. 30% of books from first-time authors; 95% from unagented writers. Pays royalty on net price. Offers (some) advance.** Publishes book 1 year after acceptance of ms. Responds in 1 month to proposals; 3 months to mss. Book catalog and ms guidelines for #10 SASE.

O→ Duquesne publishes scholarly monographs in the fields of literary studies (medieval & Renaissance), philosophy, ethics, religious studies and psychology. "We also publish a series, *Emerging Writers in Creative Nonfiction*, for first-time authors of creative nonfiction for a general readership."

Nonfiction: Scholarly, Scholarly/academic. Subjects include creative nonfiction, language/literature, philosophy, psychology, religion. "We look for quality of scholarship." For scholarly books, query or submit outline, 1 sample chapter and SASE. For creative nonfiction, submit 2 copies of ms.

Recent Title(s): *Walking My Dog, Jane*, by Ned Rozell; *The Last Settler*, by Jennifer Brice and Charles Mason.

DUTTON (ADULT TRADE), Penguin Putnam, Inc., 375 Hudson St., New York NY 10014. (212)366-2000. Website: www.penguinputnam.com. Editor-in-Chief, Editorial Director: Brian Tart. Estab. 1852. **Publishes 40 titles/year. Accepts no unsolicited manuscripts. Offers negotiable advance.** Responds in 6 months to queries.

- Dutton publishes hardcover, original, mainstream, and contemporary fiction and nonfiction in the areas of memoir, self-help, politics, psychology, and science for a general readership.

Nonfiction: Humor, reference, self-help, memoir. *Agented submissions only. No unsolicited mss.*

Fiction: Adventure, historical, literary, mainstream/contemporary, mystery, short story collections, suspense. *Agented submissions only. No unsolicited mss.*

Recent Title(s): *The Darwin Awards II*, by Wendy Northcutt (humor); *The Oath*, by John Lescroart (fiction); *Falling Angels*, by Tracy Chevalier (fiction).

Tips: "Write the complete manuscript and submit it to an agent or agents. They will know exactly which editor will be interested in a project."

DUTTON CHILDREN'S BOOKS, Penguin Putman Inc., 345 Hudson St., New York NY 10014. (212)414-3700. Fax: (212)414-3397. Website: www.penguinputnam.com. **Acquisitions:** Lucia Monfried (picture books, easy-to-read books, fiction); Stephanie Owens Lurie, president and publisher (picture books and fiction); Donna Brooks, editorial director (books for all ages with distinctive narrative style); Susan Van Metre, senior editor (character-oriented picture books and middle grade fiction); Alissa Heyman, associate editor (fiction, poetry, picture books); Jennifer Mattson, associate editor (fiction, fantasy, picture books); Meredith Mundy Wasinger, editor (picture books, fiction and nonfiction). Estab. 1852. Publishes hardcover originals as well as novelty formats. **Publishes 100 titles/year. 15% of books from first-time authors. Pays royalty. Offers advance.**

- Dutton Children's Books publishes high-quality fiction and nonfiction for readers ranging from preschoolers to young adults on a variety of subjects. Currently emphasizing picture books and middle-grade fiction that offer a fresh perspective. De-emphasizing photographic nonfiction.

Nonfiction: Children's/juvenile, For preschoolers to young adults. Subjects include animals, history (U.S.), nature/environment, science. Query with SASE.

Fiction: Picture books. Dutton Children's Books has a diverse, general interest list that includes picture books; easy-to-read books; and fiction for all ages, from "first chapter" books to young adult readers. Query with SASE and letter only.

Recent Title(s): *Miss Bindergarter Takes a Field Trip with Kindergarten*, by Joseph Slate, illustrated by Ashley Wolff (picture book); *Horace Splatty, The Cupcaked Crusader*, by Lawrence David, illustrated by Barry Gott (chapter book); *12 Again*, by Sue Corbett (novel).

EAGLE'S VIEW PUBLISHING, 6756 N. Fork Rd., Liberty UT 84310. Fax: (801)745-0903. E-mail: eglcrafts@aol.com. **Acquisitions:** Denise Knight, editor-in-chief. Estab. 1982. Publishes trade paperback originals. **Publishes 4-6 titles/year. Receives 40 queries and 20 mss/year. 90% of books from first-time authors; 100% from unagented writers. Pays 8-10% royalty on net selling price.** Publishes book 1 year or more after acceptance of ms. Accepts simultaneous submissions. Responds in 1 year to proposals. Book catalog and ms guidelines for $3.

- Eagle's View publishes primarily how-to craft books with a subject related to historical or contemporary Native American/Mountain Man/frontier crafts. Currently emphasizing bead-related craft books. De-emphasizing history except for historical Indian crafts.

Nonfiction: How-to, Indian, mountain man and American frontier (history and craft). Subjects include anthropology/archeology (Native American crafts), ethnic (Native American), history (American frontier historical patterns and books), hobbies (crafts, especially beadwork, earrings). "We are expanding from our Indian craft base to more general but related crafts. We prefer to do photography in house." Submit outline, 1-2 sample chapter(s). Reviews artwork/photos as part of ms package. Send photocopies or sample illustrations.

Recent Title(s): *Treasury of Beaded Jewelry*, by Mary Ellen Harte; *Beads and Beadwork of the American Indian*, by William C. Orchard.

Tips: "We will not be publishing any new beaded earrings books for 1-2 years. We are interested in other craft projects using seed beads, especially books that feature a variety of items, not just different designs for one item."

EAKIN PRESS/SUNBELT MEDIA, INC., P.O. Box 90159, Austin TX 78709-0159. (512)288-1771. Fax: (512)288-1813. E-mail: sales@eakinpress.com. Website: www.eakinpress.com. **Acquisitions:** Virginia Messel, publisher. Estab. 1978. Publishes hardcover and paperback originals and reprints. **Publishes 60 titles/year. Receives 1,500 submissions/year. 50% of books from first-time authors; 90% from unagented writers. Pays 10-12-15% royalty on net sales.** Publishes book 18 months after acceptance of ms. Accepts simultaneous submissions. Responds in 3 months to queries. Book catalog for $1.25; ms guidelines for #10 SASE.

Imprints: Eakin Press, Nortex Press.

- Eakin specializes in Texana and Western Americana for adults and juveniles. Currently emphasizing women's studies.

Nonfiction: Biography, cookbook (regional). Subjects include Americana (Western), business/economics, cooking/foods/nutrition, ethnic, history, military/war, regional, sports, African American studies, Civil War, Texas history, World War II. Juvenile nonfiction: includes biographies of historic personalities, prefer with Texas or regional interest, or nature studies; and easy-read illustrated books for grades 1-3. Query with SASE.

Fiction: Juvenile fiction for grades K-12, preferably relating to Texas and the Southwest or contemporary. No adult fiction. Query or submit outline/synopsis and sample chapters.

Recent Title(s): *Inside Russia*, by Inez Jeffery; *Black, Buckskin and Blue*, by Art Burton.

N EASTLAND PRESS, P.O. Box 99749, Seattle WA 98199. (206)217-0204. Fax: (206)217-0205. E-mail: info@eastlandpress.com. Website: www.eastlandpress.com. **Acquisitions:** John O'Connor, managing editor. Estab. 1981. Publishes hardcover and trade paperback originals. **Publishes 3-4 titles/year. Receives 25 queries/year. 30% of books from first-time authors; 90% from unagented writers. Pays 12-15% royalty on receipts. Offers $500-1,500 advance.** Publishes book 2 years after acceptance of ms. Accepts simultaneous submissions. Responds in 1 month to queries. Book catalog free.

- Eastland is interested in textbooks for practitioners of alternative medical therapies primarily Chinese and physical therapies and related bodywork.

Nonfiction: Reference, textbook, alternative medicine (Chinese and physical therapies and related bodywork). Subjects include health/medicine. "We prefer that a manuscript be completed or close to completion before we will consider publication. Proposals are rarely considered, unless submitted by a published author or teaching institution." Submit outline and 2-3 sample chapters. Reviews artwork/photos as part of ms package. Send photocopies.
Recent Title(s): *Cranial Sutures*, by Marc Pick; *Acupuncture in the Treatment of Children*, by Julian Scott.

EDEN PUBLISHING, P.O. Box 20176, Keizer OR 97307-0176. Phone/fax: (503)390-9013. Website: www.edenpublishing.com. **Acquisitions:** Barbara Griffin, managing editor. Publishes trade paperback originals. **Receives 1,200 queries and 10 mss/year. 40% of books from first-time authors; 100% from unagented writers. Pays royalty on retail price.** Publishes book 4-6 months after acceptance of ms. Responds in 2 weeks to queries.

- Eden Publishing is not accepting mss or queries at the moment, due to heavy publishing commitments during 2002.
- Eden publishes books with strong Christian theme. Also, recently added literary poetry to the list they market to educators and libraries.

Nonfiction: Self-help. Subjects include education, religion, spirituality (Christian only, nondenominational). Query with SASE. **All unsolicited mss returned unopened.**
Recent Title(s): *At the Foot of the Cross: Easter Dramatic Readings*, by Barbara Dan (drama); *Poetry Grand Slam Finale*, by Alan MacDougall (poetry); *Night (Die Nacht)*, by Richard Exner (bilingual text).
Tips: "Our primary target market is mainstream Christians, pastors and Christian colleges. Our secondary target market is academic libraries. We are presently working on projects into 2002."

EDUCATOR'S INTERNATIONAL PRESS, INC., 18 Colleen Rd., Troy NY 12180. (518)271-9886. Fax: (518)266-9422. E-mail: sarah@edint.com. Website: www.edint.com. **Acquisitions:** Sarah J. Biondello, publisher/acquisitions editor. Estab. 1996. Publishes hardcover and trade paperback originals and reprints. **Publishes 10-12 titles/year. Receives 50 queries and 50 mss/year. 50% of books from first-time authors; 98% from unagented writers. Pays 3-15% royalty on wholesale price.** Publishes book 1 year after acceptance of ms. Accepts simultaneous submissions. Responds in 2 months to queries; 2 months to proposals; 3 months to mss. Book catalog and ms guidelines free.

- Educator's International publishes books in all aspects of education, broadly conceived, from pre-kindergarten to postgraduate. "We specialize in texts, professional books, videos and other materials for students, faculty, practitioners and researchers. We also publish a full list of books in the areas of women's studies, and social and behavioral sciences."

Nonfiction: Textbook, supplemental texts, conference proceedings. Subjects include education, gay/lesbian, language/literature, philosophy, psychology, software, women's issues/studies. Submit table of contents, outline, 2-3 chapters, résumé with SASE. Reviews artwork/photos as part of ms package.
Recent Title(s): *Our Sons Were Labeled Behavior Disordered*, by Joy-Ruth Mickelson.
Tips: Audience is professors, students, researchers, individuals, libraries.

EDUCATORS PUBLISHING SERVICE, INC., 31 Smith Place, Cambridge MA 02138-1089. (617)547-6706. Fax: (617)547-3805. Website: www.epsbooks.com and www.lessonlogic.com. **Acquisitions:** Charles H. Heinle, vice president, Publishing Group. Estab. 1952. **Publishes 26 titles/year. Receives 400 queries and 400 mss/year. 50% of books from first-time authors; 100% from unagented writers. Pays 5-12% royalty on retail price.** Publishes book 8 months minimum after acceptance of ms. Accepts simultaneous submissions. Responds in 1 month to queries; 3 months to proposals; 3 months to mss. Book catalog and ms guidelines free.

- EPS is looking for supplementary materials for the regular K-12 and special education classroom. "We are particularly interested in workbook and text series, but will gladly consider any proposals for high-quality material that is useful to teachers and students." Currently emphasizing reading comprehension workbooks K-8.

Nonfiction: Workbooks (language arts and math) and some professional books. Subjects include education (reading comprehension, phonics and writing). supplementary texts and workbooks (reading and language arts). Query with SASE. Reviews artwork/photos as part of ms package. Send photocopies.
Recent Title(s): *Einstein's Who, What and Where*, by Carol Einstein; *Game Plan*, by Joanna Kennedy; *Educational Care*, by Mel Levine.
Tips: Teacher, students (K-adult) audiences.

EDUPRESS, INC., 208 Avenida Fabricante #200, San Clemente CA 92672. (949)366-9499. Fax: (949)366-9441. E-mail: info@edupressinc.com. Website: www.edupressinc.com. **Acquisitions:** Amanda Meinke, product coordinator.

Estab. 1979. Publishes trade paperback originals. **Publishes 40 titles/year. Receives 20 queries and 100 mss/year. 25% of books from first-time authors. Makes outright purchase.** Publishes book 1 year after acceptance of ms. Responds in 2 months to queries; 5 months to mss. Book catalog and ms guidelines free.

O→ Edupress publishes supplemental resources for classroom curriculum. Currently emphasizing more science, math, language arts emphasis than in the past.

Nonfiction: Subjects include education (resources for pre-school through middle school). Submit proposal package, including ms copy, outline, 1 sample chapter and SASE. Reviews artwork/photos as part of ms package. Send photocopies.

Recent Title(s): *Two Can Read* (2 level readers); *Crossnumber Puzzles.*

Tips: Audience is classroom teachers and homeschool parents.

EERDMANS BOOKS FOR YOUNG READERS, William B. Eerdmans Publishing Co., 255 Jefferson Ave. SE, Grand Rapids MI 49503. (616)459-4591. Fax: (616)459-6540. **Acquisitions:** Judy Zylstra, editor. Publishes picture books and middle reader and young adult fiction and nonfiction. **Publishes 12-15 titles/year. Receives 3,000 submissions/year. Pays 5-7½% royalty on retail price.** Accepts simultaneous submissions. Responds in 6 weeks to queries. Publishes middle reader and YA books 1 year after acceptance. Publishes picture books 2-3 years after acceptance. Book catalog for large SASE.

O→ "We publish books for children and young adults that deal with spiritual themes—but never in a preachy or heavy-handed way. Some of our books are clearly religious, while others (especially our novels) look at spiritual issues in very subtle ways. We look for books that are honest, wise and hopeful." Currently emphasizing general picture books (also picture book biographies), novels (middle reader and YA). De-emphasizing YA biographies, retellings of Bible stories.

Nonfiction: Children's/juvenile, picture books, middle reader, young adult nonfiction. "Do not send illustrations unless you are a professional illustrator." Submit complete mss for picture books and novels or biographies under 200 pages with SASE. For longer books, send query letter and 3 or 4 sample chapters with SASE. Reviews artwork/photos as part of ms package. Send color photocopies rather than original art.

Fiction: Juvenile, picture books, young adult, middle reader. "Do not send illustrations unless you are a professional illustrator." Submit complete mss for picture books and novels or biographies under 200 pages with SASE. For longer books, send query letter and 3 or 4 sample chapters with SASE.

Recent Title(s): *A Bird or Two: A Story about Henri Matisse*, written and illustrated by Bijou Le Tord; *When Daddy Prays*, written by Nikki Grimes, illustrated by Tim Ladwig; *Secrets in the House of Delgado*, by Gloria Miklowitz.

WILLIAM B. EERDMANS PUBLISHING CO., 255 Jefferson Ave. SE, Grand Rapids MI 49503. (616)459-4591. Fax: (616)459-6540. E-mail: sales@eerdmans.com. **Acquisitions:** Jon Pott, editor-in-chief; Charles Van Hof, managing editor (history); Judy Zylstra, children's book editor. Estab. 1911. Publishes hardcover and paperback originals and reprints. **Publishes 120-130 titles/year. Receives 3,000-4,000 submissions/year. 10% of books from first-time authors; 95% from unagented writers. Pays royalty. Offers occasional advance.** Publishes book usually within 1 year after acceptance of ms. Accepts simultaneous submissions. Responds in 6 weeks to queries. Book catalog free.

Imprints: Eerdmans Books for Young Readers (Judy Zylstra, editor).

O→ "Approximately 80% of our adult publications are religious and most of these are academic or semi-academic in character (as opposed to inspirational or celebrity books), though we also publish general trade books on the Christian life. Our nonreligious titles, most of them in regional history or on social issues, aim, similarly, at an educated audience."

Nonfiction: Children's/juvenile, reference, textbook, monographs. Subjects include history (religious), language/literature, philosophy (of religion), psychology, regional (history), religion, sociology, translation, Biblical studies, theology, ethics. "We prefer that writers take the time to notice if we have published anything at all in the same category as their manuscript before sending it to us." Query with outline, 2-3 sample chapter and SASE for return of ms. Reviews artwork/photos as part of ms package.

Recent Title(s): *Marriage—Just a Piece of Paper?*, edited by Katherine Anderson, Don S. Browning and Brian Boyer; *What Did the Biblical Writers Know and When Did They Know It?*, by William G. Dever; *David's Secret Demons*, by Baruch Halpern.

ELECTRIC WORKS PUBLISHING, 605 Ave. C.E., Bismarck ND 58501. (701)255-0356. E-mail: editors@electricpublishing.com. Website: www.electricpublishing.com. **Acquisitions:** James R. Bohe, editor-in-chief. Publishes digital books. **Publishes 50 titles/year. Receives 30 queries and 250 mss/year. 70% of books from first-time authors; 85% from unagented writers. Pays 36-40% royalty on wholesale price.** Publishes book 3 months after acceptance of ms. Accepts simultaneous submissions. Responds in 5 months to queries. Book catalog and ms guidelines online.

O→ Digital publisher offering a wide range of subjects.

Nonfiction: Biography, children's/juvenile, cookbook, how-to, humor, illustrated book, multimedia (CD-ROM, disk), reference, self-help, technical. Subjects include agriculture/horticulture, Americana, animals, anthropology/archeology, art/architecture, business/economics, child guidance/parenting, computers/electronic, cooking/foods/nutrition, creative nonfiction, education, ethnic, gardening, government/politics, health/medicine, history, hobbies, language/literature, memoirs, military/war, money/finance, multicultural, music/dance, nature/environment, philosophy, photography, psychology, recreation, regional, religion, science, sociology, software, spirituality, sports, translation, travel, women's issues/studies. *Electronic submissions only.* Submit entire ms in digital format. Reviews artwork/photos as part of ms package.

Fiction: Adventure, ethnic, experimental, fantasy, gothic, historical, horror, humor, juvenile, literary, mainstream/contemporary, military/war, multicultural, multimedia, mystery, occult, plays, poetry in translation, regional, religious, romance, science fiction, short story collections, spiritual, sports, suspense, western, young adult. *Electronic submissions only.* Submit ms in digital format.
Poetry: Submit complete ms.
Recent Title(s): *Felling of the Sons*, by Monette Bebow-Reinhard; *Marzipan*, by George Laidlaw.

ELEPHANT BOOKS, 65 Macedonia Rd., Alexander NC 28701. (828)252-9515. Fax: (828)255-8719. E-mail: sales@abooks.com. Website: abooks.com/elephant. **Acquisitions:** Pat Roberts, acquisitions editor. Publishes trade paperback originals and reprints. **Publishes 8 titles/year. Receives 100 queries and 50 mss/year. 90% of books from first-time authors; 80% from unagented writers. Pays 12-15% royalty on wholesale price. Seldom offers advance.** Publishes book 18 months after acceptance of ms. Book catalog and ms guidelines for 9×12 SASE with 5 ounces postage.
Imprints: Blue/Gray Books (contact Ralph Roberts, Civil War history).
Nonfiction: Cookbook. Subjects include cooking/foods/nutrition, history, military/war (Civil War). Query or submit outline with 3 sample chapters and proposal package, including potential marketing plans with SASE. Reviews artwork/photos as part of ms package. Send photocopies.
Recent Title(s): *Rebel Boast*, by Manly Wade Wellman.

N EMIS, INC., P.O. Box 820062, Dallas TX 75382-0062. Website: www.emispub.com. **Acquisitions:** Lynda Blake, president. Publishes trade paperback originals. **Publishes 4 titles/year. Pays 12% royalty on retail price.** Responds in 3 months to queries. Book catalog free; ms guidelines free.

- "Our books are published as a medical text designed for physicians to fit in the lab coat pocket as a quick means of locating information." Currently emphasizing infectious diseases. De-emphasizing medical program management.

Nonfiction: Reference. Subjects include health/medicine, psychology, Women's health/medicine. Submit 3 sample chapters with SASE.
Recent Title(s): *Managing Contraceptive Pill Patients.*
Tips: Audience is medical professionals and medical product manufacturers and distributors.

EMPIRE PUBLISHING SERVICE, P.O. Box 1344, Studio City CA 91614-0344. (818)789-4980. **Acquisitions:** Joseph Witt. Publishes hardcover reprints and trade paperback originals and reprints. **Publishes 40 titles/year; imprint publishes 15 titles/year. Receives 500 queries and 85 mss/year. 50% of books from first-time authors; 95% from unagented writers. Pays 6-10% royalty on retail price. Offers variable advance.** Publishes book up to 2 years after acceptance of ms. Responds in 1 month to queries; 2 months to proposals; up to 1 year to mss. Book catalog for #10 SASE; ms guidelines for $1 or #10 SASE.
Imprints: Gaslight Publications, Gaslight Books, Empire Publications, Empire Books.

- "Submit only Sherlock Holmes, performing arts and health."

Nonfiction: How-to, humor, reference, technical, textbook. Subjects include health/medicine, humor, music/dance, Sherlock Holmes. Query with SASE. Reviews artwork/photos as part of ms package. Send photocopies.
Fiction: Sherlock Holmes. Query with SASE.
Recent Title(s): *On the Scent with Sherlock Holmes*, by Jacy Tracy; *Elementary My Dear Watson*, by William Alan Landes; *The Magic of Food*, by James Cohen.

ENCOUNTER BOOKS, 665 Third St., Suite 330, San Francisco CA 94107-1951. (415)538-1460. Fax: (415)538-1461. Website: www.encounterbooks.com. **Acquisitions:** Peter Collier, publisher. Hardcover originals and trade paperback reprints. **Publishes 12-20 titles/year. Receives 500 queries and 200 mss/year. 10% of books from first-time authors; 40% from unagented writers. Pays 7-10% royalty on retail price. Offers $2,000-25,000 advance.** Publishes book 18 months after acceptance of ms. Accepts simultaneous submissions. Responds in 3 months to queries; 4 months to proposals; 4 months to mss. Book catalog and ms guidelines free or online.

- Encounter Books publishes serious nonfiction—books that can alter our society, challenge our morality, stimulate our imaginations. Currently emphasizing history, culture, social criticism and politics.

Nonfiction: Biography, reference. Subjects include child guidance/parenting, education, ethnic, government/politics, health/medicine, history, language/literature, memoirs, military/war, multicultural, nature/environment, philosophy, psychology, religion, science, sociology, women's issues/studies, gender studies. Submit proposal package, including outline and 1 sample chapter.
Recent Title(s): *Coloring the News: How Crusading for Diversity Has Corrupted American Journalism*, by William McGowan; *Heaven on Earth: The Rise and Fall of Socialism*, by Joshua Muravchik.

N ENSLOW PUBLISHERS INC., 40 Industrial Rd., Box 398, Berkeley Heights NJ 07922. (973)771-9400. Website: www.enslow.com. **Acquisitions:** Brian D. Enslow, editor. Estab. 1977. Publishes hardcover originals. **Publishes 150 titles/year. Pays royalty on net price. Offers advance.** Publishes book 1 year after acceptance of ms. Responds in 1 month to queries *Writer's Market* recommends allowing 2 months for reply to proposals. Ms guidelines for #10 SASE.

- Enslow publishes hardcover nonfiction books for young adults and school-age children, mostly as part of a series.

Nonfiction: Biography, children's/juvenile, reference. Subjects include health/medicine, history, recreation (Sports), science, sociology. Interested in new ideas for series of books for young people. No fiction, fictionalized history or dialog.

Recent Title(s): *Advertising*, by Nancy Day; *Holocaust Rescuers*, by David Lyman.
Tips: "We love to receive résumés from experienced writers with good research skills who can think like young people."

ENTREPRENEUR PRESS, 245 McCabe Way, Irvine CA 92614. (949)261-2325. Fax: (949)261-0234. E-mail: kwright @entrepreneur.com. Website: www.smallbizbooks.com. **Acquisitions:** Jere Calmes, editorial director; Kaina Wright, assistant editor. Publishes hardcover and trade paperback originals and trade paperback reprints. **Publishes 160 titles/ year. Receives 1,200 queries and 600 mss/year. 40% of books from first-time authors; 50% from unagented writers. Pays 2-30% royalty or makes $2,000-15,000 outright purchase.** Accepts simultaneous submissions. Book catalog and ms guidelines free.
Nonfiction: Humor, multimedia (e-book), reference, self-help. Subjects include business/economics, women's issues/ studies. Query with SASE or submit proposal package including outline, 2 sample chapter(s), author bio, preface or executive summary, competition. Reviews artwork/photos as part of ms package. Send transparencies.
Recent Title(s): *Start Your Own Business*, by Lesonsky; *How to Be a Teenage Millionaire*, by Beroff and Adams.
Tips: Audience is "people who are thinking about starting their own business and people who have recently started their own business. Also general business skills, including finance, marketing, presentation, leadership, etc."

EPICENTER PRESS, INC., P.O. Box 82368, Kenmore WA 98028. (425)485-6822. Fax: (425)481-8253. E-mail: info@epicenterpress.com. Website: www.epicenterpress.com. **Acquisitions:** Kent Sturgis, publisher. Estab. 1987. Publishes hardcover and trade paperback originals. **Publishes 10 titles/year. Receives 200 queries and 100 mss/year. 75% of books from first-time authors; 90% from unagented writers.** Publishes book 1-2 years after acceptance of ms. Responds in 2 months to queries. Book catalog and ms guidelines on website.
O→ "We are a regional press founded in Alaska whose interests include but are not limited to the arts, history, environment, and diverse cultures and lifestyles of the North Pacific and high latitudes.
Nonfiction: "Our focus is Alaska. We do not encourage nonfiction titles from outside Alaska." Biography, coffee table book, gift book, humor. Subjects include animals, art/architecture, ethnic, history, humor, nature/environment, photography, recreation, regional, women's issues/studies. Submit outline and 3 sample chapters. Reviews artwork/ photos as part of ms package. Send photocopies.
Recent Title(s): *Cold River Spirits*, by Jan Harper-Haines.

ETC PUBLICATIONS, 700 E. Vereda Sur, Palm Springs CA 92262-4816. (760)325-5352. Fax: (760)325-8841. **Acquisitions:** Dr. Richard W. Hostrop, publisher (education and social sciences); Lee Ona S. Hostrop, editorial director (history and works suitable below the college level). Estab. 1972. Publishes hardcover and paperback originals. **Publishes 6-12 titles/year. Receives 100 submissions/year. 75% of books from first-time authors; 90% from unagented writers. Offers 5-15% royalty, based on wholesale and retail price.** Publishes book 9 months after acceptance of ms. *Writer's Market* recommends allowing 2 months for reply to queries.
O→ ETC publishes works that "further learning as opposed to entertainment."
Nonfiction: Textbook, educational management; gifted education; futuristics. Subjects include education, translation (in above areas). Submit complete ms with SASE. *Writer's Market* recommends query first with SASE. Reviews artwork/ photos as part of ms package.
Recent Title(s): *The Internet for Educators and Homeschoolers*, by Steve Jones, Ph.D.
Tips: "Special consideration is given to those authors who are capable and willing to submit their completed work in camera-ready, typeset form. We are particularly interested in works suitable for *both* the Christian school market and homeschoolers; e.g., state history texts below the high school level with a Christian-oriented slant."

EVAN-MOOR EDUCATIONAL PUBLISHERS, 18 Lower Ragsdale Dr., Monterey CA 93940-5746. (831)649-5901. Fax: (831)649-6256. E-mail: editorial@evan-moor.com. Website: www.evan-moor.com. **Acquisitions:** Marilyn Evans, senior editor. Estab. 1979. Publishes teaching materials. **Publishes 50-60 titles/year. Receives 50 queries and 100 mss/year. 1% of books from first-time authors; 100% from unagented writers. Makes outright purchase.** Publishes book 1 year after acceptance of ms. Accepts simultaneous submissions. Responds in 3 months to queries. Book catalog and ms guidelines free or on website.
O→ "Our books are teaching ideas, lesson plans, and blackline reproducibles for grades PreK-6 in all curriculum areas except music and bilingual." Currently emphasizing writing/language arts, practice materials for home use. De-emphasizing thematic materials. We do not publish children's literature.
Nonfiction: Children's/juvenile. Subjects include education, teaching materials, grade pre-K-6. No children's literature. Submit proposal package, including outline and 3 sample chapters.
Recent Title(s): *Read and Understand Science* (6 book series); *Building Spelling Skills* (6 book series).
Tips: "Writers should know how classroom/educational materials differ from trade publications. They should request catalogs and submissions guidelines before sending queries or manuscripts. Visiting our website will give writers a clear picture of the type of materials we publish."

M. EVANS AND CO., INC., 216 E. 49th St., New York NY 10017-1502. Fax: (212)688-2810. Website: www.mevans.com. **Acquisitions:** George C. deKay, editor-in-chief (general trade); Ms. P.J. Dempsey, senior editor (general nonfiction). Estab. 1960. Publishes hardcover and trade paperback originals. **Publishes 30-40 titles/year. 5% from unagented writers. Pays negotiable royalty.** Publishes book 8 months after acceptance of ms. Responds in 2 months to queries. Book catalog for 9×12 SAE with 3 first-class stamps.
O→ Evans has a strong line of health and self-help books but is interested in publishing quality titles on a wide

variety of subject matters. "We publish a general trade list of adult nonfiction, cookbooks and semi-reference works. The emphasis is on selectivity, publishing commercial works with quality." Currently emphasizing health, relationships, nutrition.

Nonfiction: Cookbook, self-help. Subjects include cooking/foods/nutrition, general nonfiction, health/medicine, relationships. "Our most successful nonfiction titles have been related to health and the behavioral sciences. No limitation on subject." No memoirs. Query with SASE. *No unsolicited mss.*

Fiction: "Our very small general fiction list represents an attempt to combine quality with commercial potential. We publish no more than one novel per season." Query with SASE. *No unsolicited mss.*

Recent Title(s): *Dr. Atkins' Diet Revolution* (health); *The Good Girl's Guide to Bad Girl Sex*, by Barbara Keesling.

Tips: "A writer should clearly indicate what his book is all about, frequently the task the writer performs least well. His credentials, although important, mean less than his ability to convince this company that he understands his subject and that he has the ability to communicate a message worth hearing. Writers should review our website before making submissions."

EXCALIBUR PUBLICATIONS, P.O. Box 35369, Tucson AZ 85740-5369. E-mail: excalibureditor@earthlink.net. **Acquisitions:** Alan M. Petrillo, editor. Publishes trade paperback originals. **Publishes 6-8 titles/year. Pays royalty or makes outright purchase.** Responds in 2 months to mss.

O→ Excalibur publishes historical and military works from all time periods.

Nonfiction: Subjects include history (military), military/war (strategy and tactics, as well as the history of battles, firearms, arms and armour), historical personalities. "We are seeking well-researched and documented works. Unpublished writers are welcome." Query with outline, first 3 chapters, SASE. Include notes on photos, illustrations and maps.

Recent Title(s): *Howdah To High Power: A History of British Breechloading Service Pistols*, by Robert J. Maze; *Present Sabers: A History of the U.S. Horse Cavalry*, by Allan Heninger.

Tips: "Know your subject matter, and present it in a clear and precise manner. Please give us a brief description of your background or experience as it relates to your submission, as well as any marketing insight you might have on your subject."

EXCELSIOR CEE PUBLISHING, P.O. Box 5861, Norman OK 73070. (405)329-3909. Fax: (405)329-6886. **Acquisitions:** J.C. Marshall. Estab. 1989. Publishes hardcover and trade paperback originals. **Publishes 8 titles/year. Receives 400 queries/year. Pays royalty or makes outright purchase (both negotiable).** Publishes book 1 year after acceptance of ms. Accepts simultaneous submissions. Responds in 1 month to queries. Book catalog for #10 SASE.

O→ "All of our books speak to the reader through words of feeling—whether they are how-to, educational, humor or whatever genre, the reader comes away with feeling, truth and inspiration." Currently emphasizing how-to, family history, memoirs, inspiration. De-emphasizing childrens.

Nonfiction: Biography, coffee table book, gift book, how-to, humor, self-help, textbook. Subjects include Americana, education, history, hobbies, language/literature, women's issues/studies, general nonfiction, writing. Query with SASE.

Recent Title(s): *When I Want Your Opinion, I'll Tell It To You*, by Dr. Vince Orza; *How to Record Your Family History*; *Letters from the 20th Century—A History in Memories*.

Tips: "We have a general audience, book store browsers interested in nonfiction reading. We publish titles that have a mass appeal and can be enjoyed by a large reading public. We publish very few unsolicited manuscripts, and our publishing calendar is 75% full up to 1 year in advance."

EXECUTIVE EXCELLENCE PUBLISHING, 1366 E. 1120 S., Provo UT 84606. (800)304-9782. Fax: (801)377-5960. E-mail: info@eep.com. Website: www.eep.com. **Acquisitions:** Ken Shelton, editor in chief. Estab. 1984. Publishes hardcover and trade paperback originals and trade paperback reprints. **Publishes 16-20 titles/year. Receives 300 queries and 150 mss/year. 35% of books from first-time authors; 95% from unagented writers. Pays 15% on cash received and 50% of subsidary right proceeds.** Publishes book 6-9 months after acceptance of ms. Accepts simultaneous submissions. Responds in 1 month to queries; 1 month to proposals; 3 months to mss. Book catalog free or on website.

O→ Executive Excellence publishes business and self-help titles. "We help you—the busy person, executive or entrepreneur—to find a wiser, better way to live your life and lead your organization." Currently emphasizing business innovations for general management and leadership (from the personal perspective). De-emphasizing technical or scholarly textbooks on operational processes and financial management or workbooks.

Nonfiction: Self-help. Subjects include business/economics, leadership/management, entrepreneurship, career, small buisiness, motivational. Submit proposal package, including outline, 1-2 sample chapters and author bio, company information.

Recent Title(s): *Spirit of Leadership*, by Robert J. Spitzer; *Traits of Champions*, by Andrew Word.

Tips: "Executive Excellence Publishing is an established publishing house with a strong niche in the marketplace. Our magazines, *Executive Excellence*, *Sales and Marketing Excellence* and *Personal Excellence*, are distributed monthly in twelve countries across the world and give us and our authors massive market exposure. Our authors are on the cutting edge in their fields of leadership, self-help and business and organizational development. We usually publish only the biggest names in the field, but we are always looking for strong new talent with something to say, and a burning desire to say it."

FACTS ON FILE, INC., 132 W. 31st St., 17th Floor, New York NY 10001. (212)967-8800. Fax: (212)967-9196. E-mail: llikoff@factsonfile.com. Website: www.factsonfile.com. **Acquisitions:** Laurie Likoff, editorial director (science, music, history); Frank Darmstadt (science, nature, multi-volume reference); Nicole Bowen, senior editor (American history, women's studies, young adult reference); James Chambers, trade editor (health, pop culture, crime, sports); Anne Savarese, acquisitions editor (language/literature). Estab. 1941. Publishes hardcover originals and reprints. **Publishes 135 titles/year. 25% from unagented writers. Pays 10% royalty on retail price. Offers $7,000-10,000 advance.** Accepts simultaneous submissions. Responds in 2 months to queries. Book catalog free.

Imprints: Checkmark Books.

O→ Facts on File produces high-quality reference materials on a broad range of subjects for the school library market and the general nonfiction trade.

Nonfiction: "We publish serious, informational books for a targeted audience. All our books must have strong library interest, but we also distribute books effectively to the trade. Our library books fit the junior and senior high school curriculum." Reference. Subjects include contemporary culture, education, health/medicine, history, language/literature, multicultural, recreation, religion, sports, careers, entertainment, natural history, popular culture. No computer books, technical books, cookbooks, biographies (except YA), pop psychology, humor, fiction or poetry. Query or submit outline and sample chapter with SASE. No submissions returned without SASE.

Tips: "Our audience is school and public libraries for our more reference-oriented books and libraries, schools and bookstores for our less reference-oriented informational titles."

FAIRLEIGH DICKINSON UNIVERSITY PRESS, 285 Madison Ave., Madison NJ 07940. (973)443-8564. Fax: (973)443-8364. E-mail: fdupress@fdu.edu. **Acquisitions:** Harry Keyishian, director. Estab. 1967. Publishes hardcover originals. **Publishes 45 titles/year. Receives 300 submissions/year. 33% of books from first-time authors; 95% from unagented writers.** Publishes book 1 year after acceptance of ms. Responds in 2 weeks to queries. *Writer's Market* recommends allowing 2 months for reply.

- "Contract is arranged through Associated University Presses of Cranbury, New Jersey. We are a *selection* committee only." Nonauthor subsidy publishes 2% of books.

O→ Fairleigh Dickinson publishes books for the academic market.

Nonfiction: Reference, scholarly, scholarly books. Subjects include art/architecture, business/economics, film/cinema/stage, government/politics, history, music/dance, philosophy, psychology, sociology, women's issues/studies, Civil War, film, Jewish studies, literary criticism. Looking for scholarly books in all fields; no nonscholarly books. Query with outline and sample chapters. Reviews artwork/photos as part of ms package.

Recent Title(s): *Shakespeare Studies*, edited by Leeds Barroll (annual volume); *Napoleon's Italy*, by Desmond Gregory; *Future Present: Ethics and/as Science Fiction*, by Michael Pinsky.

Tips: "Research must be up to date. Poor reviews result when authors' bibliographies and notes don't reflect current research. We follow *Chicago Manual of Style* (14th edition) style in scholarly citations. We will consider collections of unpublished conference papers or essay collections, if they relate to a strong central theme and have scholarly merit."

FAIRVIEW PRESS, 2450 Riverside Ave., Minneapolis MN 55454. (800)544-8207. Fax: (612)672-4980. E-mail: press@fairview.org. Website: www.fairviewpress.org. **Acquisitions:** Lane Stiles, director; Stephanie Billecke, senior editor. Estab. 1988. Publishes hardcover and trade paperback originals and reprints. **Publishes 8-12 titles/year. Receives 3,000 queries and 1,500 mss/year. 40% of books from first-time authors; 65% from unagented writers. Advance and royalties negotiable.** Publishes book 1 year after acceptance of ms. Accepts simultaneous submissions. Responds in 6 months to proposals. Book catalog and ms guidelines free.

O→ Fairview Press currently publishes books and related materials emphasizing aging, end-of-life issues, caregiving, grief and bereavement.

Nonfiction: Reference, self-help. Subjects include health/medicine, women's issues/studies, aging, grief and bereavement, patient education, nutrition. "Manuscripts that are essentially one person's story are rarely salable." Submit proposal package including outline, 2 sample chapter(s), author bio, marketing ideas, SASE. Reviews artwork/photos as part of ms package. Send photocopies.

Tips: Audience is general reader, especially families. "Tell us what void your book fills in the market; give us an angle. Tell us who will buy your book. We have moved away from recovery books and have focused on health and medical issues."

FAITH KIDS BOOKS, Cook Communications Ministries, 4050 Lee Vance View, Colorado Springs CO 80918. (719)536-3271. Fax: (719)536-3265. **Acquisitions:** Mary McNeil, associate acquisitions editor; Heather Gemmen, senior editor. Publishes hardcover and paperback originals. **Publishes 40-50 titles/year. Receives 1,000-1,500 mss/year. Pays variable royalty on retail price or flat fee, depending on project.** Publishes book 18 months after acceptance of ms. Accepts simultaneous submissions. Responds in 6 months to queries. Ms guidelines online.

O→ Faith Kids Books publishes inspirational works for children, ages 1-12, with a strong underlying Christian theme or clearly stated biblical value, designed to foster spiritual growth in children and positive interaction between parent and child. Currently emphasizing picture books, books for the very young (under 4). De-emphasizing fiction for 8-16-year-olds.

Nonfiction: Biography, children's/juvenile. Subjects include religion (Bible stories, devotionals), picture books on nonfiction subjects. Submit proposal package including cover letter, SASE.

Fiction: Historical, juvenile, picture books, religious, toddler books. No teen fiction. Accepts proposals with SASE. Previously published or agented authors preferred.

Recent Title(s): *Tale of Three Trees*, by Angela Hunt (fiction).

FARRAR, STRAUS & GIROUX BOOKS FOR YOUNG READERS, Farrar Straus Giroux, Inc., 19 Union Square W., New York NY 10003. (212)741-6900. Fax: (212)633-2427. **Acquisitions:** Margaret Ferguson, editorial director. Estab. 1946. Publishes hardcover and trade paperback originals. **Publishes 75 titles/year. Receives 6,000 queries and mss/year. 5% of books from first-time authors; 50% from unagented writers. Pays 3-6% royalty on retail price for paperbacks, 5-10% for hardcovers. Offers $3,000-25,000 advance.** Publishes book 18 months after acceptance of ms. Accepts simultaneous submissions. Responds in 2 months to queries; 3 months to mss. Book catalog for 9×12 SAE with $1.87 postage; ms guidelines for #10 SASE.

Imprints: Aerial Fiction, Frances Foster Books, Melanie Kroupa Books, Sunburst Paperbacks.

O→ "We publish original and well-written material for all ages."

Fiction: Juvenile, picture books, young adult. "We still look at unsolicited manuscripts, but for novels we prefer synopsis and sample chapters. Always enclose SASE for any materials author wishes returned. Query status of submissions in writing—no calls, please." Query with SASE; considers complete ms.

Recent Title(s): *Holes*, by Louis Sachar (Newbery Medal Book, ages 10 and up); *Trolls*, by Polly Horvath; *Snow*, by Uri Shulevitz (Caldecott Honor Book).

Tips: Audience is full age range, preschool to young adult. Specializes in literary fiction.

FARRAR, STRAUS & GIROUX PAPERBACKS, 19 Union Square West, New York NY 10003. (212)741-6900. Publishes hardcover and trade paperback originals and reprints. **Publishes 170 titles/year. Receives 1,500-2,000 queries and mss/year.** Accepts simultaneous submissions. Responds in 2 months to queries; 2 months to proposals. Book catalog free; ms guidelines free.

Imprints: Northpoint Press; Hill and Wang; Faber and Faber Inc.

O→ Farrar, Straus & Giroux Paperbacks emphasizes literary nonfiction and fiction, as well as fiction and poetry reprints.

Nonfiction: Biography. Subjects include child guidance/parenting, education, language/literature. *No unsolicited mss.* Query with outline, 2-3 sample chapters, cv, cover letter describing project and SASE.

Fiction: Literary.

Recent Title(s): *The Corrections*, by Jonathan Franzen.

FREDERICK FELL PUBLISHERS, INC., 2131 Hollywood Blvd., Suite 305, Hollywood FL 33020. (954)925-5242. Fax: (954)925-5244. E-mail: fellpub@aol.com. Website: www.fellpub.com. **Acquisitions:** Barnara Newman, senior editor. Publishes hardcover and trade paperback originals. **Publishes 25 titles/year. Receives 4,000 queries and 1,000 mss/year. 95% of books from first-time authors; 95% from unagented writers. Pays negotiable royalty on retail price. Offers up to $10,000 advance.** Publishes book 1 year after acceptance of ms. Accepts simultaneous submissions. Responds in 1 month to queries; 3 months to proposals. Ms guidelines for #10 SASE.

O→ "Fell has just launched 14 titles in the *Know-It-All* series. We will be publishing over 125 titles in all genres. Prove to us that your title is the best in this new exciting format."

Nonfiction: "We are reviewing in all categories. Advise us of the top three competitive titles for your work and the reasons why the public would benefit by having your book published." How-to, reference, self-help. Subjects include business/economics, child guidance/parenting, education, ethnic, film/cinema/stage, health/medicine, hobbies, money/finance, spirituality. Submit proposal package, including outline, 3 sample chapters, author bio, publicity ideas, market analysis. Reviews artwork/photos as part of ms package. Send photocopies.

Recent Title(s): *Venus & Serena: My Seven Years as Hitting Coach for the Williams Sisters.*

Tips: "We are most interested in well-written, timely nonfiction with strong sales potential. We will not consider topics that appeal to a small, select audience. Learn markets and be prepared to help with sales and promotion. Show us how your book is unique or better than the competition."

THE FEMINIST PRESS AT THE CITY UNIVERSITY OF NEW YORK, 365 Fifth Ave., Suite 5406, New York NY 10016. (212)817-7915. Fax: (212)817-1593. E-mail: jcasella@gc.cuny.edu. **Acquisitions:** Jean Casella, publisher/director. Estab. 1970. Publishes hardcover and trade paperback originals and reprints. **Publishes 15-20 titles/year. Receives 1,000 submissions/year. 10% of books from first-time authors; 50% from unagented writers. Pays royalty on net receipts. Offers $250-500 advance.** Accepts simultaneous submissions. Responds in 1 month to queries; 6 months to proposals. Book catalog online; ms guidelines online.

O→ Our primary mission is to publish works of fiction by women which preserve and extend women's literary traditions. We emphasize work by multicultural/international women writers.

Nonfiction: Subjects include ethnic, gay/lesbian, government/politics, health/medicine, history, language/literature, memoirs, multicultural, music/dance, sociology, translation, women's issues/studies. "We look for nonfiction work which challenges gender-role stereotypes and documents women's historical and cultural contributions. Note that we generally publish for the college classroom as well as the trade." Children's (ages 10 and up)for two series only, *Women Changing the World* and *Girls First!*, with a special emphasis on multicultural and international characters and settings and strong female role models. No monographs. Send email queries only, limited to 200 words with **Submission** as the subject line We regret that submissions are no longer accepted through the mail and unsolicited packages will be discarded.

Fiction: "The Feminist Press publishes only fiction reprints by classic American women authors and imports and translations of distinguished international women writers. Absolutely no original fiction is considered."

Recent Title(s): *Coming to Birth*, by Marjorie Oludhe Macgoye (1986 Sinclair Prize Winner); *David's Story*, by Zoe Wicomb; *Almost Touching the Skies*, edited by Florence Howe and Jean Casella (women's coming of age stories).

Tips: We cannot accept telephone inquiries regarding proposed submissions.

FERGUSON PUBLISHING COMPANY, 200 W. Jackson, 7th Floor, Chicago IL 60606. Website: www.fergpubco.com. **Acquisitions:** Andrew Morkes, managing editor, career publications. Estab. 1940. Publishes hardcover and trade paperback originals. **Publishes 50 titles/year. Pays by project.** Responds in 6 months to queries.

O-ᴛ "We are primarily a career education publisher that publishes for schools and libraries. We need writers who have expertise in a particular career or career field (for possible full-length books on a specific career or field)."

Nonfiction: "We publish work specifically for the elementary/junior high/high school/college library reference market. Works are generally encyclopedic in nature. Our current focus is career encyclopedias. We consider manuscripts that cross over into the trade market." Reference. Subjects include careers. "No mass market, poetry, scholarly, or juvenile books, please." Query or submit an outline and 1 sample chapter.

Recent Title(s): *Ferguson Career Biographies: Colin Powell, Bill Gates, etc* (20 total books in series); *Careers in Focus: Geriatric Care, Design, etc.*

Tips: "We like writers who know the market—former or current librarians or teachers or guidance counselors."

FILTER PRESS, P.O. Box 95, Palmer Lake CO 80133-0095. (719)481-2420. Fax: (719)481-2420. E-mail: filter.press@prodigy.net. Website: www.filterpressbooks.com. **Acquisitions:** Doris Baker, president. Estab. 1956. Publishes trade paperback originals and reprints. **Publishes 4-6 titles/year. Pays 10-12% royalty on wholesale price.** Publishes book 1 year after acceptance of ms.

O-ᴛ Filter Press specializes in nonfiction of the West. De-emphasizing cooking, foods and nutrition.

Nonfiction: Subjects include Americana, anthropology/archeology, cooking/foods/nutrition, ethnic, history, memoirs, nature/environment, regional, crafts and crafts people of the Southwest. "We're interested in the history and natural history of the West." Query with outline and SASE. Reviews artwork/photos as part of ms package.

Recent Title(s): *First Governor, First Lady-John and Eliza Raitt of Colorado*, by Joyce Lohse (biography); *Bent's Fort: Crossroads of Cultures on the Santa Fe Trail*, by Mel Bacon and Dan Blegen (history).

FIRE ENGINEERING BOOKS & VIDEOS, PennWell Publishing Co., 1421 S. Sheridan Rd., Tulsa OK 74112-6600. (918)831-9420. Fax: (918)832-9319. E-mail: jaredw@pennwell.com. Website: www.pennwell-store.com. **Acquisitions:** Margaret Shake, publisher; Jared Wicklund, supervising editor. Publishes hardcover and softcover originals. **Publishes 10 titles/year. Receives 24 queries/year. 75% of books from first-time authors; 100% from unagented writers. Pays 15% royalty on net sales.** Publishes book 1 year after acceptance of ms. Does not accept simultaneous submissions. Responds in 3 months to proposals. Book catalog free.

O-ᴛ Fire Engineering publishes textbooks relevant to firefighting and training. Training firefighters and other emergency responders. Currently emphasizing strategy and tactics, reserve training, preparedness for terrorist threats, natural disasters, first response to fires and emergencies.

Nonfiction: Reference, technical, textbook. Subjects include firefighter training, public safety. Submit outline, 2 sample chapter(s), résumé, author bio, table of contents, SASE.

Recent Title(s): *Managing Major Fires*, by Skip Coleman.

Tips: "No human interest stories, technical training only."

FLORIDA ACADEMIC PRESS, P.O. Box 540, Gainesville FL 32602. (352)332-5104. Fax: (352)331-6003. E-mail: fapress@worldnet.att.net. **Acquisitions:** Max Vargas, CEO (nonfiction/self-help); Sam Decalo, managing editor (academic); Florence Dusek, assistant editor (fiction). Publishes hardcover and trade paperback originals. **Publishes 6 titles/year. Receives 200+ queries and 100+ mss/year. 80% of books from first-time authors; 100% from unagented writers. Pays 5-8% royalty on retail price. depending if paperback or hardcover.** Publishes book 3-5 months after acceptance of ms. Responds in 1-6 months to mss. Book catalog and ms guidelines free.

O-ᴛ "We are primarily an academic/scholarly publisher. We do publish self-help books if assessed as original. Our interest in fiction is secondary, and our criteria is strict. No poetry, science fiction, religious, autobiography, polemical, children's books or collections of stories."

Nonfiction: How-to, reference, scholarly, self-help. Subjects include government/politics, history, third world. Submit complete ms. Reviews artwork/photos as part of ms package. Send photocopies.

Fiction: Literary, regional. Submit complete ms.

Recent Title(s): *Complete Publishers Resource Manual*, by Linda Able (reference); *Civil-Military Relations in Africa*, by Samuel Decalo (history).

Tips: Considers complete mss only. "Manuscripts we decide to publish must be re-submitted in camera-ready form."

FLYING BOOKS, Sky Media, LLC, 121 5th Ave., NW, Suite 300, New Brighton MN 55112. (651)635-0100. Fax: (651)635-0700. E-mail: info@historicaviation.com. Website: www.historicaviation.com. **Acquisitions:** G.E. Herrick, publisher (aviation history). Publishes hardcover and trade paperback originals and reprints. **Publishes 12 titles/year; imprint publishes 2 titles/year. Receives 30 queries and 15 mss/year. 30% of books from first-time authors; 90% from unagented writers. Pays 10% royalty on wholesale price.** Responds in 1 month to queries; 1 month to proposals; 2 months to mss. Book catalog free.

O-ᴛ "Aviation and aviation history are our strong points. Illustrations, photographs and other documentation appeal to our customers. We like to see the story told: how did this aircraft 'fit,' what did it do, how did it impact peoples lives?"

Nonfiction: Subjects include history, military/war, aviation. Reviews artwork/photos as part of ms package. Send photocopies.

Recent Title(s): *Mystery Ship!*, by Edward Phillips (aviation history); *Wings of Stearman*, by Peter Bowers (aviation history); *L-Birds*, by Terry Love.
Tips: "Our buyers are interested in aviation history and aircraft in general. Of particular interest are nonfiction works covering specific aircraft types, manufacturers or military aircraft. Research and accuracy are of paramount importance."

[N] **FOCUS PUBLISHING, INC.**, P.O. Box 665, Bemidji MN 56619. (218)759-9817. Fax: (218)751-2183. E-mail: focus@paulbunyan.net. **Acquisitions:** Jan Haley, vice president. Estab. 1994. Publishes hardcover and trade paperback originals and reprints. **Publishes 4-6 titles/year. Receives 250 queries and 100 mss/year. 90% of books from first-time authors; 100% from unagented writers. Pays 7-10% royalty on retail price.** Publishes book 1 year after acceptance of ms. Responds in 2 months to queries. Book catalog free.

O→ "Focus Publishing is a small press primarily devoted to Christian books and appropriate to children and home-schooling families. Focus is on bible study books only."

Nonfiction: Children's/juvenile. Subjects include religion, women's issues/studies. Submit proposal package, including marketing ideas with SASE. Reviews artwork/photos as part of ms package. Send photocopies.
Fiction: Juvenile, picture books, religious, young adult. "We are looking for Christian books for men and young adults. Be sure to list your target audience." Query and submit synopsis.
Poetry: "We are not especially interested in poetry at this time." Query.
Recent Title(s): *Success in School*, by Vicki Caruana; *The Exemplary Husband*, by Dr. Stuart Scott.
Tips: "I prefer SASE inquiries, synopsis and target markets. Please don't send 5 lbs. of paper with no return postage. Our focus is on Christian living books for adults and children. Only Biblically-sound proposals considered."

FODOR'S TRAVEL PUBLICATIONS, INC., Random House, Inc., 280 Park Ave., New York NY 10171-0002. Website: www.fodors.com. **Acquisitions:** Karen Cure, editorial director. Estab. 1936. Publishes trade paperback originals. **Publishes 300 titles/year. Receives 100 queries and 4 mss/year. Most titles are collective works, with contributions as works for hire. Most contributions are updates of previously published volumes.** Publishes book 1 year after acceptance of ms. Accepts simultaneous submissions. Responds in 2 months to queries. Book catalog free.

O→ Fodor's publishes travel books on many regions and countries.

Nonfiction: How-to (travel), illustrated book (travel), travel guide. Subjects include travel. "We are interested in unique approaches to favorite destinations. Writers seldom review our catalog or our list and often query about books on topics that we're already covering. Beyond that, it's important to review competition and to say what the proposed book will add. Do not send originals without first querying as to our interest in the project. We're not interested in travel literature or in proposals for general travel guidebooks." Query or submit outline, sample chapter(s) and proposal package, including competition review and review of market with SASE.
Recent Title(s): *Venice and the Veneto*; *Fly Easy*; *Around Orlando with Kids*.
Tips: "In preparing your query or proposal, remember that it's the only argument Fodor's will hear about why your book will be a good one and why you think it will sell; and it's also best evidence of your ability to create the book you propose. Craft your proposal well and carefully so that it puts your best foot forward."

[N] **FOGHORN OUTDOORS**, Avalon Travel Publishing, Avalon Publishing Group, 5855 Beaudry St., Emeryville CA 94608. (510)595-3664. Website: www.foghorn.com. **Acquisitions:** Acquisitions Assistant. Estab. 1985. Publishes trade paperback originals and reprints. **Publishes 30 titles/year. Receives 500 queries and 200 mss/year. 10% of books from first-time authors; 98% from unagented writers. Pays 12% royalty on wholesale price; occasional work-for-hire.** Publishes book 18 months after acceptance of ms. Accepts simultaneous submissions. Responds in 1 month to queries; 2 months to proposals; 2 months to mss. Book catalog free.

O→ Foghorn publishes outdoor recreation guidebooks. Editorial mission is "to produce current, informative and complete travel information for specific types of travelers."

Nonfiction: Outdoor recreation guidebooks. Subjects include nature/environment, recreation (camping, biking, fishing), sports, outdoors, leisure. Query first with SASE, Attn: acquisitions assistant.
Recent Title(s): *Foghorn Outdoors: California Camping*, by Tom Stienstra.
Tips: "We are expanding our list nationally in the formats we already publish (camping, hiking, fishing, dogs) as well as developing new formats to test California."

FORDHAM UNIVERSITY PRESS, University Box L, Bronx NY 10458. Website: www.fordhampress.com. **Acquisitions:** Mary Beatrice Schulte, executive editor. Publishes hardcover and trade paperback originals and reprints. **Publishes 30 titles/year. Receives 450 queries and 100 mss/year. 25% of books from first-time authors; 100% from unagented writers. Pays 4-7% royalty on retail price.** Publishes book 6-24 months after acceptance of ms. Responds in 2 months to proposals; 2 months to mss. Book catalog and ms guidelines free.

O→ "We are a publisher in humanities, accepting scholarly monographs, collections, occasional reprints and general interest titles for consideration."

Nonfiction: Biography, textbook, scholarly. Subjects include Americana, anthropology/archeology, art/architecture, government/politics, history, language/literature, military/war (World War II), philosophy, regional (New York), religion, sociology, translation. No fiction. Submit outline, 2-5 sample chapter(s).
Recent Title(s): *Palisades: 100,000 Acres in 100 years*, by Robert Binnewies.
Tips: "We have an academic and general audience."

FOREIGN POLICY ASSOCIATION, 470 Park Ave. S., New York NY 10016. (212)481-8100. Fax: (212)481-9275. E-mail: info@fpa.org. Website: www.fpa.org. **Acquisitions:** Karen Rohan, editor-in-chief. Publishes 2 periodicals and an occasional hardcover and trade paperback original. **Publishes 5-6 titles/year. Receives 12 queries and 6 mss/year. 99% from unagented writers. Makes outright purchase of $2,500-4,000.** Publishes book 9 months after acceptance of ms. Accepts simultaneous submissions. Responds in 2 months to queries. Book catalog free.

Imprints: Headline Series (quarterly), Great Decisions (annual).

O→ "The Foreign Policy Association, a nonpartisan, not-for-profit educational organization founded in 1918, is a catalyst for developing awareness, understanding of and informed opinion on U.S. foreign policy and global issues. Through its balanced, nonpartisan publications, FPA seeks to encourage individuals in schools, communities and the workplace to participate in the foreign policy process."

Nonfiction: Reference, textbook. Subjects include government/politics, history, foreign policy, social studies. Query, submit outline.

Recent Title(s): *India: Old Civilization in a New World*, by Barbara Crossette.

Tips: Audience is students and people with an interest, but not necessarily any expertise, in foreign policy and international relations.

FORT ROSS INC. RUSSIAN-AMERICAN PUBLISHING PROJECTS, 26 Arthur Place, Yonkers NY 10701. (914)375-6448. Fax: (914)375-6439. E-mail: ftross@ix.netcom.com. **Acquisitions:** Dr. Vladimir P. Kartsev, executive director. Publishes paperback originals. **Publishes 12 titles/year. Receives 100 queries and 100 mss/year. Pays 4-7% royalty on wholesale price or makes outright purchase of $500-1,500. Offers $500 advance.** Publishes book 1 year after acceptance of ms. Accepts simultaneous submissions. Responds in 1 month to queries; 1 month to proposals; 3 months to mss.

O→ "Generally, we publish Russia-related books in English or Russian. Sometimes we publish various fiction and nonfiction books in collaboration with the East European publishers in translation. We are looking mainly for well-established authors."

Nonfiction: Biography, illustrated book (for adults and children), reference.

Fiction: Fantasy, horror, mainstream/contemporary, mystery, romance, science fiction, suspense. Query with SASE.

Recent Title(s): *Cosack Galloped Far Away*, by Nikolas Feodoroff; *Verses*, by Filip Novikov; *Bay of Cross*, by Yury Egorov (in Russian).

FORTRESS PRESS, Box 1209, Minneapolis MN 55440-1209. (612)330-3300. Website: www.fortresspress.com. **Acquisitions:** J. Michael West, editor-in-chief; Dr. K.C. Hanson, acquisitions editor. Estab. 1855. Publishes hardcover and trade paperback originals. **Publishes 60 titles/year. Receives 500-700 queries/year. 5-10% of books from first-time authors. Pays royalty on retail price.** Publishes book 1-2 years after acceptance of ms. Accepts simultaneous submissions. Responds in 3 months to proposals. Book catalog free (call 1-800-328-4648); ms guidelines online.

O→ Fortress Press publishes academic books in Biblical studies, theology, Christian ethics, church history, and professional books in pastoral care and counseling.

Nonfiction: Subjects include religion, women's issues/studies, church history, African-American studies. Query with annotated toc, brief cv, sample chapter (introduction) and SASE. Please study guidelines before submitting.

Recent Title(s): *The Writings of The New Testament*, by Luke Timothy Johnson; *The Wrath of Jonah: The Crisis of Religious Nationalism in the Israli-Palestinian Conflict*, by Rosemary Bradford Ruth and Herman J. Ruther.

FORUM, Prima Publishing, 3000 Lava Ridge Court, Roseville CA 95661. (916)787-7000. Fax: (916)787-7005. Website: www.primaforum.com. **Acquisitions:** David Richardson, editor. Publishes hardcover and trade paperback originals and reprints. **Publishes 10-15 titles/year. 25% of books from first-time authors; 5% from unagented writers. Pays variable royalty. Offers variable advance.** Publishes book 1 year after acceptance of ms. Accepts simultaneous submissions. Responds in 1 month to queries; 1 month to proposals.

O→ "Forum publishes books that contribute to the marketplace of ideas."

Nonfiction: Subjects include business/economics, contemporary culture, government/politics, history, religion, world affairs, libertarian/conservative thought, trends in business, technology and society, current affairs, individual empowerment. Query with outline, 1 sample chapter and SASE.

Recent Title(s): *Bin Ladin: The Man Who Declared War on America*, by Yossef Bodansky; *The New Thought Police*, by Tammy Bruce; *The Secret History of the CIA*, by Joseph J. Trento.

FORUM PUBLISHING COMPANY, 383 E. Main St., Centerport NY 11721. (631)754-5000. Fax: (631)754-0630. Website: www.forum123.com. **Acquisitions:** Martin Stevens. Estab. 1981. Publishes trade paperback originals. **Publishes 12 titles/year. Receives 200 queries and 25 mss/year. 75% of books from first-time authors; 75% from unagented writers. Makes outright purchase of $250-750.** Publishes book 4 months after acceptance of ms. Accepts simultaneous submissions. Responds in 1 month to mss. Book catalog free.

O→ "Forum publishes only business titles."

Nonfiction: Subjects include business/economics, money/finance. Submit outline. Reviews artwork/photos as part of ms package. Send photocopies.

Recent Title(s): *Selling Information By Mail*, by Glen Gilcrest.

FORWARD MOVEMENT PUBLICATIONS, 412 Sycamore St., Cincinnati OH 45202. (513)721-6659. Fax: (513)721-0729. E-mail: esgleason@forwarddaybyday.com. Website: www.forwardmovement.org. **Acquisitions:** The Reverend Dr. Edward S. Gleason, editor and director. Estab. 1934. Publishes trade and mass market paperback originals, trade paperback reprints and tracts. **Publishes 6 titles/year. Receives 1,000 queries and 300 mss/year. 30% of books from first-time authors; 100% from unagented writers. Pays one-time honorarium.** Responds in 1 month to queries; 1 month to proposals; 2 months to mss. Book catalog and ms guidelines free.

O→ "Forward Movement was established 'to help reinvigorate the life of the church.' Many titles focus on the life of prayer, where our relationship with God is centered, death, marriage, baptism, recovery, joy, the Episcopal Church and more." Currently emphasizing prayer/spirituality.

Nonfiction: "We publish a variety of types of books, but they all relate to the lives of Christians. We are an agency of the Episcopal Church." Biography, children's/juvenile, reference, self-help (about religion and prayer). Subjects include religion. Query with SASE or submit complete ms.

Fiction: Episcopal for middle school (ages 8-12) readers. Juvenile. Query with SASE.

Recent Title(s): *God Is Not in the Thesaurus*, by Bo Don Cox (nonfiction); *Dare to Imagine*, by Sydney Von Lehn (fiction).

Tips: Audience is primarily Episcopalians and other Christians.

FOUR WALLS EIGHT WINDOWS, 39 W. 14th St., Room 503, New York NY 10011. Fax: (212)206-8799. E-mail: edit@4w8w.com. Website: www.4w8w.com. Publisher: John Oakes. **Acquisitions:** Acquistions Editor. Estab. 1987. Publishes hardcover originals, trade paperback originals and reprints. **Publishes 35 titles/year. Receives 3,000 submissions/year. 15% of books from first-time authors; 50% from unagented writers. Pays royalty on retail or net price, depending on contract. Offers variable advance.** Publishes book 1-2 years after acceptance of ms. Responds in 2 months to queries. Book catalog for 6 X 9 SAE with 3 first-class stamps.

Imprints: No Exit, Axoplasm

O→ Emphasizing fine literature and quality nonfiction, Four Walls Eight Windows has a reputation for carefully edited and distinctive books.

Nonfiction: Subjects include history, nature/environment, science. No New Age. Query with outline and SASE. All mss without SASE discarded.

Fiction: Feminist, gay/lesbian. "No romance, popular." Query first with outline/synopsis and SASE.

Recent Title(s): *The Mystery of the Aleph*, by Amir D. Aczel (science); *Valentine*, by Lucius Shepard (fiction); *Sizzling Chops, Dazzling Spins: Ping-Pong and the Art of Staying Alive*, by Jerome Charyn (history/memoir).

FOX CHAPEL PUBLISHING, 1970 Broad St., East Petersburg PA 17520. (717)560-4703. Fax: (717)560-4702. E-mail: editors@carvingworld.com. Website: www.carvingworld.com. **Acquisitions:** Alan Giagnocavo, publisher; Ayleen Stellhorn, editor. Publishes hardcover and trade paperback originals and trade paperback reprints. **Publishes 12-20 titles/year. 80% of books from first-time authors; 100% from unagented writers. Pays royalty or makes outright purchase. Offers variable advance.** Publishes book 6-18 months after acceptance of ms. Accepts simultaneous submissions. Responds in 2 months to queries.

O→ Fox Chapel publishes woodworking and woodcarving titles for professionals and hobbyists.

Nonfiction: Subjects include woodworking, wood carving, scroll saw. Write for query submission guidelines. Reviews artwork/photos as part of ms package. Send photocopies.

Recent Title(s): *Carving the Human Face*, by Jeff Phares; *Scroll Saw Workbook*.

Tips: "We're looking for knowledgeable artists, woodworkers first, writers second to write for us. Our market is for avid woodworking hobbyists and professionals."

[N] **FRANCISCAN UNIVERSITY PRESS**, 1235 University Blvd., Steubenville OH 43852. Fax: (740)284-5454. Website: www.franuniv.edu. **Acquisitions:** Dreama Thompson. Publishes trade paperback originals and reprints. **Publishes 4 titles/year. 5% of books from first-time authors; 100% from unagented writers. Pays 5-10% royalty on retail price.** Publishes book 1 year after acceptance of ms. Responds in 3 months to proposals. Book catalog free.

O→ "We seek to further the Catholic and Franciscan mission of Franciscan University of Steubenville by publishing books in the areas of theology, biblical studies, religious education, youth ministry and prayer with a particular focus on Apologetics."

Nonfiction: Subjects include religion. Publications that will teach the Catholic faith and lend to a deeper understanding of Christian living. Query with cv and SASE or send complete ms.

Recent Title(s): *The Trinity: New and Forever*, by Father Sam Tiesi, TOR; *Liturgy of the Hours*, by Father Dominic Scotto, TOR.

[A] **THE FREE PRESS**, Simon & Schuster, 1230 Avenue of the Americas, New York NY 10020. (212)698-7000. Fax: (212)632-4989. Website: www.simonsays.com. Publisher: Martha Levin. **Acquisitions:** Bruce Nichols, vice president/senior editor (history/serious nonfiction); Philip Rapappport, editor (psychology/social work/self-help); Steven Morrow, editor (science, math, literature, art); Rachel Klayman (narrative nonfiction, literary fiction); Leslie Meredith (psychology/spirituality/self-help); Fred Hills (business/serious nonfiction); Bill Rosen (serious nonfiction/illustrated/reference); Amy Scheibe (literary fiction); Dominick Anfuso, editorial director (self-help/literary fiction). Estab. 1947. **Publishes 120 titles/year. Receives 3,000 submissions/year. 15% of books from first-time authors; 50% from unagented writers. Pays variable royalty. Offers advance.** Publishes book 1 year after acceptance of ms. Responds in 2 months to queries.

O→ The Free Press publishes a wide variety of fiction and nonfiction.

Nonfiction: Does not accept unagented submissions. Query with 1-3 sample chapters, outline before submitting mss.

Recent Title(s): *Self Matter*, by Phil McGraw; *American Jihad*, by Steven Emerson.

FREE SPIRIT PUBLISHING INC., 217 Fifth Ave. N., Suite 200, Minneapolis MN 55401-1260. (612)338-2068. Fax: (612)337-5050. E-mail: help4kids@freespirit.com. Website: www.freespirit.com. Publisher: Judy Galbraith. **Acquisitions:** Acquisitions Editor. Estab. 1983. Publishes trade paperback originals and reprints. **Publishes 30 titles/year. 25% of books from first-time authors; 50% from unagented writers. Offers advance.** Book catalog and ms guidelines free.
Imprints: Self-Help for Kids, Free Spirited Classroom Series, Self-Help for Teens.

O⊸ "We believe passionately in empowering kids to learn to think for themselves and make their own good choices."

Nonfiction: Children's/juvenile (young adult), self-help (parenting). Subjects include child guidance/parenting, education (pre-K-12, study and social skills, special needs, differentiation but not textbooks or basic skills books like reading, counting, etc.), health/medicine (mental/emotional health for/about children), psychology (for/about children), sociology (for/about children). "Many of our authors are educators, mental health professionals, and youth workers involved in helping kids and teens." No fiction or picture storybooks, poetry, single biographies or autobiographies, books with mythical or animal characters, or books with religious or New Age content. Query with cover letter stating qualifications, intent, and intended audience and how your book stands out from the field, along with outline, 2 sample chapters, résumé, SASE. Do not send original copies of work.
Recent Title(s): *Cool Women, Hot Jobs*; *Freeing Our Families from Perfectionism*; *Hands Are Not for Hitting*.
Tips: "Our books are issue-oriented, jargon-free, and solution-focused. Our audience is children, teens, teachers, parents and youth counselors. We are especially concerned with kids' social and emotional well-being and look for books with ready-to-use strategies for coping with today's issues at home or in school—written in every-day language. We are not looking for academic or religious materials, or books that analyze problem's with the nation's school systems. Instead, we want books that offer practical, positive advice so kids can help themselves and parents and teachers can help kids succeed."

FRIENDS UNITED PRESS, 101 Quaker Hill, Richmond IN 47374. (765)962-7573. Fax: (765)966-1293. Website: www.fum.org. **Acquisitions:** Barbara Bennett Mays, editor/manager. Estab. 1968. **Publishes 5 titles/year. Receives 100 queries and 80 mss/year. 50% of books from first-time authors; 99% from unagented writers. Pays 7½% royalty.** Publishes book 1 year after acceptance of ms. Accepts simultaneous submissions. Responds in 3 months to queries. Book catalog free; ms guidelines free.

O⊸ "Friends United Press publishes books that reflect Quaker religious practices and testimonies, and energize and equip Friends and others through the power of the Holy Spirit to gather people into fellowships where Jesus Christ is loved, known and obeyed 'as Teacher and Lord.' "

Nonfiction: Biography (Quaker), humor, textbook. Subjects include religion. "Authors should be Quaker and should be familiar with Quaker history, spirituality and doctrine." Submit proposal package. Reviews artwork/photos as part of ms package. Send photocopies.
Recent Title(s): *A Very Good Marriage*, by Tom Mullen (nonfiction); *New England Quaker Meetinghouses*, by Silas B. Weeks (nonfiction).
Tips: "Spirituality manuscripts must be in agreement with Quaker spirituality."

FRONT STREET, 20 Battery Park Ave., #403, Asheville NC 28801. (828)236-3097. Fax: (828)236-3098. E-mail: contactus@frontstreetbooks.com. Website: www.frontstreetbooks.com. **Acquisitions:** Joy Neaves, editor. Publishes hardcover originals. **Publishes 10-15 titles/year; imprint publishes 6-12 titles/year. Receives 1,000 queries and 2,000 mss/year. 75% of books from first-time authors; 90% from unagented writers. Pays royalty on retail price. Offers advance.** Publishes book 1 year after acceptance of ms. Accepts simultaneous submissions. Responds in 1 month to queries; 2 months to proposals; 3 months to mss. Book catalog online; ms guidelines online.
Imprints: Front Street/Lemniscant Books (Stephen Roxburgh).

O⊸ "We are an independent publisher of books for children and young adults."

Nonfiction: Biography, children's/juvenile, humor, illustrated book. Subjects include animals, creative nonfiction, ethnic, gay/lesbian, history, language/literature, memoirs, philosophy, spirituality, women's issues/studies. Reviews artwork/photos as part of ms package. Send photocopies.
Fiction: Adventure, fantasy, feminist, historical, humor, juvenile, literary, picture books, science fiction, young adult. Query with SASE.
Poetry: Submit 25 sample poems.
Recent Title(s): *Cut*, by Patricia McCormick (YA novel); *Carver: A Life in Poems*, by Marilyn Nelson (poetry); *Many Stones*, by Carolyn Coman (YA novel).

FUTURE HORIZONS, 721 W. Abram St., Arlington TX 76013. (817)277-0727. Fax: (817)277-2270. E-mail: info@futurehorizons-autism.com. Website: www.futurehorizons-autism.com. **Acquisitions:** R. Wayne Gilpin, president (autism/Asperger's syndrome); David Brown, CEO (sensory issues for special education). Publishes hardcover originals, trade paperback originals and reprints. **Publishes 10 titles/year; imprint publishes 4 titles/year. Receives 250 queries and 125 mss/year. 75% of books from first-time authors; 95% from unagented writers. Pays 10% royalty or makes outright purchase.** Publishes book 2 months after acceptance of ms. Accepts simultaneous submissions. Responds in 1 month to queries; 2 months to proposals. Book catalog and ms guidelines free on request.
Nonfiction: Children's/juvenile (pertaining to autism), cookbook (for autistic individuals), humor (about autism), self-help (detailing with autism/Asperger's syndrome). Subjects include education (about autism/Asperger's syndrome), autism. Submit proposal package including outline. Reviews artwork/photos as part of ms package. Send photocopies.

Recent Title(s): *Diagnosing Jefferson*, by Norm Ledgin (nonfiction); *Tobin Learns to Make Friends*, by Diane Murrell (childrens fiction).

Tips: Audience is parents, teachers, professionals dealing with individuals with autism or Asperger's syndrome. "Books that sell well, have practical and useful information on how to help individuals and/or care givers of individuals with autism. Personal stories, even success stories, are not helpful to others in a practical way."

FYOS ENTERTAINMENT, LLC, P.O. Box 2021, Philadelphia PA 19103. (215)972-8067. Fax: (215)972-8076. E-mail: info@fyos.com. Website: www.fyos.com. **Acquisitions:** Tonya Marie Evans, editor-in-chief (poetry, African-American fiction); Susan Borden Evans, general manager (African-American fiction). Publishes hardcover originals and trade paperback originals. **Publishes 2-3 titles/year. Receives 50-80 queries and 10-20 mss/year. Pays 10-15% royalty on retail price. or a 60 (publisher)/40 (author) split of net receipts. Will also consider outright purchase opportunities.** Publishes book 1 year after acceptance of ms. Accepts simultaneous submissions. Responds in 1-3 months to queries; 3-6 months to mss. Book catalog for #10 SASE; ms guidelines for #10 SASE.

Nonfiction: Law and self-publishing topics. Subjects include Self-Publishing. Query with SASE.

Fiction: Multicultural, poetry, romance, short story collections. "We concentrate acquisition efforts on poetry and fiction of interest primarily to the African-American reader. We are looking for thought-provoking, well-written work that offers a 'quick and entertaining' read." Query with SASE.

Poetry: "We shy away from 'rhyming form poetry' and words that are more appropriate for performance than reading." Submit 10 sample poems.

Recent Title(s): *Literary Law Guide*, by Susan Borden Evans and Tonya Evans (nonfiction/law); *Seasons of Her*, by T. Evans; *SHINE!*, by T. Evans.

Tips: African-American women, age 18-55. "Neatness counts! Present yourself and your work in a highly professional manner."

GATFPress, Graphic Arts Technical Foundation, 200 Deer Run Rd., Sewickley PA 15143-2600. (412)741-6860. Fax: (412)741-2311. E-mail: poresick@gatf.org. Website: www.gain.net. **Acquisitions:** Peter Oresick, director of publications; Tom Destree, editor in chief; Amy Woodall, managing editor (graphic arts, communication, book publishing, printing). Estab. 1924. Publishes trade paperback originals and hardcover reference texts. **Publishes 15 titles/year. Receives 25 submissions/year. 50% of books from first-time authors; 100% from unagented writers. Pays 5-15% royalty on retail price.** Publishes book 6 months after acceptance of ms. Responds in 1 month. *Writer's Market* recommends allowing 2 months for reply to queries. Book catalog for 9 × 12 SAE with 2 first-class stamps; ms guidelines for #10 SASE.

O⊸ "GATF's mission is to serve the graphic communications community as the major resource for technical information and services through research and education." Currrently emphasizing career guides for graphic communications.

Nonfiction: How-to, reference, technical, textbook. Subjects include printing/graphic communications, electronic publishing. "We primarily want textbook/reference books about printing and related technologies. However, we are expanding our reach into electronic communications." Query with SASE or submit outline, sample chapters and SASE. Reviews artwork/photos as part of ms package.

Recent Title(s): *Practical Proofreading*, by Matthew Willen; *Understanding Graphic Communication*, by Harvey Levenson; *Chemistry for the Graphic Arts*, by Nelson Eldred.

Tips: "We are publishing titles that are updated more frequently, such as *On-Demand Publishing*. Our scope now includes reference titles geared toward general audiences interested in computers, imaging, and Internet as well as print publishing."

GAY SUNSHINE PRESS and LEYLAND PUBLICATIONS, P.O. Box 410690, San Francisco CA 94141-0690. Website: www.gaysunshine.com. **Acquisitions:** Winston Leyland, editor. Estab. 1970. Publishes hardcover originals, trade paperback originals and reprints. **Publishes 6-8 titles/year. Pays royalty or makes outright purchase.** Responds in 6 weeks to queries. Book catalog for $1.

O⊸ Gay history, sex, politics, and culture are the focus of the quality books published by Gay Sunshine Press. Leyland Publications publishes books on popular aspects of gay sexuality and culture.

Nonfiction: "We're interested in innovative literary nonfiction which deals with gay lifestyles." How-to. Subjects include gay/lesbian. No long personal accounts, academic or overly formal titles. Query with SASE. **All unsolicited mss returned unopened.**

Fiction: Interested in innovative well-written novels on gay themes; also short story collections. Erotica, experimental, historical, mystery, science fiction. "We have a high literary standard for fiction." Query with SASE. **All unsolicited mss returned unopened.**

Recent Title(s): *Out of the Closet Into Our Hearts: Celebration of Our Gay/Lesbian Family Members.*

GEM GUIDES BOOK COMPANY, 315 Cloverleaf Dr., Suite F, Baldwin Park CA 91706-6510. (626)855-1611. Fax: (626)855-1610. E-mail: gembooks@aol.com. Website: www.gemguidesbooks.com. **Acquisitions:** Kathy Mayerski, editor. Estab. 1965. **Publishes 6-8 titles/year. Receives 20 submissions/year. 60% of books from first-time authors; 100% from unagented writers. Pays 6-10% royalty on retail price.** Publishes book 1 year after acceptance of ms. Accepts simultaneous submissions. Responds in 3 months to queries.

Imprints: Gembooks

"Gem Guides prefers nonfiction books for the hobbyist in rocks and minerals; lapidary and jewelry-making; travel and recreation guide books for the West and Southwest; and other regional local interest." Currently emphasizing how-to, field guides, West/Southwest regional interest. De-emphasizing stories, history, poetry.

Nonfiction: Subjects include history (Western), hobbies (lapidary and jewelry-making), nature/environment, recreation, regional (Western US), science (earth), travel. Query with outline/synopsis and sample chapters with SASE. Reviews artwork/photos as part of ms package.

Recent Title(s): *Gem Trails of Texas*, by Brad L. Cross; *Arizona Roadside Discoveries*, by Terry Hutchins; *Gem Trails of New Mexico*, by James R. Mitchell.

Tips: "We have a general audience of people interested in recreational activities. Publishers plan and have specific book lines in which they specialize. Learn about the publisher and submit materials compatible with that publisher's product line."

GENESIS PRESS, INC., 315 Third Ave. N, Columbus MS 39701. (662)329-9927. Fax: (662)329-9399. E-mail: books@genesis-press.com. Website: www.genesis-press.com. **Acquisitions:** Sharon Morgan. Publishes hardcover and trade paperback originals and reprints. **Publishes 30 titles/year. Receives 100 queries and 100-150 mss/year. 50% of books from first-time authors; 90% from unagented writers. Pays 6-12% royalty on invoice price. Offers $750-5,000 advance.** Publishes book 1 year after acceptance of ms. Responds in 2 months to queries; 4 months to mss. Ms guidelines for #10 SASE.

Genesis is interested in high quality, mainstream or literary fiction, especially by African-American authors. "We specialize in the African-American niche." Currently emphasizing African-American romance, erotica, ethnic or multicultural women's fiction, and literary. De-emphasizing nonfiction.

Nonfiction: Biography, humor. Subjects include history. Query with SASE or submit outline, 3 sample chapter(s).

Fiction: Erotica, ethnic, literary, multicultural, romance, women's. Query with SASE or submit 3 sample chapter(s), synopsis.

Recent Title(s): *Hitler, the War and the Pope*, by Ronald J. Rychlak; *Cherish the Flame*, by Beverly Clark; *No Apologies*, by Seressia Glass.

Tips: "Be professional. Always include a cover letter and SASE. Follow the submission guidelines posted on our website or send SASE for a copy."

GGC, INC./PUBLISHING, 2545 Sandbourne Lane, Herndon VA 20171. (703)793-8604. Fax: (703)793-8830. E-mail: gardner@ggcinc.com. Website: www.gogardner.com. **Acquisitions:** Garth Gardner, publisher (computer graphics, animation cartoons); Bonney Ford, editor (GGC, art, animation). Publishes trade paperback reprints. **Publishes 10 titles/year; imprint publishes 2 titles/year. Receives 50 queries and 25 mss/year. 80% of books from first-time authors; 70% from unagented writers. Pays 10-15% royalty on wholesale price or makes outright purchase.** Publishes book 3 months after acceptance of ms. Accepts simultaneous submissions. Responds in 1 month to queries. Book catalog online.

GGC publishes books on the subjects of computer graphics, animation, new media, multimedia, art, cartoons, drawing.

Nonfiction: How-to, multimedia, reference, self-help, technical, textbook. Subjects include art/architecture, education, history, computer graphics. Query with SASE or submit proposal package including 2 sample chapter(s), résumé, cover letter. Reviews artwork/photos as part of ms package. Send photocopies.

Recent Title(s): *Careers in Computer Graphics & Animation*, by Garth Gardner; *Gardner's Guide to Feature Animation Writing: The Writer's Roadmap*, by M. Webber.

GINGERBREAD HOUSE, 602 Montauk Highway, Westhampton Beach NY 11978. Website: www.gingerbreadbooks.com. Publishes hardcover and trade paperback originals and reprints. **Publishes 3-6 titles/year. Pays royalty on retail price. Offers competitive advance.** Publishes book 1 year after acceptance of ms. Does not accept simultaneous submissions. Book catalog online.

Nonfiction: Children's/juvenile, gift book. Subjects include education, religion. **All unsolicited mss returned unopened.**

Fiction: Humor, juvenile, picture books, poetry, religious, young adult. **All unsolicited mss returned unopened.**

Recent Title(s): *Grandma's Scrapbook*, by Josephine Nobisso (picture book).

Tips: "We publish high-quality books for children of all ages. Our titles must possess both universal and niche appeal. Should our 'no unsolicited mss' policy change, we will put out calls for submissions through all of the usual venues."

GLENBRIDGE PUBLISHING LTD., 19923 E. Long Ave., Aurora CO 80016. (720)870-8381. Fax: (720)870-5598. E-mail: glenbr@eazy.net. **Acquisitions:** James A. Keene, editor. Estab. 1986. Publishes hardcover originals and reprints, trade paperback originals. **Publishes 6-8 titles/year. Pays 10% royalty.** Publishes book 1 year after acceptance of ms. Accepts simultaneous submissions. Responds in 2 months to queries. Book catalog for 6X9 SAE; ms guidelines for #10 SASE.

"Glenbridge has an eclectic approach to publishing. We look for titles that have long-term capabilities."

Nonfiction: Subjects include Americana, business/economics, cooking/foods/nutrition, history, philosophy, psychology, sociology, music. Query with outline/synopsis, sample chapters and SASE.

Recent Title(s): *Three Minute Therapy: Change Your Thinking/Change Your Life*, by Dr. Michael Edelstein with David R. Steele.

THE GLOBE PEQUOT PRESS, INC., P.O. Box 480, Guilford CT 06437. (203)458-4500. Fax: (203)458-4604. Website: www.globe-pequot.com. President/Publisher: Linda Kennedy. **Acquisitions:** Shelley Wolf, submissions editor. Estab. 1947. Publishes paperback originals, hardcover originals and reprints. **Publishes 500 titles/year. Receives 2,500 submissions/year. 30% of books from first-time authors; 70% from unagented writers. Average print order for a first book is 4,000-7,500. Makes an outright purchase or pays 10% royalty on net price. Offers advance.** Publishes book 1 year after acceptance of ms. Accepts simultaneous submissions. Responds in 3 months to queries.

O→ Globe Pequot is the largest publisher of regional travel books and outdoor recreation in the United States and offers the broadest selection of travel titles of any vendor in this market.

Nonfiction: Humor (regional), regional travel guidebooks, outdoor recreation guides, natural history field guides. Subjects include cooking/foods/nutrition (regional), history (popular, regional), humor (regional), nature/environment, recreation, regional, travel. No doctoral theses, fiction, genealogies, poetry, or textbooks. Submit brief synopsis of work, table of contents or outline, sample chapter, résumé/vita, definition of target audience, and an analysis of competing titles. Reviews artwork/photos as part of ms package.

Recent Title(s): *Exploring Glacier National Park*; *Hiking Wisconsin*; *Kansas Curiosities*.

DAVID R. GODINE, PUBLISHER, INC., 9 Hamilton Place. Boston MA 02108. (617)451-9600. Fax: (617)350-0250. E-mail: info@godine.com. Website: www.godine.com. Estab. 1970. Publishes hardcover and trade paperback originals and reprints. **Publishes 35 titles/year. Pays royalty on retail price.** Publishes book 3 years after acceptance of ms. Book catalog for 5X8 SAE with 3 first-class stamps.

O→ "Our particular strengths are books about the history and design of the written word, literary essays, and the best of world fiction in translation. We also have an unusually strong list of children's books, all of them printed in their entirety with no cuts, deletions, or side-stepping to keep the political watchdogs happy."

Nonfiction: Biography, children's/juvenile, coffee table book, cookbook, illustrated book. Subjects include Americana, art/architecture, gardening, nature/environment, photography, literary criticism, current affairs. *No unsolicited mss*. Query with SASE.

Fiction: Juvenile, literary, short story collections. *No unsolicited mss*. Query with SASE.

Recent Title(s): *The Last Buffalo Hunter*, by Jake Mosher (fiction); *Easy To Remember: The Great American Songwriters and Their Songs*, by William Zinsser.

GOLLEHON PRESS, INC., 6157 28th St., SE, Grand Rapids MI 49546. (616)949-3515. Fax: (616)949-8674. Website: www.gollehonbooks.com. **Acquisitions:** Lori Adams, editor. Publishes hardcover, trade paperback and mass market paperback originals. **Publishes 6-8 titles/year. Receives 100 queries and 30 mss/year. 85% of books from first-time authors; 90% from unagented writers. Pays 7% royalty on retail price. Offers $500-1,000 advance.** Publishes book 6 months after acceptance of ms. Accepts simultaneous submissions. Responds in 1 month to queries and proposals if interested to proposals; 2 months to mss. Book catalog and ms guidelines online.

O→ Currently emphasizing how-to, self-help, pets, nutrition, gardening books for seniors. *No unsolicited mss*; brief proposals only.

Nonfiction: How-to, humor, self-help. Subjects include animals, anthropology/archeology, business/economics, gardening, health/medicine, hobbies, humor, money/finance, psychology, pets, nutrition. Submit proposal package. No SASE (we do not return mss). Reviews artwork/photos as part of ms package. Send photocopies only if requested.

Tips: "Mail brief book proposal and few sample pages only. We will request full manuscript if interested. We cannot respond to all queries. Full manuscript will be returned if we requested it and writer provides SASE. We do not return proposals. Simultaneous submissions are encouraged."

GRACIE PUBLICATIONS, Alden Enterprises, 2206 Bailey St. NW, Hartselle AL 35640-4219. E-mail: editor@poeticvoices.com. Website: www.poeticvoices.com. **Acquisitions:** Robin Travis-Murphree, executive editor. Estab. 1997. Firm publishes paperback originals. **Publishes 6-10 titles/year. Pays 8-15% royalty and 10 author's copies (out of a press run of 200).** Responds in 2 months to queries. Ms guidelines online.

Poetry: Gracie Publications seeks "to promote new and talented poets, and their work, via the publication of chapbooks of poetry. All styles of poetry are welcome. We are open to new writers, look for variety and excellence, are open to concrete forms, traditional, and free verse as well as other varieties. We do accept religious theme poems." Does not want e-mail submissions. Include cover letter with address and phone number. **Reading fee:** $10 must be included with submission. Submit complete ms.

Tips: "Make sure you read and follow guidelines. Make sure your work is neatly presented. There is nothing worse than receiving messy work or work that does not conform to the guidelines."

THE GRADUATE GROUP, P.O. Box 370351, West Hartford CT 06137-0351. (860)233-2330. Fax: (860)233-2330. E-mail: graduategroup@hotmail.com. Website: www.graduategroup.com. **Acquisitions:** Mara Whitman, president; Robert Whitman, vice president. Estab. 1964. Publishes trade paperback originals. **Publishes 50 titles/year. Receives 100 queries and 70 mss/year. 60% of books from first-time authors; 85% from unagented writers. Pays 20% royalty on retail price.** Publishes book 3 months after acceptance of ms. Accepts simultaneous submissions. Responds in 1 month to queries. Book catalog and ms guidelines free.

O→ "The Graduate Group helps college and graduate students better prepare themselves for rewarding careers and helps people advance in the workplace." Currently emphasizing test preparation, career advancement and materials for prisoners, law enforcement, books on unique careers.

Nonfiction: Reference. Subjects include business/economics, education, government/politics, health/medicine, money/finance, law enforcement. Submit complete ms and SASE with sufficient postage.
Recent Title(s): *Real Life 101: Winning Secrets You Won't Find in Class*, by Debra Yergen; *Getting In: Applicant's Guide to Graduate School Admissions*, by David Burrell.
Tips: Audience is career planning offices; college, graduate school and public libraries. "We are open to all submissions, especially those involving career planning, internships and other nonfiction titles. Looking for books on law enforcement, books for prisoners and reference books on subjects/fields students would be interested in. We want books on helping students and others to interview, pass tests, gain opportunity, understand the world of work, networking, building experience, preparing for advancement, preparing to enter business, improving personality and building relationships."

GRANITE PUBLISHING, LLC, P.O. Box 1429, Columbus NC 28756. (828)894-8444. Fax: (828)894-8454. E-mail: granitepub@5thworld.com. Website: www.5thworld.com. President: Pam Meyer. **Acquisitions:** Brian Crissey. Publishes trade paperback originals and reprints. **Publishes 3 titles/year. Receives 50 queries and 25/month mss/year. 80% of books from first-time authors; 90% from unagented writers. Pays 7½-15% royalty.** Publishes book 16 months after acceptance of ms. Accepts simultaneous submissions. Responds in 2 months to mss.
Imprints: Wild Flower Press, Swan-Raven & Co., Agents of Change

- "Granite Publishing strives to preserve the Earth by publishing books that develop new wisdom about our emerging planetary citizenship, bringing information from the outerworlds to our world." Currently emphasizing natural history, planetary healing.

Nonfiction: Multimedia. Subjects include New Age, planetary paradigm shift. Submit proposal. Reviews artwork/photos as part of ms package. Send photocopies.
Recent Title(s): *Voyagers*, by Ashayana Deane.

GRAYWOLF PRESS, 2402 University Ave., Suite 203, St. Paul MN 55114. (651)641-0077. Fax: (651)641-0036. Website: www.graywolfpress.org. Editor/Publisher: Fiona McCrae. Executive Editor: Anne Czarniecki. **Acquisitions:** Daniel Kos (poetry, nonfiction); Katie Dublinski, editor (fiction). Estab. 1974. Publishes trade cloth and paperback originals. **Publishes 16 titles/year. Receives 2,500 queries/year. 20% of books from first-time authors; 50% from unagented writers. Pays royalty on retail price. Offers $1,000-6,000 advance.** Publishes book 18 months after acceptance of ms. Does not accept simultaneous submissions. Responds in 3 months to queries. Book catalog free; ms guidelines for #10 SASE.

- Graywolf Press is an independent, nonprofit publisher dedicated to the creation and promotion of thoughtful and imaginative contemporary literature essential to a vital and diverse culture.

Nonfiction: Subjects include contemporary culture, language/literature, culture. Query with SASE.
Fiction: Literary. "Familiarize yourself with our list first."
Poetry: "We are interested in linguistically challenging work." Query with SASE.
Recent Title(s): *Antebellum Dream Book*, by Elizabeth Alexander; *Loverboy*, by Victoria Redel; *Crying at the Movies*, by Madelon Sprengnether.

GREAT QUOTATIONS PUBLISHING, 8102 Lemont Rd., #300, Woodridge IL 60517. (630)630-3903. **Acquisitions:** Diane Voreis, acquisitions editor (humor, relationships, Christian); Jan Stob, acquisitions editor (children's). Estab. 1991. **Publishes 30 titles/year. Receives 1,500 queries and 1,200 mss/year. 50% of books from first-time authors; 80% from unagented writers. Pays 3-5% royalty on net receipts.** Publishes book 6 months after acceptance of ms. Accepts simultaneous submissions. Responds in 6 months with SASE to queries. Book catalog for $2; ms guidelines for #10 SASE.

- Great Quotations seeks original material for the following general categories: children, humor, inspiration, motivation, success, romance, tributes to mom/dad/grandma/grandpa, etc. Currently emphasizing humor, Christian, relationships. De-emphasizing poetry, self-help. We publish new books twice a year, in July and in January.

Nonfiction: Humor, illustrated book, self-help. Subjects include business/economics, child guidance/parenting, humor, nature/environment, religion, sports, women's issues/studies. "We look for subjects with identifiable markets, appealing to the general public. We publish children's books or others requiring multicolor illustration on the inside. We don't publish highly controversial subject matter." Submit outline, 2 sample chapter(s). Reviews artwork/photos as part of ms package. Send photocopies or transparencies.
Poetry: "We would be most interested in upbeat and juvenile poetry."
Recent Title(s): *Secret Language of Men*; *Astrology for Cat.*
Tips: "Our books are physically small and generally a very quick read. They are available at gift shops and book shops throughout the country. We are aware that most of our books are bought on impulse and given as gifts. We need strong, clever, descriptive titles; beautiful cover art and brief, positive, upbeat text. Be prepared to submit final manuscript on computer disk, according to our specifications. (It is not necessary to try to format the typesetting of your manuscript to look like a finished book.)"

GREENE BARK PRESS, P.O. Box 1108, Bridgeport CT 06601. (203)372-4861. Fax: (203)371-5856. Website: www.greenebarkpress.com. **Acquisitions:** Thomas J. Greene, publisher; Michele Hofbauer, associate publisher. Estab. 1991. Publishes hardcover originals. **Publishes 5 titles/year. Receives 100 queries and 6,000 mss/year. 60% of books from first-time authors; 100% from unagented writers. Pays 10-15% royalty on wholesale price.** Publishes book 1 year after acceptance of ms. Accepts simultaneous submissions. Responds in 1 month to queries; 6 months to mss. Book catalog for $2; ms guidelines for SASE.

Greene Bark Press only publishes books for children and young adults, mainly picture and read-to books. "All of our titles appeal to the imagination and encourage children to read and explore the world through books. We only publish children's fiction—all subjects—but in reading picture book format appealing to ages 3-9 or all ages."

Fiction: Juvenile. Submit complete ms. No queries or ms by e-mail.

Recent Title(s): *The Magical Trunk*, by Gi Gi Tegge.

Tips: Audience is "children who read to themselves and others. Mothers, fathers, grandparents, godparents who read to their respective children, grandchildren. Include SASE, be prepared to wait, do not inquire by telephone."

GREENHAVEN PRESS, INC., 10911 Technology Place, San Diego CA 92127. Website: www.greenhaven.com. **Acquisitions:** Chandra Howard, aquisitions editor. Estab. 1970. Publishes approximately 135 anthologies/year; all anthologies are works for hire. **Makes outright purchase of $1,000-3,000.** Send query letter and resumé. No unsolicited ms to queries. Book catalog for 9×12 SAE with 3 first-class stamps or online.

Greenhaven Press publishes hard and softcover educational supplementary materials and (nontrade) nonfiction anthologies on contemporary issues, literary criticism and history for high school and college readers. These anthologies serve as supplementary educational material for high school and college libraries and classrooms. Currently emphasizing historical topics, and social-issue anthologies.

Nonfiction: Children's/juvenile. Subjects include history, social issues. "We produce tightly formatted anthologies on contemporary issues, literary criticism, and history for high school and college-level readers. We are looking for freelance book editors to research and compile these anthologies; we are not interested in submissions of single-author manuscripts. Each series has specific requirements. Potential book editors should familiarize themselves with our catalog and anthologies." Query. No unsolicited ms.

Recent Title(s): *Opposing Viewpoints: Abortion*; *Examining Pop Culture: Violence in Film and TV*; *At Issue in History: The Cuban Missle Crisis.*

GREENWILLOW BOOKS, HarperCollins Publishers, 1350 Avenue of the Americas, New York NY 10019. (212)261-6500. Website: www.harperchildrens.com. Senior Editor: Rebecca Davis. Estab. 1974. Publishes hardcover originals and reprints. **Publishes 50-60 titles/year. 1% of books from first-time authors; 30% from unagented writers. Pays 10% royalty. on wholesale price for first-time authors. Offers variable advance.** Publishes book 2 years after acceptance of ms.

Greenwillow Books publishes quality picture books and fiction for young readers of all ages, and nonfiction primarily for children under seven years of age.

Fiction: Juvenile. Fantasy, humor, literary, mystery, picture books.

Recent Title(s): *Whale Talk*, by Chris Crutcher.

Tips: "Currently not accepting unsolicited mail, mss or queries. Please call (212)261-6627 for an update."

GROLIER PUBLISHING CO., INC., Scholastic Inc., 90 Sherman Turnpike, Danbury CT 06816. (203)797-3500. Fax: (203)797-3197. Website: www.publishing.grolier.com. Estab. 1895. Publishes hardcover and trade paperback originals. Does not accept simultaneous submissions.

Imprints: Children's Press, Grolier Educational, Franklin Watts

"Grolier Publishing is a leading publisher of reference, educational and children's books. We provide parents, teachers and librarians with the tools they need to enlighten children to the pleasure of learning and prepare them for the road ahead."

GROSSET & DUNLAP PUBLISHERS, Penguin Putnam Inc., 345 Hudson St., New York NY 10014. President/Publisher: Debra Dorfman. Estab. 1898. Publishes hardcover (few) and paperback originals. **Publishes 175 titles/year. Pays royalty. Offers advance.** Publishes book 18 months after acceptance of ms. Does not accept simultaneous submissions. Responds in 2 months to queries.

Grosset & Dunlap publishes children's books that show children that reading is fun, with books that speak to their interests, and that are affordable so that children can build a home library of their own.

Nonfiction: Children's/juvenile. Subjects include nature/environment, science. *Agented submissions only.*

Fiction: Juvenile. *Agented submissions only.*

Recent Title(s): *Dragon Slayers' Academy* (series); *Zack Files* (series).

Tips: "Nonfiction that is particularly topical or of wide interest in the mass market; new concepts for novelty format for preschoolers; and very well-written easy readers on topics that appeal to primary graders have the best chance of selling to our firm."

GROUP PUBLISHING, INC., 1515 Cascade Ave., Loveland CO 80538. (970)669-3836. Fax: (970)679-4370. E-mail: kloesche@grouppublishing.com. Website: www.grouppublishing.com. **Acquisitions:** Kerri Loesche, editorial assistant. Estab. 1974. Publishes trade paperback originals. **Publishes 24 titles/year. Receives 200 queries and 50 mss/year. 40% of books from first-time authors; 95% from unagented writers. Pays up to 10% royalty on wholesale price or makes outright purchase or work for hire. Offers up to $1,000 advance.** Publishes book 18 months after acceptance of ms. Accepts simultaneous submissions. Responds in 1 month to queries; 6 months to proposals; 6 months to mss. Book catalog for 9×12 SAE with 2 first-class stamps; ms guidelines online.

"Our mission is to encourage Christian growth in children, youth and adults."

Nonfiction: Children's/juvenile, how-to, multimedia, textbook. Subjects include education, religion. "We're an interdenominational publisher of resource materials for people who work with adults, youth or children in a Christian church setting. We also publish materials for use directly by youth or children (such as devotional books, workbooks or Bibles stories). Everything we do is based on concepts of active and interactive learning as described in *Why Nobody Learns Much of Anything at Church: And How to Fix It*, by Thom and Joani Schultz. We need new, practical, hands-on, innovative, out-of-the-box ideas—things that no one's doing... yet." Query with SASE or submit proposal package including outline, 3 sample chapter(s), cover letter, introduction to book, and sample activities if appropriate.

Recent Title(s): *Aqua Church*, by Leonard Sweet (church leadership); *The Dirt on Learning*, by Thom and Joani Schultz (effective teaching and learning).

Tips: "Our audience consists of pastors, Christian education directors and Sunday school teachers."

ALDINE DE GRUYTER, Walter de Gruyter, Inc., 200 Saw Mill River Rd., Hawthorne NY 10532. (914)747-0110, ext. 19. Fax: (914)747-1326. E-mail: rkoffler@degruyterny.com. Website: www.degruyter.de. **Acquisitions:** Dr. Richard Koffler, executive editor. Publishes hardcover and academic paperback originals. **Publishes 15-25 titles/year. Receives several hundred queries and 100 mss/year. 15% of books from first-time authors; 99% from unagented writers. Pays 7½-10% royalty on net receipts.** Publishes book 9 months after acceptance of ms. Accepts simultaneous submissions. Responds in 2 months to proposals. Book catalog free; ms guidelines only after contract.

O→ Aldine de Gruyter is an academic nonfiction publisher.

Nonfiction: Scholarly, textbook (rare), course-related monographs; edited volumes. Subjects include anthropology/archeology, humanities, psychology (evolutionary), sociology, social psychology (not clinical), human services. "Aldine's authors are academics with Ph.D.'s and strong publication records. No poetry or fiction." Submit proposal package including 1-2 sample chapter(s), cv; market; competing texts; reviews of early work.

Recent Title(s): *The Politics of Medicare*, by Theodore R. Marmor.

Tips: Audience is professors and upper level and graduate students.

GRYPHON HOUSE, INC., P.O. Box 207, Beltsville MD 20704. (301)595-9500. Fax: (301)595-0051. Website: www.gryphonhouse.com. **Acquisitions:** Kathy Charner, editor-in-chief. Estab. 1971. Publishes trade paperback originals. **Publishes 12-15 titles/year. Pays royalty on wholesale price.** Does not accept simultaneous submissions. Responds in 3-6 months to queries.

O→ Gryphon House publishes books that teachers and parents of young children (birth to age 8) consider essential to their daily lives.

Nonfiction: Children's/juvenile, how-to. Subjects include child guidance/parenting, education (early childhood). Currently emphasizing reading; de-emphasizing after-school activities. Submit outline, 2-3 sample chapter(s), SASE.

Recent Title(s): *The Big Messy Art Book*, by Maryann Kohl and Jean Potter; *Games to Play with Babies, 3rd ed*, by Jackie Silberg; *Creating Readers*, by Pam Schiller.

GRYPHON PUBLICATIONS, P.O. Box 209, Brooklyn NY 11228. **Acquisitions:** Gary Lovisi, owner/publisher. Publishes trade paperback originals and reprints. **Publishes 10 titles/year. Receives 500 queries and 1,000 mss/year. 20% of books from first-time authors; 90% from unagented writers. Makes outright purchase by contract, price varies. Offers no advance.** Publishes book 1-2 years after acceptance of ms. Responds in 1 month to queries. *Writer's Market* recommends allowing 2 months for reply to queries. Book catalog and ms guidelines for #10 SASE.

Imprints: Paperback Parade Magazine, Hardboiled Magazine, Gryphon Books, Gryphon Doubles.

O→ "I publish very genre oriented work (science fiction, crime, pulps) and nonfiction on these topics, authors and artists. It's best to query with an idea first."

Nonfiction: Reference, scholarly, bibliography. Subjects include hobbies, language/literature, book collecting. "We need well-written, well-researched articles, but query first on topic and length. Writers should not submit material that is not fully developed/researched." Query with SASE. Reviews artwork/photos as part of ms package. Send photocopies; slides, transparencies may be necessary later.

Fiction: Crime, hard-boiled fiction. "We want cutting-edge fiction, under 3,000 words with impact!" For short stories, query or submit complete ms. For novels, send 1-page query letter with SASE.

Recent Title(s): *Barsom: Edgar Rice Burroughs & the Martian Myth*, by Richard A. Lysoff; *Sherlock Holmes & the Terror Out of Time*, by Ralph Vaughan.

Tips: "We are very particular about novels and book-length work. A first-timer has a better chance with a short story or article. On anything over 4,000 words *do not* send manuscript, send *only* query letter with SASE."

GUILD PRESS, EMMIS PUBLISHING, LP, Emmis Communications, 10665 Andrade Dr., Zionsville IN 46077. (317)733-4175. Fax: (317)733-4176. E-mail: sales@guildpress.com. Website: www.guildpress.com. **Acquisitions:** Nancy N. Baxter, editor (Confederate Civil War materials and regional juvenile materials). Estab. 1987. Publishes hardcover and trade paperback originals and reprints. **Publishes 20 titles/year. Receives 500+ queries and 300 mss/year. 25% of books from first-time authors; 90% from unagented writers. Pays royalty on wholesale price or retail price.** Publishes book 1 year after acceptance of ms. Does not accept simultaneous submissions. Responds in 1 month to queries; 1 month to proposals; 1 month to mss. Book catalog for #10 SASE.

Nonfiction: Biography, children's/juvenile (regional), coffee table book, humor. Subjects include history (Civil War), memoirs, regional, software (research CD-ROMs of the Official Records of the Civil War). "We are interested in nonfiction materials about Cincinnati, Atlanta, Indianapolis and cities in Texas." Query with SASE.

Fiction: Adventure, juvenile, mystery, young adult. "We do not normally accept fiction submissions."

Recent Title(s): *Legendary Hoosiers: Famous Folks From the State of Indiana*, Nelson Price; *Slander and Sweet Judgment: The Memoir of an Indiana Congressman*, Andy Jacobs, Jr.; *Indianapolis Union Station: Trains, Travelers and Changing Times*, Jim Hetherington.
Tips: Regional.

HACHAI PUBLISHING, 156 Chester Ave., Brooklyn NY 11218. (718)633-0100. Website: www.hachai.com. **Acquisitions:** Devorah Leah Rosenfeld, editor. Estab. 1988. Publishes hardcover originals. **Publishes 4 titles/year. Makes outright purchase of $800.** Accepts simultaneous submissions. Responds in 2 months to mss. Book catalog free; ms guidelines for #10 SASE.

O→ "Hachai is dedicated to producing high quality Jewish children's literature, ages 2 through 10. Story should promote universal values such as sharing, kindness, etc."

Nonfiction: Children's/juvenile. Subjects include ethnic, religion. Submit complete ms, SASE. Reviews artwork/photos as part of ms package. Send photocopies.
Recent Title(s): *Nine Spoons*, by Marci Stillerman (nonfiction); *On the Ball*, by Dina Rosenfeld (fiction).
Tips: "We are looking for books that convey the traditional Jewish experience in modern times or long ago; traditional Jewish observance such as Sabbath and Holidays and mitzvos such as mezuzah, blessings etc.; positive character traits (middos) such as honesty, charity, respect, sharing, etc. We are also interested in historical fiction and adventure tales for young readers (7-10) written with a traditional Jewish perspective and highlighting the relevance of Torah in making important choices. Please, no animal stories, romance, violence, preachy sermonizing."

HALF HALT PRESS, INC., P.O. Box 67, Boonsboro MD 21713. (301)733-7119. Fax: (301)733-7408. E-mail: hhpress@aol.com. Website: www.halfhaltpress.com. **Acquisitions:** Elizabeth Carnes, publisher. Estab. 1986. Publishes 90% hardcover and trade paperback originals and 10% reprints. **Publishes 15 titles/year. Receives 150 submissions/year. 25% of books from first-time authors; 50% from unagented writers. Pays 10-12½% royalty on retail price.** Publishes book 1 year after acceptance of ms. Does not accept simultaneous submissions. Responds in 1 month. *Writer's Market* suggests allowing 2 months for reply to queries. Book catalog for 6×9 SAE 2 first-class stamps.

O→ "We publish high-quality nonfiction on equestrian topics, books that help riders and trainers do something better."

Nonfiction: How-to. Subjects include animals (horses), sports. "We need serious instructional works by authorities in the field on horse-related topics, broadly defined." Query with SASE. Reviews artwork/photos as part of ms package.
Recent Title(s): *Dressage in Harmony*, by Walter Zettl.
Tips: "Writers have the best chance selling us well-written, unique works that teach serious horse people how to do something better. If I were a writer trying to market a book today, I would offer a straightforward presentation, letting the work speak for itself, without hype or hard sell. Allow publisher to contact writer, without frequent calling to check status. They haven't forgotten the writer but may have many different proposals at hand; frequent calls to 'touch base,' multiplied by the number of submissions, become an annoyance. As the publisher/author relationship becomes close and is based on working well together, early impressions may be important, even to the point of being a consideration in acceptance for publication."

ALEXANDER HAMILTON INSTITUTE, 70 Hilltop Rd., Ramsey NJ 07446-1119. (201)825-3377. Fax: (201)825-8696. Website: www.ahipubs.com. **Acquisitions:** Brian L.P. Zevnik, editor-in-chief; Gloria Ju, editor; Amy Knierim, editor. Estab. 1909. Publishes 3-ring binder and paperback originals. **Publishes 5-10 titles/year. Receives 50 queries and 10 mss/year. 25% of books from first-time authors; 95% from unagented writers. Pays 5-8% royalty on retail price or makes outright purchase of $3,500-7,000. Offers $3,500-7,000 advance.** Publishes book 10 months after acceptance of ms. Accepts simultaneous submissions. Responds in 1 month to queries; 2 months to mss.

O→ Alexander Hamilton Institute publishes management books for upper-level managers and executives. Currently emphasizing legal issues for HR/personnel.

Nonfiction: The main audience is US personnel executives and high-level management. Subjects include legal personnel matters. "These books combine court case research and practical application of defensible programs."
Recent Title(s): *Employer's Guide to Record-Keeping Requirements.*
Tips: "We sell exclusively by direct mail to managers and executives. A writer must know his/her field and be able to communicate legal and practical systems and programs."

HAMPTON ROADS PUBLISHING COMPANY, INC., 1125 Stoney Ridge Rd., Charlottesville VA 22902. (434)296-2772. Fax: (434)296-5096. E-mail: hrpc@hrpub.com. Website: hrpub.com. **Acquisitions:** Frank DeMarco, chief editor (metaphysical/visionary fiction); Robert S. Friedman, president (metaphysical, spiritual, inspirational, self-help); Ellen McKenna, marketing director (spiritual paths/Toltec); Richard Leviton, senior editor (alternative medicine). Estab. 1989. Publishes hardcover and trade paperback originals. **Publishes 35-40 titles/year. Receives 1,000 queries and 1,500 mss/year. 50% of books from first-time authors; 70% from unagented writers. Pays royalty. Offers $1,000-100,000 advance.** Publishes book 1 year after acceptance of ms. Accepts simultaneous submissions. Responds in 2 months to queries; 2 months to proposals; 6 months to mss.
Imprints: Young Spirit (children's spiritual).

O→ "Our reason for being is to impact, uplift and contribute to positive change in the world. We publish books that will enrich and empower the evolving consciousness of mankind."

Nonfiction: How-to, illustrated book, self-help. Subjects include New Age, spirituality. Query with SASE or submit synopsis, SASE. Reviews artwork/photos as part of ms package. Send photocopies.

Fiction: Spiritual. "Fiction should have one or more of the following themes: spiritual, inspirational, metaphysical, i.e., past life recall, out-of-body experiences, near death experience, paranormal." Query with SASE or submit synopsis or submit complete ms.

Recent Title(s): *Moments of Grace*, by Neale Donald Walsch; *Spider World: The Tower*, by Colin Wilson.

HANCOCK HOUSE PUBLISHERS, 1431 Harrison Ave., Blaine WA 98230-5005. (604)538-1114. Fax: (604)538-2262. E-mail: david@hancockwildlife.org. Website: www.hancockwildlife.org. David Hancock, publisher. **Acquisitions:** Melanie Clark, promotional manager. Estab. 1971. Publishes hardcover and trade paperback originals and reprints. **Publishes 14 titles/year. Receives 300 submissions/year. 50% of books from first-time authors; 90% from unagented writers. Pays 10% royalty.** Publishes book up to 1 year after acceptance of ms. Accepts simultaneous submissions. Book catalog free; ms guidelines online.

- Hancock House Publishers is the largest North American publisher of wildlife, and Native Indian titles. "We also cover Pacific Northwest, fishing, history, Canadiana, biographies. We are seeking agriculture, natural history, animal husbandry, conservation and popular science titles with a regional (Pacific Northwest), national or international focus." Currently emphasizing non-fiction wildlife, native history, biography, fishing. De-emphasizing cryptozoology, cowboy poetry, and guide books.

Nonfiction: "Centered around Pacific Northwest, local history, nature guide books, international ornithology and Native Americans." Biography, how-to, reference, technical, Pacific Northwest history and biography. Subjects include agriculture/horticulture, animals, ethnic, history, nature/environment, regional. Submit proposal package including outline, 3 sample chapter(s), selling points, SASE. Reviews artwork/photos as part of ms package. Send photocopies.

Recent Title(s): *Wings Across Desert (Great Motorized Crane Migration)*, by David H. Ellis; *Russell Country*, by Bette Wolf Duncan.

HANSER GARDNER PUBLICATIONS, 6915 Valley Ave., Cincinnati OH 45244. (513)527-8977. Fax: (513)527-8950. Website: www.hansergardner.com. **Acquisitions:** Woody Chapman. Estab. 1993. Publishes hardcover and paperback originals and reprints. **Publishes 5-10 titles/year. Receives 40-50 queries and 5-10 mss/year. 75% of books from first-time authors; 100% from unagented writers. Pays 10-15% royalty on net receipts.** Publishes book 10 months after acceptance of ms. Accepts simultaneous submissions. Responds in 2 weeks to queries; 1 month to proposals; 1 month to mss. Book catalog and ms guidelines free.

- Hanser Gardner publishes training and practical application titles for metalworking, machining and finishing shops/plants.

Nonfiction: "Our books are primarily basic introductory-level training books and books that emphasize practical applications. Strictly deal with subjects shown above." How-to, technical, textbook. Subjects include metalworking, machining and finishing shops/plants. Submit outline, sample chapter(s), résumé, preface and comparison to competing or similar titles. Reviews artwork/photos as part of ms package. Send photocopies.

Recent Title(s): *Industrial Painting*, by Norman R. Roobol (industrial reference).

Tips: "Our readers and authors occupy various positions within small and large metalworking, machining and finishing shops/plants. We prefer that interested individuals write, call, or fax us with their queries first, so we can send them our proposal guideline form."

HARBOR PRESS, 5713 Wollochet Dr. NW, Gig Harbor WA 98335. Fax: (253)851-5191. E-mail: info@harborpress.com. Website: www.harborpress.com. President/Publisher: Harry R. Lynn. **Acquisitions:** Deborah Young, senior editor (please direct submissions to Harbor Press, 5 Glen Dr., Plainview NY 11803). Estab. 1985. Publishes hardcover and trade paperback originals and reprints. **Publishes 4-6 titles/year. Negotiates competitive royalties on wholesale price or makes outright purchase.** Does not accept simultaneous submissions.

- Harbor Press publishes books that will help readers achieve better health and more successful lives. Currently emphasizing diet and weight loss, parenting, psychology/human relationships, successful living books. Credentialed authors only.

Nonfiction: How-to, self-help. Subjects include child guidance/parenting, cooking/foods/nutrition (diet and weight loss only), health/medicine, psychology. Query with SASE or submit proposal package including outline, 3 sample chapter(s), synopsis. Reviews artwork/photos as part of ms package. Send photocopies.

Recent Title(s): *The Prostate Diet Cookbook*, by Buffy Sanders; *Yes! Your Teen Is Crazy: Loving Your Kid Without Losing Your Mind*, by Michael Bradley.

HARCOURT, INC, Children's Books Division, 525 B St., Suite 1900, San Diego CA 92101. (619)281-6616. Fax: (619)699-6777. Website: www.harcourtbooks.com/children'sbooksdivision. Estab. 1919. Publishes hardcover originals and trade paperback reprints.

Imprints: Harcourt Children's Books, Gulliver Books, Silver Whistle, Red Wagon Books, Harcourt Young Classics, Green Light Readers, Voyager Books/Libros Viajeros, Harcourt Paperbacks, Odyssey Classics, Magic Carpet Books.

- Harcourt Inc., owns some of the world's most prestigious publishing imprints—imprints which distinguish quality products for the juvenile, educational, scientific, technical, medical, professional and trade markets worldwide.

Nonfiction: No unsolicited mss or queries accepted. No phone calls.

Fiction: No unsolicited mss or queries accepted. No phone calls.

Recent Title(s): *In My World*, by Lois Ehlert; *The Magic Hat*, by Mem Fox.

HARCOURT, INC., Trade Division, 525 B St., Suite 1900, San Diego CA 92101. (619)699-6560. Fax: (619)699-5555. Website: www.harcourtbooks.com. **Acquisitions:** David Hough, managing editor; Jane Isay, editor-in-chief (science, math, history, language); Drenka Willen, senior editor (poetry, fiction in translation, history); Walter Bode, editor (history, geography, American fiction); Ann Patty (American fiction). Publishes hardcover and trade paperback originals and trade paperback reprints. **Publishes 120 titles/year. 5% of books from first-time authors; 5% from unagented writers. Pays 6-15% royalty on retail price. Offers $2,000 minimum advance.** Accepts simultaneous submissions.
Imprints: Harvest (contact Andre Bernard).

Harcourt Inc. owns some of the world's most prestigious publishing imprints—imprints which distinguish quality products for the juvenile, educational, scientific, technical, medical, professional and trade markets worldwide. Currently emphasizing science and math.

Nonfiction: Biography, children's/juvenile, coffee table book, gift book, illustrated book, multimedia, reference, technical. Subjects include anthropology/archeology, art/architecture, child guidance/parenting, creative nonfiction, education, ethnic, gay/lesbian, general nonfiction, government/politics, health/medicine, history, language/literature, memoirs, military/war, multicultural, philosophy, psychology, religion, science, sociology, spirituality, sports, translation, travel, women's issues/studies. Published all categories *except* business/finance (university texts), cookbooks, self-help, sex. No unsolicited mss. *Agented submissions only.*

Recent Title(s): *The Best of Times*, by Haynes Johnson (nonfiction); *The Nautical Chart*, by Arturo Perez-Reverte (fiction); *The Middle of Everywhere*, by Mary Pipher (nonfiction).

HARPERCOLLINS CHILDREN'S BOOKS, HarperCollins Publishers, 1350 Avenue of the Americas, New York NY 10019. (212)261-6500. Website: www.harpercollins.com. Editor-in-Chief: Kate Morgan Jackson. **Acquisitions:** Alix Reid, editorial director; Barbara Lalichi, senior VP & editorial director; Phoebe Yeh, editorial director; Katherine Fegon, editorial director; Margaret Anastos, editorial director. Publishes hardcover originals. **Publishes 350 titles/year. Receives 200 queries and 5,000 mss/year. 5% of books from first-time authors; 25% from unagented writers. Pays 10-12½% royalty on retail price. Offers variable advance.** Publishes book 1 year (novels) or 2 years (picture books) after acceptance of ms.

Imprints: Joanna Cotler Books (Joanna Cotler, editorial director); Laura Geringer Books(Laura Geringer, editorial director); Greenwillow Books (Virginia Duncan, vice president & publisher); Harper Festival (Emily Brenner, editorial director); Avon; Harper Tempest (Elise Howard, vice president publisher); Harper Trophy (Stephen Fraser, editorial director).

Fiction: Adventure, fantasy, historical, humor, juvenile, literary, picture books, young adult. *Agented submissions only.* No unsolicited mss.

Recent Title(s): *If You Take a Mouse to the Movies*, by Laura Numeroff (picture book); *A Series of Unfortunate Events*, by Lemony Snicket (novel).

HARPERINFORMATION, HarperCollins Publishers, 10 East 53rd St., New York NY 10022. (212)207-7000. Fax: (212)207-6961. Website: www.harpercollins.com. **Acquisitions:** Megan Newman, editorial director (resource); Dave Conti, senior editor (business). Publishes hardcover originals, trade paperback originals and reprints. **10% of books from first-time authors; 0% from unagented writers.** Publishes book 1 year after acceptance of ms. Accepts simultaneous submissions. Responds in 1 month to queries; 1 month to proposals; 1 month to mss. Book catalog online.

Imprints: HarperBusiness (Adrian Zackheim); HarperResource (Megan Newman)

Nonfiction: Coffee table book, cookbook, gift book, how-to, reference, self-help. Subjects include business/economics, child guidance/parenting, computers/electronic, cooking/foods/nutrition, health/medicine, hobbies, language/literature, money/finance, sex, sociology, spirituality. *Agented submissions only.*

Recent Title(s): *The Unfinished Revolution*, by Michael Dertouzos (business); *Emeril's TV Dinners*, by Emeril Lagasse (cookbook); *A Charlie Brown Christmas*, by Charles Schultz (resource).

HARPERSANFRANCISCO, Harper Collins Publishers, 353 Sacramento St., Suite 500, San Francisco CA 94111-3653. (415)477-4400. Fax: (415)477-4444. E-mail: hcsanfrancisco@harpercollins.com. **Acquisitions:** Stephen Hanselman, senior vice president/publisher (Christian spirituality, history, biography); Liz Perle, editor-at-large (general nonfiction, women's studies, psychology, personal growth, inspiration); John Loudon, executive editor (religious studies, biblical studies, psychology/personal growth, Eastern religions, Catholic, spirituality, inspiration); Gideon Weil, editor (general nonfiction, spiritual fiction, self-help, inspiration, Judaica); Renee Sedliar, associate editor (general nonfiction, spiritual fiction, inspiration). Estab. 1977. Publishes hardcover originals, trade paperback originals and reprints. **Publishes 75 titles/year. Receives about 10,000 submissions/year. 5% of books from first-time authors. Pays royalty. Offers advance.** Publishes book within 18 months after acceptance of ms.

HarperSanFrancisco "strives to be the preeminent publisher of the most important books across the full spectrum of religion and spiritual literature, adding to the wealth of the world's wisdom by respecting all traditions."

Nonfiction: Biography, how-to, reference, self-help. Subjects include psychology (inspiration), religion, spirituality. No unsolicited mss.

Recent Title(s): *Why Religion Matters*, by Huston Smith; *The Dance*, by Oriah Mountain Dreamer; *Touching My Father's Soul*, by Jamling Tenzing Norgay.

HARTMAN PUBLISHING INC., 8529-A Indian School NE, Albuquerque NM 87112. (505)291-1274. Fax: (505)291-1284. E-mail: susan@hartmanonline.com. Website: www.hartmanonline.com. **Acquisitions:** Susan Alvare, managing editor (healthcare education). Publishes trade paperback originals. **Publishes 5-10 titles/year. Receives 50**

queries and 25 mss/year. 50% of books from first-time authors; 100% from unagented writers. Pays 6-12% royalty on wholesale or retail price or makes outright purchase of $200-600. Publishes book 4-12 months after acceptance of ms. Accepts simultaneous submissions. Responds in 1 month to proposals; 3 months to mss. Book catalog and ms guidelines free.

Imprints: Care Spring (Mark Hartman, publisher).

- We publish educational and inspirational books for employees of nursing homes, home health agencies, hospitals, and providers of eldercare.

Nonfiction: Textbook. Subjects include health/medicine. "Writers should request our books wanted list, as well as view samples of our published material." Query with SASE or submit proposal package including outline, 1 sample chapter(s) or submit complete ms. Reviews artwork/photos as part of ms package. Send photocopies or transparencies.

HARVARD BUSINESS SCHOOL PRESS, Harvard Business School Publishing Corp., 60 Harvard Way, Boston MA 02163. (617)783-7400. Fax: (617)783-7489. E-mail: bookpublisher@hbsp.harvard.edu. Website: www.hbsp.harvard.edu. Director: Carol Franco. **Acquisitions:** Jacqueline Murphy, senior editor; Suzanne Rotondo, senior editor; Kirsten Sandberg, senior editor; Melinda Adams Merino, senior editor; Hollis Heimbouch, editorial director; Jeff Kehoe, senior editor. Estab. 1984. Publishes hardcover originals. **Publishes 35-45 titles/year. Pays escalating royalty on retail price. Advances vary widely depending on author and market for the book.** Accepts simultaneous submissions. Responds in 1 month to proposals; 1 month to mss. Book catalog and ms guidelines online.

- The Harvard Business School Press publishes books for an audience of senior and general managers and business scholars. HBS Press is the source of the most influential ideas and conversations that shape business worldwide.

Nonfiction: Scholarly. Subjects include strategy, general management, leadership, marketing, finance, innovation, human resources. Submit proposal package including outline, sample chapter(s).

Recent Title(s): *Primal Leadership*, by Daniel Goleman, Richard Boyatzis, Annie McKee; *The Innovator's Dilemma*, by Clayton M. Christensen; *The Art of Possibility*, by Rosamund Stone Zander and Benjamin Zander.

Tips: "We are looking for provocative ideas that will influence the daily practices and conversations of the business world."

THE HARVARD COMMON PRESS, 535 Albany St., Boston MA 02118-2500. (617)423-5803. Fax: (617)423-0679. Website: www.harvardcommonpress.com. Publisher/President: Bruce P. Shaw. **Acquisitions:** Pamela Hoenig, executive editor. Estab. 1976. Publishes hardcover and trade paperback originals and reprints. **Publishes 16 titles/year. Receives 1,000 submissions/year. 20% of books from first-time authors; 40% from unagented writers. Pays royalty. Offers average $4,000 advance.** Publishes book 1 year after acceptance of ms. Accepts simultaneous submissions. Responds in 2 months to queries. Book catalog for 9×12 SAE with 3 first-class stamps; ms guidelines for #10 SASE.

Imprints: Gambit Books

- "We want strong, practical books that help people gain control over a particular area of their lives." Currently emphasizing cooking, child care/parenting, health. De-emphasizing general instructional books, travel.

Nonfiction: Subjects include child guidance/parenting, cooking/foods/nutrition, health/medicine. "A large percentage of our list is made up of books about cooking, child care, and parenting; in these areas we are looking for authors who are knowledgeable, if not experts, and who can offer a different approach to the subject. We are open to good nonfiction proposals that show evidence of strong organization and writing, and clearly demonstrate a need in the marketplace. First-time authors are welcome." Submit outline, 1-3 sample chapter(s). Reviews artwork/photos as part of ms package.

Recent Title(s): *Mom's Big Book of Baking*, by Lauren Chattman.

Tips: "We are demanding about the quality of proposals; in addition to strong writing skills and thorough knowledge of the subject matter, we require a detailed analysis of the competition."

[N] **HASTINGS HOUSE**, Daytrips Publishers, LINI LLC, 2601 Wells Ave., Suite 161, Fern Park FL 32730-2000. (407)339-3600. Fax: (407)339-5900. E-mail: Hhousebks@aol.com. Website: www.hastingshousebooks.com. Publisher: Peter Leers. **Acquisitions:** Earl Steinbicker, senior travel editor (biography, architecture, edits Daytrips series of guides). Publishes hardcover and trade paperback originals and reprints. **Publishes 20 titles/year. Receives 600 queries and 900 mss/year. 10% of books from first-time authors; 40% from unagented writers. Pays 8-10% royalty. on retail price on trade paperbacks. Offers $1,000-10,000 advance.** Publishes book 6-10 months after acceptance of ms. Responds in 2 months to queries.

- "We are primarily focused on expanding our Daytrips Travel Series nationally and internationally along with related travel books." Currently de-emphasizing all other subjects.

Nonfiction: Subjects include travel. Submit outline. Query.

Recent Title(s): *The Complete Book of Baseball's Negro Leagues*, by John Holway; *Extraordinary Places...Close to London*, by Elizabeth Wallace; *Red Lions & White Horses*, by Andrew Whyte.

HAWK PUBLISHING GROUP, 71075 Yale Ave., #345, Tulsa OK 74136. Website: www.hawkpub.com. Publishes hardcover and trade paperback originals. **Publishes 10-12 titles/year. 25% of books from first-time authors; 50% from unagented writers. Pays royalty.** Publishes book 9-12 months after acceptance of ms. Accepts simultaneous submissions. Ms guidelines online.

- "Please visit our website and read the submission guidelines before sending anything to us. The best way to learn what might interest us is to visit the website, read the information there, look at the books, and perhaps even read a few of them."

Nonfiction: Looking for subjects of broad appeal and interest. Queries by e-mail are welcome.
Fiction: Looking for good books of all kinds. Does not want childrens or young adult books. Queries welcome by e-mail.
Recent Title(s): *Who Really Cares?*, by Janis Ian (poetry and essays); *Goddess by Mistake*, by P.C. Cast (women's fiction); *Awash in the Blood*, by John Wooley (science fiction/fantasy).

THE HAWORTH PRESS, INC., 10 Alice St., Binghamton NY 13904. (607)722-5857. Fax: (607)722-8465. Website: www.haworthpressinc.com. **Acquisitions:** Bill Palmer, vice president, publications. Estab. 1973. Publishes hardcover and trade paperback originals. **Publishes 100 titles/year. Receives 500 queries and 250 mss/year. 60% of books from first-time authors; 98% from unagented writers. Pays 7½-15% royalty on wholesale price.** Publishes book 1 year after acceptance of ms. Responds in 2 months to proposals. Ms guidelines free.
Imprints: The Harrington Park Press, Haworth Pastoral Press, Haworth Food Products Press.
O— The Haworth Press is primarily a scholarly press.
Nonfiction: Reference, scholarly, textbook. Subjects include agriculture/horticulture, business/economics, child guidance/parenting, cooking/foods/nutrition, gay/lesbian, health/medicine, money/finance, psychology, sociology, women's issues/studies. "No 'pop' books." Submit proposal package including outline, 1-3 sample chapter(s), author bio. Reviews artwork/photos as part of ms package. Send photocopies.
Recent Title(s): *The Mental Health Diagnostic*, by Carlton Munson; *Straight Talk About Gays in the Workplace*, by Liz Winfield and Susan Spielman; *Health Care in the Black Community*, by Logan and Freeman.

HAY HOUSE, INC., P.O. Box 5100, Carlsbad CA 92018-5100. (760)431-7695. Fax: (760)431-6948. E-mail: slittrell@hayhouse.com. Website: www.hayhouse.com. **Acquisitions:** Jill Kramer, editorial director. Estab. 1985. Publishes hardcover and trade paperback originals. **Publishes 50 titles/year. Receives 1,200 submissions/year. 5% of books from first-time authors; 25% from unagented writers. Pays standard royalty.** Publishes book 12-15 months after acceptance of ms. Accepts simultaneous submissions. Responds in 2 months to mss. No e-mail submissions.
Imprints: Astro Room, Hay House Lifestyles, Mountain Movers Press.
O— "We publish books, audios and videos that help heal the planet."
Nonfiction: Biography, self-help. Subjects include cooking/foods/nutrition, education, health/medicine, money/finance, nature/environment, New Age, philosophy, psychology, sociology, women's issues/studies. "Hay House is interested in a variety of subjects as long as they have a positive self-help slant to them. No poetry, children's books or negative concepts that are not conducive to helping/healing ourselves or our planet." Query with SASE or submit outline, sample chapter(s).
Recent Title(s): *Gut Feeling*, by Carnie Wilson.
Tips: "Our audience is concerned with our planet, the healing properties of love, and general self-help principles. If I were a writer trying to market a book today, I would research the market thoroughly to make sure there weren't already too many books on the subject I was interested in writing about. Then I would make sure I had a unique slant on my idea. SASE a must! Simultaneous submissions through the mail only—no e-mail submissions."

HAZELDEN PUBLISHING AND EDUCATIONAL SERVICES, 15251 Pleasant Valley Rd., Center City MN 55012. (651)257-4010. Website: www.hazelden.org. Rebecca Post, executive editor. Estab. 1954. Publishes hardcover and trade paperback originals and trade paperback reprints. **Publishes 100 titles/year. Receives 2,500 queries and 2,000 mss/year. 30% of books from first-time authors; 50% from unagented writers. Pays 8% royalty on retail price. Offers variable advance.** Publishes book 1 year after acceptance of ms. Accepts simultaneous submissions. Responds in 6 months to queries. Book catalog and ms guidelines online.
O— Hazelden is a trade, educational and professional publisher specializing is psychology, self-help, and spiritual books that help enhance the quality of people's lives. Products include gift books, curriculum, workbooks, audio and video, computer-based products and wellness products. "We specialize in books on addiction/recovery, spirituality/personal growth and prevention topics related to chemical and mental health."
Nonfiction: Gift book, how-to, multimedia, self-help. Subjects include child guidance/parenting, gay/lesbian, health/medicine, memoirs, psychology, sex, spirituality. Query with SASE.
Recent Title(s): *Alchohol Cradle to Grave*, by Eric Newhouse; *It Will Never Happen to Me*, by Claudia Black.
Tips: Audience includes "consumers and professionals interested in the range of topics related to chemical and emotional health, including spirituality, self-help and addiction recovery."

HEALTH COMMUNICATIONS, INC., 3201 SW 15th St., Deerfield Beach FL 33442. (954)360-0909. Fax: (954)360-0034. Website: www.hci-online.com. **Acquisitions:** Christine Belleris, editorial director; Susan Tobias, editor; Allison Janse, editor; Lisa Drucker, editor. Estab. 1976. Publishes hardcover and trade paperback originals. **Publishes 40 titles/year. 20% of books from first-time authors; 80% from unagented writers. Pays 15% royalty on net price.** Publishes book 9 months after acceptance of ms. Accepts simultaneous submissions. Responds in 1 month to queries; 3 months to proposals; 3 months to mss. Book catalog for 8½×11 SASE; ms guidelines online.
O— "We are the Life Issues Publisher. Health Communications, Inc., strives to help people grow and improve their lives from physical and emotional health to finances and interpersonal relationships." Currently emphasizing books for a teenage audience with a new interest in books for active senior citizens.
Nonfiction: Gift book, self-help. Subjects include child guidance/parenting, health/medicine, psychology, sex, women's issues/studies. Submit proposal package including outline, 2 sample chapter(s), vitae, marketing study. *No phone calls*, SASE. Reviews artwork/photos as part of ms package. Send photocopies.

Recent Title(s): *We Are Not Afraid*, by Homer Hickam; *Bullies*, by Jare Middleton Moz and Mary Lee Zawadski; *Chicken Soup for the Soul of America*, by Canfield & Hansen.
Tips: Audience is composed primarily of women, aged 25-60, interested in personal growth and self-improvement. "Please do your research in your subject area. We publish general self-help books and are expanding to include new subjects such as alternative healing. We need to know why there is a need for your book, how it might differ from other books on the market and what you have to offer to promote your work."

HEALTH PRESS, P.O. Box 37470, Albuquerque NM 87176. (505)888-1394. Fax: (505)888-1521. E-mail: goodbooks@healthpress.com. Website: www.healthpress.com. **Acquisitions:** K. Frazer, editor. Estab. 1988. Publishes hardcover and trade paperback originals. **Publishes 8 titles/year. 90% of books from first-time authors; 90% from unagented writers. Pays standard royalty on wholesale price.** Publishes book 1 year after acceptance of ms. Accepts simultaneous submissions. Responds in 3 months to proposals. Book catalog free.

O━ Health Press publishes books by health care professionals on cutting-edge patient education topics.

Nonfiction: How-to, reference, self-help, textbook. Subjects include education, health/medicine. Submit proposal package including outline, 3 complete sample chapter(s), résumé. Reviews artwork/photos as part of ms package. Send photocopies.
Recent Title(s): *Keeping a Secret: A Story about Juvenile Rheumatoid Arthritis*; *Peanut Butter Jam: A Story about Peanut Allergy.*

HEALTH PROFESSIONS PRESS, P.O. Box 10624, Baltimore MD 21285-0624. (410)337-9585. Fax: (410)337-8539. E-mail: acquis@healthpropress.com. Website: www.healthpropress.com. **Acquisitions:** Mary Magnus, director of publications (aging, long-term care, health administration). Publishes hardcover and trade paperback originals. **Publishes 6-8 titles/year. Receives 70 queries and 12 mss/year. 50% of books from first-time authors; 100% from unagented writers. Pays 8-18% royalty on wholesale price.** Publishes book 10 months after acceptance of ms. Accepts simultaneous submissions. Responds in 1 month to queries; 3 months to proposals; 4 months to mss. Book catalog and ms guidelines free or online.

O━ "We are a specialty publisher. Our primary audiences are professionals, students and educated consumers interested in topics related to aging and eldercare."

Nonfiction: How-to, reference, self-help, textbook. Subjects include health/medicine, psychology. Query with SASE or submit proposal package including outline, 1-2 sample chapter(s), résumé, cover letter.
Recent Title(s): *Bon Appetit! The Joy of Dining in Long-Term Care*, by Zgola & Bordillon; *Creating Successful Dementia Care Settings (4 volumes)*, by Calkins.

HEALTHWISE PUBLICATIONS, Piccadilly Books Ltd., P.O. Box 25203, Colorado Springs CO 80936-5203. (719)550-9887. Website: www.piccadillybooks.com. Publisher: Bruce Fife. **Acquisitions:** Submissions Department. Publishes hardcover and trade paperback originals and trade paperback reprints. **Pays 10% royalty on retail price.** Publishes book within 1 year after acceptance of ms. Accepts simultaneous submissions.

O━ Healthwise specializes in the publication of books on health and fitness written with a holistic or natural health viewpoint.

Nonfiction: Subjects include cooking/foods/nutrition, health/medicine, psychology. Query with sample chapters. Responds only if interested, unless accompanied by a SASE.
Recent Title(s): *The Healing Miracles of Coconut Oil*, by Bruce Fife, N.D.

WILLIAM S. HEIN & CO., INC., 1285 Main St., Buffalo NY 14209-1987. (716)882-2600. Fax: (716)883-8100. E-mail: mail@wshein.com. **Acquisitions:** Sheila Jarrett, publications manager. Estab. 1961. **Publishes 50 titles/year. Receives 80 queries and 40 mss/year. 20% of books from first-time authors; 100% from unagented writers. Pays 10-25% royalty. on net price.** Publishes book 9 months after acceptance of ms. Accepts simultaneous submissions. Responds in 1 months to queries. Book catalog online.

O━ William S. Hein & Co. publishes reference books for law librarians, legal researchers and those interested in legal writing. Currently emphasizing legal research, legal writing and legal education.

Nonfiction: Law. Reference, scholarly. Subjects include education, government/politics, women's issues/studies, world affairs.
Recent Title(s): *Navigating the Internet: Legal Research on the World Wide Web*, by Herbert Ramy and Samantha Moppett; *Amended Criminal Procedure Law and the Criminal Court Rules of the People's Republic of China*, by Wei Luo.

HEINEMANN, Reed Elsevier (USA) Inc., 361 Hanover St., Portsmouth NH 03801. (603)431-7894. Fax: (603)431-7840. Website: www.heinemann.com. **Acquisitions:** Leigh Peake, editorial director (education); Lisa Barnett, senior editor (performing arts); William Varner, acquisitions editor (literacy); Lisa Luedeke, acquisitions editor (Boynton/Cook). Estab. 1977. Publishes hardcover and trade paperback originals. **Publishes 80-100 titles/year. 50% of books from first-time authors; 75% from unagented writers. Pays royalty on wholesale price. Offers variable advance.** Accepts simultaneous submissions. Responds in 6-8 weeks to proposals. Book catalog free; ms guidelines online.
Imprints: Boynton/Cook Publishers.

O━ Heinemann specializes in theater and education titles. "Our goal is to offer a wide selecton of books that satisfy the needs and interests of educators from kindergarten to college." Currently emphasizing literacy education, social studies, mathematics, science, K-12 education through technology.

Nonfiction: How-to, reference. Subjects include child guidance/parenting, education, film/cinema/stage, gay/lesbian, language/literature, women's issues/studies. "Our goal is to provide books that represent leading ideas within our niche markets. We publish very strictly within our categories. We do not publish classroom textbooks." Query with SASE or submit proposal package including outline, 1-2 sample chapter(s), table of contents.
Recent Title(s): *Word Matters*, by Irene Fountas and Gay-sa Pirrell.
Tips: "Keep your queries (and manuscripts!) short, study the market, be realistic and prepared to promote your book."

HELLGATE PRESS, PSI Research, P.O. Box 3727, Central Point OR 97502-0032. (541)245-6502. Fax: (541)245-6505. Website: www.psi-research.com/hellgate.htm. **Acquisitions:** Emmett Ramey, president. Estab. 1996. **Publishes 20-25 titles/year. Pays royalty.** Publishes book 6 months after acceptance of ms. Accepts simultaneous submissions. Responds in 2 months to queries. Book catalog for catalog envelope with SASE; ms guidelines for #10 SASE.

O→ Hellgate Press specializes in military history, other military topics and travel.

Nonfiction: Subjects include history, memoirs, military/war, travel. Query with SASE or submit outline, sample chapter(s). Reviews artwork/photos as part of ms package. Send photocopies.
Recent Title(s): *Code to Keep*, by Ernest Brace.

[N] **HENDRICK-LONG PUBLISHING CO., INC.**, P.O. Box 1247, Friendswood TX 77549. (281)482-6187. Fax: (281)482-6169. E-mail: hendrick-long@worldnet.att.net. Website: hendricklongpublishing.com. **Acquisitions:** Vilma Long. Estab. 1969. Publishes hardcover and trade paperback originals and hardcover reprints. **Publishes 8 titles/year. Receives 500 submissions/year. 90% from unagented writers. Pays royalty. Pays royalty on selling price. Offers advance.** Publishes book 18 months after acceptance of ms. Does not accept simultaneous submissions. 1 month to queries, 2 months if more than one query is sent to queries. Book catalog for 8½ x11 or 9×12 SASE with 4 first-class stamps; ms guidelines for #10 SASE.

O→ Hendrick-Long publishes historical fiction and nonfiction primarily about Texas and the Southwest for children and young adults.

Nonfiction: Biography, children's/juvenile. Subjects include history, regional. Query or submit outline and 2 sample chapters. Reviews artwork/photos as part of ms package. Send photocopies or No original art.
Fiction: Juvenile, young adult. Query or submit outline/synopsis and 2 sample chapters.
Recent Title(s): *Pioneer Children*, by Betsy Warren; *Maggie Houston*, by Jane Cook.

HENSLEY PUBLISHING, 6116 E. 32nd St., Tulsa OK 74135-5494. (918)664-8520. E-mail: editorial@hensleypublishing.com. Website: www.hensleypublishing.com. **Acquisitions:** Acquisitions Department. Publishes hardcover and paperback originals. **Publishes 5-10 titles/year. Receives 800 submissions/year. 50% of books from first-time authors; 50% from unagented writers.** Publishes book 18 months after acceptance of ms. Responds in 2 months to queries. Ms guidelines for #10 SASE.

O→ Hensley Publishing publishes Bible studies and curriculum that offer the reader a wide range of topics. Currently emphasizing shorter studies.

Nonfiction: Subjects include child guidance/parenting, money/finance, religion, women's issues/studies, marriage/family. "We do not want to see anything non-Christian." No New Age, poetry, plays, sermon collections. Query with synopsis and sample chapters.
Recent Title(s): *The Quest*, by Dorothy Hellstern; *God's Solutions to Life's Problems*, by Dr. Wayne Mack.
Tips: "Submit something that crosses denominational lines directed toward the large Christian market, not small specialized groups. We serve an interdenominational market—all Christian persuasions. Our goal is to get readers back into studying their Bible instead of studying about the Bible."

HERITAGE BOOKS, INC., 1540-E Pointer Ridge Place, Bowie MD 20716-1859. (301)390-7708. Fax: (301)390-7193. **Acquisitions:** Leslie Towle, editorial supervisor. Estab. 1978. Publishes hardcover and paperback originals and reprints. **Publishes 200 titles/year. Receives 300 submissions/year. 25% of books from first-time authors; 100% from unagented writers. Pays 10% royalty on list price.** Accepts simultaneous submissions. Responds in 1 month. *Writer's Market* recommends allowing 2 months for reply to queries. Book catalog for #10 SASE.

O→ "Our goal is to celebrate life by exploring all aspects of American life: settlement, development, wars and other significant events, including family histories, memoirs, etc." Currently emphasizing early American life, early wars and conflicts. De-emphasizing ancestries of contemporary people.

Nonfiction: Biography, how-to (genealogical, historical), reference, scholarly. Subjects include Americana, ethnic (origins and research guides), history, memoirs, military/war, regional (history). "Ancestries of contemporary people are not of interest. The titles should be either of general interest or restricted to Eastern U.S. and Midwest, United Kingdom, Germany." Query with SASE or submit outline. Reviews artwork/photos as part of ms package.
Tips: "The quality of the book is of prime importance; next is its relevance to our fields of interest."

HERODIAS, 185 Bridge Plaza N., Suite 308-A, Fort Lee NJ 07024. (201)944-7600. Fax: (201)944-6363. E-mail: greatblue@acninc.net. Website: www.herodias.com. **Acquisitions:** Paul Williams, editor (fiction, biography, arts). Publishes hardcover originals, trade paperback originals and reprints. **Publishes 10 titles/year. Receives 500 queries and 50 mss/year. 25% of books from first-time authors; 75% from unagented writers. Pays 7½-17½% royalty. Offers $500-2,000 advance.** Publishes book 1 year after acceptance of ms. Accepts simultaneous submissions. Responds in 2 weeks to queries; 1 month to proposals; 3 months to mss. Book catalog and writer's guidelines free or on website.
Imprints: Herodias Books for Young Readers (young adult); Little Blue Books (kids)

Nonfiction: Favors biographies/memoirs, philosophy and "ideas" books. Biography, children's/juvenile, coffee table book, cookbook, gift book, self-help. Subjects include art/architecture, cooking/foods/nutrition, language/literature, memoirs, philosophy, photography, translation. Query with SASE or submit proposal package including outline. Reviews artwork/photos as part of ms package. Send photocopies.
Fiction: Erotica, fantasy, historical, juvenile, literary, mainstream/contemporary, poetry, poetry in translation, young adult. Query with SASE or submit proposal package including synopsis.
Poetry: Poets "must be widely published in journals/good promoter." Query.
Recent Title(s): *My Lucky Star*, by Zdenka Fantlová (memoir); *The Cuttlefish*, by Maryline Desbiolles (novel); *The Bold Saboteurs*, by Chandler Brassard (novel).

HIDDENSPRING, 997 Macarthur Blvd., Mahwah NJ 07430. (201)825-7300. Fax: (201)825-8345. Website: www.hiddenspringbooks.com. **Acquisitions:** Jan-Erik Guerth, editorial director (nonfiction/spirituality). Publishes hardcover and trade paperback originals and reprints. **Publishes 10-12 titles/year. 5% of books from first-time authors; 10% from unagented writers. Royalty varies on wholesale or retail price. Offers variable advance.** Accepts simultaneous submissions. Responds in 1 month to queries.

O→ "Books should always have a spiritual angle—nonfiction with a spiritual twist."

Nonfiction: Biography, gift book, how-to, self-help. Subjects include Americana, anthropology/archeology, art/architecture, business/economics, child guidance/parenting, cooking/foods/nutrition, creative nonfiction, ethnic, gardening, gay/lesbian, government/politics, health/medicine, history, money/finance, multicultural, music/dance, nature/environment, philosophy, psychology, regional, religion, science, sex, sociology, travel, women's issues/studies. Submit proposal package including outline, 1 sample chapter(s), SASE.
Recent Title(s): *The Spiritual Traveler: New York City Sacred Water*, by Nathaniel Altman; *The Little Tern*, by Brooke Newman; *Your Soul at Work*, by Nicholas Weiler.

HIGH PLAINS PRESS, P.O. Box 123, 539 Cassa Rd., Glendo WY 82213. (307)735-4370. Fax: (307)735-4590. E-mail: editor@highplainspress.com. Website: www.highplainspress.com. **Acquisitions:** Nancy Curtis, publisher. Estab. 1986. Publishes hardcover and trade paperback originals. **Publishes 4 titles/year. Receives 300 queries and 200 mss/year. 80% of books from first-time authors; 95% from unagented writers. Pays 10% royalty on wholesale price. Offers $100-600 advance.** Publishes book 2 years after acceptance of ms. Accepts simultaneous submissions. Responds in 1 month to queries; 1 month to proposals; 3 months to mss. Book catalog and ms guidelines for 9×12 SASE.

O→ "What we sell best is history of the Old West, particularly things relating to Wyoming. We also publish one book of poetry a year in our Poetry of the American West series."

Nonfiction: "We focus on books of the American West, mainly history." Biography. Subjects include Americana, art/architecture, history, nature/environment, regional. Submit outline. Reviews artwork/photos as part of ms package. Send photocopies.
Poetry: "We only seek poetry closely tied to the Rockies. Do not submit single poems." Query or submit complete ms.
Recent Title(s): *Tom Horn: Blood on the Moon*, by Chip Carlson; *Sheepwagon: Home on the Range*, by Nancy Weidel.

HIGH TIDE PRESS, 3650 W. 183rd St., Homewood IL 60430-2603. (708)206-2054. Fax: (708)206-2044. E-mail: managing.editor@hightidepress.com. Website: www.hightidepress.com. **Acquisitions:** Diane J. Bell, managing editor. Publishes hardcover and trade paperback originals. **Publishes 8 titles/year. Receives 200 queries and 100 mss/year. 50% of books from first-time authors; 80% from unagented writers. Offers $500-1,000 advance.** Publishes book 1 year after acceptance of ms. Accepts simultaneous submissions. Responds in 1-3 months to queries; 1-3 months to proposals; 1-3 months to mss. Book catalog free or on website.
Nonfiction: Subjects include business/economics, psychology, mental illness and developmental disabilities. Reviews artwork/photos as part of ms package.
Recent Title(s): *Managed Care & Developmental Disabilities*, by Dale Mitchell, Ph.D.; *Making Money While Making a Difference*, by Richard Steckel, Ph.D.
Tips: "Our audience consists of professionals in these fields: mental health/psychology, disabilities, business, marketing, nonprofit leadership and management. You should send us a one-page query with SASE, giving a brief overview of the book, its market and your background. If we are interested, we will request a book proposal. The book proposal outlines the nature of your work, who your market is, and information about your background. Please do not send a complete manuscript unless we request one."

N HILL AND WANG, Farrar Straus & Giroux, Inc., 19 Union Square W., New York NY 10003. (212)741-6900. Fax: (212)633-9385. **Acquisitions:** Elisabeth Sifton, publisher; Lauren Osborne, senior editor; Catherine Newman, assistant editor. Estab. 1956. Publishes hardcover and trade paperbacks. **Publishes 12 titles/year. Receives 1,500 queries/year. 50% of books from first-time authors; 50% from unagented writers. Pays 10% royalty on retail price to 5,000 copies sold, 12½% to 10,000 copies, 15% thereafter on hardcover; 7½% on retail price for paperback.** Publishes book 1 year after acceptance of ms. Accepts simultaneous submissions. Book catalog free.

O→ Hill and Wang publishes serious nonfiction books, primarily in history and the social sciences.

Nonfiction: Subjects include government/politics, history (American), women's issues/studies. Submit outline, sample chapter(s). SASE and a letter explaining rationale for book.
Fiction: Not considering new fiction, drama or poetry.

Recent Title(s): *Pox Americana: The Great Smallpox Epidemic of 1775-82*, by Elizabeth A. Fenn; *1831: Year of Eclipse*, by Louis P. Masur.

LAWRENCE HILL BOOKS, Chicago Review Press, 814 N. Franklin St., Chicago IL 60610. (312)337-0747. Fax: (312)640-0542. **Acquisitions:** Yuval Taylor, editor (black interest). Publishes hardcover originals and trade paperback originals and reprints. **Publishes 3-10 titles/year. Receives 20 queries and 10 mss/year. 40% of books from first-time authors; 50% from unagented writers. Pays 7½-12½% royalty on retail price. Offers $1,500-7,500 advance.** Publishes book 1 year after acceptance of ms. Accepts simultaneous submissions. Responds in 1 month to queries; 1 month to proposals; 1 month to mss. Book catalog free.
Nonfiction: Biography, reference, general nonfiction. Subjects include ethnic, government/politics, history, multicultural. All books should appeal directly to an African American readership. Submit proposal package including outline, 2 sample chapter(s).
Recent Title(s): *Afraid of the Dark*, by Jim Myers.

HILL STREET PRESS, 191 E. Broad St., Suite 209, Athens GA 30601-2848. (706)613-7200. Fax: (706)613-7204. E-mail: editorial@hillstreetpress.com. **Acquisitions:** Judy Long, senior editor. Publishes hardcover originals, trade paperback originals and reprints. **Publishes 20 titles/year. Receives 300 queries/year. 5% of books from first-time authors; 2% from unagented writers. Pays 9-12½% royalty on wholesale price.** Publishes book 1 year after acceptance of ms. Accepts simultaneous submissions. Responds in 1 month to queries; 3 months to proposals; 6 months to mss. Book catalog and ms guidelines online.
O→ "HSP is a Southern regional press. While we are not a scholarly or academic press, our nonfiction titles must meet the standards of research for an exacting general audience."
Nonfiction: Biography, coffee table book, cookbook, gift book, humor, illustrated book. Subjects include Americana, cooking/foods/nutrition, creative nonfiction, gardening, gay/lesbian, history, memoirs, nature/environment, recreation, regional (Southern), sports, travel. Submit proposal package including outline, 3 sample chapter(s), résumé.
Fiction: Must have a strong connection with the American South. Gay/lesbian, historical, humor, literary, mainstream/contemporary, military/war, religious, sports. Submit proposal package including 3 sample chapter(s), résumé, synopsis, press clips.
Recent Title(s): *Strange Birds in the Tree of Heaven*, by Karen Salyer McElmurray (literary fiction); *The Worst Day of My Life, So Far*, by M.A. Harper (literary fiction); *How I Learned to Snap* (memoir).
Tips: "Audience is discerning with an interest in the fiction, history, current issues and food of the American South"

HIPPOCRENE BOOKS INC., 171 Madison Ave., New York NY 10016. (212)685-4371. Fax: (212)779-9338. E-mail: hippocrene.books@verizon.net. Website: www.hippocrenebooks.com. President/Publisher: George Blagowidow. **Acquisitions:** Anne E. McBride, associate editor (cooking, history, travel, nonfiction reference); Caroline Gates, associate editor (foreign language, dictionaries, language guides); Anne Kemper, associate editor (illustrated histories). Estab. 1971. Publishes hardcover and trade paperback originals. **Publishes 100 titles/year. Receives 250 submissions/year. 10% of books from first-time authors; 95% from unagented writers. Pays 6-10% royalty on retail price. Offers $2,000 advance.** Publishes book 16 months after acceptance of ms. Accepts simultaneous submissions. Responds in 2 months to queries. Book catalog for 9 x12 SAE with 5 first-class stamps; ms guidelines for #10 SASE.
O→ "We focus on ethnic-interest and language-related titles, particularly on lesser published and often overlooked ones." Currently emphasizing concise foreign language dictionaries. De-emphasizing military history.
Nonfiction: Biography, cookbook, reference. Subjects include cooking/foods/nutrition, ethnic, history, language/literature, multicultural, travel. Submit proposal package including outline, 2 sample chapter(s), table of contents.
Recent Title(s): *Chinese Frequency Dictionary*; *Cuisines of Portuguese Encounters*.
Tips: "Our recent successes in publishing general books considered midlist by larger publishers is making us more of a general trade publisher. We continue to do well with reference books like dictionaries, atlases and language studies. We ask for proposal, sample chapter, and table of contents. We then ask for material if we are interested."

HOBAR PUBLICATIONS, Finney Company, 3943 Meadowbrook Rd., Minneapolis MN 55426. (952)938-9330. Fax: (952)938-7353. E-mail: feedback@finney-hobar.com. Website: www.finney-hobar.com. **Acquisitions:** Alan E. Krysan, president. Publishes trade paperback originals. **Publishes 4-6 titles/year. Receives 30 queries and 10 mss/year. 35% of books from first-time authors; 100% from unagented writers. Pays 10% royalty on wholesale price. Offers advance.** Publishes book 6-12 months after acceptance of ms. Accepts simultaneous submissions. Responds in 3 weeks to queries.
O→ Hobar publishes agricultural and industrial technology educational materials.
Nonfiction: How-to, illustrated book, reference, technical, textbook, handbooks, field guides. Subjects include agriculture/horticulture, animals, business/economics, education, gardening, nature/environment, science, building trades. Query with SASE. Reviews artwork/photos as part of ms package.
Recent Title(s): *Reading a Ruler*, by Susan Resch.

HOBBY HOUSE PRESS, 1 Corporate Dr., Grantsville MD 21536. (301)895-3792. Fax: (301)895-5029. Website: www.hobbyhouse.com. Publishes hardcover originals. **Publishes 20 titles/year. Receives 50 queries and 25 mss/year. 85% of books from first-time authors; 100% from unagented writers. Pays 10% royalty on retail price.** Publishes book 6 months after acceptance of ms. Accepts simultaneous submissions. Responds in 2 weeks to queries; 1 month to proposals. Book catalog and ms guidelines free.

Nonfiction: Gift book, how-to, reference, price guides. Subjects include gardening, hobbies (collecting/antiques). Query with SASE or submit outline, 1 sample chapter(s), photos. Reviews artwork/photos as part of ms package. Send prints.

Recent Title(s): *In Search of Teddy*; *Ultimate Fashion Doll Makeovers*; *Collectors Guide to Antique Chocolate Molds*.

HOLIDAY HOUSE INC., 425 Madison Ave., New York NY 10017. (212)688-0085. Fax: (212)421-6134. Editor-in-Chief: Regina Griffin. **Acquisitions:** Suzanne Reinoehl, associate editor. Estab. 1935. Publishes hardcover originals. **Publishes 60 titles/year. Receives 3,000 submissions/year. 2-5% of books from first-time authors; 50% from unagented writers. Pays royalty on list price, range varies. Offers advance.** Publishes book 1-2 years after acceptance of ms. Does not accept simultaneous submissions. Ms guidelines for #10 SASE.

O→ Holiday House publishes children's and young adult books for the school and library markets. "We have a commitment to publishing first-time authors and illustrators. We specialize in quality hardcovers from picture books to young adult, both fiction and nonfiction, primarily for the school and library market." Currently emphasizing literary middle-grade novels.

Nonfiction: Biography, humor. Subjects include Americana, history, science, Judaica. Query with SASE. Reviews artwork/photos as part of ms package. Send photocopies—no originals—to Claire Counihan, art director.

Fiction: Adventure, historical. Query with SASE.

Recent Title(s): *John and Abigail Adams*, by Judith St. George; *A Child's Calendar*, by John Updike, illustrated by Trina Schart Hyman.

Tips: "We are not geared toward the mass market, but toward school and library markets. We need picture book texts with strong stories and writing. We do not publish board books or novelties."

HOLMES & MEIER PUBLISHERS, INC., East Building, 160 Broadway, New York NY 10038. (212)374-0100. Fax: (212)374-1313. E-mail: info@holmesandmeier.com. Website: www.holmesandmeier.com. Publisher: Miriam H. Holmes. **Acquisitions:** Maggie Kennedy, managing editor. Estab. 1969. Publishes hardcover and paperback originals. **Publishes 20 titles/year. Pays royalty.** Publishes book an average of 18 months after acceptance of ms. Does not accept simultaneous submissions. Responds in 6 months to queries. Book catalog free.

Imprints: Africana Publishing Company

O→ "We are noted as an academic publishing house and are pleased with our reputation for excellence in the field. However, we are also expanding our list to include books of more general interest."

Nonfiction: Biography, reference. Subjects include art/architecture, business/economics, ethnic, government/politics, history, regional, translation, women's issues/studies. Query first with outline, sample chapters, cv and idea of intended market/audience.

HENRY HOLT & COMPANY BOOKS FOR YOUNG READERS, Henry Holt & Co., Inc., 115 W. 18th St., New York NY 10011. (212)886-9200. **Acquisitions:** Laura Godwin, associate publisher and editorial director; Christy Ottaviano, executive editor; Nina Ignatowicz, senior editor; Reka Simonsen, editor; Adriane Fry, associate editor; Kate Farrell, associate editor. Estab. 1866 (Holt). Publishes hardcover originals of picture books, chapter books, middle grade and young adult novels. **Publishes 70-80 titles/year. 10% of books from first-time authors; 50% from unagented writers. Pays royalty on retail price. Offers $3,000 and up advance.** Publishes book 18 months after acceptance of ms. Does not accept simultaneous submissions. Responds in 3-4 months to queries. Book catalog for #10 SASE; ms guidelines for #10 SASE.

O→ "Henry Holt Books for Young Readers publishes highly original and cutting-edge fiction and nonfiction for all ages, from the very young to the young adult."

Nonfiction: Children's/juvenile, illustrated book. Submit complete ms.

Fiction: Adventure, fantasy, historical, humor, multicultural, mystery, picture books, sports, suspense, young adult. Juvenile: adventure, animal, contemporary, fantasy, history, humor, multicultural, sports, suspense/mystery. Picture books: animal, concept, history, humor, mulitcultural, sports. Young adult: contemporary, fantasy, history, multicultural, nature/environment, problem novels, sports. Submit complete ms.

Recent Title(s): *Visiting Langston*, by Willie Perdomo, illustrated by Bryan Collier; *The Gospel According to Larry*, by Janet Tashjian.

[N] **HENRY HOLT & COMPANY, INC.**, 115 W. 18th St., New York NY 10011. (212)886-9200. President and Publisher: John Sterling. **Acquisitions:** Jennifer Barth, editor-in-chief (adult literary fiction, narrative nonfiction); Sara Bershtel, associate publisher of Metropolitan Books (literary fiction, politics, history); Elizabeth Stein, senior editor, adult trade; David Sobel, editorial director, Times Books (science, culture, history, health); Deb Brody, senior editor, adult trade (lifestyle, health, self help, parenting). Does not accept simultaneous submissions. Query before submitting to queries.

Imprints: John Macrae Books, Metropolitan Books, Henry Holt & Company Books for Young Readers (Books by Michael Hague, Books by Bill Martin Jr. and John Archambault, Owlet Paperbacks, Redfeather Books, W5 Reference).

O→ Holt is a general interest publisher of quality fiction and nonfiction. Currently emphasizing narrative nonfiction. De-emphasizing cooking, gardening.

Recent Title(s): *M: The Man Who Became Caravaggio*; *Wild Minds*, Marc Hanser.

HOLY CROSS ORTHODOX PRESS, Hellenic College, 50 Goddard Ave., Brookline MA 02445. (617)731-3500. Fax: (617)850-1460. **Acquisitions:** Anton C. Vrame, Ph.D., managing editor. Estab. 1974. Publishes trade paperback originals. **Publishes 8 titles/year; imprint publishes 2 titles/year. Receives 10-15 queries and 10-15 mss/year. 85%**

of books from first-time authors; 100% from unagented writers. Pays 8-12% royalty on retail price. Publishes book 18 months after acceptance of ms. Accepts simultaneous submissions. Responds in 6 months to mss. Book catalog free.

Imprints: Holy Cross Orthodox Press, Hellenic College Press.

O→ Holy Cross publishes titles that are rooted in the tradition of the Eastern Orthodox Church.

Nonfiction: Academic. Subjects include ethnic, religion (Greek Orthodox). "Holy Cross Orthodox Press publishes scholarly and popular literature in the areas of Orthodox Christian theology and Greek letters. Submissions are often far too technical usually with a very limited audiences." Submit outline or submit complete ms. Reviews artwork/photos as part of ms package. Send photocopies.

Recent Title(s): *Christianity: Lineaments of a Sacred Tradition*, by Philip Sherrard.

N A **HONOR BOOKS**, P.O. Box 55388, Tulsa OK 74155. (918)523-5125. Fax: (918)523-5864. E-mail: info@honorbooks.com. Website: www.honorbooks.com. Publishes hardcover and trade paperback originals. **Publishes 60 titles/year. Pays royalty on wholesale price, makes outright purchase or assigns work for hire. Offers negotiable advance.** Publishes book 2 years after acceptance of ms.

O→ "We are a Christian publishing house with a mission to inspire and encourage people to draw near to God and to enjoy His love and grace. We are no longer accepting unsolicited mss from writers." Currently emphasizing humor, personal and spiritual growth, children's books, devotions, personal stories.

Nonfiction: Subjects include religion, Motivation, devotionals. Subjects are geared toward the "felt needs" of people. No autobiographies or teaching books.

Recent Title(s): *My Personal Promise Bibles*; *Quiet Moments with God*.

Tips: "Our books are for busy, achievement-oriented people who are looking for a balance between reaching their goals and knowing that God loves them unconditionally. Our books encourage spiritual growth, joyful living and intimacy with God. Write about what you are for and not what you are against. We look for scripts that are biblically based and which inspire readers."

HOUGHTON MIFFLIN BOOKS FOR CHILDREN, Houghton Mifflin Company, 222 Berkeley St., Boston MA 02116. (617)351-5959. Fax: (617)351-1111. Website: www.houghtonmifflinbooks.com. **Acquisitions:** Hannah Rodgers, submissions coordinator. Publishes hardcover and trade paperback originals and reprints. **Publishes 100 titles/year. Receives 5,000 queries and 14,000 mss/year. 10% of books from first-time authors; 70% from unagented writers. Pays 5-10% royalty on retail price. Offers variable advance.** Publishes book 18-24 months after acceptance of ms. Accepts simultaneous submissions. Responds in 4 months to queries. Book catalog for 9×12 SASE with 3 first-class stamps; ms guidelines for #10 SASE.

Imprints: Sandpiper Paperback Books (Eden Edwards, editor).

O→ "Houghton Mifflin gives shape to ideas that educate, inform, and above all, delight."

Nonfiction: Biography, children's/juvenile, humor, illustrated book. Subjects include animals, anthropology/archeology, art/architecture, ethnic, history, language/literature, music/dance, nature/environment, science, sports. Interested in innovative books and subjects about which the author is passionate. Query with SASE or submit sample chapter(s), synopsis. **Note:** Mss not returned without appropriate-sized SASE. Reviews artwork/photos as part of ms package. Send photocopies.

Fiction: Adventure, ethnic, historical, humor, juvenile (early readers), literary, mystery, picture books, suspense, young adult, board books. Submit complete ms with appropriate-sized SASE.

Recent Title(s): *Henry Builds a Cabin*, by D.B. Johnson; *Angelo*, by David Macaulay; *Phineas Gate: A Gruesome but True Story about Brain Science*, by John Fleischman (poetry).

Tips: "Faxed or e-mailed manuscripts and proposals are not considered."

A **HOUGHTON MIFFLIN COMPANY**, 222 Berkeley St., Boston MA 02116. (617)351-5000. Fax: (617)351-1202. Website: www.hmco.com. Executive Vice President: Wendy J. Strothman. Editor-in-Chief, Adult Books: Janet Silver. **Acquisitions:** Submissions Editor. Estab. 1832. Publishes hardcover and trade paperback originals and reprints. **Publishes 90-100 titles/year. 10% of books from first-time authors. Hardcover: pays 10-15% royalty on retail price, sliding scale or flat rate based on sales; paperback: 7½% flat fee, but negotiable. Offers variable advance.** Publishes book 1-2 years after acceptance of ms. Accepts simultaneous submissions. Responds in 3 months to proposals. Book catalog and ms guidelines free.

Imprints: Clarion Books, Walter Lorraine Books, Houghton Mifflin Books for Children, Mariner Paperbacks, Sandpiper Paperbacks, Frances Tenenbaum Books.

O→ "Houghton Mifflin gives shape to ideas that educate, inform and delight. In a new era of publishing, our legacy of quality thrives as we combine imagination with technology, bringing you new ways to know."

Nonfiction: Biography, children's/juvenile, reference, self-help. Subjects include cooking/foods/nutrition, gardening, history, nature/environment, travel, guidebooks. "We are not a mass market publisher. Our main focus is serious nonfiction. We do practical self-help but not pop psychology self-help." *Agented submissions only.*

Fiction: Literary. "We are not a mass market publisher. Study the current list." *Agented submissions only.*

Poetry: "At this point we have an established roster of poets we use. It is hard for first-time poets to get published by Houghton Mifflin."

Recent Title(s): *The Dying Animal*, by Philip Roth; *Hotel Honolulu*, by Paul Theroux; *Fast Food Nation*, by Eric Schlosser.

HOUSE OF COLLECTIBLES, Crown Publishing Group, Random House, Inc., 299 Park Ave., New York NY 10171. Website: www.randomhouse.com. **Acquisitions:** Dorothy Harris, director. Publishes trade and mass market paperback originals. **Publishes 25-28 titles/year. Receives 200 queries/year. 7% of books from first-time authors; 75% from unagented writers. Royalty on retail price varies. Offers varied advance.** Publishes book 1 year after acceptance of ms. Does not accept simultaneous submissions. Book catalog free.
Imprints: Official Price Guide series.

O→ "One of the premier publishing companies devoted to books on a wide range of antiques and collectibles, House of Collectibles publishes books for the seasoned expert and the beginning collector alike."

Nonfiction: How-to (related to collecting antiques and coins), reference. Subjects include art/architecture (fine art), sports, comic books, Civil War. **All unsolicited mss returned unopened.**
Recent Title(s): *The Official Price Guide to Vintage Fashion and Fabrics*, by Pamela Smith.
Tips: "We have been publishing price guides and other books on antiques and collectibles for over 35 years and plan to meet the needs of collectors, dealers and appraisers well into the 21st century."

HOWELL PRESS, INC., 1713-2D Allied Lane, Charlottesville VA 22903. (434)977-4006. Fax: (434)971-7204. E-mail: rhowell@howellpress.com. Website: www.howellpress.com. **Acquisitions:** Ross A. Howell, president; Meghan Mitchell, editor. Estab. 1985. **Publishes 10-13 titles/year. Receives 500 submissions/year. 10% of books from first-time authors; 80% from unagented writers. Pays 5-10% royalty. Offers advance.** Publishes book 18 months after acceptance of ms. Book catalog for 9×12 SAE with 4 first-class stamps; ms guidelines for #10 SASE.

O→ "While our aviation, history and transportation titles are produced for the enthusiast market, writing must be accessible to the general adult reader." Currently emphasizing regional (Mid-Atlantic and Southeast), travel, ghost stories, gardens, quilts and quilt history. De-emphasizing general garden guides.

Nonfiction: Illustrated book. Subjects include history, regional, aviation, transportation, gourmet, quilts. "Generally open to most ideas, as long as writing is accessible to average adult reader. Our line is targeted, so it would be advisable to look over our catalog before querying to better understand what Howell Press does." Query with SASE or submit outline, sample chapter(s). Does not return mss without SASE. Reviews artwork/photos as part of ms package.
Recent Title(s): *The Virginia Landscape*, by James Kelly and William Rasmussen.
Tips: "Focus of our program has been illustrated books, but we will also consider nonfiction manuscripts that would not be illustrated."

HOWELLS HOUSE, P.O. Box 9546, Washington DC 20016-9546. (202)333-2182. **Acquisitions:** W.D. Howells, publisher. Estab. 1988. Publishes hardcover and trade paperback originals and reprints. **Publishes 4 titles/year; imprint publishes 2-3 titles/year. Receives 2,000 queries and 300 mss/year. 50% of books from first-time authors; 60% from unagented writers. Pays 15% net royalty or makes outright purchase. May offer advance.** Publishes book 8 months after acceptance of ms. Does not accept simultaneous submissions. Responds in 2 months to proposals.
Imprints: The Compass Press, Whalesback Books.

O→ "Our interests are institutions and institutional change."

Nonfiction: Biography, illustrated book, textbook. Subjects include Americana, anthropology/archeology, art/architecture, business/economics, education, government/politics, history, photography, science, sociology, translation, women's issues/studies. Query.
Fiction: Historical, literary, mainstream/contemporary. Query.

HUDSON HILLS PRESS, INC., 1133 Broadway, Suite 1301, New York NY 10010-8001. (212)929-4994. Fax: (212)929-9051. **Acquisitions:** Paul Anbinder, president/publisher. Estab. 1978. Publishes hardcover and paperback originals. **Publishes 15 titles/year. Receives 50-100 submissions/year. 15% of books from first-time authors; 90% from unagented writers. Pays 4-6% royalty on retail price. Offers $3,500 average advance.** Publishes book 1 year after acceptance of ms. Accepts simultaneous submissions. Responds in 2 months to queries. Book catalog for 6×9 SAE with 2 first-class stamps.

O→ Hudson Hills Press publishes books about art and photography, including monographs.

Nonfiction: Subjects include art/architecture, photography. Query first, then submit outline and sample chapters. Reviews artwork/photos as part of ms package.
Recent Title(s): *Hollis Sigler's Breast Cancer Journal*, by Hollis Sigler and Susan M. Love, M.D.

HUMAN KINETICS PUBLISHERS, INC., P.O. Box 5076, Champaign IL 61825-5076. (217)351-5076. Fax: (217)351-2674. E-mail: hk@hkusa.com. Website: www.humankinetics.com. Publisher: Rainer Martens. **Acquisitions:** Ted Miller, vice president and director (trade); Martin Barnard, trade senior acquisitions editor (fitness, running, golf, tennis); Ed McNeely, trade acquisitions editor (strength training, cycling, martial arts, minor spa); Scott Wikgren, HPERD director (health, physical education, recreation, dance); Mike Bahrke, STM acquisitions editor (scientific, technical, medical); Loarn Robertson, STM acquisitions editor (biomechanics, anatomy, athletic training, cardiac rehab, test/measurement); Judy Wright, HPERD acquisitions editor (dance, motor, learning/behavior/performance/development, gymnastics, adapted physical education, older adults); Amy Clocksin, STM director. Estab. 1974. Publishes hardcover and paperback text and reference books, trade paperback originals, software and audiovisual. **Publishes 120 titles/year. Receives 300 submissions/year. 30% of books from first-time authors; 90% from unagented writers. Pays 10-15% royalty on net income.** Publishes book an average of 18 months after acceptance of ms. Accepts simultaneous submissions. Responds in 2 months to queries. Book catalog free.
Imprints: HK

O→ Human Kinetics publishes books which provide expert knowledge in sport and fitness training and techniques, physical education, sports sciences and sports medicine for coaches, athletes and fitness enthusiasts and professionals in the physical action field.

Nonfiction: How-to, multimedia, reference, self-help, technical, textbook. Subjects include education, health/medicine, psychology, recreation, sports. Submit outline, sample chapter(s). Reviews artwork/photos as part of ms package.
Recent Title(s): *Kinetic Anatomy*, by Robert Behr; *The Softball Pitching Edge*, by Cheri Kempf.

HUNTER HOUSE, P.O. Box 2914, Alameda CA 94501. (510)865-5282. Fax: (510)865-4295. E-mail: acquisitions@hunterhouse.com. Website: www.hunterhouse.com. **Acquisitions:** Jeanne Brondino, acquisitions editor; Kiran S. Rana, publisher. Estab. 1978. Publishes hardcover and trade paperback originals and reprints. **Publishes 24 titles/year. Receives 200-300 queries and 100 mss/year. 50% of books from first-time authors; 80% from unagented writers. Pays 12% royalty on net receipts, defined as selling price. Offers $500-3,000 advance.** Publishes book 1-2 years after acceptance of ms. Accepts simultaneous submissions. Responds in 2 months to queries; 3 months to proposals; 6 months to mss. Book catalog and ms guidelines for 8½×11 SAE with 3 first-class stamps.

O→ Hunter House publishes health books (especially women's health), self-help health, sexuality and couple relationships, violence prevention and intervention. De-emphasizing reference, self-help psychology.

Nonfiction: Subjects include alternative lifestyles, health/medicine, self-help, women's health, fitness, relationships, sexuality, personal growth, and violence prevention. "Health books (especially women's health) should focus on emerging health issues or current issues that are inadequately covered and be written for the general population. Family books: Our current focus is sexuality and couple relationships, and alternative lifestyles to high stress. Community topics include violence prevention/violence intervention. We also publish specialized curricula for counselors and educators in the areas of violence prevention and trauma in children." Query with proposal package, including synopsis, table of contents and chapter outline, sample chapter, target audience information, competition and what distinguishes the book. Reviews artwork/photos as part of ms package. Send photocopies, proposals generally not returned, requested mss returned with SASE. Reviews artwork/photos as part of ms package.
Recent Title(s): *The Complete Guide to Joseph H. Pilates' Techniques of Physical Conditioning*, by Allan Menezes; *Pocket Book of Foreplay*, Richard Craze; *Living Beyond Multiple Sclerosis—A Women's Guide*, by Judith Lynn Nichols.
Tips: Audience is concerned people who are looking to educate themselves and their community about real-life issues that affect them. "Please send as much information as possible about *who* your audience is, *how* your book addresses their needs, and *how* you reach that audience in your ongoing work."

HUNTER PUBLISHING, INC., 130 Campus Dr., Edison NJ 08818. Fax: (561)546-8040. E-mail: hunterp@bellsouth.net. Website: www.hunterpublishing.com. President: Michael Hunter. **Acquisitions:** Kim Andre, editor; Lissa Dailey. Estab. 1985. **Publishes 100 titles/year. Receives 300 submissions/year. 10% of books from first-time authors; 75% from unagented writers. Pays royalty. Offers negotiable advance.** Publishes book 5 months after acceptance of ms. Accepts simultaneous submissions. Responds in 3 weeks to queries; 1 month to mss. Book catalog for #10 SAE with 4 first-class stamps.
Imprints: Adventure Guides, Romantic Weekends Guides, Alive Guides.

O→ Hunter Publishing publishes practical guides for travelers going to the Caribbean, U.S., Europe, South America, and the far reaches of the globe.

Nonfiction: Reference. Subjects include regional, travel (travel guides). "We need travel guides to areas covered by few competitors: Caribbean Islands, South and Central America, regional U.S. from an active 'adventure' perspective." No personal travel stories or books not directed to travelers. Query or submit outline/synopsis and sample chapters. Reviews artwork/photos as part of ms package.
Recent Title(s): *Adventure Guide to Canada's Atlantic Provinces*, by Barbara Radcliffe-Rogers.
Tips: "Guides should be destination-specific, rather than theme-based alone. Thus, 'travel with kids' is too broad; 'Florida with Kids' is OK. Make sure the guide doesn't duplicate what other guide publishers do. We need active adventure-oriented guides and more specialized guides for travelers in search of the unusual."

IBEX PUBLISHERS, P.O. Box 30087, Bethesda MD 20824. (301)718-8188. Fax: (301)907-8707. E-mail: info@ibexpub.com. Website: www.ibexpub.com. Publishes hardcover and trade paperback originals and reprints. **Publishes 6-10 titles/year. Payment varies.** Accepts simultaneous submissions. Book catalog free.
Imprints: Iranbooks Press.

O→ IBEX publishes books about Iran and the Middle East.

Nonfiction: Biography, cookbook, reference, textbook. Subjects include cooking/foods/nutrition, language/literature. Query with SASE or submit propsal package, including outline and 2 sample chapters.
Poetry: Translations of Persian poets will be considered.

THE ICON EDITIONS, Westview Press, Perseus Books Group, 5500 Central Ave., Boulder CO 80301-2877. (303)444-3541. **Acquisitions:** Sarah Warner. Estab. 1973. Publishes hardcover and trade paperback originals. **Publishes 5 titles/year. Receives hundreds of queries/year. 25% of books from first-time authors; 70% from unagented writers. Royalty and advance vary.** Publishes book 1 year after acceptance of ms. Accepts simultaneous submissions. Book catalog free.

O→ The Icon Editions focus on books in art history, art criticism and architecture for the textbook and trade markets.

Nonfiction: Textbook, general readership titles. Subjects include art/architecture, art history, art criticism. Query with SASE. Reviews artwork/photos as part of ms package.

Recent Title(s): *Italian Renaissance Art*, by Laurie Schneider Adams.

ICONOGRAFIX, INC., 1830A Hanley Rd., P.O. Box 446, Hudson WI 54016. (715)381-9755. Fax: (715)381-9756. E-mail: iconogfx@spacestar.net. **Acquisitions:** Dylan Frautschi, acquisitions manager (transportation). Estab. 1992. Publishes trade paperback originals. **Publishes 24 titles/year. Receives 100 queries and 20 mss/year. 50% of books from first-time authors; 100% from unagented writers. Pays 8-12½% royalty on wholesale price or makes outright purchase of $1,000-3,000. Offers $1,000-3,500 advance.** Publishes book 1 year after acceptance of ms. Accepts simultaneous submissions. Responds in 1 month to queries; 3 months to proposals; 3 months to mss. Book catalog and ms guidelines free.

- Iconografix publishes special historical interest photographic books for transportation equipment enthusiasts. Currently emphasizing emergency vehicles, buses, trucks, railroads, automobiles, auto racing, construction equipment.

Nonfiction: Interested in photo archives. Coffee table book, illustrated book (photographic), photo albums. Subjects include Americana (photos from archives of historic places, objects, people), history, hobbies, military/war, transportation (older photos of specific vehicles). Query with SASE or submit proposal package, including outline. Reviews artwork/photos as part of ms package. Send photocopies.
Recent Title(s): *Greyhound Buses 1914-2000 Photo Archive*, by William A. Luke; *Indianapolis Racing Cars of Frank Kurtis, 1941-1963 Photo Archive*, by Gordon Eliot White; *Pontiac Firebird 1967-2000 Photo History*, by George W. Scala.

ICS PUBLICATIONS, Institute of Carmelite Studies, 2131 Lincoln Rd. NE, Washington DC 20002. (202)832-8489. Fax: (202)832-8967. Website: www.icspublications.org. **Acquisitions:** John Sullivan, O.C.D. Publishes hardcover and trade paperback originals and reprints. **Publishes 6 titles/year. Receives 10-20 queries and 10 mss/year. 10% of books from first-time authors; 90-100% from unagented writers. Pays 2-6% royalty on retail price or makes outright purchase. Offers $500 advance.** Publishes book 2 years after acceptance of ms. Responds in 4 months to proposals. Book catalog for 7x10 SAE with 2 first-class stamps; ms guidelines for #10 SASE.

- "Our audience consists of those interested in the Carmelite tradition and in developing their life of prayer and spirituality."

Nonfiction: "We are looking for significant works on Carmelite history, spirituality, and main figures (Saints Teresa, John of the Cross, Therese of Lisieux, etc.)." Religious (should relate to Carmelite spirituality and prayer). "Too often we receive proposals for works that merely repeat what has already been done, are too technical for a general audience, or have little to do with the Carmelite tradition and spirit." Query or submit outline and 1 sample chapter.
Recent Title(s): *The Way of Perfection*, by St. Teresa of Avila (study edition).

IDYLL ARBOR, INC., P.O. Box 720, Ravensdale WA 98051. (425)432-3231. Fax: (425)432-3726. E-mail: editors@idyllarbor.com. Website: www.idyllarbor.com. **Acquisitions:** Tom Blaschko. Publishes hardcover and trade paperback originals and trade paperback reprints. **Publishes 6 titles/year. 50% of books from first-time authors; 100% from unagented writers. Pays 8-15% royalty on wholesale price or retail price.** Publishes book 1 year after acceptance of ms. Accepts simultaneous submissions. Responds in 1 month to queries; 2 months to proposals; 4 months to mss. Book catalog and ms guidelines free.
Imprints: Issues Press, Pine Woods Press.

- Idyll Arbor publishes practical information on the current state and art of health care practice. Currently emphasizing therapies (recreational, occupational, music, horticultural), activity directors in long term care facilities, and social service professionals.

Nonfiction: Reference, technical, textbook. Subjects include agriculture/horticulture (used in long-term care activities or health care-therapy), health/medicine (for therapists, social service providers and activity directors), psychology, recreation (as therapy). "Idyll Arbor is currently developing a line of books under the imprint Issues Press, which treats emotional issues in a clear-headed manner. The first books are *Female Sex Offenders: What Therapists, Law Enforcement and Child Protective Services Need to Know* and *Sexual Addiction: My Journey from Shame to Grace*. Another series of *Personal Health* books explains a condition or a closely related set of medical or psychological conditions. The target audience is the person or the family of the person with the condition. We want to publish a book that explains a condition at the level of detail expected of the average primary care physician so that our readers can address the situation intelligently with specialists. We look for manuscripts from authors with recent clinical experience. Good grounding in theory is required, but practical experience is more important." Query preferred with outline and 1 sample chapter. Reviews artwork/photos as part of ms package. Send photocopies.
Recent Title(s): *Eating Disorders: Providing Recreational Therapy Interventions*, by Dayna Miller and Laurie Jake; *Assessment Tools for Recreational Therapy, 3rd ed*, by Joan Burlingame and Tom Blaschko.
Tips: "The books must be useful for the health practitioner who meets face to face with patients *or* the books must be useful for teaching undergraduate and graduate level classes. We are especially looking for therapists with a solid clinical background to write on their area of expertise."

ILR PRESS, Cornell University Press, Sage House, 512 E. State St., Ithaca NY 14850. (607)277-2338 ext. 232. Fax: (607)277-2374. **Acquisitions:** F. Benson, editor. Estab. 1945. Publishes hardcover and trade paperback originals and reprints. **Publishes 10-12 titles/year. Pays royalty.** Does not accept simultaneous submissions. Responds in 2 months to queries. Book catalog free.

O→ "We are interested in manuscripts with innovative perspectives on current workplace issues that concern both academics and the general public."

Nonfiction: Subjects include business/economics, government/politics, history, sociology. All titles relate to industrial relations and/or workplace issues including relevant work in the fields of history, sociology, political science, economics, human resources, and organizational behavior. Query with SASE or submit outline, sample chapter(s), cv.

Recent Title(s): *Manufacturing Advantage: Why High-Performance Systems Pay Off*, by Eileen Appelbaum, et al; *The Working Class Majority: America's Best Kept Secret*, by Michael Zweig.

Tips: "Manuscripts must be well documented to pass our editorial evaluation, which includes review by academics in related fields."

[N] **IMAGES SI INC.**, Images Publishing, 39 Seneca Loop, Staten Island NY 10314. (718)698-8305. Fax: (718)982-6145. E-mail: gina@imagesco.com. Website: www.imagesco.com. **Acquisitions:** Gina McNeil, vice president (science and tech); Dan Bianco, vice president (science fiction). Estab. 1990. Publishes hardcover originals, trade paperback originals and audio. **Publishes 5 titles/year. 10% of books from first-time authors; 75% from unagented writers. Pays 10-20% royalty on wholesale price. Offers $1,000-5,000 advance.** Publishes book 6 months after acceptance of ms. Accepts simultaneous submissions. Responds in 2 months to queries; 2 months to proposals; 2 months to mss. Book catalog online.

Nonfiction: Audiocassettes, booklets, how-to, technical. Subjects include computers/electronic, photography, science, software. Query with SASE.

Fiction: Fantasy, science fiction. "We are looking for short stories as well as full-length novels." Query with SASE.

Recent Title(s): *Kirlian Photography*, by John Iovine (photo/how-to); *Nova-Audio*, by Hoyt, Franklin, Schoen (science fiction).

IMAGINART INTERNATIONAL, INC., 307 Arizona St., Bisbee AZ 85603. (520)432-5741. Fax: (520)432-5134. E-mail: imaginart@compuserve.com. Website: www.imaginartonline.com. **Acquisitions:** Cindy Drolert, editor-in-chief. Publishes trade paperback originals. **Publishes 6 titles/year. Receives 30 queries and 10 mss/year. 70% of books from first-time authors; 100% from unagented writers. Pays 8-11% royalty on retail price.** Publishes book 9 months after acceptance of ms. Accepts simultaneous submissions. Responds in 3 months to queries; 3 months to proposals; 3 months to mss. Book catalog online; ms guidelines free.

Nonfiction: Hands-on manuals in fields of rehabilation and special education. Textbook. Subjects include speech pathology, OT, PT, special education (particularly language and autism). It is critical to have an academic degree in teaching or a field in rehabilation to be an author for us. Does not publish children's storybooks or stories about the lives of people who have a disability. Query with SASE.

Recent Title(s): *Preschool Motor Speech Evalutaion and Intervention*, by Peggy Earnest, M.A., CCC-SLP; *Sensory Motor Activities for the Young Child*, by Donna Staisiunas Hurley, P.T. (theraputic activities).

Tips: Audience consists of speech pathologists, occupational therapists, physical therapists, family members of persons with disabilities, special education teachers. "We are mostly intested in down-to-earth, hands-on materials rather than textbooks."

IMAJINN BOOKS, P.O. Box 162, Hickory Corners MI 49060-0162. (616)671-4633. Fax: (616)671-4535. E-mail: imajinn@att.net. Website: www.imajinnbooks.com. **Acquisitions:** Linda Kichline, senior editor. Publishes trade paperback originals and reprints. **Publishes 36-40 titles/year. Receives 1,500 queries and 300 submissions/year. 70% of books from first-time authors; 80% from unagented writers. Pays 6-10% royalty on retail price. Offers 25-100 advance.** Publishes book 1-3 years after acceptance of ms. Responds in 3 months to queries; 6 months to proposals; 9-12 months to mss. Book catalog and ms guidelines for #10 SASE or online.

Fiction: "We publish only alternative reality romance, i.e., paranormal, supernatural, futuristic, fantasy, time travel and children's science fiction and fantasy, ages 8-12 and 13-17." Query with SASE or submit proposal package including 3 sample chapter(s), synopsis, on request only.

Recent Title(s): *Midnight Masquerade*, by Nancy Gideon; *Dancing with the Devil*, by Keri Arthur; *Penelope Quagmire*, by Hal Lanse.

Tips: "We require certain elements to be in our books. Read several of them to determine how to ensure your book meets our needs."

IMPACT PUBLISHERS, INC., P.O. Box 6016, Atascadero CA 93423-6016. (805)466-5917. Fax: (805)466-5919. E-mail: info@impactpublishers.com. Website: www.impactpublishers.com. **Acquisitions:** Freeman Porter, acquisitions editor. Estab. 1970. Publishes trade paperback originals. **Publishes 6-10 titles/year. Receives 250 queries and 250 mss/year. 20% of books from first-time authors; 60% from unagented writers. Pays 10% royalty on net receipts. Offers advance.** Publishes book 12-18 months after acceptance of ms. Accepts simultaneous submissions. Responds in 5 months to proposals. Book catalog and ms guidelines free.

Imprints: American Source Books, Little Imp Books, Rebuilding Books, Practical Therapist series.

O→ "Our purpose is to make the best human services expertise available to the widest possible audience: children, teens, parents, couples, individuals seeking self-help and personal growth, and human service professionals." Currently emphasizing books on divorce recovery for "The Rebuilding Books Series." De-emphasizing children's books.

Nonfiction: "All our books are written by qualified human service professionals and are in the fields of mental health, personal growth, relationships, aging, families, children and professional psychology." Children's/juvenile, self-help.

Subjects include child guidance/parenting, health/medicine, psychology (professional), caregiving/eldercare. "We do not publish general fiction for children. We do not publish poetry." Submit proposal package, including short résumé or vita, book description, audience description, outline, 1-3 sample chapters and SASE.
Recent Title(s): *Making Intimate Connections: Seven Guidelines for Great Relationships and Better Communication*, by Albert Ellis, Ph.D., and Ted Crawford.
Tips: "Don't call to see if we have received your submission. Include a self-addressed, stamped postcard if you want to know if manuscript arrived safely. We prefer a non-academic, readable style. We publish only popular psychology and self-help materials written in 'everyday language' by professionals with advanced degrees and significant experience in the human services."

INCENTIVE PUBLICATIONS, INC., 3835 Cleghorn Ave., Nashville TN 37215-2532. (615)385-2934. Fax: (615)385-2967. E-mail: comments@incentivepublications.com. Website: www.incentivepublications.com. **Acquisitions:** Jean K. Signor, editor. Estab. 1970. Publishes paperback originals. **Publishes 25-30 titles/year. Receives 350 submissions/year. 25% of books from first-time authors; 100% from unagented writers. Pays royalty or makes outright purchase.** Publishes book an average of 1 year after acceptance of ms. Responds in 1 month to queries.

- Incentive publishes developmentally appropriate teacher/parent resource materials and educational workbooks for children in grades K-12. Currently emphasizing primary material. Also interested in character education, English as a second language programs, early learning, current technology, related materials.

Nonfiction: Subjects include education. Teacher resource books in pre-K through 12th grade. Query with synopsis and detailed outline.
Recent Title(s): *The BASIC/Not Boring Grade Book Series*, by Imogene Forte and Marjorie Frank (Grades 1-5); *Can We Eat the Art?*, by Paula Guhin; *Romeo & Juliet Curriculum Guide*, by Laura Maravilla.

INFO NET PUBLISHING, 25211 Longwood Lane, Lake Forest CA 92630. (949)458-9292. Fax: (949)462-9595. E-mail: infonetpublishing@home.com. Website: www.infonetpublishing.com. **Acquisitions:** Herb Wetenkamp, president. Estab. 1987. Publishes hardcover and trade paperback originals. **Publishes 6 titles/year. Receives 50 queries and 20 mss/year. 80% of books from first-time authors; 85% from unagented writers. Pays 7-10% royalty on wholesale price or makes outright purchase of $1,000-5,000. Offers $1,000-2,000 advance in some cases.** Publishes book 10 months after acceptance of ms. Accepts simultaneous submissions. Responds in 2 months to queries. Book catalog for 10×12 SAE with 2 first-class stamps; ms guidelines for #10 SASE.

- Info Net publishes for easily identified niche markets; specific markets with some sort of special interest, hobby, avocation, profession, sport or lifestyle. New emphasis on collectibles and a series of books on retailing with CD-Roms.

Nonfiction: Biography, children's/juvenile, gift book, how-to, reference, self-help, technical. Subjects include Americana (and collectibles), business/economics (retailing), history, hobbies, military/war, nature/environment (and environment), recreation, regional, science, sports, travel, women's issues/studies, aviation/aircraft archaeology. "We are looking for specific niche market books, not general titles, other than self-help. Do not repeat same formula as other books. Offer something new, in other words." Submit outline, 3 sample chapters, proposal package, including demographics, marketing plans/data with SASE. Reviews artwork/photos as part of ms package. Send photocopies.
Recent Title(s): *The Complete Guide to Bicycle Store Operations*, by Ed Benjamin.
Tips: "Please check to be sure similar titles are not already published covering the exact same subject matter. Research the book you are proposing."

INFORMATION TODAY, INC., 143 Old Marlton Pike, Medford NJ 08055. (609)654-6266. Fax: (609)654-4309. E-mail: jbryans@infotoday.com. Website: www.infotoday.com. **Acquisitions:** John B. Bryans, editor-in-chief. Publishes hardcover and trade paperback originals. **Publishes 15-20 titles/year. Receives 100 queries and 30 mss/year. 30% of books from first-time authors; 90% from unagented writers. Pays 10-15% royalty on wholesale price. Offers $500-2,500 advance.** Publishes book 9 months after acceptance of ms. Accepts simultaneous submissions. Responds in 1 month to queries; 2 months to proposals; 3 months to mss. Book catalog free or on website; ms guidelines free or via e-mail as attachment.
Imprints: ITI (academic, scholarly, library science); CyberAge Books (high-end consumer and business technology books—emphasis on Internet/www topics including online research).

- "We look for highly-focused coverage of cutting-edge technology topics, written by established experts and targeted to a tech-savvy readership. Virtually all our titles focus on how information is accessed, used, shared and transformed into knowledge that can benefit people, business and society." Currently emphasizing Internet/online technologies, including their social significance; biography, how-to, technical, reference. De-emphasizing fiction.

Nonfiction: Biography, how-to, multimedia, reference, self-help, technical, scholarly. Subjects include business/economics, computers/electronic, education, science, Internet and cyberculture, library and information science. Query with SASE. Reviews artwork/photos as part of ms package. Send photocopies.
Recent Title(s): *The Invisible Web: Uncovering Information Sources Search Engines; Can't See*, by Chris Sherman and Gary Price.
Tips: "Our readers include scholars, academics, indexers, librarians, information professionals (ITI imprint) as well as high-end consumer and business users of Internet/www/online technologies, and people interested in the marriage of technology with issues of social significance (i.e., cyberculture)."

INNER TRADITIONS, Bear & Co., P.O. Box 388, 1 Park St., Rochester VT 05767. (802)767-3174. Fax: (802)767-3726. E-mail: info@innertraditions.com. Website: www.innertraditions.com. Managing Editor: Jeanie Levitan. **Acquisitions:** Jon Graham, editor . Estab. 1975. Publishes hardcover and trade paperback originals and reprints. **Publishes 64 titles/year. Receives 7,000 submissions/year. 10% of books from first-time authors; 20% from unagented writers. Pays 8-10% royalty on net receipts. Offers $1,000 average advance.** Publishes book 1 year after acceptance of ms. Responds in 3 months to queries; 6 months to mss. Book catalog and ms guidelines free.

Imprints: Destiny Audio Editions, Destiny Books, Destiny Recordings, Healing Arts Press, Inner Traditions, Inner Traditions En Espanol, Inner Traditions India, Park Street Press, Bear & Company, Bear Cub Books, Bindu Books.

O→ Inner Traditions publishes works representing the spiritual, cultural and mythic traditions of the world and works on alternative medicine and holistic health that combine contemporary thought with the knowledge of the world's great healing traditions. Currently emphasizing sacred sexuality, indigenous spirituality, ancient history.

Nonfiction: "We are interested in the relationship of the spiritual and transformative aspects of world cultures." Children's/juvenile, self-help. Subjects include animals, art/architecture, child guidance/parenting, contemporary culture, ethnic, fashion/beauty, health/medicine (alternative medicine), history (ancient history and mythology), music/dance, nature/environment (and environment), New Age, philosophy (esoteric), psychology, religion (world religions), sex, spirituality, women's issues/studies, indigenous cultures, ethnobotany business. No fiction. Query or submit outline and sample chapters with SASE. Does not return mss without SASE. Reviews artwork/photos as part of ms package.

Recent Title(s): *Pilates on the Ball*, by Colleen Craig; *Lost Book of Enki*, by Zecharia Sitchin.

Tips: "We are not interested in autobiographical stories of self-transformation. We do accept electronic submissions (via e-mail). We are not currently looking at fiction."

☆ **INNISFREE PRESS**, 136 Roumfort Rd., Philadelphia PA 19119. (215)247-4085. Fax: (215)247-2343. E-mail: InnisfreeP@aol.com. Website: www.innisfreepress.com. **Acquisitions:** Marcia Broucek, publisher. Estab. 1996. Publishes trade paperback originals. **Publishes 6-8 titles/year. Receives 500 queries and 300 mss/year. 50% of books from first-time authors; 90% from unagented writers. Pays 10% royalty on wholesale price.** Publishes book 1 year after acceptance of ms. Accepts simultaneous submissions. Responds in 2 months to queries; 3 months to proposals; 4 months to mss. Book catalog and ms guidelines free.

O→ "Innisfree's mission is to publish spiritual classics that 'call to the deep heart's core.'" Currently emphasizing women's issues, spirituality. De-emphasizing self-help books.

Nonfiction: Spiritually focused. Subjects include religion, women's issues/studies. No poetry or children's material or fiction please. Query with proposal package, including outline, 2 sample chapters, potential audience, and what makes the book unique, with SASE. Reviews artwork/photos as part of ms package. Send photocopies.

Recent Title(s): *Red Fire*, by Paula D'arcy; *Practicing Your Path*, by Holly Whitcomb; *Give to Your Heart's Content*, by Linda R. Harper.

Tips: "Our books respond to the needs of today's seekers—people who are looking for deeper meaning and purpose in their lives, for ways to integrate spiritual depth with religious traditions."

INSTITUTE OF POLICE TECHNOLOGY AND MANAGEMENT, University of North Florida, 12000 Alumni Drive, Jacksonville FL 32224-2678. (904)620-4786. Fax: (904)620-2453. E-mail: rhodge@unf.edu. Website: www.unf.edu/iptm/. **Acquisitions:** Richard C. Hodge, editor. Estab. 1980. Publishes trade paperback originals. **Publishes 8 titles/year. Receives 30 queries and 12 mss/year. 50% of books from first-time authors; 100% from unagented writers. Pays 25% royalty on retail price or makes outright purchase of $300-2,000 (may be some combination of above).** Publishes book 6 months after acceptance of ms. Does not accept simultaneous submissions. Responds in 3 weeks to queries.

O→ "Our publications are principally for law enforcement. Our authors are almost all present or retired law enforcement officers with excellent, up-to-date knowledge." Currently emphasizing criminal investigation, management (police), security.

Nonfiction: Illustrated book, reference, technical, textbook. Subjects include law enforcement, criminal investigations, security. "Our authors are not necessarily persons whose works have been published. Manuscripts should *not* be submitted until the author has talked with the editor on the telephone. The best procedure is to have this talk before beginning to write. Articles and short handbooks are acceptable as well as longer manuals." Reviews artwork/photos as part of ms package.

Recent Title(s): *Photography and Digital Imaging in Law Enforcement*, by Kevin Mello; *Commercial Motor Vehicle Crash Investigation*, by David E. Brill.

Tips: Audience is law enforcement, private investigators, trial attorneys, insurance investigators and adjustors.

INTERCONTINENTAL PUBLISHING, 11681 Bacon Race Rd., Woodbridge VA 22192. (703)583-4800. Fax: (703)670-7825. E-mail: icpub@worldnet.att.net. **Acquisitions:** H.G. Smittenaar, publisher. Publishes hardcover and trade paperback originals. **Publishes 3-4 titles/year. Pays 5% minimum royalty.** Accepts simultaneous submissions. Responds ASAP.

O→ Intercontinental publishes mystery and suspense novels.

Fiction: Mystery, suspense. Submit proposal package, including 1-3 sample chapters, estimated word count and SASE.

Recent Title(s): *I'm Okay, You're Dead*, by Spizer (mystery); *Dekok and the Begging Death*, by Baantjer (police procedural); *Tales from Old California*, by Gerald Schiller.

Tips: "Be original, write proper English, be entertaining."

INTERCULTURAL PRESS, INC., P.O. Box 700, Yarmouth ME 04096. (207)846-5168. Fax: (207)846-5181. E-mail: books@interculturalpress.com. Website: www.interculturalpress.com. **Acquisitions:** Ms. Toby Frank, president. Estab. 1980. Publishes hardcover and paperback originals. **Publishes 8-12 titles/year. Receives 50-80 submissions/year. 50% of books from first-time authors; 95% from unagented writers. Pays royalty. Offers small advance occasionally.** Publishes book within 18 months after acceptance of ms. Accepts simultaneous submissions. Responds in 1 month to queries. Book catalog and ms guidelines free; ms guidelines online.

O→ Intercultural Press publishes materials related to intercultural relations, including the practical concerns of living and working in foreign countries, the impact of cultural differences on personal and professional relationships and the challenges of interacting with people from unfamiliar cultures, whether at home or abroad. Currently emphasizing international business.

Nonfiction: "We want books with an international or domestic intercultural or multicultural focus, including those on business operations (how to be effective in intercultural business activities), education (textbooks for teaching intercultural subjects, for instance) and training (for Americans abroad or foreign nationals coming to the United States)." Reference, textbooks, theory. Subjects include world affairs, business, education, diversity and multicultural, relocation and cultural adaptation, culture learning, training materials, country-specific guides. "Our books are published for educators in the intercultural field, business people engaged in international business, managers concerned with cultural diversity in the workplace, and anyone who works in an occupation where cross-cultural communication and adaptation are important skills. No manuscripts that don't have an intercultural focus." Accepts nonfiction translations. Submit proposals, outline.

Recent Title(s): *The Expert Expatriate: Your Guide to Successful Relocation Abroad—Moving, Living, Thriving*, by Melissa Brayer Hess and Patricia Linderman; *The New Japan: Debunking Seven Cultural Stereotypes*, by David Matsumoto; *Modern Day Vikings*, by Christina Johanssen Robinowitz and Lisa Werner Carr.

INTERLINK PUBLISHING GROUP, INC., 46 Crosby St., Northampton MA 01060. (413)582-7054. Fax: (413)582-7057. E-mail: info@interlinkbooks.com. Website: www.interlinkbooks.com. **Acquisitions:** Michel Moushabeck, publisher. Estab. 1987. Publishes hardcover and trade paperback originals. **Publishes 50 titles/year. Receives 600 submissions/year. 30% of books from first-time authors; 50% from unagented writers. Pays 6-8% royalty on retail price. Offers small advance.** Publishes book 18 months after acceptance of ms. Accepts simultaneous submissions. Responds in 1 month to queries. Book catalog free; ms guidelines online.

Imprints: Crocodile Books, USA; Interlink Books; Olive Branch Press.

O→ Interlink publishes a general trade list of adult fiction and nonfiction with an emphasis on books that have a wide appeal while also meeting high intellectual and literary standards.

Nonfiction: Subjects include world travel, world history and politics, ethnic cooking, world music. Submit outline and sample chapters.

Fiction: Ethnic, international. "Adult—We are looking for translated works relating to the Middle East, Africa or Latin America. Juvenile/Picture Books—Our list is full for the next two years." No science fiction, romance, plays, erotica, fantasy, horror. Submit outline/synopsis and sample chapters.

Recent Title(s): *House of the Winds*, by Mia Yun.

Tips: "Any submissions that fit well in our publishing program will receive careful attention. A visit to our website, your local bookstore, or library to look at some of our books before you send in your submission is recommended."

INTERNATIONAL FOUNDATION OF EMPLOYEE BENEFIT PLANS, P.O. Box 69, Brookfield WI 53008-0069. (262)786-6700. Fax: (262)786-8780. E-mail: books@ifebp.org. Website: www.ifebp.org. **Acquisitions:** Dee Birschel, senior director of publications. Estab. 1954. Publishes trade paperback originals. **Publishes 10 titles/year. Receives 20 submissions/year. 15% of books from first-time authors; 80% from unagented writers. Pays 5-15% royalty on wholesale and retail price.** Publishes book 1 year after acceptance of ms. Responds in 3 months to queries. Book catalog free; ms guidelines for #10 SASE.

O→ IFEBP publishes general and technical monographs on all aspects of employee benefits—pension plans, health insurance, etc.

Nonfiction: Subjects limited to health care, pensions, retirement planning and employee benefits and compensation. Reference, technical, textbook. Subjects include consumer information. Query with outline.

Recent Title(s): *Integrated Disability Management: An Employers Guide*, by Janet R. Douglas.

Tips: "Be aware of interests of employers and the marketplace in benefits topics, for example, how AIDS affects employers, health care cost containment."

INTERNATIONAL MARINE, The McGraw-Hill Companies, P.O. Box 220, Camden ME 04843-0220. (207)236-4838. Fax: (207)236-6314. Website: www.internationalmarine.com. Jonathan Eaton, editorial director (boating, marine nonfiction). Estab. 1969. Publishes hardcover and paperback originals. **Publishes 50 titles/year. Receives 500-700 mss/year. 30% of books from first-time authors; 80% from unagented writers. Pays standard royalties based on net price. Offers advance.** Publishes book 1 year after acceptance of ms. Responds in 2 months to queries. Ms guidelines for #10 SASE.

Imprints: Ragged Mountain Press (sports and outdoor books that take you off the beaten path).

O→ International Marine publishes "good books about boats."

Nonfiction: Publishes "a wide range of subjects include: sea stories, seamanship, boat maintenance, etc." Subjects include marine and outdoor nonfiction. All books are illustrated. "Material in all stages welcome." Query first with outline and 2-3 sample chapters. Reviews artwork/photos as part of ms package.

Recent Title(s): *Tropical Cruising Handbook*, by Mark Smacklers and Kim des Roches; *Stapleton's Powerboat Bible*, by Sid Stapleton; *PT 109: John F. Kennedy in World War II*, by Robert Donovan.

Tips: "Writers should be aware of the need for clarity, accuracy and interest. Many progress too far in the actual writing."

INTERNATIONAL MEDICAL PUBLISHING, 1516 Mintwood Drive, McLean VA 22101-0479. (703)356-2037. Fax: (703)734-8987. E-mail: contact@medicalpublishing.com. Website: www.medicalpublishing.com. **Acquisitions:** Thomas Masterson, MD, editor. Estab. 1991. Publishes mass market paperback originals. **Publishes 30 titles/year. Receives 100 queries and 20 mss/year. 5% of books from first-time authors; 100% from unagented writers. Pays royalty on gross receipts.** Publishes book 8 months after acceptance of ms. Responds in 2 months to queries.

- IMP publishes books to make life easier for doctors in training. "We're branching out to also make life easier for people with chronic medical problems."

Nonfiction: Reference, textbook. Subjects include health/medicine. "We distribute only through medical and scientific bookstores. Think about practical material for doctors-in-training. We are interested in handbooks. Online projects are of interest." Query with outline.

Recent Title(s): *Healthy People 2010*, by the US Department of Health and Human Services.

INTERNATIONAL PUBLISHERS CO., INC., 239 W. 23 St., New York NY 10011. (212)366-9816. Fax: (212)366-9820. E-mail: service@intpubnyc.com. Website: www.intpubnyc.com. **Acquisitions:** Betty Smith, president. Estab. 1924. Publishes hardcover originals, trade paperback originals and reprints. **Publishes 5-6 titles/year. Receives 50-100 mss/year. 10% of books from first-time authors. Pays 5-7½% royalty on paperbacks; 10% royalty on cloth.** Publishes book 6 months after acceptance of ms. Accepts simultaneous submissions. Responds in 1 month to queries with SASE to queries; 6 months to mss. Book catalog and ms guidelines for SAE with 55¢ postage.

- International Publishers Co., Inc. emphasizes books based on Marxist science.

Nonfiction: Subjects include art/architecture, government/politics, history, philosophy, economics, social sciences, Marxist-Leninist classics. "Books on labor, black studies and women's studies based on Marxist science have high priority." Query or submit outline, sample chapters and SASE. Reviews artwork/photos as part of ms package.

Recent Title(s): *Fiddle and Fight: A Memoir*, by Russell V. Brodine; *Afghanistan: Washington's Secret War*, by Phillip Bonosky.

Tips: No fiction or poetry.

INTERNATIONAL SOCIETY FOR TECHNOLOGY IN LEARNING (ISTE), 1787 Agate St., Eugene OR 97403-1923. (541)346-0816. E-mail: mmanweller@iste.org. Website: www.iste.org. **Acquisitions:** Mathew Manweller, acquisitions editor. Publishes trade paperback originals. **Publishes 20 titles/year. Receives 150 queries and 50 mss/year. 75% of books from first-time authors; 100% from unagented writers. Pays 12-15% royalty on retail price.** Publishes book 5 months after acceptance of ms. Accepts simultaneous submissions. Responds in 1 month to queries; 1 month to proposals; 1 month to mss. Book catalog and ms guidelines free.

- Currently emphasizing curriculum and project development books. De-emphasizing how-to books.

Nonfiction: Reference, technical, curriculum. Subjects include computers/electronic, education, software, technology. Submit proposal package including outline, 1 sample chapter(s). Reviews artwork/photos as part of ms package. Send photocopies.

Recent Title(s): *The Best Web Sites for Teachers*, by Vicki Sharp.

Tips: "Our audience is teachers, technology coordinators, administrators."

INTERNATIONAL WEALTH SUCCESS, P.O. Box 186, Merrick NY 11570-0186. (516)766-5850. Fax: (516)766-5919. **Acquisitions:** Tyler G. Hicks, editor. Estab. 1967. **Publishes 10 titles/year. Receives 100 submissions/year. 100% of books from first-time authors; 100% from unagented writers. Pays 10% royalty on wholesale or retail price. Offers usual advance of $1,000, but this varies depending on author's reputation and nature of book. Buys all rights.** Publishes book 4 months after acceptance of ms. Responds in 1 month to queries. Book catalog and ms guidelines for 9×12 SAE with 3 first-class stamps.

- "Our mission is to publish books, newsletters and self-study courses aimed at helping beginners and experienced business people start, and succeed in, their own small business in the fields of real estate, import-export, mail order, licensing, venture capital, financial brokerage, etc. The large number of layoffs and downsizings have made our publications of greater importance to people seeking financial independence in their own business, free of layoff threats and snarling bosses."

Nonfiction: How-to, self-help. Subjects include business/economics, financing, business success, venture capital, etc. "Techniques, methods, sources for building wealth. Highly personal, how-to-do-it with plenty of case histories. Books are aimed at wealth builders and are highly sympathetic to their problems. These publications present a wide range of business opportunities while providing practical, hands-on, step-by-step instructions aimed at helping readers achieve their personal goals in as short a time as possible while adhering to ethical and professional business standards." Length: 60,000-70,000 words. Query. Reviews artwork/photos as part of ms package.

Recent Title(s): *How to Buy and Flip Real Estate for a Profit*, by Rod L. Griffin.

Tips: "With the mass layoffs in large and medium-size companies there is an increasing interest in owning your own business. So we focus on more how-to hands-on material on owning—and becoming successful in—one's own business of any kind. Our market is the BWB—Beginning Wealth Builder. This person has so little money that financial planning is something they never think of. Instead, they want to know what kind of a business they can get into to make some money without a large investment. Write for this market and you have millions of potential readers. Remember—there are a lot more people *without* money than *with* money."

INTERVARSITY PRESS, P.O. Box 1400, Downers Grove IL 60515. (630)734-4000. Fax: (630)734-4200. E-mail: mail@ivpress.com. Website: www.ivpress.com. **Acquisitions:** David Zimmerman, assistant editor; Andy Le Peau, editorial director; Jim Hoover, associate editorial director (academic, reference); Cindy Bunch, editor (Bible study, Christian living); Gary Deddo, associate editor (academic); Dan Reid, editor (reference, academic); Al Hsu, associate editor (general). Estab. 1947. Publishes hardcover originals, trade paperback and mass market paperback originals. **Publishes 70-80 titles/year. Receives 1,500 queries and 1,000 mss/year. 15% of books from first-time authors; 85% from unagented writers. Pays negotiable flat fee or royalty on retail price. Offers negotiable advance.** Publishes book 1 year after acceptance of ms. Accepts simultaneous submissions. Responds in 3 months to proposals. Book catalog for 9×12 SAE and 5 first-class stamps; Ms guidelines available via e-mail or with #10 SASE.

Imprints: Academic (contact Gary Deddo); Bible Study (contact Cindy Bunch); General (contact Al Hsu); Reference (contact Dan Reid)

- InterVarsity Press publishes a full line of books from an evangelical Christian perspective targeted to an open-minded audience. "We serve those in the university, the church and the world, by publishing books from an evangelical Christian perspective."

Nonfiction: Subjects include religion. Query with SASE. *No unsolicited mss.*

Recent Title(s): *Habits of the Mind*, by James Sire; *Spritual Mentoring*, by Keith Anderson and Randy Reese.

INTERWEAVE PRESS, 201 E. Fourth St., Loveland CO 80537. (970)669-7672. Fax: (970)667-8317. Website: www.interweave.com. **Acquisitions:** Betsy Armstrong, book editorial director. Estab. 1975. Publishes hardcover and trade paperback originals. **Publishes 16-20 titles/year. Receives 50 submissions/year. 60% of books from first-time authors; 98% from unagented writers. Pays 10% royalty on net receipts.** Publishes book 1-2 years after acceptance of ms. Accepts simultaneous submissions. Responds in 2 months to queries. Book catalog and ms guidelines free.

- Interweave Press publishes instructive and inspirational titles relating to the fiber arts and beadwork topics.

Nonfiction: Subjects limited to fiber arts—basketry, spinning, knitting, dyeing and weaving—and beadwork topics. How-to, technical. Submit outline, sample chapter(s). Reviews artwork/photos as part of ms package.

Recent Title(s): *Beading in the Native American Tradition*, by David Dean.

Tips: "We are looking for very clear, informally written, technically correct manuscripts, generally of a how-to nature, in our specific fiber and beadwork fields only. Our audience includes a variety of creative self-starters who appreciate inspiration and clear instruction. They are often well educated and skillful in many areas."

IRON GATE PUBLISHING, P.O. Box 999, Niwot CO 80544-0999. (303)530-2551. Fax: (303)530-5273. E-mail: editor@irongate.com. Website: www.irongate.com; www.reunionsolutions.com. **Acquisitions:** Dina C. Carson, publisher (how-to, genealogy); Risa J. Johnson, editor (reunions). Publishes hardcover and trade paperback originals. **Publishes 6-10 titles/year; imprint publishes 2-6 titles/year. Receives 100 queries and 20 mss/year. 30% of books from first-time authors; 10% from unagented writers. Pays royalty on a case-by-case basis.** Publishes book 1 year after acceptance of ms. Accepts simultaneous submissions. Responds in 2 months to proposals. Book catalog free or on website; ms guidelines online.

Imprints: Reunion Solutions Press, KinderMed Press.

- "Our readers are people who are looking for solid, how-to advice on planning reunions or self-publishing a genealogy."

Nonfiction: How-to, multimedia, reference. Subjects include child guidance/parenting, health/medicine, hobbies. Query with SASE or submit proposal package, including outline, 2 sample chapters and marketing summary. Reviews artwork/photos as part of ms package. Send photocopies.

Recent Title(s): *The Genealogy and Local History Researcher's Self-Publishing Guide*; *Reunion Solutions: Everything You Need to Know to Plan a Family, Class, Military, Association or Corporate Reunion.*

Tips: "Please look at the other books we publish and tell us in your query letter why your book would fit into our line of books."

ITALICA PRESS, 595 Main St., Suite 605, New York NY 10044-0047. (212)935-4230. Fax: (212)838-7812. E-mail: inquiries@italicapress.com. Website: www.italicapress.com. **Acquisitions:** Ronald G. Musto and Eileen Gardiner, publishers. Estab. 1985. Publishes trade paperback originals. **Publishes 6 titles/year. Receives 600 queries and 60 mss/year. 5% of books from first-time authors; 100% from unagented writers. Pays 7-15% royalty on wholesale price.** Publishes book 1 year after acceptance of ms. Responds in 1 month to queries. Book catalog free; ms guidelines online.

- Italica Press publishes English translations of modern Italian fiction and medieval and Renaissance nonfiction.

Nonfiction: Subjects include translation. "We publish English translations of medieval and Renaissance source materials and English translations of modern Italian fiction." Query with SASE. Reviews artwork/photos as part of ms package. Send photocopies.

Poetry: Poetry titles are generally dual language.

Tips: "We are interested in considering a wide variety of medieval and Renaissance topics (not historical fiction), and for modern works we are only interested in translations from Italian fiction by well-known Italian authors."

JAIN PUBLISHING CO., P.O. Box 3523, Fremont CA 94539. (510)659-8272. Fax: (510)659-0501. E-mail: mail@jainpub.com. Website: www.jainpub.com. **Acquisitions:** M.K. Jain, editor-in-chief. Estab. 1989. Publishes hardcover and paperback originals and reprints. **Publishes 6 titles/year. Receives 300 queries/year. 100% from unagented writers. Pays up to 15% royalty on net sales.** Publishes book 1-2 years after acceptance of ms. Responds in 3 months to mss. Book catalog and ms guidelines online.

Imprints: Asian Humanities Press.

O→ Jain Publishing Company is a general trade and college textbook publisher with a diversified list. Continued emphasis on undergraduate textbooks.

Nonfiction: Reference, textbook. Subjects include general nonfiction, humanities, social sciences. "Manuscripts should be thoroughly researched and written in an 'easy to read' format. Preferably between 60,000-100,000 words." Submit proposal package including publishing history. Reviews artwork/photos as part of ms package. Send photocopies.

Recent Title(s): *Hush! Don't Say Anything to God: Passionate Poems of Rumi*, by Shahram Shiva (philosphies/religion).

ALICE JAMES BOOKS, 238 Main St., Farmington ME 04938. (207)778-7071. Fax: (207)778-7071. E-mail: ajb@umf.maine.edu. Website: www.umf.maine.edu/~ajb. **Acquisitions:** April Ossmann, director (poetry). Publishes trade paperback originals. **Publishes 4 titles/year. Receives 1,000 queries and 800 mss/year. 80% of books from first-time authors; 90% from unagented writers. Pays through competition awards.** Publishes book 9 months after acceptance of ms. Accepts simultaneous submissions. Responds in 1 month to queries; 1 month to proposals; 3 months to mss. Book catalog for free or on website; ms guidelines for #10 SASE or on website.

O→ Alice James Books is a nonprofit poetry press.

Poetry: Query.

Recent Title(s): *The Art of the Lathe*, by B.H. Fairchild; *The River at Wolf*, by Jean Valentine.

Tips: "Send SASE for contest guidelines. Do not send work before querying."

JAMESON BOOKS INC., 722 Columbus St., P.O. Box 738, Ottawa IL 61350. (815)434-7905. Fax: (815)434-7907. **Acquisitions:** Jameson G. Campaigne, publisher/editor. Estab. 1986. Publishes hardcover originals. **Publishes 6 titles/year. Receives 500 queries and 300 mss/year. 33% of books from first-time authors; 33% from unagented writers. Pays 6-15% royalty on retail price. Offers $1,000-25,000 advance.** Publishes book 1 year after acceptance of ms. Accepts simultaneous submissions. Responds in 6 months to queries.

O→ Jameson Books publishes conservative politics and economics; Chicago area history; and biographies.

Nonfiction: Biography. Subjects include business/economics, government/politics, history, regional (Chicago area). Query with SASE or submit 1 sample chapter(s). Submissions not returned without SASE.

Fiction: Interested in pre-cowboy "mountain men" in American west, before 1820 in east frontier fiction. Query with SASE or submit 1 sample chapter(s).

Recent Title(s): *Politics as a Noble Calling*, by F. Clifton White (memoirs); *Yellowstone Kelly: Gentleman and Scout*, by Peter Bowen (fiction).

JAYJO BOOKS, L.L.C., The Guidance Channel, P.O. Box 760, 135 Dupont St., Plainview NY 11803-0769. (516)349-5520. Fax: (516)349-5521. **Acquisitions:** Sally Germain, editor-in-chief (for elementary school age youth). Publishes trade paperback originals. **Publishes 8-12 titles/year. Receives 100 queries/year. 25% of books from first-time authors; 100% from unagented writers. Makes outright purchase of $500-1,000.** Publishes book 9 months after acceptance of ms. Accepts simultaneous submissions. Responds in 2 months to queries; 2 months to proposals; 2 months to mss. Book catalog and writer's guidelines for #10 SASE.

Imprints: Each book published is for a specific series. Series include: Special Family and Friends, Health Habits for Kids, Substance Free Kids, Special Kids in School. Series publish 1-5 titles/year.

Nonfiction: Children's/juvenile, illustrated book. Subjects include health/medicine (issues for children). "JayJo Books is a publisher of nonfiction books to help teachers, parents, and children cope with chronic illnesses, special needs, and health education in classroom, family, and social settings. Each JayJo series has a particular style and format it must follow. Writers should send query letter with areas of expertise or interest and suggested focus of book." No animal character books or illustrated books. Query with SASE.

Tips: "Send query letter—since we only publish books adapted to our special formats—we contact appropriate potential authors and work with them to customize manuscript."

☆ **JEWISH LIGHTS PUBLISHING**, LongHill Partners, Inc., P.O. Box 237, Sunset Farms Offices, Rt. 4, Woodstock VT 05091. (802)457-4000. Editor: Stuart Matlins. **Acquisitions:** Acquisitions Editor. Estab. 1990. Publishes hardcover and trade paperback originals, trade paperback reprints. **Publishes 30 titles/year. Receives 1,000 submissions/year. 50% of books from first-time authors; 99% from unagented writers. Pays royalty on net sales, 10% on first printing, then increases.** Publishes book 1 year after acceptance of ms. Accepts simultaneous submissions. Responds in 3 months to queries. Book catalog and ms guidelines free.

O→ "People of all faiths and backgrounds yearn for books that attract, engage, educate and spiritually inspire. Our principal goal is to stimulate thought and help all people learn about who the Jewish people are, where they come from, and what the future may hold."

Nonfiction: Children's/juvenile, illustrated book, reference, self-help. Subjects include business/economics (with spiritual slant, finding spiritual meaning in one's work), health/medicine (healing/recovery, wellness, aging, life cycle), history, nature/environment, philosophy, religion (theology), spirituality (and inspiration), women's issues/studies. "We do *not* publish haggadot, biography, poetry, or cookbooks." Submit proposal package, including cover letter, table of contents, 2 sample chapters and SASE (postage must cover weight of ms). Reviews artwork/photos as part of ms package. Send photocopies.

Recent Title(s): *Does the Soul Survive?: A Jewish Journey to Belief in Afterlife, Past Lives and Living with Purpose*, by Elie Haplan Spitz; *The Way Into Torah*, by Norman J. Cohen.

Tips: "We publish books for all faiths and backgrounds that also reflect the Jewish wisdom tradition."

JIST WORKS, INC., 8902 Otis Ave., Indianapolis IN 46216-1033. (317)613-4200. Fax: (317)613-4309. E-mail: editorial@jist.com. Website: www.jist.com. **Acquisitions:** Susan Pines, senior development editor. Estab. 1981. Publishes trade paperback originals and reprints. **Publishes 60 titles/year. Receives 150 submissions/year. 60% of books from first-time authors. Pays 5-12% royalty on wholesale price or makes outright purchase (negotiable).** Publishes book 1 year after acceptance of ms. Accepts simultaneous submissions. Responds in 3 months to queries. Book catalog and ms guidelines on website or for 9×12 SAE with 6 first-class stamps.

Imprints: Park Avenue Publications (business and self-help that falls outside of the JIST topical parameters).

- "Our purpose is to provide quality career, job search, and other living skills information, products, and services that help people manage and improve their lives—and the lives of others."

Nonfiction: How-to, multimedia, reference, self-help, textbook, video. Subjects include business/economics, computers/electronic, software, careers. Specializes in job search, self-help and career-related topics.; "We want text/workbook formats that would be useful in a school or other institutional setting. We also publish trade titles, all reading levels. Will consider books for professional staff and educators, appropriate software and videos." Query with SASE. Reviews artwork/photos as part of ms package.

Recent Title(s): *The Quick Résumé & Cover Letter Book*, by J. Michael Farr.

Tips: "Institutions and staff who work with people of all reading and academic skill levels, making career and life decisions or people who are looking for jobs are our primary audience, but we're focusing more on business and trade topics for consumers."

JOHNSON BOOKS, Johnson Publishing Co., 1880 S. 57th Court., Boulder CO 80301. (303)443-9766. Fax: (303)998-7594. E-mail: books@jpcolorado.com. **Acquisitions:** Stephen Topping, editorial director. Estab. 1979. Publishes hardcover and paperback originals and reprints. **Publishes 10-12 titles/year. Receives 500 submissions/year. 30% of books from first-time authors; 90% from unagented writers. Royalties vary.** Publishes book 1 year after acceptance of ms. Responds in 3 months to queries. Book catalog for 9×12 SAE with 5 first-class stamps.

Imprints: Spring Creek Press.

- Johnson Books specializes in books on the American West, primarily outdoor, "useful" titles that will have strong national appeal.

Nonfiction: Scholarly, guidebooks. Subjects include anthropology/archeology, general nonfiction, history, nature/environment (environmental subjects), recreation (outdoor), regional, science, translation, travel, general nonfiction, books on the West, natural history, paleontology, geology. "We are primarily interested in books for the informed popular market, though we will consider vividly written scholarly works." Looks for "good writing, thorough research, professional presentation and appropriate style. Marketing suggestions from writers are helpful." Submit outline/synopsis and 3 sample chapters.

Recent Title(s): *Women of Consequence*, by Jeanne Varnell (western biography).

JOSSEY-BASS/PFEIFFER, John Wiley & Sons, Inc., 989 Market St., San Francisco CA 94103. (415)433-1740. Fax: (415)433-0499. Website: www.josseybass.com; www.pfeiffer.com. **Acquisitions:** Paul Foster, publisher (health, education, nonprofit, psychology, religion); Cedric Crocker, publisher (business & management, Pfeiffer). **Publishes 250 titles/year. Pays variable royalties. Offers occasional advance.** Publishes book 1 year after acceptance of ms. Accepts simultaneous submissions. Responds in 2 months to queries. Ms guidelines online.

Nonfiction: Subjects include business/economics, education, health/medicine, money/finance, psychology, religion. Jossey-Bass publishes first-time and unagented authors. Publishes books on topics of interest to a wide range of readers: business & management, conflict resolution, mediation and negotiation, K-12 education, higher and adult education, healthcare management, psychology/behavioral healthcare, nonprofit & public management, religion, human resources & training. Also publishes 25 periodicals.

Recent Title(s): *Leading in a Culture of Change*, by Michael Fullan; *Fighting for Your Marriage*, by Howard J. Markman and Susan L. Blumberg; *Building Moral Intelligence*, by Michele Borba.

JOURNEYFORTH, (formerly BJU Press), 1700 Wade Hampton Blvd., Greenville SC 29614-0001. (864)242-5100, ext. 4350. E-mail: jb@bjup.com. Website: www.bjup.com. **Acquisitions:** Nancy Lohr, manuscript editor (juvenile fiction). Estab. 1974. Publishes paperback original and reprints. **Publishes 10 titles/year. Pays royalty.** Publishes book 12-18 months after acceptance of ms. Accepts simultaneous submissions. Responds in 1 month to queries; 3 months to mss. Book catalog free; ms guidelines free.

- "Small independent publisher of excellent, trustworthy novels, information books, audio tapes and ancillary materials for readers pre-school through high school. We desire to develop in our children a love for and understanding of the written word, ultimately helping them love and understand God's word."

Fiction: Adventure (children's/juvenile, young adult), historical (children's/juvenile, young adult), juvenile (animal, easy-to-read, series), mystery (children's/juvenile, young adult), sports (children's/juvenile, young adult), suspense

(young adult), western (young adult), young adult (series). "Our fiction is all based on a moral and Christian wordview." Query with SASE or submit outline, 5 sample chapter(s), Include estimated word count, short bio, Social Security number and list of publishing credits. or submit complete ms.
Recent Title(s): *Susannah and the Secret Coins*, by Elaine Schulte (historical young adult fiction); *Arby Jenkins Meets His Match*, by Sharon Hambrick (contemporary young adult); *Over the Divide*, by Catherine Farnes (young adult fiction).
Tips: "Study the publisher's guidelines. Make sure your work is suitable or you waste time for you and the publisher."

JUDAICA PRESS, 123 Ditmas Ave., Brooklyn NY 11218. (718)972-6200. Fax: (718)972-6204. E-mail: info@judaicapress.com. Website: www.judaicapress.com. **Acquisitions:** Nachum Shapiro, managing editor. Estab. 1963. Publishes hardcover and trade paperback originals and reprints. **Publishes 12 titles/year.** Responds in 3 months to queries. Book catalog online.

O→ "We cater to the traditional, Orthodox Jewish market."

Nonfiction: "Looking for very traditional Judaica, especially children's books." Biography, children's/juvenile, cookbook, textbook. Subjects include history, religion. Query with SASE or submit outline, 1 sample chapter(s).
Recent Title(s): *Friend or Foe*, by Eva Vogiel; *Living on the Edge*, by Rabbi David Goldwasser; *Locked in Time*, by M.C. Millman.

JUDSON PRESS, P.O. Box 851, Valley Forge PA 19482-0851. (610)768-2128. Fax: (610)768-2441. E-mail: judsonpress@juno.com. Website: www.judsonpress.com. Publisher: Kristy Arnesen Pullen. **Acquisitions:** Randy Frame. Estab. 1824. Publishes hardcover and paperback originals. **Publishes 20-30 titles/year. Receives 750 queries/year. Pays royalty or makes outright purchase.** Publishes book 10 months after acceptance of ms. Accepts simultaneous submissions. Responds in 3 months to queries. Book catalog for 9×12 SAE with 4 first-class stamps; ms guidelines for #10 SASE.

- Judson Press also publishes a quarterly journal, *The African American Pulpit*; call for submission guidelines.

O→ "Our audience is mostly church members and leaders who seek to have a more fulfilling personal spiritual life and want to serve Christ in their churches and other relationships. We have a large African American readership." Currently emphasizing worship resources/small group resources. De-emphasizing biography, poetry.

Nonfiction: Adult religious nonfiction of 30,000-80,000 words. Subjects include multicultural, religion. Query with SASE or submit outline, sample chapter(s).
Recent Title(s): *Journey Into Day: Meditations for New Cancer Patients*, by Rusty Freeman.
Tips: "Writers have the best chance selling us practical books assisting clergy or laypersons in their ministry and personal lives. Our audience consists of Protestant church leaders and members. Be sensitive to our workload and adapt to the market's needs. Books on multicultural issues are very welcome. Also seeking books that heighten awareness and sensitivity to issues related to the poor and to social justice."

[N] **JUSTICE HOUSE PUBLISHING, INC.**, P.O. Box 4233, Spanaway WA 98387. (253)262-0203. Fax: (253)475-2158. E-mail: rashidahreed@aol.com. Website: www.justicehouse.com. Publishes trade paperback originals. **Publishes 3-10 titles/year. Receives 5-10 queries and 1-5 mss/year. 100% of books from first-time authors; 100% from unagented writers. Pays 10-15% royalty on wholesale price.** Publishes book 2 years after acceptance of ms. Does not accept simultaneous submissions. Responds in 2-3 months to queries; 2-3 months to proposals; 3-6 months to mss. Book catalog free; ms guidelines online.
Fiction: Fantasy, feminist, gay/lesbian, mystery, romance, science fiction, short story collections. "We specialize in lesbian fiction." Submit complete ms.
Recent Title(s): *Tropical Storm*, by Melissa Good (lesbian fiction); *The Deal*, by Maggie Ryan (lesbian fiction).
Tips: Audience is comprised of 18 and older eductated lesbian females.

KALMBACH PUBLISHING CO., 21027 Crossroads Circle, P.O. Box 1612, Waukesha WI 53187-1612. (262)796-8776. Fax: (262)798-6468. E-mail: rchristianson@kalmbach.com. Website: books.kalmbachbooks.com. **Acquisitions:** Dick Christianson, editor-in-chief (model railroading, scale modeling, toy trains, railfanning); Kent Johnson, acquisitions editor (model railroading, toy trains); Philip Martin, acquisitions editor (books on writing). Estab. 1934. Publishes hardcover and paperback originals, paperback reprints. **Publishes 15-20 titles/year. Receives 100 submissions/year. 75% of books from first-time authors; 100% from unagented writers. Pays 10% royalty on net receipts. Offers $1,500 average advance.** Publishes book 18 months after acceptance of ms. Responds in 2 months to queries.

O→ Kalmbach publishes reference materials and how-to publications for serious hobbyists in the railfan, model railroading, plastic modeling and toy train collecting/operating hobbies as well as books on the art and craft of writing.

Nonfiction: How-to, illustrated book. Subjects include hobbies, science, amateur astronomy, railroading, writing. "Our book publishing effort is in railroading and hobby how-to-do-it titles *only*. I welcome telephone inquiries. They save me a lot of time, and they can save an author a lot of misconceptions and wasted work." Query first. In written query, wants detailed outline of 2-3 pages and a complete sample chapter with photos, drawings, and how-to text. Reviews artwork/photos as part of ms package.

KAMEHAMEHA SCHOOLS PRESS, Kamehameha Schools, 1887 Makuakane St., Honolulu HI 96817-1887. (808)842-8880. Fax: (808)842-8876. E-mail: kspress@ksbe.edu. Website: www.ksbe.edu/pubs/kspress/catalog.html. **Acquisitions:** Henry Bennett. Publishes hardcover and trade paperback originals and reprints. **Publishes 3-5 titles/year. 10-25% of books from first-time authors; 100% from unagented writers. Makes outright purchase.** Publishes book up to 2 years after acceptance of ms. Responds in 3 months to queries. Book catalog for #10 SASE.

Imprints: Kamehameha Schools Press, Kamehameha Schools, Kamehameha Schools Bishop Estate.

O→ "Only writers with substantial and documented expertise in Hawaiian history, Hawaiian culture, Hawaiian language, and/or Hawaiian studies should consider submitting to Kamehameha Schools Press. We prefer to work with writers available to physically meet at our Honolulu offices."

Nonfiction: Biography, children's/juvenile, reference, textbook. Subjects include education (Hawaiian), history (Hawaiian), regional (Hawaii), translation (Hawaiian). Query with SASE. Reviews artwork/photos as part of ms package. Send photocopies.

[A] **KENSINGTON PUBLISHING CORP.**, 850 Third Ave., 16th Floor, New York NY 10022. (212)407-1500. Fax: (212)935-0699. Website: www.kensingtonbooks.com. **Acquisitions:** Ann LaFarge, executive editor (romance, fiction); Kate Duffy, editorial director (historical romance, regency, romance, ballad, erotica); John Scognamiglio, editorial director (romance, regency, mystery, thrillers, pop culture, gay/lesbian); Karen Haas, editor (true crime, westerns); Amy Garvey, editor (romance, regency, historical romances); Karen Thomas, senior editor (Arabesque romance, African American fiction and nonfiction). Estab. 1975. Publishes hardcover and trade paperback originals, mass market paperback originals and reprints. **Publishes 500 titles/year; imprint publishes 3-20 titles/year. Receives 5,000 queries and 2,000 mss/year. 10% of books from first-time authors; 30% from unagented writers. Pays 8-15% royalty on retail price or makes outright purchase of $1,000-3,000. Offers $2,000-2,000,000 advance.** Publishes book 9 months after acceptance of ms. Accepts simultaneous submissions. Responds in 1 month to queries; 1 month to proposals; 4 months to mss. Book catalog online; ms guidelines for #10 SASE or online.

Imprints: Arabesque and Dafina (Karen Thomas, executive editor); Ballad, Brava and Encanto (Kate Duffy, editorial director); Citadel; Kensington; Pinnacle; Precious Gems; Twin Streams (Elaine Sparber, senior editor); Zebra.

O→ Kensington focuses on profitable niches and uses aggressive marketing techniques to support its books.

Nonfiction: Biography, cookbook, gift book, how-to, humor, illustrated book, reference, self-help. Subjects include Americana, animals, business/economics, child guidance/parenting, contemporary culture, cooking/foods/nutrition, gay/lesbian, health/medicine (alternative), history, hobbies, memoirs, military/war, money/finance, multicultural, nature/environment, philosophy, psychology, recreation, regional, sex, sports, travel, true crime, women's issues/studies, pop culture, true crime, current events. *Agented submissions only. No unsolicited mss.* Reviews artwork/photos as part of ms package. Send photocopies.

Fiction: Erotica, ethnic, gay/lesbian, historical, horror, mainstream/contemporary, multicultural, mystery, occult, romance, suspense, western (epic), thrillers; women's. *Agented submissions only. No unsolicited mss.*

Recent Title(s): *Landing It*, by Scott Hamilton (nonfiction); *Celebration*, by Fern Michaels (fiction).

Tips: Agented submissions only, except for submissions to Arabesque, Ballad, Bouquet, Encanto and Precious Gems. For those imprints, query with SASE or submit proposal package including 3 sample chapter(s), synopsis.

KENT STATE UNIVERSITY PRESS, P.O. Box 5190, Kent OH 44242-0001. (330)672-7913. Fax: (330)672-3104. **Acquisitions:** Joanna H. Craig, editor-in-chief. Estab. 1965. Publishes hardcover and paperback originals and some reprints. **Publishes 30-35 titles/year. Nonauthor subsidy publishes 20% of books. Standard minimum book contract on net sales.** Responds in 3 months to queries. Book catalog free.

O→ Kent State publishes primarily scholarly works and titles of regional interest. Currently emphasizing US history, literary criticism. De-emphasizing European history.

Nonfiction: Biography, scholarly. Subjects include anthropology/archeology, art/architecture, general nonfiction, history, language/literature, regional, true crime, literary criticism, material culture, textile/fashion studies. Especially interested in "scholarly works in history and literary studies of high quality, any titles of regional interest for Ohio, scholarly biographies, the arts, and general nonfiction. Always write a letter of inquiry before submitting manuscripts. We can publish only a limited number of titles each year and can frequently tell in advance whether or not we would be interested in a particular manuscript. This practice saves both our time and that of the author, not to mention postage costs. If interested we will ask for complete manuscript. Decisions based on inhouse readings and two by outside scholars in the field of study." Enclose return postage.

MICHAEL KESEND PUBLISHING, LTD., 1025 Fifth Ave., New York NY 10028. (212)249-5150. Publisher: Michael Kesend. **Acquisitions:** Judy Wilder, editor. Estab. 1979. Publishes hardcover and trade paperback originals and reprints. **Publishes 4-6 titles/year. Receives 300 submissions/year. 20% of books from first-time authors; 40% from unagented writers. Pays 6% royalty on wholesale price. Offers varying advance.** Publishes book 18 months after acceptance of ms. Responds in 2 months to queries. Ms guidelines for #10 SASE.

O→ Michael Kesend publishes guidebooks and other nonfiction titles for sale in bookstore chains and independents, in museum stores, parks or similar outlets. Currently emphasizing travel guidebooks. De-emphasizing health/animals/hobbies.

Nonfiction: Biography, how-to, self-help. Subjects include animals, art/architecture, gardening, health/medicine, history, hobbies, nature/environment, sports, travel (regional and national guides). Needs sports and environmental awareness guides. No photography mss. Submit outline, sample chapter(s). Reviews artwork/photos as part of ms package.

Recent Title(s): *West Coast Garden Walks*, by Alice Joyce.

Tips: "Looking for national guides, outdoor travel guides, sports nonfiction, art or garden-related guides and/or others suitable for museum stores, natural history and national or state park outlets."

DENIS KITCHEN PUBLISHING, P.O. Box 9514, North Amherst MA 01059-9514. (413)259-1627. Fax: (413)259-1812. E-mail: publishing@deniskitchen.com. Website: www.deniskitchen.com. **Acquisitions:** Denis Kitchen, publisher (graphic novels, classic comic strips, postcard books, graphics, pop culture, alternative culture). Publishes hardcover and trade paperback originals and reprints. **Publishes 4 titles/year. 15% of books from first-time authors; 50% from unagented writers. Pays 6-10% royalty on retail price. Occasionally makes deals based on percentage of wholesale if idea and/or bulk of work is done in-house. Offers $1-5,000 advance.** Publishes book 9 months after acceptance of ms. Accepts simultaneous submissions. Responds in 1 month to queries; 1 month to proposals; 1 month to mss. Book catalog and ms guidelines on website.

Nonfiction: Coffee table book, humor, illustrated book, graphic novels. Subjects include art, comic art, pop culture, alternative culture, graphic novels. Query with SASE or submit proposal package including outline, illustrative matter or submit complete ms. Reviews artwork/photos as part of ms package. Send photocopies or transparencies.

Fiction: Adventure, comic books, erotica, historical, horror, humor, literary, mystery, occult, picture books, science fiction. "We do not want pure fiction. We seek cartoonists or writer/illustrator teams who can tell compelling stories with a combination of words and pictures." No pure fiction. Query with SASE or submit sample illustrations/comic pages or submit complete ms.

Recent Title(s): *The Unsyndicated Kurtzman*, by Harvey Kurtzman; *The Grasshopper and the Ant*, by Harvey Kurtzman; *Mr. Natural Postcard Book*, by R. Crumb.

Tips: "Readers who embrace the graphic novel revolution, who appreciate historical comic strips and books, and those who follow popular and alternative culture. Readers who supported Kitchen Sink Press for three decades will find that Denis Kitchen Publishing continues the tradition and precedents established by KSP. We like to discover new talent. The artist who has a day job but a great idea is encouraged to contact us. The pop culture historial who has a new take on an important figure is likewise encouraged. We have few preconceived notions about manuscripts or ideas though we are decidedly selective. Historically we have published many first-time authors and artists, some of whom developed into award-winning creators with substantial followings. Artists or illustrators who do not have confidence in their writing should send us self-promotional postcards (our favorite way of spotting new talent)."

B. KLEIN PUBLICATIONS, P.O. Box 6578, Delray Beach FL 33482. (561)496-3316. Fax: (561)496-5546. **Acquisitions:** Bernard Klein, editor-in-chief. Estab. 1946. Publishes hardcover and paperback originals. **Publishes 5 titles/year. Pays 10% royalty on wholesale price.** Accepts simultaneous submissions. Responds in 2 months to queries. Book catalog for #10 SASE.

O→ B. Klein Publications specializes in directories, annuals, who's who books, bibliography, business opportunity, reference books. Markets books by direct mail and mail order.

Nonfiction: How-to, reference, self-help, directories; bibliographies. Subjects include business/economics, hobbies. Query with SASE or submit outline, sample chapter(s).

Recent Title(s): *Guide to American Directories*, by Bernard Klein.

ALFRED A. KNOPF, INC., Knopf Publishing Group, Random House, Inc., 299 Park Ave., New York NY 10171. (212)751-2600. Website: www.aaknopf.com. **Acquisitions:** Senior Editor. Estab. 1915. Publishes hardcover and paperback originals.. **Publishes 200 titles/year. 15% of books from first-time authors; 30% from unagented writers. Royalty and advance vary.** Publishes book 1 year after acceptance of ms. Accepts simultaneous submissions. Responds in 3 months to queries. Book catalog for 7½×10 ½ SAE with 5 first-class stamps.

O→ Knopf is a general publisher of quality nonfiction and fiction.

Nonfiction: Scholarly, Book-length nonfiction, including books of scholarly merit. Subjects include general nonfiction, general scholarly nonfiction. "A good nonfiction writer should be able to follow the latest scholarship in any field of human knowledge, and fill in the abstractions of scholarship for the benefit of the general reader by means of good, concrete, sensory reporting." **Preferred length: 50,000-150,000 words**. Query with SASE. Reviews artwork/photos as part of ms package.

Fiction: Publishes book-length fiction of literary merit by known or unknown writers. **Length: 40,000-150,000 words.** Query with SASE or submit sample chapter(s).

Recent Title(s): *The Emperor of Ocean Park*, by Stephen Carter (first novel); *Master of the Senate*, by Robert A. Caro; *Balzac and the Little Chinese Seamstress*, by Dai Sijie.

KOENISHA PUBLICATIONS, 3196 53rd St., Hamilton MI 49419-9626. (616)751-4100. Fax: (616)751-4100. E-mail: koenisha@macatawa.org. Website: www.koenisha.com. **Acquisitions:** Sharolett Koenig, publisher; Flavia Crowner, acquisition editor. Publishes trade paperback originals. **Publishes 6-10 titles/year. Receives 50 queries and 50 mss/year. 95% of books from first-time authors; 100% from unagented writers. Pays 15-25% royalty on net receipts.** Publishes book 1 year after acceptance of ms. Accepts simultaneous submissions. Responds in 1 month to queries; 2 months to proposals; 2 months to mss. Book catalog and ms guidelines free or on website.

Nonfiction: Autobiography, children's/juvenile, cookbook, how-to. Subjects include gardening, hobbies, memoirs, nature/environment. Query with SASE or submit complete ms. Reviews artwork/photos as part of ms package. Send photocopies.

Fiction: Humor, mainstream/contemporary, mystery, romance, suspense, young adult. "We do not accept manuscripts that contain unnecessary foul language, explicit sex or gratuitous violence." Query with SASE or submit proposal package including 3 sample chapter(s), synopsis.

Poetry: Submit 3 sample poems.

Recent Title(s): *My Life in Bits 'N' Pieces*, by Gene Key (autobiography); *The Iscariot Conspiracy*, by Al Blanchard (mystery); *His Spirit Within Me*, by Fannie Hawkins (inspirational poetry).

Tips: "We're NOT interested in books written to suit a particular line or house or because it's trendy. Instead write a book from your heart—the inspiration or idea that kept you going through the writing process."

N H.J. KRAMER, INC., New World Library, P.O. Box 1082, Tiburon CA 94920. (415)435-5367. Fax: (415)435-5364. E-mail: hjkramer@jps.net. **Acquisitions:** Jan Phillips, managing editor. Estab. 1984. Publishes hardcover and trade paperback originals. **Publishes 5 titles/year. Receives 1,000 queries and 500 mss/year. 20% of books from first-time authors. Advance varies.** Publishes book 18 months after acceptance of ms. Book catalog free.
Imprints: Starseed Press Children's Books.

"The books we publish are our contribution to an emerging world based on cooperation rather than on competition, on affirmation rather than on self-doubt, and on the certainty that all humanity is connected. Our goal is to touch as many lives as possible with a message of hope for a better world."

Nonfiction: Children's/juvenile, illustrated book, Spiritual themes. Subjects include health/medicine (holistic), spirituality, metaphysical.
Fiction: Juvenile. Prospective authors please note: Kramer's list is selective and is normally fully slated several seasons in advance. Submissions closed.
Recent Title(s): *Getting Real*, by Susan Campbell, Ph.D. (nonfiction); *Bless Your Heart*, by Holly Bea, illustrated by Kim Howard (fiction).
Tips: "Our books are for people who are interested in personal growth and consciousness-raising. We are not interested in personal stories unless it has universal appeal."

KRAUSE PUBLICATIONS, 700 E. State, Iola WI 54990. (715)445-2214. Website: www.krause.com. **Acquisitions:** Acquisitions Editor. Publishes hardcover and trade paperback originals. **Publishes 170 titles/year. Receives 400 queries and 40 mss/year. 10% of books from first-time authors; 90% from unagented writers. Pays 9-12% royalty on net or makes outright purchase of $2,000-10,000. Offers $1,500-4,000 advance.** Publishes book 6 months after acceptance of ms. Does not accept simultaneous submissions. Responds in 2 months to proposals; 2 months to mss. Book catalog for free or on website; ms guidelines free.

"We are the world's largest hobby and collectibles publisher."

Nonfiction: How-to, illustrated book, reference, technical, Price Guides. Subjects include hobbies (antiques, collectibles, toys), sports (outdoors, hunting, fishing), coins, stamps, firearms, knives, records, sewing, ceramics. Submit proposal package, including outline, 1-3 sample chapters and letter explaining your project's unique contributions. Reviews artwork/photos as part of ms package. Send sample photos.
Recent Title(s): *Encyclopedia of Pepsi-Cola Collectibles*, by Bob Stoddard (reference/price guide); *The Basic Guide to Dyeing and Painting Fabric*, by Cindy Walter and Jennifer Priestly (how-to); *Tying Trout Flies*, by C. Boyd Pfeiffer (how-to/reference).
Tips: Audience consists of serious hobbyists. "Your work should provide a unique contribution to the special interest."

KREGEL PUBLICATIONS, Kregel, Inc., P.O. Box 2607, Grand Rapids MI 49501. (616)451-4775. Fax: (616)451-9330. E-mail: kregelbooks@kregel.com. Website: www.kregel.com. **Acquisitions:** Dennis R. Hillman, publisher. Estab. 1949. Publishes hardcover and trade paperback originals and reprints. **Publishes 90 titles/year. Receives 400 queries and 100 mss/year. 10% of books from first-time authors; 90% from unagented writers. Pays 8-16% royalty on wholesale price. Offers $200-2,000 advance.** Publishes book 14 months after acceptance of ms. Accepts simultaneous submissions. Responds in 3 months to queries. Book catalog free; ms guidelines for #10 SASE or by e-mail.
Imprints: Editorial Portavoz

"Our mission as an evangelical Christian publisher is to provide—with integrity and excellence—trusted, biblically-based resources that challenge and encourage individuals in their Christian lives. Works in theology and biblical studies should reflect the historic, orthodox Protestant tradition."

Nonfiction: "We serve evangelical Christian readers and those in career Christian service." Biography (Christian), gift book, reference. Subjects include religion, spirituality. Query with SASE.
Fiction: Religious. Fiction should be geared toward the evangelical Christian market. Query with SASE.
Recent Title(s): *Eusebius: The Church History*, by Paul L. Maier (church history); *Joy to the World*, by Ken Osbeck (inspirational); *Lethal Harvest*, by William Cutrer (mystery).
Tips: "Our audience consists of conservative, evangelical Christians, including pastors and ministry students. Think through very clearly the intended audience for the work."

KRIEGER PUBLISHING CO., P.O. Box 9542, Melbourne FL 32902-9542. (321)724-9542. Fax: (321)951-3671. E-mail: info@krieger-publishing.com. Website: www.krieger-publishing.com. **Acquisitions:** Elaine Harland, manager/editor (natural history/sciences and veterinary medicine); Sharan Merriam, series editor (adult education); Donald M. Waltz, series editor (space sciences); David E. Kyvig, series director (local history); Hans Trefousse, series editor (history); James B. Gardner, series editor (public history). Estab. 1969. Publishes hardcover and paperback originals and reprints. **Publishes 30 titles/year. Receives 100 submissions/year. 30% of books from first-time authors; 100% from unagented writers. Pays royalty on net price.** Publishes book 18 months after acceptance of ms. Responds in 3 months to queries. Book catalog free.
Imprints: Anvil Series, Orbit Series, Public History.

"We are a short-run niche publisher providing accurate and well-documented scientific and technical titles for text and reference use, college level and higher."

Nonfiction: Reference, technical, textbook, scholarly. Subjects include agriculture/horticulture, animals, education (adult), history, nature/environment, science (space), herpetology, chemistry, physics, engineering, veterinary medicine, natural history, math. Query with SASE. Reviews artwork/photos as part of ms package.
Recent Title(s): *Amphibian Medicine & Captive Husbandry*, edited by Kevin R. Wright and Brent R. Whitaker; *A History of Christian Education: Protestant, Catholic, and Orthodox Perspectives*, by John L. Elias.

LADYBUGPRESS, 751 Laurel St. #223, San Carlos CA 94070. E-mail: ladybug@ladybugbooks.com. Website: www.ladybugbooks.com. **Acquisitions:** Publisher. Publishes trade paperback originals. **Publishes 3-4 titles/year. Receives 150 queries and 45 mss/year. 90% of books from first-time authors; 100% from unagented writers. Pays up to 15% royalty on wholesale price.** Publishes book 1 year after acceptance of ms. Accepts simultaneous submissions. Responds in 2 months to queries; 4 months to mss. Book catalog and ms guidelines online.

O━ LadybugPress publishes books focused on women's interests, books to feed the soul and fire the imagination. Currently emphasizing new technologies in book production: audio, CDs, e-books, and multimedia.

Nonfiction: Subjects include anthropology/archeology, art/architecture, business/economics, child guidance/parenting, computers/electronic, creative nonfiction, gay/lesbian, multicultural, sociology, sports, women's issues/studies. Query with SASE and e-mail address. Reviews artwork/photos as part of ms package. Send photocopies.
Fiction: Varied topics. In audio format and multimedia CD only. Query with SASE and e-mail address.
Poetry: Audio format and multimedia CD only. Query.
Recent Title(s): *Women and Disabilities: It Isn't Them and Us*, by Mona Hughes (nonfiction); *Women on a Wire, electonic edition*, edited by Georgia Jones (poetry).
Tips: "All our books include a nonprofit donation. Our focus is women but we do not discriminate against male authors. We are looking for fresh perspectives and are not afraid of taking chances. Don't send us your 'everyone said I should write a book' manuscript. We are looking for people who have something to say."

LAKE CLAREMONT PRESS, 4650 N. Rockwell St., Chicago IL 60625. (773)583-7800. Fax: (773)583-7877. E-mail: sharon@lakeclaremont.com. Website: www.lakeclaremont.com. **Acquisitions:** Sharon Woodhouse, publisher. Publishes trade paperback originals. **Publishes 5-7 titles/year. Receives 150 queries and 35 mss/year. 50% of books from first-time authors; 100% from unagented writers. Pays 10-15% royalty on wholesale price. Offers $250-2,000 advance.** Publishes book 8 months after acceptance of ms. Accepts simultaneous submissions. Responds in 1 month to queries; 2 months to proposals; 1 month to mss. Book catalog online.

O━ "We currently specialize in books on the Chicago area and its history, and would consider regional titles for other areas, especially those in the Midwest. We also like nonfiction books on ghosts, graveyards and folklore."

Nonfiction: Subjects include Americana, ethnic, history, nature/environment (regional), regional, travel, women's issues/studies, film/cinema/stage (regional), urban studies. Query with SASE or submit proposal package, including outline and 2 sample chapters, or submit complete ms (e-mail queries and proposals preferred).
Recent Title(s): *The Chicago River: A Natural and Unnatural History*, by Libby Hill; *Haunted Michigan: Recent Encounters with Active Spirits*, by Rev. Gerald S. Hunter.
Tips: "Please include a market analysis in proposals (who would buy this book & where?) and an analysis of similar books available for different regions. Please know what else is out there."

LANGENSCHEIDT PUBLISHING GROUP, 46-35 54th Rd., Maspeth NY 11378. (800)432-MAPS. Fax: (718)784-0640. E-mail: spohja@langenscheidt.com. **Acquisitions:** Sue Pohja, acquisitions; Christine Cardone, editor. Estab. 1983. Publishes hardcover and trade paperback originals. **Publishes 350 titles/year. Receives 125 queries and 50 mss/year. 100% from unagented writers. Pays royalty or makes outright purchase.** Publishes book 6 months after acceptance of ms. Accepts simultaneous submissions. Responds in 1 month to proposals. Book catalog free.
Imprints: ADC Map, American Map, Arrow Map, Creative Sales, Hagstrom Map, Hammond Map, Insight Guides, Hammond World Atlas Corp., Trakker Map, Langenscheidt Trade

O━ Langenscheidt Publishing Group publishes maps, travel guides, foreign language reference and dictionary titles, world atlases and educational materials.

Nonfiction: Reference. Subjects include education, travel, foreign language. "Any potential title that fills a gap in our line is welcome." Submit outline and 2 sample chapters (complete ms preferred).
Recent Title(s): *European Phrasebook*; *Insight Guide to Museums of London*; *Pocket Chinese Dictionary*.
Tips: "Any item related to our map, foreign language dictionary, atlas and travel lines could have potential for us. Of particular interest are titles that have a sizeable potential customer base and have little in the way of good competition."

LANGMARC PUBLISHING, P.O. Box 90488, Austin TX 78709-0488. (512)394-0989. Fax: (512)394-0829. E-mail: langmarc@booksails.com. Website: www.langmarc.com. **Acquisitions:** Lois Qualben, president (inspirational). Publishes trade paperback originals. **Publishes 3-5 titles/year; imprint publishes 1 titles/year. Receives 150 queries and 80 mss/year. 60% of books from first-time authors; 100% from unagented writers. Pays 10-13% royalty on wholesale price.** Publishes book 18 months after acceptance of ms. Accepts simultaneous submissions. Responds in 3 months to queries. Book catalog free; ms guidelines for #10 SASE.
Imprints: North Sea Press, Harbor Lights Series
Nonfiction: Self-help, inspirational; young adult. Subjects include child guidance/parenting, education, health/medicine, nature/environment. "Langmarc has contracted through mid-2002 so acceptance of new mss is unlikely." Query with SASE. Reviews artwork/photos as part of ms package. Send photocopies.
Fiction: Spiritual, inspirational. Query with SASE.

Recent Title(s): *Who's Listening Anyway?*, by Dr. John Lovitt (nonfiction/educational); *On Wings & Prayers*, Dr. Terri Wood Jerkins (novel).

LARK, Sterling Publishing, 67 Broadway, Asheville NC 28801. (828)253-0467. Fax: (828)253-7952. Website: www.larkbooks.com. Director of Publishing: Carol Taylor. **Acquisitions:** Nicole Tuggle, submissions coordinator. Estab. 1976. Publishes hardcover and trade paperback originals and reprints. **Publishes 50 titles/year. Receives 300 queries and 100 mss/year. 80% of books from first-time authors; 90% from unagented writers. Offers up to $4,000 advance.** Publishes book 1 year after acceptance of ms. Accepts simultaneous submissions. Responds in 3 months to queries.

Lark Books publishes high quality, highly illustrated books, primarily in the crafts/leisure markets celebrating the creative spirit. We work closely with bookclubs. Our books are either how-to, 'gallery' or combination books."

Nonfiction: Children's/juvenile, coffee table book, cookbook, how-to, illustrated book. Subjects include gardening, hobbies, nature/environment, crafts, occasionally cooking. Query first. If asked, submit outline and 1 sample chapter, sample projects, table of contents, visuals. Reviews artwork/photos as part of ms package. Send transparencies.
Recent Title(s): *Gorgeous Leather Crafts*.
Tips: "We publish both first-time and seasoned authors. In either case, we need to know that you have substantial expertise on the topic of the proposed book—that we can trust you to know what you're talking about. If you're great at your craft but not so great as a writer, you might want to work with us as a coauthor or as a creative consultant."

LARSON PUBLICATIONS/PBPF, 4936 Rt. 414, Burdett NY 14818-9729. (607)546-9342. Fax: (607)546-9344. E-mail: larson@lightlink.com. Website: www.larsonpublications.org. **Acquisitions:** Paul Cash, director. Estab. 1982. Publishes hardcover and trade paperback originals. **Publishes 4-5 titles/year. Receives 1,000 submissions/year. 5% of books from first-time authors. Pays variable royalty. Seldom offers advance.** Publishes book 1 year after acceptance of ms. Accepts simultaneous submissions. Responds in 4 months to queries. Visit website for book catalog.
Nonfiction: Subjects include philosophy, psychology, religion, spirituality. Query with SASE and outline.
Recent Title(s): *The Art of Napping at Work*, by William and Camille Anthony.
Tips: "We look for studies of comparative spiritual philosophy or personal fruits of independent (transsectarian viewpoint) spiritual research/practice."

LAWYERS & JUDGES PUBLISHING CO., P.O. Box 30040, Tucson AZ 85751-0040. (520)323-1500. Fax: (520)323-0055. E-mail: sales@lawyersandjudges.com. Website: www.lawyersandjudges.com. **Acquisitions:** Steve Weintraub, president. Estab. 1963. Publishes professional hardcover originals. **Publishes 15 titles/year. Receives 200 queries and 30 mss/year. 5% of books from first-time authors; 100% from unagented writers. Pays 7-10% royalty on retail price.** Publishes book 5 months after acceptance of ms. Accepts simultaneous submissions. Responds in 2 months to queries. Book catalog free.

Lawyers & Judges is a highly specific publishing company, reaching the legal and insurance fields and accident reconstruction.

Nonfiction: Reference. Subjects include law, insurance. "Unless a writer is an expert in the legal/insurance areas, we are not interested." Submit proposal package including outline, sample chapter(s).
Recent Title(s): *Human Factors in Traffic Safety*.

LEARNING PUBLICATIONS, INC., 5351 Gulf Dr., Holmes Beach FL 34217. (941)778-6651. Fax: (941)778-6818. E-mail: info@learningpublications.com. Website: www.learningpublications.com. **Acquisitions:** Ruth Erickson, editor. Estab. 1975. Publishes trade paperback originals and reprints. **Publishes 10-15 titles/year. Receives 150 queries and 50 mss/year. 50% of books from first-time authors; 100% from unagented writers. Pays 5-10% royalty.** Publishes book 1 year after acceptance of ms. Accepts simultaneous submissions. Responds in 1 month to queries; 1 month to proposals; 4 months to mss. Book catalog and ms guidelines online.

"We specifically market by direct mail to education and human service professionals materials to use with students and clients."

Nonfiction: Reference, textbook. Subjects include education, humanities, psychology, sociology, women's issues/studies. "Writers interested in submitting mss should request our guidelines first." Query with SASE or submit proposal package including outline, 1 sample chapter(s), résumé. Reviews artwork/photos as part of ms package. Send photocopies.
Tips: "Learning Publications has a limited, specific market. Writers should be familiar with who buys our books."

LEE & LOW BOOKS, 95 Madison Ave., New York NY 10016. (212)779-4400. Fax: (212)683-1894. Website: www.leeandlow.com. **Acquisitions:** Louise May, executive editor. Estab. 1991. **Publishes 12-16 titles/year. Offers advance.** Does not accept simultaneous submissions. Responds in 5 months to queries; 5 months to mss. Ms guidelines online.

"Our goals are to meet a growing need for books that address children of color, and to present literature that all children can identify with. We only consider multicultural children's picture books." Currently emphasizing material for 2-10 year olds. Sponsors a yearly New Voices Award for first-time picture book authors of color. Contest rules online at website or for SASE.

Nonfiction: Children's/juvenile, illustrated book. Subjects include ethnic, multicultural.
Fiction: Ethnic, juvenile, multicultural, illustrated.
Recent Title(s): *Rent Party Jazz*, by William Miller; *Love to Langston*, by Tony Medina.

Tips: "Of special interest are stories set in contemporary America. We are interested in fiction as well as nonfiction. We do not consider folktales, fairy tales or animal stories."

J & L LEE CO., P.O. Box 5575, Lincoln NE 68505. **Acquisitions:** Jim McKee, acquisitions editor. Publishes trade paperback originals and reprints. **Publishes 5 titles/year. Receives 25 queries and 5-10 mss/year. 20% of books from first-time authors; 60% from unagented writers. Pays 10% royalty on retail price or makes outright purchase. Offers advance.** Publishes book 18 months after acceptance of ms. Accepts simultaneous submissions. Responds in 6 months to queries; 1 month to proposals; 6 months to mss. Book catalog free.

Imprints: Salt Creek Press, Young Hearts.

O→ "Virtually everything we publish is of a Great Plains nature."

Nonfiction: Biography, reference. Subjects include Americana, history, regional. Query with SASE.

Recent Title(s): *The Good Old Days*, by Van Duling; *Bipartisan Efforts and Other Mutations*, by Paul Fell.

Tips: "We do not publish poetry."

LEGACY PRESS, Rainbow Publishers, P.O. Box 261129, San Diego CA 92196. (858)271-7600. **Acquisitions:** Christy Scannell, editor. Estab. 1997. **Publishes 20 titles/year. Receives 250 queries and 100 mss/year. 50% of books from first-time authors. Pays flat fee or royalty based on wholesale price. Offers negotiable advance.** Publishes book 1-3 years after acceptance of ms. Accepts simultaneous submissions. Book catalog for 9×12 SAE with 2 first-class stamps; ms guidelines for #10 SASE.

O→ "Legacy Press strives to publish Bible-based materials that inspire Christian spiritual growth and development in children." Currently emphasizing nonfiction for kids, particularly pre-teens and more specifically girls, although we are publishing boys and girls 2-12. No picture books, fiction without additional activities, poetry or plays.

Nonfiction: Subjects include creative nonfiction, education, hobbies, religion. Query with SASE or submit outline, 3-5 sample chapter(s), market analysis.

Recent Title(s): *The Official Christian Babysitting Guide*, by Rebecca P. Totilo; *The Ponytails*, by Bonnie Compton Hanson (5-book series).

Tips: "We are looking for Christian versions of general market nonfiction for kids, as well as original ideas."

LEGEND BOOKS, 69 Lansing St., Auburn NY 13021. (315)258-8012. **Acquisitions:** Joseph P. Berry, editor. Publishes paperback monographs, scholarly books and college textbooks. **Publishes 15 titles/year. Receives 100 queries and 60 mss/year. 50% of books from first-time authors; 100% from unagented writers. Pays 20% royalty on net sales.** Publishes book 9 months after acceptance of ms. Accepts simultaneous submissions. Responds in 2 months to queries; 2 months to proposals; 2 months to mss.

O→ Legend Books publishes a variety of books used in the college classroom, including workbooks. However, it does not publish any books on mathematics or hard sciences.

Nonfiction: Biography, scholarly, textbook, community/public affairs, speech/mass communication. Subjects include business/economics, child guidance/parenting, community, education, government/politics, health/medicine, history, humanities, philosophy, psychology, recreation, social sciences, sociology, sports, journalism, public relations, television. Query with SASE or submit complete ms (include SASE if ms is to be returned). Reviews artwork/photos as part of ms package. Send photocopies.

Recent Title(s): *The Conversion of the King of Bissau*, by Timothy Coates, Ph.D. (world history); *Community, Sport & Leisure (2nd ed.)*, by Tim Delaney, Ph.D. (sociology).

Tips: "We seek college professors who actually teach courses for which their books are designed."

LEHIGH UNIVERSITY PRESS, Linderman Library, 30 Library Dr., Lehigh University, Bethlehem PA 18015-3067. (610)758-3933. Fax: (610)758-6331. E-mail: inlup@lehigh.edu. **Acquisitions:** Philip A. Metzger, director. Estab. 1985. Publishes hardcover originals. **Publishes 10 titles/year. Receives 90-100 queries and 50-60 mss/year. 70% of books from first-time authors; 100% from unagented writers. Pays royalty.** Publishes book 18 months after acceptance of ms. Accepts simultaneous submissions. Responds in 3 months to queries. Book catalog and ms guidelines free.

O→ "Currently emphasizing works on 18th-century studies, East-Asian studies and literary criticism. Accepts all subjects of academic merit."

Nonfiction: Lehigh University Press is a conduit for nonfiction works of scholarly interest to the academic community. Biography, reference, scholarly, scholarly. Subjects include Americana, art/architecture, history, language/literature, science. Submit proposal package including 1 sample chapter(s).

Recent Title(s): *The Terror of Our Days: Four American Poets Respond to the Holocaust*, by Harriet L. Parmet; *One Woman Determined to Make a Difference: The Life of Madeleine Zabruskie Doty*, by Alice Duffy Rinehart.

LEISURE BOOKS, Dorchester Publishing Co., 276 Fifth Ave., Suite 1008, New York NY 10001-0112. (212)725-8811. Fax: (212)532-1054. E-mail: dorchedit@dorchesterpub.com. Website: www.dorchesterpub.com. **Acquisitions:** Ashley Kuehl, editorial assistant; Kate Seaver, associate editor; Alicia Condon, editorial director; Don D'Auria, senior editor (westerns, technothrillers, horror); Christopher Keeslar, editor. Estab. 1970. Publishes mass market paperback originals and reprints. **Publishes 160 titles/year. Receives thousands submissions/year. 20% of books from first-time authors; 20% from unagented writers. Pays royalty on retail price. Offers negotiable advance.** Publishes book 18 months after acceptance of ms. Does not accept simultaneous submissions. Responds in 6 months to queries. Book catalog for free (800)481-9191; ms guidelines for #10 SASE or on website.

Imprints: Love Spell (romance), Leisure (romance, western, techno, horror).

O→ Leisure Books is seeking historical and time travel romances.

Fiction: Historical, horror, romance, western, technothrillers. "We are strongly backing historical romance. All historical romance should be set pre-1900. Horrors and westerns are growing as well. No sweet romance, science fiction, erotica, contemporary women's fiction, mainstream or action/adventure." Query with SASE or submit outline, first 3 sample chapter(s), synopsis.

Recent Title(s): *Dark Guardian*, by Christine Feehan (romance).

LERNER PUBLISHING GROUP, 241 First Ave. N., Minneapolis MN 55401. (612)332-3344. Fax: (612)332-7615. Website: www.lernerbooks.com. **Acquisitions:** Jennifer Zimian. Estab. 1959. Publishes hardcover originals, trade paperback originals and reprints. **Publishes 200 titles/year. Receives 1,000 queries and 300 mss/year. 20% of books from first-time authors; 95% from unagented writers. Offers varied advance.** Accepts simultaneous submissions. Book catalog for 9×12 SAE with $3.50 postage; ms guidelines for #10 SASE.

Imprints: Carolrhoda Books; First Avenue Editions (paperback reprints for hard/soft deals only); Lerner Publications; LernerSports; LernerClassroom.

O→ "Our goal is to publish children's books that educate, stimulate and stretch the imagination, foster global awareness, encourage critical thinking and inform, inspire and entertain."

Nonfiction: Biography, children's/juvenile. Subjects include art/architecture, ethnic, history, nature/environment, science, sports. Query with SASE or submit outline, 1-2 sample chapter(s).

Recent Title(s): *Your Travel Guide to Ancient Greece*, by Nancy Day; *Alice Walker*, by Caroline Lazo.

Tips: "No alphabet, puzzle, song or text books, religious subject matter or plays. Submissions are accepted in the months of March and October only. Work received in any other month will be returned unopened. SASE required for authors who wish to have their material returned. Please allow 2-6 months for a response. No phone calls."

ARTHUR LEVINE BOOKS, Scholastic Inc., 555 Broadway, New York NY 10012. (212)343-4436. **Acquisitions:** Arthur Levine, editorial director. **Publishes 10-14 titles/year. Pays royalty on retail price. Offers variable advance.** Book catalog for 9×12 SASE.

Fiction: Juvenile, picture books, young adult. Query with SASE.

Recent Title(s): *The Hickory Chair*, by Lisa Rowe Fraustino; *The Giggler Treatment*, by Roddy Doyle; *Fighting Ruben Wolfe*, by Markus Zusak.

LIBRARIES UNLIMITED, INC., Greenwood Publishing Group, 7730 E. Belleview Ave., Suite A200, Greenwood Village CO 80111. (303)770-1220. Fax: (303)220-8843. E-mail: lu-editorial@lu.com. Website: www.lu.com. **Acquisitions:** Martin Dillon, director of acquisitions; Barbara Ittner, acquisitions editor (public library titles); Sharon Coatney (school library titles); Suzanne Barchers (teacher resources); Edward Kurdyla, general manager (academic/reference titles). Estab. 1964. Publishes hardcover originals. **Publishes 75 titles/year. Receives 400 queries and 100 mss/year. 50% of books from first-time authors; 100% from unagented writers. Pays 8-15% royalty on wholesale price.** Publishes book 1 year after acceptance of ms. Accepts simultaneous submissions. Responds in 1 month to queries; 2 months to proposals; 2 months to mss. Book catalog and ms guidelines available via website or with SASE.

Imprints: Teacher Ideas Press.

O→ Libraries Unlimited publishes resources for libraries, librarians and educators. "We are currently emphasizing readers' advisory guides, academic reference works, readers' theatre, storytelling, biographical dictionary, and de-emphasizing teacher books."

Nonfiction: Biography (collections), reference, textbook. Subjects include agriculture/horticulture, anthropology/archeology, art/architecture, business/economics, education, ethnic, health/medicine, history, language/literature, music/dance, philosophy, psychology, religion, science, sociology, women's issues/studies. "We are interested in library applications and tools for all subject areas." Submit proposal package including outline, 1 sample chapter(s), résumé. Reviews artwork/photos as part of ms package. Send photocopies.

Recent Title(s): *Women in U.S. History*, by Lyda Mary Hardy; *The Eagle on the Cactus: Traditional Stories from Mexico*, by Angel Vigil.

Tips: "We welcome any ideas that combine professional expertise, writing ability, and innovative thinking. Audience is librarians (school, public, academic and special) and teachers (K-12)."

LIGUORI PUBLICATIONS, One Liguori Dr., Liguori MO 63057. (636)464-2500. Fax: (636)464-8449. E-mail: jbauer@liguori.org. Website: www.liguori.org. Publisher: Harry Grile. **Acquisitions:** Judith A. Bauer, managing editor (Trade Group); Lisa Miller, managing editor (Pastorlink, electronic publishing). Estab. 1947. Publishes paperback originals and reprints under the Ligouri and Libros Ligouri imprints. **Publishes 30 titles/year. Pays royalty or makes outright purchase. Offers varied advance.** Publishes book 2 years after acceptance of ms. Does not accept simultaneous submissions. Responds in 2 months to queries; 2 months to proposals; 3 months to mss. Ms guidelines online.

Imprints: Faithwarerg, Libros Liguori, Liguori Books, Liguori/Triumph.

O→ Liguori Publications, faithful to the charism of Saint Alphonsus, is an apostolate within the mission of the Denver Province. Its mission, a collaborative effort of Redemptorists and laity, is to spread the gospel of Jesus Christ primarily through the print and electronic media. It shares in the Redemptorist priority of giving special attention to the poor and the most abandoned. Currently emphasizing practical spirituality, prayers and devotions, "how-to" spirituality.

Nonfiction: Manuscripts with Catholic sensibility. Self-help. Subjects include computers/electronic, religion, spirituality. Mostly adult audience; limited children/juvenile. Query with SASE or submit outline, 1 sample chapter(s).

Recent Title(s): *Francis: A Saint's Way*, by James Cowan.

LIMELIGHT EDITIONS, Proscenium Publishers, Inc., 118 E. 30th St., New York NY 10016. Fax: (212)532-5526. E-mail: limelighteditions@earthlink.net. Website: www.limelighteditions.com. **Acquisitions:** Melvyn B. Zerman, president; Roxanna Font, associate publisher. Estab. 1983. Publishes hardcover and trade paperback originals, trade paperback reprints. **Publishes 14 titles/year. Receives 150 queries and 40 mss/year. 15% of books from first-time authors; 20% from unagented writers. Pays 7½-10% royalty on retail price. Offers $500-2,000 advance.** Publishes book 10 months after acceptance of ms. Does not accept simultaneous submissions. Responds in 1 month to queries; 1 month to proposals; 3 months to mss. Book catalog and ms guidelines free.

O→ Limelight Editions publishes books on film, theater, music and dance history. "Our books make a strong contribution to their fields and deserve to remain in print for many years."

Nonfiction: "All books are on the performing arts *exclusively*." Biography, how-to (instructional), humor, illustrated book. Subjects include film/cinema/stage, history, multicultural, music/dance. Query with SASE or submit proposal package including outline, 2-3 sample chapter(s). Reviews artwork/photos as part of ms package. Send photocopies.
Recent Title(s): *You Can't Do That on Broadway!*, by Philip Rose; *Robert Mitchum: In His Own Words*, by Jerry Roberts.

LITTLE SIMON, Simon & Schuster Children's Publishing Division, Simon & Schuster, 1230 Avenue of the Americas, New York NY 10020. (212)698-1295. Fax: (212)698-2794. Website: www.simonsayskids.com. Executive Vice President/Publisher: Robin Corey. **Acquisitions:** Cindy Alvarez, vice president/editorial director; Erin Molta, senior editor. Publishes novelty books only. **Publishes 65 titles/year. 5% of books from first-time authors. Offers advance and royalties.** Publishes book 2 years after acceptance of ms. Does not accept simultaneous submissions. Responds in 8 months to queries.

O→ "Our goal is to provide fresh material in an innovative format for preschool to age eight. Our books are often, if not exclusively, format driven."

Nonfiction: "We publish very few nonfiction titles." Children's/juvenile. No picture books. Query with SASE.
Fiction: "Novelty books include many things that do not fit in the traditional hardcover or paperback format, such as pop-up, board book, scratch and sniff, glow in the dark, lift the flap, etc." Children's/juvenile. No picture books. Large part of the list is holiday-themed.
Recent Title(s): *The Cheerios Play Book*, by Lee Wade; *Easter Bugs*, by David Carter; *Knock Knock! Who's There?*, by Tad Hills.

[A] **LITTLE, BROWN AND CO., CHILDREN'S BOOKS**, Time Life Building, 1271 Avenue of the Americas, New York NY 10020. (212)522-8700. Website: www.littlebrown.com. Editorial Director/Associate Publisher: Maria Modugno. Senior Editor: Cindy Eagan. Associate Editor: Amy Hsu. **Acquisitions:** Leila Little. 3 Center Plaza, Boston MA 02108. (617)227-0730. Associate Editor: Amy Itsu. Estab. 1837. Publishes hardcover originals, trade paperback reprints. **Publishes 60-70 titles/year. Pays royalty on retail price. Offers negotiable advance.** Publishes book 2 years after acceptance of ms. Accepts simultaneous submissions. Responds in 1 month to queries; 2 months to proposals; 2 months to mss.
Imprints: Megan Tingley Books (Megan Tingley, editorial director).

O→ Little, Brown and Co. publishes board books, picture books, middle grade fiction and nonfiction YA titles. "We are looking for strong writing and presentation, but no predetermined topics."

Nonfiction: Children's/juvenile. Subjects include animals, art/architecture, ethnic, gay/lesbian, history, hobbies, nature/environment, recreation, science, sports. Writers should avoid "looking for the 'issue' they think publishers want to see, choosing instead topics they know best and are most enthusiastic about/inspired by." *Agented submissions only.*
Fiction: Adventure, ethnic, fantasy, feminist, gay/lesbian, historical, humor, juvenile, mystery, picture books, science fiction, suspense, young adult. "We are looking for strong fiction for children of all ages in any area, including multicultural. We always prefer full manuscripts for fiction." *Agented submissions only.*
Recent Title(s): *City of Bones*, by Michael Connelly; *Sea Glass*, by Anita Shreve.
Tips: "Our audience is children of all ages, from preschool through young adult. We are looking for quality material that will work in hardcover—send us your best."

LITTLE, BROWN AND CO., INC., Time Warner Inc., 1271 Avenue of the Americas, New York NY 10020. (212)522-8700. Website: twbookmark.com. Publisher/Editor-in-Chief: Michael Pietsch. **Acquisitions:** Editorial Department, Trade Division. Estab. 1837. Publishes hardcover originals and paperback originals and reprints. **Publishes 100 titles/year. Pays royalty. Offers varying advance.** Does not accept simultaneous submissions.
Imprints: Back Bay Books; Bulfinch Press; Little, Brown and Co. Children's Books.

O→ "The general editorial philosophy for all divisions continues to be broad and flexible, with high quality and the promise of commercial success as always the first considerations."

Nonfiction: Autobiography, biography, cookbook. Subjects include contemporary culture, cooking/foods/nutrition, history, memoirs, nature/environment, science, sports. No unsolicited mss or proposals. Query with SASE.
Fiction: Literary, mainstream/contemporary. No unsolicited mss. Query with SASE.
Recent Title(s): *The Tipping Point*, by Malcolm Gladwell; *A Darkness More Than Night*, by Michael Connelly.

LIVINGSTON PRESS, University of West Alabama, Station 22, Livingston AL 35470. E-mail: jwt@uwa.edu. Website: www.livingstonpress.uwa.edu. **Acquisitions:** Joe Taylor, director. Estab. 1984. Publishes hardcover and trade paperback originals. **Publishes 8-10 titles/year. 50% of books from first-time authors; 99% from unagented writers.**

Pays a choice of 12% of initial run or a combination of contributor's copies and 10% royalty of net. Publishes book 18 months after acceptance of ms. Accepts simultaneous submissions. Responds in 1 month to queries; 1 year to mss.

Imprints: Swallow's Tale Press.

O→ Livingston Press publishes topics such as Southern literature and quirky fiction. Currently emphasizing short stories. De-emphasizing poetry.

Fiction: Experimental, literary, short story collections. Query with SASE.

Poetry: "We publish very little poetry, mostly books we have asked to see." Query.

Recent Title(s): *Partita In Venice*, by Curt Leviant; *Flight From Valhalla*, by Michael Bugeja (poetry); *B. Horror and Other Stories*, by Wendell Mayo.

Tips: "Our readers are interested in literature, often quirky literature that emphasizes form and style. Our reading period runs from December to January. Please visit our website for current needs."

N **LLEWELLYN ESPAÑOL**, P.O. Box 64383, St. Paul MN 55164-0383. (651)291-1970. Fax: (651)291-1908. E-mail: lwlpc@llewellyn.com. Website: www.llewellyn.com. **Acquisitions:** Maria Bloomberg, manager. Estab. 1993. Publishes mass market and trade paperback originals and reprints. **Publishes 24 titles/year. Receives 25 queries and 100 mss/year. 25% of books from first-time authors; 90% from unagented writers. Pays 10% royalty.** Publishes book 1 year after acceptance of ms. Accepts simultaneous submissions. Responds in 3 months to queries; 3 months to proposals; 1 month to mss. Book catalog online; ms guidelines for #10 SASE.

O→ Publishes books for people of any age interested in material discussing "mind, body and spirit."

Nonfiction: Gift book, how-to, self-help, teen/young adult. Subjects include general nonfiction, health/medicine, New Age, psychology, sex, spirituality, foods/nutrition; angels; magic. "Have it edited, including all ortographic punctuation and accents." Query with SASE or submit proposal package including outline, 4 sample chapter(s) or submit complete ms. Reviews artwork/photos as part of ms package. Send photocopies.

Recent Title(s): *El Poder Milagroso de los Salmos*, by Luz Stella Rozo (self-help).

LLEWELLYN PUBLICATIONS, Llewellyn Worldwide, Ltd., P.O. Box 64383, St. Paul MN 55164-0383. (651)291-1970. Fax: (651)291-1908. E-mail: lwlpc
lewellyn.com. Website: www.llewellyn.com. **Acquisitions:** Nancy J. Mostad, acquisitions manager (New Age, metaphysical, occult, self-help, how-to books); Barbara Wright, acquisitions editor (kits and decks). Estab. 1901. Publishes trade and mass market paperback originals. **Publishes 100 titles/year. Receives 2,000 submissions/year. 30% of books from first-time authors; 90% from unagented writers. Pays 10% royalty on wholesale price or retail price.** Accepts simultaneous submissions. Responds in 3 months to queries. Book catalog for 9×12 SAE with 4 first-class stamps; ms guidelines for #10 SASE.

O→ Llewellyn publishes New Age fiction and nonfiction exploring "new worlds of mind and spirit." Currently emphasizing astrology, wicca, alternative health and healing, tarot. De-emphasizing fiction, channeling.

Nonfiction: How-to, self-help. Subjects include cooking/foods/nutrition, health/medicine, nature/environment, New Age, psychology, women's issues/studies. Submit outline, sample chapter(s). Reviews artwork/photos as part of ms package.

Fiction: "Authentic and educational, yet entertaining." Occult, spiritual (metaphysical).

Recent Title(s): *Understanding the Birth Chart*, by Kevin Burk (nonfiction).

LOCUST HILL PRESS, P.O. Box 260, West Cornwall CT 06796-0260. (860)672-0060. Fax: (860)672-4968. E-mail: locusthill@snet.net. **Acquisitions:** Thomas C. Bechtle, publisher. Estab. 1985. Publishes hardcover originals. **Publishes 12 titles/year. Receives 150 queries and 20 mss/year. 100% from unagented writers. Pays 12-18% royalty on retail price. Offers advance.** Publishes book 6 months after acceptance of ms. Accepts simultaneous submissions. Responds in 1 month to queries. Book catalog free.

O→ Locust Hill Press specializes in scholarly reference and bibliography works for college and university libraries worldwide, as well as monographs and essay collections on literary subjects.

Nonfiction: Reference. Subjects include ethnic, language/literature, women's issues/studies. "Since our audience is exclusively college and university libraries (and the occasional specialist), we are less inclined to accept manuscripts in 'popular' (i.e., public library) fields. While bibliography has been and will continue to be a specialty, our Locust Hill Literary Studies is gaining popularity as a series of essay collections and monographs in a wide variety of literary topics." Query with SASE.

Recent Title(s): *Denise Levertov: New Perspectives*, by Anne C. Little and Susie Paul.

Tips: "Remember that this is a small, very specialized academic publisher with no distribution network other than mail contact with most academic libraries worldwide. Please shape your expectations accordingly. If your aim is to reach the world's scholarly community by way of its libraries, we are the correct firm to contact. But *please*: no fiction, poetry, popular religion, or personal memoirs."

LOFT PRESS, INC., P.O. Box 126, Fort Valley VA 22652. (540)933-6210. Website: www.loftpress.com. **Acquisitions:** Ann A. Hunter, editor-in-chief. Publishes hardcover and trade paperback originals and reprints. **Publishes 12-20 titles/year; imprint publishes 2-4 titles/year. Receives 200 queries and 150 mss/year. 50% of books from first-time authors; 100% from unagented writers. Pays royalty on net receipts.** Publishes book 6 months after acceptance of ms.

Imprints: Eschat Press, Far Muse Press (both contact Stephen R. Hunter, publisher)

Nonfiction: Biography, coffee table book, how-to, technical, textbook. Subjects include Americana, art/architecture, business/economics, computers/electronic, government/politics, history, language/literature, memoirs, philosophy, regional, religion, science. Submit proposal package including outline, 1 sample chapter(s). Reviews artwork/photos as part of ms package. Send photocopies.
Fiction: Literary, plays, poetry, poetry in translation, regional, short story collections. Submit proposal package including 1 sample chapter(s), synopsis.
Poetry: Submit 5 sample poems.
Recent Title(s): *Manager's Guide to Freight Loss and Damage Claims*, by Colin Barrett (nonfiction); *The Paranoia Factor*, by Alan Peters (adventure fiction); *Vaughan*, by Josephine Barrett.

LONE EAGLE PUBLISHING CO., 1024 N. Orange Dr., Hollywood CA 90038. (323)308-3411 or 1-800-FILMBKS. E-mail: jblack@ifilm.com. Website: www.hdconline.com. **Acquisitions:** Jeff Black, editor. Estab. 1982. Publishes perfectbound and trade paperback originals. **Publishes 15 titles/year. Receives 100 submissions/year. 50% from unagented writers. Pays 10% royalty. Offers $2,500-5,000 average advance.** Publishes book 1 year after acceptance of ms. Accepts simultaneous submissions. Responds quarterly to queries. Book catalog free.

O→ Lone Eagle Publishing Company publishes reference directories that contain comprehensive and accurate credits, personal data and contact information for every major entertainment industry craft. Lone Eagle also publishes many 'how-to' books for the film production business, including books on screenwriting, directing, budgeting and producing, acting, editing, etc. Lone Eagle is broadening its base to include general entertainment titles.

Nonfiction: Biography, how-to, reference, technical. Subjects include film/cinema/stage, entertainment. "We are looking for books in film and television, related topics or biographies." Submit outline, sample chapter(s). Reviews artwork/photos as part of ms package.
Recent Title(s): *Elements of Style for Screenwriters*, by Paul Argentina; *1001: A Video Odyssey*, by Steve Tathan.
Tips: "A well-written, well-thought-out book on some technical aspect of the motion picture (or video) industry has the best chance. Pick a subject that has not been done to death, make sure you know what you're talking about, get someone well-known in that area to endorse the book and prepare to spend a lot of time publicizing the book. Completed manuscripts have the best chance for acceptance."

[A] **LONGSTREET PRESS, INC.**, 2974 Hardman Court, Atlanta GA 30305. (404)254-0110. Fax: (404)254-0116. Website: www.longstreetpress.com. **Acquisitions:** Scott Bard, president/editor. Estab. 1988. Publishes hardcover and trade paperback originals. **Publishes 45 titles/year. Receives 2,500 submissions/year. 10% of books from first-time authors. Pays royalty. Offers advance.** Publishes book 1 year after acceptance of ms. Accepts simultaneous submissions. Responds in 3 months to queries. Book catalog for 9×12 SAE with 4 first-class stamps or online; ms guidelines for #10 SASE or online.

O→ Although Longstreet Press publishes a number of genres, their strengths in the future will be general nonfiction such as business, self-help and Southern biography, guidebooks, and fiction. "As Southern publishers, we look for regional material." Currently emphasizing quality nonfiction for a wide audience (memoir, business, self-help). De-emphasizing humor, cookbooks, gift and illustrated books.

Nonfiction: Biography, coffee table book, humor, illustrated book, reference. Subjects include Americana, cooking/foods/nutrition, gardening, history, humor, language/literature, nature/environment, photography, regional, sports, women's issues/studies. "No poetry, scientific or highly technical, textbooks of any kind, erotica." *Agented submissions only.*
Fiction: Literary, mainstream/contemporary (Southern fiction). *Agented submissions only.*

LOOMPANICS UNLIMITED, P.O. Box 1197, Port Townsend WA 98368-0997. Fax: (360)385-7785. E-mail: editorial@loompanics.com. Website: www.loompanics.com. President: Michael Hoy. **Acquisitions:** Gia Cosindas, editor. Estab. 1975. Publishes trade paperback originals. **Publishes 15 titles/year. Receives 500 submissions/year. 40% of books from first-time authors; 100% from unagented writers. Pays 10-15% royalty on wholesale price or retail price or makes outright purchase of $100-1,200. Offers $500 average advance.** Publishes book 1 year after acceptance of ms. Accepts simultaneous submissions. Responds in 3 months to queries. Book catalog for $5, postage paid; ms guidelines free.

O→ "Our motto 'No more secrets-no more excuses-no more limits' says it all. Whatever the subject, our books are somewhat 'edgy'. We are the name in beat-the-system books. From computer hacking to gardening to tax avoision." Currently emphasizing unusual takes on subjects that are controversial and how-to books. Does not want anything that's already been done or New Age.

Nonfiction: "In general, we like works about outrageous topics or obscure-but-useful technology written authoritatively in a matter-of-fact way. We are looking for how-to books in the fields of espionage, investigation, the underground economy, police methods, how to beat the system, crime and criminal techniques." How-to, reference, self-help, technical. Subjects include agriculture/horticulture, Americana, anthropology/archeology, computers/electronic, government/politics, health/medicine, money/finance, psychology, science, film/cinema/stage. "We are also looking for similarly-written articles for our catalog and its supplements." Query with SASE or submit outline, sample chapter(s). Reviews artwork/photos as part of ms package.
Recent Title(s): *Surviving on the Street*, by Ace Backwords; *Last Suppers: Famous Last Meals from Death Row*, by Ty Treadwell and Michelle Vernon; *Protect Yourself Against Terrorism*, by Tony Lesce.
Tips: "Our audience is primarily young males looking for hard-to-find information on alternatives to 'The System.' Your chances for success are greatly improved if you can show us how your proposal fits in with our catalog."

LOUISIANA STATE UNIVERSITY PRESS, P.O. Box 25053, Baton Rouge LA 70894-5053. (225)578-6294. Fax: (225)578-6461. **Acquisitions:** L.E. Phillabaum, director; Maureen G. Hewitt, assistant director and editor-in-chief; John Easterly, executive editor; Sylvia Frank, acquisitions editor. Estab. 1935. Publishes hardcover originals, hardcover and trade paperback reprints. **Publishes 70-80 titles/year. Receives 800 submissions/year. 33% of books from first-time authors; 95% from unagented writers. Pays royalty.** Publishes book 1 year after acceptance of ms. Does not accept simultaneous submissions. Responds in 1 month to queries. Book catalog and ms guidelines free.
Nonfiction: Biography. Subjects include art/architecture, ethnic, government/politics, history, language/literature, music/dance, photography, regional, sociology, women's issues/studies. Query with SASE or submit outline, sample chapter(s).
Poetry: Literary.
Recent Title(s): *The Collected Poems of Robert Penn Warren* (poetry); *Lee and His Generals in War and Memory*, by Gary W. Gallagher (history).
Tips: "Our audience includes scholars, intelligent laymen, general audience."

LOVE SPELL, Dorchester Publishing Co., Inc., 276 Fifth Ave., Suite 1008, New York NY 10001-0112. (212)725-8811. Website: www.dorchesterpub.com. **Acquisitions:** Leah Hultenschmidt and Ashley Kuehl, editorial assistants; Kate Seaver, associate editor; Christopher Keeslar, senior editor. Publishes mass market paperback originals. **Publishes 48 titles/year. Receives 1,500-2,000 queries and 150-500 mss/year. 30% of books from first-time authors; 25-30% from unagented writers. Pays 4% royalty on retail price. Offers $2,000 average advance.** Publishes book 1 year after acceptance of ms. Does not accept simultaneous submissions. Responds in 6 months to mss. Book catalog for free (800)481-9191; ms guidelines online.

O‑ Love Spell publishes the quirky sub-genres of romance: time-travel, paranormal, futuristic. "Despite the exotic settings, we are still interested in character-driven plots." Love Spell has 2 humor lines including both contemporary and historical romances.

Fiction: Gothic, historical, science fiction. "Books industry-wide are getting shorter; we're interested in 90,000 words." Query with SASE or submit 3 sample chapter(s), synopsis. No material will be returned without SASE.
Recent Title(s): *Sacrament*, by Susan Squires; *Midnight Embrace*, by Amanda Ashley.

LOYOLA PRESS, 3441 N. Ashland Ave., Chicago IL 60657-1397. (773)281-1818. Fax: (773)281-0152. E-mail: editorial@loyolapress.com. Website: www.loyolapress.org. **Acquisitions:** Jim Manney, acquisitions editor (religion, spirituality). Estab. 1912. Publishes hardcover and trade paperback originals. **Publishes 30 titles/year. Receives 500 queries/year. 5% of books from first-time authors; 50% from unagented writers. Pays 15-18% royalty on wholesale price. Offers reasonable advance.** Publishes book 1 year after acceptance of ms. Accepts simultaneous submissions. Responds in 1 month to queries; 3 months to proposals. Book catalog and ms guidelines online.
Imprints: Jesuit Way
Nonfiction: Subjects include religion, spirituality, inspirational, prayer, Catholic life, grief and loss, marriage and family. *Jesuit Way* books focus on Jesuit life and history as well as on Ignatian spirituality and ministry. Query with SASE.
Recent Title(s): *Mystics and Miracles*, by Bert Ghezzi; *The Seekers Guide to Mary*, by Maria Scaperlanda; *The Loyola Kids Book of Everyday Prayers*.
Tips: "We are a trade publisher of religious books for a broad market of readers with Catholic or sacramental interests. We do not publish academic books, fiction or poetry, or books for religious professionals. We do publish in the area of Catholic faith formation. Study our guidelines."

N LUCENT BOOKS, 10911 Technology Place, San Diego CA 92127. Estab. 1988. **Publishes 180 titles/year. 10% of books from first-time authors; 90% from unagented writers. Makes outright purchase of $2,500-3,000.** Query with cover letter, résumé, list of publications, and 9×12 SAE with 3 first-class stamps for book catalog and ms guidelines.

O‑ Lucent Books is a trade publisher of nonfiction for the middle school audience providing students with resource material for academic studies and for independent learning.

Nonfiction: Children's/juvenile. Subjects include history, world affairs, cultural issues. "We produce tightly formatted books for middle grade readers. Each series has specific requirements. Potential writers should familiarize themselves with our material." ; Series deals with history, current events, social issues. All are works for hire, by assignment only. No unsolicited mss accepted.
Recent Title(s): *Tuberculosis*, Gail B. Stewart; *The Inuit*, Anne Wallace Sharp; *Flying Aces*, John F. Wukorvits.
Tips: "We expect writers to do thorough research using books, magazines and newspapers. Biased writing, whether liberal or conservative, has no place in our books. We prefer to work with writers who have experience writing nonfiction for middle grade students. We are looking for experienced writers, especially those who have written nonfiction books at young adult level."

THE LYONS PRESS, The Globe Pequot Press, Inc., 246 Goose Lane, Guilford CT 06437. (203)458-4500. Fax: (203)458-4668. Website: www.lyonspress.com. Publisher/President: Tony Lyons. **Acquisitions:** Lilly Golden, editor-at-large (fiction, memoirs, narrative nonfiction); Jay Cassell, senior editor (fishing, hunting, survival, military, history, gardening); Jay McCullogh, editor (narrative nonfiction, travelogues, adventure, military, espionage, international current events, fishing); Tom McCarthy, senior editor (sports & fitness, history, outdoor adventure, memoirs); Ann Treistman, editor (narrative nonfiction, travelogues, adventure, sports, animals, cooking); Lisa Purcell, editor-at-large (history, adventure, narrative nonfiction, cooking, gardening); Mark Weinstein, editor-at-large (major team sports, golf, history, military history, gambling, adventure); Bill Bowers, managing editor. Estab. 1984 (Lyons & Burford), 1997 (The Lyons Press). Publishes hardcover and trade paperback originals and reprints. **Publishes 240 titles/year. 50% of books from first-time authors; 30% from unagented writers. Pays 5-10% royalty on wholesale price. Offers $2,000-7,000 advance.** Publishes book 1 year after acceptance of ms. Accepts simultaneous submissions. Responds in 1 month to queries; 1 month to proposals; 2 months to mss. Book catalog online.

- The Lyons Press has teamed up to develop books with L.L. Bean, *Field & Stream*, Orvis, Outward Bound, Buckmasters and *Golf Magazine*. It was recently purchased by Globe Pequot Press.

O→ The Lyons Press publishes practical and literary books, chiefly centered on outdoor subjects—natural history, all sports, gardening, horses, fishing. Currently emphasizing adventure, sports. De-emphasizing hobbies, travel.

Nonfiction: Biography, cookbook, how-to, reference. Subjects include agriculture/horticulture, Americana, animals, anthropology/archeology, cooking/foods/nutrition, gardening, health/medicine, history, hobbies, military/war, nature/environment (environment), recreation, science, sports, travel. "Visit our website and note the featured categories." Query with SASE or submit proposal package including outline, 3 sample chapter(s). and marketing description. Reviews artwork/photos as part of ms package. Send photocopies or non-original prints.

Fiction: Historical, military/war, short story collections (fishing, hunting, outdoor, nature), sports. Query with SASE or submit proposal package including outline, 3-5 sample chapter(s).

Recent Title(s): *The Hunter, the Hammer, and Heaven*, by Robert Young Pelton (travel/adventure); *Jerusalem Creek*, by Ted Leeson (sports/fishing); *Orvis Fly-Tying Guide*, by Tom Rosenbauer (fishing).

MACADAM/CAGE PUBLISHING INC., 155 Sansome St., Suite 620, San Francisco CA 94104. (415)986-7502. Fax: (415)986-7414. E-mail: info@macadamcage.com. Website: www.macadamcage.com. Publisher: David Poindexter. **Acquisitions:** Patrick Walsh, fiction editor; Anika Streitfeld, nonfiction editor. Publishes hardcover originals. **Publishes 25 titles/year. Receives 5,000 queries and 1,500 mss/year. 75% of books from first-time authors; 50% from unagented writers.** Publishes book up to 1 year after acceptance of ms. Accepts simultaneous submissions. Responds in 4 months to queries. Ms guidelines for #10 SASE.

O→ MacAdam/Cage publishes quality works of literary fiction that are carefully crafted and tell a bold story. De-emphasizing romance, poetry, Christian or New Age mss.

Nonfiction: Biography. Subjects include history, memoirs, science, social sciences. "Narrative nonfiction that reads like fiction." No self-help or New Age. Submit proposal package including outline, up to 3 sample chapter(s), SASE.

Fiction: Historical, literary, mainstream/contemporary. No electronic or faxed submissions. Submit proposal package including up to 3 sample chapter(s), synopsis, SASE.

Recent Title(s): *Ella Minnow Pea*, by Mark Dunn (fiction); *Snow Island*, by Katherine Towler (fiction).

Tips: "We like to keep in close contact with writers. We publish for readers of quality fiction and nonfiction."

N **MAGE PUBLISHERS INC.**, 1032 29th St. NW, Washington DC 20007. (202)342-1642. Fax: (202)342-9269. E-mail: info@mage.com. Website: www.mage.com. **Acquisitions:** Amin Sepehri, assistant to publisher. Estab. 1985. Publishes hardcover originals and reprints, trade paperback originals. **Publishes 4 titles/year. Receives 40 queries and 20 mss/year. 10% of books from first-time authors; 95% from unagented writers. Pays royalty. Offers $250-1,500 advance.** Publishes book 8-16 months after acceptance of ms. Accepts simultaneous submissions. Responds in 1 month to queries; 1 month to proposals; 3 months to mss. Book catalog free.

O→ Mage publishes books relating to Persian/Iranian culture.

Nonfiction: Biography, children's/juvenile, coffee table book, cookbook, gift book, illustrated book. Subjects include anthropology/archeology, art/architecture, cooking/foods/nutrition, ethnic, history, language/literature, music/dance, sociology, translation. Query with SASE. Reviews artwork/photos as part of ms package. Send photocopies.

Fiction: Ethnic, feminist, historical, literary, mainstream/contemporary, short story collections. Must relate to Persian/Iranian culture. Query with SASE.

Poetry: Must relate to Persian/Iranian culture. Query.

Recent Title(s): *A Taste of Persia*, N. Batmanglis (cooking); *The Lion and the Throne*, Ferdowsi (mythology).

Tips: Audience is the Iranian-American community in America and Americans interested in Persian culture.

THE MAGNI GROUP, INC., 7106 Wellington Point Rd., McKinney TX 75070. (972)540-2050. Fax: (972)540-1057. E-mail: info@magnico.com. Website: www.magnico.com. **Acquisitions:** Evan Reynolds, president. Publishes hardcover originals and trade paperback reprints. **Publishes 5-10 titles/year. Receives 20 queries and 10-20 mss/year. 50% of books from first-time authors; 80% from unagented writers. Pays royalty on wholesale price or makes outright purchase. Offers advance.** Publishes book 6 months after acceptance of ms. Does not accept simultaneous submissions. Responds in 2 months to queries. Book catalog and ms guidelines online.

Imprints: Magni Publishing.

Nonfiction: Cookbook, how-to, self-help. Subjects include child guidance/parenting, cooking/foods/nutrition, health/medicine, money/finance, sex. Submit complete ms. Reviews artwork/photos as part of ms package. Send photocopies.

Recent Title(s): *Eat Like the Stars Cookbook*; *Holiday Planner*; *Birthday Planner.*

MAGNUS PRESS, P.O. Box 2666, Carlsbad CA 92018. (760)806-3743. Fax: (760)806-3689. E-mail: magnuspres@aol.com. **Acquisitions:** Warren Angel, editorial director. Publishes trade paperback originals and reprints. **Publishes 3-5 titles/year; imprint publishes 2 titles/year. 62% of books from first-time authors; 100% from unagented writers.**

Pays 6-11% royalty on retail price. Publishes book 6 months after acceptance of ms. Accepts simultaneous submissions. Responds in 1 month to queries; 2 months to proposals; 2 months to mss. Book catalog for #10 SASE; ms guidelines for #10 SASE.

Imprints: Canticle Books

Nonfiction: Inspirational; Biblical studies. Subjects include religion (from a Christian perspective.). "Writers must be well-grounded in Biblical knowledge and must be able to communicate effectively with the lay person." Query with SASE or submit proposal package including outline, 3 sample chapter(s).

Tips: Magnus Press's audience is mainly Christian lay persons, but also includes anyone interested in spirituality and/or Biblical studies and the church. "Study our listings and catalog; learn to write effectively for an average reader: read any one of our published books."

MAISONNEUVE PRESS, 6423 Adelphi Rd., University Park MD 20782. Phone/fax: (301)277-2467. E-mail: editors@maisonneuvepress.com. Website: www.maisonneuvepress.com. **Acquisitions:** Robert Merrill, editor (politics, literature, philosophy); Dennis Crow, editor (architecture, urban studies, sociology). Publishes hardcover and trade paperback originals. **Publishes 6 titles/year. 5% of books from first-time authors; 100% from unagented writers. Pays 5% royalty on cover price or $2,000 maximum outright purchase.** Publishes book 1 year after acceptance of ms. Accepts simultaneous submissions. Responds in 1 month to queries; 1 month to proposals; 1 month to mss. Book catalog free; Send letter for guidelines, individual response.

O→ "Maisonneuve provides solid, first-hand information for serious adult readers: academics and political activists."

Nonfiction: Biography. Subjects include education, ethnic, gay/lesbian, government/politics, history, language/literature, military/war, philosophy, psychology, sociology, translation, women's issues/studies, literary criticism, social theory, economics, essay collections. "We make decisions on completed mss only. Will correspond on work in progress. Some books submitted are too narrowly focused; not marketable enough. We are eager to read mss on the current crisis and war. The commercial media—TV and newspapers—are not doing a very good job of cutting through the government propaganda." Query with SASE or submit complete ms. Reviews artwork/photos as part of ms package. Send photocopies.

Recent Title(s): *Morse Peckham, Man's Rage for Chaos: Biology, Behavior and the Arts.*

MARCH STREET PRESS, 3413 Wilshire, Greensboro NC 27408. (336)282-9754. Fax: (336)282-9754. E-mail: rbixby@aol.com. Website: users.aol.com/marchst. **Acquisitions:** Robert Bixby, editor/publisher. Estab. 1988. Publishes literary chapbooks. **Publishes 6-10 titles/year. Receives 12 queries and 30 mss/year. 50% of books from first-time authors; 100% from unagented writers. Pays 15% royalty. Offers 10 copy advance.** Publishes book 6 months after acceptance of ms. Accepts simultaneous submissions. Responds in 3 months to mss. Book catalog for #10 SASE; ms guidelines for #10 SASE.

O→ March Street publishes poetry chapbooks. "We like unusual, risky, interesting things. We like to be amazed. So do our readers and writers."

Poetry: "My plans are based on the submissions I receive, not vice versa."

Recent Title(s): *Road to Alaska*, by Ray Miller; *Her Bodies*, by Elizabeth Kerlikowske.

Tips: "March Street Press is purely an act of hedonistic indulgence. The mission is to enjoy myself. Just as authors express themselves through writing, I find a creative release in designing, editing and publishing. Audience is extremely sophisticated, widely read graduates of M.A., M.F.A. and Ph.D. programs in English and fine arts. Also lovers of significant, vibrant and enriching verse regardless of field of study or endeavor. Most beginning poets, I have found, think it beneath them to read other poets. This is the most glaring flaw in their work. My advice is to read ceaselessly. Otherwise, you may be published, but you will never be accomplished."

MARINE TECHNIQUES PUBLISHING, INC., 126 Western Ave., Suite 266, Augusta ME 04330-7252. (207)622-7984. Fax: (207)621-0821. **Acquisitions:** James L. Pelletier, president/CEO (commercial marine or maritime international); Christopher S. Pelletier, vice president operations (national and international maritime related properties). **Publishes 3-5 titles/year. Receives 5-20 queries and 1-4 mss/year. 15% of books from first-time authors. Pays 25-43% royalty on wholesale or retail price.** Publishes book 6-12 months after acceptance of ms. Accepts simultaneous submissions. Responds in 2 months to queries; 4 months to proposals; 6 months to mss. Book catalog free.

O→ Publishes only books related to the commercial marine industry.

Nonfiction: Reference, self-help, technical, maritime company directories. Subjects include the commerical maritime industry only. Submit proposal package, including ms, with all photos (photocopies OK).

Fiction: Must be commercial maritime/marine related. Submit complete ms.

Poetry: Must be related to maritime/marine subject matter. Submit complete ms.

Tips: Audience consists of commercial marine/maritime firms, persons employed in all aspects of the marine/maritime commercial and recreational fields, persons interested in seeking employment in the commercial marine industry; firms seeking to sell their products and services to vessel owners, operators, and managers in the commercial marine industry worldwide, etc.

MARINER BOOKS, Houghton Mifflin, 222 Berkeley St., Boston MA 02116. (617)351-5000. Fax: (617)351-1202. Website: www.hmco.com. **Acquisitions:** Susan Canavan, managing director. Publishes trade paperback originals and reprints. **Pays royalty. Offers varing advance.** Responds in 4 months to mss.

Houghton Mifflin books give shape to ideas that educate, inform and delight. Mariner has an eclectic list that notably embraces fiction.

Nonfiction: Biography. Subjects include education, government/politics, history, nature/environment, philosophy, sociology, women's issues/studies, political thought. *Agented submissions only.*

Fiction: Literary, mainstream/contemporary. *Agented submissions only.*

Recent Title(s): *Kit's Law*, by Donna Morrissey; *The Hallelujah Side*, by Rhoda Huffey; *The Bostons*, by Carolyn Cooke.

N **MARKETSCOPE BOOKS**, 119 Richard Court, Aptos CA 95003. (831)688-7535. **Acquisitions:** Ken Albert, editor-in-chief. Estab. 1985. Publishes hardcover and trade paperback originals. **Publishes 10 titles/year. 50% of books from first-time authors; 50% from unagented writers. Pays 10-15% royalty on wholesale price.** Publishes book 1 year after acceptance of ms. Accepts simultaneous submissions. Responds in 1 week to queries *Writer's Market* recommends allowing 2 months for reply to proposals.

Nonfiction: California recreation books. Subjects include recreation (California). Query with SASE. Reviews artwork/photos as part of ms package.

MARLOR PRESS, INC., 4304 Brigadoon Dr., St. Paul MN 55126. (651)484-4600. E-mail: marlin.marlor@minn.net. **Acquisitions:** Marlin Bree, publisher. Estab. 1981. Publishes trade paperback originals. **Publishes 6 titles/year. Receives 100 queries and 25 mss/year. Pays 8-10% royalty on wholesale price.** Publishes book 1 year after acceptance of ms. Does not accept simultaneous submissions. Responds in 3-6 weeks to queries. Ms guidelines for #10 SASE.

Currently emphasizing general interest nonfiction children's books and nonfiction boating books. De-emphasizing travel.

Nonfiction: Children's/juvenile, how-to. Subjects include travel, boating. "Primarily how-to stuff." No unsolicited mss. No anecdotal reminiscences or biographical materials. No fiction or poetry. Query first; submit outline with sample chapters only when requested. Do not send full ms. Reviews artwork/photos as part of ms package.

Recent Title(s): *Going Abroad: The Bathroom Survival Guide*, by Eva Newman; *Wake of the Green Storm: A Survivor's Tale*, by Marlin Bree.

MARS PUBLISHING, INC., 6404 Wilshire Blvd., Suite 1200, Los Angeles CA 90048. (323)782-1772. Fax: (323)782-1775. E-mail: editor@marspub.com. Website: www.marspub.com. Publisher: Ed Steussy. **Acquisitions:** Lars Peterson, editor. Publishes trade paperback originals. **Publishes 15-20 titles/year; imprint publishes 12-18 titles/year. Receives 350 queries and 35-50 mss/year. 15% of books from first-time authors; 95% from unagented writers. Pays 10-15% royalty on wholesale price. Offers $3,000-5,000 advance.** Publishes book 4-6 months after acceptance of ms. Accepts simultaneous submissions. Responds in 1 month to queries; 2 months to proposals; 3 months to mss. Book catalog online; ms guidelines online.

Imprints: Parent's Guide Press.

Nonfiction: How-to, reference. Subjects include child guidance/parenting, education, health/medicine, money/finance, recreation, travel. Query with SASE or submit proposal package including outline, 2-5 sample chapter(s), author bio, marketing information. "We prefer e-mail queries."

Recent Title(s): *A Parent's Guide to the Internet*, by Ilene Raymond (compters/parenting); *A Parent's Guide to San Francisco*, by Paul Otteson (travel); *A Parent's Guide to the Best Children's Videos*, by Kids First! Editors (reference/media).

Tips: "The series informs parents and families about issues and opportunities facing them in a non-judgemental, non-biased manner; Alarmists, Ostriches need not apply. Engaging, thoughtful, humorous advice from an informed neighbor is our intended tone."

MAUPIN HOUSE PUBLISHING INC., P.O. Box 90148, Gainesville FL 32607-0148. (800)524-0634. Fax: (352)373-5546. E-mail: info@maupinhouse.com. Website: www.maupinhouse.com. **Acquisitions:** Julia Graddy, co-publisher. Publishes trade paperback originals and reprints. **Publishes 7 titles/year. Pays 5-10% royalty on retail price.** Responds in 2 months to queries.

Maupin House publishes teacher resource books for language arts teachers K-12.

Nonfiction: How-to. Subjects include education, language/literature, writing workshop, reading instruction. "We are looking for practical, in-classroom resource materials, especially in the field of language arts and writing workshops. Classroom teachers are our top choice as authors." Query with SASE.

Fiction: Juvenile (grades 3-5). "We are interested in fiction that features a child set in historical Florida."

Recent Title(s): *Primary Literacy Centers and Teaching Written Response to Text.*

MAXIMUM PRESS, 605 Silverthorn Rd., Gulf Breeze FL 32561. (850)934-0819. **Acquisitions:** Jim Hoskins, publisher. Publishes trade paperback originals. **Publishes 10-12 titles/year. Receives 10 queries and 10 mss/year. 40% of books from first-time authors; 90% from unagented writers. Pays 7½-15% royalty on wholesale price. Offers $1,000-5,000 advance.** Publishes book 3 months after acceptance of ms. Responds in 1 month to queries. *Writer's Market* recommends allowing 2 months for reply to queries. Book catalog free.

"Maximum Press is a premier publisher of books that help readers apply technology efficiently and profitably. Special emphasis is on books that help individuals and businesses increase revenue and reduce expenses through the use of computers and other low-cost information tools." Currently emphasizing e-business.

Nonfiction: How-to, technical. Subjects include business/economics, computers/electronic, Internet. Query with SASE or submit proposal package including résumé.

Recent Title(s): *Marketing on the Internet*, by Jan Zimmerman (computer/Internet); *101 Ways to Promote Your Web Site*, by Susan Sweeney (e-business).

MAYHAVEN PUBLISHING, 803 Buckthorn Cir., P.O. Box 557, Mahomet IL 61853. (217)586-4493. Fax: (217)586-6330. E-mail: ibfipone@aol.com. **Acquisitions:** Doris Wenzel, editor/publisher. Publishes hardcover and trade paperback originals. **Publishes 5-10 titles/year; imprint publishes 1 titles/year. Receives approximately 3,000 queries and 2,000 mss/year. 50% of books from first-time authors; 98% from unagented writers. Pays 7.5-20% royalty on wholesale price. Offers $100-500 advance.** Publishes book 1-2 years after acceptance of ms. Accepts simultaneous submissions. Responds in 9 months to queries; 9 months to proposals; 9 months to mss. Book catalog for $1 and SASE; ms guidelines free.
Imprints: Wild Rose

- "We established Mayhaven's Annual Awards for Fiction in 1997. Mss for awards are accepted between May 1 and December 31 each year."

Recent Title(s): *Overkill*, by Susan McBride (a Maggie Ryan mystery); *Love Matters*, by Wilfried Lippmann (short stories); *Ten Sisters: A True Story*, by Alfred, et. al. (nonfiction).
Tips: "We like variety, so we are open to many possibilities."

MBI PUBLISHING, 729 Prospect Ave., P.O. Box 1, Osceola WI 54020-0001. (715)294-3345. Fax: (715)294-4448. E-mail: mbibks@motorbooks.com. Website: www.motorbooks.com. Publishing Director: Tim Parker. **Acquisitions:** Lee Klancher, editor-in-chief; Darwin Holmstrom (motorcycles); Peter Bodensteiner (racing, how-to); Dennis Pernu (Americana, trains & boats); Josh Leventhal (promotional books). Estab. 1973. Publishes hardcover and paperback originals. **Publishes 125 titles/year. Receives 200 queries and 50 mss/year. 95% from unagented writers. Pays royalty on net receipts. Offers $5,000 average advance.** Publishes book 1 year after acceptance of ms. Accepts simultaneous submissions. Responds in 3 months to queries. Book catalog free; ms guidelines for #10 SASE.
Imprints: Bay View, Bicycle Books, Crestline, Zenith Books.

O━ MBI is a transportation-related publisher: cars, motorcycles, racing, trucks, tractors, boats, bicycles—also Americana, aviation and military history. Currently emphasizing Americana and the Civil War.

Nonfiction: Transportation-related subjects. Coffee table book, gift book, how-to, illustrated book. Subjects include Americana, history, hobbies, military/war, photography, translation (nonfiction). "State qualifications for doing book." Query with SASE. Reviews artwork/photos as part of ms package. Send photocopies.
Recent Title(s): *America's Special Forces*, by David Bohrer (modern military).

McBOOKS PRESS, 120 W. State St., Ithaca NY 14850. E-mail: mcbooks@mcbooks.com. Website: www.mcbooks.com. Publisher: Alexander G. Skutt. **Acquisitions:** (Ms.) S.K. List, editorial director. Estab. 1979. Publishes trade paperback and hardcover originals and reprints. **Publishes 20 titles/year. Pays 5-10% royalty on retail price. Offers $1,000-5,000 advance.** Responds in 1 month to queries; 2 months to proposals.

- "We are booked nearly solid for the next few years. We can only consider the highest quality projects in our narrow interest areas."

O━ Currently emphasizing nautical and military historical fiction.

Nonfiction: Subjects include regional (New York state), vegetarianism and veganism. "Authors' ability to promote a plus." No unsolicited mss. Query with SASE.
Fiction: Nautical and military historical. Query with SASE.
Recent Title(s): *Motoo Eetee*, by Irv C. Rogers; *The Boxing Register, 3rd Ed*, by James B. Roberts and Alexander G. Skutt.

McDONALD & WOODWARD PUBLISHING CO., 431-B E. Broadway, Granville OH 43023-1310. (740)321-1140. Fax: (740)321-1141. Website: www.mwpubco.com. **Acquisitions:** Jerry N. McDonald, managing partner/publisher. Estab. 1986. Publishes hardcover and trade paperback originals. **Publishes 8 titles/year. Receives 100 queries and 20 mss/year. 50% of books from first-time authors; 100% from unagented writers. Pays 10% royalty on net receipts.** Publishes book 1 year after acceptance of ms. Accepts simultaneous submissions. Responds in 2 weeks to queries. Book catalog free.

O━ "McDonald & Woodward publishes books in natural and cultural history." Currently emphasizing travel, natural and cultural history. De-emphasizing self-help.

Nonfiction: Biography, coffee table book, illustrated book. Subjects include Americana, animals, anthropology/archeology, ethnic, history, nature/environment, science, travel. Query with SASE or submit outline, sample chapter(s). Reviews artwork/photos as part of ms package. Send photocopies.
Recent Title(s): *The Carousel Keepers: An Oral History of American Carousels*, by Carrie Papa; *A Guide to Common Freshwater Invertebrates of North America*, by J. Reece Vashall; *Juan Ponce de Leon and the Spanish Discovery of Puerto Rico and Florida*, by Robert H. Fuson.
Tips: "We are especially interested in additional titles in our 'Guides to the American Landscape' series. Should consult titles in print for guidance. We want well-organized, clearly written, substantive material."

MARGARET K. McELDERRY BOOKS, Simon & Schuster Children's Publishing Division, Simon & Schuster, 1230 Sixth Ave., New York NY 10020. (212)698-2761. Fax: (212)698-2796. Website: www.simonsayskids.com. Vice President/Publisher: Brenda Bowen. **Acquisitions:** Emma D. Dryden, vice president/editorial director (books for preschoolers to 16-year-olds); Sarah Nielsen, assistant editor. Estab. 1971. Publishes quality material for preschoolers to 18-year-olds. **Publishes 25-30 titles/year. Receives 4,000 queries/year. 15% of books from first-time authors; 50%**

from unagented writers. Average print order is 4,000-6,000 for a first middle grade or young adult book; 7,500-15,000 for a first picture book. Pays royalty on hardcover retail price: 10% fiction, picture book; 5% author; 5% illustrator. Offers $5,000-8,000 advance for new authors. Publishes book up to 3 years after acceptance of ms. Ms guidelines for #10 SASE.

O→ "We are more interested in superior writing and illustration than in a particular 'type' of book." Currently emphasizing young picture books and funny middle grade fiction.

Nonfiction: Biography, children's/juvenile. Subjects include history, adventure. "Read. The field is competitive. See what's been done and what's out there before submitting. Looks for originality of ideas, clarity and felicity of expression, well-organized plot and strong characterization (fiction) or clear exposition (nonfiction); quality. Accept query letters with SASE only." No unsolicited mss.

Fiction: Adventure, fantasy, historical, mainstream/contemporary, mystery, young adult (or middle grade). No unsolicited mss. Send query letter with SASE only for picture books; query letter with first 3 chapters, SASE for middle grade and young adult novels.

Poetry: No unsolicited mss. Query or submit 3 sample poems.

Recent Title(s): *Bear Snores On*, by Karma Wilson and Jane Chapman (picture book); *Shout, Sister, Shout!*, by Roxane Orgill (nonfiction); *Stopping to Home*, by Lea Wait (middle grade fiction).

Tips: "Read! The children's book field is competitive. See what's been done and what's out there before submitting. We look for high quality: an originality of ideas, clarity and felicity of expression, a well-organized plot and strong character-driven stories."

McFARLAND & COMPANY, INC., PUBLISHERS, Box 611, Jefferson NC 28640. (336)246-4460. Fax: (336)246-5018. E-mail: info@mcfarlandpub.com. Website: www.mcfarlandpub.com. **Acquisitions:** Robert Franklin, president/editor-in-chief (chess, general); Steve Wilson, senior editor (automotive, general); Virginia Tobiassen, editor (general); Marty McGee, assistant editor; Gary Mitchem, assistant editor. Estab. 1979. Publishes hardcover and "quality" paperback originals; a "non-trade" publisher. **Publishes 225 titles/year. Receives 1,400 submissions/year. 70% of books from first-time authors; 95% from unagented writers. Pays 10-12½% royalty on net receipts.** Publishes book 10 months after acceptance of ms. Responds in 1 month to queries.

O→ McFarland publishes serious nonfiction in a variety of fields, including general reference, performing arts, sports (particularly baseball); women's studies, librarianship, literature, Civil War, history and international studies. Currently emphasizing medieval history, automotive history, Spanish-English bilingual works. De-emphasizing memoirs.

Nonfiction: Reference (and scholarly), scholarly, technical, professional monographs. Subjects include art/architecture, business/economics, contemporary culture, ethnic, film/cinema/stage, health/medicine, history, music/dance, recreation, sociology, sports (very strong), women's issues/studies (very strong), world affairs, African-American studies (very strong), chess, Civil War, drama/theater, cinema/radio/TV (very strong), librarianship (very strong), pop culture, world affairs (very strong). Reference books are particularly wanted—fresh material (i.e., not in head-to-head competition with an established title). "We prefer manuscripts of 250 or more double-spaced pages." No fiction, New Age, exposés, poetry, children's books, devotional/inspirational works, Bible studies or personal essays. Query with SASE or submit outline, sample chapter(s). Reviews artwork/photos as part of ms package.

Recent Title(s): *Encyclopedia of Capital Punishment*, by Louis J. Palmer; *Daily Life in the Middle Ages*, by Paul B. Newman.

Tips: "We want well-organized knowledge of an area in which there is not information coverage at present, plus reliability so we don't feel we have to check absolutely everything. Our market is worldwide and libraries are an important part." McFarland also publishes the *Journal of Information Ethics*.

McGAVICK FIELD PUBLISHING, 118 N. Cherry, Olathe KS 66061. (913)780-1973. Fax: (913)782-1765. E-mail: fhernan@prodigy.net. Website: www.abcnanny.com. **Publishes 4 titles/year.** Does not accept simultaneous submissions. Fax or e-mail for ms guidelines.

O→ McGavick Field publishes handbooks dealing with life situations, parent care, child care. "We are looking for books that can be published in the format of *The ABCs of Hiring a Nanny*, accompanied by a companion disk and website."

Nonfiction: Biography, how-to, humor, reference, self-help. Subjects include business/economics, child guidance/parenting, computers/electronic, government/politics, humor, women's issues/studies.

Recent Title(s): *The ABCs of Hiring a Nanny (expanded version)*, by Frances Anne Hernan (handbook for hiring child care); *I'm a Nanny, Not a Ninny*, by Frances Anne Hernan.

Tips: "We are looking for manuscripts that deal with government agencies in trying to secure parent care or help for the disabled and that will help develop programs in this modern day society."

MCGRAW-HILL/OSBORNE, The McGraw-Hill Companies, 2600 10th St., Berkeley CA 94710. (800)227-0900. Website: www.osborne.com. **Acquisitions:** Scott Rogers, editor-in-chief/vice president; Wendy Rinaldi, editorial director (programmaing and web development); Gareth Hancock, editorial director (certification); Roger Stewart, editorial director (consumer and hardware applications); Tracey Dunkelberger, editorial director of networking. Estab. 1979. Publishes computer trade paperback originals. **Publishes 250 titles/year. Receives 500 submissions/year. 25% of books from first-time authors; 50% from unagented writers. Pays 7½-15% royalty on net receipts. Offers varying advance.** Publishes book 4-8 months after acceptance of ms. Responds in 2 weeks to proposals. Book catalog online.

O→ Publishes technical computer books and software with an emphasis on emerging technologies.

Nonfiction: Reference, technical. Subjects include computers/electronic, software (and hardware). Query with SASE or submit proposal package including outline, sample chapter(s), SASE. Reviews artwork/photos as part of ms package.
Recent Title(s): *All-in-One A+ Exam Guide*, by Meyers; *Hacking Exposéd*, by McClure, Scambray and Kurtz.
Tips: "A leader in self-paced training and skills development tools on information technology and computers."

McGREGOR PUBLISHING, 4532 W. Kennedy Blvd., Suite 233, Tampa FL 33609. (813)805-2665 or (888)405-2665. Fax: (813)832-6777. E-mail: mcgregpub@aol.com. **Acquisitions:** Dave Rosenbaum, acquisitions editor. Publishes hardcover and trade paperback originals. **Publishes 15-20 titles/year. Receives 150 queries and 40 mss/year. 75% of books from first-time authors; 80% from unagented writers. Pays 10-12% royalty on retail price; 13-16% on wholesale price. Offers variable advance.** Publishes book 1 year after acceptance of ms. Accepts simultaneous submissions. Responds in 2 months to queries; 2 months to proposals; 3 months to mss. Book catalog and ms guidelines free.

- McGregor no longer publishes fiction.

O→ "We specialize in nonfiction books that 'tell the story behind the story'." Currently emphasizing true crime, sports. De-emphasizing self-help.

Nonfiction: "We're always looking for regional nonfiction titles, and especially for sports, biographies, true crime and how-to books." Biography, how-to. Subjects include business/economics, ethnic, history, money/finance, regional, sports, true crime. Query with SASE or submit outline, 2 sample chapter(s).
Recent Title(s): *Home Ice: Reflections on Frozen Ponds and Backyard Rinks*, by Jack Falls (nonfiction).
Tips: "We pride ourselves on working closely with an author and producing a quality product with strong promotional campaigns."

MEADOWBROOK PRESS, 5451 Smetana Dr., Minnetonka MN 55343. (952)930-1100. Fax: (952)930-1940. Website: www.meadowbrookpress.com. **Acquisitions:** Submissions Editor. Estab. 1975. Publishes trade paperback originals and reprints. **Publishes 20 titles/year. Receives 1,500 queries/year. 15% of books from first-time authors. Pays 10% royalty. Offers small advance.** Publishes book 1 year after acceptance of ms. Accepts simultaneous submissions. Responds in 4 months to queries. Book catalog and ms guidelines for #10 SASE.

O→ Meadowbrook is a family-oriented press which specializes in parenting and pregnancy books, party planning books and children's poetry and fiction. De-emphasizing joke, quote books, and adult poetry.

Nonfiction: How-to, humor, reference. Subjects include child guidance/parenting, cooking/foods/nutrition, pregnancy, childbirth, party planning, children's activities, relationships. "We prefer a query first; then we will request an outline and/or sample material." Send for guidelines. No children's fiction, poetry, academic or biography. Query with SASE or submit outline, sample chapter(s).
Recent Title(s): *Pregnancy, Childbirth, & the Newborn*, by Penny Simkin (pregnancy); *Instant Parties*, by Luann Grosocup and Jo Tazelaar (party planning); *Children's Busy Book*, by Trish Kuffner (parenting).
Tips: "Always send for guidelines before submitting material. We do not accept unsolicited picture book submissions."

MEDICAL PHYSICS PUBLISHING, 4513 Vernon Blvd., Madison WI 53705. (608)262-4021. Fax: (608)265-2121. E-mail: mpp@medicalphysics.org. Website: www.medicalphysics.org. **Acquisitions:** John Cameron, president; Betsey Phelps, managing editor. Estab. 1985. Publishes hardcover and trade paperback originals and reprints. **Publishes 10-12 titles/year. Receives 10-20 queries/year. 100% from unagented writers. Pays 10% royalty on wholesale price.** Publishes book 6 months after acceptance of ms. Accepts simultaneous submissions. Responds in 6 months to mss. Book catalog available via website or upon request.

O→ "We are a nonprofit, membership organization publishing affordable books in medical physics and related fields." Currently emphasizing biomedical engineering. De-emphasizing books for the general public.

Nonfiction: Reference, technical, textbook. Subjects include health/medicine, symposium proceedings in the fields of medical physics and radiology. Submit complete ms. Reviews artwork/photos as part of ms package. Send disposable copies.
Recent Title(s): *The Modern Technology of Radiation Oncology*, edited by Jacob Van Dyk; *Physics of the Body*, by John R. Cameron, James G. Skofronick and Roderick M. Grant.

MERIWETHER PUBLISHING LTD., 885 Elkton Dr., Colorado Springs CO 80907-3557. (719)594-4422. Fax: (719)594-9916. E-mail: merpcds@aol.com. **Acquisitions:** Arthur Zapel, Theodore Zapel, Rhonda Wray, editors. Estab. 1969. Publishes paperback originals and reprints. **Receives 1,200 submissions/year. 50% of books from first-time authors; 90% from unagented writers. Pays 10% royalty on retail price or makes outright purchase.** Publishes book 6 months after acceptance of ms. Accepts simultaneous submissions. Responds in 1 month to queries. Book catalog and ms guidelines for $2 postage.

O→ Meriwether publishes theater books, games and videos; speech resources; plays, skits and musicals; and resources for gifted students. "We specialize in books on the theatre arts and religious plays for Christmas, Easter and youth activities. We also publish musicals for high school performers and churches." Currently emphasizing how-to books for theatrical arts and church youth activities.

Nonfiction: "We publish unusual textbooks or trade books related to the communication or performing arts and how-to books on staging, costuming, lighting, etc." How-to, humor, reference, textbook. Subjects include film/cinema/stage, humor, music/dance, recreation, religion, theater/drama. "We prefer mainstream religion titles." Query or submit outline/synopsis and sample chapters.
Fiction: Humor, mainstream/contemporary, mystery, plays (and musicals), religious, suspense, all in playscript format.

Recent Title(s): *International Plays for Young Audiences*, by Roger Ellis; *Spontaneous Performance*, by Marsh Cassady.

Tips: "Our educational books are sold to teachers and students at college, high school and middle school levels. Our religious books are sold to youth activity directors, pastors and choir directors. Our trade books are directed at the public with a sense of humor. Another group of buyers is the professional theatre, radio and TV category. We focus more on books of plays and short scenes and textbooks on directing, staging, make-up, lighting, etc."

MERRIAM PRESS, 218 Beech St., Bennington VT 05201-2611. (802)447-0313. Fax: (305)847-5978. E-mail: ray@merriam-press.com. Website: www.merriam-press.com. Publishes hardcover originals and reprints and trade paperback originals and reprints. **Publishes 12 titles/year. Receives 100 queries and 50 mss/year. 70-90% of books from first-time authors; 95% from unagented writers. Pays 10% royalty on retail price.** Publishes book 1 year after acceptance of ms. Accepts simultaneous submissions. Responds quickly to queries; e-mail preferred to queries. Book catalog for $1 or on website; ms guidelines online.

O- Merriam Press publishes only World War II history.

Nonfiction: Biography, illustrated book, reference, technical. Subjects include military/war (World War II). Query with SASE or submit proposal package, including outline and 1 sample chapter or submit complete ms. Reviews artwork/photos as part of ms package. Send photocopies or on floppy disk/CD.

Recent Title(s): *Valor Without Arms: A History of the 316th Troop Carrier Group, 1942-1945*, by Michael N. Ingrisano, Jr.; *The Fighting Bob: A Wartime History of the USS Robely D. Evans, DD-552*, by Michael Staton; *Riflemen: On the Cutting Edge of World War II*, by Earl A. Reitan.

Tips: "Our books are geared for WWII historians, collectors, model kit builders, wargamers, veterans, general enthusiasts. We do not publish any fiction or poetry, only WWII history."

METAL POWDER INDUSTRIES FEDERATION, 105 College Rd. E., Princeton NJ 08540. (609)452-7700. Fax: (609)987-8523. E-mail: info@mpif.org. Website: www.mpif.org. **Acquisitions:** Cindy Jablonowski, publications manager; Peggy Lebedz, assistant publications manager. Estab. 1946. Publishes hardcover originals. **Publishes 10 titles/year. Pays 3-12½% royalty on wholesale or retail price. Offers $3,000-5,000 advance.** Responds in 1 month to queries.

O- Metal Powder Industries publishes monographs, textbooks, handbooks, design guides, conference proceedings, standards, and general titles in the field of powder metullary or particulate materials.

Nonfiction: Work must relate to powder metallurgy or particulate materials. Technical, textbook.

Recent Title(s): *Advances in Powder Metallurgy and Particulate Materials* (conference proceeding).

MEYERBOOKS, PUBLISHER, P.O. Box 427, Glenwood IL 60425-0427. (708)757-4950. **Acquisitions:** David Meyer, publisher. Estab. 1976. Publishes hardcover and trade paperback originals and reprints. **Publishes 5 titles/year. Pays 10-15% royalty on wholesale or retail price.** Responds in 3 months to queries.

Imprints: David Meyer Magic Books, Waltham Street Press.

O- "We are currently publishing books on stage magic history. We only consider subjects which have never been presented in book form before. We are not currently considering books on health, herbs, cookery or general Americana."

Nonfiction: Reference. Subjects include history of stage magic. Query with SASE.

Recent Title(s): *Memoirs of a Book Snake: Forty Years of Seeking and Saving Old Books*, by David Meyer (book collecting/literary memoir).

MICHIGAN STATE UNIVERSITY PRESS, 1405 S. Harrison Rd., Manly Miles Bldg., Suite 25, East Lansing MI 48823-5202. (517)355-9543. Fax: (517)432-2611. E-mail: msupress@msu.edu. Website: www.msupress.edu/unit/msupress. **Acquisitions:** Martha Bates, acquisitions editor. Estab. 1947. Publishes hardcover and softcover originals. **Publishes 35 titles/year. Receives 2,400 submissions/year. 75% of books from first-time authors; 100% from unagented writers. Pays variable royalty.** Publishes book 18 months after acceptance of ms. Does not accept simultaneous submissions. Book catalog and ms guidelines for 9×12 SASE.

Imprints: Lotus/Colleagues; University of Calgary Press; Penumbra; National Museum of Science and Industry, UK; Lynx House.

O- Michigan State University publishes scholarly books that further scholarship in their particular field. In addition they publish nonfiction that addresses, in a more contemporary way, social concerns, such as diversity, civil rights, the environment.

Nonfiction: Scholarly. Subjects include Americana (American studies), business/economics, creative nonfiction, ethnic (Afro-American studies), government/politics, history (contemporary civil rights), language/literature, regional (Great Lakes regional, Canadian studies), women's issues/studies. Reviews artwork/photos as part of ms package.

Recent Title(s): *The Low Road: A Scottish Family Memoir*, by Valerie Miller (memoir); *A Second Life: A Collected Nonfiction*, by Dan Gerber (memoir, essay); *Black Eden: The Idlewild Community*, by Lewis Walker and Benjamin C. Wilson (African-American history).

MID-LIST PRESS, 4324 12th Ave S., Minneapolis MN 55407-3218. Website: www.midlist.org. Publisher: Lane Stiles. Estab. 1989. Publishes hardcover and trade paperback originals. **Publishes 4 titles/year.** Accepts simultaneous submissions. SASE for First Series guidelines and/or general submission guidelines; also available online.

O- Mid-List Press publishes books of high literary merit and fresh artistic vision by new and emerging writers.

Recent Title(s): *Objects and Empathy*, by Arthur Saltzman (nonfiction); *Plan Z by Leslie Kove*, by Betsy Robinson (novel); *Tip to Rump*, by Katherine Starke (poetry).
Tips: Mid-List Press is an independent press. In addition to publishing the annual winners of the Mid-List Press First Series Awards, Mid-List Press publishes fiction, poetry, and creative nonfiction by established writers.

THE MIDKNIGHT CLUB, P.O. Box 25, Brown Mills NJ 08015. (609)735-9043. E-mail: info@midknightclub.net. Website: www.midknightclub.net. **Acquisitions:** Faith Ann Hotchkin, editor-in-chief. Publishes trade paperback originals and reprints. **Publishes 2-3 titles/year. Receives 300 queries and 200 mss/year. 65% of books from first-time authors; 100% from unagented writers. Pays 10-12% royalty on wholesale price. Offers advance.** Publishes book 1 year after acceptance of ms. Accepts simultaneous submissions. Responds in 2 months to queries; 4 months to proposals. Book catalog online; ms guidelines online.

O━ "We're interested in religions of the ages and occult matters that have existed for a long time. No New Age fads."

Nonfiction: How-to, self-help. Subjects include philosophy, religion, spirituality. Reviews artwork/photos as part of ms package. Send photocopies.
Recent Title(s): *Out the In Door, 2nd Ed*, by Michael Szul.

MILKWEED EDITIONS, 1011 Washington Ave. S., Suite 300, Minneapolis MN 55415. (612)332-3192. Fax: (612)215-2550. Website: www.milkweed.org and www.worldashome.org. **Acquisitions:** Emilie Buchwald, publisher; Elisabeth Fitz, first reader (fiction, children's fiction, poetry); City as Home editor (literary writing about cities); World as Home editor (literary writing about the natural world). Estab. 1980. Publishes hardcover originals and paperback originals and reprints. **Publishes 15 titles/year. Receives 3,000 submissions/year. 30% of books from first-time authors; 70% from unagented writers. Pays 7½% royalty on retail price. Offers varied advance.** Publishes book 1-2 years after acceptance of ms. Accepts simultaneous submissions. Responds in 2 months to queries; 6 months to mss. Book catalog for $1.50; ms guidelines for #10 SASE.

O━ Milkweed Editions publishes literary fiction for adults and middle grade readers, nonfiction, memoir and poetry. "Our vision is focused on giving voice to writers whose work is of the highest literary quality and whose ideas engender personal reflection and cultural action." Currently emphasizing nonfiction about the natural world.

Nonfiction: Literary. Subjects include nature/environment, human community. Submit complete ms. with SASE.
Fiction: Literary. Novels for adults and for readers 8-13. High literary quality. Submit complete ms. with SASE.
Recent Title(s): *The Prairie in Her Eyes*, by Ann Daum (nonfiction); *Hell's Bottom, Colorado*, by Laura Pritchett (fiction); *The Porcelain Apes of Moses Mendelssohn*, by Jean Nordhaus (poetry).
Tips: "We are looking for excellent writing in fiction, nonfiction, poetry, and children's novels, with the intent of making a humane impact on society. Send for guidelines. Acquaint yourself with our books in terms of style and quality before submitting. Many factors influence our selection process, so don't get discouraged. Nonfiction is focused on literary writing about the natural world, including living well in urban environments. We no longer publish children's biographies. We read poetry in January and June only."

MILKWEEDS FOR YOUNG READERS, 1011 Washington Ave. S., Suite 300, Minneapolis MN 55415. (612)332-3192. Fax: (612)215-2550. Website: www.milkweed.org. **Acquisitions:** Elizabeth Fitz, children's reader. Estab. 1984. Publishes hardcover and trade paperback originals. **Publishes 1-2 titles/year. 25% of books from first-time authors; 70% from unagented writers. Pays 7½% royalty on retail price. Offers varies advance.** Publishes book 1 year after acceptance of ms. Accepts simultaneous submissions. Responds in 2 months to queries. Book catalog for $1.50; ms guidelines for #10 SASE.

O━ "We are looking first of all for high-quality literary writitng. We publish books with the intention of making a humane impact on society." Currently emphasizing literary nonfiction about the natural world.

Fiction: For ages 8-12. Adventure, fantasy, historical, humor, mainstream/contemporary, animal, environmental. Query with SASE.
Recent Title(s): *Parents Wanted*, by George Harrar; *Emma and the Ruby Ring*, by Yvonne MacGrory.

[A] **THE MILLBROOK PRESS INC.**, 2 Old New Milford Rd., Brookfield CT 06804. Fax: (203)775-5643. Website: www.millbrookpress.com. Executive Vice President/Publisher: Jean Reynolds. Editor in Chief: Amy Shields. Senior Editors: Laura Walsh, Anita Holmes, Kristen Bettcher, Deborah Grahame. **Acquisitions:** Kristen Vibbert, manuscript coordinator. Estab. 1989. Publishes hardcover and paperback originals. **Publishes 200 titles/year. Pays varying royalty on wholesale price or makes outright purchase. Offers variable advance.** Publishes book 1 year after acceptance of ms. Does not accept simultaneous submissions.
Imprints: Twenty-First Century Books, Roaring Brook

O━ Millbrook Press publishes quality children's books of curriculum-related nonfiction for the school/library market.

Nonfiction: Children's/juvenile. Subjects include animals, anthropology/archeology, ethnic, government/politics, health/medicine, history, hobbies, multicultural, nature/environment, science, sports. Specializes in general reference, social studies, science, arts and crafts, multicultural and picutre books. *Agented submissions only. No unsolicited mss.*
Recent Title(s): *The Spring Equinox*; *Basketball Arenas*; *Body Cycles.*

MINNESOTA HISTORICAL SOCIETY PRESS, Minnesota Historical Society, 345 Kellogg Blvd. W., St. Paul MN 55102-1906. (651)296-2264. Fax: (651)297-1345. Website: www.mnhs.org/mhspress. **Acquisitions:** Gregory M. Britton, director; Ann Regan, managing editor. Estab. 1849. Publishes hardcover and trade paperback originals, trade paperback reprints. **Publishes 20 titles/year; imprint publishes 1-4 titles/year. Receives 100 queries and 25 mss/year. 50% of books from first-time authors; 85% from unagented writers. Royalties are negotiated. Offers advance.** Publishes book 14 months after acceptance of ms. Does not accept simultaneous submissions. Responds in 1 month. *Writer's Market* recommends allowing 2 months for reply to queries. Book catalog free.

Imprints: Borealis Books; Midwest Reflections (memoir and personal history); Native Voices (works by American Indians).

O-ₜ Minnesota Historical Society Press publishes both scholarly and general interest books that contribute to the understanding of the Midwest.

Nonfiction: Regional works only. Biography, coffee table book, cookbook, illustrated book, reference, scholarly. Subjects include anthropology/archeology, art/architecture, cooking/foods/nutrition, ethnic, history, memoirs, photography, regional, women's issues/studies. Query with SASE or submit proposal package including outline, 1 sample chapter(s). Reviews artwork/photos as part of ms package. Send photocopies.

Recent Title(s): *The Boys' House: New and Selected Stories*, by Jim Heynen; *Sister Nations: Native American Women Writers on Community*, edited by Heidi Erdrich and Laura Tohe; *Frank L. McGhee: A Life on the Color Line, 1861-1912*, by Paul D. Nelson.

Tips: A regional connection is required.

MITCHELL LANE PUBLISHERS, INC., P.O. Box 619, Bear DE 19701. (302)834-9646. Fax: (302)834-4164. **Acquisitions:** Barbara Mitchell, publisher. Estab. 1993. Publishes hardcover and library bound originals. **Publishes 40 titles/year. Receives 100 queries and 5 mss/year. 0% of books from first-time authors; 90% from unagented writers. Makes outright purchase on work-for-hire basis.** Publishes book 1 year after acceptance of ms. Does not accept simultaneous submissions. Responds only if interested to queries. Book catalog free.

O-ₜ "Mitchell Lane publishes multicultural biographies for children and young adults."

Nonfiction: Biography, children's/juvenile. Subjects include ethnic, multicultural. Query with SASE. **All unsolicited mss returned unopened.**

Recent Title(s): *J.K. Rowling*, by Ann Gaines (Real-Life Reader Biography); *Jonas Saek and the Polio Vaccine*, by John Barlston (unlocking the secrets of science); *Latino Entrepreneurs*, by Susan Zannos (Latinos at Work).

Tips: "We hire writers on a 'work-for-hire' basis to complete book projects we assign. Send résumé and writing samples that do not need to be returned."

MODERN LANGUAGE ASSOCIATION OF AMERICA, 26 Broadway, 3rd Floor, New York NY 10004-1789. (646)576-5000. Fax: (646)458-0030. Director of MLA Book Publications: David G. Nicholls. **Acquisitions:** Joseph Gibaldi, director of book acquisitions and development; Sonia Kane, acquisitions editor. Estab. 1883. Publishes hardcover and paperback originals. **Publishes 15 titles/year. Receives 125 submissions/year. 100% from unagented writers. Pays 5-10% royalty on net receipts.** Publishes book 1 year after acceptance of ms. Does not accept simultaneous submissions. Responds in 2 months to mss. Book catalog free.

O-ₜ The MLA publishes on current issues in literary and linguistic research and teaching of language and literature at postsecondary level.

Nonfiction: Reference, scholarly, professional. Subjects include education, language/literature, translation (with companion volume in foreign language, for classroom use). No critical monographs. Query with SASE or submit outline.

Recent Title(s): *Recovering Spain's Feminist Tradition*, edited by Lisa Vollendorf; *Nihilist Girl*, by Sofya Kovalevskaya.

MOMENTUM BOOKS, LLC, 117 W. Third St., Royal Oak MI 48067. (800)758-1870. Fax: (248)691-4531. E-mail: momentumbooks@glis.net. Website: www.momentumbooks.com. **Acquisitions:** Franklin Foxx, editor. Estab. 1987. **Publishes 6 titles/year. Receives 100 queries and 30 mss/year. 95% of books from first-time authors; 100% from unagented writers. Pays 10-15% royalty.** Does not accept simultaneous submissions.

O-ₜ Momentum Books publishes regional books and general interest nonfiction.

Nonfiction: Biography, cookbook, guides. Subjects include cooking/foods/nutrition, government/politics, history, memoirs, military/war, sports, travel, women's issues/studies. Submit proposal package including outline, 3 sample chapter(s), marketing outline.

Recent Title(s): *Thus Spake David E*, by David E. Davis, Sr. (automotive); *Rockin' Down the Dial*, by David Carson (regional history); *Offbeat Cruises & Excursions*, by Len Barnes (travel).

MOODY PRESS, Moody Bible Institute, 820 N. LaSalle Blvd., Chicago IL 60610. (312)329-8047. Fax: (312)329-2019. Website: www.moodypress.org. Vice President/Executive Editor: Greg Thornton. **Acquisitions:** Acquisitions Coordinator. Estab. 1894. Publishes hardcover, trade and mass market paperback originals and hardcover and mass market paperback reprints. **Publishes 60 titles/year; imprint publishes 5-10 titles/year. Receives 1,500 queries and 2,000 mss/year. 1% of books from first-time authors; 99% from unagented writers. Royalty varies. Offers $500-5,000 advance.** Publishes book 9-12 months after acceptance of ms. Does not accept simultaneous submissions. Responds in 2-3 months to queries. Book catalog for 9×12 SAE with 4 first-class stamps; ms guidelines online.

Imprints: Northfield Publishing, Lift Every Voice (African American interest)

O-ₜ "The mission of Moody Press is to educate and edify the Christian and to evangelize the non-Christian by ethically publishing conservative, evangelical Christian literature and other media for all ages around the world; and to help provide resources for Moody Bible Institute in its training of future Christian leaders."

Nonfiction: Children's/juvenile, gift book, general Christian living. Subjects include child guidance/parenting, money/finance, religion, spirituality, women's issues/studies. "We are no longer reviewing queries or unsolicited manuscripts unless they come to us through an agent. Unsolicited proposals will be returned only if proper postage is included. We are not able to acknowledge the receipt of your unsolicited proposal." *Agented submissions only.*

Recent Title(s): *Lies Women Believe*, by Nancy Leigh DeMoss; *The New Sugar Creek Gang series*, by Pauline Hutchens Wilson and Sandy Dengler.

Tips: "Our audience consists of general, average Christian readers, not scholars. Know the market and publishers. Spend time in bookstores researching."

THOMAS MORE PUBLISHING, Resources for Christian Living, 200 E. Bethany Dr., Allen TX 75002. (972)390-6923. Fax: (972)390-6620. E-mail: dhampton@rcl-enterprises.com. Website: www.thomasmore.com. **Acquisitions:** Debra Hampton, marketing and acquisitions director (religious publishing). Publishes hardcover, trade paperback and mass market paperback originals and reprints. **Publishes 25 titles/year. Receives 250 queries and 150 mss/year. 25% of books from first-time authors; 50% from unagented writers. Pays 8-12% royalty on wholesale price. Offers $2-10,000 advance.** Publishes book 8 months after acceptance of ms. Accepts simultaneous submissions. Responds in 3 months to proposals; 3 months to mss. Book catalog free.

Imprints: Christian Classics (contact: Debra Hampton).

O→ Thomas More specializes in self-help and religious titles.

Nonfiction: Self-help. Subjects include religion, spirituality, women's issues/studies. Submit proposal package including outline, 3 sample chapter(s). Reviews artwork/photos as part of ms package. Send photocopies.

Recent Title(s): *Forever Young: The Authorized Biography of Loretta Young*, by Joan Webster-Anderson; *Good Marriages Don't Just Happen*, by Catherine Musco Garcia-Prats and Joseph A. Garcia-Prats, M.D.

MORNINGSIDE HOUSE, INC., Morningside Bookshop, 260 Oak St., Dayton OH 45410. (937)461-6736. Fax: (937)461-4260. E-mail: msbooks@erinet.com. Website: www.morningsidebooks.com. **Acquisitions:** Robert J. Younger, publisher. Publishes hardcover and trade paperback originals. **Publishes 10 titles/year; imprint publishes 5 titles/year. Receives 30 queries and 10 mss/year. 20% of books from first-time authors; 80% from unagented writers. Pays 10% royalty on retail price. Offers $1,000-2,000 advance.** Publishes book 15 months after acceptance of ms. Accepts simultaneous submissions. Book catalog for $4 or on website.

Imprints: Morningside Press, Press of Morningside Bookshop.

O→ Morningside publishes books for readers interested in the history of the American Civil War.

Nonfiction: Subjects include history, military/war. Query with SASE or submit complete ms. Reviews artwork/photos as part of ms package. Send photocopies.

Recent Title(s): *The Mississippi Brigade of Brig. Gen. Joseph R. Davis*, by T.P. Williams.

Tips: "We are only interested in previously unpublished material."

MOUNTAIN N'AIR BOOKS, P.O. Box 12540, La Crescenta CA 91224. (818)248-9345. Website: www.mountain-n-air.com. **Acquisitions:** Gilberto d'Urso, owner. Publishes trade paperback originals. **Publishes 6 titles/year. Receives 50 queries and 35 mss/year. 75% of books from first-time authors; 100% from unagented writers. Pays 5-10% royalty on retail price or makes outright purchase.** Publishes book 6 months after acceptance of ms. Does not accept simultaneous submissions. Responds in 2 weeks to queries; 2 months to mss. Ms guidelines via website or #10 SASE.

Imprints: Bearly Cooking.

O→ Mountain N'Air publishes books for those generally interested in the outdoors and travel.

Nonfiction: Biography, cookbook, how-to. Subjects include cooking/foods/nutrition, nature/environment, recreation, travel. Submit outline, 2 sample chapter(s). Reviews artwork/photos as part of ms package. Send photocopies.

Recent Title(s): *Thinking Out Loud Through the American West*; *An Explorer's Adventures in Tibet: An 1897 Epic*; *Hiking With Your Dog*.

MOUNTAIN PRESS PUBLISHING COMPANY, P.O. Box 2399, Missoula MT 59806-2399. (406)728-1900 or (800)234-5308. Fax: (406)728-1635. E-mail: info@mtnpress.com. Website: www.mountain-press.com. **Acquisitions:** Kathleen Ort, editor (natural history/science/outdoors); Gwen McKenna, editor (history); Jennifer Carey, editor (Roadside Geology, Field Guides and Tumblweed Series). Estab. 1948. Publishes hardcover and trade paperback originals. **Publishes 15 titles/year. Receives 250 submissions/year. 50% of books from first-time authors; 90% from unagented writers. Pays 7-12% royalty on wholesale price.** Publishes book 2 years after acceptance of ms. Responds in 3 months to queries. Book catalog online.

O→ "We are expanding our Roadside Geology, Geology Underfoot and Roadside History series (done on a state by state basis). We are interested in well-written regional field guides—plants and flowers—and readable history and natural history."

Nonfiction: How-to. Subjects include animals, history (Western), nature/environment, regional, science (Earth science). "No personal histories or journals." Query with SASE or submit outline, sample chapter(s). Reviews artwork/photos as part of ms package.

Recent Title(s): *Wild Berries*, by Betty Derig and Margaret Fuller; *Dinosaurs Under the Big Sky*, by Jack Horner; *Sacagawea's Son*, by Marion Tinling.

Tips: "Find out what kind of books a publisher is interested in and tailor your writing to them; research markets and target your audience. Research other books on the same subjects. Make yours different. Don't present your manuscript to a publisher—*sell* it to him. Give him the information he needs to make a decision on a title. Please learn what we publish before sending your proposal. We are a 'niche' publisher."

THE MOUNTAINEERS BOOKS, 1001 SW Klickitat Way, Suite 201, Seattle WA 98134-1162. (206)223-6303. Fax: (206)223-6306. E-mail: mbooks@mountaineers.org. Website: www.mountaineersbooks.org. **Acquisitions:** David Emblidge, editor-in-chief. Estab. 1961. Publishes 95% hardcover and trade paperback originals and 5% reprints. **Publishes 40 titles/year. Receives 150-250 submissions/year. 25% of books from first-time authors; 98% from unagented writers. Pays royalty on net receipts. Offers advance.** Publishes book 1 year after acceptance of ms. Does not accept simultaneous submissions. Responds in 3 months to queries. Book catalog for 9×12 SAE with $1.33 postage first-class stamps.

O‑ Mountaineers Books specializes in expert, authoritative books dealing with mountaineering, hiking, backpacking, skiing, snowshoeing, kayaking, canoeing, bicycling, etc. These can be either how-to-do-it or where-to-do-it (guidebooks). Currently emphasizing regional conservation and natural history.

Nonfiction: Children's/juvenile, how-to (outdoor), guidebooks for national and international adventure travel. Subjects include nature/environment, recreation, regional, sports (non-competitive self-propelled), translation, travel, natural history, conservation. Accepts nonfiction translations. Looks for "expert knowledge, good organization." Also interested in nonfiction adventure narratives. Does *not* want to see "anything dealing with hunting, fishing or motorized travel." Submit outline, 2 sample chapter(s), author bio.

Recent Title(s): *100 Classic Hikes in Colorado*, by Warren; *Climbing: From Gym to Crag: Building Skills for Real Rock*, by Lewis and Cauthorn.

Tips: "The type of book the writer has the best chance of selling to our firm is an authoritative guidebook (*in our field*) to a specific area not otherwise covered; or a how-to that is better than existing competition (again, *in our field*)."

[N] **MOYER BELL LIMITED**, 54 Phillips St., Wickford RI 02852-5126. (401)294-0106. Fax: (401)294-1076. E-mail: info@moyerbell.com. Website: www.moyerbell.com. **Publishes 20 titles/year; imprint publishes 5 titles/year. Pays 5% royalty on retail price.** Book catalog online.

Imprints: Asphodel Press

Nonfiction: Biography, reference. Subjects include government/politics, memoirs, women's issues/studies. Query with SASE.

Fiction: Literary. Query with SASE.

MUSTANG PUBLISHING CO., P.O. Box 770426, Memphis TN 38177-0426. Website: www.mustangpublishing.com. **Acquisitions:** Rollin Riggs, editor. Estab. 1983. Publishes hardcover and trade paperback originals. **Publishes 10 titles/year. Receives 1,000 submissions/year. 50% of books from first-time authors; 90% from unagented writers. Pays 6-8% royalty on retail price. Offers advance.** Publishes book 1 year after acceptance of ms. Accepts simultaneous submissions. Responds in 1 month. *Writer's Market* recommends allowing 2 months for reply to queries. Book catalog for $2 and #10 SASE. No phone calls, please.

O‑ Mustang publishes general interest nonfiction for an adult audience.

Nonfiction: How-to, humor, self-help. Subjects include Americana, general nonfiction, hobbies, humor, recreation, sports, travel. "Our needs are very general—humor, travel, how-to, etc.—for the 18-to 60-year-old market." Query with SASE or submit outline, sample chapter(s). Reviews artwork/photos as part of ms package. Send photocopies.

Recent Title(s): *Medical School Admissions: The Insider's Guide*, by Zebala (career); *The Complete Book of Golf Games*, by Johnston (sports).

Tips: "From the proposals we receive, it seems that many writers never go to bookstores and have no idea what sells. Before you waste a lot of time on a nonfiction book idea, ask yourself, 'How often have my friends and I actually *bought* a book like this?' We are not interested in first-person travel accounts or memoirs."

[A] **THE MYSTERIOUS PRESS**, Warner Books, 1271 Avenue of the Americas, New York NY 10020. (212)522-7200. Fax: (212)522-7990. Website: www.twbookmark.com. **Acquisitions:** Sara Ann Freed, editor-in-chief. Estab. 1976. Publishes hardcover, trade paperback and mass market editions. **Publishes 36-45 titles/year. Pays standard, but negotiable, royalty on retail price. Offers negotiable advance.** Publishes book an average of 1 year after acceptance of ms. Does not accept simultaneous submissions. Responds in 2 months to queries.

O‑ The Mysterious Press publishes well-written crime/mystery/suspense fiction.

Fiction: Mystery, suspense, Crime/detective novels. No short stories. *Agented submissions only.*

Recent Title(s): *Bad News*, by Donald Westlake; *The Red Room*, by Nicci French.

THE NARRATIVE PRESS, P.O. Box 2487, Santa Barbara CA 93101. (805)884-0160. Fax: (805)884-6127. E-mail: customerservice@narrativepress.com. Website: www.narrativepress.com. **Acquisitions:** William Urschel, publisher (true first-person adventure and exploration). Publishes trade paperback originals and reprints and electronic originals and reprints. **Publishes 30 titles/year; imprint publishes 78 titles/year. Receives 100 queries and 20 submissions/year. 10% of books from first-time authors; 50% from unagented writers.** Publishes book 2 months after acceptance of ms. Accepts simultaneous submissions. Responds in 1 month to queries; 1 month to proposals; 3 months to mss. Book catalog online; ms guidelines free.

Nonfiction: Biography. Subjects include anthropology/archeology, creative nonfiction, history, memoirs, military/war, travel. Query with SASE. Reviews artwork/photos as part of ms package.

NARWHAL PRESS, INC., 1629 Meeting St., Charleston SC 29405-9408. (843)853-0510. Fax: (843)853-2528. Website: www.shipwrecks.com. **Acquisitions:** Dr. E. Lee Spence, chief editor (marine archaeology, shipwrecks); Robert Stockton, managing editor (novels, marine histories, military). Estab. 1994. Publishes hardcover and quality trade paperback originals. **75% of books from first-time authors; 95% from unagented writers. Pays 10-15% royalty on wholesale price. Offers up to $2,000 advance.** Publishes book 1 year after acceptance of ms. Accepts simultaneous submissions.

O→ Narwhal Press specializes in books about shipwrecks and marine archaeology and military history.

Nonfiction: "We are constantly searching for titles of interest to shipwreck divers, marine archaeologists, Civil War buffs, etc., but we are expanding our titles to include novels, modern naval history, World War II, Korea, Vietnam and exceptional personal memoirs." Biography, how-to, reference. Subjects include Americana, anthropology/archeology, art/architecture, history, memoirs, military/war, Civil War. Query with SASE or submit outline, sample chapter(s). Reviews artwork/photos as part of ms package. Send photocopies.

Fiction: Historical, mainstream/contemporary, military/war, dive related. "We prefer novels with a strong historical context. We invite writers to submit fiction about undersea adventures. Best to call or write first." Query with SASE or submit sample chapter(s), synopsis.

Recent Title(s): *Death's Bright Angel*, by William Kerr (award-winning author); *The Hunley*, by Mark Ragan (used in TV MOW by TNT).

Tips: "Become an expert in your subject area. Polish and proofread your writing. Don't try to format."

NATUREGRAPH PUBLISHERS, INC., P.O. Box 1047, Happy Camp CA 96039. (530)493-5353. Fax: (530)493-5240. E-mail: nature@sisqtel.net. Website: naturegraph.com. Keven Brown, editor. **Acquisitions:** Barbara Brown, editor-in-chief. Estab. 1946. Publishes trade paperback originals. **Publishes 5 titles/year. Pays 8-10% royalty on wholesale price.** Accepts simultaneous submissions. Responds in 1 month to queries; 2 months to mss. Book catalog free.

O→ "Naturegraph publishes books to help people learn about the natural world and Native American culture. Not so technically written to scare away beginners." Emphasizing natural history and Native American history (but not political).

Nonfiction: Primarily publishes nonfiction for the layman in natural history (biology, geology, ecology, astronomy); American Indian (historical and contemporary); outdoor living (backpacking, wild edibles, etc.). How-to. Subjects include ethnic, nature/environment, science (natural history: biology, geology, ecology, astronomy), crafts. "Our primary niches are nature and Native American subjects with adult level, non-technical language and scientific accuracy. First, send for our free catalog. Study what kind of books we have already published." Query with SASE or submit outline, 2 sample chapter(s).

Recent Title(s): *Alone in the Wilderness*, by Hap Gilliance.

Tips: "Please—always send a stamped reply envelope. Publishers get hundreds of manuscripts yearly; not just yours."

THE NAUTICAL & AVIATION PUBLISHING CO., 1250 Fairmont Ave., Mt. Pleasant SC 29464. (843)856-0561. Fax: (843)856-3164. E-mail: nautical.aviation.publishing@worldnet.att.net. Website: www.nauticalaviation.com. **Acquisitions:** Janet C. Matthews, acquisitions editor. Estab. 1979. Publishes hardcover originals and reprints. **Publishes 10-12 titles/year. Receives 500 submissions/year. Pays 10-14% royalty on net receipts. Offers rare advance.** Accepts simultaneous submissions. Book catalog free.

O→ The Nautical & Aviation Publishing Co. publishes naval and military history fiction and reference.

Nonfiction: Reference. Subjects include military/war (American), naval history. Query with SASE or submit 3 sample chapter(s), synopsis. Reviews artwork/photos as part of ms package.

Fiction: Historical. Submit outline, synopsis.

Recent Title(s): *A Dictionary of King Arthur's Knights*, by Pamela Ryan; *A Murder at Sea*, by William P. Mack; *The Independence Light Aircraft Carriers*, by Andrew Faltum.

Tips: "We are primarily a nonfiction publisher, but will review historical fiction of military interest with strong literary merit."

NAVAL INSTITUTE PRESS, US Naval Institute, 291 Wood Ave., Annapolis MD 21402-5035. (410)268-6110. Fax: (410)295-1084. E-mail: esecunda@usni.org. Website: www.usni.org. Press Director: Ronald Chambers. **Acquisitions:** Paul Wilderson, executive editor; Tom Cutler, senior acquisitions editor; Eric Mills, acquisitions editor. Estab. 1873. **Publishes 80-90 titles/year. Receives 700-800 submissions/year. 50% of books from first-time authors; 90% from unagented writers. Pays 5-10% royalty on net receipts.** Publishes book 1 year after acceptance of ms. Accepts simultaneous submissions. Book catalog for 9×12 SASE; ms guidelines for #10 SASE.

Imprints: Bluejacket Books (paperback reprints).

O→ The U.S. Naval Institute Press publishes general and scholarly books of professional, scientific, historical and literary interest to the naval and maritime community.

Nonfiction: "We are interested in naval and maritime subjects and in broad military topics, including government policy and funding." Biography. Subjects include government/politics, history, science, women's issues/studies, tactics, strategy, navigation, aviation, technology and others. Submit proposal package including sample chapter(s) or submit complete ms.

Fiction: Historical, military/war. Limited to fiction on military and naval themes. Very small proportion of publishing program. Submit complete ms.

Recent Title(s): *Punk's War*, by Ward Carroll (fiction); *Nelson Speaks*, by Joseph Callo (nonfiction).

NAVPRESS PUBLISHING GROUP, P.O. Box 35001, Colorado Springs CO 80935. Website: www.navpress.com. Publishes hardcover, trade paperback and mass market paperback originals and reprints. **Publishes 45 titles/year. 25% of books from first-time authors; 90% from unagented writers. Pays royalty.** Book catalog free.

Imprints: Pinion Press

Nonfiction: Reference, self-help, inspirational, Christian living, Bible studies. Subjects include business/economics, child guidance/parenting, religion, spirituality, marriage. "We dc not accept unsolicited mss. Unsolicited mss will not be acknowledged without an SASE."

NEAL-SCHUMAN PUBLISHERS, INC., 100 Varick St., New York NY 10013. (212)925-8650. Fax: (212)219-8916. E-mail: charles@neal-schuman.com. Website: www.neal-schuman.com. **Acquisitions:** Charles Harmon, director of publishing. Estab. 1976. Publishes hardcover and trade paperback originals. **Publishes 30 titles/year. Receives 500 submissions/year. 75% of books from first-time authors; 90% from unagented writers. Pays 10% royalty on net receipts. Offers infrequent advance.** Publishes book 4 months after acceptance of ms. Does not accept simultaneous submissions. Responds in 1 month to proposals. Book catalog ar.d ms guidelines free.

- "Neal-Schuman publishes books about libraries, information science and the use of information technology, especially in education and libraries."

Nonfiction: Reference, technical, textbook, professional. Subjects include computers/electronic, education, software, Internet guides, library and information science. "We are looking for many books about the Internet." Submit proposal package including outline, sample chapter(s), résumé, preface.

Recent Title(s): *Internet Power Searching, 2nd ed*, by Phil Bradley.

THOMAS NELSON, INC., Box 141000, Nashville TN 37214-1000. (615)889-9000. Website: www.thomasnelson.com. **Acquisitions:** Acquisitions Editor. **Publishes 150-200 titles/year. Pays royalty on net receipts. Rates negotiated for each project. Offers advance.** Publishes book 1-2 years after acceptance of ms. Accepts simultaneous submissions. Responds in 3 months to queries.

Imprints: Thomas Nelson Publishers, W Publishing, Rutledge Hill, J. Countryman, Cool Springs Press, Reference and Electronic Publishing, Editorial Caribe, Nelson Multimedia Group, Tommy Nelson.

- Corporate address does not accept unsolicited mss; no phone queires.
- Thomas Nelson publishes Christian lifestyle nonfiction and fiction.

Nonfiction: Reference, self-help. Subjects include business/economics (business development), health/medicine (and fitness), religion, spirituality, adult inspirational, motivational, devotional, Christian living, prayer and evangelism, Bible study, personal development. Query with SASE or submit 1 sample chapter(s), résumé, 1-page synopsis.

Fiction: Publishes commercial fiction authors who write for adults from a Christian perspective.

Recent Title(s): *Wild at Heart*, by John Eldredge; *I Hope You Dance*, by Mark D. Sanders and Tia Sillers.

TOMMY NELSON, Thomas Nelson, Inc., P.O. Box 141000, Nashville TN 37214-1000. (615)889-9000. Fax: (615)902-3330. Website: www.tommynelson.com. Publishes hardcover and trade paperback originals. **Publishes 50-75 titles/year.** Does not accept simultaneous submissions. **No unsolicited submissions**.

Imprints: Word Kids.

- Tommy Nelson publishes children's Christian nonfiction and fiction for boys and girls up to age 14. "We honor God and serve people through books, videos, software and Bibles for children that improve the lives of our customers."

Nonfiction: Children's/juvenile. Subjects include religion (Christian evangelical).

Fiction: Adventure, juvenile, mystery, picture books, religious. "No stereotypical characters."

Recent Title(s): *Hangman's Curse*, by Frank Paretti; *Prayer of Jabez for Kids*, by Bruce Wilkinson.

Tips: "Know the CBA market. Check out the Christian bookstores to see what sells and what is needed."

NEW AMERICAN LIBRARY, Penguin Putnam Inc., 375 Hudson St., New York NY 10014. (212)366-2000. Website: www.penguinputnam.com. Publisher: Kara Welsh. Editorial Director: Claire Zion. **Acquisitions:** Ellen Edwards, executive editor (commercial women's fiction—mainstream novels and contemporary romances; mysteries in a series and single title suspense; nonfiction of all types for a general audience and historical); Laura Anne Gilman, executive editor (science fiction/fantasy/horror, mystery series, New Age); Jennifer Heddle, associate editor (science fiction/fantasy, pop culture and general nonfiction, historical fiction, erotica); Audrey LaFehr, executive editor (contemporary and historical romance, women's suspense, multicultural fiction); Hilary Ross, associate executive editor (romances, Regencies); Doug Grad, senior editor (thrillers, suspense novels, international intrigue, technothrillers, military fiction and nonfiction, adventure nonfiction); Genny Ostertag, senior editor (mysteries, suspense, commerical women's fiction); Dan Slater, senior editor (historical fiction, adult westerns, thrillers, military fiction and nonfiction, true crime, media tie-ins); Cecilia Oh, associate editor (romance, Regency, commercial women's fiction, inspirational nonfiction); Jennifer Jahner, assistant editor (suspense, multicultural commercial fiction, women's fiction). Publishes mass market and trade paperback originals and reprints. **Publishes 500 titles/year. Receives 20,000 queries and 10,000 mss/year. 30-40% of books from first-time authors; 5% from unagented writers. Pays negotiable royalty. Offers negotiable advance.** Publishes book 1-2 years after acceptance of ms. Does not accept simultaneous submissions. Responds in 6 months to queries.

Imprints: Mentor, Onyx, ROC, Signet, Signet Classic, Signet Reference.

- NAL publishes commercial fiction and nonfiction for the popular audience.

Nonfiction: Biography, how-to, reference, self-help. Subjects include animals, child guidance/parenting, cooking/foods/nutrition, ethnic, health/medicine, language/literature, military/war, money/finance, psychology, sports, women's issues/studies. "Looking for reference and annual books." *Agented submissions only.*

Fiction: Erotica, ethnic, fantasy, historical, horror, mainstream/contemporary, mystery, occult, romance, science fiction, suspense, western. "Looking for writers who can deliver a book a year (or faster) of consistent quality." *Agented submissions only.*

Recent Title(s): *Suspicion of Betrayal*, by Barbara Parker; *The Medusa Stone*, by Jack DuBrul.

NEW CENTURY BOOKS, Sharon's Books, P.O. Box 7113, The Woodlands TX 77387-7113. (936)295-5357. Fax: (936)295-0409. E-mail: newcentbks@aol.com. **Acquisitions:** Thomas Fensch, publisher. Publishes hardcover and trade paperback originals and reprints. **Publishes 10-12 titles/year; imprint publishes 2-4 titles/year. Receives 300 queries and 75 mss/year. 30-40% of books from first-time authors; 100% from unagented writers. Pays 15% royalty on retail price.** Publishes book 4 months after acceptance of ms. Accepts simultaneous submissions. Responds in 1 month to proposals. Book catalog for #10 SASE.

- New Century Books published entirely using print-on-demand technology.

Nonfiction: Autobiography, biography, children's/juvenile, self-help, textbook. Subjects include Americana, child guidance/parenting, contemporary culture, creative nonfiction, general nonfiction, health/medicine, history, language/literature, memoirs, military/war, sports, women's issues/studies. Query with SASE. Reviews artwork/photos as part of ms package. Send photocopies.

Fiction: Mainstream/contemporary, mystery. "We publish 99.5% nonfiction." Query with SASE.

Recent Title(s): *A Desert Daughter's Odyssey: For All Those Whose Lives Have Been Touched by Cancer—Personally, Professionally or through a Loved One*, by Sharon Wanslee; *The Man Who Was Dr. Seuss: The Life and Work of Theodor Geisel*, by Thomas Fensch; *Somone's in the Kitchen with Dinah*, by Barbara Pearson Arau (mystery).

Tips: "Be able to prove your book is better than any others in the field; know your market, as well as writing techniques. Please do not query via e-mail or fax."

THE NEW ENGLAND PRESS, INC., P.O. Box 575, Shelburne VT 05482. (802)863-2520. Fax: (802)863-1510. E-mail: nep@together.net. Website: www.nepress.com. **Acquisitions:** Christopher A. Bray, managing editor. Estab. 1978. Publishes hardcover and trade paperback originals. **Publishes 6-8 titles/year. Receives 500 queries and 200 mss/year. 50% of books from first-time authors; 90% from unagented writers. Pays royalty on wholesale price.** Publishes book 15 months after acceptance of ms. Accepts simultaneous submissions. Responds in 3 months to queries. Book catalog free.

O→ The New England Press publishes high-quality trade books of regional northern New England interest. Currently emphasizing young adult biography. De-emphasizing railroading.

Nonfiction: Biography, illustrated book, young adult. Subjects include history, nature/environment, regional, world affairs, Vermontiana. "Nonfiction submissions must be based in Vermont and have northern New England topics. No memoirs or family histories. Identify potential markets and ways to reach them in cover letter." Query with SASE or submit outline, 2 sample chapter(s). Reviews artwork/photos as part of ms package. Send photocopies.

Fiction: Historical (Vermont, New Hampshire, Maine). "We look for very specific subject matters based on Vermont history and heritage. We are also interested in historical novels for young adults based in New Hampshire and Maine. We do not publish contemporary adult fiction of any kind." Query with SASE or submit 2 sample chapter(s), synopsis.

Recent Title(s): *Vermont Owner's Manual*, by Frank Bryan and Bill Mares (nonfiction); *Robert Frost: The People, Places, and Stones Behind His New England Poetry*, by Lea Newman (poetry).

Tips: "Our readers are interested in all aspects of Vermont and northern New England, including hobbyists (railroad books) and students (young adult fiction and biography). No agent is needed, but our market is extremely specific and our volume is low, so send a query or outline and writing samples first. Sending the whole manuscript is discouraged. We will not accept projects that are still under development or give advances."

NEW HARBINGER PUBLICATIONS, 5674 Shattuck Ave., Oakland CA 94609. (510)652-0215. Fax: (510)652-5472. E-mail: nhelp@newharbinger.com. Website: www.newharbinger.com. **Acquisitions:** Catharine Sutker, acquisitions manager; Jueli Gastwirth, senior acquisitions editor. Estab. 1979. **Publishes 50 titles/year. Receives 1,000 queries and 300 mss/year. 60% of books from first-time authors; 75% from unagented writers. Pays 10% royalty on net receipts.** Publishes book 1 year after acceptance of ms. Accepts simultaneous submissions. Responds in 1 month to queries; 1 month to proposals; 2 months to mss. Book catalog and ms guidelines free.

O→ "We look for step-by-step self-help titles on psychology, health and balanced living titles that teach the average reader how to master essential skills. Our books are also read by mental health professionals who want simple, clear explanations of important psychological techniques and health issues."

Nonfiction: Self-help (psychology/health). Subjects include health/medicine, psychology, women's issues/studies, balanced living, anger management, anxiety, coping. "Authors need to be a qualified psychotherapist or health practitioner to publish with us." Submit proposal package including outline, 2 sample chapter(s), competing titles and a compelling, supported reason why the book is unique.

Recent Title(s): *The Anxiety & Phobia Workbook, 3rd edition*, by Edmund J. Bourne; *Rosacea: A Self-Help Guide*, by Arlen Brownstein; *Brave New You*, by Mary and John Valentis.

Tips: Audience includes psychotherapists and lay readers wanting step-by-step strategies to solve specific problems. "Our definition of a self-help psychology or health book is one that teaches essential life skills. The primary goal is to train the reader so that, after reading the book, he or she can deal more effectively with health and/or psychological challenges."

NEW HOPE PUBLISHERS, Woman's Missionary Union, P.O. Box 12065, Birmingham AL 35202-2065. (205)991-8100. Fax: (205)991-4015. E-mail: new_hope@wmu.org. Website: www.newhopepubl.com. **Acquisitions:** Acquisitions Editor. **Publishes 24-27 titles/year. Receives several hundred queries/year. Large% of books from first-time authors; large% from unagented writers. Pays royalty on net receipts.** Publishes book 2 years after acceptance of ms. Responds in 6 weeks to mss. Book catalog for 9×12 SAE with 3 first-class stamps; ms guidelines for #10 SASE.
Imprints: New Hope

O→ "Our goal is to create unique books that help women and families to grow in Christ and share His hope."

Nonfiction: "We publish books dealing with all facets of Christian life for women and families, including health, discipleship, missions, ministry, Bible studies, spiritual development, parenting, and marriage. We currently do not accept adult fiction or children's picture books. We are particularly interested in niche categories (such as mission trips, domestic violence, practicing forgiveness) and books on lifestyle development and change (blended families, retirement, etc)." Children's/juvenile (religion). Subjects include child guidance/parenting (from Christian perspective), education (Christian church), health/medicine (Christian), multicultural, religion (spiritual development, Bible study, life situations from Christian perspective, ministry), women's issues/studies (Christian), church leadership, evangelism (Christian faith—must relate to missions work, cultural or multicultural issues). Prefers a query and prospectus but will evaluate a complete ms.

Recent Title(s): *A Woman's Guide to Servant Leadership*, by Rhonda H. Kelley; *Infertility: A Survival Guide for Couples and Those Who Love Them*, by Cindy Lewis Dake; *Legacy of Prayer: A Spiritual Trust Fund for the Generations*, by Jennifer Kennedy Dean.

☆ **NEW HORIZON PRESS**, P.O. Box 669, Far Hills NJ 07931. (908)604-6311. Fax: (908)604-6330. E-mail: nhp@newhorizonpressbooks.com. Website: www.newhorizonpressbooks.com. **Acquisitions:** Dr. Joan S. Dunphy, publisher (nonfiction, social cause, true crime). Estab. 1983. Publishes hardcover and trade paperback originals. **Publishes 12 titles/year. 90% of books from first-time authors; 50% from unagented writers. Pays standard royalty on net receipts. Offers advance.** Publishes book 2 years after acceptance of ms. Accepts simultaneous submissions. Book catalog and ms guidelines free.
Imprints: Small Horizons.

O→ New Horizon publishes adult nonfiction featuring true stories of uncommon heroes, true crime, social issues and self help. Introducing a new line of children's self-help.

Nonfiction: Biography, children's/juvenile, how-to, self-help. Subjects include child guidance/parenting, creative nonfiction, government/politics, health/medicine, nature/environment, psychology, women's issues/studies, true crime. Submit proposal package including outline, 3 sample chapter(s), résumé, author bio, photo, marketing information.

Recent Title(s): *Deadly Deception*, by Brenda Gunn and Shannon Richardson.

Tips: "We are a small publisher, thus it is important that the author/publisher have a good working relationship. The author must be willing to sell his book."

☆ **NEW VICTORIA PUBLISHERS**, P.O. Box 27, Norwich VT 05055-0027. (802)649-5297. Fax: (802)649-5297. E-mail: newvic@aol.com. Website: www.opendoor.com/NewVic/. Editor: ReBecca Beguin. **Acquisitions:** Claudia Lamperti, editor. Estab. 1976. Publishes trade paperback originals. **Publishes 4-6 titles/year. Receives 100 submissions/year. 50% of books from first-time authors; large% from unagented writers. Pays 10% royalty.** Publishes book 1 year after acceptance of ms. Does not accept simultaneous submissions. Book catalog free.

O→ "New Victoria is a nonprofit literary and cultural organization producing the finest in lesbian fiction and nonfiction." Emphasizing mystery. De-emphasizing coming-of-age stories.

Nonfiction: Biography. Subjects include gay/lesbian, history (feminist), women's issues/studies. "We are interested in feminist history or biography and interviews with or topics relating to lesbians." No poetry. Submit outline, sample chapter(s).

Fiction: Adventure, erotica, fantasy, feminist, historical, humor, mystery, romance, science fiction, western. "We will consider most anything if it is well written and appeals to lesbian/feminist audience. Hard copy only—no disks." Submit outline, sample chapter(s), synopsis.

Recent Title(s): *Theoretically Dead*, by Tinker Marks (mystery); *Circles of Power*, by Barbara Summerhawk.

Tips: "Try to appeal to a specific audience and not write for the general market. We're still looking for well-written, hopefully humorous, lesbian fiction and well-researched biography or nonfiction."

[N] **NEW VOICES PUBLISHING**, KidsTerrain, Inc., P.O. Box 560, Wilmington MA 01887. (978)658-2131. Fax: (978)988-8833. E-mail: rschiano@kidsterrain.com. Website: www.kidsterrain.com. **Acquisitions:** Rita Schiano, executive editor (children's books). Estab. 2000. Publishes hardcover and trade paperback originals. **Publishes 5 titles/year. Receives 30 queries and 20 mss/year. 95% of books from first-time authors; 95% from unagented writers. Pays 10-15% royalty on wholesale price.** Publishes book 1 year after acceptance of ms. Does not accept simultaneous submissions. Responds in 1 month to queries; 3 months to proposals; 3 months to mss. Book catalog online; ms guidelines online.

O→ The audience for this company is children ages 4-9.

Nonfiction: Children's/juvenile, illustrated book. Subjects include child guidance/parenting. Query with SASE. Reviews artwork/photos as part of ms package. Send photocopies.
Fiction: Juvenile. Query with SASE.
Recent Title(s): *The Magic in Me*, by Maggie Moran (children's fiction); *Aunt Rosa's House*, by Maggie Moran (children's fiction); *Last Night I Left Earth for Awhile*, by Natalie Brown-Douglas (children's fiction).
Tips: "Know, specifically, what your story/book is about."

NEW WORLD LIBRARY, 14 Pamaron Way, Novato CA 94949. (415)884-2100. Fax: (415)884-2199. E-mail: escort@nwlib.com. Website: www.neworldlibrary.com. Publisher: Marc Allen. Senior Editor: Jason Gardner. **Acquisitions:** Georgia Hughes, editorial director. Estab. 1979. Publishes hardcover and trade paperback originals and reprints. **Publishes 35 titles/year. 20% of books from first-time authors; 50% from unagented writers. Pays 12-20% royalty on wholesale price for hardcover. Offers $0-30,000 advance.** Publishes book 18 months after acceptance of ms. Accepts simultaneous submissions. Responds in 3 months to queries. Book catalog and ms guidelines free.
Imprints: Nataraj, H.J. Kramer

- NWL is dedicated to publishing books that inspire and challenge us to improve the quality of our lives and our world.

Nonfiction: Gift book, self-help. Subjects include alternative lifestyles (health), business/economics (prosperity), ethnic (African/American, Native American), health/medicine (natural), money/finance, nature/environment, psychology, religion, spirituality, women's issues/studies, nutrition, personal growth, parenting. Query with SASE or submit outline, 1 sample chapter(s), author bio, SASE. Reviews artwork/photos as part of ms package. Send photocopies.
Recent Title(s): *The Seven Whispers*, by Christina Baldwin; *Women of Spirit*, by Katherine Martin; *A Monk in the World*, by Wayne Teasdale.

NEW YORK UNIVERSITY PRESS, 838 Broadway, New York NY 10003. (212)998-2575. Fax: (212)995-3833. Website: www.nyupress.nyu.edu. **Acquisitions:** Eric Zinner (cultural studies, literature, media, history); Jennifer Hammer (Jewish studies, psychology, religion, women's studies); Stephen Magro (social sciences); Alison Waldenberg. Estab. 1916. Hardcover and trade paperback originals. **Publishes 150 titles/year. Receives 800-1,000 queries/year. 30% of books from first-time authors; 90% from unagented writers. Pays royalty on net receipts.** Publishes book 8 months after acceptance of ms. Accepts simultaneous submissions. Responds in 1 month (peer reviewed) to proposals.

- New York University Press embraces ideological diversity. "We often publish books on the same issue from different poles to generate dialogue, engender and resist pat categorizations."

Nonfiction: Subjects include anthropology/archeology, business/economics, ethnic, gay/lesbian, government/politics, history, language/literature, military/war, psychology, regional, religion, sociology, sports, women's issues/studies. Query with SASE or submit proposal package including outline, 1 sample chapter(s). Reviews artwork/photos as part of ms package. Send photocopies.

NEWMARKET PRESS, 18 E. 48th St., New York NY 10017. (212)832-3575. Fax: (212)832-3629. E-mail: mailbox@newmarketpress.com. President/Publisher: Esther Margolis. **Acquisitions:** Keith Hollaman, executive editor; Shannon Berning, assistant editor. Publishes hardcover and trade paperback originals and reprints. **Publishes 25-30 titles/year. 10% of books from first-time authors; 20% from unagented writers. Pays royalty. Offers varied advance.** Publishes book 1 year after acceptance of ms. Accepts simultaneous submissions. Responds in 3 months to queries; 3 months to proposals; 3 months to mss. Ms guidelines for #10 SASE.

- Currently emphasizing movie tie-in/companion books, health, psychology, parenting. De-emphasizing fiction.

Nonfiction: "Our focus is on parenting and health titles, and on finance books." Biography, coffee table book, self-help. Subjects include child guidance/parenting, cooking/foods/nutrition, general nonfiction, health/medicine, history, memoirs, personal finance, film/performing arts. Query with SASE or submit proposal package including outline, 1-3 sample chapter(s), author info explaining why you're the best person to write this book.
Recent Title(s): *Kids & Sports: Everything You and Your Child Need to Know About Sports, Physical Activity, and Good Health*, by Eric Small, M.D., F.A.A.P. (health and fitness/parenting); *E.T.: The Extra-Terrestrial from Concept to Classic: The Illustrated Story of the Film and Filmmakers*, by Stephen Spielberg and Melissa Mathison (film).

NO STARCH PRESS INC., 555 De Haro St., Suite 250, San Francisco CA 94107. (415)863-9900. Fax: (415)863-9950. E-mail: info@nostarch.com. Website: www.nostarch.com. **Acquisitions:** William Pollock, publisher. Estab. 1994. Publishes trade paperback originals. **Publishes 10-12 titles/year. Receives 100 queries and 5 mss/year. 80% of books from first-time authors; 90% from unagented writers. Pays 10-15% royalty on wholesale price. Offers advance.** Publishes book 4 months after acceptance of ms. Accepts simultaneous submissions. Book catalog free.
Imprints: Linux Journal Press.

- No Starch Press Inc. is an independent publishing company committed to producing easy-to-read and information-packed computer books. Currently emphasizing open source, Web development, computer security issues, programming tools, and robotics. "More stuff, less fluff."

Nonfiction: How-to, reference, technical. Subjects include computers/electronic, hobbies, software (Open Source). Submit outline, 1 sample chapter(s), author bio, market rationale. Reviews artwork/photos as part of ms package. Send photocopies.
Recent Title(s): *Steal This Computer Book 2*, by Wallace Wang; *The Linux Cookbook*, by Michael Stutz.
Tips: "No fluff—content, content, content or just plain fun. Understand how your book fits into the market. Tell us why someone, anyone, will buy your book. Be enthusiastic."

NOLO.COM, 950 Parker St., Berkeley CA 94710. (510)549-1976. Fax: (510)548-5902. E-mail: info@nolo.com. Website: www.nolo.com. **Acquisitions:** Jane Portman, managing editor. Estab. 1971. Publishes trade paperback originals. **Publishes 25 titles/year. 10% of books from first-time authors; 98% from unagented writers. Pays 10-12% royalty on net receipts.** Accepts simultaneous submissions. Responds in 2 weeks to proposals.

O→ "Our goal is to publish 'plain English' self-help law books, software and various electronic products for our consumers."

Nonfiction: How-to, reference, self-help. Subjects include business/economics, general nonfiction, money/finance, legal guides in various topics including employment, consumer, small business, intellectual property landlord/tenant and estate planning. "We do some business and finance titles, but always from a legal perspective, i.e., bankruptcy law." Query with SASE or submit outline, 1 sample chapter(s). Welcome queries but majority of titles are produced inhouse.

Recent Title(s): *Avoid Employee Lawsuits*, by Barbara Kate Repa; *Using Divorce Mediation*, by Katherine E. Stoner.

NOMAD PRESS, Nomad Communications, P.O. Box 875, Route 5 South, Norwich VT 05055. (802)649-1995. Fax: (802)649-2667. E-mail: info@nomadpress.net. Website: www.nomadpress.net. Alex Kahan, Publisher. **Acquisitions:** Lauri Berkenkamp, Acquisitions Editor. Publishes trade paperback originals. **Publishes 6+ titles/year. 60% of books from first-time authors; 90% from unagented writers. Pays royalty on retail price or makes outright purchase. Offers negotiable advance.** Publishes book 1 year after acceptance of ms. Does not accept simultaneous submissions. Responds in 1-2 months to mss. Book catalog online; ms guidelines online.

Nonfiction: Coffee table book, how-to, humor. Subjects include Americana, child guidance/parenting, creative nonfiction, hobbies, memoirs, money/finance, recreation, sports, travel. Actively seeking well-written nonfiction. No disorder-specific parenting mss, cookbooks, poetry, or technical manuals. Submit complete ms. Reviews artwork/photos as part of ms package. Send photocopies.

Recent Title(s): *Bahamas Cruising Guide Third Edition*, by Mathew Wilson (cruising/sailing guide); *Teaching Your Children Good Manners: A Go Parents! Guide* (parenting).

NORTH CAROLINA OFFICE OF ARCHIVES AND HISTORY, (formerly North Carolina Division of Archives and History), Historical Publications Section, 4622 Mail Service Center, Raleigh NC 27699-4622. (919)733-7442. Fax: (919)733-1439. E-mail: donna.kelly@ncmail.net. Website: www.ah.dcr.state.nc.us/sections/hp. **Acquisitions:** Donna E. Kelly, administrator (North Carolina and southern history). Publishes hardcover and trade paperback originals. **Publishes 4 titles/year. Receives 20 queries and 25 mss/year. 5% of books from first-time authors; 100% from unagented writers. Makes one-time payment upon delivery of completed ms.** Publishes book 2 years after acceptance of ms. Accepts simultaneous submissions. Responds in 1 week to queries; 1 week to proposals; 2 months to mss. Ms guidelines for $3.

O→ "We publish *only* titles that relate to North Carolina. The North Carolina Office of Archives and History also publishes the *North Carolina Historical Review*, a scholarly journal of history."

Nonfiction: Hardcover and trade paperback books relating to North Carolina. Subjects include history (related to NC), military/war (related to NC), regional (NC and southern history). Query with SASE. Reviews artwork/photos as part of ms package. Send photocopies.

Recent Title(s): *Tar Heels: How North Carolinians Got Their Nickname*, by Michael Taylor; *The Civil War in Coastal North Carolina*, by John S. Carbone.

Tips: Audience is public school and college teachers and students, librarians, historians, genealogists, NC citizens, tourists.

NORTH LIGHT BOOKS, F&W Publications, 4700 Galbraith Rd., Cincinnati OH 45236. Editorial Director: Greg Albert. **Acquisitions:** Acquisitions Coordinator. Publishes hardcover and trade paperback how-to books. **Publishes 40-45 titles/year. Pays 10% royalty on net receipts. Offers $4,000 advance.** Accepts simultaneous submissions. Responds in 1 month to queries. Book catalog for 9×12 SAE with 6 first-class stamps.

O→ North Light Books publishes art, craft and design books, including watercolor, drawing, colored pencil and decorative painting titles that emphasize illustrated how-to art instruction. Currently emphasizing table-top crafts using materials found in craft stores like Michael's, Hobby Lobby.

Nonfiction: Art. How-to. Subjects include computers/electronic, hobbies, watercolor, drawing, colored pencil, decorative painting, craft and graphic design instruction books. Interested in books on watercolor painting, basic drawing, pen and ink, colored pencil, decorative painting, table-top crafts, basic design, computer graphics, layout and typograpy. Do not submit coffee table art books without how-to art instruction. Query with SASE or submit outline. Send photocopies or duplicate transparencies.

Recent Title(s): *Crafting Your Own Heritage Album*, by Bev Kirschner Braun; *Rubber Stamp Extravaganza*, by Vesta Abel; *Easy Christmas Projects You Can Paint*, by Margaret Wilson and Robyn Thomas.

NORTH POINT PRESS, Farrar Straus & Giroux, Inc., 19 Union Square W., New York NY 10003. (212)741-6900. Fax: (212)633-9385. **Acquisitions:** Rebecca Saletan, editorial director; Ethan Nosowsky, editor; Katrin Wilde, assistant editor. Estab. 1980. Publishes hardcover and paperback originals. **Publishes 25 titles/year. Receives 100 queries and 100 mss/year. 20% of books from first-time authors. Pays standard royalty. Offers varied advance.** Publishes book 18 months after acceptance of ms. Accepts simultaneous submissions. Responds in 2 months to queries; 3 months to proposals; 3 months to mss. Ms guidelines for #10 SASE.

O→ "We are a broad-based literary trade publisher—high quality writing only."

Nonfiction: Subjects include history, memoirs, nature/environment, religion (no New Age), sports, travel, music, cooking/food. "Be familiar with our list. No genres." Query with SASE or submit outline, 1-2 sample chapter(s).
Recent Title(s): *The Birds of Heaven*, by Peter Matthiessen; *Rowing to Latitude*, by Jill Fredston; *Postmodern Pooh*, by Frederick Crews.

NORTHEASTERN UNIVERSITY PRESS, 360 Huntington Ave., 416CP, Boston MA 02115. (617)373-5480. Fax: (617)373-5483. Website: www.neu.edu/nupress. **Acquisitions:** William Frohlich, director (music, criminal justice); John Weingartner, senior editor (history, law and society); Elizabeth Swayze, editor (women's studies). Estab. 1977. Publishes hardcover originals and trade paperback originals and reprints. **Publishes 40 titles/year. Receives 500 queries and 100 mss/year. 50% of books from first-time authors; 90% from unagented writers. Pays 5-15% royalty on wholesale price. Offers $500-5,000 advance.** Publishes book 1 year after acceptance of ms. Accepts simultaneous submissions. Book catalog and ms guidelines free.

- Northeastern University Press publishes scholarly and general interest titles in the areas of American history, criminal justice, women's studies, music and reprints of African-American literature. Currently emphasizing American studies. De-emphasizing literary studies.

Nonfiction: Biography, scholarly, adult trade, scholarly monographs. Subjects include Americana, history, regional, women's issues/studies, music, criminal justice. Query with SASE or submit proposal package including outline, 1-2 sample chapter(s). Reviews artwork/photos as part of ms package. Send photocopies.
Recent Title(s): *The Hub: Boston Past and Present*, by Thomas H. O'Connor; *Women Pioneers for the Environment*, by Mary Joy Breton.

NORTHERN ILLINOIS UNIVERSITY PRESS, 310 N. Fifth St., DeKalb IL 60115-2854. (815)753-1826. Fax: (815)753-1845. Director/Editor-in-Chief: Mary L. Lincoln. **Acquisitions:** Martin Johnson, acquisitions editor (history, politics). Estab. 1965. **Publishes 18-20 titles/year. Pays 10-15% royalty on wholesale price. Offers advance.** Does not accept simultaneous submissions. Book catalog free.

- NIU Press publishes scholarly work and books of general interest to the informed public. "We publish mainly history, politics, anthropology, and other social sciences. We are interested also in studies on the Chicago area and midwest and in literature in translation." Currently emphasizing history, the social sciences and cultural studies.

Nonfiction: "Publishes mainly history, political science, social sciences, philosophy, literary and cultural studies, and regional studies." Subjects include anthropology/archeology, government/politics, history, language/literature, philosophy, regional, social sciences, translation, cultural studies. No collections of previously published essays, no unsolicited poetry. Query with SASE or submit outline, 1-3 sample chapter(s).
Recent Title(s): *Possessed: Women, Witches and Demons in Imperial Russia.*

[A] **NORTHFIELD PUBLISHING**, Moody Press, 215 W. Locust St., Chicago IL 60610. (800)678-8001. Fax: (312)329-2019. **Acquisitions:** Acquisitions Coordinator. **Publishes 5-10 titles/year. 1% of books from first-time authors. Pays royalty on net receipts. Offers $500-50,000 advance.** Publishes book 1 year after acceptance of ms. Does not accept simultaneous submissions. Book catalog for 9×12 SAE with 2 first-class stamps.

- "Northfield publishes a line of books for non-Christians or those exploring the Christian faith. While staying true to Biblical principles, we eliminate some of the Christian wording and Scriptual references to avoid confusion."

Nonfiction: Biography (classic). Subjects include business/economics, child guidance/parenting, money/finance, religion. *Agented submissions only.*
Recent Title(s): *The World's Easiest Guide to Finances*, by Larry Burkett with Randy Southern.

NORTHLAND PUBLISHING, LLC, P.O. Box 1389, Flagstaff AZ 86002-1389. (928)774-5251. Fax: (928)774-0592. E-mail: info@northlandpub.com. Website: www.northlandpub.com. **Acquisitions:** Tammy Gales, adult editor; Rebecca Gmez, kids editor (picture books, especially with wide appeal). Estab. 1958. Publishes hardcover and trade paperback originals. **Publishes 25 titles/year; imprint publishes 10-12 titles/year. Receives 4,000 submissions/year. 20% of books from first-time authors; 20% from unagented writers. Pays royalty. Offers advance.** Publishes book 1-2 years after acceptance of ms. Accepts simultaneous submissions. Responds in 3 months to queries. Call for book catalog and ms guidelines.
Imprints: Rising Moon (books for children). Rising Moon is no longer publishing middle-grade children's fiction.

- Rising Moon has temporarily suspended consideration of unsolicited manuscripts.
- "Northland Publishing acquires nonfiction books intended for general trade audiences on the American West and Southwest, including Native American arts, crafts, and culture; regional cookery; Western lifestyle; popular culture and history; and interior design, architecture, and gardening. Northland is not accepting poetry or fiction at this time."

Nonfiction: Coffee table book, cookbook, gift book, illustrated book. Subjects include anthropology/archeology (Native American), art/architecture, cooking/foods/nutrition (Southwest cookbooks), ethnic (Native American, Hispanic), gardening, history (Native American), hobbies (collecting/arts), nature/environment (picture books), regional (Southwestern, Western US), travel, popular culture (film, nostalgia). Query with SASE or submit outline, 2-3 sample chapter(s). No fax or e-mail submissions. Reviews artwork/photos as part of ms package. Picture books. Submit complete ms.
Recent Title(s): *Mythmakers of the West: Shaping America's Imagination*, by John A. Murray; *A Gringo's Guide to Authentic Mexican Cooking*, by Mad Coyote Joe.

Tips: "Our audience is composed of general interest readers."

NORTHWORD PRESS, Creative Publishing International, Inc., 5900 Green Oak Dr., Minnetonka MN 55343. (612)936-4700. Fax: (612)933-1456. Website: www.northwordpress.com. **Acquisitions:** Barbara K. Harold (adult books); Aimee Jackson (children's books). Estab. 1984. Publishes hardcover and trade paperback originals. **Publishes 15-20 titles/year. Receives 600 submissions/year. 25% of books from first-time authors; 50% from unagented writers. Pays 10-12% royalty on wholesale price. Offers $2,000-10,000 advance.** Publishes book 1-2 years after acceptance of ms. Accepts simultaneous submissions. Responds in 3 months to queries. Ms guidelines for #10 SASE.

O→ NorthWord Press publishes exclusively nature and wildlife titles for adults and children.

Nonfiction: Children's/juvenile, coffee table book, illustrated book, introductions to wildlife and natural history. Subjects include animals, nature/environment. Query with SASE or submit outline, sample chapter(s).

Recent Title(s): *Friendships in Nature*, by James Gary Hines II, artwork by Jan Martin McGuire (picture book; ages 5-8); *We Are Dolphins*, by Molly Grooms, illustrations by Takashi Oda (picture book; ages 4-7); *Big Cats!*, by various authors (nonfiction; ages 7-10).

Tips: "Visit our website before submitting to see if your submission is a good fit for our list."

NOVA PRESS, 11659 Mayfield Ave., Suite 1, Los Angeles CA 90049. (310)207-4078. Fax: (310)571-0908. E-mail: novapress@aol.com. Website: www.novapress.net. **Acquisitions:** Jeff Kolby, president. Estab. 1993. Publishes trade paperback originals. **Publishes 4 titles/year. Pays 10-22½% royalty on net receipts. Offers advance.** Publishes book 6 months after acceptance of ms. Does not accept simultaneous submissions. Book catalog free.

O→ Nova Press publishes only test prep books for college entrance exams (SAT, GRE, GMAT, LSAT, etc.), and closely related reference books, such as college guides and vocabulary books.

Nonfiction: How-to, self-help, technical, test prep books for college entrance exams. Subjects include education, software.

Recent Title(s): *The MCAT Chemistry Book*, by Ajikumar Aryangat.

[N] **NW WRITERS' CORPORATION**, NSpirit Cultural Newsmagazine, Ogun Books, 30620 Pacific Highway S., Suite 110, Federal Way WA 98003. (253)839-3177. Fax: (253)839-3207. E-mail: nwwriterscorp@aol.com. Website: www.nwwriterscorp.com. **Acquisitions:** Amontaine Woods, executive editor (fiction, inspirational, women); Orisade Awodola, editor (nonfiction, genealogy, history, spiritual, empowerment, black, cultural studies). Estab. 1998. Publishes hardcover and trade paperback originals and reprints. **Publishes 6-8 titles/year; imprint publishes 2-3 titles/year. Receives 600 queries and 200 mss/year. 100% of books from first-time authors; 100% from unagented writers. Pays 20-25% royalty or makes outright purchase of $1,000-2,000.** Publishes book 1 year after acceptance of ms. Accepts simultaneous submissions. Responds in 1 month to queries; 1 month to proposals; 3 months to mss. Book catalog online; ms guidelines online.

Nonfiction: Autobiography, biography, booklets, multimedia. Subjects include creative nonfiction, education, ethnic, general nonfiction, history, multicultural, psychology, religion, social sciences, sociology, spirituality, women's issues/studies, world affairs, metaphysics. Query with SASE or submit proposal package including outline, 4 sample chapter(s). Reviews artwork/photos as part of ms package. Send photocopies.

Fiction: Ethnic, historical, multicultural, multimedia, religious, spiritual. "We accept fiction mss based on marketability and review for filming potential." Query with SASE.

Recent Title(s): *Scripts of Light & Revelation*, by Dr. Harrison Matchett (metaphysics); *Ancestral Healing*, by Orisade Awodola (geneaology); *Still My Tremblin' Soul*, by Carolyn Y. Parnell (suspense).

Tips: Audience consists of educators, business leaders, college students.

OAK KNOLL PRESS, 310 Delaware St., New Castle DE 19720. (302)328-7232. Fax: (302)328-7274. E-mail: oakknoll @oakknoll.com. Website: www.oakknoll.com. Estab. 1976. Publishes hardcover and trade paperback originals and reprints. **Publishes 40 titles/year. Receives 250 queries and 100 mss/year. 50% of books from first-time authors; 100% from unagented writers.** Publishes book 12 months after acceptance of ms. Accepts simultaneous submissions.

O→ Oak Knoll specializes in books about books—preserving the art and lore of the printed word.

Nonfiction: How-to. Subjects include book arts, printing, papermaking, bookbinding, book collecting, etc. Reviews artwork/photos as part of ms package. Send photocopies.

Recent Title(s): *Historical Scripts*, by Stan Knight; *The Great Libraries*, by Stan Staikos.

[N] **OAK TREE PRESS**, 915 W. Foothill Blvd., #411, Claremont CA 91711-3356. (909)625-8400. Fax: (909)625-3930. E-mail: oaktreepub@aol.com. Website: www.oaktreebooks.com. **Acquisitions:** Sarah Wasson, acquisitions editor; Billie Johnson, publisher. Publishes hardcover, trade paperback and mass market paperback originals. **Publishes 8-10 titles/year; imprint publishes 3-4 titles/year. Receives 5,000 queries and 300 mss/year. 99% of books from first-time authors; 99% from unagented writers. Pays 20% royalty on wholesale price.** Publishes book 1 year after acceptance of ms. Accepts simultaneous submissions. Responds in 1 month to queries; 2 months to proposals; 3 months to mss. Book catalog online; ms guidelines online.

Imprints: Dark Oak Mysteries, Timeless Love.

O→ "Oak Tree books primarily target readers of commercial, rather than literary fiction, and our nonfiction targets mainstream rather than academic readers."

Nonfiction: Biography, coffee table book, gift book, how-to, humor, self-help. Subjects include Americana, art/architecture, business/economics, creative nonfiction, ethnic, health/medicine, history, memoirs, philosophy, photography, regional, sociology, travel. Query with SASE. Reviews artwork/photos as part of ms package. Send photocopies.

Fiction: Adventure, confession, feminist, humor, mainstream/contemporary, mystery, picture books, romance, suspense. Query with SASE.
Recent Title(s): *Midlife Mojo*, by Robert M. Davis, Ph.D. (self-help); *Hearts Across Forever*, by Mary Montague Sikes (romance); *Callie & the Dealer & A Dog Named Jake*, by Wendy H. Mills (mystery).
Tips: "Spell everything correctly in the query letter! Understand the business side of book publishing—or at least be willing to learn a few basics. Be eager and enthusiastic about participating in the marketing and promotion of the title."

THE OAKLEA PRESS, 6912-B Three Chopt Road, Richmond VA 23226. (804)281-5872. Fax: (804)281-5686. E-mail: jgots@oakleapress.com. Website: www.oakleapress.com. **Acquisitions:** John Gotschalk, editor (visionary fiction); S.H. Martin, publisher (self-help). Publishes hardcover and trade paperback originals. **Receives 50 queries and 25 mss/year. 25% of books from first-time authors; 100% from unagented writers. Pays 10-20% royalty on wholesale price.** Publishes book 6 months after acceptance of ms. Accepts simultaneous submissions. Responds in 1 month to queries; 1 month to proposals; 3 months to mss. Book catalog online.
Nonfiction: How-to, self-help. Subjects include psychology, spirituality, self-actualization. "Currently we are looking for books on self-improvement." Submit proposal package including outline, 1 sample chapter(s).
Fiction: Mystery, occult, suspense, visionary fiction. "We like fast-paced adventure, suspense, and mystery stories that have an underpinning of metaphysics/spirituality." Submit proposal package including 1 sample chapter(s), synopsis.
Recent Title(s): *Under a Lemon Moon*, by David Martin (fiction).

OAKWOOD PUBLISHING, P.O. Box 403, Oakwood OH 45409. (937)298-1998. **Acquisitions:** Doug Neff, managing editor. Publishes age-specific paperback originals. **Publishes 10-15 titles/year. Receives 200 queries and 50 mss/year. 90% of books from first-time authors; 100% from unagented writers. Pays 10% royalty on retail price.** Publishes book 10 months after acceptance of ms. Accepts simultaneous submissions. Responds in 2 month to queries; 3 months to proposals; 2 months to mss. Book catalog for 9×12 SAE with 2 first-class stamps; Ms guidelines for #10 SASE.
Nonfiction: Children's/juvenile, how-to, self-help. Subjects include child guidance/parenting, education, government/politics, history, religion, sex, spirituality, women's issues/studies. Subjects include motivational; social issues such as AIDS, abortion, teenage drinking; environmental issues such as the Rainforest and the ozone layer; teen sexuality, "hot youth topics," career guidance. Publishes books in the Fall. Query with SASE or submit outline, 3 sample chapter(s). Reviews artwork/photos as part of ms package. Send photocopies.
Recent Title(s): *Constitution Translated for Kids*, by Cathy Travis; *Reflections in the Mirror*, by Kayse Budd; *Wisdom of Teen Chat*, by Donna Getzinger.
Tips: Readers are students in grades 7-12 and their teachers. "We're looking for quality material on hot topics that will appeal to middle school/high school students. Submit fresh topics with logical thought and writing."

OASIS PRESS, P.O. Box 3727, Central Point OR 97502. (541)245-6502. **Acquisitions:** Harley B. Patrick. Estab. 1975. Publishes hardcover, trade paperback and binder originals. **Publishes 20-30 titles/year. Receives 90 submissions/year. 60% of books from first-time authors; 90% from unagented writers. Pays 10% royalty on the net received.** Publishes book 6 months after acceptance of ms. Accepts simultaneous submissions. Responds in 2 months (initial feedback) to queries. Book catalog and ms guidelines for #10 SASE.
Imprints: Hellgate Press.

- Oasis Press publishes books for small business or individuals who are entrepreneurs or owners or managers of small businesses (1-300 employees).

Nonfiction: How-to, reference, textbook. Subjects include business/economics, computers/electronic, education, money/finance, nature/environment, retirement, exporting, franchise, finance, marketing/public relations, relocations, environment, taxes, business start up and operation. Needs information-heavy, readable mss written by professionals in their subject fields. Interactive where appropriate. Authorship credentials less important than hands-on experience qualifications. Submit outline, sample chapter(s). Query for unwritten material or to check current interest in topic and orientation. Reviews artwork/photos as part of ms package.
Recent Title(s): *The Entrepreneur's Guide to Managing Intellectual Property*, by Paul Schaafsma.
Tips: "Best chance is with practical, step-by-step manuals for operating a business, with worksheets, checklists. The audience is made up of entrepreneurs of all types: Small business owners and those who would like to be; attorneys, accountants and consultants who work with small businesses; college students; dreamers. Make sure your information is valid and timely for its audience, also that by virtue of either its content quality or viewpoint, it distinguishes itself from other books on the market."

OCTAMERON ASSOCIATES, 1900 Mount Vernon Ave., Alexandria VA 22301. (703)836-5480. Website: www.octameron.com. **Acquisitions:** Karen Stokstad, editor. Publishes trade paperback originals. **Publishes 17 titles/year. Receives 100 submissions/year. 15% of books from first-time authors; 100% from unagented writers. Pays 7½% royalty on retail price. Offers $500-1,000 advance.** Publishes book 9 months after acceptance of ms. Accepts simultaneous submissions. Responds in 2 months to proposals. Book catalog free.
Nonfiction: Reference. Subjects include education. Submit proposal package including 2 sample chapter(s), table of contents.
Recent Title(s): *Majoring in Success*, by Anthony Arcieri and Marianne Green; *The Best 201 Colleges*, by Michael Viollt.
Tips: Audience is high school students and their parents, high school guidance counselors. "Keep the tone light."

ODD GIRLS PRESS, P.O. Box 2157, Anaheim CA 92814-0157. (800)821-0632. Fax: (419)735-2084. E-mail: publisher@oddgirlspress.com. Website: www.oddgirlspress.com. Estab. 1995. Publishes trade paperback originals. **Publishes 4 titles/year. Receives 900 queries and 250 mss/year. 25% of books from first-time authors; 95% from unagented writers. Pays 7-10% royalty on retail price.** Publishes book 1 year after acceptance of ms. Accepts simultaneous submissions. Responds in 1 month to queries; 1 month to proposals; 3 months to mss. Book catalog free; ms guidelines for #10 SASE.

Nonfiction: Autobiography, biography, humor, reference. Subjects include alternative lifestyles, gay/lesbian, women's issues/studies. Writers must know their subject well, have a written style that is accessible to many different levels of readers, i.e. not just academic. Submit complete ms.

Fiction: Fantasy, feminist, gay/lesbian, historical, literary, mystery, poetry, science fiction, suspense, western, young adult. All fiction must be lesbian-related. "We are looking for well-written material submitted in a professional manner following our guidelines. As a feminist press, we only accept writing by women." Submit complete ms.

Poetry: Submit complete ms.

Tips: "Our books are read by a wide range of readers, working class to academic. Our goal is to publish fiction and nonfiction covering topics of interest to contemporary lesbians. We will not accept mss written by men, even if the protagonist is lesbian or bisexual. We are looking for authors who know how to write and whose mss are not works in progress but finished books. Our editors work closely with the authors to polish mss and keep the author's voice intact."

OHIO UNIVERSITY PRESS, Scott Quadrangle, Athens OH 45701. (740)593-1155. Fax: (740)593-4536. Website: www.ohiou.edu/oupress/. **Acquisitions:** Gillian Berchowitz, senior editor (American history and popular culture, African studies, Appalachian studies); David Sanders, director (literature, literary criticism, midwest and frontier studies, Ohioana). Estab. 1964. Publishes hardcover and trade paperback originals and reprints. **Publishes 45-50 titles/year. Receives 500 queries and 50 mss/year. 20% of books from first-time authors; 95% from unagented writers. Pays 7-10% royalty on net receipts.** Publishes book 1 year after acceptance of ms. Responds in 1 month to queries; 1 month to proposals; 2 months to mss. Book catalog free; ms guidelines for #10 SASE.

Imprints: Ohio University Research International Studies (Gillian Berchowitz); Swallow Press (David Sanders, director).

- Ohio University Press publishes and disseminates the fruits of research and creative endeavor, specifically in the areas of literary studies, regional works, philosophy, contemporary history, African studies and frontier Americana. Its charge to produce books of value in service to the academic community and for the enrichment of the broader culture is in keeping with the university's mission of teaching, research and service to its constituents.

Nonfiction: Reference, scholarly. Subjects include Americana, anthropology/archeology, art/architecture, ethnic, gardening, government/politics, history, language/literature, military/war, nature/environment, philosophy, regional, sociology, travel, women's issues/studies, African studies. "We prefer queries or detailed proposals, rather than manuscripts, pertaining to scholarly projects that might have a general interest. Proposals should explain the thesis and details of the subject matter, not just sell a title." Query with SASE. Reviews artwork/photos as part of ms package. Send photocopies.

Recent Title(s): *Set the Ploughshare Deep: A Prairie Memoir*, by Timothy Murphy; *The Selected Letters of Yvor Winters*, edited by R.L. Barth; *Midland: Poems*, by Kwame Dawes.

Tips: "Rather than trying to hook the editor on your work, let the material be compelling enough and well-presented enough to do it for you."

THE OLIVER PRESS, INC., 5707 W. 36th St., Minneapolis MN 55416-2510. (952)926-8981. Fax: (952)926-8965. E-mail: queries@oliverpress.com. Website: www.oliverpress.com. **Acquisitions:** Denise Sterling, editor. Estab. 1991. Publishes hardcover originals. **Publishes 10 titles/year. Receives 100 queries and 20 mss/year. 10% of books from first-time authors; 100% from unagented writers.** Publishes book up to 2 years after acceptance of ms. Accepts simultaneous submissions. Responds in 6 months to queries. Book catalog for 9×12 SAE with 4 first-class stamps; ms guidelines for #10 SASE.

- "We publish collective biographies for ages 10 and up. Although we cover a wide array of subjects, all are published in this format. We are looking for titles for our Innovators series (history of technology) and Business Builders series."

Nonfiction: Collective biographies only. Children's/juvenile. Subjects include business/economics, ethnic, government/politics, health/medicine, history (history of technology), military/war, nature/environment, science. Query with SASE.

Recent Title(s): *Business Builders in Fast Food*, by Nathan Aaseng; *Women with Wings*, by Jacqueline McLean.

Tips: "Audience is primarily junior and senior high school students writing reports."

ONE ON ONE COMPUTER TRAINING, Mosaic Media, 2055 Army Trail Rd., Suite 100, Addison IL 60101. (630)628-0500. Fax: (630)628-0550. E-mail: oneonone@pincom.com. Website: www.oootraining.com. **Acquisitions:** Natalie Young, manager product development. Estab. 1976. **Publishes 10-20 titles/year. 100% from unagented writers. Makes outright purchase of $3,500-10,000. Pays 5-10% royalty (rarely). Advance offer depends on purchase contract.** Publishes book 3 months after acceptance of ms. Does not accept simultaneous submissions. Responds in 1 month to queries. Book catalog free.

Imprints: OneOnOne Computer Training, Working Smarter, Professional Training Associates

- OneOnOne Computer Training publishes ongoing computer training for computer users and office professionals. Currently emphasizing soft skills for IT professionals.

Nonfiction: How-to, self-help, technical. Subjects include computers/electronic, software, IT, Internet programming, software certification and computer security. **All unsolicited mss returned unopened.** Query.
Recent Title(s): *Problem Solving with Visual Basic*; *Managing People at Work.*

ONE WORLD BOOKS, Ballantine Publishing Group, Inc., 1540 Broadway, 11th Floor, New York NY 10036. (212)782-8378. Fax: (212)782-8442. E-mail: adiggs@randomhouse.com. **Acquisitions:** Anita Diggs, senior editor. Publishes hardcover, trade and mass market paperback originals and trade paperback reprints. **Publishes 24 titles/year. Receives 350 queries and 500 submissions/year. 50% of books from first-time authors; 5% from unagented writers. Pays 7½-15% royalty on retail price. Offers $40,000-200,000 advance.** Publishes book 18 months after acceptance of ms. Accepts simultaneous submissions. Responds in 1 month to queries; 1 month to proposals; 2 months to mss.
Nonfiction: "All One World Books must be specifically written for either an African-American, Asian or Hispanic audience. Absolutely no exceptions!" Biography, cookbook, how-to, humor, self-help. Subjects include Americana, cooking/foods/nutrition, creative nonfiction, ethnic, government/politics, history, memoirs, multicultural, philosophy, psychology, recreation, travel, women's issues/studies, African-American studies. *Agented submissions only.*
Fiction: "All One World Books must be specifically written for either an African-American, Asian or Hispanic audience. Absolutely no exceptions!" Adventure, comic books, confession, erotica, ethnic, historical, humor, literary, mainstream/contemporary, multicultural, mystery, regional, romance, suspense, strong need for commercial women's fiction. No poetry. *Agented submissions only.*
Recent Title(s): *Bill Clinton and Black America*, by Dewayne Wickham; *Bittersweet*, by Freddie Lee Johnson III.
Tips: Targets African-American, Asian and Hispanic readers. All books must be written in English.

ONJINJINKTA PUBLISHING, The Betty J. Eadie Press, P.O. Box 25490, Seattle WA 98125. Website: www.onjinjinkta.com. Publishes hardcover, trade paperback and mass market paperback originals. **Publishes 4-8 titles/year. 50% of books from first-time authors; 1% from unagented writers. Pays 10-15% royalty. Offers $1,000-5,000 advance.** Publishes book 18-24 months after acceptance of ms. Queries are accepted. Please do not send unsolicited material or ms. **Do not** send any proposal, ms, idea, etc. by mail.

O¬ "We publish books intended to bring the reader closer to God. We want to see books on spirituality and redeeming principles and about life experiences that can touch and uplift."

Nonfiction: Children's/juvenile, self-help. Subjects include creative nonfiction, history, nature/environment, philosophy, psychology, religion, spirituality, near death experiences. Submit proposal package including outline, 1 sample chapter(s), author bio, SASE.
Recent Title(s): *The Soul's Remembrance*, by Roy Mills; *The Adventures of Caterpillar Jones*, by the J.J. Brothers; *Embraced by the Light Daily Prayers and Devotions*, by Betty J. Eadie.
Tips: "Nonfiction audience is thoughtful, hopeful individuals who seek self-awareness. We can only publish a short list each year; your book must target its market forcefully, and its story must express and invoke fresh ideas. We do not publish channeled or guide inspired books. Be willing to go all out in promoting and marketing your work!"

OPEN ROAD PUBLISHING, P.O. Box 284, Cold Spring Harbor NY 11724. (631)692-7172. Fax: (631)692-7193. E-mail: Jopenroad@aol.com. Website: openroadpub.com. Publisher: Jonathan Stein. Publishes trade paperback originals. **Publishes 22-27 titles/year. Receives 200 queries and 75 mss/year. 30% of books from first-time authors; 98% from unagented writers. Pays 5-6% royalty on retail price. Offers $1,000-5,000 advance.** Publishes book 3 months after acceptance of ms. Accepts simultaneous submissions. Responds in 1 month to queries; 2 months to proposals. Book catalog and ms guidelines free.

O¬ Open Road publishes travel guides and is expanding into other areas, particularly sports/fitness and topical.

Nonfiction: How-to. Subjects include travel. Query with SASE.
Recent Title(s): *Italy Guide*, by Douglas Morris; *China Guide*, by Ruth Lor Malloy; *Southern California Guide*, by Elizabeth Borsting.

OPTIMA BOOKS, 2820 Eighth St., Berkeley CA 94710. (510)848-8708. Fax: (510)848-8737. E-mail: esl@optimabooks.com. Website: www.optimabooks.com. **Acquisitions:** Robert Graul, editor (ESL, remedial reading, writing). Estab. 1988. Publishes books for English as a second language. **Publishes 4 titles/year. Receives 8 queries and 5 mss/year. 20% of books from first-time authors; 100% from unagented writers. Makes outright purchase.** Publishes book 8 months after acceptance of ms. Accepts simultaneous submissions. Responds in 2 months to mss.

O¬ Optima publishes books dealing with English as a second language. Currently emphasizing remedial reading. Discontinuing foreign language products.

Nonfiction: Textbook, self teaching. Subjects include language/literature, ESL (English as a second language). "Books should be usable in the classroom or by the individual in a self-teaching capacity. Should be written for the non-native speaker desiring knowledge of American slang and jargon." Query with SASE. Reviews artwork/photos as part of ms package. Send photocopies.
Recent Title(s): *Robert Takes Over*, Anne Maclachlan and Lindy Ferguson; *The Dictionary of Essential American Slang*, Peter Tse; *Ya Gotta Know It!*, by Hania Hassan.

ORANGE FRAZER PRESS, INC., P.O. Box 214, Wilmington OH 45177. (937)382-3196. Fax: (937)383-3159. Website: www.orangefrazer.com. **Acquisitions:** Marcy Hawley, editor. Publishes hardcover and trade paperback originals and reprints. **Publishes 20 titles/year. Receives 50 queries and 40 mss/year. 50% of books from first-time**

authors; 99% from unagented writers. Pays 10-12% royalty on wholesale price. Offers advance. Publishes book 18 months after acceptance of ms. Accepts simultaneous submissions. Responds in 2 months to queries; 1 month to proposals; 1 month to mss. Book catalog free.

O→ Orange Frazer Press accepts Ohio-related nonfiction only; corporate histories.

Nonfiction: Accepts Ohio nonfiction only! Biography, coffee table book, cookbook, gift book, humor, illustrated book, reference, textbook. Subjects include art/architecture, cooking/foods/nutrition, education, history, memoirs, nature/environment, photography, recreation, regional (Ohio), sports, travel, women's issues/studies. Submit proposal package including outline, 1 sample chapter(s), SASE. Reviews artwork/photos as part of ms package. Send photocopies or transparencies.

Recent Title(s): *Brown's Town, 20 Famous Brown's Talk Amongst Themselves*; *Building Ohio, A Traveler's Guide to Urban Ohio*.

Tips: "We do many high-end company and corporate histories."

ORCHARD BOOKS, Scholastic, Inc., 557 Broadway, New York NY 10012. (212)343-6100. Fax: (212)343-4890. Vice President/Editorial Director: Ken Geist. **Acquisitions:** Amy Griffin, senior editor; Beth Levine, editor; Lisa Sandell, assistant editor. Estab. 1987. Publishes hardcover and trade paperback originals. **Publishes 20-30 titles/year. Receives 3,000 queries/year. 25% of books from first-time authors; 50% from unagented writers. Pays 6-10% royalty on retail price. Offers varied advance.** Publishes book 1 year after acceptance of ms. Responds in 3 months to queries.

O→ Orchard specializes in children's picture books. Currently emphasizing picture books, middle grade novels and young adult.

Nonfiction: Children's/juvenile, illustrated book. Subjects include animals, history, nature/environment. "*No unsolicited mss at this time*. Queries only! Be as specific and enlightening as possible about your book." Query with SASE. Reviews artwork/photos as part of ms package. Send photocopies.

Fiction: Picture books, young adult, middle reader; board book; novelty. No unsolicited mss, please. Query with SASE.

Recent Title(s): *Giraffes Can't Dance*, by Andreae and Parker-Rees; *Clem's Chance*, by Levitin.

Tips: "Go to a bookstore and read several Orchard Books to get an idea of what we publish. Write what you feel and query us if you think it's 'right.' It's worth finding the right publishing match."

OREGON STATE UNIVERSITY PRESS, 101 Waldo Hall, Corvallis OR 97331-6407. (541)737-3166. Fax: (541)737-3170. Website: osu.orst.edu/dept/press. **Acquisitions:** Mary Elizabeth Braun, acquiring editor. Estab. 1965. Publishes hardcover and paperback originals. **Publishes 15-20 titles/year. Receives 200 submissions/year. 75% of books from first-time authors; 100% from unagented writers. Pays royalty on net receipts.** Publishes book 1 year after acceptance of ms. Does not accept simultaneous submissions. Responds in 3 months to queries. Book catalog and ms guidelines online or for 6×9 SAE with 2 first-class stamps.

O→ Oregon State University Press publishes several scholarly and specialized books and books of particular importance to the Pacific Northwest. "OSU Press plays an essential role by publishing books that may not have a large audience, but are important to scholars, students and librarians in the region."

Nonfiction: Publishes scholarly books in history, biography, geography, literature, natural resource management, with strong emphasis on Pacific or Northwestern topics. Reference, scholarly. Subjects include regional, science. Submit outline, sample chapter(s).

Recent Title(s): *Frigid Embrace: Politics, Economics, & Environment in Alaska*, by Stephen Haycox; *Elegant Arches, Soaring Spans, & C.B. McCullough, Oregon's Master Bridge Builder*, by Robert W. Hadlow; *Crater Lake National Park: A History*, by Rick Harmon.

Tips: Send for an authors' guidelines pamphlet.

OUR SUNDAY VISITOR PUBLISHING, 200 Noll Plaza, Huntington IN 46750-4303. (219)356-8400. Fax: (219)359-9117. E-mail: booksed@osv.com. Website: osv.com. President/Publisher: Greg Erlandson. Editorial Development Manager: Jacquelyn Lindsey. **Acquisitions:** Michael Dubruiel, Beth McNamara, acquisitions editors. Estab. 1912. Publishes paperback and hardbound originals. **Publishes 30-40 titles/year. Receives 500 submissions/year. 10% of books from first-time authors; 90% from unagented writers. Pays variable royalty on net receipts. Offers $1,500 average advance.** Publishes book 1-2 years after acceptance of ms. Does not accept simultaneous submissions. Responds in 3 months to queries. Book catalog for 9×12 SAE; ms guidelines for #10 SASE or online.

O→ "We are a Catholic publishing company seeking to educate and deepen our readers in their faith." Currently emphasizing reference, apologetics and catechetics. De-emphasizing inspirational.

Nonfiction: Catholic viewpoints on family, prayer and devotional books, and Catholic heritage books. Reference. Subjects include religion. Prefers to see well-developed proposals as first submission with annotated outline and definition of intended market. Reviews artwork/photos as part of ms package.

Recent Title(s): *Our Sunday Visitor's Treasury of Catholic Stories*, by Gerald Costello.

Tips: "Solid devotional books that are not first-person, or lives of the saints and catechetical books have the best chance of selling to our firm. Make it solidly Catholic, unique, without pious platitudes."

[A] **THE OVERLOOK PRESS**, Distributed by Penguin Putnam, 141 Wooster St., New York NY 10012. (212)673-2210. Fax: (212)673-2296. Publisher: Peter Mayer. **Acquisitions:** (Ms.) Tracy Carns, publishing director. Estab. 1971. Publishes hardcover and trade paperback originals and hardcover reprints. **Publishes 40 titles/year. Receives 300 submissions/year. Pays 3-15% royalty on wholesale price or retail price. Offers advance.** Does not accept simultaneous submissions. Responds in 5 months to queries. Book catalog free.

Imprints: Elephant's Eye, Tusk Books.

Overlook Press publishes fiction, children's books and nonfiction.

Nonfiction: Biography. Subjects include art/architecture, community, contemporary culture, film/cinema/stage, history, music/dance, regional (New York State), current events, design, health/fitness, how-to, lifestyle, martial arts. No pornography. *Agented submissions only.*

Fiction: Fantasy, literary, foreign literature in translation. *Agented submissions only.*

THE OVERMOUNTAIN PRESS, P.O. Box 1261, Johnson City TN 37605. (423)926-2691. Fax: (423)929-2464. E-mail: bethw@overmtn.com. Website: www.overmtn.com. **Acquisitions:** Elizabeth L. Wright, managing editor. Estab. 1970. Publishes hardcover and trade paperback originals and reprints. **Publishes 15-20 titles/year. Receives 500 queries and 100 mss/year. 50% of books from first-time authors; 100% from unagented writers. Pays 7½-15% royalty on wholesale price.** Publishes book 1 year after acceptance of ms. Accepts simultaneous submissions. Responds in 6 months to proposals; 6 months to mss. Book catalog and ms guidelines free.

Imprints: Silver Dagger Mysteries.

The Overmountain Press publishes primarily Appalachian history. Audience is people interested in history of Tennessee, Virginia, North Carolina, Kentucky, and all aspects of this region—Revolutionary War, Civil War, county histories, historical biographies, etc. Currently emphasizing regional (Southern Appalachian) children's books, regional nonfiction, children's regional history. De-emphasizing general interest children's fiction, poetry.

Nonfiction: Regional works only. Biography, children's/juvenile, coffee table book, cookbook. Subjects include Americana, cooking/foods/nutrition, ethnic, history, military/war, nature/environment, photography, regional, women's issues/studies, Native American. Submit proposal package including outline, 3 sample chapter(s), marketing suggestions. Reviews artwork/photos as part of ms package. Send photocopies.

Fiction: Picture books.

Recent Title(s): *Textile Art from Southern Appalachia*, by Kathleen Curtis Wilson; *Soapy-Dope*, by Denvil Mullins (children's fiction).

Tips: "Please submit a proposal. Please no phone calls."

RICHARD C. OWEN PUBLISHERS INC., P.O. Box 585, Katonah NY 10536. (914)232-3903. Website: www.rcowen.com. **Acquisitions:** Janice Boland, director of children's books; Amy Finney, project editor (professional development, teacher-oriented books). Estab. 1982. Publishes hardcover and paperback originals. **Publishes 23 titles/year. Receives 50 queries and 1,000 mss/year. 99% of books from first-time authors; 100% from unagented writers.** Publishes book 2-5 years after acceptance of ms. Accepts simultaneous submissions. Responds in 1 month to queries; 1 month to proposals; 5 months to mss. Ms guidelines for SASE with 52¢ postage.

"In addition to publishing good literature, meaningful stories for 5-7-year-old children, we are also seeking mss for short, snappy stories to be included in anthologies for 7-8-year-old children. Subjects include humor, careers, mysteries, science fiction, folktales, women, fashion trends, sports, music, myths, journalism, history, inventions, planets, architecture, plays, adventure, technology, vehicles."

Nonfiction: Children's/juvenile, humor, illustrated book. Subjects include animals, art/architecture, fashion/beauty, gardening, history, music/dance, nature/environment, recreation, science, sports, women's issues/studies, contemporary culture. "Our books are for kindergarten, first and second grade children to read on their own. The stories are very brief—under 500 words—yet well structured and crafted with memorable characters, language and plots." Send for ms guidelines, then submit complete ms with SASE via mail only.

Fiction: Adventure, picture books. "Brief, strong story line, believable characters, natural language, exciting—child-appealing stories with a twist. No lists, alphabet or counting books." Send for ms guidelines, then submit full ms with SASE via mail only.

Poetry: "Poems that excite children are fun, humorous, fresh and interesting. If rhyming, must be without force or contrivance. Poems should tell a story or evoke a mood and have rhythmic language." No jingles. Submit complete ms.

Recent Title(s): *Powwow*, by Rhonda Cox (nonfiction); *Concrete*, by Ellen Javernich (fiction); *Bunny Magic*, by Suzanne Hardin (humor).

Tips: "We don't respond to queries. Please do *not* fax or e-mail us. Because our books are so brief it is better to send entire ms. We publish story books with inherent educational value for young readers—books they can read with enjoyment and success. We believe students become enthusiastic, independent, life-long learners when supported and guided by skillful teachers. The professional development work we do and the books we publish support these beliefs."

PACIFIC BOOKS, PUBLISHERS, P.O. Box 558, Palo Alto CA 94302-0558. (650)965-1980. **Acquisitions:** Henry Ponleithner, editor. Estab. 1945. **Publishes 6-12 titles/year. Pays 7½-15% royalty.** Does not accept simultaneous submissions. Responds in 1 month to queries. Book catalog for 9×12 SAE; ms guidelines for 9×12 SAE.

Pacific Books publishes general interest and scholarly nonfiction including professional and technical books, and college textbooks.

Nonfiction: General interest, professional, technical and scholarly nonfiction trade books. Reference, scholarly, technical, textbook. Subjects include Americana (western), general nonfiction, regional, translation, Hawaiiana. Looks for "well-written, documented material of interest to a significant audience." Also considers text and reference books for high school and college. Query with SASE or submit outline. Reviews artwork/photos as part of ms package.

Recent Title(s): *How to Choose a Nursery School: A Parents' Guide to Preschool Education*, by Ada Anbar.

PACIFIC PRESS PUBLISHING ASSOCIATION, Trade Book Division, P.O. Box 5353, Nampa ID 83653-5353. (208)465-2570. Fax: (208)465-2531. E-mail: booksubmissions@pacificpress.com. Website: www.pacificpress.com. **Acquisitions:** Tim Lale (children's stories, devotional, biblical, doctrinal). Estab. 1874. Publishes hardcover and trade paperback originals and reprints. **Publishes 35 titles/year. Receives 600 submissions/year. 35% of books from first-time authors; 100% from unagented writers. Pays 8-16% royalty. Offers $300-1,500 advance depending on length.** Publishes book up to 1 year after acceptance of ms. Does not accept simultaneous submissions. Responds in 3 months to queries. Ms guidelines available at website or send #10 SASE.

O→ Pacific Press is an exclusively religious publisher of the Seventh-day Adventist denomination. "We are looking for practical, how-to oriented manuscripts on religion, health, and family life that speak to human needs, interests and problems from a biblical perspective. We publish books that promote a stronger relationship with God, deeper Bible study, and a healthy, helping lifestyle."

Nonfiction: Biography, children's/juvenile, cookbook (vegetarian), how-to, self-help. Subjects include cooking/foods/nutrition (vegetarian only), health/medicine, nature/environment, religion, family living. "We can't use anything totally secular or written from other than a Christian perspective." No fiction accepted. Query or request information on how to submit a proposal. Reviews artwork/photos as part of ms package.

Recent Title(s): *Mission Pilot*, by Eileen Lantry; *Empowered Living*, by Jim Hohnberger.

Tips: "Our primary audience is members of the Seventh-day Adventist denomination. Almost all are written by Seventh-day Adventists. Books that are doing well for us are those that relate the biblical message to practical human concerns and those that focus more on the experiential rather than theoretical aspects of Christianity. We are assigning more titles, using less unsolicited material—although we still publish manuscripts from freelance submissions and proposals."

PALADIN PRESS, P.O. Box 1307, Boulder CO 80306-1307. (303)443-7250. Fax: (303)442-8741. E-mail: editorial@paladin-press.com. Website: www.paladin-press.com. President/Publisher: Peder C. Lund. **Acquisitions:** Jon Ford, editorial director. Estab. 1970. Publishes hardcover originals and paperback originals and reprints. **Publishes 50 titles/year. 50% of books from first-time authors; 100% from unagented writers. Pays 10-15% royalty on net receipts. Offers advance.** Publishes book 1 year after acceptance of ms. Accepts simultaneous submissions. Responds in 2 months to proposals. Book catalog free.

Imprints: Sycamore Island Books, Flying Machines Press.

O→ Paladin Press publishes the "action library" of nonfiction in military science, police science, weapons, combat, personal freedom, self-defense, survival.

Nonfiction: "Paladin Press primarily publishes original manuscripts on military science, weaponry, self-defense, personal privacy, financial freedom, espionage, police science, action careers, guerrilla warfare and fieldcraft." How-to, reference. Subjects include government/politics, military/war, money/finance, science. "If applicable, send sample photographs and line drawings with complete outline and sample chapters." Query with SASE.

Recent Title(s): *Techniques of Medieval Armour Reproduction*, by Brian Price.

Tips: "We need lucid, instructive material aimed at our market and accompanied by sharp, relevant illustrations and photos. As we are primarily a publisher of 'how-to' books, a manuscript that has step-by-step instructions, written in a clear and concise manner (but not strictly outline form) is desirable. No fiction, first-person accounts, children's, religious or joke books. We are also interested in serious, professional videos and video ideas (contact Michael Janich)."

PANTHEON BOOKS, Knopf Publishing Group, Random House, Inc., 299 Park Ave., New York NY 10171. (212)751-2600. Fax: (212)572-6030. Website: www.pantheonbooks.com. Editorial Director: Dan Frank. Senior Editors: Shelley Wanger, Deborah Garrison. Executive Editor: Erroll McDonald. **Acquisitions:** Adult Editorial Department. Estab. 1942. **Pays royalty. Offers advance.** Does not accept simultaneous submissions.

O→ Pantheon Books publishes both Western and non-Western authors of literary fiction and important nonfiction.

Nonfiction: Autobiography, biography, literary; international. Subjects include general nonfiction, government/politics, history, memoirs, science, travel.

Recent Title(s): *Jimmy Corrigan*, by Chris Wave; *Nigger*, by Randall Kennedy; *Three Junes*, by Julie Glass.

PARACLETE PRESS, P.O. Box 1568, Orleans MA 02653. (508)255-4685. Fax: (508)255-5705. **Acquisitions:** Editorial Review Committee. Estab. 1981. Publishes hardcover and trade paperback originals. **Publishes 16 titles/year. Receives 250 mss/year.** Publishes book up to 2 years after acceptance of ms. Accepts simultaneous submissions. Responds in 2 months to queries; 2 months to mss. Book catalog for 8½×11 SASE; ms guidelines for #10 SASE.

O→ Publisher of Christian classics, personal testimonies, devotionals, new editions of classics, compact discs and videos.

Nonfiction: Subjects include religion. No poetry or children's books. Query with SASE or submit 2-3 sample chapter(s), table of contents, chapter summaries.

Recent Title(s): *The Illumined Heart*, by Frederica Mathewes-Green; *Doors into Prayer*, by Emilie Griffin; *Surrendering to God*, by Keith Beasley-Topliffe.

PARADISE CAY PUBLICATIONS, P.O. Box 29, Arcata CA 95518-0029. (707)822-9063. Fax: (707)822-9163. E-mail: paracay@humboldt1.com. Website: www.paracay.com. **Acquisitions:** Matt Morehouse, publisher (nautical). Publishes hardcover and trade paperback originals and reprints. **Publishes 5 titles/year; imprint publishes 2 titles/year. Receives 30-40 queries and 20-30 mss/year. 10% of books from first-time authors; 100% from unagented**

writers. Pays 10-15% royalty on wholesale price or makes outright purchase of $1,000-10,000. Offers $0-2,000 advance. Publishes book 4 months after acceptance of ms. Responds in 1 month to queries; 1 month to proposals; 2 months to mss. Book catalog and ms guidelines free on request or online.

Imprints: Parday Books

Nonfiction: Cookbook, how-to, illustrated book, reference, technical, textbook. Subjects include cooking/foods/nutrition, recreation, sports, travel. Query with SASE or submit proposal package including 2-3 sample chapter(s), call first. Reviews artwork/photos as part of ms package. Send photocopies.

Fiction: Adventure (nautical, sailing), sports. All fiction must have a nautical theme. Query with SASE or submit proposal package including 2-3 sample chapter(s), synopsis.

Recent Title(s): *Heavy Weather Tactics Using Sea Anchors and Drogues*, by Earl R. Hinz (nonfiction); *Green Flash*, by L.M. Lanison (mystery).

Tips: Audience is recreational sailors and powerboaters. Call Matt Morehouse (publisher) before submitting anything.

PARAGON HOUSE PUBLISHERS, 2700 University Ave. W., Suite 200, St. Paul MN 55114-1016. (651)644-3087. Fax: (651)644-0997. E-mail: paragon@paragonhouse.com. Website: www.paragonhouse.com. **Acquisitions:** Rosemary Yo Koi, acquisitions editor. Estab. 1962. Publishes hardcover and trade paperback originals and trade paperback reprints. **Publishes 12-15 titles/year; imprint publishes 2-5 titles/year. Receives 1,500 queries and 150 mss/year. 7% of books from first-time authors; 90% from unagented writers. Offers $500-1,500 advance.** Publishes book 1 year after acceptance of ms. Accepts simultaneous submissions.

Imprints: PWPA Books (Dr. Gordon L. Anderson); Althena Books; New Era Books; ICUS Books

O‒ "We publish general interest titles and textbooks that provide the readers greater understanding of society and the world." Currently emphasizing religion, philosophy.

Nonfiction: Biography, reference, textbook. Subjects include child guidance/parenting, government/politics, memoirs, multicultural, nature/environment, philosophy, religion, sex, sociology, women's issues/studies, world affairs. Submit proposal package including outline, 2 sample chapter(s), market breakdown, SASE.

Recent Title(s): *Personal Character and National Destiny*, by Harold B. Jones; *The Woman Who Defied Kings*, by Andree Aelion Brooks; *Infinity and the Brain*, by Dudley Gould.

PARKWAY PUBLISHERS, INC., Box 3678, Boone NC 28607. (828)265-3993. Fax: (828)265-3993. E-mail: parkwaypub@hotmail.com. Website: www.parkwaypublishers.com. **Acquisitions:** Rao Aluri, president. Publishes hardcover and trade paperback originals. **Publishes 4-6 titles/year. Receives 15-20 queries and 10 mss/year. 75% of books from first-time authors; 100% from unagented writers.** Publishes book 8 months after acceptance of ms. Does not accept simultaneous submissions.

O‒ Parkway publishes books on the local history and culture of Western North Carolina. "We are located on Blue Ridge Parkway and our primary industry is tourism. We are interested in books which present the history and culture of western North Carolina to the tourist market." Will consider fiction if it highlights the region. De-emphasizing academic books and poetry books.

Nonfiction: Technical. Subjects include history, psychology, regional. Query with SASE or submit complete ms.

Recent Title(s): *Letter from James*, by Ruth Layng (historical fiction).

PARLAY INTERNATIONAL, P.O. Box 8817, Emeryville CA 94662-0817. (510)601-1000. Fax: (510)601-1008. E-mail: info@parlay.com. Website: www.parlay.com. **Acquisitions:** Maria Sundeen, director of product development. Publishes hardcover, trade paperback, mass market paperback originals and trade paperback reprints. **Publishes 6-10 titles/year. Offers advance.** Publishes book 10 months after acceptance of ms. Accepts simultaneous submissions.

O‒ Parlay International specializes in health, safety and productivity subjects.

Nonfiction: Reference, self-help, technical. Subjects include child guidance/parenting, health/medicine, money/finance, business, nutrition, productivity, safety and leadership, interpersonal skills. Query with SASE or submit proposal package including outline, 2 sample chapter(s).

Recent Title(s): *Aging & Elder Care* (book/Kopy Kit/CD-ROM packages); *Managing Work & Family* (book/Kopy Kit/CD-ROM packages).

Tips: "Parlay International publishes books for training, education and communication. Our three primary areas of information include health, safety and productivity topics. We have historically been providers of materials for educators, healthcare providers, business professionals, newsletters and training specialists. We are looking to expand our customer base to include not only business to business sales but mass market and consumer trade sales as well. Any suggested manuscript should be able to sell equally to our existing customer base as well as to the mass market, while retaining a thematic connection to our three specialty areas. Our customer base and specialty areas are very specific. Please review our website or catalogs before submitting a query."

PASSPORT PRESS, P.O. Box 1346, Champlain NY 12919-1346. **Acquisitions:** Jack Levesque, publisher. Estab. 1975. Publishes trade paperback originals. **Publishes 4 titles/year. 25% of books from first-time authors; 100% from unagented writers. Pays 6% royalty on retail price. Offers advance.** Publishes book 9 months after acceptance of ms. Does not accept simultaneous submissions.

Imprints: Travel Line Press.

O‒ Passport Press publishes practical travel guides on specific countries. Currently emphasizing offbeat countries.

Nonfiction: Subjects include travel. Especially looking for mss on practical travel subjects and travel guides on specific countries. No travelogues. Send 1-page query only. Reviews artwork/photos as part of ms package.

Recent Title(s): *Costa Rica Guide: New Authorized Edition*, by Paul Glassman.

PATHFINDER PUBLISHING OF CALIFORNIA, 3600 Harbor Blvd., #82, Oxnard CA 93035. (805)984-7756. Fax: (805)985-3267. E-mail: bmosbrook@earthlink.net. Website: www.pathfinderpublishing.com. Publishes hardcover and trade paperback originals. **Publishes 4 titles/year. Receives 100 queries and 75 mss/year. 80% of books from first-time authors; 70% from unagented writers. Pays 9-15% royalty on wholesale price. Offers $200-1,000 advance.** Publishes book 4 months after acceptance of ms. Does not accept simultaneous submissions. Responds in 1 month to queries. Book catalog free or on website.

O-ₓ Pathfinder Publishing of California was founded to seek new ways to help people cope with psychological and health problems resulting from illness, accidents, losses or crime.

Nonfiction: Self-help. Subjects include creative nonfiction, health/medicine, hobbies, psychology, sociology. Submit complete ms. "We do not open envelopes from people we do not know. We require e-mail proposals or mss now." Reviews artwork/photos as part of ms package. Send photocopies.
Recent Title(s): *Unleash the Power of Your Mind.*

N PATRON PRESS, INC., P.O. Box 241307, Mayfield Heights OH 44124. (440)646-0545. E-mail: info@patronpress.com. **Acquisitions:** Mark Ciccarelli (mark.ciccarelli@patronpress.com), publisher (religious/spiritual nonfiction). Estab. 2001. Publishes hardcover originals, and trade paperback originals and reprints. **Publishes 3-10 titles/year. Receives 225 queries and 90 mss/year. 50% of books from first-time authors; 95% from unagented writers. Pays 4-8% royalty on wholesale price.** Publishes book 6-12 months after acceptance of ms. Accepts simultaneous submissions. Responds in 2 months to queries; 2 months to proposals; 3 months to mss. Book catalog online; ms guidelines online.

O-ₓ "Patron Press is a small independent press that publishes religious and philosophical nonfiction titles. While mainstream publishers seek and acquire titles based upon commercial appeal and profitability alone, Patron Press seeks and publishes titles based upon relevancy, literary merit and contribution. Areas of interest include: mysticism, monasticism, prayer, contemplation, meditation, spiritual instruction/guidance, theological perspectives, spiritual experimentalism and proactive philosophy.

Nonfiction: Subjects include general nonfiction, philosophy, religion, spirituality. Query and mss via e-mail preferred (Adobe or MS Word). Query with SASE or submit complete ms. Reviews artwork/photos as part of ms package. Send as e-mail attachments.
Tips: "Patron Press eagerly seeks manuscripts from writers deeply committed to spiritual and philosophical enquiry."

PAULINE BOOKS & MEDIA, Daughters of St. Paul, 50 St. Paul's Ave., Jamaica Plain MA 02130-3491. (617)522-8911. Fax: (617)541-9805. Website: www.pauline.org. **Acquisitions:** Sister Patricia Edward Jablonski, acquisitions (children); Sister Madonna Ratliff, FSP, acquisitions editor (adult). Estab. 1948. Publishes trade paperback originals and reprints. **Publishes 25-35 titles/year. Receives 1,300 submissions/year. Pays 8-12% royalty on net receipts. Offers advance.** Publishes book 2-3 years after acceptance of ms. Does not accept simultaneous submissions. Responds in 3 months to queries. Book catalog for 9×12 SAE with 4 first-class stamps.

O-ₓ "As a Catholic publishing house, Pauline Books and Media publishes in the areas of faith and moral values, family formation, spiritual growth and development, children's faith formation, instruction in the Catholic faith for young adults and adults. Works consonant with Catholic theology are sought." Currently emphasizing adult faith formation. De-emphasizing teacher resources.

Nonfiction: Biography (saints), children's/juvenile, self-help, spiritual growth; faith development. Subjects include child guidance/parenting, religion (teacher resources), Scripture. No strictly secular mss. No unsolicited mss. Query with SASE.
Fiction: Juvenile. No unsolicited mss. Query only with SASE.
Recent Title(s): *Vatican II Sunday Missal, Millenium Edition*; *Lights, Camera...Faith: A Movie Lectionary*, by Peter Malone and Rose Pacatte; *Making True Love: A Guide to Lasting Relationships*, by Thomas and Donna Finn.

PAULIST PRESS, 997 MacArthur Blvd., Mahwah NJ 07430. (201)825-7300. Fax: (201)825-8345. E-mail: info@paulistpress.com. Website: www.paulistpress.com. **Acquisitions:** Lawrence Boadt, editorial director (general inquiries); Joseph Scott, editor (adult spirituality and catechetics); Christopher Bellitto, editor (academic theology); Paul Mahon, managing editor (general spirituality); Susan O'Keefe, editor (children's books). Estab. 1865. Publishes hardcover and paperback originals and paperback reprints. **Publishes 90-100 titles/year. Receives 500 submissions/year. 5-8% of books from first-time authors; 95% from unagented writers. Usually pays royalty on net, but occasionally on retail price. Offers advance.** Publishes book 18 months after acceptance of ms. Does not accept simultaneous submissions. Responds in 2 months to queries.

O-ₓ "The editorial mission of the Paulist Press is to publish books in the area of religious thought, especially but not exclusively Catholic religious thought. The major topics would be religious children's books, college theological textbooks, spirituality of prayer and religious classical works." Current areas of special interest are books that appeal to the religious and spiritual searching of unchurched people, children's books on Catholic subjects, and theology textbooks for college courses in religion. Less desired at this time are books in philosophy and biography, poetry and fiction.

Nonfiction: Self-help, textbook (religious). Subjects include philosophy, religion. "We would like to see theology (Catholic and ecumenical Christian), popular spirituality, liturgy, and religious education texts." Submit outline, 2 sample chapter(s). Reviews artwork/photos as part of ms package.
Recent Title(s): *Selling All*, by Sandra Schneiders; *St. Francis of Assisi*, by Adrian House.

N PEACHTREE CHILDREN'S BOOKS, Peachtree Publishers, Ltd., 1700 Chattahoochee Avenue, Atlanta GA 30318-2112. (404)876-8761. Fax: (404)875-2578. E-mail: hello@peachtree-online.com. Website: www.peachtree-online.com. **Acquisitions:** Helen Harriss, submissions editor. Publishes hardcover and trade paperback originals. **Publishes 20 titles/year. 25% of books from first-time authors; 25% from unagented writers. Pays royalty on retail price.; Advance varies.** Publishes book 18 months or more after acceptance of ms. Accepts simultaneous submissions. Responds in 6 months to queries; 6 months to mss. Book catalog for 6 first-class stamps; ms guidelines for #10 SASE.
Imprints: Freestone, Peachtree Jr.

O→ "We publish a broad range of subjects and perspectives, with emphasis on innovative plots and strong writing."

Nonfiction: Children's/juvenile. Subjects include agriculture/horticulture, alternative lifestyles, Americana, animals, anthropology/archeology, art/architecture, business/economics, child guidance/parenting, community, computers/electronic, contemporary culture, cooking/foods/nutrition, creative nonfiction, education, ethnic, fashion/beauty, film/cinema/stage, gardening, gay/lesbian, government/politics, health/medicine, history, hobbies, humanities, language/literature, memoirs, military/war, money/finance, multicultural, music/dance, nature/environment, New Age, philosophy, photography, psychology, recreation, regional, religion, science, sex, social sciences, sociology, software, spirituality, sports, translation, travel, true crime, women's issues/studies, world affairs. No e-mail or fax queries of mss. Submit complete ms. with SASE.
Fiction: Juvenile, picture books, young adult. No collections of poetry or short stories; no romance or sci-fi. Submit complete ms. with SASE.
Recent Title(s): *About Amphibians*, Cathryn Sill (children's picture book); *Yellow Star*, by Carmen Agra Deedy; *My Life and Death*, by Alexandra Ganarsie.

PEACHTREE PUBLISHERS, LTD., 1700 Chattahoochee Avenue, Atlanta GA 30318-2112. (404)876-8761. Fax: (404)875-2578. E-mail: hello@peachtree-online.com. Website: www.peachtree-online.com. **Acquisitions:** Helen Harriss, submissions editor. Estab. 1978. Publishes hardcover and trade paperback originals. **Publishes 20-25 titles/year. Receives 18,000 submissions/year. 25% of books from first-time authors; 75% from unagented writers. Royalty varies. Offers advance.** Publishes book 2 years or more after acceptance of ms. Accepts simultaneous submissions. Responds in 6 months to queries; 6 months to mss. Book catalog for 9×12 SAE with 6 first-class stamps.
Imprints: Peachtree Children's Books (Peachtree Jr., FreeStone).

O→ Peachtree Publishers specializes in children's books, juvenile chapter books, young adult, regional guidebooks, parenting and self-help. Currently emphasizing young adult, self-help, children's, juvenile chapter, nonfiction books.

Nonfiction: Biography, children's/juvenile, self-help. Subjects include general nonfiction, health/medicine, recreation. No technical or reference. No e-mail or fax submissions or queries. Submit outline, 4 sample chapter(s) or submit complete ms. Reviews artwork/photos as part of ms package. Send photocopies.
Fiction: Juvenile, literary, young adult. No adult fiction, fantasy, science fiction or romance. No collections of poetry or short stories. Submit complete ms. Inquires/submissions by US Mail only. E-mail and fax will not be answered.
Recent Title(s): *Around Atlanta with Children*, by Denise Black and Janet Schwartz; *Yellow Star*, by Carhen Agra Deedy; *Surviving Jamestown: The Adventures of Young Sam Collier*, by Gail Langer Karwoski.

PELICAN PUBLISHING COMPANY, P.O. Box 3110, Gretna LA 70054. (504)368-1175. Website: www.pelicanpub.com. **Acquisitions:** Nina Kooij, editor-in-chief. Estab. 1926. Publishes hardcover, trade paperback and mass market paperback originals and reprints. **Publishes 70 titles/year. Receives 5,000 submissions/year. 10% of books from first-time authors; 80% from unagented writers. Pays royalty on actual receipts. Offers advance.** Publishes book 9-18 months after acceptance of ms. Does not accept simultaneous submissions. Responds in 1 month to queries. Writer's guidelines for SASE or on website.

O→ "We believe ideas have consequences. One of the consequences is that they lead to a bestselling book. We publish books to improve and uplift the reader." Currently emphasizing business titles.

Nonfiction: Biography, children's/juvenile, coffee table book (limited), cookbook, gift book, illustrated book, self-help. Subjects include Americana (especially Southern regional, Ozarks, Texas, Florida and Southwest), art/architecture, contemporary culture, ethnic, government/politics, history (popular), multicultural, regional, religion (for popular audience mostly, but will consider others), sports, travel (regional and international), motivational (with business slant), inspirational (author must be someone with potential for large audience), Scottish, Irish, editorial cartoon. "We look for authors who can promote successfully. We require that a query be made first. This greatly expedites the review process and can save the writer additional postage expenses." No multiple queries or submissions. Query with SASE. Reviews artwork/photos as part of ms package.
Fiction: Historical, juvenile. "We publish maybe one novel a year, usually by an author we already have. Almost all proposals are returned. We are most interested in historical Southern novels." No young adult, romance, science fiction, fantasy, gothic, mystery, erotica, confession, horror, sex or violence. Submit outline, 2 sample chapter(s), synopsis, SASE.
Recent Title(s): *Events that Shaped the Nation*, by Rick Phalen (history).
Tips: "We do extremely well with cookbooks, travel, popular histories, and some business. We will continue to build in these areas. The writer must have a clear sense of the market and knowledge of the competition. A query letter should describe the project briefly, give the author's writing and professional credentials, and promotional ideas."

PENGUIN PUTNAM INC., 375 Hudson St., New York NY 10014. Website: www.penguinputnam.com. General interest publisher of both fiction and nonfiction.

Imprints: ***Adult Division***: Ace Books; Avery; Berkley Books; BlueHen Books; Dutton; G.P. Putnam's Sons; HPBooks; Jeremy P. Tarcher; Jove; New American Library [Mentor, Onyx, Signet, Signet Classics, Signet Reference]; Penguin; Putnam; Perigee; Plume; Riverhead Books; Viking; Viking Studio. ***Children's Division***: AlloyBooks; Dial Books for Young Readers; Dutton Children's Books; Firebird; Frederick Warne; G.P. Putnam's Sons; Grosset & Dunlap; Philomel; Phyllis Fogelman Books; Planet Dexter; Price Stern Sloan; Puffin Books; Viking Children's Books.

PENNSYLVANIA HISTORICAL AND MUSEUM COMMISSION, Commonwealth of Pennsylvania, Keystone Building, 400 North St., Harrisburg PA 17120-0053. (717)787-8099. Fax: (717)787-8312. Website: www.phmc.state.pa.us. **Acquisitions:** Diane B. Reed, chief, publications and sales division. Estab. 1913. Publishes hardcover and paperback originals and reprints. **Publishes 6-8 titles/year. Receives 25 submissions/year. Pays 5-10% royalty on retail price or makes outright purchase.** Publishes book 18-24 months after acceptance of ms. Accepts simultaneous submissions. Responds in 4 months to queries. Prepare ms according to the *Chicago Manual of Style*.

- "We are a public history agency and have a tradition of publishing scholarly and reference works, as well as more popularly styled books that reach an even broader audience interested in some aspect of Pennsylvania's history and heritage."

Nonfiction: All books must be related to Pennsylvania, its history or culture. "The Commission considers manuscripts on Pennsylvania, specifically on archaeology, history, art (decorative and fine), politics and biography." Illustrated book, reference, technical. Subjects include anthropology/archeology, art/architecture, government/politics, history, travel (historic). Guidelines and proposal forms available. No fiction. Query with SASE or submit outline, sample chapter(s).
Recent Title(s): *Pennsylvannia Architecture*, by Richard Webster and Deborah Stephens Burns.
Tips: "Our audience is diverse—students, specialists and generalists—all of them interested in one or more aspects of Pennsylvania's history and culture. Manuscripts must be well researched and documented (footnotes not necessarily required depending on the nature of the manuscript) and interestingly written. Manuscripts must be factually accurate, but in being so, writers must not sacrifice style."

PERFECTION LEARNING CORPORATION, 10520 New York Ave., Des Moines IA 50322-3775. (515)278-0133. Fax: (515)278-2980. Website: perfectionlearning.com. **Acquisitions:** Sue Thies, editorial director (books division); Rebecca Christian, senior editor (curriculum division). Estab. 1926. Publishes hardcover and trade paperback originals. **Publishes 50-100 fiction and informational; 25 workbooks titles/year. Pays 5-7% royalty on retail price. Offers $300-500 advance.** Does not accept simultaneous submissions. Responds in 2 months to proposals.
Imprints: Cover-to-Cover, Summit Books.

- "Perfection Learning is dedicated to publishing books and literature-based materials that enhance teaching and learning in pre-K-12 classrooms and libraries." Emphasizing hi/lo fiction and nonfiction books for reluctant readers (extreme sports, adventure fiction, etc.), high-interest novels with male protagonists.

Nonfiction: Publishes nonfiction and curriculum books, including workbooks, literature anthologies, teacher guides, literature tests, and niche textbooks for grades 3-12. "We are publishing hi-lo informational books for students in grades 2-12, reading levels 1-6." Biography. Subjects include science, social studies, high-interest topics. Query with SASE or submit outline. For curriculum books, submit proposal and writing sample with SASE.
Fiction: "We are publishing hi-lo informational books for students in grades 2-12, reading levels 1-6." No picture books. Submit 2-3 sample chapter(s), SASE.
Recent Title(s): *Into the Abyss: A Tour of Inner Peace*, by Ellen Hopkins.

PERIGEE BOOKS, Penguin Putnam Inc., 375 Hudson St., New York NY 10014. (212)366-2000. Publisher: John Duff. **Acquisitions:** Sheila Curry Oakes, executive editor (child care, health); Jennifer Repo, editor (spirituality, personal growth, personal finance, women's issues). Publishes trade paperback originals and reprints. **Publishes 55-60 titles/year. Receives hundreds queries and 300+ submissions/year. 30% of books from first-time authors; 10% from unagented writers. Pays 6-7½% royalty. Offers $5,000-150,000 advance.** Publishes book 18 months after acceptance of ms. Accepts simultaneous submissions. Responds in 2 months to queries. Book catalog free; ms guidelines given on acceptance of ms.

- Publishes in all areas of self-help and how-to with particular interest in health and child care. Currently emphasizing popular psychology, trend watching, accessible spirituality; de-emphasizing games.

Nonfiction: How-to, reference (popular), self-help, prescriptive books. Subjects include animals, business/economics, child guidance/parenting, cooking/foods/nutrition, health/medicine, hobbies, money/finance, nature/environment, psychology, sex, spirituality, sports, women's issues/studies, fashion/beauty, film/cinema/stage. Prefers agented mss, but accepts unsolicited queries. Query with SASE or submit outline.

THE PERMANENT PRESS/SECOND CHANCE PRESS, 4170 Noyac Rd., Sag Harbor NY 11963. (631)725-1101. Fax: (631)725-8215. Website: www.thepermanentpress.com. **Acquisitions:** Judith Shepard, editor. Estab. 1978. Publishes hardcover originals. **Publishes 12 titles/year. Receives 7,000 submissions/year. 60% of books from first-time authors; 60% from unagented writers. Pays 10-15% royalty on wholesale price. Offers $1,000 advance for Permanent Press books; royalty only on Second Chance Press titles.** Publishes book 18 months after acceptance of ms. Accepts simultaneous submissions. Responds in 6 months to mss. Book catalog for 8×10 SAE with 7 first-class stamps; ms guidelines for #10 SASE.

- Permanent Press publishes literary fiction. Second Chance Press devotes itself exclusively to re-publishing fine books that are out of print and deserve continued recognition. "We endeavor to publish quality writing—primarily fiction—without regard to authors' reputations or track records." Currently emphasizing literary fiction. No poetry, short story collections.

Nonfiction: Autobiography, biography, autobiography. Subjects include history, memoirs. No scientific and technical material, academic studies. Query with SASE.

Fiction: Literary, mainstream/contemporary, mystery. Especially looking for high line literary fiction, "artful, original and arresting." Query with first 20 pages.

Recent Title(s): *Lydia Cassatt Reading the Morning Paper*, by Harriett Scott Chessman; *Walking the Perfect Square*, by Reed Coleman.

Tips: "Audience is the silent minority—people with good taste. We are interested in the writing more than anything and dislike long outlines. The SASE is vital to keep track of things, as we are receiving ever more submissions. No fax queries will be answered. We aren't looking for genre fiction but a compelling, well-written story." Permanent Press does not employ readers and the number of submissions it receives has grown. If the writer sends a query or ms that the press is not interested in, a reply may take six weeks. If there is interest, it may take 3 to 6 months.

PERSPECTIVES PRESS, P.O. Box 90318, Indianapolis IN 46290-0318. (317)872-3055. E-mail: ppress@iquest.net. Website: www.perspectivespress.com. **Acquisitions:** Pat Johnston, publisher. Estab. 1982. Publishes hardcover and trade paperback originals. **Publishes 1-4 titles/year. Receives 200 queries/year. 95% of books from first-time authors; 95% from unagented writers. Pays 5-15% royalty on net receipts.** Publishes book 1 year after acceptance of ms. Does not accept simultaneous submissions. Responds in 1 month to queries. Book catalog for #10 SAE and 2 first-class stamps or on website; ms guidelines online.

- "Our purpose is to promote understanding of infertility issues and alternatives, adoption and closely-related child welfare issues, and to educate and sensitize those personally experiencing these life situations, professionals who work with such clients, and the public at large."

Nonfiction: Children's/juvenile, how-to, self-help. Subjects include child guidance/parenting, health/medicine, psychology, sociology. Must be related to infertility, adoption, alternative routes to family building. "No adult fiction!" Query with SASE.

Recent Title(s): *PCOS: The Hidden Epidemic*, by Samuel Thatcher MD; *Inside Transracial Adoption*, by Gail Steinberg and Beth Hall; *Attaching in Adoption*, by Deborah Gray.

Tips: "For adults, we are seeking infertility and adoption decision-making materials, books dealing with adoptive or foster parenting issues, books to use with children, books to share with others to help explain infertility, adoption, foster care, third party reproductive assistance, special programming or training manuals, etc. For children, we will consider adoption or foster care-related fiction manuscripts that are appropriate for preschoolers and early elementary school children. We do not consider YA. Nonfiction manuscripts are considered for all ages. No autobiography, memoir or adult fiction. While we would consider a manuscript from a writer who was not personally or professionally involved in these issues, we would be more inclined to accept a manuscript submitted by an infertile person, an adoptee, a birthparent, an adoptive parent or a professional working with any of these."

PFLAUM PUBLISHING GROUP, (formerly Hi-Time Pflaum), N90 W16890 Roosevelt Dr., Menomonee Falls WI 53051-7933. (262)502-4222. Fax: (262)502-4224. E-mail: kcannizzo@pflaum.com. **Acquisitions:** Karen A. Cannizzo, co-publisher. **Publishes 20 titles/year. Payment may be outright purchase, royalty or down payment plus royalty.** Book catalog and ms guidelines free.

- "Pflaum Publishing Group, a division of Peter Li, Inc., serves the specialized market of religious education, primarily Roman Catholic. We provide high quality, theologically sound, practical, and affordable resources that assist religious educators of and ministers to children from preschool through senior high school."

Nonfiction: Religious education programs and catechetical resources. Query with SASE.

Recent Title(s): *Activities for Teens: 77 Ways to Build Catholic Identity*; *Skits from Scripture: 10 Plays from the Old Testament*; *Skits from Scripture: 10 Plays from the New Testament*.

PHAIDON PRESS, 180 Varick St., 14th Floor, New York NY 10014. (212)652-5410. Fax: (212)652-5419. Website: www.phaidon.com. **Acquisitions:** Karen Stein, editorial director (art and architecture, design, photography). Publishes hardcover and trade paperback originals and reprints. **Publishes 100 titles/year. Receives 500 mss/year. 20% of books from first-time authors; 80% from unagented writers. Pays royalty on wholesale price. Offers advance.** Publishes book 1 year after acceptance of ms. Accepts simultaneous submissions. Responds in 3 months to proposals. Book catalog free.

Imprints: Phaidon.

Nonfiction: Subjects include art/architecture, photography. Submit proposal package including outline or submit complete ms. Reviews artwork/photos as part of ms package. Send photocopies.

PHI DELTA KAPPA EDUCATIONAL FOUNDATION, P.O. Box 789, Bloomington IN 47402. (812)339-1156. Fax: (812)339-0018. E-mail: special.pubs@pdkintl.org. Website: www.pdkintl.org. **Acquisitions:** Donovan R. Walling, director of publications and research. Estab. 1906. Publishes hardcover and trade paperback originals. **Publishes 24-30 titles/year. Receives 100 queries and 50-60 mss/year. 50% of books from first-time authors; 100% from unagented writers. Pays honorarium of $500-5,000.** Publishes book 9 months after acceptance of ms. Does not accept simultaneous submissions. Responds in 3 months to proposals. Book catalog and ms guidelines free.

O→ "We publish books for educators—K-12 and higher education. Our professional books are often used in college courses but are never specifically designed as textbooks."

Nonfiction: How-to, reference, scholarly, essay collections. Subjects include child guidance/parenting, education, legal issues. Query with SASE or submit outline, 1 sample chapter(s). Reviews artwork/photos as part of ms package.

Recent Title(s): *The ABC's of Behavior Change*, by Frank J. Sparzo; *American Overseas Schools*, edited by Robert J. Simpson and Charles R. Duke.

PHILOMEL BOOKS, Penguin Putnam Inc., 345 Hudson St., New York NY 10014. (212)414-3610. **Acquisitions:** Patricia Lee Gauch, editorial director; Michael Green, senior editor. Estab. 1980. Publishes hardcover originals. **Publishes 20-25 titles/year. Receives 2,600 submissions/year. 15% of books from first-time authors; 30% from unagented writers. Pays royalty. Offers advance.** Publishes book 1-2 years after acceptance of ms. Accepts simultaneous submissions. Book catalog for 9×12 SAE with 4 first-class stamps.

O→ "We look for beautifully written, engaging manuscripts for children and young adults."

Fiction: Historical. Children's picture books (ages 3-8); middle-grade fiction and illustrated chapter books (ages 7-10); young adult novels (ages 10-15). Particularly interested in picture book mss with original stories and regional fiction with a distinct voice. No series or activity books. Query with SASE. *No unsolicited mss*,.

Recent Title(s): *So You Want to Be President?*, by Judith St. George and David Small; *Triss*, by Brian Jacques; *Stormbreaker*, by Anthony Horowitz.

Tips: "We prefer a very brief synopsis that states the basic premise of the story. This will help us determine whether or not the manuscript is suited to our list. If applicable, we'd be interested in knowing the author's writing experience or background knowledge. We try to be less influenced by the swings of the market than in the power, value, essence of the manuscript itself."

PHILOSOPHY DOCUMENTATION CENTER, P.O. Box 7147, Charlottesville VA 22906-7147. (800)444-2419. Fax: (419)372-6987. E-mail: order@pdcnet.org. Website: www.pdcnet.org. **Acquisitions:** Dr. George Leaman, director. Estab. 1966. **Publishes 4 titles/year. Receives 4-6 queries and 4-6 mss/year. 50% of books from first-time authors. Pays 2½-10% royalty. Offers advance.** Publishes book 1 year after acceptance of ms. Does not accept simultaneous submissions. Responds in 2 months to queries. Book catalog free.

O→ The Philosophy Documentation Center works in cooperation with publishers, database producers, software developers, journal editors, authors, librarians and philosophers to create an electronic clearinghouse for philosophical publishing.

Nonfiction: Reference, textbook, guidebooks; directories in the field of philosophy. Subjects include philosophy, software. "We want to increase our range of philosophical titles and are especially interested in electronic publishing." Query with SASE or submit outline.

Recent Title(s): *Proceedings of the World Congress of Philosophy*; *2001-2002 Directory of American Philosophers*.

PICCADILLY BOOKS LTD., P.O. Box 25203, Colorado Springs CO 80936-5203. (719)550-9887. Website: www.piccadillybooks.com. Publisher: Bruce Fife. **Acquisitions:** Submissions Department. Estab. 1985. Publishes hardcover originals and trade paperback originals and reprints. **Publishes 5-8 titles/year. Receives 120 submissions/year. 70% of books from first-time authors; 95% from unagented writers. Pays 10% royalty on retail price.** Publishes book 1 year after acceptance of ms. Accepts simultaneous submissions. Responds only if interested, unless accompanied by a SASE to queries.

O→ Picadilly publishes books on humor, entertainment, performing arts, skits and sketches, and writing.

Nonfiction: How-to (on entertainment), humor. Subjects include film/cinema/stage, performing arts, writing, small business. "We have a strong interest in subjects on clowning, magic, puppetry and related arts, including comedy skits and dialogs." Query with SASE or submit sample chapter(s).

Recent Title(s): *The Sherlock Holmes Book of Magic*, by Jeff Brown.

Tips: "Experience has shown that those who order our books are either kooky or highly intelligent or both. If you like to laugh, have fun, enjoy games, or have a desire to act like a jolly buffoon, we've got the books for you."

PICTON PRESS, Picton Corp., P.O. Box 250, Rockport ME 04856-0250. (207)236-6565. Fax: (207)236-6713. E-mail: sales@pictonpress.com. Website: www.pictonpress.com. Publishes hardcover and mass market paperback originals and reprints. **Publishes 30 titles/year. Receives 30 queries and 15 mss/year. 50% of books from first-time authors; 100% from unagented writers. Pays 0-10% royalty on wholesale price or makes outright purchase. Offers advance.** Publishes book 6 months after acceptance of ms. Does not accept simultaneous submissions. Responds in 2 months to queries; 2 months to proposals; 3 months to mss. Book catalog free.

Imprints: Cricketfield Press, New England History Press, Penobscot Press, Picton Press.

O→ "Picton Press is one of America's oldest, largest and most respected publishers of genealogical and historical books specializing in research tools for the 17th, 18th and 19th centuries."

Nonfiction: Reference, textbook. Subjects include Americana, history, hobbies, genealogy, vital records. Query with SASE or submit outline.

Recent Title(s): *Nemesis At Potsdam*, by Alfred de Zayas.

THE PILGRIM PRESS, United Church of Christ, United Church Press, 700 Prospect Ave. E., Cleveland OH 44115-1100. (216)736-3755. Fax: (216)736-2207. E-mail: stavetet@ucc.org. Website: www.pilgrimpress.com. **Acquisitions:** Timothy G. Staveteig, publisher. Publishes hardcover and trade paperback originals. **Publishes 55 titles/year. 60% of**

books from first-time authors; 80% from unagented writers. Pays standard royalties. Offers advance. Publishes book an average of 18 months after acceptance of ms. Does not accept simultaneous submissions. Responds in 3 months to queries. Book catalog and ms guidelines online.

Nonfiction: Scholarly. Subjects include business/economics, gay/lesbian, government/politics, health/medicine, nature/environment, religion, social sciences, ethics, social issues with a strong commitment to justice—addressing such topics as public policy, sexuality and gender, human rights and minority liberation—primarily in a Christian context, but not exclusively.

Recent Title(s): *Coming Out Young and Faithful*, by Leanne McCall and Timothy Brown.

Tips: "We are concentrating more on academic and trade submissions. Writers should send books about contemporary social issues. Our audience is liberal, open-minded, socially aware, feminist, church members and clergy, teachers and seminary professors."

PIÑATA BOOKS, Arte Publico Press, University of Houston, Houston TX 77204-2174. (713)743-2841. Fax: (713)743-2847. Website: www.arte.uh.edu. **Acquisitions:** Nicolas Kanellos, director. Estab. 1994. Publishes hardcover and trade paperback originals. **Publishes 10-15 titles/year. 60% of books from first-time authors. Pays 10% royalty on wholesale price. Offers $1,000-3,000 advance.** Publishes book 2 years after acceptance of ms. Accepts simultaneous submissions. Responds in 1 month to queries; 6 months to mss. Book catalog and ms guidelines available via website or with #10 SASE.

O┳ Pinata Books is dedicated to the publication of children's and young adult literature focusing on US Hispanic culture by U.S. Hispanic authors.

Nonfiction: "Piñata Books specializes in publication of children's and young adult literature that authentically portrays themes, characters and customs unique to U.S. Hispanic culture." Children's/juvenile. Subjects include ethnic. Query with SASE or submit outline, 2 sample chapter(s), synopsis.

Fiction: Adventure, juvenile, picture books, young adult. Query with synopsis, 2 sample chapters and SASE.

Poetry: Appropriate to Hispanic theme. Submit 10 sample poems.

Recent Title(s): *Tun-ta-ca-tun*, by Sylvia Pena (children's poetry, preschool to young adult).

Tips: "Include cover letter with submission explaining why your manuscript is unique and important, why we should publish it, who will buy it, etc."

PINEAPPLE PRESS, INC., P.O. Box 3889, Sarasota FL 34230. (941)359-0886. **Acquisitions:** June Cussen, editor. Estab. 1982. Publishes hardcover and trade paperback originals. **Publishes 20 titles/year. Receives 1,500 submissions/year. 20% of books from first-time authors; 80% from unagented writers. Pays 6½-15% royalty on net receipts. Offers rare advance.** Publishes book 18 months after acceptance of ms. Accepts simultaneous submissions. Responds in 3 months to queries. Book catalog for 9×12 SAE with $1.25 postage.

O┳ "We are seeking quality nonfiction on diverse topics for the library and book trade markets."

Nonfiction: Biography, how-to, reference. Subjects include animals, gardening, history, nature/environment, regional (Florida). "We are seeking fiction and nonfiction suitable for Florida school-aged children. We will consider most nonfiction topics. Most, though not all, of our fiction and nonfiction deals with Florida." No pop psychology or autobiographies. Query or submit outline/brief synopsis, sample chapters and SASE.

Fiction: Historical, literary, mainstream/contemporary, regional (Florida). No romance or science fiction. Submit outline/brief synopsis and sample chapters.

Recent Title(s): *Sinkholes*, by Sandra Friend.

Tips: "Learn everything you can about book publishing and publicity and agree to actively participate in promoting your book. A query on a novel without a brief sample seems useless."

N **PINEY CREEK PRESS**, P.O. Box 227, Roaring Spring PA 16673. Phone/fax: (814)793-2260. E-mail: pineycrk@pennswoods.net. **Acquisitions:** Patty A. Wilson, executive editor (regional ghost stories, folklore collections and historical short stories); Scott Crownover, associate editor (regional ghost stories, folklore, history—particularly mid-Atlantic). Estab. 1999. Publishes mass market paperback originals and reprints. **Publishes 1-3 titles/year. Receives 250 queries and 100 mss/year. 90% of books from first-time authors; 100% from unagented writers. Offers $500-1,500 advance.** Publishes book 4-7 months after acceptance of ms. Accepts simultaneous submissions. Responds in 1-3 months to queries; 1-5 months to proposals; 1-6 months to mss. Book catalog for #10 SASE; ms guidelines for #10 SASE.

Imprints: "Currently we have our main line of ghost story collections under the main imprint of Piney Creek Press; however, we are hoping to open two new imprints this year—one for folklore collections and one for historical collections with regional themes. Be creative with these. One book slated for publication right now is *Pennsylvania Lost, True Stories of Treasures Yet to Be Recovered*."

O┳ "The audience for our books are people who have specific interests such as ghost stories or folklore and people who have a general interest in history."

Nonfiction: Subjects include Americana, history, military/war, New Age, regional, regional collections of ghost stories, folklore, historical- or war-related collections. "We are currently hoping to increase the regional collections of ghost stories, and add a line of regional folklore collections and historical collections. We will be particularly interested in any collection with an unusual theme such as ghost stories from a state along with recipes from haunted sites or historical stories all from a region that have a theme such as lost treasures or military goofs." Submit proposal package including outline, 3 sample chapter(s), photos or illustrations if there are any. Reviews artwork/photos as part of ms package. Send photocopies.

Recent Title(s): *The Pennsylvania Ghost Guide, Vol. 1 & 2*, by Patty A. Wilson.

Tips: "Know the market that you are sending to and then listen to the editor. Editors are not the enemy—they have a job to do and will help you with good advice."

PIPPIN PRESS, 229 E. 85th St., P.O. Box 1347, Gracie Station, New York NY 10028. (212)288-4920. Fax: (732)225-1562. **Acquisitions:** Barbara Francis, president and editor-in-chief; Joyce Segal, senior editor. Estab. 1987. Publishes hardcover originals. **Publishes 4-6 titles/year. Receives 1,500 queries/year. 80% from unagented writers. Pays royalty. Offers advance.** Publishes book 2 years after acceptance of ms. Does not accept simultaneous submissions. Responds in 3 weeks to queries. Book catalog for 6×9 SASE; ms guidelines for #10 SASE.

O→ Pippin publishes general nonfiction and fiction for children ages 4-12.

Nonfiction: Biography, children's/juvenile, humor, autobiography. Subjects include animals, history (American), language/literature, memoirs, nature/environment, science, general nonfiction for children ages 4-12. No unsolicited mss. Query with SASE only. Reviews artwork/photos as part of ms package. Send photocopies.

Fiction: Historical, humor, mystery, picture books. "We're especially looking for small chapter books for 7- to 11-year olds, especially by people of many cultures." Also interested in humorous fiction for ages 7-11. Query with SASE only.

Recent Title(s): *A Visit from the Leopard: Memories of a Ugandan Childhood*, by Catherine Mudiko-Piwang and Edward Frascino; *Abigail's Drum*, by John A. Minahan, illustrated by Robert Quackenbush (historical fiction).

Tips: "Read as many of the best children's books published in the last five years as you can. We are looking for multi-ethnic fiction and nonfiction for ages 7-10, as well as general fiction for this age group. I would pay particular attention to children's books favorably reviewed in *School Library Journal*, *The Booklist*, *The New York Times Book Review*, and *Publishers Weekly*."

PLANNERS PRESS, American Planning Association, 122 S. Michigan Ave., Chicago IL 60603. Fax: (312)431-9985. E-mail: slewis@planning.org. Website: www.planning.org. **Acquisitions:** Sylvia Lewis, director of publications. Estab. 1978. Publishes hardcover and trade paperback originals. **Publishes 4-6 titles/year. Receives 20 queries and 6-8 mss/year. 50% of books from first-time authors; 100% from unagented writers. Pays 7½-12% royalty on retail price. Offers advance.** Publishes book 1 year after acceptance of ms. Does not accept simultaneous submissions. Responds in 1 month to queries; 2 months to proposals; 2 months to mss. Book catalog and ms guidelines free.

O→ "Our books have a narrow audience of city planners and often focus on the tools of city planning."

Nonfiction: Technical (public policy and city planning). Subjects include government/politics. Submit 2 sample chapters and table of contents. Reviews artwork/photos as part of ms package. Send photocopies.

Recent Title(s): *Sprawl Busting: State Programs to Guide Growth*; *SafeScape*; *Planning in Plain English*.

PLANNING/COMMUNICATIONS, 7215 Oak Ave., River Forest IL 60305. (708)366-5200. E-mail: dl@jobfindersonline.com. Website: jobfindersonline.com. **Acquisitions:** Daniel Lauber, president. Estab. 1979. Publishes hardcover, trade and mass market paperback originals, trade paperback reprints. **Publishes 3-6 titles/year. Receives 30 queries and 3 mss/year. 50% of books from first-time authors; 100% from unagented writers. Pays 10-16% royalty on net receipts.** Publishes book 1 year after acceptance of ms. Accepts simultaneous submissions. Responds in 3 months to queries. Book catalog for $2 or free on website; ms guidelines online.

O→ Planning/Communications publishes books on careers, improving your life, ending discrimination, sociology, urban planning and politics.

Nonfiction: Self-help. Subjects include business/economics (careers), education, government/politics, money/finance, sociology, ending discrimination, careers, résumés, cover letters, interviewing. Submit outline, 3 sample chapter(s), SASE. Reviews artwork/photos as part of ms package. Send photocopies.

Recent Title(s): *International Job Finder*, by Daniel Lauber; *Dream It, Do It*, by Sharon Cook and Graciela Sholander; *National Job Hotline Directory*, by Sue Cubbage and Marcia Williams.

Tips: "Our editorial mission is to publish books that can make a difference in people's lives—books of substance, not glitz."

PLAYERS PRESS, INC., P.O. Box 1132, Studio City CA 91614-0132. (818)789-4980. **Acquisitions:** Robert W. Gordon, vice president, editorial. Estab. 1965. Publishes hardcover originals and trade paperback originals and reprints. **Publishes 35-70 titles/year. Receives 200-1,000 submissions/year. 15% of books from first-time authors; 80% from unagented writers. Pays royalty on wholesale price. Offers advance.** Publishes book 3 months-2 years after acceptance of ms. Does not accept simultaneous submissions. Book catalog for 9×12 SAE with 5 first-class stamps; ms guidelines for #10 SASE.

O→ Players Press publishes support books for the entertainment industries: theater, film, television, dance and technical. Currently emphasizing plays for all ages, theatre crafts, monologues and short scenes for ages 5-9, 11-15, and musicals.

Nonfiction: Children's/juvenile, theatrical drama/entertainment industry. Subjects include film/cinema/stage, performing arts, costume, theater crafts, film crafts, dance. Needs quality plays and musicals, adult or juvenile. Query with SASE. Reviews music as part of ms package.

Fiction: Plays: Subject matter includes adventure, confession, ethnic, experimental, fantasy, historical, horror, humor, mainstream, mystery, religious romance, science fiction, suspense, western. Submit complete ms for theatrical plays only. Plays must be previously produced. "No novels or story books are accepted."

Recent Title(s): *Women's Wear of the 1930's*, by Hopper/Countryman; *Rhyme Tyme*, by William-Alan Landes; *Borrowed Plumage*, by David Crawford.

Tips: "Plays, entertainment industry texts, theater, film and TV books have the only chances of selling to our firm."

PLAYHOUSE PUBLISHING, 1566 Akron-Peninsula Road, Akron OH 44313. (330)926-1313. Fax: (330)926-1315. E-mail: webmaster@playhousepublishing.com. Website: www.playhousepublishing.com. **Acquisitions:** Children's Acquisitions Editor. Publishes hardcover originals and board books. **Publishes 10-15 titles/year; imprint publishes 3-5 titles/year. Work-for-hire. Makes $150-350 outright purchase.** Publishes book 1 year after acceptance of ms. Accepts simultaneous submissions. Responds in 2 months to proposals. Book catalog online.
Imprints: Picture Me Books (board books with photos) and Nibble Me Books (board books with candy)

- Playhouse Publishing will no longer accept unsolicited mss for review. The company will not open or review any material not addressed to an individual or from a known source. The company encourages writers to submit query letters/book proposals electronically to webmaster@playhousepublishing.com. All copy must be contained in the body of an e-mail. Attachments will not be opened.

O→ "We publish juvenile fiction appropriate for children from pre-school to third grade. All Picture Me Books titles incorporate the 'picture me' concept. All Nibble Me Books titles incorporate snack foods or candy."

Fiction: Juvenile. Query with SASE.
Recent Title(s): *Bow Wow Blast Off*, by R. Jon Kapper; *Campbell's® Alphabet Soup* (Nibble Me Books); *Peek-A-Boo Farm*, by Jackie Wolf (Picture Me Books).

PLEASANT COMPANY PUBLICATIONS, 8400 Fairway Pl., Middleton WI 53562. Fax: (608)828-4768. Website: www.americangirl.com. **Acquisitions:** Erin Falligant, submissions editor. Estab. 1986. Publishes hardcover and trade paperback originals. **Publishes 50-60 titles/year. Receives 500 queries and 800 mss/year. 90% from unagented writers. Offers varying advance.** Accepts simultaneous submissions. Responds in 3 months to queries. Book catalog for #10 SASE.
Imprints: The American Girls Collection, American Girl Library, AG Fiction, History Mysteries.

O→ Pleasant Company publishes fiction and nonfiction for girls 7-12.

Nonfiction: Children's/juvenile (for girls 7-12), how-to. Subjects include Americana, history, contemporary lifestyle, activities. Query with SASE.
Fiction: Contemporary. "We are seeking strong, well-written fiction, historical and contemporary, told from the perspective of a middle-school-age girl. No romance, picture books, poetry." No picture book submissions. Query with SASE or submit complete ms.
Recent Title(s): *Smoke Screen*, by Amy Goldman Koss; *Nowhere, Now Here*, by Ann Howard Creel.

PLEXUS PUBLISHING, INC., 143 Old Marlton Pike, Medford NJ 08055-8750. (609)654-6500. Fax: (609)654-4309. E-mail: jbryans@infotoday.com. **Acquisitions:** John B. Bryans, editor-in-chief. Estab. 1977. Publishes hardcover and paperback originals. **Publishes 4-5 titles/year. Receives 30-60 submissions/year. 70% of books from first-time authors; 90% from unagented writers. Pays 10-15% royalty on net receipts. Offers $500-1,000 advance.** Accepts simultaneous submissions. Responds in 3 months to proposals. Book catalog and ms guidelines for 10×13 SAE with 4 first-class stamps.

O→ Plexus publishes mainly regional-interest (southern NJ) fiction and nonfiction including mysteries, field guides, history. Also health/medicine, biology, botany, ecology, botony, astronomy.

Nonfiction: How-to, illustrated book, reference, textbook, natural, historical references, and scholarly. Subjects include agriculture/horticulture, education, gardening, health/medicine, history (southern New Jersey), nature/environment, recreation, regional (southern NJ), science, botany, medicine, biology, ecology, astronomy. "We will consider any book on a nature/biology subject, particularly those of a reference (permanent) nature that would be of lasting value to high school and college audiences, and/or the general reading public (ages 14 and up). Authors should have authentic qualifications in their subject area, but qualifications may be by experience as well as academic training." Also interested in mss of about 20-40 pages in length for feature articles in *Biology Digest* (guidelines available for SASE). No gardening, philosophy or psychology; generally not interested in travel but will consider travel that gives sound ecological information. Query with SASE. Reviews artwork/photos as part of ms package. Send photocopies.
Fiction: Mysteries and literary novels with a strong regional (southern NJ) angle. Query with SASE.
Recent Title(s): *Down Barnegat Bay: A Nor'easter Midnight Reader*, by Robert Jahn.

POLYCHROME PUBLISHING CORPORATION, 4509 N. Francisco, Chicago IL 60625. (773)478-4455. Fax: (773)478-0786. E-mail: polypub@earthlink.net. Website: www.polychromebooks.com. Estab. 1990. Publishes hardcover originals and reprints. **Publishes 4 titles/year. Receives 3,000 queries and 7,500-8,000 mss/year. 50% of books from first-time authors; 100% from unagented writers. Pays royalty,. Offers advance.** Publishes book 2 years after acceptance of ms. Accepts simultaneous submissions. Responds in 8 months to mss. Book catalog for #10 SASE; ms guidelines for #10 SASE.
Nonfiction: Children's/juvenile. Subjects include ethnic. Subjects emphasize ethnic, particularly multicultural/Asian-American. Submit outline, 3 sample chapter(s). Reviews artwork/photos as part of ms package. Send photocopies.
Fiction: Ethnic, juvenile, multicultural (particularly Asian-American), picture books, young adult. "We do not publish fables, folktales, fairytales or anthropomorphic animal stories." Submit synopsis and 3 sample chapters, for picture books submit whole ms.
Recent Title(s): *Striking It Rich: Treasures from Gold Mountain*; *Char Siu Bad Boy*.

POPULAR CULTURE INK, P.O. Box 110, Harbor Springs MI 49740-0110. (231)439-9767. **Acquisitions:** Tom Schultheiss, publisher. Estab. 1989. Publishes hardcover originals and reprints. **Publishes 4-6 titles/year. Receives 50**

queries and 20 mss/year. 100% of books from first-time authors; 100% from unagented writers. Pays variable royalty on wholesale price. Offers variable advance. Publishes book 2 years after acceptance of ms. Accepts simultaneous submissions. Responds in 1 month to queries. Book catalog and ms guidelines free.

O‑ Popular Culture Ink publishes directories and reference books for radio, TV, music and other entertainment subjects

Nonfiction: Reference. Subjects include music/dance, popular entertainment. Query with SASE.

Recent Title(s): *Surfin' Guitars*, by Robert Dalley (1960s surf music).

Tips: Audience is libraries, avid collectors. "Know your subject backwards. Make sure your book is unique."

POPULAR WOODWORKING BOOKS, F&W Publications, 4700 Galbraith Rd., Cincinnati OH 45236. (513)531-2690. **Acquisitions:** Jim Stack, acquisitions editor. Publishes trade paperback originals and reprints. **Publishes 10-12 titles/year. Receives 30 queries and 10 mss/year. 50% of books from first-time authors; 95% from unagented writers. Pays 10-20% royalty on net receipts. Offers $3,000-5,000 advance.** Publishes book 1 year after acceptance of ms. Accepts simultaneous submissions. Responds in 1 month to queries. Book catalog for 9×12 SAE with 6 first-class stamps; ms guidelines for 9×12 SAE with 6 first-class stamps.

O‑ Popular Woodworking publishes how-to woodworking books that use photos with captions to show and tell the reader how to build projects. Technical illustrations and materials lists supply all the rest of the information needed. Currently emphasizing woodworking jigs and fixtures, furniture and cabinet projects, smaller finely crafted boxes, all styles of furniture. De-emphasizing woodturning, woodcarving, scroll saw projects.

Nonfiction: "We publish heavily illustrated how-to woodworking books that show, rather than tell, our readers how to accomplish their woodworking goals." How-to, illustrated book. Subjects include hobbies, woodworking/wood crafts. Query with SASE or submit proposal package including outline, transparencies. Reviews artwork/photos as part of ms package.

Recent Title(s): *Fast Furniture*, by Armand Sussman; *25 Essential Projects for Your Workshop*, by the editors of *Popular Woodworking*.

Tips: "Our books are for 'advanced beginner' woodworking enthusiasts."

POSSIBILITY PRESS, One Oakglade Circle, Hummelstown PA 17036-9525. (717)566-0468. Fax: (717)566-6423. E-mail: posspress@aol.com. Website: www.possibilitypress.com. **Acquisitions:** Mike Markowski, publisher; Marjorie L. Markowski, editor-in-chief. Estab. 1981. Publishes trade paperback originals. **Publishes 5-10 titles/year. Receives 1,000 submissions/year. 90% of books from first-time authors; 95% from unagented writers. Royalties vary.** Publishes book approximately 18 months after acceptance of ms. Does not accept simultaneous submissions. Responds in 2 months to queries. Ms guidelines for #10 SAE with 2 first-class stamps.

Imprints: Aviation Publishers, American Aeronautical Archives, Possibility Press.

O‑ "Our mission is to help the people of the world grow and become the best they can be, through the written and spoken word." No longer interested in health issues.

Nonfiction: How-to, self-help, inspirational. Subjects include business/economics, psychology (pop psychology), current significant events, success/motivation, inspiration, entrepreneurship, sales marketing, network and homebased business topics, and human interest success stories. Prefers submissions to be e-mailed.

Recent Title(s): *Full Speed Ahead*, by Joyce Weiss.

Tips: "Our focus is on creating and publishing short to medium length bestsellers written by authors who speak and consult. We're looking for authors who are serious about making a difference in the world."

THE POST-APOLLO PRESS, 35 Marie St., Sausalito CA 94965. **Acquisitions:** Simone Fattal, publisher. Publishes trade paperback originals and reprints. **Publishes 4 titles/year. Pays 5-7% royalty on wholesale price.** Responds in 3 months to queries. Book catalog and ms guidelines for #10 SASE.

Nonfiction: Essay, letters. Subjects include art/architecture, language/literature, translation, women's issues/studies. Query.

Fiction: Ethnic, experimental, feminist, gay/lesbian, literary (plays). Submit 1 sample chapter(s), SASE.

Poetry: Experimental/translations.

Recent Title(s): *Happily*, by Lyn Hejinian; *Some Life*, by Joanne Kyger; *Where the Rocks Started*, by Marc Atherton.

Tips: "We are interested in writers with a fresh and original vision. We often publish women who are well-known in their country, but new to the American reader."

N A **CLARKSON POTTER**, The Crown Publishing Group, Random House, Inc., 299 Park Ave., New York NY 10171. (212)751-2600. Website: www.clarksonpotter.com. **Acquisitions:** Lauren Shakely, editorial director. Estab. 1959. Publishes hardcover and trade paperback originals. Accepts agented submissions only. **Publishes 55 titles/year. 15% of books from first-time authors.**

O‑ Clarkson Potter specializes in publishing cooking books, decorating and other around-the-house how-to subjects.

Nonfiction: Biography, how-to, humor, self-help, Crafts, Cooking and Foods; Decorating; Design Gardening. Subjects include art/architecture, child guidance/parenting, cooking/foods/nutrition, humor, language/literature, memoirs, nature/environment, photography, psychology, translation. *Agented submissions only.* Query or submit outline and sample chapter with tearsheets from magazines and artwork copies (e.g.—color photocopies or duplicate transparencies).

PRAIRIE OAK PRESS, Trails Media Group, Inc., P.O. Box 317, Black Earth WI 53515. (608)767-8000. Fax: (608)767-5444. E-mail: books@wistrails.com. **Acquisitions:** Jerry Minnich, editorial consultant. Publishes hardcover originals, trade paperback originals and reprints. **Publishes 12 titles/year. Pays royalty. Offers advance.** Does not accept simultaneous submissions. Responds in 3 months to proposals.
Imprints: Prairie Classics, Acorn Guides, Trails Books.

O→ Prairie Oak publishes exclusively Midwest regional nonfiction. Currently emphasizing travel, sports, recreation.
Nonfiction: "Any work considered must have a strong tie to Wisconsin and/or the Midwest region." Subjects include art/architecture, gardening, general nonfiction, history, regional, sports, travel, folklore, general trade subjects. No poetry or fiction. Query with SASE or submit outline, 1 sample chapter(s).
Tips: "When we say we publish regional works only, we mean Wisconsin, Minnesota, Michigan, Illinois, Iowa, Indiana. Please do not submit books of national interest. We cannot consider them."

PRB PRODUCTIONS, 963 Peralta Ave., Albany CA 94706-2144. (510)526-0722. Fax: (510)527-4763. E-mail: prbprdns@aol.com. Website: www.prbpro.com; www.prbmusic.com. **Acquisitions:** Peter R. Ballinger, publisher (early and contemporary music for instruments and voices). **Publishes 10-15 titles/year. Pays 10% royalty on retail price.** Accepts simultaneous submissions. Responds in 1 month to queries; 3 months to mss. Book catalog free on request or on website.
Nonfiction: Textbook, sheet music. Subjects include music/dance. Query with SASE or submit complete ms.
Recent Title(s): *Six Sonatas for Violoncello and Basso Continuo*, by Francesco Guerini, edited by Sarah Freiberg (music score and parts); *G.P. Telemann, Fortsetzung des Harmonischen Gottesdienstes, Vol. V*, edited by Jeanne Swack (hardcover score, vocal score and 4 instrumental parts).
Tips: Audience is music schools, universities, libraries, professional music educators, and amateur/professional musicians.

PRESIDIO PRESS, 505B San Marin Dr., Suite 160, Novato CA 94945-1340. (415)898-1081 ext. 25. Fax: (415)898-0383. **Acquisitions:** Mr. E.J. McCarthy, executive editor. Estab. 1974. Publishes hardcover originals and reprints. **Publishes 24 titles/year. Receives 1,600 submissions/year. 35% of books from first-time authors; 65% from unagented writers. Pays 15-20% royalty on net receipts. Offers variable advance.** Publishes book 18 months after acceptance of ms. Does not accept simultaneous submissions. Responds in 1 month to queries. Book catalog and ms guidelines for 7½×10 ½ SAE with 4 first-class stamps.

O→ "We publish the finest and most accurate military history and military affairs nonfiction, plus entertaining and provocative fiction related to military affairs."
Nonfiction: Subjects include history, military/war (military history and military affairs). Query with SASE. Reviews artwork/photos as part of ms package. Send photocopies.
Fiction: Military/war. Query with SASE.
Recent Title(s): *Somalia on $5 a Day*, by Martin Stanton; *Beyond the Rhine*, by Donald R. Burgett.
Tips: "Study the market. Find out what publishers are publishing, what they say they want and so forth. Then write what the market seems to be asking for, but with some unique angle that differentiates the work from others on the same subject. We feel that readers of hardcover fiction are looking for works of no less than 80,000 words."

THE PRESS AT THE MARYLAND HISTORICAL SOCIETY, 201 W. Monument St., Baltimore MD 21201. (410)685-3750. Fax: (410)385-2105. E-mail: rcottom@mdhs.org. Website: www.mdhs.org. **Acquisitions:** Robert I. Cottom, publisher (Maryland-Chesapeake history); Donna B. Shear, senior editor (Maryland-Chesapeake history). Publishes hardcover and trade paperback originals and trade paperback reprints. **Publishes 6-8 titles/year. Receives 15-20 queries and 8-10 mss/year. 50% of books from first-time authors; 100% from unagented writers. Pays 6-10% royalty on retail price.** Publishes book 1 year after acceptance of ms. Accepts simultaneous submissions. Responds in 1 month to queries; 1 month to proposals; 6 months to mss. Book catalog online.

O→ The Press at the Maryland Historical Society specializes in Maryland state and Chesapeake regional subjects.
Nonfiction: Biography, children's/juvenile, illustrated book, scholarly textbook. Subjects include anthropology/archeology, art/architecture, history. Query with SASE or submit proposal package including outline, 1-2 sample chapter(s).
Recent Title(s): *The Chesapeake: An Environmental Biography*, by John R. Wennersten; *The Patapsco Valley: Cradle of the Industrial Revolution in Maryland*, by Henry K. Sharp.
Tips: "Our audience consists of intelligent readers of Maryland/Chesapeake regional history and biography."

PRESSFORWARD PUBLISHING HOUSE LLC, 4341 Doncaster Dr., Madison WI 53711-3717. (877)894-4015. E-mail: pressforward@msn.com. **Acquisitions:** Arthur W. Cran, publisher. Publishes hardcover, trade paperback and mass market paperback originals. **Publishes 3-5 titles/year. Receives 20 queries and 15 mss/year. 75% of books from first-time authors; 100% from unagented writers. Pays 10-20% royalty on retail price.** Publishes book 9 months after acceptance of ms. Accepts simultaneous submissions. Responds in 1 month to queries; 1 month to proposals; 1 month to mss. Book catalog and ms guidelines free.

O→ "We address mental health providers and consumers, as well as their families. We are beginning to accept compelling life stories of consumers."
Nonfiction: Biography, coffee table book, self-help. Subjects include education, health/medicine, nature/environment, psychology. "We like writers who have compelling life stories of overcoming disabilities of psychological or psychiatric in nature. We especially like to hear from educated mental health consumers who have new insights to share." Query with SASE or submit complete ms. Reviews artwork/photos as part of ms package. Send photocopies.

Recent Title(s): *Child Sexual Abuse: Making the Tactics Visible*, by Sam Warner.
Tips: Our audience is mental health professionals of all types; also family groups, and mental health consumers. "We want mental health consumers who have 'been through' the system and who have new stories to tell and insight to share. They should contact the publisher here at (877)894-4015. Potential writers should be skilled, well read generally and specifically and have valuable ideas about mental health treatment and recovery."

PRESTWICK HOUSE, INC., 605 Forest St., Dover DE 19904. (302)736-5614. Website: www.prestwickhouse.com. **Acquisitions:** Paul Moliken, editor. **Publishes 5-10 titles/year. Makes outright purchase of $200-1,500.**
Nonfiction: Reference, textbook, teaching supplements. Subjects include grammar, writing, test taking. Submit proposal package including outline, 1 sample chapter(s), résumé.
Recent Title(s): *Understanding the Language of Shakespeare*, by B. Kampa; *Notetaking and Outlining*, by J. Scott.
Tips: "We market our books primarily for high school English teachers. Submissions should address a direct need of grades 7-12 language arts teachers. Current and former English teachers are encouraged to submit materials developed and used by them successfully in the classroom."

PRICE STERN SLOAN, INC., Penguin Putnam Inc., 345 Hudson, New York NY 10014. (212)414-3610. Fax: (212)414-3396. **Acquisitions:** Jon Anderson, publisher. Estab. 1963. **Publishes 80 titles/year. Makes outright purchase. Offers advance.** Does not accept simultaneous submissions. Responds in 3 months to queries. Book catalog for 9×12 SAE with 5 first-class stamps; ms guidelines for #10 SASE. Address to Book Catalog or Manuscript Guidelines.
Imprints: Doodle Art, Mad Libs, Mr. Men & Little Miss, Plugged In, Serendipity, Troubador Press, Wee Sing.
O→ Price Stern Sloan publishes quirky mass market novelty series for children.
Nonfiction: Children's/juvenile, humor. "Most of our titles are unique in concept as well as execution." Do not send *original* artwork or ms. *No unsolicited mss.*
Fiction: "We publish very little in the way of fiction."
Recent Title(s): *Who's Got Mail?*, by Charles Reasoner (preschool); *What Do You Want On Your Pizza?*, by William Boniface (preschool); *Growing-Money*, by Gail Karlitz (nonfiction).
Tips: "Price Stern Sloan has a unique, humorous, off-the-wall feel."

PRIMA PUBLISHING, Random House Inc., 3000 Lava Ridge Court, Roseville CA 95661. (916)787-7000. Website: www.primapublishing.com. **Acquisitions:** *Lifestyles Division*: Alice Feinstein, editorialand publishing director; Jamie Miller, acquisitions; Jennifer Bayse Sander, acquisitions (network marketing, self-help, personal finance, cookbooks); Denise Sternad, acquisitions (girls, weddings, home, crafts); David Richardson, acquisitions (high-end business, money, investing, forum). *Prima Games Division:* Debra Kempker, publisher. Estab. 1984. Publishes hardcover originals and trade paperback originals and reprints. **Publishes 300 titles/year. Receives 750 queries/year. 10% of books from first-time authors; 30% from unagented writers. Pays 15-20% royalty on wholesale price. Offers variable advance.** Publishes book 18 months after acceptance of ms. Accepts simultaneous submissions. Responds in 1-3 months to queries. Book catalog for 9×12 SAE with 8 first-class stamps; ms guidelines for #10 SASE.
O→ "Books for the way we live, work and play." Currently emphasizing serious nonfiction, alternative health, servant leadership, practical spirituality, books for girls.
Nonfiction: Biography, self-help. Subjects include business/economics, child guidance/parenting, cooking/foods/nutrition, education, health/medicine (alternative and traditional), history, psychology, sports, entertainment, writing, crafts, pets, politics, current affairs, network marketing. "We want books with originality, written by highly qualified individuals. No fiction at this time." Query with SASE.
Recent Title(s): *Triumph*, by Harry Crocker; *Secret History of the CIA*, by Joseph Trento.
Tips: "Prima strives to reach the primary and secondary markets for each of its books. We are known for promoting our books aggressively. Books that genuinely solve problems for people will always do well if properly promoted. Try to picture the intended audience while writing the book. Too many books are written to an audience that doesn't exist."

PRINCETON BOOK COMPANY, (formerly Dance Horizons), 614 Route 130, Hightstown NJ 08520. (609)426-0602. Fax: (609)426-1344. E-mail: pbc@dancehorizons.com. Website: www.dancehorizons.com. **Acquisitions:** Charles Woodford, president (dance and health). Publishes hardcover and trade paperback originals and reprints. **Publishes 5-10 titles/year. Receives 50 queries and 25 mss/year. 80% of books from first-time authors; 100% from unagented writers. Pays negotiable royalty on retail price. Offers negotiable advance.** Publishes book 9-12 months after acceptance of ms. Accepts simultaneous submissions. Responds in 1 week to queries; 1 week to proposals. Book catalog free on request or on website; ms guidelines free.
Imprints: Dance Horizons, Elysian Editions
Nonfiction: "We publish all sorts of dance-related books including ones on fitness and health. Biography, children's/juvenile, gift book, how-to, illustrated book, reference. Subjects include music/dance. Submit proposal package including outline, 3 sample chapter(s). Reviews artwork/photos as part of ms package. Send photocopies.
Recent Title(s): *Get Stronger by Stretching with Thera-Band*, by Noa Spector-Flock; *Appreciating Dance*, by Harriet R. Lihs; *Tapworks*, by Beverly Fletcher.

N **PROFESSIONAL PUBLICATIONS, INC.**, 1250 Fifth Ave., Belmont CA 94002-3863. (650)593-9119. Fax: (650)592-4519. E-mail: amagee@ppi2pass.com. **Acquisitions:** Aline Magee, acquisitions editor. Estab. 1975. Publishes hardcover and paperback originals, video and audio cassettes, CD-ROMs. **Publishes 30 titles/year. Receives 100-200 submissions/year. Offers advance.** Publishes book 18 months after acceptance of ms. Accepts simultaneous submissions. Responds in 2 weeks to queries. Book catalog free; ms guidelines free.

O→ PPI publishes for engineering, architecture, land surveying, and interior design professionals preparing to take examinations for national licensing. Professional Publications wants only professionals practicing in the field to submit material. Currently emphasizing engineering exam review. De-emphasizing architecture exam review.

Nonfiction: Multimedia, reference, technical, textbook. Subjects include art/architecture, science, Subjects include engineering mathematics, engineering, land surveying, , interior design. Especially needs "review books for all professional licensing examinations." Query with SASE or submit sample chapter(s). Reviews artwork/photos as part of ms package.

Recent Title(s): *Civil Engineering Reference Manual for the PE Exam*, Michael R. Lindeburg, PE.

Tips: "We specialize in books for working professionals: engineers, architects, land surveyors, interior designers, etc. The more technically complex the manuscript is the happier we are. We love equations, tables of data, complex illustrations, mathematics, etc. In technical/professional book publishing, it isn't always obvious to us if a market exists. We can judge the quality of a manuscript, but the author should make some effort to convince us that a market exists. Facts, figures, and estimates about the market—and marketing ideas from the author—will help sell us on the work."

PROMETHEUS BOOKS, 59 John Glenn Dr., Amherst NY 14228-2197. (716)691-0133 ext. 207. Fax: (716)564-2711. E-mail: slmitchell@prometheusmail.com. Website: www.prometheusbooks.com. **Acquisitions:** Steven L. Mitchell, editor-in-chief (Prometheus/Humanity Books, philosophy, social science, political science, general nonfiction); Ann O'Hear, acquisitions editor (Humanity Books, scholarly and professional works in philosophy, social science, popular culture, sociology, anthropology); Linda Greenspan Regan, executive editor (Prometheus, popular science, health, psychology, criminology). Estab. 1969. Publishes hardcover originals, trade paperback originals and reprints. **Publishes 85-100 titles/year. Receives 2,500 submissions/year. 25% of books from first-time authors; 50% from unagented writers. Pays 10-15% royalty on wholesale price. Offers $0-3,000 advance.** Publishes book 18 months after acceptance of ms. Accepts simultaneous submissions. Responds in 1 month to queries; 2 months to proposals; 4 months to mss. Book catalog free or online; ms guidelines for #10 SASE or by e-mail at editorial@prometheusbooks.com.

Imprints: Humanity Books (scholarly and professionals monographs in philosophy, social science, sociology, archaeology, Marxist studies, etc.).

O→ "Prometheus Books is a leading independent publisher in philosophy, popular science and critical thinking. We publish authoritative and thoughtful books by distinguished authors in many categories. We are a niche. or specialized, publisher that features *critiques* of the paranormal and pseudoscience, critiques of religious extremism and right wing fundamentalism and creationism; Biblical and Koranic criticism: human sexuality, etc. Currently emphasizing popular science, health, psychology, social science."

Nonfiction: Biography, children's/juvenile, reference, self-help. Subjects include education, government/politics, health/medicine, history, New Age (critiques of), philosophy, psychology, religion (not religious, but critiquing), contemporary issues, current events, Islamic studies, law, popular science, critiques of the paranormal and UFO sightings, sexuality. "Ask for a catalog, go to the library, look at our books and others like them to get an idea of what our focus is." Submit proposal package including outline, synopsis and a well-developed query letter with SASE. Reviews artwork/photos as part of ms package. Send photocopies.

Recent Title(s): *Into the Buzzsaw*, by Kristina Borjesson; *It's Been a Good Life*, by Janet J. Asimov; *Cracking Cases*, by Dr. Henry C. Lee.

Tips: "Audience is highly literate with multiple degrees; an audience that is intellectually mature and knows what it wants. They are aware, and we try to provide them with new information on topics of interest to them in mainstream and related areas."

☆ **PROSTAR PUBLICATIONS INC.**, 3 Church Circle, #109, Annapolis MD 21401. (800)481-6277. Fax: (800)487-6277. Website: www.nauticalbooks.com. **Acquisitions:** Peter Griffes, president (marine-related/how-to/business/technical); Susan Willson, editor (history/memoirs). Estab. 1965. Publishes trade paperback originals. **Publishes 150 titles/year; imprint publishes 10-15 titles/year. Receives 120 queries and 50 submissions and 25 mss/year. 50% of books from first-time authors; 100% from unagented writers. Pays 15% royalty on wholesale price. Rarely offers advance.** Publishes book 1 year after acceptance of ms. Accepts simultaneous submissions. Responds in 3 months to queries; 3 months to proposals. Book catalog online.

Imprints: Lighthouse Press (Peter Griffes)

O→ "Originally, ProStar published only nautical books. At present, however, we are expanding. Any quality nonfiction book would be of interest."

Nonfiction: Coffee table book, how-to, illustrated book, technical. Subjects include history, memoirs, nature/environment, travel, nautical. Query with SASE. Reviews artwork/photos as part of ms package. Send photocopies.

Recent Title(s): *The Media Shaping the Image of a People*, by Bill Overton; *Rock Roll & Reminisce*, by Joe Andrews; *Little Known Adventures Under Sale*, by Jeff Markell.

Tips: "We prefer to work directly with the author and seldom work with agents. Please send in a well-written query letter, and we will give your book serious consideration."

PRUETT PUBLISHING, 7464 Arapahoe Rd., Suite A-9, Boulder CO 80303. (303)449-4919. Fax: (303)443-9019. E-mail: pruettbks@aol.com. **Acquisitions:** Jim Pruett, publisher. Estab. 1959. Publishes hardcover and trade paperback originals and reprints. **Publishes 10-15 titles/year. 60% of books from first-time authors; 95% from unagented writers. Pays 10-12% royalty on net receipts. Offers advance.** Publishes book 18 months after acceptance of ms. Accepts simultaneous submissions. Responds in 2 months to queries. Book catalog and ms guidelines free.

O→ "Pruett Publishing strives to convey to our customers and readers a respect of the American West, in particular the spirit, traditions, and attitude of the region. We publish books in the following subject areas: outdoor recreation, regional history, environment and nature, travel and culture. We especially need books on outdoor recreation."

Nonfiction: "We are looking for nonfiction manuscripts and guides that focus on the Rocky Mountain West." Guidebooks. Subjects include Americana (Western), anthropology/archeology (Native American), cooking/foods/nutrition (Native American, Mexican, Spanish), ethnic, history (Western), nature/environment, recreation (outdoor), regional, sports (cycling, hiking, fly fishing), travel. Submit proposal package. Reviews artwork/photos as part of ms package.

Recent Title(s): *Flyfishing the Texas Coast: Back Country Flats to Bluewater*, by Chuck Scales and Phil Shook, photography by David J. Sams; *Trout Country: Reflections on Rivers, Flyfishing & Related Addictions*, by Bob Saile; *Rocky Mountain Christmas*, by John H. Monnett.

Tips: "There has been a movement away from large publisher's mass market books and towards small publisher's regional interest books, and in turn distributors and retail outlets are more interested in small publishers. Authors don't need to have a big name to have a good publisher. Look for similar books that you feel are well produced—consider design, editing, overall quality and contact those publishers. Get to know several publishers, and find the one that feels right—trust your instincts."

PUFFIN BOOKS, Penguin Putnam Inc., 345 Hudson St., New York NY 10014-3657. (212)414-2000. Website: www.penguinputnam.com. President/Publisher: Tracy Tang. **Acquisitions:** Sharyn November, senior editor; Kristin Gilson, executive editor. Publishes trade paperback originals and reprints. **Publishes 175-200 titles/year. Receives 300 queries and 300 mss/year. 1% of books from first-time authors; 5% from unagented writers. Royalty varies. Offers variable advance.** Publishes book 18 months after acceptance of ms. Does not accept simultaneous submissions. Responds in 3 months to mss. Book catalog for 9×12 SAE with 7 first-class stamps; send request to Marketing Department.

O→ Puffin Books publishes high-end trade paperbacks and paperback reprints for preschool children, beginning and middle readers, and young adults.

Nonfiction: Biography, children's/juvenile, illustrated book, young children's concept books (counting, shapes, colors). Subjects include education (for teaching concepts and colors, not academic), history, women's issues/studies. " 'Women in history' books interest us." Query with SASE. *No unsolicited mss.*

Fiction: Picture books, young adult, Middle Grade; Easy-to-Read Grades 1-3. "We publish mostly paperback reprints. We do only a small number of original novels. We do not publish original picture books." *No unsolicited mss.*

Tips: "Our audience ranges from little children (first books) to young adult (ages 14-16). An original idea has the best luck."

[A] **G.P. PUTNAM'S SONS**, (Adult Trade), Penguin Putnam, Inc., 375 Hudson, New York NY 10014. (212)366-2000. Fax: (212)366-2666. Website: www.penguinputnam.com. Publisher: Neil Nyren. Vice President: Marian Woods. Publishes hardcover and trade paperback originals. **5% from unagented writers. Pays royalty. Offers advance.** Accepts simultaneous submissions. Responds in 6 months to queries. Request book catalog through mail order department; ms guidelines free.

Nonfiction: Biography, cookbook, self-help. Subjects include animals, business/economics, child guidance/parenting, contemporary culture, cooking/foods/nutrition, health/medicine, military/war, nature/environment, religion, science, sports, travel, women's issues/studies, celebrity-related topics. *Agented submissions only. No unsolicited mss.*

Fiction: Adventure, literary, mainstream/contemporary, mystery, suspense, Women's. Prefers agented submissions. *Agented submissions only. No unsolicited mss.*

Recent Title(s): *Lindbergh*, A. Scott Berg (nonfiction); *The Bear and the Dragon*, Tom Clancy (adventure).

QUE, Pearson Education, Indianapolis IN 46290. (317)581-3500. Website: www.quepublishing.com. Publisher: David Culverwell. **Acquisitions:** Angelina Ward, Jeff Riley, Loretta Yates, Rick Kughen, Stephanie McComb, acquisitions editors. Publishes hardcover, trade paperback and mass market paperback originals and reprints. **Publishes 100 titles/year. 80% from unagented writers. Pays variable royalty on wholesale price or makes work-for-hire arrangements. Offers varying advance.** Accepts simultaneous submissions. Responds in 1 month to proposals. Book catalog and ms guidelines online.

Nonfiction: Subjects include computers/electronic.

Recent Title(s): *Upgrading and Repairing PCs, 14th edition*, by Scott Mueller.

QUEST BOOKS, Theosophical Publishing House, 306 West Geneva Rd., Wheaton IL 60187. (630)665-0130. Fax: (630)665-8791. E-mail: questbooks@theosmail.net. Website: www.theosophical.org. **Acquisitions:** Brenda Rosen. Publishes hardcover originals and trade paperback originals and reprints. **Publishes 12-15 titles/year. Receives 500 submissions/year. 75% of books from first-time authors; 90% from unagented writers. Pays royalty. Offers varying advance.** Publishes book 20 months after acceptance of ms. Accepts simultaneous submissions. Responds in 1 month to queries. Book catalog free; ms guidelines free.

O→ "Quest Books is the imprint of the Theosophical Publishing House, the publishing arm of the Theosophical Society of America. Since 1965, Quest books has sold millions of books by leading cultural thinkers on such increasingly popular subjects as transpersonal psychology, comparative religion, deep ecology, spiritual growth, the development of creativity and alternative health practices."

Nonfiction: Biography, illustrated book, self-help. Subjects include anthropology/archeology, art/architecture, health/medicine, music/dance, nature/environment, New Age, philosophy (holistic), psychology (transpersonal), religion (Eastern and Western), science, sex, spirituality (men, women, Native American), travel, women's issues/studies, theosophy, comparative religion, men's and women's spirituality, holistic implications in science, health and healing, yoga, meditation, astrology. "Our speciality is high-quality spiritual nonfiction with a self-help aspect. Great writing is a must. We seldom publish 'personal spiritual awakening' stories. No submissions accepted that do not fit the needs outlined above." Accepts nonfiction translations. No fiction, poetry, children's books or any literature based on channeling or personal psychic impressions. Query with SASE or submit proposal package including sample chapter(s), author bio, toc. Reviews artwork/photos as part of ms package. Send photocopies.

Recent Title(s): *The Practice of Dream Healing*; *Essential Musical Intelligence*; *The Summer Solstice*.

Tips: "Our audience includes the 'New Age' community, seekers in all religions, general public, professors, and health professionals. Read a few recent Quest titles. Know our books and our company goals. Explain how your book or proposal relates to other Quest titles. Quest gives preference to writers with established reputations/successful publications."

QUILL DRIVER BOOKS/WORD DANCER PRESS, 1831 Industrial Way #101, Sanger CA 93657. (559)866-2170. Fax: (559)876-2180. E-mail: mettee@quilldriverbooks.com. **Acquisitions:** Stephen Blake Mettee, publisher. Publishes hardcover and trade paperback originals and reprints. **Publishes 10-12 (Quill Driver Books: 4/year, Word Dancer Press: 6-8/year) titles/year. 50% of books from first-time authors; 95% from unagented writers. Pays 4-10% royalty on retail price. Offers $500-5,000 advance.** Publishes book 9 months after acceptance of ms. Accepts simultaneous submissions. Responds in 1 month to queries; 1 month to proposals; 3 months to mss. Book catalog and ms guidelines for #10 SASE.

O→ "We publish a modest number of books per year, each of which, we hope, makes a worthwhile contribution to the human community, and we have a little fun along the way. We are strongly emphasizing our two new book series: The Best Half of Life series—on subjects which will serve to enhance the lifestyles, life skills, and pleasures of living for those over 50. The Fast Track Course series—short how-to or explanatory books on any subject."

Nonfiction: Biography, how-to, reference, general. Subjects include general nonfiction, regional (California), writing, aging. Query with SASE or submit proposal package. Reviews artwork/photos as part of ms package. Send photocopies.

Recent Title(s): *Answers to Satisfy the Soul: Clear, Straight Answers to 20 of Life's Most Perplexing Questions*, by Jim Denney; *The Fast Track Course on How to Write a Nonfiction Book Proposal*, by Stephen Blake Mettee.

QUITE SPECIFIC MEDIA GROUP LTD., 7 Old Fulton St., Brooklyn Heights NY 11201. (212)725-5377. Fax: (212)725-8506. E-mail: info@quitespecificmedia.com. Website: www.quitespecificmedia.com. **Acquisitions:** Ralph Pine, editor-in-chief. Editorial Office: 7373 Pyramid Place, Hollywood CA 90046. Estab. 1967. Publishes hardcover originals, trade paperback originals and reprints. **Publishes 12 titles/year. Receives 300 queries and 100 mss/year. 75% of books from first-time authors; 85% from unagented writers. Pays royalty on wholesale price. Offers varies advance.** Publishes book 18 months after acceptance of ms. Accepts simultaneous submissions. Responds to queries. Book catalog online; ms guidelines free.

Imprints: Costume & Fashion Press, Drama Publishers, By Design Press, Entertainment Pro, Jade Rabbit

O→ Quite Specific Media Group is an umbrella company of five imprints specializing in costume and fashion, theater and design.

Nonfiction: For and about performing arts theory and practice: acting, directing; voice, speech, movement; makeup, masks, wits; costumes, sets, lighting, sound; design and execution; technical theater, stagecraft, equipment; stage management; producing; arts management, all varieties; business and legal aspects; film, radio, television, cable, video; theory, criticism, reference; theater and performance history; costume and fashion. How-to, multimedia, reference, textbook, guides; manuals; directories. Subjects include fashion/beauty, film/cinema/stage, history, translation. Accepts nonfiction and technical works in translations also. Query with SASE or submit 1-3 sample chapter(s). No complete ms. Reviews artwork/photos as part of ms package.

QUORUM BOOKS, Greenwood Publishing Group, 88 Post Rd. W., Westport CT 06881. (203)226-3571. Fax: (203)222-1502. E-mail: er@greenwood.com. Website: www.greenwood.com. **Acquisitions:** Eric Valentine, publisher. **Publishes 75 titles/year. 50% of books from first-time authors. Pays 8-15% royalty on net receipts. Offers occasional advance.** Publishes book 9-12 months after acceptance of ms. Accepts simultaneous submissions. Responds in 2 weeks to queries; 1 month to proposals. Book catalog online; ms guidelines online.

Nonfiction: Scholarly and professional books. Subjects include business/economics, finance, applied economics, business law. No unsolicited mss. Query with proposal package, including content scope, organization, length of project, table of contents, intended markets, competing books, whether a complete ms is available or when it will be, cv or résumé and SASE.

Tips: "We are not a trade publisher. Our products are sold almost entirely by mail, in hardcover and at relatively high list prices, and to scholars, graduate level students and skilled professionals throughout the public and private sectors."

RAGGED MOUNTAIN PRESS, P.O. Box 220, Camden ME 04843-0220. (207)236-4837. Fax: (207)236-6314. Website: www.raggedmountainpress.com. **Acquisitions:** Jonathan Eaton, editorial director. Estab. 1969. Publishes hardcover and trade paperback originals and reprints. **Publishes 50 titles/year; imprint publishes 25 titles/year. Receives 200 queries and 100 mss/year. 30% of books from first-time authors; 90% from unagented writers. Pays 10-15% royalty on net receipts. Offers advance.** Publishes book 1 year after acceptance of ms. Accepts simultaneous submissions. Responds in 1 month to queries. Ms guidelines for #10 SASE.

O→ Ragged Mountain Press publishes books that take you off the beaten path.

Nonfiction: "Ragged Mountain publishes nonconsumptive outdoor and environmental issues books of literary merit or unique appeal." How-to (outdoor-related), humor, guidebooks; essays. Subjects include cooking/foods/nutrition, humor, nature/environment, recreation, sports, adventure, camping, fly fishing, snowshoeing, backpacking, canoeing, outdoor cookery, skiing, snowboarding, survival skills, wilderness know-how, birdwatching, natural history, climbing, kayaking. "Be familiar with the existing literature. Find a subject that hasn't been done or has been done poorly, then explore it in detail and from all angles." Query with SASE or submit outline, 1 sample chapter(s). Reviews artwork/photos as part of ms package. Send photocopies.
Recent Title(s): *Tenzing Norgay and the Sherpen of Everest*, by Tashi Tenzing; *Climber's Choice*, edited by Pat Ament; *Baseball for Everyone*, by Joe DiMaggio.

REALLY GREAT BOOKS, P.O. Box 861302, Los Angeles CA 90086. (213)624-8555. Fax: (213)624-8666. E-mail: info@reallygreatbooks.com. Website: www.reallygreatbooks.com. **Acquisitions:** Petra Frank (petra@reallygreatbooks.-com). Publishes hardcover and trade paperback originals. **Publishes 12 titles/year. Receives 100 queries and 40 mss/year. 30% of books from first-time authors; 10% from unagented writers. Pays 5-10% royalty.** Publishes book 12-18 months after acceptance of ms. Does not accept simultaneous submissions. Responds in 2 months to queries; 4 months to proposals; 6 months to mss. Book catalog for #10 SASE or online; ms guidelines for #10 SASE.
Imprints: Really Great Books, Glove Box Guides, Horny? Books.
Nonfiction: Subjects include art/architecture, creative nonfiction, ethnic, gay/lesbian, history, photography, regional, travel. "All titles we publish represent what we like to call 'the real Los Angeles.' We're interested in the city behind the facade, drawn in a compelling enough manner to appeal to a national—even a international audience." Request submission guidelines and use them to submit proposal package, including outline, 2 sample chapters and marketing proposal. Reviews artwork/photos as part of ms package. Send photocopies.
Recent Title(s): *Geography of Rage*, edited by Jervey Tervalon.

RED HEN PRESS, P.O. Box 3537, Granada Hills CA 91394. (818)831-0649. Fax: (818)831-6659. E-mail: editor@redhen.org. Website: www.redhen.org. **Acquisitions:** Mark E. Cull, publisher/editor (fiction); Katherine Gale, poetry editor (poetry, literary fiction). Estab. 1993. Publishes trade paperback originals. **Publishes 10 titles/year. Receives 2,000 queries and 500 mss/year. 10% of books from first-time authors; 90% from unagented writers.** Publishes book 1 year after acceptance of ms. Accepts simultaneous submissions. Responds in 1 month to queries; 2 months to proposals; 3 months to mss. Book catalog and ms guidelines available via website or free.

O→ Red Hen Press is a nonproft organization specializing in literary fiction and nonfiction. Currently de-emphasizing poetry.

Nonfiction: Biography, children's/juvenile, cookbook. Subjects include anthropology/archeology, cooking/foods/nutrition, ethnic, gay/lesbian, language/literature, memoirs, travel, women's issues/studies, political/social interest. Query with SASE. Reviews artwork/photos as part of ms package. Send photocopies.
Fiction: "We prefer high-quality literary fiction." Ethnic, experimental, feminist, gay/lesbian, historical, literary, mainstream/contemporary, poetry, poetry in translation, short story collections. Query with SASE.
Poetry: Query or submit 5 sample poems.
Recent Title(s): *Letters from the Underground*, by Abbie and Anita Hoffman; *Tisch*, by Stephen Dixon.
Tips: "Audience reads poetry, literary fiction, intelligent nonfiction. If you have an agent, we may be too small since we don't pay advances. Write well. Send queries first. Be willing to help promote your own book."

[N] **RED ROCK PRESS**, Suite 114, 459 Columbus Ave., New York NY 10024. Fax: (212)362-6216. E-mail: redrockprs@aol.com. Website: www.redrockpress.com. **Acquisitions:** Ilene Barth. Estab. 1998. Publishes hardcover and trade paperback originals. **Publishes 2-3 titles/year. Pays royalty on wholesale price. The amount of the advance offered depends on the project.** Does not accept simultaneous submissions. Responds in 1 month to queries; 1 month to proposals; 2 months to mss. Book catalog for #10 SASE.
Imprints: Virtue Victorious.
Nonfiction: Coffee table book, gift book, humor, illustrated book, self-help. Subjects include creative nonfiction. "The best opportunity for new writers is to submit an original, nonfiction narrative that would suit the theme of our upcoming 'Virtue Victorious' collections. These submissions go directly to each book's editor. Details can be found at www.virtuevictorious.com."

REFERENCE PRESS INTERNATIONAL, P.O. Box 4126, Greenwich CT 06831. (203)622-6860. Fax: (707)929-0282. E-mail: ckl1414@aol.com. **Acquisitions:** Cheryl Lacoff, senior editor. Publishes hardcover and trade paperback originals. **Publishes 6 titles/year. Receives 50 queries and 20 mss/year. 75% of books from first-time authors; 90% from unagented writers. Pays royalty or makes outright purchase. Offers determined by project advance.** Publishes book 6 months after acceptance of ms. Accepts simultaneous submissions. Responds in 3 months to queries.

O→ Reference Press specializes in gift books, instructional, reference and how-to titles.

Nonfiction: Gift book, how-to, illustrated book, multimedia (audio, video, CD-ROM), reference, technical, instructional. Subjects include Americana, art/architecture, business/economics, education, gardening, hobbies, money/finance, photography, anything related to the arts or crafts field. "Follow the guidelines as stated concerning subjects and types of books we're looking for." Query with SASE or submit outline, 1-3 sample chapter(s). Reviews artwork/photos as part of ms package. Send photocopies.
Recent Title(s): *Who's Who in the Peace Corps* (alumni directory).

REFERENCE SERVICE PRESS, 5000 Windplay Dr., Suite 4, El Dorado Hills CA 95762. (916)939-9620. Fax: (916)939-9626. E-mail: findaid@aol.com. Website: www.rspfunding.com. **Acquisitions:** Stuart Hauser, acquisitions editor. Estab. 1977. Publishes hardcover originals. **Publishes 10-20 titles/year. 100% from unagented writers. Pays 10% royalty. Offers advance.** Publishes book 6 months after acceptance of ms. Accepts simultaneous submissions. Responds in 2 months to queries. Book catalog for #10 SASE.

O→ Reference Service Press focuses on the development and publication of financial aid resources in any format (print, electronic, e-book, etc.). We are interested in financial aid publications aimed at specific groups (e.g., minorities, women, veterans, the disabled, undergraduates majoring in specific subject areas, specific types of financial aid, etc.).

Nonfiction: Specializes in financial aid opportunities for students in or having these characteristics: women, minorities, veterans, the disabled, etc. Reference. Subjects include agriculture/horticulture, art/architecture, business/economics, education, ethnic, health/medicine, history, religion, science, sociology, women's issues/studies, disabled. Submit outline, sample chapter(s).

Recent Title(s): *Financial Aids for African Americans, 2001-2003.*

Tips: "Our audience consists of librarians, counselors, researchers, students, re-entry women, scholars and other fund-seekers."

N A **REGAN BOOKS**, HarperCollins, 10 E. 53rd St., New York NY 10022. (212)207-7400. Fax: (212)207-6951. Website: www.harpercollins.com. **Acquisitions:** Judith Regan, president/publisher; Cal Morgan, editorial director. Estab. 1994. Publishes hardcover and trade paperback originals. **Publishes 75 titles/year. Receives 7,500 queries and 5,000 mss/year. Pays royalty on retail price. Offers variable advance.** Publishes book 1 year after acceptance of ms. Accepts simultaneous submissions. Responds in 3 months to proposals.

O→ Regan Books publishes general fiction and nonfiction: biography, self-help, style and gardening books, and is known for contemporary topics and controversial authors and titles.

Nonfiction: Biography, coffee table book, cookbook, gift book, illustrated book, reference, self-help. Subjects include agriculture/horticulture, Americana, animals, anthropology/archeology, art/architecture, business/economics, child guidance/parenting, computers/electronic, cooking/foods/nutrition, creative nonfiction, education, ethnic, gardening, gay/lesbian, government/politics, health/medicine, history, hobbies, language/literature, memoirs, military/war, money/finance, multicultural, music/dance, nature/environment, philosophy, photography, psychology, recreation, regional, religion, science, sex, sociology, software, spirituality, sports, translation, travel, women's issues/studies. No unsolicited mss. *Agented submissions only.* Reviews artwork/photos as part of ms package. Send photocopies.

Fiction: Adventure, comic books, confession, erotica, ethnic, experimental, fantasy, feminist, gay/lesbian, gothic, hi-lo, historical, horror, humor, juvenile, literary, mainstream/contemporary, military/war, multicultural, multimedia, mystery, occult, picture books, plays, poetry, poetry in translation, regional, religious, romance, science fiction, short story collections, spiritual, sports, suspense, western, young adult. No unsolicited mss. *Agented submissions only.*

Recent Title(s): *The Lost Son*, by Bernard Kerik; *Getting Over It*, by Anna Maxted.

A **REGNERY PUBLISHING, INC.**, Eagle Publishing, One Massachusetts Ave., NW, Washington DC 20001. (202)216-0600. Website: www.regnery.com. Publisher: Alfred S. Regnery. **Acquisitions:** Harry Crocker, executive editor (bestsellers); Bernadette Malone, editor; Jed Donahue, editor (biography, American history). Estab. 1947. Publishes hardcover and paperback originals and reprints. **Publishes 30 titles/year. 0% from unagented writers. Pays 8-15% royalty on retail price. Offers $0-50,000 advance.** Publishes book 1 year after acceptance of ms. Does not accept simultaneous submissions. Responds in 3 months to queries; 3 months to proposals; 3 months to mss.

Imprints: Gateway Editions, LifeLine Press, Capital Press.

O→ Regnery publishes conservative, well-written, well-produced, sometimes controversial books. Currently emphasizing health and business books.

Nonfiction: Biography, current affairs. Subjects include business/economics, government/politics, health/medicine, history, money/finance. Agented submissions only. No unsolicited mss.

Recent Title(s): *Bias: A CBS Insider Exposés How the Media Distort the News*; *Shakedown: Exposing the Real Jesse Jackson*; *The Final Days: The Last, Desparate Abuses of Power by the Clinton White House*, by Bill Sammon.

Tips: "We seek high-impact, headline-making, bestseller treatments of pressing current issues by established experts in the field."

RENAISSANCE HOUSE, 9400 Lloydcrest Drive, Beverly Hills CA 90210. (310)358-5288. Fax: (310)358-5282. Website: www.renaissancehouse.net. **Acquisitions:** Sam Laredo, publisher; Raquel Benatar, editor. Publishes hardcover and trade paperback originals. **Publishes 30 titles/year. Receives 500 queries and 100 mss/year. 25-30% of books from first-time authors; 75% from unagented writers. Pays 5-10% royalty on net receipts.** Accepts simultaneous submissions. Responds in 2 months to queries; 2 months to proposals; 2 months to mss. Book catalog free.

O→ "We specialize in highly illustrated children's books, ages 6-15. Multicultural topics and Spanish/bilingual titles are our specialty."

Nonfiction: Biography, children's/juvenile, illustrated book, Bilingual (Spanish). Subjects include animals, education, multicultural. Submit proposal package. Reviews artwork/photos as part of ms package. Send photocopies.

Fiction: Fantasy, juvenile, multicultural, picture books, legends; fables. Query with SASE.

Recent Title(s): *José Carreras, a Voice for Hope*, by César Vidal (biography); *The Spirits of the Mountain*, by Raquel Benatar (fiction).

REPUBLIC OF TEXAS PRESS, Wordware Publishing, Inc., 2320 Los Rios Blvd., Suite 200, Plano TX 75074. (972)423-0090. Fax: (972)881-9147. E-mail: gbivona@republicoftexaspress.com. Website: www.republicoftexaspress.com. **Acquisitions:** Ginnie Bivona, acquisitions editor. Publishes trade and mass market paperback originals. **Publishes 28-32 titles/year. Receives 400 queries and 300 mss/year. 95% from unagented writers. Pays 8% royalty on net receipts. Offers small advance.** Publishes book within 6 months after acceptance of ms. Accepts simultaneous submissions. Responds in 2 months to queries. Book catalog for #10 SASE; ms guidelines for #10 SASE.

O⚷ Republic of Texas Press specializes in Texas history and general Texana.

Nonfiction: Biography, humor. Subjects include ethnic, general nonfiction, history, nature/environment, regional, sports, travel, women's issues/studies, Old West, Texas military, ghost and mystery stories, trivia. Submit table of contents, 2 sample chapters, target audience, author bio and SASE.

Recent Title(s): *The Alamo Story: From Early History to Current Conflicts*, by J.R. Edmondson; *Exploring Houston with Children*, by Elaine Galit and Vikk Simmons; *A Yankee Chicks Guide to Survival in Texas*, by Sophia Dembling.

Tips: "We are interested in anything relating to Texas. From the wacky to the most informative, any nonfiction concept will be considered. Our market is adult."

[N] **RESOURCE PUBLICATIONS, INC.**, 160 E. Virginia St., Suite #290, San Jose CA 95112-5876. (408)286-8505. Fax: (408)287-8748. E-mail: info@rpinet.com. Website: www.rpinet.com/ml/. **Acquisitions:** Acquisition Director. Estab. 1973. Publishes paperback originals. **Publishes 12-18 titles/year. 30% of books from first-time authors; 99% from unagented writers. Pays 8% royalty (for a first project). Offers $250-1,000 advance.** Responds in 10 weeks to queries. Book catalog online; ms guidelines online.

O⚷ Resource Publications publishes books to help liturgists and ministers make the imaginative connection between liturgy and life.

Nonfiction: How-to, reference, self-help. Subjects include child guidance/parenting, education, music/dance, religion. Professional ministry resources for worship, education, clergy and other leaders, for use in Roman Catholic and mainline Protestant churches. Submit proposal package including résumé. Reviews artwork/photos as part of ms package.

Fiction: Fables; Anecdotes; Faith Sharing Stories; Stories useful in preaching or teaching. Query with SASE.

Recent Title(s): *Cultivating Character: Month-by-Month Resources for Parents and Teachers*; *Performing Parables*.

Tips: "We are publishers and secondarily we are book packagers. Pitch your project to us for publication first. If we can't take it on on that basis, we may be able to take it on as a packaging and production project."

RESURRECTION PRESS, LTD., 77 W. End Rd., Totowa NJ 07512-1405. (973)890-1400 Ext. 118. Fax: (973)890-2410. **Acquisitions:** Emilie Mackney, publisher. Publishes trade paperback originals and reprints. **Publishes 6-8 titles/year; imprint publishes 4 titles/year. Receives 100 queries and 100 mss/year. 25% of books from first-time authors; 100% from unagented writers. Pays 5-10% royalty. Offers $250-2,000 advance.** Publishes book 1 year after acceptance of ms. Accepts simultaneous submissions. Responds in 1 month to queries; 1 month to proposals; 2 months to mss. Book catalog and ms guidelines free.

Imprints: Spirit Life Series.

O⚷ Resurrection Press publishes religious, devotional and inspirational titles.

Nonfiction: Self-help. Subjects include religion. Query with SASE or submit outline, 2 sample chapter(s). Reviews artwork/photos as part of ms package. Send photocopies.

Recent Title(s): *Grace Notes*, by Lorraine Murray.

FLEMING H. REVELL PUBLISHING, Baker Book House, P.O. Box 6287, Grand Rapids MI 49516. Fax: (616)676-2315. Website: www.bakerbooks.com. **Acquisitions:** Lonnie Hull DuPont, interim editorial director; Bill Petersen, senior acquisitions editor; Jane Campbell, senior editor (Chosen Books); Jennifer Leep, acquisitions editor. Estab. 1870. Publishes hardcover, trade paperback and mass market paperback originals and reprints. **Publishes 50 titles/year; imprint publishes 10 titles/year. Pays 14-18% royalty on wholesale price. Offers advance.** Publishes book 1 year after acceptance of ms.

Imprints: Chosen Books, Spire Books.

O⚷ Revell publishes to the heart (rather than to the head). For 125 years, Revell has been publishing evangelical books for the personal enrichment and spiritual growth of general Christian readers.

Nonfiction: Biography, coffee table book, how-to, self-help. Subjects include child guidance/parenting, religion, Christian living.

Fiction: Religious.

Recent Title(s): *Making Children Mind Without Losing Yours*, by Dr. Kevin Leman (nonfiction); *Woman of Grace*, by Kathleen Morgan (fiction).

MORGAN REYNOLDS PUBLISHING, 620 S. Elm St., Suite 223, Greensboro NC 27406. Fax: (336)275-1152. E-mail: info@morganreynolds.com. Website: www.morganreynolds.com. **Acquisitions:** Laura Shoemaker, editor. Publishes hardcover originals. **Publishes 20-24 titles/year. Receives 250-300 queries and 100-150 mss/year. 50% of books from first-time authors; 100% from unagented writers.** Publishes book 8 months after acceptance of ms. Accepts simultaneous submissions. Responds in 3 months to queries.

O⚷ Morgan Reynolds publishes nonfiction books for juvenile and young adult readers. "We prefer lively, well-written biographies of interesting contemporary and historical figures for our biography series. Books for our

Great Events series should be insightful and exciting looks at critical periods. We are interested in more well-known subjects rather than the esoteric." Currently emphasizing great scientists, composers, philosophers, world writers. De-emphasizing sports figures.

Nonfiction: "We do not always publish the obvious subjects. Don't shy away from less popular subjects. We also publish nonfiction related to great events." Biography. Subjects include Americana (young adult/juvenile oriented), business/economics, government/politics, history, language/literature, military/war, money/finance, women's issues/studies. No children's books, picture books or fiction. Query with SASE.

Recent Title(s): *MS: The Story of Gloria Steinem*, by Elizabeth Wheaton; *Great Society: The Story of Lyndon Baines Johnson*, by Nancy Colbert.

Tips: "Request our writer's guidelines and visit our website. We will be happy to send a catalog if provided with 80 cents postage."

[N] **RICHBORO PRESS**, P.O. Box 947, Southampton PA 18966-0947. (215)355-6084. Fax: (215)364-2212. E-mail: deltaleons@yahoo.com. Website: www.richboropress.com. **Acquisitions:** George Moore, editor. Estab. 1979. Publishes hardcover, trade paperback originals and software. **Publishes 4 titles/year. Receives 500 submissions/year. 90% from unagented writers. Pays 10% royalty on retail price. Offers advance.** Publishes book 1 year after acceptance of ms. Does not accept simultaneous submissions. Responds in 2 months to queries. Book catalog free; Writer's guidelines for $1 and #10 SASE.

Nonfiction: Cookbook, how-to. Subjects include cooking/foods/nutrition, gardening, software. Query with SASE.

RISING MOON, Northland Publishing, LLC, P.O. Box 1389, Flagstaff AZ 86002-1389. (928)774-5251. Fax: (928)774-0592. E-mail: editorial@northlandpub.com. Website: www.northlandpub.com. **Acquisitions:** Rebecca Gómez, kids editor. Estab. 1958. Publishes hardcover and trade paperback originals. **Publishes 10-12 titles/year. Receives 1,000 submissions/year. 20% of books from first-time authors; 20% from unagented writers. Pays royalty. Offers advance.** Publishes book 2 years after acceptance of ms. Accepts simultaneous submissions. Responds in 3 months to queries. Call for book catalog and ms guidelines.

- Rising Moon has temporarily suspended consideration of unsolicited mss.
- Rising Moon's objective is to provide children with entertaining and informative books that follow the heart and tickle the funny bone. Rising Moon is no longer publishing middle-grade children's fiction.

Fiction: Picture books (broad subjects with wide appeal and universal themes). "We are also looking for exceptional bilingual stories (Spanish/English), activity books, fractured fairy tales, and original stories with a Southwest flavor." Submit complete ms with SASE of adequate size and postage.

Recent Title(s): *Clarence and the Great Surprise*, by Jean Ekman Adams; *Totally Polar*, by Marty Crisp and Viv Eisner.

Tips: "Our audience is composed of general interest readers."

RISING TIDE PRESS, P.O. Box 30457, Tucson AZ 85751-0457. (520)888-1140. Fax: (520)888-1123. Website: www.risingtidepress.com. **Acquisitions:** Debra Tobin, partner (mystery, adventure, nonfiction); Brenda Kazen, partner (science fiction, young adult fiction). Estab. 1991. Publishes trade paperback originals. **Publishes 10-15 titles/year. Receives 1,000 queries and 600 mss/year. 75% of books from first-time authors; 100% from unagented writers. Pays royalty on wholesale price.** Publishes book 15 months after acceptance of ms. Does not accept simultaneous submissions. Responds in 2 months to queries; 2 months to proposals; 3 months to mss. Book catalog for $1; ms guidelines for #10 SASE.

- "We are committed to publishing books by, for and about strong women and their lives.

Nonfiction: Subjects include women's issues/studies, lesbian nonfiction. Query with outline, entire ms and large SASE. Reviews artwork/photos as part of ms package. Send photocopies.

Fiction: Women's fiction only. Adventure, fantasy, historical, horror, humor, literary, mainstream/contemporary, mystery, occult, romance, science fiction, suspense, mixed genres. "Major characters must be women and stories must depict strong women characters." Query with SASE or submit synopsis or submit complete ms.

Recent Title(s): *Taking Risks*, by Judith McDaniel; *Undercurrents*, by Laurel Mills.

Tips: "We welcome unpublished authors. 2 cash prizes awarded annually. Any material submitted should be proofed. No multiple submissions."

RIVER CITY PUBLISHING, River City Publishing, LLC, 610 N. Perry St., Montgomery AL 36104. (334)265-6753. Fax: (334)265-8880. E-mail: info@rivercitypublish.com. Website: rivercitypublishing.com. **Acquisitions:** Jim Davis, managing editor; Tina Tatum, general manager; Al Newman, owner. Publishes hardcover and trade paperback originals and reprints. **Publishes 12 titles/year; imprint publishes 10 titles/year. Receives 50 queries and 300 mss/year. 20% of books from first-time authors; 90% from unagented writers. Pays 10-15% royalty on retail price. Offers 500-5,000 advance.** Publishes book 6 months after acceptance of ms. Accepts simultaneous submissions. Responds in 3 months to queries; 4 months to proposals; 1 year to mss. Book catalog and ms guidelines free.

Imprints: Starrhill Press, Black Belt Press

Nonfiction: Biography, coffee table book, illustrated book, multimedia, self-help. Subjects include art/architecture, child guidance/parenting, creative nonfiction, ethnic, gardening, gay/lesbian, government/politics, health/medicine, history, language/literature, memoirs, multicultural, music/dance, photography, regional, sports, travel. Submit proposal package including outline, 2 sample chapter(s). Reviews artwork/photos as part of ms package. Send photocopies.

Fiction: Ethnic, gay/lesbian, historical, literary, mainstream/contemporary, multicultural, poetry, regional, short story collections. Submit proposal package including 2 sample chapter(s), synopsis.
Poetry: Query.
Recent Title(s): *Turnaround*, by Tom Stoddard (sports/bio/inspirational); *These People Are Us*, by George Singleton (short stories); *The Map That Lies Between Us*, by Anne C. George (poetry).

ROC BOOKS, Penguin Putnam Inc., 375 Hudson St., New York NY 10014. (212)366-2000. Website: www.penguinputnam.com. **Acquisitions:** Laura Anne Gilman, executive editor; Jennifer Heddle, editor. Publishes mass market, trade and hardcover originals. **Publishes 36 titles/year. Receives 500 queries/year. Pays royalty. Offers negotiable advance.** Accepts simultaneous submissions. Responds in 2-3 months to queries.

O→ "We're looking for books that are a good read, that people will want to pick up time and time again."
Fiction: Fantasy, horror, science fiction. "Roc tries to strike a balance between fantasy and science fiction. We strongly discourage unsolicited submissions." Query with SASE or submit 1-2 sample chapter(s), synopsis.
Recent Title(s): *The Glasswrights' Journeyman*, by Mindy Klasky; *The Peshawer Lancers*, by S.M. Stirling.

RONIN PUBLISHING, INC., P.O. Box 522, Berkeley CA 94701. (510)420-3669. Fax: (510)420-3672. E-mail: info@roninpub.com. Website: www.roninpub.com. **Acquisitions:** Beverly Potter, publisher. Estab. 1983. Publishes trade paperback originals and reprints. **Publishes 8 titles/year. Receives 10 queries and 10 mss/year. Pays royalty on net only. Offers $500-1,000 advance.** Publishes book 1 year after acceptance of ms. Accepts simultaneous submissions. Responds in 3 months to queries. Book catalog free.

O→ "Ronin publishes book as tools for personal development, visionary alternatives and expanded consciousness."
Nonfiction: Reference, self-mastery. Subjects include agriculture/horticulture, alternative lifestyles, business/economics, cooking/foods/nutrition, gardening, health/medicine, psychology, spirituality, counterculture/psychedelia. "Our publishing purview is highly specific, as indicated in our catalog. We have rarely if ever published a book which initially arrived as an unsolicited manuscript. Please send queries only. Speak to our list." Query with SASE. *No unsolicited mss.*
Recent Title(s): *Timothy Leary: Your Brain Is God.*
Tips: "Our audience is interested in hard information and often buys several books on the same subject. Please submit query only. If on the basis of the query, we are interested in seeing the proposal or manuscript, we will let you know. No response to the query indicates that we have no interest. Become familiar with our interests through our catalog."

ROSE PUBLISHING, 4455 Torrance Blvd., #259, Torrance CA 90503. (310)370-8962. Fax: (310)370-7492. E-mail: rosepubl@aol.com. Website: www.rose-publishing.com. **Acquisitions:** Carol R. Witte, editor. **Publishes 5-10 titles/year. 5% of books from first-time authors; 100% from unagented writers. Makes outright purchase.** Publishes book 18 months after acceptance of ms. Accepts simultaneous submissions. Responds in 3 months to proposals; 2 months to mss. Book catalog free.

O→ "We publish only Bible-based materials in chart, poster or pamphlet form, easy-to-understand and appealing to children, teens or adults on Bible study, prayer, basic beliefs, Scripture memory, salvation, sharing the gospel, worship, abstinence, creation."
Nonfiction: Reference, pamphlets; group study books. Subjects include religion, science, sex, spirituality, Bible studies, Christian history, counseling aids, cults/occult, curriculum, Christian discipleship, evangelism/witnessing, Christian living, marriage, prayer, prophecy, creation, singles issues. No fiction or poetry. Submit proposal package including outline, photocopies of chart contents or poster artwork. Reviews artwork/photos as part of ms package. Send photocopies.
Recent Title(s): *Armor of God*; *Tabernacle*; *Archaeology and the Bible.*
Tips: Audience includes both church (Bible study leaders, Sunday school teachers [all ages], pastors, youth leaders) and home (parents, home schoolers, children, youth, high school and college). Open to topics that supplement Sunday School curriculum or Bible study, junior high creation materials, Tabernacle worksheets.

THE ROSEN PUBLISHING GROUP, 29 E. 21st St., New York NY 10010. Estab. 1950. Publishes nonfiction hardcover originals. **50% of books from first-time authors; 95% from unagented writers. Makes outright purchase of $200-3,000 for sale to school and public libraries.** Publishes book approximately 9 months after acceptance of ms. Does not accept simultaneous submissions. Responds in 2 months to proposals. Book catalog and ms guidelines free.
Imprints: PowerKids Press (nonfiction for grades K-4 that are supplementary to the curriculum. Topics include conflict resolution, character building, history, science, social studies and multicultural titles. Contact: Joanne Randolph, editorial director. Rosen Central (nonfiction for grades 5-8 on a wide range of topics. Topics include social issues, health, sports, self-esteem, history and science. Contact: Iris Rosoff, editorial director young adult division.
Nonfiction: Children's/juvenile, reference, self-help, textbook, young adult. Subjects include ethnic, health/medicine, history, multicultural (ethnographic studies), religion, science. Areas of particular interest include careers; coping with social, medical and personal problems; values and ethical behavior; self-esteem; social activism; social studies; high interest subjects. Submit outline, 1 sample chapter(s).
Recent Title(s): *Focus on Science and Society*; *Extreme Careers*; *Cool Careers without College.*
Tips: "The writer has the best chance of selling our firm a book on vocational guidance, personal social adjustment, a topic corellated directly to the 5-12 grade social studies or science curriculum, or high-interest, low reading-level material for teens."

ROXBURY PUBLISHING CO., P.O. Box 491044, Los Angeles CA 90049. (310)473-3312. **Acquisitions:** Claude Teweles, publisher. Estab. 1981. Publishes hardcover and paperback originals and reprints. **Publishes 15-20 titles/year. Pays royalty. Offers advance.** Accepts simultaneous submissions. Responds in 2 months to queries.

O→ Roxbury publishes college textbooks in the humanities and social sciences only.

Nonfiction: Textbook (college-level textbooks and supplements only). Subjects include humanities, social sciences, sociology, political science, family studies, criminology, criminal justice. Query with SASE or submit outline, sample chapter(s), synopsis or submit complete ms.

[N] **ROYAL FIREWORKS PUBLISHING**, 1 First Ave., P.O. Box 399, Unionville NY 10988. (845)726-4444. Fax: (845)726-3824. E-mail: rfpress@frontiernet.net. Website: www.rfpress.com. **Acquisitions:** William Neumann, editor (young adult); Myrna Kemnitz, editor (education). Estab. 1977. Publishes trade paperback originals and reprints. **Publishes 75-140 titles/year. Receives 1,000 queries and 400 mss/year. 30-50% of books from first-time authors; 98% from unagented writers. Pays 5-10% royalty on wholesale price.** Publishes book 9 months after acceptance of ms. Does not accept simultaneous submissions. Responds in 3 months to mss. Book catalog for $2.08; ms guidelines for #10 SASE.

Nonfiction: Textbook. Subjects include child guidance/parenting, education. "We do books for gifted children, their parents and teachers." Submit complete ms. Reviews artwork/photos as part of ms package. Send photocopies.

Fiction: Young adult. "We do novels for children from 8-16. We do a lot of historical fiction, science fiction, adventure, mystery, sports, etc. We are concerned about the values." No drugs, sex, swearing. Submit complete ms.

Recent Title(s): *Magic Lens*, by Michael Thompson (grammar textbook); *Keepers of the Flame*, by A. Ambler (poetry teaching manual); *Hitler's Willing Warrior*, by H. Gutsche (young adult fiction).

Tips: Audience is comprised of gifted children, their parents and teachers, and children (8-18) who read.

RUMINATOR BOOKS, 1648 Grand Ave., St. Paul MN 55105. (651)699-7038. Fax: (651)699-7190. E-mail: books@ruminator.com. Website: www.ruminator.com. **Acquisitions:** Pearl Kilbride. Publishes hardcover originals, trade paperback originals and reprints. **Publishes 8-10 titles/year. Receives 1,200 queries and 1,000 mss/year. 60% from unagented writers. Royalty varies. Offers varying advance.** Publishes book 12-18 months after acceptance of ms. Accepts simultaneous submissions. Responds in 4 months to proposals. Book catalog for 9×12 SAE with 2 first-class stamps; ms guidelines for #10 SASE.

O→ Ruminator Books is an independent press dedicated to publishing literary works from diverse voices and bringing political, social and cultural ideas to a wide and varied readership. Currently emphasizing culture studies, political, travel, memoirs, nature, history, world views. De-emphasizing spirituality, cooking, romance, mysteries, how-to, business, poetry.

Nonfiction: Subjects include government/politics, history, language/literature, memoirs, nature/environment, travel, worldviews, culture studies. No how-to, self-help/instructional, children's or poetry mss. Submit proposal package, including letter, outline and at least one sample chapter with SASE.

Fiction: Literary, adult fiction. Query with SASE or submit proposal package including outline, sample chapter(s), SASE.

Recent Title(s): *Facing the Congo*, by Jeffrey Tayler; *The Last Summer of Reason*, by Tahar Djarat; *An Algerian Childhood* (anthology).

RUTGERS UNIVERSITY PRESS, 100 Joyce Kilmer Ave., Piscataway NJ 08854-8099. (732)445-7762. Fax: (732)445-7039. E-mail: halkias@rci.rutgers.edu. Website: rutgerspress.rutgers.edu. **Acquisitions:** Leslie Mitchner, editor-in-chief/associate director (humanities); David Myers, acquiring editor (social sciences); Audra Wolfe, editor (science, health & medicine). Estab. 1936. Publishes hardcover originals and trade paperback originals and reprints. **Publishes 90 titles/year. Receives 1,500 queries and 300 mss/year. 30% of books from first-time authors; 70% from unagented writers. Pays 7½-15% royalty. Offers $1,000-10,000 advance.** Publishes book 1 year after acceptance of ms. Responds in 1 month to proposals. Book catalog and ms guidelines available via website or with SASE.

O→ "Our press aims to reach audiences beyond the academic community with accessible scholarly and regional books."

Nonfiction: Reference. Subjects include art/architecture (art history), ethnic, film/cinema/stage, gay/lesbian, government/politics, health/medicine, history, multicultural, nature/environment, regional, religion, sociology, women's issues/studies, African-American studies, Asian-American studies, history of science and technology, literature, literary criticism, human evolution, ecology, media studies. Books for use in undergraduate courses. Submit outline, 2-3 sample chapter(s). Reviews artwork/photos as part of ms package. Send photocopies.

Recent Title(s): *The Great Communication Gap: Why Americans Feel So Alone*, by Laura Pappano.

Tips: Both academic and general audiences. "Many of our books have potential for undergraduate course use. We are more trade-oriented than most university presses. We are looking for intelligent, well-written and accessible books. Avoid overly narrow topics." **50% of books from first-time authors; 80% from unagented writers. Pays 10% royalty on retail price.** Publishes book 9 months after acceptance of ms. Does not accept simultaneous submissions. Responds in 1 month to queries; 2 months to mss. Book catalog and ms guidelines online.

Fiction: Mystery, suspense, espionage; thriller. "Our needs change. Check our website." Query with SASE.

Recent Title(s): *Kafka's Fedora*, by A.J. Adler (mainstream); *Hypershot*, by Trevor Scott; *Bound to Die*, by Brian Lutterman (mystery).

Tips: "Salvo Press also sponsors the annual Mystery Novel Award. Send SASE for guidelines or check the website for them."

RUTLEDGE HILL PRESS, Thomas Nelson, P.O. Box 141000, Nashville TN 37214-1000. (615)902-2333. Fax: (615)902-2340. Website: www.rutledgehillpress.com. **Acquisitions:** Lawrence Stone, publisher. Estab. 1982. Publishes hardcover and trade paperback originals and reprints. **Publishes 40-50 titles/year. Receives 1,000 submissions/year. 40% of books from first-time authors; 80% from unagented writers. Pays royalty. Offers advance.** Publishes book 10 months after acceptance of ms. Responds in 2 months to queries. Book catalog for 9×12 SAE with 4 first-class stamps; ms guidelines for #10 SASE.

O-- "We are a publisher of market-specific books, focusing on particular genres or regions."

Nonfiction: Biography, cookbook, humor. Subjects include cooking/foods/nutrition, sports, travel (regional), women's issues/studies, Civil War history. "The book should have a unique marketing hook. Books built on new ideas and targeted to a specific U.S. region are welcome. Please, no fiction, children's, academic, poetry or religious works, and we won't even look at *Life's Little Instruction Book* spinoffs or copycats." Submit cover letter that includes brief marketing strategy and author bio, outline and sample chapters. Reviews artwork/photos as part of ms package.

Recent Title(s): *A Gentleman Entertains*, by John Bridges and Bryan Curtis; *101 Secrets a Good Dad Knows*, by Walter Browder and Sue Ellen Browder; *I Hope You Dance*, by Tia Sillers and Mark Sanders.

SAE INTERNATIONAL, Society of Automotive Engineers, 400 Commonwealth Dr., Warrendale PA 15096. (724)776-4841. **Acquisitions:** Jeff Worsinger, product manager; Martha Swiss, product manager; Lisa Moses, product manager; Kris Hattman, product manager; Tracy Fedkoe, product developer; Ed Manns, manager, product development division. Estab. 1905. Publishes hardcover and trade paperback originals, Web and CD-ROM based electronic product. **Publishes 30-40 titles/year. Receives 250 queries and 75 mss/year. 30-40% of books from first-time authors; 100% from unagented writers. Pays royalty. Offers possible advance.** Publishes book 9-10 months after acceptance of ms. Accepts simultaneous submissions. Responds in 2 months to queries. Book catalog and ms guidelines free.

O-- "Automotive means anything self-propelled. We are a professional society serving this area, which includes aircraft, spacecraft, marine, rail, automobiles, trucks and off-highway vehicles." Currently emphasizing automotive history and engineering, aerospace history and engineering.

Nonfiction: Biography, multimedia (CD-ROM, Web-based), reference, technical, textbook. Query with SASE. Reviews artwork/photos as part of ms package. Send photocopies.

Recent Title(s): *Formula Technology*; *Ford: The Dust and the Glory.*

Tips: "Audience is automotive engineers, technicians, car buffs, aerospace engineers, technicians and historians."

SAFARI PRESS, INC., 15621 Chemical Lane, Building B, Huntington Beach CA 92649-1506. (714)894-9080. Fax: (714)894-4949. E-mail: info@safaripress.com. Website: www.safaripress.com. **Acquisitions:** Jacqueline Neufeld, editor. Estab. 1984. Publishes hardcover originals and reprints and trade paperback reprints. **Publishes 20-25 titles/year. 50% of books from first-time authors; 99% from unagented writers. Pays 8-15% royalty on wholesale price.** Does not accept simultaneous submissions. Book catalog for $1.

- The editor notes that she receives many mss outside the areas of big-game hunting, wingshooting, and sporting firearms, and these are always rejected.

O-- Safari Press publishes books **only** on big-game hunting, sporting, firearms, and wingshooting; this includes African, North American, European, Asian, and South American hunting and wingshooting. Does not want books on 'outdoors' topics (hiking, camping, canoeing, etc.).

Nonfiction: Biography (of hunters), how-to (hunting and wingshooting stories), hunting adventure stories. Subjects include hunting, firearms, wingshooting, "We discourage autobiographies, unless the life of the hunter or firearms maker has been exceptional. We routinely reject manuscripts along the lines of 'Me and my buddies went hunting for... and a good time was had by all!" No outdoors topics (hiking, camping, canoeing, fishing, etc.). Query with SASE or submit outline.

Recent Title(s): *Fine European Gunmakers*; *Greatest Elk.*

SAFER SOCIETY PRESS, P.O. Box 340, Brandon VT 05733. (802)247-3132. Fax: (802)247-4233. Website: www.safersociety.org. **Acquisitions:** Theresa Milano, publications specialist. Estab. 1985. Publishes trade paperback originals. **Publishes 3-4 titles/year. Receives 15-20 queries and 15-20 mss/year. 90% of books from first-time authors; 100% from unagented writers. Pays 5% royalty on retail price.** Publishes book 1 year after acceptance of ms. Accepts simultaneous submissions. Book catalog free.

O-- "Our mission is the prevention and treatment of sexual abuse."

Nonfiction: Self-help (sex abuse prevention and treatment). Subjects include memoirs, psychology (sexual abuse). "We are a small, nonprofit, niche press. We want well-researched books dealing with any aspect of sexual abuse: treatment, prevention, understanding; works on subject in Spanish." Query with SASE, submit proposal package or complete ms. Reviews artwork/photos as part of ms package. Send photocopies.

Recent Title(s): *But He Says He Loves Me: Girls Speak Out on Dating Abuse*, by Nicole B. Sperekas, Ph.D.; *What's Happening in Our Family: Understanding Sexual Abuse through Metaphors*, by Constance M. Ostis, MSW.

Tips: Audience is persons working in mental health/persons needing self-help books. Pays small fees or low royalties.

SALEM PRESS, INC., Magill's Choice, 131 N. El Molino, Suite 350, Pasadena CA 91101. (626)584-0106. Fax: (626)584-1525. Website: www.salempress.com. **Acquisitions:** Dawn P. Dawson. **Publishes 20-22 titles/year. Receives 15 queries/year. Work-for-hire pays 5-15¢/word.** Responds in 1 month to queries; 1 month to proposals; 1 month to mss. Book catalog online.

Nonfiction: Reference. Subjects include business/economics, ethnic, government/politics, health/medicine, history, language/literature, military/war, music/dance, nature/environment, philosophy, psychology, science, sociology, women's issues/studies. "We accept vitas for writers interested in supplying articles/entries for encyclopedia-type entries in library reference books. Will also accept multi-volume book ideas from people interested in being a general editor." Query with SASE.

SALVO PRESS, P.O. Box 9095, Bend OR 97708. (541)330-8746. Fax: (541)330-8746. E-mail: info@salvopress.com. Website: www.salvopress.com. **Acquisitions:** Scott Schmidt, publisher. Publishes paperback originals (POD) and e-books in most formats. **Publishes 3 titles/year. Receives 500 queries/year. 50% of books from first-time authors; 80% from unagented writers. Pays 10% royalty on retail price.** Publishes book 9 months after acceptance of ms. Does not accept simultaneous submissions. Responds in 1 month to queries; 2 months to mss. Book catalog and ms guidelines online.
Fiction: Mystery, suspense, espionage; thriller. "Our needs change. Check our website." Query with SASE.
Recent Title(s): *Kafka's Fedora*, by A.J. Adler (mainstream); *Hypershot*, by Trevor Scott; *Bound to Die*, by Brian Lutterman (mystery).
Tips: "Salvo Press also sponsors the annual Mystery Novel Award. Send SASE for guidelines or check the website for them."

SAMS, Pearson Education, 201 W. 103rd St., Indianapolis IN 46290. (317)581-3500. Website: www.samspublishing.com. Publisher: Paul Boger. Associate Publishers: Mark Taber (web development, macromedia, Apple, Adobe, graphics, consumer topics, open source); Michael Stephens (Sun, Microsoft, programming topics). Estab. 1951. Publishes trade paperback originals. **Publishes 160 titles/year. 30% of books from first-time authors; 95% from unagented writers. Pays negotiable royalty on wholesale price. Offers negotiable advance.** Publishes book 1 year after acceptance of ms. Does not accept simultaneous submissions. Responds in 6 weeks to queries. Ms guidelines online.

O→ Sams has made a major commitment to publishing books that meet the needs of computer users, programmers, administrative and support personnel, and managers.

Nonfiction: Technical. Subjects include computers and related technologies. Accepts simultaneous submissions if noted; "however once contract is signed, Sams Publishing retains first option rights on future works on same subject." Query with SASE.
Recent Title(s): *Mac OS X Unleashed*; *ASP.NET Unleashed*.

SANTA MONICA PRESS LLC, P.O. Box 1076, Santa Monica CA 90406. Website: www.santamonicapress.com. **Acquisitions:** Acquistions Editor. Estab. 1991. Publishes trade paperback originals. **Publishes 6-10 titles/year. Receives 500+ submissions/year. 10% of books from first-time authors; 50% from unagented writers. Pays 4-10% royalty on wholesale price. Offers $500-2,500 advance.** Publishes book 6-18 months after acceptance of ms. Accepts simultaneous submissions. Responds in 1-2 months to proposals. Book catalog for 9×12 SASE with 80¢ postage; ms guidelines for #10 SASE.

O→ "At Santa Monica Press, we're not afraid to cast a wide editorial net. Our vision extends from lively and modern how-to books to offbeat looks at popular culture, from fiction to new age."

Nonfiction: Biography, gift book, how-to, humor, illustrated book, reference. Subjects include Americana, creative nonfiction, film/cinema/stage, health/medicine, language/literature, memoirs, music/dance, spirituality, sports, travel, contemporary culture, film/cinema/stage, general nonfiction, New Age. **All unsolicited mss returned unopened.** Submit proposal package, including outline, 2-3 sample chapters, biography, marketing and publicity plans, analysis of competitive titles, SASE. Reviews artwork/photos as part of ms package. Send photocopies.
Recent Title(s): *Footsteps in the Fog: Alfred Hitchcock's San Francisco*, by Jeff Kraft and Aaron Leventhal; *The Butt Hello...and Other Ways My Cats Drive Me Crazy*, by Ted Meyer; *Blues for Bird*, by Martin Gray.
Tips: "Visit our website before submitting to get a clear idea of the types of books we publish. Carefully analyze your book's competition and tell us what makes your book different—and what makes it better. Also let us know what promotional and marketing opportunities you, as the author, bring to the project."

SARABANDE BOOKS, INC., 2234 Dundee Rd., Suite 200, Louisville KY 40205. (502)458-4028. Fax: (502)458-4065. E-mail: sarabandeb@aol.com. Website: www.sarabandebooks.org. **Acquisitions:** Sarah Gorham, editor-in-chief. Publishes hardcover and trade paperback originals. **Publishes 10 titles/year. Receives 500 queries and 2,000 mss/year. 35% of books from first-time authors; 75% from unagented writers. 10% on actual income received. Offers $500-1,000 advance.** Publishes book 18 months after acceptance of ms. Accepts simultaneous submissions. Responds in 3 months to queries; 6 months to mss. Book catalog free; ms guidelines for #10 SASE.

O→ "Sarabande Books was founded to publish poetry and short fiction, as well as the occasional literary essay collection. We look for works of lasting literary value. We are actively seeking novellas, as well as essays on the writing life."

Fiction: Literary, short story collections, novellas. Queries in September only. "We do publish short novels (less than 250 pages)." Query with 1 sample story, 1 page bio, listing of publishing credits and SASE.
Poetry: "Poetry of superior artistic quality. Otherwise no restraints or specifications." Submissions in September only. Query or submit 10 sample poems.
Recent Title(s): *Bread for the Baker's Child*, by Joseph Caldwell (fiction); *Twice Removed*, by Ralph Angel (poetry).
Tips: Sarabande publishes for a general literary audience. "Know your market. Read—and buy—books of literature." Sponsors contests.

SAS PUBLISHING, SAS Campus Dr., Cary NC 27513-2414. (919)677-8000. Fax: (919)677-4444. E-mail: sasbbu@sas.com. Website: www.sas.com/pubs. **Acquisitions:** Julie M. Platt, editor-in-chief. Estab. 1976. Publishes hardcover and trade paperback originals. **Publishes 40 titles/year. Receives 30 submissions/year. 50% of books from first-time authors; 100% from unagented writers. Payment negotiable. Offers negotiable advance.** Does not accept simultaneous submissions. Responds in 2 weeks to queries. Book catalog and ms guidelines via website or with SASE.

O→ SAS publishes books for SAS software users, "both new and experienced."

Nonfiction: Technical, textbook. Subjects include software, statistics. "SAS Publishing develops and writes books inhouse. Through Books by Users Press, we also publish books by SAS users on a variety of topics relating to SAS software. We want to provide our users with additional titles to supplement our primary documentation and to enhance the users' ability to use SAS effectively. We're interested in publishing manuscripts that describe or illustrate using any of SAS products. Books must be aimed at SAS users, either new or experienced. Tutorials are particularly attractive, as are descriptions of user-written applications for solving real-life business, industry or academic problems. Books on programming techniques using SAS are also desirable. Manuscripts must reflect current or upcoming software releases, and the author's writing should indicate an understanding of SAS and the technical aspects covered in the manuscript." Query with SASE or submit outline, sample chapter(s). Reviews artwork/photos as part of ms package.

Recent Title(s): *The Little SAS Book: A Primer, Second Edition*, by Lora D. Delwiche and Susan J. Slaughter.

Tips: "If I were a writer trying to market a book today, I would concentrate on developing a manuscript that teaches or illustrates a specific concept or application that SAS users will find beneficial in their own environments or can adapt to their own needs."

SASQUATCH BOOKS, 615 Second Ave., Suite 260, Seattle WA 98104. (206)467-4300. Fax: (206)467-4301. E-mail: books@sasquatchbooks.com. Website: www.sasquatchbooks.com. President: Chad Haight. **Acquisitions:** Kate Rogers, senior editor (travel, Alaska, women's issues); Jennie McDonald, senior editor (California subjects: food and wine, gardening, history); Novella Carpenter, assistant editor (urban lifestyle, humor, women's issues). Estab. 1986. Publishes regional hardcover and trade paperback originals. **Publishes 30 titles/year. 20% of books from first-time authors; 75% from unagented writers. Pays royalty on cover price. Offers wide range advance.** Publishes book 6 months after acceptance of ms. Does not accept simultaneous submissions. Responds in 3 months to queries. Book catalog for 9×12 SAE with 2 first-class stamps.

O→ Sasquatch Books publishes books for a West Coast regional audience—Alaska to California. Currently emphasizing outdoor recreation, cookbooks and history.

Nonfiction: "We are seeking quality nonfiction works about the Pacific Northwest and West Coast regions (including Alaska to California). The literature of place includes how-to and where-to as well as history and narrative nonfiction." Reference. Subjects include animals, art/architecture, business/economics, cooking/foods/nutrition, gardening, history, nature/environment, recreation, regional, sports, travel, women's issues/studies, outdoors. Query first, then submit outline and sample chapters with SASE.

Recent Title(s): *One Hundred Demons*, by Lynda Barry; *Best Places: Northwest*; *The Northern Lights*, by Calvin Hall and Daryl Pederson.

Tips: "We sell books through a range of channels in addition to the book trade. Our primary audience consists of active, literate residents of the West Coast."

SCARECROW PRESS, INC., Rowman & Littlefield Publishing Group, 4720 Boston Way, Lanham MD 20706. (301)459-3366. Fax: (301)459-2118. Website: www.scarecrowpress.com. **Acquisitions:** Sue Easun, acquisitions editor (information studies, military history); Bruce Phillips, acquisitions editor (music, film and theatre); Tom Koerner, editorial director (educational practice and policy); Kim Tabor, acquisitions editor (curriculum resource guides, historical dictionaries); Shirley Lambert, editorial director (criminology, general reference). Estab. 1950. Publishes hardcover originals. **Publishes 175 titles/year. Receives 600-700 submissions/year. 70% of books from first-time authors; 99% from unagented writers. Pays 8% royalty on net of first 1,000 copies; 10% of net price thereafter.** Publishes book 18 months after acceptance of ms. Does not accept simultaneous submissions. Responds in 2 months to queries. Book catalog for 9×12 SAE with 4 first-class stamps.

O→ "Emphasis is on any title likely to appeal to libraries." Currently emphasizing jazz, Africana, and educational issues of contemporary interest.

Nonfiction: Academic, reference, professional/scholarly monographs. Subjects include film/cinema/stage, language/literature, religion, sports, annotated bibliographies, handbooks and biographical dictionaries in the areas of women's studies and ethnic studies, parapsychology, fine arts and handicrafts, genealogy, sports history, music, movies, stage, library and information science. Query with SASE.

Recent Title(s): *How We Will Learn in the 21st Century*, by Judy Brick; *The User's View of the Internet*, by Harry Bruce.

SCHENKMAN BOOKS, INC., 118 Main Street, Rochester VT 05767. (802)767-3702. Fax: (802)767-9528. E-mail: schenkma@sover.net. Website: www.sover.net/~schenkma/. **Acquisitions:** Joe Schenkman, editor. Estab. 1961. Publishes hardcover and trade paperback originals and reprints. **Publishes 6 titles/year. Receives 100 queries and 25 mss/year. 80% of books from first-time authors; 95% from unagented writers. Pays 10% royalty on net receipts.** Accepts simultaneous submissions. Book catalog and ms guidelines free.

O→ "Schenkman Books specializes in publishing scholarly monographs for the academic community. For almost forty years we have brought revolutionary works to the public to fuel discourse on important issues. It is our hope that the material we make available contributes to the efforts toward peace and humanitarianism throughout the world."

Nonfiction: Biography, scholarly (monographs), self-help, textbook. Subjects include anthropology/archeology, ethnic, government/politics, history, music/dance, philosophy, psychology, sociology, women's issues/studies, African studies, African-American studies, Asian studies, Caribbean studies. Query with SASE or submit outline. Reviews artwork/photos as part of ms package. Send photocopies.

Recent Title(s): *Work Abuse*, by Judith Wyatt and Chauncey Hare (self-help/management relations).

SCHOCKEN BOOKS, Knopf Publishing Group, Random House, Inc., 299 Park Ave., New York NY 10171. (212)572-2559. Fax: (212)572-6030. Website: www.schocken.com. **Acquisitions:** Altie Karper, editorial director. Estab. 1931. Publishes hardcover and trade paperback originals and reprints. **Publishes 9-12 titles/year. Small% of books from first-time authors; small% from unagented writers. Offers variable advance.** Accepts simultaneous submissions.

"Schocken publishes quality Judaica in all areas—fiction, history, biography, current affairs, spirituality and religious practices, popular culture and cultural studies."

Recent Title(s): *How To Be a Jewish Parent*, by Anita Diamont; *The Funeral Party*, by Ludmila Ulitskaya.

SCHOLASTIC PRESS, Scholastic Inc., 557 Broadway, New York NY 10012. (212)343-6100. Website: www.scholastic.com. **Acquisitions:** Elizabeth Szabla, editorial director. Publishes hardcover originals. **Publishes 50 titles/year. Receives 2,500 queries/year. 5% of books from first-time authors. Pays royalty on retail price. Offers varies advance.** Publishes book 18-24 months after acceptance of ms. Does not accept simultaneous submissions. Responds in 2 months to queries; 6-8 months to mss.

Scholastic Press publishes "fresh, literary picture book fiction and nonfiction; fresh, literary non-series or non-genre-oriented middle grade and young adult fiction." Currently emphasizing "subtly handled treatments of key relationships in children's lives; unusual approaches to commonly dry subjects, such as biography, math, history or science." De-emphasizing fairy tales (or retellings), board books, genre or series fiction (mystery, fantasy, etc.).

Nonfiction: Children's/juvenile, general interest. *Agented submissions only.*

Fiction: Juvenile, picture books. *Agented submissions only.*

Recent Title(s): *The Greatest: Muhammad Ali*, by Walter Dean Myers; *Belle Teal*, by Ann M. Martin; *The Beastly Arms*, by Patrick Jennings.

SCHOLASTIC PROFESSIONAL PUBLISHING, Scholastic Inc., 524 Broadway, New York NY 10012. Website: www.scholastic.com. Vice President/Editor-in-Chief: Terry Cooper. **Acquisitions:** Liza Charlesworth, editorial director (pre-K-grade 4 teacher resource books and materials); Virginia Dooley, editorial director (grade 4-8 teacher resource books); Wendy Murray, editorial director (teaching strategy, professional development and theory-based books). Estab. 1989. **Publishes 140+ titles/year. Offers advance.** Does not accept simultaneous submissions. Responds in 3 months to queries. Book catalog for 9×12 SASE.

"We publish a line of teacher resources to help enrich classrooms, to help meet teachers' needs." Currently emphasizing reading skills, differentiated curriculum, standards, testing.

Nonfiction: Subjects include education. Elementary and middle-school level enrichment—all subject areas, including math, science, social studies, easy art projects, phonics, writing process, management techniques, teaching strategies based on personal/professional experience in the clssroom and technology ideas. Production is limited to printed matter: resource and activity books, professional development materials, reference titles. Length: 6,000-12,000 words. Offers standard contract. Query with table of contents, outline and sample chapter.

Recent Title(s): *Irresistable ABCs*, by Joe Novelli; *Terrific Transitions*, by Ellen Booth Church; *Teaching First Grade*, by Min Hong.

Tips: "Writer should have background working in the classroom with elementary or middle school children, teaching pre-service students, and/or solid background in developing supplementary educational materials for these markets."

SCHREIBER PUBLISHING, INC., 51 Monroe St., Suite 101, Rockville MD 20850. (301)424-7737 ext. 28. Fax: (301)424-2336. E-mail: spbooks@aol.com. Website: www.schreibernet.com. President: Morry Schreiber. **Acquisitions:** Linguistics Editor; Judaica Editor. Publishes hardcover and trade paperback originals and reprints. **Publishes 8 titles/year. Receives 40 queries and 12 mss/year. 80% of books from first-time authors; 95% from unagented writers. Pays negotiable royalty on retail price.** Publishes book 6 months after acceptance of ms. Accepts simultaneous submissions. Responds in 1 month to queries; 1 month to proposals; 1 month to mss. Book catalog free or on website; ms guidelines free.

Schreiber publishes reference books and dictionaries for better language and translation work, as well as Judaica books emphasizing Jewish culture and religion. Currently emphasizing multicultural dictionaries and parochial books.

Nonfiction: Biography, children's/juvenile, coffee table book, gift book, humor, multimedia (CD-ROM), reference, textbook. Subjects include history, language/literature, memoirs, money/finance, multicultural, religion, science, translation. Query with SASE; or submit proposal package, including: outline, 1 sample chapter and table of contents. Reviews artwork/photos as part of ms package. Send photocopies.

Recent Title(s): *Questioning the Bible*, by Morry Soffer; *Spanish Business Dictionary.*

N SCHROEDER PUBLISHING CO., INC., P.O. Box 3009, Paducah KY 42002-3009. (270)898-6211. Fax: (270)898-8890. E-mail: editor@collectorbooks.com. Website: www.collectorbooks.com. Estab. 1973. Publishes hardcover and trade paperback orginals. **Publishes 95 titles/year; imprint publishes 65 (Collector Books); 30 (American Quilter's Society) titles/year. Receives 150 queries and 100 mss/year. 60% of books from first-time authors; 100% from unagented writers. Pays 5% royalty on retail price.** Publishes book 6 months after acceptance of ms. Accepts simultaneous submissions. Responds in 1 month to queries; 1 month to proposals; 1 month to mss. Book catalog online; ms guidelines online.

Imprints: Collector Books; American Quilter's Society.

Nonfiction: Coffee table book, gift book, how-to, illustrated book, reference, self-help, textbook. Subjects include general nonfiction, hobbies, antiques and collectibles. Submit proposal package including outline, 2 sample chapter(s). Reviews artwork/photos as part of ms package. Send transparencies or prints.

Recent Title(s): *Schroeder's Antiques Price Guide*, by Sharon Huxford (reference); *Vintage Golf Club Collectibles*, by Ronald John (reference); *Collector's Encyclopedia of Depression Glass*, by Gene Florence (reference).

Tips: Audience consists of collectors, garage sale and flea market shoppers, antique dealers, E-bay shoppers, and quilters.

N SCIENCE & HUMANITIES PRESS, P.O. Box 7151, Chesterfield MO 63006-7151. (636)394-4950. Fax: (636)394-1381. E-mail: pub@sciencehumanitiespress.com. Website: www.sciencehumanitiespress.com. **Acquisitions:** Dr. Bud Banis, publisher. Publishes trade paperback originals and reprints, and electronic originals and reprints. **Publishes 20-30 titles/year. Receives 200 queries and 50 mss/year. 25% of books from first-time authors; 100% from unagented writers. Pays 8% royalty on retail price.** Publishes book 6-12 after acceptance of ms. Accepts simultaneous submissions. Responds in 1 month to queries; 1 month to proposals; 3 months to mss. Book catalog online; ms guidelines online.

Imprints: Science & Humanities Press, BeachHouse Books, MacroPrintBooks (large print editions), Heuristic Books, Early Editions Books.

Nonfiction: Biography, cookbook, gift book, how-to, humor, reference, self-help, technical, textbook, medical, disabilities adaptation. Subjects include Americana, business/economics, child guidance/parenting, computers/electronic, cooking/foods/nutrition, creative nonfiction, education, government/politics, health/medicine, history, hobbies, language/literature, memoirs, military/war, money/finance, philosophy, psychology, recreation, regional, science, sex, sociology, software, spirituality, sports, travel, women's issues/studies, math/statistics, management science. "Submissions are best as brief descriptions by e-mail, including some description of the author's background/credentials, and thoughts on approach to nontraditional or specialized markets. Why is the book important and who would buy it. Prefer description by e-mail. Need not be a large format proposal."

Fiction: Adventure, fantasy, historical, humor, literary, mainstream/contemporary, military/war, mystery, plays, poetry, regional, religious, romance, science fiction, short story collections, spiritual, sports, suspense, western, young adult. "We prefer books with a theme that gives a market focus. Brief description by e-mail."

Poetry: Prefers structured poetry with a theme. "Send a brief description by e-mail with a few samples."

Recent Title(s): *To Norma Jeane with Love, Jimmie*, by Jim Dougherty/LC Van Savage (biography); *Growing Up on Route 66*, by Michael Lund (coming of age); *Ropes and Saddles*, by Andy Polson (western poems, family memories).

Tips: Sales are primarily through the Internet, special orders, reviews in specialized media, direct sales to libraries, special organizations and use as textbooks. "Our expertise is electronic publishing for continuous short-run in-house production rather than mass distribution to retail outlets. This allows us to commit to books that might not be financially successful in conventional book store environments and to keep books in print and available for extended periods of time. Books should be of types that would sell steadily over a long period of time, rather than those that require rapid rollout and bookstore shelf exposure for a short time. We consider the nurture of new talent part of our mission but enjoy experienced authors as well. We are proud that many of our books are second, third and fourth books from authors who were once our first-time authors. A good book is not a one-time accident."

A SCRIBNER, Simon & Schuster, 1230 Avenue of the Americas, New York NY 10020. (212)698-7000. Website: www.simonsays.com. **Acquisitions:** Nan Graham (literary fiction, nonfiction); Rachel Sussman (fiction, nonfiction); Brent Rumble (fiction, nonfiction); Colin Harrison (nonfiction). Publishes hardcover originals. **Publishes 70-75 titles/year. Receives thousands queries/year. 20% of books from first-time authors; 0% from unagented writers. Pays 7½-15% royalty. Offers variable advance.** Accepts simultaneous submissions. Responds in 3 months to queries.

Imprints: Rawson Associates; Lisa Drew Books; Scribner Classics (reprints only); Scribner Poetry (by invitation only); Simple Abundance Press.

Nonfiction: Biography. Subjects include education, ethnic, gay/lesbian, health/medicine, history, language/literature, nature/environment, philosophy, psychology, religion, science, criticism. *Agented submissions only.*

Fiction: Literary, mystery, suspense. *Agented submissions only.*

Recent Title(s): *From a Buick 8*, by Stephen King; *The Constant Gardener*, by John le Carre; *War in a Time of Peace*, by David Halberstan.

SCRIVENERY PRESS, P.O. Box 740969-1003, Houston TX 77274-0969. (713)665-6760. Fax: (713)665-8838. E-mail: books@scrivenery.com. Website: www.scrivenery.com. **Acquisitions:** Kevin Miller, associate editor (nonfiction); Chris Coleman, associate editor (fiction/general); Leila B. Joiner, editor (fiction/literary). Publishes hardcover originals and trade paperback originals and reprints. **Publishes 10 titles/year. Receives 2,000 queries and 30 mss/year. 25% of books from first-time authors; 50% from unagented writers. Pays 8½-15% royalty on retail price. Electronic**

and other subsidiary rights at 50% publisher's net; motion picture rights remain with author. Offers rare advance. Publishes book 10 months after acceptance of ms. Accepts simultaneous submissions. Responds in 3 months to queries; 3 months to proposals; 4 months to mss. Book catalog for $2 or on website; ms guidelines for #10 SASE or on website.

"Our primary needs are in the humanities: English literatuare (history and/or analyses); literary theory (for a general, educated audience); science, technology, and culture, and natural history (e.g., Edward O. Wilson, Stephen Jay Gould); and history, targeted at an adult, well-educated audience who seek the pleasure of expertly-wielded language. Biography (no memoirs or autobiography) is also needed; we prefer figures from arts, letters and science rather than political/military figures."

Nonfiction: Biography, how-to, self-help, humanities. Subjects include Americana, creative nonfiction, history, hobbies, language/literature, nature/environment, philosophy, science, translation. Submit proposal package including outline, 3 sample chapter(s). **All unsolicited mss returned unopened.** Reviews artwork/photos as part of ms package. Send photocopies or line-art only; no photos.

Fiction: Adventure, experimental, historical, literary, mainstream/contemporary, regional, short story collections, suspense. "Our greatest interest is in mainstream and literary fiction; we prefer literary crossover in all genres." Submit proposal package including 3 sample chapter(s), synopsis. **All unsolicited mss returned unopened.**

Recent Title(s): *Next Year in Cuba*; *Easy Reading Writing*.

Tips: "In both fiction and nonfiction, we market to an adult, educated audience who seek the pleasure of expertly-wielded language in addition to well-crafted story. Scrivenery Press is open to unpublished talent, but not writers new to the craft. Polish your manuscript as best you can; expect to be judged against seasoned pros. In fiction, we prefer polished, literate work that could be construed as a crossover between genre and literary fiction; examples would be, in mystery, Umberto Eco's *The Name of the Rose*; in mainstream, David Guterson's *Snow Falling on Cedars* or Annie Proulx's *The Shipping News*; in the history genre, Charles Frazier's *Cold Mountain*, or our recent release by E.A. Blair, *A Journey to the Interior*. In nonfiction we seek thoughtful work, but material not specifically geared to an academic market."

SEAWORTHY PUBLICATIONS, INC., 215 S. Park St., Suite #1, Port Washington WI 53074. (262)268-9250. Fax: (262)268-9208. E-mail: publisher@seaworthy.com. Website: www.seaworthy.com. **Acquisitions:** Joseph F. Janson, publisher. Publishes trade paperback originals, hardcover originals and reprints. **Publishes 8 titles/year. Receives 150 queries and 40 mss/year. 60% of books from first-time authors; 100% from unagented writers. Pays 15% royalty on wholesale price. Offers $1,000 advance.** Publishes book 6 months after acceptance of ms. Does not accept simultaneous submissions. Responds in 1 month to queries. Book catalog and ms guidelines on website or for #10 SASE.

Seaworthy Publications is a nautical book publisher that primarily publishes books of interest to recreational boaters and serious bluewater cruisers, including cruising guides, how-to and first-person adventure. Currently emphasizing guidebooks, how-to. De-emphasizing first-person adventure.

Nonfiction: Illustrated book, reference, technical. Subjects include history (nautical), hobbies (sailing, boating), regional (boating guide books), sports (sail racing), travel (world, circumnavigation). Regional guide books, first-person adventure, illustrated book, reference, technical—all dealing with boating. Query with SASE or submit 3 sample chapter(s), table of contents. Prefers electronic query via e-mail. Reviews artwork/photos as part of ms package. Send photocopies or color prints.

Recent Title(s): *Financial Freedom Afloat*, by Charles Tuller.

Tips: "Our audience consists of sailors, boaters, and those interested in the sea, sailing or long distance cruising and racing."

SEEDLING PUBLICATIONS, INC., 4522 Indianola Ave., Columbus OH 43214-2246. (614)267-7333. Fax: (614)267-4205. E-mail: sales@seedlingpub.com. Website: www.seedlingpub.com. **Acquisitions:** Josie Stewart, vice president. Estab. 1992. Publishes in an 8-, 12-, or 16-page format for beginning readers. **Publishes 8-10 titles/year. Receives 50 queries and 450 mss/year. 50% of books from first-time authors; 100% from unagented writers. Pays royalty or makes outright purchase. Offers advance.** Publishes book 1 year after acceptance of ms. Accepts simultaneous submissions. Responds in 6 months to queries. Book catalog for #10 SAE with 3 first-class stamps; ms guidelines for #10 SASE.

"We are an education niche publisher, producing books for beginning readers. Stories must include language that is natural to young children and story lines that are interesting to 5-7-year-olds and written at their beginning reading level."

Nonfiction: Children's/juvenile. Subjects include animals. Science, math or social studies concepts are considered. Does not accept mss or queries via fax or e-mail. Submit outline, SASE. Reviews artwork/photos as part of ms package. Send photocopies.

Fiction: Juvenile. Query with SASE or submit outline or submit complete ms.

Recent Title(s): *Zebras*, by Lynn Salem, Josie Stewart; *Treasure in the Attic*, by Linda Kulp.

Tips: "Follow our guidelines. Do not submit full-length picture books or chapter books. We are an education niche publisher. Our books are for children, ages 5-7, who are just beginning to read independently. We do not accept stories that rhyme or poetry at this time. Try a manuscript with young readers. Listen for spots in the text that don't flow when the child reads the story. Rewrite until the text sounds natural to beginning readers." Does not accept manuscripts or queries via email or fax.

SELF-COUNSEL PRESS, 1704 N. State St., Bellingham WA 92225. (360)676-4530. Website: www.self-counsel.com. **Acquisitions:** Richard Day, managing editor. Estab. 1971. Publishes trade paperback originals. **Publishes**

30 titles/year. Receives 1,500 queries/year. 30% of books from first-time authors; 90% from unagented writers. Pays 10% royalty on net receipts. Offers rarely advance. Publishes book 8 months after acceptance of ms. Accepts simultaneous submissions. Responds in 2 months to queries. Book catalog via website or upon request; Writer's guidelines via website or upon request.

- This publisher also has ofices in Canada.

O-ᵣ Self-Counsel Press publishes a range of quality self-help books written in practical, non-technical style by recognized experts in the fields of business, financial or legal guidance for people who want to help themselves.

Nonfiction: How-to, reference, self-help. Subjects include business/economics, computers/electronic, money/finance, Legal issues for lay people. Submit proposal package including outline, 2 sample chapter(s), résumé.

Recent Title(s): *Wills Guide for America*, by Robert C. Waters; *Simply Essential Wedding Planning Kit*, by Sharon Boglari.

SERGEANT KIRKLAND'S PRESS, 8 Yakama Trail, Spotsylvania VA 22553-2422. (540)582-6296. Fax: (540)582-8312. E-mail: seagraver@kirklands.org. Website: www.kirklands.org. **Acquisitions:** Pia S. Seagrave, Ph.D., editor-in-chief. Publishes hardcover and trade paperback originals, hardcover reprints. **Publishes 28 titles/year. Receives 200 queries and 150 mss/year. 70% of books from first-time authors; 90% from unagented writers. Pays 10% royalty.** Publishes book 6 months after acceptance of ms. Does not accept simultaneous submissions. Responds in 3 months to queries; 3 months to proposals; 4 months to mss. Book catalog and ms guidelines online.

O-ᵣ Currently emphasizing American history of academic and regional interest—colonial, African-American, Civil War, WWII and Vietnam periods.

Nonfiction: Biography, reference. Subjects include Americana, anthropology/archeology, government/politics, history, military/war, Jewish-Holocaust, slavery. Query with SASE or submit complete ms. Reviews artwork/photos as part of ms package. Send photocopies.

Recent Title(s): *Sara's Children: The Destruction of the Chmielnik*, by Suzan Hagstrom (Holocaust).

Tips: "Have your work professionally edited and be sure it meets the general standards of the *Chicago Manual of Style*."

SEVEN STORIES PRESS, 140 Watts St., New York NY 10013. (212)226-8760. Fax: (212)226-1411. E-mail: info@sevenstories.com. Website: www.sevenstories.com. **Acquisitions:** Daniel Simon; Greg Ruggiero; Jill Schoolman; Violaine Huisman. Estab. 1995. Publishes hardcover and trade paperback originals. **Publishes 20-25 titles/year. 15% of books from first-time authors; 15% from unagented writers. Pays 7-15% royalty on retail price. Offers advance.** Publishes book 1-3 years after acceptance of ms. Accepts simultaneous submissions. Responds in 3 months to queries. Book catalog and ms guidelines free.

O-ᵣ Seven Stories Press publishes literary/activist fiction and nonfiction "on the premise that both are works of the imagination and that there is no contradiction in publishing the two side by side." Currently emphasizing politics, social justice, biographies, foreign writings.

Nonfiction: Biography. Subjects include general nonfiction, general nonfiction. Responds only if interested. No unsolicited mss. Query with SASE. **All unsolicited mss returned unopened.**

Fiction: Literary. No unsolicited mss. Query with SASE. **All unsolicited mss returned unopened.**

Recent Title(s): *9/11*, by Noam Chomsky; *Lydia Cassatt Reading the Morning Paper*, by Harriet Chessman; *Poems Seven*, by Alan Dugan.

SHAW BOOKS, Waterbrook Press, 2375 Telstar Dr. #160, Colorado Springs CO 80920-1029. (719)590-4999. Fax: (719)590-8977. **Acquisitions:** Elisa Fryling Stanford, editor. Estab. 1967. Publishes mostly trade paperback originals and reprints. **Publishes 25 titles/year. Receives 1,000 submissions/year. 10-20% of books from first-time authors; 60% from unagented writers. Sometimes makes outright purchase of $375-2,500 for Bible studies. Offers advance.** Publishes book 18 months after acceptance of ms. Responds in 6 months to queries.

O-ᵣ "We are looking for unique mss from a Christian perspective on the topics below. Queries accepted but not unsolicited mss." Currently emphasizing health and wellness, family and education, literary nonfiction, Bible study guides.

Nonfiction: Subjects include cooking/foods/nutrition, creative nonfiction, education, general nonfiction, language/literature, parenting, health and wellness, Bible study, literary topics all from a Christian perspective. "We are looking for adult nonfiction with different twists—self-help manuscripts with fresh insight and colorful, vibrant writing style." No fiction, poetry or unsolicited mss. Query with SASE.

Recent Title(s): *Madeleine L'Engle Herself*, by Madeleine L'Engle; *Educational Travel on a Shoestring*, by Judith Allee and Melissa Morgan.

SHEED & WARD BOOK PUBLISHING, 7373 S. Lovers Lane Rd., Franklin WI 53132. (800)558-0580. Fax: (800)369-4448. E-mail: sheed@execpc.com. Website: www.sheedandward.com. **Acquisitions:** Jeremy W. Langford, editor-in-chief (Catholicism). Publishes hardcover and trade paperback originals. **Publishes 25-30 titles/year. Receives 600-1,000 queries and 600-1,000 mss/year. 25% of books from first-time authors; 90% from unagented writers. Pays 6-12% royalty on retail price. Offers $500-2,000 advance.** Publishes book 8 months after acceptance of ms. Does not accept simultaneous submissions. Responds in 1 month to queries; 2 months to proposals; 2 months to mss. Book catalog free or on website; Manuscript guidelines free or on website.

"We are looking for books that help our readers, most of whom are college educated, gain access to the riches of the Catholic/Christian tradition. We publish in the areas of history, biography, spirituality, prayer, ethics, ministry, justice, liturgy."

Nonfiction: Biography, gift book, reference. Subjects include religion, spirituality, family life. Submit proposal package including outline, 2 sample chapter(s), strong cover letter indicating why the project is unique and compelling. Reviews artwork/photos as part of ms package. Send photocopies.

Recent Title(s): *Seeing with Our Souls: Monastic Wisdom for Every Day*, by Joan Chittister, O.S.B.; *Professions of Faith: Living and Working as a Catholic*, edited by James Martin, S.J., and Jeremy Langford.

Tips: "We prefer that writers get our author guidelines either from our website or via mail before submitting proposals."

SHEEP MEADOW PRESS, P.O. Box 1345, Riverdale NY 10471. (718)548-5547. Fax: (718)884-0406. E-mail: sheepmdwpr@aol.com. **Acquisitions:** Stanley Moss, publisher. Publishes hardcover and trade paperback originals and reprints. **Publishes 10-12 titles/year. Pays 7-10% royalty on retail price.** Book catalog free.

Poetry: Submit complete ms.

SIERRA CLUB BOOKS, 85 Second St., San Francisco CA 94105. (415)977-5500. Fax: (415)977-5793. E-mail: danny.moses@sierraclub.org. Website: www.sierraclub.org/books. **Acquisitions:** Danny Moses, editor-in-chief; James Cohee, senior editor; Linda Gunnarson, editor. Estab. 1962. Publishes hardcover and paperback originals and reprints. **Publishes 20-30 titles/year. Receives 1,000 submissions/year. 50% from unagented writers. Pays 10-12% royalty on wholesale price. Offers $3,000-10,000 average advance.** Publishes book 1 year after acceptance of ms. Accepts simultaneous submissions. Responds in 1 month to queries; 2 months to proposals; 3 months to mss. Book catalog online.

The Sierra Club was founded to help people to explore, enjoy and preserve the nation's forests, waters, wildlife and wilderness. The books program publishes quality trade books about the outdoors and the protection of the natural world.

Nonfiction: Subjects include general nonfiction, nature/environment. A broad range of environmental subjects: outdoor adventure, women in the outdoors; literature, including travel and works on the spiritual aspects of the natural world; natural history and current environmental issues. Does *not* want "proposals for large color photographic books without substantial text; how-to books on building things outdoors; books on motorized travel; or any but the most professional studies of animals." No fiction or poetry. Query with SASE. Reviews artwork/photos as part of ms package. Send photocopies.

Recent Title(s): *Seven Wonders: Timeless Tools for a Healthier Planet*; *My Story As Told By Water*; *Forward Drive: The Race to Build "Clean" Cars for the Future.*

SILHOUETTE BOOKS, 300 E. 42nd St., New York NY 10017. (212)682-6080. Fax: (212)682-4539. Website: www.eharlequin.com. Editorial Director, Silhouette Books; Harlequin Historicals: Tara Gavin. **Acquisitions:** Mary Theresa Hussey, senior editor (Silhouette Romance); Karen Taylor Richman, senior editor (Silhouette Special Editions); Joan Marlow Golan, senior editor (Silhouette Desires); Leslie Wainger, executive senior editor (Silhouette Intimate Moments); Tracy Farrell, senior editor/editorial coordinator (Harlequin Historicals). Estab. 1979. Publishes mass market paperback originals. **Publishes over 350 titles/year. Receives approximately 4,000 submissions/year. Pays royalty. Offers advance.** Publishes book 1-3 years after acceptance of ms. Does not accept simultaneous submissions. Ms guidelines for #10 SASE.

Imprints: *Silhouette Romance* (contemporary adult romances, 53,000-58,000 words); *Silhouette Desire* (contemporary adult romances, 55,000-60,000 words); *Silhouette Intimate Moments* (contemporary adult romances, 80,000 words); *Harlequin Historicals* (adult historical romances, 95,000-105,000 words); *Silhouette Special Edition* (contemporary adult romances, 75,000-80,000 words).

Silhouette publishes contemporary adult romances.

Fiction: Romance (contemporary and historical romance for adults). "We are interested in seeing submissions for all our lines. No manuscripts other than the types outlined. Manuscript should follow our general format, yet have an individuality and life of its own that will make it stand out in the readers' minds." No unsolicited mss. Send query letter, 2 page synopsis and SASE to head of imprint.

Recent Title(s): *Cordina's Crown Jewel*, by Nora Roberts.

Tips: "The romance market is constantly changing, so when you read for research, read the latest books and those that have been recommended to you by people knowledgeable in the genre. We are actively seeking new authors for all our lines, contemporary and historical."

SILMAN-JAMES PRESS, 3624 Shannon Rd., Los Angeles CA 90027. (323)661-9922. E-mail: silmanjamespress@earthlink.net. **Acquisitions:** Gwen Feldman, Jim Fox, publishers. Publishes trade paperback originals and reprints. **Publishes 6-10 titles/year. Receives 50 queries and 40 mss/year. 50% of books from first-time authors; 80% from unagented writers. Pays 6-12% royalty on retail price.** Responds in 1 month to queries; 2 months to proposals; 3 months to mss. Book catalog free.

Nonfiction: Pertaining to film, theatre, music, peforming arts. Biography, how-to, reference, technical, textbook. Submit proposal package including outline, 1+ sample chapter(s) or submit complete ms. Reviews artwork/photos as part of ms package. Send photocopies.

Recent Title(s): *Book on Acting: Improvising Acting While Speaking Scripted Lines*, by Stephen Book; *Dealmaking in the Film and Television, 2nd Ed*, by Mark Litwak.

Tips: "Our audience ranges from people with a general interest in film (fans, etc.) to students of film and performing arts to industry professionals. We will accept 'query' phone calls."

SILVER DAGGER MYSTERIES, The Overmountain Press, P.O. Box 1261, Johnson City TN 37605. (423)926-2691. Fax: (423)232-1252. Website: www.silverdaggermysteries.com. **Acquisitions:** Alex Foster, acquisitions editor. Publishes hardcover and trade paperback originals and reprints. **Publishes 30 titles/year; imprint publishes 15 titles/year. Receives 100 queries and 50 mss/year. 50% of books from first-time authors; 50% from unagented writers. Pays 15% royalty on realized price.** Publishes book 1 year after acceptance of ms. Accepts simultaneous submissions. Responds in 1 month to queries; 3 months to proposals; 6 months to mss. Book catalog and ms guidelines online.

- Silver Dagger publishes mysteries that take place in the American South. Emphasizing cozies, police procedurals, hard-boiled detectives.

Fiction: Mystery. "We look for average-length books of 60-80,000 words." No horror or science fiction. Query with SASE or submit proposal package including 2 sample chapter(s), synopsis, author bio. **All unsolicited mss returned unopened.**

Recent Title(s): *Death's Favorite Child*, by Frankie Y. Bailey; *Voices in the Sand*, by Anne Underwood Grant.

Tips: "We publish cozies, hard-boiled and police procedural mysteries. Check the website for specific guidelines and submission dates. Due to a large number of submissions, we only review at certain times of the year."

SILVER MOON PRESS, 160 Fifth Ave., New York NY 10010. (212)242-6499. Fax: (212)242-6799. **Acquisitions:** Hope Killcoyne, managing editor. Publishes hardcover originals. **Publishes 5-8 titles/year. Receives 600 queries and 400 mss/year. 60% of books from first-time authors; 70% from unagented writers. Pays 7-10% royalty. Offers 500-1,000 advance.** Publishes book 18 months after acceptance of ms. Accepts simultaneous submissions. Responds in 2 months to queries; 2 months to proposals; 3-6 months to mss. Book catalog for 9×12 SASE; ms guidelines for #10 SASE.

- Publishes educational material for grades 3-8.

Nonfiction: Biography, test prep material. Subjects include education, history, language/literature, multicultural. Query with SASE or submit proposal package including outline, 1-3 sample chapter(s).

Fiction: Historical, multicultural, biographical. Query with SASE or submit proposal package including 1-3 sample chapter(s), synopsis.

Recent Title(s): *Thunder on the Sierra*, by Kathy Balmes (social studies, historical fiction); *Raid at Red Mill*, by Mary McGahan (historical fiction).

SIMON & SCHUSTER, 1230 Avenue of the Americas, New York NY 10020. (212)698-7000. Website: www.simonsays.com. **Pays royalty. Offers advance.**

Imprints: *Simon & Schuster Adult Publishing Group*: Simon & Schuster, Scribner (Scribner, Lisa Drew, Simple Abundance Press), The Free Press, Atria Books, Kaplan, Touchstone, Scribner Paperback Fiction, S&S Librow en Espanol, Simon & Schuster Source, Wall Street Journal Books, Pocket Books (Pocket Star, Washington Square Press, MTV Books, Sonnet Books, Star Trek, The New Folger Shakespeare, VH-1 Books, WWF Books). *Simon & Schuster Children's Publishing:* Aladdin Paperbacks, Atheneum Books for Young Readers (Anne Schwartz Books, Richard Jackson Books) Little Simon (Simon Spotlight, Rabbit Ears Books & Audio), Margaret K. McElderry Books, (Archway Paperbacks, Minstreal Books), Simon & Schuster Books for Young Readers. *Simon & Schuster New Media*: Simon & Schuster Audio (Simon & Schuster Audio Works, Simon & Schuster Sound Ideas, Pimsleur, Encore, Success), Simon & Schuster Interactive

SIMON & SCHUSTER BOOKS FOR YOUNG READERS, Simon & Schuster Children's Publishing Division, 1230 Avenue of the Americas, New York NY 10020. (212)698-7000. Fax: (212)698-2796. E-mail: childrenssubmissions@simonandschuster.com. Website: www.simonandschuster.com. **Acquisitions:** Stephen Geck, vice president/associate publisher (humorous picture books, fiction, nonfiction); Kevin Lewis, senior editor (African-American/multicultural picture books, humorous picture books, middle-grade); David Gale, editorial director (young adult/middle grade novels); Jessica Schulte, editor (picture books, young adult). Publishes hardcover originals. **Publishes 80-90 titles/year. Receives 2,500 queries and 10,000 mss/year. 5-10% of books from first-time authors; 40% from unagented writers. Pays 4-12% royalty on retail price. Offers varied advance.** Publishes book 1-3 years after acceptance of ms. Accepts simultaneous submissions. Responds in 2 months to queries. Ms guidelines for #10 SASE.

- All unsolicited mss will be returned unopened.
- "The three adjectives we use to describe our imprint are fresh, family-oriented and accessible. We're looking for writing-edge fiction, family-oriented picture books that are character-oriented." Currently emphasizing middle grade humor/adventure stories. De-emphasizing nonfiction.

Nonfiction: Children's/juvenile. Subjects include animals, ethnic, history, nature/environment. "We're looking for innovative, appealing nonfiction especially for younger readers. Please don't submit education or textbooks." **All unsolicited mss returned unopened.** Query with SASE only.

Fiction: Fantasy, historical, humor, juvenile, mystery, picture books, science fiction, young adult. "Fiction needs to be fresh, unusual and compelling to stand out from the competition. We're not looking for problem novels, stories with a moral, or rhymed picture book texts." **All unsolicited mss returned unopened.** Query with SASE only.

Poetry: "Most of our poetry titles are anthologies; we publish very few stand-alone poets." No picture book ms in rhymed verse. Query.

Recent Title(s): *Giggle, Giggle Quack*, by Doreen Cronin; *The Sissy Duckling*, by Harvey Fierstein; *Gingerbread*, by Rachel Cohn.

Tips: "We're looking for fresh, original voices and unexplored topics. Don't do something because everyone else is doing it. Try to find what they're *not* doing. We publish mainly for the bookstore market, and are looking for books that will appeal directly to kids."

SKY PUBLISHING CORP., 49 Bay State Rd., Cambridge MA 02138. (617)864-7360. Fax: (617)864-6117. E-mail: editors@skyandtelescope.com. Website: www.skyandtelescope.com. President/Publisher: Susan B. Lit. **Acquisitions:** Richard Tresch Fienberg, editor-in-chief. Estab. 1941. Publishes hardcover and trade paperback originals on topics of interest to serious amateur astronomers as well as *Sky & Telescope: The Essential Magazine of Astronomy* and *Skywatch: Your Annual Guide to Stargazing*. **Publishes 2 titles/year. Pays 10% royalty on net receipts. Magazine articles: pays 5¢/word. Offers advance on book royalties.** Does not accept simultaneous submissions. Book catalog free; magazine author and book proposal guidelines available.

O→ Sky Publishing Corporation will be an advocate of astronomy and space science through its products and services and will aggressively promote greater understanding of these disciplines among laypeople.

Nonfiction: Technical. Subjects include science (astronomy). No fiction.

Recent Title(s): *Sky Atlas 2000.0*, 2nd edition, by Wil Tirion and Roger W. Sinnott; *Deep-Sky Wonders*, by Walter Scott Houston, edited by Stephen James O'Meara.

SKYLIGHT PROFESSIONAL DEVELOPMENT, (formerly IRI/Skylight Training and Publishing, Inc.), 2626 S. Clearbrook Dr., Arlington Heights IL 60005. (800)348-4474. E-mail: info@skylightedu.com. Website: www.skylightedu.com. **Acquisitions:** Chris Jaeggi, executive editor. Estab. 1990. **Publishes 20-25 titles/year. Receives 100 queries and 60 mss/year. 40% of books from first-time authors; 100% from unagented writers. Pays 5-10% royalty on retail price.** Publishes book 1 year after acceptance of ms. Responds in 1 months to queries; 4 months to proposals; 4 months to mss. Book catalog and ms guidelines free.

O→ "We seek books that provide a bridge from the theory to practice in the classroom."

Nonfiction: Subjects include education. Educational how-to for K-12 classroom practitioners. Multiple intelligences, integrated curriculum, year-round education, multi-age clasrooms, diversity, inclusion, cooperative learning, higher-level thinking and technology in the classroom. Submit outline, sample chapter(s), brief synopsis of each chapter. Reviews artwork/photos as part of ms package. Send photocopies.

Recent Title(s): *Empowering Students with Technology*, by Alan November.

Tips: "Target K-12 classroom practitioners, staff developers, school administrators, education students. We are interested in research-based books that tell teachers in a clear, friendly, direct manner how to apply educational best practices to their classrooms. We are especially interested in books that give teachers the tools to create lessons on their own, no matter what subject area they teach."

SLACK INC., 6900 Grove Rd., Thorofare NJ 08086. (856)848-1000. Fax: (856)853-5991. E-mail: amcshane@slackinc.com. Website: www.slackinc.com. **Acquisitions:** Amy E. McShane, editorial director. Estab. 1960. Publishes hardcover and softcover originals. **Publishes 32 titles/year. Receives 80 queries and 23 mss/year. 75% of books from first-time authors; 100% from unagented writers. Pays 10% royalty. Offers advance.** Publishes book 8 months after acceptance of ms. Accepts simultaneous submissions. Responds in 4 months to queries; 1 month to proposals; 3 months to mss. Book catalog and ms guidelines free.

O→ Slack publishes academic textbooks and professional reference books on various medical topics in an expedient manner. Emphasizing more athletic training than in previous years.

Nonfiction: Multimedia (CD-ROMs), textbook (medical). Subjects include health/medicine, ophthalmology, athletic training, physical theraphy, occupational therapy, orthopedics, gastroenterology. Submit proposal package including outline, 2 sample chapter(s), market profile and cv. Reviews artwork/photos as part of ms package. Send photocopies.

Recent Title(s): *Ryan's Occupational Therapy Assistant, 3rd Edition*, by Ryan and Sladyk.

SMART COOKIE PUBLISHING, #4-2017 W. 15th Ave., Vancouver BC V6J 2L4 Canada. (604)228-1711. Fax: (604)264-1925. E-mail: kris@interchange.ubc.ca. Website: www.webspotter.com/smartcookie. **Acquisitions:** Sam Macklin, editor. Publishes trade paperback originals. **Publishes 4 titles/year. Receives 30 queries and 20 mss/year. 75% of books from first-time authors; 75% from unagented writers. Pays 5-15% royalty on retail price.** Publishes book 3 months after acceptance of ms. Accepts simultaneous submissions. Responds in 1 month to queries; 1 month to proposals; 2 months to mss. Book catalog online; ms guidelines online.

Nonfiction: Biography, children's/juvenile, illustrated book. Subjects include creative nonfiction, history, language/literature, music/dance, travel, women's issues/studies. "We're interested in nonfiction studies examining or relating to pop culture." Submit proposal package including outline, 3 sample chapter(s) or submit complete ms. Reviews artwork/photos as part of ms package. Send photocopies.

Fiction: Comic books, experimental, feminist, gay/lesbian, historical, literary, mainstream/contemporary, picture books, short story collections, young adult. "We look for works which are fun, contemporary, have an unusual perspective, and take risks." Submit proposal package including 3 sample chapter(s), synopsis or submit complete ms.

Recent Title(s): *Saugus to the Sea*, by Bill Brown (novel); *Girl on the Make*, by Kris Rothstein (short stories).

Tips: Young audience with general interest in the arts and pop culture.

SMITH AND KRAUS PUBLISHERS, INC., P.O. Box 127, Lyme NH 03768. (603)643-6431. Fax: (603) 643-1831. **Acquisitions:** Marisa Smith, president/publisher. Estab. 1990. Publishes hardcover and trade paperback originals.

Publishes 35-40 titles/year. 10% of books from first-time authors; 10-20% from unagented writers. Pays 7% royalty on retail price. Offers $500-2,000 advance. Publishes book 1 year after acceptance of ms. Does not accept simultaneous submissions. Responds in 1 month to queries; 2 months to proposals; 4 months to mss. Book catalog free.
Nonfiction: Subjects include film/cinema/stage, drama, theater. Does not return submissions. Query with SASE.
Fiction: Drama; theater. Does not return submissions. Query with SASE.
Recent Title(s): *A Shakespearean Actor Prepares*, by Adrian Brine and Michael York; *Humana Festival 2000: The Complete Plays*.

GIBBS SMITH, PUBLISHER, P.O. Box 667, Layton UT 84041. (801)544-9800. Fax: (801)544-5582. E-mail: info@gibbs-smith.com. Website: www.gibbs-smith.com. **Acquisitions:** Madge Baird, editorial director (humor, western); Gail Yngve, editor (gift books, architecture, interior decorating, poetry); Suzanne Taylor, editor (children's, rustic living, outdoor activities and picture); Linda Nimori, editor. Estab. 1969. Publishes hardcover and trade paperback originals. **Publishes 50 titles/year. Receives 1,500-2,000 submissions/year. 8-10% of books from first-time authors; 50% from unagented writers. Pays 8-14% royalty on gross receipts. Offers $2,000-3,000 advance.** Publishes book 1-2 years after acceptance of ms. Does not accept simultaneous submissions. Responds in 1 month to queries; 10 weeks to proposals; 10 weeks to mss. Book catalog for 9×12 SAE and $2.13 in postage; ms guidelines free.
Imprints: Gibbs Smith Junior.

O- "We publish books that enrich and inspire humankind." Currently emphasizing interior decorating and design, home reference. De-emphasizing novels and short stories.

Nonfiction: Humor, illustrated book, textbook, children's. Subjects include art/architecture, humor, nature/environment, regional, interior design. Query with SASE or submit outline, several completed sample chapter(s), author's cv. Reviews artwork/photos as part of ms package. Send sample illustrations if applicable.
Fiction: Only short works oriented to gift market. No novels or short stories. Submit synopsis with sample illustration, if applicable.
Poetry: "Our annual poetry contest accepts entries only in April. Charges $20 fee. Prize: $1,000." Submit complete ms.
Recent Title(s): *Timberframe Interiors* (nonfiction); *A Strong Man*, by Carol Lynn Pearson (fiction).

SOCIETY OF MANUFACTURING ENGINEERS, One SME Dr., P.O. Box 930, Dearborn MI 48121. (313)271-1500. Fax: (313)271-2861. E-mail: kingbob@sme.org. Website: www.sme.org. **Acquisitions:** Robert King, manager. Publishes hardcover and trade paperback originals. **Publishes 10 titles/year. Receives 20 queries and 10 mss/year. 90% of books from first-time authors; 100% from unagented writers. Pays 5-15% royalty on wholesale price or retail price.** Publishes book 8 months after acceptance of ms. Responds in 1 month to queries; 1 month to proposals; 1 month to mss. Book catalog and ms guidelines free or online.
Nonfiction: "Seeking manuscripts that would assist manufacturing practitioners in increasing their productivity, quality and/or efficiency." Technical, textbook. Subjects include engineering, industry. Query with SASE. Reviews artwork/photos as part of ms package. Send photocopies.
Recent Title(s): *Lean Manufacturing for Small Business*; *Electorial Discharge Machining*.
Tips: Audience is "manufacturing practitioners and management, indiviuduals wishing to advance their careers in the industry or to enhance productivity, quality, and efficiency within a manufacturing operation."

SOFT SKULL PRESS INC., 107 Norfolk St., New York NY 10002. (212)673-2502. Fax: (212)673-0787. E-mail: misshorse@softskull.com. Website: www.softskull.com. **Acquisitions:** Sander Hicks, editor; David Janik, editor; Tennessee Jones, editor; Chris Teret, editor. Publishes hardcover and trade paperback originals. **Publishes 10 titles/year. Receives 100 queries and 100 mss/year. 80% of books from first-time authors; 50% from unagented writers. Pays 7-10% royalty. Offers $100-15,000 advance.** Publishes book 6 months after acceptance of ms. Does not accept simultaneous submissions. Responds in 2 months to proposals; 3 months to mss. Book catalog free or on website; ms guidelines online.

O- "Because of our limited office space, we prefer e-mail submissions."

Nonfiction: Biography. Subjects include art/architecture, gay/lesbian, government/politics, military/war, music/dance, philosophy. Agented submissions are encouraged. Query with SASE or submit proposal package including outline, 2 sample chapter(s).
Fiction: Confession, experimental, historical, literary, mainstream/contemporary, multicultural, short story collections. Agented submissions encouraged. Query with SASE or submit proposal package including 1 sample chapter(s), synopsis.
Poetry: "We're not doing as much as we used to. Must be exceptional." Query or submit with no more than 10 sample poems.
Recent Title(s): *Cool For You*, by Eileen Myles (literary); *Why Things Burn*, by Daphne Gottlieb (poetry).
Tips: "Our audience is passionate, radical, angry, dissatisfied with the current political and cultural status quo."

SOHO PRESS, INC., 853 Broadway, New York NY 10003. (212)260-1900. Website: www.sohopress.com. **Acquisitions:** Juris Jurjevics, publisher/editor-in-chief; Laura Hruska, associate publisher. Estab. 1986. Publishes hardcover and trade paperback originals. **Publishes 40 titles/year. Receives 7,000 submissions/year. 75% of books from first-time authors; 40% from unagented writers. Pays 10-15% royalty on retail price. Offers advance.** Publishes book within 1 year after acceptance of ms. Accepts simultaneous submissions. Responds in 2 months to queries. Book catalog for 6×9 SAE with 2 first-class stamps.

O→ Soho Press publishes literate fiction and nonfiction. Currently emphasizing mystery, literary fiction, thrillers. De-emphasizing cooking, how-to.

Nonfiction: Autobiography, biography, autobiography; literary. Subjects include contemporary culture, history, memoirs, military/war, translation, travel. No self-help, how-to or cookbooks. Submit outline, sample chapter(s).

Fiction: Adventure, ethnic, feminist, historical, literary, mainstream/contemporary, mystery, suspense. Query with SASE or submit complete ms.

Recent Title(s): *The Rescue of Jerusalem: The Alliance of Africans and Hebrews in 701 BC*, by Henry Aubin; *Shadow Theater*, by Fiona Cheong.

Tips: "Soho Press publishes discerning authors for discriminating readers, finding the strongest possible writers and publishing them." Soho Press also publishes series: Hera (historical fiction reprints with accurate and strong female lead characters) and Soho Crime (mysteries set overseas, noir, procedurals); Asia200 (books about Asia).

N SOMA PUBLISHING, INC., 555 DeHaro St., Suite 220, San Francisco CA 94107. (415)252-4350 and (415)252-4360. Fax: (415)252-4352. E-mail: info@baybooks.com. **Acquisitions:** James Connolly, editorial director (james.connolly@baybooks.com). Publishes hardcover originals, trade paperback originals and reprints. **Publishes 10 titles/year. Receives 30 queries/year. 50% of books from first-time authors. Royalties vary substantially. Offers $0-25,000 advance.** Publishes book 6 months after acceptance of ms. Accepts simultaneous submissions. Responds in 3 months to queries. Book catalog for 9×12 SAE with 3 first-class stamps.

Nonfiction: Coffee table book, cookbook, gift book, how-to, illustrated book. Subjects include Americana, cooking/foods/nutrition, education, health/medicine, history, hobbies, nature/environment, travel (armchair travel). "We also publish titles related to public and cable television series" Query with SASE.

Recent Title(s): *Savor the Southwest*, by Barbara Fenzl (cooking); *Low Carb Meals in Minutes*, by Linda Gassenheimer; *Designs for a Healthy Home*, by Dan Phillips.

SOUNDPRINTS, The Trudy Corp., 353 Main Ave., Norwalk CT 06851. (203)846-2274. Fax: (203)846-1776. E-mail: soundprints@soundprints.com. Website: www.soundprints.com. **Acquisitions:** Chelsea Shriver, assistant editor. Estab. 1988. Publishes hardcover originals. **Publishes 12-14 titles/year. Receives 200 queries/year. 90% from unagented writers. Makes outright purchase.** Publishes book 2 years after acceptance of ms. Accepts simultaneous submissions. Responds in 1 month to queries. Book catalog via website or on request; ms guidelines for #10 SASE.

O→ Soundprints publishes picture books that portray a particular animal and its habitat. All books are reviewed for accuracy by curators from the Smithsonian Institution and other wildlife experts.

Nonfiction: Children's/juvenile, illustrated book. Subjects include animals, nature/environment. "We focus on worldwide wildlife and habitats. Subject animals must be portrayed realistically and must not be anthropomorphic. Meticulous research is required. All books are illustrated in full color." Query with SASE.

Fiction: Juvenile. "Most of our books are under license from the Smithsonian Institution and are closely curated fictional stories based on fact. We never do stories of anthropomorphic animals. When we publish juvenile fiction, it will be about wildlife or history and all information in the book *must* be accurate." Query with SASE.

Recent Title(s): *Bumblebee at Apple Tree Lane*, by Laura Gates Galvin; *Sockeye's Journey Home: The Story of a Pacific Salmon*, by Barbara Gaines Winkelman.

Tips: "Our books are written for children from ages four through eight. Our most successful authors can craft a wonderful story which is derived from authentic wildlife or historic facts. First inquiry to us should ask about our interest in publishing a book about a specific animal or habitat."

SOURCEBOOKS, INC., P.O. Box 4410, Naperville IL 60567. (630)961-3900. Fax: (630)961-2168. Website: www.sourcebooks.com. Publisher: Dominique Raccah. **Acquisitions:** Todd Stocke, editorial director (nonfiction trade);: Deborah Werksman (Sourcebooks Hysteria). Estab. 1987. Publishes hardcover and trade paperback originals. **Publishes 120 titles/year. 30% of books from first-time authors; 25% from unagented writers. Pays royalty on wholesale price. Offers advance.** Publishes book 1 year after acceptance of ms. Accepts simultaneous submissions. Responds in 3 months to queries. Book catalog and ms guidelines for 9×12 SASE.

Imprints: Sourcebooks Casablanca (love/relationships), Sphinx Publishing (self-help legal), Sourcebooks Hysteria (women's humor/gift book), Sourcebooks MediaFusion (multimedia).

O→ Sourcebooks publishes many forms of nonfiction titles, generally in the how-to and reference areas, including books on parenting, self-help/psychology, business and health. Focus is on practical, useful information and skills. It also continues to publish in the reference, New Age, history, current affairs and travel categories. Currently emphasizing gift, women's interest, history, reference.

Nonfiction: "We seek unique books on traditional subjects and authors who are smart and aggressive." Biography, gift book, how-to, illustrated book, multimedia, reference, self-help, technical, textbook. Subjects include art/architecture, business/economics, child guidance/parenting, history, military/war, money/finance, psychology, science, sports, women's issues/studies, contemporary culture. Books for small business owners, entrepreneurs and students. "A key to submitting books to us is to explain how your book helps the reader, why it is different from the books already out there (please do your homework) and the author's credentials for writing this book. Books likely to succeed with us are self-help, parenting and childcare, psychology, women's issues, how-to, history, reference, biography, humor, gift books or books with strong artwork." Query with SASE. 2-3 sample chapters (not the first). No complete mss. Reviews artwork/photos as part of ms package.

Recent Title(s): *Poetry Speaks*, edited by Elisa Pasoken and Rebekah Presson Moeby.

Tips: "Our market is a decidedly trade-oriented bookstore audience. We also have very strong penetration into the gift store market. Books which cross over between these two very different markets do extremely well with us. Our list is a solid mix of unique and general audience titles and series-oriented projects. In other words, we are looking for products that break new ground either in their own areas or within the framework of our series of imprints. We love to develop books in new areas or develop strong titles in areas that are already well developed."

SOUTH END PRESS, 7 Brookline St., Cambridge MA 02139. (617)547-4002. Fax: (617)547-1333. E-mail: southend@southendpress.org. Website: www.southendpress.org. Estab. 1977. Publishes library and trade paperback originals and reprints. **Publishes 10 titles/year. Receives 400 queries and 100 mss/year. 30% of books from first-time authors; 95% from unagented writers. Pays 11% royalty on wholesale price. Offers occasionally $500-2,500 advance.** Publishes book 9 months after acceptance of ms. Accepts simultaneous submissions. Responds in up to 3 months to queries; up to 3 months to proposals. Book catalog and ms guidelines free.

O→ South End Press publishes nonfiction political books with a left/feminist/multicultural perspective.

Nonfiction: Subjects include ethnic, gay/lesbian, government/politics, health/medicine, history, nature/environment (environment), philosophy, science, sociology, women's issues/studies, economics, world affairs. Query with SASE or submit 2 sample chapter(s), intro or conclusion and annotated toc. Reviews artwork/photos as part of ms package. Send photocopies.

Recent Title(s): *Marx in Soho*, by Howard Zinn; *Rogue States*, by Noam Chomsky.

SOUTHERN ILLINOIS UNIVERSITY PRESS, P.O. Box 3697, Carbondale IL 62902-3697. (618)453-2281. Fax: (618)453-1221. Website: www.siu.edu/-siupress. **Acquisitions:** Rick Stetter, director (film, criminology, trade nonfiction); Karl Kageff, senior sponsoring editor (composition, rhetoric, sports); Elizabeth Bryer, sponsoring editor (theater); Susan Wilson, associate director (American history, women's studies). Estab. 1956. Publishes hardcover and trade paperback originals and reprints. **Publishes 50-60 titles/year; imprint publishes 4-6 titles/year. Receives 800 queries and 300 mss/year. 45% of books from first-time authors; 99% from unagented writers. Pays 5-10% royalty on wholesale price. Offers rarely advance.** Publishes book 1 year after receipt of a final ms after acceptance of ms. Does not accept simultaneous submissions. Responds in 3 months to queries. Book catalog and ms guidelines free.

Imprints: Shawnee Books, Shawnee Classics (regional reprint series)

O→ "Scholarly press specializes in film and theater studies, rhetoric and composition studies, American history, aviation studies, regional and nonfiction trade, women's studies. No fiction." Currently emphasizing theater, film, American history. De-emphasizing literary criticism.

Nonfiction: Biography, reference (scholarly), textbook. Subjects include Americana, military/war, nature/environment, film/cinema/stage, true crime. Query with SASE or submit proposal package including including synopsis, table of contents, author's vita.

Recent Title(s): *The International Movie Industry*, by Gorham Kindem (film studies); *Dario Fo: Stage, Text, and Tradition*, by J. Farrell and A. Scuderi (theater); *With Lincoln in the White House*, by Michael Burlingame (American history).

SOUTHERN METHODIST UNIVERSITY PRESS, P.O. Box 750415, Dallas TX 75275-0415. Fax: (214)768-1432. Website: www.tamu.edu/upress. **Acquisitions:** Kathryn Lang, senior editor. Estab. 1937. Publishes hardcover and trade paperback originals and reprints. **Publishes 10-12 titles/year. Receives 500 queries and 500 mss/year. 75% of books from first-time authors; 95% from unagented writers. Pays up to 10% royalty on wholesale price. Offers $500 advance.** Publishes book 1 year after acceptance of ms. Does not accept simultaneous submissions. Responds in 1 week to queries; 1 month to proposals; up to 1 year to mss.

O→ Southern Methodist University publishes for the general, educated audience in the fields of literary fiction, ethics and human values, film and theater, regional studies. Currently emphasizing literary fiction. De-emphasizing scholarly, narrowly focused academic studies.

Nonfiction: Subjects include creative nonfiction, medical, ethics/human values, film/theater, regional history. Query with SASE or submit outline, 3 sample chapter(s), author bio, table of contents. Reviews artwork/photos as part of ms package. Send photocopies.

Fiction: Literary, short story collections, novels. Query with SASE.

Recent Title(s): *In the Shadow of Our House: Stories*, by Scott Blackwood; *Bombshell: A Novel*, by Liza Wieland.

THE SPEECH BIN, INC., 1965 25th Ave., Vero Beach FL 32960-3062. (561)770-0007. **Acquisitions:** Jan J. Binney, senior editor. Estab. 1984. Publishes trade paperback originals. **Publishes 10-20 titles/year. Receives 500 mss/year. 50% of books from first-time authors; 90% from unagented writers. Pays negotiable royalty on wholesale price. Offers advance.** Publishes book 1 year after acceptance of ms. Does not accept simultaneous submissions. Responds in 3 months to queries. Book catalog for 9×12 SASE.

O→ Publishes professional materials for specialists in rehabilitation, particularly speech-language pathologists and audiologists, special educators, occupational and physical therapists, and parents and caregivers of children and adults with developmental and post-trauma disabilities."

Nonfiction: Booklets, children's/juvenile (preschool-teen), how-to, illustrated book, reference, textbook, games for children and adults. Subjects include education, health/medicine, communication disorders, education for handicapped persons. Query with SASE or submit outline, sample chapter(s). Reviews artwork/photos as part of ms package. Send photocopies.

Fiction: "Booklets or books for children and adults about handicapped persons, especially with communication disorders. This is a potentially new market for The Speech Bin." Query with SASE or submit outline, sample chapter(s), synopsis.
Recent Title(s): *I Can Say S*; *I Can Say R*.
Tips: "Books and materials must be clearly presented, well written and competently illustrated. We have added books and materials for use by other allied health professionals. We are also looking for more materials for use in treating adults and very young children with communication disorders. Please do not fax manuscripts to us." The Speech Bin is increasing their number of books published per year and is especially interested in reviewing treatment materials for adults and adolescents.

[N] SPI BOOKS, 99 Spring St., 3rd Floor, New York NY 10012. (212)431-5011. Fax: (212)431-8646. E-mail: publicity@spibooks.com. Website: www.spibooks.com. **Acquisitions:** Ian Shapolsky, acquisitions editor (business, conspiracy, children's); Jill Olofsson, acquisitions editor (how-to, self-help, health). Estab. 1991. Publishes hardcover originals and reprints, trade paperback originals and reprints. **Publishes 20-30 titles/year. 5% of books from first-time authors; 50% from unagented writers. Pays 6-15% royalty on retail price. Offers $1,000-10,000 advance.** Publishes book 3-6 months after acceptance of ms. Accepts simultaneous submissions. Responds in 2 months to queries; 2 months to proposals; 2 months to mss. Book catalog online; ms guidelines free.
Nonfiction: Autobiography, biography, children's/juvenile, coffee table book, cookbook, gift book, how-to, humor, illustrated book, reference, scholarly, self-help, textbook. Subjects include alternative lifestyles, Americana, animals, anthropology/archeology, art/architecture, business/economics, child guidance/parenting, community, contemporary culture, cooking/foods/nutrition, creative nonfiction, education, ethnic, general nonfiction, government/politics, health/medicine, history, hobbies, humanities, language/literature, memoirs, military/war, money/finance, multicultural, music/dance, nature/environment, New Age, philosophy, photography, psychology, regional, religion, sex, social sciences, sociology, spirituality, sports, translation, travel, women's issues/studies, world affairs, exposé, conspiracy. "Aside from a quality editorial product, we request a marketing plan, suggested by the author, to supplement our own ideas for successfully making their book." Query with SASE or submit proposal package including outline, sample chapter(s). Reviews artwork/photos as part of ms package. Send photocopies.
Recent Title(s): *Fighting Terror: Keeping the World Safe*, by Gary Moscowitz (current affairs); *The Hypnosis Book*, by Reuben Pecarve (how-to/self-help); *Steve Martin: The Magic Years*, by Morris Walker (biography).
Tips: "Advise us how to reach the market for the legions of interested buyers of your book. Be specific if you can help us target marketing opportunities and promotional possibilities, particularly those that are not obvious. Also, let us know if there are any friends/contacts/connections you can draw upon to assist us in getting the message out about the significance of your book."

SPINSTERS INK, P.O. Box 22005, Denver CO 80222. (303)761-5552. Fax: (303)761-5284. E-mail: spinster@spinsters-ink.com. Website: www.spinsters-ink.com. Publisher: Kathy Hovis. **Acquisitions:** Sharon Silvas, editor. Estab. 1978. Publishes trade paperback originals and reprints. **Publishes 6 titles/year. Receives 400 submissions/year. 50% of books from first-time authors; 95% from unagented writers. Pays 7-11% royalty on retail price.** Publishes book 18 months after acceptance of ms. Does not accept simultaneous submissions. Responds in 4 months to queries. Book catalog free; ms guidelines for SASE or on website.

- Spinsters Ink was sold to Hovis Publishing, publisher of the monthly newspaper *Colorado Woman News*. The company plans to publish two books in 2001, six in 2002, and grow from there.

O→ "Spinsters Ink publishes novels and nonfiction works that deal with significant issues in women's lives from a feminist perspective: Books that not only name these crucial issues, but—more important—encourage change and growth. We are committed to publishing works by women writing from the periphery, fat women, Jewish women, lesbians, old women, poor women, rural women, women examining classism, women of color, women with disabilities, women who are writing books that help make the best in our lives more possible."

Nonfiction: Feminist analysis for positive change. Subjects include women's issues/studies. "We do not want to see work by men or anything that is not specific to women's lives (humor, children's books, etc.)." Query with SASE. Reviews artwork/photos as part of ms package.
Fiction: Ethnic, gay/lesbian, women's. "We do not publish poetry or short fiction. We are interested in fiction that challenges, women's language that is feminist, stories that treat lifestyles with the diversity and complexity they deserve. We are also interested in genre fiction, especially mysteries." Submit outline, sample chapter(s), synopsis.
Recent Title(s): *Those Jordan Girls*, by Jan Drury (fiction); *Deadly Embrace*, by Trudy Labovitz (murder mystery).

SPORT PUBLISHING LLC, (formerly Sagamore Publishing), 804 N. Neil St., Suite 100, Champaign IL 61820. (217)363-2072. Fax: (217)363-2073. E-mail: jbannon@sportpublishing.com. Website: sportpublishingllc.com. **Acquisitions:** Joseph Bannon, CEO (parks, recreation, leisure). Estab. 1974. Publishes hardcover and trade paperback originals. **Publishes 100 titles/year. Receives 100 queries and 100 mss/year. 40% of books from first-time authors; 100% from unagented writers. Pays 7-15% royalty.** Publishes book 6 months after acceptance of ms. Accepts simultaneous submissions. Responds in 1 month to queries. Book catalog and ms guidelines free or online.

O→ "Sagamore Publishing has been a leader in the parks and recreation field for over 20 years. We are now expanding into the areas of tourism and recreation for special populations such as people with autism or ADD/ADHD, and outdoor adventure and wildlife."

Nonfiction: Reference, textbook. Subjects include education, health/medicine, nature/environment, recreation, outdoor adventure, tourism. Submit proposal package, including outline, 1 sample chapter and market projections. Reviews artwork/photos as part of ms package. Send photocopies.
Recent Title(s): *Outdoor Recreation in American Life*, by Ken Cordell (textbook/reference).
Tips: "We strongly encourage potential authors to submit a marketing prospective with any manuscript they submit."

SQUARE ONE PUBLISHERS, INC., 16 First St., Garden City Park NY 11040. (516)535-2010. Fax: (516)535-2014. Website: www.squareonepublishers.com. Publisher: Rudy Shur. **Acquisitions:** Acquisitions Editor. Publishes trade paperback originals. **Publishes 20 titles/year. Receives 500 queries and 100 mss/year. 95% of books from first-time authors; 95% from unagented writers. Pays 10-15% royalty on wholesale price. Offers variable advance.** Publishes book 10 months after acceptance of ms. Accepts simultaneous submissions. Responds in 1 month to queries; 1 month to proposals; 1 month to mss. Book catalog and ms guidelines free or on website.
Nonfiction: Cookbook, how-to, reference, self-help. Subjects include animals, art/architecture, business/economics, child guidance/parenting, hobbies, money/finance, nature/environment, psychology, regional, religion, spirituality, sports, travel, writers' guides, cooking/foods, gaming/gambling. Query with SASE or submit proposal package including outline, author bio, introduction, synopsis, SASE. Reviews artwork/photos as part of ms package. Send photocopies.
Recent Title(s): *Losing Paradise*, by Paul Irwin (environmental/animal welfare); *Retiring Right*, by Lawrence Kaplan (personal finance); *How To Publish Your Nonfiction Book*, by Rudy Shur (writers' reference).
Tips: "We focus on making our books accessible, accurate, and interesting. They are written for people who are looking for the best place to start, and who don't appreciate the terms 'dummy,' 'idiot,' or 'fool' on the cover of their books. We look for smartly written, informative books that have a strong point of view, and that are authored by people who know their subjects well."

ST. ANTHONY MESSENGER PRESS, 28 Liberty St., Cincinnati OH 45210-1298. (513)241-5615. Fax: (513)241-0399. E-mail: books@americancatholic.org. Website: www.americancatholic.org. Publisher: The Rev. Jeremy Harrington, O.F.M. **Acquisitions:** Lisa Biedenbach, managing editor; Katie Carroll, book editor (children's); April Bolton, book editor (prayer/spirituality). Estab. 1970. Publishes trade paperback originals. **Publishes 15-25 titles/year. Receives 200 queries and 50 mss/year. 5% of books from first-time authors; 99% from unagented writers. Pays 10-12% royalty on net receipts. Offers $1,000 average advance.** Publishes book 18 months after acceptance of ms. Responds in 1 month to queries; 2 months to proposals; 2 months to mss. Book catalog for 9×12 SAE with 4 first-class stamps; ms guidelines free.

- "St. Anthony Messenger Press/Franciscan Communications seeks to communicate the word that is Jesus Christ in the styles of Saints Francis and Anthony. Through print and electronic media marketed in North America and worldwide, we endeavor to evangelize, inspire and inform those who search for God and seek a richer Catholic, Christian, human life. Our efforts help support the life, ministry and charities of the Franciscan Friars of St. John the Baptist Province, who sponsor our work." Currently emphasizing prayer/spirituality. De-emphasizing children's.

Nonfiction: Family-based religious education programs. Subjects include education, history, religion, sex, Catholic identity and teaching, prayer and spirituality resources, Scripture study. Query with SASE or submit outline. Reviews artwork/photos as part of ms package.
Recent Title(s): *Lessons from the School of Suffering: A Young Priest with Cancer Teaches Us How to Live*, by Rev. Jim Willig and Tammy Bundy; *Praying the Gospels Through Poetry: Lent to Easter*, by Peggy Rosenthal; *Can You Find Followers?: Introducing Your Child to Disciples*, by Phil Gallery and Janet Harlow.
Tips: "Our readers are ordinary 'folks in the pews' and those who minister to and educate these folks. Writers need to know the audience and the kind of books we publish. Manuscripts should reflect best and current Catholic theology and doctrine." St. Anthony Messenger Press especially seeks books which will sell in bulk quantities to parishes, teachers, pastoral ministers, etc. They expect to sell at least 5,000 to 7,000 copies of a book.

ST. AUGUSTINE'S PRESS, P.O. Box 2285, South Bend IN 46680-2285. (219)-291-3500. Fax: (219)291-3700. E-mail: bruce@staugustine.net. Website: wwwstaugustine.net. **Acquisitions:** Bruce Fingerhut, president (philosophy). Publishes hardcover originals and trade paperback originals and reprints. **Publishes 50 titles/year. Receives 200 queries and 100 mss/year. 5% of books from first-time authors; 95% from unagented writers. Pays 6-20% royalty. Offers $500-5,000 advance.** Publishes book 8 months after acceptance of ms. Accepts simultaneous submissions. Responds in 2-6 months to queries; 3-8 months to proposals; 4-8 months to mss. Book catalog free.
Imprints: Carthage Reprints.

- "Our market is scholarly in the humanities. We publish in philosophy, religion, cultural history, and history of ideas only."

Nonfiction: Biography, textbook. Subjects include history (of ideas), philosophy, religion. Query with SASE. Reviews artwork/photos as part of ms package. Send photocopies.
Recent Title(s): *Maxims*, by La Rochefoucauld (Reference); *Defamation of Pius XII*, by Ralph McInerny (history); *An Intelligent Person's Guide to Modern Culture*, by Roger Scruton (cultural history/philosophy).
Tips: Scholarly and student audience.

ST. BEDE'S PUBLICATIONS, St. Scholastica Priory, P.O. Box 545, Petersham MA 01366-0545. (978)724-3213. Fax: (978)724-3216. President: Mother Mary Clare Vincent. **Acquisitions:** Acquisitions Editor. Estab. 1977. Publishes hardcover originals, trade paperback originals and reprints. **Publishes 3-4 titles/year. Receives 100 submissions/year.**

30-40% of books from first-time authors; 98% from unagented writers. Pays 5-10% royalty on wholesale price or retail price. Publishes book 2 years after acceptance of ms. Accepts simultaneous submissions. Responds in 2 months to queries. Book catalog and ms guidelines for 9×12 SAE with 2 first-class stamps.

- St. Bede's Publications is owned and operated by the Roman Catholic nuns of St. Scholastica Priory. The publications are seen as an apostolic outreach. Their mission is to make available to everyone quality books on spiritual subjects such as prayer, scripture, theology and the lives of holy people.

Nonfiction: Textbook (theology). Subjects include history, philosophy, religion, sex, spirituality, translation, prayer, hagiography, theology, church history, related lives of saints. No submissions unrelated to religion, theology, spirituality, etc., and no poetry, fiction or children's books. Does not return submissions without adequate postage. Query or submit outline and sample chapters with SASE.

Recent Title(s): *Reading the Gospels with Gregory the Great*, translated by Santha Bhattacharji; *Why Catholic?*, by Father John Pasquini.

Tips: "There seems to be a growing interest in monasticism among lay people, and we will be publishing more books in this area. For our theology/philosophy titles our audience is scholars, colleges and universities, seminaries, etc. For our other titles (i.e. prayer, spirituality, lives of saints, etc.) the audience is above-average readers interested in furthering their knowledge in these areas."

N ✪ **ST. MARY'S PRESS**, 702 Terrace Heights, Winona MN 55987-1320. (800)533-8095. Fax: (800)344-9225. Website: www.smp.org.

Nonfiction: Subjects include religion (prayers), spirituality. Titles for Catholic youth and their parents, teachers and youth ministers. Query with SASE or submit proposal package including outline, 1 sample chapter(s). Brief author biography.

Recent Title(s): *Catholic Youth Bible*, edited by Brian Singer-Towns.

Tips: "Do research online of Saint Mary Press book lists before submitting proposal."

STACKPOLE BOOKS, 5067 Ritter Rd., Mechanicsburg PA 17055. Fax: (717)796-0412. E-mail: jschnell@stackpolebooks.com. Website: www.stackpolebooks.com. **Acquisitions:** Judith Schnell, editorial director (fly fishing, sports); Leigh Ann Berry, editor (history); Mark Allison, editor (nature); Ed Skender, editor (military guides); Kyle Weaver, editor (Pennsylvania). Estab. 1935. Publishes hardcover and paperback originals and reprints. **Publishes 75 titles/year. Offers industry standard advance.** Publishes book 1 year after acceptance of ms. Does not accept simultaneous submissions. Responds in 1 month to queries.

- "Stackpole maintains a growing and vital publishing program by featuring authors who are experts in their fields, from outdoor activities to Civil War history."

Nonfiction: Subjects include history (especially Civil War), military/war, nature/environment, photography, recreation, sports, wildlife, outdoor skills, fly fishing, paddling, climbing. Query with SASE. Does not return unsolicited mss. Reviews artwork/photos as part of ms package.

Recent Title(s): *Lee's Cavalrymen*; *Trout Flies*; *Bird Tracks and Sign*.

Tips: "Stackpole seeks well-written, authoritative manuscripts for specialized and general trade markets. Proposals should include chapter outline, sample chapter and illustrations and author's credentials."

N **STANDARD PUBLICATIONS, INC.**, P.O. Box 2226, Champaign IL 61825-2226. (217)898-7825. E-mail: spi@standardpublications.com. **Acquisitions:** Borislav Dzodo (women's content); Douglas Armstrong (men's content). Estab. 2001. publishes trade paperback originals and reprints. **Publishes 4 titles/year. Receives 20 queries and 8 mss/year. 50% of books from first-time authors; 100% from unagented writers. Pays 5-10% royalty on wholesale price or makes outright purchase of $200-10,000.** Publishes book 4 months after acceptance of ms. Accepts simultaneous submissions. Responds in 1 month to queries; 2 months to proposals; 2 months to mss.

- Publishes books for women at home, and for males interested in how-to information or technical content that is hard to find.

Nonfiction: Biography, booklets, how-to, illustrated book, reference, technical, textbook. Subjects include business/economics, child guidance/parenting, ethnic, gardening, general nonfiction, hobbies, money/finance, recreation, sex, translation. "We have three primary focuses for the next two years. In order of priority: 1. Books useful for (mostly women) who are at home. Employment and financial tips and advice are most important. We are also interested in crafts, child care, gardening, etc. 2. Content of a technical nature that is difficult to find. Usually associated with trades that often restrict their knowledge or the popular public perception of legal restrictions. Examples are locksmithing, gun maintenance, magic, legal. 3. Expanding our line of books on astrology, the occult, palm reading, horoscope, etc." Query with SASE or submit proposal package including outline, 3 sample chapter(s) or submit complete ms. Reviews artwork/photos as part of ms package. Send photocopies.

Recent Title(s): *Visual Guide to Lock Picking*, by Mark McCloud (how-to); *Nostradamus, His Works and Prophecies*, by Theodore Garencieres.

Tips: "Use Amazon.com sales rankings as a free and easy form of market research to determine the suitability of your topic matter."

STANDARD PUBLISHING, Standex International Corp., 8121 Hamilton Ave., Cincinnati OH 45231. (513)931-4050. Website: www.standardpub.com. Vice President, Church Resources: Mark Taylor; Managing Director, Church Resources: Paul Learned; Managing Director, Children's Publishing: Diane Stortz. **Acquisitions:** Ruth Frederick (children's ministry resources); Dale Reeves (Empowered Youth Products). Estab. 1866. Publishes hardcover and paperback originals and reprints. **Pays royalty.** Publishes book 18 months after acceptance of ms. Does not accept simultaneous submissions. Responds in 3 months to queries. Ms guidelines for #10 SASE, send request to Tamara Neuenschwander.

O→ Standard specializes in religious books for children and religious education. De-emphasizing board books.

Nonfiction: Children's/juvenile, illustrated book, reference. Subjects include education, religion, picture books, Christian education (teacher training, working with volunteers), quiz, puzzle, crafts (to be used in Christian education). Query with SASE.

Recent Title(s): *My Good Night Bible*, by Susan Lingo (nonfiction); *Can God See Me?*, by JoDee McConnaughhay (fiction); *Exceptional Teaching*, by Jim Pierson.

STANFORD UNIVERSITY PRESS, Stanford CA 94305-2235. (650)723-9434. Fax: (650)725-3457. Website: www.sup.org. Estab. 1925. **Publishes 120 titles/year. Receives 1,500 submissions/year. 40% of books from first-time authors; 95% from unagented writers. Pays up to 14% royalty (typically 10%, sometimes none). Offers occasional advance.** Publishes book 1 year after acceptance of ms. Does not accept simultaneous submissions. Responds in 6 weeks to queries.

O→ Stanford University Press publishes scholarly books in the humanities and social sciences, along with professional books in business, economics and management science; also high-level textbooks and some books for a more general audience.

Nonfiction: Scholarly, textbook, professional books. Subjects include anthropology/archeology, business/economics, ethnic (studies), gay/lesbian, government/politics, history, humanities, language/literature, nature/environment, philosophy, psychology, religion, science, social sciences, sociology, history and culture of China, Japan and Latin America; European history; linguistics; geology; medieval and classical studies. Query with prospectus and an outline. Reviews artwork/photos as part of ms package.

Recent Title(s): *The Selected Poetry of Robinson Jeffers.*

Tips: "The writer's best chance is a work of original scholarship with an argument of some importance."

STARBURST PUBLISHERS, P.O. Box 4123, Lancaster PA 17604. (717)293-0939. Fax: (717)293-1945. E-mail: editorial@starburstpublishers.com. Website: www.starburstpublishers.com. **Acquisitions:** Editorial Department. Estab. 1982. Publishes hardcover and trade paperback originals. **Publishes 15-20 titles/year. Receives 1,000 submissions/year. 50% of books from first-time authors; 75% from unagented writers. Pays 6-16% royalty on wholesale price. Offers varies advance.** Publishes book 1 year after acceptance of ms. Accepts simultaneous submissions. Responds in 1 month to queries. Book catalog for 9×12 SAE with 4 first-class stamps; ms guidelines for #10 SASE.

O→ Starburst publishes quality self-help, health and inspirational titles for the trade and religious markets. Currently emphasizing inspirational gift, Bible study and Bible reference, how-to and health books. De-emphasizing fiction.

Nonfiction: "We are looking for books that inspire, teach and help today's average American." Cookbook, gift book, how-to, self-help, Christian; general nonfiction. Subjects include business/economics, child guidance/parenting, cooking/foods/nutrition, education, gardening, general nonfiction, health/medicine, money/finance, nature/environment, psychology, recreation, religion, counseling/career guidance, home, real estate. Submit proposal package including outline, 3 sample chapter(s), author bio, competitive analysis. "All unsolicited queries or proposals with attached files are simply deleted, often unanswered." Reviews artwork/photos as part of ms package. Send photocopies.

Fiction: Inspirational. "We are only looking for good wholesome fiction that inspires or fiction that teaches self-help principles. We are also looking for successfully self-published fiction." Submit outline, 3 sample chapter(s), author bio.

Recent Title(s): *Learn the Word: The Bible for Teens* (nonfiction); *Stories for the Spirit-Filled Believer*, by Christine Bolley (nonfiction).

Tips: "Fifty percent of our line goes into the Christian marketplace, fifty percent into the general marketplace. We have direct sales representatives in both the Christian and general (bookstore, catalog, price club, mass merchandiser, library, health and gift) marketplace. Write on an issue that slots you on talk shows and thus establishes your name as an expert and writer."

STEEPLE HILL, Harlequin Enterprises, 300 E. 42nd St., New York NY 10017. Website: www.@harlequin.com. **Acquisitions:** Tara Gavin, editorial director; Tracy Farrell, senior editor; Ann Leslie Tuttle, associate editor; Melissa Endlich, associate editor; Kim Nadelson, all Silhouette/Harlequin Historicals editors. Estab. 1997. Publishes mass market paperback originals. **Pays royalty. Offers advance.** Does not accept simultaneous submissions. Ms guidelines for #10 SASE.

Imprints: Love Inspired.

O→ "This series of contemporary, inspirational love stories portrays Christian characters facing the many challenges of life, faith and love in today's world."

Fiction: Romance (Christian, 70,000 words). Query with SASE or submit 3 sample chapter(s), synopsis.

Recent Title(s): *Redeeming Claire*, by Cynthia Rutledge.

Tips: "Drama, humor and even a touch of mystery all have a place in this series. Subplots are welcome and should further the story's main focus or intertwine in a meaningful way. Secondary characters (children, family, friends, neighbors, fellow church members, etc.) may all contribute to a substantial and satisfying story. These wholesome tales of romance include strong family values and high moral standards. While there is no premarital sex between characters, a vivid, exciting romance that is presented with a mature perspective, is essential. Although the element of faith must clearly be present, it should be well integrated into the characterizations and plot. The conflict between the main characters should be an emotional one, arising naturally from the well-developed personalities you've created. Suitable stories should also impart an important lesson about the powers of trust and faith."

N **STEMMER HOUSE PUBLISHERS**, 2627 Caves Rd., Owings Mills MD 21117. (410)363-3690. Fax: (410)363-8459. E-mail: stemmerhouse@home.com. Website: www.stemmer.com. **Acquisitions:** Barbara Holdridge, president (design, natural history, children's books, gardening, cookbooks). Estab. 1975. Publishes hardcover and trade paperback originals. **Publishes 3-5 titles/year; imprint publishes 2 titles/year. Receives 2,000 queries and 1,500 mss/year. 50% of books from first-time authors; 90% from unagented writers. Pays 5-10% royalty on wholesale price. Offers $300 advance.** Publishes book 1-2 years after acceptance of ms. Accepts simultaneous submissions. Responds in 2 weeks to queries. Book catalog for 9×12 SAE with 3 first-class stamps; ms guidelines for #10 SASE.
Imprints: The International Design Library, The NatureEncyclopedia Series.

- Stemmer House publishes nonfiction illustrated books for adults and children in the arts and humanities, cookbooks, gardening, children's books and audio cassettes. Currently emphasizing natural history. De-emphasizing crafts.

Nonfiction: Biography, children's/juvenile, cookbook, illustrated book. Subjects include animals, art/architecture, cooking/foods/nutrition, gardening, multicultural, nature/environment. Query with SASE or submit proposal package including 3 sample chapter(s). Cover Letter. Reviews artwork/photos as part of ms package. Send photocopies or transparencies.
Recent Title(s): *A Japanese Garden Journey*, Judith D. Klingsick (nonfiction); *Will You Sting Me? Will You Bite?: The Truth About Some Scary-Looking Insects*, by Sara Swan Miller.

STENHOUSE PUBLISHERS, 477 Congress St., Suite 4B, Portland ME 04101-3417. (207)253-1600. Fax: (207)253-5121. E-mail: philippa@stenhouse.com. Website: www.stenhouse.com. **Acquisitions:** Philippa Stratton, editorial director. Estab. 1993. Publishes paperback originals. **Publishes 15 titles/year. Receives 300 queries/year. 30% of books from first-time authors; 99% from unagented writers. Pays royalty on wholesale price. Offers very modest advance.** Accepts simultaneous submissions. Responds in 1 month to queries; 3 months to mss. Book catalog and ms guidelines free or online.

- Stenhouse publishes exclusively professional books for teachers, K-12.

Nonfiction: Subjects include education (specializing in literacy). "All our books are a combination of theory and practice." No children's books or student texts. Query with SASE or submit outline. Reviews artwork/photos as part of ms package. Send photocopies.
Recent Title(s): *Read it Again*, by Brenda Parkes; *Strategies That Work: Teaching Comprehension to Enhance Understanding*, by Stephanie Harvey and Anne Goudvis.

STIPES PUBLISHING CO., P.O. Box 526, Champaign IL 61824-9933. (217)356-8391. Fax: (217)356-5753. E-mail: stipes@soltec.com. Website: www.stipes.com. **Acquisitions:** Benjamin H. Watts, (engineering, science, business); Robert Watts (agriculture, music and physical education). Estab. 1925. Publishes hardcover and paperback originals. **Publishes 15-30 titles/year. Receives 150 submissions/year. 50% of books from first-time authors; 95% from unagented writers. Pays 15% maximum royalty on retail price. Offers advance.** Publishes book 4 months after acceptance of ms. Does not accept simultaneous submissions. Responds in 2 months to queries.

- Stipes Publishing is "oriented towards the education market and educational books with some emphasis in the trade market."

Nonfiction: Technical (some areas), textbook (on business/economics, music, chemistry, CADD, agriculture/horticulture, environmental education, recreation, physical education). Subjects include agriculture/horticulture, business/economics, music/dance, nature/environment, recreation, science. "All of our books in the trade area are books that also have a college text market. No books unrelated to educational fields taught at the college level." Submit outline, 1 sample chapter(s).
Recent Title(s): *The Microstation J Workbook*, by Michael Ward.

STOEGER PUBLISHING COMPANY, 17603 Indian Head Hwy., Suite 200, Accokeek MD 20607. (301)283-6300. Fax: (301)283-6986. Website: www.stoegerindustries.com. **Acquisitions:** Jay Langston, publisher. Estab. 1925. Publishes trade paperback originals. **Publishes 12-15 titles/year. Royalty varies, depending on ms. Offers advance.** Accepts simultaneous submissions. Responds in 1 month to queries. Book catalog online.

- Stoeger publishes books on hunting, shooting sports, fishing, cooking, nature and wildlife.

Nonfiction: Specializes in reference and how-to books that pertain to hunting, fishing and appeal to gun enthusiasts. How-to, reference. Subjects include sports. Submit outline, sample chapter(s).
Recent Title(s): *Shooter's Bible 2003*; *Hounds of the World*; *Turkey Hunter's Tool Kit*.

STONE BRIDGE PRESS, P.O. Box 8208, Berkeley CA 94707. (510)524-8732. Fax: (510)524-8711. E-mail: sbp@stonebridge.com. Website: www.stonebridge.com. **Acquisitions:** Peter Goodman, publisher. Estab. 1989. Publishes hardcover and trade paperback originals. **Publishes 8 titles/year; imprint publishes 2 titles/year. Receives 100 queries and 75 mss/year. 15-20% of books from first-time authors; 90% from unagented writers. Pays royalty on wholesale price. Offers variable advance.** Publishes book 2 years after acceptance of ms. Accepts simultaneous submissions. Responds in 2 month to queries; 3 month to proposals; 4 months to mss. Book catalog free.
Imprints: The Rock Spring Collection of Japanese Literature.

- Stone Bridge Press strives "to publish and distribute high-quality informational tools about Japan." Currently emphasizing art/design, spirituality. De-emphasizing business, current affairs.

Nonfiction: How-to, reference. Subjects include art/architecture, business/economics, ethnic, language/literature, philosophy, travel, popular culture. "We publish Japan- (and some Asia-) related books only." Query with SASE. Reviews artwork/photos as part of ms package. Send photocopies.
Fiction: Experimental, fantasy, gay/lesbian. Query with SASE.
Recent Title(s): *Naikan: Gratitude, Grace, and the Japanese Art of Self-Reflection*; *The Anime Encyclopedia*; *Glyphix for Visual Journaling*.
Tips: Audience is "intelligent, worldly readers with an interest in Japan based on personal need or experience. No children's books or commercial fiction. Realize that interest in Japan is a moving target. Please don't submit yesterday's trends or rely on a view of Japan that is outmoded. Stay current!"

STONEWALL INN, St. Martin's Press, 175 Fifth Ave., New York NY 10010. (212)674-5151. Website: www.stonewallinn.com. **Acquisitions:** Keith Kahla, general editor. Publishes trade paperback originals and reprints. **Publishes 20-23 titles/year. Receives 3,000 queries/year. 40% of books from first-time authors; 25% from unagented writers. Pays standard royalty on retail price. Offers varies advance.** Publishes book 1 year after acceptance of ms. Accepts simultaneous submissions. Responds in 6 months to queries.

- Stonewall Inn is an imprint for gay and lesbian themed fiction, nonfiction and mysteries. Currently emphasizing literary fiction. De-emphasizing mysteries. No photography.

Nonfiction: Subjects include gay/lesbian, philosophy, sociology. Subjects include nearly every aspect of gay/lesbian studies. "We are looking for well-researched sociological works; author's credentials count for a great deal." Query with SASE.
Fiction: Gay/lesbian, literary, mystery. "Anybody who has any question about what a gay novel is should go out and read half a dozen. For example, there are hundreds of 'coming out' novels in print." Query with SASE.
Recent Title(s): *The Coming Storm*, by Paul Russell; *Godspeed*, by Lynn Breedlove.
Tips: Address queries to "Stonewall Inn, an Imprint of St. Martins."

STONEYDALE PRESS, 523 Main St., Stevensville MT 59870. (406)777-2729. Fax: (406)777-2521. E-mail: daleburk@montana.com. **Acquisitions:** Dale A. Burk, publisher. Estab. 1976. Publishes hardcover and trade paperback originals. **Publishes 4-6 titles/year. Receives 40-50 queries and 6-8 mss/year. 90% from unagented writers. Pays 12-15% royalty. Offers advance.** Publishes book 18 months after acceptance of ms. Does not accept simultaneous submissions. Responds in 2 months to queries. Book catalog available.

- "We seek to publish the best available source books on big game hunting, historical reminiscence and outdoor recreation in the Northern Rocky Mountain region."

Nonfiction: How-to (hunting books). Subjects include regional, sports, historical reminiscences. Query with SASE.
Recent Title(s): *Lewis & Clark on the Upper Missouri*, by Jeanne O'Neil; *Montana's Bitterroot Valley*, by Russ Lawrence.

STOREY PUBLISHING, LLC, 210 MASS MoCA Way, North Adams MA 01247. (413)346-2100. Fax: (413)346-2196. Website: www.storey.com. **Acquisitions:** Deborah Balmuth, editorial director (mind/body/spirit); Deborah Burns (horses, juvenile); Gwen Steege (gardening, crafts); Nancy Ringer (animals, building, nature); Dianne Cutillo (cooking, home reference). Estab. 1983. Publishes hardcover and trade paperback originals and reprints. **Publishes 40 titles/year. Receives 600 queries and 150 mss/year. 25% of books from first-time authors; 80% from unagented writers. Pays royalty or makes outright purchase. Offers advance.** Publishes book within 2 years after acceptance of ms. Accepts simultaneous submissions. Responds in 1 month to queries; 3 months to proposals; 3 months to mss. Book catalog and ms guidelines free or online.

- "We publish practical information that encourages personal independence in harmony with the environment."

Nonfiction: Subjects include animals, cooking/foods/nutrition, gardening, nature/environment, home, natural health and beauty, birds, beer and wine, crafts, building. Reviews artwork/photos as part of ms package.
Recent Title(s): *Deckscaping*, by Barbara Ellis; *Rosemary Gladstar's Family Herbal*; *Dream Cottages*, by Catherine Treadway.

STORY LINE PRESS, Three Oaks Farm, P.O. Box 1240, Ashland OR 97520-0055. (541)512-8792. Fax: (541)512-8793. E-mail: mail@storylinepress.com. Website: www.storylinepress.com. **Acquisitions:** Robert McDowell, publisher/editor. Estab. 1985. Publishes hardcover and trade paperback originals. **Publishes 12-16 titles/year. Receives 500 queries and 1,000 mss/year. 10% of books from first-time authors. Pays 10-15% royalty on net retail price or makes outright purchase of $250-1,500. Offers $0-3,000 advance.** Publishes book 1-2 years after acceptance of ms. Accepts simultaneous submissions. Responds in 1 month to queries; 3 months to mss. Book catalog free; ms guidelines for #10 SASE.

- "Story Line Press exists to publish the best stories of our time in poetry, fiction and nonfiction. Seventy-five percent of our list includes a wide range of poetry and books about poetry. Our books are intended for the general and academic reader. We are working to expand the audience for serious literature."

Nonfiction: Literary. Subjects include language/literature, authors. Query with SASE.
Fiction: Literary. No popular genres. Query with SASE.
Poetry: Query with SASE.
Recent Title(s): *New Expansive Poetry*, by R.S. Gwynn, editor (nonfiction); *Quit Monks Or Die!*, by Maxine Kumin (fiction); *Questions for Ecclesiastes*, by Mark Jarman (poetry).

Tips: "We strongly recommend that first-time poetry authors submit their book-length manuscripts in the Nicholas Roerich Poetry Contest, and first-time fiction authors send to the Three Oaks Fiction Contest."

STYLUS PUBLISHING, LLC, 22883 Quicksilver Dr., Sterling VA 20166. Website: styluspub.com. **Acquisitions:** John von Knorring, publisher. Estab. 1996. Publishes hardcover and trade paperback originals. **Publishes 6-10 titles/year. Receives 50 queries and 6 mss/year. 50% of books from first-time authors; 100% from unagented writers. Pays 5-10% royalty on wholesale price. Offers advance.** Publishes book 6 months after acceptance of ms. Does not accept simultaneous submissions. Responds in 1 month to queries. Book catalog free; ms guidelines online.

"We publish in higher education (diversity, professional development, distance education, teaching, administration) and training (training and development for corporate, nonprofit and government organizations)."

Nonfiction: Scholarly. Subjects include business/economics, education, training. Query or submit outline, 1 sample chapter with SASE. Reviews artwork/photos as part of ms package. Send photocopies.

Recent Title(s): *Working Virtually*; *Making It on Broken Promises*; *The Power of Problem-Based Learning*.

SUCCESS PUBLISHING, 3419 Dunham Rd., Warsaw NY 14569-9735. (716)786-5663. **Acquisitions:** Allan H. Smith, president (home-based business); Ginger Smith (business); Dana Herbison (home/craft); Robin Garretson (fiction). Estab. 1982. Publishes mass market paperback originals. **Publishes 6 titles/year. Receives 175 submissions and 10 mss/year. 90% of books from first-time authors; 100% from unagented writers. Pays 7-12% royalty. Offers $500-1,000 advance.** Publishes book 10 months after acceptance of ms. Accepts simultaneous submissions. Responds in 2 months to queries. Book catalog and ms guidelines for #10 SAE with 2 first-class stamps.

Success publishes guides that focus on the needs of the home entrepreneur to succeed as a viable business. Currently emphasizing starting a new business. De-emphasizing self-help/motivation books. Success Publishing notes that it is looking for ghostwriters.

Nonfiction: Children's/juvenile, how-to, self-help. Subjects include business/economics, child guidance/parenting, hobbies, money/finance, craft/home-based business. "We are looking for books on how-to subjects such as home business and sewing." Query with SASE.

Recent Title(s): *How to Find a Date/Mate*, by Dana Herbison.

Tips: "Our audience is made up of housewives, hobbyists and owners of home-based businesses."

SUN BOOKS/SUN PUBLISHING, P.O. Box 5588, Santa Fe NM 87502-5588. (505)471-5177. E-mail: info@sunbooks.com. Website: www.sunbooks.com. **Acquisitions:** Skip Whitson, director. Publishes trade paperback originals and reprints. **Publishes 10-15 titles/year. Receives hundreds submissions/year. 30% of books from first-time authors; 90% from unagented writers. Pays 5% royalty on retail price or makes outright purchase.** Publishes book 16 months after acceptance of ms. Responds in 2 months to queries; 2 months to proposals; 6 months to mss. Book catalog online.

Nonfiction: Biography, cookbook, how-to, humor, illustrated book, reference, self-help, technical. Subjects include Americana, anthropology/archeology, business/economics, cooking/foods/nutrition, creative nonfiction, education, government/politics, health/medicine, history, language/literature, memoirs, money/finance, multicultural, nature/environment, philosophy, psychology, regional, religion, sociology, travel, women's issues/studies, metaphysics, motivational, inspirational, Oriental studes. Query with SASE or submit proposal package including outline, sample chapter(s). Reviews artwork/photos as part of ms package. Send photocopies.

Recent Title(s): *Semakanda: Threshold Memories*; *This Mystical Life of Ours*.

SUNBELT PUBLICATIONS, 1250 Fayette St., El Cajon CA 92020. (619)258-4911. Fax: (619)258-4916. E-mail: mail@sunbeltpub.com. Website: www.sunbeltpub.com. **Acquisitions:** Jennifer Redmond, publications coordinator; Lowell Lindsay, publisher (natural history). Publishes hardcover and trade paperback originals and reprints. **Publishes 6-10 titles/year. Receives 30 queries and 20 mss/year. 80% of books from first-time authors; 100% from unagented writers. Pays 10-14% royalty.** Accepts simultaneous submissions. Responds in 1 month to queries; 1 month to proposals; 3 months to mss. Book catalog and ms guidelines free or online.

"We are interested in the cultural and natural history of the 'The Californias' in the U.S. and Mexico."

Nonfiction: "We publish multi-language pictorials, natural science and outdoor guidebooks, regional references and stories that celebrate the land and its people." Coffee table book, how-to, reference, guidebooks. Subjects include anthropology/archeology, history (regional), nature/environment (natural history), recreation, regional, travel. Query with SASE or submit proposal package including outline, 1-2 sample chapter(s) or submit complete ms. Reviews artwork/photos as part of ms package. Send photocopies.

Recent Title(s): *Baja Legends*, by Greg Niemann (history/travel); *More Adventures with Kids in San Diego*, by Judy Botello and Kt Paxton (regional guidebook).

Tips: "Our audience is interested in natural science or the cultural history of California and Baja California, Mexico. They want specific information that is accurate and up-to-date. Our books are written for an adult audience that is primarily interested in adventure and the outdoors. Our guidebooks lead to both personal and armchair adventure and travel. Authors must be willing to actively promote their book through book signings, the media, and lectures/slide shows for intended audiences."

SYBEX, INC., 1151 Marina Village Pkwy., Alameda CA 94501. (510)523-8233. Fax: (510)523-2373. E-mail: proposals@sybex.com. Website: www.sybex.com. VP/Publisher: Jordan Gold. Estab. 1976. Publishes paperback originals. **Publishes 150 titles/year. Pays standard royalties. Offers competitive advance.** Publishes book 3 months after acceptance of ms. Accepts simultaneous submissions. Responds in 1 month to queries. Book catalog online.

O→ Sybex publishes computer and software titles.

Nonfiction: "Manuscripts most publishable in the field of PC applications software, hardware, programming languages, operating systems, computer games, Internet/Web certification and networking." Technical. Subjects include computers/electronic, software. Looks for "clear writing, logical presentation of material; and good selection of material such that the most important aspects of the subject matter are thoroughly covered; well-focused subject matter; clear understanding of target audience; and well thought-out organization that helps the reader understand the material." Submit outline, 2-3 sample chapter(s), résumé. Reviews artwork/photos as part of ms package. Send disk/CD.

Recent Title(s): *Photoshop Elements Solutions*, by Mikkel Haland; *Mastering Windows 2000 Setup*, by Mark Minasi; *CCNA: Cisco Certified Network Associate Study Guide*, by Todd Lammle.

Tips: Queries/mss may be routed to other editors in the publishing group. Also seeking freelance writers for revising existing works and as contributors in multi-author projects, and freelance editors for editing works in progress.

SYSTEMS CO., INC., P.O. Box 339, Carlsborg WA 98324. (360)683-6860. **Acquisitions:** Richard H. Peetz, Ph.D., president. Estab. 1981. Publishes hardcover and trade paperback originals. **Publishes 3-5 titles/year. 50% of books from first-time authors; 100% from unagented writers. Pays 20% royalty on wholesale price after costs.** Publishes book 6 months after acceptance of ms. Accepts simultaneous submissions. Responds in 2 months to queries. Book catalog free; ms guidelines for $1.

O→ "We publish succinct and well-organized technical and how-to-do-it books with minimum filler." De-emphasizing business/economics, health/medicine.

Nonfiction: How-to, self-help, technical, textbook. Subjects include business/economics, health/medicine, money/finance, nature/environment, science, automotive, engineering. Submit outline, 2 sample chapter(s), SASE. Reviews artwork/photos as part of ms package. Send photocopies.

Recent Title(s): *Existentialism & Folklore*, by J.S. Hescher, M.D.

Tips: "Our audience consists of people in technical occupations, people interested in doing things themselves. In submitting nonfiction, writers often make the mistake of picking a common topic with lots of published books in print."

[A] **NAN A. TALESE**, Random House, Inc., 1540 Broadway, New York NY 10036. (212)782-8918. Fax: (212)782-9261. Website: www.nantalese.com. **Acquisitions:** Nan A. Talese, editorial director. Publishes hardcover originals. **Publishes 15 titles/year. Receives 400 queries and 400 mss/year. Pays variable royalty on retail price. Offers varying advance.** Publishes book 1 year after acceptance of ms. Accepts simultaneous submissions. Responds in 1 week to queries; 2 weeks to proposals; 2 weeks to mss. Agented submissions only.

O→ Nan A. Talese publishes nonfiction with a powerful guiding narrative and relevance to larger cultural interests, and literary fiction of the highest quality.

Nonfiction: Biography. Subjects include contemporary culture, history, philosophy, sociology. *Agented submissions only.*

Fiction: Well written narratives with a compelling story line, good characterization and use of language. We like stories with an edge. *Agented submissions only.*

Recent Title(s): *The Blind Assassin*, by Margaret Atwood (fiction); *Atonement*, by Ian McEwan; *London*, by Peter Ackroyd.

Tips: "Audience is highly literate people interested in story, information and insight. We want well-written material. See our website."

JEREMY P. TARCHER, INC., Penguin Putnam, Inc.,, 375 Hudson St., New York NY 10014. (212)366-2000. Website: www.penguinputnam.com. Publisher: Joel Fotinos. **Acquisitions:** Mitch Horowitz, senior editor; Wendy Hubbert, senior editor; Sara Carder, editor; Joel Fotinos, publisher. Estab. 1972. Publishes hardcover and trade paperback originals and reprints. **Publishes 40-50 titles/year. Receives 750 queries and 750 mss/year. 10% of books from first-time authors; 5% from unagented writers. Pays royalty. Offers advance.** Accepts simultaneous submissions. Book catalog free.

O→ Tarcher's vision is to publish ideas and works about human consciousness that is large enough to include all aspects of human experience.

Nonfiction: How-to, self-help. Subjects include business/economics, child guidance/parenting, gay/lesbian, health/medicine, nature/environment, philosophy, psychology, religion, women's issues/studies.

Recent Title(s): *The American Soul*, by Jacob Needleman; *Trust Us, We're Experts*, by Sheldon Rampton & John Stauber.

Tips: "Our audience seeks personal growth through books. Understand the imprint's focus and categories. We stick with the tried and true."

TCU PRESS, P.O. Box 298300, TCU, Fort Worth TX 76129. (817)257-7822. Fax: (817)257-5075. **Acquisitions:** Judy Alter, director; James Ward Lee, acquisitions consultant; A.T. Row, editor. Estab. 1966. Publishes hardcover originals, some reprints. **Publishes 12-15 titles/year. Receives 100 submissions/year. 10% of books from first-time authors; 75% from unagented writers. Pays 10% royalty on net receipts.** Publishes book 16 months after acceptance of ms. Does not accept simultaneous submissions. Responds in 3 months to queries.

O→ TCU publishes "scholarly works and regional titles of significance focusing on the history and literature of the American West." Currently emphasizing women's studies.

Nonfiction: Biography, children's/juvenile, coffee table book, scholarly. Subjects include Americana, art/architecture, contemporary culture, ethnic, history, language/literature, multicultural, regional, women's issues/studies, American studies, criticism. Query with SASE. Reviews artwork/photos as part of ms package.

Fiction: Young adult.

Recent Title(s): *From Texas to the World and Back: The Journeys of Katherine Anne Porter*, by Mark Busby & Dick Heaberlin, eds; *Tie-Fast Country*, by Robert Flynn.

Tips: "Regional and/or Texana nonfiction has best chance of breaking into our firm. Our list focuses on the history of literature of the American West, although recently we have branched out into literary criticism, women's studies and Mexican-American studies."

N **TEACHERS COLLEGE PRESS**, 1234 Amsterdam Ave., New York NY 10027. (212)678-3929. Fax: (212)678-4149. Website: www.tc.columbia.edu/tcpress. Director: Carole P. Saltz. **Acquisitions:** Brian Ellerbeck, executive acquisitions editor. Estab. 1904. Publishes hardcover and paperback originals and reprints. **Publishes 60 titles/year. Pays industry standard royalty. Offers advance.** Publishes book 1 year after acceptance of ms. Does not accept simultaneous submissions. Responds in 2 months to queries. Book catalog free.

- Teachers College Press publishes a wide range of educational titles for all levels of students: early childhood to higher education. "Publishing books that respond to, examine and confront issues pertaining to education, teacher training and school reform."

Nonfiction: Subjects include computers/electronic, education, film/cinema/stage, government/politics, history, philosophy, sociology, women's issues/studies. "This university press concentrates on books in the field of education in the broadest sense, from early childhood to higher education: good classroom practices, teacher training, special education, innovative trends and issues, administration and supervision, film, continuing and adult education, all areas of the curriculum, computers, guidance and counseling and the politics, economics, philosophy, sociology and history of education. We have recently added women's studies to our list. The Press also issues classroom materials for students at all levels, with a strong emphasis on reading and writing and social studies." Submit outline, sample chapter(s).

Recent Title(s): *Cultural Miseducation: In Search of a Democratic Solution*, by Jane Roland Martin.

TEACHING & LEARNING COMPANY, 1204 Buchanan St., P.O. Box 10, Carthage IL 62321-0010. (217)357-2591. Fax: (217)357-6789. E-mail: customerservice@teachinglearning.com. Website: www.teachinglearning.com. **Acquisitions:** Jill Day, vice president of production. Estab. 1994. **Publishes 60 titles/year. Receives 25 queries and 200 mss/year. 25% of books from first-time authors; 98% from unagented writers. Pays royalty.** Accepts simultaneous submissions. Responds in 3 months to queries; 9 months to proposals; 9 months to mss. Book catalog and ms guidelines free.

- Teaching & Learning Company publishes teacher resources (supplementary activity/idea books) for grades pre K-8. Currently emphasizing "more math for all grade levels, more primary science material."

Nonfiction: Children's/juvenile. Subjects include art/architecture, education, language/literature, science, teacher resources in language arts, reading, math, science, social studies, arts and crafts, responsibility education. No picture books or storybooks. Submit table of contents, introduction, 3 sample chapters with SASE. Reviews artwork/photos as part of ms package. Send photocopies.

Recent Title(s): *Group Project Student Role Sheets*, by Christine Boardman Moen (nonfiction); *Poetry Writing Handbook*, by Greta Barclay Lipson, Ed.D. (poetry); *Four Square Writing Methods (3 books)*, by Evan and Judith Gould.

Tips: "Our books are for teachers and parents of pre K-8th grade children."

TEMPLE UNIVERSITY PRESS, USB, 1601 N. Broad St., Philadelphia PA 19122-6099. (215)204-8787. Fax: (215)204-4719. E-mail: tempress@astro.ocis.temple.edu. Website: www.temple.edu/tempress/. **Acquisitions:** Janet Francendese, editor-in-chief; Peter Wissoker, senior acquisitions editor (communications, urban studies, geography, law); Micah Kleit, senior acquisitions editor. Estab. 1969. **Publishes 60 titles/year. Pays 10% royalty on wholesale price. Offers advance.** Publishes book 10 months after acceptance of ms. Does not accept simultaneous submissions. Responds in 2 months to queries. Book catalog free.

- "Temple University Press has been publishing useful books on Asian-Americans, law, gender issues, film, women's studies and other interesting areas for nearly 30 years for the goal of social change."

Nonfiction: Subjects include ethnic, government/politics, health/medicine, history (American), photography, regional (Philadelphia), sociology, women's issues/studies, labor studies, urban studies, Latin American, Asian American, African American, public policy. "No memoirs, fiction or poetry." Query with SASE. Reviews artwork/photos as part of ms package.

Recent Title(s): *Critical Race Theory: The Cutting Edge*, second edition, edited by Richard Delgado and Jean Stefancie.

TEN SPEED PRESS, P.O. Box 7123, Berkeley CA 94707. (510)559-1600. Fax: (510)524-1052. E-mail: info@tenspeed.com. Website: www.tenspeed.com. **Acquisitions:** Kirsty Melville, Ten Speed Press publisher; Lorena Jones, Ten Speed Press editorial director; Jo Ann Deck, Celestial Arts publisher. Estab. 1971. Publishes trade paperback originals and reprints. **Publishes 100 titles/year; imprint publishes 70 titles/year. 25% of books from first-time authors; 50% from unagented writers. Pays 15-20% royalty on net receipts. Offers $2,500 average advance.** Publishes book 1 year after acceptance of ms. Accepts simultaneous submissions. Responds in 3 months to queries. Book catalog for 9×12 SAE with 6 first-class stamps; ms guidelines for #10 SASE or on website.

Imprints: Celestial Arts, Tricycle Press

- Ten Speed Press publishes authoritative books for an audience interested in innovative ideas. Currently emphasizing cookbooks, career, business, alternative education, and offbeat general nonfiction gift books.

Nonfiction: Subjects include business/economics, child guidance/parenting, cooking/foods/nutrition, gardening, health/medicine, money/finance, nature/environment, New Age (mind/body/spirit), recreation, science. "No fiction." Query with SASE or submit proposal package including sample chapter(s).
Recent Title(s): *Charlie Trotter Cooks at Home*, by Charlie Trotter; *Hiring Smart*, by Pierre Mornell.
Tips: "We like books from people who really know their subject, rather than people who think they've spotted a trend to capitalize on. We like books that will sell for a long time, rather than nine-day wonders. Our audience consists of a well-educated, slightly weird group of people who like food, the outdoors and take a light but serious approach to business and careers. Study the backlist of each publisher you're submitting to and tailor your proposal to what you perceive as their needs. Nothing gets a publisher's attention like someone who knows what he or she is talking about, and nothing falls flat like someone who obviously has no idea who he or she is submitting to."

TEXAS A&M UNIVERSITY PRESS, College Station TX 77843-4354. (979)845-1436. Fax: (979)847-8752. E-mail: fdl@tampress.tamu.edu. Website: www.tamu.edu/upress. **Acquisitions:** Mary Lenn Dixon, editor-in-chief (presidential studies, anthropology, borderlands, western history); Shannon Davies, senior editor (natural history, agriculture); Jim Sadkovich, associate editor (military, eastern Europe, nautical archeaology). Estab. 1974. **Publishes 50 titles/year. Pays royalty. Offers advance.** Publishes book 1 year after acceptance of ms. Does not accept simultaneous submissions. Responds in 1 month to queries. Book catalog free.

O━ Texas A&M University Press publishes a wide range of nonfiction, scholarly trade and crossover books of regional and national interest, "reflecting the interests of the university, the broader scholarly community, and the people of our state and region."

Nonfiction: Subjects include agriculture/horticulture, anthropology/archeology, art/architecture, business/economics, government/politics, history (American and Western), language/literature (Texas and western), military/war, nature/environment, photography, regional (Texas and the Southwest), women's issues/studies, Mexican-US borderlands studies, nautical archaeology, ethnic studies, natural history, presidential studies, business history, veterinary medicine. Query with SASE.
Recent Title(s): *Texas Flags*, by Robert Maberry, Jr.
Tips: Proposal requirements are posted on the website.

TEXAS WESTERN PRESS, The University of Texas at El Paso, El Paso TX 79968-0633. (915)747-5688. Fax: (915)747-7515. E-mail: twp@utep.edu. Website: www.utep.edu/~twpress. Director: Dr. Jon Amastae. **Acquisitions:** Bobbi McConaughey Gonzales. Estab. 1952. Publishes hardcover and paperback originals. **Publishes 7-8 titles/year. Pays standard 10% royalty. Offers advance.** Does not accept simultaneous submissions. Responds in 2 months to queries. Book catalog and ms guidelines free; ms guidelines free.
Imprints: Southwestern Studies.

O━ Texas Western Press publishes books on the history and cultures of the American Southwest, especially historical and biographical works about West Texas, New Mexico, northern Mexico and the US-Mexico borderlands. Currently emphasizing developing border issues, economic issues of the border. De-emphasizing coffee table books.

Nonfiction: Scholarly, technical. Subjects include education, health/medicine, history, language/literature, nature/environment, regional, science, social sciences. Historic and cultural accounts of the Southwest (West Texas, New Mexico, northern Mexico and Arizona). Also art, photographic books, Native American and limited regional ficiton reprints. Occasional technical titles. "Our *Southwestern Studies* use manuscripts of up to 30,000 words. Our hardback books range from 30,000 words up. The writer should use good exposition in his work. Most of our work requires documentation. We favor a scholarly, but not overly pedantic, style. We specialize in superior book design." Query with SASE or submit outline. Follow *Chicago Manual of Style*.
Recent Title(s): *Frontier Cavalryman*, by Marcos Kinevan; *James Wiley Magoffin*, by W.H. Timmons.
Tips: Texas Western Press is interested in books relating to the history of Hispanics in the US, will experiment with photo-documentary books, and is interested in seeing more 'popular' history and books on Southwestern culture/life. "We try to treat our authors professionally, produce handsome, long-lived books and aim for quality, rather than quantity of titles carrying our imprint."

THIRD WORLD PRESS, P.O. Box 19730, Chicago IL 60619. (773)651-0700. Fax: (773)651-7286. E-mail: TWPress3@aol.com. Publisher: Haki R. Madhubuti. **Acquisitions:** Gwendolyn Mitchell, editor. Estab. 1967. Publishes hardcover and trade paperback originals and reprints. **Publishes 20 titles/year. Receives 200-300 queries and 200 mss/year. 20% of books from first-time authors; 80% from unagented writers. Pays royalty on retail price. Offers advance.** Publishes book 18 months after acceptance of ms. Accepts simultaneous submissions. Responds in 6 months to queries. Book catalog free; ms guidelines for #10 SASE.

● Third World Press is open to submissions in July only.

Nonfiction: Children's/juvenile, illustrated book, reference, self-help, textbook, African-centered; African-American materials. Subjects include anthropology/archeology, education, ethnic, government/politics, health/medicine, history, language/literature, philosophy, psychology, regional, religion, sociology, women's issues/studies, Black studies, literary criticism. Query with SASE or submit outline, 5 sample chapter(s). Reviews artwork/photos as part of ms package. Send photocopies.
Fiction: Ethnic, feminist, historical, juvenile, literary, mainstream/contemporary, picture books, plays, short story collections, young adult, African-centered; African-American materials. Query with SASE or submit 5 sample chapter(s), synopsis.

Poetry: African-centered and African-American materials. Submit complete ms.
Recent Title(s): *Special Internet*, by Chris Benson; *Tough Notes: A Healing Call for Creating Exceptional Black Men*, by Haki R. Madhubuti.

THORNDIKE PRESS, The Gale Group, 295 Kenney Memorial Dr., Waterville ME 04901. (207)859-1000. Fax: (207)859-1006. E-mail: Hazel.Rumney@gale.com. **Acquisitions:** Hazel Rumney, editor (romance, western, women's fiction); Jamie Knobloch, editorial director. Publishes hardcover originals, reprints and large print reprints. **Publishes 112 titles/year. Receives 1,000 queries and 1,000 mss/year. 60% of books from first-time authors; 75% from unagented writers. Pays royalty on wholesale price. Offers $1,000-2,000 advance.** Publishes book 8 months after acceptance of ms. Accepts simultaneous submissions. Responds in 3 months to queries; 3 months to proposals; 4-6 months to mss. Book catalog free; ms guidelines for #10 SASE.
Imprints: Five Star (contact: Hazel Rumney).
Fiction: Romance, western, women's. Submit proposal package including 3 sample chapter(s), synopsis.
Recent Title(s): *Friends and Enemies*, by Susan Oleksiw (mystery); *Desparate Acts*, by Jane Candia Coleman (romance).
Tips: Audience is intelligent readers looking for something different and satisfying. "We want highly original material that contains believable motivation, with little repetitive introspection. Show us how a character feels, rather than tell us. Humor is good; cliches are not."

THREE FORKS BOOKS, The Globe Pequot Press, P.O. Box 1718, Helena MT 59624. (406)442-6597. Fax: (406)442-0384. Website: www.falcon.com. **Acquisitions:** Megan Hiller, senior editor. Publishes hardcover and trade paperback originals. **Publishes 4 titles/year. 80% of books from first-time authors; 80% from unagented writers. Pays variable royalty.** Does not accept simultaneous submissions. Responds in 2 months to queries. Book catalog and ms guidelines free.

Three Forks specializes in regional cookbooks *or* cookbooks with a unique, non-food theme. We do not publish single-food themed cookbooks.

Nonfiction: Cookbook. Subjects include regional. Query with SASE or submit proposal package. Reviews artwork/photos as part of ms package. Send photocopies, no originals.
Recent Title(s): *Whistleberries, Stirabout, & Depression Cake* (food history); *Chocolate Snowball* (cookbook).

TIARE PUBLICATIONS, P.O. Box 493, Lake Geneva WI 53147-0493. Fax: (262)249-0299. E-mail: info@tiare.com. Website: www.tiare.com. **Acquisitions:** Gerry L. Dexter, president. Estab. 1986. Publishes trade paperback originals. **Publishes 6-12 titles/year. Receives 25 queries and 10 mss/year. 40% of books from first-time authors; 100% from unagented writers. Pays 15% royalty on wholesale price or retail price.** Publishes book 3 months after acceptance of ms. Does not accept simultaneous submissions. Responds in 1 month to queries.
Imprints: LimeLight Books, Balboa Books.

Tiare offers a wide selection of books for the radio communications enthusiast. LimeLight publishes general nonfiction on subjects ranging from crime to root beer. Balboa offers big band and jazz titles.

Nonfiction: How-to, technical, general. Subjects include computers/electronic, general nonfiction, music/dance, jazz/big bands. Query with SASE.
Recent Title(s): *Air-Ways—The Insider's Guide to Air Travel.*

TIDEWATER PUBLISHERS, Cornell Maritime Press, Inc., P.O. Box 456, Centreville MD 21617-0456. (410)758-1075. Fax: (410)758-6849. **Acquisitions:** Charlotte Kurst, managing editor. Estab. 1938. Publishes hardcover and paperback originals. **Publishes 7-9 titles/year. Receives 150 submissions/year. 41% of books from first-time authors; 99% from unagented writers. Pays 7½-15% royalty on retail price. Offers advance.** Publishes book 1 year after acceptance of ms. Does not accept simultaneous submissions. Responds in 2 months to queries. Book catalog for 10×13 SAE with 5 first-class stamps.

Tidewater Publishers issues adult nonfiction works related to the Chesapeake Bay area, Delmarva or Maryland in general. "The only fiction we handle is juvenile and must have a regional focus."

Nonfiction: Regional subjects only. Children's/juvenile, cookbook, illustrated book, reference. Subjects include cooking/foods/nutrition, history, regional. Query with SASE or submit outline, sample chapter(s). Reviews artwork/photos as part of ms package.
Fiction: Regional juvenile fiction only. Juvenile, regional. Query with SASE or submit outline, sample chapter(s), synopsis.
Recent Title(s): *Chesapeake ABC*, by Priscilla Cummings, illustrated by David Aiken; *Lost Towns of Tidewater Maryland*, by Donald G. Shomette.
Tips: "Our audience is made up of readers interested in works that are specific to the Chesapeake Bay and Delmarva Peninsula area. We do not publish personal narratives, adult fiction or poetry."

TILBURY HOUSE, PUBLISHERS, Herpswell Press, Inc., 2 Mechanic St., Gardiner ME 04345. (207)582-1899. Fax: (207)582-8227. E-mail: tilbury@tilburyhouse.com. Website: www.tilburyhouse.com. Publisher: Jennifer Elliot (New England, maritime, children's). **Acquisitions:** Audrey Maynard, children's book editor. Estab. 1990. Publishes hardcover originals, trade paperback originals. **Publishes 10 titles/year. Pays royalty.** Book catalog free; ms guidelines online.

Nonfiction: Biography, children's/juvenile, coffee table book. Subjects include animals, art/architecture, education, ethnic (children's), general nonfiction, history, memoirs, multicultural (children's), regional (New England). Submit complete ms. Reviews artwork/photos as part of ms package. Send photocopies.
Fiction: Regional (New England adult).
Recent Title(s): *Lucy's Family Tree*, by Karen Schreck (children's fiction); *Sea Soup: Zooplankton*, by Mary Cerullo (children's nonfiction); *A Doryman's Day*, by Barry Fisher (adult nonfiction).

TIMBERWOLF PRESS, INC., 202 N. Allen Dr., Suite A, Allen TX 75013. (972)359-0911. Fax: (972)359-0525. E-mail: submissions@timberwolfpress.com. Website: www.timberwolfpress.com. **Acquisitions:** Carol Woods, senior editor. Publishes trade paperback originals. **Publishes 24-30 titles/year. Receives 500+ queries and 100+ mss/year. 25% of books from first-time authors; 84% from unagented writers. Pays royalty on wholesale price. Offers industry standard advance or better.** Publishes book 6 months after acceptance of ms. Accepts simultaneous submissions. Responds in 1 month to queries; 3 months to mss. Book catalog and ms guidelines on website.
Fiction: Fantasy, military/war, mystery, science fiction, suspense. "In addition to the p-book, we present each title in fully-cast, dramatized, unabridged audio theatre, available in the usual formats; and downloadable in all formats from our website. We also stream this audio in 30-minute episodes on our website. So our stories must maintain tension and pace. Think exciting. Think breathless. Think terrific story, terrific characters, terrific writing." Query via e-mail only. Fiction only.
Recent Title(s): *Blood & Iron*, by Dan MacGregor (military/historical); *Book One of Bronwyn Etralogy: Palaces & Prisons*, by Ron Miller (fantasy).
Tips: "We accept e-queries and e-submissions only: *submissions@timberwolfpress.com* And polish that query. Grammar, punctuation, and spelling are as important in e-queries and e-submissions as they are in p-queries."

MEGAN TINGLEY BOOKS, Little, Brown & Co., Three Center Plaza, Boston MA 02108-2084. (617)227-0730. Website: www.twbookmark.com. **Acquisitions:** Megan Tingley, editorial director (picture books); Alvina Ling, assistant editor (YA novels); Mary Gruetzke, assistant editor (picture books). Publishes hardcover and trade paperback originals and reprints. **Publishes 80-100 titles/year; imprint publishes 10-20 titles/year. Receives 500-1,000 queries and 500-1,000 mss/year. 2% of books from first-time authors; 5% from unagented writers. Pays 0-15% royalty on retail price or makes outright purchase.** Publishes book 2 years after acceptance of ms. Accepts simultaneous submissions. Responds in 1 month to queries; 2-3 months to proposals; 2-3 months to mss. Book catalog for #10 SASE; ms guidelines for #10 SASE.

O→ Megan Tingley Books is an imprint of the children's book department of Little, Brown and Company. Currently emphasizing picture books for the very young. Does not want genre novels (mystery, science fiction, romance).

Nonfiction: Children's/juvenile. Subjects include animals, art/architecture, cooking/foods/nutrition, creative nonfiction, ethnic, gay/lesbian, history, hobbies, language/literature, memoirs, multicultural, music/dance, nature/environment, photography, science, sports, all juvenile interests. *Agented submissions only*, but unsolicited queries are okay. Ideally, books should be about a subject that hasn't been dealt with for children before. *Agented submissions only.* Reviews artwork/photos as part of ms package. Send photocopies or no original pieces.
Fiction: Juvenile, picture books, young adult. *Agented submissions only*, but unsolicited queries are okay. Strong, contemporary female characters preferred. No genre novels (romance, mystery, science fiction, etc.). *Agented submissions only.* Query with SASE.
Recent Title(s): *It's Okay to Be Different*, by Todd Parr; *You Read to Me, I'll Read to You*, by Mary Ann Hoberman.
Tips: "Do your research. Know our submission policy. Do not fax or call."

[N] **THE TOBY PRESS LTD.**, P.O. Box 8531, New Milford CT 06776-8531. Website: www.tobypress.com. **Acquisitions:** Editorial Director (fiction, biography). Publishes hardcover originals and paperbacks. **Publishes 20-25 titles/year. Receives 300 queries/year. 50% of books from first-time authors; 10% from unagented writers. Offers advance.** Publishes book up to 2 year after acceptance of ms. Accepts simultaneous submissions.

O→ The Toby Press publishes literary fiction.

Nonfiction: Biography.
Fiction: Literary.
Recent Title(s): *Failing Paris*, by Samantha Dunn (fiction); *Before Hiroshima*, by Joshua Barkan (fiction).

TODD PUBLICATIONS, P.O. Box 635, Nyack NY 10960. (845)358-6213. E-mail: toddpub@aol.com. Website: www.toddpublications.com. **Acquisitions:** Barry Klein, president. Estab. 1973. Publishes hardcover and trade paperback originals. **Publishes 5 titles/year. 1% of books from first-time authors. Pays 10-15% royalty on wholesale price. Offers advance.** Publishes book 3 months after acceptance of ms. Accepts simultaneous submissions. Responds in 1 month to proposals. Book catalog available via website or with SASE; ms guidelines for #10 SASE.

O→ Todd publishes and distributes reference books and directories of all types.

Nonfiction: How-to, reference, self-help, directories. Subjects include business/economics, ethnic, health/medicine, money/finance, travel. Submit 2 sample chapter(s).
Recent Title(s): *Directory Of Mastercard & Visa Credit Card Sources*; *Insider's Guide To Bank Cards With No Credit Check*; *Indian Country Address Book.*

[N] **TORAH AURA PRODUCTIONS**, 4423 Fruitland Ave., Los Angeles CA 90058. (213)585-7312. Website: www.torahaura.com. **Acquisitions:** Jane Golub. Estab. 1982. Publishes hardcover and trade paperback originals. **Publishes**

25 titles/year; imprint publishes 10 titles/year. Receives 5 queries and 10 mss/year. 2% of books from first-time authors; 100% from unagented writers. Pays 10% royalty on wholesale price. Offers advance. Publishes book 3 years after acceptance of ms. Accepts simultaneous submissions. Responds in 6 months to mss. Book catalog free.

O— Torah Aura publishes mostly educational materials for Jewish classrooms.

Nonfiction: Children's/juvenile, textbook. Subjects include language/literature (Hebrew), religion (Jewish). No picture books. Query with SASE. Reviews artwork/photos as part of ms package. Send photocopies.

Fiction: Juvenile, picture books, religious, young adult. All fiction must have Jewish interest. No picture books. Query with SASE. Reviews artwork/photos as part of ms package. Send photocopies.

Recent Title(s): *The Bible from Alef to Tav*, Penina V. Adelman.

TORCHDOG PRESS, 1032 Irving St. #514, San Francisco CA 94122-2200. (415)753-3778. E-mail: torchdog@torchdog.com. Website: www.torchdog.com. Kevin Rush, publisher. **Acquisitions:** Connor McLean, managing editor. Publishes trade paperback originals. **100% of books from first-time authors; 100% from unagented writers. Pays 6-8% royalty on retail price or makes outright purchase of $100-400.** Publishes book 6 months after acceptance of ms. Accepts simultaneous submissions. Responds in 1 month to queries; 3 months to mss. Book catalog online; ms guidelines for #10 SASE.

Fiction: Young adult. "Torchdog Press is dedicated to providing realistic, relevant and faith-filled fiction for Catholic teens aged 13-16." Prefers stories with an edge, a contemporary voice, and gently interwoven spirituality. Humor a plus. Will consider historical fiction and science fiction. Nothing heavy-handed or didactic. Submit complete ms.

Recent Title(s): *Earthquake Weather*, by Kevin Rush (young adult).

Tips: "Our audience is Catholic teens in Catholic junior high and high school. They are trying to integrate their faith into their daily lives in the real world. They face all the trials and temptations of contemporary teens." "Please, no sanitized saints leading perfect lives and making all the right decisions. Torchdog books are not for ivory tower separatists who think religion can insulate kids from the real world. Our books are for kids living in the real world, trying to figure out where their faith fits in."

TOWER PUBLISHING, 588 Saco Rd., Standish ME 04084. (207)642-5400. Fax: (207)642-5463. E-mail: info@towerpub.com. Website: www.towerpub.com. **Acquisitions:** Michael Lyons, president. Estab. 1772. Publishes hardcover originals and reprints, trade paperback originals. **Publishes 15 titles/year. Receives 60 queries and 30 mss/year. 10% of books from first-time authors; 90% from unagented writers. Pays royalty on net receipts.** Publishes book 6 months after acceptance of ms. Accepts simultaneous submissions. Responds in 1 month to queries; 2 months to proposals; 2 months to mss. Book catalog and ms guidelines on website.

O— Tower Publishing specializes in business and professional directories and legal books.

Nonfiction: Reference. Subjects include business/economics. Looking for legal books of a national stature. Query with SASE or submit outline.

TOWLEHOUSE PUBLISHING CO., 1312 Bell Grimes Lane, Nashville TN 37207. (615)366-9120. Fax: (615)366-9161. E-mail: vermonte@aol.com. Website: www.towlehouse.com. **Acquisitions:** Mike Towle, president/publisher (nonfiction, sports, gift books, pop culture, cookbooks, Christianity). Publishes hardcover, trade paperback and mass market paperback originals, hardcover and trade paperback reprints. **Publishes 10-12 titles/year. Receives 100-250 mss/year. 75% of books from first-time authors; 80% from unagented writers. Pays 8-20% royalty on wholesale price. Offers $500-2,000 advance.** Publishes book 9 months after acceptance of ms. Accepts simultaneous submissions. Responds in 4-6 months to queries.

O— "We publish nonfiction books about America that are informative and entertaining." Currently emphasizing 'potent quotables' and Good Golf! series of books. Rare exceptions. De-emphasizing cookbooks and poetry.

Nonfiction: Subjects include Americana, creative nonfiction, government/politics, history, religion, sports, insta-books dictated by headlines and milestone anniversaries of significant events. "I don't solicit children's books, poetry or non-Christian religious titles. Authors using profanity, obscenities or other vulgar or immoral language in their books need not contact me." Query with SASE or submit proposal package including outline, 2 sample chapter(s), author bio, letter containing marketing plan. Reviews artwork/photos as part of ms package. Send photocopies.

Recent Title(s): *Quotable Rudy*, by Monte Carpenter ("Potent Quotables"); *Gentlemen Only*, by Robbie Williams and Lee Heffernan (Good Golf!).

Tips: "Send one proposal for one book at a time. If you send me a query listing three, four or more 'ideas' for books, I will immediately know that you lack the commitment needed to author a book. Send a SASE for anything you send me. I don't accept fiction unless you're a bestselling fiction author."

J.N. TOWNSEND PUBLISHING, LLC, 4 Franklin St., Exeter NH 03833. (603)778-9883. Fax: (603)772-1980. E-mail: townsendpub@aol.com. Website: www.jntownsendpublishing.com. **Acquisitions:** Terri Fyler, assistant (animal). Estab. 1986. Publishes hardcover originals and trade paperback originals and reprints. **Publishes 7 titles/year. Receives 120 queries and 50 mss/year. 10% of books from first-time authors; 90% from unagented writers. Pays 7-10% royalty on retail price. Offers $500 advance.** Publishes book 1 year after acceptance of ms. Accepts simultaneous submissions. Responds in 1 month to queries; 1-2 months to proposals; 1-2 months to mss. Book catalog free; ms guidelines free.

Nonfiction: Subjects include animals, general nonfiction. Query with SASE. Reviews artwork/photos as part of ms package. Send photocopies.

Fiction: Literary, Animal-related books. Ask for a catalog and read some of the company's titles. "Call and talk to us, we're very nice." Query with SASE.
Recent Title(s): *Goat Song: My Island Angora Goat Farm*, Susan Basquin (Memoir); *Gray Dawn*, Albert Payson Terhune (Novel).
Tips: "Our audience is young and older, and mostly women who are animal and book lovers. Call us first."

TOY BOX PRODUCTIONS, 7532 Hickory Hills Court, Whites Creek TN 37189. (615)299-0822. Fax: (615)876-3931. E-mail: lori@crttoybox.com. Website: www.crttoybox.com. Estab. 1995. Publishes mass market paperback originals. **Publishes 4 titles/year. 100% of books from first-time authors; 100% from unagented writers. Pays 10-15% royalty on wholesale price.** Does not accept simultaneous submissions. Book catalog online.

- "We are not accepting new submissions at this time."

Nonfiction: Audiocassettes, biography, children's/juvenile. Subjects include Americana, education, religion. **All unsolicited mss returned unopened.**
Recent Title(s): *Holy Moses*, by Joe Loesch.

TRAFALGAR SQUARE PUBLISHING, P.O. Box 257, N. Pomfret VT 05053-0257. (802)457-1911. Fax: (802)457-1913. E-mail: tsquare@sover.net. Website: www.horseandriderbooks.com. Publisher: Caroline Robbins. **Acquisitions:** Martha Cook, managing editor. Estab. 1987. Publishes hardcover and trade paperback originals and reprints. **Publishes 10 titles/year. Pays royalty. Offers advance.** Does not accept simultaneous submissions. Responds in 2 months to queries.

"We publish high quality instructional books for horsemen and horsewomen, always with the horse's welfare in mind."

Nonfiction: "We publish books for intermediate to advanced riders and horsemen." Subjects include animals (horses). "No stories, children's books or horse biographies." Query with SASE or submit proposal package including outline, 1-2 sample chapter(s), Letter of writer's qualifications and audience for book's subject.
Recent Title(s): *Resistance Free Training*, by Richard Shrake; *You Can Train Your Horse to Do Anything!*, by Shawna and Vinton Karrasch.

TRANSNATIONAL PUBLISHERS, INC., 410 Saw Mill River Rd., Ardsley NY 10502. (914)693-5100. Fax: (914)693-4430. E-mail: info@transnationalpubs.com. Website: www.transnationalpubs.com. Publisher: Heike Fenton. **Acquisitions:** John Berger, VP/publishing director. Estab. 1980. **Publishes 45-50 titles/year. Receives 40-50 queries and 30 mss/year. 60% of books from first-time authors; 95% from unagented writers. Pays royalty.** Publishes book 6-9 months after acceptance of ms. Accepts simultaneous submissions. Responds in 1 month to queries. Book catalog and ms guidelines free.

"We provide specialized international law publications for the teaching of law and law-related subjects in law school classroom, clinic and continuing legal education settings." Currently emphasizing any area of international law that is considered a current issue/event.

Nonfiction: Reference, technical, textbook. Subjects include business/economics, government/politics, women's issues/studies, international law. Query with SASE or submit proposal package including sample chapter(s), table of contents and introduction.
Recent Title(s): *Terrorism and Business*, by Jonah Alexander and Dean Alexander; *UN Human Rights Treaty System*, by Anne F. Bayefsky; *Privatizing Reare*, by Garson Colletta.

TRAVELERS' TALES, 330 Townsend St., Suite 208, San Francisco CA 94107. (415)227-8600. Fax: (415)227-8600. E-mail: submit@travelerstales.com (submissions) or ttales@. Website: www.travelerstales.com. **Acquisitions:** James O'Reilly and Larry Habegger, series editors. Publishes anthologies, single author narratives, and consumer books. **Publishes 12-14 titles/year. Pays 10¢/word for anthology pieces. Offers advance.** Accepts simultaneous submissions. Book catalog for SASE; Ms guidelines for SASE.
Imprints: Travelers' Tales Guides, Footsteps, Travelers' Tales Classics.
Nonfiction: Subjects include travel, Personal nonfiction travel anthologies, single author narratives and consumer books.
Recent Title(s): *Travelers' Tales Cuba*, edited by Tom Miller; *Coast to Coast*, by Jan Morris.
Tips: "We publish personal, nonfiction stories and anecdotes—funny, illuminating, adventurous, frightening or grim. Stories should reflect that unique alchemy that occurs when you enter unfamiliar territory and begin to see the world differently as a result. Stories that have already been published, including book excerpts, are welcome as long as the authors retain the copyright or can obtain permission from the copyright holder to reprint the material." "We do not publish fiction."

TRICYCLE PRESS, Ten Speed Press, P.O. Box 7123, Berkeley CA 94707. (510)559-1600. Website: www.tenspeed.com. **Acquisitions:** Nicole Geiger, publisher; Abigail Samoun, assistant editor. Publishes hardcover and trade paperback originals. **Publishes 18-20 titles/year. 20% of books from first-time authors; 60% from unagented writers. Pays 15-20% royalty on wholesale price. Offers $0-9,000 advance.** Publishes book 1 year after acceptance of ms. Accepts simultaneous submissions. Responds in 4-6 months to mss. Book catalog and ms guidelines for 9×12 SAE with 3 first-class stamps.

"Tricycle Press looks for something outside the mainstream; books that encourage children to look at the world from a possibly alternative angle. We have been trying to expand into the educational market and middle grade fiction."

Nonfiction: Biography, children's/juvenile, gift book, how-to, humor, illustrated book, self-help, picture books; activity books. Subjects include animals, art/architecture, creative nonfiction, film/cinema/stage, gardening, health/medicine, multicultural, music/dance, nature/environment, photography, science, travel, geography, math. Submit complete ms for activity books; 2-3 chapters or 20 pages for others. Reviews artwork/photos as part of ms package. Send photocopies.
Fiction: Picture books. Board books and picture books: Submit complete ms. Middle grade books: Send complete outline and 2-3 sample chapters (ages 9-14). Query with synopsis and SASE for all others.
Recent Title(s): *Hey, Little Ant*, by Phillip and Hannah Hoose, illustrated by Debbie Tilley; *The Young Adventurer's Guide to Everest: From Avalanche to Zopkio*, by Jonathan Chester; *Alexandra Rambles on Book #2: Oh, and Another Thing. . .*, by Karen Salmansohn.

THE TRINITY FOUNDATION, PO Box 68, Unicoi TN 37692. (423)743-0199. Fax: (423)743-2005. E-mail: jrob 1517@aol.com. Website: www.trinityfoundation.org. **Acquisitions:** John Robbins. Publishes hardcover and paperback originals and reprints. **Publishes 5 titles/year. Makes outright purchase of $1-1,500.** Publishes book 9 months after acceptance of ms. Responds in 1 month to queries; 1 month to proposals; 3 months to mss. Book catalog online.
Nonfiction: "Only books that confirm to the philosophy and theology of the Westminster Confession of Faith." Textbook. Subjects include business/economics, education, government/politics, history, philosophy, religion, science. Query with SASE. Very few unsolicited mss meet our requirements. Read at least 1 of our books before sending a query.

TRINITY PRESS INTERNATIONAL, 4775 Linglestown Rd., Harrisburg PA 17112. **Acquisitions:** Henry Carrigan, editorial director. Estab. 1989. Publishes trade paperback originals and reprints. **Publishes 40 titles/year. Pays 10% royalty on wholesale price. Offers advance.** Publishes book 9 months after acceptance of ms. Accepts simultaneous submissions. Book catalog free.

O→ Trinity Press International is an ecumenical publisher of serious books on theology and the Bible for the religious academic community, religious professionals, and serious book readers. Currently emphasizing religion and science, ethics, Biblical studies, film and religion, and religion and culture books.

Nonfiction: Textbook. Subjects include history (as relates to the Bible), religion, Christian/theological studies. Submit outline, 1 sample chapter(s).
Recent Title(s): *Dancing with the Sacred*, by Karl Peters.

TRIUMPH BOOKS, 601 S. LaSalle St., Suite 500, Chicago IL 60605. (312)939-3330. Fax: (312)663-3557. **Acquisitions:** Thomas Bast, editorial director (sports). Publishes hardcover originals and trade paperback originals and reprints. **Publishes 24-30 titles/year. Receives 300 queries and 150 mss/year. 25% of books from first-time authors; 40% from unagented writers. Pays 10-20% royalty on wholesale price. Offers $3,000-50,000 advance.** Publishes book 1 year after acceptance of ms. Accepts simultaneous submissions. Responds in 1 month to queries; 2 months to proposals; 2 months to mss. Book catalog free.
Nonfiction: Biography, coffee table book, gift book, humor, illustrated book. Subjects include business/economics, health/medicine, recreation, sports. Query with SASE or submit proposal package including outline, 1-2 sample chapter(s). Reviews artwork/photos as part of ms package. Send photocopies.
Recent Title(s): *Competitive Leadership*, by Brian Billick with James A. Peterson, Ph.D.; *Few and Chosen*, by Whitey Ford with Phil Pope.

TRUMAN STATE UNIVERSITY PRESS, 100 E. Normal St., Kirksville MO 63501-4221. (660)785-7336. Fax: (660)785-4480. E-mail: tsup@truman.edu. Website: tsup.truman.edu. **Acquisitions:** Paula Presley, director/editor-in-chief (nonfiction); Nancy Reschly (contemporary narrative poetry); Raymond Mentzer (early modern history, literature, biography). **Publishes 8-10 titles/year. Pays 7% royalty on net receipts.**
Nonfiction: Biography, illustrated book, textbook, monographs, early modern. Subjects include Americana, history (early modern), art history, literature.
Recent Title(s): *Human Cartography*, by James Gurley (poetry); *Truman in Cartoon and Caricature*, by James Giglio (nonfiction); *Time, Space, and Women's Lives in Early Modern Europe*.

TURTLE BOOKS, 866 United Nations Plaza, Suite #525, New York NY 10017. (212)644-2020. Fax: (212)223-4387. Website: www.turtlebooks.com. **Acquisitions:** John Whitman, publisher (children's picture books). Publishes hardcover and trade paperback originals. **Publishes 6-8 titles/year. Receives 1,000 mss/year. 25% of books from first-time authors; 50% from unagented writers. Pays royalty on retail price. Offers advance.** Publishes book 12 months after acceptance of ms. Accepts simultaneous submissions.

O→ Turtle Books publishes children's picture books.

Nonfiction: Children's/juvenile, illustrated book. Subjects include animals, education, history, language/literature, multicultural, nature/environment, regional, Any subject suitable for a children's picture book. Submit complete ms. Reviews artwork/photos as part of ms package. Send photocopies, no original art.
Fiction: Adventure, ethnic, fantasy, historical, multicultural, regional, sports, western. Subjects suitable for children's picture books. "We are looking for good stories which can be illustrated as children's picture books." Submit complete ms.
Poetry: Must be suitable for an illustrated children's book format. Submit complete ms.
Recent Title(s): *Keeper of the Swamp*, by Ann Garrett; *The Crab Man*, by Patricia Van West; *Alphabet Fiesta*, by Anne Miranda (children's picture books).

Tips: "Our preference is for stories rather than concept books. We will consider only children's picture book manuscripts."

TURTLE PRESS, S.K. Productions, P.O. Box 290206, Wethersfield CT 06129-0206. (860)529-7770. Fax: (860)529-7775. E-mail: editorial@turtlepress.com. Website: www.turtlepress.com. **Acquisitions:** Cynthia Kim, editor. Publishes hardcover originals, trade paperback originals and reprints. **Publishes 4-8 titles/year. Pays 8-10% royalty. Offers $500-1,500 advance.** Does not accept simultaneous submissions. Responds in 1 month to queries.

O┳ Turtle Press publishes sports and martial arts nonfiction for a specialty niche audience. Currently emphasizing martial arts, eastern philosophy. De-emphasizing self-help.

Nonfiction: How-to, self-help. Subjects include philosophy, sports, martial arts. "We prefer tightly targeted topics on which there is little or no information available in the market, particularly for our sports and martial arts titles." Query with SASE. Query with SASE.

Recent Title(s): *Warrior Speed*, by Ted Weimann.

TUTTLE PUBLISHING, 153 Milk St., 5th Floor, Boston MA 02109. Publishing Director: Ed Walters. **Acquisitions:** Editorial Acquisitions. Estab. 1832. Publishes hardcover and trade paperback originals and reprints. **Publishes 125 titles/year. Receives 1,000 queries/year. 20% of books from first-time authors; 40% from unagented writers. Pays 5-10% royalty on net or retail price, depending on format and kind of book. Offers advance.** Publishes book 18 months after acceptance of ms. Accepts simultaneous submissions. Responds in 4 months to proposals.

O┳ "Tuttle is America's leading publisher of books on Japan and Asia."

Nonfiction: Self-help. Subjects include ethnic, health/medicine, philosophy (Eastern), religion (Eastern), Taoist. Query with SASE or submit outline. Cannot guarantee return of ms.

Recent Title(s): *St. Nadie in Winter*, by Terrance Keenan; *Bruce Lee: The Celebrated Life of the Golden Dragon*, by John Little.

[A] **TWENTY-FIRST CENTURY BOOKS**, Millbrook Press, 2 Old New Milford Rd., Brookfield CT 06804. (203)740-2220. Executive Vice President/Publisher: Jean Reynolds. Editor in Chief: Amy Shields. Senior Editors: Laura Walsh, Anita Holmes, Kristen Bettcher, Deborah Grahame. **Acquisitions:** Kirsten Vibbert, manuscript coordinator. Publishes hardcover originals. **Publishes 40 titles/year. Receives 200 queries and 50 mss/year. 20% of books from first-time authors. Pays 5-8% royalty. Offers advance.** Publishes book 18 months after acceptance of ms. Does not accept simultaneous submissions.

O┳ Twenty-First Century Books publishes nonfiction science, technology and social issues titles for children and young adults. "We no longer accept unsolicited manuscripts. Agented submissions only, please."

Nonfiction: Children's/juvenile, young adult. Subjects include government/politics, health/medicine, history, military/war, nature/environment, science, current events, social issues. "We publish primarily in series of four or more titles, for ages 12 and up, and single titles for grades 7 and up. No picture books, fiction or adult books." *Agented submissions only.*

Recent Title(s): *Tourette Syndrome*; *Handbook of the Middle East.*

TWO DOT, The Globe Pequot Press., Box 1718, Helena MT 59624. (406)442-6597. Fax: (406)442-0384. Website: www.twodotbooks.com. **Acquisitions:** Megan Hiller, editor; Charlene Patterson, editor (series nonfiction, regional history, women's history). Publishes hardcover and trade paperback originals. **Publishes 15 titles/year. 30% of books from first-time authors; 80% from unagented writers. Pays royalty on net price.** Accepts simultaneous submissions. Responds in 3 months to queries. Book catalog online; ms guidelines for #10 SASE.

O┳ "Two Dot looks for lively writing for a popular audience, well-researched, on regional themes." Currently emphasizing popular history, western history, regional history, biography collections, western Americana. De-emphasizing scholarly writings, children's books, memoirs fiction, poetry.

Nonfiction: Subjects include Americana (western), history, regional. Four state by state series of interest: *More than Petticoats* (notable women); *It Happened In ...* (state histories); *Jerks in History* (by state); and *Outlaw Tales* (by state). Submit outline, 1-2 sample chapter(s), SASE. Reviews artwork/photos as part of ms package. Send photocopies.

Recent Title(s): *Love Untamed: Romances of the Old West*, by Chris Enss and Jo Ann Chartier; *Sacagawea Speaks*, by Joyce Badgley Hunsaker; *It Happened in the Civil War*, by Michael R. Bradley.

TYNDALE HOUSE PUBLISHERS, INC., 351 Executive Dr., Carol Stream IL 60188. (630)668-8300. Website: www.tyndale.com. **Acquisitions:** Ron Beers Publishing Division. Estab. 1962. Publishes hardcover and trade paperback originals and mass paperback reprints. **Publishes 125-150 titles/year. 5% of books from first-time authors. Pays negotiable royalty. Offers negotiable advance.** Publishes book 9 months after acceptance of ms. Responds in 3 months to queries. Ms guidelines for #10 SASE.

O┳ Tyndale House publishes "practical, user-friendly Christian books for the home and family."

Nonfiction: Children's/juvenile, self-help (Christian growth). Subjects include child guidance/parenting, religion, devotional/inspirational, theology/Bible doctrine, contemporary/critical issues. Query with SASE or submit outline. *No unsolicited mss.*

Fiction: Romance. Should read romance (historical, contemporary), suspense, historical and contemporary. Christian truths must be woven into the story organically. No short story collections. Youth books: character building stories with Christian perspective. Especially interested in ages 10-14. No short story collections. Query with SASE or submit synopsis. *No unsolicited mss.*

Recent Title(s): *Unspoken*, by Francine Rivers (fiction); *Safely Home*, by Randy Alcorn; *Adolescence Isn't Terminal*, by Kevin Leman.

UCLA AMERICAN INDIAN STUDIES CENTER, 3220 Campbell Hall, Box 951548, UCLA, Los Angeles CA 90095-1548. (310)825-7315. Fax: (310)206-7060. E-mail: aiscpubs@ucla.edu. Website: www.sscnet.ucla.edu/esp/aisc. **Acquisitions:** Duane Champagne, director/editor. Publishes hardcover and trade paperback originals. **Publishes 4 titles/year. Receives 10 queries and 8 mss/year. 60% of books from first-time authors; 100% from unagented writers. Pays 8% royalty on retail price.** Publishes book 7 months after acceptance of ms. Accepts simultaneous submissions. Responds in 2 months to queries; 3 months to mss. Book catalog and ms guidelines free.

O→ "We publish nonfiction, fiction and poetry by and about Native Americans. We publish the *American Indian Culture and Research Journal*, which accepts poetry submissions.

Nonfiction: Reference, scholarly. Subjects include Americana, anthropology/archeology, ethnic, government/politics, health/medicine, history, language/literature, multicultural, religion, sociology, contemporary culture. Submit proposal package including outline, 2 sample chapter(s). Reviews artwork/photos as part of ms package. Send photocopies.
Fiction: Ethnic, plays, poetry, religious. Submit proposal package including synopsis.
Poetry: Query or submit complete ms.
Recent Title(s): *Songs from an Outcast*; *Indian Gaming: Who Wins?*; *A Sacred Path: The Way of the Muscogee Creeks.*

UNITY HOUSE, Unity School of Christianity, 1901 NW Blue Parkway, Unity Village MO 64065-0001. (816)524-3550 ext. 3190. Fax: (816)251-3552. Website: www.unityworldhq.org. **Acquisitions:** Michael Maday, editor; Raymond Teague, associate editor. Estab. 1889. Publishes hardcover and trade paperback originals and reprints. **Publishes 16 titles/year. Receives 500 submissions/year. 30% of books from first-time authors; 95% from unagented writers. Pays 10-15% royalty on net receipts. Offers advance.** Publishes book 13 months after acceptance of ms. Does not accept simultaneous submissions. Responds in 1 month to queries; 1 month to proposals; 2 months to mss. Book catalog free; ms guidelines online.

O→ "Unity House publishes metaphysical Christian books based on Unity principles, as well as inspirational books on metaphysics and practical spirituality. All manuscripts must reflect a spiritual foundation and express the Unity philosophy, practical Christianity, universal principles, and/or metaphysics."

Nonfiction: "Writers should be familiar with principles of metaphysical Christianity but not feel bound by them. We are interested in works in the related fields of holistic health, spiritual psychology and the philosophy of other world religions." Reference (spiritual/metaphysical), self-help, inspirational. Subjects include health/medicine (holistic), philosophy (perennial/New Thought), psychology (transpersonal), religion (spiritual/metaphysical Bible interpretation/modern Biblical studies). Query with book proposal, including cover letter, summarizing unique features and suggested sales and marketing strategies, toc or project outline and 1-3 sample chapters with SASE. Reviews artwork/photos as part of ms package. Send photocopies.
Fiction: Juvenile, picture books, young adult, visionary fiction. Query with SASE.
Recent Title(s): *Looking In For Number One*, by Alan Cohen; *The Vortex Shift*, by Mario DeFerrari.

THE UNIVERSITY OF AKRON PRESS, 374B Bierce Library, Akron OH 44325-1703. (330)972-5342. Fax: (330)972-8364. E-mail: uapress@uakron.edu. Website: www.uakron.edu/uapress. **Acquisitions:** Michael Carley, director. Estab. 1988. Publishes hardcover and trade paperback originals. **Publishes 8-12 titles/year. Receives 400-500 queries and 100 mss/year. 40% of books from first-time authors; 100% from unagented writers. Pays 5-10% royalty. Offers (possible) advance.** Publishes book 10-12 months after acceptance of ms. Responds in 2 months to queries; 2 months to proposals; 3 months to mss. Book catalog free; ms guidelines for #10 SASE.

O→ "The University of Akron Press strives to be the University's ambassador for scholarship and creative writing at the national and international levels." Currently emphasizing technology and the environment, Ohio history and culture, poetry, history of law, political science, and international, political, and economic history. De-emphasizing fiction.

Nonfiction: Scholarly. Subjects include history, regional, science, environment, technology, law, political science. "We publish mostly in our four nonfiction series: Technology and the Environment; Ohio History and Culture; Law, Politics and Society, and International, Political, and Economic History." Query with SASE. Reviews artwork/photos as part of ms package. Send photocopies.
Poetry: Follow the guidelines and submit manuscripts only for the contest. www.uakron.edu/uapress/poetry.html.
Recent Title(s): *Murder, Culture, and Injustice*, by Walter L. Hixson; *When Giants Roamed the Sky*, by Dale Topping.
Tips: "We have mostly an audience of general educated readers, with a more specialized audience of public historians, sociologists and political scientists for the scholarly series."

UNIVERSITY OF ALABAMA PRESS, P.O. Box 870380, Tuscaloosa AL 35487-0380. (205)348-5180. Fax: (205)348-9201. Website: www.uapress.ua.edu. **Acquisitions:** Daniel J.J. Ross, director (history, political science, regional interest); Curtis Clark, assistant director/editor-in-chief (American literature, communications, Jewish studies, public administration); Judith Knight, acquisition editor (archaeology/anthropolgy). Estab. 1945. Publishes nonfiction hardcover and paperbound originals and fiction paperback reprints. **Publishes 45-50 titles/year. Receives 300 submissions/year. 70% of books from first-time authors; 95% from unagented writers. Offers advance.** Publishes book 1 year after acceptance of ms. Responds in 2 weeks to queries. Book catalog free; ms guidelines for #10 SASE.

Nonfiction: Biography, scholarly. Subjects include anthropology/archeology, community, government/politics, history, language/literature, religion, translation. Considers upon merit almost any subject of scholarly interest, but specializes in communications, military history, political science and public administration, literary criticism and biography, history, Jewish studies and archaeology of the Southeastern US. Accepts nonfiction translations. Query with SASE. Reviews artwork/photos as part of ms package.
Fiction: Reprints of works by contemporary Southern writers.
Tips: University of Alabama Press responds to an author within 2 weeks upon receiving the manuscript. If they think it is unsuitable for Alabama's program, they tell the author at once. If the manuscript warrants it, they begin the peer-review process, which may take two to four months to complete. During that process, they keep the author fully informed.

THE UNIVERSITY OF ARKANSAS PRESS, 201 Ozark Ave., Fayetteville AR 72701-1201. (501)575-3246. Fax: (501)575-6044. E-mail: uaprinfo@cavern.uark.edu. Website: www.uapress.com. **Acquisitions:** Lawrence J. Malley, director and editor-in-chief. Estab. 1980. Publishes hardcover and trade paperback originals and reprints. **Publishes 30 titles/year. Receives 1,000 submissions/year. 30% of books from first-time authors; 95% from unagented writers. Pays royalty on net receipts. Offers advance.** Publishes book 1 year after acceptance of ms. Responds in 3 months to proposals. Book catalog on website or for 9×12 SAE with 5 first-class stamps; ms guidelines for #10 SASE.

- The University of Arkansas Press publishes series on Ozark studies, the Civil War in the West, literary studies and poetics, and sport and society.

Nonfiction: Subjects include government/politics, history (Southern), humanities, nature/environment, regional, Arkansas, African-American studies, Middle Eastern studies, poetry/poetics. Accepted mss must be submitted on disk. "Our current needs include African-American studies and history. We won't consider manuscripts for general textbooks, juvenile or anything requiring a specialized or exotic vocabulary." Query with SASE or submit outline, sample chapter(s), résumé.
Recent Title(s): *A Muslim Primer*, by Ira G. Zepp; *All Shook Up: Collected Poems About Elvis*, by Will Clemens; *Leaving Readers Behind: The Age of Corporate Newspapering*, by Gene Roberts.

UNIVERSITY OF IDAHO PRESS, P.O. Box 444416, Moscow ID 83844-4416. (208)885-3300. Fax: (208)885-3301. E-mail: uipress@uidaho.edu. Website: www.uidaho.edu/uipress. **Acquisitions:** Ivar Nelson, director. Estab. 1972. Publishes hardcover and trade paperback originals and reprints. **Publishes 8-10 titles/year. Receives 150-250 queries and 25-50 mss/year. 100% from unagented writers. Pays 10% royalty on net receipts. Offers occasional advance.** Publishes book 1 year after acceptance of ms. Accepts simultaneous submissions. Responds in 6 months to queries. Book catalog and ms guidelines free.

- Major genre published by the Press include the history of Idaho, the northern Rocky Mountains and the region; the natural history of the same area; Native American culture and history; mining history; Hemingway studies; Idaho human rights series; ecological literary criticism, resource and policy studies; and literature of the region and the West.

Nonfiction: Biography, reference, technical, textbook. Subjects include Americana, anthropology/archeology, ethnic, history, language/literature, nature/environment, recreation, regional, women's issues/studies, folklore. "Writers should contact us to discuss projects in advance. Be aware of the constraints of scholarly publishing, and avoid submitting queries and manuscripts in areas in which the press doesn't publish." Query with SASE or submit proposal package including sample chapter(s), contents and vita. Reviews artwork/photos as part of ms package. Send photocopies.
Recent Title(s): *Lewis and Clark's Mountain Wilds*, by Sharon A. Ritter; *Rediscovering Vardis Fisher*, by Joseph M. Flora.

UNIVERSITY OF ILLINOIS PRESS, 1325 S. Oak St., Champaign IL 61820-6903. (217)333-0950. Fax: (217)244-8082. E-mail: uipress@uiuc.edu. Website: www.press.uillinois.edu. **Acquisitions:** Willis Regier, director; Joan Catapano, associate director and editor-in-chief (women's studies, film, African American studies); Judy McCullon, assistant director (music, folklore, dance); Richard Martin, executive editor (philosophy, sociology, political science, law, communications, architecture); Elizabeth Dulany (American religion, anthropology, western history, Native American studies); Laurie Matheson (American history, labor history, American studies); Richard Wentworth (sport history). Estab. 1918. Publishes hardcover and trade paperback originals and reprints. **Publishes 150 titles/year. 50% of books from first-time authors; 95% from unagented writers. Pays 0-10% royalty on net receipts. Offers $1,000-1,500 (rarely) advance.** Publishes book 1 year after acceptance of ms. Responds in 1 month to queries. Book catalog for 9×12 SAE with 2 first-class stamps.

- University of Illinois Press publishes "scholarly books and serious nonfiction" with a wide range of study interests. Currently emphasizing American history, especially immigration, labor, African American, and military; American religion, music, women's studies, and film.

Nonfiction: Biography, reference, scholarly, scholarly. Subjects include Americana, animals, cooking/foods/nutrition, government/politics, history (especially American history), language/literature, military/war, music/dance (especially American music), philosophy, regional, sociology, sports, translation, film/cinema/stage. Always looking for "solid, scholarly books in American history, especially social history; books on American popular music, and books in the broad area of American studies." Query with SASE or submit outline.
Recent Title(s): *Thermin: Ether Music and Espionage*, by Albert Glinsky (nonfiction); *Fanny Herself*, by Edna Ferber (fiction); *Songs from Michael Tree*, by Michael Harper (poetry).
Tips: "Serious scholarly books that are broad enough and well-written enough to appeal to nonspecialists are doing well for us in today's market."

UNIVERSITY OF IOWA PRESS, 119 W. Park Rd., Iowa City IA 52242-1000. (319)335-2000. Fax: (319)335-2055. Website: www.uiowa.edu/~uipress. **Acquisitions:** Holly Carver, director; Prasenjit Gupta, acquisitions editor. Estab. 1969. Publishes hardcover and paperback originals. **Publishes 35 titles/year. Receives 300-400 submissions/year. 30% of books from first-time authors; 95% from unagented writers. Pays 7-10% royalty on net receipts.** Publishes book 1 year after acceptance of ms. Responds in within 6 months to queries. Book catalog online; ms guidelines free.

- "We publish authoritative, original nonfiction that we market mostly by direct mail to groups with special interests in our titles and by advertising in trade and scholarly publications."

Nonfiction: Subjects include anthropology/archeology, creative nonfiction, history (regional), language/literature, nature/environment, American literary studies. Looks for evidence of original research; reliable sources; clarity of organization; complete development of theme with documentation, supportive footnotes and/or bibliography; and a substantive contribution to knowledge in the field treated. Use *Chicago Manual of Style*. Query with SASE or submit outline. Reviews artwork/photos as part of ms package.
Fiction: Currently publishes the Iowa Short Fiction Award selections. Competition guidelines available on website.
Poetry: Currently publishes winners of the Iowa Poetry Prize Competition, Kuhl House Poets, poetry anthologies. Competition guidelines available on website.
Recent Title(s): *Embalming Mom: Essays in Life*, by Janet Burroway.
Tips: "Developing a series in creative nonfiction."

UNIVERSITY OF MAINE PRESS, 126A College Ave., Orono ME 04473. (207)866-0573. Fax: (207)866-2084. E-mail: umpress@umit.maine.edu. Website: umaine.edu/umpress. **Acquisitions:** Editorial Director. Publishes hardcover and trade paperback originals and reprints. **Publishes 4 titles/year. Receives 50 queries and 25 mss/year. 10% of books from first-time authors; 90% from unagented writers.** Publishes book 1 year after acceptance of ms.
Nonfiction: Scholarly. Subjects include history, regional, science. "We are an academic book publisher, interested in scholarly works on regional history, regional life sciences, Franco-American studies. Authors should be able to articulate their ideas on the potential market for their work." Query with SASE.
Recent Title(s): *Maine Amphibians and Reptiles*, by Hunter, Calhoun, et al.

UNIVERSITY OF MISSOURI PRESS, 2910 LeMone Blvd., Columbia MO 65201. (573)882-7641. Fax: (573)884-4498. Website: www.system.missouri.edu/upress. **Acquisitions:** (Mr.) Clair Willcox, acquisitions editor (literary criticism, short fiction, American history); Maurice Manring acquisitions editor (American history, political philosophy, general nonfiction); Beverly Jarrett, director (intellectual history, women's studies, African-American studies). Estab. 1958. Publishes hardcover and paperback originals and paperback reprints. **Publishes 55 titles/year. Receives 500 submissions/year. 40-50% of books from first-time authors; 90% from unagented writers. Pays up to 10% royalty on net receipts.** Publishes book 1 year after acceptance of ms. immediately to queries. Book catalog free.

- University of Missouri Press publishes primarily scholarly nonfiction in the humanities and social sciences and also some short fiction collections. Currently emphasizing American history, political philosophy, literary criticism, African-American studies, women's studies. De-emphasizing art history and journalism.

Nonfiction: Scholarly. Subjects include government/politics, history, regional (Missouri and the Midwest), social sciences, political science, journalism. Consult *Chicago Manual of Style*. No mathematics or hard sciences. Query with SASE or submit outline, sample chapter(s).
Fiction: "Collections of short fiction are considered throughout the year; the press does not publish novels. Queries should include sample story, a table of contents and a brief description of the manuscript that notes its length."
Recent Title(s): *Women Escaping Violence*, by Elaine Lawless; *The Voice of America and the Domestic Propaganda Battles 1945-1953*, by David Krugler.

UNIVERSITY OF NEVADA PRESS, MS 166, Reno NV 89557. (775)784-6573. Fax: (775)784-6200. E-mail: johare @unr.edu. **Acquisitions:** Joanne O'Hare, editor-in-chief (environmental arts and humanities series, western literature series, gambling series, Shepperson series in history and humanities); Sara Velez Mallea, editor (Basque studies). Estab. 1961. Publishes hardcover and paperback originals and reprints. **Publishes 35 titles/year. 20% of books from first-time authors; 99% from unagented writers. Pays 10% royalty on net receipts. Offers advance.** Publishes book 18 months after acceptance of ms. Does not accept simultaneous submissions. Responds in 2 months to queries. Book catalog and ms guidelines free.

- "We are the first university press to sustain a sound series on Basque studies—New World and Old World."

Nonfiction: Biography. Subjects include anthropology/archeology, community, ethnic (studies), history (regional and natural), language/literature, nature/environment (history), regional (history and geography), current affairs, ethno-nationalism, gambling and gaming, Basque studies. No juvenile books. Submit complete ms. *Writer's Market* recommends a query with SASE first. Reviews artwork/photos as part of ms package. Send photocopies.
Recent Title(s): *Futures at Stake: Youth, Gambling and Society*, edited by Howard J. Shaffer, Matthew N. Hall, Joni Vander Bilt, and Elizabeth M. George; *Looking for Steinbeck's Ghost*, by Jackson J. Benson; *Greening the Lyre: Environmental Poetics and Ethics*, by David W. Gilcrest.

UNIVERSITY OF NEW MEXICO PRESS, 1720 Lomas Blvd. NE, Albuquerque NM 87131-1591. (505)277-2346. E-mail: unmpress@unm.edu. **Acquisitions:** Evelyn Schlater, acquisitions (anthropology, archelogy, multicultural); David Holtby, acquisitions editor (history, Latin America); Dawn Hall, managing editor. Estab. 1929. Publishes hardcover originals and trade paperback originals and reprints. **Publishes 70 titles/year. Receives 600 submissions/year. 12% of**

books from first-time authors; 90% from unagented writers. Pays variable royalty. Offers advance. Does not accept simultaneous submissions. *Writer's Market* recommends allowing 2 months for reply to queries. Book catalog free.

O→ "The Press is well known as a publisher in the fields of anthropology, archeology, Latin American studies, photography, architecture and the history and culture of the American West, fiction, some poetry, Chicano/a studies and works by and about American Indians."

Nonfiction: Biography, children's/juvenile, illustrated book, multimedia, scholarly. Subjects include Americana, anthropology/archeology, art/architecture, creative nonfiction, ethnic, gardening, gay/lesbian, government/politics, history, language/literature, memoirs, military/war, multicultural, music/dance, nature/environment, photography, regional, religion, science, spirituality, translation, travel, women's issues/studies, contemporary culture, film/cinema/stage, true crime, New Age, general nonfiction. "No how-to, humor, juvenile, self-help, software, technical or textbooks." Query with SASE. Reviews artwork/photos as part of ms package. Send photocopies.

Recent Title(s): *Creek Indian Medicine Ways*, by David Lewis, Jr. and Ann T. Jordan; *Adventures with Ed: A Portrait of Abbey*, by Jack Loeffler.

THE UNIVERSITY OF NORTH CAROLINA PRESS, P.O. Box 2288, Chapel Hill NC 27515-2288. (919)966-3561. Fax: (919)966-3829. E-mail: uncpress@unc.edu. Website: www.uncpress.unc.edu. **Acquisitions:** Kate Torrey, director (women's history, gender studies); David Perry, editor-in-chief (regional trade, Civil War); Charles Grench, senior editor (American history, European history, law and legal studies, business and economic history, classics, political or social science); Elaine Maisner, editor (Latin American studies, religious studies, anthropology, regional trade, folklore); Sian Hunter, editor (literary studies, American studies, African American studies, social medicine, Appalachian studies, media studies); Mark Simpson-Vos, associate editor (electronic press). Publishes hardcover originals, trade paperback originals and reprints. **Publishes 90 titles/year. Receives 300 queries and 200 mss/year. 50% of books from first-time authors; 98% from unagented writers. Pays 5-15% royalty on wholesale price. Offers $1,000-10,000 advance.** Publishes book 1 year after acceptance of ms. Does not accept simultaneous submissions. Responds in 3-4 weeks to queries; 3-4 weeks to proposals; 2 weeks to mss. Book catalog and ms guidelines free or on website.

O→ "UNC Press publishes nonfiction books for academic and general audiences. We have a special interest in trade and scholarly titles about our region. We do not, however, publish original fiction, drama, or poetry, memoirs of living persons, or festshriften.

Nonfiction: Biography, cookbook, multimedia (CD-ROM). Subjects include Americana, anthropology/archeology, art/architecture, cooking/foods/nutrition, gardening, government/politics, health/medicine, history, language/literature, military/war, multicultural, music/dance, nature/environment, philosophy, photography, regional, religion, translation, women's issues/studies, African American studies, American studies, cultural studies, Latin American studies, media studies, gender studies, social medicine, Appalachian studies. Submit proposal package including outline, c.v., cover letter, abstract, and table of contenprojects within the South and by non-university authors."

Nonfiction: Scholarly, American studies only. Subjects include Americana, anthropology/archeology (historical), art/architecture (vernacular), ethnic, history, language/literature, regional, religion (history sociology, anthropology, biography only), women's issues/studies, African-American studies, Appalachian studies, folklore/folklife, material culture. Prefers "scholarly treatment and a readable style. Authors usually have Ph.D.s." Submissions in other fields, and submissions of poetry, textbooks, plays and translations are not invited. Submit outline, 2 sample chapter(s), author bio. Reviews artwork/photos as part of ms package.

Fiction: Query with SASE or submit synopsis, author bio.

Recent Title(s): *The Marriage of Anna Maye Potts*, by DeWitt Henry (fiction).

Tips: "Our market is in several groups: scholars; educated readers with special interests in given scholarly subjects; and the general educated public interested in Tennessee, Appalachia and the South. Not all our books appeal to all these groups, of course, but any given book must appeal to at least one of them."

UNIVERSITY OF NORTH TEXAS PRESS, P.O. Box 311336, Denton TX 76203-1336. Fax: (940)565-4590. E-mail: rchrisman@unt.edu or kdevinney@unt.edu. Website: www.unt.edu/untpress. Director: Ronald Chrisman. **Acquisitions:** Karen DeVinney, managing editor. Estab. 1987. Publishes hardcover and trade paperback originals and reprints. **Publishes 14-16 titles/year. Receives 500 queries/year. 95% from unagented writers. Pays 7-10% royalty on net receipts.** Publishes book 1-2 years after acceptance of ms. Does not accept simultaneous submissions. Responds in 3 months to queries. Book catalog for 8½×11 SASE.

O→ We are dedicated to producing the highest quality scholarly, academic and general interest books. We are committed to serving all peoples by publishing stories of their cultures and experiences that have been overlooked. Currently emphasizing military history, Texas history and Texas literature, Mexican-American studies.

Nonfiction: Subjects include agriculture/horticulture, Americana, ethnic, government/politics, history, language/literature, military/war, nature/environment, regional, women's issues/studies. Query with SASE. Reviews artwork/photos as part of ms package. Send photocopies.

Poetry: The only poetry we publish is the winner of the Vassar Miller Prize in Poetry, an annual, national competition with a $1,000 prize and publication of the winning manuscript each fall. Query.

Recent Title(s): *The Best of Helen Corbitt's Kitchens* (cookbook); *Combat Chaplain* (military).

Tips: "We publish series called War and the Southwest; Texas Folklore Society Publications; the Western Life Series; Literary Biographies of Texas Writers; practical guide series; Al-Filo: Mexican-American studies series."

UNIVERSITY OF PENNSYLVANIA PRESS, 4200 Pine St., Philadelphia PA 19104-4011. (215)898-6261. Fax: (215)898-0404. Website: www.upenn.edu/pennpress. Director: Eric Halpern. **Acquisitions:** Jerome Singerman, humanities editor; Peter Agree, social sciences editor; Jo Joslyn, art and architecture editor; Robert Lockhart, history editor. Estab. 1890. Publishes hardcover and paperback originals and reprints. **Publishes 75 titles/year. Receives 1,000 submissions/year. 20-50% of books from first-time authors; 95% from unagented writers. Royalty determined on book-by-book basis. Offers advance.** Publishes book 10 months after delivery of ms after acceptance of ms. Does not accept simultaneous submissions. Responds in 3 months to queries. Book catalog online.

Nonfiction: "Serious books that serve the scholar and the professional, student and general reader." Scholarly. Subjects include Americana, anthropology/archeology, art/architecture, business/economics, history (American, art), language/literature, sociology, literary criticism, cultural studies, ancient studies, medieval studies. Follow the *Chicago Manual of Style*. No unsolicited mss. Query with SASE or submit outline, résumé. Reviews artwork/photos as part of ms package. Send photocopies.

UNIVERSITY OF SCRANTON PRESS, University of Scranton, Linden and Monroe, Scranton PA 18510-4660. (570)941-4228. Fax: (570)941-4309. E-mail: richard.rousseau@scranton.edu. Website: www.scrantonpress.com. **Acquisitions:** Richard Rousseau, director. Estab. 1981. Publishes paperback originals. **Publishes 5 titles/year. Receives 200 queries and 45 mss/year. 60% of books from first-time authors; 100% from unagented writers. Pays 10% royalty.** Publishes book within 1 year after acceptance of ms. Does not accept simultaneous submissions. Book catalog and ms guidelines free.

Imprints: Ridge Row Press

O━ The University of Scranton Press, a member of the Association of Jesuit University Presses, publishes primarily scholarly monographs in theology, philosophy, and the culture and history of northeast Pennsylvania.

Nonfiction: Looking for clear editorial focus: theology/religious studies; philosophy/philosophy of religion; scholarly treatments; the culture of northeast Pennsylvania. Scholarly monographs. Subjects include art/architecture, language/literature, philosophy, regional, religion, sociology. Query with SASE or submit outline, 2 sample chapter(s).

Poetry: Only poetry related to northeast Pennsylvania.

Recent Title(s): *The Illustrated Spiritual Exercises*, edited by Jerome Nadal; *The Rise and Fall of Seranton Municipal Airport*, by William Hallstead, III; *One in a Million*, by Mary G. Clark, RN, PA-C.

UNIVERSITY OF SOUTH CAROLINA PRESS, 937 Assembly St., Carolina Plaza, 8th Floor, Columbia SC 29208. (803)777-5243. Fax: (803)777-0160. Website: www.sc.edu/uscpress. **Acquisitions:** Linda Fogle, assistant director (trade books); Barry Blose, acquisitions editor (literature, religious studies, rhetoric, communication, social work); Alexander Moore, acquisitions editor (history, regional studies). Estab. 1944. Publishes hardcover originals, trade paperback originals and reprints. **Publishes 50-55 titles/year. Receives 1,000 queries and 250 mss/year. 30% of books from first-time authors; 95% from unagented writers.** Publishes book 12-15 months after acceptance of ms. Accepts simultaneous submissions. Responds in 3 months to mss. Book catalog and ms guidelines free.

O━ "We focus on scholarly monographs and regional trade books of lasting merit."

Nonfiction: Biography, illustrated book, monograph. Subjects include art/architecture, history (American, Civil War, culinary, maritime, women's), language/literature, regional, religion, rhetoric, communication. "Do not submit entire unsolicited manuscripts or projects with limited scholarly value." Query with SASE or submit proposal package and outline and 1 sample chapter and résumé with SASE. Reviews artwork/photos as part of ms package. Send photocopies.

Recent Title(s): *Charleston in My Time: The Paintings of West Fraser*, by West Fraser; *The Jewish Confederates*, by Robert N. Rosen; *A Memory of Trains: The Boll Weevil and Others*, by Louis D. Rubin, Jr.

THE UNIVERSITY OF TENNESSEE PRESS, 110 Conference Center, Knoxville TN 37996-4108. (865)974-3321. Fax: (865)974-3724. E-mail: custserv@utpress.org. Website: www.utpress.org. **Acquisitions:** Joyce Harrison, acquisitions editor (scholarly books); Jennifer Siler, director (regional trades, fiction). Estab. 1940. **Publishes 30 titles/year. Receives 450 submissions/year. 35% of books from first-time authors; 99% from unagented writers. Pays negotiable royalty on net receipts.** Does not accept simultaneous submissions. Book catalog for 12x16 SAE with 2 first-class stamps; ms guidelines for #10 SASE.

O━ "Our mission is to stimulate scientific and scholarly research in all fields; to channel such studies, either in scholarly or popular form, to a larger number of people; and to extend the regional leadership of the University of Tennessee by stimulating research projects within the South and by non-university authors."

Nonfiction: Scholarly, American studies only. Subjects include Americana, anthropology/archeology (historical), art/architecture (vernacular), ethnic, history, language/literature, regional, religion (history sociology, anthropology, biography only), women's issues/studies, African-American studies, Appalachian studies, folklore/folklife, material culture. Prefers "scholarly treatment and a readable style. Authors usually have Ph.D.s." Submissions in other fields, and submissions of poetry, textbooks, plays and translations are not invited. Submit outline, 2 sample chapter(s), author bio. Reviews artwork/photos as part of ms package.

Fiction: Query with SASE or submit synopsis, author bio.

Recent Title(s): *The Marriage of Anna Maye Potts*, by DeWitt Henry (fiction).

Tips: "Our market is in several groups: scholars; educated readers with special interests in given scholarly subjects; and the general educated public interested in Tennessee, Appalachia and the South. Not all our books appeal to all these groups, of course, but any given book must appeal to at least one of them."

UNIVERSITY OF TEXAS PRESS, P.O. Box 7819, Austin TX 78713-7819. (512)471-7233. Fax: (512)252-7178. E-mail: utpress@uts.cc.utexas.edu. Website: www.utexas.edu/utpress/. **Acquisitions:** Theresa May, assistant director/editor-in-chief (social sciences, Latin American studies); James Burr, sponsorings editor (humanities, classics); William Bishel (sciences; Texas history). Estab. 1952. **Publishes 90 titles/year. Receives 1,000 submissions/year. 50% of books from first-time authors; 99% from unagented writers. Pays royalty on net receipts. Offers occasional advance.** Publishes book 18-24 months after acceptance of ms. Does not accept simultaneous submissions. Responds in 3 months to queries. Book catalog and ms guidelines free.

O→ "In addition to publishing the results of advanced research for scholars worldwide, UT Press has a special obligation to the people of its state to publish authoritative books on Texas. We do not publish fiction or poetry, except for some Latin American and Middle Eastern literature in translation."

Nonfiction: Biography, scholarly. Subjects include anthropology/archeology, art/architecture, ethnic, film/cinema/stage, history, language/literature, nature/environment, regional, science, translation, women's issues/studies, natural history; American, Latin American, Native American, Latino and Middle Eastern studies; classics and the ancient world, film, contemporary regional architecture, geography, ornithology, biology. Also uses specialty titles related to Texas and the Southwest, national trade titles and regional trade titles. Query with SASE or submit outline, 2 sample chapter(s). Reviews artwork/photos as part of ms package.

Fiction: Latin American and Middle Eastern translation. No poetry.

Recent Title(s): *Animals and Plants of the Ancient Maya*, by Victoria Schlesinger and Ralph W. Yarborough; *The People's Senator*, by Patrick Cox; *Small Deaths*, by Kate Breakey.

Tips: "It's difficult to make a manuscript over 400 double-spaced pages into a feasible book. Authors should take special care to edit out extraneous material. We look for sharply focused, in-depth treatments of important topics."

UNIVERSITY PRESS OF COLORADO, 5589 Arapahoe, Suite 206C, Boulder CO 80303. (720)406-8849. Fax: (720)406-3443. Director: Darrin Pratt. **Acquisitions:** Kerry Callahan, editor. Estab. 1965. Publishes hardcover and paperback originals. **Publishes 30-40 titles/year. Receives 1,000 submissions/year. 50% of books from first-time authors; 95% from unagented writers. Pays 5-15% royalty on net receipts. Offers advance.** Publishes book within 2 years after acceptance of ms. Accepts simultaneous submissions. Responds in 6 months to queries. Book catalog free.

O→ "We are a university press that publishes scholarly nonfiction in the disciplines of the American West, Native American studies, archeology, environmental studies and regional interest titles." Currently de-emphasizing fiction, poetry, biography.

Nonfiction: Scholarly. Subjects include nature/environment, regional. Length: 250-500 pages. Query with SASE. Reviews artwork/photos as part of ms package.

Recent Title(s): *Prayer on Top of the Earth*, by Kay Parker Schweinfurth; *Ancient Tollan*, by Alba Guadalupe Mastache, Robert Cobean and Dan Healan.

Tips: "We have series on the Women's West and on Mesoamerican worlds."

UNIVERSITY PRESS OF KANSAS, 2501 W. 15th St., Lawrence KS 66049-3905. (785)864-4154. Fax: (785)864-4586. E-mail: mail@newpress.upress.ukans.edu. Website: www.kansaspress.ku.edu. **Acquisitions:** Michael J. Briggs, editor-in-chief (military history, political science, law); Nancy Scott Jackson, acquisitions editor (western history, American studies, environmental studies, women's studies, philosophy); Fred M. Woodward, director, (political science, presidency, regional). Estab. 1946. Publishes hardcover originals, trade paperback originals and reprints. **Publishes 50 titles/year. Receives 600 queries/year. 20% of books from first-time authors; 98% from unagented writers. Pays 5-15% royalty on net receipts. Offers selective advance.** Publishes book 10 months after acceptance of ms. Does not accept simultaneous submissions. Responds in 1 month to proposals. Book catalog and ms guidelines free.

O→ The University Press of Kansas publishes scholarly books that advance knowledge and regional books that contribute to the understanding of Kansas, the Great Plains and the Midwest. Currently emphasizing military history.

Nonfiction: Biography, scholarly. Subjects include Americana, anthropology/archeology, government/politics, history, military/war, nature/environment, philosophy, regional, sociology, women's issues/studies. "We are looking for books on topics of wide interest based on solid scholarship and written for both specialists and informed general readers. Do not send unsolicited complete manuscripts." Submit outline, sample chapter(s), cover letter, cv, prospectus. Reviews artwork/photos as part of ms package. Send photocopies.

Recent Title(s): *States' Rights and the Union: Imperium in Imperio*, by Forrest McDonald.

UNIVERSITY PRESS OF KENTUCKY, 663 S. Limestone, Lexington KY 40508-4008. (859)257-2951. Fax: (859)323-1873. Website: www.kentuckypress.com. **Acquisitions:** Stephen Wrinn, director and editor. Estab. 1943. Publishes hardcover and paperback originals and reprints. **Publishes 60 titles/year. Royalty varies.** Publishes book 1 year after acceptance of ms. Responds in 2 months to queries. Book catalog free.

O→ "We are a scholarly publisher, publishing chiefly for an academic and professional audience, as well as books about Kentucky, the upper South, Appalachia, and the Ohio Valley."

Nonfiction: Biography, reference, scholarly (monographs). Subjects include Americana, ethnic, history (American), language/literature, military/war (history), regional, women's issues/studies, political science, film studies, American and African-American studies, folklore, Kentuckiana and regional books, Appalachian studies. "No textbooks, genealogical material, lightweight popular treatments, how-to books or books unrelated to our major areas of interest. The Press does not consider original works of fiction or poetry." Query with SASE.

UNIVERSITY PRESS OF MISSISSIPPI, 3825 Ridgewood Rd., Jackson MS 39211-6492. (601)432-6205. Fax: (601)432-6217. E-mail: press@ihl.state.ms.us. **Acquisitions:** Craig Gill, editor-in-chief (regional studies, art, folklore, fiction, memoirs); Seetha Srinivasan, director (African-American studies, popular culture, literature). Estab. 1970. Publishes hardcover and paperback originals and reprints. **Publishes 60 titles/year. Receives 750 submissions/year. 20% of books from first-time authors; 90% from unagented writers. Competitive royalties and terms. Offers advance.** Publishes book 1 year after acceptance of ms. Does not accept simultaneous submissions. Responds in 3 months to queries. Book catalog for 9×12 SAE with 3 first-class stamps.

Imprints: Muscadine Books (regional trade), Banner Books (literary reprints).

- "University Press of Mississippi publishes scholarly and trade titles, as well as special series, including: American Made Music; Conversations with Public Intellectuals; Interviews with filmmakers; Faulkner and Yoknapatawpha; Folklife in the South; Literary Conversations; Studies in Popular Culture; Understanding Health and Sickness; Writers and Their Work."

Nonfiction: Biography, scholarly. Subjects include Americana, art/architecture, ethnic (minority studies), government/politics, health/medicine, history, language/literature, music/dance, photography, regional (Southern), folklife, literary criticism, popular culture with scholarly emphasis, literary studies. "We prefer a proposal that describes the significance of the work and a chapter outline." Submit outline, sample chapter(s), cv.

Fiction: Commissioned trade editions by prominent writers.

Recent Title(s): *German Boy: A Refugee's Story*, by Wolfgang W.E. Samuel; *Kangaroo Hollow*, by Thomas Hal Phillips.

UPSTART BOOKS, (formerly Highsmith Press), P.O. Box 800, Fort Atkinson WI 53538-0800. (920)563-9571. Fax: (920)563-4801. E-mail: hpress@highsmith.com. Website: www.highsmith.com. **Acquisitions:** Matt Mulder, director of publications. Estab. 1990. Publishes hardcover and paperback originals. **Publishes 20 titles/year. Receives 500-600 queries and 400-500 mss/year. 30% of books from first-time authors; 100% from unagented writers. Pays 10-12% royalty on net receipts. Offers $250-1,000 advance.** Publishes book 6 months after acceptance of ms. Accepts simultaneous submissions. Responds in 1 month to queries; 2 months to proposals. Book catalog and ms guidelines available via website.

Imprints: Alleyside Press, Upstart Books (creative supplemental reading, library and critical thinking skills materials designed to expand the learning environment).

- Upstart Books publishes educational resources to meet the practical needs of librarians, educators, readers, library users, media specialists, schools and related institutions, and to help them fulfill their valuable functions.

Nonfiction: Children's/juvenile, reference. Subjects include education, language/literature, multicultural. "We are primarily interested in manuscripts that stimulate or strengthen reading, library and information-seeking skills and foster critical thinking." Query with outline and 1-2 sample chapters. Reviews artwork/photos as part of ms package. Send transparencies.

Fiction: "Our current emphasis is on storytelling collections for preschool-grade 6. We prefer stories that can be easily used by teachers and children's librarians, multicultural topics, and manuscripts that feature fold and cut, flannelboard, tangram, or similar simple patterns that can be reproduced. No longer accepting children's picture book mss.

Recent Title(s): *Finger Tales*, by Joan Hilyer Phelps; *Characters with Character*, by Diane Findlay.

THE URBAN LAND INSTITUTE, 1025 Thomas Jefferson St. NW, Washington DC 20007-5201. (202)624-7000. Fax: (202)624-7140. E-mail: rlevit@uli.org. Website: www.uli.org. **Acquisitions:** Rachelle Levitt, senior vice president/publisher. Estab. 1936. Publishes hardcover and trade paperback originals. **Publishes 15-20 titles/year. Receives 20 submissions/year. 2% of books from first-time authors; 100% from unagented writers. Pays 10% royalty on gross sales. Offers $1,500-2,000 advance.** Publishes book 6 months after acceptance of ms. Does not accept simultaneous submissions. Book catalog and ms. guidelines via website or 9×12 SAE.

- The Urban Land Institute publishes technical books on real estate development and land planning.

Nonfiction: Technical. Subjects include money/finance. "The majority of manuscripts are created inhouse by research staff. We acquire two or three outside authors to fill schedule and subject areas where our list has gaps. We are not interested in real estate sales, brokerages, appraisal, making money in real estate, opinion, personal point of view, or mauscripts negative toward growth and development." Query with SASE. Reviews artwork/photos as part of ms package.

Recent Title(s): *Developing Sports, Convention, and Performing Arts Centers*; *Transforming Suburban Business Districts*.

UTAH STATE UNIVERSITY PRESS, 7800 Old Main Hill, Logan UT 84322-7800. (435)797-1362. Fax: (435)797-0313. Website: www.usu.edu/usupress. **Acquisitions:** Michael Spooner, director (composition, poetry); John Alley, editor (history, folklore, fiction). Estab. 1972. Publishes hardcover and trade paperback originals and reprints. **Publishes 18 titles/year. Receives 250 submissions/year. 8% of books from first-time authors. Pays royalty on net receipts.** Publishes book 18 months after acceptance of ms. Does not accept simultaneous submissions. Responds in 1 month to queries. Book catalog free; ms guidelines online.

- Utah State University Press publishes scholarly works in the academic areas noted below. Currently interested in book-length scholarly manuscripts dealing with folklore studies, composition studies, Native American studies and history.

Nonfiction: Biography, reference, scholarly, textbook. Subjects include history (of the West), regional, folklore, the West, Native American studies, studies in composition and rhetoric. Query with SASE. Reviews artwork/photos as part of ms package. Send photocopies.

Recent Title(s): *Brigham Young's Homes*, edited by Colleen Whitley; *Disaster at the Colorado*, by Charles W. Baley; *Great Salt Lake*, edited by Gary Topping.
Tips: Utah State University Press also sponsors the annual May Swenson Poetry Award.

VAN DER PLAS PUBLICATIONS, 1282 Seventh Ave., San Francisco CA 94122-2526. (415)665-8214. Fax: (415)753-8572. **Acquisitions:** Rob van der Plas, publisher/editor. Estab. 1997. Publishes hardcover and trade paperback originals. **Publishes 6 titles/year. Receives 15 submissions/year. 10% of books from first-time authors; 100% from unagented writers. Pays 12% royalty on net receipts.** Publishes book an average of 1 year after acceptance of ms. Accepts simultaneous submissions. Responds in 3 months to queries. Book catalog and ms guidelines for #10 SASE.
Nonfiction: How-to, technical. Subjects include recreation, sports, travel. Submit complete ms. Reviews artwork/photos as part of ms package.
Recent Title(s): *Lance Armstrong's Comeback from Cancer*; *Buying a Manufactured Home.*
Tips: "Writers have a good chance selling us books with better and more illustrations and a systematic treatment of the subject. First check what is on the market and ask yourself whether you are writing something that is not yet available and wanted."

VANDAMERE PRESS, AB Associates International, Inc., P.O. Box 17446, Clearwater FL 33762. (727)556-0950. Fax: (727)556-2560. **Acquisitions:** Jerry Frank, senior acquistions editor. Estab. 1984. Publishes hardcover and trade paperback originals and reprints. **Publishes 8-15 titles/year. Receives 750 queries and 2,000 mss/year. 25% of books from first-time authors; 90% from unagented writers. Pays royalty. on revenues generated. Offers advance.** Publishes book 1-3 years after acceptance of ms. Accepts simultaneous submissions. Responds in 6 months to queries.

- Vandamere publishes high-quality work with solid, well-documented research and minimum author/political bias.

Nonfiction: Biography, coffee table book, illustrated book, reference. Subjects include Americana, education, health/medicine, history, military/war, photography, regional (Washington D.C./Mid-Atlantic), women's issues/studies, disability/healthcare issues. No New Age. Submit outline, 2-3 sample chapter(s). Send photocopies.
Fiction: Adventure, erotica, humor, mystery, suspense. Submit 5-10 sample chapter(s), synopsis.
Recent Title(s): *Nothing to Fear*, by Hugh Gregory Gallagher (nonfiction); *Cry Me a River*, by Patricia Hagan (fiction).
Tips: "Authors who can provide endorsements from significant published writers, celebrities, etc., will *always* be given serious consideration. Clean, easy-to-read, *dark* copy is essential. Patience in waiting for replies is essential. All unsolicited work is looked at, but at certain times of the year our review schedule will stop. No response without SASE."

VANDERBILT UNIVERSITY PRESS, VU Station B 351813, Nashville TN 37235. (615)322-3585. Fax: (615)343-8823. E-mail: vupress@vanderbilt.edu. Website: www.vanderbilt.edu/vupress. **Acquisitions:** Michael Ames, director. Publishes hardcover originals and trade paperback originals and reprints. **Publishes 20-25 titles/year. Receives 500 queries/year. 25% of books from first-time authors; 90% from unagented writers. Pays 8% royalty on net receipts. Offers rare advance.** Publishes book 10 months after acceptance of ms. Accepts simultaneous submissions. Responds in 2 weeks to proposals. Book catalog free.

- Also distributes for and co-publishes with Country Music Foundation.
- "Vanderbilt University Press publishes books on health care, social sciences, education and regional studies, for both academic and general audiences that are intellectually significant, socially relevant and of practical importance."

Nonfiction: Biography, scholarly, textbook. Subjects include Americana, anthropology/archeology, education, ethnic, government/politics, health/medicine, history, language/literature, multicultural, music/dance, nature/environment, philosophy, women's issues/studies. Submit prospectus, sample chapter, cv. Reviews artwork/photos as part of ms package. Send photocopies.
Recent Title(s): *A Good-Natured Riot: The Birth of the Grand Ole Opry*, by Charles K. Wolfe; *Invisible Work: Borges and Translation*, by Efrain Kristal; *Smoke in Their Eyes: Lessons Learned in Movement Leadership from the Tobacco Wars*, by Michael Pertschuk.
Tips: "Our audience consists of scholars and educated general readers."

VENTURE PUBLISHING, INC., 1999 Cato Ave., State College PA 16801. (814)234-4561. Fax: (814)234-1561. E-mail: vpublish@venturepublish.com. Website: www.venturepublish.com. **Acquisitions:** Geof Godbey, editor. Estab. 1979. Publishes hardcover and paperback originals and reprints. **Publishes 10-12 titles/year. Receives 50 queries and 20 mss/year. 40% of books from first-time authors; 100% from unagented writers. Pays royalty on wholesale price. Offers advance.** Publishes book 9 months after acceptance of ms. Does not accept simultaneous submissions. Responds in 1 month to queries; 2 months to proposals; 2 months to mss. Book catalog and ms guidelines for SASE or online.

- Venture Publishing produces quality educational publications, also workbooks for professionals, educators, and students in the fields of recreation, parks, leisure studies, therapeutic recreation and long term care.

Nonfiction: Scholarly (college academic), textbook, professional. Subjects include nature/environment (outdoor recreation management and leadership texts), recreation, sociology (leisure studies), long-term care nursing homes, therapeutic recreation. "Textbooks and books for recreation activity leaders high priority." Submit outline, 1 sample chapter(s).
Recent Title(s): *Adventure Programming*, edited by John Miles and Simon Priest; *Leisure in Your Life*, by Geof Godbey.

VGM CAREER BOOKS, McGraw-Hill Companies, Prudential Plaza, 130 E. Randolph St., Suite 900, Chicago IL 60601. Fax: (312)233-7570. **Acquisitions:** Denise Betts. Estab. 1963. Publishes paperback originals. **Publishes 35 titles/year. Receives 50-100 submissions/year. 15% of books from first-time authors; 95% from unagented writers. Pays royalty or makes outright purchase. Offers $1,000-4,000 advance.** Publishes book 1 year after acceptance of ms. Accepts simultaneous submissions. Responds in 2 months to queries. Book catalog and ms guidelines for 9×12 SAE with 5 first-class stamps.

O→ VGM publishes career-focused titles for job seekers, career planners, job changers, students and adults in education and trade markets.

Nonfiction: General trade. Subjects include business/economics, health/medicine, nature/environment. Query with SASE or submit outline, sample chapter(s).

Recent Title(s): *The Guide to Internet Job Searching 2002-2003 edition*, by Frances Roehm and Margaret Dikel.

[A] **VIKING**, Penguin Putnam Inc., 375 Hudson St., New York NY 10014. (212)366-2000. Publisher: Clare Ferraro. Publishes hardcover. **Pays royalty. Offers advance.** Publishes book 12-18 months after acceptance of ms. Accepts simultaneous submissions. Responds in 6 months to queries.

O→ Viking publishes a mix of literary and popular fiction and nonfiction.

Nonfiction: Biography. Subjects include business/economics, child guidance/parenting, cooking/foods/nutrition, health/medicine, history, language/literature, music/dance, philosophy, women's issues/studies. *Agented submissions only.*

Fiction: Literary, mainstream/contemporary, mystery, suspense. *Agented submissions only.*

Recent Title(s): *When Character Was King*, by Peggy Noonan; *Report from Ground Zero*, by Dennis Smith; *Lake Wabegon Summer 1956*, by Garrison Keillor.

VIKING CHILDREN'S BOOKS, Penguin Putnam Inc., 345 Hudson St., New York NY 10014. (212)366-2000. Regina Hayes, president/publisher. **Acquisitions:** Melanie Cecka, Elizabeth Law. Publishes hardcover originals. **Publishes 60 titles/year. Receives 7,500 queries/year. 25% of books from first-time authors; 50% from unagented writers. Pays 10% royalty on retail price. Offers negotiable advance.** Publishes book 1 year after acceptance of ms. Does not accept unsolicited submissions.

O→ Viking Children's Books publishes high-quality trade books for children including fiction, nonfiction, picture books and novelty books for pre-schoolers through young adults.

Nonfiction: Children's/juvenile. Query with SASE or submit outline, 3 sample chapter(s), SASE.

Fiction: Juvenile, picture books, young adult. Submit complete ms. for novels, picture books, chapter books with SASE.

Recent Title(s): *Baloney (Henry P.)*, by Jon Scieszka; *This Land Was Made for You and Me*, by Elizabeth Partridge; *This Lullaby*, by Sarah Dessen.

VIKING STUDIO, Penguin Putnam, Inc., 375 Hudson St., New York NY 10014. (212)366-2000. Fax: (212)366-2011. Website: www.penguinputnam.com. **Acquisitions:** Adrian Zackheil. Publishes hardcover originals. **Publishes 35-40 titles/year. Pays royalty. Offers advance.** Responds in 2 months to queries.

O→ Viking publishes high production value, quality designed books on subjects of mainstream interest that allow a compelling visual treatment. Currently emphasizing reference, history, religion.

Nonfiction: Subjects include Americana, art/architecture, contemporary culture, fashion/beauty, hobbies, New Age (and metaphysics), philosophy, photography. Query with SASE. Reviews artwork/photos as part of ms package. Send photocopies.

Recent Title(s): *My Passage from India*; *Above Hollowed Ground.*

[A] **VILLARD BOOKS**, Random House, 299 Park Ave., New York NY 10171-0002. (212)572-2600. Website: www.atrandom.com. Publisher: Ann Godoff. Estab. 1983. Publishes hardcover and trade paperback originals. **Publishes 55-60 titles/year. 5% from unagented writers. Pays negotiable royalty. Offers negotiable advance.** Accepts simultaneous submissions.

O→ "Villard Books is the publisher of savvy and sometimes quirky bestseller hardcovers and trade paperbacks."

Nonfiction: Subjects include general nonfiction, commercial nonfiction. *Agented submissions only.*

Fiction: Commercial fiction. *Agented submissions only.*

Recent Title(s): *Never Die Easy*, by Walter Payton; *The Truth Is*, by Melissa Etheridge.

VINTAGE IMAGES, P.O. Box 160, Spencerville MD 20868. (301)879-6522. Fax: (301)879-6524. E-mail: vimages@erols.com. Website: www.vintageimages.com. **Acquisitions:** Brian Smolens, president. Publishes trade paperback originals. **Publishes 8 titles/year. Pays 4-8% royalty on wholesale price.** Publishes book 5 months after acceptance of ms. Does not accept simultaneous submissions. Ms guidelines online.

O→ "We publish photographic poster books and need writers who are exceptionally creative. This is truly a creative writing exercise."

Nonfiction: Gift book, humor, illustrated book, poster books. Subjects include Americana, photography.

Recent Title(s): *Fishing Tales: A Vintage Images Poster Book.*

Tips: "We are interested in creative writers who can weave a humorous/dramatic theme around 36 vintage photos (early 1900s)."

VISIONS COMMUNICATIONS, 205 E. 10th St., 2D, New York NY 10003. (212)529-4029. Fax: (212)529-4029. E-mail: bayeun@aol.com. **Acquisitions:** Beth Bay. Estab. 1994. Visions specializes in technical and reference books. Publishes harcover originals and trade paperback originals and reprints. **Publishes 5 titles/year. Pays 5-20% royalty on retail price.** Publishes book 6 months after acceptance of ms. Responds in 1 month to queries; 3 months to mss. Ms guidelines free.

Nonfiction: Children's/juvenile, how-to, reference, self-help, technical, textbook. Subjects include art/architecture, business/economics, health/medicine, psychology, religion, science, women's issues/studies, scholarly. Submit proposal package including outline, 3 sample chapter(s).

Recent Title(s): *Illumination Engineering*, by Joe Murdoch.

VISTA PUBLISHING, INC., 422 Morris Ave., Suite #1, Long Branch NJ 07740. (732)229-6500. Fax: (732)229-9647. E-mail: czagury@vistapubl.com. Website: www.vistapubl.com. **Acquisitions:** Carolyn Zagury, president. Estab. 1991. Publishes trade paperback originals. **Publishes 12 titles/year. Receives 200 queries and 125 mss/year. 75% of books from first-time authors; 100% from unagented writers. Pays 50% royalty on wholesale price or retail price, conditions apply.** Publishes book 2-3 years after acceptance of ms. Accepts simultaneous submissions. Responds in 3 months to mss. Book catalog and ms guidelines free.

O→ Vista publishes books by nurses and allied health professionals. Currently emphasizing clinical topics. De-emphasizing fiction.

Nonfiction: Nursing, career related. Subjects include business/economics, child guidance/parenting, creative nonfiction, health/medicine, women's issues/studies (specific to nursing and allied health professionals). Submit complete ms with SASE. Reviews artwork/photos as part of ms package. Send photocopies.

Fiction: "We specialize in nurse and allied health professional authors." Horror, multicultural, mystery, poetry, short story collections, nursing, medical. Submit complete ms with SASE.

Poetry: Nursing related. Submit complete ms.

Recent Title(s): *Basics of Computers and Nursing Informatics*, by Donna Gloe, RN, Ed.D. (nonfiction); *Error in Judgement*, by Dr. Gary Birken (fiction).

Tips: "It's always worth the effort to submit your manuscript."

[N] **VITAL HEALTH PUBLISHING**, P.O. Box 544, Bloomingdale IL 60185. (630)876-0426. Fax: (630)876-0426. E-mail: vitalhealth@compuserve.com. Website: www.vitalhealth.net. **Acquisitions:** David Richard, publishing director (health, nutrition, ecology, creativity). Estab. 1997. Publishes trade paperback originals and reprints. **Publishes 10 titles/year; imprint publishes 5-6 titles/year. Receives 25 queries and 15 mss/year. 25% of books from first-time authors; 90% from unagented writers. Pays 15-20% royalty on wholesale price for top authors; pays in copies 30-40% of the time. Offers $1,000-5,000 advance.** Publishes book 6-8 months after acceptance of ms. Does not accept simultaneous submissions. Responds in 1 month to queries; 1-2 months to proposals; 1-3 months to mss. Book catalog online; Discuss with editor.

Imprints: Enhancement Books.

O→ Nonfiction books for a health-conscious, well-educated, creative audience.

Nonfiction: Audiocassettes, children's/juvenile, cookbook, self-help. Subjects include health/medicine, music/dance, New Age, philosophy, spirituality. "All titles must be related to health. Because we have a holistic philosophy, this includes nutrition, ecology, creativity and spirituality. Submit proposal package including outline, 1 sample chapter(s), cover letter describing the project. Reviews artwork/photos as part of ms package. Send photocopies or color prints.

Poetry: "Minimal poetry published and strictly related to health." Query.

Recent Title(s): *Trace Your Genes to Health*, by Chris Reading, M.D. (nonfiction); *Our Children's Health*, by Bonnie Minsky, L.C.N. and Lisa Holk, N.D. (nonfiction); *On Wings of Spirit: The American Physician's Poetry Association Anthology*, by John Graham-Pole (poetry).

Tips: "View our website to compare our titles to your manuscript."

VOLCANO PRESS, INC., P.O. Box 270, Volcano CA 95689-0270. (209)296-4991. Fax: (209)296-4995. E-mail: ruth@volcanopress.com. Website: www.volcanopress.com. **Acquisitions:** Ruth Gottstein, publisher. Estab. 1969. Publishes trade paperback originals. **Publishes 4-6 titles/year. Pays royalty on net receipts. Offers $500-1,000 advance.** Does not accept simultaneous submissions. Responds in 1 month to queries. Book catalog free.

O→ "We believe that the books we are producing today are of even greater value than the gold of yesteryear and that the sybolism of the term 'Mother Lode' is still relevant to our work."

Nonfiction: Self-help. Subjects include health/medicine, multicultural, women's issues/studies. "We publish women's health and social issues, particularly in the field of domestic violence." Query with SASE or submit outline. No e-mail or fax submissions.

Recent Title(s): *Ghost Towns of Amador*, by Andrews; *Journal and Letters from the Mines*, John Doble.

Tips: "Look at our titles on the Web or in our catalog, and submit materials consistent with what we already publish."

WALKER AND CO., Walker Publishing Co., 435 Hudson St., New York NY 10014. Fax: (212)727-0984. Publisher: George Gibson. Adult Nonfiction Editor: Jacqueline Johnson. Juvenile Publisher: Emily Easton. Juvenile Editor: Timothy Travaglini. **Acquisitions:** Submissions to Adult Nonfiction Editor limited to agents, published authors and writers wtih professional credentials in their field of expertise. Children's books to "Submissions Editor-Juvenile." Estab. 1959. Publishes hardcover and trade paperback originals. **Publishes 60 titles/year. Receives 3,500 submissions/year. Pays 7½-12% on paperback, 10-15% on hardcover. Offers competitive advance.** Responds in 3 months to queries. Book catalog for 9×12 SAE with 3 first-class stamps.

O→ Walker publishes general nonfiction on a variety of subjects as well as children's books.

Nonfiction: Adult. Subjects include health/medicine, history (science and technology), nature/environment, science (popular), sports (baseball). Query with SASE. No phone calls.
Fiction: Juvenile (fiction, nonfiction), picture books (juvenile). Query with SASE.
Recent Title(s): *Salt*, by Mark Kurlansky (history); *IQ Goes to School* (juvenile); *Lusitania*, by Diane Preston (history).

WALSWORTH PUBLISHING CO., Donning Co. Publishers, 306 N. Kansas Ave., Marceline MO 64658. (800)369-2646, ext. 3269. Fax: (660)258-7798. E-mail: steve.mull@walsworth.com. Website: www.donning.com. **Acquisitions:** Steve Mull, general manager. Publishes hardcover originals and reprints. **Publishes 40-50 titles/year. Receives 25 queries and 50 mss/year. 70% of books from first-time authors; 99% from unagented writers. Pays 5-15% royalty on wholesale price. Offers advance.** Does not accept simultaneous submissions. Ms guidelines free.

O‑ Publishes coffee table books.

Nonfiction: Coffee table book. Subjects include agriculture/horticulture, business/economics, ethnic, history (community, college, agricultural, business/economic), military/war, sports. Query with SASE.

WALTSAN PUBLISHING, LLC, 5000 Barnett St., Fort Worth TX 76103-2006. (817)654-2978. E-mail: sandra@waltsan.com. Website: www.waltsan.com. **Publishes 10-20 titles/year. Receives 1,500 queries and 1,000 mss/year. 95% of books from first-time authors; 95% from unagented writers. Pays 20% royalty on wholesale price.** Publishes book 9 months after acceptance of ms. Accepts simultaneous submissions. Responds in 1 month to queries; 1 month to proposals; 2 months to mss. Book catalog and ms guidelines online.
Nonfiction: Subjects include general nonfiction. "We look at any nonfiction subject." Query with SASE or via website or submit proposal package, including outline and 3 sample chapters or submit complete ms. Reviews artwork/photos as part of ms package. Send photocopies.
Fiction: "We look at all fiction." Full-length or collections equal to full-length only. Query with SASE or submit proposal package including 3 sample chapter(s), synopsis or submit complete ms.
Recent Title(s): *Shadows and Stones*, by Bernita Stark (dark fiction of shape changers and vampires); *Kite Paper, Papel de Barrilete*, by Sue Littleton (love poem with Spanish and English texts); *Jules Verne Classics*, edited by Walter Wellborn.
Tips: Audience is computer literate, generally higher income and intelligent. "When possible, authors record their manuscript to include audio on the CD. Check our website for guidelines and sample contract." Only publishes on CDs and other removable media.

WARNER ASPECT, Warner Books, 1271 Avenue of the Americas, New York NY 10020. (212)522-7200. Website: twbookmark.com. Editor: Jaime Levine. Publishes hardcover, trade paperback, mass market paperback originals and mass market paperback reprints. **Publishes 30 titles/year. Receives 500 queries and 350 mss/year. 5-10% of books from first-time authors; 1% from unagented writers. Pays royalty on retail price. Offers $5,000-up advance.** Publishes book 1 year after acceptance of ms. Does not accept simultaneous submissions. Responds in 3 months to mss.

O‑ "We're looking for 'epic' stories in both fantasy and science fiction. Also seeking writers of color to add to what we've already published by Octavia E. Butler, Nalo Hopkinson, Walter Mosley, etc."

Fiction: Fantasy, science fiction. "Mistake writers often make is hoping against hope that being unagented won't make a difference. We simply don't have the staff to look at unagented projects." *Agented submissions only.*
Recent Title(s): *Lion's Blood*, by Steven Barnes; *Fallen Dragon*, by Peter F. Hamilton.

WARNER BOOKS, Time & Life Building, 1271 Avenue of the Americas, New York NY 10020. (212)522-7200. Website: www.twbookmark.com. President/Time Warner Book Group: Maureen Egen. **Acquisitions:** (Ms.) Jamie Raab, senior vice president/publisher (general nonfiction and fiction); Les Pockell, associate publisher (general nonfiction); Rick Horgan, vice president/executive editor (general nonfiction and fiction, thrillers); Amy Einhorn, editorial director, trade paperback (popular culture, business, fitness, self-help); Beth de Guzman, editorial director, mass market (fiction, romance, nonfiction); Rick Wolff, vice president/executive editor (business, humor, sports); Sara Ann Freed, editor-in-chief, Mysterious Press (mysteries, suspense); Caryn Karmatz Rudy, senior editor (fiction, general nonfiction, popular culture); Rob McMahon, senior editor (fiction, business, sports); Diana Baroni, senior editor (health, fitness, general nonfiction and fiction); John Aherne, editor (popular culture, men's health, New Age, movie tie-ins, general fiction); Rolf Aettersten, vice president/Warner Faith (books for the CBA market); (Ms.) Jaime Levine, editor/Aspect (science fiction); Karen Kosztolnyik, senior editor (women's fiction); Jessica Papin, editor (general nonfiction, spirituality/New Age, memoir/biography). Estab. 1960. Publishes hardcover, trade paperback and mass market paperback originals and reprints. **Publishes 250 titles/year. Pays variable royalty. Offers variable advance.** Publishes book 2 years after acceptance of ms. Accepts no unsolicited mss to queries.
Imprints: Mysterious Press (mystery/suspense), Warner Aspect (science fiction and fantasy), Warner Vision, Warner Business, Walk Worthy Press, Warner Faith (Christian fiction and nonfiction).

O‑ Warner publishes general interest fiction and nonfiction.

Nonfiction: Biography, humor, reference, self-help. Subjects include business/economics, contemporary culture, cooking/foods/nutrition, health/medicine, history, psychology, spirituality, sports, current affairs, human potential. *No unsolicited mss.*
Fiction: Fantasy, horror, mainstream/contemporary, mystery, romance, science fiction, suspense, thrillers. *No unsolicited mss.*
Recent Title(s): *Up Country*, by Nelson DeMille; *Jack*, by John Welch, Jr. with John A. Byrne; *A Bend in the Road*, by Nicholas Sparks.

WASHINGTON STATE UNIVERSITY PRESS, Pullman WA 99164-5910. (800)354-7360. Fax: (509)335-8568. E-mail: wsupress@wsu.edu. Website: www.wsu.edu/wsupress. **Acquisitions:** Glen Lindeman, editor. Estab. 1928. Publishes hardcover originals, trade paperback originals and reprints. **Publishes 8-10 titles/year. Receives 200-250 submissions/year. 40% of books from first-time authors. Most books from unagented writers. Pays 5% royalty graduated according to sales.** Publishes book 18 months after acceptance of ms. Responds in 2 months to queries.

O─ WSU Press publishes books on the history, pre-history, culture, and politics of the West, particularly the Pacific Northwest.

Nonfiction: Biography. Subjects include cooking/foods/nutrition (history), government/politics, history, nature/environment, regional, essays. "We seek manuscripts that focus on the Pacific Northwest as a region. No poetry, novels, literary criticism, how-to books or books used specifically as classroom texts. We welcome innovative and thought-provoking titles in a wide diversity of genres, from essays and memoirs to history, archaeology and political science." Submit outline, sample chapter(s). Reviews artwork/photos as part of ms package.

Recent Title(s): *The Cayton Legacy: An African American Family*; *Washington Territory*; *The Restless Northwest: A Geographical Story.*

Tips: "We have developed our marketing in the direction of regional and local history and have attempted to use this as the base upon which to expand our publishing program. In regional history, the secret is to write a good narrative—a good story—that is substantiated factually. It should be told in an imaginative, clever way. Have visuals (photos, maps, etc.) available to help the reader envision what has happened. Tell the regional history story in a way that ties it to larger, national, and even international events. Weave it into the large pattern of history."

[N] **WATSON-GUPTILL PUBLICATIONS**, Billboard Publications, Inc., 770 Broadway, New York NY 10003. (646)654-5000. Fax: (646)654-5486. Website: www.watsonguptill.com. **Acquisitions:** Candace Raney, senior acquisitions editor (fine art, art, technique, pop culture); Bob Nirkind, senior editor (Billboard-music); Joy Acquilino, senior editor (crafts); Victoria Craven, senior editor (Amphoto-photography, lifestyle); Alison Hagge (graphic design, architecture); Julie Mazur (children's books). Publishes hardcover and trade paperback originals and reprints. **Receives 150 queries and 50 mss/year. 50% of books from first-time authors; 75% from unagented writers. Pays royalty on wholesale price.** Publishes book 9 months after acceptance of ms. Responds in 2 months to queries; 3 months to proposals. Book catalog free; ms guidelines free.

Imprints: Watson-Guptill, Amphoto, Whitney Library of Design, Billboard Books, Back Stage Books.

O─ Watson-Guptill is an arts book publisher.

Nonfiction: How-to (instructionals). Subjects include art/architecture, music/dance, photography, Lifestyle, Pop culture, Theater. "Writers should be aware of the kinds of books (arts, crafts, graphic designs, instructional) Watson-Guptill publishes before submitting. Although we are growing and will consider new ideas and approaches, we will not consider a book if it is clearly outside of our publishing program." Query with SASE or submit proposal package including outline, 1-2 sample chapter(s). Reviews artwork/photos as part of ms package. Send photocopies or transparencies.

Recent Title(s): *The Tao of Watercolor*, by Jeanne Carbonetti; *American Impressionism*, by Elizabeth Prelinger; *Manga Mania*, by Christopher Hart.

Tips: "We are an arts book publisher."

WEATHERHILL, INC., 41 Monroe Turnpike, Trumbull CT 06611. (203)459-5090. Fax: (203)459-5095. E-mail: weatherhill@weatherhill.com. Website: www.weatherhill.com. **Acquisitions:** Raymond Furse, editorial director. Estab. 1962. Publishes hardcover and trade paperback originals and reprints. **Publishes 36 titles/year. Receives 250 queries and 100 mss/year. 20% of books from first-time authors; 95% from unagented writers. Pays 12-18% royalty on wholesale price. Offers up to $10,000 advance.** Publishes book 8 months after acceptance of ms. Accepts simultaneous submissions. Responds in 1 month to proposals. Book catalog and ms guidelines free.

Imprints: Weatherhill, Tengu Books.

O─ Weatherhill publishes exclusively Asia-related nonfiction and Asian fiction and poetry in translation.

Nonfiction: Asia related topics only. Biography, coffee table book, cookbook, gift book, how-to, humor, illustrated book, reference, self-help. Subjects include anthropology/archeology, art/architecture, cooking/foods/nutrition, gardening, history, humor, language/literature, music/dance, nature/environment, photography, regional, religion, sociology, translation, travel, martial arts. Submit outline, 2 sample chapter(s), and sample illustrations (if applicable). Reviews artwork/photos as part of ms package. Send photocopies.

Fiction: "We publish only important Asian writers in translation. Asian fiction is a hard sell. Authors should check funding possibilities from appropriate sources: Japan Foundation, Korea Foundation, etc." Submit synopsis.

Poetry: Only Asian poetry in translation. Query.

Recent Title(s): *Buddha and Christ*, by Robert Elinor; *Hapkido*, by Marc Tedeschi.

WEIDNER & SONS PUBLISHING, P.O. Box 2178, Riverton NJ 08077. (856)486-1755. Fax: (856)486-7583. E-mail: weidner@waterw.com. Website: www.weidnerpublishing.com. **Acquisitions:** James H. Weidner, president. Estab. 1967. Publishes hardcover and trade paperback originals and reprints. **Publishes 10-20 titles/year; imprint publishes 10 titles/year. Receives hundreds queries and 50 mss/year. 100% of books from first-time authors; 90% from unagented writers. Pays 10% royalty on wholesale price. Offers advance.** Accepts simultaneous submissions. Responds in 1 month to queries.

Imprints: Bird Sci Books, Delaware Estuary Press, Hazlaw Books, Medlaw Books, Pulse Publications, Tycooly Publishing USA.

Weidner & Sons publishes primarily science, text and reference books for scholars, college students and researchers.

Nonfiction: Reference, technical, textbook. Subjects include agriculture/horticulture, animals, business/economics, child guidance/parenting, computers/electronic, education, gardening, health/medicine, hobbies (electronic), language/literature, nature/environment, psychology, science, ecology/environment. "At present, our needs are rather specific, and it will save authors time and money to ensure the topic is within our needs." "We do not publish fiction; never poetry. No topics in the 'pseudosciences': occult, astrology, New Age and metaphysics, etc. Suggest 2 copies of ms, double spaced, along with PC disk in Word, Write or Pagemaker." Submit outline, sample chapter(s), include e-mail address for faster response, SASE. "We prefer to receive an e-mail inquiry first as to whether we are interested in receiving the ms." Reviews artwork/photos as part of ms package. Send photocopies.

Recent Title(s): *The Huntington Sexual Behavior Scale*, by Vince Huntington (Perspectives in Psychology series).

WESCOTT COVE PUBLISHING CO., P.O. Box 130, Stamford CT 06904. (203)322-0998. Fax: (203)322-1388. **Acquisitions:** Julius M. Wilensky, president. Estab. 1968. Publishes trade paperback originals and reprints. **Publishes 4 titles/year. Receives 15 queries and 10 mss/year. 25% of books from first-time authors; 95% from unagented writers. Pays 5-10% royalty on retail price. Offers $1,000-1,500 advance.** Publishes book 1 year after acceptance of ms. Accepts simultaneous submissions. Responds in 1 week to queries. Book catalog free.

"We publish the most complete cruising guides, each one an authentic reference for the area covered."

Nonfiction: "All titles are nautical books; half of them are cruising guides. Mostly we seek out authors knowledgeable in sailing, navigation, cartography and the area we want covered. Then we commission them to write the book." How-to, humor, illustrated book, reference. Subjects include history, hobbies, regional, sports, travel, nautical. Query with SASE or submit outline, 1-2 sample chapter(s), SASE.

Recent Title(s): *Chesapeake Bay Cruising Guide Volume I, Upper Bay*, by Tom Neale.

Tips: "We publish cruising guides and nautical books."

WESLEYAN UNIVERSITY PRESS, 110 Mount Vernon St., Middletown CT 06459. (860)685-2420. Director: Tom Radko. **Acquisitions:** Suzanna Tamminen, editor-in-chief. Estab. 1957. Publishes hardcover originals and paperbacks. **Publishes 35-40 titles/year. Receives 1,500 queries and 1,000 mss/year. 10% of books from first-time authors; 80% from unagented writers. Pays 0-8% royalty. Offers up to $3,000 advance.** Publishes book 1-3 years after acceptance of ms. Accepts simultaneous submissions. Responds in 1 month to queries; 2 months to proposals; 3 months to mss. Book catalog free; ms guidelines for #10 SASE.

Wesleyan University Press is a scholarly press with a focus on poetry, music, dance and cultural studies.

Nonfiction: Biography, scholarly, textbook. Subjects include ethnic (studies), film/cinema/stage, gay/lesbian (studies), history, language/literature, music/dance, philosophy. Submit proposal package including outline, introductory letter, curriculum vitae, table of contents. Reviews artwork/photos as part of ms package. Send photocopies.

Fiction: Science fiction. "We publish very little fiction, less than 3% of our entire list."

Poetry: "Writers should request a catalog and guidelines." Submit 5-10 sample poems.

Recent Title(s): *Pleasure Dome: New and Collected Poems*, by Yusef Kommunyakaa (poetry).

WESTCLIFFE PUBLISHERS, P.O. Box 1261, Englewood CO 80150. (303)935-0900. Fax: (303)935-0903. E-mail: editor@westcliffepublishers.com. Website: www.westcliffepublishers.com. Linda Doyle, associate publisher. **Acquisitions:** Jenna Samelson, managing editor. Estab. 1981. Publishes hardcover originals, trade paperback originals and reprints. **Publishes 18 titles/year. Receives 100 queries and 60 mss/year. 50% of books from first-time authors; 100% from unagented writers. Pays royalty on retail price. Offers advance.** Publishes book 18 months after acceptance of ms. Accepts simultaneous submissions. Responds in 1 month to queries. Book catalog free; ms guidelines online.

"Westcliffe Publishers produces the highest quality in regional photography and essays for our outdoor guidebooks, coffee table-style books, and calendars. As an eco-publisher our mission is to foster environmental awareness by showing the beauty of the natural world." Strong concentration on color guide books, outdoor sports, history.

Nonfiction: Coffee table book, gift book, illustrated book, reference. Subjects include Americana, animals, gardening, history, nature/environment, photography, regional, sports (outdoor), travel. "Writers need to do their market research to justify a need in the marketplace." Submit proposal package including outline. Westcliffe will contact you for photos, writing samples.

Recent Title(s): *Colorado: 1870-2000*, by John Fielder; *Haunted Texas Vacations*, by Lisa Farwell.

Tips: Audience are nature and outdoors enthusiasts and photographers. "Just call us!"

WESTERN PSYCHOLOGICAL SERVICES, Manson Western Corp., 12031 Wilshire Blvd., Los Angeles CA 90025. (310)478-2061. Fax: (310)478-2061. E-mail: smanson@wpspublish.com. Website: www.wpspublish.com. **Acquisitions:** Susan Madden, director of marketing. Estab. 1948. Publishes trade paperback originals. **Publishes 6 titles/year. Receives 6 queries and 12 mss/year. 75% of books from first-time authors; 80% from unagented writers. Pays 5-10% royalty on wholesale price.** Publishes book 1 year after acceptance of ms. Accepts simultaneous submissions. Responds in 1 month to queries. Book catalog free.

Western Psychological Services publishes practical books used by therapists, counselors, social workers and others in the helping field working with children and adults.

Nonfiction: Self-help. Subjects include child guidance/parenting, education, multicultural, psychology. Submit complete ms. *Writer's Market* recommends a query first. Reviews artwork/photos as part of ms package. Send photocopies.
Fiction: Expressing feelings, understanding and dealing with emotional problems. Submit complete ms. *Writer's Market* recommends query first.
Recent Title(s): *Psychodiagnostics and Personality Assessment: Third Edition*, by Donald P. Ogden.

WESTERNLORE PRESS, P.O. Box 35305, Tucson AZ 85740. (520)297-5491. Fax: (520)297-1722. **Acquisitions:** Lynn R. Bailey, editor. Estab. 1941. **Publishes 6-12 titles/year. Pays standard royalty on retail price.** Does not accept simultaneous submissions. Responds in 2 months to queries.

O→ Westernlore publishes Western Americana of a scholarly and semischolarly nature.

Nonfiction: Biography, scholarly. Subjects include Americana, anthropology/archeology, history, regional, historic sights, restoration, ethnohistory pertaining to the American West. Re-publication of rare and out-of-print books. Length: 25,000-100,000 words. Query with SASE.
Recent Title(s): *The Apache Kid*, by de la Gaza (Western history); *Cochise County Stalwarts, vol. I & II.*

WESTMINSTER JOHN KNOX PRESS, Presbyterian Publishing Corporation, 100 Witherspoon St., Louisville KY 40202-1396. (502)569-5342. Fax: (502)569-5113. Website: www.wjkacademic.com. **Acquisitions:** Stephanie Egnotovich, executive editor. Publishes hardcover and trade paperback originals and reprints. **Publishes 100 titles/year. Receives 2,500 queries and 750 mss/year. 10% of books from first-time authors. Pays royalty on retail price. Offers advance.** Publishes book up to 18 months after acceptance of ms. Accepts simultaneous submissions. Book catalog and ms guidelines for #10 SASE.

O→ "All WJK books have a religious/spiritual angle, but are written for various markets—scholarly, professional, and the general reader." Westminster John Knox is affiliated with the Presbyterian Church USA.

Nonfiction: Biography, gift book, how-to, humor, illustrated book, multimedia, reference, self-help, textbook. Subjects include anthropology/archeology, child guidance/parenting, education, ethnic, gay/lesbian, history, humor, multicultural, philosophy, psychology, religion, sociology, spirituality, women's issues/studies. Submit proposal package including according to WJK book proposal guidelines.

WESTWINDS PRESS, Graphic Arts Center Publishing, P.O. Box 10306, Portland OR 97296-0306. (503)226-2402. Fax: (503)223-1410. Website: www.gacpc.com. **Acquisitions:** Tricia Brown, acquisitions editor. Estab. 1999. Publishes hardcover and trade paperback originals and reprints. **Publishes 5-7 titles/year. Receives hundreds of submissions/year. 10% of books from first-time authors; 90% from unagented writers. Pays 10-14% royalty on net receipts or makes outright purchase. Offers advance.** Publishes book an average of 2 years after acceptance of ms. Accepts simultaneous submissions. Responds in 6 months to queries. Book catalog and ms guidelines for 9×12 SAE with 6 first-class stamps.
Nonfiction: Children's/juvenile, cookbook. Subjects include history, memoirs, regional (Western regional states—nature, travel, cookbooks, Native American culture, adventure, outdoor recreation, sports, the arts and children's books), guidebooks.
Recent Title(s): *Sharkabet: A Sea of Sharks from A to Z* (children's book); *The Colorado Almanac: Facts About Colorado* (reference).
Tips: "Book proposals that are professionally written and polished with a clear market receive our most careful consideration. We are looking for originality. We publish a wide range of books for a wide audience. Some of our books are clearly for travelers, others for those interested in outdoor recreation or various regional subjects. If I were a writer trying to market a book today, I would research the competition (existing books) for what I have in mind, and clearly (and concisely) express why my idea is different and better. I would describe the book buyers (and readers)—where they are, how many of them are there, how they can be reached (organizations, publications), why they would want or need my book."

WHITE MANE BOOKS, White Mane Publishing Company Inc., 63 W. Burd St., P.O. Box 152, Shippensburg PA 17257. (717)532-2237. Fax: (717)532-6110. E-mail: editorial@whitemane.com. Website: www.whitemane.com. **Acquisitions:** Harold Collier, vice president; Alexis Handerahan, associate editor. Estab. 1987. Publishes hardcover, and trade paperback originals and reprints. **Publishes 60 titles/year; imprint publishes 12-18 titles/year. Receives 300 queries and 50 mss/year. 50% of books from first-time authors; 75% from unagented writers. Pays royalty on monies received. Offers advance.** Publishes book 18 months after acceptance of ms. Accepts simultaneous submissions. Responds in 1 month to queries; 1 month to proposals; 3 months to mss. Book catalog and ms guidelines free.
Imprints: Burd Street Press (military history, emphasis on American Civil War); Ragged Edge Press (religious); White Mane Kids (historically based children's fiction).

O→ "White Mane Publishing Company, Inc., continues its tradition of publishing the finest military history, regional, religious and children's historical fiction books." Currently emphasizing American Civil War, World War II, children's historical fiction.

Nonfiction: Children's/juvenile, reference (adult), scholarly. Subjects include history, military/war, women's issues/studies. Query with SASE. Reviews artwork/photos as part of ms package. Send photocopies.
Fiction: Historical, juvenile (middle grade), young adult. Query with SASE.
Recent Title(s): *Hawaii Goes to War: The Aftermath of Pearl Harbor*, by Wilbur and Carroll Jones (nonfiction); *Send 'Em South: Young Heroes of History Series*, by Alan Kay (fiction).

WHITEHORSE PRESS, P.O. Box 60, North Conway NH 03860-0060. (603)356-6556. Fax: (603)356-6590. **Acquisitions:** Dan Kennedy, publisher. Estab. 1988. Publishes trade paperback originals. **Publishes 10-20 titles/year. Pays 10% royalty on wholesale price.** Does not accept simultaneous submissions. Responds in 1 month to queries.
Nonfiction: "We are actively seeking nonfiction books to aid motorcyclists in topics such as motorcycle safety, restoration, repair and touring. We are especially interested in technical subjects related to motorcycling." How-to, reference. Subjects include travel. Query with SASE.
Recent Title(s): *How to Set Up Your Motorcycle Workshop*, by Charlie Masi (trade paperback).
Tips: "We like to discuss project ideas at an early stage and work with authors to develop those ideas to fit our market."

ALBERT WHITMAN AND CO., 6340 Oakton St., Morton Grove IL 60053-2723. (847)581-0033. Website: www.awhitmanco.com. **Acquisitions:** Kathleen Tucker, editor-in-chief. Estab. 1919. Publishes hardcover originals and paperback reprints. **Publishes 30 titles/year. Receives 5,000 submissions/year. 20% of books from first-time authors; 70% from unagented writers. Pays 10% royalty for novels; 5% for picture books. Offers advance.** Publishes book an average of 18 months after acceptance of ms. Accepts simultaneous submissions. Responds in 6 weeks to queries; 3-4 months to mss. Book catalog for 8×10 SAE with 3 first-class stamps; ms guidelines for #10 SASE.

O━ Albert Whitman publishes good books for children on a variety of topics: holidays (i.e., Halloween), special needs (such as diabetes) and problems like divorce. The majority of our titles are picture books with less than 1,500 words." De-emphasizing bedtime stories.

Nonfiction: All books are for ages 2-12. Children's/juvenile, illustrated book. Subjects include animals, anthropology/archeology, art/architecture, computers/electronic, cooking/foods/nutrition, ethnic, gardening, health/medicine, history, hobbies, language/literature, music/dance, nature/environment, photography, recreation, religion, science, sports, travel, social studies, math. Submit complete ms. if it is picture book length; otherwise query with SASE.
Fiction: "All books are for ages 2-12." Adventure, ethnic, fantasy, historical, humor, mystery, holiday, concept books (to help children deal with problems), family. No young adult and adult books. Submit complete ms. for picture books; for longer works submit query with outline and sample chapters.
Recent Title(s): *Pumpkin Jack*, by Will Hubbell.
Tips: "We sell mostly to libraries, but our bookstore sales are growing. We recommend you study our catalog or visit our website before submitting your work."

WHITSTON PUBLISHING CO., INC., 1717 Central Ave., Suite 201, Albany NY 12205. (518)452-1900. Fax: (518)452-1777. E-mail: whitson@capital.net. Website: www.whitston.com. **Acquisitions:** Michael Laddin, editorial director. Estab. 1969. Publishes hardcover originals. **Publishes 12 titles/year. Receives 100 submissions/year. 50% of books from first-time authors; 100% from unagented writers. Pays royalities after sale of 500 copies.** Publishes book 1 year after acceptance of ms. Does not accept simultaneous submissions. Responds in 6 months to queries.

O━ Whitston focuses on Modern American and English literature and bibliographies.

Nonfiction: "We publish nonfiction books in the humanities. We also publish reference bibliographies and indexes." Subjects include art/architecture, government/politics, health/medicine, history, language/literature, social sciences. Query with SASE. Reviews artwork/photos as part of ms package.
Recent Title(s): *The Major Essays of Henry David Thoreau*, edited by Richard Oillman; *Running with the Machine: A Journalist's Eye-Opening Plunge into Politics*, by Dan Lynch; *Living Without Fear: Understanding Cancer and the New Therapies*, by Wagner and Bugeja.

MARKUS WIENER PUBLISHERS INC., 231 Nassau St., Princeton NJ 08542. (609)921-1141. **Acquisitions:** Shelley Frisch, editor-in-chief. Estab. 1981. Publishes hardcover originals and trade paperback originals and reprints. **Publishes 20 titles/year; imprint publishes 5 titles/year. Receives 50-150 queries and 50 mss/year. Pays 10% royalty on net receipts.** Publishes book 1 year after acceptance of ms. Does not accept simultaneous submissions. Responds in 2 months to queries; 2 months to proposals. Book catalog free.
Imprints: Princeton Series on the Middle East, Topics in World History.

O━ Markus Wiener publishes textbooks in history subjects and regional world history.

Nonfiction: Textbook. Subjects include history, world affairs, Caribbean studies, Middle East, Africa.
Recent Title(s): *Afro-Cuban Music*, by Maya Roy (Middle East studies); *Cuban Legends*, by Salvador Bueno, illustrations by Sigi Kaolen; *The Levant*, by William Harris.

MICHAEL WIESE PRODUCTIONS, 11288 Ventura Blvd., Suite 621, Studio City CA 91604. (818)379-8799. E-mail: kenlee@mwp.com. Website: www.mwp.com. **Acquisitions:** Ken Lee, vice president. Estab. 1981. Publishes trade paperback originals. **Publishes 8-12 titles/year. Receives 10-15 queries/year. 90% of books from first-time authors. Pays 10% royalty on retail price. Offers $500-1,000 advance.** Publishes book 10 months after acceptance of ms. Accepts simultaneous submissions. Responds in 1 month to queries; 1 month to proposals; 2 months to mss. Book catalog online.

O━ Michael Wiese publishes how-to books for professional film or video makers, film schools and bookstores.

Nonfiction: How-to. Subjects include professional film and videomaking. Submit outline, 3 sample chapter(s). Call before submitting.
Recent Title(s): *Scripts Magic*, by Marisa D'Vari; *Freelance Writing for Hollywood*, by Scott Essman.
Tips: Audience is professional filmmakers, writers, producers, directors, actors and university film students.

WILDCAT CANYON PRESS, Circulus Publishing Group, Inc., 2716 Ninth St., Berkeley CA 94710. (510)848-3600. Fax: (510)848-1326. E-mail: info@wildcatcanyon.com. Website: www.wildcatcanyon.com. **Acquisitions:** Tamara

Traeder, publisher (relationships/lifestyle/gift books). **Publishes 10-12 titles/year. Receives 500 queries and 300 mss/year. Pays 12-16% royalty on wholesale price. Offers $1,000-3,000 advance.** Publishes book 9 months after acceptance of ms. Accepts simultaneous submissions. Responds in 6 months to queries. Book catalog and ms guidelines free.

O→ Wildcat Canyon Press publishes quality books on self-care, relationships, parenting, fashion and food.

Nonfiction: Gift book, self-help, lifestyle (fashion and food). Query with SASE or submit proposal package including outline, SASE. E-queries are accepted. Reviews artwork/photos as part of ms package. Send photocopies.

Recent Title(s): *The Hip Girl's Handbook to Home, Car and Money Stuff*; *Straight Women, Gay Men*; *Absolutely Fabulous Relationships.*

Tips: "We are looking for fun and practical book projects that work well in both the traditional bookstore and gift markets."

WILDER PUBLISHING CENTER, 919 Lafond Ave., St. Paul MN 55104. (651)659-6013. Fax: (651)642-2061. E-mail: vlh@wilder.org. Website: www.wilder.org. **Acquisitions:** Vincent Hyman, director. Publishes trade paperback originals. **Publishes 6 titles/year. Receives 30 queries and 15 mss/year. 75% of books from first-time authors; 100% from unagented writers. Pays 10% royalty on net receipts. Books are sold through direct mail; average discount is 20%. Offers $1,000-3,000 advance.** Publishes book 18 months after acceptance of ms. Does not accept simultaneous submissions. Responds in 1 month to queries; 1 month to proposals; 3 months to mss. Book catalog and ms guidelines free or online.

O→ Wilder Publishing Center emphasizes community and nonprofit organization management and development.

Nonfiction: Subjects include nonprofit management, organizational development, community building. "We are seeking mss that report 'best practice' methods using handbook or workbook formats for nonprofit and community development managers." Submit 3 sample chapter(s). Phone query OK before submitting proposal with detailed chapter outline, SASE, statement of unique selling points, identification of audience.

Recent Title(s): *The Lobbying and Advocacy Handbook for Nonprofit Organizations*; *The Wilder Nonprofit Guide to Crafting Effective Mission and Vision Statements*; *The Five Life Stages of Nonprofit Organizations.*

Tips: "Writers must be practitioners with a passion for their work in nonprofit management or community building and experience presenting their techniques at conferences. We seek practical, not academic books. Our books identify professional challenges faced by our audiences and offer practical, step-by-step solutions."

WILDERNESS PRESS, 1200 Fifth St., Berkley CA 94710. (510)558-1666. Fax: (510)558-1696. E-mail: mail@wildernesspress.com. Website: www.wildernesspress.com. **Acquisitions:** Jannie Dresser, managing editor. Estab. 1967. Publishes paperback originals. **Publishes 12 titles/year. Receives 75 submissions/year. 20% of books from first-time authors; 95% from unagented writers. Pays 5-8% royalty on retail price. Offers $1,000 average advance.** Publishes book 8 months after acceptance of ms. Does not accept simultaneous submissions. Responds in 2 months to queries. Book catalog and ms guidelines online.

O→ "We seek to publish the most accurate, reliable and useful outdoor books and maps for self-propelled outdoor activities for hikers, kayakers, skiers, snowshoers, backpackers, mountain biking."

Nonfiction: How-to (outdoors). Subjects include nature/environment, recreation, trail guides for hikers and backpackers. "We publish books about the outdoors. Most are trail guides for hikers and backpackers, but we also publish how-to books about the outdoors. The manuscript must be accurate. The author must research an area in person. If writing a trail guide, you must walk all the trails in the area your book is about. Outlook must be strongly conservationist. Style must be appropriate for a highly literate audience." Request proposal guidelines.

Recent Title(s): *Traditional Lead Climbing*; *Washington's Highest Mountains*; *The Tahoe Rim Trail.*

JOHN WILEY & SONS, INC., 111 River St., Hoboken NJ 07030. Website: www.wiley.com. Publisher: G. Helferich. **Acquisitions:** Editorial Department. Estab. 1807. Publishes hardcover originals, trade paperback originals and reprints. **Pays competitive rates. Offers advance.** Accepts simultaneous submissions. Book catalog and ms guidelines for #10 SASE.

O→ "The General Interest group publishes books for the consumer market."

Nonfiction: Biography, children's/juvenile, reference, narrative nonfiction. Subjects include history, memoirs, science (popular), African American interest, health/self-improvement. Query with SASE.

Recent Title(s): *Columbus in the Americas*, by William Least-Heat Moon; *The Chapra Center Cookbook*, by Deepak Chopra, David Simon, Leanne Backer.

WILLIAMSON PUBLISHING CO., P.O. Box 185, Church Hill Rd., Charlotte VT 05445. Website: www.williamsonbooks.com. **Acquisitions:** Susan Williamson, editorial director. Estab. 1983. Publishes trade paperback originals. **Publishes 20 titles/year. Receives 1,000 queries/year. 75% of books from first-time authors; 90% from unagented writers. Pays royalty on net receipts or makes outright purchase. Offers standard advance.** Publishes book 18 months after acceptance of ms. Does not accept simultaneous submissions. Responds in 4 months to queries. Book catalog for 8½×11 SAE with 4 first-class stamps; ms guidelines online.

- Williamson's success is based on its reputation for excellence. Its books win top awards year in and year out, including Parents Choice (3 in Fall 2001), Oppenheim, and Children's Book Council.

O→ "Our mission is to help every child fulfull his/her potential and experience personal growth through active learning. We want 'our kids' to be able to work toward a culturally rich, ethnically diverse, peaceful nation and global community." Currently emphasizing creative approaches to specific areas of science, history, cultural experiences, diversity.

Nonfiction: Biography, how-to, self-help. Subjects include animals, anthropology/archeology, art/architecture, business/economics, cooking/foods/nutrition, ethnic, government/politics, health/medicine, history, hobbies, language/literature, memoirs, money/finance, multicultural, music/dance, nature/environment, photography, psychology, science, women's issues/studies, world affairs, geography, early learning skills, careers, arts, crafts. "Williamson has five very successful children's book series: *Little Hands* (ages 2-6), *Kids Can* (ages 6-12), *Quick Starts for Kids* (64 pages, ages 8 and up), *Tales Alive* (folktales plus activities, ages 4-10) and *Kaleidoscope Kids* (96 pages, single subject, ages 8-14). They must incorporate learning through doing. *No picture books, story books, or fiction please!* Please don't call concerning your submission. It never helps your review, and it takes too much of our time. With an SASE, you'll hear from us." Query with SASE or submit 1-2 sample chapter(s), toc, SASE.
Recent Title(s): *Who Really* Discovered America, by Avery Hart (Children's Book Council Notable Trade Book, 2002); *Draw Your Own Cartoons*, by Don Mayne (Oppenheim Gold Award); *Little Italy Fingerplays and Action Songs*, by Stetson and Congdon (Parents Choice).
Tips: "Our children's books are used by kids, their parents, and educators. They encourage self-discovery, creativity and personal growth. Our books are based on the philosophy that children learn best by doing, by being involved. Our authors need to be excited about their subject area and equally important, excited about kids. Please, please, please no storybooks of any kind."

WILLOW CREEK PRESS, P.O. Box 147, 9931 Highway 70 W., Minocqua WI 54548. (715)358-7010. Fax: (715)358-2807. E-mail: andread@willowcreekpress.com. Website: www.willowcreekpress.com. **Acquisitions:** Andrea Donner, managing editor. Estab. 1986. Publishes hardcover and trade paperback originals and reprints. **Publishes 25 titles/year. Receives 400 queries and 150 mss/year. 15% of books from first-time authors; 50% from unagented writers. Pays 6-15% royalty on wholesale price. Offers $2,000-5,000 advance.** Publishes book within 18 months after acceptance of ms. Accepts simultaneous submissions. Responds in 2 months to queries.

- "We specialize in nature, outdoor, and sporting topics, including gardening, wildlife and animal books. Pets, cookbooks, and a few humor books and essays round out our titles." Currently emphasizing pets (mainly dogs and cats), wildlife, outdoor sports (hunting, fishing). De-emphasizing essays, fiction.

Nonfiction: Coffee table book, cookbook, how-to, humor, illustrated book, reference. Subjects include animals, cooking/foods/nutrition, gardening, humor, nature/environment, recreation, sports, travel, wildlife, pets. Submit outline, 1 sample chapter(s), SASE. Reviews artwork/photos as part of ms package.
Recent Title(s): *101 Uses for a Dog*; *Castwork: Reflections of Fly-Fishing Guides & the American West*; *Lab Rules: Virtues of Canine Character.*

WILLOWGATE PRESS, P.O. Box 6529, Holliston MA 01746. (508)429-8774. E-mail: willowgatepress@yahoo.com. Website: www.willowgatepress.com. **Acquisitions:** Robert Tolins, editor. Publishes trade paperback and mass market paperback originals. **Publishes 3-5 titles/year. 50% of books from first-time authors; 100% from unagented writers. Pays 5-15% royalty on retail price. Offers $500 advance.** Publishes book 6 months after acceptance of ms. Accepts simultaneous submissions. Responds in 2 months to queries; 6 months to mss. Book catalog and ms guidelines online.

- "Willowgate is a small, independent press established for the purpose of publishing good writing of the sort that the public is currently not receiving. Fundamentally, we seek to provide quality book-length fiction in all categories, and to see our titles widely promoted and kept available for longer than the brief shelf life allowed by the traditional houses. We believe that there is a need for a press whose goal is to publish quality works by new and established writers, without regard for the 'blockbuster' mentality that presently prevents more established houses from taking on such projects."

Fiction: Fantasy, gothic, historical, horror, humor, literary, mainstream/contemporary, military/war, mystery, occult, regional, science fiction, short story collections, sports. "We are not interested in children's, erotica, or experimental." Query with SASE or submit outline, plus the first ten pages and ten pages of the aurthor's choosing. Do not send cash or check in lieu of stamps for return postage.
Tips: "If a manuscript is accepted for publication, we will make every effort to avoid lengthy delays in bringing the product to market. The writer will be given a voice in all aspects of publishing, promotion, advertising and marketing, including cover art, copy, promotional forums, etc. The writer will be expected to be an active and enthusiastic participant in all stages of the publication process. We hope to attract the finest writers of contemporary fiction and to help generate similar enthusiasm in them and in their readers. Please don't send cash or a check in lieu of stamps for return postage."

WILSHIRE BOOK CO., 12015 Sherman Rd., North Hollywood CA 91605-3781. (818)765-8579. Fax: (818)765-2922. E-mail: mpowers@mpowers.com. Website: www.mpowers.com. Publisher: Melvin Powers. **Acquisitions:** Marcia Grad, senior editor. Estab. 1947. Publishes trade paperback originals and reprints. **Publishes 25 titles/year. Receives 2,000 submissions/year. 80% of books from first-time authors; 75% from unagented writers. Pays standard royalty. Offers advance.** Publishes book 6 months after acceptance of ms. Accepts simultaneous submissions. Responds in 2 months to queries. Welcomes telephone calls to discuss mss or book concepts.
Nonfiction: How-to, self-help, motivational/inspiration, recovery. Subjects include psychology, personal success, entrepreneurship, humor, Internet marketing, mail order, horsmanship, trick training for horses. Minimum 50,000 words. Query with SASE or submit outline, 3 sample chapter(s), author bio, analysis of book's competition or submit complete ms. Reviews artwork/photos as part of ms package. Send photocopies.
Fiction: Adult allegories that teach principles of psychological growth or offer guidance in living. Minimum 25,000 words. Submit 3 sample chapter(s), synopsis or submit complete ms.

Recent Title(s): *The Princess Who Believed in Fairy Tales*, by Marcia Grad; *The Knight in Rusty Armor*, by Robert Fisher; *Think & Grow Rich*, by Napoleon Hill.

Tips: "We are vitally interested in all new material we receive. Just as you hopefully submit your manuscript for publication, we hopefully read every one submitted, searching for those that we believe will be successful in the marketplace. Writing and publishing must be a team effort. We need you to write what we can sell. We suggest that you read the successful books that are similar to the manuscript you want to write. Analyze them to discover what elements make them winners. Duplicate those elements in your own style, using a creative new approach and fresh material, and you will have written a book we can catapult onto the bestseller list."

WINDSOR BOOKS, Windsor Marketing Corp., P.O. Box 280, Brightwaters NY 11718-0280. (631)321-7830. Website: www.windsorpublishing.com. **Acquisitions:** Jeff Schmidt, managing editor. Estab. 1968. Publishes hardcover and trade paperback originals, reprints, and very specific software. **Publishes 6 titles/year. Receives approximately 40 submissions/year. 60% of books from first-time authors; 90% from unagented writers. Pays 10% royalty on retail price; 5% on wholesale price (50% of total cost). Offers variable advance.** Publishes book an average of 6 months after acceptance of ms. Accepts simultaneous submissions. Responds in 2 weeks to queries. Book catalog and ms guidelines free.

O→ "Our books are for serious investors."

Nonfiction: Interested in books on strategies, methods for investing in the stock market, options market and commodities markets. How-to, technical. Subjects include business/economics (investing in stocks and commodities), money/finance, software. Query with SASE or submit outline, sample chapter(s). Reviews artwork/photos as part of ms package.

Tips: "We sell through direct mail to our mailing list and other financial lists. Writers must keep their work original; this market tends to have a great deal of information overlap among publications."

WINDSTORM CREATIVE LTD, 7419 Ebbert Dr. SE, Port Orchard WA 98367. Website: www.windstormcreative.com. **Acquisitions:** (Ms.) Cris Newport, senior editor. Estab. 1989. Publishes trade paperback originals and reprints. **Publishes 50 titles/year. Receives 5,200 queries and 15,000 mss/year. Pays 10-15% royalty on wholesale price.** Publishes book 1-2 years after acceptance of ms. Accepts simultaneous submissions. Responds in 6 months to mss.

O→ Publisher of fiction, poetry, Internet guides, episode guides, nonfiction.

Fiction: Adventure, erotica, experimental, fantasy, gay/lesbian, gothic, historical, humor, literary, science fiction, young adult. No children's books, horror, "bestseller" fiction, spy or espionage novels, "thrillers," any work which describes childhood sexual abuse or in which this theme figures prominantly. Query with cover letter and a one-page synopsis of the ms which details the major plot developments. SASE required.

Recent Title(s): *Bones Become Flowers*, by Jess Mowry (contemporary); *1001 Nights: Exotica*; *Journey of a Thousand Miles*, by Peter Kasting (gay).

Tips: "Visit website for detailed submission instructions."

WINDSWEPT HOUSE PUBLISHERS, P.O. Box 159, Mount Desert ME 04660-0159. (207)244-5027. Fax: (207)244-3369. E-mail: winswept@acadia.net. Website: www.booknotes.com/windswept. **Acquisitions:** Mavis Weinberger, owner. Publishes hardcover and trade paperback originals. **Publishes 4 titles/year. Pays up to 10% royalty.** Responds in 1 month to queries. Book catalog online; ms guidelines for #10 SASE.

Nonfiction: Biography, children's/juvenile, illustrated book. Subjects include animals, history, memoirs, nature/environment, regional. **All unsolicited mss returned unopened.** Reviews artwork/photos as part of ms package. Send photocopies.

Recent Title(s): *Tulips Under the Quarter Moon*, by Grant Judd (poetry with illustrations).

WINDWARD PUBLISHING, INC., 3943 Meadowbrook Road, Minneapolis MN 55426. (952)938-9330. Fax: (952)938-7353. E-mail: feedback@finney-hobar.com. Website: www.finney-hobar.com. **Acquisitions:** Alan E. Kryson, president. Estab. 1973. Publishes trade paperback originals. **Publishes 6-10 titles/year. Receives 50 queries and 10 mss/year. 35% of books from first-time authors; 100% from unagented writers. Pays 10% royalty on wholesale price. Offers advance.** Publishes book 6-12 months after acceptance of ms. Accepts simultaneous submissions. Responds in 3 weeks to queries.

O→ Windward publishes illustrated natural history and recreation books.

Nonfiction: Illustrated book, handbooks, field guides. Subjects include agriculture/horticulture, animals, gardening, nature/environment, recreation, science, sports, natural history. Query with SASE. Reviews artwork/photos as part of ms package.

Recent Title(s): *Birds of the Water, Sea, and Shore*, by Romashko; *Mammals of Florida*, by Brown.

WINSLOW PRESS, 115 E. 23rd St., 10th Floor, New York NY 10010. (212)254-2025. Fax: (212)254-2410. E-mail: winslow@winslowpress.com. Website: www.winslowpress.com. Publishes hardcover originals. **Publishes 30 titles/year. Receives 2,000 mss/year. 20% of books from first-time authors; 30% from unagented writers. Pays royalty. Offers advance.** Accepts simultaneous submissions. Responds in 4 months to queries. Book catalog for 8×10 SAE with 75¢ first-class stamps.

Nonfiction: Children's/juvenile only. Subjects include all but inspirational. Query with SASE. Reviews artwork/photos as part of ms package. Send photocopies.

Fiction: All juvenile subjects, except inspirational. Not accepting picture books at this time.

Poetry: Children's/juvenile only.

Tips: "We publish books for children from pre-K to young adult. We have an innovative Web program which all of our books are a part of."

WISDOM PUBLICATIONS, 199 Elm St., Somerville MA 02144. (617)776-7416 ext. 25. Fax: (617)776-7841. E-mail: editorial@wisdompubs.org. Website: www.widsompubs.org. Publisher: Timothy McNeill. **Acquisitions:** E. Gene Smith, acquisitions editor. Estab. 1976. Publishes hardcover originals, trade paperback originals and reprints. **Publishes 12-15 titles/year. Receives 240 queries/year. 50% of books from first-time authors; 95% from unagented writers. Pays 4-8% royalty on wholesale price. Offers advance.** Publishes book within 2 years after acceptance of ms. Does not accept simultaneous submissions. Book catalog and ms guidelines online.

O→ Wisdom Publications is dedicated to making available authentic Buddhist works for the benefit of all. "We publish translations, commentaries and teachings of past and contemporary Buddhist masters and original works by leading Buddhist scholars." Currently emphasizing popular applied Buddhism, scholarly titles.

Nonfiction: Reference, self-help, textbook (Buddhist). Subjects include philosophy (Buddhist or comparative Buddhist/Western), psychology, religion, Buddhism, Tibet. Query with SASE. Reviews artwork/photos as part of ms package. Send photocopies.

Poetry: Buddhist. Query.

Recent Title(s): *Engaged Buddhism in the West*, by Christopher S. Queen.

Tips: "We are basically a publisher of Buddhist books—all schools and traditions of Buddhism. Please see our catalog or our website *before* you send anything to us to get a sense of what we publish."

WISH PUBLISHING, P.O. Box 10337, Terre Haute IN 47801. (812)478-3529. Fax: (812)447-1836. E-mail: holly@wishpublishing.com. Website: www.wishpublishing.com. **Acquisitions:** Holly Kondras, president. Publishes hardcover and trade paperback originals. **Publishes 5-10 titles/year. Pays 10-18% royalty on wholesale price.** Accepts simultaneous submissions. Responds in 2 months to queries; 2 months to proposals; 2 months to mss. Book catalog and ms guidelines free or online.

Nonfiction: Biography, children's/juvenile, reference. Subjects include health/medicine, sports, women's issues/studies. Query with SASE or submit proposal package including outline, 2 sample chapter(s), author bio. Reviews artwork/photos as part of ms package. Send photocopies.

Recent Title(s): *Entering the Mother Zone* (parenting); *Tae Kwon Do for Women* (sports).

Tips: Audience is women and girls who play sports and their coaches, parents and supporters.

WIZARDS OF THE COAST, P.O. Box 707, Renton WA 98057-0707. (425)226-6500. Website: www.wizards.com. Executive Editor: Mary Kirchoff. **Acquisitions:** Peter Archer, editorial director. Publishes hardcover and trade paperback originals and trade paperback reprints. **Publishes 50-60 titles/year. Receives 600 queries and 300 mss/year. 25% of books from first-time authors; 35% from unagented writers. Pays 4-8% royalty on retail price. Offers $4,000-6,000 average advance.** Publishes book 1 year after acceptance of ms. Accepts simultaneous submissions. Responds in 4 months to queries. Ms guidelines for #10 SASE.

Imprints: Dragonlance Books; Forgotten Realms Books; Magic: The Gathering Books; Legend of the Five Rings Novels.

O→ Wizards of the Coast publishes science fiction and fantasy shared world titles. Currently emphasizing solid fantasy writers. De-emphasizing gothic fiction.

Nonfiction: "All of our nonfiction books are generated inhouse."

Fiction: Fantasy, gothic, science fiction, short story collections. "We currently publish only work-for-hire novels set in our trademarked worlds. No violent or gory fantasy or science fiction." Request guidelines, then query with outline/synopsis and 3 sample chapters.

Recent Title(s): *Dragons of a Lost Star*, by Margaret Weis and Tracy Hickman.

Tips: "Our audience largely is comprised of highly imaginative 12-30 year-old males."

WOODBINE HOUSE, 6510 Bells Mill Rd., Bethesda MD 20817. (301)897-3570. Fax: (301)897-5838. E-mail: ngray@woodbinehouse.com. Website: www.woodbinehouse.com. **Acquisitions:** Nancy Gray Paul, acquisitions editor. Estab. 1985. Publishes hardcover and trade paperback originals. **Publishes 8 titles/year. 90% from unagented writers. Pays 10-12% royalty. Offers advance.** Publishes book 18 months after acceptance of ms. Accepts simultaneous submissions. Responds in 8 months to queries. Book catalog and ms guidelines for 6×9 SAE with 3 first-class stamps.

O→ Woodbine House publishes books for or about individuals with disabilities to help those individuals and their families live fulfilling and satisfying lives in their communities.

Nonfiction: Publishes books for and about children with disabilities. Reference. Subjects include health/medicine. "I more carefully consider opening envelopes that are wrapped with excessive tape, are bulky, have return addresses that do not match the postal stamp, or display unusual handwriting. In cases such as this, I would consider returning envelopes to sender. I recommend authors send only envelopes that are clear and free of that which is described above. In addition, I would suggest authors send a SASE that is self-adhesive. Furthermore, authors can e-mail the acquisitions editors where they are sending a manuscript and inform them of the impending submission." No personal accounts or general parenting guides. Submit outline, 3 sample chapter(s). Reviews artwork/photos as part of ms package.

Fiction: Picture books (children's). Submit complete ms. with SASE.

Recent Title(s): *Activity Schedules for Children with Autism: Teaching Independent Behavior*, by Lynn McClannahan and Patricia Krantz; *Children with Fragile X Syndrome: A Parents' Guide*, by Jayne Dixon Weber, Ed.

Tips: "Do not send us a proposal on the basis of this description. Examine our catalog or website and a couple of our books to make sure you are on the right track. Put some thought into how your book could be marketed (aside from in bookstores). Keep cover letters concise and to the point; if it's a subject that interests us, we'll ask to see more."

WORDWARE PUBLISHING, INC., 2320 Los Rios Blvd., Suite 200, Plano TX 75074. (972)423-0090. Fax: (972)881-9147. E-mail: jhill@wordware.com. Website: www.wordware.com. President: Russell A. Stultz. **Acquisitions:** Jim Hill, publisher. Estab. 1983. Publishes trade paperback and mass market paperback originals. **Publishes 50-60 titles/year. Receives 100-150 queries and 50-75 mss/year. 40% of books from first-time authors; 95% from unagented writers. Pays 8% royalty on wholesale price. Offers advance.** Publishes book 6 months after acceptance of ms. Accepts simultaneous submissions. Responds in 2 months to queries. Book catalog free; ms guidelines online.
Imprints: Republic of Texas Press

O- Wordware publishes computer/electronics books covering a broad range of technologies for professional programmers and developers.

Nonfiction: Reference, technical, textbook. Subjects include computers/electronic. "Wordware publishes advanced titles for developers and professional programmers." Submit proposal package including 2 sample chapter(s), table of contents, target audience summation, competing books.
Recent Title(s): *The Tomes of Delphi Win32 Database Developers Guide*, by Warren Rachele; *Search Engine Positioning*, by Frederick Marckini.

WORKMAN PUBLISHING CO., 708 Broadway, New York NY 10003. (212)254-5900. Fax: (212)254-8098. Website: www.workman.com. Editor-in-chief: Susan Bolotin. **Acquisitions:** Suzanne Rafer, executive editor (cookbook, child care, parenting, teen interest); Ruth Sullivan, Jennifer Griffin, Margot Herrera, senior editors. Estab. 1967. Publishes hardcover and trade paperback originals. **Publishes 40 titles/year. Receives thousands of queries/year. Open to first-time authors. Pays variable royalty on retail price. Offers variable advance.** Publishes book 1 year after acceptance of ms. Accepts simultaneous submissions. Responds in 5 months to queries. Book catalog free.
Imprints: Algonquin Books of Chapel Hill, Artisan.

O- "We are a trade paperback house specializing in a wide range of popular nonfiction. We publish no adult fiction and very little children's fiction. We also publish a full range of full color wall and Page-A-Day calendars."

Nonfiction: Cookbook, gift book, how-to, humor. Subjects include child guidance/parenting, cooking/foods/nutrition, gardening, health/medicine, humor, sports, travel. Query with SASE first for guidelines. Reviews artwork/photos as part of ms package.
Recent Title(s): *Antiques Roadshow Primer*, by Carol Prisant; *The Cake Mix Doctor*, by Anne Byrn.
Tips: "No phone calls please. We do not accept submissions via fax or e-mail."

WORLD LEISURE, P.O. Box 160, Hampstead NH 03841. (617)569-1966. Fax: (617)561-7654. E-mail: wleisure@aol.com. Website: www.worldleisure.com. **Acquisitions:** Charles Leocha, president. Estab. 1977. Publishes trade paperback originals. **Publishes 3-5 titles/year. Pays royalty or makes outright purchase.** Does not accept simultaneous submissions. Responds in 2 months to queries. Book catalog and ms guidelines online.

O- World Leisure specializes in travel books, activity guidebooks and self-help titles.

Nonfiction: Self-help. Subjects include recreation, sports (skiing), travel. "We will be publishing annual updates to *Ski Europe* and *Skiing America*. Writers planning any ski stories should contact us for possible add-on assignments at areas not covered by our staff. We also will publish general travel titles such as *Travelers' Rights*, Family travel guides, guidebooks about myths and legends, the *Cheap Dates* (affordable activity guidebooks) series and self-help books such as *Getting To Know You*, and *A Woman's ABCs of Life*." Submit outline, intro sample chapter(s), annotated table of contents, SASE.
Recent Title(s): *Millionaires Handbook*, by Peter Miller.

WRITER'S DIGEST BOOKS, F&W Publications, 4700 E. Galbraith Rd., Cincinnati OH 45236. (513)531-2690, ext. 1483. Website: www.writersdigest.com. **Acquisitions:** Melanie Rigney. Estab. 1920. Publishes hardcover and paperback originals. **Publishes 14 titles/year. Receives 500 queries and 100 mss/year. 20% from unagented writers. Pays 10-20% royalty on net receipts. Offers average $5,000 and up advance.** Publishes book 18 months after acceptance of ms. Accepts simultaneous submissions. Responds in 2 months to queries. Book catalog for 9×12 SAE with 6 first-class stamps.

O- Writer's Digest Books is the premiere source for books about writing, publishing instructional and reference books for writers.

Nonfiction: How-to, reference, instructional; creativity books for writers. Subjects include language/literature, music/dance, photography. "Our instruction books stress results and how specifically to achieve them. Should be well-researched, yet lively and readable. We do *not* want to see books telling readers how to crack specific nonfiction markets: *Writing for the Computer Market* or *Writing for Trade Publications*, for instance. We are most in need of fiction technique books written by published authors. Be prepared to explain how the proposed book differs from existing books on the subject." No fiction or poetry. Query with SASE or submit outline, sample chapter(s), SASE.
Recent Title(s): *Guerilla Marketing for Writers*, by Jay Conrad Levinson and Michael Larsen; *Writing the Breakout Novel*, by Donald Maass.
Tips: Writer's Digest Books also publishes instructional books for photographers. They must instruct about the creative craft, as opposed to instructing about marketing. Contact Brad Crawford.

[N] YAHBOOKS PUBLISHING, 30799 Pinetree Rd., #356, Cleveland OH 44124. (216)233-5961. Fax: (440)247-1581. E-mail: eric@yahbooks.com. Website: www.yahbooks.com. Estab. 2001. publishes trade paperback originals. **Publishes 5 titles/year. Pays 10% royalty on wholesale price or makes outright purchase of $0-1,000.** Publishes book 0-6 months after acceptance of ms. Accepts simultaneous submissions. Responds in 1 month to queries; 1 month to proposals; 1-2 months to mss.

Nonfiction: Children's/juvenile, gift book, how-to. Subjects include computers/electronic. Submit outline, sample chapter(s) or submit complete ms. Reviews artwork/photos as part of ms package. Send photocopies.

Recent Title(s): *You Are Here College Internet Guide*, by Eric Leebow (Internet/college); *You Are Here High School Internet Guide*, by Eric Leebow (Internet/teen/high school); *You Are Here Kids & Family Internet Guide*, by Eric Leebow (Internet/family).

Tips: "We publish a book series of Internet guides. Variety of audiences."

YALE UNIVERSITY PRESS, 302 Temple St., New Haven CT 06511. (203)432-0960. Fax: (203)432-0948. Website: www.yale.edu/yup. **Acquisitions:** Jonathan Brent, editorial director (literature, Annals of Communism, Cold War studies, Judaic studies); Jean E. Thomson Black (science and medicine); Alex Schwartz (reference books); Harry Haskell (archaeology, classics, music and performing arts); Lara Heimert (English-language literary studies); Patricia Fidler (art and architectural history, geography, landscape studies); Mary Jane Peluso (languages); John Kulka (literature, poetry, philosophy, political science, and Yale Series of Younger Poets); Robert Flynn (religion, philosophy, law). Estab. 1908. Publishes hardcover and trade paperback originals. **Publishes 250 titles/year. Receives 8,000 queries and 400 mss/year. 15% of books from first-time authors; 85% from unagented writers. Pays 0-15% royalty on net receipts. Offers $500-50,000 (based on expected sales) advance.** Publishes book 1 year after acceptance of ms. Accepts simultaneous submissions. Responds in 1 month to queries; 2 months to proposals; 3 months to mss. Book catalog and ms guidelines for #10 SASE.

O→ Yale University Press publishes scholarly and general interest books.

Nonfiction: Biography, illustrated book, reference, scholarly, textbook. Subjects include Americana, anthropology/archeology, art/architecture, business/economics, education, health/medicine, history, language/literature, military/war, music/dance, philosophy, psychology, religion, science, sociology, women's issues/studies. "Our nonfiction has to be at a very high level. Most of our books are written by professors or journalists, with a high level of expertise. Submit proposals only. We'll ask if we want to see more. No unsolicited manuscripts. We won't return them." Query with SASE. Reviews artwork/photos as part of ms package. Send photocopies.

Poetry: Publishes 1 book each year. Submit to Yale Series of Younger Poets Competition. Open to poets under 40 who have not had a book previously published. Submit ms of 48-64 pages in February only! Entry fee: $15. Rules and guidelines available online or via SASE. Submit complete ms.

Recent Title(s): *Jihad*, by Ahmed Rashid; *The Coldest March*, by Susan Solomon.

Tips: "Audience is scholars, students and general readers."

YMAA PUBLICATION CENTER, 4354 Washington St., Roslindale MA 02131. (617)323-7215. Fax: (617)323-7417. E-mail: ymaa@aol.com. Website: www.ymaa.com. **Acquisitions:** David Ripianzi, director. Estab. 1982. Publishes hardcover and trade paperback originals and reprints. **Publishes 10 titles/year. Receives 50 queries and 20 mss/year. 25% of books from first-time authors; 100% from unagented writers. Pays 7-10% royalty on net receipts.** Publishes book 18 months after acceptance of ms. Accepts simultaneous submissions. Responds in 3 months to proposals. Book catalog online; ms guidelines free.

O→ "YMAA publishes books on Chinese Chi Kung (Qigong), Taijiquan, Tai Chi and Asian martial arts. We are expanding our focus to include books on healing, wellness, meditation and subjects related to Asian culture and Asian medicine." De-emphasizing fitness books.

Nonfiction: "We are most interested in Asian martial arts, Chinese medicine and Chinese Qigong. We publish Eastern thought, health, meditation, massage and East/West synthesis." How-to, multimedia, self-help. Subjects include ethnic, health/medicine (Chinese), history, philosophy, spirituality, sports, Asian martial arts, Chinese Qigong. "We no longer publish or solicit books for children. We also produce instructional videos to accompany our books on traditional Chinese martial arts, meditation, massage and Chi Kung." Submit proposal package including outline, 1 sample chapter(s), author bio, SASE. Reviews artwork/photos as part of ms package. Send photocopies and 1-2 originals to determine quality of photo/line art.

Recent Title(s): *A Woman's Qigong Guide*, by Yanling Johnson.

Tips: "If you are submitting health-related material, please refer to an Asian tradition. Learn about author publicity options as your participation is mandatory."

YUCCA TREE PRESS, 2130 Hixon Dr., Las Cruces NM 88005-3305. (505)524-2357. Fax: (505)523-8935. E-mail: yuccatree@zianet.com. Website: www.yuccatree.com. **Acquisitions:** Janie Matson, publisher. Publishes hardcover and trade paperback originals and trade paperback reprints. **Publishes 3-6 titles/year. Receives 15 queries and 10 mss/year. 75% of books from first-time authors; 100% from unagented writers. Pays 10-20% royalty on wholesale price.** Publishes book 1 year after acceptance of ms. Responds in 1 month to queries. Book catalog online; ms guidelines for #10 SASE.

Nonfiction: Military and Southwestern history only. Subjects include history (Southwestern), military/war. No fiction or historical fiction. Query with SASE. Reviews artwork/photos as part of ms package. Send photocopies.

Tips: Targets adult readers of quality history.

ZEBRA BOOKS, Kensington, 850 Third Ave., 16th Floor, New York NY 10022. (212)407-1500. Website: www.kensingtonbooks.com. **Acquisitions:** Michaela Hamilton, editor-in-chief; Ann La Farge, executive editor; Kate Duffy, editorial director (romance); John Scognamiglio, editorial director; Amy Garvey, editor; Karen Thomas, editor (African-American fiction and nonfiction); Elaine Sparber, editor (health); Bruce Bender, managing director(Citadel); Margaret Wolf, editor; Richard Ember, editor; Bob Shuman, editor; Miles Lott, editor. Publishes hardcover originals, trade paperback and mass market paperback originals and reprints. **Publishes 600 titles/year.** Publishes book 18 months after acceptance of ms. Accepts simultaneous submissions. Book catalog online; Please no queries. Send synopsis and sample chapters with SASE.

O⇁ Zebra Books is dedicated to women's fiction, which includes, but is not limited to romance.

ZONDERVAN, HarperCollins Publishers, 5300 Patterson Ave. SE, Grand Rapids MI 49530-0002. (616)698-6900. Fax: (616)698-3454. E-mail: zpub@zondervan.com. Website: www.zondervan.com. Executive VP: Scott Bolinder. **Acquisitions:** Manuscript Review Editor. Estab. 1931. Publishes hardcover and trade paperback originals and reprints. **Publishes 120 titles/year. Receives 3,000 submissions/year. 10% of books from first-time authors; 60% from unagented writers. Pays 14% royalty on net amount received on sales of cloth and softcover trade editions; 12% royalty on net amount received on sales of mass market paperbacks. Offers variable advance.** Responds in 3 months to proposals. Ms guidelines for #10 SASE.

Imprints: Zonderkidz, Inspiro (includes Bible covers, devotional calendars).

O⇁ "Our mission is to be the leading Christian communications company meeting the needs of people with resources that glorify Jesus Christ and promote biblical principles."

Nonfiction: All religious perspective (evangelical). Autobiography, biography, children's/juvenile, reference, self-help, textbook. Subjects include history, humanities, memoirs, religion, Christian living, devotional, Bible study resources, preaching, counseling, college and seminary textbooks, discipleship, worship, and church renewal for pastors, professionals and lay leaders in ministry; theological and biblical reference books. Submit outline, 1 sample chapter(s). "We only accept faxed mss."

Fiction: Some adult fiction. Refer to nonfiction. Query with SASE or submit outline, 1 sample chapter(s), synopsis.

Recent Title(s): *Soul Salsa*, by Leonard Sweet (nonfiction); *Blood of Heaven*, by Bill Myers (fiction).

Canadian & International Book Publishers

Canadian book publishers share the same mission as their U.S. counterparts—publishing timely books on subjects of concern and interest to a targetable audience. Most of the publishers listed in this section, however, differ from U.S. publishers in that their needs tend toward subjects that are specific to Canada or intended for a Canadian audience. Some are interested in submissions from Canadian writers only. There are many regional Canadian publishers that concentrate on region-specific subjects, and many Quebec publishers will only consider works in French.

U.S. writers hoping to do business with Canadian publishers should follow specific paths of research to find out as much about their intended markets as possible. The listings will inform you about what kinds of books the Canadian companies publish and tell you whether they are open to receiving submissions from nonCanadians. To further target your markets and see very specific examples of the books Canadian houses are publishing, send for catalogs from publishers or check their websites.

Once you have determined which Canadian publishers will accept your work, it is important to understand the differences that exist between U.S. mail and International mail. U.S. postage stamps are useless on mailings originating outside of the U.S. When enclosing a SASE for return of your query or manuscript from a publisher outside the U.S. (including Canada), you must include International Reply Coupons (IRCs) or postage stamps from that country. For more information on international mail process and purchasing Canadian postage stamps, see Mailing Submissions in the Getting Published section.

There has always been more government subsidy of publishing in Canada than in the U.S. However, with continued cuts in such subsidies, government support is on the decline. There are a few author-subsidy publishers in Canada and, as with author-subsidy publishers in the U.S., writers should proceed with caution when they are presented with this option.

Publishers offering author-subsidy arrangements (sometimes referred to as "joint venture," "co-publishing," or "cooperative publishing") are not listed in *Writer's Market*. If one of the publishers in this section offers you an author-subsidy contract, asks you to pay for all, or part, of the cost of any aspect of publishing (printing, marketing, etc.), or asks you to guarantee the purchase of a number of books yourself, please let us know about that company immediately.

Canadian publishers that accept manuscripts only from Canadian authors are indicated by the 🍁 symbol. Writer's interested in additional Canadian book publishing markets should consult *Literary Market Place* (R.R. Bowker & Co.) and *The Canadian Writer's Market* (McClelland & Stewart).

For a list of publishers according to their subjects of interest, see the nonfiction and fiction sections of the Book Publishers' Subject Index. Information on book publishers and producers listed in the previous edition of *Writer's Market* but not included in this edition can be found in the General Index.

A&C BLACK PUBLISHERS LTD., Bloomsbury plc, 37 Soho Square, London W1D 3QZ England. (020)7758-0200. Fax: (020)7758-0222. **Acquisitions:** Sarah Fecher, editor (children's nonfiction); Ben Seales, editor (children's fiction); Janet Murphy, editor (nautical); Sonia Wilson (sport); Linda Lambert, editor (arts and crafts); Tesni Hollands, editor (theatre, writing, reference); Nigel Redman, editor (ornithology). Publishes hardcover and trade paperback originals, trade paperback reprints. **Publishes 170 titles/year; imprint publishes 10-20 titles/year. Receives 3,000 queries and 650 mss/year. 5% of books from first-time authors; 70% from unagented writers. Pays royalty on retail price or**

net receipts; makes outright purchase very occasionally on short children's books. Offers £1,500-6,000 advance. Publishes book 9 months after acceptance of ms. Accepts simultaneous submissions. Responds in 1 month to queries; 2 months to proposals; 2 months to mss. Book catalog free.

Imprints: Adlard Coles Nautical (Janet Murphy, editor), Christopher Helm/Pica Press (Nigel Redman, editor), Herbert Press (Linda Lambert, editor).

Nonfiction: Children's/juvenile, how-to, illustrated book, reference. Subjects include art/architecture, creative nonfiction, education, multicultural, music/dance, nature/environment, recreation, sports, travel, nutrition. Query with SASE or submit proposal package including outline, 2 sample chapter(s) or submit complete ms. Reviews artwork/photos as part of ms package. Send transparencies.

Fiction: Juvenile. Submit 2 sample chapter(s), synopsis or submit complete ms.

Recent Title(s): *Raptors of the World*, by James Ferguson-Lees, et al; *Printmaking for Beginners*, by Jane Stobart; *A Cartoon History of the Earth*.

ADVENTURE BOOK PUBLISHERS, Durksen Enterprises Ltd., #712-3545-32 Ave. NE, Calgary, Alberta T1Y 6M6 Canada. (403)285-6844. E-mail: adventure@puzzlesbyshar.com. Website: www.puzzlesbyshar.com/adventurebooks. Publishes digital books. **Publishes 30-50 titles/year. Receives 1,000 queries and 400 mss/year. 100% of books from first-time authors; 100% from unagented writers. Pays 20% royalty.** Publishes book approximately 7 months after acceptance of ms. Accepts simultaneous submissions. Responds in 1 month to queries; 1 month to proposals; 5 months to mss. Book catalog online; ms guidelines provided by e-mail to invited authors.

Nonfiction: Biography, children's/juvenile, cookbook, how-to, humor, self-help. Subjects include Americana, animals, cooking/foods/nutrition, creative nonfiction, history, military/war, nature/environment. Query with synopsis via e-mail only. Reviews artwork/photos as part of ms package. GIF or JPEG images via e-mail.

Fiction: Adventure, historical, horror, humor, juvenile, mainstream/contemporary, military/war, mystery, romance, science fiction, suspense, western, young adult, children's illustrated (illustrations must be included with story). "Graphic sex/violence in excess is not necessary to tell a good or compelling story." Query with synopsis via e-mail only.

Recent Title(s): *Who! Me?*, by Sharon Kuntz (humor/nonfiction); *Star Ranger*, by Robert Blacketer (science fiction).

Tips: "We specialize in unpublished writers since they are the ones who need the most help and encouragement. As such, we do not encourage agency submissions. Manuscripts by invitation only. Materials sent via regular mail are returned only if adequate international postage is included (U.S. postage is not valid)."

THE ALTHOUSE PRESS, University of Western Ontario, Faculty of Education, 1137 Western Rd., London, Ontario N6G 1G7 Canada. (519)661-2096. Fax: (519)661-3833. E-mail: press@uwo.ca. Website: www.edu.uwo.ca/althousepress. Director: Dr. David Radcliffe. **Acquisitions:** Katherine Butson, editorial assistant. Publishes trade paperback originals and reprints. **Publishes 1-5 titles/year. Receives 30 queries and 19 mss/year. 50% of books from first-time authors; 100% from unagented writers. Pays 10% royalty. Offers $300 advance.** Publishes book 6 months after acceptance of ms. Accepts simultaneous submissions. Responds in 1 month to queries; 4 months to mss. Book catalog and ms guidelines free.

"The Althouse Press publishes both scholarly research monographs in education, and professional books and materials for educators in elementary schools, secondary schools and faculties of education." De-emphasizing curricular or instructional materials intended for use by elementary or secondary school students.

Nonfiction: Subjects include education (scholarly). "Do not send incomplete manuscripts that are only marginally appropriate to our market and limited mandate." Reviews artwork/photos as part of ms package. Send photocopies.

Recent Title(s): *Hyper Texts*, by Ellen Rose; *For the Love of Teaching*, by Brent Kilbourn.

Tips: Audience is practicing teachers and graduate education students.

AMBER LANE PRESS LTD., Church St., Charlbury 0X7 3PR United Kingdom. 01608 810024. Fax: 01608 810024. E-mail: jamberlane@aol.com. **Acquisitions:** Judith Scott, managing editor (drama/theater/music). Publishes hardcover and trade paperback originals, trade paperback reprints. **Publishes 5 titles/year. Receives 10 queries and 6 mss/year. 20% of books from first-time authors; 10% from unagented writers. Pays 7½-12% royalty. Offers £250-1,000 (sterling pounds) advance.** Publishes book 18 months after acceptance of ms. Accepts simultaneous submissions. Responds in 1 month to queries. Book catalog free.

Amber Lane Press aims "to help promote British theatre and modern drama in general."

Nonfiction: Biography, how-to, reference. Subjects include music/dance. Submit proposal package including outline, 2 sample chapter(s).

Fiction: Plays. "All plays need to be staged professionally by a major theater/theater company." Submit complete ms.

Recent Title(s): *Theatre in a Cool Climate*, Vera Gottlieb and Colin Chambers, eds; *Oroonoko*, Aphra Behn, adapted by Biyi Bandele (play); *Strindberg and Love*, by Eivor Martinus (biography).

Tips: "Explain why the book would be different from anything else already published on the subject."

ANNICK PRESS LTD., 15 Patricia Ave., Toronto, Ontario M2M 1H9 Canada. (416)221-4802. Fax: (416)221-8400. E-mail: annick@annickpress.com. Website: www.annickpress.com. **Acquisitions:** Rick Wilks, director (picturebooks, nonfiction, young adult fiction); Colleen MacMillan, associate publisher (YA, juvenile nonfiction). Publishes hardcover and trade paperback originals and mass market paperback reprints. **Publishes 25 titles/year. Receives 5,000 queries and 3,000 mss/year. 20% of books from first-time authors; 80-85% from unagented writers. Pays 10-12% royalty.**

Offers $2,000-4,000 advance. Publishes book 2 years after acceptance of ms. Does not accept simultaneous submissions. Responds in 1 month to queries; 2 months to proposals; 3 months to mss. Book catalog free or online; ms guidelines free.

O→ Annick Press maintains "a commitment to high quality books that entertain and challenge. Our publications share fantasy and stimulate imagination, while encouraging children to trust their judgment and abilities." Does not accept unsolicited mss.

Nonfiction: Children's/juvenile. Query with SASE. Reviews artwork/photos as part of ms package. Send photocopies.
Fiction: Juvenile, young adult. Query with SASE.
Recent Title(s): *Jungle Islands: My South Sea Adventure*, by Maria Coffey and Debora Pearson; *Leslie's Journal*, by Allan Stratton (young adult); *Night School*, by Loris Lesynski.

ANVIL PRESS, 204-A 175 E. Broadway, Vancouver, British Columbia V5T 1W2 Canada. (604)876-8710. Fax: (604)879-2667. E-mail: subter@portal.ca. Website: www.anvilpress.com. **Acquisitions:** Brian Kaufman. Publishes trade paperback originals. **Publishes 8-10 titles/year. Receives 300 queries/year. 80% of books from first-time authors; 70% from unagented writers. Pays 15% royalty on net receipts. Offers advance.** Publishes book 8 months after acceptance of ms. Does not accept simultaneous submissions. Responds in 2 months to queries; 2 months to proposals; 6 months to mss. Book catalog for 9×12 SAE with 2 first-class stamps; ms guidelines for #10 SASE.

O→ "Anvil Press publishes contemporary adult fiction, poetry and drama, giving voice to up-and-coming Canadian writers, exploring all literary genres, discovering, nurturing and promoting new Canadian literary talent." Currently emphasizing urban/suburban themed fiction and poetry; de-emphasizing historical novels

Fiction: Contemporary, modern literature—no formulaic or genre. Query with SASE.
Poetry: "Get our catalog, look at our poetry. We do very little poetry—maybe 1-2 titles per year." Query or submit 12 sample poems.
Recent Title(s): *Snatch*, by Judy MacInnes Jr. (poetry); *Touched*, by Jodi Lundgren (fiction).
Tips: Audience is young, informed, educated, aware, with an opinion, culturally active (films, books, the performing arts). "No U.S. authors, unless selected as the winner of our 3-Day Novel Contest. Research the appropriate publisher for your work."

ARSENAL PULP PRESS, 103, 1014 Homer St., Vancouver, British Columbia V6B 2W9 Canada. (604)687-4233. Fax: (604)669-8250. E-mail: contact@arsenalpulp.com. Website: www.arsenalpulp.com. **Acquisitions:** Linda Field, editor. Estab. 1980. Publishes hardcover and trade paperback originals and trade paperback reprints. **Publishes 16 titles/year. Receives 400 queries and 200 mss/year. 40% of books from first-time authors; 100% from unagented writers. Pays 15% royalty on wholesale price. Offers $500-1,000 advance.** Publishes book 1 year after acceptance of ms. Accepts simultaneous submissions. Responds in 1 month to queries; 4 months to proposals; 4 months to mss. Book catalog for 9×12 SAE with 2 first-class stamps or online; ms guidelines for #10 SASE or online.
Nonfiction: Cookbook, humor, illustrated book, literary, cultural studies. Subjects include art/architecture, cooking/foods/nutrition, creative nonfiction, ethnic (Canadian, aboriginal issues), gay/lesbian, history (cultural), language/literature, multicultural, music/dance (popular), regional (British Columbia), sex, sociology, travel, women's issues/studies, film. Submit proposal package including outline, 2-3 sample chapter(s). Reviews artwork/photos as part of ms package.
Fiction: Erotica, ethnic, experimental, feminist, gay/lesbian, literary, multicultural, short story collections. Submit proposal package including 2-3 sample chapter(s), synopsis.
Recent Title(s): *How It All Vegan*, by Bernard & Kramer (nonfiction-cookbook); *Carnal Nation*, by Brooks & Grubisic (fiction anthology).

BEACH HOLME PUBLISHERS LTD., 226-2040 W. 12th Ave., Vancouver, British Columbia V6J 2G2 Canada. (604)733-4868. Fax: (604)733-4860. E-mail: bhp@beachholme.bc.ca. Website: www.beachholme.bc.ca. **Acquisitions:** Michael Carroll, publisher (adult and young adult fiction, poetry, creative nonfiction); Jen Hamilton, production manager; Trisha Telep, publicity and marketing coordinator. Estab. 1971. Publishes trade paperback originals. **Publishes 14 titles/year. Receives 1,000 submissions/year. 40% of books from first-time authors; 75% from unagented writers. Pays 10% royalty on retail price. Offers $500 average advance.** Publishes book 1 year after acceptance of ms. Does not accept simultaneous submissions. Responds in 4 months to queries. Ms guidelines online.
Imprints: Porcepic Books (literary); Sandcastle Books (children's/YA); Prospect Books (nonfiction).

O→ Beach Holme seeks "to publish excellent, emerging Canadian fiction, nonfiction and poetry and to contribute to Canadian materials for children with quality young adult historical novels."

Nonfiction: Subjects include creative nonfiction. Query with SASE or submit outline, 2 sample chapter(s).
Fiction: Experimental, literary, poetry, young adult. Interested in excellent quality, imaginative writing from writers published in Canadian literary magazines. Query with SASE or submit outline, 2 sample chapter(s).
Recent Title(s): *Hail Mary Corner*, by Brian Payton; *Tiger in Trouble*, by Eric Walters.
Tips: "Make sure the manuscript is well written. We see so many that only the unique and excellent can't be put down. Prior publication is a must. This doesn't necessarily mean book-length manuscripts, but a writer should try to publish his or her short fiction or poetry."

BERG PUBLISHERS, Oxford International Publishers, 150 Cowley Rd., Oxford 0X4 1JJ United Kingdom. (44)1865-245104. Fax: (44)1865-791165. E-mail: enquiry@bergpublishers.com. Website: bergpublishers.com. **Acquisitions:** Kathryn Earle, editorial and managing director (anthropology, fashion, material culture); Kathleen May, senior commissioning editor (history & politics). Publishes hardcover and trade paperback originals. **Publishes 50 titles/year. Receives**

700 queries and 100 mss/year. 98% from unagented writers. Pays royalty on wholesale price. Publishes book 9 months after acceptance of ms. Does not accept simultaneous submissions. Responds in 2 months to queries; 2 months to proposals; 4 months to mss. Book catalog free; ms guidelines free.

O→ Berg Publishers publishes "academic books aimed at an undergraduate and postgraduate readership only." Currently emphasizing fashion, sport, material culture, leisure studies, consumption, cultural history. De-emphasizing literary studies.

Nonfiction: Textbook. Subjects include anthropology/archeology, history, sociology, sports, fashion. Submit proposal package including outline.

Recent Title(s): *'Don We Now Our Gay Apparel': Gay Men's Dress in the 20th Century*, by Shaun Cole; *The Internet: An Ethnographic Approach*, by Daniel Miller & Don Slater; *Filming Women in the Third Reich*, by Jo Fox.

BETWEEN THE LINES, 720 Bathurst St., Suite #404, Toronto, Ontario M5S 2R4 Canada. (416)535-9914. Fax: (416)535-1484. E-mail: btlbooks@web.ca. Website: www.btlbooks.com. **Acquisitions:** Paul Eprile, editorial coordinator. Publishes trade paperback originals. **Publishes 8 titles/year. Receives 150 queries and 25 mss/year. 80% of books from first-time authors; 95% from unagented writers. Pays 8% royalty.** Publishes book 1 year after acceptance of ms. Accepts simultaneous submissions. Responds in 2 months to queries; 2 months to proposals; 4 months to mss. Book catalog and ms guidelines for 8½ × 11 SAE and IRCs.

O→ "We are a small independent house concentrating on politics and public policy issues, social issues, gender issues, international development, education and the environment. We publish mainly Canadian authors."

Nonfiction: Subjects include education, gay/lesbian, government/politics, health/medicine, history, memoirs, social sciences, sociology, women's issues/studies. Submit proposal package including outline, 2-3 sample chapter(s). Reviews artwork/photos as part of ms package.

Recent Title(s): *Poor-Bashing: The Politics of Exclusion*; *Mirrors of Stone: Fragments from the Porcupine Frontier.*

THE BOOKS COLLECTIVE, 214-21, 10405 Jasper Ave., Edmonton, Alberta T5J 3S2 Canada. (780)448-0590. Fax: (780)448-0640. Publishes hardcover and trade paperback originals. **Publishes 10-12 titles/year; imprint publishes 2-5 titles/year. 30-60% of books from first-time authors; 90% from unagented writers. Pays 6-12% royalty on retail price. Offers $250-500 (Canadian) advance.** Publishes book 1 year after acceptance of ms. Does not accept simultaneous submissions. Responds in 1 month to queries; 1 month to proposals; 6 months to mss. Book catalog for 9 × 12 SAE with 4 first-class Canadian stamps or on website; ms guidelines online.

Imprints: Tesseract Books, River Books, Slipstream Books.

O→ "All nonfiction projects are developed from query letters or are developed inhouse. Always query first." Canadian authors only (expats or living abroad, landed immigrants OK). All non-Canadian submissions returned unread."

Nonfiction: Biography, multimedia. Subjects include creative nonfiction, language/literature, memoirs, multicultural. Query with SASE or submit proposal package including outline, 1-3 sample chapter(s), résumé. Reviews artwork/photos as part of ms package. Send photocopies.

Fiction: Experimental, fantasy, feminist, gay/lesbian, horror, literary, mainstream/contemporary, multicultural, multimedia, plays, poetry, regional, science fiction, short story collections. Tesseract Books publishes an annual anthology of Canadian speculative short fiction and poetry. Query with SASE or submit proposal package including 1-3 sample chapter(s), résumé, synopsis or submit complete ms.

Poetry: Query or submit 5-10 sample poems or submit complete ms.

Recent Title(s): *The Edmonton Queen: Not A Riverboat Story*, by D. Hagen (contemporary memoir); *Gypsey Messenger*, by M. Megla (poetry).

Tips: "Our books are geared for literate, intelligent readers of literary mainstream, cutting edge and speculative writing. If you do not know our titles, query first or write for guidelines. Look up our titles and study suitability of your manuscript. We are a writers' co-op—expect long timelines. Unless your manuscript is of surpassing excellence it will not survive omission of an SASE."

BOREALIS PRESS, LTD., 110 Bloomingdale St., Ottawa, Ontario K2C 4A4 Canada. (613)798-9299. Fax: (613)798-9747. E-mail: borealis@istar.ca. Website: www.borealispress.com. Frank Tierney, president. **Acquisitions:** Glenn Clever, senior editor. Estab. 1972. Publishes hardcover and paperback originals. **Publishes 10-20 titles/year. Receives 400-500 submissions/year. 80% of books from first-time authors; 95% from unagented writers. Pays 10% royalty on net receipts.** Publishes book 18 months after acceptance of ms. Does not accept simultaneous submissions. Responds in 2 months to queries. Book catalog online.

Imprints: Tecumseh Press.

O→ "Our mission is to publish work which will be of lasting interest in the Canadian book market." Currently emphasizing Canadian fiction, nonfiction, drama, poetry. De-emphasizing children's books.

Nonfiction: Biography, children's/juvenile, reference. Subjects include government/politics, history, language/literature, regional. "Only material Canadian in content." Looks for "style in tone and language, reader interest and maturity of outlook." Query with SASE or submit outline, 2 sample chapter(s). *No unsolicited mss.* Reviews artwork/photos as part of ms package.

Fiction: Adventure, ethnic, historical, literary, romance, short story collections, young adult. "Only material Canadian in content and dealing with significant aspects of the human situation." Query with SASE or submit 1-2 sample chapter(s), synopsis. *No unsolicited mss.*

Recent Title(s): *Biography of a Beagle*, by Gail MacMillan; *Who Cares Now*, by Lew Duddnidge; *A Place Called Morning*, by Anne McLaughlin.

THE BOSTON MILLS PRESS, 132 Main St., Erin, Ontario N0B 1T0 Canada. (519)833-2407. Fax: (519)833-2195. E-mail: books@bostonmillspress.com. Website: www.bostonmillspress.com. President: John Denison. **Acquisitions:** Noel Hudson, managing editor. Estab. 1974. Publishes hardcover and trade paperback originals. **Publishes 20 titles/year. Receives 100 submissions/year. 40% of books from first-time authors; 95% from unagented writers. Pays 8-15% royalty on retail price. Offers advance.** Publishes book 2 years after acceptance of ms. Accepts simultaneous submissions. Responds in 2 months to queries. Book catalog free.

Boston Mills Press publishes specific market titles of Canadian and American interest including history, transportation and regional guidebooks. "We like very focused books aimed at the North American market."

Nonfiction: Coffee table book, gift book, illustrated book. Subjects include Americana, art/architecture, cooking/foods/nutrition, creative nonfiction, gardening, history, military/war, nature/environment, photography, recreation, regional, sports, travel, Canadiana. "We're interested in anything to do with Canadian or American history—especially transportation." No autobiographies. Query with SASE. Reviews artwork/photos as part of ms package. Send photocopies.

BRICK BOOKS, Box 20081, 431 Boler Rd., London, Ontario N6K 4G6 Canada. (519)657-8579. E-mail: brick.books@sympatico.ca. Website: www.brickbooks.ca. **Acquisitions:** Don McKay, editor (poetry), Stan Dragland, editor (poetry). Publishes trade paperback originals. **Publishes 6 titles/year. Receives 60 queries and 120 mss/year. 30% of books from first-time authors; 100% from unagented writers. Pays 10% royalty in books.** Publishes book 2 years after acceptance of ms. Responds in 1 month to queries; 3 months to proposals; 5 months to mss. Book catalog and ms guidelines free or online.

- Brick Books has a reading period of January 1-April 30. Mss received outside that reading period will be returned.

Poetry: Writers must be Canadian citizens or landed immigrants. Query or submit 8-10 sample poems.

Recent Title(s): *Songs for Relinquishing the Earth*, Jan Zwicky; *Short Talks*, Anne Carson; *Rest on the Flight into Egypt*, A.F. Moritz.

Tips: "Writers without previous publications in literary journals or magazines are rarely considered by Brick Books for publication."

BROADVIEW PRESS LTD., P.O. Box 1243, Peterborough, Ontario K9J 7H5 Canada. (705)743-8990. Fax: (705)743-8353. E-mail: customerservice@broadviewpress.com. Website: www.broadviewpress.com. **Acquisitions:** Julia Gaunce, humanities editor (humanities—English, philosophy); Mical Moser, history editor; Michael Harrison, vice president (social sciences—political science, sociology, anthropology). Estab. 1985. **Publishes 50-60 titles/year. Receives 500 queries and 200 mss/year. 10% of books from first-time authors; 99% from unagented writers. Pays royalty.** Publishes book 1 year after acceptance of ms. Accepts simultaneous submissions. Responds in 1 month to queries; 2 months to proposals; 4 months to mss. Book catalog free; ms guidelines online.

"We publish in a broad variety of subject areas in the arts and social sciences. We are open to a broad range of political and philosophical viewpoints, from liberal and conservative to libertarian and Marxist, and including a wide range of feminist viewpoints."

Nonfiction: Biography, reference, textbook. Subjects include anthropology/archeology, gay/lesbian, history, language/literature, philosophy, religion, sociology, women's issues/studies. "All titles must have some potential for university or college-level course use. Crossover titles are acceptable." Query with SASE or submit proposal package. Reviews artwork/photos as part of ms package. Send photocopies.

Recent Title(s): *A Short History of the Middle Ages*, by Barbara Rosenwein.

Tips: "Our titles often appeal to a broad readership; we have many books that are as much of interest to the general reader as they are to academics and students."

BROKEN JAW PRESS, Box 596, Station A, Fredericton, New Brunswick E3B 5A6 Canada. (506)454-5127. Fax: (506)454-5127. E-mail: jblades@nbnet.nb.ca. Website: www.brokenjaw.com. Publisher: Joe Blades. **Acquisitions:** R.M. Vaughan, editor (Canadian drama); Rob McLennan, editor (Canadian poetry, critical essays). Publishes Canadian-authored trade paperback originals and reprints. **Publishes 8-12 titles/year. 50% of books from first-time authors; 100% from unagented writers. Pays 10% royalty on retail price. Offers $0-100 advance.** Publishes book 18 months after acceptance of ms. Does not accept simultaneous submissions. Responds in 1 year to mss. Book catalog for 9×12 SAE with 2 first-class Canadian stamps in Canada; ms guidelines for #10 SASE.

Imprints: Book Rat, SpareTime Editions, Dead Sea Physh Products, Maritimes Arts Projects Productions.

"We are a small, mostly literary Canadian publishing house."

Nonfiction: Illustrated book, self-help. Subjects include creative nonfiction, gay/lesbian, history, language/literature, regional, women's issues/studies, contemporary culture. Reviews artwork/photos as part of ms package.

Fiction: Literary.

Recent Title(s): *What Was Always Hers*, by Uma Parameswaran (fiction); *Bagne, or, Criteria for Heaven*, by Rob McLennan (poetry).

Tips: "We don't want unsolicited manuscripts or queries, except in the context of the New Muse Award and the Poet's Corner Award. Please see the award guidelines on our website."

THE BRUCEDALE PRESS, P.O. Box 2259, Port Elgin, Ontario N0H 2C0 Canada. (519)832-6025. Website: www.bmts.com/~brucedale. **Acquisitions:** Anne Duke Judd, editor-in-chief. Publishes hardcover and trade paperback originals.

Publishes 3 titles/year. Receives 50 queries and 30 mss/year. 75% of books from first-time authors; 100% from unagented writers. Pays royalty. Publishes book 1 year after acceptance of ms. Accepts simultaneous submissions. Book catalog and ms guidelines for #10 SASE (Canadian postage or IRC) or online.

O→ The Brucedale Press publishes books and other materials of regional interest and merit as well as literary, historical and/or pictorial works.

Nonfiction: Biography, children's/juvenile, humor, illustrated book, reference. Subjects include history, humor, language/literature, memoirs, military/war, nature/environment, photography. "Invitations to submit are sent to writers and writers' groups on The Brucedale Press mailing list when projects are in progress. Send a #10 SASE to have your name added to the list. Unless responding to an invitation to submit, query first, with outline and sample chapter for book-length submissions. Submit full manuscript of work intended for children. A brief résumé of your writing efforts and successes is always of interest, and may bring future invitations, even if the present submission is not accepted for publication." Reviews artwork/photos as part of ms package.

Fiction: Fantasy, feminist, historical, humor, juvenile, literary, mainstream/contemporary, mystery, plays, poetry, romance, short story collections, young adult.

Recent Title(s): *Barns of the Queen's Bush*, by Jon Radojkovic; *Thirty Years on Call: A Country Doctor's Family Life*, by Doris Pennington; *The Quilted Grapevine*, by Nancy-Lou Patterson.

Tips: "Our focus is very regional. In reading submissions, I look for quality writing with a strong connection to the Queen's Bush area of Ontario. Suggest all authors visit our website, get a catalog and read our books before submitting."

CANADIAN LIBRARY ASSOCIATION, 328 Frank St., Ottawa, Ontario K2P 0X8 Canada. (613)232-9625, ext. 322. Fax: (613)563-9895. E-mail: emorton@cla.ca. Website: www.cla.ca. Elizabeth Morton, editor, (feliciter/monographs). Publishes trade paperback originals. **Publishes 4 titles/year. Receives 10 queries and 5 mss/year. 50% of books from first-time authors; 100% from unagented writers. Pays 10% royalty on wholesale price.** Publishes book 6 months after acceptance of ms. Does not accept simultaneous submissions. Responds in 1 month to queries; 3 months to proposals; 3 months to mss. Book catalog and ms guidelines free.

O→ "CLA publishes practical/professional/academic materials with a Canadian focus or direct Canadian application as a service to CLA members and to contribute to the professional development of library staff."

Nonfiction: Reference, textbook. Subjects include history, language/literature, library science. Query with SASE or submit outline. Reviews artwork/photos as part of ms package. Send photocopies.

Recent Title(s): *The B2B Canadian Research Sourcebook: Your Essential Guide*; *Demystifying Copyright: A Researcher's Guide to Copyright in Canadian Libraries and Archives*.

Tips: Audience is library and information scientists.

CANADIAN PLAINS RESEARCH CENTER, University of Regina, Regina, Saskatchewan S4S 0A2 Canada. (306)585-4795. Fax: (306)585-4699. E-mail: brian.mlazgar@uregina.ca. Website: www.cprc.uregina.ca. **Acquisitions:** Brian Mlazgar, coordinator. Estab. 1973. Publishes scholarly paperback originals and some casebound originals. **Publishes 8-10 titles/year. Receives 15-20 submissions/year. 35% of books from first-time authors. Offers advance.** Publishes book 2 years after acceptance of ms. Does not accept simultaneous submissions. Responds in 6 months to queries. Book catalog and ms guidelines free.

O→ Canadian Plains Research Center publishes scholarly research on the Canadian plains.

Nonfiction: Biography, illustrated book, technical, textbook. Subjects include business/economics, government/politics, history, nature/environment, regional, sociology. "The Canadian Plains Research Center publishes the results of research on topics relating to the Canadian Plains region, although manuscripts relating to the Great Plains region will be considered. Material *must* be scholarly. Do not submit health, self-help, hobbies, music, sports, psychology, recreation or cookbooks unless they have a scholarly approach. For example, we would be interested in acquiring a pioneer manuscript cookbook, with modern ingredient equivalents, if the material relates to the Canadian Plains/Great Plains region." Query with SASE or submit complete ms. Reviews artwork/photos as part of ms package.

Recent Title(s): *Discover Saskatchewan*, by Nilson (guide to historic sites and markers).

Tips: "Pay attention to manuscript preparation and accurate footnoting, according to *Chicago Manual of Style*."

CAPALL BANN PUBLISHING, Freshfields Chieveley, Berks RG208TF United Kingdom. (0044)1635 247050. Fax: (0044)1635 247050. E-mail: capallbann1@virginbiz.com. Website: www.capallbann.co.uk. **Acquisitions:** Julia Day (MBS, healing, animals); Jon Day (MBS, religion). Publishes trade and mass market paperback originals and trade paperback and mass market paperback reprints. **Publishes 46 titles/year. Receives 400 queries and 250 mss/year. 50% of books from first-time authors; 100% from unagented writers. Pays 10% royalty on net sales.** Publishes book 8 months after acceptance of ms. Accepts simultaneous submissions. Responds in 2 weeks to queries; 2 months to proposals; 2 months to mss. Book catalog free; ms guidelines for 4 IRC's or on website.

O→ "Our mission is to publish books of real value to enhance and improve readers' lives."

Nonfiction: Illustrated book, reference, self-help, technical. Subjects include animals, anthropology/archeology, gardening, health/medicine, music/dance, nature/environment, philosophy, religion, spirituality, women's issues/studies, new age. Submit outline. Reviews artwork/photos as part of ms package. Send photocopies.

Recent Title(s): *Everything You Wanted to Know About Your Body, But So Far Nobody's Been Able to Tell You*; *Real Fairies*, by David Tame.

CARSWELL THOMSON PROFESSIONAL PUBLISHING, One Corporate Plaza 2075 Kennedy Rd., Scarborough, Ontario M1T 3V4 Canada. (416)298-5024. Fax: (416)298-5094. E-mail: ROBERT.FREEMAN@carswell.com.

Website: www.carswell.com. **Acquisitions:** Robert Freeman, vice president, legal, accounting and finance, and corporate groups. Publishes hardcover originals. **Publishes 150-200 titles/year. 30-50% of books from first-time authors. Pays 5-15% royalty on wholesale price. Offers $1,000-5,000 advance.** Publishes book 6 months after acceptance of ms. Accepts simultaneous submissions. Responds in 3 months to queries. Book catalog and ms guidelines free.

O-→ Carswell Thomson is Canada's national resource of information and legal interpretations for law, accounting, tax and business professionals.

Nonfiction: Reference (legal, tax). "Canadian information of a regulatory nature is our mandate." Submit proposal package including outline, résumé.

Tips: Audience is Canada and persons interested in Canadian information; professionals in law, tax, accounting fields; business people interested in regulatory material.

CHA PRESS, 17 York St., Ottawa, Ontario K1N 9J6 Canada. (613)241-8005, ext. 264. Fax: (613)241-5055. E-mail: chapress@canadian-healthcare.org. Website: www.canadian-healthcare.org. **Acquisitions:** Eleanor Sawyer, director of publishing. **Publishes 6-8 titles/year. Receives 5 queries and 3 mss/year. 40% of books from first-time authors; 90% from unagented writers. Pays 10-17% royalty on retail price. or makes outright purchase of $250-1,000. Offers $500-1,500 advance.** Responds in 3 months to queries. Book catalog and ms guidelines free.

O-→ CHA Press strives to be Canada's health administration textbook publisher. "We serve readers in our broad continuum of care in regional health authorities, hospitals and health care facilities and agencies, which are governed by trustees." Currently emphasizing history of regionalization; accountability of boards/executives; executives and leadership. De-emphasizing hospital-based issues of any type.

Nonfiction: How-to, textbook, guides. Subjects include health/medicine, history. Query with SASE or submit outline.

Recent Title(s): *Continuing the Care, revised edition*, coedited by Marion Stephenson and Eleanor Sawyer; *The Health-Promoting Health Care Facility*, by Ted Mauor; *Don't Shoot the Messenger*, by the Health Care Public Relations Association Canada.

Tips: Audience is healthcare facility managers (senior/middle); policy analysts/researchers; nurse practitioners and other healthcare professionals; trustees. "CHA Press is looking to expand its frontlist in 2003 to include governance, risk management, security and safety, health system reform and quality assessment. Don't underestimate amount of time it will take to write or mistake generic 'how-to' health for mass media as appropriate for CHA's specialty press."

CHARLTON PRESS, P.O. Box 94, Station Main, Thornhill, Ontario L3T 3N1 Canada. Fax: (416)488-4656. E-mail: chpress@charltonpress.com. Website: www.charltonpress.com. **Acquisitions:** Jean Dale, managing editor. Publishes trade paperback originals and reprints. **Publishes 15 titles/year. Receives 30 queries and 5 mss/year. 10% of books from first-time authors; 100% from unagented writers. Pays 10% royalty on wholesale price. or makes variable outright purchase.** Publishes book 6 months after acceptance of ms. Accepts simultaneous submissions. Responds in 1 month to queries; 1 month to proposals; 2 months to mss. Book catalog free.

Nonfiction: Reference (price guides on collectibles). Subjects include hobbies (numismatics, toys, military badges, ceramic collectibles, sports cards). Submit outline. Reviews artwork/photos as part of ms package. Send photocopies.

Recent Title(s): *Royal Doulton Figurines*, J. Dale (reference guide).

CHEMTEC PUBLISHING, 38 Earswick Dr., Toronto-Scarborough, Ontario M1E 1C6 Canada. (416)265-2603. Fax: (416)265-1399. E-mail: info@chemtec.org. Website: www.chemtec.org/. **Acquisitions:** Anna Wypych, president. Publishes hardcover originals. **Publishes 5 titles/year. Receives 10 queries and 7 mss/year. 20% of books from first-time authors. Pays 5-15% royalty on retail price.** Publishes book 6 months after acceptance of ms. Accepts simultaneous submissions. Responds in 2 months to queries; 4 months to mss. Book catalog and ms guidelines free.

O-→ Chemtec publishes books on polymer chemistry, physics and technology. "Special emphasis is given to process additives and books which treat subject in comprehensive manner."

Nonfiction: Technical, textbook. Subjects include science, environment, chemistry, polymers. Submit outline, sample chapter(s).

Recent Title(s): *Handbook of Fillers*, by George Wypych; *Handbook of Solvents*, by multiple authors.

Tips: Audience is industrial research and universities.

COACH HOUSE BOOKS, 401 Huron St. on bpNichol Lane, Toronto, Ontario M5S 2G5 Canada. (416)979-2217. Fax: (416)977-1158. E-mail: mail@chbooks.com. Website: www.chbooks.com. **Acquisitions:** Darren Wershler-Henry, poetry; Alana Wilcox, fiction. Publishes trade paperback originals. **Publishes 10 titles/year. 80% of books from first-time authors; 100% from unagented writers. Pays 10% royalty on retail price.** Publishes book 1 year after acceptance of ms. Does not accept simultaneous submissions. Responds in 6 months to queries. Book catalog and ms guidelines online.

Nonfiction: Artists' books. Query with SASE. *All unsolicited mss returned unopened.*

Fiction: Experimental, literary, plays. "Consult website for submissions policy." *All unsolicited mss returned unopened.*

Poetry: Consult website for guidelines. Query.

Recent Title(s): *Fidget*, by K. Goldsmith (poetry); *Eunoia*, by Christian Bök (poetry); *Lenny Bruce Is Dead*, by Jonathan Goldstein (fiction).

[A] **CONSTABLE PUBLISHERS**, Constable & Robinson, 3 The Lanchesters, 162 Fulham Palace Rd., London WG 9ER United Kingdom. 0208-741-3663. Fax: 0208-748-7562. **Acquisitions:** (Ms.) Carol O'Brien (biography: historical and literary, Celtic interest, pre-WWII military history, travel literature). Publishes hardcover and trade paperback originals. **Publishes 60 titles/year. Receives 3,000 queries and 1,000 mss/year. 2% of books from first-time authors;**

20% from unagented writers. Pays 7½% royalty on hardcover retail price. Offers advance. Publishes book 1 year after acceptance of ms. Accepts simultaneous submissions. Responds in 1 month to queries; 1 month to proposals; 3 months to mss. Book catalog free.

Nonfiction: Biography. Subjects include history, military/war, travel, astronomy. Query with SASE or submit 3 sample chapter(s), list of chapter titles. Reviews artwork/photos as part of ms package. Send photocopies.

Fiction: Crime/whodunnit. *Agented submissions only.*

Recent Title(s): *Hunted*, by David Fletcher (biography/travel); *Panzerkrieg*, by Mike Syron and Peter McCarthy (military history); *Chaucer: 1340-1400*, by Richard West (biography).

COTEAU BOOKS, 2206 Dewdney Ave., Suite 401, Regina, Saskatchewan S4R 1H3 Canada. (306)777-0170. Fax: (306)522-5152. E-mail: coteau@coteaubooks.com. Website: www.coteaubooks.com. **Acquisitions:** Geoffrey Ursell, publisher. Estab. 1975. Publishes trade paperback originals and reprints. **Publishes 20 titles/year. Receives 200 queries and 200 mss/year. 50% of books from first-time authors; 100% from unagented writers. Pays 10% royalty on retail price.** Publishes book 1 year after acceptance of ms. Does not accept simultaneous submissions. Responds in 2 months to queries; 6 months to mss. Book catalog free; ms guidelines online.

"Our mission is to publish the finest in Canadian fiction, nonfiction, poetry, drama and children's literature, with an emphasis on Saskatchewan and prairie writers." De-emphasizing science fiction, picture books.

Nonfiction: Coffee table book, reference. Subjects include creative nonfiction, ethnic, history, language/literature, memoirs, regional, sports, travel. Canadian authors only. Submit 3-4 sample chapter(s), author bio, SASE.

Fiction: Ethnic, fantasy, feminist, gay/lesbian, historical, humor, juvenile, literary, mainstream/contemporary, multicultural, multimedia, mystery, plays, poetry, regional, short story collections, spiritual, sports, young adult. Canadian authors only. Submit 3-4 sample chapter(s), author bio, SASE.

Poetry: Submit 20-25 sample poems or submit complete ms.

Recent Title(s): *In the Same Boat*, juvenile fiction series for ages 8 and up (promotes familiarity with other cultures); *Penelope's Way*, by Blanche Howard (novel); *Out of Her Backpack*, by Laura Cutler (short stories).

Tips: "Look at past publications to get an idea of our editorial program. We do not publish romance, horror or picture books, but are interested in juvenile and teen fiction from Canadian authors. Submissions may be made by e-mail (maximum 20 pages) with attachments."

CREATIVE BOUND, INC., Box 424, 151 Tansley Dr., Carp, Ontario K0A 1L0 Canada. (613)831-3641. Fax: (613)831-3643. E-mail: info@creativebound.com. Website: www.creativebound.com. **Acquisitions:** Gail Baird, president. Publishes trade paperback originals. **Publishes 6-8 titles/year. Receives 250 queries and 80 mss/year. 30% of books from first-time authors; 100% from unagented writers. Pays 11-15% royalty on wholesale price.** Publishes book 5 months after acceptance of ms. Accepts simultaneous submissions. Responds in 1 month to queries; 3 months to proposals; 3 months to mss. Book catalog free.

"We publish books that 'inspire, help and heal' in five categories: mind/body/spirit, personal growth, life balance, healing/recovery, parenting."

Nonfiction: Personal growth; life balance; stress management; mind/body/spirit; parenting; healing/recovery. Submit proposal package including outline, sample chapter(s). Reviews artwork/photos as part of ms package. Send photocopies.

Recent Title(s): *Vitamin C for Couples*, by Luke DeSadeleer; *It's Not About Time! Redefining Leisure in a Changing World*, by Joe Pavelka.

CRESCENT MOON PUBLISHING, P.O. Box 393, Maidstone Kent ME14 5XU United Kingdom. E-mail: jrobinson @crescentmoon.org.uk. Website: www.crescentmoon.org.uk. **Acquisitions:** Jeremy Robinson, director (arts, media, cinema, literature); Cassidy Hushes (visual arts). Publishes hardcover and trade paperback originals. **Publishes 25 titles/year. Receives 300 queries and 400 mss/year. 1% of books from first-time authors; 1% from unagented writers. Pays royalty. Offers negotiable advance.** Publishes book 18 months after acceptance of ms. Accepts simultaneous submissions. Responds in 2 months to queries; 4 months to proposals; 4 months to mss. Book catalog free; ms guidelines free.

Imprints: Joe's Press, Pagan America Magazine, Passion Magazine.

"Our mission is to publish the best in contemporary work, in poetry, fiction and critical studies and selections from the great writers." Currently emphasizing nonfiction (media, film, music, painting). De-emphasizing children's books.

Nonfiction: Biography, children's/juvenile, illustrated book, reference, scholarly (academic), textbook. Subjects include Americana, art/architecture, gardening, language/literature, music/dance, philosophy, religion, travel, women's issues/studies. Query with SASE or submit outline, 2 sample chapter(s). Reviews artwork/photos as part of ms package. Send photocopies.

Fiction: Erotica, experimental, feminist, literary. "We do not publish much fiction at present, but will consider high quality new work." Query with SASE or submit 2 sample chapter(s), synopsis.

Poetry: "We prefer a small selection of the poet's very best work at first. We prefer free or non-rhyming poetry. Do not send too much material." Query or submit 6 sample poems.

Recent Title(s): *Nuclear War in the UK* (nonfiction); *Andy Goldworthy in Close-UP* (nonfiction).

Tips: "Our audience is interested in new contemporary writing."

CRESSRELLES PUBLISHING CO. LTD., 10 Station Rd., Industrial Estate, Colwall, Malvern Worcestershire WR13 6RN United Kingdom. Phone/Fax: 01684 540154. E-mail: simonsmith@cressrelles4drama.fsbusiness.co.uk. Publishes hardcover and trade paperback originals. **Publishes 10-20 titles/year. Pays royalty on retail price.** Book catalog free.

Imprints: Kenyon-Deane; J. Garnet Miller; New Playwright's Network; Actinic Press.
Nonfiction: Subjects include drama (plays), theatre. Submit complete ms.

DUNDURN PRESS LTD., (formerly Simon & Pierre Publishing Co. Ltd.), 8 Market St., Suite 200, Toronto, Ontario M5E 1M6 Canada. (416)214-5544. Website: www.dundurn.com. **Acquisitions:** Acquisitions Editor. Estab. 1972. Publishes hardcover and trade paperback originals and reprints. **Publishes 50-60 titles/year. Receives 600 submissions/year. 50% of books from first-time authors; 85% from unagented writers. Pays 10% royalty on net receipts.** Publishes book an average of 1 year after acceptance of ms. Accepts simultaneous submissions. Responds in 3-4 months to queries. Ms guidelines free.

Dundurn publishes books by Canadian authors.

Nonfiction: Subjects include art/architecture, history (Canadian and military), music/dance (Drama), regional, art history, theatre, serious and popular nonfiction.
Fiction: Literary, mystery, young adult. Query with SASE or submit sample chapter(s), synopsis, author bio.
Recent Title(s): *Ten Good Seconds of Silence*, by Elizabeth Ruth (novel); *Queen Elizabeth, The Queen Mother 1900-2002* (illustrated biography); *Haunted: A Canadian Family's Experiences Living in a Haunted House* (popular nonfiction).

ECW PRESS, 2120 Queen St. E., Suite 200, Toronto, Ontario M4E 1E2 Canada. (416)694-3348. Fax: (416)698-9906. E-mail: info@ecwpress.com. Website: www.ecwpress.com. **Acquisitions:** Jack David, president (nonfiction); Michael Holmes, literary editor (fiction, poetry); Jennifer Hale, associate editor (pop culture, entertainment). Estab. 1979. Publishes hardcover and trade paperback originals. **Publishes 40 titles/year; imprint publishes 8 titles/year. Receives 500 queries and 300 mss/year. 30% of books from first-time authors. Pays 8-12% royalty on net receipts. Offers $300-5,000 advance.** Publishes book 18 months after acceptance of ms. Accepts simultaneous submissions. Responds in 1 month to queries; 2 months to proposals; 4 months to mss. Book catalog and ms guidelines free.

ECW publishes nonfiction about people or subjects that have a substantial fan base. Currently emphasizing books about music, Wicca, gambling, TV and movie stars.

Nonfiction: Biography (popular), humor. Subjects include business/economics, creative nonfiction, gay/lesbian, general nonfiction, government/politics, health/medicine, history, memoirs, money/finance, regional, sex, sports, women's issues/studies, contemporary culture, Wicca, gambling, TV and movie stars. Submit proposal package including outline, 4-5 sample chapter(s), IRC, SASE. Reviews artwork/photos as part of ms package. Send photocopies.
Fiction: "We publish literary fiction and poetry from Canadian authors exclusively. Literary, mystery, poetry, short story collections, suspense. Submit proposal package including 1-2 sample chapter(s), synopsis, IRC, SASE.
Poetry: "We publish Canadian poetry exclusively." Query or submit 4-5 sample poems.
Recent Title(s): *Too Close to the Falls*, by Catherine Gildiner; *Blakwidow: My First Year as a Professional Wrestler*, by Amanda Storm; *Burn*, by Paul Vermeersch (poetry).
Tips: "Visit our website *and* read a selection of our books."

EDGE SCIENCE FICTION AND FANTASY PUBLISHING, Box 1714, Calgary, Alberta T2P 2L7 Canada. (403)254-0160. Fax: (403)254-0456. E-mail: editor@edgewebsite.com. Website: www.edgewebsite.com. **Acquisitions:** Cheyenne Grewe. Publishes hardcover and trade paperback originals. **Publishes 2-4 titles/year. Receives 480 queries and 400 mss/year. 70% of books from first-time authors; 75% from unagented writers. Pays 10% royalty on wholesale price. Offers negotiable advance.** Publishes book 18 months after acceptance of ms. Does not accept simultaneous submissions. Responds in 1 month to queries; 1 month to proposals; 4-5 months to mss. Ms guidelines online.

"We want to encourage, produce and promote thought-provoking and fun-to-read science fiction and fantasy literature by 'bringing the magic alive one world at a time' with each new book released."

Fiction: Fantasy (space fantasy, sword and sorcery), science fiction (hard science/technological, soft/sociological). "We are looking for all types of fantasy and science fiction, except juvenile/young adult." Query with SASE or submit 1 sample chapter(s), synopsis.
Recent Title(s): *The Black Chalice*, by Marie Jakober (historical fantasy); *Lyskarion: The Song of the Wind*, by Janice Cullum (fantasy).
Tips: "Send us your best, polished, completed ms. Use proper ms format. Take the time before you submit to get a critique from someone who can offer you useful advice. When in doubt, visit our website for helpful resources, FAQs, and other tips."

ÉDITIONS DU NOROÎT, 6694, avenue Papineau, Montreal, Quebec H2G 2X2 Canada. (514)727-0005. Fax: (514)723-6660. E-mail: lenoroit@ca.inter.net. Website: lenoroit.multimedia.ca. **Acquisitions:** Paul Belanger, director. Publishes trade paperback originals and reprints. **Publishes 20 titles/year. Receives 500 queries and 500 mss/year. Pays 10% royalty on retail price.** Publishes book 1 year after acceptance of ms. Responds in 4 months to mss.

Éditions du Noroît publishes poetry and essays on poetry.

Poetry: Submit 40 sample poems.
Recent Title(s): *Transfiguration*, by Jacques Brault/E.D. Blodgett; *Poemes*, by Jacques Brault; *Le cercle vicieux*, by Margaret Atwood.

ÉDITIONS LA LIBERTE, INC., 3020 Chemin Ste-Foy, Ste-Foy, Quebec G1X 3V6 Canada. (418)658-3763. Fax: (418)658-3763. **Acquisitions:** Nathalie Roy, director of operations. Publishes trade paperback originals. **Publishes 4-5**

titles/year. Receives 125 queries and 100 mss/year. 75% of books from first-time authors; 90% from unagented writers. Pays 10% royalty on retail price.** Publishes book 4 months after acceptance of ms. Accepts simultaneous submissions. Book catalog free.

O→ Accepts only mss written in French. Specializes in history. De-emphasizing fiction and poetry.

Nonfiction: Biography, children's/juvenile. Subjects include Americana, animals, anthropology/archeology, child guidance/parenting, cooking/foods/nutrition, education, government/politics, history, hobbies, language/literature, music/dance, nature/environment, psychology, science, sociology. Submit proposal package including complete ms. *Writer's Market* recommends sending a query with SASE first.

Fiction: Historical, juvenile, literary, mainstream/contemporary, short story collections, young adult. Query with SASE.

Recent Title(s): *Au coeur de la Litterature D'enfance et de Jeunesse*, by Charlotte Guerette (nonfiction).

EMPYREAL PRESS, P.O. Box 1746, Place Du Parc, Montreal, Quebec HZW 2R7 Canada. Publishes trade paperback originals. **Publishes 1-2 titles/year. 50% of books from first-time authors; 90% from unagented writers.** Book catalog for #10 SASE.

O→ "Our mission is the publishing of unique Canadian literature—writing grounded in discipline and the imagination."

Fiction: Experimental, feminist, gay/lesbian, literary, short story collections. *Absolutely no unsolicited mss* due to our being an extremely small and backlogged operation.

Recent Title(s): *Winter Spring Summer Fall*, by Robert Sandiford; *The Surface of Time*, by Louis Dudek; *Saint Francis of Esplanade*, by Sonja A. Skarstedt (drama).

FERNWOOD PUBLISHING LTD., P.O. Box 9409, Station A, Halifax, Nova Scotia B3K 5S3 Canada. (902)422-3302. E-mail: info@fernwoodbooks.ca. Website: www.fernwoodbooks.ca. **Acquisitions:** Errol Sharpe, publisher (social science); Wayne Antony, editor (social science). Publishes trade paperback originals. **Publishes 12-15 titles/year. Receives 80 queries and 30 mss/year. 40% of books from first-time authors; 100% from unagented writers. Pays 7-10% royalty on wholesale price. Offers advance.** Publishes book 1 year after acceptance of ms. Accepts simultaneous submissions. Responds in 6 weeks to proposals. Book catalog and ms guidelines free.

O→ "Fernwood's objective is to publish critical works which challenge existing scholarship."

Nonfiction: Reference, textbook, scholarly. Subjects include agriculture/horticulture, anthropology/archeology, business/economics, education, ethnic, gay/lesbian, government/politics, health/medicine, history, language/literature, multicultural, nature/environment, philosophy, regional, sex, sociology, sports, translation, women's issues/studies, contemporary culture, world affairs. "Our main focus is in the social sciences and humanities, emphasizing labor studies, women's studies, gender studies, critical theory and research, political economy, cultural studies and social work—for use in college and university courses." Submit proposal package including outline, sample chapter(s). Reviews artwork/photos as part of ms package. Send photocopies.

Recent Title(s): *The Skin I'm In: Racism, Sports and Education*, by Christopher Spence.

FINDHORN PRESS, 305A The Park, Findhorn, Forres Scotland IV36 3TE United Kingdom. 01309-690582. Fax: 01309-690036. E-mail: info@findhornpress.com. Website: www.findhornpress.com. **Acquisitions:** Thierry Bogliolo, publisher. Publishes trade paperback originals. **Publishes 12 titles/year. Receives 1,000 queries/year. 50% of books from first-time authors. Pays 10-15% royalty on wholesale price.** Publishes book 1 year after acceptance of ms. Book catalog and ms guidelines online.

Nonfiction: Self-help. Subjects include health/medicine, nature/environment, spirituality. Submit proposal package including outline, 1 sample chapter(s), marketing plan.

FLICKS BOOKS, 29 Bradford Rd., Trowbridge, Wilts BA14 9AN United Kingdom. 44(1225)767728. Fax: 44(1225)760418. E-mail: flicks.books@dial.pipex.com. **Acquisitions:** Matthew Stevens, publisher (cinema/film). Publishes hardcover and trade paperback originals and reprints. **Publishes 20 titles/year. Receives 50 queries and 100 mss/year. 20% of books from first-time authors; 100% from unagented writers. Pays 10% royalty or makes outright purchase of $100-300. Offers variable advance.** Publishes book 1 year after acceptance of ms. Accepts simultaneous submissions. Responds in 1 month to queries. Book catalog free; ms guidelines free.

Nonfiction: Biography, illustrated book, reference, technical, textbook. Subjects include cinema, film, TV only. Query with SASE or submit proposal package including outline, 1 sample chapter(s) or submit complete ms. Reviews artwork/photos as part of ms package. Send photocopies.

FOULSHAM PUBLISHERS, Bennetts Close, Slough Berks SL1 5AP United Kingdom. (044)1753 526769. Fax: (044)1753 535003. Website: www.foulsham.com. **Acquisitions:** Barry Belasco, publisher (life issues/self education); Wendy Hobson, editorial director (life issues/cookery). Publishes trade paperback originals and reprints. **Publishes 60 titles/year; imprint publishes 12 titles/year. 10% of books from first-time authors; 85% from unagented writers. Pays 6-12½% royalty on wholesale price. or makes outright purchase of $5,000. Offers $1,500 advance.** Publishes book 8 months after acceptance of ms. Does not accept simultaneous submissions. Responds in 1 week to queries; 2 weeks to proposals; 2 months to mss.

Imprints: Quantum, Barry Belasco, MBS

Nonfiction: Cookbook, how-to, reference, self-help, technical. Subjects include cooking/foods/nutrition, gardening, health/medicine, psychology (popular), recreation, spirituality, travel, women's issues/studies, self education. Query with SASE. Reviews artwork/photos as part of ms package. Send photocopies.

Recent Title(s): *The New Dream Interpreter* (reference); *Classic 1,000 Low Fat Recipes* (cookery).

FOUR COURTS PRESS, Open Air, Fumbally Lane, Dublin 8 Ireland. (03531)4534668. Fax: (03531)4534672. **Acquisitions:** Martin Fanning. Publishes hardcover and trade paperback originals. **Publishes 60 titles/year. Receives 200 queries and 100 mss/year. 30% of books from first-time authors; 90% from unagented writers. Pays 10% royalty on wholesale price.** Publishes book 6 months after acceptance of ms. Does not accept simultaneous submissions. Responds in 2 months to mss. Book catalog free online; ms guidelines free.
Nonfiction: Subjects include art/architecture, health/medicine, history, military/war, philosophy, religion, spirituality, scholarly. Submit proposal package.
Recent Title(s): *Dublin Through Space and Time* (modern history); *The Irish Storyteller* (arts and literature); *The Navarre Bible: New Testament* (theology & spirituality).

GOOSE LANE EDITIONS, 469 King St., Fredericton, New Brunswick E3B 1E5 Canada. (506)450-4251. **Acquisitions:** Laurel Boone, editorial director. Estab. 1956. **Publishes 12-14 titles/year. Receives 500 submissions/year. 20% of books from first-time authors; 75% from unagented writers. Pays royalty on retail price. Offers advance.** Does not accept simultaneous submissions. Responds in 6 months to queries. Ms guidelines for #10 SASE.
Goose Lane publishes literary fiction and nonfiction from well-read and highly skilled Canadian authors.
Nonfiction: Biography, illustrated book. Subjects include art/architecture (Canadian), history, language/literature, nature/environment, regional, women's issues/studies. Query with SASE.
Fiction: Literary (novels), short story collections. Our needs in fiction never change: Substantial, character-centered literary fiction. No children's, YA, mainstream, mass market, genre, mystery, thriller, confessional or science fiction. Query with SASE.
Recent Title(s): *Strong Hollow*, by Linda Little (fiction); *Deadly Frontiers: Disaster and Rescue on Canada's Atlantic Seaboard*, by Dean Beeby (nonfiction).
Tips: "Writers should send us outlines and samples of books that show a very well-read author who, in either fiction or nonfiction, has highly developed literary skills. Our books are almost all by Canadians living in Canada. If I were a writer trying to market a book today, I would contact the targeted publisher with a query letter and synopsis, and request manuscript guidelines. Purchase a recent book from the publisher in a relevant area, if possible. Always send a SASE with IRCs or suffient return postage in Canadian stamps for reply to your query and for any material you'd like returned should it not suit our needs."

GUERNICA EDITIONS, Box 117, Station P, Toronto, Ontario M5S 2S6 Canada. (416)658-9888. Fax: (416)657-8885. E-mail: guernicaeditions@cs.com. Website: www.guernicaeditions.com. **Acquisitions:** Antonio D'Alfonso, editor/publisher (poetry, nonfiction, novels); Ken Scambray, editor (US reprints). Estab. 1978. Publishes trade paperback originals, reprints and software. **Publishes 25 titles/year. Receives 1,000 submissions and 750 mss/year. 20% of books from first-time authors; 99% from unagented writers. Pays 8-10% royalty on retail price. or makes outright purchase of $200-5,000. Offers $200-2,000 advance.** Publishes book 10 months after acceptance of ms. Does not accept simultaneous submissions. Responds in 1 month to queries; 6 months to proposals; 1 year to mss. Book catalog online.
Guernica Editions is an independent press dedicated to the bridging of cultures. "We do original and translations of fine works. We are seeking essays on authors and translations with less emphasis on poetry."
Nonfiction: Biography. Subjects include art/architecture, creative nonfiction, ethnic, film/cinema/stage, gay/lesbian, government/politics, history, language/literature, memoirs, multicultural, music/dance, philosophy, psychology, regional, religion, sex, translation, women's issues/studies. Query with SASE. *All unsolicited mss returned unopened.* Reviews artwork/photos as part of ms package. Send photocopies.
Fiction: Erotica, feminist, gay/lesbian, literary, multicultural, plays, poetry, poetry in translation. "We wish to open up into the fiction world and focus less on poetry. We specialize in European, especially Italian, translations." Query with SASE. *All unsolicited mss returned unopened.*
Poetry: Feminist, gay/lesbian, literary, multicultural, poetry in translation. "We wish to have writers in translation. Any writer who has translated Italian poetry is welcomed. Full books only. Not single poems by different authors, unless modern, and used as an anthology. First books will have no place in the next couple of years." Query.
Recent Title(s): *Red Promises*, by Halli Villegas; *A Father's Revenge*, by Pan Bouyoucas; *Of Dissonance and Shadows*, by Daniel Sloate.

HARLEQUIN ENTERPRISES, LTD., acquiring offices at: 225 Duncan Mill Rd., Don Mills Ontario M3B 3K9 Canada. (416)445-5860. Website: www.eharlequin.com. **Acquisitions:** Randall Toye, editorial director Toronto (Harlequin, Gold Eagle, Worldwide Library); Tara Gavin, editorial director New York (Silhouette, Harlequin Steeple Hill, Red Dress Ink); Karin Stoecker, editorial director UK (Harlequin, Red Dress Ink); and Diane Moggy, editorial director Toronto (MIRA). U.S.: 300 E. 42nd St., 6th Floor, New York NY 10017. (212)682-6080. UK: Eton House, 18-24 Paradise Lane, Richmond, Surrey, TW9 1SR, United Kingdom. Estab. 1949. Publishes mass market paperback originals and reprints. **Publishes 700+ titles/year. Pays royalty. Offers advance.** Publishes book 1-3 years after acceptance of ms. Does not accept simultaneous submissions. Responds in 6 weeks to queries; 2 months to mss. Ms guidelines for #10 SASE.
Imprints: Harlequin, Silhouette, MIRA, Gold Eagle, Worldwide Mysteries, Steeple Hill, Red Dress Ink.
Fiction: Adventure (heroic), mystery, romance, suspense (romantic suspense only). Query with SASE or check website.
Tips: "The quickest route to success is to follow directions for submissions: Query first. We encourage first novelists. Before sending a manuscript, read as many current Harlequin titles as you can. It's very important to know the genre and the series most appropriate for your submission."

HARPERCOLLINS PUBLISHERS LTD., 55 Avenue Rd., Suite 2900, Toronto, Ontario M5R 3L2 Canada. (416)975-9334. Vice President/Publisher/Editor-in-Chief: Iris Tupholme. Publishes hardcover and trade paperback original and reprints, mass market paperback reprints. **Publishes 45 titles/year. Pays 8-15% royalty on retail price. Offers $1,500 to over six figures advance.** Publishes book 18 months after acceptance of ms.

Nonfiction: Biography, children's/juvenile, self-help. Subjects include business/economics, gardening, gay/lesbian, government/politics, health/medicine, history, language/literature, money/finance, nature/environment, religion, travel, women's issues/studies. Query first with SASE and appropriate Canadian postage or IRCs. *No unsolicited mss.*

Fiction: Ethnic, feminist, juvenile, literary, mainstream/contemporary, picture books, religious, short story collections, young adult. Query first with SASE and appropriate Canadian postage or IRCs. *No unsolicited mss.*

Recent Title(s): *Clara Callan*, by Richard Wright; *The Corrections*, by Jonathan Franzen.

HERITAGE HOUSE PUBLISHING CO. LTD., 301-3555 Outrigger Rd., Nanoose Bay, British Columbia V9P 9K1 Canada. (250)468-5328. Fax: (250)468-5318. E-mail: publisher@heritagehouse.ca. Website: www.heritagehouse.ca. **Acquisitions:** Rodger Touchie, publisher/president. Publishes trade paperback originals. **Publishes 12-16 titles/year. Receives 200 queries and 60 mss/year. 50% of books from first-time authors; 100% from unagented writers. Pays 9% royalty. Offers advance.** Publishes book 1 year after acceptance of ms. Does not accept simultaneous submissions. Responds in 2 months to queries. Book catalog for #10 SASE.

- Heritage House is primarily a regional publisher of Western Canadiana and the Pacific Northwest. "We aim to publish and distribute good books that entertain and educate our readership regarding both historic and contemporary Western Canada and Pacific Northwest."

Nonfiction: Biography, how-to, illustrated book. Subjects include animals, anthropology/archeology, cooking/foods/nutrition, history, nature/environment, recreation, regional, sports. "Writers should include a sample of their writing, an overview sample of photos or illustrations to support the text and a brief letter describing who they are writing for." Query with SASE or submit outline, 2-3 sample chapter(s). Reviews artwork/photos as part of ms package. Send photocopies.

Fiction: Very limited. Only author/illustrator collaboration.

Recent Title(s): *Where Shadows Linger: The Untold Story of the RCMP's Olson Murders Investigation*, by W. Leslie Holmes with Bruce Northorp (police history); *Sitting Bull's Boss: Above the Medicine Line with James Morrow Walsh*, by Ian Anderson (history); *Sunshine Coast: A Place to Be*, by Rosella Lesie (travel).

Tips: "Our books appeal to residents and visitors to the northwest quadrant of the continent. Present your material only after you have done your best."

HIPPOPOTAMUS PRESS, 22 Whitewell Rd., Frome, Somerset BA11 4EL United Kingdom. 0173-466653. Fax: 01373-466653. **Acquisitions:** R. John, editor; M. Pargitter (poetry); Anna Martin (translation). Publishes hardcover and trade paperback originals. **Publishes 6-12 titles/year. 90% of books from first-time authors; 90% from unagented writers. Pays 7½-10% royalty on retail price. Offers advance.** Publishes book 10 months after acceptance of ms. Accepts simultaneous submissions. Responds in 1 month to queries. Book catalog free.

Imprints: Hippopotamus Press, *Outposts* Poetry Quarterly; distributor for University of Salzburg Press.

- Hippopotamus Press publishes first full collections of verse by those well represented in the mainstream poetry magazines of the English speaking world.

Nonfiction: Subjects include language/literature, translation. Query with SASE or submit complete ms.

Poetry: "Read one of our authors! Poets often make the mistake of submitting poetry not knowing the type of verse we publish." Query or submit complete ms.

Recent Title(s): *Mystic Bridge*, Edward Lowbury.

Tips: "We publish books for a literate audience. We have a strong link to the Modernist tradition. Read what we publish."

HORSDAL & SCHUBART PUBLISHERS LTD., #6-356 Simcoe St., Victoria, British Columbia V8V 1L1 Canada. (250)360-0829. Fax: (250)385-0829. **Acquisitions:** Marlyn Horsdal, editor. Publishes trade paperback originals and reprints. **Publishes 8-10 titles/year. 50% of books from first-time authors; 100% from unagented writers. Pays 15% royalty on wholesale price.** Publishes book 6 months after acceptance of ms. Accepts simultaneous submissions. Responds in 1 month to queries. Book catalog free.

Imprints: TouchWood Editions (creative nonfiction).

- "We concentrate on Western and Northern Canada and nautical subjects and offer useful information to give readers pause for thought, to encourage action to help heal the Earth." Currently emphasizing creative nonfiction. De-emphasizing regional histories.

Nonfiction: Biography. Subjects include anthropology/archeology, art/architecture, creative nonfiction, government/politics, history, nature/environment, recreation, regional. Query with SASE or submit outline, 2-3 sample chapter(s). Reviews artwork/photos as part of ms package. Send photocopies.

Fiction: Historical.

Recent Title(s): *Old Square-Toes and His Lady*, by John Adams; *The Promise*, by Bill Gallaber.

Tips: "Our area of interest is Western and Northern Canada. We would like more creative nonfiction and history as stories."

HOUSE OF ANANSI PRESS, 895 Don Mills Rd., 400-2 Park Centre, Toronto, Ontario M3C 1W3 Canada. (416)445-3333. Fax: (416)445-5967. E-mail: info@anansi.ca. Website: www.anansi.ca. **Acquisitions:** Martha Sharpe, publisher. Publishes hardcover and trade paperback originals. **Publishes 10-15 titles/year. Receives 750 queries/year. 5% of books from first-time authors; 99% from unagented writers. Pays 8-15% royalty on retail price. Offers $500-2,000 advance.** Publishes book 9 months after acceptance of ms. Accepts simultaneous submissions. Responds in 2 months to queries; 3 months to proposals; 4 months to mss.

O→ "Our mission is to publish the best new literary writers in Canada and to continue to grow and adapt along with the Canadian literary community, while maintaining Anansi's rich history."

Nonfiction: Biography. Subjects include anthropology/archeology, gay/lesbian, government/politics, history, language/literature, philosophy, science, sociology, women's issues/studies. "Our nonfiction list is literary, but not overly academic. Some writers submit academic work better suited for university presses or pop-psychology books, which we do not publish." Query with SASE or submit outline, 2 sample chapter(s). Reviews artwork/photos as part of ms package. Send photocopies.

Fiction: Experimental, feminist, gay/lesbian, literary, short story collections. "We publish literary fiction by Canadian authors. Authors must have been published in established literary magazines and/or journals. We only want to consider sample chapters." Query with SASE or submit 2 sample chapter(s), synopsis.

Poetry: "We only publish book-length works by Canadian authors. Poets must have a substantial résumé of published poems in literary magazines or journals. We only want samples from a manuscript." Submit 10-15 sample poems.

Recent Title(s): *The Rights Revolution*, by Michael Ignatieff (nonfiction); *This All Happened*, by Michael Winter (fiction); *A Pair of Scissors*, by Sharon Thesen (poetry).

Tips: "Submit often to magazines and journals. Read and buy other writers' work. Know and be a part of your writing community."

HOW TO BOOKS LTD., 3 Newtec Place, Magdalen Rd., Oxford OX4 1RE Great Britain. (00144)1865 793806. Fax: (00144)1865 248780. E-mail: info@howtobooks.co.uk. Website: www.howtobooks.co.uk. **Acquisitions:** Nikki Read, commissioning editor (self-help, business, careers, home & family). Publishes trade paperback originals and reprints. **Publishes 100 titles/year. Receives 200 queries and 100 mss/year. 80% of books from first-time authors; 90% from unagented writers.** Accepts simultaneous submissions. Responds in 1 month to queries; 1 month to proposals; 2 months to mss. Book catalog free or on website; ms guidelines free.

Imprints: Essentials (24 titles/year), Pathways (16 titles/year), Quick Fix (4 titles/year), Herbal Health (8 titles/year), How-To Books (100 titles/year), How To Reference (6 titles/year).

Nonfiction: How-to, reference, self-help. Subjects include business/economics, child guidance/parenting, creative nonfiction, money/finance. "Submit a proposal you feel strongly about and can write knowledgably. Have a look at our catalog/website to see what we publish. We ask authors to send a synopsis before steering them toward a specific imprint." Submit proposal package including outline, 1 sample chapter(s).

Recent Title(s): *How to Live Longer*, by Dr. Harry Alder; *Quick Fix Your Sex Life*, by Judith Verity; *Exploring Spirituality*, by Suzanne Ruthven.

Tips: "Our books are aimed at people who want to improve their lives, their careers, their general skills. Our authors have to have a passion and extensive knowledge about their subject area. Send us a proposal first; because we are a series publisher, submitted books have to fit into our format."

INSOMNIAC PRESS, 192 Spadina Ave., Suite 403, Toronto, Ontario M5T 2C2 Canada. (416)504-6270. Fax: (416)504-9313. E-mail: mike@insomniacpress.com. Website: www.insomniacpress.com. Publishes trade paperback originals and reprints, mass market paperback originals and electronic originals and reprints. **Publishes 20 titles/year. Receives 250 queries and 1,000 mss/year. 50% of books from first-time authors; 80% from unagented writers. Pays 10-15% royalty on retail price. Offers $500-1,000 advance.** Publishes book 6 months after acceptance of ms. Responds in 1 week to queries; 2 months to proposals; 2 months to mss. Book catalog and ms guidelines online.

Nonfiction: Gift book, humor, self-help. Subjects include business/economics, creative nonfiction, gay/lesbian, government/politics, health/medicine, language/literature, money/finance, multicultural, religion, true crime. Very interested in areas such as true crime and generally in well-written and well-researched nonfiction on topics of wide interest. Query via e-mail, submit proposal package including outline, 2 sample chapters, or submit complete ms. Reviews artwork/photos as part of ms package. Send photocopies.

Fiction: Comic books, ethnic, experimental, gay/lesbian, humor, literary, mainstream/contemporary, multicultural, poetry, suspense. We publish a mix of commercial (mysteries) and literary fiction. Query via e-mail, submit proposal package including synopsis or submit complete ms.

Poetry: "Our poetry publishing is limited to 2-4 books per year and we are often booked up a year or two in advance." Submit complete ms.

Recent Title(s): *Landscape with Shipwreck: First Person Cinema and the Films of Phillip Hoffman*, edited by Karyn Sandlos and Mike Hoolboom (film studies); *Pedigree Girls*, by Sherwin Tija (humor/cartoon); *Ashes Are Bone and Dust*, by Jill Battson (poetry).

Tips: "We envision a mixed readership that appreciates up-and-coming literary fiction and poetry as well as solidly researched and provocative nonfiction. Peruse our website and familiarize yourself with what we've published in the past."

INSTITUTE OF PSYCHOLOGICAL RESEARCH, INC., 34 Fleury St. W., Montreal, Quebec H3L 1S9 Canada. (514)382-3000. Fax: (514)382-3007. **Acquisitions:** Marie-Paule Chevrier, general director. Estab. 1958. Publishes hardcover and trade paperback originals and reprints. **Publishes 12 titles/year. Receives 15 submissions/year. 10% of books from first-time authors; 100% from unagented writers. Pays 10-12% royalty.** Publishes book 6 months after acceptance of ms. Responds in 2 months to queries.

O━ Institute of Psychological Research publishes psychological tests and science textbooks for a varied professional audience.

Nonfiction: Textbook. Subjects include philosophy, psychology, science, translation. "We are looking for psychological tests in French or English." Query with SASE or submit complete ms.

Recent Title(s): *épreuve individuelle d'habileté mentale*, by Jean-Marc Chevrier (intelligence test).

Tips: "Psychologists, guidance counselors, professionals, schools, school boards, hospitals, teachers, government agencies and industries comprise our audience."

ISER BOOKS, Faculty of Arts Publications, Memorial University of Newfoundland, FM 2006, St. John's, Newfoundland A1K 1A9 Canada. (709)737-8343. Fax: (709)737-7560. Website: www.mun.ca/iser/. **Acquisitions:** Al Potter, manager. Publishes trade paperback originals. **Publishes 3-4 titles/year. Receives 10-20 queries and 10 mss/year. 45% of books from first-time authors; 85% from unagented writers. Pays 6-10% royalty on wholesale price.** Publishes book 6 months after acceptance of ms. Does not accept simultaneous submissions. Responds in 1 month to queries; 2 months to proposals; 4 months to mss. Book catalog and ms guidelines free.

O━ Iser Books publishes research within such disciplines and in such parts of the world as are deemed of relevance to Newfoundland and Labrador.

Nonfiction: Biography, reference. Subjects include anthropology/archeology, ethnic, government/politics, history, multicultural, recreation, regional, sociology, translation, women's issues/studies. Query with SASE or submit proposal package including outline, 2-3 sample chapter(s).

Recent Title(s): *The Resilient Outport: Ecology, Economy, and Society in Rural Newfoundland*, by editor Rosemary Ommer.

[N] **JESPERSON PUBLISHING, LTD.**, 39 James Lane, St. John's, Newfoundland A1E 3H3 Canada. (709)753-0633. Fax: (709)753-5507. E-mail: jespersonpress@nf.aibn.com. **Acquisitions:** John Symonds, president; Jason Hurley, publishing assistant. Publishes trade paperback originals. **Publishes 10-12 titles/year. Receives 100 queries and 75 mss/year. 10% of books from first-time authors; 100% from unagented writers. Pays 10% royalty.** Publishes book 18 months after acceptance of ms. Accepts simultaneous submissions. Responds in 1 month to queries; 3 months to proposals; 3 months to mss. Book catalog and writer's guidelines free or on website.

O━ "We are interested in solid writing, a good grasp of the English language, and a Newfoundland angle." Currently emphasizing solid fiction, creative nonfiction. De-emphasizing poetry, children's books.

Nonfiction: Humor. Subjects include creative nonfiction, education, history, humor, women's issues/studies. Query with SASE. Reviews artwork/photos as part of ms package. Send photocopies.

Fiction: Experimental, feminist, historical, humor, literary, military/war, multicultural, poetry, regional, short story collections. Query with SASE.

Poetry: Query.

Recent Title(s): *Flyfishing Tips & Tactics*, Len Rich (nonfiction); *Tales From the Frozen Ocean*, Dwain Campbell (fiction); *Christ in the Pizza Place*, Clyde Rose (poetry).

Tips: "Do not send SASE with U.S. postage."

KINDRED PRODUCTIONS, 4-169 Riverton Ave., Winnipeg, Manitoba R2L 2E5 Canada. (204)669-6575. Fax: (204)654-1865. E-mail: kindred@mbconf.ca. Website: www.kindredproductions.com. **Acquisitions:** Marilyn Hudson, manager. Publishes trade paperback originals and reprints. **Publishes 3 titles/year. 1% of books from first-time authors; 100% from unagented writers. Pays 10-15% royalty on net receipts.** Publishes book 18 months after acceptance of ms. Accepts simultaneous submissions. Responds in 3 months to queries; 5 months to mss. Book catalog and ms guidelines free.

O━ "Kindred Productions publishes, promotes and markets print and nonprint resources that will shape our Christian faith and discipleship from a Mennonite Brethren perspective." Currently emphasizing inspirational with cross-over potential. De-emphasizing personal experience, biographical. No children's books or fiction.

Nonfiction: Subjects include religion, inspirational. "Our books cater primarily to our Mennonite Brethren denomination readers." Query with SASE or submit outline, 2-3 sample chapter(s).

Recent Title(s): *Liberty in Confinement*, by Johannes Reimer; *God's Orchard: Fruit of the Spirit in Action*, by Helen Lepp Friesen.

Tips: "Most of our books are sold to churches, religious bookstores and schools. We are concentrating on inspirational books. We do not accept children's manuscripts."

LAMBRECHT PUBLICATIONS, 1763 Maple Bay Rd., Duncan, British Columbia V9L 5N6 Canada. (250)748-8722. Fax: (250)748-8723. E-mail: helgal@cowichan.com. **Acquisitions:** Helga Lambrecht, publisher. Publishes hardcover, trade paperback originals and reprints. **Publishes 2 titles/year. Receives 6 queries/year. 50% of books from first-time authors. Pays 10% royalty on retail price. Offers advance.** Does not accept simultaneous submissions. Book catalog free.

O━ Lambrecht publishes local history books and cookbooks.

Nonfiction: Subjects include cooking/foods/nutrition, history, regional. *All unsolicited mss returned unopened.*

LEXISNEXIS BUTTERWORTHS, 75 Clegg Rd., Markham, Ontario L6G 1A1 Canada. (905)479-2665. Fax: (905)479-2826. E-mail: info@lexisnexis.ca. Website: www.lexisnexis.ca. **Acquisitions:** Caryl Young, publishing director. **Publishes 100 titles/year. Receives 100 queries and 10 mss/year. 50% of books from first-time authors; 100% from unagented writers. Pays 5-15% royalty on wholesale price. Offers $1,000-5,000 advance.** Publishes book 4 months after acceptance of ms. Accepts simultaneous submissions. Responds in 1 month to queries. Book catalog free.

Lexisnexis Butterworths publishes professional reference material for the legal, business and accounting markets.

Nonfiction: Multimedia (CD-ROM), reference (legal and business). Subjects include health/medicine (medical law). Query with SASE.

Recent Title(s): *The Law of Corporate Finance in Canada*, Edmund Kwaw.

Tips: Audience is legal community, business, medical, accounting professions.

LOBSTER PRESS, 1620 Sherbrooke St. W, Suites C & D, Montreal, Quebec H3H 1C9 Canada. (514)904-1100. Fax: (514)904-1101. Website: www.lobsterpress.com. **Acquisitions:** Gabriella Mancini, editorial coordinator. Publishes hardcover, trade paperback and mass market paperback originals. **Publishes 25 titles/year. Receives 200 queries and 1,500 mss/year. 90% of books from first-time authors; 75% from unagented writers. Pays 5-11% royalty on retail price. Offers $1,000-6,000 (Canadian) advance.** Publishes book 2 years after acceptance of ms. Accepts simultaneous submissions. Responds in 2 months to queries; 7 months to proposals; 10 months to mss. Book catalog for #10 SASE (IRC or Canadian postage) or online; ms guidelines online.

- Lobster Press is accepting submissions as of October 2002.

Nonfiction: Children's/juvenile, illustrated book, self-help. Subjects include child guidance/parenting, creative nonfiction, history, sex, travel. Query with SASE (IRC or Canadian postage only) or submit complete ms. Reviews artwork/photos as part of ms package. Send photocopies.

Fiction: Adventure (for children), historical (for children), juvenile, picture books, young adult. Submit complete ms.

Recent Title(s): *Going on a Journey to the Sea*, by Jane Barclay, illustrated by Doris Barrette (picture book); *Come On, Dad*, by Ed Avis, illustrated by Geneviève Després (nonfiction); *When Pigs Fly*, by Valerie Coulman, illustrated by Rogé (picture book).

LONE PINE PUBLISHING, 10145 81st Ave., Edmonton, Alberta T6E 1W9 Canada. (403)433-9333. Fax: (403)433-9646. Website: www.lonepinepublishing.com. **Acquisitions:** Nancy Foulds, editorial director. Estab. 1980. Publishes trade paperback originals and reprints. **Publishes 12-40 titles/year. Receives 800 submissions/year. 75% of books from first-time authors; 95% from unagented writers. Pays royalty.** Does not accept simultaneous submissions. Responds in 3 months to queries. Book catalog free.

Imprints: Lone Pine, Home World, Pine Candle and Pine Cone.

Lone Pine publishes natural history and outdoor recreation—including gardening—titles, and some popular history and ghost story collections by region. " 'The World Outside Your Door' is our motto—helping people appreciate nature and their own special place." Currently emphasizing ghost stories by region, popular history.

Nonfiction: Subjects include animals, gardening, nature/environment, recreation, regional. The list is set for the next year and a half, but we are interested in seeing new material. Query with SASE or submit outline, sample chapter(s). Reviews artwork/photos as part of ms package.

Recent Title(s): *Perennials for Northern California*, by Bob Tanem and Don Williamson; *Ghost Stories for Christmas*, by Jo-Anne Christensen; *Bugs of Washington & Oregon*, by John Acorn and Ian Sheldon.

Tips: "Writers have their best chance with recreational or nature guidebooks. Most of our books are strongly regional in nature."

LYNX IMAGES, INC., P.O. Box 5961, Station A, Toronto, Ontario M5W 1P4 Canada. (416)925-8422. Fax: (925)952-8352. E-mail: info@lynximages.com. Website: www.lynximages.com. **Acquisitions:** Russell Floren, president; Andrea Gutsche, director; Barbara Chisholm, producer. Publishes hardcover and trade paperback originals. **Publishes 6 titles/year. Receives 100 queries and 50 mss/year. 80% of books from first-time authors; 80% from unagented writers. Offers 40% advance.** Publishes book 1 year after acceptance of ms. Accepts simultaneous submissions.

Lynx publishes historical tourism, travel, Canadian history, Great Lakes history. Currently emphasizing travel, history, nature. De-emphasizing boating, guides.

Nonfiction: Coffee table book, gift book, multimedia. Subjects include history, nature/environment, travel. Reviews artwork/photos as part of ms package.

Recent Title(s): *Disaster Canada*; *Castles of the North*; *Disaster Great Lakes*, all by Janet Looker.

MARCUS BOOKS, P.O. Box 327, Queensville, Ontario L0G 1R0 Canada. (905)967-0219. Fax: (905)967-0216. **Acquisitions:** Tom Rieder, president. Publishes trade paperback originals and reprints. **Receives 12 queries and 6 mss/year. 90% of books from first-time authors; 100% from unagented writers. Pays 10% royalty on retail price.** Publishes book 6 months after acceptance of ms. Does not accept simultaneous submissions. Responds in 4 months to mss. Book catalog for $1.

Nonfiction: Subjects include health/medicine. "Interested in alternative health and esoteric topics." Submit outline, 3 sample chapter(s).

McCLELLAND & STEWART LTD., 481 University Ave., Suite 900, Toronto, Ontario M5G 2E9 Canada. (416)598-1114. Publishes hardcover, trade paperback and mass market paperback originals and reprints. **Publishes 80**

titles/year. Receives 1,000 queries/year. 10% of books from first-time authors; 30% from unagented writers. Pays 10-15% royalty on retail price (hardcover rates). Offers advance. Publishes book 1 year after acceptance of ms. Responds in 3 months to proposals.

Imprints: McClelland & Stewart, New Canadian Library, Douglas Gibson Books, Emblem Editions.

Nonfiction: "We publish books by Canadian authors or on Canadian subjects." Biography, coffee table book, how-to, humor, illustrated book, reference, self-help. Subjects include agriculture/horticulture, animals, art/architecture, business/economics, child guidance/parenting, cooking/foods/nutrition, education, gardening, gay/lesbian, government/politics, health/medicine, history, hobbies, language/literature, military/war, money/finance, music/dance, nature/environment, philosophy, photography, psychology, recreation, religion, science, sociology, sports, translation, travel, women's issues/studies, Canadiana. Submit outline. *All unsolicited mss returned unopened.*

Fiction: Experimental, historical, humor, literary, mainstream/contemporary, mystery, short story collections. "We publish quality fiction by prize-winning authors." *All unsolicited mss returned unopened.* Query.

Poetry: "Only Canadian poets should apply. We publish only four titles each year." Query. No unsolicted mss.

Recent Title(s): *Family Matters*, by Robinton Mistry; *Anil's Ghost*, by Michael Ondaatje; *No Great Mischief*, by Alistair MacLeod.

McGRAW-HILL RYERSON LTD., 300 Water St., Whitby, Ontario L1N 9B6 Canada. (905)430-5116. Fax: (905)430-5044. E-mail: joanh@mcgrawhill.ca. Website: www.mcgrawhill.ca. **Acquisitions:** Joan Homewood, publisher. Publishes hardcover and trade paperback originals and revisions. **Publishes 20 titles/year. 10% of books from first-time authors; 60% from unagented writers. Pays 10% royalty on retail price. Offers $4,000 average advance.** Publishes book 1 year after acceptance of ms. Accepts simultaneous submissions. Responds in 6 months to queries.

- McGraw-Hill Ryerson Ltd., publishes books on Canadian business and personal finance for the Canadian market. Currently emphasizing business/management/financial planning/investing. De-emphasizing Canadian military history.

Nonfiction: Biography (business only), how-to, reference. Subjects include business/economics, history, money/finance. "No books and proposals that are American in focus. We publish primarily for the Canadian market, but work with McGraw-Hill U.S. to distribute business, management and training titles in U.S. and internationally." Query with SASE or submit proposal package including outline.

Recent Title(s): *Make Sure It's Deductible*, Evelyn Jacks; *The Relationship-Based Enterprise*, by Ray McKenzie.

Tips: "Writers have the best chance of selling us nonfiction business and personal finance books with a distinctly Canadian focus. Proposal guidelines are available. Thorough market research on competitive titles increases chances of your proposal getting serious consideration, as does endorsement by or references from relevant professionals."

MONARCH BOOKS, Monarch Concorde House, Grenville Place, London NW7 3SA Great Britain. (44)020 8959 3668. Fax: (44)020 8959 3678. E-mail: tonyc@angushudson.com. **Acquisitions:** Tony Collins, editorial director (Christian literature). Publishes hardcover, trade paperback and mass market paperback originals and hardcover, trade paperback and mass market paperback reprints. **Publishes 33 titles/year. Receives 600-800 queries and 400 mss/year. 10% of books from first-time authors; 90% from unagented writers. Pays 10-15% royalty. Offers $1,000-4,000 advance.** Publishes book 8 months after acceptance of ms. Accepts simultaneous submissions. Responds in 2 weeks to queries. Book catalog and ms guidelines free.

Imprints: Monarch.

- "We publish primarily for the evangelical Christian market, providing tools and resources for Christian leaders." Monarch Books has recently started publishing and distributing in the US and Canada through an arrangement with Kregel Books.

Nonfiction: Biography, humor, reference, self-help. Subjects include child guidance/parenting, creative nonfiction, philosophy, psychology, religion, science, sex, sociology. Query with SASE or submit proposal package including outline, 2 sample chapter(s).

Recent Title(s): *Clash of the Worlds: What Christians Can Do in a World of Cultures in Conflict*, by David Burnett (nonfiction).

Tips: "Think about who you are writing for. What will a reader get as benefit from reading your book?"

MOOSE ENTERPRISE BOOK & THEATRE PLAY PUBLISHING, 684 Walls Side Rd., Sault Ste. Marie, Ontario P6A 5K6 Canada. (705)779-3331. Fax: (705)779-3331. **Acquisitions:** Richard Mousseau, owner/editor (fiction, history, general); Edmond Alcid, editor (poetry, children's, general). Publishes trade and mass market paperback originals. **Publishes 7-10 titles/year. Receives 10-15 queries and 10 mss/year. 60% of books from first-time authors; 100% from unagented writers. Pays 20-40% royalty on retail price.** Publishes book 6 months after acceptance of ms. Responds in 1 month to queries; 2 months to proposals; 2 months to mss. Book catalog and ms guidelines for #10 SASE.

Nonfiction: Biography, children's/juvenile. Subjects include history, memoirs, military/war. Query with SASE or submit proposal package including outline, 2 sample chapter(s), author bio. Reviews artwork/photos as part of ms package. Send photocopies.

Fiction: Adventure, historical, horror, humor, juvenile, military/war, mystery, picture books, plays, poetry, regional, science fiction, short story collections, western, young adult. Query with SASE or submit proposal package including 2 sample chapter(s), synopsis, author bio.

Poetry: Send author's bio and summary of project, typed, double spaced, one-sided. Query or submit 5 sample poems.

Recent Title(s): *A Long Exciting Trip to Peace*, by Angus Harnden (military/history); *Executor of Mercy*, by Edmond Alcid (adventure/novel); *Poems From My Heart*, by Gordon Hysen (poetry).
Tips: "Send only material that is of moral quality. Send bio of author."

NATURAL HERITAGE/NATURAL HISTORY, INC., P.O. Box 95, Station O, Toronto, Ontario M4A 2M8 Canada. (416)694-7907. Fax: (416)690-0819. E-mail: natherbooks@idirect.com. **Acquisitions:** Jane Gibson, editor-in-chief. Publishes hardcover and trade paperback originals. **Publishes 12-15 titles/year. 50% of books from first-time authors; 85% from unagented writers. Pays 8-10% royalty on retail price. Offers advance.** Publishes book 2 years after acceptance of ms. Does not accept simultaneous submissions. Responds in 4 months to queries; 6 months to proposals; 6 months to mss. Book catalog free; ms guidelines for #10 SASE.
Imprints: Natural Heritage.

Currently emphasizing heritage, history.

Nonfiction: Subjects include anthropology/archeology, art/architecture, ethnic, history, nature/environment, photography, recreation, regional, women's issues/studies. Submit outline.
Fiction: Historical, short story collections. Query with SASE.
Recent Title(s): *Superior Rendezvous-Place: Fort William in the Canadian Fur Trade*, by Jean Morrison (nonfiction); *Just a Little Later with Eevo and Slim*, by Henry Shykoff (fiction); *Let's Go to the Grand!: 100 Years of Entertainment at London's Grand Theatre*, by Sheila M. F. Johnston (nonfiction).
Tips: "We are a Canadian publisher in the natural heritage and history fields."

NEWEST PUBLISHERS LTD., 201, 8540- 109 St., Edmonton, Alberta T6G 1E6 Canada. (403)432-9427. Fax: (403)433-3179. E-mail: info@newestpress.com. Website: www.newestpress.com. **Acquisitions:** Ruth Linka, general manager. Publishes trade paperback originals. **Publishes 13-16 titles/year. Receives 200 submissions/year. 40% of books from first-time authors; 90% from unagented writers.** Accepts simultaneous submissions. Responds in 6 months to queries. Book catalog for 9×12 SASE.

NeWest publishes Western Canadian fiction, nonfiction, poetry and drama.

Nonfiction: Literary/essays (Western Canadian authors, Western Canadian and Northern themes). Subjects include ethnic, government/politics, history (Western Canada), nature/environment (northern), Canadiana. Query.
Fiction: Literary. Submit complete ms.
Recent Title(s): *Big Rig*, by Don McTavish (nonfiction).

NORBRY PUBLISHING LIMITED, 520 Aberdeen Ave., Hamilton, Ontario L8P 2S2 Canada. (905)308-9877. Fax: (905)308-9869. E-mail: norbry@norbry.com. Website: www.norbry.com. **Acquisitions:** Rebecca Pembry, president. Publishes mass market paperback originals. **Publishes 9 titles/year. 100% of books from unagented writers. Pays 10-20% royalty on retail price.** Publishes book 6 months after acceptance of ms. Accepts simultaneous submissions. Book catalog free; ms guidelines free.
Nonfiction: Multimedia (CD-ROM and network), textbook, online courseware, testing systems, assessment tools and course management systems. Subjects include business/economics, computers/electronic, education, software, accounting. Query with SASE. Reviews artwork/photos as part of ms package. Send photocopies.
Recent Title(s): *Learning Simply Accounting 8.0 for Windows*, by Harvey Freedman and Joseph Toste; *ACCPAC 4.1 for Windows*, by John Stammers; *MYOB 9.0*, by Christine Heaney.

NOVALIS, Bayard Presse, 49 Front St. E, Toronto, Ontario M5E 1B3 Canada. (416)363-3303. Fax: (416)363-9409. E-mail: cservice@novalis.ca. Website: www.novalis.ca. **Acquisitions:** Kevin Burns, commissioning editor; Michael O'Hearn, publisher; Anne Louise Mahoney, managing editor. Editorial offices: Novalis, St. Paul University, 223 Main St., Ottawa, Ontario, K1S 1C4 Canada. Phone: (613)782-3039. Fax: (613)751-4020. E-mail: kburns@ustpaul.ca. Publishes hardcover and trade paperback originals and trade paperback reprints. **Publishes 40 titles/year. 20% of books from first-time authors; 50% from unagented writers. Pays 10-15% royalty on wholesale price. Offers $300-2,000 advance.** Publishes book 9 months after acceptance of ms. Responds in 2 months to queries; 1 month to proposals; 2 months to mss. Book catalog for free or online; ms guidelines free.

"Novalis publishes books about faith, religion and spirituality in their broadest sense. Based in the Catholic tradition, our interest is strongly ecumenical. Regardless of their denominational perspective, our books speak to the heart, mind and spirit of people seeking to deepen their faith and understanding."

Nonfiction: Biography, children's/juvenile, gift book, humor, illustrated book, reference, self-help. Subjects include child guidance/parenting, education (Christian or Catholic), memoirs, multicultural, nature/environment, philosophy, religion, spirituality. Query with SASE.
Recent Title(s): *Zen Contemplation*, by Elaine Macinnes (meditation, prison ministry, autobiography); *How to Discover Your Personal Mission: The Search for Meaning*, by John Monbourquette (self-help, spirituality); *Getting It Together: Faith, Hope and Youth*, by Neil MacCarthy (young adult self-help, spirituality).

ORCA BOOK PUBLISHERS, P.O. Box 5626, Victoria, British Columbia V8R 6S4 Canada. (250)380-1229. Fax: (250)380-1892. E-mail: orca@orcabook.com. Website: www.orcabook.com. **Acquisitions:** Maggie DeVries, editor (picture books, young readers); Andrew Wooldridge, editor (juvenile fiction, teen fiction); Bob Tyrrell, publisher (YA, teen). Publishes hardcover and trade paperback originals, and mass market paperback originals and reprints. **Publishes 30 titles/year. Receives 2,500 queries and 1,000 mss/year. 20% of books from first-time authors; 75% from unagented writers. Pays royalty.** Publishes book 12-18 months after acceptance of ms. Does not accept simultaneous submissions. Responds in 1 month to queries; 1 month to proposals; 1-2 months to mss. Ms guidelines online.

Nonfiction: Subjects include multicultural, picture books. Query with SASE.
Fiction: Hi-lo, juvenile, young adult. "Ask for guidelines, find out what we publish." Submit proposal package including 2-5 sample chapter(s), synopsis, SASE.
Recent Title(s): *Before Wings*, by Beth Goobie (teen fiction); *No Two Snowflakes*, by Sheree Fitch (picture book).
Tips: "Our audience is for students in grades K-12. Know our books, and know the market."

PETER OWEN PUBLISHERS, 73 Kenway Rd., London SW5 ORE United Kingdom. 020-8373 5628. Fax: 020-8373 6760. E-mail: admin@peterowen.com. Website: www.peterowen.com. **Acquisitions:** Antonia Owen. Publishes hardcover originals and trade paperback originals and reprints. **Publishes 20-30 titles/year. Receives 1,000 queries and 200 mss/year. 70% from unagented writers. Pays 7½-10% royalty. Offers negotiable advance.** Publishes book 1 year after acceptance of ms. Accepts simultaneous submissions. Responds in 2 months to queries; 2 months to proposals; 2 months to mss. Book catalog free.

O→ "We are far more interested in proposals for nonfiction than fiction at the moment." No poetry or short stories.
Nonfiction: Biography. Subjects include art/architecture, history, language/literature, memoirs, translation, travel, women's issues/studies. Query with SASE or submit outline, 1-3 sample chapter(s). Submit complete ms with return postage.
Fiction: Literary. "No first novels and authors should be aware that we publish very little new fiction these days." Query with SASE or by e-mail.
Recent Title(s): *Almodóvar: Labrynths of Passion*, by Gwynne Edwards (nonfiction); *Doubting Thomas*, by Atle Naess (translation, novel).

PACIFIC EDUCATIONAL PRESS, Faculty of Education, University of British Columbia, Vancouver, British Columbia V6T 1Z4 Canada. Fax: (604)822-6603. E-mail: cedwards@interchange.ubc.ca. **Acquisitions:** Catherine Edwards, director. Publishes trade paperback originals and cloth reference books. **Publishes 2-4 titles/year. Receives 60 submissions/year. 15% of books from first-time authors; 100% from unagented writers.** Accepts simultaneous submissions. Responds in 6 months to mss. Book catalog and ms guidelines for 9×12 SAE with IRCs.

O→ Pacific Educational Press publishes books on the subject of education for an adult audience of teachers, scholars, librarians and parents. Currently emphasizing literature, education, social studies education, international issues, mathematics, and science.
Recent Title(s): *Teaching to Wonder: Responding to Poetry in the Secondary Classroom*, by Carl Leggo; *The Canadian Anthology of Social Studies*, by Roland Case and Penney Clark; *Teaching Shakespeare on Screen*, by Neil Bechervaise.

[N] **PEDLAR PRESS**, P.O. Box 26, Station P, Toronto, Ontario M5S 2S6 Canada. (416)534-2011. Fax: (416)535-9677. E-mail: feralgrl@interlog.com. **Acquisitions:** Beth Follett, editor (fiction, poetry). Publishes hardcover and trade paperback originals. **Publishes 4 titles/year. Receives 50-60 mss/year. 50% of books from first-time authors; 100% from unagented writers. Pays 10-15% royalty on retail price. Offers $400-800 advance.** Publishes book 1 year after acceptance of ms. Accepts simultaneous submissions. Responds in 1 month to queries; 6 months to mss. Book catalog for #10 SASE; ms guidelines for #10 SASE.

O→ Niche is marginal voices, experimental style and form. Please note: Pedlar will not consider USA authors until 2003. Currently emphasizing experimental fiction.
Nonfiction: Gift book, humor, illustrated book. Subjects include creative nonfiction, gay/lesbian, humor, language/literature, sex, women's issues/studies. Submit proposal package including outline, 5 sample chapter(s). Reviews artwork/photos as part of ms package. Send photocopies.
Fiction: Erotica, experimental, feminist, gay/lesbian, humor, literary, picture books, poetry, short story collections. Query with SASE or submit proposal package including 5 sample chapter(s), synopsis.
Recent Title(s): *Mouthing the Words*, by Camilla Gibb (fiction); *Chez 100*, by Fiona Smyth (art book).
Tips: "We select manuscripts according to our taste. Be familiar with some if not most of our recent titles."

PENGUIN BOOKS CANADA LTD., The Penguin Group, 10 Alcorn Ave., Suite 300, Toronto, Ontario M4V 3B2 Canada. (416)925-0068. **Acquisitions:** Diane Turbide, editorial director (literary nonfiction, biography, social issues); Barbara Berson, senior editor (literary fiction and nonfiction; children's and young adult fiction; history/current events); Cynthia Good, president/publisher. **Offers advance.** Does not accept simultaneous submissions.
Nonfiction: Any Canadian subject by any Canadian authors. Query with SASE. *No unsolicited mss.*
Recent Title(s): *Vinyl Café Unplugged*, by Stuart mcLean (fiction); *Diamond*, by Matthew Hart (business); *On Equilibrium*, by John Ralston Saul (philosophy).

PICASSO PUBLICATIONS, INC., Picasso Entertainment Co., 10548-115 St., Edmonton, Alberta T5H 3K6 Canada. (780)420-0417. Fax: (780)420-0475. E-mail: randolph@picassopublications.com. Website: www.picassopublications.com. **Acquisitions:** Randolph Ross Sr., director (new business development); Aaron Deines, review editor (aaron@picassopublications.com). Publishes hardcover and trade paperback originals, mass market paperback originals. **Publishes 35 titles/year; imprint publishes 5 titles/year. Receives 50,000 queries and 10,000 mss/year. 1% of books from first-time authors; 10% from unagented writers. Pays 10-12% royalty on retail price or makes outright purchase. Offers up to $1 million advance.** Publishes book approximately 9-12 months after acceptance of ms. Accepts simultaneous submissions. Responds in 2 months to queries; 1 months to proposals; 3 months to mss. Book catalog and ms guidelines free or online.
Imprints: Blink, Chronicle Fiction, Engima, Nebula, Mystic, Passion Enlightenment.

O→ Picasso Publications publishes a wide variety of books for a mass market audience.

Nonfiction: Biography, children's/juvenile, coffee table book, cookbook, gift book, how-to, humor, illustrated book, multimedia, self-help. Subjects include Americana, animals, art/architecture, child guidance/parenting, cooking/foods/nutrition, education, ethnic, gay/lesbian, government/politics, history, hobbies, language/literature, military/war, money/finance, multicultural, recreation, religion, sex, sports, women's issues/studies. Query with SASE. Reviews artwork/photos as part of ms package. Send photocopies.
Fiction: Adventure, comic books, erotica, fantasy, feminist, gay/lesbian, gothic, historical, horror, humor, juvenile, literary, mainstream/contemporary, military/war, multicultural, multimedia, mystery, regional, religious, romance, science fiction, spiritual, sports, suspense, young adult. Query with SASE.
Recent Title(s): *The Wire Fence*; *Total Man*; *Walk a Mile in My Shoes.*

PLAYWRIGHTS CANADA PRESS, 54 Wolseley St., 2nd Floor, Toronto, Ontario M5T 1A5 Canada. (416)703-0013. Fax: (416)703-0059. E-mail: angela@puc.ca. Website: www.puc.ca. **Acquisitions:** Angela Rebeiro, publisher. Estab. 1972. Publishes paperback originals and reprints of plays. **Receives 40 submissions/year. 50% of books from first-time authors; 50% from unagented writers. Pays 10% royalty on retail price.** Publishes book 6 months-1 year after acceptance of ms. Responds in 2-3 months to queries.

- Playwrights Canada Press publishes only drama by Canadian citizens or landed immigrants, which has received professional production.

Recent Title(s): *The Harps of God*, by Kent Stetson; *Building Jerusalem*, by Michael Redhill; *It's All True*, by Jason Sherman.

PONDER PUBLISHING, INC., PO Box 23037, RPO McGillivray, Winnipeg, Manitoba R3T 5S3 Canada. (204)269-2985. Fax: (204)888-7159. E-mail: service@ponderpublishing.com. Website: www.ponderpublishing.com. **Acquisitions:** Mary Barton, senior editor; Pamela Walford, assistant editor. Publishes mass market paperback originals. **Publishes 2-4 titles/year. Receives 25 queries and 300 submissions/year. 100% of books from first-time authors; 100% from unagented writers. Contracts vary and are negotiable but include signing bonuses (instead of advance) in addition to royalties.** Publishes book 1-2 years after acceptance of ms. Responds in 3-5 months to queries; 3-5 months to proposals; 3-5 months to mss. Book catalog and ms guidelines for #10 SASE or online.
Fiction: Romance. "Ponder Romance is the new voice in the genre. We are looking for contemporary romances that are relationship driven and offer an escape from the everyday through both exciting plot lines and fresh writing styles. Entertainment and humor are two key elements to the success of a Ponder Romance. We tell writers, forget what you know about writing romance, start with a dynamite story and weave the romance into it." Submit 3 sample chapter(s), synopsis.
Recent Title(s): *Oh Susannah*, by Selena Mindus; *Autumn's Eve*, by Jordanna Boston.
Tips: "Ponder Romance appeals to a wide spectrum of romance readers and has also won over many nonromance and even nonfiction readers. Read our books. Writers assume they know what we want simply because it's romance, but Ponder Romance is unique to the genre and our titles are unique to each other in a way that our writer's guidelines cannot fully convey. Ponder Romance forges a new path right down the middle between category and mainstream romance and combines the best elements of each."

PRESSES DE L'UNIVERSITÉ DE MONTREAL, Case postale 6128, Succursule Centre-ville, Montreal, Quebec M3C 3J7 Canada. (514)343-6933. Fax: (514)343-2232. E-mail: pum@umontreal.ca. Website: www.pum.umontreal.ca. **Acquisitions:** Rene Bonenfant, editor-in-chief. Street address: 3535 Queen-Mary, Suite 206, Montreal, Quebec M3V 1H8 Canada. Publishes hardcover and trade paperback originals. **Publishes 40 titles/year. Pays 8-12% royalty on net receipts.** Publishes book 6 months after acceptance of ms. Responds in 1 month to queries; 1 month to proposals; 3 months to mss. Book catalog and ms guidelines free.
Nonfiction: Reference, textbook. Subjects include education, health/medicine, history, language/literature, philosophy, psychology, sociology, translation. Submit outline, 2 sample chapter(s).

PRODUCTIVE PUBLICATIONS, P.O. Box 7200 Station A, Toronto, Ontario M5W 1X8 Canada. (416)483-0634. Fax: (416)322-7434. **Acquisitions:** Iain Williamson, owner. Estab. 1985. Publishes trade paperback originals. **Publishes 24 titles/year. Receives 160 queries and 40 mss/year. 80% of books from first-time authors; 100% from unagented writers. Pays 10-15% royalty on wholesale price.** Publishes book 6 months after acceptance of ms. Accepts simultaneous submissions. Responds in 1 month to queries; 1 month to proposals; 3 months to mss. Book catalog free.

- "Productive Publications publishes books to help readers succeed and to help them meet the challenges of the new information age and global marketplace." Interested in books on business, computer software, the Internet for business purposes, investment, stock market and mutual funds, etc. Currently emphasizing computers, software, personal finance. De-emphasizing jobs, how to get employment.

Nonfiction: How-to, reference, self-help, technical. Subjects include business/economics (small business and management), computers/electronic, hobbies, money/finance, software (business). "We are interested in small business/entrepreneurship/employment/self-help (business)/how-to—100 to 300 pages." Submit outline. Reviews artwork/photos as part of ms package. Send photocopies.
Recent Title(s): *How to Deliver Excellent Customer Service: A Step-by-Step Guide for Every Business*, by Julie Olley; *Market Your Professional Service*, by Jerome Shure.
Tips: "We are looking for books written by *knowledgable, experienced experts* who can express their ideas *clearly* and *simply.*"

PURICH PUBLISHING, Box 23032, Market Mall Post Office, Saskatoon, Saskatchewan S7J 5H3 Canada. (306)373-5311. Fax: (306)373-5315. E-mail: purich@sasktel.net. Website: www.purichpublishing.com. **Acquisitions:** Donald Purich, publisher (law, Aboriginal issues); Karen Bolstad, publisher (history). Publishes trade paperback originals. **Publishes 3-5 titles/year. 20% of books from first-time authors. Pays 8-12% royalty on retail price or makes outright purchase. Offers negotiable advance.** Publishes book within 4 months of completion of editorial work, after acceptance of ms. Accepts simultaneous submissions. Responds in 1 month to queries; 3 months to mss. Book catalog free.

O¬ Purich publishes books on law, Aboriginal/Native American issues and Western Canadian history for the academic and professional trade reference market.

Nonfiction: Reference, technical, textbook. Subjects include agriculture/horticulture, ethnic, government/politics, history. "We are a specialized publisher and only consider work in our subject areas." Query with SASE.

Recent Title(s): *Aboriginal and Treaty Rights in the Maritimes*, by Thomas Isaac.

[N] **RAINCOAST BOOK DISTRIBUTION LTD.**, 9050 Shaughnessy St., Vancouver, British Columbia V6P 6E5 Canada. Publisher: Michelle Benjamin. **Acquisitions:** Lyn Henry, executive editor. Publishes hardcover and trade paperback originals and reprints. **Publishes 60 titles/year. Receives 3,000 queries/year. 10% of books from first-time authors; 50% from unagented writers. Pays 8-12% royalty on retail price. Offers $1,000-6,000 advance.** Publishes book within 2 years after acceptance of ms. Book catalog for #10 SASE. *Does not accept unsolicited mss.*

Imprints: Raincoast Books, Polestar Books (fiction, poetry, literary nonfiction), Press Gang (lesbian and feminist nonfiction).

Nonfiction: Children's/juvenile, coffee table book, cookbook, gift book, illustrated book. Subjects include animals, art/architecture, business/economics, cooking/foods/nutrition, ethnic, history, nature/environment, photography, recreation, regional, sports, travel. *No unsolicited mss.*

Fiction: Literary, short story collections, young adult. *No unsolicited mss.*

Recent Title(s): *Mount Appetite*, by Bill Gaston (short fiction); *Love and Other Ruins*, by Karen X. Tulchinsky (fiction); *Lock Me Up or Let Me Go*, by Betty Krawczyk (memoir).

RONSDALE PRESS, 3350 W. 21st Ave., Vancouver, British Columbia V6S 1G7 Canada. Website: www.ronsdalepress.com. **Acquisitions:** Ronald B. Hatch, director (fiction, poetry, social commentary); Veronica Hatch, managing director (children's literature). Publishes trade paperback originals. **Publishes 8 titles/year. Receives 100 queries and 200 mss/year. 60% of books from first-time authors; 95% from unagented writers. Pays 10% royalty on retail price.** Publishes book 1 year after acceptance of ms. Accepts simultaneous submissions. Responds in 1 week to queries; 2 months to proposals; 3 months to mss. Book catalog for #10 SASE.

O¬ Ronsdale publishes fiction, poetry, regional history, biography and autobiography, books of ideas about Canada, as well as children's books. Currently emphasizing YA historical fiction.

Nonfiction: Biography, children's/juvenile. Subjects include history (Canadian), language/literature, nature/environment, regional.

Fiction: Short story collections, novels. Query with at least the first 80 pages.

Poetry: "Poets should have published some poems in magazines/journals and should be well-read in contemporary masters." Submit complete ms.

Recent Title(s): *Eyewitness*, by Margaret Thompson (YA historical fiction).

Tips: "Ronsdale Press is a literary publishing house, based in Vancouver, and dedicated to publishing books from across Canada, books that give Canadians new insights into themselves and their country. We aim to publish the best Canadian writers."

SAXON HOUSE CANADA, P.O. Box 6947, Station A, Toronto, Ontario M5W 1X6 Canada. (416)488-7171. Fax: (416)488-2989. **Acquisitions:** Dietrich Hummell, editor-in-chief (poetry, legends); W.H. Wallace, general manager (history, philosophy); Carla Saxon, CEO (printed music). Publishes hardcover originals and trade paperback reprints. **Publishes 4 titles/year. Receives 6 queries and 20 mss/year. 20% of books from first-time authors; 80% from unagented writers. Pays royalty on wholesale price or makes outright purchase. Offers advance.** Publishes book 15 months after acceptance of ms. Accepts simultaneous submissions. Responds in 4 months to mss.

Nonfiction: Illustrated book. Subjects include Americana, history, music/dance (printed music), philosophy, religion. Submit proposal package including 3 sample chapter(s), résumé. Reviews artwork/photos as part of ms package. Send photocopies.

Fiction: Historical, literary, poetry. Submit proposal package including 3 sample chapter(s), résumé.

Poetry: Submit 8 sample poems.

Recent Title(s): *The Journey to Canada*, by David Mills (history); *Voices From the Lake*, by E.M. Watts (illustrated ancient American Indian legend); *The Wine of Babylon*, by David Mills (epic poem).

Tips: "We want books with literary integrity. Historical accuracy and fresh narrative skills."

[A] **SCHOLASTIC CANADA LTD.**, 175 Hillmount Rd., Markham, Ontario L6C 1Z7 Canada. (905)887-7323. Fax: (905)887-1131. Website: www.scholastic.ca. Publishes hardcover and trade paperback originals. **Publishes 40 titles/year; imprint publishes 4 titles/year. 3% of books from first-time authors; 50% from unagented writers. Pays 5-10% royalty on retail price. Offers $1,000-5,000 (Canadian) advance.** Publishes book 1 year after acceptance of ms. Does not accept simultaneous submissions. Responds in 3 months to queries; 6 months to proposals. Book catalog for 8½× 11 SAE with 2 first-class stamps (IRC or Canadian stamps only).

Imprints: North Winds Press, Les editions Scholastic.

- Scholastic publishes books by Canadians and/or about Canada. Currently emphasizing junior nonfiction, Canadian interest, middle-grade fiction.

Nonfiction: Biography, children's/juvenile, how-to. Subjects include history, hobbies, nature/environment, recreation, science, sports. *Agented submissions only. No unsolicited mss.*
Fiction: Juvenile (middle grade). No unsolicited mss. *Agented submissions only.*
Recent Title(s): *Playhouse*, by Robert Munsch and Michael Martchealeo (picture book); *You Asked For It!*, by Marg Meikle (nonfiction); *With Nothing But Our Courage*, by Karleen Bradford (fiction).

[A] **SEVERN HOUSE PUBLISHERS**, 9-15 High St., Sutton, Surrey SM1 1DF United Kingdom. (0208)770-3930. Fax: (0208)770-3850. **Acquisitions:** Amanda Stewart, editorial director. Publishes hardcover and trade paperback originals and reprints. **Publishes 150 titles/year. Receives 400-500 queries and 50 mss/year. Pays 7½-15% royalty on retail price.** Does not accept simultaneous submissions. Responds in 2 months to proposals.

- Severn House is currently emphasizing suspense, romance, mystery.

Fiction: Adventure, historical, horror, mainstream/contemporary, mystery, romance, suspense. *Agented submissions only.*
Recent Title(s): *Bottled Spider*, by John Gardner; *Special Forces*, by Ted Albeury; *Another Eden*, by Julie Ellis.

SHORELINE, 23 Ste-Anne, Ste-Anne-de-Bellevue, Quebec H9X 1l1 Canada. (514)457-5733. E-mail: bookline@total.net. Website: www.shorelinepress.ca. **Acquisitions:** Judy Isherwood, editor. Publishes trade book originals. **Publishes 3-4 titles/year. Pays 10% royalty on retail price.** Publishes book 1 year after acceptance of ms. Does not accept simultaneous submissions. Responds in 1 month to queries. Book catalog for 75¢; ms guidelines online.

- "Our mission is to support new authors by publishing works of considerable merit." Currently emphasizing biographies, memoirs and local history. Do not send mss.

Recent Title(s): *Chasing Grandma*, by Barbara Young (family history); *Walk Up the Creek*, by Marjorie Ludgate (memoir/education); *This Business of Family*, by Dennis Dwyer (conflict resolution in family businesses).
Tips: "See our website for submission guide, then query by e-mail or mail query with bio and sample chapters, by post."

SNOWAPPLE PRESS, Box 66024, Heritage Postal Outlet, Edmonton, Alberta T6J 6T4 Canada. **Acquisitions:** Vanna Tessier, editor. Publishes hardcover originals, trade paperback originals and reprints, mass market paperback originals and reprints. **Publishes 5-6 titles/year. Receives 300 queries/year. 50% of books from first-time authors; 100% from unagented writers. Pays 10-50% royalty on retail price or makes outright purchase. or pays in contributor copies. Offers $100-200 advance.** Publishes book 2 years after acceptance of ms. Accepts simultaneous submissions. Responds in 1 month to queries; 3 months to proposals; 3 months to mss.

- "We focus on topics that are interesting, unusual and controversial."

Fiction: Adventure, ethnic, experimental, fantasy, feminist, historical, literary, mainstream/contemporary, mystery, picture books, short story collections, young adult. Query with SASE. *No unsolicited mss.*
Poetry: Query with IRC.
Recent Title(s): *Thistle Creek*, by Vanna Tessier (fiction); *The Last Waltz of Chopin*, by Gilberto Finzi (fiction).
Tips: "We are a small press that will publish original, interesting and entertaining fiction and poetry."

SOUND AND VISION PUBLISHING LTD., 359 Riverdale Ave., Toronto, Ontario M4J 1A4 Canada. (416)465-2828. Fax: (416)465-0755. E-mail: musicbooks@soundandvision.com. Website: www.soundandvision.com. **Acquisitions:** Geoff Savage. Publishes trade paperback originals. **Publishes 3-5 titles/year. Receives 25 queries/year. 85% of books from first-time authors; 100% from unagented writers. Pays royalty on wholesale price. Offers $500-2,000 advance.** Does not accept simultaneous submissions. Responds in 1 month to queries.

- Sound and Vision specializes in books on musical humor and quotation books.

Nonfiction: Humor. Subjects include humor, music/dance. Query with SASE.
Recent Title(s): *The Thing I've Played with the Most*, by David E. Walden; *Opera Antics and Anecdotes*, by Stephen Tanner, cartoons by Umberto Taccola.

STELLER PRESS LTD., 13-4335 W. 10th Ave., Vancouver, British Columbia V6R 2H6 Canada. (604)222-2955. Fax: (604)222-2965. E-mail: harful@telus.net. **Acquisitions:** Guy Chadsey, publisher (outdoors/gardening). Publishes trade paperback originals. **Publishes 4 titles/year. 75% of books from first-time authors; 100% from unagented writers. Pays royalty on retail price. Offers $500-2,000 advance.** Accepts simultaneous submissions. Responds in 6 months to queries.

- "All titles are specific to the Pacific Northwest." Currently emphasizing gardening, history, outdoors. De-emphasizing fiction, poetry.

Nonfiction: Subjects include gardening, history, nature/environment, regional, travel.
Recent Title(s): *Roses For the Pacific Northwest*, by Christine Allen; *Herbs For the Pacific Northwest*, by Moira Carlson.

[N] **STODDART PUBLISHING CO., LTD.**, 895 Don Mills Rd., 400-2 Park Centre, Toronto, Ontario M3C 1W3 Canada. **Acquisitions:** Donald G. Bastian, managing editor. Publishes hardcover, trade paperback and mass market paperback originals and trade paperback reprints. **Publishes 100 titles/year. Receives 800 submissions/year. 10% of**

books from first-time authors; 50% from unagented writers. Pays 8-10% royalty on retail price. Offers advance. Publishes book 1 year after acceptance of ms. Accepts simultaneous submissions. Responds in 2 months to queries. Book catalog for #10 SASE; ms guidelines for #10 SASE.

Imprints: Stoddart Kids (Kathryn Cole, publisher).

O━ Stoddart publishes "important Canadian books" for a general interest audience. Currently emphasizing money/finance, sports, business. De-emphasizing coffee table book, cookbook, gardening. Prefers queries.

Nonfiction: Biography, coffee table book, gift book, how-to, humor, illustrated book, self-help. Subjects include art/architecture, business/economics, child guidance/parenting, computers/electronic, cooking/foods/nutrition, ethnic, gardening, government/politics, history, language/literature, money/finance, nature/environment, psychology, science, sociology, sports, women's issues/studies, world affairs.

Recent Title(s): *Blue Gold: The War Against Corporate Theft of the World's Water*, by Maude Barlow and Tony Clarke; *Closer Apart: The Ardara Variations*, by Gayla Reid (fiction).

TESSERACT BOOKS, The Books Collective, 214-21 10405 Jasper Ave., Edmonton, Alberta T5J 3S2 Canada. (780)448-0590. Fax: (780)448-0640. E-mail: promo@bookscollective.com. Website: www.bookscollective.com. **Acquisitions:** Candas Jame Dorsey, editor. Publishes hardcover and trade paperback originals. **Publishes 6 titles/year. Receives 50 queries and 350 mss/year. 80% of books from first-time authors; 90% from unagented writers. Pays 8% royalty on retail price.** Publishes book 18 months after acceptance of ms. Accepts simultaneous submissions. Responds in 2 months to queries; 4 months to proposals; 6 months to mss. Book catalog for 9×12 SAE with 2 first-class stamps; ms guidelines online.

Imprints: River Books, Slipstream Books (Timothy J. Anderson, editor).

Nonfiction: Biography. Subjects include memoirs. "Our only nonfiction titles are striking, powerful memoirs." Query with SASE or submit outline, 3 sample chapter(s), SASE.

Fiction: Experimental, fantasy, poetry, science fiction, short story collections. Submit 3 sample chapter(s), synopsis, SASE.

Poetry: Query.

Recent Title(s): *Running Through the Devil's Club*, by Deborah Hurford; *Green Music*, by Ursula Pflug; *Gypsey Messenger*, by Marijan Meglin.

Tips: "Audience is people interested in unusual stories, academics, people outside the mainstream. We only publish Canadian authors."

THOMPSON EDUCATIONAL PUBLISHING, INC., 6 Ripley Ave., Suite 200, Toronto, Ontario M6S 3N9 Canada. (416)766-2763. Fax: (416)766-0398. E-mail: publisher@thompsonbooks.com. Website: www.thompsonbooks.com. **Acquisitions:** Keith Thompson, president. **Publishes 10 titles/year. Receives 15 queries and 10 mss/year. 80% of books from first-time authors; 100% from unagented writers. Pays 10% royalty on net receipts. Offers advance.** Publishes book 1 year after acceptance of ms. Does not accept simultaneous submissions. Responds in 1 month to queries. Book catalog free.

O━ Thompson Educational specializes in high-quality educational texts in the social sciences and humanities.

Nonfiction: Textbook. Subjects include business/economics, education, ethnic, government/politics, multicultural, sociology, sports, women's issues/studies. Submit outline, 1 sample chapter(s), résumé.

Recent Title(s): *Juvenile Justice Systems*, edited by N. Bala, J. Hornick, H.N. Snyder and J.J. Paetsch.

THORSONS, HarperCollins, 77-85 Fulham Palace Rd., Hammersmith, London W6 8JB England. Fax: (020)8307-4788. **Acquisitions:** Belinda Budge, publisher. Estab. 1930. Publishes paperback originals. **Publishes 150 titles/year. Pays 7½-10% royalty. Offers advance.** Does not accept simultaneous submissions. Responds in 2 months to queries. Book catalog free.

O━ Currently emphasizing color-illustrated natural therapies, popular psychology. De-emphasizing astrology.

Nonfiction: Self-help. Subjects include business/economics, health/medicine (alternative), nature/environment, philosophy, psychology, religion, sex, spirituality.

Recent Title(s): *Dynamic Yoga*, by Godfrey Devereux; *Business as Unusual*, by Anita Roddick.

TITAN BOOKS LTD., 144 Southwark St., London SE1 OUP England. Fax: (0207)620-0032. E-mail: editorial@titanemail.com. **Acquisitions:** D. Barraclough, editorial manager. Publishes trade and mass market paperback originals and reprints. **Publishes about 100 titles/year. Receives 1,000 queries and 500 mss/year. 1% of books from first-time authors; 50% from unagented writers. Pays 6-8% royalty on retail price. Offers variable advance.** Accepts simultaneous submissions. Responds in 1 month to queries; 3 months to proposals; 6 months to mss. Ms guidelines for #10 SASE.

O━ Titan Books publishes film and TV titles.

Nonfiction: Biography, how-to, illustrated books. Subjects include film/cinema/stage, film and TV. Submit outline, sample chapter(s), SASE.

Recent Title(s): *Farscape: The Illustrated Season 2 Companion*, by Paul Simpson and Ruth Thomas; *The Greatest Sci-Fi Movies Never Made*, by David Hughes.

TRADEWIND BOOKS, 2216 Stephens St., Vancouver, British Columbia V6K 3W6 Canada. (604)730-0153. Fax: (604)730-0154. E-mail: tradewindbooks@eudoramail.com. Website: www.tradewindbooks.com. **Acquisitions:** Michael Katz, publisher (picturebooks, young adult); Carol Frank, art director (picturebooks); Tiffany Stone (acquisitions editor). Publishes hardcover and trade paperback originals. **Publishes 5 titles/year. Receives 1,000 submissions/year. 10% of**

books from first-time authors; 50% from unagented writers. Pays 7% royalty on retail price. Offers variable advance. Publishes book 3 years after acceptance of ms. Accepts simultaneous submissions. Responds in 2 months to mss. Book catalog and ms guidelines online.

O→ Tradewind Books publishes juvenile picturebooks, young adult novels and nonfiction natural history. Requires that submissions include evidence that author has read at least 3 titles published by Tradewind Books.

Fiction: Juvenile. Query with SASE or submit proposal package including 2 sample chapter(s), synopsis.
Recent Title(s): *Huevos Rancheros*; *The Jade Necklace*; *Aziz: The Storyteller.*

TURNSTONE PRESS, 607-100 Arthur St., Winnipeg, Manitoba R3B 1H3 Canada. (204)947-1555. Fax: (204)942-1555. E-mail: editor@turnstonepress.mb.ca. Website: www.turnstonepress.com. **Acquisitions:** Todd Besant, managing editor. Estab. 1976. Publishes trade paperback originals. **Publishes 10-12 titles/year. Receives 1,000 mss/year. 25% of books from first-time authors; 75% from unagented writers. Pays 10% royalty on retail price. Offers advance.** Publishes book 1 year after acceptance of ms. Does not accept simultaneous submissions. Responds in 4 months to queries. Book catalog for #10 SASE.
Imprints: Ravenstone (literary genre fiction).

O→ Turnstone Press is a literary press that publishes Canadian writers with an emphasis on writers from, and writing on, the Canadian West. "We are interested in publishing experimental/literary works that mainstream publishers may not be willing to work with." Currently emphasizing nonfiction—travel, adventure travel, memoir, eclectic novels. De-emphasizing formula or mainstream work.

Nonfiction: Autobiography. Subjects include nature/environment, travel, adventure travel, cultural/social issues. Query with SASE.
Fiction: Experimental (urban), feminist, humor, literary, mainstream/contemporary, mystery, short story collections. Query with SASE.
Poetry: Submit complete ms.
Recent Title(s): *The Dead of Midnight*, by Catherine Hunter (mystery); *Beatrice*, by Monica Kidd (fiction); *Grace & Poison*, by Karen Connelly (poetry).
Tips: "Writers are encouraged to view our list and check if submissions are appropriate. Would like to see more adventure travel as well as eclectic novels. Would like to see 'nonformula' genre writing, especially *literary* mystery, urban mystery and noir for our new imprint."

THE UNIVERSITY OF ALBERTA PRESS, Ring House 2, Edmonton, Alberta T6G 2E1 Canada. (780)492-3662. Fax: (780)492-0719. E-mail: u.a.p@ualberta.ca. Website: www.ualberta.ca/~uap. Estab. 1969. **Publishes 18-25 titles/year. Receives 400 submissions/year. 60% of books from first-time authors. Pays maximum 10% royalty on net price.** Publishes book within 2 years after acceptance of ms. Does not accept simultaneous submissions. Responds in 3 months to queries. Book catalog and ms guidelines free.

O→ "Award-winning publisher the University of Alberta Press has published excellent scholarly works and fine books for general audiences. Our program is particularly strong in the areas of biography, history, language, literature, natural history and books of regional interest. Within each of those broad subject areas we have published in a variety of specific fields. We are pursuing manuscripts in our areas of strength and expertise, as listed above, and inviting submissions in several new areas including travel/adventure writing, business, health and social policy. *We do not accept unsolicited novels or poetry.* Please see our website for details."

UNIVERSITY OF CALGARY PRESS, 2500 University Dr. NW, Calgary, Alberta T2N 1N4 Canada. (403)220-7578. Fax: (403)282-0085. E-mail: whildebr@ucalgary.ca. Website: www.ucalgary.ca/ucpress. **Acquisitions:** Walter Hildebrandt, director/acquisitions editor. Publishes hardcover and trade paperback originals and reprints. **Publishes 15-20 titles/year.** Publishes book 20 months after acceptance of ms. Does not accept simultaneous submissions. Responds in 1 month to queries; 2 months to proposals; 2 months to mss. Book catalog and ms guidelines free.

O→ "University of Calgary Press is committed to the advancement of scholarship through the publication of first-rate monographs and academic and scientific journals."

Nonfiction: Scholarly. Subjects include art/architecture, philosophy, travel, women's issues/studies, world affairs. Canadian studies, post-modern studies, native studies, history and heritage of the Canadian and American heartland, 3 new series (Latin American & Caribbean, African and Northern Lights), international relations. Submit outline, 2 sample chapter(s). SASE. Reviews artwork/photos as part of ms package. Send photocopies.
Recent Title(s): *The War on Weeds in the Prairie West: An Environmental History*, by Clint Evans; *Muskox Land: Ellesmere Island in the Age of Contact*, by Lyle Dick.

N **UNIVERSITY OF MANITOBA PRESS**, 15 Gillson St. #444, Winnipeg, Manitoba R3T 2N2 Canada. (204)474-9495. Fax: (204)474-7566. Website: www.umanitoba.ca/uofmpress. **Acquisitions:** David Carr, director. Estab. 1967. Publishes nonfiction hardcover and trade paperback originals. **Publishes 4-6 titles/year. Pays 5-15% royalty on wholesale price. Offers advance.** Does not accept simultaneous submissions. Responds in 3 months to queries.
Nonfiction: Scholarly. Subjects include ethnic, history, regional, women's issues/studies. Western Canadian history. Query with SASE.
Recent Title(s): *A National Crime*, John Milloy (native/history).
Tips: "Western Canadian focus or content is important."

N **UNIVERSITY OF OTTAWA PRESS**, 542 King Edward, Ottawa, Ontario K1N 6N5 Canada. (613)562-5246. Fax: (613)562-5247. E-mail: press@uottawa.ca. Website: www.uopress.uottawa.ca. **Acquisitions:** Vicki Bennett, editor-in-chief; Professor Jean Delisle, director translation collection (translation, history of translation, teaching translation); Chad Gaffield, Guy Leclaire, directors Institute Canadian Studies (Canadian studies); Gilles Paquet, director collection (governance). Estab. 1936. **Publishes 22 titles/year. Receives 250 submissions/year. 20% of books from first-time authors; 95% from unagented writers. Pays 5-10% royalty on net receipts.** Publishes book 6-12 months after acceptance of ms. Does not accept simultaneous submissions. Responds in 1 month to queries; 6 months to mss. Book catalog free; ms guidelines free.

O→ The University Press publishes books for the scholarly and educated general audiences. They were "the first *officially* bilingual university publishing house in Canada. Our goal is to help the publication of cutting edge research—books written to be useful to active researchers but accessible to an interested public." Currently emphasizing French in North America, language rights, social justice, translation, Canadian studies. De-emphasizing medieval studies, criminology.

Nonfiction: Reference, textbook. Subjects include education, government/politics, history, language/literature, nature/environment, philosophy, regional, religion, sociology, translation, women's issues/studies. Submit outline, sample chapter(s).

Recent Title(s): *The Fallacy of Race & the Shoah*, Naomi Kramer and Ronald Headland.

Tips: "*No unrevised theses!* Envision audience of academic specialists and (for some books) educated public."

VANWELL PUBLISHING LTD., 1 Northrup Crescent, P.O. Box 2131, St. Catharines, Ontario L2R 7S2 Canada. (905)937-3100. Fax: (905)937-1760. **Acquisitions:** Angela Dobler, general editor; Simon Kooter, military editor (collections, equipment, vehicles, uniforms, artifacts); Ben Kooter, publisher (general military). Estab. 1983. Publishes trade originals and reprints. **Publishes 7-9 titles/year. Receives 100 submissions/year. 85% of books from first-time authors; 100% from unagented writers. Pays 10% royalty on retail price.** Publishes book 1 year after acceptance of ms. Does not accept simultaneous submissions. Responds in 6 months to queries. Book catalog free.

O→ Vanwell is considered Canada's leading naval heritage publisher. Currently emphasizing military aviation, biography, WWI and WWII histories.

Nonfiction: Biography, reference, scholarly. Subjects include history, military/war, regional. Query with SASE. Reviews artwork/photos as part of ms package.

Recent Title(s): *Ships of Canada's Marine Services*, by Charles Maginley and Bernard Collins; *Auro Aircraft & Cold War Aviation*, by Randall Whitcomb.

Tips: "The writer has the best chance of selling a manuscript to our firm which is in keeping with our publishing program, well written and organized. Our audience: older male, history buff, war veteran; regional tourist; students. *Canadian* only military/aviation, naval, military/history have the best chance with us. We see more interest in collective or cataloguing forms of history, also in modeling and recreating military historical artifacts."

VÉHICULE PRESS, Box 125, Place du Parc Station, Montreal, Quebec H2X 4A3 Canada. (514)844-6073. Fax: (514)844-7543. Website: www.vehiculepress.com. **Acquisitions:** Simon Dardick, president/publisher. Estab. 1973. Publishes trade paperback originals by Canadian authors only. **Publishes 15 titles/year. Receives 250 submissions/year. 20% of books from first-time authors; 95% from unagented writers. Pays 10-15% royalty on retail price. Offers $200-500 advance.** Publishes book 1 year after acceptance of ms. Responds in 4 months to queries. Book catalog for 9×12 SAE with IRCs.

Imprints: Signal Editions (poetry), Dossier Quebec (history, memoirs).

O→ "Montreal's Véhicule Press has published the best of Canadian and Quebec literature—fiction, poetry, essays, translations and social history."

Nonfiction: Autobiography, biography. Subjects include government/politics, history, language/literature, memoirs, regional, sociology. Especially looking for Canadian social history. Query with SASE. Reviews artwork/photos as part of ms package.

Poetry: Contact: Carmine Starnino.

Recent Title(s): *The Water Gods: The Inside Story of a World Bank Project in Nepal*, by Anna Paskal (nonfiction); *Araby*, by Eric Ormsby; *Through the Eyes of the Eagle: The Early Montreal Yiddish Press 1907-1916*, translated by David Rome.

Tips: "We are interested only in Canadian authors."

WALL & EMERSON, INC., 6 O'Connor Dr., Toronto, Ontario M4K 2K1 Canada. (416)467-8685. Fax: (416)352-5368. E-mail: wall@wallbooks.com. Website: www.wallbooks.com. **Acquisitions:** Byron E. Wall, president (history of science, mathematics). Estab. 1987. Publishes hardcover originals and reprints. **Publishes 3 titles/year. Receives 10 queries and 8 mss/year. 50% of books from first-time authors; 100% from unagented writers. Pays 5-12% royalty on wholesale price.** Publishes book 1 year after acceptance of ms. Accepts simultaneous submissions. Responds in 1 month to queries; 1 month to proposals; 3 months to mss. Book catalog and ms guidelines free or online.

O→ "We are most interested in textbooks for college courses that meet well-defined needs and are targeted to their audiences." Currently emphasizing adult education, engineering. De-emphasizing social work.

Nonfiction: Reference, textbook. Subjects include education, health/medicine, philosophy, science. "We are looking for any undergraduate text that meets the needs of a well-defined course in colleges in the U.S. and Canada." Submit proposal package including outline, 2 sample chapter(s).

Recent Title(s): *Princinples of Engineering Economic Analysis*; *Voices Past and Present.*

Tips: "Our audience consists of college undergraduate students and college libraries. Our ideal writer is a college professor writing a text for a course he or she teaches regularly. If I were a writer trying to market a book today, I would identify the audience for the book and write directly to the audience throughout the book. I would then approach a publisher that publishes books specifically for that audience."

N **WEIGL EDUCATIONAL PUBLISHERS LTD.**, 6325 Tenth St. SE, Calgary, Alberta T2H 2Z9 Canada. (403)233-7747. Fax: (403)233-7769. E-mail: info@weigl.com. Website: www.weigl.com. **Acquisitions:** Linda Weigl, president. Publishes hardcover originals and reprints, school library softcover. **Publishes 30 titles/year. Receives 40 queries and 20 mss/year. 5% of books from first-time authors; 100% from unagented writers. Makes outright purchase. Offers advance.** Accepts simultaneous submissions. Responds in 6 months to queries. Book catalog free; ms guidelines free.

O→ Textbook publisher catering to juvenile and young adult audience (K-12).

Nonfiction: Children's/juvenile, textbook. Subjects include animals, education, government/politics, history, nature/environment, science. Query with SASE.

Recent Title(s): *The Science of Insects* (living science series); *Forgeries, Fingerprints and Forensics: The Science of Crime*.

WHITECAP BOOKS LTD., 351 Lynn Ave., North Vancouver, British Columbia V7J 2C4 Canada. (604)980-9852. Fax: (604)980-8197. E-mail: whitecap@whitecap.ca. Website: www.whitecap.ca. **Acquisitions:** Leanne McDonald, rights and aquisitions associate. Publishes hardcover and trade paperback originals. **Publishes 24 titles/year. Receives 500 queries and 1,000 mss/year. 20% of books from first-time authors; 90% from unagented writers. Pays royalty. Offers negotiated advance.** Publishes book 18 months after acceptance of ms. Accepts simultaneous submissions. Responds in 2 months to proposals.

O→ Whitecap Books publishes a wide range of nonfiction with a Canadian and international focus. Currently emphasizing children's nonfiction, natural history. De-emphasizing children's fiction.

Nonfiction: Children's/juvenile, coffee table book, cookbook. Subjects include animals, cooking/foods/nutrition, gardening, history, nature/environment, recreation, regional, travel. "We require an annotated outline. Writers should take the time to research our list. This is especially important for children's writers." Submit outline, 1 sample chapter(s), SASE. Reviews artwork/photos as part of ms package. Send photocopies.

Recent Title(s): *Seasons In the Rockies*, by Darwin Wiggett, Tom Till, Rebecca Gambo (nonfiction); *The Queen, The Bear and The Bumblebee*, by Dini Petty (fiction).

Tips: "We want well-written, well-researched material that presents a fresh approach to a particular topic."

YORK PRESS LTD., 152 Boardwalk Dr., Toronto, Ontario M4L 3X4 Canada. E-mail: yorkpress@sympatico.ca. Website: www3.sympatico.ca/yorkpress. **Acquisitions:** Dr. S. Elkhadem, general manager/editor. Estab. 1975. Publishes trade paperback originals. **Publishes 10 titles/year. Receives 50 submissions/year. 10% of books from first-time authors; 100% from unagented writers. Pays 10-20% royalty on wholesale price. Offers advance.** Publishes book 6 months after acceptance of ms. Does not accept simultaneous submissions. Responds in 2 weeks to queries.

O→ "We publish scholarly books and creative writing of an experimental nature."

Nonfiction: Reference, scholarly, textbook. Subjects include language/literature. Query with SASE.

Fiction: Experimental. Query with SASE.

Recent Title(s): *Herman Melville: Romantic & Prophet*, C.S. Durer (scholarly literary criticism); *The Moonhare*, Kirk Hampton (experimental novel).

Tips: "If I were a writer trying to market a book today, I would spend a considerable amount of time examining the needs of a publisher *before* sending my manuscript to him. The writer must adhere to our style manual and follow our guidelines exactly."

Small Presses

"Small press" is a relative term. Compared to the dozen or so conglomerates, the rest of the book publishing world may seem to be comprised of small presses. A number of the publishers listed in the Book Publishers section consider themselves small presses and cultivate the image. For our classification, small presses are those that publish three or fewer books per year.

The publishing opportunities are slightly more limited with the companies listed here than with those in the Book Publishers section. Not only are they publishing fewer books, but small presses are usually not able to market their books as effectively as larger publishers. Their print runs and royalty arrangements are usually smaller. It boils down to money, what a publisher can afford, and in that area, small presses simply can't compete with conglomerates.

However, realistic small press publishers don't try to compete with Penguin Putnam or Random House. They realize everything about their efforts operates on a smaller scale. Most small press publishers get into book publishing for the love of it, not solely for the profit. Of course, every publisher, small or large, wants successful books. But small press publishers often measure success in different ways.

Many writers actually prefer to work with small presses. Since small publishing houses are usually based on the publisher's commitment to the subject matter, and since they necessarily work with far fewer authors than the conglomerates, small press authors and their books usually receive more personal attention than the larger publishers can afford to give them. Promotional dollars at the big houses tend to be siphoned toward a few books each season that they have decided are likely to succeed, leaving hundreds of "midlist" books underpromoted, and, more likely than not, destined for failure. Since small presses only commit to a very small number of books every year, they are vitally interested in the promotion and distribution of each one.

Just because they publish three or fewer titles per year does not mean small press editors have the time to look at complete manuscripts on spec. In fact, the editors with smaller staffs often have even less time for submissions. The procedure for contacting a small press with your book idea is exactly the same as it is for a larger publisher. Send a one-page query with SASE first. If the press is interested in your proposal, be ready to send an outline or synopsis, and/or a sample chapter or two. Be patient with their reporting times; small presses can be slower to respond than larger companies. You might consider simultaneous queries, as long as you note this, to compensate for the waiting game.

For more information on small presses, see *Novel & Short Story Writer's Market* and *Poet's Market* (Writer's Digest Books), and *The International Directory of Little Magazines and Small Presses* (Dustbooks).

For a list of publishers according to their subjects of interest, see the nonfiction and fiction sections of the Book Publishers Subject Index. Information on book publishers and producers listed in the previous edition of *Writer's Market* but not included in this edition can be found in the General Index.

aatec publications, P.O. Box 7119, Ann Arbor MI 48107. (734)995-1470. Fax: (734)995-1471. E-mail: aatecpub@mindspring.com. **Acquisitions:** Christina Bych, publisher. Publishes hardcover and trade paperback originals. **Publishes 1-3 titles/year. Receives 20 queries and 10 mss/year. 75% of books from first-time authors; 100% from unagented writers. Pays 15% royalty.** Publishes book 1 year after acceptance of ms. Does not accept simultaneous submissions. Responds in 1 month to queries. Book catalog free.

Nonfiction: How-to, technical. Subjects include history, nature/environment. "We publish—and update—the best basic books on the theory and practical use of solar electricity. Future publications should supplement or advance on this in some way." Submit outline, 2-3 sample chapter(s), publishing history. Reviews artwork/photos as part of ms package. Send photocopies.
Recent Title(s): *From Space to Earth: The Story of Solar Electricity*, by John Perlin (history).
Tips: "Audience is nontechnical, potential users of renewable energies. Review existing publications (available at many libraries). Create a book a current or potential renewable energy user would want to read."

ACME PRESS, P.O. Box 1702, Westminster MD 21158-1702. (410)848-7577. **Acquisitions:** (Ms.) E.G. Johnston, managing editor. Estab. 1991. Publishes hardcover and trade paperback originals. **Publishes 1-2 titles/year. Offers small advance.** Accepts simultaneous submissions. Responds in 2 months to mss.
Fiction: Humor. "We accept submissions on any subject as long as the material is humorous; prefer full-length novels. No cartoons or art (text only). No pornography, poetry, short stories or children's material." Submit first 3-5 chapters, synopsis, and SASE.
Recent Title(s): *SuperFan*, by Lyn A. Sherwood (funny football novel).
Tips: "We are always looking for the great comic novel."

ADAMS-HALL PUBLISHING, P.O. Box 491002, Los Angeles CA 90049. (800)888-4452. **Acquisitions:** Sue Ann Bacon, editorial director. Publishes hardcover and trade paperback originals and reprints. **Publishes 3-4 titles/year. Pays 10% royalty on net receipts. Offers negotiable advance.** Does not accept simultaneous submissions. Responds in 1 month to queries.
Nonfiction: Subjects include money/finance, business. Small successful house that aggressively promotes select titles. Only interested in business or personal finance titles with broad appeal. Submit query, title, synopsis, your qualifications, a list of 3 competitive books and how it's widely different from other books. Do not send ms or sample chapters.
Recent Title(s): *Fail Proof Your Business.*

N **ALPINE PUBLICATIONS**, 225 S. Madison Ave., Loveland CO 80537. (970)667-9317. Fax: (970)667-9157. E-mail: alpinepubl@aol.com. Website: alpinepub.com. **Acquisitions:** Ms. B.J. McKinney, publisher. Estab. 1975. Publishes hardcover and trade paperback originals and reprints. **Publishes 3 titles/year. 50% of books from first-time authors; 95% from unagented writers. Pays 8-15% royalty on wholesale price. Offers advance.** Publishes book 18 months after acceptance of ms. Accepts simultaneous submissions. Responds in 4 months to queries; 3 months to proposals; 3 months to mss. Book catalog free; ms guidelines free.
Imprints: Blue Ribbon Books.
Nonfiction: How-to, illustrated book, reference. Subjects include animals. "Alpine specializes in books that promote the enjoyment of and responsibility for companion animals with emphasis on dogs and horses." Reviews artwork/photos as part of ms package. Send photocopies.
Recent Title(s): *New Secrets of Successful Show Dog Handling*, by Peter Green and Mario Migliorini (dog); *Understanding Showmanship*, by Laurie Truskauskas (horse); *The Science and Techniques of Judging Dogs*, by Robert J. Berndt (dog).
Tips: "Our audience is pet owners, breeders and exhibitors, veterinarians, animal trainers, animal care specialists and judges. Look up some of our titles before you submit. See what is unique about our books. Write your proposal to suit our guidelines."

AMIGADGET PUBLISHING COMPANY, P.O. Box 1696, Lexington SC 29071. (803)779-3196. E-mail: jaygross@fotoartista.com. Website: www.fotoartista.com/amigadget. **Acquisitions:** Jay Gross, editor-in-chief. Publishes hardcover and trade paperback originals. **Publishes 2 titles/year. Pays royalty or makes outright purchase. Offers negotiable advance.** Does not accept simultaneous submissions. Responds in 6 months to queries.
Nonfiction: "Niche markets are our specialty. No books on Windows." Query via e-mail only.
Recent Title(s): *The Coffee Experience*, by J. Gross (travel).

ANACUS PRESS, INC., 3943 Meadowbrook Rd., Minneapolis MN 55426. (952)938-9330. Fax: (952)938-7353. E-mail: feedback@finney-hobar.com. Website: www.anacus.com. **Acquisitions:** Alan E. Krysan, publisher (bicycling guides, travel). Publishes trade paperback originals. **Publishes 3-5 titles/year. Pays 10-14% royalty on wholesale price. Offers advance.** Book catalog online.
Nonfiction: Subjects include recreation, regional, travel (travel guides, travelogue). Query with SASE.
Recent Title(s): *Bed, Breakfast & Bike Mississippi Valley*, by Dale Lally (travel guide); *The Adventure of Two Lifetimes*, by Peggy & Brian Goetz (travelogue); *Bed, Breakfast & Bike Midwest*, by Robert & Theresa Russell (travel guide).
Tips: Audience is cyclists and armchair adventurers.

ANHINGA PRESS, P.O. Box 10595, Tallahassee FL 32302. (850)521-9920. Fax: (850)442-6323. E-mail: info@anhinga.org. Website: www.anhinga.org. **Acquisitions:** Rick Campbell or Joann Gardner, editors. Publishes hardcover and trade paperback originals. **Publishes 3-4 titles/year. Pays 10% royalty on retail price. Offers Anhinga Prize of $2,000.** Accepts simultaneous submissions. Responds in 3 months to queries; 3 months to proposals; 3 months to mss. Book catalog and ms guidelines for #10 SASE or online.
Poetry: "We like good poetry." Query or submit 6 sample poems.
Recent Title(s): *Summer*, by Robert Dana; *The Secret History of Water*, by Silvia Curbelo; *Mint Snowball*, by Naomi Shihab Nye.

Tips: "We publish poetry only."

ARIADNE PRESS, 4817 Tallahassee Ave., Rockville MD 20853-3144. (301)949-2514. **Acquisitions:** Carol Hoover, president. Estab. 1976. Publishes hardcover and trade paperback originals. **Publishes 1 title/year. Pays 10% royalty on retail price.** Does not accept simultaneous submissions. Responds in 1 month to queries; 3 months to mss.
Fiction: Adventure, feminist, historical, humor, literary, mainstream/contemporary. "We look for exciting and believable plots, strong themes, and non-stereotypical characters who develop in fascinating and often unpredictable directions." Query with SASE.
Recent Title(s): *Lasting*, by Suzanne Love Harris.
Tips: "Our purpose is to promote the publication of emerging fiction writers."

AVID READER PRESS, VWI Corporation, 6705 W. Hwy 290, Suite 502-295, Austin TX 78735. (512)288-2697. Fax: (512)288-0317. E-mail: info@avidreaderpress.com. Website: www.avidreaderpress.com. **Acquisitions:** Elena Lipkowski, publisher; James Bellevue, publisher. Publishes trade paperback originals and reprints. **Publishes 3 titles/year. 50% of books from first-time authors; 90% from unagented writers. Negotiates contracts individually.** Publishes book 1 year after acceptance of ms. Accepts simultaneous submissions. Responds in 3 months to queries; 3 months to proposals; 3 months to mss. Book catalog and ms guidelines on website.
Nonfiction: Biography, coffee table book, how-to, humor, multimedia (video), self-help. Subjects include animals, health/medicine, natural health, alternative medicine. "We want to help people, and their pets, improve or maintain their health. We are seeking well written, well organized, original or unique books on Natural Health or Alternative Medicine. Books should inform consumers about health options of which they may be unaware. However, the subject matter should be supported by research. No personal accounts unless they directly relate to a general audience. We will also consider reprinting older or under-marketed titles in these areas." Submit proposal package including outline, 2 sample chapter(s), SASE. Reviews artwork/photos as part of ms package. Send photocopies.
Recent Title(s): *Improve Your Eyesight*, by James Bellevue.
Tips: When submitting a query, "include a listing of current competitive books, author qualifications, and information on how your book is unique, and potential readers of your book. We look for authors who want to actively participate in the marketing of their books."

BANDANNA BOOKS, 319-B Anacapa St., Santa Barbara CA 93101. (805)564-3559. Fax: (805)564-3559. E-mail: sasha@bandannabooks.com. Website: www.bandannabooks.com. **Acquisitions:** Sasha Newborn, publisher. Publishes trade paperback originals and reprints. **Publishes 3 titles/year. Pays royalty on net receipts. Offers up to $500 advance.** Accepts simultaneous submissions. Responds in 4 months to proposals.
Nonfiction: "We are looking for classic texts in fresh, perhaps irreverent, translations or modernized gender-conscious English. Also quick writing aids." Submit proposal package including outline, sample chapter(s), SASE.
Recent Title(s): *The Merchant of Venice*, by Shakespeare; *The First Detective, 3 Stories*, by Edgar Allan Poe.
Tips: "Our readers are college students or college age. Inventive, professional, well-thought-out presentations, please. Always include a SASE for reply."

BARDSONG PRESS, P.O. Box 775396, Steamboat Springs CO 80477-5396. (970)870-1401. Fax: (970)879-2657. E-mail: celts@bardsongpress.com. Website: www.bardsongpress.com. **Acquisitions:** Ann Gilpin, editor (Celtic history). Publishes hardcover originals and trade paperback reprints. **Publishes 1-2 titles/year. Payment method varies.** Publishes book 18 months after acceptance of ms. Accepts simultaneous submissions. Responds in 2 months to queries. Book catalog online; ms guidelines for #10 SASE.

O→ Bardsong Press publishes books on Celtic history and culture.

Nonfiction: Anthologies. Subjects include creative nonfiction, essays. Query with SASE.
Fiction: Historical, poetry. "We are looking for work that reflects the ageless culture, history, symbolism, mythology and spirituality that belongs to Celtic heritage. Settings can range from ancient times to early twentieth century and include the earliest European territories, the current nations of Wales, Scotland, Ireland, Cornwall, Isle of Man, Brittany and Galacia, as well as lands involved in the Celtic Diaspora." Query with SASE.
Poetry: "Poetry is currently only accepted through the Celtic Voice Writing contests." See Writer's Market listing under 'Contests and Awards'.
Recent Title(s): *In the Shadow of Dragons*, by Kathleen Cunningham Guler (historical fiction); *Offerings for the Green Man*, by various authors (poetry/short fiction).

BENDALL BOOKS, 145 Tyee Dr., PMB 361, Point Roberts WA 98281. (250)743-2946. Fax: (250)743-2910. E-mail: bendallbooks@islandnet.com. Website: www.islandnet.com/bendallbooks. **Acquisitions:** R. Bendall, publisher. Publishes trade paperback originals. **Publishes 1 title/year. Receives 135 queries and 10 mss/year. 50% of books from first-time authors; 100% from unagented writers. Pays 5-15% royalty on wholesale price.** Publishes book 1 year after acceptance of ms. Accepts simultaneous submissions. Book catalog free.
Nonfiction: Reference, textbook. Subjects include education. Query with SASE.
Recent Title(s): *Daily Meaning*, edited by Allan Neilsen; *Fiction Workshop Companion*, by Jon Volkmer.

[N] **BLISS PUBLISHING CO.**, P.O. Box 920, Marlborough MA 01752. (508)480-0060. **Acquisitions:** Stephen H. Clouter, publisher. Publishes hardcover and trade paperback originals. **Publishes 2-4 titles/year. Pays 10-15% royalty on wholesale price.** Does not accept simultaneous submissions. Responds in 2 months to queries.

Nonfiction: Biography, illustrated book, reference, textbook. Subjects include government/politics, history, music/dance, nature/environment, recreation, regional. Submit proposal package including outline, 3 sample chapter(s), résumé. SASE.
Recent Title(s): *Ninnuock, The Algonkian People of New England*, Steven F. Johnson.

BOOKHAVEN PRESS, LLC, P.O. Box 1243, Moon Township PA 15108. (412)494-6926. Orders: (800)782-7424. Fax: (412)494-5479. Website: www.members.aol.com/bookhaven. Editorial Manager: Victor Richards. **Acquisitions:** Dennis Damp, publisher. Publishes trade paperback originals. **Publishes 2 titles/year. Pays 7-12% royalty on wholesale price.** Does not accept simultaneous submissions. Sends form letter for rejection, destroys originals. Responds in 3 months to queries; 1 month to proposals; 2 months to mss. Book catalog free.
Nonfiction: How-to, reference. Subjects include business/economics, education, money/finance. Bookhaven Press seeks to develop complimentary titles for our existing career book line. Emphasizing health care and government employment. "We look for well-developed manuscripts from computer literate writers. All manuscripts must be available in IBM computer format (Word Perfect or Microsoft Word preferred)." Submit outline, 2 sample chapter(s).
Recent Title(s): *The Book of U.S. Government Jobs, 8th edition*; *Health Care Job Explosion! 3rd ed*, by Dennis V. Damp.

BUILDERBOOKS, (formerly Home Builder Press), National Association of Home Builders, 1201 15th St. NW, Washington DC 20005-2800. (800)368-5242 ext. 8368. Fax: (202)266-8559. E-mail: dtennyson@nahb.com. Website: www.builderbooks.com. Publisher: Eric Johnson. **Acquisitions:** Doris M. Tennyson, acquisitions editor (business and construction management for remodelers; computerization, marketing and selling for builders, remodelers, developers, suppliers, manufacturers, and their sales and marketing directors; customer relations; legal issues; seniors housing); Thersa Minch (business and construction management for builders, developers, and others; construction how-to; computerization, multifamily, safety). Publishes trade paperback originals. **Publishes 1 or more titles/year. 33% of books from first-time authors; 100% from unagented writers. Pays 10% royalty on net revenue except for sales at 50% discount or more. Usually offers a small advance.** Publishes book 6-9 months after acceptance of ms. Does not accept simultaneous submissions. Responds in 1 month to queries; 2 months to proposals; 3 months to mss. Book catalog free or on website; ms guidelines free.
Nonfiction: "We prefer a detailed outline on a strong industry topic. Our readers like step-by-step, how-to books and other products, no history or philosophy of the industry." How-to, reference, technical. Subjects include home building, remodeling, light construction industry and related topics such as business and construction management, sales and marketing, legal issues, customer service, computerization, electronic templates, multifamily, safety. Query first. E-mail queries accepted. Include electronic and hard copy artwork/photos as part of ms package. Send photocopies.
Recent Title(s): *Meetings with Clients: A Self-Study Manual for Builder's Frontline Personnel*, by Carol Smith; *Accounting and Quickbooks-Pro®*, by Diane C.O. Gilson, CPA; *Selling to Builders*, by Steve Monroe (for providers of services and materials to the industry).
Tips: "Ask for a sample outline." Audience is primarily small-, medium-, and high-volume home builders; remodelers; developers; sales and marketing directors; multifamily builders; light commercial and institutional builders (not skyscrapers), providers of services and materials for the industry employees of industry businesses; attorneys; and others in the industry.

CAROUSEL PRESS, P.O. Box 6038, Berkeley CA 94706-0038. (510)527-5849. **Acquisitions:** Carole T. Meyers, editor/publisher. Estab. 1976. Publishes trade paperback originals and reprints. **Publishes 1-2 titles/year. Pays 10-15% royalty on wholesale price. Offers $1,000 advance.** Responds in 1 month to queries.
Nonfiction: Subjects include travel. Query with SASE.
Recent Title(s): *Dream Sleeps: Castle & Palace Hotels of Europe*, by Pamela L. Barrus.

[N] **CASSANDRA PRESS**, P.O. Box 228, Boulder CO 80306. (800)527-6104. E-mail: starvibe@indra.com. **Acquisitions:** Fred Rubenfeld, president. Estab. 1985. Publishes trade paperback originals. **Publishes 3 titles/year. Receives 200 submissions/year. 50% of books from first-time authors; 50% from unagented writers. Pays 6-8% royalty on retail price. Offers rarely advance.** Publishes book 1 year after acceptance of ms. Accepts simultaneous submissions. Responds in 3 weeks to queries; 3 months to mss. Book catalog free; ms guidelines free.
Nonfiction: How-to, self-help. Subjects include cooking/foods/nutrition, government/politics, health/medicine, New Age, philosophy, psychology, religion, spirituality. "We like to do around 3 titles a year in the general New Age, metaphysical and holistic health fields." No children's books or novels. Submit outline, sample chapter(s).
Recent Title(s): *Treason the New World Order*, Gurudas (political).

[N] **COMPASS AMERICAN GUIDES INC.**, 1745 Broadway, New York NY 10019. **Acquisitions:** Daniel Mangin, editorial director; Fabrizio LaRocca, creative director. Publishes trade paperback originals. **Publishes 1-2 titles/year. Receives 20 queries and 2 mss/year. 5% of books from first-time authors; 90% from unagented writers. Makes outright purchase of $5,000-10,000. Offers $3,000-5000 advance.** Publishes book an average of 1 year after acceptance of ms. Accepts simultaneous submissions. Responds in 6 months to queries.

O→ Compass American Guides publishes guides to U.S. and Canadian states, provinces or cities.

Nonfiction: Subjects include Travel Guides. Does not accept unsolicited ms. Query this publisher about its specific format. Reviews artwork/photos as part of ms package.
Tips: "Check our titles on website."

N DISKOTECH, INC., 7930 State Line, Suite 210, Prairie Village KS 66208. (913)432-8606. Fax: (913)432-8606*51. **Acquisitions:** Jane Locke, submissions editor. Estab. 1989. Publishes multimedia nonfiction and fiction for the Internet. **Publishes 2 titles/year. Pays 10-15% royalty on wholesale price.** Does not accept simultaneous submissions. Responds in 2 months to queries.

Nonfiction: Authors must supply the multimedia, such as video, music and animation, and the work in html format. Considers most nonfiction subjects. Query with SASE.

Fiction: Authors must supply the multimedia, such as video, music and animation, and the work in html format. Considers all fiction genres. Query with SASE.

Recent Title(s): *The Martensville Nightmare CVNRG*, Karen Smith (1st multimedia true crime story on CD-Rom); *Negative Space CVNRG*, Holly Franking (computerized video novel on CD-ROM); *Celebrity Ink CVNRG* (Hypermedia Internet Tabloid).

EARTH-LOVE PUBLISHING HOUSE LTD., 3440 Youngfield St., Suite 353, Wheat Ridge CO 80033. (303)233-9660. Fax: (303)233-9354. **Acquisitions:** Laodeciae Augustine, director. Publishes trade paperback originals. **Publishes 1-2 titles/year. Pays 6-10% royalty on wholesale price.** Does not accept simultaneous submissions. Responds in 1 month to queries; 1 month to proposals; 3 months to mss.

Nonfiction: Reference. Subjects include metaphysics and minerals. Query with SASE.

Recent Title(s): *Love Is in the Earth—Kaleidoscope Pictorial Supplementz*, by Melody (mineral reference); *Loves Is in the Earth—Crystal Tarot for the Millennium*, by Melody.

EASTERN PRESS, P.O. Box 881, Bloomington IN 47402-0881. **Acquisitions:** Don Y. Lee, publisher. Estab. 1981. Publishes hardcover originals and reprints. **Publishes 3 titles/year. Pays by arrangement with author.** Does not accept simultaneous submissions. Responds in 3 months to queries.

- "Eastern Press publishes higher academic works on Asian subjects, particularly East Asia." Currently emphasizing humanities and social sciences in East Asia.

Nonfiction: Subjects include education, ethnic, language/literature. Academic books on Asian subjects and pedagogy on languages. Query with SASE or submit outline.

Recent Title(s): *History of Early Relations Between China and Tibet*, by Don Lee.

ELYSIAN EDITIONS, Princeton Book Co., 614 Route 130, Hightstown NJ 08520. (609)426-0602. Fax: (609)426-1344. E-mail: elysian@aosi.com. Website: www.dancehorizons.com/elysian. **Acquisitions:** Deborah Blok (travel, memoir, true adventure). Publishes hardcover and trade paperback originals and reprints. **Publishes 1-3 titles/year. Receives 10 queries and 10 mss/year. 25% of books from first-time authors; 100% from unagented writers. Pays royalty on retail price. Offers negotiable advance.** Publishes book 9-12 months after acceptance of ms. Accepts simultaneous submissions. Responds in 3 weeks to queries; 3 weeks to proposals; 1 month to mss. Book catalog free or on website; ms guidelines free.

Nonfiction: Biography. Subjects include memoirs, travel, true adventure. Submit proposal package including outline, 3 sample chapter(s). Reviews artwork/photos as part of ms package. Send photocopies.

Recent Title(s): *Love in Provence: Romantic Adventures in the South of France*, by Yvone Lenard (travel).

Tips: "Submit stories not only with interesting situations but interesting people." Audience is armchair travelers, people planning trips to exotic locations.

ENDLESS KNOT PRODUCTIONS, P.O. Box 230312, Boston MA 02123. (617)445-4651. Fax: (208)979-5577. E-mail: editor@endless-knot.com. Website: www.endless-knot.com. **Acquisitions:** Alexander Dwinell. Publishes trade paperback originals and reprints. **Publishes 1-2 titles/year. Pays royalty. Offers advance.** Does not accept simultaneous submissions. Responds in 2 months to queries.

Fiction: New publisher of fiction. "We are looking to publish cutting-edge fiction with a subversive kick."

Tips: "We are particularly interested in well-written stories which contain strong characters and plotting with a radical political subtext. The politics should be anti-authoritarian and anti-capitalist without being polemical."

EQUILIBRIUM PRESS, INC., 10736 Jefferson Blvd. #680, Culver City CA 90230. (310)204-3290. Fax: (310)204-3550. E-mail: info@equipress.com. Website: www.equipress.com. Publishes trade paperback originals. **Publishes 1-2 titles/year. Pays 10-15% royalty on net receipts. Offers variable advance.** Responds in 2 months to queries.

- "We're looking for books that inform and inspire—all nonfiction related to women's health and wellness for an upscale, educated audience in a wide age range. No fiction, poetry, erotica."

Nonfiction: "Personal memoirs unlikely to be acquired unless they offer something more than 'my story.'" Query with SASE or submit proposal package, including chapter-by-chapter outline, 1-3 sample chapters (including the introduction) and a letter answering the following questions in detail: How is the book unique? (i.e. what are the competing books?); who is the audience?; how will you reach that audience?; what are your credentials to write this book?; who might endorse it? *No unsolicited mss.*

Recent Title(s): *A Special Delivery: Mother-Daughter Letters from Afar*, by Mitchell & Mitchell (family/pregnancy); *The Stepmom's Guide to Simplifying Your Life*, by Goodman (family/self-help).

Tips: "Do your homework—know what other books are similar and be able to say why yours is better and/or different. Know the audience and how you will reach them. Most importantly, what are *you* prepared to do to promote the book?"

N FATHOM PUBLISHING COMPANY, P.O. Box 200448, Anchorage AK 99520-0448. (907)272-3305. Fax: (907)272-3305. E-mail: fathompub@aol.com. **Acquisitions:** Constance Taylor, publisher. Publishes 0-1 trade paperback originals/year on Alaskana history, legal issues and reference. **Pays 10-15% royalty on retail price.** Does not accept simultaneous submissions. Responds in 2 months to queries.
Nonfiction: Reference. Subjects include history, regional. Wants legal issues or related texts. Submit outline, 1 sample chapter(s).
Fiction: Wants Alaska-related fiction. Query with SASE or submit outline, 1 sample chapter(s).
Recent Title(s): *Valley of the Eagles*, Cary Anderson (natural history); *Open Meeting Laws 2d*, by Ann Taylor Schwing (legal treatise).

FIESTA CITY PUBLISHERS ASCAP, P.O. Box 5861, Santa Barbara CA 93150-5861. (805)681-9199. E-mail: fcooke3924@aol.com. **Acquisitions:** Frank E. Cooke, president; Ann Cooke, secretary/treasurer (music); Johnny Harris, consultant (music). Publishes hardcover and mass market paperback originals. **Publishes 2-3 titles/year. Pays 5-20% royalty on retail price.** Responds in 1 month to queries; 2 months to proposals. Book catalog and ms guidelines for #10 SASE.
Nonfiction: Children's/juvenile, how-to, humor. Subjects include cooking/foods/nutrition, humor. "Seeking originality." Currently emphasizing musical plays for juvenile audience. De-emphasizing cookbooks. Query with SASE or submit outline.
Fiction: Plays (musical only). "Must be original, commercially viable, preferably short, with eye-catching titles. Must be professionally done and believable. Avoid too much detail." Query with SASE or submit 1-2 sample chapter(s).
Recent Title(s): *Kids Can Write Songs, Too*, by Frank Cooke.
Tips: "Looking for material which would appeal to young adolescents in the modern society. Prefer little or no violence with positive messages. Carefully-constructed musical plays always welcome for consideration."

FINNEY COMPANY, 3943 Meadowbrook Rd., Minneapolis MN 55426. (952)938-9330. Fax: (952)938-7353. E-mail: feedback@finney-hobar.com. Website: www.finney-hobar.com. **Acquisitions:** Alan E. Krysan, president. Publishes trade paperback originals. **Publishes 2 titles/year. Pays 10% royalty on wholesale price. Offers advance.** Publishes book 1 year after acceptance of ms. Responds in 3 weeks to queries.
Nonfiction: Reference, textbook. Subjects include business/economics, education, career exploration/development. Finney publishes career development educational materials. Query with SASE. Reviews artwork/photos as part of ms package.
Recent Title(s): *Planning My Career*, by Capozziello; *Managing Students for Success in the Workplace*, by Sargent.

FLYWHEEL PUBLISHING, P.O. Box 6330, Auburn CA 95604-6330. (530)269-2020. Fax: (530)269-1728. E-mail: admin@flywheelpublishing.com. Website: www.flywheelpublishing.com. **Acquisitions:** Ben Martin, vice president. **Publishes 2-3 titles/year. Receives 100 queries/year. 75% of books from first-time authors; 95% from unagented writers. Pays 10-15% royalty on wholesale price.** Publishes book 8 months after acceptance of ms. Accepts simultaneous submissions. Responds in 1 month to queries; 1 month to proposals; 2 months to mss.
Fiction: Juvenile, literary, mainstream/contemporary, young adult. Query with SASE or submit proposal package including 3 sample chapter(s), synopsis.
Recent Title(s): *Through the Wormhole*, by Robert J. Favole (young adult fiction).

FOOTPRINT PRESS, P.O. Box 645, Fishers NY 14453-0645. (585)421-9383. Fax: (585)421-9383. E-mail: info@footprintpress.com. Website: www.footprintpress.com. **Acquisitions:** Sue Freeman, publisher (NY state recreation). Publishes trade paperback originals. **Publishes 1 title/year. Pays 10% royalty on wholesale price.** Accepts simultaneous submissions. Responds in 1 month to queries; 1 month to proposals; 2 months to mss. Book catalog and ms guidelines for #10 SASE or online.

O→ Footprint Press publishes books pertaining to outdoor recreation in New York state.

Nonfiction: How-to. Subjects include recreation, regional, sports. Query with SASE.
Recent Title(s): *Peak Experiences: Hiking the Highest Summits in New York State, County by County*, by Gary Fallesen; *Birding in Central and Western New York*, by Norman E. Wolfe; *200 Waterfalls in Central and Western New York*, by Rich and Sue Freeman.

FRONT ROW EXPERIENCE, 540 Discovery Bay Blvd., Discovery Bay CA 94514-9454. (925)634-5710. Fax: (925)634-5710. E-mail: service@frontrowexperience.com. Website: www.frontrowexperience.com. **Acquisitions:** Frank Alexander, editor. Estab. 1974. Publishes trade paperback originals and reprints. **Publishes 1-2 titles/year. Pays 10% royalty on net receipts.** Does not accept simultaneous submissions. Responds in 1 month to queries.
Imprints: Kokono

O→ Front Row publishes books on movement education and coordination activities for pre-K to 6th grade.

Nonfiction: Subjects include child guidance/parenting, education. Query.
Recent Title(s): *Perceptual-Motor Lesson Plans, Level 2.*
Tips: "Be on target—find out what we want and only submit queries."

GAMBLING TIMES, INC., 3883 W. Century Blvd., Inglewood CA 90303. (310)674-3365. Fax: (310)674-3205. E-mail: srs@gamblingtimes.com. Website: www.gamblingtimes.com. **Acquisitions:** Stanley R. Sludikoff, publisher. Publishes hardcover and trade paperback originals. **Publishes 2-4 titles/year. Pays 4-11% royalty on retail price.** Does not accept simultaneous submissions. Responds in 4 months to queries; 5 months to proposals; 6 months to mss.

Nonfiction: How-to, reference (on gambling). No longer accepts mss from first-time writers. Query with SASE or submit proposal package or submit complete ms.
Recent Title(s): *Book of Tells*, by Caro (poker).
Tips: "All of our books serve to educate the public about some aspect of gambling."

GOLDEN WEST BOOKS, P.O. Box 80250, San Marino CA 91118-8250. (626)458-8148. Fax: (626)458-8148. E-mail: trainbook@earthlink.net. Website: www.goldenwestbooks.com. **Acquisitions:** Donald Duke, publisher. Publishes hardcover originals. **Publishes 3-4 titles/year. Receives 8-10 queries and 5 mss/year. 75% of books from first-time authors; 100% from unagented writers. Pays 8-10% royalty on wholesale price. Offers no advance.** Publishes book 3 months after acceptance of ms. Does not accept simultaneous submissions. Responds in 3 months to queries. Book catalog free; ms guidelines free.

O→ Golden West Books specializes in railroad history.

Nonfiction: Illustrated book (railroad history). Subjects include Americana, history. Query with SASE. Reviews artwork/photos as part of ms package.
Recent Title(s): *The Ulster & Delaware Railroad Through the Catskills*, by Gerald M. Best; *The Streamline Era*, by Robert C. Reed; *Electric Railways Around San Francisco Bay*, by Donald Duke.

GOOD BOOK PUBLISHING COMPANY, P.O. Box 837, Kihei HI 96753-0837. (808)874-4876. Fax: (808)874-4876. E-mail: dickb@dickb.com. Website: www.dickb.com/index.shtml. **Acquisitions:** Richard G. Burns, publisher. Publishes trade paperback originals. **Publishes 1 title/year. Receives 5 queries and 5 mss/year. 100% of books from first-time authors; 100% from unagented writers. Pays 10% royalty.** Publishes book 3 months after acceptance of ms. Accepts simultaneous submissions. Responds in 1 month to queries; 1 month to mss. Book catalog free.
Nonfiction: Biography, self-help. Subjects include health/medicine, history, psychology, religion. Spiritual roots of Alcoholics Anonymous. Query with SASE.
Recent Title(s): *By the Power of God: A Guide to Early A.A. Groups and Forming Similar Groups Today*, by Dick Bo.

HEMINGWAY WESTERN STUDIES SERIES, Boise State University, 1910 University Dr., Boise ID 83725. (208)426-1999. Fax: (208)426-4373. E-mail: ttrusky@boisestate.edu. Website: www.boisestate.edu/hemingway. **Acquisitions:** Tom Trusky, editor. Publishes multiple edition artists' books which deal with Rocky Mountain political, social and environmental issues. **Offers advance.** Does not accept simultaneous submissions. Ms guidelines free.

[N] **HERBAL STUDIES LIBRARY**, 219 Carl St., San Francisco CA 94117. (415)564-6785. Fax: (415)564-6799. **Acquisitions:** J. Rose, owner. Publishes trade paperback originals. **Publishes 3 titles/year. Pays 5-10% royalty on retail price. Offers $500 advance.** Does not accept simultaneous submissions. Responds in 1 month to mss.
Nonfiction: How-to, reference, self-help. Subjects include gardening, health/medicine. No New Age. Query with SASE or submit sample chapter(s).
Recent Title(s): *The Aromatherapy Book: Applications and Inhalations*, Jeanne Rose; *375 Essential Oils and Hydrosols*, by Jeanne Rose.

ILLUMINATION ARTS, P.O. Box 1865, Bellevue WA 98009. (425)644-7185. Fax: (425)644-9274. E-mail: liteinfo@illumin.com. Website: www.illumin.com. **Acquisitions:** Ruth Thompson, editorial director, (children's books); Terri Cohlene, creative director (artwork). Publishes hardcover originals. **Publishes 2-5 titles/year. Pays royalty on wholesale price. Offers advance for artists.** Book catalog and ms guidelines free or online.

O→ Illumination Arts publishes inspirational/spiritual, children's nonfiction and fiction. Currently emphasizing adventure, humorous stories with inspirational and spiritual values. De-emphasizing Bible-based stories.

Nonfiction: Children's/juvenile. "Our books are all high quality. Send for our guidelines. Stories need to be exciting and inspirational for children." Submit complete ms with SASE. Reviews artwork/photos as part of ms package. Send photocopies.
Fiction: Juvenile, picture books, only up to 1,500 words. "All are inspirational/spiritual. Be sure story is geared toward children and has an inspirational message." No electronic submissions.
Recent Title(s): *Cassandra's Angel*; *The Whoosh of Gadoosh*; *The Tree.*
Tips: "A smart writer researches publishing companies first and then follows their submission guidelines."

INDIANA HISTORICAL SOCIETY, 450 W. Ohio St., Indianapolis IN 46202-3269. (317)232-6546. Fax: (317)233-0857. **Acquisitions:** Thomas A. Mason, vice president of publications. Estab. 1830. Publishes hardcover originals. **Publishes 3 titles/year. Pays 6% royalty on net revenue received.** Responds in 1 month to queries.
Nonfiction: Biography. Subjects include agriculture/horticulture, art/architecture, business/economics, ethnic, government/politics, history, military/war, sports. All topics must relate to Indiana. "We seek book-length manuscripts that are solidly researched and engagingly written on topics related to Indiana: biography, history, literature, music, politics, transportation, sports, agriculture, architecture." Query with SASE.
Recent Title(s): *Destination Indiana: Travels Through Hoosier History*, by Ray E. Boomhower, photographs by Darryl Jones.

IVY LEAGUE PRESS, INC., P.O. Box 3326, San Ramon CA 94583-8326. (800)IVY-PRESS. Fax: (888)IVY-PRESS. E-mail: ivyleaguepress@worldnet.att.net. **Acquisitions:** Maria Thomas, editor. Publishes hardcover, trade paperback and mass market paperback originals. **Offers advance.** Does not accept simultaneous submissions. Responds in 3 months to queries.

Nonfiction: Self-help. Subjects include ethnic, health/medicine. *No unsolicited mss.*
Fiction: Medical suspense. Query with SASE.
Recent Title(s): *Jewish Divorce Ethics*, by Bulka (nonfiction); *Allergy Shots*, by Litman (fiction).

N **JELMAR PUBLISHING CO., INC.**, P.O. Box 488, Plainview NY 11803. (516)822-6861. **Acquisitions:** Joel J. Shulman, president. Publishes hardcover and trade paperback originals. **Publishes 2-5 titles/year. Pays 25% royalty.** Does not accept simultaneous submissions. Responds in 1 week to queries.
Nonfiction: How-to, technical. Package printing and printing fields. "The writer must be a specialist and recognized expert in the field." Query with SASE.
Recent Title(s): *Graphic Design for Corrugated Packaging*, Donald G. McCaughey, Jr. (graphic design).

JOHNSTON ASSOCIATES, INTERNATIONAL (JASI), P.O. Box 313, Medina WA 98039. (425)454-3490. Fax: (425)462-1355. E-mail: jasibooks@aol.com. **Acquisitions:** Priscilla Johnston, publisher. Publishes trade paperback originals. **Publishes 3-5 titles/year. Pays 12-17½% royalty on wholesale price. Offers $500-1,500 advance.** Does not accept simultaneous submissions. Responds in 4 months to queries. Book catalog and ms guidelines for #10 SASE.
Nonfiction: Subjects include gardening, general nonfiction, recreation, regional (on any region), travel. "We are interested in books that hit unique travel niches or look at topics in new, unique ways." Query with SASE or submit proposal package including outline, sample chapter(s).
Recent Title(s): *Discover the Southwest with Kids*, by Mary Vadsudeva; *Las Vegas on the Dime*, by Michael Toole.

KALI PRESS, P.O. Box 1031, Port Townsend WA 98368. (360)385-1933. E-mail: info@kalipress.com. **Acquisitions:** Cynthia Olsen. Publishes trade paperback originals. **Publishes 3 titles/year. Pays 8-10% royalty on net receipts.** Does not accept simultaneous submissions. Responds in 1 month to queries; 6 weeks to proposals; 2 months to mss.

O→ "We specialize in complementary health which encompasses body, mind and spiritual topics." Currently emphasizing new alternative healing modalities.

Nonfiction: Subjects include health/medicine, nature/environment, spirituality. Query with SASE or submit 2 sample chapter(s). Reviews artwork/photos as part of ms package. Send photocopies.
Recent Title(s): *Australian Blue Cypress Oil: The Birth of the Blue*, by Cynthia Olsen.

LAUREATE PRESS, 2710 Ohio St., Bangor ME 04401. **Acquisitions:** Robyn Beck, editor. Publishes trade paperback originals. **Publishes 3 titles/year.** Does not accept simultaneous submissions.
Nonfiction: Fencing subjects only. How-to, technical. Query with SASE.
Recent Title(s): *The Science of Fencing*, by William Gaugler (fencing-technical); *On Fencing*, by Aldo Nadi.
Tips: Audience is recreational and competitive fencers worldwide, not martial arts or reenactment.

LIBRARY OF VIRGINIA, 800 E. Broad St., Richmond VA 23219-8000. (804)692-3999. Fax: (804)692-3736. E-mail: jkneebone@lva.lib.va.us. Website: www.lva.lib.va.us. **Acquisitions:** Gregg D. Kimball, assistant director (Virginia history and culture). Publishes hardcover originals and reprints. **Publishes 3-4 titles/year. Pays royalty on retail price or makes outright purchase.** Does not accept simultaneous submissions. Responds in 1 month to queries; 1 month to proposals; 3 months to mss. Book catalog online.
Nonfiction: The Library of Virginia publishes works that draw from the Library's collections. Biography, coffee table book, illustrated book. Subjects include history, regional. Submit proposal package including outline, 1 sample chapter(s).
Recent Title(s): *Regarding Ellen Glasgow*, by Taylor & Longest, eds. (literary essays); *Virginia in Maps*, by Stephenson & McKee, eds. (coffee table book).

LIGHTHOUSE POINT PRESS, 100 First Ave., Suite 525, Pittsburgh PA 15222-1517. (412)323-9320. Fax: (412)323-9334. E-mail: info@yearick-millea.com. **Acquisitions:** Ralph W. Yearick, publisher (business/career/general nonfiction). Publishes hardcover and trade paperback originals and trade paperback reprints. **Publishes 1-2 titles/year. Pays 5-10% royalty on retail price.** Does not accept simultaneous submissions. Responds in 6 months to queries.

O→ Lighthouse Point Press specializes in business/career nonfiction titles.

Nonfiction: Reference. Subjects include business/economics. "We are open to all types of submissions related to general nonfiction, but most interested in business/career manuscripts." Submit proposal package including outline, 1-2 sample chapter(s) or submit complete ms.
Recent Title(s): *Meetings: Do's, Don'ts and Donuts*, by Sharon M. Lippincott (reference/business).
Tips: "When submitting a manuscript or proposal, please tell us what you see as the target market/audience for the book. Also, be very specific about what you are willing to do to promote the book."

LINTEL, 24 Blake Lane, Middletown NY 10940. (845)344-1690. **Acquisitions:** Joan Dornhoefer, editorial assistant. Estab. 1978. Publishes hardcover originals and reprints and trade paperback originals. **Pays royalty. Authors get 100 copies originally, plus royalties after expenses cleared. Offers advance.** Responds in 2 months to queries; 4 months to proposals; 6 months to mss.

- Not currently accepting unsolicited mss.

Nonfiction: "So far all our nonfiction titles have been textbooks." Query with SASE.
Fiction: Experimental. Query with SASE.
Poetry: Submit 5 sample poems.
Recent Title(s): *Writing a Television Play, Second Edition*, Michelle Cousin (textbook); *June*, Mary Sanders Smith (fiction); *Love's Mainland*, by Walter James Miller.

N MENUS AND MUSIC, 1462 66th St., Emeryville CA 94608. (510)658-9100. Fax: (510)658-1605. E-mail: info@menusandmusic.com. Website: www.menusandmusic.com. **Acquisitions:** Sharon O'Connor, president (music, food, travel). Publishes trade paperback originals and reprints. **Publishes 2 titles/year. Receives 5 queries/year. Pays 7-10% royalty.** Accepts simultaneous submissions. Responds in 1 month to queries; 1 month to proposals; 3 months to mss. Book catalog free; ms guidelines free.

Nonfiction: Coffee table book, cookbook, gift book. Subjects include Americana, art/architecture, cooking/foods/nutrition, gardening, hobbies, music/dance, photography, recreation, travel. Submit proposal package including outline, 1 sample chapter(s). Reviews artwork/photos as part of ms package. Send photocopies.

Fiction: Humor (women), multimedia, poetry, poetry in translation. "We are especially interested in proposals that will appeal to women, gift buyers, or books that can be paired with music." Submit proposal package including 1 sample chapter(s), synopsis.

Poetry: Submit 3 sample poems.

Recent Title(s): *Bistro*, Sharon O'Connor.

Tips: "Our books are primarily bought by women who are interested in cooking, music and travel. We have excellent distribution in the gift industry and good distribution in the book trade. We are interested in high-quality work—we have completed books with New York's Metropolitan Opera and the San Francisco Ballet. Our books are beautiful and sell well for years."

MIDDLE ATLANTIC PRESS, 10 Twosome Dr., Box 600, Moorestown NJ 08057. (856)235-4444, ext. 314. Fax: (856)727-6914. E-mail: kdb@koen.com. Website: www.koen.com/midat/index.html. **Acquisitions:** Terence Doherty, associate publisher/acquisitions editor; Robert Koen, publisher. Publishes trade paperback originals and reprints, mass market paperback originals. **Publishes 2-3 titles/year. Pays 6-10% royalty on wholesale price. Offers $500-5,000 advance.** Responds in 3 weeks to queries. Book catalog for 9×6 SAE with 2 first-class stamps or online.

O→ Middle Atlantic Press is a regional publisher of nonfiction focusing on New York, New Jersey, Pennsylvania, Delaware and Maryland. Currently emphasizing books of information (i.e., guides, travel). De-emphasizing juvenile titles.

Nonfiction: Biography, cookbook, reference. Subjects include Americana, cooking/foods/nutrition, history, memoirs, recreation, regional, sports, travel. "M.A.P. is a regional publisher specializing in nonfiction on varied subject matter. Most everything we publish, however, to a large degree, deals with some aspect of the states to the mid-Atlantic region (NY, NJ, PA, DE and MD)." Query with general description and SASE.

Recent Title(s):*Animal Patients: 50 Years in the Life of an Animal Doctor*, by Ed Scanlon V.M.D.

N MISSOURI HISTORICAL SOCIETY PRESS, The Missouri Historical Society, P.O. Box 11940, St. Louis MO 63112-0040. (314)746-4569. Fax: (314)746-4548. E-mail: ks@mohistory.org. Website: www.mohistory.org. **Acquisitions:** Lee Sandweiss, director of publications (nonfiction with regional themes). Publishes hardcover originals and reprints and trade paperback originals and reprints. **Publishes 2-3 titles/year. Receives 40 queries and 20 mss/year. 10% of books from first-time authors; 75% from unagented writers. Pays 5-10% royalty. Offers advance.** Responds in 1 month to queries; 1 month to proposals; 2 months to mss.

Nonfiction: Biography, coffee table book, reference, textbook. Subjects include anthropology/archeology, art/architecture, history, language/literature, multicultural, regional, sports, women's issues/studies. Query with SASE.

Recent Title(s): *In Her Place: A Guide to St. Louis Women's History*, Katharine Corbett (women's history); *A Century of St. Louis Sports*, Bob Broels (sports).

Tips: "Our readers are scholars, academics and readers of regional history and related topics."

MOUNT IDA PRESS, 152 Washington Ave., Albany NY 12210. (518)426-5935. Fax: (518)426-4116. **Acquisitions:** Diana S. Waite, publisher. Publishes trade paperback original illustrated books. Does not accept simultaneous submissions.

O→ Mount Ida Press specializes in high-quality publications on regional history, architecture, and building technology.

Recent Title(s): *Albany Law School, 1851-2001: A Tradition of Change*, by Elizabeth K. Allen and Diana S. Waite.

NEW ENGLAND CARTOGRAPHICS, INC., P.O. Box 9369, North Amherst MA 01059. (413)549-4124. Fax: (413)549-3621. E-mail: geolopes@crocker.com. Website: www.necartographics.com. **Acquisitions:** Valerie Vaughan, editor; Christopher Ryan, president. Publishes trade paperback originals and reprints. **Publishes 3 titles/year. Pays 5-10% royalty on retail price.** Does not accept simultaneous submissions. Responds in 2 months to queries.

Nonfiction: Subjects include nature/environment, recreation, regional, sports. "We are interested in specific 'where to' in the area of outdoor recreation guidebooks of the northeast U.S." Topics of interest are hiking/backpacking, skiing, canoeing, rail-trails, etc. Query with SASE or submit sample chapter(s). Reviews artwork/photos as part of ms package. Send photocopies.

Recent Title(s): *Hiking Green Mountain National Forest*, by Bruce Scofield.

NEWSAGE PRESS, P.O. Box 607, Troutdale OR 97060-0607. (503)695-2211. Fax: (503)695-5406. E-mail: newsage@cascadeaccess.com. Website: www.newsagepress.com. **Acquisitions:** Maureen R. Michelson, publisher; Erica Stork, marketing communications. Estab. 1985. Publishes hardcover and trade paperback originals.

O→ "NewSage Press books address a myriad of social concerns, from environmental issues to women's issues to health issues. We focus on nonfiction books. No 'how to' books. No cynical, despairing books." Currently emphasizing books that explore the animal/human bond and are written intelligently. Photo-essay books in large format are no longer published by Newsage Press.

Nonfiction: Subjects include animals, multicultural, nature/environment, women's issues/studies.

Recent Title(s): *Singing to the Sound: Visions of Nature, Animals & Spirit*, by Brenda Peterson; *Death Without Denial, Grief Without Apology*, by Barbara K. Roberts.

NEXT DECADE, INC., 39 Old Farmstead Rd., Chester NJ 07930. (908)879-6625. Fax: (908)879-2920. E-mail: barbara@nextdecade.com. Website: www.nextdecade.com. **Acquisitions:** Barbara Kimmel, president (reference); Carol Rose, editor. Publishes trade paperback originals. **Publishes 2-4 titles/year. Pays 8-15% royalty on wholesale price.** Responds in 1 month to queries. Book catalog online.

Nonfiction: Reference. Subjects include health/medicine (women's), money/finance, multicultural, senior/retirement issues. Currently emphasizing women's health; seniors/retirement. "Due to mail security, we would prefer e-mail inquiries limited to 1-page description of the book and author background." Do not send attachments.

Recent Title(s): *Retire in Style*, by Warren Bland, Ph.D.

Tips: "We publish books that simplify complex subjects. We are a small, award-winning press that successfully publishes a handful of books each year. Do not submit if you are looking for a large advance."

OBERLIN COLLEGE PRESS, 10 N. Professor St., Oberlin College, Oberlin OH 44074. (440)775-8408. Fax: (440)775-8124. E-mail: oc.press@oberlin.edu. Website: www.oberlin.edu/~ocpress. Managing Editor: Linda Slocum. **Acquisitions:** David Young, Pamela Alexander, Martha Collins, Alberta Turner, and David Walker, editors. Publishes hardcover and trade paperback originals. **Publishes 2-3 titles/year. Pays 7½-10% royalty.** Does not accept simultaneous submissions. Responds promptly to queries; 1 month to proposals; 2 months to mss.

Imprints: *FIELD: Contemporary Poetry & Poetics*, a twice annual magazine, FIELD Translation Series, FIELD Poetry Series, FIELD Editions.

Poetry: FIELD Magazine—submit up to 5 poems with SASE for response; FIELD Translation Series—query with SASE and sample poems; FIELD Poetry Series—no unsolicited mss, enter mss in FIELD Poetry Prize held annually in May. Send SASE for guidelines after February 1.

Recent Title(s): *Here There Was Once a Country*, by Venus Khoury-Ghata, translated by Marilyn Hacker; *The Pleasure Principle*, by Jon Loomis; *Voice-Over*, by Angie Estes.

N **OCEAN VIEW BOOKS**, P.O. Box 9249, Denver CO 80209. **Acquisitions:** Lee Ballentine, editor. Publishes hardcover originals and trade paperback originals. **Publishes 2 titles/year. 100% from unagented writers. Pays royalty. Offers advance.** Does not accept simultaneous submissions. Responds to queries in 2 months, if interested.

Fiction: Literary, science fiction. "Ocean View Books is an award-winning publisher of new speculative and slipstream fiction, poetry, criticism, surrealism."

Recent Title(s): *Missing Pieces*, by Kathryn Ramtan.

OMEGA PUBLICATIONS, 256 Darrow Rd., New Lebanon NY 12125-2615. (518)794-8181. Fax: (518)794-8187. E-mail: omegapub@wisdomschild.com. Website: www.omegapub.com. **Acquisitions:** Abi'l-Khayr. Estab. 1977. Publishes hardcover and trade paperback originals and reprints. **Publishes 2-3 titles/year. Pays 12-15% royalty on wholesale price. Offers $500-1,000 advance.** Does not accept simultaneous submissions. Responds in 3 months to mss.

Nonfiction: Subjects include philosophy, religion, spirituality. "We are interested in any material related to Sufism, and only that." Query with SASE or submit 2 sample chapter(s).

Recent Title(s): *Pearl in Wine*, by Zia Inuyat Khan; *The Drunken Universe*, by P.L. Wilson.

OUGHTEN HOUSE FOUNDATION, INC., P.O. Box 1826, Coarsegold CA 93614. (937)767-9368. Fax: (937)767-1210. E-mail: info@oughtenhouse.com. Website: www.oughtenhouse.com. **Acquisitions:** Dr. Robert J. Gerard, senior acquisitions editor (alternative health and self-help). Publishes trade paperback originals. **Publishes 2 titles/year.** Does not accept simultaneous submissions. Responds in 3 months to queries. Ms guidelines online.

Nonfiction: Self-help. Subjects include child guidance/parenting, education, philosophy, psychology, sex, women's issues/studies. "We focus on self-empowerment, self-help, spiritual psychology and philosophy, alternative healthcare, and techniques for communication." Currently emphasizing self-empowerment and techniques for communication. De-emphasizing alternative healthcare. "Currently we are extremely selective due to cutbacks. Please check our website." Query with SASE. *All unsolicited mss returned unopened.*

Fiction: Humor, spiritual. Query with SASE.

Recent Title(s): *Handling Verbal Confrontation*; *Change Your DNA—Change Your Life*, both by Dr. Robert Gerard.

Tips: "We are oriented toward spirituality and alternative medicine/health. It must be unique and substantial."

OZARK MOUNTAIN PUBLISHING, INC., P.O. Box 754, Huntsville AR 72740. (479)738-2348. Fax: (479)738-2348. Website: www.ozarkmt.com. **Acquisitions:** Nancy Garrison. Publishes hardcover and trade paperback originals and mass market paperback reprints. **Publishes 3-4 titles/year. Pays 10% royalty on retail price. Offers $500 advance.** Accepts simultaneous submissions. Responds in 6 months to queries. Book catalog free or online.

Nonfiction: Subjects include New Age, spirituality (New Age/metaphysical). "No phone calls please." Query with SASE or submit proposal package including outline, 2 sample chapter(s).

Recent Title(s): *The Convoluted Universe*, by Dolores Cannon; *The Forgotten Woman*, by Arun and Sunanda Gandhi.

PACESETTER PUBLICATIONS, P.O. Box 101975, Denver CO 80250-1975. (303)722-7200. Fax: (303)733-2626. E-mail: jsabah@aol.com. Website: www.joesabah.com. **Acquisitions:** Joe Sabah, editor (how-to). Publishes trade paperback originals and reprints. **Publishes 3 titles/year. Pays 10-15% royalty. Offers $500-2,000 advance.** Does not accept simultaneous submissions. Responds in 1 month to queries.
Nonfiction: How-to, self-help. Subjects include money/finance. Query with SASE or submit proposal package including outline, 2 sample chapter(s).
Recent Title(s): *How to Get the Job You Really Want and Get Employers to Call You.*

PACIFIC VIEW PRESS, P.O. Box 2657, Berkeley CA 94702. (510)849-4213. **Acquisitions:** Pam Zumwalt, acquisitions editor. Estab. 1992. Publishes hardcover and trade paperback originals. **Publishes 3 titles/year. Pays 5-10% royalty on wholesale price. Offers $500-2,000 advance.** Responds in 2 months to queries. Book catalog free; ms guidelines for #10 SASE.
Nonfiction: Pacific View Press publishes books for persons professionally/personally aware of the growing importance of the Pacific Rim and/or the modern culture of these countries, especially China. Children's/juvenile (Asia/multicultural only), reference, textbook (Chinese medicine only). Subjects include business/economics (Asia and Pacific Rim only), health/medicine (Chinese medicine), history (Asia), multicultural, regional (Pacific Rim), travel (related to Pacific Rim), contemporary Pacific Rim affairs. "We are only interested in Pacific Rim-related issues. Do not send proposals outside of our area of interest." Query with SASE. *No unsolicited mss.*
Recent Title(s): *The Great Taiwan Bubble: The Rise and Fall of an Emerging Stock Market*, by Steven R. Champion; *A Thousand Peaks: Poems from China*, by Siyu Liu and Orel Protopopescu.
Tips: "We are currently only interested in Asia-related nonfiction for children 8-13."

THE PHOENIX GROUP, P.O. Box 20536, San Jose CA 95160. (877)594-9076. Fax: (877)594-9076. E-mail: info@tpgpub.com. Website: www.tpgpub.com. **Acquisitions:** June Rouse, editor (holistic, self-help, spiritual), Vita Goins, assistant editor (mystery, suspense, thrillers). Publishes trade paperback, mass market paperback and electronic originals. **Publishes 1-3 titles/year. Pays 8-25% royalty on retail price.** Does not accept simultaneous submissions. Responds in 6 weeks to queries; 6 weeks to proposals; 6 weeks to mss. Book catalog and ms guidlines free or online.
Nonfiction: Self-help. Subjects include business/economics, creative nonfiction, health/medicine, philosophy, sex, spirituality. Submit proposal package including outline, 3 sample chapter(s).
Fiction: Adventure, experimental, mystery, science fiction, spiritual, suspense. Submit proposal package including 3 sample chapter(s), synopsis.

PICKWICK PUBLICATION, 215 Incline Way, San Jose CA 95139. (408)224-6777. E-mail: dyh1@aol.com. Website: www.PickwickPublications.com. **Acquisitions:** Dikran Y. Hadidian, general editor (theology, Biblical studies, church history). Publishes trade paperback originals and reprints. **Publishes 3-4 titles/year. Pays 10% royalty.** Publishes book 1 year after acceptance of ms. Accepts simultaneous submissions. Responds in 2 months to queries; 4 months to proposals; 6 months to mss. Book catalog online; ms guidelines for #10 SASE.
Nonfiction: Textbook. Subjects include philosophy, religion. Query with SASE or submit outline, 2 sample chapter(s) or submit complete ms.

PONCHA PRESS, P.O. Box 280, Morrison CO 80465. (303)697-2384. Fax: (303)697-2385. E-mail: info@ponchapress.com. Website: www.ponchapress.com. **Acquisitions:** Barbara Osgood-Hartness, editor-in-chief. Publishes hardcover and trade paperback originals. **Publishes 2-3 titles/year. Receives 200 queries/year. 100% of books from first-time authors; 100% from unagented writers. Pays royalty on retail price.** Publishes book 9 months after acceptance of ms. Accepts simultaneous submissions. Responds in 1 month to queries; 3 months to mss. Book catalog and ms guidelines on website; ms guidelines online.
Nonfiction: Subjects include business/economics, cooking/foods/nutrition, regional, religion, sociology, travel, women's issues/studies. Query with SASE. **All unsolicited mss returned unopened.** Reviews artwork/photos as part of ms package. Send photocopies.
Fiction: Literary, mainstream/contemporary. Writers should consult website for submission guidelines and complete fully. Query with SASE.
Recent Title(s): *The Gold of El Negro*, by Michael C. Haley (fiction); *Gemini*, by Michael Burns (fiction).
Tips: "Only finished and polished manuscripts. No first drafts or proposals for unwritten work."

PRAKKEN PUBLICATIONS, INC., P.O. Box 8623, Ann Arbor MI 48107-8623. (313)975-2800. Fax: (313)975-2787. Publisher, George Kennedy. **Acquisitions:** Susanne Peckham, book editor. Estab. 1934. Publishes educational hardcover and paperback originals as well as educational magazines. **Publishes 3 titles/year. Pays 10% royalty on net receipts. Offers advance.** Does not accept simultaneous submissions. Responds in 2 months to queries. Book catalog for #10 SASE.

O→ "We publish books for educators in career/vocational and technology education, as well as books for the machine trades and machinists' education. Currently emphasizing machine trades.

Nonfiction: Biography (of inventors, technologists, scientists), reference. Subjects include education. "We are currently interested in manuscripts with broad appeal in any of the specific subject areas of machine trades, technology education, career-technical education, and reference for the general education field." Submit outline, sample chapter(s).
Recent Title(s): *Technology's Past, Vol.2*, by Dennis Karwatka; *Machinists' Ready Reference, 9th Ed*, by C. Weingartner.

Tips: "We have a continuing interest in magazine and book manuscripts which reflect emerging issues and trends in education, especially career-technical, industrial and technology education."

PUCKERBRUSH PRESS, 76 Main St., Orono ME 04473-1430. (207)581-3832. **Acquisitions:** Constance Hunting, publisher/editor. Estab. 1971. Publishes trade paperback originals and reprints of literary fiction and poetry. **Publishes 3-4 titles/year. Pays 10-15% royalty on wholesale price. Offers advance.** Does not accept simultaneous submissions. Responds in 1 month to queries; 2 months to proposals; 3 months to mss.
Nonfiction: Subjects include language/literature, translation, belles lettres. Query with SASE.
Fiction: Literary, short story collections.
Poetry: Highest literary quality. Submit complete ms.
Recent Title(s): *Settling*, by Patricia Ranzoni (poetry).
Tips: "No religious subjects, crime per se, tired prose. For sophisticated readers who retain love of literature. Maine writers continue to be featured." Currently emphasizing translations. De-emphasizing Maine back-to-the-land.

QED PRESS, 155 Cypress St., Fort Bragg CA 95437. (707)964-9520. Fax: (707)964-7531. E-mail: qed@mcn.org. Website: www.cypresshouse.com. President: Cynthia Frank. **Acquisitions:** Joe Shaw. Publishes hardcover and trade paperback originals and hardcover reprints. **Publishes 3 titles/year. Pays 12-15% royalty on net receipts. Offers advance.** Does not accept simultaneous submissions. Responds in 3 months to queries. Book catalog and ms guidelines free or online.
Nonfiction: Subjects include health/medicine. Publishes books about paper airplanes. Submit complete ms.
Recent Title(s): *Understanding Disease*, G.A. Langes; *Exotic Paper Airplanes*, Thay Yang.
Tips: "We're looking for well-written, user friendly manuscripts, usually under 350 pages. Target market general public with specific health issues (for example, Parkinson Disease/Diabetes/Asthma)."

RED EYE PRESS, INC., P.O. Box 65751, Los Angeles CA 90065. **Acquisitions:** James Goodwin, president. Publishes trade paperback originals. **Publishes 2 titles/year. Pays 8-12% royalty on retail price. Offers $1-2,000 advance.** Does not accept simultaneous submissions. Responds in 1 month to queries; 3 months to mss.
Nonfiction: How-to, reference. Subjects include gardening. Query with SASE or submit outline, 2 sample chapter(s).
Recent Title(s): *Great Labor Quotations—Sourcebook and Reader*, Peter Bollen.
Tips: "We publish how-to and reference works that are the standard for their genre, authoritative, and able to remain in print for many years."

RISING STAR PRESS, P.O. Box 66378, Scotts Valley CA 95066. (831)461-0604. Fax: (831)461-0445. E-mail: editor@risingstarpress.com. Website: www.risingstarpress.com. **Acquisitions:** Acquisitions Editor. Publishes hardcover originals and reprints, trade paperback originals and reprints. **Publishes 3-6 titles/year. Pays 10-15% royalty on wholesale price. Offers $1,000-8,000 advance.** Publishes book 9 months after acceptance of ms. Accepts simultaneous submissions. Responds in 2 months to proposals.
Nonfiction: Biography, reference, self-help. Subjects include education, health/medicine, language/literature, philosophy, regional, religion, sex, sociology. "Rising Star Press publishes books that cause people to think and be inspired to act in some positive and proactive way to improve their own life as well as the lives of those around them. Authors are treated as partners in the production and marketing process. Books are selected based on the combination of fit with the company mission, consistency between the author's words and life, and marketability." Currently emphasizing social and religious issues. De-emphasizing metaphysical, personal finance. "Authors need to be able to answer these questions: Who will benefit from reading this? Why? Mistakes writers often make are not identifying their target market early and shaping the work to address it." Query with SASE or submit outline, 2 sample chapter(s). Must include e-mail address with query/proposal.
Fiction: "Must illuminate topics, as listed for nonfiction submissions, for the reader is more drawn to fiction writing."
Recent Title(s): *Open Christianity—Home by Another Road*, by Jim Burklo; *And the Flames Did Not Consume Us*, by Gary Mazo.

[N] **RUSSIAN INFORMATION SERVICES**, P.O. Box 567, Montpelier VT 05601-0567. (802)223-4955. Website: solar.ini.utk.edu/rispubs/. **Acquisitions:** Stephanie Ratmeyer, vice president. Publishes trade paperback originals and reprints. **Publishes 2-3 titles/year. Receives 20-30 queries and 10 mss/year. 50% of books from first-time authors; 100% from unagented writers. Pays 8-12% royalty on retail price. Offers advance.** Publishes book 8 months after acceptance of ms. Accepts simultaneous submissions. Responds in 2 months to mss.

"Audience is business people and independent travelers to Russia and the former Soviet Union."

Nonfiction: Reference. Subjects include business/economics, language/literature, travel. "Our editorial focus is on Russia and the former Soviet Union." Submit proposal package including outline or submit complete ms. Reviews artwork/photos as part of ms package. Send photocopies.
Recent Title(s): *Survival Russian*, by Ivanov (language); *Taste of Russia* (cookbook).
Tips: RIS also publishes *Russian Life*, a monthly magazine on Russian history, travel, culture and life.

THE SIDRAN PRESS, 200 E. Joppa Rd., Suite 207, Baltimore MD 21286-3107. (410)825-8888. Fax: (410)337-0747. E-mail: sidran@sidran.org. Website: www.sidran.org. **Acquisitions:** Esther Giller, director. Estab. 1991. Publishes hardcover originals and trade paperback originals and reprints. **Publishes 2-3 titles/year. Pays 8-10% royalty on wholesale price.** Does not accept simultaneous submissions. Responds in 1 month to queries; 3 months to proposals; 6 months to mss. Book catalog and ms guidelines free.

Nonfiction: Reference, self-help, textbook, professional. Subjects include health/medicine, psychology, psychiatry, expressive therapies. Specializes in trauma/abuse/domestic violence and mental health issues. "Sidran Press is devoted to advocacy, education and research in support of people with psychiatric disabilities related to extremely traumatic life experiences." Exclusively publishes books about traumatic stress and dissociative conditions, nonfiction, practical tools for recovery, education and training materials for professionals, self-help workbooks. Currently emphasizing practical recovery tools, professional training, application of research. De-emphasizing biography, autobiography or first-person recovery narratives. Query with proposal package including outline, 2-3 sample chapters, introduction, competing titles, market information.
Recent Title(s): *Growing Beyond Survival, a Self-Help Toolkit for Managing Traumatic Stress*, by Elizabeth Vermilyea.

SLAPERING HOL PRESS, The Hudson Valley Writers' Center, 300 Riverside Dr., Sleepy Hollow NY 10591. (914)332-5953. Fax: (914)332-4825. E-mail: info@writerscenter.org. Website: www.writerscenter.org. **Acquisitions:** Stephanie Strickland and Margo Stever, co-editors (poetry). Publishes chapbooks. **Publishes 1 title/year. Receives 70 queries and 300 mss/year. 100% of books from first-time authors; 100% from unagented writers. Pays honorarium and 12 copies of book.** Publishes book 6 months after acceptance of ms. Accepts simultaneous submissions. Book catalog for #10 SASE; ms guidelines for #10 SASE.
Poetry: Unpublished poets are invited to submit a collection of poems for the annual chapbook competition. The winning poet receives a cash award, publication, copies and a reading at The Hudson Valley Writers' Center. Query.
Recent Title(s): *Freight*, by Sondra Upham; *Islands*, by Andrew Krivak; *The Landscape of Mind*, by Jianqing Zheng.
Tips: Poets should obtain the contest guidelines before submitting.

SOCRATIC PRESS, P.O. Box 66683, St. Pete Beach FL 33736-6683. (727)367-6177. Publishes hardcover, trade paperback and electronic originals and electronic reprints. **Publishes 2-3 titles/year. Pays 15-50% royalty on retail price.**
Nonfiction: How-to, humor, illustrated book, self-help. Subjects include animals, business/economics, creative nonfiction, ethnic, gay/lesbian, government/politics, health/medicine, language/literature, money/finance, nature/environment, philosophy, psychology, science, sex, social sciences, spirituality. Query with SASE or submit proposal package including outline.
Recent Title(s): *Handbook of the Coming American Revolution*, by Bryant.
Tips: Audience is "skeptical, free-thinking, libertarian, inquisitive, unihibited, curious, iconoclastic."

SOUND VIEW PRESS, 859 Boston Post Rd., Madison CT 06443. (203)245-2246. Fax: (203)245-5116. E-mail: info@falkart.com. Website: artprice.com or artistbiographies.com. **Acquisitions:** Peter Hastings Falk, president. Estab. 1985. Publishes hardcover and trade paperback originals, dictionaries and exhibition records exclusive to fine art. Does not accept simultaneous submissions.
Recent Title(s): *Who Was Who in American Art: 1564-1975*, by Peter Falk.
Tips: Currently emphasizing American art history, conservation, exhibition records.

SPECTACLE LANE PRESS, INC., P.O. Box 1237, Mt. Pleasant SC 29465-1237. (888)669-8114 (toll free). Fax: (843)971-9165. E-mail: jaskar44@aol.com. **Acquisitions:** James A. Skardon, editor. Publishes nonfiction hardcover and trade paperback originals. **Publishes 2-3 titles/year. Pays 6-10% royalty on wholesale price.** Responds in 2 weeks to queries; 1 month to mss.

- Emphasizes humor, but also interested in sports, lifestyle and celebrity-oriented books. All books should be related to subjects of strong current interest and promotable on radio and TV.

Nonfiction: "Query first. We will request an outline and 3 chapters if we are interested."
Recent Title(s): *Call Me Coach*, by George H. Baldwin (sports biography); *Money Inc*, by Joseph Farris (business cartoons).

STEEL BALLS PRESS, P.O. Box 807, Whittier CA 90608. **Acquisitions:** R. Don Steele, editor-in-chief. Publishes hardcover and trade paperback originals. "We publish only controversial self-help nonfiction." **Publishes 2-3 titles/year. Pays 10% royalty on retail price after break-even.** Guidelines available on website at http://steelballs.com.
Nonfiction: How-to, self-help. Subjects include dating, relationships, divorce, marriage, office politics. No humor, homeless, incest/molestation, save-the-world. "Query with SASE. A submission of more than 1 page will not receive a response."
Recent Title(s): *Body Language Secrets: A Guide During Courtship and Dating.*
Tips: "Write a persuasive one-page query letter. Explain who will buy and why. We attempt to provide information that will actually help an individual improve his/her romantic life."

STORMLINE PRESS, P.O. Box 593, Urbana IL 61801. **Acquisitions:** Raymond Bial, publisher. Estab. 1985. Publishes hardcover and trade paperback originals. **Publishes 1-2 titles/year. Pays 10% royalty on retail price. Offers advance.** Does not accept simultaneous submissions.
Nonfiction: Subjects include language/literature, photography, regional. Publishes photography and regional works of the highest literary quality, especially those having to do with rural and small town themes. Publication by invitation only.
Fiction: "We only publish books with rural, midwestern themes and very little fiction."
Poetry: "We publish very little poetry."

Recent Title(s): *When the Waters Recede: Rescue and Recovery During the Great Flood*, by Dan Guillory; *Silent Friends*, by Margaret Lacey (short story collection); *The Alligatory Inventions*, by Dan Guillory.
Tips: "Publishes fiction and nonfiction, generally with a Midwest connection. Publication by invitation only. We do not consider unsolicited manuscripts."

STRATA PUBLISHING, INC., P.O. Box 1303, State College PA 16804. (814)234-8545. Website: www.stratapub.com. **Acquisitions:** Kathleen Domenig, publisher (speech communication, journalism, mass communication, political science). Publishes college textbooks. **Publishes 1-3 titles/year. Pays royalty on wholesale price.** Publishes book about 1 year after acceptance of ms. Responds in 1 month to queries; 3 months to proposals; 3 months to mss. Book catalog and ms guidelines online.
Nonfiction: Textbook. Subjects include government/politics, speech, journalism, mass communication. Query with SASE or submit proposal package including outline, 2 sample chapter(s).
Recent Title(s): *Readings on the Rhetoric of Social Protest*, by Charles E. Morris III and Stephen H. Browne; *Freedom of Speech in the United States, 4th Ed*, by Thomas L. Tedford and Dale A. Herbeck; *The Why, Who and How of the Editorial Page, 3rd Ed*, by Kenneth Rystrom.
Tips: Please visit our website for a description of our publishing needs, manuscript submission guidelines.

STUDIO 4 PRODUCTIONS, P.O. Box 280400, Northridge CA 91328. (818)700-2522. Fax: (818)700-8666. Website: studio4productions.com. **Acquisitions:** Charlie Matthews, editor-in-chief; Karen Ervin-Pershing, associate editor. Publishes trade paperback originals. **Publishes 2-5 titles/year. Pays 10% royalty on retail price. Offers negotiable advance.** Does not accept simultaneous submissions. Responds in 1 month to queries; 1 month to proposals; 3 months to mss.
Nonfiction: Self-help. Subjects include child guidance/parenting, education, travel, character education, senior/aging. Query with SASE or submit outline.
Recent Title(s): *The Wisdom to Choose*, by Dixon Arnett & Wende Dawson Chan.

THE SUGAR HILL PRESS, 216 Stoddard Rd., Hancock NH 03449-5102. **Acquisitions:** L. Bickford, publisher. Estab. 1990. Publishes trade paperback originals. **Publishes 1 title/year. Pays 20% royalty on publisher's revenues.** Responds in 1 month to proposals.

- "Our books focus on helping school personnel—secretaries, guidance counselors, administrators—make the most of their school's investment in school administration software."

Nonfiction: "We publish technical manuals for users of school administrative software only. (These are supplemental materials, not the manuals which come in the box.) A successful writer will combine technical expertise with crystal-clear prose." Query with SASE.
Recent Title(s): *Perfect Attendance*, by Frances M. Kulak; *A Win School Primer*, by L. Bickford.

N TAMARACK BOOKS, INC., P.O. Box 190313, Boise ID 83719. (800)962-6657. Fax: (208)922-5880. President/Owner: Kathy Gaudry. Publishes trade paperback originals and reprints. **Publishes 3-5 titles/year. Pays 5-15% royalty. Offers advance.** Does not accept simultaneous submissions. Responds in 4 months to queries; 6 months to mss.

- "We publish nonfiction history of the American West and are avidly seeking women's books. Time period preference is for pre-1900s." Currently emphasizing "pioneer women who have made a difference, whether they have name recognition or not."

Nonfiction: Illustrated book. Subjects include history, regional. "We are looking for manuscripts for a popular audience, but based on solid research. We specialize in mountain man, women's issues and outlaw history prior to 1940 in the West, but will look at any good manuscript on Western history prior to 1940." Query with SASE or submit outline.
Recent Title(s): *Competitive Struggle, America's Western Fur Trading Posts, 1764-1865*, R.G. Robertson.
Tips: "We look for authors who want to actively participate in the marketing of their books."

TECHNICAL ANALYSIS OF STOCKS & COMMODITIES, Technical Analysis, Inc., 4757 California Ave. SW, Seattle WA 98116-4499. (206)938-0570. **Acquisitions:** Jayanthi Gopalakrishnan, editor. Estab. 1982. Publishes trade paperback originals and reprints. **Makes outright purchase.** Responds in 6 months to queries.
Nonfiction: Publishes business and economics books and software about using charts and computers to trade stocks, options, mutual funds or commodity futures. "Know the industry and the markets using technical analysis." Query with SASE.
Recent Title(s): *Charting the Stock Market*, by Hutson, Weis, Schroeder (technical analysis).
Tips: "Only traders and technical analysts really understand the industry. First consideration for publication will be given to material, regardless of topic, that presents the subject in terms that are easily understandable by the novice trader. One of our prime considerations is to instruct, and we must do so in a manner that the lay person can comprehend. This by no means bars material of a complex nature, but the author must first establish the groundwork."

N TIA CHUCHA PRESS, A Project of The Guild Complex, 1212 N. Ashland Ave. #211, Chicago IL 60622. (773)227-6117. Fax: (773)227-6159. **Acquisitions:** Luis Rodriguez, director. Publishes trade paperback originals. **Publishes 2-4 titles/year. Receives 25-30 queries and 150 mss/year. Pays 10% royalty on wholesale price. Offers $500-1,000 advance.** Publishes book 1 year after acceptance of ms. Does not accept simultaneous submissions. Responds in 9 months to mss. Book catalog free; ms guidelines free.
Poetry: "No restrictions as to style or content. We do cross-cultural and performance-oriented poetry. It has to work on the page, however." Submit complete ms.

Recent Title(s): *Rise*, by A. Van Jordan; *Bumtown*, by Tony Fitzpatrick; *Mean Days*, by Anne-Marie Cusack.
Tips: Audience is "those interested in strong, multicultural, urban poetry—the best of bar-cafe poetry. Annual manuscript deadline is June 30. Send your best work. No fillers. We read in the summer; we decide in the fall what books to publish for the following year."

VANDERWYK & BURNHAM, P.O. Box 2789, Acton MA 01720. (617)714-0287. Fax: (617)714-0268. Website: www.vandb.com. **Acquisitions:** Meredith Rutter, president. Publishes hardcover and trade paperback originals. **Publishes 1-3 titles/year. Pays royalty on retail price. Offers $500-2,000 advance.** Does not accept simultaneous submissions. Responds in 3 months to queries. Ms guidelines for #10 SASE.
Nonfiction: Subjects include education, psychology, narrative nonfiction, contemporary issues. "We publish books that make a difference in people's lives, including motivational books about admirable people and programs, and self-help books for people 50 and over." Query with SASE or submit proposal package including résumé, publishing history, synopsis.
Recent Title(s): *Are Your Parents Driving You Crazy? How to Resolve the Most Common Dilemmas with Aging Parents*; *But This Is My Mother! The Plight of Our Elderly in American Nursing Homes*.

VITESSE PRESS, PMB 367, 45 State St., Montpelier VT 05602. (802)229-4243. Fax: (802)229-6939. E-mail: dick@vitessepress.com. Website: www.vitessepress.com. **Acquisitions:** Richard H. Mansfield, editor. Estab. 1985. Publishes trade paperback originals. **Publishes 2 titles/year. Pays 10% royalty on net receipts.** Does not accept simultaneous submissions. Responds in 1 month to queries.
Nonfiction: How-to, technical, recreation. Subjects include health/medicine, regional (mountain biking guides), sports. Especially interested in cycling-related books.
Recent Title(s): *Cycling Along the Canals of New York*, by Louis Rossi.

[N] **WAYFINDER PRESS**, P.O. Box 217, Ridgway CO 81432-0217. (970)626-5452. **Acquisitions:** Marcus E. Wilson, owner. Estab. 1980. Publishes trade paperback originals. **Publishes 2 titles/year. Pays 8-10% royalty on retail price.** Does not accept simultaneous submissions. Responds in 1 month to queries.
Nonfiction: Illustrated book, reference. Subjects include Americana, government/politics, history, nature/environment, photography, recreation, regional, travel. "We are looking for books on western Colorado: history, nature, recreation, photo, and travel. No books on subjects outside our geographical area of specialization." Query with SASE or submit outline, sample chapter(s). Reviews artwork/photos as part of ms package.
Recent Title(s): *Ouray—Chief of the Utes*, P. David Smith.
Tips: "Writers have the best chance selling us tourist-oriented books. Our audience is the local population and tourists."

[N] **WESTERN NEW YORK WARES, INC.**, P.O. Box 733, Ellicott Station, Buffalo NY 14205. (716)832-6088. E-mail: waywares@gateway.net. Website: www.wnybooks.com. **Acquisitions:** Brian S. Meyer, publisher (regional history); Tom Connolly, marketing manager (sports, regional travel). Publishes trade paperback originals. **Publishes 3 titles/year. Pays 50% royalty on net receipts.** Publishes book 1 year after acceptance of ms. Accepts simultaneous submissions. Responds in 6 weeks to queries. Book catalog for free or on website; ms guidelines for #10 SASE.
Nonfiction: Subjects include art/architecture, history (on upstate Western New York), photography, regional (Buffalo, Niagra Falls, Chautauqua, Allegany), travel. No fiction. Query with SASE.
Recent Title(s): *Victorian Buffalo*, Cynthia Van Ness.

WOODBRIDGE PRESS, 12900 SW 9th St., Beaverton OR 97005. (503)626-0739. Fax: (503)644-5999. E-mail: woodpress@aol.com. Website: www.woodbridgepress.com. **Acquisitions:** Howard Weeks, editor. Estab. 1971. Publishes hardcover and trade paperback originals. **Publishes 1-2 titles/year. Pays 10-15% royalty on wholesale price. Offers advance.** Does not accept simultaneous submissions. Responds in 2 months to queries.
"We publish books by expert authors on special forms of gardening."
Nonfiction: Query with SASE. Reviews artwork/photos as part of ms package.
Recent Title(s): *Hydroponics Food Production, Sixth Edition*, by Howard M. Resh (gardening/horticulture); *Artistically Cultivated Herbs*, by Elise Felton.

WOODFIELD PRESS, 2820 Los Tomases Dr. NW, Albuquerque NM 87107-1240. (505)342-1723. **Acquisitions:** Howard J. Fried, partner. Publishes hardcover, trade paperback and mass market paperback originals. **Publishes 2 titles/year. Pays 15% royalty on wholesale price.** Publishes book 4 months after acceptance of ms. Responds in 1 month to queries; 1 month to proposals; 1 month to mss. Book catalog for #10 SASE or online.
Nonfiction: Biography, children's/juvenile. Subjects include aviation, biography. Query with SASE or submit proposal package including outline or submit complete ms.
Recent Title(s): *More Eye of Experience*, by Fried; *Still More Eye of Experience*, by Fried; *Biography of Fay Gillis Wells*.

Book Producers

Book producers provide services for book publishers, ranging from hiring writers to editing and delivering finished books. Most book producers possess expertise in certain areas and will specialize in producing books related to those subjects. They provide books to publishers who don't have the time or expertise to produce the books themselves (many produced books are highly illustrated and require intensive design and color-separation work). Some work with on-staff writers, but most contract writers on a per-project basis.

Most often a book producer starts with a proposal; contacts writers, editors, and illustrators; assembles the book; and sends it back to the publisher. The level of involvement and the amount of work to be done on a book by the producer are negotiated in individual cases. A book publisher may simply require the specialized skill of a particular writer or editor, or a producer could put together the entire book, depending on the terms of the agreement.

Writers have a similar working relationship with book producers. Their involvement depends on how much writing the producer has been asked to provide. Writers are typically paid by the hour, by the word, or in some manner other than on a royalty basis. Writers working for book producers usually earn flat fees. Writers may not receive credit (a byline in the book, for example) for their work, either. Most of the contracts require work for hire, and writers must realize they do not own the rights to writing published under this arrangement.

The opportunities are good, though, especially for writing-related work, such as fact checking, research, and editing. Writers don't have to worry about good sales. Their pay is secured under contract. Finally, writing for a book producer is a good way to broaden experience in publishing. Every book to be produced is different, and the chance to work on a range of books in a number of capacities may be the most interesting aspect of all.

Book producers most often want to see a query detailing writing experience. They keep this information on file and occasionally even share it with other producers. When they are contracted to develop a book that requires a particular writer's experience, they contact the writer. There are well over 100 book producers, but most prefer to seek writers on their own. The book producers listed in this section have expressed interest in being contacted by writers. For a list of more producers, contact the American Book Producers Association (www.abpaonline.org), 156 Fifth Ave., New York NY 10010, or look in *Literary Market Place* (R.R. Bowker).

For a list of publishers according to their subjects of interest, see the nonfiction and fiction sections of the Book Publishers Subject Index. Information on book publishers and producers listed in the previous edition of *Writer's Market* but not included in this edition can be found in the General Index.

N **BOOKWRIGHTS PRESS**, 2255 Westover Dr., Charlottesville VA 22901. (804)823-8223. Fax: (804)823-8223. E-mail: editor@bookwrights.com. Website: www.bookwrights.com. Publisher: Mayapriya Long. **Acquisitions:** Robin Field, editor. Produces hardcover and trade paperback originals. **Publishes 2 titles/year. 40% of books from first-time authors; 100% from unagented writers. Pays royalty.** Responds in 2 months to queries.

Nonfiction: How-to, self-help, technical, textbook. Subjects include regional, religion, Eastern religion. "Do not send manuscripts." Query with résumé via e-mail or mail.

Fiction: Ethnic (Asian, Indian), historical, mainstream/contemporary. Query or submit proposal.

Recent Title(s): *Sentimental Journeys*, Joe Lieberman (nonfiction); *Mandalay's Child*, Prem Sharma (fiction).

Tips: "No unsolicited manuscripts. Query first. When requested, send manuscript on disk with accompanying hard copy."

N **ALISON BROWN CERIER BOOK DEVELOPMENT, INC.**, 815 Brockton Lane N., Plymouth MN 55410. (763)449-9668. Fax: (763)449-9674. Produces hardcover and trade paperback originals. **Publishes 4 titles/year. 50%**

of books from first-time authors; 90% from unagented writers. Payment varies with project. Cannot respond to unsolicited proposals for original books but looking for experienced health and business writers for existing projects to proposals.

O→ "The vast majority of books start with our ideas or those of a publisher, not with proposals from writers. We do not act as authors' agents." Currently emphasizing health, business self-help. De-emphasizing cookbooks.

Nonfiction: How-to, reference, self-help. Subjects include business/economics, child guidance/parenting, cooking/foods/nutrition, health/medicine, sports, women's issues/studies. Query with SASE.

Recent Title(s): *AMA Complete Guide to Children's Health.*

Tips: "I often pair experts with writers and like to know about writers and journalists with co-writing experience."

COURSE CRAFTERS, INC., 44 Merrimac St., Newburyport MA 01950. (978)465-2040. Fax: (978)465-5027. E-mail: lise@coursecrafters.com. Website: www.coursecrafters.com. **Acquisitions:** Lise B. Ragan, president. Produces textbooks and educational trade materials (Spanish/ESL). **Makes outright purchase.** Manuscript guidelines vary based upon project-specific requirements.

O→ "We package materials that teach language. We are particularly looking for innovative approaches and visually appealing presentations." Special focus is on language materials.

Nonfiction: Audiocassettes, children's/juvenile, multimedia, reference, textbook (ESL, foreign language, reading/language arts). Subjects include education (preschool-adult), ethnic, language/literature, multicultural, translation. Submit résumé, publishing history, synopsis.

Tips: "Mail (or fax) résumé with list of projects related to specific experience with ESL, bilingual and/or foreign language textbook development. Also interested in storytellers and musicians for our new audio/game packages."

[N] **DESIGN PRESS**, P.O. Box 3146, Savannah GA 31402-3146. (912)525-5212. Fax: (912)525-5211. E-mail: js-hay@scad.edu.

Tips: "Design Press produces books of exceptional quality, showcasing the visual talent of the faculty, students and alumni of the Savannah College of Art and Design. A full-service book packager, Design Press takes both original and commissioned projects through the conceptual, visual, editorial and production stages. Design Press specializes in children's picture books, illustrated gift books, and specialty publications that emphasize the visual elements of art and design."

DIMI PRESS, 3820 Oak Hollow Lane, SE, Salem OR 97302-4774. (503)364-7698. Fax: (503)364-9727. E-mail: dickbook@earthlink.net. Website: www.home.earthlink.net/~dickbook. **Acquisitions:** Dick Lutz, president. Publishes trade paperback originals. **Publishes 5 titles/year. Receives 100-150 queries and 20-25 mss/year. 80% of books from first-time authors; 90% from unagented writers. Pays 10% royalty on net receipts.** Publishes book 9 months after acceptance of ms. Accepts simultaneous submissions. Responds in 1 month to queries. Book catalog for #10 SASE; ms guidelines online.

O→ "We provide accurate information about unusual things in nature." Currently de-emphasizing self-help books. No mss until requested.

Nonfiction: Subjects include animals, nature/environment, science. "Soliciting manuscripts on unusual things in nature, such as unusual animals or natural formations. Also natural disasters such as volcanic eruptions, earthquakes, or floods. Preferably of the world's 'worst.' Also related manuscripts on nature/travel/environment. No travel guides." Query with SASE or submit outline, 1 sample chapter(s). Reviews artwork/photos as part of ms package. Send photocopies.

Recent Title(s): *The Running Indians*; *Komodo, The Living Dragon*; *Hidden Amazon.*

Tips: "Audience is adults who wish to learn something and are interested in unusual travel excursions. Also assists self-publishers in producing their book. Please check guidelines before submitting."

FARCOUNTRY PRESS, P.O. Box 5630, Helena MT 59604. (406)443-2842. Fax: (406)443-5480. E-mail: prodmgr@montanamagazine.com. Website: montanamagazine.com. **Acquisitions:** Kathy Springmeyer, production director; Merle Guy, sales director. Produces soft and hardcover books devoted to travel, tourism and outdoor recreation, with special emphasis on color photography. Mostly regional titles.

Nonfiction: Coffee table book, gift book, illustrated book. Subjects include history (popular), recreation, regional, travel. Currently emphasizing Glacier and Yellowstone National Parks, Lewis and Clark Trail.

Recent Title(s): *Along the Trail with Lewis and Clark*; *Wyoming Historic Forts*; *Montana Mining Ghost Towns.*

GLEASON GROUP, INC., 6 Old Kings Hwy., Norwalk CT 06850. (203)847-6658. **Acquisitions:** Gerald Gleason, president. **Publishes 10-15 titles/year. Work-for-hire.**

Nonfiction: Textbook. Subjects include computers; application software with CD-ROMs. Submit résumé. No unsolicited mss.

Recent Title(s): *Word 2002: A Professional Approach*; *Office XP: A Professional Approach.*

Tips: "If writer is well versed in the most recent Microsoft Office software, and has written technical or software-related material before, he/she can send us their résumé."

GREEN NATURE BOOKS, Box 105, Sumterville FL 33585. (352)793-5496. Fax: (352)793-6075. Website: www.greennaturebooks.com. **Pays up to 10% royalty.**

O→ Green Nature Books specializes in books about tortoises and orchids. Query with SASE.

Recent Title(s): *Lizard Lovers' Library.*

Tips: "Contact us only if you are an expert herpetologist or wish to have a book printed privately. We are expert in small run publications, now including other fields. We arrange color content printing on demand."

LOUISE B. KETZ AGENCY, 1485 First Ave., Suite 4B, New York NY 10021. (212)535-9259. **Acquisitions:** Louise B. Ketz, president. Produces and agents hardcover and paperback originals. **Publishes 3-5 titles/year. 90% from unagented writers. Pays flat fees and honoraria to writers.** Responds in 2 months to queries.
Nonfiction: Biography, reference. Subjects include Americana, business/economics, history, science, sports. Submit proposal package.
Recent Title(s): *Quantum Leaps in the Wrong Direction*; *The McFarland Baseball Quotations Dictionary*; *Encyclopedia of American Foreign Policy, 2nd ed.*
Tips: "It is important for authors to list their credentials relevant to the book they are proposing (i.e., why they are qualified to write that nonfiction work). Also helps if author defines the market (who will buy the book and why)."

GEORGE KURIAN REFERENCE BOOKS, Box 519, Baldwin Place NY 10505. (914)962-3287. Fax: (914)962-3287. President: George Kurian. **Acquisitions:** Jeff Schultz, editor (general); Henry Sapinda, editor (religion, education, business). Produces hardcover originals. **Publishes 6 titles/year. 10% of books from first-time authors; 50% from unagented writers. Pays 10-15% royalty on net receipts.** Responds in 3 months to queries. Book catalog for 8½×11 SAE with 2 first-class stamps; ms guidelines for #10 SASE.
Imprints: International Encyclopedia Society; UN Studies Forum.

O→ "Our goal is to publish innovative reference books for the library and trade market." Currently emphasizing history, politics, international relations, religion, children's and biography. No science, art or sports.

Nonfiction: Biography, illustrated book, reference, scholarly. Subjects include Americana, business/economics, education, ethnic, government/politics, history, language/literature, memoirs, military/war, multicultural, philosophy, photography, religion, travel, women's issues/studies, contemporary culture, world affairs. Query with SASE or submit proposal package.
Recent Title(s): *Datapedia of the United States.*
Tips: "We seek to provide accurate information on issues of global interest."

LAMPPOST PRESS, INC., 710 Park Ave. #19-B, New York NY 10021-4944. (212)288-8474. **Acquisitions:** Roseann Hirsch, president. Estab. 1987. Produces hardcover, trade paperback and mass market paperback originals. **Publishes 25 titles/year. 50% of books from first-time authors; 85% from unagented writers. Pays 50% royalty or makes outright purchase.**
Nonfiction: Biography, children's/juvenile, cookbook, how-to, humor, illustrated book, self-help. Subjects include child guidance/parenting, cooking/foods/nutrition, gardening, health/medicine, money/finance, women's issues/studies. Query with SASE or submit proposal package. Reviews artwork/photos as part of ms package.

NEW ENGLAND PUBLISHING ASSOCIATES, INC., P.O. Box 5, Chester CT 06412. (860)345-READ. Fax: (860)345-3660. E-mail: nepa@nepa.com. Website: www.nepa.com. **Acquisitions:** Elizabeth Frost-Knappman, president; Edward W. Knappman, vice president/treasurer. Estab. 1983. Produces hardcover and trade paperback originals. **20% of books from first-time authors.** Responds in 6 weeks to queries.

O→ NEPA develops adult and young adult reference and information titles and series for the domestic and international markets. "Our mission is to provide personalized service to a select list of mainly nonfiction clients." Currently emphasizing history, Asian affairs, biography, crime, science, literary criticism, current events, adventure, women's topics, gay topics, reference, business amd financial. De-emphasizing fiction, young adult, scholarly women's studies, scholarly reference.

Nonfiction: Biography, how-to, reference. Subjects include Americana, anthropology/archeology, business/economics, child guidance/parenting, ethnic, gay/lesbian, government/politics, health/medicine, history, language/literature, memoirs, military/war, money/finance, multicultural, nature/environment, philosophy, science, women's issues/studies, true crime, world affairs.
Recent Title(s): *How Carlos Ghosn Rescued Nissan*, by David Magee, (HaperCollins); *Swimming with Sharks*, by Pete Klimley, (Simon & Schuster); *Blood and Whiskey: The Life and Times of Jack Daniels*, by Peter Krass, (John Wiley).
Tips: "Revise, revise, revise and do not lose hope. We don't."

PUBLICOM, INC., 60 Aberdeen Ave., Cambridge MA 02138. (617)714-0300. Fax: (617)714-0268. E-mail: info@publicom1.com. **Acquisitions:** Neil Saunders, vice president/textbook services. **Publishes 100-200 titles/year. Makes work-for-hire assignments for textbooks.**

O→ "We create leading-edge educational products and services."

Nonfiction: Textbook. Subjects include education, school disciplines K-college. Submit résumé, publishing history, synopsis.

SOMERVILLE HOUSE, INC., 24 Dinnick Crescent, Toronto, Ontario M4N 1C5 Canada. **Acquisitions:** Acquisition Department. Produces children's nonfiction. **Publishes 15 titles/year. 5% of books from first-time authors.** Responds in 4 months to queries. Manuscript guidelines for #10 SASE with postage (Canadian or IRC).

O→ Currently emphasizing science and nature.

Nonfiction: Children's/juvenile. Subjects include cooking/foods/nutrition, education, hobbies, nature/environment, science, sports. Query with SASE.

Recent Title(s): *The Titanic Book and Submersible Model*; *Bakin Brownies*, by Susan Devins.
Tips: "We accept only children's nonfiction submissions."

N **2M COMMUNICATIONS LTD.**, 121 W. 27th St., New York NY 10001. (212)741-1509. Fax: (212)691-4460. **Acquisitions:** Madeleine Morel, editorial director. Produces hardcover, trade paperback and mass market paperback originals. **Publishes 15 titles/year. 50% of books from first-time authors.** Responds in 2 weeks to queries. *Writer's Market* recommends allowing 2 months for reply to mss.
Nonfiction: Biography, cookbook, how-to, humor. Subjects include child guidance/parenting, cooking/foods/nutrition, ethnic, gay/lesbian, health/medicine, humor, psychology, women's issues/studies. Query with SASE or submit proposal package including résumé, publishing history.

VERNON PRESS, INC., 398 Columbus Ave., #355, Boston MA 02116-6008. (617)437-0388. Fax: (617)437-0894. E-mail: info@vernonpress.com. Website: www.vernonpress.com. Produces hardcover and trade paperback originals. **Publishes 8-12 titles/year.** Responds in 6 weeks to queries.

O→ Vernon Press packages illustrated nonfiction titles for trade and academic presses.

Nonfiction: Coffee table book, gift book, illustrated book. Subjects include Americana, art/architecture, gardening, history, music/dance, nature/environment, photography, regional, sports, travel. Submit query letter (2-page maximum).
Recent Title(s): *Means of Grace, Hope of Glory* (Trinity Church Boston, 2001); *Legacy of Love* (Trinity Church Boston, 2001).

THE WONDERLAND PRESS, 160 Fifth Ave., Suite 625, New York NY 10010. (212)989-2550. **Acquisitions:** John Campbell, president. Produces hardcover and trade paperback originals and mass market paperback originals. **Publishes 50 titles/year. 80% of books from first-time authors; 90% from unagented writers. Payment depends on the book: sometimes royalty with advance, sometimes work-for-hire.** Responds in 3 weeks to queries.
Nonfiction: Biography, coffee table book, how-to, humor, illustrated book, reference, self-help, TV scripts, screenplays. Subjects include art/architecture, gardening, history, psychology, pop culture. Submit proposal package including sample chapter(s). Reviews artwork/photos as part of ms package.
Recent Title(s): *The Essential Jackson Pollock*, (Abrams).
Tips: "Always submit in writing, never by telephone. Know your market intimately. Study the competition and decide whether there is a genuine need for your book, with a market base that will justify publication. Send us an enthused, authoritative, passionately written proposal that shows your mastery of the subject and that makes us say, 'Wow, we want that!'"

Consumer Magazines

Selling your writing to consumer magazines is as much an exercise of your marketing skills as it is of your writing abilities. Editors of consumer magazines are looking not only for good writing, but for good writing which communicates pertinent information to a specific audience—their readers. Why are editors so particular about the readers they appeal to? Because it is only by establishing a core of faithful readers with identifiable and quantifiable traits that magazines attract advertisers. And with many magazines earning up to half their income from advertising, it is in their own best interest to know their readers' tastes and provide them with articles and features that will keep their readers coming back.

APPROACHING THE CONSUMER MAGAZINE MARKET

Marketing skills will help you successfully discern a magazine's editorial slant and write queries and articles that prove your knowledge of the magazine's readership. The one complaint we hear from magazine editors more than any other is that many writers don't take the time to become familiar with their magazine before sending a query or manuscript. As a result, editors' desks become cluttered with inappropriate submissions.

You can gather clues about a magazine's readership—and thus establish your credibility with the magazine's editor—in a number of ways:

- Start with a careful reading of the magazine's listing in this section of *Writer's Market*. Most listings offer very straightforward information about the magazine's slant and audience.
- Study a magazine's writer's guidelines, if available. These are written by each particular magazine's editors and are usually quite specific about the magazine's needs and readership.
- Check a magazine's website. Often writer's guidelines and a selection of articles are included in a publication's online version. A quick check of archived articles lets you know if ideas you want to propose have already been covered.
- Perhaps most important, read several current issues of the target magazine.
- If possible, talk to an editor by phone. Many will not take phone queries, particularly those at the higher-profile magazines. But many editors of smaller publications will spend the time to help a writer over the phone.

Writers who can correctly and consistently discern a publication's audience and deliver stories that speak to that target readership will win out every time over writers who simply write what they write and send it where they will.

WHAT EDITORS WANT

In nonfiction, editors continue to look for short feature articles covering specialized topics. Editors want crisp writing and expertise. If you are not an expert in the area about which you are writing, make yourself one through research.

Always query before sending your manuscript. Don't e-mail or fax a query unless an editor specifically mentions openness to this in the listing. Publishing, despite all the electronic advancements, is still a very paper-oriented industry. Once a piece has been accepted, however, many publishers now prefer to receive your submission via disk or e-mail so they can avoid rekeying the manuscript.

Fiction editors prefer to receive complete short story manuscripts. Writers must keep in mind that marketing fiction is competitive and editors receive far more material than they can publish. For this reason, they often do not respond to submissions unless they are interested in using the story. Before submitting material, check the market's listing for fiction requirements to ensure your story is appropriate for that market. More comprehensive information on fiction markets can be found in *Novel & Short Story Writer's Market* (Writer's Digest Books).

Many writers make their articles do double duty, selling first or one-time rights to one publisher and second serial or reprint rights to another noncompeting market. The heading, **Reprints**, offers details when a market indicates whether they accept previously published submissions, with submission format and payment information if available.

Regardless of the type of writing you do, keep current on trends and changes in the industry. Trade magazines such as *Writer's Digest*, *Folio: The Magazine for Magazine Management*, and *Advertising Age* will keep you abreast of start-ups and shutdowns and other writing/business trends.

PAYMENT

Writers make their living by developing a good eye for detail. When it comes to marketing material, the one detail of interest to almost every writer is the question of payment. Most magazines listed here have indicated pay rates; some give very specific payment-per-word rates, while others state a range. Any agreement you come to with a magazine, whether verbal or written, should specify the payment you are to receive and when you are to receive it. Some magazines pay writers only after the piece in question has been published. Others pay as soon as they have accepted a piece and are sure they are going to use it.

In *Writer's Market*, those magazines that pay on acceptance have been highlighted with the phrase **pays on acceptance** set in bold type. Payment from these markets should reach you faster than from markets that pay on publication. There is, however, some variance in the industry as to what constitutes payment "on acceptance"—some writers have told us of two- and three-month waits for checks from markets that supposedly pay on acceptance. It is never out of line to ask an editor when you might expect to receive payment for an accepted article.

Those magazines that pay on publication have been highlighted with the phrase **pays on publication** set in bold type. Magazines that pay on publication render payment once the article is published in the periodical.

So what is a good pay rate? There are no standards; the principle of supply and demand operates at full throttle in the business of writing and publishing. As long as there are more writers than opportunities for publication, wages for freelancers will never skyrocket. Rates vary widely from one market to the next. Smaller circulation magazines and some departments of the larger magazines will pay a lower rate.

Editors know that the listings in *Writer's Market* are read and used by writers with a wide range of experience, from those as-yet unpublished writers just starting out, to those with a successful, profitable freelance career. As a result, many magazines publicly report pay rates in the lower end of their actual pay ranges. Experienced writers will be able to successfully negotiate higher pay rates for their material. Newer writers should be encouraged that as their reputation grows (along with their clip file), they will be able to command higher rates.

INFORMATION AT-A-GLANCE

In the Consumer Magazine section, symbols identify comparative payment rates (**$**–**$$$$**); new listings (N); "opportunity" markets (★) that are at least 75% freelance written, appear quarterly or more frequently, and buy a high number of manuscripts; and magazines that do not accept freelance submissions (⊘). Different sections of *Writer's Market* include other symbols; check the front and back inside covers for an explanation of all the symbols used throughout the book.

Important information is highlighted in boldface—the "quick facts" you won't find in any other market book, but should know before you submit your work. To clearly identify the editorial "point person" at each magazine, the word "**Contact:**" identifies the appropriate person to query at each magazine. We also highlight what percentage of the magazine is freelance written, how many manuscripts a magazine buys per year of nonfiction, fiction, poetry, and fillers, and respective pay rates in each category.

Information on publications listed in the previous edition of *Writer's Market* but not included in this edition may be found in the General Index.

ANIMAL

The publications in this section deal with pets, racing and show horses, and other domestic animals and wildlife. Magazines about animals bred and raised for the market are classified in the Farm category of Trade, Technical & Professional Journals. Publications about horse racing can be found in the Sports section.

$ $ AKC GAZETTE, American Kennel Club, 260 Madison Ave., New York NY 10016. Fax: (212)696-8239. E-mail: gazette@akc.org. Website: www.akc.org/love/gazet.cfm. **Contact:** Erika Mansourrian. **85% freelance written.** Monthly magazine. "Geared to interests of fanciers of purebred dogs as opposed to commercial interests or pet owners. We require solid expertise from our contributors—we are *not* a pet magazine." Estab. 1889. Circ. 60,000. Pays on publication. Publishes ms an average of 6 months after acceptance. Byline given. Offers 10% kill fee. Buys first North American serial, electronic, international rights. Submit seasonal material 6 months in advance. Accepts queries by mail. Responds in 2 months to queries. Sample copy not available. Writer's guidelines for #10 SASE.

Nonfiction: General interest, how-to, humor, interview/profile, photo feature, travel, dog art, training and canine performance sports. No poetry, tributes to individual dogs or fiction. **Buys 30-40 mss/year.** Length: 1,000-3,000 words. **Pays $300-500.** Pays expenses of writers on assignment.

Photos: Photo contest guidelines for #10 SASE. State availability with submission. Reviews color transparencies, prints. Buys one-time rights. Pays $50-200/photo. Captions, identification of subjects, model releases required.

Fiction: Annual short fiction contest only. Guidelines for #10 SASE.

The online magazine carries original content not found in the print edition. Contact: Robert Keeley.

Tips: "Contributors should be involved in the dog fancy or expert in area they write about (veterinary, showing, field trialing, obedience training, dogs in legislation, dog art or history or literature). All submissions are welcome but author must be a credible expert or be able to interview and quote the experts. Veterinary articles must be written by or with veterinarians. Humorous features or personal experiences relative to purebred dogs that have broader applications. For features generally, know the subject thoroughly and be conversant with jargon peculiar to the sport of dogs."

$ $ THE AMERICAN QUARTER HORSE JOURNAL, (formerly The Quarter Horse Journal), P.O. Box 32470, Amarillo TX 79120. (806)376-4811. Fax: (806)349-6400. E-mail: aqhajrnl@aqha.org. Website: www.aqha.com. Editor-in-Chief: Jim Jennings. **Contact:** Jim Bret Campbell, editor. **30% freelance written.** Prefers to work with published/established writers. Monthly official publication of the American Quarter Horse Association. Estab. 1948. Circ. 70,000. **Pays on acceptance.** Publishes ms an average of 3 months after acceptance. Byline given. Buys first North American serial rights. Submit seasonal material 6 months in advance. Accepts queries by mail, e-mail, fax. Responds in 2 weeks to queries.

Break in by "writing about topics tightly concentrated on the Quarter Horse industry while maintaining strong journalistic skills."

Nonfiction: Book excerpts, essays, how-to (fitting, grooming, showing, or anything that relates to owning, showing, or breeding), interview/profile (feature-type stories—must be about established horses or people who have made a contribution to the business), new product, opinion, personal experience, photo feature, technical (equine updates, new surgery procedures, etc.), travel, informational (educational clinics, current news). **Buys 40 mss/year.** Length: 800-2,000 words. **Pays $150-600.**

Photos: Reviews $2\frac{1}{4} \times 2\frac{1}{4}$, 4×5 or 35mm transparencies, 4×5 glossy prints.

The online magazine carries original content not found in the print edition. Contact: Jim Bret Campbell.

Tips: "Writers must have a knowledge of the horse business."

$ ANIMALS, Massachusetts Society for the Prevention of Cruelty to Animals, 350 S. Huntington Ave., Boston MA 02130. (617)522-7400. Fax: (617)522-4885. **Contact:** Paula Abend, editor. **90% freelance written.** Quarterly magazine covering "articles on wildlife (American and international), domestic animals, balanced treatments of controversies involving animals, conservation, animal welfare issues, pet health and pet care." Estab. 1868. Circ. 60,000. **Pays on acceptance.** Publishes ms an average of 5 months after acceptance. Byline given. Offers negotiable kill fee. Buys one-time rights, makes work-for-hire assignments. Submit seasonal material 6 months in advance. Responds in 6 weeks to queries. Sample copy for $2.95 and 9×12 SAE with 4 first-class stamps. Writer's guidelines for #10 SASE.

Nonfiction: Exposé, general interest, how-to, opinion, photo feature (animal and environmental issues and controversies), practical pet-care topics. "*Animals* does not publish breed-specific domestic pet articles or 'favorite pet' stories. Poetry and fiction are also not used." **Buys 50 mss/year.** Query with published clips. Length: 2,200 words maximum. Sometimes pays expenses of writers on assignment.
Photos: State availability with submission. Reviews contact sheets, 35 mm transparencies, 5×7 or 8×10 prints. Buys one-time rights. Payment depends on usage size and quality. Captions, identification of subjects, model releases required.
Columns/Departments: Books (reviews of books on animals and animal-related subjects), 300 words maximum; **buys 4 mss/year**. Profile (women and men who've gone to extraordinary lengths to aid animals), 800 words maximum; **buys 4 mss/year**. Query with published clips.
Tips: "Present a well-researched proposal. Be sure to include clips that demonstrate the quality of your writing. Stick to categories mentioned in *Animals'* editorial description. Combine well-researched facts with a lively, informative writing style. Feature stories are written almost exclusively by freelancers. We continue to seek proposals and articles that take a humane approach. Articles should concentrate on how issues affect animals, rather than humans."

$ $ APPALOOSA JOURNAL, Appaloosa Horse Club, 2720 West Pullman Rd., Moscow ID 83843-0903. (208)882-5578. Fax: (208)882-8150. E-mail: journal@appaloosa.com. Website: www.appaloosajournal.com. **Contact:** Robin Hendrickson, editor. **20-40% freelance written.** Monthly magazine covering Appaloosa horses. Estab. 1946. Circ. 25,000. Pays on publication. Publishes ms an average of 3 months after acceptance. Byline given. Buys first North American serial rights. Responds in 1 month to queries; 2 months to mss. Sample copy and writer's guidelines free.

- *Appaloosa Journal* no longer accepts material for columns.

Nonfiction: Historical/nostalgic, interview/profile, photo feature. **Buys 15-20 mss/year.** Query with or without published clips or send complete ms. Length: 800-2,000 words. **Pays $100-400.** Sometimes pays expenses of writers on assignment.
Photos: Send photos with submission. Payment varies. Captions, identification of subjects required.

The online magazine carries original content not found in the print edition. Contact: Michelle Berg, online editor.

Tips: "Articles by writers with horse knowledge, news sense and photography skills are in great demand. If it's a strong article about an Appaloosa, the writer has a pretty good chance of publication. A good understanding of the breed and the industry, breeders and owners is helpful. Make sure there's some substance and a unique twist."

$ $ ASPCA ANIMAL WATCH, The American Society for the Prevention of Cruelty to Animals, 315 E. 62nd St., New York NY 10021. (212)876-7700. Fax: (212)410-0087. E-mail: editor@aspca.org. Website: www.aspca.org. **Contact:** Marion Lane, editor. **40-50% freelance written.** Quarterly magazine covering animal welfare: companion animals, endangered species, farm animals, wildlife, animals in entertainment (rodeo, circus, roadside zoos), laboratory animals and humane consumerism, i.e., fur, ivory, etc. "The ASPCA's mission is to alleviate pain, fear, and suffering in all animals. As the voice of the ASPCA, *Animal Watch* is our primary means of communicating with and informing our membership. In addition to in-depth, timely coverage and original reporting on important humane issues, *Animal Watch* provides practical advice on companion animal care and the human/companion animal bond. The ASPCA promotes the adoption and responsible care of companion animals, and through the magazine we encourage stewardship in areas such as training, behavior, exercise and veterinary care." Estab. 1980. Circ. 330,000. **Pays on acceptance.** Publishes ms an average of 4 months after acceptance. Byline given. Buys first North American serial rights. Editorial lead time 6 months. Submit seasonal material 6 months in advance. Accepts queries by mail, e-mail. Accepts simultaneous submissions. Responds in 3 months to queries. Sample copy for 10×13 SAE and 4 first-class stamps.

Break in with a submission to the Animals Abroad, Animal Watchers, or Light Watch columns.

Nonfiction: Essays, exposé, historical/nostalgic, how-to, humor (respectful), interview/profile, photo feature, investigative, news, advocacy. No stories told from animals' point of view, religious stories, fiction or poetry, articles with strident animal rights messages or articles with graphic details. **Buys 25-30 mss/year.** Length: 650-2,500 words. **Pays $75-750.**
Photos: State availability with submission. Reviews transparencies, prints, digital images (300 PSI). Negotiates payment individually. Captions, identification of subjects, model releases required.
Columns/Departments: Animal Watchers (profile of celebrity, ordinary person or group doing something unique to help animals), 150-900 words; Light Watch (humor and light news), 150-300 words; Animals Abroad (first person by someone abroad), 650-700 words; Animals & the Law (balanced report on a legal or legislative subject), 650-700 words; Viewpoint (personal essay on humane subjects), 650-700 words. **Buys 10 mss/year.** Query with or without published clips. **Pays $75-225.**
Tips: "The most important assets for an *Animal Watch* contributor are familiarity with the animal welfare movement in the U.S. and the ability to write lively, well-researched articles. We are always looking for ingenious problem-solving tips as well as positive stories about people and groups and businesses who are helping to protect animals in some way and may inspire others to do the same. We know the problems—share with us some solutions, some approaches that are working. Everything we publish includes 'How you can help....' We are as likely to assign a feature as a short piece for one of the departments."

$ $ THE BARK, The Modern Dog Culture, The Bark, 2810 Eighth, Berkeley CA 94710. (510)704-0827. Fax: (510)704-0933. E-mail: editor@thebark.com. Website: www.thebark.com. **Contact:** Claudia Kawczynska, editor-in-chief. **50% freelance written.** Quarterly covering dogs in today's society. "*The Bark* brings a literate and entertaining approach to dog culture through essays, reviews, interviews and artwork. Our perspective is directed to the sophisticated reader. The point of view is topical, unsentimental, and intelligent. We are smartly designed and stylish." Estab. 1997.

Circ. 75,000. Pays on publication. Publishes ms an average of 6 months after acceptance. Byline given. Offers 20% kill fee. Buys first rights. Editorial lead time 3 months. Submit seasonal material 3 months in advance. Accepts queries by mail. Accepts previously published material. Sample copy for $4.
Nonfiction: Book excerpts, essays, exposé, historical/nostalgic, how-to, humor, interview/profile, new product, opinion, personal experience, travel. Special issues: Upcoming special issues include dogs in the visual arts and dogs in literature. No "death of a dog" pieces. **Buys 10 mss/year.** Query with published clips. Length: 600-1,700 words. **Pays $50-400.**
Photos: State availability with submission. Reviews contact sheets.
Columns/Departments: Health (holistic), 1,000 words; Training (nonaversive), 1,000 words; Behavior, 800 words. **Pays $50-300.**
Fiction: Adventure, humorous, mystery, novel excerpts, slice-of-life vignettes. No religious. **Buys 4 mss/year.** Query. Length: 400-1,200 words.
Poetry: Avant-garde, free verse, haiku, light verse, traditional. **Buys 20 poems/year.**
Fillers: Lee Forgotson, senior editor. Anecdotes, facts, gags to be illustrated by cartoonist, newsbreaks, short humor. **Buys 20/year.** Length: 100-600 words. **Pays $25-150.**
Tips: "Have a true understanding of our editorial vision and have a true appreciation for dogs. Please become familiar with our magazine before submitting."

$ $ CAT FANCY, Cat Care for the Responsible Owner, Fancy Publications, Inc., P.O. Box 6050, Mission Viejo CA 92690. (949)855-8822. Website: www.catfancy.com. **Contact:** Ellyce Rothrock, editor. **90% freelance written.** Monthly magazine covering all aspects of responsible cat ownership. Estab. 1965. Pays on publication. Buys first North American serial rights. Editorial lead time 6 months. Responds in 3 months to queries. Writer's guidelines online.
Nonfiction: Engaging presentation of expert, up-to-date information. Must be cat oriented. Not reviewing fiction at this time. How-to, humor, photo feature, behavior, health, lifestyle. **Buys 70 mss/year.** Query with published clips. Length: 1,000-2,000 words. **Pays $50-450.**
Photos: Seeking photos of happy, healthy, well-groomed cats and kittens in studio or indoor settings. Buys one-time rights. Negotiates payment individually. Captions, identification of subjects, model releases required.
Columns/Departments: Most of our columns are written by regular contributors who are recognized experts in their fields.
Tips: "No fiction or poetry. Please read recent issues to learn the kind of articles we want. Then, show us in your query how you can contribute something new and unique."

CATS USA, Guide to Buying and Caring for Purebred Kittens, Fancy Publications, P.O. Box 6050, Mission Viejo CA 92690. (949)855-8822. **Contact:** Keith Bush, editor. **90% freelance written.** Annual publication for purebred kitten buyers. Estab. 1993. Pays on publication. Buys first North American serial rights. Editorial lead time 6 months. Responds in 3 months to queries. Sample copy not available. Writer's guidelines for #10 SASE.
Nonfiction: Healthcare; training; breed information. **Buys 20 mss/year.** Query with published clips. Length: 1,000-2,000 words. **Pays $50-450.**
Photos: Looking for happy, healthy, well-groomed purebred cats and kittens in studio or indoor settings. Guidelines for #10 SASE. Buys one-time rights. Negotiates payment individually. Captions, identification of subjects, model releases required.
Tips: "No fiction or poetry. Please read a recent issue to learn the kind of articles we want. Then, show us in your query how you can contribute something new and unique."

$ $ ☆ THE CHRONICLE OF THE HORSE, P.O. Box 46, Middleburg VA 20118-0046. (540)687-6341. Fax: (540)687-3937. Website: www.chronofhorse.com. Editor: John Strassburger; Managing Editor: Nancy Comer. **Contact:** Beth Rasin, assistant editor. **80% freelance written.** Weekly magazine covering horses. "We cover English riding sports, including horse showing, grand prix jumping competitions, steeplechase racing, foxhunting, dressage, endurance riding, handicapped riding and combined training. We are the official publication for the national governing bodies of many of the above sports. We feature news, how-to articles on equitation and horse care and interviews with leaders in the various fields." Estab. 1937. Circ. 22,000. Pays for features on acceptance; news and other items on publication. Publishes ms an average of 4 months after acceptance. Byline given. Buys first North American serial rights, makes work-for-hire assignments. Submit seasonal material 3 months in advance. Accepts queries by mail, e-mail. Responds in 10 weeks to queries. Sample copy for $2 and 9×12 SAE. Writer's guidelines for #10 SASE or online.

O→ Break in by "clearing a small news assignment in your area ahead of time."

Nonfiction: General interest, historical/nostalgic (history of breeds, use of horses in other countries and times, art, etc.), how-to (trailer, train, design a course, save money, etc.), humor (centered on living with horses or horse people), interview/profile (of nationally known horsemen or the very unusual), technical (horse care, articles on feeding, injuries, care of foals, shoeing, etc.). Special issues: Steeplechase Racing (January); American Horse in Sport and Grand Prix Jumping (February); Horse Show (March); Intercollegiate (April); Kentucky 4-Star Preview (April); Junior and Pony (April); Dressage (June); Endurance issue (July); Combined Training (August); Hunt Roster (September); Vaulting and Handicapped (November); Stallion (December). No Q&A interviews, clinic reports, Western riding articles, personal experience or wild horses. **Buys 300 mss/year.** Query with or without published clips or send complete ms. Length: 6-7 pages. **Pays $150-250.**
Photos: State availability with submission. Reviews prints or color slides; accepts color for b&w reproduction. Buys one-time rights. Pays $25-30. Identification of subjects required.

Columns/Departments: Dressage, Combined Training, Horse Show, Horse Care, Racing over Fences, Young Entry (about young riders, geared for youth), Horses and Humanities, Hunting, Vaulting, Handicapped Riding, Trail Riding, 300-1,225 words; News of major competitions ("clear assignment with us first"), 1,500 words; Small local competitions, 800 words. Query with or without published clips or send complete ms. **Pays $25-200.**

Fillers: Anecdotes, newsbreaks, short humor, cartoons. **Buys 300/year.** Length: 50-175 words. **Pays $10-20.**

The online magazine carries original content not found in the print edition and includes writer's guidelines. Contact: Melinda Goslin, online editor.

Tips: "Get our guidelines. Our readers are sophisticated, competitive horsemen. Articles need to go beyond common knowledge. Freelancers often attempt too broad or too basic a subject. We welcome well-written news stories on major events, but clear the assignment with us."

$ $ DOG FANCY, Fancy Publications, Inc., P.O. Box 6050, Mission Viejo CA 92690-6050. Fax: (949)855-3045. E-mail: Sbiller@fancypubs.com. Website: www.dogfancy.com. **Contact:** Steven Biller, editor. **95% freelance written.** Monthly magazine for men and women of all ages interested in all phases of dog ownership. Estab. 1970. Circ. 286,000. Pays on publication. Publishes ms an average of 6 months after acceptance. Byline given. Offers negotiable kill fee. Buys first North American serial, nonexclusive electronic and other rights. Submit seasonal material 6 months in advance. Accepts queries by mail. Responds in 2 months to queries. Sample copy for $5.50. Writer's guidelines for #10 SASE.

Nonfiction: Book excerpts, general interest, how-to, humor, inspirational, interview/profile, new product, personal experience, photo feature, travel. "No stories written from a dog's point of view." **Buys 100 mss/year.** Query. Length: 850-1,500 words. **Pays $200-500.**

Photos: State availability with submission. Reviews contact sheets, transparencies, prints. Buys electronic rights. Offers no additional payment for photos accepted with ms.

Columns/Departments: Health and Medicine, 600-700 words; Training and Behavior, 800 words. **Buys 24 mss/year.** Query by mail only. **Pays $300-400.**

The online magazine contains original content not found in the print version. Contact: Mary McHale.

Tips: "We're looking for the unique experience that enhances the dog/owner relationship—with the dog as the focus of the story, not the owner. Medical articles are assigned to veterinarians. Note that we write for a lay audience (nontechnical), but we do assume a certain level of intelligence. Read the magazine before making a pitch. Make sure your query is clear, concise, and relevant."

$ EQUINE JOURNAL, 103 Roxbury St., Keene NH 03431-8801. (603)357-4271. Fax: (603)357-7851. E-mail: editorial@equinejournal.com. Website: www.equinejournal.com. **Contact:** Kathleen Labonville, managing editor. **90% freelance written.** Monthly tabloid covering horses—all breeds, all disciplines. "To educate, entertain and enable amateurs and professionals alike to stay on top of new developments in the field. Covers horse-related activities from all corners of New England, New York, New Jersey, Pennsylvania and the Midwest." Estab. 1988. Circ. 26,000. Pays on publication. Byline given. Buys first North American serial, electronic rights. Editorial lead time 3 months. Submit seasonal material 4 months in advance. Accepts queries by mail, e-mail, fax, phone. Responds in 2 months to queries. Writer's guidelines for #10 SASE.

Nonfiction: General interest, how-to, interview/profile. **Buys 100 mss/year.** Query with published clips or send complete ms. Length: 1,500-3,000 words.

Photos: Send photos with submission. Reviews prints. Pays $10.

Columns/Departments: Horse Health (health-related topics), 1,200-1,500 words. **Buys 12 mss/year.** Query.

Fillers: Short humor. Length: 500-1,000 words. **Pays $40-75.**

$ $ FIELD TRIAL MAGAZINE, Androscoggin Publishing, Inc., P.O. Box 98, Milan NH 03588-0098. (617)449-6767. Fax: (603)449-2462. E-mail: birddog@ncia.net. Website: www.fielddog.com/ftm. **Contact:** Craig Doherty, editor. **75% freelance written.** Quarterly magazine covering field trials for pointing dogs. "Our readers are knowledgeable sports men and women who want interesting and informative articles about their sport." Estab. 1997. Circ. 6,000. Pays on publication. Publishes ms an average of 6 months after acceptance. Byline given. Buys first North American serial rights. Editorial lead time 3 months. Submit seasonal material 6 months in advance. Accepts queries by mail, e-mail, fax. Accepts simultaneous submissions. Responds in 2 weeks to queries; 2 months to mss. Sample copy and writer's guidelines free or online.

Nonfiction: Book excerpts, essays, general interest, historical/nostalgic, how-to, interview/profile, opinion, personal experience. No hunting articles. **Buys 12-16 mss/year.** Query. Length: 1,000-3,000 words. **Pays $100-300.**

Photos: Send photos with submission. Buys one-time rights. Offers no additional payment for photos accepted with ms. Captions, identification of subjects required.

Fiction: Fiction that deals with bird dogs and field trials. **Buys 4 mss/year.** Send complete ms. Length: 1,000-2,500 words. **Pays $100-250.**

Tips: "Make sure you have correct and accurate information—we'll work with a writer who has good solid info even if the writing needs work."

$ THE GREYHOUND REVIEW, P.O. Box 543, Abilene KS 67410-0543. (785)263-4660. Fax: (785)263-4689. E-mail: nga@jc.net. Website: nga.jc.net. Editor: Gary Guccione. **Contact:** Tim Horan, managing editor. **20% freelance**

written. Monthly magazine covering greyhound breeding, training and racing. Estab. 1911. Circ. 4,000. **Pays on acceptance.** Byline given. Buys first rights. Submit seasonal material 2 months in advance. Responds in 2 weeks to queries; 1 month to mss. Sample copy for $3. Writer's guidelines free.
Nonfiction: "Articles must be targeted at the greyhound industry: from hard news, special events at racetracks to the latest medical discoveries." How-to, interview/profile, personal experience. Do not submit gambling systems. **Buys 24 mss/year.** Query. Length: 1,000-10,000 words. **Pays $85-150.**
Reprints: Send photocopy. Pays 100% of amount paid for original article.
Photos: State availability with submission. Reviews 35mm transparencies, 8×10 prints. Buys one-time rights. Pays $10-50 photo. Identification of subjects required.

$ HORSE & COUNTRY CANADA, Equine Publications, Inc., 422 Kitley Line 3, Toledo, Ontario K0E 1Y0, Canada. (613)275-1684. Fax: (613)275-1807. **Contact:** Judith H. McCartney, editor. **40% freelance written.** Bimonthly magazine covering equestrian issues. "A celebration of equestrian sport and the country way of life." Estab. 1994. Circ. 14,000. Pays on publication. Publishes ms an average of 3 months after acceptance. Byline sometimes given. Buys one-time rights. Accepts queries by mail.
Nonfiction: Book excerpts, historical/nostalgic, how-to, inspirational, new product, travel. Query with published clips. Length: 1,200-1,700 words. **Pays $25-150 for assigned articles; $25-100 for unsolicited articles.** Sometimes pays expenses of writers on assignment.
Photos: Send photos with submission. Reviews prints. Buys one-time rights. Pays $15-125/photo or negotiates payment individually. Captions required.
Columns/Departments: Back to Basics (care for horses); Ask the Experts (how-to with horses); Nutrition (for horses), all 800 words. Query with published clips. **Pays $25-150.**

$ $ $ HORSE & RIDER, The Magazine of Western Riding, Primedia, P.O. Box 4101, 741 Corporate Circle, Suite A, Golden CO 80401. (720)836-1257. Fax: (720)836-1245. E-mail: horse&rider@primediamags.com. Website: www.equisearch.com. **Contact:** René E. Riley, executive editor. **10% freelance written.** Monthly magazine covering Western horse industry, competition, recreation. "*Horse & Rider*'s mission is to educate, inform, and entertain both competitive and recreational riders with tightly focused training articles, practical stable management techniques, hands-on healthcare tips, safe trail-riding practices, well-researched consumer advice and a behind-the-scenes, you-are-there approach to major equine events." Estab. 1961. Circ. 164,000. **Pays on acceptance.** Publishes ms an average of 1 year after acceptance. Byline given. Offers $75 kill fee. Buys first North American serial rights. Editorial lead time 2 months. Submit seasonal material 6 months in advance. Accepts queries by mail. Responds in 3 months to queries; 3 months to mss. Sample copy and writer's guidelines free or on website at www.horseandrider.com.

- Does *not accept* e-mail submissions.

Nonfiction: Book excerpts, general interest, how-to (horse training, horsemanship), humor, interview/profile, new product, personal experience, photo feature, travel, horse health care, trail riding. **Buys 5-10 mss/year.** Send complete ms. Length: 1,000-3,000 words. **Pays $150-1,000.**
Photos: State availability of or send photos with submission. Buys rights on assignment or stock. Negotiates payment individually. Captions, identification of subjects, model releases required.
The online magazine carries original content not found in the print edition. Contact: René E. Riley.
Tips: Writers should have "patience, ability to accept critical editing and extensive knowledge of the Western horse industry and our publication."

$ HORSE CONNECTION, (formerly *Rocky Mountain Horse Connection*)Horse Connection, LLC, 380 Perry St., Suite 210, Castle Rock CO 80104. (303)663-1300. Fax: (303)663-1331. E-mail: hc@horseconnection.com. Website: www.horseconnection.com. **Contact:** Geoff Young, publisher. **90% freelance written.** Monthly magazine covering horse owners and riders. "Our readers are horse owners and riders. They specialize in English riding. We primarily focus on show jumping and hunters, dressage, and three-day events, with additional coverage of driving, polo, and endurance." Estab. 1995. Circ. 25,000. Pays on publication. Publishes ms an average of 1 month after acceptance. Byline given. Buys first, second serial (reprint) rights. Editorial lead time 3 months. Submit seasonal material 3 months in advance. Accepts queries by mail, e-mail. Responds in 1 month to queries. Sample copy for $3.50 or online. Writer's guidelines for #10 SASE or online.
Nonfiction: Humor, interview/profile, personal experience, event reports. No general interest stories about horses. Nothing negative. No western, racing, or breed specific articles. No "my first pony" stories. **Buys 30-50 mss/year.** Query with published clips. Length: 500-1,000 words. **Pays $25 for assigned articles; $75 for unsolicited articles.** Sometimes pays expenses of writers on assignment.
Reprints: Accepts previously published submissions.
Photos: State availability with submission. Buys one-time rights. Negotiates payment individually.
Tips: "Please read the magazine. We are currently focused on the western states and we like stories about English riders from these states."

$ $ HORSE ILLUSTRATED, The Magazine for Responsible Horse Owners, Fancy Publications, Inc., P.O. Box 6050, Mission Viejo CA 92690-6050. (949)855-8822. Fax: (949)855-3045. E-mail: horseillustrated@fancypubs.com. Website: www.horseillustratedmagazine.com. Managing Editor: Karen Keb Acevedo. **Contact:** Moira Harris, editor. **90% freelance written.** Prefers to work with published/established writers but will work with new/unpublished writers. Monthly magazine covering all aspects of horse ownership. "Our readers are adults, mostly women, between the ages of 18 and 40; stories should be geared to that age group and reflect responsible horse care." Estab. 1976. Circ. 208,000. Pays on publication. Publishes ms an average of 8 months after acceptance. Byline given. Buys one-time rights. requires first North American rights among equine publications. Submit seasonal material 6 months in advance. Accepts queries by mail, e-mail. Responds in 3 months to queries. Writer's guidelines for #10 SASE.

Nonfiction: "We are looking for authoritative, in-depth features on trends and issues in the horse industry. Such articles must be queried first with a detailed outline of the article and clips. We rarely have a need for fiction." General interest, historical/nostalgic, how-to (horse care, training, veterinary care), inspirational, photo feature. No "little girl" horse stories, "cowboy and Indian" stories or anything not *directly* relating to horses. **Buys 20 mss/year.** Query or send complete ms. Length: 1,000-2,000 words. **Pays $100-400.**

Photos: Send photos with submission. Reviews 35mm and medium format transparencies, 4×6 prints.

Tips: "Freelancers can break in at this publication with feature articles on Western and English training methods; veterinary and general care how-to articles; and horse sports articles. We rarely use personal experience articles. Submit photos with training and how-to articles whenever possible. We have a very good record of developing new freelancers into regular contributors/columnists. We are always looking for fresh talent, but certainly enjoy working with established writers who 'know the ropes' as well. We are accepting less unsolicited freelance work—much is now assigned and contracted."

$ $ THE HORSE, Your Guide to Equine Health Care, P.O. Box 4680, Lexington KY 40544-4680. (859)276-6771. Fax: (859)276-4450. E-mail: kgraetz@thehorse.com. Website: www.thehorse.com. Managing Editor: Christy West. **Contact:** Kimberly S. Graetz, editor. **75% freelance written.** Monthly magazine covering equine health and care. *The Horse* is an educational/news magazine geared toward the professional, hands-on horse owner. Estab. 1983. Circ. 40,000. **Pays on acceptance.** Publishes ms an average of 2 months after acceptance. Byline given. first world and electronic rights Accepts queries by mail, e-mail. Responds in 3 months to queries. Sample copy for $2.95 or online. Writer's guidelines free.

O→ Break in with short horse health news items.

Nonfiction: How-to, technical, topical interviews. "No first-person experiences not from professionals; this is a technical magazine to inform horse owners." **Buys 90 mss/year.** Query with published clips. Length: 500-5,000 words. **Pays $75-700 for assigned articles.**

Photos: Send photos with submission. Reviews transparencies. $35-350. Captions, identification of subjects required.

Columns/Departments: News Front (news on horse health), 100-500 words; Equinomics (economics of horse ownership); Step by Step (feet and leg care); Nutrition; Back to Basics, all 1,500-2,200 words. **Buys 50 mss/year.** Query with published clips. **Pays $50-400.**

The online magazine carries original content not found in the print edition, mostly news items.

Tips: "We publish reliable horse health information from top industry professionals around the world. Manuscript must be submitted electronically or on disk."

$ I LOVE CATS, I Love Cats Publishing, 16 Meadow Hill Lane, Armonk NY 10504. (908)222-0990. Fax: (908)222-8228. E-mail: yankee@izzy.net. Website: www.iluvcats.com. **Contact:** Lisa Allmendinger, editor. **100% freelance written.** Bimonthly magazine. "*I Love Cats* is a general interest cat magazine for the entire family. It caters to cat lovers of all ages. The stories in the magazine include fiction, nonfiction, how-to, humorous and columns for the cat lover." Estab. 1989. Circ. 100,000. Pays on publication. Publishes ms an average of 1 year after acceptance. Byline given. Must sign copyright consent form. Buys all rights. Editorial lead time 6 months. Submit seasonal material 9 months in advance. Accepts queries by mail, e-mail, phone. Responds in 3 months to queries. Sample copy for $4. Writer's guidelines for #10 SASE, online or by e-mail.

Nonfiction: Essays, general interest, how-to, humor, inspirational, interview/profile, new product, opinion, personal experience, photo feature. No poetry. **Buys 100 mss/year.** Send complete ms. Length: 500-1,500 words. **Pays $50-150, contributor copies or other premiums if requested.** Sometimes pays expenses of writers on assignment.

Photos: Please send copies; art will no longer be returned. Send photos with submission. Buys all rights. Offers no additional payment for photos accepted with ms. Identification of subjects required.

Fiction: Adventure, fantasy, historical, humorous, mainstream, mystery, novel excerpts, slice-of-life vignettes, suspense. "This is a family magazine. No graphic violence, pornography or other inappropriate material. *I Love Cats* is strictly 'G-rated.'" **Buys 100 mss/year.** Send complete ms. Length: 500-1,500 words. **Pays $50-150.**

Fillers: Anecdotes, facts, short humor. **Buys 25/year. Pays $25.**

Tips: "Please keep stories short and concise. Send complete ms with photos, if possible. I buy lots of first-time authors. Nonfiction pieces with color photos are always in short supply. With the exception of the standing columns, the rest of the magazine is open to freelancers. Be witty, humorous or take a different approach to writing."

KITTENS USA, Adopting and Caring for Your Kitten, Fancy Publications, P.O. Box 6050, Mission Viejo CA 92690. (949)855-8822. **Contact:** Keith Bush, editor. **90% freelance written.** Annual publication for kitten buyers. Estab. 1997. Pays on publication. Buys first North American serial rights. Editorial lead time 6 months. Responds in 3 months to queries. Sample copy not available. Writer's guidelines for #10 SASE.

Nonfiction: Healthcare; training; adoption. **Buys 20 mss/year.** Query with published clips. Length: 1,000-2,000 words. **Pays $50-450.**

Photos: Looking for happy, healthy, well-groomed cats and kittens in studio or indoor settings. Guidelines for #10 SASE. Buys one-time rights. Negotiates payment individually. Captions, identification of subjects, model releases required.

Tips: "No fiction or poetry. Please read recent issues to learn the kind of articles we want. Then, show us in your query how you can contribute something new and unique."

$ MINIATURE DONKEY TALK, Miniature Donkey Talk, Inc., 1338 Hughes Shop Rd., Westminster MD 21158-2911. (410)875-0118. Fax: (410)857-9145. E-mail: minidonk@qis.net. Website: www.qis.net/~minidonk/mdt.htm. Bonnie Gross, editor. **65% freelance written.** Bimonthly magazine covering miniature donkeys or donkeys, with articles on healthcare, promotion and management of donkeys for owners, breeders, or donkey lovers. Estab. 1987. Circ. 4,925. **Pays on acceptance.** Publishes ms an average of 4 months after acceptance. Byline given. Buys first, second serial (reprint) rights. Editorial lead time 2 months. Submit seasonal material 3 months in advance. Accepts queries by mail, e-mail, fax. Accepts previously published material. Responds in 2 weeks to queries; 1 month to mss. Sample copy for $5. Writer's guidelines free.

Nonfiction: Book excerpts, humor, interview/profile, personal experience. **Buys 6 mss/year.** Query with published clips. Length: 700-7,000 words. **Pays $25-150.**

Photos: State availability with submission. Reviews 3×5 prints. Buys one-time rights. Offers no additional payment for photos accepted with ms. Identification of subjects required.

Columns/Departments: Humor, 2,000 words; Healthcare, 2,000-5,000 words; Management, 2,000 words. **Buys 50 mss/year.** Query. **Pays $25-100.**

Fiction: Humorous. **Buys 6 mss/year.** Query. Length: 3,000-7,000 words. **Pays $25-100.**

Fillers: Anecdotes, facts, gags to be illustrated by cartoonist, short humor. **Buys 12/year.** Length: 200-2,000 words. **Pays $15-35.**

Tips: "Simply send your manuscript. If on topic and appropriate, good possibility it will be published. We accept the following types of material: 1) Breeder profiles—either of yourself or another breeder. The full address and/or telephone number of the breeder will not appear in the article as this would constitute advertising; 2) Coverage of nonshow events such as fairs, donkey gatherings, holiday events, etc. We do not pay for coverage of an event that you were involved in organizing; 3) Detailed or specific instructional or training material. We're always interested in people's training methods; 4) Relevant, informative equine health pieces. We much prefer they deal specifically with donkeys; however, we will consider articles specifically geared toward horses. If at all possible, substitute the word 'horse' for donkey. We reserve the right to edit, change, delete or add to health articles as we deem appropriate. Please be very careful in the accuracy of advice or treatment and review the material with a veterinarian; 5) Farm management articles; and 6) Fictional stories on donkeys."

$ $ MUSHING, Stellar Communications, Inc., P.O. Box 149, Ester AK 99725-0149. (907)479-0454. Fax: (907)479-3137. E-mail: editor@mushing.com. Website: www.mushing.com. Publisher: Todd Hoener. **Contact:** Erica Keiko Iseri, managing editor. Bimonthly magazine covering all aspects of the growing sports of dogsledding, skijoring, carting, dog packing and weight pulling. "*Mushing* promotes responsible dog care through feature articles and updates on working animal health care, safety, nutrition and training." Estab. 1987. Circ. 6,000. Pays within 60 days of publication. Publishes ms an average of 4 months after acceptance. Byline given. Buys first, second serial (reprint) rights. Submit seasonal material 4 months in advance. Accepts queries by mail, e-mail, fax, phone. Responds in 8 months to queries. Sample copy for $5, $6 US to Canada. Writer's guidelines free (call or e-mail for information) or online.

Nonfiction: "We consider articles on canine health and nutrition, sled dog behavior and training, musher profiles and interviews, equipment how-to's, trail tips, expedition and race accounts, innovations, sled dog history, current issues, personal experiences and humor." Historical/nostalgic, how-to, interview/profile. Special issues: Themes: Iditarod and long-distance racing (January/February); expeditions/peak of race season (March/April); health and nutrition (May/June); musher and dog profiles, summer activities (July/August); equipment, fall training (September/October); races and places (November/December). Query with or without published clips. Considers complete ms with SASE. Length: 1,000-2,500 words. **Pays $50-250.** Sometimes pays expenses of writers on assignment.

Photos: We look for good b&w and quality color for covers and specials. Send photos with submission. Reviews contact sheets, negatives, transparencies, prints. Buys one time and second reprint rights. Pays $20-165/photo. Captions, identification of subjects, model releases required.

Columns/Departments: Length: 500-1,000 words. Query with or without published clips or send complete ms.

Fiction: Considers short, well-written and relevant or timely fiction. Query with or without published clips or send complete ms. **Pay varies.**

Fillers: Anecdotes, facts, newsbreaks, short humor, cartoons, puzzles. Length: 100-250 words. **Pays $20-35.**

Tips: "Read our magazine. Know something about dog-driven, dog-powered sports."

N $ $ PET LIFE, Your Companion Animal magazine, Magnolia Media Group, 3451 Boston Ave., Fort Worth TX 76116. (817)560-6100. Fax: (817)560-6196. E-mail: awilson@mmgweb.com. Website: www.petlifeweb.com. **Contact:** Alexis Wilson, editor. **85% freelance written.** Bimonthly magazine. "*PetLife* is America's premier companion animal magazine featuring stories that highlight the human-animal bond." Estab. 1995. Pays on publication. Publishes ms an average of 2 months after acceptance. Byline given. Buys all rights. Editorial lead time 3 months. Submit seasonal material 6 months in advance. Accepts queries by e-mail. Accepts simultaneous submissions. Responds in 1 month to queries. Sample copy for $3.95 or online. Writer's guidelines by e-mail.

Nonfiction: How-to, humor, inspirational, interview/profile, personal experience, photo feature, technical (book reviews). "We are apolitical—although we will occasionally publish stories on the prevention of animal abuse. We focus on the human-animal bond." **Buys 30 mss/year.** Query with published clips. Length: 200-1,500 words. **Pays $50-400.**

Photos: State availability with submission. Reviews transparencies. Buys all rights. Negotiates payment individually. Identification of subjects required.

Columns/Departments: Celebrity Interviews (well-known stars who are pet owners); DogLife/CatLife (info from the experts); Vet Perspective (info on specific health issues); Odd Pets (pets other than dogs and cats). **Buys 30 mss/year.** Query. **Pays $100-300.**

Fillers: Anecdotes, facts, newsbreaks. **Buys 10/year. Pays $50.**

Tips: "**Be familiar with the magazine**. Be specific—what will the story say, who will you interview, suggest visuals. Be brief in your query. Always send a query—no unsolicited manuscripts accepted."

$ ROCKY MOUNTAIN RIDER MAGAZINE, Regional All-Breed Horse Monthly, P.O. Box 1011, Hamilton MT 59840. (406)363-4085. Fax: (406)363-1056. Website: www.rockymountainrider.com. **Contact:** Natalie Riehl, editor. **90% freelance written.** Monthly magazine "aiming to satisfy the interests of readers who enjoy horses." Estab. 1993. Circ. 14,000. Pays on publication. Publishes ms an average of 6 months after acceptance. Byline given. Buys one-time rights. Submit seasonal material 6 months in advance. Accepts simultaneous submissions. Responds in 1 month to queries; 2 months to mss. Sample copy for free. Writer's guidelines for #10 SASE.

Nonfiction: Book excerpts, essays, general interest, historical/nostalgic, humor, interview/profile, new product, personal experience, photo feature, travel, cowboy poetry. **Buys 100 mss/year.** Send complete ms. Length: 500-2,000 words. **Pays $15-90.**

Photos: Send photos with submission. Reviews 3×5 prints. Buys one-time rights. Pays $5/photo. Captions, identification of subjects required.

Poetry: Light verse, traditional. **Buys 25 poems/year.** Submit maximum 10 poems. Length: 6-36 lines. **Pays $10.**

Fillers: Anecdotes, facts, gags to be illustrated by cartoonist, short humor. Length: 200-750 words. **Pays $15.**

Tips: "*RMR* is looking for positive, human interest stories that appeal to an audience of horsepeople. We accept profiles of unusual people or animals, history, humor, anecdotes, cowboy poetry, coverage of regional events, and new products. We aren't looking for many 'how-to' or training articles, and are not currently looking at any fiction."

N $ $ TROPICAL FISH HOBBYIST MAGAZINE, The World's Most Widely Read Aquarium Monthly, TFH Publications, Inc., One TFH Plaza, Neptune City NJ 07753. (732)988-8400. Fax: (732)988-9635. E-mail: editor@tfh.com. **Contact:** Mary Sweeney, editor. **90% freelance written.** Monthly magazine covering tropical fish. Estab. 1952. Circ. 50,000. **Pays on acceptance.** Byline given. Buys all rights. Editorial lead time 3 months. Submit seasonal material 6 months in advance. Accepts queries by e-mail. Responds immediately on electronic queries to queries. Writer's guidelines by e-mail.

Nonfiction: "We cover any aspect of aquarium science, aquaculture, and the tropical fish hobby. Our readership is diverse—from neophytes to mini reef specialists. We require well-researched, well-written, and factually accurate copy, preferably with photos." **Buys 100-150 mss/year. Pays $100-250.**

Photos: State availability with submission. Reviews 2x2 transparencies. Buys multiple nonexclusive rights. Negotiates payment individually. Identification of subjects, model releases required.

Tips: "With few exceptions, all communication and submission must be electronic. We want factual, interesting, and relevant articles about the aquarium hobby written by people who are obviously knowledgeable. We publish an enormous variety of article types. Review several past issues to get an idea of the scope."

ART & ARCHITECTURE

Listed here are publications about art, art history, specific art forms and architecture written for art patrons, architects, artists, and art enthusiasts. Publications addressing the business and management side of the art industry are listed in the Art, Design & Collectibles category of the Trade section. Trade publications for architecture can be found in Building Interiors, and Construction & Contracting sections.

$ $ THE AMERICAN ART JOURNAL, Kennedy Galleries, Inc., 730 Fifth Ave., New York NY 10019. (212)541-9600. Fax: (212)977-3833. **Contact:** Jayne A. Kuchna, editor-in-chief. Prefers to work with published/established writers; works with a small number of new/unpublished writers each year. Annual magazine covering American art history of the 17th, 18th, 19th and 20th centuries, including painting, sculpture, architecture, photography, cultural history, etc., for people with a serious interest in American art, and who are already knowledgeable about the subject. Readers are scholars, curators, collectors, students of American art, or persons with a strong interest in Americana. Circ. 2,000. **Pays on acceptance.** Publishes ms an average of 6 months after acceptance. Byline given. all rights, but will reassign rights to writers. Responds in 2 months to queries. Sample copy for $18.

Nonfiction: "All articles are about some phase or aspect of American art history. No how-to articles written in a casual or 'folksy' style. Writing style must be formal and serious." Historical. **Buys 10-15 mss/year.** Length: 2,500-8,000 words. **Pays $400-600.**

Photos: Reviews b&w only. Purchased with accompanying ms. Offers no additional payment for photos. Captions required.

Tips: "Articles must be scholarly, thoroughly documented, well-researched, well-written and illustrated. Whenever possible, all manuscripts must be accompanied by b&w photographs which have been integrated into the text by the use of numbers."

$ $ AMERICAN INDIAN ART MAGAZINE, American Indian Art, Inc., 7314 E. Osborn Dr., Scottsdale AZ 85251-6401. (602)994-5445. Fax: (602)945-9533. **Contact:** Roanne P. Goldfein, editorial director. **97% freelance written.** Works with many new/unpublished writers/year. Quarterly magazine covering Native American art, historic and contemporary, including new research on any aspect of Native American art north of the US-Mexico border. Estab. 1975. Circ. 30,000. Pays on publication. Publishes ms an average of 3 months after acceptance. Byline given. Buys first, one-time rights. Responds in 3 weeks to queries; 3 months to mss. Sample copy not available. Writer's guidelines for #10 SASE.

Nonfiction: New research on any aspect of Native American art. No previously published work or personal interviews with artists. **Buys 12-18 mss/year.** Query. Length: 1,000-2,500 words. **Pays $75-300.**

Photos: An article usually requires between 8 and 15 photographs. (Photos should be glossy 8×10 prints; color photos should be transparencies; 35mm slides are acceptable.). Buys one-time rights. Fee schedules and reimbursable expenses are decided upon by the magazine and the author.

Tips: "The magazine is devoted to all aspects of Native American art. Some of our readers are knowledgeable about the field and some know very little. We seek articles that offer something to both groups. Articles reflecting original research are preferred to those summarizing previously published information."

$ $ $ AMERICANSTYLE MAGAZINE, The Rosen Group, 3000 Chestnut Ave., Suite 304, Baltimore MD 21211. (410)889-3093. Fax: (410)243-7089. E-mail: hoped@rosengrp.com. Website: www.americanstyle.com. **Contact:** Hope Daniels, editor. **80% freelance written.** Quarterly magazine covering arts, crafts, travel and interior design. "*AmericanStyle* is a full-color lifestyle publication for people who love art. Our mandate is to nurture collectors with information that will increase their passion for contemporary art and craft and the artists who create it. *AmericanStyle*'s primary audience is contemporary craft collectors and enthusiasts. Readers are college-educated, age 35+, high-income earners with the financial means to collect art and craft, and to travel to national art and craft events in pursuit of their passions." Estab. 1994. Circ. 60,000. Pays on publication. Publishes ms an average of 6 months after acceptance. Buys first North American serial rights. Editorial lead time 9 months. Submit seasonal material 1 year in advance. Accepts queries by mail, e-mail, fax. Sample copy for $3. Writer's guidelines for #10 SASE.

- *AmericanStyle* is especially interested in freelance ideas about arts travel, profiles of contemporary craft collectors, and established studio artists.

Nonfiction: Specialized arts/crafts interests. Length: 300-2,500 words. **Pays $500-800.** Sometimes pays expenses of writers on assignment.

Photos: Send photos with submission. Reviews oversized transparencies, 35mm slides. Negotiates payment individually. Captions required.

Columns/Departments: Portfolio (profiles of emerging artists); Arts Walk; Origins; One On One, all 800-1,200 words. Query with published clips. **Pays $500-700.**

Tips: "This is not a hobby-crafter magazine. Country crafts or home crafting is not our market. We focus on contemporary American craft art, such as ceramics, wood, fiber, glass, metal."

$ $ $ ART & ANTIQUES, TransWorld Publishing, Inc., 2100 Powers Ferry Rd., Atlanta GA 30339. (770)955-5656. Fax: (770)952-0669. Editor: Barbara S. Tapp. **Contact:** Patti Verbanas, managing editor. **90% freelance written.** Magazine published 11 times/year covering fine art and antique collectibles and the people who collect them and/or create them. "*Art & Antiques* is the authoritative source for elegant, sophisticated coverage of the treasures collectors love, the places to discover them, and the unique ways collectors use them to enrich their environments." Circ. 170,000. **Pays on acceptance.** Byline given. Offers 25% kill fee or $250. Buys all rights. Editorial lead time 8 months. Submit seasonal material 8 months in advance. Accepts queries by mail. Responds in 6 weeks to queries; 2 months to mss. Sample copy and writer's guidelines free.

Nonfiction: "We publish one 'interior design with art and antiques' focus feature a month." Essays, interview/profile (especially interested in profiles featuring collectors outside the Northwest and Northern California areas). Special issues: Designing with art & antiques (September and April); Asian art & antiques (February); Contemporary art (December); Latin-American art (October). **Buys 200 mss/year.** Query with or without published clips. Length: 200-1,200 words. **Pays $200-1,200 for assigned articles.** Pays expenses of writers on assignment.

Photos: Scouting shots. Send photos with submission. Reviews contact sheets, transparencies, Prints. Captions, identification of subjects required.

Columns/Departments: Art & Antiques Update (trend coverage and timely news of issues and personalities), 100-350 words; Review (thoughts and criticisms on a variety of worldwide art exhibitions throughout the year), 600-800 words; Value Judgements (experts highlight popular to undiscovered areas of collecting), 600-800 words; Emerging Artists (an artist on the cusp of discovery), 600-800 words; Collecting (profiles fascinating collectors, their collecting passions, and the way they live with their treasures), 800-900 words; Discoveries (collections in lesser-known museums and homes open to the public), 800-900 words; Studio Session (peek into the studio of an artist who is currently hot or is a revered veteran allowing the reader to watch the artist in action), 800-900 words; Then & Now (the best reproductions being created today and the craftspeople behind the work), 800-900 words; World View (major art and antiques news worldwide; visuals preferred but not necessary), 600-800 words; Travelling Collector (hottest art and antiques destinations, dictated by those on editorial calendar; visuals preferred but not necessary), 800-900 words; Essay (first-person piece tackling a topic in a nonacademic way; visuals preferred, but not necessary); Profile (profiles those who are noteworthy and describes their interests and passions; very character-driven and should reveal their personalities), 600-800 words. **Buys 200 mss/year.** Query by mail only with or without published clips. **Pays $200-800.**

Fillers: Facts, newsbreaks. **Buys 22/year.** Length: 150-300 words. **Pays $150-300.**

The online magazine carries original content not found in the print edition, though there is no payment. Contact: Bilen Mestin.

Tips: "Send scouting shots with your queries. We are a visual magazine and no idea will be considered without visuals. We are good about responding to writers in a timely fashion—excessive phone calls are not appreciated, but do check in if you haven't heard from us in 2 months. We like colorful, lively and creative writing. Have fun with your query. Multiple queries in a submission are allowed."

$ ART PAPERS, Atlanta Art Papers, Inc., P.O. Box 5748, Atlanta GA 31107-0748. (404)588-1837. Fax: (404)588-1836. E-mail: info@artpaper.org. **Contact:** Michael Pittari, editor. **95% freelance written.** Bimonthly magazine covering contemporary art and artists. "*Art Papers*, about regional and national contemporary art and artists, features a variety of perspectives on current art concerns. Each issue presents topical articles, interviews, reviews from across the US, and an extensive and informative artists' classified listings section. Our writers and the artists they cover represent the scope and diversity of the country's art scene." Estab. 1977. Circ. 12,000. Pays on publication. Publishes ms an average of 3 months after acceptance. Byline given. Not copyrighted. Buys all rights. Editorial lead time 2 months. Submit seasonal material 2 months in advance. Sample copy not available.

Nonfiction: Feature articles and reviews. **Buys 240 mss/year. Pays $40-100; unsolicited articles are on spec.**

Photos: Send photos with submission. Reviews color slides, b&w prints. Offers no additional payment for photos accepted with ms. Identification of subjects required.

Columns/Departments: Current art concerns and news. **Buys 8-10 mss/year.** Query. **Pays $30-100.**

$ $ ART SPIRIT!, Art Spirit! Inc., P.O. Box 460669, Fort Lauderdale FL 33346. (954)763-3338. Fax: (954)763-4481. E-mail: sfbiz@mindspring.com. **Contact:** Sherry Friedlander, editor. **90% freelance written.** Magazine published 3 times/year. "Art Spirit! covers music, art, drama, dance, special events." Estab. 1998. Circ. 20,000. Pays on publication. Publishes ms an average of 10 weeks after acceptance. Byline given. Buys first North American serial rights. Editorial lead time 3 months. Accepts queries by mail, e-mail, fax, phone. Accepts previously published material. Responds in 2 weeks to queries. Sample copy by e-mail. Writer's guidelines free.

Nonfiction: "Must be about arts." Interview/profile, photo feature. Length: 650-1,500 words. **Pays $100-200.**

Photos: State availability of or send photos with submission.

Tips: "Information should interest the arts group."

$ ART TIMES, A Literary Journal and Resource for All the Arts, P.O. Box 730, Mount Marion NY 12456-0730. (914)246-6944. Fax: (914)246-6944. E-mail: arttimes@ulster.net. Website: www.ulster.net/~arttimes. **Contact:** Raymond J. Steiner, editor. **10% freelance written.** Monthly tabloid covering the arts (visual, theater, dance, etc.). "*Art Times* covers the art fields and is distributed in locations most frequented by those enjoying the arts. Our copies are distributed throughout upstate New York counties as well as in most of the galleries of Soho, 57th Street and Madison Avenue in the metropolitan area; locations include theaters, galleries, museums, cultural centers and the like. Our readers are mostly over 40, affluent, art-conscious and sophisticated. Subscribers are located across U.S. and abroad (Italy, France, Germany, Greece, Russia, etc.)." Estab. 1984. Circ. 24,000. Pays on publication. Publishes ms an average of 4 years after acceptance. Byline given. Buys first rights. Submit seasonal material 8 months in advance. Accepts simultaneous submissions. Responds in 3 months to queries; 6 months to mss. Sample copy for 9×12 SAE and 6 first-class stamps. Writer's guidelines for #10 SASE or on website.

Fiction: Raymond J. Steiner, fiction editor. "We're looking for short fiction that aspires to be literary. No excessive violence, sexist, off-beat, erotic, sports, or juvenile fiction." **Buys 8-10 mss/year.** Send complete ms. Length: 1,500 words maximum. **Pays $25 maximum (honorarium) and 1 year's free subscription.**

Poetry: "We prefer well-crafted 'literary' poems. No excessively sentimental poetry." Raymond J. Steiner, poetry editor. Avant-garde, free verse, haiku, light verse, traditional, poet's niche. **Buys 30-35 poems/year.** Submit maximum 6 poems. Length: 20 lines maximum. **Offers contributor copies and 1 year's free subscription.**

Tips: "Be advised that we are presently on an approximate 4-year lead for short stories, 2-year lead for poetry. We are now receiving 300-400 poems and 40-50 short stories per month. We only publish 2-3 poems and 1 story each issue. Be familiar with *Art Times* and its special audience. *Art Times* has literary leanings with articles written by a staff of scholars knowledgeable in their respective fields. Although an 'arts' publication, we observe no restrictions (other than noted) in accepting fiction/poetry other than a concern for quality writing—subjects can cover anything and not specifically arts."

N $ $ $ ART-TALK, Box 8508, Scottsdale AZ 85252. (480)948-1799. Fax: (480)994-9284. Editor: Bill Macomber. **Contact:** Thom Romeo. **30% freelance written.** Published 9 times/year Newspaper covering fine art. "Art-Talk deals strictly with fine art, the emphasis being on the Southwest. National and international news is also covered. All editorial is of current interest/activities and written for the art collector." Estab. 1981. Circ. 42,000. **Pays on acceptance.** Publishes ms an average of 2 months after acceptance. Byline given. Buys first North American serial rights, makes work-for-hire assignments. Editorial lead time 3 months. Submit seasonal material 4 months in advance. Accepts simultaneous submissions. Responds in 2 weeks to queries; 1 month to mss. Sample copy for free.

Nonfiction: Exposé, general interest, humor, interview/profile, opinion, personal experience, photo feature. No articles on non-professional artists (e.g., Sunday Painters) or about a single commercial art gallery. **Buys 12-15 mss/year.** Length: 500-4,000 words. **Pays $75-800 for assigned articles; $50-750 for unsolicited articles.** Sometimes pays expenses of writers on assignment.

Photos: State availability with submission. Reviews transparencies, Prints. Buys one-time rights. Offers no additional payment for photos accepted with ms. Captions, identification of subjects required.
Columns/Departments: Maintains 9 freelance columnists in different cities. **Buys 38 mss/year.** Query with published clips. **Pays $100-175.**
Tips: "Good working knowledge of the art gallery/auction/artist interconnections. Should be a part of the 'art scene' in an area known for art."

N **$ARTICHOKE, Writings About the Visual Arts**, Artichoke Publishing, 208-901 Jervis St., Vancouver, British Columbia V6E 2B6, Canada. Fax: (604)683-1941. E-mail: editor@artichoke.ca. Website: www.artichoke.ca. **Contact:** Paula Gustafson, editor. **90% freelance written.** Triannual magazine. "*Artichoke* is Western Canada's visual arts magazine. Writers must be familiar with Canadian art and artists." Estab. 1989. Circ. 1,500. **Pays on acceptance.** Publishes ms an average of 6 months after acceptance. Byline given. Offers 50% kill fee. Buys one-time rights. Editorial lead time 6 months. Accepts queries by mail, e-mail, fax. Accepts simultaneous submissions. Responds in 1 week to queries; 2 weeks to mss. Sample copy and writer's guidelines free.
Nonfiction: Essays, interview/profile, opinion, critical reviews about Canadian visual art. "*Artichoke* does not publish fiction, poetry or academic jargon." **Buys 100 mss/year.** Query with or without published clips or send complete ms. Length: 1,000-2,500 words. **Pays $125.**
Photos: State availability of or send photos with submission. Reviews transparencies, prints. Buys one-time rights. Offers no additional payment for photos accepted with ms. Captions, identification of subjects required.

$ $ THE ARTIST'S MAGAZINE, F&W Publications, Inc., 4700 E. Galbraith Rd., Cincinnati OH 45236. (513)531-2690, ext. 1467. E-mail: tamedit@fwpubs.com. Website: www.artistsmagazine.com. Editor: Sandra Carpenter. **Contact:** Senior Editor. **80% freelance written.** Works with a large number of new/unpublished writers each year. Monthly magazine covering primarily two-dimensional art instruction for working artists. "Ours is a highly visual approach to teaching the serious amateur artist techniques that will help him improve his skills and market his work. The style should be crisp and immediately engaging." Circ. 200,000. Pays on publication. Publishes ms an average of 6 months after acceptance. Bionote given for feature material. Offers 25% kill fee. Buys first North American serial, second serial (reprint) rights. Responds in 3 months to queries. Sample copy for $4.50. Writer's guidelines for #10 SASE or online.

- Writers must have working knowledge of art techniques. This magazine's most consistent need is for instructional feature articles written in the artist's voice.

Nonfiction: "The emphasis must be on how the reader can learn some method of improving his artwork; or the marketing of it." Instructional only—how an artist uses a particular technique, how he handles a particular subject or medium, or how he markets his work. No unillustrated articles; no seasonal material; no travel articles; no profiles. **Buys 60 mss/year.** Length: 1,200-1,800 words. **Pays $200-350 and up.** Sometimes pays expenses of writers on assignment.
Photos: "Transparencies—in 4×5 or 35mm slide format—are required with every accepted article since these are essential for our instructional format. Full captions must accompany these." Buys one-time rights.
Tips: "Look at several current issues and read the author's guidelines carefully. Submissions must include artwork. Remember that our readers are fine artists and illustrators."

$ $ARTNEWS, ABC, 48 W. 38th St., New York NY 10018. (212)398-1690. Fax: (212)768-4002. E-mail: info@artnewsonline.com. Website: www.artnewsonline.com. **Contact:** Robin Cembalest, executive editor. Monthly "*Artnews* reports on art, personalities, issues, trends and events that shape the international art world. Investigative features focus on art ranging from old masters to contemporary, including painting, sculpture, prints and photography. Regular columns offer exhibition and book reviews, travel destinations, investment and appreciation advice, design insights and updates on major art world figures." Estab. 1902. Circ. 82,911. Accepts queries by mail, e-mail, fax, phone. Sample copy not available.

AZURE DESIGN, ARCHITECTURE AND ART, 20 Maud St., Suite 200, Toronto, Ontario M5V 2M5, Canada. (416)203-9674. Fax: (416)203-9842. E-mail: azure@azureonline.com. Website: www.azureonline.com. **Contact:** Nelda Rodger, editor. **50% freelance written.** Magazine covering design and architecture. Estab. 1985. Circ. 20,000. Pays on publication. Publishes ms an average of 1 month after acceptance. Offers variable kill fee. Buys first rights. Editorial lead time up to 45 days. Responds in 6 weeks to queries. Sample copy not available.
Nonfiction: Buys 25-30 mss/year. Length: 350-2,000 words. **Payment varies.**
Columns/Departments: RearView (essay/photo on something from a building environment); and Forms & Functions (coming exhibitions, happenings in world of design), both 300-350 words. **Buys 30 mss/year.** Query. **Payment varies.**
Tips: "Try to understand what the magazine is about. Writers must be well-versed in the field of architecture and design. It's very unusual to get something from someone I haven't worked quite closely with and gotten a sense of who the writer is. The best way to introduce yourself is by sending clips or writing samples and describing what your background is in the field."

$ $ C, international contemporary art, C The Visual Arts Foundation, P.O. Box 5, Station B, Toronto, Ontario M5T 2T2, Canada. (416)539-9495. Fax: (416)539-9903. E-mail: cmag@istar.ca. Website: www.cmagazine.com. **Contact:** Eileen Sommerman, editor. **80% freelance written.** Quarterly magazine covering international contemporary art. "*C* provides a vital and vibrant forum for the presentation of contemporary art and the discussion of issues surrounding art in our culture, including feature articles, reviews and reports, as well as original artists' projects." Estab. 1983.

Circ. 7,000. Pays on publication. Publishes ms an average of 4 months after acceptance. Byline given. Offers kill fee. Editorial lead time 3 months. Accepts queries by mail, e-mail, fax. Accepts simultaneous submissions. Responds in 6 weeks to queries; 4 months to mss. Sample copy for $10 (US). Writer's guidelines for #10 SASE.

Nonfiction: Essays, general interest, opinion, personal experience. **Buys 50 mss/year.** Length: 1,000-3,000 words. **Pays $150-500 (Canadian), $105-350 (US).**

Photos: State availability of or send photos with submission. Reviews 35mm transparencies or 8×10 prints. Buys one-time rights; shared copyright on reprints. Offers no additional payment for photos accepted with ms. Captions required.

Columns/Departments: Reviews (review of art exhibitions), 500 words. **Buys 30 mss/year.** Query. **Pays $125 (Canadian).**

N $ $ DIRECT ART MAGAZINE, Slow Art Productions, 870 Sixth Ave., New York NY 10001. (212)725-0999. E-mail: slowart@aol.com. Website: www.slowart.com. **Contact:** Paul Winslow, editor. **75% freelance written.** Semiannual fine art magazine covering alternative, anti-establishment, left-leaning fine art. Estab. 1998. Circ. 10,000. **Pays on acceptance.** Byline sometimes given. Buys one-time, electronic rights. Editorial lead time 2 months. Submit seasonal material 3 months in advance. Accepts queries by mail, e-mail. Accepts simultaneous submissions. Responds in 2 weeks to queries; 1 month to mss. Sample copy for 9×12 SAE and 10 first-class stamps. Writer's guidelines for #10 SASE.

Nonfiction: T.P. Lowens, managing editor. Essays, exposé, historical/nostalgic, how-to, humor, inspirational, interview/profile, opinion, personal experience, photo feature, technical. **Buys 4-6 mss/year.** Query with published clips. Length: 1,000-3,000 words. **Pays $100-500.**

Reprints: Accepts previously published submissions.

Photos: State availability of or send photos with submission. Reviews 35mm slide transparencies, digital files on CD (TIF format). Buys one-time rights. Negotiates payment individually.

Columns/Departments: Query with published clips. **Pays $100-500.**

N $ $ ☒ FUSE MAGAZINE, A magazine about issues of art & culture, ARTONS Publishing, 401 Richmond St. W., #454, Toronto Ontario M5V 3A8, Canada. (416)340-8026. Fax: (416)340-0494. E-mail: fuse@interlog.com. Website: www.fusemagazine.org. **Contact:** Michael Maranda, managing editor. **100% freelance written.** Quarterly magazine covering art and art criticism; analysis of cultural and political events as they impact on art production and exhibition. Estab. 1976. Circ. 3,000. Pays on publication. Publishes ms an average of 6 months after acceptance. Byline given. Offers 50% kill fee for commissioned pieces only. Buys first North American serial rights. Editorial lead time 4 months. Submit seasonal material 2 months in advance. Accepts queries by mail. Accepts simultaneous submissions. Sample copy for $5 (US funds if outside Canada). Writer's guidelines online.

Nonfiction: Essays, interview/profile, opinion, art reviews. **Buys 50 mss/year.** Length: 800-6,000 words. **Pays 10¢/word; $100 for reviews (Canadian funds).**

Photos: State availability with submission. Reviews 5×7 prints. Offers no additional payment for photos accepted with ms. Captions required.

Columns/Departments: Buys 10 mss/year. Pays 10¢/word.

Tips: Send detailed, but not lengthy, proposals with writing samples or completed manuscripts for review by the editorial board.

$ $ ☒ L.A. ARCHITECT, The Magazine of Design in Southern California, Balcony Press, 512 E. Wilson, Glendale CA 91206. (818)956-5313. Fax: (818)956-5904. E-mail: laura@balconypress.com. Website: www.laarch.com. **Contact:** Laura Hall, editor. **80% freelance written.** Bimonthly magazine covering architecture, interiors, landscape and other design disciplines. "*L.A. Architect* is interested in architecture, interiors, product, graphics and landscape design as well as news about the arts. We encourage designers to keep us informed on projects, techniques, and products that are innovative, new, or nationally newsworthy. We are especially interested in new and renovated projects that illustrate a high degree of design integrity and unique answers to typical problems in the urban cultural and physical environment." Estab. 1999. Circ. 20,000. Pays on publication. Publishes ms an average of 3 months after acceptance. Byline given. Makes work-for-hire assignments. Editorial lead time 4 months. Submit seasonal material 4 months in advance. Accepts queries by mail, e-mail, fax. Responds in 1 month to queries; 1 month to mss. Sample copy for $3. Writer's guidelines for #10 SASE or on website.

Nonfiction: Book excerpts, essays, historical/nostalgic, interview/profile, new product. "No technical; foo-foo interiors; non-Southern California subjects." **Buys 20 mss/year.** Length: 500-2,000 words. **Payment negotiable.**

Photos: State availability with submission. Buys one-time rights. Offers no additional payment for photos accepted with ms. Captions, identification of subjects, model releases required.

Tips: "Our magazine focuses on contemporary and cutting-edge work either happening in Southern California or designed by a Southern California designer. We like to find little-known talent which has not been widely published. We are not like *Architectural Digest* in flavor so avoid highly decorative subjects. Each project, product, or event should be accompanied by a story proposal or brief description and select images. Do not send original art without our written request; we make every effort to return materials we are unable to use, but this is sometimes difficult and we must make advance arrangements for original art."

$ $ THE MAGAZINE ANTIQUES, Brant Publications, 575 Broadway, New York NY 10012. (212)941-2800. Fax: (212)941-2819. **Contact:** Allison Ledes, editor. **75% freelance written.** Monthly "Articles should present new information in a scholarly format (with footnotes) on the fine and decorative arts, architecture, historic preservation and landscape architecture." Estab. 1922. Circ. 65,835. Pays on publication. Publishes ms an average of 6 months after acceptance. Byline given. Buys all rights. Editorial lead time 6 months. Submit seasonal material 6 months in advance. Responds in 3 weeks to queries; 6 months to mss. Sample copy for $10.50.

Nonfiction: Historical/nostalgic, scholarly. **Buys 50 mss/year.** Length: 2,850-3,000 words. **Pays $250-500.** Sometimes pays expenses of writers on assignment.

Photos: State availability with submission. Reviews contact sheets, negatives, transparencies, prints. Buys one-time rights. Captions, identification of subjects required.

$ $ $ $ METROPOLIS, The Magazine of Architecture and Design, Bellerophon Publications, 61 W. 23rd St., New York NY 10010. (212)627-9977. Fax: (212)627-9988. E-mail: edit@metropolismag.com. Website: www.metropolismag.com. Executive Editor: Martin Pedersen. **Contact:** Julien Devereux, managing editor. **80% freelance written.** Monthly magazine (combined issues February/March and August/September) for consumers interested in architecture and design. Estab. 1981. Circ. 45,000. Pays 60-90 days after acceptance. Publishes ms an average of 3 months after acceptance. Byline given. Makes work-for-hire assignments. Submit seasonal material 3 months in advance. Accepts queries by mail, e-mail, fax. Responds in 8 months to queries. Sample copy for $7.

Nonfiction: Martin Pedersen, executive editor. Essays (design, architecture, urban planning issues and ideas), interview/profile (of multi-disciplinary designers/architects). No profiles on individual architectural practices, information from public relations firms, or fine arts. **Buys 30 mss/year.** Length: 1,500-4,000 words. **Pays $1,500-4,000.**

Photos: Reviews contact sheets, 35mm or 4×5 transparencies, 8×10 b&w prints. Buys one-time rights. Payment offered for certain photos. Captions required.

Columns/Departments: The Metropolis Observed (architecture, design, and city planning news features), 100-1,200 words, **pays $100-1,200**; Perspective (opinion or personal observation of architecture and design), 1,200 words, **pays $1,200**; Enterprise (the business/development of architecture and design), 1,500 words, **pays $1,500**; In Review (architecture and book review essays), 1,500 words, **pays $1,500**. Direct queries to Julien Devereux, managing editor. **Buys 40 mss/year.** Query with published clips.

Tips: "Metropolis strives to tell the story of design to a lay person with an interest in the built environment, while keeping the professional designer engaged. The magazine examines the various design disciplines (architecture, interior design, product design, graphic design, planning, and preservation) and their social/cultural context. We're looking for the new, the obscure, or the wonderful. Also, be patient and don't expect an immediate answer after submission of query."

$ $ THE MODERNISM MAGAZINE, 333 N. Main St., Lambertville NJ 08530. (609)397-4104. Fax: (609)397-9377. E-mail: cgreenberg@ragoarts.com. Website: www.ragoarts.com/modmag/modmag.html. Editor: David Rago. **Contact:** Cara Greenberg, managing editor. **80% freelance written.** Quarterly magazine covering 20th century art and design. "We are interested in objects and the people who created them. Our coverage begins in the 1920s with Art Deco and related movements, and ends with 1980s Post-Modernism, leaving contemporary design to other magazines. Our emphasis is on the decorative arts—furniture, pottery, glass, textiles, metalwork and so on—but we're moving toward more coverage of painting and sculpture." Estab. 1998. Circ. 20,000. Pays on publication. Publishes ms an average of 4 months after acceptance. Byline given. Offers 25% kill fee. Buys all rights. Editorial lead time 9 months. Submit seasonal material 9 months in advance. Accepts queries by mail, e-mail, fax. Accepts previously published material. Accepts simultaneous submissions. Responds in 1 month to queries. Sample copy for $6.95. Writer's guidelines free.

Nonfiction: Book excerpts, essays, historical/nostalgic, interview/profile, new product, photo feature. "No first-person." **Buys 20 mss/year.** Query with published clips. Length: 2,000-2,500 words. **Pays $400 for assigned articles.**

Reprints: Accepts previously published submissions.

Photos: State availability of or send photos with submission. Reviews contact sheets, transparencies, prints. Buys one-time rights. Negotiates payment individually. Captions, identification of subjects required.

Tips: "Articles should be well-researched, carefully reported, and directed at a popular audience with a special interest in the Modernist movement. Please don't assume readers have prior familiarity with your subject; be sure to tell us the who, what, why, when and how of whatever you're discussing."

$ $ SOUTHWEST ART, Sabot Publishing, 5444 Westheimer Rd., Suite 1440, Houston TX 77056. (713)296-7900. Fax: (713)850-1314. E-mail: southwestart@southwestart.com. Website: www.southwestart.com. **Contact:** Editors. **60% freelance written.** Monthly magazine "directed to art collectors interested in artists, market trends and art history of the American West." Estab. 1971. Circ. 60,000. **Pays on acceptance.** Publishes ms an average of 1 year after acceptance. Byline given. Offers $125 kill fee. Not copyrighted. Submit seasonal material 8 months in advance. Accepts queries by mail, e-mail, fax. Responds in 6 months to mss. Writer's guidelines free.

Nonfiction: Book excerpts, interview/profile. No fiction or poetry. **Buys 70 mss/year.** Query with published clips. Length: 1,400-1,600 words. **Pays $600 for assigned articles.**

Photos: "Photographs, color print-outs and videotapes will not be considered." Reviews 35mm, 2°, 4×5 transparencies. Negotiates rights. Captions, identification of subjects required.

Tips: "Research the Southwest art market, send slides or transparencies with queries, send writing samples demonstrating knowledge of the art world."

$ $ U.S. ART, MSP Communications, 220 S. Sixth St., Suite 500, Minneapolis MN 55402. (612)339-7571. Fax: (612)339-5806. E-mail: tmccormick@mspcommunications.com. Publisher: Frank Sisser. **Contact:** Tracy McCormick, editor. **40% freelance written.** Monthly magazine that reflects current events and trends in the originals, original print and reproductions market and educates collectors and the trade about the market's practices and trends. Departments/ columns are staff-written. Distributed primarily through a network of 900 galleries as a free service to their customers. Circ. 50,000. **Pays on acceptance.** Publishes ms an average of 4 months after acceptance. Byline given. Offers 25% kill fee. Buys all rights for a period of 60 days following publication of article Editorial lead time 4 months. Accepts queries by mail, e-mail. Responds in 3 months to queries. Sample copy and writer's guidelines for #10 SASE.

Nonfiction: Two artist profiles per issue; an average of 6 features per issue including roundups of painters whose shared background of geographical region, heritage, or currently popular style illustrates a point; current events and exhibitions; educational topics on buying/selling practices and services available to help collectors purchase various media. **Buys 4 mss/year.** Length: 1,000-2,000 words. **Pays $300-600 for features.**

Photos: Returns material after 2 months. Reviews color transparencies.

Tips: "We are open to writers whose backgrounds are not arts-specific. We generally do not look for art critics but prefer general-assignment reporters who can present factual material with flair in a magazine format. We also are open to opinion pieces from experts (gallery owners, publishers, consultants, show promoters) withing the industry."

$ $ $ WILDLIFE ART, The Art Journal of the Natural World, Pothole Publications, Inc., 1428 E. Cliff Rd., Burnsville MN 55337. E-mail: pbarry@mail.winternet.com. Website: www.wildlifeartmag.com. Editor-in-Chief: Robert Koenke. **Contact:** Beth Mischek, editor. **80% freelance written.** Bimonthly magazine. "*Wildlife Art* is the world's largest wildlife art magazine. Features cover interviews on living artists as well as wildlife art masters, illustrators and conservation organizations. Special emphasis on landscape and plein-air paintings. Audience is publishers, collectors, galleries, museums, show promoters worldwide." Estab. 1982. Circ. 50,000. **Pays on acceptance.** Publishes ms an average of 6 months after acceptance. Byline given. Offers negotiable kill fee. Buys second serial (reprint) rights. Accepts queries by mail, phone. Responds in 6 months to queries. Sample copy for 9×12 SAE and 10 first-class stamps. Writer's guidelines for #10 SASE.

Nonfiction: General interest, historical/nostalgic, interview/profile. **Buys 40 mss/year.** Query with published clips, include artwork samples. Length: 800-5,000 words. **Pays $150-900.**

Columns/Departments: Buys 6 mss/year. Pays $100-300.

Tips: Best way to break in is to offer concrete story ideas; new talent; a new unique twist of artistic excellence.

ASSOCIATIONS

Association publications allow writers to write for national audiences while covering local stories. If your town has a Kiwanis, Lions, or Rotary Club chapter, one of its projects might merit a story in the club's magazine. If you are a member of the organization, find out before you write an article if the publication pays members for stories; some associations do not. In addition, some association publications gather their own club information and rely on freelancers solely for outside features. Be sure to find out what these policies are before you submit a manuscript. Club-financed magazines that carry material not directly related to the group's activities are classified by their subject matter in the Consumer and Trade sections.

$ AMERICA@WORK, AFL-CIO, 815 16th St. NW, Washington DC 20006. Fax: (202)508-6908. Website: www.aflcio.org. **Contact:** Tula A. Connell, editor. **10% freelance written.** Monthly magazine covering issues of interest to working families/union members. Estab. 1996. Circ. 160,000. Pays on publication. Publishes ms an average of 3 months after acceptance. Byline given. Buys first North American serial rights. Editorial lead time 2 months. Submit seasonal material 3 months in advance. Accepts queries by mail, fax. Sample copy for $2.50. Writer's guidelines not available.

Nonfiction: Essays, historical/nostalgic, how-to, interview/profile. **Buys 5-6 mss/year.** Query. Length: 600-2,000 words. **Pay varies depending on length.**

Photos: State availability with submission. Buys one-time rights. Identification of subjects, model releases required.

$ $ DAC NEWS, Official Publication of the Detroit Athletic Club, Detroit Athletic Club, 241 Madison Ave., Detroit MI 48226. (313)442-1034. Fax: (313)442-1047. E-mail: kenv@thedac.com. **Contact:** Kenneth Voyles, editor/ publisher. **10% freelance written.** Magazine published 9 times/year. "*DAC News* is the magazine for Detroit Athletic Club members. It covers club news and events, plus general interest features." Estab. 1916. Circ. 4,500. Pays on publication. Publishes ms an average of 3 months after acceptance. Byline given. Buys one-time rights, makes work-for-hire assignments. Editorial lead time 3 months. Submit seasonal material 3 months in advance. Accepts queries by mail, phone. Accepts previously published material. Responds in 1 month to queries. Sample copy for free.

Nonfiction: General interest, historical/nostalgic, photo feature. "No politics or social issues—this is an entertainment magazine. We do not acccept unsolicited mss or queries for travel articles." **Buys 2-3 mss/year.** Length: 1,000-2,000 words. **Pays $100-500.** Sometimes pays expenses of writers on assignment.

Photos: Illustrations only. State availability with submission. Reviews transparencies, 4×6 prints. Buys one-time rights. Negotiates payment individually. Captions, identification of subjects, model releases required.

Tips: "Review our editorial calendar. It tends to repeat from year to year, so a freelancer with a fresh approach to one of these topics will get our attention quickly. It helps if articles have some connection with the DAC, but this is not absolutely necessary. We also welcome articles on Detroit history, Michigan history, or automotive history."

$ $ THE ELKS MAGAZINE, 425 W. Diversey, Chicago IL 60614-6196. (773)755-4740. E-mail: elksmag@elks.org. Website: www.elks.org/elksmag. Editor: Fred D. Oakes. **Contact:** Anna L. Idol, managing editor. **25% freelance written.** Magazine published 10 times/year with basic mission of being the "voice of the Elks." All material concerning the news of the Elks is written in-house. Estab. 1922. Circ. 1,120,000. **Pays on acceptance.** Buys first North American serial rights. Responds in 1 week to queries Responds in 1 month with a yes/no on ms purchase. Sample copy and writer's guidelines for 9×12 SAE with 4 first-class stamps or online.

- Accepts queries by mail, but purchase decision is based on final mss only.

Nonfiction: "We're really interested in seeing manuscripts on business, technology, history, or just intriguing topics, ranging from sports to science." No fiction, politics, religion, controversial issues, travel, first-person, fillers, or verse. **Buys 20-30 mss/year.** Send complete ms. Length: 1,500-2,500 words. **Pays 20¢/word.**

Photos: If possible, please advise where photographs may be found. Photographs taken and submitted by the writer are paid for separately at $25 each.

Tips: "Please try us first. We'll get back to you soon."

$ $ THE KEEPER'S LOG, U.S. Lighthouse Society, 244 Kearny St., San Francisco CA 94108. (415)362-7255. **Contact:** Wayne Wheeler, editor. **20% freelance written.** Quarterly magazine covering lighthouses, lightships and human interest relating to them. "Our audience is national (some foreign members). The magazine carries historical and contemporary information (articles) relating to technical, human interest, history, etc." Estab. 1984. Circ. 11,000. Pays on publication. Publishes ms an average of 6 months after acceptance. Byline given. Buys first rights. Editorial lead time 6 months. Accepts queries by mail. Responds in 1 week to queries. Sample copy for $5. Writer's guidelines for #10 SASE.

Nonfiction: Historical/nostalgic, personal experience, photo feature, technical. Ghost stories need not apply. **Buys 1 mss/year.** Query. Length: 2,500-5,000 words. **Pays $200-400.**

Photos: State availability with submission. Reviews 5×7 prints. Offers no additional payment for photos accepted with ms. Identification of subjects required.

$ $ $ KIWANIS, 3636 Woodview Trace, Indianapolis IN 46268-3196. (317)875-8755. Fax: (317)879-0204. E-mail: cjonak@kiwanis.org. Website: www.kiwanis.org. **Contact:** Chuck Jonak, managing editor. **50% freelance written.** Magazine published 10 times/year for business and professional persons and their families. Estab. 1917. Circ. 240,000. **Pays on acceptance.** Publishes ms an average of 3 months after acceptance. Byline given. Offers 40% kill fee. Buys first rights. Accepts queries by mail, e-mail, fax. Responds in 1 month to queries. Sample copy and writer's guidelines for 9×12 SAE with 5 first class stamps. Writer's guidelines online.

Nonfiction: Articles about social and civic betterment, small-business concerns, children, science, education, religion, family, health, recreation, etc. Emphasis on objectivity, intelligent analysis, and thorough research of contemporary issues. Positive tone preferred. Concise, lively writing, absence of clichés, and impartial presentation of controversy required. When applicable, include information and quotations from international sources. Avoid writing strictly to a US audience. "We have a continuing need for articles that concern helping youth, particularly prenatal through age 5: day care, developmentally appropriate education, early intervention for at-risk children, parent education, safety and health. No fiction, personal essays, profiles, travel pieces, fillers, or verse of any kind. A light or humorous approach is welcomed where the subject is appropriate and all other requirements are observed." **Buys 40 mss/year.** Length: 1,500-2,500 words. **Pays $400-1,500.** Sometimes pays expenses of writers on assignment.

Photos: "We accept photos submitted with manuscripts. Our rate for a manuscript with good photos is higher than for one without." Buys one-time rights. Identification of subjects, model releases required.

Tips: "We will work with any writer who presents a strong feature article idea applicable to our magazine's audience and who will prove he or she knows the craft of writing. First, obtain writer's guidelines and a sample copy. Study for general style and content. When querying, present detailed outline of proposed manuscript's focus and editorial intent. Indicate expert sources to be used, as well as article's tone and length. Present a well-researched, smoothly written manuscript that contains a 'human quality' with the use of anecdotes, practical examples, quotations, etc."

$ $ THE LION, 300 W. 22nd St., Oak Brook IL 60523-8815. (630)571-5466. Fax: (630)571-8890. E-mail: rkleinfe@lionsclubs.org. Website: www.lionsclubs.org. **Contact:** Robert Kleinfelder, senior editor. **35% freelance written.** Works with a small number of new/unpublished writers each year. Monthly magazine covering service club organization for Lions Club members and their families. Estab. 1918. Circ. 520,000. **Pays on acceptance.** Publishes ms an average of 5 months after acceptance. Byline given. Buys all rights. Accepts queries by mail, e-mail, fax, phone. Responds in 1 month to queries. Sample copy and writer's guidelines free.

Nonfiction: Welcomes humor, if sophisticated but clean; no sensationalism. Prefers anecdotes in articles. Photo feature (must be of a Lions Club service project), informational (issues of interest to civic-minded individuals). No travel, biography, or personal experiences. **Buys 40 mss/year.** Length: 500-2,200 words. **Pays $100-750.** Sometimes pays expenses of writers on assignment.

Photos: Purchased with or without accompanying ms or on assignment. "Photos should be at least 5×7 glossies; color prints are preferred. Be sure photos are clear and as candid as possible." Total purchase price for ms includes payment for photos accepted with ms. Captions required.

Tips: "Send detailed description of proposed article. Query first and request writer's guidelines and sample copy. Incomplete details on how the Lions involved actually carried out a project and poor quality photos are the most frequent mistakes made by writers in completing an article assignment for us. No gags, fillers, quizzes, or poems are accepted. We are geared increasingly to an international audience. Writers who travel internationally could query for possible assignments, although only locally related expenses could be paid."

$PERSPECTIVE, Pioneer Clubs, P.O. Box 788, Wheaton IL 60189-0788. (630)876-5735. Fax: (630)293-3053. E-mail: ballenpowell@pioneerclubs.org. Website: www.pioneerclubs.org. **Contact:** Rebecca Allen-Powell, editor. **15% freelance written.** Triannual magazine for "volunteer leaders of clubs for girls and boys age 2-grade 12. Clubs are sponsored by local churches throughout North America." Estab. 1967. Circ. 24,000. **Pays on acceptance.** Publishes ms an average of 6 months after acceptance. Byline given. Buys first North American serial, second serial (reprint), all rights. Submit seasonal material 9 months in advance. Accepts queries by mail, e-mail, fax, phone. Accepts previously published material. Responds in 2 weeks to queries. Sample copy and writer's guidelines for $2.25 and 9×12 SAE with 6 first-class stamps.

- Break in by having "access to a Pioneer Clubs program in a local church and being willing to work on assignment. Almost all our articles are assigned to freelancers or to someone in a local church who runs Pioneer Clubs."

Nonfiction: How-to (relationship skills, leadership skills), inspirational, interview/profile (Christian education leaders, club leaders), personal experience (of club leaders). **Buys 0-2 mss/year.** Length: 800-1,200 words. **Pays $50-120.**
Reprints: Send photocopy of article or typed ms with rights for sale noted and information about when and where the material previously appeared.
Columns/Departments: Storehouse (game, activity, outdoor activity, service project suggestions—all related to club projects for age 2 though grade 12). **Buys 0-2 mss/year.** Send complete ms. **Pays $8-15.**
Tips: "Submit articles directly related to club work, practical in nature, i.e., ideas for leader training in communication, discipline, teaching skills. However, most of our articles are assigned. Writers who have contact with a Pioneer Clubs program in their area and who are interested in working on assignment are welcome to contact us."

$ $PERSPECTIVES IN HEALTH, Pan American Health Organization, 525 23rd St. NW, Washington DC 20037-2895. (202)974-3122. Fax: (202)974-3143. E-mail: eberwind@paho.org. Website: www.paho.org. **Contact:** Donna Eberwine, editor. **80% freelance written.** Semiannual magazine covering public health in the Americas. "*Perspectives in Health*, the popular magazine of the Pan American Health Organization (PAHO), was created in 1996 to serve as a forum on current issues in the area of international public health and human development. PAHO works with the international community, government institutions, nongovernment organizations, universities, community groups and others to strengthen national and local public health systems and to improve the health and well-being of the peoples of the Americas." Estab. 1996. Circ. 10,000. **Pays on acceptance.** Publishes ms an average of 6 months after acceptance. Byline given. Buys first North American serials rights and electronic rights to post articles on the PAHO website. Editorial lead time 2 months. Accepts queries by mail, e-mail, fax, phone. Responds in 3 weeks to queries; 1 month to mss. Sample copy and writer's guidelines free.

- Each issue of *Perspectives in Health* is published in English and Spanish.

Nonfiction: Subject matter: Culturally insightful and scientifically sound articles related to public health and human development issues and programs affecting North America, Latin America and the Caribbean. The story angle should have wide relevancy—i.e., capturing national and international concerns, even if the setting is local—and should be high in human interest content: "public health with a human face." General topics may include (but are not limited to) AIDS and other sexually transmitted diseases, maternal and child health, the environment, food and nutrition, cardiovascular diseases, cancer, mental health, oral health, violence, veterinary health, disaster preparedness, health education and promotion, substance abuse, water and sanitation, and issues related to the health and well-being of women, adolescents, workers, the elderly, and minority groups. Historical pieces on public health "trail blazers" and innovators are also welcome. General interest, historical/nostalgic, interview/profile, opinion, personal experience, photo feature. No highly technical, highly bureaucratic articles. **Buys 12 mss/year.** Query with or without published clips or send complete ms. Length: 1,500-3,000 words. **Pays $250.** Sometimes pays expenses of writers on assignment.
Photos: State availability with submission. Reviews contact sheets, negatives, transparencies, prints. Buys one-time rights. Negotiates payment individually. Captions, identification of subjects, model releases required.
Columns/Departments: Last Word, 750 words. **Buys 2 mss/year.** Query with or without published clips or send complete ms. **Pays $100.**
Tips: "*Perspectives* puts the human face on public health issues and programs. All facts must be documented. Quote people involved with the programs described. Get on-site information—not simply an Internet-research story."

$ $ RECREATION NEWS, Official Publication of the ESM Association of the Capital Region, 7339 D Hanover Pkwy., Greenbelt MD 20770. (301)474-4600. Fax: (301)474-6283. E-mail: editor@recreationnews.com. Website: www.recreationnews.com. **Contact:** Francis X. Orphe, editor. **85% freelance written.** Monthly guide to leisure-time activities for federal and private industry workers covering outdoor recreation, travel, fitness and indoor pasttimes. Estab. 1979. Circ. 104,000. Pays on publication. Publishes ms an average of 8 months after acceptance. Byline given. Buys first, second serial (reprint) rights. Submit seasonal material 10 months in advance. Accepts queries by mail, e-mail, fax, phone. Accepts previously published material. Accepts simultaneous submissions. Responds in 2 months to queries. Sample copy and writer's guidelines for 9×12 SAE with $1.05 in postage.
Nonfiction: Articles Editor. Historical/nostalgic (Washington-related), personal experience (with recreation, life in Washington), travel (mid-Atlantic travel only), sports; hobbies. Special issues: skiing (December). **Buys 45 mss/year.** Query with published clips. Length: 800-2,000 words. **Pays $50-300.**

Reprints: Send tearsheet or typed ms with rights for sale noted and information about when and where the material previously appeared. Pays $50.
Photos: Photo Editor. State availability with submission. Pays $50-125 for transparency; $25. Captions, identification of subjects required.
Tips: "Our writers generally have a few years of professional writing experience and their work runs to the lively and conversational. We like more manuscripts in a wide range of recreational topics, including the off-beat. The areas of our publication most open to freelancers are general articles on travel and sports, both participational and spectator, also historic in the DC area. In general, stories on sites visited need to include info on nearby places of interest and places to stop for lunch, to shop, etc."

$ $ $ THE ROTARIAN, Rotary International, 1560 Sherman Ave., Evanston IL 60201-4818. (847)866-3000. Fax: (847)866-9732. E-mail: rotarian@rotaryintl.org. Website: www.rotary.org. **Contact:** Janice Chambers, managing editor. **40% freelance written.** Monthly magazine for Rotarian business and professional men and women and their families, schools, libraries, hospitals, etc. "Articles should appeal to an international audience and in some way help Rotarians help other people. The organization's rationale is one of hope, encouragement, and belief in the power of individuals talking and working together." Estab. 1911. Circ. 514,565. **Pays on acceptance.** Byline sometimes given. Kill fee negotiable. Buys one-time, all rights. Accepts queries by mail, e-mail. Accepts previously published material. Sample copy for 9×12 SAE with 6 first-class stamps. Writer's guidelines for #10 SASE.
Nonfiction: General interest, humor, inspirational, photo feature, travel, sports, business, environmental. No fiction, religious, or political articles. Query with published clips. Length: about 1,500 words. **Pays negotiable rate.**
Reprints: Send tearsheet, photocopy or typed ms with rights for sale noted and information about when and where the material previously appeared. Negotiates payment.
Photos: State availability with submission. Reviews contact sheets, transparencies. Buys one-time rights.
Columns/Departments: Manager's Memo (business); Database; Health Watch; Earth Diary; Travel Tips, all 650 words. Query.
Tips: "The chief aim of *The Rotarian* is to report Rotary International news. Most of this information comes through Rotary channels and is staff written or edited. The best field for freelance articles is in the general interest category. We prefer queries with a Rotary angle. These stories run the gamut from humor pieces and 'how-to' stories to articles about such significant concerns as business management, technology, world health, and the environment."

$ $ $ SCOUTING, Boy Scouts of America, 1325 W. Walnut Hill Lane, P.O. Box 152079, Irving TX 75015-2079. (972)580-2367. Fax: (972)580-2367. E-mail: 103064.3363@compuserve.com. Website: www.scoutingmagazine.org. Executive Editor: Scott Daniels. **Contact:** Jon C. Halter, editor. **80% freelance written.** Magazine published 6 times/year covering Scouting activities for adult leaders of the Boy Scouts, Cub Scouts and Venturing. Estab. 1913. Circ. 1,000,000. **Pays on acceptance.** Publishes ms an average of 18 months after acceptance. Byline given. Offers 25% kill fee. Buys first North American serial rights. Editorial lead time 1 year. Submit seasonal material 1 year in advance. Accepts queries by mail, fax. Accepts previously published material. Accepts simultaneous submissions. Responds in 1 month to queries; 2 months to mss. Sample copy for $2.50 and 9×12 SAE with 4 first-class stamps or online. Writer's guidelines for #10 SASE or online.

- Break in with "a profile of an outstanding Scout leader who has useful advice for new volunteer leaders (especially good if the situation involves urban Scouting or Scouts with disabilities or other extraordinary roles)."

Nonfiction: Program activities, leadership techniques and styles, profiles, inspirational, occasional general interest for adults (humor, historical, nature, social issues, trends). Inspirational, interview/profile. **Buys 20-30 mss/year.** Query with published clips and SASE. Length: 600-1,200 words. **Pays $750-1,000 for major articles, $300-500 for shorter features.** Pays expenses of writers on assignment.
Reprints: Send photocopy of article and information about when and where the article previously appeared. "First-person accounts of meaningful Scouting experiences (previously published in local newspapers, etc.) are a popular subject."
Photos: State availability with submission. Reviews transparencies, prints. Buys one-time rights. Identification of subjects required.
Columns/Departments: Way It Was (Scouting history), 600-750 words; Family Talk (family—raising kids, etc.), 600-750 words. **Buys 8-12 mss/year.** Query. **Pays $300-500.**
Fillers: "Limited to personal accounts of humorous or inspirational Scouting experiences." Anecdotes, short humor. **Buys 15-25/year.** Length: 50-150 words. **Pays $25 on publication.**

- The online version carries original content not found in the print edition and includes writer's guidelines. Contact: Scott Daniels.

Tips: "*Scouting* magazine articles are mainly about successful program activities conducted by or for Cub Scout packs, Boy Scout troops, and Venturing crews. We also include features on winning leadership techniques and styles, profiles of outstanding individual leaders, and inspirational accounts (usually first person) or Scouting's impact on an individual, either as a youth or while serving as a volunteer adult leader. Because most volunteer Scout leaders are also parents of children of Scout age, *Scouting* is also considered a family magazine. We publish material we feel will help parents in strengthening their families. (Because they often deal with communicating and interacting with young people, many of these features are useful to a reader in both roles as parent and Scout leader)."

$ $ THE TOASTMASTER, Toastmasters International, 23182 Arroyo Vista, Rancho Santo Margarita CA 92688. (949)858-8255. Fax: (949)858-1207. E-mail: pubs@toastmasters.org. Website: www.toastmasters.org. **Contact:** Suzanne Frey, editor; KellyAnn LaCascia, associate editor. **50% freelance written.** Monthly magazine on public speaking, leadership, and club concerns. "This magazine is sent to members of Toastmasters International, a nonprofit educational association of men and women throughout the world who are interested in developing their communication and leadership skills. Members range from novice to professional speakers and from a wide variety of ethnic and cultural backgrounds, as Toastmasters is an international organization." Estab. 1932. Circ. 185,000. **Pays on acceptance.** Publishes ms an average of 1 year after acceptance. Byline given. Buys first, second serial (reprint), all rights. Submit seasonal material 3-4 months in advance. Accepts previously published material. Accepts simultaneous submissions. Responds in 2-3 months to queries; 2-3 months to mss. Sample copy for 9×12 SASE with 4 first-class stamps. Writer's guidelines for #10 SASE, online or by e-mail.

Nonfiction: "Toastmasters members are requested to view their submissions as contributions to the organization. Sometimes asks for book excerpts and reprints without payment, but original contribution from individuals outside Toastmasters will be paid for at stated rates." How-to, humor, interview/profile (well-known speakers and leaders), communications, leadership, language use. **Buys 50 mss/year.** Query by mail or e-mail (e-mail preferred). Length: 1,000-2,500 words. **Pays $250-350.** Sometimes pays expenses of writers on assignment.

Reprints: Send ms with rights for sale noted and information about when and where the material previously appeared. Pays 50-70% of amount paid for an original article.

Tips: "We are looking primarily for 'how-to' articles on subjects from the broad fields of communications and leadership which can be directly applied by our readers in their self-improvement and club programming efforts. Concrete examples are useful. *Avoid sexist or nationalist language and 'Americanisms' such as football examples, etc.*"

$ TRAIL & TIMBERLINE, The Colorado Mountain Club, 710 10th St., Suite 200, Golden CO 80401. (303)279-3080, ext. 105. Fax: (303)279-9690. E-mail: beckwt@cmc.org. Website: www.cmc.org. **Contact:** Tom Beckwith, editor. **80% freelance written.** Bimonthly official publication of the Colorado Mountain Club. "Articles in *Trail & Timberline* conform to the mission statement of the Colorado Mountain Club to unite the energy, interest, and knowledge of lovers of the Colorado mountains, to collect and disseminate information, to stimulate public interest, and to encourage preservation of the mountains of Colorado and the Rocky Mountain region." Estab. 1918. Circ. 10,500. Pays on publication. Publishes ms an average of 2 months after acceptance. Byline given. Buys all rights. Editorial lead time 6 months. Submit seasonal material 6 months in advance. Accepts queries by mail, e-mail. Accepts previously published material. Responds in 1 week to queries; 1 month to mss. Sample copy for $5. Writer's guidelines online.

Nonfiction: Essays, humor, personal experience, photo feature, travel. **Buys 10-15 mss/year.** Query. Length: 500-2,000 words. **Pays $50.**

Photos: Send photos with submission. Reviews contact sheets, 35mm transparencies, 3×5 or larger prints, GIF/JPG files. Buys one-time rights. Offers no additional payment for photos accepted with ms. Captions, identification of subjects, model releases required.

Columns/Departments: Wild Colorado (conservation/public lands issues), 1,000 words; Education (mountain education/natural history), 500-1,000 words. **Buys 6-12 mss/year.** Query. **Pays $50.**

Poetry: Jared Smith, associate editor, poetry. Avant-garde, free verse, traditional. **Buys 6-12 poems/year.**

Tips: "Writers should be familiar with the purposes and ethos of the Colorado Mountain Club before querying. Writer's guidelines are available and should be consulted—particularly for poetry submissions. All submissions must conform to the mission statement of the Colorado Mountain Club."

$ $ VFW MAGAZINE, Veterans of Foreign Wars of the United States, 406 W. 34th St., Kansas City MO 64111. (816)756-3390. Fax: (816)968-1169. E-mail: pbrown@vfw.org. Website: www.vfw.org. **Contact:** Rich Kolb, editor-in-chief. **40% freelance written.** Monthly magazine on veterans' affairs, military history, patriotism, defense, and current events. "*VFW Magazine* goes to its members worldwide, all having served honorably in the armed forces overseas from World War II through Bosnia." Circ. 2,000,000. **Pays on acceptance.** Byline given. Offers 50% kill fee. Buys first rights. Submit seasonal material 6 months in advance. Accepts queries by mail, fax. Responds in 2 months to queries. Sample copy for 9×12 SAE with 5 first-class stamps.

- O‐‐ Break in with "fresh and innovative angles on veterans' rights; stories on little-known exploits in U.S. military history. Will be particularly in the market for Korean War battle accounts during 2001-2003. Upbeat articles about severely disabled veterans who have overcome their disabilities; feel-good patriotism pieces; current events as they relate to defense policy; health and retirement pieces are always welcome."

Nonfiction: Veterans' and defense affairs, recognition of veterans and military service, current foreign policy, American armed forces abroad and international events affecting US national security are in demand. **Buys 25-30 mss/year.** Query with 1-page outline, résumé and published clips. Length: 1,000 words. **Pays up to $500 maximum unless otherwise negotiated.**

Photos: Send photos with submission. Reviews contact sheets, negatives, color (2×2) preferred transparencies, 5×7 or 8×10 b&w prints. Buys first North American rights. Captions, identification of subjects required.

Tips: "Absolute accuracy and quotes from relevant individuals are a must. Bibliographies useful if subject required extensive research and/or is open to dispute. Counsult *The Associated Press Stylebook* for correct grammar and punctuation. Please enclose a 3-sentence biography describing your military service and your military experience in the field in which you are writing. No phone queries."

ASTROLOGY, METAPHYSICAL & NEW AGE

Magazines in this section carry articles ranging from shamanism to extraterrestrial phenomena. The following publications regard astrology, psychic phenomena, metaphysical experiences, and related subjects as sciences or as objects of serious study. Each has an individual personality and approach to these phenomena. If you want to write for these publications, be sure to read them carefully before submitting.

$ $ $ BODY & SOUL, Balanced Living in a Busy World, (formerly *New Age*), New Age Publishing, Inc., 42 Pleasant St., Watertown MA 02472. (617)926-0200. Website: www.newage.com. Editor-in-Chief: Jennifer Cook.; Managing Editor: Elizabeth Phillips. **Contact:** Manuscript Editor. **90% freelance written.** Works with a small number of new/unpublished writers each year. Bimonthly magazine emphasizing "personal fulfillment and social change. The audience we reach is college-educated, social-service/hi-tech oriented, 25-55 years of age, concerned about social values, humanitarianism and balance in personal life." Estab. 1974. Circ. 225,000. **Pays on acceptance.** Publishes ms an average of 4 months after acceptance. Byline sometimes given. Offers 25% kill fee. Buys first North American serial, electronic rights. Editorial lead time 6 months. Submit seasonal material 6 months in advance. Accepts queries by mail. Accepts simultaneous submissions. Responds in 2 months to queries; 2 months to mss. Sample copy for $5 and 9×12 SAE. Writer's guidelines for #10 SASE or on website.

O→ No phone calls. The process of decision making takes time and involves more than one editor. An answer cannot be given over the phone.

Nonfiction: Book excerpts, essays, how-to (travel on business, select a computer, reclaim land, plant a garden), inspirational, interview/profile, new product, personal experience, religious, travel. Special issues: . **Buys 100+ mss/year.** Query with published clips. Length: 100-2,500 words. **Pays 75¢-$1/word.** Pays expenses of writers on assignment.
Reprints: Send tearsheet or photocopy.
Photos: Send photos with submission. Reviews transparencies. Buys one-time rights. Negotiates payment individually. Captions, model releases required.
Columns/Departments: Holistic Health, Food/Nutrition, Spirit, Home, Community, Travel, Life Lessons. 600-1,300 words. **Buys 50 mss/year.** Query with published clips. **Pays 75¢-$1/word.**
Tips: "Submit short, specific news items to the Upfront department. Query first with clips. A query is one to two paragraphs—if you need more space than that to *present* the idea, then you don't have a clear grip on it. The next open area is columns: Reflections often takes first-time contributors. Read the magazine and get a sense of type of writing run in column. In particular we are interested in seeing inspirational, first-person pieces that highlight an engaging idea, experience or issue. We are also looking for new cutting-edge thinking. No e-mail or phone queries, please. Begin with a query, résumé and published clips — we will contact you for the manuscript."

$ $ FATE, Llewellyn Worldwide, Ltd., P.O. Box 460, Lakeville MN 55044. E-mail: fate@fatemag.com. Website: www.fatemag.com. **Contact:** Editor. **70% freelance written.** Estab. 1948. Circ. 65,000. Pays on publication. Byline given. Buys all rights. Responds in 3 months to queries. Sample copy and writer's guidelines for $3 and 9×12 SAE with 5 first-class stamps or online.
Nonfiction: Personal psychic and mystical experiences, 350-500 words. **Pays $25.** Articles on parapsychology, Fortean phenomena, cryptozoology, spiritual healing, flying saucers, new frontiers of science, and mystical aspects of ancient civilizations, 500-3,000 words. Must include complete authenticating details. Prefers interesting accounts of single events rather than roundups. "We very frequently accept manuscripts from new writers; the majority are individual's first-person accounts of their own psychic/mystical/spiritual experiences. We do need to have all details, where, when, why, who and what, included for complete documentation. We ask for a notarized statement attesting to truth of the article." Query. **Pays 10¢/word.**
Photos: Buys slides, prints, or digital photos/illustrations with ms. Pays $10.
Fillers: Fillers are especially welcomed and must be be fully authenticated also, and on similar topics. Length: 50-300 words.
Tips: "We would like more stories about *current* paranormal or unusual events."

N MAGICAL BLEND MAGAZINE, A Primer for the 21st Century, P.O. Box 600, Chico CA 95927. (530)893-9037. Fax: (530)893-9076. E-mail: info@magicalblend.com. Website: www.magicalblend.com. **Contact:** Michael Peter Langevin, editor. **50% freelance written.** Bimonthly magazine covering social and mystical transformation. "*Magical Blend* endorses no one pathway to spiritual growth, but attempts to explore many alternative possibilities to help transform the planet." Estab. 1980. Circ. 100,000. Pays on publication. Publishes ms an average of 2 months after acceptance. Byline given. Accepts queries by mail, e-mail. Responds in 2 months to mss. Sample copy for free. Writer's guidelines for #10 SASE.

O→ Break in by "writing a great article that gives our readers something they can use in their daily lives or obtain 'name' interviews."

Nonfiction: "Articles must reflect our standards; see our magazine." Book excerpts, essays, general interest, inspirational, interview/profile, religious, travel. No poetry or fiction. **Buys 24 mss/year.** Send complete ms. Length: 1,000-5,000 words. **Pays $50-200.**
Photos: State availability with submission. Reviews transparencies. Buys all rights. Negotiates payment individually. Identification of subjects, model releases required.

Fillers: Newsbreaks. **Buys 12-20/year.** Length: 300-450 words. **Pays variable rate.**

$ NEW YORK SPIRIT MAGAZINE, 107 Sterling Place, Brooklyn NY 11217. (800)634-0989. Fax: (718)230-3459. E-mail: office@nyspirit.com. Website: www.nyspirit.com. **Contact:** Paul English, editor. Bimonthly tabloid covering spirituality and personal growth and transformation. "We are a magazine that caters to the holistic health community in New York City." Circ. 50,000. **Pays on acceptance.** Publishes ms an average of 3 months after acceptance. Byline given. Buys first rights. Editorial lead time 1 month. Accepts previously published material. Accepts simultaneous submissions. Responds in 1 month to queries. Sample copy for 8×10 SAE and 10 first-class stamps. Writer's guidelines free.

Nonfiction: Essays, how-to, humor, inspirational, interview/profile, photo feature. **Buys 30 mss/year.** Query with or without published clips. Length: 1,000-3,500 words. **Pays $150 maximum.**

Photos: State availability with submission. Model releases required.

Columns/Departments: Fitness (new ideas in staying fit), 1,500 words. **Pays $150.**

Fiction: Humorous, mainstream, inspirational. **Buys 5 mss/year.** Query with published clips. Length: 1,000-3,500 words. **Pays $150.**

Tips: "Be vivid and descriptive. We are *very* interested in hearing from new writers."

$ PANGAIA, Creating an Earth Wise Spirituality, Blessed Bee, Inc., Box 641, Point Arena CA 95468. (707)882-2052. Fax: (707)882-2793. E-mail: editor@pangaia.com. Website: www.pangaia.com. Editor-in-Chief: Anne Newkirk-Niven. **Contact:** Elizabeth Barrett, managing editor. **100% freelance written.** Quarterly journal of Earth spirituality covering Earth-based religions. "We publish articles pertinent to an Earth-loving readership. Mysticism, science, humor, tools all are described." Estab. 1997. Circ. 5,000. Pays on publication. Publishes ms an average of 6 months after acceptance. Byline given. Buys first North American serial rights. Editorial lead time 3 months. Submit seasonal material 3 months in advance. Accepts queries by mail, e-mail, fax. Responds in 1 month to queries; 1 month to mss. Sample copy for $5. Writer's guidelines for #10 SASE or on website.

Nonfiction: Book excerpts, essays, historical/nostalgic, inspirational, interview/profile, personal experience, photo feature, religious, travel. No material on unrelated topics. **Buys 30 mss/year.** Send complete ms. Length: 1,000-3,500 words. **Pays $10-100.**

Photos: State availability with submission. Reviews Reviews prints. Buys one-time rights. Negotiates payment individually. Captions, identification of subjects required.

Fiction: Adventure, ethnic, fantasy, historical, humorous, religious, science fiction. No grim or abstract stories. **Buys 4 mss/year.** Send complete ms. Length: 1,500-4,000 words. **Pays $25-50.**

Poetry: Buys 2 poems/year. Submit maximum 4 poems. Length:100 lines.

Fillers: Short humor. **Buys 2/year.** Length: 500-700 words. **Pays $10.**

Tips: "Share a spiritual insight that can enlighten others. Back up your facts with citations where relevant, and make those facts sound like the neatest thing since self-lighting charcoal. Explain how to solve a problem; offer a new way to make the world a better place. We would also like to see serious scholarship on nature religion topics, material of interest to intermediate or advanced practicioners, which is both accurate and engaging."

$ SHAMAN'S DRUM, A Journal of Experiential Shamanism, Cross-Cultural Shamanism Network, P.O. Box 270, Williams OR 97544. (541)846-1313. Fax: (541)846-1204. **Contact:** Timothy White, editor. **75% freelance written.** Quarterly educational magazine of cross-cultural shamanism. "*Shaman's Drum* seeks contributions directed toward a general but well-informed audience. Our intent is to expand, challenge, and refine our readers' and our understanding of shamanism in practice. Topics include indigenous medicineway practices, contemporary shamanic healing practices, ecstatic spiritual practices, and contemporary shamanic psychotherapies. Our overall focus is cross-cultural, but our editorial approach is culture-specific—we prefer that authors focus on specific ethnic traditions or personal practices about which they have significant firsthand experience. We are looking for examples of not only how shamanism has transformed individual lives but also practical ways it can help ensure survival of life on the planet. We want material that captures the heart and feeling of shamanism and that can inspire people to direct action and participation, and to explore shamanism in greater depth." Estab. 1985. Circ. 14,000. Publishes ms an average of 6 months after acceptance. Byline given. Buys first North American serial, first rights. Editorial lead time 1 year. Accepts previously published material. Responds in 3 months to queries. Sample copy for $7. Writer's guidelines for #10 SASE.

Nonfiction: Book excerpts, essays, interview/profile (please query), opinion, personal experience, photo feature. No fiction, poetry, or fillers. **Buys 16 mss/year.** Send complete ms. Length: 5,000-8,000 words. **Pays 5-8¢/word, depending on how much we have to edit.**

Reprints: Send ms with rights for sale noted and information about when and where the material previously appeared. Pays 50% of amount paid for an original article.

Photos: Send photos with submission. Reviews contact sheets, transparencies, All size prints. Buys one-time rights. Offers $40-50/photo. Identification of subjects required.

Columns/Departments: Judy Wells, Earth Circles. Timothy White, Reviews. Earth Circles (news format, concerned with issues, events, organizations related to shamanism, indigenous peoples, and caretaking Earth. Relevant clippings also sought. Reviews (in-depth reviews of books about shamanism or closely related subjects such as indigenous lifestyles, ethnobotany, transpersonal healing, and ecstatic spirituality), 500-1,500 words. **Buys 8 mss/year.** Query. **Pays 5¢/word.**

Tips: "All articles must have a clear relationship to shamanism, but may be on topics which have not traditionally been defined as shamanic. We prefer original material that is based on, or illustrated with, first-hand knowledge and personal experience. Articles should be well documented with descriptive examples and pertinent background information. Photographs and illustrations of high quality are always welcome and can help sell articles."

$WHOLE LIFE TIMES, P.O. Box 1187, Malibu CA 90265. (310)317-4200. Fax: (310)317-4206. E-mail: wholelifex@aol.com. Website: www.wholelifetimes.com. **Contact:** Kerri Hikida, associate editor. Monthly tabloid covering the holistic lifestyle. Estab. 1979. Circ. 58,000. Pays within 30-60 days after publication. Byline given. Buys first North American serial rights. Accepts queries by mail, e-mail, fax. Accepts previously published material. Sample copy for $3. Writer's guidelines for #10 SASE.

Nonfiction: Book excerpts, exposé, how-to, inspirational, interview/profile, travel, health, healing, spiritual, food, leading-edge information, relevant celebrity profiles. Special issues: Healing Arts, Food & Nutrition, Spirituality, New Beginnings, Relationships, Longevity, Arts/Cultures Travel, Vitamins and Supplements, Women's Issues, Sexuality, Science & Metaphysics, Environment/Simple Living. **Buys 45 mss/year.** Query with published clips or send complete ms. **Pays 5-10¢/word for feature stories only.**

Reprints: Send ms with rights for sale noted and information about when and where the material previously appeared. Pays 50% of amount paid for an original article.

Columns/Departments: Healing; Parenting; Finance; Food; Personal Growth; Relationships; Humor; Travel; Politics; Sexuality; Spirituality; and Psychology. Length: 750-1,200 words.

Tips: "Queries should show an awareness of current topics of interest in our subject area. We welcome investigative reporting and are happy to see queries that address topics in a political context. We are especially looking for articles on health and nutrition."

AUTOMOTIVE & MOTORCYCLE

Publications in this section detail the maintenance, operation, performance, racing, and judging of automobiles and recreational vehicles. Publications that treat vehicles as means of shelter instead of as a hobby or sport are classified in the Travel, Camping & Trailer category. Journals for service station operators and auto and motorcycle dealers are located in the Trade Auto & Truck section.

$$ AMERICAN IRON MAGAZINE, TAM Communications, Inc., 1010 Summer St., Stamford CT 06905. (203)425-8777. Fax: (203)425-8775. **Contact:** Chris Maida, editor. **60% freelance written.** Family-oriented magazine publishing 13 issues/year covering Harley-Davidson and other US brands with a definite emphasis on Harleys. Circ. 90,000. Pays on publication. Publishes ms an average of 6 months after acceptance. Byline given. Not copyrighted. Responds in 6 months to queries. Sample copy for $10.

Nonfiction: "Clean and nonoffensive. Stories include bike features, touring stories, how-to tech stories with step-by-step photos, historical pieces, events, opinion, and various topics of interest to the people who ride Harley-Davidsons." No fiction. **Buys 60 mss/year. Pays $250 for touring articles with slides to first-time writers.**

Photos: Send SASE for return of photos. Reviews color slides or large transparencies.

Tips: "We're not looking for stories about the top 10 biker bars or do-it-yourself tattoos. We're looking for articles about motorcycling, the people, and the machines. If you understand the Harley mystique and can write well, you've got a good chance of being published."

$AMERICAN MOTORCYCLIST, American Motorcyclist Association, 13515 Yarmouth Dr., Pickerington OH 43147. (614)856-1900. Fax: (614)856-1920. E-mail: gharrison@ama-cycle.org. Website: www.ama-cycle.org. Managing Editor: Bill Wood. **Contact:** Greg Harrison, executive editor. **10% freelance written.** Monthly magazine for "enthusiastic motorcyclists, investing considerable time and money in the sport. We emphasize the motorcyclist, not the vehicle." Estab. 1947. Circ. 260,000. Pays on publication. Byline given. Buys first North American serial rights. Editorial lead time 3 months. Submit seasonal material 4 months in advance. Accepts queries by mail, e-mail. Responds in 5 weeks to queries; 6 weeks to mss. Sample copy for $1.25. Writer's guidelines free.

Nonfiction: Interview/profile (with interesting personalities in the world of motorcycling), personal experience, travel. **Buys 8 mss/year.** Query with or without published clips or send complete ms. Length: 1,000-2,500 words. **Pays minimum $8/published column inch.**

Photos: Send photos with submission. Reviews transparencies, Prints. Buys one-time rights. Pays $50/photo minimum. Captions, identification of subjects required.

Tips: "Our major category of freelance stories concerns motorcycling trips to interesting North American destinations. Prefers stories of a timeless nature."

$ AMERICAN WOMAN ROAD & TRAVEL, 2424 Coolidge Rd., Suite 203, Troy MI 48084. (248)614-0017. Fax: (248)614-8929. E-mail: courtney@awroadandtravel.com. Website: www.awroadandtravel.com. **Contact:** Rachel L. Miller, associate editor. **80% freelance written.** Bimonthly magazine that is automotive/adventure lifestyle and service-oriented for women. Estab. 1988. Pays on publication. Publishes ms an average of 3 months after acceptance.

Byline given. Buys first, second serial (reprint) rights, makes work-for-hire assignments. Submit seasonal material 4 months in advance. Accepts queries by mail, e-mail. Accepts previously published material. Responds in 3 months to queries. Writer's guidelines online.

Nonfiction: How-to, humor, inspirational, interview/profile, new product, photo feature, lifestyle, travel, auto, and business content for upscale professional women. **Buys 30 mss/year.** Send complete ms. Length: 50-1,500 words. **Pay depends on quantity, quality and content. Byline-$100.**

Reprints: Send photocopy and information about when and where the material previously appeared.

Photos: Accepts photos via e-mail saved in JPG or GIF formats saved in Word. Photos must be 3×5 or smaller. Send photos with submission. Reviews contact sheets, Kodachrome 64. Buys all rights. Captions, identification of subjects, model releases required.

Fillers: Anecdotes, facts, gags to be illustrated by cartoonist, newsbreaks, short humor. **Buys 12/year.** Length: 25-100 words. **Pays negotiable rate.**

Tips: "The *AW Road & Travel* reader is typically career and/or family oriented, independent, and adventurous. She demands literate, entertaining, and useful information from a magazine enabling her to make educated buying decisions. It helps if the writer is into cars and trucks. We are a lifestyle type of publication more than a technical magazine. Positive attitudes wanted."

$ $ AUTO RESTORER, Fancy Publications, Inc., P.O. Box 6050, Mission Viejo CA 92690-6050. (949)855-8822, ext. 412. Fax: (949)855-3045. E-mail: tkade@fancypubs.com. **Contact:** Ted Kade, editor. **85% freelance written.** Monthly magazine covering auto restoration. "Our readers own old cars and they work on them. We help our readers by providing as much practical, how-to information as we can about restoration and old cars." Estab. 1989. Pays on publication. Publishes ms an average of 3 months after acceptance. Buys first North American serial, one-time rights. Submit seasonal material 4 months in advance. Accepts queries by mail, e-mail, fax. Responds in 2 months to queries. Sample copy for $5.50. Writer's guidelines free.

Nonfiction: How-to (auto restoration), new product, photo feature, technical, product evaluation. **Buys 60 mss/year.** Query with or without published clips. Length: 200-2,500 words. **Pays $150/published page, including photos and illustrations.**

Photos: Technical drawings that illustrate articles in black ink are welcome. Send photos with submission. Reviews contact sheets, transparencies, 5×7 prints. Offers no additional payment for photos accepted with ms.

Tips: "Query first. Interview the owner of a restored car. Present advice to others on how to do a similar restoration. Seek advice from experts. Go light on history and nonspecific details. Make it something that the magazine regularly uses. Do automotive how-tos."

$ BACKROADS, Motorcycles, Travel & Adventure, Backroads, Inc., P.O. Box 317, Branchville NJ 07826. (973)948-4176. Fax: (973)948-0823. E-mail: editor@backroadsusa.com. Website: www.backroadsusa.com. Managing Editor: Shira Kamil. **Contact:** Brian Rathjen, editor/publisher. **80% freelance written.** Monthly tabloid covering motorcycle touring. "*Backroads* is a motorcycle tour magazine geared toward getting motorcyclists on the road and traveling. We provide interesting destinations, unique roadside attractions and eateries plus Rip & Ride Route Sheets. We cater to all brands. If you really ride, you need *Backroads*." Estab. 1995. Circ. 40,000. Pays on publication. Publishes ms an average of 3 months after acceptance. Byline given. Buys one-time rights. Editorial lead time 1 month. Submit seasonal material 3 months in advance. Accepts queries by mail, e-mail, fax. Accepts previously published material. Responds in 3 weeks to queries. Sample copy for $2. Writer's guidelines free.

Nonfiction: Shira Kamil, editor/publisher. Essays (motorcycle/touring), how-to, humor, new product, opinion, personal experience, technical, travel. "No long diatribes on 'How I got into motorcycles.'" **Buys 2-4 mss/year.** Query. Length: 500-2,500 words. **Pays 5¢/word minimum for assigned articles; 2¢/word minimum for unsolicited articles.** Pays writers contributor copies or other premiums for short pieces.

Photos: Send photos with submission. Reviews contact sheets. Offers no additional payment for photos accepted with ms.

Columns/Departments: We're Outta Here (weekend destinations), 500-750 words; Great All American Diner Run (good eateries with great location), 300-800 words; Thoughts from the Road (personal opinion/insights), 250-500 words; Mysterious America (unique and obscure sights), 300-800 words; Big City Getaway (day trips), 500-750 words. **Buys 20-24 mss/year.** Query. **Pays 2¢/word-$50/article.**

Fiction: Adventure, humorous. **Buys 2-4 mss/year.** Query. Length: 500-1,500 words. **Pays 2-4¢/word.**

Fillers: Facts, newsbreaks. Length: 100-250 words.

Tips: "We prefer destination-oriented articles in a light, layman's format, with photos (negatives or transparencies preferred). Stay away from any name-dropping and first-person references."

$ $ $ $ CAR STEREO REVIEW'S MOBILE ENTERTAINMENT, Technology In Motion, Hachette Filipacchi Magazines, 1633 Broadway, 45th Floor, New York NY 10019. (212)767-6000. Fax: (212)333-2434. E-mail: mobileentertainment@bfmus.com. **Contact:** Mike Mettler, editor-in-chief. **35% freelance written.** Published 6 times/year. "*Mobile Entertainment* is geared toward the mobile-electronics enthusiast, encompassing such things as mobile video, product test reports, installation techniques, new technologies such as MP3 and navigation, and music." Estab. 1987. Circ. 140,000. **Pays on acceptance.** Publishes ms an average of 3 months after acceptance. Byline given. Offers 25% kill fee. Buys first North American serial rights. Editorial lead time 4 months. Accepts queries by mail, e-mail, fax. Responds in 6 weeks to queries; 2 months to mss. Sample copy and writers guidelines free.

Nonfiction: "As we are a highly specialized publication, we won't look at anything non-specific to our audience's needs." How-to (installation techniques), interview/profile, new product, technical. **Buys 10-20 mss/year.** Query with published clips. Length: 200-3,000 words. **Pays $40-5,000 for assigned articles; $40-2,000 for unsolicited articles.** Sometimes pays expenses of writers on assignment.
Photos: State availability with submission. Reviews contact sheets, negatives, transparencies. Buys one-time rights. Negotiates payment individually. Identification of subjects, model releases required.
Tips: "As we are experts in our field, and looked to as being the 'authority,' writers must have some knowledge of electronics, car stereo applications, and theory, especially in relation to the car environment. Our readers are not greenhorns, and expect expert opinions. Be aware of the differences between mobile and portable electronics technology versus home entertainment."

$ $ CC MOTORCYCLE NEWS, Motomag Corp., P.O. Box 808, Nyack NY 10960. (845)353-MOTO. Fax: (845)353-5240. E-mail: info@motorcyclenewsmagazine.cc. Website: www.motorcyclenewsmagazine.cc. **Contact:** Mark Kalan, publisher/editor. **50% freelance written.** Monthly magazine featuring "positive coverage of motorcycling in America—riding, travel, racing and tech." Estab. 1989. Circ. 60,000. Pays on publication. Publishes ms an average of 2 months after acceptance. Byline given. Buys one-time rights. Editorial lead time 3 months. Submit seasonal material 3 months in advance. Accepts previously published material. Accepts simultaneous submissions. Responds in 1 month to queries. Sample copy for $3. Writer's guidelines for #10 SASE.
Nonfiction: Essays, general interest, historical/nostalgic, how-to, humor, inspirational, interview/profile, new product, personal experience, photo feature, technical, travel. Special issues: Daytona Beach Blocktober Fest; Summer touring stories—travel. **Buys 12 mss/year.** Query with published clips. Length: 1,000-2,000 words. **Pays $50-250 for assigned articles; $25-125 for unsolicited articles.** Pays expenses of writers on assignment.
Reprints: Send tearsheet or photocopy. No payment.
Photos: State availability with submission. Reviews contact sheets, transparencies. Buys one-time rights. Negotiates payment individually. Captions, identification of subjects, model releases required.
Columns/Departments: Query with published clips.
Fiction: All fiction must be motorcycle related. Adventure, fantasy, historical, romance, slice-of-life vignettes. Query with published clips. Length: 1,500-2,500 words. **Pays $50-250.**
Poetry: Must be motorcycle related. Avant-garde, free verse, haiku, light verse, traditional. **Buys 6 poems/year.** Submit maximum 12 poems. Length: Length open. **Pays $10-50.**
Fillers: Anecdotes, cartoons. **Buys 12/year.** Length: 100-200 words. **Pays $10-50.**
Tips: "Ride a motorcycle and be able to construct a readable sentence!"

N $ $ CRUISING RIDER MAGAZINE, Running in Style, P.O. Box 1943, Sedona AZ 86336. (520)232-9293. E-mail: joshua@verdenet.com. **Contact:** Joshua Placa, editor. **50% freelance written.** Bimonthly coffee table magazine with national distribution for professional, affluent cruiser-style motorcycle enthusiasts. Crosses all brand lines in coverage. Query for events. Freestyle, technical, off-beat, and humorous or travel (bike included) features. Estab. 1996. Circ. 200,000. Pays on publication. Publishes ms an average of 4 months after acceptance. Byline given. Buys all rights. Editorial lead time 2 months. Submit seasonal material 6 months in advance. Accepts simultaneous submissions. Responds as soon as possible to queries.
Nonfiction: General interest, how-to, humor, interview/profile, new product, personal experience, photo feature, technical, travel. **Buys 20-30 mss/year.** Query with published clips. Length: 500-2,500 words. **Pays $150-750.** Sometimes pays expenses of writers on assignment.
Photos: Send photos with submission. Buys all rights. Negotiates payment individually.
Columns/Departments: Street Scene (industry, insurance, government, and legal news); Fashion (motor clothes/pictorial), 1,000 words; Cruise Control (riding safety), 1,000 words. **Buys some mss/year.** Query with published clips. **Pays $50-300.**
Fillers: Anecdotes, facts, news. Length: 50-200 words. **Pays $50-150.**

$ $ EASYRIDERS MAGAZINE, Paisano Publications, Inc., P.O. Box 3000, Agoura Hills CA 91301. (818)889-8740. E-mail: dnichols@easyriders.net. Website: www.easyriders.net. Editor: Keith R. Ball; Managing Editor: Lisa Pedicini. **Contact:** Cathie Stich, executive assistant. **50% freelance written.** Monthly magazine covering motorcycle events and articles for Harley-Davidson type audience. Estab. 1971. Pays on publication. Byline given. Buys first rights. Editorial lead time 3 months. Submit seasonal material 3 month in advance. Writer's guidelines free.
Nonfiction: Book excerpts, essays, exposé, general interest, historical/nostalgic, how-to, humor, inspirational, interview/profile, new product, opinion, personal experience, photo feature, technical, travel. Query. Length: 1,000-3,000 words. **Pays 25¢/word.** Sometimes pays expenses of writers on assignment.
Photos: Send photos with submission. Buys all rights. Captions, identification of subjects, model releases required.
Fiction: Adventure, erotica, experimental, fantasy, historical, humorous, suspense, western, motorcycle stories.

N $ $ FRICTION ZONE, Your Motorcycle Lifestyle Magazine, P.O. Box 530, Idyllwild CA 92549-0530. (909)659-9500. Fax: (909)659-8182. E-mail: editor@friction-zone.com. Website: www.friction-zone.com. **Contact:** Amy Holland, editor/publisher. **60% freelance written.** Monthly magazine covering motorcycles. Estab. 1999. Circ. 20,000. Pays on publication. Publishes ms an average of 1 month after acceptance. Byline given. Buys first North

American serial rights. Editorial lead time 6 weeks. Submit seasonal material 2 months in advance. Accepts queries by mail, e-mail, fax. Responds in 2 weeks to queries; 1 month to mss. Sample copy for $4.50 or on website. Writer's guidelines online.

Nonfiction: General interest, historical/nostalgic, how-to, humor, inspirational, interview/profile, new product, opinion, photo feature, technical, travel, medical (relating to motorcyclists), book reviews (relating to motorcyclists). Does not accept first-person writing. **Buys 1 mss/year.** Query. Length: 1,000-3,000 words. **Pays 10¢/word up to $300.** Sometimes pays expenses of writers on assignment.

Photos: Send photos with submission. Reviews negatives, slides. Buys one-time rights. Offers $15/published photo. Captions, identification of subjects, model releases required.

Columns/Departments: Health Zone (health issues relating to motorcyclists); Motorcycle Engines 101 (basic motorcycle mechanics); Road Trip (California destination review including hotel, road, restaurant), all 2,000 words. **Buys 60 mss/year.** Query. **Pays 10¢/word up to $300.**

Fiction: Motorcycle related. Query. Length: 2,000-3,000 words. **Pays 10¢/word up to $300.**

Fillers: Anecdotes, facts, gags to be illustrated by cartoonist, newsbreaks, short humor. Length: 2,000-3,000 words. **Pays 10¢/word up to $300.**

Tips: "Query via e-mail to editor@friction-zone.com with sample writing."

N $ $ IN THE WIND, Paisano Publications, P.O. Box 3000, Agoura Hills CA 91376-3000. (818)889-8740. Fax: (818)889-1252. E-mail: kpeterson@easyriders.net. Website: www.easyriders.com. Editor; Kim Peterson. Managing Editor: Lisa Pedicini. **Contact:** Cathie Stich, editorial assistant. **50% freelance written.** Bimonthly magazine. "Aimed at Harley-Davidson motorcycle riders and motorcycling enthusiasts, *In the Wind* is mainly a pictorial-action photos of bikes being ridden, and events, with a monthly travel piece—Travelin' Trails." Estab. 1978. Circ. 90,000. Pays on publication. Publishes ms an average of 9 months after acceptance. Byline given. Buys all rights. Editorial lead time 6 months. Accepts queries by mail, e-mail. Responds in 2 weeks to queries; 2 months to mss. Sample copy not available.

Nonfiction: Photo feature, travel. No long-winded tech articles. **Buys 6 mss/year.** Length: 1,000-2,000 words. **Pays $250-600.** Sometimes pays expenses of writers on assignment.

Photos: Send photos with submission. Reviews transparencies, digital imates, b&w, prints. Buys all rights. Identification of subjects, model releases required.

Columns/Departments: Travelin' Trails (good spots to ride to, places to stay, things to do, history), 1,200 words. **Buys 6 mss/year.** Query,. **Pays $250-600.**

Poetry: Free verse. No poetry with graphic violence or drug use. **Buys 10 poems/year.** Submit maximum 3 poems. Length: 10-100 lines.

Tips: "Know the subject. Looking for submissions from people who ride their own bikes."

$ $ $ MOTOR TREND, Petersen Publishing Co., 6420 Wilshire Blvd., Los Angeles CA 90048. (323)782-2220. Fax: (323)782-2355. E-mail: stonem@primediamag.com. Website: www.motortrend.com. **Contact:** Kevin Smith, editor. **5-10% freelance written.** Only works with published/established writers. Monthly magazine for automotive enthusiasts and general interest consumers. Circ. 1,250,000. Publishes ms an average of 3 months after acceptance. Buys all rights. Accepts queries by mail. Responds in 1 month to queries. Sample copy not available.

Nonfiction: "Automotive and related subjects that have national appeal. Emphasis on domestic and imported cars, road tests, driving impressions, auto classics, auto, travel, racing, and high-performance features for the enthusiast. Packed with facts. Freelancers should confine queries to photo-illustrated exotic drives and other feature material; road tests and related activity are handled inhouse. Fact-filled query suggested for all freelancers."

Photos: Buys photos of prototype cars and assorted automotive matter. Pays $25-500 for transparencies.

Columns/Departments: Car care (query Matt Stone, senior editor).

$ $ OUTLAW BIKER, Outlaw Biker Enterprises, Inc., 5 Marine View Plaza, Suite 207, Hoboken NJ 07030. (201)653-2700. Fax: (201)653-7892. E-mail: editor@outlawbiker.com. Website: www.outlawbiker.com. **Contact:** Chris Miller, editor. **50% freelance written.** Magazine published 6 times/year covering bikers and their lifestyle. "All writers must be insiders of biker lifestyle. Features include coverage of biker events, profiles, and humor." Estab. 1983. Circ. 150,000. Pays on publication. Publishes ms an average of 3 months after acceptance. Byline given. Buys first rights. Editorial lead time 3 months. Submit seasonal material 5 months in advance. Accepts queries by mail, e-mail, fax. Accepts previously published material. Accepts simultaneous submissions. Responds in 2 weeks to queries; 2 months to mss. Sample copy for $5.98. Writer's guidelines for #10 SASE.

Nonfiction: Historical/nostalgic, humor, new product, personal experience, photo feature, travel. Special issues: Daytona Special, Sturgis Special (annual bike runs). "No first-time experiences—our readers already know." **Buys 10-12 mss/year.** Send complete ms. Length: 100-1,000 words. **Pays $50-200.**

Photos: Send photos with submission. Reviews transparencies, prints. Buys one-time rights. Offers $0-10/photo. Captions, identification of subjects, model releases required.

Columns/Departments: Buys 10-12 mss/year. Send complete ms. **Pays $25-50.**

Fiction: Adventure, erotica, fantasy, historical, humorous, romance, science fiction, slice-of-life vignettes, suspense. No racism. **Buys 10-12 mss/year.** Send complete ms. Length: 500-2,500 words. **Pays $50-200.**

Poetry: Avant-garde, free verse, haiku, light verse, traditional. **Buys 10-12 poems/year.** Submit maximum 12 poems. Length: 2-1,000 lines. **Pays $10-25.**

Fillers: Anecdotes, facts, gags to be illustrated by cartoonist, newsbreaks, short humor. **Buys 10-12/year.** Length: 500-2,000 words. **Pays $10-25.**

The online version of *Outlaw Biker* carries original content not found in the print edition. Contact: Chris Miller.
Tips: "Writers must be insiders of the biker lifestyle. Manuscripts with accompanying photographs as art are given higher priority."

$ $ RIDER MAGAZINE, Ehlert Publishing Group, 2575 Vista Del Mar Dr., Ventura CA 93001. **Contact:** Mark Tuttle, editor. **60% freelance written.** Monthly magazine covering motorcycling. "*Rider* serves the all-brand motorcycle lifestyle/enthusiast with a slant toward travel and touring." Estab. 1974. Circ. 107,000. Pays on publication. Publishes ms an average of 6-12 months after acceptance. Byline given. Offers 25% kill fee. Buys first North American serial, electronic rights. Editorial lead time 4 months. Submit seasonal material 6 months in advance. Accepts queries by mail. Responds in 2 months to queries. Sample copy for $2.95. Writer's guidelines for #10 SASE.

"The articles we do buy often share the following characteristics: 1. The writer queried us in advance by regular mail (not by telephone or e-mail) to see if we needed or wanted the story. 2. The story was well written and of proper length. 3. The story had sharp, uncluttered photos taken with the proper film—*Rider* does not buy stories without photos."

Nonfiction: General interest, historical/nostalgic, how-to (re: motorcycling), humor, interview/profile, personal experience, travel. Does not want to see "fiction or articles on 'How I Began Motorcycling.'" **Buys 40-50 mss/year.** Query. Length: 750-2,000 words. **Pays $150-750.**
Photos: Send photos with submission. Reviews contact sheets, transparencies, 5×7 (b&w only) prints. Buys one-time and electronic rights. Offers no additional payment for photos accepted with ms. Captions required.
Columns/Departments: Favorite Rides (short trip), 850-1,100 words. **Buys 12 mss/year.** Query. **Pays $150-750.**
Tips: "We rarely accept manuscripts without photos (slides or b&w prints). Query first. Follow guidelines available on request. We are most open to feature stories (must include excellent photography) and material for 'Rides, Rallies and Clubs.' Include information on routes, local attractions, restaurants, and scenery in favorite ride submissions."

$ $ ROAD BIKE, (formerly *Motorcycle Tour & Cruiser*), TAM Communications, 1010 Summer St., Stamford CT 06905. (203)425-8777. Fax: (203)425-8775. E-mail: laurab@roadbikemag.com. **Contact:** Laura Brengelman, editor. **70% freelance written.** Monthly magazine covering motorcycling—tour and travel. Estab. 1993. Circ. 50,000. Pays on publication. Publishes ms an average of 6 months after acceptance. Byline given. Editorial lead time 4 months. Submit seasonal material 6 months in advance. Accepts queries by mail, fax. Accepts simultaneous submissions. Writer's guidelines free.
Nonfiction: How-to (motorcycle, travel, camping), interview/profile (motorcycle related), new product, photo feature (motorcycle events or gathering places with minimum of 1,000 words text), travel. No fiction. **Buys 100 mss/year.** Query with or without published clips or send complete ms. Length: 1,000-3,500 words. **Pays $150-350.**
Photos: Send photos with submission (slides preferred, prints accepted, b&w contact sheets for how-to). Buys one-time rights. Offers no additional payment for photos accepted with ms. Captions required.
Columns/Departments: Reviews (products, media, all motorcycle related), 300-750 words plus one or more photos. Query with published clips or send complete ms. **Pays $50-150.**
Fillers: Facts.

N $ $ TRUCK TREND, The SUV & Pickup Authority, Emap USA, 6420 Wilshire Blvd., Los Angeles CA 90048-5515. (323)782-2220. Fax: (323)782-2355. E-mail: trucktrend@primediacmmg.com. Website: www.trucktrend.com. Managing Editor: Jacqueline Manfredi. **Contact:** Mark Williams, editor. **60% freelance written.** Bimonthly magazine covering trucks, SUVs, minivans, vans, and travel. "*Truck Trend* readers want to know about what's new in the world of sport-utilities, pickups, and vans. What to buy, how to fix up, and where to go." Estab. 1998. Circ. 125,000. Pays on publication. Publishes ms an average of 3 months after acceptance. Byline given. Buys all rights. Editorial lead time 5 months. Submit seasonal material 6 months in advance. Accepts queries by mail. Sample copy for #10 SASE. Writer's guidelines not available.
Nonfiction: How-to, travel. Special issues: Towing; Hot Rod Truck; ½ Ton Pickup; Diesel. No personal experience, humor, or religious. **Buys 12 mss/year.** Query. Length: 500-1,800 words. **Pays $150-300/page.** Sometimes pays expenses of writers on assignment.
Photos: Send photos with submission. Reviews transparencies. Buys all rights. Offers no additional payment for photos accepted with ms. Captions, identification of subjects, model releases required.

The online magazine carries original content not found in the print edition.

Tips: "Know the subject/audience. Start by using a previous story as a template. Call editor for advice after flushing story out. Understand the editor is looking to freelancers to make life easier."

$ $ $ VELOCITY MAGAZINE, Journal of the Honda Acura Club, Honda Acura Club International, 4324 Promenade Way, Suite 109, Marina Del Rey CA 90292. (310)822-6163. Fax: (310)822-5030. E-mail: staff@hondaclub.com. Website: www.hondaclub.com. Managing Editor: Suzanne Peauralto. **Contact:** Peter Frey, editor. **50% freelance written.** Quarterly magazine covering Honda and Acura autos and products for automotive general interest and enthusiasts. Estab. 1999. Circ. 50,000. Pays on publication. Publishes ms an average of 2 months after acceptance. Byline given. Offers 50% kill fee. Buys all rights. Editorial lead time 2 months. Submit seasonal material 2 months in advance. Accepts queries by mail, fax. Accepts previously published material. Sample copy for $3. Writer's guidelines free.
Nonfiction: General interest, historical/nostalgic, new product, photo feature, automotive. **Buys 50 mss/year.** Query with published clips. Length: 400-1,000 words. **Pays 50¢/word.** Sometimes pays expenses of writers on assignment.
Reprints: Accepts previously published submissions.

Photos: Send photos with submission. Buys all rights. Negotiates payment individually. Captions, identification of subjects required.

AVIATION

Professional and private pilots and aviation enthusiasts read the publications in this section. Editors want material for audiences knowledgeable about commercial aviation. Magazines for passengers of commercial airlines are grouped in the Inflight category. Technical aviation and space journals, and publications for airport operators, aircraft dealers, and others in aviation businesses are listed under Aviation & Space in the Trade section.

N $ $ $ $ **AIR & SPACE/SMITHSONIAN MAGAZINE**, 750 9th St. NW, Washington DC 20560. (202)275-1230. Fax: (202)275-3163. E-mail: editors@airspacemag.com. Website: www.airspacemag.com. Editor: George Larson. **Contact:** Linda Shiner, executive editor (features); Pat Trenner, senior editor (departments). **80% freelance written.** Bimonthly magazine covering aviation and aerospace for a nontechnical audience. "The emphasis is on the human rather than the technological, on the ideas behind the events. Features are slanted to a technically curious, but not necessarily technically knowledgeable audience. We are looking for unique angles to aviation/aerospace stories, history, events, personalities, current and future technologies, that emphasize the human-interest aspect." Estab. 1985. Circ. 240,000. **Pays on acceptance.** Byline given. Offers kill fee. Buys first North American serial rights. Accepts queries by mail, e-mail, fax. Responds in 3 months to queries. Sample copy for $5. Guidelines for #10 SASE, on website or by e-mail.

"We're looking for 'reader service' articles—a collection of helpful hints and interviews with experts that would help our readers enjoy their interest in aviation. An example: An article telling readers how they could learn more about the space shuttle, where to visit, how to invite an astronaut to speak to their schools, what books are most informative, etc. A good place to break in is our 'Soundings' department."

Nonfiction: The editors are actively seeking stories covering space and general or business aviation. Book excerpts, essays, general interest (on aviation/aerospace), historical/nostalgic, humor, photo feature, technical. **Buys 50 mss/year.** Query with published clips. Length: 1,500-3,000 words. **Pays $1,500-3,000.** Pays expenses of writers on assignment.
Photos: Refuses unsolicited material. State availability with submission. Reviews 35 mm transparencies, digital files.
Columns/Departments: Above and Beyond (first person), 1,500-2,000 words; Flights and Fancy (whimsy), approximately 800 words. Soundings (brief items, timely but not breaking news), 500-700 words. **Buys 25 mss/year.** Query with published clips. **Pays $150-300.**

The online version carries original content not found in the print edition. Contact: Linda Shiner, Pat Trenner.

Tips: "We continue to be interested in stories about space exploration. Also, writing should be clear, accurate, and engaging. It should be free of technical and insider jargon, and generous with explanation and background. The first step every aspiring contributor should take is to study recent issues of the magazine."

$ $ **AIR LINE PILOT, The Magazine of Professional Flight Deck Crews**, Air Line Pilots Association, 535 Herndon Pkwy., P.O. Box 1169, Herndon VA 20172. (703)481-4460. Fax: (703)689-4370. E-mail: magazine@alpa.org. Website: www.alpa.org. **Contact:** Gary DiNunno, editor. **10% freelance written.** Prefers to work with published/established writers; works with a small number of new/unpublished writers each year. Bimonthly magazine for airline pilots covering commercial aviation industry information—economics, avionics, equipment, systems, safety—that affects a pilot's life in a professional sense. Also includes information about management/labor relations trends, contract negotiations, etc. Estab. 1931. Circ. 95,000. **Pays on acceptance.** Publishes ms an average of 6 months after acceptance. Offers 50% kill fee. all rights except book rights Submit seasonal material 6 months in advance. Responds in 2 months to queries. Sample copy for $2. Writer's guidelines for #10 SASE.

Nonfiction: Humor, inspirational, photo feature, technical. **Buys 20 mss/year.** Query with or without published clips or send complete ms and SASE. Length: 700-3,000 words. **Pays $100-600 for assigned articles; $50-600 for unsolicited articles.**
Reprints: Send photocopy of article or typed ms with rights for sale noted and information about when and where the material previously appeared. Pay varies.
Photos: "Our greatest need is for strikingly original cover photographs featuring ALPA flight deck crew members and their airlines in their operating environment." Send photos with submission. Reviews contact sheets, 35mm transparencies, 8×10 prints. Buys all rights for cover photos, one-time rights for inside color. Offers $10-35/b&w photo, $20-50 for color used inside and $400 for color used as cover. For cover photography, shoot vertical rather than horizontal. Identification of subjects required.
Tips: "For our feature section, we seek aviation industry information that affects the life of a professional airline pilot from a career standpoint. We also seek material that affects a pilot's life from a job security and work environment standpoint. Any airline pilot featured in an article must be an Air Line Pilot Association member in good standing. Our readers are very experienced and require a high level of technical accuracy in both written material and photographs."

$ **BALLOON LIFE**, Balloon Life Magazine, Inc., 2336 47th Ave. SW, Seattle WA 98116-2331. (206)935-3649. Fax: (206)935-3326. E-mail: tom@balloonlife.com. Website: www.balloonlife.com. **Contact:** Tom Hamilton, editor-in-chief. **75% freelance written.** Monthly magazine covering sport of hot air ballooning. Estab. 1986. Circ. 4,000. Pays on publication. Byline given. Offers 50-100% kill fee. Buys nonexclusive, all rights. Submit seasonal material 4 months in advance. Accepts previously published material. Responds in 3 weeks to queries; 1 month to mss. Sample copy for 9×12 SAE with $2 postage. Writer's guidelines for #10 SASE.

Nonfiction: Book excerpts, general interest, how-to (flying hot air balloons, equipment techniques), interview/profile, new product, technical, events/rallies; safety seminars; balloon clubs/organizations; letters to the editor. **Buys 150 mss/year.** Query with or without published clips or send complete ms. Length: 1,000-1,500 words. **Pays $50-75 for assigned articles; $25-50 for unsolicited articles.** Pays expenses of writers on assignment.

Reprints: Send tearsheet, photocopy or typed ms with rights for sale noted and information about when and where the material previously appeared. Pays 100% of amount paid for an original article or story.

Photos: Send photos with submission. Reviews transparencies, Prints. Buys nonexclusive, all rights. Offers $15/inside photos, $50/cover. Identification of subjects required.

Columns/Departments: Hangar Flying (real-life flying experience that others can learn from), 800-1,500 words; Crew Quarters (devoted to some aspect of crewing), 900 words; Preflight (a news and information column), 100-500 words; pays $50. Logbook (recent balloon events—events that have taken place in last 3-4 months), 300-500 words; pays $20. **Buys 60 mss/year.** Send complete ms. **Pays $20-50.**

Fiction: Humorous. **Buys 3-5 mss/year.** Send complete ms. Length: 800-1,500 words. **Pays $50.**

Tips: "This magazine slants toward the technical side of ballooning. We are interested in articles that help to educate and provide safety information. Also stories with manufacturers, important individuals and/or of historic events and technological advances important to ballooning. The magazine attempts to present articles that show 'how-to' (fly, business opportunities, weather, equipment). Both our Feature Stories section and Logbook section are where most manuscripts are purchased."

$ CESSNA OWNER MAGAZINE, Jones Publishing, Inc., N7450 Aanstad Rd., P.O. Box 5000, Iola WI 54945. (715)445-5000. Fax: (715)445-4053. E-mail: jenniferj@cessnaowner.org. Website: www.cessnaowner.org. **Contact:** Jennifer Julin, editor-in-chief. **50% freelance written.** Monthly magazine covering Cessna single and twin-engine aircraft. "*Cessna Owner Magazine* is the official publication of the Cessna Owner Organization (C.O.O.). Therefore, our readers are Cessna aircraft owners, renters, pilots, and enthusiasts. Articles should deal with buying/selling, flying, maintaining, or modifying Cessnas. The purpose of our magazine is to promote safe, fun, and affordable flying." Estab. 1975. Circ. 6,000. Pays on publication. Publishes ms an average of 3 months after acceptance. Byline given. Buys first, one-time, second serial (reprint) rights, makes work-for-hire assignments. Editorial lead time 1 month. Submit seasonal material 3 months in advance. Accepts queries by mail, e-mail, fax, phone. Accepts previously published material. Responds in 2 weeks to queries; 1 month to mss. Sample copy and writer's guidelines free or on website.

Nonfiction: "We are always looking for articles about Cessna aircraft modifications. We also need articles on Cessna twin-engine aircraft. April, July, and October are always big issues for us, because we attend various airshows during these months and distribute free magazines. Feature articles on unusual, highly modified, or vintage Cessnas are especially welcome during these months. Good photos are also a must." Historical/nostalgic (of specific Cessna models), how-to (aircraft repairs and maintenance), new product, personal experience, photo feature, technical (aircraft engines and airframes). Special issues: Engines (maintenance, upgrades); Avionics (purchasing, new products). **Buys 48 mss/year.** Query. Length: 1,500-3,500 words. **Pays 7-11¢/word.**

Reprints: Send mss via e-mail with rights for sale noted and information about when and where the material previously appeared.

Photos: Send photos with submission. Reviews Reviews 3×5 and larger prints. Captions, identification of subjects required.

$ GENERAL AVIATION NEWS, (formerly *Flyer*), N.W. Flyer, Inc., P.O. Box 39099, Lakewood WA 98439-0099. (253)471-9888. Fax: (253)471-9911. E-mail: kirk@generalaviationnews.com. Website: www.generalaviationnews.com. **Contact:** Kirk Gormley, editor. **30% freelance written.** Prefers to work with published/established writers. Biweekly tabloid covering general, regional, national, and international aviation stories of interest to pilots, aircraft owners, and aviation enthusiasts. Estab. 1949. Circ. 35,000. Pays 1 month after publication. Publishes ms an average of 3 months after acceptance. Byline given. Buys first North American serial, second serial (reprint) rights. Submit seasonal material 6 months in advance. Accepts queries by mail, e-mail, fax, phone. Responds in 2 months to queries. Sample copy for $3.50. Writer's guidelines for #10 SASE.

O‒ Break in by having "an aviation background, being up to date on current events, and being able to write. A 1,000-word story with good photos is the best way to see your name in print.

Nonfiction: "We stress news. A controversy over an airport, a first flight of a new design, storm or flood damage to an airport, a new business opening at your local airport—those are the sort of projects that may get a new writer onto our pages, if they arrive here soon after they happen. We are especially interested in reviews of aircraft." Personality pieces involving someone who is using his or her airplane in an unusual way, and stories about aviation safety are of interest. Query first on historical, nostalgic features, and profiles/interviews. **Buys 100 mss/year.** Query with or without published clips or send complete ms. Length: 500-2,000 words. **Pays up to $10/printed column inch.** Sometimes pays expenses of writers on assignment.

Photos: Shoot clear, up-close photos, preferably color prints or slides. Send photos with submission. Pays $10/b&w photo and $50/cover photo 1 month after publication. Captions, identification of subjects required.

Tips: "The longer the story, the less likely it is to be accepted. If you are covering controversy, send us both sides of the story. Most of our features and news stories are assigned in response to a query."

$ $ PIPERS MAGAZINE, Jones Publishing, Inc., N7450 Aanstad Rd., P.O. Box 5000, Iola WI 54945. (715)445-5000. Fax: (715)445-4053. E-mail: jenniferj@piperowner.org. Website: www.piperowner.org. **Contact:** Jennifer Julin, editor-in-chief. **50% freelance written.** Monthly magazine covering Piper single and twin engine aircraft. "*Pipers Magazine* is the official publication of the Piper Owner Society (P.O.S). Therefore, our readers are Piper aircraft owners, renters, pilots, mechanics and enthusiasts. Articles should deal with buying/selling, flying, maintaining or modifying Pipers. The purpose of our magazine is to promote safe, fun and affordable flying." Estab. 1988. Circ. 5,000. Pays on publication. Publishes ms an average of 3 months after acceptance. Buys first, one-time, second serial (reprint) rights, makes work-for-hire assignments. Editorial lead time 1 month. Submit seasonal material 3 months in advance. Accepts queries by mail, e-mail, fax, phone. Accepts previously published material. Responds in 2 weeks to queries; 1 month to mss. Sample copy for free. Writer's guidelines free.

Nonfiction: "We are always looking for articles about Piper aircraft modifications. We also are in need of articles on Piper twin engine aircraft, and late-model Pipers. April, July, and October are always big issues for us, because we attend airshows during these months and distribute free magazines." Feature articles on unusual, highly-modified, vintage, late-model, or ski/float equipped Pipers are especially welcome. Good photos are a must. Historical/nostalgic (of specific models of Pipers), how-to (aircraft repairs & maintenance), new product, personal experience, photo feature, technical (aircraft engines and airframes). **Buys 48 mss/year.** Query. Length: 1,500-3,500 words. **Pays 7-11¢/word.**

Reprints: Send mss by e-mail with rights for sale noted and information about when and where the material previously appeared.

Photos: Send photos with submission. Reviews transparencies, 3×5 and larger prints. Offers no additional payment for photos accepted. Captions, identification of subjects required.

N $ $ ✪ PLANE AND PILOT, Werner Publishing Corp., 12121 Wilshire Blvd., Suite 1200, Los Angeles CA 90025. (310)820-1500. Fax: (310)826-5008. E-mail: editors@planeandpilot.com. Website: www.planeandpilotmag.com. Editor: Lyn Freeman. **Contact:** Jenny Shearer, managing editor. **100% freelance written.** Monthly magazine covering general aviation. "We think a spirited, conversational writing style is most entertaining for our readers. We are read by private and corporate pilots, instructors, students, mechanics and technicians—everyone involved or interested in general aviation." Estab. 1964. Circ. 130,000. Pays on publication. Publishes ms an average of 3 months after acceptance. Byline given. Offers kill fee. Buys all rights. Submit seasonal material 4 months in advance. Accepts previously published material. Responds in 2 months to queries. Sample copy for $5.50. Writer's guidelines free or on website.

Nonfiction: How-to, new product, personal experience, technical, travel, Pilot Efficiency; Pilot Reports on Aircraft. **Buys 75 mss/year.** Query. Length: 1,000-1,800 words. **Pays $200-500.** Pays expenses of writers on assignment.

Reprints: Send tearsheet, photocopy or typed ms with rights for sale noted and information about when and where the material previously appeared. Pays 50% of amount paid for original article.

Photos: Submit suggested heads, decks and captions for all photos with each story. Submit b&w photos in proof sheet form with negatives or 8×10 prints with glossy finish. Submit color photos in the form of 2¼×2 ¼ or 4×5 or 35mm transparencies in plastic sleeves. Buys all rights. Offers $50-300/photo.

Columns/Departments: Readback (any newsworthy items on aircraft and/or people in aviation), 100-300 words; Jobs & Schools (a feature or an interesting school or program in aviation), 1,000-1,500 words; and Travel (any traveling done in piston-engine aircraft), 1,000-2,500 words. **Buys 30 mss/year.** Send complete ms. **Pays $200-500.**

Tips: "Pilot proficiency articles are our bread and butter. Manuscripts should be kept under 1,800 words."

$ WOMAN PILOT, Aviatrix Publishing, Inc., P.O. Box 485, Arlington Heights IL 60006-0485. (847)797-0170. Fax: (847)797-0161. E-mail: womanpilot@womanpilot.com Website: www.womanpilot. **Contact:** Editor. **80% freelance written.** Bimonthly magazine covering women who fly all types of aircraft and careers in all areas of aviation. Personal profiles, historical articles and current aviation events. Estab. 1993. Circ. 6,000. Pays on publication. Publishes ms an average of 5 months after acceptance. Byline given. Buys first North American serial rights. Accepts queries by mail, e-mail, phone. Accepts previously published material. Sample copy for $3. Writer's guidelines for #10 SASE or online.

O→ Break in with "interesting stories about women in aerospace with great photos."

Nonfiction: Book excerpts, historical/nostalgic, humor, interview/profile, new product, personal experience, photo feature. **Buys 35 mss/year.** Query with published clips or send complete ms. Length: 500-4,000 words. **Pays $20-55 for assigned articles; $20-40 for unsolicited articles.**

Reprints: Send tearsheet or typed ms with rights for sale noted and information about when and where the material previously appeared.

Photos: State availability of or send photos with submission. Buys one-time rights. Negotiates payment individually. Captions, identification of subjects, model releases required.

Fiction: Adventure, historical, humorous, slice-of-life vignettes. **Buys 4 mss/year.** Query with or without published clips. Length: 500-2,000 words. **Pays $20-35.**

Fillers: Cartoons. **Buys 6/year. Pays $10-20.**

The online version carries original content not found in the print edition and contains articles from back issues. Contact: Editor.

Tips: "If a writer is interested in writing articles from our leads, she/he should send writing samples and explanation of any aviation background. Include any writing background."

BUSINESS & FINANCE

Business publications give executives and consumers a range of information from local business news and trends to national overviews and laws that affect them. National and regional publications are listed below in separate categories. Magazines that have a technical slant are in the Trade section under Business Management, Finance, or Management & Supervision categories.

National

N $ $ DOLLARS AND SENSE: THE MAGAZINE OF ECONOMIC JUSTICE, (formerly *Dollars and Sense*), Economic Affairs Bureau, 740 Cambridge St., Cambridge MA 02141-1401. (617)876-2434. Fax: (617)876-0008. E-mail: dollars@dollarsandsense.org. Website: www.dollarsandsense.org. **Contact:** Tami J. Friedman or Alejândro Reuss, co-editors. **10% freelance written.** Bimonthly magazine covering economics, environmental, and social justice. "We explain the workings of the U.S. and international economics, and provide leftist perspectives on current economic affairs. Our audience is a mix of activists, organizers, academics, liberals, unionists, and other socially concerned people." Estab. 1974. Circ. 8,000. Pays on publication. Publishes ms an average of 4 months after acceptance. Byline given. Editorial lead time 3 months. Submit seasonal material 2 months in advance. Accepts queries by mail, e-mail, fax, phone. Sample copy for $5 or on website. Writer's guidelines online.

Nonfiction: Exposé, political economics. **Buys 6 mss/year.** Query with published clips. Length: 700-2,500 words. **Pays $0-200.** Sometimes pays expenses of writers on assignment.

Photos: State availability with submission. Buys one-time rights. Negotiates payment individually. Captions, identification of subjects required.

Tips: "Be familiar with our magazine and the types of communities interested in reading us. *Dollars and Sense* is a progressive economics magazine that explains in a popular way both the workings of the economy and struggles to change it. Articles may be on the environment, the World Bank, community organizing, urban conflict, inflation, unemployment, union reform, welfare, changes in government regulation—a broad range of topics that have an economic theme. Find samples of our latest issue on our homepage."

$ $ ENTREPRENEUR MAGAZINE, 2445 McCabe Way, Irvine CA 92614. (949)261-2325. Fax: (949)261-0234. E-mail: entmag@entrepreneur.com. Website: www.entrepreneur.com. **Contact:** Peggy Reeves Bennett, articles editor. **60% freelance written.** *Entrepreneur* readers already run their own businesses. They have been in business for several years and are seeking innovative methods and strategies to improve their business operations. They are also interested in new business ideas and opportunities, as well as current issues that affect their companies. **Pays on acceptance.** Publishes ms an average of 5 months after acceptance. Byline given. Buys first international rights. Submit seasonal material 6 months in advance. Accepts queries by mail, e-mail, fax. Responds in 3 months to queries. Sample copy for $7.20 from Order Department or on website. Writer's guidelines for #10 SASE or by e-mail.

Nonfiction: A few columns are now open to freelancers: "Smarts," "Money Buzz," "Marketing Buzz," and "Management Buzz." How-to (information on running a business, dealing with the psychological aspects of running a business, profiles of unique entrprenuers), current news/trends (and their effect on small business). **Buys 10-20 mss/year.** Query with published clips. Length: 2000 words. **Payment varies.**

Photos: "Ask for photos or transparencies when interviewing entrepreneurs; send them with the article." Buys one-time rights.

Tips: "Read several issues of the magazine! Study the feature articles versus the columns. Probably 75 percent of our freelance rejections are for article ideas covered in one of our regular columns. Go beyond the typical, flat 'business magazine query'—how to write a press release, how to negotiate with vendors, etc.—and instead investigate a current trend and develop a story on how that trend affects small business. In your query, mention companies you'd like to use to illustrate examples and sources who will provide expertise on the topic."

$ $ ENTREPRENEUR'S BIZSTARTUPS.COM, Entrepreneur Media, Inc., 2445 McCabe Way, Suite 400, Irvine CA 92614. (949)261-2083. Fax: (949)261-0234. E-mail: bsumag@entrepreneur.com. Website: www.bizstartups.com. **Contact:** Karen E. Spaeder, editor. **10% freelance written.** Monthly online magazine for young entrepreneurs (age 23 to 35). We target tech-savvy, upscale and educated readers who are preparing to start a business within the next year or have started a business within the past 2 years. Articles cover ideas for hot businesses to start; how-to advice to help new entrepreneurs run and grow their businesses; cutting-edge technology, management and marketing trends; motivational topics and more. Estab. 1989. **Pays on acceptance.** Byline given. Offers 20% kill fee. first time international rights. Submit seasonal material 6 months in advance. Accepts queries by mail, e-mail. Responds in 3 months to queries. Writer's guidelines for #10 SASE or by e-mail. No phone calls, please.

Break in by "writing like you're 25, even if you're not."

Nonfiction: "Our readers don't necessarily have tons of money, but they make up for it in attitude, energy and determination. They're seeking start-up ideas; how-to advice; cutting-edge articles to keep them on top of the latest business trends; and motivational articles to get (and keep) them psyched up. No matter what your topic, articles should be packed with real-life examples of exciting young entrepreneurs doing things in new and different ways, plus plenty of pull-outs, sidebars and tips that can be presented in an eye-catching style. Types of features we are seeking include: Psychological (staying motivated, sparking creativity, handling stress, overcoming fear, etc.); profiles of successful young entrepreneurs with original, creative, outrageous ideas and strategies others can learn from; operating articles

(how-to advice for running a business, such as finding financing, choosing a partner, marketing on a shoestring, etc.); issues (examination of how a current issue affects young entrepreneurs); industry round-ups (articles covering a particular industry and highlighting several young entrepreneurs in that industry, for example, gourmet food entrepreneurs, cigar entrepreneurs, specialty travel entrepreneurs); tech. We are always seeking people who can write interestingly and knowledgeably about technology." How-to, interview/profile, technical. Length: 1,200-1,800 words. **Pays $500 and up for features, $100 for briefs.**
Reprints: Call or e-mail for details.
Photos: State availability with submission. Identification of subjects required.
Tips: "We are looking for irreverent, creative writers who can approach topics in new ways in terms of style, format and outlook. You must write in a way our audience can relate to. They want a lot of info, fast, with specifics on where to get more info and follow up. They're skeptical and don't believe everything they read. Tone should sound like a friend giving another friend the 'inside scoop'—not like a professor lecturing from an ivory tower. Humor helps a lot. How *not* to break in: Send a résumé without a query or writing samples that are full of vague generalities."

$ $ $ INDUSTRYWEEK, Leadership in Manufacturing, Penton Media, Inc., Penton Media Building, 1300 E. 9th St., Cleveland OH 44114. (216)696-7000. Fax: (216)696-7670. E-mail: tvinas@industryweek.com. Website: www.industryweek.com. Editor-in-Chief: Patricia Panchak. **Contact:** Tonya Vinas, managing editor. **30% freelance written.** Magazine published 12 times/year. *IndustryWeek* connects marketers and manufacturers and provides information that helps manufacturers drive continuous improvement throughout the enterprise. Every issue of *IndustryWeek* is edited for the management teams of today's most competitive manufacturing companies, as well as decision-makers in the service industries that support manufacturing growth and productivity." Estab. 1970. Circ. 233,000. **Pays on acceptance.** Publishes ms an average of 2 months after acceptance. Byline given. Offers 25% kill fee. Buys all rights. Accepts queries by mail, e-mail, fax, phone. Responds in 1 month to queries. Sample copy and writer's guidelines online.
Nonfiction: Book excerpts, exposé, interview/profile. "No first-person articles." **Buys 25 mss/year.** Query with published clips. Length: 1,800-3,000 words. **Pays average of $1/word for all articles; reserves right to negotiate.** Sometimes pays expenses of writers on assignment.
Photos: Reviews contact sheets, negatives, transparencies, Prints. Buys one-time rights. Negotiates payment individually. Captions, identification of subjects required.
Tips: "Pitch wonderful ideas targeted precisely at our audience. Read, re-read, and understand the writer's guidelines. *IndustryWeek* readers are primarily senior executives—people with the title of vice president, executive vice president, senior vice president, chief executive officer, chief financial officer, chief information officer, chairman, managing director, and president. *IW*'s executive readers oversee global corporations. While *IW*'s primary target audience is a senior executive in a U.S. firm, your story should provide information that any executive anywhere in the world can use. *IW*'s audience is primarily in companies in manufacturing and manufacturing-related industries."

$ $ MYBUSINESS MAGAZINE, Hammock Publishing, 3322 W. End Ave., Suite 700, Nashville TN 37203. Fax: (615)386-9349. E-mail: lwaddle@hammock.com. Website: www.mybusinessmag.com. **Contact:** Lisa Waddle, editor. **75% freelance written.** Bimonthly magazine for small businesses. "We are a guide to small business success, however that is defined in the new small business economy. We explore the methods and minds behind the trends and celebrate the men and women leading the creation of the new small business economy." Estab. 1999. Circ. 600,000. **Pays on acceptance.** Publishes ms an average of 4 months after acceptance. Byline given. Offers 30% kill fee. Buys first North American serial, electronic rights. Editorial lead time 4 months. Submit seasonal material 5 months in advance. Accepts queries by mail, fax. Accepts simultaneous submissions. Responds in 3 weeks to queries. Sample copy and writer's guidelines free.
Nonfiction: Book excerpts, how-to (small business topics), humor, new product. **Buys 8 mss/year.** Query with published clips. Length: 200-1,800 words. **Pays $75-1,000.** Pays expenses of writers on assignment.
Fillers: Gags to be illustrated by cartoonist. **Buys 5/year.**
Tips: *MyBusiness* is sent bimonthly to the 600,000 members of the National Federation of Independent Business. "We're here to help small business owners by giving them a range of how-to pieces that evaluate, analyze, and lead to solutions."

$ THE NETWORK JOURNAL, Black Professional and Small Business News, The Network Journal Communication, 139 Fulton St., Suite 407, New York, NY 10038. (212)962-3791. Fax: (212)962-3537. E-mail: editors@tnj.com. Website: www.tnj.com. Editor: Njeru Waithaku. **Contact:** Aziz Adetimirn, publisher. **25% freelance written.** Monthly magazine covering business and career articles. *The Network Journal* caters to Black professionals and small-business owners, providing quality coverage on business, financial, technology and career news germane to the Black community. Estab. 1993. Circ. 15,000. Pays on publication. Byline given. Buys all rights. Editorial lead time 2 months. Submit seasonal material 3 months in advance. Accepts queries by mail, e-mail, fax, phone. Accepts previously published material. Accepts simultaneous submissions. Sample copy for $1 or online. Writer's guidelines for SASE or online.
Nonfiction: How-to, interview/profile. Send complete ms. Length: 1,200-1,500 words. **Pays $150-200.** Sometimes pays expenses of writers on assignment.
Photos: Send photos with submission. Buys one-time rights. Offers $25/photo. Identification of subjects required.
Columns/Departments: Book reviews, 700-800 words; career management and small business development, 800 words. **Pays $100.**

The online magazine carries original content not found in the print version and includes writer's guidelines.

Tips: "We are looking for vigorous writing and reporting for our cover stories and feature articles. Pieces should have gripping leads, quotes that actually say something and that come from several sources. Unless it is a column, please do not submit a one-source story. Always remember that your article must contain a nutgraph—that's usually the third paragraph telling the reader what the story is about and why you are telling it now. Editorializing should be kept to a minimum. If you're writing a column, make sure your opinions are well-supported."

$ $ PERDIDO, Leadership with a Conscience, High Tide Press, 3650 W. 183rd St., Homewood IL 60430-2603. (708)206-2054. Fax: (708)206-2044. E-mail: managing.editor@hightidepress.com. Website: www.perdidomagazine.com. **Contact:** Diane J. Bell, editor. **60% freelance written.** Quarterly magazine covering leadership and management as they relate to mission-oriented organizations. "We are concerned with what's happening in organizations that are mission-oriented—as opposed to merely profit-oriented. *Perdido* is focused on helping conscientious leaders put innovative ideas into practice. We seek pragmatic articles on management techniques as well as esoteric essays on social issues. The readership of *Perdido* is comprised mainly of CEOs, executive directors, vice presidents, and program directors of nonprofit and for-profit organizations. We try to make the content of *Perdido* accessible to all decision-makers, whether in the nonprofit or for-profit world, government, or academia. *Perdido* actively pursues diverse opinions and authors from many different fields." Estab. 1994. Circ. 6,000. Pays on publication. Publishes ms an average of 3 months after acceptance. Byline given. Buys first North American serial, second serial (reprint) rights. Editorial lead time 4 months. Submit seasonal material 6 months in advance. Accepts queries by mail, e-mail, fax, phone. Accepts previously published material. Accepts simultaneous submissions. Responds in 2 months to queries. Sample copy for 6×9 SASE with 2 first-class stamps or online. Writer's guidelines for #10 SASE or by e-mail.
Nonfiction: Book excerpts, essays, humor, inspirational, interview/profile. **Buys 12 mss/year.** Query with published clips. Length: 1,000-5,000 words. **Pays $70-350.**
Photos: State availability with submission. Reviews 5×7 prints. Buys one-time rights. Negotiates payment individually. Captions, identification of subjects, model releases required.
Columns/Departments: Book Review (new books on management/leadership), 800 words.
Tips: "Potential writers for *Perdido* should rely on the magazine's motto—Leadership with a Conscience—as a starting point for ideas. We're looking for thoughtful reflections or management that help people succeed. We're not asking for step-by-step recipes—'do this, do that.' In *Perdido*, we want readers to find thought-provoking, open-minded explorations of the moral dimensions of leadership from a socially aware, progressive perspective."

$ $ $ $ REPORT ON BUSINESS MAGAZINE, Globe and Mail, 444 Front St. W., Toronto, Ontario M5V 2S9, Canada. (416)585-5499. E-mail: dgoold@globeandmail.ca. Website: www.robmagazine.com. **Contact:** Douglas Goold, editor. **50% freelance written.** Monthly business magazine "covering business like *Forbes* or *Fortune* which tries to capture major trends and personalities." Circ. 300,000. **Pays on acceptance.** Publishes ms an average of 4 months after acceptance. Byline given. Offers 50% kill fee. Buys first North American serial rights. Responds in 3 weeks to queries. Sample copy for free.
Nonfiction: Book excerpts, exposé, interview/profile, new product, photo feature. Special issues: Quarterly technology report. **Buys 30 mss/year.** Query with published clips. Length: 2,000-4,000 words. **Pays $200-3,000.** Pays expenses of writers on assignment.
Tips: "For features send a one-page story proposal. We prefer to write about personalities involved in corporate events."

N $ $ TECHNICAL ANALYSIS OF STOCKS & COMMODITIES, The Traders' Magazine, Technical Analysis, Inc., 4757 California Ave. SW, Seattle WA 98116-4499. (206)938-0570. Fax: (206)938-1307. E-mail: editor@traders.com. Website: www.traders.com. Publisher: Jack K. Hutson. **Contact:** Jayanthi Gopalakrishnan, editor. **85% freelance written.** Magazine covers methods of investing and trading stocks, bonds and commodities (futures), options, mutual funds, and precious metals. Estab. 1982. Circ. 65,000. Pays on publication. Publishes ms an average of 6 months after acceptance. Byline given. Buys all rights. Accepts previously published material. Responds in 1 month to queries. Sample copy for $5. Writer's guidelines for #10 SASE or on website.

- Eager to work with new/unpublished writers.

Nonfiction: How-to (trade), humor (unusual incidents of market occurrences, cartoons), technical (trading and software aids to trading), reviews, utilities. "No newsletter-type, buy-sell recommendations. The article subject must relate to trading psychology, technical analysis, charting or a numerical technique used to trade securities or futures. Virtually requires graphics with every article." **Buys 150 mss/year.** Query with published clips or send complete ms. Length: 1,000-4,000 words. **Pays $100-500.**
Reprints: Send tearsheet with rights for sale noted and information about when and where the material previously appeared.
Photos: Christine M. Morrison, art director. State availability with submission. Buys one time and reprint rights. Pays $60-350 for b&w or color negatives with prints or positive slides. Captions, identification of subjects, model releases required.
Columns/Departments: Length: 800-1,600 words. **Buys 100 mss/year.** Query. **Pays $50-300.**
Fillers: Karen Wasserman, fillers editor. Must relate to trading stocks, bonds, options, mutual funds, commodities, or precious metals. Cartoons on investment humor. **Buys 20/year.** Length: 500 words. **Pays $20-50.**
Tips: "Describe how to use technical analysis, charting or computer work in day-to-day trading of stocks, bonds, commodities, options, mutual funds or precious metals. A blow-by-blow account of how a trade was made, including the trader's thought processes, is the very best-received story by our subscribers. One of our primary considerations is to instruct in a manner that the layperson can comprehend. We are not hypercritical of writing style."

$ $ WORKING MONEY, The Investor's Magazine, Technical Analysis, Inc., 4757 California Ave. SW, Seattle WA 98116-4499. (206)938-0570. Fax: (206)938-1307. E-mail: editor@traders.com. Website: www.working-money.com. Managing Editor: Elizabeth M.S. Flynn. **Contact:** Jayanthi Gopalakrishnan, editor. **20% freelance written.** Web-published monthly magazine covering investing. "*Working Money* is the magazine for those who have earned their money and now want to learn how to invest it." Estab. 2000. Circ. 165,000. Pays on publication. Publishes ms an average of 6 months after acceptance. Byline given. Buys all rights. Editorial lead time 3 months. Submit seasonal material 6 months in advance. Accepts queries by mail, e-mail, fax. Responds in 2 weeks to queries; 1 month to mss. Sample copy for $5. Writer's guidelines for #10 SASE or online.

Nonfiction: "How-to articles are at the core of *Working Money.* Our readers want to know how to invest their money, not just where, but how to work with the paperwork, computer programs, and institutions with which they'll need to work. How do you calculate the return on your investment? What are the dollars-and-cents implications of choosing a no-load vs. a load mutual fund? Show our readers." How-to, new product (of note to investors), personal experience (focus on lessons learned and how they will help investors), technical (features of investment-related software and hardware, etc.), mutual funds, money management, financial planning. **Buys up to 150 mss/year.** Query with published clips. Length: 1,000-2,000 words. **Pays $180/published article.**

Columns/Departments: Mutual funds (all aspects of mutual fund investing); financial planning (all aspects of financial planning); money management (as aspects of money management), all 1,000-2,000 words. **Buys 36 mss/year.** Query with published clips. **Pays $180.**

Tips: "We are not hypercritical of writing style, but accuracy is the key word. Completeness and accuracy are extremely important. Problems arising after publication will be directed to the author. Remember that *Working Money* is a how-to publication, so concentrate on instruction and elucidation."

Regional

$ $ ALASKA BUSINESS MONTHLY, Alaska Business Publishing, 501 W. Northern Lights Blvd., Suite 100, Anchorage AK 99503-2577. (907)276-4373. Fax: (907)279-2900. E-mail: editor@akbizmag.com. Website: www.akbizmag.com. **Contact:** Debbie Cutler, editor. **80% freelance written.** Magazine covering Alaska-oriented business and industry. "Our audience is Alaska businessmen and women who rely on us for timely features and up-to-date information about doing business in Alaska." Estab. 1985. Circ. 10,000. Pays on publication. Publishes ms an average of 4 months after acceptance. Byline given. Offers $50 kill fee. Buys all rights. Editorial lead time 5 months. Submit seasonal material 5 months in advance. Accepts queries by mail, e-mail, fax. Accepts previously published material. Responds in 1 month to queries. Sample copy for 9×12 SAE and 4 first-class stamps. Writer's guidelines free.

Nonfiction: General interest, how-to, interview/profile, new product (Alaska), opinion. No fiction, poetry or anything not pertinent to Alaska. **Buys approximately 130 mss/year.** Send complete ms. Length: 500-2,000 words. **Pays $150-300.** Sometimes pays expenses of writers on assignment.

Photos: State availability with submission.

Columns/Departments: Required Reading (business book reviews), Right Moves, Alaska this Month, Monthly Calendars (all Alaska related), all 500-1,200 words. **Buys 12 mss/year.** Send complete ms. **Pays $50-75.**

Tips: "Send a well-written manuscript on a subject of importance to Alaska businesses. We seek informative, entertaining articles on everything from entrepreneurs to heavy industry. We cover all Alaska industry to include mining, tourism, timber, transportation, oil and gas, fisheries, finance, insurance, real estate, communications, medical services, technology and construction. We also cover Native and environmental issues, and occasionally feature Seattle and other communities in the Pacific Northwest."

$ $ $ BC BUSINESS, Canada Wide Magazines & Communications Ltd., 4180 Lougheed Highway, 4th Floor, Burnaby, British Columbia V5C 6A7, Canada. (604)299-7311. Fax: (604)299-9188. E-mail: bcb@canadawide.com. **Contact:** Bonnie Irving, editor. **80% freelance written.** Monthly magazine covering significant issues and trends shaping the province's business environment. "Stories are lively, topical and extensively researched." Circ. 30,000. Pays 2 weeks prior to being published. Publishes ms an average of 2 months after acceptance. Byline given. Offers kill fee. Buys first rights. Editorial lead time 4 months. Submit seasonal material 4 months in advance. Accepts queries by mail, e-mail, fax, phone. Accepts simultaneous submissions. Responds in 6 weeks to queries. Writer's guidelines free.

Nonfiction: Query with published clips. Length: 800-3,000 words. **Pays 40-60¢/word, depending on length and complexity of story.** Sometimes pays expenses of writers on assignment.

Photos: State availability with submission.

$ BOULDER COUNTY BUSINESS REPORT, 3180 Sterling Circle, Suite 201, Boulder CO 80301-2338. (303)440-4950. Fax: (303)440-8954. E-mail: jwlewis@bcbr.com. Website: www.bcbr.com. **Contact:** Jerry W. Lewis, editor. **50% freelance written.** Prefers to work with local published/established writers; works with a small number of new/unpublished writers each year. Biweekly newspaper covering Boulder County business issues. Offers "news tailored to a biweekly theme and read primarily by Colorado businesspeople and by some investors nationwide. Philosophy: Descriptive, well-written articles that reach behind the scene to examine area's business activity." Estab. 1982. Circ. 10,000. Pays on publication. Publishes ms an average of 1 month after acceptance. Byline given. Buys one-time, second serial (reprint) rights. Responds in 1 month to queries; 2 weeks to mss. Sample copy for $2.

Nonfiction: Much of each issue is written around two or three special section themes. No articles are accepted in which the subject has not been pursued in-depth and both sides of an issue presented in a writing style with flair." Interview/profile, new product, explanation of competition in a particular line of business. **Buys 120 mss/year.** Query with published clips. Length: 750-1,200 words. **Pays $50-150.**

Photos: State availability with submission. Reviews b&w contact sheets. Buys one time and reprint rights. Pays $10 (maximum) for b&w contact sheet. Identification of subjects required.

Tips: "Must be able to localize a subject. In-depth articles are written by assignment. The freelancer located in the Colorado area has an excellent chance here."

BUSINESS JOURNAL OF CENTRAL NY, CNY Business Review, Inc., 231 Wallton St., Syracuse NY 13202-1230. (315)472-3104. Fax: (315)478-8166. E-mail: editor@cnybusinessjournal.com. Website: www.cnybusinessjournal.com. **Contact:** Charles McChesney, editor. **35% freelance written.** Weekly newspaper covering "business news in a 16-county area surrounding Syracuse. The audience consists of owners and managers of businesses." Estab. 1985. Circ. 8,000. Pays on publication. Publishes ms an average of 2 months after acceptance. Byline given. Offers kill fee. Buys first rights. Editorial lead time 1 month. Accepts queries by mail, e-mail, fax. Sample copy and writer's guidelines free.

Nonfiction: Humor, opinion. Query. Length: 750-2,000 words. **Pay varies.** Sometimes pays in contributor copies. Sometimes pays expenses of writers on assignment.

Photos: State availability with submission. Reviews contact sheets. Negotiates payment individually. Captions, identification of subjects, model releases required.

Columns/Departments: Query with published clips.

Fillers: Facts, newsbreaks, short humor. Length: 300-600 words. **Pays variable amount.**

The online magazine carries original content not found in the print edition.

Tips: "The audience is comprised of owners and managers. Focus on their needs. Call or send associate editor story ideas: be sure to have a Central New York 'hook.'"

$ $ $ BUSINESS LONDON, Bowes Publishers, 1174 Gainsburough Rd., London, Ontario N5Y 4X3, Canada. (519)472-7601. Fax: (519)473-7859. **Contact:** Gord Delamont, editor. **70% freelance written.** Monthly magazine covering London business. "Our audience is primarily small and medium businesses and entrepreneurs. Focus is on success stories and how to better operate your business." Estab. 1987. Circ. 14,000. Pays on publication. Publishes ms an average of 3 months after acceptance. Byline given. Offers 50% kill fee. Buys first rights. Editorial lead time 3 months. Responds in 3 months to mss. Sample copy for #10 SASE. Writer's guidelines free.

Nonfiction: How-to (business topics), humor, interview/profile, new product (local only), personal experience (must have a London connection). **Buys 30 mss/year.** Query with published clips. Length: 250-1,500 words. **Pays $125-500.**

Photos: Send photos with submission. Reviews contact sheets, transparencies. Buys one-time rights. Negotiates payment individually. Identification of subjects required.

Tips: "Phone with a great idea. The most valuable thing a writer owns is ideas. We'll take a chance on an unknown if the idea is good enough."

N $ $ BUSINESS NEW HAVEN, Second Wind Media, Ltd., 1 Church St., New Haven CT 06510. Fax: (203)781-3482. E-mail: business@businessnewhaven.com. Website: www.businessnewhaven.com. **Contact:** Michael C. Bingham, editor. **33% freelance written.** Biweekly regional business publication covering the Connecticut business community. "*Business New Haven* is a business-to-business vehicle targeted to business owners and managers." Estab. 1993. Circ. 14,000. Pays on publication. Byline given. Buys one-time, all rights. Editorial lead time 1 month. Accepts queries by mail, e-mail, fax. Sample copy online. Writer's guidelines by e-mail.

Nonfiction: How-to, interview/profile, new product, technical. **Buys 40 mss/year.** Query with published clips. Length: 500-2,500 words. **Pays $25-200.** Sometimes pays expenses of writers on assignment.

Photos: State availability with submission. Buys all rights. Negotiates payment individually. Identification of subjects required.

Tips: "We publish only stories specific to Connecticut business."

$ $ BUSINESS NH MAGAZINE, 404 Chestnut St., Suite 201, Manchester NH 03101-1831. (603)626-6354. Fax: (603)626-6359. E-mail: edit@businessnhmagazine.com. **Contact:** Matthew Mowry, editor. **50% freelance written.** Monthly magazine covering business, politics and people of New Hampshire. "Our audience consists of the owners and top managers of New Hampshire businesses." Estab. 1983. Circ. 13,000. Pays on publication. Publishes ms an average of 2 months after acceptance. Byline given. Accepts queries by e-mail, fax.

Nonfiction: How-to, interview/profile. "No unsolicited manuscripts; interested in New Hampshire writers only." **Buys 24 mss/year.** Query with published clips and résumé. Length: 750-2,500 words. **Pays $75-350.**

Photos: Both b&w and color photos used. Buys one-time rights. Pays $40-80.

Tips: "I *always* want clips and résumé with queries. Freelance stories are almost always assigned. Stories *must* be local to New Hampshire."

$ CHARLESTON REGIONAL BUSINESS JOURNAL, Setcom, Inc., P.O. Box 446, Charleston SC 29402. (843)723-7702. Fax: (843)723-7060. E-mail: info@crbj.com. Website: www.crbj.com. Publisher: William Settlemyer. **Contact:** Grady Johnson, executive editor. **20% freelance written.** Biweekly newspaper covering local business. "We publish articles of interest to small business owners in the Charleston area, preferably with a local slant." Estab. 1995.

Circ. 7,000. Pays on publication. Publishes ms an average of 1 month after acceptance. Byline given. Offers $40 kill fee. Editorial lead time 1 month. Submit seasonal material 2 months in advance. Accepts queries by mail, e-mail, fax. Accepts simultaneous submissions. Responds in 2 weeks to queries. Sample copy online.

Nonfiction: Interview/profile (business people), technical, other articles of interest to small business owners. No how-to's. **Buys 100 mss/year.** Query with published clips. Length: 400-800 words. **Pays $40-145.**

Photos: State availability with submission. Reviews Reviews e-mail photos (jpeg, 170 min resolution). Buys all rights. Offers $30/photo. Identification of subjects required.

$ $ CRAIN'S DETROIT BUSINESS, Crain Communications Inc., 1155 Gratiot, Detroit MI 48207-2997. (313)446-6000. Fax: (313)446-1687. E-mail: jmelton@crain.com. Website: www.crainsdetroit.com. Editor: Mary Kramer. Executive Editor: Cindy Goodaker. **Contact:** James Melton, special sections editor. **15% freelance written.** Weekly tabloid covering business in the Detroit metropolitan area—specifically Wayne, Oakland, Macomb, Washtenaw and Livingston counties. Estab. 1985. Circ. 150,000. Pays on publication. Publishes ms an average of 1 month after acceptance. Byline given. Buys electronic, all rights. Accepts queries by mail, e-mail. Sample copy for $1.50.

- *Crain's Detroit Business* uses only area writers and local topics.

Nonfiction: New product, technical, business. **Buys 100 mss/year.** Query with published clips. Length: 30-40 words/column inch. **Pays $10/column inch.** Pays expenses of writers on assignment.

Photos: State availability with submission.

Tips: "Contact special sections editor in writing with background and, if possible, specific story ideas relating to our type of coverage and coverage area. We only use *local* writers."

$ IN BUSINESS WINDSOR, Cornerstone Publications, Inc., 1775 Sprucewood Ave., Unit 1, LaSalle Ontario N9J 1X7, Canada. (519)250-2880. Fax: (519)250-2881. E-mail: inbiz2@mnsi.net. Website: www.inbizwin.com. **Contact:** Gary Baxter, general manager; Kelly O'Sullivan, associate editor. **70% freelance written.** Monthly magazine covering business. "We focus on issues/ideas which are of interest to businesses in and around Windsor and Essex County (Ontario). Most stories deal with business and finance; occasionally we will cover health and sports issues that affect our readers." Estab. 1988. Circ. 10,000. **Pays on acceptance.** Byline given. Buys first rights. Editorial lead time 3 months. Submit seasonal material 3 months in advance. Accepts queries by mail, e-mail, fax. Responds in 2 weeks to queries; 1 month to mss. Sample copy for $3.50.

Nonfiction: General interest, how-to, interview/profile. **Buys 25 mss/year.** Query with published clips. Length: 800-1,500 words. **Pays $70-150.** Sometimes pays expenses of writers on assignment.

$ $ INGRAM'S, Show-Me Publishing, Inc., 306 E. 12th St., Suite 1014, Kansas City MO 64106. (816)842-9994. Fax: (816)474-1111. **Contact:** Editor. **50% freelance written.** Monthly magazine covering Kansas City business/executive lifestyle for "upscale, affluent business executives and professionals. Looking for sophisticated writing with style and humor when appropriate." Estab. 1975. Circ. 26,000. Pays 30 days after publication. Publishes ms an average of 2 months after acceptance. Byline given. Buys first, electronic rights. Editorial lead time 2 months. Submit seasonal material 3 months in advance. Accepts queries by mail, fax. Responds in 6 weeks to queries. Sample copy for $3.

Nonfiction: "All articles must have a Kansas City angle. We don't accept unsolicited mss except for opinion column." General interest, how-to (business and personal finance related), interview/profile (KC execs, politicians, celebrities), opinion, technical. **Buys 30 mss/year.** Query with published clips. Length: 500-3,000 words. **Pays $175-350.** Sometimes pays expenses of writers on assignment.

Columns/Departments: Say So (opinion), 1,500 words. **Buys 12 mss/year. Pays $175 max.**

Tips: "Writers must understand the publication and the audience—knowing what appeals to a business executive, entrepreneur, or professional in Kansas City."

$ $ THE LANE REPORT, Lane Communications Group, 201 E. Main St., 14th Floor, Lexington KY 40507. (859)244-3500. Fax: (859)244-3555. E-mail: editorial@lanereport.com. Website: www.kybiz.com. **Contact:** Claude Hammond, editorial director. **50% freelance written.** Monthly magazine covering statewide business. Estab. 1986. Circ. 15,000. Pays on publication. Byline given. Buys one-time rights. Editorial lead time 6 weeks. Submit seasonal material 3 months in advance. Accepts queries by mail, e-mail, fax. Accepts previously published material. Accepts simultaneous submissions. Responds in 1 month to queries. Sample copy and writer's guidelines free.

Nonfiction: Essays, interview/profile, new product, photo feature. No fiction. **Buys 30-40 mss/year.** Query with published clips. Length: 500-2,000 words. **Pays $100-375.** Sometimes pays expenses of writers on assignment.

Photos: State availability with submission. Reviews contact sheets, negatives, transparencies, prints. Buys one-time rights. Negotiates payment individually. Identification of subjects required.

Columns/Departments: Technology and Business in Kentucky; Advertising; Exploring Kentucky; Perspective; Spotlight on the Arts, all less than 1,000 words.

The online magazine carries original content not included in the print edition. Contact: Karen Baird, online editor.

Tips: "As Kentucky's only statewide business and economics publication, we look for stories that incorporate perspectives from the Commonwealth's various regions and prominent industries—tying it into the national picture when appropriate. We also look for insightful profiles and interviews of Kentucky's entrepreneurs and business leaders."

$ $ $ LATIN TRADE, Your Business Source for Latin America, 95 Merrick Way, Suite 600, Coral Gables FL 33134. (305)358-8373. Fax: (305)358-9166. Website: www.latintrade.com. **Contact:** Mike Zellner, editor. **55% freelance written.** Monthly magazine covering Latin American business. "*Latin Trade* covers cross-border business in

Latin America for top executives doing business with the region." Estab. 1993. Circ. 105,000. Pays on publication. Publishes ms an average of 3 months after acceptance. Byline given. Offers 25% kill fee. Buys all rights, makes work-for-hire assignments. Editorial lead time 3 months. Submit seasonal material 6 months in advance. Accepts queries by mail, e-mail. Responds in 2 weeks to queries. Sample copy and writer's guidelines free.

Nonfiction: Exposé, historical/nostalgic, humor, interview/profile, travel, business news. No one-source stories or unsolicited stories. **Buys 50 mss/year.** Query with published clips. Length: 800-2,000 words. **Pays $200-1,000.** Sometimes pays expenses of writers on assignment.

Photos: State availability with submission. Reviews contact sheets. Buys one-time rights. Negotiates payment individually. Identification of subjects required.

$ $ MASS HIGH TECH, Journal of New England Technology, American City Business Journals, 529 Main St., Suite 602, Boston MA 02129. (617)242-1224. Fax: (617)242-9373. E-mail: editor@masshightech.com. Website: www.masshightech.com. Editor: Dyke Hendrickson. **Contact:** Anne Taylor, associate editor. **20% freelance written.** Weekly newspaper covering New England-based technology companies. "*Mass High Tech* is a weekly newspaper about the business deals and products of New England technology companies, read by technology executives, engineers, professors and high-tech workers." Estab. 1983. Circ. 23,000 per week. Publishes ms an average of 1 month after acceptance. Byline given. Buys all rights. Editorial lead time 2 months. Accepts queries by mail, e-mail, phone. Sample copy and writer's guidelines free.

Nonfiction: Opinion, technical. "No product reviews." Query. Length: 700-900 words.

Columns/Departments: E-commerce, Retailing, Stockwatch, Case Study, all 600 words. Query with published clips.

$ $ PACIFIC BUSINESS NEWS, 1833 Kalakaua Ave., 7th Floor, Honolulu HI 96815-1512. (808)955-8100. Fax: (808)955-8031. E-mail: pbn@lava.net. Website: pacific.bizjournals.com. **Contact:** Gina Mangieri, editor. **5% freelance written.** Weekly business newspaper. Estab. 1963. Circ. 14,500. Pays on publication. Byline given. Offers 50% kill fee. Buys all rights. Editorial lead time 1 month. Accepts queries by mail, e-mail, fax, phone. Responds in 2 weeks to queries. Sample copy for free.

Nonfiction: Opinion, feature articles. Query with published clips. Length: 750-1,000 words. **Pays $150.**

Photos: State availability with submission. Reviews negatives. Buys all rights. Offers no additional payment for photos accepted with ms. Captions required.

$ $ $ $ PROFIT, The Magazine for Canadian Entrepreneurs, Rogers Media, 777 Bay St., 5th Floor, Toronto, Ontario M5W 1A7, Canada. (416)596-5016. Fax: (416)596-5111. E-mail: profit@profitmag.ca. Website: www.profitguide.com. **Contact:** Ian Portsmouth, managing editor. **80% freelance written.** Magazine published 8 times/year covering small and medium businesses. "We specialize in specific, useful information that helps our readers manage their businesses better. We want Canadian stories only." Estab. 1982. Circ. 110,000. **Pays on acceptance.** Publishes ms an average of 2 months after acceptance. Byline given. Offers variable kill fee. Buys first North American serial, electronic rights. Submit seasonal material 6 months in advance. Accepts queries by mail, e-mail, fax, phone. Responds in 1 month to queries; 6 weeks to mss. Sample copy for 9×12 SAE with 84¢ postage. Writer's guidelines free.

Nonfiction: How-to (business management tips), strategies and Canadian business profiles. **Buys 50 mss/year.** Query with published clips. Length: 800-2,000 words. **Pays $500-2,000.** Pays expenses of writers on assignment.

Columns/Departments: Finance (info on raising capital in Canada), 700 words; Marketing (marketing strategies for independent business), 700 words. **Buys 80 mss/year.** Query with published clips. **Pays $150-600.**

The online magazine carries original content not found in the print edition. Contact: Andrea Szego, online editor.

Tips: "We're wide open to freelancers with good ideas and some knowledge of business. Read the magazine and understand it before submitting your ideas—which should have a Canadian focus."

$ ROCHESTER BUSINESS JOURNAL, Rochester Business Journal, Inc., 55 St. Paul St., Rochester NY 14604. (585)546-8303. Fax: (585)546-3398. E-mail: rackley@rbj.net. Website: www.rbjdaily.com. Editor: Paul Ericson. Managing Editor: Mike Dickinson. **Contact:** Reid Ackley, associate editor. **10% freelance written.** Weekly tabloid covering local business. "The *Rochester Business Journal* is geared toward corporate executives and owners of small businesses, bringing them leading-edge business coverage and analysis first in the market." Estab. 1984. Circ. 10,000. Pays on publication. Publishes ms an average of 1 month after acceptance. Byline given. Buys first, second serial (reprint), electronic rights. Editorial lead time 6 weeks. Accepts queries by mail, e-mail, fax. Responds in 1 week to queries. Sample copy for free or by e-mail. Writer's guidelines for #10 SASE or by e-mail.

Nonfiction: How-to (business topics), news features, trend stories with local examples. Do not query about any topics that do not include several local examples—local companies, organizations, universities, etc. **Buys 110 mss/year.** Query with published clips. Length: 1,000-2,000 words. **Pays $150.**

Tips: "The *Rochester Business Journal* prefers queries from local published writers who can demonstrate the ability to write for a sophisticated audience of business readers. Story ideas should be about business trends illustrated with numerous examples of local companies participating in the change or movement."

$ $ SACRAMENTO BUSINESS JOURNAL, American City Business Journals, Inc., 1401 21st St., Suite 200, Sacramento CA 95814-5221. (916)447-7661. Fax: (916)447-2243. E-mail: bbuchanan@bizjournals.com. Website: www.sacramento.bcentral.com. Editor: Lee Wessman. **Contact:** Bill Buchanan, managing editor. **5% freelance written.** Weekly newspaper covering the Sacramento area's economy. "Our readers are decision makers. They own or manage companies, or are community leaders who want to know what's happening. They expect sophisticated, well-researched news. And they don't read fluff." Estab. 1984. Circ. 14,000. Pays on publication. Publishes ms an average of 1 month after acceptance. Byline sometimes given. Offers 50% kill fee. Buys all rights, makes work-for-hire assignments. Editorial lead time 2 months. Submit seasonal material 2 months in advance. Accepts queries by mail, e-mail, phone. Responds in 3 weeks to queries. Sample copy for $2 and SAE with 2 first-class stamps.

- Prefers e-mail queries.

O-- Break in by sending clips that demonstrate your ability to write a complete news story.

Nonfiction: Humor, interview/profile, new product, opinion, local business news and trends. "No public relations stories on behalf of specific companies or industries. No thinly sourced stories." **Buys 60 mss/year.** Query with published clips. Length: 500-1,500 words. **Pays $125-200.** Sometimes pays expenses of writers on assignment.

Photos: State availability with submission. Reviews contact sheets, Prints. Buys one-time rights. Pays $25-50/photo. Captions, identification of subjects required.

Columns/Departments: Joe Vanacore, associate editor. Small Biz (meaningful successes or failures), 750 words. **Buys 20 mss/year.** Query. **Pays $100-175.**

Tips: "Most of our freelance work is done on assignment with a 3-week turnaround. We look for a regular stable of writers who can get an assignment, do the research, and produce a well-focused story that reflects the drama of business and doesn't avoid controversy."

$ $ TEXAS TECHNOLOGY, Dallas, Austin, Houston and San Antonio editions, (also publishes *California Technology, Colorado Technology,* and *Illinois Technology* with the same requirements and procedures), Power Media Group, 13490 TI Blvd., Suite 100, Dallas TX 75243. (972)690-6222, ext. 16. Fax: (972)690-6333. E-mail: lkline@thetechmag.com. Website: www.thetechmag.com. **Contact:** Laurie Kline, editor. **95% freelance written.** Monthly magazine covering technology. "*Texas Technology* (and sibling magazines *California Technology, Colorado Technology,* and *Illinois Technology*) are high-tech lifestyle magazines. We publish articles that discuss how technology affects our lives. Our audience is a mix of techies and mainstream consumers." Estab. 1997. Circ. 780,000 (total for all 4 publications). Pays on publication. Byline given. Offers $20 kill fee. Buys first North American serial, second serial (reprint), electronic rights, makes work-for-hire assignments. Editorial lead time 3 months. Submit seasonal material 3 months in advance. Accepts queries by mail, e-mail. Accepts simultaneous submissions. Responds in 3 weeks to queries; 2 months to mss. Sample copy and writer's guidelines free.

Nonfiction: Essays, exposé, general interest, historical/nostalgic, humor, interview/profile, new product, technical. "No computer hardware articles." **Buys 50 mss/year.** Query with published clips. Length: 1,200-3,500 words. **Pays $200-400.**

Photos: State availability with submission. Reviews contact sheets. Buys all rights. Negotiates payment individually. Captions, identification of subjects, model releases required.

$ $ UTAH BUSINESS, The Magazine for Decision Makers, Olympus Publishing, 1245 E. Brickyard Rd., Suite 90, Salt Lake City UT 84106. (801)568-0114. E-mail: editor@utahbusiness.com. Website: www.utahbusiness.com. **Contact:** Barry Scholl, editor. **95% freelance written.** Monthly magazine. "*Utah Business* is a monthly magazine focusing on the people, practices, and principles that drive Utah's economy. Audience is business owners and executives." Estab. 1986. Circ. 25,000. Pays 2 weeks after publication. Byline given. Buys first, one-time, all rights, makes work-for-hire assignments. Editorial lead time 3 months. Submit seasonal material 5 months in advance. Accepts queries by mail, e-mail, fax. Accepts previously published material. Accepts simultaneous submissions. Sample copy for $5, 8½×11 SAE and 8 first-class stamps. Writer's guidelines for #10 SASE.

O-- Break in by "reviewing our editorial calendar, then querying us with an idea for a particular column or feature 4 months in advance."

Nonfiction: How-to (business), interview/profile (business), new product, technical (business/technical), business-related articles. "Everything we publish must have a Utah angle." **Buys 150-180 mss/year.** Length: 500-2,500 words. **Pays 20¢/word.** Sometimes pays expenses of writers on assignment.

Photos: State availability with submission. Reviews contact sheets, negatives, transparencies, Prints. Buys one-time rights. Offers no additional payment for photos accepted with ms. Captions, identification of subjects, model releases required.

Columns/Departments: Query with published clips. **Pays 20¢/word.**

Tips: "Use common sense; tailor your queries and stories to this market. Use AP style and colorful leads. Read the magazine first!"

$ $ VERMONT BUSINESS MAGAZINE, 2 Church St., Burlington VT 05401-4445. (802)863-8038. Fax: (802)863-8069. E-mail: vtbizmag@together.net. Website: www.vtbusinessmagazine.com. **Contact:** Timothy McQuiston, editor. **80% freelance written.** Monthly tabloid covering business in Vermont. Circ. 8,000. Pays on publication. Publishes ms an average of 1 month after acceptance. Byline given. Buys one-time rights. Responds in 2 months to queries. Sample copy for 11×14 SAE and 7 first-class stamps.

Nonfiction: Business trends and issues. **Buys 200 mss/year.** Query with published clips. Length: 800-1,800 words. **Pays $100-200.**

Reprints: Send tearsheet and information about when and where the material previously appeared.

Photos: Send photos with submission. Reviews contact sheets. Offers $10-35/photo. Identification of subjects required.

Tips: "Read daily papers and look for business angles for a follow-up article. We look for issue and trend articles rather than company or businessman profiles. Note: Magazine accepts Vermont-specific material only. The articles must be about Vermont."

CAREER, COLLEGE & ALUMNI

Three types of magazines are listed in this section: University publications written for students, alumni, and friends of a specific institution; publications about college life for students; and publications on career and job opportunities. Literary magazines published by colleges and universities are listed in the Literary & "Little" section.

$ $ AMERICAN CAREERS, Career Communications, Inc., 6701 W. 64th St., Overland Park KS 66202. (800)669-7795. Fax: (913)362-7788. Website: www.carcom.com. **Contact:** Mary Pitchford, editor. **50% freelance written.** High school and technical school student publication covering careers, career statistics, skills needed to get jobs. "*American Careers* provides career, salary, and education information to middle school and high school students. Self-tests help them relate their interests and abilities to future careers. Articles on résumés, interviews, etc., help them develop employability skills." Estab. 1989. Circ. 500,000. **Pays on acceptance.** Byline given. Buys all rights, makes work-for-hire assignments. Accepts queries by mail. Accepts simultaneous submissions. Responds in 1 month to queries. Sample copy for $3. Writer's guidelines for #10 SASE.

Break in by "sending us query letters with samples and résumés. We want to 'meet' the writer before making an assignment."

Nonfiction: Career and education features related to career paths, including arts and communication, business, law, government, finance, construction, technology, health services, human services, manufacturing, engineering, and natural resources and agriculture. "No preachy advice to teens or articles that talk down to students." **Buys 20 mss/year.** Query by mail only with published clips. Length: 300-1,000 words. **Pays $100-450.** Pays expenses of writers on assignment.

Photos: State availability with submission. Buys all rights. Negotiates payment individually. Captions, identification of subjects, model releases required.

Tips: "Letters of introduction or query letters with samples and résumés are ways we get to know writers. Samples should include how-to articles and career-related articles. Articles written for teenagers also would make good samples. Short feature articles on careers, career-related how-to articles, and self-assessment tools (10-20 point quizzes with scoring information) are primarily what we publish."

$ $ THE BLACK COLLEGIAN, The Career & Self Development Magazine for African-American Students, iMinorities.com, Inc., 909 Poydras St., 36th Floor, New Orleans LA 70112. (504)523-0154. Fax: (504)523-0271. E-mail: robert@black-collegiate.com. Website: www.black-collegian.com. **Contact:** Robert Miller, vice president/editor. **25% freelance written.** Semiannual magazine for African-American college students and recent graduates with an interest in career and job information, African-American cultural awareness, personalities, history, trends and current events. Estab. 1970. Circ. 112,000. Pays on publication. Byline given. Buys one-time rights. Submit seasonal material 2 months in advance. Accepts queries by mail, e-mail, fax. Responds in 6 months to queries. Sample copy for $4 and 9×12 SAE. Writer's guidelines for #10 SASE.

Nonfiction: Material on careers, sports, black history, news analysis. Articles on problems and opportunities confronting African-American college students and recent graduates. Book excerpts, exposé, general interest, historical/nostalgic, how-to (develop employability), inspirational, interview/profile, opinion, personal experience. Query. Length: 900-1,900 words. **Pays $100-500 for assigned articles.**

Photos: State availability of or send photos with submission. Reviews 8×10 prints. Captions, identification of subjects, model releases required.

The online magazine carries original content in addition to what's included in the print edition. Contact: Robert Miller, online editor.

Tips: Articles are published under primarily five broad categories: job hunting information, overviews of career opportunities and industry reports, self-development information, analyses and investigations of conditions and problems that affect African Americans, and celebrations of African-American success.

$ $ $ $ BROWN ALUMNI MAGAZINE, Brown University, Box 1854, Providence RI 02912-1854. (401)863-2873. Fax: (401)863-9599. E-mail: alumni_magazine@brown.edu. Website: www.brownalumnimagazine.com. Editor: Norman Boucher. **Contact:** Ronald Dunleavy, office manager. **50% freelance written.** Bimonthly magazine covering the world of Brown University and its alumni. "We are an editorially independent, general interest magazine covering the on-campus world of Brown University and the off-campus world of its alumni." Estab. 1900. Circ. 80,000. **Pays on acceptance.** Publishes ms an average of 3 months after acceptance. Byline given. Offers 30% kill fee. Buys first North American serial rights. Editorial lead time 3 months. Submit seasonal material 4 months in advance. Accepts queries by mail, e-mail, fax. Responds in 1 month to queries; 2 months to mss. Sample copy for free. Writer's guidelines not available.

Nonfiction: Book excerpts, essays, exposé, general interest, historical/nostalgic, humor, interview/profile, opinion, personal experience, photo feature, travel, profiles. No articles unconnected to Brown or its alumni. **Buys 50 mss/year.** Query with published clips. Length: 150-4,000 words. **Pays $200-2,000 for assigned articles; $100-1,500 for unsolicited articles.** Pays expenses of writers on assignment.

Photos: State availability with submission. Reviews contact sheets, transparencies, prints. Buys one-time rights. Negotiates payment individually. Captions, identification of subjects required.

Columns/Departments: Under the Elms (news items about campus), 100-400 words; Arts & Culture (reviews of Brown-authored works), 200-500 words; Alumni P.O.V. (essays by Brown alumni), 750 words; Sports (reports on Brown sports teams and athletes), 200-500 words. **Buys 30-40 mss/year.** Query with published clips. **Pays $100-500.**

Tips: "Be imaginative and be specific. A Brown connection is required for all stories in the magazine, but a Brown connection alone does not guarantee our interest. Ask yourself: Why should readers care about your proposed story? Also, we look for depth and objective reporting, not boosterism."

$ $ CIRCLE K MAGAZINE, 3636 Woodview Trace, Indianapolis IN 46268-3196. (317)875-8755. Fax: (317)879-0204. E-mail: ckimagazine@kiwanis.org. Website: www.circlek.org. **Contact:** Amy Wiser, executive editor. **60% freelance written.** Magazine published 5 times/year. "Our readership consists almost entirely of above-average college students interested in voluntary community service and leadership development. They are politically and socially aware and have a wide range of interests." Circ. 15,000. **Pays on acceptance.** Byline given. Buys first North American serial rights. Accepts queries by mail, e-mail, fax. Responds in 2 months to queries. Sample copy and writer's guidelines for large SAE with 3 first-class stamps or on website.

Break in by offering "fresh ideas for stories dealing with college students who are not only concerned with themselves. Our readers are concerned with making their communities better."

Nonfiction: Articles published in *Circle K* are of 2 types—serious and light nonfiction. "We are interested in general interest articles on topics concerning college students and their lifestyles, as well as articles dealing with careers, community concerns, and leadership development." "No first-person confessions, family histories, or travel pieces." Query. Length: 1,500-2,000 words. **Pays $150-400.**

Photos: Purchased with accompanying ms; total price includes both photos and ms. Captions required.

Tips: "Query should indicate author's familiarity with the field and sources. Subject treatment must be objective and in-depth, and articles should include illustrative examples and quotes from persons involved in the subject or qualified to speak on it. We are open to working with new writers who present a good article idea and demonstrate that they've done their homework concerning the article subject itself, as well as concerning our magazine's style. We're interested in college-oriented trends, for example: entrepreneur schooling, high-tech classrooms, music, leisure, and health issues."

$ COLLEGE BOUND, The Magazine for High School Students By College Students, Ramholtz Publishing, Inc., 1200 South Ave., Suite 202, Staten Island NY 10314. (718)761-4800. Fax: (718)761-3300. E-mail: editorial@collegebound.net. Website: www.collegebound.net. **Contact:** Gina LaGuardia, editor-in-chief. **85% freelance written.** Bimonthly magazine "written by college students for high school students and is designed to provide an inside view of college life." Estab. 1987. Circ. 95,000. Pays on publication. Publishes ms an average of 4 months after acceptance. Byline given. Buys first North American serial, second serial (reprint), electronic rights. Editorial lead time 4 months. Submit seasonal material 4 months in advance. Accepts queries by mail, e-mail. Accepts previously published material. Responds in 5 weeks to queries. Sample copy and writer's guidelines for 9×12 SASE.

Nonfiction: How-to (apply for college, prepare for the interview, etc.), personal experience (college experiences). **Buys 30 mss/year.** Query with published clips. Length: 600-1,000 words. **Pays $70-100.**

Reprints: Send photocopy.

Photos: Send photos with submission. Reviews prints. Buys one-time rights. Offers no additional payment for photos accepted with ms.

Columns/Departments: Straight Up Strategies (think fun, service pieces: campus survival tips, admissions advice, etc.), 150-400 words; Cash Crunch (money-related tips, scholarship news, advice), 150-400 words; Personal Statement (first-person account of a college-related experience), 600-1,000 words; Debate Team (op-ed style views on college controversies), 500-600 words. **Buys 30 mss/year.** Query with published clips. **Pays $15-100.**

Fillers: Anecdotes, facts, newsbreaks, short humor. **Buys 10/year.** Length: 50-200 words. **Pays $15-25.**

The online magazine (at collegeboundmag.com) carries original content not found in the print edition.

Tips: "College students from around the country (and those young at heart) are welcome to serve as correspondents to provide our teen readership with both personal accounts and cutting-edge, expert advice on the college admissions process and beyond. We're looking for well-researched articles packed with real-life student anecdotes and expert insight on everything from dealing with dorm life, choosing the right college, and joining a fraternity or sorority, to college dating, cool campus happenings, scholarship scoring strategies, and other college issues."

$ $ COMMUNITY COLLEGE WEEK, CMA Publishing, Inc., 10520 Warwick Ave., Suite B-8, Fairfax VA 22030. (703)385-2981. Fax: (703)385-1839. E-mail: scottc@cmabiccw.com. Website: www.ccweek.com. Associate Editor: Kristina Lane. **Contact:** Scott Cech, editor. **80% freelance written.** Biweekly tabloid covering 2-year colleges. "*Community College Week* is the nation's only independent newspaper covering news, features, and trends at the country's 1,250 community, junior, and technical colleges." Circ. 6,500. Pays on publication. Byline given. Offers variable kill fee. Buys one-time print and electronic rights. Editorial lead time 2 months. Submit seasonal material 2 months in advance. Accepts queries by e-mail. Responds in 2 weeks to queries. Sample copy online. Writer's guidelines by e-mail.

Nonfiction: Exposé, interview/profile, opinion, photo feature, book reviews. **Buys 260 mss/year.** Always query by e-mail first, with published clips and résumé. Length: 400-1,500 words. **Pays 25¢/word.** Sometimes pays expenses of writers on assignment.

Photos: State availability with submission. Buys one-time rights. Negotiates payment individually. Captions required.

Columns/Departments: Pays 35¢/word.

$ $ DIVERSITY: CAREER OPPORTUNITIES AND INSIGHTS, Career Recruitment Media/CASS Communications, Inc., 1800 Sherman Ave., Suite 404, Evanston IL 60201-3769. (847)448-1019. Fax: (847)492-7373. E-mail: vicki.chung@careermedia.com. Website: www.careermedia.com. **Contact:** Vicki Chung, senior editor. **75% freelance**

written. Quarterly magazine covering "career planning and job-hunting for minorities, women, and people with disabilities, who are college or university seniors preparing to enter the workforce or graduate school. Readers will be interested in white-collar professional positions in a variety of industries." Estab. 1967. Circ. 21,000. **Pays on acceptance.** Publishes ms an average of 3 months after acceptance. Byline given. Buys first North American serial rights. Editorial lead time 3 months. Accepts queries by mail, e-mail. Responds in 3 weeks to queries; 1 month to mss. Sample copy for 10×12 SAE with 6 first-class stamps. Writer's guidelines for #10 SASE or by e-mail.

Break in with "a story targeted specifically to the concerns of women and minority college seniors who are getting ready to start their professional careers or go on to graduate school."

Nonfiction: Buys 15-20 mss/year. Query with published clips. Length: 1,500-2,000 words. **Pays $400-550 for assigned articles; $400 for unsolicited articles.** Pays phone expenses only of writers on assignment.

Photos: State availability with submission. Contact photo editor for guidelines. Identification of subjects required.

Columns/Departments: Columns are usually unpaid assignments.

Tips: "Remember our audience—college seniors who are minorities, women, and persons with disabilities. Try to appeal to today's young, hip, Internet-savvy audience. Sources interviewed should reflect diversity."

$ $ $ $ EXPERIENCE MAGAZINE, The magazine for building your career, experience.com inc., One Faneuil Hall Marketplace, Boston MA 02109. Fax: (617)305-7900. Website: www.experience.com. Editor: Danyel Barnard. **Contact:** Christopher Bordeau, associate editor. **50% freelance written.** Quarterly magazine on career development for young professionals. Estab. 1999. Circ. 1 million. Pays 45 days after acceptance. Publishes ms an average of 3 months after acceptance. Byline given. Offers 25% kill fee. Buys all rights. Editorial lead time 5 months. Accepts queries by mail, fax. Sample copy for free. Writer's guidelines for free or online.

Nonfiction: How-to, interview/profile, career-related. **Buys 20-30 mss/year.** Query with published clips. Length: 1,000-2,500 words. **Pays $500-2,500.** Sometimes pays expenses of writers on assignment.

N $ FLORIDA LEADER, (for college students), P.O. Box 14081, Gainesville FL 32604-2081. (352)373-6907. Fax: (352)373-8120. E-mail: info@studentleader.com. Website: www.floridaleader.com. Publisher: W.H. Oxendine, Jr. **Contact:** Stephanie Reck, associate editor. **10% freelance written.** Triannual magazine. College magazine, feature-oriented, especially activities, events, interests and issues pertaining to college students. Estab. 1983. Circ. 50,000. Pays on publication. Publishes ms an average of 2 months after acceptance. Byline given. Submit seasonal material 6 months in advance. Accepts queries by mail, e-mail, fax. Responds in 2 months to queries. Sample copy and writer's guidelines for $3,50, 9×12 SAE with 5 first-class stamps.

Nonfiction: Practical tips for going to college, student life and leadership development. How-to, humor, interview/profile, Feature (All multi-sourced and Florida college related). "No lengthy individual profiles or articles without primary and secondary sources of attribution." Length: 900 words. **Pays $35-75.** Sometimes pays expenses of writers on assignment.

Photos: State availability with submission. Reviews negatives, transparencies. Captions, identification of subjects, model releases required.

Columns/Departments: College Life, The Lead Role, In Every Issue (quizzes, tips), Florida Forum (features Florida high school students), 250-1,000 words. **Buys 2 mss/year.** Query.

The online magazine carries original content not found in the print edition. Contact: Stephanie Reck and Butch Oxendine, online editors.

Tips: "Read other high school and college publications for current issues, interests. Send manuscripts or outlines for review. All sections open to freelance work. Always looking for lighter, humorous articles as well as features on Florida colleges and universities, careers, jobs. Multi-sourced (5-10) articles are best."

$ $ $ $ HARVARD MAGAZINE, Harvard Magazine, Inc., 7 Ware St., Cambridge MA 02138. (617)495-5746. Fax: (617)495-0324. Website: www.harvardmagazine.com. **Contact:** John S. Rosenberg, editor. **35-50% freelance written.** Bimonthly magazine for Harvard University faculty, alumni, and students. Estab. 1898. Circ. 225,000. Pays on publication. Publishes ms an average of 4 months after acceptance. Byline given. one-time print and website rights Editorial lead time 1 year. Accepts queries by mail, fax. Responds in 1 month to queries; 1 month to mss. Sample copy online. Writer's guidelines not available.

Nonfiction: Book excerpts, essays, interview/profile, journalism on Harvard-related intellectual subjects. **Buys 20-30 mss/year.** Query with published clips. Length: 800-10,000 words. **Pays $250-2,000.** Pays expenses of writers on assignment.

$ $ $ NOTRE DAME MAGAZINE, University of Notre Dame, 538 Grace Hall, Notre Dame IN 46556-5612. (574)631-5335. Fax: (574)631-6767. E-mail: ndmag.1@nd.edu. Website: www.nd.edu/~ndmag. Managing Editor: Carol Schaal. **Contact:** Kerry Temple, editor. **75% freelance written.** Quarterly magazine covering news of Notre Dame and education and issues affecting contemporary society. "We are a university magazine with a scope as broad as that found at a university, but we place our discussion in a moral, ethical, spiritual context reflecting our Catholic heritage." Estab. 1972. Circ. 142,000. **Pays on acceptance.** Publishes ms an average of 1 year after acceptance. Byline given. Buys first, electronic rights. Accepts queries by mail, e-mail, fax. Responds in 2 months to queries. Sample copy and writer's guidelines online.

Nonfiction: Opinion, personal experience, religious. **Buys 35 mss/year.** Query with published clips. Length: 600-3,000 words. **Pays $250-1,500.** Sometimes pays expenses of writers on assignment.

Photos: State availability with submission. Reviews transparencies, 8×10 prints prints, b&w contact sheets. Buys one-time and electronic rights. Identification of subjects, model releases required.

Columns/Departments: Perspectives (essays, often written in first-person, deal with a wide array of issues—some topical, some personal, some serious, some light). Query with or without published clips or send complete ms.

The online version carries original content not found in the print edition and includes writer's guidelines. Contact: Carol Schaal.

Tips: "The editors are always looking for new writers and fresh ideas. However, the caliber of the magazine and frequency of its publication dictate that the writing meet very high standards. The editors value articles strong in storytelling quality, journalistic technique, and substance. They do not encourage promotional or nostalgia pieces, stories on sports, or essays which are sentimentally religious."

$ $ OREGON QUARTERLY, The Magazine of the University of Oregon, 5228 University of Oregon Chapman Hall, Eugene OR 97403-5228. (541)346-5048. Fax: (541)346-5571. E-mail: quarterly@oregon.uoregon.edu. Website: www.uoregon.edu/~oq. Assistant Editor: Brett Campbell. **Contact:** Guy Maynard. **50% freelance written.** Quarterly magazine covering people and ideas at the University of Oregon and the Northwest. Estab. 1919. Circ. 100,000. **Pays on acceptance.** Publishes ms an average of 3 months after acceptance. Byline given. Buys first North American serial rights. Accepts queries by mail, e-mail. Accepts previously published material. Responds in 2 months to queries. Sample copy for 9×12 SAE with 4 first-class stamps or on website.

Break in to the magazine with a profile (400 or 800 words) of a University of Oregon alumnus. Best to query first.

Nonfiction: Northwest issues and culture from the perspective of UO alumni and faculty. **Buys 30 mss/year.** Query with published clips. Length: 250-2,500 words. **Pays $100-750.** Sometimes pays expenses of writers on assignment.

Reprints: Send photocopy and information about when and where the material previously appeared. Pays 50% of amount paid for an original article.

Photos: State availability with submission. Reviews 8×10 prints. Buys one-time rights. Offers $10-25/photo. Identification of subjects required.

Fiction: Publishes novel excerpts.

Tips: "Query with strong, colorful lead; clips."

$ $ THE PENN STATER, Penn State Alumni Association, Hintz Family Alumni Center, University Park PA 16802. (814)865-2709. Fax: (814)863-5690. E-mail: pennstater@psu.edu. Website: www.alumni.psu.edu. **Contact:** Tina Hay, editor. **75% freelance written.** Bimonthly magazine covering Penn State and Penn Staters. Estab. 1910. Circ. 123,000. **Pays on acceptance.** Publishes ms an average of 4 months after acceptance. Byline given. Offers 50% kill fee. Buys first North American serial, second serial (reprint) rights. Editorial lead time 3 months. Submit seasonal material 8 months in advance. Accepts queries by mail, e-mail, fax. Accepts previously published material. Accepts simultaneous submissions. Responds in 3 months to queries. Sample copy and writer's guidelines free.

Nonfiction: Stories must have Penn State connection. Book excerpts (by Penn Staters), general interest, historical/nostalgic, interview/profile, personal experience, photo feature, book reviews, science/research. No unsolicited mss. **Buys 20 mss/year.** Query with published clips. Length: 200-3,000 words. **Pays competitive rates.** Pays expenses of writers on assignment.

Reprints: Send photocopy and information about when and where the material previously appeared. Payment varies.

Photos: Send photos with submission. Reviews transparencies, prints. Buys one-time rights. Negotiates payment individually. Captions required.

Tips: "We are especially interested in attracting writers who are savvy in creative nonfiction/literary journalism. Most stories must have a Penn State tie-in. No phone calls."

$ $ THE PURDUE ALUMNUS, Purdue Alumni Association, Purdue Memorial Union 160, 101 N. Grant St., West Lafayette IN 47906-6212. (765)494-5182. Fax: (765)494-9179. E-mail: slmartin@purdue.edu. Website: www.purdue.edu/PAA. **Contact:** Sharon Martin, editor. **50% freelance written.** Prefers to work with published/established writers; works with small number of new/unpublished writers each year. Bimonthly magazine covering subjects of interest to Purdue University alumni. Estab. 1912. Circ. 65,000. Pays on publication. Publishes ms an average of 2 months after acceptance. Byline given. Buys first rights, makes work-for-hire assignments. Submit seasonal material 6 months in advance. Accepts queries by mail. Accepts previously published material. Accepts simultaneous submissions. Responds in 3 weeks to queries. Sample copy for 9×12 SAE with 2 first-class stamps.

Nonfiction: Focus is on alumni, campus news, issues, and opinions of interest to 65,000 members of the Alumni Association. Feature style, primarily university-oriented. Issues relevant to education. General interest, historical/nostalgic, humor, interview/profile, personal experience. **Buys 12-20 mss/year.** Length: 1,500-2,500 words. **Pays $250-500 for assigned articles.** Pays expenses of writers on assignment.

Photos: State availability with submission. Reviews 5×7 prints, b&w contact sheets.

Tips: "We have more than 300,000 living, breathing Purdue alumni. If you can find a good story about one of them, we're interested. We use local freelancers to do campus pieces."

$ $ RIPON COLLEGE MAGAZINE, P.O. Box 248, Ripon WI 54971-0248. (920)748-8364. Fax: (920)748-9262. E-mail: booneL@ripon.edu. Website: www.ripon.edu. **Contact:** Loren J. Boone, editor. **15% freelance written.** Quarterly

magazine that "contains information relating to Ripon College and is mailed to alumni and friends of the college." Estab. 1851. Circ. 14,000. Pays on publication. Publishes ms an average of 3 months after acceptance. Byline given. Makes work-for-hire assignments. Accepts queries by mail, e-mail, fax, phone. Responds in 2 weeks to queries.
Nonfiction: Historical/nostalgic, interview/profile. **Buys 4 mss/year.** Query with or without published clips or send complete ms. Length: 250-1,000 words. **Pays $25-350.**
Photos: State availability with submission. Reviews contact sheets. Buys one-time rights. Offers additional payment for photos accepted with ms. Captions, model releases required.
Tips: "Story ideas must have a direct connection to Ripon College."

$ $ $ $ RUTGERS MAGAZINE, Rutgers University, Alexander Johnston Hall, New Brunswick NJ 08903. (732)932-7084, ext. 618. Fax: (732)932-8412. E-mail: rolson@ur.rutgers.edu. **Contact:** Renee Olson, editor. **30% freelance written.** Quarterly university magazine of "general interest, but articles must have a Rutgers University or alumni tie-in." Circ. 110,000. **Pays on acceptance.** Publishes ms an average of 4 months after acceptance. Byline given. Offers kill fee. Buys first North American serial rights. Submit seasonal material 8 months in advance. Accepts queries by mail, e-mail, fax. Responds in 1 month to queries. Sample copy for $3 and 9×12 SAE with 5 first-class stamps.
Nonfiction: Essays, general interest, historical/nostalgic, interview/profile, photo feature, science/research; art/humanities. No articles without a Rutgers connection. **Buys 10-15 mss/year.** Query with published clips. Length: 1,200-3,500 words. **Pays $1,200-2,200.** Pays expenses of writers on assignment.
Photos: State availability with submission. Buys one-time rights. Payment varies. Identification of subjects required.
Columns/Departments: Sports; Alumni Profiles (related to Rutgers), all 1,200-1,800 words. **Buys 4-6 mss/year.** Query with published clips. **Pays competitively.**
Tips: "Send an intriguing query backed by solid clips. We'll evaluate clips and topic for most appropriate use."

$ STUDENT LEADER, (for college students), Oxendine Publishing Inc., P.O. Box 14081, Gainesville FL 32604-2081. (352)373-6907. Fax: (352)373-8120. E-mail: jenniferl@studentleader.com. Website: www.studentleader.com. Editor: W.H. Oxendine, Jr. **Contact:** John Lamathe, associate editor. **10% freelance written.** Magazine published 3 times/year covering student government, campus leadership. Estab. 1993. Circ. 150,000. Pays on publication. Byline given. Buys all rights. Submit seasonal material 4 months in advance. Accepts queries by mail, e-mail, fax. Responds in 1 month to queries. Sample copy for 9×12 manila SASE and $3.50 check/money order to Oxendine Publishing. Writer's guidelines for #10 SASE.

O→ Visit www.studentleader.com to study our article style and previously used topics.

Nonfiction: Readers include student government officers, resident assistants, honor society leaders, volunteer coordinators, fraternity/sorority members. How-to (include details on implementing new ideas or programs on a college campus), interview/profile, personal experience, leadership development (news/tips for college students). **Buys 2 mss/year.** Query. Length: 900 words. **Pay varies.** Pays contributors copies to students or first-time writers.
Photos: State availability of or send photos with submission. Reviews contact sheets, negatives, transparencies. Buys all rights. Captions, identification of subjects required.
Fillers: Facts, newsbreaks, Tips. **Buys 2/year.** Length: 100 words/minimum. **Pays no payment for fillers.**

The online magazine carries original content not found in the print edition. Contact: John Lamathe and Butch Oxendine, online editors.

Tips: "Read other high school and college publications for current ideas, interests. Send outlines or manuscripts for review. All sections open to freelance work. Looking for practical and useful information regarding programming ideas, community-service projects, outstanding campus organizations and leadership programs."

$ ★ SUCCEED, The Magazine for Continuing Education, Ramholtz Publishing, Inc., 1200 South Ave., Suite 202, Staten Island NY 10314. (718)761-4800. Fax: (718)761-3300. E-mail: editorial@collegebound.net. **Contact:** Gina LaGuardia, editor-in-chief. **85% freelance written.** Quarterly magazine. "*SUCCEED*'s readers are interested in continuing education, whether it be for changing careers or enhancing their current career." Estab. 1994. Circ. 155,000. Pays on publication. Publishes ms an average of 4 months after acceptance. Byline given. Buys first, second serial (reprint) rights. Editorial lead time 4 months. Submit seasonal material 4 months in advance. Accepts queries by mail, e-mail. Accepts previously published material. Accepts simultaneous submissions. Responds in 5 weeks to queries. Sample copy for $1.87. Writer's guidelines for 9×12 SASE.

O→ Break in with "an up-to-date, expert-driven article of interest to our audience with personal, real-life anecdotes as support—not basis—for exploration."

Nonfiction: Essays, exposé, general interest, how-to (change careers), interview/profile (interesting careers), new product, opinion, personal experience. **Buys 25 mss/year.** Query with published clips. Length: 1,000-1,500 words. **Pays $75-150.** Sometimes pays expenses of writers on assignment.
Reprints: Send photocopy.
Photos: Send photos with submission. Reviews negatives, prints. Buys one-time rights. Offers no additional payment for photos accepted with ms. Captions, identification of subjects required.
Columns/Departments: Tech Zone (new media/technology), 300-700 words; To Be... (personality/career profile), 600-800 words; Financial Fitness (finance, money management), 100-300 words; Memo Pad (short, newsworthy items that relate to today's changing job market and continuing education); Solo Success (how readers can "do it on their own," with recommended resources, books, and software). **Buys 10 mss/year.** Query with published clips. **Pays $50-75.**
Fillers: Facts, newsbreaks. **Buys 5/year.** Length: 50-200 words.

Tips: "Stay current and address issues of importance to our readers—lifelong learners and those in career transition. They're ambitious, hands-on and open to advice, new areas of opportunity, etc."

$ $ TOMORROW'S CHRISTIAN GRADUATE, WINPress, P.O. Box 1357, Oak Park IL 60304. (708)524-5070. Fax: (708)524-5174. E-mail: winpress7@aol.com. Website: www.christiangraduate.com. **Contact:** Phillip Huber, managing editor. **85% freelance written.** Annual magazine covering seminary and graduate school planning. "*Tomorrow's Christian Graduate* is a planning guide for adults pursuing a seminary or Christian graduate education and expresses the value of a seminary or Christian graduate education." Estab. 1998. Circ. 150,000. Pays on publication. Publishes ms an average of 4 months after acceptance. Byline given. Buys first rights. Editorial lead time 4 months. Accepts queries by mail, e-mail. Sample copy for $3. Writer's guidelines free.

O-- Break in with "a well-written, researched piece that shows how readers can get into a Christian graduate school or seminary or explains some program available at such schools."

Nonfiction: First person and how-to features focus on all topics of interest to adults pursuing graduate studies. How-to, interview/profile, personal experience. No fiction or poetry. **Buys 8-10 mss/year.** Query with published clips. Length: 800-1,600 words. **Pays 12-15¢/word.**

Photos: State availability with submission. Negotiates payment individually. Captions, identification of subjects, model releases required.

Tips: "We are open to working with new/unpublished authors, especially current graduate students, graduate professors, admissions personnel, career counselors, and financial aid officers."

$ $ U.S. BLACK ENGINEER/HISPANIC ENGINEER, And Information Technology, Career Communications Group, Inc., 729 E. Pratt St., Suite 504, Baltimore MD 21202-3101. (410)244-7101. Fax: (410)752-1837. Website: www.blackfamily.net.net. **Contact:** Eric Addison, managing editor. **80% freelance written.** Quarterly magazine. "Both of our magazines are designed to bring technology issues home to people of color. We look at careers in technology and what affects career possibilities, including education. But we also look at how technology affects Black Americans and Latinos." Estab. 1976. Circ. 40,000. Pays on publication. Publishes ms an average of 1 month after acceptance. Byline given. Offers 50% kill fee. Makes work-for-hire assignments. Editorial lead time 2 months. Accepts queries by mail, e-mail, fax, phone. Responds in 2 months to queries. Sample copy for #10 SASE. Writer's guidelines for #10 SASE.

Nonfiction: How-to (plan a career, get a first job, get a good job), interview/profile, new product, technical (new technologies and people of color involved with them), Capitol Hill/federal reportage on technology and EEO issues. No opinion pieces, first-person articles, routine profiles with no news peg or grounding in science/technology issues. Length: 650-1,800 words. **Pays $250-600 for assigned articles.** Sometimes pays expenses of writers on assignment.

Photos: State availability with submission. Buys all rights. Negotiates payment individually. Captions, identification of subjects, model releases required.

Columns/Departments: Dot-Comets (rising new economy entrepreneurs); Color of Technology (Did you know that...?), 800 words; Pros on the Move (Black/Hispanic career moves), 500 words; My Greatest Challenge (up from the roots), 650 words; E-Commerce (websites of interest), 650 words; TechDollars (technology and finance), 650 words; Community News (related to science and technology), 650 words; Technology for Kids, 650 words; Technology Overseas, 650 words. **Buys 30 mss/year. Pays $250-300.**

Tips: "Call or come see me. Also contact us about covering our conferences, Black Engineer of the Year Awards and Women of Color Technology Awards."

CHILD CARE & PARENTAL GUIDANCE

Magazines in this section address the needs and interests of families with children. Some publications are national in scope, others are geographically specific. Some offer general advice for parents, while magazines such as *Catholic Parent* answer the concerns of smaller groups. Other markets that buy articles about child care and the family are included in the Religious and Women's sections and in the Trade Education and Counseling section. Publications for children can be found in the Juvenile and Teen & Young Adult sections.

$ $ ✪ ALL ABOUT KIDS MAGAZINE, Midwest Parenting Publications, 1077 Celestial St., #101, Cincinnati OH 45202. (513)684-0501. Fax: (513)684-0507. E-mail: editor@aak.com. Website: www.aak.com. **Contact:** Shelly Bucksot, editor. **100% freelance written.** Monthly magazine *All About Kids* covers a myriad of parenting topics and pieces of information relative to families and children in greater Cincinnati. Estab. 1985. Circ. 60,000. Pays on publication. Publishes ms an average of 6 months after acceptance. Byline given. Buys first, electronic rights. Editorial lead time 3 months. Submit seasonal material 6 months in advance. Accepts queries by mail. Writer's guidelines free.

Nonfiction: Exposé, general interest, historical/nostalgic, how-to (family projects, crafts), humor, inspirational, interview/profile, opinion, photo feature, travel. Special issues: Maternity (January); Special Needs Children (May). No product or book reviews. **Buys 50 mss/year.** Send complete ms. Length: 750-3,000 words. **Pays $50-250 for assigned articles; $50-100 for unsolicited articles.**

Photos: State availability with submission.

Fillers: Anecdotes, facts, gags to be illustrated by cartoonist, short humor. **Buys 20/year.** Length: 350-800 words. **Pays $50-100.**

Tips: "Submit full-text articles with query letter. Keep in mind the location of the magazine and try to include relevant sidebars, sources, etc."

$ ATLANTA PARENT/ATLANTA BABY, 2346 Perimeter Park Dr., Suite 101, Atlanta GA 30341. (770)454-7599. Fax: (770)454-7699. E-mail: atlantaparent@atlantaparent.com. Website: www.atlantaparent.com. Publisher: Liz White. **Contact:** Amy Dusek, managing editor. **50% freelance written.** Pays on publication. Publishes ms an average of 3 months after acceptance. Byline given. Buys one-time rights. Submit seasonal material 6 months in advance. Accepts queries by mail, e-mail. Accepts previously published material. Responds in 4 months to queries. Sample copy for $3.

Nonfiction: General interest, how-to, humor, interview/profile, travel. Special issues: Private School (January); Camp (February); Health and Fitness (March); Birthday Parties (February and October); Maternity and Mothering (May); Childcare (July); Back-to-School (August); Teens (September); Holidays (November/December). No first-person accounts or philosophical discussions. **Buys 60 mss/year.** Query with or without published clips or send complete ms. Length: 800-2,100 words. **Pays $30-50.** Sometimes pays expenses of writers on assignment.

Reprints: Send tearsheet or photocopy with rights for sale noted and information about when and where the material previously appeared. **Pays $30-50**.

Photos: State availability of or send photos with submission. Reviews Reviews 3×5 photos. Buys one-time rights. Offers $10/photo.

Tips: "Articles should be geared to problems or situations of families and parents. Should include down-to-earth tips and be clearly written. No philosophical discussions or first-person narratives. We're also looking for well-written humor."

$ $ $ $ BABY TALK, The Parenting Group, 530 Fifth Ave., 4th Floor, New York NY 10036. (212)522-8989. Fax: (212)522-8750. Website: www.babytalk.com. **Contact:** Brittni Boyd, editorial assistant. **Mostly freelance written**. Magazine published 10 times/year. "*Baby Talk* is written primarily for women who are considering pregnancy or who are expecting a child, and parents of children from birth through 18 months, with the emphasis on pregnancy through first six months of life." Estab. 1935. Circ. 1,725,000. Byline given. Accepts queries by mail. Responds in 2 months to queries.

Nonfiction: Features cover pregnancy, the basics of baby care, infant/toddler health, growth and development, juvenile equipment and toys, work and day care, marriage and sex, "approached from a how-to, service perspective. The message—Here's what you need to know and why—is delivered with smart, crisp style. The tone is confident and reassuring (and, when appropriate, humorous and playful), with the backing of experts. In essence, *Baby Talk* is a training manual of parents facing the day-to-day dilemmas of new parenthood." No phone calls. Query with SASE. Length: 1,000-2,000 words. **Pays $500-2,000 depending on length, degree of difficulty and the writer's experience.**

Columns/Departments: 100-1,250 words. Several departments are written by regular contributors. Query with SASE. **Pays $100-1,000.**

Tips: "Please familiarize yourself with the magazine before submitting a query. Take the time to focus your story idea; scattershot queries are a waste of everyone's time."

$ BIG APPLE PARENT/QUEENS PARENT/WESTCHESTER PARENT, Family Communications, Inc., 9 E. 38th St., 4th Floor, New York NY 10016. (212)889-6400. Fax: (212)689-4958. E-mail: hellonwheels@parentsknow.com. Website: www.parentsknow.com. **Contact:** Helen Freedman, executive editor. **90% freelance written.** Monthly tabloid covering New York City family life. "*BAP* readers live in high-rise Manhattan apartments; it is an educated, upscale audience. Often both parents are working full time in professional occupations. Child-care help tends to be one-on-one, in the home. Kids attend private schools for the most part. While not quite a suburban approach, some of our *QP* readers do have backyards (though most live in high-rise apartments). It is a more middle-class audience in Queens. More kids are in day care centers; majority of kids are in public schools. Our Westchester county edition is for suburban parents." Estab. 1985. Circ. 70,000, *Big Apple*; 68,000, *Queens Parent*; 60,000, *Westchester Parent*. Pays 2 months after publication. Byline given. Offers 50% kill fee. first New York area rights Submit seasonal material 3 months in advance. Accepts queries by mail, e-mail, fax. Accepts simultaneous submissions. Responds immediately to queries. Sample copy and writer's guidelines free.

Break in with "Commentary (op ed); newsy angles—but everything should be targeted to parents. We love journalistic pieces (as opposed to essays, which is what we mostly get.)"

Nonfiction: Book excerpts, essays, exposé, general interest, how-to, inspirational, interview/profile, opinion, personal experience, family health; education. "We're always looking for news and coverage of controversial issues." **Buys 150 mss/year.** Query with or without published clips or send complete ms. Length: 600-1,000 words. **Pays $35-50.** Sometimes pays expenses of writers on assignment.

Reprints: Send tearsheet or typed ms with rights for sale noted and information about when and where the material previously appeared. Pays same as article rate.

Photos: Reviews contact sheets, prints. Buys one-time rights. Offers $25/photo. Captions required.

Columns/Departments: Dads; Education; Family Finance. **Buys 50-60 mss/year.** Send complete ms.

Tips: "We have a very local focus; our aim is to present articles our readers cannot find in national publications. To that end, news stories and human interest pieces must focus on New York and New Yorkers. We are always looking for news and newsy pieces; we keep on top of current events, frequently giving issues that may relate to parenting a local focus so that the idea will work for us as well."

$ $ $ BOISE FAMILY MAGAZINE, Magazine for Treasure Valley Parents, 13191 W. Scotfield St., Boise ID 83713-0899. (208)938-2119. Fax: (208)938-2117. E-mail: boisefamily@cs.com. Website: www.boisefamily.com. **Contact:** Liz Buckingham, editor. **90% freelance written.** Monthly magazine covering parenting, education, child development. "Geared to parents with children 14 years and younger. Focus on education, interest, activities for children. Positive parenting and healthy families." Estab. 1993. Circ. 19,000. Pays on publication. Publishes ms an average of 3 months after acceptance. Byline given. Offers 50% kill fee. Buys first North American serial rights. Editorial lead time 3 months. Submit seasonal material 3 months in advance. Accepts queries by mail, e-mail. Accepts simultaneous submissions. Responds in 2 months to queries. Sample copy for $1.50. Writer's guidelines for #10 SASE.

Nonfiction: Essays, how-to, interview/profile, new product. Special issues: Women's Health and Maternity (January); Birthday Party Fun; Family Choice Awards (February); Education; Home & Garden (March); Summer Camps (April); Kids' Sports Guide (May); Summer, Family Travel; Fairs & Festivals (June/July); Back-to-School; the Arts (August/September); Fall Fun; Children's Health (October); Winter Family Travel; Holiday Ideas (November); Holiday Crafts and Traditions (December). No political or religious affiliation-oriented articles. **Buys 10 mss/year.** Query with published clips. Length: 900-1,300 words. **Pays $50-1,000.** Sometimes pays expenses of writers on assignment.

Reprints: Accepts previously published submissions.

Photos: State availability with submission. Reviews 3×5 prints. Buys one-time rights. Negotiates payment individually. Captions required.

Columns/Departments: Crafts, travel, finance, parenting. Length: 700-900 words. Query with published clips. **Pays $50-100.**

$ ✪ CATHOLIC PARENT, Our Sunday Visitor, 200 Noll Plaza, Huntington IN 46750-4310. (260)356-8400. Fax: (260)356-8472. E-mail: cparent@osv.com. Website: www.osv.com. **Contact:** Woodeene Koenig-Bricker, editor. **95% freelance written.** Bimonthly magazine. "We look for practical, realistic parenting articles written for a primarily Roman Catholic audience. The key is practical, not pious." Estab. 1993. Circ. 36,000. **Pays on acceptance.** Publishes ms an average of 6 months after acceptance. Byline given. Offers variable kill fee. Buys first North American serial rights. Editorial lead time 6 months. Submit seasonal material 6 months in advance. Accepts simultaneous submissions. Responds in 2 months to queries. Sample copy for $3.

- *Catholic Parent* is extremely receptive to first-person accounts of personal experiences dealing with parenting issues that are moving, emotionally engaging and uplifting for the reader. Bear in mind the magazine's mission to provide practical information for parents.

Nonfiction: Essays, how-to, humor, inspirational, personal experience, religious. **Buys 50 mss/year.** Send complete ms. Length: 850-1,200 words. **Pay varies.** Sometimes pays expenses of writers on assignment.

Photos: State availability with submission.

Columns/Departments: This Works (parenting tips), 200 words. **Buys 50 mss/year.** Send complete ms. **Pays $15-25.**

Tips: No poetry or fiction.

$ $ CHICAGO PARENT, Wednesday Journal, Inc., 141 S. Oak Park Ave., Oak Park IL 60302-2972. (708)386-5555. Fax: (708)524-8360. E-mail: chiparent@aol.com. Website: chicagoparent.com. Editor: Sharon Bloyd-Peshkin. **Contact:** Sandi Pedersen, editorial assistant. **60% freelance written.** Monthly tabloid. "*Chicago Parent* has a distinctly local approach. We offer information, inspiration, perspective and empathy to Chicago-area parents. Our lively editorial mix has a 'we're all in this together' spirit, and articles are thoroughly researched and well written." Estab. 1988. Circ. 125,000 in three zones covering the 6-county Chicago metropolitan area. Pays on publication. Publishes ms an average of 2 months after acceptance. Byline given. Offers 10-50% kill fee. Buys first, electronic rights. Editorial lead time 4 months. Submit seasonal material 4 months in advance. Accepts queries by mail. Responds in 6 weeks to queries. Sample copy for $3.95 and 11×17 SAE with $1.65 postage. Writer's guidelines for #10 SASE.

- O━ Break in by "writing 'short stuff' items (front-of-the-book short items on local people, places and things of interest to families)."

Nonfiction: Essays, exposé, how-to (parent-related), humor, interview/profile, travel, local interest; investigative features. Special issues: include Chicago Baby and Healthy Child. "No pot-boiler parenting pieces, simultaneous submissions, previously published pieces or non-local writers (from outside the 6-county Chicago metropolitan area)." **Buys 40-50 mss/year.** Query with published clips. Length: 200-2,500 words. **Pays $25-300 for assigned articles; $25-100 for unsolicited articles.** Pays expenses of writers on assignment.

Photos: State availability with submission. Reviews contact sheets, negatives, prints. Buys one-time rights. Offers $0-40/photo; negotiates payment individually. Captions, identification of subjects required.

Columns/Departments: Healthy Child (kids' health issues), 850 words; Getaway (travel pieces), up to 1,200 words; other columns not open to freelancers. **Buys 30 mss/year.** Query with published clips or send complete ms. **Pays $100.**

Tips: "We don't like pot-boiler parenting topics and don't accept many personal essays unless they are truly compelling."

$ $ $ $ ✪ CHILD, Gruner + Jahr, 375 Lexington Ave., New York NY 10017-5514. (212)499-2000. Fax: (212)499-2038. Website: www.child.com. Editor-in-Chief: Miriam Arond. Managing Editor: Polly Chevalier. **Contact:** Submissions. **95% freelance written.** Monthly magazine covering parenting. Estab. 1986. Circ. 930,000. **Pays on acceptance.** Byline given. Offers 25% kill fee. Buys all rights. Editorial lead time 5 months. Submit seasonal material 6 months in advance. Accepts queries by mail. Responds in 2 months to queries. Sample copy for $3.95. Writer's guidelines for #10 SASE.

Nonfiction: Book excerpts, essays, interview/profile, personal experience, travel, timely trend stories on topics that affect today's parents. No poetry. **Buys 50 feature, 20-30 short mss/year.** Query with published clips. Length: 650-2,500 words. **Pays $1/word and up for assigned articles.** Sometimes pays expenses of writers on assignment.
Photos: State availability with submission. Reviews transparencies. Buys one-time rights. Negotiates payment individually.
Columns/Departments: First Person (mother's or father's perspective). **Buys 10 mss/year.** Query with published clips. **Pays $1/word and up.**

The online magazine carries original content not found in the print edition. Contact: Kathleen Tripp, online editor.

Tips: "Stories should include opinions from experts as well as anecdotes from parents to illustrate the points being made. Lifestyle is key. Send a well-written query that meets our editorial needs. *Child* receives too many inappropriate submissions. Please consider your work carefully before submitting."

$ $ CHRISTIAN PARENTING TODAY, Christianity Today International, 465 Gundersen Dr., Carol Stream IL 60188-2489. (630)260-6200. Fax: (630)260-0114. E-mail: cpt@christianparenting.net. Website: www.christianparenting.net. Managing Editor: Carla Barnhill. Associate Editor: Jennifer Mangan. **Contact:** Raelynn Eickhatt, editorial coordintor. **90% freelance written.** Bimonthly magazine. "Strives to be a positive, practical magazine that targets real needs of today's family with authoritative articles based on real experience, fresh research and the timeless truths of the Bible. *CPT* provides parents information that spans birth to 14 years of age in the following areas of growth: Spiritual, social, emotional, physical, academic." Estab. 1988. Circ. 90,000. **Pays on acceptance.** Byline given. Buys first North American serial, second serial (reprint) rights. Submit seasonal material 8 months in advance. Accepts previously published material. Responds in 2 months to mss. Sample copy for 9×12 SAE with $3 postage. Writer's guidelines for #10 SASE.
Nonfiction: Feature topics of greatest interest: practical guidance in spiritual/moral development and values transfer; practical solutions to everyday parenting issues; tips on how to enrich readers' marriages; ideas for nurturing healthy family ties; family activities that focus on parent/child interaction; humorous pieces about everyday family life. Book excerpts, how-to, humor, inspirational, religious. **Buys 50 mss/year.** Length: 750-2,000 words. **Pays 12-20¢/word.**
Reprints: Send tearsheet, photocopy or typed ms with rights for sale noted and information about when and where the material previously appeared.
Photos: Do not submit photos without permission. State availability with submission. Reviews transparencies. Buys one-time rights. Model releases required.
Columns/Departments: Ideas That Work (family-tested parenting ideas from our readers), 25-100 words; Life In Our House (entertaining, true humorous stories about your family), 25-100 words; Growing Up (spiritual development topics from a Christian perspective), 420-520 words. **Pays $25-150.**
Tips: "Tell it like it is. Readers have a 'get real' attitude that demands a down-to-earth, pragmatic take on topics. Don't sugar-coat things. Give direction without waffling. If you've 'been there,' tell us. The first-person, used appropriately, is OK. Don't distance yourself from readers. They trust people who have walked in their shoes. Get reader friendly. Fill your article with nuts and bolts: developmental information, age-specific angles, multiple resources, sound-bite sidebars, real-life people and anecdotes and realistic, vividly explained suggestions."

$ $ $ CONNECT FOR KIDS, The Benton Foundation, 1625 K St., NW, Second Floor, Washington DC 20006. (202)638-5770. E-mail: julee@benton.org. Website: www.connectforkids.org. **Contact:** Julee Newberger, managing editor. **20% freelance written.** Weekly online covering issues affecting children and families. *Connect for Kids* is an information/action center for adults who want to make their communities better for kids and families. "We publish solutions-oriented journalism, specifically profiles of successful programs and public responses to issues affecting children and families." Estab. 1996. Circ. 600,000 user sessions/month. **Pays on acceptance.** Byline given. Offers 25% kill fee. Makes work-for-hire assignments. "We maintain 3 month period of exclusivity. After that time, writers may market and publish the material on their own. We also retain the right to re-publish work in other forms." Editorial lead time 2-3 months. Submit seasonal material at least 2 months in advance. Accepts queries by mail, e-mail. Accepts simultaneous submissions. Responds in 3 weeks to queries. Sample copy not available. Writer's guidelines available online at website or by e-mail.

"We look for inspiring stories of community-based action to benefit kids and families, journalism articles on issues and events facing kids and families."

Nonfiction: General interest, interview/profile. Does not want articles that fail to make a connection between the personal and the public; parenting magazine-style articles; articles that cover kids' issues but ignore the larger context of politics and community. **Buys 20 mss/year.** Query with published clips. Length: 800-1,200 words. Does not pay expenses of writers on assignment.
Photos: State availability with submission. Reviews JPEG format. Buys electronic rights. Offers no additional payment for photos accepted with ms. Negotiates payment individually. Captions, identification of subjects, model releases required.
Tips: "*Connect for Kids* has been buying high-quality freelance feature writing and book reviews since 1996. We like smart, sharp stories that emphasize community and public solutions to problems, and columns or first-person pieces from professionals and activists. Be clear, compelling and explore our website content before sending a query. We pay an average of 70¢/word for feature articles and a flat fee of $75 for book reviews, upon acceptance. We work with many members of the American Society of Journalists and Authors."

$☆ COUNTY KIDS, Journal Register Company, 877 Post Rd., Westport CT 06880. (203)226-8877. Fax: (203)221-7540. E-mail: countykids@ctcentral.com. Website: www.countykids.com. **Contact:** Linda Greco, managing editor. **70% freelance written.** Monthly tabloid for Connecticut parents. "We publish articles that are well-researched and informative, yet written in a casual tone." Estab. 1988. Circ. 44,000. Pays on publication. Byline given. Buys first North American serial, second serial (reprint), electronic rights. Editorial lead time 2 months. Submit seasonal material 3 months in advance. Accepts queries by mail, e-mail, fax. Accepts simultaneous submissions. Responds in 2 months to queries. Sample copy and writer's guidelines free.

Nonfiction: Essays, exposé, general interest, how-to, humor, interview/profile, new product, opinion, personal experience, photo feature. Special issues: Camp; Daycare Options; Back-to-School; Divorce/Single Parenting. No fiction, poetry or cute kids stories. **Buys 40 mss/year.** Query with or without published clips or send complete ms. Length: 800-2,000 words. **Pays $35-100 for assigned articles; $25-75 for unsolicited articles.**

Reprints: Accepts previously published submissions.

Photos: Send photos with submission. Reviews contact sheets, prints. Buys one-time rights. Offers no additional payment for photos accepted with ms. Identification of subjects required.

Columns/Departments: Mom's View/Dad's View (personal experience/humor), 800 words; Double Digits (tips on parenting teens), 800 words; Museum Moments (reviews of Connecticut museums), 800 words; Parentphernalia (fast facts, local news, parenting tips), 400 words. **Buys 25 mss/year.** Send complete ms. **Pays $25-35.**

Tips: "*County Kids* is looking for strong features with a Connecticut slant. We give preferences to local writers. Mom's View and Dad's View columns are a great way to get published in *County Kids*, as long as they're humorous and casual. Features sent with photos will be given priority, as will those with sidebars."

$ $☆ EXPECTING, Family Communications, 37 Hanna Ave., Suite 1, Toronto, Ontario M6K 1W9, Canada. (416)537-2604. Fax: (416)538-1794. **Contact:** Tracy Cooper, editor. **100% freelance written.** Semiannual digest-sized magazine. Writers must be Canadian health professionals. Articles address all topics relevant to expectant parents. Estab. 1995. Circ. 100,000. **Pays on acceptance.** Publishes ms an average of 6 months after acceptance. Byline given. Buys all rights. Editorial lead time 6 months. Accepts queries by mail, fax. Responds in 2 months to queries.

Nonfiction: Medical. **Buys 6 mss/year.** Query with published clips. Length: 1,000-2,000 words. **Pays $300 or more for some articles.** Sometimes pays expenses of writers on assignment.

Photos: State availability with submission. Buys all rights. Negotiates payment individually. Identification of subjects required.

$ $☆ FAMILY DIGEST, The Black Mom's Best Friend!, Family Digest Association, 696 San Ramon Valley Blvd., #349, Danville CA 94526. Fax: (925)838-4948. E-mail: editor@familydigest.com. **Contact:** John Starch, associate editor. **90% freelance written.** Quarterly magazine. "Our mission: Help black moms/female heads-of-household get more out of their roles as wife, mother, homemaker. Editorial coverage includes parenting, health, love and marriage, travel, family finances, and beauty and style. All designed to appeal to black moms." Estab. 1997. Circ. 400,000. Pays on publication. Publishes ms an average of 6 months after acceptance. Buys first North American serial, all rights. Editorial lead time 2 months. Submit seasonal material 3 months in advance. Accepts queries by e-mail. Accepts previously published material. Accepts simultaneous submissions. Responds in 1 month to queries. Writer's guidelines by e-mail.

Nonfiction: "We are not political. We do not want articles that blame others. We do want articles that improve the lives of our readers." Book excerpts, general interest (dealing with relationships), historical/nostalgic, how-to, humor, inspirational, interview/profile, personal experience. Query with published clips. Length: up to 3,000 words. **Pays $100-500.** Sometimes pays expenses of writers on assignment.

Photos: Reviews negatives, transparencies, prints. Offers no additional payment for photos accepted with ms. Captions, identification of subjects, model releases required.

Columns/Departments: A Better You!(personal development), parenting, love and marriage, health, family finances, beauty and style. **Buys 100 mss/year.** Query with published clips. **Pays $100-500.**

Fiction: Erotica, ethnic, historical, humorous, novel excerpts, romance. Query with published clips.

Fillers: Anecdotes, facts, gags to be illustrated by cartoonist, short humor. **Buys 100 mss/year.** Length: 50-250 words.

$☆ THE FAMILY DIGEST, P.O. Box 40137, Fort Wayne IN 46804. **Contact:** Corine B. Erlandson, manuscript editor. **95% freelance written.** Bimonthly magazine. "*The Family Digest* is dedicated to the joy and fulfillment of the Catholic family and its relationship to the Catholic parish." Estab. 1945. Circ. 150,000. Pays within 1-2 months of acceptance. Byline given. Buys first North American serial rights. Submit seasonal material 7 months in advance. Accepts queries by mail. Accepts previously published material. Responds in 1-2 months to queries. Sample copy and writer's guidelines for 6×9 SAE with 2 first-class stamps.

Nonfiction: Family life, parish life, prayer life, Catholic traditions. How-to, inspirational, religious. **Buys 60 unsolicited mss/year.** Send complete ms. Length: 750-1,200 words. **Pays $40-60 for accepted articles.**

Reprints: Send ms with rights for sale noted and information about when and where the material previously appeared. **Pays 5¢/word.**

Fillers: Anecdotes, tasteful humor based on personal experience. **Buys 18/year.** Length: 25-100 words. **Pays $25.**

Tips: "Prospective freelance contributors should be familiar with the publication and the types of articles we accept and publish. We are especially looking for upbeat articles which affirm the simple ways in which the Catholic faith is expressed in daily life. Articles on family and parish life, including seasonal articles, how-to pieces, inspirational, prayer, spiritual life, and Church traditions, will be gladly reviewed for possible acceptance and publication."

$$$$☆ FAMILYFUN, Disney Magazine Publishing Inc., 244 Main St., Northampton MA 01060-3107. (413)585-0444. Fax: (413)586-5724. Website: www.familyfun.com. **Contact:** Jean Graham, editorial assistant. Magazine covering activities for families with kids ages 3-12. "*Family Fun* is about all the great things families can do together. Our writers are either parents or authorities in a covered field." Estab. 1991. Circ. 1,500,000. **Pays on acceptance.** Byline sometimes given. Offers 25% kill fee. Buys simultaneous rights, makes work-for-hire assignments. Editorial lead time 6 months. Submit seasonal material 6 months in advance. Accepts simultaneous submissions. Responds in 3 months to queries. Sample copy for $3. Writer's guidelines online.

Nonfiction: Book excerpts, essays, general interest, how-to (crafts, cooking, educational activities), humor, interview/profile, personal experience, photo feature, travel. Special issues: Crafts and Holidays. **Buys dozens of mss/year.** Query with published clips. Length: 850-3,000 words. **Pays $1.25/word.** Pays expenses of writers on assignment.

Photos: State availability with submission. Reviews contact sheets, negatives, transparencies. Buys all rights. Offers $75-500/photo. Identification of subjects, model releases required.

Columns/Departments: Family Almanac, Nicole Blaserak, assistant editor (simple, quick, practical, inexpensive ideas and projects—outings, crafts, games, nature activities, learning projects, and cooking with children), 200-400 words; query or send ms; **pays $100-$200/article or $75 for ideas.** Family Traveler, Jodi Butler, (brief, newsy items about family travel, what's new, what's great, and especially, what's a good deal), 100-125 words; send ms; **pays $100, also pays $50 for ideas.** Family Ties, Kathy Whittemore, senior editor (first-person column that spotlights some aspect of family life that is humorous, inspirational, or interesting); 1,300 words; send ms; **pays $1,300.** My Great Idea, Dawn Chipman, senior editor (explains fun and inventive ideas that have worked for writer's own family); 800-1,000 words; query or send ms; **pays $750 on acceptance;** also publishes best letters from writers and readers following column, send to My Great Ideas editor, 100-150 words, **pays $25 on publication. Buys 20-25 mss/year.**

Tips: "Many of our writers break into *FF* by writing for Family Almanac or Family Traveler (front-of-the-book departments)."

$ GENESEE VALLEY PARENT MAGAZINE, 1 Grove St., Suite 204, Pittsford NY 14534. Fax: (716)264-0647. E-mail: gvparent@aol.com. **Contact:** Barbara Melnyk, managing editor. **80% freelance written.** Monthly magazine covering raising children ages infant-14. "*Genesee Valley Parent Magazine* is a publication that provides information and tips on issues related to raising young children and adolescents. We also have book reviews, a healthy family column, Teen Talk column and Growing Concerns, which addresses a range of developmental issues." Estab. 1994. Circ. 30,000. Pays on publication. Byline given. Buys one-time, second serial (reprint) rights, makes work-for-hire assignments. Editorial lead time 4 months. Submit seasonal material 4 months in advance. Accepts queries by mail, e-mail. Accepts previously published material. Accepts simultaneous submissions. Responds in 3 months to queries; 3 months to mss. Sample copy for 8½×11 SAE and $1.50 postage. Writer's guidelines for #10 SASE or by e-mail.

Nonfiction: General interest, how-to, humor, opinion, personal experience. Special issues: Baby Guide (April), Family Finances (June), Teen issue (August). **Buys 50 mss/year.** Send complete ms. Length: 550-1,200 words. **Pays $100-130 for assigned articles; $30-45 for unsolicited articles.**

Photos: Send photos with submission. Buys one-time rights. Offers no additional payment for photos accepted with ms.

Columns/Departments: Parents Exchange (opinion/personal experience related to parenting); Healthy Family (anything related to keeping family members in good health); Teen Talk (issues related to raising teens), all 550-650 words. **Buys 20 mss/year.** Send complete ms. **Pays $35.**

Tips: "Well-written, well-researched articles on current topics/issues related to raising healthy, well-adjusted children is what we run. Look for new angles, fresh approaches to age-old problems and concerns, as well as topics/issues that are more cutting edge."

$☆ HOME EDUCATION MAGAZINE, P.O. Box 1083, Tonasket WA 98855. (509)486-1351. E-mail: hem-editor@home-ed-magazine.com. Website: www.home-ed-magazine.com. **Contact:** Helen E. Hegener, managing editor. **80% freelance written.** Bimonthly magazine covering home-based education. We feature articles which address the concerns of parents who want to take a direct involvement in the education of their children—concerns such as socialization, how to find curriculums and materials, testing and evaluation, how to tell when your child is ready to begin reading, what to do when homeschooling is difficult, teaching advanced subjects, etc. Estab. 1983. Circ. 32,000. **Pays on acceptance.** Publishes ms an average of 4 months after acceptance. Byline given. Buys first North American serial, first, one-time, electronic rights. Submit seasonal material 6 months in advance. Accepts queries by mail, e-mail. Responds in 2 months to queries. Sample copy for $6.50. Writer's guidelines for #10 SASE or via e-mail.

- Break in by "reading our magazine, understanding how we communicate with our readers, having an understanding of homeschooling and being able to communicate that understanding clearly."

Nonfiction: Essays, how-to (related to home schooling), humor, interview/profile, personal experience, photo feature, technical. **Buys 40-50 mss/year.** Query with or without published clips or send complete ms. Length: 750-2,500 words. **Pays $50-100.** Sometimes pays expenses of writers on assignment.

Photos: Send photos with submission. Reviews Reviews enlargements, 35mm prints, b&w, CD-ROMs. Buys one-time rights. Pays $100/cover; $12/inside b&w photos. Identification of subjects required.

Tips: "We would like to see how-to articles (that don't preach, just present options); articles on testing, accountability, working with the public schools, socialization, learning disabilities, resources, support groups, legislation and humor. We need answers to the questions that homeschoolers ask. Please, no teachers telling parents how to teach. Personal experience with homeschooling is most preferred approach."

$ ☐ HOMESCHOOLING TODAY, S Squared Productions Inc., P.O. Box 1608, Ft. Collins CO 80524. Fax: (970)224-1824. E-mail: publisher@homeschooltoday.com. Website: www.homeschooltoday.com. **Contact:** Maureen McCaffrey, editor. **75% freelance written.** Bimonthly magazine covering homeschooling. "We are a practical magazine for homeschoolers with a broadly Christian perspective." Estab. 1992. Circ. 25,000. Pays on publication. Publishes ms an average of 1 year after acceptance. Byline given. Offers $50 kill fee. Buys first rights. Editorial lead time 6 months. Submit seasonal material 1 year in advance. Accepts queries by mail, e-mail, fax. Accepts simultaneous submissions. Responds in 1 month to queries; 2 months to mss. Sample copy and writer's guidelines free.

Nonfiction: Book excerpts, how-to, inspirational, interview/profile, new product. No fiction or poetry. **Buys 30 mss/year.** Query. Length: 500-2,500 words. **Pays 8¢/word.**

Photos: State availability with submission. Buys one-time rights. Offers no additional payment for photos accepted with ms. Captions, identification of subjects required.

$ $ ☐ METRO PARENT MAGAZINE, Metro Parent Publishing Group, 24567 Northwestern Hwy., Suite 150, Southfield MI 48075. (248)352-0990. Fax: (248)352-5066. E-mail: sdemaggio@metroparent.com. Website: www.metroparent.com. **Contact:** Susan DeMaggio, editor. **75% freelance written.** Monthly magazine covering parenting, women's health, education. "We are a local magazine on parenting topics and issues of interest to Detroit-area parents. Related issues: *Ann Arbor Parent; African/American Parent; Metro Baby Magazine.*" Circ. 85,000. Pays on publication. Publishes ms an average of 3 months after acceptance. Byline given. Buys first rights. Editorial lead time 3 months. Submit seasonal material 3 months in advance. Accepts queries by mail, e-mail. Accepts previously published material. Accepts simultaneous submissions. Responds in 2 weeks to queries; 3 months to mss. Sample copy for $2.50.

Nonfiction: Essays, humor, inspirational, personal experience. **Buys 100 mss/year.** Send complete ms. Length: 1,500-2,500 words. **Pays $50-300 for assigned articles.**

Photos: State availability with submission. Buys one-time rights. Offers $100-200/photo or negotiates payment individually. Captions required.

Columns/Departments: Women's Health (latest issues of 20-40 year olds), 750-900 words; Solo Parenting (advice for single parents); Family Finance (making sense of money and legal issues); Tweens 'N Teens (handling teen "issues"), 750-800 words. **Buys 50 mss/year.** Send complete ms. **Pays $75-150.**

$ ☐ METROKIDS MAGAZINE, The Resource for Delaware Valley Families, Kidstuff Publications, Inc., 1080 N. Delaware Ave., #702, Philadelphia PA 19125-4330. (215)291-5560. Fax: (215)291-5563. E-mail: info@metrokids.com. Website: www.metrokids.com. **Contact:** Nancy Lisagor, editor-in-chief. **80% freelance written.** Monthly tabloid providing information for parents and kids in Philadelphia, South Jersey and surrounding counties. Estab. 1990. Circ. 125,000. Pays on publication. Byline given. Buys one-time rights. Submit seasonal material 4 months in advance. Accepts queries by mail, e-mail, fax, phone. Accepts previously published material. Responds in 8 months to queries. Writer's guidelines for #10 SASE.

Nonfiction: General interest, how-to, new product, travel, Parenting; Health. Special issues: Baby First (April; pregnancy, childbirth, first baby); Camps (December-June); Special Kids (August; children with special needs); Vacations and Theme Parks (May, June); What's Happening (January; guide to events and activities); Kids 'N Care (July; guide to childcare). **Buys 40 mss/year.** Query with published clips. Length: 800-1,500 words. **Pays $1-50.** Sometimes pays expenses of writers on assignment.

Reprints: Send photocopy and information about when and where the material previously appeared. Pays $20-40.

Photos: State availability with submission. Buys one-time rights. Captions required.

Columns/Departments: Book Beat (book reviews); Bytesize (CD-ROM and website reviews); Body Wise (health); Dollar Sense (finances); all 500-700 words. **Buys 25 mss/year.** Query. **Pays $1-50.**

Tips: "Send a query letter several months before a scheduled topical issue; then follow-up with a telephone call. We are interested in feature articles (on specified topics) or material for our regular columns (with a regional/seasonal base). Articles should cite expert sources and the most up-to-date theories and facts. We are looking for a journalistic-style of writing. Editorial calendar available on request. We are also interested in finding local writers for assignments."

$ $ NORTHWEST FAMILY MAGAZINE, MMB Publications, Inc., 2275 Lake Whatcom Blvd., Suite B-1, Bellingham WA 98226-2777. (360)734-3025. Fax: (360)734-1550. E-mail: nwfamilysubmissions@earthlink.net. Website: www.nwfamily.com. **Contact:** Lisa Laskey, editor. **50% freelance written.** Monthly magazine providing information on parenting issues and helping local families to be in touch with resources, events and places in the Northwest and western Washington State. Estab. 1995. Circ. 50,000. Pays on publication. Publishes ms an average of 6 months after acceptance. Byline sometimes given. Buys one-time rights. Editorial lead time 3 months. Submit seasonal material 6 months in advance. Accepts queries by mail, e-mail. Accepts previously published material. Accepts simultaneous submissions. Responds in 3 weeks to queries; 3 months to mss. Sample copy for $1.25. Writer's guidelines for #10 SASE.

Nonfiction: Essays, general interest, how-to (relating to children), humor, inspirational, interview/profile, new product, personal experience, photo feature, travel. **Buys 40-50 mss/year.** Send complete ms. Length: 300-1,400 words. **Pays $25-45.** Sometimes pays expenses of writers on assignment.

Reprints: Accepts previously published submissions.

Photos: State availability with submission. Reviews negatives, prints (any size). Buys one-time rights. Negotiates payment individually. Model releases required.

Columns/Departments: School News (information about schools, especially local), 100-300 words; Community News (quick information for families in western Washington), 100-300 words; Reviews (videos/books/products for families), 100-300 words; Teen News (information of interest to parents of teens), 50-300 words. **Buys 8-10 mss/year.** Send complete ms. **Pays $10-20.**
Poetry: Lisa Laskey, editor. Avant-garde, free verse, haiku, light verse, traditional. "No heavy or negative content." **Buys 6 poems/year.** Submit maximum 5 poems. Length: 6-25 lines. **Pays $5-20.**
Tips: "Send entire article with word count. Topic should apply to parents (regional focus increases our need for your article) and be addressed in a positive manner—'How to' not 'How not to.'"

$ PARENTING WITH SPIRIT, Honoring the Spirituality of Children, The Institute for Spiritual Living, P.O. Box 1356, Taos NM 87571. E-mail: jfhaver@parentingwithspirit.com. Website: www.parentingwithspirit.com. Editor: Judith Costello. **Contact:** Jurgen F. Haver, managing editor. **65% freelance written.** Quarterly magazine. Estab. 1997. Circ. 1,100. **Pays on acceptance.** Publishes ms an average of 4 months after acceptance. Byline given. Buys first North American serial rights. Editorial lead time 6 months. Submit seasonal material 6 months in advance. Accepts queries by mail, e-mail. Responds in 3 weeks to queries; 2 months to mss. Sample copy for $5. Writer's guidelines for #10 SASE.
Nonfiction: Book excerpts, how-to, inspirational, opinion, personal experience, spiritual. Nothing from a conservative religious viewpoint. **Buys 10-12 mss/year.** Query or send complete ms. Length: 300-1,200 words. **Pays $10-35.**
Reprints: Accepts previously published submissions.
Photos: State availability with submission. Buys one-time rights. Offers no additional payment for photos accepted with ms.

The online magazine carries original content not found in the print edition. Contact: Jurgen F. Haver, online editor.

Tips: "Our writers are committed to the holistic and spiritual perspective of *PWS*. Many have backgrounds in journalism (with good interviewing skills), education, spiritual counseling or psychotherapy. Ask for upcoming themes. Keep articles to 1,500 words or less."

PARENTS, Gruner + Jahr, 375 Lexington Ave., New York NY 10017. (212)499-2000. Website: www.parents.com. Magazine. Responds in 6 weeks to queries. Writer's guidelines online.
Nonfiction: "Before you query us, please take a close look at our magazine at the library or newsstand. This will give you a good idea of the different kinds of stories we publish, as well as their tempo and tone. In addition, please take the time to look at the masthead to make sure you are directing your query to the correct department." Query.
Tips: "We're a national publication, so we're mainly interested in stories that will appeal to a wide variety of parents. We're always looking for compelling human-interest stories, so you may want to check your local newspaper for ideas. Keep in mind that we can't pursue stories that have appeared in competing national publications."

$ $ PARENTS' PRESS, The Monthly newspaper for Bay Area Parents, 1454 Sixth St., Berkeley CA 94710-1431. (510)524-1602. Fax: (510)524-0912. E-mail: parentsprs@aol.com. Website: www.parentspress.com. **Contact:** Dixie M. Jordan, editor. **25% freelance written.** Monthly tabloid for parents. Includes a special section for parents of teens and pre-teens. Estab. 1980. Circ. 75,000. Pays within 45 days of publication. Publishes ms an average of 4 months after acceptance. Buys all rights, including electronic, second serial (reprint) and almost always Northern California exclusive rights Submit seasonal material 6 months in advance. Accepts queries by mail, e-mail. Accepts previously published material. Accepts simultaneous submissions. Responds in 3 months to queries. Sample copy for $3. Writer's guidelines and editorial calendar for #10 SASE or online.
Nonfiction: "We require a strong Bay Area focus in almost all articles. Use quotes from experts and Bay Area parents. Please, no child-rearing tips or advice based on personal experience." Book excerpts, travel, well-researched articles on children's health; development; education; family activities. Special issues: Pregnancy, Birth & Baby, Family Travel, Back to School. **Buys 10-12 mss/year.** Send complete ms. Length: 300-1,500 words. **Pays $50-500 for assigned articles; $25-250 for unsolicited articles.**
Reprints: Send photocopy with rights for sale noted and information about when and where the material previously appeared. Pays up to $50.
Photos: State availability with submission. Reviews any size b&w prints. Buys one-time rights. Offers $15/photo. Identification of subjects, model releases required.
Tips: "We're looking for more pieces with a Bay Area focus."

$ PEDIATRICS FOR PARENTS, Pediatrics for Parents, Inc., 747 53rd, #3, Philadelphia PA 19147-3321. Fax: (419)858-7221. E-mail: rich.sagall@pobox.com. **Contact:** Richard J. Sagall, editor. **10% freelance written.** Monthly newsletter covering children's health. "*Pediatrics For Parents* emphasizes an informed, common-sense approach to childhood health care. We stress preventative action, accident prevention, when to call the doctor and when and how to handle a situation at home. We are also looking for articles that describe general, medical and pediatric problems, advances, new treatments, etc. All articles must be medically accurate and useful to parents with children—prenatal to adolescence." Estab. 1981. Circ. 1,500. Pays on publication. Publishes ms an average of 4 months after acceptance. Byline given. Buys first North American serial, electronic rights. Accepts queries by mail, e-mail, fax. Accepts previously published material. Accepts simultaneous submissions. Responds in 1 month to queries. Sample copy and writer's guidelines online.

Nonfiction: Medical. No first person or experience. **Buys 10 mss/year.** Query with or without published clips or send complete ms. Length: 200-1,000 words. **Pays $10-50.**
Reprints: Accepts previously published submissions.

$☆ SAN DIEGO FAMILY MAGAZINE, San Diego County's Leading Resource for Parents & Educators Who Care!, P.O. Box 23960, San Diego CA 92193-3960. (619)685-6970. Fax: (619)685-6978. Website: www.sandiegofamily.com. **Contact:** Claire Yezbak Fadden, editor. **75% freelance written.** Monthly magazine for parenting and family issues. "*SDFM* strives to provide informative, educational articles emphasizing positive parenting for our typical readership of educated mothers, ages 25-45, with an upper-level income. Most articles are factual and practical, a few are humor and personal experience. Editorial emphasis is uplifting and positive." Estab. 1982. Circ. 120,000. Pays on publication. Byline given. Buys first, one-time, second serial (reprint) rights. Editorial lead time 2 months. Submit seasonal material 3 months in advance. Accepts previously published material. Responds in 2 months to queries; 3 months to mss. Sample copy and writer's guidelines for $4.50 with 9×12 SAE. Writer's guidelines also available on website.

- No e-mail queries.

Nonfiction: How-to, interview/profile (influential or noted persons or experts included in parenting or the welfare of children), parenting, new baby help, enhancing education, family activities, articles of specific interest to San Diego. "No rambling, personal experience pieces." **Buys 75 mss/year.** Send complete ms. Length: 800 words maximum. **Pays $1.25/column inch.**
Reprints: Send typed ms with rights for sale noted and information about when and where the material previously appeared.
Photos: State availability with submission. Reviews contact sheets, 3½×5 or 5×7 prints. Buys one-time rights. Negotiates payment individually. Identification of subjects required.
Columns/Departments: Kids' Books (topical book reviews), 800 words. **Buys 12 mss/year.** Query. **Pays $1.25/column inch.**
Fillers: Facts, newsbreaks (specific to family market). **Buys 10/year.** Length: 50-200 words. **Pays $1.25/column inch minimum.**

$$☆ SOUTH FLORIDA PARENTING, 200 E. Las Olas Blvd., Fort Lauderdale FL 33301. (954)747-3050. Fax: (954)747-3055. E-mail: vmccash@sfparenting.com. Website: www.sfparenting.com. **Contact:** Vicki McCash Brennan, managing editor. **90% freelance written.** Monthly magazine covering parenting, family. "*South Florida Parenting* provides news, information and a calendar of events for readers in Southeast Florida. The focus is on positive parenting and things to do or information about raising children in South Florida." Estab. 1990. Circ. 110,000. Pays on publication. Byline given. Buys one-time, second serial (reprint) rights, makes work-for-hire assignments. Editorial lead time 4 months. Submit seasonal material 5 months in advance. Accepts queries by mail, e-mail, fax. Accepts previously published material. Accepts simultaneous submissions. Responds in 2 months to queries; 6 months to mss. Sample copy for 9×12 SAE with $2.95 postage. Writer's guidelines for #10 SASE.

- Preference given to writers based in South Florida.
- O⇁ Best bet to break in: "Be a local South Florida resident (particular need for writers from the Miami-Dade area) and address contemporary parenting topics and concerns."

Nonfiction: How-to (parenting issues), humor (preferably not first-person humor about kids and parents), interview/profile, personal experience, family and children's issues. Special issues: Education/Women's Health (January); Birthday Party (February); Summer Camp (March); Maternity (April); Florida/Vacation Guide (May); Kid Crown Awards (July); Back to School (August); Education (September); Holiday (December). **Buys 60+ mss/year.** Query with published clips or send complete ms. Length: 500-2,000 words. **Pays $40-300.**
Reprints: Send photocopy or e-mail on spec. **Pays $25-50.**
Photos: State availability with submission. Reviews negatives, transparencies, prints. Buys one-time rights. Sometimes offers additional payment for photos accepted with ms.
Columns/Departments: Baby Basics (for parents of infants); Family Health (child health); Preteen Power (for parents of preteens); Family Money (family finances), all 500-750 words.
Tips: "We want information targeted to the South Florida market. Multicultural and well-sourced is preferred. A unique approach to a universal parenting concern will be considered for publication. Profiles or interviews of courageous parents. Opinion pieces on child rearing should be supported by experts and research should be listed. First-person stories should be fresh and insightful. All writing should be clear and concise. Submissions can be typewritten, double-spaced, but the preferred format is on diskette or by e-mail attachment."

$$$$ TODAY'S PARENT PREGNANCY & BIRTH, 269 Richmond St. W, Toronto, Ontario M5V 1X1, Canada. (416)596-8680. Fax: (416)596-1991. Website: www.todaysparent.com. **Contact:** Editor. **100% freelance written.** Magazine published 3 times/year. "*P&B* helps, supports and encourages expectant and new parents with news and features related to pregnancy, birth, human sexuality and parenting." Estab. 1973. Circ. 200,000. **Pays on acceptance.** Publishes ms an average of 8 months after acceptance. Buys first North American serial rights. Editorial lead time 6 months. Responds in 6 weeks to queries. Sample copy and writer's guidelines for #10 SASE.
Nonfiction: Features about pregnancy, labor and delivery, post-partum issues. **Buys 12 mss/year.** Query with published clips. Length: 600-2,500 words. **Pays $350-2,000.** Sometimes pays expenses of writers on assignment.
Photos: State availability with submission. Rights negotiated individually. Pay negotiated individually.

Tips: "Our writers are professional freelance writers with specific knowledge in the childbirth field. *P&B* is written for a Canadian audience using Canadian research and sources."

$ $ TWINS, The Magazine for Parents of Multiples, The Business Word, Inc., 11211 E. Arapahoe Rd., Suite 100, Centennial CO 80114-3851. (303)290-8500 or (888)55TWINS. Fax: (303)290-9025. E-mail: twins.editor@businessword.com. Website: www.twinsmagazine.com. Editor-in-Chief: Susan J. Alt. **Contact:** Sharon Withers, managing editor. **80% freelance written.** Bimonthly magazine covering parenting multiples. "*TWINS* is an international publication that provides informational and educational articles regarding the parenting of twins, triplets and more. All articles must be multiple specific and have an upbeat, hopeful and/or positive ending." Estab. 1984. Circ. 55,000. Pays on publication. Byline given. Buys first North American serial rights. Editorial lead time 4 months. Submit seasonal material 6 months in advance. Accepts queries by mail, e-mail, fax. Accepts simultaneous submissions. Response time varies to queries. Sample copy for $5 or on website. Writer's guidelines for #10 SASE or on website.
Nonfiction: Interested in seeing twin-specific discipline articles. Personal experience (first-person parenting experience), Professional Experience as it relates to multiples. Nothing on cloning, pregnancy reduction or fertility issues. **Buys 12 mss/year.** Query with or without published clips or send complete ms. Length: 1,300 words. **Pays $25-250 for assigned articles; $25-100 for unsolicited articles.**
Photos: State availability with submission. Offers no additional payment for photos accepted with ms. Identification of subjects required.
Columns/Departments: Special Miracles (miraculous stories about multiples with a happy ending), 800-850 words. **Buys 12-20 mss/year.** Query with or without published clips or send complete ms. **Pays $40-75.**
Tips: "All department articles must have a happy ending, as well as teach a lesson helpful to parents of multiples."

$ WESTERN NEW YORK FAMILY, Western New York Family Inc., P.O. Box 265, 287 Parkside Ave., Buffalo NY 14215-0265. (716)836-3486. Fax: (716)836-3680. E-mail: wnyfamily@aol.com. Website: www.wnyfamilymagazine.com. **Contact:** Michele Miller, editor/publisher. **90% freelance written.** Monthly magazine covering parenting in Western NY. "Readership is largely composed of families with children ages newborn to 14 years. Although most subscriptions are in the name of the mother, 91% of fathers also read the publication. Strong emphasis is placed on how and where to find family-oriented events, as well as goods and services for children, in Western New York." Estab. 1984. Circ. 22,500. Pays on publication. Publishes ms an average of 3 months after acceptance. Byline given. Buys one-time, second serial (reprint), simultaneous rights. Editorial lead time 3 months. Submit seasonal material 3 months in advance. Accepts previously published material. Accepts simultaneous submissions. Responds only if interested to queries. Sample copy for $2.50 and 9×12 SAE with 3 first-class stamps. Writer's guidelines online.

- Break in with either a "cutting edge" topic that is new and different in its relevance to current parenting challenges and trends or a "timeless" topic which is "evergreen" and can be kept on file to fill last minute holes.

Nonfiction: How-to (craft projects for kids, holiday, costume, etc.), humor (as related to parenting), personal experience (parenting related), travel (family destinations). Special issues: Birthday Celebrations (January); Cabin Fever (February); Having A Baby (March); Education & Enrichment (April); Mother's Day (May); Father's Day (June); Summer Fun (July and August); Back to School (September); Halloween Happenings (October); Family Issues (November); and Holiday Happenings (December). **Buys 100 mss/year.** Send complete ms by mail or e-mail. Unsolicited e-mail attachments are not accepted; paste text of article into body of e-mail. Length: 750-3,000 words. **Pays $50-150 for assigned articles; $25-50 for unsolicited articles.** Sometimes pays expenses of writers on assignment.
Reprints: Accepts previously published submissions.
Photos: State availability with submission. Reviews 3×5 prints, JPEG files via e-mail. Buys one-time rights. Offers no additional payment for photos accepted with ms. Captions, identification of subjects, model releases required.
Fillers: Facts. **Buys 10/year.** Length: 450 words. **Pays $20.**
Tips: "We are interested in well-researched, nonfiction articles on surviving the newborn, preschool, school age and adolescent years. Our readers want practical information on places to go and things to do in the Buffalo area and nearby Canada. They enjoy humorous articles about the trials and tribulations of parenthood as well as 'how-to' articles (i.e., tips for finding a sitter, keeping your sanity while shopping with preschoolers, ideas for holidays and birthdays, etc.). Articles on making a working parent's life easier are of great interest as are articles written by fathers. We also need more material on pre-teen and young teen (13-15) issues. More material on multicultural families and their related experiences, traditions, etc., would be of interest in 2002. We prefer a warm, conversational style of writing."

$ $ $ $ WORKING MOTHER MAGAZINE, 260 Madison Ave., 3rd Floor, New York NY 10016. (212)445-6100. Fax: (212)445-6174. E-mail: editors@workingmother.com. Website: www.workingmother.com. **Contact:** Articles Department. **90% freelance written.** Prefers to work with published/established writers; works with a small number of new/unpublished writers each year. Monthly magazine for women who balance a career with the concerns of parenting. Circ. 925,000. Publishes ms an average of 4 months after acceptance. Byline given. Offers kill fee. Buys all rights. Submit seasonal material 6 months in advance. Accepts queries by mail. Sample copy for $5; available by calling (800)925-0788. Writer's guidelines online.

- *Working Mother* is exploring a sale of the magazine.

Nonfiction: Service, humor, child development, material pertinent to the working mother's predicament. Humor, service; child development; material perinent to the working mother's predicament. **Buys 9-10 mss/year.** Query. Length: 1,500-2,000 words. Pays expenses of writers on assignment.

Tips: "We are looking for pieces that help the reader. In other words, we don't simply report on a trend without discussing how it specifically affects our readers' lives and how they can handle the effects. Where can they look for help if necessary?"

COMIC BOOKS

$ $ WIZARD: THE COMICS MAGAZINE, Wizard Entertainment, 151 Wells Ave., Congers NY 10920-2036. (845)268-2000. Fax: (845)268-0053. E-mail: wizmelc@aol.com. Website: www.wizardworld.com. Editor: Brian Cunningham. Senior Editor: Joe Yanarella. **Contact:** Mel Caylo, managing editor. **50% freelance written.** Monthly magazine covering comic books, science fiction, and action figures. Estab. 1991. Circ. 209,000. Pays on publication. Publishes ms an average of 3 months after acceptance. Byline given. Offers 50% kill fee. Buys all rights. Editorial lead time 4 months. Accepts queries by mail, e-mail, fax. Responds in 6 weeks to queries. Sample copy and writer's guidelines free.

Nonfiction: Historical/nostalgic, how-to, humor, interview/profile, new product, personal experience, photo feature, first-person diary. No columns or opinion pieces. **Buys 100 mss/year.** Query with or without published clips. Length: 250-4,000 words. **Pays 15-20¢/word.** Sometimes pays expenses of writers on assignment.

Photos: State availability with submission. Buys all rights. Negotiates payment individually. Identification of subjects required.

Columns/Departments: Video Stuff (comic book, science fiction, and top-selling video games); Manga Mania (the latest news, anime, manga, toys, etc. from Japan); Coming Attractions (comic book-related movies and TV shows), 150-500 words. Query with published clips. **Pays $75-500.**

Tips: "Send plenty of samples showing the range of your writing styles. Have a good knowledge of comic books. Read a few issues to get the feel of the conversational 'Wizard Style.'"

CONSUMER SERVICE & BUSINESS OPPORTUNITY

Some of these magazines are geared to investing earnings or starting a new business; others show how to make economical purchases. Publications for business executives and consumers interested in business topics are listed under Business & Finance. Those on how to run specific businesses are classified by category in the Trade section.

$ $ ☆ HOME BUSINESS MAGAZINE, United Marketing & Research Company, Inc., 9582 Hamilton Ave. PMB 368, Huntington Beach CA 92646. Fax: (714)962-7722. E-mail: henderso@ix.netcom.com. Website: www.homebusinessmag.com. **Contact:** Stacy Henderson, online editor. **75% freelance written.** "*Home Business Magazine* covers every angle of the home-based business market including: cutting edge editorial by well-known authorities on sales and marketing, business operations, the home office, franchising, business opportunities, network marketing, mail order and other subjects to help readers choose, manage and prosper in a home-based business; display advertising, classified ads and a directory of home-based businesses; technology, the Internet, computers and the future of home-based business; home-office editorial including management advice, office set-up, and product descriptions; business opportunities, franchising and work-from-home success stories." Estab. 1993. Circ. 80,000. Pays on publication. Publishes ms an average of 6 months after acceptance. Byline given. Makes work-for-hire assignments. Editorial lead time 4 months. Submit seasonal material 6 months in advance. Accepts queries by mail, e-mail, fax. Accepts previously published material. Accepts simultaneous submissions. Sample copy for 9×12 SAE and 8 first-class stamps. Writer's guidelines for #10 SASE.

Nonfiction: Book excerpts, general interest, how-to (home business), inspirational, interview/profile, new product, personal experience, photo feature, technical, mail order; franchise; business management; internet; finance network marketing. No non-home business related topics. **Buys 40 mss/year.** Send complete ms. Length: 200-1,000 words. **Pays 20¢/word for assigned articles; $0-65 for unsolicited articles.**

Photos: Send photos with submission. Buys one-time rights. Offers no additional payment for photos accepted with ms. Identification of subjects required.

Columns/Departments: Marketing & Sales; Money Corner; Home Office; Management; Technology; Working Smarter; Franchising; Network Marketing, all 650 words. Send complete ms.

■ The online magazine carries original content not found in the print edition. Contact: Herb Wetenkamp, online editor.

Tips: "Send complete information by mail as per our writer's guidelines and e-mail if possible. We encourage writers to submit Feature Articles (2-3 pages) and Departmental Articles (1 page). Please submit polished, well-written, organized material. It helps to provide subheadings within the article. Boxes, lists and bullets are encouraged because they make your article easier to read, use and reference by the reader. A primary problem in the past is that articles do not stick to the subject of the title. Please pay attention to the focus of your article and to your title. Please don't call to get the status of your submission. We will call if we're interested in publishing the submission."

$ $ $ $ KIPLINGER'S PERSONAL FINANCE, 1729 H St. NW, Washington DC 20006. (202)887-6400. Fax: (202)331-1206. Website: www.kiplinger.com. Editor: Fred W. Frailey. **Contact:** Dayl Sanders, office manager. **10% freelance written.** Prefers to work with published/established writers. Monthly magazine for general, adult audience

intersted in personal finance and consumer information. "*Kiplinger's* is a highly trustworthy source of information on saving and investing, taxes, credit, home ownership, paying for college, retirement planning, automobile buying, and many other personal finance topics." Estab. 1947. Circ. 1,300,000. **Pays on acceptance.** Publishes ms an average of 2 months after acceptance. Buys all rights. Responds in 1 month to queries.
Nonfiction: "Most material is staff-written, but we accept some freelance. Thorough documentation is required for fact-checking." Query with published clips. Pays expenses of writers on assignment.
Tips: "We are looking for a heavy emphasis on personal finance topics."

$ $ LIVING SAFETY, A Canada Safety Council Publication for Safety in the Home, Traffic and Recreational Environments, 1020 Thomas Spratt Place, Ottawa, Ontario K1G 5L5, Canada. (613)739-1535. Fax: (613)739-1566. E-mail: jsmith@safety-council.org. Website: www.safety-council.org. **Contact:** Jack Smith, editor-in-chief. **65% freelance written.** Quarterly magazine covering off-the-job safety. "Off-the-job health and safety magazine covering topics in the home, traffic, and recreational environments. Audience is the Canadian employee and his/her family." Estab. 1983. Circ. 100,000. **Pays on acceptance.** Publishes ms an average of 2 months after acceptance. Byline given. Buys all rights. Editorial lead time 4 months. Submit seasonal material 6 months in advance. Accepts queries by mail. Accepts previously published material. Accepts simultaneous submissions. Responds in 1 month to queries. Sample copy and writer's guidelines free.
Nonfiction: General interest, how-to (safety tips, health tips), personal experience. **Buys 24 mss/year.** Query with published clips. Length: 1,000-2,500 words. **Pays $500 maximum.** Sometimes pays expenses of writers on assignment.
Reprints: Send tearsheet.
Photos: State availability with submission. Reviews contact sheets, negatives, transparencies, Prints. Offers no additional payment for photos accepted with ms. Identification of subjects required.

CONTEMPORARY CULTURE

These magazines often combine politics, current events and cultural elements such as art, literature, film and music, to examine contemporary society. Their approach to institutions is typically irreverent and investigative. Some, like *Madison*, report on alternative culture and appeal to a young adult "Generation X" audience. Others treat mainstream culture for a baby boomer generation audience.

$ $ $ $ A&U, America's AIDS Magazine, Art & Understanding, Inc., 25 Monroe St., Suite 205, Albany NY 12210-2729. (518)426-9010. Fax: (518)436-5354. E-mail: mailbox@aumag.org. Website: www.aumag.org. **Contact:** David Waggoner, editor-in-chief. **50% freelance written.** Monthly magazine covering cultural responses to AIDS/HIV. Estab. 1991. Circ. 205,000. Pays on publication. Publishes ms an average of 3 months after acceptance. Byline given. Offers 20% kill fee. Buys first North American serial rights. Editorial lead time 6 months. Accepts queries by mail, fax, phone. Accepts simultaneous submissions. Responds in 1 month to queries; 2 months to mss. Sample copy for $5. Writer's guidelines online.
Nonfiction: Book excerpts, essays, general interest, how-to, humor, interview/profile, new product, opinion, personal experience, photo feature, travel, reviews (film, theater, art exhibits, video, music, other media); Medical news. **Buys 120 mss/year.** Query with published clips. Length: 800-4,800 words. **Pays $250-2,500 for assigned articles.** Sometimes pays expenses of writers on assignment.
Photos: State availability with submission. Reviews contact sheets, up to 4×5 transparencies, 4×5 to 8×10 prints. Buys one-time rights. Offers $50-500/photo. Captions, identification of subjects, model releases required.
Columns/Departments: The Culture of AIDS (reviews of books, music, film), 800 words; Viewpoint (personal opinion), 900-1,500 words; MediaWatch (mass media opinion), 800-1,200 words. **Buys 100 mss/year.** Send complete ms. **Pays $100-250.**
Fiction: Unpublished work only; accepts prose, poetry and drama. Send complete ms. Length: 2,500-5,000 words. **Pays $50-150.**
Poetry: Any length/style (shorter works preferred). **Pays $75-150.**
The online magazine carries original content not found in the print edition. Contact: David Waggoner.
Tips: "We're looking for more articles on youth and HIV/AIDS; more international coverage; more small-town America coverage."

$ $ $ ADBUSTERS, Journal of the Mental Environment, The Media Foundation, 1243 W. 7th Ave., Vancouver, British Columbia V6H 1B7, Canada. (604)736-9401. Fax: (604)737-6021. Website: www.adbusters.org. Managing Editor: Aiden Enns. **Contact:** Kalle Lasn, editor. **50% freelance written.** Bimonthly magazine. "We are an activist journal of the mental environment." Estab. 1989. Circ. 90,000. Pays 1 month after publication. Byline given. Buys first rights. Accepts queries by mail, e-mail, fax. Accepts simultaneous submissions. Writer's guidelines online.
Nonfiction: Essays, exposé, interview/profile, opinion. **Buys variable mss/year.** Query. Length: 250-3,000 words. **Pays $100/page for unsolicited articles; 50¢/word for solicited articles.**
Fiction: Inquire about themes.
Poetry: Inquire about themes.

$ THE AMERICAN DISSIDENT, ContraOstrich Press, 1837 Main St., Concord MA 01742. E-mail: enmarge@aol.com. Website: www.geocities.com/enmarge. **Contact:** G. Tod Slone, editor. **100% freelance written.** Semiannual magazine "offering hardcore criticism of all American icons and institutions in English, French, or Spanish. Writers must be free of dogma, clear in mind, critical in outlook, and courageous in behavior." Estab. 1998. Circ. 200. Pays on publication. Publishes ms an average of 6 months after acceptance. Byline given. Buys first North American serial, one-time rights. Editorial lead time 6 months. Accepts queries by mail. Responds in 3 weeks to queries; 3 months to mss. Sample copy for $7.

Nonfiction: Essays, interview/profile, opinion, personal experience. **Buys 2-4 mss/year.** Query. Length: 250-900 words. **Pays $5 for assigned articles.** Pays in contributor's copies for poetry submissions and book reviews.

Photos: State availability with submission. Reviews prints. Buys one-time rights. Negotiates payment individually. Identification of subjects required.

Poetry: Free verse. Poetry with a message, not poetry for the sake of poetry, as in l'art pour l'art. Submit maximum 3-5 poems.

Tips: "*The American Dissident* publishes well-written dissident work (in English, French, or Spanish) that expresses some sort of visceral indignation regarding the nation. Suggested areas of criticism include, though not exclusively: Corruption in academe, poet laureates paid for by the Library of Congress, sell-out beatniks and hippies, *artistes nonengagés,* politically controlled state and national cultural councils, media whores, Medicare-bilking doctors, justice-indifferent lawyers, autocratic judges, thug cops, other dubious careerists, the "happy" culture of extreme denial and aberrant rationalization, the democratic sham masking the plutocracy and, more generally, the human veil of charade placed upon the void of the universe."

$ $ THE AMERICAN SCHOLAR, Phi Beta Kappa, 1606 New Hampshire Ave. NW, Washington DC 20009. (202)265-3808. Fax: (202)265-0083. E-mail: scholar@pbk.org. Editor: Anne Fadiman. **Contact:** Jean Stipicevic, managing editor. **100% freelance written.** Quarterly journal. "Our intent is to have articles written by scholars and experts but written in nontechnical language for an intelligent audience. Material covers a wide range in the arts, sciences, current affairs, history, and literature." Estab. 1932. Circ. 25,000. Pays on publication. Publishes ms an average of 1 year after acceptance. Byline given. Offers 50% kill fee. Buys first rights. Editorial lead time 6 months. Submit seasonal material 6 months in advance. Accepts queries by mail, e-mail, fax. Responds in 2 weeks to queries; 2 months to mss. Sample copy for $8. Writer's guidelines for #10 SASE.

Nonfiction: Essays, historical/nostalgic, humor. **Buys 40 mss/year.** Query. Length: 3,000-5,000 words. **Pays $500 maximum.**

Poetry: "We have no special requirements of length, form, or content for original poetry." Rob Farnsworth, poetry editor. **Buys 25 poems/year.** Submit maximum 3-4 poems. **Pays $50.**

$ $ $ $ ✪ BOOK, The Magazine for the Reading Life, West Egg Communications LLC, 252 W. 37th St., 5th Floor, New York NY 10018. (212)659-7070. Fax: (212)736-4455. E-mail: alanger@bookmagazine.com. Website: www.bookmagazine.com. Editor-in-Chief: Jerome Kramer. **Contact:** Adam Langer, senior editor. **80% freelance written.** Bimonthly magazine covering books and reading. Estab. 1998. Circ. 750,000. Pays 30 days after publication. Byline sometimes given. Offers kill fee. Buys first, electronic rights, makes work-for-hire assignments. Editorial lead time 3 months. Submit seasonal material 4 months in advance. Accepts queries by mail, e-mail, fax. Sample copy online.

Nonfiction: Book excerpts, essays, interview/profile. Query with published clips. Length: 1,000-4,000 words. **Pays 50¢-$1.50/word.**

Photos: Send photos with submission. Buys one-time rights. Identification of subjects required.

Columns/Departments: Shop Watch (bookstore profiles); Locations (literary travel); Group Dynamics (book-group tips, stories); Web Catches (related to books online), all 1,500 words. **Buys 36 mss/year.** Query with published clips. **Pays $500-750.**

Fiction: Literary short stories. **Buys 6 mss/year.** Send complete ms. Length: 1,000-10,000 words. **Pays $300-5,000.**

$ BOOKPAGE, Promotion, Inc., 2143 Belcourt Ave., Nashville TN 37212. (615)292-8926. Fax: (615)292-8249. E-mail: lynn@bookpage.com. Website: www.bookpage.com. **Contact:** Ms. Lynn L. Green, editor. **90% freelance written.** Monthly newspaper covering new book releases. "*BookPage* is a general interest consumer publication which covers a broad range of books. Bookstores and libraries buy *BookPage* in quantity to use as a way to communicate with their regular customers/patrons and keep them up to date on new releases. *BookPage* reviews almost every category of new books including popular and literary fiction, biography, memoir, history, science and travel. Many specialty genres (mystery, science fiction, business and finance, romance, cooking and audio books) are covered by regular columnists and are rarely assigned to other reviewers. We carry few, if any, reviews of backlist books, poetry, short story collections or scholarly books. *BookPage* editors assign all books to be reviewed, choosing from the hundreds of advance review copies we receive each month. We do not publish unsolicited reviews." Estab. 1988. Circ. 500,000. Byline given. Editorial lead time 3 months. Accepts queries by mail, e-mail, fax. Sample copy online. Writer's guidelines free.

Columns/Departments: Romance: Love, Exciting and New, 1,000 words; Business, 1,500 words; New and Good, 800 words; Mystery/Audio, 800-1,000 words. Query with published clips. **Pays $20/400-word review.**

Tips: "If you are interested in being added to our large roster of freelance reviewers, send an e-mail to the editor with a brief bio, a description of your reading interests, and samples of your writing particularly any book reviews you have written. We prefer experienced writers who can effectively communicate, with imagination and originality, what they liked about a particular book."

BOSTON REVIEW, E53-407, M.I.T., Cambridge MA 02139. (617)253-3642. E-mail: bostonreview@mit.edu. Website: bostonreview.mit.edu. Editor: Josh Cohen. **Contact:** Ian Lague, managing editor. **90% freelance written.** Bimonthly magazine of cultural and political analysis, reviews, fiction, and poetry. "The editors are committed to a society and culture that foster human diversity and a democracy in which we seek common grounds of principle amidst our many differences. In the hope of advancing these ideals, the *Review* acts as a forum that seeks to enrich the language of public debate." Estab. 1975. Circ. 20,000. Publishes ms an average of 3 months after acceptance. Byline given. Buys first North American serial rights. Responds in 6 months to queries. Sample copy for $5 or online. Writer's guidelines for #10 SASE or online.

• The *Boston Review* also offers a poetry contest. See Contests & Awards/Poetry section.

Nonfiction: Critical essays and reviews. "We do not accept unsolicited book reviews. If you would like to be considered for review assignments, please send your résumé along with several published clips." **Buys 125 mss/year.** Query with published clips.

Fiction: Jodi Daynard, fiction editor. "I'm looking for stories that are emotionally and intellectually substantive and also interesting on the level of language. Things that are shocking, dark, lewd, comic, or even insane are fine so long as the fiction is *controlled* and purposeful in a masterly way. Subtlety, delicacy, and lyricism are attractive too." **Buys 8 mss/year.** Length: 1,200-5,000 words.

Poetry: Accepting poetry mss after September 1, 2002. Mary Jo Bang and Timothy Donnelly, poetry editors.

$ $ BRUTARIAN, The Magazine of Brutiful Art, Box 210, Accokeek MD 20607. E-mail: brutarian1@juno.com. **Contact:** Dominick Salemi, publisher/editor. **100% freelance written.** Quarterly magazine covering popular and unpopular culture. "A healthy knowledge of the great works of antiquity and an equally healthy contempt for most of what passes today as culture." Estab. 1991. Circ. 5,000. Pays on publication. Publishes ms an average of 3 months after acceptance. Byline given. Buys first, one-time rights. Editorial lead time 2 months. Submit seasonal material 3 months in advance. Accepts queries by mail. Responds in 1 week to queries; 2 months to mss. Sample copy for $6.

Break in with an interview with an interesting musical group, film actor/actress or director, or unusual writer.

Nonfiction: Book excerpts, essays, exposé, general interest, historical/nostalgic, humor, interview/profile, opinion, photo feature, travel, reviews of books, film, and music. **Buys 30 mss/year.** Send complete ms. Length: 1,000-10,000 words. **Pays 5-10¢/word.** Sometimes pays expenses of writers on assignment.

Reprints: Send typed ms with rights for sale noted and information about when and where the material previously appeared. Pays 50% of amount paid for an original article.

Photos: State availability with submission. Reviews contact sheets. Buys one-time rights. Offers no additional payment for photos accepted with ms. Captions, identification of subjects, model releases required.

Columns/Departments: Celluloid Void (critiques of cult and obscure films), 500-1,000 words; Brut Library (critiques of books), 500-1,000 words. **Buys 20-30 mss/year.** Send complete ms. **Pays $50 average for book reviews; 5-10¢/word for feature articles.**

Fiction: Adventure, confessions, erotica, experimental, fantasy, horror, humorous, mystery, novel excerpts, suspense. **Buys 8-10 mss/year.** Send complete ms. Length: 1,000-10,000 words. **Pays $100-500, 10¢/word for established writers.**

Poetry: Avant-garde, free verse, traditional. **Buys 10-15 poems/year.** Submit maximum 3 poems. Length: 25-1,000 lines. **Pays $20-200.**

Tips: "Send résumé with completed manuscript. Avoid dry tone and excessive scholasticism. Do not cover topics or issues which have been done to death unless you have a fresh approach or new insights on the subject. Pays $25/illustration; $100 for cover art."

$ COMMON GROUND, Common Ground Publishing, 201-3091 W. Broadway, Vancouver, British Columbia V6K 2G9, Canada. (604)733-2215. Fax: (604)733-4415. E-mail: editor@commongroundmagazine.com. Website: www.commongroundmagazine.com. Senior Editor: Joseph Roberts. **Contact:** Robert Scheer, associate editor. **90% freelance written.** Monthly tabloid covering health, environment, spirit, creativity, and wellness. "We serve the cultural creative community." Estab. 1984. Circ. 70,000. Pays on publication. Publishes ms an average of 1 month after acceptance. Byline given. Buys one-time, second serial (reprint) rights. Editorial lead time 3 months. Submit seasonal material 3 months in advance. Accepts queries by e-mail. Accepts simultaneous submissions. Responds in 6 weeks to queries; 3 months to mss. Sample copy for $5. Writer's guidelines by e-mail.

Nonfiction: All topics must fit into "Body, Mind, Spirit" or environment themes. Book excerpts, how-to, inspirational, interview/profile, opinion, personal experience, religious, travel, call to action. **Buys 12 mss/year.** Send complete ms. Length: 500-2,500 words. **Pays 10¢/word (Canadian).**

Reprints: Accepts previously published submissions.

Photos: State availability with submission. Buys one-time rights. Offers no additional payment for photos accepted with ms. Captions required.

$ $ $ FIRST THINGS, Institute on Religion & Public Life, 156 Fifth Ave., Suite 400, New York NY 10010. (212)627-1985. Fax: (212)627-2184. E-mail: ft@firstthings.com. Website: www.firstthings.com. Editor-in-Chief: Richard John Neuhaus; Managing Editor: Matthew Berke; Associate Editor: Daniel Moloney. **Contact:** James Nuechterlein, editor. **70% freelance written.** "Intellectual journal published 10 times/year containing social and ethical commentary in broad sense, religious and ethical perspectives on society, culture, law, medicine, church and state, morality and

mores." Estab. 1990. Circ. 32,000. Pays on publication. Publishes ms an average of 4 months after acceptance. Byline given. Buys all rights. Editorial lead time 2 months. Submit seasonal material 5 months in advance. Responds in 3 weeks to mss. Sample copy and writer's guidelines for #10 SASE.
Nonfiction: Essays, opinion. **Buys 60 mss/year.** Send complete ms. Length: 1,500-6,000 words. **Pays $300-800.** Sometimes pays expenses of writers on assignment.
Poetry: Traditional. **Buys 25-30 poems/year.** Length: 4-40 lines. **Pays $50.**
Tips: "We prefer complete manuscripts (hard copy, double-spaced) to queries, but will reply if unsure."

$ $ FRANCE TODAY, FrancePress Inc., 1051 Divisadero St., San Francisco CA 94115. (415)921-5100. Fax: (415)921-0213. E-mail: info@francentral.com. Website: www.francentral.com. **Contact:** Lisel Fay, editor. **90% freelance written.** Tabloid published 10 times/year covering contemporary France. "*France Today* is a feature publication on contemporary France including sociocultural analysis, business, trends, current events and travel." Estab. 1989. Circ. 25,000. Pays on publication. Publishes ms an average of 5 months after acceptance. Byline given. Buys first North American serial, second serial (reprint) rights. Submit seasonal material 4 months in advance. Accepts queries by mail, e-mail, fax. Accepts previously published material. Responds in 3 months to queries. Sample copy for 10×13 SAE with 5 first-class stamps.
Nonfiction: Essays, exposé, general interest, historical/nostalgic, humor, interview/profile, personal experience, travel. Special issues: Paris, France on the Move, France On a Budget, Summer Travel, The French Palate, French Around the World, France Adventure. "No travel pieces about well-known tourist attractions." **Buys 50 mss/year.** Query with or without published clips or send complete ms. Length: 500-2,000 words. **Pays $150-300.**
Reprints: Send ms with rights for sale noted and information about when and where the material previously appeared. Pay varies.
Photos: Buys one-time rights. Offers $25/photo. Identification of subjects required.

$ $ $ ☆ FW MAGAZINE, FW Omni Media Corp., 296 Richmond St. West, #302, Toronto, Ontario M5V 1X2, Canada. (416)591-6537. Fax: (416)591-2390. E-mail: angela@myfw.com. Website: www.myfw.com. Managing Editor: Angela Ryan. **Contact:** P.J. Tarasuk, editorial director. **80% freelance written.** Bimonthly magazine. "We are a lifestyle magazine that is geared to both males and females. Our readership is between 18-34 years old. We focus on the hottest new trends for our readers. We profile people in their 20s doing exciting ventures." Estab. 1993. Circ. 500,000. Pays on publication. Byline given. Offers 50% kill fee. Buys first, electronic rights. Editorial lead time 2 months. Submit seasonal material 3 months in advance. Accepts queries by fax, phone. Accepts simultaneous submissions. Responds to queries in 1 month if interested to queries; 2 months to mss. Sample copy for free. Writer's guidelines by e-mail.
Nonfiction: Angela Ryan, senior editor. Exposé, general interest, how-to, interview/profile, new product, personal experience, photo feature, travel. **Buys 83 mss/year.** Query with published clips. Length: 500-3,000 words. **Pays $300-1,000.** Sometimes pays expenses of writers on assignment.
Photos: State availability with submission. Reviews contact sheets, negatives. Buys one-time rights. Negotiates payment individually. Captions, identification of subjects, model releases required.
Columns/Departments: Body (the newest trends in fitness); Travel (the new "hotspots" on a budget); Work (interesting jobs for people in their 20s); Fashion (profile new designers and trends); all 1,000 words. **Buys 50 mss/year.** Query. **Pays $300-1,000.**
The online version carries original content not found in the print edition. Contact: Angela Ryan, online editor.
Tips: "It is best to simply call P.J. Tarasuk at (416)591-6537 or Rose Cefalu at our L.A. office (323)931-3433."

$ $ $ $ ☆ MOTHER JONES, Foundation for National Progress, 731 Market St., Suite 600, San Francisco CA 94103. (415)665-6637. Fax: (415)665-6696. E-mail: query@motherjones.com. Website: www.motherjones.com. Editor: Roger Cohn. **Contact:** Alastair Paulin, managing editor; Eric Bates, investigative editor; Roger Cohn, editor-in-chief; Monika Bauerlein, features editor; Tim Dickinson, associate editor. **80% freelance written.** Bimonthly magazine covering politics, investigative reporting, social issues and pop culture. "*Mother Jones* is a 'progressive' magazine—but the core of its editorial well is reporting (i.e., fact-based). No slant required. MotherJones.com is an online sister publication." Estab. 1976. Circ. 175,000. Pays on publication. Publishes ms an average of 4 months after acceptance. Byline given. Offers 33% kill fee. Buys first North American serial, first, one-time, electronic rights. Editorial lead time 4 months. Submit seasonal material 6 months in advance. Responds in 2 months to queries. Sample copy for $6 and 9×12 SAE. Writer's guidelines for #10 SASE and online.
Nonfiction: Exposé, interview/profile, photo feature, current issues, policy, investigative reporting. **Buys 70-100 mss/year.** Query with published clips. Length: 2,000-5,000 words. **Pays $1/word.** Sometimes pays expenses of writers on assignment.
Columns/Departments: Outfront (short, newsy and/or outrageous and/or humorous items), 200-800 words; Profiles of "Hellraisers," 500 words. **Pays $1/word.**
Tips: "We're looking for hard-hitting, investigative reports exposing government cover-ups, corporate malfeasance, scientific myopia, institutional fraud or hypocrisy; thoughtful, provocative articles which challenge the conventional wisdom (on the right or the left) concerning issues of national importance; and timely, people-oriented stories on issues such as the environment, labor, the media, health care, consumer protection, and cultural trends. Send a great, short query and establish your credibility as a reporter. Explain what you plan to cover and how you will proceed with the reporting. The query should convey your approach, tone and style, and should answer the following: What are your specific qualifications to write on this topic? What 'ins' do you have with your sources? Can you provide full documentation so that your story can be fact-checked?"

$ NEW HAVEN ADVOCATE, News & Arts Weekly, New Mass Media Inc., 1 Long Wharf Dr., New Haven CT 06511-5991. (203)789-0010. Fax: (203)787-1418. E-mail: editor@newhavenadvocate.com. Website: www.newhavenadvocate.com. **Contact:** Joshua Mamis, editor. **10% freelance written.** Weekly tabloid. "Alternative, investigative, cultural reporting with a strong voice. We like to shake things up." Estab. 1975. Circ. 55,000. Pays on publication. Byline given. Buys one-time rights. Buys on speculation Editorial lead time 1 month. Submit seasonal material 2 months in advance. Accepts simultaneous submissions. Responds in 1 month to queries. Sample copy not available.
Nonfiction: Book excerpts, essays, exposé, general interest, humor, interview/profile. **Buys 15-20 mss/year.** Query with published clips. Length: 750-2,000 words. **Pays $50-150.** Sometimes pays expenses of writers on assignment.
Photos: State availability with submission. Buys one-time rights. Captions, identification of subjects, model releases required.
Tips: "Strong local focus; strong literary voice, controversial, easy-reading, contemporary, etc."

N OUTRÉ, The World of UltraMedia, Filmfax, Inc., P.O. Box 1900, Evanston IL 60204. (847)866-7155. E-mail: Filmfax@xsite.net. Website: www.filmfax.com. **Contact:** James J.J. Wilson, managing editor/story editor. **100% freelance written.** Quarterly magazine covering popular culture of the mid-20th century through the present, with an emphasis on the 1950s and 1960s. Main areas of focus are music, TV, science fiction, illustrative art, comic books, movies, books, and other pop culture icons such as drive-in movies, Route 66, etc. "Most of our features are interviews with musicians, artists, writers, actors, and the other people involved in the various areas of 20th century pop culture, although we do publish historical essays if the material is comprehensive and beyond common knowledge. We also publish reviews of current releases in video/DVD, books, and CDs relating to our general subject areas." Estab. 1994. Circ. 25,000. Pays on publication. Publishes ms an average of 6-12 months after acceptance. Byline given. Buys first North American serial rights. Editorial lead time 6-12 months. Accepts queries by mail, e-mail. Accepts previously published material. Responds in 1-2 weeks to queries; 1 month to mss. Sample copy for free. Writer's guidelines free.
Nonfiction: Book excerpts, essays, historical/nostalgic, interview/profile, new product, opinion, personal experience, photo feature. No general criticism or pieces which do not contain information not commonly known to genre film fans. **Buys 60 mss/year.** Query. Length: 300-15,000 words. **Pays 3¢/word.**
Photos: State availability with submission. Buys one-time rights. Offers no additional payment for photos accepted with ms. Identification of subjects required.
Columns/Departments: Jame J.J. Wilson, managing editor/story editor. Accepts reviews of books, CDs, and video/DVDs. **Buys 50 mss/year.** Query. **Pays 3¢/word.**
Fiction: "We publish fiction very seldom, less than 1 story/year. Inquire in advance."
Tips: "Send us an e-mail or letter describing what ideas you have that may fit our format. As a specialty publication, reading the magazine is the best way to get a feel for what we like to publish."

$ $ SHEPHERD EXPRESS, Alternative Publications, Inc., 413 N. Second St., Milwaukee WI 53203. (414)276-2222. Fax: (414)276-3312. Website: www.shepherd-express.com. **Contact:** Doug Hissou, metro editor or Dave Luhrssen, art and entertainment editor. **50% freelance written.** Weekly tabloid covering "news and arts with a progressive news edge and a hip entertainment perspective." Estab. 1982. Circ. 58,000. Pays on publication. Publishes ms an average of 2 weeks after acceptance. Submit seasonal material 1 month in advance. Accepts simultaneous submissions. Sample copy for $3.
Nonfiction: Book excerpts, essays, exposé, opinion. **Buys 200 mss/year.** Query with published clips or send complete ms. Length: 900-2,500 words. **Pays $35-300 for assigned articles; $10-200 for unsolicited articles.** Sometimes pays expenses of writers on assignment.
Photos: State availability with submission. Reviews prints. Buys one-time rights. Negotiates payment individually. Captions, identification of subjects, model releases required.
Columns/Departments: Opinions (social trends, politics, from progressive slant), 800-1,200 words; Books Reviewed (new books only: Social trends, environment, politics), 600-1,200 words. **Buys 10 mss/year.** Send complete ms.
Tips: "Include solid analysis with point of view in tight but lively writing. Nothing cute. Do not tell us that something is important, tell us why."

$ YES!, A Journal of Positive Futures, Positive Futures Network, P.O. Box 10818, Bainbridge Island WA 98110. (206)842-0216. Fax: (206)842-5208. E-mail: editors@futurenet.org. Website: www.futurenet.org. Editor: Sarah van Gelder. Quarterly magazine covering sustainability and community. "Interested in stories on building a positive future: sustainability, overcoming divisiveness, ethical business practices, etc." Estab. 1996. Circ. 14,000. Pays on publication. Byline given. Editorial lead time 4 months. Accepts queries by mail. Accepts previously published material. Accepts simultaneous submissions. Responds in 1 month to queries; 6 months to mss. Sample copy and writer's guidelines online.

O→ Break in with book reviews.

Nonfiction: "Please check website for a detailed call for submission before each issue." Book excerpts, essays, humor, interview/profile, personal experience, photo feature, technical, environmental. Query with published clips. Length: 200-3,500 words. **Pays $20-50 for assigned articles.** Pays writers with 1-year subsciption and 2 contributor copies.
Reprints: Send photocopy or typed ms with rights for sale noted and information about when and where the material previously appeared. Pays 100% of amount paid for an original article.
Photos: State availability with submission. Reviews prints. Buys one-time rights. Offers $20-75/photo. Identification of subjects required.
Columns/Departments: Query with published clips. **Pays $20-60.**

Tips: "Read and become familiar with the publication's purpose, tone and quality. We are about facilitating the creation of a better world. We are looking for writers who want to participate in that process. *Yes!* is less interested in bemoaning the state of our problems than in highlighting promising solutions. We are highly unlikely to accept submissions that simply state the author's opinion on what needs to be fixed and why. Our readers know *why* we need to move towards sustainability; they are interested in *how* to do so."

DETECTIVE & CRIME

Fans of detective stories want to read accounts of actual criminal cases, detective work, and espionage. Markets specializing in crime fiction are listed under Mystery publications.

$ P. I. MAGAZINE, America's Private Investigation Journal, 755 Bronx, Toledo OH 43609. (419)382-0967. Fax: (419)382-0967. E-mail: pimag1@aol.com. Website: www.pimag.com. **Contact:** Bob Mackowiak, editor/publisher. **75% freelance written.** "Audience includes professional investigators, attorneys, paralegals and law enforcement personnel." Estab. 1988. Circ. 5,200. Pays on publication. Publishes ms an average of 3 months after acceptance. Byline given. Buys one-time rights. Submit seasonal material 3 months in advance. Accepts simultaneous submissions. Responds in 3 months to queries; 4 months to mss. Sample copy for $6.95.

Nonfiction: Interview/profile, personal experience, accounts of real cases. **Buys 4-10 mss/year.** Send complete ms. Length: 1,000 words and up. **Pays $75 minimum.**

Photos: Send photos with submission. Buys one-time rights. May offer additional payment for photos accepted with ms. Identification of subjects, model releases required.

Tips: "The best way to get published in *P. I.* is to write a detailed story about a professional P.I.'s true-life case. Absolutely no fiction. Unsolicited fiction manuscripts will not be returned."

DISABILITIES

These magazines are geared toward disabled persons and those who care for or teach them. A knowledge of disabilities and lifestyles is important for writers trying to break in to this field; editors regularly discard material that does not have a realistic focus. Some of these magazines will accept manuscripts only from disabled persons or those with a background in caring for disabled persons.

$ $ ABILITIES, Canada's Lifestyle Magazine for People with Disabilities, Canadian Abilities Foundation, #501-489 College St., Toronto, Ontario M6G 1A5, Canada. (416)923-1885. Fax: (416)923-9829. E-mail: able@abilities.ca. Website: www.abilities.ca. Editor: Raymond Cohen. **Contact:** Lisa Bendall, managing editor. **50% freelance written.** Quarterly magazine covering disability issues. "*Abilities* provides information, inspiration and opportunity to its readers with articles and resources covering health, travel, sports, products, technology, profiles, employment, recreation and more." Estab. 1987. Circ. 45,000. Pays on publication. Publishes ms an average of 3 months after acceptance. Byline given. Offers 50% kill fee. Buys first rights. Editorial lead time 3 months. Submit seasonal material 4 months in advance. Accepts queries by mail, e-mail, fax. Responds in 3 months to queries. Sample copy for free. Writer's guidelines for #10 SASE, online or by e-mail.

Nonfiction: Book excerpts, general interest, how-to, humor, inspirational, interview/profile, new product, opinion, personal experience, photo feature, travel. Does not want "articles that 'preach to the converted'—contain info that people with disabilities likely already know, such as what it's like to have a disability." **Buys 30-40 mss/year.** Query or send complete ms. Length: 500-2,500 words. **Pays $50-400 (Canadian) for assigned articles; $50-300 (Canadian) for unsolicited articles.**

Reprints: Sometimes accepts previously published submissions (if stated as such).

Photos: State availability with submission.

Columns/Departments: The Lighter Side (humor), 600 words; Profile, 1,200 words.

Tips: "Do not contact by phone—send something in writing. Send a great idea that we haven't done before and make a case for why you'd be able to do a good job with it. Be sure to include a relevant writing sample."

$ $ $ $ ARTHRITIS TODAY, Arthritis Foundation., 1330 W. Peachtree St., Atlanta GA 30309. (404)872-7100. Fax: (404)872-9559. E-mail: atmail@arthritis.org. Website: www.arthritis.org. Editor: Cindy T. McDaniel. Managing Editor: Ben Blaney. Executive Editor: Marcy O'Koon. **Contact:** Michele Taylor, assistant editor. **50% freelance written.** Bimonthly magazine covering living with arthritis; latest in research/treatment. "*Arthritis Today* is written for the more than 43 million Americans who have arthritis and for the millions of others whose lives are touched by an arthritis-related disease. The editorial content is designed to help the person with arthritis live a more productive, independent and painfree life. The articles are upbeat and provide practical advice, information and inspiration." Estab. 1987. Circ. 700,000. **Pays on acceptance.** Byline given. Offers kill fee. Buys first North American serial, second serial (reprint) rights. Editorial lead time 6 months. Submit seasonal material 6 months in advance. Accepts queries by mail, e-mail, fax. Accepts simultaneous submissions. Responds in 2 months to queries. Sample copy for 9×11 SAE with 4 first-class stamps. Writer's guidelines for #10 SASE.

Nonfiction: General interest, how-to (tips on any aspect of living with arthiritis), inspirational, new product (arthritis-related), opinion, personal experience, photo feature, technical, travel (tips, news), service; nutrition; general health; lifestyle. **Buys 60-70 unsolicited mss/year.** Query with or without published clips or send complete ms. Length: 150-2,000 words. **Pays $150-2,000.** Pays expenses of writers on assignment.
Photos: Send photos with submission. Reviews Prints. Buys one-time rights. Negotiates payment individually. Identification of subjects required.
Columns/Departments: Research Spotlight (research news about arthritis); LifeStyle (travel, leisure), 100-300 words; Well Being (arthritis-specific medical news), 100-300 words; Hero (personal profile of people with arthritis), 100-300 words. **Buys 10 mss/year.** Query with published clips. **Pays $150-300.**
Fillers: Facts, gags to be illustrated by cartoonist, short humor. **Buys 10/year.** Length: 40-100 words. **Pays $80-150.**
Tips: "Our readers are already well-informed. We need ideas and writers that give in-depth, fresh, interesting information that truly adds to their understanding of their condition and their quality of life. Quality writers are more important than good ideas. The staff generates many of our ideas but needs experienced, talented writers who are good reporters to execute them. Please provide published clips. In addition to articles specifically about living with arthritis, we look for articles to appeal to an older audience on subjects such as hobbies, general health, lifestyle, etc."

$ $ DIABETES INTERVIEW, Kings Publishing, 3715 Balboa St., San Francisco CA 94121. (415)387-4002. Fax: (415)387-3604. E-mail: daniel@diabetesinterview.com. Website: www.diabetesinterview.com. **Contact:** Daniel Trecroci, managing editor. **40% freelance written.** Monthly tabloid covering diabetes care. "*Diabetes Interview* covers the latest in diabetes care, medications, and patient advocacy. Personal accounts are welcome as well as medical-oriented articles by MDs, RNs, and CDEs (certified diabetes educators)." Estab. 1991. Circ. 40,000. Pays on publication. Publishes ms an average of 2 months after acceptance. Byline given. Buys all rights. Editorial lead time 2 months. Submit seasonal material 2 months in advance. Accepts queries by mail, e-mail, fax, phone. Sample copy online. Writer's guidelines free.
Nonfiction: Essays, how-to, humor, inspirational, interview/profile, new product, opinion, personal experience. **Buys 25 mss/year.** Query. **Pays 20¢/word.**
Reprints: Accepts previously published submissions.
Photos: State availability of or send photos with submission. Negotiates payment individually.
Tips: "Be actively involved in the diabetes community or have diabetes. However, writers need not have diabetes to write an article, but it must be diabetes-related."

$ $ DIABETES SELF-MANAGEMENT, R.A. Rapaport Publishing, Inc., 150 W. 22nd St., Suite 800, New York NY 10011-2421. (212)989-0200. Fax: (212)989-4786. E-mail: editor@diabetes-self-mgmt.com. Website: www.diabetes-self-mgmt.com. **Contact:** Ingrid Strauch, managing editor. **20% freelance written.** Bimonthly. "We publish how-to health care articles for motivated, intelligent readers who have diabetes and who are actively involved in their own health care management. All articles must have immediate application to their daily living." Estab. 1983. Circ. 480,000. Pays on publication. Publishes ms an average of 3 months after acceptance. Byline given. Offers 20% kill fee. Buys all rights. Submit seasonal material 6 months in advance. Accepts queries by mail, e-mail, fax. Responds in 6 weeks to queries. Sample copy for $4 and 9×12 SAE with 6 first-class stamps or online. Writer's guidelines for #10 SASE.

- "We are extremely generous regarding permission to republish."

O→ Break in by having extensive knowledge of diabetes.

Nonfiction: How-to (exercise, nutrition, diabetes self-care, product surveys), technical (reviews of products available, foods sold by brand name, pharmacology), travel (considerations and prep for people with diabetes). No personal experiences, personality profiles, exposés or research breakthroughs. **Buys 10-12 mss/year.** Query with published clips. Length: 1,500-2,500 words. **Pays $400-700 for assigned articles; $200-700 for unsolicited articles.**
Tips: "The rule of thumb for any article we publish is that it must be clear, concise, useful, and instructive, and it must have immediate application to the lives of our readers. If your query is accepted, expect heavy editorial supervision."

$ DIALOGUE, Blindskills, Inc., P.O. Box 5181, Salem OR 97304-0181. (800)860-4224; (503)581-4224. Fax: (503)581-0178. E-mail: blindskl@teleport.com. Website: www.blindskills.com. **Contact:** Carol M. McCarl, editor. **60% freelance written.** Quarterly journal covering the visually impaired. Estab. 1961. Circ. 1,100. Pays on publication. Publishes ms an average of 8 months after acceptance. Byline given. Buys first rights. Editorial lead time 3 months. Accepts queries by mail, e-mail, fax. One free sample on request. Available in Braille, 4-track audio cassette, large print and disk (for compatible IBM computer). Writer's guidelines for #10 SASE.

O→ Break in by "using accurate punctuation, grammar and structure, and writing about pertinent subject matter."

Nonfiction: Features material by visually impaired writers. Essays, general interest, historical/nostalgic, how-to (life skills methods used by visually impaired people), humor, interview/profile, personal experience, sports, recreation, hobbies. No controversial, explicit sex, religious or political topics. **Buys 80 mss/year**. Send complete ms. Length: 500-1,200 words. **Pays $10-35 for assigned articles; $10-25 for unsolicited articles.**
Columns/Departments: All material should be relative to blind and visually impaired readers. Careers, 1,000 words; What Do You Do When? (dealing with sight loss), 1,000 words. **Buys 80 mss/year.** Send complete ms. **Pays $10-25.**
Fiction: Publishes material by visually impaired writers. Adventure, humorous, slice-of-life vignettes, first person experiences. No controversial, explicit sex, religious or political topics. **Buys 6-8 mss/year.** Send complete ms. Length: 800-1,200 words. **Pays $15-25.**

$✪ KALEIDOSCOPE, Exploring the Experience of Disability Through Literature and the Fine Arts, (formerly *Kaleidoscope: International magazine of Literature, Fine Arts, and Disability*), Kaleidoscope Press, 701 S. Main St., Akron OH 44311-1019. (330)762-9755. Fax: (330)762-0912. E-mail: mshiplett@udsakron.org. Website: www.udsakron.org. **Contact:** Dr. Darshan Perusek, editor-in-chief; Gail Willmott, senior editor. **75% freelance written.** Eager to work with new/unpublished writers. Semiannual magazine. Subscribers include individuals, agencies, and organizations that assist people with disabilities and many university and public libraries. Appreciates work by established writers as well. Especially interested in work by writers with a disability, but features writers both with and without disabilities. "Writers without a disability must limit themselves to our focus, while those with a disability may explore any topic (although we prefer original perspectives about experiences with disability)." Estab. 1979. Circ. 1,000. Byline given. Rights return to author upon publication. Accepts queries by mail, fax. Accepts previously published material. Responds in 3 weeks to queries. Sample copy for $5 prepaid. Writer's guidelines for #10 SASE.

O→ Submit photocopies with SASE for return of work. Please type submissions (double spaced). All submissions should be accompanied by an autobiographical sketch. May include art or photos that enhance works, prefer b&w with high contrast.

Nonfiction: Articles related to disability. Book excerpts, essays, humor, interview/profile, personal experience, book reviews, articles related to disability. Special issues: Disability and the Road Less Traveled (January 2003, deadline August 2002); Multicultural Perspectives on Disability (July 2003, deadline March 2003). **Buys 8-15 mss/year.** Length: 5,000 words maximum. **Pays $25-125 plus 2 copies.**

Reprints: Send ms with rights for sale noted and information about when and where the material previously appeared.

Photos: Send photos with submission.

Fiction: Short stories, novel excerpts. Traditional and experimental styles. Works should explore experiences with disability. Use people-first language. Length: 5,000 words maximum.

Poetry: "Do not get caught up in rhyme scheme. High quality with strong imagery and evocative language." Reviews any style. **Buys 12-20 poems/year.** Submit maximum 5 poems.

Tips: "Articles and personal experiences should be creative rather than journalistic and with some depth. Writers should use more than just the simple facts and chronology of an experience with disability. Inquire about future themes of upcoming issues. Sample copy very helpful. Works should not use stereotyping, patronizing, or offending language about disability. We seek fresh imagery and thought-provoking language."

ENTERTAINMENT

This category's publications cover live, filmed, or videotaped entertainment, including home video, TV, dance, theater, and adult entertainment. In addition to celebrity interviews, most publications want solid reporting on trends and upcoming productions. Magazines in the Contemporary Culture and General Interest sections also use articles on entertainment. For those publications with an emphasis on music and musicians, see the Music section.

$ CINEASTE, America's Leading Magazine on the Art and Politics of the Cinema, Cineaste Publishers, Inc., 304 Hudson St., 6th Floor, New York NY 10013-1015. (212)366-5720. Fax: (212)366-5724. E-mail: cineaste@cineaste.com. **Contact:** Gary Crowdus, editor-in-chief. **30% freelance written.** Quarterly magazine covering motion pictures with an emphasis on social and political perspective on cinema. Estab. 1967. Circ. 11,000. Pays on publication. Publishes ms an average of 4 months after acceptance. Byline given. Offers 50% kill fee. Buys first North American serial rights. Editorial lead time 3 months. Submit seasonal material 4 months in advance. Accepts queries by mail, e-mail, fax. Responds in 1 month to queries. Sample copy for $5. Writer's guidelines for #10 SASE.

O→ Break in by "being familiar with our unique editorial orientation—we are not just another film magazine."

Nonfiction: Book excerpts, essays, exposé, historical/nostalgic, humor, interview/profile, opinion. **Buys 20-30 mss/year.** Query with published clips. Length: 2,000-5,000 words. **Pays $30-100.**

Photos: State availability with submission. Reviews transparencies, 8×10 prints. Buys one-time rights. Offers no additional payment for photos accepted with ms. Identification of subjects required.

Columns/Departments: Homevideo (topics of general interest or a related group of films); A Second Look (new interpretation of a film classic or a re-evaluation of an unjustly neglected release of more recent vintage); Lost and Found (film that may or may not be released or otherwise seen in the US but which is important enough to be brought to the attention of our readers), all 1,000-1,500 words. Query with published clips. **Pays $50 minimum.**

Tips: "We dislike academic jargon, obtuse Marxist terminology, film buff trivia, trendy 'buzz' phrases, and show biz references. We do not want our writers to speak of how they have 'read' or 'decoded' a film, but to view, analyze, and interpret same. The author's processes and quirks should be secondary to the interests of the reader. Warning the reader of problems with specific films is more important to us than artificially 'puffing' a film because its producers or politics are agreeable. One article format we encourage is an omnibus review of several current films, preferably those not reviewed in a previous issue. Such an article would focus on films that perhaps share a certain political perspective, subject matter, or generic concerns (e.g., films on suburban life, or urban violence, or revisionist Westerns). Like individual film reviews, these articles should incorporate a very brief synopsis of plots for those who haven't seen the films. The main focus, however, should be on the social issues manifested in each film, and how it may reflect something about the current political/social/esthetic climate."

$ DANCE INTERNATIONAL, 601 Cambie St., Suite 302, Vancouver, British Columbia V6B 2P1, Canada. (604)681-1525. Fax: (604)681-7732. E-mail: danceint@direct.ca. Website: www.danceinternational.org. **Contact:** Maureen Riches, editor. **100% freelance written.** Quarterly magazine covering dance arts. "Articles and reviews on current activities in world dance, with occasional historical essays; reviews of dance films, video and books." Estab. 1973. Circ. 4,500. Pays on publication. Publishes ms an average of 3 months after acceptance. Byline given. Offers 50% kill fee. Buys one-time rights. Editorial lead time 3 months. Submit seasonal material 6 weeks in advance. Accepts queries by mail, e-mail, fax, phone. Accepts previously published material. Responds in 2 weeks to queries; 1 month to mss. Sample copy for $7. Writer's guidelines for #10 SASE.

Nonfiction: Book excerpts, essays, historical/nostalgic, interview/profile, personal experience, photo feature. **Buys 100 mss/year.** Query. Length: 1,200-2,200 words. **Pays $40-150.**

Photos: Send photos with submission. Reviews prints. Offers no additional payment for photos accepted with ms. Identification of subjects required.

Columns/Departments: Dance Bookshelf (recent books reviewed), 1,200 words; Regional Reports (events in each region), 1,200-2,000 words. **Buys 100 mss/year.** Query. **Pays $60-70.**

Tips: "Send résumé and samples of recent writings."

$ $ DANCE SPIRIT, Lifestyle Ventures, LLC, 250 W. 57th St., Suite 420, New York NY 10107. (212)265-8890. Fax: (212)265-8908. E-mail: editor@dancespirit.com. Website: www.dancespirit.com. **Contact:** Kimberly Gdula, editor. **50% freelance written.** Monthly magazine covering all dance disciplines. "*Dance Spirit* is a special interest teen magazine for girls and guys who study and perform either through a studio or a school dance performance group." Estab. 1997. Circ. 130,000. Pays on publication. Publishes ms an average of 4 months after acceptance. Byline given. Offers 25% kill fee. Buys all rights. Editorial lead time 3 months. Submit seasonal material 8 months in advance. Accepts queries by mail, e-mail, fax. Responds in 3 months to queries; 4 months to mss. Sample copy for $4.95.

Nonfiction: Personal experience, photo feature, dance-related articles only. **Buys 100 mss/year.** Query with published clips. Length: 600-1,200 words. **Pays $100-500.** Sometimes pays expenses of writers on assignment.

Photos: Reviews transparencies. Buys all rights. Negotiates payment individually. Captions, identification of subjects, model releases required.

Columns/Departments: Ballet, jazz, tap, swing, hip hop, lyrical, pom, body, beauty, city focus, choreography, stars, nutrition.

The online magazine carries original content not found in the print edition. Contact: Kimberly Gdula.

Tips: "Reading the magazine can't be stressed enough. We look for writers with a dance background and experienced dancers/choreographers to contribute; succinct writing style, hip outlook."

$ $ DIRECTED BY, The Cinema Quarterly, Visionary Media, P.O. Box 1722, Glendora CA 91740-1722. Fax: (626)963-0235. E-mail: visionarycinema@yahoo.com. Website: www.directed-by.com. **Contact:** Carsten Dau, editor. **50% freelance written.** Quarterly magazine covering the craft of filmmaking. "Our articles are for readers particularly knowledgeable about the art and history of movies. Our purpose is to communicate our enthusiasm and interest in all levels of serious filmmaking." Estab. 1998. Circ. 12,000. Pays on publication. Publishes ms an average of 3 months after acceptance. Byline given. Offers 50% kill fee. Buys all rights. Editorial lead time 3 months. Submit seasonal material 3 months in advance. Accepts queries by mail, e-mail. Accepts simultaneous submissions. Responds in 6 weeks to queries. Sample copy for $5. Writer's guidelines free or by e-mail.

Nonfiction: Essays, historical/nostalgic, interview/profile, photo feature, on-set reports. No gossip, celebrity-oriented material, or movie reviews. **Buys 12 mss/year.** Query. Length: 500-7,500 words. **Pays $50-750.** Sometimes pays expenses of writers on assignment.

Photos: State availability with submission. Reviews contact sheets. Buys all rights. Offers no additional payment for photos accepted with ms. Captions, identification of subjects required.

Columns/Departments: Trends (overview/analysis of specific moviemaking movements/genres/subjects), 1,500-2,000 words; Focus (innovative take on the vision of a director), 1,500-2,000 words; Appreciation (overview of deceased/foreign director), 1,000-1,500 words; Final Cut (spotlight interview with contemporary director), 3,000 words; Perspectives (interviews/articles about film craftspeople other than directors), 1,500-2,000 words. **Buys 12 mss/year.** Query. **Pays $50-750.**

Tips: "We are especially interested in writers who have direct access to interview a director who has not been significantly covered in previous issues of magazines."

$ $ EAST END LIGHTS, The Quarterly magazine for Elton John Fans, P.O. Box 621, Joplin MO 64802-0621. (417)437-1603. Fax: (417)206-2507. E-mail: submissions@eastendlights.com. **Contact:** Mark Norris, publisher. **90% freelance written.** Quarterly magazine covering Elton John. "In one way or another, a story must relate to Elton John, his activities or associates (past and present). We appeal to discriminating Elton fans. No gushing fanzine material. No current concert reviews." Estab. 1990. Circ. 1,700. Pays 3 weeks after publication. Publishes ms an average of 3 months after acceptance. Byline given. Offers 100% kill fee. Buys first, second serial (reprint) rights. Submit seasonal material 6 months in advance. Accepts queries by mail, e-mail, fax. Accepts previously published material. Responds in 2 months to queries. Sample copy for $2.

Nonfiction: Book excerpts, essays, exposé, general interest, historical/nostalgic, humor, interview/profile. **Buys 20 mss/year.** Query with or without published clips or send complete ms. Length: 400-1,000 words. **Pays $75-250 for assigned articles; $75-150 for unsolicited articles.** Pays in contributor copies only when author requests it.

Reprints: Send tearsheet or photocopy with rights for sale noted and information about when and where the material previously appeared. Pays 50%.
Photos: State availability with submission. Reviews negatives, 5×7 prints. Buys one-time and all rights. Offers $40-75/photo.
Columns/Departments: Clippings (non-wire references to Elton John in other publications), maximum 200 words. **Buys 12 mss/year.** Send complete ms. **Pays $20-50.**
Tips: "Approach us with a well-thought-out story idea. We prefer interviews with Elton-related personalities—past or present; try to land an interview we haven't done. We are particularly interested in music/memorabilia collecting of Elton material."

ENTERTAINMENT TODAY, L.A.'s Entertainment Weekly Since 1967, Best Publishing, Inc., 2325 W. Victory Blvd., Burbank CA 91506. Fax: (818)566-4295. E-mail: jsalazar@artnet.net. Website: www.entertainment-today.com. **Contact:** Brent Simon, editor. **40% freelance written.** Weekly print and online newspaper covering entertainment. Estab. 1967. Circ. 210,000. Pays on publication. Publishes ms an average of 3 months after acceptance. Byline given. Buys one-time rights. Editorial lead time 2 months. Submit seasonal material 2 months in advance. Accepts queries by mail, e-mail, fax, phone. Accepts previously published material. Accepts simultaneous submissions. Responds in 2 months to queries. Sample copy online. Writer's guidelines free.
Nonfiction: General interest, humor, interview/profile, opinion, photo feature, travel, any entertainment-related material. **Buys 6-12 mss/year.** Query with published clips. Length: 675-1,850 words.
Photos: State availability with submission. Offers no additional payment for photos accepted with ms. Identification of subjects required.
Columns/Departments: Book Report (book review, often entertainment-related), 415-500 words; Film Reviews, 300-600 words; Disc Domain (CD reviews), 250-400 words. **Buys 6-12 mss/year.** Query with published clips.
Fillers: Short humor.
The online publication carries original content not found in the print edition. Contact: Ginny Zoraster.

$ $ FANGORIA, Horror in Entertainment, Starlog Communications, Inc., 475 Park Ave. S., 7th Floor, New York NY 10016. (212)689-2830. Fax: (212)889-7933. Website: www.fangoria.com. **Contact:** Anthony Timpone, editor. **95% freelance written.** Works with a small number of new/unpublished writers each year. Magazine published 10 times/year covering horror films, TV projects, comics, videos, and literature, and those who create them. "We provide an assignment sheet (deadlines, info) to writers, thus authorizing queried stories that we're buying." Estab. 1979. Pays on publication. Publishes ms an average of 3 months after acceptance. Byline given. Buys all rights. Submit seasonal material 4 months in advance. Accepts queries by mail. Responds in 6 weeks to queries. Sample copy for $8 and 10×13 SAE with 4 first-class stamps. Writer's guidelines for #10 SASE.
Break in by "reading the magazine regularly and exhibiting a professional view of the genre."
Nonfiction: Book excerpts, interview/profile of movie directors, makeup FX artists, screenwriters, producers, actors, noted horror/thriller novelists and others—with genre credits; special FX and special makeup FX how-it-was-dones (on filmmaking only). Occasional "think" pieces, opinion pieces, reviews, or sub-theme overviews by industry professionals. Avoids most articles on science-fiction films. **Buys 120 mss/year.** Query with published clips. Length: 1,000-3,500 words. **Pays $100-250.** Sometimes pays expenses of writers on assignment.
Photos: State availability with submission. Reviews transparencies, prints (b&w, color). Captions, identification of subjects required.
Columns/Departments: Monster Invasion (exclusive, early information about new film productions; also mini-interviews with filmmakers and novelists). Query with published clips. **Pays $45-75.**
The online magazine carries original content not found in the print edition.
Tips: "Other than recommending that you study one or several copies of *Fangoria*, we can only describe it as a horror film magazine consisting primarily of interviews with technicians and filmmakers in the field. Be sure to stress the interview subjects' words—not your own opinions as much. We're very interested in small, independent filmmakers working outside of Hollywood. These people are usually more accessible to writers, and more cooperative. *Fangoria* is also sort of a *de facto* bible for youngsters interested in movie makeup careers and for young filmmakers. We are devoted only to *reel* horrors—the fakery of films, the imagery of the horror fiction of a Stephen King or a Clive Barker—*we do not* want nor would we *ever* publish articles on real-life horrors, murders, etc. A writer must *like* and *enjoy* horror films and horror fiction to work for us. If the photos in *Fangoria* disgust you, if the sight of (*stage*) blood repels you, if you feel 'superior' to horror (and its fans), you aren't a writer for us and we certainly aren't the market for you. We love giving new writers their *first* chance to break into print in a national magazine. We are currently looking for Vancouver-, Arizona- and Las Vegas-based correspondents."

$ $ FILM COMMENT, Film Society of Lincoln Center, 70 Lincoln Center Plaza, New York NY 10023. (212)875-5610. Fax: (212)875-5636. E-mail: filmcomment@filmlinc.com. Website: www.filmlinc.com. **Contact:** Chris Chang, associate editor. **100% freelance written.** Bimonthly magazine covering film criticism and film history, "authoritative, personal writing (not journalism) reflecting experience of and involvement with film as an art form." Estab. 1962. Circ. 30,000. Pays on publication. Publishes ms an average of 2 months after acceptance. Byline given. Offers 50% kill fee (assigned articles only). Editorial lead time 6 weeks. Accepts queries by mail, e-mail, fax, phone. Accepts simultaneous submissions. Responds in 2 weeks to queries.

Nonfiction: Essays, historical/nostalgic, interview/profile, opinion. **Buys 100 mss/year.** Send complete ms. We respond to queries, but rarely assign a writer we don't know. Length: 800-8,000 words. **There is no fixed rate, but roughly based on 3 words/$1.**
Photos: State availability with submission. Buys one-time rights. No additional payment for photos accepted with ms.
Tips: "We are more or less impervious to 'hooks,' don't worry a whole lot about 'who's hot who's not,' or tying in with next fall's surefire big hit (we think people should write about films they've seen, not films that haven't even been finished). We appreciate good writing (writing, not journalism) on subjects in which the writer has some personal investment and about which he or she has something noteworthy to say. Demonstrate ability and inclination to write FC-worthy articles. We read and consider everything we get, and we do print unknowns and first-timers. Probably the writer with a shorter submission (1,000-2,000 words) has a better chance than with an epic article that would fill half the issue."

N **FILMFAX, The Magazine of Film and Unusual Television**, Filmfax, Inc., P.O. Box 1900, Evanston IL 60204. (847)866-7155. E-mail: Filmfax@xsite.net. Website: www.filmfax.com. **Contact:** James J.J. Wilson, managing editor/story editor. **100% freelance written.** Bimonthly magazine covering films and television for the silent era through the 1970s, focusing mainly on horror, science fiction, westerns, and comedy. "Most of our features are interviews with actors, directors, writers, and the other people involved in making classic genre films, although we do publish articles on films and people if the material is comprehensive and beyond common knowledge. We also publish reviews of current releases in video/DVD, books, and CDs related to our general subject." Estab. 1986. Circ. 30,000. Pays on publication. Publishes ms an average of 6-12 months after acceptance. Byline given. Buys first North American serial rights. Editorial lead time 6-12 months. Accepts queries by mail, e-mail. Accepts previously published material. Responds in 1-2 weeks to queries; 1 month to mss. Sample copy for free. Writer's guidelines free.
Nonfiction: Book excerpts, essays, historical/nostalgic, interview/profile, new product, opinion, personal experience, photo feature. No general criticism or pieces which do not contain information not commonly known to genre film fans. **Buys 60 mss/year.** Query. Length: 300-15,000 words. **Pays 3¢/word for assigned articles; 3¢/word for unsolicited articles.**
Photos: State availability with submission. Buys one-time rights. Offers no additional payment for photos accepted with ms. Identification of subjects required.
Columns/Departments: Accepts reviews of books, CDs, and videos/DVDs. **Buys 50 mss/year.** Query. **Pays 3¢/word.**
Fiction: James J.J. WIlson, managing editor/story editor. "We publish fiction very seldom, less than one story per year. Inquire in advance."
Tips: "Send us an e-mail or letter describing what ideas you have that may fit our format. As a specialty publication, reading the magazine is the best way to get a feel for what we like to publish."

$ 5678 MAGAZINE, Champion Media, P.O. Box 8886, Gaithersburg MD 20898. (301)216-0200. Fax: (301)519-1019. E-mail: durand5678@aol.com. Website: www.5678magazine.com. **Contact:** Barry Durand, editor. **50% freelance written.** Monthly magazine covering dance: Couples, line, country, swing. "All articles with a dance or dance music slant. Interviews, reviews, features—today's social dance." Estab. 1999. Circ. 10,000. Pays on publication. Publishes ms an average of 2 months after acceptance. Byline given. Buys first rights. Editorial lead time 2 months. Accepts queries by e-mail. Sample copy for free. Writer's guidelines by e-mail.
Nonfiction: Historical/nostalgic, how-to, humor, interview/profile, photo feature. **Buys 60 mss/year.** Query. Length: 600-2,000 words. **Pays $35-100.** Sometimes pays expenses of writers on assignment.
Photos: Send photos with submission. Buys one-time rights. Negotiates payment individually. Captions, identification of subjects required.
Fiction: Humorous, slice-of-life vignettes. **Buys 10 mss/year.** Query. Length: 600-1,500 words. **Pays $35-100.**

N **$ $ KPBS ON AIR MAGAZINE, San Diego's Guide to Public Broadcasting**, KPBS Radio/TV, 5200 Campanile Dr., San Diego CA 92182-5400. (619)594-3766. Fax: (619)598-3812. Website: www.kpbs.org. **Contact:** Erin Skelton, managing editor. **15% freelance written.** Monthly magazine covering public broadcasting programming and San Diego arts. "Our readers are very intelligent, sophisticated and rather mature. Your writing should be, too." Estab. 1970. Circ. 63,000. Pays on publication. Publishes ms an average of 1 month after acceptance. Byline given. Offers 50% kill fee. Not copyrighted. Buys first North American serial rights. Submit seasonal material 3 months in advance. Accepts queries by mail, e-mail, fax, phone. Accepts previously published material. Responds in 3 months to queries. Sample copy for 9×12 SAE with 4 first-class stamps.
Nonfiction: Interview/profile of PBS personalities and/or artists performing in San Diego, opinion, profiles of public TV and radio personalities, backgrounds on upcoming programs. **Buys 60 mss/year.** Query with published clips. Length: 300-1,500 words. **Pays 20¢/word; 28¢/word if article received via modem or computer disk.** Sometimes pays expenses of writers on assignment.
Reprints: Send tearsheet or photocopy with rights for sale noted and information about when and where the material previously appeared. Pays 25¢/word.
Photos: State availability with submission. Reviews transparencies, 5×7 prints. Buys one-time rights. Offers $30-300/photo. Identification of subjects required.
Columns/Departments: On the Town (upcoming arts events in San Diego), 800 words; Short Takes (backgrounds on public TV shows), 500 words; Radio Notes (backgrounders on public radio shows), 500 words. **Buys 35 mss/year.** Query with or without published clips. **Pays 20¢/word; 28¢/word if the article is received via modem or disk.**

Tips: "Feature stories for national writers are most open to freelancers. Arts stories for San Diego writers are most open. Read the magazine, then talk to me."

N MOVIEMAKER MAGAZINE, MovieMaker Publishing Company, 2265 Westwood Blvd., #479, Los Angeles CA 90064. (310)234-9234. Fax: (310)234-9293. E-mail: jwood@moviemaker.com. Website: www.moviemaker.com. Editor: Timothy Rhys. **Contact:** Jennifer Wood, managing editor. **95% freelance written.** Quarterly magazine covering film, independent cinema, and Hollywood. "*MovieMaker*'s editorial is a progressive mix of in-depth interviews and criticism, combined with practical techniques and advice on financing, distribution, and production strategies. Behind-the-scenes discussions with Hollywood's top moviemakers, as well as independents from around the globe, are routinely found in *MovieMaker*'s pages." Estab. 1993. Circ. 50,000. Pays within one month upon publication. Publishes ms an average of 2 months after acceptance. Byline sometimes given. Offers $25 kill fee. Buys all rights. Editorial lead time 3 months. Submit seasonal material 4 months in advance. Accepts queries by mail, e-mail, fax. Accepts simultaneous submissions. Responds in 2 months to queries; 2 months to mss. Sample copy online. Writer's guidelines by e-mail.
Nonfiction: Exposé, general interest, historical/nostalgic, how-to, interview/profile, new product, technical. **Buys 10 mss/year.** Query with published clips. Length: 800-3,000 words. **Pays $75-500 for assigned articles.**
Photos: State availability with submission. Rights purchased negotiable. Offers no additional payment for photos accepted with ms. Identification of subjects required.
Columns/Departments: Documentary; Home Cinema (home video/DVD reviews); How They Did It (first-person filmmaking experiences); Cinevation (new techniques or breakthroughs in cinema/filming technology); Festival Beat (film festival reviews); World Cinema (current state of cinema from a particular country). Query with published clips. **Pays $75-300.**
Tips: "The best way to begin working with *MovieMaker* is to send a list of 'pitches' along with your résumé and clips. As we receive a number of résumés each week, we want to get an early sense of not just your style of writing, but the kinds of subjects that interest you most as they relate to film. E-mail is the preferred method of correspondence, and please allow 2-4 weeks before following up on a query or résumé."

$ $ $ PERFORMING ARTS MAGAZINE, Performing Arts Network, 10350 Santa Monica Blvd., #350, Los Angeles CA 90025. (310)551-1115. Fax: (310)551-2769. Website: www.performingartsmagazine.com. **Contact:** David Bowman, editor. **95% freelance written.** Monthly magazine covering arts and performing arts. "We cover performing arts events throughout the state of California only and articles should pertain to performances in California. Theatre-going audience." Estab. 1963. Circ. 570,000. Pays on publication. Byline given. Offers 50% kill fee. Buys all rights, makes work-for-hire assignments. Editorial lead time 3 months. Submit seasonal material 6 months in advance. Responds in 6 weeks to queries. Sample copy for 10×12 SAE with 5 first-class stamps.
Nonfiction: Interview/profile, new productions. "Do not send unsolicited mss." **Buys 75 mss/year.** Query with published clips. Length: 500-750 words. **Pays $350-500.** Sometimes pays expenses of writers on assignment.
Photos: State availability with submission. Buys all rights. Negotiates payment individually. Captions, identification of subjects required.

PREMIERE, The Interactive Movie Magazine, Hachette Filipacchi magazines, 1633 Broadway, 40th Floor, New York NY 10019. E-mail: premiere@hfnm.com. Website: www.premieremag.com. Web Group Director: Judy Koutsky. Online Producer: Nicole Perri. **Contact:** Eric Charlesworth, online editor; Doray Briskman, newsletter editor.

$ $ $ REQUEST MAGAZINE, Request Media, Inc., 10400 Yellow Circle Dr., Minnetonka MN 55343. (952)931-8740. Fax: (952)931-8490. E-mail: editors@requestmagazine.com. Website: www.requestmagazine.com. **Contact:** Heidi Raschke, editor. **70% freelance written.** Bimonthly magazine. "*Request* offers sharp, enthusiastic coverage of the latest and best in music, movies, home video and all manner of entertainment." Membership magazine for Musicland Group. Estab. 1989. Circ. 1.3 million. Pays as files go to press. Publishes ms an average of 2 months after acceptance. Byline given. Offers 50% kill fee. Buys first, electronic rights. Editorial lead time 4 months. Submit seasonal material 4 months in advance. Accepts queries by e-mail. Accepts simultaneous submissions. Sample copy for $2.95. Writer's guidelines by e-mail.
Nonfiction: Essays, general interest, humor, interview/profile, photo feature, reviews. **Buys 10-20 mss/year.** Query with published clips. Length: 150-2,500 words. **Pays $50-1,000.** Sometimes pays expenses of writers on assignment.
Photos: Send photos with submission. Reviews contact sheets. Photo rights negotiable. Negotiates payment individually. Identification of subjects required.
Columns/Departments: Reviews (short, efficient CD and video reviews), 100-200 words. Query with published clips. **Pays $50-100.**
Tips: "We prefer enthusiastic pitches on noteworthy artists or releases, ideally with a pre-determined level of interview access or research. Our core audience consists of avid music and movie lovers aged 21 to 35."

N RUE MORGUE, Horror in Culture & Entertainment, Marrs Media, Inc., 700 Queen St. E., Toronto Ontario M4M 1G9, Canada. E-mail: info@rue-morgue.com. Website: www.rue-morgue.com. Editor: Rod Gudino. Associate Editor: Mary Beth Hollyer. **Contact:** Rod Gudino. **50% freelance written.** Bimonthly magazine covering horror entertainment. "A knowledge of horror entertainment (films, books, games, toys, etc.)." Estab. 1997. Pays on publication. Publishes ms an average of 4 months after acceptance. Byline given. Buys all rights. Editorial lead time 2 months. Submit seasonal material 4 months in advance. Accepts queries by e-mail. Responds in 6 weeks to queries; 2 months to mss. Sample copy not available. Writer's guidelines by e-mail.

Nonfiction: Rod Gudino, editor. Essays, exposé, historical/nostalgic, interview/profile, new product, travel. No fiction. Reviews done by staff writers. **Buys 10 mss/year.** Query with published clips or send complete ms. Length: 500-2,000 words. **Pays $25-100.**

Columns/Departments: Rob Gudino, editor. Classic Cut (historical essays on classic horror films, books, games, comic books, music), 500-700 words. **Buys 1-2 mss/year.** Query with published clips. **Pays $25-35.**

Tips: "The editor is most responsive to hard-to-get interviews with famous horror personalities corresponding with related releases. We also are always looking out for analytical/historical essays that illuminate the reasons for the public's fascination with horror."

$ $ $ SOUND & VISION, Hachette Filipacchi Magazines, Inc., 1633 Broadway, New York NY 10019. (212)767-6000. Fax: (212)767-5615. E-mail: soundandvision@hfmag.com. Website: www.soundandvisionmag.com. Editor-in-Chief: Bob Ankosko. Entertainment Editor: Ken Richardson. **Contact:** Michael Gaughn, features editor. **50% freelance written.** Published 10 times/year. Estab. 1958. Circ. 450,000. **Pays on acceptance.** Publishes ms an average of 4 months after acceptance. Byline given. Buys first North American serial, electronic rights. Accepts queries by mail, e-mail, fax. Sample copy for 9×12 SAE and 11 first-class stamps.

Nonfiction: Home theater, audio, video and multimedia equipment plus movie and music reviews, how-to-buy and how-to-use A/V gear, interview/profile. **Buys 25 mss/year.** Query with published clips. Length: 1,500-3,000 words. **Pays $1,000-1,500.**

Tips: "Send proposals or outlines, rather than complete articles, along with published clips to establish writing ability. Publisher assumes no responsibility for return or safety of unsolicited art, photos or manuscripts."

$ $ STAGEBILL, Stagebill LLC, 823 United Plaza at 46th St., New York NY 10017. Fax: (212)949-5976. Website: www.stagebill.com. **Contact:** Robert Cashill, managing editor. **80% freelance written.** Program distributed free to performing arts audiences covering dance, theater, opera, classical music, jazz and some film. "Our editorial is geared toward an educated and sophisticated arts audience. We suggest to writers that the closest analogous publication is the *New York Times'* Sunday Arts & Leisure section." Estab. 1924. Circ. 15,000,000/year. Pays on publication. Publishes ms an average of 2 months after acceptance. Byline given. Offers 50% kill fee. Buys 90 day exclusive rights, non-exclusive after that. Editorial lead time 2 months. Submit seasonal material 3 months in advance. Accepts queries by mail, e-mail. Accepts previously published material. Responds in 2 weeks to queries; 1 month to mss. Sample copy online.

Nonfiction: Book excerpts, essays (on arts or cultural trends), humor, opinion. **Buys 200 mss/year.** Query with published clips. Length: 350-1,200 words. **Pays $250-400.** Sometimes pays expenses of writers on assignment.

Reprints: Accepts previously published submissions.

Photos: State availability with submission. Offers no additional payment for photos accepted with ms.

Columns/Departments: See/Hear (book/CD reviews), 200 words; By Design (art, design and fashion), 600-750 words; Critical Slant (opinions on culture), 350-400 words; Traveler (performing arts-oriented travel), 600-750 words; Deus Ex Machina (arts and technology), 600-750 words. **Buys 75 mss/year.** Query with published clips. **Pays $50-350.**

$ TELE REVISTA, Su Mejor Amiga, Teve Latino Publishing, Inc., P.O. Box 145179, Coral Gables FL 33114-5179. (305)445-1755. Fax: (305)445-3907. E-mail: telerevista@aol.com. Website: www.telerevista.com. **Contact:** Ana Pereiro, editor. **100% freelance written.** Monthly magazine covering Hispanic entertainment (US and Puerto Rico). "We feature interviews, gossip, breaking stories, behind-the-scenes happenings, etc." Estab. 1986. Pays on publication. Publishes ms an average of 3 months after acceptance. Byline sometimes given. Buys all rights. Editorial lead time 2 months. Submit seasonal material 3 months in advance. Accepts queries by mail, e-mail, fax. Sample copy for free.

Nonfiction: Exposé, interview/profile, opinion, photo feature. **Buys 200 mss/year.** Query. **Pays $25-75.**

Photos: State availability of or send photos with submission. Buys all rights. Negotiates payment individually. Captions required.

Columns/Departments: Buys 60 mss/year. Query. **Pays $25-75.**

Fillers: Anecdotes, facts, gags to be illustrated by cartoonist, newsbreaks, short humor.

ETHNIC & MINORITY

Ideas and concerns of interest to specific nationalities and religions are covered by publications in this category. General interest lifestyle magazines for these groups are also included. Many ethnic publications are locally oriented or highly specialized and do not wish to be listed in a national publication such as *Writer's Market*. Query the editor of an ethnic publication with which you're familiar before submitting a manuscript, but do not consider these markets closed because they are not listed in this section. Additional markets for writing with an ethnic orientation are located in the following sections: Career, College & Alumni; Juvenile; Literary & "Little"; Men's; Women's; and Teen & Young Adult.

$ AFRICAN VOICES, African Voices Communications, Inc., 270 W. 96th St., New York NY 10025. (212)865-2982. Fax: (212)316-3335. E-mail: africanvoices@aol.com. Website: www.africanvoices.com. Managing Editor: Layding Kaliba. **Contact:** Carolyn A. Butts, publisher/editor; Debbie Officer, book review editor. **85% freelance written.** Quarterly magazine covering art, film, culture. "*African Voices* is dedicated to highlighting the art, literature, and history of people of color." Estab. 1992. Circ. 20,000. Pays on publication. Byline given. Buys first North American serial rights. Editorial lead time 3 months. Submit seasonal material 3 months in advance. Accepts queries by mail. Accepts previously published material. Accepts simultaneous submissions. Responds in 3 months to queries. Sample copy for $5 or online. Writer's guidelines for #10 SASE.

Nonfiction: Book excerpts, essays, historical/nostalgic, humor, inspirational, interview/profile, photo feature, travel. Query with published clips. Length: 1,200-2,500 words. **Pays $25-100.**

Reprints: Accepts previously published submissions.

Photos: State availability with submission. Buys one-time rights. Negotiates payment individually.

Fiction: Kim Horne, fiction editor. Adventure, erotica, ethnic, experimental, fantasy, historical, horror, humorous, mainstream, mystery, novel excerpts, romance, science fiction, serialized novels, slice-of-life vignettes, suspense. **Buys 4 mss/year.** Send complete ms. Length: 500-2,500 words. **Pays $25-50.**

Poetry: Layding Kaliba, managing editor/poetry editor. Avant-garde, free verse, haiku, traditional. **Buys 10 poems/year.** Submit maximum 5 poems. Length: 5-100 lines. **Pays $10-20.**

$ AIM MAGAZINE, AIM Publishing Company, P.O. Box 1174, Maywood IL 60153. (708)344-4414. Fax: (206)543-2746. E-mail: ruthone@earthlink.net. Website: aimmagazine.org. **Contact:** Dr. Myron Apilado, editor. **75% freelance written.** Works with a small number of new/unpublished writers each year. Quarterly magazine on social betterment that promotes racial harmony and peace for high school, college and general audience. Estab. 1975. Circ. 10,000. Pays on publication. Publishes ms an average of 3 months after acceptance. Byline given. Offers 60% kill fee. Buys one-time rights. Submit seasonal material 6 months in advance. Accepts queries by mail, e-mail. Accepts simultaneous submissions. Responds in 2 months to queries. Sample copy and writer's guidelines for $4 and 9×12 SAE with $1.70 postage or online.

Nonfiction: Exposé (education), general interest (social significance), historical/nostalgic (Black or Indian), how-to (create a more equitable society), interview/profile (one who is making social contributions to community), book reviews; reviews of plays. No religious material. **Buys 16 mss/year.** Send complete ms. Length: 500-800 words. **Pays $25-35.**

Photos: Reviews b&w prints. Captions, identification of subjects required.

Fiction: "Fiction that teaches the brotherhood of man." Ethnic, historical, mainstream, suspense. **Buys 20 mss/year.** Send complete ms. Length: 1,000-1,500 words. **Pays $25-35.**

Poetry: Avant-garde, free verse, light verse. No "preachy" poetry. **Buys 20 poems/year.** Submit maximum 5 poems. Length: 15-30 lines. **Pays $3-5.**

Fillers: Anecdotes, newsbreaks, short humor. **Buys 30/year.** Length: 50-100 words. **Pays $5.**

Tips: "Interview anyone of any age who unselfishly is making an unusual contribution to the lives of less fortunate individuals. Include photo and background of person. We look at the nations of the world as part of one family. Short stories and historical pieces about Blacks and Indians are the areas most open to freelancers. Subject matter of submission is of paramount concern for us rather than writing style. Articles and stories showing the similarity in the lives of people with different racial backgrounds are desired."

$ $ AMBASSADOR MAGAZINE, National Italian American Foundation, 1860-19 St. NW, Washington DC 20009. (202)387-0600. Fax: (202)387-0800. E-mail: kevin@niaf.org. Website: www.niaf.org. **Contact:** Kevin Heitz. **50% freelance written.** Magazine for Italian-Americans covering Italian-American history and culture. "We publish nonfiction articles on little-known events in Italian-American history, and articles on Italian-American culture, traditions, and personalities living and dead." Estab. 1989. Circ. 20,000. Pays on approval of final draft. Byline given. Offers 50% or $100 kill fee. Buys second serial (reprint) rights. Editorial lead time 3 months. Accepts queries by mail, e-mail, fax. Accepts previously published material. Accepts simultaneous submissions. Responds in 1 month to queries. Sample copy and writer's guidelines free.

Nonfiction: Historical/nostalgic, interview/profile, personal experience, photo feature. **Buys 12 mss/year.** Send complete ms. Length: 1,500-2,500 words. **Pays $200.**

Photos: Send photos with submission. Reviews contact sheets, Prints. Buys one-time rights. Offers no additional payment for photos accepted with ms. Captions, identification of subjects required.

Tips: "Good photos, clear prose, and a good storytelling ability are all prerequisites."

$ $ AMERICAN VISIONS, The Magazine of Afro-American Culture, 1101 Pennsylvania Ave. NW, Suite 820, Washington DC 20004. (202)347-3820. Fax: (202)347-4096. E-mail: editor@avs.americanvisions.com. Website: www.americanvisions.com. **Contact:** Joanne Harris, executive editor. **75% freelance written.** Bimonthly magazine. "Editorial is reportorial, current, objective, 'pop-scholarly.' Audience is ages 25-54, mostly black, college educated. The scope of the magazine includes the arts, history, literature, cuisine, genealogy and travel—all filtered through the prism of the African-American experience." Estab. 1986. Circ. 125,000. Pays 30 days after publication. Publishes ms an average of 2 months after acceptance. Byline given. Offers 25% kill fee. Buys second serial (reprint), all rights. Submit seasonal material 5 months in advance. Accepts queries by mail, e-mail. Accepts previously published material. Accepts simultaneous submissions. Responds in 3 months to queries. Sample copy and writer's guidelines for #10 SASE.

Nonfiction: Publishes travel supplements—domestic, Africa, Europe, Canada, Mexico. Book excerpts, general interest, historical/nostalgic, interview/profile, photo feature, travel, literature. **Buys about 60-70 mss/year.** Query with or without published clips or send complete ms. Length: 500-2,500 words. **Pays $100-600 for assigned articles; $100-400 for unsolicited articles.** Pays expenses of writers on assignment.

Reprints: Send tearsheet or photocopy with rights for sale noted and information about when and where the material previously appeared. Pays $100.
Photos: State availability with submission. Reviews contact sheets, 3×5 transparencies, 3×5 or 8×10 prints. Buys one-time rights. Offers $15/minimum. Identification of subjects required.
Columns/Departments: Arts Scene, Books, Cuisine, Film, Music, Profile, Genealogy, Computers & Technology, Travel, 750-1,750 words. **Buys about 40 mss/year.** Send complete ms. **Pays $100-400.**
Tips: "Little-known but terribly interesting information about black history and culture is desired. Aim at an upscale audience. Send ms with credentials. Looking for writers who are enthusiastic about their topics."

$ ASIAN PAGES, Kita Associates, Inc., P.O. Box 11932, St. Paul MN 55111-1932. (952)884-3265. Fax: (952)888-9373. E-mail: asianpages@att.net. Website: www.asianpages.com. **Contact:** Cheryl Weiberg, editor-in-chief. **40% freelance written.** Biweekly newspaper covering the Asian community in the Midwest. "*Asian Pages* serves an audience of over 20 different Asian groups, including Cambodian, Chinese, Filipino, Hmong, Indian, Indonesian, Japanese, Korean, Laotian, Malaysian, Sri Lankan, Thai, Tibetan, and Vietnamese. In addition, *Asian Pages* has many nonAsian readers who, for many different reasons, have an interest in the vibrant Asian community. *Asian Pages* celebrates the achievements of the Asian community in the Midwest and promotes a cultural bridge among the many different Asian groups that the newspaper serves." Estab. 1990. Circ. 75,000. Pays on publication. Publishes ms an average of 8 months after acceptance. Byline given. Offers 50% kill fee. Buys first North American serial rights. Editorial lead time 4 months. Submit seasonal material 6 months in advance. Accepts queries by mail. Accepts simultaneous submissions. Responds in 1 month to queries; 2 months to mss. Sample copy for 9×12 SAE and 3 first-class stamps. Writer's guidelines for #10 SASE.
Nonfiction: "All articles must have an Asian slant. We're interested in articles on the Asian New Years, banking, business, finance, sports/leisure, home and garden, education, and career planning. No culturally insensitive material." Essays, general interest, humor, inspirational, interview/profile, personal experience, travel. **Buys 50-60 mss/year.** Send complete ms. Length: 500-750 words. **Pays $40.**
Photos: State availability with submission. Reviews transparencies, Prints. Buys one-time rights. Offers no additional payment for photos accepted with ms. Captions, identification of subjects required.
Columns/Departments: "Query with exceptional ideas for our market and provide 1-2 sample columns." **Buys 100 mss/year.** Query. **Pays $40.**
Fiction: Adventure, ethnic, humorous, stories based on personal experiences. No culturally insensitive material. Send complete ms. Length: 750-1,000 words. **Pays $40.**
Tips: "We look for articles that reflect a direct insight into Asian culture or being an Asian-American in today's society."

$ $ ☒ THE B'NAI B'RITH INTERNATIONAL JEWISH MONTHLY, B'nai B'rith International, 1640 Rhode Island Ave. NW, Washington DC 20036. (202)857-2708. Fax: (202)296-1092. E-mail: ijm@bnaibrith.org. Website: bnaibrith.org. Editor: Eric Rozenman. **Contact:** Stacey Freed, managing editor. **90% freelance written.** Bimonthly magazine "specializing in social, political, historical, religious, cultural, 'lifestyle,' and service articles relating chiefly to the Jewish communities of North America and Israel. Write for the American Jewish audience, i.e., write about topics from a Jewish perspective." Estab. 1886. Circ. 110,000. Pays on publication. Publishes ms an average of 6 months after acceptance. Byline given. Offers 25% kill fee. Buys first rights. Editorial lead time 3 months. Submit seasonal material 5 months in advance. Accepts queries by mail, e-mail, fax. Accepts simultaneous submissions. Responds in 2 weeks to queries; 6 weeks to mss. Sample copy for $2. Writer's guidelines for #10 SASE or by e-mail.
Nonfiction: General interest pieces of relevance to the Jewish community of US and abroad. Interview/profile, photo feature, religious, travel. "No Holocaust memoirs, no first-person essays/memoirs." **Buys 18-20 mss/year.** Query with published clips. Length: 1,000-2,500 words. **Pays $300-750 for assigned articles; $300-600 for unsolicited articles.** Sometimes pays expenses of writers on assignment.
Photos: "Rarely assigned." Buys one-time rights.
Columns/Departments: Carla Lancit, assistant editor. Up Front (book, CD reviews; small/short items with Jewish interest), 150-200 words. **Buys 3 mss/year.** Query. **Pays $50.**
Tips: "Know what's going on in the Jewish world. Look at other Jewish publications also. Writers should submit clips with their queries. Read our guidelines carefully and present a good idea expressed well. Proofread your query letter."

$ CONGRESS MONTHLY, American Jewish Congress, 15 E. 84th St., New York NY 10028. (212)879-4500. **Contact:** Jack Fischel, managing editor. **90% freelance written.** Bimonthly magazine. "*Congress Monthly*'s readership is popular, but well-informed; the magazine covers political, social, economic and cultural issues of concern to the Jewish community in general and to the American Jewish Congress in particular." Estab. 1933. Circ. 35,000. Pays on publication. Publishes ms an average of 3 months after acceptance. Byline given. Buys one-time rights. Submit seasonal material 2 months in advance. Responds in 2 months to queries.
Nonfiction: General interest ("current topical issues geared toward our audience"). Travel, book; film and theater reviews. No technical material. Query. Length: 1,000-2,500 words. **Pays amount determined by article length and author experience.**
Photos: State availability with submission. Reviews B&W prints.

$ FILIPINAS, A Magazine for All Filipinos, Filipinas Publishing, Inc., 363 El Camino Real, Suite 100, South San Francisco CA 94080. (650)872-8650. Fax: (650)872-8651. E-mail: mail@filipinasmag.com. Website: www.filipinasmag.

com. **Contact:** Mona Lisa Yuchengco, editor/publisher. Monthly magazine focused on Filipino-American affairs. "*Filipinas* answers the lack of mainstream media coverage of Filipinos in America. It targets both Filipino immigrants and American-born Filipinos, gives in-depth coverage of political, social, cultural events in the Philippines and in the Filipino-American community. Features role models, history, travel, food and leisure, issues, and controversies." Estab. 1992. Circ. 40,000. Pays on publication. Publishes ms an average of 5 months after acceptance. Byline given. Offers $10 kill fee. Buys first, all rights. Editorial lead time 2 months. Submit seasonal material 4 months in advance. Accepts queries by mail, e-mail, fax. Responds in 3 weeks to queries; 5 months to mss. Sample copy for $5. Writer's guidelines for 9½ × 4 SASE or on website.

O→ Break in with "a good idea outlined well in the query letter. Also, tenacity is key. If one idea is shot down, come up with another."

Nonfiction: Interested in seeing "more issue-oriented pieces, unusual topics regarding Filipino-Americans and stories from the Midwest and other parts of the country other than the coasts." Exposé, general interest, historical/nostalgic, inspirational, interview/profile, opinion, personal experience, travel. No academic papers. **Buys 80-100 mss/year.** Query with published clips. Length: 800-1,500 words. **Pays $50-75.**

Photos: State availability with submission. Reviews 2¼×2¼ and 4×5 transparencies. Buys one-time rights. Offers $15-35/photo. Captions, identification of subjects required.

Columns/Departments: Cultural Currents (Filipino traditions, beliefs), 1,500 words. Query with published clips. **Pays $50-75.**

$ $ GERMAN LIFE, Zeitgeist Publishing, Inc., 1068 National Hwy., LaVale MD 21502. (301)729-6190. Fax: (301)729-1720. E-mail: ccook@germanlife.com. Website: www.germanlife.com. **Contact:** Carolyn Cook, editor. **50% freelance written.** Bimonthly magazine covering German-speaking Europe. "*German Life* is for all interested in the diversity of German-speaking culture, past and present, and in the various ways that the United States (and North America in general) has been shaped by its German immigrants. The magazine is dedicated to solid reporting on cultural, historical, social, and political events." Estab. 1994. Circ. 40,000. Pays on publication. Byline given. Buys first North American serial rights. Editorial lead time 4 months. Submit seasonal material 6 months in advance. Accepts queries by mail, e-mail. Responds in 2 months to queries; 3 months to mss. Sample copy for $4.95 and SAE with 4 first-class stamps. Writer's guidelines free.

Nonfiction: General interest, historical/nostalgic, interview/profile, photo feature, travel. Special issues: Oktoberfest-related (October); Seasonal Relative to Germany, Switzerland, or Austria (December); Travel to German-speaking Europe (April). **Buys 50 mss/year.** Query with published clips. Length: 800-1,500 words. **Pays $200-500 for assigned articles; $200-350 for unsolicited articles.**

Photos: State availability with submission. Reviews color transparencies, 5×7 color or b&w prints. Buys one-time rights. Offers no additional payment for photos accepted with ms. Identification of subjects required.

Columns/Departments: German-Americana (regards specific German-American communities, organizations, and/or events past or present), 1,200 words; Profile (portrays prominent Germans, Americans, or German-Americans), 1,000 words; At Home (cuisine, etc. relating to German-speaking Europe), 800 words; Library (reviews of books, videos, CDs, etc.), 300 words. **Buys 30 mss/year.** Query with published clips. **Pays $50-150.**

Fillers: Facts, newsbreaks. Length: 100-300 words. **Pays $50-150.**

Tips: "The best queries include several informative proposals. Writers should avoid overemphasizing autobiographical experiences/stories."

$ $ HADASSAH MAGAZINE, (formerly *Hadamag Magazine*), 50 W. 58th St., New York NY 10019. (212)688-5217. Fax: (212)446-9521. E-mail: hadamag@aol.com. **Contact:** Leah Finkelshteyn, associate editor. **90% freelance written.** Monthly magazine. "*Hadassah Magazine* is a general interest Jewish feature and literary magazine. We speak to our readers on a vast array of subjects ranging from politics to parenting, to midlife crisis to Mideast crisis. Our readers want coverage on social and economic issues, Jewish women's (feminist) issues, the arts, travel and health." Circ. 300,000. Buys first rights. Sample copy and writer's guidelines for 9×12 SASE.

Nonfiction: Primarily concerned with Israel, Jewish communities around the world and American civic affairs as relates to the Jewish community. "We are also open to art stories that explore trends in Jewish art, literature, theater, etc. Will not assign/commission a story to a first-time writer for *Hadassah Magazine*." **Buys 10 unsolicited mss/year.** Query. Length: 1,500-2,000 words. Sometimes pays expenses of writers on assignment.

Photos: "We buy photos only to illustrate articles. Always interested in striking cover photos." Offers $50 for first photo, $35 for each additional photo.

Columns/Departments: "We have a family column and a travel column, but a query for topic or destination should be submitted first to make sure the area is of interest and the story follows our format."

Fiction: Short stories with strong plots and positive Jewish values. No personal memoirs, "schmaltzy" or shelter magazine fiction. Length: 1,500-2,000 words. **Pays $500 minimum.**

Tips: "We are interested in reading articles that offer an American perspective on Jewish affairs (1,500-2,000 words)."

$ ✪ HORIZONS, The Jewish Family journal, Targum Press, 22700 W. Eleven Mile Rd., Southfield MI 48034. Fax: (888)298-9992. E-mail: horizons@netvision.net.il. Website: www.targum.com. Managing Editor: Moshe Dombey. **Contact:** Miriam Zakon, chief editor. **100% freelance written.** Quarterly magazine covering the Orthodox Jewish family. "We include fiction and nonfiction, memoirs, essays, historical, and informational articles, all of interest to the Orthodox Jew." Estab. 1994. Circ. 5,000. Pays 4-6 weeks after publication. Publishes ms an average of 6 months after acceptance. Byline given. Buys one-time rights. Editorial lead time 6 months. Submit seasonal material 8 months in advance. Accepts queries by mail, e-mail, fax. Accepts simultaneous submissions. Responds in 1 week to queries; 2 months to mss. Sample copy and writer's guidelines free.

Nonfiction: Essays, historical/nostalgic, humor, inspirational, interview/profile, opinion, personal experience, photo feature, travel. **Buys 150 mss/year.** Send complete ms. Length: 350-3,000 words. **Pays $5-150.**

Photos: State availability with submission. Buys one-time rights. Offers no additional payment for photos accepted with ms.

Fiction: Historical, humorous, mainstream, slice-of-life vignettes. Nothing not suitable to Orthodox Jewish values. **Buys 10-15 mss/year.** Send complete ms. Length: 800-3,000 words. **Pays $20-100.**

Poetry: Free verse, haiku, light verse, traditional. **Buys 30-35 poems/year.** Submit maximum 4 poems. Length: 3-28 lines. **Pays $5-10.**

Fillers: Anecdotes, short humor. **Buys 20/year.** Length: 50-120 words. **Pays $5.**

Tips: "*Horizons* publishes for the Orthodox Jewish market and therefore only accepts articles that are of interest to this market. We do not accept submissions dealing with political issues or Jewish legal issues. The tone is light and friendly and we therefore do not accept submissions that are of a scholarly nature. Our writers must be very familiar with our market. Anything that is not suitable for our readership doesn't stand a chance, no matter how high its literary merit."

$ INDIAN LIFE, News from Across Native North America, Indian Life Ministries, (in Canada) P.O. Box 3765, RPO Redwood Centre, Winnipeg Manitoba R2W 3R6, Canada, (in US) P.O. Box 32, Pembina ND 58271. (204)661-9333. Fax: (204)661-3982. E-mail: jim.editor@indianlife.org. Website: www.indianlife.org. **Contact:** Jim Uttley, editor. **20% freelance written.** Bimonthly newspaper designed to help the Native North American church speak to the social, cultural, and spiritual needs of her people and reaches every province and state of English-speaking North America. *Indian Life*'s purpose is to bring hope, healing, and honor through the presentation of positive news, role models, and a Christian message. Estab. 1968. Circ. 32,000. Pays on publication. Byline given. Buys first North American serial, electronic rights. Editorial lead time 2 months. Submit seasonal material 3 months in advance. Accepts queries by mail, e-mail, fax. Responds in 1 month to queries. Sample copy for $2 or online. Writer's guidelines free.

O→ Break in with good personality pieces of people currently in the news, such as entertainers and newsmakers.

Nonfiction: Book excerpts, general interest, historical/nostalgic, inspirational, interview/profile, personal experience, photo feature, religious. **Buys 20 mss/year.** Query. Length: 300-1,500 words. **Pays $25-100.**

Photos: State availability with submission. Buys all rights. Offers $20-50/photo. Captions, identification of subjects required.

Fiction: Adventure, ethnic, historical, religious, slice-of-life vignettes. **Buys 4 mss/year.** Query. Length: 500-2,000 words. **Pays $40-175.**

Poetry: Free verse, light verse, traditional. No avant-garde or erotic. **Buys 5-10 poems/year.** Submit maximum 5 poems. Length: Maximum of 25 lines. **Pays $40.**

Fillers: Anecdotes, facts, newsbreaks. **Buys 6/year.** Length: 100 words. **Pays $20-40.**

N $ $ $ ITALIAN AMERICA, Official Publication of the Order Sons of Italy in America, Order Sons of Italy in America, 219 E St. NE, Washington DC 20002. (202)547-2900. Fax: (202)546-8168. E-mail: nationaloffice@osia.org. Website: www.osia.org. **Contact:** Dr. Dona De Sanctis, editor/deputy executive director. **50% freelance written.** Quarterly magazine. "*Italian America* strives to provide timely information about OSIA, while reporting on individuals, institutions, issues, and events of current or historical significance in the Italian-American community." Estab. 1996. Circ. 65,000. Pays on publication. Publishes ms an average of 3 months after acceptance. Byline given. Offers 50% kill fee. Buys first North American serial rights. Editorial lead time 3 months. Accepts queries by mail, e-mail, fax. Accepts simultaneous submissions. Sample copy for free. Writer's guidelines free.

Nonfiction: Essays, exposé, historical/nostalgic, interview/profile, opinion, personal experience, travel, current events. **Buys 10 mss/year.** Query with published clips. Length: 500-2,500 words. **Pays $150-1,000.** Sometimes pays expenses of writers on assignment.

Photos: State availability with submission. Reviews contact sheets. Buys one-time rights. Negotiates payment individually. Identification of subjects required.

Columns/Departments: Community Notebook (Italian-American life), 500 words; Postcard from Italy (life in Italy today), 750 words; Reviews (books, films by or about Italian-Americans), 500 words. **Buys 5 mss/year.** Query. **Pays $100-500.**

Tips: "Stories should be unique, not standard."

$ $ ☆ JEWISH ACTION, Union of Orthodox Jewish Congregations of America, 11 Broadway, 14th Floor, New York NY 10004-1302. (212)613-8146. Fax: (212)613-0646. E-mail: chabbott@ou.org. Website: www.ou.org. Editor: Nechama Carmel. **Contact:** Diane Chabbott, assistant editor. **80% freelance written.** Quarterly magazine covering a vibrant approach to Jewish issues, Orthodox lifestyle and values. Circ. 40,000. Pays 2 months after publication. Byline given. Not copyrighted. Submit seasonal material 4 months in advance. Responds in 3 months to queries. Sample copy online. Writer's guidelines for #10 SASE or by e-mail.

- Prefers queries by e-mail. Mail and fax OK.

O→ Break in with a query for "Just Between Us" column.

Nonfiction: Current Jewish issues, history, biography, art, inspirational, humor, music, book reviews. "We are not looking for Holocaust accounts. We welcome essays about responses to personal or societal challenges." **Buys 30-40 mss/year.** Query with published clips. Length: 1,000-3,000 words. **Pays $100-400 for assigned articles; $75-150 for unsolicited articles.**
Photos: Send photos with submission. Identification of subjects required.
Columns/Departments: Just Between Us (personal opinion on current Jewish life and issues), 1,000 words. **Buys 4 mss/year.**
Fiction: Must have relevance to Orthodox reader. Length: 1,000-2,000 words.
Poetry: Buys limited number poems/year. Pays $25-75.
Tips: "Remember that your reader is well educated and has a strong commitment to Orthodox Judaism. Articles on the holidays, Israel, and other common topics should offer a fresh insight. Because the magazine is a quarterly, we do not generally publish articles which concern specific timely events."

$ $ $ MOMENT, The Magazine of Jewish Culture, Politics and Religion, 4710 41st St. NW, Washington DC 20016. (202)364-3300. Fax: (202)364-2636. E-mail: editor@momentmag.com. Publisher/Editor: Hershel Shanks. **Contact:** Joshua Rolnick, managing editor. **90% freelance written.** Bimonthly magazine. "*Moment* is an independent Jewish bimonthly general interest magazine that specializes in cultural, political, historical, religious, and 'lifestyle' articles relating chiefly to the North American Jewish community and Israel." Estab. 1975. Circ. 65,000. Pays on publication. Publishes ms an average of 6 months after acceptance. Byline given. Buys first North American serial rights. Editorial lead time 3 months. Submit seasonal material 6 months in advance. Accepts queries by mail, e-mail, fax. Accepts simultaneous submissions. Responds in 1 month to queries; 3 months to mss. Sample copy for $4.50 and SAE. Writer's guidelines online.
Nonfiction: "We look for meaty, colorful, thought-provoking features and essays on Jewish trends and Israel. We occasionally publish book excerpts, memoirs, and profiles." **Buys 25-30 mss/year.** Query with published clips. Length: 2,500-4,000 words. **Pays $200-1,200 for assigned articles; $40-500 for unsolicited articles.**
Photos: State availability with submission. Buys one-time rights. Negotiates payment individually. Identification of subjects required.
Columns/Departments: 5762—snappy pieces of not more than 250 words about quirky events in Jewish communities, news and ideas to improve Jewish living; Olam (The Jewish World)—first-person pieces, humor, and colorful reportage of 600-1,500 words; Book reviews (fiction and nonfiction) are accepted but generally assigned, 400-800 words. **Buys 30 mss/year.** Query with published clips. **Pays $50-250.**
Tips: "Stories for *Moment* are usually assigned, but unsolicited manuscripts are often selected for publication. Successful features offer readers an in-depth journalistic treatment of an issue, phenomenon, institution, or individual. The more the writer can follow the principle of 'show, don't tell,' the better. The majority of the submissions we receive are about The Holocaust and Israel. A writer has a better chance of having an idea accepted if it is not on these subjects."

$ $ NA'AMAT WOMAN, Magazine of NA'AMAT USA, the Women's Labor Zionist Organization of America, NA'AMAT USA, 350 Fifth Ave., Suite 4700, New York NY 10118. (212)563-5222. Fax: (212)563-5710. **Contact:** Judith A. Sokoloff, editor. **80% freelance written.** Magazine published 4 times/year covering Jewish themes and issues, Israel, women's issues, and social and political issues. Estab. 1926. Circ. 20,000. Pays on publication. Byline given. Buys first North American serial, first, one-time, second serial (reprint) rights, makes work-for-hire assignments. Accepts queries by mail, fax. Responds in 3 months to queries. Writer's guidelines for #10 SASE.
Nonfiction: "All articles must be of particular interest to the Jewish community." Exposé, general interest (Jewish), historical/nostalgic, interview/profile, opinion, personal experience, photo feature, travel, art, music, social and political issues, Israel. **Buys 20 mss/year.** Query with or without published clips or send complete ms. **Pays 10-15¢/word.**
Photos: State availability with submission. Buys one-time rights. Pays $25-45 for 4×5 or 5×7 prints. Captions, identification of subjects required.
Columns/Departments: Film and book reviews with Jewish themes. **Buys 20 mss/year.** Query with published clips or send complete ms. **Pays 10¢/word.**
Fiction: "Intelligent fiction with Jewish slant. No maudlin nostalgia or trite humor." Historical, humorous, novel excerpts, women-oriented. **Buys 3 mss/year.** Send complete ms. Length: 2,000-3,000 words. **Pays 10¢/word.**

$ $ NATIVE PEOPLES MAGAZINE, The Arts and Lifeways, 5333 N. Seventh St., Suite C-224, Phoenix AZ 85014-2804. (602)265-4855. Fax: (602)265-3113. E-mail: editorial@nativepeoples.com. Website: www.nativepeoples.com. **Contact:** Daniel Gibson, editor. Bimonthly magazine covering Native Americans. "High-quality reproduction with full color throughout. The primary purpose of this magazine is to offer a sensitive portrayal of the arts and lifeways of Native peoples of the Americas." Estab. 1987. Circ. 50,000. Pays on publication. Byline given. Buys one-time rights. Accepts queries by mail, e-mail, fax. Responds in 2 months to queries. Writer's guidelines online.
Nonfiction: Pathways (travel section) department most open to freelancers. Looking for articles on educational, economic and political development, occasional historic pieces, Native events. Interview/profile (of interesting and leading Natives from all walks of life, with an emphasis on arts), personal experience. **Buys 35 mss/year.** Query with published clips. Length: 1,000-2,500 words. **Pays 25¢/word.**
Photos: State availability with submission. Reviews transparencies, prefers 35mm slides. Also accepts electronic photo images, inquire for details. Buys one-time rights. Offers $45-150/page rates, $250/cover photos. Identification of subjects required.

Tips: "We are focused upon authenticity and a positive portrayal of present-day Native American life and cultural practices. Our stories portray role models of Native people, young and old, with a sense of pride in their heritage and culture. Therefore, it is important that the Native American point of view be incorporated in each story."

N $ THE UKRAINIAN WEEKLY, Ukrainian National Association, 2200 Route 10, P.O. Box 280, Parsippany NJ 07054. (973)292-9800. Fax: (973)644-9510. E-mail: staff@ukrweekly.com. Website: www.ukrweekly.com. **Contact:** Roma Hadzewycz, editor-in-chief. **30% freelance written (mostly by a corps of regular contributors)**. Weekly tabloid covering news and issues of concern to Ukrainian community, primarily in North America but also around the world, and events in Ukraine. "We have a news bureau in Kyiv, capital of Ukraine." Estab. 1933. Circ. 7,000. Pays on publication. Publishes ms an average of 1 month after acceptance. Byline given. Buys first North American serial, second serial (reprint) rights, makes work-for-hire assignments. Submit seasonal material 1 month in advance. Accepts queries by mail, e-mail, fax. Responds in 1 month to mss. Sample copy for 9×12 SAE and 3 first-class stamps.

Nonfiction: Book excerpts, essays, exposé, general interest, historical/nostalgic, interview/profile, opinion, personal experience, photo feature, news events. Special issues: Easter, Christmas, anniversary of Ukraine's independence proclamation (August 24, 1991), student scholarships, anniversary of Chornobyl nuclear accident, summer events preview and year-end review of news. **Buys 80 mss/year.** Query with published clips. Length: 500-2,000 words. **Pays $50-100 for assigned articles; $25-50 for unsolicited articles.** Sometimes pays expenses of writers on assignment.

Reprints: Send typed ms with rights for sale noted and information about when and where the material previously appeared. Pays 25-50% of amount paid for an original article.

Photos: Send photos with submission. Reviews contact sheets, negatives, 3×5, 5×7 or 8×10 prints and slides. Offers no additional payment for photos accepted with ms.

Columns/Departments: News & Views (commentary on news events), 500-1,000 words. **Buys 10 mss/year.** Query. **Pays $50.**

Tips: "Become acquainted with the Ukrainian community in the U.S. and Canada. The area of our publication most open to freelancers is community news—coverage of local events and personalities."

$ $ UPSCALE MAGAZINE, Bronner Brothers, 600 Bronner Brothers Way, Atlanta GA 30310. (404)758-7467. Fax: (404)755-9892. Website: www.upscalemagazine.com. **Contact:** Joyce Davis, senior editor. Monthly magazine covering topics for "upscale Afro-American/black interests." "*Upscale* offers to take the reader to the 'next level' of life's experience. Written for the black reader and consumer, *Upscale* provides information in the realms of business, news, lifestyle, fashion and beauty, and arts and entertainment." Estab. 1989. Circ. 250,000. Pays on publication. Publishes ms an average of 4 months after acceptance. Byline given. Offers 25% kill fee. Buys first North American serial rights. Editorial lead time 3-4 months. Accepts queries by mail. Accepts simultaneous submissions. Responds in 4 weeks to queries; 2 months to mss. Sample copy online. Writer's guidelines online.

Nonfiction: Book excerpts, essays, general interest, how-to, humor, inspirational, interview/profile, opinion, personal experience, travel. Special issues: See website for editorial calendar. **Buys 315 mss/year.** Query with published clips. Length: 500-1,500 words. **Pays $200-1,000 for assigned articles; $200-600 for unsolicited articles.**

Photos: State availability with submission. Negotiates payment individually. Captions, identification of subjects, model releases required.

Columns/Departments: Constance Clemons, office manager. News & Business (factual, current); Lifestyle (travel, home, wellness, etc.); Beauty & Fashion (tips, trends, upscale fashion, hair); and Arts & Entertainment (artwork, black celebrities, entertainment). **Buys 6-10 mss/year.** Query with published clips. **Payment different for each department.**

Fiction: Humorous, novel excerpts.

Tips: "Make queries exciting. Include exciting clips. Be familiar with issues affecting black readers. Be able to write about them with ease and intelligence."

$ $ VISTA MAGAZINE, The Magazine for all Hispanics, Hispanic Publishing Corp., 999 Ponce de Leon Blvd., Suite 600, Coral Gables FL 33134. (305)442-2462. Fax: (305)443-7650. E-mail: jlobaco@hisp.com. Website: www.vistamagazine.com. **Contact:** Julia Bencomo Lobaco, editor. **50% freelance written.** Monthly magazine. "Monthly and Sunday supplement-style magazine targeting Hispanic audience. Dual-language, Spanish/English, 50/50%. Stories appear in one language or another, not both. Topics of general interest, but with a Hispanic angle." Estab. 1985. Circ. 1,000,000. Pays on publication. Publishes ms an average of 2 months after acceptance. Byline given. Offers 25% kill fee. Buys all rights. Editorial lead time 2 months. Submit seasonal material 4 months in advance. Accepts queries by mail, e-mail, fax, phone. Sample copy free or online.

Nonfiction: Exposé, general interest, historical/nostalgic, how-to (home improvement), inspirational, interview/profile, new product, photo feature, travel. "No creative writing, poems, etc." **Buys 40-50 mss/year.** Query with published clips. Length: 500-1,600 words. **Pays $250-450.** Sometimes pays expenses of writers on assignment.

Photos: State availability with submission.

Columns/Departments: In Touch (short profile of someone doing outstanding work in any area, i.e., education, business, health, etc.). **Pays $100.**

Tips: "Query by phone is usually best. Articles must be related to Hispanics, be of national interest, timely and, unless assigned by VISTA, should be 850-1,200 words—not longer."

FOOD & DRINK

Magazines appealing to gourmets, health-conscious consumers, and vegetarians are classified here. Some publications emphasize "the art and craft" of cooking for food enthusiasts who enjoy developing these skills as a leisure activity. Another popular trend stresses healthy eating and food choices. Many magazines in the Health & Fitness category present a holistic approach to well-being through nutrition and fitness for healthful living. Magazines in General Interest and Women's categories also buy articles on food topics. Journals aimed at food processing, manufacturing, and retailing are in the Trade section.

$ $ $ $ BON APPETIT, America's Food and Entertaining Magazine, Conde Nast Publications, Inc., 6300 Wilshire Blvd., Los Angeles CA 90048. (323)965-3600. Fax: (323)937-1206. Website: epicurious.com. Editor-in-Chief: Barbara Fairchild. **Contact:** Victoria von Biel, executive editor. **50% freelance written.** Monthly magazine covering fine food, restaurants, and home entertaining. "*Bon Appetit* readers are upscale food enthusiasts and sophisticated travelers. They eat out often and entertain 4-6 times a month." Estab. 1975. Circ. 1,331,853. **Pays on acceptance.** Byline given. Buys all rights. Submit seasonal material 1 year in advance. Accepts queries by mail. Responds in 6 weeks to queries. Writer's guidelines for #10 SASE.

Nonfiction: Travel (restaurant or food-related), food feature, dessert feature. "No humorous essays, cartoons, quizzes, poetry, historic food features or obscure food subjects." **Buys 50 mss/year.** Query with published clips. No phone calls or e-mails. Length: 750-2,000 words. **Pays $500-1,800.** Pays expenses of writers on assignment.

Photos: Never send photos.

Tips: "We are not interested in receiving specific queries, but we occasionally look for new good writers. They must have a good knowledge of the *Bon Appetit*-related topic (as shown in accompanying clips) and a light, lively style. Nothing long and pedantic please."

$ $ ☆ CHILE PEPPER, Cooking Zesty, River Plaza 1701 River Run #702, Ft. Worth TX 76102. (817)877-1048. Fax: (817)877-8870. E-mail: editor@chilepepper.com. **Contact:** David K. Gibson, editor. **70-80% freelance written.** Bimonthly magazine on spicy foods. "The magazine is devoted to spicy foods, and most articles include recipes. We have a very devoted readership who love their food hot!" Estab. 1986. Circ. 85,000. Pays on publication. Buys first, electronic rights. Submit seasonal material 6 months in advance. Writer's guidelines for #10 SASE.

Nonfiction: How-to (cooking and gardening with spicy foods), humor (having to do with spicy foods), interview/profiles (chefs & business people), travel (having to do with spicy foods). **Buys 50 mss/year.** Query by mail or e-mail only. Length: 1,000-3,000 words. **Pays $600 minimum for feature article.**

Reprints: Send tearsheet or photocopy and information about when and where the material previously appeared.

Photos: State availability with submission. Reviews contact sheets, negatives, transparencies, prints. Buys one-time rights. Offers $25/photo minimum. Captions, identification of subjects required.

Tips: "We're always interested in queries from *food* writers. Articles about spicy foods with six to eight recipes are just right. No fillers. No unsolicited manuscripts; queries only. E-mail queries preferred."

$ $ $ $ ☆ COOKING LIGHT, The Magazine of Food and Fitness, Southern Progress Corp., P.O. Box 1748, Birmingham AL 35201-1681. (205)445-6000. Fax: (205)445-6600. Website: cookinglight.com. **Contact:** Jill Melton, senior food editor (food) or Phillip Rhodes, senior healthy living editor (fitness/healthy lifestyle). **75% freelance written.** Magazine published 11 times/year on healthy recipes and fitness information. "*Cooking Light* is a positive approach to a healthier lifestyle. It's written for healthy people on regular diets who are counting calories or trying to make calories count toward better nutrition. Moderation, balance and variety are emphasized. The writing style is fresh, upbeat and encouraging, emphasizing that eating a balanced, varied, lower-calorie diet and exercising regularly do not have to be boring." Estab. 1987. Circ. 1,600,000. **Pays on acceptance.** Publishes ms an average of 1 year after acceptance. Byline sometimes given. Offers 33% kill fee. Submit seasonal material 1 year in advance. Accepts queries by mail. Responds in 1 year to mss.

Nonfiction: Service approaches to nutrition, healthy recipes, fitness/exercise. Backup material a must. **Buys 150 mss/year.** Must query with résumé and published clips; no unsolicited mss. Response guaranteed with SASE. Length: 400-2,000 words. **Pays $250-2,000.** Pays expenses of writers on assignment.

■ The online magazine contains original content not found in the print edition. Contact: Maelynn Cheung, managing editor, cookinglight.com.

Tips: "Emphasis should be on achieving a healthier lifestyle through food, nutrition, fitness, exercise information. In submitting queries, include information on professional background. Food writers should include examples of healthy recipes which meet the guidelines of *Cooking Light*."

GOURMET, The Magazine of Good Living, Conde Nast Publications, Inc., 4 Times Square, New York NY 10036. (212)286-2860. Fax: (212)286-2932. Website: www.gourmet.com. Editor-in-Chief: Ruth Reichl. **Contact:** John Willoughby, executive editor. Monthly magazine for sophisticated readers who have a passion for food and travel. Byline given. Offers 25% kill fee. Accepts queries by mail. Accepts simultaneous submissions. Responds in 2 months to queries. Sample copy for free.

Nonfiction: Looking for "articles on reminiscence, single foods and ethnic cuisines." **Buys 25-30 mss/year.** Query with published clips. Length: 200-3,000 words. Pays expenses of writers on assignment.

$ GOURMET FARE MAGAZINE, DRS Publishing Group, E-mail: info@gourmetfare.com. Website: www.gourmetfare.com. Editor: Diana R. Savastano. Managing Editor: Lisa D. Russo. **Contact:** Caroline North, associate editor. **50% freelance written.** Quarterly online food publication for food lovers including articles on travel, entertaining, health and more. Estab. 1993. Pays on publication. Byline given. Buys first rights. Editorial lead time 3 months. Submit seasonal material 3 months in advance. Accepts queries by e-mail. Accepts simultaneous submissions. Responds in 3 weeks to queries; 2 months to mss. Sample copy online. Writer's guidelines not available.

● Accepts queries by e-mail only.

Nonfiction: Humor, new product, travel. **Buys 20-50 mss/year.** Query. Length: 400-1,500 words. **Pays $45-150 for assigned articles; $35-75 for unsolicited articles.**

Reprints: Accepts previously published submissions.

Photos: State availability with submission.

Tips: "Review the publication for content and style. We are always looking for new and interesting articles about food, wine, and food-related products. Query via e-mail."

$ $ HOME COOKING, House of White Birches, Publishers, 306 E. Parr Rd., Berne IN 46711. (219)589-4000 ext. 396. Fax: (219)589-8093. E-mail: home_cooking@whitebirches.com. Website: www.whitebirches.com. Project Supervisor: Barb Sprunger. **Contact:** Shelly Vaughan James, editor. **55% freelance written**. Bimonthly. "*Home Cooking* delivers hundreds of kitchen-tested recipes from home cooks. Special features offer recipes, tips for today's busy cooks, techniques for food preparation, nutritional hints and more. Departments cover topics to round out the cooking experience." Circ. 75,000. Pays within 45 days after acceptance. Publishes ms an average of 8 months after acceptance. Byline given. Buys all rights. Editorial lead time 6 months. Submit seasonal material 8 months in advance. Accepts queries by mail, e-mail. Accepts simultaneous submissions. Responds in 1 month to queries. Sample copy for 6×9 SAE and 5 first-class stamps. Request editorial calendar and writer's guidelines with LSASE.

O→ Break in with a submission or query to one of *Home Cooking*'s departments.

Nonfiction: How-to, humor, new product, personal experience, Recipes, book reviews, all in food/cooking area. No health/fitness or travel articles. **Buys 60 mss/year.** Query or send complete manuscript. Length: 250-750 words plus 6-8 recipes. **Pays $50-300 for assigned articles; $50-200 for unsolicited articles.** Sometimes pays expenses of writers on assignment.

Photos: State availability with submission. Reviews prints. Buys one-time rights. Negotiates payment individually. Identification of subjects, model releases required.

Columns/Departments: Stirring Comments (book and product reviews assigned by editor), 100 words; Pinch of Sage (hints for the home cook), 200-500 words; Kitchen Know-How, 250-1,000 words. **Buys 48 mss/year.** Query or send complete manuscript. **Pays $50-200.**

Fillers: Anecdotes, facts, newsbreaks, short humor. **Buys 30/year.** Length: 10-150 words. **Pays $20-25.**

Tips: "Departments are most open to new writers. All submissions should be written specifically for our publication. Be sure to check spelling, grammar and punctuation before mailing. If that means setting aside your manuscript for two weeks to regain your objectivity, do it. A sale two weeks later beats a rejection earlier. If you follow our style in your manuscript, we know you've read our magazine. Request editorial calendar and writer's guidelines with SASE."

$ $ $ HOMETOWN COOKING, Better Homes and Gardens, Meredith Corp., 1716 Locust St., Des Moines IA 50309. (515)284-3000. Website: www.hometowncook.com. **Contact:** Joy Taylor, executive editor. **50% freelance written.** Bimonthly magazine covering food, recipes, and people. "*Hometown Cooking* provides home cooks with the very best recipes with an emphasis on those from community cookbooks." Estab. 1999. **Pays on acceptance.** Publishes ms an average of 6 months after acceptance. Byline sometimes given. Buys all rights, makes work-for-hire assignments. Editorial lead time 1 year. Submit seasonal material 18 months in advance. Accepts queries by mail. Responds in 1 month to queries; 2 months to mss. Sample copy online. Writer's guidelines not available.

Nonfiction: Book excerpts, essays, general interest, historical/nostalgic, how-to, humor, inspirational, interview/profile. **Buys 30 mss/year.** Query with published clips. Length: 500-2,000 words. **Pays $300-1,000 for assigned articles.** Sometimes pays expenses of writers on assignment.

Poetry: Light verse. **Buys 6-12 poems/year.**

Fillers: Anecdotes, short humor. Length: 50-200 words. **Pays $50-100.**

Tips: "Have an appreciation for what kinds of foods mainstream families like, and are willing to prepare."

$ $ KASHRUS MAGAZINE, The Bimonthly for the Kosher Consumer and the Trade, The Kashrus Institute, P.O. Box 204, Parkville Station, Brooklyn NY 11204. (718)336-8544. **Contact:** Rabbi Yosef Wikler, editor. **25% freelance written.** Prefers to work with published/established writers, but will work with new/unpublished writers. Bimonthly magazine covering the kosher food industry and food production. Estab. 1980. Circ. 10,000. Pays on publication. Publishes ms an average of 2 months after acceptance. Byline given. Offers 50% kill fee. Buys first, second serial (reprint) rights. Submit seasonal material 2 months in advance. Accepts queries by mail, phone. Accepts previously published material. Accepts simultaneous submissions. Responds in 1 week to queries; 2 weeks to mss. Sample copy for $3.

Nonfiction: General interest, interview/profile, new product, personal experience, photo feature, religious, technical, travel. Special issues: International Kosher Travel (October); Passover (March). **Buys 8-12 mss/year.** Query with published clips. Length: 1,000-1,500 words. **Pays $100-250 for assigned articles; up to $100 for unsolicited articles.** Sometimes pays expenses of writers on assignment.

Reprints: Send tearsheet or photocopy and information about when and where the material previously appeared. Pays 25-50% of amount paid for an original article.

Photos: No guidelines; send samples or call. State availability with submission. Buys one-time rights. Offers no additional payment for photos accepted with ms.

Columns/Departments: Book Review (cookbooks, food technology, kosher food), 250-500 words; People in the News (interviews with kosher personalities), 1,000-1,500 words; Regional Kosher Supervision (report on kosher supervision in a city or community), 1,000-1,500 words; Food Technology (new technology or current technology with accompanying pictures), 1,000-1,500 words; Travel (international, national), must include Kosher information and Jewish communities, 1,000-1,500 words; Regional Kosher Cooking, 1,000-1,500 words. **Buys 8-12 mss/year.** Query with published clips. **Pays $50-250.**

Tips: "*Kashrus Magazine* will do more writing on general food technology, production, and merchandising as well as human interest travelogs and regional writing in 2003 than we have done in the past. Areas most open to freelancers are interviews, food technology, cooking and food preparation, dining, regional reporting, and travel, but we also feature healthy eating and lifestyles, redecorating, catering, and hospitals and health care. We welcome stories on the availability and quality of kosher foods and services in communities across the U.S. and throughout the world. Some of our best stories have been by nonJewish writers about kosher observance in their region. We also enjoy humorous articles. Just send a query with clips and we'll try to find a storyline that's right for you, or better yet, call us to discuss a storyline."

$ $ RISTORANTE, Foley Publishing, P.O. Box 73, Liberty Corner NJ 07938. (908)766-6006. Fax: (908)766-6607. E-mail: barmag@aol.com. Website: www.bartender.com. **Contact:** Raymond Foley, publisher or Jaclyn Foley, editor. **75% freelance written.** Bimonthly magazine covering "Italian anything!" "*Ristorante—The magazine for the Italian Connoisseur.* For Italian restaurants and those who love Italian food, travel, wine and all things Italian!" Estab. 1994. Circ. 40,000. Pays on publication. Publishes ms an average of 3 months after acceptance. Byline sometimes given. Buys first North American serial, one-time rights. Editorial lead time 3 months. Submit seasonal material 3 months in advance. Accepts previously published material. Responds in 1 month to queries; 2 months to mss. Sample copy and writer's guidelines for 9×12 SAE and 4 first-class stamps.

- *Ristorante* is in progress to being published. It should be ready by February of 2002.

Nonfiction: Book excerpts, general interest, historical/nostalgic, how-to (prepare Italian foods), humor, new product, opinion, personal experience, travel. **Buys 25 mss/year.** Send complete ms. Length: 100-1,000 words. **Pays $100-350 for assigned articles; $75-300 for unsolicited articles.** Sometimes pays expenses of writers on assignment.

Reprints: Send tearsheet or photocopy and information about when and where the material previously appeared. Pays 25% of amount paid for an original article.

Photos: Send photos with submission. Reviews 3×5 prints. Buys one-time rights. Negotiates payment individually. Captions, model releases required.

Columns/Departments: Send complete ms. **Pays $50-200.**

Fillers: Anecdotes, facts, short humor. **Buys 10/year. Pays $10-50.**

$ $ VEGGIE LIFE, Good Food for Good Health, EGW Publishing, 1041 Shary Circle, Concord CA 94518. (510)671-9852. Fax: (510)671-0692. E-mail: veggieed@aol.com. Website: www.veggielife.com. **Contact:** Shanna Masters, editor. **90% freelance written.** Quarterly magazine covering vegetarian cooking for health. Estab. 1992. Circ. 160,000. Pays half on acceptance, half on publication. Publishes ms an average of 4 months after acceptance. Byline given. Offers 25% kill fee. Buys all rights, makes work-for-hire assignments. Editorial lead time 1 year. Submit seasonal material 1 year in advance. Accepts queries by mail, e-mail. Responds in 6 months to queries. for #10 SASE or by e-mail.

Nonfiction: Vegetarian cooking/recipes, nutrition, kitchen craft ideas. No animal rights issues/advocacy, religious/philosophical, personal opinion. **Buys 30-50 mss/year.** Query with résumé and published clips. No phone calls please; e-mail OK. **Pays 35¢/published word and $35/published recipe.** Food Features: 300-500 word intros, plus 6-8 recipes. Recipes should be delicious, low in fat, no more than 10 grams of fat/serving.

Photos: Seldom used. State availability with submission. Captions, identification of subjects, model releases required.

Tips: "Research back issues; love food, be upbeat, authoritative; no 'Why I Became a Vegetarian...' stories. Please state why you are qualified to write particular subject matter. No article with specific health claims will be considered without sufficient fact verification information."

$ $ WINE PRESS NORTHWEST, Tri-City Herald, 107 N. Cascade St., Kennewick WA 99336. (509)582-1564. Fax: (509)582-1510. E-mail: editor@winepressnw.com. Website: www.winepressnw.com. Managing Editor: Eric Degerman. **Contact:** Andy Perdue, editor. **50% freelance written.** Quarterly magazine covering Pacific Northwest wine (Washington, Oregon, British Columbia, Idaho). "We focus narrowly on Pacific Northwest wine. If we write about travel, it's where to go to drink NW wine. If we write about food, it's what goes with NW wine. No beer, no spirits." Estab. 1998. Circ. 12,000. Pays on publication. Publishes ms an average of 3 months after acceptance. Byline given. Offers 20% kill fee. Buys first North American serial, electronic rights. Editorial lead time 3 months. Submit seasonal material 3 months in advance. Accepts queries by mail, e-mail, fax. Accepts simultaneous submissions. Responds in 1 month to queries. Sample copy free or online. Writer's guidelines free.

Nonfiction: General interest, historical/nostalgic, interview/profile, new product, photo feature, travel. No "beer, spirits, non-NW (California wine, etc.)" **Buys 30 mss/year.** Query with published clips. Length: 1,500-2,500 words. **Pays $250-300.** Sometimes pays expenses of writers on assignment.

Photos: State availability with submission. Reviews contact sheets. Buys one-time rights. Negotiates payment individually. Identification of subjects required.

The online magazine carries original content not found in the print edition. Contact: Andy Perdue, online editor.

Tips: "Writers must be familiar with *Wine Press Northwest* and should have a passion for the region, its wines and cuisine."

$ $ $ WINE SPECTATOR, M. Shanken Communications, Inc., 387 Park Ave. S., New York NY 10016. (212)684-4224. Fax: (212)684-5424. E-mail: winespec@mshanken.com. Website: www.winespectator.com. **Contact:** Thomas Matthews, executive editor. **20% freelance written.** Prefers to work with published/established writers. Biweekly news magazine. Estab. 1976. Circ. 323,000. Pays within 30 days of publication. Publishes ms an average of 2 months after acceptance. Byline given. Buys all rights, makes work-for-hire assignments. Submit seasonal material 4 months in advance. Accepts queries by mail, fax. Responds in 3 months to queries. Sample copy for $5. Writer's guidelines for #10 SASE.

Nonfiction: General interest (news about wine or wine events), interview/profile (of wine, vintners, wineries), opinion, photo feature, travel, dining and other lifestyle pieces. No "winery promotional pieces or articles by writers who lack sufficient knowledge to write below just surface data." Query. Length: 100-2,000 words. **Pays $100-1,000.**

Photos: Send photos with submission. Buys all rights. Pays $75 minimum for color transparencies. Captions, identification of subjects, model releases required.

The online magazine carries original content not found in the print edition. Contact: Dana Nigro, news editor.

Tips: "A solid knowledge of wine is a must. Query letters essential, detailing the story idea. New, refreshing ideas which have not been covered before stand a good chance of acceptance. *Wine Spectator* is a consumer-oriented news magazine, but we are interested in some trade stories; brevity is essential."

$ $ WINE X MAGAZINE, Wine, Food and an Intelligent Slice of Vice, X Publishing, Inc., 880 Second St., Santa Rosa CA 95404-4611. (707)545-0992. Fax: (707)542-7062. E-mail: winex@winexwired.com. Website: www.winexwired.com. **Contact:** Darryl Roberts, editor/publisher. **100% freelance written.** Bimonthly magazine covering wine and other beverages. "*Wine X* is a lifestyle magazine for young adults featuring wine, beer, spirits, music, movies, fashion, food, coffee, celebrity interviews, health/fitness." Estab. 1997. Circ. 35,000. Pays on publication. Publishes ms an average of 3 months after acceptance. Byline given. Not copyrighted. Buys first North American and international serial, electronic rights for 3 years. Editorial lead time 3 months. Submit seasonal material 4 months in advance. Accepts queries by mail, e-mail, fax. Responds in 3 weeks to queries. Sample copy for $6. Writer's guidelines online.

Nonfiction: Essays, new product, personal experience, photo feature, travel. No restaurant reviews, wine collector profiles. **Buys 6 mss/year.** Query. Length: 500-1,500 words. **Pays $50-250 for assigned articles; $50-150 for unsolicited articles.** Sometimes pays expenses of writers on assignment.

Photos: Reviews transparencies. Buys one-time rights. Offers no additional payment for photos accepted with ms. Identification of subjects, model releases required.

Columns/Departments: Wine; Other Beverages; Lifestyle, all 1,000 words. **Buys 72 mss/year.** Query.

Fiction: Buys 6 mss/year. Query. Length: 1,000-1,500 words. **No pay for fiction.**

Poetry: Avant-garde, free verse, haiku, light verse, traditional. **Buys 2 poems/year.** Submit maximum 3 poems. Length: 10-1,500 lines.

Fillers: Short humor. **Buys 6/year.** Length: 100-500 words. **Pays $0-50.**

Tips: "See our website."

GAMES & PUZZLES

These publications are written by and for game enthusiasts interested in both traditional games and word puzzles and newer role-playing adventure, computer, and video games. Other puzzle markets may be found in the Juvenile section.

$ THE BRIDGE BULLETIN, American Contract Bridge League, 2990 Airways Blvd., Memphis TN 38116-3847. (901)332-5586, ext. 291. Fax: (901)398-7754. E-mail: editor@acbl.org. Website: www.acbl.org. Managing Editor: Paul Linxwiler. **Contact:** Brent Manley, editor. **20% freelance written.** Monthly magazine covering duplicate (tournament) bridge. Estab. 1938. Circ. 155,000. Pays on publication. Publishes ms an average of 3 months after acceptance. Byline given. Buys first, second serial (reprint) rights. Editorial lead time 2 months. Accepts queries by mail, e-mail. Accepts previously published material. Accepts simultaneous submissions.

Break in with a "humorous piece about bridge."

Nonfiction: Book excerpts, essays, how-to (play better bridge), humor, interview/profile, new product, personal experience, photo feature, technical, travel. **Buys 6 mss/year.** Query. Length: 500-2,000 words. **Pays $50/page.**

Photos: State availability with submission. Buys all rights. Negotiates payment individually. Identification of subjects required.

Tips: "Articles must relate to contract bridge in some way. Cartoons on bridge welcome."

$ $ CHESS LIFE, United States Chess Federation, 3054 US Route 9W, New Windsor NY 12553-7698. (845)562-8350, ext. 154. Fax: (845)236-4852. E-mail: magazines@uschess.org. Website: www.uschess.org. **Contact:** Peter Kurzdorfer, editor. **15% freelance written.** Works with a small number of new/unpublished writers/year. Monthly magazine.

"*Chess Life* is the official publication of the United States Chess Federation, covering news of most major chess events, both here and abroad, with special emphasis on the triumphs and exploits of American players." Estab. 1939. Circ. 70,000. Publishes ms an average of 8 months after acceptance. Byline given. Buys first rights. negotiable Submit seasonal material 8 months in advance. Accepts queries by mail, e-mail, fax, phone. Accepts simultaneous submissions. Responds in 3 months to mss. Sample copy and writer's guidelines for 9×11 SAE with 5 first-class stamps.

Nonfiction: All must have some relation to chess. General interest, historical/nostalgic, humor, interview/profile (of a famous chess player or organizer), photo feature (chess centered), technical. No "stories about personal experiences with chess." **Buys 30-40 mss/year.** Query with samples if new to publication. Length: 3,000 words maximum. **Pays $100/page (800-1,000 words).** Sometimes pays expenses of writers on assignment.

Reprints: Send tearsheet, photocopy or typed ms with rights for sale noted and information about when and where the material previously appeared.

Photos: Reviews b&w contact sheets and prints and color prints and slides. Buys all or negotiable rights. Pays $25-35 inside; $100-300 for covers. Captions, identification of subjects, model releases required.

Columns/Departments: Chess Review (brief articles on unknown chess personalities) and "Chess in Everyday Life."

Fillers: Submit with samples and clips. Buys first or negotiable rights to cartoons and puzzles. **Pays $25 upon acceptance.**

Tips: "Articles must be written from an informed point of view—not from view of the curious amateur. Most of our writers are specialized in that they have sound credentials as chess players. Freelancers in major population areas (except New York and Los Angeles, which we already have covered) who are interested in short personality profiles and perhaps news reporting have the best opportunities. We're looking for more personality pieces on chess players around the country; not just the stars, but local masters, talented youths, and dedicated volunteers. Freelancers interested in such pieces might let us know of their interest and their range. Could be we know of an interesting story in their territory that needs covering. Examples of published articles include a locally produced chess television program, a meeting of chess set collectors from around the world, chess in our prisons, and chess in the works of several famous writers."

$SCHOOL MATES, United States Chess Federation, 3054 US Route 9W, New Windsor NY 12553. (716)676-2402. Fax: (845)236-4852. E-mail: magazines@uschess.org. Website: www.uschess.org. Publication Director: Jami Anson. **Contact:** Peter Kurzdorfer, editor. **10% freelance written.** Quarterly magazine of chess for the beginning (some intermediate) player. Includes instruction, player profiles, chess tournament coverage, listings. Estab. 1987. Circ. 30,000. Pays on publication. Publishes ms an average of 6 months after acceptance. Byline given. Buys first rights. Editorial lead time 2 months. Submit seasonal material 3 months in advance. Accepts queries by mail, e-mail, fax, phone. Accepts previously published material. Accepts simultaneous submissions. Responds in 6 months to queries. Sample copy and writer's guidelines free.

Nonfiction: "We are not-for-profit; we try to make up for low pay rates with complimentary copies." Historical/nostalgic (of a famous scholastic chess personality or a scholastic chess event), how-to, humor, interview/profile (of a famous scholastic chess player or organizer), personal experience, photo feature, technical, travel, any other chess-related item. **Buys 10-20 mss/year.** Query. Length: 250-1,000 words. **Pays $50/1,000 words, $20 minimum.** Sometimes pays expenses of writers on assignment.

Reprints: Send tearsheet, photocopy or typed ms with rights for sale noted and information about when and where the material previously appeared. Pays 100% of amount paid for an original article.

Photos: Send photos with submission. Reviews prints. Buys one-time rights, pays $15 for subsequent use. Offers $25/photo for first time rights. Captions, identification of subjects required.

Columns/Departments: Test Your Tactics/Winning Chess Tactics (explanation, with diagrams, of chess tactics; 8 diagrammed chess problems, e.g., "white to play and win in 2 moves"); Basic Chess (chess instruction for beginners). Query with published clips. **Pays $50/1,000 words ($20 minimum).**

Tips: "Know your subject; chess is a technical subject, and you can't fake it. Human interest stories on famous chess players or young chess players can be 'softer,' but always remember you are writing for children, and make it lively. We use the Frye readability scale (3rd-6th grade reading level), and items written on the appropriate reading level do stand out immediately! We are most open to human interest stories, puzzles, cartoons, photos. We are always looking for an unusual angle, e.g., (wild example) a kid who plays chess while surfing, or (more likely) a blind kid and how she plays chess with her specially-made chess pieces and board, etc."

GAY & LESBIAN INTEREST

The magazines listed here cover a wide range of politics, culture, news, art, literature, and issues of general interest to gay and lesbian communities. Magazines of a strictly sexual content are listed in the Sex section.

$BAY WINDOWS, New England's Largest Gay and Lesbian Newspaper, Bay Windows, Inc., 631 Tremont St., Boston MA 02118-2034. (617)266-6670. Fax: (617)266-5973. E-mail: news@baywindows.com. Website: www.baywindows.com. **Contact:** Peter Cassels, assistant editor or Rudy Kikel (arts), or Jeff Epperly (news). **30-40% freelance written.** Weekly newspaper of gay news and concerns. "*Bay Windows* covers predominantly news of New England, but will print non-local news and features depending on the newsworthiness of the story. We feature hard news, opinion, news analysis, arts reviews and interviews." Estab. 1983. Pays within 2 months of publication. Publishes ms an average of 2 months after acceptance. Byline given. Offers 50% kill fee. Buys various rights, usually first serial rights. Submit seasonal material 3 months in advance. Accepts queries by mail, fax. Accepts previously published material. Accepts simultaneous submissions. Responds in 3 months to queries. Sample copy for $5.

Nonfiction: General interest (with a gay slant), interview/profile, opinion, photo feature, hard news. **Buys 200 mss/year.** Query with published clips or send complete ms. Length: 500-1,500 words. **Pays $25-100.**

Reprints: Send tearsheet or photocopy and information about when and where the material previously appeared. Pays 75% of amount paid for an original article.

Photos: Pays $25/published photo. Identification of subjects, model releases required.

Columns/Departments: Film, music, dance, books, art. Length: 500-1,500 words. Letters, opinion to Jeff Epperly, editor; news, features to Peter Cassels, assistant editor; arts, reviews to Rudy Kikel, arts editor. **Buys 200 mss/year. Pays $25-100.**

Poetry: All varieties. Rudy Kikel. **Buys 50 poems/year.** Length: 1-30 lines. **Pays in copies.**

Tips: "Too much gay-oriented writing is laden with the clichés and catch phrases of the movement. Writers must have intimate knowledge of gay community; however, this doesn't mean that standard English usage isn't required. We look for writers with new, even controversial perspectives on the lives of gay men and lesbians. While we assume gay is good, we'll print stories which examine problems within the community and movement. No pornography or erotica."

$ $ CURVE MAGAZINE, Outspoken Enterprises, Inc., 1 Haight St., #B, San Francisco CA 94102. Fax: (415)863-1609. E-mail: editor@curvemag.com. Website: www.curvemag.com. Editor-in-Chief: Frances Stevens. **Contact:** Gretchen Lee, managing editor. **40% freelance written.** Magazine published 8 times/year covering lesbian general interest categories. "We want dynamic and provocative articles written by, about, and for lesbians." Estab. 1991. Circ. 68,000. Pays on publication. Byline given. Offers 25% kill fee. Buys first North American serial rights. Editorial lead time 4 months. Submit seasonal material 6 months in advance. Accepts queries by mail, e-mail, fax. Sample copy for $3.95 with $2 postage. Writer's guidelines online.

Nonfiction: General interest, photo feature, travel, celebrity interview/profile. Special issues: Pride issue (June); Music issue (July/August). No essays, fiction, or poetry. **Buys 25 mss/year.** Query. Length: 200-2,500 words. **Pays $40-300.**

Photos: Send photos with submission. Buys one-time rights. Offers $50-100/photo; negotiates payment individually. Captions, identification of subjects, model releases required.

Tips: "Feature articles generally fit into one of the following categories: Celebrity profiles (lesbian, bisexual, or straight women who are icons for the lesbian community or actively involved in coalition-building with the lesbian community); community segment profiles—e.g., lesbian firefighters, drag kings, sports teams (multiple interviews with a variety of women in different parts of the country representing a diversity of backgrounds); noncelebrity profiles (activities of unknown or low-profile lesbian and bisexual activists/political leaders, athletes, filmmakers, dancers, writers, musicians, etc.); controversial issues (spark a dialogue about issues that divide us as a community, and the ways in which lesbians of different backgrounds fail to understand and support one another. We are not interested in inflammatory articles that incite or enrage readers without offering a channel for action); trends (community trends in a variety of areas, including sports, fashion, image, health, music, spirituality, and identity); and visual essays (most of our fashion and travel pieces are developed and produced in-house. However, we welcome input from freelancers and from time to time publish outside work)."

$ $ $ $ GENRE, Genre Publishing, 7080 Hollywood Blvd., #818, Hollywood CA 90028. (323)467-8300. Fax: (323)467-8365. E-mail: lfreeman@genremagazine.com. Website: www.genremagazine.com. Editor: Morris Weissinger. **Contact:** Leon Freeman, assistant editor. **60% freelance written.** Magazine published 11 times/year. "*Genre*, America's best-selling gay men's lifestyle magazine, covers entertainment, fashion, travel and relationships in a hip, upbeat, upscale voice." Estab. 1991. Circ. 50,000. Pays on publication. Publishes ms an average of 3 months after acceptance. Byline given. Offers 25% kill fee. Buys first North American serial, electronic rights. Editorial lead time 10 weeks. Submit seasonal material 10 weeks in advance. Accepts queries by mail, e-mail, fax. Sample copy for $6.95 ($5 plus $1.95 postage). Writer's guidelines for #10 SASE.

Nonfiction: Essays, exposé, general interest, historical/nostalgic, how-to, humor, inspirational, interview/profile, new product, opinion, personal experience, photo feature, religious, travel, relationships, fashion. Not interested in articles on 2 males negotiating a sexual situation or coming out stories. **Buys variable number mss/year.** Query with published clips. Length: 500-1,500 words. **Pays $150-1,600.**

Photos: State availability with submission. Reviews contact sheets, Prints (3×5 or 5×7). Buys one-time rights. Negotiates payment individually. Model releases required.

Columns/Departments: Body (how to better the body); Mind (how to better the mind); Spirit (how to better the spirit), all 700 words; Reviews (books, movies, music, travel, etc.), 500 words. **Buys variable number of mss/year.** Query with published clips or send complete ms. **Pays $200 maximum.**

Fiction: Adventure, experimental, horror, humorous, mainstream, mystery, novel excerpts, religious, romance, science fiction, slice-of-life vignettes, suspense. **Buys 10 mss/year.** Send complete ms. Length: 2,000-4,000 words.

Tips: "Like you, we take our journalistic responsibilities and ethics very seriously, and we subscribe to the highest standards of the profession. We expect our writers to represent original work that is not libelous and does not infringe upon the copyright or violate the right of privacy of any other person, firm or corporation."

$ $ GIRLFRIENDS MAGAZINE, Lesbian culture, politics, and entertainment, 3415 Cèsar Châvez, Suite 101, San Francisco CA 94110. (415)648-9464. Fax: (415)648-4705. E-mail: editorial@girlfriendsmag.com. Website: www.girlfriendsmag.com. **Contact:** Heather Findlay, editor. Monthly lesbian magazine. "*Girlfriends* provides its readers with intelligent, entertaining and visually pleasing coverage of culture, politics, and entertainment—all from an informed and critical lesbian perspective." Estab. 1994. Circ. 75,000. Pays on publication. Publishes ms an average of 6 months after acceptance. Byline given. Offers 50% kill fee. Buys first rights. use for advertising/promoting *Girlfriends* Editorial lead time 3 months. Submit seasonal material 6 months in advance. Accepts queries by mail, e-mail. Accepts simultaneous submissions. Responds in 3 weeks to queries; 2 months to mss. Sample copy for $4.95 plus $1.50 s/h or online. Writer's guidelines for #10 SASE or online.

• *Girlfriends* is not accepting fiction, poetry or fillers.

O┳ Break in by sending a letter detailing interests and story ideas, plus résumé and published samples.

Nonfiction: Book excerpts, essays, exposé, historical/nostalgic, humor, interview/profile, new product, opinion, personal experience, photo feature, religious, technical, travel, investigative features. Special issues: sex, music, bridal, sports and Hollywood issues. Special features: best lesbian restaurants in the US; best places to live. **Buys 20-25 mss/year.** Query with published clips. Length: 1,000-3,500 words. **Pays 10-25¢/word.**

Reprints: Send photocopy or typed ms with rights for sale noted and information about when and where the material previously appeared. Negotiable payment.

Photos: Send photos with submission. Reviews contact sheets, 4×5 or 2¼×2¼ transparencies, prints. Buys one-time rights. Offers $30-250/photo. Captions, identification of subjects, model releases required.

Columns/Departments: Book reviews, 900 words; Music reviews, 600 words; Travel, 600 words; Opinion pieces, 1,000 words; Humor, 600 words. Query with published clips. **Pays 15¢/word.**

Tips: "Be unafraid of controversy—articles should focus on problems and debates raised in lesbian culture, politics, and sexuality. Avoid being 'politically correct.' We don't just want to know what's happening in the lesbian world, we want to know how what's happening in the world affects lesbians."

$ $ THE GUIDE, To Gay Travel, Entertainment, Politics and Sex, Fidelity Publishing, P.O. Box 990593, Boston MA 02199-0593. (617)266-8557. Fax: (617)266-1125. E-mail: theguide@guidemag.com. Website: www.guidemag.com. **Contact:** French Wall, editor. **25% freelance written.** Monthly magazine on the gay and lesbian community. Estab. 1981. Circ. 30,000. **Pays on acceptance.** Publishes ms an average of 2 months after acceptance. Offers negotiable kill fee. Buys first rights. Submit seasonal material 2 months in advance. Accepts queries by mail, e-mail. Accepts previously published material. Accepts simultaneous submissions. Responds in 3 months to queries. Sample copy for 9×12 SAE and 8 first-class stamps. Writer's guidelines for #10 SASE.

Nonfiction: Book excerpts (if yet unpublished), essays, exposé, general interest, historical/nostalgic, humor, interview/profile, opinion, personal experience, photo feature, religious. **Buys 24 mss/year.** Query with or without published clips or send complete ms. Length: 500-5,000 words. **Pays $85-240.**

Reprints: Occasionally buys previously published submissions. Pays 100% of amount paid for an original article.

Photos: Send photos with submission. Reviews contact sheets. Buys one-time rights. Pays $15 per image used. Captions, identification of subjects, model releases required.

Tips: "Brevity, humor and militancy appreciated. Writing on sex, political analysis and humor are particularly appreciated. We purchase very few freelance travel pieces; those that we do buy are usually on less commercial destinations."

$ $ IN THE FAMILY, The Magazine for Queer People and Their Loved Ones, Family magazine, Inc., P.O. Box 5387, Takoma Park MD 20913. (301)270-4771. E-mail: lmarkowitz@aol.com. Website: www.inthefamily.com. **Contact:** Laura Markowitz, editor. **20% freelance written.** Quarterly magazine covering lesbian, gay, and bisexual family relationships. "Using the lens of psychotherapy, our magazine looks at the complexities of L/G/B family relationships as well as professional issues for L/G/B therapists." Estab. 1995. Circ. 3,000. Pays on publication. Publishes ms an average of 3 months after acceptance. Byline given. Offers 25% kill fee. Buys first rights. Editorial lead time 6 months. Submit seasonal material 4 months in advance. Responds in 1 month to queries; 3 months to mss. Sample copy for $5.50. Writers guidelines free or online.

Nonfiction: Essays, exposé, humor, opinion, personal experience, photo feature. "No autobiography or erotica." **Buys 4 mss/year.** Length: 2,500-4,000 words. **Pays $100-300 for assigned articles; $50-200 for unsolicited articles.** Sometimes pays expenses of writers on assignment.

Photos: State availability with submission. Reviews contact sheets. Buys one-time rights. Negotiates payment individually. Captions, identification of subjects, model releases required.

Columns/Departments: Ellen Elgart, senior editor. Family Album (aspects of a queer family life), 1,500 words; In the Therapy Room (clinical case presentations), 2,000 words; A Look at Research (relevant social science findings), 1,500 words; The Last Word (gentle humor), 800 words. **Buys 4 mss/year.** Send complete ms. **Pays $50-150.**

Fiction: Helena Lipstadt, fiction editor. Confessions, ethnic, slice-of-life vignettes, family life theme for G/L/BS. No erotica, science fiction, horror, romance, serialized novels, or westerns. **Buys 4 mss/year.** Send complete ms. Length: 1,000-2,500 words. **Pays $50-100.**

Poetry: Helena Lipstadt, fiction editor. Avant-garde, free verse, haiku, light verse, traditional. **Buys 4 poems/year.** Submit maximum 6 poems. Length: 10-35 lines. **Pays $50-75.**

Tips: "*In the Family* takes an in-depth look at the complexities of lesbian, gay, and bisexual family relationships, including couples and intimacy, money, sex, extended family, parenting, and more. Readers include therapists of all sexual orientations as well as family members of lesbian, gay, and bisexuals, and also queer people who are interested in what therapists have to say about such themes as how to recover from a gay bashing; how to navigate single life; how to have a good divorce; how to understand bisexuality; how to come out to children; how to understand fringe sexual practices; how to reconcile homosexuality and religion. Therapists read it to learn the latest research about working with queer families, to learn from the regular case studies and clinical advice columns. Family members appreciate the multiple viewpoints in the magazine. We look for writers who know something about these issues and who have an engaging, intelligent, narrative style. We are allergic to therapy jargon and political rhetoric."

$ $ $ METROSOURCE, MetroSource Publishing, Inc., 180 Varick St., 5th Floor, New York NY 10014. (212)691-5127. Fax: (212)741-2978. E-mail: rwalsh@metrosource.com; eandersson@metrosource.com; letters@metrosource.com. Website: www.metrosource.com. **Contact:** Richard Walsh, editor-in-chief; Eric Andersson, assistant editor; Nick Steele, fashion editor. **70% freelance written.** Magazine published 5 times/year. "*MetroSource* is an upscale, glossy, 4-color lifestyle magazine targeted to an urban, professional gay and lesbian readership." Estab. 1990. Circ. 85,000. Pays on publication. Publishes ms an average of 2 months after acceptance. Byline given. Editorial lead time 3 months. Submit seasonal material 4 months in advance. Accepts queries by mail, e-mail, fax, phone. Accepts simultaneous submissions. Sample copy for $5.

Nonfiction: Exposé, interview/profile, opinion, photo feature, travel. **Buys 20 mss/year.** Query with published clips. Length: 1,000-2,500 words. **Pays $100-900.**

Photos: State availability with submission. Negotiates payment individually. Captions, model releases required.

Columns/Departments: Book, film, television, and stage reviews; health columns; and personal diary and opinion pieces. Word lengths vary. Query with published clips. **Pays $200.**

$ MOM GUESS WHAT NEWSPAPER, 1725 L St., Sacramento CA 95814. (916)441-6397. Fax: (916)441-6422. E-mail: info@mgwnews.com. Website: www.mgwnews.com. **Contact:** Linda Birner, editor. **80% freelance written.** Works with small number of new/unpublished writers each year. Biweekly tabloid covering gay rights and gay lifestyles. A newspaper for gay men, lesbians, and their straight friends in the State Capitol and the Sacramento Valley area. First and oldest gay newspaper in Sacramento. Estab. 1977. Circ. 21,000. Publishes ms an average of 3 months after acceptance. Byline given. Buys all rights. Submit seasonal material 3 months in advance. Accepts queries by mail, e-mail. Accepts previously published material. Responds in 2 months to queries. Sample copy for $1. Writer's guidelines for 10×13 SAE with 4 first-class stamps or online.

Nonfiction: Interview/profile and photo feature of international, national or local scope. **Buys 8 mss/year.** Query. Length: 200-1,500 words. **Payment depends on article**. Pays expenses of writers on assignment.

Reprints: Send tearsheet or photocopy and information about when and where the material previously appeared. Pay varies.

Photos: Send photos with submission. Reviews 5×7 prints. Buys one-time rights. Offers no additional payment for photos accepted with ms. Captions, identification of subjects required.

Columns/Departments: News, Restaurants, Political, Health, Film, Video, Book Reviews. **Buys 12 mss/year.** Query. **Payment depends on article.**

Tips: "*MGW* is published primarily from volunteers. With some freelancers payment is made. Put requirements in your cover letter. Byline appears with each published article; photos credited. Editors reserve right to edit, crop, touch up, revise, or otherwise alter manuscripts and photos, but not to change theme or intent of the work. Enclose SASE postcard for acceptance or rejection. We will not assume responsibility for returning unsolicited material lacking sufficient return postage or lost in the mail."

OUT, 110 Greene St., Suite 600, New York NY 10012. (212)242-8100. Fax: (212)242-8338. Website: www.out.com. Editor-in-Chief: Brendan Lemon. **Contact:** Department Editor. **80% freelance written.** Monthly national magazine covering gay and lesbian general-interest topics. "Our subjects range from current affairs to culture, from fitness to finance." Estab. 1992. Circ. 120,000. Pays on publication. Publishes ms an average of 3 months after acceptance. Byline given. Offers 25% kill fee. Buys first North American serial rights. second serial (reprint) rights for anthologies (additional fee paid) and 30-day reprint rights (additional fee paid if applicable) Editorial lead time 3 months. Submit seasonal material 5 months in advance. Accepts queries by mail. Accepts simultaneous submissions. Responds in 6 weeks to queries; 2 months to mss. Sample copy for $6. Writer's guidelines for #10 SASE.

Nonfiction: Book excerpts, essays, exposé, general interest, historical/nostalgic, humor, interview/profile, new product, opinion, personal experience, photo feature, travel, fashion/lifestyle. **Buys 200 mss/year.** Query with published clips and SASE. Length: 50-1,500 words. **Pays variable rate.** Sometimes pays expenses of writers on assignment.

Photos: State availability with submission. Reviews contact sheets, transparencies, prints. Buys one-time rights. Negotiates payment individually. Captions, identification of subjects, model releases required.

Tips: "*Out*'s contributors include editors and writers from the country's top consumer titles: Skilled reporters, columnists, and writers with distinctive voices and specific expertise in the fields they cover. But while published clips and relevant experience are a must, the magazine also seeks out fresh, young voices. The best guide to the kind of stories we publish is to review our recent issues—is there a place for the story you have in mind? Be aware of our long lead time. No phone queries, please."

$ OUTSMART, Up & Out Communications, 3406 Audubon Place, Houston TX 77006. (713)520-7237. Fax: (713)522-3275. E-mail: ann@outsmartmagazine.com. Website: www.outsmartmagazine.com. **Contact:** Ann Walton Sieber, editor. **70% freelance written.** Monthly magazine covering gay, lesbian, bisexual, and transgender issues. "*OutSmart* offers vibrant and thoughtful coverage of the stories that appeal most to an educated, professional gay audience." Estab. 1994. Circ. 20,000. Pays on publication. Publishes ms an average of 2 months after acceptance. Byline given. Buys one-time, simultaneous rights. Permission to publish on website Editorial lead time 2 months. Submit

seasonal material 2 months in advance. Accepts queries by mail, e-mail, fax. Accepts previously published material. Accepts simultaneous submissions. Responds in 6 weeks to queries; 2 months to mss. Sample copy and writer's guidelines online.
Nonfiction: Historical/nostalgic, interview/profile, opinion, personal experience, photo feature, travel, health/wellness; local/national news. **Buys 24 mss/year.** Send complete ms. Length: 450-2,300 words. **Pays 5¢/word.**
Reprints: Send photocopy.
Photos: State availability with submission. Reviews 4×6 prints. Buys one-time rights. Negotiates payment individually. Identification of subjects required.
The online magazine carries original content not found in the print edition and includes writer's guidelines.
Tips: "*OutSmart* is a mainstream publication that covers culture, politics, personalities, entertainment, and health/wellness as well as local and national news and events. It is our goal to address the diversity of the lesbian, gay, bisexual, and transgender community, fostering understanding among all Houston's citizens."

$ WISCONSIN IN STEP, (formerly *In Step*), In Step, Inc., 1661 N. Water St., #411, Milwaukee WI 53202. (414)278-7840. Fax: (414)278-5868. E-mail: editor@instepnews.com. Website: www.instepnews.com. Managing Editor: Jorge Cabal. **Contact:** William Attewell, editor. **30% freelance written.** Biweekly consumer tabloid for gay and lesbian readers. Estab. 1984. Circ. 15,000. Buys first North American serial, second serial (reprint) rights. Submit seasonal material 2 months in advance. Accepts queries by mail, e-mail. Accepts simultaneous submissions. Responds in 3 weeks to queries; 1 month to mss. Sample copy for $3. Writer's guidelines for #10 SASE.
Nonfiction: Book excerpts, exposé, historical/nostalgic, interview/profile, new product, opinion, religious, travel. Query. Length: 500-2,000 words. **Pays $15-100.**
Photos: State availability with submission. Reviews 5×7 prints. Buys one-time rights. Negotiates payment individually. Captions, identification of subjects, model releases required.
The online magazine carries original content not found in the print edition. Contact: William Attewell, online editor.
Tips: "E-mail flawless copy samples to get my attention. Be patient."

GENERAL INTEREST

General interest magazines need writers who can appeal to a broad audience—teens and senior citizens, wealthy readers and the unemployed. Each magazine still has a personality that suits its audience—one that a writer should study before sending material to an editor. Other markets for general interest material are in these Consumer sections: Contemporary Culture, Ethnic/Minority, Inflight, Men's, Regional, and Women's.

$ $ THE AMERICAN LEGION MAGAZINE, P.O. Box 1055, Indianapolis IN 46206-1055. (317)630-1200. Fax: (317)630-1280. E-mail: magazine@legion.org. Website: www.legion.org. Editorial Administrator: Patricia Marschand. **Contact:** John Raughter, executive editor. **70% freelance written.** Prefers to work with published/established writers, but works with a small number of new/unpublished writers each year. Monthly magazine. "Working through 15,000 community-level posts, the honorably discharged wartime veterans of The American Legion dedicate themselves to God, country and traditional American values. They believe in a strong defense; adequate and compassionate care for veterans and their families; community service; and the wholesome development of our nation's youth. We publish articles that reflect these values. We inform our readers and their families of significant trends and issues affecting our nation, the world and the way we live. Our major features focus on the American flag, national security, foreign affairs, business trends, social issues, health, education, ethics and the arts. We also publish selected general feature articles, articles of special interest to veterans, and question-and-answer interviews with prominent national and world figures." Estab. 1919. Circ. 2,800,000. **Pays on acceptance.** Publishes ms an average of 6 months after acceptance. Byline given. Buys first North American serial rights. Accepts queries by mail, e-mail, fax. Responds in 2 months to queries. Sample copy for $3.50 and 9×12 SAE with 6 first-class stamps. Writer's guidelines for #10 SASE.
Nonfiction: Well-reported articles or expert commentaries cover issues/trends in world/national affairs, contemporary problems, general interest, sharply-focused feature subjects. Monthly Q&A with national figures/experts. General interest, interview/profile. No regional topics or promotion of partisan political agendas. No personal experiences or war stories. **Buys 50-60 mss/year.** Query with SASE should explain the subject or issue, article's angle and organization, writer's qualifications and experts to be interviewed. Length: 300-2,000 words. **Pays 40¢/word and up.**
Photos: On assignment.
Tips: "Queries by new writers should include clips/background/expertise; no longer than 1½ pages. Submit suitable material showing you have read several issues. *The American Legion Magazine* considers itself '*the* magazine for a strong America.' Reflect this theme (which includes economy, educational system, moral fiber, social issues, infrastructure, technology and national defense/security). We are a general interest, national magazine, not a strictly military magazine. We are widely read by members of the Washington establishment and other policy makers."

$ $ AMERICAN PROFILE, Publishing Group of America, 341 Cool Springs Blvd., Suite 400, Franklin TN 37067. (615)468-6000. Fax: (615)468-6100. E-mail: editorial@americanprofile.com. Website: www.americanprofile.com. Editor: Peter V. Fossel. **Contact:** Joyce Caruthers, associate editor. **95% freelance written.** Weekly magazine with national and regional editorial celebrating the people, places, and experiences of hometowns across America. The 4-color magazine is distributed through small to medium-size community newspapers. Estab. 2000. Circ. 3,000,000. **Pays on acceptance.** Byline given. Buys first, electronic, 6-month exclusive rights rights. Editorial lead time 3 months. Submit seasonal material 6 months in advance. Accepts queries by mail. Responds in 1 month to queries; 1 month to mss. Writer's guidelines online.

• In addition to a query, first-time writers should include 2-3 published clips.

Nonfiction: General interest, how-to, interview/profile. No fiction, nostalgia, poetry, essays. **Buys 250 mss/year.** Query with published clips. Length: 450-1,200 words. Pays expenses of writers on assignment.

Photos: State availability with submission. Reviews transparencies. Buys one-time rights, nonexclusive after 6 months. Negotiates payment individually. Captions, identification of subjects, model releases required.

Columns/Departments: Health; Family; Finances; Home; Gardening.

Tips: "We appreciate hard-copy submissions and 1-paragraph queries for short manuscripts (less than 500 words) on food, gardening, nature, profiles, health, and home projects for small-town audiences. Must be out of the ordinary. Please visit the website to see our writing style."

$ $ $ $ THE ATLANTIC MONTHLY, 77 N. Washington St., Boston MA 02114. Fax: (617)854-7877. Website: www.theatlantic.com. Editor: Michael Kelly. Managing Editor: Cullen Murphy. **Contact:** C. Michael Curtis, senior editor. Monthly magazine of arts and public affairs. Circ. 500,000. **Pays on acceptance.** Byline given. Buys first North American serial rights. Accepts queries by mail. Response time varies to queries.

Nonfiction: Reportage preferred. Book excerpts, essays, general interest, humor, personal experience, religious, travel. Query with or without published clips or send complete ms. All unsolicited mss must be accompanied by SASE. Length: 1,000-6,000 words. **Payment varies**. Sometimes pays expenses of writers on assignment.

Fiction: "Seeks fiction that is clear, tightly written with strong sense of 'story' and well-defined characters." Literary and contemporary fiction. **Buys 12-15 mss/year.** Send complete ms. Length: 2,000-6,000 words. **Pays $3,000.**

Poetry: Peter Davison, poetry editor. **Buys 40-60 poems/year.**

The online magazine carries original content not found in the print edition. Contact: Kate Bacon, online editor.

Tips: Writers should be aware that this is not a market for beginner's work (nonfiction and fiction), nor is it truly for intermediate work. Study this magazine before sending only your best, most professional work. When making first contact, "cover letters are sometimes helpful, particularly if they cite prior publications or involvement in writing programs. Common mistakes: melodrama, inconclusiveness, lack of development, unpersuasive characters and/or dialogue."

$ BIBLIOPHILOS, A Journal of History, Literature, and the Liberal Arts, The Bibliophile Publishing Co., Inc., 200 Security Building, Fairmont WV 26554. (304)366-8107. **Contact:** Dr. Gerald J. Bobango, editor. **65-70% freelance written.** Quarterly literary magazine concentrating on 19th century American and European history and literature. "We see ourself as a forum for new and unpublished writers, historians, philosophers, literary critics and reviewers, and those who love animals. Audience is academic-oriented, college graduate, who believes in traditional Aristotelian-Thomistic thought and education, and has a fair streak of the Luddite in him/her. Our ideal reader owns no television, has never sent nor received e-mail, and avoids shopping malls at any cost. He loves books." Estab. 1981. Circ. 400. Pays on publication. Publishes ms an average of 9 months after acceptance. Byline given. Buys first North American serial rights. Editorial lead time 6 months. Submit seasonal material 6 months in advance. Accepts queries by mail. Accepts previously published material. Accepts simultaneous submissions. Responds in 2 weeks to queries; 1 month to mss. Sample copy for $5.25. Writer's guidelines for 9½×4 SAE with 2 first-class stamps.

Break in with "either prose or poetry which is illustrative of man triumphing over and doing without technology, pure Ludditism, if need be. Send material critical of the socialist welfare state, constantly expanding federal government (or government at all levels), or exposing the inequities of affirmative action, political correctness, and the mass media packaging of political candidates. We want to see a pre-1960 worldview."

Nonfiction: Book excerpts, essays, general interest, historical/nostalgic, humor, interview/profile, opinion, personal experience, photo feature, travel, book review-essay, literary criticism. Special issues: Upcoming theme issues include an annual all book-review issue, containing 10-15 reviews and review-essays, or poetry about books and reading. Does not want to see "anything that Oprah would recommend, or that Erma Bombeck or Ann Landers would think humorous or interesting. No 'I found Jesus and it changed my life' material." **Buys 12-15 mss/year.** Query by mail only. Length: 1,500-3,000 words. **Pays $5-35.**

Photos: State availability with submission. Reviews b&w 4×6 prints. Buys one-time rights. Negotiates payment individually. Identification of subjects required.

Columns/Departments: "Features" (fiction and nonfiction, short stories), 1,500-3,000 words; "Poetry" (batches of 5, preferably thematically related), 3-150 lines; "Reviews" (book reviews or review essays on new books or individual authors, current and past), 1,000-1,500 words; "Opinion" (man triumphing over technology and technocrats, the facade of modern education, computer fetishism), 1,000-1,500 words. **Buys 15 mss/year.** Query by mail only. **Pays $25-40.**

Fiction: Adventure, ethnic, experimental, historical, humorous, mainstream, mystery, novel excerpts, romance, slice-of-life vignettes, suspense, utopian, Orwellian. "No 'I found Jesus and it turned my life around'; no 'I remember Mama, who was a saint and I miss her terribly'; no gay or lesbian topics; no drug culture material; nothing harping on political correctness; nothing to do with healthy living, HMOs, medical programs, or the welfare state, unless it is against statism in these areas." **Buys 15-20 mss/year.** Length: 1,500-3,000 words. **Pays $25-40.**

Poetry: "Formal and rhymed verse gets read first." Free verse, light verse, traditional, political satire, doggerel. "No inspirational verse, or poems about grandchildren and the cute things they do." **No poetry accepted being accepted in 2002. Buys 50-75 poems/year.** Length: 3-150 lines. **Pays $5-25.**
Fillers: Anecdotes, short humor. **Buys 5-6/year.** Length: 25-100 words. **Pays $5-10.**
Tips: "Query first, and include a large SASE and $5.25 for sample issues and guidelines. Tell us of your academic expertise, what kinds of books you can review, and swear that you will follow Turabian's bibliographic form as set forth in the guidelines and no other. Do not call us, nor fax us, nor try e-mailing, which wouldn't work anyway. Avoid the cult of relevantism and contemporaneity. Send us perfect copy, no misspellings, no grammatical errors, no trendy, PC language."

N $ $ THE CHRISTIAN SCIENCE MONITOR, 1 Norway St., Boston MA 02115. (617)450-2000. Website: www.csmonitor.com. **Contact:** Scott Armstrong (National); David Scott (International), Amelia Newcomb (Learning), Jim Bencivenga (Ideas), Gregor Lamb (Arts & Lesure), April Austin (Home Front), Clay Collins (Work & Money). Daily, except Saturdays, Sundays and holidays in North America; weekly international edition. Newspaper. Estab. 1908. Circ. 95,000. Pays on publication. all newspaper rights worldwide for 3 months following publication Accepts queries by mail, e-mail. Responds in 1 month to queries. Writer's guidelines for #10 SASE.
Nonfiction: In-depth features and essays. The newspaper includes 5 sections: Learning (education and life-long learning), Arts & Leisure, Ideas (religion, ethics, science and technology, environment, book reviews), Home Front (home and community issues) and Work & Money. Buys limited number of mss, "top quality only." Publishes original (exclusive) material only. Essays (Home Forum page). Query to appropriate section editor. **Pays Pays $200 average.** Home Forum page buys essays of 400-900 words. **Pays $150 average.** for assigned articles.
Poetry: Seeks non-religious poetry of high quality and of all lengths up to 75 lines. Free verse, traditional, Blank verse. **Pays $35-75 average.**
Tips: "Style should be bright but not cute, concise but thoroughly researched. Try to humanize news or feature writing so reader identifies with it. Avoid sensationalism. Accent constructive, solution-oriented treatment of subjects."

$ $ $ DIVERSION, 1790 Broadway, New York NY 10019. (212)969-7500. Fax: (212)969-7557. Website: www.diversion.com. **Contact:** Ed Wetschler, editor-in-chief. Monthly magazine covering travel and lifestyle, edited for physicians. "*Diversion* offers an eclectic mix of interests beyond medicine. Regular features include stories on domestic and foreign travel destinations, food and wine, sports cars, gardening, photography, books, electronic gear, and the arts. Although *Diversion* doesn't cover health subjects, it does feature profiles of doctors who excel at nonmedical pursuits or who engage in medical volunteer work." Estab. 1973. Circ. 176,000. Pays 3 months after acceptance. Byline given. Offers 25% kill fee. Editorial lead time 4 months. Responds in 1 month to queries. Sample copy for $4.50. Guidelines available.

- Break in by "querying with a brief proposal describing the focus of the story and why it would interest our readers. Include credentials and published clips."

Nonfiction: "We get so many travel and food queries that we're hard pressed to even read them all. Far better to query us on culture, the arts, sports, technology, etc." **Buys 70 mss/year.** Query with proposal, published clips, and author's credentials. Length: 1,800-2,000 words. **Pays $50-1,200.**
Columns/Departments: Travel, food & wine, photography, gardening, cars, technology. Length: 1,200 words.

$ EDUCATION IN FOCUS, Books for All Times, Inc., P.O. Box 2, Alexandria VA 22313. (703)548-0457. E-mail: staff@bfat.com. Website: www.bfat.com. **Contact:** Joe David, editor. **80% freelance written.** Semiannual Newsletter for public interested in education issues at all levels. "We are always looking for intelligent articles that provide educationally sound ideas that enhance the understanding of what is happening or what should be happening in our schools today. We are not looking for material that might be published by the Department of Education. Instead we want material from liberated and mature thinkers and writers, tamed by reason and humanitarianism." Estab. 1989. Circ. 1,000. **Pays on acceptance.** Publishes ms an average of 2 months after acceptance. Byline given. Buys first, one-time, second serial (reprint), book, newsletter and internet rights rights. Editorial lead time 2 months. Accepts queries by mail, e-mail. Accepts simultaneous submissions. Responds in 1 month to queries. Sample copy for #10 SASE.
Nonfiction: "We prefer documented, intelligent articles that deeply inform. The best way to be quickly rejected is to send articles that defend the public school system as it is today, or was!" Book excerpts, exposé, general interest. **Buys 4-6 mss/year.** Query with published clips or send complete ms. Length: 3,000 words. Some longer articles can be broken into 2 articles - one for each issue. **Pays $25-75.**
Tips: "Maintain an honest voice and a clear focus on the subject."

FANTASTIC STORIES OF THE IMAGINATION, P.O. Box 329, Brightwaters NY 11718. E-mail: fantasticstories@aol.com. Website: dnapublications.com/fantastic/index.htm. **Contact:** Edward J. McFadden III, editor.

$ $ $ FRIENDLY EXCHANGE, C-E Publishers: Publishers, Friendly Exchange Business Office, P.O. Box 2120, Warren MI 48090-2120. Publication Office: (586)753-8325. Fax: (248)447-7566. E-mail: friendlyexchange@aol.com. Website: www.friendlyexchange.com. **Contact:** Dan Grantham, editor. **80% freelance written.** Quarterly magazine for policyholders of Farmers Insurance Group of Companies exploring travel, health, home, auto, financial, lifestyle and leisure topics of interest to active families. "These are traditional families (median adult age 39) who live primarily in the area bounded by Ohio on the east and the Pacific Ocean on the west, along with Tennessee, Alabama, and Virginia." Estab. 1981. Circ. 5,700,000. **Pays on acceptance.** Publishes ms an average of 5 months after acceptance. Offers 25% kill fee. Buys all rights. Submit seasonal material 1 year in advance. Accepts simultaneous submissions. Responds in 2 months to queries. Sample copy for 9×12 SAE and 5 first-class stamps. Writer's guidelines for #10 SASE.

Nonfiction: "We provide readers with 'news they can use' through articles that help them make smart choices about lifestyle issues. We focus on home, auto, health, personal finance, travel and other lifestyle/consumer issues of interest to today's families. Readers should get a sense of the issues involved, and information that could help them make those decisions. Style is warm and colorful, making liberal use of anecdotes and quotes." **Buys 32 mss/year.** Query. Length: 200-1,200 words. **Pays $500-1,000, including expenses.**
Columns/Departments: Consumer issues, health, finances, and leisure are topics of regular columns.
Tips: "We concentrate on providing readers information relating to current trends. We prefer tightly targeted stories that provide new information to help readers make decisions about their lives. We don't take queries or mss on first-person essays or humorous articles. We prefer mail or e-mail queries."

$ $ GRIT, American Life and Traditions, Ogden Publications, 1503 SW 42nd St., Topeka KS 66609-1265. (785)274-4300. Fax: (785)274-4305. E-mail: grit@cjnetworks.com. Website: www.grit.com. **Contact:** Donna Doyle, editor-in-chief. **90% freelance written.** Open to new writers. "*Grit* is good news. As a wholesome, family-oriented magazine published for more than a century and distributed nationally, *Grit* features articles about family lifestyles, traditions, values, and pastimes. *Grit* accents the best of American life and traditions—past and present. Our readers are ordinary people doing extraordinary things, with courage, heart, determination, and imagination. Many of them live in small towns and rural areas across the country; others live in cities but share many of the values typical of small-town America." Estab. 1882. Circ. 120,000. Pays on publication. Byline given. Buys first rights. Submit seasonal material 6 months in advance. Accepts queries by mail. Sample copy and writer's guidelines for $4 and 11 × 14 SASE with 4 first-class stamps. Sample articles on website.

- *Grit* reports it is looking for articles about how soon-to-retire baby boomers are planning for retirement and how children are coping with aging parents.
- Break in through Departments such as Readers' True Stories, Pet Tales, Looking Back, Profile, Seasonal Readers Memories (Easter, Christmas, Mother's Day), Poetry.

Nonfiction: The best way to sell work is by reading each issue cover to cover. Humor, interview/profile, features (timely, newsworthy, touching but with a *Grit* angle), readers' true stories, outdoor hobbies, collectibles, gardening, crafts, hobbies, leisure pastimes. Special issues: Gardening (January-October); Health (twice a year); Travel (spring and fall); Collectibles; Pet issue; Canning Contest (essays and entries); Christmas. Query by mail only. Prefers full ms with photos. Length: Main features run 1,200-1,500 words. Department features average 800-1,000 words. **Pays up to 22¢/word for features; plays flat rate for departments.**
Photos: Professional quality photos (b&w prints or color slides) increase acceptability of articles. Send photos with submission. Pays $25-200 each in features according to quality, placement, and color/b&w. Payment for department photos included in flat rate.
Fiction: Short stories, 1,500-2,000 words; may also purchase accompanying art if of high quality and appropriate. Need serials (romance, westerns, mysteries), 3,500-10,000 words. Send ms with SASE to Fiction Dept.
Tips: "Articles should be directed to a national audience, mostly 40 years and older. Sources identified fully. Our readers are warm and loving. They want to read about others with heart. Tell us stories about someone unusual, an unsung hero, an artist of the backroads, an interesting trip with an emotional twist, a memory with a message, an ordinary person accomplishing extraordinary things. Tell us stories that will make us cry with joy." Send complete ms with photos for consideration.

N $ $ $ $ HARPER'S MAGAZINE, 666 Broadway, 11th Floor, New York NY 10012. (212)420-5720. Fax: (212)228-5889. Editor: Lewis H. Lapham. **Contact:** Ann Gollin, editor's assistant. **90% freelance written.** Monthly magazine for well-educated, socially concerned, widely read men and women who value ideas and good writing. "*Harper's Magazine* encourages national discussion on current and significant issues in a format that offers arresting facts and intelligent opinions. By means of its several shorter journalistic forms—Harper's Index, Readings, Forum, and Annotation—as well as with its acclaimed essays, fiction, and reporting, *Harper's* continues the tradition begun with its first issue in 1850: to inform readers across the whole spectrum of political, literary, cultural, and scientific affairs." Estab. 1850. Circ. 216,000. **Pays on acceptance.** Publishes ms an average of 3 months after acceptance. Offers negotiable kill fee. Vary with author and material. Accepts previously published material. Responds in 1 month to queries. Sample copy for $3.95.
Nonfiction: "For writers working with agents or who will query first only, our requirements are: public affairs, literary, international and local reporting and humor." Publishes one major report per issue. Length: 4,000-6,000 words. Publishes one major essay/issue. Length: 4,000-6,000 words. "These should be construed as topical essays on all manner of subjects (politics, the arts, crime, business, etc.) to which the author can bring the force of passionate and informed statement." Humor. No interviews; no profiles. No unsolicited poems will be accepted. **Buys 2 mss/year.** Complete ms and query must include SASE. Length: 4,000-6,000 words.
Reprints: Accepted for Readings section. Send typed ms with rights for sale noted and information about when and where the article previously appeared.
Photos: Occasionally purchased with mss; others by assignment. Stacey Clarkson, art director. State availability with submission. Pays $50-500.
Fiction: Publishes one short story/month. **Generally pays 50¢-$1/word.**
Tips: "Some readers expect their magazines to clothe them with opinions in the way that Bloomingdale's dresses them for the opera. The readers of *Harper's Magazine* belong to a different crowd. They strike me as the kind of people who would rather think in their own voices and come to their own conclusions."

$ $ $ $ ☒ HOPE MAGAZINE, How to be Part of the Solution, Hope Publishing, Inc., P.O. Box 160, Brooklin ME 04616. (207)359-4651. Fax: (207)359-8920. E-mail: info@hopemag.com. Website: www.hopemag.com. Editor-in-chief/Publisher: Jon Wilson. Editor: Kimberly Ridley. Associate Editor: Lane Fisher. Assistant Editor: Todd Nelson. **Contact:** Debbie Ramirez, editorial assistant. **90% freelance written.** Bimonthly magazine covering humanity at its best and worst. "*Hope* is a solutions-oriented journal focused on people addressing personal and societal challenges with uncommon courage and integrity. A magazine free of religious, political, or New Age affiliation, *Hope* awakens the impulse we all have—however hidden or distant—to make our world more liveable, humane, and genuinely loving. We strive to evoke empathy among readers." Estab. 1996. Circ. 22,000. Pays on publication. Publishes ms an average of 6 months after acceptance. Byline given. Offers 20% kill fee. Buys first, one-time, second serial (reprint) rights. Editorial lead time 4 months. Submit seasonal material 6 months in advance. Accepts queries by mail. Accepts simultaneous submissions. Responds in 6 months to queries. Sample copy for $5. Writer's guidelines for #10 SASE.

Nonfiction: Book excerpts, essays, general interest, interview/profile, personal experience, photo feature, features. Nothing explicitly religious, political or New Age. **Buys 50-75 mss/year.** Query with published clips or writing samples and SASE. Length: 250-3,000 words. **Pays $50-1,500.** Sometimes pays expenses of writers on assignment.

Photos: "We are very interested in and committed to the photo essay form, and enthusiastically encourage photographers and photojournalists to query us with ideas, or to submit images for thematic photo essays." State availability of or send photos with submission. Reviews contact sheets, 5×7 prints. Buys one-time rights. Negotiates payment individually. Captions, identification of subjects required.

Columns/Departments: Departments Editor. Signs of Hope (inspiring dispatches/news), 250-500 words; Arts of Hope (reviews and discussions of music, art, and literature related to hope), 1,000-2,000 words; Book Reviews (devoted primarily to nonfiction works in widely diverse subject areas related to struggle and triumph), 500-800 words. **Buys 50-60 mss/year.** Query with published clips or send complete ms and SASE. **Pays $50-150.**

Tips: "Write very personally, and very deeply. We're not looking for shallow 'feel-good' pieces. Approach uncommon subjects. Cover the ordinary in extraordinary ways. Go to the heart. Surprise us. Many stories we receive are too 'soft.' Absolutely no phone queries."

$ ☒ LIVING, For the Whole Family, Shalom Publishers, 13241 Port Republic Rd., Grottoes VA 24441. E-mail: tgether@aol.com. **Contact:** Melodie M. Davis, editor. **90% freelance written.** Quarterly newspaper. "*Living* is a quarterly 'good news' paper published to encourage and strengthen family life at all stages, directed to the general newspaper-reading public." Estab. 1992. Circ. 250,000. Pays on publication. Publishes ms an average of 9 months after acceptance. Byline given. Buys one-time, second serial (reprint) rights. Editorial lead time 6 months. Submit seasonal material 6 months in advance. Accepts previously published material. Accepts simultaneous submissions. Responds in 2 months to queries; 6 months to mss. Sample copy for 9×12 SAE and 4 first-class stamps. Writer's guidelines for #10 SASE or by e-mail.

Nonfiction: General interest, humor, inspirational, personal experience. **Buys 40-50 mss/year.** Send complete ms. Length: 300-1,000 words. **Pays $35-50.**

Photos: State availability of or send photos with submission. Reviews 3×5 or larger prints. Buys one-time rights. Offers $25/photo. Identification of subjects required.

Tips: "This paper is for a general audience in the community, but written from a Christian-value perspective. It seems to be difficult for some writers to understand our niche—*Living* is not a 'religious' periodical but handles an array of general interest family topics and mentioning Christian values or truths as appropriate. Writing is extremely competitive and we attempt to publish only high quality writing."

$ MESSENGER MAGAZINE, Everyone Learns by Reading, (formerly *African American Magazine*), Topaz Marketing & Distributing, 1014 Franklin SE, Grand Rapids MI 49507-1327. (616)243-4114, ext. 20. Fax: (616)243-6844. E-mail: wmathis@orimessenger.org. Website: www.orimessenger.org. President & CEO: Patricia E. Mathis. **Contact:** Walter L. Mathis, Sr., executive director. **50% freelance written.** Bimonthly magazine covering African Americans and other ethnic groups. "We are guided by the principles of fine press and are open to everyone regardless of their race, gender or religion." Estab. 1998. Circ. 15,000. Pays on publication. Editorial lead time 1 month. Submit seasonal material 1 month in advance. Accepts queries by mail, e-mail. Sample copy and writer's guidelines online.

Nonfiction: Book excerpts, essays, exposé, general interest, historical/nostalgic, how-to, humor, inspirational, interview/profile, new product, opinion, personal experience, photo feature, religious, technical, travel, book reviews (ethnic). **Pays negotiable rate.**

Photos: State availability of or send photos with submission. Reviews 3×5 prints. Buys one-time rights. Negotiates payment individually. Identification of subjects, model releases required.

Columns/Departments: Looking Within; Economic Focus; Positive Notes; Pastor's Perspective; Classified. **Buys 10 mss/year.** Query with published clips. **Pays negotiable rate.**

Fillers: Anecdotes, facts, newsbreaks. Length: 10-100 words.

Tips: "Dare to say what needs to be said, and to tell it like it is—whether it is 'popular' or not. Read a sample copy first and query if you have any further questions."

$ $ $ $ NATIONAL GEOGRAPHIC MAGAZINE, 1145 17th St. NW, Washington DC 20036. (202)775-7868. Fax: (202)857-7252. Website: www.nationalgeographic.com. Editor: William Allen. **Contact:** Oliver Payne, senior assistant editor, manuscripts. **60% freelance written.** Prefers to work with published/established writers. Monthly magazine for members of the National Geographic Society. "Timely articles written in a compelling, 'eyewitness' style.

Arresting photographs that speak to us of the beauty, mystery, and harsh realities of life on earth. Maps of unprecedented detail and accuracy. These are the hallmarks of *National Geographic* magazine. Since 1888, the *Geographic* has been educating readers about the world." Estab. 1888. Circ. 7,800,000.

O→ Before querying, study recent issues and check a *Geographic Index* at a library since the magazine seldom returns to regions or subjects covered within the past 10 years.

Nonfiction: Senior Assistant Editor Oliver Payne. *National Geographic* publishes general interest, illustrated articles on science, natural history, exploration, cultures and geographical regions. Of the freelance writers assigned, a few are experts in their fields; the remainder are established professionals. Fewer than 1% of unsolicited queries result in assignments. Query (500 words with clips of published articles by mail to Senior Assitant Editor Oliver Payne. Do not send mss. Length: 2,000-8,000 words. Pays expenses of writers on assignment.

Photos: Query in care of the Photographic Division.

The online magazine carries original content not included in the print edition. Contact: Valerie May, online editor.

Tips: "State the theme(s) clearly, let the narrative flow, and build the story around strong characters and a vivid sense of place. Give us rounded episodes, logically arranged."

$ $ $ THE NEW YORK TIMES, 229 W. 43rd St., New York NY 10036. (212)556-1234. Fax: (212)556-3830. *The New York Times Magazine* appears in *The New York Times* on Sunday. The *Arts and Leisure* section appears during the week. The *Op Ed* page appears daily. Sample copy not available.

Nonfiction: *Lives*: "Most articles are assigned but some unsolicited material is published, especially in the "Lives" column, a weekly personal-essay feature. Views should be fresh, lively and provocative on national and international news developments, science, education, family life, social trends and problems, arts and entertainment, personalitieis, sports and the changing American scne." Length: 900 words. **Pays $1,000**. Address unsolicited essays with SASE to the "Lives" editor. *Arts & Leisure*: Wants "to encourage imaginativeness in terms of form and approach—stressing ideas, issues, trends, investigations, symbolic reporting and stories delving deeply into the creative achievements and processes of artists and entertainers—and seeks to break away from old-fashioned gushy, fan magazine stuff." Length: 1,500-2,000 words. **Pays $100-350**, depending on length. Address unsolicited articles with SASE to the Arts & Leisure Articles Editor. *Op Ed* page: "The Op Ed page is always looking for new material and publishes many people who have never been published before. We want material of universal relevance which people can talk about in a personal way. When writing for the Op Ed page, there is no formula, but the writing itself should have some polish. Don't make the mistake of pontificating on the news. We're not looking for more political columnists." Length: 750 words. **Pays $150**.

THE NEW YORKER, The New Yorker, Inc., 4 Times Square, New York NY 10036. (212) 286-5900. Website: www.newyorker.com. Editor: David Remnick. Weekly magazine. A quality magazine of interesting, well-written stories, articles, essays and poems for a literate audience. Estab. 1925. Circ. 750,000. **Pays on acceptance.** Responds in 3 months to mss. Writer's guidelines online.

- *The New Yorker* receives approximately 4,000 submissions per month. "Despite countless hours spent on unsought stories," says fiction editor Bill Buford, "I can't recall the last writer who leapt from the crates to the page."

Fiction: Bill Buford, fiction editor. Publishes 1 ms/issue. **Payment varies.**

Poetry: Send poetry to "Poetry Department."

Tips: "Be lively, original, not overly literary. Write what you want to write, not what you think the editor would like."

$ $ $ NEWSWEEK, 251 W. 57th St., New York NY 10019. (212)445-4000. **Contact:** Pam Hamer. "*Newsweek* is edited to report the week's developments on the newsfront of the world and the nation through news, commentary and analysis." Accepts unsolicited mss for *My Turn*, a column of personal opinion. The 850-900 word essays for the column must be original, not published elsewhere and contain verifiable facts. **Payment is $1,000** on publication. Circ. 3,180,000. non-exclusive world-wide rights. Responds in 2 months only on submissions with SASE to mss.

$ $ $ THE OLD FARMER'S ALMANAC, Yankee Publishing, Inc., Main St., Dublin NH 03444. (603)563-8111. Fax: (603)563-8252. Website: www.almanac.com. **Contact:** Janice Stillman, editor. **95% freelance written.** Annual magazine covering weather, gardening, history, oddities, lore. "*The Old Farmer's Almanac* is the oldest continuously published periodical in North America. Since 1792, it has provided useful information for people in all walks of life: tide tables for those who live near the ocean; sunrise tables and planting charts for those who live on the farm or simply enjoy gardening; recipes for those who like to cook; and forecasts for those who don't like the question of weather left up in the air. The words of the *Almanac*'s founder, Robert B. Thomas, guide us still. 'Our main endeavor is to be useful, but with a pleasant degree of humour.'" Estab. 1792. Circ. 3,750,000. **Pays on acceptance.** Publishes ms an average of 9 months after acceptance. Byline given. Offers 33% kill fee. Buys first North American serial, electronic, all rights. Editorial lead time 6 months. Submit seasonal material 1 year in advance. Accepts queries by mail. Responds in 3 weeks to queries; 2 months to mss. Sample copy for $5 at bookstores or online. Writer's guidelines online.

Nonfiction: General interest, historical/nostalgic, how-to (garden, cook, save money), humor, weather, natural remedies, obscure facts, history, popular culture. No personal weather recollections/accounts, personal/family histories. Query with published clips. Length: 800-2,500 words. **Pays 65¢/word.** Sometimes pays expenses of writers on assignment.

Fillers: Anecdotes, short humor. **Buys 1-2/year.** Length: 100-200 words. **Pays 50¢/word.**

The online magazine carries original content not found in the print edition.

Tips: "Read it. Think differently. Read writer's guidelines online."

OPEN SPACES, Open Spaces Publications, Inc., PMB 134, 6327-C SW Capitol Hwy., Portland OR 97201-1937. (503)227-5764. Fax: (503)227-3401. E-mail: info@open-spaces.com. Website: www.open-spaces.com. President: Penny Harrison. Managing Editor: James Bradley. **Contact:** Elizabeth Arthur, editor. **95% freelance written.** Quarterly general interest magazine. "*Open Spaces* is a forum for informed writing and intelligent thought. Articles are written by experts in various fields. Audience is varied (CEOs and rock climbers, politicos and university presidents, etc.) but is highly educated and loves to read good writing." Estab. 1997. Pays on publication. Publishes ms an average of 6 months after acceptance. Byline given. Offers 20% kill fee. Rights purchased vary with author and material. Editorial lead time 9 months. Accepts queries by mail, fax. Accepts simultaneous submissions. Sample copy for $10 or online. Writer's guidelines for #10 SASE or online.

Nonfiction: Essays, general interest, historical/nostalgic, how-to (if clever), humor, interview/profile, personal experience, travel. **Buys 35 mss/year.** Query with published clips. Length: 1,500-2,500 words; major articles: 2,500-6,000 words. **Pays variable amount.**

Photos: State availability with submission. Buys one-time rights. Captions, identification of subjects required.

Columns/Departments: David Williams, departments editor. Books (substantial topics such as the Booker Prize, The Newbery, etc.); Travel (must reveal insight); Sports (past subjects include rowing, swing dancing and ultimate); Unintended Consequences, 1,500-2,500 words. **Buys 20-25 mss/year.** Query with published clips or send complete ms. **Pay varies.**

Fiction: Ellen Teicher, fiction editor. "Quality is far more important than type. Read the magazine." **Buys 8 mss/year.** Length: 2,000-6,000 words. **Pay varies.**

Poetry: "Again, quality is far more important than type." Susan Juve-Hu Bucharest, poetry editor. Submit maximum 3 poems with SASE.

Fillers: Anecdotes, short humor, cartoons; interesting or amusing Northwest facts; expressions, etc.

Tips: "*Open Spaces* reviews all manuscripts submitted in hopes of finding writing of the highest quality. We present a Northwest perspective as well as a national and international one. Best advice is read the magazine."

$ $ $ THE OXFORD AMERICAN, The Southern Magazine of Good Writing, The Oxford American, Inc., P.O. Box 1156, Oxford MS 38655. (662)236-1836. Fax: (662)236-3141. E-mail: oxam@watervalley.net. Website: www.oxfordamericanmag.com. Editor: Marc Smirnoff. **Contact:** Editorial Staff. **50-65% freelance written.** Bimonthly magazine covering the South. "*The Oxford American* is a general-interest literary magazine about the South." Estab. 1992. Circ. 30,000. Pays on publication. Publishes ms an average of 6 months after acceptance. Byline given. Offers 25% kill fee. Buys first North American serial, one-time rights. Editorial lead time 2 months. Submit seasonal material 4 months in advance. Accepts queries by mail. Responds in 3 weeks to queries; 3 months to mss. Sample copy for $6.50. Writer's guidelines for #10 SASE.

- Break in with "a brief, focused query highlighting the unusual, fresh aspects to your pitch, and clips. All pitches must have some Southern connection."

Nonfiction: Essays, general interest, humor, interview/profile, personal experience, Reporting; Memoirs concerning the South. **Buys 6 mss/year.** Query with published clips or send complete ms. **Pay varies.** Sometimes pays expenses of writers on assignment.

Photos: Buys one-time rights. Negotiates payment individually. Captions required.

Columns/Departments: Send complete ms. **Pay varies.**

Fiction: Novel excerpts, Short Stories. **Buys 10 mss/year.** Send complete ms. **Pay varies.**

Tips: "Like other editors, I stress the importance of being familiar with the magazine. Those submitters who know the magazine always send in better work because they know what we're looking for. To those who don't bother to at least flip through the magazine, let me point out we only publish articles with some sort of Southern connection."

$ $ $ $ PARADE, The Sunday Magazine, Parade Publications, Inc., 711 Third Ave., New York NY 10017. (212)450-7000. Fax: (212)450-7284. E-mail: steven_florio@parade.com. Website: www.parade.com. Editor: Lee Kravitz. Managing Editor: Lamar Graham. **Contact:** Steven Florio, assistant editor. **95% freelance written.** Weekly magazine for a general interest audience. Estab. 1941. Circ. 81,000,000. **Pays on acceptance.** Publishes ms an average of 5 months after acceptance. Kill fee varies in amount. Buys one-time, all rights. Editorial lead time 1 month. Accepts queries by mail, e-mail, fax. Accepts simultaneous submissions. Sample copy online. Writer's guidelines free.

Nonfiction: Publishes general interest (on health, trends, social issues or anything of interest to a broad general audience); interview/profile (of news figures, celebrities and people of national significance); and "provocative topical pieces of news value." Spot news events are not accepted, as *Parade* has a 1 month lead time. No fiction, fashion, travel, poetry, cartoons, nostalgia, regular columns, personal essays, quizzes, or fillers. Unsolicited queries concerning celebrities, politicians, sports figures, or technical are rarely assigned. **Buys 150 mss/year.** Query with published clips. Length: 1,000-1,200 words. **Pays $2,500 minimum.** Pays expenses of writers on assignment.

Tips: "If the writer has a specific expertise in the proposed topic, it increases a writer's chances for breaking in. Send a well-researched, well-written 1-page proposal and enclose a SASE. Do not submit completed manuscripts."

$ RANDOM LENGTHS, Harbor Independent News, P.O. Box 731, San Pedro CA 90733-0731. (310)519-1016. Website: www.randomlengthsnews.com. **Contact:** Mark Rosenberg, assistant editor. **30% freelance written.** Biweekly tabloid covering alternative news/features. "*Random Lengths* follows Twain's dictum of printing news 'to make people mad enough to do something about it.' Our writers do exposés, scientific, environmental, political reporting and fun, insightful, arts and entertainment coverage, for a lefty, labor-oriented, youngish crowd." Estab. 1979. Circ. 30,000. Pays in 60 days. Byline given. Offers 50% kill fee. Buys all rights. Editorial lead time 1 month. Submit seasonal material 2 months in advance. Accepts queries by mail. Accepts previously published material. Accepts simultaneous submissions. Responds in 6 weeks to queries. Sample copy for 9×13 SAE and 3 first-class stamps. Writer's guidelines free.

Nonfiction: Book excerpts, exposé, general interest, historical/nostalgic, interview/profile, opinion, photo feature. Special issues: Labor Day, triannual book edition; women and black history months. **Buys 150 mss/year.** Query. Length: 300-2,000 words. **Pays 5¢/word.** Sometimes pays expenses of writers on assignment.

Photos: State availability with submission. Reviews prints. Buys all rights. Offers $10/photo. Captions, identification of subjects required.

Columns/Departments: Community News (local angle), 300-600 words; Commentary (national/world/opinion), 600-800 words; Feature (books/music/local events), 300-600 words. **Buys 75 mss/year.** Query. **Pays 5¢/word.**

Tips: "We use mostly local material and local writers, but we are open to current-event, boffo entertaining writing. Read other alternative weeklies for reference. We are looking for regionally relevant articles. Next, entertainment stuff with a local pitch."

$ $ $ $ READER'S DIGEST, Reader's Digest Rd., Pleasantville NY 10570-7000. Website: www.readersdigest.com. **Contact:** Editorial Correspondence. Monthly general interest magazine. "We are looking for contemporary stories of lasting interest that give the magazine variety, freshness and originality." Estab. 1922. Circ. 13,000,000. **Pays on acceptance.** Byline given. Buys exclusive world periodical and electronic rights, among others. Editorial lead time 3 months. Submit seasonal material 6 months in advance. Accepts queries by mail. Accepts previously published material.

Nonfiction: Address article queries and tearsheets of published articles to the editors. Book excerpts, essays, exposé, general interest, historical/nostalgic, humor, inspirational, interview/profile, opinion, personal experience. Does not read or return unsolicited mss. **Buys 100 mss/year.** Query with published clips. Length: 1,000-2,500 words. **Original article rates generally begin at $5,000.**

Reprints: Send tearsheet or photocopy with rights for sale noted and information about when and where the material previously appeared. **Pays $1,200/*Reader's Digest*** page for World Digest rights (usually split 50/50 between original publisher and writer).

Columns/Departments: "Life's Like That contributions must be true, unpublished stories from one's own experience, revealing adult human nature, and providing appealing or humorous sidelights on the American scene. Length: 300 words maximum. **Pays $400 on publication.** True, unpublished stories are also solicited for Humor in Uniform, Campus Comedy, Virtual Hilarity and All in a Day's Work. Length: 300 words maximum. **Pays $400 on publication.** Towards More Picturesque Speech—the *first* contributor of each item used in this department is paid **$50 for original material, $35 for reprints**. For items used in Laughter, the Best Medicine, Personal Glimpses, Quotable Quotes, Notes From All Over, Points to Ponder and elsewhere in the magazine payment is as follows; to the *first* contributor of each from a published source, **$35 for original material, $30/*Reader's Digest*** two-column line." Original contributions become the property of *Reader's Digest* upon acceptance and payment. Previously published material must have source's name, date and page number. Contributions cannot be acknowledged or returned. Send complete anecdotes to *Reader's Digest*, Box 100, Pleasantville NY 10572-0100, fax to (914)238-6390 or e-mail laughlines@readersdigest.com.

Tips: "Roughly half the 20-odd articles we publish every month are reprinted from magazines, newspapers, books and other sources. The remaining 10 or so articles are original—most of them assigned, some submitted on speculation. While many of these are written by regular contributors, we're always looking for new talent and for offbeat subjects that help give our magazine variety, freshness and originality. Above all, in the writing we publish, *The Digest* demands accuracy—down to the smallest detail. Our worldwide team of 60 researchers scrutinizes every line of type, checking every fact and examining every opinion. For an average issue, they will check some 3500 facts with 1300 sources. So watch your accuracy. There's nothing worse than having an article fall apart in our research checking because an author was a little careless with his reporting. We make this commitment routinely, as it guarantees that the millions of readers who believe something simply because they saw it in *Reader's Digest* have not misplaced their trust."

$ ✪ REUNIONS MAGAZINE, P.O. Box 11727, Milwaukee WI 53211-0727. (414)263-4567. Fax: (414)263-6331. E-mail: reunions@execpc.com. Website: www.reunionsmag.com. **Contact:** Edith Wagner, editor. **75% freelance written.** Quarterly magazine covering reunions—all aspects and types. "*Reunions Magazine* is primarily for people actively involved with family, class, military, and other reunions. We want easy, practical ideas about organizing, planning, researching/searching, attending, or promoting reunions." Estab. 1990. Circ. 18,000. Pays on publication. Publishes ms an average of 1 year after acceptance. Byline given. Buys one-time rights. Editorial lead time 6 months. Submit seasonal material 1 year in advance. Accepts queries by mail, e-mail, fax. Accepts previously published material. Responds in about 1 year to queries. Sample copy free or online. Writer's guidelines for #10 SASE or online.

O⊸ Break in "by providing an exciting, instructional article about reunions."

Nonfiction: "We can never get enough about activities at reunions, particularly family reunions with multigenerational activities. We would also like more reunion food-related material." Needs reviewers for books, videos, software (include your requirements). Historical/nostalgic, how-to, humor, interview/profile, new product, personal experience, photo feature, travel. Special issues: Ethnic/African-American family reunions (Winter); food, kids stuff, theme parks, small venues (bed & breakfasts, dormitories, condos) (Summer); golf, travel and gaming features (Autumn); themes, cruises, ranch reunions and reunions in various sections of the US (Spring). **Buys 25 mss/year.** Query with published clips. Length: 500-2,500 (prefers work on the short side). **Pays $25-50.** Often rewards with generous copies.

Reprints: Send tearsheet, photocopy or typed ms with rights for sale noted and information about when and where the material previously appeared. **Usually pays $10.**

Photos: Always looking for vertical cover photos that scream: "Reunion!" Will not print mailed pictures—quality not good enough. State availability with submission. Reviews contact sheets, negatives, 35mm transparencies, prints. Buys one-time rights. Offers no additional payment for photos accepted with ms. Captions, identification of subjects, model releases required.
Fillers: Must be reunion-related. Anecdotes, facts, short humor. **Buys 20-40/year.** Length: 50-250 words. **Pays $5.**

The online magazine carries original content and includes writer's guidelines and articles. Contact: Edith Wagner, online editor.

Tips: "All copy must be reunion-related with strong reunion examples and experiences. Write a lively account of an interesting or unusual reunion, either upcoming or soon after while it's hot. Tell readers why the reunion is special, what went into planning it, and how attendees reacted. Our "Masterplan" section is a great place for a freelancer to start. Send us how-tos or tips about any aspect of reunion organizing. Open your minds to different types of reunions—they're all around!"

N **$ $ $ $ ROBB REPORT, The Magazine for the Luxury Lifestyle**, Curtco Media Labs, 1 Acton Place, Acton MA 01720. (978)264-3000. Fax: (978)264-7505. E-mail: robb@robbreport.com. Website: www.robbreport.com. Editor: Larry Bean. **Contact:** Mike Nolan. **60% freelance written.** Monthly magazine. "We are a lifestyle magazine geared toward active, affluent readers. Addresses upscale autos, luxury travel, boating, technology, lifestyles, watches, fashion, sports, investments, collectibles." Estab. 1976. Circ. 111,000. Pays on publication. Byline given. Offers 33% kill fee. Buys first North American serial, all rights. Submit seasonal material 5 months in advance. Accepts queries by mail, fax. Responds in 2 months to queries. Sample copy for $10.95 plus shipping and handling. Writer's guidelines for #10 SASE.
Nonfiction: General interest (autos, lifestyle, etc), interview/profile (prominent personalities/entrepreneurs), new product (autos, boats, consumer electronics), travel (international and domestic). Special issues: Home issue (October); Recreation (March). **Buys 60 mss/year.** Query with published clips. Length: 500-3,500 words. **Pays $150-2,000.** Sometimes pays expenses of writers on assignment.
Photos: State availability with submission. Buys one-time rights. Payment depends on article.

The online magazine carries original content not found in the print edition. Contact: Steven Castle.

Tips: "Show zest in your writing, immaculate research and strong thematic structure, and you can handle most any assignment. We want to put the reader there, whether the article is about test driving a car, fishing for marlin, touring a luxury home or profiling a celebrity. The best articles will be those that tell compelling stories. Anecdotes should be used liberally, especially for leads, and the fun should show in your writing."

SALON, 22 4th St., 16th Floor, San Francisco CA 94103. (415)645-9200. Fax: (415)645-9204. E-mail: ruth@salon.com. Website: www.salon.com. Vice President of Content/Executive Editor: Gary Kamiya. **Contact:** Ruth Henrich, associate managing editor. Monthly magazine. Accepts queries by e-mail. Responds in 3 weeks to queries. Writer's guidelines online.
Nonfiction: *Salon* does not solicit fiction or poetry submissions and will not be able to respond to such submissions. Spend some time familiarizing yourself with various sites and features. Query with published clips or send complete ms.
Tips: "We ask that you please send the text of your query or submission in plain text in the body of your e-mail, rather than as an attached file, as we may not be able to read the format of your file. Please put the words "EDITORIAL SUBMISSIONS" in the subject line of the e-mail. You can find the editor's name on our Salon Staff page. And please tell us a little about yourself—your experience and background as a writer and qualifications for writing a particular story. If you have clips you can send us via e-mail, or Web addresses of pages that contain your work, please send us a representative sampling (no more than 3 or 4, please)."

SALON.COM, 22 4th St., 16th Floor, San Francisco CA 94103. (415)645-9200. Fax: (415)645-9204. E-mail: bwyman@salon.com. Website: www.salon.com. Associate Editor: Jeff Stark. **Contact:** Bill Wyman, editor. Online. Accepts queries by e-mail. Responds in 3 weeks to queries. Writer's guidelines online.
Nonfiction: *Salon* does not solicit fiction or poetry submissions and will not be able to respond to such submissions. Spend some time familiarizing yourself with various sites and features. Query with published clips or send complete ms.
Tips: "We ask that you please send the text of your query or submission in plain text in the body of your e-mail, rather than as an attached file, as we may not be able to read the format of your file. Please put the words "EDITORIAL SUBMISSIONS" in the subject line of the e-mail. You can find the editor's name on our Salon Staff page. And please tell us a little about yourself—your experience and background as a writer and qualifications for writing a particular story. If you have clips you can send us via e-mail, or Web addresses of pages that contain your work, please send us a representative sampling (no more than 3 or 4, please)."

$ $ THE SATURDAY EVENING POST, The Saturday Evening Post Society, 1100 Waterway Blvd., Indianapolis IN 46202. (317)636-8881. Fax: (317)637-0126. E-mail: satevepst@aol.com. Website: www.satevepost.org. Travel Editor: Holly Miller. **Contact:** Patrick Perry, managing editor. **30% freelance written.** Bimonthly general interest, family-oriented magazine focusing on physical fitness, preventive medicine. "Ask almost any American if he or she has heard of *The Saturday Evening Post*, and you will find that many have fond recollections of the magazine from their childhood days. Many readers recall sitting with their families on Saturdays awaiting delivery of their *Post* subscription in the mail. *The Saturday Evening Post* has forged a tradition of 'forefront journalism.' *The Saturday Evening Post* continues to stand at the journalistic forefront with its coverage of health, nutrition, and preventive medicine." Estab. 1728. Circ. 400,000. Pays on publication. Publishes ms an average of 3 months after acceptance. Byline given. Buys second serial (reprint), all rights. Submit seasonal material 4 months in advance. Accepts queries by mail, fax. Accepts simultaneous submissions. Responds in 1 month to queries; 6 weeks to mss. Writer's guidelines for #10 SASE or online.

Nonfiction: Book excerpts, how-to (gardening, home improvement), humor, interview/profile, travel, medical; health; fitness. "No political articles or articles containing sexual innuendo or hypersophistication." **Buys 25 mss/year.** Query with or without published clips or send complete ms. Length: 750-2,500 words. **Pays $150 minumum, negotiable maximum.** Sometimes pays expenses of writers on assignment.

Photos: State availability with submission. Reviews negatives, transparencies. Buys one-time or all rights. Offers $50 minimum, negotiable maximum per photo. Identification of subjects, model releases required.

Columns/Departments: Travel (destinations); Post Scripts (well-known humorists); Post People (activities of celebrities). Length 750-1,500. **Buys 16 mss/year.** Query with published clips or send complete ms. **Pays $150 minimum, negotiable maximum.**

Poetry: Light verse.

Fillers: Post Scripts Editor: Steve Pettinga. Anecdotes, short humor. **Buys 200/year.** Length: 300 words. **Pays $15.**

Tips: "Areas most open to freelancers are Health, Fitness, Research Breakthroughs, Nutrition, Post Scripts and Travel. For travel we like text-photo packages, pragmatic tips, side bars and safe rather than exotic destinations. Query by mail, not phone. Send clips."

$ $ $ $ SMITHSONIAN MAGAZINE, MRC 951, Washington DC 20560-0951. (202)275-2000. E-mail: articles@simag.si.edu. Website: www.smithsonianmag.si.edu. Editor-in-chief: Carey Winfrey. **Contact:** Marlane A. Liddell, articles editor. **90% freelance written.** Monthly magazine for associate members of the Smithsonian Institution; 85% with college education. "*Smithsonian Magazine's* mission is to inspire fascination with all the world has to offer by featuring unexpected and entertaining editorial that explores different lifestyles, cultures and peoples, the arts, the wonders of nature and technology and much more. The highly educated, innovative readers of *Smithsonian* share a unique desire to celebrate life, seeking out the timely as well as timeless, the artistic as well as the academic and the thought-provoking as well as the humorous." Circ. 2,300,000. **Pays on acceptance.** Publishes ms an average of 6 months after acceptance. Offers 33% kill fee. Buys first North American serial rights. Editorial lead time 2 months. Submit seasonal material 3 months in advance. Responds in 2 months to queries. Sample copy for $5, c/o Judy Smith. Writer's guidelines for #10 SASE or online.

- "We consider focused subjects that fall within the general range of Smithsonian Institution interests, such as: cultural history, physical science, art and natural history. We are always looking for offbeat subjects and profiles. We do not consider fiction, poetry, political and news events, or previously published articles. We publish only twelve issues a year, so it is difficult to place an article in *Smithsonian*, but please be assured that all proposals are considered."

Nonfiction: "Our mandate from the Smithsonian Institution says we are to be interested in the same things which now interest or should interest the Institution: Cultural and fine arts, history, natural sciences, hard sciences, etc." **Buys 120-130 feature (up to 5,000 words) and 12 short (500-650 words) mss/year.** Query with published clips. **Pays various rates per feature, $1,500 per short piece.** Pays expenses of writers on assignment.

Photos: Purchased with or without ms and on assignment. "Illustrations are not the responsibility of authors, but if you do have photographs or illustration materials, please include a selection of them with your submission. In general, 35mm color transparencies or black-and-white prints are perfectly acceptable. Photographs published in the magazine are usually obtained through assignment, stock agencies, or specialized sources. No photo library is maintained and photographs should be submitted only to accompany a specific article proposal." Send photos with submission. Pays $400/full color page. Captions required.

Columns/Departments: Back Page humor, 500-650 words. **Buys 12-15 department articles/year.** Length: 1,000-2,000 words. **Pays $1,000.**

Tips: "We prefer a written proposal of one or two pages as a preliminary query. The proposal should convince us that we should cover the subject, offer descriptive information on how you, the writer, would treat the subject and offer us an opportunity to judge your writing ability. Background information and writing credentials and samples are helpful. All unsolicited proposals are sent to us on speculation and you should receive a reply within eight weeks. Please include a self-addressed stamped envelope. We also accept proposals via electronic mail at articles@simag.si.edu. If we decide to commission an article, the writer receives full payment on acceptance of the manuscript. If the article is found unsuitable, one-third of the payment serves as a kill fee."

$ $ $ THE SUN, A Magazine of Ideas, The Sun Publishing Co., 107 N. Roberson St., Chapel Hill NC 27516. (919)942-5282. Website: www.thesunmagazine.org. **Contact:** Sy Safransky, editor. **90% freelance written.** Monthly magazine. "We are open to all kinds of writing, though we favor work of a personal nature." Estab. 1974. Circ. 50,000. Pays on publication. Publishes ms an average of 6 months after acceptance. Byline given. Buys first, one-time rights. Accepts previously published material. Sample copy for $5. Writer's guidelines for SASE or online.

Nonfiction: Book excerpts, essays, general interest, interview/profile, opinion, personal experience, spiritual. **Buys 50 mss/year.** Send complete ms. Length: 7,000 words maximum. **Pays $300-1,000.** Complimentary subscription is given in addition to payment (applies to payment for *all* works, not just nonfiction).

Reprints: Send photocopy and information about when and where the material previously appeared. Pays 50% of amount paid for original article or story.

Photos: Send photos with submission. Reviews b&w prints. Buys one-time rights. Offers $50-200/photo. Model releases required.
Fiction: "We avoid stereotypical genre pieces like science fiction, romance, western, and horror. Read an issue before submitting." Literary. **Buys 20 mss/year.** Send complete ms. Length: 7,000 words maximum. **Pays $300-500.**
Poetry: Free verse, prose poems, short and long poems. **Buys 24 poems/year.** Submit maximum 6 poems. **Pays $50-200.**

TIME, Time Inc. Magazine, Time & Life Bldg., 1271 Avenue of the Americas, New York NY 10020. (212)522-1212. Fax: (212)522-0323. **Contact:** Jim Kelly, managing editor. Weekly magazine. "*Time* covers the full range of information that is important to people today—breaking news, national and world affairs, business news, societal and lifestyle issues, culture and entertainment news and reviews." Query before submitting. Estab. 1923. Circ. 4,150,000. Sample copy not available.

$ $ $ $ TOWN & COUNTRY, The Hearst Corp., 1700 Broadway, New York NY 10019. (212)903-5000. Fax: (212)262-7107. Website: www.townandcountrymag.com. **Contact:** John Cantrell, deputy editor. **40% freelance written.** Monthly lifestyle magazine. "*Town & Country* is a lifestyle magazine for the affluent market. Features focus on fashion, beauty, travel, interior design, and the arts, as well as individuals' accomplishments and contributions to society." Estab. 1846. Circ. 488,000. **Pays on acceptance.** Byline given. Offers 25% kill fee. Buys first North American serial, electronic rights. Accepts queries by mail. Responds in 1 month to queries.
Nonfiction: "We're looking for engaging service articles for a high income, well-educated audience, in numerous categories: travel, personalities, interior design, fashion, beauty, jewelry, health, city news, the arts, philanthropy." General interest, interview/profile, travel. **Buys 25 mss/year.** Query by mail only with clips before submitting. Length: column items, 100-300 words; feature stories, 800-2,000 words. **Pays $2/word.**
Tips: "We have served the affluent market for over 150 years, and our writers need to be expert in the needs and interests of that market. Most of our freelance writers start by doing short pieces for our front-of-book columns, then progress from there."

$ $ $ TROIKA, Wit, Wisdom & Wherewithal, Lone Tout Publications, Inc., P.O. Box 1006, Weston CT 06883. (203)319-0873. E-mail: submit@troikamagazine.com. Website: www.troikamagazine.com. **Contact:** Celia Meadow, editor. **95% freelance written.** Quarterly magazine covering general interest, lifestyle. "A magazine for men and women seeking a balanced, three-dimensional lifestyle: Personal achievement, family commitment, community involvement. Readers are upscale, educated, 30-50 age bracket. The *Troika* generation is a mix of what is called the X generation and the baby boomers. We are that generation. We grew up with sex, drugs and rock 'n roll, but now it really is our turn to make a difference, if we so choose." Estab. 1993. Circ. 120,000. Pays 90 days from publication. Publishes ms an average of 6 months after acceptance. Byline given. Buys first North American serial, internet rights rights. Editorial lead time 3 months. Submit seasonal material 6 months in advance. Accepts queries by mail, e-mail. Accepts previously published material. Accepts simultaneous submissions. Responds in 2 months to mss. Sample copy for $5 or online. Writer's guidelines for #10 SASE or online.
Nonfiction: Essays, exposé, general interest, how-to (leisure activities, pro bono finance), humor, inspirational, interview/profile (music related), personal experience, international affairs; environment; parenting; cultural. Celebrity profiles. **Buys 1,000 mss/year.** Query with or without published clips or send complete ms. Length: 800-3,000 words. **Pays $200-1,000 for assigned articles.**
Reprints: Send photocopy and information about when and where the material previously appeared.
Photos: State availability with submission. Reviews negatives, transparencies. Offers no additional payment for photos accepted with ms. Captions, identification of subjects, model releases required.
Columns/Departments: Literati; Pub Performances (literary, theater, arts, culture); Blueprints (architecture, interior design, fashion); Body of Facts (science); Hippocratic Horizons (health); Home Technology; Capital Commitments (personal finance); Athletics; Leisure; Mondiale (international affairs); all 750-1,200 words. **Buys 100 mss/year.** Query with or without published clips or send complete ms. **Pays $200 maximum.**
Fiction: Adventure, confessions, historical, mainstream, mystery, novel excerpts, slice-of-life vignettes, suspense, contemporary. **Buys 100 mss/year.** Send complete ms. Length: 3,000 words maximum. **Pays $200 maximum.**
The online magazine carries original content not found in the print edition and includes writer's guidelines.

$ $ THE WORLD & I, The Magazine for Lifelong Learners, News World Communications, Inc., 3600 New York Ave. NE, Washington DC 20002. (202)635-4000. Fax: (202)269-9353. E-mail: editor@worldandimag.com. Website: www.worldandi.com. Editor: Morton A. Kaplan. Executive Editor: Michael Marshall. **Contact:** Gary Rowe, editorial office manager. **90% freelance written.** Monthly magazine. "A broad interest magazine for the thinking, educated person." Estab. 1986. Circ. 30,000. Pays on publication. Publishes ms an average of 6 months after acceptance. Byline given. Offers 20% kill fee. Submit seasonal material 5 months in advance. Accepts queries by mail. Accepts previously published material. Responds in 6 weeks to queries; 10 weeks to mss. Sample copy for $5 and 9×12 SASE. Writer's guidelines for #10 SASE.
Nonfiction: "Description of Sections: Current Issues: Politics, economics and strategic trends covered in a variety of approaches, including special report, analysis, commentary and photo essay. The Arts: International coverage of music, dance, theater, film, television, craft, design, architecture, photography, poetry, painting and sculpture—through reviews, features, essays, opinion pieces and a 6-page Gallery of full-color reproductions. Life: Surveys all aspects of life in 22 rotating subsections which include: Travel and Adventure (first person reflections, preference given to authors who

provide photographic images), Profile (people or organizations that are 'making a difference'), Food and Garden (must be accompanied by photos), Education, Humor, Hobby, Family, Consumer, Trends, and Health. Send SASE for complete list of subsections. Natural Science: Covers the latest in science and technology, relating it to the social and historical context, under these headings: At the Edge, Impacts, Nature Walk, Science and Spirit, Science and Values, Scientists: Past and Present, Crucibles of Science and Science Essay. Book World: Excerpts from important, timely books (followed by commentaries) and 10-12 scholarly reviews of significant new books each month, including untranslated works from abroad. Covers current affairs, intellectual issues, contemporary fiction, history, moral/religious issues and the social sciences. Currents in Modern Thought: Examines scholarly research and theoretical debate across the wide range of disciplines in the humanities and social sciences. Featured themes are explored by several contributors. Investigates theoretical issues raised by certain current events, and offers contemporary reflection on issues drawn from the whole history of human thought. Culture: Surveys the world's people in these subsections: Peoples (their unique characteristics and cultural symbols), Crossroads (changes brought by the meeting of cultures), Patterns (photo essay depicting the daily life of a distinct culture), Folk Wisdom (folklore and practical wisdom and their present forms), and Heritage (multicultural backgrounds of the American people and how they are bound to the world). Photo Essay: Patterns, a 6- or 8-page photo essay, appears monthly in the Culture section. Emphasis is placed on comprehensive photographic coverage of a people or group, their private or public lifestyle, in a given situation or context. Accompanying word count: 300-500 words. Photos must be from existing stock, no travel subsidy. Life & Ideals, a 6- or 8-page photo essay, occasionally appears in the Life section. First priority is given to those focused on individuals or organizations that are 'making a difference.' Accompanying word count: 700-1,000 words." No *National Enquirer*-type articles. **Buys 1,200 mss/year.** Query with published clips. Length: 1,000-5,000 words. **Pays per article basis for assigned articles.** Seldom pays expenses of writers on assignment.

Reprints: Send typed ms with rights for sale noted and information about when and where the material previously appeared.

Photos: State availability with submission. Reviews contact sheets, transparencies, prints. Buys one-time rights. Payment negotiable. Identification of subjects, model releases required.

Fiction: Novel excerpts.

Poetry: Arts Editor. Avant-garde, free verse, haiku, light verse, traditional. **Buys 4-6 poems/year.** Submit maximum 5 poems. **Pays $30-75.**

Tips: "We accept articles from journalists, but also place special emphasis on scholarly contributions. It is our hope that the magazine will enable the best of contemporary thought, presented in accessible language, to reach a wider audience than would normally be possible through the academic journals appropriate to any given discipline."

HEALTH & FITNESS

The magazines listed here specialize in covering health and fitness topics for a general audience. Health and fitness magazines have experienced a real boom lately. Most emphasize developing healthy lifestyle choices in exercise, nutrition and general fitness. Many magazines offer alternative healing and therapies that are becoming more mainstream, such as medicinal herbs, health foods and a holistic mind/body approach to well-being. As wellness is a concern to all demographic groups, publishers have developed editorial geared to specific audiences: African-American women, older readers, men, women. Also see the Sports/Miscellaneous section where publications dealing with health and particular sports may be listed. For magazines that cover healthy eating, refer to the Food & Drink section. Many general interest publications are also potential markets for health or fitness articles. Health topics from a medical perspective are listed in the Medical category of Trade.

$ $ ☐ AMERICAN FITNESS, 15250 Ventura Blvd., Suite 200, Sherman Oaks CA 91403. (818)905-0040. Fax: (818)990-5468. Website: www.afaa.com. Publisher: Roscoe Fawcett. **Contact:** Dr. Meg Jordan, editor. **75% freelance written.** Bimonthly magazine covering exercise and fitness, health, and nutrition. "We need timely, in-depth, informative articles on health, fitness, aerobic exercise, sports nutrition, age-specific fitness, and outdoor activity." Absolutely no first-person accounts. Need well-reserched articles for professional readers. Circ. 42,000. Pays 6 weeks after publication. Publishes ms an average of 6 months after acceptance. Byline given. Submit seasonal material 4 months in advance. Accepts queries by mail, fax. Accepts previously published material. Accepts simultaneous submissions. Responds in 6 weeks to queries. Sample copy for $3 and SAE with 6 first-class stamps.

Nonfiction: Needs include health and fitness, including women's issues (pregnancy, family, pre- and post-natal, menopause, and eating disorders); new research findings on exercise techniques and equipment; aerobic exercise; sports nutrition; sports medicine; innovations and trends in aerobic sports; tips on teaching exercise and humorous accounts of fitness motivation; physiology; youth and senior fitness. Historical/nostalgic (history of various athletic events), inspirational, interview/profile (fitness figures), new product (plus equipment review), personal experience (successful fitness story), photo feature (on exercise, fitness, new sport), travel (activity adventures). No articles on unsound nutritional practices, popular trends, or unsafe exercise gimmicks. **Buys 18-25 mss/year.** Query with published clips or send complete ms. Length: 800-1,200 words. **Pays $200 for features, $80 for news.** Sometimes pays expenses of writers on assignment.

Photos: Sports, action, fitness, aquatic aerobics competitions, and exercise class. "We are especially interested in photos of high-adrenalin sports like rock climbing and mountain biking." Reviews transparencies, prints. Usually buys all rights; other rights purchased depend on use of photo. Pays $35 for transparencies. Captions, identification of subjects, model releases required.

Columns/Departments: Research (latest exercise and fitness findings); Alternative paths (nonmainstream approaches to health, wellness, and fitness); Strength (latest breakthroughs in weight training); Clubscene (profiles and highlights of fitness club industry); Adventure (treks, trails, and global challenges); Food (low-fat/nonfat, high-flavor dishes); Homescene (home-workout alternatives); Clip 'n' Post (concise exercise research to post in health clubs, offices, or on refrigerators). Length: 800-1,000 words. Query with published clips or send complete ms. **Pays $100-140.**

Tips: "Make sure to quote scientific literature or good research studies and several experts with good credentials to validate exercise trend, technique, or issue. Cover a unique aerobics or fitness angle, provide accurate and interesting findings, and write in a lively, intelligent manner. Please, no first-person accouts of 'How I lost weight or discovered running.' *AF* is a good place for first-time authors or regularly published authors who want to sell spin-offs or reprints."

$ $ $ ▣ AMERICAN HEALTH & FITNESS, CANUSA Publishing, 5775 McLaughlin Rd., Mississauga, Ontario L5R 3P7, Canada. (905)507-3545. Fax: (905)507-2372. E-mail: editorial@ahfmag.com. Website: www.ahfmag.com. Publisher: Robert Kennedy. **Contact:** Kerrie-Lee Brown, editor-in-chief. **85% freelance written.** Bimonthly magazine. "*American Health & Fitness* is designed to help male fitness buffs (18-39) to keep fit, strong, virile and healthy through sensible diet and exercise." Estab. 2000. Circ. 350,000. **Pays on acceptance.** Publishes ms an average of 4 months after acceptance. Byline given. Offers $500 kill fee. Buys all rights. Editorial lead time 4 months. Submit seasonal material 5 months in advance. Accepts queries by mail. Responds in 1 month to queries; 6 months to mss. Sample copy for $5.

Nonfiction: Exposé, general interest, how-to, humor, inspirational, interview/profile, new product, personal experience, photo feature, travel, bodybuilding and weight training, health & fitness tips, diet, medical advice, profiles, workouts, nutrition. **Buys 80-100 mss/year.** Send complete ms. Length: 1,400-2,000 words. **Pays $350-1,500 for assigned articles; $350-1,000 for unsolicited articles.** Sometimes pays expenses of writers on assignment.

Photos: Send photos with submission. Reviews 35mm transparencies, 8×10 prints. Buys all rights. Offers $50-1,000/photo. Captions, identification of subjects required.

Columns/Departments: Chiropractic; Personal Training; Strength & Conditioning; Dental; Longevity; Natural Health. **Buys 40 mss/year.** Send complete ms. **Pays $100-1,000.**

Fillers: Anecdotes, facts, gags to be illustrated by cartoonist, newsbreaks, short humor. **Buys 50-100/year.** Length: 100-200 words. **Pays $50-100.**

▣ The online magazine carries original content not found in the print edition. Contact: Kerrie-Lee Brown.

$ $ BETTER HEALTH, Better Health Magazine, 1450 Chapel St., New Haven CT 06511-4440. (203)789-3972. Fax: (203)789-4053. **Contact:** Cynthia Wolfe Boynton, editor/publishing director. **90% freelance written.** Prefers to work with published/established writers; will consider new/unpublished writers. Query first, do not send article. Bimonthly magazine devoted to health, wellness and medical issues. Estab. 1979. Circ. 500,000. **Pays on acceptance.** Byline given. Offers 20% kill fee. Buys first rights. Sample copy for $2.50. Writer's guidelines for #10 SASE.

Nonfiction: Wellness/prevention issues are of primary interest. New medical techniques or nonmainstream practices are not considered. No fillers, poems, quizzes, seasonal, heavy humor, inspirational or personal experience. Length: 1,500-3,000 words. **Pays $300-700.**

N $ $ BETTER NUTRITION, SABOT Publishing, 301 Concourse Blvd., Richmond VA 23059. (804)346-0990. Fax: (804)346-2281. E-mail: editorial@betternutrition.com. Website: www.betternutrition.com. **Contact:** Jerry Shaver, managing editor; Marshall Norton, special sections editor. **20% freelance written.** Monthly magazine covering nutritional news and approaches to optimal health. "The new *Better Nutrition* helps people (men, women, families, old and young) integrate nutritious food, the latest and most effective dietary supplements, and exercise/personal care into healthy lifestyles." Estab. 1938. Circ. 480,000. Pays on publication. Publishes ms an average of 2 months after acceptance. Byline given. Buys varies according to article rights. Editorial lead time 3 months. Accepts queries by mail, e-mail. Sample copy for free.

Nonfiction: Each issue has multiple features, clinical research crystallized into accessible articles on nutrition, health, alternative medicine, disease prevention. **Buys 120-180 mss/year.** Query. Length: 400-1,200 words. **Pays $400-1,000.**

Photos: State availability with submission. Reviews 4×5 transparencies, 3×5 prints. Buys one time rights or nonexclusive reprint rights. Negotiates payment individually. Captions, identification of subjects, model releases required.

Columns/Departments: Health Watch; Nutrition News; Women's Health; Earth Medicine; Healing Herbs; Better Hair, Skin & Nails; Herb Update; Health in Balance; Book Zone; Supplement Update; Natural Energy; Children's Health; Sports Nutrition; Earth Watch; Homeopathy; Botanical Medicine; Meatless Meals; Trim Time; Healthier Pets; Ayurvedic Medicine; Longevity; Healing Herbs; Frontiers of Science.

Tips: "Be on top of what's newsbreaking in nutrition and supplementation. Interview experts. Fact-check, fact-check, fact-check. Send in a résumé (including Social Security/IRS number), a couple of clips and a list of article possibilities."

$ $ DELICIOUS LIVING!, Feel Good/Live Well, New Hope Natural Media, 1401 Pearl St., Suite 200, Boulder CO 80302. E-mail: delicious@newhope.com. Website: www.healthwell.com. Editorial Director: Karen Raterman. **Contact:** Lara Evans, managing editor. **85% freelance written.** Monthly magazine covering natural products, nutrition, alternative medicines, herbal medicines. "*Delicious Living!* magazine empowers natural foods store shoppers to make health-conscious choices in their lives. Our goal is to improve consumers' perception of the value of natural methods in achieving health. To do this, we educate consumers on nutrition, disease prevention, botanical medicines and natural personal care products." Estab. 1985. Circ. 420,000. **Pays on acceptance.** Publishes ms an average of 6 months after acceptance. Byline given. Offers 20% kill fee. Editorial lead time 6 months. Submit seasonal material 8 months in advance. Accepts simultaneous submissions. Responds in 3 months to queries. Sample copy and writer's guidelines free.

Nonfiction: Book excerpts, how-to, interview/profile, personal experience (regarding natural or alternative health), health nutrition; herbal medicines; alternative medicine; environmental. **Buys 150 mss/year.** Query with published clips. Length: 500-2,000 words. **Pays $100-700 for assigned articles; $50-300 for unsolicited articles.**

Photos: State availability with submission. Reviews 3×5 prints. Buys one-time rights. Offers no additional payment for photos accepted with ms. Identification of subjects required.

Columns/Departments: Herbs (scientific evidence supporting herbal medicines), 1,500 words; Nutrition (new research on diet for good health), 1,200 words; Dietary Supplements (new research on vitamins/minerals, etc.), 1,200 words. Query with published clips. **Pays $100-500.**

The online magazine carries original content not found in the print edition. Contact: Kim Stewart, online editor.

Tips: "Highlight any previous health/nutrition/medical writing experience. Demonstrate a knowledge of natural medicine, nutrition, or natural products. Health practitioners who demonstrate writing ability are ideal freelancers."

$ $ FIT, Goodman Media Group, Inc., 419 Park Ave. S., 18th Floor, New York NY 10016. (212)541-7100. Fax: (212)245-1241. **Contact:** Rita Trieger, editor. **50% freelance written.** Works with a small number of new/unpublished writers each year. Bimonthly magazine covering fitness and health for active, young women. Circ. 125,000. Pays on publication. Publishes ms an average of 5 months after acceptance. Byline given. Offers 20% kill fee. Buys all rights. Submit seasonal material 6 months in advance. Accepts queries by mail, e-mail. Responds in 1 month if rejecting ms, longer if considering for publication to mss.

Break in by sending writing samples (preferably published) and a long list of queries/article ideas. The magazine reports it is looking for first-person accounts of new and interesting sports, adventures, etc.

Nonfiction: "We get many queries on how to treat/handle many physical and mental ailments—we wouldn't do an entire article on an illness that only 5% or less of the population suffers from." Health; Fitness; Sports; Beauty; Psychology; Relationships; Athletes; Nutrition. **Buys 20 mss/year.** Query with published clips. No phone queries. Length: 1,000-1,500 words.

Photos: Reviews contact sheets, transparencies, prints. Buys all rights. Identification of subjects, model releases required.

Columns/Departments: Finally Fit Contest. Readers can submit "before and after" success stories along with color slides or photos.

Tips: "We strive to provide the latest health and fitness news in an entertaining way—that means coverage of real people (athletes, regular women, etc.) and/or events (fitness shows, marathons, etc.), combined with factual information. First-person is okay. Looking for stories that are fun to read, revealing, motivational and informative."

$ $ $ $ FITNESS MAGAZINE, 15 E. 26th St., New York NY 10010. (212)499-2000. Fax: (212)499-1568. **Contact:** Elizabeth Goodman, articles editor. Monthly magazine for women in their twenties and thirties who are interested in fitness and living a healthy life. "Do not call." **Pays on acceptance.** Byline given. Offers 20% kill fee. Buys first North American serial rights. Responds in 2 months to queries. Writer's guidelines for #10 SASE.

Nonfiction: "We need timely, well-written nonfiction articles on exercise and fitness, beauty, health, diet/nutrition, and psychology. We always include boxes and sidebars in our stories." **Buys 60-80 mss/year.** Query. Length: 1,500-2,500 words. **Pays $1,500-2,500.** Pays expenses of writers on assignment.

Reprints: Send photocopy. Negotiates fee.

Columns/Departments: Length:600-1,200 words. **Buys 30 mss/year.** Query. **Pays $800-1,500.**

Tips: "Our pieces must get inside the mind of the reader and address her needs, hopes, fears and desires. *Fitness* acknowledges that getting and staying fit is difficult in an era when we are all time-pressured."

N **$ $ $ $ HEALTH**, Time, Inc., Southern Progress Corp., 2100 Lakeshore Dr., Birmingham AL 35209. Fax: (205)445-5123. Website: www.healthmag.com. Vice President/Editor: Doug Crichton. **Contact:** Sara Weeks, editorial assistant. Published 10 times/year Magazine covering health, fitness and nutrition. "Our readers are predominantly college-educated women in their 30s, 40s and 50s. Edited to focus not on illness, but on wellness events, ideas, and people." Estab. 1987. Circ. 1,350,000. **Pays on acceptance.** Byline given. Offers 33% kill fee. Buys first publication and online rights rights. Accepts queries by mail, fax. Accepts simultaneous submissions. Responds in 2 months to queries to mss. Sample copy for $5 to Back Issues. Writer's guidelines for #10 SASE.

- *Health* has joined other Time Inc. Southern Progress magazines such as *Cooking Light*, *Southern Accents* and *Coastal Living*.

Nonfiction: No unsolicited mss. **Buys 25 mss/year.** Query with published clips and SASE. Length: 1,200 words. **Pays $1-1.50/word.** Pays expenses of writers on assignment.

Columns/Departments: Food, Mind, Healthy Looks, Fitness, Relationships.

Tips: "We look for well-articulated ideas with a narrow focus and broad appeal. A query that starts with an unusual local event and hooks it legitimately to some national trend or concern is bound to get our attention. Use quotes, examples and statistics to show why the topic is important and why the approach is workable. We need to see clear evidence of credible research findings pointing to meaningful options for our readers. Stories should offer practical advice and give clear explanations."

$ $ HEPATITIS, Management and Treatment - A Practical Guide for Patients, Families and Friends, Quality Publishing Inc., 523 N. Sam Houston Tollway E, Suite 300, Houston TX 77060. (281)272-2744. E-mail: editor@hepatitismag.com. Website: www.hepatitismag.com. **Contact:** Brian J. Todd, managing editor. **70-80% freelance written.** Bimonthly magazine covering Hepatitis health news. Estab. 1999. Circ. 25,000. Pays on publication. Publishes ms an average of 2 months after acceptance. Byline given. Buys first North American serial, electronic rights. Editorial lead time 6 months. Submit seasonal material 4 months in advance. Accepts queries by mail, e-mail. Accepts simultaneous submissions. Responds in 6 weeks to queries. Sample copy and writer's guidelines free.

Nonfiction: Inspirational, interview/profile, new product, personal experience. "We do not want any one-source or no-source articles." **Buys 42-48 mss/year.** Query with or without published clips. Length: 1,500-2,500 words. Sometimes pays expenses of writers on assignment.

Photos: Send photos with submission. Reviews transparencies, prints, GIF/JPEG files. Rights negotiated, usually purchases one-time rights. Offers no additional payment for photos accepted with ms. Identification of subjects required.

Columns/Departments: An Apple a Day (general news or advice on Hepatitis written by a doctor or healthcare professional), 1,500-2,000 words. **Buys 12-18 mss/year.** Query. **Pays $$375-500.**

Tips: "Be specific in your query. Show me that you know the topic you want to write about. And show me that you can write a solid, well-rounded story."

$ $ $ $ INTOUCH, The Good Health Guide to Cancer Prevention and Treatment, PRR, Inc., 48 S. Service Rd., Suite 310, Melville NY 11747. Fax: (631)777-8700. E-mail: randi@cancernetwork.com. Website: www.intouchlive.com. **Contact:** Randi Londer Gould, managing editor. **90% freelance written.** Bimonthly magazine focusing on cancer prevention and treatment. "*InTouch* offers comprehensive, authoritative, up-to-date information on cancer prevention and treatment. Written for the layman with an upbeat, positive tone." Estab. 1999. Circ. 150,000. **Pays on acceptance.** Publishes ms an average of 1 year after acceptance. Byline given. Offers 25% kill fee. Purchases all rights for 6 months. Editorial lead time 6 months. Submit seasonal material 8 months in advance. Accepts queries by e-mail. Accepts simultaneous submissions. Responds in 6 weeks to queries. Sample copy and writer's guidelines free.

Nonfiction: Essays, interview/profile, health. Does not want personal stories of dealing with cancer unless it's a particularly good 600-word essay. **Buys 50 mss/year.** Query. Length: 1,000-3,000 words. **Pays $1/word.** Pays expenses of writers on assignment.

Photos: All photos are commissioned to professional photographers.

Columns/Departments: InSync (the mind/body connection. These stories usually focus on a type of complementary treatment such as biofeedback or meditation. Query.). InSight (an essay page at the back of the book. We're looking for emotional stories that pull readers in and leave them with something to ponder.), 600 words, send complete ms. The InTouch Interview (a one-on-one, in-person interview with a prominent figure in the oncology community. No query required, but do contact us with your idea before interviewing the subject). An InTouch Report (a comprehensive treatment of a specific cancer).

Tips: "We look for lively, concise writing in the active voice. Look at our website to get a sense of topics we've covered. We welcome brief queries by e-mail. If it's a topic we'd like to assign, we ask for a longer query in the format described in our writer's guidelines."

$ $ $ ☐ MAMM MAGAZINE, Courage, Respect & Survival, MAMM L.L.C., 54 W. 22nd St., 4th Floor, New York NY 10010. (212)242-2163. Fax: (212)675-8505. E-mail: elsieh@mamm.com. Website: www.mamm.com. Managing Editor: Craig Moskowitz. **Contact:** Gwen Darien, editor. **100% freelance written.** Magazine published 10 times/year covering cancer prevention, treatment and survival for women. "*MAMM* gives its readers the essential tools and emotional support they need before, during and after diagnosis of breast, ovarian and other female reproductive cancers. We offer a mix of survivor profiles, conventional and alternative treatment information, investigative features, essays and cutting-edge news." Estab. 1997. Circ. 100,000. Pays within 45 days of acceptance. Publishes ms an average of 5 months after acceptance. Byline given. Offers 20% kill fee. Buys exclusive rights up to 90 days after publishing, first rights after that Editorial lead time 4 months. Submit seasonal material 4 months in advance. Accepts simultaneous submissions. Sample copy and writer's guidelines free.

Nonfiction: Book excerpts, essays, exposé, historical/nostalgic, how-to, humor, inspirational, interview/profile, opinion, personal experience, photo feature. **Buys 90 mss/year.** Query with published clips. Length: 200-3,000 words. **Pays $50-1,000.** Sometimes pays expenses of writers on assignment.

Photos: Send photos with submission. Reviews contact sheets, negatives. Buys first rights. Negotiates payment individually. Identification of subjects required.

Columns/Departments: Cancer Girl (humor/experience); Opinion (cultural/political); International Dispatch (experience), all 600 words. **Buys 30 mss/year.** Query with published clips. **Pays $250-300. Buys 6 mss/year.** Query with published clips.

Poetry: Avant-garde, free verse, haiku, light verse, traditional. **Buys 6 poems/year.** Submit maximum 3 poems. Length: 10-40 lines. **Pays $100-150.**

Fillers: Anecdotes, facts, gags to be illustrated by cartoonist, newsbreaks. **Buys 30/year.** Length: 50-150 words. **Pays $50-75.**

$ $ $ $ MEN'S HEALTH, Rodale, 33 E. Minor St., Emmaus PA 18098. (610)967-5171. Fax: (610)967-7725. E-mail: TedSpiker@rodale.com. Website: www.menshealth.com. Editor-in-Chief: David Zinczenko; Editor: Greg Gutfeld; Executive Editor: Peter Moore. **Contact:** Ted Spiker, senior editor. **50% freelance written.** Magazine published 10 times/year covering men's health and fitness. "*Men's Health* is a lifestyle magazine showing men the practical and positive actions that make their lives better, with articles covering fitness, nutrition, relationships, travel, careers, grooming and health issues." Estab. 1986. Circ. 1,600,000. **Pays on acceptance.** Offers 25% kill fee. Buys all rights. Accepts queries by mail, fax. Responds in 3 weeks to queries. Writer's guidelines for #10 SASE.

O→ Freelancers have the best chance with the front-of-the-book piece, Malegrams.

Nonfiction: "Authoritative information on all aspects of men's physical and emotional health. We rely on writers to seek out the right experts and to either tell a story from a first-person vantage or get good anecdotes." **Buys 30 features/year; 360 short mss/year.** Query with published clips. Length: 1,200-4,000 words for features, 100-300 words for short pieces. **Pays $1,000-5,000 for features; $100-500 for short pieces.**

Columns/Departments: Length: 750-1,500 words. **Buys 80 mss/year. Pays $750- 2,000.**

The online magazine carries original content not included in the print edition. Contact: Fred Zahradnick, online associate.

Tips: "We have a wide definition of health. We believe that being successful in every area of your life is being healthy. The magazine focuses on all aspects of health, from stress issues to nutrition to exercise to sex. It is 50% staff written, 50% from freelancers. The best way to break in is not by covering a particular subject, but by covering it within the magazine's style. There is a very particular tone and voice to the magazine. A writer has to be a good humor writer as well as a good service writer. Prefers mail queries. No phone calls, please."

$ $ $ MUSCLE & FITNESS, The Science of Living Super-Fit, Weider Health & Fitness, 21100 Erwin St., Woodland Hills, CA 91367. (818)884-6800. Fax: (818)595-0463. Website: www.muscle-fitness.com. **Contact:** Vincent Scalisi, editorial director; Bill Geiger, executive editor (training and other articles); Jo Ellen Krumm, managing editor (nutrition and food articles). **50% freelance written.** Monthly magazine covering bodybuilding and fitness for healthy, active men and women. It contains a wide range of features and monthly departments devoted to all areas of bodybuilding, health, fitness, injury prevention and treatment, and nutrition. Editorial fulfills 2 functions: information and entertainment. Special attention is devoted to how-to advice and accuracy. Estab. 1950. Circ. 500,000. Pays on publication. Publishes ms an average of 2 months after acceptance. Editorial lead time 5 months. Submit seasonal material 6 months in advance. Accepts queries by mail. Accepts previously published material. Responds in 1 month to queries.

Nonfiction: Bill Geiger, executive editor. "All features and departments are written on assignment." Book excerpts, how-to (training), humor, interview/profile, photo feature. **Buys 120 mss/year.** Does not accept unsolicited mss. Length: 800-1,800 words. **Pays $400-1,000 for assigned articles.** Pays expenses of writers on assignment.

Reprints: Send photocopy with rights for sale noted and information about when and where the material previously appeared. Payment varies.

Photos: State availability with submission.

Tips: "Know bodybuilders and bodybuilding. Read our magazine regularly (or at least several issues), come up with new information or a new angle on our subject matter (bodybuilding training, psychology, nutrition, diets, fitness, etc.), then pitch us in terms of providing useful, unique, how-to information for our readers. Send a 1-page query letter (as described in *Writer's Market*) to sell us on your idea and on you as the best writer for that article. Send a sample of your published work."

NEW LIVING, New Living, Inc., 1212 Rt. 25A, Suite 1B, Stony Brook NY 11790. (631)751-8819. Fax: (631)751-8910. E-mail: newliving@aol.com. Website: www.newliving.com. **Contact:** Christine Lynn Harvey, editor. **10% freelance written.** Monthly newspaper. "Holistic health and fitness consumer news magazine covering herbal medicine, clinical nutrition, mind/body medicine, fitness, healthy recipes, product reviews, energy healing (reiki, chakra, and sound), hypnosis, past life regression." Estab. 1991. Circ. 100,000. Pays on publication. Byline given. Makes work-for-hire assignments. Editorial lead time 2 months. Submit seasonal material 2 months in advance. Accepts queries by e-mail. Responds in 6 weeks to queries. Sample copy for 9×12 SAE with $1.21 postage. Writer's guidelines for #10 SASE.

Nonfiction: Needs only feature articles on holistic/natural health topics. Query. Length: 800-1,700 words. **Pays $25-100.**

Photos: State availability of or send photos with submission. Reviews contact sheets. Buys all rights. Offers $25-100/photo. Identification of subjects required.

Tips: "If you are going to send an article on herbal medicine please be an herbalist or author of a book on this topic; please see our website to see the kinds of articles we publish."

$ $ $ $ POZ, POZ Publishing L.L.C., One Little W. 12th St., 6th Floor, New York NY 10014. (212)242-2163. Fax: (212)675-8505. E-mail: poz-editor@poz.com. Website: www.poz.com. Managing Editor: Jennifer Hsu. **Contact:** Walter Armstrong, editor. **100% freelance written.** Monthly national magazine for people impacted by HIV and AIDS. "*POZ* is a trusted source of conventional and alternative treatment information, investigative features, survivor profiles, essays and cutting-edge news for people living with AIDS and their caregivers. *POZ* is a lifestyle magazine with both health and cultural content." Estab. 1994. Circ. 91,000. Pays 45 days after acceptance. Publishes ms an average of 3 months after acceptance. Byline given. Offers 20% kill fee. Buys first rights. Editorial lead time 4 months. Submit seasonal material 4 months in advance. Accepts simultaneous submissions. Sample copy and writer's guidelines free.

Nonfiction: Book excerpts, essays, exposé, historical/nostalgic, how-to, humor, inspirational, interview/profile, opinion, personal experience, photo feature. **Buys 180 mss/year.** Query with published clips. "We take unsolicited mss on speculation only." Length: 200-3,000 words. **Pays $50-1,000.** Sometimes pays expenses of writers on assignment.
Photos: Send photos with submission. Reviews contact sheets, negatives. Buys first rights. Negotiates payment individually. Identification of subjects required.
Columns/Departments: Life (personal experience); Back Page (humor); Data Dish (opinion/experience/information), all 600 words. **Buys 120 mss/year.** Query with published clips. **Pays $200-3,000.**
Fiction: Buys 10 mss/year. Send complete ms. Length: 700-2,000 words. **Payment negotiable.**
Poetry: Avant-garde, free verse, haiku, light verse, traditional. **Buys 12 poems/year.** Submit maximum 3 poems. Length: 10-40 lines. **Payment negotiable.**
Fillers: Anecdotes, facts, gags to be illustrated by cartoonist, newsbreaks, short humor. **Buys 90/year.** Length: 50-150 words. **Pays $50-75.**

$ $ $ $ SHAPE MAGAZINE, Weider Publications Inc., 21100 Erwin St., Woodland Hills CA 91367. (818)595-0593. Fax: (818)704-7620. Website: www.shapemag.com. Editor-in-Chief: Barbara Harris. **Contact:** Anne Russell, editorial director. **70% freelance written.** Prefers to work with published/established writers. Monthly magazine covering women's health and fitness. "*Shape* reaches women who are committed to the healthful, active lifestyles. Our readers are participating in a variety of sports and fitness related activities, in the gym, at home and outdoors, and they are also proactive about their health and are nutrition conscious." Estab. 1981. Circ. 900,000. **Pays on acceptance.** Offers 33% kill fee. Buys second serial (reprint), all rights. Submit seasonal material 8 months in advance. Responds in 2 months to queries. Sample copy for 9×12 SAE and 4 first-class stamps.
Nonfiction: "We use some health and fitness articles written by professionals in their specific fields." Book excerpts, exposé (health, fitness, nutrition related), how-to (get fit), interview/profile (of fit women), health/fitness; recipes. Special issues: Every September is an anniversary issue. "No articles that haven't been queried first." **Buys 27 features/year and 36-54 short mss/year.** Query by mail only with published clips. Length: 3,000 words for features, 1,000 words for shorter pieces. **Pays $1/word.**
Photos: Submit slides or photos with photographer's name or institution to be credited. Captions, model releases required.
Tips: "Review a recent issue of the magazine. Provide source verification materials and sources for items readers may buy, including 800 numbers. Not responsible for unsolicited material. We reserve the right to edit any article."

$ $ ✪ VIBRANT LIFE, A Magazine for Healthful Living, Review and Herald Publishing Assn., 55 W. Oak Ridge Dr., Hagerstown MD 21740-7390. (301)393-4019. Fax: (301)393-4055. E-mail: vibrantlife@rhpa.org. Website: www.vibrantlife.com. **Contact:** Larry Becker, editor. **80% freelance written.** Enjoys working with published/established writers; works with a small number of new/unpublished writers each year. Bimonthly magazine covering health articles (especially from a prevention angle and with a Christian slant). "The average length of time between acceptance of a freelance-written manuscript and publication of the material depends upon the topics: some immediately used; others up to 2 years." Estab. 1885. Circ. 50,000. **Pays on acceptance.** Byline given. Offers 50% kill fee. Buys first serial, first world serial, or sometimes second serial (reprint) rights. Submit seasonal material 9 months in advance. Accepts queries by mail, e-mail, fax. Accepts previously published material. Responds in 1 month to queries. Sample copy for $1. Writer's guidelines for #10 SASE or online.
Nonfiction: "We seek practical articles promoting better health and a more fulfilled life. We especially like features on breakthroughs in medicine, and most aspects of health. We need articles on how to integrate a person's spiritual life with their health. We'd like more in the areas of exercise, nutrition, water, avoiding addictions of all types and rest—all done from a wellness perspective." Interview/profile (with personalities on health). **Buys 50-60 feature articles/year and 6-12 short mss/year.** Send complete ms. Length: 500-1,500 words for features, 25-250 words for short pieces. **Pays $75-300 for features, $50-75 for short pieces.**
Reprints: Send tearsheet and information about when and where the material previously appeared. Pays 50% of amount paid for an original article.
Photos: Not interested in b&w photos. Send photos with submission. Reviews 35mm transparencies.
Columns/Departments: Buys 12-18 department articles/year. Length: 500-650 words. **Pays $75-175.**
Tips: "*Vibrant Life* is published for baby boomers, particularly young professionals, age 40-55. Articles must be written in an interesting, easy-to-read style. Information must be reliable; no faddism. We are more conservative than other magazines in our field. Request a sample copy, and study the magazine and writer's guidelines."

$ $ $ $ VIM & VIGOR, America's Family Health Magazine, 1010 E. Missouri Ave., Phoenix AZ 85014-2601. (602)395-5850. Fax: (602)395-5853. E-mail: careyj@mcmurry.com. Website: www.vigormagazine.com. **Contact:** Carey Jones, associate publisher/editor. **75% freelance written.** Quarterly magazine covering health and healthcare. Estab. 1985. Circ. 1,100,000. **Pays on acceptance.** Publishes ms an average of 3 months after acceptance. Byline given. Buys all rights. Sample copy for 9×12 SAE with 8 first-class stamps or online. Writer's guidelines for #10 SASE.
Nonfiction: "Absolutely no complete manuscripts will be accepted/returned. All articles are assigned. Send published samples for assignment consideration. Any queries regarding story ideas will be placed on the following year's conference agenda and will be addressed on a topic-by-topic basis." Health; disease; medical breakthroughs; exercise/fitness trends; wellness; healthcare. **Buys 12 mss/year.** Send published clips by mail or e-mail. Length: 500-1,500 words. **Pays 75¢-$1.20/word.** Pays expenses of writers on assignment.
Tips: "Writers must have consumer healthcare experience."

N $ $ $ ☐ WEIGHT WATCHERS MAGAZINE, W/W Publishing Group, 747 3rd Ave., 24th Floor, New York NY 10017. (212)207-8800. Fax: (212)588-1733. Editor-in-Chief: Nancy Gagliarch; Senior Editor: GeriAnne Fennessey; Food Editor: Rebecca Adams; Publishing Assistant: Jerry Laboy-Bruce. **70% freelance written.** Bimonthly magazine mostly for women interested in weight loss, including healthy lifestyle/behavior information/advice, news on health, nutrition, fitness, beauty, fashion, psychology and food/recipes. Weight loss success and before-and-after stories also welcome. Estab. 1968. Circ. 500,000. **Pays on acceptance.** Offers 25% kill fee. Buys first North American serial rights. Editorial lead time 3-12 months. Accepts queries by mail.

Nonfiction: Covers diet, nutrition, motivation/psychology, food, spas, beauty, fashion and products for both the kitchen and an active lifestyle. Articles have an authoritative yet friendly tone. How-to and service information crucial for all stories. Query with published clips. Length: 700-1,500 words.

Columns/Departments: Accepts editorial in health, fitness, diet, inspiration, nutrition.

Tips: "Well developed, tightly written queries always a plus, as are trend pieces. We're always on the lookout for a fresh angle on an old topic. Sources must be reputable; we prefer subjects to be medical professionals with university affiliations who are published in their field of expertise. Lead times require stories to be seasonal, long-range and forward-looking. We're looking for fresh, innovative stories that yield worthwhile information for women interested in losing weight—the latest exercise alternatives, a suggestion of how they can reduce stress, nutritional information that may not be common knowledge, reassurance about their lifestyle or health concerns, etc. Familiarity with the Weight Watchers philosophy/program is a plus."

$ $ $ $ ☐ YOGA JOURNAL, 2054 University Ave., Suite 600, Berkeley CA 94704-1082. (510)841-9200. E-mail: nisaacs@yogajournal.com. Website: www.yogajournal.com. **Contact:** Matthew Solan, senior editor; Todd Jones, senior editor; Phil Catalfo, senior editor; Nora Isaacs, managing editor; Vesela Simic, copy editor. **75% freelance written.** Bimonthly magazine covering the practice and philosophy of yoga. Estab. 1975. Circ. 130,000. Pays within 90 days of acceptance. Publishes ms an average of 10 months after acceptance. Byline given. Offers kill fee on assigned articles. Buys first North American serial rights. Submit seasonal material 4 months in advance. Accepts queries by mail. Accepts previously published material. Responds in 3 months to queries. Sample copy for $4.99. Writer's guidelines online.

Nonfiction: "Yoga is a main concern, but we also highlight other conscious living/New Age personalities and endeavors (nothing too 'woo-woo'). In particular we welcome articles on the following themes: 1. Leaders, spokepersons, and visionaries in the yoga community; 2. The practice of hatha yoga; 3. Applications of yoga to everyday life; 4. Hatha yoga anatomy and kinesiology, and therapeutic yoga; 5. Nutrition and diet, cooking, and natural skin and body care." Book excerpts, how-to (yoga, exercise, etc.), inspirational, interview/profile, opinion, photo feature, travel (yoga-related). Does not want unsolicited poetry or cartoons. "Please avoid New Age jargon and in-house buzz words as much as possible." **Buys 50-60 mss/year.** Query with SASE. Length: 2,500-6,000 words. **Pays $800-2,000.**

Reprints: Send tearsheet or photocopy with rights for sale noted and information about when and where the material previously appeared.

Columns/Departments: Health (self-care; well-being); Body-Mind (hatha Yoga; other body-mind modalities; meditation; yoga philosophy; Western mysticism); Community (service; profiles; organizations; events), Length: 1,500-2,000 words. **Pays $400-800.** Living (books; video; arts; music), 800 words. **Pays $200-250.** World of Yoga, Spectrum (brief yoga and healthy living news/events/fillers), 150-600 words. **Pays $50-150**. "We encourage a well-written query letter outlining your subject and describing its appeal."

Tips: "Please read our writer's guidelines before submission. Do not e-mail or fax unsolicited manuscripts."

$ $ ☐ YOUR HEALTH & FITNESS, General Learning Communications, 900 Skokie Blvd., Northbrook IL 60062-1574. (847)205-3000. Fax: (847)564-8197. Website: www.glcomm.com. **Contact:** Debb Bastian, editorial director. **90% freelance written.** Prefers to work with published/established writers. Quarterly magazine. Needs "general, educational material on health, fitness, and safety that can be read and understood easily by the lay person. We also have a need for more technical health-related material written for a general audience, such as information on specific procedures and diseases." Estab. 1969. Circ. 1,000,000. Pays after publication. Publishes ms an average of 6 months after acceptance. No byline given (contributing editor status given in masthead). Buys all rights.

O→ "All article topics assigned. No queries; if you're interested in writing for the magazine, send a cover letter, résumé, curriculum vitae, and writing samples. All topics are determined approximately 1 year in advance of publication by editors. No unsolicited manuscripts."

Nonfiction: All article topics are assigned. General interest (health-related). **Buys approximately 65 mss/year.** Send a résumé and cover letter accompanied by several published writing samples on health and/or health-related topics. Length: 300-1,000 words. **Pay varies, commensurate with experience.**

Tips: "Write to a general audience with only a surface knowledge of health and fitness topics. Possible subjects include exercise and fitness, psychology, nutrition, safety, disease, drug data, and health concerns. No phone queries."

HISTORY

Listed here are magazines and other periodicals written for historical collectors, genealogy enthusiasts, historic preservationists and researchers. Editors of history magazines look for fresh accounts of past events in a readable style. Some publications cover an era, while others may cover a region or subject area, such as aviation history.

$ $ AMERICA'S CIVIL WAR, Primedia History Group, 741 Miller Dr., SE, Suite D-2, Leesburg VA 20175-8920. (703)771-9400. Fax: (703)779-8345. E-mail: americascivilwar@thehistorynet.com. Website: www.thehistorynet.com. Managing Editor: Carl von Wodtke. **Contact:** Dana Shoaf, editor. **95% freelance written.** Bimonthly magazine covering "popular history and straight historical narrative for both the general reader and the Civil War buff covering strategy, tactics, personalities, arms and equipment." Estab. 1988. Circ. 78,000. Pays on publication. Publishes ms an average of 2 years after acceptance. Byline given. Buys all rights. Accepts queries by mail, e-mail, fax. Responds in 3 months to queries; 6 months to mss. Sample copy for $5. Writer's guidelines for #10 SASE or online.

Nonfiction: Historical/nostalgic, book notices; preservation news. No fiction or poetry. **Buys 24 mss/year.** Query. Length: 3,500-4,000 words and should include a 500-word sidebar. **Pays $300 and up.**

Photos: Send photos with submission or cite sources. "We'll order." Captions, identification of subjects required.

Columns/Departments: Personality (profiles of Civil War personalities); Men & Material (about weapons used); Commands (about units); Eyewitness to War (historical letters and diary excerpts). Length: 2,000 words. **Buys 24 mss/year.** Query. **Pays $150 and up.**

The online magazine carries original content not found in the print edition and includes writer's guidelines. Contact: Roger Vance.

Tips: "All stories must be true. We do not publish fiction or poetry. Write an entertaining, well-researched, informative and unusual story that grabs the reader's attention and holds it. Include suggested readings in a standard format at the end of your piece. Manuscript must be typed, double-spaced on one side of standard white 8½×11, 16 to 30 pound paper—no onion skin paper or dot matrix printouts. All submissions are on speculation. Prefer subjects to be on disk (IBM- or Macintosh-compatible floppy disk) as well as a hard copy. Choose stories with strong art possibilities."

AMERICAN HERITAGE, 90 Fifth Ave., New York NY 10011. (212)367-3100. Fax: (212)367-3149. E-mail: mail@americanheritage.com. Website: www.americanheritage.com. **Contact:** Richard Snow, editor. **70% freelance written.** Magazine published 8 times/year. "*American Heritage* writes from a historical point of view on politics, business, art, current and international affairs, and our changing lifestyles. The articles are written with the intent to enrich the reader's appreciation of the sometimes nostalgic, sometimes funny, always stirring panorama of the American experience." Circ. 300,000. **Pays on acceptance.** Publishes ms an average of 6-12 months after acceptance. Byline given. Buys first North American serial, all rights. Submit seasonal material 1 year in advance. Responds in 2 months to queries. Writer's guidelines for #10 SASE.

- Before submitting material, "check our index to see whether we have already treated the subject."

Nonfiction: Wants "historical articles by scholars or journalists intended for intelligent lay readers rather than for professional historians." Emphasis is on authenticity, accuracy and verve. "Interesting documents, photographs and drawings are always welcome. Style should stress readability and accuracy." Historical/nostalgic. **Buys 30 unsolicited mss/year.** Query. Length: 1,500-6,000 words. **Pay varies.** Sometimes pays expenses of writers on assignment.

Tips: "We have over the years published quite a few 'firsts' from young writers whose historical knowledge, research methods and writing skills met our standards. The scope and ambition of a new writer tell us a lot about his or her future usefulness to us. A major article gives us a better idea of the writer's value. Everything depends on the quality of the material. We don't really care whether the author is 20 and unknown, or 80 and famous, or vice versa. No phone calls, please."

$ $ AMERICAN HISTORY, 6405 Flank Dr., Harrisburg PA 17112-2750. (717)657-9555. Website: www.thehistorynet.com. **Contact:** Tom Huntington, editor. **60% freelance written.** Bimonthly magazine of cultural, social, military, and political history published for a general audience. Estab. 1966. Circ. 95,000. **Pays on acceptance.** Byline given. Buys first rights. Responds in 10 weeks to queries. Sample copy and guidelines for $5 (includes 3rd class postage) or $4 and 9×12 SAE with 4 first-class stamps. Writer's guidelines for #10 SASE or online.

Nonfiction: Features events in the lives of noteworthy historical figures and accounts of important events in American history. Also includes pictorial features on artists, photographers, and graphic subjects. "Material is presented on a popular rather than a scholarly level." **Buys 20 mss/year.** Query by mail only with published clips and SASE. Length: 2,000-4,000 words depending on type of article. **Pays $500-600.**

Photos: Welcomes suggestions for illustrations.

The online magazine occasionally carries some original content not included in the print edition. Contact: Christine Techky, managing editor.

Tips: "Key prerequisites for publication are thorough research and accurate presentation, precise English usage, and sound organization, a lively style, and a high level of human interest. Unsolicited manuscripts not considered. Inappropriate materials include: fiction, book reviews, travelogues, personal/family narratives not of national significance, articles about collectibles/antiques, living artists, local/individual historic buildings/landmarks, and articles of a current editorial nature. Currently seeking articles on significant Civil War subjects. No phone, fax, or e-mail queries, please."

$ THE ARTILLERYMAN, Historical Publications, Inc., 234 Monarch Hill Rd., Tunbridge VT 05077. (802)889-3500. Fax: (802)889-5627. E-mail: mail@civilwarnews.com. **Contact:** Kathryn Jorgensen, editor. **60% freelance written.** Quarterly magazine covering antique artillery, fortifications, and crew-served weapons 1750-1900 for competition shooters, collectors, and living history reenactors using artillery. "Emphasis on Revolutionary War and Civil War but includes everyone interested in pre-1900 artillery and fortifications, preservation, construction of replicas, etc." Estab. 1979. Circ. 2,000. Pays on publication. Publishes ms an average of 6 months after acceptance. Byline given. Not copyrighted.

Buys one-time rights. Accepts queries by mail, e-mail, fax. Accepts previously published material. Accepts simultaneous submissions. Responds in 3 weeks to queries. Sample copy and writer's guidelines for 9×12 SAE with 4 first-class stamps.

O‑ Break in with a historical or travel piece featuring artillery—the types and history of guns and their use.

Nonfiction: Interested in "artillery *only*, for sophisticated readers. Not interested in other weapons, battles in general." Historical/nostalgic, how-to (reproduce ordnance equipment/sights/implements/tools/accessories, etc.), interview/profile, new product, opinion (must be accompanied by detailed background of writer and include references), personal experience, photo feature, technical (must have footnotes), travel (where to find interesting antique cannon). **Buys 24-30 mss/year.** Send complete ms. Length: 300 words minimum. **Pays $20-60.** Sometimes pays expenses of writers on assignment.

Reprints: Send tearsheet or photocopy and information about when and where the material previously appeared. Pays 100% of amount paid for an original article.

Photos: Send photos with submission. Pays $5 for 5×7 and larger b&w prints. Captions, identification of subjects required.

Tips: "We regularly use freelance contributions for Places-to-Visit, Cannon Safety, The Workshop, and Unit Profiles departments. Also need pieces on unusual cannon or cannon with a known and unique history. To judge whether writing style and/or expertise will suit our needs, writers should ask themselves if they could knowledgeably talk *artillery* with an expert. Subject matter is of more concern than writer's background."

$ $ AVIATION HISTORY, Primedia History Group, 741 Miller Dr., SE, Suite D-2, Leesburg VA 20175-8920. (703)771-8400. Fax: (703)779-8345. E-mail: AviationHistory@thehistorynet.com. Website: www.thehistorynet.com. Managing Editor: Carl von Wodtke. **Contact:** Arthur Sanfelici, editor. **95% freelance written.** Bimonthly magazine covering military and civilian aviation from first flight to the jet age. It aims to make aeronautical history not only factually accurate and complete, but also enjoyable to varied subscriber and newsstand audience. Estab. 1990. Circ. 60,000. Pays on publication. Publishes ms an average of 2 years after acceptance. Byline given. Buys all rights. Editorial lead time 6 months. Submit seasonal material 1 year in advance. Accepts queries by mail, e-mail, fax. Accepts simultaneous submissions. Responds in 3 months to queries; 6 months to mss. Sample copy for $5. Writer's guidelines for #10 SASE or online.

Nonfiction: Book excerpts, historical/nostalgic, interview/profile, personal experience, travel. **Buys 24 mss/year.** Query. Length: Feature articles should be 3,500-4,000 words, each with a 500-word sidebar, author's biography and book suggestions for further reading. **Pays $300.**

Photos: State availability of art and photos with submissions, cite sources. "We'll order." Reviews contact sheets, negatives, transparencies. Buys one-time rights. Identification of subjects required.

Columns/Departments: People and Planes; Enduring Heritage; Aerial Oddities; Art of Flight, all 2,000 words. **Pays $150**. Book reviews, 300-750 words, **pays minimum $40**.

The online magazine carries original content not found in the print edition and includes writer's guidelines. Contact: Roger Vance.

Tips: "Choose stories with strong art possibilities. Include a hard copy as well as an IBM- or Macintosh-compatible floppy disk. Write an entertaining, informative and unusual story that grabs the reader's attention and holds it. All stories must be true. We do not publish fiction or poetry."

$ CHRONICLE OF THE OLD WEST, P.O. Box 2859, Show Low AZ 85902. (928)532-2875. Fax: (928)532-5170. E-mail: OldPress@RavenHeart.com. Website: www.chronicleoftheoldwest.com. **Contact:** Dakota Livesay. **50% freelance written.** Monthly 1800s newspaper for the Old West enthusiast. Pays 30 days after publication. Publishes ms an average of 2 months after acceptance. Buys one-time rights. Accepts queries by mail, e-mail, fax, phone. Responds in 1 month to queries. Sample copy on request. Writer's guidelines for #10 SASE.

Nonfiction: Newspaper focuses on people and events of the 1800s written as if the event just happened and the writer is a reporter to the paper. No fiction. Query with or without published clips or send complete ms. Length: 500-1,500 words. **Pays 5-8¢/word.**

Photos: Photos are encouraged. Send photos with submission.

Columns/Departments: The Old West on Celluloid (how current and past western movies portray the Old West); The Old West Today (descriptions of places and events where people can go to experience the Old West today. This needs to be submitted 4 months prior to the event).

Tips: "We are looking for the real flavor and atmosphere of the Old West, not technical or dry scholarly accounts. Articles should be written as if the author is a reporter for *Chronicle of the Old West* writing about a current event. We want to give the reader the feeling the event just took place, and the reader is at the time and location of the subject of the article."

$ $ GATEWAY HERITAGE, Missouri Historical Society, P.O. Box 11940, St. Louis MO 63112-0040. (314)746-4557. Fax: (314)746-4548. E-mail: jstevens@mohistory.org. Website: www.mohistory.org. **Contact:** Josh Stevens, editor. **75% freelance written.** Quarterly magazine covering Missouri history. "*Gateway Heritage* is a popular history magazine which is sent to members of the Missouri Historical Society. Thus, we have a general audience with an interest in history." Estab. 1980. Circ. 9,000. Pays on publication. Publishes ms an average of 6 months after acceptance. Byline given. Offers $75 kill fee. Buys first North American serial rights. Editorial lead time 6 months. Submit seasonal material 1 year in advance. Accepts queries by mail, e-mail, fax. Responds in 2 weeks to queries; 2 months to mss. Sample copy for 9×12 SAE and 7 first-class stamps. Writer's guidelines for #10 SASE.

Nonfiction: Book excerpts, interview/profile, photo feature, historical, scholarly essays, Missouri biographies, viewpoints on events, first-hand historical accounts, regional architectural history, literary history. No genealogies. **Buys 12-15 mss/year.** Query with published clips. Length: 3,500-5,000 words. **Pays $200 (average).**
Photos: State availability with submission.
Columns/Departments: Literary Landmarks (biographical sketches and interviews of famous Missouri literary figures), 1,500-2,500 words; Missouri Biographies (biographical sketches of famous and interesting Missourians), 1,500-2,500 words; Gateway Album (excerpts from diaries and journals), 1,500-2,500 words. **Buys 6-8 mss/year.** Query with published clips. **Pays $250-500.**
Tips: "Ideas for our departments are a good way to break in to *Gateway Heritage*."

$ GOOD OLD DAYS, America's Premier Nostalgia Magazine, House of White Birches, 306 E. Parr Rd., Berne IN 46711. (219)589-4000. E-mail: editor@goodolddaysonline.com. E-mail: editor@goodolddaysonline.com. Website: www.goodolddays-magazine.com. **Contact:** Ken Tate, editor. **75% freelance written.** Monthly magazine of first person nostalgia, 1900-1955. "We look for strong narratives showing life as it was in the first half of this century. Our readership is comprised of nostalgia buffs, history enthusiasts and the people who actually lived and grew up in this era." Pays on publication. Publishes ms an average of 8 months after acceptance. Byline given. Prefers all rights, but will negotiate for First North American serial and one-time rights Submit seasonal material 10 months in advance. Responds in 2 months to queries. Sample copy for $2. Writer's guidelines online.
Nonfiction: Regular features: Good Old Days on Wheels (transportation auto, plane, horse-drawn, tram, bicycle, trolley, etc.); Good Old Days In the Kitchen (favorite foods, appliances, ways of cooking, recipes); Home Remedies (herbs and poultices, hometown doctors, harrowing kitchen table operations). Historical/nostalgic, humor, interview/profile, personal experience, photo feature, favorite food/recipes; year-round seasonal material; biography; memorable events; fads; fashion; sports; music; literature; entertainment. No fiction accepted. **Buys 350 mss/year.** Query or send complete ms. Length: 500-1,500 words. **Pays $15-75, depending on quality and photos.**
Photos: Send photos with submission. Identification of subjects required.
Tips: "Most of our writers are not professionals. We prefer the author's individual voice, warmth, humor and honesty over technical ability."

$$$$ MHQ, The Quarterly journal of Military History, Primedia History Group, 741 Miller Dr. SE, Suite D-2, Leesburg VA 20175-8920. (703)771-9400. Fax: (703)779-8345. E-mail: mhq@thehistory.net.com. Website: www.thehistorynet.com. Editor: Rod Paschall. Managing Editor: Carl von Wodtke. **Contact:** Richard Latture, associate editor. **100% freelance written.** Quarterly journal covering military history. "*MHQ* offers readers in-depth articles on the history of warfare from ancient times into the 20th century. Authoritative features and departments cover military strategies, philosophies, campaigns, battles, personalities, weaponry, espionage and perspectives, all written in a lively and readable style. Articles are accompanied by classical works of art, contemporary illustrations, photographs and maps. Readers include serious students of military tactics, strategy, leaders and campaigns, as well as general world history enthusiasts. Many readers are currently in the military or retired officers." Estab. 1988. Circ. 30,000. Pays on publication. Byline given. Buys all rights. Editorial lead time 10 months. Submit seasonal material 1 year in advance. Accepts queries by mail, e-mail, fax. Accepts simultaneous submissions. Responds in 3 months to queries; 6 months to mss. Sample copy for $23 (hardcover), $13 (softcover); some articles on website. Writer's guidelines for #10 SASE or online.
Nonfiction: Historical/nostalgic, personal experience, photo feature. No fiction or stories pertaining to collectibles or reenactments. **Buys 50 mss/year.** Query preferred; also accepts complete ms. Length: 1,000-5,000 words. **Pays $800-2,000 for assigned articles; $400-2,000 for unsolicited articles.**
Photos: Send photos with submission. Reviews transparencies, prints. Buys all rights. Negotiates payment individually. Identification of subjects required.
Columns/Departments: Artists on War (description of artwork of a military nature); Experience of War (first-person accounts of military incidents); Strategic View (discussion of military theory, strategy); Arms & Men (description of military hardware or unit), all up to 3,000 words. **Buys 20 mss/year.** Send complete ms. **Pays $400-800.**

The online magazine carries original content not included in the print edition and includes writer's guidelines. Contact: Roger Vance.

Tips: "All stories must be true—we publish no fiction. Although we are always looking for variety, some subjects—World War II, the American Civil War, and military biography, for instance—are the focus of so many proposals that we are forced to judge them by relatively rigid criteria. We are always glad to consider articles on these subjects. However, less common ones—medieval, Asian, or South American military history, for example—are more likely to attract our attention. The likelihood that articles can be effectively illustrated often determines the ultimate fate of manuscripts. Many otherwise excellent articles have been rejected due to a lack of suitable art or photographs. Regular departments—columns on strategy, tactics, and weaponry—average 1,500 words. Our contributing editors provide most departments, but we often consider unsolicited proposals, especially for 'Experience of War,' which is personal reminiscence. These stories need not be combat experiences per se, but must be true first-person narratives. While the information we publish is scholarly and substantive, we prefer writing that is light, anecdotal, and above all, engaging, rather than didactic."

$$ MILITARY HISTORY, Primedia History Group, 741 Miller Dr., SE, Suite D-2, Leesburg VA 20175-8920. (703)771-9400. Fax: (703)779-8345. E-mail: MilitaryHistory@thehistorynet.com. Website: www.thehistorynet.com. Managing Editor: Carl von Wodtke. **Contact:** Jon Guttman, editor. **95% freelance written.** "We'll work with anyone, established or not, who can provide the goods and convince us as to its accuracy." Bimonthly magazine covering all military history of the world. "We strive to give the general reader accurate, highly readable, ofter narrative popular history, richly accompanied by period art." Circ. 105,000. Pays on publication. Publishes ms an average of 2 years after acceptance. Byline given. Buys all rights. Submit seasonal material 1 year in advance. Accepts queries by mail, e-mail, fax. Responds in 3 months to queries; 6 months to mss. Sample copy for $5. Writer's guidelines for #10 SASE or online.

Nonfiction: Historical/nostalgic, interview/profile (military figures of commanding interest), personal experience (only occasionally). **Buys 24 mss/year.** Query with published clips. "Submit a short, self-explanatory query summarizing the story proposed, its highlights and/or significance. State also your own expertise, access to sources or proposed means of developing the pertinent information." Length: 4,000 words with a 500-word sidebar. **Pays $400.**

Columns/Departments: Intrigue, Weaponry, Perspectives, Personality and review of books, video, CD-ROMs, software—all relating to military history. Length: 2,000 words. **Buys 24 mss/year.** Query with published clips. **Pays $200.**

The online magazine contains content not found in the print edition and includes writer's guidelines. Contact: Roger Vance.

Tips: "We would like journalistically 'pure' submissions that adhere to basics, such as full name at first reference, same with rank, and definition of prior or related events, issues cited as context or obscure military 'hardware.' Read the magazine, discover our style, and avoid subjects already covered. Pick stories with strong art possibilities (real art and photos), send photocopies, tell us where to order the art. Avoid historical overview; focus upon an event with appropriate and accurate context. Provide bibliography. Tell the story in popular but elegant style. Include a hard copy as well as an IBM- or Macintosh-compatible floppy disk."

$ $ PERSIMMON HILL, National Cowboy and Western Heritage Museum, 1700 NE 63rd St., Oklahoma City OK 73111. (405)478-6404. Fax: (405)478-4714. E-mail: editor@nationalcowboymuseum.org. Website: www.nationalcowboymuseum.org. **Contact:** M.J. Van Deventer, editor. **70% freelance written.** Prefers to work with published/established writers; works with a small number of new/unpublished writers each year. Quarterly magazine for an audience interested in Western art, Western history, ranching and rodeo, including historians, artists, ranchers, art galleries, schools, and libraries. Estab. 1970. Circ. 15,000. Pays on publication. Publishes ms an average of 2 years after acceptance. Byline given. Buys first rights. Responds in 3 months to queries. Sample copy for $10.50, including postage. Writer's guidelines for #10 SASE or on website.

- The editor of *Persimmon Hill* reports: "We need more material on rodeo, both contemporary and historical. And we need more profiles on contemporary working ranches in the West."

Nonfiction: Historical and contemporary articles on famous Western figures connected with pioneering the American West, Western art, rodeo, cowboys, etc. (or biographies of such people), stories of Western flora and animal life and environmental subjects. "We want thoroughly researched and historically authentic material written in a popular style. May have a humorous approach to subject." "No broad, sweeping, superficial pieces; i.e., the California Gold Rush or rehashed pieces on Billy the Kid, etc." **Buys 35-50 mss/year.** Query by mail only with clips. Length: 1,500 words. **Pays $150-250.**

Photos: Purchased with ms or on assignment. Reviews color transparencies, Glossy b&w prints. Pays according to quality and importance for b&w and color photos. Captions required.

Tips: "Send us a story that captures the spirit of adventure and indvidualism that typifies the Old West or reveals a facet of the Western lifestyle in comtemporary society. Excellent illustrations for articles are essential! We lean towards scholarly, historical, well-researched articles. We're less focused on Western celebrities than some of the other contemporary Western magazines."

$ $ $ $ PRESERVATION MAGAZINE, National Trust for Historic Preservation, 1785 Massachusetts Ave. NW, Washington DC 20036. (202)588-6388. Fax: (202)588-6266. E-mail: preservation@nthp.org. Website: preservationonline.org. **Contact:** Sudip Bose, associate editor. **75% freelance written.** Prefers to work with published/established writers. Bimonthly magazine covering preservation of historic buildings in the US. "We cover subjects related in some way to place. Most entries are features, department, or opinion pieces." Circ. 250,000. Pays on publication. Publishes ms an average of 1 month after acceptance. Byline given. Offers variable kill fee. Buys one-time rights. Accepts queries by mail, e-mail, fax. Responds in 2 months to queries.

Nonfiction: Book excerpts, essays, historical/nostalgic, humor, interview/profile, new product, opinion, photo feature, travel, features, news. **Buys 30 mss/year.** Query with published clips. Length: 500-3,500 words. Sometimes pays expenses of writers on assignment, but not long-distance travel.

The online magazine carries original content not found in the print edition. Contact: Margaret Foster.

Tips: "Do not send or propose histories of buildings, descriptive accounts of cities or towns or long-winded treatises. Best bet for breaking in is via Preservation Online, Preservation News (news features, 500-1,000 words), Bricks & Mortar (brief profile or article, 250-500 words)."

$ $ $ TIMELINE, Ohio Historical Society, 1982 Velma Ave., Columbus OH 43211-2497. (614)297-2360. Fax: (614)297-2367. E-mail: timeline@ohiohistory.org. **Contact:** Christopher S. Duckworth, editor. **90% freelance written.** Works with a small number of new/unpublished writers each year. Bimonthly magazine covering history, prehistory, and the natural sciences, directed toward readers in the Midwest. Estab. 1885. Circ. 19,000. **Pays on acceptance.** Publishes ms an average of 1 year after acceptance. Byline given. Offers $75 minimum kill fee. Buys first North American serial, all rights. Submit seasonal material 6 months in advance. Accepts queries by mail, e-mail, fax. Responds in 3 weeks to queries; 6 weeks to mss. Sample copy for $6 and 9×12 SAE. Writer's guidelines for #10 SASE.

Nonfiction: Topics include the traditional fields of political, economic, military, and social history; biography; the history of science and technology; archaeology and anthropology; architecture; the fine and decorative arts; and the natural sciences including botany, geology, zoology, ecology, and paleontology. Book excerpts, essays, historical/nostalgic, interview/profile (of individuals), photo feature. **Buys 22 mss/year.** Query. Length: 1,500-6,000 words. Also vignettes of 500-1,000 words. **Pays $100-900.**
Photos: Submissions should include ideas for illustration. Send photos with submission. Reviews contact sheets, transparencies, 8×10 prints. Buys one-time rights. Captions, identification of subjects, model releases required.
Tips: "We want crisply written, authoritative narratives for the intelligent lay reader. An Ohio slant may strengthen a submission, but it is not indispensable. Contributors must know enough about their subject to explain it clearly and in an interesting fashion. We use high-quality illustration with all features. If appropriate illustration is unavailable, we can't use the feature. The writer who sends illustration ideas with a manuscript has an advantage, but an often-published illustration won't attract us."

$ $ TRACES OF INDIANA AND MIDWESTERN HISTORY, Indiana Historical Society, 450 W. Ohio St., Indianapolis IN 46202-3269. (317)232-1877. Fax: (317)233-0857. E-mail: rboomhower@indianahistory.org. Website: www.indianahistory.org/traces.htm. Executive Editor: Thomas A. Mason. **Contact:** Ray E. Boomhower, managing editor. **80% freelance written.** Quarterly magazine on Indiana and Midwestern history. "Conceived as a vehicle to bring to the public good narrative and analytical history about Indiana in its broader contexts of region and nation, *Traces* explores the lives of artists, writers, performers, soldiers, politicians, entrepreneurs, homemakers, reformers, and naturalists. It has traced the impact of Hoosiers on the nation and the world. In this vein, the editors seek nonfiction articles that are solidly researched, attractively written, and amenable to illustration, and they encourage scholars, journalists, and freelance writers to contribute to the magazine." Estab. 1989. Circ. 11,000. **Pays on acceptance.** Publishes ms an average of 6 months after acceptance. Byline given. Buys one-time rights. Submit seasonal material 1 year in advance. Responds in 3 months to mss. Sample copy and writer's guidelines for $5.25 (make checks payable to Indiana Historical Society) and 9×12 SAE with 7 first-class stamps or on website. Writer's guidelines for #10 SASE.
Nonfiction: Book excerpts, historical essays, historical photographic features on topics of biography, literature, folklore, music, visual arts, politics, economics, industry, transportation and sports. **Buys 20 mss/year.** Send complete ms. Length: 2,000-4,000 words. **Pays $100-500.**
Photos: Send photos with submission. Reviews contact sheets, transparencies, photocopies, prints. Buys one-time rights. Pays "reasonable photographic expenses." Captions, identification of subjects, permissions required.
Tips: "Freelancers should be aware of prerequisites for writing history for a broad audience. Should have some awareness of this magazine and other magazines of this type published by Midwestern historical societies. Preference is given to subjects with an Indiana connection and authors who are familiar with *Traces*. Quality of potential illustration is also important."

$ ☒ TRUE WEST, True West Publishing, Inc., P.O. Box 8008, Cave Creek AZ 85327. (888)587-1881. Fax: (480)575-1903. E-mail: editor@truewestmagazine.com. Website: www.truewestmagazine.com. Executive Editor: Bob Boze Bell. **Contact:** Mare Rosenbaum, associate editor. **80% freelance written.** Works with a small number of new/unpublished writers each year. Monthly magazine covering Western American history from prehistory to 1930. "We want reliable research on significant historical topics written in lively prose for an informed general audience. More recent topics may be used if they have a historical angle or retain the Old West flavor of trail dust and saddle leather." Estab. 1953. Circ. 50,000. **Pays on acceptance.** Publishes ms an average of 6 months after acceptance. Byline given. Buys first North American serial rights. Editorial lead time 3 months. Submit seasonal material 6 months in advance. Accepts queries by mail, e-mail. Responds in 6 weeks to queries; 2 months to mss. Sample copy for $2 and 9×12 SAE. Writer's guidelines for #10 SASE.

O→ "We are looking for historically accurate stories on the Old West that make you go 'What happens next?' Think and write outside of the box. History should be fun. If you have a passion for the West and can write creatively, we will probably publish you."

Nonfiction: Book excerpts, historical/nostalgic, humor, interview/profile, travel. No fiction or unsupported, undocumented tales. **Buys 110 mss/year.** Query. Length: 1,200-5,000 words. **Pays $50-800.**
Photos: State availability with submission. Reviews contact sheets, negatives, 4×5 transparencies, 4×5 prints. Buys one-time rights. Offers $10-75/photo. Captions, identification of subjects, model releases required.
Columns/Departments: Bob Boze Bell, executive editor. True Reviews (book reviews), 300-800 words. **Buys 50 mss/year.** Query. **Pays $50-200.**
Fillers: Bob Boze Bell, executive editor. Anecdotes, facts, gags to be illustrated by cartoonist, newsbreaks, short humor. **Buys 30/year.** Length: 50-600 words. **Pays $30-250.**
Tips: "Do original research on fresh topics. Stay away from controversial subjects unless you are truly knowledgeable in the field. Read our magazines and follow our guidelines. A freelancer is most likely to break in with us by submitting thoroughly researched, lively prose on relatively obscure topics. First-person accounts rarely fill our needs. Historical accuracy and strict adherence to the facts are essential. We much prefer material based on primary sources (archives, court records, documents, contemporary newspapers and first-person accounts) to those that rely mainly on secondary sources (published books, magazines, and journals). Note: We are currently trying to take *True West* and *Old West* back to their 'roots' by publishing shorter pieces. Ideal length is between 1,500-3,000 words."

$ $ VIETNAM, Primedia History Group, 741 Miller Dr., SE, #D-2, Leesburg VA 20175-8920. (703)779-9400. Fax: (703)779-8345. E-mail: Vietnam@thehistorynet.com. Website: www.thehistorynet.com. Managing Editor: Carl von

Wodtke. **Contact:** David T. Zabecki, editor. **90% freelance written.** Bimonthly magazine providing in-depth and authoritative accounts of the many complexities that made the war in Vietnam unique, including the people, battles, strategies, perspectives, analysis and weaponry. Estab. 1988. Circ. 52,000. Pays on publication. Publishes ms an average of 2 years after acceptance. Byline given. Buys all rights. Accepts queries by mail, e-mail, fax. Responds in 3 months to queries; 6 months to mss. Sample copy for $5. Writer's guidelines for #10 SASE.

Nonfiction: Book excerpts (if original), historical/nostalgic (military), interview/profile, personal experience. "Absolutely no fiction or poetry; we want straight history, as much personal narrative as possible, but not the gung-ho, shoot-'em-up variety, either." **Buys 24 mss/year.** Query. Length: 4,000 words maximum; sidebars 500 words. **Pays $300 for features.**

Photos: Send photos with submission or state availability and cite sources. Identification of subjects required.

Columns/Departments: Arsenal (about weapons used, all sides); Personality (profiles of the players, all sides); Fighting Forces (various units or types of units: air, sea, rescue); Perspectives. Length: 2,000 words. Query. **Pays $150.**

The online magazine contains content not found in the print edition and includes writer's guidelines. Contact: Roger Vance.

Tips: "Choose stories with strong art possibilities. Send hard copy plus an IBM- or Macintosh-compatible floppy disk. All stories must be true. We do not publish fiction or poetry. All stories should be carefully researched, third-person articles or firsthand accounts that give the reader a sense of experiencing historical events."

$ $ WILD WEST, Primedia History Group, 741 Miller Dr., SE, Suite D-2, Leesburg VA 20175-8920. (703)771-9400. Fax: (703)779-8345. E-mail: wildwest@thehistorynet.com. Website: www.thehistorynet.com. Managing Editor: Carl von Wodtke. **Contact:** Gregory Lalire, editor. **95% freelance written.** Bimonthly magazine covering the history of the American frontier, from its eastern beginnings to its western terminus. "*Wild West* covers the popular (narrative) history of the American West—events, trends, personalities, anything of general interest." Estab. 1988. Circ. 83,500. Pays on publication. Publishes ms an average of 2 years after acceptance. Byline given. Not copyrighted. Buys all rights. Editorial lead time 6 months. Submit seasonal material 1 year in advance. Accepts queries by mail, e-mail. Accepts simultaneous submissions. Responds in 3 months to queries; 6 months to mss. Sample copy for $5. Writer's guidelines for #10 SASE or online.

Nonfiction: Historical/nostalgic (Old West). No excerpts, travel, etc. Articles can be "adapted from" book. No fiction or poetry—nothing current. **Buys 36 mss/year.** Query. Length: 3,500 words with a 500-word sidebar. **Pays $300.**

Photos: State availability with submission. Reviews negatives, transparencies. Buys one-time rights. Offers no additional payment for photos accepted with ms. Captions, identification of subjects required.

Columns/Departments: Gunfighters & Lawmen, 2,000 words; Westerners, 2,000 words; Warriors & Chiefs; Western Lore, 2,000 words; Guns of the West, 1,500 words; Artists West, 1,500 words; Books Reviews, 250 words. **Buys 36 mss/year.** Query. **Pays $150 for departments; book reviews paid by the word, minimum $40.**

The online magazine carries original content not found in the print edition. Contact: Roger Vance, online editor.

Tips: "Always query the editor with your story idea. Successful queries include a description of sources of information and suggestions for color and black-and-white photography or artwork. The best way to break into our magazine is to write an entertaining, informative and unusual story that grabs the reader's attention and holds it. We favor carefully researched, third-person articles that give the reader a sense of experiencing historical events. Include a hard copy as well as an IBM- or Macintosh-compatible floppy disk."

$ $ WORLD WAR II, Primedia History Group, 741 Miller Dr., SE, Suite D-2, Leesburg VA 20175-8920. (703)771-9400. Fax: (703)779-8345. E-mail: worldwarii@thehistorynet.com. Website: www.thehistorynet.com. Managing Editor: Carl von Wodtke. **Contact:** Christopher Anderson, editor. **95% freelance written.** Prefers to work with published/established writers. Bimonthly magazine covering "military operations in World War II—events, personalities, strategy, national policy, etc." Estab. 1986. Circ. 146,000. Pays on publication. Publishes ms an average of 2 years after acceptance. Byline given. Buys all rights. Accepts queries by mail, e-mail, fax. Responds in 3 months to queries; 6 months to mss. Sample copy for $5. Writer's guidelines for #10 SASE or online.

Nonfiction: World War II military history. Submit anniversary-related material 1 year in advance. No fiction. **Buys 24 mss/year.** Query. Length: Length: 4,000 words with a 500-word sidebar. **Pays $300 and up.**

Photos: For photos and other art, send photocopies and cite sources. "We'll order." State availability with submission. Captions, identification of subjects required.

Columns/Departments: Undercover (espionage, resistance, sabotage, intelligence gathering, behind the lines, etc.); Personality (WWII personalities of interest); Armament (weapons, their use and development); Commands (unit histories); One Man's War (personal profiles), all 2,000 words. Book reviews, 300-750 words. **Buys 30 (plus book reviews) mss/year.** Query. **Pays $150 and up.**

The online magazine contains content not found in the print edition and includes writer's guidelines. Contact: Roger Vance.

Tips: "List your sources and suggest further readings in standard format at the end of your piece—as a bibliography for our files in case of factual challenge or dispute. All submissions are on speculation. Include a hard copy as well as an IBM- or Macintosh-compatible floppy disk. All stories must be true. We do not publish fiction or poetry. Stories should be carefully researched."

HOBBY & CRAFT

Magazines in this category range from home video to cross-stitch. Craftspeople and hobbyists who read these magazines want new ideas while collectors need to know what is most valuable and why. Collectors, do-it-yourselfers, and craftspeople look to these magazines for inspiration and information. Publications covering antiques and miniatures are also listed here. Publications covering the business side of antiques and collectibles are listed in the Trade Art, Design & Collectibles section.

$ ANTIQUE JOURNAL, Krause Publications/Antique Trader Publications, P.O. Box 12589, El Cajon CA 92022. (619)593-2925. Fax: (619)447-7187. E-mail: editorialnow@aol.com. Website: www.collect.com. **Contact:** Alison Ashton, managing editor. **45% freelance written.** Monthly newspaper covering antiques and collectibles. *Antique Journal* reaches antique collectors situated in Northern California, Nevada, Oregon and Washington. Estab. 1991. Circ. 28,000. **Pays on acceptance.** Publishes ms an average of up to 1 year after acceptance. Byline given. Buys first, electronic rights. Editorial lead time 1 month. Accepts queries by mail, e-mail. Accepts simultaneous submissions. Sample copy and writer's guidelines free.

Nonfiction: General interest, how-to, interview/profile, photo feature. **Buys 2 mss/year.** Query. Length: 500-1,200 words. **Pays $25-60.**

Photos: Send photos with submission. Reviews contact sheets. Buys all rights. Negotiates payment individually. Captions required.

Tips: "Be knowledgable in antiques and collecting and have good photos."

$ $ ANTIQUE TRADER, (formerly *The Antique Trader Weekly*), 700 E. State St., Iola WI 54990-0001. (715)445-2214. Fax: (715)445-4087. E-mail: korbecks@krause.com. Website: www.collect.com. **Contact:** Sharon Korbeck, editor. **90% freelance written.** Works with many new/unpublished writers each year. Weekly newspaper for collectors, dealers and auction houses dealing with antiques and collectibles. Estab. 1957. Circ. 60,000. Pays on publication. Publishes ms an average of 2-8 months after acceptance. Buys exclusive rights for *Antique Trader.* Writer's guidelines online.

Nonfiction: "We're looking for well-researched stories about the current market for particular antiques/collectibles areas (like Carnival glass, art pottery, postcards, etc.). Stories must include current market trends, values and quotes from appropriate dealers, collectors and other sources." Also looking for interesting, topical profiles of interesting collectors, dealers and others in the industry. **Buys 100-150 mss/year.** Query or submit story on spec. Length: 750-1,000 words plus sidebars. **Pays $100-200 for features.**

Photos: Reviews transparencies, color, b&w prints, slides, digital images (at least 150 dpi). Payment for photos is included with purchase of mss.

Tips: "We don't want the same historical 'textbook' approach seen in other antiques publications. We want articles brimming with personality, style, fun trivia, interesting sidebars and lively quotes. Make antiquing come alive through vibrant writing and clear photos."

N $ ANTIQUE & COLLECTABLES NEWSMAGAZINE, Krause Publications, P.O. Box 12589, El Cajon CA 92022. (619)593-2926. Fax: (619)447-7187. E-mail: editorialnow@aol.com. Website: www.collect.com. **Contact:** Alison Ashton, managing editor. **45% freelance written.** Monthly magazine covering antiques and collectibles. *Antique & Collectables* reaches antique collectors situated in Southern California, Nevada and Arizona. Estab. 1979. Circ. 27,500. **Pays on acceptance.** Publishes ms an average of 1 year after acceptance. Byline given. Buys first, electronic rights. Editorial lead time 1 month. Accepts queries by mail, e-mail. Accepts simultaneous submissions. Sample copy for free. Writer's guidelines free.

Nonfiction: General interest, how-to, interview/profile, photo feature. Query. Length: 500-1,200 words. **Pays $25-60.**

Photos: Send photos with submission. Reviews contact sheets. Buys all rights. Negotiates payment individually. Captions required.

Tips: "Be knowledgable in antiques and collecting and have good photos."

$ $ ANTIQUES & COLLECTING MAGAZINE, 1006 S. Michigan Ave., Chicago IL 60605. (312)939-4767. Fax: (312)939-0053. E-mail: acmeditor@interaccess.com. **Contact:** Frances Graham, editor. **80% freelance written.** Monthly magazine covering antiques and collectibles. Estab. 1931. Circ. 20,000. Pays on publication. Publishes ms an average of 3 months after acceptance. Byline given. Buys first rights. Editorial lead time 2 months. Submit seasonal material 3 months in advance. Accepts queries by mail, e-mail, fax, phone. Responds in 3 weeks to queries; 2 months to mss. Sample copy for free. Writer's guidelines for free or by e-mail.

Nonfiction: Book excerpts, general interest, historical/nostalgic, how-to, interview/profile, opinion, personal experience, photo feature, features about antiques and collectibles made before 1970. **Buys 40-50 mss/year.** Query. Length: 1,000-1,600 words. **Pays $150-250 plus 4 copies.**

Photos: Send photos with submission. Reviews transparencies, prints. Buys one-time rights. Offers no additional payment for photos accepted with ms. Captions, identification of subjects required.

Fillers: Anecdotes, facts.

$ ☆ AUTOGRAPH COLLECTOR, Odyssey Publications, 510-A South Corona Mall, Corona CA 92879-1420. (909)734-9636. Fax: (909)371-7139. E-mail: dbtogi@aol.com. Website: www.autographcollector.com. **Contact:** Ev Phillips, editor. **80% freelance written.** Monthly magazine covering the autograph collecting hobby. "The focus of

Autograph Collector is on documents, photographs or any collectible item that has been signed by a famous person, whether a current celebrity or historical figure. Articles stress how and where to locate celebrities and autograph material, authenticity of signatures and what they are worth." Byline given. Offers negotiable kill fee. Buys all rights. Editorial lead time 2 months. Submit seasonal material 3 months in advance. Accepts queries by mail, e-mail, fax, phone. Responds in 2 weeks to queries. Sample copy and writer's guidelines free.

Nonfiction: "Articles must address subjects that appeal to autograph collectors and should answer six basic questions: Who is this celebrity/famous person? How do I go about collecting this person's autograph? Where can I find it? How scarce or available is it? How can I tell if it's real? What is it worth?" Historical/nostalgic, how-to, interview/profile, personal experience. **Buys 25-35 mss/year.** Query. Length: 1,600-2,000 words. **Pays 5¢/word.** Sometimes pays expenses of writers on assignment.

Photos: State availability with submission. Reviews transparencies, prints. Buys one-time rights. Offers $3/photo. Captions, identification of subjects required.

Columns/Departments: "*Autograph Collector* buys 8-10 columns per month written by regular contributors." **Buys 90-100 mss/year.** Query. **Pays $50 or as determined on a per case basis.**

Fillers: Anecdotes, facts. **Buys 20-25/year.** Length: 200-300 words. **Pays $15.**

Tips: "Ideally writers should be autograph collectors themselves and know their topics thoroughly. Articles must be well-researched and clearly written. Writers should remember that *Autograph Collector* is a celebrity-driven magazine and name recognition of the subject is important."

$ BEAD & BUTTON, Kalmbach Publishing, 21027 Crossroads Circle, Waukesha WI 53186. (262)796-8776. E-mail: akorach@beadandbutton.com. Website: www.beadandbutton.com. Editor: Alice Korach. **Contact:** Lora Groszkiewicz, editorial assistant. **50% freelance written.** "*Bead & Button* is a bimonthly magazine devoted to techniques, projects, designs and materials relating to beads, buttons, and accessories. Our readership includes both professional and amateur bead and button makers, hobbyists, and enthusiasts who find satisfaction in making beautiful things." Estab. 1994. Circ. 80,000. **Pays on acceptance.** Publishes ms an average of 4 months after acceptance. Byline given. Offers $75 kill fee. Buys all rights. Accepts queries by mail, e-mail, fax. Writer's guidelines free, online or by e-mail.

Nonfiction: Historical/nostalgic (on beaded jewelry history), how-to (make beaded jewelry and accessories), humor (or inspirational —1 endpiece for each issue), interview/profile. **Buys 24-30 mss/year.** Send complete ms. Length: 750-3,000 words. **Pays $75-300.**

Photos: Send photos with submission. Offers no additional payment for photos accepted with ms. Identification of subjects required.

Columns/Departments: Chic & Easy (fashionable jewelry how-to); Beginner (easy-to-make jewelry how-to); Simply Earrings (fashionable earring how-to); Fun Fashion (trendy jewelry how-to), all 1,500 words. **Buys 12 mss/year.** Send complete ms. **Pays $75-150.**

Tips: "*Bead & Button* magazine primarily publishes how-to articles by the artists who have designed the piece. We publish one profile and one historical piece per issue. These would be the only applicable articles for non-artisan writers. Also our humorous and inspirational endpiece might apply."

$ $ BLADE MAGAZINE®, The World's #1 Knife Publication, Krause Publications, 700 E. State St., Iola WI 54990. (715)445-2214. Fax: (715)445-4087. E-mail: blademagazine@krause.com. Website: www.blademag.com. Editor: Steve Shackleford. **Contact:** Joe Kertzman, managing editor. **60% freelance written.** Monthly magazine for knife enthusiasts who want to know as much as possible about quality knives and edged tools, hand-made and factory knife industries, antique knife collecting, etc. *Blade* is designed to highlight the romance and history of man's oldest tool, the knife. Our readers are into any and all knives used as tools/collectibles. Estab. 1973. Circ. 75,000. Pays on publication. Publishes ms an average of 1 year after acceptance. Byline given. Offers $20 kill fee. Buys all rights. Editorial lead time 4 months. Submit seasonal material 4 months in advance. Accepts queries by mail, e-mail, fax, phone. Responds in 3 months to queries. Sample copy for #10 SASE.

Nonfiction: "We would like to see articles on knives in adventuresome lifesaving situations." Book excerpts, exposé, general interest, historical/nostalgic (on knives), how-to, humor, new product, personal experience, photo feature, technical, travel, adventure (on a knife theme), celebrities who own knives, knives featured in movies with shots from the movie, etc. No articles on how to use knives as weapons. No poetry. **Buys 50 mss/year.** Query. Length: 1,000-1,500 words. **Pays $125-300. "We will pay top dollar in the knife market."** Sometimes pays expenses of writers on assignment.

Photos: State availability of or send photos with submission. Offers no additional payment for photos accepted with ms. Captions, identification of subjects required.

Columns/Departments: Buys 60 mss/year. Query. **Pays $150-250.**

Fillers: Anecdotes, facts, newsbreaks. **Buys 1-2/year.** Length: 50-200 words. **Pays $25-50.**

Tips: "We are always willing to read submissions from anyone who has read a few copies and studied the market. The ideal article for us is a piece bringing out the romance, legend, and love of man's oldest tool—the knife. We like articles that place knives in peoples' hands—in life saving situations, adventure modes, etc. (Nothing gory or with the knife as the villain.) People and knives are good copy. We are getting more and better written articles from writers who are reading the publication beforehand. That makes for a harder sell for the quickie writer not willing to do his homework. Go to knife shows and talk to the makers and collectors. Visit knifemakers' shops and knife factories. Read anything and everything you can find on knives and knifemaking."

$ BREW YOUR OWN, The How-to Homebrew Beer Magazine, Battenkill Communications, 5053 Main St., Suite A, Manchester Center VT 05255. (802)362-3981. Fax: (802)362-2377. E-mail: edit@byo.com. Website: www.byo.com. **Contact:** Kathleen Ring, editor. **85% freelance written.** Monthly magazine covering home brewing. "Our mission is to provide practical information in an entertaining format. We try to capture the spirit and challenge of brewing while helping our readers brew the best beer they can." Estab. 1995. Circ. 42,000. **Pays on acceptance.** Publishes ms an average of 4 months after acceptance. Byline given. Offers 25% kill fee. Buys all rights. Editorial lead time 3 months. Submit seasonal material 3 months in advance. Accepts queries by mail, e-mail, fax. Responds in 2 months to queries. Writer's guidelines for #10 SASE.

Break in by "sending a detailed query in one of two key areas: how to brew a specific, interesting style of beer (with step-by-step recipes) or how to build your own specific piece of brewing equipment."

Nonfiction: Informational pieces on equipment, ingredients and brewing methods. Historical/nostalgic, how-to (home brewing), humor (related to home brewing), interview/profile (of professional brewers who can offer useful tips to home hobbyists), personal experience, trends. **Buys 75 mss/year.** Query with published clips or description of brewing expertise. Length: 800-3,000 words. **Pays $50-150, depending on length, complexity of article and experience of writer.** Sometimes pays expenses of writers on assignment.

Photos: State availability with submission. Reviews contact sheets, transparencies, 5×7 prints, slides and electronic images. Buys all rights. Negotiates payment individually. Captions required.

Columns/Departments: News (humorous, unusual news about homebrewing), 50-250 words; Last Call (humorous stories about homebrewing), 700 words. **Buys 12 mss/year.** Query with or without published clips. **Pays $50.**

Tips: "*Brew Your Own* is for anyone who is interested in brewing beer, from beginners to advanced all-grain brewers. We seek articles that are straightforward and factual, not full of esoteric theories or complex calculations. Our readers tend to be intelligent, upscale, and literate."

N $ CERAMICS MONTHLY, The American Ceramic Society, P.O. Box 6102, Westerville OH 43086. (614)523-1660. Fax: (614)891-8960. E-mail: editorial@ceramicsmonthly.org. Website: www.ceramicsmonthly.org. **Contact:** Renée Fairchild, editorial assistant. **50% freelance written.** Monthly except July and August Magazine covering the ceramic art and craft field. "Technical and business information for potters and ceramic artists." Estab. 1953. Circ. 39,000. Pays on publication. Byline given. Editorial lead time 3 months. Submit seasonal material 6 months in advance. Accepts queries by mail, e-mail, fax, phone. Responds in 6 weeks to queries; 2 months to mss. Writer's guidelines for #10 SASE or on website.

Nonfiction: Essays, how-to, interview/profile, opinion, personal experience, technical. **Buys 100 mss/year.** Send complete ms. Length: 500-3,000 words. **Pays 7¢/word.**

Photos: Send photos with submission. Reviews 2¼ x 2¼ or 4×5 transparencies. Offers $15 for black and white; $25 for color photos. Captions required.

Columns/Departments: Up Front (workshop/exhibition review), 500-1,000 words. **Buys 20 mss/year.** Send complete ms. **Pays 7¢/word.**

$ $ CLASSIC TOY TRAINS, Kalmbach Publishing Co., 21027 Crossroads Circle, Waukesha WI 53187. (262)796-8776. Fax: (262)796-1142. E-mail: editor@classtrain.com. Website: www.classtrain.com. **Contact:** Neil Besougloff, editor. **80% freelance written.** Magazine published 9 times/year covering collectible toy trains (O, S, Standard, G scale, etc.) like Lionel, American Flyer, Marx, Dorfan, etc. "For the collector and operator of toy trains, *CTT* offers full-color photos of layouts and collections of toy trains, restoration tips, operating information, new product reviews and information, and insights into the history of toy trains." Estab. 1987. Circ. 72,000. **Pays on acceptance.** Publishes ms an average of 1 year after acceptance. Byline given. Buys all rights. Editorial lead time 3 months. Submit seasonal material 6 months in advance. Accepts queries by mail, e-mail. Responds in 3 weeks to queries; 1 month to mss. Sample copy for $4.95 plus s&h. Writer's guidelines for #10 SASE or on website.

Nonfiction: General interest, historical/nostalgic, how-to (restore toy trains; design a layout; build accessories; fix broken toy trains), interview/profile, personal experience, photo feature, technical. **Buys 90 mss/year.** Query. Length: 500-5,000 words. **Pays $75-500.** Sometimes pays expenses of writers on assignment.

Photos: Send photos with submission. Reviews 4×5 transparencies, 5×7 prints preferred. Buys all rights. Offers no additional payment for photos accepted with ms or $15-75/photo. Captions required.

Fillers: Uses cartoons. **Buys 6/year. Pays $30.**

The online magazine carries original content not found in the print edition and includes writer's guidelines. Contact: Mike Williams and Jim Schulz, online editors.

Tips: "It's important to have a thorough understanding of the toy train hobby; most of our freelancers are hobbyists themselves. One-half to two-thirds of *CTT*'s editorial space is devoted to photographs; superior photography is critical."

$ COLLECTIBLES CANADA, Canada's Guide to Contemporary Collectible Art, Trajan Publishing, 103 Lakeshore Rd., Suite 202, St. Catharines, Ontario L2N 2T6, Canada. (905)646-7744, ext. 229. Fax: (905)646-0995. E-mail: mccauley@trajan.com. Website: www.collectiblescanada.ca. Editor: Mary Lynn McCauley. **90% freelance written.** Quarterly magazine covering contemporary collectible art. "We provide news and profiles of limited edition collectible art from a positive perspective. We are an informational tool for collectors who want to read about the products they love." Circ. 12,000. Pays 1 month after publication. Publishes ms an average of 3 months after acceptance. Byline given. Buys first North American serial rights. Editorial lead time 3 months. Submit seasonal material 3 months in advance. Accepts queries by mail, e-mail, fax. Responds in 1 month to queries. Sample copy for $3.95 (Canadian) and $2.50 IRC. Writer's guidelines for #10 SASE.

Nonfiction: Historical/nostalgic (collectibles), interview/profile, new product, technical, collectible art such as figurines, dolls, bears, prints, etc. No articles on antique-related subjects (we cover contemporary collectibles). No articles about stamp, coin, or sports collecting. **Buys 16 mss/year.** Query with published clips. Length: 500-1,200 words. **Pays $75-120 (Canadian).** Sometimes pays expenses of writers on assignment.

Photos: State availability with submission. Reviews negatives, transparencies, prints. Buys one-time rights. Negotiates payment individually. Identification of subjects required.

Columns/Departments: Book reviews (positive slant, primarily informational). Length: 500-800 words.

Tips: "Read the magazine first. Writers who can offer an article with a unique angle based on collectibles. Examples of past article ideas: 'The history of Fabergé,' 'Crossing the Lines: how collectibles go from art print to figurine, to plate to doll.' Send an e-mail with your idea and I'll evaluate it promptly."

$ $ COLLECTOR'S MART, Contemporary Collectibles, Gifts & Home Decor, Krause Publications, 700 E. State St., Iola WI 54990. (715)445-2214. Fax: (715)445-4087. E-mail: collectorsmart@krause.com. Website: www.collectorsmart.net. **Contact:** Mary L. Sieber, editor. **50% freelance written.** Bimonthly magazine covering contemporary collectibles, gifts, and home decor for collectors of all types. Estab. 1976. Circ. 90,000. Pays on publication. Publishes ms an average of 6 months after acceptance. Byline given. perpetual nonexclusive rights. Editorial lead time 2 months. Submit seasonal material 4 months in advance. Accepts queries by mail, e-mail, fax. Responds in 1 month to mss. Writer's guidelines available.

- Break in with "exciting, interesting theme topics for collections, i.e., seaside, fun and functional, patio decor, etc."

Nonfiction: Inspirational, interview/profile (artists of collectibles), new product. **Buys 20-30 mss/year.** Send complete ms. Length: 750-1,500 words. **Pays $50-300.**

Photos: Send only color photos with submission. Reviews transparencies, Prints, electronic images. Buys one-time rights. Offers no additional payment for photos accepted with ms. Captions required.

- The online magazine carries original content not found in the print edition. Contact: Mary L. Sieber.

Tips: "We're looking for more pieces on unique Christmas theme collectibles, i.e., tree toppers. Also includes giftware and home decor."

$ $ COLLECTORS NEWS, P.O. Box 306, Grundy Center IA 50638. (319)824-6981. Fax: (319)824-3414. E-mail: collectors@collectors-news.com. Website: collectors-news.com. **Contact:** Linda Kruger, managing editor. **20% freelance written.** Works with a small number of new/unpublished writers each year. Monthly magazine-size publication on offset, glossy cover, covering antiques, collectibles, and nostalgic memorabilia. Estab. 1959. Circ. 7,000. Pays on publication. Publishes ms an average of 1 year after acceptance. Byline given. Buys first rights, makes work-for-hire assignments. Submit seasonal material 3 months in advance. Accepts queries by mail, e-mail, fax, phone. Responds in 2 weeks to queries; 6 weeks to mss. Sample copy for $4 and 9×12 SAE. Writer's guidelines free.

- Break in with articles on collecting online; history and values of collectibles and antiques; collectors with unique and/or extensive collections; using collectibles in the home decor; music collectibles; transportation collectibles; advertising collectibles; bottles; glass, china, and silver; primitives; furniture; jewelry; lamps; western; textiles; toys; black memorabilia; political collectibles; movie memorabilia, and any 20th century and timely subjects.

Nonfiction: General interest (any subject re: collectibles, antique to modern), historical/nostalgic (relating to collections or collectors), how-to (display your collection, care for, restore, appraise, locate, add to, etc.), interview/profile (covering individual collectors and their hobbies, unique or extensive; celebrity collectors, and limited edition artists), technical (in-depth analysis of a particular antique, collectible, or collecting field), travel ("hot" antiquing places in the US). Special issues: 12-month listing of antique and collectible shows, flea markets, and conventions, (January includes events January-December; June includes events June-May); Care & Display of Collectibles (September); holidays (October-December). **Buys 36 mss/year.** Query with sample of writing. Length: 800-1,000 words. **Pays $1.10/column inch.**

Photos: "Articles must be accompanied by photographs for illustration." A selection of 2-8 images is suggested. "Articles are eligible for full-color front page consideration when accompanied by quality color prints, color slides, high res electronic images and/or color transparencies. Only 1 article is highlighted on the cover/month. Any article providing a color photo selected for front page use receives an additional $25." Reviews color or b&w images. Buys first rights. Payment for photos included in payment for ms. Captions required.

Tips: "Present a professionally written article with quality illustrations—well-researched and documented information."

$ $ CRAFTS MAGAZINE, 14901 S. Heritagecrest Way, Bluffdale UT 84065. **Contact:** Valerie Pingree, editor-in-chief. Magazine published 10 times/year designed to help readers make creative and rewarding handmade crafts. The main focus is fresh, craft-related projects our reader can make and display in her home or give as gifts. Estab. 1978. Circ. 345,000. **Pays on acceptance.** Byline given. Buys all rights. Editorial lead time 6 months. Accepts queries by mail, e-mail. Responds in 1 month to queries. Writer's guidelines for #10 SASE.

Nonfiction: How-to. **Buys 300 mss/year.** Query with photo or sketch of how-to project. Do not send the actual project until request. **Pays $100-500 for assigned articles.**

Tips: "We are looking for projects that are fresh, innovative, and in sync with today's trends. We accept projects made with a variety of techniques and media. Projects can fall in several categories, ranging from home decor to gifts, garden accessories to jewelry, and other seasonal craft projects. Submitted projects must be original, never-before-published, copyright-free work that use readily available materials."

$ $ CRITICAL CERAMICS, c/o Bennington College, Route 67A, Bennington VT 05201. E-mail: editor@criticalceramics.org. Website: www.criticalceramics.org. Editor: Thomas J. Wallace. **Contact:** Forrest Snyder, editor. **100% freelance written.** Online magazine covering contemporary ceramic art. Nonprofit. Estab. 1997. Circ. 5,000. Pays on publication. Publishes ms an average of 1 month after acceptance. Byline given. Buys Buys non-exclusive rights in perpetuity rights. Editorial lead time 1 month. Submit seasonal material 1 month in advance. Accepts queries by mail, e-mail. Accepts simultaneous submissions. Responds in 1 week to queries; 1 month to mss. Sample copy online. Writer's guidelines online or by e-mail.

Nonfiction: Book excerpts, essays, exposé, interview/profile, opinion, personal experience, photo feature, travel, cross-cultural dialog. **Buys 12-24 mss/year.** Query. Length: 750-1,500 words. **Pays $75-500 for assigned articles; $50-350 for unsolicited articles.** Sometimes pays expenses of writers on assignment.

Photos: State availability with submission. Reviews transparencies, 4×6 prints. Buys non-exclusive electronic rights in perpetuity. Negotiates payment individually. Captions, identification of subjects required.

Columns/Departments: Exhibition (reviews); Book Reviews; Video Reviews. **Buys 12-24 mss/year.** Query. **Pays $20-150.**

Tips: "Show enthusiasm for contemporary art with a unique view of subject area. This is a publication for professional contemporary ceramic artists."

$ $ CROCHET WORLD, House of White Birches, P.O. Box 776, Henniker NH 03242. Fax: (219)589-8093. Website: www.whitebirches.com. **Contact:** Susan Hankins, editor. **100% freelance written.** Bimonthly magazine covering crochet patterns. "*Crochet World* is a pattern magazine devoted to the art of crochet. We also feature a Q&A column, letters (swap shop) column, and occasionally nonpattern manuscripts, but it must be devoted to crochet." Estab. 1978. Circ. 75,000. Pays on publication. Byline given. Buys all rights. Editorial lead time 4 months. Submit seasonal material 6 months in advance. Responds in 1 month to queries. Sample copy for $2. Writer's guidelines free.

Nonfiction: How-to (crochet). **Buys 0-2 mss/year.** Send complete ms. Length: 500-1,500 words. **Pays $50.**

Columns/Departments: Touch of Style (crocheted clothing); It's a Snap! (quick 1-night simple patterns); Pattern of the Month, first and second prize each issue. **Buys dozens of mss/year.** Send complete pattern. **Pays $40-300.**

Poetry: Strictly crochet-related. **Buys 0-5 poems/year.** Submit maximum 2 poems. Length: 6-20 lines. **Pays $10-20.**

Fillers: Anecdotes, facts, short humor. **Buys 0-10/year.** Length: 25-200 words. **Pays $5-30.**

Tips: "Be aware that this is a pattern-generated magazine for crochet designs. I prefer the actual item sent along with complete directions/graphs etc., over queries. In some cases a photo submission or good sketch will do. Crocheted designs must be well-made and original and directions must be complete. Write for Designer's Guidelines which detail how to submit designs. Noncrochet items, such as fillers, poetry *must* be crochet-related, not knit, not sewing, etc."

$ DANCING USA, The Art of Ballroom Dance, Dancing USA LLC, 200 N. York Rd., Elmhurst IL 60126-2750. (630)782-1260. Fax: (630)617-9950. E-mail: ballroom@dancingusa.com. Website: www.dancingusa.com. **Contact:** Michael Fitzmaurice, editor. **60% freelance written.** Works with new writers. Bimonthly magazine covering ballroom, swing and Latin dance: how-tos, technique, floor craft; source for dance videos, CDs, shoes, where to dance. Estab. 1983. Circ. 20,000. Pays on publication. Publishes ms an average of 6 months after acceptance. Byline given. Buys first North American serial rights. Editorial lead time 3 months. Submit seasonal material 4 months in advance. Accepts queries by mail, e-mail, fax. Responds in 2 months to queries; 2 months to mss. Sample copy for free.

Nonfiction: Book excerpts, exposé, historical/nostalgic, how-to, humor, inspirational, interview/profile, new product, personal experience, photo feature, travel, commentary, all dance related. **Buys 30-40 mss/year.** Send complete ms. Length: 1,000-2,000 words. **Pays $25-75 for assigned articles; $10-50 for unsolicited articles.**

Photos: Send photos with submission. No additional payment.

Fiction: Looking for any type of fiction that includes a style of ballroom, Latin, or swing dance, or the industry or enjoyment of ballroom dance as a main theme.

Tips: "Works with new writers. Hot Stuff department features new dance-related products, books, and music. Four to 8 features/issue from freelancers include dancer profiles, history of dancers, entertainers, expert dance advice, promoting dance. Each issue tries to include a city dance guide, a style of dance, dance functions, a major dance competition, and a celebrity profile. Example: Denver, Tango, Weddings, U.S. Championships, and Rita Moreno."

$ $ DECORATIVE ARTIST'S WORKBOOK, F&W Publications, Inc., 4700 E. Galbraith Rd., Cincinnati OH 45236. (513)531-2690, ext. 1461. E-mail: dawedit@fwpubs.com. Website: www.decorativeartist.com. **Contact:** Anne Hevener, editor. **75% freelance written.** Bimonthly magazine covering decorative painting projects and products of all sorts. Offers "straightforward, personal instruction in the techniques of decorative painting." Estab. 1987. Circ. 90,000. **Pays on acceptance.** Byline given. Offers 25% kill fee. Buys first North American serial rights. Submit seasonal material 8 months in advance. Accepts queries by mail, e-mail. Responds in 2 weeks to queries. Sample copy for $4.65 and 9×12 SAE with 5 first-class stamps.

Nonfiction: How-to (related to decorative painting projects), new product, technique. **Buys 30 mss/year.** Query with slides or photos. Length: 1,200-1,800 words. **Pays 15-25¢/word.**

The online magazine carries original content not found in the print edition. Contact: Anne Hevener, online editor.

Tips: "Create a design, surface or technique that is fresh and new to decorative painting. I'm looking for experts in the field who, through their own experience, can artfully describe the techniques involved. How-to articles are most open to freelancers skilled in decorative painting. Be sure to query with photo/slides, and show that you understand the extensive graphic requirements for these pieces and can provide painted progressives—painted illustrations that show works in progress."

$ DOLL WORLD, The Magazine for Doll Lovers, House of White Birches, 306 E. Parr Rd., Berne IN 46711. (260)589-4000. Fax: (260)589-8093. E-mail: doll_world@whitebirches.com. Website: www.dollworldmagazine.com. **Contact:** Vicki Steensma, editor. **90% freelance written.** Bimonthly magazine covering doll collecting, restoration. "Interested in informative articles about doll history, interviews with doll artists and collectors, how-to articles, nostalgic and first-person stories about dolls." Estab. 1976. Circ. 65,000. Pays pre-publication. Byline given. Buys all rights. Submit seasonal material 9 months in advance. Accepts queries by e-mail, fax, phone. Responds in 2 months to queries. Writer's guidelines for #10 SASE or by e-mail.

Nonfiction: "Subjects with broad appeal to the 'boomer' generation." The editor reports an interest in seeing features on dolls of the 1930s-1970s. **Pays $50 and up** depending on published length of article, and presentation of article and accompanying graphics. Historical/nostalgic (about dolls and collecting), how-to (about dolls—collecting, care, display, sell, buy), humor (about dolls), inspirational, interview/profile (those in the doll industry), new product, personal experience (dolls), photo feature (dolls), religious (dolls), technical (dolls), travel (dolls). **Buys 50 mss/year.** Send complete ms.

Photos: Send top-quality photos or disk images (hi-res TIFF Mac format). Send photos with submission. Captions, identification of subjects required, written separate from ms required.

Tips: "Choose a specific manufacturer or artist and talk about his dolls or a specific doll—modern or antique—and explore its history and styles made. Be descriptive, but do not overuse adjectives. Use personal conversational tone. Be interested enough in the magazine to have looked at an issue before submitting."

$ $ DOLLHOUSE MINIATURES, Kalmbach Publishing Co., 21027 Crossroads Circle, Waukesha WI 53187-1612. (262)796-8776. Fax: (262)796-1383. E-mail: cstjacques@dhminiatures.com. Website: www.dhminiatures.com. Editor: Candice St. Jacques. **50% freelance written.** Monthly magazine covering dollhouse scale miniatures. "*Dollhouse Miniatures* is America's best-selling miniatures magazine and the definitive resource for artisans, collectors, and hobbyists. It promotes and supports the large national and international community of miniaturists through club columns, short reports, and by featuring reader projects and ideas." Estab. 1971. Circ. 35,000. **Pays on acceptance.** Byline given. Offers 10% kill fee. Buys all rights. Editorial lead time 6 months. Submit seasonal material 6 months in advance. Accepts queries by mail, e-mail. Responds in 1 month to queries; 2 months to mss. Sample copy free (1 copy). Contact: Customer Service (800)533-6644 or customerservice@kalmbach.com. Writer's guidelines for #10 SASE or online.

Nonfiction: How-to (miniature projects of various scales in variety of media), interview/profile (artisans, collectors), photo feature (dollhouses, collections, museums). No articles on miniature shops or essays. **Buys 50-60 mss/year.** Query with or without published clips or send complete ms. Length: 500-1,500 words. **Pays $50-350 for assigned articles; $0-200 for unsolicited articles.** Pays expenses of writers on assignment.

Photos: Send photos with submission. Reviews 35mm slides and larger, 3×5 prints. Buys all rights. Photos are paid for with ms. Seldom buys individual photos. Captions, identification of subjects required.

Tips: "Familiarity with the miniatures hobby is very helpful. Accuracy to scale is extremely important to our readers. A complete package (manuscripts/photos) has a better chance of publication."

N $ DOLLMAKING, Your Resource for Creating & Costuming Modern Porcelain Dolls, Jones Publishing, N7450 Aanstad Rd., P.O. Box 5000, Iola WI 54945. (715)377-9780. Fax: (715)445-4053. E-mail: dolledit@pressenter.com. Website: www.dollmakingartisan.com. **Contact:** Stacy D. Carlson, editor. **50% freelance written.** Bimonthly magazine covering porcelain dollmaking. "*Dollmaking*'s intent is to entertain and inform porcelain and sculpted modern doll artists and costumers with the newest projects and techniques. It is meant to be a resource for hobby enthusiasts." Estab. 1985. Circ. 15,000. Pays on publication. Byline sometimes given. Buys all rights. Editorial lead time 4 months. Submit seasonal material 4 months in advance. Accepts queries by mail, e-mail, fax, phone. Sample copy online. Writer's guidelines free.

Nonfiction: Inspirational, interview/profile, personal experience. **Buys 12 mss/year.** Query. Length: 800 words. **Pays $75-150 for assigned articles.**

Photos: State availability with submission. Reviews 2½ x 2½ transparencies. Buys all rights. Negotiates payment individually.

Columns/Departments: Sewing Q&A (readers write in with sewing questions), 1,600 words. **Buys 2-3 mss/year.** Query. **Pays $75.**

Fillers: Anecdotes. **Buys 6/year.** Length: 500-800 words. **Pays $55-75.**

Tips: "The best way to break in is to send a manuscript of something the author has written concerning porcelain dollmaking and costuming. The article may be a personal story, a special technique used when making a doll, a successful doll fundraiser, sewing tips for dolls, or anything that would be of interest to a serious doll artisan. If no manuscript is available, at least send a letter of interest."

$ $ $ FAMILY TREE MAGAZINE, Discover, Preserve & Celebrate Your Family's History, F&W Publications, 4700 E. Galbraith Rd., Cincinnati OH 45236. (513)531-2690. Fax: (513)531-2902. E-mail: ftmedit@fwpubs.com. Website: www.familytreemagazine.com. **Contact:** David A. Fryxell, editor-in-chief. **75% freelance written.** Bimonthly magazine covering family history, heritage, and genealogy. "*Family Tree Magazine* is a general-interest consumer magazine that helps readers discover, preserve, and celebrate their family's history. We cover genealogy, ethnic heritage, personal history, genealogy websites and software, scrapbooking, photography and photo preservation, and other ways that families connect with their past." Estab. 1999. Circ. 85,000. **Pays on acceptance.** Publishes ms an average of 6 months after acceptance. Byline given. Offers 25% kill fee. Buys first, electronic rights. Editorial lead time 8 months. Submit seasonal material 8 months in advance. Accepts queries by mail, e-mail. Responds in 1 month to queries. Sample copy for $6.25 or on website. Writer's guidelines for #10 SASE or on website.

O→ Break in by suggesting a "useful, timely idea for our Toolkit section on a resource that our readers would love to discover."

Nonfiction: "Articles are geared to beginners but never talk down to the audience. We emphasize sidebars, tips, and other reader-friendly 'packaging,' and each article aims to give the reader the resources necessary to take the next step in his or her quest for their personal past." Book excerpts, historical/nostalgic, how-to (genealogy), new product (photography, computer), technical (genealogy software, photography equipment), travel (with ethnic heritage slant). **Buys 60 mss/year.** Query with published clips. Length: 500-3,500 words. **Pays $150-800.** Sometimes pays expenses of writers on assignment.

Photos: State availability with submission. Reviews color transparencies. Buys one-time rights. Negotiates payment individually. Captions required.

The online magazine carries original content not found in the print edition and includes writer's guidelines. Contact: Susan Wenner, managing editor.

Tips: "We see too many broad, general stories on genealogy or records, and personal accounts of 'How I found great-aunt Sally' without how-to value."

$ $ FIBERARTS, The Magazine of Textiles, Altamont Press, 67 Broadway, Asheville NC 28801. (828)253-0467. Fax: (828)236-2869. E-mail: editor@fiberartsmagazine.com. Website: www.fiberartsmagazine.com. **Contact:** Sunita Patterson, editor. **90% freelance written.** Magazine published 5 times/year covering textiles as art and craft (contemporary trends in fiber sculpture, weaving, quilting, surface design, stitchery, papermaking, basketry, felting, wearable art, knitting, fashion, crochet, mixed textile techniques, ethnic dying, fashion, eccentric tidbits, etc.) for textile artists, craftspeople, hobbyists, teachers, museum and gallery staffs, collectors and enthusiasts. Estab. 1975. Circ. 23,745. Pays 30 days after publication. Publishes ms an average of 4 months after acceptance. Byline given. Buys first rights. Accepts queries by mail. Sample copy for $5. Writer's guidelines for #10 SAE with 2 first-class stamps.

Nonfiction: "Please be very specific about your proposal. Also, an important consideration in accepting an article is the kind of photos that you can provide as illustration. We like to see photos in advance." Essays, historical/nostalgic (ethnic), interview/profile (artist), opinion, personal experience, photo feature, technical, education; trends; exhibition reviews; textile news; book reviews. Query with brief outline, prose synopsis, SASE and visuals. No phone or e-mail queries. Length: 250-2,000 words. **Pays $70-550.**

Photos: Color slides or b&w glossies must accompany every article. The more photos to choose from, the better. Please include a separate, number-keyed caption sheet. The names and addresses of those mentioned in the article or to whom the visuals are to be returned are necessary. Captions required.

Columns/Departments: Commentary (thoughtful opinion on a topic of interest to our readers), 400 words; Swatches (new ideas for fiber, unusual or offbeat subjects, work spaces, resources and marketing, techniques, materials, equipment, design and trends), 450 words and 2-4 photos; Profile (focuses on one artist), 450 words and 1 photo; Reviews (exhibits and shows; summarize quality, significance, focus and atmosphere, then evaluate selected pieces for aesthetic quality, content and technique—because we have an international readership, brief biographical notes or quotes might be pertinent for locally or regionally known artists), 500 words and 3-5 photos. (Do not cite works for which visuals are unavailable; you are not eligible to review a show in which you have participated as an artist, organizer, curator or juror.). **Pays $100-150.**

Tips: "Our writers are very familiar with the textile field, and this is what we look for in a new writer. Familiarity with textile techniques, history or events determines clarity of an article more than a particular style of writing. The writer should also be familiar with *Fiberarts* magazine. While the professional is essential to the editorial depth of *Fiberarts*, and must find timely information in the pages of the magazine, this is not our greatest audience. Our editorial philosophy is that the magazine must provide the non-professional textile enthusiast with the inspiration, support, useful information and direction to keep him or her excited, interested and committed. Although we address serious issues relating to the fiber arts as well as light, we're looking for an accessible rather than overly scholarly tone."

$ FIBRE FOCUS, Magazine of the Ontario Handweavers and Spinners, 217 Maki Ave., Sudbury, Ontario P3E 2P3, Canada. E-mail: karend@vianet.on.ca. Website: www.ohs.on.ca. **Contact:** Karen Danielson, editor. **90% freelance written.** Quarterly magazine covering handweaving, spinning, basketry, beading, and other fibre arts. "Our readers are weavers and spinners who also do dyeing, knitting, basketry, feltmaking, papermaking, sheep raising, and craft supply. All articles deal with some aspect of these crafts." Estab. 1957. Circ. 1,000. Pays within 30 days after publication. Byline given. Buys one-time rights. Editorial lead time 6 months. Submit seasonal material 6 months in advance. Accepts previously published material. Responds in 1 month to queries. Sample copy for $5 Canadian.

Nonfiction: How-to, interview/profile, new product, opinion, personal experience, technical, travel, book reviews. **Buys 40-60 mss/year.** Length: Varies. **Pays $25 Canadian/published page.**

Photos: Send photos with submission. Reviews 4×6 color prints. Buys one-time rights. Offers additional payment for photos accepted with ms. Captions, identification of subjects required.

Fiction: Humorous, slice-of-life vignettes. **Pays $25 Canadian/published page.**

Tips: "Visit the OHS website for current information."

$ $ FINE TOOL JOURNAL, Antique & Collectible Tools, Inc., 27 Fickett Rd., Pownal ME 04069. (207)688-4962. Fax: (207)688-4831. E-mail: ceb@finetoolj.com. Website: www.finetoolj.com. **Contact:** Clarence Blanchard, president. **90% freelance written.** Quarterly magazine specializing in older or antique hand tools from all traditional trades. Readers are primarily interested in woodworking tools, but some subscribers have interests in such areas as leatherworking, wrenches, kitchen and machinist tools. Readers range from beginners just getting into the hobby to advanced collectors and organizations. Estab. 1970. Circ. 2,500. Pays on publication. Publishes ms an average of 6 months after acceptance. Byline given. Offers $50 kill fee. Buys first, second serial (reprint) rights. Editorial lead time 9 months. Submit seasonal material 6 months in advance. Accepts queries by mail. Accepts previously published material. Responds in 2 months to queries; 3 months to mss. Sample copy for $5. Writer's guidelines for #10 SASE.

Nonfiction: "We're looking for articles about tools from all trades. Interests include collecting, preservation, history, values and price trends, traditional methods and uses, interviews with collectors/users/makers, etc. Most articles published will deal with vintage, pre-1950, hand tools. Also seeking articles on how to use specific tools or how a specific trade was carried out. However, how-to articles must be detailed and not just of general interest. We do on occasion run articles on modern toolmakers who produce traditional hand tools." General interest, historical/nostalgic, how-to (make, use, fix and tune tools), interview/profile, personal experience, photo feature, technical. **Buys 24 mss/year.** Send complete ms. Length: 400-2,000 words. **Pays $50-200.** Pays expenses of writers on assignment.

Photos: Send photos with submission. Reviews 4×5 prints. Buys all rights. Negotiates payment individually. Identification of subjects, model releases required.

Columns/Departments: Stanley Tools (new finds and odd types), 300-400 words; Tips of the Trade (how to use tools), 100-200 words. **Buys 12 mss/year.** Send complete ms. **Pays $30-60.**

Tips: "The easiest way to get published in the *Journal* is to have personal experience or know someone who can supply the detailed information. We are seeking articles that go deeper than general interest and that knowledge requires experience and/or research. Short of personal experience, find a subject that fits our needs and that interests you. Spend some time learning the ins and outs of the subject and with hard work and a little luck you will earn the right to write about it."

$ $ FINE WOODWORKING, The Taunton Press, P.O. Box 5506, Newtown CT 06470-5506. (203)426-8171. Fax: (203)270-6753. E-mail: fw@taunton.com. Website: www.taunton.com. Publisher: Tim Schreiner. **Contact:** Anatole Burkin, executive editor. Bimonthly magazine on woodworking in the small shop. "All writers are also skilled woodworkers. It's more important that a contributor be a woodworker than a writer. Our editors (also woodworkers) will provide assistance." Estab. 1975. Circ. 270,000. **Pays on acceptance.** Byline given. Offers variable kill fee. Buys first rights. Rights to republish in anthologies and use in promo pieces Submit seasonal material 6 months in advance. Accepts simultaneous submissions. Responds in 2 months to queries. Writer's guidelines free and online.

> "We're looking for good articles on almost all aspects of woodworking from the basics of tool use, stock preparation and joinery to specialized techniques and finishing. We're especially keen on articles about shop-built tools, jigs and fixtures or any stage of design, construction, finishing and installation of cabinetry and furniture. Whether the subject involves fundamental methods or advanced techniques, we look for high-quality workmanship, thoughtful designs, safe and proper procedures."

Nonfiction: How-to (woodworking). "No specs—our editors would rather see more than less." **Buys 120 mss/year.** Query with proposal letter. **Pays $150/magazine page for assigned articles.** Sometimes pays expenses of writers on assignment.

Photos: Send photos with submission. Reviews contact sheets, negatives, transparencies, prints. Buys one-time rights. Captions, identification of subjects, model releases required.

Columns/Departments: Notes & Comment (topics of interest to woodworkers); Question & Answer (woodworking Q&A); Methods of Work (shop tips); Tools & Materials (short reviews of new tools). **Buys 400 mss/year. Pays $10-150/published page.**

> The online magazine carries original content not found in the print edition. Contact: Tim Sams, online editor.

Tips: "Send for authors guidelines and follow them. Stories about woodworking reported by non-woodworkers are *not* used. Our magazine is essentially reader-written by woodworkers."

$ $ FINESCALE MODELER, Kalmbach Publishing Co., 21027 Crossroads Circle, P.O. Box 1612, Waukesha WI 53187. (414)796-8776. Fax: (414)796-1383. E-mail: tthompson@finescale.com. Website: www.finescale.com. **Contact:** Paul Boyer. **80% freelance written.** Eager to work with new/unpublished writers. Magazine published 10 times/year "devoted to how-to-do-it modeling information for scale model builders who build non-operating aircraft, tanks, boats, automobiles, figures, dioramas, and science fiction and fantasy models." Circ. 60,000. **Pays on acceptance.** Publishes ms an average of 14 months after acceptance. Byline given. Buys all rights. Responds in 6 weeks to queries; 3 months to mss. Sample copy for 9×12 SAE and 3 first-class stamps.

- *Finescale Modeler* is especially looking for how-to articles for car modelers.

Nonfiction: How-to (build scale models), technical (research information for building models). Query or send complete ms. Length: 750-3,000 words. **Pays $55 published page minimum.**

Photos: Send photos with submission. Reviews transparencies, color prints. Buys one-time rights. Pays $7.50 minimum for transparencies and $5 minimum for color prints. Captions, identification of subjects required.

Columns/Departments: *FSM* Showcase (photos plus description of model); *FSM* Tips and Techniques (model building hints and tips). **Buys 25-50 mss/year.** Send complete ms. **Pays $25-50.**

Tips: "A freelancer can best break in first through hints and tips, then through feature articles. Most people who write for *FSM* are modelers first, writers second. This is a specialty magazine for a special, quite expert audience. Essentially, 99% of our writers will come from that audience."

$ $ GENEALOGICAL COMPUTING, Ancestry, Inc., 360 W. 4800 N., Provo UT 84604. (801)705-7000. Fax: (801)705-7001. E-mail: gceditor@ancestry.com. Website: www.ancestry.com. **Contact:** Elizabeth Kelly Kerstens, managing editor. **85% freelance written.** Quarterly magazine covering genealogy and computers. Estab. 1980. Circ. 32,000. Pays on publication. Publishes ms an average of 4 months after acceptance. Byline given. Buys all rights. Editorial lead time 4 months. Submit seasonal material 4 months in advance.
Nonfiction: How-to, interview/profile, new product, technical. **Buys 40 mss/year.** Query. Length: 1,500-2,500 words. **Pays $75-500.**
Reprints: Accepts previously published submissions. Pays 75% of amount paid for an original article.

$ $ THE HOME SHOP MACHINIST, 2779 Aero Park Dr., Traverse City MI 49686. (616)946-3712. Fax: (616)946-3289. E-mail: jrice@villagepress.com. Website: www.villagepress.com. **Contact:** Joe D. Rice, editor. **95% freelance written.** Bimonthly magazine covering machining and metalworking for the hobbyist. Circ. 34,000. Pays on publication. Publishes ms an average of 2 years after acceptance. Byline given. Buys first North American serial rights. Responds in 2 months to queries. Sample copy for free. Writer's guidelines for 9×12 SASE.
Nonfiction: How-to (projects designed to upgrade present shop equipment or hobby model projects that require machining), technical (should pertain to metalworking, machining, drafting, layout, welding or foundry work for the hobbyist). No fiction or "people" features. **Buys 40 mss/year.** Query with or without published clips or send complete ms. Length: open—"whatever it takes to do a thorough job." **Pays $40/published page, plus $9/published photo.**
Photos: Send photos with submission. Pays $9-40 for 5×7 b&w prints; $70/page for camera-ready art; $40 for b&w cover photo. Captions, identification of subjects required.
Columns/Departments: Book Reviews; New Product Reviews; Micro-Machining; Foundry. Length: 600-1,500 words. "Become familiar with our magazine before submitting." **Buys 25-30 mss/year.** Query. **Pays $40-70.**
Fillers: Machining tips/shortcuts. **Buys 12-15/year.** Length: 100-300 words. **Pays $30-48.**
Tips: "The writer should be experienced in the area of metalworking and machining; should be extremely thorough in explanations of methods, processes—always with an eye to safety; and should provide good quality b&w photos and/or clear dimensioned drawings to aid in description. Visuals are of increasing importance to our readers. Carefully planned photos, drawings and charts will carry a submission to our magazine much farther along the path to publication."

$ $ KITPLANES, For designers, builders and pilots of experimental aircraft, A Primedia Publication, 8745 Aero Dr., Suite 105, San Diego CA 92123. (858)694-0491. Fax: (858)694-8147. E-mail: dave@kitplanes.com. Website: www.kitplanes.com. Managing Editor: Mary Bernard. **Contact:** Dave Martin, editor. **80% freelance written.** Eager to work with new/unpublished writers. Monthly magazine covering self-construction of private aircraft for pilots and builders. Estab. 1984. Circ. 72,000. Pays on publication. Publishes ms an average of 3 months after acceptance. Byline given. exclusive complete serial rights Submit seasonal material 6 months in advance. Accepts queries by mail, e-mail. Responds in 2 weeks to queries; 6 weeks to mss. Sample copy for $6. Writer's guidelines free.
Nonfiction: "We are looking for articles on specific construction techniques, the use of tools, both hand and power, in aircraft building, the relative merits of various materials, conversions of engines from automobiles for aviation use, installation of instruments and electronics." General interest, how-to, interview/profile, new product, personal experience, photo feature, technical. No general-interest aviation articles, or "My First Solo" type of articles. **Buys 80 mss/year.** Query. Length: 500-3,000 words. **Pays $70-600 including story photos for assigned articles.**
Photos: State availability of or send photos with submission. Buys one-time rights. Pays $300 for cover photos. Captions, identification of subjects required.
Tips: "*Kitplanes* contains very specific information—a writer must be extremely knowledgeable in the field. Major features are entrusted only to known writers. I cannot emphasize enough that articles must be directed at the individual aircraft builder. We need more 'how-to' photo features in all areas of homebuilt aircraft."

$ KNITTING DIGEST, House of White Birches, 306 E. Parr Rd., Berne IN 46711. (260)589-4000. Fax: (219)589-8093. E-mail: knitting_digest@whitebirches.com. Website: www.whitebirches.com. **Contact:** Jeanne Stauffer, editor. **100% freelance written.** Bimonthly magazine covering knitting designs and patterns. "We print only occasional articles, but are always open to knitting designs and proposals." Estab. 1993. Circ. 50,000. Pays within 6 months. Publishes ms an average of 11 months after acceptance. Byline given. Offers 100% kill fee. Buys all rights. Accepts queries by mail, e-mail. Accepts simultaneous submissions. Responds in 2 months to queries; 6 months to mss. Sample copy not available. Writer's guidelines for #10 SASE.
Nonfiction: How-to (knitting skills), technical (knitting field). **Buys 4-6 mss/year.** Send complete ms. Length: 500 words maximum. **Pays variable amount. Also pays in contributor copies.**
Tips: "Clear concise writing. Humor is appreciated in this field, as much as technical tips. The magazine is a digest, so space is limited. All submissions must be typed and double-spaced."

$ $ KNIVES ILLUSTRATED, The Premier Cutlery Magazine, 265 S. Anita Dr., Suite 120, Orange CA 92868-3310. (423)894-8319. Fax: (423)892-7254. E-mail: knivesillustrated@yahoo.com. Website: www.knivesillustrated.com. **Contact:** Bruce Voyles, editor. **40-50% freelance written.** Bimonthly magazine covering high-quality factory and custom knives. "We publish articles on different types of factory and custom knives, how-to make knives, technical articles, shop tours, articles on knife makers and artists. Must have knowledge about knives and the people who use and make them. We feature the full range of custom and high tech production knives, from miniatures to swords, leaving nothing untouched. We're also known for our outstanding how-to articles and technical features on equipment, materials and knife making supplies. We do not feature knife maker profiles as such, although we do spotlight some makers by featuring a variety of their knives and insight into their background and philosophy." Estab. 1987. Circ. 35,000. Pays on publication. Byline given. Editorial lead time 3 months. Accepts queries by mail, e-mail, fax. Responds in 2 weeks to queries. Sample copy available. Writer's guidelines for #10 SASE.

Nonfiction: General interest, historical/nostalgic, how-to, interview/profile, new product, photo feature, technical. **Buys 35-40 mss/year.** Query. Length: 400-2,000 words. **Pays $100-500.**

Photos: Send photos with submission. Reviews 35mm, $2\frac{1}{4} \times 2\frac{1}{4}$, 4×5 transparencies, 5×7 prints prints, electronic images in TIF, GIP or JPG Mac format. Negotiates payment individually. Captions, identification of subjects, model releases required.

Tips: "Most of our contributors are involved with knives, either as collectors, makers, engravers, etc. To write about this subject requires knowledge. A 'good' writer can do OK if they study some recent issues. If you are interested in submitting work to *Knives Illustrated* magazine, it is suggested you analyze at least two or three different editions to get a feel for the magazine. It is also recommended that you call or mail in your query to determine if we are interested in the topic you have in mind. While verbal or written approval may be given, all articles are still received on a speculation basis. We cannot approve any article until we have it in hand, whereupon we will make a final decision as to its suitability for our use. Bear in mind we do not suggest you go to the trouble to write an article if there is doubt we can use it promptly."

LAPIDARY JOURNAL, 60 Chestnut Ave., Suite 201, Devon PA 19333-1312. (610)964-6300. Fax: (610)293-0977. E-mail: lj_editorial@primediasi.com. Website: www.lapidaryjournal.com. Editor: Merle White. **Contact:** Hazel Wheaton, managing editor. **70% freelance written.** Monthly magazine covering gem, bead and jewelry arts. "Our audience is hobbyists who usually have some knowledge of and proficiency in the subject before they start reading. Our style is conversational and informative. There are how-to projects and profiles of artists and materials." Estab. 1947. Circ. 53,000. **Pays on acceptance.** Publishes ms an average of 4 months after acceptance. Byline given. one-time and worldwide rights. Editorial lead time 3 months. Accepts queries by mail, e-mail. Sample copy online.

Nonfiction: Looks for conversational and lively narratives with quotes and anecdotes; Q&A's; interviews. How-to (jewelry/craft), interview/profile, new product, personal experience, technical, travel. Special issues: Bead Annual, Gemstone Annual, Jewelry Design issue. **Buys 100 mss/year.** Query. Length: 1,500-2,500 words preferred; 1,000-3,500 words acceptable; longer works occasionally published serially. Pays some expenses of writers on assignment.

Reprints: Send photocopy.

Tips: "Some knowledge of jewelry, gemstones and/or minerals is a definite asset. *Jewelry Journal* is a section within *Lapidary Journal* that offers illustrated, step-by-step instruction in gem cutting, jewelry making, and beading. Please request a copy of the *Jewelry Journal* guidelines for greater detail."

$ $ ☒ THE LEATHER CRAFTERS & SADDLERS JOURNAL, 331 Annette Court, Rhinelander WI 54501-2902. (715)362-5393. Fax: (715)362-5391. E-mail: journal@newnorth.net. Managing Editor: Dorothea Reis. **Contact:** William R. Reis, publisher. **100% freelance written.** Bimonthly magazine. "A leather-working publication with how-to, step-by-step instructional articles using full-size patterns for leathercraft, leather art, custom saddle, boot and harness making, etc. A complete resource for leather, tools, machinery, and allied materials, plus leather industry news." Estab. 1990. Circ. 9,000. Pays on publication. Publishes ms an average of 2 months after acceptance. Byline given. Buys first North American serial, second serial (reprint) rights. Submit seasonal material 6 months in advance. Accepts queries by mail, e-mail, fax, phone. Accepts previously published material. Accepts simultaneous submissions. Responds in 1 month to mss. Sample copy for $5. Writer's guidelines for #10 SASE.

O→ Break in with a how-to, step-by-step leather item article from beginner through masters and saddlemaking.

Nonfiction: "I want only articles that include hands-on, step-by-step, how-to information." How-to (crafts and arts, and any other projects using leather). **Buys 75 mss/year.** Send complete ms. Length: 500-2,500 words. **Pays $20-250 for assigned articles; $20-150 for unsolicited articles.**

Reprints: Send tearsheet or photocopy. Pays 50% of amount paid for an original article.

Photos: Send good contrast color print photos and full-size patterns and/or full-size photo-carve patterns with submission. Lack of these reduces payment amount. Captions required.

Columns/Departments: Beginners; Intermediate; Artists; Western Design; Saddlemakers; International Design; and Letters (the open exchange of information between all peoples). Length: 500-2,500 words on all. **Buys 75 mss/year.** Send complete ms. **Pays 5¢/word.**

Fillers: Anecdotes, facts, gags to be illustrated by cartoonist, newsbreaks. Length: 25-200 words. **Pays $5-20.**

Tips: "We want to work with people who understand and know leathercraft and are interested in passing on their knowledge to others. We would prefer to interview people who have achieved a high level in leathercraft skill."

$ LINN'S STAMP NEWS, Amos Press, 911 Vandemark Rd., P.O. Box 29, Sidney OH 45365. (937)498-0801. Fax: (800)340-9501. E-mail: linns@linns.com. Website: www.linns.com. Editor: Michael Laurence. **Contact:** Michael Schreiber, managing editor. **50% freelance written.** Weekly tabloid on the stamp collecting hobby. All articles must be about philatelic collectibles. Our goal at *Linn's* is to create a weekly publication that is indispensable to stamp collectors. Estab. 1928. Circ. 51,000. Pays within one month of publication. Publishes ms an average of 3 months after acceptance. Byline given. Buys first rights. first worldwide serial rights Submit seasonal material 2 months in advance. Responds in 6 weeks to queries. Sample copy for free. Writer's guidelines by e-mail.

Nonfiction: General interest, historical/nostalgic, how-to, interview/profile, technical, club and show news, current issues, auction realization and recent discoveries. "No articles merely giving information on background of stamp subject. Must have philatelic information included." **Buys 50 mss/year.** Send complete ms. Length: 500 words maximum. **Pays $50.** Sometimes pays expenses of writers on assignment.
Photos: Good illustrations a must. Provide captions on a separate sheet of paper. Send scans with submission. Reviews digital color at twice actual size (300 dpi). Buys all rights. Offers no additional payment for photos accepted with ms. Captions required.
Tips: "Check and double check all facts. Footnotes and bibliographies are not appropriate to newspaper style. Work citation into the text. Even though your subject might be specialized, write understandably. Explain terms. *Linn's* features are aimed at a broad audience of relatively novice collectors. Keep this audience in mind. Provide information in such a way to make stamp collecting more interesting to more people."

$ ☆ LOST TREASURE, INC., P.O. Box 451589, Grove OK 74345. Fax: (918)786-2192. E-mail: managingeditor osttreasure.com. Website: www.losttreasure.com. **Contact:** Patsy Beyerl, managing editor. **75% freelance written.** Monthly and annual magazines covering lost treasure. Estab. 1966. Circ. 55,000. Pays on publication. Byline given. Buys all rights. Accepts queries by mail, e-mail, fax. Responds in 1 month to queries; 2 months to mss. Sample copy for #10 SASE. Writer's guidelines for 10×13 SAE with $1.47 postage or online.
Nonfiction: *Lost Treasure*, a monthly, is composed of lost treasure stories, legends, folklore, how-to articles, treasure hunting club news, who's who in treasure hunting, tips. Length: 500-1,500 words. *Treasure Cache*, an annual, contains stories about documented treasure caches with a sidebar from the author telling the reader how to search for the cache highlighted in the story. **Buys 225 mss/year.** Query on *Treasure Cache* only. Length: 1,000-2,000 words. **Pays 4¢/word.**
Photos: Black & white or color prints, hand-drawn or copied maps, art with source credit with mss will help sell your story. We are always looking for cover photos with or without accompanying ms. Pays $100/published cover photo. Must be 35mm color slides, vertical. Pays $5/published photo. Captions required.
Tips: "We are only interested in treasures that can be found with metal detectors. Queries welcome but not required. If you write about famous treasures and lost mines, be sure we haven't used your selected topic recently and story must have a new slant or new information. Source documentation required. How-tos should cover some aspect of treasure hunting and how-to steps should be clearly defined. If you have a *Treasure Cache* story we will, if necessary, help the author with the sidebar telling how to search for the cache in the story. *Lost Treasure* articles should coordinate with theme issues when possible."

$ $ MEMORY MAKERS, The First Source for Scrapbooking Ideas, Satellite Press, 12365 Huron St., Suite 500, Denver CO 80234. (303)452-1968. Fax: (303)452-2164. E-mail: editorial@memorymakersmagazine.com. Website: www.memorymakersmagazine.com. **Contact:** Deborah Mock, editor. **50% freelance written.** Bimonthly magazine covering creative scrapbook ideas and craft techniques. "*Memory Makers* is an international magazine that showcases ideas and stories of scrapbookers. It includes articles with information, instructions, and products that apply to men and women who make creative scrapbooks." Estab. 1996. Circ. 225,000. Pays on project completion. Publishes ms an average of 6 months after acceptance. Byline given. Buys first rights. Editorial lead time 6 months. Submit seasonal material 6 months in advance. Accepts queries by mail, e-mail. Accepts simultaneous submissions. Writer's guidelines for #10 SASE or on website.

O→ Break in with articles on "unique craft techniques that can apply to scrapbooking, and personal stories of how scrapbooking has impacted someone's life."

Nonfiction: Historical/nostalgic, how-to (scrapbooking), inspirational, interview/profile, new product, personal experience, photography. No "all-encompassing how-to scrapbook" articles. **Buys 6-10 mss/year.** Query with published clips. Length: 1,000-1,500 words. **Pays $500-750.**
Columns/Departments: Keeping It Safe (issues surrounding the safe preservation of scrapbooks); Scrapbooking 101 (how-to scrapbooking techniques for beginners); Photojournaling (new and useful ideas for improving scrapbook journaling); Modern Memories (computer and modern technology scrapbooking issues), all 600-800 words. Query with published clips. **Pays $200-350.**

$ MINIATURE QUILTS, Chitra Publications, 2 Public Ave., Montrose PA 18801. (570)278-1984. Fax: (570)278-2223. E-mail: chitraed@epix.net. Website: www.quilttownusa.com. **Contact:** Joyce Libal, senior editor. **40% freelance written.** Bimonthly magazine on miniature quilts. "We seek articles of an instructional nature (all techniques), profiles of talented quiltmakers, and informational articles on all aspects of miniature quilts. Miniature is defined as quilts made up of blocks smaller than 5 inches." Estab. 1990. Circ. 70,000. Pays on publication. Publishes ms an average of 6 months after acceptance. Byline given. Buys second serial (reprint) rights. Submit seasonal material 8 months in advance. Accepts queries by mail, fax. Responds in 2 months to queries. Writer's guidelines for SASE or online.

O→ "Best bet—a quilter writing about a new or unusual quilting technique."

Nonfiction: How-to, interview/profile (quilters who make small quilts), photo feature (about noteworthy miniature quilts or exhibits). Query. Length: 1,500 words maximum. **Pays $75/published page of text.**
Photos: Send photos with submission. Reviews 35mm slides and larger transparencies. Offers $20/photo. Captions, identification of subjects, model releases required.
Tips: "We're looking for articles (with slides or transparencies) on quilts in museum collections."

$ $ MODEL RAILROADER, P.O. Box 1612, Waukesha WI 53187. Fax: (262)796-1142. E-mail: mrmag@mrmag.c om. Website: www.trains.com. **Contact:** Russ Larson, editor/publisher. Monthly magazine for hobbyists interested in scale model railroading. "We publish articles on all aspects of model-railroading and on prototype (real) railroading as a subject for modeling." Byline given. exclusive rights Accepts queries by mail, e-mail, fax. Responds in 2 months to queries.

O→ "Study publication before submitting material." First-hand knowledge of subject almost always necessary for acceptable slant.

Nonfiction: Wants construction articles on specific model railroad projects (structures, cars, locomotives, scenery, benchwork, etc.). Also photo stories showing model railroads. Query. **Pays base rate of $90/page.**

Photos: Buys photos with detailed descriptive captions only. Pays $15 and up, depending on size and use. Full color cover earns $200.

Tips: "Before you prepare and submit any article, you should write us a short letter of inquiry describing what you want to do. We can then tell you if it fits our needs and save you from working on something we don't want."

$ $ MONITORING TIMES, Grove Enterprises, Inc., 7540 Hwy. 64 W., Brasstown NC 28902-0098. (828)837-9200. Fax: (828)837-2216. E-mail: mteditor@grove-ent.com. Website: www.grove-ent.com. Publisher: Robert Grove. **Contact:** Rachel Baughn, editor. **15% freelance written.** Monthly magazine for radio hobbyists. Estab. 1982. Circ. 25,000. Pays on publication. Publishes ms an average of 4 months after acceptance. Byline given. Buys first North American serial, second serial (reprint) rights. Submit seasonal material 4 months in advance. Accepts queries by mail, e-mail. Accepts previously published material. Responds in 1 month to queries. Sample copy and writer's guidelines for 9×12 SAE and 9 first-class stamps.

O→ Break in with a shortwave station profile or topic, or scanning topics of broad interest.

Nonfiction: General interest, how-to, humor, interview/profile, personal experience, photo feature, technical. **Buys 50 mss/year.** Query. Length: 1,500-3,000 words. **Pays average of $50/published page.**

Reprints: Send photocopy and information about when and where the material previously appeared. Pays 25% of amount paid for an original article.

Photos: Send photos with submission. Buys one-time rights. Captions required.

Columns/Departments: "Query managing editor."

Tips: "Need articles on radio communications systems and shortwave broadcasters. We are accepting more technical projects."

$ THE NUMISMATIST, American Numismatic Association, 818 N. Cascade Ave., Colorado Springs CO 80903-3279. (719)632-2646. Fax: (719)634-4085. E-mail: anaedi@money.org. **Contact:** Barbara Gregory, editor/publisher. Monthly magazine covering numismatics (study of coins, tokens, medals, and paper money). Estab. 1888. Circ. 28,500. Pays on publication. Publishes ms an average of 1 year after acceptance. Byline given. Buys perpetual, but nonexclusive rights. Editorial lead time 2 months. Sample copy for free.

Nonfiction: "Submitted material should present new information and/or constitute a contribution to numismatic education for the experienced collector and beginner alike." Book excerpts, essays, historical/nostalgic, opinion, technical. Special issues: First Strike, a supplement for young or new collectors, is published twice yearly, in December and June. **Buys 60 mss/year.** Query or send complete ms. Length: 3,500 words maximum. **Pays $3/column inch.** Sometimes pays expenses of writers on assignment.

Photos: Send photos with submission. Negotiates payment individually. Captions, identification of subjects required.

Columns/Departments: Send complete ms. **Pays $25-100.**

PACK-O-FUN, Projects For Kids & Families, Clapper Communications, 2400 Devon Ave., Des Plaines IL 60018-4618. (847)635-5800. Fax: (847)635-6311. Website: www.craftideas.com. Editor: Billie Ciancio. **Contact:** Irene Mueller, managing editor. **85% freelance written.** Bimonthly magazine covering crafts and activities for kids and those working with kids. Estab. 1951. Circ. 102,000. Pays 45 days after signed contract. Byline given. Buys all rights. Editorial lead time 6 months. Submit seasonal material 8 months in advance. Accepts queries by mail, fax. Accepts previously published material. Accepts simultaneous submissions. Responds in 2 months to queries. Sample copy for $3.50 or online.

Nonfiction: "We request quick and easy, inexpensive crafts and activities. Projects must be original, and complete instructions are required upon acceptance." **Payment negotiable.**

Reprints: Send tearsheet and information about when and where the material previously appeared.

Photos: Photos of project may be submitted in place of project at query stage.

Tips: "*Pack-O-Fun* is looking for original how-to projects for kids and those working with kids. Write simple instructions for crafts to be done by children ages 5-13 years. We're looking for recyclable ideas for throwaways. We accept fiction if accompanied by a craft or in skit form (appropriate for classrooms, scouts or Bible school groups). It would be helpful to check out our magazine before submitting."

$ $ PIECEWORK MAGAZINE, Interweave Press, Inc., 201 E. Fourth St., Loveland CO 80537-5655. (970)669-7672. Fax: (970)667-8317. E-mail: piecework@interweave.com. Website: www.interweave.com. Editor: Jeane Hutchins. **Contact:** Jake Rexus, assistant editor. **90% freelance written.** Bimonthly magazine covering needlework history. "*PieceWork* celebrates the rich tradition of needlework and the history of the people behind it. Stories and projects on embroidery, cross-stitch, knitting, crocheting and quilting, along with other textile arts, are featured in each issue." Estab. 1993. Circ. 60,000. Pays on publication. Byline given. Offers 30% kill fee. Buys first North American serial rights. Editorial lead time 6 months. Submit seasonal material 6 months in advance. Accepts queries by mail, e-mail, fax, phone. Responds in 6 months to queries. Sample copy and writer's guidelines free.

Nonfiction: Book excerpts, historical/nostalgic, how-to, interview/profile, new product. No contemporary needlework articles. **Buys 25-30 mss/year.** Send complete ms. Length: 1,000-2,000 words. **Pays $100/printed page.**
Photos: State availability of or send photos with submission. Reviews transparencies, prints. Buys one-time rights. Captions, identification of subjects, model releases required.
Tips: "Submit a well-researched article on a historical aspect of needlework complete with information on visuals and suggestion for accompanying project."

$ $ $ POPTRONICS, Gernsback Publications, Inc., 275-G Marcus Blvd., Hauppauge NY 11788. (631)592-6720. Fax: (631)592-6723. E-mail: clamorte@gernsback.com or popeditor@gernsback.com. Website: www.gernsback.com. **Contact:** Chris LaMorte, editor. **75% freelance written.** Monthly magazine on electronics technology and electronics construction, such as communications, computers, test equipment, components, video and audio. 92 year history in electronic publications. The new magazine *Poptronics* is a combination of 2 older publications, one of which began in 1929. Estab. 2000. Circ. 104,000. Publishes ms an average of 6 months after acceptance. Byline given. Buys all rights. Submit seasonal material 6 months in advance. Accepts queries by mail, e-mail. Responds in 2 months to queries; 4 months to mss. Times vary for unsolicited mss. Sample copy and writer's guidelines free or online.
Nonfiction: How-to (electronic project construction), new product. **Buys 150-200 mss/year.** Send complete ms. Length: 1,000-10,000 words. **Pays $150-700 for assigned articles; $100-700 for unsolicited articles.**
Photos: Send photos with submission. Buys all rights. Offers no additional payment for photos accepted with ms. Captions, identification of subjects, model releases required.

$ POPULAR COMMUNICATIONS, CQ Communications, Inc., 25 Newbridge Rd., Hicksville NY 11801. (516)681-2922. Fax: (516)681-2926. E-mail: popularcom@aol.com. Website: www.popular-communications.com. **Contact:** Harold Ort, editor. **25% freelance written.** Monthly magazine covering the radio communications hobby. Estab. 1982. Circ. 40,000. Pays on publication. Publishes ms an average of 6 months after acceptance. Byline given. Buys first North American serial rights. Editorial lead time 3 months. Submit seasonal material 6 months in advance. Accepts queries by mail, e-mail. Responds in 1 month to queries; 2 months to mss. Sample copy for free. Writer's guidelines for #10 SASE.
Nonfiction: General interest, how-to (antenna construction), humor, new product, photo feature, technical. **Buys 6-10 mss/year.** Query. Length: 1,800-3,000 words. **Pays $35/printed page.**
Photos: State availability with submission. Negotiates payment individually. Captions, identification of subjects, model releases required.
Tips: "Either be a radio enthusiast or know one who can help you before sending us an article."

$ $ $ $ POPULAR MECHANICS, Hearst Corp., 810 Seventh Ave., 6th Floor, New York NY 10019. (212)649-2000. Fax: (212)586-5562. E-mail: popularmechanics@hearst.com. Website: www.popularmechanics.com. **Contact:** Joe Oldham, editor-in-chief; Sarah Deem, managing editor. **up to 50% freelance written.** Monthly magazine on automotive, home improvement, science, boating, outdoors, electronics. "We are a men's service magazine that tries to address the diverse interests of today's male, providing him with information to improve the way he lives. We cover stories from do-it-yourself projects to technological advances in aerospace, military, automotive and so on." Estab. 1902. Circ. 1,400,000. **Pays on acceptance.** Publishes ms an average of 6 months after acceptance. Byline given. Offers 25% kill fee. Buys all rights. Submit seasonal material 6 months in advance. Responds in 3 weeks to queries; 1 month to mss. Writer's guidelines for SASE or online.
Nonfiction: General interest, how-to (shop projects, car fix-its), new product, technical. Special issues: Boating Guide (February); Home Improvement Guide (April); Consumer Electronics Guide (May); New Cars Guide (October); Woodworking Guide (November). No historical, editorial, or critique pieces. **Buys 2 mss/year.** Query with or without published clips or send complete ms. Length: 500-1,500 words. **Pays $500-1,500 for assigned articles; $300-1,000 for unsolicited articles.** Sometimes pays expenses of writers on assignment.
Photos: Usually assigns a photographer. "If you have photos, send with submission." Reviews prints, slides. Buys all rights. Offers no additional payment for photos accepted with ms. Captions, identification of subjects, model releases required.
Columns/Departments: New Cars (latest and hottest cars out of Detroit and Europe), Car Care (Maintenance basics, How It Works, Fix-Its and New products: send to Don Chaikin. Electronics, Audio, Home Video, Computers, Photography: send to Tobey Grumet. Boating (new equipment, how-tos, fishing tips), Outdoors (gear, vehicles, outdoor adventures): send to Cliff Gromer. Home & Shop Journal: send to Steve Willson. Science (latest developments), Tech Update (breakthroughs) and Aviation (sport aviation, homebuilt aircraft, new commercial aircraft, civil aeronautics): send to Jim Wilson. All columns are about 800 words.

The online magazine contains material not found in the print edition. Contact: Ken Juran, online editor.

$ $ POPULAR WOODWORKING, F&W Publications, 4700 E. Galbraith Rd., Cincinnati OH 45236. (513)531-2690, ext 1407. E-mail: popwood@fwpubs.com. Website: www.popularwoodworking.com. Editor: Steve Shanesy. **Contact:** Christopher Schwarz, senior editor. **45% freelance written.** Bimonthly magazine. "*Popular Woodworking* invites woodworkers of all levels into a community of professionals who share their hard-won shop experience through in-depth projects and technique articles, which help the readers hone their existing skills and develop new ones. Related stories increase the readers' understanding and enjoyment of their craft. Any project submitted must be aesthetically pleasing, of sound construction and offer a challenge to readers. On the average, we use four freelance features per issue. Our primary needs are 'how-to' articles on woodworking. Our secondary need is for articles that will inspire discussion concerning woodworking. Tone of articles should be conversational and informal, as if the writer is speaking directly to the reader. Our readers are the woodworking hobbyist and small woodshop owner. Writers should have an extensive knowledge of woodworking, or be able to communicate information gained from woodworkers." Estab. 1981. Circ. 200,000. **Pays on acceptance.** Publishes ms an average of 10 months after acceptance. Byline given. Buys first world rights. Submit seasonal material 6 months in advance. Accepts queries by mail, e-mail, fax, phone. Accepts previously published material. Responds in 2 months to queries. Sample copy for $4.50 and 9×12 SAE with 6 first-class stamps or online.

- "The project must be well designed, well constructed, well built and well finished. Technique pieces must have practical application."

Nonfiction: How-to (on woodworking projects, with plans), humor (woodworking anecdotes), technical (woodworking techniques). Special issues: Workshop issue, tool buying guide. No tool reviews. **Buys 40 mss/year.** Query with or without published clips or send complete ms. **Pay starts at $150/published page**.

Reprints: Send photocopy with rights for sale noted and information about when and where the material previously appeared. Pays 25% of amount paid for an original article.

Photos: Photographic quality affects acceptance. Need sharp close-up color photos of step-by-step construction process. Send photos with submission. Reviews color only, slides and transparencies, 3×5 glossies acceptable. Captions, identification of subjects required.

Columns/Departments: Tricks of the Trade (helpful techniques), Out of the Woodwork (thoughts on woodworking as a profession or hobby, can be humorous or serious), 500-1,500 words. **Buys 20 mss/year.** Query.

- The online version of this publication contains material not found in the print edition. Contact: Christopher Schwarz.

Tips: "Write an 'Out of the Woodwork' column for us and then follow up with photos of your projects. Submissions should include materials list, complete diagrams (blueprints not necessary), and discussion of the step-by-step process. We have become more selective on accepting only practical, attractive projects with quality construction. We are also looking for more original topics for our other articles."

$ THE PYSANKA, Starwind Press, P.O. Box 98, Ripley OH 45167. (937)392-4549. E-mail: susannah@techgallery.com. **Contact:** Susannah West, editor. **90% freelance written.** Quarterly newsletter covering wax-resist egg decoration. "*The Pysanka* examines the art of wax-resist egg decoration (pysanky). Its audience is artists and hobbysists who create this style egg." Estab. 2000. Circ. 100. **Pays on acceptance.** Publishes ms an average of 3 months after acceptance. Byline given. Offers 100% kill fee. Buys first North American serial rights. Editorial lead time 3 months. Submit seasonal material 3 months in advance. Accepts queries by mail, e-mail. Accepts previously published material. Responds in 2 months to queries; 2 months to mss. Sample copy for $3. Writer's guidelines for #10 SASE.

Nonfiction: Historical/nostalgic, how-to, interview/profile, new product, opinion, personal experience, photo feature, travel. **Buys 16-20 mss/year.** Query or send complete ms. Length: 900-2,000 words. **Pays $10.**

Reprints: Accepts previously published submissions.

Photos: State availability with submission. Negotiates payment individually. Identification of subjects required.

Columns/Departments: Around and About (reviews of interesting places to visit related to the craft), 500-1,000 words; Passing the Torch (workshop experiences), 200-500 words; On the Pysanky Bookshelf (book reviews), 100-200 words. **Buys 8-12 mss/year.** Query. **Pays $5-10.**

Fiction: Ethnic. **Buys 4 mss/year.** Send complete ms. Length: 2,000-5,000 words. **Pays 1¢/word.**

Tips: "The writer should be familiar with the wax-resist style of egg decoration, ideally an artist or hobbyist who makes this style of egg."

$ QUILT WORLD, House of White Birches, 306 E. Parr Rd., Berne IN 46711. (219)589-4000. Fax: (207)794-3290. E-mail: hatch@agate.net. **Contact:** Sandra L. Hatch, editor. **100% freelance written.** Works with a small number of new/unpublished writers each year. Bimonthly magazine covering quilting. "*Quilt World* is a general quilting publication. We accept articles about special quilters, techniques, coverage of unusual quilts at quilt shows, special interest quilts, human interest articles and patterns. We include 5-8 patterns in every issue. Reader is 30-70 years old, midwestern." Circ. 130,000. Pays 45 days after acceptance. Byline given. Buys first, one-time, all rights. Submit seasonal material 10 months in advance. Accepts queries by mail, e-mail. Responds in 3 months to queries. Writer's guidelines for #10 SASE.

Nonfiction: How-to, interview/profile (quilters), new product (quilt products), photo feature, technical. **Buys 18-24 mss/year.** Query or send complete ms. Length: Open. **Pays $50-100.**

Reprints: Send photocopy and information about when and where the material previously appeared.

Photos: Send photos with submission. Reviews transparencies, prints. Buys all or one-time rights. Offers $15/photo (except covers). Identification of subjects required.

Tips: "Read several recent issues for style and content."

$ $ QUILTING TODAY MAGAZINE, Chitra Publications, 2 Public Ave., Montrose PA 18801. (570)278-1984. Fax: (570)278-2223. E-mail: chitraed@epix.net. Website: www.quilttownusa.com. **Contact:** Joyce Libal, senior editor. **50% freelance written.** Bimonthly magazine on quilting, traditional and contemporary. "We seek articles that will cover 1 or 2 full pages (800 words each); informative to the general quilting public, present new ideas, interviews, instructional, etc." Estab. 1986. Circ. 70,000. Pays on publication. Publishes ms an average of 6 months after acceptance. Byline given. Buys second serial (reprint) rights. Submit seasonal material 8 months in advance. Accepts queries by mail, fax. Responds in 1 month to queries; 2 months to mss. Writer's guidelines for SASE or online.

O→ "Best bet—a quilter writing about a new or unusual quilting technique."

Nonfiction: Book excerpts, essays, how-to (for various quilting techniques), humor, interview/profile, new product, opinion, personal experience, photo feature. **Buys 20-30 mss/year.** Query or send complete ms. Length: 800-1,600 words. **Pays $75/full page of published text.**

Reprints: Send photocopy with rights for sale noted and information about when and where the material previously appeared. **Pays $75/published page.**

Photos: Send photos with submission. Reviews transparencies, 35mm slides. Offers $20/photo. Captions, identification of subjects required.

Tips: "Our publication appeals to traditional quilters. We're interested in articles (with slides or transparencies) on quilts in museum collections."

$ $ $ RAILMODEL JOURNAL, Golden Bell Press, 2403 Champa St., Denver CO 80205. **Contact:** Robert Schleicher, editor. **80% freelance written.** Monthly magazine "for advanced model railroaders. 100% photojournalism. We use step-by-step how-to articles with photos of realistic and authentic models." Estab. 1989. Circ. 16,000. Pays on publication. Byline given. Offers 100% kill fee. Buys first, second serial (reprint) rights. Editorial lead time 6 months. Submit seasonal material 6 months in advance. Responds in 4 months to queries; 8 months to mss. Sample copy for $5.50. Writer's guidelines free.

Nonfiction: Historical/nostalgic, how-to, photo feature, technical. "No beginner articles or anything that could even be mistaken for a toy train." **Buys 70-100 mss/year.** Query. Length: 200-5,000 words. **Pays $60-800.** Sometimes pays expenses of writers on assignment.

Photos: Send photos with submission. Reviews contact sheets, 35mm transparencies, 5×7 prints. Buys one-time and reprint rights. Captions, identification of subjects, model releases required.

Tips: "Writers must understand dedicated model railroaders who recreate 100% of their model cars, locomotives, buildings, and scenes from specific real-life prototypes. Close-up photos a must."

$ RENAISSANCE MAGAZINE, division of Queue, Inc., 338 Commerce Dr., Fairfield CT 06432. (800)232-2224. Fax: (800)775-2729. E-mail: renaissance@queueinc.com. Website: www.renaissancemagazine.com. **Contact:** Kim Guarnaccia, managing editor. **90% freelance written.** Quarterly magazine covering the history of the Middle Ages and the Renaissance. "Our readers include historians, reenactors, roleplayers, medievalists, and Renaissance Faire enthusiasts." Estab. 1996. Circ. 33,000. Pays on publication. Publishes ms an average of 1 year after acceptance. Byline given. Buys first North American serial rights. Editorial lead time 6 months. Submit seasonal material 4 months in advance. Accepts queries by mail, e-mail, fax, phone. Accepts previously published material. Responds in 3 weeks to queries; 2 months to mss. Sample copy for $9. Writer's guidelines for #10 SASE or online.

- The editor reports an interest in seeing costuming "how-to" articles; and Renaissance Festival "insider" articles.

O→ Break in by submitting short (500-1,000 word) articles as fillers or querying on upcoming theme issues.

Nonfiction: Essays, exposé, historical/nostalgic, how-to, interview/profile, new product, opinion, photo feature, religious, travel. **Buys 25 mss/year.** Query or send ms. Length: 1,000-5,000 words. **Pays 7¢/word.**

Photos: State availability with submission. Reviews contact sheets, negatives, transparencies, prints. Buys all rights. Offers no additional payment for photos accepted with ms or negotiates payment separately. Captions, identification of subjects, model releases required.

Columns/Departments: Book reviews, 500 words. Include original or good copy of book cover. "For interested reviewers, books can be supplied for review; query first." **Pays 7¢/word.**

Tips: "Send in all articles in the standard manuscript format with photos/slides or illustrations for suggested use. Writers *must* be open to critique, and all historical articles should also include a recommended reading list. A SASE must be included to receive a response to any submission."

$ $ ✪ ROCK & GEM, The Earth's Treasures, Minerals and Jewelry, Miller Magazines, Inc., 4880 Market St., Ventura CA 93003-7783. (805)644-3824, ext. 29. Fax: (805)644-3875. E-mail: rockgemmag@aol.com. Website: www.rockngem.com. **Contact:** Lynn Varon, managing editor. **99% freelance written.** Monthly magazine covering rockhounding field trips, how-to lapidiary projects, minerals, fossils, gold prospecting, mining, etc. "This is not a scientific journal. Its articles appeal to amateurs, beginners, and experts, but its tone is conversational and casual, not stuffy. It's for hobbyists." Estab. 1971. Circ. 55,000. Pays on publication. Byline given. Buys first North American serial rights. Editorial lead time 4 months. Submit seasonal material 6 months in advance. Accepts queries by mail. Writer's guidelines for SASE or online.

Nonfiction: General interest, how-to, humor, personal experience, photo feature, travel. Does not want to see "The 25th Anniversary of the Pet Rock," or anything so scientific that it could be a thesis. **Buys 156-200 mss/year.** Send complete ms. Length: 2,000-4,000 words. **Pays $100-250.**

Photos: Accepts prints, slides or digital art on disk or CD only (provide thumbnails). Send photos with submission. Offers no additional payment for photos accepted with ms. Captions required.

Tips: "We're looking for more how-to articles and field trips with maps. Read writers guidelines very carefully and follow all instructions in them. Then be patient. Your manuscript may be published within a month or even a year from date of submission."

$ $ RUG HOOKING MAGAZINE, Stackpole Magazines, 1300 Market St., Suite 202, Lemoyne PA 17043-1420. (717)234-5091. Fax: (717)234-1359. E-mail: rughook@paonline.com. Website: www.rughookingonline.com. Editor: Wyatt Myers. **Contact:** Editorial Assistant. **75% freelance written.** Published 5 times/year Magazine covering the craft of rug hooking. "This is the only magazine in the world devoted exclusively to rug hooking. Our readers are both novices and experts. They seek how-to pieces, features on fellow artisans and stories on beautiful rugs new and old." Estab. 1989. Circ. 11,000. **Pays on acceptance.** Publishes ms an average of 1 year after acceptance. Byline given. Buys all rights. Editorial lead time 6 months. Submit seasonal material 6 months in advance. Accepts queries by mail, e-mail, fax. Responds in 2 months to queries. Sample copy for $5.

Nonfiction: Also buys 2 100-page books/year. How-to (hook a rug or a specific aspect of hooking), personal experience. Also publishes 2 100-page books. **Buys 30 mss/year.** Query with published clips. Length: 825-2,475 words. **Pays $74.25-222.75.** Sometimes pays expenses of writers on assignment.

Reprints: Send photocopy and information about when and where the material previously appeared.

Photos: Send photos with submission. Reviews 2×2 transparencies, 3×5 prints. Buys all rights. Negotiates payment individually. Identification of subjects required.

$ $ SCALE AUTO ENTHUSIAST, Kalmbach Publishing Co., 21027 Crossroads Circle, P.O. Box 1612, Waukesha WI 53187-1612. (262)796-8776. Fax: (262)796-1383. E-mail: pmulligan@kalmbach.com. Website: www.scaleautomag.com. **Contact:** Patrick Mulligan, managing editor. **70% freelance written.** Magazine published 8 times/year covering model car building. "We are looking for model builders, collectors and enthusiasts who feel their models and/or modeling techniques and experiences would be of interest and benefit to our readership." Estab. 1979. Circ. 35,000. Pays on publication. Publishes ms an average of 1 year after acceptance. Byline given. Buys all rights. Editorial lead time 4 months. Submit seasonal material 4 months in advance. Accepts queries by mail, e-mail, fax, phone. Responds in 3 months to queries; 3 months to mss. Sample copy and writer's guidelines free or on website.

Nonfiction: Book excerpts, historical/nostalgic, how-to (build models, do different techniques), interview/profile, personal experience, photo feature, technical. Query or send complete ms. Length: 750-3,000 words. **Pays $75-100/published page.**

Photos: When writing how-to articles be sure to take photos *during* the project. Send photos with submission. Reviews negatives, 35mm color transparencies, color glossy. Buys all rights. Negotiates payment individually. Captions, identification of subjects, model releases required.

Columns/Departments: Buys 50 mss/year. Query. **Pays $75-100.**

Tips: "First and foremost, our readers like how-to material: how-to paint, how-to scratchbuild, how-to chop a roof, etc. Basically, our readers want to know how to make their own models better. Therefore, any help or advice you can offer is what modelers want to read. Also, the more photos you send, taken from a variety of views, the better choice we have in putting together an outstanding article layout. Send us more photos than you would ever possibly imagine we could use. This permits us to pick and choose the best of the bunch."

$ $ SEW NEWS, The Fashion Magazine for People Who Sew, Primedia Enthusiast Group, 741 Corporate Circle, Suite A, Golden CO 80401. (303)278-1010. Fax: (303)277-0370. E-mail: sewnews@sewnews.com. Website: www.sewnews.com. **Contact:** Linda Turner Griepentrog, editor. **90% freelance written.** Works with a small number of new/unpublished writers each year. Monthly magazine covering fashion-sewing. "Our magazine is for the beginning home sewer to the professional dressmaker. It expresses the fun, creativity and excitement of sewing." Estab. 1980. Circ. 175,000. **Pays on acceptance.** Publishes ms an average of 6 months after acceptance. Byline given. Buys all rights. Submit seasonal material 6 months in advance. Accepts queries by mail, e-mail, fax. Responds in 2 months to mss. Sample copy for $5.99. Writer's guidelines for #10 SAE with 2 first-class stamps or online.

- All stories submitted to *Sew News* must be on disk or by e-mail.

Nonfiction: How-to (sewing techniques), interview/profile (interesting personalities in home-sewing field). **Buys 200-240 mss/year.** Query with published clips if available. Length: 500-2,000 words. **Pays $25-500 for assigned articles.**

Photos: Prefers color photos or slides. Send photos with submission. Buys all rights. Payment included in ms price. Identification of subjects required.

The online magazine carries some original content not found in the print edition and includes writer's guidelines. *Sew News* has a free online newsletter.

Tips: "Query first with writing sample and outline of proposed story. Areas most open to freelancers are how-to and sewing techniques; give explicit, step-by-step instructions plus rough art. We're using more home decorating content."

$ SPORTS COLLECTORS DIGEST, Krause Publications, 700 E. State St., Iola WI 54990. (715)445-2214. Fax: (715)445-4087. E-mail: kpsports@aol.com. Website: www.krause.com. **Contact:** T.S. O'Connell, editor. **25% freelance written.** Works with a small number of new/unpublished writers each year. Weekly magazine covering sports memorabilia. "We serve collectors of sports memorabilia—baseball cards, yearbooks, programs, autographs, jerseys, bats, balls, books, magazines, ticket stubs, etc." Estab. 1952. Circ. 38,000. Pays after publication. Publishes ms an average of 3 months after acceptance. Byline given. Buys first North American serial rights. Submit seasonal material 3 months in advance. Responds in 5 weeks to queries; 2 months to mss. Sample copy for free.

Nonfiction: General interest (new card issues, research older sets), historical/nostalgic (old staduims, old collectibles, etc.), how-to (buy cards, sell cards and other collectibles, display collectibles, ways to get autographs, jerseys and other memorabilia), interview/profile (well-known collectors, ball players—but must focus on collectibles), new product (new card sets), personal experience (what I collect and why-type stories). No sports stories. "We are not competing with *The Sporting News*, *Sports Illustrated* or your daily paper. Sports collectibles only." **Buys 50-75 mss/year.** Query. Length: 300-3,000 words. **Pays $100-150.**

Reprints: Send tearsheet. Pays 100% of amount paid for an original article.

Photos: Unusual collectibles. Send photos with submission. Buys all rights. Pays $25-150 for b&w prints. Identification of subjects required.
Columns/Departments: Length: 500-1,500 words. "We have all the columnists we need but welcome ideas for new columns." **Buys 100-150 mss/year.** Query. **Pays $90-150.**
Tips: "If you are a collector, you know what collectors are interested in. Write about it. No shallow, puff pieces; our readers are too smart for that. Only well-researched articles about sports memorabilia and collecting. Some sports nostalgia pieces are OK. Write only about the areas you know about."

$ STAMP COLLECTOR, Krause Publications, 700 E. State St., Iola WI 54990-0001. (715)445-2214. Fax: (715)445-4612. E-mail: baumannf@krause.com. Website: www.stampcollector.net. **Contact:** Fred Baumann, associate editor. **10% freelance written.** Biweekly tabloid covering philately (stamp collecting). "For stamp collectors of all ages and experience levels." Estab. 1931. Circ. 17,941. Pays on publication. Publishes ms an average of 6 months after acceptance. Byline given. Buys first North American serial rights. Editorial lead time 1 month. Submit seasonal material 3 months in advance. Accepts queries by mail, e-mail. Accepts simultaneous submissions. Responds in 1 week to queries; 1 month to mss. Sample copy for free.
Nonfiction: How-to (collecting stamps). Special issues: Upcoming specialty guides include world and US stamps, postal history, holiday gift guide, topical stamps, other specialty areas. Send complete ms. Length: 150-950 words. **Pays $25-100.** Sometimes pays writers with subscriptions and hobby books. Sometimes pays expenses of writers on assignment.
Photos: State availability with submission. Reviews prints. Buys one-time rights. Offers no additional payment for photos accepted with ms. Captions, identification of subjects required.
Columns/Departments: Postal History (a detailed look at how a particular stamp or cover played a role in moving the mail), 500-950 words. **Buys 6-10 mss/year.** Query. **Pays $25-75.**
Tips: "Submissions are pretty much limited to writers with stamp collecting experience and/or interest."

$ SUNSHINE ARTIST, America's Premier Show & Festival Publication, Palm House Publishing Inc., 3210 Dade Ave., Orlando FL 32804. (407)539-1399. Fax: (407)539-1499. E-mail: business@sunshineartist.com. Website: www.sunshineartist.com. Publisher: David Cook. **Contact:** Amy Detwiler, editor. Monthly magazine covering art shows in the US. "We are the premier-marketing/reference magazine for artists and crafts professionals who earn their living through art shows nationwide. We list more than 2,000 shows monthly, critique many of them and publish articles on marketing, selling and other issues of concern to professional show circuit artists." Estab. 1972. Circ. 12,000. Pays on publication. Publishes ms an average of 3 months after acceptance. Byline given. Buys first North American serial rights. Responds in 2 months to queries. Sample copy for $5.
Nonfiction: "We publish articles of interest to artists and crafts professionals who travel the art show circuit. Current topics include marketing, computers and RV living." No how-to. **Buys 5-10 freelance mss/year.** Query with or without published clips or send complete ms. Length: 1,000-2,000 words. **Pays $50-150.**
Reprints: Send photocopy and information about when and where the material previously appeared.
Photos: Send photos with submission. Offers no additional payment for photos accepted with ms. Captions, identification of subjects, model releases required.

$ $ TATTOO REVUE, Art & Ink Enterprises, Inc., 5 Marine View Plaza, Suite 207, Hoboken NJ 07030. (201)653-2700. Fax: (201)653-7892. E-mail: inked@skinartmag.com. Website: tattoorevue.com. Editor: Jean Chris Miller. **Contact:** Jean Lavalle, managing editor. **25% freelance written.** Interview and profile magazine published 10 times/year covering tattoo artists, their art and lifestyle. "All writers must have knowledge of tattoos. Features include interviews with tattoo artists and collectors." Estab. 1990. Circ. 100,000. Pays on publication. Publishes ms an average of 3 months after acceptance. Byline given. Buys one-time rights. Editorial lead time 3 months. Submit seasonal material 5 months in advance. Accepts queries by mail, e-mail, fax. Accepts previously published material. Accepts simultaneous submissions. Responds in 2 weeks to queries. Sample copy for $5.98. Writer's guidelines for #10 SASE.
Nonfiction: Book excerpts, historical/nostalgic, humor, interview/profile, photo feature. Special issues: Publishes special convention issues—dates and locations provided upon request. "No first-time experiences—our readers already know." **Buys 10-30 mss/year.** Query with published clips or send complete ms. Length: 500-2,500 words. **Pays $50-200.**
Photos: Send photos with submission. Reviews transparencies, prints. Buys one-time rights. Offers $0-10/photo. Captions, identification of subjects, model releases required.
Columns/Departments: **Buys 10-30 mss/year.** Query with or without published clips or send complete ms. **Pays $25-50.**
Fiction: Adventure, erotica, fantasy, historical, humorous, science fiction, suspense. "No stories featuring someone's tattoo coming to life!" **Buys 10-30 mss/year.** Query with published clips or send complete ms. Length: 500-2,500 words. **Pays $50-100.**
Poetry: Avant-garde, free verse, haiku, light verse, traditional. **Buys 10-30 poems/year.** Submit maximum 12 poems. Length: 2-1,000 lines. **Pays $10-25.**
Fillers: Anecdotes, facts, gags to be illustrated by cartoonist, newsbreaks, short humor. **Buys 10-20/year.** Length: 50-2,000 words.
The online magazine carries original content not found in the print edition. Contact: Chris Miller.
Tips: "All writers must have knowledge of tattoos! Either giving or receiving."

$ TOY CARS & MODELS, Krause Publications, 700 E. State St., Iola WI 54990-0001. (715)445-2214. Fax: (715)445-4087. Website: www.toycarsmag.com. **Contact:** Merry Dudley, editor. **90% freelance written.** Monthly 4-color, glossy magazine covering toy vehicles/models. "We cover the hobby market for collectors of die-cast models, model kit builders and fans of all types of vehicle toys." Estab. 1998. Circ. 20,000. Pays on publication. Publishes ms an average of 1 year after acceptance. Byline given. perpetual non-exclusive rights Editorial lead time 4 months. Submit seasonal material 6 months in advance. Accepts queries by mail, e-mail, phone. Accepts simultaneous submissions. Responds in 2 weeks to queries; 2 months to mss. Sample copy for $4.50 or online. Writer's guidelines for SASE or online.

Break in with "great color photos."

Nonfiction: Interested in seeing histories of obscure companies/toy lines/scale model/kits. General interest, historical/nostalgic, how-to (building or detailing models), interview/profile, new product, personal experience, photo feature, technical. **Buys 25 mss/year.** Query with published clips. Length: 800-1,500 words. **Pays $30-150.** Sometimes pays expenses of writers on assignment.

Photos: Send photos with submission. Reviews negatives, 3×5 transparencies, 3×5 prints. Buys one-time rights. No additional payment for photos accepted with ms. Captions, identification of subjects, model releases required.

Columns/Departments: The Checkered Flag (nostalgic essays about favorite toys), 500-800 words; Helpful Hints (tips about model kit buildings, etc.), 25-35 words; Model Reviews (reviews of new die-cast and model kits), 100-350 words. **Buys 25 mss/year.** Query with published clips. **Pays $30-100.**

The online magazine carries original content not found in the print version. Contact: Merry Dudley, online editor.

Tips: "Our magazine is for serious hobbyists looking for info about kit building, model quality, new product info and collectible value."

$ $ TOY FARMER, Toy Farmer Publications, 7496 106 Ave. SE, LaMoure ND 58458-9404. (701)883-5206. Fax: (701)883-5209. E-mail: zekesez@aol.com. Website: www.toyfarmer.com. President/Publisher: Cathy Scheibe. **Contact:** Cheryl Hegvik, editorial assistant. **65% freelance written.** Monthly magazine covering farm toys. Estab. 1978. Circ. 27,000. Pays after acceptance. Byline given. Buys first North American serial rights. Editorial lead time 3 months. Submit seasonal material 3 months in advance. Accepts queries by mail, e-mail, fax, phone. Accepts previously published material. Responds in 1 month to queries; 2 months to mss. Sample copy for $4. Writer's guidelines available upon request.

- Youth involvement is strongly encouraged.

Nonfiction: General interest, historical/nostalgic, humor, interview/profile, new product, personal experience, technical, book introductions. **Buys 100 mss/year.** Query with published clips. Length: 800-1,500 words. **Pays 10¢/word.** Sometimes pays expenses of writers on assignment.

Photos: Must be 35mm originals. State availability with submission. Reviews transparencies. Buys one-time rights. Offers no additional payment for photos accepted with ms.

Columns/Departments: "We have regular monthly columns; so freelance work should not duplicate column subjects."

$ $ TOY SHOP, Krause Publications, 700 E. State St., Iola WI 54990. (715)445-2214. Fax: (715)445-4087. E-mail: korbecks@krause.com. Website: www.toyshopmag.com. **Contact:** Sharon Korbeck, editorial director. **85-90% freelance written.** Biweekly tabloid covering toy collecting. "We cover primarily vintage collectible toys from the 1930s-present. Stories focus on historical toy companies, the collectibility of toys, and features on prominent collections." Estab. 1988. Circ. 40,000. Pays on publication. Publishes ms an average of 8-30 months after acceptance. Byline given. perpetual nonexclusive rights Editorial lead time 6 months. Submit seasonal material 1 year in advance. Accepts queries by mail, e-mail. Accepts simultaneous submissions. Responds in 2 months to queries. Sample copy for $4.50 (plus first-class postage). Writer's guidelines online.

Nonfiction: Historical/nostalgic (toys, toy companies), interview/profile (toy collectors), new product (toys), photo feature, features on old toys. No opinion, broad topics, or poorly researched pieces. **Buys 100 mss/year.** Query. Length: 500-1,500 words. **Pays $50-200.** Contributor's copies included in payment. Sometimes pays expenses of writers on assignment.

Reprints: Send photocopy and information about when and where the material previously appeared.

Photos: State availability of or send photos with submission. Reviews negatives, transparencies, 3×5 prints, and electronic photos. Rights purchased with ms rights. Negotiates payment individually. Captions, identification of subjects, model releases required.

Columns/Departments: Collector Profile (profile of toy collectors), 700-1,000 words. **Buys 25 mss/year.** Query. **Pays $50-150.**

Tips: "Articles must be specific. Include historical info, quotes, values of toys, and photos with story. Talk with toy dealers and get to know the market."

$ $ TOY TRUCKER & CONTRACTOR, Toy Farmer Publications, 7496 106th Ave. SE, LaMoure ND 58458-9404. (701)883-5206. Fax: (701)883-5209. E-mail: zekesez@aol.com. Website: www.toytrucker.com. President/Publisher: Cathy Scheibe. **Contact:** Cheryl Hegvik, editorial assistant. **75% freelance written.** Monthly magazine covering collectible toys. "We are a magazine on hobby and collectible toy trucks and construction pieces." Estab. 1990. Circ.

6,500. **Pays on acceptance.** Byline given. Buys first North American serial rights. Editorial lead time 3 months. Submit seasonal material 3 months in advance. Accepts queries by mail, e-mail, fax, phone. Accepts previously published material. Responds in 1 month to queries; 2 months to mss. Sample copy for $4. Writer's guidelines available on request.

Nonfiction: Historical/nostalgic, interview/profile, new product, personal experience, technical. **Buys 35 mss/year.** Query. Length: 800-2,400 words. **Pays 10¢/word.** Sometimes pays expenses of writers on assignment.

Photos: Must be 35mm originals. Send photos with submission. Offers no additional payment for photos accepted with ms. Captions, identification of subjects, model releases required.

Tips: "Send sample work that would apply to our magazine. Also, we need more articles on collectors or builders. We have regular columns, so a feature should not repeat what our columns do."

$ $ TRADITIONAL QUILTWORKS, The Pattern Magazine for Traditional Quilters, Chitra Publications, 2 Public Ave., Montrose PA 18801. (570)278-1984. Fax: (570)278-2223. E-mail: chitraed@epix.net. Website: www.quilttownusa.com. **Contact:** Joyce Libal, senior editor. **50% freelance written.** Bimonthly magazine on quilting. "We seek articles of an instructional nature, profiles of talented teachers, articles on the history of specific areas of quiltmaking (patterns, fiber, regional, etc.)." Estab. 1988. Circ. 70,000. Pays on publication. Publishes ms an average of 6 months after acceptance. Byline given. Buys second serial (reprint) rights. Submit seasonal material 8 months in advance. Accepts queries by mail, fax. Responds in 2 months to queries. Writer's guidelines for #10 SASE or online.

O→ "Best bet—a quilter writing about a new or unusual quilting technique."

Nonfiction: Historical, instructional, quilting education. **Buys 12-18 mss/year.** Query or send complete ms. Length: 1,500 words maximum. **Pays $75/published page of text.**

Reprints: Send photocopy and information about when and where the material previously appeared.

Photos: Send photos with submission. Reviews 35mm slides and larger transparencies (color). Offers $20/photo. Captions, identification of subjects, model releases required.

Tips: "Our publication appeals to traditional quilters."

$ $ WEEKEND WOODCRAFTS, EGW Publishing Inc., 1041 Shary Circle, Concord CA 94518. (925)671-9852. Fax: (925)671-0692. E-mail: rjoseph@egw.com. Website: www.weekendwoodcrafts.com. **Contact:** Robert Joseph, editor. Bimonthly magazine covering woodworking/crafts. "Projects that can be completed in one weekend." Estab. 1992. Circ. 91,000. Pays half on acceptance and half on publication. Publishes ms an average of 3 months after acceptance. Byline given. Buys first rights. Editorial lead time 2 months. Submit seasonal material 2 months in advance. Accepts queries by mail, e-mail. Accepts simultaneous submissions. Responds in 2 months to mss. Sample copy online. Writer's guidelines free.

Nonfiction: How-to (tips and tech), woodworking projects. **Buys 10 mss/year.** Send complete ms. Length: 400-1,500 words. **Pays $100-500.**

Photos: Send photos with submission. Reviews contact sheets, 4×6 prints. Buys all rights. Offers no additional payment for photos accepted with ms.

Tips: "Build simple and easy weekend projects, build one- to two-hour projects."

$ $ WOODSHOP NEWS, Soundings Publications Inc., 35 Pratt St., Essex CT 06426-1185. (860)767-8227. Fax: (860)767-0645. E-mail: editorial@woodshopnews.com. Website: www.woodshopnews.com. **Contact:** A.J. Hamler, editor. **20% freelance written.** Monthly tabloid "covering woodworking for professionals and hobbyists. Solid business news and features about woodworking companies. Feature stories about interesting professional and amateur woodworkers. Some how-to articles." Estab. 1986. Circ. 100,000. Pays on publication. Publishes ms an average of 6 months after acceptance. Byline given. Offers 25% kill fee. Buys first North American serial rights. Submit seasonal material 4 months in advance. Accepts queries by mail, e-mail, fax. Responds in 1 month to queries. Sample copy online. Writer's guidelines free.

- *Woodshop News* needs writers in major cities in all regions except the Northeast. Also looking for more editorial opinion pieces.

Nonfiction: How-to (query first), interview/profile, new product, opinion, personal experience, photo feature. Key word is "newsworthy." No general interest profiles of "folksy" woodworkers. **Buys 15-25 mss/year.** Query with published clips or send complete ms. Length: 100-1,200 words. **Pays $50-500 for assigned articles; $40-250 for unsolicited articles.** Pays expenses of writers on assignment.

Photos: Send photos with submission. Reviews contact sheets, prints. Buys one-time rights. Offers $20-35/color photo; $250/color cover, usually with story. Captions, identification of subjects required.

Columns/Departments: Pro Shop (business advice, marketing, employee relations, taxes, etc. for the professional written by an established professional in the field);Finishing (how-to and techniques, materials, spraybooths, staining; written by experienced finishers), both 1,200-1,500 words. **Buys 18 mss/year.** Query. **Pays $200-300.**

Fillers: Small filler items, briefs, or news tips that are followed up by staff reporters. **Pays $10.**

Tips: "The best way to start is a profile of a business or hobbyist woodworker in your area. Find a unique angle about the person or business and stress this as the theme of your article. Avoid a broad, general-interest theme that would be more appropriate to a daily newspaper. Our readers are woodworkers who want more depth and more specifics than would a general readership. If you are profiling a business, we need standard business information such as gross annual earnings/sales, customer base, product line and prices, marketing strategy, etc. Color 35 mm photos are a must. We need more freelance writers from the Mid-Atlantic, Midwest and West Coast."

$ $ WOODWORK, A Magazine For All Woodworkers, Ross Periodicals, 42 Digital Dr., #5, Novato CA 94949. (415)382-0580. Fax: (415)382-0587. E-mail: woodwork@rossperiodicals.com. Publisher: Tom Toldrian. **Contact:** John Lavine, editor. **90% freelance written.** Bimonthly magazine covering woodworking. "We are aiming at a broad audience of woodworkers, from the enthusiast to professional. Articles run the range from intermediate to complex. We cover such subjects as carving, turning, furniture, tools old and new, design, techniques, projects, and more. We also feature profiles of woodworkers, with the emphasis being always on communicating woodworking methods, practices, theories, and techniques. Suggestions for articles are always welcome." Estab. 1986. Circ. 50,000. Pays on publication. Byline given. Buys first North American serial, second serial (reprint) rights. Accepts queries by mail, e-mail, fax. Sample copy for $5 and 9×12 SAE with 6 first-class stamps. Writer's guidelines for #10 SASE.

Nonfiction: How-to (simple or complex, making attractive furniture), interview/profile (of established woodworkers that make attractive furniture), photo feature (of interest to woodworkers), technical (tools, techniques). "Do not send a how-to unless you are a woodworker." Query. Length: 1,500-2,000 words. **Pays $150/published page.**

Photos: Send photos with submission. Reviews 35mm slides. Buys one-time rights. Pays higher page rate for photos accepted with ms. Captions, identification of subjects required.

Columns/Departments: Tips and Techniques column, **pays $35-75.** Interview/profiles of established woodworkers (bring out woodworker's philosophy about the craft, opinions about what is happening currently). Good photos of attractive furniture a must. Section on how-to desirable. Query with published clips.

Tips: "Our main requirement is that each article must directly concern woodworking. If you are not a woodworker, the interview/profile is your best, really only chance. Good writing is essential as are good photos. The interview must be entertaining, but informative and pertinent to woodworkers' interests. Include sidebar written by the profile subject."

HOME & GARDEN

The baby boomers' turn inward, or "cocooning," has caused an explosion of publications in this category. Gardening magazines in particular have blossomed, as more people are developing leisure interests at home. Some magazines here concentrate on gardens; others on the how-to of interior design. Still others focus on homes and gardens in specific regions of the country. Be sure to read the publication to determine its focus before submitting a manuscript or query.

$ THE ALMANAC FOR FARMERS & CITY FOLK, Greentree Publishing, Inc., #319, 840 S. Rancho Dr., Suite 4, Las Vegas NV 89106. (702)387-6777. Website: www.thealmanac.com. **Contact:** Lucas McFadden, editor. **40% freelance written.** Annual almanac of "down-home, folksy material pertaining to farming, gardening, homemaking, animals, etc." Deadline: March 31. Estab. 1983. Circ. 800,000. Pays on publication. Publishes ms an average of 6 months after acceptance. Byline given. Buys first North American serial rights. Sample copy for $4.99. Writer's guidelines not available.

O-- Break in with short, humorous, gardening, or how-to pieces.

Nonfiction: Essays, general interest, historical/nostalgic, how-to (any home or garden project), humor. No fiction or controversial topics. "Please, no first-person pieces!" **Buys 30 mss/year.** No queries please. Send complete ms by mail. Length: 350-1,400 words. **Pays $45/page.**

Poetry: Buys 1-4 poems/year. Pays $45 for full pages, otherwise proportionate share thereof.

Fillers: Anecdotes, facts, short humor, gardening hints. **Buys 60/year.** Length: 125 words maximum. **Pays $10-45.**

Tips: "Typed submissions essential as we scan in manuscript. Short, succinct material is preferred. Material should appeal to a wide range of people and should be on the 'folksy' side, preferably with a thread of humor woven in. No first-person pieces."

$ $ THE AMERICAN GARDENER, A Publication of the American Horticultural Society, 7931 E. Boulevard Dr., Alexandria VA 22308-1300. (703)768-5700. Fax: (703)768-7533. E-mail: editor@ahs.org. Website: www.ahs.org. Managing Editor: Mary Yee. **Contact:** David J. Ellis, editor. **75% freelance written.** Bimonthly magazine covering gardening and horticulture. "*The American Gardener* is the official publication of the American Horticultural Society (AHS), a national, nonprofit, membership organization for gardeners, founded in 1922. AHS is dedicated to educating and inspiring people of all ages to become successful, environmentally responsible gardeners by advancing the art and science of horticulture." Estab. 1922. Circ. 26,000. Pays on publication. Publishes ms an average of 6 months after acceptance. Byline given. Offers 25% kill fee. Buys first North American serial rights. Also buys limited rights to run articles on members-only website. Editorial lead time 4 months. Submit seasonal material at least 1 year in advance. Accepts queries by mail. Responds in 3 months to queries. Sample copy for $5. Writer's guidelines for #10 SASE.

Nonfiction: "Feature-length articles include in-depth profiles of individual plant groups, profiles of prominent American horticulturists and gardeners (living and dead); profiles of unusual public or private gardens; descriptions of historical developments in American gardening; descriptions of innovative landscape design projects (especially relating to use of regionally native plants or naturalistic gardening); and descriptions of important plant breeding and research programs tailored to a lay audience. We run a few how-to articles; these should address relatively complex or unusual topics that most other gardening magazines won't tackle—photography needs to be provided." **Buys 30 mss/year.** Query with published clips. Length: 1,500-2,500 words. **Pays $300-500, depending on complexity and author's experience.**

Reprints: Rarely purchases second rights. Send photocopy of article with information about when and where the material previously appeared. Pay varies.

Photos: Must be accompanied by postage-paid return mailer. State availability with submission. Reviews transparencies. Buys one-time rights, plus limited rights to run article on member's-only website. Offers $40-300/photo. Identification of subjects required.
Columns/Departments: Natural Connections (explains a natural phenomenon—plant and pollinator relationships, plant and fungus relationships, parasites—that may be observed in nature or in the garden), 750-1,200 words; Regional Happenings (events that directly affect gardeners only in 1 area, but are of interest to others: an expansion of a botanical garden, a serious new garden pest, the launching of a regional flower show, a hot new gardening trend), 250-300 words. **Buys 15 mss/year.** Query with published clips. **Pays $50-250.**
Tips: "Our readers are advanced, passionate amateur gardeners; about 20 percent are horticultural professionals. Most prefer not to use synthetic chemical pesticides. Our articles are intended to bring this knowledgeable group new information, ranging from the latest scientific findings that affect plants to in-depth profiles of specific plant groups, and the history of gardening and gardens in America."

$ ARIZONA GARDEN, J & J Publishing, 429 S. Tiago Dr., Gilbert AZ 85233. (480)539-1955. Fax: (480)539-1955. E-mail: senly926@aol.com; jdward9@aol.com. **Contact:** Jennifer Ward-Seney, editor; Josie Ward, managing editor. **90% freelance written.** Bimonthly magazine covering gardening in Arizona, using native and non-native plants. "We focus on gardening in Arizona. Writers do not have to be Arizona residents but must research our zones to know planting care and instructions." Estab. 2001. Circ. 2,500. Pays on publication. Publishes ms an average of 3-6 months after acceptance. Byline sometimes given. Offers 10% kill fee. Buys one-time rights. Editorial lead time 1-3 months. Submit seasonal material 3-4 months in advance. Accepts queries by mail, e-mail. Accepts previously published material. Accepts simultaneous submissions. Responds in 1 month to queries; 1 month to mss. Sample copy for 9×12 SAE with 5 first-class stamps or for $3. Writer's guidelines for #10 SASE.
O‑ All articles should be slanted to gardening.
Nonfiction: Book excerpts, historical/nostalgic, how-to, humor, new product, personal experience, photo feature, travel. **Buys 90 mss/year.** Query with or without published clips or send complete ms. Length: 300-1,200 words.
Photos: State availability with submission. Reviews contact sheets, transparencies, Slides; GIF/JPEG files. Buys one-time rights. Identification of subjects, model releases, must have photographer's name and address on each slide/contact sheet required.
Columns/Departments: Book Review (garden books), 300 words; Vegetable Gardening, 600-800 words; Cooking from the Garden (recipes using herbs and vegetables from the garden), 2-3 recipes. Query with or without published clips or send complete ms. **Pays 12¢/word.**
Fiction: Humorous. **Buys 6 mss/year.** Query with or without published clips or send complete ms. Length: 300-500 words. **Pays 12¢/word.**
Fillers: Facts, newsbreaks (only in garden industry), Planting Tips. **Buys 12-15/year.** Length:300 words. **Pays 12¢/word.**
Tips: "We're looking for writers who will write for planting in the Arizona climate. Our focus is to be informative for the beginning and intermediate gardener. We do not focus on only desert landscaping but want articles on plants that are not native but will grow in our climate. Please e-mail for a list of current topics."

$ $ ATLANTA HOMES AND LIFESTYLES, Weisner Publishing LLC, 1100 Johnson Ferry Rd., Suite 595, Atlanta GA 30342. (404)252-6670. Fax: (404)252-6673. Website: www.atlantahomesmag.com. **Contact:** Oma Blaise, editor. **65% freelance written.** Magazine published 8 times/year. "*Atlanta Homes and Lifestyles* is designed for the action-oriented, well-educated reader who enjoys his/her shelter, its design and construction, its environment, and living and entertaining in it." Estab. 1983. Circ. 33,091. Pays on publication. Publishes ms an average of 6 months after acceptance. Byline given. Buys all rights. Accepts queries by mail, fax. Responds in 3 months to queries. Sample copy for $3.95. Writer's guidelines online.
Nonfiction: Interview/profile, new product, photo feature, well-designed homes, gardens, local art, remodeling, food, preservation, entertaining. "We do not want articles outside respective market area, not written for magazine format, or that are excessively controversial, investigative or that cannot be appropriately illustrated with attractive photography." **Buys 35 mss/year.** Query with published clips. Length: 500-1,200 words. **Pays $400.** Sometimes pays expenses of writer on assignment.
Photos: Most photography is assigned. State availability with submission. Reviews transparencies. Buys one-time rights. Pays $40-50/photo. Captions, identification of subjects, model releases required.
Columns/Departments: Short Takes (newsy items on home and garden topics); Quick Fix (simple remodeling ideas); Cheap Chic (stylish decorating that is easy on the wallet); Digging In (outdoor solutions from Atlanta's gardeners); Big Fix (more extensive remodeling projects); Real Estate News. Length: 350-500 words. Query with published clips. **Pays $50-200.**
Tips: "Query with specific new story ideas rather than previously published material."

$ $ AUSTIN HOME & LIVING, Publications & Communications, Inc., 505 Cypress Creek, Suite B, Cedar Park TX 78613. (512)926-4663. Fax: (512)331-3950. E-mail: bronas@pcinews.com. Website: www.austinhomeandliving.com. **Contact:** Brona Stockton, associate publisher. **75% freelance written.** Bimonthly magazine. "*Austin Home & Living* showcases the homes found in Austin and provides tips on food, gardening, and decorating." Estab. 1994. Circ. 20,000. Pays on publication. Publishes ms an average of 4 months after acceptance. Byline given. Offers 100% kill fee. Buys all rights. Editorial lead time 4 months. Submit seasonal material 6 months in advance. Accepts queries by mail, e-mail, fax. Responds in 1 month to queries; 2 months to mss. Sample copy and writer's guidelines free.

Nonfiction: How-to, interview/profile, new product, travel. **Buys 18 mss/year.** Query with published clips. Length: 500-2,000 words. **Pays $200 for assigned articles.** Pays expenses of writers on assignment.
Photos: State availability of or send photos with submission. Reviews negatives, transparencies, prints. Buys all rights. Offers no additional payment for photos accepted with ms. Captions required.

$ BACKHOME, Your Hands-On Guide to Sustainable Living, Wordsworth Communications, Inc., P.O. Box 70, Hendersonville NC 28793. (828)696-3838. Fax: (828)696-0700. E-mail: backhome@ioa.com. Website: www.backhomemagazine.com. **Contact:** Lorna K. Loveless, editor. **80% freelance written.** Bimonthly magazine. *BackHome* encourages readers to take more control over their lives by doing more for themselves: productive organic gardening; building and repairing their homes; utilizing alternative energy systems; raising crops and livestock; building furniture; toys and games and other projects; creative cooking. *BackHome* promotes respect for family activities, community programs, and the environment. Estab. 1990. Circ. 26,000. Pays on publication. Publishes ms an average of 1 year after acceptance. Byline given. Offers $25 kill fee at publisher's discretion. Buys first North American serial rights. Editorial lead time 3 months. Submit seasonal material 6 months in advance. Accepts queries by mail, e-mail, fax, phone. Accepts previously published material. Responds in 6 weeks to queries; 2 months to mss. Sample copy $5 or online. Writer's guidelines for SASE or online.

- The editor reports an interest in seeing "more alternative energy experiences, *good* small houses, workshop projects (for handy persons, not experts), and community action others can copy."
- Break in by writing about personal experience (especially in overcoming challenges) in fields in which *Backhome* focuses.

Nonfiction: How-to (gardening, construction, energy, homebusiness), interview/profile, personal experience, technical, self-sufficiency. No essays or old-timey reminiscences. **Buys 80 mss/year.** Query. Length: 750-5,000 words. **Pays $35 (approximately)/printed page.**
Reprints: Send photocopy and information about when and where the material previously appeared. Pays $35/printed page.
Photos: Send photos with submission. Reviews 35mm slides, color prints, and JPG photo attachments of 300 dpi. Buys one-time rights. Offers additional payment for photos published. Identification of subjects required.
Tips: "Very specific in relating personal experiences in the areas of gardening, energy, and homebuilding how-to. Third-person approaches to others' experiences are also acceptable but somewhat less desirable. Clear color photo prints, especially those in which people are prominent, help immensely when deciding upon what is accepted."

$$$$ BETTER HOMES AND GARDENS, 1716 Locust St., Des Moines IA 50309-3023. (515)284-3044. Fax: (515)284-3763. Website: www.bhg.com. Editor-in-Chief: Karol DeWulf Nickell; Editor (Building): Shawn Gilliam; Editor (Food & Nutrition): Nancy Aepking; Editor (Garden/Outdoor Living): Mark Kane; Editor (Health): Catherine Hamrick; Editor (Education & Parenting): Richard Sowienski; Editor (Money Management, Automotive, Electronics): Lamont Olson; Editor (Features & Travel): Becky Mollenkamp; Editor (Interior Design): Sarah Egge. **10-15% freelance written.** Magazine "providing home service information for people who have a serious interest in their homes." "We read all freelance articles, but much prefer to see a letter of query rather than a finished manuscript." Estab. 1922. Circ. 7,605,000. **Pays on acceptance.** Buys all rights. Sample copy not available. Writer's guidelines not available.
Nonfiction: Travel, Education, gardening, health, cars, home, entertainment. "We do not deal with political subjects or with areas not connected with the home, community, and family." No poetry or fiction. **Pay rates.**
Tips: Most stories published by this magazine go through a lengthy process of development involving both editor and writer. Some editors will consider *only* query letters, not unsolicited manuscripts. Direct queries to the department that best suits your story line.

$$ CALIFORNIA HOMES, The Magazine of Architecture, the Arts and Distinctive Design, McFadden-Bray Publishing Corp., P.O. Box 8655, Newport Beach CA 92658. (949)640-1484. Fax: (949)640-1665. E-mail: edit@calhomesmagazine.com. **Contact:** Susan McFadden, editor. **80% freelance written.** Bimonthly magazine covering California interiors, architecture, some food, travel, history, current events in the field. Estab. 1997. Circ. 50,000. Pays on publication. Publishes ms an average of 3 months after acceptance. Byline given. Offers 50% kill fee. Buys first North American serial rights. Editorial lead time 3 months. Submit seasonal material 6 months in advance. Accepts queries by mail, e-mail, fax. Responds in 1 month to queries; 2 months to mss. Sample copy for $3.95. Writer's guidelines for #10 SASE.
Nonfiction: Query. Length: 500-1,000 words. **Pays $250-500.** Sometimes pays expenses of writers on assignment.
Photos: State availability with submission. Buys one-time rights. Negotiates payment individually. Captions required.

$$$ CANADIAN GARDENING MAGAZINE, Avid Media, Inc., 340 Ferrier St., Suite 210, Markham, Ontario L3R 2Z5, Canada. (905)475-8440. Fax: (905)475-9246. E-mail: satterthwaite@canadiangardening.com. Website: www.canadiangardening.com. Managing Editor: Christina Selby. **Contact:** Aldona Satterthwaite, editor. **100% freelance written.** Magazine published 7 times/year covering Canadian gardening. "*Canadian Gardening* is a national magazine aimed at the avid home gardener. Our readers are city gardeners with tiny lots, country gardeners with rolling acreage, indoor gardeners, rooftop gardeners, and enthusiastic beginners and experienced veterans. Estab. 1990. Circ. 140,000. **Pays on acceptance.** Byline given. Offers 25-50% kill fee. Buys electronic rights. Editorial lead time 3 months. Submit seasonal material 3 months in advance. Accepts queries by mail, e-mail, fax, phone. Accepts simultaneous submissions. Responds in 3 months to queries. Sample copy and writer's guidelines free.

Nonfiction: How-to (planting and gardening projects), humor, personal experience, technical, plant and garden profiles, practical advice. **Buys 100 mss/year.** Query. Length: 200-2,000 words. **Pays $50-1,550.** Sometimes pays expenses of writers on assignment.

Photos: Send photos with submission. Reviews color transparencies. Negotiates payment individually.

$ $ $ CANADIAN HOME WORKSHOP, The Do-It-Yourself Magazine, Avid Media Inc., 340 Ferrier St., Suite 210, Markham, Ontario L3R 2Z5, Canada. (905)475-8440. Fax: (905)475-9246. E-mail: letters@canadianhomeworkshop.com. Website: www.canadianhomeworkshop.com. **Contact:** Douglas Thomson, editor. **90% freelance written.** Half of these are assigned. Magazine published 10 times/year covering the "do-it-yourself" market including woodworking projects, renovation, restoration and maintenance. Circ. 120,000. Pays 1 month after receipt. Byline given. Offers 50% kill fee. Rights are negotiated with author. Submit seasonal material 6 months in advance. Responds in 6 weeks to queries. Sample copy for 9×12 SAE. Writer's guidelines for #10 SASE.

Nonfiction: How-to (home maintenance, renovation, woodworking projects and features). **Buys 40-60 mss/year.** Query with published clips. Length: 1,500-2,500 words. **Pays $800-1,200.** Pays expenses of writers on assignment.

Photos: Send photos with submission. Payment for photos, transparencies negotiated with the author. Captions, identification of subjects, model releases required.

Tips: "Freelancers must be aware of our magazine format. Products used in how-to articles must be readily available across Canada. Deadlines for articles are four months in advance of cover date. How-tos should be detailed enough for the amateur but appealing to the experienced. Articles must have Canadian content: sources, locations, etc."

$ $ CANADIAN HOMES & COTTAGES, (formerly *Homes & Cottages*), The In-Home Show Ltd., 6557 Mississauga Rd., Suite D, Mississauga, Ontario L5N 1A6, Canada. (905)567-1440. Fax: (905)567-1442. E-mail: jadair@homesandcottages.com. Website: www.homesandcottages.com. Editor: Janice Naisby. **Contact:** Jim Adair, editor-in-chief. **75% freelance written.** Magazine published 6 times/year covering building and renovating; "technically comprehensive articles." Estab. 1987. Circ. 64,000. Pays on publication. Publishes ms an average of 2 months after acceptance. Byline given. Offers 10% kill fee. Buys first North American serial rights. Editorial lead time 3 months. Submit seasonal material 3 months in advance. Accepts queries by mail. Sample copy for SAE. Writer's guidelines for #10 SASE.

Nonfiction: Looking for how-to projects and simple home improvement ideas. Humor (building and renovation related), new product, technical. **Buys 32 mss/year.** Query. Length: 1,000-2,000 words. **Pays $300-750.** Sometimes pays expenses of writers on assignment.

Photos: Send photos with submission. Reviews transparencies, prints. Buys one-time rights. Negotiates payment individually. Captions, identification of subjects required.

Tips: "Read our magazine before sending in a query. Remember that you are writing to a Canadian audience."

$ $ COLORADO HOMES & LIFESTYLES, Wiesner Publishing, LLC, 7009 S. Potomac St., Englewood CO 80112-4029. (303)662-5204. Fax: (303)662-5307. E-mail: emcgraw@coloradohomesmag.com. Website: www.coloradohomesmag.com. Managing Editor: Danielle Fox. **Contact:** Evalyn McGraw, editor-in-chief. **75% freelance written.** Upscale shelter magazine published 9 times/year containing beautiful homes, gardens, travel articles, art and artists, food and wine, architecture, calendar, antiques, etc. All of Colorado is included. Geared toward home-related and lifestyle areas, personality profiles, etc. Estab. 1981. Circ. 35,000. **Pays on acceptance.** Publishes ms an average of 3 months after acceptance. Byline given. Offers 15% kill fee. Buys first North American serial rights. Editorial lead time 3 months. Submit seasonal material 1 year in advance. Accepts queries by mail, e-mail. Accepts simultaneous submissions. Responds in 2 months to queries. Sample copy and writer's guidelines for SASE.

- The editor reports that *Colorado Homes & Lifestyles* is doing many more lifestyle articles and needs more unusual and interesting worldwide travel stories.

Nonfiction: Fine homes and furnishings, regional interior design trends, interesting personalities and lifestyles, gardening and plants—all with a Colorado slant. Book excerpts, general interest, historical/nostalgic, new product, photo feature, travel. Special issues: Mountain Homes and Lifestyles (people, etc., January/February); Great Bathrooms & Remodels (March); Sourcebook Guide (April); Designer Showhouse (May); Decorating & Remodeling (June/July); Home of the Year Contests & Kitchens (August); Second Homes (September); Million-Dollar Homes (October); Holidays (November-December). No personal essays, religious, humor, technical. **Buys 50-75 mss/year.** Query with published clips. Length: 1,200-1,500 words. **Pays $200-300.** Sometimes pays expenses of writers on assignment.

Reprints: Send photocopy or typed ms with rights for sale noted and information about when and where the material previously appeared. Pays 35-50% of amount paid for an original article.

Photos: Send photos with submission. Reviews 35mm, 4×5 and 2×2 color transparencies, b&w glossy prints. Identification of subjects, title and caption suggestions appreciated. please include photographic credits required.

Columns/Departments: Gardening (informative); Artisans (profile of Colorado artisans/craftspeople and work); Travel (worldwide, personal experience preferred); Architecture (Colorado), all 1,100-1,300 words. **Buys 60-75 mss/year.** Query with published clips. **Pays $175-250.**

The online magazine carries original content not found in the print edition. Contact: Danielle Fox, assistant editor.

Tips: "Send query, lead paragraph, clips (published and unpublished, if possible). Send ideas for story or stories. Include some photos, if applicable. The more interesting and unique the subject the better. A frequent mistake made by writers is failure to provide material with a style and slant appropriate for the magazine, due to poor understanding of the focus of the magazine."

$ $ CONCRETE HOMES, Publications and Communications Inc. (PCI), 9101 Burnet Rd., Suite 207, Austin TX 78758. Fax: (512)331-3950. E-mail: homes@pcinews.com. Website: concretehomesmagazine.com. Editor: Eugene Morgan. **Contact:** Brona Stockton, associate publisher . **85% freelance written.** Bimonthly magazine covering homes built with concrete. "*Concrete Homes* is a publication designed to be informative to consumers, builders, contractors, architects, etc., who are interested in concrete homes. The magazine profiles concrete home projects (they musy be complete) and offers how-to and industry news articles." Estab. 1999. Circ. 25,000. Pays on publication. Publishes ms an average of 2 months after acceptance. Byline given. Offers 100% kill fee. Buys all rights. Editorial lead time 2 months. Submit seasonal material 3-4 months in advance. Accepts queries by mail, e-mail. Accepts simultaneous submissions. Responds in 1 month to queries; 1 month to mss. Sample copy online. Writer's guidelines online.
Nonfiction: Brona Stockton, associate publisher. How-to, interview/profile, new product, technical. **Buys 30-40 mss/year.** Query or query with published clips. Length: 800-2,000 words. **Pays $200-250.** Sometimes pays expenses of writers on assignment.
Photos: State availability with submission. Reviews 8×10 transparencies, prints, GIF/JPEG files. Buys all rights. Offers no additional payment for photos accepted with ms. Captions required.
Tips: "Demonstrate awareness of concrete homes and some knowledge of the construction/building industry."

$ $ $ $ COTTAGE LIFE, Quarto Communications, 54 St. Patrick St., Toronto, Ontario M5T 1V1, Canada. (416)599-2000. Fax: (416)599-4070. E-mail: editorial@cottagelife.com. Website: www.cottagelife.com. Managing Editor: Catherine Collins. **Contact:** Penny Caldwell, editor. **80% freelance written.** Bimonthly magazine. "*Cottage Life* is written and designed for the people who own and spend time at waterfront cottages throughout Canada and bordering U.S. states, with a strong focus on Ontario. The magazine has a strong service slant, combining useful 'how-to' journalism with coverage of the people, trends, and issues in cottage country. Regular columns are devoted to boating, fishing, watersports, projects, real estate, cooking, nature, personal cottage experience, and environmental, political, and financial issues of concern to cottagers." Estab. 1988. Circ. 70,000. **Pays on acceptance.** Publishes ms an average of 2 months after acceptance. Byline given. Offers 50-100% kill fee. Buys first North American serial rights. Sample copy not available. Writer's guidelines free.
Nonfiction: Book excerpts, exposé, historical/nostalgic, how-to, humor, interview/profile, personal experience, photo feature, technical. **Buys 90 mss/year.** Query with published clips and SAE with Canadian postage or IRCs. Length: 1,500-3,500 words. **Pays $100-2,200 for assigned articles; $50-1,000 for unsolicited articles.** Sometimes pays expenses of writers on assignment.
Columns/Departments: On the Waterfront (front department featuring short news, humor, human interest, and service items). Length: 400 words maximum. Pays $100. Cooking, Real Estate, Fishing, Nature, Watersports, Personal Experience and Issues. Length: 150-1,200 words. Query with published clips and SAE with Canadian postage or IRCs. **Pays $100-750.**
Tips: "If you have not previously written for the magazine, the 'On the Waterfront' section is an excellent place to break in."

$ $ $ COUNTRY HOME, Meredith Corp., 1716 Locust St., Des Moines IA 50309-3023. (515)284-2015. Fax: (515)284-2552. E-mail: countryh@mdp.com. Website: www.countryhome.com. Editor-in-Chief: Carol Sama Sheehan. **Contact:** Christine Hofmann-Bourque, assignments editor. Magazine published 8 times/year for people interested in the country way of life. "*Country Home* magazine is a lifestyle publication created for readers who share passions for American history, style, craftsmanship, tradition, and cuisine. These people, with a desire to find a simpler, more meaningful lifestyle, live their lives and design their living spaces in ways that reflect those passions." Estab. 1979. Circ. 1,000,000. Pays on completion of assignment. Publishes ms an average of 5 months after acceptance. Byline given. Submit seasonal material 6 months in advance. Accepts queries by mail. Responds in 6 weeks to queries. Sample copy for $4.95. Writer's guidelines not available.

"We are not responsible for unsolicited manuscripts, and we do not encourage telephone queries."
Nonfiction: Architecture and Design, Families at Home, Travel, Food and Entertaining, Art and Antiques, Gardens and Outdoor Living, Personal Reflections. Query by mail only with writing samples and SASE. Length: 750-1,500 words. **Pays $500-1,500.**
Columns/Departments: Length: 500-750 words. Include SASE. Query with published clips. **Pays $300-500.**

The online magazine carries original content not found in the print edition. Contact: Lori Blachford, online editor.

$ $ $ COUNTRY LIVING, The Hearst Corp., 224 W. 57th St., New York NY 10019. (212)649-3509. E-mail: countryliving@women.com. **Contact:** Marjorie Gage, senior editor. Monthly magazine covering home design and interior decorating with an emphasis on country style. "A lifestyle magazine for readers who appreciate the warmth and traditions associated with American home and family life. Each monthly issue embraces American country decorating and includes features on furniture, antiques, gardening, home building, real estate, cooking, entertaining and travel." Estab. 1978. Circ. 1,600,000. Sample copy not available. Writer's guidelines not available.
Nonfiction: Most open to freelancers: Antiques articles from authorities, personal essay. **Buys 20-30 mss/year.** Send complete ms and SASE. **Payment varies.**
Columns/Departments: Most open to freelancers: Readers Corner. Include SASE. Send complete ms. **Payment varies.**
Tips: "Know the magazine, know the market and know how to write a good story that will interest *our* readers."

$ $ COUNTRY SAMPLER, Country Sampler, Inc., 707 Kautz Rd., St. Charles IL 60174. (630)377-8000. Fax: (630)377-8194. Website: www.sampler.com. Publisher: Margaret Borst. **Contact:** Paddy Kalahar Buratto, editor. Bimonthly magazine. "*Country Sampler* is a country decorating, antiques and collectibles magazine and a country product catalog." Estab. 1984. Circ. 462,263. Accepts queries by mail, fax. Sample copy not available.

Nonfiction: "Furniture, accessories and decorative accents created by artisans throughout the country are displayed and offered for purchase directly from the maker. Fully decorated room settings show the readers how to use the items in their homes to achieve the warmth and charm of the country look."

Tips: "Send photos and story idea for a country style house tour. Story should be regarding decorating tips and techniques."

N $ $ COUNTRY SAMPLER DECORATING IDEAS, Emmis Communications, 707 Kautz Rd., St. Charles IL 60174. Fax: (630)377-8194. E-mail: decideas@sampler.emmis.com. Website: www.decoratingideas.com. Managing Editor: Rita M. Woker. **Contact:** Mike Morris, editor. **60% freelance written.** Bimonthly magazine on home decor and home improvement. "This magazine is devoted to providing do-it-yourself decorating solutions for the average homeowner, through step-by-step projects, topical articles, and real-life feature stories that inspire readers to create the country home of their dreams." **Pays on acceptance.** Publishes ms an average of 6 months after acceptance. Byline given. Makes work-for-hire assignments. Editorial lead time 4 months. Submit seasonal material 6 months in advance. Accepts queries by mail, e-mail, fax. Responds in 1 month to queries; 3 months to mss. Sample copy not available. Writer's guidelines free.

Nonfiction: Book excerpts, how-to (decorating projects), interview/profile, photo feature, house tours. Special issues: Decorate With Paint (February, July, and November); Kitchen & Bath Makeovers (May); Window & Wall Treatments (August). No opinion or fiction. **Buys 50 mss/year.** Query with published clips. Length: 500-1,500 words. **Pays $250-350.** Sometimes pays expenses of writers on assignment.

Photos: State availability with submission. Reviews transparencies, 3×5 prints. Buys negotiable rights. Negotiates payment individually. Captions, identification of subjects, model releases required.

Tips: "Query letters accompanied by published clips are your best bet. We do not accept unsolicited articles, but pay on acceptance for assigned articles. So it is best to sell us on an article concept and support that concept with similar published articles."

$ $ $ DECORATING IDEAS, Woman's Day Special Interest Publications, Hachette-Filipacchi Magazines, 1633 Broadway, New York NY 10019. (212)767-6000. Fax: (212)767-5618. Website: www.womansday.com/specials. Editors: Jean Nayar, Jane Chesnutt, Olivia Monjo, Kitty Cox. **Contact:** Amanda Rock, assistant managing editor. Magazine published 4 times/year covering home decorating. "This magazine aims to inspire and teach readers how to create a beautiful home." **Pays on acceptance.** Publishes ms an average of 3 months after acceptance. Byline given. Offers up to 25% kill fee. Buys all rights. Editorial lead time 6 months. Submit seasonal material 10 months in advance. Accepts queries by mail, fax. Responds in 2 months to mss. Sample copy not available. Writer's guidelines for #10 SASE.

Nonfiction: Book excerpts, general interest, how-to (home decor projects for beginner/intermediate skill levels—sewing, woodworking, painting, etc.), interview/profile, new product, photo feature, technical, collectibles, hard-to-find services, unique stores. Query with published clips. Length: 250-1,000 words. **Payment varies based on length, writer, importance**. Sometimes pays expenses of writers on assignment.

Photos: Send representative photos with query. Buys one-time rights. Model releases required.

Columns/Departments: Step by Step (how-to instructions for 1 or 2 relevant projects that can be completed in a day or two), 400-800 words; Collecting; Furniture Finds; Spotlight On...; Style Notes; Swatches; Where to Find It; Let's Go Shopping; Finishing Touches. **Payment varies based on length, writer, and level/amount of research required.**

The online magazine carries original content not found in the print edition. Contact: Amanda Rock.

Tips: "Send a brief, clear query letter with recent, relevant (published) clips, and be patient. Before and after photos are very helpful, as are photos of ideas for Step by Step column. In addition to specific ideas and projects (for which how-to information is provided), we look at decorating trends, provide advice on how to get the most design for your money (with and without help from a professional), and highlight noteworthy new products and services." No phone queries please. Part of Woman's Day Special Interest Publications.

$ $ DESIGN TIMES, The Art of Interiors, Regis Publishing Co., Inc., 1 Design Center Place, Suite 249, Boston MA 02210. (617)443-0636 ext. 227. Fax: (617)443-0637. E-mail: louis@designtimes.net. Website: www.designtimes.com. **Contact:** Louis Postel. **75% freelance written.** Bimonthly magazine covering high-end residential interior design nationwide. "Show, don't tell. Readers want to look over the shoulders of professional interior designers. Avoid cliche. Love design." Estab. 1988. Circ. 100,000. Pays on publication. Publishes ms an average of 4 months after acceptance. Byline given. Offers 10% kill fee. Buys all rights. Editorial lead time 3 months. Submit seasonal material 6 months in advance. Accepts queries by mail, e-mail, fax. Accepts simultaneous submissions. Responds in 1 month to queries. Sample copy for 10 X 13 SAE with 10 first-class stamps or on website. Writer's guidelines not available.

Nonfiction: Residential interiors. **Buys 25 mss/year.** Query with published clips. Length: 1,200-3,000 words. **Payment varies.** Sometimes pays expenses of writers on assignment.

Photos: State availability with submission. Reviews 4 X 5 transparencies, Prints 9 X 10. Buys one-time rights. Negotiates payment individually. Captions, identification of subjects, model releases required.

Columns/Departments: Pays $100-150.

Tips: "A home owned by a well-known personality or designer would be a good feature query. Since the magazine is so visual, great photographs are a big help. We're also looking for before/after 'design emergency' stories."

$ $ EARLY AMERICAN LIFE, Celtic Moon Publishing, Inc., 207 House Ave., Suite 103, Camp Hill PA 17011. (717)730-6263. Fax: (717)730-7385. E-mail: ginnys@celticmooninc.com. Website: www.earlyamericanlife.com. **Contact:** Virginia Stimmel, editor. **20% freelance written.** Bimonthly magazine for "people who are interested in capturing the warmth and beauty of the 1600-1840 period and using it in their homes and lives today. They are interested in antiques, traditional crafts, architecture, restoration, and collecting." Estab. 1970. Circ. 130,000. **Pays on acceptance.** Publishes ms an average of 1 year after acceptance. Byline given. worldwide rights Accepts queries by mail, e-mail, fax. Responds in 3 months to queries. Sample copy and writer's guidelines for 9×12 SAE with 4 first-class stamps.

- Break in "by offering highly descriptive, entertaining, yet informational articles on social culture, decorative arts, antiques, or well-restored and appropriately furnished homes that reflect middle-class American life prior to 1850."

Nonfiction: "Social history (the story of the people, not epic heroes and battles), travel to historic sites, antiques and reproductions, restoration, architecture, and decorating. We try to entertain as we inform. We're always on the lookout for good pieces on any of our subjects. Would like to see more on how real people did something great to their homes." **Buys 40 mss/year.** Query with or without published clips or send complete ms. Length: 750-3,000 words. **Pays $100-600.**

Tips: "Our readers are eager for ideas on how to bring early America into their lives. Conceive a new approach to satisfy their related interests in arts, crafts, travel to historic sites, and especially in houses decorated in the Early American style. Write to entertain and inform at the same time. Be prepared to help us with sources for illustrations."

N $ $ $ FINE GARDENING, Taunton Press, 63 S. Main St., P.O. Box 5506, Newtown CT 06470-5506. (203)426-8171. Fax: (203)426-3434. E-mail: fg@taunton.com. Website: www.finegardening.com. **Contact:** Todd Meier, executive editor. Bimonthly magazine. "High-value magazine on landscape and ornamental gardening. Articles written by avid gardeners—first person, hands-on gardening experiences." Estab. 1988. Circ. 200,000. **Pays on acceptance.** Publishes ms an average of 6 months after acceptance. Byline given. Buys all rights. Editorial lead time 1 year. Submit seasonal material 1 year in advance. Accepts queries by mail, e-mail, fax. Sample copy not available. Writer's guidelines free.

Nonfiction: How-to, personal experience, photo feature, Book review. **Buys 60 mss/year.** Query. Length: 1,000-3,000 words. **Pays $300-1,200.**

Photos: Send photos with submission. Prefers digital. Serial rights.

Columns/Departments: Book, video and software reviews (on gardening); Last Word (essays/serious, humorous, fact or fiction). Length: 250-500 words. **Buys 30 mss/year.** Query. **Pays $50- 200.**

Tips: "It's most important to have solid first-hand experience as a gardener. Tell us what you've done with your own landscape and plants."

$ $ FINE HOMEBUILDING, The Taunton Press, 63 S. Main St., P.O. Box 5506, Newtown CT 06470-5506. (800) 926-8776. Fax: (203) 270-6751. E-mail: fh@taunton.com. Website: www.taunton.com. **Contact:** Kevin Ireton, editor-in-chief. Bimonthly magazine for builders, architects, contractors, owner/builders and others who are seriously involved in building new houses or reviving old ones. Estab. 1981. Circ. 300,000. Pays half on acceptance, half on publication. Publishes ms an average of 1 year after acceptance. Byline given. Offers on acceptance payment as kill fee. Buys first rights. Reprint rights Responds in 1 month to queries. Sample copy not available. Writer's guidelines for SASE and on website.

Nonfiction: "We're interested in almost all aspects of home building, from laying out foundations to capping cupolas." Query with outline, description, photographs, sketches and SASE. **Pays $150/published page.**

Photos: "Take lots of work-in-progress photos. Color print film, ASA 400, from either Kodak or Fuji works best. If you prefer to use slide film, use ASA 100. Keep track of the negatives; we will need them for publication. If you're not sure what to use or how to go about it, feel free to call for advice."

Columns/Departments: Tools & Materials, Reviews, Questions & Answers, Tips & Techniques, Cross Section, What's the Difference?, Finishing Touches, Great Moments, Breaktime, Drawing Board (design column). Query with outline, description, photographs, sketches and SASE. **Payment varies.**

Tips: "Our chief contributors are home builders, architects and other professionals. We're more interested in your point of view and technical expertise than your prose style. Adopt an easy, conversational style and define any obscure terms for non-specialists. We try to visit all our contributors and rarely publish building projects we haven't seen, or authors we haven't met."

$ $ FLOWER AND GARDEN MAGAZINE, 51 Kings Highway W., Haddonfield NJ 08033-2114. (856)354-5034. Fax: (856)354-5147. E-mail: kcpublishing@earthlink.net. Website: flowerandgardenmag.com. **Contact:** Senior Editor. **80% freelance written.** Works with a small number of new/unpublished writers each year. Bimonthly picture magazine. "*Flower & Garden* focuses on ideas that can be applied to the home garden and outdoor environs; primarily how-to, but also historical and background articles are considered if a specific adaptation can be obviously related to home gardening." Estab. 1956. Circ. 250,000. **Pays on acceptance.** Publishes ms an average of 1 year after acceptance. Byline sometimes given. Buys first-time nonexclusive, reprint rights Accepts queries by mail, e-mail, fax. Responds in 2 months to queries. Sample copy for $3. Writer's guidelines for #10 SASE.

- The editor tells us good quality photos accompanying articles are more important than ever.

Nonfiction: Interested in illustrated articles on how to do certain types of gardening and descriptive articles about individual plants. Flower arranging, landscape design, house plants and patio gardening are other aspects covered. "The approach we stress is practical (how-to-do-it, what-to-do-it-with). We emphasize plain talk, clarity and economy of words. An article should be tailored for a national audience." **Buys 20-30 mss/year.** Query. Length: 500-1,000 words. **Pays variable rates depending on quality and kind of material and author's credentials, $200-500.**

Reprints: Send typed ms with rights for sale noted and information about when and where the material previously appeared.

Photos: Color slides and transparencies preferred, 35mm and larger but 35mm slides or prints not suitable for cover. Submit cover photos as 2¼×2¼ or larger transparencies. In plant or flower shots, indicate which end is up on each photo. Photos are paid for on publication, $60-175 inside, $300 for covers. An accurate packing list with appropriately labeled photographs and numbered slides with description sheet (including latin botanical and common names) is required required.

Tips: "The prospective author needs good grounding in gardening practice and literature. Offer well-researched and well-written material appropriate to the experience level of our audience. Photographs help sell the story. Describe special qualifications for writing the particular proposed subject."

$ $ GARDENING HOW-TO, North American Media Group, 12301 Whitewater Dr., Minnetonka MN 55343. (952)936-9333. Fax: (952)936-9755. E-mail: justin@gardeningclub.com. Website: www.gardeningclub.com. **Contact:** Justin W. Hancock, horticulture editor. **40% freelance written.** Bimonthly magazine covering gardening/horticulture. "*Gardening How-To* is the bimonthly publication of the National Home Gardening Club, headquartered in Minnetonka, Minnesota. As the primary benefit of membership in the Club, the magazine's aim is to provide timely, interesting, and inspiring editorial that will appeal to our audience of intermediate- to advanced-level home gardeners." Estab. 1996. Circ. 600,000. **Pays on acceptance.** Publishes ms an average of 4 months after acceptance. Byline given. Offers 25% kill fee. Buys one-time rights. Editorial lead time 6 months. Submit seasonal material 6 months in advance. Accepts queries by mail, e-mail, fax. Sample copy for $3. Writer's guidelines for free or by e-mail.

Nonfiction: How-to (gardening/horticulture). **Buys 36 mss/year.** Query with published clips. Length: 1,000-2,000 words. **Pays $200-1,000.** Sometimes pays expenses of writers on assignment.

Photos: State availability with submission. Buys one-time rights. Negotiates payment individually.

$ $ THE HERB COMPANION, Herb Companion Press, 243 E. Fourth St., Loveland CO 80537. (970)663-0831. Fax: (970)663-0909. E-mail: herbcompanion@hcpress.com. Website: www.discoverherbs.com. **Contact:** Dawna Edwards, editor. **80% freelance written.** Bimonthly magazine about herbs: Culture, history, culinary, crafts and some medicinal use for both experienced and novice herb enthusiasts. Circ. 180,000. Pays on publication. Byline given. Buys all rights. Editorial lead time 4 months. Accepts queries by mail, e-mail, fax. Responds in 2 months to queries. Sample copy for $6. Writer's guidelines for #10 SASE.

Nonfiction: Practical horticultural, original recipes, historical, herbal crafts, helpful hints and book reviews. How-to, interview/profile. Submit by mail only detailed query or ms. Length: 4 pages or 1,000 words. **Pays according to length, story type and experience.**

Photos: Returns photos and artwork. Send photos with submission. Reviews Prefers transparencies.

Tips: "New approaches to familiar topics are especially welcome. If you aren't already familiar with the content, style and tone of the magazine, we suggest you read a few issues. Technical accuracy is essential. Please use scientific as well as popular names for plants and cover the subject in depth while avoiding overly academic presentation. Information should be made accessible to the reader, and we find this is best accomplished by writing from direct personal experience where possible and always in an informal style."

$ HOME DIGEST, Your Guide to Home and Life Improvement, Home Digest International, Inc., 268 Lakeshore Rd. E., Unit 604, Oakville, Ontario L6J 7S4, Canada. (905)844-3361. Fax: (905)849-4618. E-mail: homedigest@canada.com. Website: www.home-digest.com. **Contact:** William Roebuck, editor. **25% freelance written.** Quarterly magazine covering house, home, and life management for families in stand-alone houses in the greater Toronto region. "*Home Digest* has a strong service slant, combining useful how-to journalism with coverage of the trends and issues of home ownership and family life. In essence, our focus is on the concerns of families living in their own homes." Estab. 1995. Circ. 522,000. Pays on publication. Publishes ms an average of 3 months after acceptance. Byline given. Buys first North American serial rights and the rights to archive articles on the magazine's website. Editorial lead time 3 months. Submit seasonal material 5 months in advance. Accepts queries by mail, e-mail, fax. Accepts previously published material. Accepts simultaneous submissions. Responds in 1 month to queries. Sample copy for 9×6 SAE and 2 Canadian first-class stamps. Writer's guidelines for #10 SASE or online.

Nonfiction: General interest, how-to (household hints, basic home renovation, decorating), humor (living in Toronto), inspirational. No opinion, fashion, or beauty. **Buys 8 mss/year.** Query. Length: 350-700 words. **Pays $35-100 (Canadian).**

Photos: Send photos with submission. Reviews prints. Buys one-time rights. Pays $10-20/photo. Captions, identification of subjects, model releases required.

Columns/Departments: Household Hints (tested tips that work); Health & Fitness News (significant health/body/fitness news); both 300-350 words. **Buys 4-6 mss/year.** Query. **Pays $40-50 (Canadian).**

Tips: "Base your ideas on practical experiences. We're looking for 'uncommon' advice that works."

$ $ $ HORTICULTURE, Gardening at Its Best, 98 N. Washington St., Boston MA 02114. (617)742-5600. Fax: (617)367-6364. E-mail: tfischer@primediasi.com. Website: www.hortmag.com. **Contact:** Thomas Fischer, executive editor. Magazine published 8 times/year. "*Horticulture*, the country's oldest gardening magazine, is designed for active amateur gardeners. Our goal is to offer a blend of text, photographs and illustrations that will both instruct and inspire readers." Circ. 250,000. Byline given. Offers kill fee. Buys first North American serial, one-time rights. Submit seasonal material 10 months in advance. Accepts queries by mail, e-mail, fax. Responds in 3 months to queries. Sample copy not available. Writer's guidelines for SASE or by e-mail.
Nonfiction: "We look for an encouraging personal experience, anecdote and opinion. At the same time, a thorough article should to some degree place its subject in the broader context of horticulture." Include disk where posisble. **Buys 15 mss/year.** Query with published clips, subject background material and SASE. Length: 1,000-2,000 words. **Pays $600-1,500.** Pays expenses of writers on assignment if previously arranged with editor.
Columns/Departments: Length: 100-1,500 words. Query with published clips, subject background material and SASE. Include disk where possible. **Pays $50-750.**
Tips: "We believe every article must offer ideas or illustrate principles that our readers might apply on their own gardens. No matter what the subject, we want our readers to become better, more creative gardeners."

$ $ LAKESTYLE, Celebrating life on the water, Bayside Publications, Inc., P.O. Box 170, Excelsior MN 55331. (952)470-1380. Fax: (952)470-1389. E-mail: editor@lakestyle.com. Website: www.lakestyle.com. **Contact:** Nancy Jahnke, editor. **50% freelance written.** Quarterly magazine. "*Lakestyle* is committed to celebrating the lifestyle chosen by lake home and cabin owners." Estab. 2000. Circ. 40,000. Pays on publication. Publishes ms an average of 3 months after acceptance. Byline given. Offers 10% kill fee. Buys all rights. Editorial lead time 2 months. Submit seasonal material 3 months in advance. Accepts queries by mail, e-mail, fax, phone. Accepts previously published material. Responds in 3 weeks to queries; 1 month to mss. Sample copy for $5. Writer's guidelines free.
Nonfiction: Essays, historical/nostalgic, how-to, humor, inspirational, interview/profile, new product, photo feature. No direct promotion of product. **Buys 15 mss/year.** Query with or without published clips or send complete ms. Length: 500-2,500 words. **Pays 25-50¢/word for assigned articles; 10-25¢/word for unsolicited articles.** Sometimes pays expenses of writers on assignment.
Photos: State availability of or send photos with submission. Rights purchased vary. Offers no additional payment for photos accepted with ms. Captions, identification of subjects, model releases required.
Columns/Departments: Lakestyle Entertaining (entertaining ideas); Lakestyle Gardening (gardening ideas); On the Water (boating/playing on the lake); Hidden Treasures (little known events); At the Cabin (cabin owner's information); all approximately 1,000 words. **Buys 10 mss/year.** Query with or without published clips or send complete ms. **Pays 10-25¢/word.**
Tips: "*Lakestyle* is interested in enhancing the lifestyle chosen by our readers, a thorough knowledge of cabin/lake home issues helps writers fulfill this goal."

$ $ LOG HOME LIVING, Home Buyer Publications, Inc., 4200-T Lafayette Center Dr., Chantilly VA 20151. (703)222-9411. Fax: (703)222-3209. E-mail: plobred@homebuyerpubs.com. Website: www.loghomeliving.com. **Contact:** Peter Lobred, editor. **50% freelance written.** Monthly magazine for enthusiasts who are dreaming of, planning for, or actively building a log home. Estab. 1989. Circ. 132,000. **Pays on acceptance.** Publishes ms an average of 6 months after acceptance. Byline given. Offers $100 kill fee. Buys first, second serial (reprint) rights. Editorial lead time 6 months. Submit seasonal material 6 months in advance. Accepts queries by mail. Accepts previously published material. Responds in 6 weeks to queries. Sample copy for $4. Writer's guidelines for #10 SASE.
Nonfiction: Book excerpts, how-to (build or maintain log home), interview/profile (log home owners), personal experience, photo feature (log homes), technical (design/decor topics), travel. "We do not want historical/nostalgic material." **Buys 6 mss/year.** Query. Length: 1,000-2,000 words. **Pays $250-500.** Pays expenses of writers on assignment.
Reprints: Send tearsheet or photocopy and information about when and where the material previously appeared. Pays 50% of amount paid for an original article.
Photos: State availability with submission. Reviews contact sheets, 4×5 transparencies, 4×6 prints. Buys one-time rights. Negotiates payment individually.
Tips: "*Log Home Living* is devoted almost exclusively to modern manufactured and handcrafted kit log homes. Our interest in historical or nostalgic stories of very old log cabins, reconstructed log homes, or one-of-a-kind owner-built homes is secondary and should be queried first."

$ $ MOUNTAIN LIVING, Wiesner Publishing, 7009 S. Potomac St., Englewood CO 80112. (303)397-7600. Fax: (303)397-7619. E-mail: irawlings@mountainliving.com. Website: www.mountainliving.com. **Contact:** Irene Rawlings, editor. **50% freelance written.** Bimonthly magazine covering "shelter and lifestyle issues for people who live in, visit, or hope to live in the mountains." Estab. 1994. Circ. 35,000. **Pays on acceptance.** Publishes ms an average of 4 months after acceptance. Byline given. Offers 15% kill fee. Buys all rights. Editorial lead time 6 months. Submit seasonal material 6 months in advance. Accepts queries by mail, e-mail, phone. Accepts simultaneous submissions. Responds in 6 weeks to queries; 2 months to mss. Sample copy for $5 or on website. Writer's guidelines for #10 SASE. "The best guidelines are to read the magazine."
Nonfiction: Book excerpts, interview/profile, photo feature, travel, home features. **Buys 30 mss/year.** Query with published clips. Length: 1,200-2,000 words. **Pays $250-500.** Sometimes pays expenses of writers on assignment.
Photos: Provide photos (slides, transparencies, or on disk, saved as TIFF and at least 300 dpi). State availability with submission. Buys one-time rights. Negotiates payment individually.

Columns/Departments: Architecture; Art; Sporting Life; Travel; Off the Beaten Path (out-of-the-way mountain areas in US); History; Cuisine; Environment; Destinations (an art-driven department featuring a beautiful mountain destination in US—must be accompanied by quality photograph). Length: 300-1,500 words. **Buys 35 mss/year.** Query with published clips. **Pays $50-500.**
Tips: "A deep understanding of and respect for the mountain environment is essential. Think out of the box. We love to be surprised. Write a brilliant, short query and always send clips."

$ $ $ $ ORGANIC GARDENING, Rodale, 33 E. Minor, Emmaus PA 18098. (610)967-8363. Fax: (610)967-7846. E-mail: Sandra.Weida@Rodale.com. Website: www.organicgardening.com. **Contact:** Sandra Weida, office coordinator. **75% freelance written.** Bimonthly magazine. "*Organic Gardening* is for gardeners who garden, who enjoy gardening as an integral part of a healthy lifestyle. Editorial shows readers how to grow anything they choose without chemicals. Editorial details how to grow flowers, edibles and herbs, as well as information on ecological landscaping. Also organic topics including soil building and pest control." Circ. 700,000. Pays between acceptance and publication. Byline given. Buys all rights. Accepts queries by mail, fax. Responds in 3 months to queries. Sample copy not available.
Nonfiction: "The natural approach to the whole home landscape." Query with published clips and outline. **Pays up to $1/word for experienced writers.**

The online magazine carries original content not found in the print edition. Contact: Scott Meyer, online editor.
Tips: "If you have devised a specific technique that's worked in your garden, have insight into the needs and uses of a particular plant or small group of plants, or have designed whole gardens that integrate well with their environment, and, if you have the capacity to clearly describe what you've learned to other gardeners in a simple but engaging manner, please send us your article ideas. Read a recent issue of the magazine thoroughly before you submit your ideas. The scope and tone of our content has changed dramatically in the last year—be sure your ideas and your approach to presenting them jibe with the magazine as it is now. If you have an idea that you believe fits with our content, send us a one-page description of it that will grab our attention in the same manner you intend to entice readers into your article. Be sure to briefly explain why your idea is uniquely suited to our magazine. (We will not publish an article that has already appeared elsewhere. Also, please tell us if you are simultaneously submitting your idea to another magazine.) Tell us about the visual content of your idea—that is, what photographs or illustrations would you suggest be included with your article to get the ideas and information across to readers? If you have photographs, let us know. If you have never been published before, consider whether your idea fits into our Gardener to Gardener department. The shorter, narrowly focused articles in the department and its conversational tone make for a more accessible avenue into the magazine for inexperienced writers."

PEOPLE, PLACES & PLANTS, P.O. Box 6131, Falmout ME 04105. (207)878-4953. Fax: (207)878-4957. E-mail: paul@ppplants.com. Website: newenglandgardening.com. Paul Tukey, editor-in-chief. **50% freelance written.** Published 5 times/year Gardening magazine focused on New England. Circ. 52,000. **Pays on acceptance.** Publishes ms an average of 3 months after acceptance. Buys first rights. Responds in 1 month to queries. Sample copy by e-mail. Writer's guidelines by e-mail.
Nonfiction: Know the subject at hand; anecdotes help get readers interested in stories. Query. **Pays $50-500.**
Photos: Reviews Slides. $50-500.

$ $ ROMANTIC HOMES, Y-Visionary Publishing, 265 Anita Dr., Suite 120, Orange CA 92868. (714)939-9991. Fax: (714)939-9909. Website: www.romantichomesmag.com. Editor: Ellen Paulin. **Contact:** Catherine Yarnovich, executive managing editor. **60% freelance written.** Monthly magazine covering home decor. "*Romantic Homes* is the magazine for women who want to create a warm, intimate, and casually elegant home—a haven that is both a gathering place for family and friends and a private refuge from the pressures of the outside world. The *Romantic Homes* reader is personally involved in the decor of her home. Features offer unique ideas and how-to advice on decorating, home furnishings, and gardening. Departments focus on floor and wall coverings, paint, textiles, refinishing, architectural elements, artwork, travel, and entertaining. Every article responds to the reader's need to create a beautiful, attainable environment, providing her with the style ideas and resources to achieve her own romantic home." Estab. 1994. Circ. 140,000. **Pays on acceptance.** Publishes ms an average of 2 months after acceptance. Byline given. Buys all rights. Editorial lead time 5 months. Submit seasonal material 6 months in advance. Accepts queries by mail, fax. Accepts simultaneous submissions. Responds in 2 weeks to queries; 2 months to mss. Writer's guidelines for #10 SASE.
Nonfiction: "Not just for dreaming, *Romantic Homes* combines unique ideas and inspirations with practical how-to advice on decorating, home furnishings, remodeling, and gardening for readers who are actively involved in improving their homes. Every article responds to the reader's need to know how to do it and where to find it." Essays, how-to, new product, personal experience, travel. **Buys 150 mss/year.** Query with published clips. Length: 1,000-1,200 words. **Pays $500.**
Photos: State availability of or send photos with submission. Reviews transparencies. Buys all rights. Captions, identification of subjects, model releases required.
Columns/Departments: Departments cover antiques, collectibles, artwork, shopping, travel, refinishing, architectural elements, flower arranging, entertaining, and decorating. Length: 400-600 words. **Pays $250.**
Tips: "Submit great ideas with photos."

$ $ SEATTLE HOMES AND LIFESTYLES, Wiesner Publishing LLC, 1221 East Pike St., Suite 204, Seattle WA 98122-3930. (206)322-6699. Fax: (206)322-2799. E-mail: falbert@seattlehomesmag.com. Website: www.seattlehomesmag.com. **Contact:** Fred Albert, editor. **60% freelance written.** Magazine published 8 times/year covering home design and lifestyles. "*Seattle Homes and Lifestyles* showcases the finest homes and gardens in the Northwest, and the personalities and lifestyles that make this region special. We try to help our readers take full advantage of the resources the region has to offer with in-depth coverage of events, travel, entertaining, shopping, food, and wine. And we write about it with a warm, personal approach that underscores our local perspective." Estab. 1996. Circ. 30,000. **Pays on acceptance.** Publishes ms an average of 2 months after acceptance. Byline given. Offers 25% kill fee. Buys first, electronic rights. Editorial lead time 3 months. Submit seasonal material 4 months in advance. Accepts queries by mail. Accepts previously published material. Accepts simultaneous submissions. Responds in 4 months to queries. Writer's guidelines for #10 SASE, online, or by e-mail.

Nonfiction: General interest, how-to (decorating, cooking), interview/profile, photo feature, travel. "No essays, journal entries, sports coverage." **Buys 95 mss/year.** Query with published clips. Length: 300-1,500 words. **Pays $125-375.**

Photos: State availability with submission. Reviews contact sheets, transparencies, prints. Buys one-time rights. Negotiates payment individually. Captions, identification of subjects, model releases required.

Columns/Departments: Profiles (human interest/people making contribution to community), 300 words; Design Watch (consumer pieces related to home design), 1,200 words; Taking Off (travel to a region, not 1 sole destination), 1,500 words; Artisan's Touch (craftperson producing work for the home), 400 words. **Buys 70 mss/year.** Query with published clips. **Pays $125-275.**

Tips: "We're always looking for experienced journalists with clips that demonstrate a knack for writing engaging, informative features. We're also looking for writers knowledgeable about architecture and decorating who can communicate a home's flavor and spirit through the written word. Since all stories are assigned by the editor, please do not submit manuscripts. Send a résumé and 3 published samples of your work. Story pitches are not encouraged. Please mail all submissions—do not e-mail or fax. Please don't call—we'll call you if we have an assignment. Writers from the Seattle area only (except travel)."

$ $ $ SOUTHERN ACCENTS, Southern Progress Corp., 2100 Lakeshore Dr., Birmingham AL 35209. (205)445-6000. Fax: (205)445-6990. Website: www.southernaccents.com. **Contact:** Frances MacDougall, managing editor. "*Southern Accents* celebrates the best of the South." Estab. 1977. Circ. 370,000. Accepts queries by mail. Responds in 2 months to queries.

Nonfiction: "Each issue features the finest homes and gardens along with a balance of features that reflect the affluent lifestyles of its readers, including architecture, antiques, entertaining, collecting and travel." Query by mail with SASE, clips, and photos.

The online magazine carries original content not found in the print edition. Contact: Rex Perry, online editor.

Tips: "Query us only with specific ideas targeted to our current columns."

N $ $ $ STYLE AT HOME, Transcontinental Media, Inc., 25 Sheppard Ave. W., Suite 100, Toronto, Ontario M2N 6S7, Canada. (416)733-7600. Fax: (416)218-3632. E-mail: letters@styleathome.com. Managing Editor: Laurie Grassi. **Contact:** Gail Johnston Habs, editor. **85% freelance written.** Magazine published 9 times/year. "The number one magazine choice of Canadian women aged 25 to 54 who own a home and have a serious interest in decorating. Provides an authoritative, stylish collection of inspiring and accessible interiors, decor projects; reports on style design trends." Estab. 1997. Circ. 195,000. **Pays on acceptance.** Publishes ms an average of 4 months after acceptance. Byline given. Offers 50% kill fee. Buys first, electronic rights. Editorial lead time 4 months. Submit seasonal material 6 months in advance. Accepts queries by mail, e-mail. Responds in 1 month to queries; 2 weeks to mss. Writer's guidelines by e-mail.

Break in by "familiarizing yourself with the type of interiors we show. Be very up-to-date with the design and home decor market in Canada. Provide a lead to a fabulous home or garden."

Nonfiction: Interview/profile, new product. "No how-to; these are planned in-house." **Buys 80 mss/year.** Query with published clips; include scouting shots with interior story queries. Length: 300-700 words. **Pays $300-1,000.** Sometimes pays expenses of writers on assignment.

Columns/Departments: Humor (fun home decor/renovating experiences), 500 words. Query with published clips. **Pays $250-500.**

$ $ TIMBER FRAME HOMES, Home Buyer Publications, 4200-T Lafayette Center Dr., Chantilly VA 20151. Fax: (703)222-3209. E-mail: editor@timberframehomes.com. Website: www.timberframehomes.com. **Contact:** Tracy M. Ruff, editor. **50% freelance written.** Quarterly magazine for people who own or are planning to build contemporary timber frame homes. It is devoted exclusively to timber frame homes that have a freestanding frame and wooden joinery. Our interest in historical, reconstructed timber frames and one-of-a-kind owner-built homes is secondary and should be queried first. Estab. 1991. Circ. 92,500. **Pays on acceptance.** Publishes ms an average of 3 months after acceptance. Byline given. Offers $100 kill fee. Buys first rights. Accepts queries by mail, e-mail. Sample copy for $4. Writer's guidelines for #10 SASE.

Nonfiction: Book excerpts, general interest, how-to, interview/profile, new product, photo feature, technical. No historical articles. **Buys 15 mss/year.** Query with published clips. Length: 1,200-1,400 words. **Pays $300-500.** Sometimes pays expenses of writers on assignment.

Photos: State availability with submission. Reviews contact sheets, transparencies, prints. Buys one-time rights. Negotiates payment individually.

Columns/Departments: Constructive Advice (timber frame construction); Interior Elements (decorating); Drawing Board (design), all 1,200-1,400 words. **Buys 6 mss/year.** Query with published clips. **Pays $300-500.**

$ $ UNIQUE HOMES MAGAZINE, Network Communications, 327 Wall St., Princeton NJ 08540. Fax: (609)688-0201. E-mail: lkim@uniquehomes.com. Website: www.uniquehomes.com. Editor: Kathleen Carlin-Russell. **Contact:** Lauren Baier Kim, managing editor. **20% freelance written.** Bimonthly magazine covering luxury real estate for consumers and the high-end real estate industry. "Our focus is the luxury real estate market, i.e., trends and luxury homes (including luxury home architecture, interior design, and landscaping)." Pays on publication. Publishes ms an average of 3 months after acceptance. Byline given. Makes work-for-hire assignments. Editorial lead time 3 months. Submit seasonal material 5 months in advance. Accepts queries by mail, e-mail, fax. Responds in 1 month to queries. Sample copy online. Writer's guidelines not available.

Nonfiction: Looking for luxury interiors, architecture and landscaping, high-end luxury real estate profiles on cities and geographical regions. Special issues: Waterfront Properties; Golf issue; Ski issue; Outlook issue. **Buys 32 mss/year.** Query with published clips and résumé. Length: 300-1,500 words. **Pays $150-550.** Sometimes pays expenses of writers on assignment.

Photos: State availability of or send photos with submission. Reviews transparencies, prints. Buys one-time rights. Negotiates payment individually. Captions required.

Columns/Departments: News and Reviews (timely shorts on real estate news and trends), 100 words; Creating Style (luxury interiors), 300-600 words; Creating Structure (luxury architecture), 300-600 words; Creating Scenery (luxury landscaping), 300-600 words. **Buys 18 mss/year.** Query with published clips and résumé. **Pays $150-550.**

Tips: "Always looking for creative and interesting story ideas on interior decorating, architecture, and landscaping for the luxury home. For profiles on specific geographical areas, seeking writers with an in-depth personal knowledge of the luxury real estate trends in those locations."

$ $ VICTORIAN HOMES, Y-Visionary Publishing L.P., 265 S. Anita Dr., Suite 120, Orange CA 92868-3310. (714)939-9991 ext. 332. Fax: (714)939-9909. E-mail: ekotite@pacbell.net. Website: www.victorianhomesmag.com. Managing Editor: Cathy Yarnovich. **Contact:** Erika Kotite, editor. **90% freelance written.** Bimonthly magazine covering Victorian home restoration and decoration. "*Victorian Homes* is read by Victorian home owners, restorers, house museum management and others interested in the Victorian revival. Feature articles cover home architecture, interior design, furnishings and the home's history. Photography is *very* important to the feature." Estab. 1981. Circ. 100,000. **Pays on acceptance.** Publishes ms an average of 1 year after acceptance. Byline given. Offers $50 kill fee. Buys first North American serial, one-time rights. Editorial lead time 4 months. Submit seasonal material 1 year in advance. Accepts queries by mail, e-mail, fax. Accepts simultaneous submissions. Responds in 6 weeks to queries; 2 months to mss. Sample copy and writer's guidelines for SAE.

O¬ Break in with "access to good photography and reasonable knowledge of the Victorian era."

Nonfiction: "Article must deal with structures—no historical articles on Victorian people or lifestyles." How-to (create period style curtains, wall treatments, bathrooms, kitchens, etc.), photo feature. **Buys 30-35 mss/year.** Query. Length: 800-1,800 words. **Pays $300-500.** Sometimes pays expenses of writers on assignment.

Photos: State availability with submission. Reviews $2\frac{1}{4} \times 2\frac{1}{4}$ transparencies. Buys one-time rights. Negotiates payment individually. Captions required.

$ $ WATER GARDENING, The Magazine for Pondkeepers, The Water Gardeners, Inc., P.O. Box 607, St. John IN 46373. (219)374-9419. Fax: (219)374-9052. E-mail: editor@watergardening.com. Website: www.watergardening.com. **Contact:** Sue Speichert, editor. **50% freelance written.** Bimonthly magazine. *Water Gardening* is for hobby water gardeners. "We prefer articles from a first-person perspective." Estab. 1996. Circ. 25,000. Pays on publication. Publishes ms an average of 6 months after acceptance. Byline given. Offers 50% kill fee. Buys first North American serial rights. Editorial lead time 6 months. Submit seasonal material 6-12 months in advance. Accepts queries by mail, e-mail, fax. Responds in 1 month to queries; 3 months to mss. Sample copy for $3. Writer's guidelines for #10 SASE.

Nonfiction: Sue Speichert. How-to (construct, maintain, improve ponds, water features), interview/profile, new product, personal experience, photo feature. **Buys 18-20 mss/year.** Query. Length: 600-1,500 words.

Photos: State availability with submission. Reviews contact sheets, 3×5 transparencies, 3×5 prints. Buys one-time rights. Negotiates payment individuallly. Captions, identification of subjects, model releases required.

HUMOR

Publications listed here specialize in gaglines or prose humor, some for readers and others for performers or speakers. Other publications that use humor can be found in nearly every category in this book. Some have special needs for major humor pieces; some use humor as fillers; many others are interested in material that meets their ordinary fiction or nonfiction requirements but also has a humorous slant. The majority of humor articles must be submitted as complete manuscripts or speculation because editors usually can't know from a query whether or not the piece will be right for them.

$ COMEDY WRITERS ASSOCIATION NEWSLETTER, P.O. Box 605, Times Plaza Station, 542 Atlantic Ave., Brooklyn NY 11217-0605. (718)855-5057. E-mail: makinsonrobert@hotmail.com. **Contact:** Robert Makinson, editor.

10% freelance written. Semiannual newsletter on comedy writing for association members. Estab. 1989. **Pays on acceptance.** Publishes ms an average of 3 months after acceptance. Byline given. Buys all rights. Accepts queries by mail, e-mail. Responds in 2 weeks to queries; 1 month to mss. Sample copy for $5. Writer's guidelines for #10 SASE.
Nonfiction: "You may submit articles and byline will be given if used, but at present payment is only made for jokes. Emphasis should be on marketing, not general humor articles." How-to (articles about marketing, directories, Internet, new trends). Query. Length: 250-500 words.
Tips: "The easiest way to be mentioned in the publication is to submit short jokes. (Payment is $1-3/joke). Jokes for professional speakers preferred. Include SASE when submitting jokes."

$ FUNNY TIMES, A Monthly Humor Review, Funny Times, Inc., P.O. Box 18530, Cleveland Heights OH 44118. (216)371-8600. Fax: (216)371-8696. E-mail: ft@funnytimes.com. Website: www.funnytimes.com. **Contact:** Raymond Lesser, Susan Wolpert, editors. **10% freelance written.** Monthly tabloid for humor. "*Funny Times* is a monthly review of America's funniest cartoonists and writers. We are the *Reader's Digest* of modern American humor with a progressive/peace-oriented/environmental/politically activist slant." Estab. 1985. Circ. 58,000. Pays on publication. Publishes ms an average of 3 months after acceptance. Byline given. Buys one-time, second serial (reprint) rights. Editorial lead time 2 months. Accepts previously published material. Accepts simultaneous submissions. Responds in 3 months to mss. Sample copy for $3 or 9×12 SAE with 4 first-class stamps. Writer's guidelines online.
Nonfiction: "We only publish humor or interviews with funny people (comedians, comic actors, cartoonists, etc.). Everything we publish is very funny. If your piece isn't extremely funny then don't bother to send it. Don't send us anything that's not outrageously funny. Don't send anything that other people haven't already read and told you they laughed so hard they peed their pants." Essays (funny), humor, interview/profile, opinion (humorous), personal experience (absolutely funny). **Buys 36 mss/year.** Send complete ms. Length: 500-700 words. **Pays $50 minimum.**
Reprints: Accepts previously published submissions.
Columns/Departments: Query with published clips.
Fiction: Humorous. **Buys 6 mss/year.** Query with published clips. Length: 500 words. **Pays $50-150.**
Fillers: Short humor. **Buys 6/year. Pays $20.**
Tips: "Send us a small packet (1-3 items) of only your very funniest stuff. If this makes us laugh we'll be glad to ask for more. We particularly welcome previously published material that has been well-received elsewhere."

INFLIGHT

Most major inflight magazines cater to business travelers and vacationers who will be reading during the flight, about the airline's destinations and other items of general interest.

$ $ $ $ ATTACHÉ MAGAZINE, Pace Communications, 1301 Carolina St., Greensboro NC 27401. (336)378-6065. Fax: (336)378-8278. E-mail: attacheair@aol.com. Website: www.attachemag.com. Editor: Lance Elko. **Contact:** Submissions Editor. **75% freelance written.** Monthly magazine for travelers on U.S. Airways. "We focus on 'the best of the world' and use a humorous view." Estab. 1997. Circ. 441,000. **Pays on acceptance.** Publishes ms an average of 4 months after acceptance. Byline given. Offers kill fee. Buys first global serial rights. Editorial lead time 3 months. Accepts queries by mail, e-mail. Responds in 6 weeks to queries; 1 month to mss. Sample copy for $7.50 or online. Writer's guidelines for #10 SASE or online.
Nonfiction: Features are highly visual, focusing on some unusual or unique angle of travel, food, business, or other topic approved by an *Attaché* editor." Book excerpts, essays, general interest, personal experience, travel, food; lifestyle; sports. **Buys 50-75 mss/year.** Query with published clips. Length: 350-2,500 words. **Pays $350-2,500.** Sometimes pays expenses of writers on assignment.
Photos: State availability with submission. Reviews contact sheets, negatives, transparencies. Buys one-time rights. Negotiates payment individually. Identification of subjects, model releases required.
Columns/Departments: Passions includes several topics such as "Vices," "Food," "Golf," "Sporting," "Shelf Life," and "Things That Go"; Paragons features short lists of the best in a particular field or category, as well as 400-word pieces describing the best of something—for example, the best home tool, the best ice cream in Paris, and the best reading library. Each piece should lend itself to highly visual art. Informed Sources are departments of expertise and first-person accounts; they include "How It Works," "Home Front," "Improvement," and "Genius at Work." **Buys 50-75 mss/year.** Query. **Pays $500-2,000.**
Tips: "We look for cleverly written, entertaining articles with a unique angle, particularly pieces that focus on 'the best of' something. Study the magazine for content, style and tone. Queries for story ideas should be to the point and presented clearly. Any correspondence should include SASE."

$ $ $ HEMISPHERES, Pace Communications for United Airlines, 1301 Carolina St., Greensboro NC 27401. (336)383-5800. E-mail: hemiedit@aol.com. Website: www.hemispheresmagazine.com. **Contact:** Mr. Selby Bateman, senior editor. **95% freelance written.** Monthly magazine for the educated, sophisticated business and recreational frequent traveler on an airline that spans the globe. Estab. 1992. Circ. 500,000. **Pays on acceptance.** Publishes ms an average of 3 months after acceptance. Byline given. Offers 20% kill fee. Buys first worldwide rights. Editorial lead time 8 months. Submit seasonal material 8 months in advance. Accepts queries by mail. Responds in 2 months to queries; 4 months to mss. Sample copy for $7.50. Writer's guidelines for #10 SASE.

Nonfiction: "Keeping 'global' in mind, we look for topics that reflect a modern appreciation of the world's cultures and environment. No 'What I did (or am going to do) on a trip to. . . .' " General interest, humor, personal experience. Query with published clips. Length: 500-3,000 words. **Pays 50¢/word and up.**

Photos: State availability with submission. Reviews transparencies "only when we request them." Buys one-time rights. Negotiates payment individually. Captions, identification of subjects, model releases required.

Columns/Departments: Making a Difference (Q&A format interview with world leaders, movers, and shakers. A 500-600 word introduction anchors the interview. We want to profile an international mix of men and women representing a variety of topics or issues, but all must truly be making a difference. No puffy celebrity profiles.); 15 Fascinating Facts (A snappy selection of 1- or 2-sentence obscure, intriguing, or travel-service-oriented items that the reader never knew about a city, state, country, or destination.); Executive Secrets (Things that top executives know); Case Study (Business strategies of international companies or organizations. No lionizations of CEOs. Strategies should be the emphasis. "We want international candidates."); Weekend Breakway (Takes us just outside a major city after a week of business for several activities for a physically active, action-packed weekend. This isn't a sedentary "getaway" at a "property."); Roving Gourmet (Insider's guide to interesting eating in major city, resort area, or region. The slant can be anything from ethnic to expensive; not just "best." The 4 featured eateries span a spectrum from "hole in the wall," to "expense account lunch," and on to "big deal dining."); Collecting (Occasional 800-word story on collections and collecting that can emphasize travel.); Eye on Sports (Global look at anything of interest in sports.); Vintage Traveler (Options for mature, experienced travelers.); Savvy Shopper (Insider's tour of best places in the world to shop. Savvy Shopper steps beyond all those stories that just mention the great shopping at a particular destination. A shop-by-shop, gallery-by-gallery tour of the best places in the world.); Science and Technology (Substantive, insightful stories on how technology is changing our lives and the business world. Not just another column on audio components or software. No gift guides!); Aviation Journal (For those fascinated with aviation. Topics range widely.); Terminal Bliss (A great airports guide series.); Grape And Grain (Wine and spirits with emphasis on education, not one-upmanship.); Show Business (Films, music, and entertainment); Musings (Humor or just curious musings.); Quick Quiz (Tests to amuse and educate.); Travel Trends (Brief, practical, invaluable, global, trend-oriented.); Book Beat (Tackles topics like the Wodehouse Society, the birth of a book, the competition between local bookshops and national chains. Please, no review proposals.); What the World's Reading (Residents explore how current bestsellers tell us what their country is thinking.). Length: 1,400 words. Query with published clips. **Pays 50¢/word and up.**

Fiction: Adventure, humorous, mainstream, explorations of those issues common to all people but within the context of a particular culture. **Buys 14 mss/year.** Query. Length: 1,000-4,000 words. **Pays 50¢/word and up.**

Tips: "We increasingly require writers of 'destination' pieces or departments to 'live whereof they write.' Increasingly want to hear from U.S., U.K., or other English-speaking/writing journalists (business & travel) who reside outside the U.S. in Europe, South America, Central America, and the Pacific Rim—all areas that United flies. We're not looking for writers who aim at the inflight market. *Hemispheres* broke the fluffy mold of that tired domestic genre. Our monthly readers are a global mix on the cutting edge of the global economy and culture. They don't need to have the world filtered by U.S. writers. We want a Hong Kong restaurant writer to speak for that city's eateries, so we need English-speaking writers around the globe. That's the 'insider' story our readers respect. We use resident writers for departments such as Roving Gourmet, Savvy Shopper, On Location, 3 Perfect Days, and Weekend Breakaway, but authoritative writers can roam in features. Sure we cover the U.S., but with a global view: No 'in this country' phraseology. 'Too American' is a frequent complaint for queries. We use UK English spellings in articles that speak from that tradition and we specify costs in local currency first before U.S. dollars. Basically, all of above serves the realization that today, 'global' begins with respect for 'local.' That approach permits a wealth of ways to present culture, travel, and business for a wide readership. We anchor that with a reader-service mission that grounds everything in 'how to do it.'"

$ $ HORIZON AIR MAGAZINE, Paradigm Communications Group, 2701 First Ave., Suite 250, Seattle WA 98121. Fax: (206)448-6939. **Contact:** Michele Andrus Dill, editor. **90% freelance written.** Monthly inflight magazine covering travel, business, and leisure in the Pacific Northwest. "*Horizon Air Magazine* serves a sophisticated audience of business and leisure travelers. Stories must have a Northwest slant." Estab. 1990. Circ. 425,000/month. Pays on publication. Publishes ms an average of 1 year after acceptance. Byline given. Offers 33% kill fee. Buys first North American serial, electronic rights. Editorial lead time 6 months. Submit seasonal material 5 months in advance. Accepts queries by mail, fax. Sample copy for 10×12 SASE. Writer's guidelines for #10 SASE.

Nonfiction: Essays (personal), general interest, historical/nostalgic, how-to, humor, interview/profile, personal experience, photo feature, travel, business. Special issues: Meeting planners' guide, golf, gift guide. No material unrelated to the Pacific Northwest. **Buys approximately 36 mss/year.** Query with published clips or send complete ms. Length: 1,500-3,000 words. **Pays $300-700.** Sometimes pays expenses of writers on assignment.

Photos: State availability with submission. Reviews transparencies, prints. Buys one-time rights. Negotiates payment individually. Captions, identification of subjects, model releases required.

Columns/Departments: Region (Northwest news/profiles), 200-400 words; Air Time (personal essays), 700 words. **Buys 15 mss/year.** Query with published clips. **Pays $100 (Region), $250 (Air Time).**

$ $ MERIDIAN, Adventure Media, 3983 S. McCarran Blvd., Suite 434, Reno NV 89502. (775)856-3532. Fax: (775)829-2457. E-mail: meridian@adventuremedia.com. Website: www.adventuremedia.com. **Contact:** Lisa Wogan, editor. **80% freelance written.** Monthly inflight magazine. "All queries must have a connection to the cities where Midway flies (mostly East Coast destinations). We're interested in things to see and do that are not on every tourism brochure: think off-the-beaten path. Also, we want to meet the people behind the story, whether it's a business short or a feature." Circ. 220,000. Pays 30 days after publication. Publishes ms an average of 3 months after acceptance. Byline given. Offers 25% kill fee. Buys first North American serial rights. Editorial lead time 3 months. Submit seasonal material 6 months in advance. Accepts queries by mail, e-mail. Accepts simultaneous submissions. Responds in 2 months to queries; 3 months to mss. Sample copy for $2. Writer's guidelines for #10 SASE or by e-mail.

Nonfiction: Essays, general interest, interview/profile, travel. No nostalgia, how-to or technical. Query with published clips. Length: 250-2,000 words. **Pays 25-35¢/word for assigned articles; 20-25¢/word for unsolicited articles.** Sometimes pays expenses of writers on assignment.

Photos: State availability with submission. Buys one-time rights. Negotiates payment individually. Identification of subjects, model releases required.

Columns/Departments: Departments include business, tech and dining.

Tips: "Start with front-of-the-book and back-of-the-book departments (business profiles, restaurant profiles, unusual event previews). If you can do a good job with a 300-word story, we'll feel more comfortable assigning longer pieces. Query by mail with one or two well-thought ideas, explaining why they'd work for our magazine."

$ MIDWEST EXPRESS MAGAZINE, Paradigm Communications Group, 2701 First Ave., Suite 250, Seattle WA 98121. **Contact:** Steve Hansen, managing editor. **90% freelance written.** Bimonthly magazine for Midwest Express Airlines. "Positive depiction of the changing economy and culture of the US, plus travel and leisure features." Estab. 1993. Circ. 35,000. Pays on publication. Byline given. Buys first North American serial rights. Editorial lead time 9 months. Accepts queries by mail. Responds in 6 weeks to queries. Sample copy for 9×12 SASE. Writer's guidelines free.

• *Midwest Express* continues to look for *sophisticated* travel and golf writing.

Nonfiction: Travel, business, sports and leisure. Special issues: "Need good ideas for golf articles in spring." No humor, how-to, or fiction. **Buys 20-25 mss/year.** Query by mail only with published clips and résumé. Length: 250-3,000 words. **Pays $100 minimum.** Sometimes pays expenses of writers on assignment.

Columns/Departments: Preview (arts and events), 200-400 words; Portfolio (business), 200-500 words. **Buys 12-15 mss/year.** Query with published clips. **Pays $100-150.**

Tips: "Article ideas *must* encompass areas within the airline's route system. We buy quality writing from reliable writers. Editorial philosophy emphasizes innovation and positive outlook. Do not send manuscripts unless you have no clips."

$ $ $ $ SOUTHWEST AIRLINES SPIRIT, 4333 Amon Carter Blvd., Fort Worth TX 76155-9616. (817)967-1804. Fax: (817)967-1571. E-mail: john.clark@spiritmag.com. Website: www.spiritmag.com. **Contact:** John Clark, editorial director. Monthly magazine for passengers on Southwest Airlines. Estab. 1992. Circ. 350,000. **Pays on acceptance.** Byline given. Buys first North American serial, electronic rights. Responds in 1 month to queries.

Nonfiction: "Seeking accessible, entertaining, relevant and timely glimpses of people, places, products and trends in the regions Southwest Airlines serves. Newsworthy/noteworthy topics; well-researched and multiple source only. Experienced magazine professionals only. Business, travel, technology, sports and lifestyle (food, fitness and culture) are some of the topics covered in *Spirit*." **Buys 40 mss/year.** Query by mail only with published clips. Length: 1,800 words. **Pays $1/word.** Pays expenses of writers on assignment.

Columns/Departments: Length: 800 to 1,000 words. **Buys 21 mss/year.** Query by mail only with published clips. **Pay varies.**

Fillers: Buys 12/year. Length: 250 words. **Pays variable amount.**

Tips: "*Southwest Airlines Spirit* magazine reaches nearly 2.1 million readers every month aboard Southwest Airlines. Our median reader is a college-educated, 38-year-old business person with a household income of nearly $100,000. Our stories tap the vitality of life through accessible, entertaining and oftentimes unconventional glimpses of people, places, products and trends in the regions that Southwest Airlines serves. Business, travel, technology, sports and lifestyle (food, fitness and culture) are some of the topics covered in *Spirit*."

$ $ SPIRIT OF ALOHA, The Inflight Magazine of Aloha Airlines and Island Air, Honolulu Publishing Co., Ltd., 36 Merchant St., Honolulu HI 96813. (808)524-7400. Fax: (808)531-2306. E-mail: jotaguro@honpub.com. Website: www.spiritofaloha.com. **Contact:** Janice Otaguro, editor. **50% freelance written.** Bimonthly magazine covering visitor activities/destinations and Hawaii culture and history. "Although we are an inflight magazine for an inter-island airline, we try to keep our editorial as fresh and lively for residents as much as for visitors." Estab. 1978. Circ. 60,000. **Pays on acceptance.** Publishes ms an average of 2 months after acceptance. Byline given. Buys first rights. Editorial lead time 2 months. Submit seasonal material 2 months in advance. Accepts queries by mail, e-mail. Responds in 2 months to queries. Sample copy and writer's guidelines free.

Nonfiction: All must be related to Hawaii. Book excerpts, general interest, historical/nostalgic, interview/profile, photo feature, travel. No poetry or "How I spent my vacation in Hawaii" type pieces. **Buys 24 mss/year.** Query with published clips. Length: 1,500-2,500 words. **Pays $500.** Sometimes pays expenses of writers on assignment.

Photos: State availability with submission. Reviews transparencies. Buys one-time rights. Negotiates payment individually. Captions, identification of subjects, model releases required.

$ $ $ WASHINGTON FLYER MAGAZINE, 1707 L St., NW, Suite 800, Washington DC 20036. Fax: (202)331-2043. E-mail: readers@themagazinegroup.com. Website: www.fly2dc.com. **Contact:** Michael McCarthy, editor-in-chief. **60% freelance written.** Bimonthly magazine for business and pleasure travelers at Washington National and Washington Dulles International airports INSI. "Primarily affluent, well-educated audience that flies frequently in and out of Washington,

DC." Estab. 1989. Circ. 182,000. **Pays on acceptance.** Byline given. Offers 25% kill fee. Buys first North American serial rights. Submit seasonal material 4 months in advance. Accepts queries by mail, e-mail, fax. Responds in 10 weeks to queries. Sample copy and writer's guidelines for 9×12 SAE with $2 postage.

O‑‑ "First understand the magazine—from the nuances of its content to its tone. Best departments to get your foot in the door are 'Washington Insider' and 'Mini Escapes.' The former deals with new business, the arts, sports, etc. in Washington. The latter: getaways that are within four hours of Washington by car. Regarding travel, we're less apt to run stories on sedentary pursuits (e.g., inns, B&Bs, spas). Our readers want to get out and discover an area, whether it's DC or Barcelona. Action-oriented activities work best. Also, the best way to pitch is via e-mail. Our mail is sorted by interns, and sometimes I never get queries. E-mail is so immediate, and I can give a more personal response."

Nonfiction: One international destination feature per issue, determined 6 months in advance. One feature per issue on aspect of life in Washington. General interest, interview/profile, travel, business. No personal experiences, poetry, opinion or inspirational. **Buys 20-30 mss/year.** Query with published clips. Length: 800-1,200 words. **Pays $500-900.**

Photos: State availability with submission. Reviews negatives, almost always color transparencies. Buys one-time rights. Considers additional payment for top-quality photos accepted with ms. Identification of subjects required.

Columns/Departments: Washington Insider, Travel, Hospitality, Airports and Airlines, Restaurants, Shopping, all 800-1,200 words. Query. **Pays $500-900.**

Tips: "Know the Washington market and issues relating to frequent business/pleasure travelers as we move toward a global economy. With a bimonthly publication schedule it's important that stories remain viable as possible during the magazine's two-month 'shelf life.' No telephone calls, please and understand that most assignments are made several months in advance. Queries are best sent via e-mail."

$ $ ZOOM! MAGAZINE, Valley Media, LLC, 503 West 2600 South, Bountiful UT 84010-7717. (801)693-7300. Fax: (801)693-7310. E-mail: mildredevans@qwest.net. Website: www.zoominflight.com. **Contact:** Mildred Evans, editor. **75% freelance written.** Bimonthly magazine covering general interest, places and events in cities on Vanguard Airlines' schedules. Estab. 1996. Circ. 15,000; issue readership 200,000. Pays on publication. Publishes ms an average of 6 months after acceptance. Byline given. Offers $50 kill fee. Buys one-time rights. Editorial lead time 3 months. Submit seasonal material 3 months in advance. Accepts queries by mail, e-mail. Responds in 1 month to queries; 3 months to mss. Sample copy for $2. Writer's guidelines free.

Nonfiction: General interest, historical/nostalgic, interview/profile, new product, travel. No articles on business, humor, Internet or health. **Buys 12 mss/year.** Query with or without published clips. Length: 1,000-2,500 words. **Pays $100-250.**

Tips: "Submit previously published clips with a specific idea."

JUVENILE

Just as children change and grow, so do juvenile magazines. Children's magazine editors stress that writers must read recent issues. A wide variety of issues are addressed in the numerous magazines for the baby boom echo. Respecting nature, developing girls' self-esteem, and establishing good healthy habits all find an editorial niche. This section lists publications for children up to age 12. Magazines for young people 13-19 appear in the Teen and Young Adult category. Many of the following publications are produced by religious groups and, where possible, the specific denomination is given. For additional juvenile/young adult markets, see our sister publication *Children's Writer's & Illustrator's Market* (Writer's Digest Books).

$ $ $ ARCHAEOLOGY'S DIG MAGAZINE, Cobblestone Publishing, 30 Grove St., Suite C, Peterborough NH 03458-1454. (603)924-7209. Fax: (603)924-7380. E-mail: cfbakerIII@meganet.net. Website: www.digonsite.com. **Contact:** Rosalie Baker, editor. **50% freelance written.** Bimonthly magazine covering archaeology for kids ages 8-13. Estab. 1999. Circ. 35,000. Pays on publication. Publishes ms an average of 4 months after acceptance. Byline given. Offers 25% kill fee. Buys all rights. Editorial lead time 6 months. Submit seasonal material 3 months in advance. Accepts queries by mail, e-mail, fax. Responds in several months to queries; 1 month to mss. Sample copy for $4.95 with 8×11 SASE or $9 without SASE. Writer's guidelines online.

- Does *not* accept unsolicited material. Cobblestone Publishing, a division of The Cricket Magazine Group, recently purchased *Dig*, moving the offices from New York to New Hampshire. Rosalie Baker, editor of *Calliope*, is the new editor.

Nonfiction: Personal experience, photo feature, travel, archaeological excavation reports. No fiction. Occasional paleontology stories accepted. **Buys 12 mss/year.** Query with published clips. Length: 100-1,000 words. **Pays 20-25¢/word.**

Photos: State availability with submission. Buys one-time rights. Negotiates payment individually. Identification of subjects required.

Tips: "Please remember that this is a children's magazine for kids ages 8-13 so the tone is light-hearted, but scholarly, and as kid-friendly as possible."

$ BABYBUG, Carus Publishing Co., P.O. Box 300, Peru IL 61354. (815)224-6656. Editor-in-Chief: Marianne Carus. **Contact:** Paula Morrow, editor. **50% freelance written.** Board-book magazine published monthly except for combined

May/June and July/August issues. "*Babybug* is 'the listening and looking magazine for infants and toddlers,' intended to be read aloud by a loving adult to foster a love of books and reading in young children ages 6 months-2 years." Estab. 1994. Circ. 45,000. Pays on publication. Publishes ms an average of 18 months after acceptance. Byline given. Buys variable rights. Editorial lead time 10 months. Submit seasonal material 1 year in advance. Accepts simultaneous submissions. Sample copy for $5. Writer's guidelines for #10 SASE.

Nonfiction: General interest. **Buys 10-20 mss/year.** Send complete ms. Length: 1-10 words. **Pays $25.**

Fiction: Anything for infants and toddlers. Adventure, humorous. **Buys 10-20 mss/year.** Send complete ms. Length: 2-8 short sentences. **Pays $25 and up.**

Poetry: Buys 8-10 poems/year. Submit maximum 5 poems. Length: 2-8 lines. **Pays $25.**

Tips: "Imagine having to read your story or poem—out loud—50 times or more! That's what parents will have to do. Babies and toddlers demand, 'Read it again'—your material must hold up under repetition."

$ $ $ BOYS' LIFE, Boy Scouts of America, P.O. Box 152079, Irving TX 75015-2079. Fax: (972)580-2079. Website: www.bsa.scouting.org. **Contact:** Michael Goldman, senior editor. **75% freelance written.** Prefers to work with published/established writers; works with small number of new/unpublished writers each year. Monthly magazine covering activities of interest to all boys ages 6-18. Most readers are Boy Scouts or Cub Scouts. Estab. 1911. Circ. 1,300,000. **Pays on acceptance.** Publishes ms an average of 1 year after acceptance. Buys one-time rights. Accepts queries by mail, fax. Responds in 2 months to queries. Sample copy for $3 and 9×12 SAE. Writer's guidelines for #10 SASE or online.

Nonfiction: Subject matter is broad, everything from professional sports to American history to how to pack a canoe. Look at a current list of the BSA's more than 100 merit badge pamphlets for an idea of the wide range of subjects possible. Uses strong photo features with about 500 words of text. Separate payment or assignment for photos. How-to, photo feature, hobby and craft ideas. **Buys 60 mss/year.** Query with SASE. No phone queries. Length: Major articles run 500-1,500 words; preferred length is about 1,000 words, including sidebars and boxes. **Pays $400-1,500.** Pays expenses of writers on assignment.

Columns/Departments: Rich Haddaway, associate editor. "Science, nature, earth, health, sports, space and aviation, cars, computers, entertainment, pets, history, music are some of the columns for which we use 300-750 words of text. This is a good place to show us what you can do." **Buys 75-80 mss/year.** Query. **Pays $250-300.**

Fiction: Fiction Editor. Include SASE. Adventure, humorous, mystery, science fiction. **Buys 12-15 mss/year.** Send complete ms. Length: 1,000-1,500 words. **Pays $750 minimum.**

Fillers: Freelance comics pages and scripts.

Tips: "We strongly recommend reading at least 12 issues of the magazine before you submit queries. We are a good market for any writer willing to do the necessary homework."

$ BREAD FOR GOD'S CHILDREN, Bread Ministries, Inc., P.O. Box 1017, Arcadia FL 34265. (863)494-6214. Fax: (863)993-0154. E-mail: bread@sunline.net. Editor: Judith M. Gibbs. **Contact:** Susan Callahan, editorial secretary. **10% freelance written.** Published 8 times/year. "An interdenominational Christian teaching publication published 8 times/year written to aid children and youth in leading a Christian life." Estab. 1972. Circ. 10,000. Pays on publication. Publishes ms an average of 6 months after acceptance. Byline given. Buys first rights. Accepts queries by mail. Accepts simultaneous submissions. Responds in 6 months to mss. Three sample copies for 9×12 SAE and 5 first-class stamps. Writer's guidelines for #10 SASE.

- Break in with a good story about a 6-10 year old gaining insight into a spiritual principle—without an adult preaching the message to him.

Reprints: Send tearsheet and information about when and where the material previously appeared.

Columns/Departments: Let's Chat (children's Christian values), 500-700 words; Teen Page (youth Christian values), 600-800 words; Idea Page (games, crafts, Bible drills). **Buys 5-8 mss/year.** Send complete ms. **Pays $30.**

Fiction: "We are looking for writers who have a solid knowledge of Biblical principles and are concerned for the youth of today living by those principles. Our stories must be well written, with the story itself getting the message across—no preaching, moralizing, or tag endings." No fantasy, science fiction, or nonChristian themes. **Buys 15-20 mss/year.** Send complete ms. Length: 600-800 words (young children), 900-1,500 words (older children). **Pays $40-50.**

Tips: "We're looking for more submissions on healing miracles and reconciliation/restoration. Follow usual guidelines for careful writing, editing, and proofreading. We get many manuscripts with misspellings, poor grammar, careless typing. Know your subject—writer should know the Lord to write about the Christian life. Study the publication and our guidelines."

$ $ CALLIOPE, Exploring World History, Cobblestone Publishing Co., 30 Grove St., Suite C, Peterborough NH 03458-1454. (603)924-7209. Fax: (603)924-7380. E-mail: editorial@cobblestone.mv.com. Website: www.cobblestonepub.com. Editors: Rosalie and Charles Baker. **Contact:** Rosalie F. Baker, editor. **More than 50% freelance written.** Magazine published 9 times/year covering world history (East and West) through 1800 AD for 8- to 14-year-olds. Articles must relate to the issue's theme. Circ. 11,000. Pays on publication. Byline given. Buys all rights. Sample copy for $4.50 and 7½×10½ SASE with 4 first-class stamps or online. Writer's guidelines for SASE or online.

- Break in with a "well-written query on a topic that relates directly to an upcoming issue's theme, a writing sample that is well-researched and concise and a bibliography that includes new research."

Nonfiction: Articles must relate to the theme. Essays, general interest, historical/nostalgic, how-to (activities), humor, interview/profile, personal experience, photo feature, technical, travel, recipes. No religious, pornographic, biased or sophisticated submissions. **Buys 30-40 mss/year.** Query by mail only with published clips. Length: 700-800 words for feature articles; 300-600 words for supplemental nonfiction. **Pays 20-25¢/printed word.**
Photos: State availability with submission. Reviews contact sheets, Color slides and b&w prints. Buys one-time rights. Pays $15-100 (color cover negotiated).
Columns/Departments: Activities (crafts, recipes, projects); up to 700 words. Query by mail only with published clips. **Pays on individual basis.**
Fiction: All fiction must be theme-related. **Buys 10 mss/year.** Length: 1,000 words maximum. **Pays 20-25¢/word.**
Fillers: Puzzles and games (no word finds); crossword and other word puzzles using the vocabulary of the issue's theme; mazes and picture puzzles that relate to the theme. **Pays on individual basis.**
Tips: "A query must consist of all of the following to be considered (please use non-erasable paper): a brief cover letter stating the subject and word length of the proposed article; a detailed one-page outline explaining the information to be presented in the article; an extensive bibliography of materials the author intends to use in preparing the article; a self-addressed stamped envelope. (Authors are urged to use primary resources and up-to-date scholarly resources in their bibliography.) Writers new to *Calliope* should send a writing sample with the query. In all correspondence, please include your complete address as well as a telephone number where you can be reached."

$ CELEBRATE, WordAction Publishing Co., 6401 The Paseo, Kansas City MO 64131. (816)333-7000, ext. 2358. Fax: (816)333-4439. E-mail: mhammer@nazarene.org. Website: www.wordaction.com. **Contact:** Melissa Hammer, early childhood curriculum editor. Weekly newspaper featuring a children's Sunday school theme. "*Celebrate* is a full-color story paper for 3-6 year olds which correlates directly with the WordAction Sunday school curriculum. It is designed to connect Sunday school learning with the daily living experiences and growth of the child." Circ. 12,000. Pays on publication. Publishes ms an average of 1 year after acceptance. Byline given. multi-use rights Editorial lead time 1 year. Submit seasonal material 1 year in advance. Accepts queries by mail, e-mail. Accepts simultaneous submissions. Responds in 2 weeks to queries; 1 month to mss. Writer's guidelines and theme list for #10 SASE.

- This story paper replaces *Together Time* and *Listen*, published by WordAction. Debut issue was September 2001.

Columns/Departments: Songs; Rhymes; Crafts; Fingerplays; Recipes; Simple (20 pt.) Dot-to-Dot picture ideas; Simple puzzle or maze ideas. **Buys 30 mss/year.** Send complete ms. **Pays 25¢/line-$15.**
Poetry: "We prefer rhythmic, pattern poems, but will accept free-verse if thought and 'read aloud' effect flow smoothly. Include word pictures of subject matter relating to everyday experiences. Avoid portrayal of extremely precocious, abnormally mature children." **Buys 20 poems/year.** Submit maximum 5 poems. Length: 4-8 lines. **Pays 25¢/line; $2 minimum.**
Tips: "We're looking for activities and poems on specific Bible characters like Daniel, Ruth and Naomi, David, Samuel, Paul. We need activities and crafts based on our Bible themes. Write on a 3- to 6-year-old level of understanding. We are currently in need of recipes that children can do successfully with adult supervision. We specifically need freelance submissions focused at the kindergarten age level."

$ $ CHICKADEE MAGAZINE, Discover a World of Fun, The Owl Group, Bayard Press Canada, 49 Front St. E., 2nd Floor, Toronto, Ontario M5E 1B3, Canada. (416)340-2700. Fax: (416)340-9769. E-mail: owl@owlkids.com. Website: www.owlkids.com. **Contact:** Angela Keenlyside, managing editor. **25% freelance written.** Magazine published 9 times/year for 6- to 9-year-olds. "We aim to interest children in the world around them in an entertaining and lively way." Estab. 1979. Circ. 110,000 Canada and US. Pays on publication. Byline given. Buys all rights. Accepts queries by mail, e-mail, fax. Responds in 3 months to queries. Sample copy for $4 and SAE ($2 money order or IRCs). Writer's guidelines for SAE ($2 money order or IRCs).
Nonfiction: How-to (easy and unusual arts and crafts), personal experience (real children in real situations). No articles for older children; no religious or moralistic features.
Photos: Send photos with submission. Reviews 35mm transparencies. Identification of subjects required.
Fiction: Adventure, humorous. No talking animal stories or religious articles. **Pays $200 (US).**
Tips: "A frequent mistake made by writers is trying to teach too much—not enough entertainment and fun."

$ $ ☆ CHILDREN'S PLAYMATE, Children's Better Health Institute, P.O. Box 567, Indianapolis IN 46206-0567. (317)636-8881 ext. 267. Fax: (317)684-8094. Website: www.cbhi.org/magazines/childrensplaymate/. **Contact:** (Ms.) Terry Harshman, editor. **40% freelance written.** Eager to work with new/unpublished writers. Magazine published 8 times/year for children ages 6-8. "We are looking for articles, poems, and activities with a health, fitness, or nutrition oriented theme. We try to present our material in a positive light, and we try to incorporate humor and a light approach wherever possible without minimizing the seriousness of what we are saying." Estab. 1929. Pays on publication. Byline given. Buys all rights. Submit seasonal material 8 months in advance. Responds in 3 months to queries. Sample copy for $1.75. Writer's guidelines for #10 SASE.

- May hold mss for up to 1 year before acceptance/publication.

O→ Include word count. Material will not be returned unless accompanied by a SASE.

Nonfiction: "A feature may be an interesting presentation on good health, exercise, proper nutrition and safety as well as science and historical breakthroughs in medicine." **Buys 25 mss/year.** Send complete ms. Length: 500 words maximum. **Pays up to 17¢/word.**
Fiction: Not buying much fiction right now except for rebus stories of 100-300 words and occasional poems. Vocabulary suitable for ages 6-8. Include word count. Send complete ms. **Pays minimum of 17¢/word.**

Fillers: Recipes, puzzles, dot-to-dots, color-ins, hidden pictures, mazes. Prefers camara-ready activities. Activity guidelines for #10 SASE. **Buys 25/year. Payment varies.**

Tips: "We need more historical nonfiction on medicine, medical breakthroughs (vaccines, etc.) and simple science articles with occasional experiments. We're especially interested in materials about health, nutrition, science, medicine, fitness, and fun."

$ $ CLUBHOUSE MAGAZINE, Focus on the Family, 8605 Explorer Dr., Colorado Springs CO 80920. Fax: (719)531-3499. Website: www.clubhousemagazine.org. Editor: Jesse Florea. **Contact:** Suzanne Hadley, assistant editor. **25% freelance written.** Monthly magazine geared for Christian kids ages 8-12. Estab. 1987. Circ. 118,000. **Pays on acceptance.** Byline given. Buys one-time rights. Editorial lead time 5 months. Submit seasonal material 7 months in advance. Sample copy for $1.50 with 9×12 SASE. Writer's guidelines for #10 SASE.

- Break in by "Being familiar with content and style. Well-written retellings of Bible stories with a different point of view are always a need."

Nonfiction: Essays, general interest, historical/nostalgic, how-to, inspirational, interview/profile, personal experience, photo feature, religious experience. **Buys 3 mss/year.** Send complete ms. Length: 800-1,200 words. **Pays 10-25¢/word.** Sometimes pays expenses of writers on assignment.

Photos: Send photos with submission. Reviews contact sheets. Negotiates payment individually. Captions, identification of subjects, model releases required.

Columns/Departments: Lookout (news/kids in community), 50 words. **Buys 5 mss/year.** Send complete ms. **Pays $75-150.**

Fiction: Fantasy, historical, humorous, mystery, religious, western, holiday, children's literature (Christian). Avoid contemporary, middle-class family settings (existing authors meet this need), poems (rarely printed), stories dealing with boy-girl relationships. **Buys 10 mss/year.** Send complete ms. Length: 400-1,600 words. **Pays $200-450.**

Fillers: Facts, newsbreaks. **Buys 2/year.** Length: 40-100 words. **Pays $50-150.**

$ $ COBBLESTONE, Discover American History, Cobblestone Publishing, 30 Grove St., Suite C, Peterborough NH 03458-1457. (603)924-7209. Fax: (603)924-7380. Website: www.cobblestonepub.com. **Contact:** Meg Chorlian, editor. Monthly magazine (September-May) covering American history for children ages 8-14. **100% freelance written** (except letters and departments); approximately 1 issue/year is by assignment. Prefers to work with published/established writers "Each issue presents a particular theme, making it exciting as well as informative. Half of all subscriptions are for schools." All material must relate to monthly theme. Circ. 30,000. Pays on publication. Publishes ms an average of 4 months after acceptance. Byline given. Offers 50% kill fee. Buys all rights. Editorial lead time 8 months. Accepts queries by mail, fax. Accepts simultaneous submissions. Responds in 4 months to queries. Sample copy for $4.95 and 7½×10½ SAE with 4 first-class stamps. Writer's guidelines and query deadlines with SASE.

Nonfiction: "Request a copy of the writer's guidelines to find out specific issue themes in upcoming months." Historical/nostalgic, interview/profile, personal experience, plays, biography, recipes, activities. No material that editorializes rather than reports. **Buys 80 mss/year.** Query by mail with published clips, outline, and bibliography. Length: Feature articles 600-800 words; supplemental nonfiction 300-500 words. **Pays 20-25¢/printed word.**

Photos: Photos must relate to theme. State availability with submission. Reviews contact sheets, transparencies, prints. Buys one-time rights. Offers $15-50 for nonprofessional quality, up to $100 for professional quality. Captions, identification of subjects required.

Columns/Departments: Puzzles and Games (no word finds); crosswords and other word puzzles using the vocabulary of the issue's theme.

Fiction: Adventure, ethnic, historical, biographical fiction relating to theme. Has to be very strong and accurate. **Buys 5 mss/year.** Query with published clips. Length: 500-800 words. **Pays 20-25¢/word.**

Poetry: Must relate to theme. Free verse, light verse, traditional. **Buys 5 poems/year.** Length: Up to 50 lines.

Tips: "Review theme lists and past issues of magazine to see what we look for."

$ $ CRICKET, Carus Publishing Co., P.O. Box 300, Peru IL 61354-0300. (815)224-6656. **Contact:** Marianne Carus, editor-in-chief. Monthly magazine for children ages 9-14. Estab. 1973. Circ. 73,000. Pays on publication. Byline given. Buys all rights. Submit seasonal material 1 year in advance. Accepts previously published material. Responds in 3 months to mss. Sample copy for $5 and 9×12 SAE. Writer's guidelines for #10 SASE.

- *Cricket* is looking for more fiction and nonfiction for the older end of its 9-14 age range. It also seeks humorous stories and mysteries (*not* detective spoofs), fantasy and original fairy tales, stand-alone excerpts from unpublished novels, and well-written/researched science articles.

Nonfiction: A short bibliography is required for all nonfiction articles. Travel, adventure, biography, foreign culture, geography, history, natural science, science, social science, sports, technology. Send complete ms. Length: 200-1,500 words. **Pays 25¢/word maximum.**

Reprints: Send typed ms with rights for sale noted and information about when and where the material previously appeared. Pays 50% of amount paid for an original article.

Fiction: Adventure, ethnic, fantasy, historical, humorous, mystery, novel excerpts, science fiction, suspense, western, fairy tales. No didactic, sex, religious, or horror stories. **Buys 75-100 mss/year.** Send complete ms. Length: 200-2,000 words. **Pays 25¢/word maximum.**

Poetry: Buys 20-30 poems/year. Length: 25 lines maximum. **Pays $3/line maximum.**

$ CRUSADER MAGAZINE, P.O. Box 7259, Grand Rapids MI 49510-7259. Website: www.calvinistcadets.org. **Contact:** G. Richard Broene, editor. **40% freelance written.** Works with a small number of new/unpublished writers each year. Magazine published 7 times/year. "*Crusader Magazine* shows boys 9-14 how God is at work in their lives and in the world around them." Estab. 1958. Circ. 10,000. **Pays on acceptance.** Publishes ms an average of 8 months after acceptance. Byline given. Buys first North American serial, one-time, second serial (reprint), simultaneous rights. Rights purchased vary with author and material. Accepts simultaneous submissions. Responds in 2 months to queries. Sample copy for 9×12 SASE. Writer's guidelines for #10 SASE.

• Accepts queries and submissions by mail.

Nonfiction: Articles about young boys' interests: sports (articles about athletes and developing Christian character through sports; b&w photos appreciated), outdoor activities (camping skills, nature study, survival exercises; practical 'how to do it' approach works best. 'God in nature' themes also appreciated if done without preachiness), science, crafts (made with easily accessible materials; must provide clear, accurate instructions), and problems. Emphasis is on a Christian perspective, but no simplistic moralisms. How-to, humor, inspirational, interview/profile, personal experience, informational. Special issues: Write for new themes list in February. **Buys 20-25 mss/year.** Send complete ms. Length: 500-1,500 words. **Pays 2-5¢/word.**

Reprints: Send typed ms with rights for sale noted. Pay varies.

Photos: Pays $4-25 for photos purchased with mss.

Columns/Departments: Project Page (uses simple projects boys 9-14 can do on their own).

Fiction: "Considerable fiction is used. Fast-moving stories that appeal to a boy's sense of adventure or sense of humor are welcome. Avoid preachiness. Avoid simplistic answers to complicated problems. Avoid long dialogue and little action." Length: 900-1,500 words. **Pays 2¢/word minimum.**

Fillers: Short humor, any type of puzzles.

Tips: "Best time to submit stories/articles is early in calendar year—in March or April. Also remember readers are boys ages 9-14. Stories must reflect or add to the theme of the issue."

$ $ ☐ CURRENT HEALTH 1, The Beginning Guide to Health Education, General Learning Communications, 900 Skokie Blvd., Suite 200, Northbrook IL 60062-4028. (847)205-3141. Fax: (847)564-8197. E-mail: crubenstein @glcomm.com. **Contact:** Carole Rubenstein, senior editor. **95% freelance written.** An educational health periodical published monthly, September-April/May. "Our audience is 4th-7th grade health education students. Articles should be written at a 5th grade reading level. The information should be accurate, timely, accessible and highly readable." Estab. 1976. Circ. 152,000. Pays on publication. Publishes ms an average of 4 months after acceptance. Buys all rights. Sample copy available with 80¢ postage.

Nonfiction: Health curriculum. **Buys 64 mss/year.** Query with introductory letter, résumé and clips. *No unsolicited mss. Articles are on assignment only.* Length: 950-2,000 words. **Pays $150-450.**

Tips: "We are looking for good writers with preferably an education and/or health background, who can write for the age group in a scientifically accurate and engaging way. Ideally, the writer should be an expert in the area in which he or she is writing. All topics are open to freelancers: disease, drugs, fitness and exercise, psychology, nutrition, first aid and safety, relationships and personal health."

$ ☐ DISCOVERIES, Word Action Publishing Co., 6401 The Paseo, Kansas City MO 64131. (816)333-7000, ext. 2728. Fax: (816)333-4439. E-mail: khendrixson@nazarene.org. Editor: Virginia Folsom. **Contact:** Katherine Hendrixson, editorial assistant. **80% freelance written.** Weekly Sunday school take-home paper. "Our audience is third and fourth graders. We require that the stories relate to the Sunday school lesson for that week." Circ. 18,000. **Pays on acceptance.** Publishes ms an average of 1 year after acceptance. Byline given. multi-use rights Accepts queries by mail, e-mail. Accepts previously published material. Accepts simultaneous submissions. Responds in 6 weeks to queries; 2 months to mss. Sample copy and writer's guidelines for #10 SASE.

O┳ "Follow theme list and guidelines. Make sure content is Biblically correct and relevant where necessary."

Reprints: Send typed ms with rights for sale noted and information about when and where the material previously appeared.

Fiction: Submit contemporary, true-to-life portrayals of 8- to 10-year-olds, written for a third- to fourth-grade reading level. Religious themes. Must relate to our theme list. No fantasy, science fiction, abnormally mature or precocious children, personification of animals. **Buys 50 mss/year.** Send complete ms. Length: 400-500 words. **Pays 5¢/word.**

Fillers: Gags to be illustrated by cartoonist, puzzles, trivia (any miscellaneous area of interest to 8- to 10-year-olds, including hobbies, fun activities, weird information, etc.). We accept spot cartoons *only.* **Buys 130/year.** Length: 50-200 words. **Pays 5¢/word.**

Tips: "Follow our theme list, read the Bible verses that relate to the theme. September 2002 begins our new curriculum."

$ ☐ DISCOVERY TRAILS, Gospel Publishing House, 1445 N. Boonville Ave., Springfield MO 65802-1894. (417)831-8000. Fax: (417)862-6059. E-mail: rl-discoverytrails@gph.com. Website: www.radiantlife.org. **Contact:** Sinda S. Zinn, editor. **98% freelance written.** Weekly 4-page Sunday school take-home paper. *Discovery Trails* is written for boys and girls 10-12 (slanted toward older group). Fiction, adventure stories showing children applying Christian principles in everyday living are used in the paper. **Pays on acceptance.** Publishes ms an average of 18 months after acceptance. Byline given. Buys one-time, second serial (reprint), simultaneous rights. Editorial lead time 18 months. Submit seasonal material 18 months in advance. Accepts simultaneous submissions. Responds in 1 month to queries. Sample copy and writer's guidelines for #10 SASE.

Nonfiction: Wants articles with reader appeal, emphasizing some phase of Christian living or historical, scientific, or natural material which includes a spiritual lesson. Submissions should include a bibliography of facts. **Buys 15-20 mss/year.** Send complete ms. Length: 500 words maximum. **Pays 7-10¢/word.**
Reprints: Send typed ms with rights for sale noted and information about when and where the material previously appeared. Pays 7¢/word.
Fiction: Wants fiction that presents realistic characters working out their problems according to Bible principles, presenting Christianity in action without being preachy. Serial stories acceptable. Adventure, historical, humorous, mystery. No Bible fiction, "Halloween," or "Santa Claus" stories. **Buys 80-90 mss/year.** Send complete ms. Length: 1,000 words (except for serial stories). **Pays 7-10¢/word.**
Poetry: Light verse, traditional. **Buys 10 poems/year.** Submit maximum 2-3 poems. **Pays $5-15.**
Fillers: Bits & Bytes of quirky facts, puzzles, interactive activities, quizzes, word games, and fun activities that address social skills on a focused topic with accurate research, vivid writing, and spiritual emphasis. Crafts, how-to articles, recipes should be age appropriate, safe and cheap, express newness/originality and accuracy, a clear focus, and an opening that makes kids want to read and do it. **Buys 8-10/year.** Length: 300 words maximum.
Tips: "Follow the guidelines, remember the story should be interesting—carried by dialogue and action rather than narration—and appropriate for a Sunday school take-home paper. Don't send groups of stories in 1 submission."

$ $ ☒ FACES, People, Places and Cultures, Cobblestone Publishing, 30 Grove St., Peterborough NH 03458. (603)924-7209. Fax: (603)924-7380. E-mail: faces@cobblestonepub.com. Website: www.cobblestonepub.com. **Contact:** Elizabeth Carpentiere, editor. **90-100% freelance written.** Monthly magazine published during school year. "*Faces* covers world culture for ages 9-14. It stands apart from other children's magazines by offering a solid look at one subject and stressing strong editorial content, color photographs throughout and original illustrations. *Faces* offers an equal balance of feature articles and activities, as well as folktales and legends." Estab. 1984. Circ. 15,000. Pays on publication. Publishes ms an average of 4 months after acceptance. Byline given. Offers 50% kill fee. Buys all rights. Editorial lead time 1 year. Accepts queries by mail, e-mail. Accepts simultaneous submissions. Sample copy for $4.95 and 7½× 10½ (or larger) SAE with $2 postage or online. Writer's guidelines for #10 SASE.

O→ All material must relate to the theme of a specific upcoming issue in order to be considered. Writers new to *Faces* should send a writing sample with the query.

Nonfiction: Historical/nostalgic, humor, interview/profile, personal experience, photo feature, travel, recipes, activities, puzzles, mazes. All must relate to theme. **Buys 45-50 mss/year.** Query with published clips. Length: 800 words for feature articles; 300-600 for supplemental nonfiction; up to 700 words for activities. **Pays 20-25¢/word.**
Photos: State availability of photos with submission or send copies of related images for photo researcher. Reviews contact sheets, transparencies, prints. Buys one-time rights. Captions, identification of subjects, model releases required.
Fiction: Ethnic, historical, retold legends or folktales. Depends on theme. Query with published clips. Length: Up to 800 words. **Pays 20-25¢/word.**
Poetry: Avant-garde, free verse, haiku, light verse, traditional. Length: 100 words maximum.
Tips: "Freelancers should send for a sample copy of magazine and a list of upcoming themes and writer's guidelines. The magazine is based on a monthly theme (upcoming themes include Kalahari Life, Poland, Prairie Provinces of Canada, Palestinians). We appreciate professional queries that follow our detailed writer's guidelines."

$ $ ☒ THE FRIEND, 50 E. North Temple, Salt Lake City UT 84150-3226. Fax: (801)240-2270. **Contact:** Vivian Paulsen, managing editor. **50% freelance written.** Eager to work with new/unpublished writers as well as established writers. Monthly publication of The Church of Jesus Christ of Latter-Day Saints for children ages 3-11. Circ. 275,000. **Pays on acceptance.** Buys all rights. Submit seasonal material 8 months in advance. Responds in 2 months to mss. Sample copy and writer's guidelines for $1.50 and 9×12 SAE with 4 first-class stamps.
Nonfiction: "*The Friend* is particularly interested in stories based on true experiences." Special issues: Christmas, Easter. Submit complete ms with SASE. No queries please. Length: 1,000 words maximum. **Pays 10¢/word minimum.**
Poetry: Serious, humorous, holiday. Any form with child appeal. **Pays $25 minimum.**
Tips: "Do you remember how it feels to be a child? Can you write stories that appeal to children ages 3-11 in today's world? We're interested in stories with an international flavor and those that focus on present-day problems. Send material of high literary quality slanted to our editorial requirements. Let the child solve the problem—not some helpful, all-wise adult. No overt moralizing. Nonfiction should be creatively presented—not an array of facts strung together. Beware of being cutesy."

$ $ $ GIRL'S LIFE, Monarch Publishing, 4517 Harford Rd., Baltimore MD 21214. Fax: (410)254-0991. Website: www.girlslife.com. Editor: Karen Bokram. **Contact:** Kelly A. White, executive editor. Bimonthly magazine covering girls ages 9-15. Estab. 1994. Circ. 2,000,000. Pays on publication. Publishes ms an average of 3 months after acceptance. Byline given. Buys first exclusive North American serial or all rights. Editorial lead time 4 months. Submit seasonal material 5 months in advance. Accepts queries by mail. Responds in 1 month to queries. Sample copy for $5 or online. Writer's guidelines for #10 SASE.
Nonfiction: Book excerpts, essays, general interest, how-to, humor, inspirational, interview/profile, new product, travel, beauty, relationship, sports. Special issues: Back to School (August/September); Fall, Halloween (October/November); Holidays, Winter (December/January); Valentine's Day, Crushes (February/March); Spring, Mother's Day (April/May); and Summer, Father's Day (June/July). **Buys 40 mss/year.** Query by mail with published clips. Submit complete mss on spec only. Length: 700-2,000 words. **Pays $150-800.**

Photos: State availability with submission. Reviews contact sheets, negatives, transparencies. Negotiates payment individually. Captions, identification of subjects, model releases required.
Columns/Departments: Sports; Try It! (new trends, celeb interviews); both 1,200 words. **Buys 20 mss/year.** Query with published clips. **Pays $150-450.**
Tips: Send queries with published writing samples and detailed résumé. "Have new ideas, a voice that speaks to our audience—not *down* to our audience—and supply artwork source (i.e. color slides)."

$ GUIDE, True Stories Pointing to Jesus, Review and Herald Publishing Association, 55 W. Oak Ridge Dr., Hagerstown MD 21740. (301)393-4038. Fax: (301)393-4055. E-mail: guide@rhpa.org. Website: www.guidemagazine.org. **Contact:** Randy Fishell, editor, or Helen Lee, assistant editor. **90% freelance written.** Weekly magazine featuring all-true stories showing God's involvement in 10- to 14-year-olds' lives. Estab. 1953. Circ. 33,000. **Pays on acceptance.** Publishes ms an average of 6 months after acceptance. Byline given. Buys first North American serial rights. Editorial lead time 8 months. Submit seasonal material 8 months in advance. Accepts queries by mail, e-mail, fax. Responds in 1 month to queries. Sample copy for SAE and 2 first-class stamps. Writer's guidelines for #10 SASE or online.

Break in with "a true story that shows in a clear way that God is involved in a 10- to 14-year-old's life."
Nonfiction: Religious. "No fiction. Non-fiction should set forth a clearly evident spiritual application." **Buys 300 mss/year.** Send complete ms. Length: 750-1,500 words. **Pays $25-125.**
Reprints: Send photocopy. Pays 50% of usual rates.
Fillers: Games, puzzles, religious. **Buys 75/year. Pays $25-40.**
Tips: "The majority of 'misses' are due to the lack of a clearly evident (not 'preachy') spiritual application."

$ $ GUIDEPOSTS FOR KIDS ON THE WEB, Guideposts, 1050 Broadway, Suite 6, Chesterton IN 46304. Fax: (219)926-3839. E-mail: gp4k@guideposts.org; send queries to rtolin@guideposts.org. Website: www.gp4k.com. Editor: Mary Lou Carney. **Contact:** Rosanne Tolin, managing editor. **90% freelance written.** Online publication for kids 6-11. "*Guideposts for Kids on the Web* is an interactive, entertaining, and empowering place for kids to learn and play." Estab. 2001. Circ. 60,000 visitors/month. **Pays on acceptance.** Byline given. Buys electronic rights. Non-exclusive print rights Editorial lead time 3 months. Submit seasonal material 6 months in advance. Accepts queries by mail, e-mail, fax. Accepts simultaneous submissions. Responds in 6 weeks to queries; 2 months to mss. Sample copy online. Writer's guidelines for #10 SASE or online.
Nonfiction: General interest, historical/nostalgic, how-to, humor, inspirational, interview/profile. Does not want preachy stories that have really religious overtones. **Buys 60 mss/year.** Query with or without published clips or send complete ms. Length: 150-500 words. **Pays $100-400 for assigned articles; $50-300 for unsolicited articles.** Pays expenses of writers on assignment.
Photos: State availability of or send photos with submission. Buys all rights. Negotiates payment individually. Identification of subjects required.
Columns/Departments: Tips from the Top (tips from celebrity athletes who are good role models), 500 words; Cool Kids (profiles of kids 6-11 doing volunteer work), 200-500 words; Stories and poems (fiction), 300-1,000 words; Animals, Animals! (animal pieces), 100-400 words; God's Mysterious Ways (miraculous, true stories of God's power with a child as the protaganist), 150-300 words; Arts and Crafts and What's Cooking, 100-300 words. **Buys 85 mss/year.** Query with or without published clips. **Pays $50-500.**
Fiction: Adventure, ethnic, fantasy, historical, humorous, mainstream, mystery, science fiction, serialized novels, suspense, From a child's perspective, avoid the adult voice. Does not want "stories about Bible-toting kids, stories where adults have all the answers." **Buys 15 mss/year.** Send complete ms. Length: 300-1,000 words. **Pays $100-400.**
Poetry: Avant-garde, free verse, haiku, light verse, traditional. **Buys 5-10 poems/year.** Submit maximum 6 poems. **Pays $25-50.**
Fillers: Facts, newsbreaks. **Buys 12-25/year. Pays $50-250.**
Tips: "Break in with our Cool Kids department or animal pieces. Make sure your kid voice is at work—don't be stiff in your approach when writing for gp4k.com. Think like a kid, use writing that will capture a child's attention. Keep copy tight, use subheads. Links to other great websites with more information on a particular subject are also essential."

$ HIGHLIGHTS FOR CHILDREN, 803 Church St., Honesdale PA 18431-1824. (570)253-1080. Fax: (570)251-7847. Website: www.highlights.com. Editor: Christine French Clark. **Contact:** Manuscript Submissions. **80% freelance written.** Monthly magazine for children ages 2-12. Estab. 1946. Circ. 3,000,000. **Pays on acceptance.** Buys all rights. Accepts queries by mail. Responds in 2 months to queries. Sample copy for free. Writer's guidelines for #10 SASE.
Nonfiction: "We need articles on science, technology, and nature written by persons with strong backgrounds in those fields. Contributions always welcomed from new writers, especially engineers, scientists, historians, teachers, etc., who can make useful, interesting facts accessible to children. Also writers who have lived abroad and can interpret the ways of life, especially of children, in other countries in ways that will foster world brotherhood. Sports material, biographies and articles of general interest to children. Direct, original approach, simple style, interesting content, not rewritten from encyclopedias. State background and qualifications for writing factual articles submitted. Include references or sources of information. Articles geared toward our younger readers (3-7) especially welcome, up to 400 words. Also buys original party plans for children ages 4-12, clearly described in 300-600 words, including drawings or samples of items to be illustrated. Also, novel but tested ideas in crafts, with clear directions and made-up models. Projects must require only free or inexpensive, easy-to-obtain materials. Especially desirable if easy enough for early primary grades. Also,

fingerplays with lots of action, easy for very young children to grasp and to dramatize. Avoid wordiness. We need creative-thinking puzzles that can be illustrated, optical illusions, brain teasers, games of physical agility, and other 'fun' activities." Query. Length: 900 words maximum. **Pays $50 for party plans; $25 for craft ideas; $25 for fingerplays.**
Photos: Reviews color 35mm slides, photos, or art reference materials that are helpful and sometimes crucial in evaluating mss.
Fiction: Unusual, meaningful stories appealing to both girls and boys, ages 2-12. "Vivid, full of action. Engaging plot, strong characterization, lively language." Prefers stories in which a child protagonist solves a dilemma through his or her own resources. Seeks stories that the child ages 8-12 will eagerly read, and the child ages 2-7 will begin to read and/or will like to hear when read aloud (400-900 words). "We publish stories in the suspense/adventure/mystery, fantasy and humor category, all requiring interesting plot and a number of illustration possiblities. Also need rebuses (picture stories 125 words or under), stories with urban settings, stories for beginning readers (100-400 words), sports and humorous stories and mysteries. We also would like to see more material of 1-page length (300-500 words), both fiction and factual. War, crime, and violence are taboo." **Pays $100 minimum.**

The online magazine carries original content not found in the print edition.
Tips: "We are pleased that many authors of children's literature report that their first published work was in the pages of *Highlights*. It is not our policy to consider fiction on the strength of the reputation of the author. We judge each submission on its own merits. With factual material, however, we do prefer that writers be authorities in their field or people with first-hand experience. In this manner we can avoid the encyclopedic article that merely restates information readily available elsewhere. We don't make assignments. Query with simple letter to establish whether the nonfiction subject is likely to be of interest. A beginning writer should first become familiar with the type of material that *Highlights* publishes. Include special qualifications, if any, of author. Write for the child, not the editor. Write in a voice that children understand and relate to. Speak to today's kids, avoiding didactic, overt messages. Even though our general principles haven't changed over the years, we are contemporary in our approach to issues. Avoid worn themes."

$ $ HUMPTY DUMPTY'S MAGAZINE, Children's Better Health Institute, P.O. Box 567, Indianapolis IN 46206-0567. (317)636-8881. **Contact:** Nancy S. Axelrad, editor. **25% freelance written.** Magazine published 8 times/year covering health, nutrition, hygiene, fitness, and safety for children ages 4-6. "Our publication is designed to entertain and to educate young readers in healthy lifestyle habits. Fiction, poetry, pencil activities should have an element of good nutrition or fitness." Estab. 1948. Circ. 350,000. Pays on publication. Publishes ms an average of 8 months after acceptance. Byline given. Buys all rights. Editorial lead time 8 months. Submit seasonal material 10 months in advance. Accepts simultaneous submissions. Responds in 3 months to queries. Sample copy for $1.75. Writer's guidelines for #10 SASE.
Nonfiction: "Material must have a health theme—nutrition, safety, exercise, hygiene. We're looking for articles that encourage readers to develop better health habits without preaching. Very simple factual articles that creatively teach readers about their bodies. We use several puzzles and activities in each issue—dot-to-dot, hidden pictures, and other activities that promote following instructions, developing finger dexterity, and working with numbers and letters." Include word count. **Buys 3-4 mss/year.** Send complete ms. Length: 300 words maximum. **Pays 22¢/word.**
Photos: Send photos with submission. Buys all rights. Offers no additonal payment for photos accepted with ms.
Columns/Departments: Mix & Fix (no-cook recipes), 100 words. All ingredients must be nutritious—low fat, no sugar, etc.—and tasty. **Buys 8 mss/year.** Send complete ms. **Payment varies.**
Fiction: "We use some stories in rhyme and a few easy-to-read stories for the beginning reader. All stories should work well as read-alouds. Currently we need health/sports/fitness stories. We try to present our health material in a positive light, incorporating humor and a light approach wherever possible. Avoid stereotyping. Characters in contemporary stories should be realistic and reflect good, wholesome values." Include word count. **Buys 4-6 mss/year.** Send complete ms. Length: 350 words maximum. **Pays 22¢/word.**
Tips: "We are not currently buying new material. Inquire before submitting manuscripts."

$ $ JACK AND JILL, Children's Better Health Institute, P.O. Box 567, Indianapolis IN 46206-0567. (317)636-8881. Fax: (317)684-8094. **Contact:** Daniel Lee, editor. **50% freelance written.** Magazine published 8 times/year for children ages 7-10. "Material will not be returned unless accompanied by SASE with sufficient postage." No queries. May hold material being seriously considered for up to 1 year. Estab. 1938. Circ. 200,000. Pays on publication. Publishes ms an average of 8 months after acceptance. Byline given. Buys all rights. Submit seasonal material 8 months in advance. Responds in 10 weeks to mss. Sample copy for $1.25. Writer's guidelines for #10 SASE.

Break in with nonfiction about ordinary kids with a news hook—something that ties in with current events, matters the kids are seeing on television and in mainstream news—i.e., space exploration, scientific advances, sports, etc.

Nonfiction: "Because we want to encourage youngsters to read for pleasure and for information, we are interested in material that will challenge a young child's intelligence *and* be enjoyable reading. Our emphasis is on good health, and we are in particular need of articles, stories, and activities with health, safety, exercise and nutrition themes. We try to present our health material in a positive light—incorporating humor and a light approach wherever possible without minimizing the seriousness of what we are saying. Straight factual articles are OK if they are short and interestingly written. We would rather see, however, more creative alternatives to the straight factual article. Items with a news hook will get extra attention. We'd like to see articles about interesting kids involved in out-of-the-ordinary activities. We're also interested in articles about people with unusual hobbies for our Hobby Shop department." **Buys 10-15 mss/year.** Send complete ms. Length: 500-800 words. **Pays 17¢/word minimum.**

Photos: When appropriate, photos should accompany ms. Reviews sharp, contrasting b&w glossy prints. Sometimes uses color slides, transparencies or good color prints. Buys one-time rights. Pays $15/photo.

Fiction: May include, but is not limited to, realistic stories, fantasy, adventure—set in past, present, or future. "All stories need a well-developed plot, action and incident. Humor is highly desirable. Stories that deal with a health theme need not have health as the primary subject." **Buys 20-25 mss/year.** Send complete ms. Length: 500-800 words. **Pays 15¢/word minimum.**

Fillers: Puzzles (including various kinds of word and crossword puzzles), poems, games, science projects, and creative craft projects. "We get a lot of these. To be selected, an item needs a little extra spark and originality. Instructions for activities should be clearly and simply written and accompanied by models or diagram sketches. We also have a need for recipes. Ingredients should be healthful; avoid sugar, salt, chocolate, red meat and fats as much as possible. In all material, avoid references to eating sugary foods, such as candy, cakes, cookies and soft drinks."

Tips: "We are constantly looking for new writers who can tell good stories with interesting slants—stories that are not full of out-dated and time-worn expressions. We like to see stories about kids who are smart and capable, but not sarcastic or smug. Problem-solving skills, personal responsibility and integrity are good topics for us. Obtain *current* issues of the magazine and *study* them to determine our present needs and editorial style."

$ $ LADYBUG, The Magazine for Young Children, Carus Publishing Co., P.O. Box 300, Peru IL 61354-0300. (815)224-6656. Editor-in-Chief: Marianne Carus. **Contact:** Paula Morrow, editor. Monthly magazine for children ages 2-6. "We look for quality writing—quality literature, no matter the subject." Estab. 1990. Circ. 134,000. Pays on publication. Byline given. Rights purchased vary. Submit seasonal material 1 year in advance. Responds in 3 months to mss. Sample copy and guidelines for $5 and 9×12 SAE. Guidelines only for #10 SASE.

- *Ladybug* needs imaginative activities based on concepts and interesting, appropriate nonfiction. See sample issues. Also needs articles and parent-child activities for its online parent's companion at www.ladybugforparents.com.

Nonfiction: Can You Do This?, 1-2 pages; The World Around You, 2-4 pages; activities based on concepts (size, color, sequence, comparison, etc.), 1-2 pages. "Most *Ladybug* nonfiction is in the form of illustration. We'd like more simple science, how-things-work, and behind-the-scenes on a preschool level." **Buys 35 mss/year.** Send complete ms; no queries. Length: 250-300 words. **Pays 25¢/word.**

Fiction: Adventure, ethnic, fantasy, humorous, mainstream, mystery, folklore. **Buys 30 mss/year.** Send complete ms. Length: 850 words maximum. **Pays 25¢/word.**

Poetry: Light verse, traditional, humorous. **Buys 20 poems/year.** Submit maximum 5 poems. Length: 20 lines maximum. **Pays $3/line, with $25 minimum.**

Fillers: "We welcome interactive activities: rebuses, up to 100 words; *original* fingerplays and action rhymes (up to 8 lines)." Anecdotes, facts, short humor. **Buys 10/year.** Length: 250 words maximum. **Pays 25¢/word.**

Tips: "Reread manuscript *before* sending in. Keep within specified word limits. Study back issues before submitting to learn about the types of material we're looking for. Writing style is paramount. We look for rich, evocative language and a sense of joy or wonder. Remember that you're writing for preschoolers—be age-appropriate but not condescending. A story must hold enjoyment for both parent and child through repeated read-aloud sessions. Remember that people come in all colors, sizes, physical conditions, and have special needs. Be inclusive!"

$ MY FRIEND, The Catholic Magazine for Kids, Pauline Books & Media/Daughters of St. Paul, 50 St. Paul's Ave., Jamaica Plain, Boston MA 02130-3495. (617)522-8911. Fax: (617)541-9805. E-mail: myfriend@pauline.org. Website: www.myfriendmagazine.com. Editor-in-Chief: Sister Donna Williams Giaimo. **Contact:** Sister Maria Grace Dateno, editor. **25% freelance written.** Magazine published 10 times/year for children ages 6-12. "*My Friend* is a 32-page monthly Catholic magazine for boys and girls. Its goal is to celebrate the Catholic Faith—as it is lived by today's children and as it has been lived for centuries." Theme list available. Send a SASE to the above address. Circ. 11,000. **Pays on acceptance.** worldwide publication rights. Sample copy for $2.95. Writer's guidelines for #10 SASE.

- Break in with "well-written fiction that grabs imagination and gently teaches a lesson—stories of real kids making a difference."

Nonfiction: "We are looking for innovative ideas and new approaches to values." How-to, interview/profile, religious, technical, media-related articles, real-life features. Send complete ms. Length: 150-800 words. **Pays $35-100.** Pays in contributor copies by prior arrangement with an author "who wishes to write as a form of sharing our ministry."

Photos: Send photos with submission.

Fiction: "We are looking for stories that immediately grab the imagination of the reader. Good dialogue, realistic character development, current lingo are necessary. A child protagonist must resolve a dilemma through his or her own resources. We prefer seeing a sample or submission of a story. Often we may not be able to use a particular story, but the author will be asked to write another for a specific issue based on his or her experience, writing ability, etc. At this time we especially desire stories that deal with the following: communication within the family; respect for all human life; the meaning of our baptism today; God's providence; reaching out to others; and the eucharist as a meal and a sacrifice." **Pays $75-150.**

Tips: "For fiction, we prefer the submission of manuscripts to query letters. If you are not sure whether a story would be appropriate for *My Friend*, please request our complete guidelines, theme list, and a sample issue (see above). For nonfiction articles, you may query by e-mail, but most are written by staff and contributing authors."

$ NATURE FRIEND, Carlisle Press, 2673 TR 421, Sugarcreek OH 44681. (330)852-1900. Fax: (330)852-3285. Managing Editor: Elaine Troyer. **Contact:** Marvin Wengerd, editor. **80% freelance written.** Monthly magazine covering nature. "*Nature Friend* includes stories, puzzles, science experiments, nature experiments—all submissions need to honor God as creator." Estab. 1983. Circ. 10,000. Pays on publication. Publishes ms an average of 10 months after acceptance. Byline given. Buys first, one-time rights. Editorial lead time 4 months. Submit seasonal material 3 months in advance. Accepts simultaneous submissions. Responds in 4 months to mss. Sample copy for $2.50 postage paid. Writer's guidelines for $4 postage paid.

O— Break in with a "conversational story about a nature subject that imparts knowledge and instills Christian values."

Nonfiction: How-to (nature, science experiments), photo feature, articles about interesting/unusual animals. No poetry, evolution, animals depicted in captivity. **Buys 50 mss/year.** Send complete ms. Length: 250-900 words. **Pays 5¢/word.**

Photos: Send photos with submission. Reviews prints. Buys one-time rights. Offers $35-50/photo. Captions, identification of subjects required.

Columns/Departments: Learning By Doing, Hands on! Hands on! Hands on! (anything about nature), 500-900 words. **Buys 20 mss/year.** Send complete ms.

Fillers: Facts, puzzles, short essays on something current in nature. **Buys 35/year.** Length: 150-250 words. **Pays 5¢/word.**

Tips: "We want to bring joy to children by opening the world of God's creation to them. We endeavor to educate with science experiments, stories, etc. We endeavor to create a sense of awe about nature's creator and a respect for His creation. I'd like to see more submissions on hands-on things to do with a nature theme (not collecting rocks or leaves—real stuff). Also looking for good stories that are accompanied by good photography."

$ $ NEW MOON, The Magazine for Girls & Their Dreams, New Moon Publishing, Inc., P.O. Box 3620, Duluth MN 55803-3620. (218)728-5507. Fax: (218)728-0314. E-mail: girl@newmoon.org. Website: www.newmoon.org. **Contact:** Deb Mylin, managing editor. **25% freelance written.** Bimonthly magazine covering girls ages 8-14, edited by girls aged 8-14. "In general, all material should be pro-girl and feature girls and women as the primary focus. *New Moon* is for every girl who wants her voice heard and her dreams taken seriously. *New Moon* celebrates girls, explores the passage from girl to woman and builds healthy resistance to gender inequities. The *New Moon* girl is true to herself and *New Moon* helps her as she pursues her unique path in life, moving confidently into the world." Estab. 1992. Circ. 30,000. Pays on publication. Publishes ms an average of 1 year after acceptance. Byline given. Buys all rights. Editorial lead time 6 months. Submit seasonal material 8 months in advance. Accepts queries by mail, e-mail, fax. Accepts previously published material. Accepts simultaneous submissions. Responds in 2 months to mss. Sample copy for $6.50 or online. Writer's guidelines for SASE or online.

O— Adult writers can break in with "*Herstory* articles about less well-known women from all over the world, especially if it relates to one of our themes. Same as *Women's Work* articles. Girls can break in with essays and articles (non-fiction) that relate to a theme."

Nonfiction: Essays, general interest, humor, inspirational, interview/profile, opinion, personal experience (written by girls), photo feature, religious, travel, multicultural/girls from other countries. No fashion, beauty, or dating. **Buys 20 mss/year.** Query with or without published clips or send complete ms. Length: 600 words. **Pays 6-12¢/word.**

Reprints: Send ms with rights for sale noted and information about when and where the material previously appeared. Negotiates fee.

Photos: State availability with submission. Buys one-time rights. Negotiates payment individually. Captions, identification of subjects required.

Columns/Departments: Women's Work (profile of a woman and her job(s) relating the the theme), 600 words; Herstory (historical woman relating to theme), 600 words. **Buys 10 mss/year.** Query. **Pays 6-12¢/word.**

Fiction: Prefers girl-written material. All girl-centered. Adventure, fantasy, historical, humorous, slice-of-life vignettes. **Buys 6 mss/year.** Send complete ms. Length: 900-1,200 words. **Pays 6-12¢/word.**

Poetry: No poetry by adults.

Tips: "We'd like to see more girl-written feature articles that relate to a theme. These can be about anything the girl has done personally, or she can write about something she's studied. Please read *New Moon* before submitting to get a sense of our style. Writers and artists who comprehend our goals have the best chance of publication. We love creative articles—both nonfiction and fiction—that are not condescending to our readers. Keep articles to suggested word lengths; avoid stereotypes. Refer to our guidelines and upcoming themes."

$ ON THE LINE, Mennonite Publishing House, 616 Walnut Ave., Scottdale PA 15683-1999. (724)887-8500. Fax: (724)887-3111. E-mail: mary@mph.org. **Contact:** Mary Clemens Meyer, editor. **90% freelance written.** Works with a small number of new/unpublished writers each year. Monthly Christian magazine for children ages 9-14. "*On the Line* helps upper elementary and junior high children understand and appreciate God, the created world, themselves, and others." Estab. 1908. Circ. 5,500. **Pays on acceptance.** Publishes ms an average of 1 year after acceptance. Byline given. Buys one-time rights. Submit seasonal material 6 months in advance. Accepts simultaneous submissions. Responds in 1 month to mss. Sample copy for 9×12 SAE and 2 first-class stamps.

Nonfiction: How-to (things to make with easy-to-get materials including food recipes), informational (300-500 word articles on wonders of nature, people who have made outstanding contributions). **Buys 95 mss/year.** Send complete ms. **Pays $15-35.**

Reprints: Send typed ms with rights for sale noted and information about when and where the material previously appeared. Pays 75% of amount paid for an original article.

Photos: Limited number of photos purchased with or without ms. Total purchase price for ms includes payment for photos. Pays $25-50 for 8×10 b&w or color photos.

Fiction: Adventure, humorous, religious, everyday problems. **Buys 50 mss/year.** Send complete ms. Length: 1,000-1,800 words. **Pays 3-5¢/word.**
Poetry: Light verse, religious. Length: 3-12 lines. **Pays $10-25.**
Fillers: Appropriate puzzles, cartoons, and quizzes.
Tips: "Study the publication first. We need short, well-written how-to and craft articles; also more puzzles. Don't send query; we prefer to see the complete manuscript."

$ $ OWL MAGAZINE, The Discovery Magazine for Children, Owl Group (owned by Bayard Press), 49 Front St. E., 2nd Floor, Toronto, Ontario M5E 1B3, Canada. (416)340-2700. Fax: (416)340-9769. E-mail: owl@owl.on.ca. Website: www.owlkids.com. **Contact:** Mary Beth Leatherdale, editor. **25% freelance written.** Works with small number of new writers each year. Magazine published 9 times/year covering science and nature. Aims to interest children in their environment through accurate, factual information about the world presented in an easy, lively style. Estab. 1976. Circ. 75,000. Pays on publication. Byline given. Buys all rights. Submit seasonal material 1 year in advance. Accepts queries by mail, fax. Responds in 3 months to queries. Sample copy for $4.28. Writer's guidelines for SAE (large envelope if requesting sample copy) and money order for $1 postage (no stamps please).
Nonfiction: Book excerpts, general interest, how-to, humor, personal experience (real life children in real situations), photo feature (natural science, international wildlife and outdoor features), science, nature and environmental features. No problem stories with drugs, sex or moralistic views, or talking animal stories. **Buys 6 mss/year.** Query with published clips. Length: 500-1,500 words. **Pays $200-500 (Canadian).**
Photos: Send for photo package before submitting material. State availability with submission. Reviews 35mm transparencies. Identification of subjects required.
Tips: "Write for editorial guidelines first. Review back issues of the magazine for content and style. Know your topic and approach it from an unusual perspective. Our magazine never talks down to children. Our articles have a very light conversational tone and this must be reflected in any writing that we accept. We would like to see more articles about science and technology that aren't too academic."

$ $ POCKETS, The Upper Room, 1908 Grand Ave., P.O. Box 340004, Nashville TN 37203-0004. (615)340-7333. Fax: (615)340-7267. E-mail: pockets@upperroom.org. Website: www.pockets.org. Editor: Janet R. Knight. **Contact:** Lynn Gilliam, associate editor. **60% freelance written.** Monthly (except February) magazine covering children's and families' spiritual formation. "We are a Christian, inter-denominational publication for children 6-11 years of age. Each issue reflects a specific theme." Estab. 1981. Circ. 94,000. **Pays on acceptance.** Byline given. Buys first North American serial rights. Submit seasonal material 1 year in advance. Responds in 6 weeks to mss. Sample copy for 8½×11 or larger SAE and 4 first-class stamps. Writer's guidelines for #10 SASE or online.

- *Pockets* publishes fiction and poetry, as well as short, short stories (no more than 600 words) for children 4-7. They publish one of these stories/issue. Eager to work with new/unpublished writers.

Nonfiction: Each issue reflects a specific theme; themes available for #10 SASE. Interview/profile, personal experience, religious (retold scripture stories). No violence or romance. **Buys 5 mss/year.** Length: 400-1,000 words. **Pays 14¢/word.**
Reprints: Accepts one-time previously published submissions. Send typed ms with rights for sale noted and information about when and where the material previously appeared.
Photos: No photos unless they accompany an article. Send photos with submission. Reviews contact sheets, transparencies, prints. Buys one-time rights. Pays $25/photo.
Columns/Departments: Refrigerator Door (poetry and prayer related to themes), maximum 24 lines; Pocketsful of Love (family communications activities), 300 words; Peacemakers at Work (profiles of children working for peace, justice, and ecological concerns), 300-800 words. **Pays 14¢/word**. Activities/Games (related to themes). **Pays $25 and up**. Kids Cook (simple recipes children can make alone or with minimal help from an adult). **Pays $25**. **Buys 20 mss/year.**
Fiction: "Submissions do not need to be overtly religious. They should reflect daily living, lifestyle, and problem-solving based on living as faithful disciples. They should help children experience the Christian life that is not always a neatly wrapped moral package but is open to the continuing revelation of God's will for their lives." Adventure, ethnic, slice-of-life vignettes. **Buys 44 mss/year.** Length: 600-1,400 words. **Pays 14¢/word.**
Poetry: Buys 22 poems/year. Length: 4-24 lines. **Pays $2/line, $25 minimum.**

The online magazine carries original content not found in the print edition and includes writer's guidelines, themes, and fiction-writing contest guidelines. Contact: Lynn Gilliam, associate editor.

Tips: "Theme stories, role models, and retold scripture stories are most open to freelancers. We are also looking for nonfiction stories about children involved in peace/justice/ecology efforts. Poetry is also open. It is very helpful if writers send for themes. These are *not* the same as writer's guidelines. We have an annual fiction writing contest. Contest guidelines available with #10 SASE or on our website."

$ SHINE BRIGHTLY, (formerly *Shine*), GEMS Girls' Clubs, P.O. Box 7259, Grand Rapids MI 49510. (616)241-5616. Fax: (616)241-5558. E-mail: sara@gemsgc.org. Website: www.gospelcom.net/gems. Editor: Jan Boone. **Contact:** Sara Lynne Hilton, managing editor. **80% freelance written.** Works with new and published/established writers. Monthly magazine "to show girls ages 9-14 how God is at work in their lives and in the world around them. Our readers are mainly girls from Christian homes who belong to GEMS Girls' Clubs, a relationship-building club program available through churches. The May/June issue annually features material written by our readers." Estab. 1971. Circ. 13,000.

Pays on publication. Publishes ms an average of 1 year after acceptance. Byline given. Buys first North American serial, second serial (reprint) rights. Submit seasonal material 1 year in advance. Accepts simultaneous submissions. Responds in 2 months to queries. Sample copy for 9×12 SAE with 3 first class stamps and $1. Writer's guidelines for #10 SASE.

Nonfiction: "Because our magazine is published around a monthly theme, requesting the letter we send out twice a year to our established freelancers would be most helpful. We do not want easy solutions or quick character changes from good to bad. No pietistic characters. No 'new girl at school starting over after parents' divorce' stories. Constant mention of God is not necessary if the moral tone of the story is positive. We do not want stories that always have a happy ending." Needs include: biographies and autobiographies of "heroes of the faith," informational (write for issue themes), multicultural materials. Humor (need much more), inspirational, interview/profile, personal experience (avoid the testimony appraoch), photo feature (query first), religious, travel. Special issues: School Skills Needed (September); Danger Ahead! Join the Rescue Squad (October); Lost and Found (November); Rescuing Christmas (December); Dial 9-1-1 (January); I'm Lonely...Rescue Me! (February); Danger...Beware! (March); Team Up With Mother Earth (April); You Want Me to Join What? (May/June). **Buys 10 unsolicited mss/year.** Send complete ms. Length: 200-800 words. **Pays $10-20, plus 2 copies.**

Reprints: Send typed ms with rights for sale noted and information about when and where the material previously appeared.

Photos: Purchased with or without ms. Appreciate multicultural subjects. Reviews 5×7 or 8×10 clear color glossy prints. Pays $25-50 on publication.

Columns/Departments: How-to (crafts); puzzles and jokes; quizzes. Length: 200-400 words. Send complete ms. **Pay varies.**

Fiction: Adventure, historical, humorous, mystery, religious, romance, slice-of-life vignettes, suspense. **Buys 20 mss/year.** Send complete ms. Length: 400-1,000 words. **Pays $20-50.**

Poetry: Free verse, haiku, light verse, traditional. **Buys 5 poems/year.** Length: 15 lines maximum. **Pays $5-15 minimum.**

Tips: "Prefers not to see anything on the adult level, secular material, or violence. Writers frequently oversimplify the articles and often write with a Pollyanna attitude. An author should be able to see his/her writing style as exciting and appealing to girls ages 9-14. The style can be fun, but also teach a truth. Subjects should be current and important to *Shine Brightly* readers. Use our theme update as a guide. We would like to receive material with a multicultural slant."

$ $ ✪ SPIDER, The Magazine for Children, Cricket Magazine Group, P.O. Box 300, Peru IL 61354. (815)224-6656. Fax: (815)224-6615. Editor: Heather Delabre. **Contact:** Submissions Editor. **80% freelance written.** Monthly magazine covering literary, general interest. "*Spider* introduces 6- to 9-year-old children to the highest quality stories, poems, illustrations, articles, and activities. It was created to foster in beginning readers a love of reading and discovery that will last a lifetime. We're looking for writers who respect children's intelligence." Estab. 1994. Circ. 87,000. Pays on publication. Publishes ms an average of 2-3 years after acceptance. Byline given. Buys first North American serial, second serial (reprint), all rights. Editorial lead time 9 months. Accepts previously published material. Accepts simultaneous submissions. Responds in 4 months to mss. Sample copy for $5. Writer's guidelines for #10 SASE.

Nonfiction: A bibliography is required with all nonfiction submissions. Nature, animals, science & technology, environment, foreign culture, history. **Buys 6-8 mss/year.** Send complete ms. Length: 300-800 words. **Pays 25¢/word.**

Reprints: Send photocopy with rights for sale noted and information about when and where the material previously appeared.

Photos: Send photos with submission. Reviews contact sheets, 35mm to 4×4 transparencies, 8×10 prints. Buys one-time rights. Offers $35-50/photo. Captions, identification of subjects, model releases required.

Fiction: Adventure, ethnic, fantasy, historical, humorous, mystery, science fiction, suspense, realistic fiction, folk tales, fairy tales. No romance, horror, religious. **Buys 15-20 mss/year.** Send complete ms. Length: 300-1,000 words. **Pays 25¢/word.**

Poetry: Free verse, traditional, nonsense, humorous, serious. No forced rhymes, didactic. **Buys 10-20 poems/year.** Submit maximum 5 poems. Length: 20 lines maximum. **Pays $3/line maximum.**

Fillers: Puzzles, crafts, recipes, mazes, games, brainteasers, engaging math and word activities. **Buys 15-20/year. Payment depends on type of filler.**

Tips: "We'd like to see more of the following: Engaging nonfiction, fillers, and 'takeout page' activities, folktales, fairy tales, science fiction, and humorous stories. Most importantly, do not write down to children."

N $ $ $ SPORTS ILLUSTRATED FOR KIDS, Time-Warner, Time & Life Building, 1271 Sixth Ave., New York NY 10020. (212)522-3112. Fax: (212)522-0120. Website: www.sikids.com. **Contact:** Editorial Administrator. **20% freelance written.** Monthly magazine on sports for children 8 years old and up. Content is divided 20/80 between sports as played by kids, and sports as played by professionals. Estab. 1989. **Pays on acceptance.** Publishes ms an average of 3 months after acceptance. Byline given. Offers 25% kill fee. Buys all rights. Accepts queries by mail, fax. For sample copy call (800)992-0196. Writer's guidelines for #10 SASE.

Nonfiction: General interest, how-to, humor, inspirational, interview/profile, photo feature, Games, puzzles. **Buys 15 mss/year.** Query with published clips. Length: 100-1,500 words. **Pays $75-1,000 for assigned articles; $75-800 for unsolicited articles.** Pays expenses of writers on assignment.

Photos: State availability with submission. Buys one-time rights.

Columns/Departments: The Worst Day I Ever Had (tells about day in pro athlete's life when all seemed hopeless), 150 words.

The online magazine carries original content not found in the print edition. Contact: Peter Kay, Director of New Media.

$ STONE SOUP, The Magazine by Young Writers and Artists, Children's Art Foundation, P.O. Box 83, Santa Cruz CA 95063-0083. (831)426-5557. Fax: (831)426-1161. E-mail: editor@stonesoup.com. Website: www.stonesoup.com. **Contact:** Ms. Gerry Mandel, editor. **100% freelance written.** Bimonthly magazine of writing and art by children, including fiction, poetry, book reviews, and art by children through age 13. Audience is children, teachers, parents, writers, artists. "We have a preference for writing and art based on real-life experiences; no formula stories or poems." Estab. 1973. Pays on publication. Publishes ms an average of 3 months after acceptance. Buys all rights. Submit seasonal material 6 months in advance. Sample copy for $4 or online. Writer's guidelines for SASE or online.

- Don't send queries, just submissions.

Nonfiction: Historical/nostalgic, personal experience, book reviews. **Buys 12 mss/year. Pays $35.**
Fiction: Adventure, ethnic, experimental, fantasy, historical, humorous, mystery, science fiction, slice-of-life vignettes, suspense. "We do not like assignments or formula stories of any kind." **Buys 60 mss/year.** Send complete ms. **Pays $35 for stories.** Authors also receive 2 copies and discounts on additional copies and on subscriptions.
Poetry: Avant-garde, free verse. **Buys 12 poems/year. Pays $35/poem.**

The online magazine carries original content not found in the print edition and includes writer's guidelines. Contact: Ms. Gerry Mandel, online editor.

Tips: "All writing we publish is by young people ages 13 and under. We do not publish any writing by adults. We can't emphasize enough how important it is to read a couple of issues of the magazine. We have a strong preference for writing on subjects that mean a lot to the author. If you feel strongly about something that happened to you or something you observed, use that feeling as the basis for your story or poem. Stories should have good descriptions, realistic dialogue, and a point to make. In a poem, each word must be chosen carefully. Your poem should present a view of your subject, and a way of using words that are special and all your own."

$ STORY FRIENDS, Mennonite Publishing House, 616 Walnut Ave., Scottdale PA 15683-1999. (724)887-3753. Fax: (724)887-3111. E-mail: rstutz@mph.org. **Contact:** Rose Mary Stutzman, editor. **80% freelance written.** Monthly magazine for children ages 4-9. "*Story Friends* is planned to nurture faith development in 4-9 year olds." Estab. 1905. Circ. 7,000. **Pays on acceptance.** Publishes ms an average of 1 year after acceptance. Byline given. Buys one-time, second serial (reprint) rights. Submit seasonal material 6 months in advance. Accepts simultaneous submissions. Responds in 2 months to queries. Sample copy for 9×12 SAE and 2 first-class stamps. Writer's guidelines for #10 SASE.
Nonfiction: How-to (craft ideas for young children), photo feature. **Buys 20 mss/year.** Length: 300-500 words. **Pays 3-5¢/word.**
Reprints: Send photocopy with rights for sale noted and information about when and where the material previously appeared. Pays 100% of amount paid for an original article.
Photos: Send photos with submission. Reviews 8½×11 b&w prints. Buys one-time rights. Offers $20-25/photo. Model releases required.
Fiction: Buys 50 mss/year. Send complete ms. Length: 300-800 words. **Pays 3-5¢/word.**
Poetry: Traditional. **Buys 20 poems/year.** Length: 4-16 lines. **Pays $10/poem.**
Tips: "Send stories that children from a variety of ethnic backgrounds can relate to; stories that deal with experiences similar to all children. Send stories with a humorous twist. We're also looking for well-planned puzzles that challenge and promote reading readiness."

$ $ TURTLE MAGAZINE FOR PRESCHOOL KIDS, Children's Better Health Institute, P.O. Box 567, Indianapolis IN 46206-0567. (317)636-8881. Fax: (317)684-8094. Website: www.turtlemag.com. **Contact:** (Ms.) Terry Harshman, editor. **40% freelance written.** Bimonthly (monthly March, June, September, December) magazine. General interest, interactive magazine with the purpose of helping preschoolers develop healthy minds and bodies. Circ. 300,000. Pays on publication. Byline given. Buys all rights. Submit seasonal material 8 months in advance. Responds in 3 months to queries. Sample copy for $1.75. Writer's guidelines for #10 SASE.

- May hold mss for up to 1 year before acceptance/publication.

Nonfiction: "We use very simple science experiments. These should be pretested. We also publish simple, healthful recipes." **Buys 20 mss/year.** Length: 100-300 words. **Pays up to 22¢/word.**
Fiction: "Not buying much fiction right now except for rebus stories. All material should have a health or fitness slant. We no longer buy stories about 'generic' turtles because we now have PokeyToes, our own trade-marked turtle character. All should 'move along' and lend themselves well to illustration. Writing should be energetic, enthusiastic and creative—like preschoolers themselves. No queries, please." **Buys 20 mss/year.** Length: 150-300 words. **Pays up to 22¢/word.**
Poetry: "We're especially looking for action rhymes to foster creative movement in preschoolers. We also use short verse on our inside front cover and back cover."
Tips: "We are looking for more easy science experiments and simple, nonfiction health articles. We are trying to include more material for our youngest readers. Stories must be age-appropriate for two- to five-year-olds, entertaining and written from a healthy lifestyle perspective."

$ $ U.S. KIDS, A Weekly Reader Magazine, Children's Better Health Institute, P.O. Box 567, Indianapolis IN 46206-0567. (317)636-8881. **Contact:** Daniel Lee, editor. **50% freelance written.** Magazine published 8 times/year featuring "kids doing extraordinary things, especially activities related to health, sports, the arts, interesting hobbies, the environment, computers, etc." Estab. 1987. Circ. 230,000. Pays on publication. Publishes ms an average of 4 months after acceptance. Byline given. Buys all rights. Editorial lead time 6 months. Submit seasonal material 6 months in advance. Responds in 4 months to mss. Sample copy for $2.95 or online. Writer's guidelines for #10 SASE.

• *U.S. Kids* is being retargeted for a younger audience.

Nonfiction: Especially interested in articles with a health/fitness angle. General interest, how-to, interview/profile, science, kids using computers, multicultural. **Buys 16-24 mss/year.** Send complete ms. Length: 400 words maximum. **Pays up to 25¢/word.**

Photos: State availability with submission. Reviews contact sheets, negatives, transparencies, color photocopies, or prints. Buys one-time rights. Negotiates payment individually. Captions, identification of subjects, model releases required.

Columns/Departments: Real Kids (kids doing interesting things); Fit Kids (sports, healthy activities); Computer Zone. Length: 300-400 words. Send complete ms. **Pays up to 25¢/word.**

Fiction: Buys very little fictional material. **Buys 1-2 mss/year.** Send complete ms. Length: 400 words. **Pays up to 25¢/word.**

Poetry: Light verse, traditional, kid's humorous, health/fitness angle. **Buys 6-8 poems/year.** Submit maximum 6 poems. Length: 8-24 lines. **Pays $25-50.**

Fillers: Facts, newsbreaks, short humor, puzzles, games, activities. Length: 200-500 words. **Pays 25¢/word.**

Tips: "We are retargeting magazine for first-, second-, and third-graders, and looking for fun and informative articles on activities and hobbies of interest to younger kids. Special emphasis on fitness, sports, and health. Availability of good photos a plus."

$ $ WILD OUTDOOR WORLD (W.O.W.), Joy Publications, LLC, P.O. Box 1329, Helena MT 59624. (406)449-1335. Fax: (406)449-9197. E-mail: wowgirl@qwest.net. **Contact:** Carolyn Zieg Cunningham, editorial director. **75% freelance written.** Magazine published 5 times/year covering North American wildlife for children ages 8-12. "*W.O.W.* emphasizes the conservation of North American wildlife and habitat and the importance of recycling to conserve our natural resources. Articles reflect sound principles of ecology and environmental education. It stresses the 'web of life,' nature's balance and the importance of habitat." Estab. 1993. Circ. 150,000. **Pays on acceptance.** Publishes ms an average of 18 months after acceptance. Byline given. Buys first North American serial, electronic rights. Editorial lead time 4 months. Submit seasonal material 8 months in advance. Accepts queries by mail, e-mail, fax. Accepts simultaneous submissions. Responds in 2 months to queries. Sample copy for 9×12 SAE and 3 first-class stamps. Writer's guidelines for #10 SASE.

Break in with scientific accuracy, strong habitat focus; both educational and fun to read.

Nonfiction: Looking for life histories and habitat needs of wild animals. How-to (children's outdoor-related projects, camping, hiking, other healthy outdoor pursuits), interview/profile, personal experience. No anthropomorphism, no domestic animal stories. **Buys 24-30 mss/year.** Query. Length: 600-850 words. **Pays $100-300 maximum.**

Photos: *No unsolicited photos.* State availability with submission. Reviews 35mm transparencies. Buys one-time rights. Offers $50-250/photo. Captions, identification of subjects, model releases required.

Columns/Departments: Making a Difference (kids' projects that improve their environment and surrounding habitat), 500 words; Short Stuff (short items, puzzles, games, interesting facts about nature), 300 words. **Buys 25-30 mss/year.** Query. **Pays $50-100.**

Fillers: Facts. **Buys 15-20/year.** Length: 300 words maximum. **Pays $50-100.**

Tips: "Because our publisher is a nonprofit whose mission is to conserve habitat for wildlife, we look for a gentle conservation/habitat/outdoor ethics message. Stories should be scientifically accurate because the magazine is used in many classrooms. We also look for a hopeful, light-hearted, fun style."

LITERARY & "LITTLE"

Fiction, poetry, essays, book reviews, and scholarly criticism comprise the content of the magazines listed in this section. Some are published by colleges and universities, and many are regional in focus.

Everything about "little" literary magazines is different than other consumer magazines. Most carry few or no ads, and many do not seek them. Circulations under 1,000 are common. And sales often come more from the purchase of sample copies than from the newsstand.

The magazines listed in this section cannot compete with the pay rates and exposure of the high-circulation general interest magazines also publishing fiction and poetry. But most "little" literary magazines don't try. They are more apt to specialize in publishing certain kinds of fiction or poetry: traditional, experimental, works with a regional sensibility, or the fiction and poetry of new and younger writers. For that reason, and because fiction and poetry vary so widely in style, writers should *always* invest in the most recent copies of the magazines they aspire to publish in.

Many "little" literary magazines pay contributors only in copies of the issues in which their works appear. *Writer's Market* lists only those that pay their contributors in cash. However, *Novel & Short Story Writer's Market* includes nonpaying fiction markets, and has in-depth information about fiction techniques and markets. The same is true of *Poet's Market* for nonpaying poetry markets (both books are published by Writer's Digest Books). Many literary agents and book editors regularly read these magazines in search of literary voices not found in mainstream writing. There are also more literary opportunities listed in the Contests & Awards section.

ACM (ANOTHER CHICAGO MAGAZINE), Left Field Press, 3709 N. Kenmore, Chicago IL 60613. Website: www.anotherchicagomag.com. **Contact:** Barry Silesky, poetry editor. Biannual magazine with an emphasis on quality, experimental, politically aware prose, fiction, poetry, reviews, cross-genre work, and essays. Estab. 1977. Circ. 2,000. Buys first North American serial rights. Accepts simultaneous submissions. Responds in 3 months to queries; 6 months to mss.

Nonfiction: Essays.

Fiction: Experimental.

Poetry: Appreciates traditional to experimental verse with an emphasis on message, especially poems with strong voices articulating social or political concerns. Barry Silesky. No religious verse. Submit 3-4 typed poems at a time.

Tips: "Buy a copy—subscribe and support your own work."

$ACORN, A Journal of Contemporary Haiku, redfox press, P.O. Box 186, Philadelphia PA 19105. E-mail: missias@earthlink.net. Website: home.earthlink.net/~missias/acorn.html. **Contact:** A.C. Missias, editor. Biannual magazine dedicated to publishing "the best of contemporary English language haiku, and in particular to showcasing individual poems that reveal the extraordinary moments found in everyday life." Estab. 1998. Publishes ms an average of 1-6 months after acceptance. Buys first, one-time rights. Accepts queries by mail, e-mail. Responds in 3 weeks to mss.

Poetry: Decisions made by editor on a rolling basis. Poems judged purely on their own merits, not dependent on other work taken. Sometimes acceptance conditional on minor edits. Often comments on rejected poems. Accepts poetry written by children. Haiku. Does not want epigrams, musings, and overt emotion poured into 17 syllables; surreal, science fiction, or political commentary 'ku;' strong puns or raunchy humor. Syllable counting generally discouraged. Submit 5-25 poems at a time. Length: 1-5 lines.

Tips: "This is primarily a journal for those with a focused interest in haiku, rather than an outlet for the occasional short jottings of longer-form poets. It is a much richer genre than one might surmise from many of the recreational websites that claim to promote 'haiku' and bound to appeal to many readers and writers, especially those attuned to the world around them."

$AFRICAN AMERICAN REVIEW, St. Louis University, Shannon Hall SLU, 220 N. Grand Blvd., St. Louis MO 63105-2007. Fax: (314)977-3649. E-mail: keenanam@slu.edu. Website: aar.slu.edu. Managing Editor: Roxanne Schwab. **Contact:** Alienne Keenan, editorial assistant. **65% freelance written.** Quarterly magazine covering African-American literature and culture. "Essays on African-American literature, theater, film, art and culture generally; interviews; poetry and fiction by African-American authors; book reviews." Estab. 1967. Circ. 3,137. Pays on publication. Publishes ms an average of 1 year after acceptance. Byline given. Buys first North American serial rights. Editorial lead time 1 year. Responds in 1 month to queries; 3 months to mss. Sample copy for $8. Writer's guidelines for #10 SASE.

Nonfiction: Essays, interview/profile. **Buys 30 mss/year.** Query. Length: 3,500-6,000 words. **Pays $50-150.** Pays in contributors copies upon request.

Photos: State availability with submission. Pays $100 for covers. Captions required.

Fiction: Ethnic. **Buys 4 mss/year.** Send complete ms. Length: 2,500-5,000 words. **Pays $50-150.**

$AGNI, Dept. WM, Boston University 236 Bay State Rd., Boston, MA 02215. (617)353-7135. Fax: (617)353-7134. E-mail: agni@bu.edu. Website: www.bu.edu/agni. **Contact:** Eric Grunwald, managing editor. Biannual magazine. "*AGNI* publishes poetry, fiction and essays. Also regularly publishes translations and is committed to featuring the work of emerging writers. We have published Derek Walcott, Joyce Carol Oates, Sharon Olds, John Updike, Ha Jin, John Keene, Jhumpa Lahiri, Robert Pinsky, and many others." Next reading period is October 1, 2002 to February 15, 2003. Estab. 1972. Circ. 2,000. Pays on publication. Publishes ms an average of 6 months after acceptance. Byline given. Buys first North American serial rights. Rights to reprint in *AGNI* anthology (with author's consent). Editorial lead time 1 year. Accepts queries by mail. Accepts simultaneous submissions. Responds in 2 weeks to queries; 4 months to mss. Sample copy for $9 or online. Writer's guidelines for #10 SASE.

Fiction: Short stories. **Buys 6-12 mss/year. Pays $20-150.**

Poetry: Buys more than 140 poems/year. Submit maximum 5 poems. with SASE **Pays $20-150.**

The online magazine carries original content not found inthe print edition. Contact: Askold Melnyczuk, online editor.

Tips: "We're looking for extraordinary translations from little-translated languages. It is important to look at a copy of *AGNI* before submitting, to see if your work might be compatible. Please write for guidelines or a sample."

$ $ ALASKA QUARTERLY REVIEW, ESB 208, University of Alaska-Anchorage 3211 Providence Dr., Anchorage AK 99508. (907)786-6916. E-mail: ayaqr@uaa.alaska.edu. Website: www.uaa.alaska.edu/aqr. **Contact:** Ronald Spatz, executive editor. **95% freelance written.** Semiannual magazine publishing fiction, poetry, literary nonfiction and short plays in traditional and experimental styles. Estab. 1982. Circ. 2,200. Honorariums on publication when funding permits. Publishes ms an average of 6 months after acceptance. Byline given. Buys first North American serial rights. Upon request, rights will be transferred back to author after publication. Accepts queries by mail, e-mail. Responds in 4 months to queries; 4 months to mss. Sample copy for $6. Writer's guidelines for SASE or on website.

• *Alaska Quarterly* reports they are always looking for freelance material and new writers.

Nonfiction: Literary nonfiction: essays and memoirs. **Buys 0-5 mss/year.** Query. Length: 1,000-20,000 words. **Pays $50-200 subject to funding.** Pays in contributor's copies and subscription when funding is limited.

Fiction: Experimental and traditional literary forms. No romance, children's or inspirational/religious. Publishes novel excerpts. **Buys 20-26 mss/year**. Also publishes drama: Experimental and traditional one-act plays. **Buys 0-2 mss/year.** Send complete ms. Length: up to 20,000 words. **Pays $50-200 subject to funding; pays in contributor's copies and subscriptions when funding is limited.**

Poetry: Avant-garde, free verse, traditional. No light verse. **Buys 10-30 poems/year.** Submit maximum 10 poems. **Pays $10-50 subject to availability of funds;** pays in contributor's copies and subscriptions when funding is limited.

The online magazine carries original content not found in the print edition and includes writer's guidelines.

Tips: "All sections are open to freelancers. We rely almost exclusively on unsolicited manuscripts. *AQR* is a nonprofit literary magazine and does not always have funds to pay authors."

ALTERNATE REALITIES WEBZINE, Alternate Realities, 5026 NE 57th Ave., Portland OR 97218. (503)249-7125. Fax: (503)249-2758. E-mail: Fanwrite@aol.com. Website: www.alternaterealitieszine.com. **Contact:** Joan M. McCarty, senior editor/publisher. **100% freelance written.** Bimonthly online webzine covering fantasy, science fiction, horror, mysteries, thrillers, intrigues, genre art, and poetry. "We like cutting edge fiction, not the usual, overdone subjects. Tell the story with a new slant and character driven. Be familiar with both the guidelines and the magazine itself. Also, if your story is already on the Web, even if it is on your own personal site, it is considered a reprint and must be offline for no less than 6 months before we will take it." Estab. 1998. Circ. 2,000-3,000 visits/issue. Pays on second month of appearance. Byline given. Buys electronic rights. Editorial lead time 2 months. Submit seasonal material 1-2 months in advance. Accepts queries by mail, e-mail. Accepts previously published material. Accepts simultaneous submissions. Responds in 1 month to queries; 1-2 months to mss. Writer's guidelines online.

Nonfiction: Joan M. McCarty, senior editor. Book excerpts, general interest, historical/nostalgic, how-to, humor, genre-specific articles, book, movie, and TV reviews. "No content outside the genres we represent or outside of how to write fiction." **Buys 2-6 mss/year.** Query. Length: Flexible. **Pays $5-15.** Sometimes pays expenses of writers on assignment.

Fiction: Senior Editor. Fantasy, horror, mystery, science fiction, serialized novels, suspense. No overdone story plots (e.g., elves, dragons, serial killers, Roswell, etc.), anything outside specified genres, or romance. **Buys 60-150 mss/year.** Send complete ms. Length: 1,000-5,000 words. **Pays $5-15.**

Poetry: Fantasy/Poetry Editor. Free verse, light verse, traditional. No mundane poetry or anything that does not fit the genres the publication covers. **Buys 30 poems/year.** Submit maximum 3 poems. E-mail: Lorkiff@earthlink.net. Length: 3-Epic lines. **Pays $1-3.**

Tips: "Read the genres that you are writing in, choose the unusual plotlines, and be professional. Not only read the guidelines, but follow them. We have specific editors that handle the different genres if you do not send your work to the right editor, it can and will often times delay your work. Know the rules of the genres before attempting to break them. And, for goodness sake, know your grammar and the industry standards."

$ ANTIETAM REVIEW, 41 S. Potomac, Hagerstown MD 21740-5512. (301)791-3132. Fax: (240)420-1754. E-mail: winnie@washingtoncountyaas.com. **Contact:** Winnie Wagaman, managing editor. **90% freelance written.** Annual magazine covering fiction (short stories), poetry and b&w photography. Estab. 1982. Circ. 1,500. Pays on publication. Byline given. Accepts queries by mail, phone. Responds in 4 months to queries. Sample copy for $6.30 (current issue). Writer's guidelines for #10 SASE.

Fiction: Novel excerpts, short stories of a literary quality. No religious, romance, erotica, confession, horror or condensed novels. **Buys 9 mss/year.** Query with published clips or send complete ms. Length: 5,000 words. **Pays $100.**

Poetry: Paul Grant. Avant-garde, free verse, traditional. Does not want to see haiku, religious and most rhyme. **Buys 20-25 poems/year.** Submit maximum 3 poems. **Pays $25.**

Tips: "Spring annual issue will need fiction, poetry and b&w photography not previously published. Still seeking high quality work from both published and emerging writers. Also, we now have a summer Literary Contest. We consider materials from September 1 through February 1. Offers cash prize and publication in *Antietam*"

$ THE ANTIGONISH REVIEW, St. Francis Xavier University, P.O. Box 5000, Antigonish, Nova Scotia B2G 2W5, Canada. (902)867-3962. Fax: (902)867-5563. E-mail: tar@stfx.ca. Managing Editor: Josephine Mensch. **Contact:** B. Allan Quigley, editor. **100% freelance written.** Quarterly magazine. Estab. 1970. Circ. 850. Pays on publication. Publishes ms an average of 4 months after acceptance. Byline given. Offers variable kill fee. Rights retained by author rights. Editorial lead time 4 months. Submit seasonal material 4 months in advance. Accepts queries by mail, e-mail, fax. Responds in 1 month to queries; 4 months to mss. Sample copy for $4 or online. Writer's guidelines for #10 SASE or online.

Nonfiction: Essays, interview/profile, book reviews/articles. No academic pieces. **Buys 15-20 mss/year.** Query. Length: 1,500-5,000 words. **Pays $50-150.**

Fiction: Literary. No erotica. **Buys 35-40 mss/year.** Send complete ms. Length: 500-5,000 words.

Poetry: Buys 100-125 poems/year. Submit maximum 5 poems. **Pays in copies.**

Tips: "Send for guidelines and/or sample copy. Send ms with cover letter and SASE with submission."

$ANTIOCH REVIEW, P.O. Box 148, Yellow Springs OH 45387-0148. Website: www.antioch.edu/review. **Contact:** Robert S. Fogarty, editor. Quarterly magazine for general, literary, and academic audience. Estab. 1941. Circ. 5,100. Pays on publication. Publishes ms an average of 10 months after acceptance. Byline given. Rights revert to author upon publication rights. Accepts queries by mail. Sample copy for $6. Writer's guidelines for #10 SASE.

- Responds in 3 months.

Nonfiction: "Contemporary articles in the humanities and social sciences, politics, economics, literature, and all areas of broad intellectual concern. Somewhat scholarly, but never pedantic in style, eschewing all professional jargon. Lively, distinctive prose insisted upon. We *do not* read simultaneous submissions." Length: 2,000-8,000 words. **Pays $10/printed page.**

Fiction: "Quality fiction only, distinctive in style with fresh insights into the human condition." No science fiction, fantasy, or confessions. **Pays $10/printed page.**

Poetry: No light or inspirational verse.

$ARC, Canada's National Poetry Magazine, Arc Poetry Society, Box 7368, Ottawa, Ontario K1L 8E4, Canada. **Contact:** John Barton, Rita Donovan, co-editors. Semiannual magazine featuring poetry, poetry-related articles, and criticism. "Our focus is poetry, and Canadian poetry in general, although we do publish writers from elsewhere. We are looking for the best poetry from new and established writers. We often have special issues. SASE for upcoming special issues and contests." Estab. 1978. Circ. 1,000. Pays on publication. Publishes ms an average of 6 months after acceptance. Byline given. Buys one-time rights. Responds in 4 months to queries. Writer's guidelines for #10 SASE.

Nonfiction: Essays, interview/profile, book reviews. Query first. Length: 1,000-4,000 words. **Pays $30/printed page (Canadian) and 2 copies.**

Photos: Query first. Buys one-time rights. Pays $300 for 10 photos.

Poetry: Avant-garde, free verse. **Buys 40 poems/year.** Submit maximum 6 poems. **Pays $30/printed page (Canadian).**

Tips: "Please include brief biographical note with submission."

THE BARCELONA REVIEW, Correu Vell 12-2, Barcelona 08002, Spain. E-mail: editor@barcelonareview.com. Website: www.barcelonareview.com. **Contact:** Jill Adams, editor. Sample copy not available.

$BELLINGHAM REVIEW, Signpost Press, Mail Stop 9053, Western Washington University, Bellingham WA 98225. (360)650-4863. E-mail: bhreview@cc.wwu.edu. Website: www.wwu.edu/~bhreview. Editor: Brenda Miller. **Contact:** Poetry, Fiction, or Creative Nonfiction editor. **100% freelance written.** Semiannual nonprofit magazine. *Bellingham Review* seeks literature of palpable quality; stories, essays, and poems that nudge the limits of form, or execute traditional forms exquisitely. Estab. 1977. Circ. 1,600. Pays on publication. Publishes ms an average of 6 months after acceptance. Byline given. Buys first North American serial rights. Editorial lead time 6 months. Accepts simultaneous submissions. Responds in 3 months to mss. Sample copy for $7. Writer's guidelines for #10 SASE or on website.

Nonfiction: Nonfiction Editor. Essays, personal experience. Does not want anything nonliterary. **Buys 4-6 mss/year.** Send complete ms. Length: 9,000 words maximum. **Pays up to $200, as funds allow, plus contributor copies.**

Fiction: Fiction Editor. Literary short fiction. Does not want anything nonliterary. **Buys 4-6 mss/year.** Send complete ms. Length: 9,000 words maximum. **Pays up to $200, as funds allow.**

Poetry: Poetry Editor. Avant-garde, free verse, traditional. Will not use light verse. **Buys 10-30 poems/year.** Submit maximum 3 poems. **Pays up to $50.**

Tips: "Open submission period is from October 1 through February 1. Manuscripts arriving between February 2 and September 30 will be returned unread." The *Bellingham Review* holds 3 annual contests: the 49th Parallel Poetry Award, the Annie Dillard Award in Nonfiction, and the Tobias Wolff Award in Fiction. Submissions December 1-March 15. See the individual listings for these contests under Contests & Awards for full details.

$BLACK WARRIOR REVIEW, P.O. Box 862936, Tuscaloosa AL 35486-0027. (205)348-4518. Website: www.webdelsol.com/bwr. **90% freelance written.** Semiannual magazine of fiction, poetry, essays and reviews. Estab. 1974. Circ. 2,000. Pays on publication. Publishes ms an average of 6 months after acceptance. Byline given. Buys first rights. Responds in 2 weeks to queries; 3 months to mss. Sample copy for $8. Writer's guidelines for #10 SASE or online.

- Consistently excellent magazine. Placed stories and poems in recent *Best American Short Stories*, *Best American Poetry* and *Pushcart Prize* anthologies.

Nonfiction: David Mitchell-Goldberg, editor. Interview/profile, book reviews; literary/personal essays. **Buys 5 mss/year.** No queries; send complete ms. **Pays up to $100 and 2 contributor's copies.**

Fiction: Matt Maki, fiction editor. Publishes novel excerpts if under contract to be published. One story/chapter per envelope, please. **Buys 12 mss/year. Pays up to $150 and 2 contributor's copies.**

Poetry: Molly Oberlin, poetry editor. **Buys 35 poems/year.** Submit maximum 3-6 poems. **Pays up to $75 and 2 contributor's copies.**

Tips: "Read the *BWR* before submitting; editors change each year. Send us your best work. Submissions of photos and/or artwork is encouraged. We sometimes choose unsolicited photos/artwork for the cover. Address all submissions to the appropriate genre editor."

$$ BOULEVARD, Opojaz, Inc., 6614 Clayton Rd., PMB 325, Richmond Heights MO 63117. (314)862-2643. Fax: (314)781-7250. Website: www.richardburgin.com. **Contact:** Richard Burgin, editor. **100% freelance written.** Triannual magazine covering fiction, poetry, and essays. "*Boulevard* is a diverse literary magazine presenting original creative work by well-known authors, as well as by writers of exciting promise." Estab. 1985. Circ. 3,500. Pays on publication. Publishes ms an average of 9 months after acceptance. Byline given. Offers no kill fee. Buys first North American serial rights. Accepts queries by mail, phone. Accepts simultaneous submissions. Responds in 2 weeks to queries; 2 months to mss. Sample copy for $7. Writer's guidelines for #10 SASE.

O→ Break in with "a touching, intelligent, and original story, poem or essay."

Nonfiction: Book excerpts, essays, interview/profile, opinion, photo feature. "No pornography, science fiction, children's stories, or westerns." **Buys 10 mss/year.** Send complete ms. Length: 8,000 words. **Pays $50-250 (sometimes higher).**

Fiction: Confessions, experimental, mainstream, novel excerpts. "We do not want erotica, science fiction, romance, western, or children's stories." **Buys 20 mss/year.** Send complete ms. Length: 8,000 words. **Pays $150-300.**

Poetry: Avant-garde, free verse, haiku, traditional. "Do not send us light verse." **Buys 80 poems/year.** Submit maximum 5 poems. Length: 200 lines. **$25-250 (sometimes higher).**

Tips: "Read the magazine first. The work *Boulevard* publishes is generally recognized as among the finest in the country. We continue to seek more good literary or cultural essays. Send only your best work."

N ▣ BOVINE FREE WYOMING,. E-mail: submissions@bovinefreewyoming.com. Website: www.bovinefreewyoming.com. Managing Editor: Danny C. Knestaut. **Contact:** Vickie L. Knestaut, editor. **100% freelance written.** Quarterly online literary magazine. "We are looking for quality literature that will appeal to the general public." Estab. 2000. Circ. 2,000 unique visits/year. **Pays on acceptance.** Publishes ms an average of 3 months after acceptance. Byline given. Offers 100% kill fee. Buys electronic rights. Editorial lead time 3 months. Submit seasonal material 3 months in advance. Accepts queries by e-mail. Accepts previously published material. Accepts simultaneous submissions. Responds in 2 weeks to queries; 1 month to mss. Sample copy by e-mail. Writer's guidelines online.

Nonfiction: Vickie L. Knestaut, editor. Essays, general interest, historical/nostalgic, humor, opinion. No articles that appeal only to specialized fields. Send complete ms. Length: 7,500 word maximum. **Pays $10.**

Photos: State availability with submission. Reviews GIF/JPEG files. Buys electronic rights. Offers $10/photo.

Fiction: Vickie L. Knestaut, editor. "We are a general interest publication, therefore, we do not care to see pornography or erotica that is done in poor taste." **Buys 12 mss/year.** Send complete ms. Length: 7,500 word maximum. **Pays $10.**

Poetry: "We are open to all poetic forms." Vickie L. Knestaut, editor. No author-centric poetry that makes no attempt to relate the reader to the poem. **Buys 20 poems/year.** Submit maximum 5 poems.

Tips: "The greatest advice I have heard about writing is: 'No one cares about you.' It may sound callous, but we find that the writing we enjoy most is the writing that concerns itself with the reader, and not solely with the talents and/or cleverness of the author."

$ $ BRICK, A Literary Journal, Brick, Box 537, Station Q, Toronto, Ontario M4T 2M5, Canada. E-mail: info@brickmag.com. Website: www.brickmag.com. Editor: Linda Spalding. **Contact:** Michael Redhill, managing/contributing editor. **90% freelance written.** Semiannual magazine covering literature and the arts. "We publish literary nonfiction of a very high quality on a range of arts and culture subjects." Estab. 1975. Circ. 3,000. Pays on publication. Publishes ms an average of 3 months after acceptance. Byline given. Buys first North American serial, one-time rights. Editorial lead time 5 months. Accepts queries by mail, e-mail. Responds in 6 weeks to queries; 4 months to mss. Sample copy for $12. Writer's guidelines for free, online, or by e-mail.

Nonfiction: Essays, historical/nostalgic, interview/profile, opinion, travel. No fiction, poetry, personal real-life experience, or book reviews. **Buys 30-40 mss/year.** Send complete ms. Length: 250-6,000 words. **Pays $75-500 (Canadian).**

Photos: State availability with submission. Reviews transparencies, prints, GIF/JPEG files. Buys one-time rights. Offers $25-50/photo.

Tips: "Brick is interested in polished work by writers who are widely read and in touch with contemporary culture. The magazine is serious, but not fusty. We like to feel the writer's personality in the piece, too."

$ BUTTON, New England's Tiniest Magazine of Poetry, Fiction and Gracious Living, Box 26, Lunenburg MA 01462. E-mail: buttonx26@aol.com. **Contact:** Sally Cragin, editor. **10% freelance written.** Annual literary magazine. "*Button* is New England's tiniest magazine of poetry, fiction, and gracious living, published once a year. As 'gracious living' is on the cover, we like wit, brevity, cleverly-conceived essay/recipe, poetry that isn't sentimental or song lyrics. I started *Button* so that a century from now, when people read it in landfils or, preferably, libraries, they'll say, 'Gee, what a great time to have lived. I wish I lived back then.'" Estab. 1993. Circ. 1,500. Pays on publication. Byline given. Buys first North American serial rights. Editorial lead time 6 months. Responds in 2 months to mss. Sample copy for $2 and 1 34¢ stamp. Writer's guidelines for #10 SASE.

Nonfiction: Personal experience, cooking stories. Does not want "the tired, the trite, the sexist, the multiply-folded, the single-spaced, the sentimental, the self-pitying, the swaggering, the infantile (i.e., coruscated whimsy and self-conscious quaint), poems about Why You Can't Be Together and stories about How Complicated Am I. Before you send us anything, sit down and read a poem by Stanley Kunitz or a story by Evelyn Waugh, Louisa May Alcott, or anyone who's visited the poles, and if you still think you've written a damn fine thing, have at it. A word-count on the top of the page is fine—a copyright or 'all rights reserved' reminder makes you look like a beginner." **Buys 1-2 mss/year.** Length: 300-2,000 words. **Pays $25 honorarium, plus copies.**

Fiction: Seeking quality fiction. **Buys 1-2 mss/year.** Send complete ms. Length: 300-2,000 words. **Pays $25.**

Poetry: Seeking quality poetry. Free verse, traditional. **Buys 2-4 poems/year.** Submit maximum 3 poems. **Pays $10-25.**

Tips: "*Button* writers have been widely published elsewhere, in virtually all the major national magazines. They include, Ralph Lombreglia, Lawrence Millman, They Might Be Giants, Combustible Edison, Sven Birkerts, Stephen McCauley,

Amanda Powell, Wayne Wilson, David Barber, Romayne Dawnay, Brendan Galvin, and Diana DerHovanessian. It's 2 bucks for a sample, which seems reasonable. Follow the guidelines, make sure you read your work aloud, and don't inflate or deflate your publications and experience. We've published plenty of new folks, but on the merits of the work."

$ $ THE CAPILANO REVIEW, 2055 Purcell Way, North Vancouver, British Columbia V7J 3H5, Canada. E-mail: tcr@capcollege.bc.ca. Website: www.capcollege.bc.ca/dept/tcr/tcr. **Contact:** Sharon Thesen, editor. **100% freelance written.** "Triannual visual and literary arts magazine that publishes only what the editors consider to be the very best fiction, poetry, drama, or visual art being produced. *TCR* editors are interested in fresh, original work that stimulates and challenges readers. Over the years, the magazine has developed a reputation for pushing beyond the boundaries of traditional art and writing. We are interested in work that is new in concept and in execution." Estab. 1972. Circ. 900. Pays on publication. Byline given. Buys first North American serial rights. Accepts queries by mail. Responds in 1 month to queries; 5 months to mss. Sample copy not available. Writer's guidelines for #10 SASE with IRC or Canadian stamps or online.

Fiction: Query by mail or send complete ms with SASE and Canadian postage or IRCs. Novel excerpts, literary. **Buys 10-15 mss/year.** Length: 6,000 words. **Pays $50-200.**

Poetry: Submit maximum 5-10 poems (with SASE). Avant-garde, free verse. **Buys 40 poems/year. Pays $50-200.**

$ THE CHARITON REVIEW, Truman State University, Kirksville MO 63501-9915. (660)785-4499. Fax: (660)785-7486. **Contact:** Jim Barnes, editor. **100% freelance written.** Semiannual (fall and spring) magazine covering contemporary fiction, poetry, translation, and book reviews. Circ. 600. Pays on publication. Publishes ms an average of 6 months after acceptance. Byline given. Buys first North American serial rights. Accepts queries by mail. Responds in 1 week to queries; 1 month to mss. Sample copy for $5 and 7x10 SAE with 4 first-class stamps.

Nonfiction: Essays (essay reviews of books). **Buys 2-5 mss/year.** Send complete ms. Length: 1,000-5,000 words. **Pays $15.**

Fiction: Ethnic, experimental, mainstream, novel excerpts, traditional. "We are not interested in slick or sick material." **Buys 6-10 mss/year.** Send complete ms. Length: 1,000-6,000 words. **Pays $5/page (up to $50).**

Poetry: Avant-garde, traditional. **Buys 50-55 poems/year.** Submit maximum 5 poems. Length: Open. **Pays $5/page.**

Tips: "Read *Chariton*. Know the difference between good literature and bad. Know what magazine might be interested in your work. We are not a trendy magazine. We publish only the best. All sections are open to freelancers. Know your market or you are wasting your time—and mine. Do *not* write for guidelines; the only guideline is excellence."

$ THE CHATTAHOOCHEE REVIEW, Georgia Perimeter College, 2101 Womack Rd., Dunwoody GA 30338-4497. (770)551-3019. Website: www.chattahoochee-review.org. **Contact:** Lawrence Hetrick, editor. Quarterly magazine. "We publish a number of Southern writers, but *Chattahoochee Review* is not by design a regional magazine. All themes, forms, and styles are considered as long as they impact the whole person: heart, mind, intuition, and imagination." Estab. 1980. Circ. 1,350. Pays on publication. Publishes ms an average of 3 months after acceptance. Byline given. Buys first rights. Accepts queries by mail. Responds in 2 weeks to queries; 4 months to mss. Sample copy for $6. Writer's guidelines for #10 SASE.

Nonfiction: "We look for distinctive, honest personal essays and creative nonfiction of any kind, including the currently popular memoiristic narrative. We publish interviews with writers of all kinds: literary, academic, journalistic, and popular. We also review selected current offerings in fiction, poetry, and nonfiction, including works on photography and the visual arts, with an emphasis on important southern writers and artisits. We do not often, if ever, publish technical, critical, theoretical, or scholarly work about literature although we are interested in essays written for general readers about writers, their careers, and their work." Essays (interviews with authors, reviews). **Buys 10 mss/year.** Send complete ms. Length: 5,000 words maximum.

Photos: State availability with submission. Buys one-time rights. Negotiates payment individually. Identification of subjects required.

Fiction: Accepts all subject matter except science fiction and romance. **Buys 12 mss/year.** Send complete ms. Length: 6,000 words maximum. **Pays $20/page.**

Poetry: Avant-garde, free verse, haiku, light verse, traditional. **Buys 60 poems/year.** Submit maximum 5 poems. **Pays $50/poem.**

Tips: "Become familiar with our journal and the type of work we regularly publish."

$ CHELSEA, Chelsea Associates, P.O. Box 773 Cooper Station, New York NY 10276-0773. **Contact:** Alfredo de Palchi, editor. **70% freelance written.** Semiannual magazine. "We stress style, variety, originality. No special biases or requirements. Flexible attitudes, eclectic material. We take an active interest, as always, in cross-cultural exchanges, superior translations, and are leaning toward cosmopolitan, interdisciplinary techniques, but maintain no strictures against traditional modes." Estab. 1958. Circ. 1,800. Pays on publication. Publishes ms an average of 6 months after acceptance. Byline given. Buys first North American serial rights. Accepts queries by mail. Responds in 6 months to mss. Sample copy for $6. Writer's guidelines for #10 SASE.

- *Chelsea* also sponsors fiction and poetry contests. Send SASE for guidelines.

Nonfiction: Essays, book reviews (query first with sample). **Buys 6 mss/year.** Send complete ms with SASE. Length: 6,000 words. **Pays $15/page.**

Fiction: Mainstream, novel excerpts, literary. **Buys 12 mss/year.** Send complete ms. Length: 5,000-6,000 words. **Pays $15/page.**

Poetry: Avant-garde, free verse, traditional. **Buys 60-75 poems/year. Pays $15/page.**

Tips: "We only accept written correspondence. We are looking for more super translations, first-rate fiction, and work by writers of color. No need to query; submit complete manuscript. We suggest writers look at a recent issue of *Chelsea*."

CHICKEN SOUP FOR THE SOUL, 101 Stories to Open the Heart and Rekindle the Spirit, Chicken Soup for the Soul Enterprises, Inc., P.O, Box 30880, Santa Barbara CA 93130. (805)682-6311. Fax: (805)563-2945. E-mail: nautio@chickensoup.com. Website: www.chickensoup.com. Managing Editor: Heather McNamara. **Contact:** Nancy Mitchell-Autio, acquisitions editor. **95% freelance written.** Paperback with 8-12 publications/year featuring inspirational, heartwarming, uplifting short stories. Estab. 1993. Circ. Over 40 titles; 60 million books in print. Pays on publication. Publishes ms an average of 8 months after acceptance. Byline given. Buys all rights. Accepts queries by mail, e-mail, fax. Accepts previously published material. Accepts simultaneous submissions. Responds upon consideration to queries. Sample copy not available. Writer's guidelines online.

Nonfiction: Humor, inspirational, personal experience, religious. Special issues: Traveling sisterhood, Mother-Daughter stories, Christian teen, Christmas stories, stories by and/or about men, on love, kindness, parenting, family, Nascar racing, athletes, teachers, fishing, adoption, volunteers. No sermon, essay, eulogy, term paper, journal entry, political, or controversial issues. **Buys 1,000 mss/year.** Send complete ms. Length: 300-1,200 words. **Pays $300.**

Poetry: Traditional. No controversial poetry. **Buys 50 poems/year.** Submit maximum 5 poems. **Pays $300.**

Fillers: Anecdotes, facts, gags to be illustrated by cartoonist, short humor. **Buys 50/year. Pays $300.**

Tips: "We prefer submissions to be sent via our website at www.chickensoup.com. Print submissions should be on 8½×11 paper in 12 point Times New Roman font. Type authors contact information appears on the first page of story. Stories are to be nonfiction. No anonymous or author unknown submissions are accepted. We do not return submissions."

$ CIMARRON REVIEW, Oklahoma State University, 205 Morrill Hall, OSU, Stillwater OK 74078-0135. (405)744-9476. E-mail: cimarronreview@hotmail.com. **Contact:** E.P. Walkiewicz, editor. **85% freelance written.** Quarterly magazine. "We publish short fiction, poetry, and essays of serious literary quality by writers often published, seldom published and previously unpublished. We have no bias with respect to subject matter, form (traditional or experimental), or theme. Though we appeal to a general audience, many of our readers are writers themselves or members of a university community." Estab. 1967. Circ. 500. Pays on publication. Publishes ms an average of 6 months after acceptance. Byline given. Buys first North American serial rights. Responds in 3 months to mss. Sample copy for $7.

Nonfiction: Essays, general interest, historical/nostalgic, interview/profile, opinion, personal experience, travel, literature, and arts. "We are not interested in highly subjective personal reminiscences; obscure or arcane articles; or short, light 'human interest' pieces." **Buys 9-12 mss/year.** Send complete ms. Length: 1,000-7,500 words. **Pays $50, plus 1-year's subscription.**

Fiction: Mainstream, novel excerpts. No juvenile or genre fiction. **Buys 12-17 mss/year.** Send complete ms. Length: 1,250-7,000 words. **Pays $50.**

Poetry: Free verse, traditional. No haiku, light verse, or religious poems. **Buys 55-70 poems/year.** Submit maximum 6 poems.

Tips: "For prose, submit legible, double-spaced typescript with name and address on manuscript. Enclose a SASE and brief cover letter. For poetry, same standards apply, but single-spaced is conventional. Be familiar with high quality, contemporary writing. Evaluate your own work cafefully."

$ COLORADO REVIEW, Center for Literary Publishing, Department of English, Colorado State University, Fort Collins CO 80523. (970)491-5449. E-mail: creview@colostate.edu. Website: www.coloradoreview.com. Managing Editor: Stephanie G'Schwind. **Contact:** David Milofsky, editor. Literary magazine published 3 times/year. Estab. 1972. Circ. 1,300. Pays on publication. Publishes ms an average of 1 year after acceptance. Byline given. Buys first North American serial rights. Editorial lead time 1 year. Accepts queries by mail. Responds in 2 months to mss. Sample copy for $10. Writer's guidelines for #10 SASE.

Nonfiction: Stephanie G'Schwind, managing editor. Essays (personal). **Buys 3-5 mss/year.** Send complete ms. **Pays $5/page.**

Fiction: Short fiction. No genre fiction. **Buys 15-20 mss/year.** Send complete ms. **Pays $5/page.**

Poetry: Considers poetry of any style. Don Revell or Jorie Graham, poetry editors. **Buys 60-100 poems/year. Pays $5/page.**

Tips: Manuscripts are read from September 1 to April 30. Manuscripts recieved between May 1 and August 30 will be returned unread.

$ $ ☐ CONFRONTATION, A Literary Journal, Long Island University, Brookville NY 11548. (516)299-2720. Fax: (516)299-2735. E-mail: mtucker@liu.edu. Assistant to Editor: Michael Hartnett. **Contact:** Martin Tucker, editor-in-chief. **75% freelance written.** Semiannual magazine. "We are eclectic in our taste. Excellence of style is our dominant concern." Estab. 1968. Circ. 2,000. Pays on publication. Publishes ms an average of 1 year after acceptance. Byline given. Offers kill fee. Buys first North American serial, first, one-time, all rights. Accepts queries by mail, e-mail, phone. Accepts simultaneous submissions. Responds in 3 weeks to queries; 2 months to mss. Sample copy for $3. Writer's guidelines not available.

Nonfiction: Essays, personal experience. **Buys 15 mss/year.** Send complete ms. Length: 1,500-5,000 words. **Pays $100-300 for assigned articles; $15-300 for unsolicited articles.**

Photos: State availability with submission. Buys one-time rights. Offers no additional payment for photos accepted with ms.

Fiction: Jonna Semeiks. "We judge on quality, so genre is open." Experimental, mainstream, novel excerpts, slice-of-life vignettes. **Buys 60-75 mss/year.** Send complete ms. Length: 6,000 words. **Pays $25-250.**
Poetry: Michael Hartnett. Avant-garde, free verse, haiku, light verse, traditional. **Buys 60-75 poems/year.** Submit maximum 6 poems. Length: Open. **Pays $10-100.**
Tips: "Most open to fiction and poetry. Study our magazine."

$ THE CONNECTICUT POETRY REVIEW, The Connecticut Poetry Review Press, P.O. Box 818, Stonington CT 06378. Managing Editor: Harley More. **Contact:** J. Claire White. **60% freelance written.** Annual magazine covering poetry/literature. Estab. 1981. Circ. 500. **Pays on acceptance.** Byline sometimes given. Buys first rights. Editorial lead time 4 months. Submit seasonal material 4 months in advance. Accepts queries by mail. Responds in 1 month to queries; 3 months to mss. Sample copy for $3.50 and #10 SASE. Writer's guidelines for #10 SASE.
Nonfiction: Book excerpts, essays. **Buys 18 mss/year.**
Fiction: Experimental.
Poetry: Avant-garde, free verse, haiku, traditional. No light verse. **Buys 20-30 poems/year.** Submit maximum 4 poems. Length: 3-25 lines. **Pays $5-10.**

$ CREATIVE NONFICTION, Creative Nonfiction Foundation, 5501 Walnut St., Suite 202, Pittsburgh PA 15232. (412)688-0304. Fax: (412)683-9173. E-mail: info@creativenonfiction.org. Website: www.creativenonfiction.org. Managing Editor: Leslie Aizenman. **Contact:** Lee Gutkind, editor. **100% freelance written.** Magazine published 3 times/year covering nonfiction—personal essay, memoir, literary journalism. "*Creative Nonfiction* is the first journal to focus exclusively upon the genre of creative nonfiction. It publishes personal essay, memoir, and literary journalism on a broad range of subjects. Interviews with prominent writers and commentary about the genre also appear on its pages." Estab. 1993. Circ. 4,000. Pays on publication. Publishes ms an average of 1 year after acceptance. Byline given. Buys all rights. Editorial lead time 3 months. Accepts queries by mail, e-mail, fax, phone. Accepts simultaneous submissions. Responds in 3 weeks to queries; 6 months to mss. Sample copy for $10.
Nonfiction: Book excerpts, essays, interview/profile, personal experience, reviews of books. Does not want poetry, fiction, self-involved narratives that do not have larger meaning. **Buys 30 mss/year.** Send complete ms. Length: 5,000 words maximum. **Pays $10/page—more if grant money available for assigned articles.**
Tips: "Points to remember when submitting to *Creative Nonfiction:* strong reportage; well-written prose, attentive to language, rich with detail and distinctive voice; an informational quality or 'teaching element' offering the reader something to learn; a compelling, focused, sustained narrative that's well-structured, makes sense, and conveys a meaning. Manuscripts will not be accepted via fax."

$ DESCANT, Descant Arts & Letters Foundation, P.O. Box 314, Station P, Toronto, Ontario M5S 2S8, Canada. (416)593-2557. E-mail: descant@web.net. Website: www.descant.on.ca. Editor: Karen Mulhallen. **Contact:** Mary Newberry, managing editor. Quarterly journal. Estab. 1970. Circ. 1,200. Pays on publication. Publishes ms an average of 16 months after acceptance. Editorial lead time 4 months. Accepts queries by mail. Sample copy for $8. Writer's guidelines for #10 SASE or by e-mail.

- Accepts queries by mail only. Pays $100 honorarium, plus 1-year's subscription for accepted submissions of any kind.

Nonfiction: Book excerpts, essays, interview/profile, personal experience, historical.
Photos: State availability with submission. Reviews contact sheets, prints. Buys one-time rights. Offers no additional payment for photos accepted with ms.
Fiction: Short stories or book excerpts. Maximum length 6,000 words; 3,000 words or less preferred. Send complete ms.
Poetry: Free verse, light verse, traditional. Submit maximum 10 poems.
Tips: "Familiarize yourself with our magazine before submitting."

$ $ $ DOUBLETAKE, 55 Davis Square, Somerville MA 02144. (617)591-9389. Website: www.doubletakemagazine.org. **Contact:** Fiction Editor. Pays on publication. Byline given. Buys first North American serial rights. Accepts simultaneous submissions. Responds in 3 months to mss. Sample copy for $12. Writer's guidelines for #10 SASE.
Fiction: "We accept realistic fiction in all of its variety. We look for stories with a strong narrative voice and an urgency in the writing." **Buys 12 mss/year.** Send complete ms. Length: No preferred length. **Pays competitively.**

The online magazine carries original content not found in the print edition and includes writer's guidelines.

Tips: "*Doubletake* looks for writing distinguished by economy, directness, authenticity, and heart."

$ DREAMS & VISIONS, New Frontiers in Christian Fiction, Skysong Press, 35 Peter St. S., Orillia, Ontario L3V 5A8, Canada. (705)329-1770. Fax: (705)329-1770. E-mail: skysong@bconnex.net. Website: www.bconnex.net/~skysong. **Contact:** Steve Stanton, editor. **100% freelance written.** Semiannual magazine. "Innovative literary fiction for adult Christian readers." Estab. 1988. Circ. 200. Pays on publication. Publishes ms an average of 1 year after acceptance. Byline given. Buys first North American serial, second serial (reprint) rights. Editorial lead time 1 year. Accepts queries by mail, e-mail. Accepts simultaneous submissions. Responds in 6 weeks to queries; 6 months to mss. Sample copy for $4.95. Writer's guidelines for #10 SASE or online.
Fiction: Experimental, fantasy, humorous, mainstream, mystery, novel excerpts, religious, science fiction, slice-of-life vignettes. "We do not publish stories that glorify violence or perversity." **Buys 10 mss/year.** Send complete ms. Length: 2,000-6,000 words. **Pays ½¢/word.**

$ DREAMS OF DECADENCE, P.O. Box 2988, Radford VA 24143-2988. (540)763-2925. Fax: (540)763-2924. E-mail: dreamsofdecadence@dnapublications.com. Website: www.dnapublications.com/dreams. **Contact:** Angela Kessler, editor. Quarterly magazine featuring vampire fiction and poetry. Pays on publication. Publishes ms an average of 6 months after acceptance. Buys first North American serial rights. Accepts simultaneous submissions. Responds in 1 month to queries; 1 month to mss. Sample copy for $5. Writer's guidelines for #10 SASE or online.

Fiction: "I like elegant prose with a Gothic feel. The emphasis is on dark fantasy rather than horror. No vampire feeds, vampire has sex, someone becomes a vampire pieces." **Buys 30-40 mss/year.** Send complete ms. Length: 1,000-15,000 words. **Pays 1-5¢/word.**

Poetry: "Looking for all forms; however, the less horrific and the more explicitly vampiric a poem is, the more likely it is to be accepted." **Pays $3/short poem; $5/long poem; $20/featured poet.**

Tips: "We look for atmospheric, well-written stories with original ideas, not rehashes."

$ EPOCH, Cornell University, 251 Goldwin Smith Hall, Cornell University, Ithaca NY 14853. (607)255-3385. Fax: (607)255-6661. Editor: Michael Koch. **Contact:** Joseph Martin, senior editor. **100% freelance written.** Magazine published 3 times/year. "Well-written literary fiction, poetry, personal essays. Newcomers always welcome. Open to mainstream and avant-garde writing." Estab. 1947. Circ. 1,000. Pays on publication. Byline given. Offers 100% kill fee. Buys first North American serial rights. Editorial lead time 6 months. Submit seasonal material 8 months in advance. Accepts queries by mail. Responds in 2 weeks to queries; 6 weeks to mss. Sample copy for $5. Writer's guidelines for #10 SASE.

Nonfiction: Send complete ms. Essays, interview. No inspirational. **Buys 6-8 mss/year.** Send complete ms. Length: Open. **Pays $5-10/printed page.**

Photos: Send photos with submission. Reviews contact sheets, transparencies, any size prints. Buys one-time rights. Negotiates payment individually.

Fiction: Experimental, mainstream, novel excerpts, literary short stories. **Buys 25-30 mss/year.** Send complete ms. Length: Open. **Pays $5 and up/printed page.**

Poetry: Nancy Vieira Couto. Avant-garde, free verse, haiku, light verse, traditional, all types. **Buys 30-75 poems/year.** Submit maximum 7 poems.

Tips: "Tell your story, speak your poem, straight from the heart. We are attracted to language and to good writing, but we are most interested in what the good writing leads us to, or where."

$ $ EVENT, Douglas College, P.O. Box 2503, New Westminster, British Columbia V3L 5B2, Canada. (604)527-5293. Fax: (604)527-5095. E-mail: event@douglas.bc.ca. Website: event.douglas.bc.ca. **Contact:** Ian Cockfield, managing editor. **100% freelance written.** Magazine published 3 times/year containing fiction, poetry, creative nonfiction, and reviews. "We are eclectic and always open to content that invites involvement. Generally, we like strong narrative." Estab. 1971. Circ. 1,250. Pays on publication. Publishes ms an average of 8 months after acceptance. Byline given. Buys first North American serial rights. Accepts queries by mail, e-mail, fax, phone. Accepts simultaneous submissions. Responds in 1 month to queries; 6 months to mss. Sample copy for $5. Writer's guidelines for #10 SASE (Canadian postage/IRCs only).

- *Event* does not read mss in July, August, December, and January. No e-mail submissions. All submissions must include SASE (Canadian postage or IRCs only).

Fiction: Christine Dewar, fiction editor. "We look for readability, style, and writing that invites involvement." Submit maximum 2 stories. **Buys 12-15 mss/year.** Send complete ms. Length: 5,000 words maximum. **Pays $22/page to $500.**

Poetry: "We tend to appreciate the narrative and sometimes the confessional modes." Gillian Harding-Russell, poetry editor. Free verse, prose. No light verse. **Buys 30-40 poems/year.** Submit maximum 10 poems. **Pays $25-500.**

Tips: "Write well and read some past issues of *Event*."

$ FIELD, Contemporary Poetry & Poetics, Oberlin College Press, 10 N. Professor St., Oberlin OH 44074-1095. (440)775-8408. Fax: (440)775-8124. E-mail: oc.press@oberlin.edu. Website: www.oberlin.edu/~ocpress. **Contact:** Linda Slocum, managing editor. **60% freelance written.** Semiannual magazine of poetry, poetry in translation, and essays on contemporary poetry by poets. No electronic submissions. Estab. 1969. Circ. 1,500. Pays on publication. Byline given. Buys first rights. Editorial lead time 4 months. Accepts queries by mail, e-mail, fax, phone. Responds in 6 weeks to mss. Sample copy for $7. Writer's guidelines online.

Poetry: Buys 100 poems/year. Submit maximum 5 poems with SASE. **Pays $15/page.**

Tips: "Submit 3-5 of your best poems with a cover letter. No simultaneous submissions and include a SASE. Keep trying! Submissions are read year-round."

THE FIRST LINE, K Street Ink, P.O. Box 0382, Plano TX 75025-0382. E-mail: info@thefirstline.com. Website: www.thefirstline.com. Co-editors: David LaBounty and Jeff Adams. **Contact:** Robin LaBounty, manuscript coordinator. **95% freelance written.** Quarterly magazine. *The First Line* is a magazine that explores the different directions writers can take when they start from the same place. All stories must be written with the first line provided by the magazine. Estab. 1999. Circ. 100. Pays on publication. Publishes ms an average of 1 month after acceptance. Byline given. Buys first North American serial, electronic rights. Editorial lead time 2 months. Accepts queries by mail, e-mail. Accepts simultaneous submissions. Responds in 1 week to queries; 2 months to mss. Sample copy for $3. Writer's guidelines free.

Nonfiction: David LaBounty, editor. Essays, interview/profile, book reviews. **Buys 4-8 mss/year.** Query. Length: 300-1,000 words. **Pays $5 for assigned articles; $5 for unsolicited articles.**

Fiction: Robin LaBounty, manuscript coordinator. Adventure, ethnic, experimental, fantasy, historical, horror, humorous, mainstream, mystery, romance, science fiction, suspense, western. No stories that do not start with the issue's first sentence. **Buys 40-60 mss/year.** Send complete ms. Length: 300-1,500 words. **Pays $5.**

Tips: Start your stories with these sentences: (Spring issue, deadline February 1) The first thing I saw when I woke was Chris' face; (Summer issue, deadline May 1) The incident on the island is the stuff of legend, but let me tell you the real story; (Fall issue, deadline August 1) Jimmy Hanson was a sallow man who enjoyed little in life save for his blank (you fill in the blank); and (Winter issue, deadline November 1) I can't believe I just heard that.

FLASHQUAKE, An Online Quarterly journal of Flash Literature, River Road Studios, P.O. Box 2154, Albany NY 12220-0154. E-mail: dorton@flashquake.org. Website: www.flashquake.org. **Contact:** Debi Orton, publisher/editor. **90% freelance written.** Quarterly online literary journal covering flash literature. "Our specialty is flash literature—complete stories with beginnings, middles, ends, conflicts, resolutions, characters—in the most compact form possible. We look for new ideas, fresh perspectives, interesting situations, and compelling characters." Estab. 2001. Circ. 1,500 hits/month. **Pays on acceptance.** Publishes ms an average of 1-3 months after acceptance. Byline given. Buys first, electronic rights. Editorial lead time 1-3 months. Submit seasonal material 1-3 months in advance. Accepts queries by mail, e-mail. Accepts previously published material. Accepts simultaneous submissions. Responds in 1 week to queries; 1-3 months to mss. Sample copy online. Writer's guidelines online.

Nonfiction: Essays, general interest, humor, inspirational, personal experience. No religious-themed or politically-slanted nonfiction. No rants. **Buys 24 mss/year.** Send complete ms. Length: 1,000 words maximum. **Pays $5-25 for unsolicited personal essays and memoirs.** "We pay cash ($5-25) for up to 3 contributors/issue (6 contributors beginning with the Fall 2002 issue); all writers receive CD copy of issue."

Photos: State availability with submission. Buys one-time rights. Offers no additional payment for photos accepted with ms. Captions, identification of subjects required.

Columns/Departments: "We publish flash plays, i.e., plays of less than 10 minutes in duration when performed. We pay cash **($5-25)** for up to 3 contributors/issue (6 contributors beginning with the Fall 2002 issue); all writers receive CD copy of issue." Send complete ms.

Fiction: "We pay cash **($5-25)** for up to 3 contributors/issue (6 contributors beginning with the Fall 2002 issue); all writers receive CD copy of issue." Adventure, ethnic, experimental, fantasy, horror, humorous, mainstream, mystery, science fiction, suspense. No religious or romantic. **Buys 24 mss/year.** Send complete ms. Length: 1,000 words maximum.

Poetry: "We pay cash **($5-25)** for up to 3 contributors/issue (6 contributors beginning with the Fall 2002 issue); all writers receive CD copy of issue." Avant-garde, free verse, haiku, light verse, traditional, prose poetry. No religious or romantic. **Buys 24 poems/year.** Submit maximum 3 poems. Length: 35 line maximum.

Tips: "Proofread your work thoroughly. We will instantly reject your work for spelling and grammar errors. Save your document as plain text and paste it into an e-mail message. We will not open attachments. We want work that the reader will think about long after reading it. We want stories that compel the reader to continue reading them. We like experimental work, but that should not be construed as a license to forget narrative clarity, plot, character development, or reader satisfaction."

$ FRANK, An International Journal of Contemporary Writing & Art, Association Frank, 32 rue Edouard Vaillant, Montreuil, France. (33)(1)48596658. Fax: (33)(1)48596668. E-mail: dapplefield@readfrank.com. Website: www.readfrank.com or www.frank.ly. **Contact:** David Applefield, editor. **80% freelance written.** Magazine covering contemporary writing of all genres. Bilingual. "Writing that takes risks and isn't ethnocentric is looked upon favorably." Estab. 1983. Circ. 4,000. Pays on publication. Publishes ms an average of 1 year after acceptance. Byline given. Buys one-time rights. Editorial lead time 6 months. Responds in 1 month to queries; 2 months to mss. Sample copy for $10. Writer's guidelines for #10 SASE or online.

Nonfiction: Interview/profile, travel. **Buys 2 mss/year.** Query. **Pays $100 for assigned articles.**

Photos: State availability with submission. Buys one-time rights. Negotiates payment individually.

Fiction: Experimental, novel excerpts, international. **Buys 8 mss/year.** Send complete ms. Length: 1,000-3,000 words. **Pays $10/printed page.**

Poetry: Avant-garde, translations. **Buys 20 poems/year.** Submit maximum 10 poems. **Pays $20.**

Tips: "Suggest what you do or know best. Avoid query form letters—we won't read the manuscript. Looking for excellent literary/cultural interviews with leading American writers or cultural figures. Very receptive to new Foreign Dossiers of writing from a particular country."

$ $ THE GEORGIA REVIEW, The University of Georgia, 012 Gilbert Hall, University of Georgia, Athens GA 30602-9009. (706)542-3481. Fax: (706)542-0047. E-mail: garev@uga.edu. Website: www.uga.edu/garev. Managing Editor: Annette Hatton. **Contact:** T.R. Hummer, editor. **99% freelance written.** Quarterly journal. "Our readers are educated, inquisitive people who read a lot of work in the areas we feature, so they expect only the best in our pages. All work submitted should show evidence that the writer is at least as well-educated and well-read as our readers. Essays should be authoritative but accessible to a range of readers." Estab. 1947. Circ. 5,000. Pays on publication. Publishes ms an average of 6 months after acceptance. Byline given. Buys first North American serial rights. Accepts queries by mail. Responds in 2 weeks to queries; 3 months to mss. Sample copy for $7. Writer's guidelines for #10 SASE.

- No simultaneous or electronic submissions.

Nonfiction: Essays. "For the most part we are not interested in scholarly articles that are narrow in focus and/or overly burdened with footnotes. The ideal essay for *The Georgia Review* is a provocative, thesis-oriented work that can engage both the intelligent general reader and the specialist." **Buys 12-20 mss/year.** Send complete ms. **Pays $40/published page.**
Photos: Send photos with submission. Reviews 5×7 prints or larger. Buys one-time rights. Offers no additional payment for photos accepted with ms.
Fiction: "We seek original, excellent writing not bound by type. Ordinarily we do not publish novel excerpts or works translated into English and we strongly discourage authors from submitting these." **Buys 12-20 mss/year.** Send complete ms. **Pays $40/published page.**
Poetry: "We seek original, excellent poetry." **Buys 60-75 poems/year.** Submit maximum 5 poems. **Pays $3/line.**
Tips: "Unsolicited manuscripts will not be considered during the months of June, July, and August; all such submissions received during that period will be returned unread."

$ THE GETTYSBURG REVIEW, Gettysburg College, Gettysburg PA 17325. (717)337-6770. Fax: (717)337-6775. Website: www.gettysburgreview.com. **Contact:** Peter Stitt, editor. Quarterly magazine. "Our concern is quality. Manuscripts submitted here should be extremely well written." Reading period September-May. Estab. 1988. Circ. 4,000. Pays on publication. Byline given. Buys first North American serial rights. Editorial lead time 1 year. Submit seasonal material 9 months in advance. Accepts queries by mail, fax. Responds in 1 month to queries; 3 months to mss. Sample copy for $7. Writer's guidelines for #10 SASE.
Nonfiction: Essays. **Buys 20 mss/year.** Send complete ms. Length: 3,000-7,000 words. **Pays $25/page.**
Fiction: High quality, literary. Novel excerpts. **Buys 20 mss/year.** Send complete ms. Length: 2,000-7,000 words. **Pays $25/page.**
Poetry: Buys 50 poems/year. Submit maximum 3 poems. **Pays $2/line.**

$ $ GLIMMER TRAIN STORIES, Glimmer Train Press, Inc., 710 SW Madison St., #504, Portland OR 97205. (503)221-0836. E-mail: assistance@glimmertrain.com. Website: www.glimmertrain.com. **Contact:** Linda Swanson-Davies, co-editor. **90% freelance written.** Quarterly magazine of literary short fiction. "We are interested in well-written, emotionally-moving short stories published by unknown, as well as known, writers." Estab. 1991. Circ. 16,000. **Pays on acceptance.** Byline given. Buys first rights. Accepts queries by e-mail. Responds in 3 months to mss. Sample copy for $9.95 or on website. Writer's guidelines online.
Fiction: "Open to stories of all themes, all subjects." **Buys 32 mss/year. Pays $500.**
Tips: To submit a story, use the form on the website. All stories should be submitted via this electronic format. See *Glimmer Train*'s contest listings in Contest and Awards section.

$ GRAIN LITERARY MAGAZINE, Saskatchewan Writers Guild, P.O. Box 67, Saskatoon, Saskatchewan S7K 3K1, Canada. (306)244-2828. Fax: (306)244-0255. E-mail: grain@sasktel.net. Website: www.skywriter.com/grain. Buisiness Administrator: Jennifer Still. **Contact:** Elizabeth Philips, editor. **100% freelance written.** Quarterly magazine covering poetry, fiction, creative nonfiction, drama. "*Grain* publishes writing of the highest quality, both traditional and innovative in nature. The *Grain* editors' aim: To publish work that challenges readers; to encourage promising new writers; and to produce a well-designed, visually interesting magazine." Estab. 1973. Circ. 1,600. Pays on publication. Publishes ms an average of 11 months after acceptance. Byline given. Buys first rights, Canadian, serial. Editorial lead time 6 months. Accepts queries by mail, e-mail, fax, phone. Responds in 1 month to queries; 4 months to mss. Sample copy for $8 or online. Writer's guidelines for #10 SASE or online.
Nonfiction: Interested in creative nonfiction.
Photos: Submit 12-20 slides and b/w prints, short statement (200 words) and brief résumé. Reviews transparencies, prints. Pays $100 for front cover art, $30/photo.
Fiction: Literary fiction of all types. "No romance, confession, science fiction, vignettes, mystery." **Buys 40 mss/year. Pays $40-175.**
Poetry: "High quality, imaginative, well-crafted poetry. Submit maximum 10 poems and SASE with postage or IRC's. Avant-garde, free verse, haiku, traditional. No sentimental, end-line rhyme, mundane." **Buys 78 poems/year. Pays $40-175.**
Tips: "Sweat the small stuff. Pay attention to detail, credibility. Make sure you have researched your piece and that the literal and metaphorical support one another."

N $ $ $ $ GRANTA, The Magazine of New Writing, Granta Publications, 2/3 Hanover Yard, Noel Rd., London NI 8BE, England. (44)(0)20 7704 9776. E-mail: editorial@granta.com. Website: www.granta.com. Editor: Ian Jack. **Contact:** Fatema Ahmed, editorial assistant. **100% freelance written.** Quarterly 256-page paperback book. Estab. 1979. Circ. 80,000. Pays on publication. Byline given. Offers kill fee, amount determined by arrangement. Buys world English language rights, first serial rights (minimum). "We hold more rights in pieces we commission." Editorial lead time 3 months. Accepts simultaneous submissions. Responds in 3 months to mss. Sample copy for $12.95. Writer's guidelines available by e-mail or online at website.

- Queries not necessary.

Nonfiction: Ian Jack, editor. No articles or reporting whose relevancy will not last the life span of the magazine. The pieces we publish should last for several years (as the issues themselves do).
Fiction: Ian Jack, editor. **Buys no more than 2 short stories or synopsis and first chapter of a novel.** Novel excerpts, literary. No genre fiction. Length: No limits on length. **Payment varies.**

Tips: "You must be familiar with the magazine and ask yourself honestly if you feel your piece meets our criteria. We receive many submissions every day, many of which are completely unsuitable for *Granta* (however well written).

$ HAPPY, 240 E. 35th St., Suite 11A, New York NY 10016. E-mail: bayardx@aol.com. **Contact:** Bayard, editor. Pays on publication. Byline given. Buys one-time rights. Accepts queries by mail, e-mail. Accepts simultaneous submissions. Responds in 1 month to queries. Sample copy for $15. Writer's guidelines for #10 SASE.
Fiction: "We accept anything that's beautifully written. Genre isn't important. It just has to be incredible writing." Novel excerpts, short stories. **Buys 100-130 mss/year.** Send complete ms. Length: 6,000 words maximum. **Pays 1-5¢/word.**
Tips: "Don't bore us with the mundane—blast us out of the water with the extreme!"

$ HARPUR PALATE, a literary journal at Binghamton University, English Department, P.O. Box 6000, Binghamton University, Binghamton NY 13902-6000. (607)355-4761. E-mail: tfinley@binghamton.edu. Website: go.to/hpjournal.com; harpurpalate.binghamton.edu. **Contact:** Toiya Kristen Finley, fiction editor; Catherine Dent and Anne Rashid, poetry editors. **100% freelance written.** Semiannual literary magazine. "We believe writers should explore different genres to tell their stories. *Harpur Palate* accepts pieces regardless of genre, as long as the works pay attention to craft, structure, language, and the story well told." Estab. 2000. Circ. 400. Pays on publication. Publishes ms an average of 1-2 months after acceptance. Byline given. Buys first North American serial, electronic rights. Editorial lead time 3 months. Accepts queries by mail, e-mail. Accepts simultaneous submissions. Responds in 1 week to queries; 3 months to mss. Sample copy for $7.50, plus $1.18 shipping and handling, or on website. Writer's guidelines for #10 SASE or on website.
Fiction: "We believe that journals published by creative writing programs should reflect the work of the students in the programs. Creative writing students at Binghamton express themselves in a spectrum of styles and genres, and *Harpur Palate* believes that writers who explore the boundaries of genre should have the opportunity to place their work in a literary journal. We're open to pieces that may have a hard time fitting in other venues." Adventure, ethnic, experimental, fantasy, historical, humorous, mainstream, mystery, novel excerpts, science fiction, suspense, literary, fabulism, magical realism, metafiction, slipstream (genre blending). "No solipistic or self-centered fiction or autobiography pretending to be fiction. No pornography, excessive profanity, or shock value for shock value's sake." **Buys 20-30 mss/year.** Length: 250-8,000 words. **Pays $5-20.**
Poetry: "We are open to speculative as well as realistic themes in poetry." Avant-garde, free verse, haiku, traditional, experimental, blank verse, long poems, lyrical, narrative, prose poems, sonnets, tanka, villanelles. No poems longer than 10 pages. No pornography, excessive profanity, or shock value for shock value's sake. No response without SASE. **Buys 40-50 poems/year.** Submit maximum 3-5 poems. **Pays $5-10.**
Tips: "Send a cover letter and short bio along with your manuscript. If you have an e-mail address, please include with your cover letter. Reading period for Winter issue: August 1-October 15; reading period for Summer issue: January 1-March 15. Submissions sent between reading periods will not be read. *Harpur Palate* sponsors a fiction contest during the spring and a poetry contest during the fall. The Winter issue also contains a Writing By Degrees Conference supplement. The editorial boards choose manuscripts during final selection committees after the deadline. If we would like to hold your fiction or poetry manuscript for final selection, we will inform you. Wherever you submit, always send a professional cover letter and mansucript. First impressions are of the utmost importance."

$ HAYDEN'S FERRY REVIEW, Arizona State University, Box 871502, Arizona State University, Tempe AZ 85287-1502. (480)965-1243. Fax: (480)965-2229. E-mail: hfr@asu.edu. Website: www.haydensferryreview.org. **Contact:** Fiction, Poetry, or Art Editor. **85% freelance written.** Semiannual magazine. "*Hayden's Ferry Review* publishes best quality fiction, poetry, and creative nonfiction from new, emerging, and established writers." Estab. 1986. Circ. 1,300. Pays on publication. Publishes ms an average of 6 months after acceptance. Byline given. Buys first North American serial rights. Editorial lead time 3 months. Accepts queries by mail. Accepts simultaneous submissions. Responds in 2 weeks to queries; 3 months to mss. Sample copy for $6. Writer's guidelines for #10 SASE.

- No electronic submissions.

Nonfiction: Essays, interview/profile, personal experience. **Buys 2 mss/year.** Send complete ms. Length: Open. **Pays $25-100.**
Photos: Send photos with submission. Reviews slides. Buys one-time rights. Offers $25/photo.
Fiction: Ethnic, experimental, humorous, slice-of-life vignettes. **Buys 10 mss/year.** Send complete ms. Length: Open. **Pays $25-100.**
Poetry: Avant-garde, free verse, haiku, light verse, traditional. **Buys 60 poems/year.** Submit maximum 6 poems. Length: Open. **Pays $25-100.**

$ HIGH PLAINS LITERARY REVIEW, 180 Adams St., Suite 250, Denver CO 80206. (303)320-6828. Fax: (303)320-0463. Managing Editor: Phyllis A. Harwell. **Contact:** Robert O. Greer, Jr, editor-in-chief. **80% freelance written.** Triannual magazine. "The *High Plains Literary Review* publishes short stories, essays, poetry, reviews, and interviews, bridging the gap between commercial quarterlies and academic reviews." Estab. 1986. Circ. 1,200. Pays on publication. Byline given. Buys first North American serial rights. Accepts simultaneous submissions. Responds in 3 months to queries; 3 months to mss. Sample copy for $4. Writer's guidelines for #10 SASE.

- Its unique editorial format—between commercial and academic—makes for lively reading. Could be good market for that "in between" story.

Nonfiction: Essays, reviews. **Buys 20 mss/year.** Send complete ms. Length: 10,000 words maximum. **Pays $5/page.**

Fiction: Ethnic, historical, humorous, mainstream. **Buys 12 mss/year.** Send complete ms. Length: 10,000 words maximum. **Pays $5/page.**
Poetry: Buys 45 poems/year. Pays $10/page.

$ THE HOLLINS CRITIC, P.O. Box 9538, Hollins University, Roanoke VA 24020-1538. E-mail: acockrell@hollins.edu. Website: www.hollins.edu/academics/critic. Editor: R.H.W. Dillard. Managing Editor: Amanda Cockrell. **Contact:** Cathryn Hankla, poetry editor. **100% freelance written.** Magazine published 5 times/year. Estab. 1964. Circ. 400. Pays on publication. Publishes ms an average of 2 years after acceptance. Byline given. Buys first North American serial rights. Accepts queries by mail. Accepts simultaneous submissions. Responds in 2 months to mss. Sample copy for $1.50. Writer's guidelines for #10 SASE.

- No e-mail submissions. Send complete ms.

Poetry: Avant-garde, free verse, traditional. **Buys 16-20 poems/year.** Submit maximum 5 poems. **Pays $25.**
Tips: "We accept unsolicited poetry submissions; all other content is by prearrangement."

$ THE HUDSON REVIEW, A magazine of literature and the arts, The Hudson Review, Inc., 684 Park Ave., New York NY 10021. Fax: (212)774-1911. Managing Editor: Ronald Koury. **Contact:** Paula Deitz, editor. **100% freelance written.** Quarterly magazine publishing fiction, poetry, essays, book reviews; criticism of literature, art, theatre, dance, film and music; and articles on contemporary cultural developments. Estab. 1948. Circ. 5,000. Pays on publication. Publishes ms an average of 6 months after acceptance. Byline given. Only assigned reviews are copyrighted. Editorial lead time 3 months. Accepts queries by mail. Responds in 2 months to queries; 3 months to mss. Sample copy for $8. Writer's guidelines for #10 SASE.
Nonfiction: Paula Deitz. Essays, general interest, historical/nostalgic, opinion, personal experience, travel. **Buys 4-6 mss/year.** Send complete ms between January 1 and March 31 only; book reviews should be queried. Length: 3,500 words maximum. **Pays 2½¢/word.**
Fiction: Ronald Koury. Read between September 1 and November 30 only. **Buys 4 mss/year. Pays 2½¢/word.**
Poetry: Jonathan Mooallem, associate editor. Read poems only between April 1 and June 30. **Buys 12-20 poems/year.** Submit maximum 8-10 poems. **Pays 50¢/line.**
Tips: "We do not specialize in publishing any particular 'type' of writing; our sole criterion for accepting unsolicited work is literary quality. The best way for you to get an idea of the range of work we publish is to read a current issue. We do not consider simultaneous submissions. Unsolicted mss submitted outside of specified reading times will be returned unread."

N HUNGER MOUNTAIN, The Vermont College Journal of Arts & Letters, Vermont College/Union Institute & University, 36 College St., Montpelier VT 05602. Fax: (802)828-8649. E-mail: hungermtn@tui.edu. Website: www.hungermtn.org. **Contact:** Caroline Mercurio, managing editor. **Approx. 30% freelance written.** Semiannual perfect-bound journal covering high quality fiction, poetry, creative nonfiction, interviews, photography, and artwork reproductions. Literary perfect-bound journal that accepts high quality work from unknown, emerging, or successful writers and artists. No genre fiction, drama, children's writing, or academic articles, please. Estab. 2002. Pays on publication. Publishes ms an average of no more than 6 months after acceptance. Byline given. Buys first North American serial rights. Submit seasonal material 6 months in advance. Accepts queries by mail, e-mail, fax. Accepts simultaneous submissions. Responds in 1 month to queries; 3 months to mss. Sample copy for $10. for free, online at website, or by e-mail.
Nonfiction: Creative nonfiction only. All book reviews and interviews will be solicited. Book excerpts, essays, opinion, personal experience, photo feature, religious, travel. Special issues: "We will publish special issues, hopefully yearly, but we do not know yet the themes of these issues." No informative or instructive articles, please. Query with published clips. **Pays $25-100.** Sometimes pays expenses of writers on assignment.
Photos: Send photos with submission. Reviews contact sheets, transparencies, prints, GIF/JPEG files. Slides preferred. Buys one-time rights. Negotiates payment individually. Query with published clips. **Pays $25-100.**
Poetry: Avant-garde, free verse, haiku, traditional, nature, narrative, experimental, etc. No light verse, humor/quirky/catchy verse, greeting card verse. **Buys 10 poems/year.**
Tips: "We want high quality work! Submit in duplicate. Manuscripts must be typed, prose double-spaced. Poets submit at least 3 poems. Multiple genre submissions discouraged. We love b&w photography and short shorts. Fresh viewpoints and human interest are very important, as is originality. We are committed to publishing an outstanding journal of arts & letters. Do not send entire novels, manuscripts, or short story collections. Do not send previously published work."

$ THE ICONOCLAST, 1675 Amazon Rd., Moliegan Lake NY 10547-1804. **Contact:** Phil Wagner, editor. **90% freelance written.** Bimonthly literary magazine. "Aimed for a literate general audience with interests in fine (but accessible) fiction and poetry." Estab. 1992. Circ. 600. **Pays on acceptance.** Publishes ms an average of 9-12 months after acceptance. Byline given. Buys first North American serial rights. Editorial lead time 1-2 months. Accepts queries by mail. Responds in 2 weeks to queries; 1 month to mss. Sample copy for $2.50. Writer's guidelines for #10 SASE.
Nonfiction: Essays, humor, reviews, literary/cultural matters. Does not want "anything that would be found in the magazines on the racks of supermarkets or convenience stores." **Buys 6-10 mss/year.** Query. Length: 250-2,500 words. **Pays 1¢/word.** Pays in contributor copies for previously published articles.
Photos: Line drawings preferred. State availability with submission. Reviews 4×6, b&w only prints. Buys one-time rights. Negotiates payment individually.
Columns/Departments: Book reviews (fiction/poetry), 250-500 words. **Buys 6 mss/year.** Query. **Pays 1¢/word.**

Fiction: Buys more fiction and poetry than anything else. Ethnic, experimental, fantasy, humorous, mainstream, novel excerpts, science fiction, literary. No character studies, slice-of-life, pieces strong on attitude/weak on plot. **Buys 25 mss/year.** Send complete ms. Length: 250-3,000 words. **Pays 1¢/word.**
Poetry: Avant-garde, free verse, haiku, light verse, traditional. No religious, greeting card, beginner rhyming. **Buys 75 poems/year.** Submit maximum 4 poems. Length: 2-50 lines. **Pays $2-5.**
Tips: "Professional conduct and sincerity help. Know it's the best you can do on a work before sending it out. Skill is the luck of the prepared. Everything counts. We love what we do, and are serious about it—and expect you to share that attitude. If writing is a casual hobby, time filler, or résumé-builder, please direct your efforts toward a more appropriate publication."

$ INDIANA REVIEW, Indiana University, Ballantine Hall 465, 1020 E. Kirkwood, Bloomington IN 47405-7103. (812)855-3439. Website: www.indiana.edu/~inreview/ir.html. **Contact:** David Daniels, editor. **100% freelance written.** Biannual magazine. "*Indiana Review*, a nonprofit organization run by IU graduate students, is a journal of previously unpublished poetry and fiction. Literary interviews and essays also considered. We publish innovative fiction and poetry. We're interested in energy, originality, and careful attention to craft. While we publish many well-known writers, we also welcome new and emerging poets and fiction writers." Estab. 1976. Circ. 2,000. Pays on publication. Byline given. Buys first North American serial rights. Accepts queries by mail, e-mail, phone. Accepts simultaneous submissions. Responds in 2 weeks to queries; 3 months to mss. Sample copy for $8. Writer's guidelines for #10 SASE or online.

O→ Break in with 500-1,000 word book reviews of fiction, poetry, nonfiction, and literary criticism published within the last 2 years, "since this is the area in which there's the least amount of competition."

Nonfiction: Essays, interview/profile, creative nonfiction, reviews. No "coming of age/slice of life pieces." **Buys 5-7 mss/year.** Send complete ms. Length: 9,000 words maximum. **Pays $5/page, plus 2 contributor's copies.**
Fiction: "We look for daring stories which integrate theme, language, character, and form. We like polished writing, humor, and fiction which has consequence beyond the world of its narrator." Ethnic, experimental, mainstream, novel excerpts, literary, short fictions, translations. No genre fiction. **Buys 14-18 mss/year.** Send complete ms. Length: 250-15,000 words. **Pays $5/page, plus 2 contributor's copies.**
Poetry: Looks for inventive and skillful writing. Avant-garde, free verse. **Buys 80 poems/year.** Submit maximum 6 poems. Length: 5 lines minimum. **Pays $5/page, plus 2 contributor's copies.**
Tips: "We're always looking for nonfiction essays that go beyond merely autobiographical revelation and utilize sophisticated organization and slightly radical narrative strategies. We want essays that are both lyrical and analytical where confession does not mean nostalgia. Read us before you submit. Often reading is slower in summer and holiday months. Only submit work to journals you would proudly subscribe to, then subscribe to a few. Take care to read the latest 2 issues and specifically mention work you identify with and why. Submit work that 'stacks up' with the work we've published." Offers annual poetry, fiction prizes. See website for details.

$ THE IOWA REVIEW, 308 EPB, The University of Iowa, Iowa City IA 52242. (319)335-0462. Fax: (319)335-2535. E-mail: iareview@blue.weeg.uiowa.edu. Website: www.uiowa.edu/~iareview/. **Contact:** David Hamilton, editor. Triannual magazine. Estab. 1970. Buys first North American serial rights. Nonexclusive anthology, classroom, and online serial rights. Responds in 3 months to queries; 3 months to mss. Sample copy for $7 and online. Writer's guidelines online.

● This magazine uses the help of colleagues and graduate assistants. Its reading period is September 1-March 1.

Tips: "We publish essays, reviews, novel excerpts, stories, and poems, and would like for our essays not always to be works of academic criticism. We have no set guidelines as to content or length, but strongly recommend that writers read a sample issue before submitting." **Buys 65-80 unsolicited ms/year**. Submit complete ms with SASE. **Pays $20/page for verse; $10/page for prose**.

$ JAPANOPHILE PRESS, P.O. Box 7977, 415 N. Main St., Ann Arbor MI 48107. E-mail: japanophile@aol.com. Website: www.japanophile.com. **Contact:** Madeleine Vala, associate editor. **80% freelance written.** Works with a small number of new/unpublished writers each year. Semiannual magazine for literate people interested in Japanese culture anywhere in the world. Estab. 1974. Pays on publication. Publishes ms an average of 3 months after acceptance. Byline given. Buys first North American serial rights. Accepts queries by mail, e-mail. Accepts previously published material. Responds in 3 months to queries; 3 months to mss. Sample copy for $7, postpaid, or on website. Writer's guidelines for #10 SASE or on website.

O→ Break in with "nonfiction articles or short personal essays. We're also looking for nonfiction with photos, movie reviews, short short stories, and Japan-related illustration."

Nonfiction: "We want material on Japanese culture in *North America or anywhere in the world*, even Japan. We want articles, preferably with photos, about persons engaged in arts of Japanese origin: a Virginia naturalist who is a haiku poet, a potter who learned raku in Japan, a vivid 'I was there' account of a Go tournament in California. We would like to hear more about what it's like to be a Japanese in the U.S. Our particular slant is a certain kind of culture wherever it is in the world: Canada, the U.S., Europe, Japan. The culture includes flower arranging, haiku, sports, religion, travel, art, photography, fiction, etc. It is important to study the magazine." Humor, interview/profile, opinion. **Buys 8 mss/year.** Query. Length: 1,800 words maximum. **Pays $8-25.**
Reprints: Send information about when and where the material previously appeared Pays 100% of amount paid for original article.
Photos: Pays $10-50 for glossy prints. "We prefer b&w people pictures."

Columns/Departments: Regular columns and features are Tokyo Topics and Japan in North America. "We also need columns about Japanese culture in various American cities." Length: 1,000 words. Query. **Pays $1-25.**

Fiction: Themes should relate to Japan or Japanese culture. Annual contest pays $100 to best short story (contest reading fee $5). Should include 1 or more Japanese and nonJapanese characters in each story. Adventure, experimental, historical, humorous, mainstream, mystery, romance. Length: 1,000-4,000 words. **Pays up to $25.**

Poetry: It must either relate to Japanese culture or be in a Japanese form such as haiku. Avant-garde, haiku, light verse, traditional. Length: 3-50 lines. **Pays $1-20.**

Fillers: Newsbreaks, short humor, clippings. Length: 200 words maximum. **Pays $1-5.**

Tips: "We want to see more articles about Japanese culture worldwide, including unexpected places, but especially U.S., Canada, and Europe. Lack of convincing fact and detail is a frequent mistake." Publication deadlines are September 1 (Winter issue) and March 1 (Summer issue).

$ THE JOURNAL, The Ohio State University, 421 Denney Hall, 164 W. 17th Ave., Columbus OH 43210. (614)292-4076. Fax: (614)292-7816. E-mail: thejournal05@postbox.acs.ohio-state.edu. Website: www.english.ohiostate.edu/journals/the_journal. **Contact:** Fiction Editor, Poetry Editor, Nonfiction Editor, Poetry Review Editor. **100% freelance written.** Semiannual magazine. "We're open to all forms; we tend to favor work that gives evidence of a mature and sophisticated sense of the language." Estab. 1972. Circ. 1,500. Pays on publication. Byline given. Buys first North American serial rights. Accepts queries by mail. Accepts simultaneous submissions. Responds in 2 weeks to queries; 2 months to mss. Sample copy for $7 or online. Writer's guidelines for #10 SASE or online.

Nonfiction: Essays, interview/profile. **Buys 2 mss/year.** Query. Length: 2,000-4,000 words. **Pays $30 maximum.**

Columns/Departments: Reviews of contemporary poetry, 2,000-4,000 words. **Buys 2 mss/year.** Query. **Pays $30.**

Fiction: Novel excerpts, literary short stories. **Pays $30.**

Poetry: Avant-garde, free verse, traditional. **Buys 100 poems/year.** Submit maximum 5 poems. **Pays $30.**

$ KALLIOPE, a journal of women's literature & art, Florida Community College at Jacksonville, 3939 Roosevelt Blvd., Jacksonville FL 32205. (904)381-3511. Website: www.fccj.org/kalliope. **Contact:** Mary Sue Koeppel, editor. **100% freelance written.** Biannual magazine. "*Kalliope* publishes poetry, short fiction, reviews, and b&w art, usually by women artists. We look for artistic excellence." Estab. 1978. Circ. 1,600. Pays on publication. Publishes ms an average of 3 months after acceptance. Byline given. Buys first rights. Accepts queries by mail. Responds in 1 week to queries. Sample copy for $7 (recent issue) or $4 (back copy), or see sample issues on website. Writer's guidelines for #10 SASE or on website.

- *Kalliope's* reading period is September-April.
- Break in with a "finely crafted poem or short story or a Q&A with an established, well-published woman poet or literary novelist."

Nonfiction: Interview/profile (Q&A), reviews of new works of poetry and fiction. **Buys 6 mss/year.** Send complete ms. Length: 500-2,000 words. **Pays $10 honorarium if funds are available, otherwise 2 copies or subscription.**

Photos: "Visual art should be sent in groups of 4-10 works. We require b&w professional quality, glossy prints made from negatives. Please supply photo credits, model releases, date of work, title, medium, and size on the back of each photo submitted. Include artist's résumé where applicable. We welcome an artist's statement of 50-75 words."

Fiction: Ethnic, experimental, novel excerpts, literary. **Buys 12 mss/year.** Send complete ms. Length: 100-2,000 words. **Pays $10 honorarium if funds are available, otherwise 2 copies or subscription.**

Poetry: Avant-garde, free verse, haiku, traditional. **Buys 75 poems/year.** Submit maximum 3-5 poems. Length: 2-120 lines. **Pays $10 honorarium if funds are available, otherwise 2 copies or subscription.**

Tips: "We publish the best of the material submitted to us each issue. (We don't build a huge backlog and then publish from that backlog for years.) Although we look for new writers and usually publish several with each issue alongside already established writers, we love it when established writers send us their work. We've recently published Tess Gallagher, Enid Shomer, and one of the last poems by Denise Levertov. Send a bio with all submissions."

$ THE KENYON REVIEW, Kenyon College, Gambier OH 43022. (740)427-5208. Fax: (740)427-5417. E-mail: kenyonreview@kenyon.edu. Website: www.kenyonreview.org. **Contact:** David H. Lynn, editor. **100% freelance written.** Triannual magazine covering contemporary literature and criticism. An international journal of literature, culture, and the arts dedicated to an inclusive representation of the best in new writing (fiction, poetry, essays, interviews, criticism) from established and emerging writers. Estab. 1939. Circ. 5,000. Pays on publication. Publishes ms an average of 1 year after acceptance. Byline given. Buys first rights. Editorial lead time 1 year. Submit seasonal material 1 year in advance. Accepts queries by mail. Responds in 3-4 months to queries. Sample copy for $9 or on website. Writer's guidelines for 4×9 SASE or on website.

$ THE KIT-CAT REVIEW, 244 Halstead Ave., Harrison NY 10528. (914)835-4833. **Contact:** Claudia Fletcher, editor. **100% freelance written.** Quarterly magazine. "*The Kit-Cat Review* is named after the 18th Century Kit-Cat Club, whose members included Addison, Steele, Congreve, Vanbrugh, and Garth. Its purpose is to promote/discover excellence and originality. Some issues are part anthology." The Winter issue includes the winner of the annual Gavin Fletcher Memorial Prize for Poetry of $1,000. The winning poem is published shortly thereafter in a *Kit-Cat Review* ad in the *American Poetry Review*. Estab. 1998. Circ. 500. **Pays on acceptance.** Byline given. Buys one-time rights. Accepts queries by mail, phone. Responds in 1 week to queries; 1 month to mss. Sample copy for $7, payable to Claudia Fletcher.

Nonfiction: "Shorter pieces stand a better chance of publication." Book excerpts, essays, general interest, historical/nostalgic, humor, interview/profile, personal experience, travel. **Buys 4 mss/year.** Send complete ms with brief bio and SASE. Length: 5,000 words maximum. **Pays $25-100.**
Fiction: Experimental, novel excerpts, slice-of-life vignettes. No stories with "O. Henry-type formula endings. Shorter pieces stand a better chance of publication." **Buys 20 mss/year.** Send complete ms. Length: 5,000 words maximum. **Pays $25-100.**
Poetry: Free verse, traditional. No excessively obscure poetry. **Buys 100 poems/year. Pays $10-100.**
Tips: "Obtaining a sample copy is strongly suggested. Include a short bio, SASE, and word count for fiction and nonfiction submissions."

$ $ THE MALAHAT REVIEW, The University of Victoria, P.O. Box 1700, STN CSC, Victoria, British Columbia V8W 2Y2, Canada. (250)721-8524. E-mail: malahat@uvic.ca (for queries only). Website: web.uvic.ca/malahat. **Contact:** Marlene Cookshaw, editor. **100% freelance written.** Eager to work with new/unpublished writers. Quarterly magazine covering poetry, fiction, and reviews. Estab. 1967. Circ. 1,000. **Pays on acceptance.** Publishes ms an average of 6 months after acceptance. Byline given. Offers 100% kill fee. Buys second serial (reprint) rights, first world rights. Accepts queries by mail, e-mail. Responds in 2 weeks to queries; 3 months to mss. Sample copy for $10 (US). Writer's guidelines online.
Nonfiction: "Query first about review articles, critical essays, interviews, and visual art, which we generally solicit." Include SASE with Canadian postage or IRCs. **Pays $30/magazine page.**
Fiction: Buys 20 mss/year. Send complete ms. Length: 20 pages maximum. **Pays $30/magazine page.**
Poetry: Avant-garde, free verse, traditional. **Buys 100 poems/year.** Length: 5-10 pages. **Pays $30/magazine page.**
Tips: "Please do not send more than 1 manuscript (the one you consider your best) at a time. See *The Malahat Review's* long poem and novella contests in Contest & Awards section."

$ THE MASSACHUSETTS REVIEW, South College, University of Massachusetts, Amherst MA 01003-9934. (413)545-2689. Fax: (413)577-0740. E-mail: massrev@external.umass.edu. Website: www.massreview.org. **Contact:** Corwin Ericson, managing editor; Mary Heath, Paul Jenkins, David Lenson, editors. Quarterly magazine. Estab. 1959. Pays on publication. Publishes ms an average of 18 months after acceptance. Buys first North American serial rights. Accepts queries by mail, e-mail, fax. Responds in 3 months to queries; 3 months to mss. Sample copy for $7. Sample articles and writer's guidelines online.

- Does not respond to mss without SASE.

Nonfiction: Articles on all subjects. No reviews of single books. Send complete ms or query with SASE. Length: 6,500 words maximum. **Pays $50.**
Fiction: Buys 10 mss/year. Length: 25-30 pages maximum. **Pays $50.**
Poetry: Submit maximum 6 poems. **Pays 35¢/line to $10 maximum.**
Tips: "No manuscripts are considered June-October. No fax or e-mail submissions. No simultaneous submissions."

$ MICHIGAN QUARTERLY REVIEW, 3032 Rackham Bldg., 915 E. Washington, University of Michigan, Ann Arbor MI 48109-1070. (734)764-9265. E-mail: dorisk@umich.edu. Website: www.umich.edu/~mqr. **Contact:** Laurence Goldstein, editor. **75% freelance written.** Quarterly magazine. Estab. 1962. Circ. 1,500. Pays on publication. Publishes ms an average of 1 year after acceptance. Byline given. Buys first serial rights. Accepts queries by mail. Responds in 2 months to queries; 2 months to mss. Sample copy for $4. Writer's guidelines available on website or for #10 SASE.

- The Lawrence Foundation Prize is a $1,000 annual award to the best short story published in the *Michigan Quarterly Review* during the previous year. Prefers to work with published/established writers.

Nonfiction: "*MQR* is open to general articles directed at an intellectual audience. Essays ought to have a personal voice and engage a significant subject. Scholarship must be present as a foundation, but we are not interested in specialized essays directed only at professionals in the field. We prefer ruminative essays, written in a fresh style and which reach interesting conclusions. We also like memoirs and interviews with significant historical or cultural resonance." **Buys 35 mss/year.** Query. Length: 2,000-5,000 words. **Pays $100-150.**
Fiction: No restrictions on subject matter or language. "We are very selective. We like stories which are unusual in tone and structure, and innovative in language." **Buys 10 mss/year.** Send complete ms. **Pays $10/published page.**
Poetry: Buys 10 poems/year. Pays $10/published page.
Tips: "Read the journal and assess the range of contents and the level of writing. We have no guidelines to offer or set expectations; every manuscript is judged on its unique qualities. On essays—query with a very thorough description of the argument and a copy of the first page. Watch for announcements of special issues which are usually expanded issues and draw upon a lot of freelance writing. Be aware that this is a university quarterly that publishes a limited amount of fiction and poetry that it is directed at an educated audience, one that has done a great deal of reading in all types of literature."

$ MID-AMERICAN REVIEW, Department of English, Bowling Green State University, Bowling Green OH 43403. (419)372-2725. Fax: (419)372-6805. Website: www.bgsu.edu/midamericanreview. **Contact:** Michael Czyzniejewski, editor-in-chief. Willing to work with new/unpublished writers. Semiannual magazine of "the highest quality fiction, poetry, and translations of contemporary poetry and fiction." Also publishes critical articles and book reviews of contemporary literature. Estab. 1981. Pays on publication when funding is available. Publishes ms an average of 6 months after acceptance. Byline given. Buys one-time rights. Accepts queries by mail, phone. Responds in 4 months to mss. Sample copy for $7 (current issue), $5 (back issue); rare back issues $10.

"Grab our attention with something original—even experimental—but most of all, well-written."
Nonfiction: Essays (articles focusing on contemporary authors and topics of current literary interest), short book reviews (500-1,000 words). **Pays $10/page up to $50, pending funding.**
Fiction: Character-oriented, literary, experimental, short short. **Buys 12 mss/year. Pays $10/page up to $50, pending funding.**
Poetry: Karen Craigo; poetry editor. Strong imagery and sense of vision. **Buys 60 poems/year. Pays $10/page up to $50, pending funding.**
Tips: "We are seeking translations of contemporary authors from all languages into English; submissions must include the original. We would also like to see more creative nonfiction. Write great original work."

$ $ THE MISSOURI REVIEW, 1507 Hillcrest Hall, University of Missouri, Columbia MO 65211. (573)882-4474. Fax: (573)884-4671. E-mail: missouri_@missouri.edu. Website: www.missourireview.org. Associate Editor: Evelyn Somers. Poetry Editor: Marta Ferguson. **Contact:** Speer Morgan, editor. **90% freelance written.** Triannual magazine. "We publish contemporary fiction, poetry, interviews, personal essays, cartoons, special features—such as 'History as Literature' series and 'Found Text' series—for the literary and the general reader interested in a wide range of subjects." Estab. 1978. Circ. 5,500. Offers signed contract. Byline given. Editorial lead time 6 months. Accepts queries by mail, e-mail, phone. Responds in 2 weeks to queries; 3 months to mss. Sample copy for $8 or online. Writer's guidelines for #10 SASE or online.
Nonfiction: Evelyn Somers, associate editor. Book excerpts, essays. No literary criticism. **Buys 10 mss/year.** Send complete ms. **Pays $30/printed page, up to $750.**
Fiction: Mainstream, novel excerpts, literary. No genre fiction. **Buys 25 mss/year.** Send complete ms. **Pays $30/printed page up to $750.**
Poetry: Publishes 3-5 poetry features of 6-12 pages per issue. "Please familiarize yourself with the magazine before submitting poetry." Marta Ferguson, poetry editor. **Buys 50 poems/year. Pays $125-250.**
The online magazine carries original content not found in the print edition and includes writer's guidelines. Contact: Hoa Ngo, online editor.
Tips: "Send your best work."

$ MODERN HAIKU, An Independent Journal of Haiku and Haiku Studies, P.O. Box 1752, Madison WI 53701-1752. (608)233-2738. Website: www.family-net.net/~brooksbooks/modernhaiku. **Contact:** Robert Spiess, editor. **85% freelance written.** Magazine published 3 times/year. "*Modern Haiku* publishes high quality material only. Haiku and related genres, articles on haiku, haiku book reviews, and translations compose its contents. It has an international circulation and is widely subscribed to by university, school, and public libraries. Estab. 1969. Circ. 625. Pays on acceptance for poetry; on publication for prose. Publishes ms an average of 3 months after acceptance. Byline given. Buys first North American serial rights. Editorial lead time 4 months. Accepts queries by mail, phone. Responds in 1 week to queries; 2 weeks to mss. Sample copy for $6.65. Writer's guidelines for #10 SASE.
Nonfiction: Essays (anything related to haiku). **Buys 40 mss/year.** Send complete ms. **Pays $5/page.**
Columns/Departments: Haiku & Senryu; Haibun; Articles (on haiku and related genres); book reviews (books of haiku or related genres), 4 pages maximum. **Buys 15 mss/year.** Send complete ms. **Pays $5/page.**
Poetry: Haiku, senryu. Does not want "general poetry, sentimental, and pretty-pretty haiku or overtly pornographic." **Buys 800 poems/year.** Submit maximum 24 poems. **Pays $1.**
Tips: "Study the history of haiku, read books about haiku, learn the aesthetics of haiku and methods of composition. Write about your sense perceptions of the suchness of entities, avoid ego-centered interpretations."

NEOTROPE, P.O. Box 6305, Santa Barbara CA 93160. E-mail: apowell10@hotmail.com. Website: www.brokenboulder.com. **Contact:** Adam Powell, fiction editor.

$ NEW ENGLAND REVIEW, Middlebury College, Middlebury VT 05753. (802)443-5075. E-mail: nereview@middlebury.edu. Website: www.middlebury.edu/~nereview/. Editor: Stephen Donadio. Managing Editor: Jodee Stanley Rubins. **Contact:** On envelope: Poetry, Fiction, or Nonfiction Editor; on letter: Stephen Donadio. Quarterly magazine. Serious literary only. Reads September 1 to May 31 (postmarked dates). Estab. 1978. Circ. 2,000. Pays on publication. Publishes ms an average of 6 months after acceptance. Byline given. Buys first North American serial rights. Accepts simultaneous submissions. Responds in 2 weeks to queries; 3 months to mss. Sample copy for $7. Writer's guidelines for #10 SASE.
Nonfiction: Serious literary only. Rarely accepts previously published submissions (out of print or previously published abroad only.) **Buys 20-25 mss/year.** Send complete ms. Length: 7,500 words maximum, though exceptions may be made. **Pays $10/page ($20 minimum), and 2 copies.**
Fiction: Send 1 story at a time. Serious literary only, novel excerpts. **Buys 25 mss/year.** Send complete ms. **Pays $10/page ($20 minimum), and 2 copies.**
Poetry: Buys 75-90 poems/year. Submit maximum 6 poems. **Pays $10/page or $20, and 2 copies.**
Tips: "We consider short fiction, including shorts, short-shorts, novellas, and self-contained extracts from novels. We consider a variety of general and literary, but not narrowly scholarly, nonfiction; long and short poems; speculative, interpretive, and personal essays; book reviews; screenplays; graphics; translations; critical reassessments; statements by artists working in various media; interviews; testimonies; and letters from abroad. We are committed to exploration of all forms of contemporary cultural expression in the United States and abroad. With few exceptions, we print only work not published previously elsewhere."

$ NEW LETTERS, University of Missouri-Kansas City, University House, 5101 Rockhill Rd., Kansas City MO 64110-2499. (816)235-1168. Fax: (816)235-2611. E-mail: newletters@umkc.edu. Website: umkc.edu/newletters. Managing Editor: Robert Stewart. **Contact:** James McKinley, editor. **100% freelance written.** Quarterly magazine. "*New Letters* is intended for the general literate reader. We publish literary fiction, nonfiction, essays, poetry. We also publish art." Estab. 1934. Circ. 1,800. Pays on publication. Publishes ms an average of 5 months after acceptance. Byline given. Buys first North American serial rights. Editorial lead time 6 months. Submit seasonal material 6 months in advance. Accepts queries by mail, e-mail. Accepts simultaneous submissions. Responds in 1 month to queries; 3 months to mss. Sample copy for $5.50 (current issue) or sample articles on website. Writer's guidelines for #10 SASE or on website.

- Submissions are not read between May 15 and October 15.

Nonfiction: Essays. No self-help, how-to, or nonliterary work. **Buys 6-8 mss/year.** Send complete ms. Length: 5,000 words maximum. **Pays $40-100.**

Photos: Send photos with submission. Reviews contact sheets, 2 X 4 transparencies, prints. Buys one-time rights. Pays $10-40/photo.

Fiction: No genre fiction. **Buys 12 mss/year.** Send complete ms. Length: 5,000 words maximum. **Pays $30-75.**

Poetry: Avant-garde, free verse, haiku, traditional. No light verse. **Buys 40 poems/year.** Submit maximum 3 poems. Length: Open. **Pays $10-25.**

Tips: "We aren't interested in essays that are footnoted, essays usually described as scholarly or critical. Our preference is for creative nonfiction or personal essays. We prefer shorter stories and essays to longer ones (an average length is 3,500-4,000 words). We have no rigid preferences as to subject, style, or genre, although commercial efforts tend to put us off. Even so, our only fixed requirement is on *good* writing."

$ THE NEW QUARTERLY, new directions in Canadian writing, St. Jerome's University, 200 University Ave. W., Waterloo, Ontario N2L 3G3, Canada. (519)884-8111, ext. 290. E-mail: newquart@watarts.uwaterloo.ca. Website: www.newquarterly.uwaterloo.ca. Editor: Kim Jernigan. **95% freelance written.** Quarterly book covering Canadian fiction and poetry. "Emphasis on emerging writers and genres, but we publish some traditional stuff as well if the language and narrative structure are fresh." Estab. 1980. Circ. 700. Pays on publication. Publishes ms an average of 4 months after acceptance. Byline given. Buys first Canadian rights. Editorial lead time 6 months. Accepts queries by mail, e-mail. Accepts simultaneous submissions. Responds in 2 weeks to queries; 4 months to mss. Sample copy for $10 (cover price, plus mailing). Writer's guidelines for #10 SASE or online.

Fiction: Kim Jernigan, Rae Crossman, Pat Skinner, fiction editors. Canadian work only. We are not interested in genre fiction. We are looking for innovative, beautifully crafted, deeply felt literary fiction. **Buys 20-25 mss/year.** Send complete ms. Length: 20 pages maximum. **Pays $150/story.**

Poetry: Randi Patterson, John Vardon, Mark Spielmacher, Lesley Elliott, poetry editors. Avant-garde, free verse, traditional, Canadian work only. **Buys 60-80 poems/year.** Submit maximum 5 poems. Length: 4½ inches typeset.

Tips: "Reading us is the best way to get our measure. We don't have preconceived ideas about what we're looking for other than that it must be Canadian work (Canadian writers, not necessarily Canadian content). We want something that's fresh, something that will repay a second reading, something in which the language soars and the feeling is complexly rendered. Narrative innovation a plus."

$ $ NEW YORK STORIES, LaGuardia/CUNY, 31-10 Thomson Ave., Long Island City NY 11101. (718)482-5673. E-mail: nystories@lagcc.cuny.edu. Website: www.newyorkstories.org. **Contact:** Daniel Caplice Lynch, editor-in-chief. **100% freelance written.** Magazine published 3 times/year. "Our purpose is to publish quality short fiction and New York centered nonfiction. We look for fresh approaches, artistic daring and story telling talent. We are especially interested in work that explores NYC's diversity—ethnic, social, sexual, psychological, economic and geographical." Circ. 1,500. Pays on publication. Publishes ms an average of 6 months after acceptance. Byline given. Buys first North American serial rights. Editorial lead time 6 months. Submit seasonal material 6 months in advance. Accepts queries by mail, e-mail. Accepts simultaneous submissions. Responds in 2 weeks to queries; 6 months to mss. Sample copy for $4. Writer's guidelines for #10 SASE, online or by e-mail.

Nonfiction: Essays, personal experience, all must be related to New York City. **Buys 25-30 mss/year.** Send complete ms. Length: 300-6,000 words. **Pays $100-750.**

Photos: Send photos with submission. Buys one-time rights. Negotiates payment individually. Model releases required.

Fiction: Seeks quality above all; also minority writers, New York City themes. Ethnic, experimental. **Buys 25 mss/year.** Send complete ms. Length: 300-6,000 words. **Pays $100-750.**

Tips: "Send your best work. Try briefer pieces, cultivate a fresh approach. For the NYC nonfiction pieces, look on your doorstep. Fresh angles of vision and psychological complexity are the hallmarks of our short stories."

$ THE NORTH AMERICAN REVIEW, University of Northern Iowa, Cedar Falls IA 50614-0516. (319)273-6455. Fax: (319)273-4326. E-mail: nar@uni.edu. Website: webdelsol.com/NorthAmReview/NAR/. **Contact:** Vince Gotera, editor. **90% freelance written.** Bimonthly magazine. Circ. under 5,000. Pays on publication. Publishes ms an average of 9 months after acceptance. Byline given. Buys first rights. Accepts queries by mail, e-mail, fax, phone. Responds in 3 months to queries; 3 months to mss. Sample copy for $5.

- This is the oldest literary magazine in the country and one of the most prestigious. Also one of the most entertaining—and a tough market for the young writer.

O→ Break in with the "highest quality poetry, fiction, and nonfiction on any topic, but particularly interested in the environment, gender, race, ethnicity, and class."

Nonfiction: No restrictions; highest quality only. Length: Open. **Pays $5/350 words; $20 minimum, $100 maximum.**

Fiction: No restrictions; highest quality only. Length: Open. **$5/350 words; $20 minimum, $100 maximum.**
Poetry: No restrictions; highest quality only. Length: Open. **Pays $1/line; $20 minimum, $100 maximum.**
Tips: "We like stories that start quickly and have a strong narrative arc. Poems that are passionate about subject, language, and image are welcome, whether they are traditional or experimental, whether in formal or free verse (closed or open form). Nonfiction should combine art and fact with the finest writing. We do not accept simultaneous submissions; these will be returned unread. We read poetry, fiction, and nonfiction year-round."

$ $ NORTH CAROLINA LITERARY REVIEW, A Magazine of Literature, Culture, and History, English Dept., East Carolina University, Greenville NC 27858-4353. (252)328-1537. Fax: (252)328-4889. E-mail: bauerm@mail.ecu.edu. Website: www.ecu.edu/nclr. **Contact:** Margaret Bauer, editor. Annual magazine published in fall covering North Carolina writers, literature, culture, history. "Articles should have a North Carolina slant. First consideration is always for quality of work. Although we treat academic and scholarly subjects, we do not wish to see jargon-laden prose; our readers, we hope, are found as often in bookstores and libraries as in academia. We seek to combine best elements of magazine for serious readers with best of scholarly journal." Estab. 1992. Circ. 750. Pays on publication. Publishes ms an average of 1 year after acceptance. Byline given. Buys first North American serial rights. Rights returned to writer on request. Editorial lead time 6 months. Accepts queries by mail, e-mail. Responds in 1 month to queries; 6 months to mss. Sample copy for $10-15. Writer's guidelines for SASE or via e-mail.

O→ Break in with an article related to the special feature topic. Check the website for upcoming topics and deadlines.

Nonfiction: North Carolina-related material only. Book excerpts, essays, exposé, general interest, historical/nostalgic, humor, interview/profile, opinion, personal experience, photo feature, travel, reviews, short narratives, surveys of archives. "No jargon-laden academic articles." **Buys 25-35 mss/year.** Query with published clips. Length: 500-5,000 words. **Pays $50-300.**
Photos: State availability with submission. Reviews 5×7 or 8×10 prints; snapshot size or photocopy OK. Buys one-time rights. Pays $25-250. Captions and identification of subjects required; releases when appropriate required.
Columns/Departments: NC Writers (interviews, biographical/bibliographic essays); Reviews (essay reviews of North Carolina-related (fiction, creative nonfiction, poetry). Query with published clips. **Pays $50-300.**
Fiction: Must be North Carolina related—either by a NC-connected writer or set in NC. **Buys 3-4 mss/year.** Query. Length: 5,000 words maximum. **Pays $50-300.**
Poetry: NC poets only. **Buys 8-10 poems/year.** Length: 30-150 lines. **Pays $25-50.**
Fillers: Buys 2-10/year. Length: 50-300 words. **Pays $25-50.**
Tips: "By far the easiest way to break in is with special issue sections. We are especially interested in reports on conferences, readings, meetings that involve North Carolina writers, and personal essays or short narratives with strong sense of place. See back issues for other departments. These are the only areas in which we encourage unsolicited manuscripts; but we welcome queries and proposals for all others. Interviews are probably the other easiest place to break in; no discussions of poetics/theory, etc., except in reader-friendly (accessible) language; interviews should be personal, more like conversations, that explore connections between a writer's life and his/her work."

$ NORTHWEST FLORIDA REVIEW, Okaloosa Island Press-The Gavis Corp., P.O. Box 8122, Ft. Walton Beach FL 32548. E-mail: nwfreview@cs.com. Editor: Mario A. Petaccia. **Contact:** Marie Liberty, fiction; Lola Haskins, poetry. **100% freelance written.** Semiannual magazine. "No special slant or philosophy. Just good writing in fiction, poetry, and articles." Estab. 2001. Circ. 1,500. Pays on publication. Byline given. Buys first North American serial rights. Editorial lead time 3 months. Submit seasonal material 9 months in advance. Accepts queries by mail, e-mail. Accepts simultaneous submissions. Responds in 1 month to queries; 3 months to mss. Sample copy for $5. Writer's guidelines for #10 SASE.
Nonfiction: Book excerpts, essays, humor, interview/profile. No religious, technical, travel, or how-to. **Buys 2 mss/year.** Send complete ms. Length: 1,000-3,000 words. **Pays $20.**
Photos: Buys one-time rights. Offers no additional payment for photos accepted with ms. Identification of subjects required.
Fiction: Experimental, humorous, mainstream, novel excerpts. **Buys 8 mss/year.** Send complete ms. Length: 1,500-5,000 words. **Pays $20.**
Poetry: Free verse. No haiku or light verse. **Buys 40-50 poems/year.** Submit maximum 3-5 poems. Length: 10-50 lines. **Pays $5.**
Tips: "Read the best magazine or subscribe to *NWFR* to see what we like."

$ NOSTALGICALLY, (formerly *Nostalgia*), P.O. Box 2224, Orangeburg SC 29116. E-mail: cnostalgia@aol.com. **Contact:** Connie L. Martin, editor. **100% freelance written.** Quarterly magazine (every season) for "true, personal experiences that relate faith, struggle, hope, success, failure, and rising above problems common to all." Estab. 1986. Circ. 500. Pays on publication. Publishes ms an average of 1 year after acceptance. Byline given. Buys one-time rights. Submit seasonal material 6 months in advance. Accepts queries by mail. Accepts previously published material. Responds in 6 weeks to queries. Sample copy for $2. Writer's guidelines for #10 SASE.

O→ The editor reports an interest in seeing "more humorous, funny experiences in life; need heartwarming more than sad. I would appreciate not receiving material all about Mom, Dad, Uncle, Aunt, or siblings or pets. I need true personal experience."

Nonfiction: General interest, historical/nostalgic, humor, inspirational, opinion, personal experience, photo feature, religious, travel. Does not want to see anything with profanity or sexual references. **Buys 20 mss/year.** Send complete ms. Length: 1,500 words. **Payment varies.** Pays contributor's copies if preferred.

Reprints: Send tearsheet and information about when and where the material previously appeared. Payment varies.
Photos: State availability with submission. Offers no additional payment for photos with ms.
Poetry: Free verse, haiku, light verse, traditional, modern prose. "No ballads; no profanity; no sexual references." Submit maximum 3 poems. Length: 45-50 lines maximum.
Tips: "Study newsletter."

N ONE STORY, One Story LLC, P.O. Box 1326, New York NY 10156. E-mail: submissions@one-story.com. Website: www.one-story.com. Publisher: Maribeth Batcha. Editor: Hannah Tinti. **Contact:** Maribeth Batcha and Hannah Tinti. **100% freelance written.** Bimonthly literary magazine covering one short story. "*One-Story* is a literary magazine that contains, simply, **one story**. It is a subscription-only magazine. Approximately every 2 weeks, subscribers will be sent 1 story in the mail. This story will be an amazing read. It will be artfully designed, lightweight, easy to carry, and ready to entertain on buses, in bed, in subways, in cars, in the park, in the bath, in the waiting rooms of doctor's, on the couch, or on line at the supermarket. Subscribers will also receive a good-looking case that each of these stories will fit in, creating a collection of exciting and original new work. Subscribers will also have access to a website, www.one-story.com, where they can post their reactions to the stories they have received, learn more about *One-Story* authors, and hear about *One-Story* readings and events. We believe that short stories are best read alone. They should not be sandwiched in between a review and an exposé on liposuction, or placed after another work of fiction that is so sad or funny or long that the reader is worn out by the time they turn it. The experience of reading a story by itself is usually found only in MFA programs or writing workshops. This is a shame. Besides, there is always time to read one story." Estab. 2002. Pays on publication. Publishes ms an average of 3-6 months after acceptance. Byline given. Buys first North American serial rights. Buys the rights to publish excerpts on website and in promotional materials. Editorial lead time 3-4 months. Accepts queries by mail, e-mail. Accepts simultaneous submissions. Responds in 2-3 months to mss. Sample copy for $5. Writer's guidelines for #10 SASE or online at website.
Fiction: Maribeth Batcha and Hannah Tinti, editors. Literary short stories. *One-Story* only accepts short stories. Do not send excerpts. Do not send more than 1 story at a time. **Buys 18 mss/year.** Send complete ms. Length: 3,000-10,000 words. **Pays $100.**
Tips: "*One-Story* is looking for stories that are strong enough to stand alone. Therefore they must be very good. We want the best you can give. We want our socks knocked off."

$ $ THE PARIS REVIEW, 541 E. 72nd St., New York NY 10021. (212)861-0016. Fax: (212)861-4504. Website: www.parisreview.com. **Contact:** George A. Plimpton, editor. Quarterly magazine. Pays on publication. Buys first English-language rights. Accepts queries by mail. Sample copy for $15 (includes postage). Writer's guidelines for #10 SASE.

- Response time varies. Address submissions to proper department.

Fiction: Study the publication. Annual Aga Khan Fiction Contest award of $1,000. Query. Length: No length limit. **Payment varies depending on length.**
Poetry: Study the publication. Richard Howard, poetry editor.

$ $ PARNASSUS, Poetry in Review, Poetry in Review Foundation, 205 W. 89th St., #8-F, New York NY 10024. (212)362-3492. Fax: (212)875-0148. E-mail: parnew@aol.com. Managing Editor: Ben Downing. **Contact:** Herbert Leibowitz, editor. Semiannual magazine covering poetry and criticism. Estab. 1972. Circ. 1,500. Pays on publication. Publishes ms an average of 5 months after acceptance. Byline given. Buys one-time rights. Accepts queries by mail. Responds in 2 months to mss. Sample copy for $15. Writer's guidelines not available.
Nonfiction: Essays. **Buys 30 mss/year.** Query with published clips. Length: 1,500-7,500 words. **Pays $50-300.** Sometimes pays writers in contributor copies or other premiums rather than a cash payment upon request.
Poetry: Accepts most types of poetry. Avant-garde, free verse, traditional. **Buys 3-4 unsolicited poems/year.**
Tips: "Be certain you have read the magazine and are aware of the editor's taste. Blind submissions are a waste of everybody's time. We'd like to see more poems that display intellectual acumen and curiosity about history, science, music, etc., and fewer trivial lyrical poems about the self, or critical prose that's academic and dull. Prose should sing."

PEEKS & VALLEYS, A New England Fiction Journal, Davis Publications, P.O. Box 708, Newport NH 03773-0708. (603)863-5896. Fax: (603)863-8198. E-mail: hotdog@nhvt.net. Website: www.peeksandvalleys.com. **Contact:** Cindy Davis, editor. **100% freelance written.** Quarterly magazine covering short stories. "We especially would like to see submissions by children." Estab. 1999. **Pays on acceptance.** Publishes ms an average of 8 months after acceptance. Byline given. Not copyrighted. Buys one-time, second serial (reprint) rights. Editorial lead time 4 months. Submit seasonal material 6 months in advance. Accepts queries by mail, e-mail, fax. Accepts previously published material. Accepts simultaneous submissions. Responds in 1 month to queries; 2 months to mss. Sample copy for $4. Writer's guidelines for #10 SASE.
Fiction: Adventure, ethnic, fantasy, historical, horror, humorous, mainstream, mystery, religious, romance, science fiction, slice-of-life vignettes, suspense, western. No talking animals, sex, or obscenity. **Buys 30 mss/year.** Send complete ms. Length: 3,000 words. **Pays $5 and up.**
Poetry: Light verse, traditional. **Buys 5 poems/year.** Submit maximum 2 poems. Length: 30 lines.

$ PLEIADES, Pleiades Press, Department of English & Philosophy, Central Missouri State University, Warrensburg MO 64093. (660)543-4425. Fax: (660)543-8544. E-mail: kdp8106@cmsu2.cmsu.edu. **Contact:** R.M. Kinder, editor (fiction, essays); Kevin Prufer, editor (poetry, reviews); Susan Steinberg, editor (fiction, essays). **100% freelance written.** Semiannual journal. "We publish contemporary fiction, poetry, interviews, literary essays, special-interest personal essays, reviews for a general and literary audience." (5½×8½ perfect bound). Estab. 1991. Circ. 3,000. Pays on publication. Publishes ms an average of 9 months after acceptance. Byline given. Buys first North American serial, second serial (reprint) rights. Occasionally requests rights for TV, radio reading, website) Editorial lead time 9 months. Accepts queries by mail, e-mail, phone. Accepts simultaneous submissions. Responds in 2 months to queries; 2 months to mss. Sample copy for $5 (back issue), $6 (current issue). Writer's guidelines for #10 SASE.

- "We also sponsor the Lena-Miles Wever Todd Poetry Series competition, a contest for the best book manuscript by an American poet. The winner receives $1,000, publication by Pleiades Press, and distribution by Louisiana State University Press. Deadline September 15. Send SASE for guidelines."

Nonfiction: Book excerpts, essays, interview/profile, reviews. "Nothing pedantic, slick, or shallow." **Buys 4-6 mss/year.** Send complete ms. Length: 2,000-4,000 words. **Pays $10.**
Fiction: R.M. Kinder, editor. Ethnic, experimental, humorous, mainstream, novel excerpts, magic realism. No science fiction, fantasy, confession, erotica. **Buys 16-20 mss/year.** Send complete ms. Length: 2,000-6,000 words. **Pays $10.**
Poetry: Kevin Prufer, editor. Avant-garde, free verse, haiku, light verse, traditional. "Nothing didactic, pretentious, or overly sentimental." **Buys 40-50 poems/year.** Submit maximum 6 poems. **Pays $3/poem, and contributor copies.**
Tips: "Show care for your material and your readers—submit quality work in a professional format. Include cover letter with brief bio and list of publications. Include SASE."

$ $ PLOUGHSHARES, Emerson College, Department M, 120 Boylston St., Boston MA 02116. Website: www.pshares.org. **Contact:** Don Lee, editor. Triquarterly magazine for "readers of serious contemporary literature." Circ. 6,000. Pays on publication. Publishes ms an average of 6 months after acceptance. Buys first North American serial rights. Accepts simultaneous submissions. Responds in 5 months to mss. Sample copy for $9 (back issue). Writer's guidelines for #10 SASE.

- A competitive and highly prestigious market. Rotating and guest editors make cracking the line-up even tougher, since it's difficult to know what is appropriate to send. The reading period is August 1-March 31.

Nonfiction: Essays (personal and literary; accepted only occasionally). Length: 6,000 words maximum. **Pays $25/printed page, $50-250.**
Fiction: Mainstream, literary. **Buys 25-35 mss/year.** Length: 300-6,000 words. **Pays $25/printed page, $50-250.**
Poetry: Avant-garde, free verse, traditional, blank verse. Length: Open. **Pays $25/printed page, $50-250.**
Tips: "We no longer structure issues around preconceived themes. If you believe your work is in keeping with our general standards of literary quality and value, submit at any time during our reading period."

POETIC VOICES MAGAZINE, Gracie Publications, 2206 Bailey St. NW, Hartselle AL 35640-4219. E-mail: editor@poeticvoices.com. Website: members.aol.com/gracieami/arch.htm. **Contact:** Robin Travis-Murphree, executive editor. Monthly online. *Poetic Voices* is "informational and educational in content. Articles include feature interviews, columns on mechanics of writing, questions on writing and publishing, information on organizations useful to poets, contest and award opportunities, publishing opportunities, workshops and conferences, book reviews, and more. The magazine can be accessed at http://members.aol.com/gracieami/arch.htm." Estab. 1997. Circ. 10,000. Buys one-time rights. Accepts queries by e-mail. Accepts previously published material. Accepts simultaneous submissions. Responds in 2 months to queries. Writer's guidelines online.
Nonfiction: Essays, how-to, interview/profile, technical.
Poetry: "We are open to most forms, styles, and subjects." Often comments on rejected poems. Accepts poetry written by children. Ursula T. Gibson, poetry editor (poetryeditor@poeticvoices.com). Does not want pornography, scatology, racial slurs, or dehumanizing poems. Submit up to 4 poems/month by e-mail, text in body of message.
Tips: "Make sure you read and follow guidelines. Make sure your work is neatly presented. There is nothing worse than receiving messy work or work that does not conform to the guidelines."

$ POETRY, Modern Poetry Association, 60 W. Walton St., Chicago IL 60610. Fax: (312)255-3702. E-mail: poetry@poetrymagazine.org. Website: www.poetrymagazine.org. Editor: Joseph Parisi. Managing Editor: Helen Klaviter. **Contact:** Stephen Young, senior editor. **100% freelance written.** Monthly magazine. Estab. 1912. Circ. 10,000. Pays on publication. Publishes ms an average of 9 months after acceptance. Byline given. Buys all rights. Copyright returned to author on request. Accepts queries by mail. Responds in 1 month to queries; 4 months to mss. Sample copy for $5.50 or online at website. Writer's guidelines for #10 SASE or online at website.
Nonfiction: Reviews (most are solicited). **Buys 14 mss/year.** Query. Length: 1,000-2,000 words. **Pays $50/page.**
Poetry: All styles and subject matter. **Buys 180-250 poems/year.** Submit maximum 4 poems. Length: Open. **Pays $2/line.**

PRAIRIE SCHOONER, 201 Andrews Hall, P.O. Box 880334, Lincoln NE 68588-0334. E-mail: eflanagan2@unl.edu. Website: www.unl.edu/schooner/psmain.htm. **Contact:** Hilda Raz, editor.

$ PRISM INTERNATIONAL, Department of Creative Writing, Buch E462-1866 Main Mall, University of British Columbia, Vancouver, British Columbia V6T 1Z1, Canada. (604)822-2514. Fax: (604)822-3616. E-mail: prism@interchange.ubc.ca. Website: prism.arts.ubc.ca. Executive Editor: Michael Kissinger. **Contact:** Abigail Kinch, editor. **100% freelance written.** Eager to work with new/unpublished writers. Quarterly magazine emphasizing contemporary literature, including translations, for university and public libraries, and private subscribers. Estab. 1959. Circ. 1,200. Pays on publication. Publishes ms an average of 4 months after acceptance. Buys first North American serial rights. Accepts queries by mail, e-mail, fax, phone. Responds in 4 months to queries; 4 months to mss. Sample copy for $7 or on website. Writer's guidelines for #10 SAE with 1 first-class Canadian stamp (Canadian entries) or 1 IRC (US entries), or on website.

O→ Break in by "sending unusual or experimental work (we get mostly traditional submissions) and playing with forms (e.g., nonfiction, prose poetry, etc.)."

Nonfiction: "*Creative* nonfiction that reads like fiction. Nonfiction pieces should be creative, exploratory, or experimental in tone rather than rhetorical, academic, or journalistic." No reviews, tracts, or scholarly essays. **Pays $20/printed page.**

Fiction: For Drama: One-acts preferred. Also interested in seeing dramatic monologues. **Buys 3-5 mss/year**. Send complete ms. Length: 25 pages maximum. **Pays $20/printed page**. Experimental, novel excerpts, traditional. **Buys 12-16 mss/year.** Send complete ms. Length: 25 pages maximum. **Pays $20/printed page, and 1-year subscription.**

Poetry: Buys 20 poems/issue. Avant-garde, traditional. Submit maximum 6 poems. **Pays $40/printed page, and 1-year subscription.**

Tips: "We are looking for new and exciting fiction. Excellence is still our No. 1 criterion. As well as poetry, imaginative nonfiction and fiction, we are especially open to translations of all kinds, very short fiction pieces and drama which work well on the page. Translations must come with a copy of the original language work. We pay an additional $10/printed page to selected authors whose work we place on our online version of *Prism*."

$ $ QUARTERLY WEST, University of Utah, 200 S. Central Campus Dr., Room 317, Salt Lake City UT 84112-9109. (801)581-3938. Website: www.utah.edu/quarterlywest. **Contact:** David Hawkins, editor. Semiannual magazine. "We publish fiction, poetry, and nonfiction in long and short formats, and will consider experimental as well as traditional works." Estab. 1976. Circ. 1,900. Pays on publication. Publishes ms an average of 6 months after acceptance. Buys all rights. Accepts queries by mail. Accepts simultaneous submissions. Responds in 6 months to mss. Sample copy for $7.50 or online. Writer's guidelines for #10 SASE or online.

Nonfiction: Essays, interview/profile, personal experience, travel, book reviews. **Buys 2-3 mss/year.** Send complete ms. Length: 10,000 words maximum. **Pays $25.**

Fiction: Jeff Chapman. No preferred lengths; interested in longer, fuller short stories and short shorts. Ethnic, experimental, humorous, mainstream, novel excerpts, slice-of-life vignettes, short shorts, translations. **Buys 6-10 mss/year.** Send complete ms.

Poetry: Nicole Walker. Avant-garde, free verse, traditional. **Buys 40-50 poems/year.** Submit maximum 5 poems. **Pays $15-100.**

Tips: "We publish a special section of short shorts every issue, and we also sponsor a biennial novella contest. We are open to experimental work—potential contributors should read the magazine! Don't send more than 1 story/submission. Biennial novella competition guidelines available upon request with SASE. We prefer work with interesting language and detail—plot or narrative are less important. We don't do Western themes, or religious work."

$ $ QUEEN'S QUARTERLY, A Canadian Review, Queen's University, Kingston Ontario K7L 3N6, Canada. (613)533-2667. Fax: (613)533-6822. E-mail: qquarter@post.queensu.ca. Website: info.queensu.ca/quarterly. **Contact:** Joan Harcourt, literary editor. **95% freelance written.** Quarterly magazine covering a wide variety of subjects, including science, humanities, arts and letters, politics and history for the educated reader. Estab. 1893. Circ. 3,000. Publishes ms an average of 6-12 months after acceptance. Byline given. Buys first North American serial rights. Responds in 2-3 months to queries. *Writer's Market* recommends allowing 2 months for reply to mss. Does not accept simultaneous submissions. Sample copy online. Writer's guidelines online.

- No reply/return without IRC.

O→ Submissions can be sent as e-mail attachment or on hard copy with a SASE (Canadian postage).

Fiction: Novel excerpts, short stories. Length: 2,500 words.

Poetry: Buys 25 poems/year. Submit maximum 6 poems.

$ RAIN CROW, Rain Crow Publishing, P.O. Box 11013, Chicago IL 60611. Fax: (503)214-6615. E-mail: rcp@rain-crow.com. Website: www.rain-crow.com/. **Contact:** Michael S. Manley, editor. Triannual magazine featuring well-crafted, original, entertaining fiction. "We publish new and established writers in many styles and genres. We are a publication for people passionate about the short story form." Estab. 2001. Circ. 500. Pays on publication. Publishes ms an average of 4 months after acceptance. Byline given. Buys one-time, electronic rights. Editorial lead time 4 months. Submit seasonal material 8 months in advance. Accepts queries by mail, e-mail. Accepts previously published material. Accepts simultaneous submissions. Responds in 3 weeks to queries; 4 months to mss. Sample copy for $5. Writer's guidelines for #10 SASE, online, or by e-mail.

Fiction: Erotica, experimental, mainstream, science fiction, literary. "No propaganda, pornography, juvenile, formulaic." **Buys 30 mss/year.** Send complete ms. Length: 250-8,000 words. **Pays $5-150.**

Tips: "Write to the best of your abilities, submit your best work. Present yourself and your work professionally. When we evaluate a submission, we ask, 'Is this something we would like to read again? Is this something we would give to someone else to read?' A good manuscript makes the reader forget they are reading a manuscript. We look for attention to craft: Voice, language, character, and plot working together to maximum effect. Unique yet credible settings and situations that entertain get the most attention."

$ RARITAN, A Quarterly Review, 31 Mine St., New Brunswick NJ 08903. (732)932-7887. Fax: (732)932-7855. Editor: Jackson Lears. **Contact:** Stephanie Volmer, managing editor. Quarterly magazine covering literature, history, fiction, and general culture. Estab. 1981. Circ. 3,500. Pays on publication. Publishes ms an average of 1 year after acceptance. Byline given. Buys first North American serial rights. Editorial lead time 5 months. Accepts queries by mail. Sample copy not available. Writer's guidelines not available.

• *Raritan* no longer accepts previously published or simultaneous submissions.

Nonfiction: Book excerpts, essays. **Buys 50 mss/year.** Send complete ms. Length: 15-30 pages.

$ RIVER STYX, Big River Association, 634 N. Grand Blvd., 12th Floor, St. Louis MO 63103. Website: www.riverstyx.org. Senior Editors: Quincy Troupe and Michael Castro. **Contact:** Richard Newman, editor. Triannual magazine. "*River Styx* publishes the highest quality fiction, poetry, interviews, essays, and visual art. We are an internationally distributed multicultural literary magazine." Manuscripts read May-November. Estab. 1975. Pays on publication. Publishes ms an average of 1 year after acceptance. Byline given. Buys one-time rights. Accepts queries by mail. Accepts simultaneous submissions. Responds in 4 months to mss. Sample copy for $7. Writer's guidelines for #10 SASE or online.

Nonfiction: Essays, interview/profile. **Buys 2-5 mss/year.** Send complete ms. **Pays 2 contributor copies, plus 1 year subscription; pays $8/page if funds are available**.

Photos: Send photos with submission. Reviews 5 X 7 or 8 X 10 b&w and color prints and slides. Buys one-time rights. Pays 2 contributor copies, plus 1-year subscription; $8/page if funds are available.

Fiction: Novel excerpts, short stories, literary. **Buys 6-9 mss/year.** Send complete ms. **Pays 2 contributor copies, plus 1-year subscription; $8/page if funds are available.**

Poetry: Avant-garde, free verse, formal. No religious. **Buys 40-50 poems/year.** Submit maximum 3-5 poems. **Pays 2 contributor copies, plus a 1-year subscription; $8/page if funds are available.**

$ $ ☆ ROSEBUD, The Magazine For People Who Enjoy Good Writing, Rosebud, Inc., P.O. Box 459, Cambridge WI 53523. (608)423-4750. Website: www.rsbd.net. **Contact:** Rod Clark, editor. **100% freelance written.** Quarterly magazine "for people who love to read and write. Our readers like good storytelling, real emotion, a sense of place and authentic voice." Estab. 1993. Circ. 9,000. Pays on publication. Publishes ms an average of 2 months after acceptance. Byline given. Buys first, one-time, second serial (reprint) rights. Editorial lead time 3 months. Submit seasonal material 3 months in advance. Accepts previously published material. Accepts simultaneous submissions. Sends acknowledgement postcard upon receipt of submission and responds in 5 months to queries. Sample copy for $6.95 or sample articles online. Writer's guidelines for SASE or online.

• Charges $1.00 reading fee.

Nonfiction: Book excerpts, essays, general interest, historical/nostalgic, humor, interview/profile, personal experience, travel, memoirs that have a literary sensibility. "No editorializing." Send complete ms. Length: 1,200-1,800 words. **Pays $45-195, and 3 contributor copies.**

Reprints: Send tearsheet or photocopy. Pays 100% of amount paid for an original article.

Photos: State availability with submission. Buys one-time rights. Offers no additional payment for photos accepted with ms. Captions, identification of subjects, model releases required.

Fiction: Ethnic, experimental, historical, humorous, mainstream, novel excerpts, slice-of-life vignettes, suspense. "No formula pieces." **Buys 80 mss/year.** Send complete ms. Length: 1,200-1,800 words. **Pays $15-50.**

Poetry: Avant-garde, free verse, traditional. No inspirational poetry. **Buys 36 poems/year.** Submit maximum 5 poems. Length: Open. **Pays 3 contributor copies.**

Tips: "Something has to 'happen' in the pieces we choose, but what happens inside characters is much more interesting to us than plot manipulation. We prefer to respond with an individualized letter (send SASE for this) and recycle submitted manuscripts. We will return your manuscript only if you send sufficient postage. As of June 2001, only manuscripts accompanied by a $1 fee will be read."

$ THE SAINT ANN'S REVIEW, A Journal of Contemporary Arts and Letters, Saint Ann's School, 129 Pierrepont St., Brooklyn NY 11201. E-mail: sareview@saintanns.k12.ny.us. Website: www.saintannsreview.com. **Contact:** Beth Bosworth, Editor. **100% freelance written.** Semiannual literary magazine. "We seek fully realized work, distinguished by power and craft." Estab. 2000. Circ. 2,000. Pays on publication. Publishes ms an average of 4 months after acceptance. Byline given. Buys first North American serial rights. Submit seasonal material 4 months in advance. Accepts queries by mail. Responds in 1 month to queries; 4 months to mss. Sample copy for $10. Writer's guidelines for #10 SASE, by e-mail, or on website.

Nonfiction: Book excerpts (occasionally), essays, humor, interview/profile, personal experience, photo feature. **Buys 6 mss/year.** Query with or without published clips or send complete ms. Length: 7,500 words maximum. **Pays $50/published page.**

Photos: Send photos with submission. Reviews transparencies, prints, GIF/JPEG files; black and white art. Buys one-time rights. Offers $200/photo page or art page.

Columns/Departments: Book reviews, 1,500 words. **Buys 4 mss/year.** Send complete ms by mail only. **Pays $50/published page.**

Fiction: Ethnic, experimental, fantasy, historical, humorous, mainstream, slice-of-life vignettes, translations. **Buys 15 mss/year.** Length: 7,500 words maximum. **Pays $50/published page.**

Poetry: Avant-garde, free verse, haiku, light verse, traditional, translations. **Buys 30 poems/year.** Submit maximum 5 poems. **Pays $100/page, $300 maximum.**

$ SHORT STUFF, for Grown-ups, Bowman Publications, 712 W. 10th St., Loveland CO 80537. (970)669-9139. E-mail: shortstf89@aol.com. **Contact:** Donnalee Bowman, editor. **98% freelance written.** Bimonthly magazine. "We are perhaps an enigma in that we publish only clean stories in any genre. We'll tackle any subject, but don't allow obscene language or pornographic description. Our magazine is for grown-ups, *not* X-rated 'adult' fare." Estab. 1989. Circ. 10,400. Payment and contract upon publication. Byline given. Buys first North American serial rights. Editorial lead time 3 months. Submit seasonal material 3 months in advance. Responds in 6 months to mss. Sample copy for $1.50 and 9×12 SAE with 5 first-class stamps. Writer's guidelines for #10 SASE.

O→ Break in with "a good, tight story. Cover letters stating what a great story is enclosed really turn me off, just a personal bit about the author is sufficient."

Nonfiction: Most nonfiction is staff written. Humor. Special issues: "We are holiday oriented and each issue reflects the appropriate holidays. **Buys 30 mss/year.** Send complete ms. Length: 500-1,500 words. **Pays $10-50.**

Photos: Send photos with submission. Buys one-time rights. Offers no additional payment for photos accepted with ms. Identification of subjects required.

Fiction: Adventure, historical, humorous, mainstream, mystery, romance, science fiction, suspense, western. **Buys 144 mss/year.** Send complete ms. Length: 500-1,500 words. **Pays $10-50.**

Fillers: Anecdotes, short humor. **Buys 200/year.** Length: 20-500 words. **Pays $1-5.**

Tips: "Don't send floppy disks or cartridges. Do include cover letter about the author, not a synopsis of the story. We are holiday oriented; mark on *outside* of envelope if story is for Easter, Mother's Day, etc. We receive 500 manuscripts each month. This is up about 200%. Because of this, I implore writers to send one manuscript at a time. I would not use stories from the same author more than once an issue and this means I might keep the others too long. Please don't e-mail your stories! If you have an e-mail address, please include that with cover letter so we can contact you. If no SASE, we destroy ms."

$ THE SOUTHERN REVIEW, 43 Allen Hall, Louisiana State University, Baton Rouge LA 70803-5001. (225)578-5108. Fax: (225)578-5098. E-mail: bmacon@lsu.edu. Website: www.lsu.edu/thesouthernreview. **Contact:** Michael Griffith, associate editor. **100% freelance written.** Works with a moderate number of new/unpublished writers each year. Quarterly magazine "with emphasis on contemporary literature in the United States and abroad, and with special interest in Southern culture and history." No queries. Reading period: September-May. Estab. 1935. Circ. 3,100. Pays on publication. Publishes ms an average of 6 months after acceptance. Byline given. Buys first North American serial rights. Accepts queries by mail. Responds in 2 months to mss. Sample copy for $8. Writer's guidelines for #10 SASE or online.

Nonfiction: Essays with careful attention to craftsmanship, technique and seriousness of subject matter. "Willing to publish experimental writing if it has a valid artistic purpose. Avoid extremism and sensationalism. Essays should exhibit thoughtful and sometimes severe awareness of the necessity of literary standards in our time." Emphasis on contemporary literature, especially southern culture and history. No footnotes. **Buys 25 mss/year.** Length: 4,000-10,000 words. **Pays $12/page.**

Fiction: Short stories of lasting literary merit, with emphasis on style and technique; novel excerpts. Length: 4,000-8,000 words. **Pays $12/page.**

Poetry: Length: 1-4 pages. **Pays $20/page.**

$ THE SPIRIT THAT MOVES US, The Spirit That Moves Us Press, Inc., P.O. Box 720820WM, Jackson Heights NY 11372-0820. (718)426-8788. **Contact:** Morty Sklar, editor. Annual book of literary works. "We don't push any 'schools'; we're open to many styles and almost any subject matter. We favor work that expresses feeling, whether subtle or passionate. Irregularly we publish *Editor's Choice: Fiction, Poetry & Art from the U.S. Small Press*, which consists of selections from nominations made by other small literary publishers. When writers see our open call for nominations for this anthology, they should encourage their publishers to nominate their and other people's work." Estab. 1975. Pays on publication. Publishes ms an average of 3 months after acceptance. Byline given. Buys first North American serial, second serial (reprint) rights. Accepts queries by mail. Accepts simultaneous submissions. Sample copy for $5.75 for *15th Anniversary Issue*, $10.75 for *Editor's Choice* to readers of *Writer's Market*.

- In 2003, The Spirit That Moves Us Press will bring out its first novel and won't be reading unsolicited mss during that time. Responds in 2 weeks to queries, 3 months after deadline date on mss (nothing is accepted until everything is read).

Nonfiction: Buys 20-30 mss for special issues/year. Essays. Query for current theme. Length: 8,500 words maximum. **Pays $15-25, plus contributor's copy for assigned articles.** Pays in contributor copies if so requested by author. "Royalty set-up for single-author books, with a cash advance."

Reprints: Accepts previously published submissions (only for those collections that we specify). Send tearsheet or photocopy, and information about when and where the material previously appeared. Pays 100% of amount paid for original article.

Photos: "Photos are considered for artistic merit, and not just illustrative function. All art that we use has to stand on its own." Reviews contact sheets, 8×10 prints. Buys one-time rights. Offers $15/photo; $100 for cover photos, plus a free copy and 40% off additional copies.

Fiction: "Nothing slick or commercial." **Buys 15-30 mss/year.** Length: 8,500 words maximum. **Pays $15-25, plus a free copy and 40% off additional copies.**

Poetry: "Not interested in work that just tries to be smart, flashy, sensational; if it's technically skilled but conveys no feeling, we don't care about it for publication. We were the first U.S. publisher to bring out a collection by the Czech poet Nobel Laureate of 1984, Jaroslav Seifert—and before he won the Nobel prize." **Buys 50-100 poems/year. Pays $15 (depending on length and funding/sales obtained), plus a free copy and 40% off additional copies.**

Tips: "Writers and visual artists should query first to see what we're working on if they haven't seen our latest call for manuscripts in *Poets & Writers* magazine or elsewhere. Send #10 SASE for themes and time frames."

$STAND MAGAZINE, Department of English, VCU, Richmond VA 23284-2005. (804)828-1331. E-mail: dlatane@vcu.edu. Website: www.people.vcu.edu. Managing Editor: Jon Glover. **Contact:** David Latané, US editor. **75% freelance written.** Quarterly magazine covering short fiction, poetry, criticism, and reviews. "*Stand Magazine* is concerned with what happens when cultures and literatures meet, with translation in its many guises, with the mechanics of language, with the processes by which the policy receives or disables its cultural makers. *Stand* promotes debate of issues that are of radical concern to the intellectual community worldwide." Estab. 1952. Circ. 3,000 worldwide. Pays on publication. Publishes ms an average of 10 months after acceptance. Byline given. Buys first world rights. Editorial lead time 2 months. Accepts queries by mail. Responds in 6 weeks to queries; 3 months to mss. Sample copy for $12. Writer's guidelines for #10 SASE with sufficient number of IRCs or online.
Nonfiction: "Reviews are commissioned from known freelancers." Reviews of poetry/fiction. **Buys 8 mss/year.** Query. Length: 200-5,000 words. **Pays $30/1,000 words.**
Fiction: Adventure, ethnic, experimental, historical, mainstream. "No genre fiction." **Buys 12-14 mss/year.** Send complete ms. Length: 8,000 words maximum. **Payment varies.**
Poetry: Avant-garde, free verse, traditional. **Buys 100-120 poems/year.** Submit maximum 6 poems. **Pays $37.50/poem.**
Tips: "Poetry/fiction areas are most open to freelancers. *Stand* is published in England and reaches an international audience. North American writers should submit work to the U.S. address. While the topic or nature of submissions does not have to be 'international,' writers may do well to keep in mind the range of *Stand*'s audience."

STORYQUARTERLY, 431 Sheridan Rd., Kenilworth IL 60043. E-mail: storyquarterly@yahoo.com. **Contact:** M.M.M. Hayes, publisher/editor. An annual, all-fiction international collection.

$THE STRAIN, Interactive Arts Magazine, 11702 Webercrest, Houston TX 77048. **Contact:** Norman Clark Stewart, Jr., editor. **80% freelance written.** Monthly magazine. Estab. 1987. Pays on publication. Publishes ms an average of 3 years after acceptance. Byline given. Buys first, one-time, second serial (reprint) rights, makes work-for-hire assignments. Accepts previously published material. Responds in 2 years to queries; 2 years to mss.
Nonfiction: Alicia Alder, articles editor. Essays, exposé, how-to, humor, photo feature, technical. **Buys 2-20 mss/year.** Send complete ms. **Pays $5 minimum.**
Reprints: Send typed ms with rights for sale noted and information about when and where the material previously appeared.
Photos: Send photos with submission. Reviews transparencies, Prints. Buys one-time rights. Identification of subjects, model releases required.
Columns/Departments: Charlie Mainze, editor. Multimedia performance art. Send complete ms. **Pays $5 minimum.**
Fiction: Michael Bond, editor. **Buys 1-35 mss/year.** Send complete ms. **Pays $5 minimum.**
Poetry: Annas Kinder, editor. Avant-garde, free verse, light verse, traditional. **Buys 100 poems/year.** Submit maximum 5 poems. **Pays $5 minimum.**

$THE STRAND MAGAZINE, P.O. Box 1418, Birmingham MI 48012-1418. (800)300-6652. Fax: (248)874-1046. E-mail: strandmag@worldnet.att.net. **Contact:** A.F. Gulli, managing editor. Quarterly magazine covering mysteries, short stories, essays, book reviews. "Mysteries and short stories written in the classic tradition of this century's great authors." Estab. 1998. Pays on publication. Publishes ms an average of 4 months after acceptance. Byline given. Buys first North American serial rights. Responds in 1 month to queries; 4 months to mss. Sample copy not available. Writer's guidelines for #10 SASE.
Fiction: Horror, humorous, mystery, suspense, tales of the unexpected. Send complete ms. Length: 2,000-6,000 words. **Pays $50-175.**
Tips: "No gratuitous violence, sexual content, or explicit language, please."

$TAMPA REVIEW, University of Tampa Press, 401 W. Kennedy Blvd., Tampa FL 33606. (813)253-6266. Website: tampareview.ut.edu. **Contact:** Richard B. Mathews, editor. Semiannual magazine published in hardback format. An international literary journal publishing art and literature from Florida and Tampa Bay as well as new work and translations from throughout the world. Estab. 1988. Circ. 500. Pays on publication. Publishes ms an average of 10 months after acceptance. Byline given. Buys first North American serial rights. Editorial lead time 18 months. Accepts queries by mail. Responds in 5 months to mss. Sample copy for $7. Writer's guidelines for #10 SASE.
Nonfiction: Elizabeth Winston, nonfiction editor. General interest, interview/profile, personal experience, creative nonfiction. No "how-to" articles, fads, journalistic reprise, etc. **Buys 6 mss/year.** Send complete ms. Length: 250-7,500 words. **Pays $10/printed page.**
Photos: State availability with submission. Reviews contact sheets, negatives, transparencies, prints, digital files. Buys one-time rights. Offers $10/photo. Captions, identification of subjects required.
Fiction: Lisa Birnbaum and Kathleen Ochshorn, fiction editors. Literary. **Buys 6 mss/year.** Send complete ms. Length: 200-5,000 words. **Pays $10/printed page.**
Poetry: Don Morrill and Martha Serpas, poetry editors. Avant-garde, free verse, haiku, light verse, traditional, visual/experimental. No greeting card verse, hackneyed, sing-song, rhyme-for-the-sake-of-rhyme. **Buys 45 poems/year.** Submit maximum 10 poems. Length: 2-225 lines.

Tips: "Send a clear cover letter stating previous experience or background. Our editorial staff considers submissions between September and December for publication in the following year."

$ THEMA, Box 8747, Metairie LA 70011-8747. (504)887-1263. E-mail: thema@cox.net. **Contact:** Virginia Howard, editor. **100% freelance written.** Triannual magazine covering a different theme for each issue. Upcoming themes for SASE. "*Thema* is designed to stimulate creative thinking by challenging writers with unusual themes, such as 'laughter on the steps' and 'jogging on ice.' Appeals to writers, teachers of creative writing and general reading audience." Estab. 1988. Circ. 350. **Pays on acceptance.** Byline given. Buys one-time rights. Accepts queries by mail, e-mail. Accepts previously published material. Responds in 5 months to mss. Sample copy for $8. Writer's guidelines for #10 SASE.

Reprints: Send typed ms with rights for sale noted and information about when and where the material previously appeared. Pays the same amount paid for original.

Fiction: Special Issues: An Unlikely Alliance (November 1, 2002); Off on a Tangent (March 1, 2003); The Middle Path (July 1, 2003). Adventure, ethnic, experimental, fantasy, historical, humorous, mainstream, mystery, novel excerpts, religious, science fiction, slice-of-life vignettes, suspense, western. "No erotica." **Buys 30 mss/year. Pays $10-25.**

Poetry: Avant-garde, free verse, haiku, light verse, traditional. "No erotica." **Buys 27 poems/year.** Submit maximum 3 poems. Length: 4-50 lines. **Pays $10.**

Tips: "Be familiar with the themes. *Don't submit* unless you have an upcoming theme in mind. Specify the target theme on the first page of your manuscript or in a cover letter. Put your name on *first* page of manuscript only. (All submissions are judged in blind review after the deadline for a specified issue.) Most open to fiction and poetry. Don't be hasty when you consider a theme—mull it over and let it ferment in your mind. We appreciate interpretations that are carefully constructed, clever, subtle, well thought out."

$ $ ✪ THE THREEPENNY REVIEW, P.O. Box 9131, Berkeley CA 94709. (510)849-4545. Website: www.threepennyreview.com. **Contact:** Wendy Lesser, editor. **100% freelance written.** Works with small number of new/unpublished writers each year. Quarterly tabloid. "We are a general interest, national literary magazine with coverage of politics, the visual arts, and the performing arts as well." Estab. 1980. Circ. 9,000. **Pays on acceptance.** Publishes ms an average of 1 year after acceptance. Byline given. Buys first North American serial rights. Responds in 1 month to queries; 2 months to mss. Sample copy for $10 or online. Writer's guidelines for SASE or online.

- Does not read mss in summer months.

Nonfiction: Essays, exposé, historical/nostalgic, personal experience, book, film, theater, dance, music, and art reviews. **Buys 40 mss/year.** Query with or without published clips or send complete ms. Length: 1,500-4,000 words. **Pays $200.**

Fiction: No fragmentary, sentimental fiction. **Buys 10 mss/year.** Send complete ms. Length: 800-4,000 words. **Pays $200.**

Poetry: Free verse, traditional. No poems "without capital letters or poems without a discernible subject." **Buys 30 poems/year.** Submit maximum 5 poems. **Pays $100.**

Tips: "Nonfiction (political articles, memoirs, reviews) is most open to freelancers."

$ $ TIN HOUSE, McCormack Communications, Box 10500, Portland OR 97296. Website: www.tinhouse.com. Editor-in-Chief: Win McCormack. Managing Editor: Holly Macarthur. Editors: Rob Spillman, Elissa Schappell. **Contact:** Lee Montgomery. **90% freelance written.** Quarterly magazine. "We are a general interest literary quarterly. Our watchword is quality. Our audience is people interested in literature in all its aspects, from the mundane to the exalted." Estab. 1998. Circ. 5,000. Pays on publication. Publishes ms an average of 6 months after acceptance. Byline given. Buys first North American serial rights, anthology rights. Editorial lead time 6 months. Submit seasonal material 6 months in advance. Accepts queries by mail. Accepts simultaneous submissions. Responds in 6 weeks to queries; 3 months to mss. Sample copy for $15. Writer's guidelines for #10 SASE.

Nonfiction: Book excerpts, essays, interview/profile, personal experience. Send complete ms. Length: 5,000 words maximum. **Pays $50-800 for assigned articles; $50-500 for unsolicited articles.** Sometimes pays expenses of writers on assignment.

Columns/Departments: Lost and Found (mini-reviews of forgotten or under appreciated books), up to 500 words; Readable Feasts (fiction or nonfiction literature with recipes), 2,000-3,000 words; Pilgrimage (journey to a personally significant place, especially literary), 2,000-3,000 words. **Buys 15-20 mss/year.** Send complete ms. **Pays $50-500.**

Fiction: Experimental, mainstream, novel excerpts, literary. **Buys 15-20 mss/year.** Send complete ms. Length: 5,000 words maximum. **Pays $200-800.**

Poetry: Amy Bartlett, poetry editor. Avant-garde, free verse, traditional. No prose masquerading as poetry. **Buys 40 poems/year.** Submit maximum 5 poems. **Pays $50-150.**

Tips: "Remember to send a SASE with your submission."

$ TRIQUARTERLY, 2020 Ridge Ave., Northwestern University, Evanston IL 60208-4302. (847)491-3490. Fax: (847)467-2096. **Contact:** Susan Firestone Hahn, editor. **70% freelance written.** Triannual magazine of fiction, poetry and essays, as well as artwork. Estab. 1964. Pays on publication. Publishes ms an average of 1 year after acceptance. Buys first North American serial rights, nonexclusive reprint rights. Responds in 3 months to queries; 3 months to mss. Sample copy for $5. Writer's guidelines for #10 SASE.

- *TriQuarterly* has had several stories published in the *O. Henry Prize* anthology and *Best American Short Stories* as well as poetry in *Best American Poetry.* Eager to work with new/unpublished writers.

Nonfiction: Essays. No scholarly or critical essays except in special issues. Query.

Fiction: No prejudice against style or length of work; only seriousness and excellence are required. Does not accept or read mss between April 1 and September 30. **Buys 20-50 unsolicited mss/year. Payment varies depending on grant support.**
Poetry: Buys 20-50 poems/year. Payment varies depending on grant support.

N **UTOPIA DEL SUR, The Latin American Literary Journal**, Utopia del Sur Foundation, Pedro de Mendoza 155, 14 "A", Buenos Aires, Argentina 1156. E-mail: utopiadelsur@hotmail.com. Website: www.utopiadelsur.org. Managing Editor: Macarena Zorraquin. **Contact:** Kevin Carrel Footer, editor. **90% freelance written.** Semiannual magazine. "*Utopia del Sur: The Latin American Literary Journal* publishes the finest writing from or about Latin America. All writers who draw their inspiration from Latin America may submit their work for consideration. We publish both established writers and new voices in creative nonfiction, fiction and poetry. *Utopia del Sur* tells the vibrant, complex story of Latin America today through good writing and daring photography. We look forward to seeing your best work." Estab. 2000. Circ. 500. Pays on publication. Publishes ms an average of 6 months after acceptance. Byline given. Not copyrighted. Buys first, second serial (reprint), electronic rights. Rights purchased varies. Editorial lead time 3 months. Accepts queries by e-mail. Accepts previously published material. Accepts simultaneous submissions. Responds in 2 weeks to queries; 3 months to mss. Sample copy online. Writer's guidelines online.
Nonfiction: Kevin Carrel Footer, editor. "Send your best work and we will gladly review it." Book excerpts, essays, interview/profile, literary essays; literary travel; literary journalism; book reviews and excerpts. **Buys 10 mss/year.** Length: varies. **Pays $100 maximum.**
Photos: State availability with submission. Reviews GIF/JPEG files. Buys one-time rights. Negotiates payment individually.
Fiction: John Fernandes, fiction editor. "Send your best work and we will be glad to review it." Literary fiction in all its forms. **Buys 10 mss/year.** Send complete ms. Length: varies. **Pays $100 maximum.**
Poetry: Maria Volonté, poetry editor. **Buys 10 poems/year.** Submit maximum 5 poems. Length: varies.
Tips: "*Utopia del Sur* looks for the best writing and photography on the Latin American experience. New writers have as good a chance as established writers in breaking in to our publication if their work is well-crafted and true. Quality matters to us above all, so submit your best work. We accept manuscripts in English, Spanish and Portuguese, though we publish in English whenever possible. We prefer electronic submissions."

VESTAL REVIEW, Vestal Review, 2609 Dartmouth Dr., Vestal NY 13850. E-mail: editor@stny.rr.com. Website: www.vestalreview.net. Editor-in-Chief: Mark Budman. **Contact:** Mark Budman. **100% freelance written.** Quarterly online covering flash fiction. Estab. 2000. Circ. 2,000. Pays 30 days after publication. Publishes ms an average of 3 months after acceptance. Byline given. Offers 100% kill fee. Buys electronic rights. Editorial lead time 3 months. Submit seasonal material 3 months in advance. Accepts queries by e-mail. Accepts simultaneous submissions. Responds in 1 week to queries; 2 months to mss. Sample copy free or on website. Writer's guidelines free or on website.
Fiction: Editor. Erotica, ethnic, experimental, fantasy, historical, horror, humorous, mainstream, mystery, science fiction, suspense, flash fiction. No children's stories. **Buys 32 mss/year.** Send complete ms. Length: 500 words or less. **Pays $6-25 and 1 contributor's copy.**

$ VIRGINIA QUARTERLY REVIEW, University of Virginia, One West Range, P.O. Box 400223, Charlottesville VA 22904-4223. (434)924-3124. Fax: (434)924-1397. Website: www.virginia.edu/vqr. **Contact:** Staige D. Blackford, editor. Quarterly magazine. "A national journal of literature and thought." Estab. 1925. Circ. 4,000. Pays on publication. Publishes ms an average of 1 year after acceptance. Byline given. Buys first rights. Editorial lead time 6 months. Submit seasonal material 6 months in advance. Responds in 2 weeks to queries; 2 months to mss. Sample copy for $5. Writer's guidelines for #10 SASE or online.
Nonfiction: Book excerpts, essays, general interest, historical/nostalgic, humor, inspirational, personal experience, travel. Send complete ms. Length: 2,000-4,000 words. **Pays $10/page maximum.**
Fiction: Adventure, ethnic, historical, humorous, mainstream, mystery, novel excerpts, romance. Send complete ms. Length: 2,000-4,000 words. **Pays $10/page maximum.**
Poetry: Gregory Orr, poetry editor. All type. Submit maximum 5 poems. **Pays $1/line.**

$ VISIONS-INTERNATIONAL, Black Buzzard Press, 1007 Ficklen Rd., Fredericksburg VA 22405. (540)310-0730. **Contact:** B.R. Strahan, editor. **95% freelance written.** Magazine published 2 times/year featuring poetry, essays and reviews. Estab. 1979. Circ. 750. Pays on publication. Publishes ms an average of 6 months after acceptance. Byline given. Buys first North American serial rights. Editorial lead time 4 months. Accepts queries by mail. Responds in 3 weeks to queries; 2 months to mss. Sample copy for $4.95. Writer's guidelines for #10 SASE.
Nonfiction: Essays (by assignment after queryreviews). No sentimental, self-serving or religious submissions. Query. Length: 1 page maximum. **Pays $10 and complimentary copies.** Pays with contributor copies when grant money is unavailable.
Poetry: Avant-garde, free verse, traditional. No sentimental, religious, scurrilous, sexist, racist, amaturish, or over 3 pages. **Buys 110 poems/year.** Submit 3-6 poems Length: 2-120 lines.
Tips: "Know your craft. We are not a magazine for amateurs. We also are interested in translation from *modern* poets writing in any language into English."

WEB DEL SOL. E-mail: submissions@webdelsol.com. Website: www.webdelsol.com. **Contact:** Fiction Editor. Sample copy online.

● E-mail submissions only. No lower limit on words, upper limit 3,500. Short stories and stand-alone excerpts. Nothing previously published.

$WEST BRANCH, Bucknell Hall, Bucknell University, Lewisburg PA 17837-2029. (570)577-1853. Fax: (570)577-3760. E-mail: westbranch@bucknell.edu. Website: www.departments.bucknell.edu/stadler_center/westbranch. Managing Editor: Andrew Ciotola. **Contact:** Paula Closson Buck, editor. Semiannual literary magazine. "*West Branch* is an aesthetic conversation between the traditional and the innovative in poetry, fiction and nonfiction. It brings writers, new and established, to the rooms where they will be heard, and where they will, no doubt, rearrange the furniture." Pays on publication. Byline given. Buys first North American serial rights. Accepts queries by mail. Accepts simultaneous submissions. Sample copy for $3. Writer's guidelines for #10 SASE or on website.
Nonfiction: Book excerpts, essays, general interest, historical/nostalgic, opinion, personal experience, travel, literary. **Buys 4-5 mss/year.** Send complete ms. **Pays $20-100 ($10/page).**
Fiction: Experimental, historical, humorous, novel excerpts, serialized novels, slice-of-life vignettes, literary. No genre fiction. **Buys 10-12 mss/year.** Send complete ms. **Pays $20-100 ($10/page).**
Poetry: Avant-garde, free verse, haiku, traditional, formal, experimental. **Buys 30-40 poems/year.** Submit maximum 6 poems.
Tips: "Please send only one submission at a time and do not send another work until you have heard about the first. Send no more than 6 poems or 30 pages of prose at once. We accept simultaneous submissions if they are clearly marked as such, and if we are notified immediately upon acceptance elsewhere. Manuscripts must be accompanied by the customary return materials; we cannot respond by e-mail or postcard. All manuscripts should be typed, with the author's name on each page; prose must be double-spaced. We recommend that you acquaint yourself with the magazine before submitting."

WEST COAST LINE, A Journal of Contemporary Writing & Criticism, West Coast Review Publishing Society, 2027 EAA, Simon Fraser University, Burnaby British Columbia V5A 1S6, Canada. (604)291-4287. Fax: (604)291-4622. E-mail: wcl@sfu.ca. Website: www.sfu.ca/west-coast-line. **Contact:** Roger Farr, managing editor. Triannual magazine of contemporary literature and criticism. Estab. 1990. Circ. 500. Pays on publication. Buys one-time rights. Editorial lead time 4 months. Accepts queries by mail, e-mail. Responds in 1 month; up to 6 months to mss. Sample copy for $10. Writer's guidelines for SASE (US must include IRC).
Nonfiction: Essays (literary/scholarly/critical), experimental prose. "No journalistic articles or articles dealing with nonliterary material." **Buys 8-10 mss/year.** Send complete ms. Length: 1,000-5,000 words. **Pays $8/page, 2 contributor's copies and a year's free subscription.**
Fiction: Experimental, novel excerpts. **Buys 3-6 mss/year.** Send complete ms. Length: 1,000-7,000 words. **Pays $8/page.**
Poetry: Avant-garde. "No light verse, traditional." **Buys 10-15 poems/year.** Submit maximum maximum 5-6 poems.
Tips: "Submissions must be either scholarly or formally innovative. Contributors should be familiar with current literary trends in Canada and the U.S. Scholars should be aware of current schools of theory. All submissions should be accompanied by a brief cover letter; essays should be formatted according to the MLA guide. The publication is not divided into departments. We accept innovative poetry, fiction, experimental prose and scholarly essays."

$WESTERN HUMANITIES REVIEW, University of Utah, English Department, 255 S. Central Campus Dr., Room 3500, Salt Lake City UT 84112-0494. (801)581-6070. Fax: (801)585-5167. E-mail: whr@mail.hum.utah.edu. Website: www.hum.utah.edu/whr. **Contact:** Samantha Ruckman, managing editor. Biannual magazine for educated readers. Estab. 1947. Circ. 1,000. Pays on publication. Publishes ms an average of 1 year after acceptance. Buys all rights. Accepts simultaneous submissions. Sample copy for $8. Writer's guidelines not available.

● "We read manuscripts between September 1 and May 1. Manuscripts sent outside of these dates will be returned unread."

Nonfiction: Barry Weller, editor-in-chief. Authoritative, readable articles on literature, art, philosophy, current events, history, religion, and anything in the humanities. Interdisciplinary articles encouraged. Departments on films and books. **Buys 4-5 unsolicited mss/year.** Send complete ms. **Pays $5/published page.**
Fiction: Karen Brennan, fiction editor. Experimental. **Buys 8-12 mss/year.** Send complete ms. **Pays $5/published page.**
Poetry: Richard Howard, poetry editor.
Tips: "Because of changes in our editorial staff, we urge familiarity with *recent* issues of the magazine. Inappropriate material will be returned without comment. We do not publish writer's guidelines because we think that the magazine itself conveys an accurate picture of our requirements. Please, *no* e-mail submissions."

$WHETSTONE, Barrington Area Arts Council, Box 1266, Barrington IL 60011. (847)382-5626. Fax: (847)382-3685. **Contact:** Dale Griffith, editor-in-chief; Lanny Ori, Charles White, associate editors. **100% freelance written.** Annual magazine featuring fiction, creative nonfiction, and poetry. "We publish work by emerging and established authors for readers hungry for poetry and prose of substance." Estab. 1982. Circ. 800. Pays on publication. Publishes ms an average of 14 months after acceptance. Byline given. Not copyrighted. Buys first North American serial rights. Accepts queries by mail. Accepts simultaneous submissions. Responds in 5 months to mss. Sample copy and writer's guidelines for $5.

O-- To break in, "send us your best work after it has rested long enough for you to forget it and therefore can look at it objectively to fine-tune before submitting."

Nonfiction: Essays (creative). "No articles." **Buys 0-3 mss/year.** Send complete ms. Length: 500-5,000 words. **Pays 2 copies, and variable cash payment.**

Fiction: Novel excerpts, short stories. **Buys 10-12 mss/year.** Send complete ms. Length: 500-5,000 words. **Pays 2 copies, and variable cash payment.**

Poetry: Free verse, traditional. "No light verse, for children, political poems." **Buys 10-20 poems/year.** Submit maximum 7 poems. **Pays 2 copies, and variable cash payment.**

Tips: "We look for fresh approaches to material. We appreciate careful work. Send us your best. We welcome unpublished authors. Though we pay in copies and small monetary amounts that depend on the generosity of our patrons and subscribers, we offer prizes for work published in *Whetstone*. These prizes total $1,000, and are given to 3 or more writers. The editors make their decisions at the time of publication. This is not a contest. In addition, we nominate authors for *Pushcart*; *Best American Short Stories*; *Poetry and Essays*; *O. Henry Awards*; *Best of the South*; Illinois Arts Council Awards; and other prizes and anthologies as they come to our attention. Though our press run is moderate, we work for our authors and offer a prestigious vehicle for their work."

$ WILLOW SPRINGS, 705 W. First Ave., Eastern Washington University, Spokane WA 99201. (509)623-4349. E-mail: cnhowell@mail.ewu.edu. **Contact:** Christopher Howell, editor. **100% freelance written.** Semiannual magazine. "We publish quality contemporary poetry, fiction, nonfiction, and works in translation." Estab. 1977. Circ. 1,500. Publishes ms an average of 4 months after acceptance. Byline given. Buys first rights. Editorial lead time 2 months. Responds in 2 months to queries; 2 months to mss. Sample copy for $5.50. Writer's guidelines for #10 SASE.

- A magazine of growing reputation. Takes part in the AWP Intro Award program.

Nonfiction: Essays. **Buys 4 mss/year.** Send complete ms. **Pays 2 contributor copies.**

Fiction: Literary fiction only. "No genre fiction, please." **Buys 5-8 mss/year.** Send complete ms.

Poetry: Avant-garde, free verse. "No haiku, light verse, or religious." **Buys 50-80 poems/year.** Submit maximum 6 poems. Length: 12 pages maximum.

Tips: "We do not read manuscripts in June, July, and August, and we do not accept multiple submissions."

WORLD WIDE WRITERS, P.O. Box 3229, Bournemouth BH1 1ZS, England. E-mail: writintl@globalnet.co.uk. Website: www.worldwriters.net. **Contact:** Frederick E. Smith, editor. Sample copy not available.

N ▣ WOULD THAT IT WERE, The Internet's Premier Magazine of Historical SF, Small Potatoes Press, 509 Elm St., Suite 603, Dallas TX 75202. E-mail: editor@wouldthatitwere.com. Website: www.wouldthatitwere.com. **Contact:** Don Muchow, editor/publisher. **90% freelance written.** Quarterly online magazine covering Victorian science fiction. "*Would That It Were* specializes in science fiction written in the style made popular by H.G. Wells, Jules Verne, Mary Shelley, and Robert Louis Stevenson. We are looking for original stories up to 5,000 words (we prefer less than 3,000) that are set in the period ranging roughly from 1830-1930." Estab. 1999. Circ. 1,000 readers/issue. Pays on publication. Byline given. Offers 100% kill fee. Buys electronic rights. Editorial lead time 2 months. Submit seasonal material 2 months in advance. Accepts queries by e-mail. Accepts previously published material. Accepts simultaneous submissions. Responds in 1 week to queries; 1 month to mss. Sample copy online. Writer's guidelines online.

Nonfiction: Don Muchow, editor. "We do want alternate-history (1830-1930), SteamPunk, unpublished Victorian manuscripts, and like-themed submissions." Historical/nostalgic, interview/profile. Special issues: Planned "Best of" print anthology for 2002/2003 time frame. "No religious, inspirational, modern-day themed (after all, our magazine is Victorian science fiction), modern science fiction, horror, westerns, ghost story theme, war, romance, or anything that does not fit the genteel and inquisitive spirit of Victorian science and science fiction." **Buys 4 mss/year.** Send Complete ms with intro, bio, and head shot. Length: 1,000-3,000 words. **Pays $100-300 for assigned articles; $100-300 for unsolicited articles.**

Photos: Send photos with submission. Reviews GIF/JPEG files. Buys nonexclusive electronic rights for duration of issue, plus right to archive images online in "Past Issues" area. Offers no additional payment for photos accepted with ms. Captions, identification of subjects, model releases required.

Columns/Departments: Don Muchow, editor. Articles (articles of interest to period or theme), 3,000 words. **Buys 4 mss/year.** Query. **Pays $50-250.**

Fiction: Don Muchow, editor; Jeff Robinson, editor. "We want alternate-history (1830-1930), SteamPunk, unpublished Victorian manuscripts, and like-themed submissions." Historical, science fiction. "No religious, inspirational, modern-day themed (after all, our magazine is Victorian science fiction), modern science fiction, horror, westerns, ghost stories, war stories, romance." **Buys 25 mss/year.** Send complete ms. Length: 1,000-5,000 words. **Pays $50-250.**

Poetry: "We rarely buy poetry, but are fond of sonnets, articles about Victorian poets, and the occasional Don Marquis pastiche." Don Muchow, editor. Period-related or humorous. **Buys 2 poems/year.** Submit maximum 1 poems. Length: No limit. **Pays per agreement.**

Fillers: Don Muchow, editor. Facts. Length: 100-300 words. **Pays by arrangement.**

Tips: "Read our guidelines. The fastest way to get rejected is by sending us a story about September 11, 2001, or anything else not Victorian science fiction. E-mail submissions only, no snail mail. Subject line of e-mail must include author, story title, and word length; should include bio and head shot with submission. We respond to all submissions within 1 quarter of receiving them. Query only for terms, guidelines, or special arrangements, not for story status. We are ordinary folks and not too hung up on protocol, but we don't have a lot of time to spend on each story. Make sure your communications are brief, clear, and effective. A short plug for your story, or a reminder that your material has previously appeared in our magazine, is never a bad idea. Learn to use your word processor. We hate, for instance, removing 12 spaces in a row just because you don't know how to use the Tab key. Do not hard-break lines or use other formatting that will make it difficult to transfer copy to HTML."

$ $ THE YALE REVIEW, Blackwell Publishing, Inc., Yale University, P.O. Box 208243, New Haven CT 06520-8243. (203)432-0499. Website: www.yale.edu. Managing Editor: Susan Bianconi. **Contact:** J.D. McClatchy, editor. **20% freelance written.** Quarterly magazine. "No writer's guidelines available. Consult back issues." Estab. 1911. Circ. 7,000. Pays prior to publication. Publishes ms an average of 1 year after acceptance. Buys one-time rights. Responds in 2 months to queries; 2 months to mss. Sample copy not available. Writer's guidelines not available.

- *The Yale Review* has published work chosen for the Pushcart anthology, *The Best American Poetry*, and the O. Henry Award.

Nonfiction: Authoritative discussions of politics, literature, and the arts. No previously published submissions. Send complete ms with cover letter and SASE. Length: 3,000-5,000 words. **Pays $100-500.**
Fiction: Buys quality fiction. Length: 3,000-5,000 words. **Pays $100-500.**

$ $ $ ZOETROPE: ALL STORY, AZX Publications, The Sentinel Bldg., 916 Kearny St., San Francisco CA 94133. (415)788-7500. E-mail: info@all-story.com. Website: www.all-story.com. **Contact:** Francis Ford Coppola, publisher. Quarterly magazine specializing in high caliber short fiction. "*Zoetrope: All Story* presents a new generation of classic stories. Inspired by the Coppola heritage of independence and creativity, the magazine is at once innovative and deeply traditional. *Zoetrope: All Story* explores the intersection of fiction and film, and anticipates some of its stories becoming memorable films." Estab. 1997. Circ. 20,000. Publishes ms an average of approximately 6 months after acceptance. Byline given. Buys first North American serial rights. 2-year film option Accepts queries by mail. Accepts simultaneous submissions. Responds in 5 months (if SASE included) to mss. Sample copy for $7.50. Writer's guidelines for SASE or online.
Fiction: Literary short stories, one-act plays. No excerpts or reprints. **Buys 32-40 mss/year.** Send complete ms. **Pays $1,500.**

Current and select back issues can be found online. "The website also features up-to-date information on news, events, contests, workshops, writer's guidelines, and more. In addition, the site links to Francis Ford Coppola's virtual studio, which is host to an online workshop for short story writers. Each month several virtual studio submissions are featured in the online supplement, *All-Story Extra*."

ZUZU'S PETALS QUARTERLY, P.O. Box 4853, Ithaca NY 14852. E-mail: fiction@zuzu.com. Website: www.zuzu.com. **Contact:** Doug DuCap, fiction editor.

$ ZYZZYVA, The Last Word: West Coast Writers & Artists, P.O. Box 590069, San Francisco CA 94159-0069. (415)752-4393. Fax: (415)752-4391. E-mail: editor@zyzzyva.org. Website: www.zyzzyva.org. **Contact:** Howard Junker, editor. **100% freelance written.** Works with a small number of new/unpublished writers each year. Magazine published in March, August, and November. "We feature work by West Coast writers only. We are essentially a literary magazine, but of wide-ranging interests and a strong commitment to nonfiction." Estab. 1985. Circ. 4,000. **Pays on acceptance.** Publishes ms an average of 3 months after acceptance. Byline given. First North American serial and one-time anthology rights Accepts queries by mail, e-mail, fax, phone. Responds in 1 week to queries; 1 month to mss. Sample copy for $7 or online. Writer's guidelines online.
Nonfiction: Book excerpts, general interest, historical/nostalgic, humor, personal experience. **Buys 50 mss/year.** Query by mail or e-mail. Length: Open. **Pays $50.**
Photos: Reviews copies or slides only.
Fiction: Ethnic, experimental, humorous, mainstream. **Buys 20 mss/year.** Send complete ms. Length: Open. **Pays $50.**
Poetry: Buys 20 poems/year. Submit maximum 5 poems. Length: 3-200 lines. **Pays $50.**
Tips: "West Coast writers means those currently living in California, Alaska, Washington, Oregon, or Hawaii."

MEN'S

Magazines in this section offer features on topics of general interest primarily to men. Magazines that also use material slanted toward men can be found in Business & Finance, Child Care & Parental Guidance, Ethnic/Minority, Gay & Lesbian Interest, General Interest, Health & Fitness, Military, Relationships and Sports sections. Magazines featuring pictorial layouts accompanied by stories and articles of a sexual nature, both gay and straight, appear in the Sex section.

$ $ $ CIGAR AFICIONADO, M. Shanken Communications, Inc., 387 Park Ave. S., New York NY 10016. (212)684-4224. Fax: (212)684-5424. Website: www.cigaraficionado.com. Editor: Marvin Shanken. **Contact:** Gordon Mott, executive editor. **75% freelance written.** Bimonthly magazine covering cigars and men's lifestyle. Estab. 1992. Circ. 300,000. **Pays on acceptance.** Publishes ms an average of 9 months after acceptance. Byline given. Offers 25% kill fee. Buys all rights. Editorial lead time 3 months. Submit seasonal material 3 months in advance. Accepts queries by mail, fax. Responds in 2 months to queries. Sample copy and writer's guidelines for SASE.
Nonfiction: Buys 80-100 mss/year. Query. Length: 2,000 words. **Pay varies.** Sometimes pays expenses of writers on assignment.

Columns/Departments: Length: 1,000 words. **Buys 20 mss/year. Payment varies.**

The online magazine carries original content not found in the print edition. Contact: Dave Savona, online editor.

$ $ $ $ ESQUIRE, 250 W. 55th St., New York NY 10019. (212)649-4020. Editor-in-Chief: David Granger. Senior Editor: A.J. Jacobs. Monthly magazine covering the ever-changing trends in American culture. Monthly magazine for smart, well-off men. General readership is college educated and sophisticated, between ages 30 and 45. Written mostly by contributing editors on contract. Rarely accepts unsolicited manuscripts. Estab. 1933. **Pays on acceptance.** Publishes ms an average of 2 months after acceptance. Retains first worldwide periodical publication rights for 90 days from cover date Editorial lead time at least 2 months.

Nonfiction: Focus is the ever-changing trends in American culture. Topics include current events and politics, social criticism, sports, celebrity profiles, the media, art and music, men's fashion. Queries must be sent by letter. **Buys 4 features and 12 shorter mss/year.** Length: Columns average 1,500 words; features average 5,000 words; short front of book pieces average 200-400 words. **Payment varies.**

Photos: Nancy Iacoi, photo editor. Uses mostly commissioned photography. Payment depends on size and number of photos.

Fiction: Adrienne Miller, literary editor. "Literary excellence is our only criterion." Accepts work chiefly from literary agencies. Novel excerpts, short stories, some poetry, memoirs, and plays.

Tips: "A writer has the best chance of breaking in at *Esquire* by querying with a specific idea that requires special contacts and expertise. Ideas must be timely and national in scope."

$ GC MAGAZINE, LPI Publishing, P.O. Box 331775, Fort Worth TX 76163. (817)640-1306. Fax: (817)633-9045. E-mail: cabaret@flash.net. Managing Editor: Thomas Foss. **Contact:** Jon Keeyes, editor. **80% freelance written.** Monthly magazine. "*GC Magazine* is a general entertainment magazine for men. We include entertainment celebrity interviews (movies, music, books) along with general interest articles for adult males." Estab. 1994. Circ. 53,000. Pays on publication. Publishes ms an average of 3 months after acceptance. Buys one-time rights. Editorial lead time 3 months. Submit seasonal material 6 months in advance. Accepts queries by mail, e-mail, fax. Accepts previously published material. Accepts simultaneous submissions. Responds in 1 month to queries. Sample copy for $1.50. Writer's guidelines for #10 SASE.

Nonfiction: Book excerpts, essays, exposé, general interest, historical/nostalgic, how-to, humor, interview/profile, opinion, personal experience, technical, travel, dating tips. No religious or "feel good" articles. **Buys 100 mss/year.** Query. Length: 1,000-3,000 words. **Pays 2¢/word.** Sometimes pays expenses of writers on assignment.

Reprints: Accepts previously published submissions.

Photos: State availability with submission. Reviews 3×5 prints, GIF/JPEG files. Buys one-time rights. Offers no additional payment for photos accepted with ms. Model releases required.

Columns/Departments: Actress feature (film actress interviews), 2,500 words; Author feature (book author interviews), 1,500 words; Music feature (singer or band interviews), 1,500 words. **Buys 50 mss/year.** Query. **Pays 2¢/word.**

Fiction: Adventure, erotica, experimental, fantasy, historical, horror, humorous, mainstream, mystery, science fiction, suspense, western. No romance. **Buys 12 mss/year.** Send complete ms. Length: 1,000-3,000 words. **Pays 1¢/word plus contributor copies.**

Tips: "Submit material typed and free of errors. Writers should think of magazines like *Maxim* and *Details* when determining article ideas for our magazine. Our primary readership is adult males and we are seeking original and unique articles."

$ $ $ HEARTLAND USA, UST Publishing, 100 W. Putnam Ave., Greenwich CT 06830-5316. (203)622-3456. Fax: (203)863-7296. E-mail: husaedit@att.net. **Contact:** Brad Pearson, editor. **95% freelance written.** Bimonthly magazine for working men. "*HUSA* is a general interest lifestyle magazine for adult males—active outdoorsmen. The editorial mix includes hunting, fishing, sports, automotive, how-to, country music, human interest and wildlife." Estab. 1991. Circ. 901,000. **Pays on acceptance.** Byline given. Offers 20% kill fee. Buys first North American serial, second serial (reprint) rights. Submit seasonal material 1 year in advance. Accepts queries by mail, e-mail, fax. Accepts previously published material. Accepts simultaneous submissions. Responds in 1 month to queries. Sample copy for free. Writer's guidelines for #10 SASE.

Nonfiction: Book excerpts, general interest, historical/nostalgic, how-to, humor, inspirational, interview/profile, new product, personal experience, photo feature, technical, travel. "No fiction or dry expository pieces." **Buys 30 mss/year.** Query with or without published clips or send complete ms. Length: 350-1,200 words. **Pays 50-80¢/word for assigned articles; 25-80¢/word for unsolicited articles.** Sometimes pays expenses of writers on assignment.

Reprints: Send photocopy and information about when and where the material previously appeared. Pays 25% of amount paid for an original article.

Photos: Send photos with submission. Reviews transparencies. Buys one-time rights. Identification of subjects required.

Tips: "Features with the possibility of strong photographic support are open to freelancers, as are our departments. We look for a relaxed, jocular, easy-to-read style, and look favorably on the liberal use of anecdote or interesting quotations. Our average reader sees himself as hardworking, traditional, rugged, confident, uncompromising, and daring."

$ $ HOUSE OF ROSES, Universal Entertainment for Men, House of Roses, Inc., P.O. Box 93759, Los Angeles CA 90093. (323)930-4770. Fax: (323)930-4771. E-mail: branyon@houseofroses.com. Website: www.houseofroses.com. Managing Editor: Brandon Thomas. **Contact:** Branyon Davis, executive editor. **50% freelance written.** Bimonthly magazine covering all things that interest young males, including but not limited to gadgets, music, sports, money, brew, movies, gear, and women. Writing must be cutting edge, humorous, irreverent, and interesting. Estab. 2001. Circ. 500,000. Pays on publication. Publishes ms an average of 2 months after acceptance. Byline sometimes given. Buys first, second serial (reprint) rights. Editorial lead time 2 months. Submit seasonal material 4 months in advance. Accepts queries by mail, e-mail. Accepts previously published material. Accepts simultaneous submissions. Responds in 2 weeks to queries. Writer's guidelines by e-mail.

Nonfiction: Exposé, general interest, how-to, humor, interview/profile. Does not want to see lengthy, rambling, personally relevant stories with no clear audience. **Buys 100 mss/year.** Query with published clips. Length: 200-1,000 words. **Pays $50-200 for assigned articles; $50-100 for unsolicited articles.** Sometimes pays expenses of writers on assignment.

Photos: State availability with submission. Reviews contact sheets. Negotiates payment individually.

Fillers: Facts, gags to be illustrated by cartoonist, short humor. **Buys 60/year.** Length: 20-150 words. **Pays $20-50.**

Tips: "Be professional, funny, interesting, and off-the-wall."

$ $ $ $ THE INTERNATIONAL, The Magazine of Adventure and Pleasure for Men, Tomorrow Enterprises, 2228 E. 20th St., Oakland CA 94606. (510)532-6501. Fax: (510)536-5886. E-mail: tonyattomr@aol.com. **Contact:** Mr. Anthony L. Williams, managing editor. **70% freelance written.** Monthly magazine covering "bush and seaplane flying, seafaring, pleasure touring, etc. with adventure stories from all men who travel on sexual tours to Asia, Latin America, The Caribbean, and the Pacific." Estab. 1997. Circ. 5,000. Pays on publication. Publishes ms an average of 2 months after acceptance. Buys first rights. Editorial lead time 2 months. Submit seasonal material 3 months in advance. Accepts queries by mail, e-mail. Accepts simultaneous submissions. Responds in 2 weeks to queries; 2 months to mss. Writer's guidelines free.

Nonfiction: Seafaring storis of all types published with photos. Military and veteran stories also sought as well as expats living abroad. Especially interested in airplane flying stories with photos. Exposé, general interest, historical/nostalgic, humor, interview/profile, opinion, personal experience, photo feature, travel. No pornography, no family or "honeymoon" type travel. **Buys 40-50 mss/year.** Send complete ms. Length: 700 words maximum. **Pays $100-2,000 for assigned articles; $25-1,000 for unsolicited articles.** Sometimes pays expenses of writers on assignment.

Photos: Send photos with submission. Reviews negatives, 3×5 prints. Buys one-time or all rights. Offers no additional payment for photos accepted with ms. Identification of subjects required.

Columns/Departments: Asia/Pacific Beat; Latin America/Caribbean Beat (Nightlife, Adventure, Air & Sea), 450 words; Lifestyles Abroad (Expatriate Men's Doings Overseas), 600-1,000 words. **Buys 25 mss/year.** Send complete ms. **Pays $25-1,000.**

Fillers: Anecdotes, facts, gags to be illustrated by cartoonist, newsbreaks, short humor. **Buys 25/year.** Length: 200-600 words. **Pays $25-100.**

Tips: "If a single male lives in those parts of the world covered, and is either a pleasure tourist, pilot or seafarer, we are interested in his submissions. He can visit our upcoming website or contact us directly. Stories from female escorts or party girls are also welcomed."

$ $ $ MEN'S JOURNAL, Wenner Media, Inc., 1290 Avenue of the Americas, New York NY 10104-0298. (212)484-1616. Fax: (212)767-8213. Website: www.mensjournal.com. Editor: Sid Evans. **Contact:** Sarah Griffin, assistant editor. Magazine published 10 times/year covering general lifestyle for men, ages 25-49. "*Men's Journal* is for active men with an interest in participatory sports, travel, fitness, and adventure. It provides practical, informative articles on how to spend quality leisure time." Estab. 1992. Circ. 550,000. Accepts queries by mail, fax.

- *Men's Journal* won the National magazine Award for Personal Service.

Nonfiction: Features and profiles 2,000-7,000 words; shorter features of 400-1,200 words; equipment and fitness stories, 400-1,800 words. Book excerpts, essays, exposé, general interest, historical/nostalgic, how-to, humor, new product, personal experience, photo feature, travel. Query with SASE. **Payment varies.**

$ ▣ SHARPMAN.COM, The Ultimate Guide's to Men's Living, SharpMan Media LLC, 11718 Barrington Court, No. 702, Los Angeles CA 90049-2930. (310)446-7915. Fax: (310)446-7965. E-mail: EMF@SharpMan.com. Website: www.sharpman.com. Editor: Y.M. Reiss. **Contact:** Elizabeth Felicetti, managing editor. **50% freelance written.** Weekly online. "*SharpMan.com* is an online community for professional men, ages 18-35. The *SharpMan.com* magazine is designed to be 'the Ultimate Men's Guide to SharpLiving.' In articles on wardrobe, work, grooming, dating, health, toys, and more, *SharpMan.com* attempts to provide meaningful instruction on where to go, what to do, how to dress, and what to buy." Estab. 1998. Circ. approximately 60,000. Pays on publication. Byline given. Buys all rights. exclusive rights to version posted (negotiable on excerpts from existing ms published for promotional purposes) Editorial lead time 2 months. Submit seasonal material 4 months in advance. Accepts queries by e-mail. Responds in 1 month to queries; 2 months to mss. Sample copy online. Writer's guidelines by e-mail.

Nonfiction: *Sharpman.com* frequently features writers who publish for the purpose of gaining professional recognition or promotion for published mss and other services. Where a writer seeks to promote a product, remuneration is provided by way of a link to their desired URL, in lieu of cash. Men's interest: SharpDating, SharpWork, SharpTravel, SharpHealth, SharpGrooming, SharpToys (all in "how-to" form). Book excerpts, exposé, how-to, interview/profile, new product, technical, travel. **Buys 100 mss/year.** Query with published clips. Length: 600-2,000 words. **Pays $50.** Sometimes pays expenses of writers on assignment. Accepts submissions in a modified form with SharpMan Media, LLC retaining rights to modified product.

Photos: "Must be a 'legal' use of the photo provided." State availability with submission. Negotiates payment individually. Captions, identification of subjects, model releases required.

Columns/Departments: SharpTravel (for business and leisure travelers); SharpWork (oriented towards young professionals); and SharpDating (slanted towards men in their 20s-30s), all 600-2,000 words; SharpToys, 300-1,500 words; SharpHealth, 600-1,500 words; and SharpGrooming. We also publish a "Tip of the Week," generally 100-300 words. **Buys 100 mss/year.** Query with published clips. **Pays $50.**

Fillers: Facts. Length: 25-100 words. **Pays $5.**

Tips: "Familiarize yourself with our magazine's topics and tone. We write for a very specific audience. The Editorial Team prefers content written in the 'SharpMan Tone,' a fast, male-oriented tone that provides specific information on the subject at hand. Ideally, each article features 'top tips' or step-by-step 'how-to' language delivering specific information that can be easily and immediately implemented by the reader. *SharpMan.com* content is nonerotic in nature, and articles may not include any inappropriate language."

$ $ $ SMOKE MAGAZINE, Life's Burning Desires, Lockwood Publications, 26 Broadway, Floor 9M, New York NY 10004. (212)391-2060. Fax: (212)827-0945. E-mail: editor@smokemag.com. Website: www.smokemag.com. Senior Editor: Mark Bernardo. **Contact:** Alyson Boxman Levine, editor-in-chief. **75% freelance written.** Quarterly magazine covering cigars and men's lifestyle issues. "A large majority of *Smoke's* readers are affluent men, ages 28-50; active, educated, and adventurous." Estab. 1995. Circ. 175,000. Pays 2 months after publication. Publishes ms an average of 3 months after acceptance. Byline given. Offers 25% kill fee. Buys first rights. Editorial lead time 2 months. Submit seasonal material 6 months in advance. Accepts queries by mail, e-mail. Accepts simultaneous submissions. Responds in 6 weeks to queries; 3 months to mss. Sample copy for $4.99.

O‑ Break in with "good nonfiction that interests guys—beer, cuisine, true-crime, sports, cigars, of course. Be original."

Nonfiction: Essays, exposé, general interest, historical/nostalgic, how-to, humor, interview/profile, opinion, personal experience, photo feature, technical, travel, true crime. **Buys 25 mss/year.** Query with published clips. Length: 1,500-3,000 words. **Pays $500-1,500.** Sometimes pays expenses of writers on assignment.

Photos: State availability with submission. Reviews 2¼×2¼ transparencies. Negotiates payment individually. Identification of subjects required.

Columns/Departments: Smoke Undercover, Smoke Slant (humor); What Lew Says (cigar industry news); Workin' Stiffs (world's best jobs), all 1,500 words. **Buys 20 mss/year.** Query with published clips. **Pays $500-1,500.**

Fillers: Anecdotes, facts, gags to be illustrated by cartoonist, newsbreaks, short humor. **Buys 12 fillers/year.** Length: 200-500 words. **Pays $200-500.**

The online magazine carries original content not found in the print edition.

Tips: "Send a short, clear query with clips. Go with your field of expertise: cigars, sports, music, true crime, etc."

$ $ UMM (URBAN MALE MAGAZINE), Canada's Only Lifestyle and Fashion Magazine for Men, UMM Publishing Inc., 6 Antares Dr., Phase 1, Unit 7, Nepean Ontario K2E 8A9, Canada. (613)723-6216. E-mail: editor@umm.ca. Website: www.umm.ca. Editor: Abbis Mahmoud. **Contact:** David Sachs, senior editor. **100% freelance written.** Bimonthly magazine covering men's interests. "Our audience is young men, aged 18-24. We focus on Canadian activities, interests, and lifestyle issues. Our magazine is fresh and energetic and we look for original ideas carried out with a spark of intelligence and/or humour (and you'd better spell humour with a 'u')." Estab. 1998. Circ. 90,000. Pays 1 month after publication. Publishes ms an average of 3 months after acceptance. Byline given. Buys first North American serial rights. Editorial lead time 3 months. Submit seasonal material 4 months in advance. Accepts queries by e-mail. Accepts simultaneous submissions. Responds in 6 weeks to queries; 6 weeks to mss.

Nonfiction: Book excerpts, exposé, general interest, historical/nostalgic, how-to, humor, interview/profile, new product, personal experience, travel, adventure; cultural; sports; music. **Buys 80 mss/year.** Query with published clips. Length: 1,200-3,500 words. **Pays $100-400.** Sometimes pays expenses of writers on assignment.

Photos: State availability with submission. Reviews contact sheets, prints. Buys one-time rights. Negotiates payment individually.

Fillers: Anecdotes, facts, short humor. **Buys 35/year.** Length: 100-500 words. **Pays $50-150.**

Tips: "Be familiar with our magazine before querying. We deal with all subjects of interest to young men, especially those with Canadian themes. We are very open-minded. Original ideas and catchy writing are key."

MILITARY

These publications emphasize military or paramilitary subjects or other aspects of military life. Technical and semitechnical publications for military commanders, personnel, and planners, as well as those for military families and civilians interested in Armed Forces activities are listed here. Publications covering military history can be found in the History section.

N **$ $ AIR FORCE TIMES**, Army Times Publishing Co., 6883 Commercial Dr., Springfield VA 22159. (703)750-8646. Fax: (703)750-8601. Website: www.airforcetimes.com. **Contact:** Lance Bacon, managing editor. Weeklies edited separately for Army, Navy, Marine Corps, and Air Force military personnel and their families. They contain career information such as pay raises, promotions, news of legislation affecting the military, housing, base activities, and features of interest to military people. Estab. 1940. **Pays on acceptance.** Byline given. Offers kill fee. Buys first rights. Accepts queries by mail, e-mail, phone. Accepts simultaneous submissions. Responds in 1 month to queries. Sample copy for #10 SASE. Writer's guidelines for #10 SASE.

Nonfiction: Features of interest to career military personnel and their families. No advice pieces. **Buys 150-175 mss/year.** Query. Length: 750-2,000 words. **Pays $100-500.**
Columns/Departments: Length: 500-900. **Buys 75 mss/year. Pays $75-125.**

The online magazines carry original content not found in the print editions. Websites: www.armytimes.com; www.navytimes.com; www.airforcetimes.com; www.marinecorpstimes.com. Contact: Neff Hudson, online editor.

Tips: Looking for "stories on active duty, reserve and retired military personnel; stories on military matters and localized military issues; stories on successful civilian careers after military service."

$ $ ARMY MAGAZINE, 2425 Wilson Blvd., Arlington VA 22201-3385. (703)841-4300. Fax: (703)841-3505. E-mail: armymag@ausa.org. Website: www.ausa.org. **Contact:** Mary Blake French, editor. **70% freelance written.** Prefers to work with published/established writers. Monthly magazine emphasizing military interests. Estab. 1904. Circ. 90,000. Pays on publication. Publishes ms an average of 5 months after acceptance. Byline given. Buys all rights. Submit seasonal material 3 months in advance. Accepts queries by mail. Sample copy for 9×12 SAE with $1 postage or online. Writer's guidelines for 9×12 SAE with $1 postage or online.

• *Army Magazine* looks for shorter articles.

Nonfiction: "We would like to see more pieces about little-known episodes involving interesting military personalities. We especially want material lending itself to heavy, contributor-supplied photographic treatment. The first thing a contributor should recognize is that our readership is very savvy militarily. 'Gee-whiz' personal reminiscences get short shrift, unless they hold their own in a company in which long military service, heroism and unusual experiences are commonplace. At the same time, *Army* readers like a well-written story with a fresh slant, whether it is about an experience in a foxhole or the fortunes of a corps in battle." Historical/nostalgic (military and original), humor (military feature-length articles and anecdotes), interview/profile, new product, personal experience (dealing especially with the most recent conflicts in which the US Army has been involved: Desert Storm, Panama, Grenada), photo feature, technical. No rehashed history. No unsolicited book reviews. **Buys 8 mss/year.** Submit complete ms (hard copy and disk). Length: 1,000-1,500 words. **Pays 12-18¢/word.**
Photos: Send photos with submission. Reviews transparencies, prints, slides. Buys all rights. Pays $50-100 for 8×10 b&w glossy prints; $50-350 for 8×10 color glossy prints or 2¼ × 2¼ transparencies; will also accept 35mm. Captions required.
Columns/Departments: Military news, books, comment (*New Yorker*-type "Talk of the Town" items). **Pays $40-150.**

$ $ ARMY TIMES, Times News Group, Inc., 6883 Commercial Dr., Springfield VA 22159. (703)750-9000. Fax: (703)750-8622. E-mail: features@atpco.com. Website: www.armytimes.com. **Contact:** Chuck Vinch, managing editor. Weekly for Army military personnel and their families containing career information such as pay raises, promotions, news of legislation affecting the military, housing, base activities and features of interest to military people. Estab. 1940. Circ. 230,000. **Pays on acceptance.** Byline given. Offers kill fee. Makes work-for-hire assignments. Accepts queries by mail, e-mail. Accepts simultaneous submissions. Responds in 1 month to queries. Sample copy and writer's guidelines for #10 SASE.

Break in by "proposing specific feature stories that only you can write—things we wouldn't be able to get from 'generic' syndicated or wire material. The story must contain an element of mystery and/or surprise, and be entertaining as well as informative. Above all, your story must have a direct connection to military people's needs and interests."

Nonfiction: Features of interest to career military personnel and their families: food, relationships, parenting, education, retirement, shelter, health, and fitness, sports, personal appearance, community, recreation, personal finance, entertainment. No advice please. **Buys 150-175 mss/year.** Query. Length: 750-2,000 words. **Pays $100-500.**
Columns/Departments: Length: 500-900 words. **Buys 75 mss/year. Pays $75-125.**

The online magazines carry original content not found in the print editions. Contact: Kent Miller, online editor.

Tips: Looking for "stories on active duty, reserve and retired military personnel; stories on military matters and localized military issues; stories on successful civilian careers after military service."

N **$ $ $ MARINE CORPS TIMES**, Army Times Publishing Co., 6883 Commercial Dr., Springfield VA 22159. (703)750-9000. Fax: (703)750-8767. E-mail: marinelet@atpco.com. Website: www.marinecorpstimes.com. **Contact:** Chris Lawson, managing editor, *Army Times*; Alex Neil, managing editor, *Navy Times*; Julie Bird, managing editor, *Air Force Times*; Rob Colenso, managing editor, *Marine Corps Times*. Weeklies edited separately for Army, Navy, Marine Corps, and Air Force military personnel and their families. They contain career information such as pay raises, promotions, news of legislation affecting the military, housing, base activities and features of interest to military people. Estab. 1940. Circ. 230,000 (combined). Pays on publication. Byline given. Offers kill fee. Buys first rights. Accepts queries by mail, e-mail, phone. Accepts simultaneous submissions. Responds in 1 month to queries. Sample copy for #10 SASE. Writer's guidelines for #10 SASE.

Nonfiction: Features of interest to career military personnel and their families, including stories on current military operations and exercises. No advice pieces. **Buys 150-175 mss/year.** Query. Length: 750-2,000 words. **Pays $100-500.**
Columns/Departments: Length: 500-900 words. **Buys 75 mss/year. Pays $75-125.**

The online magazines carry original content not found in the print editions. Websites: www.armytimes.com; www.navytimes.com; www.airforcetimes.com. Contact: Kent Miller, online editor.

Tips: Looking for "stories on active duty, reserve and retired military personnel; stories on military matters and localized military issues; stories on successful civilian careers after military service."

$ $ MILITARY TIMES, Times News Group, Inc. (subsidiary of Gannett Corp.), 6883 Commercial Dr., Springfield VA 22159. Fax: (703)750-8781. E-mail: features@atpco.com. Website: www.militarycity.com. Managing Editor: David Craig. **Contact:** G.E. Willis, features editor. **25% freelance written.** Weekly tabloid covering lifestyle topics for active, retired and reserve military members and their families. "Features need to have real military people in them, and appeal to readers in all the armed services. Our target audience is 90% male, young, fit and adventurous, mostly married and often with young children. They move frequently. Writer queries should approach ideas with those demographics and facts firmly in mind." Circ. 300,000. **Pays on acceptance.** Publishes ms an average of 2 months after acceptance. Byline given. Offers 25% kill fee. Buys first, electronic rights. Editorial lead time 2 months. Submit seasonal material 3 months in advance. Accepts queries by mail, e-mail, fax. Accepts simultaneous submissions. Responds in 6 weeks to queries. Sample copy for $2.25 or online. Writer's guidelines for SAE with 1 first-class stamp or by e-mail.

O→ "Greatest need is in the adventure categories of sports, recreation, outdoor, personal fitness and running. Personal finance features are especially needed, but they must be specifically tailored to our military audience's needs and interests."

Nonfiction: Book excerpts, how-to, interview/profile, new product, photo feature, technical, travel, Sports, recreation, entertainment, health, personal fitness, self-image (fashion, trends), relationships, personal finance, food. "No poems, war memoirs or nostalgia, fiction, travel pieces that are too upscale (luxury cruises) or too focused on military monuments/museums." **Buys 110 mss/year.** Query with published clips. Length: 300-1,500 words. **Pays $100-500.** Sometimes pays expenses of writers on assignment.

Photos: State availability with submission. Reviews transparencies. Offers work-for-hire. Offers $75/photo. Captions, identification of subjects required.

Columns/Departments: Slices of Life (human-interest shorts), 300 words; Running (how-to for experienced runners, tips, techniques, problem-solving), 500 words; Personal Fitness (how-to, tips, techniques for working out, improving fitness), 500 words. **Buys 40 mss/year.** Query. **Pays $100-200.**

Tips: "Our *Lifelines* section appears every week with a variety of services, information and entertainment articles on topics that relate to readers' off-duty lives; or to personal dimensions of their on-duty lives. Topics include food, relationships, parenting, education, retirement, shelter, health and fitness, sports, personal appearances, community, recreation, personal finance and entertainment. We are looking for articles about military life, its problems and how to handle them, as well as interesting things people are doing, on the job and in their leisure. Keep in mind that our readers come from all of the military services. For instance, a story can focus on an Army family, but may need to include families or sources from other services as well. The editorial 'voice' of the section is familiar and conversational; good-humored without being flippant; sincere without being sentimental; savvy about military life but in a relevant and subtle way, never forgetting that our readers are individuals first, spouses or parents or children second, and service members third."

N $ $ NAVAL HISTORY, US Naval Institute, 291 Wood Rd., Annapolis MD 21402-5034. (410)295-1079. Fax: (410)295-1049. E-mail: fschultz@usni.org. Website: www.navalinstitute.org. Associate Editors: Colin Babb and Giles Roblyer. **Contact:** Fred L. Schultz, editor-in-chief. **90% freelance written.** Bimonthly magazine covering naval and maritime history, worldwide. "We are committed, as a publication of the 127-year-old US Naval Institute, to presenting the best and most accurate short works in international naval and maritime history. We do find a place for academicians, but they should be advised that a good story generally wins against a dull topic, no matter how well researched." Estab. 1988. Circ. 40,000. **Pays on acceptance.** Publishes ms an average of 2 years after acceptance. Byline given. Buys all rights. Editorial lead time 6 months. Submit seasonal material 6 months in advance. Accepts queries by mail, e-mail, fax, phone. Responds in 1 month to queries; 2 months to mss. Sample copy for $3.95 and SASE, or on website. Writer's guidelines for #10 SASE or on website.

Nonfiction: Book excerpts, essays, historical/nostalgic, humor, inspirational, interview/profile, personal experience, photo feature, technical. **Buys 50 mss/year.** Query. Length: 1,000-3,000 words. **Pays $300-500 for assigned articles; $75-400 for unsolicited articles.**

Photos: State availability with submission. Reviews contact sheets, transparencies, 4×6 or larger prints, and digital submissions or CD-ROM. Buys one-time rights. Offers $10 minimum. Captions, identification of subjects, model releases required.

Fillers: Anecdotes, newsbreaks (naval-related), short humor. **Buys 40-50/year.** Length: 50-1,000 words. **Pays $10-50.**

Tips: "A good way to break in is to write a good, concise, exciting story supported by primary sources and substantial illustrations. Naval history-related news items (ship decommissionings, underwater archaeology, etc.) are also welcome. Because our story bank is substantial, competition is severe. Tying a topic to an anniversary many times is an advantage. We still are in need of Korean and Vietnam War-era material."

$ $ NAVY TIMES, Army Times Publishing Co., 6883 Commercial Dr., Springfield VA 22159. (703)750-8636. Fax: (703)750-8767. E-mail: navylet@atpco.com. Website: www.navytimes.com. **Contact:** Keely Goss, assistant editor. Weekly newspaper covering sea services. News and features of men and women in the Navy, Coast Guard and Marine Corps. Estab. 1950. Circ. 90,000. Pays on publication. Byline given. Buys all rights. Submit seasonal material 2 months in advance. Accepts previously published material. Writer's guidelines free.

Nonfiction: Historical/nostalgic, opinion, news, features. **Buys 100 mss/year.** Query. Length: 500-1,000 words. **Payment negotiable.**

Reprints: Send tearsheet.

$ PARAMETERS, U.S. Army War College Quarterly, US Army War College, 122 Forbes Ave., Carlisle PA 17013-5238. (717)245-4943. E-mail: parameters@awc.carlisle.army.mil. Website: www.carlisle.army.mil/usawc/parameters. **Contact:** Col. Robert H. Taylor, USA Ret., editor. **100% freelance written.** Prefers to work with published/established writers or experts in the field. Readership consists of senior leaders of US defense establishment, both uniformed and civilian, plus members of the media, government, industry and academia. Subjects include national and international security affairs, military strategy, military leadership and management, art and science of warfare, and military history with contemporary relevance. Estab. 1971. Circ. 13,500. Pays on publication. Publishes ms an average of 6 months after acceptance. Byline given. Buys first North American serial rights. Accepts queries by mail, e-mail, phone. Responds in 6 weeks to queries. Sample copy and writer's guidelines free or online.

Nonfiction: Prefers articles that deal with current security issues, employ critical analysis and provide solutions or recommendations. Liveliness and verve, consistent with scholarly integrity, appreciated. Theses, studies and academic course papers should be adapted to article form prior to submission. Documentation in complete endnotes. Send complete ms. Length: 4,500 words average. **Pays $150 average.**

Tips: "Make it short; keep it interesting; get criticism and revise accordingly. Write on a contemporary topic. Tackle a subject only if you are an authority. No fax submissions." Encourage e-mail submissions.

$ $ PROCEEDINGS, U.S. Naval Institute, 291 Wood Rd., Annapolis MD 21402-5034. (410)268-6110. Fax: (410)295-1049. Website: www.usni.org. Editor: Fred H. Rainbow. **Contact:** Gordon Keiser, senior editor. **80% freelance written.** Monthly magazine covering Navy, Marine Corps, Coast Guard issues. Estab. 1873. Circ. 100,000. **Pays on acceptance.** Publishes ms an average of 9 months after acceptance. Byline given. Buys all rights. Editorial lead time 3 months. Responds in 2 months to queries. Sample copy for $3.95. Writer's guidelines free.

Nonfiction: Essays, historical/nostalgic, interview/profile, photo feature, technical. **Buys 100-125 mss/year.** Query with or without published clips or send complete ms. Length: 3,000 words. **Pays $60-150/printed page for unsolicited articles.**

Photos: State availability of or send photos with submission. Reviews transparencies, prints. Buys one-time rights. Offers $25/photo maximum.

Columns/Departments: Comment & Discussion (letters to editor), 750 words; Commentary (opinion), 900 words; Nobody Asked Me, But... (opinion), less than 1,000 words. **Buys 150-200 mss/year.** Query or send complete ms. **Pays $34-150.**

Fillers: Anecdotes. **Buys 20/year.** Length: 100 words. **Pays $25.**

$ $ $ $ THE RETIRED OFFICER MAGAZINE, 201 N. Washington St., Alexandria VA 22314-2539. (800)245-8762. Fax: (703)838-8179. E-mail: editor@troa.org. Website: www.troa.org. Editor: Col. Warren S. Lacy, USA-Ret. Managing Editor: Molly Wyman. **Contact:** Molly Wyman. **60% freelance written.** Prefers to work with published/established writers. Monthly magazine for officers of the seven uniformed services and their families. "*The Retired Officer Magazine* covers topics such as current military/political affairs, military history, travel, finance, hobbies, health and fitness, and military family and retirement lifestyles." Estab. 1945. Circ. 389,000. **Pays on acceptance.** Publishes ms an average of 1 year after acceptance. Byline given. Buys first North American serial rights. Accepts queries by mail, e-mail, fax. Responds in 3 months to queries. Sample copy and writer's guidelines for 9×12 SAE with 6 first-class stamps or online.

Nonfiction: Current military/political affairs, health and wellness, recent military history, travel, military family lifestyle. Emphasis now on current military and defense issues. "We rarely accept unsolicited manuscripts." **Buys 48 mss/year.** Query with résumé, sample clips and SASE. Length: 800-2,500 words. **Pays up to $1,700.**

Photos: Query with list of stock photo subjects. Original slides and transparencies must be suitable for color separation. Reviews transparencies. Pays $20 for each 8×10 b&w photo (normal halftone) used. Pays $75-250 for inside color; $300 for cover.

The online magazine carries original content not found in the print edition and includes writer's guidelines. Contact: Ronda Reid, online editor.

$ $ $ $ SOLDIER OF FORTUNE, The Journal of Professional Adventurers, Omega Group, Ltd., 5735 Arapahoe Ave., Suite A-5, Boulder CO 80306-0693. (303)449-3750. Fax: (303)444-5617. E-mail: editor@sofmag.com. Website: www.sofmag.com. Managing Editor: Dwight Swift. Deputy Editor: Tom Reisinger. **Contact:** Marty Kufus, assistant editor. **50% freelance written.** Monthly magazine covering military, paramilitary, police, combat subjects and action/adventure. "We are an action-oriented magazine; we cover combat hot spots around the world. We also provide timely features on state-of-the-art weapons and equipment; elite military and police units; and historical military operations. Readership is primarily active-duty military, veterans and law enforcement." Estab. 1975. Circ. 175,000. Byline given. Offers 25% kill fee. Buys all rights; will negotiate Submit seasonal material 5 months in advance. Responds in 3 weeks to queries; 1 month to mss. Sample copy for $5. Writer's guidelines for #10 SASE.

Nonfiction: Exposé, general interest, historical/nostalgic, how-to (on weapons and their skilled use), humor, interview/profile, new product, personal experience, photo feature (number one on our list), technical, travel, novel excerpts; combat reports; military unit reports and solid Vietnam and Operation Desert Storm articles. "No 'How I won the war' pieces; no op-ed pieces unless they are fully and factually backgrounded; no knife articles (staff assignments only). All

submitted articles should have good art; art will sell us on an article." **Buys 75 mss/year.** Query with or without published clips or send complete ms. Send mss to articles editor; queries to managing editor. Length: 2,000-3,000 words. **Pays $150-250/page.** Sometimes pays expenses of writers on assignment.
Reprints: Send disk copy, photocopy of article and information about when and where the material previously appeared. Pays 25% of amount paid for an original article.
Photos: Send photos with submission. Reviews contact sheets, transparencies. Buys one-time rights. Pays $500 for cover photo. Captions, identification of subjects required.
Columns/Departments: Combat craft (how-to military and police survival skils); I Was There (first-person account of the arcane or unusual based in a combat or law-enforcement environment), both 600-800 words. **Buys 16 mss/year.** Send complete ms. **Pays $150.**
Fillers: Bulletin Board editor. Newsbreaks (military/paramilitary related has to be documented). Length: 100-250 words. **Pays $50.**
Tips: "Submit a professionally prepared, complete package. All artwork with cutlines, double-spaced typed manuscript with 5.25 or 3.5 IBM-compatible disk, if available, cover letter including synopsis of article, supporting documentation where applicable, etc. Manuscript must be factual; writers have to do their homework and get all their facts straight. One error means rejection. We will work with authors over the phone or by letter, tell them if their ideas have merit for an acceptable article, and help them fine-tune their work. I Was There is a good place for freelancers to start. Vietnam features, if carefully researched and art heavy, will always get a careful look. Combat reports, again, with good art, are number one in our book and stand the best chance of being accepted. Military unit reports from around the world are well received as are law-enforcement articles (units, police in action). If you write for us, be complete and factual; pros read *Soldier of Fortune*, and are very quick to let us know if we (and the author) err."

MUSIC

Music fans follow the latest industry news in these publications that range from opera to hip hop. Types of music and musicians or specific instruments are the sole focus of some magazines. Publications geared to the music industry and professionals can be found in the Trade Music section. Additional music and dance markets are found in the Contemporary Culture and Entertainment sections.

$ $ AMERICAN RECORD GUIDE, Record Guide Productions, 4412 Braddock St., Cincinnati OH 45204. (513)941-1116. E-mail: rightstar@aol.com. **Contact:** Donald Vroon, editor. **90% freelance written.** Bimonthly 6×9 book covering classical music for music lovers and record collectors. Estab. 1935. Circ. 10,000. Pays on publication. Publishes ms an average of 2 months after acceptance. Byline given. Buys all rights. Editorial lead time 2 months. Accepts queries by mail, e-mail. Accepts previously published material. Accepts simultaneous submissions. Sample copy for $7. Writer's guidelines free.
Nonfiction: Essays. **Buys 30-45 full-length mss and hundreds of reviews mss/year.** Query. **Pays $50-350 for assigned articles; $50-150 for unsolicited articles.**

$ AMERICAN SONGWRITER MAGAZINE, 1009 17th Ave. S., Nashville TN 37212-2201. (615)321-6096. Fax: (615)321-6097. E-mail: info@AmericanSongwriter.com. Website: www.AmericanSongwriter.com. Managing Editor: Lou Heffernan. **Contact:** Vernell Hackett, editor. **30% freelance written.** Bimonthly magazine about songwriters and the craft of songwriting for many types of music, including pop, country, rock, metal, jazz, gospel, and r&b. Estab. 1984. Circ. 5,000. Pays on publication. Publishes ms an average of 2 months after acceptance. Offers 25% kill fee. Buys first North American serial rights. Accepts previously published material. Responds in 2 months to queries. Sample copy for $4. Writer's guidelines for #10 SASE.
Nonfiction: General interest, interview/profile, new product, technical, home demo studios, movie and TV scores, performance rights organizations. **Buys 20 mss/year.** Query with published clips. Length: 300-1,200 words. **Pays $25-60.**
Reprints: Send tearsheet or photocopy and information about when and where the material previously appeared. Pays same amount as paid for an original article.
Photos: Send photos with submission. Reviews 3×5 prints. Buys one-time rights. Offers no additional payment for photos accepeted with ms. Identification of subjects required.
Tips: "*American Songwriter* strives to present articles which can be read a year or two after they were written and still be pertinent to the songwriter reading them."

$ $ BLUEGRASS UNLIMITED, Bluegrass Unlimited, Inc., P.O. Box 771, Warrenton VA 20188-0771. (540)349-8181 or (800)BLU-GRAS. Fax: (540)341-0011. E-mail: editor@bluegrassmusic.com. Website: www.bluegrassmusic.com. Editor: Peter V. Kuykendall. **Contact:** Sharon Watts, managing editor. **60% freelance written.** Prefers to work with published/established writers. Monthly magazine covering bluegrass, acoustic, and old-time country music. Estab. 1966. Circ. 27,000. Pays on publication. Publishes ms an average of 4 months after acceptance. Byline given. Offers negotiated kill fee. Buys first North American serial, one-time, second serial (reprint), all rights. Submit seasonal material 4 months in advance. Accepts queries by mail, e-mail, fax. Responds in 2 weeks to queries; 2 months to mss. Sample copy for free. Writer's guidelines for #10 SASE.

Nonfiction: General interest, historical/nostalgic, how-to, interview/profile, personal experience, photo feature, travel. No "fan"-style articles. **Buys 60-70 mss/year.** Query with or without published clips. Length: Open. **Pays 8-10¢/word.**
Reprints: Send photocopy with rights for sale noted and information about when and where the material previously appeared. Payment is negotiable.
Photos: State availability of or send photos with submission. Reviews 35mm transparencies and 3×5, 5×7 and 8×10 b&w and color prints. Buys all rights. Pays $50-175 for transparencies; $25-60 for b&w prints; $50-250 for color prints. Identification of subjects required.
Fiction: Ethnic, humorous. **Buys 3-5 mss/year.** Query. Length: Negotiable. **Pays 8-10¢/word.**
Tips: "We would prefer that articles be informational, based on personal experience or an interview with lots of quotes from subject, profile, humor, etc."

$ $ CHAMBER MUSIC, Chamber Music America, 305 Seventh Ave., New York NY 10001-6008. (212)242-2022. Fax: (212)242-7955. E-mail: kkrenz@chamber-music.org. Website: www.chamber-music.org/magazine. **Contact:** Karissa Krenz, editor. Bimonthly magazine covering chamber music. Estab. 1977. Circ. 13,000. Pays on publication. Publishes ms an average of 5 months after acceptance. Byline given. Offers kill fee. Buys first rights. Editorial lead time 4 months. Accepts queries by mail, phone.
Nonfiction: Book excerpts, essays, humor, opinion, personal experience, issue-oriented stories of relevance to the chamber music fields written by top music journalists and critics, or music practitioners. No artist profiles, no stories about opera or symphonic work. **Buys 35 mss/year.** Query with published clips. Length: 2,500-3,500 words. **Pays $500 minimum.** Sometimes pays expenses of writers on assignment.
Photos: State availability with submission. Offers no payment for photos accepted with ms.

$ $ $ $ ✪ GUITAR ONE, The Magazine You Can Play, 6 E. 32nd St., 11th Floor, New York NY 10016. Fax: (212)251-0840. E-mail: editors@guitaronemag.com. Website: www.guitaronemag.com. **Contact:** Troy Nelson, editor-in-chief. **75% freelance written.** Monthly magazine covering guitar news, artists, music, gear. Estab. 1996. Circ. 140,000. Pays on publication. Publishes ms an average of 1 month after acceptance. Byline given. Offers 50% kill fee. Buys one-time rights. Editorial lead time 3 months. Accepts queries by mail, e-mail, fax. Accepts simultaneous submissions. Sample copy online.
Nonfiction: Interview/profile (with guitarists). **Buys 15 mss/year.** Query with published clips. Length: 2,000-5,000 words. **Pays $300-1,200 for assigned articles; $150-800 for unsolicited articles.** Sometimes pays expenses of writers on assignment.
Photos: State availability with submission. Reviews negatives, transparencies, prints. Buys one-time rights. Negotiates payment individually.
Columns/Departments: Opening Axe (newsy items on artists), 450 words; Soundcheck (records review), 200 words; Gear Box (equipment reviews), 800 words.
Tips: "Find an interesting feature with a nice angle that pertains to guitar enthusiasts. Submit a well-written draft or samples of work."

$ $ GUITAR PLAYER MAGAZINE, The Music Player Group, 2800 Campus Dr., San Mateo CA 94403. (650)513-4400. E-mail: guitplyr@musicplayer.com. Website: www.guitarplayer.com. **Contact:** Michael Molenda, editor-in-chief. **50% freelance written.** Monthly magazine for persons "interested in guitars, guitarists, manufacturers, guitar builders, equipment, careers, etc." Circ. 150,000. **Pays on acceptance.** Publishes ms an average of 3 months after acceptance. Byline given. Buys first serial and all reprint rights Responds in 6 weeks to queries. Writer's guidelines for #10 SASE.
Nonfiction: Publishes "wide variety of articles pertaining to guitars and guitarists: interviews, guitar craftsmen profiles, how-to features—anything amateur and professional guitarists would find fascinating and/or helpful. In interviews with 'name' performers, be as technical as possible regarding strings, guitars, techniques, etc. We're not a pop culture magazine, but a magazine for musicians. The essential question: What can the reader take away from a story to become a better player?" **Buys 30-40 mss/year.** Query. Length: Open. **Pays $250-450.** Sometimes pays expenses of writers on assignment.
Photos: Reviews 35 mm color transparencies, b&w glossy prints. Buys one-time rights. Payment varies.

$ $ MODERN DRUMMER, 12 Old Bridge Rd., Cedar Grove NJ 07009. (201)239-4140. Fax: (201)239-7139. Editorial Director: William F. Miller. Senior Editor: Rick Van Horn. **Contact:** Ronald Spagnardi, editor-in-chief. **60% freelance written.** Monthly magazine for "student, semipro and professional drummers at all ages and levels of playing ability, with varied specialized interests within the field." Circ. 102,000. Pays on publication. Publishes ms an average of 3 months after acceptance. Buys all rights. Accepts previously published material. Responds in 2 weeks to queries. Sample copy for $4.99. Writer's guidelines for #10 SASE.
Nonfiction: "All submissions must appeal to the specialized interests of drummers." How-to, interview/profile, new product, personal experience, technical, informational. **Buys 40-50 mss/year.** Query with published clips or send complete ms. Length: 5,000-8,000 words. **Pays $200-500.**
Reprints: Send photocopy with rights for sale noted and information about when and where the material previously appeared.
Photos: Reviews color transparencies, 8×10 b&w prints. Purchased with accompanying ms.
Columns/Departments: Jazz Drummers Workshop; Rock Perspectives; Rock 'N' Jazz Clinic; Driver's Seat (Big Band); In The Studio; Show Drummers Seminar; Teachers Forum; Drum Soloist; The Jobbing Drummer; Strictly

Technique; Shop Talk; Latin Symposium. Book Reviews; Record Reviews; Video Reviews. Profile columns: Portraits; Up & Coming; From the Past. Length: 500-1,000 words. "Technical knowledge of area required for most columns." **Buys 40-50 mss/year.** Send complete ms. **Pays $50-150.**
Tips: "*MD* is looking for music journalists rather than music critics. Our aim is to provide information, not to make value judgments. Therefore, keep all articles as objective as possible. We are interested in how and why a drummer plays a certain way; the readers can make their own decisions about whether or not they like it."

$ MUSIC FOR THE LOVE OF IT, 67 Parkside Dr., Berkeley CA 94705. (510)654-9134. Fax: (510)654-4656. E-mail: tedrust@musicfortheloveofit.com. Website: www.musicfortheloveofit.com. **Contact:** Ted Rust, editor. **20% freelance written.** Bimonthly newsletter covering amateur musicianship. "A lively, intelligent source of ideas and enthusiasm for a musically literate audience of adult amateur musicians." Estab. 1988. Circ. 600. Pays on publication. Publishes ms an average of 2 months after acceptance. Byline given. Buys one-time rights. Editorial lead time 1 month. Submit seasonal material 1 month in advance. Accepts queries by mail, e-mail, fax, phone. Responds in 1 week to queries; 1 month to mss. Sample copy for $6. Writer's guidelines free, online, or by e-mail.
Break in with "a good article, written from a musician's point of view, with at least 1 photo."
Nonfiction: Essays, historical/nostalgic, how-to, personal experience, photo feature. No concert reviews, star interviews, CD reviews. **Buys 6 mss/year.** Query. Length: 500-1,500 words. **Pays $50 or gift subscriptions.**
Photos: State availability with submission. Reviews 4×6 prints or larger. Buys one-time rights. Offers no additional payment for photos accepted with ms. Identification of subjects required.
Tips: "We're looking for more good how-to articles on musical styles. Love making music. Know something about it."

$ $ PROFILE, Vox Publishing, 3670 Central Pike, Suite J, Hermitage TN 37076. (615)872-8080, ext. 3312. Fax: (615)872-9786. E-mail: profile@profilemagazine.com. Website: www.profilemagazine.com. **Contact:** Chris Well, editor-in-chief. **70% freelance written.** Bimonthly magazine covering Christian books, music, art and more. "*Profile* is the only magazine of its kind, covering the spectrum of Christian products from books and music to children's resources and gifts. It reaches the core Christian retail customer—females between the ages of 21 and 50." Estab. 1998. Circ. 95,000. Pays within 30 days after publication. Publishes ms an average of 2 months after acceptance. Byline sometimes given. Buys first North American serial, electronic rights. Editorial lead time 6 months. Submit seasonal material 4 months in advance. Accepts queries by mail, e-mail, fax. Sample copy for $5.
Nonfiction: Interview/profile (artists), religious. No essays, inspirational pieces. **Buys 20-30 mss/year.** Query with published clips. Length: 500-2,500 words. **Pays 6-10¢/word for assigned articles.** Sometimes pays expenses of writers on assignment.
Photos: State availability with submission. Buys one-time rights. Offers no additional payment for photos accepted with ms. Identification of subjects required.
Columns/Departments: Noteworthy (brief profiles of Christian music artists), 400-600 words; Snapshots (brief profiles of people writing/making books), 400-600 words; Showcase (reviews of Christian books and music), 250 words. **Buys 30 mss/year.** Query with published clips. **Pays 6-10¢/word.**
Tips: "We're looking for people who can exhibit working knowledge of the authors, books and artists we cover. We also want to be convinced that they've read our magazine."

$ RELIX MAGAZINE, Music for the Mind, 180 Varick St., 5th Floor, New York NY 10014. (646)230-0100. Website: www.relix.com. **Contact:** Aeve Baldwin, managing editor. **40% freelance written.** Bimonthly magazine focusing on new and independent bands, classic rock, lifestyles, and music alternatives such as roots, improvisational music, psychedelia, and jambands. Estab. 1974. Circ. 100,000. Pays on publication. Publishes ms an average of 4 months after acceptance. Byline given. Buys all rights. Accepts queries by mail, e-mail. Accepts previously published material. Responds in 6 months to queries. Sample copy for $5.
Nonfiction: Feature topics include jambands, reggae, Grateful Dead, bluegrass, jazz, country, rock, experimental, electronic, and world music; also deals with environmental, cultural, and lifestyle issues. Historical/nostalgic, humor, interview/profile, new product, photo feature, technical, live reviews, new artists, hippy lifestyles, food, mixed media, books. Query by mail with published clips if available or send complete ms. Length: 300-1,500 words. **Pays variable rates.**
Photos: "Whenever possible, submit complete artwork with articles."
Columns/Departments: Query with published clips or send complete ms. **Pays variable rates.**
Tips: "The best part of working with freelance writers is discovering new music we might never have stumbled across."

SPIN, 205 Lexington Ave., 3rd Floor, New York NY 10016. (212)231-7400. Fax: (212)231-7300. Website: www.spin.com. Publisher: Jon Chalon. **Contact:** Sia Michel, editor-in-chief. Monthly magazine covering music and popular culture. "*Spin* covers progressive rock as well as investigative reporting on issues from politics, to pop culture. Editorial includes reviews, essays, profiles and interviews on a wide range of music from rock to jazz. It also covers sports, movies, politics, humor, fashion and issues—from AIDS research to the environment. The editorial focuses on the progressive new music scene and young adult culture more from an 'alternative' perspective as opposed to mainstream pop music. The magazine discovers new bands as well as angles for the familiar stars." Estab. 1985. Circ. 540,000.
Nonfiction: Features are not assigned to writers who have not established a prior relationship with *Spin.* Cultural, political or social issues. New writers: submit complete ms with SASE. Established writers: query specific editor with published clips.

Columns/Departments: Most open to freelancers: Exposure (short articles on popular culture, TV, movies, books), 200-500 words, query Maureen Callahan, associate editor; Reviews (record reviews), 100 words, queries/mss to Alex Pappademas, senior editor; Noise (music and new artists), query Tracey Pepper, senior associate editor. Query before submitting.

Tips: "The best way to break into the magazine is the Exposure and Reviews sections. We primarily work with seasoned, professional writers who have extensive national magazine experience and very rarely make assignments based on unsolicited queries."

$ $ SYMPHONY, American Symphony Orchestra League, 33 W. 60th St., Fifth Floor, New York NY 10023-7905. (212)262-5161, ext. 247. Fax: (212)262-5198. E-mail: editor@symphony.org. Website: www.symphony.org. **Contact:** Melinda Whiting, editor-in-chief. **50% freelance written.** Bimonthly magazine for the orchestra industry and classical music enthusiasts covering classical music, orchestra industry, musicians. Writers should be knowledgeable about classical music and have critical or journalistic/repertorial approach. Circ. 18,500. **Pays on acceptance.** Publishes ms an average of 2 months after acceptance. Byline given. Buys first, one-time rights. Editorial lead time 6 months. Submit seasonal material 8 months in advance. Accepts queries by mail, e-mail, phone. Accepts simultaneous submissions. Writer's guidelines online.

Nonfiction: Book excerpts, essays, inspirational, interview/profile, opinion, personal experience (rare), photo feature (rare), issue features, trend pieces (by assignment only; pitches welcome). Does not want to see reviews, interviews. **Buys 30 mss/year.** Query with published clips. Length: 900-3,500 words. **Pays $150-600.** Sometimes pays expenses of writers on assignment.

Photos: State availability of or send photos with submission. Reviews contact sheets, negatives, prints, electronic photos. Buys one-time rights. Offers no additional payment for photos accepted with ms. Captions, identification of subjects required.

Columns/Departments: Repertoire (orchestral music—essays); Comment (personal views and opinions); Currents (electronic media developments); In Print (books); On Record (CD, DVD, video), all 1,000 words. **Buys 4 mss/year.** Query with published clips.

Tips: "We need writing samples before assigning pieces. We prefer to craft the angle with the writer, rather than adapt an existing piece. Pitches and queries should demonstrate a clear relevance to the American orchestra industry and should be timely."

$ $ $ $ VIBE, 215 Lexington Ave., 6th Floor, New York NY 10016. (212)448-7300. Fax: (212)448-7430. Website: www.vibe.com. Managing Editor: Jacklyn Monk. **Contact:** Individual editors as noted. Monthly magazine covering urban music and culture. "*Vibe* chronicles and celebrates urban music and the youth culture that inspires and consumes it." Estab. 1993. Circ. 800,000. Pays on publication. Buys first North American serial rights. Editorial lead time 4 months. Responds in 2 months to queries. Sample copy available on newsstands. Writer's guidelines for #10 SASE.

Nonfiction: Robert Simpson, deputy editor; Shani Saxon, music editor. Cultural, political or social issues. Query with published clips, résumé and SASE. Length: 800-3,000 words. **Pays $1/word.**

Columns/Departments: Start (introductory news-based section), 350-740 words, send queries to Brett Johnson, senior editor. Revolutions (music reviews), 100-800 words, send queries to Craig Seymour, associate music editor. Book reviews, send queries Robert Morales, senior editor. Query with published clips, résumé and SASE. **Pays $1/word.**

Tips: "A writer's best chance to be published in *Vibe* is through the Start or Revolutions Sections. Keep in mind that *Vibe* is a national magazine, so ideas should have a national scope. People in Cali should care as much about the story as people in NYC. Also, *Vibe* has a four-month lead time. What we work on today will appear in the magazine four or more months later. Stories must be timely with respect to this fact."

MYSTERY

These magazines buy fictional accounts of crime, detective work, mystery and suspense. Skim through other sections to identify markets for fiction; some will consider mysteries. Markets for true crime accounts are listed under Detective & Crime.

$ HARDBOILED, Gryphon Publications, P.O. Box 209, Brooklyn NY 11228. Website: www.gryphonbooks.com. **Contact:** Gary Lovisi, editor. **100% freelance written.** Semiannual book covering crime/mystery fiction and nonfiction. "Hard-hitting crime fiction and private-eye stories—the newest and most cutting-edge work and classic reprints." Estab. 1988. Circ. 1,000. Pays on publication. Publishes ms an average of 18 months after acceptance. Byline given. Offers 100% kill fee. Buys one-time rights. Editorial lead time 1 year. Submit seasonal material 9 months in advance. Accepts queries by mail. Accepts previously published material. Responds in 2 weeks to queries; 1 month to mss. Sample copy for $8 or double issue for $20 (add $1.50 book postage). Writer's guidelines for #10 SASE.

Nonfiction: Book excerpts, essays, exposé. **Buys 4-6 mss/year.** Query. Length: 500-3,000 words. **Pays 1 copy.**

Reprints: Query first.

Photos: State availability with submission.

Columns/Departments: Occasional review columns/articles on hardboiled writers. **Buys 2-4 mss/year.** Query.

Fiction: Mystery, hardboiled crime, and private-eye stories, all on the cutting edge. **Buys 40 mss/year.** Send complete ms. Length: 500-3,000 words. **Pays $5-50.**

Tips: Best bet for breaking in is short hard crime fiction filled with authenticity and brevity.

$ ALFRED HITCHCOCK'S MYSTERY MAGAZINE, Dell magazines, 475 Park Ave. S., 11th Floor, New York NY 10016. Website: www.themysteryplace.com. Editor: Linda Landrigan. **100% freelance written.** Monthly magazine featuring new mystery short stories. Circ. 615,000. **Pays on acceptance.** Byline given. Buys first rights. Foreign Rights Submit seasonal material 7 months in advance. Responds in 2 months to queries. Sample copy for $5. Writer's guidelines for #10 SASE.

Fiction: "Because this is a mystery magazine, the stories we buy must fall into that genre in some sense or another. We are interested in nearly every kind of mystery, however: stories of detection of the classic kind, police procedurals, private eye tales, suspense, courtroom dramas, stories of espionage, and so on. We ask only that the story be about crime (or the threat or fear of one). We sometimes accept ghost stories or supernatural tales, but those also should involve a crime." Original and well-written mystery and crime fiction. Length: Up to 14,000 words. **Pays 8¢/word.**

Tips: "No simultaneous submissions, please. Submissions sent to *Alfred Hitchcock's Mystery Magazine* are not considered for or read by *Ellery Queen's Mystery Magazine*, and vice versa."

$ THE MYSTERY REVIEW, A Quarterly Publication for Mystery Readers, C. von Hessert & Associates, P.O. Box 233, Colborne, Ontario K0K 1S0, Canada. E-mail: mystrev@reach.net. Website: www.themysteryreview.com. **Contact:** Barbara Davey, editor. **80% freelance written.** Quarterly magazine covering mystery and suspense. "Our readers are interested in mystery and suspense books, films. All topics related to mystery—including real life unsolved mysteries." Estab. 1992. Circ. 8,500 (80% of distribution is in US). Pays on publication. Publishes ms an average of 6 months after acceptance. Byline given. Buys first North American serial rights. Editorial lead time 6 months. Submit seasonal material 6 months in advance. Accepts queries by mail, e-mail, fax. Responds in 6 weeks to queries; 1 month to mss. Sample copy for $6. Writer's guidelines online.

Nonfiction: Interview/profile, true life mysteries. Query. Length: 2,000-5,000 words. **Pays $30 maximum.**

Photos: Send photos with submission. Buys all rights. Offers no additional payment for photos accepted with ms. Identification of subjects, model releases required.

Columns/Departments: Book reviews (mystery/suspense titles only), 500 words; Truly Mysterious ("unsolved," less-generally-known, historical, or contemporary cases; photos/illustrations required), 2,000-5,000 words; Book Shop Beat (bookstore profiles; questionnaire covering required information available from editor), 500 words. **Buys 50 mss/year.** Query with published clips. **Pays $10-30.**

Fillers: Puzzles, trivia, shorts (items related to mystery/suspense). **Buys 4/year.** Length: 100-500 words. **Pays $10-20.**

$ ELLERY QUEEN'S MYSTERY MAGAZINE, Dell magazines Fiction Group, 475 Park Ave. S., 11th Floor, New York NY 10016. (212)686-7188. Fax: (212)686-7414. E-mail: elleryqueen@dellmagazines.com. Website: www.themysteryplace.com. **Contact:** Janet Hutchings, editor. **100% freelance written.** Magazine published 11 times/year featuring mystery fiction. Estab. 1941. Circ. 500,000 readers. **Pays on acceptance.** Publishes ms an average of 6 months after acceptance. Byline given. Buys first North American serial rights. Accepts simultaneous submissions. Responds in 3 months to mss. Sample copy for $5. Writer's guidelines for #10 SASE.

Fiction: "We publish every type of mystery: the suspense story, the psychological study, the private-eye story, the deductive puzzle—the gamut of crime and detection from the realistic (including stories of police procedure) to the more imaginative (including 'locked rooms' and 'impossible crimes'). We always need detective stories. Special consideration given to anything timely and original. No sex, sadism, or sensationalism-for-the-sake-of-sensationalism, no gore or horror. Seldom publishes parodies or pastiches." **Buys up to 120 mss/year.** Send complete ms. Length: Most stories 3,000-10,000 words. Accepts longer and shorter submissions—including minute mysteries of 250 words, and novellas of up to 20,000 words from established authors. **Pays 5-8¢/word, occasionally higher for established authors.**

Poetry: Short mystery verses, limericks. Length: 1 page, double spaced maximum.

Tips: "We have a Department of First Stories to encourage writers whose fiction has never before been in print. We publish an average of 11 first stories every year."

NATURE, CONSERVATION & ECOLOGY

These publications promote reader awareness of the natural environment, wildlife, nature preserves, and ecosystems. Many of these "green magazines" also concentrate on recycling and related issues, and a few focus on environmentally-conscious sustainable living. They do not publish recreation or travel articles except as they relate to conservation or nature. Other markets for this kind of material can be found in the Regional; Sports (Hiking & Backpacking in particular); and Travel, Camping & Trailer categories, although magazines listed there require that nature or conservation articles be slanted to their specialized subject matter and audience.

$ $ ALTERNATIVES JOURNAL, Environmental Thought, Policy and Action, Alternatives, Inc., Faculty of Environmental Studies, University of Waterloo, Waterloo, Ontario N2L 3GL, Canada. (519)888-4442. Fax: (519)746-0292. E-mail: altsed@fes.uwaterloo.ca. Website: www.alternativesjournal.ca. Editor: Robert Gibson. **Contact:** Ray Tomalty, senior editor. **90% freelance written.** Quarterly magazine covering environmental issues. Estab. 1971. Circ. 4,800. Pays on publication. Publishes ms an average of 5 months after acceptance. Byline given. Offers 50% kill fee. Buys first rights. Editorial lead time 7 months. Submit seasonal material 5 months in advance. Accepts queries by mail, e-mail, fax. Accepts simultaneous submissions. Sample copy for free. Writer's guidelines free.

Nonfiction: Book excerpts, essays, exposé, humor, interview/profile, opinion. **Buys 50 mss/year.** Query with published clips. Length: 800-3,000 words. **Pays $50-150 for assigned articles; $50-150 for unsolicited articles.** All contributors receive a free subscription in addition to payment. Sometimes pays expenses of writers on assignment.
Photos: State availability with submission. Buys one-time rights. Offers $35-75/photo. Identification of subjects required.

$ $ $ ☆ AMC OUTDOORS, The Magazine of the Appalachian Mountain Club, Appalachian Mountain Club, 5 Joy St., Boston MA 02108. (617)523-0655. Fax: (617)523-0722. E-mail: meno@amcinfo.org. Website: www.outdoors.org. **Contact:** Madeleine Eno, editor/publisher. **90% freelance written.** Monthly magazine covering outdoor recreation and conservation issues in the Northeast. Estab. 1907. Circ. 85,000. Pays on publication. Byline given. Offers 25% kill fee. Buys all rights. Editorial lead time 3 months. Accepts queries by e-mail. Responds in 1 month to queries; 2 months to mss. Sample copy for 9×12 SASE. Writer's guidelines free or online.
Nonfiction: Looking for writing familiar to particularities of Northeast—landscape and conservation issues. Book excerpts, essays, exposé, general interest, historical/nostalgic, how-to, interview/profile, opinion, personal experience, photo feature, technical, travel. Special issues: Northern Forest Report (April) featuring the northern areas of New York, New Hampshire, Vermont, and Maine, and protection efforts for these areas. No "how hiking changed my life" or first-person outdoor adventure without a hook. Query with or without published clips. Length: 500-3,000 words. Pays minimal expenses.
Photos: State availability with submission. Reviews contact sheets, transparencies, prints. Identification of subjects, model releases required.
Columns/Departments: Jane Roy Brown. News (environmental/outdoor recreation coverage of Northeast), 1,300 words. **Buys 40 mss/year.** Query. **Pays $250-1,200.**

$ $ $ AMERICAN FORESTS, American Forests, P.O. Box 2000, Washington DC 20013. (202)955-4500. Fax: (202)887-1075. E-mail: mrobbins@amfor.org. Website: www.americanforests.org. **Contact:** Michelle Robbins, editor. **75% freelance written.** (mostly assigned). Quarterly magazine "of trees and forests, published by a nonprofit citizens' organization that strives to help people plant and care for trees for ecosystem restoration and healthier communities." Estab. 1895. Circ. 25,000. **Pays on acceptance.** Publishes ms an average of 8 months after acceptance. Byline given. Buys one-time rights. Submit seasonal material 5 months in advance. Accepts queries by mail, e-mail. Accepts previously published material. Responds in 2 months to queries. Sample copy for $2. Writer's guidelines for SASE or online.

O┯ Break in with "stories that resonate with city dwellers who love trees, or small, forestland owners (private). This magazine is looking for more urban and suburban-oriented pieces.

Nonfiction: All articles should emphasize trees, forests, forestry and related issues. General interest, historical/nostalgic, how-to, humor, inspirational. **Buys 8-12 mss/year.** Query. Length: 1,200-2,000 words. **Pays $250-1,000.**
Reprints: Send tearsheet or typed ms with rights for sale noted and information about when and where the material previously appeared. Pays 50% of amount paid for original article.
Photos: Originals only. Send photos with submission. Reviews 35mm or larger transparencies, Glossy color prints. Buys one-time rights. Offers no additional payment for photos accompanying ms. Captions required.
Tips: "We're looking for more good urban forestry stories, and stories that show cooperation among disparate elements to protect/restore an ecosystem. Query should have honesty and information on photo support. We *do not* accept fiction or poetry at this time."

$ $ APPALACHIAN TRAILWAY NEWS, Appalachian Trail Conference, P.O. Box 807, Harpers Ferry WV 25425-0807. (304)535-6331. Fax: (304)535-2667. E-mail: editor@appalachiantrail.org. **Contact:** Robert A. Rubin, editor. **40% freelance written.** Bimonthly magazine. Estab. 1925. Circ. 35,000. **Pays on acceptance.** Byline given. Buys first North American serial, second serial (reprint) rights. Responds in 2 months to queries. Sample copy and writer's guidelines for $2.50. Writer's guidelines only for SASE.

- Articles must relate to Appalachian Trail.

Nonfiction: Publishes but does not pay for "hiking reflections." Essays, general interest, historical/nostalgic, how-to, humor, inspirational, interview/profile, photo feature, technical, travel. **Buys 15-20 mss/year.** Query with or without published clips, or send complete ms. Prefers e-mail queries. Length: 250-3,000 words. **Pays $25-300.** Pays expenses of writers on assignment.
Reprints: Send photocopy with rights for sale noted and information about when and where the material previously appeared.
Photos: State availability with submission. Reviews contact sheets, 5×7 prints, slides, digital images. Offers $25-125/photo; $300/cover. Identification of subjects required.
Tips: "Contributors should display a knowledge of or interest in the Appalachian Trail. Those who live in the vicinity of the Trail may opt for an assigned story and should present credentials and subject of interest to the editor."

$ $ $ $ AUDUBON, The Magazine of the National Audubon Society, National Audubon Society, 700 Broadway, New York NY 10003-9501. Fax: (212)477-9069. E-mail: editor@audubon.org. Website: www.audubon.org. **Contact:** Editor. **15% freelance written.** Bimonthly magazine "reflecting nature with joy and reverence and reporting the issues that affect and endanger the delicate balance and life on this planet." Estab. 1887. Circ. 460,000. **Pays on acceptance.** Byline given. Buys all rights. Accepts queries by mail, fax. Responds in 3 months to queries. Sample copy for $5 and postage or online. Writer's guidelines for #10 SASE or online.

- "No phone calls, please."

Nonfiction: "We are interested in nature/environmental articles with an emphasis on science and conservation." Do not send complete mss, *accepts queries only.* Essays, exposé, interview/profile, investigative. No humor, poetry or book excerpts. Query with published clips. Unsolicited mss will not be returned. Virtually all pieces are written in-house; unsolicited story ideas rarely accepted. Length: 150-3,000 words. **Pays $100-3,000.** Pays some expenses of writers on assignment.
Tips: "*Audubon* articles deal with the natural and human environment. They cover the remote as well as the familiar. What they all have in common, however, is that they have a story to tell, one that will not only interest *Audubon* readers, but that will interest everyone with a concern for the affairs of humans and nature. We want good solid journalism. We want stories of people and places, good news and bad: humans and nature in conflict, humans and nature working together, humans attempting to comprehend, restore and renew the natural world. We are looking for new voices and fresh ideas. Among the types of stories we seek: Profiles of individuals whose life and work illuminate some issues relating to natural history, the environment, conservation, etc.; balanced reporting on environmental issues and events here in North America; environmental education; advocacy; "citizen science"; analyses of events, policies, and issues from fresh points of view. We do not publish fiction or poetry. We're not seeking first-person meditations on 'nature,' accounts of wild animal rescue or taming, or birdwatching articles."

$ THE BEAR DELUXE MAGAZINE, Orlo, P.O. Box 10342, Portland OR 97296. (503)242-1047. Fax: (503)243-2645. E-mail: bear@teleport.com. Website: www.orlo.org. **Contact:** Tom Webb, editor. **80% freelance written.** Quarterly magazine. "*The Bear Deluxe Magazine* provides a fresh voice amid often strident and polarized environmental discourse. Street level, solution-oriented, and nondogmatic, *The Bear Deluxe* presents lively creative discussion to a diverse readership." Estab. 1993. Circ. 19,000. Pays on publication. Publishes ms an average of 2 months after acceptance. Byline given. Offers 25% kill fee. Buys first rights. Editorial lead time 3 months. Submit seasonal material 4 months in advance. Accepts queries by mail, e-mail. Accepts previously published material. Responds in 3 months to queries; 6 months to mss. Sample copy for $3. Writer's guidelines for #10 SASE or online at www.orlo.org.
Nonfiction: Book excerpts, essays, exposé, general interest, interview/profile, new product, opinion, personal experience, photo feature, travel, artist profiles. Special issues: Publishes 1 theme/year. **Buys 40 mss/year.** Query with published clips. Length: 250-4,500 words. **Pays 5¢/word.** Sometimes pays expenses of writers on assignment.
Photos: State availability with submission. Reviews contact sheets, transparencies, 8×10 prints. Buys one-time rights. Offers $30/photo. Identification of subjects, model releases required.
Columns/Departments: Reviews (almost anything), 300 words; Hands-On (individuals or groups working on eco-issues, getting their hands dirty), 1,200 words; Talking Heads (creative first person), 500 words; News Bites (quirk of eco-news), 300 words; Portrait of an Artist (artist profiles), 1,200 words. **Buys 16 mss/year.** Query with published clips. **Pays 5¢/word, subscription, and copies.**
Fiction: "Stories must have some environmental context." Adventure, condensed novels, historical, humorous, mystery, novel excerpts, science fiction, western. **Buys 8 mss/year.** Send complete ms. Length: 750-4,500 words. **Pays 5¢/word.**
Poetry: Avant-garde, free verse, haiku, light verse, traditional. **Buys 16-20 poems/year.** Submit maximum 5 poems. Length: 50 lines maximum. **Pays $10, subscription, and copies.**
Fillers: Facts, newsbreaks, short humor. **Buys 10/year.** Length: 100-750 words. **Pays 5¢/word, subscription, and copies.**
Tips: "Offer to be a stringer for future ideas. Get a copy of the magazine and guidelines, and query us with specific nonfiction ideas and clips. We're looking for original, magazine-style stories, not fluff or PR. Fiction, essay, and poetry writers should know we have an open and blind review policy and should keep sending their best work even if rejected once. Be as specific as possible in queries."

$ $ BIRD WATCHER'S DIGEST, Pardson Corp., P.O. Box 110, Marietta OH 45750. (740)373-5285. E-mail: editor@birdwatchersdigest.com. Website: www.birdwatchersdigest.com. **Contact:** William H. Thompson III, editor. **60% freelance written.** Works with a small number of new/unpublished writers each year. Bimonthly magazine covering natural history—birds and bird watching. "*BWD* is a nontechnical magazine interpreting ornithological material for amateur observers, including the knowledgeable birder, the serious novice and the backyard bird watcher; we strive to provide good reading and good ornithology." Estab. 1978. Circ. 90,000. Pays on publication. Publishes ms an average of 2 years after acceptance. Byline given. Buys one-time, second serial (reprint) rights. Submit seasonal material 6 months in advance. Accepts previously published material. Responds in 2 months to queries. Sample copy for $3.99 or online. Writer's guidelines for #10 SASE or online.
Nonfiction: "We are especially interested in fresh, lively accounts of closely observed bird behavior and displays and of bird-watching experiences and expeditions. We often need material on less common species or on unusual or previously unreported behavior of common species." Book excerpts, how-to (relating to birds, feeding and attracting, etc.), humor, personal experience, travel (limited, we get many). No articles on pet or caged birds; none on raising a baby bird. **Buys 75-90 mss/year.** Send complete ms. Length: 600-3,500 words. **Pays from $100.**
Photos: Send photos with submission. Reviews transparencies, prints. Buys one-time rights. Pays $75 minimum for transparencies.

The online magazine carries content not found in the print edition and includes writer's guidelines.
Tips: "We are aimed at an audience ranging from the backyard bird watcher to the very knowledgeable birder; we include in each issue material that will appeal at various levels. We always strive for a good geographical spread, with material from every section of the country. We leave very technical matters to others, but we want facts and accuracy, depth and quality, directed at the veteran bird watcher and at the enthusiastic novice. We stress the joys and pleasures of bird watching, its environmental contribution, and its value for the individual and society."

$ $ BIRDER'S WORLD, Enjoying Birds at Home and Beyond, Kalmbach Publishing Co., P.O. Box 1612, Waukesha WI 53187-1612. Fax: (262)798-6468. E-mail: mail@birdersworld.com. Website: www.birdersworld.com. Editor: Charles J. Hagner. Managing Editor: Diane Jolie. Associate Editor: Matt Schlag-Mendenhall. **Contact:** Rosemary Nowak, editorial assistant. Bimonthly magazine covering wild birds and birdwatching. "*Birder's World* is a magazine designed for people with a broad interest in wild birds and birdwatching. Our readers are curious and generally well-educated with varying degrees of experience in the world of birds. No poetry, fiction, or puzzles please." Estab. 1987. Circ. 70,000. **Pays on acceptance.** Byline given. Offers $100 kill fee. Buys one-time rights. Accepts queries by mail. Writer's guidelines for #10 SASE or by e-mail.

Nonfiction: Essays, how-to (attracting birds), interview/profile, personal experience, photo feature (bird photography), travel (birding trips in North America), book reviews, product reviews/comparisons, bird biology, endangered or threatened birds. No poetry, fiction, or puzzles. **Buys 60 mss/year.** Query with published clips or send complete ms. Length: 500-2,400 words. **Pays $200-450.** Sometimes pays expenses of writers on assignment.

Photos: State availability with submission. Buys one-time rights. Identification of subjects required.

$ $ $ CALIFORNIA WILD, Natural Science for Thinking Animals, California Academy of Sciences, Golden Gate Park, San Francisco CA 94118. (415)750-7117. Fax: (415)221-4853. E-mail: kkhowell@calacademy.org. Website: www.calacademy.org/calwild. **Contact:** Keith Howell, editor. **75% freelance written.** Quarterly magazine covering natural sciences and the environment. "Our readers' interests range widely from ecology to geology, from endangered species to anthropology, from field identification of plants and birds to armchair understanding of complex scientific issues." Estab. 1948. Circ. 32,000. Pays prior to publication. Publishes ms an average of 3 months after acceptance. Byline given. Offers 50% kill fee; maximum $200. Buys first North American serial, one-time rights. Editorial lead time 3 months. Submit seasonal material 6 months in advance. Accepts queries by mail, fax. Responds in 6 weeks to queries; 6 months to mss. Sample copy for 9×12 SASE or on website. Writer's guidelines for #10 SASE or on website.

Nonfiction: Personal experience, photo feature, biological, and earth sciences. Special issues: Mostly California pieces, but also from Pacific Ocean countries. No travel pieces. **Buys 20 mss/year.** Query with published clips. Length: 1,000-3,000 words. **Pays $250-1,000 for assigned articles; $200-800 for unsolicited articles.** Sometimes pays expenses of writers on assignment.

Photos: State availability with submission. Reviews transparencies. Buys one-time rights. Offers $75-150/photo. Identification of subjects, model releases required.

Columns/Departments: A Closer Look (unusual places); Wild Lives (description of unusual plant or animal); In Pursuit of Science (innovative student, teacher, young scientist), all 1,000-1,500 words; Skywatcher (research in astronomy), 2,000-3,000 words. **Buys 12 mss/year.** Query with published clips. **Pays $200-400.**

Fillers: Facts. **Pays $25-50.**

Tips: "We are looking for unusual and/or timely stories about California environment or biodiversity."

$ $ $ CANADIAN WILDLIFE, Tribute Publishing, 71 Barber Greene Rd., Don Mills, Ontario M3C 2A2, Canada. (416)445-0544. Fax: (416)445-2894. E-mail: wild@tribute.ca. Editor: Kendra Toby. **Contact:** Gillian Girodat, assistant editor. **90% freelance written.** Magazine published 5 times/year covering wildlife conservation. Includes topics pertaining to wildlife, endangered species, conservation, and natural history. When possible, it is beneficial if articles have a Canadian slant or the topic has global appeal. Estab. 1995. Circ. 25,000. **Pays on acceptance.** Publishes ms an average of 3 months after acceptance. Byline given. Offers 15% kill fee. Buys first North American serial rights. Editorial lead time 3 months. Submit seasonal material 4 months in advance. Accepts queries by mail, e-mail, fax. Responds in 3 weeks to queries; 2 months to mss. Sample copy for $3.25 (Canadian). Writer's guidelines free.

Nonfiction: Book excerpts, interview/profile, photo feature, science/nature. Special issues: Oceans issue (every June). No standard travel stories. **Buys 20 mss/year.** Query with published clips. Length: 800-2,500 words. **Pays $500-1,200 for assigned articles; $300-1,000 for unsolicited articles.** Sometimes pays expenses of writers on assignment.

Photos: Send photos with submission. Reviews transparencies. Buys one-time rights. Negotiates payment individually. Captions, identification of subjects, model releases required.

Columns/Departments: Vistas (science news), 200-500 words; Book Reviews, 100-150 words. **Buys 15 mss/year.** Query with published clips. **Pays $50-250.**

Tips: "*Canadian Wildlife* is a benefit of membership in the Canadian Wildlife Federation. Nearly 25,000 people currently receive the magazine. The majority of these men and women are already well versed in topics concerning the environment and natural science; writers, however, should not make assumptions about the extent of a reader's knowledge of topics."

$ CONSCIOUS CHOICE, The Journal of Ecology & Natural Living, Dragonfly Chicago LLC, 920 N. Franklin, Suite 202, Chicago IL 60610-3179. Fax: (312)751-3973. E-mail: james@consciouschoice.com. Website: www.consciouschoice.com. Editor: Ross Thompson. Managing Editor: James Faber. **Contact:** James Faber, managing editor. **95% freelance written.** Monthly tabloid covering the environment, natural health, and natural foods. Estab. 1988. Circ. 50,000. Pays on publication. Publishes ms an average of 6 months after acceptance. Byline given. Offers 50% kill fee. Buys first North American serial, electronic rights. Editorial lead time 6 months. Submit seasonal material 6 months in advance. Accepts queries by mail, e-mail. Accepts simultaneous submissions. Responds in 6 weeks to queries; 1 month to mss. Sample copy online. Writer's guidelines free, online, or by e-mail.

Nonfiction: General interest, inspirational, interview/profile, new product, personal experience, technical. **Buys 5 mss/year.** Query with published clips. Length: 1,500 words. **Pays $75-150.** Sometimes pays expenses of writers on assignment.

$ $ ✪ E THE ENVIRONMENTAL MAGAZINE, Earth Action Network, P.O. Box 5098, Westport CT 06881-5098. (203)854-5559. Fax: (203)866-0602. E-mail: info@emagazine.com. Website: www.emagazine.com. **Contact:** Jim Motavalli, editor. **60% freelance written.** Bimonthly magazine. "*E Magazine* was formed for the purpose of acting as a clearinghouse of information, news, and commentary on environmental issues." Estab. 1990. Circ. 50,000. Pays on publication. Byline given. Buys first North American serial rights. Editorial lead time 3 months. Submit seasonal material 6 months in advance. Accepts queries by mail, e-mail, fax. Accepts simultaneous submissions. Sample copy for $5 or online. Writer's guidelines for #10 SASE.

• The editor reports an interest in seeing more investigative reporting.

Nonfiction: On spec or free contributions welcome. Exposé (environmental), how-to, new product, book review, feature (in-depth articles on key natural environmental issues). **Buys 100 mss/year.** Query with published clips. Length: 100-4,000 words. **Pays 30¢/word.**

Photos: State availability with submission. Reviews printed samples, e.g., magazine tearsheets, postcards, etc. to be kept on file. Buys one-time rights. Negotiates payment individually. Identification of subjects required.

Columns/Departments: In Brief/Currents (environmental news stories/trends), 400-1,000 words; Conversations (Q&As with environmental "movers and shakers"), 2,000 words; Tools for Green Living; Your Health; Eco-Travel; Eco-Home; Eating Right; Green Business; Consumer News (each 700-1,200 words). On spec or free contributions welcome. Query with published clips.

▣ Contact: Jim Motavalli, online editor.

Tips: "Contact us to obtain writer's guidelines and back issues of our magazine. Tailor your query according to the department/section you feel it would be best suited for. Articles must be lively, well researched, balanced, and relevant to a mainstream, national readership." On spec or free contributions welcome.

$ $ HOOKED ON THE OUTDOORS, 2040 30th St., Suite A, Boulder CO 80301. (406)582-8173. Fax: (406)522-3744. E-mail: nancy@ruhooked.com. Website: www.ruhooked.com. Editor: John Byorth. **Contact:** Nancy Coulter-Parker, managing editor. **60% freelance written.** "*Hooked on the Outdoors* magazine is a bimonthly travel and gear guide for outdoorsy folk of all ages, shapes, sizes, religions, and mantras. No matter the background, all have the North American backyard in common. *Hooked* is the outdoor guide for readers who are multi-sport oriented and, just the same, people new to the outdoors, providing affordable, close to home destinations and gear alternative." Estab. 1998. Circ. 165,000. Pays within 30 days of publication. Publishes ms an average of 4 months after acceptance. Byline given. Offers 15% kill fee. Buys first North American serial rights. Editorial lead time 3 months. Submit seasonal material 6 months in advance. Accepts queries by mail, e-mail. Accepts simultaneous submissions. Responds in 6 weeks to queries; 2 months to mss. Sample copy for $5 and SAE with $1.75 postage. Writer's guidelines online.

Nonfiction: Book excerpts, essays, exposé, general interest, humor, interview/profile, new product, opinion, personal experience, photo feature, travel. Special issues: Travel Special (February 2002); Grassroots (conservation, clubs, outdoor schools, events; April 2002). **Buys 4 mss/year.** Query with published clips. Length: 350-1,800 words. **Pays 35-50¢/word.** Sometimes pays expenses of writers on assignment.

Photos: State availability with submission. Reviews contact sheets. Buys one-time rights. Offers $25-290. Captions, model releases required.

Columns/Departments: Nancy Coulter-Parker, executive editor. Outtakes/News & Issues (conservation, outdoor sports, etc), 300 words; Birds Bees Trees (essays on human relationships), 650 words. **Buys 30 mss/year.** Query with published clips. **Pays 35-50¢/word.**

Fillers: Mark Miller, assistant editor. Anecdotes, facts, gags to be illustrated by cartoonist, newsbreaks, short humor. **Buys 50/year.** Length: 25-100 words. **Pays 25¢/word.**

Tips: "Send well thought out, complete queries reflective of research. Writers ought not query on topics already covered."

$ $ $ MINNESOTA CONSERVATION VOLUNTEER, Minnesota Department of Natural Resources, 500 Lafeyette Rd., St. Paul MN 55155-4046. (651)296-0894. Fax: (651)296-0902. E-mail: greg.breining@dnr.state.mn.us. Website: www.dnr.state.mn.us. Editor: Kathleen Weflen. **Contact:** Greg Breining, managing editor. **50% freelance written.** Bimonthly magazine covering Minnesota natural resources, wildlife, natural history, outdoor recreation, and land use. "As the masthead says, *Minnesota Conservation Volunteer* is a donor-supported magazine advocating conservation and wise use of Minnesota's natural resources. But don't confuse us with so-called 'wise-use' movements. Material must reflect an appreciation of nature and an ethic of care for the environment. At the same time, we are interested in points of view that challenge the orthodoxy of environmental groups or of the Department of Natural Resources itself. To dispel any impression that we are simply a 'house organ' of the Department of Natural Resources, we try to maintain healthy skepticism and to rely on a variety of sources in our reporting. More than 120,000 Minnesota households, businesses, schools, and other groups subscribe to this conservation magazine." Estab. 1940. Circ. 120,000. **Pays on acceptance.** Publishes ms an average of 1 month after acceptance. Byline given. Offers 30% kill fee. Buys first North American serial, rights to post to website, and archive rights. Editorial lead time 8 months. Submit seasonal material 8 months in advance. Accepts queries by mail, e-mail, fax. Accepts previously published material. Accepts simultaneous submissions. Responds in 1 month to queries; 2 months to mss. Sample copy free or on website. Writer's guidelines free.

Nonfiction: Book excerpts, essays, exposé, general interest, historical/nostalgic, humor, interview/profile, opinion, personal experience, photo feature, travel, "Young Naturalist" for children. Does not publish "poetry, essays with an 'aint's Nature grand!' tone or theme, uncritical advocacy." **Buys 10 mss/year.** Query with published clips. Length: 1,500-2,200 words. **Pays $750-1,000 for full-length feature articles.** Pays expenses of writers on assignment.

Photos: State availability with submission. Reviews 35mm or large format transparencies. Buys one-time rights, will negotiate for Web use separately. Offers $75/photo.
Columns/Departments: Close Encounters (unusual, exciting, or humorous personal wildlife experience in Minnesota), 1,000-1,500 words; Sense of Place (first- or third-person essay developing character of a Minnesota place), 1,500-2,200 words; Viewpoint (well-researched and well-reasoned opinion piece), 1,000-1,500 words; Minnesota Profile (concise description of emblematic state species or geographic feature), 400 words. **Buys 10 mss/year.** Query with published clips. **Pays 50¢/word.**
Tips: "In submitting queries, look beyond topics to *stories:* What is someone doing and why? How does the story end? In submitting a query addressing a particular issue, think of the human impacts and the sources you might consult. Summarize your idea, the story line, and sources in 2 or 3 short paragraphs. While topics must have relevance to Minnesota and give a Minnesota character to the magazine, feel free to round out your research with out-of-state sources."

$ $ $ NATIONAL PARKS, 1300 19th St. NW, Suite 300, Washington DC 20036. (202)223-6722. Fax: (202)659-0650. E-mail: npmag@npca.org. Website: www.npca.org/. Editor-in-chief: Linda Rancourt. **Contact:** Jenell Talley, publications coordinator. **60% freelance written.** Prefers to work with published/established writers. Bimonthly magazine for a largely unscientific but highly educated audience interested in preservation of National Park System units, natural areas and protection of wildlife habitat. Estab. 1919. Circ. 325,000. **Pays on acceptance.** Publishes ms an average of 2 months after acceptance. Offers 33% kill fee. Responds in 5 months to queries. Sample copy for $3 and 9×12 SASE or online. Writer's guidelines for #10 SASE.
Nonfiction: All material must relate to U.S. national parks. Exposé (on threats, wildlife problems in national parks), descriptive articles about new or proposed national parks and wilderness parks; natural history pieces describing park geology, wildlife or plants; new trends in park use; legislative issues. No poetry, philosophical essays or first-person narratives. No unsolicited mss. Length: 1,500 words. **Pays $1,300 for full-length features; $750 for service articles.**
Photos: No color prints or negatives. Send for guidelines. Not responsible for unsolicited photos. Send photos with submission. Reviews color slides. Pays $150-350 inside; $525 for covers. Captions required.
Tips: "Articles should have an original slant or news hook and cover a limited subject, rather than attempt to treat a broad subject superficially. Specific examples, descriptive details, and quotes are always preferable to generalized information. The writer must be able to document factual claims, and statements should be clearly substantiated with evidence within the article. *National Parks* does not publish fiction, poetry, personal essays, or 'My trip to...' stories."

$ $ $ $ NATIONAL WILDLIFE, National Wildlife Federation, 11100 Wildlife Center Dr., Reston VA 20190. (703)438-6524. Fax: (703)438-6544. E-mail: pubs@nwf.org. Website: www.nwf.org/natlwild. **Contact:** Mark Wexler, editor. **75% freelance written.** Assigns almost all material based on staff ideas. Assigns few unsolicited queries. Bimonthly magazine. "Our purpose is to promote wise use of the nation's natural resources and to conserve and protect wildlife and its habitat. We reach a broad audience that is largely interested in wildlife conservation and nature photography." Estab. 1963. Circ. 660,000. **Pays on acceptance.** Publishes ms an average of 1 year after acceptance. Offers 25% kill fee. Buys all rights. Submit seasonal material 8 months in advance. Accepts queries by mail, e-mail, fax. Responds in 6 weeks to queries. Writer's guidelines for #10 SASE.
Nonfiction: General interest (2,500 word features on wildlife, new discoveries, behavior, or the environment), how-to (an outdoor or nature related activity), interview/profile (people who have gone beyond the call of duty to protect wildlife and its habitat, or to prevent environmental contamination and people who have been involved in the environment or conservation in interesting ways), personal experience (outdoor adventure), photo feature (wildlife), short 700-word features on an unusual individual or new scientific discovery relating to nature. "Avoid too much scientific detail. We prefer anecdotal, natural history material." **Buys 50 mss/year.** Query with or without published clips. Length: 750-2,500 words. **Pays $800-3,000.** Sometimes pays expenses of writers on assignment.
Photos: John Nuhn, photo editor. Send photos with submission. Reviews Kodachrome or Fujichrome transparencies. Buys one-time rights.
Tips: "Writers can break in with us more readily by proposing subjects (initially) that will take only 1 or 2 pages in the magazine (short features)."

$ $ $ $ NATURAL HISTORY, Natural History Magazine, Central Park W. at 79th St., New York NY 10024. (212)769-5500. E-mail: nhmag@amnh.org. **Contact:** Ellen Goldensohn, editor-in-chief. **15% freelance written.** Magazine published 10 times/year for well-educated audience: professional people, scientists, and scholars. Circ. 225,000. **Pays on acceptance.** Publishes ms an average of 3 months after acceptance. Byline given. Buys first North American serial rights. Becomes an agent for second serial (reprint) rights Submit seasonal material 6 months in advance.
Nonfiction: "We are seeking new research on mammals, birds, invertebrates, reptiles, ocean life, anthropology, astronomy, preferably written by principal investigators in these fields. Our slant is toward unraveling problems in behavior, ecology, and evolution." **Buys 60 mss/year.** Query by mail or send complete ms. Length: 1,500-3,000 words. **Pays $500-2,500.**
Photos: Rarely uses 8×10 b&w glossy prints; pays $125/page maximum. Much color is used; pays $300 for inside, and up to $600 for cover. Buys one-time rights.
Columns/Departments: Journal (reporting from the field); Findings (summary of new or ongoing research); Naturalist At Large; The Living Museum (relates to the American Museum of Natural History); Discovery (natural or cultural history of a specific place).

Tips: "We expect high standards of writing and research. We do not lobby for causes, environmental, or other. The writer should have a deep knowledge of his subject, then submit original ideas either in query or by manuscript."

N NORTHERN WOODLANDS MAGAZINE, Vermont Woodlands Magazine, Inc., 1776 Center Rd., P.O. Box 471, Corinth VT 05039-0471. (802)439-6292. Fax: (802)439-6296. E-mail: sue@northernwoodlands.com. Website: www.northernwoodlands.com. Editors: Stephen Long and Virginia Barlow. **Contact:** Sue Kashanski, assistant editor. **40-60% freelance written.** Quarterly magazine covering natural history, conservation, and forest management in the Northeast. "*Northern Woodlands* strives to inspire landowners' sense of stewardship by increasing their awareness of the natural history and the principles of conservation and forestry that are directly related to their land. We also hope to increase the public's awareness of the social, economic, and environmental benefits of a working forest." Estab. 1994. Circ. 12,000. **Pays on acceptance.** Publishes ms an average of 6 months after acceptance. Byline given. Buys one-time rights. Editorial lead time 6 months. Submit seasonal material 6 months in advance. Accepts queries by mail, e-mail. Accepts previously published material. Accepts simultaneous submissions. Responds in 2 weeks to queries; 1½ months to mss. Sample copy online. Writer's guidelines online at website or by e-mail.
Nonfiction: Stephen Long, editor. Book excerpts, essays, how-to (related to woodland management), interview/profile. No product reviews, first-person travelogues, cute animal stories, opinion, or advocacy pieces. **Buys 15-20 mss/year.** Query with published clips. Length: 500-3,000 words. **Pays 10¢/word.** Sometimes pays expenses of writers on assignment.
Photos: State availability with submission. Reviews transparencies, prints. Buys one-time rights. Offers $25-75/photo. Identification of subjects required.
Columns/Departments: Stephen Long, editor. A Place in Mind (essays on places of personal significance), 600-800 words. **Pays $100**. Knots and Bolts (seasonal natural history items or forest-related news items), 300-600 words. **Pays 10¢/word**. Wood Lit (book reviews), 600 words. **Pays $25**. Field Work (profiles of people who work in the woods, the wood-product industry, or conservation field), 1,500 words. **Pays 10¢/word**. **Buys 30 mss/year.** Query with published clips.
Poetry: Jim Schley, poetry editor. Free verse, light verse, traditional. **Buys 4 poems/year.** Submit maximum 5 poems. **Pays $25.**
Tips: "We will work with subject-matter experts to make their work suitable for our audience."

$ $ $ ☆ ONEARTH, The Natural Resources Defense Council, 40 W. 20th St., New York NY 10011. Fax: (212)727-1773. E-mail: amicus@nrdc.org. Website: www.nrdc.org. **Contact:** Kathrin Day Lassila, editor. **75% freelance written.** Quarterly magazine covering national and international environmental issues. "*The Amicus Journal* is intended to provide the general public with a journal of thought and opinion on environmental affairs, particularly those relating to policies of national and international significance." Estab. 1979. Circ. 250,000. Pays on publication. Publishes ms an average of 6 months after acceptance. Byline given. Offers variable kill fee. Buys first North American serial, simultaneous, electronic rights. Submit seasonal material 6 months in advance. Accepts queries by mail, e-mail. Responds in 3 months to queries. Sample copy for $5. Writer's guidelines for #10 SASE.
Nonfiction: Environmental features. **Buys 12 mss/year.** Query with published clips. Length: 3,000. **Pays 50¢/word.** Sometimes pays expenses of writers on assignment.
Photos: State availability with submission. Reviews contact sheets, color transparencies, 8×10 b&w prints. Buys one-time rights. Negotiates payment individually. Captions, identification of subjects, model releases required.
Columns/Departments: News & Comment (summary reporting of environmental issues, tied to topical items), 700-2,000 words; International Notebook (new or unusual international environmental stories), 700-2,000 words; People, 2,000 words; Reviews (in-depth reporting on issues and personalities, well-informed essays on books of general interest to environmentalists interested in policy and history), 500-1,000 words. Query with published clips. **Pay negotiable.**
Poetry: All poetry should be rooted in nature. Brian Swann, poetry editor. Avant-garde, free verse, haiku. **Buys 12 poems/year.** Length: 1 ms page. **Pays $75.**
Tips: "Please stay up to date on environmental issues, and review *OnEarth* before submitting queries. Except for editorials all departments are open to freelance writers. Queries should precede manuscripts, and manuscripts should conform to the *Chicago Manual of Style*. *Amicus* needs interesting environmental stories—of local, regional or national import—from writers who can offer an on-the-ground perspective. Accuracy, high-quality writing, and thorough knowledge of the environmental subject are vital."

N ORION, The Orion Society, 187 Main St., Great Barrington MA 01230. E-mail: orion@orionsociety.org. Website: www.oriononline.org. Managing Editor: H. Emerson Blake. **Contact:** Aina Barten, associate editor. **30% freelance written.** Quarterly magazine covering the environment. "*Orion* is a quarterly magazine that explores the relationship between people and nature, examines human communities and how they fit into the larger natural community, and strives to renew our spiritual connection to the world. It is a forum of many voices that, collectively, seek to create a philosophy that guides our relationships with nature. *Orion* publishes literary nonfiction, short stories, interviews, poetry, reviews, and visual images related to this exploration. *Orion* is meant as a lively, personal, informative, and provocative dialogue. We look for compelling, reflective writing that connects readers to important issues by heightening awareness of the interconnections between humans and nature. We generally do not select material that is academic or theoretical, nor do we select material that is overly journalistic or overly topical. Literary journalism is welcome." Estab. 1982. Circ. 20,000. Pays on publication. Publishes ms an average of 8 months after acceptance. Byline given. Buys first North

American serial rights. Editorial lead time 4 months. Submit seasonal material 6 months in advance. Accepts queries by mail, e-mail. Accepts simultaneous submissions. Responds in 4-8 weeks to queries; 4-6 months to mss. Sample copy online. Writer's guidelines online.

Nonfiction: Essays, exposé, historical/nostalgic, humor, personal experience, photo feature, travel. No "What I learned during my walk in the woods"; personal hiking adventure/travel anecdotes; writing that deals with the natural world in only superficial ways. **Buys 8-20 mss/year.** Send complete ms. Length: 600-5,000 words. **Pays 10-20¢/word.** Pays in contributor copies if requested.

Photos: State availability with submission. Reviews contact sheets, prints. Buys one-time rights. Negotiates payment individually.

Columns/Departments: Features (any subject or slant), 2,500-5,000 words; Arts and the Earth (ways in which the arts are expressing and changing our thinking about nature), 1,200-2,500 words; Profile (stories of individuals working for a healthy world), 1,200-2,500 words; Natural Excursions (encounters with the natural world), 1,200-2,500 words; Deep Green (our spiritual relationship with nature and how it is being re-established), 1,200-2,500 words; Book Reviews (dealing with the context as well as content of environmental texts), 600-800 words; Coda (our endpaper), 600 words. **Buys 5-10 mss/year.** Send complete ms. **Pays 10-20¢/word; $100/book review.**

Fiction: Adventure, ethnic, historical, humorous, mainstream, slice-of-life vignettes. No manuscripts that don't carry an environmental message or involve the landscape/nature as a major character. **Buys 0-1 mss/year.** Send complete ms. Length: 1,200-4,000 words. **Pays 10-20¢/word.**

Poetry: Cheryl Daigle, poetry editor. Avant-garde, free verse, haiku, light verse, traditional. No cliché nature poetry. **Buys 20-30 poems/year.** Submit maximum 8 poems.

Tips: "It is absolutely essential that potential submitters read at least one issue of *Orion* before sending work. We are not your typical environmental magazine, and we approach things rather differently than, say, *Sierra* or *Audobon*. We are most impressed by and most likely to work with writers whose submissions show that they know our magazine."

$ $ $ OUTDOOR AMERICA, Izaak Walton League of America, 707 Conservation Lane, Gaithersburg MD 20878. (301)548-0150. Fax: (301)548-9409. E-mail: oa@iwla.org. Website: www.iwla.org. **Contact:** Jason McGarvey, editor. Quarterly magazine covering national conservation efforts/issues. "*Outdoor America*, one of the nation's most established conservation magazines, has been published by the Izaak Walton League, a national conservation organization, since 1922. A quarterly 4-color publication, *Outdoor America* is received by approximately 40,000 League members, as well as representatives of Congress and the media. Our audience, located predominantly in the midwestern and mid-Atlantic states, enjoys traditional recreational pursuits, such as fishing, hiking, hunting and boating. All have a keen interest in protecting the future of our natural resources and outdoor recreation heritage." Estab. 1922. Circ. 40,000. **Pays on acceptance.** Publishes ms an average of 2 months after acceptance. Accepts queries by mail, e-mail. Sample copy for $2.50. Writer's guidelines online.

Nonfiction: Conservation and natural resources issue stories with national implications. Query or send ms for short items (500 words or less). Features are planned 6-12 months in advance. Length: 350-3,000 words. **Pays $150-1,000.**

N PLANET VERMONT QUARTERLY, A Journal of Earth, Spirit, and Healing, P.O. Box 587, Winooski VT 05404-0587. (802)654-8024. Fax: (802)654-8024. E-mail: pvq@planetvermont.com. Website: www.Planetvermont.com. Managing Editor: Greg Guma. **Contact:** Dian Mueller, designing editor. **75% freelance written.** Quarterly tabloid covering Earth-honoring spirituality, community building, and health. "*Planet Vermont Quarterly* is an independent publication with a bioregional emphasis and a global perspective. Our mission is to present thoughtful information that challenges people to keep their minds and hearts open and contribute their best toward a better world; to provide an appealing, low-cost venue for information on innovative, holistically-oriented activities, good and services in the region; and to foster a sense of community centered on these ideals. As much as possible, we allow themes to emerge based on submissions, so that we can tap into the issues that are inspiring the community at large. Although the focus is somewhat bioregional—centering on Vermont—just about any topic can be addressed so long as there it has a connection to honoring the Earth, building community, healing, and/or living life with a spiritual approach." Estab. 1992. Circ. 20,000. Pays within one month of publication. Byline given. Buys one-time, electronic rights. Editorial lead time 2 months. Submit seasonal material 2 months in advance. Accepts queries by mail, e-mail. Accepts previously published material. Accepts simultaneous submissions. Responds in 1 month to queries; 1 month to mss. Sample copy for $4. Writer's guidelines online.

Nonfiction: Dian Mueller, editor. Book excerpts, essays, historical/nostalgic, how-to, inspirational, interview/profile, opinion, personal experience, photo feature, religious, book and provider reviews. Special issues: November issue includes a section on parenting. No preachy manuscripts. **Buys 48 mss/year.** Send complete ms. Length: 250-3,000 words. **Pays 2-5¢/word for unsolicited articles.**

Photos: Send photos with submission. Reviews prints, GIF/JPEG files. Buys one-time rights. Offers $10-35/photo. Captions, identification of subjects required.

Columns/Departments: Dian Mueller, editor. Pathways (personal narratives, reviews, how-to's), up to 1,200 words; Musings (reflections on regional life; poetry), up to 1,000 words; Vermont News (relevant short news), up to 800 words. **Buys 12 mss/year.** Send complete ms. **Pays 2-5¢/word.**

Fiction: Dian Mueller, editor. Fiction must fit within the overall theme of the publication. Experimental, fantasy, historical, novel excerpts, religious, science fiction, slice-of-life vignettes. **Buys 4 mss/year.** Query. Length: 500-2,000 words. **Pays 2-5¢/word.**

Poetry: Dian Mueller, editor. Avant-garde, free verse, haiku, light verse, traditional. **Buys 16 poems/year.** Submit maximum 10 poems. Length: 50 line maximum.

Tips: "Write about experiences and ideas that are compelling and inspiring to you in a way that respects the readers' intelligence without becoming too heavy."

$ $ $ $ SIERRA, 85 Second St., 2nd Floor, San Francisco CA 94105-3441. (415)977-5656. Fax: (415)977-5794. E-mail: sierra.letters@sierraclub.org. Website: www.sierraclub.org. Editor-in-chief: Joan Hamilton. Senior Editors: Reed McManus, Paul Rauber. **Contact:** Robert Schildgen, managing editor. Works with a small number of new/unpublished writers each year. Bimonthly magazine emphasizing conservation and environmental politics for people who are well educated, activist, outdoor-oriented, and politically well informed with a dedication to conservation. Estab. 1893. Circ. 695,000. **Pays on acceptance.** Publishes ms an average of 4 months after acceptance. Byline given. Offers negotiable kill fee. Buys first North American serial rights. Accepts queries by mail, fax. Accepts previously published material. Responds in 2 months to queries. Sample copy for $3 and SASE, or online. Writer's guidelines online.

- The editor reports an interest in seeing pieces on environmental "heroes," thoughtful features on new developments in solving environmental problems, and outdoor adventure stories with a strong environmental element.

Nonfiction: Exposé (well-documented articles on environmental issues of national importance such as energy, wilderness, forests, etc.), general interest (well-researched nontechnical pieces on areas of particular environmental concern), interview/profile, photo feature (photo essays on threatened or scenic areas), journalistic treatments of semitechnical topic (energy sources, wildlife management, land use, waste management, etc.). No "My trip to ..." or "Why we must save wildlife/nature" articles; no poetry or general superficial essays on environmentalism; no reporting on purely local environmental issues. **Buys 30-36 mss/year.** Query with published clips. Length: 800-3,000 words. **Pays $450-4,000.**
Reprints: Send photocopy with rights for sale noted and information about when and where the material previously appeared. Reprints pay negotiable.
Photos: Tanuja Mehrotra, art and production manager. Send photos with submission. Buys one-time rights. Pays maximum $300 for transparencies; more for cover photos.
Columns/Departments: Food for Thought (food's connection to environment); Good Going (adventure journey); Hearth & Home (advice for environmentally sound living); Body Politics (health and the environment); Profiles (biographical look at environmentalists); Hidden Life (exposure of hidden environmental problems in everyday objects); Lay of the Land (national/international concerns), 500-700 words; Mixed Media (essays on environment in the media; book reviews), 200-300 words. **Pays $50-500.**

The online magazine carries original content not found in the print edition and includes writer's guidelines.

Tips: "Queries should include an outline of how the topic would be covered and a mention of the political appropriateness and timeliness of the article. Statements of the writer's qualifications should be included."

$ SNOWY EGRET, The Fair Press, P.O. Box 9, Bowling Green IN 47833. (812)829-1910. Editor: Philip C. Repp. Managing Editor: Ruth C. Acker. **Contact:** Editors. **95% freelance written.** Semiannual literary magazine featuring nature writing. "We publish works which celebrate the abundance and beauty of nature, and examine the variety of ways in which human beings interact with landscapes and living things. Nature writing from literary, artistic, psychological, philosophical, and historical perspectives." Estab. 1922. Circ. 400. Pays on publication. Publishes ms an average of 6 months after acceptance. Byline given. Buys first North American serial rights. one-time anthology rights, or reprints rights Editorial lead time 2 months. Accepts queries by mail. Accepts simultaneous submissions. Responds in 1 month to queries; 2 months to mss. Sample copy for 9×12 SASE and $8. Writer's guidelines for #10 SASE.

Break in with "an essay, story, or short description based on a closely observed first-hand encounter with some aspect of the natural world."

Nonfiction: Essays, general interest, interview/profile, personal experience, travel. **Buys 10 mss/year.** Send complete ms. Length: 500-10,000 words. **Pays $2/page.**
Columns/Departments: Jane Robertson, Woodnotes editor. Woodnotes (short descriptions of personal encounters with wildlife or natural settings), 200-2,000 words. **Buys 12 mss/year. Pays $2/page.**
Fiction: Nature-oriented works (in which natural settings, wildlife, or other organisms and/or characters who identify with the natural world are significant components. "No genre fiction, e.g., horror, western romance, etc." **Buys 4 mss/year.** Send complete ms. Length: 5,000-10,000 words. **Pays $2/page.**
Poetry: Avant-garde, free verse, traditional. **Buys 30 poems/year.** Submit maximum 5 poems. **Pays $4/poem or page.**
Tips: "The writers we publish invariably have a strong personal identification with the natural world, have examined their subjects thoroughly, and write about them sincerely. They know what they're talking about and show their subjects in detail, using, where appropriate, detailed description and dialogue."

$ WHOLE EARTH, Point Foundation, 1408 Mission Ave., San Rafael CA 94901. (415)256-2800. Fax: (415)256-2808. E-mail: editor@wholeearthmag.com. Website: www.wholeearthmag.com. Editor: Mike Stone. Associate Editor: Emily Polk. **Contact:** Attn. Submissions. **70% freelance written.** "Quarterly periodical, descendent of the Whole Earth Catalog. Evaluates tools, ideas, and practices to sow the seeds for a long-term, viable planet." Estab. 1971. Circ. 30,000. Pays on publication. Publishes ms an average of 6 months after acceptance. Byline given. one-time rights to articles; all rights for reviews Editorial lead time 3 months. Accepts previously published material. Accepts simultaneous submissions. Responds in 1 month (no promises) to mss. Sample copy online. Writer's guidelines for SASE or online.
Nonfiction: Essays, exposé, general interest, how-to, humor, interview/profile, new product, personal experience, photo feature, religious, travel, historical; book reviews. "No dull repeats of old ideas or material; no 'goddess' material, spiritual, New Age or 'Paths to...'" Send complete ms (queries are discouraged). Length: 500-3,000 words. **Pays negotiable rates for assigned articles.**
Photos: State availability with submission. Buys one-time rights. Negotiates payment individually.

Fiction: Rarely publishes fiction. **Buys 2-4 mss/year.**
Poetry: Avant-garde, free verse, haiku, light verse, traditional. No long works. **Buys 1-4 poems/year.** Length: 100 lines maximum. **Payment negotiable.**
Tips: "We like your personal voice: intimate, a lively conversation with an attentive friend. We like ideas, thoughts and events to appear to stand independent and clear of the narrator. Don't send a variation on an old idea. Show us you did your homework."

$ $ $ $ WILDLIFE CONSERVATION, 2300 Southern Blvd., Bronx NY 10460. E-mail: nsimmons@wcs.org. Website: www.wcs.org. **Contact:** Nancy Simmons, senior editor. Bimonthly magazine for environmentally aware readers. Offers 25% kill fee. Buys first North American serial rights. Accepts simultaneous submissions. Responds in 1 month to queries. Sample copy for $5.95 (includes postage). Writer's guidelines available for SASE or via e-mail.
Nonfiction: "We want well-reported articles on conservation issues, conservation successes, and straight natural history based in author's research." **Buys 30 mss/year.** Query with published clips. Length: 300-2,000 words. **Pays $1/word for features and department articles, and $150/short piece.**

PERSONAL COMPUTERS

Personal computer magazines continue to evolve. The most successful have a strong focus on a particular family of computers or widely-used applications and carefully target a specific type of computer use. Although as technology evolves, some computers and applications fall by the wayside. Be sure you see the most recent issue of a magazine before submitting material.

$ $ ☒ COMPUTOREDGE, San Diego, Denver, and Albuquerque's Computer Magazine, The Byte Buyer, Inc., P.O. Box 83086, San Diego CA 92138. (858)573-0315. Fax: (858)573-0205. E-mail: submissions@computoredge.com. Website: www.computoredge.com. Executive Editor: Leah Steward. **Contact:** Patricia Smith, editor. **90% freelance written.** "We are the nation's largest regional computer weekly, providing San Diego, Denver, and Albuquerque with entertaining articles on all aspects of computers. We cater to the novice/beginner/first-time computer buyer. Humor is welcome." Published as *Computer Edge* in San Diego and Denver; published as *Computer Scene* in Albuquerque. Estab. 1983. Circ. 175,000. Pays 30 days after publication. Byline given. Offers $15 kill fee. Buys first North American serial rights. One-week exclusive and 6 months non-exclusive Web rights. Submit seasonal material 2 months in advance. Accepts queries by e-mail. Responds in 2 months to queries. Sample copy for SAE with 7 first-class stamps or on website. Writer's guidelines online.

- Accepts electronic submissions only.

Nonfiction: General interest (computer), how-to, humor, personal experience. **Buys 150 mss/year.** Send complete ms. Length: 900-1,200 words. **Pays $100-200.**
Columns/Departments: Beyond Personal Computing (a reader's personal experience); Mac Madness (Macintosh-related); I Don't Do Windows (alternative operating systems). Length: 700-800 words. **Buys 80 mss/year.** Send complete ms. **Pays $50-145.**
Fiction: Confessions, fantasy, slice-of-life vignettes. **Buys 20 mss/year.** Send complete ms. Length: 900-1,200 words. **Pays $100-200.**
Tips: "Be relentless. Convey technical information in an understandable, interesting way. We like light material, but not fluff. Write as if you're speaking with a friend. Avoid the typical 'Love at First Byte' and the 'How My Grandmother Loves Her New Computer' article. We do not accept poetry. Avoid sexual innuendoes/metaphors. Reading a sample issue is advised."

$ $ $ LAPTOP, Bedford Communications, 1410 Broadway, 21st Floor, New York NY 10018. (212)807-8220. E-mail: jmckenna@bedfordmags.com. Website: www.bedfordmags.com. Editor-in-Chief: David. A. Finck. **Contact:** Jessica McKenna, managing editor. **60% freelance written.** Monthly magazine covering mobile computing, such as laptop computer hardware, software and peripherals; industry trends. "Publication is geared toward the mobile technology laptop computer buyer, with an emphasis on the small office." Estab. 1991. Pays on publication. Publishes ms an average of 3 months after acceptance. Byline given. Offers 20% kill fee. Buys all rights. Editorial lead time 4 months. Accepts queries by mail, e-mail. Responds in 4 months to queries. Sample copy online. Writer's guidelines not available.
Nonfiction: How-to (e.g., how to install a CD-ROM drive), technical, hands-on reviews, features. **Buys 80-100 mss/year.** Length: 600-4,500 words. **Pays $150-1,250.** Sometimes pays expenses of writers on assignment.
Tips: "Send résumé with feature-length clips (technology-related, if possible) to editorial offices. Unsolicited manuscripts are not accepted or returned."

$ $ $ $ MACADDICT, Imagine Media, 150 North Hill Dr., Brisbane CA 94005. (415)468-4684. Fax: (415)468-4686. E-mail: editor@macaddict.com. Website: www.macaddict.com. Managing Editor: Jennifer Morgan. **Contact:** Rik Myslewski, editor-in-chief. **35% freelance written.** Monthly magazine covering Macintosh computers. "*MacAddict* is a magazine for Macintosh computer enthusiasts of all levels. Writers must know, love and own Macintosh computers." Estab. 1996. Circ. 180,000. Pays on publication. Publishes ms an average of 3 months after acceptance. Byline given. Buys all rights. Editorial lead time 3 months. Submit seasonal material 2 months in advance. Accepts queries by mail, e-mail. Responds in 1 month to queries.

Nonfiction: How-to, new product, technical. No humor, case studies, personal experience, essays. **Buys 20 mss/year.** Query with or without published clips. Length: 250-7,500 words. **Pays $50-2,500.**

Columns/Departments: Reviews (always assigned), 300-750 words; How-to's (detailed, step-by-step), 500-2,500 words; features, 1,000-2,500 words. **Buys 30-40 mss/year.** Query with or without published clips. **Pays $50-2,500.**

Fillers: Narasu Rebbapragada, editor. Get Info. **Buys 20/year.** Length: 50-500 words. **Pays $25-200.**

The online magazine carries original content not found in the print edition. Contact: Niko Coucouvanis, online editor.

Tips: "Send us an idea for a short one to two page how-to and/or send us a letter outlining your publishing experience and areas of Mac expertise so we can assign a review to you (reviews editor is Niko Coulo). Your submission should have great practical hands-on benefit to a reader, be fun to read in the author's natural voice, and include lots of screenshot graphics. We require electronic submissions. Impress our reviews editor with well-written reviews of Mac products and then move up to bigger articles from there."

N **$ $ $ SMART COMPUTING**, Sandhills Publishing, 131 W. Grand Dr., Lincoln NE 68521. (800)544-1264. Fax: (402)479-2104. E-mail: editor@smartcomputing.com. Website: www.smartcomputing.com. Managing Editor: Chris Trumble. **Contact:** Ron Kobler, editor-in-chief or Lesa Scarborough. **45% freelance written.** Monthly magazine. "We focus on plain-English computing articles with an emphasis on tutorials that improve productivity without the purchase of new hardware." Estab. 1990. Circ. 300,000. **Pays on acceptance.** Publishes ms an average of 2 months after acceptance. Byline given. Offers 25% kill fee. Buys all rights. Editorial lead time 4 months. Submit seasonal material 4 months in advance. Accepts queries by mail, e-mail. Accepts simultaneous submissions. Responds in 1 month to queries. Sample copy for $7.99. Writer's guidelines for #10 SASE.

Break in with "any article containing little-known tips for improving software and hardware performance and Web use. We're also seeking clear reporting on key trends changing personal technology."

Nonfiction: How-to, new product, technical. No humor, opinion, personal experience. **Buys 250 mss/year.** Query with published clips. Length: 800-3,200 words. **Pays $240-960.** Pays expenses of writers on assignment up to $75.

Photos: Send photos with submission. Buys all rights. Offers no additional payment for photos accepeted with ms. Captions required.

The online magazine carries original content not found in the print edition. Contact: Corey Russmand, online editor.

Tips: "Focus on practical, how-to computing articles. Our readers are intensely productivity-driven. Carefully review recent issues. We receive many ideas for stories printed in the last 6 months."

$ $ $ WIRED MAGAZINE, Condé Nast Publications, 520 Third St., 3rd Floor, San Francisco CA 94107-1815. (415)276-5000. Fax: (415)276-5150. E-mail: submit@wiredmag.com. Website: www.wired.com. Publisher: Dean Shutte. Editor-in-chief: Chris Anderson. **Contact:** Chris Baker, editorial assistant. **95% freelance written.** Monthly magazine covering technology and digital culture. "We cover the digital revolution and related advances in computers, communications, and lifestyles." Estab. 1993. Circ. 500,000. **Pays on acceptance.** Publishes ms an average of 3 months after acceptance. Byline given. Offers 25% kill fee. all rights for items less than 1,000 words, first North American serial rights for pieces over 1,000 words Editorial lead time 3 months. Responds in 3 weeks to queries. Sample copy for $4.95. Writer's guidelines by e-mail.

Nonfiction: Essays, interview/profile, opinion. "No poetry or trade articles." **Buys 85 features, 130 short pieces, 200 reviews, 36 essays, and 50 other mss/year.** Query. Pays expenses of writers on assignment.

Tips: "Send query letter with clips to Chris Baker. Read the magazine. We get too many inappropriate queries. We need quality writers who understand our audience, and who understand how to query."

PHOTOGRAPHY

Readers of these magazines use their cameras as a hobby and for weekend assignments. To write for these publications, you should have expertise in photography. Magazines geared to the professional photographer can be found in the Professional Photography section.

$ NATURE PHOTOGRAPHER, Nature Photographer Publishing Co., Inc., P.O. Box 690518, Quincy MA 02269. (617)847-0091. Fax: (617)847-0952. E-mail: nature_photographer@yahoo.com. Website: www.naturephotographermag.com. **Contact:** Helen Longest-Saccone and Evamarie Mathaey, co-editors-in-chief/photo editors. **100% freelance written.** Quarterly magazine written by field contributors and editors; write to above address to become a "Field Contributor." *Nature Photographer* emphasizes nature photography that uses low-impact and local less-known locations, techniques and ethics. Articles include how-to, travel to worldwide wilderness locations, and how nature photography can be used to benefit the environment and environmental education of the public. Estab. 1990. Circ. 25,000. Pays on publication. Buys one-time rights. Submit seasonal material 8 months in advance. Accepts queries by mail, e-mail. Accepts simultaneous submissions. Responds in 2 months to queries. Sample copy for 9×12 SAE and 6 first-class stamps. Writer's guidelines for #10 SASE or online.

Nonfiction: How-to (underwater, exposure, creative techniques, techniques to make photography easier, low-impact techniques, macro photography, large-format wildlife), photo feature, technical, travel. No articles about photographing in zoos or on game farms. **Buys 56-72 mss/year.** Query with published clips or writing samples. Length: 750-2,500 words. **Pays $75-150.**

Reprints: Send photocopy and information about when and where the material previously appeared. Pays 75% of amount *Nature Photographer* pays for an original article.

Photos: Send photos upon request. Do not send with submission. Reviews 35mm, 2¼×2¼ and 4×5 transparencies. Buys one-time rights. Offers no additional payment for photos accepted with ms. Identification of subjects required.

Tips: "Query with original, well-thought-out ideas and good writing samples. Make sure you send a SASE. Areas most open are travel, how-to, and conservation articles with dramatic slides to illustrate the articles. Must have good, solid research and knowledge of subject. Be sure to obtain guidelines by sending a SASE with request before submitting query. If you have not requested guidelines within the last year, request an updated version, because *Nature Photographer* is now written by editors and field contributors and guidelines will outline how you can become a field contributor."

$ $ PC PHOTO, Werner Publishing Corp., 12121 Wilshire Blvd., Suite 1200, Los Angeles CA 90025. Fax: (310)826-5008. Website: www.pcphotomag.com. Managing Editor: Chris Robinson. **Contact:** Rob Sheppard, editor. **60% freelance written.** Bimonthly magazine covering digital photography. "Our magazine is designed to help photographers better use digital technologies to improve their photography." Estab. 1997. Circ. 175,000. Pays on publication. Publishes ms an average of 4 months after acceptance. Byline given. Buys one-time rights. Editorial lead time 6 months. Submit seasonal material 6 months in advance. Accepts queries by mail. Responds in 1 month to queries. Sample copy for #10 SASE or online.

Nonfiction: How-to, personal experience, photo feature. **Buys 30 mss/year.** Query. Length: 1,200 words. **Pays $500 for assigned articles; approximately $400 for unsolicited articles.**

Photos: Send photos with submission. Reviews contact sheets, inkjet prints. Do not send original transparencies or negatives. Buys one-time rights. Offers $100-200/photo.

Tips: "Since *PCPHOTO* is a photography magazine, we must see photos before any decision can be made on an article, so phone queries are not appropriate. Ultimately, whether we can use a particular piece or not will depend greatly on the photographs and how they fit in with material already in our files. We take a fresh look at the modern photographic world by encouraging photography and the use of new technologies. Editorial is intended to demystify the use of modern equipment by emphasizing practical use of the camera and the computer, highlighting the technique rather than the technical."

$ $ PHOTO LIFE, Canada's Photography Magazine, Apex Publications, Inc., One Dundas St. W., Suite 2500, P.O. Box 84, Toronto, Ontario M5G 1Z3, Canada. (800)905-7468. Fax: (800)664-2739. E-mail: editor@photolife.com. Website: www.photolife.com. **Contact:** Mark A. Price, editor-in-chief. **15% freelance written.** Bimonthly magazine. "*Photo Life* is geared to a Canadian and U.S. audience of advanced amateur photographers. *Photo Life* is not a technical magazine per se, but techniques should be explained in enough depth to make them clear." Estab. 1976. Circ. 73,500. Pays on publication. Publishes ms an average of 1 year after acceptance. Byline given. Buys one-time rights. Editorial lead time 4 months. Submit seasonal material 6 months in advance. Accepts queries by mail, e-mail. Accepts simultaneous submissions. Responds in 3 months to queries. Sample copy for $5.50. Writer's guidelines free via email.

Nonfiction: How-to (photo tips, technique), inspirational, photo feature, technical, travel. **Buys 10 mss/year.** Query with published clips or send complete ms. **Pays $100-600 (Canadian).**

Photos: Reviews transparencies, prints. Buys one-time rights. Negotiates payment individually. Captions, model releases required.

Tips: "We will review any relevant submissions that include a full text or a detailed outline of an article proposal. Accompanying photographs are necessary, as the first decision of acceptance will be based upon images. Most of the space available in the magazine is devoted to our regular contributors. Therefore, we cannot guarantee publication of other articles within any particular period of time. Currently, we are overflowing with travel articles. You are still welcome to submit to this category, but the waiting period may be longer than expected (up to 1½ years). You may, however, use your travel photography to explain photo techniques. A short biography is optional."

$ $ $ PHOTO TECHNIQUES, Preston Publications, Inc., 6600 W. Touhy Ave., Niles IL 60714. (847)647-2900. Fax: (847)647-1155. E-mail: jwhite@phototechmag.com. Website: www.phototechmag.com. Publisher: S. Tinsley Preston III. Editor: Joe White. **50% freelance written.** Prefers to work with experienced photographer-writers; happy to work with excellent photographers whose writing skills are lacking. Bimonthly publication covering photochemistry, lighting, optics, processing, and printing, Zone System, digital imaging/scanning/printing, special effects, sensitometry, etc. Aimed at serious amateurs. Article conclusions should be able to be duplicated by readers. Estab. 1979. Circ. 35,000. Pays within 3 weeks of publication. Publishes ms an average of 8 months after acceptance. Byline given. Buys one-time rights. Sample copy for $5. Writer's guidelines for #10 SASE.

Nonfiction: How-to, photo feature, technical (product review), special interest articles within the above listed topics. Query or complete ms. Length: Open, but most features run approximately 2,500 words or 3-4 magazine pages. **Pays $150-750 for well-researched technical articles.**

Photos: Photographers have a much better chance of having their photos published if the photos accompany a written article. Prefers JPGs scanned at 300 dpi and sent via e-mail or CD-ROM, or prints, slides, and transparencies. Buys one-time rights. Manuscript payment includes payment for photos. Captions, technical information required.

Tips: "Study the magazine! Virtually all writers we publish are readers of the magazine. We are now more receptive than ever to articles about photographers, history, aesthetics, and informative backgrounders about specific areas of the photo industry or specific techniques. Successful writers for our magazine are doing what they write about."

$ TODAY'S PHOTOGRAPHER INTERNATIONAL, The Make Money With Your Camera Magazine, P.O. Box 777, Lewisville NC 27023. (336)945-9867. Fax: (336)945-3711. Website: www.aipress.com. Editor: Vonda H. Blackburn. **Contact:** Sarah Hinshaw, associate editor. **100% freelance written.** Bimonthly magazine addressing "how to make money—no matter where you live—with the equipment that you currently own." Editor's sweepstakes pays $500 for the best story in each issue. Estab. 1986. Circ. 78,000. Publishes ms an average of 6 months after acceptance. Byline given. Buys one-time rights. Editorial lead time 6 months. Submit seasonal material 6 months in advance. Accepts simultaneous submissions. Responds in 3 weeks to queries; 3 months to mss. Sample copy for $2, 9×12 SAE, and 4 first-class stamps or for $3. Writer's guidelines free.
Nonfiction: How-to, new product, opinion, personal experience, photo feature, technical, travel. No "What I did on my summer vacation" stories.
Photos: State availability with submission. Reviews transparencies, prints. Buys one-time rights. Offers no additional payment for photos accepted with ms. Captions, identification of subjects, model releases required.
Columns/Departments: Vonda Blackburn, editor. Books (how-to photography), 200-400 words; Sports (how-to photograph sports), 1,000 words. **Buys 40 mss/year.** Query. **Pay negotiable.**
Tips: Present a complete submission package containing: your manuscript, photos (with captions, model releases and technical data) and an inventory list of the submission package.

POLITICS & WORLD AFFAIRS

These publications cover politics for the reader interested in current events. Other publications that will consider articles about politics and world affairs are listed under the Business & Finance, Contemporary Culture, Regional, and General Interest sections. For listings of publications geared toward the professional, see Government & Public Service in the Trade section.

$ $ $ CALIFORNIA JOURNAL, 2101 K St., Sacramento CA 95816. (916)444-2840. Fax: (916)444-2339. E-mail: edit@statenet.com. Editor: David Lesher. **Contact:** Kathleen Les, managing editor **20% freelance written.** Monthly magazine "with nonpartisan coverage aimed at a literate, well-informed, well-educated readership with strong involvement in California issues, politics, or government." Estab. 1970. Circ. 12,000. Pays on publication. Publishes ms an average of 3 months after acceptance. Byline given. Buys all rights. Accepts queries by mail, fax. Responds in 2 weeks to queries; 2 months to mss.
Nonfiction: Political analysis. Interview/profile (of state and local government officials), opinion (on politics and state government in California). No outright advocacy pieces, fiction, poetry, product pieces. **Buys 10 unsolicited mss/year.** Query. Length: 800-2,000 words. **Pays $300-2,000.** Sometimes pays expenses of writers on assignment.
Photos: State availability with submission. Reviews contact sheets. Buys all rights. Negotiates payment individually. Identification of subjects required.
Columns/Departments: Soapbox (opinion on current affairs), 800 words. **Does not pay.**
Tips: "Be well versed in political and environmental affairs as they relate to California."

$ $ CHURCH & STATE, Americans United for Separation of Church and State, 518 C St. NE, Washington DC 20002. (202)466-3234. Fax: (202)466-3353. E-mail: americansunited@au.org. Website: www.au.org. **Contact:** Joseph Conn, editor. **10% freelance written.** Monthly magazine emphasizing religious liberty and church/state relations matters. Strongly advocates separation of church and state. Readership is well-educated. Estab. 1947. Circ. 33,000. **Pays on acceptance.** Publishes ms an average of 2 months after acceptance. Buys all rights. Accepts queries by mail. Accepts simultaneous submissions. Responds in 2 months to queries. Sample copy and writer's guidelines for 9×12 SAE with 3 first-class stamps.
Nonfiction: Exposé, general interest, historical/nostalgic, interview/profile. **Buys 11 mss/year.** Query. Length: 800-1,600 words. **Pays $150-300 for assigned articles.** Sometimes pays expenses of writers on assignment.
Reprints: Send tearsheet, photocopy or typed ms with rights for sale noted and information about when and where the material previously appeared.
Photos: Send photos with submission. Buys one-time rights. Pays negotiable fee for b&w prints. Captions required.
Tips: "We're looking for feature articles on underreported local church-state controversies. We also consider 'viewpoint' essays that offer a unique or personal take on church-state issues. We are not a religious magazine. You need to see our magazine before you try to write for it."

$ COMMONWEAL, A Review of Public Affairs, Religion, Literature, and the Arts, Commonweal Foundation, 475 Riverside Dr., Room 405, New York NY 10115. (212)662-4200. Fax: (212)662-4183. E-mail: commonweal@commonwealmagazine.org. Website: www.commonwealmagazine.org. Editor: Margaret O'Brien-Steinfels. **Contact:** Patrick Jordan, managing editor. Biweekly journal of opinion edited by Catholic lay people, dealing with topical issues of the day on public affairs, religion, literature and the arts. Estab. 1924. Circ. 20,000. Pays on publication. Byline given. Buys all rights. Submit seasonal material 2 months in advance. Responds in 2 months to queries. Sample copy for free.
Nonfiction: Essays, general interest, interview/profile, personal experience, religious. **Buys 30 mss/year.** Query with published clips. Length: 2,000-2,500 words. **Pays $75-100.**
Columns/Departments: Upfronts (brief, newsy reportorials, giving facts, information, and some interpretation behind the headlines of the day), 750-1,000 words; Last Word (usually of a personal nature, on some aspect of the human condition: spiritual, individual, political, or social), 800 words.

Poetry: Rosemary Deen, poetry editor. Free verse, traditional. **Buys 20 poems/year. Pays 75¢/line.**
Tips: "Articles should be written for a general but well-educated audience. While religious articles are always topical, we are less interested in devotional and churchy pieces than in articles which examine the links between 'worldly' concerns and religious beliefs."

$ DISASTER NEWS NETWORK, Villagelife.org Inc., 7855 Rappahannock Ave., Suite 200, Jessup MD 20794. (443)755-9999. Fax: (443)755-9990. E-mail: susank@disasternews.net. Website: www.disasternews.net. **Contact:** Susan Kim, news director. **100% freelance written.** Daily magazine. "The Disaster News Network is a comprehensive Internet site of timely news and information about U.S. disaster response and volunteer opportunities. DNN has been designed to be the primary first source of public information about U.S. disaster response efforts. Its news content is unusual because 100% of our content is original—DNN does not subscribe to any wire services or syndicates. The DNN news staff is located across the country, but meet regularly by telephone. All of the writers have previous daily news experience." Estab. 1998. Pays at end of the month. Publishes ms an average of 1 day after acceptance. Byline given. Buys all rights, makes work-for-hire assignments. Accepts queries by e-mail. Writer's guidelines free online or by e-mail.
Nonfiction: Religious, disaster response features. **Buys 600 mss/year.** Query with published clips. **Pays $85-100.** Pays expenses of writers on assignment.
Photos: Send photos with submission. Reviews prints. Buys all rights. Negotiates payment individually. Captions required.
Columns/Departments: Query. **Pays $85-100.**
Tips: "Daily news background/experience is helpful."

$ $ EMPIRE STATE REPORT, The Independent Magazine of Politics, Policy and the Business of Government, P.O. Box 9001, Mount Vernon NY 10552-9001. (914)699-2020. Fax: (914)699-2025. E-mail: sacunto@cinn.com. Website: www.empirestatereport.com. **Contact:** Stephen Acunto, Jr., associate publisher/executive editor. Monthly magazine with "timely and independent information on politics, policy and governance for local and state officials throughout New York State." Estab. 1974. Circ. 16,000. Pays up to 2 months after publication. Byline given. Buys first North American serial rights. Accepts queries by mail, e-mail, fax, phone. Responds in 1 month to queries; 2 months to mss. Sample copy for $4.50 with 9×12 SASE or online. Writer's guidelines online.

- Specifically looking for journalists with a working knowledge of legislative issues in New York State and how they affect businesses, municipalities, and all levels of government.

Nonfiction: Essays, exposé, interview/profile, opinion, analysis. Special issues: Editorial calendar available. **Buys 48 mss/year.** Query with published clips. Length: 500-4,500 words. **Pays $100-700.** Sometimes pays expenses of writers on assignment.
Photos: Send photos with submission. Reviews any size prints. Identification of subjects required.
Columns/Departments: Empire State Notebook (short news stories about state politics), 300-900 words; Perspective (opinion pieces), 800-850 words. Perspectives does not carry remuneration.

- The online magazine carries original content not found in the print edition and includes writer's guidelines. Contact: Stephen Acunto Jr.

Tips: "We are seeking journalists and nonjournalists from throughout New York State who can bring a new perspective and/or forecast on politics, policy, and the business of government. Query first for columns."

$ $ EUROPE, Delegation of the European Commission, 2300 M St. NW, 3rd Floor, Washington DC 20037. (202)862-9555. Fax: (202)429-1766. Website: www.eurunion.org. Managing Editor: Peter Gwin. **Contact:** Robert Guttman, editor-in-chief. **50% freelance written.** Monthly magazine for anyone with a professional or personal interest in Europe and European/US relations. Estab. 1963. Circ. 75,000. Pays on publication. Publishes ms an average of 3 months after acceptance. Byline given. Offers 50% kill fee. Buys first, all rights. Editorial lead time 2 months. Submit seasonal material 4 months in advance. Accepts queries by mail, e-mail, fax, phone. Responds in 6 months to queries. Sample articles and writer's guidelines online.
Nonfiction: General interest, historical/nostalgic, interview/profile, interested in current affairs (with emphasis on economics, business and politics), the Single Market and Europe's relations with the rest of the world. Publishes monthly cultural travel pieces, with European angle. **Buys 20 mss/year.** Length: 600-1,500 words. **Pays $50-500 for assigned articles; $50-400 for unsolicited articles.**
Photos: Photos purchased with or without accompanying mss. Buys b&w and color. Pays $25-35 for b&w print, any size; $100 for inside use of transparencies; $450 for color used on cover; per job negotiable.
Columns/Departments: Art & Leisure (book, art, movie reviews, etc.), 200-800 words. **Pays $50-250.**
Tips: "We are always interested in stories that connect Europe to the U.S.—especially business stories. Company profiles, a U.S. company having success or vice versa, are a good bet. Also interested in articles on the 'euro' and good, new and different travel pieces."

N $ $ IDEAS ON LIBERTY, 30 S. Broadway, Irvington-on-Hudson NY 10533. (914)591-7230. Fax: (914)591-8910. E-mail: srichman@cfee.org. Website: www.fee.org. Publisher: Foundation for Economic Education. **Contact:** Sheldon Richman, editor. **85% freelance written.** Monthly publication for "the layman and fairly advanced students of liberty." Estab. 1946. Pays on publication. Publishes ms an average of 5 months after acceptance. Byline given. Buys all rights, including reprint rights. Sample copy for 7½×10 ½ SASE with 4 first-class stamps.

- Eager to work with new/unpublished writers.

Nonfiction: "We want nonfiction clearly analyzing and explaining various aspects of the free market, private property, limited-government philosophy. Though a necessary part of the literature of freedom is the exposure of collectivistic cliches and fallacies, our aim is to emphasize and explain the positive case for individual responsibility and choice in a free-market economy. We avoid name-calling and personality clashes. Ours is an intelligent analysis of the principles underlying a free-market economy. No political strategies or tactics." **Buys 100 mss/year.** Query with SASE. Length: 3,500 words. **Pays 10¢/word.** Sometimes pays expenses of writers on assignment.
Tips: "It's most rewarding to find freelancers with new insights, fresh points of view. Facts, figures and quotations cited should be fully documented, to their original source, if possible."

$ THE LABOR PAPER, Serving Southern Wisconsin, Union-Cooperative Publishing, 3030 39th Ave., Suite 110, Kenosha WI 53144. (262)657-6116. Fax: (262)657-6153. Website: www.laborpaper.homepage.com. **Contact:** Mark T. Onosko, publisher. **30% freelance written.** Weekly tabloid covering union/labor news. Estab. 1935. Circ. 12,000. Pays on publication. Publishes ms an average of 2 months after acceptance. Byline given. Buys all rights. Editorial lead time 1 month. Submit seasonal material 1 month in advance. Accepts queries by mail, fax. Accepts simultaneous submissions. Sample copy and writer's guidelines free.
Nonfiction: Exposé, general interest, historical/nostalgic, humor, inspirational. **Buys 4 mss/year.** Query with published clips. Length: 300-1,000 words. **Pays $25.** Sometimes pays expenses of writers on assignment.
Photos: State availability with submission. Negotiates payment individually. Captions required.

$ $ THE NATION, 33 Irving Place, 8th Floor, New York NY 10003. (212)209-5400. Fax: (212)982-9000. E-mail: submissions@thenation.com. Website: www.thenation.com. **Contact:** Peggy Suttle, assistant to editor. **75% freelance written.** Works with a small number of new/unpublished writers each year. Weekly magazine "firmly committed to reporting on the issues of labor, national politics, business, consumer affairs, environmental politics, civil liberties, foreign affairs and the role and future of the Democratic Party." Estab. 1865. Pays on other. Buys first rights. Accepts queries by mail, e-mail, fax. Sample copy for free. Writer's guidelines for 6×9 SASE.
Nonfiction: "We welcome all articles dealing with the social scene, from an independent perspective." Queries encouraged. **Buys 100 mss/year. Pays $225-300.** Sometimes pays expenses of writers on assignment.
Columns/Departments: Editorial, 500-700 words. **Pays $100.**
Poetry: *The Nation* publishes poetry of outstanding aesthetic quality. Send poems with SASE. Grace Shulman, poetry editor. **Payment negotiable.**

The online magazine carries original content not found in the print edition and includes writer's guidelines. Contact: Katrina Vanden Heuvel, editor.

Tips: "We are a journal of left/liberal political opinion covering national and international affairs. We are looking both for reporting and for fresh analysis. On the domestic front, we are particularly interested in civil liberties; civil rights; labor, economics, environmental and feminist issues and the role and future of the Democratic Party. Because we have readers all over the country, it's important that stories with a local focus have real national significance. In our foreign affairs coverage we prefer pieces on international political, economic and social developments. As the magazine which published Ralph Nader's first piece (and there is a long list of *Nation* "firsts"), we are seeking new writers."

NATIONAL REVIEW, 215 Lexington Ave., New York NY 10016. (212)679-7330. E-mail: richardlowry@hotmail.com. Website: www.nationalreview.com. **Contact:** Rich Lowry, editor. Magazine.

Contact: Jonah Goldberg, online editor (jonahemail@aol.com).

N $ $ THE NATIONAL VOTER, League of Women Voters, 1730 M St. NW, #1000, Washington DC 20036. (202)429-1965. Fax: (202)429-0854. E-mail: nationalvoter@lwv.org. Website: www.lwv.org. **Contact:** Bob Adams, editor. Quarterly magazine. "*The National Voter* provides background, perspective, and commentary on public policy issues confronting citizens and their leaders at all levels of government. And it empowers people to make a difference in their communities by offering guidance, maturation and models for action." Estab. 1951. Circ. 100,000. Pays on publication. Byline given. Makes work-for-hire assignments. Editorial lead time 2 months. Accepts queries by mail, e-mail, fax, phone. Sample copy for free.
Nonfiction: Exposé, general interest, interview/profile. No essays, personal experience, religious, opinion. **Buys 6 mss/year.** Query with published clips. Length: 200-4,000 words. **Payment always negotiated.** Pays expenses of writers on assignment.
Photos: State availability with submission. Reviews contact sheets. Buys one-time rights. Offers no additional payment for photos accepted with ms. Captions, identification of subjects required.

THE NEW REPUBLIC, 1331 H St. NW, Suite 700, Washington DC 20005. (202)508-4444. Fax: (202)628-9383. E-mail: tnr@aol.com. Website: www.thenewrepublic.com. Editor-in-Chief, Chairman: Martin Peretz. Executive Editor: Christopher Orr. **Contact:** Asher Price, assistant editor; Leon Wieseltier, literary editor. Magazine.

Contact: Christiane Culhane, assistant editor; Jonathan Cohn, editor.

$ $ THE PROGRESSIVE, 409 E. Main St., Madison WI 53703-2899. (608)257-4626. Fax: (608)257-3373. E-mail: editorial@progressive.org. Website: www.progressive.org. **Contact:** Matthew Rothschild, editor. **75% freelance written.** Monthly Estab. 1909. Pays on publication. Publishes ms an average of 6 weeks after acceptance. Byline given. Buys all rights. Accepts queries by mail. Responds in 1 month to queries. Sample copy for 9×12 SAE with 4 first-class stamps or sample articles online. Writer's guidelines for #10 SASE.

Nonfiction: Investigative reporting (exposé of corporate malfeasance and governmental wrongdoing); electoral coverage (a current electoral development that has national implications); social movement pieces (important or interesting event or trend in the labor movement, or the GLBT movement, or in the area of racial justice, disability rights, the environment, women's liberation); foreign policy pieces (a development of huge moral importance where the US role may not be paramount); interviews (a long Q&A with a writer, activist, political figure, or musician who is widely known or doing especially worthwhile work); activism (highlights the work of activists and activist groups; increasingly, we are looking for good photographs of a dynamic or creative action, and we accompany the photos with a caption); book reviews (cover two or three current titles on a major issue of concern). Primarily interested in articles which interpret, from a progressive point of view, domestic and world affairs. Occasional lighter features. "*The Progressive* is a *political* publication. General interest is inappropriate." "We do not want editorials, satire, historical pieces, philosophical peices or columns." Query. Length: 500-4,000 words. **Pays $250-500.**
Poetry: publishes one original poem a month. "We prefer poems that connect up—in one fashion or another, however obliquely—with political concerns. **Pays $150.**
Tips: "Sought-after topics include electoral coverage, social movement, foreign policy, activism and book reviews."

$PROGRESSIVE POPULIST, Journal from America's Heartland, P.O. Box 150517, Austin TX 78715-0517. (512)447-0455. Fax: (603)649-7871. E-mail: populist@usa.net. Website: www.populist.com. Managing Editor: Art Cullen. **Contact:** Jim Cullen, editor. **90% freelance written.** Biweekly tabloid covering politics and economics. "We cover issues of interest to workers, small businesses, and family farmers and ranchers." Estab. 1995. Circ. 6,000. Pays on publication. Publishes ms an average of 1 month after acceptance. Byline given. Buys first North American serial, second serial (reprint) rights. Editorial lead time 3 weeks. Submit seasonal material 1 month in advance. Accepts queries by mail, e-mail, fax, phone. Accepts previously published material. Accepts simultaneous submissions. Sample copy and writer's guidelines free.
Nonfiction: "We cover politics and economics. We are interested not so much in the dry reporting of campaigns and elections, or the stock markets and GNP, but in how big business is exerting more control over both the government and ordinary people's lives, and what people can do about it." Essays, exposé, general interest, historical/nostalgic, humor, interview/profile, opinion. "We are not much interested in 'sound-off' articles about state or national politics, although we accept letters to the editor. We prefer to see more 'journalistic' pieces, in which the writer does enough footwork to advance a story beyond the easy realm of opinion." **Buys 400 mss/year.** Query. Length: 600-2,500 words. **Pays $15-50.** Pays writers with contributor copies or other premiums if preferred by writer.
Reprints: Send photocopy with rights for sale noted and information about when and where the material previously appeared.
Photos: State availability with submission. Buys one-time rights. Negotiates payment individually. Identification of subjects required.
Tips: "We do prefer submissions by e-mail. I find it's easier to work with e-mail and for the writer it probably increases the chances of getting a response."

[N] **$$$$REASON, Free Minds and Free Markets**, Reason Foundation, 3415 S. Sepulveda Blvd., Suite 400, Los Angeles CA 90034. (310)391-2245. Fax: (310)390-8986. E-mail: jwalker@reason.com. Website: www.reason.com. **Contact:** Jesse Walker, associate editor. **30% freelance written.** Monthly magazine covering politics, current events, culture, ideas. "*Reason* covers politics, culture and ideas from a dynamic libertarian perspective. It features reported works, opinion pieces, and book reviews." Estab. 1968. Circ. 55,000. **Pays on acceptance.** Byline given. Offers kill fee. Buys first North American serial, first, all rights. Editorial lead time 2 months. Submit seasonal material 3 months in advance. Accepts queries by mail, e-mail. Responds in 6 weeks to queries; 2 months to mss. Sample copy for $4. Writer's guidelines for #10 SASE.
Nonfiction: Book excerpts, essays, exposé, general interest, humor, interview/profile, opinion. No products, personal experience, how-to, travel. **Buys 50-60 mss/year.** Query with published clips. Length: 1,000-5,000 words. **Pays $300-2,000.** Sometimes pays expenses of writers on assignment.

The online magazine carries original content not found in the print edition and includes writer's guidelines. Contact: Nick Gillespie.

Tips: "We prefer queries of no more than one or two pages with specifically developed ideas about a given topic rather than more general areas of interest. Enclosing a few published clips also helps."

$$TOWARD FREEDOM, A Progressive Perspective on World Events, Toward Freedom, Inc., P.O. Box 468, Burlington VT 05422-0468. (802)654-8024. E-mail: info@towardfreedom.com. Website: www.towardfreedom.com. **Contact:** Greg Guma, editor. **75% freelance written.** Magazine published 8 times/year covering politics/culture, focus on Third World, Europe, and global trends. "*Toward Freedom* is an internationalist journal with a progressive perspective on political, cultural, human rights, and environmental issues around the world. Also covers the United Nations, the post-nationalist movements and U.S. foreign policy." Estab. 1952. Circ. 3,500. Pays on publication. Byline given. Buys first North American serial, one-time rights. Editorial lead time 1 month. Accepts queries by mail, e-mail. Responds in 3 months to queries. Sample copy for $3. Writer's guidelines for #10 SASE or on website.

Break in with "a clear, knowledgeable, and brief query, either by e-mail or U.S. mail, along with the basis of your knowledge about the subject. We're also looking for a new hook for covering subjects we follow, as well as comparisons between the U.S. and other places. We're also eager to break stories that are being 'censored' in mainstream media."

Nonfiction: Essays, interview/profile, opinion, personal experience, travel, features, book reviews, foreign, political analysis. Special issues: Women's Visions (March); Global Media (December/January). **Buys 50-75 mss/year.** Query. Length: 700-2,500 words.
Photos: Send photos with submission. Reviews prints. Buys one-time rights. Offers $35 maximum/photo. Identification of subjects required.
Columns/Departments: *TF* Reports (from foreign correspondents); UN; Beyond Nationalism; Art and Book Reviews; 800-1,200 words. **Buys 10-20 mss/year.** Query. **Pays up to 10¢/word.** Last Word (creative commentary), 900 words. **Buys 8 mss/year.** Query. **Pays $100.**

The online magazine carries original content not found in the print edition and includes guidelines. Contact: Greg Guma.

Tips: "We're looking for articles linking politics and culture; effective first-person storytelling; proposals for global solutions with realistic basis and solid background; provocative viewpoints within the progressive tradition; political humor. We receive too many horror stories about human rights violations, lacking constructive suggestions and solutions; knee-jerk attacks on imperialism."

$ $ WASHINGTON MONTHLY, The Washington Monthly Co., 733 15th St. NW, Suite 1000, Washington DC 20005. (202)393-5155. Fax: (202)332-8413. E-mail: editors@washingtonmonthly.com. Website: www.washingtonmonthly.com. Editor: Paul Glastris. **Contact:** Stephanie Mencimer, editor, or Nicholas Thompson, editor. **50% freelance written.** Monthly magazine covering politics, policy, media. "We are a neo-liberal publication with a long history and specific views—please read our magazine before submitting." Estab. 1969. Circ. 20,000. Pays on publication. Publishes ms an average of 2 months after acceptance. Byline given. Buys all rights. Editorial lead time 2 months. Submit seasonal material 4 months in advance. Accepts queries by mail, e-mail, fax, phone. Responds in 3 weeks to queries; 2 months to mss. Sample copy for 11×17 SAE with 5 first-class stamps or by e-mail. Writer's guidelines for #10 SASE, online, or by e-mail.
Nonfiction: Book excerpts, essays, exposé, general interest, historical/nostalgic, interview/profile, opinion, personal experience, technical, first-person political. "No humor, how-to, or generalized articles." **Buys 10 mss/year.** Query with or without published clips or send complete ms. Length: 1,500-5,000 words. **Pays 10¢/word.**
Photos: State availability with submission. Reviews contact sheets, prints. Buys one-time rights. Negotiates payment individually.
Columns/Departments: Memo of the Month (memos); On Political Books, Booknotes (both reviews of current political books), 1,500-3,000 words. **Buys 10 mss/year.** Query with published clips or send complete ms. **Pays 10¢/word.**
Tips: "Call our editors to talk about ideas. Always pitch articles showing background research. We're particularly looking for first-hand accounts of working in government. We also like original work showing that the government is or is not doing something important. We have writer's guidelines, but do your research first."

$ $ $ WORLD POLICY JOURNAL, World Policy Institute, 66 Fifth Ave., 9th Floor, New York NY 10011. (212)229-5808. Fax: (212)807-1294. E-mail: wrigleyl@newschool.edu. Website: www.worldpolicy.org. Editor: Karl E. Meyer. **Contact:** Linda Wrigley, managing editor. **10% freelance written.** Quarterly journal covering international politics, economics, and security isssues, as well as historical and cultural essays, book reviews, profiles, and first-person reporting from regions not covered in the general media. "We are eager to work with new or unpublished writers as well as more established writers. We hope to bring principle and proportion, as well as a sense of reality and direction to America's discussion of its role in the world." Circ. 8,000. Pays on publication. Publishes ms an average of 3 months after acceptance. Byline given. Buys all rights. Accepts queries by mail, e-mail, fax. Manuscripts by mail only. Responds in 3 months to queries. Sample copy for $7.95 and 9×12 SASE with 10 first-class stamps.
Nonfiction: Articles that "define policies that reflect the shared needs and interests of all nations of the world." Query. Length: 2,500-4,500 words. **Pays variable commission rate.**

PSYCHOLOGY & SELF-IMPROVEMENT

These publications focus on psychological topics, how and why readers can improve their own outlooks, and how to understand people in general. Many General Interest, Men's, and Women's publications also publish articles in these areas. Magazines treating spiritual development appear in the Astrology, Metaphysical & New Age section, as well as in Religion, while markets for holistic mind/body healing strategies are listed in the Health & Fitness section.

$ $ PERSONAL JOURNALING MAGAZINE, F&W Publications, Inc., 4700 E. Galbraith Rd., Cincinnati OH 45236. E-mail: journaling@fwpubs.com. Website: www.journalingmagazine.com. **Contact:** Editor. **70% freelance written.** Bimonthly magazine covering personal writing—letters, journals, memoirs. Estab. 1999. **Pays on acceptance.** Publishes ms an average of 4-6 months after acceptance. Byline and bionote given. Buys electronic, first world serial rights. Editorial lead time 6 months. Sample copy online. Writer's guidelines online.
Nonfiction: *How-to*: Easy-to-read how-to articles on keeping a journal that are original in style and fresh in content. *First person*: How has keeping a journal affected you personally and emotionally? Does your experience resonate with other journal-writers, yet it's a unique experience that no one else has gone through? If you can convey the experience

clearly and compellingly, and within 1,500 words, send us your revised, polished first-person journal-writing essay. We'd be happy to take a look!" Book excerpts, essays, how-to, new product, personal experience, personal writing experience. **Buys 30 mss/year.** Query for features; send complete ms for first-person essays. Length: 1,000-1,500 words. **Pays 30-45¢/word.**

Columns/Departments: "Columns are not open for submission; however, we have 3 departments that are open for submission: Writing Ways (no more than 1 page, double-spaced creative journal-keeping ideas). **Pays $50**. A Journaler's Life (500-600 word essay on the impact of journaling on a life). **Pays $200**. My Favorite Entry (no more than 2 pages, double-spaced, real-life journal excerpts). **Pays $100**. We also have rotating call-for-responses each issue that are open for submission."

$$$$ PSYCHOLOGY TODAY, Sussex Publishers, Inc., 49 E. 21st St., 11th Floor, New York NY 10010. (212)260-7210. Fax: (212)260-7445. E-mail: psychtoday@aol.com. Website: www.psychologytoday.com. **Contact:** Carin Gorrell, senior editor. Bimonthly magazine. "*Psychology Today* explores every aspect of human behavior, from the cultural trends that shape the way we think and feel to the intricacies of modern neuroscience. We're sort of a hybrid of a science magazine, a health magazine and a self-help magazine. While we're read by many psychologists, therapists and social workers, most of our readers are simply intelligent and curious people interested in the psyche and the self." Estab. 1967. Circ. 331,400. Pays on publication. Publishes ms an average of 3 months after acceptance. Byline given. Buys first North American serial rights. Editorial lead time 5 months. Accepts queries by mail. Responds in 1 month to queries. Sample copy for $3.50. Writer's guidelines for #10 SASE.

Nonfiction: "Nearly any subject related to psychology is fair game. We value originality, insight and good reporting; we're not interested in stories or topics that have already been covered *ad nauseum* by other magazines unless you can provide a fresh new twist and much more depth. We're not interested in simple-minded 'pop psychology.'" No fiction, poetry or first-person essays on "How I Conquered Mental Disorder X." **Buys 20-25 mss/year.** Query with published clips. Length: 1,500-4,000 words. **Pays $1,000-2,500.**

Columns/Departments: News Editor. News & Trends (short pieces, mostly written by staff, occasionally by freelancers), 150-300 words. Query with published clips. **Pays $150-300.**

$ ROSICRUCIAN DIGEST, Rosicrucian Order, AMORC, 1342 Naglee Ave., San Jose CA 95191-0001. (408)947-3600. Website: www.rosicrucian.org. **Contact:** Robin M. Thompson, editor-in-chief. Quarterly magazine (international) emphasizing mysticism, science, philosophy, and the arts for educated men and women of all ages seeking alternative answers to life's questions. **Pays on acceptance.** Publishes ms an average of 6 months after acceptance. Byline given. Buys first, second serial (reprint) rights. Accepts queries by mail, phone. Responds in 3 months to queries. Sample copy for free. Writer's guidelines for #10 SASE.

Nonfiction: How to deal with life—and all it brings us—in a positive and constructive way. Informational articles—new ideas and developments in science, the arts, philosophy, and thought. Historical sketches, biographies, human interest, psychology, philosophical, and inspirational articles. "We are always looking for good articles on the contributions of ancient civilizations to today's civilizations, the environment, ecology, inspirational (nonreligious) subjects. Know your subject well and be able to capture the reader's interest in the first paragraph. Be willing to work with the editor to make changes in the manuscript." No religious, astrological, or political material, or articles promoting a particular group or system of thought. Most articles are written by members or donated, but we're always open to freelance submissions. No book-length mss. Query. Length: 1,500-2,000 words. **Pays 6¢/word.**

Reprints: Prefers typed ms with rights for sale noted and information about when and where the article previously appeared, but tearsheet or photcopy acceptable. Pays 50% of amount paid for an original article.

Tips: "We're looking for more pieces on these subjects: our connection with the past—the important contributions of ancient civilizations to today's world and culture and the relevance of this wisdom to now; how to channel teenage energy/angst into positive, creative, constructive results (preferably written by teachers or others who work with young people—written for frustrated parents); and the vital necessity of raising our environmental consciousness if we are going to survive the coming millennium or even century."

$ SCIENCE OF MIND MAGAZINE, 3251 W. Sixth St., P.O. Box 75127, Los Angeles CA 90075-0127. (213)388-2181. Fax: (213)388-1926. E-mail: edit@scienceofmind.com. Website: www.scienceofmind.com. Publisher: Randall Friesen. Senior Editor: Kathy Juline. **Contact:** Jim Shea, assistant editor. **30% freelance written.** Monthly magazine featuring articles on spirituality, self-help, and inspiration. "Our publication centers on oneness of all life and spiritual empowerment through the application of Science of Mind principles." Pays on publication. Publishes ms an average of 5 months after acceptance. Byline given. Buys first North American serial rights. Submit seasonal material 6 months in advance. Writer's guidelines for SASE or online.

Nonfiction: Book excerpts, essays, inspirational, interview/profile, personal experience (of Science of Mind), spiritual. **Buys 35-45 mss/year.** Length: 750-2,000 words. **Payment varies. Pays in copies for some features written by readers.**

Photos: Inspirational, *Science of Mind* oriented. Reviews 35mm transparencies, 5×7, or 8×10 b&w prints. Buys one-time rights.

The online version contains material not found in the print edition.

Tips: "We are interested in first-person experiences of a spiritual nature having to do with Science of Mind principles."

REGIONAL

Many regional publications rely on staff-written material, but others accept work from freelance writers who live in or know the region. The best regional publication to target with your submissions is usually the one in your hometown, whether it's a city or state magazine or a Sunday supplement in a newspaper. Since you are familiar with the region, it is easier to propose suitable story ideas.

Listed first are general interest magazines slanted toward residents of, and visitors to, a particular region. Next, regional publications are categorized alphabetically by state, followed by Canada. Publications that report on the business climate of a region are grouped in the regional division of the Business & Finance category. Recreation and travel publications specific to a geographical area are listed in the Travel, Camping & Trailer section. Keep in mind also that many regional publications specialize in specific areas and are listed according to those sections. Regional publications are not listed if they only accept material from a select group of freelancers in their area or if they did not want to receive the number of queries and manuscripts a national listing would attract. If you know of a regional magazine that is not listed, approach it by asking for writer's guidelines before you send unsolicited material.

General

$$ BLUE RIDGE COUNTRY, Leisure Publishing, P.O. Box 21535, Roanoke VA 24018-9900. (540)989-6138. Fax: (540)989-7603. E-mail: info@leisurepublishing.com. Website: www.blueridgecountry.com. **Contact:** Kurt Rheinheimer, editor-in-chief. **75% freelance written.** Bimonthly magazine. "The magazine is designed to celebrate the history, heritage, and beauty of the Blue Ridge region. It is aimed at adult, upscale readers who enjoy living or traveling in the mountain regions of Virginia, North Carolina, West Virginia, Maryland, Kentucky, Tennessee, South Carolina, and Georgia." Estab. 1988. Circ. 80,000. Pays on publication. Publishes ms an average of 8 months after acceptance. Byline given. Offers $50 kill fee for commissioned pieces only. Buys first, second serial (reprint) rights. Submit seasonal material 6 months in advance. Accepts queries by mail, e-mail, fax. Responds in 2 months to queries; 2 months to mss. Sample copy for 9×12 SAE with 6 first-class stamps or online. Writer's guidelines for #10 SASE.

Nonfiction: "Looking for more backroads travel, history and legend/lore pieces." General interest, historical/nostalgic, personal experience, photo feature, travel. **Buys 25-30 mss/year.** Query with or without published clips or send complete ms. Length: 750-2,000 words. **Pays $50-250 for assigned articles; $25-250 for unsolicited articles.**

Photos: Send photos with submission. Reviews transparencies. Buys one-time rights. Pays $25-50/photo. Identification of subjects required.

Columns/Departments: Country Roads (shorts on people, events, travel, ecology, history, antiques, books); Mountain Inns (reviews of inns); Mountain Delicacies (cookbooks and recipes). **Buys 30-42 mss/year.** Query. **Pays $10-40.**

Tips: "Would like to see more pieces dealing with contemporary history (1940s-70s). Freelancers needed for regional departmental shorts and 'macro' issues affecting whole region. Need field reporters from all areas of Blue Ridge region. Also, we need updates on the Blue Ridge Parkway, Appalachian Trail, national forests, ecological issues, preservation movements."

$ CHRONOGRAM, Luminary Publishing, P.O. Box 459, New Paltz NY 12561. Fax: (914)256-0349. E-mail: info@chronogram.com. Website: www.chronogram.com. **Contact:** Brian K. Mahoney, editor. **50% freelance written.** Monthly magazine covering regional arts and culture. "*Chronogram* features accomplished, literary writing on issues of cultural, spiritual, and idea-oriented interest." Estab. 1994. Circ. 20,000. Pays on publication. Publishes ms an average of 3 months after acceptance. Byline given. Buys one-time rights. Editorial lead time 2 months. Submit seasonal material 3 months in advance. Accepts queries by mail, e-mail. Accepts simultaneous submissions. Responds in 2 weeks to queries; 6-8 weeks to mss. Sample copy and writer's guidelines online.

Nonfiction: Book excerpts, essays, exposé, general interest, historical/nostalgic, humor, interview/profile, opinion, personal experience, photo feature, religious, travel. "No health practitioners writing about their own healing modality." **Buys 24 mss/year.** Query with published clips. Length: 1,000-3,500 words. **Pays $75-150.**

Photos: State availability with submission. Reviews contact sheets. Buys one-time rights. Negotiates payment individually. Captions required.

Poetry: Franci Levine Grater, poetry editor. Avant-garde, free verse, haiku, traditional.

Tips: "The editor's ears are always open for new voices and all story ideas are invited for pitching. *Chronogram* welcomes all voices and viewpoints as long as they are expressed well. We discriminate solely based on the quality of the writing, nothing else. Clear, thoughtful writing on any subject will be considered for publication in *Chronogram*. We publish a good deal of introspective first-person narratives and find that in the absence of objectivity, subjectivity at least is a quantifiable middle ground between ranting opinion and useless facts."

$$$$ COWBOYS & INDIANS MAGAZINE, The Premier Magazine of the West, Dusty Spur Publishing, 8214 Westchester Dr., Suite 800, Dallas TX 75225. (214)750-8222. Fax: (214)750-4522. E-mail: mail@cowboysindians.

com. Website: www.cowboysindians.com. Editor: Eric O'Keefe. **Contact:** Melissa Flynn. **60% freelance written.** Magazine published 8 times/year covering people and places of the American West. "The Premier Magazine of the West, *Cowboys & Indians* captures the romance, drama, and grandeur of the American frontier—both past and present—like no other publication. Undeniably exclusive, the magazine covers a broad range of lifestyle topics: art, home interiors, travel, fashion, Western film, and Southwestern cuisine." Estab. 1993. Circ. 101,000. Pays on publication. Publishes ms an average of 2 months after acceptance. Byline given. Offers 20% kill fee. Buys first North American serial, electronic rights. Editorial lead time 4 months. Submit seasonal material 6 months in advance. Accepts queries by mail, e-mail, fax. Responds in 1 month to queries; 1 month to mss. Sample copy for $5. Writer's guidelines for free or by e-mail.

Nonfiction: Book excerpts, exposé, general interest, historical/nostalgic, interview/profile, photo feature, travel, art. No essays, humor, or opinion. **Buys 60-75 mss/year.** Query. Length: 500-3,000 words. **Pays $250-5,000 for assigned articles; $250-1,000 for unsolicited articles.** Sometimes pays expenses of writers on assignment.

Photos: State availability with submission. Reviews contact sheets, 2×2 transparencies. Buys one-time rights. Negotiates payment individually. Captions, identification of subjects required.

Columns/Departments: Art; Travel; Music; Home Interiors, all 1,000 words. **Buys 50 mss/year.** Query. **Pays $250-1,500.**

Tips: "Our readers are educated, intelligent, and well-read Western enthusiasts, many of whom collect Western Americana, read other Western publications, attend shows, and have discerning tastes. Therefore, articles should assume a certain level of prior knowledge of Western subjects on the part of the reader. Articles should be readable and interesting to the novice and general interest reader as well. Please keep your style lively, above all things, and fast-moving, with snappy beginnings and endings. Wit and humor are always welcome."

$ $ GUESTLIFE, Monterey Bay/New Mexico/El Paso/St. Petersburg/Clearwater/Houston/Vancouver, Desert Publications, Inc., 303 N. Indian Canyon Dr., Palm Springs CA 92262. (760)325-2333. Fax: (760)325-7008. E-mail: edit@palmspringslife.com. Website: www.guestlife.com. **Contact:** Olga Reyes, managing editor. **95% freelance written.** Annual prestige hotel room magazine covering history, highlights, and activities of the area named (i.e., *Monterey Bay GuestLife*). "*GuestLife* focuses on its respective area and is placed in hotel rooms in that area for the affluent vacationer." Estab. 1979. Pays on publication. Publishes ms an average of 9 months after acceptance. Byline given. Offers 25% kill fee. Buys electronic, all rights. Editorial lead time 4 months. Submit seasonal material 3 months in advance. Accepts queries by e-mail. Responds in 1 month to queries; 1 month to mss. Sample copy for $10. Writer's guidelines not available.

Nonfiction: General interest (regional), historical/nostalgic, photo feature, travel. **Buys 3 mss/year.** Query with published clips. Length: 300-1,500 words. **Pays $100-500.**

Photos: State availability with submission. Reviews contact sheets. Buys all rights. Negotiates payment individually. Identification of subjects required.

Fillers: Facts. **Buys 3/year.** Length: 50-100 words. **Pays $50-100.**

$ $ NOW AND THEN, The Appalachian Magazine, Center for Appalachian Studies and Services, P.O. Box 70556-ETSU, Johnson City TN 37614-0556. (423)439-6173. Fax: (423)439-6340. E-mail: woodsidj@etsu.edu. Website: cass.etsu.edu/n&t/. Managing Editor: Nancy Fischman. **Contact:** Jane Harris Woodside, editor-in-chief. **80% freelance written.** Triannual magazine covering Appalachian region from Southern New York to Northern Mississippi. "*Now & Then* accepts a variety of writing genres: fiction, poetry, nonfiction, essays, interviews, memoirs, and book reviews. All submissions must relate to Appalachia and to the issue's specific theme. Our readership is educated and interested in the region." Estab. 1984. Circ. 1,000. Pays on publication. Publishes ms an average of 4 months after acceptance. Byline given. Buys all rights. Editorial lead time 6 months. Accepts queries by mail, e-mail, fax. Accepts simultaneous submissions. Responds in 5 months to queries; 5 months to mss. Sample copy for $7.50. Writer's guidelines for #10 SASE or online.

Nonfiction: Book excerpts, essays, general interest, historical/nostalgic, humor, interview/profile, opinion, personal experience, photo feature, book reviews from and about Appalachia. "We don't consider articles which have nothing to do with Appalachia; articles which blindly accept and employ regional stereotypes (dumb hillbillies, poor and downtrodden hillfolk, and miners)." Query with published clips. Length: 1,000-2,500 words. **Pays $15-250 for assigned articles; $15-100 for unsolicited articles.** Sometimes pays expenses of writers on assignment.

Reprints: Send ms with rights for sale noted and information about when and where the material previously appeared. Pays 100% of amount paid for original article (typically $15-60).

Photos: State availability with submission. Buys one-time rights. Offers no additional payment for photos accepted with ms. Captions, identification of subjects required.

Fiction: "Fiction has to relate to Appalachia and to the issue's theme in some way." Adventure, ethnic, experimental, fantasy, historical, humorous, mainstream, slice-of-life vignettes. **Buys 3-4 mss/year.** Send complete ms. Length: 750-2,500 words. **Pays $15-100.**

Poetry: Free verse, haiku, light verse, traditional. "No stereotypical work about the region. I want to be surprised and embraced by the language, the ideas, even the form." **Buys 25-30 poems/year.** Submit maximum 5 poems. **Pays $10.**

Tips: "Get a copy of the magazine and read it. Then make sure your submission has a connection to Appalachia (check out http://cass.etsu.edu/cass/apregion.htm) and fits in with an upcoming theme."

$ $ $ $ SUNSET MAGAZINE, Sunset Publishing Corp., 80 Willow Rd., Menlo Park CA 94025-3691. (650)321-3600. Fax: (650)327-7537. E-mail: travelquery@sunset.com. Website: www.sunset.com. Editor-in-Chief: Katie Tamony.

Contact: Peter Fish, senior travel editor; Kathleen Brenzel, senior garden editor. Monthly magazine covering the lifestyle of the Western states. "*Sunset* is a Western lifestyle publication for educated, active consumers. Editorial provides localized information on gardening and travel, food and entertainment, home building and remodeling." Freelance articles should be timely and only about the 13 Western states. Garden section accepts queries by mail. Travel section prefers queries by e-mail. **Pays on acceptance.** Byline given. Sample copy not available. Guidelines for freelance travel items for #10 SASE addressed to Editorial Services.

Nonfiction: "Travel items account for the vast majority of *Sunset's* freelance assignments, although we also contract out some short garden items. However *Sunset* is largely staff-written." Travel (in the West). **Buys 50-75 mss/year.** Query. Length: 550-750 words. **Pays $1/word.**

Columns/Departments: Building & Crafts; Food; Garden; Travel. Travel Guide length: 300-350 words. Direct queries to specific editorial department.

Tips: "Here are some subjects regularly treated in *Sunset*'s stories and Travel Guide items: outdoor recreation (i.e., bike tours, bird-watching spots, walking or driving tours of historic districts); indoor adventures (i.e., new museums and displays, hands-on science programs at aquariums or planetariums, specialty shopping); special events (i.e., festivals that celebrate a region's unique social, cultural, or agricultural heritage). Also looking for great weekend getaways, backroad drives, urban adventures and culinary discoveries such as ethnic dining enclaves. Planning and assigning begins a year before publication date."

$ $ ☆ VILLAGE PROFILE, Community Maps, Guides, and Directories, Progressive Publishing, Inc., 33 N. Geneva, Elgin IL 60120. (800)600-0134, ext. 221. E-mail: dave@villageprofilemail.com. Website: www.villageprofile.com. **Contact:** David Gall, managing editor. **50% freelance written.** Annual local community guides covering 40 states. "We publish community guides and maps for (primarily) chambers of commerce across the U.S. Editorial takes on a factual, yet upbeat, positive view of communities. Writers need to be able to make facts and figures 'friendly,' to present information to be used by residents as well as businesses, as guides are used for economic development." Publishes 350 projects/year. Estab. 1988. **Pays on acceptance.** Publishes ms an average of 4 months after acceptance. Byline given. Buys electronic, all rights, makes work-for-hire assignments. Editorial lead time 2 months. Accepts queries by mail, e-mail. Sample copy for 9×12 SASE. Writer's guidelines free.

Nonfiction: Buys 100 mss/year. Query with published clips and geographic availability. Length: 1,000-4,000 words. **Pays $200-500 for assigned articles.** Sometimes pays expenses of writers on assignment.

Photos: State availability with submission. Negotiates payment individually. Identification of subjects required.

Tips: "Writers must meet deadlines, know how to present a positive image of a community without going overboard with adjectives and adverbs! Know how to find the info you need if our contact (typically a busy chamber executive) needs your help doing so. Availability to 'cover' a region/area is a plus."

$ $ $ YANKEE, Yankee Publishing Inc., P.O. Box 520, Dublin NH 03444-0520. (603)563-8111. Fax: (603)563-8252. E-mail: queries@yankeepub.com. Website: www.newengland.com. Editor: Michael Carlton. **Contact:** (Ms.) Sam Darley, editorial assistant. **75% freelance written.** Monthly magazine covering New England. "Our mission is to express and perhaps, indirectly, preserve the New England culture—and to do so in an entertaining way. Our audience is national and has one thing in common—it loves New England." Estab. 1935. Circ. 500,000. Pays within 30 days of acceptance. Publishes ms an average of 10 months after acceptance. Byline given. Offers 33% kill fee. Buys first rights. Submit seasonal material 6 months in advance. Accepts queries by mail. Responds in 2 months to queries. Writer's guidelines for #10 SASE.

O-- Break in with a short item for the "Snippets" section.

Nonfiction: Essays, general interest, humor, interview/profile, personal experience. "No 'good old days' pieces, no dialect humor and nothing outside New England!" **Buys 30 mss/year.** Query with published clips and SASE. Length: 250-2,500 words. **Pays $100-1,500.** Pays expenses of writers on assignment.

Photos: Send photos with submission. Reviews contact sheets, transparencies. Buys one-time rights. Offers $50-150/photo. Identification of subjects required.

Columns/Departments: Snippets (short bits on interesting people, anecdotes, historical oddities), 100-400 words, **pays $50-200.** Great New England Cooks (profile recipes), 500 words, **pays $800.** Recipe with a History (family favorites that have a story behind them), 100-200 words plus recipe, **pays $50.** Travel, 25-200 words, query first, **pays $25-250**. **Buys 80 mss/year.** Query with published clips and SASE. **Pays $25-800. Buys 4 mss/year.** Send complete ms. Length: 500-2,500 words. **Pays $1,000.** "We don't choose poetry by type. We look for the best." Jean Burden, poetry editor. "No inspirational, holiday-oriented, epic, limericks, etc." **Buys 40 poems/year.** Submit maximum 3 poems. Length: 2-20 lines. **Pays $50.**

The online magazine carries original content not found in the print edition. Contact: Erica Bollerud, online editor.

Tips: "Submit lots of ideas. Don't censor yourself—let *us* decide whether an idea is good or bad. We might surprise you. Remember we've been publishing for 65 years, so chances are we've already done every 'classic' New England subject. Try to surprise us—it isn't easy. These departments are most open to freelancers: Snippets and Recipe with a History. Study the ones we publish—the format should be apparent. It is to your advantage to read several issues of the magazine before sending us a query or a manuscript. *Yankee* will not publish fiction or poetry beginning with the July 2002 issue."

Alabama

[N] $ $ ALABAMA HERITAGE, University of Alabama, Box 870342, Tuscaloosa AL 35487-0342. (205)348-7467. Fax: (205)348-7473. Website: www.AlabamaHeritage.com. **Contact:** T.J. Beitelman, editor. **50% freelance written.** "*Alabama Heritage* is a nonprofit historical quarterly published by the University of Alabama and the University of Alabama at Birmingham for the intelligent lay reader. We are interested in lively, well-written, and thoroughly researched articles on Alabama/Southern history and culture. Readability and accuracy are essential." Estab. 1986. Pays on publication. Byline given. Buys first, second serial (reprint) rights. Accepts queries by mail. Responds in 1 month to queries; 1 month to mss. Sample copy for $6. Writer's guidelines for #10 SASE.

Nonfiction: Historical. "We do not want fiction, poetry, book reviews, articles on current events or living artists, and personal/family reminiscences." **Buys 10 mss/year.** Query. Length: 1,500-4,000 words. **Pays $200.** Sends 10 copies to each author, plus 1-year subscription.

Photos: Reviews contact sheets. Buys one-time rights. Identification of subjects required.

Tips: "Authors need to remember that we regard history as a fascinating subject, not as a dry recounting of dates and facts. Articles that are lively and engaging, in addition to being well researched, will find interested readers among our editors. No term papers, please. All areas are open to freelance writers. Best approach is a written query."

$ ALABAMA LIVING, Alabama Rural Electric Association, P.O. Box 244014, Montgomery AL 36124. (334)215-2732. Fax: (334)215-2733. E-mail: dgates@areapower.com. Website: alabamaliving.com. Darryl Gates, editor. **10% freelance written.** Monthly magazine covering rural electric consumers. "Our magazine is an editorially balanced, informational and educational service to members of rural electric cooperatives. Our mix regularly includes Alabama history, nostalgia, gardening, outdoor and consumer pieces." Estab. 1948. Circ. 350,000. **Pays on acceptance.** Byline given. Not copyrighted. Editorial lead time 4 months. Submit seasonal material 4 months in advance. Accepts queries by mail, e-mail. Accepts simultaneous submissions. Responds in 1 month to queries. Sample copy for free.

- Break in with a bit of history or nostalgia about Alabama or the Southeast and pieces about "little-known" events in Alabama history or "little-known" sites.

Nonfiction: Historical/nostalgic (rural-oriented), inspirational, personal experience (Alabama). Special issues: Gardening (March); Holiday Recipes (December). **Buys 6 mss/year.** Send complete ms. Length: 300-750 words. **Pays $100 minimum for assigned articles; $50 minimum for unsolicited articles.**

Reprints: Send ms with rights for sale noted. Pays $50.

[N] $ $ BIRMINGHAM WEEKLY, Magnolia Media, 2257 Highland Ave. S., Birmingham AL 35205. (205)939-4030. E-mail: editor@bhamweekly.com. **Contact:** Darin Powell, editor. **40% freelance written.** Weekly. "We are an alternative newsweekly; alternative in the sense that we're an alternative to daily papers and TV news. We are edgy, hip, well written but based in solid journalism. Our audience is 18-54, educated with disposable income and an irreverant but intelligent point of view." Estab. 1997. Circ. 30,000. Pays on publication. Publishes ms an average of 2 weeks after acceptance. Byline given. Editorial lead time 3 weeks. Submit seasonal material 2 months in advance. Accepts queries by mail, e-mail. Accepts simultaneous submissions. Responds in 2 weeks to queries. Sample copy for free. Writer's guidelines not available.

Nonfiction: "We are strictly interested in stories that have a Birmingham connection, except in reviews, where the requirement is for readers to be able to buy the CD or book or see the film in Birmingham." Essays, exposé, general interest, historical/nostalgic, humor, interview/profile. "No opinion columns, i.e., op-ed stuff." Query with or without published clips. Length: 100-1,000 words. **Pays 5¢/word.** Sometimes pays expenses of writers on assignment.

Columns/Departments: Sound Advice (CD reviews), 100 words; Book Reviews, 300 words. Query with or without published clips. **Pays 5 ¢/ word.**

$ $ MOBILE BAY MONTHLY, PMT Publishing, P.O. Box 66200, Mobile AL 36660. (251)473-6269. Fax: (251)479-8822. E-mail: deblina@pmtpublishing.com. **Contact:** Deblina Chakraborty, assistant editor. **25% freelance written.** "*Mobile Bay Monthly* is a monthly lifestyle magazine for the South Alabama/Gulf Coast region focusing on the people, ideas, issues, arts, homes, food, culture, and businesses that make Mobile Bay an interesting place." Estab. 1990. Circ. 10,000. Pays on publication. Publishes ms an average of 4 months after acceptance. Byline given. Buys first rights. Editorial lead time 4 months. Submit seasonal material 6 months in advance. Accepts queries by mail, e-mail, fax. Sample copy for $2. Writer's guidelines not available.

Nonfiction: General interest, historical/nostalgic, how-to (home renovations, etc.), interview/profile, personal experience, photo feature, travel (must be along the Gulf Coast). Accepts queries by mail, fax, e-mail. **Buys 10 mss/year.** Query with published clips. Length: 1,200-3,000 words. **Pays $100-300.**

Photos: State availability with submission. Buys one-time rights. Negotiates payment individually. Identification of subjects required.

Tips: "We use mostly local writers. Strong familiarity with the Mobile area is a must. No phone calls; please send query letters with writing samples."

Alaska

$ $ $ ALASKA, Exploring Life on the Last Frontier, 619 E. Ship Creek Ave., Suite 329, Anchorage AK 99501. (907)272-6070. Fax: (907)258-5360. Website: www.alaskamagazine.com. **Contact:** Donna Rae Thompson, editorial assistant. **70% freelance written.** Eager to work with new/unpublished writers. Magazine published 10 times year covering topics "uniquely Alaskan." Estab. 1935. Circ. 180,000. Pays on publication. Publishes ms an average of 6 months after acceptance. Byline given. Buys first, one-time rights. Submit seasonal material 1 year in advance. Accepts queries by mail. Responds in 2 months to queries; 2 months to mss. Sample copy for $3 and 9×12 SAE with 7 first-class stamps. Writer's guidelines for #10 SASE.

O→ Break in by "doing your homework. Make sure a similar story has not appeared in the magazine within the last five years. It must be about Alaska."

Nonfiction: Historical/nostalgic, humor, interview/profile, personal experience, photo feature, travel, adventure, outdoor recreation (including hunting, fishing), Alaska destination stories. No fiction or poetry. **Buys 40 mss/year.** Query. Length: 100-2,500 words. **Pays $100-1,250.**

Photos: Send photos with submission. Reviews 35mm or larger transparencies, slides labeled with your name. Captions, identification of subjects required.

Tips: "We're looking for top-notch writing—original, well-researched, lively. Subjects must be distinctly Alaskan. A story on a mall in Alaska, for example, won't work for us; every state has malls. If you've got a story about a Juneau mall run by someone who is also a bush pilot and part-time trapper, maybe we'd be interested. The point is *Alaska* stories need to be vivid, focused and unique. Alaska is like nowhere else—we need our stories to be the same way."

Arizona

$ $ ARIZONA FOOTHILLS MAGAZINE, Media That Deelivers, Inc., 8132 N. 87th Place, Scottsdale AZ 85258. (480)460-5203. Fax: (480)443-1517. E-mail: reneedee@azfoothillsmag.com. Website: www.azfoothillsmag.com. Editor: Renee Dee. **Contact:** Karen Werner, executive editor. **30% freelance written.** Monthly magazine covering Arizona lifesyle. Estab. 1996. Circ. 60,000. Pays on publication. Publishes ms an average of 6 months after acceptance. Byline given. Editorial lead time 6 months. Submit seasonal material 4 months in advance. Accepts queries by mail, e-mail. Responds in 1 month to queries; 1 month to mss. Sample copy and writer's guidelines for #10 SASE.

O→ Break in by "submitting a story with a local angle and having several reader-service sidebars in mind."

Nonfiction: Renee Dee, publisher. General interest, how-to (decorate, paint, outdoor recreation), inspirational, interview/profile, new product, personal experience, photo feature, travel, fashion, decor, arts. **Buys 30 mss/year.** Query with published clips. Length: 900-2,000 words. **Pays 15-20¢/word for assigned articles; 10¢/word for unsolicited articles.** Sometimes pays expenses of writers on assignment.

Photos: Send photos with submission. Reviews contact sheets, transparencies. Buys one-time rights. Negotiates payment individually. Captions, identification of subjects, model releases required.

Columns/Departments: Travel, dining, fashion, home decor, design, architecture, wine, shopping, golf, performance & visual arts.

Tips: "We prefer stories that appeal to my audience written with an upbeat, contemporary approach and reader service in mind."

$ $ $ ARIZONA HIGHWAYS, 2039 W. Lewis Ave., Phoenix AZ 85009-9988. (602)712-2024. Fax: (602)254-4505. Website: www.arizonahighways.com. **Contact:** Beth Deveny, managing editor. **100% freelance written.** Magazine that is state-owned, designed to help attract tourists into and through Arizona. Estab. 1925. Circ. 425,000. **Pays on acceptance.** Buys first North American serial rights. Accepts queries by mail, e-mail, fax. Responds in 1 month to queries; 1 month to mss. Sample copy not available. Writer's guidelines for #10 SASE.

O→ Break in with "a concise query written with flair, backed by impressive clips that reflect the kind of writing that appears in *Arizona Highways*. The easiest way to break into the magazine for writers new to us is to propose short items for the Off-ramp section, contribute short humor anecdotes for the Humor page, or submit 650-word pieces for the Along the Way column."

Nonfiction: Feature subjects include narratives and exposition dealing with history, anthropology, nature, wildlife, armchair travel, out of the way places, small towns, Old West history, Indian arts and crafts, travel, etc. Travel articles are experience-based. All must be oriented toward Arizona. "We deal with professionals only, so include a list of current credits." **Buys 50 mss/year.** Query with a lead paragraph and brief outline of story. Length: 600-1,800 words. **Pays $1/word.** Pays expenses of writers on assignment.

Photos: "We use transparencies of medium format, 4×5, and 35mm when appropriate to the subject matter, or they display exceptional quality or content. We prefer 35mm at 100 ISO or slower. Each transparency must be accompanied by information attached to each photograph: where, when, what. No photography will be reviewed by the editors unless the photographer's name appears on each and every transparency." Peter Ensenberger, photo editor. Buys one-time rights. Pays $100-600.

Columns/Departments: Focus on Nature (short feature in first or third person dealing with the unique aspects of a single species of wildlife), 800 words; Along the Way (short essay dealing with life in Arizona, or a personal experience keyed to Arizona), 800 words; Back Road Adventure (personal back-road trips, preferably off the beaten path and outside major metro areas), 1,000 words; Hike of the Month (personal experiences on trails anywhere in Arizona), 500 words; Arizona Humor (amusing short anecdotes about Arizona), 200 words maximum. **Pays $50-1,000, depending on department.**

The online magazine carries original content not found in the print edition. Contact: Robert J. Early, editor.

Tips: "Writing must be of professional quality, warm, sincere, in-depth, well peopled and accurate. Avoid themes that describe first trips to Arizona, the Grand Canyon, the desert, Colorado River running, etc. Emphasis is to be on Arizona adventure and romance as well as flora and fauna, when appropriate, and themes that can be photographed. Double check your manuscript for accuracy. Our typical reader is a 50-something person with the time, the inclination, and the means to travel."

$ CAREFREE ENTERPRISE MAGAZINE, Serving Arizona Since 1963, Carefree Enterprise Magazine, Inc., P.O. Box 1145, Carefree AZ 85377. E-mail: staff@carefreeenterprise.com. Website: www.carefreeenterprise.com. Editor: Fran Barbano. **Contact:** Susan Smyth, assistant editor. **35% freelance written.** Magazine published 11 times/year. "*CEM* is a good news publication. We dwell on the positive, uplifting, and inspiring influences of life. We promote our areas and people." Circ. 3,000. Usually pays within 3 months after publication. Publishes ms an average of 1 year after acceptance. Byline given. Buys first North American serial, first, one-time, second serial (reprint) rights. Editorial lead time up to 1 year. Submit seasonal material 6 months in advance. Accepts queries by mail, e-mail. Accepts previously published material. Responds in 4 months to queries; 4 months to mss. Sample copy for $2 with 9½×12½ SAE with $1.39 postage, or $4, includes postage. Writer's guidelines for #10 SASE.

Nonfiction: General interest, historical/nostalgic, humor, inspirational, personal experience, photo feature, travel, health, alternative medicine. "Nothing negative or controversial." **Buys 50 mss/year.** Query with or without published clips or send complete ms. Length: 300-1,500 words. **Pays $50 for assigned articles; $5-50 for unsolicited articles.**

Photos: State availability with submission. Reviews transparencies, prints (up to 8×10). Buys one-time rights. Pays $5/photo. Captions, identification of subjects, model releases required.

Columns/Departments: Stephanie Bradley, assistant editor. Health, 100-300 words. **Buys 36 mss/year.** Query with or without published clips or send complete ms. **Pays $5-35.**

Fiction: Pays $50 maximum for features. Serial pays $50 maximum for each part.

Poetry: "Nothing negative, controversial, or unacceptable to families."

Fillers: Anecdotes, facts, short humor. **Buys 12-50/year.** Length: 50-300 words. **Pays $15-35.**

Tips: "We are easy to work with. New and established writers should be familiar with our publication and audience. Our youngest columnist is a 17-year-old blind girl who writes from a teen's point of view and often touches on blindness, and how others interact with handicapped individuals. We are open and receptive to any/all good news, upbeat, family-oriented material. We could use more humor, inspiration, travel (regional and worldwide), and positive solutions to everyday challenges. We like to feature profiles of outstanding people (no politics, no commercials) who are role model material. Be familiar with this publication. New articles on eldercare covering dementia to diapers. Particularly need problem-solving articles (How did you handle it or cope?). People caring for aging parents need guidance, support, encouragement."

$ $ CITY AZ, City AZ Publishing LLC, 342 E. Thomas Rd., Phoenix AZ 85012. (602)667-9798. Fax: (602)508-9454. E-mail: info@cityaz.com. Website: www.cityaz.com. **Contact:** Leigh Flayton, editor. **75% freelance written.** Bimonthly lifestyle and culture magazine "with an emphasis on modern design, culinary trends, cultural trends, fashion, great thinkers of our time and entertainment." Estab. 1997. Circ. 40,000. Pays 30 days after publication. Byline given. Offers 50% kill fee. Buys first, electronic rights. Editorial lead time 3 months. Submit seasonal material 3 months in advance. Accepts queries by mail, e-mail, fax, phone. Responds in 3 weeks to queries; 2 months to mss. Sample copy for e-mail request. Writer's guidelines not available.

Nonfiction: General interest, interview/profile, new product, photo feature, travel, architecture. Query with published clips. Length: 300-2,000 words. **Pays $25-400.**

Photos: State availability with submission. Reviews contact sheets, negatives, transparencies, prints. Buys one-time or electronic rights. Negotiates payment individually. Identification of subjects, model releases required.

Columns/Departments: Design (articles on industrial/product design and firms) 2,000 words. **Buys 100 mss/year.** Query with published clips.

$ $ $ PHOENIX MAGAZINE, (formerly *Phoenix*), Cities West Publishing, Inc., 4041 N. Central Ave., Suite 530, Phoenix AZ 85012. (602)234-0840. Fax: (602)604-0169. E-mail: phxmag@citieswestpub.com. **Contact:** Kathy Khoury, managing editor. **70% freelance written.** Monthly magazine covering regional issues, personalities, events, customs, and history of metro Phoenix. Estab. 1966. Circ. 60,000. Pays on publication. Publishes ms an average of 3 months after acceptance. Byline given. Buys first North American serial rights. Submit seasonal material 1 year in advance. Accepts queries by mail, e-mail. Responds in 2 months to queries; 2 months to mss. Sample copy for $3.95 and 9×12 SASE with 5 first-class stamps. Writer's guidelines for #10 SASE.

> O━ Break in with "short pieces of 150-300 words for the PHX-files highlighting local trends and personalities, or with other short features of 750-1,000 words on same topics. Avoid the obvious. Look for the little-known, the funky, and the offbeat."

Nonfiction: General interest, interview/profile, investigative, historical, service pieces (where to go and what to do around town). "No material dealing with travel outside the region or other subjects that don't have an effect on the area. No sports, politics, business, fiction, or personal essays, please." **Buys 50 mss/year.** Query with published clips. Length: 150-2,000 words.

Tips: "Our audience consists of well-educated, affluent Phoenicians. Articles must have strong local connection, vivid, lively writing, and present new information or a new way of looking at things."

SCOTTSDALE LIFE, The City Magazine, CitiesWest, 4041 N. Central, #A-100, Phoenix AZ 85012. (602)234-0840. Fax: (602)277-7857. E-mail: sdalelife@citieswestpub.com. **Contact:** Linda Groenemann, editor. **50% freelance written.** Monthly magazine covering city and lifestyle, art, entertaining, people, business, society, dining. Estab. 1998. Circ. 40,000. **Pays on acceptance.** Byline given. Offers 10% kill fee. Buys electronic, all rights. Editorial lead time 2 months. Submit seasonal material 4 months in advance. Accepts queries by mail, e-mail. Responds in 1 month to queries. Sample copy for free. Editorial calendars are available.

Nonfiction: All relating to the Arizona reader. Essays, exposé, general interest, historical/nostalgic, how-to, humor, inspirational, interview/profile, new product, personal experience, photo feature, travel. Special issues: Real Estate, Beauty & Health, Art, Golf, Lifestyle. **Buys 20 mss/year.** Query with published clips. Length: 1,000-2,000 words. **Payment varies.**

Photos: State availability with submission. Reviews transparencies, prints. Buys all rights. Negotiates payment individually. Captions, identification of subjects, model releases required.

Columns/Departments: City (briefs, mini-profiles); Artful Diversions (gallery reviews), both 300-500 words; Good Taste (dining reviews), 700 words. **Buys 50 mss/year.** Query with published clips. **Payment varies.**

Poetry: Cowboy poetry. **Buys 2-5 poems/year.**

Tips: "No idea is a bad idea. Do not fax or phone unless you have written first. Look for the local angle or a way to make the idea relevant to the Phoenix/Scottsdale reader. Suggest photo possibilities."

$ $ TUCSON LIFESTYLE, Conley Publishing Group, Ltd., Suite 12, 7000 E. Tanque Verde Rd., Tucson AZ 85715-5318. (520)721-2929. Fax: (520)721-8665. E-mail: tucsonlife@aol.com. **Contact:** Scott Barker, executive editor. **90% freelance written.** Prefers to work with published/established writers. Monthly magazine covering Tucson-related events and topics. Estab. 1982. Circ. 32,000. **Pays on acceptance.** Publishes ms an average of 6 months after acceptance. Byline given. Buys first North American serial rights. Submit seasonal material 1 year in advance. Accepts queries by mail, e-mail, fax. Responds in 2 months to queries; 3 months to mss. Sample copy for $2.95 plus $3 postage. Writer's guidelines free.

O‑‑ Features are not open to freelancers.

Nonfiction: All stories need a Tucson angle. "Avoid obvious tourist attractions and information that most residents of the Southwest are likely to know. No anecdotes masquerading as articles. Not interested in fish-out-of-water, Easterner-visiting-the-Old-West pieces." **Buys 20 mss/year. Pays $50-500.**

Photos: Query about electronic formats. Reviews contact sheets, $2\frac{1}{4} \times 2\frac{1}{4}$ transparencies, 5×7 prints. Buys one-time rights. Pays $25-100/photo. Identification of subjects required.

Columns/Departments: Lifestylers (profiles of interesting Tucsonans). Query. **Pays $100-200.**

Tips: "Style is not of paramount importance; good, clean copy with an interesting lead is a must."

California

$ ANGELENO MAGAZINE, Modern Luxury, 5455 Wilshire Blvd., Suite 1412, Los Angeles CA 90036. (323)930-9400 ext. 2375. Fax: (323)930-9402. **Contact:** Alexandria Abramian. Bimonthly magazine covering luxury lifestyle. "We cover the good things in life—fashion, fine dining, home design, the arts—from a sophisticated, cosmopolitan, well-to-do perspective." Estab. 1999. Circ. 80,000. Pays 2 months after receipt of invoice. Buys first, all rights. Submit seasonal material 6 months in advance. Responds in 2 months to queries. Sample copy for $7.15 for current issue; $8.20 for back issue. Writer's guidelines for #10 SASE.

Nonfiction: "All articles must be focused on LA except travel." General interest, how-to (culinary, home design), interview/profile, photo feature (occasional), travel. No fiction; no unsolicited mss. Query with published clips. Length: 500-4,500 words. Pays expenses of writers on assignment.

Photos: State availability with submission. Reviews transparencies, prints, digital (300+ dpi). Buys one-time rights.

$ $ BRNTWD MAGAZINE, PTL Productions, 2118 Wilshire Blvd., #1060, Santa Monica CA 90403. (310)390-0251. Fax: (310)390-0261. E-mail: dylan@brntwdmagazine.com. Website: www.brntwdmagazine.com. **Contact:** Dylan Nugent, editor-in-chief. **100% freelance written.** Bimonthly magazine covering entertainment, business, lifestyles, reviews. "Wanting in-depth interviews with top entertainers, politicians, and similar individuals. Also travel, sports, adventure." Estab. 1995. Circ. 70,000. Pays on publication. Byline given. Editorial lead time 3 months. Submit seasonal material 3 months in advance. Accepts queries by mail, e-mail, phone. Accepts simultaneous submissions. Sample copy for $5. Writer's guidelines available.

O‑‑ Break in with "strong editorial pitches on unique personalities, trends, or travel destinations."

Nonfiction: Book excerpts, exposé, general interest, historical/nostalgic, humor, interview/profile, new product, opinion, personal experience, photo feature, travel. **Buys 80 mss/year.** Query with published clips. Length: 1,000-2,500 words. **Pays 10-15¢/word.**

Photos: State availability with submission. Reviews contact sheets, negatives, prints. Offers no additional payment for photos accepted with ms. Captions, identification of subjects required.

Columns/Departments: Reviews (film/books/theater/museum), 100-500 words; Sports (Southern California angle), 200-600 words. **Buys 20 mss/year.** Query with or without published clips or send complete ms. **Pays 15¢/word.**

Tips: "Los Angeles-based writers preferred for most articles."

$ $ $ $ DIABLO MAGAZINE, The Magazine of the East Bay, Diablo Publications, 2520 Camino Diablo, Walnut Creek CA 94596. (925)943-1111. Fax: (925)943-1045. E-mail: d-mail@diablopubs.com. Website: www.diablomag.com. Editor: Susan Safipour. **Contact:** Robert Strohmeyer, managing editor. **50% freelance written.** Monthly magazine covering regional travel, food, homestyle, and profiles in Contra Costa and southern Alameda counties and selected areas of Oakland and Berkeley. Estab. 1979. Circ. 45,000. **Pays on acceptance.** Publishes ms an average of 3 months after acceptance. Byline given. Offers 25% kill fee. Buys first rights. Editorial lead time 3 months. Submit seasonal material 5 months in advance. Accepts queries by mail, e-mail, fax. Sample copy online. Writer's guidelines free.

Nonfiction: General interest, interview/profile, new product, photo feature, technical, travel. No restaurant profiles, out of country travel, nonlocal topics. **Buys 60 mss/year.** Query with published clips. Length: 600-3,000 words. **Pays $300-2,000.** Sometimes pays expenses of writers on assignment.

Photos: State availability with submission. Buys one-time rights. Negotiates payment individually.

Columns/Departments: Tech; Parenting; Homestyle; Food; Books; Health; Profiles; Local Politics, all 1,000 words. Query with published clips.

Tips: "We prefer San Francisco Bay area writers who are familiar with the area."

$ $ ☆ THE EAST BAY MONTHLY, The Berkeley Monthly, Inc., 1301 59th St., Emeryville CA 94608. (510)658-9811. Fax: (510)658-9902. E-mail: editorial@themonthly.com. **Contact:** Kira Halpern, editor. **95% freelance written.** Monthly tabloid. "We feature distinctive, intelligent articles of interest to *East Bay* readers." Estab. 1970. Circ. 80,000. Pays on publication. Byline given. Buys first, second serial (reprint) rights. Editorial lead time 2+ months. Submit seasonal material 3 months in advance. Accepts queries by mail, e-mail. Accepts simultaneous submissions. Responds in 1 month to queries; 1 month to mss. Sample copy for $1. Writer's guidelines for #10 SASE.

Nonfiction: Essays (first-person), exposé, general interest, humor, interview/profile, personal experience, photo feature, arts, culture, lifestyles. No fiction or poetry. Query with published clips. Length: 1,500-3,000 words. **Pays $350-700.**

Reprints: Send tearsheet and information about when and where the material previously appeared.

Photos: State availability with submission. Negotiates payment individually. Identification of subjects required.

Columns/Departments: Shopping Around (local retail news), 2,000 words; First Person, 2,000 words. Query with published clips.

$ $ L.A. WEEKLY, 6715 Sunset Blvd., Los Angeles CA 90020. (323)465-9909. Fax: (323)465-3220. Website: www.laweekly.com. Editor: Laurie Ochoa. Managing Editor: Kateri Butler. **Contact:** Janet Duckworth, features editor; Tom Christie, arts editor; Alan Mittelstaedt, news editor. **30% freelance written.** Weekly newspaper. "*L.A. Weekly* provides a fresh, alternative look at Los Angeles. We have arts coverage, news analysis, and investigative reporting and a comprehensive calendar section." Estab. 1978. Circ. 225,000. Pays on publication. Byline given. Offers 33% kill fee. Buys first North American serial, electronic rights. Accepts queries by mail, e-mail, fax. Responds in 1 month to queries; 4 months to mss. Sample copy online. Writer's guidelines not available.

Nonfiction: Essays, exposé, interview/profile. "We assign many articles to freelancers but accept very few unsolicited manuscripts." Query with published clips. No submissions through website. **Pays 37¢/word.**

Photos: State availability with submission.

Columns/Departments: Query with published clips. **Pays 37¢/word basic rate.**

LOS ANGELES TIMES MAGAZINE, Los Angeles Times, 202 W. First St., Los Angeles CA 90012. (213)237-7811. Fax: (213)237-7386. **Contact:** Alice Short, editor. **50% freelance written.** Weekly magazine of regional general interest. Circ. 1,384,688. Payment schedule varies. Publishes ms an average of 2 months after acceptance. Byline given. Buys first North American serial rights. Submit seasonal material 3 months in advance. Accepts simultaneous submissions. Responds in 2 months to queries; 2 months to mss. Sample copy and writer's guidelines free.

Nonfiction: Covers California, the West, the nation and the world. Essays (reported), general interest, interview/profile, investigative and narrative journalism. Query with published clips. Length: 2,500-4,500 words.

Photos: Query first; prefers to assign photos. Reviews color transparencies, b&w prints. Buys one-time rights. Payment varies. Captions, identification of subjects, model releases required.

Tips: "Prospective contributors should know their subject well and be able to explain why a story merits publication. Previous national magazine writing experience preferred."

$ $ METRO SANTA CRUZ, Metro Newspapers, 115 Cooper St., Santa Cruz CA 95060. (831)457-9000. Fax: (831)457-5828. E-mail: kluker@metcruz.com. Website: www.metroactive.com. **Contact:** Kelly Luker, interim-editor. **20-30% freelance written.** Weekly newspaper. "*Metro* is for a sophisticated coastal university town audience—stories must be more in-depth with an unusual slant not covered in daily newspapers." Estab. 1994. Circ. 55,000. Pays on publication. Publishes ms an average of 2-5 weeks after acceptance. Byline given. Offers kill fee only with assignment memorandum signed by editor. Buys first North American serial, second serial (reprint), nonexclusive rights. Submit seasonal material 3 months in advance. Responds in 2 months to queries; 4 months to mss. Sample copy not available. Writer's guidelines not available.

Nonfiction: Features include a cover story of 3,000-3,500 words and a hometown story of 1,000-1,200 words about an interesting character. Some local angle needed. Book excerpts, essays (personal), exposé, interview/profile (particularly entertainment oriented), music; personal essay. **Buys 75 mss/year.** Query with published clips. Length: 500-4,000 words. **Pays $50-500.**

Reprints: Send photocopy and information about when and where the material previously appeared. Pays $25-200.

Photos: Send photos with submission. Reviews contact sheets, negatives, any size transparencies, prints, digital (tiff 180dpi). Buys one-time rights. Pays $25-50/photo, more if used on cover. Captions, identification of subjects, model releases required.

Columns/Departments: MetroGuide (entertainment features, interviews), 500-3,000 words. Query with published clips. **Pays $25-200.**

Tips: "Seasonal features are most likely to be published, but we take only the best stuff. Local stories or national news events with a local angle will also be considered. Preferred submission format is by e-mail. We are enthusiastic about receiving freelance inquiries. What impresses us most is newsworthy writing, compellingly presented. We define news broadly and consider it to include new information about old subjects as well as a new interpretation of old information. We like stories which illustrate broad trends by focusing in detail on specific examples."

$ $ $ ORANGE COAST MAGAZINE, The Magazine of Orange County, Orange Coast Kommunications Inc., 3701 Birch St., Suite 100, Newport Beach CA 92660-2618. (949)862-1133. Fax: (949)862-0133. E-mail: agenda@orangecoastmagazine.com. Website: www.orangecoastmagazine.com. **Contact:** Anastacia Grenda, managing editor. **90% freelance written.** Monthly magazine "designed to inform and enlighten the educated, upscale residents of Orange County, California; highly graphic and well researched." Estab. 1974. Circ. 50,000. Pays on publication. Publishes ms an average of 4 months after acceptance. Byline given. Offers 20% kill fee. Buys one-time rights. Submit seasonal material 6 months in advance. Accepts queries by mail. Accepts simultaneous submissions. Responds in 2 months to queries; 2 months to mss. Sample copy for $2.95 and 10×12 SAE with 8 first-class stamps. Writer's guidelines for #10 SASE.

O→ Break in with Short Cuts (topical briefs of about 100 words), pays $50-75; Escape (Pacific time zone travel pieces of about 600 words), pays $250.

Nonfiction: Absolutely no phone queries. Exposé (Orange County government, politics, business, crime), general interest (with Orange County focus), historical/nostalgic, interview/profile (prominent Orange County citizens), travel, guides to activities and services. Special issues: Health and Fitness (January); Dining and Entertainment (March); National & International Travel (April); Home and Garden (June); Local Travel (October); Holiday (December). **Buys 100 mss/year.** Query with published clips. Length: 1,200-3,000 words. **Pays $350-700 for assigned articles.**

Columns/Departments: Most columns are not open to freelancers. Length: 1,000-2,000 words. **Buys 200 mss/year.** Query with published clips or send complete ms. **Pays $200 maximum.**

Fiction: Buys only under rare circumstances. Send complete ms. Length: 1,000-5,000 words. **Pays $250.**

The online magazine carries original content not found in the print edition. Contact: Nancy Cheever, online editor.

Tips: "We're looking for more local personality profiles, analysis of current local issues, local takes on national issues. Most features are assigned to writers we've worked with before. Don't try to sell us 'generic' journalism. *Orange Coast* prefers articles with specific and unusual angles focused on Orange County. A lot of freelance writers ignore our Orange County focus. We get far too many generalized manuscripts."

$ $ PALM SPRINGS LIFE, The California Prestige Magazine, Desert Publications, Inc., 303 N. Indian Canyon, Palm Springs CA 92262. (760)325-2333. Fax: (760)325-7008. Editor: Stewart Weiner. **Contact:** Sarah Hagerty, executive editor. **75% freelance written.** Monthly magazine covering "affluent resort/southern California/Palm Springs desert resorts. *Palm Springs Life* is a luxurious magazine aimed at the affluent market." Estab. 1958. Circ. 20,000. Pays on publication. Publishes ms an average of 3 months after acceptance. Byline given. Offers 25% kill fee. Buys all rights. Negotiable Submit seasonal material 6 months in advance. Responds in 3 weeks to queries. Sample copy for $3.95. Writer's guidelines not available.

• Increased focus on desert region and business writing opportunities.

Nonfiction: Book excerpts, essays, interview/profile. Query with published clips. Length: 500-2,500 words. **Pays $50-750 for assigned articles; $25-500 for unsolicited articles.**

Photos: State availability with submission. Reviews contact sheets. Buys all rights. Pays $5-125/photo. Captions, identification of subjects, model releases required.

Columns/Departments: Around Town (local news), 50-250 words. **Buys 12 mss/year.** Query with or without published clips. **Pays $5-200.**

N $ PALO ALTO WEEKLY, Embarcadero Publishing Co., 703 High St., P.O. Box 1610, Palo Alto CA 94301. (650)326-8210. Fax: (650)326-3928. Website: www.PaloAltoOnline.com. **Contact:** Tyler Hanley, editorial assistant. **5% freelance written.** Semiweekly tabloid focusing on local issues and local sources. Estab. 1979. Circ. 48,000. Pays on publication. Publishes ms an average of 1 month after acceptance. Byline given. Offers 50% kill fee. Buys first rights. Submit seasonal material 2 months in advance. Accepts queries by mail. Responds in 2 weeks to queries. Sample copy for 9×12 SAE and 2 first-class stamps. Writer's guidelines not available.

• *Palo Alto Weekly* covers sports and has expanded its arts and entertainment coverage. It is still looking for stories in Palo Alto/Stanford area or features on people from the area.

Nonfiction: General interest, historical/nostalgic, interview/profile, photo feature. Special issues: Together (weddings—mid-February); Interiors (May, October). Nothing that is not local; no travel. **Buys 25 mss/year.** Query with published clips. Length: 700-1,000 words. **Pays $35-60.** Payment is negotiable.

Photos: Send photos with submission. Reviews contact sheets, prints 5×7. Buys one-time rights. Pays $10 minimum/photo. Captions, identification of subjects, model releases required.

Tips: "Writers have the best chance if they live within circulation area and know publication and area well. DON'T send generic, broad-based pieces. The most open sections are food, interiors, and sports. Longer 'cover story' submissions may be accepted. Keep it LOCAL."

$ $ SACRAMENTO MAGAZINE, Sacramento Magazines Corp., 706 56th St., Suite 210, Sacramento CA 95819. (916)452-6200. Fax: (916)452-6061. E-mail: krista@sacmag.com. Website: www.sacmag.com. Managing Editor: Darlena Belushin McKay. **Contact:** Krista Minard, editor. **100% freelance written.** Works with a small number of new/unpublished writers each year. Monthly magazine with a strong local angle on local issues, human interest and consumer items for readers in the middle to high income brackets. Estab. 1975. Circ. 29,000. Pays on publication. Publishes ms an average of 3 months after acceptance. Generally buys first North American serial rights and electronic rights, rarely second serial (reprint) rights. Accepts queries by mail. Responds in 2 months to queries; 2 months to mss. Sample copy for $4.50. Writer's guidelines for #10 SASE.

O→ Break in with submissions to City Lights.

Nonfiction: Local isues vital to Sacramento quality of life. "No e-mail, fax or phone queries will be answered." **Buys 5 unsolicited feature mss/year.** Query. Length: 1,500-3,000 words, depending on author, subject matter and treatment. **Pays $250 and up.** Sometimes pays expenses of writers on assignment.

Photos: Send photos with submission. Buys one-time rights. Payment varies depending on photographer, subject matter and treatment. Captions, identification of subjects, location and date required.

Columns/Departments: Business, home and garden, first person essays, regional travel, gourmet, profile, sports, city arts (1,000-1,800 words); City Lights (250-300 words). **Pays $50-400.**

$ $ SACRAMENTO NEWS & REVIEW, Chico Community Publishing, 1015 20th St., Sacramento CA 95814. (916)498-1234. Fax: (916)498-7920. E-mail: stevenj@newsreview.com or jacksong@newsreview.com. Website: www.newsreview.com. **Contact:** Steven T. Jones, news editor; Jackson Griffith, arts and lifestyle editor. **25% freelance written.** Magazine. "We are an alternative news and entertainment weekly. We maintain a high literary standard for submissions; unique or alternative slant. Publication aimed at a young, intellectual audience; submissions should have an edge and strong voice." Estab. 1989. Circ. 95,000. Pays on publication. Publishes ms an average of 2 months after acceptance. Byline given. Offers 10% kill fee. Buys first, electronic rights. Editorial lead time 2 months. Submit seasonal material 2 months in advance. Accepts queries by mail, e-mail, fax, phone. Accepts simultaneous submissions. Responds in 1 month to queries; 2 months to mss. Sample copy for 50¢.

Nonfiction: Essays, exposé, general interest, humor, interview/profile, personal experience. Special issues: Publishes holiday gift guides (November/December). Does not want to see travel, product stories, business profile. **Buys 20-30 mss/year.** Query with published clips. Length: 750-5,000 words. **Pays $40-500.** Sometimes pays expenses of writers on assignment.

Photos: State availability with submission. Reviews 8×10 prints. Buys one-time rights. Negotiates payment individually. Identification of subjects required.

Columns/Departments: In the Mix (CD/TV/book reviews), 150-750 words. **Buys 10-15 mss/year.** Query with published clips. **Pays $10-300.**

$ $ $ $ SAN FRANCISCO, Focus on the Bay Area, 243 Vallejo St., San Francisco CA 94111. (415)398-2800. Fax: (415)398-6777. E-mail: ltrottier@sanfran.com. Website: www.sanfran.com. **Contact:** Lisa Trottier, managing editor. **50% freelance written.** Prefers to work with published/established writers. Monthly city/regional magazine. Estab. 1968. Circ. 180,000. Pays on publication. Publishes ms an average of 2 months after acceptance. Byline given. Offers 25% kill fee. Submit seasonal material 5 months in advance. Responds in 2 months to queries; 2 months to mss. Sample copy for $3.95.

Nonfiction: All stories should relate in some way to the San Francisco Bay Area (travel excepted). Exposé, interview/profile, travel, arts; politics; public issues; sports; consumer affairs. Query with published clips. Length: 200-4,000 words. **Pays $100-2,000 and some expenses.**

N $ VENTURA COUNTY REPORTER, 1567 Spinnaker Dr., Suite 202, Ventura CA 93001. (805)658-2244. Fax: (805)658-7803. E-mail: editor@vcreporter.com. **Contact:** David Rolland, editor. **35% freelance written.** Weekly tabloid covering local news. Circ. 35,000. Pays on publication. Publishes ms an average of 2 weeks after acceptance. Byline given. Buys first North American serial rights. Accepts queries by mail, e-mail, fax. Responds in 3 weeks to queries. Sample copy not available. Writer's guidelines not available.

- Works with a small number of new/unpublished writers each year.

Nonfiction: Ventura County slant predominates. General interest (local slant), humor, interview/profile, travel (local-within 500 miles). Length: 2,000-3,000 words. **Payment varies.**

Photos: Send photos with submission. Reviews b&w contact sheet.

Columns/Departments: Entertainment, Dining News, News, Feature, Culture. Send complete ms. **Payment varies.**

Tips: "As long as topics are up-beat with local slant, we'll consider them."

Colorado

$ $ $ ASPEN MAGAZINE, Ridge Publications, 720 E. Durant Ave., Suite E-8, Aspen CO 81611. (970)920-4040, ext. 25. Fax: (970)920-4044. E-mail: edit@aspenmagazine.com. Website: www.aspenmagazine.com. Editor: Janet C. O'Grady. **Contact:** Dana R. Butler, managing editor. **30% freelance written.** Bimonthly magazine covering Aspen and the Roaring Fork Valley. "All things Aspen, written in a sophisticated, insider-oriented tone." Estab. 1974. Circ. 20,000. Pays within 30 days of publication. Byline sometimes given. Offers 10% kill fee. Buys first North American serial, electronic rights. Editorial lead time 2 months. Accepts queries by mail, e-mail, fax. Accepts simultaneous submissions. Responds in 2 months to queries; 6 months to mss. Sample copy for 9×12 SAE and 10 first-class stamps. Writer's guidelines for #10 SASE.

Nonfiction: Essays, new product, photo feature, historical, environmental and local issues, architecture and design, sports and outdoors, arts. "We do not publish general interest articles without a strong Aspen hook. We do not publish 'theme' (skiing in Aspen) or anniversary (40th year of Aspen Music Festival) articles, fiction, poetry, or prewritten manuscripts." **Buys 30-60 mss/year.** Query with published clips. Length: 50-4,000 words. **Pays $50-1,000.** Sometimes pays expenses of writers on assignment.

Photos: State availability with submission. Reviews contact sheets, negatives, transparencies, prints. Identification of subjects, model releases required.

$ $ RELOCATING TO THE VAIL VALLEY, Showcase Publishing, Inc., P.O. Box 8680, Prairie Village KS 66208. (913)648-5757. Fax: (913)648-5783. Editor: Dave Leathers. **Contact:** Liz Murray, associate editor. Annual relocation guides, free for people moving to the area. Pays on publication. Publishes ms an average of 6 months after acceptance. Byline given. Buys one-time rights. Editorial lead time 4 months. Submit seasonal material 4 months in advance. Accepts queries by mail, fax. Accepts simultaneous submissions. Responds in 1 month to queries; 1 month to mss. Sample copy for $5.

Nonfiction: Historical/nostalgic, travel, local issues. **Buys 8 mss/year.** Query with published clips. Length: 600-1,000 words. **Pays $60-350.** Sometimes pays expenses of writers on assignment.

Reprints: Accepts previously published submissions.

Photos: State availability of or send photos with submission. Reviews transparencies. Buys one-time rights. Offers no additional payment for photos accepted with ms. Identification of subjects required.

Tips: "Really read and understand our audience."

$ $ STEAMBOAT MAGAZINE, Sundance Plaza, 1250 S. Lincoln Ave., P.O. Box 881659, Steamboat Springs CO 80488. (970)871-9413. Fax: (970)871-1922. E-mail: deb@steamboatmagazine.com. Website: www.steamboatmagazine.com. **Contact:** Deborah Olsen, editor. **80% freelance written.** Semiannual magazine "showcasing the history, people, lifestyles, and interests of Northwest Colorado. Our readers are generally well-educated, well-traveled, upscale, active people visiting our region to ski in winter and recreate in summer. They come from all 50 states and many foreign countries. Writing should be fresh, entertaining, and informative." Estab. 1978. Circ. 30,000. Pays 50% on acceptance, 50% on publication. Publishes ms an average of 6 months after acceptance. Byline given. Buys exclusive rights. Submit seasonal material 1 year in advance. Accepts queries by mail, e-mail, fax, phone. Responds in 3 months to queries. Sample copy for $3.95 and SAE with 10 first-class stamps. Writer's guidelines free.

Nonfiction: Book excerpts, essays, general interest, historical/nostalgic, humor, interview/profile, photo feature, travel. **Buys 10-15 mss/year.** Query with published clips. Length: 150-1,500 words. **Pays $50-300 for assigned articles.** Sometimes pays expenses of writers on assignment.

Photos: State availability with submission. Reviews transparencies. Buys one-time rights. Pays $50-250/photo. Captions, identification of subjects, model releases required.

Tips: "Western lifestyles, regional history, nature (including environmental subjects), sports and recreation are very popular topics for our readers. We're looking for new angles on ski/snowboard stories and activity-related stories. Please query first with ideas to make sure subjects are fresh and appropriate. We try to make subjects and treatments 'timeless' in nature because our magazine is a 'keeper' with a multi-year shelf life."

$ $ VAIL/BEAVER CREEK MAGAZINE, P.O. Box 1414, Vail CO 81658. (970)949-9170. Fax: (970)949-9176. E-mail: bergerd@vail.net. **Contact:** Don Berger, editor. **80% freelance written.** Semiannual magazine "showcasing the lifestyles and history of the Vail Valley. We are particularly interested in personality profiles, home and design features, the arts, winter and summer recreation and adventure stories, and environmental articles." Estab. 1975. Circ. 30,000. **Pays on acceptance.** Publishes ms an average of 6 months after acceptance. Byline given. Offers 100% kill fee. Buys one-time rights. Editorial lead time 1 year. Submit seasonal material 1 year in advance. Accepts queries by mail, e-mail. Accepts simultaneous submissions. Responds in 1 month to queries; 2 months to mss. Sample copy for $5.95 and SAE with 10 first-class stamps. Writer's guidelines free.

Nonfiction: Essays, general interest, historical/nostalgic, humor, interview/profile, personal experience, photo feature. **Buys 20-25 mss/year.** Query with published clips. Length: 500-3,000 words. **Pays 20-30¢/word.** Sometimes pays expenses of writers on assignment.

Reprints: Send ms with rights for sale noted and information about when and where the material previously appeared.

Photos: State availability with submission. Reviews transparencies. Buys one-time rights. Offers $50-250/photo. Captions, identification of subjects, model releases required.

Tips: "Be familiar with the Vail Valley and its 'personality.' Approach a story that will be relevant for several years to come. We produce a magazine that is a 'keeper.' "

Connecticut

$ $ $ ☒ CONNECTICUT MAGAZINE, Journal Register Company, 35 Nutmeg Dr., Trumbull CT 06611. (203)380-6600. Fax: (203)380-6610. E-mail: cmonagan@connecticutmag.com. Website: www.connecticutmag.com.

Editor: Charles Monagan. **Contact:** Dale Salm, managing editor. **75% freelance written.** Prefers to work with published/established writers who know the state and live/have lived here. Monthly magazine "for an affluent, sophisticated, suburban audience. We want only articles that pertain to living in Connecticut." Estab. 1971. Circ. 93,000. Pays on publication. Publishes ms an average of 4 months after acceptance. Byline given. Offers 20% kill fee. Buys first North American serial rights. Submit seasonal material 4 months in advance. Accepts queries by mail, e-mail, fax. Responds in 6 weeks to queries. Sample copy not available. Writer's guidelines for #10 SASE.

O→ Freelancers can best break in with "First" (short, trendy pieces with a strong Connecticut angle); find a story that is offbeat and write it in a lively, interesting manner.

Nonfiction: Interested in seeing hard-hitting investigative pieces and strong business pieces (not advertorial). Book excerpts, exposé, general interest, interview/profile, topics of service to Connecticut readers. Special issues: Dining/entertainment, northeast/travel, home/garden and Connecticut bride twice/year. Also, business (January) and healthcare once/year. No personal essays. **Buys 50 mss/year.** Query with published clips. Length: 3,000 words maximum. **Pays $600-1,200.** Sometimes pays expenses of writers on assignment.

Photos: Send photos with submission. Reviews contact sheets, transparencies. Buys one-time rights. Pays $50 minimum/photo. Identification of subjects, model releases required.

Columns/Departments: Business; Health; Politics; Connecticut Calendar; Arts; Dining Out; Gardening; Environment; Education; People; Sports; Media; From the Field (quirky, interesting regional stories with broad appeal). Length: 1,500-2,500 words. **Buys 50 mss/year.** Query with published clips. **Pays $400-700.**

Fillers: Short pieces about Connecticut trends, curiosities, interesting short subjects, etc. Length: 150-400 words. **Pays $75-150.**

The online magazine carries original content not found in the print edition. Contact: Charles Monagan, online editor.

Tips: "Make certain your idea has not been covered to death by the local press and can withstand a time lag of a few months. Again, we don't want something that has already received a lot of press."

$ $ DELAWARE TODAY, 3301 Lancaster Pike, Suite 5C, Wilmington DE 19805. (302)656-1809. Fax: (302)656-5834. E-mail: editors@delawaretoday.com. Website: www.delawaretoday.com. **Contact:** Marsha Mah, editor. **50% freelance written.** Monthly magazine geared toward Delaware people, places and issues. "All stories must have Delaware slant. No pitches such as Delawareans will be interested in a national topic." Estab. 1962. Circ. 25,000. Pays on publication. Publishes ms an average of 4 months after acceptance. Byline given. Offers 50% kill fee. all rights for 1 year. Editorial lead time 3 months. Submit seasonal material 6 months in advance. Responds in 2 months to queries. Sample copy for $2.95.

Nonfiction: Historical/nostalgic, interview/profile, photo feature, lifestyles, issues. Special issues: Newcomer's Guide to Delaware. **Buys 40 mss/year.** Query with published clips. Length: 100-3,000 words. **Pays $50-750 for assigned articles.** Sometimes pays expenses of writers on assignment.

Photos: State availability with submission. Buys one-time rights. Negotiates payment individually. Identification of subjects required.

Columns/Departments: Business, Health, History, People, all 1,500 words. **Buys 24 mss/year.** Query with published clips. **Pays $150-250.**

Fillers: Anecdotes, newsbreaks, short humor. **Buys 10/year.** Length: 100-200 words. **Pays $50-75.**

Tips: "No story ideas that we would know about, i.e., a profile of the governor. Best bets are profiles of quirky/unique Delawareans that we'd never know about or think of."

District of Columbia

$ $ WASHINGTON CITY PAPER, 2390 Champlain St. NW, Washington DC 20009. (202)332-2100. Fax: (202)332-8500. E-mail: tscocca@washingtoncitypaper.com. Website: www.washingtoncitypaper.com. Editor: Erik Wemple. **Contact:** Tom Scocca. **50% freelance written.** "Relentlessly local alternative weekly in nation's capital covering city and regional politics, media, and arts. No national stories." Estab. 1981. Circ. 93,000. Pays on publication. Publishes ms an average of 6 weeks after acceptance. Byline given. Offers 10% kill fee for assigned stories. Buys first rights. Editorial lead time 7-10 days. Responds in 1 month to queries. Writer's guidelines for #10 SASE.

Nonfiction: Tom Scocca (district line); Erik Wemple. "Our biggest need for freelancers is in the District Line section of the newspaper: short, well-reported and local stories. These range from carefully-drawn profiles to sharp, hooky approaches to reporting on local institutions. We don't want op-ed articles, fiction, poetry, service journalism, or play-by-play accounts of news conferences or events. We also purchase, but more infrequently, longer 'cover-length' stories that fit the criteria stated above. Full guide to freelance submissions can be found on website." **Buys 100 mss/year.** Query with published clips or send complete ms. Length: District Line: 800-2,500 words; Covers: 4,000-10,000 words. **Pays 10-40¢/word.** Sometimes pays expenses of writers on assignment.

Photos: Make appointment to show portfolio to Jandos Rothstein, art director. Pays minimum of $75.

Columns/Departments: Leonard Roberge, arts editor. Music Writing (eclectic). **Buys 100 mss/year.** Query with published clips or send complete ms. **Pays 10-40¢/word.**

Tips: "Think local. Great ideas are a plus. We are willing to work with anyone who has a strong idea, regardless of vita."

$ $ $ THE WASHINGTON POST, 1150 15th St. NW, Washington DC 20071. (202)334-7750. Fax: (202)912-3609. **Contact:** K.C. Summers, travel editor. **40% freelance written.** Prefers to work with published/established writers. Weekly newspaper travel section (Sunday). Pays on publication. Publishes ms an average of 6 months after acceptance. Byline given. Buys first North American serial rights. Responds in 1 month to queries. Does not respond to unsolicited mss.

- "We are now emphasizing staff-written articles as well as quality writing from other sources. Stories are rarely assigned; all material comes in on speculation; there is no fixed kill fee." Travel must not be subsidized in any way.

Nonfiction: Emphasis is on travel writing with a strong sense of place, color, anecdote, and history. Query with published clips. Length: 1,500-2,500 words, plus sidebar for practical information.
Photos: State availability with submission.

Florida

$ $ BOCA RATON MAGAZINE, JES Publishing, 6413 Congress Ave., Suite 100, Boca Raton FL 33487. (561)997-8683. Fax: (561)997-8909. E-mail: lisao@bocamag.com. Website: www.bocamag.com. **Contact:** Lisa Ocker, editor. **70% freelance written.** Bimonthly lifestyle magazine "devoted to the residents of South Florida, featuring fashion, interior design, food, people, places, and issues that shape the affluent South Florida market." Estab. 1981. Circ. 20,000. Pays on publication. Publishes ms an average of 3 months after acceptance. Byline given. Buys second serial (reprint) rights. Submit seasonal material 7 months in advance. Accepts simultaneous submissions. Responds in 1 month to queries. Sample copy for $4.95 and 10×13 SAE with 10 first-class stamps. Writer's guidelines for #10 SASE.
Nonfiction: General interest, historical/nostalgic, humor, interview/profile, photo feature, travel. Special issues: Interior Design (September-October); Beauty (January-February); Health (July-August). Query with published clips or send complete ms. Length: 800-2,500 words. **Pays $50-600 for assigned articles; $50-300 for unsolicited articles.**
Reprints: Send tearsheet. Payment varies.
Photos: Send photos with submission.
Columns/Departments: Body & Soul (health, fitness and beauty column, general interest), 1,000 words; Hitting Home (family and social interactions), 1,000 words. Query with published clips or send complete ms. **Pays $50-250.**
Tips: "We prefer shorter manuscripts, highly localized articles, excellent art/photography."

$ $ FLORIDA MONTHLY MAGAZINE, (formerly *Florida Living Magazine*), Florida Media, Inc., 102 Drennen Rd., Suite C-5, Orlando FL 32806. (407)816-9596. Fax: (407)816-9373. E-mail: editor@floridamagazine.com. Website: www.floridamagazine.com. Publisher: E. Douglas Cifers. **Contact:** Deborah Pacuch. Monthly lifestyle magazine covering Florida travel, food and dining, heritage, homes and gardens, and all aspects of Florida lifestyle. Full calendar of events each month. Estab. 1981. Circ. 225,235. Pays on publication. Publishes ms an average of 6 months after acceptance. Byline given. Buys first rights. Editorial lead time 3 months. Submit seasonal material 6 months in advance. Accepts queries by mail, e-mail, fax. Responds in 2 months to queries. Sample copy for $5. Writer's guidelines for #10 SASE.

- Interested in material on areas outside of the larger cities.
- Break in with stories specific to Florida showcasing the people, places, events, and things that are examples of Florida's rich history and culture.

Nonfiction: Historical/nostalgic, interview/profile, travel, general Florida interest, out-of-the-way Florida places, dining, attractions, festivals, shopping, resorts, bed & breakfast reviews, retirement, real estate, business, finance, health, recreation, sports. **Buys 50-60 mss/year.** Query with published clips. Length: 500-2,500 words. **Pays $100-400 for assigned articles; $50-250 for unsolicited articles.**
Photos: Send photos with submission. Reviews 3×5 color prints and slides. Offers $6/photo. Captions required.
Columns/Departments: Golf; Homes & Gardenings; Heritage (all Florida-related); 750 words. **Buys 24 mss/year.** Query with published clips. **Pays $75-250.**

$ FT. MYERS MAGAZINE, And Pat, LLC, 15880 Summerlin Road, Suite 189, Fort Myers FL 33908. Fax: (516)771-4482. E-mail: ftmyers@optonline.net. Managing Editor: Andrew Elias. **Contact:** Pat Simms-Elias, editor. **90% freelance written.** Bimonthly magazine covering media, arts, recreation, lifestyles in Fort Myers and southwest Florida. Audience: 25- to 55-year-old educated, active, successful males and females. Content: Arts, media, design, technology, sports, health, travel, home and garden. Estab. 2001. Circ. 20,000. Pays on publication. Publishes ms an average of 3 months after acceptance. Byline given. Offers 50% kill fee. Buys one-time, second serial (reprint) rights. Editorial lead time 3 months. Submit seasonal material 3 months in advance. Accepts queries by mail, e-mail, fax. Accepts previously published material. Accepts simultaneous submissions. Responds in 3 months to queries; 3 months to mss. Writer's guidelines for #10 SASE or by e-mail.
Nonfiction: Book excerpts, essays, exposé, general interest, historical/nostalgic, how-to, humor, interview/profile, new product, opinion, personal experience, technical, travel. **Buys 60-75 mss/year.** Query with or without published clips or send complete ms. Length: 300-1,500 words. **Pays $40-150.** Will pay in copies or in ad barter at writer's request. Sometimes pays expenses of writers on assignment.
Reprints: Accepts previously published submissions.
Photos: State availability of or send photos with submission. Reviews 4×5 to 8×10 prints. Buys one-time rights. Negotiates payment individually; generally offers $10-50/photo. Captions, identification of subjects required.

Columns/Departments: Media: books, music, video, film, theater, Internet, software (news, previews, reviews, interviews, profiles), 300-1,500 words. Lifestyles: art & design, science & technology, house & garden, health & nutrition, sports & recreation, travel & leisure, food & drink (news, interviews, previews, reviews, profiles, advice), 300-1,500 words. **Buys 60 mss/year.** Query with or without published clips or send complete ms. **Pays $40-150.**

Fiction: Humorous, slice-of-life vignettes. **Buys 5 mss/year.** Query with or without published clips or send complete ms. Length: 300-1,500 words. **Pays $40-150.**

$ $ $ GULFSHORE LIFE, 9051 North Tamiami Trail N., Suite 202, Naples FL 34108. (239)594-9980. Fax: (239)594-9986. E-mail: info@gulfshorelifemag.com. Website: www.gulfshorelifemag.com. **Contact:** Bob Morris, editor. **75% freelance written.** Magazine published 10 times/year for "southwest Florida, the workings of its natural systems, its history, personalities, culture and lifestyle." Estab. 1970. Circ. 35,000. Pays on publication. Publishes ms an average of 4 months after acceptance. Byline given. Buys first North American serial rights. Submit seasonal material 8 months in advance. Accepts queries by mail, e-mail, fax. Accepts simultaneous submissions. Sample copy for 9×12 SAE and 10 first-class stamps.

Nonfiction: All articles must be related to southwest Florida. Historical/nostalgic, interview/profile, issue/trend. **Buys 100 mss/year.** Query with published clips. Length: 500-3,000 words. **Pays $100-1,000.**

Photos: Send photos with submission. Reviews 35mm transparencies, 5×7 prints. Buys one-time rights. Pays $50-100. Identification of subjects, model releases required.

Tips: "We buy superbly written stories that illuminate southwest Florida personalities, places. and issues. Surprise us!"

$ $ JACKSONVILLE, White Publishing Co., 1032 Hendricks Ave., Jacksonville FL 32207. (904)396-8666. Fax: (904)396-0926. **Contact:** Joseph White, editor. **50% freelance written.** Monthly magazine covering life and business in northeast Florida "for upwardly mobile residents of Jacksonville and the Beaches, Orange Park, St. Augustine and Amelia Island, Florida." Estab. 1985. Circ. 25,000. Pays on publication. Byline given. Offers 25-33% kill fee to writers on assignment. Buys first North American serial, second serial (reprint) rights. Editorial lead time 3 months. Submit seasonal material 4 months in advance. Responds in 6 weeks to queries; 1 month to mss. Sample copy for $5 (includes postage).

Nonfiction: All articles *must* have relevance to Jacksonville and Florida's First Coast (Duval, Clay, St. John's, Nassau, Baker counties). Book excerpts, exposé, general interest, historical/nostalgic, how-to (service articles), humor, interview/profile, personal experience, photo feature, travel, commentary, local business successes, trends, personalities, community issues, how institutions work. **Buys 50 mss/year.** Query with published clips. Length: 1,200-3,000 words. **Pays $50-500 for feature length pieces.** Sometimes pays expenses of writers on assignment.

Reprints: Send photocopy. Payment varies.

Photos: State availability with submission. Reviews contact sheets, transparencies. Buys one-time rights. Negotiates payment individually. Captions, model releases required.

Columns/Departments: Business (trends, success stories, personalities), 1,000-1,200 words; Health (trends, emphasis on people, hopeful outlooks), 1,000-1,200 words; Money (practical personal financial advice using local people, anecdotes and examples), 1,000-1,200 words; Real Estate/Home (service, trends, home photo features), 1,000-1,200 words; Travel (weekends, daytrips, excursions locally and regionally), 1,000-1,200 words; occasional departments and columns covering local history, sports, family issues, etc. **Buys 40 mss/year. Pays $150-250.**

Tips: "We are a writer's magazine and demand writing that tells a story with flair."

$ $ TALLAHASSEE MAGAZINE, Rowland Publishing Inc., 1932 Miccosokee Rd., Tallahassee FL 32308. (850)878-0554. Fax: (850)656-1871. E-mail: jbettinger@rowland.com. Website: www.rowland.com. **Contact:** Julie Bettinger, editor. **50% freelance written.** Bimonthly magazine covering Tallahassee area-North Florida and South Georgia. "*Tallahassee Magazine* is dedicated to reflecting the changing needs of a capital city challenged by growth and increasing economic, political, and social diversity." Estab. 1979. Circ. 17,300. **Pays on acceptance.** Publishes ms an average of 3 months after acceptance. Byline given. Buys one-time rights. Editorial lead time 3 months. Submit seasonal material 4 months in advance. Accepts queries by mail, e-mail, fax. Accepts simultaneous submissions. Responds in 1 month to queries. Sample copy for $2.95 and #10 SAE with 4 first-class stamps; sample articles online. Writer's guidelines for #10 SASE.

Nonfiction: General interest, historical/nostalgic, how-to, humor, inspirational, interview/profile, personal experience, photo feature, travel, politics, sports, lifestyles, must deal with region. **Buys 10 mss/year.** Query or submit ms with SASE. Length: 1,000-1,500 words. **Pays $100-250.**

Reprints: Send ms with rights for sale noted and information about when and where the material previously appeared. Pays $100-350.

Photos: State availability with submission. Reviews 35mm transparencies, 3×5 prints. Buys one-time rights. Offers no additional payment for photos accepted with ms. Identification of subjects, model releases required.

Columns/Departments: Humor; Cooking; People; and Social, all 850 words or less. **Buys 12-18 mss/year.** Query with published clips. **Pays $100.**

Tips: "Know the area we cover. This area is unusual in terms of the geography and the people. We are a Southern city, not a Florida city, in many ways. Know what we have published recently and don't try to sell us on an idea that we have published within three years of your query. Be lucid and concise and take enough time to get your facts straight. Make submissions on disk, either in Microsoft Word or Word Perfect."

Georgia

$$$$ ATLANTA, 1330 W. Peachtree St., NE, Suite 450, Atlanta GA 30309. (404)872-3100. Fax: (404)870-6219. E-mail: sfreeman@atlantamag.emmis.com. Website: www.atlantamagazine.com. **Contact:** Scott Freeman, senior editor. Monthly magazine that explores people, pleasures, useful information, regional happenings, restaurants, shopping, etc., for a general adult audience in Atlanta, including subjects in government, sports, pop culture, urban affairs, arts and entertainment. "*Atlanta* magazine articulates the special nature of Atlanta and appeals to an audience that wants to understand and celebrate the uniqueness of the region. The magazine's mission is to serve as a tastemaker by virtue of in-depth information and authoritative, provocative explorations of issues, personalities, and lifestyles." Circ. 69,000. **Pays on acceptance.** Byline given. Offers 25% kill fee. Buys first North American serial rights. Accepts queries by mail, e-mail, phone. Responds in 2 months to queries. Sample copy online.

Nonfiction: "*Atlanta* magazine articulates the special nature of Atlanta and appeals to an audience that wants to understand and celebrate the uniqueness of the region. The magazine's mission is to serve as a tastemaker by virtue of in-depth information and authoritative, provocative explorations of issues, personalities and lifestyles." General interest, interview/profile, travel. **Buys 36-40 mss/year.** Query with published clips. Length: 1,500-5,000 words. **Pays $300-2,000.** Pays expenses of writers on assignment.

Columns/Departments: Essay, travel. **Length:** 1,000-1,500 words. **Buys 30 mss/year.** Query with published clips. **Pays $500.**

Fiction: Novel excerpts.

Fillers: Buys 80/year. Length: 75-175 words. **Pays $50-100.**

Tips: "Writers must know what makes their piece a story rather than just a subject."

$ ☆ FLAGPOLE MAGAZINE, Flagpole, P.O. Box 1027, Athens GA 30603. (706)549-9523. Fax: (706)548-3981. E-mail: editor@flagpole.com. Website: www.flagpole.com. **Contact:** Pete McCommons, editor. **75% freelance written.** Local "alternative" weekly with a special emphasis on popular (and unpopular) music. "Will consider stories on national, international musicians, authors, politicians, etc., even if they don't have a local or regional news peg. However, those stories should be original, irreverent enough to justify inclusion. Of course, local/Southern news features stories are best. We like reporting, storytelling more than opinion pieces." Estab. 1987. Circ. 16,000. Pays on publication. Publishes ms an average of 1 month after acceptance. Byline given. Makes work-for-hire assignments. Editorial lead time 2 months. Submit seasonal material 2 months in advance. Responds in 2 weeks to queries; 1 month to mss. Sample copy online.

Nonfiction: Book excerpts, essays, exposé, interview/profile, new product, personal experience. **Buys 5? mss/year.** Query by e-mail. Length: 600-2,000 words.

Reprints: Send tearsheet, photocopy or typed ms with rights for sale noted and information about when and where the material previously appeared.

Photos: State availability with submission. Reviews prints. Buys all rights. Negotiates payment individually. Captions required.

Columns/Departments: Lit. (book reviews), 800 words. **Buys 30 mss/year.** Send complete ms. **Pays 7¢/word.**

Tips: "Read our publication online before querying, but don't feel limited by what you see. We can't afford to pay much, so we're open to young/inexperienced writer-journalists looking for clips. Fresh, funny, insightful voices make us happiest, as does reportage over opinion. If you've ever succumbed to the temptation to call a pop record 'ethereal' we probably won't bother with your music journalism. No faxed submissions, please."

$$ GEORGIA MAGAZINE, Georgia Electric Membership Corp., P.O. Box 1707, Tucker GA 30085. (770)270-6950. Fax: (770)270-6995. E-mail: ann.orowski@georgiaemc.com. Website: www.Georgiamagazine.org. **Contact:** Ann Orowski, editor. **50% freelance written.** "We are a monthly magazine for and about Georgians, with a friendly, conversational tone and human interest topics." Estab. 1945. Circ. 444,000. Pays on publication. Publishes ms an average of 4 months after acceptance. Byline given. Buys first North American serial, electronic rights. Editorial lead time 2 months. Submit seasonal material 6 months in advance. Accepts simultaneous submissions. Responds in 1 month to subjects of interest to queries. Sample copy for $2. Writer's guidelines for #10 SASE.

Nonfiction: General interest (Georgia-focused), historical/nostalgic, how-to (in the home and garden), humor, inspirational, interview/profile, photo feature, travel. **Buys 24 mss/year.** Query with published clips. Length: 800-1,000 words; 500 words for smaller features and departments. **Pays $50-300.**

Photos: State availability with submission. Reviews contact sheets, transparencies, prints. Buys one-time rights. Negotiates payment individually. Identification of subjects, model releases required.

$$ KNOW ATLANTA MAGAZINE, New South Publishing, 1303 Hightower Trail, Suite 101, Atlanta GA 30350. (770)650-1102. Fax: (770)650-2848. E-mail: editor1@knowatlanta.com. Website: www.knowatlanta.com. **Contact:** Geoff Kohl, editor. **80% freelance written.** Quarterly magazine covering the Atlanta area. "Our articles offer information on Atlanta that would be useful to newcomers—homes, schools, hospitals, fun things to do, anything that makes their move more comfortable." Estab. 1986. Circ. 192,000. Pays on publication. Byline given. Offers 100% kill fee. Buys first North American serial rights. Editorial lead time 2 months. Submit seasonal material 2 months in advance. Accepts queries by mail, e-mail, fax. Accepts previously published material. Sample copy for free.

- "Know the metro Atlanta area, especially hot trends in real estate. Writers who know about international relocation trends and commercial real estate topics are hot."

Nonfiction: General interest, how-to (relocate), interview/profile, personal experience, photo feature. No fiction. **Buys 20 mss/year.** Query with clips. Length: 1,000-2,000 words. **Pays $100-500 for assigned articles; $100-300 for unsolicited articles.** Sometimes pays expenses of writers on assignment.
Reprints: Accepts previously published submissions.
Photos: Send photos with submission, if available. Reviews contact sheets. Buys one-time rights. Negotiates payment individually. Captions, identification of subjects required.

$ $ NORTH GEORGIA JOURNAL, Legacy Communications, Inc., P.O. Box 127, Roswell GA 30077. (770)642-5569. Fax: (770)642-1415. E-mail: northgeorgiajournal@georgiahistory.ws. Website: www.georgiahistory.ws. **Contact:** Olin Jackson, publisher. **70% freelance written.** Quarterly magazine "for readers interested in travel, history, and lifestyles in Georgia." Estab. 1984. Circ. 18,861. Pays on publication. Publishes ms an average of 5 months after acceptance. Byline given. Offers 25% kill fee. Usually buys all rights. Rights negotiable. Editorial lead time 3 months. Submit seasonal material 6 months in advance. Accepts queries by mail, e-mail, fax. Sample copy for 9×12 SAE and 3 first-class stamps, or online. Writer's guidelines for #10 SASE.
Nonfiction: Historical/nostalgic, how-to (survival techniques; mountain living; do-it-yourself home construction and repairs, etc.), interview/profile (celebrity), personal experience (anything unique or unusual pertaining to Georgia history), photo feature (any subject of a historic nature which can be photographed in a seasonal context, i.e., old mill with brilliant yellow jonquils in foreground), travel (subjects highlighting travel opportunities in north Georgia). Query with published clips. **Pays $75-350.**
Photos: Send photos with submission. Reviews contact sheets, transparencies. Rights negotiable. Negotiates payment individually. Captions, identification of subjects, model releases required.
Fiction: Novel excerpts.
Tips: "Good photography is crucial to acceptance of all articles. Send written queries then *wait* for a response. *No telephone calls, please*. The most useful material involves a first-person experience of an individual who has explored a historic site or scenic locale and *interviewed* a person or persons who were involved with or have first-hand knowledge of a historic site/event. Interviews and quotations are crucial. Articles should be told in writer's own words."

N POINTS NORTH MAGAZINE, Serving Atlanta's Stylish Northside, All Points Interactive Media Corp., 568 Peachtree Pkwy., Suite 116, Cumming GA 30041-6820. (770)844-0969. Fax: (770)844-0968. E-mail: managingeditor@ptsnorth.com. Website: www.ptsnorth.com. Managing Editor: Carolyn WIlliams. **Contact:** Managing Editor. **75% freelance written.** Monthly magazine covering lifestyle (regional). "*Points North* is a first-class lifestyle magazine for affluent residents of suburban communities in north metro Atlanta." Estab. 2000. Circ. 50,000. **Pays on acceptance.** Publishes ms an average of 1 month after acceptance. Byline given. Offers negotiable (for assigned articles only) kill fee. Buys electronic, first serial (in the southeast with a 6 month moratorium) rights. Editorial lead time 2 months. Submit seasonal material 5 months in advance. Accepts queries by mail, e-mail, fax. Accepts previously published material. Responds in 6-8 weeks to queries; 6-8 months to mss. Sample copy for $3. Online at website or by e-mail.
Nonfiction: General interest, historical/nostalgic, interview/profile, travel, area-specific topics. No political, controversial, advertorial, new age, health and fitness, sports (particularly golf). **Buys 50-60 mss/year.** Query with published clips. Length: 1,200-2,500 words. **Pays $350-500.**
Photos: "We do not accept photos until article acceptance. Do not send photos with query." State availability with submission. Reviews slide transparencies, 4×6 prints, GIF/JPEG files. Offers no additional payment for photos accepted with ms. Captions, identification of subjects, model releases required.
Columns/Departments: Grand Designs: Gardening (gardening tips), 1,200-1,500 words; Grand Designs: Home (home-improvement tips), 1,200-1,500 words; Northside Shopper (where to shop in the Atlanta area for specific goods), 1,200-1,500 words. Indulgence (unique escapes for the affluent), 1,200-1,500 words. **Buys 25-35 mss/year.** Query with published clips. **Pays $300-500.**
Tips: "The best way for a freelancer, who is interested in being published, is to get a sense of the types of articles we're looking for by reading the magazine."

$ $ SUN VALLEY MAGAZINE, Valley Publishing LLC, 12 E. Bullion, Suite B, Hailey ID 83333. (208)788-0770. Fax: (208)788-3881. E-mail: info@sunvalleymag.com. Website: www.sunvalleymag.com. **Contact:** Laurie C. Sammis, editor. **95% freelance written.** Quarterly magazine covering the lifestyle of the Sun Valley area. *Sun Valley Magazine* "presents the lifestyle of the Sun Valley area and the Wood River Valley, including recreation, culture, profiles, history and the arts." Estab. 1973. Circ. 17,000. Pays on publication. Publishes ms an average of 5 months after acceptance. Byline given. Buys first North American serial, electronic rights. Editorial lead time 1 year. Submit seasonal material 14 months in advance. Accepts queries by mail. Accepts previously published material. Accepts simultaneous submissions. Responds in 5 weeks to queries; 2 months to mss. Sample copy for $4.95 and $3 postage. Writer's guidelines for #10 SASE.
Nonfiction: "All articles are focused specifically on Sun Valley, the Wood River Valley and immediate surrounding areas." Historical/nostalgic, interview/profile, photo feature, travel. Special issues: Sun Valley home design and architecture, Spring; Sun Valley weddings/wedding planner, summer. Query with published clips. **Pays $40-500.** Sometimes pays expenses of writers on assignment.
Reprints: Only occasionally purchases reprints.
Photos: State availability with submission. Reviews transparencies. Buys one-time rights and some electronic rights. Offers $60-275/photo. Identification of subjects, model releases required.

Columns/Departments: Conservation issues, winter/summer sports, health & wellness, mountain-related activities and subjects, home (interior design), garden. All columns must have a local slant. Query with published clips. **Pays $40-300.**

Tips: "Most of our writers are locally based. Also, we rarely take submissions that are not specifically assigned, with the exception of fiction. However, we always appreciate queries."

Illinois

$ $ $ $ CHICAGO MAGAZINE, 500 N. Dearborn, Suite 1200, Chicago IL 60610-4901. Fax: (312)222-0699. E-mail: shane_tritsch@primediamags.com. Website: www.chicagomag.com. **Contact:** Shane Tritsch, managing editor. **50% freelance written.** Prefers to work with published/established writers. Monthly magazine for an audience which is "95% from Chicago area; 90% college educated; upper income, overriding interests in the arts, politics, dining, good life in the city and suburbs. Most are in 25-50 age bracket, well-read and articulate." Estab. 1968. Circ. 175,000. **Pays on acceptance.** Publishes ms an average of 3 months after acceptance. Buys first rights. Submit seasonal material 4 months in advance. Accepts queries by mail, e-mail. Responds in 1 month to queries. For sample copy, send $3 to Circulation Dept. Writer's guidelines for #10 SASE.

Nonfiction: "On themes relating to the quality of life in Chicago: Past, present, and future." Writers should have "a general awareness that the readers will be concerned, influential, longtime Chicagoans. We generally publish material too comprehensive for daily newspapers." Exposé, humor, personal experience, think pieces, profiles, spot news, historical articles. **Buys 100 mss/year.** Query; indicate specifics, knowledge of city and market, and demonstrable access to sources. Length: 200-6,000 words. **Pays $100-3,000 and up.** Pays expenses of writers on assignment.

Photos: Usually assigned separately, not acquired from writers. Reviews 35mm transparencies, color and b&w glossy prints.

The online editor is Deborah Wilk.

Tips: "Submit detailed queries, be business-like and avoid clichéd ideas."

$ $ $ $ CHICAGO READER, Chicago's Free Weekly, Chicago Reader, Inc., 11 E. Illinois, Chicago IL 60611. (312)828-0350. Fax: (312)828-9926. E-mail: mail@chicagoreader.com. Website: www.chicagoreader.com. Editor: Alison True. **Contact:** Kiki Yablon, managing editor. **50% freelance written.** Weekly Alternative tabloid for Chicago. Estab. 1971. Circ. 136,000. Pays on publication. Publishes ms an average of 3 months after acceptance. Byline given. No kill fee. Buys one-time rights. Editorial lead time up to 6 months. Accepts queries by mail, e-mail, fax. Accepts previously published material. Accepts simultaneous submissions. Responds if interested to queries. Sample copy for free. Writer's guidelines free or online.

Nonfiction: Book excerpts, essays, exposé, general interest, historical/nostalgic, humor, interview/profile, opinion, personal experience, photo feature. No celebrity interviews, national news or issues. **Buys 500 mss/year.** Send complete ms. Length: 4,000-50,000 words. **Pays $100-3,000.** Sometimes pays expenses of writers on assignment.

Reprints: Accepts previously published submissions.

Columns/Departments: Reading, First Person, Cityscape, Neighborhood News, all 1,500-2,500 words; arts and entertainment reviews, up to 1,200 words; calendar items, 400-1,000 words.

Tips: "Our greatest need is for full-length magazine-style feature stories on Chicago topics. We're *not* looking for: hard news (What the Mayor Said About the Schools Yesterday); commentary and opinion (What I Think About What the Mayor Said About the Schools Yesterday); poetry. We are not particularly interested in stories of national (as opposed to local) scope, or in celebrity for celebrity's sake (â la *Rolling Stone*, *Interview*, etc.). More than half the articles published in the *Reader* each week come from freelancers, and once or twice a month we publish one that's come in 'over the transom'—from a writer we've never heard of and may never hear from again. We think that keeping the *Reader* open to the greatest possible number of contributors makes a fresher, less predictable, more interesting paper. We not only publish unsolicited freelance writing, we depend on it. Our last issue in December is dedicated to original fiction."

$ $ $ CS, (formerly *Chicago Social*), Modern Luxury Inc., 727 N. Hudson Ave., #001, Chicago IL 60610. (312)787-4600. Fax: (312)787-4628. Publisher: Michael Blaise Kong. Editor-in-Chief: Royaa G. Silver. **Contact:** Gina Bazer, senior editor. **70% freelance written.** Monthly luxury lifestyle magazine. "We cover the good things in life—fashion, fine dining, the arts, etc.—from a sophisticated, cosmopolitan, well-to-do perspective." Circ. 75,000. Pays 2 months after receipt of invoice. Byline given. Offers kill fee. first rights and all rights in this market. Editorial lead time 6 months. Submit seasonal material 3-6 months in advance. Responds in 1 month to queries. Sample copy for $7.15 for current issue; $8.20 for back issue. Writer's guidelines not available.

Nonfiction: General interest, how-to (gardening, culinary, home design), interview/profile, photo feature (occasional), travel. No fiction. *No unsolicited mss.* Query with published clips only. Length: 500-4,500 words. **Pays $50-900.** Pays expenses of writers on assignment.

Photos: State availability with submission. Reviews transparencies, prints. Buys one-time rights. We pay for film and processing only.

Columns/Departments: Few Minutes With (Q&A), 800 words; City Art, Home Design, 2,000 words. Query with published clips only. **Pays $150-400.**

Tips: "Send résumé, clips and story ideas. Mention interest and expertise in cover letter. We need writers who are knowledgeable about home design, architecture, art, culinary arts, entertainment, fashion and retail."

$ ILLINOIS ENTERTAINER, Chicago's Music Monthly, Roberts Publishing, Inc., 124 W. Polk, #103, Chicago IL 60605. (312)922-9333. Fax: (312)922-9369. E-mail: ieeditors@aol.com. Website: www.illinoisentertainer.com. **Contact:** Althea Legaspi, editor. **80% freelance written.** Monthly free magazine covering "popular and alternative music, as well as other entertainment: film, media." Estab. 1974. Circ. 75,000. Pays on publication. Publishes ms an average of 2 months after acceptance. Byline given. Offers 50% kill fee. Buys first North American serial rights. Editorial lead time 2 months. Submit seasonal material 2 months in advance. Accepts queries by mail. Accepts simultaneous submissions. Responds in 2 months to queries. Sample copy for $5.

Nonfiction: Exposé, how-to, humor, interview/profile, new product, reviews. No personal, confessional, inspirational articles. **Buys 75 mss/year.** Query with published clips. Length: 600-2,600 words. **Pays $15-160.** Sometimes pays expenses of writers on assignment.

Reprints: Send ms with rights for sale noted and information about when and where the material previously appeared. Pays 100% of amount paid for an original article.

Photos: Send photos with submission. Reviews contact sheets, transparencies, 5×7 prints. Buys one-time rights. Offers $20-200/photo. Captions, identification of subjects, model releases required.

Columns/Departments: Spins (LP reviews), 250-300 words. **Buys 200-300 mss/year.** Query with published clips. **Pays $15.**

The online version contains material not found in the print edition. Contact: Althea Legaspi.

Tips: "Send clips, résumé, etc. and be patient. Also, sending queries that show you've seen our magazine and have a feel for it greatly increases your publication chances. Don't send unsolicited material. No e-mail solicitations or queries of any kind."

$ NEAR WEST/SOUTH GAZETTE, (formerly *Near West Gazette*), Near West Gazette Publishing Co., 1335 W. Harrison St., Chicago IL 60607. (312)243-4288. Editor: Mark J. Valentino. **Contact:** William S. Bike and Gail Mansfield, associate editors. **50% freelance written.** Works with new/unpublished writers. Monthly newspaper covering Near West Side of Chicago, West Loop and South Loop/Dearborn Park community. News and issues for residents, students, and faculty of the neighborhood bordering the University of Illinois of Chicago. Estab. 1983. Circ. 10,000. Pays on publication. Publishes ms an average of 1 month after acceptance. Byline given. Buys one-time, simultaneous rights. Submit seasonal material 2 months in advance. Accepts queries by mail. Accepts simultaneous submissions. Responds in 5 weeks to queries. Sample copy for 11×14 SAE and 4 first-class stamps.

Nonfiction: Essays, exposé, general interest, historical/nostalgic, humor, inspirational, interview/profile, opinion, personal experience, religious, sports (must be related to Near West Side/West Loop/South Loop communities). Special issues: Christmas. No product promotions. **Buys 60 mss/year.** Length: 300-1,800 words. **Pays $60 for assigned articles.** Sometimes pays expenses of writers on assignment.

Reprints: Send photocopy and information about when and where the material previously appeared. Pays $60.

Photos: Send photos with submission. Reviews 5×7 prints. Buys one-time rights. Offers no additional payment for photos accepted with ms. Identification of subjects required.

Columns/Departments: Forum (opinion), 750 words; Streets (Near West Side/West Loop/South Loop history), 500 words. **Buys 12 mss/year.** Query. **Pays $60.**

Tips: "Must pertain directly to our neighborhood."

$ $ NEWCITY, Chicago's News and Arts Weekly, New City Communications, Inc., 770 N. Halsted, Chicago IL 60622. (312)243-8786. Fax: (312)243-8802. E-mail: elaine@newcitynet.com. Website: www.newcitychicago.com. Editor: Brian Hieggelke. **Contact:** Elaine Richardson, managing editor. **50% freelance written.** Weekly magazine. Estab. 1986. Circ. 70,000. Pays 2-4 months after publication. Publishes ms an average of 1 month after acceptance. Byline given. Offers 20% kill fee in certain cases... first rights and non-exclusive electronic rights. Editorial lead time 2 months. Submit seasonal material 2 months in advance. Accepts queries by e-mail. Responds in 1 month to mss. Sample copy for $3. Writer's guidelines for #10 SASE.

Nonfiction: Essays, exposé, general interest, interview/profile, personal experience, travel (related to traveling from Chicago and other issues particularly affecting travelers from this area), service. **Buys 100 mss/year.** Query by e-mail only. Length: 100-4,000 words. **Pays $15-450.** Rarely pays expenses of writers on assignment.

Photos: State availability with submission. Reviews contact sheets. Buys one-time rights. Captions, identification of subjects, model releases required.

Columns/Departments: Lit (literary supplement), 300-2,000 words; Music, Film, Arts (arts criticism), 150-800 words; Chow (food writing), 300-2,000 words. **Buys 50 mss/year.** Query by e-mail. **Pays $15-300.**

The online magazine carries origianl content not found in the print edition. Contact: Elaine Richardson, online editor.

Tips: "E-mail a solid, sharply written query that has something to do with what our magazine publishes."

Indiana

$ $ EVANSVILLE LIVING, Tucker Publishing Group, 100 NW Second St., Suite 203, Evansville IN 47715-5725. (812)426-2115. Fax: (812)426-2134. E-mail: ktucker@evansvillelivingmagazine.com. Website: www.evansvillelivingmagazine.com. **Contact:** Kristen Tucker, editor/publisher; Shellie Benson, managing editor (sbenson@evansvillelivingmagazine.com). **80-100% freelance written.** Bimonthly magazine covering Evansville, Indiana, and the greater area. "*Evansville Living* is the only full-color, glossy, 100+ page city magazine for the Evansville, Indiana, area. Regular departments include: Home Style, Garden Style, Day Tripping, Sporting Life, and Local Flavor (menus)." Estab. 2000. Circ. 50,000. **Pays on acceptance.** Publishes ms an average of 3 months after acceptance. Byline given. Buys all rights. Editorial lead time 6 months. Submit seasonal material 6 months in advance. Accepts queries by mail, e-mail, fax. Accepts previously published material. Sample copy for $5 or online. Writer's guidelines for free or by e-mail.

Nonfiction: Essays, general interest, historical/nostalgic, photo feature, travel. **Buys 60-80 mss/year.** Query with published clips. Length: 200-600 words. **Pays $100-300.** Sometimes pays expenses of writers on assignment.

Reprints: Accepts previously published submissions.

Photos: State availability with submission. Reviews contact sheets, negatives, transparencies, prints. Buys all rights. Negotiates payment individually. Captions, identification of subjects required.

Columns/Departments: Home Style (home); Garden Style (garden); Sporting Life (sports); Local Flavor (menus), all 1,500 words. Query with published clips. **Pays $100-300.**

$ $ INDIANAPOLIS MONTHLY, Emmis Publishing Corp., 40 Monument Circle, Suite 100, Indianapolis IN 46204. (317)237-9288. Fax: (317)684-2080. Website: www.indianapolismonthly.com. **Contact:** Rebecca Poynor Burns, editor. **30% freelance written.** Prefers to work with published/established writers. "*Indianapolis Monthly* attracts and enlightens its upscale, well-educated readership with bright, lively editorial on subjects ranging from personalities to social issues, fashion to food. Its diverse content and attention to service make it the ultimate source by which the Indianapolis area lives." Estab. 1977. Circ. 45,000. **Pays on acceptance.** Publishes ms an average of 2 months after acceptance. Byline given. Offers negotiable kill fee. Buys first North American serial, one-time rights. Editorial lead time 3 months. Submit seasonal material 3 months in advance. Accepts queries by mail, e-mail. Accepts simultaneous submissions. Responds in 3 weeks to queries. Sample copy for $6.10.

- This magazine is using more first-person essays, but they must have a strong Indianapolis or Indiana tie. It will consider nonfiction book excerpts of material relevant to its readers.

Nonfiction: Must have a strong Indianapolis or Indiana angle. Book excerpts (by Indiana authors or with strong Indiana ties), essays, exposé, general interest, interview/profile, photo feature. No poetry, fiction, or domestic humor; no "How Indy Has Changed Since I Left Town," "An Outsider's View of the 500," or generic material with no or little tie to Indianapolis/Indiana. **Buys 35 mss/year.** Query by mail with published clips. Length: 200-3,000 words. **Pays $50-1,000.**

Reprints: Send typed ms with rights for sale noted and information about when and where the material previously appeared *Accepts reprints only from noncompeting markets.*

Photos: State availability with submission. Buys one-time rights. Negotiates payment individually. Captions, identification of subjects, model releases required.

Tips: "Our standards are simultaneously broad and narrow: broad in that we're a general interest magazine spanning a wide spectrum of topics, narrow in that we buy only stories with a heavy emphasis on Indianapolis (and, to a lesser extent, Indiana). Simply inserting an Indy-oriented paragraph into a generic national article won't get it: All stories must pertain primarily to things Hoosier. Once you've cleared that hurdle, however, it's a wide-open field. We've done features on national celebrities—Indianapolis native David Letterman and *Mir* astronaut David Wolf of Indianapolis, to name 2—and we've published 2-paragraph items on such quirky topics as an Indiana gardening supply house that sells insects by mail. Query with clips showing lively writing and solid reporting. No phone queries please."

Kansas

$ $ KANSAS!, Kansas Department of Commerce and Housing, 1000 SW Jackson St., Suite 100, Topeka KS 66612-1354. (785)296-3479. Fax: (785)296-6988. E-mail: ksmagazine@kansascommerce.com. **90% freelance written.** Quarterly magazine emphasizing Kansas travel attractions and events. Estab. 1945. Circ. 52,000. **Pays on acceptance.** Publishes ms an average of 1 year after acceptance. Byline given. Buys one-time rights. Submit seasonal material 8 months in advance. Accepts queries by mail. Responds in 2 months to queries. Sample copy and writer's guidelines available.

Nonfiction: "Material must be Kansas-oriented and have good potential for color photographs. The focus is on travel with articles about places and events that can be enjoyed by the general public. In other words, events must be open to the public, places also. Query letter should clearly outline story. We are especially interested in Kansas freelancers who can supply their own quality photos." General interest, photo feature, travel. Query by mail. Length: 750-1,250 words. **Pays $200-400.** Pays mileage and lodging of writers on assignment.

Photos: "We are a full-color photo/manuscript publication." Send photos (original transparencies only) with query. Pays $50-75 (generally included in ms rate) for 35mm or larger format transparencies. Captions required.

Tips: "History and nostalgia stories do not fit into our format because they can't be illustrated well with color photos. Submit a query letter describing one appropriate idea with outline for possible article and suggestions for photos."

Kentucky

$ BACK HOME IN KENTUCKY, Back Home in Kentucky, Inc., P.O. Box 710. Clay City KY 40312-0710. (606)663-1011. Fax: (606)663-1808. E-mail: backhome@mis.net. **Contact:** Jerlene Rose, editor/publisher. **50% freelance written.** Magazine published 10 times/year "covering Kentucky heritage, people, places, events. We reach Kentuckians and 'displaced' Kentuckians living outside the state." Estab. 1977. Circ. 8,000. Pays on publication. Publishes ms an average of 6 months after acceptance. Byline given. Buys first North American serial rights. Submit seasonal material 6 months in advance. Responds in 2 months to queries. Sample copy for $3 and 9×12 SAE with $1.23 postage affixed. Writer's guidelines for #10 SASE.

● Interested in profiles of Kentucky gardeners, cooks, craftspeople.

Nonfiction: Historical/nostalgic (Kentucky-related eras or profiles), photo feature (Kentucky places and events), travel (unusual/little-known Kentucky places), profiles (Kentucky cooks, gardeners, and craftspersons), memories (Kentucky related). No inspirational or religion. **Buys 25 mss/year.** Query with or without published clips or send complete ms. Length: 500-2,000 words. **Pays $50-150 for assigned articles; $25-75 for unsolicited articles.** "In addition to normal payment, writers receive 2 copies of issue containing their article."

Reprints: Send tearsheet and information about when and where the material previously appeared. Pays 50% of amount paid for an original article.

Photos: Looking for color transparencies for covers (inquire for specific topics). Vertical format. Pays $50-150. Photo credits given. For inside photos, send photos with submission. Reviews transparencies, 4×6 prints. Rights purchased depends on situation. Occasionally offers additional payment for photos accepted with ms. Identification of subjects, model releases required.

Columns/Departments: Travel, crafts, gardeners, and cooks (all Kentucky related), 500-750 words. **Buys 10-12 mss/year.** Query with published clips. **Pays $15-40.**

Tips: "We work mostly with unpublished writers who have a feel for Kentucky's people, places, and events. Areas most open are little known places in Kentucky, unusual history, and profiles of interesting Kentuckians, and Kentuckians with unusual hobbies or crafts."

$ $ KENTUCKY LIVING, P.O. Box 32170, Louisville KY 40232-0170. (502)451-2430. Fax: (502)459-1611. **Contact:** Paul Wesslund, editor. Mostly freelance written. Prefers to work with published/established writers. Monthly Feature magazine primarily for Kentucky residents. Estab. 1948. Circ. 450,000. **Pays on acceptance.** Publishes ms an average of 12 months after acceptance. Byline given. first serial rights for Kentucky. Submit seasonal material at least 6 months in advance. Accepts previously published material. Accepts simultaneous submissions. Responds in 1 month to queries. Sample copy for 9×12 SAE and 4 first-class stamps.

Nonfiction: Kentucky-related profiles (people, places or events), recreation, travel, leisure, lifestyle articles, book excerpts. **Buys 18-24 mss/year.** Query with or without published clips or send complete ms. **Pays $75-125 for "short" features (600-800 words); pays $150-350 for major articles (750-1,500 words).** Sometimes pays expenses of writers on assignment.

Photos: State availability of or send photos with submission. Reviews Color slides and prints. Payment for photos included in payment for ms. Identification of subjects required.

Tips: "The quality of writing and reporting (factual, objective, thorough) is considered in setting payment price. We prefer general interest pieces filled with quotes and anecdotes. Avoid boosterism. Well-researched, well-written feature articles are preferred. All articles must have a strong Kentucky connection."

$ $ KENTUCKY MONTHLY, Vested Interest Publications, 213 St. Clair St., Frankfort KY 40601. (502)227-0053. Fax: (502)227-5009. E-mail: membry@kentuckymonthly.com or smvest@kentuckymonthly.com. Website: www.kentuckymonthly.com. Editor: Stephen M. Vest. **Contact:** Michael Embry, executive editor. **75% freelance written.** Monthly magazine. "We publish stories about Kentucky and Kentuckians, including those who live elsewhere." Estab. 1998. Circ. 30,000. Pays within 90 days of publication. Publishes ms an average of 3 months after acceptance. Byline given. Buys first North American serial rights. Editorial lead time 3 months. Submit seasonal material 4 months in advance. Accepts queries by mail, e-mail, fax. Accepts simultaneous submissions. Responds in 2 weeks to queries; 1 month to mss. Sample copy and writer's guidelines online.

Nonfiction: Book excerpts, general interest, historical/nostalgic, how-to, humor, interview/profile, photo feature, religious, travel, all with a Kentucky angle. **Buys 60 mss/year.** Query with or without published clips. Length: 300-2,000 words. **Pays $25-350 for assigned articles; $20-100 for unsolicited articles.**

Photos: State availability with submission. Reviews negatives. Buys all rights. Captions required.

Fiction: Adventure, historical, mainstream, novel excerpts. **Buys 10 mss/year.** Query with published clips. Length: 1,000-5,000 words. **Pays $50-100.**

Tips: "We're looking for more fashion, home, and garden, first-person experience, mystery. Please read the magazine to get the flavor of what we're publishing each month. We accept articles via e-mail, fax, and mail."

$ $ LOUISVILLE MAGAZINE, 137 W. Muhammad Ali Blvd., Suite 101, Louisville KY 40202-1438. (502)625-0100. Fax: (502)625-0109. E-mail: loumag@loumag.com. Website: www.louisville.com. **Contact:** Bruce Allar, editor. **60% freelance written.** Monthly magazine "for and generally about people of the Louisville Metro area. Routinely covers arts, entertainment, business, sports, dining and fashion. Features range from news analysis/exposé to humorous commentary. We like lean, clean prose, crisp leads." Estab. 1950. Circ. 20,000. Publishes ms an average of 3 months after acceptance. Byline given. Offers 20% kill fee. Buys first North American serial rights. Editorial lead time 6 weeks. Submit seasonal material 6 months in advance. Accepts queries by mail, e-mail, fax. Responds in 3 months to queries. Sample copy online.

Nonfiction: Essays, exposé, general interest, historical/nostalgic, interview/profile, photo feature. Special issues: City Guide (January); Kentucky Derby (April); EATS (September); Louisville Bride (December). **Buys 75 mss/year.** Query. Length: 500-3,500 words. **Pays $50-600 for assigned articles.**

Photos: State availability with submission. Buys one-time rights. Offers $25-50/photo. Identification of subjects required.
Columns/Departments: End Insight (essays), 750 words. **Buys 10 mss/year.** Send complete ms. **Pays $100-150.**

Louisiana

N $ $ SUNDAY ADVOCATE MAGAZINE, P.O. Box 588, Baton Rouge LA 70821-0588. (225)383-1111, ext. 350. Fax: (225)388-0351. E-mail: glangley@theadvocate.com. Website: www.theadvocate.com. **Contact:** Tim Belehrad, news/features editor. **5% freelance written.** Estab. 1925. Pays on publication. Publishes ms an average of 3 months after acceptance. Byline given. Buys one-time rights.

- "Freelance features are put on our website."
- Break in with travel articles.

Nonfiction: Well-illustrated, short articles; must have local, area, or Louisiana angle, in that order of preference. **Buys 24 mss/year. Pays $100-200.**
Reprints: Send tearsheet or typed ms with rights for sale noted and information about when and where the material previously appeared. Pays $100-200.
Photos: Photos purchased with ms. Pays $30/published color photo.
Tips: "Style and subject matter vary. Local interest is most important. No more than 4 to 5 typed, double-spaced pages."

Maine

N $ MAINE MAGAZINE, The Magazine of Maine's Treasures, County Wide Communications, Inc., 78 River St., Dover-Foxcroft ME 04426. (207)564-7548. Website: www.mainemagazine.com. Editor: Bob Bertu. **Contact:** Lester J. Reynolds, managing editor. **30% freelance written.** Monthly magazine and online covering Maine and its people. Estab. 1977. Circ. 16,000. Pays on acceptance or publication (negotiable). Byline sometimes given. Offers 100% kill fee. Buys electronic, all rights. Editorial lead time 9 months. Submit seasonal material 9 months in advance. Accepts queries by mail. Accepts simultaneous submissions. Responds in 30 days to queries. Sample copy and writer's guidelines for $4 or online at website.
Nonfiction: "First person not interesting unless you're related to a rich and famous or unique Mainer." Book excerpts, essays, how-to, humor, inspirational, interview/profile, new product, personal experience, photo feature, religious, travel. Query. Length: 1,000-2,000 words. **Pays $25-50.** Sometimes pays expenses of writers on assignment.
Photos: Reviews contact sheets, negatives, transparencies. Buys all rights. Offers $15/photo or negotiates payment individually. Captions, identification of subjects required.
Columns/Departments: "We are unusually set here with Maine writers." **Buys 10 or fewer mss/year.** Query. **Pays $10-20.**
Poetry: "Many are submitted by readers who love Maine." **Buys 10 or fewer poems/year. Pays $5.**
Tips: "We're looking for work that is unique and about Maine—unusual people, places. We always want Stephen King interviews—good luck. We can give you his office address."

$ $ MAINE TIMES, Maine Times Publishing Co., P.O. Box 2129, Bangor ME 04402. (207)947-4410. Fax: (207)947-4458. E-mail: mainetimes@mainetimes.com. Website: www.mainetimes.com. **Contact:** Jay Davis, editor. **50% freelance written.** Weekly tabloid covering the state of Maine. "*Maine Times* is a newspaper with stories long and short on the environment, politics, events, the arts, the Maine lifestyle. We look for good writing. For assigned stories we buy the material but follow a liberal reprint policy. For submitted pieces we pay for one-time rights." Estab. 1968. Circ. 7,500. Pays on publication. Byline given. Offers negotiable kill fee. Submit seasonal material 2 months in advance. Accepts queries by mail, e-mail, fax. Sample copy for free. Writer's guidelines not available.
Nonfiction: Essays, opinion, personal experience, reviews. All articles must be queried in advance. **Buys 100 mss/year. Pays $50-800.**
Columns/Departments: Back of the Book (personal essays about Maine—high standard), 700-1,000 words; Other Voices (opinion pieces), 700-1,000 words; Reviews (books, plays, etc.), 400-600 words. **Buys 100 mss/year.** Query or send complete ms. **Pays $50-75.**
Poetry: Wes McNair, poetry editor. Accepts all good poetry. **Buys 30 poems/year. Pays $50.**
Tips: "*Maine Times* is a lively, well-written weekly that explores Maine in its many forums. We love to publish fine personal essays and opinion pieces that inform our appreciation of Maine."

Maryland

$ $ $ $ BALTIMORE MAGAZINE, Inner Harbor East 1000 Lancaster St., Suite 400, Baltimore MD 21202. (410)752-4200. Fax: (410)625-0280. Website: www.baltimoremag.net. **Contact:** Ken Iglehart, managing editor. **50-60% freelance written.** Monthly magazine. "Pieces must address an educated, active, affluent reader and must have a very strong Baltimore angle." Estab. 1907. Circ. 70,000. Pays within 1 month of publication. Byline given. Buys first rights in all media. Submit seasonal material 4 months in advance. Accepts queries by mail, e-mail. Sample copy for $4.45. Writer's guidelines online.

- Break in through "Baltimore Inc. and B-Side—these are our shortest, newsiest sections and we depend heavily on tips and reporting from strangers. Please note that we are exclusively local. Submissions without a Baltimore angle may be ignored."

Nonfiction: Book excerpts (Baltimore subject or author), essays, exposé, general interest, historical/nostalgic, humor, interview/profile (with a Baltimorean), new product, personal experience, photo feature, travel (local and regional to Maryland *only*). "Nothing that lacks a strong Baltimore focus or angle." Query by mail with published clips or send complete ms. Length: 1,000-3,000 words. **Pays 30-40¢/word.** Sometimes pays expenses of writers on assignment.

Columns/Departments: Hot Shot, Health, Education, Sports, Parenting, Politics. Length: 1,000-2,500 words. "The shorter pieces are the best places to break into the magazine." Query with published clips.

- The online magazine carries original content not found in the print edition. Contact: Mary-Rose Nelson, online editor.

Tips: "Writers who live in the Baltimore area can send résumé and published clips to be considered for first assignment. Must show an understanding of writing that is suitable to an educated magazine reader and show ability to write with authority, describe scenes, help reader experience the subject. Too many writers send us newspaper-style articles. We are seeking: 1) *Human interest features*—strong, even dramatic profiles of Baltimoreans of interest to our readers. 2) *First-person accounts* of experience in Baltimore, or experiences of a Baltimore resident. 3) *Consumer*—according to our editorial needs, and with Baltimore sources. Writers should read/familiarize themselves with style of *Baltimore Magazine* before submitting."

CHESAPEAKE LIFE MAGAZINE, Lund Media Ventures, Ltd., 1040 Park Ave., Suite 200, Baltimore MD 21201. (443)451-6023. Fax: (443)451-6027. E-mail: editor@chesapeakelifemag.com. Website: www.chesapeakelifemag.com. **Contact:** Kessler Burnett, editor. **99% freelance written.** Bimonthly magazine covering restaurant reviews, travel, book reviews, regional calendar of events, feature articles, gardening, sailing. "*Chesapeake Life* is a regional magazine covering the Chesapeake areas of Maryland, Virginia and Southern Delaware." Estab. 1995. Circ. 85,000. Pays on publication. Byline given. Buys first North American serial rights. Editorial lead time 2 months. Accepts queries by mail, e-mail, fax, phone. Writer's guidelines free.

Nonfiction: Book excerpts, general interest, historical/nostalgic, interview/profile, photo feature, travel. Query with published clips. Length: Length: open.

Photos: Send photos with submission. Buys one-time rights. Negotiates payment individually.

Massachusetts

BOSTON GLOBE MAGAZINE, Boston Globe, P.O. Box 2378, Boston MA 02107. (617)929-2900. Website: www.globe.com/globe/magazine. Assistant Editors: Catherine Foster, Jan Freeman. **Contact:** Nick King, editor-in-chief. **50% freelance written.** Weekly magazine. Circ. 726,830. Pays on publication. Publishes ms an average of 2 months after acceptance. Buys non exclusive electronic rights Editorial lead time 2 months. Submit seasonal material 3 months in advance. Sample copy for 9×12 SAE and 2 first-class stamps.

Nonfiction: Book excerpts (first serial rights only), essays (variety of issues including political, economic, scientific, medical, and the arts), interview/profile (not Q&A). No travelogs, poetry, personal essays or fiction. **Buys up to 100 mss/year.** Query; SASE must be included with ms or queries for return. Length: 1,500-4,000 words. **Payment negotiable.**

Photos: Purchased with accompanying ms or on assignment. Reviews contact sheets. Pays standard rates according to size used. Captions required.

$$$$ BOSTON MAGAZINE, 300 Massachusetts Ave., Boston MA 02115. (617)262-9700. Fax: (617)267-1774. Website: www.bostonmagazine.com. **Contact:** Jon Marcus, editor. **10% freelance written.** Monthly magazine covering the city of Boston. Estab. 1962. Circ. 125,000. Pays on publication. Publishes ms an average of 3 months after acceptance. Byline given. Offers 20% kill fee. Buys first North American serial rights. Editorial lead time 2 months. Submit seasonal material 4 months in advance. Accepts queries by mail, fax. Responds in 2 weeks to queries.

Nonfiction: Book excerpts, exposé, general interest, interview/profile, politics, crime, trends, fashion. **Buys 20 mss/year.** Query. *No unsolicited mss.* Length: 1,200-12,000 words. Pays expenses of writers on assignment.

Photos: State availability with submission. Buys one-time rights. Negotiates payment individually.

Columns/Departments: Dining; Finance; City Life; Personal Style; Politics; Ivory Tower; Media; Wine; Boston Inc. Books; Music. Query.

Tips: "Read *Boston*, and pay attention to the types of stories we use. Suggest which column/department your story might best fit, and keep your focus on the city and its environs. We like a strong narrative style, with a slightly 'edgy' feel—we rarely do 'remember when' stories. Think *city* magazine."

$$ CAPE COD LIFE, including Martha's Vineyard and Nantucket, Cape Cod Life, Inc., P.O. Box 1385, Pocasset MA 02559-1385. (508)564-4466. Fax: (508)564-4470. Website: www.capecodlife.com. Editor: Brian F. Shortsleeve. **Contact:** Laurel Kornhiser, editorial director. **80% freelance written.** Magazine published 7 times/year focusing on "area lifestyle, history and culture, people and places, business and industry, and issues and answers for year-round and summer residents of Cape Cod, Nantucket and Martha's Vineyard as well as non-residents who spend their leisure time here." Circ. 45,000. Pays 30 days after publication. Byline given. Offers 20% kill fee. Buys first North American serial rights, makes work-for-hire assignments. Submit seasonal material 6 months in advance. Accepts queries by mail. Responds in 3 months to queries; 3 months to mss. Sample copy for $5. Writer's guidelines for #10 SASE.

Nonfiction: Book excerpts, general interest, historical/nostalgic, interview/profile, new product, photo feature, travel, gardening, marine, nautical, nature, arts, antiques. **Buys 20 mss/year.** Query with or without published clips. Length: 1,000-3,000 words. **Pays $100-500.**

Photos: Photo guidelines for #10 SASE. Buys first rights with right to reprint. Pays $25-225. Captions, identification of subjects required.

The online magazine carries original material not found in the print edition.

Tips: "Freelancers submitting *quality* spec articles with a Cape Cod and Islands angle have a good chance at publication. We like to see a wide selection of writer's clips before giving assignments. We accept more spec work written about Cape Cod and Islands history than any other subject. We also publish *Cape Cod Home: Living and Gardening on the Cape and Islands* covering architecture, landscape design and interior design with a Cape and Islands focus."

$ $ PROVINCETOWN ARTS, Provincetown Arts, Inc., 650 Commercial St., Provincetown MA 02657. (508)487-3167. Fax: (508)487-8634. Website: www.capecodaccess.com. **Contact:** Christopher Busa, editor. **90% freelance written.** Annual magazine covering contemporary art and writing. "*Provincetown Arts* focuses broadly on the artists and writers who inhabit or visit the Lower Cape, and seeks to stimulate creative activity and enhance public awareness of the cultural life of the nation's oldest continuous art colony. Drawing upon a 75-year tradition rich in visual art, literature, and theater, *Provincetown Arts* offers a unique blend of interviews, fiction, visual features, reviews, reporting, and poetry." Estab. 1985. Circ. 8,000. Pays on publication. Publishes ms an average of 4 months after acceptance. Offers 50% kill fee. Buys one-time, second serial (reprint) rights. Editorial lead time 6 months. Submit seasonal material 6 months in advance. Responds in 3 weeks to queries; 2 months to mss. Sample copy for $10. Writer's guidelines for #10 SASE.

Nonfiction: Book excerpts, essays, humor, interview/profile. **Buys 40 mss/year.** Send complete ms. Length: 1,500-4,000 words. **Pays $150 minimum for assigned articles; $125 minimum for unsolicited articles.**

Photos: Send photos with submission. Reviews 8×10 prints. Buys one-time rights. Offers $20-$100/photo. Identification of subjects required.

Fiction: Mainstream, novel excerpts. **Buys 7 mss/year.** Send complete ms. Length: 500-5,000 words. **Pays $75-300.**

Poetry: Buys 25 poems/year. Submit maximum 3 poems. **Pays $25-150.**

$ $ WORCESTER MAGAZINE, 172 Shrewsbury St., Worcester MA 01604-4636. (508)755-8004. Fax: (508)755-4734. E-mail: editorial@worcestermag.com. Website: www.worcestermag.com. **Contact:** Michael Warshaw, editor. **10% freelance written.** Weekly tabloid emphasizing the central Massachusetts region, especially the city of Worcester. Estab. 1976. Circ. 40,000. Pays on publication. Publishes ms an average of 3 weeks after acceptance. Byline given. Buys all rights. Submit seasonal material 2 months in advance. Accepts queries by mail, e-mail, fax.

● Does not respond to unsolicited material.

O╼ Break in with "back of the book arts and entertainment articles."

Nonfiction: "We are interested in any piece with a local angle." Essays, exposé (area government, corporate), general interest, historical/nostalgic, humor, opinion (local), personal experience, photo feature, religious, interview (local). **Buys less than 75 mss/year.** Length: 500-1,500 words. **Pays 10¢/ word.**

Michigan

$ $ $ ANN ARBOR OBSERVER, Ann Arbor Observer Co., 201 E. Catherine, Ann Arbor MI 48104. Fax: (734)769-3375. E-mail: hilton@aaobserver.com. Website: www.arborweb.com. **Contact:** John Hilton, editor. **50% freelance written.** Monthly magazine. "We depend heavily on freelancers and we're always glad to talk to new ones. We look for the intelligence and judgment to fully explore complex people and situations, and the ability to convey what makes them interesting. We've found that professional writing experience is not a good predictor of success in writing for the *Observer*. So don't let lack of experience deter you. Writing for the *Observer* is, however, a demanding job. Our readers range from U-M faculty members to hourly workers at GT Products. That means articles have to be both accurate and accessible." Estab. 1976. Circ. 63,000. Pays on publication. Publishes ms an average of 2 months after acceptance. Byline given. Accepts queries by mail, e-mail, fax, phone. Responds in 3 weeks to queries; several months to mss. Sample copy for 12½×15 SAE with $3 postage. Writer's guidelines for #10 SASE.

Nonfiction: Historical, investigative features, profiles, brief vignettes. Must pertain to Ann Arbor. **Buys 75 mss/year.** Length: 100-7,000 words. **Pays up to $1,000.** Sometimes pays expenses of writers on assignment.

Columns/Departments: Inside Ann Arbor (short, interesting tidbits), 300-500 words. **Pays $125.** Around Town (unusual, compelling ancedotes), 750-1,500 words. **Pays $150-200.**

Tips: "If you have an idea for a story, write a 100-200-word description telling us why the story is interesting. We are open most to intelligent, insightful features of up to 5,000 words about interesting aspects of life in Ann Arbor."

$ HOUR DETROIT, Hour Media LLC, 117 W. Third St., Royal Oak MI 48067. (248)691-1800. Fax: (248)691-4531. E-mail: editorial@hourdetroit.com. Managing Editor: George Bulanda. Senior Editor: Rebecca Powers. **Contact:** Ric Bohy, editor. **50% freelance written.** Monthly magazine. "General interest/lifestyle magazine aimed at a middleto upper-income readership aged 17-70." Estab. 1996. Circ. 45,000. **Pays on acceptance.** Publishes ms an average of 2 months after acceptance. Byline given. Offers 30% kill fee. Buys first North American serial rights. Editorial lead time 6 weeks. Submit seasonal material 1 year in advance. Accepts queries by mail, e-mail, fax. Sample copy for $6.

Nonfiction: Book excerpts, exposé, general interest, historical/nostalgic, interview/profile, new product, photo feature, technical, travel. **Buys 150 mss/year.** Query with published clips. Length: 300-2,500 words. Sometimes pays expenses of writers on assignment.

Photos: State availability with submission.

$ $ TRAVERSE, Northern Michigan's Magazine, Prism Publications, 148 E. Front St., Traverse City MI 49684. Fax: (231)941-8391. E-mail: traverse@traversemagazine.com. Website: www.traversemagazine.com. **Contact:** Jeff Smith, editor. **20% freelance written.** Monthly magazine covering northern Michigan life. "*Traverse* is a celebration of the life and environment of northern Michigan." Estab. 1981. Circ. 30,000. **Pays on acceptance.** Byline given. Offers 10% kill fee. Buys first North American serial rights. Editorial lead time 1 year. Submit seasonal material 1 year in advance. Accepts queries by mail, e-mail, fax, phone. Accepts simultaneous submissions. Responds in 2 months to queries. Sample copy for $3. Writer's guidelines for #10 SASE.

Nonfiction: Book excerpts, essays, general interest, historical/nostalgic, humor, interview/profile, personal experience, photo feature, travel. No fiction or poetry. **Buys 24 mss/year.** Query with published clips or send complete ms. Length: 1,000-3,200 words. **Pays $150-500.** Sometimes pays expenses of writers on assignment.

Photos: State availability with submission. Buys one-time rights. Negotiates payment individually.

Columns/Departments: Up in Michigan Reflection (essays about northern Michigan); Reflection on Home (essays about northern homes), both 700 words. **Buys 18 mss/year.** Query with published clips or send complete ms. **Pays $100-200.**

Tips: "When shaping an article for us, consider first that it must be strongly rooted in our region. The lack of this foundation element is one of the biggest reasons for our rejecting material. If you send us a piece about peaches, even if it does an admirable job of relaying the history of peaches, their medicinal qualities, their nutritional magnificence, and so on, we are likely to reject if it doesn't include local farms as a reference point. We want sidebars and extended captions designed to bring in a reader not enticed by the main subject. We cover the northern portion of the Lower Peninsula and to a lesser degree the Upper Peninsula. General categories of interest include nature and the environment, regional culture, personalities, the arts (visual, performing, literary), crafts, food & dining, homes, history, and outdoor activities (e.g., fishing, golf, skiing, boating, biking, hiking, birding, gardening). We are keenly interested in environmental and land-use issues but seldom use material dealing with such issues as health care, education, social services, criminal justice, and local politics. We use service pieces and a small number of how-to pieces, mostly focused on small projects for the home or yard. Also, we value research. We need articles built with information. Many of the pieces we reject use writing style to fill in for information voids. Style and voice are strongest when used as vehicles for sound research."

Minnesota

$ $ ✪ LAKE COUNTRY JOURNAL MAGAZINE, Evergreen Press of Brainerd, 1863 Design Dr., Baxter MN 56425. Fax: (218)825-7816. E-mail: jodi@lakecountryjournal.com. Website: www.lakecountryjournal.com. **Contact:** Jodi Schwen, editor. **90% freelance written.** Bimonthly magazine covering central Minnesota's lake country. "We target a specific geographical niche in central Minnesota. The writer must be familiar with our area. We promote positive family values, foster a sense of community, increase appreciation for our natural and cultural environments, and provide ideas for enhancing the quality of our lives." Estab. 1996. Circ. 14,500. Pays on publication. Publishes ms an average of 6 months after acceptance. Byline given. Offers 25% kill fee. Buys first North American serial, second serial (reprint), electronic rights. Submit seasonal material 1 year in advance. Accepts queries by mail, e-mail. Responds in 2 months to queries; 3 months to mss. Sample copy for $5.

- Break in by "submitting department length first—they are not scheduled as far in advance as features. Always in need of original fillers."

Nonfiction: Essays, general interest, how-to, humor, interview/profile, personal experience, photo feature. "No articles that come from writers who are not familiar with our target geographical location." **Buys 30 mss/year.** Query with or without published clips. Length: 1,000-1,500 words. **Pays $100-175.** Sometimes pays expenses of writers on assignment.

Reprints: Accepts previously published submissions.

Photos: State availability with submission. Reviews transparencies. Buys one-time rights. Negotiates payment individually. Identification of subjects, model releases required.

Columns/Departments: Profile-People from Lake Country, 800 words; Essay, 800 words; Health (topics pertinent to central Minnesota living), 500 words; Family Fun, 500 words. **Buys 40 mss/year.** Query with published clips. **Pays $50-75.**

Fiction: Adventure, humorous, mainstream, slice-of-life vignettes, literary, also family fiction appropriate to Lake Country and seasonal fiction. **Buys 6 mss/year.** Length:1,500 words. **Pays $100-175.**

Poetry: Free verse. "Never use rhyming verse, avant-garde, experimental, etc." **Buys 20 poems/year.** Submit maximum 4 poems. Length: 8-32 lines. **Pays $25.**

Fillers: Anecdotes, short humor. **Buys 20/year.** Length: 100-500 words. **Pays $25.**

Tips: "Most of the people who will read your articles live in the north central Minnesota lakes area. All have some significant attachment to the area. We have readers of various ages, backgrounds, and lifestyles. After reading your article, we hope to have a deeper understanding of some aspect of our community, our environment, ourselves, or humanity in general. Tell us something new. Show us something we didn't see before. Help us grasp the significance of your topic. Use analogies, allusions, and other literary techniques to add color to your writing. Add breadth by making the subject relevant to all readers—especially those who aren't already interested in your subject. Add depth by connecting your subject with timeless insights. If you can do this without getting sappy or didactic or wordy or dull, we're looking for you."

$ $ LAKE SUPERIOR MAGAZINE, Lake Superior Port Cities, Inc., P.O. Box 16417, Duluth MN 55816-0417. (218)722-5002. Fax: (218)722-4096. E-mail: edit@lakesuperior.com. Website: www.lakesuperior.com. **Contact:** Konnie LeMay, editor. **60% freelance written.** Works with a small number of new/unpublished writers each year. Please include phone number and address with e-mail queries. Bimonthly magazine covering contemporary and historic people, places and current events around Lake Superior. Estab. 1979. Circ. 20,000. Pays on publication. Publishes ms an average of 10 months after acceptance. Byline given. Buys first North American serial, second serial (reprint) rights. Submit seasonal material 1 year in advance. Accepts queries by mail, e-mail. Responds in 3 months to queries. Sample copy for $3.95 and 5 first-class stamps. Writer's guidelines for #10 SASE.

Nonfiction: Book excerpts, general interest, historical/nostalgic, humor, interview/profile (local), personal experience, photo feature (local), travel (local), city profiles, regional business, some investigative. **Buys 45 mss/year.** Query with published clips. Length: 300-2,200 words. **Pays $60-600.** Sometimes pays expenses of writers on assignment.

Photos: "Quality photography is our hallmark." Send photos with submission. Reviews contact sheets, 2×2 and larger transparencies, 4×5 prints. Offers $40/image; $125 for covers. Captions, identification of subjects, model releases required.

Columns/Departments: Current events and things to do (for Events Calendar section), less than 300 words; Around The Circle (media reviews; short pieces on Lake Superior; Great Lakes environmental issues; themes, letters and short pieces on events and highlights of the Lake Superior Region); I Remember (nostalgic lake-specific pieces), up to 1,100 words; Life Lines (single personality profile with photography), up to 900 words. Other headings include Destinations; Nature; Wilderness Living; Heritage; Shipwreck; Chronicle; Lake Superior's Own; House for Sale. **Buys 20 mss/year.** Query with published clips. **Pays $60-90.**

Fiction: Ethnic, historic, humorous, mainstream, novel excerpts, slice-of-life vignettes, ghost stories. Must be targeted regionally. **Buys 2-3 mss/year.** Query with published clips. Length: 300-2,500 words. **Pays $1-125.**

The online magazine carries original content not found in the print edition. Contact: Konnie Lemay, online editor.

Tips: "Well-researched queries are attended to. We actively seek queries from writers in Lake Superior communities. We prefer manuscripts to queries. Provide enough information on why the subject is important to the region and our readers, or why and how something is unique. We want details. The writer must have a thorough knowledge of the subject and how it relates to our region. We prefer a fresh, unused approach to the subject which provides the reader with an emotional involvement. Almost all of our articles feature quality photography, color or black and white. It is a prerequisite of all nonfiction. All submissions should include a *short* biography of author/photographer; mug shot sometimes used. Blanket submissions need not apply."

$ $ MINNESOTA MONTHLY, 10 S. Fifth St., Suite 1000, Minneapolis MN 55402. Fax: (612)371-5801. E-mail: phnettleton@mnmo.com. Website: www.mnmo.com. **Contact:** Pamela Hill Nettleton, editor. **50% freelance written.** "*Minnesota Monthly* is a regional lifestyle publication written for a sophisticated, well-educated audience living in the Twin Cities area and in greater Minnesota." Estab. 1967. Circ. 80,000. **Pays on acceptance.** Accepts queries by mail, e-mail. Writer's guidelines online.

"The Journey column/department (2,000 words) is probably the best break-in spot for freelancers. Submit, in its entirety, a diary or journal of a trip, event, or experience that changed your life. Past journeys: being an actress on a cruise ship, a parent's death, making a movie."

Nonfiction: Regional issues, arts, services, places, people, essays, exposé, general interest, historical/nostalgia, interview/profile, new product, photo feature, travel in Minnesota. "We want exciting, excellent, compelling writing with a strong Minnesota angle." Query with résumé, published clips, and SASE. Length: 1,000-4,000 words. **Pay is negotiable.**

Columns/Departments: Portrait (photo-driven profile), 360 words; Just Asking (sassy interview with a Minnesota character or celebrity), 900 words; Midwest Traveler, 950-2,000 words; Postcards (chatty notes from Midwest towns), 300 words; Journey (diary/journal of a life-changing experience), 2,000 words. Query with résumé, published clips, and SASE. **Pay negotiable.**

Fiction: Fiction in the June issue, and a November fiction contest, The Tamarack Awards. Complete information about The Tamarack Awards is available in the Contests & Awards section of *Writer's Market*.

Tips: "Our readers are bright, artsy, and involved in their communities. Writing should reflect that. Stories must all have a Minnesota angle. If you can write well, try us!"

Mississippi

$ $ MISSISSIPPI MAGAZINE, DownHome Publications, 5 Lakeland Circle, Jackson MS 39216. (601)982-8418. Fax: (601)982-8447. **Contact:** Jennifer Ellis, editor. **90% freelance written.** Bimonthly magazine covering Mississippi—the state and its lifestyles. "We are interested in positive stories reflecting Mississippi's rich traditions and heritage, and focusing on the contributions the state and its natives have made to the arts, literature and culture. In each issue we showcase homes and gardens, lifestyle issues, food, design, art and more." Estab. 1982. Circ. 30,000. Pays on publication. Publishes ms an average of 6 months after acceptance. Byline given. Offers 50% kill fee. Buys first North American serial rights. Editorial lead time 6 months. Submit seasonal material 1 year in advance. Accepts queries by mail, fax. Accepts simultaneous submissions. Responds in 3 months to queries. Sample copy and writer's guidelines for #10 SASE.

Nonfiction: General interest, historical/nostalgic, how-to (home decor), interview/profile, personal experience, travel. "No opinion, political, essay, book reviews, exposé." **Buys 15 mss/year.** Query. Length: 900-1,800 words. **Pays $150-350 for assigned articles; $75-200 for unsolicited articles.**

Photos: Send photos with query. Reviews transparencies, Prints. Buys one-time rights. Negotiates payment individually. Captions, identification of subjects, model releases required.

Columns/Departments: Gardening (short informative article on a specific plant or gardening technique), 750-1,000 words; Culture Center (story about an event or person relating to Mississippi's art, music, theatre, or literature), 750-1,000 words; On Being Southern (personal essay about life in Mississippi. Only ms submissions accepted), 750 words. **Buys 6 mss/year.** Query. **Pays $150-225.**

Missouri

$ $ KANSAS CITY HOMES & GARDENS, Showcase Publishing, Inc., P.O. Box 8680, Prairie Village KS 66208. (913)648-5757. Fax: (913)648-5783. E-mail: spublishingco@kc.rr.com. Editor: Dave Leathers. **Contact:** Liz Murray, associate editor. Bimonthly magazine. "Since 1986, Kansas City residents (mainly women) have embraced a local publication that speaks to them. Their home, lifestyle, and family are featured with emphasis on high-quality, upscale decorating, building, and living." Estab. 1986. Pays on publication. Byline given. Buys one-time rights. Editorial lead time 4 months. Submit seasonal material 4 months in advance. Accepts queries by mail, e-mail, fax. Accepts previously published material. Accepts simultaneous submissions. Responds in 1 month to queries; 1 month to mss. Sample copy for $7.50 or online. Writer's guidelines online.

Nonfiction: Travel, home and garden. **Buys 8 mss/year.** Query with published clips. Length: 600-1,000 words. **Pays $60-350.** Sometimes pays expenses of writers on assignment.

Reprints: Accepts previously published submissions.

Photos: State availability of or send photos with submission. Reviews transparencies. Buys one-time rights. Offers no additional payment for photos accepted with ms. Identification of subjects required.

Columns/Departments: Time Away (places to take vacations to), 600 words. Query with published clips. **Pays $60-350.**

Tips: "Really read and understand our audience. Who are they and what do they want?"

$ $ MISSOURI LIFE, Missouri Life, Inc., P.O. Box 421, Fayette MO 65248-0421. (660)248-3489. Fax: (660)248-2310. E-mail: info@missourilife.com. Website: www.missourilife.com. Editor-in-Chief: Danita Allen Wood. **Contact:** Tricia Mosser, managing editor. **70% freelance written.** Bimonthly magazine covering the state of Missouri. "*Missouri Life*'s readers are mostly college-educated people with a wide range of travel and lifestyle interests. Our magazine discovers the people, places, and events—both past and present—that make Missouri a good place to live and/or visit." Estab. 1998. Circ. 50,000. **Pays on acceptance.** Byline given. Offers negotiable kill fee. Buys all, non-exclusive rights. Editorial lead time 3 months. Submit seasonal material 6 months in advance. Accepts queries by mail, fax. Responds in 1 month to queries; 2 months to mss. Sample copy online. Writer's guidelines for #10 SASE or online.

Nonfiction: General interest, historical/nostalgic, interview/profile, travel, all Missouri-related. **Buys 18 feature length mss/year.** Query. Length: 300-2,000 words. **Pays $50-600; 20¢/word.**

Photos: State availability with submission. Reviews transparencies. Buys all non-exclusive rights. Offers $50-150/photo. Captions, identification of subjects, model releases required.

Columns/Departments: Best of Missouri (people and places, past and present, written in an almanac style), 300 words maximum; Missouri Artist (features a Missouri artist), 500 words; Made in Missouri (products and businesses native to Missouri), 500 words; Missouri Memory (a personal memory of Missouri gone by), 500 words; Missouri Hands (crafts and other items by Missouri artists that don't fall into 'fine art' category), 500 words; Day Trip (on museum event, etc., accompanied by sidebar listing specialty restaurants and other areas of interest close to featured spot), 300-500 words; Missouri Homes (on home of particular historic or other interest—preferably open to public), 500-600 words. **Pays $50-200.**

$ $ RELOCATING IN KANSAS CITY, Showcase Publishing, Inc., P.O. Box 8680, Prairie Village KS 66208. (913)648-5757. Fax: (913)648-5783. Editor: Dave Leathers. **Contact:** Liz Murray, associate editor. Annual relocation guides, free for people moving to the area. Pays on publication. Byline given. Buys one-time rights. Editorial lead time 4 months. Submit seasonal material 4 months in advance. Accepts queries by mail, fax. Accepts previously published material. Accepts simultaneous submissions. Responds in 1 month to queries; 1 month to mss. Sample copy for $5.

Nonfiction: Historical/nostalgic, travel, local issues. **Buys 8 mss/year.** Query with published clips. Length: 600-1,000 words. **Pays $60-350.** Sometimes pays expenses of writers on assignment.

Reprints: Accepts previously published submissions.

Photos: Reviews transparencies. Buys one-time rights. Offers no additional payment for photos accepted with ms. Identification of subjects required.
Tips: "Really read and understand our audience."

$ $ RELOCATING TO THE LAKE OF THE OZARKS, Showcase Publishing, Inc., P.O. Box 8680, Prairie Village KS 66208. (913)648-5757. Fax: (913)648-5783. Editor: Dave Leathers. **Contact:** Liz Murray, associate editor. Annual relocation guides, free for people moving to the area. Pays on publication. Publishes ms an average of 6 months after acceptance. Byline given. Buys one-time rights. Editorial lead time 4 months. Submit seasonal material 4 months in advance. Accepts queries by mail, fax. Accepts previously published material. Accepts simultaneous submissions. Responds in 1 month to queries; 1 month to mss. Sample copy for $5.
Nonfiction: Historical/nostalgic, travel, local issues. **Buys 8 mss/year.** Query with published clips. Length: 600-1,000 words. **Pays $60-350.** Sometimes pays expenses of writers on assignment.
Reprints: Accepts previously published submissions.
Photos: State availability of or send photos with submission. Reviews transparencies. Buys one-time rights. Offers no additional payment for photos accepted with ms. Identification of subjects required.
Tips: "Really read and understand our audience."

$ RIVER HILLS TRAVELER, Todd Publishing, Route 4, Box 4396, Piedmont MO 63957. (573)223-7143. Fax: (573)223-2117. E-mail: btodd@semo.net. Website: www.deepozarks.com. **Contact:** Bob Todd, online editor. **50% freelance written.** Monthly tabloid covering "outdoor sports and nature in the southeast quarter of Missouri, the east and central Ozarks. Topics like those in *Field & Stream* and *National Geographic*." Estab. 1973. Circ. 7,500. Pays on publication. Publishes ms an average of 2 months after acceptance. Byline given. Buys one-time rights. Editorial lead time 2 months. Submit seasonal material 1 year in advance. Accepts queries by e-mail. Accepts simultaneous submissions. Responds in 2 months to queries. Sample copy and writer's guidelines for SAE or online.
Nonfiction: Historical/nostalgic, how-to, humor, opinion, personal experience, photo feature, technical, travel. "No stories about other geographic areas." **Buys 80 mss/year.** Query with writing samples. Length: 1,500 word maximum. **Pays $15-50.** Sometimes pays expenses of writers on assignment.
Reprints: Send typed ms with rights for sale noted and information about when and where the material previously appeared.
Photos: Send photos with submission. Buys one-time rights. Negotiates payment individually. Pays $25 for covers.

■ The online magazine carries original content not found in the print edition and includes writer's guidelines. Contact: Bob Todd, online editor.

Tips: "We are a 'poor man's' *Field & Stream* and *National Geographic*—about the eastern Missouri Ozarks. We prefer stories that relate an adventure that causes a reader to relive an adventure of his own or consider embarking on a similar adventure. Think of an adventure in camping or cooking, not just fishing and hunting. How-to is great, but not simple instructions. We encourage good first-person reporting."

Montana

$ $ MONTANA MAGAZINE, Lee Enterprises, P.O. Box 5630, Helena MT 59604-5630. (406)443-2842. Fax: (406)443-5480. E-mail: editor@montanamagazine.com. Website: www.montanamagazine.com. **Contact:** Beverly R. Magley, editor. **90% freelance written.** Bimonthly magazine. "Strictly Montana-oriented magazine that features community profiles, contemporary issues, wildlife and natural history, travel pieces." Estab. 1970. Circ. 40,000. Publishes ms an average of 1 year after acceptance. Byline given. Buys one-time rights. Submit seasonal material 1 year in advance. Accepts simultaneous submissions. Responds in 6 months to queries. Sample copy for $5 or online. Writer's guidelines for #10 SASE or online.

- Accepts queries by e-mail. No phone calls.

Nonfiction: Query by September for summer material; March for winter material. Essays, general interest, interview/profile, photo feature, travel. Special issues: Special features on summer and winter destination points. No 'me and Joe' hiking and hunting tales; no blood-and-guts hunting stories; no poetry; no fiction; no sentimental essays. **Buys 30 mss/year.** Query with samples and SASE. Length: 300-3,000 words. **Pays 15¢/word.** Sometimes pays expenses of writers on assignment.
Reprints: Send photocopy of article with rights for sale noted and information about when and where the material previously appeared. Pays 50% of amount paid for an original article.
Photos: Send photos with submission. Reviews contact sheets, 35mm or larger format transparencies, 5×7 prints. Buys one-time rights. Offers additional payment for photos accepted with ms. Captions, identification of subjects, model releases required.
Columns/Departments: Memories (reminisces of early-day Montana life), 800-1,000 words; Outdoor Recreation, 1,500-2,000 words; Community Festivals, 500 words, plus b&w or color photo; Montana-Specific Humor, 800-1,000 words. Query with samples and SASE.
Tips: "We avoid commonly known topics so Montanans won't ho-hum through more of what they already know. If it's time to revisit a topic, we look for a unique slant."

Nevada

$ $ NEVADA MAGAZINE, 401 N. Carson St., Carson City NV 89701-4291. (775)687-5416. Fax: (775)687-6159. E-mail: editor@nevadamagazine.com. Website: www.nevadamagazine.com. Editor: David Moore. **Contact:** Joyce Hollister, associate editor. **50% freelance written.** Works with a small number of new/unpublished writers each year. Bimonthly magazine published by the state of Nevada to promote tourism. Estab. 1936. Circ. 80,000. Pays on publication. Publishes ms an average of 8 months after acceptance. Byline given. Buys first North American serial rights. Submit seasonal material 6 months in advance. Accepts queries by mail, e-mail. Responds in 1 month to queries. Sample copy for $1. Writer's guidelines for #10 SASE.

O→ Break in with shorter departments, rather than trying to tackle a big feature. Good bets are Dining Out, Recreation, Casinoland, Side Trips, and Roadside Attractions.

Nonfiction: "We welcome stories and photos on speculation." Nevada topics only. Historical/nostalgic, humor, interview/profile, personal experience, photo feature, travel, recreational, think pieces. **Buys 40 unsolicited mss/year.** Send complete ms or query. Length: 500-1,800 words. **Pays $50-500.**

Photos: Send photo material with accompanying ms. Name, address, and caption should appear on each photo or slide. Denise Barr, art director. Buys one-time rights. Pays $20-100 for color transparencies and glossy prints.

Tips: "Keep in mind the magazine's purpose is to promote Nevada tourism. Keys to higher payments are quality and editing effort (more than length). Send cover letter; no photocopies. We look for a light, enthusiastic tone of voice without being too cute; articles bolstered by facts and thorough research; and unique angles on Nevada subjects."

$ $ RELOCATING TO LAS VEGAS, Showcase Publishing, Inc., P.O. Box 8680, Prairie Village KS 66208. (913)648-5757. Fax: (913)648-5783. Editor: Dave Leathers. **Contact:** Liz Murray, associate editor. Annual relocation guides, free for people moving to the area. Pays on publication. Publishes ms an average of 6 months after acceptance. Byline given. Buys one-time rights. Editorial lead time 4 months. Submit seasonal material 4 months in advance. Accepts queries by mail, e-mail. Responds in 1 month to queries; 1 month to mss. Sample copy for $5.

Nonfiction: Historical/nostalgic, travel, local issues. **Buys 8 mss/year.** Query with published clips. Length: 650-1,000 words. **Pays $60-350.** Sometimes pays expenses of writers on assignment.

Reprints: Accepts previously published submissions.

Photos: State availability with submission. Reviews transparencies. Buys one-time rights. Offers no additional payment for photos accepted with ms. Identification of subjects required.

Tips: "Really read and understand our audience."

New Hampshire

$ $ NEW HAMPSHIRE MAGAZINE, McLean Communications, Inc., 150 Dow St., Manchester NH 03101. (603)624-1442. E-mail: editor@nhmagazine.com. Website: www.nhmagazine.com. **Contact:** Rick Broussard, editor. **50% freelance written.** Monthly magazine devoted to New Hampshire. "We want stories written for, by, and about the people of New Hampshire with emphasis on qualities that set us apart from other states. We feature lifestyle, adventure, and home-related stories with a unique local angle." Estab. 1986. Circ. 24,000. Pays on publication. Byline given. Offers 25% kill fee. Buys all rights. Editorial lead time 3 months. Submit seasonal material 3 months in advance. Accepts queries by mail, e-mail, fax. Accepts simultaneous submissions. Responds in 2 months to queries; 3 months to mss.

Nonfiction: Essays, general interest, historical/nostalgic, photo feature, business. **Buys 30 mss/year.** Query with published clips. Length: 800-2,000 words. **Pays $50-300.** Sometimes pays expenses of writers on assignment.

Photos: State availability with submission. Rights purchased vary. Possible additional payment for photos accepted with ms. Captions, identification of subjects, model releases required.

■ The online magazine carries original content not found in the print edition. Contact: Rick Broussard, online editor.

Tips: Network Publications publishes 1 monthly magazine entitled *New Hampshire Magazine* and a "specialty" publication called *Destination New Hampshire*. "In general, our articles deal with the people of New Hampshire—their lifestyles and interests. We also present localized stories about national and international issues, ideas, and trends. We will only use stories that show our readers how these issues have an impact on their daily lives. We cover a wide range of topics, including healthcare, politics, law, real-life dramas, regional history, medical issues, business, careers, environmental issues, the arts, the outdoors, education, food, recreation, etc. Many of our readers are what we call 'The New Traditionalists'—aging Baby Boomers who have embraced solid American values and contemporary New Hampshire lifestyles."

New Jersey

$ $ $ $ NEW JERSEY MONTHLY, The Magazine of the Garden State, New Jersey Monthly LLC, 55 Park Place, P.O. Box 920, Morristown NJ 07963-0920. (973)539-8230. Fax: (973)538-2953. E-mail: editor@njmonthly.com. Website: www.njmonthly.com. Editor: Nancy Nusser. **Contact:** Christopher Hann, senior editor. **75-80% freelance written.** Monthly magazine covering "just about anything to do with New Jersey, from news, politics and sports to decorating trends and lifestyle issues. Our readership is well-educated, affluent, and on average our readers have lived in New Jersey 20 years or more." Estab. 1976. Circ. 95,000. Pays on completion of fact-checking. Publishes ms an average of 3 months after acceptance. Byline given. Offers 20% kill fee. Buys first North American serial rights. Editorial lead time 3 months. Submit seasonal material 6 months in advance. Accepts queries by mail, e-mail, fax, phone. Accepts simultaneous submissions. Responds in 2 months to queries. Writer's guidelines for $2.95.

- This magazine continues to look for strong investigative reporters with novelistic style and solid knowledge of New Jersey issues.

Nonfiction: Book excerpts, essays, exposé, general interest, historical/nostalgic, humor, interview/profile, personal experience, photo feature, travel (within New Jersey). "No experience pieces from people who used to live in New Jersey or general pieces that have no New Jersey angle." **Buys 90-100 mss/year.** Query with published magazine clips and SASE. Length: 1,200-3,500 words. **Pays $750-2,000.** Pays reasonable expenses of writers on assignment with prior approval.
Photos: State availability with submission. Reviews transparencies, prints. Buys one-time rights. Payment negotiated. Identification of subjects, model releases required.
Columns/Departments: Exit Ramp (back page essay usually originating from personal experience but told in such a way that it tells a broader story of statewide interest), 1,400 words. **Buys 12 mss/year.** Query with published clips. **Pays $200-400.**
Fillers: Anecdotes. **Buys 12-15/year.** Length: 200-250 words. **Pays $100.**
Tips: "The best approach: Do your homework! Read the past year's issues to get an understanding of our well-written, well-researched articles that tell a tale from a well-established point of view."

$ $ NEW JERSEY OUTDOORS, New Jersey Department of Environmental Protection, P.O. Box 402, Trenton NJ 08625. (609)777-4182. Fax: (609)292-3198. E-mail: njo@dep.state.nj.us. Website: www.state.nj.us/dep/njo/. **Contact:** Denise Damiano Mikics, editor. **75% freelance written.** Quarterly magazine highlighting New Jersey's natural and historic resources and activities related to them. Estab. 1950. Circ. 13,000. Pays on publication. Byline given. Buys one-time rights. Editorial lead time 1 year. Submit seasonal material 1 year in advance. Accepts queries by mail, e-mail, fax. Responds in 6 months to queries. Sample copy for $4.25. Writer's guidelines for #10 SASE or on website.
Nonfiction: "*New Jersey Outdoors* is not interested in articles showing disregard for the environment or in items demonstrating unskilled people taking extraordinary risks." Note: All should be about the conservation and enjoyment of natural and historic resources (e.g., fishing, hunting, hiking, camping, skiing, boating, gardening, trips to/activities in specific New Jersey locations.) General interest, how-to, personal experience, photo feature. **Buys 30-40 mss/year.** Query with published clips. Length: 600-2,000 words. **Pays $100-450.** Sometimes pays expenses of writers on assignment.
Reprints: Rarely accepts previously published submsisions. Send typed ms with rights for sale noted, and information about when and where the material previously appeared. Pays up to 100% of amount paid for the original article.
Photos: State availability with submission. Reviews duplicate transparencies, prints (duplicate). Buys one-time rights. Offers $20-125/photo.
Tips: "*New Jersey Outdoors* generally publishes season-specific articles, planned a year in advance. Topics should be fresh, and stories should be accompanied by *great* photography. Articles and photos *must* relate to New Jersey. Also, we'd like to see more personal experience stories of enjoying New Jersey's outdoor and historic resources."

$ $ NEW JERSEY SAVVY LIVING, CTB, LLC, P.O. Box 607, Short Hills NJ 07078-0607. (973)379-7749. Fax: (973)379-4116. Website: www.njsavvyliving.com. **Contact:** Elaine Davis, editor. **90% freelance written.** Magazine published 5 times/year covering New Jersey residents with affluent lifestyles. "*Savvy* is a regional magazine for an upscale audience, ages 35-65. We focus on lifestyle topics such as decorating, fashion, people, travel, and gardening." Estab. 1997. Circ. 60,000. Pays on publication. Publishes ms an average of 3 months after acceptance. Byline given. Offers $50 kill fee. variable rights. Editorial lead time 3 months. Accepts queries by mail. Accepts previously published material. Accepts simultaneous submissions. Response time varies to queries. Sample copy for 9×12 SAE.
Nonfiction: General interest, historical/nostalgic, how-to, humor, inspirational, interview/profile, photo feature, travel, home/decorating. Special issues: Home (April). No investigative, fiction, personal experience, and nonNew Jersey topics (excluding travel). **Buys 50 mss/year.** Query with published clips. Length: 900-2,000 words. **Pays $250-500.**
Reprints: Accepts previously published submissions (nonconflicting markets only).
Photos: State availability with submission. Reviews contact sheets, negatives, transparencies, prints. Buys one-time rights. Offers no additional payment for photos accepted with ms. Captions, identification of subjects, model releases required.
Columns/Departments: Wine & Spirits (wine trends); Savvy Shoppers (inside scoop on buying); Intrepid Diner (restaurant review); Home Gourmet (from food to hostess gifts at home), all 900-1,000 words. **Buys 25 mss/year.** Query with published clips. **Pays $250.**
Fillers: Lydia Gnau, assistant editor. Facts, newsbreaks. Length: 125-250 words. **Pays $25-50.**
Tips: "Offer ideas of interest to an upscale New Jersey readership. We love articles that utilize local sources and are well-focused. Trends are always a good bit, so come up with a hot idea and make us believe you can deliver."

$ $ THE SANDPAPER, Newsmagazine of the Jersey Shore, The SandPaper, Inc., 1816 Long Beach Blvd., Surf City NJ 08008-5461. (609)494-5900. Fax: (609)494-1437. E-mail: lbinews@hotmail.com. **Contact:** Jay Mann, managing editor. **10% freelance written.** Weekly tabloid covering subjects of interest to Jersey shore residents and visitors. "*The SandPaper* publishes 2 editions covering many of the Jersey Shore's finest resort communities including Long Beach Island and Ocean City, New Jersey. Each issue includes a mix of news, human interest features, opinion columns, and entertainment/calendar listings." Estab. 1976. Circ. 60,000. Pays on publication. Publishes ms an average of 1 month after acceptance. Byline given. Offers 100% kill fee. Buys first, all rights. Submit seasonal material 3 months in advance. Accepts queries by mail, e-mail, fax, phone. Accepts simultaneous submissions. Responds in 1 month to queries. Sample copy for 9×12 SAE with 8 first-class stamps.

O▬ "The opinion page and columns are most open to freelancers."

Nonfiction: Must pertain to New Jersey shore locale. Essays, general interest, historical/nostalgic, humor, opinion, arts, entertaining news, reviews; also environmental submissons relating to the ocean, wetlands, and pinelands. **Buys 10 mss/year.** Send complete ms. Length: 200-2,000 words. **Pays $25-200.** Sometimes pays expenses of writers on assignment.

Reprints: Send photocopy and information about when and where the material previously appeared. Pays 25-50% of amount paid for an original article.

Photos: Send photos with submission. Buys one-time or all rights. Offers $8-25/photo.

Columns/Departments: Speakeasy (opinion and slice-of-life, often humorous); Commentary (forum for social science perspectives); both 1,000-1,500 words, preferably with local or Jersey Shore angle. **Buys 50 mss/year.** Send complete ms. **Pays $30.**

Tips: "Anything of interest to sun worshippers, beach walkers, nature watchers, and water sports lovers is of potential interest to us. There is an increasing coverage of environmental issues. We are steadily increasing the amount of entertainment-related material in our publication. Articles on history of the shore area are always in demand."

New York

$ $ ADIRONDACK LIFE, P.O. Box 410, Jay NY 12941-0410. (518)946-2191. Fax: (518)946-7461. E-mail: aledit@adirondacklife.com. Website: www.adirondacklife.com. **Contact:** Elizabeth Folwell, editor or Galen Crane, managing editor. **70% freelance written.** Prefers to work with published/established writers. Magazine published 8 issues/year, including special Annual Outdoor Guide, emphasizes the Adirondack region and the North Country of New York State in articles covering outdoor activities, history, and natural history directly related to the Adirondacks. Estab. 1970. Circ. 50,000. Pays 45 days after acceptance. Publishes ms an average of 6 months after acceptance. Byline given. Buys first North American serial rights. Submit seasonal material 1 year in advance. Accepts queries by mail, e-mail. Sample copy for $3 and 9×12 SAE. Writer's guidelines for #10 SASE or online.

O▬ "For new writers, the best way to break into the magazine is through departments."

Nonfiction: "*Adirondack Life* attempts to capture the unique flavor and ethos of the Adirondack mountains and North Country region through feature articles directly pertaining to the qualities of the area." Special issues: Outdoors (May); Single-topic Collector's issue (September). **Buys 20-25 unsolicited mss/year.** Query with published clips. Length: 2,500-5,000 words. **Pays 25¢/word.** Sometimes pays expenses of writers on assignment.

Photos: All photos must have been taken in the Adirondacks. Each issue contains a photo feature. Purchased with or without ms on assignment. All photos must be individually identified as to the subject or locale and must bear the photographer's name. Send photos with submission. Reviews color transparencies, prints (b&w). Pays $125 for full page, b&w, or color; $300 for cover (color only, vertical in format). Credit line given.

Columns/Departments: Special Places (unique spots in the Adirondack Park); Watercraft; Barkeater (personal to political essays); Wilderness (environmental issues); Working (careers in the Adirondacks); Home; Yesteryears; Kitchen; Profile; Historic Preservation; Sporting Scene. Length: 1,200-2,400 words. Query with published clips. **Pays 25¢/word.**

Fiction: Considers first-serial novel excerpts in its subject matter and region.

Tips: "Do not send a personal essay about your meaningful moment in the mountains. We need factual pieces about regional history, sports, culture, and business. We are looking for clear, concise, well-organized manuscripts that are strictly Adirondack in subject. Check back issues to be sure we haven't already covered your topic. Please do not send unsolicited manuscripts via e-mail. Check out our guidelines online."

$ $ $ AVENUE, 823 United Nations Plaza, New York NY 10017. (212)476-0640. Fax: (212)758-7395. Editor-in-chief: Jill Brooke. **Contact:** Maileen Celis, managing editor. **25% freelance written.** Monthly magazine covering New York art, fashion, restaurants; business, design and travel. "As *Avenue* is intended for readers on Manhattan's Upper East Side our subject matter is generally high end, and most pieces focus on a New York personality." Estab. 1976. Circ. 80,000. Pays 60 days after publication. Publishes ms an average of 2 months after acceptance. Byline given. Offers 15% kill fee. Buys all rights. Editorial lead time 3 months. Submit seasonal material 3 months in advance. Accepts queries by mail, fax.

Nonfiction: Essays, general interest, historical/nostalgic, interview/profile, personal experience, travel. **Buys 30 mss/year.** Query with published clips. Length: 150-1,800 words. **Pays $150-1,500.** Pays expenses of writers on assignment.

Photos: State availability with submission. Reviews prints. Buys one-time rights. Negotiates payment individually. Identification of subjects, model releases required.

Tips: "Send submission by mail or fax after looking over a recent issue to familiarize yourself with our format."

$ BUFFALO SPREE MAGAZINE, David Laurence Publications, Inc., 5678 Main St., Buffalo NY 14221. (716)634-0820. Fax: (716)810-0075. E-mail: info@buffalospree.com. Website: www.buffalospree.com. **Contact:** Elizabeth Licata, editor. **90% freelance written.** Bimonthly city regional magazine. Estab. 1967. Circ. 25,000. Pays on publication. Publishes ms an average of 1 month after acceptance. Byline given. Buys first North American serial rights. Accepts queries by mail, e-mail, fax. Responds in 6 months to queries. Sample copy for $3.95 and 9×12 SAE with 9 first-class stamps.

Nonfiction: "Most articles are assigned not unsolicited." Interview/profile, travel, issue-oriented features, arts, living, food, regional. **Buys 5-10 mss/year.** Query with résumé and published clips. Length: 1,000-2,000 words. **Pays $125-250.**

Tips: "Send a well-written, compelling query or an interesting topic, and *great* clips. We no longer regularly publish fiction or poetry. Prefers material that is Western New York related."

$ POLICE OFFICER'S QUARTERLY .38 SPECIAL MAGAZINE, (formerly *Police Officer's Quarterly*), 47-01 Greenpoint Ave., Columbus Circle Station #114, Sunnyside NY 11104-1709. (212)699-3825, ext. 4827. Fax: (212)699-3825, ext. 4827. E-mail: 38special@onebox.com. **Contact:** Liz Martinez DeFranco, editor. Quarterly magazine. *POQ .38 Special* is distributed to police officers, peace officers, federal agents, corrections officers, auxiliary police officers, probation and parole officers, civilian employees of law enforcement agencies, etc., in the New York metropolitan area. Estab. 2001. Buys one-time rights. Accepts queries by e-mail. Accepts previously published material. Accepts simultaneous submissions. Sample copy for $5, plus a 9×12 SASE. Writer's guidelines by e-mail.

Nonfiction: "We are seeking stories on travel; law enforcement product/news; books with a LE hook; movies and other entertainment that our readers would enjoy knowing about; worthy LE-related Internet sites; the latest developments in forensics and technology; health articles with a LE spin; investigation techniques; innovative international, national, regional, or local (inside and outside of the New York area) approaches to LE or crime prevention issues; other topics of interest to our reader population. General interest. "We see too many pieces that are dry and not enjoyable to read. Even if the topic is serious or scientific, present the material as though you were telling a friend about it." Query. Length: 1,000-1,500 words. **Pays $100.**

Photos: Photos are very helpful and much appreciated; however, there is no additional pay for photos. Inclusion of photos does increase chances of publication.

Columns/Departments: Book'Em (book reviews/excerpts/author interviews); Internet Guide; Screening Room (movie reviews); Your Finances; Management in Focus; Health Department; Forensics Lab; Technology. Query. **Pays $75.**

Tips: "Writers should keep in mind that this is a lifestyle magazine whose readers happen to be cops, not a cop magazine with some lifestyle topics in it."

$ $ SYRACUSE NEW TIMES, A. Zimmer, Ltd., 1415 W. Genesee St., Syracuse NY 13204. Fax: (315)422-1721. E-mail: editorial@syracusenewtimes.com. Website: newtimes.rway.com. **Contact:** Molly English, editor. **50% freelance written.** Weekly tabloid covering news, sports, arts and entertainment. "*Syracuse New Times* is an alternative weekly that can be topical, provocative, irreverent, and intensely local." Estab. 1969. Circ. 46,000. Pays on publication. Publishes ms an average of 1 month after acceptance. Byline given. Buys one-time rights. Editorial lead time 3 months. Submit seasonal material 3 months in advance. Accepts simultaneous submissions. Responds in 2 weeks to queries; 1 month to mss. Sample copy for 9×12 SAE and 2 first-class stamps. Writer's guidelines for #10 SASE.

Nonfiction: Essays, general interest. **Buys 200 mss/year.** Query by mail with published clips. Length: 250-2,500 words. **Pays $25-200.**

Photos: State availability of or send photos with submission. Reviews 8×10 prints, color slides. Buys one-time rights. Offers $10-25/photo or negotiates payment individually. Identification of subjects required.

Tips: "Move to Syracuse and query with strong idea."

$ $ TIME OUT NEW YORK, Time Out New York Partners, LP, 627 Broadway, 7th Floor, New York NY 10012. (212)539-4444. Fax: (212)253-1174. E-mail: letters@timeoutny.com. Website: www.timeoutny.com. Editor-in-Chief: Cyndi Stivers. **Contact:** Annie Bell, editorial assistant. **20% freelance written.** Weekly magazine covering entertainment in New York City. "Those who want to contribute to *Time Out New York* must be intimate with New York City and its environs." Estab. 1995. Circ. 120,000. Pays on publication. Publishes ms an average of 1 month after acceptance. Byline sometimes given. Offers 25% kill fee. Makes work-for-hire assignments. Accepts queries by mail, fax, phone. Responds in 2 months to queries.

O→ Pitch ideas to the editor of the section to which you would like to contribute (i.e., film, music, dance, etc.). Be sure to include clips or writing samples with your query letter.

Nonfiction: Essays, general interest, how-to, humor, interview/profile, new product, travel (primarily within NYC area), reviews of various entertainment topics. No essays, articles about trends, unpegged articles. Query with published clips. Length: 250-1,500 words. **Pays 20¢/word for b&w features and $300/page for color features.**

Columns/Departments: Around Town (Billie Cohen); Art (Tim Griffin); Books & Poetry (Maureen Shelly); Technology (Adam Wisnieski); Cabaret (H. Scott Jolley); Check Out (Zoe Wolff); Clubs (Bruce Tantum); Comedy (Joe Grossman); Dance (Gia Kourlas); Eat Out (Salma Abdelnour); Film; Gay & Lesbian (Les Simpson); Kids (Barbara Aria); Music: Classical & Opera (Steve Smith); Music: Rock, Jazz, etc. (Elisabeth Vincentelli); Radio (Ian Landau); Sports (Brett Martin); Television (Michael Freidson); Theater (Jason Zinoman); Video (Michael Freidson).

▣ The online magazine carries original content not found in the print edition. Contact: Amy Brill, online editor.

Tips: "We're always looking for quirky, less-known news about what's going on in New York City."

North Carolina

$ $ AAA CAROLINAS GO MAGAZINE, 6600 AAA Dr., Charlotte NC 28212. Fax: (704)569-7815. Website: www.aaacarolinas.com. Managing Editor: Jacquie Hughett. **Contact:** Tom Crosby, editor. **20% freelance written.**

Member publication for the American Automobile Association covering travel, auto-related issues. "We prefer stories that focus on travel and auto safety in North and South Carolina and surrounding states." Estab. 1922. Circ. 750,000. Pays on publication. Byline given. Buys all rights. Editorial lead time 2 months. Accepts queries by mail. Sample copy and writer's guidelines for #10 SASE.

Nonfiction: Travel (auto-related). Length: 750 words. **Pays 15¢/word.**

Photos: Send photos with submission. Reviews slides. Buys all rights. Offers no additional payment for photos accepted with ms. Identification of subjects required.

The online magazine carries original content not found in the print edition. Contact: Jacquie Hughett, editor.

Tips: "Submit regional stories relating to Carolinas travel."

$ $ $ CHARLOTTE MAGAZINE, Abarta Media, 127 W. Worthington Ave., Suite 208, Charlotte NC 28203. (704)335-7181. Fax: (704)335-3739. E-mail: editor@charlottemag.com. Website: www.charlottemag.com. **Contact:** Richard H. Thurmond, editorial director. **75% freelance written.** Monthly magazine covering Charlotte life. "This magazine tells its readers things they didn't know about Charlotte, in an interesting, entertaining, and sometimes provocative style." Circ. 30,000. Pays within 30 days of acceptance. Publishes ms an average of 3 months after acceptance. Byline given. Offers 25% kill fee. Buys first North American serial rights. Editorial lead time 3 months. Submit seasonal material 6 months in advance. Accepts queries by mail, e-mail. Accepts simultaneous submissions. Responds in 6 months to mss. Sample copy for 8 1/2×11 SAE and $2.09.

Nonfiction: Book excerpts, exposé, general interest, historical/nostalgic, interview/profile, photo feature, travel. **Buys 90-100 mss/year.** Query with published clips. Length: 200-3,000 words. **Pays 25-50¢/word.** Sometimes pays expenses of writers on assignment.

Photos: State availability with submission. Buys one-time rights. Negotiates payment individually. Identification of subjects required.

Columns/Departments: Buys 35-50 mss/year. Pays 25¢-50¢/word.

Tips: "A story for *Charlotte* magazine could only appear in *Charlotte* magazine. That is, the story and its treatment are particularly germane to this area."

$ $ OUR STATE, Down Home in North Carolina, Mann Media, P.O. Box 4552, Greensboro NC 27404. (336)286-0600. Fax: (336)286-0100. E-mail: editorial@ourstate.com. Website: www.ourstate.com. **Contact:** Mary Ellis, editor. **95% freelance written.** Monthly magazine covering North Carolina. "*Our State* is dedicated to providing editorial about the history, destinations, out-of-the-way places, and culture of North Carolina." Estab. 1933. Circ. 81,000. Pays on publication. Publishes ms an average of 6-24 months after acceptance. Byline given. Buys first North American serial rights. Editorial lead time 4 months. Submit seasonal material 4 months in advance. Accepts queries by mail, fax. Responds in 6 weeks to queries; 2 months to mss. Sample copy for $3.95. Writer's guidelines for #10 SASE.

Nonfiction: Book excerpts, historical/nostalgic, how-to, humor, personal experience, photo feature, travel. **Buys 60 mss/year.** Send complete ms. Length: 1,000-1,500 words. **Pays $125-300 for assigned articles; $50-125 for unsolicited articles.** Sometimes pays expenses of writers on assignment.

Photos: State availability with submission. Reviews 35mm or 4×6 transparencies. Buys one-time rights. Negotiates payment individually. Pays $15-350/photo, depending on size; $125-50 for photos assigned to accompany specific story; $500 maximum for cover photos. Identification of subjects required.

Columns/Departments: Tar Heel Memories (remembering something specific about North Carolina), 1,200 words; Tar Heel Profile (profile of interesting North Carolinian), 1,500 words; Tar Heel Literature (review of books by North Carolina writers and about North Carolina), 300 words. **Buys 40 mss/year.** Send complete ms. **Pays $50-300.**

Tips: "We are developing a style for travel stories that is distinctly *Our State*. That style starts with outstanding photographs, which not only depict an area, but interpret it and thus become an integral part of the presentation. Our stories need not dwell on listings of what can be seen. Concentrate instead on the experience of being there, whether the destination is a hiking trail, a bed and breakfast, a forest, or an urban area. What thoughts and feelings did the experience evoke? We want to know why you went there, what you experienced, and what impressions you came away with. With at least 1 travel story an issue, we run a short sidebar called, "If you're going." It explains how to get to the destination; rates or admission costs if there are any; a schedule of when the attraction is open or list of relevant dates; and an address and phone number for readers to write or call for more information. This sidebar eliminates the need for general-service information in the story."

Ohio

$ BEND OF THE RIVER MAGAZINE, P.O. Box 859, Maumee OH 43537. (419)893-0022. **Contact:** R. Lee Raizk, publisher. **90% freelance written.** This magazine reports that it is eager to work with new/unpublished writers. "We buy material that we like whether it is by an experienced writer or not." Monthly magazine for readers interested in northwestern Ohio history and nostalgia. Estab. 1972. Circ. 7,500. Pays on publication. Publishes ms an average of 6 months after acceptance. Byline given. Buys one-time rights. Submit seasonal material 2 months in advance. Responds in 1 month to queries. Sample copy for $1.25. Writer's guidelines not available.

Nonfiction: "We deal heavily with Northwestern Ohio history and nostalgia. We are looking for old snapshots of the Toledo area to accompany articles, personal reflection, etc." Historical/nostalgic. Special issues: Deadline for holiday issue is November 1. **Buys 75 unsolicited mss/year.** Query with or without published clips or send complete ms. Length: 1,500 words. **Pays $25 on up.**

Reprints: Send tearsheet and information about when and where the material previously appeared. Pays 100% of the amount paid for the original article.

Photos: Purchases b&w or color photos with accompanying ms. Pays $5 minimum. Captions required.

Tips: "Any Toledo area, well-researched nostalgia, local history will be put on top of the heap. If you send a picture with manuscript, it gets an A+! We pay a small amount but usually use our writers often and through the years. We're loyal."

$ $ $ CINCINNATI MAGAZINE, One Centennial Plaza, 705 Central Ave., Suite 175, Cincinnati OH 45202. (513)421-4300. Fax: (513)562-2746. **Contact:** Kitty Morgan, editor. Monthly magazine emphasising Cincinnati living. Circ. 30,000. Pays on publication. Byline given. Buys first rights. Sample copy not available. Writer's guidelines not available.

Nonfiction: Articles on personalities, business, sports, lifestyle, history relating to Cincinnati. Seeking to expand coverage of local authors. **Buys 12 mss/year.** Query. Length: 2,500-3,500 words. **Pays $500-1,000.**

Columns/Departments: Cincinnati dining, media, arts and entertainment, people, homes, politics, sports. Length: 1,000-1,500 words. **Buys 10-15 mss/year.** Query. **Pays $300-400.**

Tips: "Freelancers may find a market in At Home section (bimonthly), special advertising sections on varying topics from golf to cardiac care (query Special Projects Managing Editor Mary Beth Crocker). Always query in writing, with clips. All articles have a Cincinnati base. No generics, please. Also: no movie, book, theater reviews, poetry or fiction."

CLEVELAND MAGAZINE, City Magazines, Inc., 1422 Euclid Ave., #730Q, Cleveland OH 44115. (216)771-2833. Fax: (216)781-6318. E-mail: editorial@clevelandmagazine.com. Website: www.clevelandmagazine.com. **Contact:** Steve Gleydura, editorial director. **60% freelance written.** Mostly by assignment. Monthly magazine with a strong Cleveland/Northeast Ohio angle. Estab. 1972. Circ. 50,000. Pays on publication. Publishes ms an average of 3 months after acceptance. Byline given. Buys first, second serial (reprint), electronic rights. Editorial lead time 6 months. Submit seasonal material 8 months in advance. Accepts queries by mail, e-mail, fax. Accepts simultaneous submissions. Responds in 2 months to queries. Sample copy not available.

Nonfiction: Book excerpts, general interest, historical/nostalgic, humor, interview/profile, travel, home and garden. Query with published clips. Length: 800-4,000 words. **Pays $250-1,000.**

Columns/Departments: My Town (Cleveland first-person stories), 1,500 words. Query with published clips. **Pays $300.**

N **DARKE COUNTY PROFILE**, 4952 Bishop Rd., Greenville OH 45331. (937)547-0048. Fax: (937)547-9503. E-mail: dcprofile@erinet.com. **Contact:** Diana J. Linder, editor. **15% freelance written.** Monthly magazine covering people and places in the Darke County area. Estab. 1994. Circ. 500. Pays on publication. Publishes ms an average of 3-6 months after acceptance. Byline given. Buys one-time rights. Editorial lead time 3 months. Submit seasonal material 3 months in advance. Accepts previously published material. Responds in 3-6 months to mss. Sample copy for $2. Writer's guidelines by e-mail.

Nonfiction: Diana J. Linder. General interest, how-to (crafts), humor, inspirational, personal experience, travel. No foul language, graphic violence, or pornography. **Buys 10-12 mss/year.** Send complete ms. Length: 500-1,500 words. **; Pays $15-20.** Pays in contributor copies for work published for the first time in the *Profile*.

Photos: Send photos with submission. Buys one-time rights. Pays $3.50/photo. Captions required.

Fiction: Diana J. Linder. Adventure, condensed novels, humorous, mainstream, mystery, romance, suspense, western. No violence, foul language, or sexually explicit material. **Buys 12-14 mss/year.** Send complete ms. Length: 500-1,500 words. **Pays $15-20.**

Fillers: Diana J. Linder. Anecdotes, facts, short humor. **Buys 6-12/year.** Length: 250-500 words. **Pays $5-10.**

Tips: Write tight and send neatly typed mss with a SASE.

$ $ NORTHERN OHIO LIVE, LIVE Publishing Co.11320 Juniper Rd., Cleveland OH 44106. (216)721-1800. Fax: (216)721-2525. E-mail: bgleisser@livepub.com. **Contact:** Benjamin Gleisser, managing editor. **70% freelance written.** Monthly magazine covering Northern Ohio news, politics, business, arts, entertainment, education, and dining. "Reader demographic is mid-30s to 50s, though we're working to bring in the late 20s. Our readers are well educated, many with advanced degrees. They're interested in Northern Ohio's cultural scene and support it." Estab. 1980. Circ. 32,000. Pays on 20th of publication month. Publishes ms an average of 1 month after acceptance. Byline given. Offers 33% kill fee. Buys first North American serial rights. Editorial lead time 3 months. Submit seasonal material 4 months in advance. Responds in 3 weeks to queries; 2 months to mss. Sample copy for $3. Writer's guidelines not available.

Nonfiction: All should have a Northern Ohio slant. Essays, exposé, general interest, humor, interview/profile, photo feature, travel. Special issues: Gourmet Guide (restaurants) (May). **Buys 100 mss/year.** Query with published clips. Length: 1,000-3,500 words. **Pays $100-1,000.** Sometimes pays expenses of writers on assignment.

Reprints: Send photocopy and information about when and where the material previously appeared.

Photos: State availability with submission. Reviews contact sheets, 4×5 transparencies, 3×5 prints. Buys one-time rights. Negotiates payment individually. Identification of subjects required.

Columns/Departments: News & Reviews (arts previews, personality profiles, general interest), 800-1,800 words. **Pays $200-300.** Time & Place (personal essay), 400-450 words. **Pays $100**. Must be local authors. **Buys 60-70 mss/year.** Query with published clips.

Fiction: Novel excerpts.

Tips: "Don't send submissions not having anything to do with Northern Ohio. Must have some tie to the Northeast Quadrant of Ohio."

$ $ $ OHIO MAGAZINE, Great Lakes Publishing Co., 62 E. Broad St., Columbus OH 43215-3522. (614)461-5083. Fax: (614)461-8504. E-mail: editorial@ohiomagazine.com. Website: www.ohiomagazine.com. **Contact:** Nicole Gabriel, managing editor. **50% freelance written.** Monthly magazine emphasizing Ohio-based travel, news, and feature material that highlights what's special and unique about the state. Estab. 1978. Circ. 95,000. Pays on publication. Publishes ms an average of 6 months after acceptance. Byline given. Buys first North American serial, one-time, second serial (reprint), all rights. First serial rights Submit seasonal material 6 months in advance. Accepts queries by mail, e-mail, fax. Responds in 3 months to queries; 3 months to mss. Sample copy for $3 and 9×12 SAE or online. Writer's guidelines for #10 SASE.

O→ Break in by "knowing the magazine—read it thoroughly for several issues. Send good clips—that show your ability to write on topics we cover. We're looking for thoughtful stories on topics that are more contextual and less shallow. I want queries that show the writer has some passion for the subject."

Nonfiction: Length: 1,000-3,000 words. **Pays $600-1,800.** Sometimes pays expenses of writers on assignment.

Reprints: Send tearsheet or photocopy and information about when and where the material previously appeared. Pays 50% of amount paid for an original article.

Photos: Rob McGarr, art director. Rate negotiable.

Columns/Departments: Length: 100-1,500 words. **Buys minimum 20 unsolicited mss/year. Pays $50-500.**

Tips: "Freelancers should send all queries in writing, not by telephone. Successful queries demonstrate an intimate knowledge of the publication. We are looking to increase our circle of writers who can write about the state in an informative and upbeat style. Strong reporting skills are highly valued."

$ $ OVER THE BACK FENCE, Southern Ohio's Own Magazine, Back Fence Publishing, Inc., P.O. Box 756, Chillicothe OH 45601. (740)772-2165. Fax: (740)773-7626. E-mail: backfenc@bright.net. Website: www.backfence.com. Sarah Williamson, managing editor. Quarterly magazine. "We are a regional magazine serving 20 counties in Southern Ohio. *Over The Back Fence* has a wholesome, neighborly style. It appeals to readers from young adults to seniors, showcasing art and travel opportunities in the area." Estab. 1994. Circ. 15,000. Pays on publication. Publishes ms an average of 2 years after acceptance. Byline given. Buys one-time North American serial rights. Makes work-for-hire assignments. Editorial lead time 1 year. Submit seasonal material 1 year in advance. Accepts queries by mail. Accepts simultaneous submissions. Responds in 3 months to queries. Sample copy for $4 or on website. Writer's guidelines for #10 SASE or on website.

O→ Break in with personality profiles (1,000 words), short features, columns (600 words), and features (1,000 words).

Nonfiction: General interest, historical/nostalgic, humor, inspirational, interview/profile, personal experience, photo feature, travel. **Buys 9-12 mss/year.** Query with or without published clips or send complete ms. Length: 750-1,000 words. **Pays 10¢/word minimum, negotiable depending on experience.**

Reprints: Send photocopy of article or short story and typed ms with rights for sale noted, and information about when and where the material previously appeared. Payment negotiable.

Photos: "If sending photos as part of a text/photo package, please request our photo guidelines and submit color transparencies." Reviews color, 35mm or larger transparencies, prints 3.20 X 5. Buys one-time rights. $25-100/photo. Captions, identification of subjects, model releases required.

Columns/Departments: The Arts, 750-1,000 words; History (relevant to a designated county), 750-1,000 words; Inspirational (poetry or short story), 600-850 words; Profiles From Our Past, 300-600 words; Sport & Hobby, 750-1,000 words; Our Neighbors (i.e., people helping others), 750-1,000 words. All must be relevant to Southern Ohio. **Buys 24 mss/year.** Query with or without published clips or send complete ms. **Pays 10¢/word minimum, negotiable depending on experience.**

Fiction: Humorous. **Buys 4 mss/year.** Query with published clips. Length: 300-850 words. **Pays 10¢/word minimum, negotiable depending on experience.**

Poetry: Wholesome, traditional free verse, light verse, and rhyming. **Buys 4 poems/year.** Submit maximum 4 poems. Length: 4-32 lines. **Pays 10¢/word or $25 minimum.**

Tips: "Our approach can be equated to a friendly and informative conversation with a neighbor about interesting people, places, and events in Southern Ohio (counties: Adams, Athens, Clark, Clinton, Fayette, Fairfield, Gallia, Greene, Highland, Hocking, Jackson, Lawrence, Meigs, Muskingum, Perry, Pickaway, Pike, Ross, Scioto, Vinton, Warren, and Washington)."

$ $ PLAIN DEALER SUNDAY MAGAZINE, Plain Dealer Publishing Co., Plain Dealer Plaza, 1801 Superior Ave., Cleveland OH 44114. (216)999-4546. Fax: (216)515-2039. E-mail: eburbach@plaind.com. **Contact:** Ellen Stein Burbach, editor. **50% freelance written.** Weekly newspaper focusing on Cleveland and Northeastern Ohio. Circ. 500,000. Pays on publication. Publishes ms an average of 2 months after acceptance. Byline given. Buys first, one-time rights. all Web rights Submit seasonal material 3 months in advance. Accepts queries by mail, e-mail, fax. Responds in 1 month to queries; 2 months to mss. Sample copy for $1.

O→ "Start small, with North by Northeast pieces."

Nonfiction: Must include focus on northeast Ohio people, places and issues. Book excerpts, essays, exposé, general interest, historical/nostalgic, humor, inspirational, interview/profile, new product, personal experience, photo feature, travel (only personal essays or local ties). **Buys 50-100 (feature) mss/year.** Query with published clips or send complete ms. Length: 800-4,000 words. **Pays $150-650 for assigned articles.**

Reprints: Send typed ms with rights for sale noted and information about when and where the material previously appeared.

Columns/Departments: North by Northeast (short upfront pieces), **pays $20-70**; Essays (personal perspective, memoir OK), **pays $150-200**, 900 words maximum; The Back Burner (food essays with recipe), **pays $200.**

Tips: "We're always looking for superior writers and great stories."

Oklahoma

$ $ OKLAHOMA TODAY, P.O. Box 53384, Oklahoma City OK 73152-9971. Fax: (405)522-4588. E-mail: mccune@oklahomatoday.com. Website: www.oklahomatoday.com. **Contact:** Louisa McCune, editor-in-chief. **80% freelance written.** Works with approximately 25 new/unpublished writers each year. Bimonthly magazine covering people, places, and things Oklahoman. "We are interested in showing off the best Oklahoma has to offer; we're pretty serious about our travel slant but regularly run history, nature, and personality profiles." Estab. 1956. Circ. 45,000. Pays on publication. Publishes ms an average of 6 months after acceptance. Byline given. first worldwide serial rights. Submit seasonal material 1 year in advance. Accepts queries by mail, e-mail. Responds in 4 months to queries. Sample copy for $3.95 and 9×12 SASE or online. Writer's guidelines for #10 SASE or online.

- *Oklahoma Today* has won Magazine of the Year, awarded by the International Regional magazine Association, 4 out of the last 10 years, and in 1999 won *Folio* magazine's Editorial Excellence Award for Best Regional magazine.

O‒ "Start small. Look for possibilities for The Range. Even letters to the editor are good ways to 'get some ink.' "

Nonfiction: Book excerpts (on Oklahoma topics), historical/nostalgic (Oklahoma only), interview/profile (Oklahomans only), photo feature (in Oklahoma), travel (in Oklahoma). No phone queries. **Buys 20-40 mss/year.** Query with published clips. Length: 250-3,000 words. **Pays $25-750.**

Photos: "We are especially interested in developing contacts with photographers who live in Oklahoma or have shot here. Send samples." Photo guidelines for SASE. Reviews 4×5, 2¼×2¼, and 35mm color transparencies, high-quality transparencies, slides, and b&w prints. Buys one-time rights to use photos for promotional purposes. Pays $50-750 for color. Captions, identification of subjects required.

Fiction: Novel excerpts, occasionally short fiction.

Tips: "The best way to become a regular contributor to *Oklahoma Today* is to query us with 1 or more story ideas, each developed to give us an idea of your proposed slant. We're looking for *lively*, concise, well-researched and reported stories, stories that don't need to be heavily edited and are not newspaper style. We have a 3-person full-time editorial staff, and freelancers who can write and have done their homework get called again and again."

Oregon

$ $ OREGON COAST, 4969 Highway 101 N. #2, Florence OR 97439-0130. (541)997-8401, ext. 115 or (800)348-8401, ext. 115. Fax: (541)902-0400. E-mail: judy@ohwy.com. Website: www.ohwy.com. **Contact:** Stefani Blair, managing editor. **65% freelance written.** Bimonthly magazine covering the Oregon Coast. Estab. 1982. Circ. 50,000. Pays after publication. Publishes ms an average of up to 1 year after acceptance. Byline given. Offers 33% (on assigned stories only, not on stories accepted on spec) kill fee. Buys first North American serial rights. Submit seasonal material 6 months in advance. Accepts queries by mail, e-mail. Responds in 3 months to queries. Sample copy for $4.50. Writer's guidelines for #10 SASE.

- This company also publishes *Northwest Travel.*

O‒ Break in with "great photos with a story that has a great lead and no problems during fact-checking. Like stories that have a slightly different take on 'same-old' subjects and have good anecdotes and quotes. Stories should have satisfying endings."

Nonfiction: "A true regional with general interest, historical/nostalgic, humor, interview/profile, personal experience, photo feature, travel, and nature as pertains to Oregon Coast." **Buys 55 mss/year.** Query with published clips. Length: 500-1,500 words. **Pays $75-250, plus 2-5 contributor copies.**

Reprints: Send tearsheet or photocopy and information about when and where the material previously appeared. Pays an average of 60% of the amount paid for an original article.

Photos: Photo submissions with no ms or stand alone or cover photos. Send photos with submission. Reviews 35mm or larger transparencies. Buys one-time rights. Captions, identification of subjects, model releases (for cover), photo credits required.

Fillers: Newsbreaks (no-fee basis).

Tips: "Slant article for readers who do not live at the Oregon Coast. At least 1 historical article is used in each issue. Manuscript/photo packages are preferred over manuscripts with no photos. List photo credits and captions for each historic print or color slide. Check all facts, proper names, and numbers carefully in photo/manuscript packages. Need stories with great color photos—could be photo essays. Must pertain to Oregon Coast somehow."

Pennsylvania

$ $ BERKS COUNTY LIVING, West Lawn Graphic Communications, 801 Commerce St., P.O. Box 2195, Sinking Spring PA 19608. (610)678-2798. Fax: (610)678-2799. E-mail: treed@berkscountyliving.com. Website: www.berkscountyliving.com. **Contact:** Terry Scott Reed, editor. **90% freelance written.** Bimonthly magazine covering topics of interest to people living in Berks County, Pennsylvania. Estab. 2000. Circ. 36,000. Pays on publication. Publishes ms an average of 4 months after acceptance. Byline given. Offers 25% kill fee. Buys first North American serial rights. Editorial lead time 6 months. Submit seasonal material 4 months in advance. Accepts queries by mail, e-mail, fax. Accepts previously published material. Accepts simultaneous submissions. Responds in 1 week to queries; 1 month to mss. Sample copy for 9×12 SAE and 2 first-class stamps. Writer's guidelines for #10 SASE or online at www.berkscountyliving.com/writers.

Nonfiction: Articles must be associated with Berks County, Pennsylvania. Exposé, general interest, historical/nostalgic, how-to, humor, inspirational, interview/profile, new product, photo feature, travel, food, health. **Buys 25 mss/year.** Query. Length: 750-2,000 words. **Pays $150-400.** Sometimes pays expenses of writers on assignment.

Reprints: Accepts previously published submissions.

Photos: State availability with submission. Reviews 35mm or greater transparencies, any size prints. Buys one-time rights. Negotiates payment individually. Captions, identification of subjects, model releases required.

$ $ CENTRAL PA, WITF, Inc., P.O. Box 2954, Harrisburg PA 17105-2954. (717)221-2800. Fax: (717)221-2630. E-mail: centralpa@centralpa.org. Website: www.centralpa.org. **Contact:** Steve Kennedy, senior editor. **90% freelance written.** Monthly magazine covering life in Central Pennsylvania. Estab. 1982. Circ. 42,000. Pays on publication. Publishes ms an average of 4 months after acceptance. Offers 20% kill fee. Buys first North American serial rights. Editorial lead time 3 months. Submit seasonal material 6 months in advance. Accepts queries by mail, e-mail, fax. Accepts simultaneous submissions. Responds in 6 weeks to queries. Sample copy for $3.50 and SASE. Writer's guidelines for #10 SASE.

O┳ Break in through Central Stories, Thinking Aloud, blurbs, and accompanying events calendar.

Nonfiction: Essays, general interest, historical/nostalgic, how-to, humor, interview/profile, opinion, personal experience, photo feature, travel. Special issues: Dining/Food (January); Regional Insider's Guide (July); Best of Central PA (December). **Buys 50 mss/year.** Query with published clips or send complete ms. Length: 800-3,000 words. **Pays $200-750 for assigned articles; $50-500 for unsolicited articles.** Sometimes pays expenses of writers on assignment.

Photos: State availability with submission. Reviews contact sheets, transparencies, prints. Buys one-time rights. Negotiates payment individually. Identification of subjects required.

Columns/Departments: Central Stories (quirky, newsy, regional), 300 words; Thinking Aloud (essay), 1,200 words; Cameo (interview), 800 words. **Buys 90 mss/year.** Query with published clips or send complete ms. **Pays $50-100.**

Tips: "Wow us with something you wrote, either a clip or a manuscript on spec. If it's off target but shows you can write well and know the region, we'll ask for more. We're looking for creative nonfiction, with an emphasis on conveying valuable information through near literary-quality narrative."

$ $ ☆ PENNSYLVANIA, Pennsylvania Magazine Co., P.O. Box 755, Camp Hill PA 17001-0755. (717)697-4660. E-mail: pamag@aol.com. Publisher: Albert E. Holliday. **Contact:** Matt Holliday, editor. **90% freelance written.** Bimonthly magazine covering people, places, events, and history in Pennsylvania. Estab. 1981. Circ. 33,000. Pays on acceptance except for articles (by authors unknown to us) sent on speculation. Publishes ms an average of 9 months after acceptance. Byline given. 25% kill fee for assigned articles. Buys first North American serial, one-time rights. Submit seasonal material 9 months in advance. Accepts queries by mail, e-mail. Responds in 1 month to queries. Sample copy for $2.95. Writer's guidelines for #10 SASE.

O┳ Break in with "a text/photo package—learn to take photos or hook up with a photographer who will shoot for our rates."

Nonfiction: Features include general interest, historical, photo feature, vacations and travel, people/family success stories, consumer-related inventions, serious statewide issues—all dealing with or related to Pennsylvania. Will not consider without illustrations; send photocopies of possible illustrations with query or mss. Include SASE. Nothing on Amish topics, hunting, or skiing. **Buys 75-120 mss/year.** Query. Length: 750-2,500 words. **Pays 10-15¢/word.**

Reprints: Send photocopy with rights for sale noted and information about when and where the material previously appeared. Pays 5¢/word.

Photos: No original slides or transparencies. Americana Photo Journal includes 1-4 interesting photos and a 250-word caption; Photography Essay highlights annual photo essay contest entries. Reviews 35mm 2¼×2¼ color transparencies, 5×7 to 8×10 color and b&w prints. Buys one-time rights. $15-25 for inside photos; up to $100 for covers. Captions required.

Columns/Departments: Panorama (short items about people, unusual events, family and individually owned consumer-related businesses), 250-900 words; Almanac (short historical items), 1,000-2,500 words; Museums, 400-500 words. All must be illustrated. Include SASE. Query. **10-15¢/word.**

Tips: "Our publication depends upon freelance work—send queries."

$ $ PENNSYLVANIA HERITAGE, Pennsylvania Historical and Museum Commission and the Pennsylvania Heritage Society, Commonwealth Keystone Bldg., Plaza Level, 400 North St., Harrisburg PA 17120-0053. (717)787-7522. Fax: (717)787-8312. E-mail: miomalley@state.pa.us. Website: www.paheritage.org. **Contact:** Michael J. O'Malley III, editor. **90% freelance written.** Prefers to work with published/established writers. Quarterly magazine. "*Pennsylvania*

Heritage introduces readers to Pennsylvania's rich culture and historic legacy, educates and sensitizes them to the value of preserving that heritage and entertains and involves them in such a way as to ensure that Pennsylvania's past has a future. The magazine is intended for intelligent lay readers." Estab. 1974. Circ. 10,000. Pays on publication. Publishes ms an average of 1 year after acceptance. Byline given. Buys all rights. Accepts queries by mail, e-mail. Responds in 10 weeks to queries; 8 months to mss. Sample copy for $5 and 9×12 SAE or online. Writer's guidelines for #10 SASE or online.

- *Pennsylvania Heritage* is now considering freelance submissions that are shorter in length (2,000-3,000 words), pictorial/photographic essays, biographies of famous (and not-so-famous) Pennsylvanians, and interviews with individuals who have helped shape, make, preserve the Keystone State's history and heritage.

Nonfiction: "Our format requires feature-length articles. Manuscripts with illustrations are especially sought for publication. We are now looking for shorter (2,000 words) manuscripts that are heavily illustrated with *publication-quality* photographs or artwork. We are eager to work with experienced travel writers for destination pieces on historical sites and museums that make up 'The Pennsylvania Trail of History.'" Art, science, biographies, industry, business, politics, transportation, military, historic preservation, archaeology, photography, etc. No articles which in no way relate to Pennsylvania history or culture. **Buys 20-24 mss/year.** Prefers to see mss with suggested illustrations. Length: 2,000-3,500 words. **Pays $100-500.**

Photos: State availability of or send photos with submission. Buys one-time rights. $25-200 for transparencies; $5-75 for b&w photos. Captions, identification of subjects required.

Tips: "We are looking for well-written, interesting material that pertains to any aspect of Pennsylvania history or culture. Potential contributors should realize that, although our articles are popularly styled, they are not light, puffy, or breezy; in fact they demand strident documentation and substantiation (sans footnotes). The most frequent mistake made by writers in completing articles for us is making them either too scholarly or too sentimental or nostalgic. We want material which educates, but also entertains. Authors should make history readable and enjoyable. Our goal is to make the Keystone State's history come to life in a meaningful, memorable way."

$ $ PHILADELPHIA MAGAZINE, 1818 Market St., 36th Floor, Philadelphia PA 19103. (215)564-7700. Fax: (215)656-3502. Website: www.phillymag.com. President/Publisher: David R. Lipson. **Contact:** Duane Swierczynski, senior editor. Monthly magazine. "*Philadelphia* is edited for the area's community leaders and their families. It provides in-depth reports on crucial and controversial issues confronting the region—business trends, political analysis, metropolitan planning, sociological trends—plus critical reviews of the cultural, sports, and entertainment scene." Estab. 1908. Circ. 133,083. **Pays on acceptance.** Accepts queries by mail. Sample copy not available. Writer's guidelines not available.

O━ Break in by sending queries along with clips. "Remember that we are a general interest magazine that focuses exclusively on topics of interest in the Delaware Valley."

Nonfiction: "Articles range from law enforcement to fashion, voting trends to travel, transportation to theater, also includes the background studies of the area newsmakers." Query with clips and SASE.

Tips: "*Philadelphia Magazine* readers are an affluent, interested, and influential group who can afford the best the region has to offer. They're the greater Philadelphia area residents who care about the city and its politics, lifestyles, business, and culture."

$ $ $ PITTSBURGH MAGAZINE, WQED Pittsburgh, 4802 Fifth Ave., Pittsburgh PA 15213. (412)622-1360. Website: www.pittsburghmag.com. **Contact:** Michelle Pilecki, executive editor. **70% freelance written.** Monthly magazine. "*Pittsburgh* presents issues, analyzes problems, and strives to encourage a better understanding of the community. Our region is Western Pennsylvania, Eastern Ohio, Northern West Virginia, and Western Maryland." Estab. 1970. Circ. 75,000. Pays on publication. Publishes ms an average of 2 months after acceptance. Byline given. Offers kill fee. Buys first North American serial, second serial (reprint) rights. Submit seasonal material 6 months in advance. Accepts queries by mail. Responds in 2 months to queries. Sample copy for $2 (old back issues). Writer's guidelines online or via SASE.

- The editor reports a need for more hard news and stories targeting readers in their 30s and 40s, especially those with young families. Prefers to work with published/established writers. The monthly magazine is purchased on newsstands and by subscription, and is given to those who contribute $40 or more/year to public TV in western Pennsylvania.

Nonfiction: "Without exception—whether the topic is business, travel, the arts, or lifestyle—each story is clearly oriented to Pittsburghers of today and to the greater Pittsburgh region of today." Must have greater Pittsburgh angle. No fax, phone, or e-mail queries. No complete mss. Exposé, lifestyle, sports, informational, service, business, medical, profile. "We have minimal interest in historical articles and we do not publish fiction, poetry, advocacy, or personal reminiscence pieces." Query in writing with outline and clips. Length: 3,500 words maximum. **Pays $300-1,500+.**

Photos: Query. Pays prenegotiated expenses of writer on assignment. Model releases required.

Columns/Departments: The Front (short, front-of-the-book items). Length: 300 words maximum. **Pays $50-150.**

The online magazine carries original content not found in the print edition. Contact: Michelle Pilecki, executive editor.

Tips: "Best bet to break in is through hard news with a region-wide impact or service pieces or profiles with a regional interest. The point is that we want more stories that reflect our region, not just a tiny part. And we *never* consider any story without a strong regional focus. We do not respond to fax and e-mail queries."

N **$ $ WESTSYLVANIA**, Allegheny Heritage Development Corp., P.O. Box 565, 105 Zee Plaza, Hollidaysburg PA 16648-0565. (814)696-9380. Fax: (814)696-9569. E-mail: jschumacher@westsylvania.org. Website: www.westsylva

nia.com. **Contact:** Jerilynn Schumacher, editor. **90% freelance written.** Quarterly magazine covering regional heritage in southwestern Pennsylvania. "*Westsylvania* magazine celebrates the heritage and lifestyles of south-central and southwestern Pennsylvania. Articles must reflect the region's natural and/or cultural heritage in some fashion. This is not a history magazine, but articles should show how the region's history has influenced the contemporary scene." Estab. 1997. Circ. 12,000. Pays on publication. Publishes ms an average of 4 months after acceptance. Byline given. Offers $50 kill fee. Buys first North American serial rights. Editorial lead time 2 months. Submit seasonal material 2 months in advance. Accepts queries by mail, e-mail, fax. Accepts simultaneous submissions. Sample copy for 9×12 SAE and 6 first-class stamps.

O- Break in with "a query with a strong southwestern Pennsylvania heritage angle—the broader the angle, the better. I like features that have region-wide perspectives."

Nonfiction: Book excerpts, essays, general interest, historical/nostalgic, humor, inspirational, interview/profile, photo feature, religious, travel (regional pieces only). "No unsolicited manuscripts." **Buys 30 mss/year.** Query with published clips. Length: 1,000-2,500 words. **Pays $75-150 for assigned articles.** Sometimes pays writers with contributor copies or other premiums rather than a cash payment by personal arrangement.
Photos: State availability with submission. Reviews contact sheets, transparencies. Buys one-time rights. Negotiates payment individually. Captions, identification of subjects, model releases required.
Columns/Departments: First Person (oral histories), 1,000 words; Foodways (recipes), Book Reviews (informational), both 500 words. **Buys 15 mss/year.** Query with published clips. **Pays $50-100.**
Fillers: Anecdotes, facts, short humor. Length: 50-500 words. **Pays $25-100.**
Tips: Poorly written queries will receive no response. "Striving for people oriented stories with lively active verbs."

$ $ WHERE & WHEN, Pennsylvania Travel Guide, The Barash Group, 403 S. Allen St., State College PA 16801. (800)326-9584. Fax: (814)238-3415. E-mail: arupe@barashgroup.com. Website: www.whereandwhen.com. **Contact:** Anissa Ruppert, editor. **75% freelance written.** Quarterly magazine covering travel and tourism in Pennsylvania. "*Where & When* presents things to see and do in Pennsylvania." Circ. 100,000. Pays on publication. Byline given. Offers 50% kill fee. Buys first North American serial rights. Editorial lead time 6 months. Submit seasonal material 6 months in advance. Responds in 1 month to queries. Sample copy and writer's guidelines free.
Nonfiction: Travel. **Buys 20-30 mss/year.** Query. Length: 800-2,500 words. **Pays $150-400.**
Photos: State availability with submission. Reviews transparencies, prints, Slides. Buys one-time rights. Negotiates payment individually. Captions, identification of subjects required.
Columns/Departments: Bring the Kids (children's attractions); Heritage Traveler (state heritage parks); Small Town PA (villages and hamlets in Pennsylvania); On the Road Again (attractions along a particular road); all 800-1,200 words. **Buys 10 mss/year.** Query. **Pays $100-250.**

Rhode Island

$ $ $ RHODE ISLAND MONTHLY, The Providence Journal Company, 280 Kinsley Ave., Providence RI 02903. (401)421-8200. Fax: (401)277-8080. E-mail: paula_bodah@rimonthly.com. Website: www.rimonthly.com. Editor: Paula M. Bodah. **Contact:** Sarah Francis, managing editor. **80% freelance written.** Monthly magazine. "*Rhode Island Monthly* is a general interest consumer magazine with a strict Rhode Island focus." Estab. 1988. Circ. 41,000. **Pays on acceptance.** Publishes ms an average of 3 months after acceptance. Byline given. Offers 20% kill fee. Buys all rights for 90 days from date of publication. Editorial lead time 3 months. Submit seasonal material 6 months in advance. Accepts queries by mail, e-mail, fax. Responds in 6 weeks to queries; 1 month to mss. Sample copy online. Writer's guidelines not available.
Nonfiction: Exposé, general interest, interview/profile, photo feature. **Buys 40 mss/year.** Query with published clips. Length: 1,800-3,000 words. **Pays $600-1,200.** Sometimes pays expenses of writers on assignment.

South Carolina

$ $ ☐ CHARLESTON MAGAZINE, P.O. Box 1794, Mt. Pleasant SC 29465-1794. (843)971-9811. Fax: (843)971-0121. E-mail: dshankland@charlestonmag.com. Website: charlestonmag.com. **Contact:** Darcy Shankland, editor. **80% freelance written.** Bimonthly magazine covering current issues, events, arts and culture, leisure pursuits, travel, and personalities, as they pertain to the city of Charleston and surrounding areas. "A Lowcountry institution for 30 years, *Charleston Magazine* captures the essence of Charleston and her surrounding areas—her people, arts and architecture, culture and events, and natural beauty." Estab. 1976. Circ. 22,000. Pays 30 days after publication. Byline given. Buys one-time rights. Submit seasonal material 4 months in advance. Accepts queries by mail, e-mail, fax. Responds in 1 month to queries. Sample copies may be ordered at cover price from office. Writer's guidelines for #10 SASE.
Nonfiction: "Must pertain to the Charleston area and its present culture." General interest, humor, interview/profile, opinion, photo feature, travel, food, architecture, sports, current events/issues, art. "Not interested in 'Southern nostalgia' articles or gratuitous history pieces." **Buys 40 mss/year.** Query with published clips and SASE. Length: 150-1,500 words. **Payment negotiated.** Sometimes pays expenses of writers on assignment.
Reprints: Send photocopy and information about when and where the material previously appeared. Pay negotiable.
Photos: Send photos with submission. Reviews contact sheets, transparencies, Slides. Buys one-time rights. Identification of subjects required.

Columns/Departments: Channel Markers (general local interest), 50-400 words; Local Seen (profile of local interest), 250-300 words; In Good Taste (restaurants and culinary trends in the city), 1,000-1,200 words, plus recipes; Chef at Home (profile of local chefs), 1,200 words, plus recipes; On the Road (travel opportunities near Charleston), 1,000-1,200 words; Southern View (personal experience about Charleston life), 750 words; Doing Business (profiles of exceptional local businesses), 1,000-1,200 words; Native Talent (local profiles), 1,000-1,200 words; Top of the Shelf (reviews of books with Southern content or by a Southern author), 750 words.

Tips: "Charleston, although a city with a 300-year history, is a vibrant, modern community with a tremendous dedication to the arts and no shortage of newsworthy subjects. We're looking for the freshest stories about Charleston—and those don't always come from insiders, but also outsiders who are keenly observant."

$ $ HILTON HEAD MONTHLY, Voice of the Community, Frey Media, Inc., 2 Park Lane, Hilton Head Island SC 29928. Fax: (843)785-2778. E-mail: hhmeditor@hargray.com. **Contact:** Rob Kaufman, editor. **75% freelance written.** Monthly magazine covering the business, people and lifestyle of Hilton Head, SC. "Our mission is to provide fresh, upbeat reading about the residents, lifestyle and community affairs of Hilton Head Island, an upscale, intensely pro-active resort community on the Eastern seaboard. We are not even remotely 'trendy,' but we like to see how national trends/issues play out on a local level. Especially interested in: home design and maintenance, entrepreneurship, nature, area history, golf/tennis/boating, volunteerism." Circ. 28,000. **Pays on acceptance.** Publishes ms an average of 6 months after acceptance. Byline given. Offers 50% kill fee. Buys first North American serial rights, makes work-for-hire assignments. Editorial lead time 3 months. Submit seasonal material 4 months in advance. Accepts queries by mail, e-mail, fax. Accepts previously published material. Accepts simultaneous submissions. Responds in 1 week to queries; 4 months to mss. Sample copy for $3.

Nonfiction: Essays (short, personal), general interest, historical/nostalgic (history only), how-to (home related), humor, interview/profile (Hilton Head residents only), opinion (general humor or Hilton Head Island community affairs), personal experience, travel. No "exposé interviews with people who are not Hilton Head residents; profiles of people, events or businesses in Beaufort, SC, Savannah, GA, Charleston or other surrounding cities, unless it's within a travel piece." **Buys 225-250 mss/year.** Query with published clips. Length: 800-2,000 words. **Pays 10¢/word.**

Photos: State availability with submission. Reviews contact sheets, prints, slides; any size. Buys one-time rights. Negotiates payment individually.

Columns/Departments: Wellness (any general healthcare topic, especially for an older audience), 800-1,100 words; Focus (profile of Hilton Head Island personality/community leader), 1,000-1,300 words; Community (profile of Hilton Head Island volunteer organization), 800-1,100 words. Query with published clips. **Pays 10¢/word minimum.**

Tips: "Give us concise, bullet-style descriptions of what the article covers (in the query letter); choose upbeat, pro-active topics; delight us with your fresh (not trendy) description and word choice."

$ $ SANDLAPPER, The Magazine of South Carolina, The Sandlapper Society, Inc., P.O. Box 1108, Lexington SC 29071-1108. (803)359-9941. Fax: (803)359-0629. E-mail: aida@sandlapper.org. Website: www.sandlapper.org. Editor: Robert P. Wilkins. **Contact:** Aida Rogers, managing editor. **60% freelance written.** Quarterly magazine focusing on the positive aspects of South Carolina. "*Sandlapper* is intended to be read at those times when people want to relax with an attractive, high-quality magazine that entertains and informs them about their state." Estab. 1989. Circ. 18,000 with a readership of 60,000. Pays during the dateline period. Publishes ms an average of 1 year after acceptance. Byline given. Buys first North American serial rights, right to reprint. Submit seasonal material 6 months in advance. Accepts queries by mail, e-mail, fax. Sample copy online. Writer's guidelines for #10 SASE.

Nonfiction: Feature articles and photo essays about South Carolina's interesting people, places, cuisine, things to do. Occasional history articles. Essays, general interest, humor, interview/profile, photo feature. Query with clips and SASE. Length: 500-2,500 words. **Pays $100/published page.** Sometimes pays expenses of writers on assignment.

Photos: "*Sandlapper* buys b&w prints, color transparencies and art. Photographers should submit working cutlines for each photograph." No digital at this time. Pays $25-75, $100 for cover or centerspread photo.

The online version contains material not found in the print edition. Contact: Dan Harmon.

Tips: "We're not interested in articles about topical issues, politics, crime or commercial ventures. Avoid first-person nostalgia and remembrances of places that no longer exist. We look for top-quality literature. Humor is encouraged. Good taste is a standard. Unique angles are critical for acceptance. Dare to be bold, but not too bold."

South Dakota

$ DAKOTA OUTDOORS, South Dakota, Hipple Publishing Co., P.O. Box 669, 333 W. Dakota Ave., Pierre SD 57501-0669. (605)224-7301. Fax: (605)224-9210. E-mail: office@capjournal.com. Editor: Kevin Hipple. **Contact:** Rachel Engbrecht, managing editor. **85% freelance written.** Monthly magazine on Dakota outdoor life, focusing on hunting and fishing. Estab. 1974. Circ. 7,000. Pays on publication. Publishes ms an average of 2 months after acceptance. Byline given. Submit seasonal material 3 months in advance. Accepts queries by mail, e-mail. Accepts simultaneous submissions. Responds in 3 months to queries. Sample copy for 9 × 12 SAE and 3 first-class stamps. Writer's guidelines not available.

Nonfiction: "Topics should center on fishing and hunting experiences and advice. Other topics such as boating, camping, hiking, environmental concerns, and general nature will be considered as well." General interest, how-to, humor, interview/profile, personal experience, technical (all on outdoor topics—prefer in the Dakotas). **Buys 120 mss/year.** Send complete ms. Length: 500-2,000 words. **Pays $5-50.** Sometimes pays in contributor's copies or other premiums (inquire).

Reprints: Send typed ms with rights for sale noted and information about when and where the material previously appeared. 50% of amount paid for an original article.

Photos: Send photos with submission. Reviews 3×5 or 5×7 prints. Buys one-time rights. Offers no additonal payment for photos accepted with ms or negotiates payment individually. Identification of subjects required.

Columns/Departments: Kids Korner (outdoors column addressing kids 12-16 years of age). Length: 50-500 words. **Pays $5-15.**

Fiction: Adventure, humorous. **Buys 15 mss/year.** Send complete ms.

Fillers: Anecdotes, facts, gags to be illustrated by cartoonist, newsbreaks, short humor, line drawings of fish and game. Prefers 5×7 prints. **Buys 10/year.**

Tips: "Submit samples of manuscript or previous works for consideration; photos or illustrations with manuscript are helpful."

Texas

$ $ $ PAPERCITY, Dallas Edition, Urban Publishers, 3303 Lee Pkwy., #340, Dallas TX 75219. (214)521-3439. Fax: (214)521-3178. E-mail: rebecca@papercitymag.com. **Contact:** Rebecca Sherman, Dallas editor; Holly Moore, Houston editor. **10% freelance written.** Monthly magazine. "*Papercity* covers fashion, food, entertainment, home design and decoratives for urban Dallas and Houston. Our writing is lively, brash, sexy—it's where to read about the hottest restaurants, great chefs, where to shop, what's cool to buy, where to go, and the chicest places to stay—from sexy, small hotels in New York, Los Angeles, London, and Morocco, to where to buy the newest trends in Europe. We cover local parties with big photo spreads, and a hip nightlife column." Estab. 1994 (Houston); and 1998 (Dallas). Circ. 85,000 (Dallas). Pays on publication. Publishes ms an average of 1 month after acceptance. Byline given. Offers 10% kill fee. Buys first North American serial rights. Editorial lead time 2 months. Submit seasonal material 4 months in advance. Accepts queries by mail, e-mail, fax. Accepts simultaneous submissions. Responds in 3 weeks to queries; 1 month to mss. Sample copy for 9×12 SAE with $1.50 in first-class stamps. Writer's guidelines for #10 SASE or by e-mail.

Nonfiction: General interest, interview/profile, new product, travel, home decor, food. Special issues: Bridal (February); Travel (April); Restaurants (August). No straight profiles on anyone, especially celebrities. **Buys 10-12 mss/year.** Query with published clips. Length: 150-3,000 words. **Pays 35-50¢/word.**

Photos: State availability with submission. Reviews contact sheets, transparencies, prints. Buys one-time rights. Negotiates payment individually.

Tips: "Read similar publications such as *W*, *Tattler*, *Wallpaper*, *Martha Stewart Living* for new trends, style of writing, hip new restaurants. We try to be very 'of the moment' so give us something in Dallas, Houston, New York, Los Angeles, London, etc. that we haven't heard yet. Chances are if other hip magazines are writing about it so will we."

$ $ $ TEXAS HIGHWAYS, The Travel magazine of Texas, Box 141009, Austin TX 78714-1009. (512)486-5858. Fax: (512)486-5879. E-mail: editors@texashighways.com. Website: www.texashighways.com. **Contact:** Jill Lawless, managing editor. **80% freelance written.** Monthly magazine "encourages travel within the state and tells the Texas story to readers around the world." Estab. 1974. Circ. 300,000. **Pays on acceptance.** Publishes ms an average of 1 year after acceptance. Buys first North American serial, electronic rights. Accepts queries by mail. Responds in 2 months to queries. Writer's guidelines for SASE or online.

Nonfiction: "Subjects should focus on things to do or places to see in Texas. Include historical, cultural, and geographic aspects if appropriate. Text should be meticulously researched. Include anecdotes, historical references, quotations, and, where relevant, geologic, botanical, and zoological information." Query with description, published clips, additional background materials (charts, maps, etc.), and SASE. Length: 1,200-1,500 words. **Pays 40-50¢/word.**

Tips: "We like strong leads that draw in the reader immediately and clear, concise writing. Be specific and avoid superlatives. Avoid overused words. Don't forget the basics—who, what, where, why and how."

$ $ $ TEXAS PARKS & WILDLIFE, 3000 South I.H. 35, Suite 120, Austin TX 78704. (512)912-7000. Fax: (512)707-1913. Website: www.tpwmagazine.com. Managing Editor: Mary-Love Bigony. **Contact:** Elaine Robbins, executive editor. **80% freelance written.** Monthly magazine featuring articles about Texas hunting, fishing, birding, outdoor recreation, game and nongame wildlife, state parks, environmental issues. All articles must be about Texas. Estab. 1942. Circ. 150,000. **Pays on acceptance.** Publishes ms an average of 6 months after acceptance. Byline given. Kill fee determined by contract, usually $200-250. Buys first rights. Submit seasonal material 6 months in advance. Accepts queries by mail. Responds in 1 month to queries; 3 months to mss. Sample copy and writer's guidelines online.

• *Texas Parks & Wildlife* needs more hunting and fishing material.

Nonfiction: General interest (Texas only), how-to (outdoor activities), photo feature, travel (state parks). **Buys 60 mss/year.** Query with published clips. Length: 500-2,500 words.

Photos: Send photos to photo editor. Reviews transparencies. Buys one-time rights. Offers $65-350/photo. Captions, identification of subjects required.

Tips: "Read outdoor pages of statewide newspapers to keep abreast of news items that can lead to story ideas. Feel free to include more than 1 story idea in one query letter. All areas are open to freelancers. All articles must have a Texas focus."

N $ $ WHERE DALLAS MAGAZINE, Abarta Media, 4809 Cole Ave., Suite 165, Dallas TX 75205. (214)522-0050. Fax: (214)522-0504. E-mail: pfelps@abartapub.com. **Contact:** Paula Felps, editor. **75% freelance written.** Monthly magazine. "*WHERE Dallas* is part of the *WHERE Magazine International* network, the world's largest publisher of travel magazines. Published in more than 46 cities around the world, travelers trust *WHERE* to guide them to the best in shopping, dining, nightlife and entertainment." Estab. 1996. Circ. 45,000. Pays on publication. Publishes ms an average of 2 months after acceptance. Byline given. Buys all rights. Editorial lead time 2 months. Submit seasonal material 2 months in advance. Accepts queries by mail, e-mail. Accepts simultaneous submissions. Sample copy for $3.

O→ Break in with "a solid idea—solid meaning the local Dallas angle is *everything*. We're looking for advice and tips that would/could only come from those living in the area."

Nonfiction: General interest, historical/nostalgic, photo feature, travel, special events. **Buys 20 mss/year.** Query with published clips. Length: 650-1,000 words. **Pays $200-300.** Sometimes pays expenses of writers on assignment.

Photos: Send photos with submission. Reviews transparencies. Buys one time rights, all rights on cover photos. Captions, identification of subjects, model releases required.

Columns/Departments: Pays $100-450.

Tips: "To get our attention, send clips with clever, punchy writing, like you might find in a society or insider column in the newspaper. We're also looking for writers with an expertise in shopping, with knowledge of fashion/art/antiques/collectibles."

Vermont

$ $ VERMONT LIFE MAGAZINE, 6 Baldwin St., Montpelier VT 05602-2109. (802)828-3241. Fax: (802)828-3366. E-mail: tslayton@life.state.vt.us. Website: www.vtlife.com. **Contact:** Thomas K. Slayton, editor-in-chief. **90% freelance written.** Prefers to work with published/established writers. Quarterly magazine. "*Vermont Life* is interested in any article, query, story idea, photograph, or photo essay that has to do with Vermont. As the state magazine, we are most favorably impressed with pieces that present positive aspects of life within the state's borders." Estab. 1946. Circ. 85,000. Publishes ms an average of 9 months after acceptance. Byline given. Offers kill fee. Buys first North American serial rights. Submit seasonal material 1 year in advance. Accepts queries by mail, e-mail, fax. Responds in 1 month to queries. Writer's guidelines for #10 SASE.

O→ Break in with "short humorous Vermont anecdotes for our 'Postboy' column."

Nonfiction: Wants articles on today's Vermont, those which portray a typical or, if possible, unique aspect of the state or its people. Style should be literate, clear and concise. Subtle humor favored. No "Vermont clichés"—maple syrup, town meetings, or stereotyped natives. **Buys 60 mss/year.** Query by letter essential. Length: 1,500 words average. **Pays 25¢/word.**

Photos: Buys photos with mss; buys seasonal photographs alone. Prefers b&w contact sheets to look at first on assigned material. Color submissions must be 4×5 or 35mm transparencies. Gives assignments but only with experienced photographers. Query in writing. Buys one-time rights. Pays $75-200 inside color; $500 for cover. Captions, identification of subjects, model releases required.

The online version contains material not found in the print edition. Contact: Andrew Jackson.

Tips: "Writers who read our magazine are given more consideration because they understand that we want authentic articles about Vermont. If a writer has a genuine working knowledge of Vermont, his or her work usually shows it. Vermont is changing and there is much concern here about what this state will be like in years ahead. It is a beautiful, environmentally sound place now and the vast majority of residents want to keep it so. Articles reflecting such concerns in an intelligent, authoritative, non-hysterical way will be given very careful consideration. The growth of tourism makes us interested in intelligent articles about specific places in Vermont, their history and attractions to the traveling public."

Virginia

$ $ THE ROANOKER, Leisure Publishing Co., 3424 Brambleton Ave., P.O. Box 21535, Roanoke VA 24018-9900. (540)989-6138. Fax: (540)989-7603. E-mail: info@leisurepublishing.com. Website: www.theroanoker.com. **Contact:** Kurt Rheinheimer, editor. **75% freelance written.** Works with a small number of new/unpublished writers each year. Magazine published 6 times/year. "*The Roanoker* is a general interest city magazine for the people of Roanoke, Virginia, and the surrounding area. Our readers are primarily upper-income, well-educated professionals between the ages of 35 and 60. Coverage ranges from hard news and consumer information to restaurant reviews and local history." Estab. 1974. Circ. 12,000. Pays on publication. Publishes ms an average of 4 months after acceptance. Byline given. Buys all rights, makes work-for-hire assignments. Submit seasonal material 4 months in advance. Accepts queries by mail, e-mail, fax. Responds in 2 months to queries. Sample copy for $2 and 9×12 SAE with 5 first-class stamps or online.

Nonfiction: "We're looking for more photo feature stories based in western Virginia. We place special emphasis on investigative and exposé articles." Exposé, historical/nostalgic, how-to (live better in western Virginia), interview/profile (of well-known area personalities), photo feature, travel (Virginia and surrounding states), periodic special sections on fashion, real estate, media, banking, investing. **Buys 30 mss/year.** Query with published clips or send complete ms. Length: 1,400 words maximum. **Pays $35-200.**

Reprints: Rarely accepts previously published submissions. Send tearsheet. Pays 50% of amount paid for an original article.

Photos: Send photos with submission. Reviews color transparencies. Rights purchased vary. Pays $5-10 for 5×7 or 8×10 b&w prints; $10-50 for color transparencies. Captions, model releases required.

Columns/Departments: Skinny (shorts on people, Roanoke-related books, local issues, events, arts and culture).

Tips: "We're looking for more pieces on contemporary history (1930s-70s). It helps if freelancer lives in the area. The most frequent mistake made by writers in completing an article for us is not having enough Roanoke-area focus: use of area experts, sources, slants, etc."

Washington

N NSPIRIT CULTURAL NEWS MAGAZINE, NW Writers' Corp., 30620 Pacific Hwy. S., #110, Federal Way WA 98003-4888. Fax: (253)839-3207. E-mail: nwwriterscorp@aol.com. Website: www.nwwriterscorp.com. Editor: Amontaine Woods. Managing Editor: Orisade Awodola. **Contact:** Amontaine Woods. **80% freelance written.** Monthly magazine covering cultural issues. "*NSpirit Cultural NewsMAGAZINE* is a family-oriented, 32-page, color glossy consumer magazine. Its focus is to provide empowering articles, essays, literary works, and visual art, for purposes of education and economic development in the King County, Greater Puget Sound, and parts of Pierce County areas." Estab. 1998. Circ. 50,000. Pays on publication. Publishes ms an average of 1 month after acceptance. Byline given. Buys first North American serial rights. Editorial lead time 2 months. Submit seasonal material 3 months in advance. Accepts queries by mail, e-mail, fax. Accepts simultaneous submissions. Responds in 1 month to queries; 2 months to mss. Sample copy for #10 SASE. Writer's guidelines for #10 SASE.

Nonfiction: Della Westerfield, senior editor. Book excerpts, general interest, inspirational, interview/profile, personal experience. Special issues: Christmas/Hanukkah (December); Martin Luther King, Jr. Birthday (January); Festival Sundiata, Giraffe Project (February); Bill & Melinda Gates, Millennium Scholarship Fund (March); Earth Day/Environmental (April); Mother's Day/Mental Health Month (May); Father's Day/Graduations (June); Independence Day/America (July); Salvation Army/US Peace Corps (September); Cancer Awareness Month (October); Thanksgiving (November). No politics, violence, racial/discrimination. **Buys 6-8 mss/year.** Query with published clips. Length: 750 words. **Pays $50-250 for assigned articles.** Sometimes pays expenses of writers on assignment.

Photos: State availability of or send photos with submission. Reviews contact sheets, GIF/JPEG files. Buys one-time rights. Offers no additional payment for photos accepted with ms. Identification of subjects required.

$ $ SEATTLE MAGAZINE, Tiger Oak Publications, Inc., 423 Third Ave. W., Seattle WA 98119. (206)284-1750. Fax: (206)284-2550. E-mail: rachel@seattlemag.com. Website: www.seattlemag.com. **Contact:** Rachel Hart, editor. Monthly magazine "serving the Seattle metropolitan area. Articles should be written with our readers in mind. They are interested in social issues, the arts, politics, homes and gardens, travel, and maintaining the region's high quality of life." Estab. 1992. Circ. 45,000. Pays on or about 30 days after publication. Publishes ms an average of 3 months after acceptance. Byline given. Offers 25% kill fee. Buys first rights. Editorial lead time 6 months. Submit seasonal material 6 months in advance. Accepts queries by e-mail, fax. Responds in 2 months to queries. Sample copy for #10 SASE. Writer's guidelines online.

O⇁ Break in by "suggesting short, newsier stories with a strong Seattle focus."

Nonfiction: Book excerpts (local), essays, exposé, general interest, humor, interview/profile, photo feature, travel, local/regional interest. No longer accepting queries by mail. Query with published clips. Length: 100-2,000 words. **Pays $50 minimum.** Sometimes pays expenses of writers on assignment.

Photos: State availability with submission. Buys one-time rights. Negotiates payment individually.

Columns/Departments: Scoop, Urban Safari; Voice; Trips; People; Environment; Hot Button; Fitness; Fashion; Eat and Drink. Query with published clips. **Pays $100-300.**

Tips: "The best queries include some idea of a lead and sources of information, plus compelling reasons why the article belongs specifically in *Seattle Magazine*. In addition, queries should demonstrate the writer's familiarity with the magazine. New writers are often assigned front- or back-of-the-book contents, rather than features. However, the editors do not discourage writers from querying for longer articles and are especially interested in receiving trend pieces, in-depth stories with a news hook and cultural criticism with a local angle."

N $ $ $ SEATTLE WEEKLY, Village Voice, 1008 Western Ave., Suite 300, Seattle WA 98104. (206)623-0500. Fax: (206)467-4377. E-mail: editorial@seattleweekly.com. **Contact:** Audrey van Buskirk. **20% freelance written.** Weekly tabloid covering arts, politics, food, business and books with local and regional emphasis. Estab. 1976. Circ. 105,000. Pays on publication. Publishes ms an average of 1 month after acceptance. Byline given. Offers variable kill fee. Buys first North American serial rights. Submit seasonal material 2 months in advance. Responds in 1 month to queries. Sample copy for $3. Writer's guidelines for #10 SASE.

Nonfiction: Book excerpts, exposé, general interest, historical/nostalgic (Northwest), humor, interview/profile, opinion. **Buys 6-8 mss/year.** Query with cover letter, résumé, published clips and SASE. Length: 500-3,000 words. **Pays $50-800.** Sometimes pays expenses of writers on assignment.

Reprints: Send tearsheet. Payment varies.

Tips: "The *Seattle Weekly* publishes stories on Northwest politics and art, usually written by regional and local writers, for a mostly upscale, urban audience; writing is high-quality magazine style."

Wisconsin

$ $ $ MILWAUKEE MAGAZINE, 417 E. Chicago St., Milwaukee WI 53202. (414)273-1101. Fax: (414)273-0016. E-mail: John.Fennell@qg.com. Website: www.milwaukeemagazine.com. **Contact:** John Fennell, editor. **40% freelance written.** Monthly magazine. "We publish stories about Milwaukee, of service to Milwaukee-area residents and exploring the area's changing lifestyle, business, arts, politics, and dining." Circ. 40,000. Pays on publication. Publishes ms an average of 2 months after acceptance. Byline given. Offers 20% kill fee. Buys first rights. Submit seasonal material 6 months in advance. Accepts queries by mail, e-mail. Responds in 6 weeks to queries. Sample copy for $4.

Nonfiction: Essays, exposé, general interest, historical/nostalgic, interview/profile, photo feature, travel, food and dining, and other services. "No articles without a strong Milwaukee or Wisconsin angle." Length: 2,500-6000 words for full-length features; 800 words for 2-page "breaker" features (short on copy, long on visuals). **Buys 30-50 mss/year.** Query with published clips. **Pays $400-1,000 for full-length, $150-400 for breaker.** Sometimes pays expenses of writers on assignment.

Columns/Departments: Insider (inside information on Milwaukee, exposé, slice-of-life, unconventional angles on current scene), up to 500 words; Mini Reviews for Insider, 125 words. Query with published clips.

Tips: "Pitch something for the Insider, or suggest a compelling profile we haven't already done. Submit clips that prove you can do the job. The department most open is Insider. Think short, lively, offbeat, fresh, people-oriented. We are actively seeking freelance writers who can deliver lively, readable copy that helps our readers make the most out of the Milwaukee area. Because we're only human, we'd like writers who can deliver copy on deadline that fits the specifications of our assignment. If you fit this description, we'd love to work with you."

$ $ WISCONSIN TRAILS, P.O. Box 317, Black Earth WI 53515-0317. (608)767-8000. Fax: (608)767-5444. E-mail: lkearney@wistrails.com. Website: www.wistrails.com. **Contact:** Laura Kearney, assistant editor. **40% freelance written.** Bimonthly magazine for readers interested in Wisconsin and its contemporary issues, personalities, recreation, history, natural beauty, and arts. Estab. 1960. Circ. 55,000. Pays on publication. Publishes ms an average of 6 months after acceptance. Byline given. Buys first North American serial, one-time rights. Submit seasonal material 1 year in advance. Accepts queries by mail, e-mail, fax. Responds in 4 months to queries. Sample copy for $4.95. Writer's guidelines for #10 SASE.

> O─ "We're looking for active articles about people, places, events, and outdoor adventures in Wisconsin. We want to publish 1 in-depth article of state-wide interest or concern/issue, and several short (600-1,500 words) articles about short trips, recreational opportunities, personalities, restaurants, inns, history, and cultural activities. We're looking for more articles about out-of-the-way Wisconsin places that are exceptional in some way and engaging pieces on Wisconsin's little-known and unique aspects."

Nonfiction: "Our articles focus on some aspect of Wisconsin life: an interesting town or event, a person or industry, history or the arts, and especially outdoor recreation. We do not use first-person essays or biographies about people who were born in Wisconsin but made their fortunes elsewhere. No poetry. No articles that are too local for our regional audience, or articles about obvious places to visit in Wisconsin. We need more articles about the new and little-known." **Buys 3 unsolicited mss/year.** Query or send outline. Length: 1,000-3,000 words. **Pays 25¢/word for assigned articles.** Sometimes pays expenses of writers on assignment.

Photos: Photographs purchased with or without mss, or on assignment. Color photos usually illustrate an activity, event, region, or striking scenery. Prefer photos with people in scenery. Reviews 35mm or larger transparencies. Pays $65-125 for inside color; $250 for covers. Captions, labels with photographer's name required.

Tips: "When querying, submit well-thought-out ideas about stories specific to people, places, events, arts, outdoor adventures, etc., in Wisconsin. Include published clips with queries. Do some research—many queries we receive are pitching ideas for stories we recently have published. Know the tone, content, and audience of the magazine. Refer to our writers' guidelines, or request them, if necessary."

Wyoming

$ WYOMING RURAL ELECTRIC NEWS (WREN), 340 West B St., Suite 101, Casper WY 82601. (307)682-7527. Fax: (307)682-7528. E-mail: wren@coffey.com. **Contact:** Kris Wendtland, editor. **20% freelance written.** Monthly magazine for audience of small town residents, vacation-home owners, farmers, and ranchers. Estab. 1955. Circ. 35,000. Pays on publication. Publishes ms an average of 1 month after acceptance. Byline given. Buys one-time rights. Submit seasonal material 2 months in advance. Accepts queries by mail, e-mail, fax, phone. Responds in 3 months to queries. Sample copy for $2.50 and 9×12 SASE. Writer's guidelines for #10 SASE.

> O─ "You have just learned something. It is so amazing you just have to find out more. You call around. You search on the Web. You go to the library. Everything you learn about it makes you want to know more. In a matter of days, all your friends are aware that you are into something. You don't stop talking about it. You're totally confident that they find it interesting too. Now, write it down and send it to us. We are excited just wondering what you find so amazing! Come on, tell us! Tell us!"

Nonfiction: "We print science, ag, how-to, and human interest but not fiction. Topics of interest in general include: hunting, cooking, gardening, commodities, sugar beets, wheat, oil, coal, hard rock mining, beef cattle, electric technologies such as lawn mowers, car heaters, air cleaners and assorted gadgets, surge protectors, pesticators, etc." Wants science articles with question/answer quiz at end—test your knowledge. Buys electrical appliance articles. Articles welcome that put present and/or future in positive light. No nostalgia. No sad stories. **Buys 4-10 mss/year.** Send complete ms. Length: 500-800 words. **Pays up to $140, plus 4 copies.**
Reprints: Send tearsheet or photocopy and information about when and where the material previously appeared.
Photos: Color only.
Tips: "Always looking for fresh, new writers, original perspectives. Submit entire manuscript. Don't submit a regionally set story from some other part of the country. Photos and illustrations (if appropriate) are always welcomed. We don't care if you misspell words. We don't care if your grammar is poor. We want factual articles that are blunt, to the point, accurate."

Canadian/International

$ $ ABACO LIFE, Caribe Communications, P.O. Box 37487, Raleigh NC 27627. (919)859-6782. Fax: (919)859-6769. E-mail: jimkerr@mindspring.com. Website: www.abacolife.com. Managing Editor: Cathy Kerr. **Contact:** Jim Kerr, editor/publisher. **50% freelance written.** Quarterly magazine covering Abaco, an island group in the Northeast Bahamas. "*Abaco Life* editorial focuses entirely on activities, history, wildlife, resorts, people and other subjects pertaining to the Abacos. Readers include locals, vacationers, second home owners and other visitors whose interests range from real estate and resorts to scuba, sailing, fishing and beaches. The tone is upbeat, adventurous, humorous. No fluff writing for an audience already familiar with the area." Estab. 1979. Circ. 10,000. Pays on publication. Publishes ms an average of 2 months after acceptance. Byline given. Offers 40% kill fee. Buys one-time rights. Editorial lead time 2 months. Submit seasonal material 4 months in advance. Accepts queries by mail, e-mail. Accepts simultaneous submissions. Responds in 2 weeks to queries; 2 months to mss. Sample copy for $2. Writer's guidelines free.
Nonfiction: General interest, historical/nostalgic, how-to, interview/profile, personal experience, photo feature, travel. "No general first-time impressions. Articles must be specific, show knowledge and research of the subject and area—'Abaco's Sponge Industry'; 'Diving Abaco's Wrecks'; 'The Hurricane of '36.'" **Buys 8-10 mss/year.** Query or send complete ms. Length: 400-2,000 words. **Pays $150-350.**
Photos: State availability of or send photos with submission. Reviews transparencies, prints. Buys one-time rights. Offers $25-100/photo. Negotiates payment individually. Captions, identification of subjects, model releases required.
■ The online magazine carries original content not found in the print edition. Contact: Jim Kerr, online editor.
Tips: "Travel writers must look deeper than a usual destination piece, and the only real way to do that is spend time in Abaco. Beyond good writing, which is a must, we like submissions on Microsoft Word or Works, but that's optional. Color slides are also preferred over prints, and good ones go a long way in selling the story. Read the magazine to learn its style."

$ $ $ ALBERTAVIEWS, The Magazine About Alberta for Albertans, Local Perspectives Publishing, Inc., #602, 815 First St. SW, Calgary, Alberta T2P 1N3, Canada. (403)243-5334. Fax: (403)243-8599. E-mail: contactus@albertaviews.ab.ca. Website: www.albertaviews.ab.ca. Publisher/Editor: Jackie Flanagan. **Contact:** Renee Groves, associate editor. **50% freelance written.** Bimonthly magazine covering Alberta culture: politics, economy, social issues, and art. "We are a regional magazine providing thoughtful commentary and background information on issues of concern to Albertans. Most of our writers are Albertans." Estab. 1997. Circ. 30,000. Pays on publication. Publishes ms an average of 3 months after acceptance. Byline given. Offers 50% kill fee. Buys first North American serial, electronic rights. Editorial lead time 3 months. Submit seasonal material 3 months in advance. Accepts queries by e-mail. Responds in 6 weeks to queries; 2 months to mss. Sample copy for free. Writer's guidelines free, online, or by e-mail.
Nonfiction: Does not want anything not directly related to Alberta. Essays. **Buys 18 mss/year.** Query with published clips. Length: 3,000-5,000 words. **Pays $1,000-1,500 for assigned articles; $350-750 for unsolicited articles.** Sometimes pays expenses of writers on assignment.
Photos: State availability with submission. Buys one-time rights, Web rights. Negotiates payment individually.
Fiction: Only fiction by Alberta writers. **Buys 6 mss/year.** Send complete ms. Length: 2,500-4,000 words. **Pays $1,000 maximum.**

$ ATLANTIC BOOKS TODAY, Atlantic Provinces Book Review Society, 1657 Barrington St., #502, Halifax, Nova Scotia B3J 2A1, Canada. (902)429-4454. E-mail: booksatl@istar.ca. **Contact:** Elizabeth Eve, managing editor. **50% freelance written.** Quarterly tabloid covering books and writers in Atlantic Canada. "We only accept written inquiries for stories pertaining to promoting interest in the culture of the Atlantic region." Estab. 1992. Circ. 20,000. Pays on publication. Byline given. Offers $25 kill fee. Buys one-time rights. Editorial lead time 6 months. Submit seasonal material 3 months in advance. Accepts queries by mail. Accepts simultaneous submissions. Responds in 1 month to queries. Sample copy and writer's guidelines for #10 SASE.
Nonfiction: Book excerpts, general interest. Query with published clips. Length: 1,000 words maximum. **Pays $120 maximum for assigned articles.** Sometimes pays expenses of writers on assignment.

$ $ THE ATLANTIC CO-OPERATOR, Promoting Community Ownership, Atlantic Co-operative Publishers, 123 Halifax St., Moncton, New Brunswick E1C 8N5, Canada. Fax: (506)858-6615. E-mail: coop@nbnet.nb.ca.

Contact: Cynthia Boudreau, editor. **95% freelance written.** Tabloid published 9 times/year covering co-operatives. "We publish articles of interest to the general public, with a special focus on community ownership and community economic development in Atlantic Canada." Estab. 1933. Pays on publication. Publishes ms an average of 2 months after acceptance. Byline given. Editorial lead time 2 months. Submit seasonal material 2 months in advance. Accepts queries by mail, e-mail, fax. Accepts simultaneous submissions. Responds in 3 weeks to queries. Sample copy not available.

Nonfiction: Exposé, general interest, historical/nostalgic, interview/profile. No political stories, economical stories, sports. **Buys 90 mss/year.** Query with published clips. Length: 500-2,000 words. **Pays 20¢/word.** Pays expenses of writers on assignment.

Reprints: Accepts previously published submissions.

Photos: State availability with submission. Reviews prints, GIF/JPEG files. Buys one-time rights. Offers $25/photo. Identification of subjects required.

Columns/Departments: Health and Lifestyle (anything from recipes to travel), 800 words; International Page (co-operatives in developing countries, good ideas from around the world). **Buys 10 mss/year.** Query with published clips. **Pays 15¢/word.**

$ $ BEAUTIFUL BRITISH COLUMBIA, 302-3939 Quadra St., Victoria, British Columbia V8X 1J5, Canada. Fax: (250)384-9926. E-mail: ed@beautifulbc.ca. Website: www.beautifulbc.ca. Managing Editor: Anita Willis. **Contact:** Bryan McGill, editor. **80% freelance written.** Quarterly magazine covering British Columbia subjects. "A quarterly scenic geographic and travel magazine of British Columbia. Primary subjects: wildlife, parks and wilderness, travel, outdoor adventure, geography, history, eco-tourism, native culture, environment, heritage preservation." Estab. 1959. Circ. 170,000. **Pays on acceptance.** Publishes ms an average of 1 year after acceptance. Byline given. Offers 50% kill fee. first worldwide rights Editorial lead time 1 year. Submit seasonal material 1 year in advance. Accepts queries by mail. Responds in 1 month to queries; 1 month to mss. Sample copy for $5.95 (Canadian). Writer's guidelines for #10 SASE (Canadian postage).

Nonfiction: No poetry, fiction, people profiles; nothing unrelated to British Columbia." **Buys 20 mss/year.** Query with published clips. Length: 1,000-3,500 words. **Pays 50¢/word.** Sometimes pays expenses of writers on assignment.

Photos: Send photos with submission. Reviews transparencies. Buys one-time rights. Offers $100-500. Captions, identification of subjects, model releases required.

Fillers: Facts, newsbreaks, short humor. **Buys 20/year.** Length: 10-250 words. **Pays 50¢/word.**

Tips: "We do not encourage submissions from contributors who live outside British Columbia. In our experience, only resident writers/photographers are able to provide the kind of in-depth, fresh, surprising perspectives on British Columbia that our readers demand."

$ $ $ THE BEAVER, Canada's History Magazine, Canada's National History Society, 478-167 Lombard Ave., Winnipeg, Manitoba R3B 0T6, Canada. (204)988-9300. Fax: (204)988-9309. E-mail: cnhs@historysociety.ca. Website: www.historysociety.ca. Associate Editor: Doug Whiteway. **Contact:** Annalee Greenberg, editor. **65% freelance written.** Bimonthly magazine covering Canadian history. Estab. 1920. Circ. 41,000. **Pays on acceptance.** Byline given. Offers $200 kill fee. Buys first North American serial, electronic rights. Editorial lead time 4 months. Submit seasonal material 8 months in advance. Accepts queries by mail. Accepts simultaneous submissions. Responds in 6 weeks to queries; 2 months to mss. Sample copy for 9×12 SAE and 2 first-class stamps. Writer's guidelines for #10 SASE or online.

O‑ Break in with a "new interpretation based on solid new research; entertaining magazine style."

Nonfiction: Photo feature (historical), historical (Canadian focus). Does not want anything unrelated to Canadian history. **Buys 30 mss/year.** Query with published clips. Length: 600-4,000 words. **Pays $400-1,000 for assigned articles; $300-600 for unsolicited articles.** Sometimes pays expenses of writers on assignment.

Photos: State availability with submission. Buys one-time rights. Offers no additional payment for photos accepted with ms. Identification of subjects, model releases required.

Columns/Departments: Book and other media reviews and Canadian history subjects, 600 words ("These are assigned to freelancers with particular areas of expertise, i.e., women's history, labour history, French regime, etc."). **Buys 15 mss/year. Pays $125.**

Tips: "*The Beaver* is directed toward a general audience of educated readers, as well as to historians and scholars. We are in the market for lively, well-written, well-researched, and informative articles about Canadian history that focus on all parts of the country and all areas of human activity. Subject matter covers the whole range of Canadian history, with particular emphasis on social history, politics, exploration, discovery and settlement, aboriginal peoples, business and trade, war, culture and sport. Articles are obtained through direct commission and by submission. Queries should be accompanied by a stamped, self-addressed envelope. *The Beaver* publishes articles of various lengths, including long features (from 1,500-4,000 words) that provide an in-depth look at an event, person or era; short, more narrowly focused features (from 600-1,500 words). Longer articles may be considered if their importance warrants publication. Articles should be written in an expository or interpretive style and present the principal themes of Canadian history in an original, interesting and informative way."

$ BRAZZIL, Brazzil, P.O. Box 50536, Los Angeles CA 90050. (323)255-8062. Fax: (323)257-3487. E-mail: brazzil@brazzil.com. Website: www.brazzil.com. **Contact:** Rodney Mello, editor. **60% freelance written.** Monthly magazine covering Brazilian culture. Estab. 1989. Circ. 12,000. Pays on publication. Publishes ms an average of 2 months after acceptance. Byline given. Offers 10% kill fee. Buys one-time rights. Editorial lead time 2 months. Submit seasonal material 2 months in advance. Accepts queries by mail, e-mail, fax, phone. Accepts simultaneous submissions. Responds in 2 weeks to queries. Sample copy free or online.

Nonfiction: "All subjects have to deal in some way with Brazil and its culture. We assume our readers know very little or nothing about Brazil, so we explain everything." Book excerpts, essays, exposé, general interest, historical/nostalgic, humor, interview/profile, opinion, personal experience, travel. **Buys 15 mss/year.** Query. Length: 800-5,000 words. **Pays $20-50.** Pays writers with contributor copies or other premiums by mutual agreement.

Reprints: Send photocopy with rights for sale noted and information about when and where the material previously appeared. Pays 50% of amount paid for an original article.

Photos: State availability with submission. Reviews prints. Buys one-time rights. Offers no additional payment for photos accepted with ms. Identification of subjects required.

The online version of *Brazzil* contains content not included in the print edition. Contact: Leda Mello, online editor.

Tips: "We are interested in anything related to Brazil: politics, economy, music, behavior, profiles. Please document material with interviews and statistical data if applicable. Controversial pieces are welcome."

$ $ $ CANADIAN GEOGRAPHIC, 39 McArthur Ave., Ottawa, Ontario K1L 8L7, Canada. (613)745-4629. Fax: (613)744-0947. E-mail: editorial@canadiangeographic.ca. Website: www.canadiangeographic.ca. **Contact:** Rick Boychuk, editor. **90% freelance written.** Works with a small number of new/unpublished writers each year. Bimonthly magazine. "*Canadian Geographic*'s colorful portraits of our ever-changing population show readers just how important the relationship between the people and the land really is." Estab. 1930. Circ. 240,000. **Pays on acceptance.** Publishes ms an average of 3 months after acceptance. first Canadian rights Accepts queries by mail, e-mail, fax. Responds in 1 month to queries. Sample copy for $5.95 Canadian and 9×12 SAE or online.

- *Canadian Geographic* reports a need for more articles on earth sciences.

Nonfiction: Buys authoritative geographical articles, in the broad geographical sense, written for the average person, not for a scientific audience. Predominantly Canadian subjects by Canadian authors. **Buys 30-45 mss/year.** Query. Length: 1,500-3,000 words. **Pays 80¢/word minimum.** Sometimes pays expenses of writers on assignment.

Photos: Pays $75-400 for color photos, depending on published size.

$ $ OUTDOOR CANADA MAGAZINE, 340 Ferrier St., Suite 210, Markham, Ontario L3R 2Z5, Canada. (905)475-8440. Fax: (905)475-9246. E-mail: editorial@outdoorcanada.ca. Website: www.outdoorcanada.ca. **Contact:** Patrick Walsh, editor-in-chief. **90% freelance written.** Works with a small number of new/unpublished writers each year. Magazine published 8 times/year emphasizing noncompetitive outdoor recreation in Canada *only*. Estab. 1972. Circ. 95,000. Pays on publication. Publishes ms an average of 8 months after acceptance. Byline given. Buys first rights. Submit seasonal material 1 year in advance. Accepts queries by mail, e-mail. Responds in 1 month to queries. Writer's guidelines online.

Nonfiction: How-to, fishing, hunting, outdoor issues, outdoor destinations in Canada. **Buys 35-40 mss/year.** Query. Length: 2,500 words. **Pays $500 and up for assigned articles.**

Reprints: Send information about when and where the article previously appeared. Payment varies.

Photos: Emphasize people in the Canadian outdoors. Pays $100-250 for 35mm transparencies and $400/cover. Captions, model releases required.

Fillers: Short news pieces. **Buys 30-40/year.** Length: 100-500 words. **Pays $50 and up.**

The online magazine carries original content not found in the print edition. Contact: Aaron Kylie, online editor.

$ $ $ TORONTO LIFE, 59 Front St. E., Toronto, Ontario M5E 1B3, Canada. (416)364-3333. Fax: (416)955-4982. E-mail: editorial@torontolife.com. Website: www.torontolife.com. **Contact:** John Macfarlane, editor. **95% freelance written.** Prefers to work with published/established writers. Monthly magazine emphasizing local issues and social trends, short humor/satire, and service features for upper income, well-educated and, for the most part, young Torontonians. Circ. 92,574. **Pays on acceptance.** Publishes ms an average of 4 months after acceptance. Byline given. Pays 50% kill fee for commissioned articles only. Buys first North American serial rights. Responds in 3 weeks to queries. Sample copy for $4.50 with SAE and IRCs.

Nonfiction: Uses most types of articles. **Buys 17 mss/issue**. Query with published clips and SASE. Length: 1,000-6,000 words. **Pays $500-5,000.**

Columns/Departments: "We run about 5 columns an issue. They are all freelanced, though most are from regular contributors. They are mostly local in concern and cover politics, business, performing arts, media, design, and food." Length: 2,000 words. Query with published clips and SASE. **Pays $2,000.**

Tips: "Submissions should have strong Toronto orientation."

$ $ UP HERE, Life at the Top of the World, OUTCROP: The Northern Publishers, P.O. Box 1350, Yellowknife, Northwest Territories X1A 2N9, Canada. (867)920-4367. Fax: (867)873-2844. E-mail: cooper@uphere.ca. Website: www.uphere.ca. **Contact:** Cooper Langford, editor. **70% freelance written.** Magazine published 8 times/year covering general interest about Canada's North. "We publish features, columns, and shorts about people, wildlife, native cultures, travel, and adventure in Yukon, Northwest Territories, and Nunavut. Be informative, but entertaining." Estab. 1984. Circ. 35,000. Pays on publication. Byline given. Offers 50% kill fee. Buys first North American serial rights. Editorial lead time 6 months. Accepts queries by mail, e-mail, fax. Sample copy for $3.50 (Canadian) and 9×12 SASE with $1.45 Canadian postage. Writer's guidelines for legal-sized SASE and 45¢ Canadian postage.

O⊸ Break in with "precise queries with well-developed focuses for the proposed story."

Nonfiction: Essays, general interest, how-to, humor, interview/profile, new product, personal experience, photo feature, technical, travel, lifestyle/culture, historical. **Buys 25-30 mss/year.** Query. Length: 1,500-3,000 words. **Fees are negotiable.**

Photos: "*Please* do not send unsolicited original photos, slides. Photocopies are sufficient." Send photos with submission. Reviews transparencies, Prints. Buys one-time rights. Captions, identification of subjects required.

Columns/Departments: Write for updated guidelines, visit website, or e-mail. **Buys 25-30 mss/year.** Query with published clips.

The online magazine carries original content not found in the print edition. Contact: Cooper Langford or Mifi Purvis, online editors.

Tips: "We like well-researched, concrete adventure pieces, insights about Northern people and lifestyles, readable natural history. Features are most open to freelancers—travel, adventure, and so on. We don't want a comprehensive 'How I spent my summer vacation' hour-by-hour account. We want stories with angles, articles that look at the North through a different set of glasses. Photos are important; you greatly increase your chances with top-notch images." XZ

$ $ $ VANCOUVER MAGAZINE, Transcontinental Publications, Inc., 555 W. 12th Ave., Suite 300, East Tower, Vancouver, British Columbia V5Z 4L4, Canada. (604)877-7732. Fax: (604)877-4823. E-mail: mail@vancouvermagazine.com. Website: www.vancouvermagazine.com. **Contact:** Nick Rockel, editor. **70% freelance written.** Monthly Magazine covering the city of Vancouver. Estab. 1967. Circ. 65,000. **Pays on acceptance.** Byline given. Offers negotiable kill fee. Buys first North American serial rights. Editorial lead time 2 months. Submit seasonal material 6 months in advance. Accepts queries by mail, e-mail, fax, phone. Accepts simultaneous submissions. Responds in 2 weeks to queries; 1 month to mss. Sample copy for $5. Writer's guidelines for #10 SASE or by e-mail.

Nonfiction: "We prefer to work with writers from a conceptual stage and have a 6-week lead time. Most stories are under 1,500 words. Please be aware that we don't publish poetry and rarely publish fiction." Book excerpts, essays, historical/nostalgic, humor, interview/profile, new product, personal experience, photo feature, travel. **Buys 200 mss/year.** Query. Length: 200-3,000 words. **Pays 50¢/word.** Sometimes pays expenses of writers on assignment.

Photos: State availability with submission. Reviews contact sheets, negatives, transparencies, prints, GIF/JPEG files. Buys negotiable rights. Negotiates payment individually. Captions, identification of subjects, model releases required.

Columns/Departments: Sport; Media; Business; City Issues, all 1,500 words. Query. **Pays 50¢/word.**

Tips: "Read back issues of the magazine, or visit our website. Almost all of our stories have a strong Vancouver angle. Submit queries by e-mail. Do not send complete stories."

$ $ $ WESTWORLD MAGAZINE, Canada Wide Magazines and Communications, 4180 Lougheed Hwy., 4th Floor, Burnaby, British Columbia V5C 6A7, Canada. Fax: (604)299-9188. E-mail: arose@canadawide.com. **Contact:** Anne Rose, editor. **80% freelance written.** Quarterly Magazine distributed to members of The Canadian Automobile Association, with a focus on local (British Columbia), regional and international travel. Estab. 1983. Circ. 500,000. Pays on publication. Byline given. Offers 50% kill fee. Buys first North American serial, second serial (reprint) rights. Editorial lead time 6 months. Submit seasonal material 1 year in advance. Accepts simultaneous submissions. Writer's guidelines currently under revision.

• Editorial lineup for following year determined in June; queries held for consideration at that time. No phone calls.

Nonfiction: Travel (domestic and international). "No purple prose." **Buys 6 mss/year.** Query with published clips. Length: 800-1,500 words. **Pays 35-50¢/word.**

Reprints: send photocopy and information about when and where the material previously appeared. Pays 50% of amount paid for an original article.

Photos: State availability of photos with submission, do not send photos until requested. Review. Buys one-time rights. Offers $35-75/photo. Captions, identification of subjects, model releases required.

Columns/Departments: Query with published clips. **Pays 35-50¢/word.**

Tips: "Don't send gushy, travelogue articles. We prefer stories that are informative with practical, useful tips that are well written and researched. Approach an old topic/destination in a fresh/original way."

RELATIONSHIPS

These publications focus on lifestyles and relationships of single adults. Other markets for this type of material can be found in the Women's category. Magazines of a primarily sexual nature, gay or straight, are listed under the Sex category. The Gay & Lesbian Interest section contains general interest editorial targeted to that audience.

$ $ CONVERSELY, Conversely, Inc., PMB #121, 3053 Fillmore St., San Francisco CA 94123-4009. E-mail: writers@conversely.com. Website: www.conversely.com. **Contact:** Alejandro Gutierrez, editor. **60-80% freelance written.** Quarterly online literary magazine covering relationships between women and men. "*Conversely* is dedicated to exploring relationships between women and men—every stage, every aspect—through different forms of writing: essays, memoirs, fiction. Our audience is both female and male, mostly in the 18-35 year age range. We look for writing that is intelligent, provocative, and witty; we look for topics that are original and appealing to our readers." Estab. 2000. Pays on publication. Publishes ms an average of 3 months after acceptance. Byline given. Offers negotiable kill fee. electronic rights (90 days exclusive; nonexclusive thereafter). Also buys one-time, nonexclusive anthology rights. Editorial lead time 3 months. Submit seasonal material 3 months in advance. Accepts queries by e-mail. Accepts simultaneous submissions. Responds in 2 weeks to queries; 2 months to mss. Sample copy and writer's guidelines online.

• Only accepts e-mail queries.

O→ Break in with "personal opinion essays for our 'Antidote' department."

Nonfiction: Essays, opinion, personal experience. "No how-to or anything that very overtly tries to teach or tell readers what to do or how to behave. No explicit sex." **Buys 15-20 mss/year.** Send complete ms. Length: 750-3,000 words. **Pays $100-200.** Sometimes pays expenses of writers on assignment.

Photos: State availability with submission. Negotiates payment individually.

Fiction: Mainstream. No erotica, science fiction, gothic, romance. **Buys 5-10 mss/year.** Send complete ms. Length: 750-3,000 words. **Pays $100-200.**

Tips: "We value writing that is original in its choice of subject and/or its approach to it. We prefer work that explores different and/or unconventional, yet engaging, aspects of relationships. We seek writing that achieves a balance between 'intelligent,' 'provocative,' and 'witty.' Intelligent, as in complex and sophisticated. Provocative, as in it challenges the reader by presenting unexpected or nontraditional viewpoints. Witty, as in it uses clever humor, and the writing doesn't take itself too seriously. We turn down many otherwise fine submissions that discuss clichéd topics. We also turn down many well-written pieces in which the 'voice' is not right for us."

$ $ DIVORCE MAGAZINE, Segue Esprit, Inc., 145 Front St., Suite 301, Toronto, Ontario M5A 1E3, Canada. E-mail: editors@divorcemag.com. Website: www.DivorceMagazine.com. **Contact:** Diana Shepherd, editor. Quarterly magazine covering separation and divorce. "We have 4 quarterly editions: New York/New Jersey, Illinois, Southern California, and Ontario. *Divorce Magazine* is designed to help people cope with the difficult transition of separation and divorce. Our mandate is to provide a unique, friendly resource of vital information and timely advice to help our readers survive—even thrive—during their divorce." Estab. 1996. Circ. 104,000. Pays on publication.

The online version contains material not found in the print edition.

$ $ MARRIAGE PARTNERSHIP, Christianity Today International, 465 Gundersen Dr., Carol Stream IL 60188. Fax: (630)260-0114. E-mail: mp@marriagepartnership.com. Website: www.marriagepartnership.com. Executive Editor: Michael G. Maudlin; Managing Editor: Ginger E. Kolbaba. **Contact:** Raelinn Eickhoff, editorial coordinator. **50% freelance written.** Quarterly magazine covering Christian marriages. "Our readers are married Christians. Writers must understand our readers." Estab. 1988. Circ. 55,000. **Pays on acceptance.** Publishes ms an average of 1 month after acceptance. Byline given. Offers 50% kill fee. Buys first North American serial rights. Editorial lead time 6 months. Submit seasonal material 1 year in advance. Accepts queries by mail, e-mail, fax. Responds in 10 weeks to queries; 2 months to mss. Sample copy for $5 or online. Writer's guidelines free.

Nonfiction: Book excerpts, essays, how-to, humor, inspirational, interview/profile, opinion, personal experience, religious. **Buys 20 mss/year.** Query with or without published clips. Length: 1,200-2,300 words. **Pays 15-30¢/word for assigned articles; 15¢/word for unsolicited articles.** Pays expenses of writers on assignment.

Columns/Departments: View Point (opinion), 1,000 words; Soul to Soul (inspirational), 1,500 words; Work It Out (problem-solving), 1,000 words. **Buys 10 mss/year.** Query with or without published clips. **Pays 15-30¢/word.**

Tips: "Think of topics with a fresh slant. Be ever mindful of our readers. Writers who can communicate with freshness, clarity, and insight will receive serious consideration. We are looking for writers who are willing to candidly speak about their own marriages. We strongly urge writers who are interested in contributing to *Marriage Partnership* to read several issues to become thoroughly acquainted with our tone and slant."

RELIGIOUS

Religious magazines focus on a variety of subjects, styles, and beliefs. Most are sectarian, but a number approach topics such as public policy, international affairs, and contemporary society from a nondenominational perspective. Fewer religious publications are considering poems and personal experience articles, but many emphasize special ministries to singles, seniors or other special interest groups. Such diversity makes reading each magazine essential for the writer hoping to break in. Educational and inspirational material of interest to church members, workers and leaders within a denomination or religion is needed by the publications in this category. Religious magazines for children and teenagers can be found in the Juvenile and Teen & Young Adult sections. Other religious publications can be found in the Contemporary Culture and Ethnic/Minority sections as well. Spiritual topics are also addressed in the Astrology, Metaphysical and New Age section as well as in the Health & Fitness section. Publications intended to assist professional religious workers in teaching and managing church affairs are classified in Church Administration & Ministry in the Trade section.

$ALIVE NOW, 1908 Grand Ave., P.O. Box 340004, Nashville TN 37203-0004. Website: www.alivenow.org. Bimonthly thematic magazine for a general Christian audience interested in reflection and meditation. Circ. 70,000. Writer's guidelines and themes available on website or with SASE.
Poetry: Avant-garde, free verse. Length: 10-45 lines.

$AMERICA, 106 W. 56th St., New York NY 10019. (212)581-4640. Fax: (212)399-3596. E-mail: articles@americamagazine.org. Website: www.americamagazine.org. **Contact:** The Rev. Thomas J. Reese, editor. Published weekly for adult, educated, largely Roman Catholic audience. Estab. 1909. **Pays on acceptance.** Byline given. Buys all rights. Responds in 3 weeks to queries. Writer's guidelines free, by mail or online.
Nonfiction: "We publish a wide variety of material on religion, politics, economics, ecology, and so forth. We are not a parochial publication, but almost all pieces make some moral or religious point." Articles on theology, spirituality, current political, social issues. "We are not interested in purely informational pieces or personal narratives which are self-contained and have no larger moral interest." Length: 1,500-2,000 words. **Pays $50-300.**
Poetry: Only 10-12 poems published a year, thousands turned down. Paul Mariani, poetry editor. **Buys 10-12 poems/year.** Length: 15-30 lines.

$$☆ ANGELS ON EARTH, Guideposts, 16 E. 34th St., New York NY 10016. (212)251-8100. E-mail: angelsedtr@guideposts.org. **Contact:** Colleen Hughes, editor-in-chief. **90% freelance written.** Bimonthly magazine. "*Angels on Earth* publishes true stories about God's messengers at work in today's world. We are interested in stories of heavenly angels and stories involving humans who have played angelic roles in daily life." Estab. 1995. Circ. 550,000. Pays on publication. Buys all rights. Editorial lead time 6 months. Submit seasonal material 6 months in advance. Accepts queries by mail. Responds in 3 months to queries.
Nonfiction: True, inspirational, personal experience (most stories are first-person experiences but can be ghost-written). Nothing that directly preaches, no how-to's. **Buys 100 mss/year.** Send complete ms with SASE. Length: 100-2,000 words. **Pays $25-500.**
Photos: State availability with submission. Buys one-time rights. Offers no additional payments for photos accepted with ms.
Columns/Departments: Meg Belviso, departments editor. Earning Their Wings (unusual stories of good deeds worth imitating); Only Human? (Is the angelic character a human being? The narrator is pleasantly unsure and so is the reader), both 350 words. **Pays $50-100**. Messages (brief, mysterious happenings, or letters describing how a specific article helped you). **Pays $25. Buys 50 mss/year.** Send complete ms with SASE.

$THE ANNALS OF SAINT ANNE DE BEAUPRÉ, Redemptorist Fathers, P.O. Box 1000, St. Anne De Beaupré, Quebec G0A 3C0, Canada. (418)827-4538. Fax: (418)827-4530. Editor: Father Bernard Mercier, CSs.R. **Contact:** Father Roch Achard, managing editor. **20% freelance written.** Monthly religious magazine. "Our mission statement includes dedication to Christian family values and devotion to St. Anne." Estab. 1885. Circ. 45,000. **Pays on acceptance.** Buys first rights. Editorial lead time 6 months. Submit seasonal material 6 months in advance. Responds in 1 month to queries. Sample copy and writer's guidelines for 8½×11 SAE and IRCs.
Nonfiction: Inspirational, religious. **Buys 150 mss/year.** Send complete ms. Length: 500-1,500 words. **Pays 3-4¢/word, plus 3 copies.**
Fiction: Religious, inspirational. "No senseless mockery." **Buys 100 mss/year.** Send complete ms. Length: 500-1,500 words. **Pays 3-4¢/word.**
Tips: "Write something inspirational with spiritual thrust. Reporting rather than analysis is simply not remarkable. Each article must have a spiritual theme. Please only submit first North American rights manuscripts with the rights clearly stated. We maintain an article bank and pick from it for each month's needs which loosely follows the religious themes for each month. Right now, our needs lean toward nonfiction of approximately 1,100 words."

$THE ASSOCIATE REFORMED PRESBYTERIAN, Associate Reformed Presbyterian General Synod, 1 Cleveland St., Suite 110, Greenville SC 29601-3696. (864)232-8297, ext. 237. Fax: (864)271-3729. E-mail: arpmaged@arpsynod.org. Website: www.arpsynod.org. **Contact:** Ben Johnston, editor. **5% freelance written.** Works with a small number of new/unpublished writers each year. Christian magazine serving a conservative, evangelical, and Reformed denomination. Estab. 1976. Circ. 6,000. **Pays on acceptance.** Publishes ms an average of 4 months after acceptance. Byline given. Not copyrighted. Buys first, one-time, second serial (reprint) rights. Submit seasonal material 4 months in advance. Accepts queries by mail, e-mail, fax. Accepts simultaneous submissions. Responds in 1 month to queries. Sample copy for $1.50. Writer's guidelines for #10 SASE.
Nonfiction: Book excerpts, essays, inspirational, opinion, personal experience, religious. **Buys 10-15 mss/year.** Query. Length: 400-2,000 words. **Pays $25-75.**
Reprints: Send information about when and where the article previously appeared. Pays 100% of amount paid for an original article.
Photos: State availability with submission. Buys one-time rights. Offers $25 maximum/photo. Captions, identification of subjects required.
Fiction: Religious, children's. "Currently overstocked." **Pays $50 maximum.**
Tips: "Feature articles are the area of our publication most open to freelancers. Focus on a contemporary problem and offer Bible-based solutions to it. Provide information that would help a Christian struggling in his daily walk. Writers should understand that we are denominational, conservative, evangelical, Reformed, and Presbyterian. A writer who appreciates these nuances would stand a much better chance of being published here than one who does not."

$ BIBLE ADVOCATE, Bible Advocate Press, Church of God (Seventh Day), P.O. Box 33677, Denver CO 80233. (303)452-7973. E-mail: BibleAdvocate@cog7.org/BA/. Website: www.cog7.org/BA/. Editor: Calvin Burrell. **Contact:** Sherri Langton, associate editor. **25% freelance written.** Religious magazine published 10 times/year. "Our purpose is to advocate the Bible and represent the Church of God (Seventh Day) to a Christian audience." Estab. 1863. Circ. 13,500. Pays on publication. Publishes ms an average of 9 months after acceptance. Byline given. Offers 50% kill fee. Buys first, second serial (reprint), electronic rights. Editorial lead time 3 months. Submit seasonal material 6 months in advance. Accepts queries by mail, e-mail. Accepts simultaneous submissions. Responds in 2 months to queries. Sample copy for 9×12 SAE and 3 first-class stamps. Writer's guidelines online.

Nonfiction: Inspirational, opinion, personal experience, religious, Biblical studies. No articles on Christmas or Easter. **Buys 20-25 mss/year.** Send complete ms and SASE. Length: 1,500 words. **Pays $25-55.**

Reprints: Send typed ms with rights for sale noted.

Photos: Send photos with submission. Reviews prints. Offers payment for photos accepted with ms. Identification of subjects required.

Columns/Departments: Viewpoint (opinion), 600-700 words. **Buys 3 mss/year.** Send complete ms and SASE. **No payment for opinion pieces.**

Poetry: Free verse, traditional. No avant-garde. **Buys 10-12 poems/year.** Submit maximum 5 poems. Length: 5-20 lines. **Pays $20.**

Fillers: Anecdotes, facts. **Buys 5/year.** Length: 50-400 words. **Pays $10-20.**

Tips: "Be fresh, not preachy! We're trying to reach a younger audience now, so think how you can cover contemporary and biblical topics with this audience in mind. Articles must be in keeping with the doctrinal understanding of the Church of God (Seventh Day). Therefore, the writer should become familiar with what the Church generally accepts as truth as set forth in its doctrinal beliefs. We reserve the right to edit manuscripts to fit our space requirements, doctrinal stands and church terminology. Significant changes are referred to writers for approval. No fax or handwritten submissions, please."

$ $ CATHOLIC FORESTER, Catholic Order of Foresters, 355 Shuman Blvd., P.O. Box 3012, Naperville IL 60566-7012. Fax: (630)983-3384. E-mail: cofpr@aol.com. Website: www.catholicforester.com. Editor: Mary Ann File. **Contact:** Patricia Baron, associate editor. **20% freelance written.** Bimonthly magazine for members of the Catholic Order of Foresters, a fraternal insurance benefit society. *Catholic Forester* articles cover varied topics to create a balanced issue for the purpose of informing, educating, and entertaining our readers. Circ. 100,000. **Pays on acceptance.** Buys first North American serial rights. Editorial lead time 6 months. Submit seasonal material 6 months in advance. Responds in 3 months to mss. Sample copy for 9×12 SAE and 4 first-class stamps. Writer's guidelines for #10 SASE.

Nonfiction: Inspirational, religious, travel, health, parenting, financial, money management, humor. **Buys 12-16 mss/year.** Send complete ms by mail or fax. Rejected material will not be returned without accompanying SASE. Length: 500-1,500 words. **Pays 20¢/word.**

Photos: State availability with submission. Reviews transparencies. Buys one-time rights. Negotiates payment individually.

Fiction: Humorous, religious. **Buys 12-16 mss/year.** Length: 500-1,500 words. **Pays 20¢/word.**

Poetry: Light verse, traditional. **Buys 3 poems/year.** Length: 15 lines maximum. **Pays 20¢/word.**

Tips: "Our audience includes a broad age spectrum, ranging from youth to seniors. Nonfiction topics that appeal to our members include health and wellness, money management and budgeting, parenting and family life, interesting travels, insurance, nostalgia, and humor. A good children's story with a positive lesson or message would rate high on our list."

$ $ CATHOLIC NEAR EAST MAGAZINE, Catholic Near East Welfare Association, 1011 First Ave., New York NY 10022-4195. (212)826-1480. Fax: (212)826-8979. Website: www.cnewa.org. Executive Editor: Michael La Civita. **Contact:** Helen C. Packard, assistant editor. **50% freelance written.** Bimonthly magazine for a Catholic audience with interest in the Near East, particularly its current religious, cultural, and political aspects. Estab. 1974. Circ. 100,000. Pays on publication. Publishes ms an average of 6 months after acceptance. Byline given. Buys all rights. Accepts queries by mail, fax. Responds in 2 months to queries. Sample copy and writer's guidelines for 7½×10½ SAE with 2 first-class stamps.

Nonfiction: "Cultural, devotional, political, historical material on the Near East, with an emphasis on the Eastern Christian churches. Style should be simple, factual, concise. Articles must stem from personal acquaintance with subject matter, or thorough up-to-date research." Length: 1,200-1,800 words. **Pays 20¢/edited word.**

Photos: "Photographs to accompany manuscript are welcome; they should illustrate the people, places, ceremonies, etc. which are described in the article. We prefer color transparencies but occasionally use b&w." Pay varies depending on use—scale from $50-300.

Tips: "We are interested in current events in the Near East as they affect the cultural, political, and religious lives of the people."

$ CATHOLIC SENTINEL, Oregon Catholic Press, P.O. Box 18030, Portland OR 97218. (503)281-1191. Fax: (503)282-3486. E-mail: sentinel@ocp.org. Website: www.sentinel.org. **Contact:** Bob Pfohman, editor. **10% freelance written.** "Catholic diocesan newspaper about and for the Catholic community in Oregon. All articles must have Catholic and Oregon connections." Estab. 1870. Circ. 17,000. Pays on publication. Publishes ms an average of 1 month after acceptance. Byline given. Offers 100% kill fee. Not copyrighted. Buys first rights. Editorial lead time 1 month. Submit seasonal material 2 months in advance. Accepts queries by mail, e-mail, fax, phone. Responds in 6 weeks to mss. Sample copy for 75¢ and SAE with 3 first-class stamps.

Nonfiction: Historical/nostalgic (Oregon Catholic history), interview/profile (Oregon Catholics), opinion (no payment), personal experience, photo feature, religious, travel (no payment). **Buys 5-10 mss/year.** Query for features and personal experiences; send complete ms for opinion pieces. Length: 750-1,500 words. **Pays $25-150 for assigned articles; $10-50 for unsolicited articles.** Sometimes pays expenses of writers on assignment.

Reprints: Accepts previously published submissions.

Photos: State availability with submission. Reviews prints. Buys one-time rights. Negotiates payment individually. Captions, identification of subjects required.

Columns/Departments: Buys 10-15 mss/year. Query or send complete ms. **Pays $0-25.**

N $ $ **CELEBRATE LIFE**, American Life League, P.O. Box 1350, Stafford VA 22555. (540)659-4171. Fax: (540)659-2586. E-mail: clmag@all.org. Website: www.all.org/. Editor: Elizabeth Daub. **Contact:** Suzanne Bergeron, assistant editor. **50% freelance written.** Bimonthly educational magazine covering pro-life education and human interest. "We are a religious-based publication specializing in pro-life education through human-interest stories and investigative exposés. Our purpose is to inspire, encourage, motivate, and educate pro-life individuals and activists." Estab. 1979. Circ. 70,000. Pays on publication. Byline given. Offers 25% kill fee. Buys first, second serial (reprint) rights, or makes work-for-hire assignments. Submit seasonal material 4 months in advance. Accepts queries by mail, e-mail, fax. Accepts previously published material. Accepts simultaneous submissions. Responds in 6 months to mss. Sample copy for 9×12 SAE SAE and 4 first-class stamps. Writer's guidelines free.

Break in with "interview-based human interest or investigative exposés."

Nonfiction: "No fiction, book reviews, poetry, allegory, devotionals." **Buys 40 mss/year.** Query with published clips or send complete ms. Length: 300-1,500 words.

Photos: Buys one-time rights. Identification of subjects required.

Fillers: Newsbreaks. **Buys 5/year.** Length: 75-200 words. **Pays $10.**

Online version of magazine: www.all.org/celebrate-life/indexht.

Tips: "We look for inspiring, educational, or motivational human-interest stories. We are religious based and no exceptions pro-life. All articles must have agreement with the principles expressed in Pope John Paul II's encyclical *Evangelium Vitae*. Our common themes include: abortion, post-abortion healing, sidewalk counseling, adoption, and contraception."

$ $ **THE CHRISTIAN CENTURY**, Christian Century Foundation, 104 S. Michigan Ave., Suite 700, Chicago IL 60605-1150. (312)263-7510. Fax: (312)263-7540. E-mail: main@christiancentury.org. Website: www.christiancentury.org. **Contact:** David Heim, executive editor. **90% freelance written.** Eager to work with new/unpublished writers. Biweekly magazine for ecumenically-minded, progressive Protestant church people, both clergy and lay. "Authors must have a critical and analytical perspective on the church and be familiar with contemporary theological discussion." Estab. 1884. Circ. 30,000. Pays on publication. Publishes ms an average of 3 months after acceptance. Byline given. Buys all rights. Editorial lead time 1 month. Submit seasonal material 4 months in advance. Accepts queries by mail. Accepts simultaneous submissions. Responds in 1 week to queries; 2 months to mss. Sample copy for $3. Writer's guidelines online.

Nonfiction: "We use articles dealing with social problems, ethical dilemmas, political issues, international affairs, and the arts, as well as with theological and ecclesiastical matters. We focus on issues of church and society, and church and culture." Essays, humor, interview/profile, opinion, religious. No inspirational. **Buys 150 mss/year.** Send complete ms; query appreciated, but not essential. Length: 1,000-3,000 words. **Pays $75-200 for assigned articles; $75-150 for unsolicited articles.**

Photos: State availability with submission. Reviews any size prints. Buys one-time rights. Offers $25-100/photo.

Fiction: Humorous, religious, slice-of-life vignettes. No moralistic, unrealistic fiction. **Buys 4 mss/year.** Send complete ms. Length: 1,000-3,000 words. **Pays $75-200.**

Poetry: Jill Pelaez Baumgaertner, poetry editor. Avant-garde, free verse, haiku, traditional. No sentimental or didactic poetry. **Buys 50 poems/year.** Length: 20 lines. **Pays $50.**

Tips: "We seek manuscripts that articulate the public meaning of faith, bringing the resources of religious tradition to bear on such topics as poverty, human rights, economic justice, international relations, national priorities, and popular culture. We are equally interested in articles that probe classical theological themes. We welcome articles that find fresh meaning in old traditions and which adapt or apply religious traditions to new circumstances. Authors should assume that readers are familiar with main themes in Christian history and theology; are unthreatened by the historical-critical study of the Bible; and are already engaged in relating faith to social and political issues. Many of our readers are ministers or teachers of religion at the college level."

$ **CHRISTIAN COURIER**, Reformed Faith Witness, 4-261 Martindale Rd., St. Catharines, Ontario L2W 1A1, Canada. (905)682-8311. Fax: (905)682-8313. E-mail: cceditor@aol.com. **Contact:** Harry Der Nederlanden, editor. **20% freelance written.** Biweekly newspaper covering news of importance to Christians, comments, and features. "We assume a Christian perspective which acknowledges that this world belongs to God and that human beings are invited to serve God in every area of society." Estab. 1945. Circ. 4,000. Pays 30 days after publication. Publishes ms an average of 2 months after acceptance. Byline given. Not copyrighted. Editorial lead time 1 month. Submit seasonal material 3 months in advance. Accepts previously published material. Accepts simultaneous submissions. Responds only if material accepted.

O→ Break in by "addressing issues from a clearly Biblical worldview without becoming moralistic, pietistic, or didactic."

Nonfiction: Essays, historical/nostalgic, humor, inspirational, interview/profile, opinion, personal experience, religious, ideas, trends, developments in science and technology. **Buys 40 mss/year.** Send complete ms. Length: 500-1,500 words. **Pays $50-100 for assigned articles; $25-75 for unsolicited articles.**

Photos: State availability with submission. Pays $20/photo.

$ $ CHRISTIAN HOME & SCHOOL, Christian Schools International, 3350 E. Paris Ave. SE, Grand Rapids MI 49512. (616)957-1070, ext. 239. Fax: (616)957-5022. E-mail: RogerS@CSIonline.org. Website: www.CSIonline.org/chs. Executive Editor: Gordon L. Bordewyk. **Contact:** Roger Schmurr, senior editor. **30% freelance written.** Works with a small number of new/unpublished writers each year. Bimonthly magazine covering family life and Christian education. "*Christian Home & School* is designed for parents in the United States and Canada who send their children to Christian schools and are concerned about the challenges facing Christian families today. These readers expect a mature, Biblical perspective in the articles, not just a Bible verse tacked onto the end." Estab. 1922. Circ. 65,000. Pays on publication. Publishes ms an average of 4 months after acceptance. Byline given. Buys first North American serial rights. Submit seasonal material 4 months in advance. Accepts queries by mail, e-mail. Responds in 1 month to queries. Sample copy and writer's guidelines for 9×12 SAE with 4 first-class stamps. Writer's guidelines only for #10 SASE or online.

● The editor reports an interest in seeing articles on how to experience and express forgiveness in your home, raise polite kids in a rude world, and good educational practices in Christian schools.

O→ Break in by picking a contemporary parenting situation/problem, and writing to Christian parents.

Nonfiction: "We publish features on issues that affect the home and school and profiles on interesting individuals, providing that the profile appeals to our readers and is not a tribute or eulogy of that person." Book excerpts, interview/profile, opinion, personal experience, articles on parenting and school life. **Buys 40 mss/year.** Send complete ms. Length: 1,000-2,000 words. **Pays $125-200.**

Photos: "If you have any color photos appropriate for your article, send them along."

Tips: "Features are the area most open to freelancers. We are publishing articles that deal with contemporary issues that affect parents. Use an informal easy-to-read style rather than a philosophical, academic tone. Try to incorporate vivid imagery and concrete, practical examples from real life. We look for manuscripts with a mature Christian perspective."

$ $ CHRISTIAN READER, Stories of Faith, Hope, and God's Love, Christianity Today, 465 Gundersen Dr., Carol Stream IL 60188. (630)260-6200. Fax: (630)260-0114. E-mail: creditor@christianreader.net. Website: www.christianreader.net. Managing Editor: Bonne Steffen. **Contact:** Cynthia Thomas, editorial coordinator. **25% freelance written.** Bimonthly magazine for adult evangelical Christian audience. Estab. 1963. Circ. 185,000. Pays on acceptance; on publication for humor pieces. Byline given. Editorial lead time 5 months. Submit seasonal material 8 months in advance. Accepts queries by mail. Accepts simultaneous submissions. Responds in 1 month to queries. Sample copy for 5×8 SAE and 4 first-class stamps. Writer's guidelines for #10 SASE.

Nonfiction: Book excerpts, general interest, historical/nostalgic, humor, inspirational, interview/profile, personal experience, photo feature, religious. **Buys 100-125 mss/year.** Query with or without published clips or send complete ms. Length: 250-1,500 words. **Pays $125-600 depending on length.** Pays expenses of writers on assignment.

Reprints: Send tearsheet, photocopy or typed ms with rights for sale noted and information about when and where the material previously appeared. Pays 35-50% of amount paid for an original article.

Photos: Send photos with submission. Reviews transparencies, prints. Buys one-time rights. Negotiates payment individually. Identification of subjects required.

Columns/Departments: Lite Fare (adult church humor), 50-200 words; Kids of the Kingdom (kids say and do funny things), 50-200 words; Rolling Down the Aisle (humorous wedding tales), 50-200 words. **Buys 50-75 mss/year.** Send complete ms. **Pays $25-35.**

Fillers: Anecdotes, short fillers. **Buys 10-20/year.** Length: 100-250 words. **Pays $35.**

Tips: "Most of our articles are reprints or staff-written. Freelance competition is keen, so tailor submissions to meet our needs by observing the following: The *Christian Reader* audience is truly a general interest one, including men and women, urban professionals and rural homemakers, adults of every age and marital status, and Christians of every church affiliation. We seek to publish a magazine that people from the variety of ethnic groups in North America will find interesting and relevant."

$ THE CHRISTIAN RESPONSE, A Newsletter for Concerned Christians, HAPCO Industries, P.O. Box 125, Staples MN 56479-0125. (218)894-1165. E-mail: hapco@brainerd.net. Website: www.brainerd.net/~hapco/. **Contact:** Hap Corbett, editor. **10% freelance written.** Bimonthly newsletter "responding to anti-Christian bias from a Christian perspective." Estab. 1993. Circ. 300. **Pays on acceptance.** Publishes ms an average of 2 months after acceptance. Byline given. Buys one-time rights. Editorial lead time 2 months. Submit seasonal material 6 months in advance. Accepts queries by mail, e-mail, phone. Responds in 2 weeks to queries. Sample copy for $1 (or 3 first-class stamps). Writer's guidelines for #10 SASE.

Nonfiction: Examples of anti-Christian bias in America. **Buys 4-6 mss/year.** Send complete ms. Length: 200-750 words. **Pays $5-20.**

Fillers: Anecdotes, facts, newsbreaks. **Buys 2-4/year/year.** Length: 150 words. **Pays $5-20.**
Tips: "We want exposés of anti-Christian bias or denial of civil rights to people because of religious beliefs."

$ $ CHRISTIANITY TODAY, 465 Gundersen Dr., Carol Stream IL 60188-2498. (630)260-6200. Fax: (630)260-8428. E-mail: CTEditor@ChristianityToday.com. Website: www.christianitytoday.com. **Contact:** Mark Galli, managing editor. **80% freelance written.** Works with a small number of new/unpublished writers each year. Biweekly magazine emphasizing orthodox, evangelical religion, "covers Christian doctrine, issues, trends, and current events and news from a Christian perspective. It provides a forum for the expression of evangelical conviction in theology, evangelism, church life, cultural life, and society. Special features include issues of the day, books, films, missions, schools, music, and services available to the Christian market." Estab. 1956. Circ. 154,000. Publishes ms an average of 6 months after acceptance. Buys first rights. Submit seasonal material at least 8 months in advance. Accepts queries by mail, e-mail, fax. Responds in 3 months to queries. Sample copy and writer's guidelines for 9×12 SAE with 3 first-class stamps.
Nonfiction: Book excerpts, essays, interview/profile, opinion, theological, ethical, historical, informational (not merely inspirational). **Buys 96 mss/year.** *Query only.* Unsolicited mss not accepted and not returned. Length: 1,000-4,000 words. **Pays negotiable rates.** Sometimes pays expenses of writers on assignment.
Reprints: Accepts previously published submissions. Pays 25% of amount paid for an original article.
Columns/Departments: The CT Review (books, the arts, and popular culture). Length: 900-1,000 words. **Buys 7 mss/year.** *Query only.*
■ The online magazine carries original content not found in the print edition. Contact: Ted Olsen, online editor.
Tips: "We are developing more of our own manuscripts and requiring a much more professional quality from others. Queries without SASE will not be answered and manuscripts not containing SASE will not be returned."

$ $ CHRYSALIS READER, R.R. 1, Box 4510, Dillwyn VA 23936. E-mail: chrysalis@hovac.com. Website: www.swedenborg.com. Managing Editor: Susanna van Rensselaer. **Contact:** Richard Butterworth, editorial associate. **90% freelance written.** Annual literary magazine on spiritually related topics. "*It is very important to send for writer's guidelines and sample copies before submitting.* Content of fiction, articles, reviews, poetry, etc., should be directly focused on that issue's theme and directed to the educated, intellectually curious reader." Estab. 1985. Circ. 3,000. Pays at page-proof stage. Publishes ms an average of 9 months after acceptance. Byline given. Buys first rights, makes work-for-hire assignments. Accepts queries by mail, e-mail. Responds in 1 month to queries; 4 months to mss. Sample copy for $10 and 8½×11 SAE. Writer's guidelines and copy deadlines for SASE or by e-mail.
• E-mail for themes and guidelines (no mss will be accepted by e-mail).
Nonfiction: Upcoming themes: Serendipity (2002); Spiritual Well-Being (2003); Letting Go (2004). Essays, interview/profile. **Buys 20 mss/year.** Query. Length: 2,500-3,500 words. **Pays $50-250 for assigned articles; $50-150 for unsolicited articles.**
Photos: Send suggestions for illustrations with submission. Buys original artwork for cover and inside copy; b&w illustrations related to theme; **pays $25-150**. Buys one-time rights. Offers no additional payment for photos accepted with ms. Captions, identification of subjects required.
Fiction: Robert Tucker, fiction editor. Short fiction more likely to be published. Adventure, experimental, historical, mainstream, mystery, science fiction. **Buys 10 mss/year.** Query. Length: 2,500-3,500 words. **Pays $50-150.**
Poetry: Rob Lawson, senior editor. Avant-garde and traditional, *but not religious.* **Buys 15 poems/year.** Submit maximum 6 poems. **Pays $25.**

$ $ COLUMBIA, 1 Columbus Plaza, New Haven CT 06510. (203)772-2130. Fax: (203)777-0114. E-mail: tim.hickey@kofc-supreme.com. Website: www.kofc.org. **Contact:** Tim S. Hickey, editor. Monthly magazine for Catholic families. Caters primarily to members of the Knights of Columbus. Estab. 1921. Circ. 1,500,000. **Pays on acceptance.** Buys first North American serial rights. Accepts queries by mail, e-mail, fax. Sample copy and writer's guidelines free.
Nonfiction: Fact articles directed to the Catholic layman and his family dealing with current events, social problems, Catholic apostolic activities, education, ecumenism, rearing a family, literature, science, arts, sports and leisure. No reprints, poetry, or cartoons. **Buys 20 mss/year.** Query with SASE. Length: 1,000-1,500 words. **Pays $300-600.**
■ The online magazine carries original content not found in the print edition. Contact: Tim S. Hickey, online editor.
Tips: "Few unsolicited manuscripts are accepted."

$ CONSCIENCE, A Newsjournal of Prochoice Catholic Opinion, Catholics for a Free Choice, 1436 U St. NW, Suite 301, Washington DC 20009-3997. (202)986-6093. E-mail: conscience@catholicsforchoice.org. Website: www.catholicsforchoice.org. **Contact:** Editor. **60% freelance written.** Sometimes works with new/unpublished writers. Quarterly newsjournal covering reproductive health and rights, including but not limited to abortion rights in the church, and church-state issues in US and worldwide. "A feminist, pro-choice perspective is a must, and knowledge of Christianity and specifically Catholicism is helpful." Estab. 1980. Circ. 12,000. Pays on publication. Publishes ms an average of 4 months after acceptance. Byline given. Buys first North American serial rights, makes work-for-hire assignments. Accepts queries by mail, e-mail. Responds in 4 months to queries. Sample copy for 9×12 SAE and 4 first-class stamps. Writer's guidelines for #10 SASE.
Nonfiction: Especially needs material that recognizes the complexity of reproductive issues and decisions, and offers original, honest insight. "Writers should be aware that we are a nonprofit organization." Book excerpts, interview/profile, opinion, personal experience (a small amount), issue analysis. **Buys 4-8 mss/year.** Query with published clips or send complete ms. Length: 1,500-3,500 words. **Pays $150-200.**

Reprints: Send typed ms with rights for sale noted and information about when and where the material previously appeared. Pays 20-30% of amount paid for an original article.

Photos: Prefers b&w prints. State availability with submission. Identification of subjects required.

Columns/Departments: Book reviews, 600-1,200 words. **Buys 4-8 mss/year. Pays $50-75.**

Tips: "Say something new on the issue of abortion, or sexuality, or the role of religion or the Catholic church, or women's status in the church. Thoughtful, well-researched, and well-argued articles needed. The most frequent mistakes made by writers in submitting an article to us are lack of originality and wordiness."

$ $ CORNERSTONE, Cornerstone Communications, Inc., 939 W. Wilson, Chicago IL 60640-5718. (773)561-2450 ext. 2080. Fax: (773)989-2076. E-mail: poetry@cornerstonemag.com. Website: www.cornerstonemag.com. Editor: Jon Trott. **Contact:** Submissions Editor. **10% freelance written.** Eager to work with new/unpublished writers. Irregularly published magazine covering contemporary issues in the light of Evangelical Christianity. Estab. 1972. Pays after publication. Byline given. Buys first North American serial rights. Submit seasonal material 6 months in advance. Accepts simultaneous submissions. Does not return mss. Sample copy and writer's guidelines for 8½ × 11 SAE with 5 first-class stamps.

- "We will contact you *only* if your work is accepted for possible publication. We *encourage* simultaneous submissions because we take so long to get back to people! E-mail all poetry submissions to poetry@cornerstonemag.com (if e-mail is unavailable to you, we accept hard copies). Send no queries."

Poetry: "No limits *except* for epic poetry ("We've not the room!"). Avant-garde, free verse, haiku, light verse, traditional. **Buys 5-10 poems/year.** Submit maximum 5 poems. **Payment negotiated. 1-15 lines: $10; over 15 lines: $25.**

The online version carries original content not found in the print edition. Contact: Jon Trott, online editor.

Tips: "A display of creativity which expresses a biblical world view without clichés or cheap shots at non-Christians is the ideal. We are known as one of the most avant-garde magazines in the Christian market, yet attempt to express orthodox beliefs in today's language. *Any* writer who does this well may be published by *Cornerstone*."

$ THE COVENANT COMPANION, Covenant Publications of the Evangelical Covenant Church, 5101 N. Francisco Ave., Chicago IL 60625. (773)784-3000. Fax: (773)784-4366. E-mail: communication@covchurch.org. Website: www.covchurch.org. **Contact:** Jane K. Swanson-Nystrom, editor. **10-15% freelance written.** "As the official monthly periodical of the Evangelical Covenant Church, we seek to inform the denomination we serve and encourage dialogue on issues within the church and in our society." Circ. 20,000. Publishes ms an average of 2 months after acceptance. Byline given. Submit seasonal material 4 months in advance. Accepts queries by mail, e-mail. Accepts simultaneous submissions. Writer's guidelines for #10 SASE.

Nonfiction: Inspirational, religious, Contemporary issues. **Buys 40 mss/year.** Send complete ms. Unused mss returned only if accompanied by SASE. Length: 500-2,000 words. **Pays $50-100 for assigned articles.**

Reprints: Send tearsheet, photocopy or typed ms with rights for sale noted and information about when and where the material previously appeared.

Photos: Send photos with submission. Reviews prints. Buys one-time rights. Offers no additional payment for photos accepted with ms. Identification of subjects required.

$ $ DECISION, Billy Graham Evangelistic Association, 1300 Harmon Place, Minneapolis MN 55403-1988. (612)338-0500. Fax: (612)335-1299. E-mail: submissions@bgea.org. Website: www.decisionmag.org. Editor: Kersten Beckstrom. **Contact:** Bob Paulson, associate editor. **10% freelance written.** Works each year with small number of new/unpublished writers, as well as a solid stable of experienced writers. Monthly magazine with a mission "to set forth to every reader the Good News of salvation in Jesus Christ with such vividness and clarity that he or she will be drawn to make a commitment to Christ; to encourage, teach, and strengthen Christians." Estab. 1960. Circ. 1,400,000. Pays on publication. Publishes ms an average of up to 18 months after acceptance. Byline given. Offers 50% kill fee. Buys first rights. Assigns work-for-hire mss, articles, projects. Editorial lead time 1 year. Submit seasonal material 10 months in advance. Responds in 3 months to mss. Sample copy for 9×12 SAE and 4 first-class stamps. Writer's guidelines for #10 SASE.

- Include telephone number with submission.

"The best way to break into our publication is to submit an article that has some connection to the Billy Graham Evangelistic Association or Samaritan's Purse, but also has strong takeaway for the personal lives of the readers."

Nonfiction: How-to, inspirational, personal experience, religious, motivational. **Buys approximately 20 mss/year.** Send complete ms. Length: 400-1,500 words. **Pays $30-260.** Pays expenses of writers on assignment.

Photos: State availability with submission. Reviews prints. Buys one-time rights. Captions, identification of subjects, model releases required.

Columns/Departments: Where Are They Now? (people who have become Christians through Billy Graham Ministries), 500-600 words. **Buys 12 mss/year.** Send complete ms. **Pays $85.**

Poetry: Amanda Knoke, assistant editor. Free verse, light verse, traditional. **Buys 6 poems/year.** Submit maximum 7 poems. Length: 4-16 lines. **Pays 60¢/word.**

Fillers: Anecdotes. **Buys 50/year.** Length: 300-500 words. **Pays $25-75.**

Tips: "Articles should have some connection to the ministry of Billy Graham or Franklin Graham. For example, you may have volunteered in one of these ministries or been touched by them. The article does not need to be entirely about that connection, but it should at least mention the connection. Testimonies and personal experience articles should show how God intervened in your life, and how you have been transformed by God. SASE required with submissions."

$ $ DISCIPLESHIP JOURNAL, NavPress, a division of The Navigators, P.O. Box 35004, Colorado Springs CO 80935-0004. (719)531-3514. Fax: (719)598-7128. E-mail: sue.kline@navpress.com. Website: www.discipleshipjournal.com. **Contact:** Sue Kline, editor. **90% freelance written.** Works with a small number of new/unpublished writers each year. Bimonthly magazine. "The mission of *Discipleship Journal* is to help believers develop a deeper relationship with Jesus Christ, and to provide practical help in understanding the scriptures and applying them to daily life and ministry. We prefer those who have not written for us before begin with nontheme articles about almost any aspect of Christian living. We'd like more articles that explain a Bible passage and show how to apply it to everyday life, as well as articles about developing a relationship with Jesus; reaching the world; growing in some aspect of Christian character; or specific issues related to leadership and helping other believers grow." Estab. 1981. Circ. 130,000. **Pays on acceptance.** Publishes ms an average of 6 months after acceptance. Byline given. Buys first North American serial, second serial (reprint), electronic rights. Submit seasonal material 6 months in advance. Accepts queries by mail, e-mail, fax. Responds in 6 weeks to queries. Sample copy and writer's guidelines for $2.56 and 9×12 SAE or online.

O→ Break in through departments (On the Home Front, Getting into God's Word, DJ Plus) and with nontheme feature articles.

Nonfiction: "We'd like to see more articles that encourage involvement in world missions; help readers in personal evangelism, follow-up, and Christian leadership; or show how to develop a real relationship with Jesus." Book excerpts (rarely), how-to (grow in Christian faith and disciplines; help others grow as Christians; serve people in need; understand and apply the Bible), inspirational, interpretation/application of the Bible. No personal testimony, humor, anything not directly related to Christian life and faith, politically partisan articles. **Buys 80 mss/year.** Query with published clips and SASE only. Length: 500-2,500 words. **Pays 25¢/word for first rights.** Sometimes pays expenses of writers on assignment.

Reprints: Send tearsheet and information about when and where the material previously appeared. Pays 5¢/word for reprints.

Tips: "Our articles are meaty, not fluffy. Study writer's guidelines and back issues and try to use similar approaches. Don't preach. Polish before submitting. About half of the articles in each issue are related to one theme. We are looking for more practical articles on ministering to others and more articles on growing in Christian character. Be vulnerable. Show the reader that you have wrestled with the subject matter in your own life. We can no longer accept unsolicited manuscripts. Query first."

$ $ THE DOOR, P.O. Box 1444, Waco TX 76703-1444. (214)827-2625. Fax: (254)752-4915. E-mail: robert_darden@baylor.edu. Website: www.thedoormagazine.com. **Contact:** Robert Darden, senior editor. **90% freelance written.** Works with a large number of new/unpublished writers each year. Bimonthly magazine. "*The Door* is the world's only, oldest and largest religious humor and satire magazine." Estab. 1969. Circ. 7,500. Pays on publication. Publishes ms an average of 1 year after acceptance. Buys first rights. Accepts queries by mail. Responds in 3 months to mss. Sample copy for $5.95. Writer's guidelines for #10 SASE.

O→ Read several issues of the magazine first! Get the writer's guidelines.

Nonfiction: Looking for humorous/satirical articles on church renewal, Christianity and organized religion. Exposé, humor, interview/profile, religious. No book reviews or poetry. **Buys 45-50 mss/year.** Send complete ms. Length: 1,500 words maximum; 750-1,000 preferred. **Pays $50-250.** Sometimes pays expenses of writers on assignment.

Reprints: Send typed ms with rights for sale noted and information about when and where the material previously appeared.

The online magazine carries original content not found in the print edition. Contact: Robert Darden.

Tips: "We look for someone who is clever, on our wave length, and has some savvy about the evangelical church. We are very picky and highly selective. The writer has a better chance of breaking in with our publication with short articles since we are a bimonthly publication with numerous regular features and the magazine is only 52 pages. The most frequent mistake made by writers is that they do not understand satire. They see we are a humor magazine and consequently come off funny/cute (like *Reader's Digest*) rather than funny/satirical (like *National Lampoon*)."

$ DOVETAIL, A Journal By and For Jewish/Christian Families, Dovetail Institute for Interfaith Family Resources, 775 Simon Greenwell Lane, Boston KY 40107. (502)549-5499. Fax: (502)549-3543. E-mail: di-ifr@bardstown.com. Website: www.dovetailpublishing.com. **Contact:** Mary Helene Rosenbaum, editor. **75% freelance written.** Bimonthly newsletter for interfaith families. "All articles must pertain to life in an interfaith (primarily Jewish/Christian) family. We are broadening our scope to include other sorts of interfaith mixes. We accept all kinds of opinions related to this topic." Estab. 1992. Circ. 1,500. Pays on publication. Publishes ms an average of 9 months after acceptance. Byline given. Buys first, one-time, second serial (reprint) rights. Editorial lead time 6 months. Submit seasonal material 6 months in advance. Accepts queries by mail, e-mail, fax, phone. Accepts previously published material. Accepts simultaneous submissions. Responds in 3 months to queries. Sample copy for 9×12 SAE and 3 first-class stamps. Writer's guidelines free.

O→ Break in with "a fresh approach to standard interfaith marriage situations."

Nonfiction: Book reviews, 500 words. **Pays $15, plus 2 copies**. Book excerpts, interview/profile, opinion, personal experience. No fiction. **Buys 5-8 mss/year.** Send complete ms. Length: 800-1,000 words. **Pays $25, plus 2 copies.**

Photos: Send photos with submission. Reviews 5×7 prints. Buys one-time rights. Offers no additional payment for photos accepted with ms. Identification of subjects, model releases required.
Fillers: Anecdotes, short humor. **Buys 1-2/year.** Length: 25-100 words. **Pays $10.**
Tips: "Write on concrete, specific topics related to Jewish/Christian or other dual-faith intermarriage: no proselytizing, sermonizing, or general religious commentary. Successful freelancers are part of an interfaith family themselves, or have done solid research/interviews with members of interfaith families. We look for honest, reflective personal experience. We're looking for more on alternative or nontraditional families, e.g., interfaith gay/lesbian, single parent raising child in departed partner's faith."

$ EVANGEL, Free Methodist Publishing House, P.O. Box 535002, Indianapolis IN 46253-5002. (317)244-3660. **Contact:** Julie Innes, editor. **100% freelance written.** Weekly take-home paper for adults. Estab. 1897. Circ. 20,000. Pays on publication. Publishes ms an average of 1 year after acceptance. simultaneous, second serial (reprint) or one-time rights. Submit seasonal material 9-12 months in advance. Accepts queries by mail. Responds in 4-6 weeks to queries. Sample copy and writer's guidelines for #10 SASE.
Nonfiction: Interview (with ordinary person who is doing something extraordinary in his community, in service to others); profile (of missionary or one from similar service profession who is contributing significantly to society); personal experience (finding a solution to a problem common to young adults; coping with handicapped child, for instance, or with a neighborhood problem. Story of how God-given strength or insight saved a situation). **Buys 125 mss/year.** Send complete ms. Length: 300-1,000 words. **Pays 4¢/word.**
Reprints: Send typed ms with rights for sale noted and information about when and where the material previously appeared.
Photos: Purchased with accompanying ms. Captions helpful with photographer credit required.
Fiction: Religious themes dealing with contemporary issues from a Christian frame of reference. Story must "go somewhere." **Buys 50 mss/year.** Send complete ms.
Poetry: Free verse, light verse, traditional, religious. **Buys 20 poems/year.** Submit maximum 5 poems. Length: 4-24 lines. **Pays $10.**
Tips: "Seasonal material will get a second look. Write an attention-grabbing lead followed by an article that says something worthwhile. Relate the lead to some of the universal needs of the reader—promise in that lead to help the reader in some way. Lack of SASE brands author as a nonprofessional."

$ THE EVANGELICAL BAPTIST, Fellowship of Evangelical Baptist Churches in Canada, 18 Louvigny, Lorraine, Quebec J6Z 1T7, Canada. (450)621-3248. Fax: (450)621-0253. E-mail: eb@fellowship.ca. Website: www.fellowship.ca. **Contact:** Ginette Cotnoir, managing editor. **30% freelance written.** Magazine published 5 times/year covering religious, spiritual, Christian living, denominational, and missionary news. "We exist to enhance the life and ministry of the church leaders of our association of churches—including pastors, elders, deacons, and all the men and women doing the work of the ministry in local churches." Estab. 1953. Circ. 3,000. Pays on publication. Publishes ms an average of 6 months after acceptance. Byline given. Buys one-time, second serial (reprint) rights. Editorial lead time 4 months. Accepts queries by mail, e-mail. Accepts previously published material. Accepts simultaneous submissions. Sample copy for 9×12 SAE with $1.50 in Canadian first-class stamps. Writer's guidelines for #10 SASE (Canadian stamps only).

Break in with items for "Church Life (how-to and how-we articles about church ministries, e.g., small groups, worship, missions) or Columns (Joy in the Journey, View from the Pew)."

Nonfiction: Religious. No poetry, fiction, puzzles. **Buys 12-15 mss/year.** Send complete ms. Length: 500-2,400 words. **Pays $25-50.**
Photos: State availability with submission. Reviews prints. Buys one-time rights. Offers no additional payment for photos accepted with ms. Captions required.
Columns/Departments: Church Life (practical articles about various church ministries, e.g., worship, Sunday school, missions, seniors, youth, discipleship); Joy in the Journey (devotional article re: a lesson learned from God in everyday life); View from the Pew (light, humorous piece with spiritual value on some aspect of Christian living), all 600-800 words. **Buys 10 mss/year.** Send complete ms. **Pays $25-50.**
Tips: "Columns and departments are the best places for freelancers. Especially looking for practical articles for Church Life from writers who are themselves involved in a church ministry. Looking for 'how-to' and 'how-we' approach."

$ $ EVANGELIZING TODAY'S CHILD, Child Evangelism Fellowship, Inc., Box 348, Warrenton MO 63383-0348. (636)456-4321. Fax: (636)456-4321. E-mail: etceditor@cefonline.com. Website: www.cefonline.com/etcmag. **Contact:** Elsie Lippy, editor. **50% freelance written.** Bimonthly magazine. "Our purpose is to equip Christians to win the world's children to Christ and disciple them. Our readership is Sunday school teachers, Christian education leaders, and children's workers in every phase of Christian ministry to children 4-12 years old." Estab. 1942. Circ. 18,000. Pays within 60 days of acceptance. Publishes ms an average of 6 months after acceptance. Byline given. Offers kills fee if assigned. Buys first North American serial, electronic rights. Submit seasonal material 6 months in advance. Accepts queries by mail, e-mail, fax. Responds in 2 months to queries. Sample copy for $2. Writer's guidelines for #10 SASE.
Nonfiction: Unsolicited articles welcomed from writers with Christian education training or current experience in working with children. **Buys 35 mss/year.** Query. Length: 900 words. **Pays 10-14¢/word.**
Reprints: Send photocopy and information about when and where the material previously appeared. Pays 35% of amount paid for an original article.

$ THE FIVE STONES, Newsletter for Small Churches, 69 Weymouth St., Providence RI 02906. (401)861-9405. E-mail: pappas@tabcom.org. **Contact:** Tony Pappas, editor. **33% freelance written.** Quarterly newsletter covering issues related to small church life. "*The Five Stones* is the only journal for the issues small congregations face. First-person articles and accounts of positive experiences best." Circ. 750. Pays on publication. Byline given. Not copyrighted. Editorial lead time 1 year. Submit seasonal material 1 year in advance. Accepts queries by mail, e-mail, fax, phone. Accepts simultaneous submissions. Responds in 1 month to queries; 4 months to mss. Sample copy for 9×12 SAE and 3 first-class stamps. Writer's guidelines for #10 SASE.

Nonfiction: Book excerpts, essays, general interest, historical/nostalgic, how-to, humor, inspirational, interview/profile, new product, personal experience, religious. **Buys 8-12 mss/year.** Send complete ms. Length: 1,500 words maximum. **Pays $5.**

Reprints: Accepts previously published submissions.

$ FORWARD IN CHRIST, The Word from the WELS, WELS, 2929 N. Mayfair Rd., Milwaukee WI 53222-4398. (414)256-3888. Fax: (414)256-3899. E-mail: fic@sab.wels.net. Website: www.wels.net. **Contact:** Gary P. Baumler, editor. **5% freelance written.** Monthly magazine covering WELS news, topics, issues. The material usually must be written by or about WELS members. Estab. 1913. Circ. 56,000. Pays on publication. Publishes ms an average of 6 months after acceptance. Byline given. Buys one-time rights. Editorial lead time 3 months. Submit seasonal material 4 months in advance. Accepts queries by mail, e-mail, fax. Responds in 2 months to queries. Sample copy and writer's guidelines free.

Nonfiction: Julie Tessmer, senior communications assistant. Personal experience, religious. Query. Length: 550-1,200 words. **Pays $75/page, $125 for every 2 pages.** Sometimes pays expenses of writers on assignment.

Photos: State availability with submission. Reviews contact sheets. Buys one-time rights, plus 1 month on Web. Negotiates payment individually. Captions, identification of subjects, model releases required.

Fillers: Gary Baumler, editor.

Tips: "Topics should be of interest to the majority of the members of the synod—the people in the pews. Articles should have a Christian viewpoint, but we don't want sermons. We suggest you carefully read at least 5 or 6 issues with close attention to the length, content, and style of the features."

$ FOURSQUARE WORLD ADVANCE, International Church of the Foursquare Gospel, 1910 W. Sunset Blvd., Suite 200, P.O. Box 26902, Los Angeles CA 90026-0176. Website: www.foursquare.org. **Contact:** Ronald D. Williams, editor. **5% freelance written.** Bimonthly magazine covering devotional/religious material, denominational news. "The official publication of the International Church of the Foursquare Gospel is distributed without charge to members and friends of the Foursquare Church." Estab. 1917. Circ. 98,000. Pays on publication. Publishes ms an average of 2 months after acceptance. Byline given. Buys first, one-time, second serial (reprint), simultaneous rights. Editorial lead time 6 months. Submit seasonal material 6 months in advance. Accepts queries by mail, e-mail. Accepts previously published material. Responds in 2 weeks to queries. Sample copy and writer's guidelines free.

Nonfiction: Inspirational, interview/profile, personal experience, religious. **Buys 2-3 mss/year.** Send complete ms. Length: 800-1,200 words. **Pays $100.**

Photos: State availability with submission. Reviews 4×6 prints. Buys one-time rights. Offers no additional payment for photos accepted with ms. Captions, identification of subjects, model releases required.

The online version carries original content not found in the print edition. Contact: Ron Williams.

$ GOD ALLOWS U-TURNS, True Stories of Hope and Healing. An ongoing book series project, The God Allows U-Turns Project, P.O. Box 717, Faribault MN 55021-0717. Fax: (507)334-6464. E-mail: editor@godallowsuturns.com. Website: www.godallowsuturns.com. **Contact:** Allison Gappa Bottke, editor. **100% freelance written.** Christian inspirational book series. "Each anthology contains approximately 100 uplifting, encouraging, and inspirational true stories written by contributors from all over the world. Multiple volumes are planned." Published by Barbour Publishing under the Promise Press imprint in association with Alive Communications, Inc. Estab. 2000. Pays on publication. Byline given. Accepts previously published material. Accepts simultaneous submissions. Writer's guidelines online or for #10 SASE.

- Accepts stories by mail, e-mail, fax. Prefers submissions via website or e-mail, but *does not accept stories as e-mail attachments*. Responds *only* when a story is selected for publication. For a list of current *God Allows U-Turns* books open to submissions, as well as related opportunities, go to www.godallowsuturns.com. Timelines vary, so send stories any time as they may fit another volume. You may submit the same story to more than 1 volume, but you must send a separate copy to each. When submitting, indicate which volume it is for.

Nonfiction: "Open to well-written personal inspirational pieces showing how faith in God can inspire, encourage, and heal. True stories that must touch our emotions." Essays, historical/nostalgic, humor, inspirational, interview/profile, personal experience, religious. **Buys 100+ mss/year. Pays $50, plus 1 copy of anthology.**

Tips: "Read a current volume. See the website for a sample story. Keep it real. Ordinary people doing extraordinary things with God's help. These true stories must touch our emotions. Our contributors are a diverse group with no limits on age or denomination."

$ $ GROUP MAGAZINE, Group Publishing Inc., 1515 Cascade Ave., Loveland CO 80538. (970)669-3836. Fax: (970)669-3269. E-mail: kdieterich@youthministry.com. Website: www.groupmag.com. Publisher: Tim Gilmour; Departments Editor: Kathy Dieterich. **Contact:** Rick Lawrence, editor. **60% freelance written.** Bimonthly magazine covering youth ministry. "Writers must be actively involved in youth ministry. Articles we accept are practical, not theoretical,

and focused for local church youth workers." Estab. 1974. Circ. 57,000. **Pays on acceptance.** Publishes ms an average of 6 months after acceptance. Byline given. Offers $20 kill fee. Buys all rights. Submit seasonal material 7 months in advance. Responds in 2 months to queries. Sample copy for $2 and 9×12 SAE. Writer's guidelines for SASE or online.
Nonfiction: How-to (youth ministry issues). No personal testimony, theological or lecture-style articles. **Buys 50-60 mss/year.** Query. Length: 250-2,200 words. **Pays $40-250.** Sometimes pays expenses of writers on assignment.
Tips: "Submit a youth ministry idea to one of our mini-article sections—we look for tried-and-true ideas youth ministers have used with kids."

$ $ GUIDEPOSTS MAGAZINE, 16 E. 34th St., New York NY 10016-4397. (212)251-8100. Website: www.guideposts.org. **Contact:** Mary Ann O'Roark, executive editor. **30% freelance written.** Works with a small number of new/unpublished writers each year. Monthly magazine. "*Guideposts* is an inspirational monthly magazine for people of all faiths, in which men and women from all walks of life tell in true, first-person narrative how they overcame obstacles, rose above failures, handled sorrow, gained new spiritual insight, and became more effective people through faith in God." Estab. 1945. Pays on publication. Publishes ms an average of several months after acceptance. Offers 20% kill fee. Buys all rights.

- "Many of our stories are ghosted articles, so the writer would not get a byline unless it was his/her own story. Because of the high volume of mail the magazine receives, we regret we *cannot* return manuscripts, and will contact writers only if their material can be used."

Nonfiction: Articles and features should be true stories written in simple, anecdotal style with an emphasis on human interest. Short mss of approximately 250-750 words (pays $100-250) considered for such features as "Angels Among Us," "His Mysterious Ways," and general 1-page stories. Address short items to Celeste McCauley. For full-length mss, 750-1,500 words, pays $250-500. All mss should be typed, double-spaced, and accompanied by e-mail address, if possible. Annually awards scholarships to high school juniors and seniors in writing contest. **Buys 40-60 unsolicited mss/year.** Length: 250-1,500 words. **Pays $100-500.** Pays expenses of writers on assignment.
Tips: "Study the magazine before you try to write for it. Each story must make a single spiritual point that readers can apply to their own daily lives. And it may be easier to just sit down and write them than to have to go through the process of preparing a query. They should be warm, well written, intelligent, and upbeat. We require personal narratives that are true and have some spiritual aspect, but the religious element can be subtle and should *not* be sermonic. A writer succeeds with us if he or she can write a true article using short-story techniques with scenes, drama, tension, and a resolution of the problem presented."

$ HOME TIMES, A Good Little Newspaper for God & Country, Neighbor News, Inc., 3676 Collin Dr., #16, West Palm Beach FL 33406. (561)439-3509. Fax: (561)968-1758. E-mail: hometimes2@aol.com. Website: www.hometimes.org. **Contact:** Dennis Lombard, publisher/editor. **50% freelance written.** Weekly tabloid of conservative, pro-Christian news and views. "*Home Times* is a conservative newspaper written for the general public but with a Biblical worldview and family-values slant. It is not religious or preachy." Estab. 1988. Circ. 8,000. Pays on publication. Publishes ms an average of 3 months after acceptance. Byline given. Buys one-time rights. Editorial lead time 2 months. Submit seasonal material 2 months in advance. Accepts simultaneous submissions. Sample copy for $3. Writer's guidelines for #10 SASE.
Nonfiction: Essays, general interest, historical/nostalgic, how-to, humor, inspirational, interview/profile, opinion, personal experience, photo feature, religious, travel, current events. "Nothing preachy, moralistic, or with churchy slant." **Buys 25 mss/year.** Send complete ms. No queries. Length: 500-900 words. **Pays $5 minimum for assigned articles.** Pays contributor's copies or subscriptions on mutual agreement.
Reprints: Send tearsheet or photocopy and information about when and where the material previously appeared. Pays $5-10.
Photos: Send photos with submission. Reviews any size prints. Buys one-time rights. Offers $5/photo used. Captions, identification of subjects, model releases required.
Columns/Departments: Buys 50 mss/year. Send complete ms. **Pays $5-15.**
Fiction: Historical, humorous, mainstream, religious, issue-oriented contemporary. "Nothing preachy, moralistic." **Buys 5 mss/year.** Send complete ms. Length: 500-900 words. **Pays $5-25.**
Poetry: Free verse, light verse, traditional. **Buys 12 poems/year.** Submit maximum 3 poems. Length: 2-24 lines. **Pays $5.**
Fillers: Anecdotes, facts, short humor, good quotes. **Buys 25/year.** Length: 100 word maximum. **Pays 3-6 issues on acceptance.**
Tips: "We encourage new writers. We are different from ordinary news or religious publications. We strongly suggest you read guidelines and sample issues. (Writer's subscription 12 issues for $12, regularly $16.) We are most open to material for new columns; journalists covering hard news in major news centers—with conservative slant. Also, lots of letters and short op-eds though we pay only in issues (3-6) for them. We're also looking for good creative nonfiction, especially historical, conservative, and/or humorous."

$ $ INSIDE JOURNAL, The Hometown Newspaper of America's Prisoners, Prison Fellowship Ministries, P.O. Box 17429, Washington DC 20041-0429. (703)478-0100. Fax: (703)318-0235. E-mail: jpeck@pfm.org. **Contact:** Jeff Peck, managing editor. **5% freelance written.** Bimonthly newspaper covering prisons, prison life, surviving prison. "*IJ* is a Christian newspaper written exclusively for prisoners. All content is passed through a Christian worldview to inspire hope and aid inmates in their present circumstances. Material must have direct influence on prison life with practical takeaway value for the readers." Estab. 1990. Circ. 400,000. Pays on publication. Publishes ms an average of

2 months after acceptance. Byline given. Buys first, second serial (reprint), simultaneous rights. Editorial lead time 2 months. Submit seasonal material 2 months in advance. Accepts queries by mail, e-mail. Accepts previously published material. Accepts simultaneous submissions. Responds in 2 months to queries; 8 months to mss. Sample copy and writer's guidelines free.

Nonfiction: How-to (survive in prison, find a job, fight depression), humor, inspirational, interview/profile, religious. No fiction or Bible studies. **Buys 5 mss/year.** Send complete ms. Length: 500-1,500 words. **Pays $50-200.** Pays prisoners in contributor copies.

Photos: State availability of or send photos with submission. Reviews contact sheets, transparencies, prints. Buys one-time rights. Negotiates payment individually. Identification of subjects required.

Columns/Departments: Shortimer (preparing for release from prison); Especially for Women (how women cope with prison); Fatherly Advice (how to be a father in prison), all 750 words. **Buys 3 mss/year.** Send complete ms.

Tips: "Visit a prison, find out firsthand what inmates are dealing with. Or find an ex-prisoner who is making it on the outside. Interview person for 'How are you successful' tips. What are they doing differently to avoid returning to prison? Also, we need more celebrity interviews with people of Christian faith."

N **JEWISH FRONTIER**, Labor Zionist Letters, POB 4013, Amity Station, New Haven CT 06525. (203)397-4903. Fax: (203)397-4903. E-mail: Jewish-frontier@yahoo.com. Website: www.jewishfrontier.org/frontier. **Contact:** Bennett Lovett-Graff, managing editor. **100% freelance written.** Bimonthly intellectual journal covering progressive Jewish issues. "Reportage, essays, reviews, and occasional fiction and poetry, with a progressive Jewish perspective, and a particular interest in Israeli and Jewish-American affairs." Estab. 1934. Circ. 2,600. **Pays on acceptance.** Publishes ms an average of 4 months after acceptance. Byline given. Buys first, second serial (reprint), electronic rights. Editorial lead time 4 months. Submit seasonal material 2 months in advance. Accepts queries by mail, e-mail. Accepts previously published material. Accepts simultaneous submissions. Responds in 1 month to queries; 2 months to mss. Sample copy for 9×12 SASE and 3 first-class stamps, and online at website. Writer's guidelines online.

Nonfiction: Bennett Lovett-Graff, managing editor. Must have progressive Jewish focus, or will not be considered. Book excerpts, essays, exposé, historical/nostalgic, interview/profile, opinion, personal experience. **Buys 20 mss/year.** Query. Length: 1,000-2,500 words. **Pays 5¢/word.**

Photos: State availability with submission. Buys all rights. Offers no additional payment for photos accepted with ms. Captions, identification of subjects required.

Columns/Departments: Bennett Lovett-Graff, managing editor. Essays (progressive Jewish opinion), 1,000-2,500 words; Articles (progressive Jewish reportage), 1,000-2,500 words); Reviews, 500-1,000 words. **Buys 12 mss/year.** Query. **Pays 5¢/word.**

Poetry: Bennett Lovett-Graff, managing editor. Avant-garde, free verse, haiku, traditional. **Buys 12 poems/year.** Submit maximum 3 poems. Length: 7-25 lines. **Pays 5¢/word.**

Tips: "Send queries with strong ideas first. *Jewish Frontier* particularly appreciates original thinking on its topics related to progressive Jewish matters."

N $ **LEADERS IN ACTION**, (formerly *Brigade Leader*), CSB Ministries, P.O. Box 150, Wheaton IL 60189. (630)582-0630. Fax: (630)582-0623. E-mail: dchristensen@csbministries.org. Website: CSBministries.org. **Contact:** Deborah Christensen, editor. Magazine published 3 times/year covering leadership issues for CSB Ministries leaders. "*Leaders in Action* is distributed to leaders with CSB Ministries across North America. CSB is a nonprofit, nondenominational agency dedicated to winning and training boys and girls to serve Jesus Christ. Hundreds of churches throughout the U.S. and Canada make use of our wide range of services." Estab. 1960. Circ. 6,000. Pays on publication. Publishes ms an average of 3 months after acceptance. Byline given. Offers $35 kill fee. Buys first, second serial (reprint) rights. Editorial lead time 3 months. Responds in 1 week to queries. Sample copy for $1.50 and 10×13 SAE with 4 first-class stamps. Writer's guidelines for #10 SASE.

Nonfiction: Religious leadership. **Buys 8 mss/year.** Query. Length: 500-1,500 words. **Pays 5-10¢/word.** Sometimes pays expenses of writers on assignment.

Reprints: Send typed ms with rights for sale noted. Pays 50% of amount paid for an original article.

Photos: State availability with submission. Buys one-time rights. Negotiates payment.

Tips: "We're looking for writers who can encourage and inspire leaders of children and youth, and work within a tight deadline. We work by assignment."

$ **LIFEGLOW**, Christian Record Services, P.O. Box 6097, Lincoln NE 68506. (402)488-0981. Fax: (402)488-7582. Website: www.christianrecord.org. **Contact:** Gaylena Gibson, editor. **95% freelance written.** Large print Christian publication for sight-impaired over 25 covering health, handicapped people, uplifting articles. Estab. 1984. Circ. 32,700. **Pays on acceptance.** Publishes ms an average of 3 years after acceptance. Byline given. Buys one-time rights. Accepts previously published material. Accepts simultaneous submissions. Responds in 1 year to mss. Sample copy for 7×10 SAE and 5 first-class stamps. Writer's guidelines for #10 SASE.

"Write for an interdenominational Christian audience."

Nonfiction: Essays, general interest, historical/nostalgic, humor, inspirational, interview/profile, personal experience, travel, adventure, biography, careers, handicapped, health, hobbies, marriage, nature. **Buys 40 mss/year.** Send complete ms. Length: 200-1,400 words. **Pays 4-5¢/word, and complimentary copies.**

Photos: Send photos with submission. Buys one-time rights. Negotiates payment individually.

Columns/Departments: Baffle U! (puzzle), 150 words, **pays $15-25/puzzle**; Vitality Plus (current health topics), length varies, **pays 4¢/word**. **Buys 10 mss/year.** Send complete ms.

Poetry: Light verse. **Buys very few poems/year.** Length: 12 lines. **Pays $10-20.**
Fillers: Anecdotes, facts, short humor. **Buys very few/year.** Length: 300 words maximum. **Pays 4¢/word.**
Tips: "Make sure manuscript has a strong ending that ties everything together and doesn't leave us dangling. Pretend someone else wrote it—would it hold your interest? Draw your readers into the story by being specific rather than abstract or general."

$LIGHT AND LIFE MAGAZINE, Free Methodist Church of North America, P.O. Box 535002, Indianapolis IN 46253-5002. (317)244-3660. Fax: (317)248-9055. E-mail: llmauthors@fmcna.org. **Contact:** Doug Newton, editor. Works with a small number of new/unpublished writers each year. Bimonthly magazine emphasizing evangelical Christianity with Wesleyan slant for a cross section of adults. Also includes discipleship guidebook and national/international and denominational religion news. Estab. 1868. Circ. 19,000. Pays on publication. Byline given. Buys first North American serial rights. Accepts queries by mail. Sample copy for $4. Writer's guidelines for #10 SASE.
Nonfiction: Send complete ms. Length: varies. **Pays 9¢/word, 10¢/word if submitted on disk.**

$$LIGUORIAN, One Liguori Dr., Liguori MO 63057-9999. (636)464-2500. Fax: (636)464-8449. E-mail: aweinert iguori.org. Website: www.liguorian.org. Managing Editor: Cheryl Plass. **Contact:** Fr. Allan Weinert, CSSR, editor-in-chief. **25% freelance written.** Prefers to work with published/established writers. Magazine published 10 times/year for Catholics. "Our purpose is to lead our readers to a fuller Christian life by helping them better understand the teachings of the gospel and the church and by illustrating how these teachings apply to life and the problems confronting them as members of families, the church, and society." Estab. 1913. Circ. 220,000. **Pays on acceptance.** Buys all rights but will reassign rights to author after publication upon written request. Submit seasonal material 8 months in advance. Accepts queries by mail, e-mail, fax, phone. Responds in 4 months to mss. Sample copy and writer's guidelines for 9×12 SAE with 3 first-class stamps or online.
Nonfiction: "Pastoral, practical, and personal approach to the problems and challenges of people today." "No travelogue approach or unresearched ventures into controversial areas. Also, no material found in secular publications—fad subjects that already get enough press, pop psychology, negative or put-down articles." **Buys 40-50 unsolicited mss/year.** Length: 400-2,000 words. **Pays 10-12¢/word.** Sometimes pays expenses of writers on assignment.
Photos: Photographs on assignment only unless submitted with and specific to article.

$THE LIVING CHURCH, Living Church Foundation, 816 E. Juneau Ave., P.O. Box 514036, Milwaukee WI 53203. (414)276-5420. Fax: (414)276-7483. E-mail: tlc@livingchurch.org. Managing Editor: John Schuessler. **Contact:** David Kalvelage, editor. **50% freelance written.** Weekly magazine on the Episcopal Church. News or articles of interest to members of the Episcopal Church. Estab. 1878. Circ. 9,000. Does not pay unless article is requested. Publishes ms an average of 3 months after acceptance. Byline given. Buys one-time rights. Editorial lead time 3 weeks. Submit seasonal material 1 month in advance. Accepts queries by mail, e-mail, fax. Responds in 2 weeks to queries; 1 month to mss. Sample copy for free. Writer's guidelines online.
Nonfiction: Opinion, personal experience, photo feature, religious. **Buys 10 mss/year.** Send complete ms. Length: 1,000 words. **Pays $25-100.** Sometimes pays expenses of writers on assignment.
Photos: Send photos with submission. Reviews any size prints. Buys one-time rights. Offers $15-50/photo.
Columns/Departments: Benediction (devotional), 250 words; Viewpoint (opinion), under 1,000 words. Send complete ms. **Pays $50 maximum.**
Poetry: Light verse, traditional.

$LIVING LIGHT NEWS, Living Light Ministries, 5306 89th St., #200, Edmonton Alberta T6E 5P9, Canada. (780)468-6397. Fax: (780)468-6872. E-mail: shine@livinglightnews.org. Website: www.livinglightnews.org. **Contact:** Jeff Caporale, editor. **100% freelance written.** Bimonthly tabloid covering evangelical Christianity. "Our publication is a seeker-sensitive evangelical outreach oriented newspaper focusing on glorifying God and promoting a personal relationship with Him." Estab. 1985. Circ. 24,000. Pays on publication. Publishes ms an average of 2 months after acceptance. Byline sometimes given. Offers 100% kill fee. Buys first North American serial, first, one-time, second serial (reprint), simultaneous, all rights, makes work-for-hire assignments. Editorial lead time 2 months. Submit seasonal material 3 months in advance. Accepts queries by mail, e-mail, phone. Accepts previously published material. Accepts simultaneous submissions. Responds in 2 months to queries; 2 months to mss. Sample copy for 10×13 SAE with $2.10 in IRCs. Writer's guidelines for #10 SASE with 1 IRC, online or by e-mail.

O→ Break in with "a story about a well-known Christian in sports or entertainment."

Nonfiction: General interest, humor, inspirational, interview/profile, religious, sports. Special issues: "We have a special Christmas issue focused on the traditional meaning of Christmas and a special Christian college supplement called New Horizons each spring." No issue-oriented, controversial stories. **Buys 50 mss/year.** Query with published clips. Length: 300-1,000 words. **Pays $30-100 for assigned articles; $10-100 for unsolicited articles.** Sometimes pays expenses of writers on assignment.
Reprints: Send tearsheet, photocopy or typed ms with rights for sale noted and information about when and where the material previously appeared. Pays 5¢/word.
Photos: State availability with submission. Reviews 3×5 prints, GIF/JPEG files. Buys all rights. Offers $20/photo. Identification of subjects required.
Columns/Departments: Relationships, 600 words; Parenting (positive, helpful, punchy, humorous, Biblically based parenting pointers), 650 words; Humor (light-hearted anecdotes about God and the current culture in the world today), 600 words. **Buys 40 mss/year.** Query with published clips. **Pays $10-25.**

Fiction: "We only want to see Christmas-related fiction." No Victorian-era, strongly American fiction. "We are a Northern Canadian publication." **Buys 10 mss/year.** Query with published clips. Length: 300-1,250 words. **Pays $10-100.**

Tips: "Please visit our website for a sample of our publication. All of our stories must be of interest to both Christians and non-Christians. We look for lively writing styles that are friendly, down-to-earth and engaging. We especially like celebrity profiles."

$ $ THE LOOKOUT, For Today's Growing Christian, Standard Publishing, 8121 Hamilton Ave., Cincinnati OH 45231-9981. (513)931-4050. Fax: (513)931-0950. E-mail: lookout@standardpub.com. Website: www.standardpub.com. Administrative Assistant: Sheryl Overstreet. **Contact:** Shawn McMullen, editor. **50% freelance written.** Weekly magazine for Christian adults, with emphasis on spiritual growth, family life, and topical issues. "Our purpose is to provide Christian adults with practical, Biblical teaching and current information that will help them mature as believers." Estab. 1894. Circ. 100,000. **Pays on acceptance.** Publishes ms an average of 1 year after acceptance. Byline given. Offers 33% kill fee. Buys first, one-time rights. Editorial lead time 6 months. Submit seasonal material 6 months in advance. Accepts queries by mail, e-mail, fax. Accepts previously published material. Accepts simultaneous submissions. Responds in 3 weeks to queries; 2 months to mss. Sample copy and guidelines for 75¢. Writer's guidelines for #10 SASE.

- Audience is mainly conservative Christians.

Nonfiction: "Writers need to send for current theme list. We also use inspirational short pieces." Inspirational, interview/profile, opinion, personal experience, religious. No fiction or poetry. **Buys 100 mss/year.** Query with or without published clips or send complete ms. Length: 350-800 words. **Pays 5-12¢/word.** Sometimes pays expenses of writers on assignment.

Reprints: Accepts previously published submissions. Pays 60% of amount paid for an original article.

Photos: State availability with submission. Buys one-time rights. Offers no additional payment for photos accepted with ms. Identification of subjects required.

Tips: "*The Lookout* publishes from a theologically conservative, nondenominational, and noncharismatic perspective. It is a member of the Evangelical Press Association. We have readers in every adult age group, but we aim primarily for those aged 35-55. Most readers are married and have older elementary to young adult children. But a large number come from other home situations as well. Our emphasis is on the needs of ordinary Christians who want to grow in their faith, rather than on trained theologians or church leaders. As a Christian general-interest magazine, we cover a wide variety of topics—from individual discipleship to family concerns to social involvement. We value well-informed articles that offer lively and clear writing as well as strong application. We often address tough issues and seek to explore fresh ideas or recent developments affecting today's Christians."

$ ☆ THE LUTHERAN DIGEST, The Lutheran Digest, Inc., P.O. Box 4250, Hopkins MN 55343. (952)933-2820. Fax: (952)933-5708. E-mail: tldi@lutherandigest.com. Website: www.lutherandigest.com. **Contact:** David L. Tank, editor. **95% freelance written.** Quarterly magazine covering Christianity from a Lutheran perspective. "Articles frequently reflect a Lutheran Christian perspective, but are not intended to be sermonettes. Popular stories show how God has intervened in a person's life to help solve a problem." Estab. 1953. Circ. 110,000. **Pays on acceptance.** Publishes ms an average of 6 months after acceptance. Byline given. Buys first, second serial (reprint) rights. Editorial lead time 9 months. Submit seasonal material 9 months in advance. Accepts queries by mail. Accepts previously published material. Accepts simultaneous submissions. Responds in 1 month to queries; 4 months to mss. Sample copy for $3.50. Writer's guidelines online.

O¬ Break in with "reprints from other publications that will fill less than three pages of *TLD*. Articles of one or two pages are even better. As a digest, we primarily look for previously published articles to reprint, however, we do publish about twenty to thirty percent original material. Articles from new writers are always welcomed and seriously considered."

Nonfiction: General interest, historical/nostalgic, how-to (personal or spiritual growth), humor, inspirational, personal experience, religious, nature, God's unique creatures. Does not want to see "personal tributes to deceased relatives or friends. They are seldom used unless the subject of the article is well-known. We also avoid articles about the moment a person finds Christ as his or her personal savior." **Buys 50-60 mss/year.** Send complete ms. Length: 1,500 words. **Pays $25-50.**

Reprints: Accepts previously published submissions. We prefer this as we are a digest and 70-80% of our articles are reprints.

Photos: "We seldom print photos from outside sources." State availability with submission. Buys one-time rights.

Tips: "An article that tugs on the 'heart strings' just a little and closes leaving the reader with a sense of hope is a writer's best bet to breaking into *The Lutheran Digest*."

$ THE LUTHERAN JOURNAL, 7317 Cahill Rd., Suite 201, Minneapolis MN 55439-2081. (952)562-1234. Fax: (952)941-3010. Publisher: Michael L. Beard. **Contact:** Editorial Assistant. Magazine published 3 times/year for Lutheran Church members, middle age and older. Estab. 1938. Circ. 130,000. Pays on publication. Byline given. Buys one-time rights. Accepts simultaneous submissions. Responds in 4 months to queries. Sample copy for 9×12 SAE with 80¢ postage.

Nonfiction: Historical/nostalgic, how-to, humor, inspirational, interview/profile, personal experience, religious, interesting or unusual church projects, think articles. **Buys 25-30 mss/year.** Send complete ms. Length: 1,500 words maximum; occasionally 2,000 words. **Pays 1-4¢/word.**

Reprints: Send tearsheet, photocopy or typed ms with rights for sale noted and information about when and where the material previously appeared. Pays up to 50% of amount paid for an original article.

Photos: Send photocopies of b&w and color photos with accompanying ms. Please do not send original photos.

Poetry: Buys 2-3 poems/issue, as space allows. Pays $5-30.

Tips: "We strongly prefer a warm, personal style of writing that speaks directly to the reader. In general, writers should seek to convey information rather than express personal opinion, though the writer's own personality should be reflected in the article's style. Send submissions with SASE so we may respond."

$ LUTHERAN PARTNERS, Augsburg Fortress, Publishers, ELCA (DM), 8765 W. Higgins Rd., Chicago IL 60631-4195. (773)380-2875. Fax: (773)380-2829. E-mail: lpartmag@elca.org. Website: www.elca.org/lp. Managing Editor: William A. Decker. **Contact:** Carl E. Linder, editor. **15-20% freelance written.** Bimonthly magazine covering issues of religious leadership. "We are a leadership magazine for the ordained and rostered lay ministers of the Evangelical Lutheran Church in America (ELCA), fostering an exchange of opinions on matters involving theology, leadership, mission, and service to Jesus Christ. Know your audience: ELCA congregations and the various kinds of leaders who make up this church and their prevalent issues of leadership." Estab. 1979. Circ. 20,000. Pays on publication. Publishes ms an average of 6 months after acceptance. Byline given. Buys first, one-time, second serial (reprint), electronic rights. Editorial lead time 6 months. Submit seasonal material 6 months in advance. Accepts queries by mail, e-mail, fax, phone. Accepts previously published material. Accepts simultaneous submissions. Responds in 1 month to queries; 6 months to mss. Sample copy for $2. Writer's guidelines free or online.

- The editor reports an interest in seeing articles on various facets of ministry from the perspectives of ethnic authors (Hispanic, African-American, Asian, Native American, Arab-American).
- Break in through "Jottings" (practical how-to articles involving congregational ministry ideas, 500 words maximum)."

Nonfiction: Historical/nostalgic, how-to (leadership in faith communities), humor (religious cartoon), inspirational, opinion (religious leadership issues), religious, book reviews (query book review editor). "No exposés, no articles primarily promoting products/services; no anti-religion." **Buys 15-20 mss/year.** Query with published clips or send complete ms. Length: 500-2,000 words. **Pays $25-170.** Pays in copies for book reviews.

Photos: State availability with submission. Buys one-time rights. Generally offers no additional payment for photos accepted with ms. Captions, identification of subjects required.

Columns/Departments: Review Editor. Partners Review (book reviews), 700 words. Query or submit ms. **Pays in copies.**

Fiction: Rarely accepts religious fiction. Query.

Poetry: Free verse, haiku, light verse, traditional, hymns. **Buys 6-10 poems/year.** Submit maximum 10 poems. **Pays $50-75.**

Fillers: Practical ministry (education, music, youth, social service, administration, worship, etc.) in congregation. **Buys 3-6/year.** Length: 500 words. **Pays $25.**

Tips: "Know congregational life, especially from the perspective of leadership, including both ordained pastor and lay staff. Think current and future leadership needs. It would be good to be familiar with ELCA rostered pastors, lay ministers, and congregations."

$ MENNONITE BRETHREN HERALD, 3-169 Riverton Ave., Winnipeg, Manitoba R2L 2E5, Canada. (204)669-6575. Fax: (204)654-1865. E-mail: mbherald@mbconf.ca. Website: www.mbherald.com. **Contact:** Jim Coggins, editor; Susan Brandt, managing editor. **25% freelance written.** Biweekly family publication "read mainly by people of the Mennonite Brethren faith, reaching a wide cross section of professional and occupational groups, including many homemakers. Readership includes people from both urban and rural communities. It is intended to inform members of events in the church and the world, serve personal and corporate spiritual needs, serve as a vehicle of communication within the church, serve conference agencies, and reflect the history and theology of the Mennonite Brethren Church." Estab. 1962. Circ. 16,500. Pays on publication. Publishes ms an average of 6 months after acceptance. Byline given. Not copyrighted. Buys one-time rights. Accepts queries by e-mail, fax. Responds in 6 months to queries. Sample copy for $1 and 9×12 SAE with 2 IRCs. Writer's guidelines not available.

- "Articles and manuscripts not accepted for publication will be returned if a SASE (Canadian stamps or IRCs) is provided by the writers."

Nonfiction: Articles with a Christian family orientation, youth directed, Christian faith and life, and current issues. Wants articles critiquing the values of a secular society, attempting to relate Christian living to the practical situations of daily living; showing how people have related their faith to their vocations. Send complete ms. Length: 250-1,500 words. **Pays $30-40.** Pays expenses of writers on assignment.

Reprints: Send tearsheet, photocopy or typed ms with rights for sale noted and information about when and where the material previously appeared. Pays 70% of amount paid for an original article.

Photos: Photos purchased with ms.

Columns/Departments: Viewpoint (Christian opinion on current topics), 850 words. Crosscurrent (Christian opinion on music, books, art, TV, movies), 350 words.

Poetry: Length: 25 lines maximum.

Tips: "We like simple style, contemporary language, and fresh ideas. Writers should take care to avoid religious clichés."

$ MESSAGE MAGAZINE, Review and Herald Publishing Association, 55 W. Oak Ridge Dr., Hagerstown MD 21740. (301)393-4099. Fax: (301)393-4103. E-mail: message@rhpa.org. Website: www.messagemagazine.org. Editor: Ron C. Smith. Associate Editor: Dwain Esmond. **Contact:** Pat Sparks Harris, administrative secretary. **10-20% freelance written.** Bimonthly magazine. "*Message* is the oldest religious journal addressing ethnic issues in the country. Our audience is predominantly black and Seventh-day Adventist; however, *Message* is an outreach magazine geared to the unchurched." Estab. 1898. Circ. 120,000. **Pays on acceptance.** Publishes ms an average of 1 year after acceptance. Byline given. Buys first North American serial rights Editorial lead time 6 months. Submit seasonal material 6 months in advance. Responds in 9 months to queries. Sample copy and writer's guidelines free.

Nonfiction: General interest (to a Christian audience), how-to (overcome depression; overcome defeat; get closer to God; learn from failure, etc.), inspirational, interview/profile (profiles of famous African Americans), personal experience (testimonies), religious. **Buys 10 mss/year.** Send complete ms. Length: 800-1,200 words. **Payment varies.**

Photos: State availability with submission. Buys one-time rights. Identification of subjects required.

Columns/Departments: Voices in the Wind (community involvement/service/events/health info); Message, Jr. (stories for children with a moral, explain a Biblical or moral principle); Recipes (no meat or dairy products—12-15 recipes and an intro); Healthspan (health issues); all 500 words. **Buys 12-15 mss/year.** Send complete ms for Message, Jr. and Healthspan. Query editorial assistant with published clips for Voices in the Wind and Recipes. **Pays $50-300.**

Fillers: Anecdotes, facts, newsbreaks. **Buys 1-5/year.** Length: 200-500 words. **Payment varies.**

The online version contains material not found in the print edition.

Tips: "Please look at the magazine before submitting manuscripts. *Message* publishes a variety of writing styles as long as the writing style is easy to read and flows—please avoid highly technical writing styles."

$ THE MESSENGER OF THE SACRED HEART, Apostleship of Prayer, 661 Greenwood Ave., Toronto, Ontario M4J 4B3, Canada. (416)466-1195. **Contact:** Rev. F.J. Power, S.J., editor. **20% freelance written.** Monthly magazine for "Canadian and U.S. Catholics interested in developing a life of prayer and spirituality; stresses the great value of our ordinary actions and lives." Estab. 1891. Circ. 15,000. **Pays on acceptance.** Byline given. Buys first rights. Submit seasonal material 5 months in advance. Responds in 1 month to queries. Sample copy for $1 and 7½×10½ SAE. Writer's guidelines for #10 SASE.

Fiction: Religious/inspirational; stories about people, adventure, heroism, humor, drama. **Buys 12 mss/year.** Length: 750-1,500 words. **Pays 6¢/word.**

Tips: "Develop a story that sustains interest to the end. Do not preach, but use plot and characters to convey the message or theme. Aim to move the heart as well as the mind. Before sending, cut out unnecessary or unrelated words or sentences. If you can, add a light touch or a sense of humor to the story. Your ending should have impact, leaving a moral or faith message for the reader."

$ $ MINNESOTA CHRISTIAN CHRONICLE, Beard Communications, 7317 Cahill Rd., Suite 201, Edina MN 55439. (952)562-1213. Fax: (952)941-3010. E-mail: editor@mcchronicle.com. Website: www.mcchronicle.com. **Contact:** Dave Bohon, editor. **10% freelance written.** Biweekly newspaper covering Christian community in Minnesota. "Our readers tend to be conservative evangelicals with orthodox Christian beliefs and conservative social and political views." Estab. 1978. Circ. 21,000. Pays 1 month following publication. Publishes ms an average of 2 months after acceptance. Byline given. Buys one-time rights. Editorial lead time 1 month. Submit seasonal material 2 months in advance. Accepts queries by mail, e-mail. Accepts simultaneous submissions. Responds in 1 month to queries. Sample copy for $2. Writer's guidelines for #10 SASE.

Nonfiction: Exposé, general interest, historical/nostalgic, how-to, humor (Christian humor, satire, clean), inspirational, interview/profile, new product, personal experience, photo feature, religious. Special issues: Higher education guide, Christmas section, Christian school directory, Life Resource Guide, Christian Ministries Directory. **Buys 36 mss/year.** Query. Length: 500-2,000 words. **Pays $20-200.**

Reprints: Send typed ms with rights for sale noted. Pays 50% of amount paid for an original article.

Photos: State availability with submission. Reviews contact sheets. Buys one-time rights. Negotiates payment individually. Captions required.

Tips: "Stories for the *Minnesota Christian Chronicle* must have a strong Minnesota connection and a clear hook for the Christian community. We do not publish general nonreligious stories or devotionals. We rarely buy from writers who are not in Minnesota."

$ THE MIRACULOUS MEDAL, 475 E. Chelten Ave., Philadelphia PA 19144-5785. (215)848-1010. **Contact:** Rev. William J. O'Brien, C.M., editor. **40% freelance written.** Quarterly magazine. Estab. 1915. **Pays on acceptance.** Publishes ms an average of 2 years after acceptance. Buys first North American serial rights. Accepts queries by mail. Responds in 3 months to queries. Sample copy for 6×9 SAE and 2 first-class stamps.

- Buys articles only on special assignment.

Fiction: Wants good general fiction—not necessarily religious, but if religion is basic to the story, the writer should be sure of his facts. Only restriction is that subject matter and treatment must not conflict with Catholic teaching and practice. Can use seasonal material, Christmas stories. Should not be pious or sermon-like. Length: 2,000 words maximum. Occasionally uses short-shorts from 1,000-1,250 words. **Pays 2¢/word minimum.**

Poetry: Preferably about the Virgin Mary or at least with a religious slant. Length: 20 lines maximum. **Pays 50¢/line minimum.**

$ $ MOODY MAGAZINE, Moody Bible Institute, 820 N. LaSalle Blvd., Chicago IL 60610. (312)329-2164. Fax: (312)329-2149. E-mail: moodyedit@moody.edu. Website: www.moody.edu. **Contact:** Andrew Scheer, managing editor. **62% freelance written.** Bimonthly magazine for evangelical Christianity. "Our readers are conservative, evangelical Christians highly active in their churches and concerned about applying their faith in daily living." Query first for all submissions by mail, but not by phone. Unsolicited mss will be returned unread. Estab. 1900. Circ. 112,000. **Pays on acceptance.** Publishes ms an average of 9 months after acceptance. Byline given. Buys first North American serial rights. Submit seasonal material 9 months in advance. Responds in 2 months to queries. Sample copy for 9×12 SAE with $2 first-class postage. Writer's guidelines for #10 SASE.

O-ᴛ Break in with "noncover, freestanding narrative articles."

Nonfiction: Personal narratives (on living the Christian life); a few reporting articles. "No biographies, historical articles, or studies of Bible figures." **Buys 55 mss/year.** Query. Length: 1,200-2,200 words. **Pays 15¢/word for queried articles; 20¢/word for assigned articles.** Sometimes pays expenses of writers on assignment.

Columns/Departments: First Person (the only article written for nonChristians; a personal conversion testimony written by the author [will accept "as told to's"]; the objective is to tell a person's testimony in such a way that the reader will understand the gospel and want to receive Christ as Savior), 800-900 words; News Focus (in-depth, researched account of current news or trend), 1,000-1,400 words. **Buys 12 mss/year.** May query by fax or e-mail for New Focus only. **Pays 15¢/word.**

Fiction: Will consider well-written contemporary stories that are directed toward spiritual application. Avoid clichéd salvation accounts, biblical fiction, parables, and allegories. Length: 1,200-2,000 words. **Pays 15¢/word.**

Tips: "We want articles that cover a broad range of topics, but with 1 common goal: To foster application by a broad readership of specific Biblical principles. *Moody* especially seeks narrative accounts showing one's realization and application of specific, scriptural principles in daily life. In generating ideas for such articles, we recommend a writer consider: What has God been 'working on' in your life in the past few years? How have you been learning to apply a new realization of what Scripture is commanding you to do? What difference has this made for you and those around you? By publishing accounts of people's spiritual struggles, growth and discipleship, our aim is to encourage readers in their own obedience to Christ. We're also looking for some pieces that use an anecdotal reporting approach."

$ $ MY DAILY VISITOR, Our Sunday Visitor, Inc., 200 Noll Plaza, Huntington IN 46750. (219)356-8400. E-mail: mdvisitor@osv.com. **Contact:** Catherine M. Odell, editor. **99% freelance written.** Bimonthly magazine of Scripture meditations based on the day's Catholic Mass readings. Circ. 30,000. **Pays on acceptance.** Publishes ms an average of 6 months after acceptance. Byline given. Not copyrighted. Buys one-time rights. Accepts queries by mail, e-mail. Responds in 2 months to queries. Sample copy and writer's guidelines for #10 SAE with 2 first-class stamps.

• "Guest editors write on assignment basis only."

Nonfiction: Inspirational, personal experience, religious. **Buys 12 mss/year.** Query with published clips. Length: 150-160 words times the number of days in month. **Pays $500 for 1 month (28-31) of meditations, and 5 free copies.**

Tips: "Previous experience in writing Scripture-based meditations or essays is helpful."

$ NORTH AMERICAN VOICE OF FATIMA, Barnabite Fathers-North American Province, National Shrine Basilica of Our Lady of Fatima, 1023 Swann Rd., P.O. Box 167, Youngstown NY 14174-0167. (716)754-7489. Fax: (716)754-9130. E-mail: voice@fatimashrine.com. Website: www.fatimashrine.com. **Contact:** Rev. Peter M. Calabrese, CRSP, editor. **90% freelance written.** Quarterly magazine covering Catholic spirituality. "The Barnabite Fathers wish to share the joy and challenge of the Gospel and to foster devotion to Our Lady, Mary, the Mother of the Redeemer and Mother of the Church who said at Cana: 'Do whatever He tells you.'" Estab. 1961. Circ. 1,200. Pays on publication. Publishes ms an average of 3 months after acceptance. Byline given. Buys first North American serial, one-time, second serial (reprint) rights, makes work-for-hire assignments. Editorial lead time 2 months. Submit seasonal material 2 months in advance. Accepts queries by mail, e-mail. Accepts simultaneous submissions. Responds in 3 weeks to queries Does not return unsolicited mss. Sample copy for free. Writer's guidelines for #10 SASE.

Nonfiction: Inspirational, personal experience, religious. **Buys 32 mss/year.** Send complete ms. Length: 500-1,250 words. **Pays 5¢/word.**

Photos: Send photos with submission. Buys one-time rights. Offers no additional payment for photos accepted with ms. Identification of subjects required.

Columns/Departments: Book Reviews (religious), 500 words or less. Send complete ms. **Pays 5¢/word.**

Poetry: Free verse, traditional. **Buys 16-20 poems/year.** Length: 4 lines minimum. **Pays $10-25.**

Tips: "We are a Catholic spirituality magazine that publishes articles on faith-based themes—also inspirational or uplifting stories. While Catholic we also publish articles by nonCatholic Christians."

$ ▣ NOW WHAT?, Bible Advocate Press/Church of God (Seventh Day), P.O. Box 33677, Denver CO 80233. (303)452-7973. Fax: (303)452-0657. E-mail: BibleAdvocate@cog7.org. Website: nowwhat.cog7.org. Editor: Calvin Burrell. **Contact:** Sherri Langton, associate editor. **100% freelance written.** "Online religious publication covering social and religious topics; more inclusive of nonChristians." Estab. 1996. Pays on publication. Publishes ms an average of 6-9 months after acceptance. Byline given. Offers 50% kill fee. Buys first, second serial (reprint), electronic rights. Editorial lead time 3 months. Submit seasonal material 6 months in advance. Accepts queries by mail, e-mail. Accepts simultaneous submissions. Responds in 3 weeks to queries. Sample copy for 9×12 SAE and 2 first-class stamps. Writer's guidelines for #10 SASE and online.

O-ᴛ "For the online magazine, write for the 'felt needs' of the reader and come up with creative ways for communicating to the unchurched."

Nonfiction: Inspirational, personal experience, religious. No Christmas or Easter pieces. **Buys 10-20 mss/year.** Send complete ms and SASE. Length: 1,500-1,800 words. **Pays $35-55.**
Reprints: Send typed ms with rights for sale noted and information about when and where the material previously appeared. Pays $35-55.
Photos: Send photos with submission. Buys one-time rights. Offers additional payment for photos accepted with ms. Identification of subjects required.
Fillers: Facts, resources. **Buys 6-10/year.** Length: 50-250 words. **Pays $10-20.**
Tips: "Be vulnerable in your personal experiences. Show, don't tell! Delete Christian jargon and write with the nonChristian in mind. Significant changes are referred to writers for approval. No fax or handwritten submissions, please."

$ OBLATES, Missionary Association of Mary Immaculate, 9480 N. De Mazenod Dr., Belleville IL 62223-1160. (618)398-4848. Fax: (618)398-8788. Website: www.snows.org. Managing Editor: Christine Portell. **Contact:** Mary Mohrman, manuscripts editor. **15% freelance written.** Prefers to work with published writers. Bimonthly magazine. Inspirational magazine for Christians; audience mainly Catholic adults. Circ. 500,000. **Pays on acceptance.** Publishes ms an average of 2 years after acceptance. Byline given. Buys first North American serial rights. Submit seasonal material 6 months in advance. Responds in 2 months to mss. Sample copy and writer's guidelines for 6×9 or larger SAE with 2 first-class stamps.
Nonfiction: Inspirational and personal experience with positive spiritual insights. No preachy, theological, or research articles. Avoid current events and controversial topics. Send complete ms. Length: 500-600 words. **Pays $150.**
Poetry: "Emphasis should be on inspiration, insight, and relationship with God." Light verse—reverent, well-written, perceptive, with traditional rhythm and rhyme. Submit maximum 2 poems. Length: 8-12 lines. **Pays $50.**
Tips: "We're looking for pieces offering comfort, encouragement, and a positive sense of applicable Christian direction to their lives. Focus on sharing of personal insight to problem (i.e., death or change), but must be positive, uplifting. We have well-defined needs for an established market but are always on the lookout for exceptional work. No queries."

$ $ ON MISSION, North American Mission Board, SBC, 4200 North Point Pkwy., Alpharetta GA 30022-4176. (770)410-6284. Fax: (770)410-6105. E-mail: onmission@namb.net. Website: www.onmission.com. **Contact:** Carolyn Curtis, editor. **50% freelance written.** Bimonthly lifestyle magazine that popularizes evangelism and church planting. "*On Mission*'s primary purpose is to help readers and churches become more intentional about personal evangelism. *On Mission* equips Christians for leading people to Christ and encourages churches to reach new people through new congregations." Estab. 1997. Circ. 100,000. **Pays on acceptance.** Publishes ms an average of 6 months after acceptance. Byline given. Buys first, electronic, first north american rights. Editorial lead time 9 months. Submit seasonal material 9 months in advance. Accepts queries by mail, e-mail. Responds in 6 months to queries; 6 months to mss. Sample copy free or online. Writer's guidelines free, online, or by e-mail.

O‑ Break in with a 600-word how-to article.

Nonfiction: How-to, humor, personal experience (stories of sharing your faith in Christ with a nonChristian). **Buys 30 mss/year.** Query with published clips. Length: 350-1,200 words. **Pays 25¢/word, more for cover stories.** Pays expenses of writers on assignment.
Photos: Most are shot on assignment. Buys one-time rights. Captions, identification of subjects required.
Columns/Departments: My Mission (personal evangelism), 700 words. **Buys 2 mss/year.** Query. **Pays 25¢/word.**
Tips: "Readers might be intimidated if those featured appear to be 'super Christians' who seem to live on a higher spiritual plane. Try to introduce subjects as three-dimensional, real people. Include anecdotes or examples of their fears and failures, including ways they overcame obstacles. In other words, take the reader inside the heart of the *On Mission* Christian and reveal the inevitable humanness that makes that person not only believable, but also approachable. We want the reader to feel encouraged to become *On Mission* by identifying with people like them who are featured in the magazine."

OUR SUNDAY VISITOR, Our Sunday Visitor, Inc., 200 Noll Plaza, Huntington IN 46750. (219)356-8400. Fax: (219)356-8472. E-mail: oursunvis@osv.com. Website: www.osv.com. Managing Editor: Richard G. Beemer. **Contact:** Gerald Korson, editor. **10% freelance written.** (Mostly assigned). Weekly tabloid covering world events and culture from a Catholic perspective. Estab. 1912. Circ. 70,000. **Pays on acceptance.** Publishes ms an average of 1 month after acceptance. Byline given. Buys first rights. Accepts queries by mail, e-mail.

$ PENTECOSTAL EVANGEL, The General Council of the Assemblies of God, 1445 N. Boonville, Springfield MO 65802-1894. (417)862-2781. Fax: (417)862-0416. E-mail: pe@ag.org. Website: www.pe.ag.org. Editor: Hal Donaldson. **5% freelance written.** Works with a small number of new/unpublished writers each year. Weekly magazine emphasizing news of the Assemblies of God for members of the Assemblies and other Pentecostal and charismatic Christians. Estab. 1913. Circ. 258,000. **Pays on acceptance.** Publishes ms an average of 6 months after acceptance. Byline given. Buys first North American serial, second serial (reprint), electronic rights. Submit seasonal material 6 months in advance. Accepts queries by mail, e-mail, fax, phone. Responds in 3 months to queries. Sample copy and writer's guidelines $1 or online.
Nonfiction: Inspirational, personal experience, informational (articles on homelife that convey Christian teaching), news, human interest, evangelical, current issues, seasonal. Send complete ms. Length: 500-1,200 words. **Pays up to $150.**
Photos: Photos purchased without accompanying ms. Pays $30 for 8×10 b&w glossy prints; $50 for 35mm or larger color transparencies. Total purchase price for ms includes payment for photos.

Tips: "We publish first-person articles concerning spiritual experiences; that is, answers to prayer for help in a particular situation, of unusual conversions or healings through faith in Christ. All articles submitted to us should be related to religious life. We are Protestant, evangelical, Pentecostal, and any doctrines or practices portrayed should be in harmony with the official position of our denomination (Assemblies of God)."

$THE PENTECOSTAL MESSENGER, Messenger Publishing House, P.O. Box 850, Joplin MO 64802-0850. (417)624-7050. Fax: (417)624-7102. E-mail: pm@pcg.org. Website: www.pcg.org. **Contact:** John Mallinak, editor. Will accept freelance material occasionally. Monthly magazine dedicated to encourgaing and informing ministers and lay leaders. "*The Pentecostal Messenger* is the official organ of the Pentecostal Church of God. It goes to ministers and church members." Estab. 1919. Circ. 5,000. Pays on publication. Byline given. Buys second serial (reprint), simultaneous rights. Accepts queries by mail, e-mail, phone. Accepts simultaneous submissions. Sample copy for 9×12 SAE and 2 first-class stamps. Writer's guidelines free.

Nonfiction: Interested in articles that deal with leadership issues, church growth, and how-to articles in regard to church programs and outreach, etc. Send complete ms. Length: 400-1,200 words. **Pays 2¢/word.**

Reprints: Send tearsheet, photocopy or typed ms with rights for sale noted and information about when and where the material previously appeared.

PIME WORLD, PIME Missionaries, 17330 Quincy St., Detroit MI 48221-2765. (313)342-4066. Fax: (313)342-6816. E-mail: pimeworld@pimeusa.org. Website: www.pimeusa.org. **Contact:** Cari Hartman, publications manager. **10% freelance written.** Bimonthly magazine supplemented with a newsletter, *PIME World's North America*. "Our focus is on educating North American Catholics on the missionary nature of the Church and inviting them to realize their call to be missionaries. The magazine and newsletter also serve the purpose of introducing the missionaries by emphasizing the IR activities throughout the world. Our audience is largely high school educated, conservative in both religion and politics." Estab. 1954. Circ. 16,000. Pays on publication. Publishes ms an average of 5 months after acceptance. Byline given. Buys one-time rights. Editorial lead time 2 months. Submit seasonal material 2 months in advance. Accepts queries by mail, e-mail, fax, phone. Accepts simultaneous submissions. Responds in 2 weeks to queries; 2 months to mss. Sample copy for free. Writer's guidelines for #10 SASE.

Nonfiction: Missionary activities of the Catholic church in the world, especially in Bangladesh, Brazil, Myanmar, Cameroon, Guinea Bissau, Hong Kong, India, Ivory Coast, Japan, Papua New Guinea, the Philippines, and Thailand. Query or send complete ms. Length: 200-500 words. **Pays $15 flat rate upon publication; 501-1,000 words pays $25 flat rate upon publication.**

Reprints: Accepts previously published submissions.

Photos: State availability of or send photos with submission. Buys one-time rights. Pays $10/color photo. Identification of subjects required.

Tips: "Articles produced from a faith standpoint dealing with current issues of social justice, evangelization, witness, proclamation, pastoral work in the foreign missions, etc. Interviews of missionaries, both religious and lay, welcome. Good quality color photos greatly appreciated."

$$☆ THE PLAIN TRUTH, Renewing Faith & Values, Plain Truth Ministries, 300 W. Green St., Pasadena CA 91129. Fax: (626)304-8172. E-mail: phyllis_duke@ptm.org. Website: www.ptm.org. Editor: Greg Albrecht. **Contact:** Phyllis Duke, assistant editor. **90% freelance written.** Bimonthly magazine. "We seek to reignite the flame of shattered lives by illustrating the joy of a new life in Christ." Estab. 1935. Circ. 70,000. Pays on publication. Publishes ms an average of 8 months after acceptance. Byline given. Offers $50 kill fee. Buys all-language rights for *The Plain Truth* and its affiliated publications Editorial lead time 6 months. Submit seasonal material 6 months in advance. Accepts queries by mail, e-mail. Accepts simultaneous submissions. Sample copy for 9×12 SAE and 5 first-class stamps. Writer's guidelines for #10 SASE or online.

Nonfiction: Inspirational, interview/profile, personal experience, religious. **Buys 48-50 mss/year.** Query with published clips and SASE. *No unsolicited mss.* Length: 750-2,500 words. **Pays 25¢/word.**

Reprints: Send tearsheet or photocopy of article or typed ms with rights for sale noted and information about when and where the article previously appeared with SASE for response. Pays 15¢/word.

Photos: State availability with submission. Reviews transparencies, prints. Buys one-time rights. Negotiates payment individually. Captions required.

The online magazine carries original content not found in the print edition and includes writer's guidelines.

Tips: "Material should offer Biblical solutions to real-life problems. Both first-person and third-person illustrations are encouraged. Articles should take a unique twist on a subject. Material must be insightful and practical for the Christian reader. All articles must be well researched and Biblically accurate without becoming overly scholastic. Use convincing arguments to support your Christian platform. Use vivid word pictures, simple and compelling language, and avoid stuffy academic jargon. Captivating anecdotes are vital."

$PRAIRIE MESSENGER, Catholic Journal, Benedictine Monks of St. Peter's Abbey, P.O. Box 190, Muenster, Saskatchewan S0K 2Y0, Canada. (306)682-1772. Fax: (306)682-5285. E-mail: pm.canadian@stpeters.sk.ca. Website: www.stpeters.sk.ca/prairie_messenger. Editor: Rev. Andrew Britz, OSB. **Contact:** Maureen Weber, associate editor. **10% freelance written.** Weekly Catholic journal with strong emphasis on social justice, Third World, and ecumenism. Estab. 1904. Circ. 7,300. Pays on publication. Publishes ms an average of 4 months after acceptance. Byline given. Not copyrighted. Buys first North American serial, first, one-time, second serial (reprint), simultaneous rights. Submit seasonal material 3 months in advance. Accepts queries by mail, e-mail, fax, phone. Responds in 2 months to queries. Sample copy and writer's guidelines for 9×12 SAE with $1 Canadian postage or IRCs.

Nonfiction: Interview/profile, opinion, religious. "No articles on abortion." **Buys 15 mss/year.** Send complete ms. Length: 250-600 words. **Pays $40-60.** Sometimes pays expenses of writers on assignment.

Photos: Send photos with submission. Reviews 3×5 prints. Buys all rights. Offers $15/photo. Captions required.

$ PRESBYTERIAN RECORD, 50 Wynford Dr., Toronto, Ontario M3C 1J7, Canada. (416)444-1111. Fax: (416)441-2825. E-mail: pcrecord@presbyterian.ca. Website: www.presbyterian.ca/record. **Contact:** The Rev. John Congram, editor. **50% freelance written.** Eager to work with new/unpublished writers. Monthly magazine for a church-oriented, family audience. Circ. 50,000. Pays on publication. Publishes ms an average of 4 months after acceptance. Buys first North American serial, one-time, simultaneous rights. Submit seasonal material 3 months in advance. Accepts queries by mail, e-mail, fax. Sample copy and guidelines for 9×12 SAE with $1 Canadian postage or IRCs or online.

- Responds in 2 months on accepted ms; returns rejected material in 3 months.

Nonfiction: Check a copy of the magazine for style. Inspirational, interview/profile, personal experience, religious. Special issues: evangelism; spirituality; education. No material solely or mainly American in context. No sermons, accounts of ordinations, inductions, baptisms, receptions, church anniversaries, or term papers. **Buys 15-20 unsolicited mss/year.** Query. Length: 600-1,500 words. **Pays $60 (Canadian).** Sometimes pays expenses of writers on assignment.

Reprints: Send tearsheet, photocopy or typed ms with rights for sale noted and information about when and where the material previously appeared.

Photos: When possible, photos should accompany ms; e.g., current events, historical events, and biographies. Pays $15-20 for glossy photos.

Columns/Departments: Vox Populi (items of contemporary and often controversial nature), 700 words; Mission Knocks (new ideas for congregational mission and service), 700 words.

The online magazine carries original content not found in the print edition and includes writer's guidelines. Contact: Tom Dickey, online editor.

Tips: "There is a trend away from maudlin, first-person pieces redolent with tragedy and dripping with simplistic, pietistic conclusions. Writers often leave out those parts which would likely attract readers, such as anecdotes and direct quotes. Using active rather than passive verbs also helps most manuscripts."

$ $ PRESBYTERIANS TODAY, Presbyterian Church (U.S.A.), 100 Witherspoon St., Louisville KY 40202-1396. (502)569-5637. Fax: (502)569-8632. E-mail: today@pcusa.org. Website: www.pcusa.org/today. **Contact:** Eva Stimson, editor. **45% freelance written.** Prefers to work with published/established writers. Denominational magazine published 10 times/year covering religion, denominational activities, and public issues for members of the Presbyterian Church (U.S.A.). "The magazine's purpose is to increase understanding and appreciation of what the church and its members are doing to live out their Christian faith." Estab. 1867. Circ. 70,000. **Pays on acceptance.** Publishes ms an average of 6 months after acceptance. Byline given. Offers 50% kill fee. Buys first North American serial rights. Editorial lead time 3 months. Submit seasonal material 3 months in advance. Accepts queries by mail, e-mail, fax, phone. Responds in 2 weeks to queries; 1 month to mss. Sample copy and writer's guidelines free.

Break in with a "short feature for our 'Spotlight' department (300 words)."

Nonfiction: "Most articles have some direct relevance to a Presbyterian audience; however, *Presbyterians Today* also seeks well-informed articles written for a general audience that help readers deal with the stresses of daily living from a Christian perspective." How-to (everyday Christian living), inspirational, Presbyterian programs, issues, peoples. **Buys 20 mss/year.** Send complete ms. Length: 1,000-1,800 words. **Pays $300 maximum for assigned articles; $75-300 for unsolicited articles.**

Photos: State availability with submission. Reviews contact sheets, transparencies, b&w prints. Buys one-time rights. Negotiates payment individually. Identification of subjects required.

$ PRESERVING CHRISTIAN HOMES, General Youth Division, 8855 Dunn Rd., Hazelwood MO 63042. (314)837-7304. Fax: (314)837-4503. E-mail: youth@upci.org. Website: www.upci.org/youth. **Contact:** Todd Gaddy, editor and general youth director of promotions. **40% freelance written.** Bimonthly magazine covering Christian home and family. "All submissions must conform to Christian perspective." Estab. 1970. Circ. 4,500. Pays on publication. Publishes ms an average of 9 months after acceptance. Byline sometimes given. Buys one-time, simultaneous rights. Editorial lead time 6 months. Submit seasonal material 6 months in advance. Accepts queries by mail. Accepts simultaneous submissions. Responds in 2 weeks to queries; 2 months to mss. Sample copy for 10×13 SAE and 2 first-class stamps.

- No e-mail submissions will be accepted.

Nonfiction: General interest, humor, inspirational, personal experience, religious. Special issues: Mothers Day/Fathers Day. No "editorial or political." **Buys 15 mss/year.** Send complete ms. Length: 500-1,500 words. **Pays $30-40.**

Photos: State availability with submission. Buys all rights. Negotiates payment individually.

Fiction: Humorous, religious, slice-of-life vignettes. **Buys 6 mss/year.** Send complete ms. Length: 500-1,500 words. **Pays $30-40.**

Poetry: Free verse, light verse, traditional. **Buys 3 poems/year.** Submit maximum 5 poems. Length: 10-40 lines. **Pays $20-25.**

Fillers: Anecdotes, facts, short humor. **Buys 2/year.** Length: 50-200 words. **Pays $10-20.**

Tips: "Be relevant to today's Christian families!"

$ $ PRISM MAGAZINE, America's Alternative Evangelical Voice, Evangelicals for Social Action, 10 E. Lancaster Ave., Wynnewood PA 19096. (610)645-9391. Fax: (610)649-8090. E-mail: kristyn@esa-online.org. Website: www.esa-online.org. **Contact:** Kristyn Komarnicki, editor. **50% freelance written.** Bimonthly magazine covering Christianity and social justice. For holistic, Biblical, socially-concerned, progressive Christians. Estab. 1993. Circ. 7,000. Pays on publication. Publishes ms an average of 4-6 months after acceptance. Byline given. Buys first North American serial rights. Editorial lead time 4 months. Submit seasonal material 4 months in advance. Accepts queries by mail, e-mail. Responds in 1 month to queries; 3 months to mss. Sample copy for $3. Writer's guidelines free.

- "We're a nonprofit, some writers are pro bono." Occasionally accepts previously published material.

Nonfiction: Book excerpts (to coincide with book release date), essays, inspirational, opinion, personal experience. **Buys 10-12 mss/year.** Send complete ms. Length: 500-3,000 words. **Pays $75-300 for assigned articles; $25-200 for unsolicited articles.**

Photos: Send photos with submission. Reviews prints. Buys one-time rights. Pays $25/photo published; $150 if photo used on cover.

Tips: "We look closely at stories of holistic ministry. It's best to request a sample copy to get to know *PRISM*'s focus/style before submitting—we receive so many submissions that are not appropriate."

$ ☆ PURPOSE, 616 Walnut Ave., Scottdale PA 15683-1999. (724)887-8500. Fax: (724)887-3111. E-mail: horsch@mph.org. Website: www.mph.org. **Contact:** James E. Horsch, editor. **95% freelance written.** Weekly magazine "for adults, young and old, general audience with varied interests. My readership is interested in seeing how Christianity works in difficult situations." Estab. 1968. Circ. 11,000. **Pays on acceptance.** Publishes ms an average of 8 months after acceptance. Buys one-time rights. Submit seasonal material 6 months in advance. Accepts simultaneous submissions. Responds in 3 months to queries. Sample copy and writer's guidelines for 6×9 SAE and 2 first-class stamps.

Nonfiction: Inspirational stories from a Christian perspective. "I want upbeat stories that deal with issues faced by believers in family, business, politics, religion, gender, and any other areas—and show how the Christian faith resolves them. *Purpose* conveys truth through quality fiction or true life stories. Our magazine accents Christian discipleship. Christianity affects all of life, and we expect our material to demonstate this. I would like story-type articles about individuals, groups and organizations who are intelligently and effectively working at such problems as hunger, poverty, international understanding, peace, justice, etc., because of their faith. Essays and how-to-do-it pieces must include a lot of anecdotal, life-exposure examples." **Buys 130 mss/year.** Send complete ms. Length: 750 words. **Pays 5¢/word maximum. Buys one-time rights only.**

Reprints: Send tearsheet, photocopy or typed ms with rights for sale noted and information about when and where the material previously appeared.

Photos: Photos purchased with ms must be sharp enough for reproduction; requires prints in all cases. Pays $20. Captions required.

Fiction: "Produce the story with specificity so that it appears to take place somewhere and with real people." Historical, humorous, religious.

Poetry: Free verse, light verse, traditional, blank verse. **Buys 130 poems/year.** Length: 12 lines. **Pays $7.50-20/poem depending on length and quality. Buys one-time rights only.**

Fillers: Anecdotal items up to 599 words. **Pays 4¢/word maximum.**

Tips: "We are looking for articles which show the Christian faith working at issues where people hurt; stories need to be told and presented professionally. Good photographs help place material with us."

$ QUEEN OF ALL HEARTS, Montfort Missionaries, 26 S. Saxon Ave., Bay Shore NY 11706-8993. (631)665-0726. Fax: (631)665-4349. E-mail: pretre@worldnet.att.net. Website: www.montfortmissionaries.com. **Contact:** Roger Charest, S.M.M., managing editor. **50% freelance written.** Bimonthly magazine covering "Mary, Mother of Jesus, as seen in the sacred scriptures, tradition, history of the church, the early Christian writers, lives of the saints, poetry, art, music, spiritual writers, apparitions, shrines, ecumenism, etc." Estab. 1950. Circ. 2,000. **Pays on acceptance.** Publishes ms an average of 6 months after acceptance. Byline given. Not copyrighted. Submit seasonal material 6 months in advance. Accepts queries by mail, e-mail, fax, phone. Responds in 2 months to queries. Sample copy for $2.50.

Nonfiction: Essays, inspirational, interview/profile, personal experience, religious (Marialogical and devotional). **Buys 25 mss/year.** Send complete ms. Length: 750-2,500 words. **Pays $40-60.**

Photos: Send photos with submission. Reviews transparencies. Buys one-time rights. Pay varies.

Fiction: Religious. **Buys 6 mss/year.** Send complete ms. Length: 1,500-2,500 words. **Pays $40-60.**

Poetry: Joseph Tusiani, poetry editor. Free verse. **Buys approximately 10 poems/year.** Submit maximum 2 poems. **Pays in contributor copies.**

$ ☆ THE QUIET HOUR, Cook Communications Ministries, 4050 Lee Vance View, Colorado Springs CO 80918. (719)536-0100. E-mail: gwilde@mac.com. Managing Editor: Doug Schmidt. **Contact:** Gary Wilde, editor. **100% freelance written.** Devotional booklet published quarterly featuring daily devotions. "*The Quiet Hour* is the adult-level quarterly devotional booklet published by David C. Cook. The purpose of *The Quiet Hour* is to provide Bible-based devotional readings for Christians who are in the process of growing toward Christlikeness. Most often, *The Quiet Hour* is used at home, either in the morning or evening, as part of a devotional period. It may be used by individuals, couples, or families. For those studying with our Bible-in-Life curriculum, it also helps them prepare for the upcoming Sunday school lesson." **Pays on acceptance.** Publishes ms an average of 14 months after acceptance. Byline given. Makes work-for-hire assignments. Editorial lead time 14 months. Responds in 3 months to queries. Writer's guidelines free.

Nonfiction: Daily devotionals. **Buys 52 mss/year.** Query by mail only with résumé and/or list of credits. **Pays $15-25/devotional.**

Tips: "Send list of credits with query—especially other devotional writing. Do not send samples. We will assign the scripture passages to use."

$ $ REFORM JUDAISM, Union of American Hebrew Congregations, 633 Third Ave., New York NY 10017-6778. (212)650-4240. Website: www.uahc.org/rjmag/. Editor: Aron Hirt-Manheimer. **Contact:** Joy Weinberg, managing editor. **30% freelance written.** Quarterly magazine of Reform Jewish issues. "*Reform Judaism* is the official voice of the Union of American Hebrew Congregations, linking the institutions and affiliates of Reform Judaism with every Reform Jew. *RJ* covers developments within the Movement while interpreting events and Jewish tradition from a Reform perspective." Pays on publication. Publishes ms an average of 3 months after acceptance. Byline given. Offers kill fee for commissioned articles. Buys first North American serial rights. Submit seasonal material 6 months in advance. Accepts previously published material. Responds in 2 months to queries; 2 months to mss. Sample copy for $3.50. Writer's guidelines for SASE or online.

Nonfiction: Book excerpts, exposé, general interest, historical/nostalgic, inspirational, interview/profile, opinion, personal experience, photo feature, travel. **Buys 30 mss/year.** Submit complete ms with SASE. Length: Cover stories: 2,500-3,500 words; major feature: 1,800-2,500 words; secondary feature: 1,200-1,500 words; department (e.g., Travel): 1,200 words; letters: 200 words maximum; opinion: 525 words maximum. **Pays 30¢/word.** Sometimes pays expenses of writers on assignment.

Reprints: Send tearsheet, photocopy or typed ms with rights for sale noted and information about when and where the material previously appeared. Usually does not publish reprints.

Photos: Send photos with submission. Reviews 8×10/color or slides and b&w prints. Buys one-time rights. Pays $25-75. Identification of subjects required.

Fiction: Sophisticated, cutting-edge, superb writing. **Buys 4 mss/year.** Send complete ms. Length: 600-2,500 words. **Pays 30¢/word.**

The online magazine carries original content not found in the print edition and includes writer's guidelines.

Tips: "We prefer a stamped postcard including the following information/checklist: __Yes, we are interested in publishing; __No, unfortunately the submission doesn't meet our needs; __Maybe, we'd like to hold on to the article for now. Submissions sent this way will receive a faster response."

$ $ THE REPORTER, Women's American ORT, Inc., 315 Park Ave. S., 17th Floor, New York NY 10010. (800)51-WAORT, ext. 265. Fax: (212)674-3057. E-mail: editor@waort.org. **Contact:** Dana Asher, editor. **85% freelance written.** Semiannual nonprofit journal published by Jewish women's organization covering Jewish women celebrities, issues of contemporary Jewish culture, Israel, anti-Semitism, women's rights, Jewish travel, and the international Jewish community. Estab. 1966. Circ. 65,000. Payment time varies. Publishes ms an average of 1 year after acceptance. Byline given. Buys first North American serial rights. Submit seasonal material 6 months in advance. Accepts queries by mail, e-mail. Responds in 3 months to queries. Sample copy for 9×12 SAE and 3 first-class stamps. Writer's guidelines for #10 SASE.

Break in with "a different look at a familiar topic, i.e., 'Jews without God' (Winter 2000). Won't consider handwritten or badly-typed queries. Unpublished writers are welcome. Others, include credits."

Nonfiction: Cover feature profiles a dynamic Jewish woman making a difference in Judaism, women's issues, education, entertainment, profiles, business, journalism, arts. Essays, exposé, humor, inspirational, opinion, personal experience, photo feature, religious, travel. Query. Length: 1,800 words maximum. **Pays $200 and up.**

Photos: Send photos with submission. Identification of subjects required.

Columns/Departments: Education Horizon; Destination (Jewish sites/travel); Inside Out (Advocacy); Women's Business; Art Scene (interviews, books, films); Lasting Impression (uplifting/inspirational).

Fiction: Publishes novel excerpts and short stories as part of Lasting Impressions column. Length: 800 words. **Pays $150-300.**

Tips: "Send query only by e-mail or postal mail. Show us a fresh look, not a rehash. Particularly interested in stories of interest to younger readers."

$ REVIEW FOR RELIGIOUS, 3601 Lindell Blvd., Room 428, St. Louis MO 63108-3393. (314)977-7363. Fax: (314)977-7362. E-mail: review@slu.edu. Website: www.reviewforreligious.org. **Contact:** David L. Fleming, S.J., editor. **100% freelance written.** Bimonthly magazine for Roman Catholic priests, brothers, and sisters. Estab. 1942. Pays on publication. Publishes ms an average of 9 months after acceptance. Byline given. Buys first North American serial rights. Rarely buys second serial (reprint) rights. Accepts queries by mail, fax. Responds in 2 months to queries.

Nonfiction: Spiritual, liturgical, canonical matters only. Not for general audience. Length: 1,500-5,000 words. **Pays $6/page.**

Tips: "The writer must know about religious life in the Catholic Church and be familiar with prayer, vows, community life, and ministry."

N SCP JOURNAL and SCP NEWSLETTER, Spiritual Counterfeits Project, P.O. Box 4308, Berkeley CA 94704-4308. (510)540-0300. Fax: (510)540-1107. E-mail: scp@scp-inc.org. Website: www.scp-inc.org/. **Contact:** Tal Brooke, editor. **5-10% freelance written.** Prefers to work with published/established writers. "The *SCP Journal* and *SCP Newsletter* are quarterly publications geared to reach demanding nonbelievers while giving Christians authentic insight into the very latest spiritual and cultural trends." Targeted audience is the educated lay reader. Estab. 1975. Circ. 18,000.

Pays on publication. Publishes ms an average of 6 months after acceptance. Byline given. Buys negotiable rights. Accepts simultaneous submissions. Responds in 3 months to queries. Sample copy for $8.75. Writer's guidelines for #10 SASE.

- Less emphasis on book reviews and more focus on specialized "single issue" topics.

Nonfiction: Book excerpts, essays, exposé, interview/profile, opinion, personal experience, religious. Query by telephone. Length: 2,500-3,500 words. **Pay negotiated by phone.**
Reprints: Call for telephone inquiry first. Payment is negotiated.
Photos: State availability with submission. Reviews contact sheets, prints, slides. Buys one-time rights. Offers no additional payment for photos accepted with ms. Captions, identification of subjects, model releases required.
Tips: "The area of our publication most open to freelancers is specialized topics covered by *SCP*. Do not send unsolicited samples of your work until you have checked with us by phone to see if it fits *SCP*'s area of interest and publication schedule. The usual profile of contributors is that they are published within the field, have advanced degrees from top ranked universities, as well as experience that makes their work uniquely credible."

N $ SEEK, Standard Publishing, 8121 Hamilton Ave., Cincinnati OH 45231. (513)931-4050, ext. 365. Fax: (513)931-0950. Website: www.standardpub.com. **Contact:** Eileen H. Wilmoth, editor. **98% freelance written.** Prefers to work with published/established writers. Quarterly Sunday school paper in weekly issues for young and middle-aged adults who attend church and Bible classes. Circ. 45,000. **Pays on acceptance.** Publishes ms an average of 1 year after acceptance. Byline given. Buys first North American serial, second serial (reprint) rights. Submit seasonal material 1 year in advance. Responds in 3 months to queries. Sample copy and writer's guidelines for 6×9 SAE with 2 first-class stamps.
Nonfiction: "We look for articles that are warm, inspirational, devotional, or personal or human interest; that deal with controversial matters, timely issues of religious, ethical, or moral nature, or first-person testimonies, true-to-life happenings, vignettes, emotional situations or problems; communication problems and example of answered prayers. Article must deliver its point in a convincing manner but not be patronizing or preachy. It must appeal to either men or women, must be alive, vibrant, sparkling, and have a title that demands the article be read. We always need stories about families, marriages, problems on campus, and life testimonies." **Buys 150-200 mss/year.** Send complete ms. Length: 400-1,200 words. **Pays 5¢/word.**
Reprints: Send tearsheet, photocopy or typed ms with rights for sale noted and information about when and where the material previously appeared. Pays 50% of amount paid for an original article.
Photos: B&W photos purchased with or without mss. Pays $20 minimum for good 8×10 glossy prints.
Fiction: Religious fiction and religiously slanted historical and humorous fiction. No poetry. Length: 400-1,200 words. **Pays 5¢/word.**
Tips: "Submit manuscripts which tell of faith in action or victorious Christian living as central theme. We select manuscripts as far as 1 year in advance of publication. Complimentary copies are sent to our published writers immediately following printing."

$ $ SHARING THE VICTORY, Fellowship of Christian Athletes, 8701 Leeds Rd., Kansas City MO 64129. (816)921-0909. Fax: (816)921-8755. E-mail: stv@fca.org. Website: www.fca.org. Editor: David Smale. **50% freelance written.** Prefers to work with published/established writers, but works with a growing number of new/unpublished writers each year. Published 9 times/year. "We seek to encourage and enable athletes and coaches at all levels to take their faith seriously on and off the 'field.'" Estab. 1959. Circ. 80,000. Pays on publication. Publishes ms an average of 4 months after acceptance. Byline given. Buys first rights. Submit seasonal material 6 months in advance. Responds in 3 months to queries; 3 months to mss. Sample copy for $1 and 9×12 SAE with 3 first-class stamps. Writer's guidelines free for #10 SASE or by e-mail.
Nonfiction: Inspirational, interview/profile (with name athletes and coaches solid in their faith), personal experience, photo feature. No "sappy articles on 'I became a Christian and now I'm a winner.'" **Buys 5-20 mss/year.** Query. Length: 500-1,000 words. **Pays $100-200 for unsolicited articles, more for the exceptional profile.**
Reprints: Send typed ms with rights for sale noted. Pays 50% of amount paid for an original article.
Photos: State availability with submission. Reviews contact sheets. Buys one-time rights. Pay depends on quality of photo but usually a minimum of $50. Model releases for required.
Tips: "Profiles and interviews of particular interest to coed athlete, primarily high school and college age. Our graphics and editorial content appeal to youth. The area most open to freelancers is profiles on or interviews with well-known athletes or coaches (male, female, minorities) and offbeat but interscholastic team sports."

$ $ SIGNS OF THE TIMES, Pacific Press Publishing Association, P.O. Box 5353, Nampa ID 83653-5353. (208)465-2579. Fax: (208)465-2531. E-mail: mmoore@pacificpress.com. **Contact:** Marvin Moore, editor. **40% freelance written.** Works with a small number of new/unpublished writers each year. Monthly magazine. "We are a monthly Seventh-day Adventist magazine encouraging the general public to practice the principles of the Bible." Estab. 1874. Circ. 200,000. **Pays on acceptance.** Publishes ms an average of 6-18 months after acceptance. Byline given. Offers kill fee. Buys first North American serial, one-time, second serial (reprint) rights. Editorial lead time 1 year. Submit seasonal material 1 year in advance. Responds in 1 month to queries; 2-3 months to mss. Sample copy and writer's guidelines for 9×12 SAE with 3 first-class stamps. Writer's guidelines online.
Nonfiction: "We want writers with a desire to share the good news of reconciliation with God. Articles should be people-oriented, well-researched, and should have a sharp focus. Gospel articles deal with salvation and how to experience it. While most of our gospel articles are assigned or picked up from reprints, we do occasionally accept unsolicited

manuscripts in this area. Gospel articles should be 1,250 words. Christian lifestyle articles deal with the practical problems of everyday life from a Biblical and Christian perspective. These are typically 1,000-1,200 words. We request that authors include sidebars that give additional information on the topic whenever possible. First-person stories must illuminate a spiritual or moral truth that the individual in the story learned. We especially like stories that hold the reader in suspense or that have an unusual twist at the end. First-person stories are typically 1,000 words long." General interest, how-to, humor, inspirational, interview/profile, personal experience, religious. **Buys 75 mss/year.** Query by mail only with or without published clips or send complete ms. Length: 500-1,500 words. **Pays 10-20¢/word.**
Reprints: Send tearsheet, photocopy or typed ms with rights for sale noted and information about when and where the material previously appeared. Pays 50% of amount paid for an original article.
Photos: Merwin Stewart, photo editor. Reviews b&w contact sheets, 35mm color transparencies, 5×7 or 8×10 b&w prints. Buys one-time rights. Pays $35-300 for transparencies; $20-50 for prints. Captions, identification of subjects, model releases required.
Columns/Departments: Send complete ms. **Pays $25-150.**
Fillers: "Short fillers can be inspirational/devotional, Christian lifestyle, stories, comments that illuminate a Biblical text—in short, anything that might fit in a general Christian magazine." Length: 500-600 words.
Tips: "The audience for *Signs of the Times* includes both Christians and nonChristians of all ages. However, we recommend that our authors write with the nonChristian in mind, since most Christians can easily relate to articles that are written from a nonChristian perspective, whereas many nonChristians will have no interest in an article that is written from a Christian perspective. While *Signs* is published by Seventh-day Adventists, we mention even our own denominational name in the magazine rather infrequently. The purpose is not to hide who we are but to make the magazine as attractive to nonChristian readers as possible. We are especially interested in articles that respond to the questions of everyday life that people are asking and the problems they are facing. Since these questions and problems nearly always have a spiritual component, articles that provide a Biblical and spiritual response are especially welcome. Any time you can provide us with 1 or more sidebars that add information to the topic of your article, you enhance your chance of getting our attention. Two kinds of sidebars seem to be especially popular with readers: Those that give information in lists, with each item in the list consisting of only a few words or at the most a sentence or 2; and technical information or long explanations that in the main article might get the reader too bogged down in detail. Whatever their length, sidebars need to be part of the total word count of the article. We like the articles in *Signs of the Times* to have interest-grabbing introductions. One of the best ways to do this is with anecdotes, particularly those that have a bit of suspense or conflict."

$ SOCIAL JUSTICE REVIEW, 3835 Westminster Place, St. Louis MO 63108-3472. (314)371-1653. Fax: (314)371-0889. E-mail: centbur@juno.com. Website: www.socialjusticereview.org. **Contact:** The Rev. John H. Miller, C.S.C., editor. **25% freelance written.** Works with a small number of new/unpublished writers each year. Bimonthly magazine. Estab. 1908. Publishes ms an average of 1 year after acceptance. Not copyrighted, however special articles within the magazine may be copyrighted, or an occasional special issue has been copyrighted due to author's request. Buys first North American serial rights. Accepts queries by mail. Sample copy for 9×12 SAE and 3 first-class stamps.
Nonfiction: Scholarly articles on society's economic, religious, social, intellectual, political problems with the aim of bringing Catholic social thinking to bear upon these problems. Query by mail only with SASE. Length: 2,500-3,000 words. **Pays about 2¢/word.**
Reprints: Send typed ms with rights for sale noted and information about when and where the material previously appeared. Pays about 2¢/word.
Tips: "Write moderate essays completely compatible with papal teaching and readable to the average person."

$ SPIRITUAL LIFE, 2131 Lincoln Rd. NE, Washington DC 20002-1199. (202)832-8489. Fax: (202)832-8967. E-mail: edodonnell@aol.com. Website: www.Spiritual-Life.org. **Contact:** Br. Edward O'Donnell, O.C.D., editor. **80% freelance written.** Prefers to work with published/established writers. Quarterly magazine for "largely Christian, well-educated, serious readers." Circ. 12,000. **Pays on acceptance.** Publishes ms an average of 1 year after acceptance. Buys first North American serial rights. Responds in 2 months to queries. Sample copy and writer's guidelines for 7×10 or larger SAE with 5 first-class stamps.
Nonfiction: Serious articles of contemporary spirituality and its pastoral application to everday life. High quality articles about our encounter with God in the present day-world. Language of articles should be college level. Technical terminology, if used, should be clearly explained. Material should be presented in a postive manner. Buys inspirational and think pieces. "Brief autobiographical information (present occupation, past occupations, books and articles published, etc.) should accompany article." Sentimental articles or those dealing with specific devotional practices not accepted. No fiction or poetry. **Buys 20 mss/year.** Length: 3,000-5,000 words. **Pays $50 minimum, and 2 contributor's copies.**

$ $ ST. ANTHONY MESSENGER, 28 W. Liberty St., Cincinnati OH 45210-1298. (513)241-5615. Fax: (513)241-0399. E-mail: stanthony@americancatholic.org. Website: www.AmericanCatholic.org. **Contact:** Father Jack Wintz, O.F.M., editor. **55% freelance written.** Monthly general interest magazine for a national readership of Catholic families, most of which have children or grandchildren in grade school, high school, or college. Circ. 340,000. **Pays on acceptance.** Publishes ms an average of 9 months after acceptance. Byline given. Buys electronic rights. First worldwide serial rights. Submit seasonal material 6 months in advance. Accepts queries by mail, e-mail, fax. Responds in 3 weeks to queries; 2 months to mss. Sample copy and writer's guidelines for 9×12 SAE with 4 first-class stamps.

Nonfiction: How-to (on psychological and spiritual growth, problems of parenting/better parenting, marriage problems/marriage enrichment), humor, inspirational, interview/profile, opinion (limited use; writer must have special qualifications for topic), personal experience (if pertinent to our purpose), photo feature, informational, social issues. **Buys 35-50 mss/year.** Query with published clips. Length: 1,500-2,500 words. **Pays 16¢/word.** Sometimes pays expenses of writers on assignment.
Fiction: Mainstream, religious. **Buys 12 mss/year.** Send complete ms with SASE. Length: 2,000-2,500 words. **Pays 16¢/word.**
Poetry: "Our poetry needs are very limited." Submit maximum 4-5 poems. Length: Up to 20-25 lines; the shorter, the better. **Pays $2/line; $20 minimum.**
Tips: "The freelancer should consider why his or her proposed article would be appropriate for us, rather than for *Redbook* or *Saturday* We treat human problems of all kinds, but from a religious perspective. Articles should reflect Catholic theology, spirituality, and employ a Catholic terminology and vocabulary. We need more articles on prayer, scripture, Catholic worship. Get authoritative information (not merely library research); we want interviews with experts. Write in popular style; use lots of examples, stories, and personal quotes. Word length is an important consideration."

$ STANDARD, Nazarene International Headquarters, 6401 The Paseo, Kansas City MO 64131. (816)333-7000, ext. 2555. E-mail: Evlead@nazarene.org. **Contact:** Everett Leadingham, editor. **100% freelance written.** Works with a small number of new/unpublished writers each year. Weekly inspirational paper with Christian reading for adults. Estab. 1936. Circ. 160,000. **Pays on acceptance.** Publishes ms an average of 18 months after acceptance. Byline given. Buys one-time, second serial (reprint) rights. Submit seasonal material 6 months in advance. Accepts queries by mail, e-mail. Responds in 10 weeks to queries. Sample copy for free. Writer's guidelines for SAE with 2 first-class stamps.
Reprints: Send tearsheet.
Fiction: Prefers fiction-type stories *showing* Christianity in action. Send complete ms. Length: 500-1,200 words. **Pays 3½¢/word for first rights; 2¢/word for reprint rights.**
Poetry: Free verse, haiku, light verse, traditional. **Buys 50 poems/year.** Submit maximum 5 poems. Length: 50 lines. **Pays 25¢/line.**
Tips: "Stories should express Christian principles without being preachy. Setting, plot, and characterization must be realistic."

$ $ THE STANDARD, Magazine of the Baptist General Conference, Baptist General Conference, 2002 S. Arlington Heights Rd., Arlington Heights IL 60005. Fax: (847)228-5376. E-mail: jhanning@baptistgeneral.org. Website: www.bgcworld.org. **Contact:** Jodi Hanning, developmental and managing editor. **65% freelance written.** Nonprofit, religious, evangelical Christian magazine published 10 times/year covering the Baptist General Conference. "*The Standard* is the official magazine of the Baptist General Conference (BGC). Articles related to the BGC, our churches, or by/about BGC people receive preference." Estab. early 1900. Circ. 9,000. Pays on publication. Byline given. Offers 50% kill fee. Buys first rights. Editorial lead time 6 months. Submit seasonal material 6 months in advance. Accepts queries by e-mail. Responds in 1 month to queries; 2 months to mss. Sample copy for #10 SASE. Writer's guidelines free.
Nonfiction: Book excerpts, general interest, how-to, inspirational, interview/profile, photo feature, religious, travel, sidebars related to theme. No sappy religious pieces, articles not intended for our audience. Ask for a sample instead of sending anything first. **Buys 20-30 mss/year.** Query with published clips. Length: 300-2,000 words. **Pays $50-240.** Sometimes pays expenses of writers on assignment.
Photos: State availability with submission. Reviews prints. Buys one-time rights. Offers $15/photo. Captions, identification of subjects, model releases required.
Columns/Departments: Bob Putman, associate editor. Around the BGC (blurbs of news happening in the BGC), 50-150 words. Send complete ms. **Pays $15-20.**
Tips: "Please study the magazine and the denomination. We will send sample copies to interested freelancers and give further information about our publication needs upon request. Freelancers who are interested in working an assignment are welcome to express their interest."

$ THESE DAYS, Presbyterian Publishing Corp., 100 Witherspoon St., Louisville KY 40202-1396. (502)569-5102. Fax: (502)569-5113. E-mail: vpatton@presbypub.com. **Contact:** Vince Patton, editor. **95% freelance written.** Quarterly magazine covering religious devotionals. "*These Days* is published especially for the Cumberland Presbyterian Church, The Presbyterian Church in Canada, The Presbyterian Church (U.S.A.), The United Churches of Canada, and The United Church of Christ as a personal, family, and group devotional guide." Estab. 1970. Circ. 200,000. **Pays on acceptance.** Publishes ms an average of 8 months after acceptance. Byline given. Buys all rights, makes work-for-hire assignments. Editorial lead time 10 months. Submit seasonal material 1 year in advance. Accepts queries by mail, e-mail. Responds in 6 months to queries; 10 months to mss. Sample copy for 6×9 SAE and 3 first-class stamps. Writer's guidelines for #10 SASE.
Nonfiction: "Use freelance in all issues. Only devotional material will be accepted. Send for application form and guidelines. Enclose #10 SASE." Publishes very few unsolicited devotionals. Devotions and devotional aids in our format. **Buys 365 mss/year.** Query with or without published clips. Length: Devotionals, 250 words; These Moments, 500 words; These Times, 750 words. **Pays $14.25 for devotions; $30 for These Moments, and $45 for These Times.**
Poetry: Buys 2-4 poems/year. Submit maximum 5 poems. Length: 3-20 lines. **Pays $15.**

Tips: "The best way to be considered is to send a 1-page query that includes your religious affiliation and your religious, writing-related experience, plus a sample devotion in our format and/or published clips of similar material. Read a current issue devotionally to get a feel for the magazine. We would also like to see more minority and Canadian writers."

$ TOGETHER, Shalom Publishers, Box 656, Route 2, Grottoes VA 24441. E-mail: tgether@aol.com. **Contact:** Melodie M. Davis, editor. **95% freelance written.** "*Together* is used quarterly by churches as an outreach paper to encourage readers to faith in Christ and God and participation in a local church. In addition to testimonies of spiritual conversion or journey, we publish general inspirational or family-related articles." Estab. 1986. Circ. 180,000. Pays on publication. Publishes ms an average of 9 months after acceptance. Byline given. Buys one-time, second serial (reprint) rights. Editorial lead time 6 months. Submit seasonal material 9 months in advance. Accepts previously published material. Accepts simultaneous submissions. Responds in 2 months to queries; 6 months to mss. Sample copy for 9×12 SAE and 4 first-class stamps. Writer's guidelines for #10 SASE or by e-mail.
Nonfiction: Inspirational, personal experience (testimony), religious. **Buys 22-24 mss/year.** Send complete ms. Length: 300-1,000 words. **Pays $35-50.**
Photos: State availability with submission. Reviews 3×5 prints. Buys one-time rights. Offers $25/photo. Identification of subjects required.
Tips: "We can use good contemporary conversion stories (to Christian faith) including as-told-to's. Read other stuff that is being published and then ask if your writing is up to the level of what is being published today."

$ $ $ TRICYCLE, The Buddhist Review, The Buddhist Ray, Inc, 92 Vandam St., New York NY 10013. (212)645-1143. Fax: (212)645-1493. E-mail: editorial@tricycle.com. Website: www.tricycle.com. Editor-in-Chief: James Shaheen. **Contact:** Caitlin Van Dusen, assistant editor. **80% freelance written.** Quarterly magazine covering the impact of Buddhism on Western culture. "*Tricycle* readers tend to be well-educated and open-minded." Estab. 1991. Circ. 65,000. Pays on publication. Byline given. Offers 25% kill fee. Buys one-time rights. Editorial lead time 3 months. Accepts queries by mail, e-mail, fax. Accepts simultaneous submissions. Responds in 1 month to queries; 3 months to mss. Sample copy for $7.50 or online at website. Writer's guidelines free.
Nonfiction: Book excerpts, essays, general interest, historical/nostalgic, humor, inspirational, interview/profile, personal experience, photo feature, religious, travel. **Buys 4-6 mss/year.** Send complete ms. Length: 1,000-5,000 words. **Pays $300-1,000.**
Photos: State availability with submission. Reviews contact sheets. Buys one-time rights. Negotiates payment individually. Captions, identification of subjects required.
Columns/Departments: Reviews (film, books, tapes), 600 words; Science and Gen Next, both 700 words. **Buys 6-8 mss/year.** Query. **Pays $0-300.**
Poetry: *Tricycle* reports that they publish "very, very little poetry" and do not encourage unsolicited submissions.
Tips: "*Tricycle* is a Buddhist magazine, and nearly every unsolicited manuscript that interests us is Buddhist-related."

$ $ U.S. CATHOLIC, Claretian Publications, 205 W. Monroe St., Chicago IL 60606. (312)236-7782. Fax: (312)236-8207. E-mail: editors@uscatholic.org. Website: www.uscatholic.org. Editor: Mark J. Brummel, CMF. Editorial Director: Anne Spencer Ellis. Executive Editor: Meinrad Scherer-Emunds. **Contact:** Fran Hurst, editorial assistant. **100% freelance written.** Monthly magazine covering Roman Catholic spirituality. "*U.S. Catholic* is dedicated to the belief that it makes a difference whether you're Catholic. We invite and help our readers explore the wisdom of their faith tradition and apply their faith to the challenges of the 21st century." Estab. 1935. Circ. 50,000. **Pays on acceptance.** Publishes ms an average of 3 months after acceptance. Byline given. Buys first North American serial rights. Editorial lead time 8 months. Submit seasonal material 6 months in advance. Accepts queries by mail, e-mail, fax, phone. Responds in 1 month to queries; 2 months to mss. Sample copy for large SASE. Writer's guidelines for #10 SASE.
Nonfiction: Essays, inspirational, opinion, personal experience, religious. **Buys 100 mss/year.** Send complete ms. Length: 2,500-3,500 words. **Pays $250-600.** Sometimes pays expenses of writers on assignment.
Photos: State availability with submission.
Columns/Departments: Pays $250-600.
Fiction: Maureen Abood, literary editor. Mainstream, religious, slice-of-life vignettes. **Buys 4-6 mss/year.** Send complete ms. Length: 2,500-3,000 words. **Pays $300.**
Poetry: Maureen Abood, literary editor. Free verse. "No light verse." **Buys 12 poems/year.** Submit maximum 5 poems. Length: 50 lines. **Pays $75.**

THE UNITED CHURCH OBSERVER, 478 Huron St., Toronto, Ontario M5R 2R3, Canada. (416)960-8500. Fax: (416)960-8477. E-mail: general@ucobserver.org. Website: www.ucobserver.org. **Contact:** Muriel Duncan, editor. **20% freelance written.** Prefers to work with published/established writers. Monthly newsmagazine for people associated with The United Church of Canada. Deals primarily with events, trends, and policies having religious significance. Most coverage is Canadian, but reports on international or world concerns will be considered. Pays on publication. Publishes ms an average of 4 months after acceptance. Byline usually given. first serial rights and occasionally all rights. Accepts queries by mail, e-mail, fax.
Nonfiction: Occasional opinion features only. Extended coverage of major issues is usually assigned to known writers. Submissions should be written as news, no more than 1,200 words length, accurate, and well-researched. No opinion pieces or poetry. Queries preferred. **Rates depend on subject, author, and work involved.** Pays expenses of writers on assignment as negotiated.

Reprints: Send tearsheet or photocopy and information about when and where the material previously appeared. Payment negotiated.

Photos: Buys photographs with mss. Color or b&w, electronic mail. Payment varies.

Tips: "The writer has a better chance of breaking in at our publication with short articles; this also allows us to try more freelancers. Include samples of previous *news* writing with query. Indicate ability and willingness to do research, and to evaluate that research. The most frequent mistakes made by writers in completing an article for us are organizational problems, lack of polished style, short on research, and a lack of inclusive language."

$ THE UPPER ROOM, Daily Devotional Guide, P.O. Box 340004, Nashville TN 37203-0004. (615)340-7252. Fax: (615)340-7267. E-mail: theupperroommagazine@upperroom.org. Website: www.upperroom.org. Editor and Publisher: Stephen D. Bryant. **Contact:** Marilyn Beaty, editorial assistant. **95% freelance written.** Eager to work with new/unpublished writers. Bimonthly magazine "offering a daily inspirational message which includes a Bible reading, text, prayer, 'Thought for the Day,' and suggestion for further prayer. Each day's meditation is written by a different person and is usually a personal witness about discovering meaning and power for Christian living through scripture study which illuminates daily life." Circ. 2.2 million (US); 385,000 outside US. Pays on publication. Publishes ms an average of 1 year after acceptance. Byline given. Buys first North American serial rights, translation rights. Submit seasonal material 14 months in advance. Sample copy and writer's guidelines with a 4×6 SAE and 2 first-class stamps. Guidelines only for #10 SASE or online.

- "Manuscripts are not returned. If writers include a stamped, self-addressed postcard, we will notify them that their writing has reached us. This does not imply acceptance or interest in purchase. Does not respond unless material is accepted for publication."

Nonfiction: Inspirational, personal experience, Bible-study insights. Special issues: Lent and Easter 2003; Advent 2003. No poetry, lengthy "spiritual journey" stories. **Buys 365 unsolicited mss/year.** Send complete ms by mail or e-mail. Length:300 words. **Pays $25 per meditation.**

Tips: "The best way to break into our magazine is to send a well-written manuscript that looks at the Christian faith in a fresh way. Standard stories and sermon illustrations are immediately rejected. We very much want to find new writers and welcome good material. We are particularly interested in meditations based on Old Testament characters and stories. Good repeat meditations can lead to work on longer assignments for our other publications, which pay more. A writer who can deal concretely with everyday situations, relate them to the Bible and spiritual truths, and write clear, direct prose should be able to write for *The Upper Room*. We want material that provides for more interaction on the part of the reader—meditation suggestions, journaling suggestions, space to reflect and link personal experience with the meditation for the day. Meditations that are personal, authentic, exploratory and full of sensory detail make good devotional writing."

$ $ THE UU WORLD, Unitarian Universalist Association, 25 Beacon St., Boston MA 02108-2800. (617)742-2100. Fax: (617)742-7025. E-mail: world@uua.org. Website: www.uuworld.org. Editor-in-Chief: Tom Stites. **Contact:** Robert Tarutis. **50% freelance written.** Bimonthly magazine "to promote and inspire denominational self-reflection; to inform readers about the wide range of Unitarian Universalist values, purposes, activities, aesthetics, and spiritual attitudes, and to educate readers about the history, personalities, and congregations that comprise UUism; to enhance its dual role of leadership and service to member congregations." Estab. 1987. Circ. 120,000. **Pays on acceptance.** Publishes ms an average of 1 year after acceptance. Byline given. Buys one-time rights. Editorial lead time 3 months. Submit seasonal material 3 months in advance. Accepts queries by mail, e-mail, fax. Responds in 2 months to queries; 3 months to mss. Sample copy and writer's guidelines for 9×12 SAE or online.

Nonfiction: All articles must have a clear UU angle. Essays, historical/nostalgic (Unitarian or Universalist focus), inspirational, interview/profile (with UU individual or congregation), photo feature (of UU congregation or project), religious. Special issues: "We are planning issues on family, spirituality and welfare reform." No unsolicited poetry or fiction. **Buys 5 mss/year.** Query with published clips. Length: 1,500-3,500 words. **Pays $400 minimum for assigned articles.** Sometimes pays expenses of writers on assignment.

Photos: State availability with submission. Reviews contact sheets. Buys one-time rights. Offers no additional payment for photos accepted with ms. Captions, identification of subjects, model releases required.

Columns/Departments: Living the Faith (profiles of UUs and UU congregations). **Pays $250-500 for assigned articles.**

$ $ THE WAR CRY, The Salvation Army, 615 Slaters Lane, Alexandria VA 22313. Fax: (703)684-5539. E-mail: war_cry@usn.salvationarmy.org. Website: www.christianity.com/salvationarmyusa. Managing Editor: Jeff McDonald. **Contact:** Lt. Colonel Marlene Chase, editor-in-chief. **10% freelance written.** Biweekly magazine covering army news and Christian devotional writing. Estab. 1881. Circ. 400,000. **Pays on acceptance.** Publishes ms an average of 2 months-1 year after acceptance. Byline given. Buys one-time rights. Editorial lead time 6 weeks. Submit seasonal material 1 year in advance. Responds in 4-6 weeks to queries. Sample copy, theme list and writer's guidelines free or online.

- "A best bet would be a well-written profile of an exemplary Christian or a recounting of a person's experiences that deepened the subject's faith and showed God in action. Most popular profiles are of Salvation Army programs and personnel."

Nonfiction: Humor, inspirational, interview/profile, personal experience, religious. No missionary stories, confessions. **Buys 40 mss/year.** Send complete ms. **Pays up to 20¢/word for assigned articles; 15-20¢/word for unsolicited articles.** Sometimes pays expenses of writers on assignment.

Reprints: Send typed ms with rights for sale noted and information about when and where the material previously appeared. Pays 12¢/word.
Photos: Buys one-time rights. Offers $35-200/photo. Identification of subjects required.
Fiction: Religious. **Buys 5-10 mss/year.** Send complete ms. Length: 1,200-1,500 words. **Pays up to 20¢/word.**
Poetry: Free verse. **Buys 10-20/year poems/year.** Submit maximum 5 poems. Length:16 lines. **Pays $20-50.**
Fillers: Anecdotes (inspirational). **Buys 10-20/year.** Length: 200-500 words. **Pays 15-20¢/word.**
Tips: "We are soliciting more short fiction, inspirational articles and poetry, interviews with Christian athletes, evangelical leaders and celebrities, and theme-focused articles."

$ THE WESLEYAN ADVOCATE, The Wesleyan Publishing House, P.O. Box 50434, Indianapolis IN 46250-0434. (317)570-5204. Fax: (317)570-5260. E-mail: communications@wesleyan.org. Executive Editor: Dr. Norman G. Wilson. **Contact:** Jerry Brecheisen, managing editor. Monthly magazine of The Wesleyan Church. Estab. 1842. Circ. 20,000. Pays on publication. Byline given. Buys first rights or simultaneous rights (prefers first rights). Submit seasonal material 6 months in advance. Accepts simultaneous submissions. Responds in 2 weeks to queries. Sample copy for $2. Writer's guidelines for #10 SASE.
Nonfiction: Humor, inspirational, religious. No poetry accepted. Send complete ms. Length: 500-700 words. **Pays $25-150.**
Reprints: Send photocopy of article and typed ms with rights for sale noted and information about when and where the material previously appeared.
Tips: "Write for a guide."

$ $ ✪ WHISPERS FROM HEAVEN, Publications International, Ltd., 7373 N. Cicero, Lincolnwood IL 60712. Fax: (847)329-5387. E-mail: vsmith@pubint.com. Editor: Julie Greene. Managing Editor: Becky Bell. **Contact:** Vicki Smith, acquisitions editor. **100% freelance written.** Bimonthly magazine covering inspirational human-interest. "We're looking for real-life experiences (personal and otherwise) that lift the human spirit and illuminate positive human traits and values: Though many stories may deal with (the overcoming of) tragedy and/or difficult times, descriptions shouldn't be too visceral and the emphasis should be on adversity overcome with a positive result. *Whispers*, though inspiring, is not overtly religious." Estab. 1999. Circ. 50,000. **Pays on acceptance.** Publishes ms an average of 5 months after acceptance. Byline given. Buys all rights. Editorial lead time 5 months. Submit seasonal material 5 months in advance. Accepts queries by mail, e-mail, fax. Writer's guidelines free.
Nonfiction: Essays, general interest, inspirational, personal experience, religious. "Nothing overtly religious or anything that explores negative human characteristics." **Buys 150 mss/year.** Query with or without published clips. Length: 800-1,200 words. **Pays $100-225.** Pays expenses of writers on assignment.
Tips: "We are particularly fond of stories (when warranted) that have a 'twist' at the end—an extra bit of surprising information that adds meaning and provides an emotional connecting point to the story itself."

$ WOMAN'S TOUCH, Assemblies of God Women's Ministries Department (GPH), 1445 Boonville Ave., Springfield MO 65802-1894. (417)862-2781. Fax: (417)862-0503. E-mail: womanstouch@ag.org. Website: www.ag.org/womanstouch. **Contact:** Darla Knoth, managing editor. **50% freelance written.** Willing to work with new/unpublished writers. Bimonthly inspirational magazine for women. "Articles and contents of the magazine should be compatible with Christian teachings as well as human interests. The audience is women of all walks of life." Estab. 1977. Circ. 15,000. Pays on publication. Publishes ms an average of 10 months after acceptance. Byline given. Buys first, second, or one-time and electronic rights. Editorial lead time 10 months. Submit seasonal material 10 months in advance. Accepts queries by mail, e-mail, fax. Responds in 3 months to queries. Sample copy for 9½×11 SAE with 3 first-class stamps or online. Writer's guidelines for #10 SASE or online.
Nonfiction: Book excerpts, general interest, inspirational, personal experience, religious, health. No fiction, poetry. **Buys 30 mss/year.** Send complete ms. Length: 200-600 words. **Pays $10-50 for assigned articles; $10-35 for unsolicited articles.**
Reprints: Send photocopy and information about when and where the material previously appeared. Pays 50-75% of amount paid for an original article.
Columns/Departments: A Final Touch (inspirational/human interest), 400 words; A Better You (health/wellness), 400 words; A Lighter Touch (true, unpublished anecdotes), 100 words.

The online magazine carries original content not found in the print edition and includes writer's guidelines. Contact: Darla Knoth, online editor.

Tips: "Submit manuscripts on current issues of interest to women. Familiarize yourself with *Woman's Touch* by reading 2 issues before submitting an article."

$ ✪ WORLD CHRISTIAN, Global Activists for the Cause of Christ, WINPress, P.O. Box 1357, Oak Park IL 60304. (708)524-5070. Fax: (708)524-5174. E-mail: WINPress7@aol.com. **Contact:** Phillip Huber, managing editor. Quarterly magazine covering religious missions and evangelism. Estab. 1982. Circ. 30,000 (March, June, September), 150,000 (December). Pays on publication. Publishes ms an average of 6 months after acceptance. Byline given. Buys first, all rights. Editorial lead time 6 months. Accepts queries by mail, e-mail. Sample copy for $4. Writer's guidelines free.

- The editor reports an interest in seeing good profiles of average Christians making a difference around the world.
- Break in with well-written articles that show evidence of careful research from multiple sources, about interesting or unusual aspects of missions and evangelism.

Nonfiction: Book excerpts, essays, general interest, how-to, inspirational, interview/profile, opinion, personal experience, photo feature, religious, some sidebars. "No fiction, poetry, or feel-good, warm, fuzzy stories about how God is important in a person's life." **Buys 50-60 mss/year.** Query with published clips. Length: 600-2,000 words. **Pays 6-15¢/word.** Sometimes pays expenses of writers on assignment.
Photos: State availability with submission. Negotiates payment individually. Captions, identification of subjects, model releases required.

RETIREMENT

On January 1, 1996, the first baby boomer turned 50. With peak earning power and increased leisure time, this generation is able to pursue varied interests while maintaining active lives. More people are retiring in their 50s, while others are starting a business or traveling and pursuing hobbies. These publications give readers specialized information on health and fitness, medical research, finances, and other topics of interest, as well as general articles on travel destinations and recreational activities.

$ ALIVE!, A Magazine for Christian Senior Adults, Christian Seniors Fellowship, P.O. Box 46464, Cincinnati OH 45246-0464. (513)825-3681. Editor: J. David Lang. **Contact:** A. June Lang, office editor. **60% freelance written.** Bimonthly magazine for senior adults 50 and older. "We need timely articles about Christian seniors in vital, productive lifestyles, travel or ministries." Estab. 1988. Pays on publication. Byline given. Buys first, second serial (reprint) rights. Submit seasonal material 6 months in advance. Accepts ms by mail. Responds in 2 months to mss. Sample copy for 9×12 SAE with 3 first-class stamps. Writer's guidelines for #10 SASE.

- Membership $18/year. Organization membership may be deducted from payment at writer's request.

Nonfiction: General interest, humor, inspirational, interview/profile, photo feature, religious, travel. **Buys 25-50 mss/year.** Send complete ms and SASE. Length: 600-1,200 words. **Pays $18-75.**
Reprints: Send tearsheet, photocopy or typed ms with rights for sale noted and information about when and where the material previously appeared. Pays 60-75% of amount paid for an original article.
Photos: State availability with submission. Buys one-time rights. Offers $10-25. Identification of subjects, model releases required.
Columns/Departments: Heart Medicine (humorous personal anecdotes; prefer grandparent/granchild stories or anecdotes re: over-55 persons), 10-100 words. **Buys 50 mss/year.** Send complete ms and SASE. **Pays $2-25.**
Fiction: Adventure, humorous, religious, romance, slice-of-life vignettes, motivational, inspirational. **Buys 12 mss/year.** Send complete ms. Length: 600-1,200 words. **Pays $20-60.**
Fillers: Anecdotes, facts, gags to be illustrated by cartoonist, short humor. **Buys 15/year.** Length: 50-500 words. **Pays $2-15.**
Tips: "Include SASE and information regarding whether manuscript is to be returned or tossed."

N FIFTY SOMETHING MAGAZINE, Jet Media, 7533-C Tyler Blvd., Mentor OH 44060. (440)953-2200. Fax: (440)953-2202. E-mail: linde@apk.net. **Contact:** Linda Lindeman DeCarlo, publisher. **80% freelance written.** Quarterly magazine covering nostalgia. "We are focusing on the 50-and-better reader." Estab. 1990. Circ. 10,000. Pays on publication. Publishes ms an average of 6 months after acceptance. Byline given. Offers 5% kill fee. Buys one-time, second serial (reprint), simultaneous rights. Editorial lead time 6 months. Submit seasonal material 6 months in advance. Accepts queries by mail, e-mail. Accepts previously published material. Accepts simultaneous submissions. Responds in 3 months to queries; 3 months to mss. Sample copy for 9×12 SAE and 4 first-class stamps. Writer's guidelines for #10 SASE.
Nonfiction: Book excerpts, essays, exposé, general interest, historical/nostalgic, how-to, humor, inspirational, interview/profile, new product, opinion, personal experience, photo feature, travel. **Buys 10 mss/year.** Length: 500-1,500 words. **Pays $10-100 for assigned articles; $10-100 for unsolicited articles.** Sometimes pays expenses of writers on assignment.
Photos: Send photos with submission. Reviews 4×6 prints, GIF/JPEG files. Buys one-time rights. Negotiates payment individually. Captions, identification of subjects, model releases required.
Columns/Departments: Health & Fitness (good news/tips), 500 words; Travel (unique trips), 1,000 words; Humor (aging issues), 500 words; Finance (tips), 500 words. **Buys 10 mss/year.** Send complete ms. **Pays $10-100.**
Fiction: Adventure, confessions, ethnic, experimental, fantasy, historical, humorous, mainstream, mystery, novel excerpts, romance, slice-of-life vignettes, suspense, western. No erotica or horror. **Buys 10 mss/year.** Send complete ms. Length: 500-1,500 words. **Pays $10-100.**
Poetry: Avant-garde, free verse, light verse, traditional. **Buys 10 poems/year.** Submit maximum 5 poems. Length: 10-25 lines.
Fillers: Anecdotes, facts, gags to be illustrated by cartoonist, newsbreaks, short humor. **Buys 10/year.** Length: 50-150 words. **Pays $10-100.**

$ MATURE LIVING, A Magazine for Christian Senior Adults, LifeWay Press of the Southern Baptist Convention, 1 LifeWay Plaza, Nashville TN 37234-0175. (615)251-2485. Fax: (615)277-8272. E-mail: matureliving@lifeway.com. **Contact:** Judy Pregel, editor. **70% freelance written.** Monthly leisure magazine for senior adults 55 and older.

Estab. 1977. Circ. 350,000. **Pays on acceptance.** Byline given. Prefers to purchase all rights if writer agrees. Submit seasonal material 1 year in advance. Responds in 3 months to mss. Sample copy for 9×12 SAE with 4 first-class stamps. Writer's guidelines for #10 SASE.

Nonfiction: General interest, historical/nostalgic, how-to, humor, inspirational, interview/profile, personal experience, photo feature, travel, crafts. No pornography, profanity, occult, liquor, dancing, drugs, gambling. **Buys 100 mss/year.** Length: 600-1,200 words. **Pays 5 1/2¢/word; $75 minimum.**

Photos: State availability with submission. Offers $10-25/photo. Pays on publication.

Columns/Departments: Cracker Barrel (brief, humorous, original quips and verses),**pays $15**; Grandparents' Brag Board (something humorous or insightful said or done by your grandchild or great-grandchild),**pays $15**; Inspirational (devotional items), pays $25; Food (introduction and 4-6 recipes),**pays $50**; Over the Garden Fence (vegetable or flower gardening), **pays $40**; Crafts (step-by-step procedures),**pays $40**; Game Page (crossword or word-search puzzles and quizzes),**pays $40**.

Fiction: No reference to liquor, dancing, drugs, gambling; no pornography, profanity or occult. **Buys 12 mss/year.** Send complete ms.

Poetry: Buys 30/year poems/year. Submit maximum 5 poems. Length: open. **Pays $25.**

$ MATURE YEARS, The United Methodist Publishing House, 201 Eighth Ave. S., Nashville TN 37202-0801. Fax: (615)749-6512. E-mail: matureyears@umpublishing.org. **Contact:** Marvin W. Cropsey, editor. **50% freelance written.** Prefers to work with published/established writers. Quarterly magazine "designed to help persons in and nearing the retirement years understand and appropriate the resources of the Christian faith in dealing with specific problems and opportunities related to aging." Estab. 1954. Circ. 70,000. **Pays on acceptance.** Publishes ms an average of 1 year after acceptance. Buys first North American serial rights. Submit seasonal material 14 months in advance. Responds in 2 weeks to queries; 2 months to mss. Sample copy for $5 and 9×12 SAE. Writer's guidelines for #10 SASE.

Nonfiction: Especially important are opportunities for older adults to read about service, adventure, fulfillment, and fun. How-to (hobbies), inspirational, religious, travel (special guidelines), older adult health, finance issues. **Buys 75-80 mss/year.** Send complete ms; e-mail submissions preferred. Length: 900-2,000 words. **Pays $45-125.** Sometimes pays expenses of writers on assignment.

Reprints: Send tearsheet, photocopy or typed ms with rights for sale noted and information about when and where the material previously appeared. Pays at same rate as for previously unpublished material.

Photos: Send photos with submission. Buys one-time rights. Negotiates pay individually. Captions, model releases required.

Columns/Departments: Health Hints (retirement, health), 900-1,500 words; Going Places (travel, pilgrimage), 1,000-1,500 words; Fragments of Life (personal inspiration), 250-600 words; Modern Revelations (religious/inspirational), 900-1,500 words; Money Matters (personal finance), 1,200-1,800 words; Merry-Go-Round (cartoons, jokes, 4-6 line humorous verse); Puzzle Time (religious puzzles, crosswords). **Buys 4 mss/year.** Send complete ms. **Pays $25-45.**

Fiction: Religious, slice-of-life vignettes, retirement years. **Buys 4 mss/year.** Send complete ms. Length: 1,000-2,000 words. **Pays $60-125.**

Poetry: Free verse, haiku, light verse, traditional. **Buys 24 poems/year poems/year.** Submit maximum 6 poems. Length: 3-16 lines. **Pays $5-20.**

$ $ $ $ MODERN MATURITY, American Association of Retired Persons, 601 E St. NW, Washington DC 20049. (202)434-6880. Website: www.aarp.org. **Contact:** Hugh Delehanty, editor. **50% freelance written.** Prefers to work with published/established writers. Bimonthly magazine. "*Modern Maturity* is devoted to the varied needs and active life interests of AARP members, age 50 and over, covering such topics as financial planning, travel, health, careers, retirement, relationships, and social and cultural change. Its editorial content serves the mission of AARP seeking through education, advocacy and service to enhance the quality of life for all by promoting independence, dignity, and purpose." Circ. 17,800,000. **Pays on acceptance.** Publishes ms an average of 6 months after acceptance. Byline given. exclusive worldwide publication rights Submit seasonal material 6 months in advance. Responds in 3 months to queries. Sample copy and writer's guidelines free.

Nonfiction: Careers, workplace, practical information in living, financial and legal matters, personal relationships, consumerism. Query first by mail only. *No unsolicited mss.* Length: up to 2,000 words. **Pays up to $3,000.** Sometimes pays expenses of writers on assignment.

Photos: Photos purchased with or without accompanying mss. Pays $250 and up for color; $150 and up for b&w.

Fiction: Very occasional short fiction.

Tips: "The most frequent mistake made by writers in completing an article for us is poor follow-through with basic research. The outline is often more interesting than the finished piece. We do not accept unsolicited manuscripts."

$ ✪ PLUS, 3565 S. Higuera St., San Luis Obispo CA 93401. (805)544-8711. Fax: (805)544-4450. E-mail: plusmag@fix.net. Publisher: Gary D. Suggs. **Contact:** George Brand, editor. **60% freelance written.** Monthly magazine covering seniors to inform and entertain the "over-50" but young-at-heart audience. Estab. 1981. Circ. 60,000. Pays on publication. Publishes ms an average of 2 months after acceptance. Byline given. Buys one-time rights. Editorial lead time 2 months. Submit seasonal material 2 months in advance. Accepts queries by mail. Accepts simultaneous submissions. Responds in 2 weeks to queries; 1 month to mss. Sample copy for 9×12 SAE with $2 postage.

Nonfiction: Historical/nostalgic, humor, interview/profile, personal experience, travel, book reviews, entertainment, health. Special issues: Going Back to School; Christmas (December); Travel (October, April). No finance, automotive, heavy humor, poetry or fiction. **Buys 60-70 mss/year.** Query with SASE or send complete ms. Length: 900-1,200 words. **Pays $1.50/inch.**
Photos: Send photos with submission. Reviews transparencies, 5×7 prints. Offers $5-15/photo.
Tips: "Request and read a sample copy before submitting."

$ SENIOR LIVING NEWSPAPERS, Metropolitan Radio Group, 318 E. Pershing St., Springfield MO 65806. (417)862-0852. Fax: (417)862-9079. E-mail: elefantwalk@msn.com. **Contact:** Joyce Yonker O'Neal, managing editor. **25-50% freelance written.** Monthly newspaper covering active seniors in retirement. "For people 55+. Positive and upbeat attitude on aging, prime-of-life times. Slant is directed to mid-life and retirement lifestyles. Readers are primarily well-educated and affluent retirees, homemakers, and career professionals. *Senior Living* informs; health, fitness-entertains; essays, nostalgia, humor, etc." Estab. 1995. Circ. 40,000. Pays 30 days after publication. Publishes ms an average of 2 months after acceptance. Byline given. Buys first, second serial (reprint), electronic rights. Editorial lead time 3 months. Submit seasonal material 4 months in advance. Accepts queries by mail, e-mail. Responds in 2 weeks to queries; 1 month to mss. Sample copy for 9×12 SAE with 5 first-class stamps. Writer's guidelines for #10 SASE.
Nonfiction: Essays, general interest, historical/nostalgic, humor, inspirational, interview/profile, personal experience, photo feature, religious, travel, health-related. No youth-oriented, preachy, sugar-coated, technical articles. **Buys 65 mss/year.** Send complete ms. Length: Maximum 600 words. **Pays $20-35 for assigned articles; $5-35 for unsolicited articles.**
Photos: Send photos with submission. Buys one-time rights. Offers $5/photo. Captions, identification of subjects, model releases required.
Fillers: Anecdotes, facts, short humor. **Buys 15/year.** Length: 150-250 words. **Pays $5-10.**
Tips: "Beginning writers who are in need of byline clips stand a good chance if they indicate that they do not require payment for article. A query letter is not necessary, but a cover letter telling a bit about yourself is nice."

ROMANCE & CONFESSION

Listed here are publications that need stories of romance ranging from ethnic and adventure to romantic intrigue and confession. Each magazine has a particular slant; some are written for young adults, others to family-oriented women. Some magazines also are interested in general interest nonfiction on related subjects.

$ THE BLACK ROMANCE GROUP, Black Confessions, Black Romance, Black Secrets, Bronze Thrills, Jive, Sterling/McFadden Partnership, 233 Park Ave. S., 6th Floor, New York NY 10003. (212)979-4915. Fax: (212)979-4825. Website: www.sterlingmacfadden.com. **Contact:** Takesha Powell or Lisa Finn, editors. **100% freelance written.** Eager to work with new/unpublished writers. Bimonthly magazine of romance and love. Pays on publication. Publishes ms an average of 2 months after acceptance. Byline given on special feature articles only but not short stories. Buys all property rights of stories. Accepts queries by mail, phone. Responds in 4 months to mss. Sample copy for 9×12 SAE with 5 first-class stamps. Writer's guidelines free.
Nonfiction: "We like our articles to have a down-to-earth flavor. They should be written in the spirit of sisterhood, fun and creativity. Come up with an original idea that our readers may not have thought of but will be dying to try out." How-to (relating to romance and love), feature articles on any aspect of relationships. Query with published clips. Length: 3-5 typed pages. **Pays $125.**
Fiction: Romance confessional stories told from an African-American female perspective. Stories should include two love scenes, alluding to sex. Include spicy, sexual topics of forbidden love, but not graphic detail. Stories must include a conflict between the heroine and her love interest. The age of characters can range from mid-teenage years through late thirties. Make stories exciting, passionate (uninhibited sexual fantasies) and romantic. Send complete ms. Length: 5,000 words. **Pays $100.**
Tips: "Follow our writer's guidelines and read a few sample copies before submitting your manuscript. Use a romance writer's phrase book as a guide when writing stories, especially love scenes. Submit stories with original, modern conflicts. Incorporate romance and sex in manuscripts, uninhibitedly—making the stories an exciting, passionate escape for readers to imagine fulfilling their secret desires."

N $ TRUE CONFESSIONS, Macfadden Women's Group, 233 Park Ave. S., New York NY 10003. (212)979-4898. Fax: (212)979-4825. E-mail: trueconfessions@sterlingmacfadden.com. **Contact:** Pat Byrdsong, editor. **100% freelance written.** Monthly magazine for high-school-educated, working class women, teens through maturity. Circ. 200,000. Pays 1 month after publication. Publishes ms an average of 4 months after acceptance. Buys all rights. Submit seasonal material 8 months in advance. Responds in 15 months to mss.

- Eager to work with new/unpublished writers.
- "If you have a strong story to tell, tell it simply and convincingly. We always have a need for 4,000-word stories with dramatic impact about dramatic events." Asian-, Latina-, Native- and African-American stories are encouraged.

Nonfiction: Timely, exciting, true emotional first-person stories on the problems that face today's women. The narrators should be sympathetic, and the situations they find themselves in should be intriguing, yet realistic. Many stories may have a strong romantic interest and a high moral tone; however, personal accounts or "confessions," no matter how controversial the topic, are encouraged and accepted. Careful study of current issue is suggested. Send complete ms. No simultaneous submissions. SASE required. Length: 4,000 to 7,000 words and mini stories 1,000-1,500 words. **Pays 5¢/word.**

Columns/Departments: Family Zoo (pet feature), 50 words or less, **pays $50 for pet photo and story.** All other features are 200-300 words: My Moment With God (a short prayer); Incredible But True (an incredible/mystical/spiritual experience); My Man (a man who has been special in your life); Woman to Woman (a point of view about a contemporary subject matter or a woman overcoming odds). **Pays $65** for all features; **$75** for My Moment with God. Send complete ms and SASE.

Poetry: Poetry should rhyme. Length: 4-20 lines. **Pays $10 minimum.**

Tips: "Our magazine is almost 100% freelance. We purchase all stories that appear in our magazine. Read 3-4 issues before sending submissions. Do not talk down to our readers. We prefer manuscripts on disk as well as hard copy."

$✪ TRUE ROMANCE, Sterling/MacFadden Partnership, 333 Seventh Ave., 11th Floor, New York NY 10003. (212)979-4800. Fax: (212)780-3555. E-mail: pvitucci@sterlingmacfadden.com. Website: www.truestorymail.com. **Contact:** Pat Vitucci, editor. **100% freelance written.** Monthly magazine for women, teens through retired, offering compelling confession stories based on true happenings, with reader identification and strong emotional tone. No third-person material. Estab. 1923. Circ. 225,000. Pays 1 month after publication. Buys all rights. Submit seasonal material 6 months in advance. Accepts queries by mail, e-mail, fax. Responds in 8 months to queries.

Nonfiction: Confessions, true love stories, mini-adventures: problems and solutions; dating and marital, and child-rearing difficulties. Realistic yet unique stories dealing with current problems, everyday events; strong emotional appeal. **Buys 180 mss/year.** Submit ms. Length: 6,000-9,000 words. **Pays 3¢/word; slightly higher rates for short-shorts.**

Columns/Departments: That's My Child (photo and 50 words); Loving Pets (photo and 50 words), **both pay $50;** Cupid's Corner (photo and 500 words about you and spouse), **pays $100;** Passages(2,000-4,000 words about a unique experience), **pays 3¢/word**; As I Lived It (3,000-5,000 words for literary short stories in first and third person), **pays 3¢/word**.

Poetry: Light romantic poetry. Length: 24 lines maximum. **Pays $10-30.**

Tips: "A timely, well-written story that is told by a sympathetic narrator who sees the central problem through to a satisfying resolution is *all* important to break into *True Romance*. We are always looking for interesting, emotional, identifiable stories."

N $✪ TRUE STORY, Sterling/Macfadden Partnership, 233 Park Ave. S., New York NY 10003. (212)979-4825. Fax: (212)979-7342. E-mail: hdalton@sterlingmacfadden.com. Website: www.truestorymail.com. **Contact:** Tina Pappalardo or Heather Dalton, editors. **80% freelance written.** Monthly magazine for young married, blue-collar women, 20-35; high school education; increasingly broad interests; home-oriented, but looking beyond the home for personal fulfillment. Circ. 580,000. Pays 1 month after publication. Byline given. Buys all rights. Submit seasonal material 1 year in advance. Responds in 1 year to queries. Writer's guidelines online.

- Subject matter can range from light romances to sizzling passion, from all-out tearjerkers to happily-ever-after endings, and everything in between.

Nonfiction: "First-person stories covering all aspects of women's interest: love, marriage, family life, careers, social problems,etc. The best direction a new writer can be given is to carefully study several issues of the magazine; then submit a fresh, exciting, well-written true story. We have no taboos. It's the handling and believability that make the difference between a rejection and an acceptance." **Buys about 125 full-length mss/year.** Submit only complete mss and disk for stories. Length: 2,000-8,000 words. **Pays 5¢/word; $100 minimum. Pays a flat rate for columns or departments, as announced in the magazine.**

Tips: "*True Story* is unique because all of our stories are written from the hearts of real people, and deal with all of the issues that affect us today—parenthood, relationships, careers, family affairs, and social concerns. All of our stories are written in first person, and should be no less than 2,000 words and no more than 8,000. If you have access to a computer, we require you to send your submission on a disk, along with a clean hard copy of the story. Please keep in mind, all files must be saved as rich text format (RTF)."

RURAL

These publications draw readers interested in rural lifestyles. Surprisingly, many readers are from urban centers who dream of or plan to build a house in the country. Magazines featuring design, construction, log homes, and "country" style interior decorating appear in Home & Garden.

$ $ THE COUNTRY CONNECTION, Ontario's Green Magazine, Pinecone Publishing, P.O. Box 100, Boulter, Ontario K0L 1G0, Canada. (613)332-3651. E-mail: magazine@pinecone.on.ca. Website: www.pinecone.on.ca. **Contact:** Gus Zylstra, editor. **100% freelance written.** Magazine published 3 times/year covering nature, environment, history and nostalgia, "the arts" and "green travel." "*The Country Connection* is a magazine for true nature lovers and the rural adventurer. Building on our commitment to heritage, cultural, artistic, and environmental themes, we continually add new topics to illuminate the country experience of people living within nature. Our goal is to chronicle rural life in its many aspects, giving 'voice' to the countryside." Estab. 1989. Circ. 10,000. Pays on publication. Publishes ms an average of 4 months after acceptance. Byline given. Buys first rights. Editorial lead time 4 months. Accepts queries by mail, e-mail, phone. Sample copy for $4.55. Writer's guidelines for #10 SASE (in Canada) or SAE and IRC (in US), or online.

Nonfiction: General interest, historical/nostalgic, humor, opinion, personal experience, travel, lifestyle, leisure, art and culture, vegan recipes. No hunting, fishing, animal husbandry, or pet articles. **Buys 50 mss/year.** Send complete ms. Length: 500-2,000 words. **Pays 7-10¢/word.**

Photos: Send photos with submission. Reviews transparencies, prints. Buys one-time rights. Offers $10-50/photo. Captions required.

Columns/Departments: Pays 7-10¢/word.

Fiction: Adventure, fantasy, historical, humorous, slice-of-life vignettes, country living. **Buys 4 mss/year.** Send complete ms. Length: 500-1,500 words. **Pays 7-10¢/word.**

The online magazine carries original content not found in the print edition. Contact: Gus Zylstra.

Tips: "Canadian content only. Send manuscript with appropriate support material such as photos, illustrations, maps, etc. Do not send U.S. stamps."

$ COUNTRY FOLK, Salaki Publishing & Design, HC77, Box 608, Pittsburg MO 65724. (417)993-5944. Fax: (417)993-5944. E-mail: salaki@countryfolkmag.com. Website: www.countryfolkmag.com. **Contact:** Susan Salaki, editor. **100% freelance written.** Bimonthly magazine. "*Country Folk* publishes true stories and history of the Ozarks." Estab. 1994. Circ. 6,200. Pays on publication. Publishes ms an average of 3 months after acceptance. Byline given. Buys first rights. Editorial lead time 2 months. Submit seasonal material 3 months in advance. Accepts queries by mail, e-mail, fax, phone. Responds in 1 month to queries; 2 months to mss. Sample copy for $4.75. Writer's guidelines for #10 SASE.

• *Country Folk* has increased from quarterly to bimonthly and doubled its circulation.

Nonfiction: Historical/nostalgic, how-to, humor, inspirational, personal experience, photo feature, true ghost stories of the Ozarks. **Buys 10 mss/year.** Prefers e-mail submissions. Length: 750-1,000 words. **Pays $5-20.** Pays writers with contributor copies or other premiums if we must do considerable editing to the work.

Photos: Send photos with submission. Buys one-time rights.

Fiction: Historical, humorous, mystery, novel excerpts. **Buys 10 mss/year.** Send complete ms. Length: 750-1,000 words. **Pays $5-50.**

Poetry: Haiku, light verse, traditional. **Buys 25 poems/year.** Submit maximum 3 poems. **Pays $1-5.**

Fillers: Anecdotes, facts, gags to be illustrated by cartoonist, newsbreaks, short humor. **Buys 25/year. Pays $1-5.**

Tips: "We want material from people who are born and raised in the country, especially the Ozark region. We accept submissions in any form, handwritten or typed. Many of the writers and poets whose work we publish are first-time submissions. Most of the work we publish is written by older men and women who have heard stories from their parents and grandparents about how the Ozark region was settled in the 1800s. Almost any writer who writes from the heart about a true experience from his or her youth will get published. Our staff edits for grammar and spelling errors. All the writer has to be concerned about is conveying the story."

$ $ FARM & RANCH LIVING, Reiman Publications, 5925 Country Lane, Greendale WI 53129. (414)423-0100. Fax: (414)423-8463. E-mail: editors@farmandranchliving.com. Website: www.farmandranchliving.com. **Contact:** Nick Pabst, editor. **30% freelance written.** Eager to work with new/unpublished writers. Bimonthly magazine aimed at families that farm or ranch full time. "*F&RL* is *not* a 'how-to' magazine—it focuses on people rather than products and profits." Estab. 1978. Circ. 400,000. Pays on publication. Publishes ms an average of 6 months after acceptance. Byline given. Buys first, one-time rights. Submit seasonal material 6 months in advance. Accepts queries by mail, e-mail, fax. Responds in 6 weeks to queries. Sample copy for $2. Writer's guidelines for #10 SASE.

Break in with "photo-illustrated stories about present-day farmers and ranchers."

Nonfiction: Humor (rural only), inspirational, interview/profile, personal experience (farm/ranch related), photo feature, nostalgia, prettiest place in the country (photo/text tour of ranch or farm). No how-to articles or stories about "hobby farmers" (doctors or lawyers with weekend farms); no issue-oriented stories (pollution, animal rights, etc.). **Buys 30 mss/year.** Query with or without published clips or send complete ms. Length: 600-1,200 words. **Pays up to $200 for text/photo package. Payment for Prettiest Place negotiable.**

Reprints: Send photocopy with rights for sale noted. Payment negotiable.

Photos: Scenic. State availability with submission. Buys one-time rights. Pays $75-200 for 35mm color slides.

Fillers: Anecdotes, short humor (with farm or ranch slant), jokes. **Buys 10/year.** Length: 50-150 words. **Pays $10-25.**

Tips: "Our readers enjoy stories and features that are upbeat and positive. A freelancer must see *F&RL* to fully appreciate how different it is from other farm publications—ordering a sample is strongly advised (not available on newsstands). Photo features (about interesting farm or ranch families) and personality profiles are most open to freelancers."

$ FARM TIMES, 504 Sixth St., Rupert ID 83350. (208)436-1111. Fax: (208)436-9455. E-mail: farmtimeseditor@safelink.net. Website: www.farmtimes.com. **Contact:** Terri McAffee, managing editor. **50% freelance written.** Monthly tabloid for agriculture-farming/ranching. "*Farm Times* is dedicated to rural living in the Intermountain and Pacific Northwest. Stories related to farming and ranching in the states of Idaho, Montana, Nevada, Oregon, Utah, Washington, and Wyoming are our mainstay, but farmers and ranchers do more than just work. Human interest articles that appeal to rural readers are used on occasion." Estab. 1987. Pays on publication. Byline given. Editorial lead time 1 month. Submit seasonal material 3 months in advance. Accepts queries by mail, e-mail. Responds in 2 months to queries. Sample copy for $2.50 or online. Writer's guidelines for #10 SASE.

• The editor reports an interest in seeing articles about global agriculture issues and trends that affect the Pacific Northwest and Intermountain West agriculture producer, rural health care, and Western water issues.

O─ Break in by writing tight, and including photos, charts, or graphs, if possible.

Nonfiction: Always runs 1 feature article of interest to women. Exposé, general interest, how-to, interview/profile, new product (few), opinion, farm or ranch issues, late breaking news. Special issues: Irrigation, Chemical/Fertilizer, Potato Production. No humor, essay, first person, personal experience, or book excerpts. **Buys 200 mss/year.** Query with published clips or send complete ms. Length: 500-800 words. **Pays $1.50/column inch.**

Reprints: Send typed ms with rights for sale noted and information about when and where the material previously appeared. Pays 100% of amount paid for an original article.

Photos: Send photos with submission. Reviews 3×5 or larger prints, contact sheets with negatives, 300 dpi TIFF files. Buys one-time rights. Offers $7/b&w or color photos inside, $35/color front page A Section cover. Captions, identification of subjects, model releases required.

Columns/Departments: Horse (horse care/technical), 500-600 words; Rural Religion (interesting churches/missions/religious activities), 600-800 words; Dairy (articles of interest to dairy farmers), 600-800 words. **Buys 12 mss/year.** Query. **Pays $1.50/column inch.**

Tips: "Ag industry-related articles should have a Pacific Northwest and Intermountain West slant (crops, production techniques, etc.), or how they pertain to the global market. Write tight, observe desired word counts. Feature articles can vary between agriculture and rural living. Good quality photos included with manuscript increase publication chances. Articles should have farm/ranch/rural slant on various topics: health, travel (farmers vacation, too), financial, gardening/landscape, etc."

$ $ MOTHER EARTH NEWS, Ogden Publications, 1503 SW 42nd St., Topeka KS 66609-1265. (785)274-4300. E-mail: letters@motherearthnews.com. Website: www.motherearthnews.com. Managing Editor: K.C. Compton. **Contact:** Cheryl Long, editor. Mostly written by staff and team of established freelancers. Bimonthly magazine emphasizing country living, country skills, natural health and sustainable technologies for both long-time and would-be ruralists. "*Mother Earth News* is dedicated to presenting information that helps readers be more self-sufficient, financially independent, and environmentally aware." Circ. 350,000. Pays on publication. Byline given. Submit seasonal material 5 months in advance. Responds in 6 months to mss. Sample copy for $5. Writer's guidelines for #10 SASE.

• *Mother Earth News* was recently purchased by Ogden Publications, publishers of *Grit* and *Capper's*.

Nonfiction: How-to, alternative energy systems; organic gardening; home building; home retrofit and maintenance; energy-efficient structures; seasonal cooking; home business. No fiction, please. **Buys 35-50 mss/year.** Query. "Sending us a short, to-the-point paragraph is often enough. If it's a subject we don't need at all, we can answer it immediately. If it tickles our imagination, we'll ask to take a look at the whole piece." Length: 300-3,000 words. **Payment negotiated.**

Photos: "Although not essential, we very much encourage contributors to send good, usable photos with their mss." Include type of film, speed and lighting used. Reviews any size color transparencies transparencies, 8×10 b&w glossies prints. Total purchase price for ms includes payment for photos. Captions, photo credits required.

Columns/Departments: Country Lore (down-home solutions to everyday problems); Bits & Pieces (snippets of news, events and silly happenings); Herbs & Remedies (home healing, natural medicine); Energy & Environment (ways to conserve energy while saving money; also alternative energy).

Tips: "Probably the best way to break in is to study our magazine, digest our writer's guidelines, and send us a concise article illustrated with color transparencies that we can't resist. When folks query and we give a go-ahead on speculation, we often offer some suggestions. Failure to follow those suggestions can lose the sale for the author. We want articles that tell what real people are doing to take charge of their own lives. Articles should be well-documented and tightly written treatments of topics we haven't already covered."

$ ☆ RURAL HERITAGE, 281 Dean Ridge Lane, Gainesboro TN 38562-5039. (931)268-0655. E-mail: editor@ruralheritage.com. Website: www.ruralheritage.com. Publisher: Allan Damerow. **Contact:** Gail Damerow, editor. **98% freelance written.** Willing to work with a small number of new/unpublished writers. Bimonthly magazine devoted to the training and care of draft animals. Estab. 1976. Circ. 4,500. Pays on publication. Publishes ms an average of 6 months after acceptance. Byline given. first English language rights Submit seasonal material 6 months in advance. Accepts queries by mail, e-mail. Responds in 3 months to queries. Sample copy for $8. Writer's guidelines online at www.wuralheritage.com/business_office.

Nonfiction: How-to (farming with draft animals), interview/profile (people using draft animals), photo feature. No articles on *mechanized* farming. **Buys 100 mss/year.** Query or send complete ms. Length: 1,200-1,500 words. **Pays 5¢/word.**

Photos: Six covers/year (color transparency or 5×7 horizontal print), animals in harness $100. Photo guidelines for #10 SASE or on website. Send photos with submission. Buys one-time rights. Pays $10. Captions, identification of subjects required.

Poetry: Traditional. **Pays $5-25.**

Tips: "Thoroughly understand our subject: working draft animals in harness. We'd like more pieces on plans and instructions for constructing various horse-drawn implements and vehicles. Always welcome are: 1.) Detailed descriptions and photos of horse-drawn implements, 2.) Prices and other details of draft animal and implement auctions and sales."

$ $ RURALITE, P.O. Box 558, Forest Grove OR 97116-0558. (503)357-2105. Fax: (503)357-8615. E-mail: ruralite@ruralite.org. Website: www.ruralite.org. **Contact:** Curtis Condon, editor-in-chief. **80% freelance written.** Works with new, unpublished writers. Monthly magazine aimed at members of consumer-owned electric utilities throughout 10 western states, including Alaska. Publishes 48 regional editions. Estab. 1954. Circ. 325,000. **Pays on acceptance.** Byline given. Buys first, sometimes reprint rights. Accepts queries by mail. Responds in 1 month to queries. Sample copy and writer's guidelines for 10×13 SAE with 4 first-class stamps; guidelines also online.

Nonfiction: Looking for well-written nonfiction, dealing primarily with human interest topics. Must have strong Northwest perspective and be sensitive to Northwest issues and attitudes. Wide range of topics possible, from energy-related subjects to little-known travel destinations to interesting people living in areas served by consumer-owned electric utilities. Family-related issues, Northwest history (no encyclopedia rewrites), people and events, unusual tidbits that tell the Northwest experience are best chances for a sale. Special issues: Gardening (February 2001). **Buys 50-60 mss/year.** Query first; unsolicited manuscripts submitted without request rarely read by editors. Length: 300-2,000 words. **Pays $50-450.**

Reprints: Send typed ms with rights for sale noted and information about when and where the material previously appeared. Pays 50% of amount paid for an original article.

Photos: "Illustrated stories are the key to a sale. Stories without art rarely make it. Black-and-white prints, color slides, all formats accepted."

Tips: "Study recent issues. Follow directions when given an assignment. Be able to deliver a complete package (story and photos). We're looking for regular contributors to whom we can assign topics from our story list after they've proven their ability to deliver quality mss."

SCIENCE

These publications are published for laymen interested in technical and scientific developments and discoveries, applied science, and technical or scientific hobbies. Publications of interest to the personal computer owner/user are listed in the Personal Computers section. Journals for scientists and engineers are listed in Trade in various sections.

$ $ AD ASTRA, The Magazine of the National Space Society, 600 Pennsylvania Ave. SE, Suite 201, Washington DC 20003-4316. (202)543-1900. Fax: (202)546-4189. E-mail: adastraed@aol.com. Website: www.nss.org/adastra. **Contact:** Frank Sietzen, Jr., editor-in-chief. **90% freelance written.** Bimonthly magazine covering the space program. "We publish non-technical, lively articles about all aspects of international space programs, from shuttle missions to planetary probes to plans for the future." Estab. 1989. Circ. 38,800. Pays on publication. Byline given. Buys first North American serial rights. Responds when interested to queries. Sample copy for 9×12 SASE.

Nonfiction: Book excerpts, essays, exposé, general interest, interview/profile, opinion, photo feature, technical. No science fiction or UFO stories. Query with published clips. Length: 1,600-3,200 words. **Pays $400-450 for features.**

Photos: State availability with submission. Reviews color prints, digital, JPEG-IS, GISS. Buys one-time rights. Negotiates pay. Identification of subjects required.

Tips: "We require manuscripts to be in Word or text file formats. Know the field of space technology, programs and policy. Know the players. Look for fresh angles. And, please, know how to write!"

$ $ $ AMERICAN ARCHAEOLOGY, The Archaeological Conservancy, 5301 Central Ave. NE, #402, Albuquerque NM 87108-1517. (505)266-9668. Fax: (505)266-0311. E-mail: archcons@nm.net. Website: www.americanarchaeology.org. Assistant Editor: Tamara Stewart. **Contact:** Michael Bawaya, editor. **60% freelance written.** Quarterly magazine. "We're a popular archaeology magazine. Our readers are very interested in this science. Our features cover important digs, prominent archaeologists, and most any aspect of the science. We only cover North America." Estab. 1997. Circ. 35,000. **Pays on acceptance.** Publishes ms an average of 3 months after acceptance. Byline given. Offers 20% kill fee. Buys one-time, electronic rights. Editorial lead time 3 months. Accepts queries by mail, e-mail, fax. Responds in 3 weeks to queries; 1 month to mss.

Nonfiction: Archaeology. No fiction, poetry, humor. **Buys 12 mss/year.** Query with published clips. Length: 2,000-2,500 words. **Pays $700-1,000.** Sometimes pays expenses of writers on assignment.

Photos: State availability with submission. Reviews transparencies, Prints. Buys one-time rights. Offers $300-1,000/photo. Negotiates payment individually. Identification of subjects required.

Tips: "Read the magazine. Features must have a considerable amount of archaeological detail."

$ $ ARCHAEOLOGY, Archaeological Institute of America, 36-36 33rd St., Long Island NY 11106. (718)472-3050. Fax: (718)472-3051. E-mail: peter@archaeology.org. Website: www.archaeology.org. **Contact:** Peter A. Young, editor-in-chief. **5% freelance written.** Magazine. "*Archaeology* combines worldwide archaeological findings with photography, specially rendered maps, drawings, and charts. Articles cover current excavations, recent discoveries, and special studies of ancient cultures. Regular features: Newsbriefs, film and book reviews, current museum exhibits. We generally commission articles from professional archaeologists. The only magazine of its kind to bring worldwide archaeology to the attention of the general public." Estab. 1948. Circ. 200,000. **Pays on acceptance.** Byline given. Offers 25% kill fee. Buys first North American serial rights. Submit seasonal material 6 months in advance. Accepts queries by mail, e-mail, fax. Accepts simultaneous submissions. Sample copy and writer's guidelines free.

Nonfiction: Essays, general interest. **Buys 6 mss/year.** Query preferred. Length: 1,000-3,000 words. **Pays $750 maximum.** Sometimes pays expenses of writers on assignment.
Photos: Send photos with submission. Reviews 4×5 color transparencies, 35mm color slides. Identification of subjects, credits required.

The online magazine carries original content not found in the print edition. Contact: Mark Rose, online editor.
Tips: "We reach nonspecialist readers interested in art, science, history, and culture. Our reports, regional commentaries, and feature-length articles introduce readers to recent developments in archaeology worldwide."

N $ $ **ASTRONOMY**, Kalmbach Publishing, 21027 Crossroads Circle, P.O. Box 1612, Waukesha WI 53187-1612. (262)796-8776. Fax: (262)798-6468. E-mail: astro@astronomy.com. Editor: Bonnie Gordon. Managing Editor: David J. Eicher. **75% of articles submitted and written by science writers; includes commissioned and unsolicited.** Monthly magazine covering the science and hobby of astronomy. "Half of our magazine is for hobbyists (who may have little interest in the heavens in a scientific way); the other half is directed toward armchair astronomers who may be intrigued by the science." Estab. 1973. Circ. 185,000. **Pays on acceptance.** Byline given. Buys first North American serial, one-time, all rights. Responds in 1 month to queries to queries. Responds in 3 months (unsolicited mss) to mss. Writer's guidelines for #10 SASE or online.

- "We are governed by what is happening in the space program and the heavens. It can be up to a year before we publish a manuscript." Query for electronic submissions.

Nonfiction: Book excerpts, new product (announcements), photo feature, technical, space, astronomy. **Buys 25 mss/year.** Query. Length: 500-4,500 words. **Pays $50-500.**
Photos: Send photos with submission. Pays $25/photo. Captions, identification of subjects, model releases required.
Tips: "Submitting to *Astronomy* could be tough. (Take a look at how technical astronomy is.) But if someone is a physics teacher (or math or astronomy), he or she might want to study the magazine for a year to see the sorts of subjects and approaches we use, and then submit a proposal."

$ $ **THE ELECTRON**, 1776 E. 17th St., Cleveland OH 44114-3679. (216)781-9400. Fax: (216)781-0331. Website: www.cie-wc.edu. Managing Editor: Michael Manning. **Contact:** Ted Sheroke, advertising manager. **80% freelance written.** Quarterly tabloid on development and trends in electronics and high technology. Estab. 1934. Circ. 25,000. Pays on publication. Publishes ms an average of 2 months after acceptance. Byline given. Buys all rights. Responds as soon as possible to mss. Sample copy and writer's guidelines for 8½×11 SASE.
Nonfiction: All submissions must be electronics/technology related. Photo feature, technical (tutorial and how-to), technology news and feature; career and educational. Query with letter/proposal and published clips. Length: 800 words. **Pays $50-500.**
Reprints: Send photocopy of article or typed ms with rights for sale noted and information about when and where the material previously appeared. Does not pay for reprints.
Photos: State availability with submission. Reviews 8×10 and 5×7 b&w prints. Captions, identification of subjects required.
Tips: "We would like to receive educational electronics/technical articles. They must be written in a manner understandable to the beginning-intermediate electronics student. We are also seeking news/feature-type articles covering timely developments in high technology."

$ $ $ **POPULAR SCIENCE, The What's New Magazine**, Time4Media, 2 Park Ave., New York NY 10016. (212)779-5000. Fax: (212)779-5103. E-mail: emily.laber@Time4.com. Website: www.popsci.com. Editor-in-Chief: Scott Mowbray. **Contact:** William G. Phillips, executive editor. **50% freelance written.** Monthly magazine for the well-educated adult, interested in science, technology, new products. "*Popular Science* is devoted to exploring (and explaining) to a nontechnical, but knowledgeable, readership the technical world around us. We cover all of the sciences, engineering and technology, and above all, products. We are largely a 'thing'-oriented publication: things that fly or travel down a turnpike, or go on or under the sea, or cut wood, or reproduce music, or build buildings, or make pictures. We are especially focused on the new, the ingenious, and the useful. Contributors should be as alert to the possibility of selling us pictures and short features as they are to major articles. Freelancers should study the magazine to see what we want and avoid irrelevant submissions." Estab. 1872. Circ. 1,550,000. **Pays on acceptance.** Byline given. Offers 25% kill fee. Buys first North American serial, second serial (reprint) rights. Editorial lead time 3 months. Accepts queries by mail, e-mail, fax. Responds in 1 month to queries. Writer's guidelines for #10 SASE or on website.
Tips: "Probably the easiest way to break in here is by covering a news story in science and technology that we haven't heard about yet. We need people to be acting as scouts for us out there and we are willing to give the most leeway on these performances. We are interested in good, sharply focused ideas in all areas we cover. We prefer a vivid, journalistic style of writing, with the writer taking the reader along with him, showing the reader what he saw, through words."

$ $ $ $ **SCIENTIFIC AMERICAN**, 415 Madison Ave., New York NY 10017. (212)754-0550. Fax: (212)755-1976. E-mail: editors@sciam.com. Website: www.sciam.com. **Contact:** Philip Yam, news editor. Monthly magazine covering developments and topics of interest in the world of science. Query before submitting. "*Scientific American* brings its readers directly to the wellspring of exploration and technological innovation. The magazine specializes in first-hand accounts by the people who actually do the work. Their personal experience provides an authoritative perspective on future growth. Over 100 of our authors have won Nobel Prizes. Complementing those articles are regular departments written by *Scientific American*'s staff of professional journalists, all specialists in their fields. *Scientific American* is the authoritative source of advance information. Authors are the first to report on important breakthroughs, because they're the people who make them. It all goes back to *Scientific American*'s corporate mission: to link those who use knowledge with those who create it." Estab. 1845. Circ. 710,000.

Nonfiction: Freelance opportunities mostly in the news scan section; limited opportunity in feature well. **Pays $1/word average.** Pays expenses of writers on assignment.

$ $ SKY & TELESCOPE, The Essential magazine of Astronomy, Sky Publishing Corp., 49 Bay State Rd., Cambridge MA 02138. (617)864-7360. Fax: (617)576-0336. E-mail: editors@skyandtelescope.com. Website: skyandtelescope.com. Editor: Richard Tresch Fienberg. **Contact:** Bud Sadler, managing editor. **15% freelance written.** Monthly magazine covering astronomy. "*Sky & Telescope* is the magazine of record for astronomy. We cover amateur activities, research news, equipment, book and software reviews. Our audience is the amateur astronomer who wants to learn more about the night sky." Estab. 1941. Circ. 125,000. Pays on publication. Publishes ms an average of 6 months after acceptance. Byline given. Buys first rights. Editorial lead time 4 months. Submit seasonal material 1 year in advance. Accepts queries by mail, e-mail, fax. Responds in 3 weeks to queries; 1 month to mss. Sample copy for $4.99. Writer's Guidelines free by e-mail request to auguide@skyandtelescope.com, online or for #10 SASE.

Nonfiction: Essays, historical/nostalgic, how-to, opinion, personal experience, photo feature, technical. No poetry, crosswords, new age or alternative cosmologies. **Buys 10 mss/year.** Query. Length: 1,500-4,000 words. **Pays at least 25¢/word.** Sometimes pays expenses of writers on assignment.

Photos: Send photos with submission. Reviews contact sheets. Buys one-time rights. Negotiates payment individually. Identification of subjects required.

Columns/Departments: Focal Point (opinion), 850 words; Books & Beyond (reviews), 800 words; Amateur Astronomers (profiles), 1,500 words. **Buys 20 mss/year.** Query. **Pays 25¢/word.**

Tips: "Good artwork is key. Keep the text lively and provide captions."

$ $ WEATHERWISE, The Magazine About the Weather, Heldref Publications, 1319 18th St. NW, Washington DC 20036. (202)296-6267. Fax: (202)296-5149. E-mail: ww@heldref.org. Website: www.weatherwise.org. Associate Editor: Kimbra Cutlip. Assistant Editor: Ellen Fast. **Contact:** Doyle Rice, managing editor. **75% freelance written.** Bimonthly magazine covering weather and meteorology. "*Weatherwise* is America's only magazine about the weather. Our readers range from professional weathercasters and scientists to basement-bound hobbyists, but all share a common craving for information about weather as it relates to the atmospheric sciences, technology, history, culture, society, art, etc." Estab. 1948. Circ. 32,000. Pays on publication. Publishes ms an average of 6 months after acceptance. Byline given. Buys all rights. Editorial lead time 6-9 months. Submit seasonal material 9 months in advance. Accepts queries by mail, e-mail, fax, phone. Responds in 2 months to queries. Sample copy for $4 and 9×12 SAE with 10 first-class stamps. Writer's guidelines for #10 SASE or online.

"First, familiarize yourself with the magazine by taking a close look at the most recent 6 issues. (You can also visit our website, which features the full text of many recent articles.) This will give you an idea of the style of writing we prefer in *Weatherwise*. Then, read through our writer's guidelines (available from our office or on our website) which detail the process for submitting a query letter. As for the subject matter, keep your eyes and ears open for the latest research and/or current trends in meteorology and climatology that may be appropriate for the general readership of *Weatherwise*. And always keep in mind weather's awesome power and beauty—its 'fun, fury, and fascination' that so many of our readers enjoy."

Nonfiction: Book excerpts, essays, general interest, historical/nostalgic, how-to, interview/profile, new product, opinion, personal experience, photo feature, technical, travel. Special issues: Photo Contest (September/October deadline June 1). "No blow-by-blow accounts of the biggest storm to ever hit your backyard." **Buys 15-18 mss/year.** Query with published clips. Length: 1,500-2,500 words. **Pays $200-500 for assigned articles; $0-300 for unsolicited articles.** Sometimes pays expenses of writers on assignment.

Photos: Reviews contact sheets, negatives, prints, electronic files. Buys one-time rights. Negotiates payment individually. Captions, identification of subjects required.

Columns/Departments: Front & Center (news, trends, opinion), 300-400 words; Weather Talk (folklore and humor), 1,000 words. **Buys 12-15 mss/year.** Query with published clips. **Pays $0-200.**

Tips: "Don't query us wanting to write about broad types like the Greenhouse Effect, the Ozone Hole, El Niño, etc. Although these are valid topics, you can bet you won't be able to cover it all in 2,000 words. With these topics and all others, find the story within the story. And whether you're writing about a historical storm or new technology, be sure to focus on the human element—the struggles, triumphs, and other anecdotes of individuals."

SCIENCE FICTION, FANTASY & HORROR

These publications often publish experimental fiction and many are open to new writers. More information on these markets can be found in the Contests & Awards section under the Fiction heading.

$ ABSOLUTE MAGNITUDE, Science Fiction Adventures, DNA Publications, P.O. Box 2988, Radford VA 24143. E-mail: absolutemagnitude@dnapublications.com. Website: www.dnapublications.com/. Warren Lapine, editor-in-chief. **95% freelance written.** Quarterly magazine featuring science fiction short stories. "We specialize in action/adventure science fiction with an emphasis on hard science fiction short stories." Estab. 1993. Circ. 6,000. Pays on publication. Publishes ms an average of 6 months after acceptance. Byline given. Buys first rights. First English language serial rights. Editorial lead time 6 months. Accepts simultaneous submissions. Responds in 1 month to mss. Sample copy for $5. Writer's guidelines for #10 SASE.

- This editor is still looking for tightly plotted stories that are character driven. He is now purchasing more short stories than before. "Do not query—send complete manuscript."

Fiction: Buys 40 mss/year. Send complete ms. Length: 1,000-25,000 words. **Pays 3-7¢/word.**

Poetry: Any form. Best chance with light verse. **Buys 4 poems/issue.** Submit maximum 5 poems. Length: Up to 25,000 words. **Pays $10/poem.**

Tips: "We are very interested in working with new writers, but we are not interested in 'drawer-cleaning' exercises. There is no point in sending less than your best effort if you are interested in a career in writing. We do not use fantasy, horror, satire, or funny science fiction. We're looking for character-driven, action/adventure-based Technical Science Fiction. We want tightly plotted stories with memorable characters. Characters should be the driving force behind the action of the story; they should not be thrown in as an afterthought. We need to see both plot development and character growth. Stories which are resolved without action on the protagonist's part do not work for us; characters should not be spectators in situations completely beyond their control or immune to their influence. Some of our favorite writers are Roger Zelazny, Frank Herbert, Robert Silverberg, and Fred Saberhagen."

$ $ ANALOG SCIENCE FICTION & FACT, Dell magazine Fiction Group, 475 Park Ave. S, 11th Floor, New York NY 10016. (212)686-7188. Fax: (212)686-7414. E-mail: analog@dellmagazines.com. Website: www.analogsf.com. **Contact:** Dr. Stanley Schmidt, editor. **100% freelance written.** Eager to work with new/unpublished writers. Monthly magazine for general future-minded audience. Accepts queries for serials and fact articles only; query by mail. Estab. 1930. **Pays on acceptance.** Publishes ms an average of 10 months after acceptance. Byline given. Buys first North American serial rights. Nonexclusive foreign serial rights Responds in 1 month to queries (send queries for serials and fact articles only to queries. Sample copy for $5. Writer's guidelines for #10 SASE or online.

- Break in by telling an "unforgettable story in which an original, thought-provoking, plausible idea plays an indispensible role."

Nonfiction: Looking for illustrated technical articles dealing with subjects of not only current but future interest, i.e., topics at the present frontiers of research whose likely future developments have implications of wide interest. **Buys 11 mss/year.** Query by mail only. Length: 5,000 words. **Pays 6¢/word.**

Fiction: "Basically, we publish science fiction stories. That is, stories in which some aspect of future science or technology is so integral to the plot that, if that aspect were removed, the story would collapse. The science can be physical, sociological or psychological. The technology can be anything from electronic engineering to biogenetic engineering. But the stories must be strong and realistic, with believable people doing believable things—no matter how fantastic the background might be." **Buys 60-100 unsolicited mss/year.** Length: 2,000-80,000 words. **Pays 4¢/word for novels; 5-6¢/word for novelettes; 6-8¢/word for shorts under 7,500 words; $450-600 for intermediate lengths.**

Tips: "In query give clear indication of central ideas and themes and general nature of story line—and what is distinctive or unusual about it. We have no hard-and-fast editorial guidelines, because science fiction is such a broad field that I don't want to inhibit a new writer's thinking by imposing 'Thou Shalt Not's.' Besides, a really good story can make an editor swallow his preconceived taboos. I want the best work I can get, regardless of who wrote it—and I need new writers. So I work closely with new writers who show definite promise, but of course it's impossible to do this with every new writer. No occult or fantasy."

$ ANOTHEREALM, 33537 N. Evergreen Dr., Gages Lake IL 60030. (847)543-4126. E-mail: editor@anotherealm.com. Website: http://anotherealm.com. **Contact:** Gary A. Markette, senior editor. **100% freelance written.** Semi-monthly magazine covering science fiction, fantasy, and horror. "An e-zine of short (5,000 words and under) science fiction, fantasy, and horror." Estab. 1998. Circ. 5,000/week. Pays on publication. Byline given. first Internet rights Editorial lead time 3 months. Submit seasonal material 3 months in advance.

- No queries necessary. Story submissions accepted any time, but evaluated only during October-November reading period.

Fiction: When submitting "paste plain text (ASCII) in e-mail; do not attach files to e-mail. *Anotherealm* downloads no attachments from e-mails to avoid possible viruses." Fantasy, horror, science fiction. No experimental, stream-of-consciousness, avante-garde or vampire stories. **Buys 24-30 mss/year.** Send complete ms. Length: Maximum 5,000 words. **Pays $10 on publication.**

Tips: "Visit our website. Read our guidelines, our BBS, and a few of the stories. That way, you'll have a better idea about what we like to publish. We never get enough hard science fiction stories (hint, hint)."

$ ASIMOV'S SCIENCE FICTION, Dell magazine Fiction Group, 475 Park Avenue S., 11th Floor, New York NY 10016. (212)686-7188. Fax: (212)686-7414. E-mail: asimovs@dellmagazines.com. Executive Editor: Sheila Williams. **Contact:** Gardner Dozois, editor. **98% freelance written.** Works with a small number of new/unpublished writers each year. Magazine published 11 times a year, including 1 double issue. Estab. 1977. Circ. 50,000. **Pays on acceptance.** Buys first North American serial rights; nonexclusive foreign serial rights; reprint rights occasionally. Accepts queries by mail. Responds in 2 months to queries. Sample copy for $5. Writer's guidelines for #10 SASE or online.

Fiction: Science fiction primarily. Some fantasy and humor but no "Sword and Sorcery." No explicit sex or violence that isn't integral to the story. "It is best to read a great deal of material in the genre to avoid the use of some *very* old ideas." **Buys 10mss/issue.** Send complete ms and SASE with *all* submissions. Length: 750-15,000 words. **Pays 5-8¢/word.**

Poetry: Length: 40 lines maximum. **Pays $1/line.**

Tips: "In general, we're looking for 'character-oriented' stories, those in which the characters, rather than the science, provide the main focus for the reader's interest. Serious, thoughtful, yet accessible fiction will constitute the majority of our purchases, but there's always room for the humorous as well. Borderline fantasy is fine, but no Sword & Sorcery, please. A good overview would be to consider that all fiction is written to examine or illuminate some aspect of human existence, but that in science fiction the backdrop you work against is the size of the universe. Please do not send us submissions on disk or via e-mail. We've bought some of our best stories from people who have never sold a story before."

N $ CENTURY, Century Publishing, Inc., P.O. Box 336, Hastings-on-Hudson NY 10706. E-mail: editor@centurymag.com. Website: www.centurymag.com. **Contact:** Robert K.J. Killheffer, editor. **100% freelance written.** Biannual magazine covering speculative fiction (science fiction, fantasy, horror). "We're looking for speculative fiction with a high degree of literary accomplishment—ambitious work which can appeal not only to the genre's regular audience but to readers outside the genre as well." Estab. 1994. Circ. 2,000. **Pays on acceptance.** Publishes ms an average of 1 year after acceptance. Byline given. Buys first world English rights; nonexclusive reprint rights Responds in 3 months to mss. Sample copy for $7.00. Writer's guidelines for #10 SASE or on website.

Fiction: Experimental, fantasy, horror, science fiction. **Buys 16-20 mss/year.** Send complete ms. Length: 250-20,000 words. **Pays 4¢/word.**

$ CHALLENGING DESTINY, New Fantasy & Science Fiction, Crystalline Sphere Publishing, RR #6, St. Marys, Ontario N4X 1C8, Canada. (519)885-6012. E-mail: csp@golden.net. Website: home.golden.net/~csp/. **Contact:** Dave Switzer, editor. **80% freelance written.** Quarterly magazine covering science fiction and fantasy. Estab. 1997. Circ. 200. Pays on publication. Publishes ms an average of 5 months after acceptance. Byline given. Buys first North American serial rights. Accepts queries by mail, e-mail. Accepts simultaneous submissions. Responds in 1 week to queries; 1 month to mss. Sample copy for $7.50 (Canadian), $6.50 (US). Writer's guidelines for #10 SASE or online.

Fiction: Fantasy, science fiction. **Buys 24 mss/year.** Send complete ms. Length: 2,000-10,000 words. **Pays $1¢/word (Canadian).**

Tips: "We're interested in stories where violence is rejected as a means for solving problems. We're also interested in stories with philosophical, political, or religious themes. We're not interested in stories where the good guys kill the bad guys and then live happily ever after. Read an issue to see what kind of stories we publish. Many of the stories we publish are between 4,000 and 8,000 words and have interesting characters, ideas, and plot."

N $ CHAMPAGNE SHIVERS, Champagne Productions, 2419 Klein Place, Regina, Saskatchewan S4V 1M4, Canada. E-mail: champagneshivers@hotmail.com. **Contact:** Cathy Buburuh, editor. **90% freelance written.** Quarterly online horror magazine. Estab. 2002. Pays prior to publication. Publishes ms an average of 3 months after acceptance. Byline given. Offers 100% kill fee. Buys first rights. Editorial lead time 3 months. Submit seasonal material 3 months in advance. Accepts queries by e-mail. Responds in 2 days to queries; 1 week to mss. Sample copy for free. Writer's guidelines free.

Nonfiction: Special features (horror-related), interviews with horror celebrities, horror writers, etc. **Buys 4-6 mss/year.** Send complete ms. Length: 1,000-2,000 words. **Pays $5.** Prizes for best contribution each issue.

Photos: Send photos with submission. Buys one-time rights. Pays $5. Captions, identification of subjects required.

Columns/Departments: Open to ideas for special features (must have a horror slant). **Pays $5. Buys 30 mss/year.** Send complete ms. Length: 2,000 words. **Pays $5.**

Poetry: Non-rhyming poetry stands the best chance for acceptance. Avant-garde, free verse, haiku, light verse, traditional, horror-related only; also buys demented nursery rhymes. **Buys 30 poems/year.** Submit maximum 1 poems. Length: 20-100 lines.

Tips: "I prefer well-written suspenseful horror to blood, guts and gore. Poetic language scores points with this editor. Read the guidelines online for more tips and find out why I call the magazine *Champagne Shivers*."

$ THE CRYSTAL BALL, The Starwind Press, P.O. Box 98, Ripley OH 45167. (937)392-4549. E-mail: marlene@techgallery.com. **Contact:** Marlene Powell, editor. **90% freelance written.** Quarterly magazine covering science fiction and fantasy for young adult readers. "We are especially targeting readers of middle school age." Estab. 1997. **Pays on acceptance.** Publishes ms an average of 6 months after acceptance. Byline given. Offers 100% kill fee. Buys first, second serial (reprint) rights. Editorial lead time 4 months. Accepts queries by mail, e-mail, phone. Sample copy for 9×12 SASE and $3. Writer's guidelines for #10 SASE.

Nonfiction: How-to (science), interview/profile, personal experience, book reviews; science information. **Buys 4-6 mss/year.** Query. Length: 900-3,000 words. **Pays ¼¢/word.**

Reprints: Send typed ms with rights for sale noted and information about when and where the material previously appeared. Pays 100% of amount paid for an original article.

Photos: Send photos with submission. Negotiates payment individually. Captions, identification of subjects required.

Columns/Departments: Book Reviews (science fiction and fantasy), 100-200 words or less; museum reviews (science & technology, museums & centers, children's museums), 900 words. **Buys 10-15 mss/year.** Query. **Pays ¼¢/word.**

Fiction: Fantasy, science fiction. **Buys 10-12 mss/year.** Send complete ms. Length: 1,000-5,000 words. **Pays ¼¢/word.**
Tips: "Have a good feel for writing for kids. Don't 'write down' to your audience because they're kids. We look for articles of scientific and technological interest."

DRAGONS, KNIGHTS, AND ANGELS, The Magazine of Christian Fantasy and Science Fiction, Creative Mental Programming Ent. LLC, 5461 W. 4605 S., West Valley City Utah 84120. E-mail: dkamagazine@quixnet.net. Website: www.dkamagazine.net. **Contact:** Rebecca Shelley, executive editor. **90% freelance written.** Quarterly online publication. *DKA Magazine* is a family friendly magazine of Christian fantasy and science fiction featuring short stories, poetry, and art. Estab. January 2000. Circ. 1,000 hits/issue. **Pays on acceptance.** Publishes ms an average of 3 months after acceptance. Byline given. Not copyrighted. Buys one-time, electronic rights. Editorial lead time 1 month. Accepts previously published material. Accepts simultaneous submissions. Responds in 1 month (we prefer e-mail submissions) to mss. Sample copy and writer's guidelines online.

- Send complete ms, no queries. Reading periods January, April, July, and October.

Fiction: "*DKA* magazine is founded on the idea that the power of God is the greatest magic of all. While the stories we publish do not need to have an obvious moral, the protagonists must be motivated by moral values, or learn some moral value by the end of the story. This is a family magazine, so keep that in mind regarding language and content of the stories you submit." Fantasy, religious, science fiction. "Absolutely no erotica, gay/lesbian, excessive violence, or foul language." **Buys 16 mss/year.** Send complete ms. Length: 500-4,000 words. **Pays ½¢/word.**
Poetry: Free verse, light verse, traditional. No erotic, dark, occult, or gory poems. **Buys 12 poems/year.** Submit maximum 5 poems. Length: 4-500 lines. **Pays $10.**
Tips: "We're getting too many mushy 'not-plots.' Remember, a short story needs a clear beginning, middle, and end, and must have a conflict. The battle between good and evil is an integral part of fantasy. Don't be afraid to use it. Please refer to guidelines on our site before submitting."

$ FLESH AND BLOOD, 121 Joseph St., Bayville NJ 08721. E-mail: HorrorJack@aol.com. Website: zombie.horrorseek.com/horror/fleshnblood/. **Contact:** Jack Fisher, editor. **90% freelance written.** Triannual magazine covering horror/dark fantasy. Estab. 1997. Circ. 500. Pays within 3 months of acceptance. Publishes ms an average of 10 months after acceptance. Editorial lead time 1 month. Accepts queries by mail, e-mail. Responds in 2 weeks to queries; 2 months to mss. Sample copy for $4.50 (check payable to John Fisher). Writer's guidelines for #10 SASE or online.

- The editor reports an interest in seeing powerful vignettes/stories with surrealism-avante-garde(ism) to them and original, unique ghost stories. The magazine recently won Best Magazine of the Year Award in the Jobs in Hell newsletter contest.

Fiction: Horror, slice-of-life vignettes, dark fantasy. "No garden-variety work, or work where the main character is a 'nut' killer, etc." **Buys 18-24 mss/year.** Length: 500-4,000 words. **1-2¢/word.**
Poetry: Avant-garde, free verse, horror/dark fantasy surreal, bizarre. "No rhyming, love pieces." **Buys 15-20 poems/year.** Submit maximum 5 poems. Length: 3-25 lines. **Pays $5-10.**
Tips: "We like light horror over gore. Don't let the title deceive you. Surreal, bizarre, eccentric tales have a good chance. We especially like dark fantasy pieces and vignettes."

$ THE MAGAZINE OF FANTASY & SCIENCE FICTION, Spilogale, Inc., P.O. Box 3447, Hoboken NJ 07030. (201)876-2551. Fax: (201)876-2551. E-mail: gordonfsf@aol.com. Website: www.fsfmag.com. **Contact:** Gordon Van Gelder, editor. **100% freelance written.** Monthly magazine covering fantasy fiction and science fiction. "*The Magazine of Fantasy and Science Fiction* publishes various types of science fiction and fantasy short stories and novellas, making up about 80% of each issue. The balance of each issue is devoted to articles about science fiction, a science column, book and film reviews, cartoons, and competitions." Estab. 1949. Circ. 80,000. **Pays on acceptance.** Byline given. Buys first North American serial, foreign serial rights. Submit seasonal material 8 months in advance. Accepts previously published material. Responds in 2 months to queries. Sample copy for $5. Writer's guidelines for #10 SASE or online.
Columns/Departments: Curiosities (forgotten books), 250 words. **Buys 11 mss/year. Pays $50.**
Fiction: Prefers character-oriented stories. Fantasy, horror, science fiction. No electronic submissions. **Buys 70-100 mss/year.** Send complete ms. Length: 2,000-25,000 words. **Pays 5-8¢/word.**
Tips: "We need more hard science fiction and humor."

SCI FICTION, SCIFI.COM, PMB 391, 511 Avenue of the Americas, New York NY 10011-8436. Website: www.scifi.com/scifiction. **Contact:** Ellen Datlow, fiction editor. **100% freelance written.** Weekly webzine covering science fiction. Estab. 2000. Pays on signature of contract. Publishes ms an average of 3 months after acceptance. Byline given. Buys first, electronic, use in print rights. Editorial lead time 2 months. Accepts queries by e-mail. Responds in 2 months to mss. Sample copy online. Writer's guidelines online.

- Accepts queries by e-mail only through the publication's website.

Fiction: Ellen Datlow, fiction editor. Fantasy, science fiction. **Buys 48 mss/year.** Send complete ms. Length: 2,000-22,000 words. **Pays $20¢/word-3,500.**

$ $ STARLOG MAGAZINE, The Science Fiction Universe, Starlog Group, 475 Park Ave. S., 7th Floor, New York NY 10016-1689. Fax: (212)889-7933. E-mail: allan.dart@starloggroup.com. Website: www.starlog.com. **Contact:** David McDonnell, editor. **90% freelance written.** Monthly magazine covering "the science fiction-fantasy genre: its films, TV, books, art and personalities. We often provide writers with a list of additional questions for them to ask interviewees. Manuscripts *must* be submitted by e-mail or on computer disk." Estab. 1976. Pays after publication.

Publishes ms an average of 3 months after acceptance. Byline given. Offers kill fee only to manuscripts. Buys all rights. Accepts queries by mail, e-mail, fax. Responds in 1 month to queries. Sample copy for $7. Writer's guidelines for #10 SASE.

- "We are somewhat hesitant to work with unpublished writers. We concentrate on interviews with actors, directors, writers, producers, special effects technicians and others. Be aware that 'sci-fi' and 'Trekkie' are seen as derogatory terms by our readers and by us."

O→ Break in by "doing something fresh, imaginative or innovative—or all three. Or by getting an interview we can't get or didn't think of. The writers who sell to us try *hard* and manage to meet one or more challenges."

Nonfiction: "We also sometimes cover science fiction/fantasy animation. We prefer article format as opposed to Q&A interviews." Book excerpts (having directly to do with SF films, TV or literature), interview/profile (actors, directors, screenwriters—who've done science fiction films—and science fiction novelists), movie/TV set visits. No personal opinion think pieces/essays. *No* first person. Avoid articles on horror films/creators. Query first with published clips. Length: 500-3,000 words. **Pays $35 (500 words or less); $50-75 (sidebars); $150-275 (1,000-4,000 words).** Pays $50 for *each* reprint in each foreign edition or such.

Photos: "No separate payment for photos provided by film studios or TV networks." State availability with submission. Buys all rights. Photo credit given. Pays $15-25 for color slide transparencies depending on quality. Captions, identification of subjects, credit line required.

Columns/Departments: Booklog (book reviews by assignment only). **Buys 150 reviews/year.** Book review, 125 words maximum. No kill fee. Query with published clips. **Pays $15 each.**

▣ This online magazine carries original content not found in the print edition. Contact: David McDonnell, online editor.

Tips: "Absolutely *no fiction*. We do *not* publish it and we throw away fiction manuscripts from writers who *can't* be bothered to include SASE. Nonfiction only please! We are always looking for *fresh* angles on the various *Star Trek* shows and *Star Wars*. Read the magazine more than once and don't just rely on this listing. Know something about science fiction films, TV and literature. Most full-length major assignments go to freelancers with whom we're already dealing, but if we like your clips and ideas, it's possible we'll give *you* a chance. No phone calls for *any* reason please—we *mean* that!"

SEX

Magazines featuring pictorial layouts accompanied by stories and articles of a sexual nature, both gay and straight, are listed in this section. Dating and single lifestyle magazines appear in the Relationships section. Other markets for articles relating to sex can be found in the Men's and Women's sections.

$☆ CHEATERS CLUB, Hounds of Hell Publishing, P.O. Box 1319, Hudson, Quebec J0P 1H0, Canada. (450)458-1934. Fax: (450)458-2977. **Contact:** Editor. **100% freelance written.** Monthly men's magazine covering "swingers, lesbians, couples who invite others to join them; threesomes, foursomes, and moresomes." "All Hounds of Hell Publishing titles deal with hardcore sex." Estab. 1996. Circ. 40,000. Pays on 60-day terms. Publishes ms an average of 3 months after acceptance. Byline sometimes given. Buys all rights. Editorial lead time 3 months. Accepts queries by mail, e-mail, fax, phone. Accepts simultaneous submissions. Sample copy for $5 (US)/issue. Writer's guidelines for #10 SASE or by e-mail.

Fiction: "We will not accept anything to do with violence, children, nonconsenting sex, or degradation." **Buys 64 mss/year.** Send complete ms. Length: 1,300-2,000 words. **Pays $10-15/1,000 words.**

Tips: "Story length should not exceed 2,000 words. Cut the introduction—get straight to the sex. Stories of 800-1,200 words are needed. Open with a bang—is it interesting? Does it excite the reader? Be very descriptive and very graphic, but not violent. Be explicitly descriptive. We want to smell leather, taste the skin, and feel the action as it takes place. But the sex must be enjoyable for all participants; nobody does anything in these stories against their will."

$☆ FIRST HAND, Experiences For Loving Men, Firsthand, Ltd., 310 Cedar Lane, Teaneck NJ 07666. (201)836-9177. Fax: (201)836-5055. E-mail: firsthand3@aol.com. Publisher: Jackie Lewis. **Contact:** Don Dooley, editor. **75% freelance written.** Eager to work with new/unpublished writers. Magazine published 12 times/year covering homosexual erotica. Estab. 1980. Circ. 70,000. Pays on publication. Publishes ms an average of 8 months after acceptance. Byline given. Buys all rights (exceptions made) and second serial (reprint) rights. Submit seasonal material 10 months in advance. Responds in 4 months to mss. Sample copy for $5. Writer's guidelines for #10 SASE.

Reprints: Send photocopy. Pays 50% of amount paid for original articles.

Fiction: "We prefer fiction in the first person which is believable—stories based on the writer's actual experience have the best chance. We're not interested in stories which involve underage characters in sexual situations. Other taboos include bestiality, rape—except in prison stories, as rape is an unavoidable reality in prison—and heavy drug use. Writers with questions about what we can and cannot depict should write for our guidelines, which go into this in more detail. We print mostly self-contained stories; we will look at novel excerpts, but only if they stand on their own." Erotica. Length: Up to 5,000 words; average 2,000-3,000 words.

Tips: "*First Hand* is a very reader-oriented publication for gay men. Half of each issue is made up of letters from our readers describing their personal experiences, fantasies, and feelings. Our readers are from all walks of life, all races and ethnic backgrounds, all classes, all religious and political affiliations, and so on. They are very diverse, and many live in far-flung rural areas or small towns; for some of them, our magazines are the primary source of contact with gay life, in some cases the only support for their gay identity. Our readers are very loyal and save every issue. We return that loyalty by trying to reflect their interests—for instance, by striving to avoid the exclusively big-city bias so common to national gay publications. So bear in mind the diversity of the audience when you write."

$ IN TOUCH/INDULGE FOR MEN, In Touch International, Inc., 13122 Saticoy St., North Hollywood CA 91605-3402. (818)764-2288. Fax: (818)764-2307. E-mail: michael@intouchformen.com. Website: www.intouchformen.com. **Contact:** Michael W. Jimenez, editor. **80% freelance written.** Works with a small number of new/unpublished writers each year. Monthly magazine covering the gay male lifestyle, gay male humor and erotica. Estab. 1973. Circ. 70,000. Pays on publication. Byline given, pseudonym OK. Buys one-time rights. Accepts queries by mail, e-mail, fax. Accepts simultaneous submissions. Responds in 2 months to queries. Sample copy for $6.95. Writer's guidelines for #10 SASE or online.

Break in with "a clear, solid story that can be sent on disk or sent via e-mail."

Nonfiction: Rarely buys nonfiction. Send complete ms. Length: 3,000-3,500 words. **Pays $25-75.**

Photos: Send photos with submission. Reviews contact sheets, transparencies, prints. Buys one-time rights. Offers $25/photo. Captions, identification of subjects, model releases required.

Fiction: Gay male erotica. **Buys 82 mss/year.** Send complete ms. Length: 3,000-3,500 words. **Pays $75 maximum.**

Fillers: Short humor. **Buys 12/year.** Length: 1,500-2,500 words. **Pays $25-50.**

Tips: "Our publications feature male nude photos plus three fiction pieces, several articles, cartoons, humorous comments on items from the media, photo features. We try to present positive aspects of the gay lifestyle, with an emphasis on humor. Humorous pieces may be erotic in nature. We are open to all submissions that fit our gay male format; the emphasis, however, is on humor and the upbeat. We receive many fiction manuscripts but not nearly enough unique, innovative, or even experimental material."

$ KEY CLUB, Hounds of Hell Publishing, P.O. Box 1319, Hudson, Quebec J0P 1H0, Canada. (450)458-1934. Fax: (450)458-2977. **Contact:** Editor. **100% freelance written.** Monthly Men's magazine covering "first time anal virgins, new partners, new toys, new experiences. All Hounds of Hell Publishing titles deal with hardcore sex." Estab. 1996. Circ. 40,000. Pays on 60-day terms. Publishes ms an average of 3 months after acceptance. Byline sometimes given. Buys all rights. Editorial lead time 3 months. Accepts queries by mail, e-mail, fax, phone. Accepts simultaneous submissions. Sample copy for $5 (US)/issue. Writer's guidelines for #10 SASE.

Fiction: Erotica. "We will not accept anything to do with violence, children, nonconsenting sex, or degradation." **Buys 64 mss/year.** Send complete ms. Length: 1,300-2,000 words. **Pays $10-15/1,000 words.**

Tips: "Story length should not exceed 2,000 words. Cut the introduction—get straight to the sex. Stories of 800-1,200 words are needed. Open with a bang—is it interesting? Does it excite the reader? Be very descriptive and very graphic, but not violent. Be explicitly descriptive. We want to smell leather, taste the skin, and feel the action as it takes place. But the sex must be enjoyable for all participants; nobody does anything in these stories against their will."

$ OPTIONS, AJA Publishing, P.O. Box 392, White Plains NY 10602. E-mail: Dianaedt@bellsouth.net. Editor: Don Stone. **Contact:** Diana Sheridan, associate editor. **Mostly freelance written**. Sexually explicit magazine published 10 times/year for and about bisexuals and to a lesser extent homosexuals. "Stories and letters about bisexuality. Positive approach. Safe-sex encounters unless the story clearly pre-dates the AIDS situation." Estab. 1977. Circ. 100,000. Pays on publication. Publishes ms an average of 10 months after acceptance. Byline given, usually pseudonymous. Buys all rights. Accepts queries by mail, e-mail. Sample copy for $2.95 and 6×9 SAE with 5 first-class stamps. Writer's guidelines for #10 SASE or by e-mail.

- Buys almost no seasonal material. Accepts queries, but prefers to receive complete ms. Generally responds to postal mail queries in 3 weeks, and usually replies overnight to e-mail submissions.

Fiction: "We don't usually get enough true first-person stories and need to buy some from writers. They must be bisexual, mostly man/man, hot, and believable. They must not read like fiction." **Buys 80 mss/year.** Send complete ms. Length: 2,000-3,000 words. **Pays $100.**

Tips: "We use many more male/male pieces than female/female. No longer buying 'letters'. We get enough real ones."

$$$$ PENTHOUSE, General Media, 11 Penn Plaza, 12th floor, New York NY 10001. (212)702-6000. Fax: (212)702-6279. Website: www.penthousemag.com. Editor: Peter Bloch. **Contact:** Heidi Handman. Monthly magazine. "*Penthouse* is for the sophisticated male. Its editorial scope ranges from outspoken contemporary comment to photography essays of beautiful women. *Penthouse* features interviews with personalities, sociological studies, humor, travel, food and wines, and fashion and grooming for men." Estab. 1969. Circ. 1,100,000. Pays 2 months after acceptance. Byline given. Offers 25% kill fee. Buys all rights. Editorial lead time 3 months. Accepts simultaneous submissions. Writer's guidelines for #10 SASE.

Nonfiction: Exposé, general interest (to men), interview/profile. **Buys 50 mss/year.** Query with published clips or send complete ms. Length: 4,000-6,000 words. **Pays $3,000.**

Columns/Departments: Length: 1,000 words. **Buys 25 mss/year.** Query with published clips or send complete ms. **Pays $500.**

Tips: "Because of our long lead time, writers should think at least 6 months ahead. We take chances. Go against the grain; we like writers who look under rocks and see what hides there."

$ $ ☒ PENTHOUSE VARIATIONS, (formerly *Variations*), General Media Communications, Inc., 11 Penn Plaza, 12th Floor, New York NY 10001. (212)702-6000. E-mail: variations@generalmedia.com. **Contact:** Barbara Pizio, executive editor. **100% freelance written.** Monthly erotica magazine. "*Variations* offers readers a window into the sex lives of America's most exciting couples. Each issue is an elegantly erotic package of healthy sexual fact and fantasy reflecting the rich color in the rainbow of human delight." Estab. 1978. Circ. 300,000. **Pays on acceptance.** Publishes ms an average of 14 months after acceptance. Buys all rights. Editorial lead time 7 months. Submit seasonal material 10 months in advance. Responds in 1 month to queries; 2 months to mss. Sample copy from (888)312-BACK. Writer's guidelines for #10 SASE or by e-mail.

Nonfiction: Book excerpts, interview/profile, personal experience. "No humor, no poetry, no children, no one under 21, no relatives, no pets, no coercion." **Buys 50 mss/year.** Query by mail only or send complete ms. Length: 3,000-3,500 words. **Pays $400 maximum.**

Fiction: "*Variations* publishes couple-oriented narratives in which a person fully describes his or her favorite sex scenes squarely focused within 1 of the magazine's usual categories, in highly explicit erotic detail, using the best possible language." Erotica. Length: 3,000-3,500 words. **Pays $400 maximum.**

Tips: "Read the magazine to familiarize yourself with our voice, style, and categories. Write about what you're familiar with and the most comfortable discussing. We're looking for focused manuscripts which are carefully crafted by excellent writers. We are always glad to work with new writers who choose to go the distance to write successful stories for us."

$ $ $ $ PLAYBOY MAGAZINE, 680 N. Lake Shore Dr., Chicago IL 60611. (312)751-8000. E-mail: articles@playboy.com. Website: www.playboy.com. **Contact:** Jonathan Black. Monthly magazine. "As the world's largest general interest lifestyle magazine for men, *Playboy* spans the spectrum of contemporary men's passions. From hard-hitting investigative journalism to light-hearted humor, the latest in fashion and personal technology to the cutting edge of the popular culture, *Playboy* is and always has been guidebook and dream book for generations of American men...the definitive source of information and ideas for over 10 million readers each month. In addition, *Playboy*'s 'Interview' and '20 Questions' present profiles of politicians, athletes and today's hottest personalities." Estab. 1953. Circ. 3,283,000. Buys first North American serial rights. Editorial lead time 6 months. Accepts queries by mail. Responds in 1 month to queries. Writer's guidelines for #10 SASE or online at website.

- *Playboy* does not consider poetry, plays, story outlines or novel-length mss.

Nonfiction: Articles Editor. "*Playboy* regularly publishes nonfiction articles on a wide range of topics—sports, politics, music, topical humor, personality profiles, business and finance, science, technology, and other topics that have a bearing on our readers' lifestyles. You can best determine what we're looking for by becoming familiar with the nonfiction we are currently publishing. We frequently reject ideas and articles simply because they are inappropriate to our publication." General interest, humor, interview/profile. Does not accept unsolicited poetry. Mss should be typed, double-spaced and accompanied by a SASE. Writers who submit mss without a SASE will receive neither the ms nor a printed rejection. Submit brief query that outlines idea, explains why it's right for *Playboy*, and "tells us something about yourself." Length: 4,000-5,000 words. **Pays $3,000.**

Fiction: Fiction Department. "*Playboy* is considered one of the top fiction markets in the world. We publish serious contemporary stories, mystery, suspense, humor, science fiction and sports stories. It pays to take a close look at the magazine before submitting material; we often reject stories of high quality because they are inappropriate to our publication." Humorous, mainstream, mystery, science fiction, suspense. Does not consider poetry, plays, story outlines or novel-length mss. Writers should remember that the magazine's appeal is chiefly to a well-informed, young male audience. Fairy tales, extremely experimental fiction and out-right pornography all have their place, but it is not in *Playboy.* Handwritten submissions will be returned unread. Writers who submit mss without including a SASE will receive neither the ms nor a printed rejection. "We will not consider stories submitted electronically or by fax." Length: 1,000-6,000 words. **Pays $2,000-5,000.**

Tips: "A bit of advice for writers: Please bear in mind that *Playboy* is not a venue where beginning writers should expect to be published. Nearly all of our writers have long publication histories, working their way up through newspapers and regional publications. Aspiring writers should gain experience and an extensive file of by-lined features before approaching *Playboy.* Please don't call our offices to ask how to submit a story or to explain a story. Don't ask for sample copies, a statement of editorial policy, a reaction to an idea for a story, or a detailed critique. We are unable to provide these, as we receive dozens of submissions daily."

$ $ $ ☒ PLAYGIRL, 801 Second Ave., New York NY 10017. (212)661-7878. Fax: (212)697-6343. E-mail: mzipp@bluehrzn.com. Editor-in-Chief: Michelle Zipp. **25% freelance written.** Prefers to work with published/established writers. Monthly magazine. "*PLAYGIRL* addresses the needs, interests and desires of women 18 years of age and older. We provide something no other American women's magazine can: An uninhibited approach to exploring sexuality and fantasy that empowers, enlightens, and entertains. We publish features articles of all sorts: interviews with top celebrities; essays and humor pieces on sexually related topics; first-person accounts of sensual adventures; articles on the latest trends in sex, love, romance, and dating; and how-to stories that give readers sexy news they can use. We also publish erotic fiction and reader fantasies from a woman's perspective. The common thread—besides, of course, good, lively writing and scrupulous research—is a fresh, open-minded, inquisitive attitude." Circ. 500,000. Pays within 6 weeks of acceptance. Publishes ms an average of 5 months after acceptance. Byline given. Buys all rights. Submit seasonal material 6 months in advance. Accepts queries by mail, fax. Responds in 3 months to mss. Sample copy not available. Writer's guidelines for #10 SASE.

O→ Break in with pieces for Fantasy Forum. "This section is devoted to female fantasies and pleasures of the flesh. Be creative, wild, and uninhibited in your writings. Write what turns you on, not what you think turns other people on. All submissions considered must be sexually explorative fantasies that empower, enlighten, and entertain. Any fantasies that involve pain, degradation, or extreme negativity will not be published." Send complete ms and mark 'Fantasy Forum' on the envelope.

Nonfiction: Average issue: 3 articles; 1 celebrity interview. Essays, exposé (related to women's issues), general interest, interview/profile (Q&A format with major celebrities—pitch first), new product, articles on sexuality, medical breakthroughs, relationships, insightful, lively articles on current issues, investigative pieces particularly geared to *PLAYGIRL*'s focus on sex/dating/relationships. **Buys 6 mss/year.** Query with published clips. Length: 1,500-2,000 for Fantasy Forum; 1,600-2,500 for articles. **Pays $300-1,000 (varies); $25 for some fantasies, much more for celeb interviews.** Sometimes pays expenses of writers on assignment.

Tips: "Best bet for first-time writers: Fantasy Forum. No phone calls, please."

$ STICKY BUNS, Hounds of Hell Publishing, P.O. Box 1319, Hudson, Quebec J0P 1H0, Canada. (450)458-1934. Fax: (450)458-2977. **Contact:** Editor. **100% freelance written.** Monthly Men's magazine covering "the anal fetish as well as S&M and bondage. All Hounds of Hell Publishing titles deal with hardcore sex." Estab. 1996. Circ. 40,000. Pays on 60-day terms. Publishes ms an average of 3 months after acceptance. Byline sometimes given. Buys all rights. Editorial lead time 3 months. Accepts queries by mail, e-mail, fax, phone. Accepts simultaneous submissions. Sample copy for $5 (US)/issue. Writer's guidelines for #10 SASE.

Fiction: Looking for "anal adventures; very sticky, lots of wet descriptions, oils, etc." "We will not accept anything to do with violence, children, nonconsenting sex, or degradation." **Buys 64 mss/year.** Send complete ms. Length: 1,300-2,000 words. **Pays $10-15/1,000 words.**

Tips: "Story length should not exceed 2,000 words. Cut the introduction—get straight to the sex. Stories of 800-1,200 words are needed. Open with a bang—is it interesting? Does it excite the reader? Be very descriptive and very graphic, but not violent. Be explicitly descriptive. We want to smell leather, taste the skin, and feel the action as it takes place. But the sex must be enjoyable for all participants; nobody does anything in these stories against their will."

$ ✪ WICKED FETISHES, Hounds of Hell Publishing, P.O. Box 1319, Hudson, Quebec J0P 1H0, Canada. (450)458-1934. Fax: (450)458-2977. **Contact:** Editor. **100% freelance written.** Monthly "men's sophisticate" digest covering "fetish, domination/submission, feet, etc.—within the law. All Hounds of Hell Publishing titles deal with hardcore sex." Estab. 1996. Circ. 40,000. Pays on 60-day terms. Publishes ms an average of 3 months after acceptance. Byline sometimes given. Buys all rights. Editorial lead time 3 months. Accepts queries by mail, e-mail, fax, phone. Accepts simultaneous submissions. Sample copy for $5 (US)/issue. Writer's guidelines for #10 SASE.

Fiction: "We will not accept anything to do with violence, children, nonconsenting sex, or degradation." **Buys 64 mss/year.** Send complete ms. Length: 1,300-2,000 words. **Pays $10-15/1,000 words.**

Tips: "Story length should not exceed 2,000 words. Cut the introduction—get straight to the sex. Stories of 800-1,200 words are needed. Open with a bang—is it interesting? Does it excite the reader? Be very descriptive and very graphic, but not violent. Be explicitly descriptive. We want to smell leather, taste the skin, and feel the action as it takes place. But the sex must be enjoyable for all participants; nobody does anything in these stories against their will."

SPORTS

A variety of sports magazines, from general interest to sports medicine, are covered in this section. For the convenience of writers who specialize in one or two areas of sport and outdoor writing, the publications are subcategorized by the sport or subject matter they emphasize. Publications in related categories (for example, Hunting & Fishing; Archery & Bowhunting) often buy similar material. Writers should read through this entire section to become familiar with the subcategories. Publications on horse breeding and hunting dogs are classified in the Animal section, while horse racing is listed here. Publications dealing with automobile or motorcycle racing can be found in the Automotive & Motorcycle category. Markets interested in articles on exercise and fitness are listed in the Health & Fitness section. Outdoor publications that promote the preservation of nature, placing only secondary emphasis on nature as a setting for sport, are in the Nature, Conservation & Ecology category. Regional magazines are frequently interested in sports material with a local angle. Camping publications are classified in the Travel, Camping & Trailer category.

Archery & Bowhunting

$ $ ✪ BOW & ARROW HUNTING, Y-Visionary Publishing, LP, 265 S. Anita Dr., Suite 120, Orange CA 92868-3310. (714)939-9991. Fax: (714)939-9909. E-mail: editorial@bowandarrowhunting.com. Website: www.bowandarrowhunting.com. **Contact:** Joe Bell, editor. **70% freelance written.** Magazine published 9 times/year covering bowhunting. "Dedicated to serve the serious bowhunting enthusiast. Writers must be willing to share their secrets so our readers can become better bowhunters." Estab. 1962. Circ. 90,000. Pays on publication. Publishes ms an average of 2 months after acceptance. Byline given. Buys all rights. Submit seasonal material 6 months in advance. Accepts queries by mail. Accepts simultaneous submissions. Responds in 1 month to queries; 6 weeks to mss. Sample copy and writer's guidelines free.

Nonfiction: How-to, humor, interview/profile, opinion, personal experience, technical. **Buys 60 mss/year.** Send complete ms. Length: 1,700-3,000 words. **Pays $200-450.**

Photos: Send photos with submission. Reviews contact sheets, 35mm and 2×2 transparencies, 5×7 prints. Buys one-time or all rights. Offers no additional payment for photos accepted with ms. Captions required.

Fillers: Facts, newsbreaks. **Buys 12/year.** Length: 500 words. **Pays $20-100.**

Tips: "Inform readers how they can become better at the sport, but don't forget to keep it fun! Sidebars are recommended with every submission."

$ $ BOWHUNTER, The Number One Bowhunting Magazine, Primedia Enthusiast Publications, 6405 Flank Dr., Harrisburg PA 17112. (717)657-9555. Fax: (717)657-9552. E-mail: bowhunter@cowles.com. Website: www.bowhunter.com. Founder/Editor-in-Chief: M.R. James. **Contact:** Jeff Waring, managing editor. **50% freelance written.** Bimonthly magazine covering hunting big and small game with bow and arrow. "We are a special-interest publication, produced by bowhunters for bowhunters, covering all aspects of the sport. Material included in each issue is designed to entertain and inform readers, making them better bowhunters." Estab. 1971. Circ. 181,455. **Pays on acceptance.** Publishes ms an average of 1 year after acceptance. Byline given. Buys first North American serial, one-time rights. Submit seasonal material 8 months in advance. Accepts queries by mail, e-mail. Responds in 1 month to queries; 5 weeks to mss. Sample copy for $2. Writer's guidelines free.

Nonfiction: "We publish a special 'Big Game' issue each Fall (September) but need all material by mid-March. Another annual publication, Whitetail Bowhunter, is staff written or by assignment only. Our latest special issue is the Gear Guide, which highlights the latest in equipment. We don't want articles that graphically deal with an animal's death. And, please, no articles written from the animal's viewpoint." General interest, how-to, interview/profile, opinion, personal experience, photo feature. **Buys 60 plus mss/year.** Query. Length: 250-2,000 words. **Pays $500 maximum for assigned articles; $100-400 for unsolicited articles.** Sometimes pays expenses of writers on assignment.

Photos: Send photos with submission. Reviews 35mm and 2¼×2¼ transparencies, 5×7 and 8×10 prints. Buys one-time rights. Offers $75-250/photo. Captions required.

Tips: "A writer must know bowhunting and be willing to share that knowledge. Writers should anticipate *all* questions a reader might ask, then answer them in the article itself or in an appropriate sidebar. Articles should be written with the reader foremost in mind; we won't be impressed by writers seeking to prove how good they are—either as writers or bowhunters. We care about the reader and don't need writers with 'I' trouble. Features are a good bet because most of our material comes from freelancers. The best advice is: Be yourself. Tell your story the same as if sharing the experience around a campfire. Don't try to write like you think a writer writes."

$ $ BOWHUNTING WORLD, Ehlert Publishing Group, 6420 Sycamore Lane N., #100, Maple Grove MN 55369. E-mail: mstrandlund@affinitygroup.com. **Contact:** Mike Strandlund, editor. **50% freelance written.** Bimonthly magazine with 3 additional issues for bowhunting and archery enthusiasts who participate in the sport year-round. Estab. 1952. Circ. 130,000. **Pays on acceptance.** Publishes ms an average of 5 months after acceptance. Byline given. Buys first, second serial (reprint) rights. Responds in 1 week to e-mail queries; 6 weeks to mss. Sample copy for $3 and 9×12 SAE with 10 first-class stamps. Writer's guidelines for #10 SASE.

- Accepts queries by mail, but prefers e-mail.

Nonfiction: How-to articles with creative slants on knowledgeable selection and use of bowhunting equipment and bowhunting methods. Articles must emphasize knowledgeable use of archery or hunting equipment, and/or specific bowhunting techniques. Contributors must be authorities in the areas of archery and bowhunting. Straight hunting adventure narratives and other types of articles now appear only in special issues. Equipment-oriented aricles must demonstrate wise and insightful selection and use of archery equipment and other gear related to the archery sports. Some product-review, field-test, equipment how-to, and technical pieces will be purchased. We are not interested in articles whose equipment focuses on random mentioning of brands. Technique-oriented aricles most sought are those that briefly cover fundamentals and delve into leading-edge bowhunting or recreational archery methods. **Buys 60 mss/year.** Query with or without published clips or send complete ms. Length: 1,500-3,000 words. **Pays $350-500.**

Photos: "We are seeking cover photos that depict specific behavioral traits of the more common big game animals (scraping whitetails, bugling elk, etc.) and well-equipped bowhunters in action. Must include return postage."

Tips: "Writers are strongly advised to adhere to guidelines and become familiar with our format, as our needs are very specific. Writers are urged to query by e-mail. We prefer detailed outlines of 6 or so article ideas/query. Assignments are made for the next 18 months."

Basketball

$ $ $ ✪ SLAM, Petersen Publications, 1115 Broadway, 8th Floor, New York NY 10010. E-mail: susan@harris-pub.com. Website: www.slamonline.com. **Contact:** Susan Price, managing editor. **70% freelance written.** Magazine published 10 times/year covering basketball; sports journalism with a hip-hop sensibility targeting ages 13-24. Estab. 1994. Circ. 200,000. Pays on publication. Publishes ms an average of 3 months after acceptance. Byline given. Offers 25% kill fee. Buys all rights. Accepts queries by mail, e-mail, fax. Writer's guidelines free.

Nonfiction: Interview/profile, team story. **Buys 150 mss/year.** Query with published clips. Length: 200-3,000 words. **Pays $100-1,000 for assigned articles.** Sometimes pays expenses of writers on assignment.
Photos: State availability with submission. Buys one-time rights. Negotiates payment individually.

The online magazine carries original content not found in the print edition. Contact: Lang Whitaker, online editor.

Tips: "Pitch profiles of unknown players; send queries, not manuscripts; do not try to fake a hip-hop sensibility. Never contact the editor-in-chief. Story meetings are held every 6-7 weeks at which time all submissions are considered."

Bicycling

$ $ $ ADVENTURE CYCLIST, Adventure Cycling Assn., Box 8308, Missoula MT 59807. (406)721-1776. Fax: (406)721-8754. E-mail: ddambrosio@adv-cycling.org. Website: www.adv-cycling.org. **Contact:** Daniel D'Ambrosio, editor. **75% freelance written.** Magazine published 9 times/year for Adventure Cycling Association members. Estab. 1975. Circ. 30,000. Pays on publication. Byline given. Buys first rights. Submit seasonal material 3 months in advance. Accepts previously published material. Sample copy and guidelines for 9×12 SAE with 4 first-class stamps.
Nonfiction: How-to, humor, interview/profile, photo feature, technical, travel, U.S. or foreign tour accounts; special focus (on tour experience). **Buys 20-25 mss/year.** Query with or without published clips or send complete ms. Length: 800-2,500 words. **Pays $450-1,200.**
Reprints: Send photocopy.
Photos: Bicycle, scenery, portraits. State availability with submission. Reviews color transparencies. Identification of subjects, model releases required.

$ $ $ BICYCLING, Rodale Press, Inc., 135 N. Sixth St., Emmaus PA 18098. (610)967-5171. Fax: (610)967-8960. E-mail: bicycling@rodale.com. Website: www.bicycling.com. Publisher: Nicholas Freedman. **Contact:** Doug Donaldson, associate editor. **50% freelance written.** Magazine published 11 times/year. "*Bicycling* features articles about fitness, training, nutrition, touring, racing, equipment, clothing, maintenance, new technology, industry developments, and other topics of interest to committed bicycle riders. Editorially, we advocate for the sport, industry, and the cycling consumer." Estab. 1961. Circ. 280,000. **Pays on acceptance.** Byline given. Buys all rights. Submit seasonal material 6 months in advance. Accepts previously published material. Responds in 2 months to queries. Sample copy for $3.50. Writer's guidelines for #10 SASE.

"There are 2 great break-in opportunities for writers: 1.) 'Noblest Invention' (750-word column) offers writers a chance to tell us why the bicycle is the greatest bit of machinery ever created. 2.) 'Ask the Wrench' maintenance feature showcases a local bike mechanic's know-how. If you know a great mechanic, this is a chance to get in the magazine."

Nonfiction: "We are a cycling lifestyle magazine. We seek readable, clear, well-informed pieces that show how cycling is part of our readers' lives. We sometimes run articles that are inspirational, and inspiration might flavor even our most technical pieces. No fiction or poetry." How-to (on all phases of bicycle touring, repair, maintenance, commuting, new products, clothing, riding technique, nutrition for cyclists, conditioning), photo feature (on cycling events), technical (opinions about technology), travel (bicycling must be central here), fitness. **Buys 10 unsolicited mss/year.** Query. **Payment varies.** Sometimes pays expenses of writers on assignment.
Reprints: Send tearsheet or photocopy and information about when and where the material previously appeared.
Photos: State availability of or send photos with submission. Pays $15-250/photo. Captions, model releases required.
Fillers: Anecdotes.
Tips: "Don't send us travel pieces about where you went on summer vacation. Travel/adventure stories have to be about something larger than just visiting someplace on your bike and meeting quirky locals."

$ $ BIKE MAGAZINE, EMAP USA, 33046 Calle Aviador, San Juan Capistrano CA 92675. (949)496-5922. Fax: (949)496-7849. **Contact:** Ron Ige, editor. **35% freelance written.** Magazine publishes 10 times/year covering mountain biking. Estab. 1993. Circ. 160,000. Pays on publication. Publishes ms an average of 2 months after acceptance. Byline given. Offers 25% kill fee. Buys first North American serial rights. Editorial lead time 4 months. Submit seasonal material 6 months in advance. Responds in 2 months to queries. Sample copy for $8. Writer's guidelines for #10 SASE.

Bike receives many travel-related queries and is seeking more investigative journalism on matters that affect mountain bikers. Writers have a much better chance of publication if they tackle larger issues that affect mountain bikers, such as trail access or sport controversies (i.e., drugs in cycling). If you do submit a travel article, know that a great location is not a story in itself—there must also be a theme. Examine back issues before submitting a travel story; if *Bike* has covered your location before, they won't again (for at least 4-5 years).

Nonfiction: Writers should submit queries in March (April 1 deadline) for consideration for the following year's editions. All queries received by April 1 will be considered and editors will contact writers about stories they are interested in. Queries should include word count. Humor, interview/profile, personal experience, photo feature, travel. **Buys 20 mss/year.** Length: 1,000-2,500 words. **Pays 50¢/word.** Sometimes pays expenses of writers on assignment.
Photos: David Reddick, photo editor. Send photos with submission. Reviews color transparencies, b&w prints. Buys one-time rights. Negotiates payment individually. Captions, identification of subjects required.
Columns/Departments: Splatter (news), 300 words; Urb (details a great ride within 1 hour of a major metropolitan area), 600-700 words. Query year-round for Splatter and Urb. **Buys 20 mss/year. Pays 50¢/word.**

Tips: "Remember that we focus on hard core mountain biking, not beginners. We're looking for ideas that deliver the excitement and passion of the sport in ways that aren't common or predictable. Ideas should be vivid, unbiased, irreverent, probing, fun, humorous, funky, quirky, smart, good. Great feature ideas are always welcome, especially features on cultural matters or issues in the sport. However, you're much more likely to get published in *Bike* if you send us great ideas for short articles. In particular we need stories for our Splatter, a front-of-the-book section devoted to news, funny anecdotes, quotes, and odds and ends. These stories range from 50 to 300 words. We also need personality profiles of 600 words or so for our People Who Ride section. Racers are OK but we're more interested in grassroots people with interesting personalities—it doesn't matter if they're Mother Theresas or scumbags, so long as they make mountain biking a little more interesting. Short descriptions of great rides are very welcome for our Urb column; the length should be from 600-700 words."

$ CRANKMAIL, Cycling in Northeastern Ohio, P.O. Box 33249, Cleveland OH 44133-0249. Fax: (440)877-0373. E-mail: editor@crankmail.com. Website: www.crankmail.com. **Contact:** James Guilford, editor/publisher. Monthly magazine covering bicycling in all aspects. "Our publication serves the interests of bicycle enthusiasts established, accomplished adult cyclists. These individuals are interested in reading about the sport of cycling, bicycles as transportation, ecological tie-ins, sports nutrition, the history and future of bicycles and bicycling." Estab. 1977. Circ. 1,000. Pays on publication. Byline given. Buys one-time, second serial (reprint) rights. Editorial lead time 1 month. Submit seasonal material 3 months in advance. Sample copy for $1. Writer's guidelines for #10 SASE.

Nonfiction: Essays, historical/nostalgic, how-to, humor, interview/profile, personal experience, technical, travel. "No articles encouraging folks to start bicycling—our readers are already cyclists." Send complete ms. Length: 600-1,800 words. **Pays $10 minimum for unsolicited articles.**

Reprints: Send typed ms with rights for sale noted and information about when and where the material previously appeared.

Fiction: Publishes very short novel excerpts.

Fillers: Cartoons. **Pays $5-10.**

▣ The online magazine carries original content, and content not found in the print edition. Contact: James Guilford, online editor.

$ USA CYCLING MAGAZINE, One Olympic Plaza, Colorado Springs CO 80909. (719)866-4581. Fax: (719)866-4596. E-mail: media@usacycling.org or joe@tpgsports.com. Website: www.usacycling.org or www.tpgsports.com. Editor: Patrice Quintero. **Contact:** Joseph Oberle, publications manager, (763)595-0808. **25% freelance written.** Bimonthly magazine covering reportage and commentary on American bicycle racing, personalities, and sports physiology for USAC licensed cyclists. Estab. 1980. Circ. 49,000. Pays on publication. Publishes ms an average of 2 months after acceptance. Byline given. Accepts queries by e-mail. Accepts previously published material. Responds in 2 weeks to queries. Sample copy for 10×12 SAE and 2 first-class stamps.

Nonfiction: How-to (train, prepare for a bike race), inspirational, interview/profile, personal experience, photo feature. No comparative product evaluations. **Buys 15 mss/year.** Length: 800-1,200 words. **Pays $50-75.**

Reprints: Send photocopy.

Photos: State availability with submission. Buys one-time rights. Captions required.

▣ The online magazine carries original content not found in the print edition. Contact: Patrice Quintero, online editor.

Tips: "We do not want race reports. We want features from 800-1,200 words on American cycling activities. First-person stories that put the reader in the action are preferred. Please do not send product reviews."

Boating

$ $ BOATING LIFE, World Publications Inc., 460 N. Orlando Ave., Suite 200, Winter Park FL 32789-2988. (407)628-4802. Fax: (407)628-7061. E-mail: boatlife@worldzine.com. Website: www.boatinglifemag.com. Executive Editor: Robert Stephens. Managing Editor: Sue Whitney. **Contact:** Randy Vance, editor. **40% freelance written.** Magazine published 7 times/year covering powerboats under 36 feet, lifestyle, news, technology, maneuvers, operation, travel. "We are a product-related and lifestyle title. As such, we focus on people, fun, boating skills and technical subjects or product reviews. We demand a high caliber of writing and want our writers to 'think and write outside the box' to bring color and excitement to the water." Estab. 1997. Circ. 103,000. Pays on publication. Byline given. Buys all rights. Editorial lead time 6 months. Submit seasonal material 6 months in advance. Accepts simultaneous submissions. Responds in 2 weeks to queries.

O‑‑ Break in with 100-500 word boating news and travel stories involving trends, great places to take your boat, and buying, maintenance and handling tips.

Nonfiction: How-to, humor, new product, photo feature, technical, travel. "No stories on sailing or sailboats." **Buys 40 mss/year.** Query. Length: 400-2,500 words. **Pays $125-750.**

Photos: State availability with submission. Buys all North American and Internet rights. Offers $50-500/photo, bonus for cover shots. Identification of subjects required.

Columns/Departments: On Maneuvers (tips on operating a powerboat); Family Boating (tips for family boating); Owner's Manual (tips on everything from buying to selling), all 500-600 words. **Buys 12 mss/year.** Query. **Pays $125-350.**

Fillers: Facts, newsbreaks. **Buys 6/year.** Length: 50-125 words. **Pays $50-100.**

Tips: "We avoid travelogues and lean toward boating activities narratives. We prefer tories to cover someone else's experience, not the writer's. Premium photography highlighting new or nearly new boats is key to any article sale. The general tone is light and conversational. All articles should in some way engage the reader in the fun of the boating lifestyle."

$ $ ☒ CANOE & KAYAK MAGAZINE, Canoe America Associates, 10526 NE 68th St., Suite 3, Kirkland WA 98033. (425)827-6363. Fax: (425)827-1893. E-mail: editor@canoekayak.com. Website: www.canoekayak.com. Editor: Tim Jackson. **Contact:** Robin Stanton, managing editor. **75% freelance written.** Bimonthly magazine. "*Canoe & Kayak Magazine* is North America's #1 paddlesports resource. Our readers include flatwater and whitewater canoeists and kayakers of all skill levels. We provide comprehensive information on destinations, technique and equipment. Beyond that, we cover canoe and kayak camping, safety, the environment, and the history of boats and sport." Estab. 1972. Circ. 70,000. Pays on publication. Publishes ms an average of 6 months after acceptance. Byline given. first international rights, which includes electronic and anthology rights Editorial lead time 4 months. Submit seasonal material 6 months in advance. Accepts queries by mail, e-mail. Responds in 2 months to queries. Sample copy and writer's guidelines for 9×12 SAE with 7 first-class stamps.

O― Break in with good destination or Put-In (news) pieces with excellent photos. "Take a good look at the types of articles we publish before sending us any sort of query."

Nonfiction: Historical/nostalgic, how-to (canoe, kayak camp; load boats; paddle whitewater, etc.), personal experience, photo feature, technical, travel. Special issues: Whitewater Paddling; Beginner's Guide; Kayak Touring; Canoe Journal. "No cartoons, poems, stories in which bad judgement is portrayed, or 'Me and Molly' articles." **Buys 25 mss/year.** Query with or without published clips or send complete ms. Length: 400-2,500 words. **Pays $25-800 for assigned articles; $25-450 for unsolicited articles.**

Photos: "Some activities we cover are canoeing, kayaking, canoe fishing, camping, canoe sailing or poling, backpacking (when compatible with the main activity) and occasionally inflatable boats. We are not interested in groups of people in rafts, photos showing disregard for the environment, gasoline-powered, multi-horsepower engines unless appropriate to the discussion, or unskilled persons taking extraordinary risks." State availability with submission. Reviews 35mm transparencies, 4×6 prints. Buys one-time rights. Offers $25-500/photo. Captions, identification of subjects, model releases required.

Columns/Departments: Put In (environment, conservation, events), 650 words; Destinations (canoe and kayak destinations in US, Canada), 1,500 words; Traditions (essays: traditional paddling), 750 words. **Buys 40 mss/year.** Send complete ms. **Pays $100-350.**

Fillers: Anecdotes, facts, newsbreaks. **Buys 20/year.** Length: 200-500 words. **Pays $25-50.**

Tips: "Start with Put-In articles (short featurettes) or short, unique equipment reviews. Or give us the best, most exciting article we've ever seen—with great photos. Read the magazine before submitting."

$ $ $ CHESAPEAKE BAY MAGAZINE, Boating at Its Best, Chesapeake Bay Communications, 1819 Bay Ridge Ave., Annapolis MD 21403. (410)263-2662. Fax: (410)267-6924. E-mail: editor@cbmmag.net. Managing Editor: Jane Meneely. **Contact:** Wendy Mitman Clarke, executive editor. **60% freelance written.** Monthly magazine covering boating and the Chesapeake Bay. "Our readers are boaters. Our writers should know boats and boating. Read the magazine before submitting." Estab. 1972. Circ. 46,000. Pays within 60 days after acceptance. Publishes ms an average of 1 year after acceptance. Byline given. Buys first North American serial rights. Editorial lead time 1 year. Submit seasonal material 1 year in advance. Accepts queries by mail, e-mail, fax, phone. Accepts simultaneous submissions. Responds in 2 months to queries; 3 months to mss. Sample copy for $5.19 prepaid.

O― "Read our Channel 9 column and give us some new ideas. These are short news items, profiles, and updates: 200-800 words."

Nonfiction: Destinations, boating adventures, how-to, marina reviews, history, nature, environment, lifestyles, personal and institutional profiles, boat-type profiles, boatbuilding, boat restoration, boating anecdotes, boating news. **Buys 30 mss/year.** Query with published clips. Length: 300-3,000 words. **Pays $100-1,000.** Pays expenses of writers on assignment.

Photos: Buys one-time rights. Offers $45-150/photo, $350/day rate for assignment photography. Captions, identification of subjects required.

Tips: "Send us unedited writing samples (not clips) that show the writer can write, not just string words together. We look for well-organized, lucid, lively, intelligent writing."

$ $ $ CRUISING WORLD, The Sailing Company, 5 John Clarke Rd., Newport RI 02840-0992. (401)845-5100. Fax: (401)845-5180. Website: www.cruisingworld.com. Editor: Herb McCormick. Managing Editor: Elaine Lembo. **Contact:** Tim Murphy, executive editor. **60% freelance written.** Monthly magazine covering sailing, cruising/adventuring; do-it-yourself boat improvements. "*Cruising World* is a publication by and for sailboat owners who spend time in home waters as well as voyaging the world. Its readership is extremely loyal, savvy and driven by independent thinking." Estab. 1974. Circ. 155,000. **Pays on acceptance for articles;** on publication for photography. Publishes ms an average of 18 months after acceptance. Byline given. Buys 6-month, all-world, first time rights (amendable). Editorial lead time 3 months. Submit seasonal material 1 year in advance. Accepts queries by mail. Responds in 1 month to queries; 4 months to mss. Sample copy for free. Writer's guidelines online.

Nonfiction: Book excerpts, essays, exposé, general interest, historical/nostalgic, how-to, humor, interview/profile, new product, opinion, personal experience, photo feature, technical, travel. No travel articles that have nothing to do with cruising aboard sailboats from 20-50 feet in length. **Buys dozens of mss/year.** Send complete ms. **Pays $50-1,500 for assigned articles; $50-1,000 for unsolicited articles.** Sometimes pays expenses of writers on assignment.
Photos: Send photos with submission. Reviews negatives, transparencies, color slides preferred. Buys one-time rights. Negotiates payment individually. Also buys stand-alone photos. Captions required.
Columns/Departments: Shoreline (sailing news, people and short features; contact Nim Marsh), 500 words maximum; Hands-on Sailor (refit, voyaging, seamanship, how-to; contact Darrell Nicholson), 1,000-1,500 words. **Buys dozens of mss/year.** Query with or without published clips or send complete ms. **Pays $100-700.**
Tips: "*Cruising World's* readers know exactly what they want to read, so our best advice to freelancers is to carefully read the magazine and envision which exact section or department would be the appropriate place for proposed submissions."

$ $☆ HEARTLAND BOATING, The Waterways Journal, Inc., 319 N. Fourth St., Suite 650, St. Louis MO 63102. (314)241-4310 or (800)366-9630. Fax: (314)241-4207. E-mail: info@heartlandboating.com. Website: www.heartlandboating.com. **Contact:** H. Nelson Spencer, editor/publisher. **70% freelance written.** Magazine published 9 times/year covering recreational boating on the inland waterways of mid-America, from the Great Lakes south to the Gulf of Mexico and over to the east. "Our writers must have experience with, and a great interest in, boating, particularly in the area described above. *Heartland Boating*'s content is both informative and humorous—describing boating life as the heartland boater knows it. We are boaters and enjoy the outdoor, water-oriented way of life. The content reflects the challenge, joy, and excitement of our way of life afloat. We are devoted to both power and sailboating enthusiasts throughout middle America; houseboats are included. The focus is on the freshwater inland rivers and lakes of the heartland, primarily the waters of the Tennessee, Cumberland, Ohio, Missouri, and Mississippi rivers, the Tennessee-Tombigbee Waterway, and the lakes along these rivers." Estab. 1989. Circ. 16,000. Pays on publication. Publishes ms an average of 3 months after acceptance. Byline given. Buys first North American serial, first, electronic rights. Editorial lead time 3 months. Submit seasonal material 6 months in advance. Accepts queries by mail, e-mail, fax, phone. Accepts previously published material. Responds in 1 month to queries. Sample copy and writer's guidelines free.
Nonfiction: How-to (articles about navigation information and making time spent aboard easier and more comfortable), humor, personal experience (sharing expericenes aboard and on cruises in our coverage area), technical (boat upkeep and maintenance), travel (along the rivers and on the lakes in our coverage area and on-land stops along the way). Special issues: Annual Boat Show/New Products issue in December looks at what is coming out on the market for the coming year. **Buys 110 mss/year.** Query with published clips or send complete ms. Length: 850-1,500 words. **Pays $100-300.**
Reprints: Send tearsheet, photocopy or typed ms and information about when and where the material previously appeared. Pays 50% of amount paid for original article.
Photos: Send photos with submission. Reviews transparencies, prints. Buys one-time rights. Offers no additional payment for photos accepted with ms.
Columns/Departments: Food Afloat (recipes easy to make when aboard), Books Aboard (book reviews), Handy Hints (small boat improvement projects), Waterways History (on-water history tidbits), all 850 words. **Buys 45 mss/year.** Query with published clips or send complete ms. **Pays $75-150.**
Tips: "We usually plan an editorial schedule for the coming year in August. Submitting material between May and July will be most helpful for the planning process, although we accept submissions year-round."

$ $ HOUSEBOAT MAGAZINE, The Family magazine for the American Houseboater, Harris Publishing, Inc., 360 B St., Idaho Falls ID 83402. Fax: (208)522-5241. E-mail: hbeditor@houseboatmagazine.com. Website: www.houseboatmagazine.com. **Contact:** Steve Smede, editor. **40% freelance written.** Monthly magazine for houseboaters, who enjoy reading everything that reflects the unique houseboating lifestyle. If it is not a houseboat-specific article, please do not query. Estab. 1990. Circ. 25,000. Pays on publication. Publishes ms an average of 3 months after acceptance. Byline given. Offers 25% kill fee. Buys first North American serial, electronic rights. Editorial lead time 6 months. Submit seasonal material 6 months in advance. Accepts simultaneous submissions. Responds in 1 month to queries; 2 months to mss. Sample copy for $5. Writer's guidelines free.

- No unsolicited mss. Accepts queries by mail and fax, but e-mail strongly preferred.

Nonfiction: How-to, interview/profile, new product, personal experience, travel. **Buys 36 mss/year.** Query. Length: 1,000-1,200 words. **Pays $150-300.**
Photos: Often required as part of submission package. Color prints discouraged. Digital prints are unacceptable. Seldom purchases photos without mss, but occasionally buys cover photos. Reviews transparencies, high-resolution electronic images. Buys one-time rights. Offers no additional payment for photos accepted with ms. Captions, model releases required.
Columns/Departments: Pays $100-200.
Tips: "As a general rule, how-to articles are always in demand. So are stories on unique houseboats or houseboaters. You are less likely to break in with a travel piece that does not revolve around specific people or groups. Personality profile pieces with excellent supporting photography are your best bet."

$ LAKELAND BOATING, The Magazine for Great Lakes Boaters, O'Meara-Brown Publications, 500 Davis St., Suite 1000, Evanston IL 60201-4802. (847)869-5400. Fax: (847)869-5989. E-mail: lb@omeara-brown.com. Associate Editor: Dave Mull. **Contact:** Matthew Wright, editor. **50% freelance written.** Magazine covering Great Lakes boating. Estab. 1946. Circ. 60,000. Pays on publication. Byline given. Buys first North American serial rights. Responds in 4 months to queries. Sample copy for $5.50 and 9×12 SAE with 6 first-class stamps. Writer's guidelines free.

Nonfiction: Book excerpts, historical/nostalgic, how-to, interview/profile, personal experience, photo feature, technical, travel, must relate to boating in Great Lakes. No inspirational, religious, exposé or poetry. **Buys 20-30 mss/year.** Length: 800-3,00 words. **Pays $100-600.**

Photos: State availability with submission. Reviews prefers 35mm transparencies. Buys one-time rights. Captions required.

Columns/Departments: Bosun's Locker (technical or how-to pieces on boating), 100-1,000 words. **Buys 40 mss/year.** Query. **Pays $30-100.**

$ $ ☆ OFFSHORE, Northeast Boating at its Best, Offshore Communications, Inc., 220 Reservoir St., Suite 9, Needham MA 02494. (781)449-6204. Fax: (781)449-9702. E-mail: editors@offshoremag.net. Website: www.offshoremag.net. **Contact:** Lisa Fabian, production editor. **80% freelance written.** Monthly magazine covering power and sailboating on the coast from Maine to New Jersey. Estab. 1976. Circ. 35,000. **Pays on acceptance.** Publishes ms an average of 5 months after acceptance. Byline given. Offers 50% kill fee. Buys first North American serial rights. Submit seasonal material 6 months in advance. Accepts queries by mail. Accepts simultaneous submissions. Writer's guidelines for #10 SASE.

Nonfiction: Articles on boats, boating, New York, New Jersey, and New England coastal places and people, Northeast coastal history. **Buys 90 mss/year.** Query with or without published clips or send complete ms. Length: 1,200-2.500 words. **Pays $350-500 for features, depending on length.**

Photos: Reviews 35mm slides. Buys one-time rights. Pays $150-300. Identification of subjects required.

Tips: "Writers must demonstrate a familiarity with boats and with the Northeast coast. Specifically we are looking for articles on boating destinations, boating events (such as races, rendezvous, and boat parades), on-the-water boating adventures, boating culture, maritime museums, maritime history, boating issues (such as safety and the environment), seamanship, fishing, how-to stories, and essays. Note: Since *Offshore* is a regional magazine, all stories must focus on the area from New Jersey to Maine. We are always open to new people, the best of whom may gradually work their way into regular writing assignments. Important to ask for (and follow) our writer's guidelines if you're not familiar with our magazine."

$ $ ☆ PACIFIC YACHTING, Western Canada's Premier Boating Magazine, OP Publishing Ltd., 1080 Howe St., Suite 900, Vancouver, British Columbia V6Z 2T1, Canada. (604)606-4644. Fax: (604)687-1925. E-mail: editor@pacificyachting.com. Website: www.pacificyachting.com. **Contact:** Simon Hill, editor. **90% freelance written.** Monthly magazine covering all aspects of recreational boating on British Columbia's coast. "The bulk of our writers and photographers not only come from the local boating community, many of them were long-time *PY* readers before coming aboard as a contributor. The *PY* reader buys the magazine to read about new destinations or changes to old haunts on the British Columbia coast and to learn the latest about boats and gear." Circ. 19,000. Pays on publication. Publishes ms an average of 6 months after acceptance. Byline given. Buys first North American serial, simultaneous rights. Editorial lead time 4 months. Submit seasonal material 6 months in advance. Accepts queries by mail, e-mail, fax. Sample copy for $4.95, plus postage charged to credit card. Writer's guidelines free.

Nonfiction: Historical/nostalgic (British Columbia coast only), how-to, humor, interview/profile, personal experience, technical (boating related), travel, cruising, and destination on the British Columbia coast. "No articles from writers who are obviously not boaters!" Query. Length: 1,500-2,000 words. **Pays $150-500.** Pays expenses of writers on assignment.

Photos: Send photos with submission. Reviews transparencies, 4×6 prints, and slides. Buys one-time rights. Offers no additional payment for photos accepted with ms. Offers $25-300 for photos accepted alone. Identification of subjects required.

Columns/Departments: Currents (current events, trade and people news, boat gatherings, and festivities), 50-250 words. Reflections, Cruising, 800-1,000 words. Query. **Pay varies.**

Tips: "We strongly encourage queries before submission (written with SAE and IRCs, or by phone or e-mail). While precise nautical information is important, colorful anecdotes bring your cruise to life. Both are important. In other words, our reader wants you to balance important navigation details with first-person observations, blending the practical with the romantic. Write tight, write short, write with the reader in mind, write to inform, write to entertain. Be specific, accurate, and historic."

$ $ PONTOON & DECK BOAT, Harris Publishing, Inc., 360 B. St., Idaho Falls ID 83402. (208)524-7000. Fax: (208)522-5241. E-mail: brady@pdbmagazine.com. Website: www.pdbmagazine.com. **Contact:** Brady L. Kay, editor. **15% freelance written.** Magazine published 8 times/year. "We are a boating niche publication geared toward the pontoon and deck boating lifestyle and consumer market. Our audience is comprised of people who utilize these boats for varied family activities and fishing. Our magazine is promotional of the PDB industry and its major players. We seek to give the reader a 2-fold reason to read our publication: To celebrate the lifestyle, and to do it aboard a first-class craft." Estab. 1995. Circ. 84,000. Pays on publication. Byline given. Buys one-time rights. Editorial lead time 2 months. Submit seasonal material 3 months in advance. Accepts simultaneous submissions. Responds in 6 weeks to queries; 3 months to mss. Sample copy and writer's guidelines free.

Nonfiction: How-to, personal experience, technical, remodeling, rebuilding. "We are saturated with travel pieces, no general boating, no humor, no fiction, poetry." **Buys 15 mss/year.** Query with or without published clips or send complete ms. Length: 600-2,000 words. **Pays $50-300.** Sometimes pays expenses of writers on assignment.
Photos: State availability with submission. Reviews transparencies. Rights negotiable. Captions, model releases required.
Columns/Departments: No Wake Zone (short, fun quips); Better Boater (how-to). **Buys 6-12 mss/year.** Query with published clips. **Pays $50-150.**
Tips: "Be specific to pontoon and deck boats. Any general boating material goes to the slush pile. The more you can tie together the lifestyle, attitudes, and the PDB industry, the more interest we'll take in what you send us."

$ $ $ POWER & MOTORYACHT, Primedia, 260 Madison Ave., 8th Floor, New York NY 10016. (917)256-2200. Fax: (917)256-2282. E-mail: dbyrne@primediasi.com. Editor: Richard Thiel. **Contact:** Diane M. Byrne, executive editor. **20% freelance written.** Monthly magazine covering powerboating. "*Power & Motoryacht* is devoted exclusively to the high-end powerboat market, those boats 24-feet or larger. Every reader owns at least 1 powerboat in this size range. Our magazine reaches virtually every U.S. owner of a 40-foot or larger powerboat—the only publication that does so. For our readers, boating is not a hobby, it's a lifestyle." Estab. 1985. Circ. 157,000. **Pays on acceptance.** Publishes ms an average of 6 months after acceptance. Byline given. Offers 33% kill fee. Buys first North American serial and permanent electronic rights. Editorial lead time 1 year. Submit seasonal material 6 months in advance. Accepts queries by mail, e-mail, fax. Accepts simultaneous submissions. Responds in 1 month to queries. Sample copy for 10×12 SASE. Writer's guidelines for #10 SASE.

O→ Break in by "knowing the boat business—know which manufacturers specialize in cruising boats vs. sportfishing boats, for example, and know the difference between production-built and semi-custom vessels. Be an authority on the subject you're pitching—our readers can spot uninformed writers!"

Nonfiction: How-to (how to fix things, install things, shop for boats and accessories smarter, etc.), humor, interview/profile, personal experience, technical, travel. **Buys 10-15 mss/year.** Query with published clips. Length: 800-1,400 words. **Pays $500-1,200.** Sometimes pays expenses of writers on assignment.
Photos: State availability with submission; unsolicited images will not be returned. Reviews original slides and original 4×5 transparencies. Buys one-time rights. Payment for ms will include payment for photos if requested as package. Captions, identification of subjects required.
Tips: "Writers must be authorities on the subject matter they write about—our readers have an average of 31 years' experience on the water, so they want experts to provide advice and information. Some of our regular feature themes are seamanship (rules of the road and boating protocol techniques); cruising (places readers can take their own boats for a few days' enjoyment); maintenance (tips on upkeep and repair); engines (innovations that improve efficiency and/or lessen environmental impact)."

$ $ POWER BOATING CANADA, 1020 Brevik Place, Suites 4 & 5, Mississauga, Ontario L4W 4N7, Canada. (905)624-8218. Fax: (905)624-6764. E-mail: editor@powerboating.com. Website: www.powerboating.com. **Contact:** Steve Fennell, editor. **70% freelance written.** Bimonthly magazine covering recreational power boating. "*Power Boating Canada* offers boating destinations, how-to features, boat tests (usually staff written), lifestyle pieces—with a Canadian slant—and appeal to recreational power boaters across the country." Estab. 1984. Circ. 42,000. Pays on publication. Publishes ms an average of 3 months after acceptance. Byline given. Buys first North American serial rights. Editorial lead time 2 months. Submit seasonal material 3 months in advance. Accepts previously published material. Responds in 1 month to queries; 2 months to mss. Sample copy for free.
Nonfiction: "Any articles related to the sport of power boating, especially boat tests." Historical/nostalgic, how-to, interview/profile, personal experience, travel (boating destinations). No general boating articles or personal anectdotes. **Buys 40-50 mss/year.** Query. Length: 1,200-2,500 words. **Pays $150-300 (Canadian).** Sometimes pays expenses of writers on assignment.
Reprints: Send photocopy with rights for sale noted and information about when and where the material previously appeared.
Photos: Send photos with submission. Reviews contact sheets, negatives, transparencies, prints. Buys one-time rights. Payment varies; no additional payment for photos accepted with ms. Captions, identification of subjects required.

$ $ $ SAIL, 98 N. Washington St., 2nd Floor, Boston MA 02114. (617)720-8600. Fax: (617)723-0912. E-mail: sailmail@primediasi.com. Website: www.sailmagazine.com or www.sailbuyersguide.com. Editor: Peter Nielsen. **Contact:** Amy Ullrich, managing editor. **30% freelance written.** Monthly magazine "written and edited for everyone who sails—aboard a coastal or bluewater cruiser, trailerable, one-design or offshore racer, or daysailer. How-to and technical articles concentrate on techniques of sailing and aspects of design and construction, boat systems, and gear; the feature section emphasizes the fun and rewards of sailing in a practical and instructive way." Estab. 1970. Circ. 180,000. **Pays on acceptance.** Publishes ms an average of 1 year after acceptance. Byline given. Buys first North American serial rights. Accepts queries by mail, e-mail, fax. Responds in 3 months to queries. Writer's guidelines for SASE or online (download).
Nonfiction: How-to, personal experience, technical, distance cruising, destinations. Special issues: "Cruising, chartering, commissioning, fitting-out, special race (e.g., America's Cup), Top Ten Boats, FKP Awards." **Buys 50 mss/year.** Query. Length: 1,500-3,000 words. **Pays $200-800.** Sometimes pays expenses of writers on assignment.
Photos: Prefers transparencies. Pay varies, up to $700 if photo used on cover. Captions, identification of subjects, credits required.

Columns/Departments: Sailing Memories (short essay); Sailing News (cruising, racing, legal, political, environmental); Under Sail (human interest). Query. **Pays $25-400.**

The online magazine carries original content not found in the print edition and includes writer's guidelines. Contact: Kimball Livingston, online editor.

Tips: "Request an article's specification sheet. We look for unique ways of viewing sailing. Skim old issues of *Sail* for ideas about the types of articles we publish. Always remember that *Sail* is a sailing magazine. Stay away from gloomy articles detailing all the things that went wrong on your boat. Think constructively and write about how to avoid certain problems. You should focus on a theme or choose some aspect of sailing and discuss a personal attitude or new philosophical approach to the subject. Notice that we have certain issues devoted to special themes—for example, chartering, electronics, commissioning, and the like. Stay away from pieces that chronicle your journey in the day-by-day style of a logbook. These are generally dull and uninteresting. Select specific actions or events (preferably sailing events, not shorebound activities), and build your articles around them. Emphasize the sailing."

$ $ $ SAILING MAGAZINE, 125 E. Main St., Port Washington WI 53074-0249. (262)284-3494. Fax: (262)284-7764. E-mail: sailingmag@ameritech.net. Website: www.sailingonline.com. Publisher: William F. Schanen. **Contact:** Gregory O. Jones, editor. Monthly magazine for the experienced sailor. Estab. 1966. Circ. 52,000. Pays on publication. Buys one-time rights. Accepts queries by mail, e-mail. Responds in 2 months to queries.

"Let us get to know your writing with short, newsy, sailing-oriented pieces with good slides for our Splashes section. Query for upcoming theme issues; read the magazine; writing must show the writer loves sailing as much as our readers. We are always looking for fresh stories on new destinations with vibrant writing and top-notch photography. Always looking for short (100-1,500 word) articles or newsy items."

Nonfiction: "Experiences of sailing, cruising, and racing or cruising to interesting locations, whether a small lake near you or islands in the Southern Ocean, with first-hand knowledge and tips for our readers. Top-notch photos with maps, charts, cruising information complete the package. No regatta sports unless there is a story involved." Book excerpts, how-to (tech pieces on boats and gear), interview/profile, personal experience, travel (by sail). **Buys 15-20 mss/year.** Length: 750-2,500 words. **Pays $100-800.**

Photos: Reviews color transparencies. Pays $50-400. Captions required.

Tips: Prefers text in Word on disk for Mac or to e-mail address. "No attached files, please."

$ $ SEA KAYAKER, Sea Kayaker, Inc., P.O. Box 17029, Seattle WA 98107-0729. (206)789-1326. Fax: (206)781-1141. E-mail: editor@seakayakermag.com. Website: www.seakayakermag.com. Editor: Christopher Cunningham. **Contact:** Karin Redmond, executive editor. **95% freelance written.** Bimonthly publication. "*Sea Kayaker* is a bimonthly publication with a worldwide readership that covers all aspects of kayak touring. It is well-known as an important source of continuing education by the most experienced paddlers." Estab. 1984. Circ. 28,000. Pays on publication. Publishes ms an average of 6 months after acceptance. Byline given. Offers 10% kill fee. Buys first North American serial rights. Editorial lead time 4 months. Submit seasonal material 4 months in advance. Accepts queries by mail, e-mail, fax, phone. Responds in 2 months to queries. Sample copy for $5.75. Writer's guidelines for SASE.

Nonfiction: Essays, historical/nostalgic, how-to (on making equipment), humor, interview/profile, new product, opinion, personal experience, technical, travel. **Buys 50 mss/year.** Query with or without published clips or send complete ms. Length: 1,500-5,000 words. **Pays 18-20¢/word for assigned articles; 12-15¢/word for unsolicited articles.**

Photos: Send photos with submission. Reviews transparencies, prints. Buys one-time rights. Offers $15-400. Captions, identification of subjects required.

Columns/Departments: Technique, Equipment, Do-It-Yourself, Food, Safety, Health, Environment, Book Reviews; 1,000-2,500 words. **Buys 40-45 mss/year.** Query. **Pays 12-20¢/word.**

Tips: "We consider unsolicited manuscripts that include a SASE, but we give greater priority to brief descriptions (several paragraphs) of proposed articles accompanied by at least two samples—published or unpublished—of your writing. Enclose a statement as to why you're qualified to write the piece and indicate whether photographs or illustrations are available to accompany the piece."

N $ $ TRAILER BOATS MAGAZINE, Poole Publications, Inc., 20700 Belshaw Ave., Carson CA 90746-3510. (310)537-6322. Fax: (310)537-8735. E-mail: editors@trailerboats.com. Website: www.trailerboats.com. Executive Editor: Ron Eldridge. **Contact:** Jim Henricks, editor. **50% freelance written.** Monthly magazine covering legally trailerable power boats and related powerboating activities. Estab. 1971. Circ. 100,000. **Pays on acceptance.** Publishes ms an average of 3 months after acceptance. Byline given. Buys all rights. Editorial lead time 4 months. Submit seasonal material 5 months in advance. Responds in 1 month to queries. Sample copy for 9×12 SAE with 7 first-class stamps.

Nonfiction: General interest (trailer boating activities), historical/nostalgic (places, events, boats), how-to (repair boats, installation, etc.), humor (almost any power boating-related subject), interview/profile, personal experience, photo feature, technical, travel (boating travel on water or highways), product evaluations. Special issues: Annual new boat review. No "How I Spent My Summer Vacation" stories, or stories not directly connected to trailerable boats and related activities. **Buys 70-80 unsolicited mss/year.** Query. Length: 1,000-2,500 words. **Pays $150-1,000.** Sometimes pays expenses of writers on assignment.

Photos: Send photos with submission. Reviews 2¼×2¼ and 35mm slides transparencies. Buys all rights. Captions, identification of subjects, model releases required.

Columns/Departments: Over the Transom (funny or strange boating photos); Watersports (boat-related); Marine Electronics (what and how to use); Boating Basics (elementary boating tips), all 1,000-1,500 words. **Buys 60-70 mss/year.** Query. **Pays $250-450.**

Tips: "Query should contain short general outline of the intended material; what kind of photos; how the photos illustrate the piece. Write with authority, covering the subject with quotes from experts. Frequent mistakes are not knowing the subject matter or the audience. The writer may have a better chance of breaking in at our publication with short articles and fillers if they are typically hard-to-find articles. We do most major features inhouse, but try how-to stories dealing with smaller boats, installation and towing tips, boat trailer repair. Good color photos will win our hearts every time."

N $ $ **WATERWAY GUIDE**, 326 First St., Suite 400A, Annapolis MD 21403. (443)482-9377. Website: www.waterwayguide.com. **Contact:** Jay Livingston, managing editor. **90% freelance written.** Triannual magazine covering intracoastal waterway travel for recreational boats. "Writer must be knowledgeable about navigation and the areas covered by the guide." Estab. 1947. Circ. 30,000. Pays on publication. Publishes ms an average of 3 months after acceptance. Byline given. Buys first North American serial, electronic rights. Makes work-for-hire assignments. Editorial lead time 4 months. Submit seasonal material 3 months in advance. Accepts queries by mail, phone. Responds in 6 weeks to queries; 2 months to mss. Sample copy for $39.95 with $3 postage.

Nonfiction: Essays, historical/nostalgic, how-to, photo feature, technical, travel. **Buys 6 mss/year.** Query with or without published clips or send complete ms. Length: 250-5,000 words. **Pays $50-500.** Pays in contributor copies or other premiums for helpful tips and useful information.

Photos: Send photos with submission. Reviews transparencies, 3×5 prints. Buys all rights. Offers $25-50/photo. Captions, identification of subjects required.

Tips: "Must have on-the-water experience and be able to provide new and accurate information on geographic areas covere dby *Waterway Guide*."

$ **WAVELENGTH PADDLING MAGAZINE**, Wave-Length Communications, Inc., 2735 North Rd., Gabriola Island, British Columbia V0R 1X7, Canada. (250)247-9789. Fax: (250)247-9789. E-mail: wavenet@island.net. Website: www.wavelengthmagazine.com. **Contact:** Alan Wilson, editor. **75% freelance written.** Bimonthly magazine covering sea kayaking. "We promote safe paddling, guide paddlers to useful products and services and explore coastal environmental issues." Estab. 1991. Circ. 60,000 print and electronic readers. Pays on publication. Publishes ms an average of 4 months after acceptance. Byline given. Offers 10% kill fee. Buys first North American serial, electronic rights. Print and electronic material remains perpetually on website. Editorial lead time 4 months. Submit seasonal material 4 months in advance. Accepts queries by mail, e-mail, phone. Responds in 2 months to queries. Sample copy online. Writer's guidelines online.

O→ "Sea kayaking content, even if from a beginner's perspective, is essential. We like a light approach to personal experiences and humor is appreciated. Good detail (with maps and pics) for destinations material. Write to our feature focus."

Nonfiction: Book excerpts, how-to (paddle, travel), humor, interview/profile, new product, opinion, personal experience, technical, travel, trips; advice. **Buys 25 mss/year.** Query. Length: 1,000-2,000 words. **Pays $50-100.**

Photos: State availability with submission. Reviews 4×6 prints. Buys first and electronic rights. Offers $25-50/photo. Captions, identification of subjects required.

Fillers: Anecdotes, facts, gags to be illustrated by cartoonist, newsbreaks, short humor. **Buys 8-10/year.** Length: 25-250 words. **Pays $25-50.**

Tips: "You must know paddling—although novice paddlers are welcome. A strong environmental or wilderness appreciation component is advisable. We are willing to help refine work with flexible people. E-mail queries preferred. Check out our Editorial Calendar for our upcoming features."

$ $ **WOODENBOAT MAGAZINE, The Magazine for Wooden Boat Owners, Builders, and Designers**, WoodenBoat Publications, Inc., P.O. Box 78, Brooklin ME 04616. (207)359-4651. Fax: (207)359-8920. Website: www.woodenboat.com. Editor-in-Chief: Jonathan A. Wilson. Senior Editor: Mike O'Brien. Associate Editor: Tom Jackson. **Contact:** Matthew P. Murphy, editor. **50% freelance written.** Bimonthly magazine for wooden boat owners, builders, and designers. "We are devoted exclusively to the design, building, care, preservation, and use of wooden boats, both commercial and pleasure, old and new, sail and power. We work to convey quality, integrity, and involvement in the creation and care of these craft, to entertain, inform, inspire, and to provide our varied readers with access to individuals who are deeply experienced in the world of wooden boats." Estab. 1974. Circ. 106,000. Pays on publication. Publishes ms an average of 1 year after acceptance. Byline given. Offers variable kill fee. Buys first North American serial rights. Accepts previously published material. Accepts simultaneous submissions. Responds in 2 months to queries; 2 months to mss. Sample copy for $4.50. Writer's guidelines for #10 SASE.

Nonfiction: Technical (repair, restoration, maintenance, use, design, and building wooden boats). No poetry, fiction. **Buys 50 mss/year.** Query with published clips. Length: 1,500-5,000 words. **Pays $200-250/1,000 words.** Sometimes pays expenses of writers on assignment.

Reprints: Send tearsheet or typed ms with rights for sale noted and information about when and where the material previously appeared.

Photos: Send photos with submission. Reviews negatives. Buys one-time rights. Pays $15-75 b&w, $25-350 color. Identification of subjects required.

Columns/Departments: On the Waterfront pays for information on wooden boat-related events, projects, boatshop activities, etc. Uses same columnists for each issue. Length: 250-1,000 words. Send complete information. **Pays $5-50.**

Tips: "We appreciate a detailed, articulate query letter, accompanied by photos, that will give us a clear idea of what the author is proposing. We appreciate samples of previously published work. It is important for a prospective author to become familiar with our magazine. Most work is submitted on speculation. The most common failure is not exploring the subject material in enough depth."

$ $ $ YACHTING, 18 Marshall St., Suite 114, South Norwalk CT 06854. (203)299-5900. Fax: (203)299-5901. E-mail: kwooten@yachtingnet.com. Website: www.yachtingmagazine.com. Publisher: Peter Beckenbach. Editor-in-Chief: Kenny Wooton. **30% freelance written.** Monthly magazine. "Monthly magazine written and edited for experienced, knowledgeable yachtsmen." Estab. 1907. Circ. 132,000. **Pays on acceptance.** Byline given. Buys first North American serial, electronic rights. Editorial lead time 2 months. Submit seasonal material 6 months in advance. Accepts queries by mail, e-mail, fax. Responds in 1 month to queries; 3 months to mss. Sample copy for free. Writer's guidelines online.
Nonfiction: Personal experience, technical. **Buys 50 mss/year.** Query with published clips. Length: 750-800 words. **Pays $150-1,500.** Pays expenses of writers on assignment.
Photos: Send photos with submission. Reviews transparencies. Negotiates payment individually. Captions, identification of subjects, model releases required.
Tips: "We require considerable expertise in our writing because our audience is experienced and knowledgeable. Vivid descriptions of quaint anchorages and quainter natives are fine, but our readers want to know how the yachtsmen got there, too. They also want to know how their boats work. *Yachting* is edited for experienced, affluent boatowners—power and sail—who don't have the time or the inclination to read sub-standard stories. They love carefully crafted stories about places they've never been or a different spin on places they have, meticulously reported pieces on issues that affect their yachting lives, personal accounts of yachting experiences from which they can learn, engaging profiles of people who share their passion for boats, insightful essays that evoke the history and traditions of the sport and compelling photographs of others enjoying the game as much as they do. They love to know what to buy and how things work. They love to be surprised. They don't mind getting their hands dirty or saving a buck here and there, but they're not interested in learning how to make a masthead light out of a mayonnaise jar. If you love what they love and can communicate like a pro (that means meeting deadlines, writing tight, being obsessively accurate and never misspelling a proper name), we'd love to hear from you."

Gambling

$ $ CHANCE MAGAZINE, The Best of Gaming, ARC Publishing, LLC, 16 E. 41st St., 2nd Floor, New York NY 10017. Fax: (212)889-3630. E-mail: bphillips@chancemag.com. Website: www.chancemag.com. **Contact:** Buster Phillips, managing editor. **50% freelance written.** Bimonthly magazine covering gambling lifestyle, upscale resorts, food, wine, spas, etc. "*Chance* is an upscale magazine for readers interested in getting the most out of a gambling vacation. From travel, resorts and spas, to tips and advice on gaming, *Chance* is a smartly written and fun guide for the gaming connoisseur." Circ. 190,000. Pays on publication. Publishes ms an average of 3 months after acceptance. Byline given. Offers 25% kill fee. Buys first North American serial rights. Editorial lead time 6 months. Submit seasonal material 6 months in advance. Accepts queries by mail, e-mail, fax. Sample copy online.
Nonfiction: General interest, how-to, interview/profile, personal experience, photo feature, anything gambling related. No systems or self-promotion. **Buys 50 mss/year.** Query with published clips or send complete ms. Length: 1,200-3,500 words. **Pays $150-600 for assigned articles.** Sometimes pays expenses of writers on assignment.
Photos: State availability with submission. Payment negotiated individually.
Columns/Departments: The Intelligent Player (advanced advice for the serious gambler), 2,000 words; Ante (short, quick upfront pieces), 300-600 words. **Buys 12 mss/year.** Send complete ms. **Pays $150-500.**
Tips: "Either be a gambling fan with specific knowledge or be familiar with the life of a high roller—luxuries that somehow tie in to casinos and gaming. Above all, be a good writer with experience."

$ $ PLAYERS' GUIDE TO SPORTS BOOKS, (formerly *Players' Guide to Las Vegas Sports Books With Off Shore Betting Guide*), Players Guide, 11000 S. Eastern Ave., #1618, Henderson NV 89052-2965. (702)361-4602. Fax: (702)361-4605. E-mail: buzzdaly@aol.com. Website: www.buzzdaly.com. **Contact:** Buzz Daly, editor. **20-50% freelance written.** Annual magazine, weekly tabloid, and website covering sports wagering and online gaming. "We address the needs and interests of people who bet on sports. We focus on legal activities in Las Vegas and off shore, and do features on bookmakers, oddsmakers, professional bettors, etc. Although many readers are casual/recreationally, we do not 'dumb down' our coverage. Our readers are regular bettors who do not apologize for this activity." Estab. 1994. Circ. 75,000. **Pays on acceptance.** Byline given. Offers 10% or 100% kill fee. Buys first, electronic rights. Editorial lead time 2 months. Accepts queries by mail, e-mail. Responds in 2 weeks to queries; 1 week to mss. Sample copy for $3.95.
Nonfiction: "Our magazine is an annual. Our period for obtaining stories is from mid-March to early June. But our website uses material all year long." Book excerpts, interview/profile, new product. No exposés, handicapping tips, stories about losing, getting stiffed, etc. We have no interest in stories based on trite material or clichés." **Buys variable mss/year.** Query with published clips. Length: 300-1,500 words. **Pays $50-400.** Sometimes pays expenses of writers on assignment.
Photos: Send photos with submission. Reviews contact sheets, prints. Buys one-time rights. Offers no additional payment for photos accepted with ms. Identification of subjects, model releases required.

Tips: "A writer must be a bettor to be considered as a contributor. He does not need to state it, we can tell by the material. We look for fresh insight and original story ideas. However, an old idea presented imaginatively and with sophistication will be considered. For instance, the ups and downs of being or dealing with a local bookmaker, with revealing anecdotes, falls within our parameters. We have no interest in hard luck stories, bad beats, etc."

General Interest

$ $ ROCKY MOUNTAIN SPORTS MAGAZINE, Rocky Mountain Sports, Inc., 2525 15th St., #1A, Denver CO 80211. (303)477-9770. Fax: (303)477-9747. E-mail: rheaton@rockymountainsports.com. Website: www.rockymountainsports.com. Publisher: Mary Thorne. **Contact:** Rebecca Heaton, editor. **50% freelance written.** Monthly magazine covering nonteam-related sports in Colorado. "*Rocky* is a magazine for sports-related lifestyles and activities. Our mission is to reflect and inspire the active lifestyle of Rocky Mountain residents." Estab. 1986. Circ. 80,000. Pays on publication. Publishes ms an average of 2 months after acceptance. Byline given. Buys second serial (reprint) rights. Editorial lead time 3 months. Submit seasonal material 5 months in advance. Accepts queries by mail, e-mail, fax. Accepts previously published material. Responds in 3 weeks to queries; 2 months to mss. Sample copy and writer's guidelines for #10 SASE.

- The editor says she wants to see mountain outdoor sports writing *only*. No ball sports, hunting, or fishing.

O→ Break in with "Rocky Mountain angle—off-the-beaten-path."

Nonfiction: How-to, humor, inspirational, interview/profile, new product, opinion, personal experience, photo feature, travel. Special issues: Skiing & Snowboarding (November); Nordic (December) Snowshoeing (January); Running (March); Adventure Travel (April); Triathlon (May); Paddling and Climbing (June); Road Cycling & Camping (July); Mountain Biking & Hiking (August); Women's Sports & Marathon (September); Health Club (October). No articles on football, baseball, basketball, or other sports covered in depth by newspapers. **Buys 24 mss/year.** Query with published clips. Length: 1,500 words maximum. **Pays $150 minimum.**

Reprints: Send photocopy and information about when and where the material previously appeared. Pays 20-25% of amount paid for original article.

Photos: State availability with submission. Reviews transparencies, prints. Buys one-time rights. Captions, identification of subjects required.

Columns/Departments: Starting Lines (short newsy items); Running, Cycling, Climbing, Triathalon, Fitness, Nutrition, Sports Medicine, Off the Beaten Path (sports we don't usually cover). **Buys 20 mss/year.** Query. **Pays $25-300.**

Tips: "Have a Colorado angle to the story, a catchy cover letter, good clips, and demonstrate that you've read and understand our magazine and its readers."

$ SILENT SPORTS, Waupaca Publishing Co., P.O. Box 152, Waupaca WI 54981-9990. (715)258-5546. Fax: (715)258-8162. E-mail: info@silentsports.net. Website: www.silentsports.net. **Contact:** Greg Marr, editor. **75% freelance written.** Monthly magazine covering running, cycling, cross-country skiing, canoeing, kayaking, snowshoeing, in-line skating, camping, backpacking, and hiking aimed at people in Wisconsin, Minnesota, northern Illinois, and portions of Michigan and Iowa. "Not a coffee table magazine. Our readers are participants from rank amateur weekend athletes to highly competitive racers." Estab. 1984. Circ. 10,000. Pays on publication. Publishes ms an average of 3 months after acceptance. Byline given. Offers 20% kill fee. Buys one-time rights. Submit seasonal material 4 months in advance. Accepts queries by mail, e-mail, fax. Accepts previously published material. Responds in 3 months to queries. Sample copy and writer's guidelines for 10×13 SAE with 7 first-class stamps.

- The editor needs local angles on in-line skating, recreation bicycling, and snowshoeing.

Nonfiction: All stories/articles must focus on the Upper Midwest. General interest, how-to, interview/profile, opinion, technical, travel. **Buys 25 mss/year.** Query. Length: 2,500 words maximum. **Pays $15-100.** Sometimes pays expenses of writers on assignment.

Reprints: Send typed ms with rights for sale noted and information about when and where the material previously appeared. Pays 50% of amount paid for an original article.

Photos: State availability with submission. Reviews transparencies. Buys one-time rights. Pays $5-15 for b&w story photos; $50-100 for color covers.

Tips: "Where-to-go and personality profiles are areas most open to freelancers. Writers should keep in mind that this is a regional, Midwest-based publication. We want only stories/articles with a focus on our region."

$ SPORTS ETC, The Northwest's Outdoor Magazine, Sports Etc, 11715 Greenwood Ave. N, Seattle WA 98133. (206)418-0747. Fax: (206)418-0746. E-mail: staff@sportsetc.com. Website: www.sportsetc.com. **Contact:** Carolyn Price, editor. **80% freelance written.** Monthly magazine covering outdoor recreation in the Pacific Northwest. "Writers must have a solid knowledge of the sport they are writing about. They must be doers." Estab. 1988. Circ. 40,000. Pays on publication. Publishes ms an average of 3 months after acceptance. Byline given. Buys first rights. Editorial lead time 2 months. Submit seasonal material 4 months in advance. Accepts queries by mail, e-mail, fax. Accepts previously published material. Accepts simultaneous submissions. Sample copy and writer's guidelines for $3.

Nonfiction: Interview/profile, new product, travel. Query with published clips. Length: 750-1,500 words. **Pays $10-50.** Sometimes pays expenses of writers on assignment.

Photos: Send photos with submission. Reviews negatives, transparencies. Buys all rights. Captions, identification of subjects, model releases required.

Columns/Departments: Your Health (health and wellness), 750 words. **Buys 10-12 mss/year.** Query with published clips. **Pays $40-50.**

Tips: "*Sports Etc* is written for the serious Pacific Northwest outdoor recreationalist. The magazine's look, style and editorial content actively engage the reader, delivering insightful perspectives on the sports it has come to be known for—alpine skiing, bicycling, hiking, in-line skating, kayaking, marathons, mountain climbing, Nordic skiing, running and snowboarding. *Sports Etc* magazine wants vivid writing, telling images and original perspectives to produce its smart, entertaining monthly."

$ $ $ $ SPORTS ILLUSTRATED, Time Inc. Magazine Co., Sports Illustrated Building, 135 W. 50th St., New York NY 10020. (212)522-1212. E-mail: story_queries@simail.com. **Contact:** Chris Hunt, articles editor; Mark Marvic, senior editor. Weekly magazine. "*Sports Illustrated* reports and interprets the world of sport, recreation and active leisure. It previews, analyzes and comments upon major games and events, as well as those noteworthy for character and spirit alone. It features individuals connected to sport and evaluates trends concerning the part sport plays in contemporary life. In addition, the magazine has articles on such subjects as sports gear and swim suits. Special departments deal with sports equipment, books and statistics." Estab. 1954. Circ. 3,339,000. Accepts queries by mail. Responds in 4-6 weeks to queries.

- Do not send photos or graphics.

Golf

$ $ ARIZONA, THE STATE OF GOLF, Arizona Golf Association, 7226 N. 16th St., Suite 200, Phoenix AZ 85020. (602)944-3035. Fax: (602)944-3228. E-mail: rchrist@azgolf.org. Website: www.azgolf.org. **Contact:** Russ Christ, editor. **50% freelance written.** Bimonthly magazine covering golf in Arizona, the official publication of the Arizona Golf Association. Estab. 1999. Circ. 45,000. **Pays on acceptance.** Byline given. Buys all rights. Editorial lead time 6 months. Submit seasonal material 3 months in advance. Accepts queries by mail. Accepts previously published material. Accepts simultaneous submissions. Sample copy and writer's guidelines free.

Nonfiction: Book excerpts, essays, historical/nostalgic, how-to (golf), humor, inspirational, interview/profile, new product, opinion, personal experience, photo feature. **Buys 20-30 mss/year.** Query with or without published clips. Length: 500-2,000 words. **Pays $50-500.** Sometimes pays expenses of writers on assignment.

Reprints: Accepts previously published submissions.

Photos: State availability with submission. Reviews contact sheets. Rights purchased varies. Negotiates payment individually. Captions, identification of subjects required.

Columns/Departments: Short Strokes (golf news and notes), Improving Your Game (golf tips), Out of Bounds (guest editorial—800 words). Query.

$ $ CHICAGO DISTRICT GOLFER, TPG Sports, Inc., 1710 Douglas Dr. N., Golden Valley MN 55422. (763)595-0808. Fax: (763)595-0016. E-mail: joe@tpgsports.com. Website: www.tpgsports.com or www.cdga.org. **Contact:** Joseph Oberle, publications manager. **90% freelance written.** Bimonthly magazine covering golf in Illinois, the official publication of the Chicago District Golf Association and Golf Association of Illinois. Estab. 1922. Circ. 71,000. Pays on acceptance or publication. Byline given. Buys all rights. Editorial lead time 2 months. Submit seasonal material 3 months in advance. Accepts queries by mail, e-mail. Accepts previously published material. Accepts simultaneous submissions. Sample copy and writer's guidelines free.

Nonfiction: General interest, historical/nostalgic, how-to (golf), humor, interview/profile, opinion, personal experience, travel. **Buys 25-35 mss/year.** Query with or without published clips. Length: 500-5,000 words. **Pays $50-500.** Sometimes pays expenses of writers on assignment.

Reprints: Accepts previously published submissions.

Photos: State availability with submission. Reviews contact sheets. Negotiates payment individually. Captions, identification of subjects required.

Columns/Departments: CDGA/GAI Update (news and notes); Club Profile; Friends of the Game; Chicago District Lesson. Query.

$ $ $ GOLF CANADA, Official magazine of the Royal Canadian Golf Association, RCGA/Relevant Communications, 2070 Hadwen Rd., Mississauga, Ontario L5K 2T3, Canada. (905)849-9700. Fax: (905)845-7040. E-mail: golfcanada@rcga.org. Website: www.rcga.org. **Contact:** John Tenpenny, editor. **80% freelance written.** Magazine published 4 times/year covering Canadian golf. "*Golf Canada* is the official magazine of the Royal Canadian Golf Association, published to entertain and enlighten members about RCGA-related activities and to generally support and promote amateur golf in Canada." Estab. 1994. Circ. 150,000. **Pays on acceptance.** Byline given. Offers 100% kill fee. Buys first translation, electronic rights. Editorial lead time 3 months. Submit seasonal material 6 months in advance. Accepts queries by mail, e-mail, fax, phone. Accepts previously published material. Sample copy for free.

Nonfiction: Historical/nostalgic, interview/profile, new product, opinion, photo feature, travel. No professional golf-related articles. **Buys 42 mss/year.** Query with published clips. Length: 750-3,000 words. **Pays 60¢/word including electronic rights.** Sometimes pays expenses of writers on assignment.

Photos: State availability with submission. Reviews contact sheets, negatives, transparencies, prints. Buys all rights. Negotiates payment individually. Captions required.

Columns/Departments: Guest Column (focus on issues surrounding the Canadian golf community), 700 words. Query. **Pays 60¢/word including electronic rights.**

Tips: "Keep story ideas focused on Canadian competitive golf."

$ $ $ GOLF TIPS, The Game's Most In-Depth Instruction & Equipment Magazine, Werner Publishing Corp., 12121 Wilshire Blvd., Suite 1200, Los Angeles CA 90025. (310)820-1500. Fax: (310)826-5008. E-mail: editors@golftipsmag.com. Website: www.golftipsmag.com. Senior Editor: Mike Chwasky. Editor at Large: Tom Ferrell. **Contact:** David DeNunzio, editor. **95% freelance written.** Magazine published 9 times/year covering golf instruction and equipment. "We provide mostly concise, very clear golf instruction pieces for the serious golfer." Estab. 1986. Pays on publication. Publishes ms an average of 2 months after acceptance. Byline given. Offers 33% kill fee. Buys first, second serial (reprint) rights. Editorial lead time 3 months. Submit seasonal material 4 months in advance. Accepts previously published material. Responds in 1 month to queries. Sample copy and writer's guidelines free.

Nonfiction: Book excerpts, how-to, interview/profile, new product, photo feature, technical, travel, all golf related. "Generally golf essays rarely make it." **Buys 125 mss/year.** Send complete ms. Length: 250-2,000 words. **Pays $300-1,000 for assigned articles; $300-800 for unsolicited articles.** Occassionally negotiates other forms of payment. Sometimes pays expenses of writers on assignment.

Photos: State availability with submission. Reviews 2×2 transparencies. Buys all rights. Negotiates payment individually. Captions, identification of subjects required.

Columns/Departments: Stroke Saver (very clear, concise instruction), 350 words; Lesson Library (book excerpts—usually in a series), 1,000 words; Travel Tips (formatted golf travel), 2,500 words. **Buys 40 mss/year.** Query with or without published clips or send complete ms. **Pays $300-850.**

The online magazine carries original content not found in the print edition. Contact: Tom Ferrell, online editor.

Tips: "Contact a respected PGA Professional and find out if they're interested in being published. A good writer can turn an interview into a decent instruction piece."

$ $ GOLF TRAVELER, Official Publication of Golf Card International, Affinity Group, Inc., 2575 Vista del Mar, Ventura CA 93001. Fax: (805)667-4217. E-mail: golf@golfcard.com. Website: www.golfcard.com. **Contact:** Valerie Law, editorial director. **50% freelance written.** Quarterly magazine and monthly e-newsletter "are the membership publications for the Golf Card, an organization that offers its members reduced or waived greens fees at 3,500 affiliated golf courses in North America." Estab. 1976. Circ. 100,000. **Pays on acceptance.** Byline given. Offers 33% kill fee. Buys first North American serial, electronic rights. Editorial lead time 3 months. Submit seasonal material 5 months in advance. Accepts queries by mail, e-mail, fax. Accepts previously published material. Accepts simultaneous submissions. Responds in 1 month to queries. Sample copy for $2.50, plus 9×12 SASE.

Nonfiction: Book excerpts, essays, how-to, interview/profile, new product, personal experience, photo feature, technical. No poetry or cartoons. **Buys 12 mss/year.** Query with published clips or send complete ms. Length: 500-2,500 words. **Pays $75-500.**

Reprints: Accepts previously published submissions.

Photos: Send photos with submission. Reviews transparencies. Buys one-time rights. Negotiates payment individually. Identification of subjects, model releases required.

The online magazine carries original content not found in the print edition. Contact: Ken Cohen.

$ $ MINNESOTA GOLFER, 6550 York Ave. S., Suite 211, Edina MN 55435. (952)927-4643. Fax: (952)927-9642. E-mail: editor@mngolf.org. Website: www.mngolf.org. **Contact:** W.P. Ryan, editor. **75% freelance written.** Bimonthly magazine covering golf in Minnesota, the official publication of the Minnesota Golf Association. Estab. 1975. Circ. 72,500. Pays on acceptance or publication. Byline given. Buys all rights. Editorial lead time 3 months. Accepts queries by mail, fax. Accepts simultaneous submissions.

Nonfiction: Book excerpts, essays, historical/nostalgic, how-to (golf), humor, inspirational, interview/profile, new product, opinion, personal experience, photo feature. **Buys 18-20 mss/year.** Query with published clips. Length: 500-2,500 words. **Pays $50-500.** Sometimes pays expenses of writers on assignment.

Photos: State availability with submission. Reviews contact sheets, transparencies. Rights purchased varies. Negotiates payment individually. Captions, identification of subjects required.

Columns/Departments: Punch shots (golf news and notes). Magazine features rotating departments on the following: Women's Page; Golf Business News; Rules, etiquette and news for beginning golfers; New Equipment; Travel; Opinion; Golf players and personalities with links to Minnesota. Query.

$ $ PACIFIC GOLF, Canada Wide Magazines & Communications Ltd., 4180 Lougheed Hwy., 4th Floor, Burnaby, British Columbia V5C 6A7, Canada. (604)299-7311. Fax: (604)299-9188. E-mail: acollette@canadawide.com. **Contact:** Ann Collette, editor. **80% freelance written.** Quarterly magazine. "*Pacific Golf* appeals to British Columbia's golfers and reflects the West Coast golf experience. We concentrate on the new, the influential, Canadian golfers, and subject matter based in British Columbia." Circ. 20,000. Pays on publication. Publishes ms an average of 2 months after acceptance. Byline given. Offers variable kill fee. first Canadian rights. Editorial lead time 4 months. Submit seasonal material 4 months in advance. Responds in 6 weeks to mss. Sample copy not available.

Nonfiction: Query with published clips. Length: 500-1,800 words. **Pays 40-50¢/word.** Sometimes pays expenses of writers on assignment.

Photos: State availability with submission.

$ $ VIRGINIA GOLFER, TPG Sports Inc., 1710 Douglas Dr. N., Golden Valley MN 55422. (763)595-0808. Fax: (763)595-0016. E-mail: info@tpgsports.com. **Contact:** Andrew Blair, editor. **65% freelance written.** Bimonthly magazine covering golf in Virginia, the official publication of the Virginia Golf Association. Estab. 1983. Circ. 33,000. Pays on publication. Byline given. Buys all rights. Editorial lead time 6 months. Submit seasonal material 3 months in advance. Accepts queries by mail, e-mail. Accepts previously published material. Accepts simultaneous submissions. Sample copy and writer's guidelines free.

Nonfiction: Book excerpts, essays, historical/nostalgic, how-to (golf), humor, inspirational, interview/profile, personal experience, photo feature, technical (golf equipment), where to play, golf business. **Buys 30-40 mss/year.** Query with or without published clips or send complete ms. Length: 500-2,500 words. **Pays $50-500.** Sometimes pays expenses of writers on assignment.

Reprints: Accepts previously published submissions.

Photos: State availability with submission. Reviews contact sheets. Rights purchased varies. Negotiates payment individually. Captions, identification of subjects required.

Columns/Departments: Chip ins & Three Putts (news notes); Rules Corner (golf rules explanations and discussion); Pro Tips, Golf Travel (where to play); Golf Business (what's happening?). Query.

Guns

$ $ THE ACCURATE RIFLE, Precision Shooting, Inc., 222 McKee St., Manchester CT 06040-4800. (860)645-8776. Fax: (860)643-8215. Website: www.theaccuraterifle.com. **Contact:** Dave Brennan, editor. **30-35% freelance written.** Monthly magazine covering "the specialized field of 'extreme rifle accuracy' excluding rifle competition disciplines." Estab. 2000. Circ. 8,000. Pays on publication. Publishes ms an average of 3 months after acceptance. Byline given. Buys first North American serial rights. Editorial lead time 2 months. Submit seasonal material 3 months in advance. Accepts queries by mail, fax. Responds in 2 weeks to queries; 1 month to mss. Sample copy for free. Writer's guidelines not available.

Nonfiction: General interest, historical/nostalgic, how-to, humor, interview/profile, personal experience. "Nothing common to newsstand firearms publications. This has a very sophisticated and knowledgable readership." **Buys 36 mss/year.** Query. Length: 1,800-3,000 words. **Pays $200-500.**

Photos: Send photos with submission. Reviews 4×6 prints. Buys one-time rights. Offers no additional payment for photos accepted with ms. Captions required.

Tips: "Call the editor first and tell him what topic you propose to write about. Could save time and effort."

$ $ GUN DIGEST, DBI Books, Inc., Division of Krause Publications, 700 E. State St., Iola WI 54990. (888)457-2873. Fax: (715)445-4087. **Contact:** Ken Ramage, editor-in-chief. **50% freelance written.** Prefers to work with published/established writers, but works with a small number of new/unpublished writers each year. Annual journal covering guns and shooting. Estab. 1944. **Pays on acceptance.** Publishes ms an average of 20 months after acceptance. Byline given. Buys all rights. Accepts queries by mail. Responds as time allows to queries.

Nonfiction: Buys 25 mss/year. Query. Length: 500-5,000 words. **Pays $100-600 for text/art package.**

Photos: Prefers 8X10 b&w prints. Slides, transparencies OK. No digital. State availability with submission. Payment for photos included in payment for ms. Captions required.

Tips: Award of $1,000 to author of best article (juried) in each issue.

$ $ MUZZLE BLASTS, National Muzzle Loading Rifle Association, P.O. Box 67, Friendship IN 47021. (812)667-5131. Fax: (812)667-5137. E-mail: nmlra@nmlra.org. Website: www.nmlra.org. Editor: Eric A. Bye. **Contact:** Terri Trowbridge, director of publications. **65% freelance written.** Monthly magazine. "Articles must relate to muzzleloading or the muzzleloading era of American history." Estab. 1939. Circ. 23,000. Pays on publication. Publishes ms an average of 6 months after acceptance. Byline given. Offers $50 kill fee. Buys first North American serial, one-time, second serial (reprint) rights. Editorial lead time 4 months. Submit seasonal material 6 months in advance. Responds in 1 month to mss. Sample copy and writer's guidelines free.

Nonfiction: Book excerpts, general interest, historical/nostalgic, how-to, humor, interview/profile, new product, personal experience, photo feature, technical, travel. "No subjects that do not pertain to muzzleloading." **Buys 80 mss/year.** Query. Length: 2,500 words. **Pays $150 minimum for assigned articles; $50 minimum for unsolicited articles.**

Photos: Send photos with submission. Reviews 5×7 prints. Buys one-time rights. Negotiates payment individually. Captions, model releases required.

Columns/Departments: Buys 96 mss/year. Query. **Pays $50-200.**

Fiction: Must pertain to muzzleloading. Adventure, historical, humorous. **Buys 6 mss/year.** Query. Length: 2,500 words. **Pays $50-300.**

Fillers: Facts. **Pays $50.**

$ $ PRECISION SHOOTING, Precision Shooting, Inc., 222 McKee St., Manchester CT 06040-4800. (860)645-8776. Fax: (860)643-8215. Website: www.precisionshooting.com. **Contact:** Dave Brennan, editor. **30-35% freelance written.** Monthly magazine covering "the specialized field of 'extreme rifle accuracy' including rifle competition disciplines." Estab. 1956. Circ. 17,500. Pays on publication. Publishes ms an average of 3 months after acceptance. Byline given. Buys first North American serial rights. Editorial lead time 2 months. Submit seasonal material 3 months in advance. Accepts queries by mail, fax. Responds in 2 weeks to queries; 1 month to mss. Sample copy for free. Writer's guidelines not available.

Nonfiction: General interest, historical/nostalgic, how-to, humor, interview/profile, personal experience. "Nothing common to newsstand firearms publications. This has a very sophisticated and knowledgeable readership." **Buys 36 mss/year.** Query. Length: 1,800-3,000 words. **Pays $200-500.**

Photos: Send photos with submission. Reviews 4×6 prints. Buys one-time rights. Offers no additional payment for photos accepted with ms. Captions required.

Tips: "Call the editor first and tell him what topic you propose to write about. Could save time and effort."

$ $ ☆ SHOTGUN NEWS, Primedia, Box 1790, Peoria IL 61656. (309)679-5408. Fax: (309)679-5476. E-mail: sgnews@primediasi.com. Website: www.shotgunnews.com. **Contact:** Robert W. Hunnicutt, general manager/editor. **95% freelance written.** Tabloid published every 10 days covering firearms, accessories, ammunition and militaria. "The nation's oldest and largest gun sales publication. Provides up-to-date market information for gun trade and consumers." Estab. 1946. Circ. 100,000. **Pays on acceptance.** Publishes ms an average of 3 months after acceptance. Byline given. Buys first North American serial rights. Editorial lead time 1 month. Submit seasonal material 3 months in advance. Responds in 1 month to queries. Sample copy for free.

Nonfiction: Historical/nostalgic, how-to, technical. No political pieces, fiction or poetry. **Buys 50 mss/year.** Query. Length: 1,000-3,000 words. **Pays $200-500 for assigned articles.** Sometimes pays expenses of writers on assignment.

Photos: Send photos with submission. Reviews prints. Buys one-time rights. Offers no additional payment for photos accepted with ms. Captions required.

Hiking & Backpacking

$ $ $ $ BACKPACKER, Rodale, 33 E. Minor St., Emmaus PA 18098-0099. (610)967-8296. Fax: (610)967-8181. E-mail: jdorn@backpacker.com. Website: www.backpacker.com. **Contact:** Jon Dorn, executive editor. **50% freelance written.** Magazine published 9 times/year covering wilderness travel for backpackers. Estab. 1973. Circ. 285,000. **Pays on acceptance.** Byline given. Buys one-time, all rights. Accepts queries by mail, e-mail, fax. Responds in 1 month to queries. Writer's guidelines for #10 SASE or online.

Nonfiction: "What we want are features that let us and the readers 'feel' the place, and experience your wonderment, excitement, disappointment, or other emotions encountered 'out there.' If we feel like we've been there after reading your story, you've succeeded." Essays, exposé, historical/nostalgic, how-to (expedition planner), humor, inspirational, interview/profile, new product, opinion, personal experience, technical, travel. No step-by-step accounts of what you did on your summer vacation—stories that chronicle every rest stop and gulp of water. Query with published clips. Length: 750-4,000 words. **Pays $400-2,000.**

Photos: State availability with submission. Buys one-time rights. Pay varies.

Columns/Departments: Signpost, "News From All Over" (adventure, environment, wildelife, trails, techniques, organizations, special interests—well-written, entertaining, short, newsy item), 50-500 words; Body Language (in-the-field health column), 750-1,200 words; Moveable Feast (food-related aspects of wilderness: nutrition, cooking techniques, recipes, products, and gear), 500-750 words; Weekend Wilderness (brief but detailed guides to wilderness areas, providing thorough trip-planning information, only enough anecdote to give a hint, then the where/when/hows), 500-750 words; Know How (ranging from beginner to expert focus, written by people with solid expertise, details ways to improve performance, how-to-do-it instructions, information on equipment manufacturers, and places readers can go), 300-1,000 words; and Backcountry (personal perspectives, quirky and idiosyncratic, humorous critiques, manifestos and misadventures, interesting angle, lesson, revelation, or moral), 750-1,200 words. **Buys 50-75 mss/year.** Query with published clips. No phone calls regarding story ideas. Written or e-mail queries only. **Pays $200-1,000.**

▣ The online magazine carries original content not found in the print edition.

Tips: "Our best advice is to read the publication—most freelancers don't know the magazine at all. The best way to break in is with an article for the Backcountry, Weekend Wilderness, or Signpost Department."

$ $ $ $ ☆ OUTSIDE, Mariah Media Inc., Outside Plaza, 400 Market St., Santa Fe NM 87501. (505)989-7100. Website: www.outsidemag.com. Editor: Hal Espen. **Contact:** Assistant to the Editor. **90% freelance written.** Monthly magazine. "*Outside* is a monthly national magazine for active, educated, upscale adults who love the outdoors and are concerned about its preservation." Estab. 1977. Circ. 550,000. Pays after acceptance. Publishes ms an average of 3 months after acceptance. Byline given. Offers 25% kill fee. Buys first North American serial rights. Submit seasonal material 5 months in advance. Writer's guidelines for #10 SASE.

Nonfiction: Book excerpts, essays, general interest, how-to, interview/profile (major figures associated with sports, travel, environment, outdoor), photo feature (outdoor photography), technical (reviews of equipment, how-to), travel (adventure, sports-oriented travel). Do not want to see articles about sports that we don't cover (basketball, tennis, golf, etc.). **Buys 40 mss/year.** Query with published clips. Length: 1,500-4,000 words. **Pays $1/word.** Pays expenses of writers on assignment.

Photos: "Do not send photos; if we decide to use a story, we may ask to see the writer's photos." Reviews transparencies. Buys one-time rights. Captions, identification of subjects required.

Columns/Departments: Dispatches (news, events, short profiles relevant to outdoors), 200-1,000 words; Destinations (places to explore, news, and tips for adventure travelers), 250-400 words; Review (evaluations of products), 200-1,500 words. **Buys 180 mss/year.** Query with published clips.

The online magazine carries original content not found in the print edition. Contact: Amy Marr, online editor.

Tips: "Prospective writers should study the magazine before querying. Look at the magazine for our style, subject matter and standards." The departments are the best areas for freelancers to break in.

Hockey

$ $ $ AMERICAN HOCKEY INC., Official Publication of USA Hockey, c/o TPG Sports, Inc., 1710 Douglas Dr. N., #201, Golden Valley MN 55422. (763)595-0808. Fax: (763)595-0016. E-mail: joe@tpgsports.com. Editor: Harry Thompson. **Contact:** Joseph Oberle, publications manager. **60% freelance written.** Magazine published 10 times/year covering amateur hockey in the US. "The world's largest hockey magazine, *AHM* is the official magazine of USA Hockey, Inc., the national governing body of hockey." Estab. 1980. Circ. 444,000. Pays on acceptance or publication. Byline given. Buys all rights. Editorial lead time 6 months. Submit seasonal material 4 months in advance. Accepts previously published material. Accepts simultaneous submissions. Sample copy and writer's guidelines free.

Nonfiction: Essays, general interest, historical/nostalgic, how-to (play hockey), humor, inspirational, interview/profile, new product, opinion, personal experience, photo feature, travel, hockey camps, pro hockey, juniors, college, NCAA hockey championships, Olympics, youth, etc. **Buys 20-30 mss/year.** Query. Length: 500-5,000 words. **Pays $50-750.** Pays expenses of writers on assignment.

Reprints: Accepts previously published submissions.

Photos: State availability with submission. Reviews contact sheets. Rights purchased varies. Negotiates payment individually. Captions, identification of subjects required.

Columns/Departments: Short Cuts (news and notes); Coaches' Corner (teaching tips); USA Hockey; Inline Notebook (news and notes). **Pays $150-250.**

Fiction: Adventure, humorous, slice-of-life vignettes. **Buys 10-20 mss/year. Pays $150-1,000.**

Fillers: Anecdotes, facts, gags to be illustrated by cartoonist, newsbreaks, short humor. **Buys 20-30/year.** Length: 10-100 words. **Pays $25-250.**

Tips: Writers must have a general knowledge and enthusiasm for hockey, including ice, inline, street, and other. The primary audience is youth players in the US.

$ $ MINNESOTA HOCKEY JOURNAL, Official Publication of Minnesota Hockey, Inc., c/o TPG Sports, Inc., 1710 Douglas Dr. N., Golden Valley MN 55422. (763)595-0808. Fax: (763)595-0016. E-mail: joe@tpgsports.com. Website: www.tpgsports.com. Editor: Greg Anzlec. **Contact:** Joseph Oberle, publications manager. **50% freelance written.** Journal published 4 times/year. Estab. 2000. Circ. 40,000. Pays on publication. Byline given. Buys all rights. Editorial lead time 6 months. Submit seasonal material 4 months in advance. Accepts previously published material. Accepts simultaneous submissions. Sample copy and writer's guidelines free.

Nonfiction: Essays, general interest, historical/nostalgic, how-to (play hockey), humor, inspirational, interview/profile, new product, opinion, personal experience, photo feature, travel, hockey camps, pro hockey, juniors, college, Olympics, youth, etc. **Buys 5-10 mss/year.** Query. Length: 500-5,000 words. **Pays $100-500.** Sometimes pays expenses of writers on assignment.

Reprints: Accepts previously published submissions.

Photos: State availability with submission. Reviews contact sheets. Rights purchased vary. Negotiates payment individually. Captions, identification of subjects required.

Columns/Departments: Hot Shots (news and notes); Open Ice (opinion). **Pays $50-250.**

Fillers: Anecdotes, facts, gags to be illustrated by cartoonist, newsbreaks, short humor, game page with puzzles. **Buys 5-10 mss/year.** Length: 10-100 words. **Pays $25-250.**

Horse Racing

$ $ AMERICAN TURF MONTHLY, Star Sports Corp., 306 Broadway, Lynbrook NY 11563. (516)599-2121. Fax: (516)599-0451. E-mail: editor@americanturf.com. Website: www.americanturf.com. **Contact:** James Corbett, editor-in-chief. **90% freelance written.** Monthly magazine covering Thoroughbred racing, handicapping, and wagering. "Squarely focused on Thoroughbred handicapping and wagering. *ATM* is a magazine for horseplayers, not owners, breeders, or 12-year-old girls enthralled with ponies." Estab. 1946. Circ. 28,000. Pays on publication. Publishes ms an average of 4 months after acceptance. Byline given. Makes work-for-hire assignments. Editorial lead time 2 months. Submit seasonal material 2 months in advance. Accepts queries by mail, e-mail. Responds in 1 month to queries. Sample copy and writer's guidelines free.

Nonfiction: Handicapping and wagering features. Special issues: Triple Crown/Kentucky Derby (May); Saratoga/Del Mar (August); Breeder's Cup (November). No historical essays, bilious 'guest editorials,' saccharine poetry, fiction. **Buys 50 mss/year.** Query. Length: 800-2,000 words. **Pays $75-300 for assigned articles; $100-500 for unsolicited articles.**

Photos: Send photos with submission. Reviews 3×5 transparencies, Prints. Buys one-time rights. Offers $25 interior; $150 for cover. Identification of subjects required.

Fillers: Newsbreaks, short humor. **Buys 5/year.** Length: 400 words. **Pays $25.**

The online magazine carries original content not found in the print version. Contact: Dana Romick, online editor.

Tips: "Send a good query letter specifically targeted at explaining how this contribution will help our readers to cash a bet at the track!"

N $ $ THE BACKSTRETCH, United Thoroughbred Trainers of America, Inc., P.O. Box 7065, Louisville KY 40257-0065. (800)325-3487. Fax: (502)893-0026. E-mail: bstretch@couriernet.infi.net. Website: www.thebackstretch.com. **Contact:** Kevin Baker, copy editor and designer. **90% freelance written.** Bimonthly magazine directed chiefly to Thoroughbred trainers but also to owners, fans, and others working in or involved with the racing industry. Estab. 1962. Circ. 10,000. Pays on publication. Publishes ms an average of 3 months after acceptance. Accepts queries by mail, e-mail, fax, phone. Accepts previously published material. Sample copy on request.

Break in with "an outline and samples with your query; be available for questions regarding manuscript; try to provide photos and adhere to electronic format for submissions."

Nonfiction: Profiles of trainers, owners, jockeys, horses, and other personalities who make up the world of racing; analysis of industry issues; articles on paritcular tracks or races, veterinary topics; information on legal or business aspects of owning, training, or racing horses; and historical perspectives. Opinions should be informed by expertise on the subject treated. Noncommissioned articles are accepted on a speculation basis. Length: 1,500-2,500 words. **Pays $150-450.**

Reprints: Send typed ms with rights for sale noted and information about when and where the material previously appeared. Payment negotiable.

Photos: It is advisable to include photo illustrations when possible, or these can be arranged for separately.

The online magazine carries original content not found in the print edition.

Tips: "If an article is a simultaneous submission, this must be stated and we must be advised if it is accepted elsewhere. Articles should be double spaced and may be submitted by mail, fax, or e-mail on 3½-inch disk saved in text or in program compatible with QuarkXPress for Macintosh."

$ $ HOOF BEATS, United States Trotting Association, 750 Michigan Ave., Columbus OH 43215. (614)224-2291. Fax: (614)222-6791. **Contact:** Dean A. Hoffman, editor; Nicole Kraft, associate editor. **50% freelance written.** Monthly magazine covering harness racing for the participants of the sport of harness racing. "We cover all aspects of the sport—racing, breeding, selling, etc." Estab. 1933. Circ. 14,000. Pays on publication. Publishes ms an average of 3 months after acceptance. Byline given. Buys negotiable rights. Submit seasonal material 4 months in advance. Responds in 1 months to mss. Free sample copy postpaid.

Nonfiction: General interest, historical/nostalgic, humor, inspirational, interview/profile, new product, personal experience, photo feature, horse care. **Buys 15-20 mss/year.** Length: Open. **Pays $100-400.** Negotiable.

Photos: State availability with submission. Reviews prints, electronic images. Buys one-time rights. Negotiates payment individually. Identification of subjects required.

Hunting & Fishing

$ $ ALABAMA GAME & FISH, *Game & Fish*, P.O. Box 741, Marietta GA 30061. **Contact:** Jimmy Jacobs, editor. See *Game & Fish*.

N $ $ AMERICAN ANGLER, the Magazine of Fly Fishing & Fly Tying, Morris Communications Corp., 160 Benmont Ave., Bennington VT 05201. Fax: (802)447-2471. **Contact:** Philip Monahan, editor. **95% freelance written.** Bimonthly magazine covering fly fishing. "*American Angler* is dedicated to giving fly fishers practical information they can use—wherever they fish, whatever they fish for." Estab. 1976. Circ. 60,000. Pays on publication. Publishes ms an average of 6 months after acceptance. Byline given. Buys first North American serial, one-time rights. Editorial lead time 3 months. Submit seasonal material 5 months in advance. Accepts queries by mail, fax. Accepts previously published material. Accepts simultaneous submissions. Responds in 6 weeks to queries; 2 months to mss. Sample copy for $6. Writer's guidelines for #10 SASE.

Nonfiction: How-to (most important), personal experience, photo feature (seldom), technical. No promotional flack for pay back free trips or freebies, no superficial, broad-brush coverage of subjects. **Buys 45-60 mss/year.** Query with published clips. Length: 800-2,200 words. **Pays $200-400.**

Reprints: Send information about when and where the material previously appeared. Pay negotiable.

Photos: "Photographs are important. A fly-tying submission should always include samples of flies to send to our staff photographer, even if photos of the flies are included." Send photos with submission. Reviews contact sheets, transparencies. Buys one-time rights. Offers no additional payment for photos accepted with ms. Captions, identification of subjects required.

Columns/Departments: One-page shorts (problem solvers), 350-750 words. Query with published clips. **Pays $100-300.**

Tips: "If you are new to this editor, please submit complete queries."

$ $ ARKANSAS SPORTSMAN, Game & Fish, P.O. Box 741, Marietta GA 30061. (770)953-9222. Fax: (770)933-9510. E-mail: ken_duke@primediamags.com. Website: ArkansasSportsmanMag.com. **Contact:** Ken Duke, editor. See *Game & Fish*. Accepts queries by mail, e-mail.

$ $ BASSMASTER MAGAZINE, B.A.S.S. Publications, 5845 Carmichael Pkwy., Montgomery AL 36117. (334)272-9530. Fax: (334)396-8230. E-mail: editorial@bassmaster.com. Website: www.bassmaster.com. **Contact:** Dave Precht, editor. **80% freelance written.** Magazine published 10 times/year about largemouth, smallmouth, and spotted bass, offering "how-to" articles for dedicated beginning and advanced bass fishermen, including destinations and new product reviews. Estab. 1968. Circ. 600,000. **Pays on acceptance.** Publishes ms an average of 1 year after acceptance. Byline given. Buys electronic rights. Editorial lead time 2 months. Submit seasonal material 6 months in advance. Accepts queries by mail, e-mail. Responds in 2 months to queries. Sample copy for $2. Writer's guidelines for #10 SASE.

- Needs destination stories (how to fish a certain area) for the Northwest and Northeast.

Nonfiction: Historical/nostalgic, how-to (patterns, lures, etc.), interview/profile (of knowledgeable people in the sport), new product (reels, rods, and bass boats), travel (where to go fish for bass), conservation related to bass fishing. "No first-person, personal experience-type articles." **Buys 100 mss/year.** Query. Length: 500-2,500 words. **Pays $100-500.**

Photos: Send photos with submission. Reviews transparencies. Buys all rights. Offers no additional payment for photos accepted with ms, but pays $700 for color cover transparencies. Captions, model releases required.

Columns/Departments: Short Cast/News/Views/Notes/Briefs (upfront regular feature covering news-related events such as new state bass records, unusual bass fishing happenings, conservation, new products, and editorial viewpoints). Length: 250-400 words. **Pays $100-3,000.**

Fillers: Anecdotes, newsbreaks. **Buys 4-5/year.** Length: 250-500 words. **Pays $50-100.**

Tips: "Editorial direction continues in the short, more direct how-to article. Compact, easy-to-read information is our objective. Shorter articles with good graphics, such as how-to diagrams, step-by-step instruction, etc., will enhance a writer's articles submitted to *Bassmaster Magazine*. The most frequent mistakes made by writers in completing an article for us are poor grammar, poor writing, poor organization, and superficial research. Send in detailed queries outlining specific objectives of article, obtain writer's guidelines. Be as concise as possible."

$ $ BC OUTDOORS SPORT FISHING, OP Publishing, 1080 Howe St., Suite 900, Vancouver, British Columbia V6Z 2T1, Canada. (604)606-4644. Fax: (604)687-1925. E-mail: outdoorsgroupeditorial@oppublishing.com. Website: www.oppublishing.com. Editor: George Gruenfeld. **Contact:** Roegan Lloyd, managing editor. **80% freelance written.** Magazine published 6 times/year covering fresh and saltwater fishing, camping and backroads. Pays on publication. Publishes ms an average of 3 months after acceptance. Byline given. Offers negotiable kill fee. Buys first North American serial rights. Sample copy and writer's guidelines for 8×10 SAE with 7 Canadian first-class stamps or IRC.

Nonfiction: "We would like to receive how-to, where-to features dealing with fishing in British Columbia." How-to (new or innovative articles on fishing subjects), personal experience (outdoor adventure), outdoor topics specific to British Columbia. **Buys 60 mss/year.** Query. Length: 1,700-2,000 words. **Pays $300-500.**

Photos: State availability with submission. Buys one-time rights; buys other rights for cover photo. Pays $25-75 on publication for 5×7 b&w prints; $35-150 for color 35mm transparencies. Captions, identification of subjects required.

Tips: "Wants in-depth information, professional writing only. Emphasis on environmental issues. Those pieces with a conservation component have a better chance of being published. Subject must be specific to British Columbia. We receive many manuscripts written by people who obviously do not know the magazine or market. The writer has a better chance of breaking in with short, lesser-paying articles and fillers, because we have a stable of regular writers who produce most main features."

$ $ THE BIG GAME FISHING JOURNAL, Offshore Informational Publications, 1800 Bay Ave., Point Pleasant NJ 08742. (732)840-4900. Fax: (732)223-2449. E-mail: captlen@aol.com. Website: www.bgf-journal.com. Senior Publisher: Leonard Belcaro. **Contact:** Chris Bohlman, managing editor. **90% freelance written.** Bimonthly magazine covering big game fishing. "We require highly instructional articles prepared by qualified writers/fishermen." Estab. 1994. Circ. 45,000. Pays on publication. Byline given. Offers 50% kill fee. Buys first North American serial rights. Editorial lead time 3 months. Submit seasonal material 3 months in advance. Accepts queries by mail, e-mail. Accepts simultaneous submissions. Responds in 2 weeks to queries; 1 month to mss. Sample copy not available. Writer's guidelines free.

Nonfiction: How-to, interview/profile, technical. **Buys 50-70 mss/year.** Send complete ms. Length: 2,000-3,000 words. **Pays $200-400.** Sometimes pays expenses of writers on assignment.

Photos: Send photos with submission. Reviews transparencies. Buys one-time rights. Offers no additional payment for photos accepted with ms. Captions required.

Tips: "Our format is considerably different than most publications. We prefer to receive articles from qualified anglers on their expertise—if the author is an accomplished writer, all the better. We require highly instructional articles that teach both novice and expert readers."

$ $ BUGLE, Elk Country and the Hunt, Rocky Mountain Elk Foundation, 2291 W. Broadway, Missoula MT 59808. (406)523-4570. Fax: (406)543-7710. E-mail: bugle@rmef.org. Website: www.elkfoundation.org. Editor: Dan Crockett. **Contact:** Lee Cromrich, assistant editor. **50% freelance written.** Bimonthly magazine covering elk conservation and elk hunting. "*Bugle* is the membership publication of the Rocky Mountain Elk Foundation, a nonprofit wildlife conservation group. Our readers are predominantly hunters, many of them conservationists who care deeply about protecting wildlife habitat. Hunting stories and essays should celebrate the hunting experience, demonstrating respect for wildlife, the land, and the hunt. Articles on elk behavior or elk habitat should include personal observations and entertain as well as educate." Estab. 1984. Circ. 132,000. **Pays on acceptance.** Publishes ms an average of 9 months after acceptance. Byline given. Offers variable kill fee. Buys one-time rights. Editorial lead time 6 months. Submit seasonal material 6 months in advance. Accepts queries by mail, e-mail, fax, phone. Accepts previously published material. Responds in 1 month to queries; 3 months to mss. Sample copy for $5. Writer's guidelines for #10 SASE.

O→ Preparation: "Read as many issues of *Bugle* as possible to know what the Elk Foundation and magazine are about. Then write a strong query with those things in mind. Send it with clips of other published or unpublished pieces representative of story being proposed."

Nonfiction: Book excerpts, essays, general interest (elk related), historical/nostalgic, humor, interview/profile, opinion, personal experience, photo feature. No how-to, where-to. **Buys 20 mss/year.** Query with or without published clips or send complete ms. Length: 1,500-4,500 words. **Pays 20¢/word and 3 contributor copies; more issues at cost.**

Reprints: Send typed ms with rights for sale noted and information about when and where the material previously appeared. Pays 75% of amount paid for original article.

Columns/Departments: Situation Ethics, 1,000-2,000 words; Thoughts & Theories, 1,500-4,000 words; Women in the Outdoors, 1,000-2,500 words. **Buys 13 mss/year.** Query with or without published clips or send complete ms. **Pays 20¢/word.**

Fiction: Adventure, historical, humorous, novel excerpts, slice-of-life vignettes, western. No fiction that doesn't pertain to elk or elk hunting. **Buys 4 mss/year.** Query with or without published clips or send complete ms. Length: 1,500-4,500 words. **Pays 20¢/word.**

Poetry: Free verse. **Buys 6 poems/year.** Submit maximum 6 poems.

Tips: "Creative queries (250-500 words) that showcase your concept and your style remain the most effective approach. We're hungry for submissions for 3 specific columns: Situation Ethics, Thoughts & Theories, and Women in the Outdoors. Send a SASE for guidelines. We also welcome strong, well-reasoned opinion pieces on topics pertinent to hunting and wildlife conservation, and humorous pieces about elk behavior or encounters with elk (hunting or otherwise). We'd also like to see more humor; more natural history pertaining to elk and elk country; more good, thoughtful writing from women."

$ $ ☐ CALIFORNIA GAME & FISH, *Game & Fish*, Box 741, Marietta GA 30061. **Contact:** Burt Carey, editor. See *Game & Fish*.

$ $ ☐ DEER & DEER HUNTING, Krause Publications, 700 E. State St., Iola WI 54990-0001. Fax: (715)445-4087. **Contact:** Dan Schmidt, editor. **95% freelance written.** Magazine published 9 times/year covering white-tailed deer and deer hunting. "Readers include a cross section of the deer hunting population—individuals who hunt with bow, gun, or camera. The editorial content of the magazine focuses on white-tailed deer biology and behavior, management principle and practices, habitat requirements, natural history of deer, hunting techniques, and hunting ethics. We also publish a wide range of 'how-to' articles designed to help hunters locate and get close to deer at all times of the year. The majority of our readership consists of 2-season hunters (bow and gun) and approximately one-third camera hunt." Estab. 1977. Circ. 140,000. **Pays on acceptance.** Byline given. Editorial lead time 6 months. Submit seasonal material 6 months in advance. Accepts queries by mail. Responds in 3 months to queries. Sample copy for 9×12 SASE. Writer's guidelines free.

Nonfiction: General interest, historical/nostalgic, how-to, inspirational, photo feature. No "Joe and me" articles. **Buys 30-50 mss/year.** Query. Length: 750-3,000 words. **Pays $150-525 for assigned articles; $150-325 for unsolicited articles.** Sometimes pays expenses of writers on assignment.

Photos: Send photos with submission. Reviews transparencies. Negotiates payment individually. Captions, identification of subjects, model releases required.

Fiction: "Mood" deer hunting pieces. **Buys 9 mss/year.** Send complete ms.

Fillers: Facts, newsbreaks. **Buys 40-50/year.** Length: 100-500 words. **Pays $15-150.**

Tips: "Feature articles dealing with deer biology or behavior should be documented by scientific research (the author's or that of others) as opposed to a limited number of personal observations."

$ $ $ $ FIELD & STREAM, 2 Park Ave., New York NY 10016-5695. Editor: Slaton White. **Contact:** David E. Petzal, managing editor. **50% freelance written.** Monthly magazine. "Broad-based service magazine for the hunter and fisherman. Editorial content consists of articles of penetrating depth about national hunting, fishing, and related activities. Also humor and personal essays, nostalgia, and 'mood pieces' on the hunting or fishing experience and profiles on outdoor people." Estab. 1895. Circ. 1,790,400. **Pays on acceptance.** Byline given. Buys first rights. Accepts queries by mail. Responds in 2 weeks to queries. Sample copy not available. Writer's guidelines for #10 SASE.

Nonfiction: Length: 1,500 words for features. Payment varies depending on the quality of work, importance of the article. **Pays $800 and up to $1,000 and more on a sliding scale for major features. Query by mail only.**

Photos: Send photos with submission. Reviews slides (prefers color). Buys first rights. When purchased separately, pays $450 minimum for color.

Fillers: Buys short pieces for the "Up Front" section that run the gamut from natural history to conservation news, anecdotal humor, short tips, and carefully crafted opinion pieces (word length: 25-400).

☐ Online version of magazine carries original content not contained in the print edition. Contact: Elizabeth Burnham.

Tips: "Writers are encouraged to submit queries on article ideas. These should be no more than a paragraph or 2, and should include a summary of the idea, including the angle you will hang the story on, and a sense of what makes this piece different from all others on the same or a similar subject. Many queries are turned down because we have no idea what the writer is getting at. Be sure that your letter is absolutely clear. We've found that if you can't sum up the point of the article in a sentence or 2, the article doesn't have a point. Pieces that depend on writing style, such as humor, mood, and nostalgia or essays often can't be queried and may be submitted in manuscript form. The same is true of short tips. All submissions to *Field & Stream* are on an on-spec basis. Before submitting anything, however, we encourage you to *study*, not simply read, the magazine. Many pieces are rejected because they do not fit the tone or style of the magazine, or fail to match the subject of the article with the overall subject matter of *Field & Stream*. Above all, study the magazine before submitting anything."

$ $ THE FISHERMAN, LIF Publishing Corp., 14 Ramsey Rd., Shirley NY 11967-4704. (631)345-5200. Fax: (631)345-5304. E-mail: melfish@aol.com. Publisher: Fred Golofaro. Associate Publisher: Pete Barrett. **Contact:** Tom Melton, managing editor. **75% freelance written.** Weekly magazine covering fishing with an emphasis on saltwater. Circ. 110,000. Pays on publication. Byline given. Offers variable kill fee. Submit seasonal material 2 months in advance. Accepts queries by mail, e-mail. Responds in 6 weeks to queries. Sample copy and writer's guidelines free.
Nonfiction: General interest, historical/nostalgic, how-to, interview/profile, personal experience, photo feature, technical, travel. Special issues: Boat & Motor Buyer's Guide and Winter Workbench (January); Inshore Fishing (April); Saltwater Fly, Party Boat, Black Bass (May); Offshore Fishing (June); Surf Fishing (August); Striped Bass (October). "No 'Me and Joe' tales. We stress how, when, where, and why." **Buys 300 mss/year.** Length: 1,000-1,500 words. **Pays $110-150.**
Photos: Send photos with submission. Offers no additional payment for photos accepted with ms, but offers $50-100 for single color cover photos. Identification of subjects required.
Tips: "Focus on specific how-to and where-to subjects within each region."

$ FISHING & HUNTING NEWS, Outdoor Empire Publishing, 424 N. 130th St., Seattle WA 98133. (206)624-3845. Fax: (206)695-8512. E-mail: staff@fishingandhuntingnews.com. Website: www.fhnews.com/. **Contact:** John Marsh, managing editor. **5% freelance written.** Bimonthly magazine covering fishing and hunting. "We focus on upcoming fishing and hunting opportunities in your area—where to go and what to do once you get there." Estab. 1954. Circ. 112,500. Pays on publication. Publishes ms an average of 1 month after acceptance. Byline given. Buys first North American serial, second serial (reprint) rights, reprint rights for Outdoor Empire Publishing. Editorial lead time 1 month. Submit seasonal material 2 months in advance. Accepts queries by mail, e-mail. Sample copy and writer's guidelines free.
Nonfiction: How-to (local fishing and hunting), where-to. **Buys 30 mss/year.** Query with published clips. Length: 1,500-2,000 words. **Pays $125 and up.** Seldom pays expenses of writers on assignment.
Photos: State availability with submission. Buys all rights. Captions required.
Tips: "*F&H News* is published in 8 local editions across the western U.S., Great Lakes, and mid-Atlantic states. We are looking for technique- or strategy-related articles that can be used by anglers and hunters in these areas."

$ $ FLORIDA GAME & FISH, *Game & Fish*, Box 741, Marietta GA 30061. (770)953-9222. **Contact:** Jimmy Jacobs, editor. See *Game & Fish*.

N $ FLORIDA WILDLIFE, Florida Game & Fresh Water Fish Commission, 620 S. Meridian St., Tallahassee FL 32399-1600. (850)488-5563. Fax: (850)488-8974. E-mail: dick.sublette@fwc.state.fl.us. Website: www.floridaconservation.org. **Contact:** Dick Sublette, editor. **50% freelance written.** Bimonthly magazine covering hunting, natural history, fishing, endangered species, and wildlife conservation. "In outdoor sporting articles we seek themes of wholesome recreation. In nature articles we seek accuracy and conservation purpose." Estab. 1947. Circ. 20,000. Pays on publication. Byline given. Buys first North American serial, second serial (reprint) rights. Published stories may appear on website for up to 4 months. Submit seasonal material 6 months in advance. Accepts simultaneous submissions. Responds in 2 months to queries. Sample copy for $3.50. Writer's guidelines for #10 SASE.
Nonfiction: "We buy general interest hunting, fishing, and nature stories. No stories that humanize animals, or opinionated stories not based on confirmable facts." General interest (bird watching, hiking, camping, boating), how-to (hunting and fishing), humor (wildlife related; no anthropomorphism), inspirational, personal experience (wildlife, hunting, fishing, outdoors), photo feature (Florida species: game, nongame, botany), technical (rarely purchased, but open to experts), nature appreciation, and outdoor ethics. Special issues: Annual Florida Fishing edition (March/April); Hunting season (September/October and November/December). **Buys 40-50 mss/year.** Send complete ms; double space text or submit on Word disc. Length: 500-1,500 words. **Generally pays, $55/published page, plus per photo disbursement.**
Photos: State availability with submission. Reviews transparencies. Buys one-time rights. Pays $35-80/inside photos, $150/front cover photos, $100/back cover. Captions required.
Fiction: "We rarely buy fiction, and then only if it is true to life and directly related to good sportsmanship and conservation. No fairy tales, erotica, profanity, or obscenity." **Buys 1-2 mss/year.** Send complete ms. Length: 500-1,200 words. **Generally pays $55/published page.**
Tips: "Read and study recent issues for subject matter, style, and examples of our viewpoint, philosophy and treatment. We look for wholesome recreation, ethics, safety, and good outdoor experience more than bagging the game in our stories. We usually need well-written hunting, saltwater, and freshwater fishing articles that are entertaining and informative, and that describe places to hunt and fish in Florida. We do not publish articles that feature a commercial interest or a specific brand name product. Use the active rather than the passive voice. Our readership varies from schoolchildren to senior citizens, and a large number of subscribers reside in urban areas and in all 50 states."

$ $ FLY FISHING IN SALT WATERS, World Publications, Inc., 460 N. Orlando Ave., Suite 200, Winter Park FL 32789-7061. (407)628-4802. Fax: (407)628-7061. E-mail: editor@flyfishinsalt.com. Website: www.flyfishinsalt.c

om. **Contact:** David Ritchie, editor. **90% freelance written.** Bimonthly magazine covering fly fishing in salt waters anywhere in the world. Estab. 1994. Circ. 44,000. Pays on publication. Publishes ms an average of 1 year after acceptance. Byline given. Buys first North American serial, electronic rights. Editorial lead time 3 months. Submit seasonal material 2 months in advance. Accepts queries by mail, e-mail. Responds in 1 month to queries; 2 months to mss. Sample copy for $3, plus $1 S&H. Writer's guidelines for #10 SASE.

O━ Break in with "well written original material that is oriented toward teaching a new idea, concept, location, technique, etc."

Nonfiction: Book excerpts, essays, historical/nostalgic, how-to, interview/profile, new product, personal experience, photo feature, technical, travel, resource issues (conservation). **Buys 40-50 mss/year.** Query with or without published clips. Length: 1,500-2,500 words. **Pays $400-500.**

Photos: Send photos with submission. Reviews 35mm color transparencies. Buys one-time rights. Offers no additional payment for photos accepted with ms; pays $80-300/photo if purchased separately. Captions, identification of subjects required.

Columns/Departments: Legends/Reminiscences (history-profiles-nostalgia), 2,000-2,500 words; Resource (conservation issues), 1,000-1,500 words; Fly Tier's Bench (how to tie saltwater flies), 1,000-1,500 words, photos or illustrations critical; Boating (technical how-to), 2,000-2,500 words; Saltwater 101 (for beginners, tackle tips and techniques), 1,000-2,000 words. **Buys 25-30 mss/year.** Query. **Pays $400-500.**

Fiction: Adventure, humorous, mainstream, all dealing with fly fishing. **Buys 2-3 mss/year.** Send complete ms. Length: 2,000-3,000 words. **Pays $500.**

Fillers: Most fillers are staff written.

▣ The online magazine carries content not found in the print edition. Contact: David Ritchie, online editor.

Tips: "Follow up on your inquiry with a phone call."

$ $ FLYFISHING & TYING JOURNAL, A Compendium for the Complete Fly Fisher, Frank Amato Publications, 4040 SE Wister, Portland OR 97222. (503)653-8108. Fax: (503)653-2766. E-mail: kim@amatobooks.com. Website: www.amatobooks.com. **Contact:** Kim Koch, editor. **70% freelance written.** Quarterly magazine covering flyfishing and fly tying for both new and veteran anglers. Every issue is seasonally focused: Spring, summer, fall and winter. Estab. 1980. Circ. 60,000. Pays on publication. Byline given. Buys first rights. Editorial lead time up to 1 year. Submit seasonal material up to 1 year in advance. Accepts queries by mail. Responds in 1 month to queries; 2 months to mss. Writer's guidelines for #10 SASE. Attn: Kim Koch.

Nonfiction: How-to, personal experience. **Buys 55-60 mss/year.** Query. Length: 1,000-2,000 words. **Pays $200-600.**

Photos: State availability with submission. Reviews transparencies. Buys one-time rights. Offers no additional payment for photos accepted with ms. Captions, identification of subjects, model releases required.

$ FUR-FISH-GAME, 2878 E. Main, Columbus OH 43209-9947. **Contact:** Mitch Cox, editor. **65% freelance written.** Monthly magazine for outdoorsmen of all ages who are interested in hunting, fishing, trapping, dogs, camping, conservation, and related topics. Estab. 1900. Circ. 111,000. **Pays on acceptance.** Publishes ms an average of 7 months after acceptance. Byline given. Buys first, all rights. Responds in 2 months to queries. Sample copy for $1 and 9×12 SAE. Writer's guidelines for #10 SASE.

Nonfiction: "We are looking for informative, down-to-earth stories about hunting, fishing, trapping, dogs, camping, boating, conservation, and related subjects. Nostalgic articles are also used. Many of our stories are 'how-to' and should appeal to small-town and rural readers who are true outdoorsmen. Some recents articles have told how to train a gun dog, catch big-water catfish, outfit a bowhunter, and trap late-season muskrat. We also use personal experience stories and an occasional profile, such as an article about an old-time trapper. 'Where-to' stories are used occasionally if they have broad appeal." Query. Length: 500-3,000 words. **Pays $50-150 or more for features depending upon quality, photo support, and importance to magazine.**

Photos: Send photos with submission. Reviews transparencies, color prints (5×7 or 8×10). Pays $25 for separate freelance photos. Captions, credits required.

Tips: "We are always looking for quality how-to articles about fish, game animals, or birds that are popular with everyday outdoorsmen but often overlooked in other publications, such as catfish, bluegill, crappie, squirrel, rabbit, crows, etc. We also use articles on standard seasonal subjects such as deer and pheasant, but like to see a fresh approach or new technique. Instructional trapping articles are useful all year. Articles on gun dogs, ginseng, and do-it-yourself projects are also popular with our readers. An assortment of photos and/or sketches greatly enhances any manuscript, and sidebars, where applicable, can also help. No phone queries, please."

$ $ ✪ GAME & FISH, 2250 Newmarket Pkwy., Suite 110, Marietta GA 30067. (770)953-9222. Fax: (770)933-9510. Website: GameandFish.About.com. **Contact:** Ken Dunwoody, editorial director. **90% freelance written.** Publishes 30 different monthly outdoor magazines, each one covering the fishing and hunting opportunities in a particular state or region (see individual titles and editors). Estab. 1975. Circ. 575,000. Pays 60 days prior to cover date of issue. Publishes ms an average of 7 months after acceptance. Byline given. Offers negotiable kill fee. Buys first North American serial rights. Submit seasonal material 8 months in advance. Accepts queries by mail, fax. Responds in 3 months to queries. Sample copy for $3.50 and 9×12 SASE. Writer's guidelines for #10 SASE.

Nonfiction: Prefers queries over unsolicited mss. Length: 1,500-2,400 words. **Pays $125-300; additional payment made for electronic rights.**

Photos: Reviews transparencies, B&W prints. Buys one-time rights. Cover photos $250, inside color $75, and b&w $25. Captions, identification of subjects required.

Fiction: Humorous, nostalgia pertaining to hunting and fishing. Length: 1,100-2,500 words. **Pays $125-250; additional payment made for electronic rights.**

Online magazine occasionally carries original content not found in the print edition. Contact: Dave Schaefer.

Tips: "Our readers are experienced anglers and hunters, and we try to provide them with useful, specific articles about where, when, and how to enjoy the best hunting and fishing in their state or region. We also cover topics concerning game and fish management. Most articles should be tightly focused and aimed at outdoorsmen in 1 particular state. After familiarizing themselves with our magazine(s), writers should query the appropriate state editor (see individual listings) or send to Ken Dunwoody."

$ $ GEORGIA SPORTSMAN, *Game & Fish*, Box 741, Marietta GA 30061. (770)953-9222. **Contact:** Jimmy Jacobs, editor. See *Game & Fish*.

$ $ GREAT PLAINS GAME & FISH, *Game & Fish*, Box 741, Marietta GA 30061. (770)953-9222. **Contact:** Nick Gilmore, editor. See *Game & Fish*.

$ $ ILLINOIS GAME & FISH, *Game & Fish*, Box 741, Marietta GA 30061. (770)953-9222. **Contact:** Dennis Schmidt, editor. See *Game & Fish*.

$ $ INDIANA GAME & FISH, *Game & Fish*, Box 741, Marietta GA 30061. (770)953-9222. **Contact:** Ken Freel, editor. See *Game & Fish*.

$ $ IOWA GAME & FISH, *Game & Fish*, Box 741, Marietta GA 30061. (770)953-9222. **Contact:** Nick Gilmore, editor. See *Game & Fish*.

$ $ KENTUCKY GAME & FISH, *Game & Fish*, Box 741, Marietta GA 30061. (770)953-9222. **Contact:** Ken Freel, editor. See *Game & Fish*.

$ $ LOUISIANA GAME & FISH, *Game & Fish*, Box 741, Marietta GA 30061. (770)953-9222. Fax: (770)933-9510. E-mail: ken_duke@primediamags.com. Website: LAgameandfish.com. **Contact:** Ken Duke, editor. See listing for *Game & Fish*. Accepts queries by e-mail.

$ $ MARLIN, The International Sportfishing Magazine, Marlin Magazine, a division of World Publications, LLC., P.O. Box 8500, Winter Park FL 32790. (407)628-4802. Fax: (407)628-7061. E-mail: editor@marlinmag.com. Website: www.marlinmag.com. **Contact:** David Ritchie, editor. **90% freelance written.** Bimonthly magazine. "*Marlin* covers the sport of big game fishing (billfish, tuna, dorado and wahoo). Our readers are sophisticated, affluent, and serious about their sport—they expect a high-class, well-written magazine that provides information and practical advice." Estab. 1982. Circ. 50,000. **Pays on acceptance.** Publishes ms an average of 3 months after acceptance. Byline given. Buys first North American serial rights. Submit seasonal material 3 months in advance. Accepts previously published material. Sample copy and writer's guidelines free with SASE.

Nonfiction: General interest, how-to (bait-rigging, tackle maintenance, etc.), new product, personal experience, photo feature, technical, travel. "No freshwater fishing stories. No 'Me & Joe went fishing' stories." **Buys 30-50 mss/year.** Query with published clips. Length: 800-3,000 words. **Pays $250-500.**

Reprints: Send photocopy and information about when and where the material previously appeared. Pays 50-75% of amount paid for original article.

Photos: State availability with submission. Reviews original slides. Buys one-time rights. Offers $50-300 for inside use, $1,000 for a cover.

Columns/Departments: Tournament Reports (reports on winners of major big game fishing tournaments), 200-400 words; Blue Water Currents (news features), 100-400 words. **Buys 25 mss/year.** Query. **Pays $75-250.**

Tips: "Tournament reports are a good way to break in to *Marlin*. Make them short but accurate, and provide photos of fishing action or winners' award shots (*not* dead fish hanging up at the docks). We always need how-tos and news items. Our destination pieces (travel stories) emphasize where and when to fish, but include information on where to stay also. For features: Crisp, high action stories with emphasis on exotic nature, adventure, personality, etc.—nothing flowery or academic. Technical/how-to: Concise and informational—specific details. News: Again, concise with good details—watch for legislation affecting big game fishing, outstanding catches, new clubs and organizations, new trends and conservation issues."

$ MICHIGAN OUT-OF-DOORS, P.O. Box 30235, Lansing MI 48909. (517)371-1041. Fax: (517)371-1505. E-mail: dknick@mucc.org. Website: www.mucc.org. **Contact:** Dennis C. Knickerbocker, editor. **75% freelance written.** Monthly magazine emphasizing Michigan outdoor recreation, especially hunting and fishing, conservation, nature, and environmental affairs. Estab. 1947. Circ. 100,000. **Pays on acceptance.** Publishes ms an average of 6 months after acceptance. Byline given. Buys first North American serial rights. Submit seasonal material 6 months in advance. Accepts queries by mail, phone. Responds in 1 month to queries. Sample copy for $3.50. Writer's guidelines for free or on website.

Break in by "writing interestingly about an *unusual* aspect of Michigan natural resources and/or outdoor recreation.

Nonfiction: "Stories must have a Michigan slant unless they treat a subject of universal interest to our readers." Exposé, historical/nostalgic, how-to, interview/profile, opinion, personal experience, photo feature. Special issues: Archery Deer

Hunting (October); Firearm Deer Hunting (November); Cross-country Skiing and Early-ice Lake Fishing (December or January). No humor or poetry. **Buys 96 mss/year.** Send complete ms. Length: 1,000-2,000 words. **Pays $90 minimum for feature stories.**

Photos: Buys one-time rights. Offers no additional payment for photos accepted with ms; others $20-175. Captions required.

Tips: "Top priority is placed on true accounts of personal adventures in the out-of-doors—well-written tales of very unusual incidents encountered while hunting, fishing, camping, hiking, etc."

$ $ MICHIGAN SPORTSMAN, *Game & Fish*, Box 741, Marietta GA 30061. (770)953-9222. **Contact:** Dennis Schmidt, editor. See *Game & Fish*.

$ MID WEST OUTDOORS, Mid West Outdoors, Ltd., 111 Shore Dr., Burr Ridge IL 60527-5885. (630)887-7722. Fax: (630)887-1958. E-mail: glaulunen@midwestoutdoors.com. Website: www.MidWestOutdoors.com. **Contact:** Gene Laulunen, editor. **100% freelance written.** Monthly tabloid emphasizing fishing, hunting, camping, and boating. Estab. 1967. Circ. 45,000. Pays on publication. Publishes ms an average of 3 months after acceptance. Byline given. Buys simultaneous rights. Submit seasonal material 2 months in advance. Accepts previously published material. Accepts simultaneous submissions. Responds in 3 weeks to queries. Sample copy for $1 or online. Writer's guidelines for #10 SASE or online.

- Submissions may be e-mailed to info@midwestoutdoors.com (Microsoft Word format preferred).

Nonfiction: How-to (fishing, hunting, camping in the Midwest), where-to-go (fishing, hunting, camping within 500 miles of Chicago). "We do not want to see any articles on 'my first fishing, hunting or camping experiences,' 'cleaning my tackle box,' 'tackle tune-up,' 'making fishing fun for kids,' or 'catch and release.'" **Buys 1,800 unsolicited mss/year.** Send complete ms. Length: 1,000-1,500 words. **Pays $15-30.**

Reprints: Send tearsheet.

Photos: Reviews slides and b&w prints. Buys all rights. Offers no additional payment for photos accompanying ms. Captions required.

Columns/Departments: Fishing; Hunting. Send complete ms. **Pays $30.**

Tips: "Break in with a great unknown fishing hole or new technique within 500 miles of Chicago. Where, how, when, and why. Know the type of publication you are sending material to."

$ $ MID-ATLANTIC GAME & FISH, *Game & Fish*, Box 741, Marietta GA 30061. (770)953-9222. **Contact:** Ken Freel, editor. See *Game & Fish*.

$ $ MINNESOTA SPORTSMAN, *Game & Fish*, Box 741, Marietta GA 30061. (770)953-9222. **Contact:** Dennis Schmidt, editor. See *Game & Fish*.

$ $ MISSISSIPPI GAME & FISH, *Game & Fish*, Box 741, Marietta GA 30061. (770)953-9222. **Contact:** Jimmy Jacobs, editor. See listing for *Game & Fish*.

Nonfiction: How-to (hunting and fishing).

$ $ MISSOURI GAME & FISH, *Game & Fish*, Box 741, Marietta GA 30061. (770)953-9222. Fax: (770)933-9510. E-mail: ken_duke@primediamags.com. Website: MissouriGameandFish.com. **Contact:** Ken Duke, editor. See listing for *Game & Fish*.

$ $ MUSKY HUNTER MAGAZINE, P.O. Box 340, St. Germain WI 54558. (715)477-2178. Fax: (715)477-8858. Editor: Jim Saric. **Contact:** Steve Heiting. **90% freelance written.** Bimonthly magazine on musky fishing. "Serves the vertical market of musky fishing enthusiasts. We're interested in how-to where-to articles." Estab. 1988. Circ. 34,000. Pays on publication. Publishes ms an average of 4 months after acceptance. Byline given. Buys first, one-time rights. Submit seasonal material 4 months in advance. Responds in 2 months to queries. Sample copy for 9×12 SAE with $1.93 postage. Writer's guidelines for #10 SASE.

Nonfiction: Historical/nostalgic (related only to musky fishing), how-to (modify lures, boats, and tackle for musky fishing), personal experience (must be musky fishing experience), technical (fishing equipment), travel (to lakes and areas for musky fishing). **Buys 50 mss/year.** Send complete ms. Length: 1,000-2,500 words. **Pays $100-300 for assigned articles; $50-300 for unsolicited articles.** Payment of contributor copies or other premiums negotiable.

Photos: Send photos with submission. Reviews 35mm transparencies, 3×5 prints. Buys one-time rights. Offers no additional payment for photos accepted with ms. Identification of subjects required.

$ $ NEW ENGLAND GAME & FISH, *Game & Fish*, Box 741, Marietta GA 30061. (770)953-9222. **Contact:** Steve Carpenteri, editor. See *Game & Fish*.

$ $ NEW YORK GAME & FISH, Game & Fish, Box 741, Marietta GA 30061. (770)953-9222. **Contact:** Steve Carpenteri, editor. See *Game & Fish*.

$ $ NORTH AMERICAN WHITETAIL, The Magazine Devoted to the Serious Trophy Deer Hunter, *Game & Fish*, 2250 Newmarket Pkwy., Suite 110, Marietta GA 30067. (770)953-9222. Fax: (770)933-9510. **Contact:** Gordon Whittington, editor. **70% freelance written.** Magazine published 8 times/year about hunting trophy-class white-tailed deer in North America, primarily the US. "We provide the serious hunter with highly sophisticated information about trophy-class whitetails and how, when, and where to hunt them. We are not a general hunting magazine or a magazine for the very occasional deer hunter." Estab. 1982. Circ. 130,000. Pays 65 days prior to cover date of issue.

Publishes ms an average of 6 months after acceptance. Byline given. Offers negotiable kill fee. Buys first North American serial rights. Submit seasonal material 10 months in advance. Accepts queries by mail, fax, phone. Responds in 3 months to mss. Sample copy for $3.50 and 9×12 SAE with 7 first-class stamps. Writer's guidelines for #10 SASE.
Nonfiction: How-to, interview/profile. **Buys 50 mss/year.** Query. Length: 1,000-3,000 words. **Pays $150-400.**
Photos: Send photos with submission. Reviews 35mm transparencies, 8×10 prints. Buys one-time rights. Offers no additional payment for photos accepted with ms. Captions, identification of subjects required.
Columns/Departments: Trails and Tails (nostalgic, humorous, or other entertaining styles of deer-hunting material, fictional or nonfictional), 1,200 words. **Buys 8 mss/year.** Send complete ms. **Pays $150.**
Tips: "Our articles are written by persons who are deer hunters first, writers second. Our hard-core hunting audience can see through material produced by nonhunters or those with only marginal deer-hunting expertise. We have a continual need for expert profiles/interviews. Study the magazine to see what type of hunting expert it takes to qualify for our use, and look at how those articles have been directed by the writers. Good photography of the interviewee and his hunting results must accompany such pieces."

$ $ NORTH CAROLINA GAME & FISH, *Game & Fish*, Box 741, Marietta GA 30061. (770)953-9222. Fax: (770)933-9510. **Contact:** David Johnson, editor. See *Game & Fish*.

$ $ OHIO GAME & FISH, *Game & Fish*, Box 741, Marietta GA 30061. (770)953-9222. **Contact:** Steve Carpenteri, editor. See *Game & Fish*.

$ $ OKLAHOMA GAME & FISH, *Game & Fish*, Box 741, Marietta GA 30061. (770)953-9222. Fax: (770)933-9510. **Contact:** Nick Gilmore, editor. See *Game & Fish*.

$ $ ONTARIO OUT OF DOORS, Roger's Media, 777 Bay St., 28th Floor, Toronto, Ontario M5W 1A7, Canada. (416)596-5815. Fax: (416)596-2517. E-mail: jkerr@rmpublishing.com. Website: www.fishontario.com. Editor: Burt Myers. **Contact:** John Kerr, managing editor. **90% freelance written.** Magazine published 10 times/year covering the outdoors (hunting, fishing, camping). Estab. 1968. Circ. 93,865. **Pays on acceptance.** Publishes ms an average of 6 months after acceptance. Byline given. Buys first, electronic rights. Editorial lead time 6 months. Submit seasonal material 6 months in advance. Accepts queries by mail, e-mail, fax. Responds in 3 months to queries. Sample copy and writer's guidelines free.
Nonfiction: Book excerpts, essays, exposé, how-to (fishing and hunting), humor, inspirational, interview/profile, new product, opinion, personal experience, photo feature, technical, travel (where-to), wildlife management; environmental concerns. "No 'Me and Joe' features or articles written from a woman's point of view on how to catch a bass." **Buys 100 mss/year.** Length: 500-2,500 words. **Pays $750 maximum for assigned articles; $700 maximum for unsolicited articles.** Sometimes pays expenses of writers on assignment.
Photos: Send photos with submission. Reviews transparencies. Buys one-time and electronic rights. Pays $450-750 for covers. Captions required.
Columns/Departments: Trips & Tips (travel pieces), 50-150 words; Short News, 50-500 words. **Buys 30-40 mss/year.** Query. **Pays $50-250.**
Fiction: Humorous, novel excerpts. **Buys 6 mss/year.** Send complete ms. Length: 1,000 words. **Pays $500 maximum.**
Fillers: Facts, newsbreaks. **Buys 40/year.** Length: 25-100 words. **Pays $15-50.**
Tips: "With the exception of short news stories, it is suggested that writers query prior to submission."

$ $ $ $ OUTDOOR LIFE, The Sportsman's Authority Since 1898, Time 4 Media, Inc., 2 Park Ave., New York NY 10016. (212)779-5000. Fax: (212)779-5366. E-mail: olmagazine@aol.com. Website: www.outdoorlife.com. Editor: Todd W. Smith. Managing Editor: Camille Cozzone Rankin. **Contact:** Colin Moore, executive editor. **60% freelance written.** Magazine published 9 times/year covering hunting and fishing in North America. "*Outdoor Life* is a major national source of information for American and Canadian hunters and anglers. It offers news, regional reports, adventure stories, how-to, regular advice from experts, profiles, and equipment tests." Estab. 1898. Circ. 1,350,000. **Pays on acceptance.** Publishes ms an average of 6 months after acceptance. Byline given. Buys first North American serial, electronic rights. Editorial lead time 4 months. Submit seasonal material 5 months in advance. Accepts queries by mail, e-mail, fax. Responds in 1 month to queries; 2 months to mss. Sample copy for 9×12 SAE, plus proper postage. Writer's guidelines for #10 SASE.
Nonfiction: All articles must pertain to hunting and fishing pursuits. How-to, personal experience, interesting/wild news stories, adventure stories. Query with published clips. Length: 100-2,000 words. **Pays $500-3,000.**
Photos: Do not send photos until requested.
Columns/Departments: Frank Minter, senior associate editor (gear); Colin Moore, executive editor (hunting/fishing, bonus sections). Regionals, 150-300 words; Snap Shots, 150 words; Private Lessons, 500-700 words. **Buys 200 mss/year.** Query with published clips. **Pays $75-500.**
Fillers: John Snow, articles editor for Snap Shots section. Facts, newsbreaks. **Buys 40-50/year.** Length: 150 words. **Pays $75.**
Tips: "If someone catches a record fish or takes a record game animal, or has a great adventure/survival story, they may try to submit a full-length feature, but the story must be exceptional."

$ THE OUTDOORS MAGAZINE, For the Better Hunter, Angler & Trapper, Elk Publishing, Inc., 181 S. Union St., Burlington VT 05401. (802)860-0003. Fax: (802)860-0003. E-mail: OutdoorMagazine@aol.com. Website: www.outdoorsmagazine.net. **Contact:** James Ehlers, editor. **80% freelance written.** Monthly magazine covering wildlife conservation. "New England hunting, fishing, and trapping magazine with a focus on environmental and conservation issues." Estab. 1996. Circ. 9,500. Pays on publication. Publishes ms an average of 1 year after acceptance. Byline given. Offers 10% kill fee. Buys first North American serial rights. Editorial lead time 1 year. Submit seasonal material 6 months in advance. Accepts queries by mail. Accepts previously published material. Responds in 1 month to queries; 3 month to mss. Sample copy online or by e-mail. Writer's guidelines free.

Nonfiction: Book excerpts, essays, exposé, general interest, historical/nostalgic, how-to, interview/profile, new product, opinion, personal experience, technical. **Buys 200 mss/year.** Query with published clips. Length: 750-2,500 words. **Pays $20-150 for assigned articles.**

Photos: State availability with submission. Reviews contact sheets. Buys one-time rights. Pays $15-75/photo. Identification of subjects required.

Columns/Departments: Buys 100 mss/year. Query with published clips. **Pays $20-60.**

Fillers: Anecdotes, facts.

Tips: "*Know* the publication, not just read it, so you understand the audience. Patience and thoroughness will go a long way."

$ $ PENNSYLVANIA ANGLER & BOATER, Pennsylvania Fish and Boat Commission, P.O. Box 67000, Harrisburg PA 17106-7000. (717)705-7844. E-mail: amichaels@state.pa.us. Website: www.fish.state.pa.us. **Contact:** Art Michaels, editor. **80% freelance written.** Bimonthly magazine covering fishing, boating, and related conservation topics in Pennsylvannia. Circ. 30,000. Pays 2 months after acceptance. Publishes ms an average of 8 months after acceptance. Byline given. Buys varying rights. Submit seasonal material 8 months in advance. Responds in 1 month to queries; 2 months to mss. Sample copy for 9×12 SAE with 9 first-class stamps. Writer's guidelines for #10 SASE.

Nonfiction: How-to (and where-to), technical. No saltwater or hunting material. **Buys 100 mss/year.** Query. Length: 500-2,500 words. **Pays $25-300.**

Photos: Send photos with submission. Reviews 35mm and larger transparencies. Rights purchased vary. Offers no additional payment for photos accompanying mss. Captions, identification of subjects, model releases required.

$ $ PENNSYLVANIA GAME & FISH, *Game & Fish*, Box 741, Marietta GA 30061. (770)953-9222. **Contact:** Steve Carpenteri, editor. See *Game & Fish*.

$ $ PETERSEN'S HUNTING, 6420 Wilshire Blvd., Los Angeles CA 90048. (323)782-2173. Fax: (323)782-2477. **Contact:** J. Scott Rupp, editor. **10% freelance written.** Magazine published 10 times/year covering sport hunting. "We are a 'how-to' magazine devoted to all facets of sport hunting, with the intent to make our readers more knowledgeable, more successful and safer hunters." Circ. 350,000. Pays on scheduling. Publishes ms an average of 9 months after acceptance. Byline given. Buys all rights. Responds in 1 month to queries. Writer's guidelines on request.

Nonfiction: General interest, how-to (on hunting techniques), travel. **Buys 15 mss/year.** Query. Length: 2,400 words. **Pays $350 minimum.**

Photos: Send photos with submission. Reviews 35mm transparencies. Buys one-time rights. Captions, identification of subjects, model releases required.

$ $ RACK MAGAZINE, Adventures in Trophy Hunting, Buckmasters Ltd., P.O. Box 244022, Montgomery AL 36124-4022. (800)240-3337. Fax: (334)215-3535. E-mail: mhandley@buckmasters.com. Website: www.rackmag.com. **Contact:** Mike Handley, editor. **10-15% freelance written.** Hunting magazine published monthly (August-January). "*Rack Magazine* caters to deer hunters and chasers of other big game animals who prefer short stories detailing the harvests of exceptional specimens. There are no how-to, destination, or human interest stories; only pieces describing particular hunts." Estab. 1999. Circ. 125,000. Pays on publication. Publishes ms an average of 11 months after acceptance. Byline given. Buys first North American serial, second serial (reprint) rights. Editorial lead time 9 months. Accepts queries by e-mail, phone. Accepts previously published material. Accepts simultaneous submissions. Responds in 1 month to queries. Sample copy for free. Writer's guidelines by e-mail.

Nonfiction: Interview/profile, personal experience. *Rack Magazine* does not use how-to, destination, humor, general interest, or hunter profiles. **Buys 35-40 mss/year.** Query. Length: 500-1,500 words. **Pays $250.**

Reprints: Accepts previously published submissions.

Photos: Send photos with submission. Reviews transparencies. Captions, identification of subjects required.

Tips: "We're only interested in stories about record book animals (those scoring high enough to qualify for BTR, B&C, P&Y, SCI, or Longhunter). Whitetails must be scored by a certified BTR/Buckmasters measurer and their antlers must register at least 160-inches on the BTR system. Deer scoring 190 or better on the B&C or P&Y scales would be candidates, but the hunter would have to have his or her buck scored by a BTR measurer."

$ $ ROCKY MOUNTAIN GAME & FISH, Game & Fish, Box 741, Marietta GA 30061. Fax: (770)933-9510. **Contact:** Burt Carey, editor. See *Game & Fish*.

$ $ SAFARI MAGAZINE, The Journal of Big Game Hunting, Safari Club International, 4800 W. Gates Pass Rd., Tucson AZ 85745. (520)620-1220. Fax: (520)618-3555. E-mail: sskinner@safariclub.org. Website: www.safariclub.org. Director of Publications/Editor: Steve Comus. **Contact:** Stan Skinner, managing editor. **90% freelance written.** Bimonthly journal covering international big game hunting and wildlife conservation. Circ. 40,000. Pays on publication. Publishes ms an average of 18 months after acceptance. Byline given. Buys first, all rights. Submit seasonal material 1 year in advance. Accepts queries by mail, e-mail. Responds in 2 weeks to queries; 6 weeks to mss. Sample copy for $4. Writer's guidelines for #10 SASE.

O━ Break in with "engaging, suspenseful, first-person stories of big-game hunts that involve unique circumstances or unusual regions and animals. Conservation stories should include reputable, known sources in the field, plenty of facts, and be supported by scientific data."

Nonfiction: Photo feature (wildlife), travel (firearms, hunting techniques, etc.). **Buys 72 mss/year.** Query with or without published clips or send complete ms. Length: 2,000 words. **Pays $300 for professional writers, less if not professional.**

Photos: State availability of or send photos with submission. Buys first rights. Payment depends on size in magazine. Pays up to $45 for b&w; $100 color. Captions, identification of subjects, model releases required.

Tips: "Study the magazine. Send complete manuscript and photo package. Make it appeal to knowledgeable, world-traveled big game hunters. Features on conservation contributions from big game hunters around the world are open to freelancers. We have enough stories on first-time African safaris. We need North and South American, European, and Asian hunting stories, plus stories dealing with wildlife conservation, especially as it applies to our organization and members."

$ $ ✪ SALT WATER SPORTSMAN MAGAZINE, 263 Summer St., Boston MA 02210. (617)303-3660. Fax: (617)303-3661. E-mail: editor@saltwatersportsman.com. Website: www.saltwatersportsman.com. **Contact:** Barry Gibson, editor. **85% freelance written.** Monthly magazine. "*Salt Water Sportsman* is edited for serious marine sport fishermen whose lifestyle includes the pursuit of game fish in US waters and around the world. It provides information on fishing trends, techniques and destinations, both local and international. Each issue reviews offshore and inshore fishing boats, high-tech electronics, innovative tackle, engines, and other new products. Coverage also focuses on sound fisheries management and conservation." Circ. 165,000. **Pays on acceptance.** Publishes ms an average of 5 months after acceptance. Byline given. Offers 100% kill fee. Buys first North American serial rights. Submit seasonal material 8 months in advance. Accepts queries by mail, e-mail, fax. Accepts previously published material. Responds in 1 month to queries. Sample copy and writer's guidelines for #10 SASE.

Nonfiction: "Readers want solid how-to, where-to information written in an enjoyable, easy-to-read style. Personal anecdotes help the reader identify with the writer." How-to, personal experience, technical, travel (to fishing areas). **Buys 100 mss/year.** Query. Length: 1,200-2,000 words. **Pays $300-750.**

Reprints: Send tearsheet. Pays up to 50% of amount paid for original article.

Photos: Reviews color slides. Pays $1,500 minimum for 35mm, $2\frac{1}{4} \times 2\frac{1}{4}$ or 8×10 transparencies for cover. Offers additional payment for photos accepted with ms. Captions required.

Columns/Departments: Sportsman's Tips (short, how-to tips and techniques on salt water fishing, emphasis is on building, repairing, or reconditioning specific items or gear). Send complete ms.

Tips: "There are a lot of knowledgeable fishermen/budding writers out there who could be valuable to us with a little coaching. Many don't think they can write a story for us, but they'd be surprised. We work with writers. Shorter articles that get to the point which are accompanied by good, sharp photos are hard for us to turn down. Having to delete unnecessary wordage—conversation, clichés, etc.—that writers feel is mandatory is annoying. Often they don't devote enough attention to specific fishing information."

$ $ ✪ SHOTGUN SPORTS MAGAZINE, P.O. Box 6810, Auburn CA 95604. (530)889-2220. Fax: (530)889-9106. E-mail: shotgun@shotgunsportsmagazine.com. **Contact:** Linda Martin, production coordinator. **50% freelance written.** Welcomes new writers. Magazine published 11 times/year. "We cover all the shotgun sports and shotgun hunting—sporting clays, trap, skeet, hunting, gunsmithing, shotshell patterning, shotsell reloading, mental training for the shotgun sports, shotgun tests, anything 'shotgun.'" Pays on publication. Publishes ms an average of 1-6 months after acceptance. Buys all rights. Sample copy and writer's guidelines available by contacting Linda Martin, production coordinator.

• Responds within 3 weeks. Subscription: $31 (US); $38 (Canada); $66 (foreign).

Nonfiction: "Current needs: Anything with a 'shotgun' subject. Tests, think pieces, roundups, historical, interviews, etc." "No articles promoting a specific club or sponsored hunting trip, etc." Submit query or complete ms, with photos by mail with SASE. Can query by e-mail. Length: 1,000-5,000 words. **Pays $50-200.**

Photos: "5×7 or 8×10 b&w or 4-color with appropriate captions. On disk or e-mailed at least 5-inches and 300 dpi (contact Graphics Artist for details)." Reviews transparencies (35 mm or larger), b&w, or 4-color. Send photos with submission.

Tips: "Do not fax manuscript. Send good photos. Take a fresh approach. Create a professional, yet friendly article. Send diagrams, maps, and photos of unique details, if needed. For interviews, more interested in 'words of wisdom' than a list of accomplishments. Reloading articles must include source information and backup data. Check your facts and data! If you can't think of a fresh approach, don't bother. If it's not about shotguns or shotgunners, don't send it. Never say, 'You don't need to check my data; I never make mistakes.'"

$ $ ✪ SOUTH CAROLINA GAME & FISH, *Game & Fish*, Box 741, Marietta GA 30061. (770)953-9222. **Contact:** David Johnson, editor. See *Game & Fish*.

$ $ ✪ SOUTH CAROLINA WILDLIFE, P.O. Box 167, Rembert Dennis Bldg., Columbia SC 29202-0167. (803)734-3972. E-mail: scwmed@scdnr.state.sc.us. Editor: Linda Renshaw. **Contact:** Caroline Foster, managing editor. **75% freelance written.** Bimonthly magazine for South Carolinans interested in wildlife and outdoor activities. Estab. 1954. Circ. 60,000. **Pays on acceptance.** Publishes ms an average of 6 months after acceptance. Byline given. Buys first rights. Responds in 2 months to queries. Sample copy for free.

Nonfiction: "Realize that the topic must be of interest to South Carolinans and that we must be able to justify using it in a publication published by the state department of natural resources—so if it isn't directly about outdoor recreation, a certain plant or animal, it must be somehow related to the environment and conservation. Readers prefer a broad mix of outdoor related topics (articles that illustrate the beauty of South Carolina's outdoors and those that help the reader get more for his/her time, effort, and money spent in outdoor recreation). These 2 general areas are the ones we most need. Subjects vary a great deal in topic, area and style, but must all have a common ground in the outdoor resources and heritage of South Carolina. Review back issues and query with a 1-page outline citing sources, giving ideas for photographs, explaining justification, and giving an example of the first 2 paragraphs." Does not need any column material. Generally does not seek photographs. The publisher assumes no responsibility for unsolicited material. **Buys 25-30 mss/year.** Query. Length: 1,000-3,000 words. **Pays $200-400.**

Tips: "We need more writers in the outdoor field who take pride in the craft of writing and put a real effort toward originality and preciseness in their work. Query on a topic we haven't recently done. Frequent mistakes made by writers in completing an article are failure to check details and go in-depth on a subject."

$ $ $ SPORT FISHING, The Magazine of Saltwater Fishing, 460 N. Orlando Ave., Suite 200, Winter Park FL 32789-7061. (407)571-4576. Fax: (407)571-4577. E-mail: doug.olander@worldpub.net. **Contact:** Doug Olander, editor-in-chief. **50% freelance written.** Magazine covering saltwater sports fishing. Estab. 1986. Circ. 150,000. Pays within 6 weeks of acceptance. Byline given. Offers $100 kill fee. Buys first North American serial, one-time rights. Submit seasonal material 5 months in advance. Accepts queries by mail, e-mail, fax. Responds in 2 weeks to queries. Sample copy for #10 SASE. Writer's guidelines for #10 SASE or by e-mail.

O→ Break in with freelance pieces for the "Tips & Techniques News" and "Fish Tales" departments.

Nonfiction: How-to (rigging & techniques tips), technical, conservation, where-to (all on sport fishing). **Buys 32-40 mss/year.** Query. Length: 2,000-3,000 words. **Pays $500-600.**

Photos: Send photos with submission. Reviews Reviews transparencies and returns within 1 week. Buys one-time rights. Pays $75-300 inside; $1,000 cover.

Columns/Departments: Fish Tales (humorous sport fishing anecdotes); Rigging (how-to rigging for sport fishing); Technique (how-to technique for sport fishing), 800-1,200 words. **Buys 8-24 mss/year.** Send complete ms. **Pays $250.**

Tips: "Don't query unless you are familiar with the magazine; note—*salt water only.* Find a fresh idea or angle to an old idea. We welcome the chance to work with new/unestablished writers who know their stuff—and how to say it."

$ $ ✪ TENNESSEE SPORTSMAN, *Game & Fish*, Box 741, Marietta GA 30061. (770)953-9222. **Contact:** David Johnson, editor. See *Game & Fish.*

$ $ ✪ TEXAS SPORTSMAN, *Game & Fish*, Box 741, Marietta GA 30061. (770)953-9222. **Contact:** Nick Gilmore, editor. See *Game & Fish.*

$ $ TIDE MAGAZINE, Coastal Conservation Association, 6919 Portwest Dr., Suite 100, Houston TX 77024. (713)626-4222. Fax: (713)626-5852. E-mail: tide@joincca.org. **Contact:** Doug Pike, editor. Bimonthly magazine on saltwater fishing and conservation of marine resources. Estab. 1977. Circ. 60,000. Pays on publication. Byline given. Buys one-time rights. Submit seasonal material 6 months in advance. Responds in 1 month to queries.

Nonfiction: Essays, exposé, general interest, historical/nostalgic, humor, opinion, personal experience, travel, Related to saltwater fishing and Gulf/Atlantic coastal habitats. **Buys 40 mss/year.** Query with published clips. Length: 1,200-1,500 words. **Pays $250-350 for ms/photo package.**

Photos: Reviews negatives, 35mm transparencies, color prints. Buys one-time rights. Pays $50-100. Captions required.

$ $ ✪ TRAPPER & PREDATOR CALLER, Krause Publications Inc., 700 E. State St., Iola WI 54990. (715)445-2214. Fax: (715)445-4087. E-mail: waitp@krause.com. Website: www.trapperpredatorcaller.com. **Contact:** Paul Wait, editor. **90% freelance written.** Monthly tabloid covering trapping, predator calling and muzzleloading. "Our editorial goal is to entertain and educate our readers with national and regional articles that promote trapping and predator calling." Estab. 1975. Circ. 41,000. Pays on publication. Buys first North American serial rights. Submit seasonal material 6 months in advance. Sample copy and writer's guidelines free.

Nonfiction: How-to, humor, interview/profile, new product, opinion, personal experience. **Buys 100 mss/year.** Query with or without published clips or send complete ms. Length: 1,200-2,500 words. **Pays $80-250 for assigned articles; $40-200 for unsolicited articles.**

Photos: Send photos with submission. Reviews prints. Buys one-time rights. Offers no additional payment for photos accepted with ms. Captions, identification of subjects required.

The online version contains material not found in the print edition. Contact: Paul Wait.

Tips: "Detailed how-to articles receive strongest consideration."

$ $ ✪ TURKEY & TURKEY HUNTING, Krause Publications, 700 E. State St., Iola WI 54990-0001. (715)445-2214. Fax: (715)445-4087. E-mail: schlenderj@krause.com. Website: www.turkeyandturkeyhunting.com. **Contact:** Jim Schlender, editor. **90% freelance written.** Bimonthly magazine covering turkey hunting and turkey biology. "*Turkey & Turkey Hunting* is for serious, experienced turkey hunters." Estab. 1983. Circ. 45,000. **Pays on acceptance.** Publishes ms an average of 1 year after acceptance. Byline given. Offers 50% kill fee. Buys first North American serial rights. Editorial lead time 1 year. Submit seasonal material 1 year in advance. Accepts queries by mail. Sample copy and writer's guidelines free.

Nonfiction: How-to, personal experience. **Buys 45 mss/year.** Query with published clips. Length: 2,000 words. **Pays $275-300.**

Photos: Send photos with submission. Reviews transparencies. Buys one-time rights. Offers $75-300/photo, depending on size. Pays on publication for photos.

Tips: "Have a thorough knowledge of turkey hunting and the hunting industry. Send fresh, informative queries, and indicate topics you'd feel comfortable covering on assignment."

$ $ TURKEY CALL, Wild Turkey Center, P.O. Box 530, Edgefield SC 29824-0530. (803)637-3106. Fax: (803)637-0034. E-mail: scrowder@nwtf.net or dhowlett@nwtf.net. Editor: Doug Howlett. **Contact:** Stephanie Crowder, publishing assistant; Russ Lumpkin, managing editor. **50-60% freelance written.** Eager to work with new/unpublished writers and photographers. Bimonthly educational magazine for members of the National Wild Turkey Federation. Estab. 1973. Circ. 150,000. Pays on acceptance for assigned articles, on publication for unsolicited articles. Publishes ms an average of 6 months after acceptance. Byline given. Buys one-time rights. Accepts queries by mail, e-mail. Accepts previously published material. Responds in 6 weeks to queries. Sample copy for $3 and 9×12 SAE. Writer's guidelines for #10 SASE or online.

- Queries required. Submit complete package if article is assigned. Wants original mss only.

O-w Break in with a knowledgeable, fresh point of view. Articles must be tightly written.

Nonfiction: Feature articles dealing with the hunting and management of the American wild turkey. Must be accurate information and must appeal to national readership of turkey hunters and wildlife management experts. May use some fiction that educates or entertains in a special way. Length: Up to 2,500 words. **Pays $100 for short fillers of 600-700 words, $200-500 for features.**

Reprints: Send photocopy and information about when and where the material previously appeared. Pays 50% of amount paid for the original article.

Photos: "We want quality photos submitted with features." Art illustrations also acceptable. "We are using more and more inside color illustrations." No typical hunter-holding-dead-turkey photos or setups using mounted birds or domestic turkeys. Photos with how-to stories must make the techniques clear (example: how to make a turkey call; how to sculpt or carve a bird in wood). Reviews transparencies. Buys one-time rights. Pays $35 minimum for b&w photos and simple art illustrations; up to $175 for inside color, reproduced any size; $200-400 for covers.

Tips: "The writer should simply keep in mind that the audience is 'expert' on wild turkey management, hunting, life history, and restoration/conservation history. He/she *must know the subject*. We are buying more third person, more fiction, more humor—in an attempt to avoid the 'predictability trap' of a single subject magazine."

$ $ ✪ VIRGINIA GAME & FISH, *Game & Fish*, Box 741, Marietta GA 30061. (770)953-9222. **Contact:** David Johnson, editor. See *Game & Fish*.

$ $ ✪ WASHINGTON-OREGON GAME & FISH, *Game & Fish*, Box 741, Marietta GA 30061. **Contact:** Burt Carey, editor. See *Game & Fish*.

$ $ ✪ WEST VIRGINIA GAME & FISH, *Game & Fish*, Box 741, Marietta GA 30061. (770)953-9222. **Contact:** Ken Freel, editor. See *Game & Fish*.

$ $ ✪ WISCONSIN OUTDOOR JOURNAL, Krause Publications, 700 E. State St., Iola WI 54990-0001. (715)445-2214. Fax: (715)445-4087. E-mail: waitp@krause.com. Website: www.wisoutdoorjournal.com. **Contact:** Paul Wait, editor. **95% freelance written.** Magazine published 8 times/year covering Wisconsin hunting, fishing, trapping, and wildlife. "*Wisconsin Outdoor Journal* is more than a straight hook-and-bullet magazine. Though *WOJ* carries how-to and where-to information, it also prints narratives, nature features, and state history pieces to give our readers a better appreciation of Wisconsin's outdoors." Estab. 1987. Circ. 48,000. **Pays on acceptance.** Publishes ms an average of 1 year after acceptance. Byline given. Buys first North American serial rights. Editorial lead time 1 year. Submit seasonal material 1 year in advance. Accepts queries by mail, fax. Responds in 2 months to queries. Sample copy and writer's guidelines for #10 SASE. Writer's guidelines for #10 SASE.

Nonfiction: The best bet for breaking in is through mood pieces. "We use at least 1 'fireside' piece/issue." Book excerpts, essays, historical/nostalgic, how-to, interview/profile, personal experience, photo feature. No stories focusing on out-of-state topics; no general recreation (hiking, biking, skiing) features. **Buys 65 mss/year.** Query with published clips. Length: 1,600-2,000 words. **Pays $150-250.** Pays expenses of writers on assignment.

Photos: Send photos with submission. Reviews transparencies. Buys one-time rights. Offers $75-275/photo.

Columns/Departments: Wisconsin Field Notes (anecdotes, outdoor news items not extensively covered by newspapers, interesting outdoor occurrences, all relevant to Wisconsin; may include photos), 50-750 words. **Pays $5-75 on publication.**

Fiction: Adventure, historical, nostalgic. "No eulogies of a good hunting dog." **Buys 10 mss/year.** Send complete ms. Length: 1,500-2,000 words. **Pays $100-250.**

Tips: "Don't submit personal hunting and fishing stories. Seek fresh, new topics, such as an analysis of long-term outdoor issues. Writers need to know Wisconsin intimately—stories that appear as regionals in other magazines probably won't be printed within *WOJ's* pages."

$ $ ✪ WISCONSIN SPORTSMAN, *Game & Fish*, Box 741, Marietta GA 30061. (770)953-9222. **Contact:** Dennis Schmidt, editor. See *Game & Fish*.

Martial Arts

$ $ INSIDE KUNG-FU, The Ultimate In Martial Arts Coverage!, CFW Enterprises, 4201 Vanowen Place, Burbank CA 91505. (818)845-2656. Fax: (818)845-7761. E-mail: davecater@cfwenterprises.com. **Contact:** Dave Cater, editor. **90% freelance written.** Monthly magazine for those with "traditional, modern, athletic and intellectual tastes. The magazine slants toward little-known martial arts, and little-known aspects of established martial arts." Estab. 1973. Circ. 125,000. Pays on publication date on magazine cover. Publishes ms an average of 6 months after acceptance. Byline given. Buys first North American serial rights. Editorial lead time 6 months. Submit seasonal material 6 months in advance. Accepts simultaneous submissions. Responds in 1 month to queries; 2 months to mss. Sample copy for $5.95 and 9×12 SAE with 5 first class stamps. Writer's guidelines for #10 SASE.

Nonfiction: "Articles must be technically or historically accurate." *Inside Kung-Fu* is looking for external type articles (fighting, weapons, multiple hackers). Book excerpts, essays, exposé (topics relating to martial arts), general interest, historical/nostalgic, how-to (primarily technical materials), inspirational, interview/profile, new product, personal experience, photo feature, technical, travel, cultural/philosophical. No "sports coverage, first-person articles or articles which constitute personal aggrandizement." **Buys 120 mss/year.** Query or send complete ms. Length: 1,500-3,000 words (8-10 pages, typewritten and double-spaced). **Pays $125-175.**

Reprints: Send tearsheet or typed ms with rights for sale noted and information about when and where the material previously appeared. No payment.

Photos: State availability of or send photos with submission. Reviews contact sheets, negatives, 5×7 or 8×10 color prints. Buys all rights. No additional payment for photos. Captions, identification of subjects, model releases required.

Fiction: "Fiction must be short (1,000-2,000 words) and relate to the martial arts. We buy very few fiction pieces." Adventure, historical, humorous, mystery, novel excerpts, suspense. **Buys 2-3 mss/year.**

Tips: "See what interests the writer. May have a better chance of breaking in at our publication with short articles and fillers since smaller pieces allow us to gauge individual ability, but we're flexible—quality writers get published, period. The most frequent mistakes made by writers in completing an article for us are ignoring photo requirements and model releases (always number one—and who knows why? All requirements are spelled out in writer's guidelines)."

N $ $ JOURNAL OF ASIAN MARTIAL ARTS, Via Media Publishing Co., 821 W. 24th St., Erie PA 16502-2523. (814)455-9517. E-mail: info@goviamedia.com. Website: www.goviamedia.com. **Contact:** Michael A. DeMarco, editor. **90% freelance written.** Quarterly magazine covering "all historical and cultural aspects related to Asian martial arts, offering a mature, well-rounded view of this uniquely fascinating subject. Although the journal treats the subject with academic accuracy (references at end), writing need not lose the reader!" Estab. 1991. Pays on publication. Publishes ms an average of 1 year after acceptance. Byline given. Buys first, second serial (reprint) rights. Submit seasonal material 6 months in advance. Responds in 1 month to queries; 2 months to mss. Sample copy for $10. Writer's guidelines for #10 SASE.

Nonfiction: "All articles should be backed with solid, reliable reference material." Essays, exposé, historical/nostalgic, how-to (martial art techniques and materials, e.g., weapons), interview/profile, personal experience, photo feature (place or person), religious, technical, travel. "No articles overburdened with technical/foreign/scholarly vocabulary, or material slanted as indirect advertising or for personal aggrandizement." **Buys 30 mss/year.** Query with short background and martial arts experience. Length: 2,000-10,000 words. **Pays $150-500.** and information about when and where the material previously appeared. Pays 50% of amount paid for an original article.

Photos: State availability with submission. Reviews contact sheets, negatives, transparencies, prints. Buys one-time and reprint rights. Offers no additional payment for photos accepted with ms. Identification of subjects, model releases required.

Columns/Departments: Location (city, area, specific site, Asian or nonAsian, showing value for martial arts, researchers, history); Media Review (film, book, video, museum for aspects of academic and artistic interest). Length: 1,000-2,500 words. **Buys 16 mss/year.** Query. **Pays $50-200.**

Fiction: Adventure, historical, humorous, slice-of-life vignettes, translation. No material that does not focus on martial arts culture. **Buys 1 mss/year.** Query. Length: 1,000-10,000 words. **Pays $50-500, or copies.**

Poetry: Avant-garde, free verse, haiku, light verse, traditional, translation. "No poetry that does not focus on martial arts culture." **Buys 2 poems/year.** Submit maximum 10 poems. **Pays $10-100, or copies.**

Fillers: Anecdotes, facts, gags to be illustrated by cartoonist, newsbreaks, short humor. **Buys 2/year.** Length: 25-500 words. **Pays $1-50, or copies.**

Tips: "Always query before sending a manuscript. We are open to varied types of articles; most however require a strong academic grasp of Asian culture. For those not having this background, we suggest trying a museum review, or interview, where authorities can be questioned, quoted, and provide supportive illustrations. We especially desire articles/reports from Asia, with photo illustrations, particularly of a martial art style, so readers can visually understand the unique attributes of that style, its applications, evolution, etc. 'Location' and media reports are special areas that writers may consider, especially if they live in a location of martial art significance."

$ KUNGFU QIGONG, Wisdom for Body and Mind, TC Media, 40748 Encyclopedia Circle, Fremont CA 94538. (510)656-5100. Fax: (510)656-8844. E-mail: info@kungfumagazine.com. Website: www.kungfumagazine.com. **Contact:** Gene Ching, associate publisher. **70% freelance written.** Bimonthly magazine covering Chinese martial arts and culture. "*Kungfu Qigong* covers the full range of Kungfu culture, including healing, philosophy, meditation, yoga, Fengshui, Buddhism, Taoism, history, and the latest events in art and culture, plus insightful features on the martial

arts." Circ. 50,000. Pays on publication. Byline given. Buys first North American serial, electronic rights. Editorial lead time 4 months. Submit seasonal material 4 months in advance. Accepts queries by mail, e-mail, fax, phone. Responds in 2 months to queries; 3 months to mss. Sample copy for $3.99 or online. Writer's guidelines free or online.
Nonfiction: Book excerpts, exposé, general interest, historical/nostalgic, how-to, interview/profile, personal experience, photo feature, religious, technical, travel, cultural perspectives. No poetry or fiction. **Buys 100 mss/year.** Query. Length: 500-2,500 words. **Pays $35-125.**
Photos: Send photos with submission. Reviews 5×7 prints, GIF/JPEG files. Buys one-time rights. Offers no additional payment for photos accepted with ms. Captions, identification of subjects required.
Tips: "Check out our website and get an idea of past articles."

$ $ T'AI CHI, Leading International magazine of T'ai Chi Ch'uan, Wayfarer Publications, P.O. Box 39938, Los Angeles CA 90039. (323)665-7773. Fax: (323)665-1627. E-mail: taichi@tai-chi.com. Website: www.tai-chi.com. **Contact:** Marvin Smalheiser, editor. **90% freelance written.** Bimonthly magazine covering T'ai Chi Ch'uan as a martial art and for health and fitness. "Covers T'ai Chi Ch'uan and other internal martial arts, plus qigong and Chinese health, nutrition, and philosophical disciplines. Readers are practitioners or laymen interested in developing skills and insight for self-defense, health, and self-improvement." Estab. 1977. Circ. 30,000. Pays on publication. Publishes ms an average of 3 months after acceptance. Byline given. Buys first North American serial rights. Editorial lead time 3 months. Submit seasonal material 6 months in advance. Accepts queries by mail, e-mail, fax. Responds in 3 weeks to queries; 3 months to mss. Sample copy for $3.95. Writer's guidelines for #10 SASE or online.

Break in by "understanding the problems our readers have to deal with learning and practicing T'ai Chi, and developing an article that deals with 1 or more of those problems.

Nonfiction: Book excerpts, essays, how-to (on T'ai Chi Ch'uan, qigong, and related Chinese disciplines), interview/profile, personal experience. "Do not want articles promoting an individual, system, or school." **Buys 50-60 mss/year.** Query with or without published clips or send complete ms. Length: 1,200-4,500 words. **Pays $75-500.** Sometimes pays expenses of writers on assignment.
Photos: Send photos with submission. Reviews color transparencies, color or b&w 4×6 or 5×7 prints. Buys one-time and reprint rights. Offers no additional payment for photos accepted with ms, but overall payment takes into consideration the number and quality of photos. Captions, identification of subjects, model releases required.
Tips: "Think and write for practitioners and laymen who want information and insight, and who are trying to work through problems to improve skills and their health. No promotional material."

Miscellaneous

$ ACTION PURSUIT GAMES, CFW Enterprises, Inc., 4201 Vanowen Place, Burbank CA 91505. (818)845-2656. Fax: (818)845-7761. E-mail: editor@actionpursuitgames.com. Website: www.actionpursuitgames.com. **Contact:** Daniel Reeves, editor. **60% freelance written.** Monthly magazine covering paintball. Estab. 1987. Circ. 85,000. Pays on publication. Publishes ms an average of 2 months after acceptance. Byline given. Buys electronic rights. print rights Editorial lead time 3 months. Submit seasonal material 6 months in advance. Accepts queries by e-mail. Sample copy for 9×12 SAE and 5 first-class stamps. Writer's guidelines online.
Nonfiction: Essays, exposé, general interest, historical/nostalgic, how-to, humor, interview/profile, new product, opinion, personal experience, technical, travel, all paintball-related. No sexually oriented material. **Buys 100+ mss/year.** Length: 500-1,000 words. **Pays $100.** Sometimes pays expenses of writers on assignment.
Photos: Send photos with submission. Reviews transparencies, prints. Buys all rights, Web and print. Negotiates payment individually. Captions, identification of subjects, model releases required.
Columns/Departments: Guest Commentary, 400 words; TNT (tournament news), 500-800 words; Young Guns, 300 words; Scenario Game Reporting, 300-500 words. **Buys 24 mss/year.** Send complete ms. **Pays $100.**
Fiction: Adventure, historical, must be paintball related. **Buys 1-2 mss/year.** Send complete ms. Length: 500 words. **Pays $100.**
Poetry: Avant-garde, free verse, haiku, light verse, traditional, must be paintball related. **Buys 1-2 poems/year.** Submit maximum 1 poem. Length: 20 lines.
Fillers: Anecdotes, gags to be illustrated by cartoonist. **Buys 2-4/year.** Length: 20-50 words. **Pays $25.**
Tips: "Good graphic support is critical. Read writer's guidelines at website; read website, www.actionpursuitgames.com, and magazine."

$ $ AMERICAN CHEERLEADER, Lifestyle Ventures, 250 W. 57th St., Suite 420, New York NY 10107. (212)265-8890. Fax: (212)265-8908. E-mail: editors@americancheerleader.com. Website: www.americancheerleader.com. Editorial Director: Julie Davis. **Contact:** Sheila Noone, editor. **50% freelance written.** Bimonthly magazine covering high school and college cheerleading. Estab. 1995. Circ. 200,000. Pays on publication. Publishes ms an average of 2 months after acceptance. Byline given. Buys all rights. Editorial lead time 4 months. Submit seasonal material 4 months in advance. Accepts queries by mail, e-mail, fax. Responds in 3 weeks to queries; 2 months to mss. Writer's guidelines for #10 SASE.
Nonfiction: How-to (cheering techniques, routines, pep songs, etc.), interview/profile, new product, personal experience. **Buys 20 mss/year.** Query with published clips. Length: 750-2,000 words. **Pays $75-300.** Sometimes pays expenses of writers on assignment.

Photos: State availability with submission. Reviews transparencies, 5×7 prints. Buys all rights. Offers no additional payment for photos accepted with ms. Captions, identification of subjects, model releases required.

Columns/Departments: Ask Us (expert advice on readers' cheer, stunt, and tumble questions); Cheer-O-Scope (cheer-y horoscope forecasts); Coach to Coach (helpful hints from experienced cheer coaches); College Spotlight (the lowdown on great college cheer programs); Cool Stuff (product picks, usually with cheerleading/sports themes); Eating Smart (nutritious tidbits for the active cheerleader); Fab Fundraising (fundraising ideas with originality and pizzazz to keep the cash rolling in); Gameday Beauty (makeovers, cosmetics, hair products, beauty tips); Healthy Athlete (anything from PMS to how to buy running shoes to athletic training tips); Squad of the Month (highlighting the country's coolest high school and all-star cheer squads); Star Struck (celebs who cheered, and what cheering has brought to their current careers); Stunt School (technical know-how and step-by-step instruction on tumbling, jumping, stunting, and more); What's Going On (cheer news in bite-size newsy paragraphs).

The online magazine carries original content not found in the print edition.

Tips: "We invite proposals from freelance writers who are involved in or have been involved in cheerleading—i.e. coaches, sponsors, or cheerleaders. Our writing style is upbeat and 'sporty' to catch and hold the attention of our teenaged readers. Articles should be broken down into lots of sidebars, bulleted lists, Q&As, etc."

$ CANADIAN RODEO NEWS, Canadian Rodeo News, Ltd., #223, 2116 27th Ave. NE, Calgary, Alberta T2E 7A6, Canada. (403)250-7292. Fax: (403)250-6926. E-mail: crn@rodeocanada.com. Website: www.rodeocanada.com. **Contact:** Jennifer Jones, editor. **60% freelance written.** Monthly tabloid covering "Canada's professional rodeo (CPRA) personalities and livestock. Read by rodeo participants and fans." Estab. 1964. Circ. 4,000. Pays on publication. Publishes ms an average of 1 month after acceptance. Byline given. Buys first, second serial (reprint) rights. Editorial lead time 1 month. Submit seasonal material 1 month in advance. Accepts queries by mail, e-mail, fax. Accepts simultaneous submissions. Responds in 1 month to queries; 2 months to mss. Sample copy and writer's guidelines free with SASE.

Nonfiction: General interest, historical/nostalgic, interview/profile. **Buys 70-80 mss/year.** Query. Length: 500-1,200 words. **Pays $30-60.**

Reprints: Send photocopy of article or typed ms with rights for sale noted and information about when and where the material previously appeared. Pays 100% of amount paid for an original article.

Photos: Send photos with submission. Reviews 4×6 prints. Buys one-time rights. Offers $15-25/cover photo.

Tips: "Best to call first with the story idea to inquire if it is suitable for publication. Readers are very knowledgeable of the sport, so writers need to be as well."

$ FENCERS QUARTERLY MAGAZINE, P.O. Box 69, Peace Valley MO 65788. (417)866-4370. E-mail: evange1@atlascomm.net or ale368s@smsu.edu. Editor-in-Chief: Nick Evangelista. **Contact:** Anita Evangelista, managing editor. **60% freelance written.** Quarterly magazine covering fencing, fencers, history of sword/fencing/dueling, modern techniques and systems, controversies, personalities of fencing, personal experience. "This is a publication for all fencers and those interested in fencing; we favor the grassroots level rather than the highly-promoted elite. Readers will have a grasp of terminology of the sword and refined fencing skills—writers must be familiar with fencing and current changes and controversies. We are happy to air any point of view on any fencing subject, but the material must be well-researched and logically presented." Estab. 1996. Circ. 5,000. Pays prior to or at publication. Publishes ms an average of 6 months after acceptance. Byline given. Offers 25% kill fee. Buys first North American serial, second serial (reprint), electronic rights, makes work-for-hire assignments. Editorial lead time 3 months. Submit seasonal material 6 months in advance. Accepts queries by mail, e-mail. Accepts simultaneous submissions. Sample copy for $2, 8×10 SAE, and 2 first-class stamps. Writer's guidelines for #10 SASE or by e-mail.

- Responds in 1 week or less for e-mail; 1 month for snail mail if SASE; no reply if no SASE and material not usable.

Nonfiction: "All article types acceptable—however, we have seldom used fiction or poetry (though will consider if has special relationship to fencing)." How-to should reflect some aspect of fencing or gear. Personal experience welcome. No articles "that lack logical progression of thought, articles that rant, 'my weapon is better than your weapon' emotionalism, puff pieces, or public relations stuff." **Buys 100 mss/year.** Query with or without published clips or send complete ms. Length: 100-4,000 words. **Pays $100-200 (rarely) for assigned articles; $10-60 for unsolicited articles.**

Photos: Send photos by mail or as e-mail attachment. Prefers prints, all sizes. Buys all rights. Negotiates payment individually. Captions, identification of subjects, model releases required.

Columns/Departments: Cutting-edge news (sword or fencing related), 100 words; Reviews of books/films, 300 words; Fencing Generations (profile), 200-300 words; Tournament Results (veteran events only, please), 200 words. **Buys 40 mss/year.** Send complete ms. **Pays $10-20.**

Fiction: Will consider all as long as strong fencing/sword slant is major element. No erotica. Query with or without published clips or send complete ms. Length: 1,500 words maximum. **Pays $25-100.**

Poetry: Will consider all which have distinct fencing/sword element as central. No erotica. Submit maximum 10 poems. Length: Up to 100 lines. **Pays $10.**

Fillers: Anecdotes, facts, gags to be illustrated by cartoonist, newsbreaks. **Buys 30/year.** Length: 100 words maximum. **Pays $5.**

Tips: "We love new writers! Professionally presented work impresses us. We prefer complete submissions, and e-mail or disk (in rich text format .rtf, please) are our favorites. Ask for our writer's guidelines. Always aim your writing to knowledgeable fencers who are fascinated by this subject, take their fencing seriously, and want to know more about its history, current events, and controversies. Action photos should show proper form—no flailing or tangled-up images, please. We want to know what the 'real' fencer is up to these days, not just what the Olympic contenders are doing. If we don't use your piece, we'll tell you why not."

$ $POLO PLAYERS' EDITION, Rizzo Management Corp., 3500 Fairlane Farms Rd., Suite 9, Wellington FL 33414. (561)793-9524. Fax: (561)793-9576. E-mail: info@poloplayersedition.com. Website: www.poloplayersedition.com. **Contact:** Gwen Rizzo, editor. Monthly magazine on polo—the sport and lifestyle. "Our readers are affluent, well-educated, well read and highly sophisticated." Circ. 6,150. **Pays on acceptance.** Publishes ms an average of 2 months after acceptance. Kill fee varies. Buys first North American serial rights, makes work-for-hire assignments. Submit seasonal material 3 months in advance. Accepts queries by mail, e-mail, fax. Accepts simultaneous submissions. Responds in 3 months to queries. Writer's guidelines for #10 SAE with 2 stamps.

Nonfiction: Historical/nostalgic, interview/profile, personal experience, photo feature, technical, travel. Special issues: Annual Art Issue/Gift Buying Guide; Winter Preview/Florida Supplement. **Buys 20 mss/year.** Query with published clips or send complete ms. Length: 800-3,000 words. **Pays $150-400 for assigned articles; $100-300 for unsolicited articles.** Sometimes pays expenses of writers on assignment.

Reprints: Send tearsheet or typed ms with rights for sale noted and information about when and where the material previously appeared. Pays 50% of amount paid for an original article.

Photos: State availability of or send photos with submission. Reviews contact sheets, transparencies, prints. Buys one-time rights. Offers $20-150/photo. Captions required.

Columns/Departments: Yesteryears (historical pieces), 500 words; Profiles (clubs and players), 800-1,000 words. **Buys 15 mss/year.** Query with published clips. **Pays $100-300.**

Tips: "Query us on a personality or club profile or historic piece or, if you know the game, state availability to cover a tournament. Keep in mind that ours is a sophisticated, well-educated audience."

$PRIME TIME SPORTS & FITNESS, GND Prime Time Publishing, P.O. Box 6097, Evanston IL 60204. (847)784-1194. Fax: (847)784-1194. E-mail: dadorner@aol.com. Website: www.bowldtalk.com. Managing Editor: Steven Ury. **Contact:** Dennis A. Dorner, editor. **80% freelance written.** Monthly magazine covering seasonal pro sports, health club sports, and fitness. Estab. 1974. Circ. 35,000. Pays on publication. Publishes ms an average of 6 months after acceptance. Byline given. all rights; will assign back to author in 85% of cases. Submit seasonal material 6 months in advance. Accepts queries by mail, e-mail. Accepts simultaneous submissions. Responds in 6 months to queries. Sample copy on request. Writer's guidelines online.

O→ Break in with a 400-600-word fiction piece or a 400-word instructional article.

Nonfiction: "We love short articles that get to the point. Nationally oriented big events and national championships." Book excerpts (fitness and health), exposé (in tennis, fitness, racquetball, health clubs, diets), general interest, historical/nostalgic, how-to (expert instructional pieces on any area of coverage), humor (large market for funny pieces on health clubs and fitness), inspirational, interview/profile, new product, opinion (only from recognized sources who know what they are talking about), personal experience (definitely humor), photo feature (on related subjects), technical (on exercise and sport), travel (related to fitness, tennis camps, etc.), adult (slightly risqué and racy fitness); news reports (on racquetball, handball, tennis, running events). Special issues: Swimwear (March); Baseball Preview (April); Summer Fashion (July); Pro Football Preview (August); Aerobic Wear (September); Fall Fashion (October); Ski Issue (November); Workout and Diet Routines (December/January). "No articles on local-only tennis and racquetball tournaments without national appeal." **Buys 150 mss/year.** Length: 2,000 words maximum. **Pays $50-200.** Sometimes pays expenses of writers on assignment.

Reprints: Send tearsheet, photocopy or typed ms with rights for sale noted and information about when and where the material previously appeared. Pays 20% of amount paid for an original article or story.

Photos: Specifically looking for fashion photo features. Nancy Thomas, photo editor. Send photos with submission. Buys all rights. Pays $20-75 for b&w prints. Captions, identification of subjects, model releases required.

Columns/Departments: George Thomas, column/department editor. New Products; Fitness Newsletter; Handball Newsletter; Racquetball Newsletter; Tennis Newsletter; News & Capsule Summaries; Fashion Spot (photos of new fitness and bathing suits and ski equipment). Length: 50-250 words ("more if author has good handle to cover complete columns"). "We want more articles with photos and we are searching for one woman columnist, Diet and Nutrition." **Buys 100 mss/year.** Send complete ms. **Pays $25-50.**

Fiction: Judy Johnson, fiction editor. "Upbeat stories are needed." Erotica, fantasy, humorous, novel excerpts, religious, romance. **Buys 20 mss/year.** Send complete ms. Length: 500-2,500 words maximum. **Pays $100-250.**

Poetry: Free verse, haiku, light verse, traditional, *on related subjects only.* Length: Up to 150 words. **Pays $25-50.**

The online magazine carries original content not found in the print edition and includes writer's guidelines. Contact: Bob Eres, online editor.

Tips: "Send us articles dealing with court club sports, exercise, and nutrition that exemplify an upbeat 'you can do it' attitude. Pro sports previews 3-4 months ahead of their seasons are also needed. Good short fiction or humorous articles can break in. Expert knowledge of any related subject can bring assignments; any area is open. We consider everything as a potential article, but are turned off by credits, past work, and degrees. We have a constant demand for well-written articles on instruction, health, and trends in both. Other articles needed are professional sports training techniques, fad diets, tennis and fitness resorts, photo features with aerobic routines. A frequent mistake made by writers is in length—articles are too long. When we assign an article, we want it newsy if it's news and opinion if opinion."

N $ ★ RUGBY MAGAZINE, Rugby Press Limited, 2350 Broadway, New York NY 10024. (212)787-1160. Fax: (212)595-0934. E-mail: rugbymag@aol.com. Website: www.rugbymag.com. Editor: Ed Hagerty. **Contact:** Ed Hagerty. **75% freelance written.** Monthly tabloid. "*Rugby Magazine* is the journal of record for the sport of rugby in the U.S. Our demographics are among the best in the country." Estab. 1975. Circ. 10,000. Pays on publication. Publishes ms an average of 2 months after acceptance. Byline given. Buys all rights. Editorial lead time 1 month. Submit seasonal material 2 months in advance. Accepts queries by mail, e-mail, fax, phone. Accepts simultaneous submissions. Responds in 2 weeks to queries; 1 month to mss. Sample copy for $3. Writer's guidelines free.

Nonfiction: Book excerpts, essays, general interest, historical/nostalgic, how-to, humor, interview/profile, new product, opinion, personal experience, photo feature, technical, travel. **Buys 15 mss/year.** Send complete ms. Length: 600-2,000 words. **Pays $50 minimum.** Pays expenses of writers on assignment.

Reprints: Send tearsheet or typed ms with rights for sale noted and information about when and where the material previously appeared. Pay varies.

Photos: Send photos with submission. Reviews negatives, transparencies, Prints. Buys all rights. Offers no additional payment for photos accepted with ms.

Columns/Departments: Nutrition, athletic nutrition, 900 words; Referees' Corner, 1,200 words. **Buys 2-3 mss/year.** Query with published clips. **Pays $50 maximum.**

Fiction: Condensed novels, humorous, novel excerpts, slice-of-life vignettes. **Buys 1-3 mss/year.** Query with published clips. Length: 1,000-2,500 words. **Pays $100.**

Tips: "Give us a call. Send along your stories or photos; we're happy to take a look. Tournament stories are a good way to get yourself published in *Rugby Magazine.*"

$ $ TENNIS WEEK, Tennis News, Inc., 15 Elm Place, Rye NY 10580. (914)967-4890. Fax: (914)967-8178. **Contact:** Heather H. Holland, managing editor. **10% freelance written.** Biweekly magazine covering tennis. "For readers who are either tennis fanatics or involved in the business of tennis." Estab. 1974. Circ. 80,000. Pays on publication. Byline given. Buys all rights. Editorial lead time 1 month. Submit seasonal material 1 month in advance. Responds in 1 month to queries. Sample copy for $3.

Nonfiction: Buys 15 mss/year. Query with or without published clips. Length: 1,000-2,000 words. **Pays $300.**

Motor Sports

$ $ SAND SPORTS MAGAZINE, Wright Publishing Co., Inc., P.O. Box 2260, Costa Mesa CA 92628. (714)979-2560, ext. 107. Fax: (714)979-3998. Website: www.sandsports.net. **Contact:** Michael Sommer, editor. **20% freelance written.** Bimonthly magazine covering vehicles for off-road and sand dunes. Estab. 1995. Circ. 25,000. Pays on publication. Byline given. Buys first, one-time rights. Editorial lead time 3 months. Submit seasonal material 6 months in advance. Accepts queries by mail. Sample copy and writer's guidelines free.

Nonfiction: How-to (technical-mechanical), photo feature, technical. **Buys 20 mss/year.** Query. Length: 1,500 words minimum. **Pays $125-175/page.** Sometimes pays expenses of writers on assignment.

Photos: Send photos with submission. Reviews contact sheets, transparencies, 5×7 prints. Buys one-time rights. Negotiates payment individually. Captions, identification of subjects, model releases required.

$ $ ★ SPEEDWAY ILLUSTRATED, Performance Media LLC, 107 Elm St., Salisbury MA 01952. (978)465-9099. Fax: (978)465-9033. E-mail: rsneddon@speedwayillustrated.com. Website: www.speedwayillustrated.com. Executive Editor: Dick Berggren. **Contact:** Rob Sneddon, editor. **80% freelance written.** Monthly magazine covering stock car racing. Estab. 2000. Circ. 125,000. Pays on publication. Byline given. Buys first rights. Editorial lead time 6 weeks. Accepts queries by mail, e-mail, fax. Responds in 2 weeks to queries. Sample copy and writer's guidelines free.

Nonfiction: Interview/profile, opinion, personal experience, photo feature, technical. **Buys 300 mss/year.** Query. **Pays variable rate.**

Photos: Send photos with submission. Reviews transparencies, digital. Buys all rights. Offers $40-250/photo. Captions, identification of subjects, model releases required.

Columns/Departments: We seek short items with photos. **Buys 100 mss/year. Pays $25-200.**

Tips: "We pay for everything that is published and aggressively seek short, high-interest value pieces that are accompanied by strong photography."

Olympics

$ USA GYMNASTICS, 201 S. Capitol Ave., Suite 300, Pan American Plaza, Indianapolis IN 46225. (317)237-5050. Fax: (317)237-5069. E-mail: lpeszek@usa-gymnastics.org. Website: www.usa-gymnastics.org. **Contact:** Luan Peszek, editor. **10% freelance written.** Bimonthly magazine covering gymnastics—national and international competitions. Designed to educate readers on fitness, health, safety, technique, current topics, trends, and personalities related to the gymnastics/fitness field. Readers are gymnasts ages 7-18, parents, and coaches. Estab. 1981. Circ. 80,000. Pays on publication. Publishes ms an average of 4 months after acceptance. Byline given. Buys all rights. Submit seasonal material 4 months in advance. Accepts queries by e-mail, fax. Accepts simultaneous submissions. Responds in 2 months to queries. Sample copy for $5.

Nonfiction: General interest, how-to (related to fitness, health, gymnastics), inspirational, interview/profile, opinion (Open Floor section), photo feature. **Buys 3 mss/year.** Query. Length: 1,500 words maximum. **Pay negotiable.**
Reprints: Send photocopy.
Photos: Send photos with submission. Buys all rights. Offers no additional payment for photos accepted with ms. Identification of subjects required.
Tips: "Any articles of interest to gymnasts (men, women, rhythmic gymnastics, trampoline, and tumbling), coaches, judges, and parents, are what we're looking for. This includes nutrition, toning, health, safety, trends, techniques, timing, etc."

Running

$ $ $ $ RUNNER'S WORLD, Rodale, 135 N. 6th St., Emmaus PA 18098. (610)967-5171. Fax: (610)967-8883. E-mail: rwedit@rodale.com. Website: www.runnersworld.com. Deputy Editor: Bob Wischnia. **Contact:** Adam Bean, managing editor. **5% freelance written.** Monthly magazine on running, mainly long-distance running. "The magazine for and about distance running, training, health and fitness, nutrition, motivation, injury prevention, race coverage, personalities of the sport." Estab. 1966. Circ. 500,000. Pays on publication. Publishes ms an average of 6 months after acceptance. Byline given. Buys all rights. Submit seasonal material 6 months in advance. Accepts queries by mail. Responds in 2 months to queries. Writer's guidelines for #10 SASE.

O→ Break in through columns *Women's Running*, *Human Race* and *Finish Line*. Also *Warmups*, which mixes international running news with human interest stories. If you can send us a unique human interest story from your region, we will give it serious consideration.

Nonfiction: How-to (train, prevent injuries), interview/profile, personal experience. No "my first marathon" stories. No poetry. **Buys 5-7 mss/year.** Query. **Pays $1,500-2,000.** Pays expenses of writers on assignment.
Photos: State availability with submission. Buys one-time rights. Identification of subjects required.
Columns/Departments: Finish Line (back-of-the-magazine essay, personal experience—humor); Women's Running (essay page written by and for women). **Buys 24 mss/year.** Send complete ms. **Pays $300.**

The online magazine carries original content not found in the print edition. Contact: Marty Post.

Tips: "We are always looking for 'Adventure Runs' from readers—runs in wild, remote, beautiful and interesting places. These are rarely race stories but more like backtracking/running adventures. Great color slides are crucial, 2,000 words maximum."

$ $ RUNNING TIMES, The Runner's Best Resource, Fitness Publishing, Inc., 213 Danbury Rd., Wilton CT 06897. (203)761-1113. Fax: (203)761-9933. E-mail: editor@runningtimes.com. Website: www.runningtimes.com. Managing Editor: Marc Chalufour. **Contact:** Jonathan Beverly, editor. **40% freelance written.** Magazine published 10 times/year covering distance running and racing. "*Running Times* is the national magazine for the experienced running participant and fan. Our audience is knowledgeable about the sport and active in running and racing. All editorial relates specifically to running: improving performance, enhancing enjoyment, or exploring events, places, and people in the sport." Estab. 1977. Circ. 75,000. Pays on publication. Publishes ms an average of 3 months after acceptance. Byline given. Buys first North American serial, second serial (reprint), electronic rights. Editorial lead time 4 months. Submit seasonal material 6 months in advance. Accepts queries by mail, e-mail. Responds in 1 month to queries; 2 months to mss. Sample copy for $5. Writer's guidelines for #10 SASE.
Nonfiction: Book excerpts, essays, historical/nostalgic, how-to (training), humor, inspirational, interview/profile, new product, opinion, personal experience (with theme, purpose, evidence of additional research and/or special expertise), photo feature, travel, news, reports. No basic, beginner how-to, generic fitness/nutrition, or generic first-person accounts. **Buys 25 mss/year.** Query. Length: 1,500-3,000 words. **Pays $200-500 for assigned articles; $100-300 for unsolicited articles.** Sometimes pays expenses of writers on assignment.
Photos: State availability with submission. Buys one-time rights. Negotiates payment individually. Identification of subjects required.
Columns/Departments: Training (short topics related to enhancing performance), 1,000 words; Sports-Med (application of medical knowledge to running), 1,000 words; Nutrition (application of nutritional principles to running performance), 1,000 words; Cool Down (lighter toned essay on an aspect of the running life), 400 words. **Buys 15 mss/year.** Query. **Pays $50-200.**
Fiction: Any genre, with running-related theme or characters. **Buys 1-2 mss/year.** Send complete ms. Length: 1,500-3,000 words. **Pays $100-500.**
Tips: "Thoroughly get to know runners and the running culture, both at the participant level and the professional, elite level."

$ $ TRAIL RUNNER, The Magazine of Running Adventure, North South Publications, 5455 Spine Rd., Mezz. A, Boulder CO 80301. (303)499-8410. Fax: (303)530-3729. E-mail: editor@trailrunnermag.com. Website: www.trailrunnermag.com. **Contact:** Brian Metzler, editor. **65% freelance written.** Bimonthly magazine covering all aspects of off-road running. "The only nationally circulated 4-color glossy magazine dedicated to covering trail running." Estab. 1999. Circ. 40,000. Pays on publication. Publishes ms an average of 2 months after acceptance. Byline given. Offers $50 kill fee. Buys first North American serial, electronic rights. Editorial lead time 3 months. Submit seasonal material 5 months in advance. Accepts queries by mail, e-mail. Accepts simultaneous submissions. Responds in 3 weeks to queries; 2 months to mss. Sample copy for $3. Writer's guidelines free, online, or by e-mail.

Nonfiction: Essays, exposé, general interest, historical/nostalgic, how-to, humor, inspirational, interview/profile, new product, opinion, personal experience, photo feature, technical, travel, racing. No gear reviews, race results. **Buys 30-40 mss/year.** Query with published clips. Length: 800-2,000 words. **Pays 30-40¢/word.** Sometimes pays expenses of writers on assignment.
Photos: Send photos with submission. Reviews 35mm transparencies, prints. Buys one-time rights. Offers $50-250/photo. Identification of subjects, model releases required.
Columns/Departments: Monique Cole, senior editor. Training (race training, altitude training, etc.), 800 words; Adventure (off-beat aspects of trail running), 600-800 words; Wanderings (personal essay on any topic related to trail running), 600 words; Urban Escapes (urban trails accessible in and around major US sites), 800 words; Personalities (profile of a trail running personality), 1,000 words. **Buys 5-10 mss/year.** Query with published clips. **Pays 30-40¢/word.**
Fiction: Adventure, fantasy, slice-of-life vignettes. **Buys 1-2 mss/year.** Query with published clips. Length: 1,000-1,500 words. **Pays 25-35¢/word.**
Fillers: Anecdotes, facts, gags to be illustrated by cartoonist, newsbreaks, short humor. **Buys 50-60/year.** Length: 75-400 words. **Pays 25-35¢/word.**
The online version contains material not found in the print edition. Contact: Phil Mislinski.
Tips: "Best way to break in is with interesting and unique trail running news, notes, and nonsense from around the world. Also, check the website for more info."

$ $ TRIATHLETE MAGAZINE, The World's Largest Triathlon Magazine, Triathlon Group of North America, 2037 San Elijo, Cardiff CA 92007. (760)634-4100. Fax: (760)634-4110. E-mail: cgandolfo@triathletemag.com. Website: www.triathletemag.com. **Contact:** Christina Gandolfo, editor. **50% freelance written.** Monthly magazine. "In general, articles should appeal to seasoned triathletes, as well as eager newcomers to the sport. Our audience includes everyone from competitive athletes to people considering their first event." Estab. 1983. Circ. 50,000. Pays on publication. Byline given. Buys second serial (reprint), all rights. Editorial lead time 3 months. Submit seasonal material 6 months in advance. Accepts queries by mail, e-mail. Accepts simultaneous submissions. Sample copy for $5.
Nonfiction: How-to, interview/profile, new product, photo feature, technical. "No first-person pieces about your experience in triathlon or my-first-triathlon stories." **Buys 36 mss/year.** Query with published clips. Length: 1,000-3,000 words. **Pays $200-600.** Sometimes pays expenses of writers on assignment.
Photos: State availability with submission. Reviews transparencies. Buys first North American rights. Offers $50-300/photo.
Tips: "Writers should know the sport and be familiar with the nuances and history. Training-specific articles that focus on new, but scientifically based, methods are good, as are seasonal training pieces."

Skiing & Snow Sports

$ SKATING, United States Figure Skating Association, 20 First St., Colorado Springs CO 80906-3697. (719)635-5200. Fax: (719)635-9548. E-mail: lfawcett@usfsa.org. **Contact:** Laura Fawcett, editor. Official publication of the USFSA published 10 times/year. "*Skating* magazine is the official publication of U.S. Figure Skating, and thus we cover skating at both the championship and grass roots level." Estab. 1923. Circ. 48,000. Pays on publication. Publishes ms an average of 3 months after acceptance. Byline given. Buys first rights. Accepts queries by mail, e-mail, fax.
The best way for a writer to break in is through the "Ice Time with—..." department, which features USFSA members (skaters, volunteers, etc.) who have unique or interesting stories to tell. This is a feature that highlights members and their accomplishments and stories on and off the ice (800-1,500 words).
Nonfiction: General interest, historical/nostalgic, how-to, interview/profile (background and interests of skaters, volunteers, or other USFSA members), photo feature, technical and competition reports, figure skating issues and trends, sports medicine. **Buys 10 mss/year.** Query. Length: 500-2,500 words. **Payment varies.**
Photos: Photos purchased with or without accompanying ms. Query. Pays $15 for 8×10 or 5×7 b&w glossy prints, and $35 for color prints or transparencies.
Columns/Departments: Ice Breaker (news briefs); Foreign Competition Reports; Ice Time With... (features on USFSA members); Sports Medicine; In Synch (synchronized skating news); On the Lookout (up-and-coming athletes). Length: 500-2,000 words.
Tips: "We want writing by experienced persons knowledgeable in the technical and artistic aspects of figure skating with a new outlook on the development of the sport. Knowledge and background in technical aspects of figure skating is helpful, but not necessary to the quality of writing expected. We would like to see articles and short features on USFSA volunteers, skaters, and other USFSA members who normally wouldn't get recognized, as opposed to features on championship-level athletes, which are usually assigned to regular contributors. Good quality color photos are a must with submissions. Also would be interested in seeing figure skating 'issues and trends' articles, instead of just profiles. No professional skater material. Synchronized skating and adult skating are the 2 fastest growing aspects of the USFSA. We would like to see more stories dealing with these unique athletes."

$ $ $ SKI MAGAZINE, Times Mirror Magazines, 929 Pearl St., Suite 200, Boulder CO 80302. (303)448-7600. Fax: (303)448-7638. E-mail: mdrummey@skimag.com. Website: www.skimag.com. Editor-in-Chief: Andy Bigford. **Contact:** Maureen Drummey, assistant editor. **15% freelance written.** Monthly magazine. "*Ski* is a ski-lifestyle publication written and edited for recreational skiers. Its content is intended to help them ski better (technique), buy better (equipment and skiwear), and introduce them to new experiences, people, and adventures." Estab. 1936. Circ. 430,000.

Pays on acceptance. Publishes ms an average of 3 months after acceptance. Byline given. Offers 15% kill fee. Buys first North American serial rights. Submit seasonal material 8 months in advance. Accepts queries by mail, e-mail. Responds in 1 month to queries. Sample copy for 9×12 SAE and 5 first-class stamps.

Nonfiction: Essays, historical/nostalgic, how-to, humor, interview/profile, personal experience. **Buys 5-10 mss/year.** Send complete ms. Length: 1,000-3,500 words. **Pays $500-1,000 for assigned articles; $300-700 for unsolicited articles.** Pays expenses of writers on assignment.

Photos: Send photos with submission. Buys one-time rights. Offers $75-300/photo. Captions, identification of subjects, model releases required.

Columns/Departments: See magazine.

Fillers: Facts, short humor. **Buys 10/year.** Length: 60-75 words. **Pays $50-75.**

Online magazine carries original content not found in the print edition. Contact: Doug Sabanosh.

Tips: "Writers must have an extensive familiarity with the sport and know what concerns, interests, and amuses skiers. Start with short pieces ('hometown hills,' 'dining out,' 'sleeping in'). Columns are most open to freelancers."

$ $ $ $SKIING, Times Mirror Magazines, Inc., 929 Pearl St., Suite 200, Boulder CO 80302. (303)448-7600. Fax: (303)448-7676. E-mail: editors@skiingmag.com. Website: www.skiingmag.com. Editor-in-Chief: Perkins Miller. **Contact:** Helen Olsson, executive editor. Magazine published 7 times/year for skiers who deeply love winter, who live for travel, adventure, instruction, gear and news. "*Skiing* is the user's guide to winter adventure. It is equal parts jaw-dropping inspiration and practical information, action and utility, attitude and advice. It relates the lifestyles of dedicated skiers and captures their spirit of daring and exploration. Dramatic photography transports readers to spine-tingling mountains with breathtaking immediacy. Reading *Skiing* is almost as much fun as being there." Estab. 1948. Circ. 400,000. Byline given. Offers 40% kill fee.

Nonfiction: Buys 10-15 feature (1,500-2,000 words) and 12-24 short (100-500 words) mss/year. Query. **Pays $1,000-2,500/feature; $100-500/short piece.**

Columns/Departments: Length: 200-1,000 words. **Buys 2-3 mss/year.** Query. **Pays $150-1,000.**

The online magazine carries original content not found in the print edition. Contact: Adam Hirshfield, online editor.

Tips: "Consider less obvious subjects: smaller ski areas, specific local ski cultures, unknown aspects of popular resorts. Be expressive, not merely descriptive! We want readers to feel the adventure in your writing—to tingle with the excitement of skiing steep powder, of meeting intriguing people, of reaching new goals or achieving dramatic new insights. We want readers to have fun, to see the humor in and the lighter side of skiing and their fellow skiers."

$ $SNOW GOER, Ehlert Publishing Group, 6420 Sycamore Lane, Maple Grove MN 55369. Fax: (763)383-4499. E-mail: eskogman@affinitygroup.com. Website: www.snowmobilenews.com. **Contact:** Eric Skogman, editor. **5% freelance written.** Magazine published 6 times/year covering snowmobiling. "*Snow Goer* is a hard-hitting, tell-it-like-it-is magazine designed for the ultra-active snowmobile enthusiast. It is fun, exciting, innovative, and on the cutting edge of technology and trends." Estab. 1967. Circ. 76,000. Pays on publication. Publishes ms an average of 5 months after acceptance. Byline given. Buys first, one-time rights. Editorial lead time 5 months. Submit seasonal material 6 months in advance. Accepts queries by mail, e-mail, fax. Accepts simultaneous submissions. Responds in 3 months to queries. Sample copy for 8×10 SAE and 4 first-class stamps.

Nonfiction: General interest, how-to, interview/profile, new product, personal experience, photo feature, technical, travel. **Buys 6 mss/year.** Query. Length: 500-4,000 words. **Pays $50-500.** Sometimes pays expenses of writers on assignment.

Photos: State availability with submission. Reviews contact sheets, prints. Buys one-time rights or all rights. Negotiates payment individually. Captions, identification of subjects required.

$ $SNOW WEEK, The Snowmobile Racing Authority, Ehlert Publishing Group, 6420 Sycamore Lane N., Maple Grove MN 55369. (763)383-4400. Fax: (763)383-4499. E-mail: eskogman@affinitygroup.com. Website: www.snowmobilenews.com. **Contact:** Eric Skogman, editor. **15% freelance written.** Magazine published 16 times/year covering snowmobile racing. "We cover snowmobile racing from coast to coast for hardcore fans. We get in the pits, inside the race trailers, and pepper our race coverage with behind the scenes details." Estab. 1973. Circ. 26,000. Pays on publication. Publishes ms an average of 2 months after acceptance. Byline given. Buys first, one-time, simultaneous rights. Editorial lead time 2 weeks. Accepts queries by mail, e-mail, fax, phone. Sample copy for 8×11 SAE and 4 first-class stamps.

Nonfiction: Technical, race coverage. **Buys 20 mss/year.** Query. Length: 500-4,000 words. **Pays 50-450.** Sometimes pays expenses of writers on assignment.

Photos: State availability with submission. Reviews contact sheets, prints. Buys one-time rights. Offers no additional payment for photos accepted with ms. Captions, identification of subjects required.

Tips: "Writers should also be fans of the sport, know how to write and photograph races."

$ $SNOWEST MAGAZINE, Harris Publishing, 360 B St., Idaho Falls ID 83402. (208)524-7000. Fax: (208)522-5241. E-mail: lindstrm@snowest.com. Publisher: Steve Janes. **Contact:** Lane Lindstrom, editor. **10-25% freelance written.** Monthly magazine. "*SnoWest* covers the sport of snowmobiling, products, and personalities in the western states. This includes mountain riding, deep powder, and trail riding, as well as destination pieces, tech tips, and new model reviews." Estab. 1972. Circ. 160,000. Pays on publication. Publishes ms an average of 2 months after acceptance. Byline given. Buys first North American serial rights. Editorial lead time 6 months. Submit seasonal material 3 months in advance. Sample copy and writer's guidelines free.

Nonfiction: How-to (fix a snowmobile, make it high performance), new product, technical, travel. **Buys 3-5 mss/year.** Query with published clips. Length: 500-1,500 words. **Pays $150-300.**

Photos: Send photos with submission. Buys one-time rights. Negotiates payment individually. Captions, identification of subjects required.

N $ $ $ TRANSWORLD STANCE, Transworld Media, 353 Airport Rd., Oceanside CA 92054. (760)722-7777. Fax: (760)722-0653. **Contact:** Kevin Imamura, editor; Ted Newsome, editor-in-chief; Chandra Conway, managing editor; Nolan Woodrell, associate editor. **50-75% freelance written.** Bimonthly magazine geared toward teen males. "*Stance* is a lifestyle magazine written from the perspective of skateboarders and snowboarders. The main focus is celebrities (from our world as well as everywhere else), products, music, and fashion." Estab. 2000. Circ. 100,000. Pays on publication. Publishes ms an average of 4 months after acceptance. Byline given. Offers 50% kill fee. Makes work-for-hire assignments. Editorial lead time 4 months. Submit seasonal material 6 months in advance. Accepts queries by mail, e-mail, fax. Sample copy for 8×11 SAE and 4 first-class stamps.

Nonfiction: Historical/nostalgic, how-to (customize cars, buy a car), humor, interview/profile, new product, technical, travel (how to travel cross country and through Europe for cheap). Length: 25-1,500 words. **Pays 60¢/word minimum.** Sometimes pays expenses of writers on assignment.

Photos: Send photos with submission. Reviews contact sheets. Buys one-time rights. Negotiates payment individually. Identification of subjects, model releases required.

Columns/Departments: Nolan Woodrell, associate editor. Product Fix (product reviews); Now Playing (video game reviews), 100-150 words; Media Injection (book/video/magazine reviews), 100 words. Query. **Pays 60¢/word.**

Fillers: Facts, gags to be illustrated by cartoonist.

Tips: "We like to include as many how-to's and service-oriented pieces as possible."

Soccer

$ $ SOCCER NOW, Official Publication of the American Youth Soccer Organization, American Youth Soccer Organization, 12501 S. Isis Ave., Hawthorne CA 90250. (800)USA-AYSO or (310)643-6455. Fax: (310)643-5310. E-mail: soccernow@ayso.org. Website: www.soccer.org. **Contact:** David Brown, editor. Quarterly magazine covering soccer (AYSO and professional). "For AYSO members, both players (age 5-18) and their parents. Human interest about AYSO players and adult volunteers, or professional players (especially if they played in AYSO as kids)." Estab. 1976. Circ. 470,000. Pays on publication. Publishes ms an average of 3 months after acceptance. Byline given. Makes work-for-hire assignments. Editorial lead time 3 months. Accepts queries by mail, e-mail, fax. Responds in 1 month to queries. Sample copy free on request.

Nonfiction: General interest (soccer), historical/nostalgic, how-to (playing tips subject to approval by Director of Coaching), interview/profile, personal experience, photo feature. Query. Length: 400-1,000 words. **Pays $50-200.** Sometimes pays expenses of writers on assignment.

Photos: Send photos with submission. Reviews contact sheets, transparencies, prints. Buys one-time rights. Offers $0-50/photo. Identification of subjects required.

Columns/Departments: Headlines (news); Team Tips (instructional); Game Zone (games for kids—e.g., soccer-related word puzzles). Query. **Pays $0-50.**

Water Sports

DIVER, Seagraphic Publications, Ltd., Box 1312, Station A, Delta, British Columbia V4M 3Y8 Canada. (604)948-9937. Fax: (604948-9985. E-mail barbroy@direct.ca. Website: www.divermag.com. Publisher: Peter Vassilopoulos. **Contact:** Barb Roy, editor. Magazine published 9 times/year emphasizing scuba diving, ocean science, and technology for a well-educated, outdoor-oriented readership. Circ. 17,500. Payment follows publication. Publishes ms an average of up to 1 year after acceptance. Byline given. Buys first North American serial rights. Accepts queries by mail, e-mail, fax, phone. Responds in up to 3 months to queries.

- "articles are subject to being accepted for use in supplement issues on tabloid." Travel features considered only August through October for use following year.

Nonfiction: General interest (underwater oriented), historical/nostalgic (shipwrecks, treasure artifacts, archaeological), how-to (underwater activities such as photography), humor, interview/profile (underwater personalities in all spheres—military sports, scientific, or commercial), personal experience (related to diving), photo feature (marine life), technical (related to oceanography, commercial/military diving, etc.), travel (dive resorts). No subjective product reports. Submit complete ms with SAE and IRCs. Length: 800-1,000 words. Does not pay for travel articles.

Photos: "Features are mostly those describing dive sites, experiences, etc. Photo features are reserved more as specials, while almost all articles must be well illustrated with color or b&w prints supplemented by color transparencies." Submit original photo material with accompanying ms. Buys one-time rights. Pays $15 minimum for 5×7 or 8×10 b&w glossy prints; $20 minimum for 35mm color transparencies. Captions, model releases required.

Columns/Departments: Book reviews. Length: 200 words maximum. Send complete ms. **No payment.**

Fillers: Anecdotes, newsbreaks, short humor. **Buys 8-10 /year.** Length 50-150 words. **Pays no payment for news items.**

Tips: "No phone calls about status of manuscript. Write if no response within reasonable time. Only brief, to-the-point correspondence will be answered. Lengthy communications will probably result in return of work unused. Publisher assumes no liability to use material even after lengthy waiting period. Acceptances subject to final and actual use."

$ $ IMMERSED MAGAZINE, The International Technical Diving Magazine, Immersed LLC, FDR Station, P.O. Box 947, New York NY 10150-0947. (201)792-1331. Fax: (212)259-9310. E-mail: bob@immersed.com. Website: www.immersed.com. **Contact:** Bob Sterner, publisher/editor. **60% freelance written.** Quarterly magazine covering scuba diving. "Advances on the frontier of scuba diving are covered in theme-oriented issues that examine archeology, biology, history, gear, and sciences related to diving. We emphasize training, education, and safety." Estab. 1996. Circ. 25,000. Pays on publication. Byline given. Offers kill fee. Buys one-time, electronic rights. Editorial lead time 6 months. Accepts queries by mail, e-mail, fax, phone. Sample copy online. Writer's guidelines for #10 SASE.

O→ Break in with "how-to equipment rigging stories or travel stories on unusual but accessible destinations."

Nonfiction: Historical/nostalgic, how-to, interview/profile, new product, personal experience, photo feature, technical, travel. No poetry, opinion diatribes, axe-grinding exposés. **Buys 30 mss/year.** Query. Length: 500-2,000 words. **Pays $150-250.** Sometimes pays expenses of writers on assignment.

Photos: Send photos with submission. Reviews transparencies, prints. Buys one-time and promotional website rights. Offers no additional payment for photos accepted with ms. Captions required.

Columns/Departments: Technically Destined (travel), 1,200 words; Rigging For Success (how-to, few words/heavily illustrated); Explorer (personality profile), 2,000 words; Tech Spec (product descriptions), 1,000 words; New Products (product press releases), 200 words; Book Review (book review), 800 words. **Buys 12 mss/year.** Query. **Pays $150-250.**

Fillers: Newsbreaks. **Pays 35¢/word.**

Tips: "Query first with a short, punchy paragraph that describes your story and why it would be of interest to our readers. There's bonus points for citing which feature or department would be most appropriate for your story."

$ $ PADDLER MAGAZINE, World's No. 1 Canoeing, Kayaking and Rafting Magazine, Paddlesport Publishing, P.O. Box 775450, Steamboat Springs CO 80477-5450. (970)879-1450. Fax: (970)870-1404. E-mail: bieline@paddlermagazine.com. Website: www.paddlermagazine.com. Editor: Eugene Buchanan. **Contact:** Tom Bie, managing editor. **70% freelance written.** Bimonthly magazine covering paddle sports. "*Paddler* magazine is written by and for those knowledgeable about river running, flatwater canoeing and sea kayaking. Our core audience is the intermediate to advanced paddler, yet we strive to cover the entire range from beginners to experts. Our editorial coverage is divided between whitewater rafting, whitewater kayaking, canoeing and sea kayaking. We strive for balance between the Eastern and Western U.S. paddling scenes and regularly cover international expeditions. We also try to integrate the Canadian paddling community into each publication." Estab. 1991. Circ. 80,000. Pays on publication. Publishes ms an average of 6 months after acceptance. Byline given. Buys first North American serial rights. One-time electronic rights Editorial lead time 3 months. Submit seasonal material 6 months in advance. Accepts queries by mail, e-mail. Responds in 6 months to queries. Sample copy for $3 with 8æ×11 SASE. Writer's guidelines for #10 SASE.

O→ Break in through "The Hotline section at the front of the magazine."

Nonfiction: Book excerpts, essays, general interest, historical/nostalgic, how-to, humor, inspirational, interview/profile, new product, opinion, personal experience, photo feature, technical, travel (must be paddlesport related). **Buys 75 mss/year.** Query. Length: 100-3,000 words. **Pays 10-25¢/word (more for established writers) for assigned articles; 10-20¢/word for unsolicited articles.** Sometimes pays expenses of writers on assignment.

Photos: Submissions should include photos or other art. State availability with submission. Reviews contact sheets, negatives, transparencies. Buys one-time rights. Offers $25-200/photo.

Columns/Departments: Hotline (timely news and exciting developments relating to the paddling community. Stories should be lively and newsworthy), 150-750 words; Paddle People (unique people involved in the sport and industry leaders), 600-800 words; Destinations (informs paddlers of unique places to paddle—we often follow regional themes and cover all paddling disciplines); submissions should include map and photo, 800 words. Marketplace (gear reviews, gadgets and new products, and is about equipment paddlers use, from boats and paddles to collapsible chairs, bivy sacks and other accessories), 250-800 words. Paddle Tales (short, humorous anecdotes), 75-300 words. Skills (a "How-to" forum for experts to share tricks of the trade, from playboating techniques to cooking in the backcountry), 250-1,000 words. Query. **Pays 20-25¢/word.**

Tips: "We prefer queries, but will look at manuscripts on speculation. No phone queries please. Be familiar with the magazine and offer us unique, exciting ideas. Most positive responses to queries are on spec, but we will occasionally make assignments."

$ $ ☆ SPORT DIVER, World Publications, 460 N. Orlando Ave., Suite 200, Winter Park FL 32789-2988. (407)571-4584. Fax: (407)571-4585. E-mail: kirk.brown@worldpub.net. Website: www.sportdiver.com. Kirk Brown, managing editor. **75% freelance written.** Bimonthly magazine covering scuba diving. "We portray the adventure and fun of diving—the reasons we all started diving in the first place." Estab. 1993. Circ. 175,000. Pays on publication, sometimes on acceptance. Byline given. Offers 25% kill fee. Buys first North American serial rights. Editorial lead time 3 months. Submit seasonal material 4 months in advance. Accepts queries by e-mail. Responds in 2 weeks to queries; 3 months to mss. Writer's guidelines for #10 SASE.

Nonfiction: Personal experience, travel, diving. No nondiving related articles. **Buys 150 mss/year.** Query with SASE. Length: 800-2,000 words. **Pays $300-500.**

Photos: State availability with submission. Reviews transparencies. Buys one-time rights. Offers $50-200/photo; $1,000 for covers. Captions required.
Columns/Departments: Divebriefs (shorts), 150-450 words. Query. **Pays $50-250.**

The online magazine carries original content not included in the print edition. Contact: Paul Tzimoulis, online editor.

Tips: "Know diving, and even more importantly, know how to write. It's getting much more difficult to break into the market due to a recent series of takeovers."

$ $ WAKE BOARDING MAGAZINE, World Publications, Inc., P.O. Box 2456, Winter Park FL 32790. Fax: (407)628-7061. E-mail: editor@wakeboardingmag.com. Website: www.wakeboardingmag.com. Editor: Jeff Barton. **Contact:** Kevin Michael, managing editor. **10% freelance written.** Magazine published 9 times/year covering wakeboarding. "*Wake Boarding Magazine* is the leading publication for wakeboarding in the world. Articles must focus on good riding, first and foremost, then good fun and good times. Covers competition, travel, instruction, personalities, and humor." Estab. 1994. Circ. 65,000. Pays on publication. Publishes ms an average of 3 months after acceptance. Byline given. Buys all rights. Editorial lead time 4 months. Submit seasonal material 4 months in advance. Accepts queries by mail, e-mail. Accepts simultaneous submissions. Responds in 1 week to queries; 1 month to mss. Sample copy and writer's guidelines free.
Nonfiction: General interest, how-to (wakeboarding instruction), humor, interview/profile, new product, photo feature, travel. "No Weekend Wallys having fun on the lake. Serious riders only. Nothing to do with water skiing or barefooting." **Buys 6-8 mss/year.** Send complete ms. Length: 1,000-2,500 words. **Pays $200-500.**
Photos: Send photos with submission. Reviews slide transparencies. Buys all rights. Negotiates payment individually. Captions, identification of subjects required.
Columns/Departments: Random Notes (events, travel stories), 600-750 words. **Buys 6-8 mss/year.** Send complete ms. **Pays $50-200.**
Tips: "Contact us first before presuming article is worthy. What may be cool to you might not fit our readership. Remember, *WBM*'s readership is made up of a lot of teenagers, so buck authority every chance you get."

$ THE WATER SKIER, USA Water Ski, 1251 Holy Cow Rd., Polk City FL 33868-8200. (863)324-4341. Fax: (863)325-8259. E-mail: satkinson@usawaterski.org. Website: www.usawaterski.org. Scott Atkinson, editor. **10-20% freelance written.** Magazine published 9 times/year. "*The Water Skier* is the membership magazine of USA Water Ski, the national governing body for organized water skiing in the United States. The magazine has a controlled circulation and is available only to USA Water Ski's membership, which is made up of 20,000 active competitive water skiers and 10,000 members who are supporting the sport. These supporting members may participate in the sport but they don't compete. The editorial content of the magazine features distinctive and informative writing about the sport of water skiing only." Estab. 1951. Circ. 30,000. Byline given. Offers 30% kill fee. Editorial lead time 4 months. Submit seasonal material 6 months in advance. Responds in 2 weeks to queries. Sample copy for $3.50. Writer's guidelines for #10 SASE.

Most open to material for feature articles (query editor with your idea).

Nonfiction: Historical/nostalgic (has to pertain to water skiing), interview/profile (call for assignment), new product (boating and water ski equipment), travel (water ski vacation destinations). **Buys 10-15 mss/year.** Query. Length: 1,500-3,000 words. **Pays $100-150.**
Reprints: Send photocopy. Pay negotiable.
Photos: State availability with submission. Reviews contact sheets. Buys all rights. Negotiates payment individually. Captions, identification of subjects required.
Columns/Departments: The Water Skier News (small news items about people and events in the sport), 400-500 words. Other topics include safety, training (3-event, barefoot, disabled, show ski, ski race, kneeboard, and wakeboard); champions on their way; new products. Query. **Pays $50-100.**

The online magazine carries original content not found in the print edition. Contact: Scott Atkinson, online editor.

Tips: "Contact the editor through a query letter (please, no phone calls) with an idea. Avoid instruction, these articles are written by professionals. Concentrate on articles about the people of the sport. We are always looking for interesting stories about people in the sport. Also, short news features which will make a reader say to himself, 'Hey, I didn't know that.' Keep in mind that the publication is highly specialized about the sport of water skiing."

TEEN & YOUNG ADULT

Publications in this category are for teens (13-19). Publications for college students are in the Career, College & Alumni section. Those for younger children are inthe Juvenile section.

$ $ CAMPUS LIFE, Christianity Today, Inc., 465 Gundersen Dr., Carol Stream IL 60188. (630)260-6200. Fax: (630)260-0114. E-mail: clmag@campuslife.com. Website: www.campuslife.net. **Contact:** Chris Lutes, editor. **35% freelance written.** Magazine published 9 times/year for the Christian life as it relates to today's teen. "*Campus Life* is a magazine for high-school and early college-age teenagers. Our editorial slant is not overtly religious. The indirect style is intended to create a safety zone with our readers and to reflect our philosophy that God is interested in all of life. Therefore, we publish 'message stories' side by side with general interest, humor, etc. We are also looking for stories that help high school students consider a Christian college education." Estab. 1942. Circ. 100,000. **Pays on**

acceptance. Publishes ms an average of 5 months after acceptance. Byline given. Offers 50% kill fee. Buys first, one-time rights. Editorial lead time 4 months. Accepts queries by mail, fax. Responds in 5 weeks to queries. Sample copy for $3 and 8×10 SAE with 3 first-class stamps. Writer's guidelines for #10 SASE or online.

- No unsolicited mss.

Nonfiction: Humor, personal experience, photo feature. **Buys 15-20 mss/year.** Query with published clips. Length: 750-1,500 words. **Pays 15-20¢/word minimum.**

Reprints: Send tearsheet, photocopy or typed ms with rights for sale noted and information about when and where the material previously appeared. Pays $50.

Fiction: Buys 1-5 mss/year. Query. Length: 1,000-2,000 words. **Pays 15-20¢/word.**

Tips: "The best way to break in to *Campus Life* is through writing first-person or as-told-to first-person stories. We want stories that capture a teen's everyday 'life lesson' experience. A first-person story must be highly descriptive and incorporate fictional technique. While avoiding simplistic religious answers, the story should demonstrate that Christian values or beliefs brought about a change in the young person's life. But query first with theme information telling the way this story would work for our audience."

$ ENCOUNTER, Standard Publishing, 8121 Hamilton Ave., Cincinnati OH 45231-2323. (513)931-4050. Fax: (513)931-0950. E-mail: kcarr@standardpub.com. **Contact:** Kelly Carr, editor. **90% freelance written.** Weekly magazine for "teens, age 13-19, from Christian backgrounds who generally receive this publication in their Sunday School classes or through subscriptions." "We use freelance material in every issue. Our theme list is available on a quarterly basis. Writers need only give us their name and address (or e-mail address) in order to be added to our mailing list." **Pays on acceptance.** Publishes ms an average of 1 year after acceptance. Byline given. Buys first, second serial (reprint) rights. Submit seasonal material 1 year in advance. Accepts queries by mail, e-mail. Responds in 2 months to queries. Sample copy and writer's guidelines for 9×12 SAE with 2 first-class stamps.

Nonfiction: "We want articles that promote Christian values and ideals." No puzzles. General interest (school, church, family, dating, sports, part-time jobs), humor, inspirational, interview/profile, personal experience, religious. Submit complete ms. Include Social Security number on ms. Length: 800-1,100 words. **Pays 6-8¢/word.**

Reprints: Send typed ms with rights for sale noted. Pays 6¢/word.

Fiction: "All fiction should have some message for the modern Christian teen. Fiction should deal with all subjects in a forthright manner, without being preachy and without talking down to teens. No tasteless manuscripts that promote anything adverse to the Bible's teachings." Adventure, humorous, religious, suspense. Send complete ms. Length: 900-1,100 words. **Pays 6-8¢/word.**

Tips: "Don't be trite. Use unusual settings or problems. Use a lot of illustrations, a good balance of conversation, narration, and action. Style must be clear, fresh—no sermonettes or sickly-sweet fiction. Take a realistic approach to problems. Be willing to submit to editorial policies on doctrine; knowledge of the Bible a must. Also, be aware of teens today, and what they do. Language, clothing, and activities included in manuscripts should be contemporary. We are also looking for articles about real teens who are making a difference in their school, community or church. Articles for this feature should be approx. 900 words in length. We would also like a picture of the teen or group of teens to run with the article."

N $ FLORIDA LEADER, (for high school students), Oxendine Publishing, Inc., P.O. Box 14081, Gainesville FL 32604-2081. (352)373-6907. Fax: (352)373-8120. E-mail: info@studentleader.com. Website: www.floridaleader.com. Editor: W. H. Oxendine, Jr. **Contact:** Stephanie Rectz, associate editor. Triannual magazine covering high school and pre-college youth. Estab. 1983. Circ. 50,000. Pays on publication. Publishes ms an average of 3 months after acceptance. Buys all rights. Submit seasonal material 4 months in advance. Accepts queries by mail, e-mail, fax. Accepts simultaneous submissions. Responds in 2 months to queries. Sample copy for $3.50 and 8×11 SAE, with 3 first-class stamps. For query response and/or writer's guidelines send #10 SASE.

Nonfiction: Practical tips for going to college, student life, and leadership development. "No lengthy individual profiles or articles without primary and secondary sources of attribution." How-to, new product. Length: 250-1,000 words. **Payment varies. Pays students or first-time writers with contributor's copies.**

Photos: Send photos with submission. Reviews contact sheets, negatives, transparencies. Buys all rights. Offers $50/photo maximum. Captions, identification of subjects, model releases required.

Columns/Departments: College Life, The Lead Role, In Every Issue (quizzes, tips), Florida Forum (features Florida high school students), 250-1,000 words. **Buys 2 mss/year.** Query. **Pays $35-75.**

Fillers: Facts, newsbreaks, tips, book reviews. Length: 100-300 words. **Pays no payment.**

Tips: "Read other high school and college publications for current issues, interests. Send manuscripts or outlines for review. All sections open to freelance work. Always looking for lighter, humorous articles as well as features on Florida colleges and universities, careers, jobs. Multi-sourced (5-10) articles are best."

$ $ GUIDEPOSTS FOR TEENS, Guideposts, 1050 Broadway, Suite 6, Chesterton IN 46304. (219)929-4429. Fax: (219)926-3839. E-mail: gp4t@guideposts.org. Website: www.gp4teens.com. Editor-in-Chief: Mary Lou Carney. **Contact:** Betsy Kohn, editor. **90% freelance written.** Bimonthly magazine serving as an inspiration for teens. "*Guideposts for Teens* is a 4-color, value-centered magazine that offers teens ages 12-18 true, first-person stories packed with adventure and inspiration. Our mission is to empower teens through lively, positive, thought-provoking content: music reviews, how-tos, advice, volunteer opportunities, news, quizzes, profiles of positive role models—both celebrity and ordinary teens. *Guideposts for Teens* helps our readers discover sound values that will enable them to lead successful, hope-filled lives." Estab. 1998. Circ. 250,000. **Pays on acceptance.** Byline sometimes given. Offers 25% kill fee. Buys all rights. Editorial lead time 6 months. Submit seasonal material 6 months in advance. Accepts queries by mail, e-mail. Accepts simultaneous submissions. Responds in 1 month to queries; 2 months to mss. Sample copy for $4.50. Writer's guidelines for #10 SASE.

Nonfiction: Nothing written from an adult point of view. How-to, humor, inspirational, interview/profile, personal experience, religious. **Buys 80 mss/year.** Query. Length: 700-2,000 words. **Pays $175-500 for assigned articles; $150-400 for unsolicited articles.** Pays expenses of writers on assignment.

Photos: State availability with submission. Buys one-time rights. Negotiates payment individually. Identification of subjects required.

Columns/Departments: Quiz (teen-relevant topics, teen language), 1,000 words; How-to (strong teen voice/quotes, teen topics), 750-1,000 words; Profiles (teens who initiate change/develop service projects), 300-500 words. **Buys 40 mss/year.** Query with published clips. **Pays $175-400.**

The online magazine carries original content not found in the print edition. Contact: Chris Lyon, managing editor.

Tips: "We are eagerly looking for a number of things: teen how-to pieces, quizzes, humor. Most of all, though, we are about TRUE STORIES in the *Guideposts* tradition. Teens in dangerous, inspiring, miraculous situations. These first-person (ghostwritten) true narratives are the backbone of *GP4T*—and what sets us apart from other publications."

$ $ KEYNOTER, Key Club International, 3636 Woodview Trace, Indianapolis IN 46268-3196. E-mail: keynoter@kiwanis.org. Website: www.keyclub.org. **Contact:** Amy L. Wiser, executive editor. **65% freelance written.** Monthly magazine for youth (December/January combined issue), distributed to members of Key Club International, a high school service organization for young men and women. Estab. 1946. Circ. 171,000. **Pays on acceptance.** Publishes ms an average of 5 months after acceptance. Byline given. Buys first North American serial rights. Submit seasonal material 7 months in advance. Accepts queries by mail, e-mail. Accepts simultaneous submissions. Responds in 2 months to queries. Sample copy for 65¢ and 8½ × 11 SAE. Writer's guidelines for SASE.

Nonfiction: "We would like to receive self-help and school-related nonfiction on leadership, community service, and teen issues." Book excerpts (included in articles), general interest (for intelligent teen audience), historical/nostalgic (generally not accepted), how-to (advice on how teens can enhance the quality of lives or communities), humor (accepted if adds to story), interview/profile (rarely purchased), new product (affecting teens), photo feature (if subject is right), technical (understandable and interesting to teen audience), travel (must apply to club travel schedule), academic, self-help, subjects that entertain and inform teens on topics that relate directly to their lives. "*Please, no first-person confessions, fiction, or articles that are written down to our teen readers. No filler, or book, movie, or music reviews.*" **Buys 10-15 mss/year.** Query with SASE. Length: 1,200-1,500 words. Sometimes pays expenses of writers on assignment.

Reprints: Send tearsheet or photocopy and information about when and where the material previously appeared.

Photos: State availability with submission. Reviews negatives, color contact sheets. Buys one-time rights. Payment for photos included in payment for ms. Identification of subjects required.

Tips: "We want to see articles written with attention to style and detail that will enrich the world of teens. Articles must be thoroughly researched and must draw on interviews with nationally and internationally respected sources. Our readers are 13-18, mature, and dedicated to community service. We are very committed to working with good writers, and if we see something we like in a well-written query, we'll try to work it through to publication."

$ LISTEN MAGAZINE, The Health Connection, 55 W. Oak Ridge Dr., Hagerstown MD 21740. (301)393-4010. Fax: (301)393-4055. E-mail: listen@healthconnection.org. Editor: Anita Jacobs. **Contact:** Anita Jacobs, editor. **50% freelance written.** Monthly magazine specializing in tobacco, drug, and alcohol prevention, presenting positive alternatives to various tobacco, drug, and alcohol dependencies. "*Listen* is used in many high school classes and by professionals: medical personnel, counselors, law enforcement officers, educators, youth workers, etc." Circ. 40,000. **Pays on acceptance.** Publishes ms an average of 6 months after acceptance. Byline given. first rights for use in *Listen*, reprints, and associated material. Accepts queries by mail, e-mail, fax. Accepts previously published material. Accepts simultaneous submissions. Responds in 2 months to queries. Sample copy for $1 and 9×12 SASE. Writer's guidelines for SASE.

Break in with "a fresh approach with a surprise ending."

Nonfiction: Seeks articles that deal with causes of drug use such as poor self-concept, family relations, social skills, peer pressure. Especially interested in youth-slanted articles or personality interviews encouraging nonalcoholic and nondrug ways of life and showing positive alternatives. Also interested in good activity articles of interest to teens; an activity that teens would want to do instead of taking abusive substances because they're bored. Teenage point of view is essential. Also seeks narratives which portray teens dealing with youth conflicts, especially those related to the use of or temptation to use harmful substances. Growth of the main character should be shown. "Submit an article with an ending that catches you by surprise. We don't want typical alcoholic story/skid-row bum, or AA stories. We are also being inundated with drunk-driving accident stories. Unless yours is unique, consider another topic." **Buys 30-50 unsolicited mss/year.** Query. Length: 1,000-1,200 words. **Pays 5-10¢/word.** Sometimes pays expenses of writers on assignment.

Reprints: Send photocopy of article or typed ms with rights for sale noted and information about when and where the material previously appeared. Pays their regular rates.

Photos: Color photos preferred, but b&w acceptable. Purchased with accompanying ms. Captions required.

Fillers: Word square/general puzzles are also considered. **Pays $15.**

Tips: "True stories are good, especially if they have a unique angle. Other authoritative articles need a fresh approach. In query, briefly summarize article idea and logic of why you feel it's good. Make sure you've read the magazine to understand our approach."

$ LIVE, A Weekly journal of Practical Christian Living, Gospel Publishing House, 1445 N. Boonville Ave., Springfield MO 65802-1894. (417)862-2781. Fax: (417)862-6059. E-mail: rl-live@gph.org. Website: www.radiantlife.org. **Contact:** Paul W. Smith, senior editor, adult resources. **100% freelance written.** Quarterly magazine for weekly distribution covering practical Christian living. "*LIVE* is a take-home paper distributed weekly in young adult and adult Sunday school classes. We seek to encourage Christians in living for God through fiction and true stories which apply Biblical principles to everyday problems." Estab. 1928. Circ. 115,000. **Pays on acceptance.** Publishes ms an average of 18 months after acceptance. Byline given. Buys first, second serial (reprint) rights. Editorial lead time 12 months. Submit seasonal material 18 months in advance. Accepts queries by mail, e-mail, fax, phone. Accepts simultaneous submissions. Responds in 2 weeks to queries; 2 months to mss. Sample copy and writer's guidelines for #10 SASE or writer's guidelines *only* on website.

Break in with "true stories that demonstrate how the principles in the Bible work in every day circumstances as well as crises."

Nonfiction: Inspirational, religious. No preachy articles or stories that refer to religious myths (e.g., Santa Claus, Easter Bunny, etc.). **Buys 50-100 mss/year.** Send complete ms. Length: 400-1,500 words. **Pays 7-10¢/word.**

Reprints: Send tearsheet, photocopy or typed ms with rights for sale noted and information about when and where the material previously appeared. Pays 7¢/word.

Photos: Send photos with submission. Reviews 35mm transparencies and 3×4 prints or larger. Buys one-time rights. Offers $35-60/photo. Identification of subjects required.

Fiction: Religious, inspirational. No preachy fiction, fiction about Bible characters, or stories that refer to religious myths (e.g., Santa Claus, Easter Bunny, etc.). No science or Bible fiction. **Buys 50 mss/year.** Send complete ms. Length: 800-1,600 words. **Pays 7-10¢/word.**

Poetry: Free verse, haiku, light verse, traditional. **Buys 15-24 poems/year.** Submit maximum 3 poems. Length: 12-25 lines. **Pays $35-60.**

Fillers: Anecdotes, short humor. **Buys 12-36/year.** Length: 300-600 words. **Pays 7-10¢/word.**

Tips: "Don't moralize or be preachy. Provide human interest articles with Biblical life application. Stories should consist of action, not just thought-life; interaction, not just insight. Heroes and heroines should rise above failures, take risks for God, prove that scriptural principles meet their needs. Conflict and suspense should increase to a climax! Avoid pious conclusions. Characters should be interesting, believable, and realistic. Avoid stereotypes. Characters should be active, not just pawns to move the plot along. They should confront conflict and change in believable ways. Describe the character's looks and reveal his personality through his actions to such an extent that the reader feels he has met that person. Readers should care about the character enough to finish the story. Feature racial, ethnic, and regional characters in rural and urban settings."

$$$$ SEVENTEEN, 1440 Broadway, 13th Floor, New York NY 10018. (212)204-4300. Fax: (212)204-3972 or (212)204-3973. Website: www.seventeen.com. Editor-in-Chief: Annemarie Iverson. **Contact:** Darcy Jacobs, senior editor. **20% freelance written.** Monthly magazine. "*Seventeen* is a young woman's first fashion and beauty magazine. Tailored for young women in their teens and early twenties, *Seventeen* covers fashion, beauty, health, fitness, food, college, entertainment, fiction, plus crucial personal and global issues." Circ. 2,400,000. **Pays on acceptance.** Publishes ms an average of 6 months after acceptance. Byline given. Offers 25% kill fee. Buys one-time rights. Accepts queries by mail. Responds in 3 months to queries. Sample copy not available. Writer's guidelines available.

Break in with the Who Knew section, which contains shorter items, or *Quiz*.

Nonfiction: Articles and features of general interest to young women who are concerned with intimate relationships and how to realize their potential in the world; strong emphasis on topicality and service. Send brief outline and query, including typical lead paragraph, summing up basic idea of article, with clips of previously published works. Articles are commissioned after outlines are submitted and approved. Length: 1,200-2,500 words. **Pays $1/word, occasionally more for assigned articles.** Pays expenses of writers on assignment.

Photos: Photos usually by assignment only. Loraine Pavich, photo editor.

Fiction: Thoughtful, well-written stories on subjects of interest to girls between the ages of 12 and 21. Avoid formula stories—"She's blonde and pretty; I'm not"—no heavy moralizing or condescension of any sort. We also have an annual fiction contest. Length: 1,000-3,000 words. **Pays $500-2,000.**

The online magazine carries original content not found in the print edition. Contact: Lauren Weedon, online editor.

Tips: "Writers have to ask themselves whether or not they feel they can find the right tone for a *Seventeen* article—a tone which is empathetic, yet never patronizing; lively, yet not superficial. Not all writers feel comfortable with, understand, or like teenagers. If you don't like them, *Seventeen* is the wrong market for you. An excellent way to break in to the magazine is by contributing ideas for quizzes or the 'My Story' (personal essay) column."

$$ SPIRIT, Lectionary-based Weekly for Catholic Teens, Good Ground Press, 1884 Randolph Ave., St. Paul MN 55105-1700. (651)690-7010. Fax: (651)690-7039. E-mail: jmcsj9@aol.com. Managing Editor: Therese Sherlock, CSJ. **Contact:** Joan Mitchell, CSJ, editor. **50% freelance written.** Weekly newsletter for religious education of Catholic high schoolers. "We want realistic fiction and nonfiction that raises current ethical and religious questions and that deals with conflicts that teens face in multi-racial contexts. The fact we are a religious publication does *not* mean we want pious, moralistic fiction." Estab. 1981. Circ. 26,000. Pays on publication. Publishes ms an average of 6 months after acceptance. Byline given. Buys all rights. Editorial lead time 6 months. Submit seasonal material 6 months in advance. Accepts queries by mail, e-mail, fax. Accepts simultaneous submissions. Responds in 1 month to queries. Sample copy and writer's guidelines free.

Nonfiction: "No Christian confessional, born-again pieces." Interview/profile, personal experience, religious, Roman Catholic leaders, human interest features, social justice leaders, projects, humanitarians. **Buys 4 mss/year.** Query with published clips or send complete ms. Length: 1,000-1,200 words. **Pays $200-225 for assigned articles; $150 for unsolicited articles.**
Photos: State availability with submission. Reviews 8×10 prints. Buys one-time rights. Offers $85-125/photo. Identification of subjects required.
Fiction: "We want realistic pieces for and about teens—nonpedantic, nonpious. We need good Christmas stories that show spirit of the season, and stories about teen relationship conflicts (boy/girl, parent/teen)." Conflict vignettes. **Buys 10 mss/year.** Query with published clips or send complete ms. Length: 1,000-1,200 words. **Pays $150-200.**
Tips: "Writers must be able to write from and for teen point of view rather than adult or moralistic point of view. In nonfiction, interviewed teens must speak for themselves. Query to receive call for stories, spec sheet, sample issues."

$ $ TEENSFORJC.COM, (formerly *Setmag.com*), PLGK, Inc., Suite 760-355, Lawrenceville-Suwanee Rd., Suwane GA 30024. (770)831-8622. E-mail: uvaldes@aol.com. Website: www.teensforjc.com. Managing Editor: Ryder Stuart. **Contact:** Quentin Plair, editor. **90% freelance written.** Online publication covering Christian teen life. "TeensforJC.com salutes the exhiliration and fun of being a Christian teen. Our publication stays positive without becoming idealistic. Many subjects and viewpoints are explored in our open forums, but the endless exploration of teen negatives is left to other teen sites. Our goal is to celebrate all the wonderful things that make being a Christian teen great and provide the information that teens need to lay a foundation for success in life." Estab. 2001. Circ. 5,000 hits/month. Pays on publication. Publishes ms an average of 6 months after acceptance. Byline given. Buys one-time rights. Editorial lead time 4 months. Submit seasonal material 4 months in advance. Accepts queries by mail, e-mail, phone. Accepts previously published material. Accepts simultaneous submissions. Responds in 7 weeks to queries; 2 months to mss. Sample copy online. Writer's guidelines for #10 SASE.
Nonfiction: Book excerpts, essays, humor, inspirational, interview/profile (celebrities), opinion (current or teen issues), personal experience, photo feature, travel (vacations). Special issues: "We will need Spring/Prom short stories and articles by January 15 each year. Summer Fun articles/short stories and poetry by April 15 each year. Back to School stories by June 15 of each year. College Search and Scholarship information by Sept. 15 of each year." **Buys 1 mss/year.** Send complete ms. **Pays $25-250.** Sometimes pays expenses of writers on assignment.
Reprints: Accepts previously published submissions.
Photos: Send photos with submission. Reviews 8×10 prints, GIF/JPEG files. Buys one-time rights. Offers $15-30/photo. Identification of subjects, model releases required.
Columns/Departments: School Tips (helpful tips for high school students), Speak Out (opinion articles written by teens), both 500-1,500 words. **Buys 10 mss/year.** Send complete ms. **Pays $25-250.**
Fiction: Adventure, experimental, fantasy, historical, horror, humorous, mainstream, mystery, romance, science fiction, suspense. **Buys 10 mss/year.** Send complete ms. **Pays $25-250.**
Poetry: All appropriate poetry submissions are posted as long as the author is between 12 and 19 years of age. Electronic submissions are encouraged. Avant-garde, free verse, haiku, light verse, traditional. **No payment for poetry.**
Fillers: Anecdotes, facts, short humor. **Buys 40/year.** Length: 10-500 words. **Pays $15-50.**

$ TODAY'S CHRISTIAN TEEN, Marketing Partners, Inc., P.O. Box 100, Morgantown PA 19543. (610)856-6830. Fax: (610)856-6831. E-mail: tcpubs@mkpt.com. Editor: Jerry Thacker. **Contact:** Elaine Williams, assistant editor. **75% freelance written.** Quarterly magazine covering teen issues from a Biblical perspective. "*Today's Christian Teen* is designed to deal with issues in the life of Christian teenagers from a conservative perspective." Estab. 1990. Circ. 100,000. Pays on publication. Publishes ms an average of 1 year after acceptance. Byline sometimes given. Buys simultaneous rights. Editorial lead time 1 year. Submit seasonal material 1 year in advance. Accepts queries by mail, e-mail, fax. Accepts previously published material. Accepts simultaneous submissions. Responds in 1 month to queries; 3 months to mss. Sample copy for 9×12 SAE with 4 first-class stamps. Writer's guidelines for #10 SASE.

"Make your article practical, using principles from KJV Bible."

Nonfiction: Inspirational, personal experience, religious. **Buys 10 mss/year.** Send complete ms. Length: 800-1,200 words. **Pays $150.**
Reprints: Accepts previously published submissions.
Photos: Offers no additional payment for photos accepted with ms.

$ $ TRANSCENDMAG.COM, PLGK, Inc., Suite 760-355, 2855 Lawrenceville-Suwanee Rd., Suwanee GA 30024. (770)831-8622. E-mail: uvaldes@aol.com. Website: www.transcendmag.com. Managing Editor: Travis Lucas. **Contact:** Quentin Plair, editor. **75% freelance written.** Monthly online publication for African-American teens. This is a "publication for African-American teens which salutes the fun and exhiliration of being a teen. *Transcendmag* embraces the fact that in the 21st century there is no limit to the potential of this generation. We hope to bolster that potential by providing timely tips and information." Estab. 2000. Circ. 10,000 hits/month. Pays on publication. Publishes ms an average of 2 months after acceptance. Byline given. Buys one-time rights. Editorial lead time 3 months. Submit seasonal material 4 months in advance. Accepts queries by mail, e-mail, phone. Accepts previously published material. Accepts simultaneous submissions. Responds in 6 weeks to queries; 3 months to mss. Sample copy online. Writer's guidelines for #10 SASE or on website.
Nonfiction: Book excerpts (teen focused), essays (current or teen issues), how-to (makeup, hair, dating, skin care, tanning, sports), humor, inspirational, interview/profile (role models, celebrities), opinion (current or teen issues), per-

sonal experience, photo feature. Special issues: Black History/Prom Preparation, January 2002; Graduation/Summer Fun, May 2002; Back to School/Scholarships/College Planning, September 2002. Will not print articles that are not teen related. **Buys 2 mss/year.** Send complete ms. **Pays $25-250.** Sometimes pays expenses of writers on assignment.
Reprints: Accepts previously published submissions.
Photos: Send photos with submission. Reviews GIF/JPEG files. Buys one-time rights. Offers $10-25/photo. Captions, identification of subjects, model releases required.
Columns/Departments: School tips (helpful tips for high school students), Speak Out (opinion articles written by teens), both 500-1,500 words. **Buys 12 mss/year.** Send complete ms. **Pays $25-250.**
Fiction: Adventure, ethnic, fantasy, humorous, romance, science fiction. **Buys 4 mss/year.** Send complete ms. **Pays $25-250.**
Poetry: All appropriate poetry is printed as long as the poet is age 12-19. Avant-garde, free verse, haiku, light verse, traditional. **No payment for poetry.**
Fillers: Anecdotes, facts, short humor. **Buys 50/year.** Length: 500 words maximum. **Pays $20.**

$ $ $ $ TWIST, Bauer Publishing, 270 Sylvan Ave., Englewood Cliffs NJ 07632. Fax: (201)569-4458. E-mail: twistmail@aol.com. Website: www.twistmagazine.com. Editor: Richard Spencer. **Contact:** Kristin McKeon, deputy editor. **5% freelance written.** Monthly entertainment magazine targeting 14- to 19-year-old girls. Estab. 1997. Circ. 700,000. **Pays on acceptance.** Publishes ms an average of 3 months after acceptance. Byline given. Offers 20% kill fee. Buys first North American serial rights. Editorial lead time 3 months. Submit seasonal material 4 months in advance. Accepts queries by mail. Accepts simultaneous submissions. Responds in 1 month to queries.
Nonfiction: "No articles written from an adult point of view about teens—i.e., a mother's or teacher's personal account." Personal experience (real teens' experiences, preferably in first person). **Pays minimum $50 for short item; up to $1/word for longer pieces.** Pays expenses of writers on assignment.
Photos: State availability with submission. Negotiates payment individually. Identification of subjects, model releases required.

■ The online magazine carries original content not found in the print edition. Contact: Kristin McKeon, online editor.

Tips: "Tone must be conversational, neither condescending to teens nor trying to be too slangy. If possible, send clips that show an ability to write for the teen market. We are in search of real-life stories, and writers who can find teens with compelling real-life experiences (who are willing to use their full names and photographs in the magazine). Please refer to a current issue to see examples of tone and content. No e-mail queries or submissions, please."

$ $ WHAT MAGAZINE, What! Publishers Inc., 108-93 Lombard Ave., Winnipeg, Manitoba R3B 3B1, Canada. (204)985-8160. Fax: (204)957-5638. E-mail: what@whatmagazine.ca. **Contact:** Barbara Chabai, editor/publisher. **40% freelance written.** Magazine published 5 times during the school year covering teen issues and pop culture. "*What Magazine* is distributed to high school students across Canada. We produce a mag that is empowering, interactive and entertaining. We respect the reader—today's teens are smart and creative (and critical)." Estab. 1987. Circ. 250,000. Pays 30 days after publication. Publishes ms an average of 3 months after acceptance. Byline given. Offers negotiable kill fee. Buys first North American serial rights. Editorial lead time 5 months. Submit seasonal material 5 months in advance. Accepts queries by mail, e-mail, fax. Responds in 2 months to queries; 1 month to mss. Sample copy for 9×12 SAE with Canadian postage. Writer's guidelines for #10 SAE with Canadian postage.
Nonfiction: General interest, interview/profile, issue-oriented features. No cliché teen material. **Buys 6-10 mss/year.** Query with published clips. Length: 700-1,900 words. **Pays $175-400 (Canadian).** Sometimes pays expenses of writers on assignment.
Photos: Send photos with submission. Reviews transparencies, 4×6 prints. Negotiates payment individually. Identification of subjects required.
Tips: "We have an immediate need for savvy freelancers to contribute features, short articles, interviews and reviews that speak to our intelligent teen audience. Looking for fresh talent and new ideas in the areas of entertainment, pop culture, teen issues, international events as they relate to readers, celebs and 'real people' profiles, lifestyle articles, extreme sports and any other stories of relevance to today's Canadian teen."

$ WITH, The Magazine for Radical Christian Youth, Faith and Life Press, 722 Main St., P.O. Box 347, Newton KS 67114-0347. (316)283-5100. Fax: (316)283-0454. E-mail: carold@mennoniteusa.org. Website: www.withonline.org. **Contact:** Carol Duerksen, editor. **60% freelance written.** Magazine published 6 times/year for teenagers. "We are a Christian youth magazine that strives to help youth be radically commited to a personal relationship with Jesus Christ, to peace and justice, and to sharing God's good news through word and action." Circ. 4,000. **Pays on acceptance.** Byline given. Buys one-time rights. Submit seasonal material 6 months in advance. Accepts queries by mail, fax. Accepts simultaneous submissions. Responds in 1 month to queries; 2 months to mss. Sample copy for 9×12 SAE with 4 first-class stamps. Writer's guidelines and theme list for #10 SASE. Additional detailed guidelines for first-person stories, how-to articles, and/or fiction available for #10 SASE.

O→ Break in with "well-written true stories from teen's standpoint."

Nonfiction: How-to, humor, personal experience, religious, youth. **Buys 15 mss/year.** Send complete ms. Length: 400-1,800 words. **Pays 5¢/word for simultaneous rights; higher rates for articles written on assignment; 3¢/word for reprint rights and for unsolicited articles.** Sometimes pays expenses of writers on assignment.
Reprints: Send ms with rights for sale noted and information about when and where the material previously appeared. Pays 60% of amount paid for an original article.

Photos: Send photos with submission. Reviews 8×10 color prints. Buys one-time rights. Offers $10-50/photo. Identification of subjects required.
Fiction: Humorous, religious, youth, parables. **Buys 15 mss/year.** Send complete ms. Length: 500-2,000 words. **Payment same as nonfiction.**
Poetry: Avant-garde, free verse, haiku, light verse, traditional. **Buys 0-2 poems/year. Pays $10-25.**
Tips: "We're looking for more wholesome humor, not necessarily religious—fiction, nonfiction, cartoons, light verse. Christmas and Easter material has a good chance with us because we receive so little of it."

$ YOUNG & ALIVE, Christian Record Services, P.O. Box 6097, Lincoln NE 68506. Website: www.christianrecord.org. **Contact:** Gaylena Gibson, editor. **95% freelance written.** Large-print Christian material for sight-impaired people age 12-25 (also in braille), covering health, handicapped people, uplifting articles. "Write for an interdenominational Christian audience—we also like to portray handicapped individuals living normal lives or their positive impact on those around them." Submit seasonal material anytime. Estab. 1976. Circ. 25,000 large print; 3,000 braille. **Pays on acceptance.** Publishes ms an average of 3 years after acceptance. Byline given. Buys one-time rights. Accepts simultaneous submissions. Responds in 1 year to mss. Sample copy for 7×10 SAE with 5 first-class stamps. Writer's guidelines for #10 SASE or included with sample copy.
Nonfiction: Essays, general interest, historical/nostalgic, humor, inspirational, personal experience, travel, adventure (true), biography, camping, careers, handicapped, health, hobbies, holidays, nature, sports. **Buys 40 mss/year.** Send complete ms. Length: 200-1,400 words. **Pays 4-5¢/word. "We do provide complimentary copies in addition to payment."**
Photos: Send photos with submission. Reviews 3×5 to 10×12 prints. Buys one-time rights. Negotiates payment individually. Model releases required.
Fillers: Anecdotes, facts, short humor. Length: 300 words maximum. **Pays 4¢/word.**
Tips: "Make sure article has a strong ending that ties everything together. Pretend someone else wrote it—would it hold your interest? Draw your readers into the story by being specific rather than abstract or general."

N $ $ YOUNG SALVATIONIST, The Salvation Army, P.O. Box 269, Alexandria VA 22313-0269. (703)684-5500. Fax: (703)684-5539. E-mail: ys@usn.salvationarmy.org. Website: publications.salvationarmyusa.org. **Contact:** Tim Clark, managing editor. **80% freelance written.** Monthly magazine for high school teens. . "Only material with Christian perspective with practical real-life application will be considered." Circ. 48,000 **Pays on acceptance.** Publishes ms an average of 6 months after acceptance. Byline given. Buys first North American serial, first, one-time, second serial (reprint) rights. Submit seasonal material 6 months in advance. Accepts queries by mail, e-mail. Responds in 2 months to queries. Sample copy for 9×12 SAE with 3 first-class stamps or on website. Writer's guidelines and theme list for #10 SASE or on website.

- Works with a small number of new/unpublished writers each year.
- "Our greatest need is for nonfiction pieces based in real life rather than theory or theology. Practical living articles are especially needed. We receive many fiction submissions but few good nonfiction."

Nonfiction: "Articles should deal with issues of relevance to teens (high school students) today; avoid 'preachiness' or moralizing." How-to, humor, inspirational, interview/profile, personal experience, photo feature, religious. **Buys 60 mss/year.** Send complete ms. Length: 1,000-1,500 words. **Pays 15¢/word for first rights.**
Reprints: Send tearsheet, photocopy or typed ms with rights for sale noted and information about when and where the material previously appeared. Pays 10¢/word for reprints.
Fiction: Only a small amount is used. Adventure, fantasy, humorous, religious, romance, science fiction, (all from a Christian perspective). **Buys few mss/year.** Length: 500-1,200 words. **Pays 15¢/word.**
Tips: "Study magazine, familiarize yourself with the unique 'Salvationist' perspective of *Young Salvationist*; learn a little about the Salvation Army; media, sports, sex and dating are strongest appeal."

$ $ YOUTH UPDATE, St. Anthony Messenger Press, 28 W. Liberty St., Cincinnati OH 45210-1298. (513)241-5615. Fax: (513)241-0399. E-mail: carolann@americancatholic.org. Website: www.americancatholic.org. **Contact:** Carol Ann Morrow, editor. **90% freelance written.** Monthly newsletter of faith life for teenagers. *Youth Update* is "designed to attract, instruct, guide, and challenge Catholics of high school age by applying the Gospel to modern problems/situations." Circ. 23,000. **Pays on acceptance.** Publishes ms an average of 6 months after acceptance. Byline given. Responds in 3 months to queries. Sample copy and writer's guidelines for #10 SASE.
Nonfiction: Inspirational, practical self help, spiritual. No fiction. **Buys 12 mss/year.** Query or send outline. "Identify yourself on the envelope; don't use lots of stamps, but have your envelope weighed and postage neatly affixed." **Pays $400-475.**

The online magazine mirrors the print edition. Contact: Carol Ann Morrow.

Tips: "Write for a 15-year-old with a C+ average."

TRAVEL, CAMPING & TRAILER

Travel magazines give travelers in-depth information about destinations, detailing the best places to go, attractions in the area, and sites to see—but they also keep them up to date about potential negative aspects of these destinations. Publications in this category tell tourists and campers the where-tos and how-tos of travel. This category is extremely competitive, demanding quality writing, background information, and professional photography. Each publication has its own slant. Sample copies should be studied carefully before sending submissions.

$AAA GOING PLACES, Magazine for Today's Traveler, AAA Auto Club South, 1515 N. Westshore Blvd., Tampa FL 33607. (813)289-5923. Fax: (813)289-6245. E-mail: pzeno@aaasouth.com. Phyllis Zeno, editor-in-chief. **50% freelance written.** Bimonthly magazine on auto tips, cruise travel, and tours. Estab. 1982. Circ. 2,500,000. Pays on publication. Publishes ms an average of 6 months after acceptance. Byline given. Buys one-time rights. Submit seasonal material 9 months in advance. Accepts simultaneous submissions. Responds in 2 months to queries; 2 months to mss. Sample copy not available. Writer's guidelines for SAE.

Nonfiction: Travel stories feature domestic and international destinations with practical information and where to stay, dine and shop, as well as personal anecdotes and historical background; they generally relate to tours currently offered by AAA Travel Agency. Historical/nostalgic, how-to, humor, interview/profile, personal experience, photo feature, travel. Special issues: Cruise Guide and Europe Issue. **Buys 15 mss/year.** Send complete ms. Length: 500-1,500 words. **Pays $50/printed page.**

Photos: State availability with submission. Reviews 2×2 transparencies. Offers no additional payment for photos accepted with ms. Captions required.

Columns/Departments: AAAway We Go (local attractions in Florida, Georgia or Tennessee).

Tips: "We prefer lively, upbeat stories that appeal to a well-traveled, sophisticated audience, bearing in mind that AAA is a conservative company."

$ $AAA MIDWEST TRAVELER, AAA Auto Club of Missouri, 12901 N. 40 Dr., St. Louis MO 63141. (314)523-7350 ext. 6301. Fax: (314)523-6982. E-mail: dreinhardt@aaamissouri.com. Website: www.aaamissouri.com/travelermagazines. Editor: Michael J. Right. **Contact:** Deborah Reinhardt, managing editor. **80% freelance written.** Bimonthly magazine covering travel and automotive safety. "We provide members with useful information on travel, auto safety and related topics." Estab. 1901. Circ. 440,000. **Pays on acceptance.** Byline given. Offers $50 kill fee. Not copyrighted. Buys first North American serial, second serial (reprint), electronic rights. Editorial lead time 1 year. Submit seasonal material 6 months in advance. Accepts queries by mail, e-mail, fax. Accepts simultaneous submissions. Responds in 1 month to queries; 1 month to mss. Sample copy for 10×13 SAE and 4 first-class stamps. Writer's guidelines for #10 SASE.

Nonfiction: Travel. No humor, fiction, poetry or cartoons. **Buys 20-30 mss/year.** Query with published clips the first time. Length: 800-1,200 words. **Pays $250-350.**

Photos: State availability with submission. Reviews transparencies, prints. Buys one-time and electronic rights. Offers no additional payment for photos accepted with ms. Captions required.

Tips: "Send queries between December and February, as we plan our calendar for the following year. Request a copy. Serious writers ask for media kit to help them target their piece. Travel destinations and tips are most open to freelancers; all departments and auto-related news handled by staff. We see too many 'Here's a recount of our family vacation' manuscripts. Go easy on first-person accounts."

$ $AAA TODAY, 1515 N. Westshore Blvd., Tampa FL 33607. (813)289-1391. Fax: (813)288-7935. E-mail: sklim@aaasouth.com. Sandy Klim, editor. **25% freelance written.** Bimonthly magazine covering travel destinations. Estab. 1960. Circ. 4,000,000. Pays on publication. Publishes ms an average of 6 months after acceptance. Byline given. Editorial lead time 1 year. Submit seasonal material 1 year in advance. Accepts queries by mail. Sample copy and writer's guidelines free.

Nonfiction: Travel. **Buys 18 mss/year.** Query with published clips. Length: 500-1,500 words. **Pays $250.**

Photos: State availability with submission.

$ $☐ ARUBA NIGHTS, Nights Publications, Inc., 1831 Rene Levesque Blvd. W., Montreal, Quebec H3H 1R4, Canada. (514)931-1987. Fax: (514)931-6273. E-mail: editor@nightspublications.com. Website: www.nightspublications.com. Managing Editor: Zelly Zuskin. **Contact:** Sonya Plowman, editor. **90% freelance written.** Annual magazine covering the Aruban vacation lifestyle experience with an upscale, upbeat touch. Estab. 1988. Circ. 225,000. **Pays on acceptance.** Publishes ms an average of 9 months after acceptance. Byline given. Buys first North American serial, first Caribbean rights. Editorial lead time 1 month. Accepts queries by mail, e-mail, fax. Responds in 2 weeks to queries; 1 month to mss. Sample copy for $5 (make checks payable to Nights Publications, Inc.). Writer's guidelines by e-mail.

O-- *Aruba Nights* is looking for more articles on nightlife experiences.

Nonfiction: General interest, historical/nostalgic, how-to (relative to Aruba vacationers), humor, inspirational, interview/profile, opinion, personal experience, photo feature, travel, Eco-tourism, Aruban culture, art, activities, entertainment, topics relative to vacationers in Aruba. "No negative pieces or stale rewrites." **Buys 5-10 mss/year.** Send complete ms, include SAE with Canadian postage or IRC. Length: 250-750 words. **Pays $75-250.**

Photos: State availability with submission. Reviews transparencies. Buys one-time rights. Pays $50/photo. Captions, identification of subjects, model releases required.

Tips: "Demonstrate your voice in your query letter. Be descriptive, employ vivid metaphors. Stories should immerse the reader in a sensory adventure. Focus on individual aspects of the Aruban lifestyle and vacation experience (e.g., art, music, culture, a colorful local character, a personal experience, etc.), rather than generalized overviews. Provide an angle that will be entertaining to vacationers who are already there. E-mail submissions accepted."

$ $ ASU TRAVEL GUIDE, ASU Travel Guide, Inc., 1525 Francisco Blvd. E., San Rafael CA 94901. (415)459-0300. Fax: (415)459-0494. E-mail: chris@asutravelguide.com. Website: www.asutravelguide.com. **Contact:** Christopher Gil, managing editor. **80% freelance written.** Quarterly guidebook covering international travel features and travel discounts for well-traveled airline employees. Estab. 1970. Circ. 50,000. **Pays on acceptance.** Publishes ms an average of 4 months after acceptance. Byline given. Buys first North American serial, first, second serial (reprint) rights. Submit seasonal material 6 months in advance. Accepts previously published material. Accepts simultaneous submissions. Responds in 1 year to queries; 1 year to mss. Sample copy for 6×9 SAE and 5 first-class stamps. Writer's guidelines for #10 SASE.

Nonfiction: International travel articles "similar to those run in consumer magazines. Not interested in amateur efforts from inexperienced travelers or personal experience articles that don't give useful information to other travelers." Destination pieces only; no "Tips on Luggage" articles. Unsolicited mss or queries without SASE will not be acknowledged. No telephone queries. Travel (international). **Buys 16 mss/year.** Length: 1,800 words. **Pays $200.**

Reprints: Send tearsheet and information about when and where the material previously appeared. Pays 100% of amount paid for an original article.

Photos: "Interested in clear, high-contrast photos." Reviews 5×7 and 8×10 b&w or color prints. Payment for photos is included in article price; photos from tourist offices are acceptable.

Tips: "Query with samples of travel writing and a list of places you've recently visited. We appreciate clean and simple style. Keep verbs in the active tense and involve the reader in what you write. Avoid 'cute' writing, coined words and stale cliches. The most frequent mistakes made by writers in completing an article for us are: 1) Lazy writing—using words to describe a place that could describe any destination such as 'there is so much to do in (fill in destination) that whole guidebooks have been written about it'; 2) Including fare and tour package information—our readers make arrangements through their own airline."

$ $ BONAIRE NIGHTS, Nights Publications, Inc., 1831 René Levesque Blvd. W., Montreal, Quebec H3H 1R4, Canada. (514)931-1987. Fax: (514)931-6273. E-mail: editor@nightspublications.com. Managing Editor: Zelly Zuslein. **Contact:** Sonya Plowman, editor. **90% freelance written.** Annual magazine covering Bonaire vacation experience. "Upbeat entertaining lifestyle articles: Colorful profiles of locals, eco-tourism; lively features on culture, activities (particularly scuba and snorkeling), special events, historical attractions, how-to features. Audience is North American tourists." Estab. 1993. Circ. 65,000. **Pays on acceptance.** Publishes ms an average of 9 months after acceptance. Byline given. Buys first North American serial, first Caribbean rights. Editorial lead time 1 month. Accepts queries by mail, e-mail, fax. Responds in 2 weeks to queries; 1 month to mss. Sample copy for $5 (make check payable to Night Publications, Inc). Writer's guidelines by e-mail.

Nonfiction: General interest, historical/nostalgic, how-to, humor, inspirational, interview/profile, opinion, personal experience, photo feature, travel, lifestyle, local culture, art, activities, scuba diving, snorkling, eco-tourism. **Buys 6-9 mss/year.** Query. Length: 250-750 words. **Pays $75-250.**

Photos: State availability with submission. Reviews transparencies. Pays $50/slide. Captions, identification of subjects, model releases required.

Tips: "Demonstrate your voice in your query letter. Focus on the Bonaire lifestyle, what sets it apart from other islands. We want personal experience, not generalized overviews. Be positive and provide an angle that will appeal to vacationers who are already there. Our style is upbeat, friendly, fluid and descriptive."

$ CAMPERS MONTHLY, Mid Atlantic Edition—New York to Virginia; Northeast Edition—Maine to New York, P.O. Box 260, Quakertown PA 18951. (215)536-6420. Fax: (215)536-6509. E-mail: werv2@aol.com. **Contact:** Paula Finkbeiner, editor. **50% freelance written.** Monthly (except December) tabloid. "With the above emphasis, we want to encourage our readers to explore all forms of outdoor recreation using a tent or recreational vehicle as a 'home away from home.' Travel—places to go, things to do and see." Estab. 1991 (Mid-Atlantic), 1993 (Northeast). Circ. 35,000 (Mid-Atlantic), 25,000 (Northeast). Pays on publication. Publishes ms an average of 2 months after acceptance. Byline given. Buys simultaneous rights. Editorial lead time 2 months. Submit seasonal material 4 months in advance. Accepts queries by mail, e-mail. Accepts simultaneous submissions. Responds in 2 months to mss. Sample copy and writer's guidelines for 10×13 SASE.

O━ Break in by finding a "little-known" destination in either of the regions covered.

Nonfiction: Historical/nostalgic (tied in to a camping trip), how-to (selection, care, maintenance of RV's, tents, accessories, etc.), humor, personal experience, technical, travel (camping in the Mid-Atlantic or Northeast region). Special issues: Snowbird Issue (October)—geared toward campers heading South; Christmas Gift Ideas (November). "This is generally the only time we accept articles on areas outside our coverage area." **Buys 20-40 mss/year.** Send complete ms. Length: 800-2,000 words. **Pays $90-150 for assigned articles; $50 or more for unsolicited articles.** Sometimes pays expenses of writers on assignment.

Reprints: Send photocopy with rights for sale noted and information about when and where the material previously appeared. Pays 50% of amount paid for an original article.

Photos: Send photos with submission. Reviews 5×7 or 8×10 glossy b&w and color prints. Offers $3-5/photo. Don't send snapshots or polaroids.

Columns/Departments: Campground Cook (ideas for cooking in RV's, tents and over campfires; include recipes), 500-1,000 words; Tales From the Road (humorous stories of "on-the-road" travel), 350-800 words; Tech Tips (technical pieces on maintenance and enhanced usage of RV-related equipment), 350-1,800 words; Cybersite (websites of interest to RVer's), 500-1,000 words. **Buys 10-15 mss/year.** Send complete ms. **Pays $40-60.**

Fiction: Humorous, slice-of-life vignettes. **Buys 10 mss/year.** Query. Length: 300-1,000 words. **Pays $60-75.**

Fillers: Facts, short humor (must be RV-oriented). **Buys 8/year.** Length: 30-350 words. **Pays $20-35.**

Tips: Most open to freelancers are "destination pieces focusing on a single attraction or activity or closely clustered attractions are always needed. General interest material, technical or safety ideas (for RVs) is an area we're always looking for pieces on. Off-the-beaten track destinations always get priority. We're always looking for submissions for destination pieces for our Mid-Atlantic edition."

CAMPERWAYS, CAMP-ORAMA, CAROLINA RV TRAVELER, FLORIDA RV TRAVELER, NORTHEAST OUTDOORS, SOUTHERN RV & TEXAS RV, Woodall Publications Corp., 2575 Vista Del Mar Dr., Ventura CA 93001. (800)323-9076. Fax: (805)667-4122. E-mail: editor@woodallpub.com. Website: www.woodalls.com. **Contact:** Melinda Baccanari, senior managing editor. **75% freelance written.** Monthly tabloid covering RV lifestyle. "We're looking for articles of interest to RVers. Lifestyle articles, destinations, technical tips, interesting events and the like make up the bulk of our publications. We also look for region-specific travel and special interest articles." Circ. 30,000. **Pays on acceptance.** Byline given. Offers 50% kill fee. Buys first North American serial rights. Submit seasonal material 4 months in advance. Accepts queries by mail, e-mail. Responds in 3 weeks to queries; 1 month to mss. Sample copy for free. Writer's guidelines for #10 SASE.

Nonfiction: How-to, humor, inspirational, interview/profile, new product, opinion, personal experience, technical, travel. No "Camping From Hell" articles. **Buys 1,000 mss/year.** Query with published clips. Length: 500-2,000 words. **Payment varies.**

Photos: Prefers slides. State availability with submission. Reviews negatives, 4×5 transparencies, 4×5 prints. Buys first North American serial rights. Pays $5/photo. Captions, identification of subjects required.

Columns/Departments: Gadgets & Gears (new product reviews), 600 words; RV Renovations (how-to building/renovations project), 1,000 words; Stopping Points (campground reviews), 1,000 words. **Buys 100 mss/year.** Query with published clips. **Payment negotiable.**

Tips: "Be an expert in RVing. Make your work readable to a wide variety of readers, from novices to full-timers."

$ $ CAMPING CANADA'S RV LIFESTYLES, 1020 Brevik Place, Mississauga, Ontario L4W 4N7, Canada. (905)624-8218. Fax: (905)624-6764. Website: www.rvlifemag.com. **Contact:** Norm Rosen, vice president special projects. **50% freelance written.** Magazine published 7 times/year (monthly January-June and November). "*Camping Canada's RV Lifestyles* is geared to readers who enjoy travel/camping. Upbeat pieces only. Readers vary from owners of towable trailers or motorhomes to young families and entry-level campers (no tenting)." Estab. 1971. Circ. 51,000. Pays on publication. Byline given. Buys first North American serial rights. Editorial lead time 2 months. Responds in 1 month to queries; 2 months to mss. Sample copy for free. Writer's guidelines not available.

Nonfiction: How-to, personal experience, technical, travel. No inexperienced, unresearched or too general pieces. **Buys 20-30 mss/year.** Query. Length: 1,200-2,000 words. **Payment varies.**

Photos: Send photos with submission. Buys one-time rights. Offers no additional payment for photos accepted with ms.

Tips: "Pieces should be slanted toward RV living. All articles must have an RV slant. Canadian content regulations require 95% Canadian writers."

$ CAMPING TODAY, Official Publication of the Family Campers & RVers, 126 Hermitage Rd., Butler PA 16001-8509. (724)283-7401. **Contact:** DeWayne Johnston, June Johnston, editors. **30% freelance written.** Monthly official membership publication of the FCRV. *Camping Today* is "the largest nonprofit family camping and RV organization in the United States and Canada. Members are heavily oriented toward RV travel, both weekend and extended vacations. Concentration is on member activities in chapters. Group is also interested in conservation and wildlife. The majority of members are retired." Estab. 1983. Circ. 25,000. Pays on publication. Publishes ms an average of 6 months after acceptance. Byline given. Buys one-time rights. Submit seasonal material 3 months in advance. Accepts simultaneous submissions. Responds in 2 months to queries; 2 months to mss. Sample copy and guidelines for 4 first-class stamps. Writer's guidelines for #10 SASE.

Nonfiction: Humor (camping or travel related), interview/profile (interesting campers), new product, technical (RDs related), travel (interesting places to visit by RV, camping). **Buys 10-15 mss/year.** Query by mail only or send complete ms with photos. Length: 750-2,000 words. **Pays $50-150.**

Reprints: Send typed ms with rights for sale noted and information about when and where the material previously appeared. Pays 35-50% of amount paid for original article.

Photos: "Need b&w or sharp color prints inside (we can make prints from slides) and vertical transparencies for cover." Send photos with submission. Captions required.

Tips: "Freelance material on RV travel, RV maintenance/safety, and items of general camping interest throughout the United States and Canada will receive special attention. Good photos increase your chances."

$ $ CHICAGO TRIBUNE, Travel Section, 435 N. Michigan Ave., Chicago IL 60611. (312)222-3999. Fax: (312)222-0234. E-mail: rcurwen@tribune.com. **Contact:** Randy Curwen, editor. Weekly newspaper Sunday 22-page travel section aimed at vacation travelers. Circ. 1,100,000. Pays on publication. Publishes ms an average of 6 weeks after acceptance. Byline given. Buys one-time rights. Microfilm, online, and CD-ROM useage. Submit seasonal material 2 months in advance. Accepts simultaneous submissions. Responds in 1 month to mss. Sample copy for large SAE and $1.50 postage. Writer's guidelines for #10 SASE.

Nonfiction: Essays, general interest, historical/nostalgic, how-to (travel, pack), humor, opinion, personal experience, photo feature, travel. Special issues: "There will be 16 special issues in the next 18 months." **Buys 150 mss/year.** Send complete ms. Length: 500-2,000 words. **Pays $150-500.**
Photos: State availability with submission. Reviews 35mm transparencies, 8×10 or 5×7 prints. Buys one-time rights. Pays $100/color photo; $25/b&w; $100 for cover. Captions required.
Tips: "Be professional. Use a word processor. Make the reader want to go to the area being written about. Only 1% of manuscripts make it."

$ CLUBMEX, 3450 Bonita Rd., Suite 103, Chula Vista CA 91910-5200. (619)422-3022. Fax: (619)422-2671. **Contact:** Chuck Stein, publisher/editor. **75% freelance written.** Bimonthly newsletter. "Our readers are travelers to Baja California and Mexico, and are interested in retirement, RV news, fishing, and tours. They are knowledgeable but are always looking for new places to see." Estab. 1975. Circ. 5,000. Pays on publication. Publishes ms an average of 2 months after acceptance. Byline given. Buys first North American serial rights. Submit seasonal material 3 months in advance. Responds in 1 month to queries; 1 month to mss. Sample copy and writer's guidelines for 9×12 SAE with 2 first-class stamps.

- *Clubmex* accepts articles dealing with all of Mexico. They want upbeat, positive articles about Mexico which motivate readers to travel there by car.

Nonfiction: Historical/nostalgic, humor, interview/profile, personal experience, travel. **Buys 36-50 mss/year.** Send complete ms. Length: 900-1,500 words. **Pays $65 for the cover story; $50 for other articles used; $25 for informative short pieces.**
Reprints: Send tearsheet, photocopy or typed ms with rights for sale noted and information about when and where the material previously appeared. Pays 100% of amount paid for original article.
Photos: State availability with submission. Reviews 3×5 prints. Buys one-time rights. Offers no additional payment for photos accepted with ms. Captions required.

$ $ COAST TO COAST MAGAZINE, Affinity Group, Inc., 2575 Vista Del Mar Dr., Ventura CA 93001-3920. Fax: (805)667-4217. E-mail: vlaw@affinitygroup.com. Website: www.rv.net. **Contact:** Valerie Law, editorial director. **80% freelance written.** Magazine published 8 times/year for members of Coast to Coast Resorts. "*Coast to Coast* focuses on travel, recreation, and good times, with most stories targeted to recreational vehicle owners." Estab. 1982. Circ. 200,000. **Pays on acceptance.** Publishes ms an average of 5 months after acceptance. Byline given. Offers 33% kill fee. Buys first North American serial rights. Submit seasonal material 5 months in advance. Responds in 1 month to queries; 2 months to mss. Sample copy for $4 and 9×12 SASE. Writer's guidelines available.
Nonfiction: Book excerpts, essays, general interest, historical/nostalgic, how-to, humor, inspirational, interview/profile, new product, opinion, personal experience, photo feature, technical, travel. No poetry, cartoons. **Buys 50 mss/year.** Query with published clips. Length: 500-2,500 words. **Pays $75-600.**
Reprints: Send photocopy and information about when and where the material previously appeared. Pays approximately 50% of amount paid for original article.
Photos: Send photos with submission. Reviews transparencies. Buys one-time rights. Pays $50-600/photo. Identification of subjects required.
Tips: "Send clips or other writing samples with queries, or story ideas will not be considered."

$ $ CURACAO NIGHTS, Nights Publications, Inc., 1831 Rene Levesque Blvd. W., Montreal, Quebec H3H 1R4, Canada. (514)931-1987. Fax: (514)931-6273. E-mail: editor@nightspublications.com. Managing Editor: Zelly Zuskin. **Contact:** Sonya Plowman, editor. **90% freelance written.** Annual magazine covering the Curacao vacation experience. "We are seeking upbeat, entertaining lifestyle articles; colorful profiles of locals; lively features on culture, activities, nightlife, eco-tourism, special events, gambling; how-to features; humor. Our audience is North American vacationers." Estab. 1989. Circ. 155,000. **Pays on acceptance.** Publishes ms an average of 9 months after acceptance. Byline given. Buys first North American serial, first Caribbean rights. Editorial lead time 1 month. Accepts queries by mail, e-mail, fax. Responds in 2 weeks to queries; 1 month to mss. Sample copy for $5 (check payable to Nights Publications Inc.). Writer's guidelines by e-mail.
Nonfiction: General interest, historical/nostalgic, how-to (help a vacationer get the most from their vacation), humor, inspirational, interview/profile, opinion, personal experience, photo feature, travel, eco-tourism, lifestyle, local culture, art, activities, night life, topics relative to vacationers in Curacao. "No negative pieces, generic copy, or stale rewrites." **Buys 5-10 mss/year.** Query with published clips, include SASE and either Canadian postage or IRC. Length: 250-750 words. **Pays $75-250.**
Photos: State availability with submission. Reviews transparencies. Buys one-time rights. Pays $50/photo. Captions, identification of subjects, model releases required.
Tips: "Demonstrate your voice in your query letter. Focus on individual aspects of the island lifestyle and vacation experience (e.g., art, music, culture, a colorful local character, a personal experience, etc.), rather than a generalized overview. Provide an angle that will be entertaining to vacationers who are already on the island. Our style is upbeat, friendly, fluid, and descriptive."

$ $ $ ENDLESS VACATION MAGAZINE, Endless Vacation, 9998 N. Michigan Rd., Carmel IN 46032-9640. (317)805-8120. Fax: (317)805-9507. Website: www.rci.com. **Contact:** Julie Woodard, senior editor. Prefers to work with published/established writers. Bimonthly magazine. "*Endless Vacation* is the vacation-idea magazine edited for people who love to travel. Each issue offers articles for America's dedicated and frequent leisure travelers—time-share owners. Articles and features explore the world through a variety of vacation opportunities and options for travelers who average 4 weeks of leisure travel each year." Estab. 1974. Circ. 1,219,393. **Pays on acceptance.** Publishes ms an average of 6 months after acceptance. Byline given. Buys first North American serial rights. Accepts queries by mail, fax. Accepts simultaneous submissions. Responds in 2 months to queries; 2 months to mss. Sample copy for $5 and 9×12 SAE with 5 first-class stamps. Writer's guidelines for #10 SASE.

Nonfiction: Senior Editor. Most articles are from established writers already published in *Endless Vacation. Accepts very few unsolicited pieces.* Essays. **Buys 24 mss/year.** Query with published clips via mail (no phone calls). Length: 1,500-2,000 words. **Pays $500-1,000 for assigned articles; $250-800 for unsolicited articles.** Sometimes pays expenses of writers on assignment.

Photos: Reviews transparencies, 35mm slides. Buys one-time rights. Pays $300-1,300/photo. Identification of subjects required.

Columns/Departments: Weekender (on domestic weekend vacation travel); Healthy Traveler; Family Vacationing; Taste (on food-related travel topics), 800-1,000 words. Also news items for Facts, Fads and Fun Stuff column on travel news, products, and the useful and unique in travel, 100-200 words. Query with published clips via mail (no phone calls). **Pays $300-800.**

Tips: "We will continue to focus on travel trends and timeshare resort destinations. Articles must be packed with pertinent facts and applicable how-tos. Information—addresses, phone numbers, dates of events, costs—must be current and accurate. We like to see a variety of stylistic approaches, but in all cases the lead must be strong. A writer should realize that we require first-hand knowledge of the subject and plenty of practical information. For further understanding of *Endless Vacation*'s direction, the writer should study the magazine and writer's guidelines."

$ ESCAPEES MAGAZINE, Sharing the RV Lifestyle, Escapees Inc., 100 Rainbow Dr., Livingston TX 77351-9300. (936)327-8873. Fax: (936)327-4388. E-mail: editor@escapees.com. Website: www.escapees.com. Editor: Janice Lasko. **Contact:** Ann Rollo or Tammy Johnson, editorial assistants. **90% freelance written.** Bimonthly magazine published for members of Escapees RV Club. "Articles must be RV related. *Escapees Magazine* readers are seeking RVing knowledge beyond what is found in conventional RV magazines." Estab. 1978. Circ. 35,000. Pays on publication. Publishes ms an average of 6 months after acceptance. Byline given. Buys first North American serial, first, one-time, second serial or electronic rights. Editorial lead time 6 months. Submit seasonal material 6 months in advance. Accepts previously published material. Sample copy for $3. Writer's guidelines free.

Nonfiction: All articles must be RV related. General interest, historical/nostalgic, how-to, humor, inspirational, interview/profile, new product, personal experience, photo feature, technical, travel, mechanical; finances; working; volunteering; boondocking. Travelogues, consumer advocacy issues, poetry and recipes are not generally published. **Buys 100-125 mss/year.** Send complete ms. Length: 1,400 words maximum. **Pays $150 maximum.**

Reprints: Accepts previously published submissions.

Photos: Send photos with submission. Reviews contact sheets, transparencies, prints. Buys one-time rights. Negotiates payment individually. Captions required.

Fiction: All fiction must be RV related. Adventure, historical, humorous, mainstream, mystery, slice-of-life vignettes, western. **Buys 2-6 mss/year.** Send complete ms. Length: 1,400 words maximum. **Pays $150 maximum.**

Tips: "Please do not send queries. Send complete manuscripts."

$ $ FAMILY MOTOR COACHING, Official Publication of the Family Motor Coach Association, 8291 Clough Pike, Cincinnati OH 45244-2796. (513)474-3622. Fax: (513)388-5286. E-mail: magazine@fmca.com. Website: www.fmca.com. Director of Communications: Pamela Wisby Kay. **Contact:** Robbin Gould, editor. **80% freelance written.** "We prefer that writers be experienced RVers." Monthly magazine emphasizing travel by motorhome, motorhome mechanics, maintenance and other technical information. "*Family Motor Coaching* magazine is edited for the members and prospective members of the Family Motor Coach Association who own or are about to purchase self-contained, motorized recreational vehicles known as motorhomes. Featured are articles on travel and recreation, association news and activities, plus articles on new products and motorhome maintenance and repair. Approximately ⅓ of editorial content is devoted to travel and entertainment, ⅓ to association news, and ⅓ to new products, industry news and motorhome maintenance." Estab. 1963. Circ. 133,000. **Pays on acceptance.** Publishes ms an average of 8 months after acceptance. Byline given. Buys first North American serial rights. Submit seasonal material 4 months in advance. Accepts queries by mail, e-mail, fax. Responds in 3 months to queries. Sample copy for $3.99. Writer's guidelines for #10 SASE.

Nonfiction: How-to (do-it-yourself motor home projects and modifications), humor, interview/profile, new product, technical, motorhome travel (various areas of North America accessible by motorhome), bus conversions, nostalgia. **Buys 90-100 mss/year.** Query with published clips. Length: 1,000-2,000 words. **Pays $100-500.**

Photos: State availability with submission. Prefers North American serial rights but will consider one-time rights on photos only. Offers no additional payment for b&w contact sheets, 35mm or 2¼×2¼ color transparencies. Captions, model releases, photo credits required.

Tips: "The greatest number of contributions we receive are travel; therefore, that area is the most competitive. However, it also represents the easiest way to break in to our publication. Articles should be written for those traveling by self-contained motorhome. The destinations must be accessible to motorhome travelers and any peculiar road conditions should be mentioned."

$ $ FRONTIER MAGAZINE, Adventure Media, 3983 S. McCarran Blvd., No. 434, Reno NV 89502. (775)856-3532. Fax: (775)829-2457. E-mail: info@frontiermag.com. Website: adventuremedia.com. **Contact:** M. Susan Wilson, managing editor. **60% freelance written.** Monthly magazine covering travel, with special emphasis on the Rocky Mountain states. "*Frontier Magazine* is a sophisticated yet fun-to-read magazine that celebrates the Rocky Mountain lifestyle. It celebrates those attitudes, traditions and issues that define the modern west." Estab. 1998. Circ. 250,000. Pays on publication. Publishes ms an average of 4 months after acceptance. Byline given. Offers 25% kill fee. Buys first North American serial rights. Editorial lead time 4 months. Submit seasonal material 4 months in advance. Accepts queries by mail, e-mail. Responds in 2 months to queries; 2 months to mss. Sample copy for $2 (shipping and handling). Writer's guidelines for #10 SASE.

Nonfiction: Essays, general interest, historical/nostalgic, humor (essays), interview/profile, photo feature, travel. Special issues: Golf guide (October); and Ski guide (November). "We do not accept fiction, religious or how-to articles." **Buys 15 mss/year.** Query with published clips. Length: 350-1,500 words. **Pays 25-50¢/word.**

Photos: State availability with submission. Reviews duplicate slides only. Buys one-time rights. Negotiates payment individually. Identification of subjects required.

Columns/Departments: Nancy Alton, senior editor. Local Color (tourist-oriented events around the route system), 50-500 words; Creature Comforts (hotel/restaurant reviews), 700 words; Local Flavor (restaurants, chefs or specialty cuisine along the Frontier Airline route system). **Buys 30 mss/year.** Query with published clips. **Pays $50-150.**

Tips: "Know the airline's route system—we accept stories only from/about these areas. Submit clips with all queries."

$ $ GO MAGAZINE, AAA Carolinas, P.O. Box 29600, Charlotte NC 28229-9600. (704)569-7733. Fax: (704)569-7815. E-mail: trcrosby@aaa.qa.com. Website: www.aaacarolinas.com. **Contact:** Jacquie Hughett, assistant editor. **10% freelance written.** Bimonthly newspaper covering travel, automotive, safety (traffic) and insurance. "Consumer-oriented membership publication providing information on complex or expensive subjects—car buying, vacations, traffic safety problems, etc." Estab. 1928. Circ. 750,000. Pays on publication. Publishes ms an average of 3 months after acceptance. Makes work-for-hire assignments. Editorial lead time 2 months. Submit seasonal material 2 months in advance. Accepts queries by mail, fax. Responds in 6 weeks to queries; 3 months to mss. Sample copy for SAE with 4 first-class stamps. Writer's guidelines for #10 SASE.

Nonfiction: How-to (fix auto, travel safety, etc.), travel, automotive insurance, traffic safety. **Buys 12-14 mss/year.** Query with published clips. Length: 600-900 words. **Pays 15¢/published word.**

Photos: Send photos with submission. Buys one-time rights. Offers no additional payment for photos accepted with ms.

$ ☆ HEALING RETREATS & SPAS, 5036 Carpinteria Ave., Carpinteria CA 93013. (805)745-5413. Fax: (805)745-5643. E-mail: editorial@healingretreats.com. Website: www.healingretreats.com. Publisher: J.K. Spencer. Editor: Melissa Scott. **90% freelance written.** Bimonthly magazine covering retreats, spas, health, and lifestyle issues. "We try to present healing and nurturing *alternatives* for the global community, and provide a bridge between travel, health, and New Age magazine material." Estab. 1996. Circ. 45,000. Pays on publication. Publishes ms an average of 1 year after acceptance. Byline given. Buys one-time rights. Editorial lead time 2 months. Submit seasonal material 9 months in advance. Accepts queries by mail, e-mail, fax. Responds in 6 weeks to queries; 2 months to mss. Writer's guidelines by e-mail.

Nonfiction: Book excerpts, general interest, how-to (at-home therapies), interview/profile, new product, photo feature, travel (spas and retreats only), health alternatives. **Buys 50 mss/year.** Query with published clips. Length: 700-3,000 words. **Pays $100-500 depending on length, experience and availability, and quality of images.** Pays writers with contributor copies or other premiums if they want 20 or more copies for self-promotion.

Photos: Send photos with submission. Reviews transparencies. Buys one-time rights. Offers no additional payment for photos accepted with ms. Captions required.

Columns/Departments: Buys 40 mss/year. Send complete ms. **Pays $25-150.**

Tips: "Writers can break in with well-written, first-hand knowledge of an alternative health issue or therapy. Even our travel pieces require this type of knowledge. Once a writer proves capable, other assignments can follow. We're particularly looking for stories on religious retreats—ashrams, monasteries, zen centers. Please, no more 'I was stressed out from my life, I went to a spa, now I feel great, the end.'"

$ $ HIGHWAYS, The Official Publication of the Good Sam Club, TL Enterprises, Inc., 2575 Vista Del Mar, Ventura CA 93001. (805)667-4100. Fax: (805)667-4454. E-mail: goodsam@goodsamclub.com. Website: www.goodsamclub.com/highways. **Contact:** Ronald H. Epstein, associate publisher. **40% freelance written.** Monthly magazine (November/December issues combined) covering recreational vehicle lifestyle. "All of our readers—since we're a membership publication—own or have a motorhome, trailer, camper or van conversion. Thus, our stories include road-travel conditions and terms and information about campgrounds and locations." Estab. 1966. Circ. 950,000. **Pays on acceptance.** Publishes ms an average of 6 months after acceptance. Byline given. Offers 50% kill fee. Buys first North American serial, electronic rights. Editorial lead time 15 weeks. Submit seasonal material 5 months in advance. Accepts queries by mail, e-mail, fax. Responds in 3 weeks to queries; 2 months to mss. Sample copy and writer's guidelines free or online.

Nonfiction: How-to (repair/replace something on an RV), humor, technical, travel (all RV related). **Buys 15-25 mss/year.** Query. Length: 1,000-2,000 words.

Photos: Send photos with submission. Reviews contact sheets, negatives, transparencies, prints. Buys one-time rights. No additional payment for photos accepted with ms. Captions, identification of subjects, model releases required.

Columns/Departments: Beginners (people buying an RV for the first time), 1,200 words; View Points (issue related), 750 words. Query. **Pays $200-250.**

Tips: "Understand RVs and RVing. It's a unique lifestyle and different than typical traveling. Aside from that, we welcome good writers!"

$ $ INTERNATIONAL LIVING, Agora Ireland Ltd., 5 Catherine St., Waterford Ireland. 353-51-304-557. Fax: 353-51-304-561. E-mail: lsheridan@internationalliving.com. Website: www.InternationalLiving.com. Managing Editor: Robin Finlay. **Contact:** Laura Sheridan, assistant editor. **50% freelance written.** Monthly newsletter covering retirement, travel, investment, and real estate overseas. "We do not want descriptions of how beautiful places are. We want specifics, recommendations, contacts, prices, names, addresses, phone numbers, etc. We want offbeat locations and off-the-beaten-track spots." Estab. 1981. Circ. 500,000. Pays on publication. Publishes ms an average of 3 months after acceptance. Byline given. Offers 25-50% kill fee. Buys all rights. Editorial lead time 2 months. Submit seasonal material 3 months in advance. Accepts queries by mail, e-mail, fax. Accepts simultaneous submissions. Responds in 2 months to mss. Sample copy for #10 SASE. Writer's guidelines free.

Break in by writing about something real. If you find it a chore to write the piece you're sending us, then chances are, we don't want it.

Nonfiction: How-to (get a job, buy real estate, get cheap airfares overseas, start a business, etc.), interview/profile (entrepreneur abroad), new product (travel), personal experience, travel, shopping, cruises. Special issues: "We produce special issues each year focusing on Asia, Eastern Europe, and Latin America." No descriptive, run-of-the-mill travel articles. **Buys 100 mss/year.** Send complete ms. Length: 500-2,000 words. **Pays $200-500 for assigned articles; $100-400 for unsolicited articles.**

Photos: State availability with submission. Reviews contact sheets, negatives, transparencies, prints. Buys all rights. Offers $50/photo. Identification of subjects required.

Fillers: Facts. **Buys 20/year.** Length: 50-250 words. **Pays $25-100.**

The online magazine carries original content not found in the print version. Contact: Len Galvin, online editor (lgalvin@internationalliving.com).

Tips: "Make recommendations in your articles. We want first-hand accounts. Tell us how to do things: how to catch a cab, order a meal, buy a souvenir, buy property, start a business, etc. *International Living*'s philosophy is that the world is full of opportunities to do whatever you want, whenever you want. We will show you how."

$ $ INTERVAL WORLD, 6262 Sunset Dr., Miami FL 33143. E-mail: intervaleditors@interval-intl.com. Website: www.intervalworld.com. Editor: Elizabeth Willard. **Contact:** Amy Drew Teitler, managing editor. **34% freelance written.** Quarterly magazine covering travel. *Interval World* magazine is distributed to Interval International members in the US, Canada, and Caribbean. Estab. 1980. Circ. 800,000. **Pays on acceptance.** Publishes ms an average of 3 months after acceptance. Byline given. Editorial lead time 6 months. Accepts queries by mail, e-mail. Sample copy and writer's guidelines not available.

Nonfiction: How-to, new product, photo feature, travel, health, pastimes, adventure travel. **Buys 20-25 mss/year. Pays 25¢/word.**

Photos: State availability with submission. Reviews transparencies. Buys print and electronic rights. Negotiates payment individually. Captions, identification of subjects, model releases required.

Tips: "Send résumé, cover letter, and several clips (preferably travel). Do not send unsolicited submissions/articles."

$ $ $ $ ISLANDS, An International magazine, Islands Media Corp., P.O. Box 4728, Santa Barbara CA 93140-4728. (805)745-7100. Fax: (805)745-7102. E-mail: editorial@islands.com. Website: www.islands.com. **Contact:** James Badham, editor. **95% freelance written.** Magazine published 8 times/year covering "accessible and once-in-a-lifetime islands from many different perspectives: travel, culture, lifestyle. We ask our authors to give us the essence of the island and do it with literary flair." Estab. 1981. Circ. 220,000. **Pays on acceptance.** Publishes ms an average of 8 months after acceptance. Byline given. Offers 25% kill fee. Buys all rights. Accepts queries by mail, e-mail, fax. Responds in 2 months to queries; 6 weeks to mss. Sample copy for $6. Writer's guidelines for #10 SASE or online.

Nonfiction: "Each issue contains 4-5 feature articles and numerous departments. Any authors who wish to be commissioned should send a detailed proposal for an article, an estimate of costs (if applicable), and samples of previously published work. The majority of our feature manuscripts are commissioned." Book excerpts, essays, general interest, interview/profile, personal experience, photo feature, travel, island-related material. No service stories. **Buys 25 feature mss/year.** Query with published clips or send complete ms. Length: 2,000-4,000 words. **Pays $1,000-4,000.** Sometimes pays expenses of writers on assignment.

Photos: "Fine color photography is a special attraction of *Islands*, and we look for superb composition, technical quality, and editorial applicability." Label slides with name and address, include captions, and submit in protective plastic sleeves. Reviews 35mm transparencies. Buys one-time rights. Pays $75-300 for 35mm transparencies. Identification of subjects required.

Columns/Departments: Horizons section and ArtBeat (all island related), 200-600 words; Crossroads (columns and experiences that highlight island life), 500-1,500 words; IslandWise (travel experiences, classic island hotel, classic island eatery, great enrichment experience), 700-1,000 words; Insiders (list 10 things to do in well-visited islands), 800 words. **Buys 50 mss/year.** Query with published clips. **Pays $25-1,000.**

Tips: "A freelancer can best break in to our publication with front- or back-of-the-book stories. Stay away from general, sweeping articles. We will be using big name writers for major features; will continue to use newcomers and regulars for columns and departments."

$ KAFENIO, Where Europe Is Only a Mouseclick Away, Meier & Jacobson, Box 142, Karpathos 85700, Greece. (+30)2450 31716. Fax: (+30)2450 31716. E-mail: editor@kafeniocom.com. Website: www.kafeniocom.com. Publisher: Alf B. Meier. **Contact:** Roberta Beach Jacobson, editor. **60-65% freelance written.** Monthly magazine covering European life and culture. "*Kafenio*, focusing on European life and culture, has adult readers in North America, Europe, Africa, and Australia." Estab. 2000. Circ. 25,300. **Pays on acceptance.** Publishes ms an average of 2 months after acceptance. Byline given. Buys one-month electronic rights rights. Editorial lead time 2 months. Submit seasonal material 2 months in advance. Responds in 3 days to queries; 3 days to mss.

- Accepts queries by e-mail only. No archives.

Nonfiction: essay@kafeniocom.com. Nonfiction for Speakers Table department only. Essays, humor, inspirational, opinion, personal experience, travel (all first person only), sports. Send complete ms. Length: 600 words maximum. **Pays $100.**

Reprints: Accepts previously published submissions.

Tips: "Know something about Europe. Have a little fun with your writing. If you don't enjoy it, others won't either. Remember, our readers either live in or travel to Europe."

$ $ MICHIGAN LIVING, AAA Michigan, 2865 Waterloo, Troy MI 48084. (248)816-9265. Fax: (248)816-2251. E-mail: michliving@aol.com. **Contact:** Ron Garbinski, editor. **50% freelance written.** Monthly magazine. "*Michigan Living* is edited for the residents of Michigan and contains information about travel and lifestyle activities in Michigan, the U.S. and around the world. Articles also cover automotive developments, highway safety. Regular features include a car care column, a calendar of coming events, restaurant and overnight accomodations reviews and news of special interest to Auto Club members." Estab. 1922. Circ. 1,099,000. Pays on publication. Publishes ms an average of 6 months after acceptance. Byline given. Offers 20% kill fee. Buys first North American serial rights. Submit seasonal material 9 months in advance. Accepts queries by e-mail. Responds in 6 weeks to queries.

Nonfiction: Travel articles on US and Canadian topics. **Buys few unsolicited mss/year.** Query. Length: 200-1,000 words. **Pays $75-600 for assigned articles.**

Photos: Photos purchased with accompanying ms. Reviews transparencies. Pays $450 for cover photos; $50-400 for color transparencies. Captions required.

Tips: "In addition to descriptions of things to see and do, articles should contain accurate, current information on costs the traveler would encounter on his trip. Items such as lodging, meal and entertainment expenses should be included, not in the form of a balance sheet but as an integral part of the piece. We want the sounds, sights, tastes, smells of a place or experience so one will feel he has been there and knows if he wants to go back. Requires travel-related queries via e-mail."

$ $ MOTORHOME, TL Enterprises, 2575 Vista Del Mar Dr., Ventura CA 93001. (805)667-4100. Fax: (805)667-4484. Website: www.motorhomemagazine.com. Editorial Director: Barbara Leonard. **Contact:** Sherry McBride, senior managing editor. **60% freelance written.** Monthly magazine. "*MotorHome* is a magazine for owners and prospective buyers of self-propelled recreational vehicles who are active outdoorsmen and wide-ranging travelers. We cover all aspects of the RV lifestyle; editorial material is both technical and nontechnical in nature. Regular features include tests and descriptions of various models of motorhomes, travel adventures and hobbies pursued in such vehicles, objective analysis of equipment and supplies for such vehicles and do-it-yourself articles. Guides within the magazine provide listings of manufacturers, rentals and other sources of equipment and accessories of interest to enthusiasts. Articles must have an RV slant and excellent transparencies accompanying text." Estab. 1968. Circ. 144,000. **Pays on acceptance.** Publishes ms an average of within 1 year after acceptance. Byline given. Offers 30% kill fee. Buys first North American serial, electronic rights. Editorial lead time 4 months. Submit seasonal material 6 months in advance. Accepts queries by mail, fax, phone. Responds in 1 month to queries; 2 months to mss. Sample copy for free. Writer's guidelines for #10 SASE.

Break in with *Crossroads* items.

Nonfiction: General interest, historical/nostalgic, how-to, humor, interview/profile, new product, personal experience, photo feature, technical, travel, celebrity profiles; recreation; lifestyle; legislation, all RV related. No diaries of RV trips or negative RV experiences. **Buys 120 mss/year.** Query with or without published clips. Length: 250-2,500 words. **Pays $300-600.**

Photos: Send photos with submission. Reviews 35mm slides. Buys one-time rights. Offers no additional payment for art accepted with ms. Pays $500+ for covers. Captions, identification of subjects, model releases required.

Columns/Departments: Crossroads (offbeat briefs of people, places and events of interest to travelers), 100-200 words; Keepers (tips, resources). Query with or without published clips or send complete ms. **Pays $100.**

The online magazine carries original content not found in the print version. Contact: Sherry McBride, online editor.

Tips: "If a freelancer has an idea for a good article, it's best to send a query and include possible photo locations to illustrate the article. We prefer to assign articles and work with the author in developing a piece suitable to our audience. We are in a specialized field with very enthusiastic readers who appreciate articles by authors who actually enjoy motorhomes. The following areas are most open: Crossroads—brief descriptions of places to see or special events, with one photo/slide, 100-200 words; travel—places to go with a motorhome, where to stay, what to see, etc.; we prefer not to use travel articles where the motorhome is secondary; and how-to—personal projects on author's motorhomes to make travel easier, unique projects, accessories. Also articles on unique personalities, motorhomes, humorous experiences. Be sure to submit appropriate photography (35mm slides) with at least one good motorhome shot to illustrate travel articles. No phone queries, please."

$ $ $ $ NATIONAL GEOGRAPHIC TRAVELER, National Geographic Society, 1145 17th St. NW, Washington DC 20036. Website: nationalgeographic.com/traveler. Editor: Keith Bellows. Executive Editor: Paul Martin. **Contact:** Scott Stuckey or Sheila Buckmaster, senior editors. **90% freelance written.** Published 8 times/year. "*National Geographic Traveler* is filled with practical information and detailed maps designed to encourage readers to explore and travel. Features domestic and foreign destinations, photography, the economics of travel, adventure trips, and weekend getaways to help readers plan a variety of excursions. Our writers need to equip our readers with inspiration to travel. We want lively writing—personal anecdotes with telling details, not an A to Z account of a destination." Estab. 1984. Circ. 720,000. **Pays on acceptance.** Publishes ms an average of 3-12 months after acceptance. Byline given. Offers 30% kill fee. Buys one-time, electronic rights. Editorial lead time 3-12 months. Submit seasonal material ideas 1 year in advance. Accepts queries by mail. Responds in 6 weeks to queries. Writer's guidelines for #10 SASE.

Nonfiction: Each issue of the magazine contains 5 or more features, roughly balanced between US and foreign subjects. "Generally, we are interested in places accessible to most travelers, not just the intrepid or wealthy. The types of destinations we cover vary widely, from mainstream to adventure travel." Essays, general interest, historical/nostalgic, how-to, humor, inspirational, new product (travel oriented), opinion, personal experience, photo feature, travel. "We do not want to see general, impersonal, fact-clogged articles. We do not want to see any articles similar to those we, or our competitors, have run recently." **Buys 80-100 mss/year.** Query with published clips. Length: 250-2,500 words. **Pays 50¢/word minimum.** Pays expenses of writers on assignment.

Columns/Departments: Smart Traveler—Norie Quintos, editor (travel trends, sources, strategies, and solutions); 48 Hours—Susan O'Keefe, editor (the best of a city); Room Check (unique and special places to stay). **Buys 150-200 mss/year.** Query with published clips. **Pays 50¢/word minimum.**

Tips: "Familiarize yourself with our magazine—not only the types of stories we run, but the types of stories we've run in the past. Formulate a story idea, and then send a detailed query, recent clips, and contact information to the editor responsible for the section you'd like to be published in. We prefer that our readers be allowed to experience a destination directly through the words and actions of people the writer encounters, not just through the writer's narrative. Write a title and deck for your idea. Your piece must have a hook. We do not read unsolicited manuscripts except for essays submitted for our Journeys section." No unsolicited photographs.

$ NATURALLY, Nude Recreation Travel, Internaturally, Inc. Publishing Co., P.O. Box 317, Newfoundland NJ 07435-0317. (973)697-3552. Fax: (973)697-8313. Website: www.internaturally.com. **Contact:** Bernard Loibl, editor. **90% freelance written.** Quarterly magazine covering wholesome family nude recreation and travel locations. "*Naturally* nude recreation looks at why millions of people believe that removing clothes in public is a good idea, and at places specifically created for that purpose—with good humor, but also in earnest. *Naturally* nude recreation takes you to places where your personal freedom is the only agenda, and to places where textile-free living is a serious commitment." Estab. 1981. Circ. 35,000. Pays on publication. Byline given. Buys first, one-time rights. Editorial lead time 4 months. Submit seasonal material 4 months in advance. Accepts queries by mail, e-mail, fax. Accepts simultaneous submissions. Sample copy for $9. Writer's guidelines free.

Nonfiction: Frequent contributors and regular columnists, who develop a following through *Naturally*, are paid from the Frequent Contributors Budget. Payments increase on the basis of frequency of participation. General interest, interview/profile, personal experience, photo feature, travel. **Buys 12 mss/year.** Send complete ms. Length: 2 pages. **Pays $70/published page, including photos.**

Reprints: Accepts previously published submissions.

Photos: Send photos with submission. Reviews contact sheets, negatives, transparencies, prints. Buys one-time rights. Payment for photos included in payment forms.

Fillers: Cheryl Hanenberg, associate editor. Anecdotes, facts, gags to be illustrated by cartoonist, newsbreaks, short humor.

Tips: "*Naturally* nude recreation invokes the philosophies of naturism and nudism, but also activities and beliefs in the mainstream that express themselves, barely: spiritual awareness, New Age customs, pagan and religious rites, alternative and fringe lifestyle beliefs, artistic expressions, and many individual nude interests. Our higher purpose is simply to help restore our sense of self. Although the term 'nude recreation' may, for some, conjure up visions of sexual frivolities inappropriate for youngsters—because that can also be technically true—these topics are outside the scope of *Naturally* magazine. Here the emphasis is on the many varieties of human beings, of all ages and backgrounds, recreating in their most natural state, at extraordinary places, their reasons for doing so, and the benefits they derive."

$ $ NORTHWEST TRAVEL, Northwest Regional magazines, 4969 Hwy. 101 N., Suite 2, Florence OR 97439. (541)997-8401or (800)348-8401. Fax: (541)902-0400. E-mail: judy@ohwy.com. Website: www.ohwy.com. **Contact:** Stefani Blair, managing editor. **60% freelance written.** Bimonthly magazine. "We like energetic writing about popular activities and destinations in the Pacific Northwest. *Northwest Travel* aims to give readers practical ideas on where to go in the region. Magazine covers Oregon, Washington, Idaho, British Columbia, and western Montana; occasionally Alaska." Estab. 1991. Circ. 50,000. Pays after publication. Publishes ms an average of 8 months after acceptance. Buys first North American serial rights. Submit seasonal material 6 months in advance. Accepts queries by mail, e-mail. Responds in 3 months to queries; 3 months to mss. Sample copy for $4.50. Writer's guidelines for #10 SASE.

- Have good slides to go with a story that is lively with compelling leads, quotes, anecdotes, and no grammar problems.

Nonfiction: Book excerpts, general interest, historical/nostalgic, interview/profile (rarely), photo feature, travel (only in Northwest region). "No cliché-ridden pieces on places that everyone covers." **Buys 40 mss/year.** Query with or without published clips. Length: 1,250-2,000 words. **Pays $100-350 for feature articles, and 2-5 contributor copies.**

Reprints: Send photocopy and information about when and where the material previously appeared. Pays 50% of amount paid for original article.
Photos: "Put who to credit and model releases needed on cover photos—will pay extra for those needing and having model releases." State availability with submission. Reviews transparencies, prefers dupes. Buys one-time rights. Captions, identification of subjects required.
Columns/Departments: Worth a Stop (brief items describing places "worth a stop"), 300-350 words. **Pays $50.** Back Page (photo and text package on a specific activity, season, or festival with some technical photo info), 80 words and 1 slide. **Pays $75. Buys 25-30 mss/year.** Send complete ms.
Tips: "Write fresh, lively copy (avoid clichés), and cover exciting travel topics in the region that haven't been covered in other magazines. A story with stunning photos will get serious consideration. The department most open to freelancers is the Worth a Stop department. Take us to fascinating and interesting places we might not otherwise discover."

$ PATHFINDERS, Travel Information for People of Color, 6424 N. 13th St., Philadelphia PA 19126. (215)927-9950. Fax: (215)927-3359. E-mail: blaktravel@aol.com. Website: www.pathfinderstravel.com. **Contact:** Joseph P. Blake, managing editor. **75% freelance written.** Quarterly magazine covering travel for people of color, primarily African-Americans. "We look for lively, original, well-written stories that provide a good sense of place, with useful information and fresh ideas about travel and the travel industry. Our main audience is African-Americans, though we do look for articles relating to other persons of color: Native Americans, Hispanics and Asians." Estab. 1997. Circ. 50,000. Pays on publication. Byline given. Buys first North American serial, electronic rights. Accepts queries by mail, e-mail. Responds in 2 months to queries; 2 months to mss. Sample copy at bookstores (Barnes & Noble, Borders, Waldenbooks). Writer's guidelines online.

- Break in through *Looking Back*, 600-word essay on travel from personal experience that provides a historical perspective and US travel with cultural perspective.

Nonfiction: Interested in seeing more Native American stories, places that our readers can visit and rodeos (be sure to tie-in African-American cowboys). Essays, historical/nostalgic, how-to, personal experience, photo feature, travel (all vacation travel oriented). "No more pitches on Jamaica." **Buys 16-20 mss/year.** Send complete ms. Length: 1,200-1,400 words for cover stories; 1,000-1,200 words for features. **Pays $125.**
Photos: State availability with submission.
Columns/Departments: Chef's Table, Post Cards from Home, 500-600 words. Send complete ms. **Pays $100.**
Tips: "We prefer seeing finished articles rather than queries. All articles are submitted on spec. Articles should be saved in either WordPerfect of Microsoft Word, double-spaced and saved as a text-only file. Include a hard copy. E-mail articles are accepted only by request of the editor. No historical articles."

$ $ PILOT GETAWAYS MAGAZINE, Airventure Publishing LLC, P.O. Box 550, Glendale CA 91209-0550. (818)241-1890. Fax: (818)241-1895. E-mail: editor@pilotgetaways.com. Website: www.pilotgetaways.com. **Contact:** John Kounis, editor. **90% freelance written.** Quarterly magazine covering aviation travel for private pilots. "*Pilot Getaways* is a travel magazine for private pilots. Our articles cover destinations that are easily accessible by private aircraft, including details such as airport transportation, convenient hotels, and attractions. Other regular features include Fly-in dining, Flying Tips, and Bush Flying." Estab. 1998. Circ. 20,000. Pays on publication. Byline given. Buys first North American serial, electronic rights. Editorial lead time 4 months. Submit seasonal material 9 months in advance. Accepts queries by mail, e-mail, fax, phone. Accepts simultaneous submissions. Responds in 2 weeks to queries; 2 months to mss. Sample copy and writer's guidelines free.
Nonfiction: Travel (specifically travel guide articles). "We rarely publish articles about events that have already occurred, such as travel logs about trips the authors have taken or air show reports." **Buys 30 mss/year.** Query. Length: 1,000-3,500 words. **Pays $100-500.**
Reprints: Accepts previously published submissions.
Photos: State availability with submission. Reviews contact sheets, negatives, 35mm transparencies, prints, GIF/JPEG files. Buys one-time rights. Negotiates payment individually. Captions, identification of subjects required.
Columns/Departments: Weekend Getaways (short fly-in getaways), 2,000 words; Fly-in Dining (reviews of airport restaurants), 1,200 words; Flying Tips (tips and pointers on flying technique), 1,000 words; Bush Flying (getaways to unpaved destinations), 1,500 words. **Buys 20 mss/year.** Query. **Pays $100-500.**
Tips: "*Pilot Getaways* follows a specific format, which is factual and informative. We rarely publish travel logs that chronicle a particular journey. Rather, we prefer travel guides with phone numbers, addresses, prices, etc., so that our readers can plan their own trips. The exact format is described in our writer's guidelines."

$ $ $ PORTHOLE CRUISE MAGAZINE, Panoff Publishing, 4517 NW 31st Ave., Wingate Commons, Ft. Lauderdale FL 33309-3403. (954)377-7777. Fax: (954)377-7000. E-mail: jrush@ppigroup.com. Website: www.porthole.com. Editorial Director: Dale Rim. **Contact:** Jill Rush, managing editor. **90% freelance written.** Bimonthly magazine covering the cruise industry. "*Porthole Cruise Magazine* entices its readers into taking a cruise vacation by delivering information that is timely, accurate, colorful, and entertaining." Estab. 1992. Circ. 35,000. Pays on publication. Publishes ms an average of 6 months after acceptance. Byline given. Offers 35% kill fee. Buys second serial (reprint), electronic, first international serial rights. Editorial lead time 8 months. Submit seasonal material 5 months in advance. Accepts queries by mail, e-mail, fax. Accepts simultaneous submissions. Responds in 2 months to queries; 6 months to mss. Sample copy for 8×11 SAE and $3 postage. Writer's guidelines for #10 SASE.
Nonfiction: Book excerpts, essays (your cruise experience), exposé, general interest (cruise related), historical/nostalgic, how-to (pick a cruise, not get seasick, travel tips), humor, interview/profile (crew on board or industry executives),

new product, personal experience, photo feature, travel (off-the-beaten path, adventure, ports, destinations, cruises), onboard fashion, spa articles, duty-free shopping port shopping, ship reviews. Special issues: Cuba, Europe. No articles on destinations that can't be reached by ship. "Please, please do not send us accounts of your lovely, spectacular, or breathtaking family cruise vacations from the point of embarkation to debarkation. Concentrate on vivid details, personal experiences, and go beyond the normal, 'We cruised to . . . ' Include out-of-the-ordinary subject matter. Try to transport the reader from the pages to the places you traveled rather than simply giving a laundry list of what you saw. Please don't write asking for a cruise so that you can do an article! You must be an experienced cruise writer to do a ship review." **Buys 75 mss/year.** Query with published clips or send complete ms. Length: 1,000-3,000 words. **Pays $400-1,200 for assigned articles; $250-1,000 for unsolicited articles.** Pays expenses of writers on assignment.

Reprints: Send photocopy of article or typed ms with rights for sale noted and information about when and where the material previously appeared. Negotiates payment.

Photos: Linda Douthat, creative director. State availability with submission. Reviews transparencies, prints. Buys one-time rights. Negotiates payment individually. Captions, identification of subjects, model releases required.

Columns/Departments: Deckadence (luxury); Ombudsman (investigative), "My" Port City (personal accounts of experiences in certain destination), both 1,200 words; Beautiful Thing (spa service on board), 700 words; Brass Tacks (consumer-oriented travel tips, short bits); Personality Plus (intriguing travel-oriented profiles); Fashion File (onboard fashion), all 400 words. Also humor, cruise cuisine, shopping, photo essays. **Buys 50 mss/year.** Query with published clips or send complete ms. **Pays $400-1,200.**

Fillers: Facts, gags to be illustrated by cartoonist, newsbreaks, short humor. **Buys 30/year.** Length: 25-200 words. **Pays 25¢/word.**

The online magazine carries original content not found in the print edition and includes writer's guidelines.

Tips: "We prefer to be queried via e-mail. Submit an outline showing how you will incorporate anecdotes and dialogue. Clips are not necessary. Offbeat, original travel stories are preferred. Tie-ins to celebrity culture, pop culture, arts/entertainment, politics, cuisine, architecture, are highly regarded."

$ $ THE SOUTHERN TRAVELER, AAA Auto Club of Missouri, 12901 N. Forty Dr., St. Louis MO 63141. (314)523-7350. Fax: (314)523-6982. Editor: Michael J. Right. **Contact:** Deborah Klein, managing editor. **80% freelance written.** Bimonthly magazine. Estab. 1997. Circ. 130,000. **Pays on acceptance.** Byline given. Not copyrighted. Buys first North American serial, second serial (reprint) rights. Accepts simultaneous submissions. Responds in 1 month to queries; 1 month to mss. Sample copy for 12½X 9½ SAE and 3 first-class stamps. Writer's guidelines for #10 SASE.

Query, with best chance for good reception January-March for inclusion in following year's editorial calendar.

Nonfiction: "We feature articles on regional and world travel, area history, auto safety, highway and transportation news." **Buys 30 mss/year.** Query. Length: 2,000 words maximum. **Pays $250 maximum.**

Reprints: Send typed ms with rights for sale noted and information about when and where the material previously appeared. Pays $125-150.

Photos: State availability with submission. Reviews transparencies. One-time photo reprint rights. Offers no additional payment for photos accepted with ms. Captions required.

Tips: "Editorial schedule is set 18 months in advance. Request a copy. Serious writers ask for media kit to help them target their story. Some stories available throughout the year, but most are assigned early. Travel destinations and tips are most open to freelancers; auto-related topics handled by staff. Make story bright and quick to read. We see too many 'Here's what I did on my vacation' manuscripts. Go easy on first-person accounts."

$ $ $ $ SPA, Healthy Living, Travel & Renewal, Islands Media, 6309 Carpinteria Ave., Carpinteria CA 93013. (805)745-7100. Fax: (805)745-7102. Website: www.spamagazine.com. **Contact:** Liz Mazurski, editor-in-chief. Bimonthly magazine covering health spas: treatments, travel, cuisine, fitness, beauty. "Approachable and accessible, yet authoritative and full of advice, *Spa* is the place to turn for information and tips on nutrition, spa cuisine/recipes, beauty, health, skin care, travel (to spas), fitness, wellness, and renewal. Sometimes humorous and light, sometimes thoughtful and introspective, *Spa* is always helpful, insightful and personal." Byline given. Offers 25% kill fee. Buys first North American serial, all rights. Editorial lead time 3 months. Accepts queries by mail. Sample copy for $6.

Nonfiction: Essays, how-to (beauty), humor, personal experience, travel. Does not want "a general article on a spa you have visited." **Buys 30 mss/year.** Query with published clips. Length: 1,500-3,000 words. **Pays $1,125-2,500.** Sometimes pays expenses of writers on assignment.

Columns/Departments: Being Well (news and trends on health and healing, wellness and workouts); Spa Talk (new spas, spa programs, treatments); Lotions & Potions (beauty, fragrance); Living Wardrobe (personal style, fashion); Living Well (home, garden, books, music, internet). **Buys 60 mss/year.** Query with published clips. **Pays $100-1,500.**

$ $ ST. MAARTEN NIGHTS, Nights Publications, Inc., 1831 Rene Levesque Blvd. W., Montreal, Quebec H3H 1R4, Canada. (514)931-1987. Fax: (514)931-6273. E-mail: editor@nightspublications.com. Website: www.nightspublications.com. Managing Editor: Zelly Zuskin. **Contact:** Sonya Plowman, editor. **90% freelance written.** Annual magazine covering the St. Maarten/St. Martin vacation experience seeking "upbeat entertaining lifestyle articles." "Our audience is the North American vacationer." Estab. 1981. Circ. 225,000. **Pays on acceptance.** Publishes ms an average of 9 months after acceptance. Byline given. Buys first North American serial rights. first Caribbean rights Editorial lead time 1 month. Accepts queries by mail, e-mail, fax, phone. Responds in 2 weeks to queries; 1 month to mss. Sample copy for $5 (make checks payable to Nights Publications, Inc.). Writer's guidelines by e-mail.

"Let the reader experience the story; utilize the senses; be descriptive."

Nonfiction: Lifestyle with a lively, upscale touch. Include SASE with Canadian postage or IRC. General interest, historical/nostalgic, how-to (gamble), humor, inspirational, interview/profile, opinion, personal experience, photo feature, travel, colorful profiles of islanders, sailing, ecological, eco-tourism, local culture, art, activities, entertainment, night life, special events, topics relative to vacationers in St. Maarten/St. Martin. "No negative pieces or stale rewrites or cliché copy." **Buys 8-10 mss/year.** Query with published clips. Length: 250-750 words. **Pays $75-250.**
Photos: State availability with submission. Reviews transparencies. Buys one-time rights. Pays $50/photo. Captions, identification of subjects, model releases required.
Tips: "Our style is upbeat, friendly, fluid and descriptive. Our magazines cater to tourists who are already at the destination, so ensure your story is of interest to this particular audience. We welcome stories that offer fresh angles to familiar tourist-related topics."

$ $ TIMES OF THE ISLANDS, The International magazine of the Turks & Caicos Islands, Times Publications, Ltd., P.O. Box 234, Caribbean Place, Providenciales Turks & Caicos Islands, British West Indies. (649)946-4788. Fax: (649)941-3402. E-mail: timespub@tciway.tc. Website: www.timespub.tc. **Contact:** Kathy Borsuk, editor. **60% freelance written.** Quarterly magazine covering The Turks & Caicos Islands. "*Times of the Islands* is used by the public and private sector to inform visitors and potential investors/developers about the Islands. It goes beyond a superficial overview of tourist attractions with in-depth articles about natural history, island heritage, local personalities, new development, offshore finance, sporting activities, visitors' experiences, and Caribbean fiction." Estab. 1988. Circ. 6,000-9,000. Pays on publication. Publishes ms an average of 6 months after acceptance. Byline given. Buys second serial (reprint) rights. Publication rights for 6 months with respect to other publications distributed in Caribbean. Editorial lead time 4 months. Submit seasonal material at least 4 months in advance. Accepts queries by mail, fax. Accepts simultaneous submissions. Responds in 6 weeks to queries; 2 months to mss. Sample copy for $6. Writer's guidelines for #10 SASE or on website.
Nonfiction: Book excerpts, essays, general interest (Caribbean art, culture, cooking, crafts), historical/nostalgic, humor, interview/profile (locals), personal experience (trips to the Islands), photo feature, technical (island businesses), travel, book reviews, nature, ecology, business (offshore finance), watersports. **Buys 20 mss/year.** Query. Length: 500-3,000 words. **Pays $200-600.**
Reprints: Send photocopy and information about when and where the material previously appeared. Payment varies.
Photos: Send photos with submission. Reviews slides, prints, digital photos. Offers no additional payment for photos accepted with ms. Pays $15-100/photo. Identification of subjects required.
Columns/Departments: On Holiday (unique experiences of visitors to Turks & Caicos), 500-1,500 words. **Buys 4 mss/year.** Query. **Pays $200.**
Fiction: Adventure, ethnic, historical, humorous, mystery, novel excerpts. **Buys 2-3 mss/year.** Query. Length: 1,000-3,000 words. **Pays $250-400.**
Tips: "Make sure that the query/article specifically relates to the Turks and Caicos Islands. The theme can be general (ecotourism, for instance), but the manuscript should contain specific and current references to the Islands. We're a high-quality magazine, with a small budget and staff, and are very open-minded to ideas (and manuscripts). Writers who have visited the Islands at least once would probably have a better perspective from which to write."

$ TRANSITIONS ABROAD, P.O. Box 1300, Amherst MA 01004-1300. (413)256-3414. Fax: (413)256-0373. E-mail: editor@transitionsabroad.com. Website: www.transitionsabroad.com. Editor/Publisher: Clay Hubbs. **Contact:** Max Hartshorne, managing editor. **80-90% freelance written.** Bimonthly magazine resource for low-budget international travel, often with an educational or work component. Focus is on the alternatives to mass tourism. Estab. 1977. Circ. 20,000. Pays on publication. Byline given. Buys first, second serial (reprint) rights. Accepts queries by mail, e-mail. Responds in 1 month to queries; 1 month to mss. Sample copy for $6.45. Writer's guidelines for #10 SASE or online.

Break in by sending "a fascinating article (1,000 words) with very updated pratical information and color slides or prints with people in them, or an article on a job you got overseas and how someone else could do it."

Nonfiction: Lead articles (up to 1,500 words) provide first-hand practical information on independent travel to featured country or region (see topics schedule). **Pays $75-150**. Also, how to find educational and specialty travel opportunities, practical information (evaluation of courses, special interest and study tours, economy travel), travel (new learning and cultural travel ideas). Foreign travel only. Few destination ("tourist") pieces or first-person narratives. *Transitions Abroad* is a resource magazine for independent, educated, and adventurous travelers, not for armchair travelers or those addicted to packaged tours or cruises. Emphasis on information—which must be usable by readers—and on interaction with people in host country. **Buys 20 unsolicited mss/year.** Query with credentials and SASE. Include author's bio and e-mail with submissions. Length: 500-1,500 words. **Pays $25-150.**
Photos: Photos increase likelihood of acceptance. Send photos with submission. Buys one-time rights. Pays $10-45 for color prints or color slides, $150 for covers (color slides only). Captions, identification of subjects required.
Columns/Departments: Worldwide Travel Bargains (destinations, activities, and accomodations for budget travelers—featured in every issue); Tour and Program Notes (new courses or travel programs); Travel Resources (new information and ideas for independent travel); Working Traveler (how to find jobs and what to expect); Activity Vacations (travel opportunities that involve action and learning, usually by direct involvement in host culture); Responsible Travel (information on community-organized tours). Length: 1,000 words maximum. **Buys 60 mss/year.** Send complete ms. **Pays $20-50.**

Fillers: Info Exchange (information, preferably first hand—having to do with travel, particularly offbeat educational travel and work or study abroad). **Buys 10/year.** Length: 750 words maximum. **Pays complimentary 1-year subscription.**

The online magazine carries original content not found in the print edition and includes writer's guidelines.

Tips: "We like nuts and bolts stuff, practical information, especially on how to work, live, and cut costs abroad. Our readers want usable information on planning a travel itinerary. Be specific: names, addresses, current costs. We are very interested in educational and long-stay travel and study abroad for adults and senior citizens. *Overseas Travel Planner* published each year in July provides best information sources on work, study, and independent travel abroad. Each bimonthly issue contains a worldwide directory of educational and specialty travel programs."

$ $ $ $ TRAVEL + LEISURE, American Express Publishing Corp., 1120 Avenue of the Americas, New York NY 10036. (212)382-5600. E-mail: tlquery@amexpub.com. Website: www.travelandleisure.com. Editor-in-Chief: Nancy Novogrod. Executive Editor: Barbara Peck. Managing Editor: Mark Orwoll. **Contact:** Editor. **80% freelance written.** "*Travel + Leisure* is a monthly magazine edited for affluent travelers. It explores the latest resorts, hotels, fashions, foods, and drinks." Circ. 925,000. **Pays on acceptance.** Byline given. Offers 25% kill fee. Buys first world rights. Accepts queries by mail, e-mail. Responds in 6 weeks to queries; 6 weeks to mss. Sample copy for $5.50 from (800)888-8728 or P.O. Box 2094, Harlan IA 51537-4094. Writer's guidelines for #10 SASE.

O→ There is no single editorial contact for *Travel + Leisure*. It is best to find the name of the editor of each section, as appropriate for your submission.

Nonfiction: Travel. **Buys 40-50 feature (3,000-5,000 words) and 200 short (125-500 words) mss/year.** Query (e-mail preferred). **Pays $4,000-6,000/feature; $100-500/short piece.** Pays expenses of writers on assignment.

Photos: Discourages submission of unsolicited transparencies. Buys one-time rights. Payment varies. Captions required.

Columns/Departments: Length: 1,200-2,500 words. **Buys 125-150 mss/year. Pays $1,000-2,500.**

Tips: "Queries should not be generic, but suggest ideas for specific departments in the magazine."

$ $ TRAVEL AMERICA, The U.S. Vacation Magazine, World Publishing Co., 990 Grove St., Evanston IL 60201-4370. (847)491-6440. Editor-in-Chief/Associate Publisher: Bob Meyers. **Contact:** Randy Mink, managing editor. **80% freelance written.** Bimonthly magazine covering US vacation travel. Estab. 1985. Circ. 300,000. Byline given. Buys first North American serial rights. Submit seasonal material 6 months in advance. Accepts queries by mail. Responds in 1 month to queries; 6 weeks to mss. Sample copy for $5 and 9×12 SASE with $1.60 postage.

Nonfiction: Primarily destination-oriented travel articles and resort/hotel profiles and roundups, but will consider essays, how-to, humor, nostalgia, Americana. "U.S. destination travel features must have personality and strong sense of place, developed through personal experiences, quotes, humor, human interest, local color. We prefer people-oriented writing, not dry guidebook accounts and brochure-style fluff. Always in the market for nationwide roundup stories—past roundups have included U.S. Gambling Meccas and Top 10 Amusement Parks. Also short slices of Americana focusing on nostalgia, collectibles and crafts, ethnic communities and celebrations, special events. It is best to study current contents and query by mail only first." **Buys 60 mss/year.** Length: 1,000 words. **Pays $150-300.**

Reprints: Send typed ms with rights for sale noted. Payment varies.

Photos: Top-quality original color slides preferred. Prefers photo feature package (ms, plus slides), but will purchase slides only to support a work-in-progress. Buys one-time rights. Captions required.

Tips: "Because we are heavily photo-oriented, superb slides are our foremost concern. The most successful approach is to send 2-3 sheets of slides with the query or complete manuscript. Include a list of other subjects you can provide as a photo feature package."

N $ TRAVEL SMART, Communications House, Inc., Dobbs Ferry NY 10522. (800)327-3633. Fax: (914)693-8731. E-mail: travelsmartnews@aol.com. Website: www.travelsmartnews.com. **Contact:** Nancy Dunnan, managing editor. Monthly newsletter covering information on "good-value travel." Estab. 1976. Pays on publication. Buys all rights. Accepts queries by mail, e-mail. Responds in 6 weeks to queries; 6 weeks to mss. Sample copy for 9×12 SAE and 3 first-class stamps. Writer's guidelines for 9×12 SAE with 3 first-class stamps.

Nonfiction: "Interested primarily in bargains or little-known deals on transportation, lodging, food, unusual destinations that are really good values. No destination stories on major Caribbean islands, London, New York, no travelogs, 'my vacation,' poetry, fillers. No photos or illustrations other than maps. Just hard facts. We are not part of 'Rosy fingers of dawn...' school." Write for guidelines, then query. Length: 100-1,500 words. **Pays $150 maximum.**

Tips: "When you travel, check out small hotels offering good prices, good restaurants, and send us brief rundown (with prices, phone numbers, addresses). Information must be current. Include your phone number with submission, because we sometimes make immediate assignments."

$ $ $ VOYAGEUR, The Magazine of Carlson Hospitality Worldwide, Pace Communications, 1301 Carolina St., Greensboro NC 27401. (336)378-6065. Fax: (336)378-8272. Editor: Jaci H. Ponzoni. **Contact:** Sarah Lindsay, senior editor. **90% freelance written.** Quarterly in-room magazine for Radisson hotels and affiliates. "*Voyageur* is an international magazine published quarterly for Carlson Hospitality Worldwide and distributed in the rooms of Radisson Hotels & Resorts, Park Plaza and Park Inn hotels, and Country Inns & Suites By Carlson throughout North and South America, Europe, Australia, Africa, Asia, and the Middle East. All travel-related stories must be in destinations where Radisson, Country Inns & Suites, or Park have hotels." Estab. 1992. Circ. 160,000. Pays on publication. Publishes ms an average of 2 months after acceptance. Offers 25% kill fee. Buys first North American serial rights. Editorial lead time 4 months. Submit seasonal material 6 months in advance. Accepts queries by mail. Responds in 2 months to queries; 2 months to mss. Sample copy for $5. Writer's guidelines for #10 SASE.

O-→ Break in with a "well-thought-out, well-written, well-researched query on a city or area the writer lives in or knows well—one where Carlson has a presence (Radisson, Country Inns, or Park)."

Nonfiction: The cover story is an authoritative, yet personal profile of a destination where Radisson has a major presence, featuring a mix of standard and off-the-beaten-path activities and sites including sightseeing, recreation, restaurants, shopping, and cultural attractions. Length: 1,200 words plus At a Glance, a roundup of useful and intriguing facts for travelers. The Cultural Feature brings to life some aspect of a country's or region's arts and culture, including performing, culinary, visual, and folk arts. The successful article combines a timely sample of activities for travelers with a sense of the destination's unique spirit or personality as reflected in the arts. Must be a region where Radisson has a major presence. Length: 900 words. Travel. Query with published clips. **Pays $800-1,200.** Sometimes pays expenses of writers on assignment.

Photos: State availability with submission. Reviews contact sheets, transparencies, prints. Buys one-time rights. Negotiates payment individually. Identification of subjects, model releases required.

Columns/Departments: A place-specific shopping story with cultural context and upscale attitude, 250 words and 50-word mini-sidebar; an action-oriented, first-person story focusing on travel involving sports such as biking, kayaking, scuba diving, hiking, or sailing, 250 words, plus 50-word mini-sidebar; Agenda (insights into conducting business and traveling for business internationally), 250 words with 50-word mini-sidebar; Au Revoir (an evocative, first-person look back at an appealing Carlson destination), 350 words. **Buys 24 mss/year.** Query with published clips. **Pays $300-400.**

Tips: "We look for authoritative, energetic, and vivid writing to inform and entertain business and leisure travelers, and we are actively seeking writers with an authentic European, Asian, Latin American, African, or Australian perspective. Travel stories should be authoritative yet personal."

$ $ WOODALL'S REGIONALS, 2575 Vista Del Mar Dr., Ventura CA 93001. E-mail: editor@woodallpub.com. Website: www.woodalls.com. **Contact:** Dee Reed, assistant editor. Monthly magazine for RV and camping enthusiasts. Woodall's Regionals include *Camper Ways*, *Midwest RV Traveler*, *Northeast Outdoors*, *Florida RV Traveler*, *Southern RV*, *Texas RV*, and *Southwest RV Traveler*. Byline given. Buys first rights. Accepts queries by mail, e-mail. Responds in 1-2 months to queries. Sample copy for free. Writer's guidelines free.

Nonfiction: "We need interesting and tightly focused feature stories on RV travel and lifestyle, campground spotlights and technical articles that speak to both novices and experienced RVers." **Buys 500 mss/year.** Query with published clips. Length: 500-1,700 words. **Pays $250-400/feature; $75-150/department article and short piece.**

WOMEN'S

Women have an incredible variety of publications available to them. A number of titles in this area have been redesigned to compete in the crowded marketplace. Many have stopped publishing fiction and are focusing more on short, human interest nonfiction articles. Magazines that also use material slanted to women's interests can also be found in the following categories: Business & Finance; Child Care & Parental Guidance; Contemporary Culture; Food & Drink; Gay & Lesbian Interest; Health & Fitness; Hobby & Craft; Home & Garden; Relationships; Religious; Romance & Confession; and Sports.

$ $ BBW, Real Women, Real Beauty, Aeon Publishing Group, Inc., P.O. Box 1297, Elk Grove CA 95759-1297. Fax: (916)684-7628. E-mail: sesmith@bbwmagazine.com. Website: www.bbwmagazine.com. **Contact:** Sally E. Smith, editor-in-chief. **50% freelance written.** Bimonthly magazine covering fashion and lifestyle for women size 16+. "*BBW* strives to inspire women all sizes of large to celebrate their beauty and enrich their lives by providing them with affirming information and resources in the areas of fashion and beauty, health and well-being, entertainment and romance, and work and leisure." Estab. 1979. Circ. 100,000. Pays on publication. Publishes ms an average of 2 months after acceptance. Byline given. Offers 20% kill fee. Buys all rights. Editorial lead time 4 months. Accepts queries by mail, e-mail, fax. Responds in 3 months to queries; 3 months to mss. Sample copy for $5. Writer's guidelines for #10 SASE, online, or by e-mail.

Nonfiction: Book excerpts, essays, exposé, general interest, how-to (beauty/style), humor, new product, opinion, photo feature, travel. "No first-person narratives, poetry, fiction." **Buys 18 mss/year.** Query with published clips. Length: 800-2,500 words. **Pays $125-500.**

Photos: State availability with submission. Reviews contact sheets, negatives, 2¼×2¼ transparencies, slides. Buys all rights. Offers no additional payment for photos accepted with ms. Captions, model releases required.

Columns/Departments: Personal Best (improve well-being), 1,200 words; Careers (tools to manage/enhance careers), 1,500 words; Finance (increase financial security), 1,200 words; Perspectives (male perspective), 800 words; Last Word (humorous end page), 700 words; Destinations (travel within US), 1,200 words; Entertaining, 1,000 words. **Buys 30 mss/year.** Query with published clips. **Pays $125-250.**

Fillers: Anecdotes, facts (products, trends, style, fashion, reviews). **Buys 12/year.** Length: 100-200 words. **Pays $25.**

Tips: "Pitch specific articles/topics—2-3 sentences summarizing your proposed topic, and communicating how the piece will be written, i.e., interviews, sidebars, etc."

$✪ BOOK CLUB TODAY, Upbeat & Innovative Publication for Book Club Members, Book Club Today, Inc., P.O Box 210165, Cleveland OH 44121-7165. Fax: (216)382-0644. E-mail: bookclubtoday@aol.com. Website: www.bookclubtoday.com. **Contact:** Bonnie Eaver, editor. **50% freelance written.** Bimonthly magazine covering information for reading groups. "We are looking for positive, upbeat articles to enhance book club and reading group meetings: book reviews, discussion questions and author profiles. Books reviewed must stimulate lively discussions." Estab. 1999. Pays on publication. Publishes ms an average of 6 months after acceptance. Byline sometimes given. Buys first rights. Editorial lead time 4 months. Submit seasonal material 4 months in advance. Accepts queries by mail, e-mail, fax. Responds in 2 months to queries; 3 months to mss. Sample copy online.

Nonfiction: Interview/profile. No negative book reviews or satire. **Buys 60 mss/year.** Query or send complete ms. Length: 250-1,000 words. **Pays $15-50.** Sometimes pays expenses of writers on assignment.

Photos: State availability with submission.

Columns/Departments: Book Reviews (classics and new releases), 250-750 words, **pays $15-50**; Discussion Questions (for book club meetings), 10-15 questions/book, **pays $10-30**; Author Profiles (personal and professional information), 250-750 words, **pays $15-50**; Meeting of the Month (interview with book club member), 500-1,000 words, **pays $25-50**; Book Suggestion Column (interview author or librarian), 250-350 words, **pays $10-20**; Test Your Knowledge Literary Quiz (by assignment only), 10-15 questions and answers, **pays $25-50**; Biblio Basics (helpful hints for reading groups), 250-350 words, **pays $10-30**.

Tips: "Please review a sample issue first. Submit positive, upbeat, fun articles."

$ $ $ BRIDAL GUIDE, R.F.P., LLC, 3 E. 54th St., 15th Floor, New York NY 10022. (212)838-7733. Fax: (212)308-7165. Website: www.bridalguidemag.com. Editor-in-Chief: Diane Forden. **Contact:** Denise Schipani, executive editor; Laurie Bain Wilson, travel editor for travel features. **50% freelance written.** Bimonthly magazine covering relationships, sexuality, fitness, wedding planning, psychology, finance, travel. Prefers to work with experienced/published writers. **Pays on acceptance.** Accepts queries by mail. Responds in 3 months to queries; 3 months to mss. Sample copy for $5 and SAE with 4 first-class stamps. Writer's guidelines available.

Nonfiction: "Please do not send queries concerning beauty and fashion, since we produce them in-house. We do not accept personal wedding essays, fiction, or poetry. Address travel queries to travel editor." All correspondence accompanied by an SASE will be answered. **Buys 100 mss/year.** Query with published clips. Length: 1,000-2,000 words. **Pays 50¢/word.**

Photos: Photography and illustration submissions should be sent to the art department. Robin Zachary, art director; Kelly Roberts, associate art director.

Columns/Departments: The only columns written by freelancers cover finance and wedding-planning issues.

Tips: "We are looking for service-oriented, well-researched pieces that are journalistically written. Writers we work with use at least 3 expert sources, such as physicians, book authors, and business people in the appropriate field. Our tone is conversational yet authoritative. Features are also generally filled with real-life anecdotes. We also do features that are completely real-person based—such as roundtables of bridesmaids discussing their experiences, or grooms-to-be talking about their feelings about getting married. In queries, we are looking for a well thought-out idea, the specific angle of focus the writer intends to take, and the sources he or she intends to use. Queries should be brief and snappy—and titles should be supplied to give the editor an even better idea of the direction the writer is going in."

$ $ BRIDE AGAIN, The Only magazine Designed for Second Time Brides, 1240 N. Jefferson Ave., Suite G, Anaheim CA 92807. (714)632-7000. Fax: (714)632-5405. E-mail: editor@brideagain.com. Website: www.brideagain.com. **Contact:** Beth Ramirez, editor. Quarterly magazine for the encore bride. "*Bride Again* is targeted primarily to women ages 35-45 and secondarily to those 45 and over. They have been married at least once before, and most likely have children from a previous marriage or will be marrying someone with children. They have a career and income of over $45,000 per year, and are more mature and sophisticated than the 26-year-old first-time bride." Estab. 1997. Circ. 125,000. Pays on publication. Byline given. Writer's guidelines for #10 SASE.

Nonfiction: "Topics can be on, but not limited to: Remarriage, blending families, becoming a stepmother, combining households, dealing with children in the wedding party, children—his, mine and ours, joint custody, dealing with difficult ex-spouses, real dresses for real women, legal aspects of remarriage, pre- and post-nuptial agreements, alternatives to the wedding veil, unusual wedding and/or honeymoon locations." Interfaith marriages; handling extended step families; having another child together. How-to, humor, inspirational, interview/profile, personal experience. No queries please. Send complete ms. Length: 1,000 words. **Pays 35¢/word.**

Photos: Does not purchase photos.

Columns/Departments: Finances, Blending Families, Religion, Groom's Viewpoint, Unusual Honeymoon Locations, Beauty for Ages 30+/40+/50+, Remarriage, Fashion; all 800-1,000 words. Book reviews (on the feature topics listed above), 250 words. Send complete ms. **Pays 35¢/word.**

Tips: "All articles must be specific to encore brides."

$ $ $ $ CHATELAINE, 777 Bay St., #800, Toronto, Ontario M5W 1A7, Canada. (416)596-5000. Fax: (416)596-5516. E-mail: editors@chatelaine.com. Website: www.chatelaine.com. **Contact:** Kim Pittaway, managing editor. Monthly magazine. "*Chatelaine* is edited for Canadian women ages 25-49, their changing attitudes and lifestyles. Key editorial ingredients include health, finance, social issues and trends, as well as fashion, beauty, food and home decor. Regular departments include Health pages, Entertainment, Humour, How-to." **Pays on acceptance.** Byline given. Offers 25-100% kill fee. Buys first, electronic rights. Accepts queries by mail. Sample copy not available. Writer's guidelines for #10 SASE with postage.

Nonfiction: Seeks "agenda-setting reports on national issues and trends as well as pieces on health, careers, personal finance and other facts of Canadian life." **Buys 50 mss/year.** Query with published clips and SASE. Length: 1,000-2,500 words. **Pays $1,000-2,500.** Pays expenses of writers on assignment.

Columns/Departments: Length: 500-1,000 words. Query with published clips and SASE. **Pays $500-750.**

The online magazine carries original content not found in the print edition. Contact: Trish Snyder, online editor.

$ CINCINNATI WOMAN MAGAZINE, Niche Publishing and Media L.L.C., P.O. Box 8170, West Chester OH 45069-8170. (513)851-8916. Fax: (513)851-8916. E-mail: cincinnatiwoman@cinci.rr.com. Editor: Cathy Habes. **Contact:** Alicia Wiehe, publisher. **90% freelance written.** Monthly magazine covering women's issues and needs. "Dedicated exclusively to capturing the spirit of Cincinnati-area women, we are committed to providing our readers with information as well as inspiration." Estab. 1998. Circ. 35,000. Pays on publication. Publishes ms an average of 4 months after acceptance. Byline given. Buys one-time rights. Editorial lead time 2 months. Submit seasonal material 3 months in advance. Accepts queries by mail, e-mail. Accepts simultaneous submissions. Responds in 2 weeks to queries. Sample copy for 8×10 SAE and 3 first-class stamps. Writer's guidelines for #10 SASE.

Nonfiction: Book excerpts, essays, general interest, how-to, humor, inspirational, interview/profile, new product, opinion, personal experience, photo feature, travel, health/beauty. **Buys 50 mss/year.** Query with published clips or send complete ms. Length: 500-1,000 words. **Pays $80 maximum for assigned articles; $30 maximum for unsolicited articles.**

Reprints: Send photocopy of article or typed ms with rights for sale noted and information about when and where the material previously appeared.

Photos: State availability with submission. Reviews transparencies, 4×6 prints. Buys one-time rights. Offers no additonal payment for photos accepted with ms. Captions, identification of subjects required.

Columns/Departments: Body Shop (health/beauty nuggets), 700 words; *CWM* Cooks (entertaining and recipes), 700 words; *CWM* Style (women's fashion), 700 words; *CWM* Travel, 700 words. **Buys 30 mss/year.** Query with published clips or send complete ms. **Pays $30.**

Fiction: Adventure, confessions, horror, humorous, mainstream, mystery, religious, romance, slice-of-life vignettes. **Buys 20 mss/year.** Query with published clips or send complete ms. Length: 700-1,200 words. **Pays $30.**

Poetry: Avant-garde, free verse, light verse, traditional. **Buys 5 poems/year.** Submit maximum 3 poems. Length: 5-60 lines. **Pays $20.**

Fillers: Anecdotes, facts, newsbreaks, short humor. **Buys 5/year.** Length: 50-100 words. **Pays $15.**

Tips: "We're looking for material on 20-something, dating, fashion, first-time mom experiences, holistic health, cooking, short personal essays."

$ $ COMPLETE WOMAN, For All The Women You Are, Associated Publications, Inc., 875 N. Michigan Ave., Suite 3434, Chicago IL 60611-1901. (312)266-8680. Editor: Bonnie L. Krueger. **Contact:** Lora Wintz, executive editor. **90% freelance written.** Bimonthly magazine. "Manuscripts should be written for today's busy women, in a concise, clear format with useful information. Our readers want to know about the important things: sex, love, relationships, career, and self-discovery. Examples of true-life anecdotes incorporated into articles work well for our readers, who are always interested in how other women are dealing with life's ups and downs." Estab. 1980. Circ. 350,000. Pays 45 days after acceptance. Publishes ms an average of 6 months after acceptance. Byline given. Buys first North American serial, second serial (reprint), simultaneous rights. Editorial lead time 6 months. Submit seasonal material 5 months in advance. Accepts queries by mail. Accepts simultaneous submissions. Responds in 2 months to queries; 2 months to mss. Sample copy not available. Writer's guidelines for #10 SASE.

"Break in with writing samples that relate to the magazine. Also, the editor reports a need for more relationship stories."

Nonfiction: "We want self-help articles written for today's woman. Articles that address dating, romance, sexuality, and relationships are an integral part of our editorial mix, as well as inspirational and motivational pieces." Book excerpts, exposé (of interest to women), general interest, how-to (beauty/diet-related), humor, inspirational, interview/profile (celebrities), new product, personal experience, photo feature, sex, love, relationship advice. **Buys 60-100 mss/year.** Query with published clips or send complete ms. Length: 800-2,000 words. **Pays $160-400.** Sometimes pays expenses of writers on assignment.

Reprints: Send tearsheet, photocopy or typed ms with rights for sale noted and information about when and where the material previously appeared.

Photos: Photo features with little or no copy should be sent to Gail Mitchell. Send photos with submission. Reviews 2.25 or 35mm transparencies, 5×7 prints. Buys one-time rights. Pays $35-100/photo. Captions, identification of subjects, model releases required.

Tips: "Freelance writers should review publication, review writer's guidelines, then submit their articles for review. We're looking for new ways to explore the usual topics, written in a format that will be easy for our readers (24-40+ women) to understand. We also like sidebar information that readers can review quickly before or after reading the article. Our focus is relationship-driven, with an editorial blend of beauty, health, and career."

$ $ $ $ CONDÉ NAST BRIDE'S, Condé Nast, 4 Times Square, 6th Floor, New York NY 10036. Fax: (212)286-8331. Website: www.brides.com. Editor-in-Chief: Millie Bratten. **Contact:** Sally Kilbridge, managing editor. **75% freelance written.** Bimonthly magazine covering all things related to the bride—engagement, the wedding and marriage. All articles are written for the engaged woman planning her wedding. Estab. 1934. Circ. 500,000. **Pays on acceptance.**

Publishes ms an average of 6 months after acceptance. Byline given. Offers 15% kill fee. Buys all rights. Editorial lead time 6 months. Submit seasonal material 1 year in advance. Accepts queries by mail. Responds in 3 months to queries. Sample copy not available. Writer's guidelines for #10 SASE.

Nonfiction: Topic (1) Personal essays on wedding planning, aspects of weddings or marriage. Length: 800 words. Written by brides, grooms, attendants, family members, friends in the first person. The writer's unique experience qualifies them to tell this story. (2) Articles on specific relationship and lifestyle issues. Length: 800 words. Select a specialized topic in the areas of relationships, religion, in-laws, second marriage, finances, careers, health, fitness, nutrition, sex, decorating, or entertaining. Written either by experts (attorneys, doctors, financial planners, marriage counselors, etc) or freelancers who interview and quote experts and real couples. (3) In-depth explorations of relationship and lifestyle issues. Length: 2,000-3,000 words. Well-researched articles on finances, health, sex, wedding and marriage trends. Should include statistics, quotes from experts and real couples, a resolution of the issues raised by each couple. Book excerpts, essays, how-to, personal experience. No humor. **Buys 36 mss/year.** Query with published clips. Length: 800-2,000 words. **Pays $1/word for assigned articles.** Pays expenses of writers on assignment.

Photos: State availability with submission. Negotiates payment individually.

Columns/Departments: Length: 750 words. Query with published clips. **Pays $1/word.**

Tips: "We look for relationship pieces that will help a newlywed couple adjust to marriage. Wedding planning articles are usually written by experts or depend on a lot of interviews with experts. Writers should have a good idea of what we would and would not do: Read the 3 or 4 most recent issues. What separates us from the competition is quality writing, photographs, amount of information. All articles are assigned with some consumer slant, with the exception of personal essays."

N **$ $ ESSENCE**, 1500 Broadway, New York NY 10036. (212)642-0600. Fax: (212)921-5173. Website: www.essence.com. Publication director: Susan L. Taylor. **Contact:** Diane Weathers, editor-in-chief. Monthly magazine. "*Essence* is the magazine for today's Black women. Edited for career-minded, sophisticated and independent achievers, *Essence*'s editorial is dedicated to helping its readers attain their maximum potential in various lifestyles and roles. The editorial content includes career and educational opportunities; fashion and beauty; investing and money management; health and fitness; parenting; information on home decorating and food; travel; cultural reviews; fiction; and profiles of achievers and celebrities." Estab. 1970. Circ. 1,000,000. **Pays on acceptance.** Byline given. Offers 25% kill fee. Makes assignments on a one-time serial rights basis. Editorial lead time 6 months. Submit seasonal material 6 months in advance. Accepts queries by mail, fax. Accepts previously published material. Responds in 2 months to queries; 2 months to mss. Sample copy for $3.25. Writer's guidelines for #10 SASE.

Nonfiction: Book excerpts, novel excerpts. **Buys 200 mss/year.** Query. Length: will be given upon assignment. **Pays by the word.**

Reprints: Send tearsheet and information about when and where the material previously appeared. Pays 50% of the amount paid for the original article.

Photos: "We particularly would like to see photographs for our travel section that feature Black travelers." Jan de Chabert, creative director. State availability with submission. Pays from $200 up depending on the size of the image. Model releases required.

Columns/Departments: Query department editors: Lifestyle (food, lifestyle, travel, parenting, consumer information): Jorge Avange; Entertainment: Elayne Fluker; Health & Fitness: Sharon Boone. Word length will be given upon assignment. Query. **Pays by the word.**

The online magazine carries original content not found in the print edition.

Tips: "Please note that *Essence* no longer accepts unsolicited mss for fiction or nonfiction, except for the Brothers, Where There's a Will, Making Love Work, Our World, Back Talk and Interiors columns. So please only send query letters for nonfiction story ideas."

$ $ $ $ FAMILY CIRCLE MAGAZINE, Gruner & Jahr, 375 Lexington Ave., New York NY 10017-5514. (212)499-2000. Fax: (212)499-1987. E-mail: nclark@familycircle.com. Website: www.familycircle.com. Editor-in-Chief: Susan Ungaro. **Contact:** Nancy Clark, deputy editor. **80% freelance written.** Magazine published every 3 weeks. "We are a national women's service magazine which covers many stages of a woman's life, along with her everyday concerns about social, family, and health issues." Estab. 1932. Circ. 5,000,000. Byline given. Offers 20% kill fee. Buys one-time, all rights. Editorial lead time 4 months. Submit seasonal material 4 months in advance. Responds in 2 months to queries; 2 months to mss. Sample copy not available. Writer's guidelines for #10 SASE.

Break in with "Women Who Make A Difference." Send queries to Marilyn Balamaci, senior editor.

Nonfiction: "We look for well-written, well-reported stories told through interesting anecdotes and insightful writing. We want well-researched service journalism on all subjects." Essays, humor, opinion, personal experience, women's interest subjects such as family and personal relationships, children, physical and mental health, nutrition and self-improvement. No fiction or poetry. **Buys 200 mss/year.** Query with SASE. Length: 1,000-2,500 words. **Pays $1/word.** Pays expenses of writers on assignment.

Columns/Departments: Women Who Make a Difference (profiles of volunteers who have made a significant impact on their community), 1,500 words; Profiles in Courage/Love (dramatic narratives about women and families overcoming adversity), 2,000 words; Full Circle (opinion/point of view on current issue/topic of general interest to our readers), 750 words; Humor, 750 words. **Buys 200 mss/year.** Query with published clips and SASE. **Pays $1/word.**

Tips: "Query letters should be concise and to the point. Also, writers should keep close tabs on *Family Circle* and other women's magazines to avoid submitting recently run subject matter."

$$$$ FLARE MAGAZINE, 777 Bay St., 7th Floor, Toronto ON M5W 1AL, Canada. E-mail: editors@flare.com. Website: www.flare.com. **Contact:** Rita Silvan, features editor. Monthly magazine for women ages 17-34. Byline given. Offers 50% kill fee. Buys first North American serial, electronic rights. Accepts queries by e-mail. Response time varies to queries. Sample copy for #10 SASE. Writer's guidelines available.
Nonfiction: Looking for "women's fashion, beauty, health, sociological trends and celebrities." **Buys 24 mss/year.** Query. Length: 200-1,200 words. **Pays $1/word.** Pays expenses of writers on assignment.

GLAMOUR, Conde Nast Publications, Inc., 4 Times Square, 16th floor, New York NY 10036. (212)286-2860. Fax: (212)286-8336. Website: www.glamour.com. Monthly magazine covering subjects ranging from fashion, beauty and health, personal relationships, career, travel, food and entertainment. *Glamour* is edited for the contemporary woman, and informs her of the trends and recommends how she can adapt them to her needs, and motivates her to take action. Estab. 1939.
Nonfiction: Personal experience (relationships), travel.

$$$$ HARPER'S BAZAAR, The Hearst Corp., 1700 Broadway, New York, NY 10019. (212)903-5000. Editor-in-Chief: Glenda Bailey. **Contact:** Features Department. "*Harper's Bazaar* is a monthly specialist magazine for women who love fashion and beauty. It is edited for sophisticated women with exceptional taste. *Bazaar* offers ideas in fashion and beauty, and reports on issues and interests relevant to the lives of modern women." Estab. 1867. Circ. 711,000. Pays on publication. Byline given. Offers 25% kill fee. Buys worldwide rights. Responds in 2 months to queries. Sample copy not available. Writer's guidelines not available.
Nonfiction: Buys 36 mss/year. Query with published clips. Length: 2,000-3,000 words. **Payment negotiable.**
Columns/Departments: Length: 500-700 words. **Payment negotiable.**

$ I DO FOR BRIDES, Pinnacle Publishing Co., 4798 Long Island Dr. NW, Atlanta GA 30342. (404)255-1234. Fax: (404)255-2575. E-mail: editorial.ppc@mindspring.com. Website: www.idoforbrides.com. **Contact:** Lissa Poirot, editor. **60% freelance written.** Quarterly magazine covering the bridal industry. The magazine includes tips for wedding preparation, bridal attire, honeymoon and wedding destinations. Publishes 4 regional versions: Alabama; Atlanta; Tennessee; and Washington DC, Maryland, and Virginia. Estab. 1996. Circ. 160,000. Pays on other. Publishes ms an average of 8 months after acceptance. Byline given. Buys all rights. Editorial lead time 8 months. Submit seasonal material 8 months in advance. Accepts queries by mail, e-mail. Accepts simultaneous submissions.
Nonfiction: Book excerpts, essays, general interest, historical/nostalgic, how-to (bridal-related), humor, inspirational, interview/profile, new product, opinion, personal experience, photo feature, religious, travel. **Buys 8 mss/year.** Query. Length: 300-1,000 words. **Pays variable rate.**

$$$$ LADIES' HOME JOURNAL, Meredith Corporation, 125 Park Ave., 20th Floor, New York NY 10017-5516. (212)557-6600. Fax: (212)455-1313. Website: www.lhj.com. **Contact:** Myrna Blyth, publishing director/editor-in-chief. **50% freelance written.** Monthly magazine focusing on issues of concern to women 30-45. They cover a broader range of news and political issues than many women's magazines. "*Ladies' Home Journal* is for active, empowered women who are evolving in new directions. It addresses informational needs with highly focused features and articles on a variety of topics including beauty and fashion, food and nutrition, health and medicine, home decorating and design, parenting and self-help, personalities and current events." Circ. 5,000,000. **Pays on acceptance.** Offers 25% kill fee. Rights bought vary with submission. Accepts queries by mail. Responds in 3 months to queries. Sample copy not available. Writer's guidelines for #10 SASE, Attention: Writer's Guidelines on the envelope.
Nonfiction: Submissions on the following subjects should be directed to the editor listed for each: investigative reports, news-related features, psychology/relationships/sex (Pam O'Brien, executive editor); celebrities/entertainment (Jim Brosseau). Query with published clips. Length: 2,000-3,000 words. **Pays $2,000-4,000.** Pays expenses of writers on assignment.
Photos: *LHJ* arranges for its own photography almost all the time. State availability with submission. Rights bought vary with submission. Offers variable payment for photos accepted with ms. Captions, identification of subjects, model releases required.
Columns/Departments: Query the following editor or box for column ideas. First Person (Pam O'Brien, executive editor). Query. **Pays $750-2,000.**
Fiction: Shana Aborn, senior editor, books. Only short stories and novels submitted by an agent or publisher will be considered. No poetry of any kind. **Buys 12 mss/year.**
■ The online magazine carries original content not found in the print edition. Contact: Mary Farrell, online director.

$ THE LINK & VISITOR, Baptist Women's Missionary Society of Ontario and Quebec, 30 Arlington Ave., Toronto, Ontario M6G 3K8, Canada. (416)651-7192. Fax: (416)651-0438. E-mail: linkvis@idirect.com. **Contact:** Editor. **50% freelance written.** Magazine published 6 times/ year "designed to help Baptist women grow their world, faith, relationships, creativity, and mission vision-evangelical, egalitarian, Canadian." Estab. 1878. Circ. 4,000. Pays on publication. Publishes ms an average of 6 months after acceptance. Byline given. Buys one-time, second serial (reprint), simultaneous rights, makes work-for-hire assignments. Editorial lead time 2 months. Submit seasonal material 3 months in advance. Accepts simultaneous submissions. Sample copy for 9×12 SAE with 2 first-class Canadian stamps. Writer's guidelines free.
Nonfiction: "Articles must be biblically literate. No easy answers, American mindset or U.S. focus, retelling of Bible stories, sermons." Inspirational, interview/profile, religious. **Buys 30-35 mss/year.** Send complete ms. Length: 750-2,000 words. **Pays 5-10¢/word (Canadian).** Sometimes pays expenses of writers on assignment.

Photos: State availability with submission. Reviews prints. Buys one-time rights. Offers no additional payment for photos accepted with ms. Captions required.
Tips: "We cannot use unsolicited manuscripts from non-Canadian writers. When submitting by e-mail, please send stories as messages, not as attachments."

LONG ISLAND WOMAN, Maraj, Inc., P.O. Box 309, Island Park NY 11558. Fax: (516)889-6983. E-mail: editor@liwomanonline.com. Website: www.liwomanonline.com. **Contact:** Jane Lane, managing editor. **60% freelance written.** Monthly magazine covering issues of importance to women—health, family, finance, arts, entertainment, fitness, travel, home. Estab. 2001. Circ. 35,000. Pays within 30 days of publication. Publishes ms an average of 3 months after acceptance. Byline given. Offers 50% kill fee. Buys one-time rights for print and online use. Editorial lead time 3 months. Submit seasonal material 3 months in advance. Accepts queries by mail, e-mail. Accepts previously published material. Accepts simultaneous submissions. Responds in 6 weeks to queries; 3 months to mss. Sample copy for $3. Writer's guidelines for free, online or by e-mail.
Nonfiction: Book excerpts, general interest, how-to, humor, interview/profile, new product, opinion, personal experience, travel, reviews. **Buys 75-100 mss/year.** Query with published clips or send complete ms. Length: 300-1,500 words. **Pays $50-150 for assigned articles; $35-120 for unsolicited articles.**
Reprints: Accepts previously published submissions.
Photos: State availability of or send photos with submission. Reviews 5×7 prints. Buys one-time rights. Offers $10-25/photo. Captions, identification of subjects, model releases required.
Columns/Departments: Humor, Health Issues, Family Issues, Financial and Business Issues, Book Reviews and Books, Arts and Entertainment, Travel and Leisure, Home and Garden, all 500-1,000 words. **Buys 75-100 mss/year.** Query with published clips or send complete ms. **Pays $50-100.**

$ $ $ MODERN BRIDE, Conde Nast Publications, 4 Times Square, New York NY 10036. Website: www.modernbride.com. Editor-in-Chief: Antonia van der Meer. **Contact:** Christina Cush, executive editor. "*Modern Bride* is designed as the bride-to-be's guide to planning her wedding, honeymoon, and first home or apartment. Issues cover: (1) bridal fashion (including grooms, attendants, and mothers-of-the-bride), travel trousseau and lingerie; (2) home furnishings (tableware, furniture, linens, appliances, housewares, accessories, etc.); (3) honeymoon travel (covering the honeymoon hotspots around the world). Additional regular features include beauty, sex, health and fitness; wedding gifts; wedding planning tips; relationships; financial advice; and shopping information." Estab. 1949. Circ. 400,000. **Pays on acceptance.** Byline given. Offers 25% kill fee. Buys first periodical rights. Editorial lead time 6 months. Accepts queries by mail. Responds in 6 weeks to queries.
Nonfiction: Personal experience, relationship/sex articles; planning articles. **Buys 10 unsolicited mss/year.** Query with published clips. Length: 500-2,000 words. **Pays according to experience of writer and difficulty/length of assignment.** Sometimes pays expenses of writers on assignment.
Reprints: Send tearsheet of article or short story. Pays 50% of amount paid for original article.
Columns/Departments: Voices and On His Mind (personal experiences of bride and groom).

The online magazine carries original content not found in the print edition. Contact: Christine Ford, online content editor.

$ $ MORE MAGAZINE, Meredith Corp., 125 Park Ave., New York NY 10017. Fax: (212)455-1433. Website: www.lhj.com/more/. Editor-in-Chief: Susan Crandell. **Contact:** Stephanie Woodard, articles editor. **90% freelance written.** Magazine published 10 times/year covering smart, sophisticated 40- to 60-year-old women. Estab. 1998. Circ. 700,000. **Pays on acceptance.** Publishes ms an average of 3 months after acceptance. Byline given. Offers 25% kill fee. Buys first North American serial, first, all rights. Editorial lead time 4 months. Submit seasonal material 6 months in advance. Accepts queries by mail, fax. Responds in 3 months to queries; 3 months to mss. Sample copy not available. Writer's guidelines for #10 SASE.
Nonfiction: Essays, exposé, general interest, interview/profile, personal experience, travel, crime, food. **Buys 50 mss/year.** Query with published clips. Length: 300-2,500 words. **Pays variable rate depending on writer/story length.** Pays expenses of writers on assignment.
Photos: State availability with submission. Negotiates payment individually. Captions, identification of subjects, model releases required.
Columns/Departments: Buys 20 mss/year. Query with published clips. **Pays $300.**

$ $ $ $ MS. MAGAZINE, Liberty Media for Women, UC, 20 Exchange Place, 22nd Floor, New York NY 10005. (212)509-2092. Fax: (212)509-2407. E-mail: info@msmagazine.com. Website: www.msmagazine.com. Editor-in-Chief: Marcia Gillespie. Editor: Gloria Jacobs. **Contact:** Manuscripts Editor. **30% freelance written.** Bimonthly magazine on women's issues and news. Estab. 1972. Circ. 150,000. Byline given. Offers 30% kill fee. Buys first North American serial rights. Responds in 2 months to queries; 2 months to mss. Sample copy for $9. Writer's guidelines for #10 SASE.
Nonfiction: International and national (US) news, the arts, books, popular culture, feminist theory and scholarship, ecofeminism, women's health, spirituality, political and economic affairs. Photo essays. **Buys 4-5 feature (3,500 words) and 4-5 short (500 words) mss/year.** Query with published clips. Length: 300-3,500 words. **Pays $1/word.** Pays expenses of writers on assignment.
Reprints: Send tearsheet or typed ms with rights for sale noted and information about when and where the material previously appeared. Pays 50% of amount paid for original article.
Photos: State availability with submission. Buys one-time rights. Identification of subjects, model releases required.

Columns/Departments: Length: 3,000 words maximum. **Buys 4-5 mss/year. Pays $1/word.**
Tips: Needs "international and national women's news, investigative reporting, personal narratives, humor, world-class fiction and poetry, and prize-winning journalists and feminist thinkers."

$ $ ☆ GRACE ORMONDE WEDDING STYLE, Elegant Publishing Inc., P.O. Box 89, Barrington RI 02806. (401)245-9726. Fax: (401)245-5371. E-mail: yanni@weddingstylemagazine.com. Website: www.weddingstylemagazine.com. Editor: Grace Ormonde. **Contact:** Yannis Tzoumas, editorial director/publisher. Annual magazine covering wedding and special event planning resource. "*Grace Ormonde Wedding Style* is a wedding and special event planning magazine with editorial covering home and home decorating, women's health issues, cooking, beauty and travel." Estab. 1997. Circ. 225,000. Pays on publication. Publishes ms an average of 4 months after acceptance. Accepts queries by mail, e-mail, fax. Sample copy not available. Writer's guidelines not available.
Nonfiction: General interest, how-to, interview/profile, personal experience, travel. **Buys 35 mss/year.** Query. Length: 300-3,500 words. **Pays $100-300.** Sometimes pays expenses of writers on assignment.
Photos: State availability with submission. Reviews transparencies. Negotiates payment individually.
Columns/Departments: Wedding related (flowers, beauty, etc.), 450 words, buys 25 mss/year; Women's Health, 3,000 words, buys 1 ms/year; Home Decorating/Cooking, 400 words, buys 5 mss/year; Travel, 350 words, buys 3 mss/year. Query. **Pays $100-300.**
Poetry: Avant-garde, free verse, light verse, traditional. **Buys 10 poems/year.** Length: 4-28 lines.
Fillers: Anecdotes, facts.
Tips: "All stories are assigned and involve an interview with one or more experts in a given field."

$ $ $ REDBOOK MAGAZINE, 224 W. 57th St., New York NY 10019. Website: www.redbookmag.com. Editor-in-chief: Ellen Kunes. Monthly magazine. "*Redbook* addresses young married women between the ages of 28 and 42. Most of our readers are married with children 10 and under; over 60 percent work outside the home. The articles entertain, educate and inspire our readers to confront challenging issues. Each article must be timely and relevant to *Redbook* readers' lives." Estab. 1903. Circ. 3,200,000. **Pays on acceptance.** Publishes ms an average of 6 months after acceptance. Rights purchased vary with author and material. Responds in 3 months to queries; 3 months to mss. Sample copy not available. Writer's guidelines online.

O→ "Please review at least the past six issues of *Redbook* to better understand subject matter and treatment."

Nonfiction: Articles Department. Subjects of interest: social issues, parenting, sex, marriage, news profiles, true crime, dramatic narratives, health. Query with published clips and SASE. Length: Articles: 2,500-3,000 words; short articles, 1,000-1,500 words.
Tips: "Most *Redbook* articles require solid research, well-developed anecdotes from on-the-record sources, and fresh, insightful quotes from established experts in a field that pass our 'reality check' test. Articles must apply to women in our demographics."

$ $ TODAY'S CHRISTIAN WOMAN, 465 Gundersen Dr., Carol Stream IL 60188-2498. (630)260-6200. Fax: (630)260-0114. E-mail: tcwedit@christianitytoday.com. Website: www.todayschristianwoman.net. Editor: Jane Johnson Struck. Associate Editor: Camerin Courtney. **Contact:** Amy Tatum, assistant editor. **50% freelance written.** Bimonthly magazine for Christian women of all ages, single and married, homemakers, and career women. "*Today's Christian Woman* seeks to help women deal with the contemporary issues and hot topics that impact their lives, as well as provide depth, balance, and a Biblical perspective to the relationships they grapple with daily in the following arenas: family, friendship, faith, marriage, single life, self, work, and health." Estab. 1979. Circ. 250,000. **Pays on acceptance.** Publishes ms an average of 6 months after acceptance. Byline given. Buys first rights. Submit seasonal material 9 months in advance. Accepts queries by mail, e-mail, fax. Responds in 2 months to queries; 2 months to mss. Sample copy for $5. Writer's guidelines for #10 SASE or online.
Nonfiction: How-to, narrative, inspirational. *Practical* spiritual living articles, 1,500-1,800 words. Humor (light, first-person pieces that include some spiritual distinctive), 1,000-1,500 words. Issues (third-person, anecdotal articles that report on scope of trends or hot topics, and provide perspective and practical take away on issues, plus sidebars), 1,800 words. How-to, inspirational. Query. No unsolicited mss. "The query should include article summary, purpose, and reader value, author's qualifications, suggested length, date to send, and SASE for reply." **Pays 20-25¢/word.**
Columns/Departments: Faith @ Work (recent true story of how you shared your faith with someone on the job), 100-200 words; **pays $25.** My Favorite Web Site (a short description of a website you've found particularly helpful or interesting), 100 words; **pays $25.** Readers' Picks (a short review of your current favorite CD or book, and why), 200 words; **pays $25.** My Story (first-person, true-life dramatic story of how you solved a problem or overcame a difficult situation), 1,500-1,800 words; **pays $300.** Small Talk (true humorous or inspirational anecdotes about children), 50-100 words; **pays $25.** Does not return or acknowledge submissions to these departments.
Tips: "Articles should be practical and contain a distinct evangelical Christian perspective. While *TCW* adheres strictly to this underlying perspective in all its editorial content, articles should refrain from using language that assumes a reader's familiarity with Christian or church-oriented terminology. Bible quotes and references should be used selectively. All Bible quotes should be taken from the New International Version if possible. All articles should be highly anecdotal, personal in tone, and universal in appeal."

$ $ WEDDINGBELLS, (Canada), WEDDINGBELLS, Inc., 50 Wellington St. E., Suite 200, Toronto, Ontario M5E 1C8, Canada. (416)862-8479. Fax: (416)862-2184. E-mail: info@weddingbells.com. Website: www.weddingbells.com. Editor: Alison McGill. **Contact:** Anne Gibson, managing editor. **10% freelance written.** Semiannual magazine covering bridal, wedding, setting up home. Estab. 1985. Circ. 107,000 (Canada), 325,000 (USA). Pays on completion of assignment. Publishes ms an average of 6 months after acceptance. Offers 25% kill fee. Buys first North American serial, second serial (reprint), electronic rights. Accepts queries by mail, fax. Responds in 2 months to queries; 2 months to mss. Sample copy not available. Writer's guidelines not available.

Nonfiction: Book excerpts, bridal service pieces. **Buys 22 mss/year.** Query with published clips. **Pays variable rates for assigned articles.** Sometimes pays expenses of writers on assignment.

N $ $ **WEDDINGBELLS, (U.S.)**, WEDDINGBELLS, Inc., 34 King St. E., Suite 800, Toronto, Ontario M5C 2X8, Canada. (416)363-1574. Fax: (416)363-6004. E-mail: info@weddingbells.com. Website: www.weddingbells.com. Editor: Crys Stewart. **Contact:** Michael Killingsworth, managing editor. **10% freelance written.** Semiannual magazine covering bridal, wedding, setting up home. Estab. 2000. Circ. 350,000. Pays on completion of assignment. Publishes ms an average of 6 months after acceptance. Byline sometimes given. Offers 25% kill fee. Buys first North American serial, second serial (reprint), electronic rights. Accepts queries by mail, fax. Responds in 2 months to queries; 2 months to mss.

Nonfiction: Book excerpts, bridal service pieces. **Buys 22 mss/year.** Query with published clips. **Pays variable rates for assigned articles.** Sometimes pays expenses of writers on assignment.

$ $ $ $ **WOMAN'S DAY**, 1633 Broadway, 42nd Floor, New York NY 10019. (212)767-6000. Fax: (212)767-5610. Website: www.womansday.com. **Contact:** Stephanie Abarbanel, senior articles editor. **75% freelance written.** Magazine published 17 issues/year. "*Woman's Day* is written and edited for the contemporary woman. *Woman's Day* editorial package covers the various issues that are important to women today: food & nutrition, health & fitness, beauty & fashion, as well as the traditional values of home, family, and children. The changing needs of women are also addressed with articles and more in-depth *WD* Reports that focus on religion, money management, at-home business, law, and relationships." Circ. 6,000,000. **Pays on acceptance.** Byline given. Offers 25% kill fee. Accepts queries by mail. Responds in 1 month to queries. Sample copy not available.

Nonfiction: Uses articles on all subjects of interest to women—family life, childrearing, education, homemaking, money management, careers, family health, work, and leisure activities. Also interested in fresh, dramatic narratives of women's lives and concerns. "These must be lively to read with a high emotional content." **Payment varies** depending on length, type, writer, and whether it's for regional or national use, but rates are high. Pays a bonus fee in addition to regular rate for articles based on writer's ideas (as opposed to assigned story.) **Bonus fee is an additional 20% of fee (up to $500).** "We no longer accept unsolicited manuscripts except for Back Talk essays of 750 words—and cannot return or be responsible for those that are sent to us." Length: 500-1,500 depending on material. Pays expenses of writers on assignment.

Columns/Departments: "We welcome short (750 words), thought-provoking spirited essays on controversial topics for Back Talk page. We prefer to cover significant issues that concern a large number of women and families rather than the slight or trivial or those that affect only a few. Essays are usually based on personal experience and always written in the first person, but they must have reader identification." Submit completed essays only, no queries, with SASE. **Pays $2,000.**

Fillers: Neighbors columns **pay $75/each** for brief practical suggestions on homemaking, childrearing, and relationships. Address to the editor of the section.

Tips: "Our primary need is for ideas with broad appeal that can be featured on the cover. These include diet stories, organizing tips, and money saving information. We're buying more short pieces. Submissions must be double spaced and must include a SASE and clips. Faxes and e-mails will not be read."

$ $ **WOMAN'S LIFE**, A Publication of Woman's Life Insurance Society, 1338 Military St., P.O. Box 5020, Port Huron MI 48061-5020. (810)985-5191, ext. 181. Fax: (810)985-6970. E-mail: wkrabach@womanslifeins.com. Website: www.womanslifeins.com. Editor: Janice U. Whipple. **Contact:** Wendy L. Krabach, director of communications and fraternal services. **30% freelance written.** Quarterly magazine published for a primarily female-membership to help them care for themselves and their families. Estab. 1892. Circ. 32,000. Pays on publication. Publishes ms an average of 1 year after acceptance. Byline given. Not copyrighted. Buys one-time, second serial (reprint), simultaneous rights. Submit seasonal material 6 months in advance. Accepts queries by mail, e-mail, fax. Accepts simultaneous submissions. Responds in 1 year to queries; 1 year to mss. Sample copy for 9×12 SAE and 4 first-class stamps. Writer's guidelines for #10 SASE.

- Works only with published/established writers.

Nonfiction: Looking primarily for general interest stories for women aged 25-55 regarding physical, mental and emotional health and fitness; and financial/fiscal health and fitness. "We would like to see more creative financial pieces that are directed at women." **Buys 4-10 mss/year.** Send complete ms. Length: 1,000-2,000 words. **Pays $150-500.**

Reprints: Send tearsheet, photocopy or typed ms with rights for sale noted and information about when and where the material previously appeared. Pays 15% of amount paid for an original article.

Photos: Only interested in photos included with ms. Identification of subjects, model releases required.

$ $ $ **WOMAN'S WORLD**, The Woman's Weekly, Heinrich Bauer North America, Inc., 270 Sylvan Ave., Englewood Cliffs NJ 07632. Fax: (201)569-3584. Editor-in-Chief: Stephanie Saible. **Contact:** Kathy Fitzpatrick and Johnene Granger, features editors. **95% freelance written.** Weekly magazine covering "human interest and service pieces of interest to family-oriented women across the nation. *Woman's World* is a women's service magazine. It offers a blend of fashion, food, parenting, beauty, and relationship features coupled with the true-life human interest stories." **Pays**

on acceptance. Publishes ms an average of 4 months after acceptance. Buys first North American Serial rights for 6 months. Submit seasonal material 4 months in advance. Accepts queries by mail. Responds in 6 weeks to queries; 2 months to mss. Sample copy not available. Writer's guidelines for #10 SASE.

• Ranked as one of the best markets for fiction writers in *Writer's Digest* magazine's "Fiction 50," June 2001.

Nonfiction: Dramatic personal women's stories and articles on self-improvement, medicine, and health topics. Please specify "Real-Life Story" on envelope. Features include Emergency (real-life drama); My Story; Medical Miracle; Triumph; Courage; My Guardian Angel; Happy Ending (queries to Kathy Fitzpatrick). Also service stories on parenting, marriage, and work (queries to Irene Daria). **Pays $500/1,000 words.**

Fiction: Johnene Granger, fiction editor. Short story, romance, and mainstream of 1,500 words and mini-mysteries of 1,000 words. "Each of our stories has a light romantic theme and can be written from either a masculine or feminine point of view. Women characters may be single, married, or divorced. Plots must be fast moving with vivid dialogue and action. The problems and dilemmas inherent in them should be contemporary and realistic, handled with warmth and feeling. The stories must have a positive resolution." Specify "Fiction" on envelope. Always enclose SASE. Responds in 4 months. No phone or fax queries. Pays $1,000 for romances on acceptance for North American serial rights for 6 months. "The 1,000 word mini-mysteries may feature either a 'whodunnit' or 'howdunnit' theme. The mystery may revolve around anything from a theft to murder. However, we are not interested in sordid or grotesque crimes. Emphasis should be on intricacies of plot rather than gratuitous violence. The story must include a resolution that clearly states the villain is getting his or her come-uppance." Submit complete mss. Specify "Mini-Mystery" on envelope. Enclose SASE. Stories slanted for a particular holiday should be sent at least 6 months in advance. No phone queries. Not interested in science fiction, fantasy, historical romance, or foreign locales. No explicit sex, graphic language, or seamy settings. Send complete ms. **Pays $500-1,400.**

Tips: "Come up with good queries. Short queries are best. We have a strong emphasis on well-researched material. Writers must send research with manuscript including book references and phone numbers for double checking. The most frequent mistakes made by writers in completing an article for us are sloppy, incomplete research, not writing to the format, and not studying the magazine carefully enough beforehand."

$ WOMEN ALIVE, Encouraging Excellence in Holy Living, Women Alive, Inc., P.O. Box 4683, Overland Park KS 66204. (913)649-8583. Fax: (913)649-8583. E-mail: ahinthorn@kc.rr.com. Website: www.womenalivemagazine.org. Managing Editor: Jeanette Littleton. **Contact:** Aletha Hinthorn, editor. **50% freelance written.** Bimonthly magazine covering Christian living. "*Women Alive* encourages and equips women to live holy lives through teaching them to live out Scripture." Estab. 1984. Circ. 4,000. Pays on publication. Publishes ms an average of 6 months after acceptance. Byline given. Buys first North American serial, first, one-time, second serial (reprint), simultaneous rights. Editorial lead time 4 months. Submit seasonal material 4 months in advance. Accepts queries by mail, e-mail. Accepts simultaneous submissions. Responds in 6 weeks to mss. Sample copy for 9×12 SAE and 4 first-class stamps. Writer's guidelines not available.

Nonfiction: Inspirational, opinion, personal experience, religious. **Buys 30 mss/year.** Send complete ms. Length: 500-1,500 words.

Photos: State availability with submission. Offers no additional payment for photos accepted with ms.

$ $ WOMEN IN BUSINESS, American Business Women's Association (The ABWA Company, Inc.), 9100 Ward Pkwy., P.O. Box 8728, Kansas City MO 64114-0728. (816)361-6621. Fax: (816)361-4991. E-mail: abwa@abwahq.org. Website: www.abwa.org. **Contact:** Kathleen Isaacson, editor. **30% freelance written.** Bimonthly magazine covering issues affecting working women. "How-to features for career women on business trends, small-business ownership, self-improvement, and retirement issues. Profiles of ABWA members only." Estab. 1949. Circ. 47,000. **Pays on acceptance.** Publishes ms an average of 3 months after acceptance. Byline given. Buys first North American serial rights. Editorial lead time 3 months. Accepts queries by mail, e-mail, fax. Accepts simultaneous submissions. Responds in 3 weeks to queries; 2 months to mss. Sample copy for 9×12 SAE and 4 first-class stamps. Writer's guidelines for #10 SASE.

O‑‑ Break in by "having knowledge of the business world and how women fit into it."

Nonfiction: How-to, interview/profile (ABWA members only), computer/Internet. No fiction or poetry. **Buys 3% of submitted mss/year.** Query. Length: 500-1,000 words. **Pays variable rates.**

Photos: State availability with submission. Reviews 3×5 prints. Buys all rights. Offers no additional payment for photos accepted with ms. Identification of subjects required.

Columns/Departments: Life After Business (concerns of retired business women); It's Your Business (entrepreneurial advice for business owners); Tech Talk (new work-related technology and training); Health Spot (health issues that affect women in the work place). Length: 315-700 words. Query. **Payment varies.**

Trade, Technical & Professional Journals

Many writers who pick up *Writer's Market* for the first time do so with the hope of selling an article or story to one of the popular, high-profile consumer magazines found on newsstands and in bookstores. Many of those writers are surprised to find an entire world of magazine publishing that exists outside the realm of commercial magazines and that they may have never known about—trade journals. Writers who *have* discovered trade journals have found a market that offers the chance to publish regularly in subject areas they find interesting, editors who are typically more accessible than their commercial counterparts, and pay rates that rival those of the big-name magazines.

Trade journal is the general term for any publication focusing on a particular occupation or industry. Other terms used to describe the different types of trade publications are business, technical, and professional journals. They are read by truck drivers, bricklayers, farmers, fishermen, heart surgeons, and just about everyone else working in a trade or profession. Trade periodicals are sharply angled to the specifics of the professions on which they report. They offer business-related news, features, and service articles that will foster their readers' professional development.

Trade magazine editors tell us their readers are a knowledgeable and highly interested audience. Writers for trade magazines have to either possess knowledge about the field in question or be able to report it accurately from interviews with those who do. Writers who have or can develop a good grasp of a specialized body of knowledge will find trade magazine editors who are eager to hear from them. And since good writers with specialized knowledge are a somewhat rare commodity, trade editors tend, more than typical consumer magazine editors, to cultivate ongoing relationships with writers. If you can prove yourself as a writer who "delivers," you will be paid back with frequent assignments and regular paychecks.

An ideal way to begin your foray into trade journals is to write for those that report on your present profession. Whether you've been teaching dance, farming, or working as a paralegal, begin by familiarizing yourself with the magazines that serve your occupation. After you've read enough issues to have a feel for the kinds of pieces the magazines run, approach the editors with your own article ideas. If you don't have experience in a profession but can demonstrate an ability to understand (and write about) the intricacies and issues of a particular trade that interests you, editors will still be willing to hear from you.

Photographs help increase the value of most stories for trade journals. If you can provide photos, mention that in your query. Since selling photos with a story usually means a bigger paycheck, it's worth any freelancer's time to develop basic camera skills.

Query a trade journal as you would a consumer magazine. Most trade editors like to discuss an article with a writer first and will sometimes offer names of helpful sources. Mention any direct experience you may have in the industry in your query letter. Send a résumé and clips if they show you have some background or related experience in the subject area. Read each listing carefully for additional submission guidelines.

To stay abreast of new trade magazines starting up, watch for news in *Folio: The Magazine for Magazine Management* and *Advertising Age* magazines. Another source for information about trade publications is the *Business Publication Advertising Source*, published by Standard

Rate and Data Service (SRDS) which is available in most libraries. Designed primarily for people who buy ad space, the volume provides names and addresses of thousands of trade journals, listed by subject matter.

Information on trade publications listed in the previous edition of *Writer's Market* but not included in this edition can be found in the General Index.

ADVERTISING, MARKETING & PR

Trade journals for advertising executives, copywriters, and marketing and public relations professionals are listed in this category. Those whose main focus is the advertising and marketing of specific products, such as home furnishings, are classified under individual product categories. Journals for sales personnel and general merchandisers can be found in the Selling & Merchandising category.

[N] BIG IDEA, Detroit's Connection to the Communication Arts, Big Idea, 1900 Hilton, Ferndale MI 48220. Fax: (248)544-7745. E-mail: info@bigideaweb.com. Website: www.bigideaweb.com. **Contact:** Conny Coon, vice president-editorial (send e-mail queries to ccoon@bigideaweb.com). **75% freelance written.** Monthly magazine covering creative and communication arts in Southeastern Michigan. "We are a trade magazine specifically for creative professionals in the advertising, marketing and communication arts industry in Southeastern Michigan. Detroit is the third largest advertising market in the US. We are the resource for anyone in the agency, film and video, printing, post production, interactive, art and design, illustration, or photography." Estab. 1994. Circ. 10,000. **Pays on acceptance.** Publishes ms an average of 2 months after acceptance. Byline sometimes given. Offers 100% kill fee. Editorial lead time 2 months. Accepts queries by mail, e-mail, fax. Accepts previously published material. Responds in 6 weeks to queries. and 4 first-class stamps.

Nonfiction: Conny Coon, VP Editorial. **Buys 10-12 mss/year.** Query with published clips. Length: 1,500-2,500 words. **Pays $100-350 for assigned articles.** Sometimes pays expenses of writers on assignment.

Photos: State availability with submission. Reviews GIF/JPEG files. Offers no additional payment for photos accepted with ms. Captions, identification of subjects, model releases required.

$ $ $ BRAND PACKAGING, Stagnito Communications, 210 S. Fifth St., St. Charles IL 60174. (630)377-0100. Fax: (630)377-1688. E-mail: bswientek@stagnito.com. Website: www.brandpackaging.com. Senior Editor: Jim George. **Contact:** Bob Swientek, editor. **15% freelance written.** Bimonthly magazine covering how packaging can be a marketing tool. "We publish strategies and tactics to make products stand out on the shelf. Our market is brand managers who are marketers but need to know something about packaging." Estab. 1997. Circ. 33,000. **Pays on acceptance.** Publishes ms an average of 2 months after acceptance. Byline given. Makes work-for-hire assignments. Editorial lead time 3 months. Submit seasonal material 3 months in advance. Accepts queries by mail, fax. Sample copy for free.

Nonfiction: How-to, interview/profile, new product. **Buys 30 mss/year.** Send complete ms. Length: 600-2,400 words. **Pays 40-50¢/word.**

Photos: State availability with submission. Reviews contact sheets, 35mm transparencies, 4×5 prints. Buys one-time rights. Negotiates payment individually. Identification of subjects required.

Columns/Departments: Whatever happened to... (packaging failures); New Technology (new packaging technology), both 600 words. **Buys 20 mss/year.** Query. **Pays $150-400.**

The online version of this publication contains material not found in the print edition.

Tips: "Be knowledgeable on marketing techniques and be able to grasp packaging techniques. Be sure you focus on packaging as a marketing tool. Use concrete examples. We are not seeking case histories at this time."

$ DECA DIMENSIONS, 1908 Association Dr., Reston VA 20191. (703)860-5000. Fax: (703)860-4013. E-mail: deca_dimensions@deca.org. Website: www.deca.org. **Contact:** Cindy Sweeney, editor. **30% freelance written.** Quarterly magazine covering marketing, professional development, business, career training during school year (no issues published May-August). "*Deca Dimensions* is the membership magazine for DECA—The Association of Marketing Students—primarily ages 15-19 in all 50 states, the U.S. territories, Germany and Canada. The magazine is delivered through the classroom. Students are interested in developing professional, leadership and career skills." Estab. 1947. Circ. 160,000. Pays on publication. Byline given. Buys first, second serial (reprint) rights. Editorial lead time 3 months. Submit seasonal material 4 months in advance. Accepts queries by mail, e-mail, fax, phone. Accepts simultaneous submissions. Sample copy for free.

Nonfiction: "Interested in seeing trends/forecast information of interest to audience (how do you forecast? why? what are the trends for the next 5 years in fashion or retail?)." Essays, general interest, how-to (get jobs, start business, plan for college, etc.), interview/profile (business leads), personal experience (working), leadership development. **Buys 10 mss/year.** Send complete ms. Length: 800-1,000 words. **Pays $125 for assigned articles; $100 for unsolicited articles.**

Reprints: Send typed ms and information about when and where the material previously appeared. Pays 85% of amount paid for an original article.

Columns/Departments: Professional development, leadership, 350-500 words. **Buys 6 mss/year.** Send complete ms. **Pays $75-100.**

MEDIA INC., Pacific Northwest Media, Marketing and Creative Services News, P.O. Box 24365, Seattle WA 98124-0365. (206)382-9220. Fax: (206)382-9437. E-mail: media@media-inc.com. Website: www.media-inc.com. Publisher: James Baker. **Contact:** David Drury, editor. **30% freelance written.** Quarterly magazine covering Northwest US media, advertising, marketing and creative-service industries. Audience is Northwest ad agencies, marketing professionals, media and creative-service professionals. Estab. 1987. Circ. 10,000. Byline given. Responds in 1 month to queries. Sample copy for 9×12 SAE and 6 first-class stamps.
Tips: "It is best if writers live in the Pacific Northwest and can report on local news and events in Media Inc.'s areas of business coverage."

N $ $ $ PROMO MAGAZINE, Insights and Ideas for Building Brands, Primedia, 11 Riverbend Dr., Stamford CT 06907. (203)358-9900. Fax: (203)358-5834. E-mail: pbreen@primediabusiness.com. Website: www.promomagazine.com. **Contact:** Peter Breen, editor. **5% freelance written.** Monthly magazine covering promotion marketing. "*Promo* serves marketers and stories must be informative, well-written, and familiar with the subject matter." Estab. 1987. Circ. 25,000. Pays on publication. Publishes ms an average of 2 months after acceptance. Byline given. Offers 25% kill fee. Buys first North American serial rights. Editorial lead time 3 months. Submit seasonal material 3 months in advance. Responds in 1 month to queries. Sample copy for $5.
Nonfiction: Exposé, general interest, how-to (marketing programs), interview/profile, new product (promotion). "No general marketing stories not heavily involved in promotions." Generally does not accept unsolicited mss, query first. **Buys 6-10 mss/year.** Query with published clips. Length: variable. **Pays $1,000 maximum for assigned articles; $500 maximum for unsolicited articles.** Sometimes pays expenses of writers on assignment.
Photos: State availability with submission. Reviews contact sheets, negatives. Negotiates payment individually. Captions, identification of subjects, model releases required.
Tips: "Understand that our stories aim to teach marketing professionals about successful promotion strategies. Case studies or new promos have the best chance."

N $ $ SIGN BUILDER ILLUSTRATED, America's How-To Sign Magazine, Summons-Boardman Publishing Corp., 345 Hudson St., 12th Floor, New York NY 10014. (252)355-5806. Fax: (252)355-5690. E-mail: jwooten@sbpub.com. Website: www.signshop.com. **Contact:** Jeff Wooten, editor. **40% freelance written.** Monthly magazine covering sign and graphic industry. "*Sign Builder Illustrated* targets sign professionals where they work: on the shop floor. Our topics cover the broadest spectrum of the sign industry, from design to fabrication, installation, maintenance and repair. Our readers own a similarly wide range of shops, including commercial, vinyl, sign erection and maintenance, electrical and neon, architectural, and awnings." Estab. 1974. Circ. 14,500. **Pays on acceptance.** Publishes ms an average of 3 months after acceptance. Byline given. Offers 25% kill fee. Buys all rights. Editorial lead time 3 months. Submit seasonal material 4 months in advance. Accepts queries by mail, e-mail, fax, phone. Accepts simultaneous submissions. Responds in 1 month to queries. Sample copy for free. Writer's guidelines free.
Nonfiction: Historical/nostalgic, how-to, humor, interview/profile, photo feature, technical. **Buys 50-60 mss/year.** Query. Length: 1,500-2,500 words. **Pays $250-550 for assigned articles.** Sometimes pays expenses of writers on assignment.
Photos: Send photos with submission. Reviews 3×5 prints. Buys all rights. Negotiates payment individually. Captions, identification of subjects required.
Tips: "Be very knowledgeable about a portion of the sign industry you are covering. We want our readers to come away from each article with at least one good idea, one new technique, or one more 'trick of the trade.' At the same time, we don't want a purely textbook listing of 'do this, do that.' Our readers enjoy *Sign Builder Illustrated* because the publication speaks to them in a clear and lively fashion, from one sign professional to another. We want to engage the reader who has been in the business for some time. While there might be a place for basic instruction in new techniques, our average paid subscriber has been in business over twenty years, employs over seven people, and averages of $800,000 in annual sales. These people aren't neophytes content with retread articles they can find anywhere. It's important for our writers to use anecdotes and examples drawn from the daily sign business."

$ $ SIGNCRAFT, The Magazine for Today's Sign Maker, SignCraft Publishing Co., Inc., P.O. Box 60031, Fort Myers FL 33906. (941)939-4644. Fax: (941)939-0607. E-mail: signcraft@signcraft.com. Website: www.signcraft.com. **Contact:** Tom McIltrot, editor. **10% freelance written.** Bimonthly magazine covering the sign industry. "Like any trade magazine, we need material of direct benefit to our readers. We can't afford space for material of marginal interest." Estab. 1980. Circ. 14,000. Pays on publication. Publishes ms an average of 6 months after acceptance. Byline given. Offers negotiable kill fee. Buys first North American serial, all rights. Accepts queries by mail, e-mail, fax. Responds in 1 month to queries. Sample copy and writer's guidelines for $3.
Nonfiction: "All articles should be directly related to quality commercial signs. If you are familiar with the sign trade, we'd like to hear from you." Interview/profile. **Buys 10 mss/year.** Query with or without published clips. Length: 500-2,000 words.

$ $ SIGNS OF THE TIMES, The Industry Journal Since 1906, ST Publications, Dept. WM, 407 Gilbert Ave., Cincinnati OH 45202-2285. (513)421-2050. Fax: (513)421-5144. E-mail: sconner@stpubs.com. Website: www.signweb.com. **Contact:** Susan Conner, senior editor. **15-30% freelance written.** Monthly magazine covering the sign and outdoor advertising industries. Estab. 1906. Circ. 17,000. Pays on publication. Publishes ms an average of 3 months after acceptance. Byline given. variable rights. Accepts queries by mail, e-mail, fax, phone. Responds in 3 months to queries. Sample copy and writer's guidelines for 9×12 SAE with 10 first-class stamps.

Nonfiction: Historical/nostalgic (regarding the sign industry), how-to (carved signs, goldleaf, etc.), interview/profile (focusing on either a signshop or a specific project), photo feature (query first), technical (sign engineering, etc.). Nothing "nonspecific on signs, an example being a photo essay on 'signs I've seen.' We are a trade journal with specific audience interests." **Buys 15-20 mss/year.** Query with published clips. **Pays $150-500.**

Reprints: Send tearsheet or typed ms with rights for sale noted and information about when and where the material previously appeared. Payment is negotiated.

Photos: "Sign industry-related photos only. We sometimes accept photos with funny twists or misspellings." Send photos with submission.

Fillers: Open to queries; request rates.

The online version contains material not found in the print edition.

Tips: "Be thoroughly familiar with the sign industry, especially in the CAS-related area. Have an insider's knowledge plus an insider's contacts."

ART, DESIGN & COLLECTIBLES

The businesses of art, art administration, architecture, environmental/package design, and antiques/collectibles are covered in these listings. Art-related topics for the general public are located in the Consumer Art & Architecture category. Antiques and collectibles magazines for enthusiasts are listed in Consumer Hobby & Craft. (Listings of markets looking for freelance artists to do artwork can be found in *Artist's and Graphic Designer's Market*, Writer's Digest Books.)

$ AIRBRUSH ACTION MAGAZINE, Action, Inc., 3209 Atlantic Ave., P.O. Box 438, Allenwood NJ 08720. (732)223-7078. Fax: (732)223-2855. E-mail: cstieglitz@monmouth.com. Website: www.airbrushaction.com. **Contact:** Kate Priest, editor. **80% freelance written.** Bimonthly magazine covering the spectrum of airbrush applications: Illustration, t-shirt airbrushing, fine art, automotive and sign painting, hobby/craft applications, wall murals, fingernails, temporary tattoos, artist profiles, reviews and more. Estab. 1985. Circ. 60,000. Pays on publication. Publishes ms an average of 6 months after acceptance. Byline given. Buys all rights. Editorial lead time 6 months. Submit seasonal material 6 months in advance. Accepts queries by mail, e-mail, fax, phone. Accepts simultaneous submissions.

Nonfiction: How-to, humor, inspirational, interview/profile, new product, personal experience, technical. Nothing unrelated to airbrush. Query with published clips. **Pays 10¢/word.** Sometimes pays expenses of writers on assignment.

Photos: Send photos with submission. Buys all rights. Negotiates payment individually. Captions, identification of subjects, model releases required.

Columns/Departments: Query with published clips.

The online version contains material not found in the print edition. Contact: Cliff Stieglitz.

Tips: "Send bio and writing samples. Send well-written technical information pertaining to airbrush art. We publish a lot of artist profiles—they all sound the same. Looking for new pizzazz!"

N $ $ ANTIQUEWEEK, DMG World Media (USA), P.O. Box 90, Knightstown IN 46148-0090. (765)345-5133. Fax: (800)695-8153. E-mail: connie@antiqueweek.com. Website: www.antiqueweek.com. Managing Editor: Connie Swaim. **Contact:** Tom Hoepf, central edition editor. **80% freelance written.** Weekly tabloid covering antiques and collectibles with 2 editions: Eastern and Central. "We also have a new monthly, *Antiques West*. *AntiqueWeek* has a wide range of readership from dealers and auctioneers to collectors, both advanced and novice. Our readers demand accurate information presented in an entertaining style." Estab. 1968. Circ. 64,000. Pays on publication. Byline given. Offers 10% kill fee or $25. Buys first, second serial (reprint) rights. Submit seasonal material 1 month in advance. Accepts queries by mail, e-mail, fax. Sample copy for free. Writer's guidelines for #10 SASE.

Nonfiction: Historical/nostalgic, how-to, interview/profile, opinion, personal experience, antique show and auction reports, feature articles on particular types of antiques and collectibles. **Buys 400-500 mss/year.** Query with or without published clips or send complete ms. Length: 1,000-2,000 words. **Pays $50-250.**

Reprints: Send tearsheet or typed ms with rights for sale noted and information about when and where the material previously appeared.

Photos: Send photos with submission. Identification of subjects required.

The online magazine carries original content not found in the print edition. Contact: Connie Swaim, online editor.

Tips: "Writers should know their topics thoroughly. Feature articles must be well-researched and clearly written. An interview and profile article with a knowledgeable collector might be the break for a first-time contributor. We seek a balanced mix of information on traditional antiques and 20th century collectibles."

$ THE APPRAISERS STANDARD, New England Appraisers Association, 5 Gill Terrace, Ludlow VT 05149-1003. (802)228-7444. Fax: (802)228-7444. E-mail: llt44@ludl.tds.net. Website: www.newenglandappraisers.net. **Contact:** Linda L. Tucker, publisher/editor. **50% freelance written.** Works with a small number of new/unpublished writers each year. Quarterly publication covering the appraisals of antiques, art, collectibles, jewelry, coins, stamps and real estate. "The writer should be knowledgeable on the subject, and the article should be written with appraisers in mind, with prices quoted for objects, good pictures and descriptions of articles being written about.'. Estab. 1980. Circ. 1,300. Pays on publication. Publishes ms an average of 1 year after acceptance. Short bio and byline given. first and simultaneous rights. Submit seasonal material 2 months in advance. Accepts queries by mail, e-mail. Accepts simultaneous submissions. Responds in 1 month to queries; 2 months to mss. Sample copy for 9×12 SAE with 78¢ postage. Writer's guidelines for #10 SASE.

Nonfiction: "All geared toward professional appraisers." Interview/profile, personal experience, technical, travel. Query with or without published clips or send complete ms. Length: 700 words. **Pays $50.**

Reprints: Send ms with rights for sale noted and information about when and where the material previously appeared.

Photos: Send photos with submission. Reviews negatives, prints. Buys one-time rights. Offers no additional payment for photos accepted with ms. Identification of subjects required.

Tips: "Interviewing members of the association for articles, reviewing, shows and large auctions are all ways for writers who are not in the field to write articles for us. Articles should be geared to provide information which will help the appraisers with ascertaining value, detecting forgeries or reproductions, or simply providing advice on appraising the articles.

$ $ $ $ ARCHITECTURAL RECORD, McGraw-Hill, 2 Penn Plaza, 9th Floor, New York NY 10121. (212)904-2594. Fax: (212)904-4256. Website: www.architecturalrecord.com. Editor: Robert Ivy, FAIA; Managing Editor: Ingrid Whitehead. **Contact:** Linda Ransey. **50% freelance written.** Monthly magazine covering architecture and design. "Our readers are architects, designers and related professionals." Estab. 1891. Circ. 106,000. Pays on publication. Publishes ms an average of 2 months after acceptance. Byline given. Offers 25% kill fee. Buys all rights. Editorial lead time 2 months. Submit seasonal material 2 months in advance. Accepts queries by mail. Responds in 2 weeks to queries; 2 months to mss. Sample copy and writer's guidelines online.

N $ $ ART MATERIALS RETAILER, Fahy-Williams Publishing, 171 Reed St., P.O. Box 1080, Geneva NY 14456-8080. (315)789-0458. Fax: (315)789-4263. E-mail: tmanzer@fwpi.com. Website: www.artmaterialsretailer.com. **Contact:** Tina Manzer, editor. **10% freelance written.** Quarterly magazine. Estab. 1998. Pays on publication. Byline given. Buys one-time rights. Editorial lead time 2 months. Submit seasonal material 3 months in advance. Accepts simultaneous submissions. Responds in 3 weeks to queries; 3 months to mss. Sample copy for free. Writer's guidelines free.

Nonfiction: Book excerpts, how-to, interview/profile, personal experience. **Buys 2 mss/year.** Send complete ms. Length: 1,500-3,000 words. **Pays $50-250.** Sometimes pays expenses of writers on assignment.

Photos: State availability with submission. Reviews transparencies. Buys one-time rights. Offers no additional payment for photos accepted with ms. Identification of subjects required.

Fillers: Anecdotes, facts, newsbreaks. **Buys 5/year.** Length: 500-1,500 words. **Pays $50-125.**

Tips: "We like to review mss rather than queries. Artwork (photos, drawings, etc.) is real plus. We enjoy (our readers enjoy) practical, nuts and bolts, news-you-can-use articles."

$ ARTS MANAGEMENT, 110 Riverside Dr., Suite 4E, New York NY 10024. (212)579-2039. **Contact:** A.H. Reiss, editor. **2% freelance written.** Magazine published 5 times/year for cultural institutions. Estab. 1962. Circ. 6,000. Pays on publication. Byline given. Buys all rights. Accepts queries by mail. Responds in 2 months to queries. Writer's guidelines for #10 SASE.

- *Arts Management* is almost completely staff-written and uses very little outside material.

Nonfiction: Short articles, 400-900 words, tightly written, expository, explaining how arts administrators solved problems in publicity, fund raising and general administration; actual case histories emphasizing the how-to. Also short articles on the economics and sociology of the arts and important trends in the nonprofit cultural field. Must be fact-filled, well-organized and without rhetoric. No photographs or pictures. **Pays 2-4¢/word.**

$ $ $ HOW, Design Ideas at Work, F&W Publications, Inc., 4700 E. Galbraith Rd., Cincinnati OH 45236. (513)531-2222. Fax: (513)531-2902. E-mail: editorial@howdesign.com. Website: www.howdesign.com. **Contact:** Bryn Mooth, editor. **75% freelance written.** Bimonthly magazine covering graphic design and illustration business. "*HOW: Design Ideas at Work* strives to serve the business, technological and creative needs of graphic-design professionals. The magazine provides a practical mix of essential business information, up-to-date technological tips, the creative whys and hows behind noteworthy projects, and profiles of professionals who are impacting design. The ultimate goal of *HOW* is to help designers, whether they work for a design firm or for an inhouse design department, run successful, creative, profitable studios." Estab. 1985. Circ. 38,000. **Pays on acceptance.** Byline given. Buys first North American serial rights. Responds in 6 weeks to queries. Sample copy for cover price plus $1.50 (cover price varies per issue). Writer's guidelines for #10 SASE.

Nonfiction: Interview/profile, new product, business tips, environmental graphics, digital design, hot design markets. Special issues: Self-Promotion Annual (September/October); Business Annual (November/December); International Annual of Design (March/April); Creativity/Paper/Stock Photography (May/June); Digital Design Annual (July/August). No how-to articles for beginning artists or fine-art-oriented articles. **Buys 40 mss/year.** Query with published clips and samples of subject's work, artwork or design. Length: 1,500-2,000 words. **Pays $700-900.** Sometimes pays expenses of writers on assignment.

Photos: State availability with submission. Reviews Information updated and verified. Buys one-time rights. Captions required.

Columns/Departments: Design Disciplines (focuses on lucrative fields for designers/illustrators); Production (ins, outs and tips on production); Digital Design (behind the scenes of electronically produced design projects); Tech Review and Workspace (takes an inside look at the design of creatives' studios). Other columns include Legal Ease (legal issues for designers) and Biz Tips (business issues that impact design studios), 1,200-1,500 words. **Buys 35 mss/year.** Query with published clips. **Pays $250-400.**

Tips: "We look for writers who can recognize graphic designers on the cutting-edge of their industry, both creatively and business-wise. Writers must have an eye for detail, and be able to relay *HOW*'s step-by-step approach in an interesting, concise manner—without omitting any details. Showing you've done your homework on a subject—and that you can go beyond asking 'those same old questions'—will give you a big advantage."

N $ INTERIOR BUSINESS MAGAZINE, The Lawn & Landscape Media Group, 4012 Bridge Ave., Cleveland OH 44113. (800)456-0707. Fax: (216)961-0364. Website: www.interiorbusinessonline.com. Publisher: Cindy Code. **Contact:** Ali Cybulski, managing editor. **5-10% freelance written.** Magazine covering interior landscaping. "*Interior Business* addresses the concerns of the professional interior landscape contractor. It's devoted to the business management needs of interior landscape professionals." Estab. 2000. Circ. 6,000. Pays on publication. Publishes ms an average of 3 months after acceptance. Editorial lead time 3 months. Submit seasonal material 5 months in advance. Responds in 1 week to queries.

Nonfiction: Interior landscaping. "No articles oriented to the consumer or homeowner." **Buys 2 mss/year.** Length: 1,000-2,500 words. **Pays $250-500.**

Tips: "Know the audience. It's the professional business person, not the consumer."

N $ MANHATTAN ARTS INTERNATIONAL E-ZINE, (formerly *Manhattan Arts International Magazine*), Manhattan Arts International, 200 E. 72nd St., Suite 26L, New York NY 10021. (212)472-1660. Fax: (212)794-0324. E-mail: info@manhattanarts.com. Website: manhattanarts.com. Editor-in-Chief: Renee Phillips. **Contact:** Michael Jason, managing editor. Bimonthly magazine covering fine art. Audience is comprised of art professionals, artists and collectors. Educational, informative, easy-to-read style, making art more accessible. Highly promotional of new artists. Estab. 1983. Circ. 50,000. Pays on publication. Publishes ms an average of 1 month after acceptance. Byline given. Makes work-for-hire assignments. Submit seasonal material 3 months in advance. Accepts queries by e-mail. Accepts simultaneous submissions. Responds in 3 months to queries.

Nonfiction: New writers receive byline and promotion, art books. Book excerpts (art), essays (art world), general interest (collecting art), inspirational, interview/profile (major art leaders), new product (art supplies), technical (art business). **Buys 30 mss/year.** Sometimes pays expenses of writers on assignment.

Tips: "A knowledge of the current, contemporary art scene is a must. We are not actively seeking new writers at this time."

$ $ TEXAS ARCHITECT, Texas Society of Architects, 816 Congress Ave., Suite 970, Austin TX 78701. (512)478-7386. Fax: (512)478-0528. E-mail: editor@texasarchitect.org. Website: www.texasarchitect.org. **Contact:** Stephen Sharpe, editor. **30% freelance written.** Mostly written by unpaid members of the professional society. Bimonthly journal covering architecture and architects of Texas. "*Texas Architect* is a highly visually-oriented look at Texas architecture, design and urban planning. Articles cover varied subtopics within architecture. Readers are mostly architects and related building professionals." Estab. 1951. Circ. 12,000. Pays on publication. Publishes ms an average of 3 months after acceptance. Byline given. Buys one-time, all rights, makes work-for-hire assignments. Submit seasonal material 4 months in advance. Accepts queries by mail, e-mail. Responds in 6 weeks to queries. Sample copy and writer's guidelines free or online at website.

Nonfiction: Interview/profile, photo feature, technical, Book reviews. Query with published clips. Length: 100-2,000 words. **Pays $50-100 for assigned articles.**

Photos: Send photos with submission. Reviews contact sheets, 35mm or 4×5 transparencies, 4×5 prints. Buys one-time rights. Offers no additional payment for photos accepted with ms. Identification of subjects required.

Columns/Departments: News (timely reports on architectural issues, projects and people), 100-500 words. **Buys 10 mss/year.** Query with published clips. **Pays $50-100.**

AUTO & TRUCK

These publications are geared to automobile, motorcycle, and truck dealers; professional truck drivers; service department personnel; or fleet operators. Publications for highway planners and traffic control experts are listed in the Government & Public Service category.

$ $ AUTOINC., Automotive Service Association, 1901 Airport Freeway, Bedford TX 76021. (817)283-6205. Fax: (817)685-0225. E-mail: editor@asashop.org. Website: www.autoinc.org. Managing Editor: Levy Joffrion. **Contact:** Angie Wilson, editor. **25% freelance written.** Monthly magazine covering independent automotive repair. "The mission of *AutoInc.*, ASA's official publication, is to be the informational authority for ASA and industry members nationwide. Its purpose is to enhance the professionalism of these members through management, technical and legislative articles, researched and written with the highest regard for accuracy, quality and integrity." Estab. 1952. Circ. 16,000. Pays on publication. Publishes ms an average of 2 months after acceptance. Byline given. Buys all rights. Editorial lead time 2 months. Accepts queries by mail, e-mail, fax. Accepts simultaneous submissions. Responds in 6 weeks to queries; 2 months to mss. Sample copy for $5 or online. Writer's guidelines online or by e-mail.

Nonfiction: How-to (automotive repair), technical. No book reviews, product or company-oriented material. **Buys 10 mss/year.** Query with published clips. Length: 1,200-1,700 words. **Pays $250-500.** Sometimes pays expenses of writers on assignment.

Photos: State availability of or send photos with submission. Reviews 2×3 transparencies, 3×5 prints. Buys one-time and electronic rights. Negotiates payment individually. Captions, identification of subjects, model releases required.

Tips: "Learn about the automotive repair industry, specifically the independent shop segment. Understand the high-tech requirements needed to succeed today."

$ $ BUSINESS FLEET, Managing 10-50 Company Vehicles, Bobit Publishing, 21061 S. Western Ave., Torrance CA 90501-1711. (310)533-2592. Fax: (310)533-2503. E-mail: steve.elliott@bobit.com. Website: www.businessfleet.com. **Contact:** Steve Elliott, executive editor. **30% freelance written.** Bimonthly magazine covering businesses which operate 10-50 company vehicles. "While it's a trade publication aimed at a business audience, *Business Fleet* has a lively, conversational style. The best way to get a feel for our 'slant' is to read the magazine." Estab. 2000. Circ. 100,000. Pays on publication. Publishes ms an average of 2 months after acceptance. Byline given. Offers 25% kill fee. Buys first, second serial (reprint), electronic rights. Editorial lead time 2 months. Submit seasonal material 2 months in advance. Accepts queries by mail, e-mail, fax. Responds in 2 weeks to queries; 2 months to mss. Sample copy and writer's guidelines free.

Nonfiction: How-to, interview/profile, new product, personal experience, photo feature, technical. **Buys 16 mss/year.** Query with published clips. Length: 500-2,000 words. **Pays $100-400.** Pays with contributor copies or other premiums by prior arrangement. Sometimes pays expenses of writers on assignment.

Photos: State availability with submission. Reviews 3×5 prints. Buys one-time, reprint and electronic rights. Negotiates payment individually. Captions required.

The online magazine carries original content not included in the print edition. Contact: Steve Elliott, online editor.

Tips: "Our mission is to educate our target audience on more economical and efficient ways of operating company vehicles, and to inform the audience of the latest vehicles, products, and services available to small commercial companies. Be knowledgeable about automotive and fleet-oriented subjects."

$ $ FLEET EXECUTIVE, The Magazine of Vehicle Management, The National Association of Fleet Administrators, Inc., 100 Wood Ave. S., Suite 310, Iselin NJ 08830-2716. (732)494-8100. Fax: (732)494-6789. E-mail: publications@nafa.org. Website: www.nafa.org. **Contact:** Jessica Sypniewski, managing editor. **50% freelance written.** Monthly magazine covering automotive fleet management. "*NAFA Fleet Executive* focuses on car, van and light-duty truck management in U.S. and Canadian corporations, government agencies and utilities. Editorial emphasis is on general automotive issues; improving jobs skills, productivity and professionalism; legislation and regulation; alternative fuels; safety; interviews with prominent industry personalities; technology; Association news; public service fleet management; and light-duty truck fleet management." Estab. 1957. Circ. 4,000. Pays on publication. Publishes ms an average of 4 months after acceptance. Buys all rights. Editorial lead time 2 months. Accepts queries by mail, e-mail, fax. Accepts simultaneous submissions. Responds in 1 month to queries. Sample copy online. Writer's guidelines free.

Nonfiction: "NAFA hosts its Fleet Management Institute, an educational conference and trade show, which is held in a different city in the U.S. and Canada each year. *Fleet Executive* would consider articles on regional attractions, particularly those that might be of interest to those in the automotive industry, for use in a conference preview issue of the magazine. The preview issue is published one month prior to the conference. Information about the conference, its host city, and conference dates in a given year may be found on NAFA's website, www.nafa.org, or by calling the association at (732)494-8100." Interview/profile, technical. **Buys 12 mss/year.** Query with published clips. Length: 500-3,000 words. **Pays $500 maximum.**

Photos: State availability with submission. Reviews electronic images.

Tips: "The sample articles online at www.nafa.org/admenu.htm should help writers get a feel of the journalistic style we require."

$ $ GLASS DIGEST, Ashlee Publishing, 18 E. 41st St., New York NY 10017. (212)376-7722. Fax: (212)376-7723. E-mail: michael@ashlee.com. Website: www.ashlee.com. **Contact:** Michael J. McSweeney, editor. **15% freelance written.** Monthly magazine covering flat glass, glazing, auto glass. Estab. 1921. Pays on publication. Publishes ms an average of 2 months after acceptance. Byline given. Buys first, all rights, makes work-for-hire assignments. Editorial lead time 3 months. Accepts queries by mail, e-mail, fax. Accepts simultaneous submissions.

Nonfiction: Photo feature, technical. "No reports on stained glass hobbyists or art glass." **Buys 16-20 mss/year.** Query. Length: 1,000-2,000 words. **Pays $100-400.** Sometimes pays expenses of writers on assignment.

Photos: State availability with submission. Negotiates payment individually. Identification of subjects required.

Tips: "Architecturally interesting projects with good photography make excellent features for *Glass Digest*."

$ $ NEW ENGLAND MECHANIC, P.O. Box M, Franklin MA 02038. (508)528-6211. **Contact:** M. Zingraff, managing editor. **40% freelance written.** Bimonthly newspaper covering automotive repair, testing, maintenance. "Our slant on technical information is both for advanced technician and apprentice. We cover news on laws and regulations, some management information and profiles of shops and wholesales." Estab. 1996. Circ. 5,000. **Pays on acceptance.** Byline given. Offers 50% kill fee on assignments only. Buys one-time, second serial (reprint) rights. Editorial lead time 1 month. Responds in 2 months to queries. Writer's guidelines for #10 SASE.

Nonfiction: General interest, how-to, interview/profile, technical. **Buys 18 mss/year.** Query with published clips. Length: 500-1,500 words. **Pays $100-200 for assigned articles; $35-100 for unsolicited articles.**

Photos: State availability with submission. Reviews contact sheets, 3×5 or larger prints. Buys one-time rights. Pays $25 for first photo, $10 each additional photos in series. Captions, identification of subjects required.

Columns/Departments: Query.

Fillers: Facts. **Buys 6/year.** Length: 150 words. **Pays $25-50.**

N **NORTHWEST MOTOR, Journal for the Automotive Industry**, Northwest Automotive Publishing Co., P.O. Box 46937, Seattle WA 98146-0937. (206)935-3336. Fax: (206)937-9732. E-mail: nwmotor@quest.net. **Contact:** J.B. Smith, editor. **5% freelance written.** Monthly magazine covering the automotive industry. Estab. 1909. Circ. 11,500. Pays on publication. Byline given. Offers 10% kill fee. Buys all rights. Editorial lead time 1 month. Submit seasonal material 2 months in advance. Accepts queries by mail, e-mail. Accepts simultaneous submissions. Sample copy for $2. Writer's guidelines for #10 SASE.

O-т Break in by sending a listing of available articles.

Nonfiction: Interested in seeing automotive environmental articles. Book excerpts, general interest, how-to, new product, photo feature, technical. **Buys 6 mss/year.** Query. Length: 250-1,200 words. **Payment varies.** Sometimes pays expenses of writers on assignment.

Photos: Send photos with submission. Reviews 3×5 prints. Buys all rights. Negotiates payment individually.

Columns/Departments: Buys 4-6 mss/year. Query. **Payment varies.**

Fillers: Anecdotes, facts. **Buys 4-9/year.** Length: 15-100 words. **Pays variable amount.**

N **OLD CARS WEEKLY, News & Marketplace**, Krause Publications, 700 E. State St., Iola WI 54990-0001. (715)445-4612. Fax: (715)445-4087. E-mail: mathiowetzk@@krause.com. Website: www.oldcarsweekly.com. Editor: Keith Mathiowetz. **Contact:** Angelo Van Dogart, associate editor. **50% freelance written.** Weekly tabloid covering old cars. Estab. 1971. Circ. 65,000. Pays in the month after publication date. Publishes ms an average of 6 months after acceptance. Byline given. Buys perpetual but nonexclusive rights. For sample copy call circulation department. Writer's guidelines for #10 SASE.

Nonfiction: How-to, technical, auction prices realized lists. No "Grandpa's Car," "My First Car" or "My Car" themes. **Buys 1,600 mss/year.** Send complete ms. Length: 400-1,600 words. **Payment varies.**

Photos: Send photos with submission. Buys perpetual but non-exclusive rights. Pays $5/photo. Offers no additional payment for photos accepted with ms. Captions, identification of subjects required.

Tips: "Ninety percent of our material is done by a small group of regular contributors. Many new writers break in here, but we are *usually overstocked* with material and *never* seek nostalgic or historical pieces from new authors. Our big need is for well-written items that fit odd pieces in a tabloid page layout. Budding authors should try some short, catchy items that help us fill odd-ball 'news holes' with interesting writing. Authors with good skills can work up to longer stories. A weekly keeps us too busy to answer mail and phone calls. The best queries are 'checklists' where we can quickly mark a 'yes' or 'no' to article ideas."

$ $ OVERDRIVE, The Voice of the American Trucker, Randall Publishing Co./Overdrive, Inc., 3200 Rice Mine Rd., Tuscaloosa AL 35406. (205)349-2990. Fax: (205)750-8070. E-mail: mheine@randallpub.com. Website: www.etrucker.net. Editor: Linda Longton. **Contact:** Max Heine, editorial director. **5% freelance written.** Monthly magazine for independent truckers. Estab. 1961. Circ. 140,000. Pays on publication. Publishes ms an average of 2 months after acceptance. Byline given. Offers 10% kill fee. all North American rights, including electronic rights. Responds in 2 months to queries. Sample copy and writer's guidelines for 9×12 SASE.

Nonfiction: All must be related to independent trucker interest. Essays, exposé, how-to (truck maintenance and operation), interview/profile (successful independent truckers), personal experience, photo feature, technical. Query with or without published clips or send complete ms. Length: 500-2,000 words. **Pays $200-1,000 for assigned articles.**

Photos: Send photos with submission. Reviews transparencies, prints and slides. Buys all rights. Offers $25-150/photo.

Tips: "Talk to independent truckers. Develop a good knowledge of their concerns as small-business owners, truck drivers and individuals. We prefer articles that quote experts, people in the industry and truckers to first-person expositions on a subject. Get straight facts. Look for good material on truck safety, on effects of government regulations, and on rates and business relationships between independent truckers, brokers, carriers and shippers."

$ $ ROAD KING MAGAZINE, For the Professional Driver, Hammock Publishing, Inc., 3322 West End Ave., Suite 700, Nashville TN 37203. (615)690-3403. Fax: (615)690-3401. E-mail: roadking@hammock.com. Website: www.roadking.com. Editor: Tom Berg. **Contact:** Bill Hudgins, editor-in-chief. **80% freelance written.** Bimonthly magazine. "*Road King* is published bimonthly for long-haul truckers. It celebrates the lifestyle and work and profiles interesting and/or successful drivers. It also reports on subjects of interest to our audience, including outdoors, vehicles, music and trade issues." Estab. 1963. Circ. 229,900. **Pays on acceptance.** Publishes ms an average of 4 months after acceptance. Byline given. Offers negotiable kill fee. Buys first North American serial, electronic rights. Editorial lead time 3 months. Submit seasonal material 4 months in advance. Accepts queries by mail, e-mail. Responds in 2 months to queries. Sample copy for 9×12 SAE and 5 first-class stamps. Writer's guidelines for #10 SASE.

Nonfiction: How-to (trucking-related), humor, interview/profile, new product, personal experience, photo feature, technical, travel. Special issues: Road Gear (the latest tools, techniques and industry developments to help truckers run a smarter, more efficient trucking business); Haul of Fame (salutes drivers whose work or type of rig makes them unique); At Home on the Road ("creature comfort" products, services and information for the road life, including what's new, useful, interesting or fun for cyber-trucking drivers); Fleet Focus (asks fleet management about what their companies offer, and drivers about why they like it there); Weekend Wheels (from Harleys to Hondas, most drivers have a passion for their "other" set of wheels. This section looks at this aspect of drivers' lives). "No fiction, poetry." **Buys 20 mss/year.** Query with published clips. Length: 850-2,000 words. **Payment negotiable.** Sometimes pays expenses of writers on assignment.
Photos: State availability with submission. Reviews contact sheets. Buys negotiable rights. Negotiates payment individually. Identification of subjects, model releases required.
Columns/Departments: Lead Driver (profile of outstanding trucker), 250-500 words; Roadrunner (new products, services suited to the business of trucking or to truckers' lifestyles), 100-250 words. **Buys 6-10 mss/year.** Query. **Payment negotiable.**
Fillers: Anecdotes, facts, gags to be illustrated by cartoonist, short humor. Length: 100-250 words. **Pays $50.**

The online magazine of *Road King* carries original content not found in the print edition. Contact: Bill Hudgins.

$ $ RV TRADE DIGEST, Your Source for Management, Marketing and Production Information, Cygnus Business Media Inc., 1233 Janeville Ave., Fort Atkinson WI 53538. (800)547-7377 ext. 349. Fax: (920)563-1702. E-mail: editor@rvtradedigest.com. Website: www.rvtradedigest.com. **Contact:** Greg Gerber, editor. **25% freelance written.** Monthly magazine. "RV Trade Digest seeks to help RV dealers become more profitable and efficient. We don't want fluff and theory. We want tested and proven ideas other dealers can apply to their own businesses. We believe sharing best practices helps everyone in the industry stay strong." Estab. 1980. Circ. 17,000. Pays 30 days after publication. Publishes ms an average of 3 months after acceptance. Byline given. Buys first North American serial rights. Editorial lead time 3 months. Submit seasonal material 4 months in advance. Accepts queries by mail, e-mail. Accepts simultaneous submissions. Responds in 2 months to queries. Sample copy for free. Writer's guidelines free.
Nonfiction: How-to (install, service parts, accessories), interview/profile (of industry leaders or successful RV dealers), new product (with emphasis on how to best sell and market the product), technical, business subjects, mobile electronics. Does not want articles about RV travel experience. **Buys 8-12 mss/year.** Length: 1,000-2,000 words. **Pays $300-500.** Pays expenses of writers on assignment.
Photos: Send photos with submission. Reviews transparencies, Prints. Buys one-time rights. Negotiates payment individually. Model releases required.
Columns/Departments: Dealer Pro-File, Profit Central, Modern Manager, Shop Talk, Industry Insider.
Tips: "Send complete manuscript. Propose an idea that will have broad appeal to the RV industry in that it will be interesting and useful to RV dealers, manufacturers and suppliers. Queries must include background/experience and published clips."

$ $ SPORT TRUCK & SUV ACCESSORY BUSINESS, Covering the Light Truck-Van-SUV Aftermarket, Cygnus Business Media, 1233 Janesville Ave., Ft. Atkinson WI 53533. (920)563-6388. Fax: (920)563-1702. E-mail: peter.hubbard@cygnuspub.com. **Contact:** Peter A. Hubbard, editor. **25% freelance written.** "*Sport Truck & SUV Accessory Business* is a bimonthly trade magazine designed to provide light truck accessory dealers and installers with advice on improving their retail business practices, plus timely information about industry trends and events. Each issue's editorial package includes a dealer profile, plus features aimed at meeting the distinct needs of store owners, managers and counter sales people. The magazine also provides aftermarket, OEM and trade association news, three separate new product sections, plus an analysis of light truck sales." Estab. 1996. Circ. 15,000. Pays 30 days after publication. Publishes ms an average of 3 months after acceptance. Byline given. Buys first North American serial rights. Editorial lead time 3 months. Submit seasonal material 4 months in advance. Accepts simultaneous submissions. Responds in 1 month to queries. Sample copy, writer's guidelines free.

Break in with "a feature on a top truck or SUV retailer in your area."
Nonfiction: General interest, interview/profile, new product, technical, Considers cartoons. No travel, installation how-to's. **Buys 20-30 mss/year.** Query. Length: 1,000-2,000 words. **Pays $300-500.**
Photos: Send photos with submission. Reviews transparencies, prints. Buys one-time rights. Negotiates payment individually. Model releases required.
Tips: "Send query with or without completed manuscripts. Background/experience and published clips are required."

$ $ TODAY'S TRUCKING, New Communications Group, 130 Belfield Rd., Toronto, Ontario M9W 1G1, Canada. (416)614-2200. Fax: (416)614-8861. E-mail: editors@todaystrucking.com. Website: www.todaystrucking.com. Editor: Stephen Petit. **Contact:** Rolf Lockwood. **15% freelance written.** Monthly magazine covering the trucking industry in Canada. "We reach nearly 30,000 fleet owners, managers, owner-operators, shop supervisors, equipment dealers, and parts distributors across Canada. Our magazine has a strong service slant, combining useful how-to journalism with analysis of news, business issues, and heavy-duty equipment trends. Before you sit down to write, please take time to become familiar with *Today's Trucking*. Read a few recent issues." Estab. 1987. Circ. 30,000. **Pays on acceptance.** Byline given. Buys first North American serial, second serial (reprint) rights. Editorial lead time 2 months. Submit seasonal material 3 months in advance. Accepts queries by mail, e-mail, fax. Sample copy and writer's guidelines free.
Nonfiction: How-to, interview/profile, technical. **Buys 20 mss/year.** Query with published clips. Length: 500-2,000 words. **Pays 40¢/word.** Sometimes pays expenses of writers on assignment.

Photos: State availability with submission.
Columns/Departments: Pays 40¢/word.

N **$ $ WESTERN CANADA HIGHWAY NEWS**, Craig Kelman & Associates, 3C-2020 Portage Ave., Winnipeg, Manitoba R3J 0K4, Canada. (204)985-9785. Fax: (204)985-9795. E-mail: kelmantr@videon.wave.ca. **Contact:** Terry Ross, managing editor. **30% freelance written.** Quarterly magazine covering trucking. "The official magazine of the Alberta, Saskatchewan and Manitoba trucking associations." Estab. 1995. Circ. 4,000. Pays on publication. Publishes ms an average of 2 months after acceptance. Byline given. Buys one-time rights. Editorial lead time 3 months. Submit seasonal material 3 months in advance. Accepts simultaneous submissions. Responds in 2 months to queries; 4 months to mss. Sample copy for 10×13 SAE with 1 IRC. Writer's guidelines for #10 SASE.
Nonfiction: Essays, general interest, how-to (run a trucking business), interview/profile, new product, opinion, personal experience, photo feature, technical, profiles in excellence (bios of trucking or associate firms enjoying success). **Buys 8-10 mss/year.** Query. Length: 500-3,000 words. **Pays 18-25¢/word.** Sometimes pays expenses of writers on assignment.
Reprints: Send tearsheet, photocopy or typed ms and information about when and where the material previously appeared. Pays 60% of amount paid for an original article.
Photos: State availability with submission. Reviews Reviews 4×6 prints. Buys one-time rights. Identification of subjects required.
Columns/Departments: Safety (new safety innovation/products), 500 words; Trade Talk (new products), 300 words. Query. **Pays 18-25¢/word.**
Tips: "Our publication is fairly time-sensitive re: issues affecting the trucking industry in Western Canada. Current 'hot' topics are international trucking (NAFTA-induced changes), deregulation, driver fatigue, health and safety, emissions control and national/international highway systems."

AVIATION & SPACE

In this section are journals for aviation business executives, airport operators, and aviation technicians. Publications for professional and private pilots are in the Consumer Aviation section.

$ $ AIRCRAFT MAINTENANCE TECHNOLOGY, Cygnus Business Media, 1233 Janesville Ave., Fort Atkinson WI 53538. (920)563-6388. Fax: (920)563-1702. E-mail: editor@amtonline.com. Website: www.amtonline.com. Editor: Joe Escobar. **10% freelance written.** Magazine published 10 times/year covering aircraft maintenance. "*Aircraft Maintenance Technology* provides aircraft maintenance professionals world-wide with a curriculum of technical, professional, and managerial development information that enables them to more efficiently and effectively perform their jobs. Estab. 1989. Circ. 41,500 worldwide. Pays on publication. Publishes ms an average of 2 months after acceptance. Byline given. Offers $50 kill fee. Buys all rights, makes work-for-hire assignments. Editorial lead time 3 months. Submit seasonal material 6 months in advance. Accepts queries by mail, e-mail, fax. Accepts simultaneous submissions. Responds in 2 weeks to queries; 1 month to mss. Sample copy for free. Writer's guidelines for #10 SASE or by e-mail.
Nonfiction: How-to, technical, safety; human factors. Special issues: Aviation career issue (August). No travel/pilot-oriented pieces. **Buys 10-12 mss/year.** Query with published clips. Length: 600-1,500 words, technical articles 2,000 words. **Pays $200.**
Photos: State availability with submission. Buys one-time rights. Offers no additional payment for photos accepted with ms. Captions, identification of subjects, model releases required.
Columns/Departments: Professionalism, 1,000-1,500 words; Safety Matters, 600-1,000 words; Human Factors, 600-1,000 words. **Buys 10-12 mss/year.** Query with published clips. **Pays $200.**
Tips: "This is a technical magazine, which is approved by the FAA and Transport Canada for recurrency training for technicians. Freelancers should have a strong background in aviation, particularly maintenance, to be considered for technical articles. Columns/Departments: freelancers still should have a strong knowledge of aviation to slant professionalism, safety and human factors pieces to that audience."

$ $ AVIATION INTERNATIONAL NEWS, The Newsmagazine of Corporate, Business and Regional Aviation, The Convention News Co., P.O. Box 277, 214 Franklin Ave., Midland Park NJ 07432. (201)444-5075. Fax: (201)444-4647. E-mail: editor@ainonline.com. Website: www.ainonline.com. Editor-AIN Monthly Edition: Nigel Moll. **Contact:** R. Randall Padfield, editor-in-chief. **30-40% freelance written.** Monthly magazine (with onsite issues published at three conventions and two international air shows each year) covering business and commercial aviation with news features, special reports, aircraft evaluations and surveys on business aviation worldwide, written for business pilots. "While the heartbeat of *AIN* is driven by the news it carries, the human touch is not neglected. We pride ourselves on our people stories about the industry's 'movers and shakers' and others in aviation who make a difference." Estab. 1972. Circ. 40,000. **Pays on acceptance** or upon receipt of writer's invoice. Publishes ms an average of 2 months after acceptance. Byline given. Offers variable kill fee. first North American serial and second serial (reprint) rights and makes work-for-hire assignments. Editorial lead time 2 months. Submit seasonal material 3 months in advance. Accepts queries by mail, e-mail, fax. Responds in 6 weeks to queries; 2 months to mss. Sample copy for $10. Writer's guidelines for 9×12 SAE with 3 first-class stamps.

Break in with "local news stories relating to business, commercial and regional airline aviation—think turbine-powered aircraft (no stories about national airlines, military aircraft, recreational aviation or history."

Nonfiction: "We hire freelancers to work on our staff at three aviation conventions and two international airshows each year. Must have strong reporting and writing skills and knowledge of aviation." How-to (aviation), interview/profile, new product, opinion, personal experience, photo feature, technical. No puff pieces. "Our readers expect serious, real news. We don't pull any punches." **Buys 150-200 mss/year.** Query with published clips. Length: 200-3,000 words. **Pays 30¢/word to first timers, higher rates to proven AIN freelancers.** Pays expenses of writers on assignment.
Photos: Send photos with submission. Reviews contact sheets, transparencies, prints, TIFF files (300 dpi). Buys one-time rights. Negotiates payment individually. Captions required.

"AIN Alerts, our online mini-newsletter, is posted on our website twice a week and carries original content not found in our print publications. It includes 10-12 news items or about 100 words each week." Contact: Gordon Gilbert, ggilbert@ainonline.com.

Tips: "Our core freelancers are professional pilots with good writing skills, good journalists and reporters with an interest in aviation (some with pilot licenses) or technical experts in the aviation industry. The ideal *AIN* writer has an intense interest in and strong knowledge of aviation, a talent for writing news stories and journalistic cussedness. Hit me with a strong news story relating to business aviation that takes me by surprise—something from your local area or area of expertise. Make it readable, fact-filled and in the inverted-pyramid style. Double-check facts and names. Interview the right people. Send me good, clear photos and illustrations. Send me well-written, logically ordered copy. Do this for me consistently and we may take you along on our staff to one of the conventions in the U.S. or an airshow in Paris, Singapore, London or Dubai."

$ $ AVIATION MAINTENANCE, PBI Media LLC, 1201 Seven Locks Rd., Suite 300, Potomac MD 20854. (301)354-1831. Fax: (301)340-8741. E-mail: am@pbimedia.com. Website: www.aviationmx.com. **Contact:** Matt Thurber, editor. **60% freelance written.** Monthly magazine covering aircraft maintenance from small to large aircraft. Aviation Maintenance delivers news and information about the aircraft maintenance business for mechanics and management at maintenance shops, airlines, and corporate flights departments. Estab. 1982. Circ. 38,000. **Pays on acceptance.** Publishes ms an average of 2 months after acceptance. Byline given. Kill fee varies. Buys all rights. Editorial lead time 3 months. Submit seasonal material 3 months in advance. Accepts queries by mail, e-mail, fax, phone. Responds in 1 week to queries; 1 month to mss. Sample copy online. Writer's guidelines free.
Nonfiction: Exposé, interview/profile, technical. No fiction, technical how-to or poetry. **Buys 50 mss/year.** Query with or without published clips. Length: 700-1,500 words. **Pays 35¢/word.** Pays expenses of writers on assignment.
Photos: State availability with submission. Buys all rights. Negotiates payment individually. Captions, identification of subjects required.
Columns/Departments: Intelligence (news), 200-500 words; Postflight (profile of aircraft mechanic), 800 words plus photo. **Buys 12 mss/year.** Query with or without published clips. **Pays $200-250.**
Tips: "Writer must be intimately familiar with or involved in aviation, either as a pilot or preferably a mechanic or a professional aviation writer. Best place to break in is in the Intelligence News section or with a Postflight profile of an interesting mechanic."

$ $ GSE TODAY, Cygnus Business Media, 1233 Janesville Ave., Fort Atkinson WI 53538. (920)563-1622. Fax: (920)563-1699. E-mail: editor@gsetoday.com. Website: www.gsetoday.com. **Contact:** Michelle Garetson, editor. **20% freelance written.** Magazine published 10 times/year. "Our readers are those aviation professionals who are involved in ground support—the equipment manufacturers, the suppliers, the ramp operators, ground handlers, airport and airline managers. We cover issues of interest to this community—deicing, ramp safety, equipment technology, pollution, etc." Estab. 1993. Circ. 15,000. Pays on publication. Publishes ms an average of 2 months after acceptance. Buys all rights. Editorial lead time 2 months. Accepts queries by mail, e-mail, fax. Responds in 3 weeks to queries; 3 months to mss. Sample copy for 9×11 SAE and 5 first-class stamps.
Nonfiction: How-to (use or maintain certain equipment), interview/profile, new product, opinion, photo feature, technical aspects of ground support and issues, industry events, meetings, new rules and regulations. **Buys 12-20 mss/year.** Send complete ms. Length: 500-2,000 words. **Pays $100-300.**
Reprints: Send photocopy or typed ms with rights for sale noted and information about when and where the article previously appeared. Pays 50% of the amount paid for an original article.
Photos: Send photos with submission. Reviews 35mm prints, electronic preferred, slides. Buys all rights. Offers no additional payment for photos accepted with ms. Identification of subjects required.
Tips: "Write about subjects that relate to ground services. Write in clear and simple terms—personal experience is always welcome. If you have an aviation background or ground support experience, let us know."

N $ $ $ PROFESSIONAL PILOT, Queensmith Communications, 3014 Colvin St., Alexandria VA 22314. (703)370-0606. Fax: (703)370-7082. E-mail: editorial@propilotmag.com. Website: www.propilotmag.com. **Contact:** Lori Ranson, managing editor. **75% freelance written.** Monthly magazine covering regional airline, corporate and various other types of professional aviation. "The typical reader has a sophisticated grasp of piloting/aviation knowledge and is interested in articles that help him/her do the job better or more efficiently." Estab. 1967. Circ. 44,000. Pays on publication. Publishes ms an average of 2-3 months after acceptance. Byline given. Kill fee negotiable. Buys all rights. Accepts queries by mail, e-mail, fax, phone.

"Affiliation with an active flight department, weather activity of Air Traffic Control (ATC) is helpful. Our readers want tool tech stuff from qualified writers with credentials."

Nonfiction: "Typical subjects include new aircraft design, new product reviews (especially avionics), pilot techniques, profiles of regional airlines, fixed base operations, profiles of corporate flight departments and technological advances."

All issues have a theme such as regional airline operations, maintenance, avionics, helicopters, etc. **Buys 40 mss/year.** Query. Length: 750-2,500 words. **Pays $200-1,000, depending on length. A fee for the article will be established at the time of assignment.** Sometimes pays expenses of writers on assignment.
Photos: Send photos with submission. Reviews Prefers transparencies or slides. Buys all rights. Additional payment for photos negotiable. Captions, identification of subjects required.
Tips: Query first. "Freelancer should be a professional pilot or have background in aviation. Authors should indicate relevant aviation experience and pilot credentials (certificates, ratings and hours). We place a greater emphasis on corporate operations and pilot concerns."

BEAUTY & SALON

$ $ AMERICAN SALON, Advanstar, One Park Ave., LBBY 2, New York NY 10016. (212)951-6600. Fax: (212)951-6624. Website: www.advanstar.com. **Contact:** Robbin McClain, editor. **5% freelance written.** Monthly Magazine covering "business stories of interest to salon owners and stylists, distributors and manufacturers of professional beauty products." Estab. 1878. Circ. 132,000. **Pays on acceptance.** Publishes ms an average of 3 months after acceptance. Byline given. Buys first North American serial, first rights. Editorial lead time 3 months. Accepts queries by mail. Sample copy for free. Writer's guidelines free.

O━ Break in with "extensive experience (in writing and the beauty industry); topic of article must be relevant. Very hard to get into our mag."

$ $ BEAUTY STORE BUSINESS, Creative Age Communications, 7628 Densmore Ave., Van Nuys CA 91406-2042. (818)782-7328, ext. 353. Fax: (818)782-7450. E-mail: mbirenbaum@creativeage.com. **Contact:** Marc Birenbaum, executive editor. **60% freelance written.** Magazine published 10 times/year covering beauty store business management. "The publication is read by owners and managers of nearly all types of beauty stores, including open-to-the-public general and multicultural market-oriented specialty retailers with or without salon services and exclusive-line distributors' professional-only stores." Estab. 1994. Circ. 15,000. **Pays on acceptance.** Publishes ms an average of 3 months after acceptance. Byline given. Offers negotiable kill fee. Buys all rights. Editorial lead time 3 months. Submit seasonal material 4 months in advance. Accepts queries by mail, e-mail, fax. Responds in 1 week to queries; 2 weeks to mss, if interested. Sample copy for free.
Nonfiction: How-to (business management, merchandising, e-commerce, retailing), interview/profile (industry leaders). "No business articles available in general-circulation publications. Want industry specific pieces." **Buys 6-8 mss/year.** Query. Length: 1,500-2,500+ words. **Pays $250-525 for assigned articles.** Sometimes pays expenses of writers on assignment.
Photos: Do not send computer art electronically. State availability with submission. Reviews transparencies, computer art (artists work on Macs, request 300 dpi, 133 LS, on CD or Zip Disk, saved as JPEG, TIFF or EPS). Buys all rights. Negotiates payment individually. Captions, identification of subjects required.

$ $ COSMETICS, Canada's Business Magazine for the Cosmetics, Fragrance, Toiletry and Personal Care Industry, Rogers, 777 Bay St., Suite 405, Toronto, Ontario M5W 1A7, Canada. (416)596-5817. Fax: (416)596-5179. E-mail: rwood@rmpublishing.com. Website: www.cosmeticsmag.com. **Contact:** Ronald A. Wood, editor. **10% freelance written.** Bimonthly magazine. "Our main reader segment is the retail trade—department stores, drugstores, salons, estheticians—owners and cosmeticians/beauty advisors; plus manufacturers, distributors, agents and suppliers to the industry." Estab. 1972. Circ. 13,000. **Pays on acceptance.** Publishes ms an average of 3 months after acceptance. Byline given. Offers 50% kill fee. Buys all rights. Editorial lead time 4 months. Submit seasonal material 4 months in advance. Accepts queries by mail. Responds in 1 month to queries. Sample copy for $6 (Canadian) and 8% GST.
Nonfiction: General interest, interview/profile, photo feature. **Buys 10 mss/year.** Query. Length: 250-1,200 words. **Pays 25¢/word.** Sometimes pays expenses of writers on assignment.
Photos: Send photos with submission. Reviews 2½ up to 8×10 transparencies, 4×6 up to 8×10 prints, 35mm slides. Buys all rights. Offers no additional payment for photos accepted with ms. Captions, identification of subjects, model releases required.
Columns/Departments: "All articles assigned on a regular basis from correspondents and columnists that we know personally from the industry."

▣ The online magazine carries original content not found in the print edition. Contact: Jim Hicks, publisher/online editor.

Tips: "Must have broad knowledge of the Canadian cosmetics, fragrance and toiletries industry and retail business. 99.9% of freelance articles are assigned by the editor to writers involved with the Canadian cosmetics business."

$ $ DAYSPA, For the Salon of the Future, Creative Age Publications, 7628 Densmore Ave., Van Nuys CA 91406. (818)782-7328. Fax: (818)782-7450. E-mail: dayspa@creativeage.com. Website: wwwdayspamagazine.com. Managing Editor: Linda Kossoff. **Contact:** Linda Lewis, executive editor. **60% freelance written.** Bimonthly magazine covering the business of day spas, skin care salons, wellness centers. "*Dayspa* includes only well targeted business articles directed at the owners and managers of high-end, multi-service salons, day spas, resort spas and destination spas." Estab. 1996. Circ. 31,000. **Pays on acceptance.** Publishes ms an average of 4 months after acceptance. Byline given. Buys first, one-time rights. Editorial lead time 4 months. Submit seasonal material 4 months in advance. Accepts queries by mail, e-mail, fax, phone. Responds in 2 months to queries. Sample copy for $5.

Nonfiction: Book excerpts, how-to, interview/profile, photo feature. **Buys 40 mss/year.** Query. Length: 1,200-3,000 words. **Pays $150-500.**
Photos: Send photos with submission. Buys one-time rights. Negotiates payment individually. Identification of subjects, model releases required.
Columns/Departments: Legal Pad (legal issues affecting salons/spas); Money Matters (financial issues), both 1,200-1,500 words. **Buys 20 mss/year.** Query. **Pays $150-300.**

$ $ DERMASCOPE MAGAZINE, The Encyclopedia of Aesthetics & Spa Therapy, Geneva Corporation, 2611 N. Belt Line Rd., Suite 140, Sunnyvale TX 75182. (972)226-2309. Fax: (972)226-2339. E-mail: dermascope@aol.com. Website: www.dermascope.com. **Contact:** Saundra Wallens, editor-in-chief. Monthly magazine covering aesthetics (skin care) and body and spa therapy. "Our magazine is a source of practical advice and continuing education for skin care, body and spa therapy professionals. Our main readers are salon, day spa and destination spa owners, managers or technicians." Estab. 1976. Circ. 15,000. Pays on publication. Publishes ms an average of 6 months after acceptance. Byline given. Buys all rights. Editorial lead time 3 months. Submit seasonal material 6 months in advance. Accepts queries by mail, fax. Responds in 1 month to queries; 6 months to mss. Sample copy online.
Nonfiction: Interested in seeing non-product specific how-to articles with photographs. Book excerpts, general interest, historical/nostalgic, how-to, inspirational, personal experience, photo feature, technical. **Buys 6 mss/year.** Query with published clips. Length: 1,500-2,500 words. **Pays $50-250.**
Photos: State availability with submission. Reviews 4×5 prints. Buys all rights. Offers no additional payment for photos accepted by ms. Captions, identification of subjects, model releases required.
Tips: "Write from the practitioner's point of view. Step-by-step how-to's that show the skin care and body and spa therapist practical methodology are a plus. Would like more business and finance ideas, applicable to the industry."

$ $ DERMATOLOGY INSIGHTS, A Patient's Guide to Healthy Skin, Hair and Nails, American Academy of Dermatology, 930 N. Meacham Rd., Schaumburg IL 60173. (847)330-0230. E-mail: dmonti@aad.org. Website: www.aad.org. Managing Editor: Lara Lowery. **Contact:** Dean Monti, editor. **60% freelance written.** Semiannual magazine covering dermatology. *Dermatology Insights* contains "educational and informative articles for consumers about dermatological subjects." Estab. 2000. **Pays on acceptance.** Publishes ms an average of 4 months after acceptance. Byline given. Buys all rights, makes work-for-hire assignments. Editorial lead time 4 months. Submit seasonal material 4 months in advance. Accepts queries by mail, e-mail. Responds in 3 weeks to queries; 1 month to mss. Sample copy for free. Writer's guidelines not available.
Nonfiction: General interest, how-to, interview/profile, new product, personal experience, photo feature, technical. **Buys 10-15 mss/year.** Query. Length: 750 words maximum. **Pays flat rate of $40/hour.** Sometimes pays expenses of writers on assignment.
Photos: State availability with submission. Buys all rights. Negotiates payment individually. Identification of subjects required.
Columns/Departments: Patient Perspective (patient's first hand account). **Buys 2-3 mss/year.** Query. **Pays flat rate of $40/hour.**

MASSAGE & BODYWORK, Associated Bodywork & Massage Professionals, 1271 Sugarbush Dr., Evergreen CO 80439-9766. (303)674-8478 or (800)458-2267. Fax: (303)674-0859. E-mail: editor@abmp.com. Website: www.massageandbodywork.com. **Contact:** Karrie Mowen, editor. **85% freelance written.** Bimonthly magazine covering therapeutic massage/bodywork. "A trade publication for the massage therapist, bodyworker and skin care professionals. An all-inclusive publication encompassing everything from traditional Swedish massage to energy work to other complementary therapies (i.e.-homeopathy, herbs, aromatherapy, etc.)." **Pays on acceptance.** Publishes ms an average of 6 months after acceptance. Buys first North American serial, one-time, electronic rights. Editorial lead time 6 months. Submit seasonal material 6 months in advance. Accepts queries by mail, e-mail, fax, phone. Responds in 1 month to queries; 5 months to mss. Writer's guidelines free.
Nonfiction: Essays, exposé, how-to (technique/modality), interview/profile, opinion, personal experience, technical, travel. No fiction. **Buys 60-75 mss/year.** Query with published clips. Length: 1,000-3,000 words.
Reprints: Accepts previously published submissions.
Photos: State availability with submission. Reviews contact sheets. Buys one-time rights. Negotiates payment individually. Captions, identification of subjects, model releases required.
Columns/Departments: Buys 20 mss/year.
Tips: "Know your topic. Offer suggestions for art to accompany your submission. *Massage & Bodywork* looks for interesting, tightly-focused stories concerning a particular modality or technique of massage, bodywork, somatic and skin care therapies. The editorial staff welcomes the opportunity to review manuscripts which may be relevant to the field of massage, bodywork and skin care practices, in addition to more general pieces pertaining to complementary and alternative medicine. This would include the widely varying modalities of massage and bodywork, (from Swedish massage to Polarity therapy), specific technique articles and ancillary therapies, including such topics as biomagnetics, aromatherapy and facial rejuvenation. Reference lists relating to technical articles should include the author, title, publisher and publication date of works cited. Word count: 1,500 to 4,000 words; longer articles negotiable."

$ $ MASSAGE MAGAZINE, Exploring Today's Touch Therapies, 200 7th Ave., #240, Santa Cruz CA 95062. (831)477-1176. E-mail: edit@massagemag.com. Website: www.massagemag.com. **Contact:** Karen Menehan, editor. **25% freelance written.** Bimonthly magazine covering massage and other touch therapies. Estab. 1985. Circ. 80,000.

Pays on acceptance. Publishes ms an average of 1 year after acceptance. Byline given. Buys first North American serial rights. Accepts queries by mail, e-mail. Responds in 2 months to queries; 3 months to mss. Sample copy and writer's guidelines free.

Nonfiction: Book excerpts, essays, general interest, how-to, inspirational, interview/profile, personal experience, photo feature, technical, experiential. Length: 600-2,000 words. **Pays $50-300 for assigned articles.**

Reprints: Send tearsheet of article and typed ms with rights for sale noted and information about when and where the material previously appeared. Pays 50-75% of amount paid for an original article.

Photos: Send photos with submission. Buys one-time rights. Offers $25-75/photo. Identification of subjects, identification of photographer required.

Columns/Departments: Profiles; Table Talk (news briefs); Practice Building (business); Technique; Body/mind. Length: 800-1,200 words. **Pays $100.**

Fillers: Facts, newsbreaks. Length: 100- 800 words. **Pays $125 maximum.**

Tips: "Our readers seek practical information on how to help their clients, improve their techniques and/or make their businesses more successful, as well as feature articles that place massage therapy in a positive or inspiring light. Since most of our readers are professional therapists, we do not publish articles on topics like 'How Massage Can Help You Relax.' Please study a few back issues so you know what types of topics and tone we're looking for."

N $ $ NAILPRO, The Magazine for Nail Professionals, Creative Age Publications, 7628 Densmore Ave., Van Nuys CA 91406. (818)782-7328. Fax: (818)782-7450. E-mail: nailpro@aol.com. Website: www.nailpro.com. **Contact:** Jodi Mills, executive editor. **75% freelance written.** Monthly magazine written for manicurists and nail technicians working in full-service salons or nails-only salons. It covers technical and business aspects of working in and operating a nail-care service, as well as the nail-care industry in general. Estab. 1989. Circ. 65,000. **Pays on acceptance.** Publishes ms an average of 6 months after acceptance. Byline given. Offers 50% kill fee. Buys first North American serial rights. Editorial lead time 3 months. Submit seasonal material 3 months in advance. Accepts queries by mail, e-mail, fax. Accepts simultaneous submissions. Responds in 6 weeks to queries. Sample copy for $2 and 8½×11 SASE.

Nonfiction: Book excerpts, how-to, humor, inspirational, interview/profile, personal experience, photo feature, technical. No general interest articles or business articles not geared to the nail-care industry. **Buys 50 mss/year.** Query. Length: 1,000-3,000 words. **Pays $150-450.**

Reprints: Send typed ms with rights for sale noted and information about when and where the material previously appeared. Pays 25-50% of amount paid for an original article.

Photos: Send photos with submission. Reviews transparencies, prints. Buys one-time rights. Negotiates payment individually. Identification of subjects, model releases required.

Columns/Departments: Building Business (articles on marketing nail services/products), 1,200-2,000 words; Shop Talk (aspects of operating a nail salon), 1,200-2,000 words. **Buys 50 mss/year.** Query. **Pays $200-300.**

The online magazine carries original content not found in the print edition. Contact: Jodi Mills.

N $ $ NAILS, Bobit Publishing, 21061 S. Western Ave., Torrance CA 90501-1711. (310)533-2400. Fax: (310)533-2504. E-mail: nailsmag@bobit.com. Website: www.nailsmag.com. **Contact:** Cyndy Drummey, editor. **10% freelance written.** Monthly magazine. "*NAILS* seeks to educate its readers on new techniques and products, nail anatomy and health, customer relations, working safely with chemicals, salon sanitation, and the business aspects of running a salon." Estab. 1983. Circ. 55,000. **Pays on acceptance.** Byline given. Buys all rights. Submit seasonal material 4 months in advance. Accepts queries by mail, e-mail, fax. Responds in 3 months to queries. Sample copy for #10 SASE. Writer's guidelines for #10 SASE.

Nonfiction: Historical/nostalgic, how-to, inspirational, interview/profile, personal experience, photo feature, technical. "No articles on one particular product, company profiles or articles slanted toward a particular company or manufacturer." **Buys 20 mss/year.** Query with published clips. Length: 1,200-3,000 words. **Pays $200-500.** Sometimes pays expenses of writers on assignment.

Photos: State availability with submission. Reviews contact sheets, transparencies, prints (any standard size acceptable). Buys all rights. Offers $50-200/photo. Captions, identification of subjects, model releases required.

The online version contains material not found in the print edition. Contact: Hannah Lee.

Tips: "Send clips and query; *do not send unsolicited manscripts.* We would like to see ideas for articles on a unique salon or a business article that focuses on a specific aspect or problem encountered when working in a salon. The Modern Nail Salon section, which profiles nail salons and full-service salons, is most open to freelancers. Focus on an innovative business idea or unique point of view. Articles from experts on specific business issues—insurance, handling difficult employees, cultivating clients—are encouraged."

$ $ SKIN INC. MAGAZINE, The Complete Business Guide for Face & Body Care, Allured Publishing Corp., 362 S. Schmale Rd., Carol Stream IL 60188. (630)653-2155. Fax: (630)653-2192. E-mail: taschetta-millane@allured.com. Website: www.skininc.com. Publisher: Marian Raney. **Contact:** Melinda Taschetta-Millane, associate publisher/editor. **30% freelance written.** Magazine published 12 times/year. "Manuscripts considered for publication that contain original and new information in the general fields of skin care and makeup, dermatological and esthetician-assisted surgical techniques. The subject may cover the science of skin, the business of skin care and makeup, and plastic surgeons on healthy (i.e., non-diseased) skin. Subjects may also deal with raw materials, formulations and regulations concerning claims for products and equipment." Estab. 1988. Circ. 16,000. Pays on publication. Publishes ms an average of 6 months after acceptance. Byline given. Buys all rights. Editorial lead time 6 months. Submit seasonal material 1 year in advance. Accepts queries by mail, e-mail, fax, phone. Responds in 2 weeks to queries; 1 month to mss. Sample copy for free. Writer's guidelines free.

Nonfiction: General interest, how-to, interview/profile, personal experience, technical. **Buys 6 mss/year.** Query with published clips. Length: 2,000 words. **Pays $100-300 for assigned articles; $50-200 for unsolicited articles.**

Photos: State availability with submission. Reviews 3×5 prints. Buys one-time rights. Offers no additional payment for photos accepted with ms. Captions, identification of subjects, model releases required.

Columns/Departments: Finance (tips and solutions for managing money), 2,000-2,500 words; Personnel (managing personnel), 2,000-2,500 words; Marketing (marketing tips for salon owners), 2,000-2,500 words; Retail (retailing products and services in the salon environment), 2,000-2,500 words. Query with published clips. **Pays $50-200.**

Fillers: Facts, newsbreaks. **Buys 6/year.** Length: 250-500 words. **Pays $50-100.**

Tips: "Have an understanding of the skin care industry."

BEVERAGES & BOTTLING

Manufacturers, distributors, and retailers of soft drinks and alcoholic beverages read these publications. Publications for bar and tavern operators and managers of restaurants are classified in the Hotels, Motels, Clubs, Resorts & Restaurants category.

BAR & BEVERAGE BUSINESS MAGAZINE, Mercury Publications Ltd., 1839 Inkster Blvd., Winnipeg, Manitoba R2X 1R3, Canada. (204)954-2085. Fax: (204)954-2057. E-mail: mp@mercury.mb.ca. Website: www.mercury.mb.ca/. Editor: Kelly Gray. **Contact:** Kristi Balon, editorial production manager. **33% freelance written.** Bimonthly magazine providing information on the latest trends, happenings, buying-selling of beverages and product merchandising. Estab. 1998. Circ. 16,077. Pays 30-45 days from receipt of invoice. Byline given. Offers 33% kill fee. Buys all rights. Submit seasonal material 3 months in advance. Accepts queries by mail, e-mail, fax. Accepts simultaneous submissions. Responds in 2 weeks to queries. Sample copy and writer's guidelines free or by e-mail.

Nonfiction: How-to (making a good drink, training staff, etc.), interview/profile. Industry reports, profiles on companies. Query with published clips. Length: 500-9,000 words. **Pays 25-35¢/word.** Sometimes pays expenses of writers on assignment.

Photos: State availability with submission. Reviews negatives, transparencies, 3×5 prints, JPEG, EPS or TIFF files. Buys all rights. Negotiates payment individually. Captions required.

Columns/Departments: Out There (bar & bev news in various parts of the country), 100-500 words. Query. **Pays $0-100.**

Tips: "Send an e-mailed, faxed or mailed query outlining their experience, interests and pay expectations. A requirement also is clippings."

$ BEER, WINE & SPIRITS BEVERAGE RETAILER, The Marketing & Merchandising Magazine for Off-Premise Innovators, Oxford Publishing Company, 307 W. Jackson Ave., Oxford MS 38655-2154. (662)236-5510. Fax: (662)236-5541. E-mail: brenda@oxpub.com. Website: www.beverage-retailer.com. **Contact:** Brenda Owen, editor. **2-5% freelance written.** Magazine published 6 times a year covering alcohol beverage retail industry (off-premise). "Our readership of off-premise beverage alcohol retailers (owners and operators of package liquor stores, wine cellars, beer barns, etc.) appreciates our magazine's total focus on helping them increase their revenue and profits. We particulary emphasize stories on retailers' own ideas and efforts to market their products and their stores' images." Estab. 1997. Circ. 20,000. **Pays on acceptance.** Publishes ms an average of 7 months after acceptance. Byline given. Buys first North American serial rights. Editorial lead time 6 months. Submit seasonal material 6 months in advance. Accepts queries by mail. Responds in 2 weeks to queries; 1 month to mss. Sample copy for $5 or online at website.

O→ Break in with a "successful retailer" profile or product feature that shows your grasp on moneymaking tips, marketing and merchandising ideas.

Nonfiction: General interest, how-to, interview/profile, industry commentary. "No book reviews; no product stories narrowly focused on one manufacturer's product; no general stories on beverage categories (Scotch, tequila, etc.) unless trend-oriented." **Buys 4-6 mss/year.** Query with published clips or send complete ms. Length: 350-800 words. **Pays $100 for assigned articles.** Pays phone expenses only of writers on assignment.

Photos: State availability of or send photos with submission. Reviews contact sheets, all sizes transparencies, prints (all sizes). Buys all rights. Offers no additional payment for photos accepted with ms on most features. Negotiates payment individually on cover stories and major features. Captions, identification of subjects, model releases required.

Columns/Departments: Successful Retailers (what business practice, unique facility feature or what other quality makes this business so successful?), 350-400 words; Marketing & Merchandising (*brief* stories of innovative efforts by retailers [displays, tastings and other events, celebrity appearances, special sales, etc.]) 50-350 words. Query with published clips or send complete ms. **Pays $25-100.**

Tips: "Rely solely on off-premise beverage alcohol retailers (and, in some cases, leading industry experts) as your sources. Make certain every line of your story focuses on telling the reader how to improve his business' revenue and profits. Keep your story short, and include colorful, intelligent and concise retailer quotes. Include a few *relevant* and irresistible statistics. We particularly appreciate trend or analysis stories when we get them early enough to publish them in a timely fashion."

$ $ THE BEVERAGE JOURNAL, Michigan Edition, MI Licensed Beverage Association, 920 N. Fairview Ave., Lansing MI 48912. (518)374-9611. Fax: (517)374-1165. E-mail: ashock@mlba.org. Website: www.mlba.org. **Contact:** Amy Shock, editor. **40-50% freelance written.** Monthly magazine covering hospitality industry. "A monthly trade magazine devoted to the beer, wine and spirits industry in Michigan. It is dedicated to serving those who make their living serving the public and the state through the orderly and responsible sale of beverages." Estab. 1983. Circ. 4,200. Pays on publication. Buys one-time, second serial (reprint) rights, makes work-for-hire assignments. Editorial lead time 3 months. Submit seasonal material 3 months in advance. Accepts queries by mail, e-mail. Responds in 2 weeks to queries; 1 month to mss. Sample copy for $5 or online.

Nonfiction: Essays, general interest, historical/nostalgic, how-to (make a drink, human resources, tips, etc.), humor, interview/profile, new product, opinion, personal experience, photo feature, technical. **Buys 24 mss/year.** Send complete ms. Length:1,000 words. **Pays $20-200.**

Reprints: Accepts previously published submissions.

Columns/Departments: Interviews (legislators, others), 750-1,000 words; personal experience (waitstaff, customer, bartenders), 500 words. "Open to essay content ideas." **Buys 12 mss/year.** Send complete ms. **Pays $25-100.**

Tips: "We are particularly interested in nonfiction concerning responsible consumption/serving of alcohol. We are looking for product reviews, company profiles, personal experiences, food-related articles that would benefit our audience. Our audience is a busy group of business owners and hospitality professionals striving to obtain pertinent information that is not too wordy."

N $ $ PATTERSON'S CALIFORNIA BEVERAGE JOURNAL, Interactive Color, Inc., 4910 San Fernando Rd., Glendale CA 91204. (818)291-1125. Fax: (818)547-4607. E-mail: nswords@interactivecolor.com. **Contact:** Meridith May. **25% freelance written.** Monthly magazine covering the alcohol, beverage and wine industries. "Patterson's reports on the latest news in product information, merchandising, company appointments, developments in the wine industry and consumer trends. Our readers can be informed, up-to-date and confident in their purchasing decisions." Estab. 1962. Circ. 20,000. Byline given. Offers 50% kill fee. Editorial lead time 1 month. Submit seasonal material 1 month in advance. Accepts queries by mail, e-mail, fax. Accepts simultaneous submissions. Sample copy for free. Writer's guidelines free.

Nonfiction: Interview/profile, new product, market reports. "No consumer-oriented articles or negative slants on industry as a whole." **Buys 200 mss/year.** Query with published clips. Length: 600-1,800 words. **Pays $60-200.**

Photos: State availability with submission. Reviews transparencies. Buys all rights. Offers no additional payment for photos accepted with ms. Captions, identification of subjects required.

Columns/Departments: Query with published clips.

$ $ VINEYARD & WINERY MANAGEMENT, 3535 Industrial Dr., Suite A3, Santa Rosa CA 95403. (707)566-3810. Fax: (707)566-3815. E-mail: gparnell@vwm-online.com. Website: www.vwm-online.com. **Contact:** Graham Parnell, managing editor. **80% freelance written.** Bimonthly magazine of professional importance to grape growers, winemakers and winery sales and business people. Estab. 1975. Circ. 4,500. Pays on publication. Byline given. Buys first North American serial, simultaneous rights. Accepts queries by e-mail. Responds in 3 weeks to queries; 1 month to mss. Sample copy for free. Writer's guidelines for #10 SASE.

Nonfiction: Subjects are technical in nature and explore the various methods people in these career paths use to succeed, and also the equipment and techniques they use successfully. Business articles and management topics are also featured. The audience is national with western dominance. How-to, interview/profile, new product, technical. **Buys 30 mss/year.** Query. Length: 300-5,000 words. **Pays $30-1,000.** Sometimes pays expenses of writers on assignment.

Photos: State availability with submission. Reviews contact sheets, negatives, transparencies. Black & white often purchased for $20 each to accompany story material; 35mm and/or 4×5 transparencies for $50 and up; 6/year of vineyard and/or winery scene related to story. Identification of subjects required.

Tips: "We're looking for long-term relationships with authors who know the business and write well. Electronic submissions required; query for formats."

BOOK & BOOKSTORE

Publications for book trade professionals from publishers to bookstore operators are found in this section. Journals for professional writers are classified in the Journalism & Writing category.

$ BLOOMSBURY REVIEW, A Book Magazine, Dept. WM, Owaissa Communications Co., Inc., P.O. Box 8928, Denver CO 80201. (303)455-3123. Fax: (303)455-7039. E-mail: bloomsb@aol.com. **Contact:** Marilyn Auer, editor. **75% freelance written.** Bimonthly tabloid covering books and book-related matters. "We publish book reviews, interviews with writers and poets, literary essays and original poetry. Our audience consists of educated, literate, *nonspecialized* readers." Estab. 1980. Circ. 50,000. Pays on publication. Publishes ms an average of 4 months after acceptance. Byline given. Buys first, one-time rights. Accepts queries by mail. Responds in 4 months to queries. Sample copy for $5 and 9×12 SASE. Writer's guidelines for #10 SASE.

Nonfiction: "Summer issue features reviews, etc., about the American West. *We do not publish fiction.*" Essays, interview/profile, book reviews. **Buys 60 mss/year.** Query with published clips or send complete ms. Length: 800-1,500 words. **Pays $10-20. Sometimes pays writers with contributor copies or other premiums "if writer agrees."**

Reprints: Considered but not encouraged. Send photocopy of article and information about when and where the article previously appeared.
Photos: State availability with submission. Reviews prints. Buys one-time rights. Offers no additional payment for photos accepted with ms.
Columns/Departments: Book reviews and essays, 500-1,500 words. **Buys 6 mss/year.** Query with published clips or send complete ms. **Pays $10-20.**
Poetry: Ray Gonzalez, poetry editor. Avant-garde, free verse, haiku, traditional. **Buys 20 poems/year.** Submit maximum 5 poems. **Pays $5-10.**
Tips: "We appreciate receiving published clips and/or completed manuscripts. Please—no rough drafts. Book reviews should be of new books (within 6 months of publication)."

$ $ FOREWORD MAGAZINE, ForeWord Magazine Inc., 129½ E. Front St., Traverse City MI 49684. (231)933-3699. Fax: (231)933-3899. E-mail: alexmoorereviews@traverse.com. Website: www.forewordmagazine.com. **Contact:** Alex Moore, managing editor. **95% freelance written.** Bimonthly magazine covering independent and university presses for booksellers and librarians with articles, news, book reviews. Estab. 1998. Circ. 15,000. Pays 2 months after publication. Publishes ms an average of 2-3 month after acceptance. Byline given. Buys all rights. Editorial lead time 3 months. Submit seasonal material 5 months in advance. Accepts queries by mail, e-mail, fax. Responds in 1 month to queries; 1 month to mss. Sample copy for 8×10 SASE.
Nonfiction: Book excerpts, essays, opinion. Query with published clips or send complete ms. Length: 600-2,000 words. **Pays $40-100 for assigned articles.**
Photos: State availability with submission. Reviews prints. Buys all rights. Offers no additional payment for photos accepted with ms. Captions required.
Columns/Departments: Pays $40-100.
Tips: "Be knowledgeable about the needs of booksellers and librarians—remember we are an industry trade journal, not a how-to or consumer publication. We review books prior to publication, so book reviews are always assigned—but send us a note telling subjects you wish to review in as well as a résumé."

$ THE HORN BOOK MAGAZINE, The Horn Book, Inc., 56 Roland St., Suite 200, Boston MA 02129. (617)628-0225. Fax: (617)628-0882. E-mail: magazine@hbook.com. Website: www.hbook.com. **Contact:** Roger Sutton, editor-in-chief. **75% freelance written.** Prefers to work with published/established writers. Bimonthly magazine covering children's literature for librarians, booksellers, professors, teachers and students of children's literature. Estab. 1924. Circ. 21,500. Pays on publication. Publishes ms an average of 4 months after acceptance. Byline given. Submit seasonal material 6 months in advance. Accepts queries by mail, e-mail, fax. Accepts simultaneous submissions. Responds in 2 months to queries. Sample copy and writer's guidelines online.
Nonfiction: Interested in seeing strong, authoritative pieces about children's books and contemporary culture. Writers should be familiar with the magazine and its contents. Interview/profile (children's book authors and illustrators), topics of interest to the children's bookworld. **Buys 20 mss/year.** Query or send complete ms. Length: 1,000-2,800 words. **Pays honorarium upon publication.**
▣ The online magazine carries original content not found in the print edition and includes writer's guidelines.
Tips: "Writers have a better chance of breaking into our publication with a query letter on a specific article they want to write."

$ ▣ INDEPENDENT PUBLISHER, The Jenkins Group, 400 W. Front St., #4A, Traverse City MI 49684. (231)933-0445. Fax: (231)933-0448. E-mail: jimb@bookpublishing.com. Website: www.independentpublisher.com. **Contact:** Jim Barnes, managing editor. **25% freelance written.** Monthly online. "*Independent Publisher* is a monthly online trade journal for small and independent publishing companies. We focus on marketing, promoting and producing books and how independent publishers can compete in this competitive industry. We also run profiles of successful publishers, an awards section and new title listings." Estab. 1983. Circ. 30,000. Pays on publication. Publishes ms an average of 1 month after acceptance. Byline given. Editorial lead time 2 months. Submit seasonal material 4 months in advance. Accepts queries by e-mail. Accepts simultaneous submissions. Responds in 3 weeks to queries; 1 month to mss. Sample copy and writer's guidelines free.
Nonfiction: Book excerpts, essays, exposé, how-to, interview/profile, opinion. "No consumer-oriented stories. We are a trade magazine for publishers." **Buys 12 mss/year.** Query with published clips. Length: 1,000-4,000 words.
Photos: State availability with submission. Reviews transparencies, prints. Buys one-time rights. Offers no additional payment for photos accepted with ms. Identification of subjects required.
Columns/Departments: Book Biz; Industry Update; Calendar of Events; Passageways to Profit (distribution strategies); PublishItRight.com (how-to); Inklings (writing for books, film and stage); For Love of Books (book arts), all 1,200-1,600 words. **Buys 6 mss/year.** Query with published clips. **Pays $50-100.**
Tips: "We're looking for in-depth profiles of publishers who find new ways to market their books."

BRICK, GLASS & CERAMICS

These publications are read by manufacturers, dealers, and managers of brick, glass, and ceramic retail businesses. Other publications related to glass and ceramics are listed in the Consumer Art & Architecture and Consumer Hobby & Craft sections.

$ $ GLASS MAGAZINE, For the Architectural Glass Industry, National Glass Association, 8200 Greensboro Dr., McLean VA 22102-. (703)442-4890. Fax: (703)442-0630. E-mail: charles@glass.org. Website: www.glass.org. **Contact:** Charles Cumpston, editor. **10% freelance written.** Prefers to work with published/established writers. Monthly magazine covering the architectural glass industry. Circ. 23,291. **Pays on acceptance.** Publishes ms an average of 6 months after acceptance. Byline given. Kill fee varies. Buys first rights. Accepts queries by mail, e-mail, fax. Responds in 2 months to mss. Sample copy for $5 and 9×12 SAE with 10 first-class stamps.

Nonfiction: Interview/profile (of various glass businesses; profiles of industry people or glass business owners), new product, technical (about glazing processes). **Buys 5 mss/year.** Query with published clips. Length: 1,000 words minimum. **Pays $150-300 for assigned articles.**

Photos: State availability with submission.

Tips: *Glass Magazine* is doing more inhouse writing; freelance cut by half. "Do *not* send in general glass use stories. Research the industry first, then query."

$ STAINED GLASS, Stained Glass Association of America, 10009 E. 62nd St., Raytown MO 64133. (800)438-9581. Fax: (816)737-2801. E-mail: sgaa@stainedglass.org. Website: www.stainedglass.org. **Contact:** Richard Gross, editor. **70% freelance written.** Quarterly magazine. "Since 1906, *Stained Glass* has been the official voice of the Stained Glass Association of America. As the oldest, most respected stained glass publication in North America, *Stained Glass* preserves the techniques of the past as well as illustrates the trends of the future. This vital information, of significant value to the professional stained glass studio, is also of interest to those for whom stained glass is an avocation or hobby." Estab. 1906. Circ. 8,000. Pays on publication. Publishes ms an average of 1 year after acceptance. Byline given. Buys one-time rights. Editorial lead time 6 months. Submit seasonal material 8 months in advance. Accepts queries by mail, e-mail, fax. Responds in 3 months to queries. Sample copy and writer's guideline free.

O→ Break in with "excellent photography and in-depth stained glass architectural knowledge."

Nonfiction: Strong need for technical and how to create architectural type stained glass. Glass etching, use of etched glass in stained glass compositions, framing. How-to, humor, interview/profile, new product, opinion, photo feature, technical. **Buys 9 mss/year.** Query or send complete ms but must include photos or slides—very heavy on photos. **Pays $125/illustrated article; $75/non-illustrated.**

Reprints: Accepts previously published submissions from non-stained glass publications only. Send tearsheet of article. Payment negotiable.

Photos: Send photos with submission. Reviews 4×5 transparencies, send slides with submission. Buys one-time rights. Pays $75 for non-illustrated. Pays $125 plus 3 copies for line art or photography. Identification of subjects required.

Columns/Departments: Teknixs (technical, how-to, stained and glass art), word length varies by subject. "Columns must be illustrated." **Buys 4 mss/year.** Query or send complete ms, but must be illustrated.

Tips: "We need more technical articles. Writers should be extremely well versed in the glass arts. Photographs are extremely important and must be of very high quality. Submissions without photographs or illustrations are seldom considered unless something special and writer states that photos are available. However, prefer to see with submission."

$ $ US GLASS, METAL & GLAZING, Key Communications Inc., P.O. Box 569, Garrisonville VA 22463. (540)720-5584. Fax: (540)720-5687. E-mail: egiard@glass.com. Website: www.usglassmag.com. **Contact:** Ellen Giard, editor. **25% freelance written.** Monthly magazine for companies involved in the flat glass trades. Estab. 1966. Circ. 27,000. Pays on publication. Publishes ms an average of 3 months after acceptance. Byline given. Buys all rights. Editorial lead time 3 months. Submit seasonal material 2 months in advance. Accepts queries by mail, e-mail, fax. Accepts simultaneous submissions. Responds in 1 month to queries; 2 months to mss. Sample copy and writer's guidelines on website.

Nonfiction: Buys 12 mss/year. Query with published clips. **Pays $300-600 for assigned articles.** Sometimes pays expenses of writers on assignment.

Photos: State availability with submission. Reviews contact sheets. Buys first North American rights. Offers no additional payment for photos accepted with ms. Captions, identification of subjects required.

The online magazine carries original content not found in the print edition. Contact: Holly Carter.

BUILDING INTERIORS

Owners, managers, and sales personnel of floor covering, wall covering, and remodeling businesses read the journals listed in this category. Interior design and architecture publications may be found in the Consumer Art, Design & Collectibles category. For journals aimed at other construction trades see the Construction & Contracting section.

$ $ PWC, Painting & Wallcovering Contractor, Finan Publishing Co. Inc., 107 W. Pacific Ave., St. Louis MO 63119-2323. (314)961-6644. Fax: (314)961-4809. E-mail: jbeckner@finan.com. Website: www.paintstore.com. **Contact:** Jeffery Beckner, editor. **90% freelance written.** Bimonthly magazine. "*PWC* provides news you can use: Information helpful to the painting and wallcovering contractor in the here and now." Estab. 1928. Circ. 30,000. Pays 30 days after acceptance. Publishes ms an average of 1 month after acceptance. Byline given. Offers variable kill fee. Buys first North American serial rights. Editorial lead time 2 months. Submit seasonal material 2 months in advance. Accepts simultaneous submissions. Responds in 2 weeks to queries. Sample copy for free.

Nonfiction: Essays, exposé, how-to (painting and wallcovering), interview/profile, new product, opinion, personal experience. **Buys 40 mss/year.** Query with published clips. Length: 1,500-2,500 words. **Pays $300 minimum.** Pays expenses of writers on assignment.
Reprints: Send photocopy and information about when and where the material previously appeared. Negotiates payment.
Photos: State availability of or send photos with submission. Reviews contact sheets, negatives, transparencies, digital prints. Buys all rights. Offers no additional payment for photos accepted with ms. Identification of subjects required.
Columns/Departments: Anything of interest to the small businessman, 1,250 words. **Buys 2 mss/year.** Query with published clips. **Pays $50-100.**
Tips: "We almost always buy on an assignment basis. The way to break in is to send good clips, and I'll try and give you work."

N $ $ QUALIFIED REMODELER, The Business Management Tool for Professional Remodelers, Cygnus Business Media, 1233 Janesville Ave., Fort Atkinson WI 53538. Website: www.qualifiedremodeler.com. Editor: Roger Stanley. **Contact:** Jonathan Sweet, managing editor. **15% freelance written.** Monthly magazine covering residential remodeling. Estab. 1975. Circ. 92,500. **Pays on acceptance.** Publishes ms an average of 1 month after acceptance. Byline given. Buys all rights. Editorial lead time 3 months. Submit seasonal material 2 months in advance. Accepts queries by mail, e-mail, fax, phone. Sample copy online.
Nonfiction: How-to (business management), new product, photo feature, best practices articles, innovative design. **Buys 12 mss/year.** Query with published clips. Length: 1,200-2,500 words. **Pays $300-600 for assigned articles; $200-400 for unsolicited articles.** Sometimes pays expenses of writers on assignment.
Photos: Send photos with submission. Reviews negatives, transparencies. Buys one-time rights. Negotiates payment individually.
Columns/Departments: Query with published clips. **Pays $200-400.**
The online version contains material not found in the print edition.
Tips: "We focus on business management issues faced by remodeling contractors. For example, sales, marketing, liability, taxes and just about any matter addressing small business operation."

$ $ REMODELING, Hanley-Wood, LLC, One Thomas Circle NW, Suite 600, Washington DC 20005. (202)452-0800. Fax: (202)785-1974. E-mail: hartman@hanley-wood.com. Website: www.remodelingmagazine.com. Editor-in-Chief: Sal Alfano. **Contact:** Christine Hartman, managing editor. **10% freelance written.** Monthly magazine covering residential and light commercial remodeling. "We cover the best new ideas in remodeling design, business, construction and products." Estab. 1985. Circ. 80,000. Pays on publication. Publishes ms an average of 3 months after acceptance. Byline given. Offers 5¢/word kill fee. Buys first North American serial rights. Accepts queries by mail, e-mail, fax. Responds in 1 month to queries. Sample copy for free.
Nonfiction: Interview/profile, new product, technical, small business trends. **Buys 6 mss/year.** Query with published clips. Length: 250-1,000 words. **Pays 50¢/word.** Sometimes pays expenses of writers on assignment.
Photos: State availability with submission. Reviews 4×5 transparencies, slides, 8×10 prints. Buys one-time rights. Offers $25-125/photo. Captions, identification of subjects, model releases required.
The online magazine carries original content not included in the print edition. Contact: John Butterfield, online editor.
Tips: "We specialize in service journalism for remodeling contractors. Knowledge of the industry is essential."

$ $ WALLS & CEILINGS, Dept. SMM, 755 W. Big Beaver Rd., Troy MI 48084. (248)244-1735. Fax: (248)362-5103. E-mail: mazures@bnp.com. Website: www.wconline.com. **Contact:** Nick Moretti, editor. **20% freelance written.** Monthly magazine for contractors involved in lathing and plastering, drywall, acoustics, fireproofing, curtain walls, movable partitions together with manufacturers, dealers, and architects. Estab. 1938. Circ. 30,000. Pays on publication. Publishes ms an average of 6 months after acceptance. Byline given. Buys all rights. Submit seasonal material 4 months in advance. Accepts queries by mail, e-mail, phone. Accepts simultaneous submissions. Responds in 6 months to queries. Sample copy for 9×12 SAE with $2 postage. Writer's guidelines for #10 SASE.
Break in with technical expertise in drywall, plaster, stucco.
Nonfiction: How-to (drywall and plaster construction and business management), technical. **Buys 20 mss/year.** Query or send complete ms. Length: 1,000-1,500 words. **Pays $50-500.** Sometimes pays expenses of writers on assignment.
Reprints: Send tearsheet or photocopy with rights for sale noted and information about when and where the material previously appeared. Pays 50% of the amount paid for an original article.
Photos: Send photos with submission. Reviews contact sheets, negatives, transparencies, Prints. Buys one-time rights. Captions, identification of subjects required.
The online magazine carries original content not included in the print edition.

BUSINESS MANAGEMENT

These publications cover trends, general theory, and management practices for business owners and top-level business executives. Publications that use similar material but have a less technical slant are listed in the Consumer Business & Finance section. Journals for middle management, including supervisors and office managers, appear in the Management & Supervision section.

Those for industrial plant managers are listed under Industrial Operations and under sections for specific industries, such as Machinery & Metal. Publications for office supply store operators are included in the Office Environment & Equipment section.

$ $ ACCOUNTING TODAY, Accountants Media Group, 395 Hudson St., 5th Floor, New York NY 10014. (212)337-8444. **Contact:** Bill Carlino. Biweekly newspaper. "*Accounting Today* is the newspaper of record for the accounting industry." Estab. 1987. Circ. 35,000. Pays on publication. Publishes ms an average of 1 month after acceptance. Byline given. Buys all rights. Editorial lead time 3 weeks. Responds in 1 month to queries. Sample copy for $7.
Nonfiction: Essays, exposé, how-to, interview/profile. **Buys 35 mss/year.** Query with published clips. Length: 500-1,500 words. **Pays 25-65¢/word for assigned articles.** Pays expenses of writers on assignment.
Photos: State availability with submission. Negotiates payment individually.

$ $ $ ACROSS THE BOARD, The Conference Board Magazine, The Conference Board, 845 Third Ave., New York NY 10022-6679. (212)759-0900. Fax: (212)836-3828. E-mail: atb@conference-board.org. Website: www.acrosstheboardmagazine.com. Editor: Al Vogl. Managing Editor: Matthew Budman. **Contact:** Vadim Liberman, assistant editor. **60% freelance written.** Bimonthly magazine covering business—focuses on higher management. "*Across the Board* is a nonprofit magazine of ideas and opinions for leaders in business, goverment and other organizations. The editors present business perspectives on timely issues, including management practices, foreign policy, social issues, and science and technology. *Across the Board* is neither an academic business journal not a 'popular' manual. That means we aren't interested in highly technical articles about business strategy. It also means we don't publish oversimple 'how-to' articles. We are an idea magazine, but the ideas should have practical overtones. We let *Forbes, Fortune* and *Business Week* do most of the straight reporting, while we do some of the critical thinking; that is, we let writers explore the implications of the news in depth. *Across the Board* tries to provide different angles on important topics, and to bring to its readers' attention issues that they might otherwise not devote much thought to." Circ. 30,000. Pays on publication. Publishes ms an average of 4 months after acceptance. Byline given. Offers 20% kill fee. Buys first rights. Editorial lead time 6 months. Submit seasonal material 6 months in advance. Accepts queries by mail, e-mail, fax. Accepts simultaneous submissions. Responds in 3 weeks to queries. Sample copy for free. Writer's guidelines for #10 SASE or online.
Nonfiction: Book excerpts, essays, humor, opinion, personal experience. No new product information. **Buys 30 mss/year.** Query with published clips or send complete ms. Length: 500-4,000 words. **Pays $50-2,500.** Sometimes pays expenses of writers on assignment.
Photos: State availability with submission. Reviews contact sheets. Buys one-time or all rights. Negotiates payment individually. Captions, identification of subjects required.
Tips: "We emphasize the human side of organizational life at all levels. We're as concerned with helping managers who are 'lonely at the top' as with motivating workers and enhancing job satisfaction."

$ $ AMERICAN DRYCLEANER/COIN-OP/CLEAN CAR/AMERICAN LAUNDRY NEWS, American Trade Magazines/Crain Communications Inc., 500 N. Dearborn, Chicago IL 60610. (312)337-7700. Fax: (312)337-8654. E-mail: drycleaner@crain.com. **Contact:** Ian Murphy, managing editor. **20% freelance written.** Monthly tabloid covering drycleaning, coin laundry, coin car cleaning, institutional laundry. Estab. 1934. Circ. 25,000. Pays on publication. Publishes ms an average of 1 month after acceptance. Byline given. Offers 10% kill fee. Buys first, second serial (reprint), all rights. Editorial lead time 2 months. Submit seasonal material 2 months in advance. Accepts queries by mail, e-mail, fax, phone. Accepts simultaneous submissions. Responds in 1 month to queries; 4 months to mss. Sample copy for 6×9 SAE and 2 first-class stamps.
Nonfiction: How-to (general biz, industry-specific), interview/profile, new product, personal experience, technical. No inspirational, consumer-geared. **Buys 12-15 mss/year.** Query. Length: 600-2,000 words. **Pays $50-500 for assigned articles; $25-250 for unsolicited articles.** Sometimes pays expenses of writers on assignment.
Photos: State availability with submission. Reviews contact sheets, negatives, 4×5 or slide transparencies, 3×5-5×7 prints. Buys one-time rights. Negotiates payment individually. Identification of subjects required.
Columns/Departments: General Business, 1,200 words. **Buys 72 mss/year.** Send complete ms. **Pays $50-150.**
Tips: "Each magazine is geared toward small-business owners in these specific industries. Writers will find professional experience in the industry is a plus; general small-business articles are often used, but tailored to each magazine's audience."

$ $ BEDTIMES, The Business Journal for the Sleep Products Industry, International Sleep Products Association, 501 Wythe St., Alexandria VA 22304-1917. (703)683-8371. Fax: (703)683-4503. E-mail: kburns@sleepproducts.org. Website: www.sleepproducts.org. **Contact:** Kathleen Burns, editor. **20-40% freelance written.** Monthly magazine covering the mattress manufacturing industry. "Our news and features are straight forward—we are not a lobbying vehicle for our association. No special slant or philosophy." Estab. 1917. Circ. 4,000. **Pays on acceptance.** Publishes ms an average of 4 months after acceptance. Byline sometimes given. Buys first North American serial rights. Editorial lead time 2 months. Accepts queries by e-mail, fax. Accepts simultaneous submissions. Responds in 1 month to queries. Sample copy for $4. Writer's guidelines free for #10 SASE or by e-mail.

O╼ Break in with "Headlines"—short news stories. We also use freelancers for our monthly columns on "New Products," "Newsmakers," and "Snoozebriefs." Query first.

Nonfiction: Interview/profile, photo feature. "No pieces that do not relate to business in general or mattress industry in particular." **Buys 15-25 mss/year.** Query with published clips. Length: 500-3,500 words. **Pays 25-50¢/word for short features; $1,000 for cover story.**
Photos: State availability with submission. Buys one-time rights. Negotiates payment individually. Identification of subjects required.
Columns/Departments: Millennium Milestones (companies marking anniversaries from 25 to 150 years), 1,000 words. **Buys 10-12 mss/year.** Query with 3 published clips. **Pays $350 or more depending on length and degree of difficulty in getting the story.**
Tips: "Cover stories are a major outlet for freelance submissions. Once a story is written and accepted, the author is encouraged to submit suggestions to the graphic designer of the magazine regarding ideas for the cover illustration as well as possible photos/graphs/charts, etc. to be used with the story itself. Topics have included annual industry forecast; physical expansion of industry facilities; e-commerce; flammability and home furnishings; the risks and rewards of marketing overseas; the evolving family business; the shifting workplace environment; and what do consumers really want?"

$ CA MAGAZINE, Canadian Institute of Chartered Accountants, 277 Wellington St. W, Toronto, Ontario M5V 3H2, Canada. (416)977-3222. Fax: (416)204-3409. E-mail: camagazine@cica.ca. Website: www.camagazine.com. **Contact:** Christian Bellavance, editor-in-chief. **30% freelance written.** Magazine published 10 times/year covering accounting. "CA Magazine is the leading accounting publication in Canada and the preferred information source for chartered accountants and financial executives. It provides a forum for discussion and debate on professional, financial and other business issues." Estab. 1911. Circ. 74,834. **Pays on acceptance.** Publishes ms an average of 3 months after acceptance. Byline given. Offers 30% kill fee. Buys all rights. Editorial lead time 4 months. Accepts queries by e-mail. Responds in 1 month to queries. Sample copy and writer's guidelines online.
Nonfiction: Book excerpts, financial/accounting business. **Buys 30 mss/year.** Query. Length: 2,500-3,500 words. **Pays honorarium for chartered accountants; freelance rate varies.**

$ $ CONTRACT MANAGEMENT, National Contract Management Association, 1912 Woodford Rd, Vienna VA 22182. Fax: (703)448-0939. E-mail: cm@ncmahq.org. Website: www.ncmahq.org. **Contact:** Amy Miedema, editor-in-chief. **10% freelance written.** Monthly magazine covering contract and business management. "Most of the articles published in *Contract Management (CM)* are written by members, although one does not have to be an NCMA member to be published in the magazine. Articles should concern some aspect of the contract management profession, whether at the level of a beginner or that of the advanced practitioner." Estab. 1960. Circ. 23,000. Pays on publication. Publishes ms an average of 3 months after acceptance. Byline given. Buys one-time rights. Editorial lead time 10 weeks. Submit seasonal material 3 months in advance. Accepts queries by mail, e-mail, fax, phone. Accepts previously published material. Accepts simultaneous submissions. Responds in 2 weeks to queries; 1 month to mss. Sample copy and writer's guidelines free.
Nonfiction: Essays, general interest, how-to, humor, inspirational, new product, opinion, technical. No company or CEO profiles—please read a copy of publication before submitting. **Buys 6-10 mss/year.** Query with published clips. Length: 1,000-2,500 words. **Pays $300, association members paid in 3 copies.**
Reprints: Accepts previously published submissions.
Photos: State availability with submission. Buys one-time rights. Offers no additional payment for photos accepted with ms. Captions, identification of subjects required.
Columns/Departments: Professional Development (self-improvement in business), 1,000-1,500 words; Back to Basics (basic how-tos and discussions), 1,500-2,000 words. **Buys 2 mss/year.** Query with published clips. **Pays $300.**
Tips: "Query and read at least one issue. Visit website to better understand our audience."

$ $ CONTRACTING PROFITS, Trade Press Publishing, 2100 W. Florist Ave., Milwaukee WI 53209. (414)228-7701. E-mail: dianna.b@tradepress.com. Website: www.cleanlink.com/cp. **Contact:** Dianna Bisswurm, editor. **40% freelance written.** Magazine published 11 times/year covering "building service contracting, business management advice." "We are the pocket MBA for this industry—focusing not only on cleaning-specific topics, but also discussing how to run businesses better and increase profits through a variety of management articles." Estab. 1995. Circ. 32,000. Pays within 30 days of acceptance. Byline given. Buys all rights. Editorial lead time 2 months. Submit seasonal material 3 months in advance. Accepts queries by mail, e-mail. Sample copy online. Writer's guidelines free.
Nonfiction: Exposé, how-to, interview/profile, technical. "No product-related reviews or testimonials." **Buys 30 mss/year.** Query with published clips. Length: 1,200-3,000 words. **Pays $100-500.** Sometimes pays expenses of writers on assignment.
Columns/Departments: Query with published clips.
Tips: "Read back issues on our website and be able to understand some of those topics prior to calling."

$ CONVENTION SOUTH, Covey Communications Corp., 2001 W. First St., P.O. Box 2267, Gulf Shores AL 36547-2267. (251)968-5300. Fax: (251)968-4532. E-mail: info@conventionsouth.com. Website: www.conventionsouth.com. Editor: J. Talty O'Connor. **Contact:** Kristen McIntosh, executive editor. **50% freelance written.** Monthly business journal for meeting planners who plan events in the South. Topics relate to the meetings industry—how-to articles, industry news, destination spotlights. Estab. 1983. Circ. 16,000. Pays on publication. Publishes ms an average of 2 months after acceptance. Byline given. Buys first, second serial (reprint) rights. Editorial lead time 3 months. Submit seasonal material 4 months in advance. Accepts queries by mail, e-mail, fax. Accepts simultaneous submissions. Responds in 2 months to queries. Sample copy for free. Writer's guidelines for #10 SASE.

Nonfiction: How-to (relative to meeting planning/travel), interview/profile, photo feature, technical, travel. **Buys 50 mss/year.** Query. Length: 750-1,250 words. **Payment negotiable.** Pays in contributor copies or other premiums if arranged in advance. Sometimes pays expenses of writers on assignment.

Reprints: Send photocopy and information about when and where the material previously appeared. Pay negotiable.

Photos: Send photos with submission. Reviews 5×7 prints. Buys one-time rights. Offers no additional payment for photos accepted with ms. Captions, identification of subjects required.

Columns/Departments: How-to (related to meetings), 700 words. **Buys 12 mss/year.** Query with published clips. **Payment negotiable.**

Tips: "Know who our audience is and make sure articles are appropriate for them."

N $ $ EXECUTIVE UPDATE, Greater Washington Society of Association Executives, Reagan Building & International Trade Center, 1300 Pennsylvania Ave. NW, Washington DC 20004. Fax: (202)326-0960. E-mail: sbriscoe@gwsae.org. Website: www.executiveupdate.com. **Contact:** Scott Briscoe, editor. **60% freelance written.** Monthly magazine "exploring a broad range of association management issues and for introducing and discussing management and leadership philosophies. It is written for individuals at all levels of association management, with emphasis on senior staff and CEOs." Estab. 1979. Circ. 14,000. **Pays on acceptance.** Publishes ms an average of 6 months after acceptance. Byline given. Offers 20% kill fee. Buys first rights. Editorial lead time 3 months. Submit seasonal material 6 months in advance. Accepts queries by mail, e-mail, fax, phone. Accepts simultaneous submissions. Responds in 1 month to queries; 2 months to mss. Sample copy and writer's guidelines free.

Nonfiction: How-to, humor, interview/profile, opinion, personal experience, travel, management and workplace issues. **Buys 24-36 mss/year.** Query with published clips. Length: 1,750-2,250 words. **Pays $500-700.** Pays expenses of writers on assignment.

Columns/Departments: Intelligence (new ways to tackle day-to-day issues), 500-700 words; Off the Cuff (guest column for association executives). Query. **Pays $100-200.**

$ $ EXPANSION MANAGEMENT MAGAZINE, Growth Strategies for Companies On the Move, Penton Media, Inc., 9500 Nall, Suite 400, Overland Park KS 66207. (913)381-4800. Fax: (913)381-8858. Editor: Bill King. **Contact:** Lance Yoder, managing editor. **75% freelance written.** Monthly magazine covering economic development. Estab. 1986. Circ. 45,000. **Pays on acceptance.** Publishes ms an average of 1 month after acceptance. Byline given. Buys all rights, makes work-for-hire assignments. Editorial lead time 2 months. Sample copy for $7. Writer's guidelines free.

Nonfiction: "*Expansion Management* presents articles and industry reports examining relocation trends, strategic planning, work force hiring, economic development agencies, relocation consultants and state, province and county reviews and profiles to help readers select future expansions and relocation sites." **Buys 120 mss/year.** Query with published clips. Length: 1,000-1,500 words. **Pays $200-400 for assigned articles.** Sometimes pays expenses of writers on assignment.

Photos: Send photos with submission. Buys one-time rights. Offers no additional payment for photos accepted with ms. Captions required.

Tips: "Send clips first, then call me."

$ $ $ EXPO, Atwood Publishing LLC, 11600 College Blvd., Overland Park KS 66210. (913)469-1185. Fax: (913)469-0806. E-mail: eingram@expoweb.com. Website: www.expoweb.com. **Contact:** Elizabeth Ingram, editor-in-chief. **80% freelance written.** Magazine covering expositions. "*EXPO* is the information and education resource for the exposition industry. It is the only magazine dedicated exclusively to the people with direct responsibility for planning, promoting and operating trade and consumer shows. Our readers are show managers and their staff, association executives, independent show producers and industry suppliers. Every issue of *EXPO* contains in-depth, how-to features and departments that focus on the practical aspects of exposition management, including administration, promotion and operations." Pays on publication. Byline given. Offers 50% kill fee. Buys first North American serial rights. Editorial lead time 3 months. Accepts queries by mail, e-mail, fax. Responds in 3 weeks to queries. Sample copy for free. Writer's guidelines free or online at website.

Nonfiction: How-to, interview/profile. Query with published clips. Length: 600-2,400 words. **Pays 50¢/word.** Pays expenses of writers on assignment.

Photos: State availability with submission.

Columns/Departments: Profile (personality profile), 650 words; Exhibitor Matters (exhibitor issues) and EXPOTech (technology), both 600-1,300 words. **Buys 10 mss/year.** Query with published clips.

Tips: "*EXPO* now offers shorter features and departments, while continuing to offer in-depth reporting. Editorial is more concise, using synopsis, bullets and tidbits whenever possible. Every article needs sidebars, call-outs, graphs, charts, etc., to create entry points for readers. Headlines and leads are more provocative. And writers should elevate the level of shop talk, demonstrating that *EXPO* is the leader in the industry. We plan our editorial calendar about one year in advance, but we are always open to new ideas. Please query before submitting a story to *EXPO*—tell us about your idea and what our readers would learn. Include your qualifications to write about the subject and the sources you plan to contact."

$ $ IN TENTS, The Magazine for the Tent Rental and Fabric Structure Industries, Industrial Fabrics Association International, 1801 County Rd. B W., Roseville MN 55113-4061. (612)225-6970. Fax: (612)225-6966. E-mail: intents@ifai.com. Website: www.ifai.com. **Contact:** John Gehner, editor. **50% freelance written.** Quarterly magazine covering tent-rental and fabric structure industries. Estab. 1994. Circ. 12,000. **Pays on acceptance.** Publishes ms an average of 2 months after acceptance. Byline given. Buys all rights. Editorial lead time 3 months. Accepts queries by mail, e-mail, fax. Sample copy and writer's guidelines free.

- Break in with familiarity of tent rental, special events, tent manufacturing and fabric structure industries. Or lively, intelligent writing on technical subjects.

Nonfiction: How-to, interview/profile, new product, photo feature, technical. **Buys 10-12 mss/year.** Query. Length: 800-2,000 words. **Pays $100-500.** Sometimes pays expenses of writers on assignment.
Photos: State availability with submission. Reviews contact sheets, negatives, transparencies, prints, Digital images. Buys one-time rights. Negotiates payment individually. Captions, identification of subjects, model releases required.
Tips: "We look for lively, intelligent writing that makes technical subjects come alive."

$ $ MEETINGS MEDIA, 550 Montgomery St., #750, San Francisco CA 94111. Fax: (415)788-0301. E-mail: tyler.davidson@meetings411.com. Website: www.meetings411.com. **Contact:** Tyler Davidson, editor. **75% freelance written.** Monthly tabloid covering meeting, event and conference planning. Estab. 1986. Circ. Meetings East 22,000; Meetings South 22,000; Meetings West 26,000. Pays one month after publication. Publishes ms an average of 1 month afer acceptance. Byline given. Buys first North American serial electronic rights. Editorial lead time 3 months. Submit seasonal material 3 months in advance. Accepts queries by mail, e-mail, fax. Responds in 3 weeks to queries. Sample copy for 9×13 SAE and 5 first-class stamps.

- Queries and pitches are accepted on columns & cover stories ONLY. All other assignments (Features and Site Inspections) are based exclusively on editorial calendar (www.meetings411.com/editorialcal_main.asp.). Interested writers should send a resume and two/three relevant clips—which MUST show familiarity with meetings/conventions topics—by mail.

Nonfiction: How-to, travel (as it pertains to meetings and conventions. "No first-person fluff. We are a business magazine." **Buys 150 mss/year.** Query with published clips. Length: 1,200-2,000 words. **Pays $500 flat rate per package.**
Photos: State availability with submission. Buys one-time rights. Offers no additional payment for photos accepted with ms. Identification of subjects required.
Tips: "We're always looking for freelance writers who are local to our destination stories. For Site Inspections, get in touch in late September or early October, when we usually have the following year's editorial calendar available.

$ $ NORTHEAST EXPORT, A Magazine for New England Companies Engaged in International Trade, Commerce Publishing Company, Inc., P.O. Box 254, Northborough MA 01532. (508)351-2925. Fax: (508)351-6905. E-mail: editor@northeast-export.com. Website: www.northeast-export.com. **Contact:** Carlos Cunha, editor. **30% freelance written.** Bimonthly business-to-business magazine. "*Northeast Export* is the only publication directly targeted at New England's international trade community. All stories relate to issues affecting New England companies and feature only New England-based profiles and examples. Estab. 1997. Circ. 13,500. **Pays on acceptance.** Byline given. Offers 10% kill fee. Buys all rights. Editorial lead time 2 months. Accepts queries by mail, e-mail, fax. Sample copy for free.
Nonfiction: How-to, interview/profile, travel, industry trends/analysis. "We will not take unsolicited articles. Query first with clips." **Buys 10-12 mss/year.** Query with published clips and SASE. No unsolicited material. Length: 800-2,000 words. **Payment varies.**
Photos: State availability of or send photos with submission. Reviews 2¼ transparencies, 5×7 prints. Buys one-time rights. Negotiates payment individually. Captions, identification of subjects, model releases required.
Tips: "We're looking for writers with availability; the ability to write clearly about tough, sometimes very technical subjects; the fortitude to slog through industry jargon to get the story straight; a knowledge of international trade issues and/or New England transportation infrastructure. We're interested in freelancers with business writing and magazine experience, especially those with contacts in the New England manufacturing, finance and transportation communities."

$ $ PORTABLE RESTROOM OPERATOR, Rangoon Moon Inc., P.O. Box 904, Dahlonega GA 30533. (706)864-6838. Fax: (706)864-9851. E-mail: sesails@yahoo.com. Website: www.1promag.com. Managing Editor: M.A. Watson. **Contact:** Kevin Gralton, editor. **50% freelance written.** Magazine published 9 times/year covering portable sanitation. Estab. 1998. **Pays on acceptance.** Publishes ms an average of 2 months after acceptance. Byline given. Editorial lead time 1 month. Submit seasonal material 2 months in advance. Accepts queries by mail, e-mail, fax.
Nonfiction: Quality articles that will be of interest to our readers. Studies on governmental changes, OSHA regulations, and sanitation articles that deal with portable restrooms are of strong interest. Exposé (government relations, OSHA, EPS associated, trends, public attitudes, etc.), general interest (state portable restroom associations, conventions, etc.), historical/nostalgic, humor, inspirational, new product, personal experience, technical. Query or send complete ms. Length: Length is not important. **Pays 15¢/word.**
Photos: No negatives. "We need good contrast." Send photos with submission. Buys one-time rights. Pays $15 for b&w and color prints that are used. Captions, model releases required.
Tips: "Material must pertain to portable sanitation industry."

$ $ $ $ PROFESSIONAL COLLECTOR, Pohly & Partners, 27 Melcher St., 2nd Floor, Boston MA 02210-1516. (617)451-1700. Fax: (617)338-7767. E-mail: procollector@pohlypartners.com. Website: www.pohlypartners.com.

Contact: Karen English, editor. **90% freelance written.** Quarterly magazine published for Western Union's Financial Services Inc.'s Quick Collect Service, covering debt collection business/lifestyle issues. "We gear our articles directly to the debt collectors and their managers. Each issue offers features covering the trends and players, the latest technology, and other issues affecting the collections industry. It's all designed to help collectors be more productive and improve their performance." Estab. 1993. Circ. 161,000. Pays on publication. Byline given. Buys first North American serial rights. Editorial lead time 9 months. Submit seasonal material 9 months in advance. Accepts queries by mail, e-mail, fax. Sample copy and writer's guidelines free.

Nonfiction: General interest, how-to (tips on good collecting), humor, interview/profile, new product, book reviews. **Buys 10-15 mss/year.** Query with published clips. Length: 400-2,000 words. **Payment negotiable for assigned articles.** Sometimes pays expenses of writers on assignment.

Photos: State availability with submission. Reviews contact sheets, 3×5 prints. Buys one-time rights. Negotiates payment individually. Captions, identification of subjects, model releases required.

Columns/Departments: Industry Roundup (issues within industry), 500-1,000 words; Tips, 750-1,000 words; Q&A (questions & answers for collectors), 1,500 words. **Buys 15-20 mss/year.** Query with published clips. **Payment negotiable.**

Tips: "Writers should be aware that *Professional Collector* is a promotional publication, and that its content must support the overall marketing goals of Western Union. It helps to have extensive insider knowledge about the debt collection industry."

$ $ PROGRESSIVE RENTALS, The Voice of the Rental-Purchase Industry, Association of Progressive Rental Organizations, 1504 Robin Hood Trail, Austin TX 78703. (800)204-2776. Fax: (512)794-0097. E-mail: jsherrier@apro-rto.com. Website: www.apro-rto.com. **Contact:** Julie Stephen Sherrier, editor. **50% freelance written.** Bimonthly magazine covering the rent-to-own industry. "*Progressive Rentals* is the only publication representing the rent-to-own industry and members of APRO. The magazine covers timely news and features affecting the industry, association activities and member profiles. Awarded best 4-color magazine by the American Society of Association Executives in 1999." Estab. 1980. Circ. 5,500. **Pays on acceptance.** Publishes ms an average of 2 months after acceptance. Byline given. Offers 25% kill fee. Buys first North American serial rights. Editorial lead time 2 months. Submit seasonal material 4 months in advance. Accepts queries by mail, e-mail, fax, phone. Accepts simultaneous submissions. Responds in 1 month to queries; 2 months to mss. Sample copy for free.

Nonfiction: Exposé, general interest, how-to, inspirational, interview/profile, technical, industry features. **Buys 12 mss/year.** Query with published clips. Length: 1,200-2,500 words. **Pays $150-700.** Sometimes pays expenses of writers on assignment.

$ $ RENTAL MANAGEMENT, American Rental Association, 1900 19th St., Moline IL 61265. (309)764-2475. Fax: (309)764-1533. E-mail: brian.alm@ararental.org. Website: www.rentalmanagementmag.com. Managing Editor: Tamera Bonnicksen. **Contact:** Brian R. Alm, editor. **30% freelance written.** Monthly magazine for the equipment rental industry worldwide (*not* property, real estate, appliances, furniture or cars), emphasizing management topics in particular but also marketing, merchandising, technology, etc. Estab. 1970. Circ. 19,300. **Pays on acceptance.** Publishes ms an average of 3 months after acceptance. Byline sometimes given. Buys first North American serial rights. Editorial lead time 2 months. Submit seasonal material 3 months in advance. Accepts queries by mail, e-mail, fax.

Nonfiction: Business management and marketing. **Buys 20-25 mss/year.** Query with published clips. Does not respond to unsolicited work unless being considered for publication. Length: 600-1,500 words. **Payment negotiable.** Sometimes pays expenses of writers on assignment.

Reprints: Send tearsheet or typed ms with rights for sale noted and information about when and where the material previously appeared.

Photos: State availability with submission. Reviews contact sheets, negatives, 35mm or 2¼ transparencies, Any size prints. Buys one-time rights. Negotiates payment individually. Identification of subjects required.

Columns/Departments: "We are adequately served by existing columnists and have a long waiting list of others to use pending need." **Buys 20 mss/year.** Query with published clips. **Payment negotiable.**

Tips: "Show me you can write maturely, cogently and fluently on management matters of direct and compelling interest to the small-business owner or manager in a larger operation; no sloppiness, no unexamined thoughts, no stiffness or affectation—genuine, direct and worthwhile English. Knowledge of the equipment rental industry is a distinct plus."

N $ $ SBN, Pittsburgh edition, SBN Inc., 800 Vinial St., Suite B-208, Pittsburgh PA 15212. (412)321-6050. Fax: (412)321-6058. E-mail: pittsburgh@sbnnet.com. Website: www.sbn-online.com. **Contact:** Ray Marano, editor. **5% freelance written.** Monthly magazine. "We provide information and insight designed to help companies grow. Our focus is on local companies with 50-250 employees and their successful business strategies, with the ultimate goal of educating entrepreneurs. Our target audience is business owners and other top executives." Estab. 1994. Circ. 16,000. Pays on publication. Publishes ms an average of 2 months after acceptance. Byline given. Buys all rights, makes work-for-hire assignments. Editorial lead time 2 months. Submit seasonal material 4 months in advance. Accepts queries by mail, e-mail, fax. Responds in 1 month to queries. Sample copy for $3. Writer's guidelines free.

Nonfiction: Book excerpts, how-to, interview/profile, opinion, annual energy and telecommunication supplements, among others. "No basic profiles about 'interesting' companies or stories about companies with no ties to Pittsburgh." Query with published clips. Length: 250-1,000 words. **Pays $150-300 for assigned articles.**

Reprints: Accepts reprints (mainly columns from business professionals). Send photocopy of article or short story and information about when and where the article previously appeared.

Photos: State availability with submission. Reviews negatives, transparencies. Buys one-time or all rights. Negotiates payment individually. Identification of subjects required.
Tips: "Have articles localized to the Pittsburgh and surrounding areas. We look for articles that will help our readers, educate them on a business strategy that another company may be using that can help our readers' companies grow."

SBN MAGAZINE, Smart Business Network Inc., 14725 Detroit Ave., #200, Cleveland OH 44107. (216)228-6397. Fax: (216)529-8924. E-mail: editor@sbnonline.com. Website: www.sbnonline.com. **Contact:** Dustin S. Klein, editor. **5% freelance written.** Monthly business magazine with an audience made up of business owners and top decision makers. "*SBN* is smart ideas for growing companies. Best practices, winning strategies. The pain—and joy—of running a business. Every issue delves into the minds of the most innovative executives in Northeast Ohio and across the nation to report on how market leaders got to the top and what strategies they use to stay there." Estab. 1989. Pays on publication. Publishes ms an average of 2 months after acceptance. Byline given. Offers 50% kill fee. Buys first North American serial, second serial (reprint), electronic rights. Editorial lead time 3 months. Submit seasonal material 3 months in advance. Accepts queries by mail, e-mail. Responds in 2 weeks to queries; 1 month to mss. Sample copy online. Writer's guidelines by e-mail.
Nonfiction: How-to, interview/profile. No breaking news or straight personality profiles. **Buys 2-5 mss/year.** Query with published clips. Length: 450-1,500 words. **Pays $200-500.** Sometimes pays expenses of writers on assignment.
Reprints: Accepts previously published submissions.
Photos: State availability with submission. Reviews negatives, prints. Buys one-time, reprint or web rights. Offers no additional payment for photos accepted with ms. Identification of subjects required.
Columns/Departments: Another View (business management related), 500-700 words. **Buys 6-8 mss/year.** Query.
The online magazine carries original content not found in the print edition. Contact: Dustin S. Klein, editor.
Tips: "The best way to submit to *SBN* is to read us—either online or in print. Remember, our audience is made up of top level business executives and owners."

N $ $ SECURITY DEALER, Cygnus Publishing, 445 Broad Hollow Rd., Melville NY 11747. (516)845-2700. Fax: (516)845-7109. E-mail: susan.brady@cygnuspub.com. **Contact:** Susan A. Brady, editor. **25% freelance written.** Monthly magazine for electronic alarm dealers, burglary and fire installers, with technical, business, sales and marketing information. Circ. 25,000. Pays 3 weeks after publication. Publishes ms an average of 4 months after acceptance. Byline sometimes given. Buys first North American serial rights. Accepts simultaneous submissions.
Nonfiction: How-to, interview/profile, technical. No consumer pieces. Query by mail only. Length: 1,000-3,000 words. **Pays $300 for assigned articles; $100-200 for unsolicited articles.** Sometimes pays expenses of writers on assignment.
Photos: State availability with submission. Reviews contact sheets, transparencies. Offers $25 additional payment for photos accepted with ms. Captions, identification of subjects required.
Columns/Departments: Closed Circuit TV, Access Control (both on application, installation, new products), 500-1,000 words. **Buys 25 mss/year.** Query by mail only. **Pays $100-150.**
Tips: "The areas of our publication most open to freelancers are technical innovations, trends in the alarm industry and crime patterns as related to the business as well as business finance and management pieces."

$ $ STAMATS MEETINGS MEDIA, (formerly *Meetings Media*), 550 Montgomery St., #750, San Francisco CA 94111. Fax: (415)788-0301. E-mail: tyler.davidson@meetings411.com. Website: www.meetings411.com. Destinations Editor: Anita Epler. **Contact:** Tyler Davidson, editor (columnists, cover stories). **75% freelance written.** Monthly tabloid covering meeting, event and conference planning. Estab. 1986. Circ. *Meetings East* and *Meetings South* 22,000; *Meetings West* 26,000. Pays one month after publication. Publishes ms an average of 1 month after acceptance. Byline given. Buys first North American serial, electronic rights. Editorial lead time 3 months. Submit seasonal material 3 months in advance. Accepts queries by mail, e-mail, fax. Responds in 3 weeks to queries. Sample copy for 9×13 SAE and 5 first-class stamps.

Queries and pitches are accepted on columns, cover stories only. All other assignments (Features and Site Inspections) are based exclusively on editorial calendar (www.meetings411.com/editorial_main.asp). Interested writers should send a résumé and 2-3 relevant clips, which must show familiarity with meetings/conventions topics—by e-mail.

Nonfiction: How-to, travel (as it pertains to meetings and conventions). "No first-person fluff. We are a business magazine." **Buys 150 mss/year.** Query with published clips. Length: 1,200-2,000 words. **Pays $500 flat rate/package.**
Photos: State availability with submission. Buys one-time rights. Offers no additional payment for photos accepted with ms. Identification of subjects required.
Tips: "We're always looking for freelance writers who are local to our destination stories. For Site Inspections, get in touch in late September or early October, when we usually have the following year's editorial calendar available."

$ THE STATE JOURNAL, The State Journal Corp., 904 Virginia St. E., Charleston WV 25301. (304)344-1630. Fax: (304)345-2721. E-mail: sjeditor@aol.com. Website: www.statejournal.com. **Contact:** Jack Bailey, editor. **30% freelance written.** "We are a weekly journal dedicated to providing stories of interest to the business community in West Virginia." Estab. 1984. Circ. 12,000. Pays on publication. Publishes ms an average of 2 months after acceptance. Byline given. Buys first rights. Editorial lead time 2 months. Submit seasonal material 4 months in advance. Accepts queries by mail, e-mail, fax. Responds in 3 weeks to queries; 2 months to mss. Sample copy for #10 SASE. Writer's guidelines for #10 SASE.

Nonfiction: General interest, interview/profile, new product, opinion, (All business related). **Buys 150 mss/year.** Query. Length: 250-1,500 words. **Pays $50.** Sometimes pays expenses of writers on assignment.
Photos: State availability with submission. Reviews contact sheets. Buys one-time rights. Offers $15/photo. Captions required.
Columns/Departments: Business related, especially slanted toward WV. **Buys 25 mss/year.** Query. **Pays $50.**
Tips: "Localize your work—mention West Virginia specifically in the article; or talk to business people in West Virginia.

$ $ UDM, Upholstery Design & Management, Chartwell Communications, 380 E. Northwest Hwy., Suite 300, Des Plaines IL 60016-2208. (847)795-7690. Fax: (847)390-7100. E-mail: mchazin@chartcomm.com. Website: www.udmonline.com. **Contact:** Michael Chazin, editor/associate publisher. **10% freelance written.** Monthly business-to-business magazine covering upholstered furniture/industry management. "*UDM* targets suppliers, manufacturers and retailers/resellers of upholstered furniture for the home, office, institution. Because we are highly specialized, we need writers with a knowledge of the furniture industry and familiarity and ability to identify new style trends." Estab. 1989. Circ. 8,600. Pays on publication. Publishes ms an average of 2 months after acceptance. Byline usually given. Buys first North American serial rights. Accepts queries by mail, e-mail. Responds in 2 weeks to queries; 2 months to mss. Sample copy for free.
Nonfiction: Interview/profile. **Buys 6-10 mss/year.** Query. Length: 500-2,500 words. **Pays $250-700.** Sometimes pays expenses of writers on assignment.
Photos: Reviews transparencies, prints. Offers no additional payment for photos accepted with ms. Captions, identification of subjects required.
Tips: "Writers must have inside knowledge of furniture/upholstery or be privy to knowledge. We try to stay on the leading edge of color and style trends—12-18 months before they hit retail stores."

N UNFINISHEDBUSINESS, Official Voice of the Unfinished Furniture Association, Association Headquarters, Inc., 17000 Commerce Pkwy., Mount Laurel NJ 08054. (856)439-0500, ext. 3064. Fax: (856)439-0525. E-mail: jbertonazzi@ahint.com. Website: www.unfinishedfurniture.org. **Contact:** Judy Bertonazzi, editor. **17% freelance written.** Bimonthly magazine covering unfinished furniture retailing, manufacturing and selling. "*UnfinishedBUSINESS* is a bimonthly trade publication serving the unfinished furniture industry. Our main mission is to uphold the beliefs and values of the Unfinished Furniture Association (UFA) while providing our readers with information and news that is important for their daily business activities. The UFA wishes to promote the common business interests of the unfinished furniture industry, encourage the most efficient and professional organization and administration of firms in the unfinished furniture industry, and conduct meetings and educational programs. The UFA also has a goal of collecting and publishing information about the unfinished furniture industry that is relevant to their business needs in today's business world." Estab. 1996. Circ. 3,500. Pays on publication. Publishes ms an average of 4 months after acceptance. Byline given. Offers $400 kill fee. Buys second serial (reprint) rights. Editorial lead time 2 months. Submit seasonal material 2 months in advance. Accepts queries by mail, e-mail, fax. Accepts previously published material. Accepts simultaneous submissions. Responds in 2 weeks to queries; 2 months to mss. Sample copy online. Writer's guidelines by e-mail.
Nonfiction: Interview/profile. Special issues: Furniture and Design Trends (January/February issue and July/August issue every year). No fiction, personal experience essays, historical. **Buys 6-8 mss/year.** Query. Length: 1,200-3,000 words. **Pays $400 for assigned articles.**
Photos: Send photos with submission. Reviews GIF/JPEG files (300 dpi). Buys one-time rights. Offers no additional payment for photos accepted with ms. Captions, identification of subjects required.
Tips: "Get to know professionals in the industry."

N VENECONOMY/VENECONOMÍA, VenEconomía, Edificio Gran Sabana, Piso 1, Avendia Abraham Lincoln, Sabana Grande, Caracas, Venezuela DF. (+58)212-761-8121. Fax: (+58)212-762-8160. E-mail: editor@veneconía.com. Website: www.veneconomía.com or www.veneconomy.com. Managing Editor: Robert Bottome. **Contact:** Francisco Toro, political editor. **70% freelance written.** Monthly business magazine covering business, political and social issues in Venezuela. "*VenEconomy*'s subscribers are mostly businesspeople, both Venezuelans and foreigners doing business in Venezuela. Some academics and diplomats also read our magazine. The magazine is published monthly both in English and Spanish—freelancers may query us in either language. Our slant is decidedly pro-business, but not dogmatically conservative. Development, human rights, political and environmental issues are covered from a business-friendly angle." Estab. 1983. Pays on publication. Publishes ms an average of 1 month after acceptance. Byline given. Offers 50% kill fee. Makes work-for-hire assignments. Editorial lead time 1-2 months. Submit seasonal material 1 month in advance. Accepts queries by e-mail. Accepts simultaneous submissions. Responds in 2 weeks to queries; 4 months to mss. Sample copy by e-mail.
Nonfiction: Essays, exposé, interview/profile, new product, opinion. No first-person stories or travel articles. **Buys 50 mss/year.** Query. Length: 1,100-3,200 words. **Pays 10-15¢/word for assigned articles.** Sometimes pays expenses of writers on assignment.
Tips: "A Venezuela tie-in is absolutely indispensable. While most of our readers are businesspeople, *VenEconomy* does not limit itself strictly to business-magazine fare. Our aim is to give our readers a sophisticated understanding of the main issues affecting the country as a whole. Stories about successful Venezuelan companies, or foreign companies doing business successfully with Venezuela are particularly welcome. Stories about the oil-sector, especially as it relates to Venezuela, are useful. Other promising topics for freelancers outside Venezuela include international trade and trade negotiations, U.S.-Venezuela bilateral diplomatic relations, international investors' perceptions of business prospects in Venezuela, and international organizations' assessments of environmental, human rights, or democracy and development

issues in Venezuela, etc. Both straight reportage and somewhat more opinionated pieces are acceptable, articles that straddle the borderline between reportage and opinion are best. Before querying, ask yourself: Would this be of interest to me if I was doing business in or with Venezuela?"

N $ $ $ WORLD TRADE, "For the Executive with Global Vision", BNP, 23211 S. Pointe Dr., Suite 101, Laguna Hills CA 92653. Fax: (949)830-1328. Website: www.worldtrademag.com. Editor: Patrick Burnson. **Contact:** Jack Sweet, managing editor. **50% freelance written.** Monthly magazine covering international business. Estab. 1988. Circ. 75,000. Pays on publication. Publishes ms an average of 1 month after acceptance. Byline given. Buys all rights. Editorial lead time 3 months. Accepts queries by mail, fax.

Nonfiction: "See our editorial calendar online at wwww.worldtrademag.com." Interview/profile, technical, finance, logistics. **Buys 40-50 mss/year.** Query with published clips. Length: 450-1,500 words. **Pays 50¢/word.**

Photos: State availability with submission. Reviews transparencies, Prints. Buys all rights. Negotiates payment individually. Identification of subjects required.

Columns/Departments: International Business Services, 800 words; Shipping, Supply Chain Management, Logistics, 800 words; Software & Technology, 800 words; Economic Development (US, International), 800 words. **Buys 40-50 mss/year. Pays 50¢/word.**

Tips: "We seek writers with expertise in their subject areas, as well as solid researching and writing skills. We want analysts more than reporters. We don't accept unsolicited manuscripts, and we don't want phone calls— Please read *World Trade* before sending a query."

CHURCH ADMINISTRATION & MINISTRY

Publications in this section are written for clergy members, church leaders, and teachers. Magazines for lay members and the general public are listed in the Consumer Religious section.

$ THE AFRICAN AMERICAN PULPIT, Judson Press, 588 N. Gulph Rd., King of Prussia PA 19406. (610)768-2128. Fax: (610)768-2441. E-mail: Victoria.McGoey@abc-usa.org. Website: www.judsonpress.com/TAAP. Editors: Martha Simmons, Frank A. Thomas. **Contact:** Victoria McGoey, project manager. **100% freelance written.** Quarterly magazine covering African American preaching. "*The African American Pulpit* is a quarterly journal that serves as a repository for the very best of African American preaching and provides practical and creative resources for persons in ministry." Estab. 1997. Circ. 2,000. Pays on publication. Publishes ms an average of 6 months after acceptance. Byline always given. Editorial lead time 9 months. Submit seasonal material 1 year in advance. Accepts queries by mail, e-mail, fax, phone. Accepts simultaneous submissions. Writer's guidelines online or by e-mail.

Nonfiction: Sermons/articles relating to African American preaching and the African American Church. Book excerpts, essays, how-to (craft a sermon), inspirational, interview/profile, opinion, religious. **Buys 60 mss/year.** Send complete ms. Length: 1,500-3,000 words.

$ CE CONNECTION COMMUNIQUE, Creative Christian Ministries, P.O. Box 12624, Roanoke VA 24027. Fax: (540)342-7511. E-mail: ccmbbr@juno.com. **Contact:** Betty Robertson, editor. **25% freelance written.** Monthly e-newsletter, "a vehicle of communication for pastors, local church Christian education leaders and volunteer teachers." Estab. 1995. **Pays on acceptance.** Publishes ms an average of 6 months after acceptance. Byline given. Buys one-time rights. Editorial lead time 6 months. Submit seasonal material 6 months in advance. Accepts simultaneous submissions. Responds in 6 months to queries. Writer's guidelines for #10 SASE.

Nonfiction: How-to, new product. **Buys 12 mss/year.** Send complete ms. Length: 100-600 words. **Pays $5-10.**

N $ THE CHRISTIAN COMMUNICATOR, 9731 N. Fox Glen Dr., #6F, Niles IL 60714-4222. (847)296-3964. Fax: (847)296-0754. E-mail: linjohnson@compuserve.com. **Contact:** Lin Johnson, editor. **90% freelance written.** Monthly magazine covering Christian writing and speaking. Circ. 4,000. Pays on publication. Publishes ms an average of 6-12 months after acceptance. Byline given. Buys first, one-time, second serial (reprint) rights. Editorial lead time 3 months. Submit seasonal material 9 months in advance. Accepts queries by e-mail. Responds in 4-6 weeks to queries; 4-6 weeks to mss. Sample copy free with SAE and 5 first-class stamps. Writer's guidelines free with SASE or by e-mail.

Nonfiction: Book excerpts, essays, how-to, inspirational, interview/profile, opinion, personal experience. **Buys 90 mss/year.** Query or send complete ms. Length: 300-1,000 words. **Pays $10.** Reviews contact sheets. Offers no additional payment for photos accepted with ms. Identification of subjects required.

Columns/Departments: Speaker's Corner (speaking), 650-1,000 words. **Buys 11 mss/year.** Query. **Pays $10.**

Poetry: Free verse, light verse, traditional. **Buys 11 poems/year.** Submit maximum 3 poems. Contact: Gretchen Sousa, poetry editor (gretloriat@earthlink.net) Length: 4-20 lines. **Pays $5.** Anecdotes, facts, newsbreaks, short humor. **Buys 10-30/year.** Length: 50-300 words. **Pays $10.**

Tips: "We primarily use 'how to' articles, personal experience articles, and personality features on experienced writers and editors. However, we're willing to look at any other pieces or fillers geared to the writing life."

$ CHURCH EDUCATOR, Educational Ministries, Inc., 165 Plaza Dr., Prescott AZ 86303. (520)771-8601. Fax: (520)771-8621. E-mail: edmin2@aol.com. **Contact:** Linda Davidson, editor. **95% freelance written.** Monthly magazine covering resources for Christian educators. "*Church Educator* has programming ideas for the Christian educator in the mainline Protestant church. We are *not* on the conservative, fundamental side theologically, so slant articles to the liberal side. Programs should offer lots of questions and not give pat answers." Estab. 1978. Circ. 4,500. Pays 60 days after publication. Publishes ms an average of 2 months after acceptance. Byline given. Buys first rights. Editorial lead time 3 months. Submit seasonal material 7 months in advance. Accepts queries by mail, e-mail, fax, phone. Accepts simultaneous submissions. Responds in 2 weeks to queries; 4 months to mss. Sample copy for 9×12 SAE and 4 first-class stamps. Writer's guidelines free.

Nonfiction: How-to, religious. Special issues: How to recruit volunteers; Nurturing faith development of children. No testimonials. **Buys 200 mss/year.** Send complete ms. Length: 500-2,000 words. **Pays 3¢/word.**

Fiction: Religious. "No 'How God Saved My Life' or 'How God Answers Prayers.'" **Buys 10 mss/year.** Send complete ms. Length: 500-1,500 words. **Pays 3¢/word.**

Tips: "We are always looking for material on the seasons of the church year: Advent, Lent, Pentecost, Epiphany. Write up a program for one of those seasons directed toward children, youth, adults or intergenerational."

$ CREATOR MAGAZINE, Bimonthly magazine of Balanced Music Ministries, P.O. Box 480, Healdsburg CA 95448. (707)837-9071. E-mail: creator@creatormagazine.com. **Contact:** Rod Ellis, editor. **35% freelance written.** Bimonthly magazine. "Most readers are church music directors and worship leaders. Content focuses on the spectrum of worship styles from praise and worship to traditional to liturgical. All denominations subscribe. Articles on worship, choir rehearsal, handbells, children's/youth choirs, technique, relationships, etc." Estab. 1978. Circ. 6,000. Pays on publication. Publishes ms an average of 3 months after acceptance. Byline given. Buys first, one-time, second serial (reprint) rights. Occasionally buys no rights. Editorial lead time 3 months. Submit seasonal material 4 months in advance. Accepts queries by mail. Accepts simultaneous submissions. Sample copy for 9×12 SAE and 5 first-class stamps. Writer's guidelines free.

Nonfiction: Essays, how-to (be a better church musician, choir director, rehearsal technician, etc.), humor (short personal perspectives), inspirational, interview/profile (call first), new product (call first), opinion, personal experience, photo feature, religious, technical (choral technique). Special issues: July/August is directed toward adult choir members, rather than directors. **Buys 20 mss/year.** Query or send complete ms. Length: 1,000-10,000 words. **Pays $30-75 for assigned articles; $30-60 for unsolicited articles.** Pays expenses of writers on assignment.

Photos: State availability of or send photos with submission. Reviews negatives, 8×10 prints. Buys one-time rights. Offers no additional payment for photos accepted with ms. Captions required.

Columns/Departments: Hints & Humor (music ministry short ideas, anecdotes [cute] ministry experience), 75-250 words; Inspiration (motivational ministry stories), 200-500 words; Children/Youth (articles about specific choirs), 1,000-5,000 words. **Buys 15 mss/year.** Query or send complete ms. **Pays $20-60.**

▣ The online magazine carries original content not found in the print edition.

Tips: "Request guidelines and stick to them. If theme is relevant and guidelines are followed, we'll probably publish."

$ CROSS & QUILL, The Christian Writers Newsletter, Christian Writers Fellowship International, 1624 Jefferson Davis Rd., Clinton SC 29325-6401. (864)697-6035. E-mail: cwfi@cwfi-online.org. Website: www.cwfi-online.org. **Contact:** Sandy Brooks, editor/publisher. **75% freelance written.** Bimonthly journal featuring information and encouragement for writers. "We serve Christian writers and others in Christian publishing. We like informational and how-to articles." Estab. 1976. Circ. 1,000. Pays on publication. Publishes ms an average of 6 months after acceptance. Byline given. Buys first, second serial (reprint) rights. Editorial lead time 6 months. Submit seasonal material 6 months in advance. Accepts queries by mail. Responds in 2 weeks to queries; 2 months to mss. Sample copy for $2 with 9×11 SAE and 2 first-class stamps. Writer's guidelines for #10 SASE.

- Break in by writing "good informational, substantive how-to articles. Right now we're particularly looking for articles on juvenile writing and owning and operating writers groups—successes and learning experiences; also organizing and operating writers workshops and conferences."

Nonfiction: How-to, humor, inspirational, interview/profile, new product, technical. **Buys 25 mss/year.** Send complete ms. Length: 300-800 words. **Pays $10-25.** Sometimes pays in contributor copies or other premiums for fillers, poetry.

Photos: State availability with submission.

Poetry: Free verse, haiku, light verse, traditional. **Buys 6 poems/year.** Submit maximum 3 poems. Length: 12 lines. **Pays $5.**

Tips: "Study guidelines and follow them. No philosophical, personal reflection or personal experiences."

$ $ GROUP MAGAZINE, Group Publishing, Inc., 1515 Cascade Ave., Loveland CO 80538. (970)669-3836. Fax: (970)679-4372. E-mail: greditor@grouppublishing.com. Website: www.youthministry.com. Editor: Rick Lawrence. **Contact:** Kathy Dieterich, assistant editor. **50% freelance written.** Bimonthly magazine for Christian youth workers. "*Group* is the interdenominational magazine for leaders of Christian youth groups. *Group*'s purpose is to supply ideas, practical help, inspiration and training for youth leaders." Estab. 1974. Circ. 55,000. **Pays on acceptance.** Byline sometimes given. Buys all rights. Editorial lead time 4 months. Submit seasonal material 5 months in advance. Accepts queries by mail, e-mail, fax. Responds in 6 weeks to queries; 2 months to mss. Sample copy for $2 plus 10×12 SAE and 3 first-class stamps. Writer's guidelines for #10 SASE.

Nonfiction: Inspirational, personal experience, religious. No fiction. **Buys 30 mss/year.** Query. Length: 175-2,000 words. **Pays $125-300.** Sometimes pays expenses of writers on assignment.

Columns/Departments: Try This One (short ideas for group use), 300 words; Hands-On-Help (tips for youth leaders), 175 words; Strange But True (profiles remarkable youth ministry experience), 500 words. **Pays $40.**

$ KIDS' MINISTRY IDEAS, Review and Herald Publishing Association, 55 W. Oak Ridge Dr., Hagerstown MD 21740. (301)393-4115. Fax: (301)393-4055. E-mail: kidsmin@rhpa.org. Managing Editor: Tamara Michelenko Terry. **Contact:** Patricia Fritz, editor. **95% freelance written.** "A quarterly resource for those leading children to Jesus, *Kids' Ministry Ideas* provides affirmation, pertinent and informative articles, program ideas, resource suggestions, and answers to questions from a Seventh-day Adventist Christian perspective." Estab. 1991. Circ. 5,000. **Pays on acceptance.** Publishes ms an average of 3 months after acceptance. Byline given. Offers variable kill fee. Buys first North American serial, electronic rights. Editorial lead time 3 months. Submit seasonal material 3 months in advance. Accepts queries by mail, e-mail, fax. Responds in 3 weeks to queries; 3 months to mss. Sample copy and writer's guidelines free.

Nonfiction: Inspirational, new product (related to children's ministry), articles fitting the mission of *Kids' Ministry Ideas*. **Buys 40-60 mss/year.** Send complete ms. Length: 300-1,000 words. **Pays $100 for assigned articles; $80 for unsolicited articles.**

Photos: State availability with submission. Buys one-time rights. Captions required.

Columns/Departments: Buys 20-30 mss/year. Query. **Pays $30-100.**

Tips: "Request writers' guidelines and a sample issue."

$ $ LEADERSHIP, A Practical Journal for Church Leaders, Christianity Today International, 465 Gundersen Dr., Carol Stream IL 60188. (630)260-6200. Fax: (630)260-0114. E-mail: ljeditor@leadershipjournal.net. Website: www.leadershipjournal.net. Editor: Marshall Shelley. Managing Editor: Eric Reed. **Contact:** Dawn Zemke, editorial coordinator. **75% freelance written.** Works with a small number of new/unpublished writers each year. Quarterly magazine. Writers must have a "knowledge of and sympathy for the unique expectations placed on pastors and local church leaders. Each article must support points by illustrating from real life experiences in local churches." Estab. 1980. Circ. 65,000. **Pays on acceptance.** Publishes ms an average of 6 months after acceptance. Byline given. Offers 33% kill fee. Buys first, electronic rights. Editorial lead time 6 months. Submit seasonal material 6 months in advance. Accepts queries by mail, e-mail, fax. Responds in 3 weeks to queries; 2 months to mss. Sample copy for $5 or online. Writer's guidelines free with SASE or online.

Nonfiction: How-to, humor, interview/profile, personal experience, Sermon Illustrations. "No articles from writers who have never read our journal." **Buys 60 mss/year.** Query. Length: 300-3,000 words. **Pays $35-400.** Sometimes pays expenses of writers on assignment.

Photos: Send photos with submission. Reviews contact sheets. Buys one-time rights. Offers $25-250/photo. Captions, identification of subjects, model releases required.

Columns/Departments: Eric Reed, managing editor. Growing Edge (book/software reviews); Ministry Staff (stories from church staffers), both 500 words. **Buys 8 mss/year.** Query. **Pays $100-200.**

Tips: "Every article in *Leadership* must provide practical help for problems that church leaders face. *Leadership* articles are not essays expounding a topic or editorials arguing a position or homilies explaining biblical principles. They are how-to articles, based on first-person accounts of real-life experiences in ministry. They allow our readers to see 'over the shoulder' of a colleague in ministry who then reflects on those experiences and identifies the lessons learned. As you know, a magazine's slant is a specific personality that readers expect (and it's what they've sent us their subscription money to provide). Our style is that of friendly conversation rather than directive discourse—what I learned about local church ministry rather than what you need to do."

N $ MOMENTUM, Official Journal of the National Catholic Educational Association, National Catholic Educational Association, 1077 30th St. NW, Suite 100, Washington DC 20007-3852. (202)337-6232. Fax: (202)333-6706. E-mail: momentum@ncea.org. Website: www.ncea.org. **Contact:** Brian E. Gray, editor. **65% freelance written.** Quarterly educational journal covering educational issues in Catholic schools, parishes and private schools. "*Momentum* is a membership journal of the National Catholic Educational Association. The audience is educators and administrators in Catholic and private schools K-12, and parish programs." Estab. 1970. Circ. 28,000. Pays on publication. Publishes ms an average of 3 months after acceptance. Byline given. Buys first rights. Accepts queries by e-mail. Sample copy for $5 SASE and 8 first-class stamps. Writer's guidelines free.

Nonfiction: Educational trends, issues, research. No articles unrelated to educational and catechesis issues. **Buys 40-60 mss/year.** Query and send complete ms. Length: 1,500 words. **Pays $75 maximum.**

Photos: State availability with submission. Reviews Prints. Offers no additional payment for photos accepted with ms. Captions, identification of subjects required.

Columns/Departments: From the Field (practical application in classroom), 700 words; Justice and Peace Education (examples); DRE Direction (parish catechesis), all 900 words. **Buys 10 mss/year.** Query and send complete ms. **Pays $50.**

$ PASTORAL LIFE, Society of St. Paul, P.O. Box 595, Canfield OH 44406-0595. (330)533-5503. Fax: (330)533-1076. E-mail: plmagazine@hotmail.com. Website: www.albahouse.org. **Contact:** Rev. Matthew Roehrig, editor. **66% freelance written.** Works with new/unpublished writers. "Monthly magazine designed to focus on the current problems, needs, issues and all important activities related to all phases of Catholic pastoral work and life." Estab. 1953. Circ. 2,000. Pays on publication. Publishes ms an average of 4 months after acceptance. Byline given. Buys first rights. Accepts queries by mail, e-mail, fax, phone. Responds in 1 month to queries. Sample copy and writer's guidelines for 6×9 SAE and 4 first-class stamps.

Nonfiction: "*Pastoral Life* is a professional review, principally designed to focus attention on current problems, needs, issues and important activities related to all phases of pastoral work and life." **Buys 30 unsolicited mss/year.** Query with outline before submitting ms. Length: 1,000-3,500 words. **Pays 4¢/word minimum.**

Tips: "Articles should have application for priests and Christian leadership to help them in their ministries and lives."

$ $ THE PRIEST, Our Sunday Visitor, Inc., 200 Noll Plaza, Huntington IN 46750-4304. (260)356-8400. Fax: (260)356-8472. E-mail: tpriest@osv.com. Website: www.osv.com. Editor: Msg. Owen F. Campion. **Contact:** Murray Hubley, associate editor. **55% freelance written.** Monthly magazine. "We run articles that will aid priests in their day-to-day ministry. Includes items on spirituality, counseling, administration, theology, personalities, the saints, etc." **Pays on acceptance.** Byline given. Buys first North American serial rights. Editorial lead time 3 months. Submit seasonal material 4 months in advance. Accepts queries by mail, e-mail, fax, phone. Responds in 5 weeks to queries; 3 months to mss. Sample copy and writer's guidelines free.

Nonfiction: Essays, historical/nostalgic, humor, inspirational, interview/profile, opinion, personal experience, photo feature, religious. **Buys 96 mss/year.** Send complete ms. Length: 1,500-5,000 words. **Pays $200 minimum for assigned articles; $50 minimum for unsolicited articles.**

Photos: Send photos with submission. Reviews transparencies, prints. Buys one-time rights. Negotiates payment individually. Captions, identification of subjects required.

Columns/Departments: Viewpoint (whatever applies to priests and the Church), 1,000 words. **Buys 36 mss/year.** Send complete ms. **Pays $50-100.**

Tips: "Say what you have to say in an interesting and informative manner and stop. Freelancers are most often published in 'Viewpoints.' Please do not stray from the magisterium of the Catholic Church."

$ $ REV., Group Publishing, Inc., 1515 Cascade Ave., Loveland CO 80538-8681. (970)669-3836. Fax: (970)679-4392. E-mail: rector@onlinerev.com. Website: www.onlinerev.com. Editor: Paul Allen. **Contact:** Kristi Rector, associate editor. **25% freelance written.** Bimonthly magazine for pastors. "We offer practical solutions to revolutionize and revitalize ministry." Estab. 1997. Circ. 30,000. **Pays on acceptance.** Publishes ms an average of 6 months after acceptance. Byline given. Makes work-for-hire assignments. Editorial lead time 6 months. Submit seasonal material 8 months in advance. Accepts queries by mail, e-mail. Responds in 2 months to queries. Writer's guidelines for #10 SASE or online.

O→ Break in with short, practical department pieces.

Nonfiction: Ministry, leadership and personal articles with practical application. "No devotions, articles for church members, theological pieces." **Buys 18-24 mss/year.** Query or send complete ms. Length: 1,800-2,000 words. **Pays $300-400.**

Columns/Departments: Preaching & Teaching (preparation & techniques); Worship (all aspects of the worship service); Personal Growth (personal or spiritual growth); Team Work (working with staff and volunteer leaders); Family Ministry (helping families including singles and elderly); Outreach (local and missions); Discipleship (small groups and one-on-one); Current Trends (trends that affect the church), Home Front (pastor's family), Church Biz (leadership and administration), all 250-300 words. **Buys 25 mss/year.** Send complete ms. **Pays $35-50.**

Fillers: Cartoons. **Buys 12/year. Pays $50.**

Tips: "We're most open to submissions for our departments. Remember that we focus on practical articles with an edgy tone."

$ TEACHERS INTERACTION, Concordia Publishing House 3558 S. Jefferson Ave., St. Louis MO 63118-3968. (314)268-1083. Fax: (314)268-1329. E-mail: tom.nummela@cph.org. Editorial Associate: Jean Muser. **Contact:** Tom Nummela, editor. **20% freelance written.** Quarterly magazine of practical, inspirational, theological articles for volunteer Sunday school teachers. Material must be true to the doctrines of the Lutheran Church—Missouri Synod. Estab. 1960. Circ. 12,000. Pays on publication. Publishes ms an average of 1 year after acceptance. Byline given. Buys all rights. Submit seasonal material 1 year in advance. Accepts queries by mail, e-mail, fax. Responds in 3 months to mss. Sample copy for $3.99. Writer's guidelines for #10 SASE.

Nonfiction: How-to (practical help/ideas used successfully in own classroom), inspirational, personal experience (of a Sunday School classroom nature—growth). No theological articles. **Buys 6 mss/year.** Send complete ms. Length: 1,200 words. **Pays up to $110.**

Fillers: "*Teachers Interaction* buys short Interchange items—activities and ideas planned and used successfully in a church school classroom." **Buys 48/year.** Length: 200 words maximum. **Pays $20.**

Tips: "Practical or 'it happened to me' experiences articles would have the best chance. Also short items—ideas used in classrooms; seasonal and in conjunction with our Sunday school material, Our Life in Christ. Our format emphasizes volunteer Sunday school teachers."

$ $ TODAY'S CATHOLIC TEACHER, The Voice of Catholic Education, Peter Li Education Group, 2621 Dryden Rd., Suite 300, Dayton OH 45439. (937)293-1415. Fax: (937)293-1310. E-mail: mnoschang@peterli.com. Website: www.catholicteacher.com. **Contact:** Mary C. Noschang, editor. **60% freelance written.** Magazine published 6 times/year during school year covering Catholic education for grades K-12. "We look for topics of interest and practical help to teachers in Catholic elementary schools in all curriculum areas including religion technology, discipline, motivation." Estab. 1972. Circ. 50,000. Pays on publication. Publishes ms an average of 2 months after acceptance. Byline given. first and all rights and makes work-for-hire assignments Editorial lead time 3 months. Submit seasonal material 6 months in advance. Accepts queries by mail, e-mail, fax. Accepts simultaneous submissions. Responds in 1 month to queries; 3 months to mss. Sample copy for $3 or on website. Writer's guidelines online.

Nonfiction: Interested in articles detailing ways to incorporate Catholic values into academic subjects other than religion class. Essays, how-to, humor, interview/profile, personal experience. "No articles pertaining to public education." **Buys 15 mss/year.** Query or send complete ms. Length: 1,500-3,000 words. **Pays $150-300.** Sometimes pays expenses of writers on assignment.
Photos: State availability with submission. Reviews transparencies, prints. Buys one-time rights. Offers $20-50/photo. Captions, identification of subjects, model releases required.
Tips: "Although our readership is primarily classroom teachers, *Today's Catholic Teacher* is read also by principals, supervisors, superintendents, boards of education, pastors, and parents. *Today's Catholic Teacher* aims to be for Catholic educators a source of information not available elsewhere. The focus of articles should span the interests of teachers from early childhood through junior high. Articles may be directed to just one age group yet have wider implications. Preference is given to material directed to teachers in grades four through eight. The desired magazine style is direct, concise, informative and accurate. Writing should be enjoyable to read, informal rather than scholarly, lively, and free of educational jargon."

$WORLD PULSE, Evangelism and Missions Information Service/Wheaton College, P.O. Box 794, Wheaton IL 60189. (630)752-7158. Fax: (630)752-7155. E-mail: pulsenews@aol.com. **Contact:** Managing Editor. **60% freelance written.** Semimonthly newsletter covering mission news and trends. "We provide current information about evangelical Christian missions and churches around the world. Most articles are news-oriented, although we do publish some features and interviews." Estab. 1965. Circ. 5,000. Pays on publication. Publishes ms an average of 2 months after acceptance. Byline given. Buys first, all rights. Editorial lead time 2 months. Accepts queries by mail, e-mail, fax, phone. Responds in 2 weeks to queries; 1 month to mss. Sample copy and writer's guidelines free.

O→ Break in with "coverage of the subjects requested, bringing to the task both the topic's essential components, but with a dash of style, as well."

Nonfiction: Interview/profile, photo feature, religious, technical. Does not want anything that does not cover the world of evangelical missions. **Buys 50-60 mss/year.** Query with published clips. Length: 300-1,000 words. **Pays $25-100.** Sometimes pays expenses of writers on assignment.
Photos: Send photos with submission. Reviews contact sheets. Buys all rights. Negotiates payment individually. Identification of subjects required.
Tips: "Have a knowledge of and appreciation for the evangelical missions community, as well as for cross-cultural issues. Writing must be economical, with a judicious use of quotes and examples."

$ $YOUR CHURCH, Helping You With the Business of Ministry, Christianity Today, Inc., 465 Gundersen Dr., Carol Stream IL 60188. (630)260-6200. Fax: (630)260-0114. E-mail: yceditor@yourchurch.net. Website: www.yourchurch.net. **Contact:** Cynthia Thomas, editorial coordinator. **80% freelance written.** Bimonthly magazine. "Articles pertain to the business aspects of ministry pastors are called upon to perform: administration, purchasing, management, technology, building, etc." Estab. 1955. Circ. 150,000. **Pays on acceptance.** Publishes ms an average of 4 months after acceptance. Byline given. Buys one-time rights. Submit seasonal material 5 months in advance. Accepts queries by mail, e-mail, fax, phone. Accepts simultaneous submissions. Responds in 1 month to queries; 2 months to mss. Sample copy and writer's guidelines for 9×12 SAE with 5 first-class stamps.
Nonfiction: How-to, new product, technical. Special issues: Church Management, Construction. **Buys 25 mss/year.** Send complete ms. Length: 900-1,500 words. **Pays about 15¢/word.**
Reprints: Send photocopy and information about when and where the material previously appeared. Pays 30% of the amount paid for an original article.
Photos: State availability with submission. Reviews 4×5 transparencies, 5×7 or 8×10 prints. Buys one-time rights. Offers no additional payment for photos accepted with ms. Captions, identification of subjects, model releases required.
Tips: "The editorial is generally geared toward brief and helpful articles dealing with some form of church business. Concise, bulleted points from experts in the field are typical for our articles."

$YOUTH AND CHRISTIAN EDUCATION LEADERSHIP, Pathway Press, 1080 Montgomery Ave., P.O. Box 2250, Cleveland TN 37320-2250. (423)478-7599. Fax: (423)478-7616. E-mail: Ann.Steely@PathwayPress.org. Editor: Tony P. Lane. **Contact:** Ann Steely, editorial assistant. **25% freelance written.** Quarterly magazine covering Christian education. "*Youth and Christian Education Leadership* is written for teachers, youth pastors, children's pastors, and other local Christian education workers." Estab. 1976. Circ. 10,000. **Pays on acceptance.** Publishes ms an average of 6 months after acceptance. Buys one-time rights. Editorial lead time 6 months. Submit seasonal material 6 months in advance. Accepts queries by mail, e-mail. Accepts simultaneous submissions. Responds in 3 months to mss. Sample copy for $1 and 9×12 SASE. Writer's guidelines free.
Nonfiction: How-to, humor (in-class experience), inspirational, interview/profile, motivational; seasonal short skits. **Buys 16 mss/year.** Send complete ms; include SSN. Send SASE for return of ms. Length: 400-1,200 words. **$25-45.**
Reprints: Send typed, double-spaced ms with rights for sale noted and information about when and where the material previously appeared. Pays 80% of amount paid for an original article.
Photos: State availability with submission. Reviews contact sheets, transparencies. Buys one-time rights. Negotiates payment individually.
Columns/Departments: Sunday School Leadership, Reaching Out (creative evangelism), The Pastor and Christian Education, Preschool, Elementary, Teen, Adult, Drawing Closer, Kids Church; all 500 words. Send complete ms with SASE. **Pays $25-45.**

Tips: "Become familiar with the publication's content and submit appropriate material. We are continually looking for 'fresh ideas' that have proven to be successful."

CLOTHING

N **BOBBIN**, 1500 Hampton St., Suite 150, Columbia SC 29201. (803)771-7500. Fax: (803)799-1461. Website: www.bobbin.com. Editor-in-Chief: Kathleen DesMarteau. **25% freelance written.** Monthly magazine for CEO's and top management in apparel and soft goods businesses including manufacturers and retailers. Circ. 19,000. Pays on receipt of article. Byline given. Buys all rights. Responds in 2 weeks to queries. Sample copy for free. Writer's guidelines free.
Columns/Departments: R&D; Winning Strategies; International Watch; Best Practices; Retail Strategies; Production Solutions.
Tips: "Articles should be written in a style appealing to busy top managers and should in some way foster thought or new ideas, or present solutions/alternatives to common industry problems/concerns. CEOs are most interested in quick read pieces that are also informative and substantive. Articles should not be based on opinions but should be developed through interviews with industry manufacturers, retailers or other experts, etc. Sidebars may be included to expand upon certain aspects within the article. If available, illustrations, graphs/charts, or photographs should accompany the article."

$ $ EMB-EMBROIDERY/MONOGRAM BUSINESS, VNU Business Publications, 1115 Northmeadows Pkwy., Roswell GA 30076. (800)241-9034. Fax: (770)569-5105. E-mail: mtalkington@embmag.com. Website: www.embmag.com. **Contact:** Mario Talkington, senior editor. **30% freelance written.** Monthly magazine covering computerized embroidery and digitizing design. "Readable, practical business and/or technical articles that show our readers how to succeed in their profession." Estab. 1994. Circ. 26,000. **Pays on acceptance.** Publishes ms an average of 3 months after acceptance. Byline given. Buys all rights. Editorial lead time 3 months. Submit seasonal material 6 months in advance. Accepts queries by mail, e-mail. Accepts simultaneous submissions. Sample copy for $10. Writer's guidelines not available.
Nonfiction: How-to (embroidery, sales, marketing, design, general business info), interview/profile, new product, photo feature, technical (computerized embroidery). **Buys 4-6 mss/year.** Query. Length: 800-2,000 words. **Pays $200 and up for assigned articles.**
Photos: Send photos with submission. Reviews transparencies, Prints. Negotiates payment individually.
Tips: "Show us you have specified knowledge, experience or contacts in the embroidery industry or a related field."

$ $ MADE TO MEASURE, Halper Publishing Company, 830 Moseley Rd., Highland Park IL 60035. (847)780-2900. Fax: (847)780-2902. E-mail: mtm@halper.com. Website: www.halper.com. **Contact:** Rick Levine, editor/publisher. **50% freelance written.** Semiannual magazine covering uniforms and career apparel. "A semi-annual magazine/buyers' reference containing leading sources of supply, equipment and services of every description related to the Uniform, Career Apparel, and allied trades, throughout the entire U.S." Estab. 1930. Circ. 25,000. **Pays on acceptance.** Publishes ms an average of 2 months after acceptance. Byline given. Buys first North American serial rights. Editorial lead time 4 months. Submit seasonal material 4 months in advance. Accepts queries by mail, e-mail. Accepts simultaneous submissions. Responds in 3 weeks to queries. Sample copy free or online at website.
Nonfiction: "Please only consider sending queries related to stories to companies that wear or make uniforms, career apparel or identifying apparel." Historical/nostalgic, interview/profile, new product, personal experience, photo feature, technical. **Buys 12-15 mss/year.** Query with published clips. Length: 1,000-3,000 words. **Pays $400-1,200.** Sometimes pays expenses of writers on assignment.
Photos: State availability with submission. Reviews contact sheets, any prints. Buys one-time rights. Negotiates payment individually.
Tips: "We look for features about large and small companies who wear uniforms (restaurants, hotels, industrial, medical, public safety, etc.)."

N **$ $ TEXTILE WORLD**, (formerly *ATI*), Billian Publishing Co., 2100 Powers Ferry Rd., Atlanta GA 30339. (770)955-5656. Fax: (770)952-0669. Website: www.textileindustries.com. **Contact:** Rachel Dunn, associate editor. **10% freelance written.** Monthly magazine covering "the business of textile, apparel and fiber industries with considerable technical focus on products and processes. No puff pieces pushing a particular product." Estab. 1887. Pays on publication. Byline given. Buys first North American serial rights.
Nonfiction: Technical, business. **Buys 10 mss/year.** Query. Length: 500 words minimum. **Pays $200/published page.**
Photos: Send photos with submission. Reviews prints. Buys one-time rights. Offers no additional payment for photos accepted with ms. Captions required.

CONFECTIONERY & SNACK FOODS

These publications focus on the bakery, snack, and candy industries. Journals for grocers, wholesalers, and other food industry personnel are listed in Groceries & Food Products.

$ $ PACIFIC BAKERS NEWS, 3155 Lynde St., Oakland CA 94601. (510)532-5513. **Contact:** C.W. Soward, publisher. **30% freelance written.** Eager to work with new/unpublished writers. Monthly newsletter for commercial bakeries in the western states. Estab. 1961. Pays on publication. No byline given; uses only 1-paragraph news items.

Nonfiction: Uses bakery business reports and news about bakers. Buys only brief "boiled-down news items about bakers and bakeries operating only in Alaska, Hawaii, Pacific Coast and Rocky Mountain states. We welcome clippings. We need monthly news reports and clippings about the baking industry and the donut business." No pictures, jokes, poetry or cartoons. Length: 10-200 words. **Pays 10¢/word for news and 6¢/word for clips.**

CONSTRUCTION & CONTRACTING

Builders, architects, and contractors learn the latest industry news in these publications. Journals targeted to architects are also included in the Consumer Art & Architecture category. Those for specialists in the interior aspects of construction are listed under Building Interiors.

$ $ ADVANCED MATERIALS & COMPOSITES NEWS AND COMPOSITES eNEWS, International Business & Technology Intelligence on High Performance M&P, Composites Worldwide Inc., 991C Lomas Santa Fe Dr., MC469, Solana Beach CA 92075-2141. (858)755-1372. Fax: (858)755-5271. E-mail: info@compositesnews.com. Website: www.compositesnews.com. Managing Editor: Susan Loud. **Contact:** Steve Loud, editor. **5% freelance written.** Bimonthly newsletter covering advanced materials and fiber-reinforced composites. *Advanced Materials and Composites News* "covers markets, materials, processes and organization for all sectors of the global hi-tech materials world. Audience is management, academics, government, suppliers and fabricators. Focus on news about growth opportunities." Estab. 1978. Circ. 10,000. Pays on publication. Publishes ms an average of 1 months after acceptance. Byline sometimes given. Buys all rights. Editorial lead time 2 weeks. Submit seasonal material 3 months in advance. Accepts queries by e-mail. Responds in 1 week to queries; 1 month to mss. Sample copy for #10 SASE. Writer's guidelines not available.
Nonfiction: New product, technical. **Buys 4-6 mss/year.** Query. Length: 100-700 words. **Pays $100-400.**
Photos: State availability with submission. Reviews 4×5 transparencies, prints, 35mm slides, JPEGs. Buys all rights. Offers no additional payment for photos accepted with ms. Captions, identification of subjects, model releases required.

$ $ AUTOMATED BUILDER, CMN Associates, Inc., 1445 Donlon St., Suite 16, Ventura CA 93003. (805)642-9735. Fax: (805)642-8820. E-mail: info@automatedbuilder.com. Website: www.automatedbuilder.com. Editor-in-Chief: Don Carlson. **Contact:** Bob Mendel. **10% freelance written.** Monthly magazine specializing in management for industrialized (manufactured) housing and volume home builders. "Our material is technical in content, and concerned with new technologies or improved methods for in-plant building and components related to building. Online content is uploaded from the monthly print material." Estab. 1964. Circ. 25,000. **Pays on acceptance.** Publishes ms an average of 3 months after acceptance. Byline given. Buys first North American serial rights. Editorial lead time 2 months. Submit seasonal material 2 months in advance. Accepts queries by mail, e-mail, fax. Responds in 2 weeks to queries. Sample copy for free.
Nonfiction: Case history articles on successful home building companies which may be 1) production (big volume) home builders; 2) mobile home manufacturers; 3) modular home manufacturers; 4) prefabricated (panelized) home manufacturers; 5) house component manufacturers; or 6) special unit (in-plant commercial building) manufacturers. Also uses interviews, photo features and technical articles. "No architect or plan 'dreams'. Housing projects must be built or under construction." **Buys 6-8 mss/year.** Query. Phone queries OK. Length: 250-500 words. **Pays $300.**
Photos: State availability with submission. Reviews 35mm or larger—35mm preferred transparencies, Wants 4×5, 5×7 or 8×10 glossies. No additional payment. Captions, identification of subjects required.
Tips: "Stories often are too long, too loose; we prefer 500 to 750 words. We prefer a phone query on feature articles. If accepted on query, article usually will not be rejected later."

$ $ CAM MAGAZINE, Construction Association of Michigan, 43636 S. Woodward, Bloomfield Hills MI 48302-3204. (248)972-1000. Fax: (248)972-1001. E-mail: brooks@cam-online.com. Website: www.cam-online.com. **Contact:** Phyllis L. Brooks, editor. **5% freelance written.** Monthly magazine covering all facets of the construction industry. "*CAM Magazine* is devoted to the growth and progress of individuals and companies serving and servicing the industry. It provides a forum on new construction-related technology, products and services, plus publishes information on industry personnel changes and advancements." Estab. 1978. Circ. 5,000. Pays on publication. Byline given. Buys all rights. Editorial lead time 2 months. Submit seasonal material 3 months in advance. Accepts queries by mail, e-mail, fax, phone. Sample copy and editorial subject calendar with query and SASE.
Nonfiction: Construction-related only. **Buys 3 mss/year.** Query with published clips. Length: Features: 1,000-2,000 words; will also review short pieces. **Pays $250-500.**
Photos: Send photos with submission. Reviews contact sheets, negatives, transparencies, Color or b&w prints. Buys one-time rights. Offers no additional payment for photos accepted with ms.
Tips: "Anyone having *current* knowledge or expertise on trends and innovations related to construction is welcome to submit articles. Our readers are construction experts."

$ $ CONCRETE CONSTRUCTION, Hanley-Wood, LLC., 426 S. Westgate St., Addison IL 60101. (630)543-0870. Fax: (630)543-5399. E-mail: cceditor@hanley-wood.com. Website: www.worldofconcrete.com. Editor: William Palmer. **Contact:** Pat Reband, managing editor. **20% freelance written.** Monthly magazine for concrete contractors, engineers, architects, specifiers and others who design and build residential, commercial, industrial and public works, cast-in-place concrete structures. It also covers job stories and new equipment in the industry. Estab. 1956. Circ. 80,000.

Pays on acceptance. Publishes ms an average of 4 months after acceptance. Byline given. Editorial lead time 4 months. Submit seasonal material 4 months in advance. Accepts queries by mail, e-mail, fax. Responds in 2 weeks to queries; 1 month to mss. Sample copy for free. Writer's guidelines free.

Nonfiction: How-to, new product, personal experience, photo feature, technical, job stories. **Buys 7-10 mss/year.** Query with published clips. Length: 2,000 words maximum. **Pays $250 or more for assigned articles; $200 minimum for unsolicited articles.** Pays expenses of writers on assignment.

Photos: Send photos with submission. Reviews contact sheets, negatives, transparencies, prints. Buys one-time rights. Offers no additional payment for photos accepted with ms. Captions required.

Tips: "Have a good understanding of the concrete construction industry. How-to stories accepted only from industry experts. Job stories must cover procedures, materials, and equipment used as well as the project's scope."

$ $ $ THE CONCRETE PRODUCER, Hanley-Wood LLC, 426 S. Westgate St., Addison IL 60101. (630)705-2601. Fax: (630)543-3112. E-mail: ryelton@hanley-wood.com. Website: www.worldofconcrete.com. **Contact:** Rick Yelton, editor. **30% freelance written.** Monthly magazine covering concrete production. "Our audience consists of producers who have succeeded in making concrete the preferred building material through management, operating, quality control, use of the latest technology, or use of superior materials." Estab. 1982. Circ. 18,000. **Pays on acceptance.** Publishes ms an average of 2 months after acceptance. Byline given. Buys second serial (reprint) rights. Editorial lead time 4 months. Accepts queries by mail, e-mail, fax, phone. Responds in 1 week to queries; 2 months to mss. Sample copy for $4. Writer's guidelines free.

Nonfiction: How-to (promote concrete), new product, technical. **Buys 10 mss/year.** Send complete ms. Length: 500-2,000 words. **Pays $200-1,000.** Sometimes pays expenses of writers on assignment.

Photos: Scan photos at 300 dpi. State availability with submission. Reviews transparencies, prints. Offers no additional payment for photos accepted with ms. Captions, identification of subjects required.

$ CONSTRUCTION EQUIPMENT GUIDE, 470 Maryland St., Ft. Washington PA 19034. (800)523-2200 or (215)885-2900. Fax: (215)885-2910. E-mail: editorial@constructionequipguide.com. **Contact:** Craig Mongeau, editor-in-chief. **30% freelance written.** Biweekly newspaper. "We are looked at as the primary source of information in the construction industry by equipment manufacturers, sellers and users. We cover the Midwest, Northeast, Southwest and Southeast states with our 4 editions published biweekly. We give the latest news on current construction projects, legislative actions, political issues, mergers and acquisitions, new unique applications of equipment and in-depth features." Estab. 1957. Circ. 120,000. Pays on publication. Publishes ms an average of 1 month after acceptance. Byline given. Buys all rights. Accepts queries by mail, e-mail, fax, phone. Sample copy for free. Writer's guidelines free.

Nonfiction: General interest, historical/nostalgic, how-to (winterizing construction equipment, new methods of construction applications), interview/profile, new product, personal experience, photo feature, technical. **Buys 200-600 mss/year.** Query with published clips. Length: 150-1,200 words. **Negotiates payment individually.**

Photos: Send photos with submission. Negotiates payment individually. Captions, identification of subjects required.

Tips: "Keep an eye out for commercial construction in your area. Take note of the name of the contractors on site. Then give us a call to see if you should follow up with a full story and photos. Pay attention to large and small jobs right around you. Read articles in *Construction Equipment Guide* to learn what information is important to our readers, who are equipment users, sellers and makers."

$ $ EQUIPMENT JOURNAL, Canada's National Equipment Newspaper, 5160 Explorer Dr., Unit 6, Mississauga, Ontario L4W 4T7, Canada. (800)667-8541. Fax: (905)629-7988. E-mail: editor@equipmentjournal.com. Website: www.equipmentjournal.com. **Contact:** Michael Anderson, editor. **10% freelance written.** Journal published 17 times/year covering heavy equipment used in construction, mining and forestry industries. Estab. 1966. Circ. 25,000. Pays on publication. Byline given. Makes work-for-hire assignments. Editorial lead time 1 month. Submit seasonal material 1 month in advance. Accepts queries by mail, e-mail, fax, phone. Accepts simultaneous submissions. Sample copy for free.

Nonfiction: Interview/profile, new product, technical. "No material that falls outside of *EJ*'s mandate—the Canadian equipment industry." **Buys 10 mss/year.** Query. Length: 500-1,000 words. **Pays $200 (Canadian).** Sometimes pays expenses of writers on assignment.

Photos: State availability with submission. Reviews 4×6 prints. Buys all rights. Negotiates payment individually. Identification of subjects required.

Tips: "Provide an idea for a story that is uniquely Canadian."

$ HARD HAT NEWS, Lee Publications, Inc., 6113 State Highway 5, Palatine Bridge NY 13428. (518)673-3237. Fax: (518)673-2381. E-mail: rdecamp@leepub.com. Website: www.leepub.com. **Contact:** Ralph DeCamp, editor. **80% freelance written.** Biweekly tabloid covering heavy construction, equipment, road and bridge work. "Our readers are contractors and heavy construction workers involved in excavation, highways, bridges, utility construction and underground construction." Estab. 1980. Circ. 58,000. Byline given. Editorial lead time 2 weeks. Submit seasonal material 2 weeks in advance. Accepts queries by mail, e-mail, fax, phone. Sample copy and writer's guidelines free.

O→ "We especially need writers with some knowledge of heavy construction, although anyone with good composition and interviewing skills is welcome. Focus on major construction in progress in your area."

Nonfiction: Also 'Job Stories,' (a brief overall description of the project, the names and addresses of the companies and contractors involved, and a description of the equipment used, including manufacturers' names and model numbers.

Quotes from the people in charge, as well as photos, are important, as are the names of the dealers providing the equipment). Interview/profile, new product, opinion, photo feature, technical. Send complete ms. Length: 50-800 words. **Pays $2.50/inch.** Sometimes pays expenses of writers on assignment.
Photos: Send photos with submission. Reviews Prints; Slides. Offers $15/photo. Captions, identification of subjects required.
Columns/Departments: New Products; Association News; Parts and Repairs; Attachments; Trucks and Trailers; People on the Move.
Tips: "Every issue has a focus—see our editorial calender. Special consideration is given to a story that coincides with the focus. A color photo is necessary for the front page. Vertical shots work best. We need more writers in metro NY area. Also, we are expanding our distribution into the Mid-Atlantic states and need writers in Virginia, Tennessee, North Carolina and South Carolina."

$ $ HEAVY EQUIPMENT NEWS, Vulcan Publications, 33 Inverness Center Parkway, Suite 300, Birmingham AL 35243. Fax: (205)380-1384. E-mail: akizzire@vulcanpub.com. Website: www.heavyequipmentnews.com. **Contact:** Ashley Kizzire, editor-in-chief. **30-40% freelance written.** Monthly magazine covering construction equipment and construction industry. "*Heavy Equipment News* is an editorial-driven publication for the construction contractor, focusing on job sites, asphalt-road building, concrete, business management, equipment selection and material handling." Estab. 1995. Circ. 63,000. **Pays on acceptance.** Publishes ms an average of 3 months after acceptance. Byline given. Offers 10% kill fee. Buys first North American serial, second serial (reprint), electronic rights. Editorial lead time 6 months. Submit seasonal material 6 months in advance. Accepts queries by mail, e-mail, fax. Responds in 2 weeks to queries; 1 month to mss. Sample copy for #10 SASE. Writer's guidelines free.
Nonfiction: How-to, interview/profile, new product, personal experience, technical. **Buys 24 mss/year.** Query with published clips. Length: 1,200-1,500 words. **Pays $500.**
Photos: Reviews transparencies, prints. Buys all rights. Offers no additional payment for photos accepted with ms. Captions, identification of subjects required.
Columns/Departments: Asphalt Road, Concrete Batch, The Trenches, In the Field, Technology Report, Business Sense, Point of View, Truck Stop. Query with published clips. **Pays $300.**

N $ $ JOINERS' QUARTERLY, Journal of Timber Framing & Traditional Building, Fox Maple Press, Inc., P.O. Box 249, Brownfield ME 04010. (207)935-3720. E-mail: foxmaple@foxmaple.com. Website: www.foxmaple.com. **Contact:** Steve K. Chappell, editor. **75% freelance written.** Quarterly magazine covering traditional building, timber framing, natural and sustainable construction. Estab. 1982. Circ. 10,000. Pays on publication. Publishes ms an average of 9 months after acceptance. Byline given. Buys all rights. Editorial lead time 9 months. Submit seasonal material 6 months in advance. Accepts queries by mail. Accepts simultaneous submissions. Responds in 1 month to queries; 2 months to mss. Sample copy for $4.50. Writer's guidelines for #10 SASE.
Nonfiction: Historical/nostalgic (building techniques), how-to (timber frame, log build, sustainable materials, straw building), inspirational, new product, technical (alternative building techniques). **Buys 12 mss/year.** Query. Length: 500-2,500 words. **Pays $50/published page.** Sometimes pays expenses of writers on assignment.
Reprints: Send photocopy of article or short story and information about when and where the article previously appeared. Pays 50-100% of amount paid for an original article.
Photos: Send photos with submission. Reviews transparencies, prints. Buys all rights. Offers no additional payment for photos accepted with ms. Identification of subjects required.
Tips: "We're looking for articles on sustainable construction, especially from a timber framing aspect. Architects, builders and owner/builders are our primary readers and writers. We also like to feature natural and historical home building techniques such as straw/clay, roof thatching, sod home, etc. We need clean and concise articles with photos and/or artwork."

$ $ MC MAGAZINE, The Voice of the Manufactured Concrete Products Industry, National Precast Concrete Association, 10333 N. Meridian St., Suite 272, Indianapolis IN 46290. (317)571-9500. Fax: (317)571-0041. E-mail: rhyink@precast.org. Website: www.precast.org. **Contact:** Ron Hyink, managing editor. **75% freelance written.** Quarterly magazine covering manufactured concrete products. "*MC Magazine* is a publication for owners and managers of factories that produce concrete materials used in construction. We publish business articles, technical articles, company profiles, safety articles and project profiles with the intent of educating our readers in order to increase the quality and use of precast concrete." Estab. 1995. Circ. 8,500. **Pays on acceptance.** Publishes ms an average of 6 months after acceptance. Byline given. Buys first North American serial, second serial (reprint), all rights. Editorial lead time 3 months. Accepts queries by mail, e-mail, fax. Accepts simultaneous submissions. Responds in 1 month to queries; 2 months to mss. Sample copy online.
Nonfiction: How-to (business), interview/profile, technical (concrete manufacturing). "No humor, essays, fiction or fillers." **Buys 12-16 mss/year.** Query or send complete ms. Length: 1,500-2,500 words. **Pays $250-700.** Sometimes pays expenses of writers on assignment.
Photos: State availability with submission. Buys all rights. Offers no additional payment for photos accepted with ms. Captions required.
Tips: "Understand the audience and the purpose of the magazine. We have an ongoing need for business-related articles that would be pertinent to small- to mid-sized manufacturers. Understanding audience interests and needs is important and expressing a willingness to tailor a subject to get the right slant is critical. Our primary freelance needs are about general business or technology topics. Of course, if you are an engineer or a writer specializing in industry, construction

or manufacturing technology, other possibilities would certainly exist. Writing style should be concise, yet lively and entertaining. Avoid cliches. We require a third-person perspective, encourage a positive tone and active voice. For stylistic matters, follow the *AP Style Book*."

MICHIGAN CONTRACTOR & BUILDER, CMD Group, 40000 Grand River, Suite 404, Novi MI 48375-2147. (248)471-5811. Fax: (248)471-6103. E-mail: akalousdian@cahners.com. **Contact:** Aram Kalousdian. **25% freelance written.** Weekly magazine covering the commercial construction industry in Michigan (no home building). "*Michigan Contractor & Builder's* audience is contractors, equipment suppliers, engineers and architects. The magazine reports on construction projects in Michigan. It does not cover homebuilding. Stories should focus on news or innovative techniques or materials in construction." Estab. 1907. Circ. 3,700. Pays 30 days after publication. Byline given. Buys all rights. Accepts queries by mail, e-mail, fax, phone. Sample copy for free.

Nonfiction: Michigan construction projects. **Buys 52 mss/year.** Query with published clips. Length: 1,500 words with 5-7 photos. **Payment negotiable.**

Photos: Send photos with submission. Reviews original prints. Buys all rights. Offers no additional payment for photos accepted with ms. Captions required.

$ $ NW BUILDER MAGAZINE, Pacific NW Sales & Marketing, Inc., 500 W. 8th St., Suite 270, Vancouver WA 98660. (360)906-0793. Fax: (360)906-0794. E-mail: mgreditor@nwbuildermagazine.com. Website: www.nwbuildermagazine.com. **Contact:** Curt Hopkins, editor. **10-50% freelance written.** Monthly journal covering NW residential and commercial building. "Articles must address pressing topics for builders in our region with a special emphasis on the business aspects of construction." Estab. 1996. Circ. 25,000. Pays on acceptance of revised ms. Publishes ms an average of 1 month after acceptance. Byline given. Buys first North American serial, electronic rights. Editorial lead time 2 months. Submit seasonal material 3 months in advance. Accepts queries by mail, e-mail, fax. Responds in 1 week to queries; 1 month to mss. Sample copy for free or online. Writer's guidelines free.

Nonfiction: How-to, interview/profile, new product, technical. No personal bios unless they teach a valuable lesson to those in the building industry. **Buys 40 mss/year.** Query. Length: 500-1,500 words. **Pays $50-300.** Sometimes pays expenses of writers on assignment.

Photos: State availability with submission. Buys first North American serial and electronic rights. Offers no additional payment for photos accepted with ms. Captions, identification of subjects, model releases required.

Columns/Departments: Engineering; Construction; Architecture & Design; Tools & Materials; Heavy Equipment; Business & Economics; Legal Matters; E-build; Building Green, all 750-1,000 words. Query.

Tips: Writers should "email an intro as to why he/she should write for us. A thorough knowledge of our publication is crucial. Also, must be a Northwest slant."

$ $ PENNSYLVANIA BUILDER, Pennsylvania Builders Association, 600 N. 12th St., Lemoyne PA 17043. (717)730-4380. Fax: (717)730-4396. E-mail: scornbower@pahomes.org. Website: www.pahomes.org. **Contact:** Susan H. Cornbower, director of publications. **10% freelance written.** "Quarterly trade publication for builders, remodelers, subcontractors and other affiliates of the home building industry in Pennsylvania." Estab. 1988. Circ. 12,200. Pays on publication. Publishes ms an average of 1 year after acceptance. Byline given. Buys one-time rights. Editorial lead time 3 months. Submit seasonal material 9 months in advance. Accepts queries by mail, e-mail. Accepts simultaneous submissions. Responds in 2 weeks to queries; 3 months to mss. Sample copy for free. Writer's guidelines by e-mail.

Nonfiction: General interest, how-to, new product, technical. No personnel or company profiles. **Buys 1-2 mss/year.** Send complete ms. Length: 800-1,200 words. **Pays $250.** Sometimes pays expenses of writers on assignment.

Reprints: Accepts previously published submissions.

Photos: Send photos with submission. Reviews negatives, transparencies, prints. Buys one-time rights. Negotiates payment individually. Captions, identification of subjects required.

$ $ PERMANENT BUILDINGS & FOUNDATIONS (PBF), R.W. Nielsen Co., 350 E. Center St., Suite 201, Provo UT 84606-3276. (801)373-0013. E-mail: rnielsen@pbf.org. Website: www.permanentbuildings.com. Managing Editor: Carolyn R. Nielsen. **Contact:** Roger W. Nielsen, editor. **15% freelance written.** Magazine published 8 times/year. "*PBF* readers are contractors who build residential and light commercial concrete buildings. Editorial focus is on materials that last: Concrete and new technologies to build solid, energy efficient structures, insulated concrete walls and tilt-up construction, waterproofing, underpinning, roofing and the business of contracting and construction." Estab. 1989. Circ. 30,000. Pays on publication. Byline given. Buys first North American serial rights. Editorial lead time 1 month. Submit seasonal material 2 months in advance. Accepts queries by mail, e-mail. Responds in 2 weeks to queries; 1 month to mss. Sample copy for 9×12 SASE or online. Writer's guidelines free or online.

Nonfiction: How-to (construction methods, management techniques), humor, interview/profile, new product, technical, book reviews, tool reviews. Special issues: Water proofing February, Insulated Concrete Forming supplement April. Special issues: Water proofing (February); Insulated Concrete Forming supplement (April). **Buys 5-10 mss/year.** Query. Length: 500-1,500 words. **Pays $150-600 for assigned articles; $50-500 for unsolicited articles.** Sometimes pays expenses of writers on assignment.

Photos: State availability with submission. Reviews contact sheets. Buys one-time rights. Offers no additional payment for photos accepted with ms. Captions, identification of subjects required.

Columns/Departments: Marketing Tips, 250-500 words; Q&A (solutions to contractor problems), 200-500 words. Query. **Pays $50-500.**

■ The online magazine carries original content not found in the print edition. Contact: Roger Nielsen.

$ $ REEVES JOURNAL, Business News Publishing Co., 23211 South Pointe Dr., Suite 101, Laguna Hills CA 92653. Fax: (949)859-7845. E-mail: scott@reeves-journal.com. Website: www.reevesjournal.com. **Contact:** Scott Marshutz, editor. **25% freelance written.** Monthly magazine covering building subcontractors—plumbers, HVAC contractors. Estab. 1920. Circ. 13,800. Pays on publication. Byline given. Buys first North American serial, electronic rights. Editorial lead time 3 months. Accepts queries by mail, e-mail, fax. Responds in 1 month to queries; 2 months to mss. Sample copy for free. Writer's guidelines for #10 SASE.

- "Knowledge of building construction, water science, engineering is extremely helpful. Even better—former plumbing, HVAC experience, and a great command of the English language."

Nonfiction: "Only articles applicable to plumbing/HVAC subcontracting trade in the western US." How-to, interview/profile, new product, technical. Query with published clips. Length: 500-1,500 words. **Pays $100-350.** Pays phone expenses.

Photos: State availability with submission. Buys all rights. Negotiates payment individually. Captions, identification of subjects required.

The online magazine carries original content not found in the print edition. Contact: Scott Marshutz.

Tips: "Know the market—we're not just another builder publication. Our target audience is the plumbing, HVAC contractor—new construction, mechanical, and service and repair. We cover the western U.S. (plus Texas)."

$ $ UNDERGROUND CONSTRUCTION, Oildom Publishing Co. of Texas, Inc., P.O. Box 941669, Houston TX 77094-8669. (281)558-6930. Fax: (281)558-7029. E-mail: rcarpenter@oildompublishing.com. Website: www.oildompublishing.com. **Contact:** Robert Carpenter, editorial director. **35% freelance written.** Monthly magazine covering underground oil and gas pipeline, water and sewer pipeline, cable construction for contractors and owning companies. Circ. 34,500. Publishes ms an average of 6 months after acceptance. Buys first North American serial rights. Accepts queries by mail, e-mail, fax, phone. Responds in 1 month to mss.

Nonfiction: How-to, job stories. Query with published clips. Length: 1,000-2,000 words. **Pays $3-500.** Sometimes pays expenses of writers on assignment.

Photos: Send photos with submission. Reviews color prints and slides. Buys one-time rights. Captions required.

Tips: "We supply guidelines outlining information we need." The most frequent mistake made by writers in completing articles is unfamiliarity with the field.

DRUGS, HEALTHCARE & MEDICAL PRODUCTS

$ $ SUNWEAR VISION, Frames Data, P.O. Box 1945, Big Bear Lake CA 92315. (909)866-5590. Fax: (909)866-5577. E-mail: cwalker@framesdata.com. Website: www.framesdata.com. **Contact:** Christie Walker, editor. **20% freelance written.** Magazine published 3 times/year for the eye wear industry. "*Sunwear Vision* brings readers current information on all the latest designs and innovations available in the field of fashion and sports sunwear." Estab. 1970. Circ. 30,000. Pays 1 month prior to publication. Publishes ms an average of 3 months after acceptance. Byline given. Buys first North American serial rights. Editorial lead time 3 months. Submit seasonal material 3 months in advance. Accepts simultaneous submissions. Responds in 1 week to queries. Sample copy for 8×10 SAE and 2 first-class stamps.

Nonfiction: How-to, new product. **Buys 10 mss/year.** Query with published clips. Length: 800-1,600 words. **Pays $300-500.**

Photos: Send photos with submission. Buys one-time rights. Offers no additional payment for photos accepted with ms. Captions, identification of subjects required.

Tips: "Write for the doctor. How can doctors make more money selling sunwear?"

$ $ $ VALIDATION TIMES, Washington Information Source Co., 6506 Old Stage Rd., Suite 100, Rockville MD 20852-4326. (301)770-5553. Fax: (301)468-0475. E-mail: wis@fdainfo.com. Website: www.fdainfo.com. **Contact:** Kenneth Reid, publisher. Monthly newsletter covering regulation of pharmaceutical and medical devices. "We write to executives who have to keep up on changing FDA policies and regulations, and on what their competitors are doing at the agency." Estab. 1992. Pays on publication. Publishes ms an average of 1 month after acceptance. Byline given. Makes work-for-hire assignments. Editorial lead time 1 month. Submit seasonal material 1 month in advance. Accepts queries by mail. Responds in 1 month to queries. Sample copy and writer's guidelines free.

Nonfiction: How-to, technical, regulatory. No lay interest pieces. **Buys 50-100 mss/year.** Query. Length: 600-1,500 words. **Pays $100/half day; $200 full day "to cover meetings and same rate for writing."** Sometimes pays expenses of writers on assignment.

Tips: "If you're covering a conference for non-competing publications, call me with a drug or device regulatory angle."

EDUCATION & COUNSELING

Professional educators, teachers, coaches, and counselors—as well as other people involved in training and education—read the journals classified here. Many journals for educators are non-profit forums for professional advancement; writers contribute articles in return for a byline and contributor's copies. *Writer's Market* includes only educational journals that pay freelancers for articles. Education-related publications for students are included in the Consumer Career, College & Alumni; and Teen & Young Adult sections. Listings in the Childcare & Parental Guidance and Psychology & Self-Improvement sections of Consumer Magazines may also be of interest.

$ $ ARTS & ACTIVITIES, Publishers' Development Corporation, Dept. WM, 591 Camino de la Reina, Suite 200, San Diego CA 92108-3104. (619)819-4530. Fax: (619)297-5353. Website: www.artsandactivities.com. **Contact:** Maryellen Bridge, editor-in-chief. **95% freelance written.** Eager to work with new/unpublished writers. Monthly (except July and August) magazine covering art education at levels from preschool through college for educators and therapists engaged in arts and crafts education and training. Estab. 1932. Circ. 20,000. Pays on publication. Publishes ms an average of 1 year after acceptance. Byline given. Buys first North American serial rights. Submit seasonal material 6 months in advance. Accepts queries by mail. Responds in 3 months to queries. Sample copy for 9×12 SAE and 8 first-class stamps. Writer's guidelines for #10 SASE.

- Editors here are seeking more materials for upper elementary and secondary levels on printmaking, ceramics, 3-dimensional design, weaving, fiber arts (stitchery, tie-dye, batik, etc.), crafts, painting and multicultural art.

Nonfiction: Historical/nostalgic (arts, activities, history), how-to (classroom art experiences, artists' techniques), interview/profile (of artists), opinion (on arts activities curriculum, ideas of how to do things better, philosophy of art education), personal experience (this ties in with the how-to, we like it to be personal, no recipe style), articles of exceptional art programs. **Buys 80-100 mss/year.** Length: 200-2,000 words. **Pays $35-150.**

Tips: "Frequently in unsolicited manuscripts, writers obviously have not studied the magazine to see what style of articles we publish. Send for a sample copy to familiarize yourself with our style and needs. The best way to find out if his/her writing style suits our needs is for the author to submit a manuscript on speculation. We prefer an anecdotal style of writing, so that readers will feel as though they are there in the art room as the lesson/project is taking place. Also, good quality photographs of student artwork are important. We are a *visual* art magazine!"

$ THE ATA MAGAZINE, The Alberta Teachers' Association, 11010 142nd St., Edmonton, Alberta T5N 2R1, Canada. (780)447-9400. Fax: (780)455-6481. E-mail: postmaster@teachers.ab.ca. Website: www.teachers.ab.ca. Editor: Tim Johnston. **Contact:** Raymond Gariepy, associate editor. Quarterly magazine covering education. Estab. 1920. Circ. 39,500. Pays on publication. Publishes ms an average of 4 months after acceptance. Byline given. Offers $25 kill fee. Buys one-time rights. Editorial lead time 2 months. Submit seasonal material 2 months in advance. Accepts queries by mail, e-mail, fax, phone. Accepts simultaneous submissions. Responds in 2 months to queries. Sample copy and writer's guidelines free.

Nonfiction: Education-related topics. Query with published clips. Length: 500-1,250 words. **Pays $75 Canadian.**

Photos: Send photos with submission. Reviews 4×6 prints. Negotiates rights. Negotiates payment individually. Captions required.

$ $ ATHLETIC MANAGEMENT, Momentum Media Sports Publishing, 2488 N. Triphammer Rd., Ithaca NY 14850. (607)257-6970, ext. 18. Fax: (607)257-7328. E-mail: info@momentummedia.com. Website: www.athleticsearch.com. **Contact:** Eleanor Frankel, editor. **20% freelance written.** Bimonthly magazine covering management of high school and college athletics. "The magazine is written for athletic directors. Articles are how-to and must be well-organized." Estab. 1988. Circ. 30,000. Pays on publication. Publishes ms an average of 2 months after acceptance. Byline given. Buys first North American serial, first, second serial (reprint), electronic, all rights, makes work-for-hire assignments. Editorial lead time 3 months. Accepts queries by mail, e-mail, fax. Responds in 2 weeks to queries. Sample copy for #10 SASE.

Nonfiction: How-to. Query with published clips. Length: 1,500-3,000 words. **Pays $400-800.** Sometimes pays expenses of writers on assignment.

Tips: "Provide writing samples that show you can write a well-organized, how-to article."

$ $ $ CHILDREN'S VOICE, Child Welfare League of America, 440 First St. NW, 3rd Floor, Washington DC 20001-2085. (202)638-2952. Fax: (202)638-4004. E-mail: voice@cwla.org. Website: www.cwla.org/pubs. **Contact:** Steve Boehm, editor-in-chief. **10% freelance written.** Bimonthly magazine covering "issues of importance for children, youth and families; professionals who work with children, youth and families at risk; and advocates and policymakers who work in their behalf. Sample topics include fostercare and adoption, child abuse and neglect, juvenile justice, pregnant and parenting teens, childcare and early child and early childhood development, troubled youth, homeless youth, etc." Estab. 1991. Circ. 40,000. Pays on publication. Publishes ms an average of 6 months after acceptance. Byline given. Buys all rights. Editorial lead time 6 months. Submit seasonal material 6 months in advance. Accepts queries by mail, e-mail, fax. Responds in 2 weeks to queries; 2 months to mss. Sample copy for 9×12 SAE and 3 first-class stamps. Writer's guidelines online.

Nonfiction: Essays, general interest, interview/profile, opinion, personal experience, successful programs. No poetry, advertisements for products or services disguised as feature articles. **Buys 6-10 mss/year.** Query. Length: 1,800-2,800 words. **Pays 25-50¢/word. Generally does not pay cash for professionals in the field of child welfare.** Sometimes pays expenses of writers on assignment.

Photos: State availability with submission. Reviews contact sheets. Buys all rights. Negotiates payment individually. Captions, identification of subjects, model releases required.

Tips: "Writers must know the field of child welfare or have intimate knowledge of an aspect that is unique, insightful, studied and authoritative. Material that promotes a product or service is not suitable."

$ CLASS ACT, Class Act, Inc., P.O. Box 802, Henderson KY 42419. E-mail: classact@henderson.net. Website: www.henderson.net/~classact. **Contact:** Susan Thurman, editor. **50% freelance written.** Newsletter published 9 times/year covering English/language arts education. "Our writers must know English as a classroom subject and should be familiar with writing for teens. If you can't make your ms interesting to teenagers, we're not interested." Estab. 1993. Circ. 300. **Pays on acceptance.** Publishes ms an average of 6 months after acceptance. Byline given. Offers 100% kill fee. Buys all rights. Editorial lead time 2 months. Submit seasonal material 3 months in advance. Accepts queries by mail, e-mail. Accepts simultaneous submissions. Responds in 1 month to queries. Sample copy for $3. Writer's guidelines online.

O→ Break in with "an original, ready-for-classroom-use article that provides tips for writing (but geared to a teenage audience)."

Nonfiction: How-to (games, puzzles, assignments relating to English education). "No Masters theses; no esoteric articles; no poetry; no educational theory or jargon." **Buys 12 mss/year.** Send complete ms. Length: 100-2,000 words. **Pays $10-40.**

Columns/Departments: Writing assignments (innovative, thought-provoking for teens), 500-1,500 words; puzzles, games (English education oriented), 200 words; teacher tips (bulletin boards, time-saving devices), 100 words. "E-mailed mss (not attachments) are encouraged. Articles on disk (MS Word or Works) also are encouraged." Send complete ms. **Pays $10-40.**

Fillers: Teacher tips. **Pays $10.**

Tips: "Please know the kind of language used by junior/senior high students. Don't speak above them. Also, it helps to know what these students *don't* know, in order to explain or emphasize the concepts. Clip art is sometimes used but is not paid extra for. We like material that's slightly humorous while still being educational. We are especially open to innovative writing assignments, educational puzzles and games, and instructions on basics. Again, be familiar with this age group. Remember we are geared for English teachers."

$ $ HISPANIC OUTLOOK IN HIGHER EDUCATION, 210 Rt 4 East, Ste 310, Paramus NJ 07652. (201)587-8800, ext 100. Fax: (201)587-9105. E-mail: sloutlook@aol.com. Website: www.hispanicoutlook.com. Editor: Adalyn Hixson. **Contact:** Sue Lopez-Isa, managing editor. **50% freelance written.** Biweekly magazine. "We're looking for higher education story articles, with a focus on Hispanics and the advancements made by and for Hispanics in higher education." Circ. 28,000. Pays on publication. Publishes ms an average of 2 months after acceptance. Byline given. Editorial lead time 2 months. Submit seasonal material 3 months in advance. Accepts queries by mail, e-mail, fax. Accepts simultaneous submissions. Sample copy for free.

O→ Break with "issues articles such as new laws in higher education."

Nonfiction: Historical/nostalgic, interview/profile (of academic or scholar), opinion (on higher education), personal experience, all regarding higher education only. **Buys 20-25 mss/year.** Query with published clips. Length: 1,750-2,000 words. **Pays $400 minimum for assigned articles.** Pays expenses of writers on assignment.

Photos: Send photos with submission. Reviews b&w or color prints. Offers no additional payment for photos accepted with ms.

Tips: "Articles explore the Hispanic experience in higher education. Special theme issues address sports, law, health, corporations, heritage, women, and a wide range of similar issues; however, articles need not fall under those umbrellas."

$ $ $ PTO TODAY, The Magazine for Parent Group Leaders, PTO Today, Inc., 844 Franklin St., Unit 8, Wrentham MA 02093. (508)541-9130. Fax: (508)384-6108. E-mail: cprato@ptotoday.com. Website: www.ptotoday.com. **Contact:** Cate Prato, managing editor. **40% freelance written.** Bimonthly magazine covering the work of school parent-teacher groups. "We celebrate the work of school parent volunteers and provide resources to help them do that work more effectively." Estab. 1999. Circ. 80,000. Pays on publication. Publishes ms an average of 2 months after acceptance. Byline given. Offers 40% kill fee. Buys first North American serial, electronic, all rights. Editorial lead time 4 months. Submit seasonal material 4 months in advance. Accepts queries by e-mail. Sample copy online. Writer's guidelines by e-mail.

Nonfiction: Exposé, general interest, historical/nostalgic, how-to (anything related to PTO/PTA), interview/profile, new product, personal experience. **Buys 14 mss/year.** Query. Length: 800-3,000 words. **Pays 30¢-$1/word for assigned articles; $100-500 for unsolicited articles.** Sometimes pays expenses of writers on assignment.

Photos: State availability with submission. Buys one-time rights. Negotiates payment individually. Identification of subjects required.

Tips: "It's difficult for us to find talented writers with strong experience with parent groups. This experience is a big plus. Also, it helps to review our writer's guidelines before querying."

$ SCHOOL ARTS MAGAZINE, 50 Portland St., Worcester MA 01608-9959. Fax: (610)683-8229. Website: www.davis-art.com. **Contact:** Eldon Katter, editor. **85% freelance written.** Monthly magazine (September-May), serving arts and craft education profession, K-12, higher education and museum education programs written by and for art teachers. Estab. 1901. Pays on publication. Publishes ms an average of 3 months after acceptance. Buys all rights. Accepts queries by mail, phone. Responds in 3 months to queries. Sample copy and writer's guidelines free.

O→ Break in with "professional quality photography to illustrate art lessons."

Nonfiction: Articles on art and craft activities in schools. Should include description and photos of activity in progress, as well as examples of finished artwork. Query or send complete ms and SASE. Length: 600-1,400 words. **Pays $30-150.**

▣ The online version contains material not found in the print edition.

Tips: "We prefer articles on actual art projects or techniques done by students in actual classroom situations. Philosophical and theoretical aspects of art and art education are usually handled by our contributing editors. Our articles are reviewed and accepted on merit and each is tailored to meet our needs. Keep in mind that art teachers want practical tips, above all—more hands-on information than academic theory. Write your article with the accompanying photographs in hand." The most frequent mistakes made by writers are "bad visual material (photographs, drawings) submitted with articles, or a lack of complete descriptions of art processes; and no rationale behind programs or activities. Familiarity with the field of art education is essential. Review recent issues of *School Arts*."

$ $ $ TEACHER MAGAZINE, Editorial Projects in Education, 6935 Arlington Rd., Bethesda MD 20814. Fax: (301)280-3150. E-mail: info@teachermagazine.org. Website: www.teachermagazine.org. Managing Editor: Samantha Stainburn. **Contact:** Rich Shea, executive editor. **40% freelance written.** Magazine published 8 times/year covering the teaching profession. "One of the major thrusts of the current school reform movement is to make teaching a true profession. *Teacher Magazine* plays a central role in that effort. It is a national communications network that provides teachers with the information they need to be better practitioners and effective leaders." Estab. 1989. Circ. 120,000. Pays on publication. Publishes ms an average of 1 month after acceptance. Byline given. Offers 25% kill fee. Buys first North American serial, electronic rights. Editorial lead time 3 months. Submit seasonal material 4 months in advance. Accepts queries by mail, e-mail, fax. Responds in 2 months to queries. Sample copy online. Writer's guidelines free.
Nonfiction: Book excerpts, essays, interview/profile, personal experience, photo feature, investigative. No "how-to" articles. **Buys 56 mss/year.** Query with published clips. Length: 1,000-5,000 words. **Pays 50¢/word.** Sometimes pays expenses of writers on assignment.
Photos: State availability with submission. Reviews contact sheets, transparencies, prints. Buys one-time rights. Negotiates payment individually. Identification of subjects, model releases required.
Columns/Departments: Current events, forum. Query with published clips. **Pays 50¢/word.**
Tips: "Sending us a well-researched query letter accompanied by clips that demonstrate you can tell a good story is the best way to break into *Teacher Magazine.* Describe the characters in your proposed article. What scenes do you hope to include in the piece?"

N $ TEACHER'S DISCOVERY, English, Foreign Language, Social Studies and Science editions, American Eagle, 2676 Paldan Dr., Auburn Hills MI 48326-1824. (248)340-7220 ext. 219. Fax: (248)276-1652. E-mail: science@teachersdiscovery.cnchost.com. **10-20% freelance written.** Semiannual educational materials catalogues covering English, foreign language, social studies and science. Estab. 1969. Circ. 2,000,000. Pays on publication. Byline given. Buys first, electronic, all rights. Editorial lead time 2 months. Submit seasonal material 6 months in advance. Accepts queries by mail, e-mail, fax. Accepts simultaneous submissions. Responds in 1 month to queries. Sample copy for $5.
Nonfiction: How-to articles with concrete examples, practical suggestions, first-person accounts of classroom experiences, quick teacher tips and ideas, seasonal and curriculum-related activities and projects, school humor, jokes, anecdotes, quips or quotes. **Buys 10 mss/year.** Query. Length: 100 words minimum. **Pays $25 minimum.**
Photos: State availability with submission. Buys one-time or all rights. Negotiates payment individually. Identification of subjects, model releases required.
Fiction: Adventure, condensed novels, confessions, ethnic, experimental, historical, humorous, mainstream, novel excerpts, religious, slice-of-life vignettes, suspense. No erotica. **Buys 2 mss/year.** Query. Length: 100 words minimum. **Pays $25 minimum.**
Poetry: Avant-garde, free verse, haiku, light verse, traditional. No erotica. **Buys 5 poems/year.** Submit maximum 5 poems. Length: 1-13 lines. **Pays $25 minimum.**
Fillers: Anecdotes, facts, gags to be illustrated by cartoonist, newsbreaks, short humor. **Buys 100/year.** Length: 10-50 words. **Pays $25.**
Tips: "We like material that is slightly humorous while still being educational. All contributions must be original and not previously published. If you send your item electronically, remember to include your name, address and other information."

$ TEACHERS OF VISION, Christian Educators Association, P.O. Box 41300, Pasadena CA 91114. (626)798-1124. Fax: (626)798-2346. E-mail: judy@ceai.org. Website: www.ceai.org. Editor: Forrest L. Turpen. **Contact:** Judy Turpen, contributing editor. **30% freelance written.** Bimonthly newsletter for Christian teachers in public education. "*Teachers of Vision*'s articles inspire, inform and equip teachers and administrators in the educational arena. Readers look for teacher tips, integrating faith & work, and general interest education articles. Topics include union issues, religious expression and activity in public schools and legal rights of Christian educators. Our audience is primarily public school educators. Other readers include teachers in private schools, university professors, school administrators, parents and school board members." Estab. 1953. Circ. 10,000. Pays on publication. Publishes ms an average of 6 months after acceptance. Byline given. Buys first North American serial, second serial (reprint) rights. Editorial lead time 6 months. Submit seasonal material 6 months in advance. Accepts queries by mail, e-mail, fax, phone. Accepts simultaneous submissions. Responds in 1 month to queries; 6 months to mss. Sample copy for 9×12 SAE and 4 first-class stamps. Writer's guidelines for #10 SASE or on website.
Nonfiction: How-to, humor, inspirational, interview/profile, opinion, personal experience, religious. "Nothing preachy." **Buys 15-20 mss/year.** Query or send complete ms if 2,000 words or less. Length: 600-2,500 words. **Pays $30-40.**
Reprints: Accepts previously published submissions.

Photos: State availability with submission. Buys one-time and reprint rights. Offers no additional payment for photos accepted with ms.
Columns/Departments: Query. **Pays $10-30.**
Fillers: Send with SASE—must relate to public education.
Tips: "We are looking for material on living out one's faith in appropriate, legal ways in the public school setting."

$ $ TEACHING THEATRE, Educational Theatre Association, 2343 Auburn Ave., Cincinnati OH 45219-2819. (513)421-3900. Fax: (513)421-7077. E-mail: jpalmarini@edta.org. Website: www.edta.org. **Contact:** James Palmarini, editor. **65% freelance written.** Quarterly magazine covering education theater K-12, primary emphasis on middle and secondary level education. "*Teaching Theatre* emphasizes the teaching, theory, philosophy issues that are of concern to teachers at the elementary, secondary, and—as they relate to teaching K-12 theater—college levels. We publish work that explains specific approaches to teaching (directing, acting, curriculum development and management, etc.); advocates curriculum reform; or offers theories of theater education." Estab. 1989. Circ. 3,500. **Pays on acceptance.** Publishes ms an average of 3 months after acceptance. Byline given. Buys one-time, electronic rights. Editorial lead time 2 months. Submit seasonal material 3 months in advance. Accepts previously published material. Accepts simultaneous submissions. Responds in 1 month to queries; 3 months to mss. Sample copy for $2. Writer's guidelines for #10 SASE.
Nonfiction: "*Teaching Theatre*'s audience is well-educated and most have considerable experience in their field; *generalist* articles are discouraged; readers already *possess* basic skills." Book excerpts, essays, how-to, interview/profile, opinion, technical theater. **Buys 20 mss/year.** Query. **Pays $100-300.**
Photos: State availability with submission. Reviews contact sheets, 5×7 and 8×10 transparencies, Prints. Offers no additional payment for photos accepted with ms.
Tips: Wants articles that address the needs of the busy but experienced high school theater educators. "Fundamental pieces, on the value of theater education are *not* of value to us—our readers already know that."

$ $ $ $ TEACHING TOLERANCE, The Southern Poverty Law Center, 400 Washington Ave., Montgomery AL 36104. (334)956-8200. Fax: (334)956-8484. E-mail: cpon@splcenter.org. Website: www.teachingtolerance.org. **Contact:** Cynthia Pon, research editor. **65% freelance written.** Semiannual magazine. "*Teaching Tolerance* is dedicated to helping K-12 teachers promote tolerance and understanding between widely diverse groups of students. Includes articles, teaching ideas, and reviews of other resources available to educators." Estab. 1991. Circ. 600,000. **Pays on acceptance.** Byline given. Buys all rights. Editorial lead time 6 months. Submit seasonal material 6 months in advance. Accepts queries by mail, fax. Sample copy and writer's guidelines free or online.
Nonfiction: Essays, how-to (classroom techniques), personal experience (classroom), photo feature. "No jargon, rhetoric or academic analysis. No theoretical discussions on the pros/cons of multicultural education." **Buys 6-8 mss/year.** Query with published clips. Length: 1,000-3,000 words. **Pays $500-3,000 for assigned articles.** Pays expenses of writers on assignment.
Photos: State availability with submission. Reviews contact sheets, transparencies. Buys one-time rights. Captions, identification of subjects required.
Columns/Departments: Essays (personal reflection, how-to, school program), 400-800 words; Idea Exchange (special projects, successful anti-bias activities), 250-500 words; Student Writings (short essays dealing with diversity, tolerance & justice), 300-500 words. **Buys 8-12 mss/year.** Query with published clips. **Pays $50-1,000.**
The online magazine carries original content not found in the print edition and includes writer's guidelines. Contact: Tim Walker, online editor.
Tips: "We want lively, simple, concise writing. The writing style should be descriptive and reflective, showing the strength of programs dealing successfully with diversity by employing clear descriptions of real scenes and interactions, and by using quotes from teachers and students. We ask that prospective writers study previous issues of the magazine and writer's guidelines before sending a query with ideas. Most open to articles that have a strong classroom focus. We are interested in approaches to teaching tolerance and promoting understanding that really work—approaches we might not have heard of. We want to inform our readers; we also want to inspire and encourage them. We know what's happening nationally; we want to know what's happening in your neighborhood classroom."

$ TECH DIRECTIONS, Prakken Publications, Inc., P.O. Box 8623, Ann Arbor MI 48107-8623. (734)975-2800. Fax: (734)975-2787. E-mail: tom@techdirections.com. Website: www.techdirections.com. **Contact:** Tom Bowden, managing editor. **100% freelance written.** Eager to work with new/unpublished writers. Monthly (except June and July) magazine covering issues, trends and activities of interest to science, technical and technology educators at the elementary through post-secondary school levels. Estab. 1934. Circ. 43,000. Pays on publication. Publishes ms an average of 1 year after acceptance. Byline given. Buys all rights. Responds in 1 month to queries. Sample copy for $5. Writer's guidelines for #10 SASE or online.
Nonfiction: Uses articles pertinent to the various teaching areas in science and technology education (woodwork, electronics, drafting, physics, graphic arts, computer training, etc.). Prefers authors who have direct connection with the field of science and/or technical education. "The outlook should be on innovation in educational programs, processes or projects that directly apply to the technical education area." Main focus: Technical career and education. General interest, how-to, personal experience, technical, think pieces. **Buys 50 unsolicited mss/year.** Length: 2,000-3,000 words. **Pays $50-150.**
Photos: Send photos with submission. Reviews color prints. Payment for photos included in payment for ms. Will accept electronic art as well.

Columns/Departments: Direct from Washington (education news from Washington DC); Technology Today (new products under development); Technologies Past (profiles the inventors of last century); Mastering Computers, Technology Concepts (project orientation).

Tips: "We are most interested in articles written by science and technical educators about their class projects and their ideas about the field. We need more and more technology-related articles, especially written for the community college level."

ELECTRONICS & COMMUNICATION

These publications are edited for broadcast and telecommunications technicians and engineers, electrical engineers, and electrical contractors. Included are journals for electronic equipment designers and operators who maintain electronic and telecommunication systems. Publications for appliance dealers can be found in Home Furnishings & Household Goods.

$ THE ACUTA JOURNAL OF TELECOMMUNICATIONS IN HIGHER EDUCATION, ACUTA, 152 W. Zandale Dr., Suite 200, Lexington KY 40503-2486. (859)278-3338. Fax: (859)278-3268. E-mail: pscott@acuta.org. Website: www.acuta.org. **Contact:** Patricia Scott, communications manager. **20% freelance written.** Quarterly professional association journal covering telecommunications in higher education. "Our audience includes, primarily, middle to upper management in the telecommunications department on college/university campuses. They are highly skilled, technology-oriented professionals who provide data, voice and video communications services for residential and academic purposes." Estab. 1997. Circ. 2,200. Pays on publication. Publishes ms an average of 6 months after acceptance. Byline given. Buys first rights. Editorial lead time 6 months. Accepts queries by mail, e-mail, fax, phone. Responds in 1 month to queries; 2 months to mss. Sample copy for 9×12 SAE and 6 first-class stamps. Writer's guidelines free.

O→ Break in with a campus study or case profile. "Contact me with your idea for a story. Convince me that you can handle the level of technical depth required."

Nonfiction: "Each issue has a focus. Available with writer's guidelines. We are only interested in articles described in article types." How-to (telecom), technical (telecom), case study, college/university application of technology. **Buys 6-8 mss/year.** Query. Length: 1,200-4,000 words. **Pays 8-10¢/word.** Sometimes pays expenses of writers on assignment.

Photos: State availability with submission. Reviews prints. Offers no additional payment for photos accepted with ms. Captions, model releases required.

Tips: "Our audience expects every article to be relevant to telecommunications on the college/university campus, whether it is related to technology, facilities, or management. Writers must read back issues to understand this focus and the level of technicality we expect."

$ $ DIGITAL OUTPUT, The Business Guide for Electronic Publishers, The Doyle Group, 5150 Palm Valley Road, Suite 103, Ponte Vedra Beach FL 32082. (904)285-6020. Fax: (904)285-9944. E-mail: tmurphy@digitaloutput.net. Website: www.digitaloutput.net. **Contact:** Terry Murphy, editor. **50% freelance written.** Monthly magazine covering electronic prepress, desktop publishing and digital imaging, with articles ranging from digital capture and design to electronic prepress and digital printing. "*Digital Output* is a national business publication for electronic publishers and digital imagers, providing monthly articles which examine the latest technologies and digital methods and discuss how to profit from them. Our readers include service bureaus, prepress and reprographic houses, designers, commercial printers, wide-format printers, ad agencies, corporate communications and others." Estab. 1994. Circ. 30,000. Pays on publication. Publishes ms an average of 2 months after acceptance. Byline given. Offers 10-20% kill fee. one-time rights including electronic rights for archival posting. Editorial lead time 3 months. Submit seasonal material 3 months in advance. Accepts queries by mail, e-mail. Responds in 3 weeks to queries; 1 month to mss. Sample copy for $4.50 or online.

Nonfiction: How-to, interview/profile, technical, case studies. **Buys 36 mss/year.** Query with published clips or hyperlinks to posted clips. Length: 1,500-4,000 words. **Pays $250-600.**

Photos: State availability with submission.

Tips: "Our readers are graphic arts professionals. Freelance writers we use are deeply immersed in the technology of commercial printing, desktop publishing, digital imaging, color management, PDF workflow, inkjet printing and similar topics."

$ $ ELECTRONIC SERVICING & TECHNOLOGY, The Professional magazine for Electronics and Computer Servicing, P.O. Box 12487, Overland Park KS 66282-2487. (913)492-4857. Fax: (913)492-4857. E-mail: cpersedit@aol.com. **Contact:** Conrad Persson, editor. **80% freelance written.** Monthly magazine for service technicians, field service personnel, and avid servicing enthusiasts, who service audio, video, and computer equipment. Estab. 1950. Circ. 15,000. Pays on publication. Publishes ms an average of 4 months after acceptance. Byline given. Buys one-time rights. Editorial lead time 2 months. Accepts queries by mail, e-mail, fax, phone. Accepts simultaneous submissions. Responds in 1 month to queries; 2 months to mss. Sample copy for free. Writer's guidelines free.

O→ Break in by knowing how to service consumer electronics products and being able to explain it in writing in good English.

Nonfiction: Book excerpts, how-to (service consumer electronics), new product, technical. **Buys 40 mss/year.** Query or send complete ms. **Pays $50/page.**

Reprints: Send ms with rights for sale noted and information about when and where the material previously appeared.

Photos: Send photos with submission. Buys one-time rights. Offers no additional payment for photos accepted with ms.

Columns/Departments: Business Corner (business tips); Computer Corner (computer servicing tips); Video Corner (understanding/servicing TV and video), all 1,000-2,000 words. **Buys 30 mss/year.** Query or send complete ms. **Pays $100-300.**

Tips: "Writers should have a strong background in electronics, especially consumer electronics servicing. Understand the information needs of consumer electronics service technicians, and be able to write articles that address specific areas of those needs."

N $ $ $ SOUND & VIDEO CONTRACTOR, Intertec Publishing, 9800 Metcalf Ave., Overland Park KS 66212-2286. (913)341-1300. Fax: (913)967-1905 or (818)780-6040. E-mail: nat_hecht@intertec.com. **Contact:** Nathaniel Hecht, editor. **60% freelance written.** Monthly magazine covering "professional audio, video, security, acoustical design, sales and marketing." Estab. 1983. Circ. 24,000. **Pays on acceptance.** Publishes ms an average of 3 months after acceptance. Byline given. Buys one-time, all rights. Editorial lead time 3 months. Accepts queries by mail, e-mail, fax, phone. Accepts simultaneous submissions. Responds ASAP to queries and to mss. Sample copy and writer's guidelines free.

Nonfiction: Historical/nostalgic, how-to, photo feature, technical, professional audio/video applications, installations. No product reviews, opinion pieces, advertorial, interview/profile, exposé/gossip. **Buys 60 mss/year.** Query. Length: 1,000-2,500 words. **Pays $200-1,200 for assigned articles; $200-650 for unsolicited articles.**

Reprints: Accepts previously published submissions.

Photos: Send photos with submission. Reviews transparencies, prints. Offers no additional payment for photos accepted with ms. Identification of subjects required.

Columns/Departments: Security Technology Review (technical install information); Sales & Marketing (techniques for installation industry); Video Happenings (Pro video/projection/storage technical info), all 1,500 words. **Buys 30 mss/year.** Query. **Pays $200-350.**

Tips: "We want materials and subject matter that would be of interest to audio/video/security/low-voltage product installers/contractors/designers professionals. If the piece allows our readers to save time, money and/or increases their revenues, then we have reached our goals. Highly technical is desirable."

ENERGY & UTILITIES

People who supply power to homes, businesses, and industry read the publications in this section. This category includes journals covering the electric power, natural gas, petroleum, sola,r and alternative energy industries.

N $ $ ALTERNATIVE ENERGY RETAILER, Zackin Publications, Inc., P.O. Box 2180, Waterbury CT 06722-2180. (203)755-0158. Fax: (203)755-3480. E-mail: griffin@sme-online.com. Website: www.aer-online.com/aer/. **Contact:** Michael Griffin, editor. **5% freelance written.** Prefers to work with published/established writers. Monthly Magazine on selling home hearth products—chiefly solid fuel and gas-burning appliances. "We seek detailed how-to tips for retailers to improve business. Most freelance material purchased is about retailers and how they succeed." Estab. 1980. Circ. 10,000. Pays on publication. Publishes ms an average of 2 months after acceptance. Buys first North American serial rights. Submit seasonal material 4 months in advance. Accepts queries by mail, e-mail, fax, phone. Responds in 2 weeks to queries. Sample copy for 9×12 SAE and 4 first-class stamps. Writer's guidelines for #10 SASE.

- Submit articles that focus on hearth market trends and successful sales techniques.

Nonfiction: How-to (improve retails profits and business know-how), interview/profile (of successful retailers in this field). No "general business articles not adapted to this industry." **Buys 10 mss/year.** Query. Length: 1,000 words. **Pays $200.**

Photos: State availability with submission. Reviews color transparencies. Buys one-time rights. Pays $25-125 maximum for 5×7 b&w prints. Identification of subjects required.

Tips: "A freelancer can best break into our publication with features about readers (retailers). Stick to details about what has made this person a success."

$ $ ELECTRICAL APPARATUS, The Magazine of Electromechanical & Electronic Application & Maintenance, Barks Publications, Inc., 400 N. Michigan Ave., Chicago IL 60611-4198. (312)321-9440. Fax: (312)321-1288. Senior Editor: Kevin N. Jones. **Contact:** Elsie Dickson, editorial director. Monthly magazine for persons working in electrical and electronic maintenance, chiefly in industrial plants, who install and service electrical motors, transformers, generators, controls and related equipment. Estab. 1967. Circ. 17,000. **Pays on acceptance.** Publishes ms an average of 3 months after acceptance. Byline given. all rights unless other arrangements made. Accepts queries by mail, fax. Responds in 1 week to queries; 1 month to mss. Sample copy for $4.

Nonfiction: Technical. Length: 1,500-2,500 words. **Pays $250-500 for assigned articles.**

Tips: "All feature articles are assigned to staff and contributing editors and correspondents. Professionals interested in appointments as contributing editors and correspondents should submit résumé and article outlines, including illustration suggestions. Writers should be competent with a camera, which should be described in résumé. Technical expertise is absolutely necessary, preferably an E.E. degree, or practical experience. We are also book publishers and some of the material in *EA* is now in book form, bringing the authors royalties. Also publishes an annual directory, subtitled *ElectroMechanical Bench Reference*."

$ $ NATIONAL PETROLEUM NEWS, 250 S. Wacker Dr., Suite 1150, Chicago IL 60606. (312)977-0999. Fax: (312)980-3135. E-mail: dwight@mail.aip.com. Website: www.npn-net.com. **Contact:** Darren Wight, editor. **3% freelance written.** Prefers to work with published/established writers. Monthly magazine for decision-makers in the petroleum marketing and convenience store industry. Estab. 1909. Circ. 38,000. Pays on acceptance if done on assignment. Publishes ms an average of 2 months after acceptance. Buys variable rights, depending upon author and material; usually buys all rights. Accepts queries by mail, e-mail, fax. Sample copy not available.

• This magazine is particularly interested in articles on national industry-related material.

Nonfiction: Material related directly to developments and issues in the petroleum marketing and convenience store industry and "how-to" and "what-with" case studies. "No unsolicited copy, especially with limited attribution regarding information in story." **Buys 9-10 mss/year.** Length: 2,500 words maximum. **Pays $50-150/printed page.** Sometimes pays expenses of writers on assignment.

Reprints: Send typed ms on disk with rights for sale noted and information about when and where the article previously appeared.

Photos: Pays $150/printed page. Payment for color and b&w photos.

The online magazine carries original content not found in the print edition. Contact: Darren Wight, online editor.

$ $ PUBLIC POWER, Dept. WM, 2301 M St. NW, Washington DC 20037-1484. (202)467-2948. Fax: (202)467-2910. E-mail: jlabella@appanet.org. Website: www.appanet.org. **Contact:** Jeanne LaBella, editor. **60% freelance written.** Prefers to work with published/established writers. Bimonthly trade journal. Estab. 1942. **Pays on acceptance.** Publishes ms an average of 3 months after acceptance. Byline given. Accepts queries by mail, e-mail, fax. Responds in 6 months to queries. Sample copy and writer's guidelines free.

Nonfiction: Features on municipal and other local publicly owned electric utilities. **Pays $400 and up.**

Photos: Reviews transparencies, slides and prints.

Tips: "We look for writers who are familiar with energy policy issues."

$ $ $ TEXAS CO-OP POWER, Texas Electric Cooperatives, Inc., 2550 S. IH-35, Austin TX 78704. (512)454-0311. Website: www.texascoopower.com. Editor: Kaye Northcott. Managing Editor: Carol Moczygemba. **50% freelance written.** Monthly magazine covering rural Texas life, people and places. "*Texas Co-op Power* provides 825,000 households and businesses educational and technical information about electric cooperatives in a high-quality and entertaining format to promote the general welfare of cooperatives, their member-owners and the areas in which they serve." Estab. 1948. Circ. 800,000. **Pays on acceptance.** Publishes ms an average of 6 months after acceptance. Byline given. Buys first, electronic rights. Editorial lead time 3 months. Submit seasonal material 6 months in advance. Accepts queries by mail, e-mail, fax. Accepts simultaneous submissions. Responds in 1 month to queries; 2 months to mss. Sample copy online. Writer's guidelines for #10 SASE.

Nonfiction: General interest, historical/nostalgic, interview/profile, photo feature, travel. **Buys 30 mss/year.** Query with published clips. Length: 1,000-2,000 words. **Pays $400-1,000.** Sometimes pays expenses of writers on assignment.

Photos: State availability with submission. Reviews transparencies, prints. Buys one-time rights. Negotiates payment individually. Identification of subjects, model releases required.

Tips: "We're looking for Texas-related, rural-based articles, often first-person, always lively and interesting."

N $ UTILITY FLEETS, (formerly *Utility and Telephone Fleets*), Practical Communications, Inc., 2615 Three Oaks Rd., Cary IL 60013-0183. (847)639-2200. Fax: (847)639-9542. E-mail: curtis@pracom.com. Website: www.utilityfleets.com. **Contact:** Curt Marquardt, editor. **20% freelance written.** Magazine published 8 times/year for fleet managers and maintenance supervisors for electric gas and water utilities, telephone, interconnect and cable TV companies, public works departments and related contractors. "Case history/application features are also welcome." Estab. 1987. Circ. 18,000. Pays on publication. Publishes ms an average of 1 month after acceptance. Byline given. Buys all rights. Submit seasonal material 2 months in advance. Responds in 2 months to mss. Sample copy and writer's guidelines free.

Nonfiction: How-to (ways for performing fleet maintenance/improving management skills/vehicle tutorials), technical, case history/application features. No advertorials in which specific product or company is promoted. **Buys 4-5 mss/year.** Query with published clips. Length: 1,000-2,800 words. **Pays 30¢/word if experienced in auto writing; 20¢/word if not.**

Photos: Send photos with submission. Reviews contact sheets, negatives, 3×5 transparencies, prints. Buys one-time rights. Offers no additional payment for photos accepted with ms. Captions required.

Tips: "Working with a utility or telephone company and gathering information about a construction, safety or fleet project is the best approach for a freelancer."

ENGINEERING & TECHNOLOGY

Engineers and professionals with various specialties read the publications in this section. Publications for electrical, electronics, and telecommunications engineers are classified separately under Electronics & Communication. Magazines for computer professionals are in the Information Systems section.

[N] CANADIAN CONSULTING ENGINEER, Business Information Group, 1450 Don Mills Rd., Toronto, Ontario M3B 2X7, Canada. (416)442-2266. E-mail: bledger@corporate.southam.ca. Website: www.canadianconsultingengineer.com. **Contact:** Bronwen Ledger, editor. **20% freelance written.** Bimonthly magazine covering consulting engineering in private practice. Estab. 1958. Circ. 8,900. Pays on publication. Publishes ms an average of 4 months after acceptance. Byline given depending on length of story. Offers 50% kill fee. Buys first North American serial rights. Editorial lead time 6 months. Responds in 3 months to mss. Sample copy for free.

Nonfiction: Historical/nostalgic, new product, technical. **Buys 8-10 mss/year.** Length: 300-1,500 words. **Pays $200-1,000 (Canadian).** Sometimes pays expenses of writers on assignment.

Photos: State availability with submission. Buys one-time rights. Negotiates payment individually.

Columns/Departments: Export (selling consulting engineering services abroad); Management (managing consulting engineering businesses); On-Line (trends in CAD systems); Employment. Length: 800 words. **Buys 4 mss/year.** Query with published clips,. **Pays $250-400.**

$ $ CABLING SYSTEMS, Southam Inc., 1450 Don Mills Rd., Don Mills Ontario M3B 2X7, Canada. (416)442-2124. Fax: (416)442-2214. E-mail: jstrom@cablingsystems.com. Website: www.cablingsystems.com. **Contact:** Janine Strom, editor. **50% freelance written.** Magazine published 8 times/year covering structured cabling/telecommunications industry. "*Cabling Systems* is written for engineers, designers, contractors, and end users who design, specify, purchase, install, test and maintain structured cabling and telecommunications products and systems." Estab. 1998. Circ. 11,000. Pays on publication. Publishes ms an average of 1 month after acceptance. Byline given. Buys all rights. Editorial lead time 3 months. Submit seasonal material 1 month in advance. Accepts queries by mail, e-mail, phone. Accepts simultaneous submissions. Sample copy online. Writer's guidelines free.

Nonfiction: Technical (case studies, features). "No reprints or previously written articles. All articles are assigned by editor based on query or need of publication." **Buys 12 mss/year.** Query with published clips. Length: 1,500-2,500 words. **Pays 40-50¢/word.** Sometimes pays expenses of writers on assignment.

Photos: State availability with submission. Reviews contact sheets, prints. Negotiates payment individually. Captions, identification of subjects required.

Columns/Departments: Focus on Engineering/Design, Focus on Installation, Focus on Maintenance/Testing, all 1,500 words. **Buys 7 mss/year.** Query with published clips. **Pays 40-50¢/word.**

Tips: "Visit our website to see back issues, and visit links on our website for background."

$ $ FLOW CONTROL, The Magazine of Fluid Handling Systems, Witter Publishing Corp., 84 Park Ave., Flemington NJ 08822. (908)788-0343 ext. 141. Fax: (908)788-8416. E-mail: flowcontrol@witterpublishing.com. Website: www.flowcontrolnetwork.com. Managing Editor: Mary Beth Schwartz. **Contact:** Ron Piechota, editor. **90% freelance written.** Monthly magazine covering fluid handling systems. "*Flow Control* is the technology resource for the fluid handling industry's critical disciplines of control, containment and measurement. *Flow Control* provides solutions for system design, operational and maintenance challenges in all process and OEM applications." Estab. 1995. Circ. 40,000. Pays on publication. Publishes ms an average of 1 month after acceptance. Byline given. Buys all rights. Accepts queries by mail, e-mail, fax, phone.

Nonfiction: How-to (design or maintenance), technical. No glorified product releases. **Buys 18 mss/year.** Query with published clips or send complete ms. Length: 1,000-2,500 words. **Pays $250-350.** Sometimes pays writers with contributor copies or other premiums.

Photos: Review. Offers no additional payment for photos accepted with ms. Captions, identification of subjects required.

Columns/Departments: Query with published clips or send complete ms. **Pays $250.**

Tips: "Anyone involved in flow control technology and/or applications may submit a manuscript for publication. Articles should be informative and analytical, containing sufficient technical data to support statements and material presented. Articles should not promote any individual product, service, or company. Case history features, describing the use of flow control technologies in specific applications, are welcomed."

LASER FOCUS WORLD MAGAZINE, PennWell, 98 Spit Brook Rd., Nashua NH 03062-2801. (603)891-0123. Fax: (603)891-0574. E-mail: carols@pennwell.com. Website: www.optoelectronics-world.com. Publisher: Christine Shaw. Group Editorial Director: Stephen G. Anderson. **Contact:** Carol Settino, managing editor. **1% freelance written.** Monthly magazine for physicists, scientists and engineers involved in the research and development, design, manufacturing and applications of lasers, laser systems and all other segments of optoelectronic technologies. Estab. 1968. Circ. 66,000. Publishes ms an average of 6 months after acceptance. Byline given unless anonymity requested. all rights. Accepts queries by mail, e-mail, fax, phone. Responds in 1 month to queries. Sample copy and writer's guidelines free.

Nonfiction: Lasers, laser systems, fiberoptics, optics, detectors, sensors, imaging and other optoelectronic materials, components, instrumentation and systems. "Each article should serve our reader's need by either stimulating ideas, increasing technical competence or improving design capabilities in the following areas: natural light and radiation sources, artificial light and radiation sources, light modulators, optical materials and components, image detectors, energy detectors, information displays, image processing, information storage and processing, subsystem and system testing, support equipment and other related areas. No flighty prose, material not written for our readership or irrelevant material. Query first with a clear statement and outline of why the article would be important to our readers.

Photos: Drawings: Rough drawings acceptable, are finished by staff technical illustrator. Send photos with submission. Reviews 4×5 color transparencies, 8×10 b&w glossies.

Tips: "The writer has a better chance of breaking in at our publication with short articles because shorter articles are easier to schedule, but must address more carefully our requirements for technical coverage. Most of our submitted materials come from technical experts in the areas we cover. The most frequent mistake made by writers in completing articles for us is that the articles are too commercial, i.e., emphasize a given product or technology from one company. Also articles are not the right technical depth, too thin or too scientific."

$ $ LIGHTING DESIGN & APPLICATION, Illuminating Engineering Society of North America, 120 Wall St., 17th Floor, New York NY 10005-4001. (212)248-5000, ext. 108. Fax: (212)248-5017. E-mail: cbeardsley@iesna.org. Website: www.iesna.org. **Contact:** Chuck Beardsley, editor. **20% freelance written.** Monthly magazine. "*LD&A* is geared to professionals in lighting design and the lighting field in architecture, retail, entertainment, etc. From designers to educators to sales reps, *LD&A* has a very unique, dedicated and well-educated audience." Estab. 1971. Circ. 10,000. **Pays on acceptance.** Publishes ms an average of 4 months after acceptance. Byline given. Buys first rights. Editorial lead time 4 months. Submit seasonal material 6 months in advance. Accepts queries by mail, e-mail, fax, phone. Accepts simultaneous submissions. Responds in 2 weeks to queries. Sample copy for free.

Nonfiction: "Every year we have entertainment, outdoor, retail and arts and exhibits issues. Historical/nostalgic, how-to, opinion, personal experience, photo feature, technical. "No articles blatantly promoting a product, company or individual." **Buys 6-10 mss/year.** Query. Length: 1,500-2,200 words. **Pays $300-400 for assigned articles.**

Photos: Send photos with submission. Reviews 4×5 transparencies. Offers no additional payment for photos accepted with ms. Captions required.

Columns/Departments: Essay by Invitation (industry trends), 1,200 words. Query. **Does not pay for columns.**

Tips: "Most of our features detail the ins and outs of a specific lighting project. From Ricky Martin at the Grammys to the Getty Museum, *LD&A* gives its readers an in-depth look at how the designer(s) reached their goals."

$ $ THE PEGG, The Association of Professional Engineers, Geologists & Geophysicists of Alberta, 1500 Scotia One, 10060 Jasper Ave. NW, Edmonton, Alberta T5J 4A2, Canada. Fax: (780)425-1722. E-mail: glee@apegga.org. Website: www.apegga.org. **Contact:** George W. Lee, managing editor. **30% freelance written.** Monthly (except August and December) newspaper covering regional (Alberta) engineering and geoscience. The official publication of the self-regulating organization of engineers and geoscientists. Nontechnical journal of association news and features of interest to engineers and geoscientists, and their families. Estab. 1970. Circ. 39,000. **Pays on acceptance.** Publishes ms an average of 1-2 months after acceptance. Byline given. Offers variable kill fee. Buys exclusive first rights, nonexclusive reprint rights, including electronic rights. Editorial lead time 1 month. Accepts queries by mail, e-mail, fax. Responds in 2 weeks to queries; 1 month to mss. Sample copy for large SAE with Canadian postage. Writer's guidelines by e-mail.

Nonfiction: Essays (by professionals in appropriate disciplines only), historical/nostalgic, interview/profile, new product, opinion (by professionals in appropriate disciplines only), technical (by professionals in appropriate disciplines only). **Buys 30-50 mss/year.** Query with published clips. Length: 300-1,000 words. **Pays $200-400.** Pays in contributor copies for non-professional writers (i.e., members). Sometimes pays expenses of writers on assignment.

Photos: Send photos with submission. Reviews prints, GIF/JPEG files. Buys one-time rights. Offers no additional payment for photos accepted with ms. Captions, identification of subjects required.

Tips: "Stories must involve Alberta APEGGA members or material of interest to them. Write as if the reader is a lay person, but a well-educated one. We like 'golly gee whiz' stories, heavy on anecdotes and analogies, to make complex information inviting and palatable."

$ $ PROGRESSIVE ENGINEER, RR 3, Box 356, Lewisburg PA 17837. (570)568-8444. E-mail: progress@jdweb.com. Website: www.ProgressiveEngineer.com. **Contact:** Tom Gibson, editor. **75% freelance written.** Monthly online magazine. "*Progressive Engineer* is written for all disciplines of engineers in the Mid-Atlantic and northeast regions (VA, NC, MD, WV, DE, DC, PA, NJ, CT, RI, MA, VT, NH, ME). We take a less technical slant than most engineering magazines and cover the engineers behind the technology as well as the technology itself. Promotes the profession of engineering by writing about engineers, projects and related activities." Estab. 1997. Pays on publication. Publishes ms an average of 4 months after acceptance. Byline given. Offers $25 kill fee. Buys first North American serial, second serial (reprint) rights. Editorial lead time 6 months. Accepts queries by mail, e-mail. Accepts simultaneous submissions. Responds in 3 weeks to queries; 1 month to mss. Writer's guidelines on request.

Nonfiction: The editor reports a need for more profiles of engineers. General interest, interview/profile, technical, travel, historical. **Buys 30 mss/year.** Query with published clips. Length: 800-2,000 words. **Pays $150-300.** Sometimes pays expenses of writers on assignment.

Reprints: Send tearsheet, photocopy or typed ms with rights for sale noted and information about when and where the material previously appeared. Pays 50% of amount paid for original article.

Photos: State availability with submission. Reviews contact sheets, transparencies, prints, digital images. Buys one-time rights. Offers $25. Captions, identification of subjects required.

Columns/Departments: Profiles (individual engineers), 1,000 words; Business/Career Topics (affecting engineers), 1,000 words; Travel, Places to Visit (see technology in action), 1,000 words. Query with published clips. **Pays $150.**

Tips: "If you know of an engineer or company (project) doing something interesting or unique in your area, we'd like to hear about it."

ENTERTAINMENT & THE ARTS

The business of the entertainment/amusement industry in arts, film, dance, theater, etc., is covered by these publications. Journals that focus on the people and equipment of various music specialties are listed in the Music section, while art and design business publications can be found in Art, Design & Collectibles. Entertainment publications for the general public can be found in the Consumer Entertainment section.

N **AMERICAN CINEMATOGRAPHER, The International Journal of Film & Digital Production Techniques**, American Society of Cinematographers, 1782 N. Orange Dr., Hollywood CA 90028. (323)969-4333. Fax: (323)876-4973. E-mail: stephen@theasc.com. Website: cinematographer.com. Senior Editor: Rachael Bosley. **Contact:** Stephen Pizzello, editor. **90% freelance written.** Monthly magazine covering cinematography (motion picture, TV, music video, commercial). "*American Cinematographer* is a trade publication devoted to the art and craft of cinematography. Our readers are predominantly film-industry professionals." Estab. 1919. Circ. 45,000. Pays on publication. Publishes ms an average of 2-3 months after acceptance. Byline given. Offers 50% kill fee. Buys all rights. Editorial lead time 2 months. Submit seasonal material 3 months in advance. Accepts queries by mail, e-mail, phone. Responds in 2 weeks to queries; 2 months to mss. Sample copy and writer's guidelines free.

Nonfiction: Interview/profile, new product, technical. No reviews, opinion pieces. **Buys 20-25 mss/year.** Query with published clips. Length: 1,500-4,000 words. **Pays $600-1,200.** Pays in contributor copies if the writer is promoting his/her own product or company. Sometimes pays expenses of writers on assignment.

Tips: "Familiarity with the technical side of film production and the ability to present that information in an articulate fashion to our audience are crucial."

$ $ BOXOFFICE MAGAZINE, RLD Publishing Co., 155 S. El Molino Ave., Suite 100, Pasadena CA 91101. (626)396-0250. Fax: (626)396-0248. E-mail: boxoffice@earthlink.net. Website: www.boxoffice.com. Editor-in-chief: Kim Williamson. **Contact:** Christine James, managing editor. **15% freelance written.** Monthly magazine about the motion picture industry for members of the film industry: theater owners, film producers, directors, financiers and allied industries. Estab. 1920. Circ. 8,000. Pays on publication. Publishes ms an average of 4 months after acceptance. Byline given. all rights, including electronic publishing. Submit seasonal material 4 months in advance. Accepts queries by mail, e-mail, fax.

"*Boxoffice* magazine is particularly interested in freelance writers who can write business articles on the exhibition industry or technical writers who are familiar with projection/sound equipment and new technologies such as digital cinema."

Nonfiction: "We are a general news magazine about the motion picture and theatre industry and are looking for stories about trends, developments, problems or opportunities facing the industry. Almost any story will be considered, including corporate profiles, but we don't want gossip or celebrity coverage." Book excerpts, essays, historical/nostalgic, interview/profile, new product, personal experience, photo feature, technical, investigative "all regarding movie theatre business." Query with published clips. Length: 800-2,500 words. **Pays 10¢/word.**

Photos: State availability with submission. Reviews prints, slides. Pays $10 maximum. Captions required.

The online version of this magazine carries original content. Contact: Kim Williamson.

Tips: "Request a sample copy, indicating you read about *Boxoffice* in *Writer's Market.* Write a clear, comprehensive outline of the proposed story and enclose a résumé and clip samples."

$ CALLBOARD, Monthly Theatre Trade Magazine, Theatre Bay Area, 870 Market St., #375, San Francisco CA 94102-3002. (415)430-1140. Fax: (415)430-1145. E-mail: tba@theatrebayarea.org. Website: www.theatrebayarea.org. **Contact:** Karen McKevitt, editor. **50% freelance written.** Monthly magazine for local theater in the SF Bay area. "We publish news, views, essays and features on the Northern California theater industry. We also include listings, audition notices and job resources." Estab. 1976. Circ. 5,000. Pays on publication. Publishes ms an average of 4 months after acceptance. Byline given. Offers 50% kill fee. Buys first rights. Editorial lead time 6 weeks. Submit seasonal material 2 months in advance. Accepts queries by mail, e-mail, phone. Accepts simultaneous submissions. Responds in 1 month to queries. Sample copy for $6.

Nonfiction: Book excerpts, essays, opinion, personal experience, technical (theater topics only), features. No reviews or profiles of actors. **Buys 12-15 mss/year.** Query with published clips. Length: 800-2,000 words. **Pays $100-200 for assigned articles; $35-75 for department articles.** Pays expenses of writers on assignment.

Reprints: Send tearsheet or typed ms with rights for sale noted and information about when and where the material previously appeared. Pays 25% of amount paid for an original article.

Photos: State availability with submission. Reviews contact sheets, 5×7 prints. Buys one-time rights. Offers no additional payment for photos accepted with ms. Identification of subjects required.

$ CAMPUS ACTIVITIES, Cameo Publishing Group, P.O. Box 509, Prosperity SC 29127. (800)728-2950. Fax: (803)321-2049. E-mail: cameopublishing@mac.com. Website: www.campusactivitiesmagazine.com. Editor: Lisa Lackey. Managing Editor: Kappy Griffith. **Contact:** WC Kirby, publisher. **75% freelance written.** Magazine published 8 times/year covering entertainment on college campuses. *Campus Activities* goes to entertainment buyers on every campus in the US. Features stories on artists (national and regional), speakers and the programs at individual schools. Estab. 1991. Circ. 5,912. Pays on publication. Publishes ms an average of 2 months after acceptance. Byline given. Offers 15% kill fee if accepted and not run. Buys first, second serial (reprint), electronic rights. Editorial lead time 2 months. Submit seasonal material 2 months in advance. Accepts queries by mail, e-mail, fax. Accepts simultaneous submissions. Responds in 1 month to queries; 2 months to mss. Sample copy for $3.50. Writer's guidelines free.

Nonfiction: Interview/profile, photo feature. Accepts no unsolicited articles. **Buys 40 mss/year.** Query. Length: 1,400-3,000 words. **Pays $250.** Sometimes pays expenses of writers on assignment.

Photos: State availability with submission. Reviews contact sheets, negatives, 3×5 transparencies, 8×10 prints, electronic media at 300 dpi or higher. Buys one-time rights. Negotiates payment individually. Identification of subjects required.

Tips: "Writers who have ideas, proposals and special project requests should contact the publisher prior to any commitment to work on such a story. The publisher welcomes innovative and creative ideas for stories and works with writers on such proposals which have significant impact on our readers."

$ $ DANCE TEACHER, The Practical magazine of Dance, Lifestyle Ventures, 250 W. 57th St., Suite 420, New York NY 10107. (212)265-8890, ext. 20. Fax: (212)265-8908. E-mail: csims@lifestyleventures.com. Website: www.dance-teacher.com. **Contact:** Caitlin Sims, editor. **80% freelance written.** Monthly magazine. "Our readers are professional dance educators, business persons and related professionals in all forms of dance." Estab. 1979. Circ. 8,000. Pays on publication. Publishes ms an average of 3 months after acceptance. Byline given. Negotiates rights and permission to reprint on request. Submit seasonal material 6 months in advance. Accepts queries by mail, e-mail, fax, phone. Responds in 3 months to mss. Sample copy for 9×12 SAE and 6 first-class stamps. Writer's guidelines free by mail or on website.

Nonfiction: How-to (teach, business), interview/profile, new product, personal experience, photo feature. Special issues: Auditions (January); Summer Programs (February); Music & More (July); Costumes and Production Preview (November); College/Training Schools (December). No PR or puff pieces. All articles must be well researched. **Buys 50 mss/year.** Query. Length: 700-2,000 words. **Pays $100-250.**

Photos: Send photos with submission. Reviews contact sheets, negatives, transparencies, prints. Limited photo budget.

The online magazine carries original content. Contact: Caitlin Sims.

Tips: "Read several issues—particularly seasonal. Stay within writer's guidelines."

$ $ DRAMATICS MAGAZINE, Educational Theatre Association, 2343 Auburn Ave., Cincinnati OH 45219-2815. (513)421-3900. Fax: (513)421-7077. E-mail: dcorathers@edta.org. Website: www.edta.org. **Contact:** Donald Corathers, editor-in-chief. **70% freelance written.** Monthly magazine for theater arts students, teachers and others interested in theater arts education. "*Dramatics* is designed to provide serious, committed young theatre students and their teachers with the skills and knowledge they need to make better theatre; to be a resource that will help high school juniors and seniors make an informed decision about whether to pursue a career in theatre, and about how to do so; and to prepare high school students to be knowledgeable, appreciative audience members for the rest of their lives." Estab. 1929. Circ. 37,000. **Pays on acceptance.** Publishes ms an average of 3 months after acceptance. Byline given. Buys first North American serial rights. Submit seasonal material 3 months in advance. Accepts queries by mail, e-mail, fax. Accepts previously published material. Accepts simultaneous submissions. Responds in 3 months to queries longer than 3 months on unsolicited mss to mss. Sample copy for 9×12 SAE with 5 first-class stamps. Writer's guidelines free.

"The best way to break in is to know our audience—drama students, teachers and others interested in theater—and to write for them."

Nonfiction: How-to (technical theater, directing, acting, etc.), humor, inspirational, interview/profile, photo feature, technical. **Buys 30 mss/year.** Send complete ms. Length: 750-3,000 words. **Pays $50-400.** Sometimes pays expenses of writers on assignment.

Reprints: Send tearsheet, photocopy or typed ms with rights for sale noted and information about when and where the material previously appeared. Pays up to 75% of amount paid for original.

Photos: Query. Purchased with accompanying ms. Reviews transparencies. Total price for ms usually includes payment for photos.

Fiction: Drama (one-act and full-length plays). Prefers unpublished scripts that have been produced at least once. "No plays for children, Christmas plays or plays written with no attention paid to the conventions of theater." **Buys 5-9 mss/year.** Send complete ms. **Pays $100-400.**

Tips: "Writers who have some practical experience in theater, especially in technical areas, have a leg-up here, but we'll work with anybody who has a good idea. Some freelancers have become regular contributors. Others ignore style suggestions included in our writer's guidelines."

$ $ $ EMMY MAGAZINE, Academy of Television Arts & Sciences, 5220 Lankershim Blvd., North Hollywood CA 91601-3109. (818)754-2800. Fax: (818)761-8524. E-mail: emmymag@emmys.org. Website: www.emmys.org. **Contact:** Gail Polevoi, editor. **90% freelance written.** Prefers to work with published/established writers. Bimonthly magazine on television for TV professionals. Circ. 14,000. Pays on publication or within 6 months. Publishes ms an average of 4 months after acceptance. Byline given. Offers 25% kill fee. Buys first North American serial rights. Accepts queries by mail, e-mail, fax. Responds in 1 month to queries. Sample copy for 9×12 SAE and 6 first-class stamps. Writer's guidelines online.

Nonfiction: Articles on contemporary issues, trends, and VIPs (especially those behind the scenes) in broadcast and cable TV; programming and new technology. "Looking for profiles of fascinating people who work 'below the line' in television. Also, always looking for new writers who understand technology and new media and can writer about it in an engaging manner. We require TV industry expertise and clear, lively writing." Query with published clips. Length: 1,700 words. **Pays $900-1,000.**

Columns/Departments: Most written by regular contributors, but newcomers can break into Labors of Love. Length: 500-1,500 words, depending on department. Query with published clips. **Pays $250-750.**

Tips: "Please review recent issues before querying us. Query with published, television-related clips. No fanzine, academic or nostalgic approaches, please. Demonstrate experience in covering the business of television and your ability to write in a lively and compelling manner about programming trends and new technology. Identify fascinating people behind the scenes, not just in the executive suites but in all ranks of the industry."

$ $ RELEASE PRINT, The Magazine of Film Arts Foundation, Film Arts Foundation, 145 9th St., San Francisco CA 94103. (415)552-8760. Fax: (415)552-0882. Website: www.filmarts.org. **Contact:** Chuleenan Svetvilas, editor. **80% freelance written.** Monthly magazine covering U.S. independent filmmaking. "We have a knowledgeable readership of film and videomakers. They are interested in the financing, production, exhibition and distribution of independent films and videos. They are interested in practical and technical issues and, to a lesser extent, aesthetic ones." Estab. 1977. Circ. 5,000. Pays on publication. Publishes ms an average of 3 months after acceptance. Byline given. all rights for commissioned works. For works submitted on spec, buys first rights and requests acknowledgement of Release Print in any subsequent publication. Editorial lead time 4 months. Accepts queries by mail. Responds in 3 weeks to queries; 2 months to mss. Writer's guidelines for 9×12 SASE with $1.47 postage.

O→ Break in with a proposal for an article or interview of an American experimental, documentary or very low budget feature film/video maker with ties to the San Francisco Bay area (or an upcoming screening in this area). Submit at least 4 months prior to publication date.

Nonfiction: Interview/profile, personal experience, technical, Book Reviews. No film criticism or reviews. **Buys 30-35 mss/year.** Query. Length: 300-1,800 words. **Pays 10¢/word.** Sometimes pays expenses of writers on assignment.
Photos: Send photos with submission. Reviews prints. Buys one-time rights. Offers no additional payment for photos accepted with ms. Identification of subjects required.
Columns/Departments: Book Reviews (independent film & video), 800-1,000 words. **Buys 4 mss/year.** Query. **Pays 10¢/word.**

N $ SCREEN MAGAZINE, Screen Enterprises Inc., 222 W. Ontario St., Suite 500, Chicago IL 60610. (312)640-0800. Fax: (312)640-1928. E-mail: editorial@screenmag.com. Website: www.screenmag.com. **Contact:** Claire Weingarden, managing editor. **10% freelance written.** Biweekly Chicago-based trade magazine covering advertising and film production in the Midwest and national markets. "*Screen* is written for Chicago-area producers (and other creatives involved) of commercials, AV, features, independent corporate and multimedia." Estab. 1979. Circ. 15,000. Pays on publication. Publishes ms an average of a few weeks after acceptance. Byline given. Offers 50% kill fee. Makes work-for-hire assignments. Accepts queries by mail, e-mail, fax. Responds in 3 weeks to queries. Sample copy online.
Nonfiction: Interview/profile, new product, technical. "No general AV; specific to other markets; no-brainers and opinion." **Buys 50 mss/year.** Query with published clips. Length: 535-750 words. **Pays $100-150.** Sometimes pays expenses of writers on assignment.
Photos: Send photos with submission. Reviews prints. Offers no additional payment for photos accepted with ms. Captions required.
Tips: "Our readers want to know facts and figures. They want to know the news about a company or an individual. We provide exclusive news of this market, in as much depth as space allows without being boring, with lots of specific information and details. We write knowledgably about the market we serve. We recognize the film/video-making process is a difficult one because it 1) is often technical, 2) has implications not immediately discerned."

$ SOUTHERN THEATRE, Southeastern Theatre Conference, P.O. Box 9868, Greensboro NC 27429-0868. E-mail: publications@setc.org. Website: www.setc.org. **Contact:** Deanna Thompson, editor. **100% freelance written.** Quarterly magazine covering theatre. "*Southern Theatre* is *the* magazine covering all aspects of theatre in the Southeast, from innovative theatre companies to important trends to people making a difference in the region. All stories must be written in a popular magazine style but with subject matter appropriate for theatre professionals (not the general public). The audience includes members of the Southeastern Theatre Conference, founded in 1949 and the nation's largest regional theatre organization. These members include individuals involved in professional, community, college/university, children's and secondary school theatre. The magazine also is purchased by more than 100 libraries." Estab. 1962. Circ. 3,600. **Pays on acceptance.** Publishes ms an average of 3 months after acceptance. Byline given. Buys first North American serial, first, one-time, second serial (reprint), electronic rights. Editorial lead time 3 months. Submit seasonal material 6 months in advance. Accepts queries by mail, e-mail. Responds in 6 weeks to queries; 3 months to mss. Sample copy for $6. Writer's guidelines for free, online or by e-mail.
Nonfiction: Looking for stories on design/technology, playwriting, acting, directing, all with a Southeastern connection. General interest (innovative theatres and theatre programs; trend stories), interview/profile (people making a difference in Southeastern theatre). Special issues: Playwriting (fall issue, all stories submitted by January 1). No scholarly articles. **Buys 15-20 mss/year.** Query with or without published clips or send complete ms. Length: 1,000-3,000 words. **Pays $25 for features stories.** Pays in contributor copies for book reviews, sidebars and other short stories.
Photos: State availability of or send photos with submission. Reviews transparencies, prints. Offers no additional payment for photos accepted with ms. Captions, identification of subjects, model releases required.
Columns/Departments: Outside the Box (innovative solutions to problems faced by designers and technicians), 800-1,000 words; Words, words, words (reviews of books on theatre), 400-550 words. **Buys 2-4 mss/year.** Query or send complete ms. **No pay for columns.**
Tips: "Look for a theatre or theatre person in your area that is doing something different or innovative that would be of interest to others in the profession, then write about that theatre or person in a compelling way. We also are looking

for well-written trend stories (talk to theatres in your area about trends that are affecting them), and we especially like stories that help our readers do their jobs more effectively. Send an e-mail detailing a well-developed story idea, and ask if we're interested."

FARM

The successful farm writer focuses on the business side of farming. For technical articles, editors feel writers should have a farm background or agricultural training, but there are opportunities for the general freelancer too. The following farm publications are divided into seven categories, each specializing in a different aspect of farming: equipment; crops & soil management; dairy farming; livestock; management; miscellaneous; and regional.

Agricultural Equipment

$ $ IMPLEMENT & TRACTOR, Agri USA, 2302 W. First St., Cedar Falls IA 50613. (319)277-3599. Fax: (319)277-3783. E-mail: rvanzoorhis@cfu.net@cfu.net. Website: www.ag-implement.com. **Contact:** Bob VanZoorhis, editor. **15% freelance written.** Bimonthly magazine covering farm equipment, light construction, commercial turf and lawn and garden equipment. "*Implement & Tractor* offers technical and business news for equipment dealers, manufacturers, consultants and others involved as suppliers to the industry. Writers must know US and global machinery and the industry trends." Estab. 1895. Circ. 7,500. Pays on publication. Publishes ms an average of 6 months after acceptance. Byline given. Buys all rights. Editorial lead time 4 months. Accepts queries by mail, e-mail, fax. Responds in 2 months to queries. Sample copy for $6.

Nonfiction: Interview/profile (dealer or manufacturer), new product, photo feature, technical. No lightweight technical articles, general farm machinery articles or farmer profiles articles. Query with published clips. Length: 200-600 words. **Pays $100-250.** Sometimes pays expenses of writers on assignment.

Photos: State availability with submission. Reviews contact sheets. Buys one-time rights. Offers no additional payment for photos accepted with ms. Captions, identification of subjects required.

Tips: "Know the equipment industry, have an engineer's outlook for analyzing machinery and a writer's skills to communicate that information. Technical background is helpful, as is mechanical aptitude."

Crops & Soil Management

$ $ AMERICAN FRUIT GROWER, Meister Publishing, 37733 Euclid Ave., Willoughby OH 44094. (440)942-2000. Fax: (440)942-0662. E-mail: afg_edit@meisternet.com. Website: www.fruitgrower.com. **Contact:** Brian Sparks, managing editor. **10% freelance written.** Annual magazine covering commercial fruit growing. "How-to" articles are best. Estab. 1880. Circ. 44,000. Pays on publication. Publishes ms an average of 4 months after acceptance. Byline given. Buys first rights. Editorial lead time 2 months. Submit seasonal material 4 months in advance. Accepts queries by mail, e-mail, fax, phone. Responds in 2 weeks to queries; 2 months to mss. Sample copy for free. Writer's guidelines free.

Nonfiction: How-to (better grow fruit crops). **Buys 6-10 mss/year.** Query with published clips or send complete ms. Length: 800-1,200 words. **Pays $200-250.** Sometimes pays expenses of writers on assignment.

Photos: Send photos with submission. Reviews prints; slides. Buys one-time rights. Negotiates payment individually.

$ $ COTTON GROWER MAGAZINE, Meister Publishing Co., 65 Germantown Court, #220, Cordova TN 38018. (901)756-8822. Fax: (901)756-8879. Editor: Bill Sepencer. **Contact:** Frank Giles, senior editor. **5% freelance written.** Monthly magazine covering cotton production, cotton markets and related subjects. Readers are mostly cotton producers who seek information on production practices, equipment and products related to cotton. Estab. 1901. Circ. 45,000. **Pays on acceptance.** Publishes ms an average of 2 months after acceptance. Byline given. Buys first rights. Editorial lead time 2 months. Submit seasonal material 2 months in advance. Accepts queries by mail, e-mail, fax, phone. Accepts simultaneous submissions. Sample copy for free. Writer's guidelines not available.

Nonfiction: Interview/profile, new product, photo feature, technical. No fiction or humorous pieces. **Buys 5-10 mss/year.** Query with published clips. Length: 500-800 words. **Pays $200-400.** Pays expenses of writers on assignment.

Photos: State availability with submission. Reviews transparencies. Buys all rights. Offers no additional payment for photos accepted with ms. Captions, identification of subjects required.

$ $ $ CPM, Crop Production Magazine, Media Products Inc./United Agri Products, P.O. Box 1-B, Eugene OR 97440. (541)687-2315 or (800)874-3276. Fax: (541)686-0248. E-mail: editor@CPMmagazine.com. Website: www.CPMmagazine.com. **Contact:** Denise Wendt, editor. **80% freelance written.** Magazine published 6 times/year covering agriculture and crop production. "*CPM* provides practical information on crop production strategies and tools. We publish how-to, solution-oriented information for large, commercial farmers. Our editorial scope includes timely, national issues of interest to farmers. Our goal is to provide information that will help farmers produce a better crop, save money

or improve their bottom line." Estab. 1987. Circ. 150,000. Pays 60 days prior to publication. Publishes ms an average of 6 months after acceptance. Byline given. Buys all rights. Submit seasonal material 8 months in advance. Accepts queries by mail, e-mail, fax, phone. Sample copy and writer's guidelines available on request.
Nonfiction: How-to (crop production/farm management), interview/profile, new product, technical (sprayer technology, equipment updates), success stories. Query with published clips. Length: 500-1,500 words. **Pays $500-1,000.**
Photos: Send slides with submission. Articles without photos will be returned. Buys all rights. Offers no additional payment for photos accepted with manuscript. Captions, identification of subjects, model releases required.
Columns/Departments: From the Field, Market News, New Products and Label Updates.
Tips: "We're looking for stories that provide farmers with practical information they can take to the field. We need established ag writers with a good understanding of issues important to farmers. Flexibility in working with editors to shape stories is important."

$ $ THE FRUIT GROWERS NEWS, Great American Publishing, P.O. Box 128, Sparta MI 49345. (616)887-9008. Fax: (616)887-2666. E-mail: gentry@iserv.net. Website: www.fruitgrowersnews.com. Publisher: Matt McCallum. **Contact:** Karen Gentry, associate editor. **25% freelance written.** Monthly tabloid covering agriculture. "Our objective is to provide commercial fruit growers of all sizes information to help them succeed." Estab. 1970. Circ. 28,000. Pays on publication. Publishes ms an average of 2 months after acceptance. Makes work-for-hire assignments. Editorial lead time 1 month. Submit seasonal material 1 month in advance. Accepts queries by mail, e-mail, fax, phone. Accepts simultaneous submissions. Responds in 2 weeks to queries; 1 month to mss. Sample copy for free.
Nonfiction: Essays, general interest, how-to, interview/profile, new product, opinion, technical. No advertorials, other "puff pieces." **Buys 72 mss/year.** Query with published clips. Length: 800-1,100 words. **Pays $100-125.** Sometimes pays expenses of writers on assignment.
Photos: Send photos with submission. Reviews prints. Buys one-time rights. Offers $15/photo. Captions required.

$ GRAIN JOURNAL, Country Publications, Inc., 3065 Pershing Ct., Decatur IL 62526. (217)877-8660. Fax: (217)877-6647. E-mail: ed@grainnet.com. Website: www.grainnet.com. **Contact:** Ed Zdrojewski, editor. **5% freelance written.** Bimonthly magazine covering grain handling and merchandising. "*Grain Journal* serves the North American grain industry, from the smallest country grain elevators and feed mills to major export terminals." Estab. 1972. Circ. 12,000. Pays on publication. Publishes ms an average of 2 months after acceptance. Byline sometimes given. Buys first rights. Editorial lead time 2 months. Submit seasonal material 2 months in advance. Accepts simultaneous submissions. Sample copy for free.
Nonfiction: How-to, interview/profile, new product, technical. Query. Length: 750 words maximum. **Pays $100.**
Photos: Send photos with submission. Reviews contact sheets, negatives, transparencies, 3×5 prints. Buys one-time rights. Offers $50-100/photo. Captions, identification of subjects required.
Tips: "Call with your idea. We'll let you know if it is suitable for our publication."

$ GRAINEWS, Farm Business Communications (division of Agricore United), P.O. Box 6600, Winnipeg, Manitoba R3C 3A7, Canada. (204)944-5587. Fax: (204)944-5416. E-mail: asirski@fbc.agricoreunited.com. **Contact:** Andy Sirski, editor-in-chief or David Bedard, managing editor (dbedard@fbc.agricoreunited.com). **80% freelance written.** Newspaper published 17 times/year covering agriculture/agribusiness. **Pays on acceptance.** Publishes ms an average of 1 month after acceptance. Byline given. Buys first rights. Editorial lead time 1 month. Submit seasonal material 1 month in advance. Accepts queries by mail, e-mail, fax, phone. Responds in 2 weeks to queries. Sample copy for free.
Nonfiction: Indepth how-to articles on various aspects of farming. "Every article should be written from the farmer's perspective." General interest, historical/nostalgic, humor, new product, opinion, personal experience, technical. Query. **Pays $150 for assigned articles; $25 for unsolicited articles.** Sometimes pays expenses of writers on assignment.
Photos: State availability with submission. Buys one-time rights. Offers no additional payment for photos accepted with ms. Captions, identification of subjects required.
Tips: "We want writers who are farmers. We love 'how-to' articles on farm-related repairs, etc. Ask yourself how your story will help or entertain other farmers, and if it doesn't, don't send it."

$ $ GRAPE GROWER MAGAZINE, Western Ag Publishing Co., 4969 E. Clinton Way #104, Fresno CA 93727. (559)252-7000. Fax: (559)252-7387. E-mail: editorial@westagpubco.com. **Contact:** Randy Bailey, associate publisher. **20% freelance written.** Monthly magazine covering viticulture and wineries. Estab. 1968. Circ. 12,000. Pays on publication. Publishes ms an average of 4 months after acceptance. Byline sometimes given. Buys all rights, makes work-for-hire assignments. Editorial lead time 2 months. Submit seasonal material 3 months in advance. Accepts queries by mail, e-mail, fax, phone. Accepts simultaneous submissions. Responds in 2 weeks to queries; 1 month to mss. Sample copy free by e-mail.
Nonfiction: How-to, interview/profile, new product, personal experience. Query or send complete ms. Length: 900-1,500 words. Sometimes pays expenses of writers on assignment.
Photos: Send photos with submission. Reviews transparencies, prints. Buys all rights.

$ ONION WORLD, Columbia Publishing, P.O. Box 9036, Yakima WA 98909-0036. (509)248-2452, ext. 152. Fax: (509)248-4056. E-mail: brent@freshcut.com. Website: www.onionworld.net. **Contact:** Brent Clement, managing editor. **50% freelance written.** Monthly magazine covering the world of onion production and marketing for onion growers and shippers. Estab. 1985. Circ. 5,500. Pays on publication. Publishes ms an average of 1 month after acceptance.

Byline given. Not copyrighted. Buys first North American serial rights. Submit seasonal material 1 month in advance. Accepts queries by mail, e-mail, fax, phone. Accepts simultaneous submissions. Responds in 1 month to queries. Sample copy for 9×12 SAE and 5 first-class stamps.

• Columbia Publishing also produces *Fresh Cut, The Tomato Magazine, Potato Country and Carrot Country.*

Nonfiction: General interest, historical/nostalgic, interview/profile. **Buys 30 mss/year.** Query. Length: 1,200-1,250 words. **Pays $5/column inch for assigned articles.**

Reprints: Send photocopy and information about when and where the material previously appeared. Pays 50% of amount paid for an original article.

Photos: Send photos with submission. Buys all rights. Offers no additional payment for photos accepted with ms unless it's a cover shot. Captions, identification of subjects required.

Tips: "Writers should be familiar with growing and marketing onions. We use a lot of feature stories on growers, shippers and others in the onion trade—what they are doing, their problems, solutions, marketing plans, etc."

$ $ RICE JOURNAL, SpecCom International, Inc., 5808 Faringdon Place, Raleigh NC 27609. (919)872-5040. Fax: (919)876-6531. E-mail: editor@ricejournal.com. Website: www.ricejournal.com. **contact:** Mary Ann Rood, editor. **5% freelance written.** Monthly (January-June) magazine covering rice farming. "Articles must discuss rice production practices. Readers are rice farmers. Include on-farm interview with one or more farmers who use the featured agronomic practice. Must include photo of the farmer involved in a farming activity." Estab. 1897. Circ. 10,000. Pays on publication. Byline given. Buys first rights. Editorial lead time 2 months. Accepts queries by mail, e-mail, fax. Responds in 2 weeks to queries; 2 months to mss. Sample copy online. Writer's guidelines for #10 SASE.

Nonfiction: How-to, personal experience, photo feature, technical, farmer production tips. Special issues: January: land preparation; February: water management; March: weed control; April: rice diseases and management; May: insect control, tracked vehicles; June: harvest, curing. No recipes, cooking. **Buys 2 mss/year.** Query. Length: 600-2,000 words. **Pays $50-400.**

Photos: State availability with submission. Buys one-time rights. Offers no additional payment for photos accepted with ms. Captions, identification of subjects required.

$ $ THE VEGETABLE GROWERS NEWS, Great American Publishing, P.O. Box 128, Sparta MI 49345. (616)887-9008. Fax: (616)887-2666. E-mail: gentry@iserv.net. Website: www.vegetablegrowersnews.com. Publisher: Matt McCallum. **Contact:** Karen Gentry, associate editor. **25% freelance written.** Monthly tabloid covering agriculture. "Our objective is to provide commercial vegetable growers of all sizes information to help them succeed." Estab. 1970. Circ. 28,000. Pays on publication. Publishes ms an average of 2 months after acceptance. Makes work-for-hire assignments. Editorial lead time 1 month. Submit seasonal material 1 month in advance. Accepts queries by mail, e-mail, fax, phone. Accepts simultaneous submissions. Responds in 2 weeks to queries; 1 month to mss. Sample copy for free.

Nonfiction: Essays, general interest, how-to, interview/profile, new product, opinion, technical. No advertorials, other "puff pieces." **Buys 72 mss/year.** Query with published clips. Length: 800-1,100 words. **Pays $100-125.** Sometimes pays expenses of writers on assignment.

Photos: Send photos with submission. Reviews prints. Buys one-time rights. Offers $15/photo. Captions required.

Dairy Farming

$ DAIRY GOAT JOURNAL, P.O. Box 10, 128 E. Lake St., Lake Mills WI 53551. (920)648-8285. Fax: (920)648-3770. **Contact:** Dave Thompson, editor. **45% freelance written.** Monthly journal. "We are looking for clear and accurate articles about dairy goat owners, their herds, cheesemaking, and other ways of marketing products. Some readers own two goats; others own 1,500 and are large commercial operations." Estab. 1917. Circ. 8,000, including copies to more than 70 foreign countries. Pays on publication. Byline given.

Nonfiction: Information on personalities and on public issues affecting dairy goats and their owners. How-to articles with plenty of practical information. Health and husbandry articles should be written with appropriate experience or academic credentials. **Buys 100 mss/year.** Query with published clips. Length: 750-2,500 words. **Pays $50-150.** Pays expenses of writers on assignment.

Photos: Color or b&w. Vertical or horizontal for cover. Goats and/or people. Pays $100 maximum for 35mm slides for covers; $20-70 for inside use or for b&w. Identification of subjects required.

Tips: "We love good articles about dairy goats and will work with beginners, if you are cooperative."

N $ $ HOARD'S DAIRYMAN, W.D. Hoard and Sons, Co., 28 Milwaukee Ave. W, Fort Atkinson WI 53538-0801. (920)563-5551. Fax: (920)563-7298. E-mail: hoards@hoards.com. Website: www.hoards.com. Editor: W.D. Knox. **Contact:** Steven A. Larson, managing editor. published 20 times/year Tabloid covering dairy industry. "We publish semi-technical information published for dairy-farm families and their advisors." Estab. 1885. Circ. 100,000. **Pays on acceptance.** Publishes ms an average of 4 months after acceptance. Byline given. Buys first rights. Editorial lead time 2 months. Submit seasonal material 3 months in advance. Accepts queries by mail, e-mail, fax. Responds in 2 weeks to queries; 1 month to mss. Sample copy for 12x15 SAE and $3. Writer's guidelines for #10 SASE.

Nonfiction: How-to, technical. **Buys 60 mss/year.** Query. Length: 800-1,500 words. **Pays $150-350.**

Photos: Send photos with submission. Reviews 2x2 transparencies. Offers no additional payment for photos accepted with ms.

$ $ WESTERN DAIRYBUSINESS, Dept. WM, Heritage Complex, 4500 S. Laspina, Tulare CA 93274. (559)687-3160. Fax: (559)687-3166. E-mail: tfitchette@dairybusiness.com. Website: www.dairybusiness.com. **Contact:** Todd Fitchette, editor; Shana Davis, managing editor (sdavis@dairybusiness.com). **10% freelance written.** Prefers to work with published/established writers. Monthly magazine dealing with large herd commercial dairy industry. Rarely publishes information about non-Western producers or dairy groups and events. Estab. 1922. Circ. 17,000. Pays on publication. Publishes ms an average of 3 months after acceptance. Byline given. Buys first North American serial rights. Submit seasonal material 3 months in advance. Accepts queries by mail, e-mail. Responds in 1 month to queries. Sample copy for 9×12 SAE and 4 first-class stamps.

Nonfiction: Special emphasis on: Environmental stewardship, herd management systems, business management, facilities/equipment, forage/cropping. Interview/profile, new product, opinion, industry analysis. "No religion, nostalgia, politics or 'mom and pop' dairies." Query or send complete ms. Length: 300-1,500 words. **Pays $25-400 for assigned articles.**

Reprints: Seldom accepts previously published submissions. Send information about when and where the article previously appeared. Pays 50% of amount paid for an original article.

Photos: Photos are a critical part of story packages. Send photos with submission. Reviews contact sheets, 35mm or 2¼×2 ¼ transparencies. Buys one-time rights. Pays $25 for b&w; $50-100 for color. Captions, identification of subjects required.

Tips: "Know the market and the industry, be well-versed in large-herd dairy management and business."

Livestock

$ $ ANGUS BEEF BULLETIN, Angus Productions, Inc., 3201 Frederick Ave., St. Joseph MO 64506. (816)383-5200. Fax: (816)233-6575. E-mail: shermel@angus.org. Website: www.angusebeefbulletin.com. **Contact:** Shauna Hermel, editor. **45% freelance written.** Tabloid published 4 times/year covering commercial cattle industry. "The *Bulletin* is mailed free to commercial cattlemen who have purchased an Angus bull, and had the registration transferred to them within the last 3 years." Estab. 1985. Circ. 67,000. Pays on publication. Publishes ms an average of 3 months after acceptance. Byline given. Buys first, electronic rights. Editorial lead time 3 months. Submit seasonal material 3 months in advance. Accepts queries by mail, e-mail. Accepts simultaneous submissions. Responds in 3 weeks to queries; 3 months to mss. Sample copy for $5. Writer's guidelines for #10 SASE.

Nonfiction: How-to (cattle production), interview/profile, technical (cattle production). **Buys 10 mss/year.** Query with published clips. Length: 800-2,500 words. **Pays $50-600.** Pays expenses of writers on assignment.

Photos: Send photos with submission. Reviews 5×7 transparencies, 5×7 glossy prints. Buys all rights. Offers $25/photo. Identification of subjects required.

Tips: "Read the publication *Angus Journal* and have a firm grasp of the commercial cattle industry and how the Angus breeds fit in that industry."

$ $ $ ANGUS JOURNAL, Angus Productions Inc., 3201 Frederick Ave., St. Joseph MO 64506-2997. (816)383-5200. Fax: (816)233-6575. E-mail: shermel@angusjournal.com. Website: www.angusjournal.com. **Contact:** Shauna Hermel, editor. **40% freelance written.** Monthly magazine covering Angus cattle. "The *Angus Journal* is the official magazine of the American Angus Association. Its primary function as such is to report to the membership association activities and information pertinent to raising Angus cattle." Estab. 1919. Circ. 22,000. Pays on publication. Publishes ms an average of 3 months after acceptance. Byline given. Buys first, electronic rights. Editorial lead time 2 months. Submit seasonal material 3 months in advance. Accepts queries by mail, e-mail, fax. Accepts simultaneous submissions. Responds in 3 weeks to queries; 2 months to mss. Sample copy for $5. Writer's guidelines for #10 SASE.

Nonfiction: How-to (cattle production), interview/profile, technical (related to cattle). **Buys 20-30 mss/year.** Query with published clips. Length: 800-3,500 words. **Pays $50-1,000.** Pays expenses of writers on assignment.

Photos: Send photos with submission. Reviews 5×7 glossy prints. Buys all rights. Offers $25-400/photo. Identification of subjects required.

The online magazine carries original content not included in the print edition. Contact: Shauna Hermel, online editor.

Tips: "Read the magazine and have a firm grasp of the cattle industry."

$ $ FEED LOT MAGAZINE, Feed Lot Magazine Inc., P.O. Box 850, Dighton KS 67839. (620)397-2838. Fax: (620)397-2839. E-mail: feedlot@st-tel.net. Website: www.feedlotmagazine.com. **Contact:** Robert A. Strong, editor (rstrong@st-tel.net). **40% freelance written.** Bimonthly magazine. "The editorial information content fits a dual role: large feedlots and their related cow/calf, operations, and large 500pl cow/calf, 100pl stocker operations. The information covers all phases of production from breeding, genetics, animal health, nutrition, equipment design, research through finishing fat cattle. *Feed Lot* publishes a mix of new information and timely articles which directly affect the cattle industry." Estab. 1993. Circ. 12,000. Pays on publication. Publishes ms an average of 2 months after acceptance. Byline given. Offers 50% kill fee. Buys all rights. Editorial lead time 2 months. Submit seasonal material 6 months in advance. Accepts queries by mail, e-mail, fax. Responds in 1 month to queries. Sample copy and writer's guidelines for $1.50.

Nonfiction: Interview/profile, new product (cattle-related), photo feature. Send complete ms. Length: 100-400 words. **Pays 20¢/word.**

Reprints: Send tearsheet or typed ms with rights for sale noted and information about when and where the material previously appeared. Pays 50% of amount paid for an original article.

Photos: State availability of or send photos with submission. Reviews contact sheets. Buys all rights. Negotiates payment individually. Captions, model releases required.
Tips: "Know what you are writing about—have a good knowledge of the subject."

$SHEEP! MAGAZINE, P.O. Box 10, 128 E. Lake St., Lake Mills WI 53551. (920)648-8285. Fax: (920)648-3770. **Contact:** Dave Thompson, editor. **35% freelance written.** Prefers to work with published/established writers. Monthly magazine. "We're looking for clear, concise, useful information for sheep raisers who have a few sheep to a 1,000 ewe flock." Estab. 1980. Circ. 15,000. Pays on publication. Byline given. Offers $30 kill fee. Buys all rights or makes work-for-hire assignments Submit seasonal material 3 months in advance.
Nonfiction: Information (on personalities and/or political, legal or environmental issues affecting the sheep industry). Health and husbandry articles should be written be someone with extensive experience or appropriate credentials (i.e., a veterinarian or animal scientist); features (on small businesses that promote wool products and stories about local and regional sheep producers' groups and their activities); first-person narratives. Book excerpts, how-to (on innovative lamb and wool marketing and promotion techniques, efficient record-keeping systems or specific aspects of health and husbandry), interview/profile (on experienced sheep producers who detail the economics and management of their operation), new product (of value to sheep producers; should be written by someone who has used them), technical (on genetics health and nutrition). **Buys 80 mss/year.** Query with published clips or send complete ms. Length: 750-2,500 words. **Pays $45-150.** Pays expenses of writers on assignment.
Reprints: Send tearsheet or photocopy. Pays 40% of amount paid for an original article.
Photos: Color—vertical compositions of sheep and/or people—for cover. Use only b&w inside magazine. Black & white, 35mm photos or other visuals improve chances of a sale. Buys all rights. Pays $100 maximum for 35mm color transparencies; $20-50 for 5×7 b&w prints. Identification of subjects required.
Tips: "Send us your best ideas and photos! We love good writing!"

WESTERN LIVESTOCK REPORTER, Western Livestock Reporter, Inc., P.O. Box 30758, Billings MT 59107. (406)259-4589. Fax: (406)259-6888. E-mail: wlrpubs@imt.net. Website: www.cattleplus.com. **Contact:** Jamie Lane, editor. Weekly newspaper. "Our audience is professional cattle and sheep producers. Material must speak to people who have been in the business for years. We print stories on livestock news, industry news, health issues in cattle, and others intended for our readers." Estab. 1940. Circ. 13,000. Pays on publication. Publishes ms an average of 1 month after acceptance. Byline given. Buys first, one-time, second serial (reprint) rights. Editorial lead time 1 week. Submit seasonal material 2 months in advance. Accepts queries by mail, e-mail. Accepts previously published material. Accepts simultaneous submissions. Sample copy online.
Nonfiction: How-to, humor, interview/profile. Special issues: Performance issues last 2 weeks in March. Does not want those which are new accounts of issues the industry has been working on for years. **Buys 52 mss/year.** Send complete ms. Length: 750 words. **Pays $35-150.** Sometimes pays expenses of writers on assignment.
Photos: Send photos with submission. Reviews prints. Buys one-time rights. Offers $7.50/photo. Captions, identification of subjects required.
Poetry: Cowboy poetry. **Buys 3-4 poems/year.** Submit maximum 4 poems. Length: 36.

Management

$AG JOURNAL, Arkansas Valley Publishing, P.O. Box 500, La Junta CO 81050-0500. (800)748-1997. Fax: (719)384-2867. E-mail: journal@ria.net. Website: www.agjournalonline.com. **Contact:** Jeanette Larson, managing editor. **20% freelance written.** Weekly journal covering agriculture. "The Ag Journal covers people, issues and events relevant to ag producers in our seven state region (Colorado, Kansas, Oklahoma, Texas, Wyoming, Nebraska, New Mexico)." Estab. 1949. Circ. 11,000. Pays on publication. Publishes ms an average of 2 weeks after acceptance. Byline given. Buys first, one-time rights, makes work-for-hire assignments. Editorial lead time 1 month. Submit seasonal material 1 month in advance. Accepts queries by e-mail. Accepts previously published material. Responds in 2 weeks to queries. Sample copy and writer's guidelines free.
Nonfiction: How-to, interview/profile, new product, opinion, photo feature, technical. Query by e-mail only. **Pays $1-1.50/printed column inch for assigned articles.** Sometimes pays expenses of writers on assignment.
Photos: State availability with submission. Buys one-time rights. Offers $4.50-25/photo. Captions, identification of subjects required.
Tips: "Query by e-mail."

$AGVENTURES, Schatz Publishing Group, 11950 W. Highland Ave., Blackwell OK 74631-9511. (580)628-4551. Fax: (580)628-2011. E-mail: agventures@aol.com. Website: www.agventures.com. **Contact:** Sheree Lewis, manager. **95% freelance written.** Bimonthly business-to-business Magazine covering agricultural business opportunities. Estab. 1997. Circ. 2,500. Pays on publication. Publishes ms an average of 3 months after acceptance. Byline sometimes given. Offers 50% kill fee. Buys all rights. Editorial lead time 3 months. Submit seasonal material 3 months in advance. Accepts queries by mail, e-mail, fax, phone. Accepts simultaneous submissions. Responds in 2 weeks to queries; 1 month to mss. Sample copy for $4. Writer's guidelines free.
Nonfiction: Interview/profile (research). "No personal experience (nothing in the first person)." **Buys 30-40 mss/year.** Send complete ms. Length: 2,000-3,000 words. **Pays $75-150.**

Photos: Send photos with submission. Reviews 4×6 prints. Buys all rights. Pays $20/photo. Captions, model releases required.
Tips: "We want ideas on how people are making money on their small acreage and articles that tell how they do it. The best way to get accepted is to imitate the format of existing articles."

$ $ NEW HOLLAND NEWS, P.O. Box 1895, New Holland PA 17557-0903. Website: www.newholland.com/na. **Contact:** Gary Martin, editor. **60% freelance written.** Works with a small number of new/unpublished writers each year. Magazine published 8 times/year covering agriculture; designed to entertain and inform farm families. Estab. 1960. **Pays on acceptance.** Publishes ms an average of 10 months after acceptance. Byline given. Offers negotiable kill fee. Buys first North American serial rights. Submit seasonal material 6 months in advance. Accepts queries by mail. Responds in 2 months to queries. Sample copy and writer's guidelines for 9×12 SAE with 2 first-class stamps.

O-- Break in with an "agricultural 'economic' success story with all the management details."
Nonfiction: "We need strong photo support for articles of 1,200-1,700 words on farm management and farm human interest." Inspirational, photo feature. **Buys 40 mss/year.** Query. **Pays $700-900.** Pays expenses of writers on assignment.
Photos: Send photos with submission. Reviews color transparencies. Buys one-time rights. Pays $50-300, $500 for cover shot. Captions, identification of subjects, model releases required.
Tips: "The writer must have an emotional understanding of agriculture and the farm family and must demonstrate in the article an understanding of the unique economics that affect farming in North America. We want to know about the exceptional farm managers, those leading the way in agriculture. Use anecdotes freely."

N $ SMALL FARM TODAY, The How-to Magazine of Alternative and Traditional Crops, Livestock, and Direct Marketing, Missouri Farm Publishing, Inc., Ridge Top Ranch 3903 W. Ridge Trail Rd., Clark MO 65243-9525. (573)687-3525. Fax: (573)687-3148. E-mail: smallfarm@socket.net. Website: www.smallfarmtoday.com. Editor: Ron Macher. **Contact:** Paul Berg, managing editor. Bimonthly magazine "for small farmers and small-acreage landowners interested in diversification, direct marketing, alternative crops, horses, draft animals, small livestock, exotic and minor breeds, home-based businesses, gardening, vegetable and small fruit crops." Estab. 1984 as *Missouri Farm Magazine*. Circ. 12,000. Pays 60 days after publication. Publishes ms an average of 6 months after acceptance. Byline given. Buys first serial and nonexclusive reprint rights (right to reprint article in an anthology) Submit seasonal material 4 months in advance. Accepts queries by mail, e-mail, fax. Responds in 3 months to queries. Sample copy for $3. Writer's guidelines available.

O-- Break in with a detailed "how-to" story with budget information on a specific crop or animal.
Nonfiction: Practical and how-to (small farming, gardening, alternative crops/livestock). Special issues: Poultry (January); Wool & Fiber (March); Aquaculture (July); Equipment (November). Query letters recommended. Length: 1,200-2,600 words.
Reprints: Send tearsheet, photocopy or typed ms with rights for sale noted and information about when and where the material previously appeared. Pays 57% of amount paid for an original article.
Photos: Send photos with submission. Buys one-time and nonexclusive reprint rights (for anthologies). Offers $6 for inside photos and $10 for cover photos. Pays $4 for negatives or slides. Captions required.
Tips: "No poetry or humor. Your topic must apply to the small farm or acreage. It helps to provide more practical and helpful information without the fluff. We need 'how-to' articles (how to grow, raise, market, build, etc.), as well as articles about small farmers who are experiencing success through diversification, specialty/alternative crops and livestock, and direct marketing."

Regional

$ AGRI-TIMES NORTHWEST, Sterling Ag LLC, 124 S. Main, P.O. Box 1626, Pendleton OR 97801. (541)276-6202. Fax: (541)278-4778. **Contact:** Sterling Allen, publisher. **50% freelance written.** Biweekly newspaper covering agriculture in western Idaho, eastern Oregon and eastern Washington. "News, features about regional farmers/agribusiness only." Estab. 1983. Circ. 4,000. Pays on 15th of month after publication. Publishes ms an average of 1 month after acceptance. Byline given. Buys one-time rights. Submit seasonal material 1 months in advance. Accepts simultaneous submissions. Responds in 1 month to queries. Sample copy for 50¢ and 8×10 SAE with 4 first-class stamps. Writer's guidelines for #10 SASE.
Nonfiction: How-to (regional farming and ranching), humor (regional farming and ranching), interview/profile (regional farmers/ranchers), photo feature (regional agriculture), technical (regional farming and ranching). **Buys 25 mss/year.** Query with or without published clips or send complete ms. Length: 750 words maximum. **Pays 75¢/column inch.**
Reprints: Send typed ms with rights for sale noted and information about when and where the material previously appeared.
Photos: Send photos with submission. Reviews contact sheets, negatives, prints. Buys one-time rights. Offers $5-10/photo. Captions, identification of subjects required.
Tips: "Focus on our region's agriculture. Be accurate."

N $ FARM WORLD, (formerly *Farmweek*), DMG World Media, P.O. Box 90, Knightstown IN 46148-1242. (800)876-5133. Fax: (800)318-1055. E-mail: davidb@farmworldonline.com. Website: www.farmworldonline.com. **Contact:** David Blower, editor. **40-50% freelance written.** Weekly newspaper covering agriculture. Estab. 1955. Circ.

36,000. Pays on 10th of month following publication. Byline given. Buys first, electronic rights, makes work-for-hire assignments. Editorial lead time 1 month. Submit seasonal material 6 months in advance. Accepts queries by mail, e-mail, fax. Response time varies; up to 1 year to queries. Sample copy free or online at website. Writer's guidelines free or online at website.

Nonfiction: "We've seen a lot but we are always looking for ways farmers are able to succeed in the current crisis." New issues include GMOs, and other biotech; trade; marketing; and farm land preservation. The environment and new regulations are also of concern to farmers. General interest (agriculture), interview/profile (ag leaders), new product, photo feature (agriculture), technical. "We don't want first-person accounts. No unsolicited columns, no opinion, no humor, no nostalgia." **Buys 400 mss/year.** Query. Length: 1,000 words maximum. **Pays $50 (less than 300 words); $75 (more than 300 words); and an additional $25 if put on website.** Pays expenses of writers on assignment.

Photos: Reviews prints. Buys one-time rights. Offers $5 maximum/photo. Front page photos: $15 each. Captions, identification of subjects required.

Tips: "We want feature stories about farmers and agribusiness operators. How do they operate their businesses? Keys to success? Etc. Best thing to do is call us first with idea, or write. Could also be a story about some pressing issue in agriculture nationally that affects farmers everywhere."

$ $ FLORIDA GROWER, The Oldest Spokesman For Florida Agriculture, Meister Publishing Co., 1555 Howell Branch Rd., Suite C-204, Winter Park FL 32789. (407)539-6552. E-mail: flg_edit@meisternet.com. Website: www.floridagrower.net. Editor: Michael Allen. **Contact:** Michael Allen. **10% freelance written.** Monthly magazine "edited for the Florida farmer with commercial production interest primarily in citrus, vegetables, and other ag endeavors." "Our goal is to provide articles which update and inform on such areas as production, ag financing, farm labor relations, technology, safety, education and regulation." Estab. 1907. Circ. 14,500. Pays on publication. Byline given. Buys all rights. Editorial lead time 2 months. Submit seasonal material 3 months in advance. Accepts queries by mail, e-mail, fax, phone. Responds in 1 month to queries. Sample copy for 9×12 SAE and 5 first-class stamps. Writer's guidelines free.

Nonfiction: Interview/profile, photo feature, technical. Query with published clips. Length: 750-1,000 words. **Pays $150-250.**

Photos: Send photos with submission.

N $ FLORIDAGRICULTURE, Florida Farm Bureau Federation, 5700 SW 34th St., Gainesville FL 32608. (352)374-1521. Fax: (352)374-1530. E-mail: ealbanesi@sfbcic.com. Website: www.fb.com/flfb. **Contact:** Ed Albanesi, editor. **Less than 5% freelance written.** Monthly tabloid covering Florida agriculture. Promotes agriculture to its 125,000 members families. Estab. 1943. Circ. 125,000. **Pays on acceptance.** Publishes ms an average of 3 months after acceptance. Byline sometimes given. Buys all rights. Editorial lead time 3 months. Submit seasonal material 3 months in advance. Accepts queries by mail, e-mail. Responds in 1 week to queries; 1 month to mss. Sample copy for $3.

Nonfiction: Sportsmen articles with a Florida connection. **Buys fewer than 2 mss/year.** Query. Length: 500-1,500 words. **Pays $50-100 for assigned articles.**

Photos: State availability with submission. Buys up to 3 uses. Negotiates payment individually. Captions, identification of subjects required.

N $ THE LAND, Minnesota's Favorite Ag Publication, Free Press Co., P.O. Box 3169, Mankato MN 56002-3169. (507)345-4523. E-mail: kschulz@the-land.com. Website: www.the-land.com. **Contact:** Kevin Schulz, editor. **40% freelance written.** Weekly tabloid covering farming in Minnesota. "Although we're not tightly focused on any one type of farming, our articles must be of interest to farmers. In other words, will your article topic have an impact on people who live and work in rural areas?" Prefer to work with Minnesota writers. Estab. 1976. Circ. 40,000. **Pays on acceptance.** Publishes ms an average of 2 months after acceptance. Byline given. Buys first North American serial rights. Editorial lead time 2 months. Submit seasonal material 2 months in advance. Accepts queries by mail, e-mail. Responds in 3 weeks to queries; 2 months to mss. Sample copy for free. Writer's guidelines for #10 SASE.

Nonfiction: General interest (ag), how-to (crop, livestock production, marketing). "Nothing that doesn't pertain to Minnesota agricultural or rural life." **Buys 80 mss/year.** Query. Length: 500-750 words. **Pays $30-60 for assigned articles.**

Photos: Send photos with submission. Reviews contact sheets. Buys one-time rights. Negotiates payment individually.

Columns/Departments: Query. **Pays $10-50.**

Tips: "Be enthused about rural Minnesota life and agriculture and be willing to work with our editors. We try to stress relevance. When sending me a query, convince me the story belongs in a Minnesota farm publication."

$ $ MAINE ORGANIC FARMER & GARDENER, Maine Organic Farmers & Gardeners Association, 662 Slab City Rd., Lincolnville ME 04849. (207)763-3043. E-mail: jenglish@midcoast.com. Website: www.mofga.org. **Contact:** Jean English, editor. **40% freelance written.** Prefers to work with published/established local writers. Quarterly Magazine. "*MOF&G* promotes and encourages sustainable agriculture and environmentally sound living. Our primary focus is organic farming, gardening and forestry, but we also deal with local, national and international agriculture, food and environmental issues." Estab. 1976. Circ. 10,000. Pays on publication. Publishes ms an average of 8 months after acceptance. Byline and bio offered. Buys first North American serial, first, one-time, second serial (reprint) rights. Submit seasonal material 1 year in advance. Accepts queries by mail, e-mail. Accepts simultaneous submissions. Responds in 2 months to queries. Sample copy for $2 and SAE with 7 first-class stamps. Writer's guidelines free.

Nonfiction: Book reviews; how-to based on personal experience, research reports, interviews. Profiles of farmers, gardeners, plants. Information on renewable energy, recycling, nutrition, health, non-toxic pest control, organic farm management and marketing. "We use profiles of New England organic farmers and gardeners and news reports (500-1,000 words) dealing with US/international sustainable ag research and development, rural development, recycling projects, environmental and agricultural problems and solutions, organic farms with broad impact, cooperatives and community projects." **Buys 30 mss/year.** Query with published clips or send complete ms. Length: 250-3,000 words. **Pays $20-200.**
Reprints: Send ms with rights for sale noted and information about when and where the material previously appeared. Pays 50% of amount paid for an original article.
Photos: State availability of b&w photos with query; send 3×5 b&w photos with ms. State availability with submission. Buys one-time rights. Captions, identification of subjects, model releases required.
Tips: "We are a nonprofit organization. Our publication's primary mission is to inform and educate, but we also want readers to enjoy the articles."

FINANCE

These magazines deal with banking, investment, and financial management. Publications that use similar material but have a less technical slant are listed under the Consumer Business & Finance section.

$ $ AMERICA'S COMMUNITY BANKER, 900 19th St. NW, Suite 400, Washington DC 20006. (202)857-3100. Fax: (202)857-5581. E-mail: lmarjamaa@acbankers.org. Website: www.acbankers.org. **Contact:** Leigh Marjamaa, editor. **25% freelance written.** Monthly magazine. "*America's Community Banker* is written for senior managers and executives of community financial institutions. The magazine covers all aspects of financial institution management, with an emphasis on strategic business issues and trends. Recent features have included bank marketing tactics on a budget, trends in home mortgage finance and alternative bank funding." Circ. 14,000. **Pays on acceptance.** Publishes ms an average of 2 months after acceptance. Byline given. Offers 20% kill fee. Buys first North American serial rights. Editorial lead time 3 months. Submit seasonal material 6 months in advance. Responds in 1 month to queries. Sample copy and writer's guidelines free.
Nonfiction: "Articles must be well-researched and backed up by a variety of sources, preferably senior managers of financial institutions or experts associated with the banking industry." How-to (articles on various aspects of a financial institution's operations). **Buys 6 mss/year.** Query with published clips. Length: 1,000-2,700 words. **Pays 50¢/word.**
Photos: Send photos with submission. Reviews contact sheets, negatives, prints. Buys one-time rights. Identification of subjects required.
Columns/Departments: Nationwide News (news items on banking and finance), 100-500 words; Technology Report (news on techology for community bankers); and Surveys and Trends (information on the banking business and business in general). **Buys 25 mss/year.** Query with published clips.
Tips: "The best way to develop a relationship with *America's Community Banker* is through our two departments, Nationwide News and Technology Report. If writers can prove themselves reliable there first, major feature assignments may follow."

$ $ $ $ BANKING STRATEGIES, Bank Administration Institute (BAI), Chicago IL. E-mail: kcline@bai.org. Website: www.bai.org/bankingstrategies. **Contact:** Kenneth Cline, senior editor. **70% freelance written.** Magazine covering banking and financial services. "Magazine covers banking from a strategic and managerial perspective for its senior financial executive audience. Each issue includes in-depth trend articles and interviews with influential executives." Offers variable kill fee. Buys all rights. Accepts queries by e-mail. Responds almost immediately to queries.
Nonfiction: How-to (articles that help institutions be more effective and competitive in the marketplace), interview/profile (executive interviews). "No topic queries, we assign stories to freelancers. I'm looking for qualifications as opposed to topic queries. I need experienced writers/reporters." **Buys 30 mss/year.** E-queries preferred. **Pays $1.25/word for assigned articles.**
Tips: "Demonstrate ability and financial services expertise. I'm looking for freelancers who can write according to our standards, which are quite high."

$ $ $ $ BLOOMBERG WEALTH MANAGER, Bloomberg L.P., P.O. Box 888, Princeton NJ 08542-0888. (609)279-3000. Fax: (917)369-7915. E-mail: wealthmanager@bloomberg.net. Website: www.wealth.bloomberg.com. Editor: Robert Casey. **Contact:** Mary Ann McGuigan, executive editor. **90% freelance written.** published 10 times/year Magazine for financial advisors. "Stories should provide insight and information for the financial adviser. Put yourself on the adviser's side of the table and cover the issues thoroughly from his/her perspective. The piece should delve beneath the surface. We need specific examples, professional caveats, advice from professionals." Estab. 1999. Circ. 45,000. **Pays on acceptance.** Publishes ms an average of 3 months after acceptance. Byline given. Offers 30% kill fee. Buys first North American serial rights. Editorial lead time 2 months. Submit seasonal material 2 months in advance. Accepts queries by mail, e-mail, fax, phone. Responds in 1 month to queries.
Nonfiction: Book excerpts, interview/profile, technical. Do not submit anything that does not deal with financial planning issues or the financial markets. **Buys 30-40 mss/year.** Query with published clips. Length: 1,500-3,000 words. **Pays $1.50-2/word for assigned articles.** Sometimes pays expenses of writers on assignment.

Columns/Departments: Expertly Speaking, Tax Strategies, Retirement, Executive Compensation (all financial planning), all 1,900 words. **Buys 10-15 mss/year.** Query with published clips. **Pays $1.50-2/word.**

The online version contains material not found in the print edition. Contact: Linda Hayes.

Tips: "*Wealth Manager* is a trade magazine. All pieces should be written from the perspective of a financial adviser who has wealthy clients."

$ $ $ $ BUSINESS CREDIT MAGAZINE, The Publication for Credit and Financial Professionals, The National Association of Credit Management, 8840 Columbia, 100 Parkway, Columbia MD 21045. (410)740-5560. Fax: (410)740-5574. E-mail: normah@nacm.org. Website: www.nacm.org. **Contact:** Norma J. Heim, managing editor. **95% freelance written.** published 10 times/year Magazine covering business credit. Membership consists of 52 US affiliated associations and an international arm: Finance, Credit, and International Business that operates in Europe and throughout the world, and consists of 800 multinational firms in the US and 30 countries. Articles are directed at the interchange of credit information, practices and methods as well as articles concerning bankruptcy cases and laws. Estab. 1898. Circ. 32,000. Pays on publication. Publishes ms an average of 6 months after acceptance. Byline given. Offers 100% kill fee. Buys all rights, makes work-for-hire assignments. Accepts queries by mail, e-mail, fax, phone. Accepts previously published material. Responds in 2 weeks to queries; 2 months to mss. Sample copy for $7. Writer's guidelines by e-mail or fax.

Nonfiction: "We have numerous conferences all over the globe throughout the year. We try to find local writers and photographers to cover them." Interview/profile, technical. **Buys 36 mss/year.** Send complete ms. Length: 1,500-3,000 words. **Pays $1/word-$2,500.** Sometimes pays expenses of writers on assignment.

Photos: Review. Offers no additional payment for photos accepted with ms unless by prior arrangement.

Columns/Departments: Professional at Work (business/office/credit), 1,500 words. Personnel Matters (personnel/collections), 1,500 words. Business Law (retention/forfeiting/bankruptcy), 2000 words. **Buys 20 mss/year.** Send complete ms.

Fillers: Gags to be illustrated by cartoonist. **Pays $350 maximum.**

Tips: "Read the magazine. If you are qualified to write for *BC* in terms of content, submit articles by fax, e-mail, or mail. Content more important than writer's ability: we clean up all manuscripts to greater or lesser degree."

$ $ CREDIT UNION MANAGEMENT, Credit Union Executives Society, 5510 Research Park Dr., Madison WI 53711. (608)271-2664. Fax: (608)271-2303. E-mail: editors@cues.org. Website: www.cumanagement.org. **Contact:** Mary Arnold or Theresa Sweeney, editors. **44% freelance written.** Monthly magazine covering credit union, banking trends management, HR, marketing issues. "Our philosophy mirrors the credit union industry of cooperative financial services." Estab. 1978. Circ. 7,413. **Pays on acceptance.** Publishes ms an average of 2 months after acceptance. Editorial lead time 3 months. Submit seasonal material 4 months in advance. Accepts queries by mail, e-mail, fax, phone. Accepts simultaneous submissions. Responds in 2 weeks to queries; 1 month to mss. Sample copy and writer's guidelines free.

Nonfiction: Book excerpts, how-to (be a good mentor/leader, recruit, etc.), interview/profile, technical. **Buys 74 mss/year.** Query with published clips. Length: 700-2,400 words. **Pays $250-350.** Pays phone expenses only of writers on assignment.

Columns/Departments: Management Network (book/web reviews, briefs), 300 words; Trends (marketing trends), 700 words; Point of Law, 700 words; Plugged In (new technology/operations trends), 700 words. Query with published clips. **Pays $250-350.**

Tips: "The best way is to e-mail an editor; include résumé. Follow up with mailing cover letter and clips. Knowledge of financial services is very helpful."

$ $ EQUITIES MAGAZINE LLC, 160 Madison Ave., 3rd Floor, New York NY 10016. (212)213-1300. Fax: (212)213-5872. E-mail: equitymag@aol.com. Website: www.equitiesmagazine.com. **Contact:** Robert J. Flaherty, editor. **50% freelance written.** "We are a seven-issues-a-year financial magazine covering the fastest-growing public companies in the world. We study the management of companies and act as critics reviewing their performances. We aspire to be 'The Shareholder's Friend.' We want to be a bridge between quality public companies and sophisticated investors." Estab. 1951. Circ. 18,000. Pays on publication. Publishes ms an average of 2 months after acceptance. Byline given. Buys all rights. Accepts queries by mail. Sample copy for 9×12 SAE and 5 first-class stamps.

Nonfiction: "We must know the writer first as we are careful about whom we publish. A letter of introduction with résumé and clips is the best way to introduce yourself. Financial writing requires specialized knowledge and a feel for people as well, which can be a tough combination to find." Carries guest columns by famous money managers who are not writing for cash payments, but to showcase their ideas and approach. Exposé, new product, technical. **Buys 30 mss/year.** Query with published clips. Length: 300-1,500 words. **Pays $250-750 for assigned articles, more for very difficult or investigative pieces.** Pays expenses of writers on assignment.

Photos: Send color photos with submission. Reviews contact sheets, negatives, transparencies, prints. Offers no additional payment for photos accepted with ms. Identification of subjects required.

Columns/Departments: Pays $25-75 for assigned items only.

Tips: "Give us an idea for a story on a specific publically-owned company, whose stock is traded on NASDAQ, the NYSE, or American Stock Exchange. Anyone who enjoys analyzing a business and telling the story of the people who started it, or run it today, is a potential *Equities* contributor. But to protect our readers and ourselves, we are careful about who writes for us. We do not want writers who are trading the stocks of the companies they profile. Business writing is an exciting area and our stories reflect that. If a writer relies on numbers and percentages to tell his story, rather than the individuals involved, the result will be numbingly dull."

$ $ $ THE FEDERAL CREDIT UNION, National Association of Federal Credit Unions, 3138 N. 10th St., Arlington VA 22201. (703)522-4770. Fax: (703)524-1082. E-mail: tfcu@nafcu.org. Website: www.nafcu.org. Executive Editor: Patrick M. Keefe. **Contact:** Robin Johnston, publisher/managing editor. **30% freelance written.** "Looking for writers with financial, banking or credit union experience, but will work with inexperienced (unpublished) writers based on writing skill. Published bimonthly, *The Federal Credit Union* is the official publication of the National Association of Federal Credit Unions. The magazine is dedicated to providing credit union management, staff and volunteers with in-depth information (HR, technology, security, board management, etc.) they can use to fulfill their duties and better serve their members. The editorial focus includes coverage of management issues, operations, technology as well as volunteer-related issues." Estab. 1967. Circ. 8,000. Pays on publication. Publishes ms an average of 3 months after acceptance. Byline given. Buys first North American serial rights. Submit seasonal material 5 months in advance. Accepts queries by mail, e-mail, fax. Accepts simultaneous submissions. Responds in 2 months to queries. Sample copy for 10×13 SAE and 5 first-class stamps. Writer's guidelines for #10 SASE.

- Break in with "pithy, informative, thought-provoking items for our 'Management Insight' section (for free or a small fee of $50-100)."

Nonfiction: Humor, inspirational, interview/profile. Query with published clips and SASE. Length: 1,200-2,000 words. **Pays $400-1,000.**

Photos: Send photos with submission. Reviews 35mm transparencies, 5×7 prints. Buys all rights. Offers no additional payment for photos accepted with ms. Pays $50-500. Identification of subjects, model releases required.

- The online magazine carries original content not found in the print edition. Contact: Robin Johnston.

Tips: "We would like more articles on how credit unions are using technology to serve their members and more articles on leading-edge technologies they can use in their operations. If you can write on current trends in technology, human resources, or strategic planning, you stand a better chance of being published than if you wrote on other topics."

$ $ $ FINANCIAL PLANNING, Thomson Financial, 11 Penn Plaza, 17th Floor, New York NY 10001. (212)631-1468. Fax: (212)631-9731. E-mail: thomas.johnson@tfn.com. Website: www.financial-planning.com. **Contact:** Thomas W. Johnson, editor-in-chief. **30-40% freelance written.** Monthly magazine covering investment strategies, estate planning, practice management and other issues facing professional financial planners and money managers. Estab. 1971. Circ. 100,000. Pays on publication. Publishes ms an average of 3 months after acceptance. Byline given. Offers 15% kill fee. Buys all rights. Editorial lead time 3 months. Submit seasonal material 4 months in advance. Accepts queries by mail, e-mail. Responds in 3 weeks to queries; 1 month to mss. Sample copy for $10. Writer's guidelines free.

Nonfiction: Book excerpts, how-to, interview/profile, new product, opinion, technical. No product endorsements. **Buys 25-30 mss/year.** Query (e-mail preferred). Length: 1,800-2,500 words. **Pays 50¢/word.** Sometimes pays expenses of writers on assignment.

Photos: State availability with submission. Reviews contact sheets, any size prints. Offers no additional payment for photos accepted with ms. Identification of subjects required.

- The online magazine carries original content not included in the print edition. Contact: John Whelan, online editor.

Tips: "Avoid articles that are too general—ours is a professional readership who require thoughtful, in-depth analysis of financial issues. A submission that includes charts, graphs and statistical data is much more likely to pique our interest than overviews of investing."

ILLINOIS BANKER, Illinois Bankers Association, 133 S. Fourth St., Suite 300, Springfield IL 62701. (217)789-9340. Fax: (217)789-5410. **Contact:** Debbie Jemison, editor. "Our audience is approximately 3,000 bankers and vendors related to the banking industry. The purpose of the publication is to educate and inform readers on major public policy issues affecting banking today, as well as provide new ideas that can be applied to day-to-day operations and management. Writers may not sell or promote a product or service." Estab. 1891. Circ. 2,500. Publishes ms an average of 3 months after acceptance. Byline given. Buys first North American serial rights. Editorial lead time 2 months. Accepts simultaneous submissions. Responds in 3 months to queries. Sample copy and writer's guidelines free.

Nonfiction: "It is *IBA* policy that writers do not sell or promote a particular product, service or organization within the content of an article written for publication." Essays, historical/nostalgic, interview/profile, new product, opinion, personal experience. Query. Length: 1,000-1,500 words.

Photos: State availability with submission. Reviews contact sheets, negatives, transparencies, prints. Captions, identification of subjects required.

Tips: "Articles published in *Illinois Banker* address current issues of key importance to the banking industry in Illinois. Our intention is to keep readers informed of the latest industry news, developments and trends, as well as provide necessary technical information. We publish articles on any topic that affects the banking industry, provided the content is in agreement with Association policy and position. Because we are a trade association, most articles need to be reviewed by an advisory committee before publication; therefore, the earlier they are submitted the better. Some recent topics include: agriculture, bank architecture, commercial and consumer credit, marketing, operations/cost control, security and technology. In addition, articles are also considered on the topics of economic development and business/banking trends in Illinois and the Midwest region."

N INVESTMENT NEWS, Crain Communications, 711 Third Ave., New York NY 10017-4014. (212)210-0750. Fax: (212)210-0444. E-mail: kgirard@crain.com. Website: www.investmentnews.com. **Contact:** Keith Girard, editor. **10% freelance written.** Weekly magazine, newsletter, tabloid covering financial planning and investing. "It covers the business of personal finance to keep its audience of planners, brokers and other tax investment professionals informed

of the latest news about their industry." Estab. 1997. Circ. 60,000. Pays on publication. Publishes ms an average of 1 month after acceptance. Byline given. Negotiate kill fee. Buys all rights, makes work-for-hire assignments. Editorial lead time 2 weeks. Submit seasonal material 1 month in advance. Sample copy for free. Writer's guidelines free.
Tips: "Come to us with a specific pitch-preferably based on a news tip. We prefer to be contacted by fax or e-mail."

$ $ $ $ MORTGAGE BANKING, The Magazine of Real Estate Finance, Mortgage Bankers Association of America, 1919 Pennsylvania Ave., NW, Washington DC 20006. (202)557-2853. Fax: (202)721-0245. E-mail: janet_hewitt@mbaa.org. Website: www.mbaa.org. Associate Editor: Lesley Hall. **Contact:** Janet Reilley Hewitt, editor-in-chief. Monthly magazine covering real estate finance. "Timely examinations of major news and trends in the business of mortgage lending for both commercial and residential real estate." Estab. 1939. Circ. 10,000. **Pays on acceptance.** Publishes ms an average of 2 months after acceptance. Byline given. Negotiates kill fee. Buys one-time rights, makes work-for-hire assignments. Editorial lead time 2 months. Submit seasonal material 3 months in advance. Accepts queries by mail, e-mail, fax. Accepts simultaneous submissions. Responds in 1 month to queries; 4 months to mss. Sample copy and writer's guidelines free.
Nonfiction: Book excerpts, essays, interview/profile, opinion. Special issues: Commercial real estate special supplemental issue (February); Internet guide supplemental issue (September). **Buys 30 mss/year.** Query. Length: 3,000-4,000 words. **Pays $1,000-3,000.** Sometimes pays expenses of writers on assignment.
Photos: State availability with submission. Reviews prints. Buys one-time rights. Negotiates payment individually. Identification of subjects, model releases required.
Columns/Departments: Book reviews (current, relevant material), 300 words; executive essay (industry executive's personal views on relevant topic), 750-1,000 words. **Buys 2 mss/year.** Query. **Pay negotiated.**
Tips: "Trends in technology, current and upcoming legislation that will affect the mortgage industry are good focus."

N $ $ $ $ ON WALL STREET, Thomson Media, 40 W. 57th St., New York NY 10019. (212)631-1400. Fax: (212)631-9731. E-mail: evan.cooper@tfn.com. Website: www.onwallstreet.com. **Contact:** Evan Cooper, editor-in-chief. **50% freelance written.** Monthly magazine for stockbrokers. "We help 95,000 stockbrockers build their business." Estab. 1991. Circ. 95,000. Pays on publication. Publishes ms an average of 1 month after acceptance. Byline given. Offers 50% kill fee. Buys first North American serial rights. Editorial lead time 2 months. Submit seasonal material 2 months in advance. Accepts queries by mail, e-mail. Accepts simultaneous submissions. Responds in 1 week to queries; 1 month to mss. Sample copy and writer's guidelines free.
Nonfiction: How-to, interview/profile. "No investment-related articles about hot stocks, nor funds or hot alternative investments." **Buys 30 mss/year.** Query. Length: 1,000-3,000 words. **Pays $1/word.**
Photos: State availability with submission. Reviews contact sheets. Buys one-time rights. Negotiates payment individually. Identification of subjects required.
Tips: "Writers should know what stockbrokers need to expand their business—industry-specific knowledge of cold-calling, selling investment ideas."

$ $ SERVICING MANAGEMENT, The Magazine for Loan Servicing Professionals, Zackin Publications, P.O. Box 2180, Waterbury CT 06722-2180. (800)325-6745 ext. 241. Fax: (203)755-3480. E-mail: lepore@sm-online.com. Website: www.sm-online.com. **Contact:** Connie Lepore, editor. **15% freelance written.** Monthly magazine covering residential mortgage servicing. Estab. 1989. Circ. 20,000. **Pays on acceptance.** Publishes ms an average of 2 months after acceptance. Byline given. Buys all rights. Accepts queries by mail, e-mail, fax. Responds in 2 weeks to queries. Sample copy and writer's guidelines free.

O→ Break in by "submitting a query for Servicing Reports, a monthly department featuring news and information about mortgage servicing and the industry. It should be informative, topical and include comments by industry professionals."

Nonfiction: How-to, interview/profile, new product, technical. **Buys 10 mss/year.** Query. Length: 1,500-2,500 words. Will pay industry experts with contributor copies or other premiums rather than a cash payment.
Photos: State availability with submission. Reviews contact sheets. Buys all rights. Offers no additional payment for photos accepted with ms. Identification of subjects required.
Columns/Departments: Buys 5 mss/year. Query. **Pays $200.**

$ $ $ TRADERS MAGAZINE, Thomson Media Group, 1110 Plaza, 17th Floor, New York NY 10001. (212)465-7124. Fax: (212)631-9770. E-mail: byrnej@tfn.com. Website: www.tradersmagazine.com. **Contact:** John Aidan Byrne, editor. **35% freelance written.** Monthly magazine plus 2 specials covering equity trading and technology. "Provides comprehensive coverage of how institutional trading is performed on NASDAQ and the New York Stock Exchange." Circ. 6,000 (controlled). Pays on publication. Publishes ms an average of 2 months after acceptance. Byline given. Buys all rights. Editorial lead time 2 months. Submit seasonal material 3 months in advance. Accepts queries by mail, e-mail, phone. Sample copy free to writers on assignment.

O→ Needs more "buy-side" stories (on mutual fund, pension fund traders, etc.)

Nonfiction: Book excerpts, exposé, general interest, historical/nostalgic, how-to, humor, interview/profile, new product, opinion, personal experience, religious, technical. Special issues: Correspondent clearing (every market) and market making survey of broker dealers. No stories that are related to fixed income and other non-equity topics. **Buys 12-20 mss/year.** Query with published clips or send complete ms. Length: 750-2,800 words. **Pays 50¢-$1/word.**
Columns/Departments: Special Features (market regulation and human interest), 1600 words; Trading & Technology, 1,600 words; Washington Watch (market regulation), 750 words. Query with published clips. **Pays 50¢-$1/word.**

Fiction: Ethnic, historical, humorous, mystery, science fiction, slice-of-life vignettes. No erotica. **Buys 1 mss/year.** Query with or without published clips or send complete ms. Length: 2,100-2,800 words. **Pays 50¢-$2/word.**

The online magazine carries original content not found in the print edition. "We welcome controversy in both mediums."

Tips: "Boil it all down and don't bore the hell out of readers. Advice from a distinguished scribe which we pass along. Learn to explain equity market making and institutional trading in a simple, direct manner. Don't waffle. Have a trader explain the business to you if necessary. The *Traders Magazine* is highly regarded among Wall Street insiders, trading honchos, and Washington Pundits alike."

FISHING

$$ PACIFIC FISHING, FIS North America, 4209 21st Ave., Suite 402, Seattle WA 98199. (206)216-0111. Fax: (206)216-0222. E-mail: Brad@pfmag.com. Website: www.pfmag.com. **Contact:** Brad Warren, editor. **75% freelance written.** Works with some new/unpublished writers. Monthly magazine for commercial fishermen and others in the commercial fishing industry throughout Alaska, the west coast, and the Pacific. "*Pacific Fishing* views the fisherman as a small businessman and covers all aspects of the industry, including harvesting, processing and marketing." Estab. 1979. Circ. 10,000. Pays on publication. Publishes ms an average of 2 months after acceptance. Byline given. Buys first North American serial rights. Accepts queries by mail, e-mail, fax, phone. Variable response time to queries. Sample copy and writer's guidelines for 9×12 SAE with 10 first-class stamps.

Study the magazine before querying. "We also manage North American content for www.fis.com, the leading online provider of global news and market intelligence for the commercial fishing and seafood industry. Study the site and e-mail us for details if interested."

Nonfiction: "Articles must be concerned specifically with commercial fishing. We view fishermen as small business operators and professionals who are innovative and success-oriented. To appeal to this reader, *Pacific Fishing* offers 4 basic features: Technical, how-to articles that give fishermen hands-on tips that will make their operation more efficient and profitable; practical, well-researched business articles discussing the dollars and cents of fishing, processing and marketing; profiles of a fisherman, processor or company with emphasis on practical business and technical areas; and in-depth analysis of political, social, fisheries management and resource issues that have a direct bearing on commercial fishermen." Editors here are putting more focus on local and international seafood marketing, technical coverage of gear and vessels. Interview/profile, technical (usually with a business book or slant). **Buys 20 mss/year.** Query noting whether photos are available, and enclosing samples of previous work and SASE. Length: varies, one-paragraph news items to 3,000-word features. **Pays 20¢/word for most assignments.** Sometimes pays expenses of writers on assignment.

Reprints: Send photocopy and information about when and where the material previously appeared. Pays 100% of the amount paid for an original article.

Photos: "We need good, high-quality photography, especially color, of commercial fishing. We prefer 35mm color slides or JPEG files of at least 300 dpi." Our rates are $200 for cover; $50-100 for inside color; $25-75 for b&w and $10 for table of contents.

FLORISTS, NURSERIES & LANDSCAPERS

Readers of these publications are involved in growing, selling, or caring for plants, flowers, and trees. Magazines geared to consumers interested in gardening are listed in the Consumer Home & Garden section.

$$ DIGGER, Oregon Association of Nurserymen, 2780 S.E. Harrison, Suite 102, Milwaukie OR 97222. (503)653-8733. Fax: (503)653-3956. E-mail: csivesind@oan.org. Website: www.nurseryguide.com. **Contact:** Cam Sivesind, manager of publications and communications. **50% freelance written.** Monthly magazine covering nursery and greenhouse industry. "Our readers are mainly nursery and greenhouse operators and owners who propagate nursery stock/crops, so we write with them in mind." Circ. 5,000. Pays on receipt of copy. Publishes ms an average of 2 months after acceptance. Byline given. Offers 100% kill fee. Buys first North American serial rights. Editorial lead time 6 weeks. Submit seasonal material 2 months in advance. Accepts queries by mail, e-mail, fax, phone. Sample copy and writer's guidelines free.

Nonfiction: General interest, how-to (propagation techniques, other crop-growing tips), interview/profile, personal experience, technical. Special issues: Farwest Magazine (August)—this is a triple-size issues that runs in tandem with our annual Trade Show (11,500 circulation for this issue). "No articles not related or pertinent to nursery and greenhouse industry." **Buys 20-30 mss/year.** Query. Length: 800-2,000 words. **Pays $125-400 for assigned articles; $100-300 for unsolicited articles.** Sometimes pays expenses of writers on assignment.

Photos: State availability with submission. Reviews negatives, 5×7 prints, slides. Buys one-time rights. Offers $25-150/photo. Captions, identification of subjects required.

Tips: "Our best freelancers are familiar with or have experience in the horticultural industry. Some 'green' knowledge is a definite advantage."

$ GROWERTALKS, Ball Publishing, 335 N. River St., P.O. Box 9, Batavia IL 60510. (630)208-9080. Fax: (630)208-9350. E-mail: beytes@growertalks.com. Website: www.growertalks.com. **Contact:** Chris Beytes, editor. **50% freelance written.** Monthly magazine. "*GrowerTalks* serves the commercial greenhouse grower. Editorial emphasis is on floricultural crops: bedding plants, potted floral crops, foliage and fresh cut flowers. Our readers are growers, managers and owners. We're looking for writers who've had experience in the greenhouse industry." Estab. 1937. Circ. 9,500. Pays on publication. Publishes ms an average of 3 months after acceptance. Byline given. Buys first North American serial rights. Editorial lead time 4 months. Submit seasonal material 3 months in advance. Accepts queries by mail, e-mail, fax. Responds in 1 month to queries. Sample copy and writer's guidelines free.

Nonfiction: How-to (time- or money-saving projects for professional flower/plant growers), interview/profile (ornamental horticulture growers), personal experience (of a grower), technical (about growing process in greenhouse setting). "No articles that promote only one product." **Buys 36 mss/year.** Query. Length: 1,200-1,600 words. **Pays $125 minimum for assigned articles; $75 minimum for unsolicited articles.**

Photos: State availability with submission. Reviews 2½×2½ slides and 3×5 prints. Buys one-time rights. Negotiates payment individually. Captions, identification of subjects, model releases required.

The online magazine carries original content not included in the print edition. Contact: Chris Beytes, online editor.

Tips: "Discuss magazine with ornamental horticulture growers to find out what topics that have or haven't appeared in the magazine interest them."

$ $ THE GROWING EDGE, New Moon Publishing, Inc., 341 SW Second St., Corvallis OR 97333. (541)757-2511. Fax: (541)757-0028. E-mail: doug@growingedge.com. Website: www.growingedge.com. **Contact:** Doug Peckenpaugh, editor. **85% freelance written.** Bimonthly magazine covering indoor and outdoor high-tech gardening techniques and tips. Estab. 1980. Circ. 20,000. Pays on publication. Publishes ms an average of 3 months after acceptance. Byline given. first serial and reprint rights Submit seasonal material 6 months in advance. Accepts queries by mail, e-mail. Responds in 3 months to queries. Sample copy for $3. Writer's guidelines online.

Break in with "a detailed, knowledgeable e-mail story pitch."

Nonfiction: How-to, interview/profile, personal experience (must be technical), book reviews, general horticulture and agriculture. Query. Length: 500-3,500 words. **Pays 20¢/word (10¢ for first rights, 5¢ for non-exclusive reprint and non-exclusive electronic rights).**

Reprints: Send tearsheet, photocopy or typed ms with rights for sale noted and information about when and where the material previously appeared. Payment negotiable.

Photos: Buys first and reprint rights. Pays $25-175. Pays on publication. Credit line given.

Tips: Looking for more hydroponics articles and information that will give the reader/gardener/farmer the "growing edge" in high-tech gardening and farming on topics such as high intensity grow lights, water conservation, drip irrigation, advanced organic fertilizers, new seed varieties and greenhouse cultivation.

$ $ ORNAMENTAL OUTLOOK, Your Connection To The South's Horticulture Industry, Meister Publishing Co., 1555 Howell Branch Rd., Suite C204, Winter Park FL 32789. (407)539-6552. Fax: (407)539-6544. E-mail: oo_edit@meisternet.com. Website: www.ornamentaloutlook.com. **Contact:** Michael Allen, managing editor. **50% freelance written.** Monthly magazine. "*Ornamental Outlook* is written for commercial growers of ornamental plants in the Southeast U.S. Our goal is to provide interesting and informative articles on such topics as production, legislation, safety, technology, pest control, water management and new varieties as they apply to Southeast growers." Estab. 1991. Circ. 12,500. Pays 30 days after publication. Publishes ms an average of 4 months after acceptance. Byline given. Buys all rights. Editorial lead time 2 months. Submit seasonal material 3 months in advance. Accepts queries by mail, e-mail, fax, phone. Responds in 3 months to queries. Sample copy for 9×12 SAE and 5 first-class stamps. Writer's guidelines free.

Nonfiction: Interview/profile, photo feature, technical. "No first-person articles. No word-for-word meeting transcripts or all-quote articles." Query with published clips. Length: 750-1,000 words. **Pays $250/article including photos.**

Photos: Send photos with submission. Reviews contact sheets, transparencies, prints. Buys one-time rights. Captions, identification of subjects required.

Tips: "I am most impressed by written queries that address specific subjects of interest to our audience, which is the *Southeast* grower of *commercial* horticulture. Our biggest demand is for features, about 1,000 words, that follow subjects listed on our editorial calendar (which is sent with guidelines). Please do not send articles of national or consumer interest."

$ $ TREE CARE INDUSTRY MAGAZINE, National Arborist Association, 3 Perimeter Rd. Unit 1, Manchester NH 03103-3341. (800)733-2622 or (603)314-5380. E-mail: garvin@natlarb.com. Website: www.natlarb.com. Mark Garvin, editor. **50% freelance written.** Monthly magazine covering tree care and landscape maintenance. Estab. 1990. Circ. 28,500. Pays within 30 days of publication. Publishes ms an average of 3 months after acceptance. Byline given. Buys first North American serial rights. Editorial lead time 10 weeks. Submit seasonal material 3 months in advance. Accepts queries by mail, e-mail, fax, phone. Responds in 2 weeks to queries; 2 months to mss. Sample copy for 9×12 SAE and 6 first-class stamps. Writer's guidelines free.

Nonfiction: Book excerpts, historical/nostalgic, interview/profile, new product, technical. **Buys 40 mss/year.** Query with published clips. Length: 900-3,500 words. **Pays negotiable rate.**

Photos: Send photos with submission. Reviews prints. Buys one-time and web rights. Negotiate payment individually. Captions, identification of subjects required.

Columns/Departments: Management Exchange (business management-related); 1,200-1,800 words; Industry Innovations (inventions), 1,200 words; From The Field (OP/ED from practitioners), 800 words. **Buys 40 mss/year.** Send complete ms. **Pays $100 and up.**

Tips: "Preference is given to writers with background and knowledge of the tree care industry; our focus is relatively narrow. Preference is also given to photojournalists willing to work on speculation."

GOVERNMENT & PUBLIC SERVICE

Listed here are journals for people who provide governmental services at the local, state, or federal level or for those who work in franchised utilities. Journals for city managers, politicians, bureaucratic decision makers, civil servants, firefighters, police officers, public administrators, urban transit managers, and utilities managers are listed in this section.

$ AMERICAN FIRE JOURNAL, Fire Publications, Inc., 9072 Artesia Blvd., Bellflower CA 90706. (562)866-1664. Fax: (562)867-6434. E-mail: afjm@accessl.net. Website: www.americanfirejournal.com. Editor: Carol Carlsen Brooks. **Contact:** John Ackerman, publisher. **90% freelance written.** Monthly magazine covering fire service. "Written by firefighters for firefighters." Estab. 1940s. Circ. 6,000. Pays on publication. Publishes ms an average of 6 months after acceptance. Byline given. Buys first rights. Editorial lead time 3 months. Submit seasonal material 3 months in advance. Accepts queries by mail, e-mail, fax, phone. Responds in 2 weeks to queries; 2 months to mss. Sample copy for $3.50. Writer's guidelines free.
Nonfiction: Historical/nostalgic, how-to, new product, opinion, photo feature, technical. **Buys 50 mss/year.** Send complete ms. Any length. **Pays $150 maximum.**
Photos: Send photos with submission. Reviews contact sheets, negatives, transparencies, Prints (any size). Buys one-time rights. Offers $5-50/photo. Captions required.
Columns/Departments: Hot Flashes (news/current events), 100-300 words; Innovations (new firefighting tricks and techniques), 300-1,000 words. **Buys 2-4 mss/year.** Send complete ms. **Pays $10 maximum.**
Fillers: Anecdotes, facts, newsbreaks. **Buys 2-4/year.** Length: 300-1,000 words. **Pays $25 maximum.**
Tips: "Content of articles is generally technical, tactical, educational or related to fire service legislation, current events or recent emergency incidents. We do not publish fiction or people profiles. We do, however, accept manuscripts for a monthly column of fire-service-related humor. Your punctuation, grammar and spelling are not our primary concerns. We have editors to correct these. We are more interested in your expertise, knowledge and experience in fire service subjects. However, it is important to spell names, places and organizations correctly, as our editors may not be familiar with them. Do not include opinions (unless you are submitting a Guest Editorial), unsubstantiated statements or untested tactics in your article. Accuracy is essential. Be sure of your facts, and always attribute information and identify sources."

$ CHIEF OF POLICE MAGAZINE, National Association of Chiefs of Police, 3801 Biscayne Blvd., Miami FL 33137. (305)573-0070. Fax: (305)573-9819. E-mail: policeinfo@aphf.org. Website: www.aphf.org. **Contact:** Jim Gordon, executive editor. Bimonthly journal for law enforcement commanders (command ranks). Circ. 13,500. **Pays on acceptance.** Publishes ms an average of 6 months after acceptance. Byline given. Buys first rights. Submit seasonal material 6 months in advance. Accepts queries by mail, e-mail, fax. Accepts simultaneous submissions. Responds in 2 weeks to queries. Sample copy for $3 and 9×12 SAE with 5 first-class stamps. Writer's guidelines for #10 SASE.

O→ Break in with "a story concerning command officers or police family survivors."

Nonfiction: "We want stories about interesting police cases and stories on any law enforcement subject or program that is positive in nature." General interest, historical/nostalgic, how-to, humor, inspirational, interview/profile, new product, personal experience, photo feature, religious, technical. "No exposé types or anti-police." **Buys 50 mss/year.** Send complete ms. Length: 600-2,500 words. **Pays $25-75 for assigned articles; $25-100 for unsolicited articles.** Sometimes pays expenses of writers on assignment.
Photos: Send photos with submission. Reviews 5×6 prints. Buys one-time rights. Pays $5-10 for b&w; $10-25 for color. Captions required.
Columns/Departments: New Police (police equipment shown and tests), 200-600 words. **Buys 6 mss/year.** Send complete ms. **Pays $5-25.**
Fillers: Anecdotes, short humor, law-oriented cartoons. **Buys 100/year.** Length: 100-1,600 words. **Pays $5-25.**
Tips: "Writers need only contact law enforcement officers right in their own areas and we would be delighted. We want to recognize good commanding officers from sergeant and above who are involved with the community. Pictures of the subject or the department are essential and can be snapshots. We are looking for interviews with police chiefs and sheriffs on command level with photos."

$ $ CORRECTIONS TECHNOLOGY & MANAGEMENT, Hendon Publishing, Inc., 130 Waukegan Rd., Deerfield IL 60015. (847)444-3300. Fax: (847)444-3333. E-mail: tcaestecker@hendonpub.com. Website: www.ctmmag.com. **Contact:** Tom Caestecker, assistant editor. **40% freelance written.** Magazine covering correctional facility management. "We focus on positive stories of corrections professionals doing their job. For stories...lots of quotes, dramatic photos. Make it real. Make it useful." Estab. 1997. Circ. 15,000. Pays 30 days after publication. Publishes ms an average of 3 months after acceptance. Byline given. Buys first North American serial rights. Editorial lead time 4 months. Submit seasonal material 6 months in advance. Responds in 1 month to mss. Sample copy for 9×12 SAE and 6 first-class stamps.
Nonfiction: Facility design; technology; management; health care; food services, safety; trainings; interview/profile; photo features. "Nothing 'general market.' Must be corrections-specific." **Buys 30 mss/year.** Query with published clips. Length: 2,000-2,500 words.

Photos: Send photos with submission. Reviews transparencies, 8×10 prints. Buys all rights. Negotiates payment individually. Captions, identification of subjects, model releases required.

Columns/Departments: Corrections Profile (spotlight on one facility), 2,000 words; Tactical Profile (products in corrections tactics), 1,000 words. **Buys 3 mss/year.** Query with published clips. **Pays 10-15¢/word.**

$ $ COUNTY, Texas Association of Counties, P.O. Box 2131, Austin TX 78768. (512)478-8753. Fax: (512)481-1240. E-mail: jiml@county.org. Website: www.county.org. **Contact:** Jim Lewis, editor. **15% freelance written.** Bimonthly magazine covering county and state government in Texas. "We provide elected and appointed county officials with insights and information that helps them do their jobs and enhances communications among the independent office-holders in the courthouse." Estab. 1988. Circ. 5,500. **Pays on acceptance.** Publishes ms an average of 2 months after acceptance. Byline given. Makes work-for-hire assignments. Editorial lead time 2 months. Submit seasonal material 4 months in advance. Accepts queries by mail, e-mail, phone. Responds in 2 weeks to queries; 1 month to mss. Sample copy and writer's guidelines for 8×10 SAE with 3 first-class stamps.

Nonfiction: Historical/nostalgic, photo feature, government innovations. **Buys 5 mss/year.** Query with published clips. Length: 1,000-3,000 words. **Pays $300-500.** Sometimes pays expenses of writers on assignment.

Photos: State availability with submission. Buys all rights. Negotiates payment individually. Captions, identification of subjects, model releases required.

Columns/Departments: Safety; Human Resources; Risk Management (all directed toward education of Texas county officials), maximum length 1,000 words. **Buys 2 mss/year.** Query with published clips. **Pays $300.**

Tips: "Identify innovative practices or developing trends that affect Texas county officials and have the basic journalism skills to write a multi-sourced, informative feature."

$ $ FIRE CHIEF, Primedia Business, 29 N. Wacker Dr., Chicago IL 60606. (312)726-2574. Fax: (312)726-2812. E-mail: jwilmoth@primediabusiness.com. Website: www.firechief.com. **Contact:** Janet Wilmoth, editor. **90% freelance written.** Monthly magazine. "*Fire Chief* is the management magazine of the fire service, addressing the administrative, personnel, training, prevention/education, professional development and operational issues faced by chiefs and other fire officers, whether in paid, volunteer or combination departments. We're potentially interested in any article that can help them do their jobs better, whether that's as incident commanders, financial managers, supervisors, leaders, trainers, planners, or ambassadors to municipal officials or the public." Estab. 1956. Circ. 50,000. Pays on publication. Publishes ms an average of 6 months after acceptance. Byline given. Kill fee negotiable. Buys first, one-time, second serial (reprint), all rights. Editorial lead time 2 months. Submit seasonal material 4 months in advance. Accepts queries by mail, e-mail, fax. Responds in 1 month to queries; 2 months to mss. Sample copy and writer's guidelines free or online.

Nonfiction: "If your department has made some changes in its structure, budget, mission or organizational culture (or really did reinvent itself in a serious way), an account of that process, including the mistakes made and lessons learned, could be a winner. Similarly, if you've observed certain things that fire departments typically could do a lot better and you think you have the solution, let us know." How-to, technical. **Buys 50-60 mss/year.** Query with published clips. Length: 1,500-8,000 words. **Pays $50-400.** Sometimes pays expenses of writers on assignment.

Photos: State availability with submission. Reviews transparencies, Prints. Buys one-time or reprint rights. Captions, identification of subjects required.

Columns/Departments: Training Perspectives, EMS Viewpoints, Sound Off, Volunteer Voice, 1,000-1,800 words.

Tips: "Writers who are unfamiliar with the fire service are very unlikely to place anything with us. Many pieces that we reject are either too unfocused or too abstract. We want articles that help keep fire chiefs well informed and effective at their jobs."

$ $ FIREHOUSE MAGAZINE, Cygnus Business Media, 445 Broad Hollow Rd., Suite 21, Melville NY 11747. (631)845-2700. Fax: (631)845-7109. E-mail: peter@firehouse.com. Website: www.firehouse.com. Editor-in-Chief: Harvey Eisner. **Contact:** Peter Matthews, assistant editor. **85% freelance written.** Works with a small number of new/unpublished writers each year. Monthly magazine. "*Firehouse* covers major fires nationwide, controversial issues and trends in the fire service, the latest firefighting equipment and methods of firefighting, historical fires, firefighting history and memorabilia. Fire-related books, fire safety education, hazardous materials incidents and the emergency medical services are also covered." Estab. 1976. Circ. 127,000. Pays on publication. Byline given. Accepts queries by mail, e-mail, fax. Sample copy for 9×12 SAE and 8 first-class stamps. Writer's guidelines free or online.

Nonfiction: Book excerpts (of recent books on fire, EMS and hazardous materials), historical/nostalgic (great fires in history, fire collectibles, the fire service of yesteryear), how-to (fight certain kinds of fires, buy and maintain equipment, run a fire department), technical (on almost any phase of firefighting, techniques, equipment, training, administration), trends in the fire service. No profiles of people or departments that are not unusual or innovative, reports of nonmajor fires, articles not slanted toward firefighters' interests. No poetry. **Buys 100 mss/year.** Query with or without published clips. Length: 500-3,000 words. **Pays $50-400 for assigned articles.**

Photos: Send photos with submission. Pays $25-200 for transparencies and color prints. Cannot accept negatives. Captions, identification of subjects required.

Columns/Departments: Training (effective methods); Book Reviews; Fire Safety (how departments teach fire safety to the public); Communicating (PR, dispatching); Arson (efforts to combat it). Length: 750-1,000. **Buys 50 mss/year.** Query or send complete ms. **Pays $100-300.**

Tips: "Have excellent fire service credentials and be able to offer our readers new information. Read the magazine to get a full understanding of the subject matter, the writing style and the readers before sending a query or manuscript. Send photos with manuscript or indicate sources for photos. Be sure to focus articles on firefighters."

$ FOREIGN SERVICE JOURNAL, 2101 E St. NW, Washington DC 20037-2990. (202)944-5511. Fax: (202)338-8244. E-mail: journal@afsa.org. Website: www.afsa.org. **Contact:** Steve Honley, editor. **75% freelance written.** Monthly magazine for Foreign Service personnel and others interested in foreign affairs and related subjects. Estab. 1924. Pays on publication. Publishes ms an average of 3 months after acceptance. Byline given. Buys first North American serial rights. Accepts queries by mail, e-mail, fax. Responds in 1 month to queries. Sample copy for $3.50 and 10×12 SAE with 6 first-class stamps. Writer's guidelines for #10 SASE.

O‐ Break in through "Postcard from Abroad—short items (600 words) on life abroad."

Nonfiction: Uses articles on "diplomacy, professional concerns of the State Department and Foreign Service, diplomatic history and articles on Foreign Service experiences. Much of our material is contributed by those working in the profession. Informed outside contributions are welcomed, however." Essays, exposé, humor, opinion, personal experience. **Buys 15-20 unsolicited mss/year.** Query. Length: 1,000-3,000 words. **Offers honoraria.**

Tips: "We're more likely to want your article if it has something to do with diplomacy or U.S. foreign policy."

$ $ THE JOURNAL OF SAFE MANAGEMENT OF DISRUPTIVE AND ASSAULTIVE BEHAVIOR, Crisis Prevention Institute, Inc., 3315-K N. 124th S, Brookfield WI 53005. Fax: (262)783-5906. E-mail: info@crisisprevention.com. Website: www.crisisprevention.com. **Contact:** Diana B. Kohn, editor/advertising manager. **20% freelance written.** Semi-annual journal covering safe management of disruptive and assaultive behavior. "Our audience is human service and business professionals concerned about workplace violence issues. *CPI* is the world leader in violence prevention training." Estab. 1980. Circ. 12,000. Pays on publication. Publishes ms an average of 6 months after acceptance. Byline given. Offers 50% kill fee. Buys one-time, second serial (reprint) rights. Editorial lead time 6 months. Submit seasonal material 3 months in advance. Responds in 1 month to queries. Sample copy and writer's guidelines free.

Nonfiction: "Each issue is specifically devoted to one topic. Inquire about topics by e-mail." Interview/profile, new product, opinion, personal experience, research. Inquire for editorial calendar. **Buys 5-10 mss/year.** Query. Length: 1,500-3,000 words. **Pays $50-300 for assigned articles; $50-100 for unsolicited articles.**

Tips: "For more information on CPI, please refer to our website."

$ LAW AND ORDER, Hendon Co., 130 Waukegan Road, Deerfield IL 60015. (847)444-3300. Fax: (847)444-3333. E-mail: esanow@hendonpub.com. Website: www.lawandordermag.com. **Contact:** Ed Sanow, editor-in-chief. **90% freelance written.** Prefers to work with published/established writers. Monthly magazine covering the administration and operation of law enforcement agencies, directed to police chiefs, sheriffs, and supervisors. Estab. 1953. Circ. 42,000. Pays on publication. Publishes ms an average of 6 months after acceptance. Byline given. Buys first North American serial rights. Submit seasonal material 3 months in advance. Accepts queries by mail, e-mail, fax, phone. Responds in 1 month to queries. Sample copy for 9×12 SAE. Writer's guidelines free.

Nonfiction: General police interest. How-to (do specific police assignments), new product (how applied in police operation), technical (specific police operation). Special issues: Weapons (January); Buyers Guide (February); S.W.A.T. (March); Community Relations (April); Science & Technology (May); Training (June); Mobile Patrol (July); Communications (August); Uniforms (September); IACP (October); Investigative (November); Computing & the Internet (December). No articles dealing with courts (legal field) or convicted prisoners. No nostalgic, financial, travel or recreational material. **Buys 150 mss/year.** Query; no simultaneous queries. Length: 2,000-3,000 words. **Pays 10-25¢/word.**

Photos: Send photos with submission. Reviews transparencies, prints. Buys all rights. Pays $25-40/photo. Identification of subjects required.

Tips: "*L&O* is a respected magazine that provides up-to-date information that police chiefs can use. Writers must know their subject as it applies to this field. Case histories are well received. We are upgrading editorial quality—stories *must* show some understanding of the law enforcement field. A frequent mistake is not getting photographs to accompany article."

N $ $ LAW ENFORCEMENT TECHNOLOGY, Cygnus Business Media, P.O. Box 803, 1233 Janesville Ave., Fort Atkinson WI 53538-0803.. (920)563-1726. Fax: (920)563-1702. E-mail: ronnie.garrett@cygnuspubs.com. Editor: Ronnie Garrett. **50% freelance written.** Monthly magazine covering police management and technology. Estab. 1974. Circ. 35,000. Pays on publication. Publishes ms an average of 6 months after acceptance. Byline given. Offers 25% kill fee. Buys first North American serial rights. Editorial lead time 6 months. Submit seasonal material 6 months in advance. Responds in 1 month to queries; 2 months to mss. and 6 first-class stamps. Writer's guidelines for #10 SASE.

Nonfiction: Book excerpts, how-to, interview/profile, photo feature, police management and training. **Buys 15 mss/year.** Query. Length: 800-1,800 words. **Pays $75-400 for assigned articles.**

Reprints: Send ms with rights for sale noted and information about when and where the material previously appeared. Payment negotiable.

Photos: Send photos with submission. Reviews contact sheets, negatives, 5×7 or 8×10 prints. Buys one-time rights. Offers no additional payment for photos accepted with ms. Captions required.

Tips: "Writer should have background in police work or currently work for a police agency. Most of our articles are technical or supervisory in nature. Please query first after looking at a sample copy."

$ $ NATIONAL FIRE & RESCUE, SpecComm International, Inc., 5808 Faringdon Place, Suite 200, Raleigh NC 27609. (919)872-5040. Fax: (919)876-6531. E-mail: editor@nfrmag.com. Website: www.nfrmag.com. **Contact:** Phil Powell, editor. **80% freelance written.** Bimonthly magazine. "*National Fire & Rescue* is a bimonthly magazine devoted to informing the nation's fire and rescue services, with special emphasis on fire departments serving communities of less than 100,000. It is the *Popular Science* for fire and rescue with easy-to-understand information on science, technology and training." Estab. 1980. Circ. 30,000. Pays on publication. Publishes ms an average of 5 months after acceptance. Byline given. Offers 50% kill fee. Buys first North American serial rights. Editorial lead time 2 months. Submit seasonal material 3 months in advance. Accepts simultaneous submissions. Responds in 1 month to queries. Call for writer's guidelines.

Nonfiction: Book excerpts, how-to, humor, inspirational, interview/profile, new product, personal experience, photo feature. No pieces marketing specific products or services. **Buys 40 mss/year.** Query with published clips. Length: 600-2,000 words. **Pays $100-350 for assigned articles; $100-200 for unsolicited articles.** Pays expenses of writers on assignment.

Photos: State availability with submission. Buys one-time rights. Offers $50-200/photo. Identification of subjects required.

Columns/Departments: Leadership (management); Training; Special Operations, all 800 words. **Buys 16 mss/year.** Send complete ms. **Pays $100-200.**

Tips: "Discuss your story ideas with the editor."

$ $ $ $ NFPA JOURNAL, National Fire Protection Association, P.O. Box 9101, Quincy MA 02269-9101. (617)984-7562. Fax: (617)984-7090. E-mail: nfpajournal@nfpa.org. Website: www.nfpa.org. Publisher: Kathie Robinson. **Contact:** Denise Laitinen, managing editor. **50% freelance written.** Bimonthly magazine covering fire safety, fire science, fire engineering. "The *NFPA Journal*, the official journal of the NFPA, reaches all of the association's various fire safety professionals. Covering major topics in fire protection and suppression, the bimonthly *Journal* carries investigation reports; special NFPA statistical studies on large-loss and multiple-death fires, fire fighter deaths and injuries, and other annual reports; articles on fire protection advances and public education; and information of interest to NFPA members. Fire fighting techniques and fire department management are also covered." Estab. 1969. Circ. 74,000. **Pays on acceptance.** Publishes ms an average of 1 year after acceptance. Byline given. Buys all rights. Editorial lead time 6 months. Accepts queries by e-mail, fax. Sample copy and writer's guidelines free.

Nonfiction: Technical. No fiction, product pieces or human interest. **Buys 10 mss/year.** Query. Length: 2,000-5,000 words. **Pays $1,200-1,800 for assigned articles.** Sometimes pays expenses of writers on assignment.

Photos: State availability with submission. Buys one-time rights. Negotiates payment individually. Captions, identification of subjects, model releases required.

Tips: "Query or call. Be familiar with our publication and audience. We happily send out sample issues and guidelines. Because we are a peer-reviewed journal, we can not endorse or promote particular products—no infomercials please! We appreciate and value quality writers who can provide well-written material on technical subjects related to fire and life safety."

$ $ 9-1-1 MAGAZINE, Official Publications, Inc., 18201 Weston Place, Tustin CA 92780-2251. (714)544-7776. Fax: (714)838-9233. E-mail: publisher@9-1-1magazine.com. Website: www.9-1-1magazine.com. **Contact:** Randall Larson, editor. **85% freelance written.** Bimonthly magazine for knowledgeable emergency communications professionals and those associated with this respectful profession. "Serving law enforcement, fire and emergency medical services, *9-1-1 Magazine* provides valuable information to readers in all aspects of the public safety communications and response community. Each issue contains a blending of product-related, technical, operational and people-oriented stories, covering the skills, training and equipment which these professionals have in common." Estab. 1989. Circ. 20,000. Pays on publication. Publishes ms an average of 4-6 months after acceptance. Byline given. Offers 20% kill fee. Buys one-time, second serial (reprint) rights. Accepts queries by mail, e-mail, fax. Responds in 1 month to queries; 2 months to mss. Sample copy for 9×12 SAE and 5 first-class stamps. Writer's guidelines for #10 SASE.

Nonfiction: New product, photo feature, technical, Incident report. **Buys 20-30 mss/year.** Query with SASE or by e-mail. We prefer queries, but will look at manuscripts on speculation. Most positive responses to queries are considered on spec, but occasionally we will make assignments. Length: 1,000-2,500 words. **Pays 10¢/word.**

Photos: Send photos with submission. Reviews color transparencies, prints, hi-res digital (300 dpi). Buys one-time rights. Offers $50-100/interior, $300/cover. Captions, identification of subjects required.

Fillers: Cartoons. **Buys 6/year. Pays $25.**

The online version of this magazine contains material not found in the print version.

Tips: "We are looking for writers knowledgable in this field. As a trade magazine, stories should be geared for professionals in the emergency services and dispatch field, not the lay public. We seldom use poetry or fiction. Our primary considerations in selecting material are: quality, appropriateness of material, brevity, knowledge of our readership, accuracy, accompanying photography, originality, wit and humor, a clear direction and vision, and proper use of language."

$ $ $ PLANNING, American Planning Association, 122 S. Michigan Ave., Suite 1600, Chicago IL 60603. (312)431-9100. Fax: (312)431-9985. E-mail: slewis@planning.org. Website: www.planning.org. **Contact:** Sylvia Lewis, editor. **25% freelance written.** Monthly magazine emphasizing urban planning for adult, college-educated readers who are regional and urban planners in city, state or federal agencies or in private business or university faculty or students. Estab. 1972. Circ. 30,000. Pays on publication. Publishes ms an average of 2 months after acceptance. Byline given. Buys all rights. Accepts queries by mail, e-mail, fax. Responds in 2 months to queries. Sample copy and writer's guidelines for 9×12 SAE with 5 first-class stamps.

Nonfiction: "It's best to query with a fairly detailed, one-page letter or e-mail. We'll consider any article that's well written and relevant to our audience. Articles have a better chance if they are timely and related to planning and land use and if they appeal to a national audience. All articles should be written in magazine feature style." Exposé (on government or business, but topics related to planning, housing, land use, zoning), general interest (trend stories on cities, land use, government), how-to (successful government or citizen efforts in planning, innovations, concepts that have been applied), technical (detailed articles on the nitty-gritty of planning, zoning, transportation but no footnotes or mathematical models). Special issues: Also needs news stories up to 500 words. **Buys 36 features and 24 news story mss/year.** Length: 500-2,000 words. **Pays $150-1,000.**

Photos: "We prefer that authors supply their own photos, but we sometimes take our own or arrange for them in other ways." State availability with submission. Buys one-time rights. Pays $100 minimum for photos used on inside pages and $300 for cover photos. Captions required.

$ $ POLICE AND SECURITY NEWS, DAYS Communications, Inc., 1208 Juniper St., Quakertown PA 18951-1520. (215)538-1240. Fax: (215)538-1208. E-mail: jdevery@policeandsecuritynews.com. **Contact:** James Devery, editor. **40% freelance written.** Bimonthly tabloid on public law enforcement and private security. "Our publication is designed to provide educational and entertaining information directed toward management level. Technical information written for the expert in a manner that the non-expert can understand." Estab. 1984. Circ. 22,000. Pays on publication. Publishes ms an average of 2 months after acceptance. Byline given. Buys first North American serial rights. Accepts queries by mail, e-mail, fax, phone. Accepts simultaneous submissions. Sample copy and writer's guidelines for 9×12 SAE with $2.18 postage.

Nonfiction: Al Menear, articles editor. Exposé, historical/nostalgic, how-to, humor, interview/profile, opinion, personal experience, photo feature, technical. **Buys 12 mss/year.** Query. Length: 200-4,000 words. **Pays 10¢/word. Sometimes pays in trade-out of services.**

Reprints: Send tearsheet, photocopy or typed ms with rights for sale noted and information about when and where the material previously appeared.

Photos: State availability with submission. Reviews 3×5 prints. Buys one-time rights. Offers $10-50/photo.

Fillers: Facts, newsbreaks, short humor. **Buys 6/year.** Length: 200-2,000 words. **Pays 10¢/word.**

$ POLICE TIMES, American Federation of Police & Concerned Citizens, Inc., 3801 Biscayne Blvd., Miami FL 33137. (305)573-0070. Fax: (305)573-9819. **Contact:** Jim Gordon, executive editor. **80% freelance written.** Eager to work with new/unpublished writers. Quarterly magazine covering "law enforcement (general topics) for men and women engaged in law enforcement and private security, and citizens who are law and order concerned." Circ. 55,000. **Pays on acceptance.** Publishes ms an average of 6 months after acceptance. Byline given. Buys second serial (reprint) rights. Submit seasonal material 4 months in advance. Accepts queries by mail, fax. Accepts simultaneous submissions. Sample copy for $2.50 and 9×12 SAE with 3 first-class stamps. Writer's guidelines for #10 SASE.

Nonfiction: Book excerpts, essays (on police science), exposé (police corruption), general interest, historical/nostalgic, how-to, humor, interview/profile, new product, personal experience (with police), photo feature, technical (all police related). Special issues: "We produce a special edition on police killed in the line of duty. It is mailed May 15 so copy must arrive six months in advance. Photos required." No anti-police materials. **Buys 50 mss/year.** Send complete ms. Length: 200-4,000 words. **Pays $25-100. Payment includes right to publish on organization's website.**

Photos: Send photos with submission. Reviews 5×6 prints. Buys all rights. Offers $5-25/photo. Identification of subjects required.

Columns/Departments: Legal Cases (lawsuits involving police actions); New Products (new items related to police services); Awards (police heroism acts). Length: 200-1,000. **Buys variable number of mss/year.** Send complete ms. **Pays $25-75.**

Fillers: Fillers are usually humorous stories about police officer and citizen situations. Special stories on police cases, public corruptions, etc., are most open to freelancers. Anecdotes, facts, newsbreaks, short humor, cartoons. **Buys 100/year.** Length: 50-100 words. **Pays $5-10.**

GROCERIES & FOOD PRODUCTS

In this section are publications for grocers, food wholesalers, processors, warehouse owners, caterers, institutional managers, and suppliers of grocery store equipment. See the section on Confectionery & Snack Foods for bakery and candy industry magazines.

N $ AUTOMATIC MERCHANDISER MAGAZINE, Cygnus Business Media, 36 S. 3rd St., Fort Atkinson WI 53538. (800)547-7377. Fax: (920)563-1702. E-mail: stacey.meacham@amonline.com. Website: www.amonline.com. Editor: Elliot Maras. **Contact:** Stacey Meacham, managing editor. **30% freelance written.** Monthly magazine covering vending and office coffee. Estab. 1940. Circ. 16,000. **Pays on acceptance.** Byline given. Buys first rights. Editorial lead time 1 months. Accepts queries by mail, e-mail, fax. Accepts simultaneous submissions. Sample copy online.

$ $ $ DISTRIBUTION CHANNELS, AWMA's Magazine for Candy, Tobacco, Grocery and General Merchandise Marketers, American Wholesale Marketers Association, 1128 16th St. NW, Washington DC 20036. (202)463-2124. Fax: (202)467-0559. E-mail: tracic@awmanet.org. Website: www.awmanet.org. **Contact:** Traci Carneal, editor-in-chief. **75% freelance written.** Magazine published 10 times/year. "We cover trends in candy, tobacco, groceries, beverages, snacks and other product categories found in convenience stores, grocery stores and drugstores, plus distribution topics. Contributors should have prior experience writing about the food, retail and/or distribution industries.

Editorial includes a mix of columns, departments and features (2-6 pages). We also cover AWMA programs." Estab. 1948. Circ. 10,000. **Pays on acceptance.** Publishes ms an average of 2 months after acceptance. Byline given. Editorial lead time 4 months. Accepts queries by mail, e-mail, fax.

Nonfiction: How-to, technical, Industry trends; also profiles of distribution firms. No comics, jokes, poems or other fillers. **Buys 80 mss/year.** Query with published clips. Length: 1,200-3,600 words. **Pays $200-1,200 generally.** Sometimes pays industry members who author articles. Pays expenses of writers on assignment.

Photos: Authors must provide artwork (with captions) with articles.

Tips: "We're looking for reliable, accurate freelancers with whom we can establish a long-term working relationship. We need writers who understand this industry. We accept very few articles on speculation. Most are assigned. To consider a new writer for an assignment, we must first receive his or her résumé, at least two writing samples and references. We only work with full-time freelancers."

N $ $ FOODSERVICE DIRECTOR, VNU Business Media, 770 Broadway, New York NY 10003. (646)654-7403. Fax: (646)654-7410. Executive Editor: James Pond; Feature Editor: Karen Weisberg; News Editor: Amanda Chater. **Contact:** Walter J. Schruntek, editor. **20% freelance written.** Monthly tabloid covering non-commercial foodservice operations for operators of kitchens and dining halls in schools, colleges, hospitals/health care, office and plant cafeterias, military, airline/transportation, correctional institutions. Estab. 1988. Circ. 45,000. Pays on publication. Byline sometimes given. Buys all rights. Submit seasonal material 3 months in advance. Accepts simultaneous submissions. Sample copy for free.

Nonfiction: How-to, interview/profile. **Buys 60-70 mss/year.** Query with published clips. Length: 700-900 words. **Pays $250-500.** Sometimes pays expenses of writers on assignment.

Photos: Send photos with submission. Reviews transparencies. Buys all rights. Offers no additional payment for photos accepted with ms. Identification of subjects required.

Columns/Departments: Equipment (case studies of kitchen/serving equipment in use), 700-900 words; Food (specific category studies per publication calendar), 750-900 words. **Buys 20-30 mss/year.** Query. **Pays $250-500.**

$ $ FRESH CUT MAGAZINE, The Magazine for Value-added Produce, Columbia Publishing, 417 N. 20th Ave., Yakima WA 98902. (509)248-2452. Fax: (509)248-4056. E-mail: ken@freshcut.com. **Contact:** Ken Hodge, editor. **40% freelance written.** Monthly magazine covering minimally processed fresh fruits and vegetables, packaged salads, etc. "We want informative articles about processing produce. We also want stories about how these products are sold at retail, in restaurants, etc." Estab. 1993. Circ. 18,464. Pays on publication. Publishes ms an average of 2 months after acceptance. Byline given. Buys all rights. Editorial lead time 2 months. Submit seasonal material 3 months in advance. Accepts queries by mail, e-mail, fax, phone. Responds in 1 month to queries; 2 months to mss. Sample copy for 9×12 SAE. Writer's guidelines for #10 SASE.

Nonfiction: Historical/nostalgic, new product, opinion, technical. Special issues: Retail (May); Foodservice (February, July); Packaging Technology (December). **Buys 2-4 mss/year.** Query with published clips. **Pays $5/column inch for assigned articles; $75-125 for unsolicited articles.**

Reprints: Send tearsheet with rights for sale noted and information about when and where the material previously appeared. Pays 50% of amount paid for an original article.

Photos: Send photos with submission. Reviews transparencies. Buys one-time rights. Offers no additional payment for photos accepted with ms. Identification of subjects required.

Columns/Departments: Packaging; Food Safety; Processing/Engineering. **Buys 20 mss/year.** Query. **Pays $125-200.**

Fillers: Facts. Length: 300 words maximum. **Pays $25-50.**

$ $ HEALTH PRODUCTS BUSINESS, CYGNUS Business Media Inc., 445 Broad Hollow Rd., Suite 21, Melville NY 11747. (631)845-2700. Fax: (631)845-2723. Website: www.healthproductsbusiness.com. **Contact:** Michael Schiavetta, managing editor. **70% freelance written.** Monthly magazine covering natural health products. "The business magazine for natural products retailers." Estab. 1954. Circ. 16,000. Pays on publication. Publishes ms an average of 3 months after acceptance. Byline given. Buys first North American serial rights. Editorial lead time 4 months. Submit seasonal material 3 months in advance. Accepts queries by mail, fax. Sample copy for $3. Writer's guidelines free.

Nonfiction: Store profile. Query. **Pays $200-250.**

Photos: State availability with submission.

The online version of this publication contains material not found in the print edition. Contact: Michael Schiavetta, managing editor.

Tips: "We are always looking for well-written store profiles with a lot of detailed information, but new writers should always query first to receive writer's guidelines and other necessary information. We prefer writers with industry experience/interest."

$ $ PRODUCE MERCHANDISING, Vance Publishing Corp., 10901 W. 84th Terrace, Lenexa KS 66214. (913)438-8700. Fax: (913)438-0691. E-mail: jkresin@producemerchandising.com. Website: www.producemerchandising.com. **Contact:** Janice M. Kresin, editor. **33% freelance written.** Monthly magazine. "The magazine's editorial purpose is to provide information about promotions, merchandising and operations in the form of ideas and examples. *Produce Merchandising* is the only monthly journal on the market that is dedicated solely to produce merchandising information for retailers." Circ. 12,000. **Pays on acceptance.** Publishes ms an average of 3 months after acceptance. Byline given. Buys all rights. Editorial lead time 3 months. Accepts queries by mail. Responds in 2 weeks to queries. Sample copy for free.

Nonfiction: How-to, interview/profile, new product, photo feature, technical (contact the editor for a specific assignment). **Buys 48 mss/year.** Query with published clips. Length: 1,000-1,500 words. **Pays $200-600.** Pays expenses of writers on assignment.

Photos: State availability of or send photos with submission. Reviews color slides and 3×5 or larger prints. Buys all rights. Offers no additional payment for photos accepted with ms. Captions, identification of subjects, model releases required.

Columns/Departments: Contact editor for a specific assignment. **Buys 30 mss/year.** Query with published clips. **Pays $200-450.**

Tips: "Send in clips and contact the editor with specific story ideas. Story topics are typically outlined up to a year in advance."

$ $ THE SERVER FOODSERVICE NEWS, Business Communications, Inc., 157 S. 26th St., Pittsburgh PA 15203. (412)381-5029. Fax: (412)381-5205. E-mail: editorial@theservernews.com. Website: www.theservernews.com. **Contact:** Lori Monahan, executive editor. **10-15% freelance written.** Monthly tabloid covering food service, restaurant industry, C-stores, supermarket chains. "*The Server Foodservice News* is edited for the food service industry. It is edited for restaurant personnel, liquor licenses, chain operation, personnel, etc. *The Server* provides pertinent data about new products, trends and other vital information. *The Server Foodservice News* is a national publication with a regional focus and a local flair. Michigan, Ohio, West Virginia, Maryland, Delaware, New Jersey, New York, and Pennsylvania are states that are covered with editorial features, current events and the people who make them happen in the foodservice industry." Estab. 1979. Circ. 25,000. Pays on publication. Byline given. Buys all rights. Accepts queries by mail, e-mail, fax. Sample copy for $3.95. Writer's guidelines free.

Nonfiction: General interest, historical/nostalgic, interview/profile, new product. No restaurant reviews. Query. Length: 400-800 words. **Pays 10-15¢/word.**

Photos: Send photos with submission. Reviews contact sheets. Buys all rights. Offers $5/photo. Captions, identification of subjects, model releases required.

The online version contains materials not found in the print edition. Contact: Lori Monahan.

WESTERN GROCER MAGAZINE, Mercury Publications Ltd., 1839 Inkster Blvd., Winnipeg, Manitoba R2X 1R3, Canada. (204)954-2085. Fax: (204)954-2057. E-mail: mp@mercury.mb.ca. Website: www.mercury.mb.ca/. Editor: Frank Yeo. **Contact:** Kristi Balon, editorial production manager. **75% freelance written.** Bimonthly magazine covering the grocery industry. Reports profiles on independent food stores, supermarkets, manufacturers and food processors, brokers, distributors and wholesalers. Estab. 1916. Circ. 15,500. Pays 30-45 days from receipt of invoice. Byline given. Offers 33% kill fee. Buys all rights. Submit seasonal material 3 months in advance. Accepts queries by mail, e-mail, fax. Accepts simultaneous submissions. Responds in 2 weeks to queries. Sample copy and writer's guidelines free or by e-mail.

Nonfiction: How-to, interview/profile. Industry reports and profiles on companies. Query with published clips. Length: 500-9,000 words. **Pays 25-35¢/word.** Sometimes pays expenses of writers on assignment.

Photos: State availability with submission. Reviews negatives, transparencies, 3×5 prints, JPEG, EPS or TIF files. Buys all rights. Negotiates payment individually. Captions required.

Fillers: Facts. Length: 100 words.

Tips: "Send an e-mailed, faxed or mailed query outlining your experience, interests and pay expectations. A requirement also is clippings."

HOME FURNISHINGS & HOUSEHOLD GOODS

Readers rely on these publications to learn more about new products and trends in the home furnishings and appliance trade. Magazines for consumers interested in home furnishings are listed in the Consumer Home & Garden section.

$ FINE FURNISHINGS INTERNATIONAL, G&W McNamara Publishing, 4215 White Bear Parkway, Suite 100, St. Paul MN 55110. Fax: (651)653-4308. E-mail: ffiedit@gwmcnamara.com. Website: www.ffimagazine.com. **Contact:** Esther De Hollander, managing editor. Bimonthly magazine covering the high-end furniture industry. Estab. 1997. Circ. 22,400. Pays on publication. Publishes ms an average of 3 months after acceptance. Byline given. Offers $150-250 kill fee. Buys all rights. Editorial lead time 2 months. Submit seasonal material 3 months in advance. Accepts queries by mail, e-mail. Sample copy for $6. Writer's guidelines free.

Nonfiction: Historical/nostalgic, how-to, interview/profile, technical. Query. **Pays $150.** Sometimes pays expenses of writers on assignment.

Tips: "The most helpful experience is if a writer has knowledge of interior design or, specifically, fine furniture. We already have a pool of journalists, although we welcome clips from writers who would like to be considered for assignments. Particularly if they have a profile of a high-end interior designer. Our style is professional business writing—no flowery prose. Articles tend to be to the point as our readers are busy professionals who read for information, not for leisure."

$ $ $ HOME FURNISHINGS RETAILER, (formerly *Home Furnishings Executive*), National Home Furnishings Association (NHFA), P.O. Box 2396, High Point NC 27261. (336)801-6152. Fax: (336)801-6102. E-mail: tkemerly@nhfa.org. **Contact:** Trisha Kemerly, editor. **75% freelance written.** Monthly magazine published by NHFA covering the home furnishings industry. "We hope that home furnishings retailers view our magazine as a profitability tool. We want each issue to help them make money or save money." Estab. 1927. Circ. 17,000. **Pays on acceptance.** Publishes ms an average of 6 weeks after acceptance. Byline given. Buys first North American serial rights. Editorial lead time 3 months. Accepts queries by mail, e-mail. Responds in 1 month to queries. Sample copy available with proper postage. Writer's guidelines for #10 SASE.

- Break in by "e-mailing queries that pertain to our market - furniture retailers. We publish articles that give our readers tangible ways to improve their business."

Nonfiction: Query with published clips. Length: Features: 3,000-5,000 words. **Pays $350-500 for assigned articles.**
Photos: State availability with submission. Reviews transparencies. Buys one-time rights. Negotiates payment individually. Identification of subjects required.
Columns/Departments: Columns cover business and product trends that shape the home furnishings industry; Advertising and Marketing; Finance; Technology; Training; Creative Leadership; Law; Style and Operations. Length: 1,200-1,500 words. Query with published clips.
Tips: "Our readership includes owners of small 'ma and pa' furniture stores, executives of medium-sized chains (two to ten stores), and executives of big chains. Articles should be relevant to retailers and provide them with tangible information, ideas, and products to better their business."

N $ HOME LIGHTING & ACCESSORIES, P.O. Box 2147, Clifton NJ 07015. (973)779-1600. Fax: (973)779-3242. Website: www.homelighting.com. **Contact:** Linda Longo, editor. **25% freelance written.** Prefers to work with published/established writers. Monthly magazine for lighting showrooms/department stores. Estab. 1923. Circ. 10,000. Pays on publication. Publishes ms an average of 6 months after acceptance. Buys first rights. Submit seasonal material 6 months in advance. Accepts queries by mail, e-mail. Responds in 2 months to queries. Sample copy for 9×12 SAE and 4 first-class stamps.
Nonfiction: Interview/profile (with lighting retailers), personal experience (as a businessperson involved with lighting), technical (concerning lighting or lighting design), Profile (of a successful lighting retailer/lamp buyer). Special issues: Outdoor (March); tribute to Tiffanies (August). **Buys less than 10 mss/year.** Query.
Reprints: Send tearsheet and information about when and where the material previously appeared.
Photos: State availability with submission. Offers no additional payment for 5×7 or 8×10 b&w glossy prints. Captions required.
Tips: "Have a unique perspective on retailing lamps and lighting fixtures. We often use freelancers located in a part of the country where we'd like to profile a specific business or person. Anyone who has published an article dealing with any aspect of home furnishings will have high priority."

$ THE WALL PAPER, G&W McNamara Publishing, 4215 White Bear Parkway, Suite 100, St. Paul MN 55110-7635. Fax: (651)653-4308. E-mail: twpedit@gwmcnamara.com. Website: www.thewallpaper.com. **Contact:** Kate Lundquist. Tabloid published 10 times/year on the wall coverings industry. Estab. 1979. Circ. 16,700. Pays on publication. Byline given. Offers $150-250 kill fee. Buys all rights. Editorial lead time 2 months. Submit seasonal material 3 months in advance. Accepts queries by mail, e-mail. Responds in 2 months to queries. Sample copy for $4. Writer's guidelines free.
Nonfiction: Historical/nostalgic, how-to, interview/profile. Query with published clips. **Pays $150.** Sometimes pays expenses of writers on assignment.
Photos: State availability with submission. Reviews 4×6 or larger transparencies, 4×6 or 8×10 prints. Buys all rights. Offers no additional payment for photos accepted with ms. Captions required.
Tips: "Most of all we need creative ideas and approaches to topics in the field of furniture and interior design. A writer needs to be knowledgeable in the field because our readers would know if information was inaccurate. We are looking mostly for features on specific topics or on installation or design."

HOSPITALS, NURSING & NURSING HOMES

In this section are journals for medical and nonmedical nursing home personnel, clinical and hospital staffs, and medical laboratory technicians and managers. Journals publishing technical material on medical research and information for physicians in private practice are listed in the Medical category.

N HOSPITALS & HEALTH NETWORKS, Health Forum, One N. Franklin, 29th Floor, Chicago IL 60606. E-mail: bsantamour@healthforum.com. Website: www.hhnmag.com. **Contact:** Bill Santamour, managing editor. **25% freelance written.** Monthly magazine covering hospitals. "We are a business publication for hospital and health system executives. We use only writers who are thoroughly familiar with the hospital field. Submit résumé and up to five samples of health care-related articles. We assign all articles and do not consider manuscripts." Estab. 1926. Circ. 85,000. **Pays on acceptance.** Publishes ms an average of 3 months after acceptance. Byline given. Offers variable kill fee. Buys all rights. Editorial lead time 2-3 months. Accepts queries by e-mail. Responds in 2-4 months to queries.

Nonfiction: Interview/profile, technical. Query with published clips. Length: 350-2,000 words. **Pays $300-1,500 for assigned articles.**

Tips: "If you demonstrate via published clips that you are thoroughly familiar with the business issues facing health-care executives, and that you are a polished reporter and writer, we will consider assigning you an article for our InBox section to start out. These are generally 350 words on a specific development of interest to hospitals and health system executives. Persistence does not pay with us. Once you've sent your résumé and clips, we will review them. If we have no assignment at that time, we will keep promising freelance candidates on file for future assignments."

$JOURNAL OF CHRISTIAN NURSING, Nurses Christian Fellowship, InterVarsity Christian Fellowship, P.O. Box 7895, Madison WI 53707-7895. (608)274-4823, ext. 401. E-mail: jcn@ivcf.org. Website: www.ncf-jcn.org. Editor: Judith Allen Shelly. **Contact:** Cathy Walker, managing editor. **30% freelance written.** Quarterly magazine covering spiritual care, ethics, crosscultural issues, etc. "Our target audience is Christian nurses in the U.S., and we are nondenominational in character. We are prolife in position. We strive to help Christian nurses view nursing practice through the eyes of faith. Articles must be relevant to Christian nursing and consistent with our statement of faith." Estab. 1984. Circ. 8,000. **Pays on acceptance.** Publishes ms an average of 1-2 years after acceptance. Byline given unless subject matter requires pseudonym. Offers 50% kill fee. Buys first, second serial (reprint) rights. rarely; all rights, only multiple-authored case studies. Editorial lead time up to 2 years. Submit seasonal material 1 year in advance. Accepts queries by mail, e-mail, fax. Responds in 1 month to queries; 2 months to mss. Sample copy for $5 and SAE with 4 first-class stamps. Writer's guidelines for #10 SASE or online.

Nonfiction: How-to, humor, inspirational, interview/profile, opinion, personal experience, photo feature, religious, all must be appropriate for Christian nurses. Poetry not accepted. No purely academic articles, subjects not appropriate for Christian nurses, devotionals, Bible study. **Buys 20-30 mss/year.** Send complete ms. Length: 6-12 pages (typed, double spaced). **Pays $25-80 and up to 8 complimentary copies.**

Reprints: Send tearsheet or photocopy and information about when and where the material previously appeared.

Photos: State availability of or send photos with submission. No rights purchased; all photos returned. Offers no additional payment for photos accepted with ms. Identification of subjects, model releases required.

Columns/Departments: Book Reviews (Resources). **No payment for Book Reviews.**

Tips: "Unless an author is a nurse, it will be unlikely that he/she will have an article accepted—unless it's a very interesting story about a nurse who is involved in creative ministry with a strong faith dimension."

$ $ $LONG TERM CARE, The Ontario Long Term Care Association, 345 Renfrew Dr., Suite 102-202, Markham, Ontario L3R 9S9, Canada. (905)470-8995. Fax: (905)470-9595. E-mail: heather_runtz@sympatico.ca. Website: www.oltca.com. Assistant Editor: Tracey Ann Schofield. **Contact:** Heather Runtz, editor. Quarterly magazine covering "practical articles of interest to staff working in a long term care setting (nursing home, retirement home); professional issues; information must be applicable to a Canadian setting; focus should be on staff and for resident well-being." Estab. 1990. Circ. 6,000. Pays on publication. Publishes ms an average of 4 months after acceptance. Byline given. Buys one-time rights. Editorial lead time 3 months. Submit seasonal material 5 months in advance. Responds in 3 months to queries. Sample copy for free. Writer's guidelines free.

Nonfiction: General interest, how-to (practical, of use to long term care practitioners), inspirational, interview/profile. No product-oriented articles. Query with published clips. Length: 800-1,500 words. **Pays up to $1,000 (Canadian).**

Reprints: Send tearsheet, photocopy or typed ms and information about when and where the material previously appeared. Pays 50% of amount paid for an original article.

Photos: Send photos with submission. Reviews contact sheets, 5×5 prints. Buys one-time rights. Offers no additional payment for photos accepted with ms. Captions, model releases required.

Columns/Departments: Resident Health (nursing, rehabilitation, food services); Resident Life (activities, volunteers, spiritual and pastoral care); Environment (housekeeping, laundry, maintenance, safety, landscape and architecture, staff health and well being), all 800 words. Query with published clips. **Pays up to $1,000 (Canadian).**

Tips: "Articles must be positive, upbeat, and contain helpful information that staff and managers working in the long term care field can use. Focus should be on staff and resident well being. Articles that highlight new ways of doing things are particularly useful. Please call the editor to discuss ideas. Must be applicable to Canadian settings."

NURSEWEEK, NurseWeek Publishing, 1156-C Aster Ave., Sunnyvale CA 94086. (800)859-2091. Fax: (408)249-3756. E-mail: carolb@nurseweek.com. Website: www.nurseweek.com. **Contact:** Carol Bradley, editor. Magazine. *NurseWeek* is an independent biweekly news magazine supported by advertising revenue, sales of continuing education, and trade shows. Its editorial mission is to provide nurses with the latest news, resources, and opportunities to help them succeed in their lives and careers. Byline given. Five regional editions: California, Mountain West, South Central, Midwest, and Great Lakes. Assigns articles. **Pays on acceptance.**

NurseWeek.com is updated daily with news content and posts new job listings on a daily basis.

$ $NURSEZONE.COM, AMN Healthcare Inc., 12235 El Camino Real, Suite 200, San Diego CA 92130. (858)720-6227. Fax: (866)510-1905. E-mail: carol.burke@nursezone.com. Website: www.nursezone.com. **Contact:** Carol Burke, editorial director. **50% freelance written.** Daily online publication covering the professional and personal lives of nurses. Estab. 2000. Circ. 21,000 visits/month. Pays on publication. Byline given. Offers variable kill fee. Buys second serial (reprint), electronic, all rights, makes work-for-hire assignments. Editorial lead time up to 1 month. Submit seasonal material 1 month in advance. Accepts queries by mail, e-mail. Accepts previously published material. Responds in 1 month to queries. Writer's guidelines for #10 SASE.

Nonfiction: Book excerpts, exposé, general interest, historical/nostalgic, humor, inspirational, interview/profile, new product, personal experience, photo feature, technical, travel, career-related for nurses; finance; news by specialty; medical news; holistic approaches to medicine. No consumer-related health articles. **Buys variable mss/year.** Query with published clips. Length: 600-1,000 words. **Pays $100-300.** Sometimes pays expenses of writers on assignment.
Photos: State availability with submission. Reviews contact sheets, 5×7 prints, GIF/JPEG/TIFF formats. Buys all and electronic rights. Negotiates payment individually. Captions, identification of subjects, model releases required.
Columns/Departments: Nursing News (medical news relevant to working nurses); Devices and Technology (latest news affecting working nurses); Career Advice (unique stories about nurses, information for career nurses); Travel Stories (how this might relate to nurses); Travel Tips (suggestions for travelers); Nursing Conferences (coverage of news), all 300-800 words; Realistic Stories (stories about nurses working in today's industry), 600-2,000 words; Your Finances (financial news, information, tips relevant to today's nurses), 300-1,000 words. Query. **Pays $100-300.**
Fiction: Nancy Fagan, content manager. Condensed novels, historical, humorous, novel excerpts, romance, slice-of-life vignettes, anything related to nurses or written by nurses. **Buys variable number of mss/year.** Query with published clips. Length: 500-2,500 words. **Pays $100-300.**
Tips: "Find an angle unique to nurses; personal stories by or about nurses are always welcome; try to have a nurse in the byline."

$ $ $ NURSING SPECTRUM, Florida Edition, Nursing Spectrum, 1001 W. Cypress Creek Rd., Ste. 300, Ft. Lauderdale FL 33309. (954)776-1455. Fax: (954)776-1456. E-mail: pclass@nursingspectrum.com. Website: www.nursingspectrum.com. **Contact:** Phyllis Class, RN, editorial director. **80% freelance written.** Biweekly magazine covering registered nursing. "We support and recognize registered nurses. All articles must have at least one RN in byline. We prefer articles that feature nurses in our region, but articles of interest to all nurses are welcome, too. We look for substantive, yet readable articles. Our bottom line—timely, relevant, and compelling articles that support nurses and help them excel in their clinical and professional careers." Estab. 1991. Circ. 53,928. Pays on publication. Byline given. Buys all rights. Editorial lead time 3 months. Submit seasonal material 4 months in advance. Accepts queries by mail, e-mail, fax, phone. Responds in 1 month to queries; 4 months to mss. Sample copy and writer's guidelines free.

O→ "Having an original idea is paramount and the first step in writing an article. We are looking for success stories, nurses to be proud of, and progress that is helping patients. If you and your colleagues have dealt with and learned from a thorny issue, tell us how. What is new in your field? Consider your audience: all RNs, well-educated, and of various specialties. Will they relate, be inspired, learn something? The best articles are both interesting and informative."

Nonfiction: General interest, how-to (career management), humor, interview/profile, personal experience, photo feature. Special issues: Critical Care, nursing management. "No articles that do not have at least one RN on the byline." **Buys 125 plus mss/year.** Length: 700-1,200 words. **Pays $50-800 for assigned articles.** Sometimes pays expenses of writers on assignment.
Photos: Review. Buys one-time rights. Negotiates payment individually. Captions, identification of subjects, model releases required.
Columns/Departments: Perspectives in Leadership (nurse managers); Advanced Practice (advanced practice nurses); Humor Infusion (cartoon, amusing anecdotes); Career Fitness (career tips, types of careers). **Buys 75 mss/year.** Query with published clips. **Pays $50-120.**
Tips: "Write in 'magazine' style—as if talking to another RN. Use to-the-point, active language. Narrow your focus. Topics such as 'The Future of Nursing' or 'Dealing With Change' are too broad and non-specific. Use informative but catchy titles and subheads (we can help with this). If quoting others be sure quotes are meaningful and add substance to the piece. To add vitality, you may use statistics and up-to-date references. Try to paint a complete picture, using pros and cons. Be both positive and realistic."

[N] **$ $ $ NURSING SPECTRUM, Greater Philadelphia/Tri-State edition**, Nursing Spectrum, 2002 Renaissance Blvd., Suite 250, King of Prussia PA 19406. (610)292-8000. Fax: (610)292-0179. E-mail: gstrassberg@nursingspectrum.com. Website: www.nursingspectrum.com. **Contact:** Gary Strassberg, managing editor. **80% freelance written.** Biweekly magazine covering registered nursing. "We support and recognize registered nurses. All articles must have at least one RN in byline. We prefer articles that feature nurses in our region, but articles of interest to all nurses are welcome, too. We look for substantive, yet readable articles. Our bottom line—timely, relevant, and compelling articles that support nurses and help them excel in their clinical and professional careers." Estab. 1992. Circ. 71,500. Byline given.

- See *Nursing Spectrum, Florida Edition* for article needs.

$ $ $ NURSING SPECTRUM, New England edition, Nursing Spectrum, 1050 Waltham St., Suite 510, Waltham MA 02421. (781)863-2300. Fax: (781)863-6277. E-mail: jborgatti@nursingspectrum.com. Website: www.nursingspectrum.com. **Contact:** Joan Borgatti, RN, editor. **80% freelance written.** Biweekly magazine covering registered nursing. "We support and recognize registered nurses. All articles must have at least one RN in byline. We prefer articles that feature nurses in our region, but articles of interest to all nurses are welcome, too. We look for substantive, yet readable articles. Our bottom line—timely, relevant, and compelling articles that support nurses and help them excel in their clinical and professional careers." Estab. 1997. Circ. 114,555. Byline given. Accepts queries by mail, e-mail, fax, phone.

- See *Nursing Spectrum, Florida Edition* for article needs.

▣ The online version carries original content not found in the print edition. Contact: Cynthia Saver, RN, editor.

$ $ $ NURSING SPECTRUM, Washington, DC/Baltimore edition, Nursing Spectrum, 803 W. Broad St., Suite 500, Falls Church VA 22046. (703)237-6515. Fax: (703)237-6299. E-mail: csaver@nursingspectrum.com. Website: www.nursingspectrum.com. **Contact:** Cindy Saver, RN, editor. **80% freelance written.** Biweekly journal covering registered nursing. "We support and recognize registered nurses. All articles must have at least one RN in byline. We prefer articles that feature nurses in our region, but articles of interest to all nurses are welcome, too. We look for substantive, yet readable articles. Our bottom line—timely, relevant, and compelling articles that support nurses and help them excel in their clinical and professional careers." Estab. 1990. Circ. 71,170.

• See *Nursing Spectrum, Florida Edition* for article needs.

N $ $ NURSING2003, (formerly *Nursing2000*), Springhouse Corporation, 1111 Bethlehem Pike, P.O. Box 908, Springhouse PA 19477-0908. (215)646-8700. Fax: (215)653-0826. E-mail: nursing@springnet.com. Website: www.springnet.com. Vice President Journals and Continuing. Editor-in-Chief: Cheryl L. Mee, RN, BC, MSN. Managing Editor: Jane Benner. **Contact:** Pat Wolf, editorial dept. **100% freelance written.** Monthly magazine "Written by nurses for nurses; we look for practical advice for the direct caregiver that reflects the author's experience. Any form acceptable, but focus must be nursing." Estab. 1971. Circ. over 300,000. Pays on publication. Publishes ms an average of 18 months after acceptance. Byline given. Offers 50% kill fee. Buys all rights. Submit seasonal material 8 months in advance. Responds in 2 weeks to queries; 3 months to mss. Sample copy for $4. Writer's guidelines online.
Nonfiction: Book excerpts, exposé, how-to (specifically as applies to nursing field), inspirational, new product, opinion, personal experience, photo feature. No articles from patients' point of view, poetry, etc. **Buys 100 mss/year.** Query. Length: 100 words minimum. **Pays $50-400 for assigned articles.**
Reprints: Send photocopy and information about when and where the material previously appeared. Pays 50% of amount paid for an original articles.
Photos: State availability with submission. Buys all rights. Offers no additional payment for photos accepted with ms. Model releases required.
Tips: "Basically, *Nursing2003* is a how-to journal, full of hands-on, practical articles. We look for the voice of experience from authors and for articles that help our readers deal with problems they face. We're always interested in taking a look at manuscripts that fall into the following categories: clinical articles, drug articles, charting/documentation, emotional problems, legal problems, ethical dilemnas, difficult ot challenging cases."

HOTELS, MOTELS, CLUBS, RESORTS & RESTAURANTS

These publications offer trade tips and advice to hotel, club, resort, and restaurant managers, owners, and operators. Journals for manufacturers and distributors of bar and beverage supplies are listed in the Beverages & Bottling section.

$ $ BARTENDER MAGAZINE, Foley Publishing, P.O. Box 158, Liberty Corner NJ 07938. (908)766-6006. Fax: (908)766-6607. E-mail: barmag@aol.com. Website: www.bartender.com. Editor: Jaclyn M. Wilson. **Contact:** Jackie Foley, publisher. **100% freelance written.** Prefers to work with published/established writers; eager to work with new/unpublished writers. Quarterly magazine emphasizing liquor and bartending for bartenders, tavern owners and owners of restaurants with full-service liquor licenses. Circ. 147,000. Pays on publication. Publishes ms an average of 3 months after acceptance. Byline given. Buys first North American serial, first, one-time, second serial (reprint), simultaneous, all rights. Submit seasonal material 3 months in advance. Accepts simultaneous submissions. Responds in 2 months to mss. Sample copy for 9×12 SAE and 4 first-class stamps.
Nonfiction: General interest, historical/nostalgic, how-to, humor, interview/profile (with famous bartenders or ex-bartenders), new product, opinion, personal experience, photo feature, travel, Nostalgia; Unique bars; New techniques; New drinking trends; Bar sports; Bar magic tricks. Special issues: Annual Calendar and Daily Cocktail Recipe Guide. Send complete ms and SASE. Length: 100-1,000 words.
Reprints: Send tearsheet and information about when and where the material previously appeared. Pays 25% of amount paid for an original article.
Photos: Send photos with submission. Pays $7.50-50 for 8×10 b&w glossy prints; $10-75 for 8×10 color glossy prints. Captions, model releases required.
Columns/Departments: Bar of the Month; Bartender of the Month; Drink of the Month; Creative Cocktails; Bar Sports; Quiz; Bar Art; Wine Cellar; Tips from the Top (from prominent figures in the liquor industry); One For the Road (travel); Collectors (bar or liquor-related items); Photo Essays.; **Length:** 200-1,000 words. Query by mail only with SASE. **Pays $50-200.**
Fillers: Anecdotes, newsbreaks, short humor, Clippings; Jokes; Gags. Length: 25-100 words. **Pays $5-25.**
Tips: "To break in, absolutely make sure that your work will be of interest to all bartenders across the country. Your style of writing should reflect the audience you are addressing. The most frequent mistake made by writers in completing an article for us is using the wrong subject."

$ $ CHEF, The Food Magazine for Professionals, Talcott Communications Corp., 20 N. Wacker Dr., Suite 1865, Chicago IL 60606. (312)849-2220. Fax: (312)849-2174. E-mail: chef@talcott.com. Website: www.chefmagazine.com. **Contact:** Brent T. Frei, editor-in-chief. **40% freelance written.** Monthly magazine covering chefs in all food-service segments. "*Chef* is the one magazine that communicates food production to a commercial, professional audience in a meaningful way." Circ. 42,000. **Pays on acceptance.** Byline given. Offers 10% kill fee. Buys first North American serial, second serial (reprint) rights. Editorial lead time 2 months. Submit seasonal material 4 months in advance. Accepts queries by mail, e-mail, fax. Responds in 3 weeks to queries; 2 months to mss. Sample copy and writer's guidelines free.

Nonfiction: Book excerpts, essays, exposé, general interest, historical/nostalgic, how-to (create a dish or perform a technique), humor, inspirational, interview/profile, new product, opinion, personal experience, photo feature, technical. **Buys 30-50 mss/year.** Query. Length: 750-1,500 words. **Pays $250-500.** Sometimes pays expenses of writers on assignment.

Reprints: Accepts previously published submissions.

Photos: State availability with submission. Reviews transparencies. Buys one-time rights. Negotiates payment individually. Captions, identification of subjects required.

Columns/Departments: Flavor (traditional and innovative applications of a particular flavor) 1,000-1,200 words; Dish (professional chef profiles), 1,000-1,200 words; Savor (themed recipes), 1,000-1,500 words; Spin (menu trends), 750-1,250 words. **Buys 12-18 mss/year.** Query. **Pays $250-500.**

Tips: "Know food and apply it to the business of chefs. Always query first, *after* you've read our magazine. Tell us how your idea can be used by our readers to enhance their businesses in some way."

$ $ CHRISTIAN CAMP & CONFERENCE JOURNAL, Christian Camping International U.S.A., P.O. Box 62189, Colorado Springs CO 80962-2189. (719)260-9400. Fax: (719)260-6398. E-mail: editor@cciusa.org. Website: www.cciusa.org. **Contact:** Natalee Roth, editor. **75% freelance written.** Prefers to work with published/established writers. Bimonthly magazine emphasizing the broad scope of organized camping with emphasis on Christian camping. "All who work in youth camps and adult conferences read our magazine for inspiration and to get practical help in ways to serve in their operations." Estab. 1963. Circ. 7,500. Pays on publication. Publishes ms an average of 4 months after acceptance. Byline given. negotiable rights Submit seasonal material 6 months in advance. Accepts queries by mail, e-mail. Responds in 1 month to queries. Sample copy for $2.25 plus 9×12 SASE. Writer's guidelines for #10 SASE.

Nonfiction: General interest (trends in organized camping in general, Christian camping in particular), how-to (anything involved with organized camping from motivating staff, to programming, to record keeping, to camper follow-up), inspirational, interview/profile (with movers and shakers in Christian camping; submit a list of basic questions first). **Buys 20-30 mss/year.** Query required. Length: 500-3,000 words. **Pays 16¢/word.**

Reprints: Send photocopy and information about when and where the material previously appeared. Pays 50% of amount paid for an original article.

Photos: Review. Price negotiable for 35mm color transparencies.

▣ The online version of this publication contains material not found in the print edition. Contact: Natalee Roth, online editor.

Tips: "The most frequent mistake made by writers is that they send articles unrelated to our readers. Ask for our publication guidelines first. Profiles/interviews are the best bet for freelancers."

CLUB MANAGEMENT, The Resource for Successful Club Operations, Finan Publishing Company, 107 W. Pacific Ave., St. Louis MO 63119-2323. (314)961-6644. Fax: (314)961-4809. E-mail: tfinan@finan.com. Website: www.club-mgmt.com. **Contact:** Tom Finan, editor. Bimonthly magazine covering club management, private club market, hospitality industry. Estab. 1925. Circ. 16,702. Pays on publication. Publishes ms an average of 2 months after acceptance. Buys first North American serial, electronic rights. Accepts queries by mail, e-mail, fax.

Nonfiction: General interest, historical/nostalgic, how-to, interview/profile, personal experience, photo feature, technical, travel. **Buys 100 mss/year.** Query with published clips. Length: 1,500-2,500 words.

Photos: State availability with submission.

Columns/Departments: Sports (private club sports: golf, tennis, yachting, fitness, etc.).

Tips: "We don't accept blind submissions. Please submit a résumé and clips of writer's work."

$ $ EL RESTAURANTE MEXICANO, P.O. Box 2249, Oak Park IL 60303-2249. (708)445-9454. Fax: (708)445-9477. E-mail: kfurore@yahoo.com. **Contact:** Kathleen Furore, editor. Magazine published 5 times/year covering Mexican restaurants. "*El Restaurante Mexicano* offers features and business-related articles that are geared specifically to owners and operators of Mexican, Tex-Mex, Southwestern, and Latin cuisine restaurants." Estab. 1997. Circ. 25,000. Pays on publication. Publishes ms an average of 3 months after acceptance. Byline given. Buys first North American serial rights. Responds in 2 months to queries. Sample copy for free.

Nonfiction: Looking for stories about unique Mexican restaurants and about business issues that affect Mexican restaurant owners. "No specific knowledge of food or restaurants is needed; the key qualification is to be a good reporter who knows how to slant a story toward the Mexican restaurant operator." **Buys 2-4 mss/year.** Query with published clips. Length: 800-1,500 words. **Pays $225.** Pays expenses of writers on assignment.

Tips: "Query with a story idea and tell how it pertains to Mexican restaurants."

$ $ FLORIDA HOTEL & MOTEL JOURNAL, The Official Publication of the Florida Hotel & Motel Association, Accommodations, Inc., P.O. Box 1529, Tallahassee FL 32302-1529. (850)224-2888. Fax: (850)222-3462. E-mail: journal@fhma.net. Website: www.flahotel.com. **Contact:** Lytha Page Belrose, editor and director of communications. **10% freelance written.** Prefers to work with published/established writers. Monthly except combination August/September and December/January issues. Magazine acting as a reference tool for managers and owners of Florida's hotels, motels and resorts. Estab. 1978. Circ. 8,500. Pays on publication. Publishes ms an average of 1-2 months after acceptance. Byline given. Buys first rights. Editorial lead time 1-9 months. Submit seasonal material 4-5 months in advance. Accepts queries by mail. Accepts previously published material. Responds in 2-4 months to queries. Sample copy and writer's guidelines free.

- Preference is given to articles that include references to member properties and general managers affiliated with the Florida Hotel and Motel Association. Since the association acquires new members weekly, queries may be made prior to the scheduling of interviews. This does not preclude the use of materials or ideas based on non-member properties, but member property sources are preferable.

Nonfiction: How-to (pertaining to hotel management), interview/profile, new product, personal experience, technical. No travel tips or articles aimed at the traveling public, and no promotion of individual property or destination. Query with published clips. Length: 500-2,000 words. **Pays 10¢/published word for assigned articles; 10¢/published word for unsolicited articles.** Pays in contributor copies if the article is reprinted with persmission, or the author is a paid representative of a company which is publicized in some manner through the article. Sometimes pays expenses of writers on assignment.

Photos: State availability with submission. Buys all rights. Offers no additional payment for photos accepted with ms. Captions, identification of subjects, model releases required.

Columns/Departments: Management Monograph, 1,000 words (expert information for hotel and motel management); Florida Scene, 700 words (Florida-specific, time-sensitive information for hotel managers or owners); National Scene, 1,000 words (USA-specific, time-sensitive information for hotel managers or owners); Fillers and Features, 1,000 words (information specific to editorial focus for the issue). Query. **Pays 10¢/word.**

Fillers: Anecdotes, facts, short humor. Length: 50-1,000 words. **Pays 10¢/word.**

Tips: "We use press releases provided to this office that fit the profile of our magazine's departments, targeting items of interest to the general managers of Florida's lodging operations. Feature articles are written based on an editorial calendar. We also publish an annual buyer's guide that provides a directory of all FH&MA member companies and allied member companies."

$ $ HOSPITALITY TECHNOLOGY, Edgell Communications, 4 Middlebury Blvd., Randolph NJ 07869. (973)252-0100. Fax: (973)252-9020. E-mail: jskorupa@edgellmail.com. Website: www.htmagazine.com. **Contact:** Joe Skorupa, editor. **70% freelance written.** Magazine published 9 times/year. "We cover the technology used in foodservice and lodging. Our readers are the operators, who have significant IT responsibilities." Estab. 1996. Circ. 16,000. **Pays on acceptance.** Publishes ms an average of 1 month after acceptance. Byline given. Buys all rights, makes work-for-hire assignments. Editorial lead time 2 months. Accepts queries by mail, e-mail, fax, phone. Responds in 2 weeks to queries.

Nonfiction: How-to, interview/profile, new product, technical. Special issues: "We publish two studies each year, the Restaurant Industry Technology Study and the Lodging Industry Technology Study." No unsolicited mss. **Buys 40 mss/year.** Query with published clips. Length: 800-1,200 words. **Pays $1/word.** Sometimes pays expenses of writers on assignment.

$ $ HOTELIER, Kostuch Publications, 23 Lesmill Rd., Suite 101, Toronto, Ontario M3B 3P6, Canada. (416)447-0888. Fax: (416)447-5333. E-mail: rcaira@foodservice.ca. Website: www.foodserviceworld.com. Associate Editor: Carol Neshevich. **Contact:** Rosanna Caira, editor. **40% freelance written.** Bimonthly magazine covering the Canadian hotel industry. Estab. 1989. Circ. 9,000. Pays on publication. Byline given. Buys first North American serial rights. Editorial lead time 3 months. Submit seasonal material 2 months in advance. Accepts queries by mail, fax. Sample copy and writer's guidelines free.

Nonfiction: How-to, new product. No case studies. **Buys 30-50 mss/year.** Query with or without published clips. Length: 700-1,500 words. **Pays 35¢/word (Canadian).** Sometimes pays expenses of writers on assignment.

Photos: Send photos with submission. Offers $30-75/photo.

$ $ $ PIZZA TODAY, The Monthly Professional Guide to Pizza Profits, Macfadden Protech, LLC, P.O. Box 1347, New Albany IN 47151. (812)949-0909. Fax: (812)941-9711. E-mail: jwhite@pizzatoday.com. Website: www.pizzatoday.com. **Contact:** Jeremy White, executive editor. **30% freelance written.** Works only with publishes/established writers. Monthly magazine for the pizza industry, covering trends, features of successful pizza operators, business and management advice, etc. Estab. 1983. Circ. 40,000. **Pays on acceptance.** Publishes ms an average of 2 months after acceptance. Byline given. Offers 10-30% kill fee. Buys all rights. Submit seasonal material 3 months in advance. Accepts queries by mail, e-mail, fax. Responds in 2 months to queries; 3 weeks to mss. Sample copy for 10×13 SAE and 6 first-class stamps. Writer's guidelines for #10 SASE.

Nonfiction: Interview/profile, entrepreneurial slants, pizza production and delivery, employee training, hiring, marketing and business management. No fillers, humor or poetry. **Buys 50 mss/year.** Length: 1,000-1,500 words. **Pays 50¢/word, occasionally more.** Sometimes pays expenses of writers on assignment.

Photos: Reviews contact sheets, negatives, transparencies, color slides, 5×7 prints. Captions required.

Tips: "We currently need more helpful, quality marketing pieces."

$ $ WESTERN HOTELIER MAGAZINE, Mercury Publications Ltd., 1839 Inkster Blvd., Winnipeg, Manitoba R2X 1R3, Canada. (204)954-2085. Fax: (204)954-2057. E-mail: mp@mercury.mb.ca. Website: www.mercury.mb.ca/. Editor: Kelly Gray. **Contact:** Kristi Balon, editorial production manager. **45% freelance written.** Quarterly magazine

covering the hotel industry. Circ. 4,342. Pays 30-45 days from receipt of invoice. Byline given. Offers 33% kill fee. Buys all rights. Submit seasonal material 3 months in advance. Accepts queries by mail, e-mail, fax. Accepts simultaneous submissions. Responds in 2 weeks to queries. Sample copy and writer's guidelines free or by e-mail.
Nonfiction: How-to (train staff), interview/profile. Industry reports and profiles on companies. Query with published clips. Length: 500-9,000 words. **Pays 25-35¢/word.** Sometimes pays expenses of writers on assignment.
Photos: State availability with submission. Reviews negatives, transparencies, 3×5 prints, JPEG, EPS or TIF files. Buys all rights. Negotiates payment individually. Captions required.
Columns/Departments: Across the West (hotel news from various parts of Western Canada), 100-500 words. Query. **Pays $0-100.**
Fillers: Facts. Length: 100 words.
Tips: "Send an e-mailed, faxed or mailed query outlining your experience, interests and pay expectations. A requirement also is clippings."

$ $ WESTERN RESTAURANT NEWS, Mercury Publications Ltd., 1839 Inkster Blvd., Winnipeg, Manitoba R2X 1R3, Canada. (204)954-2085. Fax: (204)954-2057. E-mail: mp@mercury.mb.ca. Website: www.mercury.mb.ca. Editor: Kelly Gray. **Contact:** Kristi Balon, editorial production manager. **33% freelance written.** Bimonthly magazine covering the restaurant trade. Reports profiles and industry reports on associations, regional business developments etc. Estab. 1994. Circ. 14,532. Pays 30-45 days from receipt of invoice. Byline given. Offers 33% kill fee. Buys all rights. Submit seasonal material 3 months in advance. Accepts queries by mail, e-mail, fax. Accepts simultaneous submissions. Sample copy and writer's guidelines free or by e-mail.
Nonfiction: How-to, interview/profile. Industry reports and profiles on companies. Query with published clips. Length: 500-9,000 words. **Pays 25-35¢/word.** Sometimes pays expenses of writers on assignment.
Photos: State availability with submission. Reviews negatives, transparencies, 3×5 prints, JPEG, EPS or TIF files. Buys all rights. Negotiates payment individually. Captions required.
Columns/Departments: Across the West (restaurant news from Western Canada), 100-500 words. Query. **Payment varies.**
Fillers: Facts. Length: 100 words.
Tips: "Send an e-mailed, faxed or mailed query outlining your experience, interests and pay expectations. A requirement also is clippings."

INDUSTRIAL OPERATIONS

Industrial plant managers, executives, distributors, and buyers read these journals. Some industrial management journals are also listed under the names of specific industries. Publications for industrial supervisors are listed in Management & Supervision.

$ $ COMMERCE & INDUSTRY, Mercury Publications Ltd., 1839 Inkster Blvd., Winnipeg, Manitoba R2X 1R3, Canada. (204)954-2085. Fax: (204)954-2057. E-mail: mp@mercury.mb.ca. Website: www.mercury.mb.ca/. Editor: Frank Yeo. **Contact:** Kristi Balon, editorial production manager. **75% freelance written.** Bimonthly magazine covering the business and industrial sectors. Industry reports and company profiles provide readers with an indepth insight into key areas of interest in their profession. Estab. 1947. Circ. 18,876. Pays 30-45 days from receipt of invoice. Byline given. Offers 33% kill fee. Buys all rights. Submit seasonal material 3 months in advance. Accepts queries by mail, e-mail, fax. Accepts simultaneous submissions. Responds in 2 weeks to queries. Sample copy and writer's guidelines free or by e-mail.
Nonfiction: How-to, interview/profile. Industry reports and profiles on companies. Query with published clips. Length: 500-9,000 words. **Pays 25-35¢/word.** Sometimes pays expenses of writers on assignment.
Photos: State availability with submission. Reviews negatives, transparencies, 3×5 prints, JPEG, EPS or TIF files. Buys all rights. Negotiates payment individually. Captions required.
Tips: "Send an e-mailed, faxed or mailed query outlining your experience, interests and pay expectations. A requirement also is clippings."

INDUSTRIAL FABRIC PRODUCTS REVIEW, Industrial Fabrics Association International, 1801 County Rd. B W, Roseville MN 55113-4061. (651)222-2508. Fax: (651)225-6966. E-mail: gdnordstrom@ifai.com. Website: www.ifai.com. **Contact:** Galynn Nordstrom, editorial director. **50% freelance written.** staff- and industry-written. Monthly magazine covering industrial textiles and products made from them for company owners, salespeople and researchers in a variety of industrial textile areas. Estab. 1915. Circ. 11,000. Pays on publication. Publishes ms an average of 2 months after acceptance. Byline given. Buys all rights. Accepts queries by mail, e-mail, phone. Responds in 1 month to queries.

> O→ Break in by "researching the industry/magazine audience and editorial calendar. The editorial calendar is available on our website at ifai.com. We rarely buy material not directed specifically at our markets."

Nonfiction: Technical, marketing and other topics related to any aspect of industrial fabric industry from fiber to finished fabric product. Special issues: new products, new fabrics and equipment. No historical or apparel-oriented articles. **Buys 8-10 mss/year.** Query with phone number. Length: 1,200-3,000 words.
Tips: "We encourage freelancers to learn our industry and make regular, solicited contributions to the magazine. We do not buy photography."

[N] $ $ INDUSTRIAL WASTEWATER, An Official Publication of the Water Environment Foundation, InterMarket Publishing LLC, 10244 Timber Ridge Dr., Ashland VA 23005. (804)550-0323. Fax: (804)550-2181. E-mail: editor@industrialwastewater.net. **Contact:** Susan L. Schaibly, managing editor. **40% freelance written.** Bimonthly magazine covering wastewater treatment for industrial facilities. *Industrial Wastewater* is edited to provide information on the practical application of science and technology in industrial wastewater treatment. *Industrial Wastewater* serves industrial personnel, consultants and others involved in all aspects of the design, management, operation, treatment, and disposal of wastewater. Estab. 1993. Circ. 38,117. Pays on publication. Byline given. Buys first, one-time, electronic rights, makes work-for-hire assignments. May purchase all rights. Rights purchased depends on the writer and the article. Editorial lead time 2 months. Submit seasonal material 2 months in advance. Accepts queries by mail, e-mail, fax, phone. Accepts previously published material. Accepts simultaneous submissions. Sample copy online. Writer's guidelines free.
Nonfiction: New product, technical, case study. **Buys 10 mss/year.** Query with published clips. Length: 1,000-4,500 words. **Pays $500.** Call editors to discuss circumstances under which writers are paid in contributor copies.
Photos: State availability with submission. Reviews 3×5 prints. Buys one time rights and Web rights. Negotiates payment individually. Captions, identification of subjects required.
Columns/Departments: News (regulatory issues), 1,500 words; Tech Talk (techincal developments in wastewater), 1,000 words; Problem Solvers (problem/solution articles), 1,500 words. **Buys 4 mss/year.** Query with published clips. **Pays $0-400.**
Tips: "Provide unique environmental or industry-oriented articles. Articles are technical in nature, written for professionals in the field."

$ $ $ PEM PLANT ENGINEERING & MAINTENANCE, Clb Media, Inc., 3228 S. Service Rd., 2nd Floor, West Wing, Burlington Ontario L7N 3H8, Canada. (905)634-2100. Fax: (905)634-2238. E-mail: editor@industrialsourcebook.com. Website: www.pem-mag.com. **Contact:** Nathan Mallett, editor. **30% freelance written.** Bimonthly magazine looking for "informative articles on issues that affect plant floor operations and maintenance." Circ. 18,500. Pays on publication. Publishes ms an average of 3 months after acceptance. Byline given. Buys one-time rights. Editorial lead time 4 months. Submit seasonal material 4 months in advance. Accepts simultaneous submissions. Responds in 3 weeks to queries; 1 month to mss. Sample copy and writer's guidelines free.
Nonfiction: How-to (how-to keep production downtime to a minimum, how-to better operate an industrial operation), new product, technical. **Buys 6 mss/year.** Query with published clips. Length: 750-4,000 words. **Pays $500-1,400 (Canadian).** Sometimes pays expenses of writers on assignment.
Photos: State availability with submission. Reviews transparencies, prints. Buys one-time rights. Negotiates payment individually. Captions required.
Tips: "Information can be found at our website. Call us for sample issues, ideas, etc."

$ $ QUALITY DIGEST, 40 Declaration Dr., Suite 100, Chico CA 95973. (530)893-4095. Fax: (530)893-0395. E-mail: editorial@qualitydigest.com. Website: www.qualitydigest.com. **Contact:** Scott M. Paton, editor-in-chief. **75% freelance written.** Monthly magazine covering quality improvement. Estab. 1981. Circ. 75,000. **Pays on acceptance.** Byline given. Buys all rights. Submit seasonal material 4 months in advance. Accepts queries by mail, e-mail, fax. Accepts simultaneous submissions. Responds in 3 months to mss. Sample copy and writer's guidelines free.
Nonfiction: Book excerpts, how-to (implement quality programs and solve problems for benefits, etc.), interview/profile, opinion, personal experience, technical. **Buys 2-5 mss/year.** Query with or without published clips or send complete ms. Length: 800-3,000 words. **Pays $200-600 for assigned articles. Pays in contributor copies for unsolicited mss**. Sometimes pays expenses of writers on assignment.
Reprints: Send tearsheet and information about when and where the material previously appeared.
Photos: Send photos with submission. Reviews any size prints. Buys one-time rights. Offers no additional payment for photos accepted with ms. Captions, identification of subjects, model releases required.

The online magazine carries original content not found in the print edition and includes writer's guidelines. Contact: Dirk Dusharme.

Tips: "Please be specific in your articles. Explain what the problem was, how it was solved and what the benefits are. Tell the reader how the technique described will benefit him or her. We feature shorter, tighter, more focused articles than in the past. This means we have more articles in each issue. We're striving to present our readers with concise, how-to, easy-to-read information that makes their job easier."

[N] $ $ WAREHOUSING MANAGEMENT, Cahners Business Information, 275 Washington St., Newton MA 02458. (617)558-4569. E-mail: warehousing@cahners.com. Website: www.warehousemag.com. **Contact:** John Johnson, chief editor. **40% freelance written.** Magazine published 11 times/year covering warehousing, distribution centers, inventory. "*Warehousing Management* is an 11 times-a-year glossy national magazine read by managers of warehouses and distribution centers. We focus on lively, well-written articles telling our readers how they can achieve maximum facility productivity and efficiency. Heavy management components. We cover technology, too." Estab. 1994. Circ. 42,000. Pays on acceptance (allow 4-6 weeks for invoice processing). Publishes ms an average of 1 month after acceptance. Byline given. Editorial lead time 3 months. Accepts queries by mail, e-mail, fax. Sample copy for free. Writer's guidelines free.
Nonfiction: Articles must be on-point, how-to pieces for managers. How-to, new product, technical. Special issues: State-of-the-Industry Report, Peak Performer, Salary and Wage survey, Warehouse of the Year. Doesn't want to see anything that doesn't deal with our topic—warehousing. No general-interest profiles or interviews. **Buys 25 mss/year.** Query with published clips. **Pays $300-650.**

Photos: State availability with submission. Reviews negatives, transparencies, Prints. Buys all rights. Offers no additional payment for photos accepted with ms. Captions, identification of subjects required.

The online magazine carries original content not found in the print edition and includes writer's guidelines.

Tips: "Learn a little about warehousing, distributors and write well. We typically don't accept specific article queries, but welcome introductory letters from journalists to whom we can assign articles. But authors are welcome to request an editorial calendar and develop article queries from it."

$ $ WEIGHING & MEASUREMENT, WAM Publishing Co., P.O. Box 2247, Hendersonville TN 37077. (615)824-6920. Fax: (615)824-7092. E-mail: dwam34@inwave.com. Website: www.weighingandmeasurement.com. **Contact:** David M. Mathieu, editor. Bimonthly magazine for users of industrial scales. Estab. 1914. Circ. 13,900. **Pays on acceptance.** Byline given. Offers 20% kill fee. Buys all rights. Accepts queries by mail, e-mail, fax, phone. Responds in 2 weeks to queries. Sample copy for $2.

Nonfiction: Interview/profile (with presidents of companies), personal experience (guest editorials on government involvement in business, etc.), technical, Profile (about users of weighing and measurement equipment); Product reviews. **Buys 15 mss/year.** Query on technical articles; submit complete ms for general interest material. Length: 1,000-2,500 words. **Pays $175-300.**

INFORMATION SYSTEMS

These publications give computer professionals more data about their field. Consumer computer publications are listed under Personal Computers.

N $ $ COMPUTER GRAPHICS WORLD, PennWell, 98 Spit Brook Rd., Nashua NH 03062-2801. (603)891-0123. Fax: (603)891-0539. E-mail: phill@pennwell.com. Website: www.cgw.com. **Contact:** Phil Lo Piccolo, editor. **25% freelance written.** Monthly magazine. "*Computer Graphics World* specializes in covering computer-aided 3D modeling, animation, and visualization and their uses in entertainment, engineering, and scientific applications." Estab. 1978. Circ. 60,000. **Pays on acceptance.** Publishes ms an average of 3 months after acceptance. Byline given. Offers 20% kill fee. Buys all rights. Editorial lead time 4 months. Submit seasonal material 3 months in advance. Sample copy for free.

Nonfiction: New product, opinion, technical, user application stories, professional-user, techonology innovations. "We do not want to run articles that are geared to computer programmers. Our focus as a magazine is on users involved in specific applications." **Buys 20-25 mss/year.** Query with published clips. Length: 1,200-2,000 words. **Pays $500 minimum.**

Columns/Departments: Technology stories (describes innovation and its implication for computer graphics users), 750-1,000 words; Reviews (offers hands-on review of important new products), 750 words; and Application Stories (highlights unique use of the technology by a single user), 400 words. **Buys 24 mss/year.** Query with published clips. **Pays $300-500.**

Tips: "Freelance writers will be most successful if they have some familiarity with computers and know how to write from a user's perspective. They do not need to be computer experts, but they do have to understand how to explain the impact of the technology and the applications in which a user is involved. Our feature section, and our application story section are open to freelancers. The trick to winning acceptance for your story is to have a well-developed idea that highlights a fascinating new trend or development in computer graphics technology or profiles a unique and fascinating use of the technology by a single user or a specific class of users."

$ $ $ DESKTOP ENGINEERING, Complete Computing Resource for Engineers, Helmers Publishing, P.O. Box 874, Peterborough NH 03458. (603)924-9631. Fax: (603)924-4004. E-mail: de-editors@helmers.com. Website: www.deskeng.com. **Contact:** Jennifer M. Runyon, managing editor. **90% freelance written.** Monthly magazine covering microcomputer hardware/software for hands-on design and mechanical engineers and engineering management. Estab. 1995. Circ. 62,000. Pays on publication. Publishes ms an average of 4 months after acceptance. Byline given. Buys all rights. Editorial lead time 3 months. Accepts queries by mail, e-mail, fax, phone. Responds in 6 weeks to queries; 6 months to mss. Sample copy free; editorial calendar online.

Nonfiction: How-to, new product, technical, reviews. "No fluff." **Buys 120 mss/year.** Query. Length: 750-3,000 words. **Pays 60¢/word for assigned articles; negotiable for unsolicited articles.** Sometimes pays expenses of writers on assignment.

Photos: Send photos with submission. Negotiates payment individually. Captions required.

Columns/Departments: Product Briefs (new products), 50-100 words; Reviews (software, hardware, books), 500-1,500 words. **Buys 30 mss/year.** Query. **Payment varies.**

The online magazine carries original content not found in the print edition. Contact: Jennifer M. Runyon.

Tips: "Call the editors or e-mail them for submission tips."

N $ $ $ GAME DEVELOPER, CMP Media LLC, 600 Harrison St., San Francisco CA 94107. (415)947-6000. Fax: (415)947-6090. E-mail: editors@gdmag.com. Website: www.gdmag.com. Managing Editor: Everard Strong. **Contact:** Jennifer Olsen, editor-in-chief. **90% freelance written.** Monthly magazine covering computer game development. Estab. 1994. Circ. 35,000. Pays on publication. Publishes ms an average of 3-6 months after acceptance. Byline given. Buys first North American serial, first, electronic, all rights. Editorial lead time 3 months. Submit seasonal material 4 months in advance. Accepts queries by e-mail. Sample copy for free. Writer's guidelines online.

Nonfiction: How-to, personal experience, technical. **Buys 50 mss/year.** Query. Length: 3,000-5,000 words. **Pays $150/page.**

Photos: State availability with submission.

The online magazine carries original content not found in the print edition and includes writer's guidelines. Contact: Daniel Huebner, online editor.

Tips: "We're looking for writers who are professional game developers with published game titles. We do not target the hobbyist or amateur market."

$ $ $ $ GOVERNMENT COMPUTER NEWS, Post Newsweek Tech Media, 10 G St., NE, Suite 500, Washington DC 20002. (202)772-2500. Fax: (202)772-2511. E-mail: editor@gcn.com. Website: www.gcn.com. **Contact:** Thomas Temin, editorial director. Biweekly for government information technology managers. **Pays on acceptance.** Byline given. Offers variable kill fee. Buys all rights. Responds in 1 month to queries. Sample copy for free. Writer's guidelines for #10 SASE.

Nonfiction: Buys 30 mss/year. Query. Length: 700-1,200 words. **Pays $800-2,000.** Pays expenses of writers on assignment.

Columns/Departments: Length: 400-600 words. No freelance columns accepted. **Buys 75 mss/year.** Query. **Pays $250-400.**

Fillers: Buys 10/year. Length: 300-500 words. **Pays $250-450.**

Tips: Needs "technical case histories of applications of computers to governmental missions and trends in information technology."

$ $ $ $ INFORMATION WEEK, 600 Community Dr., Manhasset NY 11030. (516)562-5000. Fax: (516)562-5036. E-mail: iweekletters@cmp.com. Website: www.informationweek.com. Editor-in-Chief: Bob Evans. **Contact:** Frances Witkowski, office coordinator. **20% freelance written.** Weekly magazine for information systems managers. Estab. 1985. Circ. 440,000. **Pays on acceptance.** Publishes ms an average of 1 month after acceptance. Byline given. Offers 25% kill fee. Buys first rights. Non-exclusive serial rights Accepts simultaneous submissions. Responds in 1 month to mss. Sample copy for free.

Nonfiction: Book excerpts, how-to, interview/profile, new product, technical, News analysis, company profiles. **Buys 30 mss/year.** Query with published clips. Length: 1,500-4,000 words. **Pays $1.10/word minimum.** Pays expenses of writers on assignment.

Reprints: Considers prviously published submissions.

Tips: Needs "feature articles on technology trends—all with a business angle. We look at implementations by users, new products, management issues, intranets, the Internet, web, networks, PCs, objects, workstations, sewers, etc. Our competitors are tabloids—we're better written, more selective, and more analytical."

$ $ iSERIES NEWS, (formerly *News/400*), Penton Technology Media, 221 E. 29th St., Loveland CO 80538. (970)663-4700. Fax: (970)663-3285. E-mail: editors@as400network.com. Website: www.iseriesnetwork.com. **Contact:** Lori Piotrowski, senior acquisitions editor. **40% freelance written.** Magazine published 14 times/year. "Programming, networking, IS management, technology for users of IBM AS/400 platform." Estab. 1982. Circ. 30,000 (international). Pays on publication. Publishes ms an average of 3 months after acceptance. Byline given. Offers 50% kill fee. Buys first, second serial (reprint), all rights. Editorial lead time 4 months. Submit seasonal material 4 months in advance. Accepts queries by mail, e-mail, fax, phone. Responds in 3 weeks to queries; 5 weeks to mss. Writer's guidelines online.

Nonfiction: Book excerpts, opinion, technical. **Buys 70 mss/year.** Query. Length: 1,500-2,500 words. **Pays 17-50¢/word for assigned articles.** Pays in contributor copies upon request of the author. Sometimes pays expenses of writers on assignment.

Reprints: Send photocopy. Payment negotiable.

Photos: State availability with submission. Offers no additional payment for photos accepted with ms.

Columns/Departments: Dialog Box (computer industry opinion), 1,500 words; Load'n'go (complete utility). **Buys 24 mss/year.** Query. **Pays $250-1,000.**

The online magazine carries original content not found in the print edition and includes writer's guidelines. Contact: Lori Piotrowski.

Tips: "Be familiar with IBM AS/400 computer platform."

$ JOURNAL OF INFORMATION ETHICS, McFarland & Co., Inc., Publishers, 720 Fourth Ave. S., St., Cloud State University, St. Cloud MN 56301. (320)255-4822. Fax: (320)255-4778. E-mail: hauptman@stcloudstate.edu. **Contact:** Robert Hauptman, LRTS, editor. **90% freelance written.** Semiannual Scholarly journal. "Addresses ethical issues in all of the information sciences with a deliberately interdisciplinary approach. Topics range from electronic mail monitoring to library acquisition of controversial material. The journal's aim is to present thoughtful considerations of ethical dilemmas that arise in a rapidly evolving system of information exchange and dissemination." Estab. 1992. Circ. 500. Pays on publication. Publishes ms an average of 9 months after acceptance. Byline given. Buys all rights. Submit seasonal material 8 months in advance. Accepts queries by mail, e-mail, fax, phone. Sample copy for $21. Writer's guidelines free.

Nonfiction: Essays, opinion, book reviews. **Buys 10 mss/year.** Send complete ms. Length: 500-3,500 words. **Pays $25-50 depending on length.**

Tips: "Familiarize yourself with the many areas subsumed under the rubric of information ethics, e.g., privacy, scholarly communication, errors, peer review, confidentiality, e-mail, etc. Present a well-rounded discussion of any fresh, current or evolving ethical topic within the information sciences, or involving real-world information collection/exchange."

SYS ADMIN, CMP Media, Inc., 1601 W. 23rd St., Suite 200, Lawrence KS 66046. (785)838-7555. Fax: (785)841-2047. E-mail: rendsley@cmp.com. Website: www.sysadminmag.com. Editor-in-Chief: Amber Ankerholz. **Contact:** Rikki Endsley, associate managing editor. **90% freelance written.** Monthly magazine. "*Sys Admin* is written for UNIX systems administrators. Articles are practical and technical. Our authors are practicing UNIX systems administrators." Estab. 1992. Circ. 60,000. Pays on publication. Publishes ms an average of 6 months after acceptance. Byline given. Offers $150 kill fee. Buys all rights. Editorial lead time 4 months. Accepts queries by mail, e-mail, fax, phone. Accepts simultaneous submissions. Responds in 1 month to queries. Sample copy for free.
Nonfiction: Technical. **Buys 40-60 mss/year.** Query. Length: 1,000 words. **Payment varies.**

N **WINDOWS DEVELOPER MAGAZINE**, CMP Media, Suite 200, 1601 W. 23rd St., Lawrence KS 66046. (785)838-7552. Fax: (785)841-2047. E-mail: wdletter@cmp.com. Website: www.wd-mag.com. Editor: John Dorsey. **Contact:** Pam VanSchmus, managing editor. **90% freelance written.** Monthly magazine. "*WD* is written for advanced Windows programmers. Articles are practical, advanced, code-intensive, and not product-specific. We expect our authors to be working Windows programmers." Estab. 1990. Circ. 23,000. **Pays on acceptance.** Publishes ms an average of 6 months after acceptance. Byline given. Offers $150 kill fee. Buys all rights. Editorial lead time 3 months. Accepts simultaneous submissions. Responds in 2 weeks to queries. Sample copy for free. Writer's guidelines free.
Nonfiction: Technical. **Buys 70-80 mss/year.** Query. Length: Varies. **Payment varies.**

INSURANCE

$ $ $ BUSINESS & HEALTH INSTITUTE, Keys to Workforce Productivity, (formerly *Business & Health*), Thomson/Medical Economics, 5 Paragon Dr., Montvale NJ 07645-1742. (201)358-7208. E-mail: rick.service@medec.com. Website: www.businessandhealth.com. **Contact:** Richard Service, editor. **60% freelance written.** E-magazine with special print editions. "*B&H* carries articles about how employers can cut their health care costs and improve the quality of care they provide to workers. We also write about health care policy at the federal, state and local levels." Estab. 1983. Circ. 45,000. **Pays on acceptance.** Publishes ms an average of 2 months after acceptance. Byline given. Offers 20% kill fee. Buys all rights. Editorial lead time 2 months. Submit seasonal material 4 months in advance. Accepts queries by mail, e-mail. Responds in 3 months to mss.
Nonfiction: How-to (cut health care benefits costs, provide better care), Case studies (of successful employer-led efforts); trend piece on broad issues such as 24-hour coverage or benefits for retirees. **Buys approximately 50 mss/year.** Query with published clips and SASE. Length: 2,000-3,500 words. **Pays $1,200-2,000 for features.** Pays expenses of writers on assignment.
Columns/Departments: Primarily staff written but will consider queries.
Tips: "Please be familiar with *B&H*. Articles should combine a business angle with a human interest approach and address both cost-containment and quality of care. Include cost-benefit analysis data and material for charts or graphs whenever possible."

$ $ GEICO DIRECT, K.L. Publications, 2001 Killebrew Dr., Suite 105, Bloomington MN 55425-1879. (952)854-0155. Fax: (952)854-9440. E-mail: klpub@aol.com. **Contact:** Jan Brenny, editor. **60% freelance written.** Semiannual magazine published for the government Employees Insurance Company (GEICO) policyholders. Estab. 1988. Circ. 4,000,000. **Pays on acceptance.** Byline given. Buys first North American serial rights. Accepts queries by mail. Responds in 3 months to queries. Writer's guidelines for #10 SASE.

- Break in by "submitting an idea (or editorial approach) for auto/home safety or themed regional travel—one theme with several destinations around the country—that is unique, along with proof of research and writing ability."

Nonfiction: Americana, home and auto safety, car care, financial, lifestyle. General interest (for 50 plus audience), how-to (auto/home related only), technical (auto), travel. Query with published clips. Length: 1,000-2,200 words. **Pays $300-650.**
Photos: Reviews 35mm transparencies. Payment varies.
Columns/Departments: Moneywise, Your Car. Length: 500-600 words. Query with published clips. **Pays $175-350.**
Tips: "We prefer work from published/established writers, especially those with specialized knowledge of the insurance industry, safety issues and automotive topics."

JEWELRY

$ $ AJM: THE AUTHORITY ON JEWELRY MANUFACTURING, Manufacturing Jewelers and Suppliers of America, 45 Royal Little Dr., Providence RI 02904. (401)274-3840. Fax: (401)274-0265. E-mail: ajm@ajm-magazine.com. Website: www.ajm-magazine.com. **Contact:** Tina Wojtkielo, editor. **75% freelance written.** Monthly magazine. "*AJM* is a monthly magazine providing technical, marketing and business information for finished jewelry manufacturers and supporting industries." Estab. 1956. **Pays on acceptance.** Publishes ms an average of 6 months after acceptance.

Byline given. all rights for limited period of 18 months Editorial lead time 1 year. Submit seasonal material 6 months in advance. Accepts queries by mail, e-mail, fax. Responds in 2 months to mss. Sample copy and writer's guidelines free.

Nonfiction: All articles should focus on jewelry manufacturing techniques, especially how-to and technical articles. How-to, new product, technical. "No generic articles for a wide variety of industries, articles for hobbyists, or articles written for a consumer audience. Our focus is professional jewelry manufacturers and designers, and articles for AJM should be carefully targeted for this audience." **Buys 40 mss/year.** Query. Length: 2,500-3,000 words. **Pays $300-500 for assigned articles.** Sometimes pays expenses of writers on assignment.

Reprints: Occasionally accepts previously published submissions. Query.

Photos: State availability with submission. Buys one-time rights. Negotiates payment individually. Captions required.

Tips: "Because our editorial content is highly focused and specific, we assign most article topics rather than relying on outside queries. We are, as a result, always seeking new writers comfortable with business and technical topics who will work with us long term and whom we can develop into 'experts' in jewelry manufacturing. We invite writers to send an introductory letter and clips highlighting business and technical writing skills if they would like to be considered for a specific assignment."

$ THE DIAMOND REGISTRY BULLETIN, 580 Fifth Ave., #806, New York NY 10036. (212)575-0444. Fax: (212)575-0722. E-mail: diamond58@aol.com. Website: www.diamondregistry.com. **Contact:** Joseph Schlussel, editor-in-chief. **50% freelance written.** Monthly Newsletter. Estab. 1969. Pays on publication. Buys all rights. Submit seasonal material 1 month in advance. Accepts queries by mail, e-mail. Accepts simultaneous submissions. Responds in 3 weeks to mss. Sample copy for $5.

Nonfiction: How-to (ways to increase sales in diamonds, improve security, etc.), interview/profile (of interest to diamond dealers or jewelers), prevention advice (on crimes against jewelers). Send complete ms. Length: 50-500 words. **Pays $75-150.**

Tips: "We seek ideas to increase sales of diamonds."

N $ $ THE ENGRAVERS JOURNAL, P.O. Box 318, Brighton MI 48116. (810)229-5725. Fax: (810)229-8320. E-mail: sdavis@engraversjournal.com. Website: www.engraversjournal.com. Publisher: Michael J. Davis. **Contact:** Sonja Davis, general manager. **60% freelance written.** Monthly magazine covering the recognition and identification industry (engraving, marking devices, awards, jewelry, and signage.). "We provide practical information for the education and advancement of our readers, mainly retail business owners." Estab. 1975. **Pays on acceptance.** Publishes ms an average of 1 year after acceptance. Byline given. Buys one-time rights, makes work-for-hire assignments. Accepts queries by mail, e-mail, fax. Responds in 2 weeks to mss. Sample copy and writer's guidelines free.

O→ To break in, submit well written, fairly in-depth general business articles. Topics and article style should focus on the small retail business owner, and should be helpful and informative.

Nonfiction: General interest (industry related), how-to (small business subjects, increase sales, develop new markets, use new sales techniques, etc.), technical. No general overviews ofthe industry. Length: 1,000-5,000 words. **Pays $200 and up.**

Reprints: Send tearsheet, photocopy or typed ms with rights for sale noted and information about when and where the material previously appeared. Pays 50-100% of amout paid for original article.

Photos: Send photos with submission. Pays variable rate. Captions, identification of subjects, model releases required.

Tips: "Articles should always be down to earth, practical and thoroughly cover the subject with authority. We do not want the 'textbook' writing approach, vagueness, or theory—our readers look to us for sound practical information. We use an educational slant, publishing both trade-oriented articles and general business topics of interest to a small retail-oriented readership."

$ $ FASHION ACCESSORIES, S.C.M. Publications, Inc., P.O. Box 859, Mahwah NJ 07430-0859. (201)684-9222. Fax: (201)684-9228. **Contact:** Samuel Mendelson, publisher. Monthly newspaper covering costume or fashion jewelry. Published for executives in the manufacturing, wholesaling and retail buying of fashion jewelry and accessories. Estab. 1951. Circ. 9,500. **Pays on acceptance.** Byline given. Not copyrighted. Buys first rights. Submit seasonal material 3 months in advance. Sample copy for $2 and 9×12 SAE with 4 first-class stamps.

Nonfiction: Essays, general interest, historical/nostalgic, interview/profile, new product. **Buys 20 mss/year.** Query with published clips. Length: 1,000-2,000 words. **Pays $100-300.**

Photos: Send photos with submission. Reviews 4×5 prints. Buys one-time rights. Offers no additional payment for photos accepted with ms.

Columns/Departments: Fashion Report (interviews and reports of fashion news), 1,000-2,000 words.

Tips: "We are interested in anything that will be of interest to costume jewelry buyers."

$ $ LUSTRE, The Jeweler's Magazine on Design & Style, Cygnus Publishing Company, 24 Mountain Ridge Dr., Cedar Grove NJ 07009. (631)845-2700. Fax: (631)845-7109. E-mail: loraine. depasque@cygnuspub.com. Website: www.lustremag.com. Managing Editor: Matthew Kramer. **Contact:** Lorraine DePasque, editor-in-chief. Bimonthly Trade magazine covering fine jewelry and related accessories. "*LUSTRE* is dedicated to helping the retail jeweler stock, merchandise, sell and profit from upscale, high-quality brand name and designer jewelry. Many stories are how-to. We also offer sophisticated graphics to showcase new products." Estab. 1997. Circ. 12,200. Pays on publication. Publishes ms an average of 4 months after acceptance. Byline given. Offers 50% kill fee. Buys all rights. Editorial lead time 4 months. Submit seasonal material 4 months in advance. Accepts queries by mail. Responds in 4 weeks to queries. Sample copy for free.

Nonfiction: How-to, new product. **Buys 18 mss/year.** Query with published clips. Length: 1,000-2,500 words. **Pays $500.** Sometimes pays expenses of writers on assignment.

Photos: State availability with submission. Buys one-time rights plus usage for one year after publication date (but not exclusive usage). Offers no additional payment for photos accepted with ms. Captions, identification of subjects required.

Columns/Departments: Celebrity Link (tie in designer jewelry with celebrity), 500 words; Details (news about designer jewelry), 500 words; International Eye, 500 words. **Buys 8 mss/year.** Query. **Pays $500.**

Tips: "Step 1: Request an issue sent to them; call (212) 921-1091; ask for assistant. Step 2: Write a letter to Lorraine with clips. Step 3: Lorraine will call back. Background in jewelry is helpful."

JOURNALISM & WRITING

Journalism and writing magazines cover both the business and creative sides of writing. Writing publications offer inspiration and support for professional and beginning writers. Although there are many valuable writing publications that do not pay, we list those that pay for articles.

$ $ $ $ AMERICAN JOURNALISM REVIEW, 1117 Journalism Bldg., University of Maryland, College Park MD 20742. (301)405-8803. Fax: (301)405-8323. E-mail: editor@ajr.org. Website: www.ajr.org. Editor: Rem Rieder. **Contact:** Lori Robertson, managing editor. **80% freelance written.** Monthly magazine covering print, broadcast and online journalism. "Mostly journalists subscribe. We cover ethical issues, trends in the industry, coverage that falls short." Circ. 27,000. Pays within 30 days after publication. Publishes ms an average of 2 months after acceptance. Byline given. Offers 25% kill fee. Buys first North American serial, electronic rights. Editorial lead time 1 month. Accepts queries by mail, e-mail, fax. Responds in 3 weeks to queries. Sample copy for $4.95 pre-paid or online. Writer's guidelines for free or online.

Nonfiction: Exposé, humor, interview/profile, personal experience, ethical issues. **Buys many mss/year.** Query with published clips or send complete ms. Length: 2,000-4,000 words. **Pays $1,500-2,000.** Pays expenses of writers on assignment.

Fillers: Jill Rosen, assistant managing editor. Anecdotes, facts, short humor, short pieces. Length: 150-1,000 words. **Pays $100-250.**

Tips: "Write a short story for the front-of-the-book section. We prefer queries to completed articles. Include in a page what you'd like to write about, who you'll interview, why it's important and why you should write it."

$ AUTHORSHIP, National Writers Association, 3140 S. Peoria, PMB #295, Aurora CO 80014. (303)841-0246. E-mail: sandywrter@aol.com. Website: www.nationalwriters.com. Editor: Sandy Whelchel. **Contact:** Kathe Gustafson. Quarterly magazine covering writing articles only. "Association magazine targeted to beginning and professional writers. Covers how-to, humor, marketing issues." Disk and e-mail submissions given preference. Estab. 1950s. Circ. 4,000. **Pays on acceptance.** Byline given. Buys first North American serial, second serial (reprint) rights. Editorial lead time 3 months. Submit seasonal material 6 months in advance. Accepts simultaneous submissions. Responds in 2 months to queries. Sample copy for #10 SASE.

Nonfiction: Writing only. Poetry (January/February). **Buys 25 mss/year.** Query or send complete ms. Length: 900 words. **Pays $10 or discount on memberships and copies.**

Photos: State availability with submission. Reviews 5×7 prints. Buys one-time rights. Offers no additional payment for photos accepted with ms. Identification of subjects, model releases required.

Tips: "Members of National Writers Association are given preference. Writing conference in Denver every June."

$ BOOK DEALERS WORLD, North American Bookdealers Exchange, P.O. Box 606, Cottage Grove OR 97424. (541)258-2625. Fax: (541)258-2625. Website: www.bookmarketingprofits.com. **Contact:** Al Galasso, editorial director. **50% freelance written.** Quarterly magazine covering writing, self-publishing and marketing books by mail. Circ. 20,000. Pays on publication. Publishes ms an average of 3 months after acceptance. Byline given. Buys first North American serial, second serial (reprint) rights. Accepts simultaneous submissions. Responds in 1 month to queries. Sample copy for $3.

Nonfiction: Book excerpts (writing, mail order, direct mail, publishing), how-to (home business by mail, advertising), interview/profile (of successful self-publishers), positive articles on self-publishing, new writing angles, marketing. **Buys 10 mss/year.** Send complete ms. Length: 1,000-1,500 words. **Pays $25-50.**

Reprints: Send typed ms with rights for sale noted and information about when and where the material previously appeared. Pays 80% of amount paid for an original article.

Columns/Departments: Print Perspective (about new magazines and newsletters); Self-Publisher (on successful self-publishers and their marketing strategy). Length: 250-1,000 words. **Buys 20 mss/year.** Send complete ms. **Pays $5-20.**

Fillers: Fillers concerning writing, publishing or books. **Buys 6/year.** Length: 100-250 words. **Pays $3-10.**

Tips: "Query first. Get a sample copy of the magazine."

$ BRIDGES ROMANCE MAGAZINE, Bridges Romance Magazine, P.O. Box 150099, Denver CO 80215-0099. Fax: (303)984-0051. E-mail: becci@bridgesmagazine.info. Website: www.bridgesmagazine.info. **Contact:** Becci Davis, editor-in-chief/managing editor. **65% freelance written.** Bimonthly magazine covering women's fiction reading and writing. "We are printed in a flip-format. One half of the magazine is geared toward readers of women's fiction (book reviews, author profiles, etc.) while the other half is geared toward authors. We need writing how-to's, editor/publisher profiles, researching articles, etc." Estab. 2000. Pays on publication. Publishes ms an average of 2 months after acceptance. Byline given. Buys first North American serial, one-time, second serial (reprint) rights. Editorial lead time 3 months. Submit seasonal material 4 months in advance. Accepts queries by e-mail. Accepts previously published material. Accepts simultaneous submissions. Responds in 6 weeks to queries; 3 months to mss. Sample copy for 9×12 SAE and 4 first-class stamps. Writer's guidelines for #10 SASE or by e-mail.

Nonfiction: How-to (writing technique), interview/profile, opinion. "All special projects are assigned. We don't accept freelance submissions for this purpose." Book reviews are done inhouse. **Buys 50 mss/year.** Query. Length: 500-2,000 words. **Pays 1-10¢/word for assigned articles; 1-5¢/word for unsolicited articles.**

Photos: State availability with submission. Buys one-time rights. Offers no additional payment for photos accepted with ms.

Tips: "Please make sure your topic is well researched and your ideas are clearly conveyed. Our readers don't just want to know why you think something is important, but also how your experience or expertise can benefit them. Target authors—our reader's portion is almost completely done by *Bridges* staff."

$BYLINE, P.O. Box 5240, Edmond OK 73083-5240. (405)348-5591. E-mail: mpreston@bylinemag.com. Website: www.bylinemag.com. **Contact:** Marcia Preston, editor/publisher. **80% freelance written.** Eager to work with new/unpublished writers or experienced ones. Magazine published 11 times/year for writers and poets. Estab. 1981. **Pays on acceptance.** Publishes ms an average of 3 months after acceptance. Byline given. Buys first North American serial rights. Editorial lead time 3-4 months. Submit seasonal material 6 months in advance. Accepts queries by mail, e-mail. Accepts simultaneous submissions. Responds in 2 months or less to queries. Sample copy for $4 postpaid. Writer's guidelines online.

- Please *do not send* complete mss by e-mail.

O→ "First $ale is probably the easiest way to break in. Do not submit full ms by e-mail."

Nonfiction: "We're always searching for appropriate, well-written features on topics we haven't covered for a couple of years." Needs articles of 1,500-1,800 words connected with writing and selling. No profiles of writers. **Buys approximately 75 mss/year.** Prefers queries; will read complete mss. Send SASE. Length: 1,500-1,800 words. **Pays $75.**

Columns/Departments: End Piece (humorous, philosophical or motivational personal essay related to writing), 700 words, pays $35; First Sale (account of a writer's first sale), 250-300 words, pays $20; Only When I Laugh (writing-related humor), 50-600 words; pays $15-25; Great American Bookstores (unique, independent bookstores), 500-600 words. Send complete ms. **Pays $30-40.**

Fiction: Mainstream, genre; literary. No science fiction, erotica or extreme violence. **Buys 11 mss/year.** Send complete ms. Length: 2,000-4,000 words. **Pays $100.**

Poetry: "All poetry should connect in some way with the theme of writing or the creative process." Sandra Soli, poetry editor. Free verse, haiku, light verse, traditional. **Buys 100 poems/year.** Submit maximum 3 poems. Length: Under 30 lines. **Pays $10 plus free issue.**

Tips: "We're open to freelance submissions in all categories. We're always looking for clear, concise feature articles on topics that will help writers write better, market smarter, and be more successful. Strangely, we get many more short stories than we do features, but we buy more features. If you can write a friendly, clear and helpful feature on some aspect of writing better or selling more work, we'd love to hear from you."

$CANADIAN WRITER'S JOURNAL, P.O. Box 5180, New Liskeard, Ontario P0J 1P0, Canada. (705)647-5424. Fax: (705)647-8366. E-mail: cwj@cwj.ca. Website: www.cwj.ca. **Contact:** Carole Roy, managing editor. **75% freelance written.** Bimonthly magazine for writers. Accepts well-written articles by inexperienced writers. Estab. 1984. Circ. 350. Pays on publication. Publishes ms an average of 9 months after acceptance. Byline given. Buys one-time rights. Accepts queries by mail, e-mail, fax, phone. Responds in 2 months to queries. Sample copy for $8, including postage. Writer's guidelines for #10 SAE and IRC or online.

Nonfiction: Looking for articles on how to break into niche markets. How-to (articles for writers). **Buys 200 mss/year.** Query optional. **Pays $5/published magazine page (approx. 450 words).**

Reprints: Send typed ms with rights for sale noted and information about when and where the material previously appeared.

Fiction: Requirements currently being met by annual contest. Send SASE for rules, or see guidelines on website.

Poetry: Short poems or extracts used as part of articles on the writing of poetry.

Tips: "We prefer short, tightly written, informative how-to articles. U.S. writers note that U.S. postage cannot be used to mail from Canada. Obtain Canadian stamps, use IRCs or send small amounts in cash."

$FELLOW SCRIPT, InScribe Christian Writers' Fellowship, 333 Hunter's Run, Edmonton Alberta T6R 2N9, Canada. (780)988-5622. Fax: (780)430-0139. E-mail: submissions@inscribe.org. Website: www.inscribe.org. **Contact:** Elsie Montgomery, editor. **100% freelance written.** Quarterly Writers' newsletter featuring Christian writing. "Our readers are Christians with a commitment to writing. Among our readership are best-selling authors and unpublished beginning writers. Submissions to us should include practical information, something the reader can put into practice the same day she reads it." Estab. 1980. Circ. 250. Pays on publication. Publishes ms an average of 2 months after acceptance.

Byline given. Buys one-time rights. Editorial lead time 3 months. Submit seasonal material 4 months in advance. Accepts queries by mail, e-mail, fax, phone. Accepts simultaneous submissions. Responds in 1 month to queries; 2 months to mss. Sample copy for 9×12 SAE and 2 first-class stamps or IRCs. Writer's guidelines online.

O━ "The best bet to break in at FellowScript is to write something very specific that will be useful to writers. We receive far too many 'general' submissions which try to cover too much territory in one article. Choose your topic and keep a narrow focus."

Nonfiction: Essays, exposé, how-to (for writers), inspirational, interview/profile, new product, personal experience, photo feature, religious. "Does not want poetry, fiction or think piece, commentary articles." **Buys 30-45 mss/year.** Send complete ms. Length: 250-900 words. **Pays 2 1/2¢/word, Canadian funds.**

Photos: State availability with submission. Reviews 4×6 prints. Buys one-time rights. Negotiates payment individually. Captions, identification of subjects required.

Columns/Departments: Book reviews, 150-300 words; market updates and profiles, 50-300 words (both for writers). **Buys 1-3 mss/year.** Send complete ms. **Pays 1 copy.**

Fillers: Facts, newsbreaks. **Buys 5-10/year.** Length: 25-75 words. **Pays 1 copy.**

Tips: "Send your complete manuscript by post or e-mail. E-mail is preferred. Tell us a bit about yourself. Write in a casual, first-person, anecdotal style. Be sure your article is full of practical material, something that can be applied. Most of our accepted freelance submissions fall into the 'how-to' category, and involve tasks, crafts or procedures common to writers, as our magazine is solely devoted to instructing and encouraging writers. Please do not swamp us with inspirational articles (e.g., 'How I sold My First Story'), as we receive too many of these already."

$ FICTION FIX, CoffeehouseForWriters.com, W242-A Madison Ave., Oconomowoc WI 53066. E-mail: articles @coffeehouseforwriters.com. Website: www.coffeehouseforwriters.com/news.html. **Contact:** Miranda Fuller. **90% freelance written.** Monthly online publication covering writing and publishing. "As an ezine specifically for fiction writers, we aim to present nuts and bolts how-to articles with a personable, often humorous style. Share techniques as if you're sitting down with a group of writer friends and saying, 'Hey, I've learned something wonderful about writing. Let me share it with you.'" Estab. 1997. Circ. 3,000 unique visits/month, 5,000 e-mail subscribers. Pays on publication. Byline given. Offers $10 kill fee. electronic rights, including non-exclusive ability to archive (removed at writer's request). Editorial lead time 4 months. Submit seasonal material 4 months in advance. Accepts queries by e-mail. Responds in 1 month to queries; 1 month to mss. Sample copy and writer's guidelines online.

Nonfiction: How-to (on the craft of writing fiction), opinion, personal experience (writing/how-to related). No fiction, poetry or essays. No articles that are thinly veiled attempts to sell a product. Book, software and website reviews are generally staff written. **Buys 24-30 mss/year.** Query. Length: 800-1,000 words. **Pays $20-30 for original feature articles.**

Columns/Departments: E-mail: karen@coffeehouseforwriters.com. This Writer's Opinion (opinion pieces, either humorous or hard-hitting), 500 words. **Buys 4-6 mss/year.** Send complete ms. **Pays $10.**

Tips: "We appreciate how-to articles that are lively and personable, as opposed to dry and clinical. Don't be affraid to share your personal writing experiences, or tell us more about how you learned to integrate a particular writing technique. We favor writers who send us queries that are well-written, professional and not too informal."

$ $ FREELANCE WRITER'S REPORT, CNW Publishing, Inc., Main St., P.O. Box A, North Stratford NH 03590-0167. (603)922-8338. Fax: (603)922-8339. E-mail: danakcnw@ncia.net. Website: www.writers-editors.com. **Contact:** Dana K. Cassell, editor. **25% freelance written.** Monthly Newsletter. "*FWR* covers the marketing and business/office management aspects of running a freelance writing business. Articles must be of value to the established freelancer; nothing basic." Estab. 1982. Pays on publication. Publishes ms an average of 6 months after acceptance. Byline given. Buys one-time rights. Editorial lead time 2 months. Submit seasonal material 2 months in advance. Accepts queries by mail, e-mail. Accepts simultaneous submissions. Responds in 1 week to queries; 1 month to mss. Sample copy for 6×9 SAE with 2 first-class stamps (for back copy); $4 for current copy. Writer's guidelines online.

Nonfiction: Book excerpts, how-to (market, increase income or profits). No articles about the basics of freelancing. **Buys 50 mss/year.** Send complete ms. Length: up to 900 words. **Pays 10¢/word.**

Reprints: Accepts previously published submissions.

The online magazine carries original content not found in the print edition and includes writer's guidelines.

Tips: "Write in a terse, newsletter style."

$ INSCRIPTIONS MAGAZINE, 500 Seventh Ave., 8th Floor, New York NY 10018. E-mail: editor@inscriptions magazine.com. Website: www.inscriptionsmagazine.com. **Contact:** Jade Walker, editor. **100% freelance written.** Weekly E-zine covering writing, editing, publishing. "*Inscriptions* is the weekly e-zine for professional writers. Our focus is to help working writers and editors find work, paying markets and contests offering cash prizes." Estab. 1998. Pays on publication. Publishes ms an average of 2 months after acceptance. Byline given. Buys one-time, electronic rights. Editorial lead time 3 months. Submit seasonal material 3 months in advance. Accepts queries by e-mail. Responds in 2 weeks to queries. Sample copy for free. Writer's guidelines online.

Nonfiction: "Authors can opt for advertising in lieu of payments." Book excerpts, how-to, humor, interview/profile. **Buys 150 mss/year.** Query. Length: 500-1,500 words. **Pays $5-40.**

Fillers: Buys 50/year. Length: 25-300 words. **Pays nothing for fillers.**

Tips: "Articles must focus on writing or publishing-related issues (including interviews, how-to's, troubleshooting, etc.). *Inscriptions* does not publish fiction, poetry or other nonfiction articles, unless the submissions have won our sponsored monthly contest. Interviews should be conducted with working writers, authors, writing teachers, editors, agents or publishers. All interviews must be approved in advance. *Inscriptions* accepts reprints of writing-related articles. The publication where the article originally appeared will be credited. However, you must hold the copyright to the article, in order to submit it to us."

$ MAINE IN PRINT, Maine Writers and Publishers Alliance, 14 Maine St., Suite 416, Brunswick ME 04011. (207)729-8808. Fax: (207)725-1014. Website: www.mainewriters.org. Editor: Pat Sims. Bimonthly Newsletter for writers, editors, teachers, librarians, etc., focusing on Maine literature and the craft of writing. Estab. 1975. Circ. 3,000. Pays on publication. Publishes ms an average of 2 months after acceptance. Byline given. Buys one-time rights. Editorial lead time 2 months. Accepts queries by mail. Accepts simultaneous submissions. Sample copy and writer's guidelines free.

Nonfiction: Essays, how-to (writing), interview/profile, technical. No creative writing, fiction or poetry. **Buys 20 mss/year.** Query with published clips. Length: 400-1,500 words. **Pays $25-75 for assigned articles.**

Reprints: Send tearsheet and information about when and where the material previously appeared. Pays $25.

Photos: State availability with submission. Offers no additional payment for photos accepted with ms.

Columns/Departments: Front-page articles (writing related), 500-1,500 words. **Buys 20 mss/year.** Query. **Pays $25 minimum.**

Tips: "Become a member of Maine Writers & Publishers Alliance. Become familiar with Maine literary scene."

$ $ $ MASTHEAD, The Magazine About Magazines, North Island Publishing, 1606 Sedlescomb Dr., Unit 8, Mississauga, Ontario L4X 1M6, Canada. (905)625-7070. Fax: (905)625-4856. E-mail: wshields@masthead.ca. Website: www.mastheadonline.com. **Contact:** William Shields, editor. **40% freelance written.** Journal published 10 times/year covering the Canadian magazine industry. "With its lively mix of in-depth features, news stories, service pieces, surveys, tallies and spirited commentary, this independent journal provides detailed coverage and analysis of the events, issues, personalities and technologies shaping Canada's magazine industry." Estab. 1987. Circ. 4,200. Pays on publication. Publishes ms an average of 2 months after acceptance. Byline given. Offers 50% kill fee. Buys first North American serial rights. Editorial lead time 1 month. Accepts queries by mail. Accepts simultaneous submissions. Responds in 2 weeks to queries; 1 month to mss. Sample copy for free. Writer's guidelines free or by e-mail.

Nonfiction: "We generally pay $600-850 for a cover story running 2,000-2,500 words, depending on the amount of research, etc. required. For the most part, *Masthead* generates feature ideas in-house and then assigns the stories to regular contributors. When space permits, we sometimes run shorter features or service pieces (1,000-1,500 words) for a flat rate of $350." Book excerpts, essays, exposé, historical/nostalgic, how-to, humor, interview/profile, new product, opinion, personal experience, technical. No articles that have nothing to do with Canadian magazines. Length: 100-3,000 words. **Pays $30-850 (Canadian).** Sometimes pays expenses of writers on assignment.

Photos: State availability with submission. Negotiates payment individually. Identification of subjects required.

Columns/Departments: Back of the Book, the guest column pays freelancers a flat rate of $350 and runs approximately 950 words. Back of the Book columns examine and/or comment on issues or developments relating to any department: editorial, art, production, circulation, publishing, advertising, etc. **Buys 10 mss/year.** Query with published clips. **Pays $350 (Canadian).**

Fiction: Novel excerpts. No excerpts that have nothing to do with Canadian magazines. Query with published clips.

The online magazine carries original content. Contact: William Shields.

Tips: "Have a solid understanding of the Canadian magazine industry. A good way to introduce yourself is to propose small articles on new magazines."

$ NEW WRITER'S MAGAZINE, Sarasota Bay Publishing, P.O. Box 5976, Sarasota FL 34277-5976. (941)953-7903. E-mail: newriters@aol.com. Website: www.newriters.com. **Contact:** George S. Haborak, editor. **95% freelance written.** Bimonthly magazine. "*New Writer's Magazine* believes that *all* writers are *new* writers in that each of us can learn from one another. So, we reach pro and non-pro alike." Estab. 1986. Circ. 5,000. Pays on publication. Byline given. Buys first rights. Accepts queries by mail. Responds in 1 month to queries; 1 month to mss. Sample copy for $3. Writer's guidelines for #10 SASE.

Nonfiction: General interest, how-to (for new writers), humor, interview/profile, opinion, personal experience (with pro writer). **Buys 50 mss/year.** Send complete ms. Length: 700-1,000 words. **Pays $10-50.**

Photos: Send photos with submission. Reviews 5×7 prints. Offers no additional payment for photos accepted with ms. Captions required.

Fiction: Experimental, historical, humorous, mainstream, slice-of-life vignettes. "Again we do *not* want anything that does not have a tie-in with the writing life or writers in general." **Buys 2-6 mss/year.** Send complete ms. Length: 700-800 words. **Pays $20-40.**

Poetry: Free verse, light verse, traditional. Does not want anything *not* for writers. **Buys 10-20 poems/year.** Submit maximum 3 poems. Length: 8-20 lines. **Pays $5 minimum.**

Fillers: For cartoons, writing lifestyle slant. Buys 20-30/year. Pays $10 maximum. Anecdotes, facts, newsbreaks, short humor. **Buys 5-15/year.** Length: 20-100 words. **Pays $5 maximum.**

Tips: "Any article *with photos* has a good chance, especially an *up close and personal* interview with an established professional writer offering advice, etc. Short profile pieces on new authors also receive attention."

$ OHIO WRITER, Poets' & Writers' League of Greater Cleveland, P.O. Box 91801, Cleveland OH 44101. (216)421-0403. Fax: (216)791-1727. E-mail: pwlgc@msn.com. **Contact:** Stephen and Gail Bellamy, editors. **75% freelance written.** Bimonthly magazine covering writing and Ohio writers. Estab. 1987. Pays on publication. Publishes ms an average of 4 months after acceptance. Byline given. Buys one-time, second serial (reprint) rights. Editorial lead time 4 months. Submit seasonal material 4 months in advance. Accepts queries by mail, e-mail, fax, phone. Responds in 6 weeks to mss. Sample copy for S2.50. Writer's guidelines for #10 SASE.

Nonfiction: "All articles must related to the writing life or Ohio writers, or Ohio publishing scene." Essays, how-to, humor, inspirational, interview/profile, opinion, personal experience. **Buys 24 mss/year.** Send complete ms and SASE. Length: 2,000-2,500 words. **Pays $25 minimum, up to $50 for lead article, other payment under arrangement with writer.**

Reprints: Send typed ms with rights for sale noted and information about when and where the material previously appeared. Pays 50% of amount paid for an original article.

Columns/Departments: Subjectively Yours (opinions, controversial stance on writing life), 1,500 words; Reveiws (Ohio writers, publishers or publishing), 400-600 words; Focus on (Ohio publishing scene, how to write/publish certain kind of writing, e.g., travel), 1,500 words. **Buys 6 mss/year.** Send complete ms. **Pays $25-50; $5/book review.**

Tips: "We look for articles about writers and writing, with a special emphasis on activities in our state. However, we publish articles by writers throughout the country that offer something helpful about the writing life. Profiles and interviews of writers who live in Ohio are always needed. *Ohio Writer* is read by both beginning and experienced writers and hopes to create a sense of community among writers of different genres, abilities and backgrounds. We want to hear a personal voice, one that engages the reader. We're looking for intelligent, literate prose that isn't stuffy."

$ THE WIN INFORMER, The Professional Association for Christian Writers, (formerly *Writers Information Network*), Writers Information Network, P.O. Box 11337, Bainbridge Island WA 98110. (206)842-9103. Fax: (206)842-0536. E-mail: writersinfonetwork@juno.com. Website: www.bluejaypub.com/win. **Contact:** Elaine Wright Colvin, editor. **33⅓% freelance written.** Bimonthly magazine covering religious publishing industry. Estab. 1983. Circ. 1,000. **Pays on acceptance.** Publishes ms an average of 1-4 months after acceptance. Byline given. Buys first North American serial rights. Editorial lead time 2 months. Submit seasonal material 2 months in advance. Accepts queries by e-mail. Responds in 1 month to mss. Sample copy for $5, 9×12 SAE with 4 first-class stamps. Writer's guidelines for #10 SASE.

O→ Break in by "getting involved in the Christian publishing (CBA) industry; interview CBA published authors, CBA editors or CBA bookstore managers."

Nonfiction: Submit material in the body of e-mail only. How-to (writing), humor, inspirational, interview/profile, new product, opinion, personal experience (for advanced/professional writers only), religious, technical. No beginners basics material used. Send complete ms. Length: 50-800 words. **Pays $5-50, sometimes pays other than cash.** Sometimes pays expenses of writers on assignment.

Columns/Departments: Industry News, Market News, Changes in the Industry, Watch on the World, Poetry News, Speakers Microphone, Conference Schedule, Look Over My Shoulder, new books reviewed or announced, Bulletin Board, Computer Corner. Send complete ms in body of e-mail or as an e-mail attachment.

N $ THE WRITE MARKETS REPORT, Monthly Paying Markets, Deep South Publishing Co., P.O. Box 2399, Bangor ME 04402-2399. E-mail: angela@writersweekly.com. Website: www.writersweekly.com/index-twmr.htm. Angela Adair-Hoy, editor. **40% freelance written.** Monthly online writing and publishing. "Features new paying markets received from editors 2 weeks prior to issue's release, as well as articles on how to make more money writing." Estab. 1997. Circ. 200,000 visits/month. **Pays on acceptance.** Byline given. Offers 100% kill fee. Buys electronic rights. first or one-time electronic rights Editorial lead time 2 months. Submit seasonal material 2 months in advance. Accepts queries by e-mail. Accepts previously published material. Accepts simultaneous submissions. Sample copy and writer's guidelines online.

Nonfiction: Book excerpts, how-to, interview/profile, personal experience. "We do *not* want how-to-write articles. We only want how-to-sell-your-writing articles." **Buys 18 mss/year.** Length: 600-1,000 words. **Pays $50.** Pays expenses of writers on assignment.

Photos: State availability with submission. Reviews 90x130 GIFS or JPEGS. One-time electronic rights. Offers no additional payment for photos accepted with manuscript. Model releases required.

Columns/Departments: Book excerpts (freelance income topics). "We run writing-related book excerpts for authors with byline and ordering info, but we don't pay for these." **Buys 12 mss/year.** Query.

Tips: "Our audience is comprised of professional writers, most of them freelance fulltime. No newbie articles. All articles must target professionals, teaching them marketing tips and new ideas while not talking down to them. We are only interested in articles that teach writers how to make more money writing."

$ $ WRITER'S DIGEST, 4700 E. Galbraith Rd., Cincinnati OH 45236. (513)531-2690 ext. 1483. E-mail: wdsubmissions@fwpubs.com. Website: www.writersdigest.com. **Contact:** Kelly Nickell, features editor. **70% freelance written.** Monthly magazine about writing and publishing. "Our readers write fiction, nonfiction, plays and scripts. They're interested in improving writing skills and the ability to sell their work and find new outlets for their talents." Estab. 1920. Circ. 150,000. **Pays on acceptance.** Publishes ms an average of 6-9 months after acceptance. Byline given. Offers 25% kill fee. first world serial rights for one-time editorial use, possible electronic posting, microfilm/microfiche use and magazine promotional use. Pays 25% reprint fee and 10% for electronic use in fee-charging mediums. Submit seasonal material 8 months in advance. Writer's guidelines online.

- *Writer's Digest* strongly prefers e-queries and responds in 3 weeks to e-queries; 3 months mail queries w/SASE. The magazine does not accept or read e-queries with attachments.

O→ "Break in through Markets Spotlight, or with a 500-1,000 word 'how-to' article."

Nonfiction: "What we need is the how-to article: How to write compelling leads and conclusions, how to improve your character descriptions, how to become more efficient and productive. We like plenty of examples, anecdotes and details in our articles. On how-to technique articles, we prefer to work with writers with a proven track record of success. For example, don't pitch us an article on creating effective dialog if you've never had a work of fiction published. Don't query about setting up a book tour if you've never done one. We like our articles to speak directly to the reader through the use of the first-person voice. We are seldom interested in author interviews and 'evergreen' topics are not accepted unless they are timely and address industry trends. Must have fax to receive galleys. "Don't send articles today that would have fit in WD five years ago. No articles titled 'So You Want to Be a Writer,' and no first-person pieces without something readers can learn from in the sharing of the story. Avoid the 'and then I wrote' article that is a promotional vehicle for you without tips on how others can put your experience to work." **Buys 60 mss/year.** We only accept electronic final manuscripts. Length: 500-1,800 words. **Pays 25-40¢/word.** Sometimes pays expenses of writers on assignment.

Tips: "Two-thirds of assignments are based on staff-generated ideas. Only about 25 unsolicited queries for features are assigned per year. Note that our standing columns and departments are not open to freelance submissions. Further, we buy at most five interviews/profiles per year; nearly all that we publish are staff-written. Candidates for First Success interviews (all of which are conducted in-house) should send galleys and information about themselves at least five months before their book's pubilcation date to Jerry Jackson at the address above."

$ WRITER'S FORUM, Writer's Digest School, 4700 E. Galbraith Rd., Cincinnati OH 45236. (513)531-2690, ext. 1343. E-mail: wdsforum@fwpubs.com. Website: www.writersdigestschool.com. **Contact:** Maria Altevers, editor. **100% freelance written.** Tri-annual newsletter covering writing techniques, marketing and inspiration for students enrolled in fiction and nonfiction writing courses offered by Writer's Digest School. Estab. 1970. Circ. 10,000. **Pays on acceptance.** Publishes ms an average of 6 months after acceptance. Byline given. Buys first, second serial (reprint) rights. Accepts queries by mail, e-mail. Accepts simultaneous submissions. Sample copy for free.

- Break in with something "how-to" oriented that is geared toward beginning writers and/or writers just breaking into print.

Nonfiction: How-to (write or market short stories, or articles, novels and nonficiton books). **Buys 12 mss/year.** Prefers complete mss to queries. Length: 500-1,000 words. **Pays $25.**

$ WRITER'S GUIDELINES & NEWS, The Who, What, When, and Where Magazine for Writers, P.O. Box 310647, Jamaica NY 11431-0647. (718)380-0800. E-mail: WGandNews@aol.com. **Contact:** Christopher L. Buono, editor-in-chief. **60% freelance written.** Quarterly magazine covering writing. "We consider ourselves 'the friend of the writer,' so we are very flexible. We will consider anything, well-written, with a writing slant for beginning as well as professional writers." Estab. 1988. Circ. 2,500. Pays on publication. Publishes ms an average of 6 months after acceptance. Byline given. Buys first North American serial rights. Editorial lead time 4 months. Submit seasonal material 4 months in advance. Accepts queries by mail, e-mail. Responds in 1 month to queries; 4 months to mss. Sample copy for $5. Writer's guidelines for #10 SASE.

- Break in with "articles about writers or the writing profession. Inform and entertain. Write for writers. Surprise us with your inventiveness and talent."

Nonfiction: All submissions must include an SASE for reply and/or return. Essays, general interest, how-to (on writing), humor, inspirational, interview/profile, opinion, personal experience. "No articles without a writing slant." **Buys 50 mss/year.** Send complete ms. Length: 750-1,500 words. **Pays $5-25.** Some work (e.g., fillers, news items, poetry and short pieces) receives payment in magazine copies.

Photos: Review. Buys one-time rights.

$ WRITERS' JOURNAL, The Complete Writer's Magazine, Val-Tech Media, P.O. Box 394, Perham MN 56573-0394. (218)346-7921. Fax: (218)346-7924. E-mail: writersjournal@lakesplus.com. Website: www.writersjournal.com. Managing Editor: John Ogroske. **Contact:** Leon Ogroske, editor. **90% freelance written.** Bimonthly Trade magazine covering writing. "*Writers' Journal* is read by thousands of aspiring writers whose love of writing has taken them to the next step: Writing for money. We are an instructional manual giving writers the tools and information necessary to get their work published. We also print works by authors who have won our writing contests." Estab. 1980. Circ. 26,000. Pays on publication. Publishes ms an average of 10 months after acceptance. Byline given. Buys one-time rights. Editorial lead time 8 months. Submit seasonal material 8 months in advance. Accepts queries by mail, e-mail, fax, phone. Accepts simultaneous submissions. Responds in 6 weeks to queries; 6 months to mss. Sample copy for $5.

Nonfiction: Looking for articles on fiction writing (plot development, story composition, character development, etc.) and writing "how-to." Book excerpts, essays, exposé, general interest (to writers), humor, inspirational, interview/profile, new product, opinion, personal experience, photo feature, technical. No erotica. **Buys 45 mss/year.** Send complete ms. Length: 800-2,500 words. Pays in contributor copies or other premiums if author agrees.

Photos: State availability with submission. Reviews contact sheets, Prints. Buys one-time rights. Negotiates payment individually. Model releases required.

Columns/Departments: For Beginners Only (helpful advice to beginners), 800-2,500 words. **Buys 30 mss/year.** Send complete ms. **Pays $20, plus contributor copies.**

Fiction: "We only publish winners of our fiction contests—16 contests/year."

Poetry: Esther Leiper-Jefferson, poetry editor. No erotica. **Buys 25 poems/year.** Submit maximum 4 poems. Length: 25 lines. **Pays $5.**

Fillers: Anecdotes, facts, short humor, cartoons. **Buys 20/year.** Length: 200 words. **Pays $10.**

Tips: "Appearance must be professional with no grammatical or spelling errors submitted on white paper, double spaced with easy-to-read font. We want articles that will help writers improve technique in writing, style, editing, publishing, and story construction. We are interested in how writers use new and fresh angles to break into the writing markets."

$ WRITING THAT WORKS, The Business Communications Report, 7481 Huntsman Blvd., #720, Springfield VA 22153-1648. E-mail: inq@writingthatworks.com. Website: www.writingthatworks.com/wtw.htm. **Contact:** John De Lellis, editor/publisher. Monthly Newsletter on business writing and communications. "Our readers are company writers, editors, communicators and executives. They need specific, practical advice on how to write well as part of their job." Estab. 1983. Pays within 45 days of acceptance. Publishes ms an average of 3 months after acceptance. Byline sometimes given. Buys all rights. Editorial lead time 2 months. Accepts queries by mail, e-mail. Responds in 1 month to queries. Sample copy and writer's guidelines online.

Nonfiction: Practical, short, how-to articles and quick tips on business writing techniques geared to company writers, editors, publication staff and communicators. "We're always looking for shorts—how-to tips on business writing." How-to. **Buys 120 mss/year.** Accepts electronic final mss. Length: 100-500 words. **Pays $35-150.**

Columns/Departments: Writing Techniques (how-to business writing advice); Style Matters (grammar, usage and editing); Online Publishing (writing, editing and publishing for the Web); Managing Publications; PR & Marketing (writing).

Fillers: Short tips on writing or editing. Mini-reviews of communications websites for business writers, editors and communicators. Length: 100-150 words. **Pays $35.**

Tips: "We do not use material on how to get published or how to conduct a freelancing business. Format your copy to follow *Writing That Works* style. Include postal and e-mail addresses, phone numbers and website URLs and prices for products/services mentioned in articles."

$$$$ WRITTEN BY, The Magazine of the Writers Guild of America, West, 7000 W. Third St., Los Angeles CA 90048. (323)782-4803. Fax: (323)782-4802. E-mail: writtenby@wga.org. Website: www.wga.org. **Contact:** Richard Stayton, editor. **40% freelance written.** Monthly magazine. "*Written By* is the premier monthly magazine written by and for America's screen and TV writers. We focus on the craft of screenwriting and cover all aspects of the entertainment industry from the perspective of the writer. We are read by all screenwriters and most entertainment executives." Estab. 1987. Circ. 17,000. **Pays on acceptance.** Publishes ms an average of 2 months after acceptance. Byline given. Offers 10% kill fee. Buys first North American serial, electronic rights. Editorial lead time 4 months. Submit seasonal material 4 months in advance. Accepts queries by mail, e-mail, fax. Writer's guidelines for #10 SASE.

Break in with "an exclusive profile or Q&A with a major TV or screenwriter."

Nonfiction: Book excerpts, essays, historical/nostalgic, humor, interview/profile, opinion, personal experience, photo feature, technical (software). No "how to break into Hollywood," "how to write scripts"-type beginner pieces. **Buys 20 mss/year.** Query with published clips. Length: 500-3,500 words. **Pays $500-3,500 for assigned articles.** Sometimes pays expenses of writers on assignment.

Photos: State availability with submission. Reviews transparencies. Buys one-time rights. Offers no additional payment for photos accepted with ms. Captions, identification of subjects, model releases required.

Columns/Departments: Pays $1,000 maximum.

The online version of this publication contains material not found in the print edition.

Tips: "We are looking for more theoretical essays on screenwriting past and/or present. Also the writer must *always* keep in mind that our audience is made up primarily of working writers who are inside the business, therefore all articles need to have an 'insider' feel and not be written for those who are still trying to break in to Hollywood. We prefer a hard copy submission or e-mail."

LAW

While all of these publications deal with topics of interest to attorneys, each has a particular slant. Be sure that your subject is geared to a specific market—lawyers in a single region, law students, paralegals, etc. Publications for law enforcement personnel are listed under Government & Public Service.

$$$$ ABA JOURNAL, The Lawyer's Magazine, American Bar Association, 750 N. Lake Shore Dr., Chicago IL 60611. (312)988-6018. E-mail: abajournal@abanet.org. Website: www.abajournal.com. Editor: Danial J. Kim. **Contact:** Debra Cassens, managing editor. **10% freelance written.** Monthly magazine covering law. "The *ABA Journal* is an independent, thoughtful and inquiring observer of the law and the legal profession. The magazine is edited for members of the American Bar Association." Circ. 389,000. **Pays on acceptance.** Byline given. Makes work-for-hire assignments. Accepts queries by mail, e-mail. Sample copy and writer's guidelines free.

Nonfiction: Legal features. "We don't want anything that does not have a legal theme. No poetry or fiction." **Buys 5 mss/year.** Query with published clips. Length: 700-3,500 words. **Pays $400-2,000 for assigned articles.**

Columns/Departments: Law Beat (reports on legal news and trends), 700-1,400 words; Solo Network (advice for solo practitioners), 1,000 words; In the Office (life on the job for lawyers), 700-1,400 words; In re Technology (technology for lawyers), 700-1,400 words. **Buys 25 mss/year.** Query with published clips. **Pays $350-1,200.**

$ $ $ $ CALIFORNIA LAWYER, Daily journal Corporation, 1145 Market St., 8th Floor, San Francisco CA 94103. (415)252-0500. Fax: (415)252-2482. E-mail: peter_allen@dailyjournal.com. Website: www.dailyjournal.com. Managing Editor: Tema Goodwin. **Contact:** Peter Allen, editor. **30% freelance written.** Monthly magazine of law-related articles and general-interest subjects of appeal to lawyers and judges. "Our primary mission is to cover the news of the world as it affects the law and lawyers, helping our readers better comprehend the issues of the day and to cover changes and trends in the legal profession. Our readers are all 140,000 California lawyers, plus judges, legislators and corporate executives. Although we focus on California and the West, we have subscribers in every state. *California Lawyer* is a general interest magazine for people interested in law. Our writers are journalists." Estab. 1981. Circ. 140,000. **Pays on acceptance.** Publishes ms an average of 3 months after acceptance. Byline given. Offers 25% kill fee. Buys first North American serial, electronic rights. Editorial lead time 3 months. Accepts queries by mail, e-mail, fax. Sample copy and writer's guidelines for #10 SASE.

O→ Break in by "showing us clips—we usually start people out on short news stories."

Nonfiction: Essays, general interest, interview/profile, News and feature articles on law-related topics. "We are interested in concise, well-written and well-researched articles on issues of current concern, as well as well-told feature narratives with a legal focus. We would like to see a description or outline of your proposed idea, including a list of possible sources." **Buys 12 mss/year.** Query with or without published clips or send complete ms. Length: 500-5,000 words. **Pays $50-2,000.** Pays expenses of writers on assignment.

Photos: Jake Flaherty, art director. State availability with submission. Reviews prints. Identification of subjects, model releases required.

Columns/Departments: California Esq. (current legal trends). 300 words. **Buys 6 mss/year.** Query with or without published clips. **Pays $50-250.**

COLORADO JOURNAL, Daily journal Corp., 717 17th St., Suite 2710, Denver CO 80202. (303)222-3202. Fax: (303)292-5821. E-mail: charles_ashby@dailyjournal.com. Website: www.dailyjournal.com. Editor: Katrina Dewey. **Contact:** Charles Ashby, Denver bureau chief. **20-30% freelance written.** Weekly tabloid covering legal issues. Estab. 1996. Circ. 2,000. Pays on publication. Byline given. Buys all rights. Editorial lead time 1 month. Submit seasonal material 1 month in advance. Accepts queries by mail, e-mail, fax, phone. Responds in 1 month to queries. Sample copy and writer's guidelines free.

Nonfiction: Exposé, general interest, how-to, interview/profile, photo feature, technical. Query. Length: 1,200-2,000 words. Sometimes pays expenses of writers on assignment.

Photos: State availability with submission. Reviews contact sheets. Buys all rights. Negotiates payment individually. Identification of subjects required.

Columns/Departments: Mark McDougal, managing editor. Query.

$ $ $ $ CORPORATE LEGAL TIMES, 656 W. Randolph St., #500-E, Chicago IL 60661-2114. (312)654-3500. E-mail: info@cltmag.com. Website: www.corporatelegaltimes.com. **Contact:** Robert Vosper, managing editor. **50% freelance written.** Monthly tabloid. "*Corporate Legal Times* is a monthly national magazine that gives general counsel and inhouse attorneys information on legal and business issues to help them better manage corporate law departments. It routinely addresses changes and trends in law departments, litigation management, legal technology, corporate governance and inhouse careers. Law areas covered monthly include: Intellectual property, international, technology, project finance, e-commerce and litigation. All articles need to be geared toward the inhouse attorney's perspective." Estab. 1991. Circ. 45,000. Pays on publication. Publishes ms an average of 3 months after acceptance. Byline given. Buys all rights. Editorial lead time 3 months. Submit seasonal material 3 months in advance. Accepts queries by mail, e-mail. Responds in 3 weeks to queries. Sample copy for $17. Writer's guidelines for #10 SASE.

Nonfiction: Interview/profile, news about legal aspects of business issues and events. **Buys 12-25 mss/year.** Query with published clips. Length: 500-3,000 words. **Pays $500-2,000.**

Photos: Freelancers should state availability of photos with submission. State availability with submission. Reviews color transparencies, b&w prints. Buys all rights. Offers $25-150/photo. Identification of subjects required.

Tips: "Our publication targets general counsel and inhouse lawyers. All articles need to speak to them—not to the general attorney population. Query with clips and a list of potential inhouse sources."

$ $ $ JOURNAL OF COURT REPORTING, National Court Reporters Association, 8224 Old Courthouse Rd., Vienna VA 22182. (703)556-6272. Fax: (703)556-6291. E-mail: pwacht@ncrahq.org. **Contact:** Peter Wacht, editor. **20% freelance written.** Monthly (bimonthly July/August and November/December) Magazine. "The *Journal of Court Reporting* has two complementary purposes: to communicate the activities, goals and mission of its publisher, the National Court Reporters Association; and, simultaneously, to seek out and publish diverse information and views on matters significantly related to the information/court reporting profession." Estab. 1905. Circ. 34,000. **Pays on acceptance.** Publishes ms an average of 3 months after acceptance. Byline given. Buys one-time rights, makes work-for-hire assignments. Editorial lead time 3 months. Accepts simultaneous submissions. Sample copy for $5. Writer's guidelines free.

Nonfiction: Essays, historical/nostalgic, how-to, interview/profile, new product, technical. **Buys 10 mss/year.** Query. Length: 1,200 words. words. **Pays $55-1,000.** Sometimes pays expenses of writers on assignment.

Photos: State availability with submission. Buys one-time rights. Offers no additional payment for photos accepted with ms. Captions, identification of subjects, model releases required.

$ $ $ LAW OFFICE COMPUTING, James Publishing, 3505 Cadillac Ave., Suite H, Costa Mesa CA 92626. (714)755-5450. Fax: (714)751-5508. E-mail: editorloc@jamespublishing.com. Website: www.lawofficecomputing.com. **Contact:** Amanda Clifford, managing editor. **90% freelance written.** Bimonthly magazine covering legal technology industry. "*Law Office Computing* is a magazine written for attorneys and other legal professionals. It covers the legal technology field and features software reviews, profiles of prominent figures in the industry and 'how-to' type articles." Estab. 1991. Circ. 8,000. Pays on publication. Publishes ms an average of 2 months after acceptance. Byline given. Buys first North American serial rights. Editorial lead time 4 months. Submit seasonal material 4 months in advance. Accepts queries by mail, e-mail, fax. Sample copy for free. Writer's guidelines online.

Nonfiction: How-to, interview/profile, new product, technical. Looking for Macintosh and Linux articles. **Buys 30 mss/year.** Query. Length: 2,000-4,000 words. **Pays on a case-by-case basis.** Sometimes pays expenses of writers on assignment.

Photos: State availability with submission.

Columns/Departments: Tech profile (profile firm using technology), 1,200 words; My Solution, 1,500 words; Software reviews: Short reviews (a single product), 400-800 words; Software Shootouts (2 or 3 products going head-to-head), 1,000-1,500 words; Round-Ups/Buyer's Guides (8 to 15 products), 300-500 words per product. Each type of software review article has its own specific guidelines. Request the appropriate guidelines from editor. **Buys 6 mss/year.** Query. **Pays on a case-by-case basis.**

Tips: "If you are a practicing attorney, legal MIS or computer consultant, try the first-person My Solution column or a short review. If a professional freelance writer, technology profiles or a news story regarding legal technology are best; since most of our other copy is written by legal technology professionals."

N LEGAL ASSISTANT TODAY, James Publishing, Inc., 3505 Cadillac Ave., Suite H, Costa Mesa CA 92626. (714)755-5468. Fax: (714)755-5508. E-mail: editorlat@jamespublishing.com. Website: www.legalassistanttoday.com. **Contact:** Rod Hughes, editor/publisher. Bimonthly magazine "geared toward all legal assistants/paralegals throughout the United States and Canada, regardless of specialty (litigation, corporate, bankruptcy, environmental law, etc.). How-to articles to help paralegals perform their jobs more effectively are most in demand, as is career and salary information, and timely news and trends pieces." Estab. 1983. Circ. 10,000. Pays on publication. Byline given. Buys first North American serial, electronic rights. non-exclusive electronic/Internet right and non-exclusive rights to use the article, author's name, image and biographical data in advertising and promotion. Editorial lead time 10 weeks. Submit seasonal material 3 months in advance. Accepts queries by mail, e-mail, fax. Accepts simultaneous submissions. Responds in 2 month to mss. Sample copy and writer's guidelines free.

Nonfiction: Interview/profile (unique and interesting paralegals in unique and particular work-related situations), news (brief, hard news topics regarding paralegals). Features: present information to help paralegals advance their careers.

Photos: Send photos with submission.

Tips: "Fax a detailed outline of a 3,000 to 4,500-word feature about something useful to working legal assistants. Writers *must* understand our audience. There is some opportunity for investigative journalism as well as the usual features, profiles and news. How-to articles are especially desired. If you are a great writer who can interview effectively, and really dig into the topic to grab readers' attention, we need you."

N LOS ANGELES DAILY JOURNAL, Daily journal Corporation, 915 E. First St., Los Angeles CA 90012. (213)229-5300. Fax: (213)625-0945. Website: www.dailyjournal.com. **Contact:** Katrina Dewey, editor. **5% freelance written.** Daily newspaper covering legal affairs. "Must be of interest to lawyers and others interested in legal and governmental affairs." Estab. 1877. Circ. 17,500. Pays on publication. Byline given. Offers variable kill fee. Buys first, electronic rights, makes work-for-hire assignments. Accepts queries by mail, e-mail, fax, phone. Accepts simultaneous submissions.

Nonfiction: Book excerpts, essays, exposé, humor, interview/profile, opinion. **Buys variable number of mss/year.** Query with published clips. Length: 500-5,000 words. **Payment varies (individually negotiated).** Sometimes pays expenses of writers on assignment.

Photos: State availability with submission. Buys all rights. Negotiates payment individually. Captions, identification of subjects required.

$ $ THE NATIONAL JURIST, Crittenden Magazines, P.O. Box 939039, San Diego CA 92193. (858)503-7562. Fax: (858)503-7588. **Contact:** Keith Carter, managing editor. **5% freelance written.** Bimonthly magazine covering law literature. Estab. 1991. Circ. 100,000. Pays on publication. Buys all rights. Accepts queries by mail, e-mail, fax, phone.

Nonfiction: General interest, how-to, humor, interview/profile. **Buys 4 mss/year.** Query. Length: 750-3,000 words. **Pays $100-500 for assigned articles.**

Photos: State availability with submission. Reviews contact sheets. Negotiates payment individually.

Columns/Departments: Pays $100-500.

$ $ THE PENNSYLVANIA LAWYER, Pennsylvania Bar Association, P.O. Box 186, 100 South St., Harrisburg PA 17108-0186. E-mail: editor@pabar.org. Executive Editor: Marcy Carey Mallory. Editor: Geoff Yuda. **Contact:** Donald C. Sarvey, editorial director. **25% freelance written.** Prefers to work with published/established writers. Bimonthly magazine published as a service to the legal profession and the members of the Pennsylvania Bar Association.

Estab. 1979. Circ. 30,000. **Pays on acceptance.** Publishes ms an average of 6 months after acceptance. Byline given. Buys first, one-time rights. Submit seasonal material 6 months in advance. Accepts queries by mail, e-mail. Responds in 2 months to queries; 2 months to mss. Sample copy for $2. Writer's guidelines for #10 SASE or by e-mail.
Nonfiction: All features must relate in some way to Pennsylvania lawyers or the practice of law in Pennsylvania. How-to, interview/profile, law-practice management, technology. **Buys 8-10 mss/year.** Query. Length: 1,200-2,000 words. **Pays $50 for book reviews; $75-400 for assigned articles; $150 for unsolicited articles.** Sometimes pays expenses of writers on assignment.
Photos: State availability with submission. Reviews contact sheets. Buys one-time rights. Negotiates payment individually. Identification of subjects required.

$ $ $ STUDENT LAWYER, The Magazine of the Law Student Division, American Bar Association, 750 N. Lake Shore Dr., Chicago IL 60611. (312)988-6048. Fax: (312)988-6081. E-mail: abastulawyer@abanet.org. Website: www.abanet.org/lsd. **Contact:** Ira Pilchen, editor. **85% freelance written.** Works with a small number of new writers each year. Monthly magazine. "*Student Lawyer* is a legal-affairs features magazine that competes for a share of law students' limited spare time, so the articles we publish must be informative, lively, well-researched good reads." Estab. 1972. Circ. 35,000. **Pays on acceptance.** Publishes ms an average of 3 months after acceptance. Byline given. Buys first rights. Editorial lead time 5 months. Submit seasonal material 6 months in advance. Accepts queries by mail, e-mail, phone. Writer's guidelines online.
Nonfiction: Essays (on legal affairs), interview/profile (prominent person in law-related fields), opinion (on matters of current legal interest). No fiction, please. **Buys 25 mss/year.** Query with published clips. Length: 2,500-4,000 words. **Pays $500-1,200 for features.** Sometimes pays expenses of writers on assignment.
Columns/Departments: Profile (profiles out-of-the ordinary lawyers), 1,200 words; Coping (dealing with law school), 1,200 words; Online (Internet and the law), 1,200 words; Leagal-ease (language and legal writing), 1,200 words; Jobs (marketing to legal employers), 1,200 words; Opinion (opinion on legal issue), 800 words. **Buys 45 mss/year.** Query with published clips. **Pays $200-500.**
Tips: "*Student Lawyer* actively seeks good new reporters and writers eager to prove themselves. Legal training definitely not essential; writing talent is. The writer should not think we are a law review; we are a features magazine with the law (in the broadest sense) as the common denominator. Find issues of national scope and interest to write about; be aware of subjects the magazine—and other media—have already covered and propose something new. Write clearly and well. Expect to work with editor to polish manuscripts to perfection. We do not make assignments to writers with whose work we are not familiar. If you're interested in writing for us, send a detailed, thought-out query with 3 previously published clips. We are always willing to look at material on spec. Sorry, we don't return manuscripts."

LUMBER

$ $ BUILDING MATERIAL DEALER, National Lumber & Building Material Dealers Association, 1405 Lilac Dr. N, Minneapolis MN 55422. Fax: (763)582-3024. Website: www.dealer.org. **Contact:** Carla Waldemar, editor. **10% freelance written.** Monthly magazine covering the lumber and building center industry. Estab. 1985. Circ. 30,000. Pays on publication. Publishes ms an average of 2 months after acceptance. Byline given. Buys one-time rights. Editorial lead time 3 months. Submit seasonal material 3 months in advance. Accepts queries by mail, fax. Accepts simultaneous submissions. Responds in 2 months to queries; 1 month to mss. Sample copy for $5.
Nonfiction: New product, technical. No general business, interviews/profiles. **Buys 24 mss/year.** Query with published clips. Length: 600-2,500 words. **Pays $100-300.**
Reprints: Accepts previously published submissions.
Photos: State availability with submission. Buys one-time rights. Offers no additional payment for photos accepted with ms. Identification of subjects required.

[N] PALLET ENTERPRISE, Industrial Reporting Inc., 10244 Timber Ridge Dr., Ashland VA 23005. (804)550-0323. Fax: (804)550-2181. E-mail: editor@ireporting.com. Website: www.palletenterprise.com. Managing Editor: Chaille Brindley. **Contact:** Tim Cox, editor. **40% freelance written.** Monthly magazine covering lumber and pallet operations. Articles should offer technical, solution-oriented information. Anti-forest articles are not accepted. Articles should focus on machinery and unique ways to improve profitability/make money. Estab. 1981. Circ. 14,500. Pays on publication. Buys first, one-time, electronic rights, makes work-for-hire assignments. May buy all rights. Rights purchased depends on the writer and the article. Editorial lead time 2 months. Submit seasonal material 2 months in advance. Accepts queries by mail, e-mail, fax, phone. Accepts previously published material. Accepts simultaneous submissions. Sample copy online. Writer's guidelines free.
Nonfiction: "We only want articles of interest to pallet manufacturers, pallet recyclers, and lumber companies/sawmills." Interview/profile, new product, opinion, technical, industry news; environmental; forests operation/plant features. No lifestyle, humor, general news, etc. **Buys 20 mss/year.** Query with published clips. Length: 1,000-3,000 words. **Pays $200-400 for assigned articles; $100-400 for unsolicited articles.** Call editor to discuss circumstances under which writers are paid in contributor copies. Sometimes pays expenses of writers on assignment.
Photos: State availability with submission. Reviews 3×5 prints. Buys one time rights and Web rights. Negotiates payment individually. Captions, identification of subjects required.
Columns/Departments: Green Watch (environmental news/opinion affecting U.S. forests), 1,500 words. **Buys 12 mss/year.** Query with published clips. **Pays $200-400.**

Tips: "Provide unique environmental or industry-oriented articles. Many of our freelance articles are company features of sawmills, pallet manufacturers, pallet recyclers, and wood waste processors."

$ $ SOUTHERN LUMBERMAN, Hatton-Brown Publishers, P.O. Box 681629, Franklin TN 37068-1629. (615)791-1961. Fax: (615)591-1035. E-mail: southernlumberman@forestind.com. Website: www.southernlumberman.com. **Contact:** Nanci P. Gregg, editor. **20% freelance written.** Works with a small number of new/unpublished writers each year. Monthly journal for the sawmill industry. Estab. 1881. Circ. 15,000. Pays on publication. Publishes ms an average of 3 months after acceptance. Byline given. Buys first North American serial rights. Submit seasonal material 6 months in advance. Responds in 1 month to queries; 2 months to mss. Sample copy for $3 and 9×12 SAE with 5 first-class stamps. Writer's guidelines for #10 SASE.
Nonfiction: How-to (sawmill better), technical, equipment analysis, sawmill features. **Buys 10-15 mss/year.** Query with or without published clips or send complete ms. Length: 500-2,000 words. **Pays $150-350 for assigned articles; $100-250 for unsolicited articles.** Sometimes pays expenses of writers on assignment.
Reprints: Send tearsheet or photocopy of article and information about when and where the article previously appeared. Pays 25-50% of amount paid for an original article.
Photos: Always looking for news feature types of photos featuring forest products, industry materials or people. Send photos with submission. Reviews transparencies, 4×5 color prints. Pays $10-25/photo. Captions, identification of subjects required.
Tips: "Like most, we appreciate a clearly-worded query listing merits of suggested story—what it will tell our readers they need/want to know. We want quotes, we want opinions to make others discuss the article. Best hint? Find an interesting sawmill operation owner and start asking questions—I bet a story idea develops. We need color photos too. Find a sawmill operator and ask questions—what's he doing bigger, better, different. We're interested in new facilities, better marketing, improved production."

N TIMBERLINE, Timber Industry Newsline/Trading Post, Industrial Reporting Inc., 10244 Timber Ridge Dr., Ashland VA 23005. (804)550-0323. Fax: (804)550-2181. E-mail: editor@ireporting.com. Website: www.timberlinemag.com. Managing Editor: Chaille Brindley. **Contact:** Tim Cox, editor. **50% freelance written.** Monthly tabloid covering the forest products industry. Articles should offer technical, solution-oriented information. Anti-forest products, industry articles are not accepted. Articles should focus on machinery and unique ways to improve profitability and make money. Estab. 1994. Circ. 30,000. Pays on publication. Byline given. Buys first, one-time, electronic rights, makes work-for-hire assignments. May purchase all rights. Rights purchased depends on the writer and the article. Editorial lead time 2 months. Submit seasonal material 2 months in advance. Accepts queries by mail, e-mail, fax, phone. Accepts previously published material. Accepts simultaneous submissions. Sample copy online. Writer's guidelines free.
Nonfiction: "We only want articles of interest to loggers, sawmills, wood treatment facilities, etc. Readers tend to be pro-industry/conservative, and opinion pieces must be written to appeal to them." Historical/nostalgic, interview/profile, new product, opinion, technical, Industry News; Environmental Operation/Plant Features. No lifestyles, humor, general news, etc. **Buys 25 mss/year.** Query with published clips. Length: 1,000-3,000 words. **Pays $200-400 for assigned articles; $100-400 for unsolicited articles.** Call editor to discuss circumstances under which writers are paid in contributor copies. Sometimes pays expenses of writers on assignment.
Photos: State availability with submission. Reviews 3×5 prints. Buys one time rights and Web rights. Negotiates payment individually. Captions, identification of subjects required.
Columns/Departments: From the Hill (legislative news impacting the forest products industry), 1,800 words; Green Watch (environmental news/opinion affecting U.S. forests), 1,500 words. **Buys 12 mss/year.** Query with published clips. **Pays $200-400.**
Tips: "Provide unique environmental or industry-oriented articles. Many of our freelance articles are company features of logging operations or sawmills."

MACHINERY & METAL

$ ANVIL MAGAZINE, Voice of the Farrier & Blacksmith, P.O. Box 1810, 2770 Sourdough Flat, Georgetown CA 95634. (530)333-2142. Fax: (530)333-2906. E-mail: anvil@anvilmag.com. Website: www.anvilmag.com. Publisher/Editor: Rob Edwards. **Contact:** Mimi Clark, senior editor. **40% freelance written.** Monthly magazine covering "how-to articles on hoof care and horseshoeing and blacksmithing, tips on running your own farrier or blacksmith business and general articles on those subjects." Estab. 1978. Circ. 4,000. Pays on publication. Publishes ms an average of 1 year after acceptance. Byline sometimes given. Buys first North American serial rights. Editorial lead time 3 months. Submit seasonal material 6 months in advance. Accepts queries by mail, e-mail, fax. Accepts simultaneous submissions. Sample copy for $6. Writer's guidelines free.
Nonfiction: Material has to be specific to the subjects of horseshoeing, hoof care, farrier interests, blacksmithing interest. General interest, historical/nostalgic, how-to, humor, interview/profile, new product, opinion, photo feature, technical, Book reviews of farrier/blacksmithing publications. **Buys 8-10 mss/year.** Send complete ms. Length: 1,200-1,600 words. **Pays $25-200.** Sometimes pays expenses of writers on assignment.
Photos: Send photos with submission. Reviews transparencies, prints. Buys one-time rights. Offers $25 additional payment for photos accepted with ms. Negotiates payment individually if photos only, such as for a how-to article. Identification of subjects required.

Poetry: Traditional on blacksmithing and farriery subjects only. No cowboy poetry. **Buys 5-6 poems/year.** Submit maximum 1-2 poems. Length: 20-40 lines lines. **Pays $25.**

Tips: "Write clearly and concisely. Our readers are professionals. Stay away from generic topics or general horsemanship. Our most popular features are "how to's" and interviews. For interviews, don't be bashful—ask the tough questions."

$ $ $ CUTTING TOOL ENGINEERING, CTE Publications, 400 Skokie Blvd., Suite 395, Northbrook IL 60062-7903.. (847)498-9100. Fax: (847)559-4444. Website: www.ctemag.com. **Contact:** Don Nelson, editorial director. **50% freelance written.** Monthly magazine covering industrial metal cutting tools and metal cutting operations. "*Cutting Tool Engineering* serves owners, managers and engineers who work in manufacturing, specifically manufacturing that involves cutting or grinding metal or other materials. Writing should be geared toward improving manufacturing processes." Circ. 35,000. Pays 1 week before publication. Publishes ms an average of 2 months after acceptance. Byline given. Offers 50% kill fee. Buys all rights. Editorial lead time 2 months. Accepts queries by mail, fax. Accepts simultaneous submissions. Responds in 2 months to mss. Sample copy and writer's guidelines free.

Nonfiction: How-to, interview/profile, opinion, personal experience, technical. "No fiction, articles that don't relate to manufacturing." **Buys 30 mss/year.** Length: 1,500-3,000 words. **Pays $450-1,000.** Pays expenses of writers on assignment.

Photos: State availability with submission. Reviews transparencies, prints. Buys all rights. Negotiates payment individually. Captions required.

Columns/Departments: Talking Points (interview with industry subject), 600 words; Cutting Remarks (opinion piece), 900 words; Manager's Desk (shop owner), 700 words; Back To Basics (tool review), 500 words. **Buys 28 mss/year.** Query with published clips. **Pays $150-300.**

Tips: "For queries, write two clear paragraphs about how the proposed article will play out. Include sources that would be in the article."

$ $ $ THE FABRICATOR, The Croydon Group, Ltd., 833 Featherstone Rd., Rockford IL 61107. (815)399-8700. Fax: (815)484-7700. E-mail: miked@thefabricator.com. Website: www.thefabricator.com. **Contact:** Mike Dorcey, managing editor. **15% freelance written.** Monthly magazine covering metal forming and fabricating. Our purpose is to disseminate information about modern metal forming and fabricating techniques, machinery, tooling and management concepts for the metal fabricator. Estab. 1971. Circ. 55,000. Pays on publication. Byline given. Buys all rights. Editorial lead time 6 months. Accepts queries by mail, e-mail. Responds in 2 weeks to queries; 1 month to mss. Sample copy and writer's guidelines free.

Nonfiction: How-to, technical, company profile. Special issues: Forecast issue (January). No unsolicited case studies. Query with published clips. Length: 800-1,200 words. **Pays 40-80¢/word.** Sometimes pays expenses of writers on assignment.

Photos: Request guidelines for digital images. State availability with submission. Reviews transparencies, prints. Rights purchased depends on photographer requirements. Negotiates payment individually. Captions, identification of subjects required.

Columns/Departments: Eye on Europe (metal fabricating in Europe); Asia Chronicle (metal fabricating in Asia), both 800 words. **Buys 10 mss/year.** Query. **Pays 40-80¢/word.**

The online magazine carries original content not found in the print edition. Contact: Lincoln Brunner.

$ MATERIAL HANDLING WHOLESALER, Specialty Publications International, Inc., P.O. Box 725, Dubuque IA 52004-0725. (877)638-6190 or (563)557-4495. Fax: (563)557-4499. E-mail: dmillius@mhwmag.com. Website: www.mhwmag.com. **Contact:** Hilary Hawley, editor. **100% freelance written.** Monthly magazine covering material handling industry. *MHW* is published monthly for new and used equipment dealers, equipment manufacturers, manufacturer reps, parts suppliers and service facilities serving the material handling industry. Estab. 1979. Circ. 13,000. Pays on publication. Publishes ms an average of 2 months after acceptance. Byline given. Buys first rights. Editorial lead time 1 month. Submit seasonal material 2 months in advance. Accepts queries by mail, e-mail, fax. Accepts simultaneous submissions. Sample copy for $29 annually-3rd class. Writer's guidelines free.

Nonfiction: General interest, how-to, inspirational, new product, opinion, personal experience, photo feature, technical, material handling news.

Photos: Send photos with submission. Reviews 3×5 prints. Buys all rights. Offers no additional payment for photos accepted with ms.

Columns/Departments: Aftermarket (aftermarket parts and service); Battery Tech (batteries for lifts-MH equipment; Marketing Matters (sales trends in MH industry); Internet at Work (internet trends), all 1,200 words. **Buys 3 mss/year.** Query. **Pays $0-50.**

The online version of this publication contains material not found in the print edition. Contact: Jan Day, online editor.

N $ $ MODERN MACHINE SHOP, Gardner Publications, Inc., 6915 Valley Ave., Cincinnati OH 45244-3029. (513)527-8800. Fax: (513)527-8801. E-mail: malbert@mmsonline.com. Website: www.mmsonline.com. **Contact:** Mark Albert, editor-in-chief. **5% freelance written.** Monthly Estab. 1928. Pays 1 month following acceptance. Publishes ms an average of 6 months after acceptance. Byline given. Accepts queries by mail, e-mail, fax, phone. Responds in 1 month to mss. Call for sample copy. Writer's guidelines online.

O— Advances in metalworking technology are occurring rapidly. Articles that show how this new technology, as embodied in specific products, is being implemented in shops and plants are sought after. Writers are strongly encouraged to call to discuss an idea.

Nonfiction: Uses only articles dealing with all phases of metalworking, manufacturing and machine shop work, with photos. "Ours is an industrial publication, and contributing authors should have a working knowledge of the metalworking industry. We regularly use contributions from machine shop owners, engineers, other technical experts, and suppliers to the metalworking industry. Almost all of these contributors pursue these projects to promote their own commercial interests." **Buys 5 or fewer unsolicited mss/year.** Query. Length: 1,000-3,500 words. **Pays current market rate.**

The online magazine carries original content not found in the print edition. Contact: A.J. Sweatt (ajsweatt@mmsonline.com).

Tips: "Articles that review basic metalworking/machining processes, especially if they include a rethinking or reevaluation of these processes in light of today's technical trends, are always welcome."

$ $ $ MSI, (formerly *Manufacturing Systems*), Reed Business Information, 2000 Clearwater Dr., Oak Brook IL 60523-8809. (630)320-7041. Fax: (630)320-7088. E-mail: rmichel@cahners.com. Website: www.manufacturingsystems.com. **Contact:** Roberto Michel, editor. Monthly magazine. "*Manufacturing Systems* is about the use of information technology to improve productivity in discrete manufacturing and process industries." Estab. 1984. Circ. 105,000. Pays on publication. Publishes ms an average of 3 months after acceptance. Byline sometimes given. Buys all rights. Editorial lead time 3 months. Submit seasonal material 4 months in advance. Accepts queries by e-mail. Sample copy for free.

Nonfiction: Technical, features about supply chain management software. **Buys 9 mss/year.** Query.

Photos: No additional payment for photos. Captions required.

$ $ ORNAMENTAL AND MISCELLANEOUS METAL FABRICATOR, National Ornamental And Miscellaneous Metals Association, 532 Forest Pkwy., Suite A, Forest Park GA 30297. Fax: (404)363-2857. E-mail: todd@nomma.org. **Contact:** Todd Daniel, editor. **20% freelance written.** Bimonthly magazine "to inform, educate and inspire members of the ornamental and miscellaneous metalworking industry." Estab. 1959. Circ. 8,500. Pays when article is received. Byline given. Buys one-time rights. Editorial lead time 2 months. Accepts queries by mail, e-mail, fax. Responds in 1 month to queries. Sample copy for 9×12 SAE and 6 first-class stamps. Writer's guidelines for $1.

Nonfiction: Book excerpts, essays, exposé, general interest, historical/nostalgic, how-to, humor, inspirational, interview/profile, new product, opinion, personal experience, photo feature, technical. **Buys 5-7 mss/year.** Query. Length: 1,200-2,000 words. **Pays $300-350 for assigned articles; $150 for unsolicited articles.** Pays expenses of writers on assignment.

Reprints: Send tearsheet, photocopy or typed ms with rights for sale noted and information about when and where the material previously appeared. Pays 100% of amount paid for an original article.

Photos: State availability with submission. Reviews contact sheets, negatives, transparencies, prints. May offer additonal payment for photos accepted with ms. Model releases required.

Tips: "Make article relevant to our industry. Don't write in passive voice."

$ $ $ PRACTICAL WELDING TODAY, The Croydon Group, Ltd., 833 Featherstone Rd., Rockford IL 61107-6302. (815)227-8282. Fax: (815)484-7715. E-mail: stephaniev@thefabricator.com. Website: www.thefabricator.com. Managing Editor: Mike Dorcey. **Contact:** Stephanie Vaughan, associate editor. **15% freelance written.** Bimonthly magazine covering welding. "We generally publish how-to, educational articles that teach people about a process or how to do something better." Estab. 1997. Circ. 40,000. Pays on publication. Byline given. Buys all rights. Editorial lead time 6 months. Accepts queries by mail, e-mail. Responds in 2 weeks to queries; 2 months to mss. Sample copy and writer's guidelines free.

Nonfiction: How-to, technical, company profiles. Special issues: Forecast issue on trends in welding (January/February). No promotional, one-sided, persuasive articles, unsolicited case studies. **Buys 5 mss/year.** Query with published clips. Length: 800-1,200 words. **Pays 40-80¢/word.** Sometimes pays expenses of writers on assignment.

Photos: State availability with submission. Reviews contact sheets. Rights purchased depends on photographer requirements. Negotiates payment individually. Captions, identification of subjects required.

Columns/Departments: Inspection Connection (inspecting welds), 700 words. **Buys 1-2 mss/year.** Query with published clips. **Pays 40-80¢/word.**

Tips: "Follow our author guidelines and editorial policies to write a how-to piece from which our readers can benefit."

$ $ SPRINGS, The Magazine of Spring Technology, Spring Manufacturing Institute, 2001 Midwest Rd., Suite 106, Oak Brook IL 60523-1335. (630)495-8588. Fax: (630)495-8595. **Contact:** Rita Schauer, editor. **10% freelance written.** Bimonthly magazine covering precision mechanical spring manufacture. Articles should be aimed at spring manufacturers." Estab. 1962. Circ. 8,900. Pays on publication. Publishes ms an average of 6 months after acceptance. Byline given. Buys first rights. Editorial lead time 4 months. Accepts simultaneous submissions. Sample copy and writer's guidelines free.

Nonfiction: General interest, how-to, interview/profile, opinion, personal experience, technical. **Buys 4-6 mss/year.** Length: 2,000-10,000 words. **Pays $100-600 for assigned articles; $50-300 for unsolicited articles.**

Photos: State availability with submission. Reviews transparencies, prints. Buys one-time rights. Offers no additional payment for photos accepted with ms. Captions required.

Fillers: Facts, newsbreaks. **Buys 4/year.** Length: 200-1,000 words. **Pays $25-50.**

Tips: "Call the editor. Contact springmakers and spring industry suppliers and ask about what interests them. Include interviews/quotes from people in the spring industry in the article. The editor can supply contacts."

$ $ STAMPING JOURNAL, The Croydon Group, Ltd., 833 Featherstone Rd., Rockford IL 61107. (815)227-8285. Fax: (815)484-7783. E-mail: katm@thefabricator.com. Website: www.thefabricator.com. Managing Editor: Mike Dorcey. **Contact:** Kathleen McLaughlin, associate editor. **15% freelance written.** Bimonthly magazine covering metal stamping. "We look for how-to, educational articles—non-promotional." Estab. 1989. Circ. 35,000. Pays on publication. Byline given. Buys all rights. Editorial lead time 6 months. Accepts queries by mail, e-mail, fax, phone. Responds in 2 weeks to queries; 2 months to mss. Sample copy and writer's guidelines free.
Nonfiction: How-to, technical, company profile. Special issues: Forecast issue (January). No unsolicited case studies. **Buys 5 mss/year.** Query with published clips. Length: 1,000 words. **Pays 40-80¢/word.** Sometimes pays expenses of writers on assignment.
Photos: State availability with submission. Reviews contact sheets. Rights purchased depends on photographer requirements. Negotiates payment individually. Captions, identification of subjects required.

The online magazine contains material not found in the print edition. Contact: Lincoln Brunner, online editor.
Tips: "Articles should be impartial and should not describe the benefits of certain products available from certain companies. They should not be biased toward the author's or against a competitor's products or technologies. The publisher may refuse any article that does not conform to this guideline."

$ $ $ TPJ—THE TUBE & PIPE JOURNAL, The Croydon Group, Ltd., 833 Featherstone Rd., Rockford IL 61107. (815)227-8262. Fax: (815)484-7713. E-mail: ericl@thefabricator.com. Website: www.thefabricator.com. Managing Editor: Michael Dorcey. **Contact:** Eric Lundin, associate editor. **15% freelance written.** Magazine published 8 times/year covering metal tube and pipe. Educational perspective—emphasis is on "how-to" articles to accomplish a particular task or how to improve on a process. New trends and technologies are also important topics. Estab. 1990. Circ. 30,000. Pays on publication. Byline given. Buys all rights. Editorial lead time 6 months. Accepts queries by mail, e-mail. Responds in 2 weeks to queries; 2 months to mss. Sample copy and writer's guidelines free.
Nonfiction: Any new or improved tube production or fabrication process—includes manufacturing, bending and forming tube (metal tube only). How-to, technical, company profile. Special issues: Forecast issue (January). No unsolicited case studies. **Buys 5 mss/year.** Query with published clips. Length: 800-1,200 words. **Pays 40-80¢/word.** Sometimes pays expenses of writers on assignment.
Photos: State availability with submission. Reviews contact sheets. Rights purchased depends on photographer requirements. Negotiates payment individually. Captions, identification of subjects required.
Columns/Departments: Manager's Notebook (management tips, information news), 1,000 words. **Pays 40¢/word.**
Tips: "Submit a detailed proposal, including an article outline, to the editor."

$ $ WIRE ROPE NEWS & SLING TECHNOLOGY, VS Enterprises, P.O. Box 871, Clark NJ 07066. (908)486-3221. Fax: (732)396-4215. E-mail: vsent@aol.com. Website: www.wireropenews.com. Editor: Barbara McGrath. Managing Editor: Conrad Miller. **Contact:** Edward J. Bluvias, publisher. **100% freelance written.** Bimonthly magazine "published for manufacturers and distributors of wire rope, chain, cordage, related hardware, and sling fabricators. Content includes technical articles, news and reports describing the manufacturing and use of wire rope and related products in marine, construction, mining, aircraft and offshore drilling operations." Estab. 1979. Circ. 3,400. **Pays on acceptance.** Publishes ms an average of 6 months after acceptance. Byline sometimes given. Buys all rights. Editorial lead time 2 months. Submit seasonal material 2 months in advance. Accepts queries by mail, fax. Accepts simultaneous submissions.
Nonfiction: General interest, historical/nostalgic, interview/profile, photo feature, technical. **Buys 30 mss/year.** Send complete ms. Length: 2,500-5,000 words. **Pays $300-500.**
Photos: Send photos with submission. Reviews contact sheets, 5×7 prints. Buys all rights. Offers no additional payment for photos accepted with ms. Identification of subjects required.

MAINTENANCE & SAFETY

N $ $ AMERICAN WINDOW CLEANER MAGAZINE, Voice of the Professional Window Cleaner, P.O. 70888, Port Richmond CA 94807. (510)233-4011. Fax: (510)233-4111. E-mail: awcmag@aol.com. Website: www.awcmag.com. **Contact:** Richard Fabry, editor. **20% freelance written.** Bimonthly magazine window cleaning. "Articles to help window cleaners become more profitable, safe, professional and feel good about what they do." Estab. 1986. Circ. 8,000. **Pays on acceptance.** Publishes ms an average of 4 months after acceptance. Byline given. Offers 33% kill fee. Buys first rights. Editorial lead time 2 months. Submit seasonal material 3 months in advance. Responds in 2 weeks to queries; 1 month to mss. Sample copy for free. Writer's guidelines free.
Nonfiction: How-to, humor, inspirational, interview/profile, personal experience, photo feature, technical. Special issues: Covering a window cleaner, convention in February 2001 in Washington, DC. "Do not want PR-driven pieces. Want to educate no push a particular product." **Buys 20 mss/year.** Query. Length: 500-5,000 words. **Pays $50-250.** Sometimes pays expenses of writers on assignment.
Photos: State availability with submission. Reviews contact sheets, transparencies, 4×6 Prints. Buys one-time rights. Offers $10 per photo. Captions required.

Columns/Departments: Window Cleaning Tips (tricks of the trade); 1,000-2,000 words; Humor-anecdotes-feel good-abouts (window cleaning industry); Computer High-tech (tips on new technology), all 1,000 words. **Buys 12 mss/year.** Query. **Pays $50-100.**

Tips: "*American Window Cleaner Magazine* covers an unusual niche that gets peoples' curiosity. What could possibly be covered in the international magazine for window cleaners? We are open to a wide varietyof articles as long as they are in some way connected to our industry. This would include: window cleaning unusual buildings, landmarks; working for well-known people/celebrities; window cleaning in resorts/casinos/unusual cities; humor or satire about our industry or the public's perception of it. If you have a good idea for a story, there is a good chance we will be interested in you writing it. At some point, we make phone contact and chat to see if our interests are compatible."

$ BREATHING AIR DIGEST, Sub-Aquatics, Inc., Publications Division, 8855 E. Broad St., Reynoldsburg OH 43068. (614)864-1235. Fax: (614)864-0071. E-mail: rlauer@breathingair.com. Website: www.breathingair.com. Editor: Richard Lauer. **Contact:** William McBride, managing editor. **25% freelance written.** Semiannual magazine. "Our audience is primarily those involved with the production, handling, and use of high-pressure pure breathing air, particularly fire and safety departments, dive stores, etc. We are interested in articles of 500-1,500 words related to tips, experiences, technology and applications." Estab. 1989. Circ. 12,000. Pays on publication. Publishes ms an average of 1 year after acceptance. Byline given. Buys first, one-time rights. Editorial lead time 1 year. Accepts queries by mail, e-mail, fax, phone. Accepts simultaneous submissions. Responds in 6 weeks to queries; 2 months to mss. Sample copy for 9×12 SAE and 4 first-class stamps.

Nonfiction: How-to, humor, new product, personal experience, photo feature, technical, accidents and near miss. "We are not interested in brand-specific promotional material." **Buys 3-6 mss/year.** Send complete ms. Length: 500-1,500 words. **Pays $50-70.**

Photos: Send photos with submission. Reviews negatives, transparencies, prints. Buys one-time rights. Offers no additional payment for photos accepted with ms.

Columns/Departments: Send complete ms. **Pays $50-70.**

Tips: "We most want articles that will be of use to others in this field. Often, the relating of 'bad' experiences can be helpful."

$ $ $ CANADIAN OCCUPATIONAL SAFETY, CLB Media, Inc., 3228 S. Service Rd., Suite 209, Burlington, Ontario L7N 3H8, Canada. (905)634-2100 ext. 35. Fax: (905)634-2238. E-mail: mgault@cos-mag.com. Website: www.cos-mag.com. **Contact:** Michelle Gault, editor. **40% freelance written.** Bimonthly magazine. "We want informative articles dealing with issues that relate to occupational health and safety in Canada." Estab. 1989. Circ. 14,000. Pays on publication. Publishes ms an average of 3 months after acceptance. Byline given. Buys one-time rights. Editorial lead time 4 months. Submit seasonal material 4 months in advance. Accepts queries by mail, e-mail, fax, phone. Responds in 3 weeks to queries; 1 month to mss. Sample copy and writer's guidelines free.

Nonfiction: How-to, interview/profile. **Buys 30 mss/year.** Query with published clips. Length: 500-2,000 words. **Payment varies.** Sometimes pays expenses of writers on assignment.

Photos: State availability with submission. Reviews transparencies. Buys one-time rights. Negotiates payment individually. Captions required.

Tips: "Present us with an idea for an article that will interest workplace health and safety professionals, with cross-Canada appeal."

$ CLEANING BUSINESS, P.O. Box 1273, Seattle WA 98111. Fax: (206)622-6876. E-mail: bills@cleaningconsultants.com. Website: www.cleaningconsultants.com. William R. Griffin, Publisher. **Contact:** Bill Sieckowski, editor. **80% freelance written.** Quarterly magazine. "We cater to those who are self-employed in any facet of the cleaning and maintenance industry and seek to be top professionals in their field. *Cleaning Business* is published for self-employed cleaning professionals, specifically carpet, upholstery and drapery cleaners; janitorial and maid services; window washers; odor, water and fire damage restoration contractors. Our readership is small but select. We seek concise, factual articles, realistic but definitely upbeat." Circ. 6,000. Pays 1 month after publication. Publishes ms an average of 3 months after acceptance. Byline given. Buys first North American serial, second serial (reprint), all rights, makes work-for-hire assignments. Submit seasonal material 6 months in advance. Responds in 3 months to mss. Sample copy for $3 and 8×10 SAE with 3 first-class stamps. Writer's guidelines for #10 SASE.

Nonfiction: Exposé (safety/health business practices), how-to (on cleaning, maintenance, small business management), humor (clean jokes, cartoons), interview/profile, new product (must be unusual to rate full article—mostly obtained from manufacturers), opinion, personal experience, technical. Special issues: "What's New?" (February). No "wordy articles written off the top of the head, obviously without research, and needing more editing time than was spent on writing." **Buys 40 mss/year.** Query with or without published clips. Length: 500-3,000 words.

Photos: "Magazine size is 8½×11—photos need to be proportionate. Also seeks full-color photos of relevant subjects for cover." State availability with submission. Buys one-time rights. Pays $5-25 for. Captions, identification of subjects, model releases required.

Columns/Departments: "Ten regular columnists now sell four columns per year to us. We are interested in adding Safety & Health and Fire Restoration columns (related to cleaning and maintenance industry). We are also open to other suggestions—send query." **Buys 36 mss/year.** Query with or without published clips. **Pays $15-85.**

Fillers: Anecdotes, gags to be illustrated by cartoonist, newsbreaks, short humor, Jokes, Gags. **Buys 40/year.** Length: 3-200 words. **Pays $1-20.**

Tips: "We are constantly seeking quality freelancers from all parts of the country. A freelancer can best break in to our publication with fairly technical articles on how to do specific cleaning/maintenance jobs; interviews with top professionals covering this and how they manage their business; and personal experience. Our readers demand concise, accurate information. Don't ramble. Write only about what you know and/or have researched. Editors don't have time to rewrite your rough draft. Organize and polish before submitting."

$ $ EXECUTIVE HOUSEKEEPING TODAY, The International Executive Housekeepers Association, 1001 Eastwind Dr., Suite 301, Westerville OH 43081. (614)895-7166. Fax: (614)895-1248. E-mail: avance@ieha.org. Website: www.ieha.org. **Contact:** Andi Vance, editor. **95% freelance written.** Monthly magazine for "nearly 8,000 decision makers responsible for housekeeping management (cleaning, grounds maintenance, laundry, linen, pest control, waste management, regulatory compliance, training) for a variety of institutions: hospitality, healthcare, education, retail, government." Estab. 1930. Circ. 5,500. **Pays on acceptance.** Publishes ms an average of 6 months after acceptance. Byline given. Buys first North American serial rights. Editorial lead time 2 months. Submit seasonal material 3 months in advance. Accepts queries by mail, e-mail, fax, phone. Sample copy and writer's guidelines free.

Nonfiction: General interest, interview/profile, new product (related to magazine's scope), personal experience (in housekeeping profession), technical. **Buys 30 mss/year.** Query with published clips. Length: 500-1,500 words. **Pays $150-250.**

Photos: State availability with submission. Reviews negatives. Buys one-time rights. Offers no additional payment for photos accepted with ms. Identification of subjects required.

Columns/Departments: Federal Report (OSHA/EPA requirements), 1,000 words; Industry News; Management Perspectives (industry specific), 500-1,500 words. Query with published clips. **Pays $150-250.**

Tips: "Have a background in the industry or personal experience with any aspect of it."

$ $ PEST CONTROL MAGAZINE, 7500 Old Oak Blvd., Cleveland OH 44130. (440)243-8100. Fax: (440)891-2683. Website: www.pestcontrolmag.com. **Contact:** Susan Porter, associate publisher/executive editor. Monthly Magazine for professional pest management professionals and sanitarians. Estab. 1933. Circ. 20,000. Pays on publication. Submit seasonal material 3 months in advance. Accepts queries by mail, e-mail, phone. Responds in 1 month to mss. Sample copy not available.

- Break in with "information directly relating to the field—citing sources that are either industry experts (university or otherwise) or direct quotes from pest/management professionals."

Nonfiction: All articles must have trade or business orientation. How-to, humor, inspirational, interview/profile, new product, personal experience (stories about pest management operations and their problems), case histories, new technological breakthroughs. No general information type of articles desired. **Buys 3 mss/year.** Query only. Length: 1,000-1,400 words. **Pays $150-400 minimum.**

Photos: Certain digital photos accepted; please query on specs. State availability with submission. Pays $50-500 for 8×10 color or transparencies for front cover graphics. No additional payment for photos used with ms.

Columns/Departments: Regular columns use material oriented to this profession. Length: 550 words.

The online magazine carries original material not found in the print edition. Contact: Heather Gooch.

MANAGEMENT & SUPERVISION

This category includes trade journals for middle management business and industrial managers, including supervisors and office managers. Journals for business executives and owners are classified under Business Management. Those for industrial plant managers are listed in Industrial Operations.

$ $ HR MAGAZINE, On Human Resource Management, Society for Human Resource Management, 1800 Duke St., Alexandria VA 22314-3499. (703)548-3440. Fax: (703)535-6488. E-mail: hrmag@shrm.org. Website: www.shrm.org. Editor: Patrick Mirza. **Contact:** Karen Caldwell, editorial assistant. **70% freelance written.** Monthly magazine covering human resource management professions with special focus on business news that affects the workplace including compensation, benefits, recruiting, training and development, management trends, court decisions, legislative actions and government regulations. Estab. 1948. Circ. 165,000. **Pays on acceptance.** Publishes ms an average of 2 months after acceptance. Byline given. Buys all rights. Editorial lead time 4 months. Accepts queries by mail, e-mail, fax. Responds in 1 month to queries. Sample copy for free.

- Break in by having "relevant writing experience and a sharp, narrowly-focused article idea on something new or not well-covered elsewhere."

Nonfiction: Technical, expert advice and analysis, news features. **Buys 50 mss/year.** Query. Length: 1,800-2,500 words. Pays expenses of writers on assignment.

Photos: State availability with submission. Buys one-time rights. Identification of subjects, model releases required.

Tips: "Readers are members of the Society for Human Resource Management (SHRM), mostly HR managers with private employers."

N $ $ $ HUMAN RESOURCE EXECUTIVE, LRP Publications Magazine Group, 747 Dresher Rd., P.O. Box 980, Dept. 500, Dresher PA 19044. (215)784-0910. Fax: (215)784-0275. E-mail: dshadovitz@lrp.com. Website: www.hrexecutive.com. **Contact:** David Shadovitz, editor. **30% freelance written.** Monthly magazine. "Monthly magazine serving the information needs of chief human resource professionals/executives in companies, government agencies and nonprofit institutions with 500 or more employees." Estab. 1987. Circ. 60,000. **Pays on acceptance.** Publishes ms an average of 2 months after acceptance. Byline given. Pays 50% kill fee on assigned stories. Buys first, all rights. including reprint rights Accepts queries by mail, e-mail, fax. Responds in 1 month to mss.

Nonfiction: Book excerpts, interview/profile. **Buys 16 mss/year.** Query with published clips. Length: 1,800 words. **Pays $200-900.** Sometimes pays expenses of writers on assignment.

Photos: State availability with submission. Reviews contact sheets. Buys first and repeat rights. Offers no additional payment for photos accepted with ms. Identification of subjects required.

$ $ INCENTIVE, VNU Business Publications, Dept. WM, 770 Broadway, New York NY 10003. (646)654-7646. Fax: (646)654-7650. E-mail: lestelle@incentivemag.com. Website: www.incentivemag.com. **Contact:** Libby Estell, managing editor. Monthly magazine covering sales promotion and employee motivation: managing and marketing through motivation. Estab. 1905. Circ. 41,000. **Pays on acceptance.** Publishes ms an average of 3 months after acceptance. Byline given. Buys all rights. Accepts queries by mail, e-mail, fax. Responds in 1 month to queries; 2 months to mss. Sample copy for 9×12 SAE.

Nonfiction: General interest (motivation, demographics), how-to (types of sales promotion, buying product categories, using destinations), interview/profile (sales promotion executives), travel (incentive-oriented), Corporate case studies. **Buys 48 mss/year.** Query with published clips. Length: 1,000-2,000 words. **Pays $250-700 for assigned articles; Does not pay for unsolicited articles.** Pays expenses of writers on assignment.

Reprints: Send tearsheet and information about when and where the material previously appeared. Pays 50% of the amount paid for an original article.

Photos: Send photos with submission. Reviews contact sheets, transparencies. Offers some additional payment for photos accepted with ms. Identification of subjects required.

Tips: "Read the publication, then query."

$ MANAGE, 2210 Arbor Blvd., Dayton OH 45439. (937)294-0421. Fax: (937)294-2374. E-mail: doug@nma1.org. Website: www.nma1.org. **Contact:** Douglas E. Shaw, editor-in-chief. **60% freelance written.** Works with a small number of new/unpublished writers each year. Quarterly magazine for first-line and middle management and scientific/technical managers. Estab. 1925. Circ. 30,000. **Pays on acceptance.** Publishes ms an average of 6 months after acceptance. Buys first North American serial rights. Reprint privileges; book rights remain with the author Responds in 3 months to queries. Sample copy and writer's guidelines for 9×12 SAE and 3 first-class stamps.

Nonfiction: "All material published by *Manage* is in some way management-oriented. Most articles concern one or more of the following categories: Communications, executive abilities, human relations, job status, leadership, motivation and productivity and professionalism. Articles should be specific and tell the manager how to apply the information to his job immediately. Be sure to include pertinent examples, and back up statements with facts." *Manage* does not want essays or academic reports, but interesting, well-written and practical articles for and about management. Length: 600-1,000 words. **Pays 5¢/word.**

Reprints: Send photocopy. Pays 100% of amount paid for an original article.

Tips: "Keep current on management subjects; submit timely work. Include word count on first page of manuscript."

$ SUPERVISION, 320 Valley, Burlington IA 52601. Publisher: Michael S. Darnall. **Contact:** Teresa Levinson, editor. **95% freelance written.** Monthly magazine for first-line foremen, supervisors and office managers. "*Supervision*'s objective is to provide informative articles which develop the attitudes, skills, personal and professional qualities of supervisory staff, enabling them to use more of their potential to maximize productivity, minimize costs, and achieve company and personal goals." Estab. 1939. Circ. 2,620. Pays on publication. Publishes ms an average of 6 months after acceptance. Buys all rights. Accepts queries by mail. Responds in 1 month to mss. Sample copy and writer's guidelines for 9×12 SAE with 4 first-class stamps; mention *Writer's Market* in request.

Nonfiction: How-to (cope with supervisory problems, discipline, absenteeism, safety, productivity, goal setting, etc.), personal experience (unusual success story of foreman or supervisor). No sexist material written from only a male viewpoint. **Buys 12 mss/year.** Include biography and/or byline with ms submissions. Length: 1,500-1,800 words. **Pays 4¢/word.**

Tips: "Following AP stylebook would be helpful." Uses no advertising. Send correspondence to Editor.

MARINE & MARITIME INDUSTRIES

$ $ MARINE BUSINESS JOURNAL, The Voice of the Marine Industries Nationwide, 330 N. Andrews Ave., Ft. Lauderdale FL 33301. (954)522-5515. Fax: (954)522-2260. E-mail: sboating@southernboating.com. Website: www.southernboating.com. **Contact:** Timothy Banse, executive editor. **25% freelance written.** Bimonthly magazine that covers the recreational boating industry. "*The Marine Business Journal* is aimed at boating dealers, distributors and manufacturers, naval architects, yacht brokers, marina owners and builders, marine electronics dealers, distributors and manufacturers, and anyone involved in the US marine industry. Articles cover news, new product technology and public affairs affecting the industry." Estab. 1986. Circ. 26,000. Pays on publication. Publishes ms an average of 1 month after acceptance. Byline given. Buys first North American serial, one-time, second serial (reprint) rights. Accepts queries by mail, e-mail. Responds in 2 weeks to queries. Sample copy for $2.50, 9×12 SAE with 7 first-class stamps. Writer's guidelines for #10 SASE.

Nonfiction: **Buys 20 mss/year.** Query with published clips. Length: 500-2,000 words. **Pays $100-200.** Sometimes pays expenses of writers on assignment.
Photos: State availability with submission. Reviews 35mm or larger transparencies, Prints, 5×7. Buys one-time rights. Offers $25-50/photo. Captions, identification of subjects, model releases required.
Tips: "Query with clips. It's a highly specialized field, written for professionals by professionals, almost all on assignment or by staff."

$ $ PROFESSIONAL MARINER, Journal of the Maritime Industry, Navigator Publishing, 58 Fore St., Portland ME 04112. (207)822-4350. Fax: (207)772-2879. E-mail: editors@professionalmariner.com. Website: www.professionalmariner.com. **Contact:** John Gormley, editor. **75% freelance written.** Bimonthly magazine covering professional seamanship and maritime industry news. Estab. 1993. Circ. 29,000. Pays on publication. Byline given. Buys all rights. Editorial lead time 3 months. Accepts queries by mail, e-mail, fax, phone. Accepts simultaneous submissions.
Nonfiction: For professional mariners on vessels and ashore. Seeks submissions on industry news, regulations, towing, piloting, technology, engineering, business, maritime casualties and feature stories about the maritime industry. Does accept "sea stories" and personal professional experiences as correspondence pieces. **Buys 15 mss/year.** Query. Length: Varies; short clips to long profiles/features. **Pays 20¢/word.** Sometimes pays expenses of writers on assignment.
Photos: Send photos with submission. Reviews Slides; Prints. Buys one-time rights. Negotiates payment individually. Captions, identification of subjects required.
Tips: "Remember that our audience is professional mariners and other marine professionals. Stories must be written at a level that will benefit this group."

MEDICAL

Through these journals, physicians, therapists, and mental health professionals learn how other professionals help their patients and manage their medical practices. Publications for nurses, laboratory technicians, and other medical personnel are listed in the Hospitals, Nursing and Nursing Home section. Publications for drug store managers and drug wholesalers and retailers, as well as hospital equipment suppliers, are listed with Drugs, Health Care and Medical Products. Publications for consumers that report trends in the medical field are found in the Consumer Health and Fitness categories.

$ $ $ AMA ALLIANCE TODAY, American Medical Association Alliance, Inc., 515 N. State St., Chicago IL 60610. (312)464-4470. Fax: (312)464-5020. E-mail: amaa@ama-assn.org. Website: www.ama-assn.org/alliance. **Contact:** Chrissy McShane, editor. **25% freelance written.** Magazine published 3 times/year for physicians' spouses. Works with both established and new writers. Estab. 1965. Circ. 60,000. **Pays on acceptance.** Publishes ms an average of 6 months after acceptance. Buys first rights. Accepts queries by mail, e-mail, fax. Accepts simultaneous submissions. Sample copy for 9×12 SAE and 2 first-class stamps.

O→ Break in with a "solid understanding of issues affecting physicians and their families with a special emphasis on the perspective of the physician's spouse or child."

Nonfiction: All articles must be related to the experiences of physicians' spouses. Current health issues; financial topics, physicians' family circumstances, business management and volunteer leadership how-to's. Query with clear outline of article—what points will be made, what conclusions drawn, what sources will be used. Length: 1,000 words. **Pays $300-800.**
Photos: Uses all color visuals. State availability with submission.
Tips: "Emphasize trends in healthcare as they affect the spouses and children of physicians."

$ $ $ AMERICA'S PHARMACIST, National Community Pharmacists Association, 205 Daingerfield Rd., Alexandria VA 22314. (703)683-8200. Fax: (703)683-3619. E-mail: deleisa.johnson@ncpanet.org. Website: www.ncpanet.org. **Contact:** Deleisa Johnson, editor. **10% freelance written.** Monthly magazine. "*America's Pharmacist* publishes business and management information and personal profiles of independent community pharmacists, the magazine's principal readers." Estab. 1904. Circ. 25,000. Pays on publication. Publishes ms an average of 3 months after acceptance. Byline given. Offers 20% kill fee. Buys all rights. Editorial lead time 3 months. Submit seasonal material 3 months in advance. Accepts queries by mail, e-mail, fax. Accepts simultaneous submissions. Responds in 1 week to queries; 2 weeks to mss. Sample copy and writer's guidelines free.
Nonfiction: Interview/profile, business information. **Buys 3 mss/year.** Query. Length: 1,500-2,500 words. **Pays $500-1,000.** Sometimes pays expenses of writers on assignment.
Photos: State availability with submission. Reviews contact sheets. Buys one-time rights. Negotiates payment individually. Captions, identification of subjects, model releases required.

N $ $ CONTINUING CARE, Stevens Publishing, 5151 Beltline Rd., Dallas TX 75254. (972)687-6786. Fax: (972)687-6770. E-mail: sbienkowski@stevenspublishing.com. Website: www.ccareonline.com. **Contact:** Sandra Bienkowski, editor. **10% freelance written.** Monthly journal covering care management. "*Continuing Care* provides practical information for managed care professionals in case management and discharge planning of high-risk, high-cost patient cases in home health care, rehabilitation and long-term care settings. *Continuing Care* encourages practical articles on case management, focusing on quality outcome of patient care at a cost-effective price to the health care payer. The magazine also informs readers on professional and business news, insurance and reimbursement issues and legal and legislative news." Estab. 1971. Circ. 22,000. Pays on publication. Byline given. Offers no kill fee. Buys all rights. Editorial lead time 4 months. Submit seasonal material 4 months in advance. Accepts queries by mail, e-mail, fax, phone. Accepts simultaneous submissions. Sample copy for free. Writer's guidelines free.

Nonfiction: Essays, exposé, general interest, new product, opinion, technical. **Buys 4 mss/year.** Query with published clips. Length: 1,500-2,000 words. **Pays $0-500.** Sometimes pays in contributor copies.

Photos: Send photos with submission. Offers $0-500/photo. Captions, identification of subjects required.

Columns/Departments: Managed Care, 2,000 words. **Buys 3 mss/year.** Query with published clips. **Pays $0-50.**

EVERY SECOND COUNTS, The Emergency Response Magazine, National Safety Council, 1121 Spring Lake Dr., Itasca IL 60143-3201. Fax: (630)775-2285. E-mail: parkerj@nsc.org. Website: www.nsc.org. Editor: Jennifer Grow. **Contact:** James Parker, associate editor. **40% freelance written.** Bimonthly magazine about EMTs, firefighters, paramedics and first-aid instructors. Estab. 1999. Circ. 150,000. **Pays on acceptance.** Publishes ms an average of 2 months after acceptance. Byline given. Buys all rights. Submit seasonal material 6 months in advance. Accepts queries by mail, e-mail, fax. Responds in 4 months to queries; 4 months to mss. Sample copy for 8×10 SASE. Writer's guidelines for #10 SASE.

Nonfiction: Exposé, general interest, historical/nostalgic, how-to, interview/profile, new product, opinion, personal experience, photo feature. **Buys 20 mss/year.** Query with published clips. Length: 2,000-3,000 words. **Payment determined on a per assignment basis.**

Photos: Send photos with submission. Reviews contact sheets, transparencies, prints, GIF/JPEG files. Buys one-time rights. Offers $50/photo. Identification of subjects, model releases required.

$ $ $ HEALTHPLAN, American Association of Health Plans, 1129 20th St. NW, Suite 600, Washington DC 20036. (202)778-3246. Fax: (202)331-7487. E-mail: gfauntleroy@aahp.org. Website: www.aahp.org. Editor: Louise Kertesz. **Contact:** Glenda Fauntleroy, managing editor. **75% freelance written.** Bimonthly magazine. "*Healthplan* is geared toward administrators in HMOs, PPOs, and similar health plans. Articles should inform and generate interest and discussion about topics on anything from patient care to regulatory issues." Estab. 1990. Circ. 7,000. Pays within 30 days of acceptance of article in final form. Publishes ms an average of 2 months after acceptance. Byline given. Offers 30% kill fee. Buys all rights. Editorial lead time 2 months. Submit seasonal material 4 months in advance. Accepts queries by mail, e-mail, fax. Accepts simultaneous submissions. Sample copy for free.

Nonfiction: Book excerpts, how-to (how industry professionals can better operate their health plans), opinion. "We do not accept stories that promote products." Query with published clips or send complete ms. Length: 1,800-2,500 words. **Pays 65¢/word minimum for assigned articles.** Pays phone expenses of writers on assignment.

Tips: "Look for health plan success stories in your community; we like to include case studies on a variety of topics—including patient care, provider relations, regulatory issues—so that our readers can learn from their colleagues. Our readers are members of our trade association and look for advice and news. Topics relating to the quality of health plans are the ones more frequently assigned to writers, whether a feature or department. We also welcome story ideas. Just send us a letter with the details."

$ $ JEMS, The Journal of Emergency Medical Services, Jems Communications, 1947 Camino Vida Roble, Suite 200, Carlsbad CA 92008-2789. (760)431-9797. Fax: (760)930-9567. Website: www.jems.com. **Contact:** A.J. Heightman, editor. **95% freelance written.** Monthly magazine directed to personnel who serve the pre-hospital emergency medicine industry: Paramedics, EMTs, emergency physicians and nurses, administrators, EMS consultants, etc. Estab. 1980. Circ. 45,000. Pays on publication. Publishes ms an average of 6 months after acceptance. Byline given. all North American serial rights Submit seasonal material 6 months in advance. Accepts queries by mail, e-mail, fax. Responds in 2-3 months to queries. Sample copy and writer's guidelines free.

Nonfiction: Essays, exposé, general interest, how-to, humor, interview/profile, new product, opinion, personal experience, photo feature, technical, continuing education. **Buys 50 mss/year.** Query. **Pays $200-400.**

Photos: State availability with submission. Reviews 4×6 prints. Buys one-time rights. Offers $25 minimum per photo. Identification of subjects, model releases required.

Columns/Departments: Length: 850 words maximum. "Columns and departments are staff-written with the exception of commentary on EMS issues and practices." Query with or without published clips. **Pays $50-250.**

Tips: "Please submit a one-page query letter before you send a manuscript. Your query should answer these questions: 1) What specifically are you going to tell *JEMS* readers? 2) Why do *JEMS* readers need to know this? 3) How will you make your case (i.e., literature review, original research, interviews, personal experience, observation)? Your query should explain your qualifications, as well as include previous writing samples."

$ $ MANAGED CARE, 780 Township Line Rd., Yardley PA 19067-4200. (267)685-2784. Fax: (267)685-2966. E-mail: editors@managedcaremag.com. Website: www.managedcaremag.com. **Contact:** John Marcille, managing editor. **50% freelance written.** Monthly magazine. "We emphasize practical, usable information that helps the physician or HMO administrator cope with the options, challenges and hazards in the rapidly changing health care industry. Our regular readers understand that 'health care reform' isn't a piece of legislation; it's an evolutionary process that's already well under way. But we hope to help our readers also keep the faith that led them to medicine in the first place." Estab.

1992. Circ. 60,000. **Pays on acceptance.** Publishes ms an average of 1 month after acceptance. Byline given. Offers 20% kill fee. Buys all rights. Editorial lead time 3 months. Submit seasonal material 4 months in advance. Accepts queries by mail, e-mail, fax. Responds in 3 weeks to queries; 2 months to mss. Sample copy for free.

Nonfiction: "I strongly recommend submissions via e-mail. You'll get a faster response." Book excerpts, general interest (trends in health-care delivery and financing, quality of care, and employee concerns), how-to (deal with requisites of managed care, such as contracts with health plans, affiliation arrangements, accredidation, computer needs, etc.), original research and review articles that examine the relationship between health care delivery and financing. Also considered occasionally are personal experience, opinion, interview/profile and humor pieces, but these must have a strong managed care angle and draw upon the insights of (if they are not written by) a knowledgeable MD or managed care professional. **Buys 40 mss/year.** Query with published clips. Length: 1,000-3,000 words. **Pays 50-60¢/word.** Pays expenses of writers on assignment.

Photos: State availability with submission. Reviews contact sheets, negatives, transparencies, Prints. Buys first-time rights. Negotiates payment individually.

Columns/Departments: Michael Dalzell. News/Commentary (usually staff-written, but factual anecdotes involving managed care's effect on providers are welcome), 100-300 words; Employer Update, 800-1,000 words. **Pays $100-600.**

Tips: "Know our audience (physicians and health plan executives) and their needs. Study our website to see what we cover. We work with many first-time contributors."

$ $ $ $ MEDICAL ECONOMICS, 5 Paragon Dr., Montvale NJ 07645-1742. (201)358-7367. Fax: (201)722-2688. E-mail: helen.mckenna@medec.com. Website: www.memag.com. **Contact:** Helen A. McKenna, outside copy editor. Semimonthly magazine (24 times/year). "*Medical Economics* is a national business magazine read by M.D.s and D.O.s in office-based practice. Our purpose is to be informative and useful to practicing physicians in the professional and financial management of their practices. We look for contributions from writers who know—or will make the effort to learn—the non-clinical concerns of today's physician. These writers must be able to address those concerns in feature articles that are clearly written and that convey authoritative information and advice. Our articles focus very narrowly on a subject, and explore it in depth." Circ. 162,000. **Pays on acceptance.** Offers 25% kill fee. first world publication rights Accepts queries by mail, e-mail, fax. Sample copy for free.

Nonfiction: Articles about private physicians in innovative, pioneering and/or controversial situations affecting medical care delivery, patient relations or malpractice prevention/litigation; personal finance topics. "We do not want overviews or pieces that only skim the surface of a general topic. We address physician readers in a conversational, yet no-nonsense tone, quoting recognized experts on office management, personal finance, patient relations and medical-legal issues." **Buys 40-50 mss/year.** Query with published clips. Length: 1,500-2,500 words. **Pays $1,200-2,500 for assigned articles.** Pays expenses of writers on assignment.

Photos: Review. Will negotiate an additional fee for photos accepted for publication.

Tips: "We look for articles about physicians who run high-quality, innovative practices suited to the age of managed care. We also look for how-to service articles—on practice-management and personal-finance topics—which must contain anecdotal examples to support the advice. Read the magazine carefully, noting its style and content. Then send detailed proposals or outlines on subjects that would interest our mainly primary-care physician readers."

$ $ MEDICAL IMAGING, 295 Promenade St., Suite 2, Providence RI 02908. (401)455-0555. Fax: (401)455-1551. E-mail: mtierney@mwc.com. Website: www.medicalimagingmag.com. **Contact:** Mary Tierney, editor. **60% freelance written.** Monthly magazine covering diagnostic imaging equipment. Estab. 1986. Circ. 20,000. Pays on publication. Publishes ms an average of 2 months after acceptance. Byline given. Buys all rights. Editorial lead time 2 months. Responds to queries. Sample copy for $10 prepaid.

Nonfiction: Interview/profile, technical. "No general interest/human interest stories about healthcare. Articles *must* deal with our industry, diagnostic imaging." **Buys 6 mss/year.** Query with published clips. Length: 1,500-2,500 words. Sometimes pays expenses of writers on assignment.

Photos: State availability with submission. Reviews negatives. Buys all rights. Offers no additional payment for photos accepted with ms. Identification of subjects, model releases required.

Tips: "Send a letter with an interesting story idea that is applicable to our industry, diagnostic imaging. Then follow up with a phone call. Areas most open to freelancers are features and technology profiles. You don't have to be an engineer or doctor but you have to know how to talk and listen to them."

$ $ ▣ MODERN PHYSICIAN, Essential Business News for the Executive Physician, Crain Communications, 360 N. Michigan Ave., Chicago IL 60601. E-mail: jconn@crain.com. Website: www.modernphysician.com. **Contact:** Joseph Conn, editor. **40% freelance written.** Biweekly magazine covering business and management news for doctors. "*Modern Physician* offers timely topical news features with lots of business information—revenues, earnings, financial data." Estab. 1997. Circ. 32, 552. **Pays on acceptance.** Publishes ms an average of 2 months after acceptance. Byline given. Buys all rights. Editorial lead time 2 months. Accepts queries by mail, e-mail. Responds in 6 weeks to queries. Sample copy for free. Writer's guidelines sent after query.

O‑‑ Break in with a regional story involving business or physicians.

Nonfiction: Length: 1,000-2,000 words. **Pays 40-50¢/word.**

▣ The online magazine carries original content not found in the print edition. Contact: Joseph Conn.

Tips: "Read the publication, know our audience, come up with a good story idea that we haven't thought of yet."

$ $ THE NEW PHYSICIAN, 1902 Association Dr., Reston VA 20191. **Contact:** Rebecca Sernett, editor. **50% freelance written.** Magazine published 9 times/year for medical students, interns, residents and educators. Circ. 30,000. **Pays on acceptance.** Publishes ms an average of 2 months after acceptance. Accepts simultaneous submissions. Responds in 2 months to mss. Sample copy for 10×13 SAE and 5 first-class stamps. Writer's guidelines for #10 SASE.

Nonfiction: Articles on social, political, economic issues in medical education/health care. **Buys 14 mss/year.** Query or send complete ms. Length: 800-3,000 words. **Pays 25-50¢/word; higher fees for selected pieces.** Sometimes pays expenses of writers on assignment.

Reprints: Send photocopy and information about when and where the material previously appeared. Pay varies.

Tips: "Although we are published by an association (the American Medical Student Association), we are not a 'house organ.' We are a professional magazine for readers with a progressive view on health care issues and a particular interest in improving medical education and the health care system. Our readers demand sophistication on the issues we cover. Freelancers should be willing to look deeply into the issues in question and not be satisfied with a cursory review of those issues."

$ $ PHYSICIAN, Focus on the Family, 8605 Explorer Dr., Colorado Springs CO 80920. (719)531-3400. Fax: (719)531-3499. E-mail: physician@macmail.fotf.org. Website: www.family.org. Managing Editor: Charles Johnson. **Contact:** Susan Stevens, editor. **20% freelance written.** Bimonthly magazine. "The goal of our magazine is to encourage physicians in their faith, family and medical practice. Writers should understand the medical lifestyle." Estab. 1989. Circ. 89,000. **Pays on acceptance.** Publishes ms an average of 6 months after acceptance. Byline given. Buys first North American serial rights. Editorial lead time 1 year. Accepts queries by mail, e-mail, fax. Responds in 2 months to queries. Sample copy for SASE.

Nonfiction: General interest, interview/profile, personal experience, religious, technical. "No patient's opinions of their doctor." **Buys 20-30 mss/year.** Query. Length: 900-2,400 words. **Pays $100-500 for assigned articles.** Sometimes pays expenses of writers on assignment. Accepts previously published submissions.

Photos: State availability with submission. Reviews transparencies. Buys one-time rights. Negotiates payment individually.

Tips: "Most writers are M.D.'s."

N $ $ $ THE PHYSICIAN AND SPORTSMEDICINE, McGraw-Hill, 4530 W. 77th St., Edina MN 55435. (952)835-3222. Fax: (952)835-3460. E-mail: psmmanuscripts@mcgraw-hill.com. Website: www.physsportsmed.com. **Contact:** James R. Wappes, executive editor. **5% freelance written.** Monthly magazine covering medical aspects of sports and exercise. Prefers to work with published/established writers. "We publish articles that are of practical, clinical interest to our physician audience." Estab. 1973. Circ. 115,000. **Pays on acceptance.** Publishes ms an average of 4 months after acceptance. Byline given. Buys all rights. Responds in 2 months to queries. Sample copy for $10. Writer's guidelines for #10 SASE or on website.

- This publication is relying more heavily on the clinical component of the journal, meaning review articles written by physicians who have expertise in a specific specialty.

Nonfiction: New developments and issues in sports medicine. Query. Length: 250-2,500 words. **Pays $150-1,800.**

Photos: Mary Schill, photo editor. State availability with submission.

N $ $ $ PHYSICIANS' TRAVEL & MEETING GUIDE, Quadrant HealthCom, Inc., 26 Main St., Chatham NJ 07928. Fax: (973)701-8895. E-mail: ptmg@qho.com. Website: www.ptmg.com. Managing Editor: Eileen Cassidy. **Contact:** Bea Riemschneider, editor-in-chief. **60% freelance written.** Monthly magazine covering travel for physicians and their families. *Physicians' Travel & Meeting Guide* supplies continuing medical education events listings and extensive travel coverage of international and national destinations. Circ. 142,541. **Pays on acceptance.** Byline given. Buys first North American serial rights. Submit seasonal material 4-6 months in advance. Accepts queries by mail, e-mail. Responds in 3 months to queries.

Nonfiction: Photo feature, travel. **Buys 25-35 mss/year.** Query with published clips. Length: 450-3,000 words. **Pays $150-1,000 for assigned articles.**

Photos: State availability of or send photos with submission. Reviews 35mm; 4×5 transparencies. Buys one-time rights. Captions, identification of subjects required.

$ $ PODIATRY MANAGEMENT, Kane Communications, Inc., P.O. Box 750129, Forest Hills NY 11375. (718)897-9700. Fax: (718)896-5747. E-mail: bblock@prodigy.net. Website: www.podiatrym.com. Publisher: Scott C. Borowsky. **Contact:** Barry Block, editor. Magazine published 9 times/year for practicing podiatrists. "Aims to help the doctor of podiatric medicine to build a bigger, more successful practice, to conserve and invest his money, to keep him posted on the economic, legal and sociological changes that affect him." Estab. 1982. Circ. 13,500. Pays on publication. Byline given. Buys first North American serial, second serial (reprint) rights. Submit seasonal material 4 months in advance. Accepts queries by e-mail. Accepts simultaneous submissions. Responds in 2 weeks to queries. Sample copy for $3 and 9×12 SAE. Writer's guidelines for #10 SASE.

Nonfiction: Book excerpts, general interest (taxes, investments, estate, estate planning, recreation, hobbies), how-to (establish and collect fees, practice management, organize office routines, supervise office assistants, handle patient relations), interview/profile (about interesting or well-known podiatrists), personal experience. Special issues: "These subjects are the mainstay of the magazine, but offbeat articles and humor are always welcome." **Buys 25 mss/year.** Length: 1,000-2,500 words. **Pays $150-600.**

Reprints: Send photocopy. Pays 33% of amount paid for an original article.

Photos: State availability with submission. Buys one-time rights. Pays $15 for b&w contact sheet.
Tips: "We have been persuading writers to use e-mail for the past few years because of the speed, ease of editing, and general efficiency of the process. The tragic events of 9/11/01 along with the anthrax issue now make the policy mandatory...and the trees will also appreciate it!"

$ $ STITCHES, The Journal of Medical Humour, Stitches Publishing Inc., 16787 Warden Ave., R.R. #3, Newmarket, Ontario L3Y 4W1, Canada. (905)853-1884. Fax: (905)853-6565. **Contact:** Simon Hally, editor. **90% freelance written.** Monthly magazine covering humor for physicians. "*Stitches* is read primarily by physicians in Canada. Stories with a medical slant are particularly welcome, but we also run a lot of non-medical material. It must be funny and, of course, brevity is the soul of wit." Estab. 1990. Circ. 37,500. Pays on publication. Publishes ms an average of 2 months after acceptance. Byline given. Buys first North American serial, electronic rights. Editorial lead time 1 month. Submit seasonal material 4 months in advance. Responds in 6 weeks to queries; 2 months to mss. Sample copy and writer's guidelines free.
Nonfiction: Humor, personal experience. **Buys 30 mss/year.** Send complete ms. Length: 200-2,000 words. **Pays 40¢/word (Canadian).**
Fiction: Humorous. **Buys 40 mss/year.** Send complete ms. Length: 200-2,000 words. **Pays 40¢/word (Canadian).**
Poetry: Humorous. **Buys 5 poems/year.** Submit maximum 5 poems. Length: 2-30 lines. **Pays 50¢/word (Canadian).**
Fillers: Gags to be illustrated by cartoonist, short humor. **Pays negotiable rate.**
Tips: "Due to the nature of humorous writing, we have to see a completed manuscript, rather than a query, to determine if it is suitable for us. Along with a short cover letter, that's all we require."

$ $ ☒ STRATEGIC HEALTH CARE MARKETING, Health Care Communications, 11 Heritage Lane, P.O. Box 594, Rye NY 10580. (914)967-6741. Fax: (914)967-3054. E-mail: healthcomm@aol.com. Website: www.strategichealthcare.com. **Contact:** Michele von Dambrowski, editor. **90% freelance written.** Monthly Newsletter covering health care marketing and management in a wide range of settings including hospitals, medical group practices, home health services, and managed care organizations. Emphasis is on strategies and techniques employed within the health care field and relevant applications from other service industries. Works with published/established writers only. Estab. 1984. Pays on publication. Publishes ms an average of 2 months after acceptance. Byline given. Offers 25% kill fee. Buys first North American serial rights. Accepts queries by mail, e-mail. Responds in 1 month to queries. Sample copy for 9×12 SAE and 3 first-class stamps. Guidelines sent with sample copy only.

- *Strategic Health Care Marketing* is specifically seeking writers with expertise/contacts in managed care, patient satisfaction and e-health.

Nonfiction: "Preferred format for feature articles is the case history approach to solving marketing problems. Crisp, almost telegraphic style." How-to, interview/profile, new product, technical. **Buys 50 mss/year.** *No unsolicited mss.* Length: 700-3,000 words. **Pays $100-500.** Sometimes pays expenses of writers on assignment with prior authorization.
Photos: Photos, unless necessary for subject explanation, are rarely used. State availability with submission. Reviews contact sheets. Buys one-time rights. Offers $10-30/photo. Captions, model releases required.

The online magazine carries original content not found in the print edition. Contact: Mark Gothberg.

Tips: "Writers with prior experience on business beat for newspaper or newsletter will do well. We require a sophisticated, in-depth knowledge of health care and business. This is not a consumer publication—the writer with knowledge of both health care and marketing will excel. Absolutely no unsolicited manuscripts; any received will be returned or discarded unread."

$ $ $ $ UNIQUE OPPORTUNITIES, The Physician's Resource, U O Inc., 455 S. Fourth Ave., Suite 1236, Louisville KY 40202. Fax: (502)587-0848. E-mail: bett@uoworks.com. Website: www.uoworks.com. Editor: Mollie Vento Hudson. **Contact:** Bett Coffman, associate editor. **45% freelance written.** Bimonthly magazine covering physician relocation and career development. "Published for physicians interested in a new career opportunity. It offers physicians useful information and first-hand experiences to guide them in making informed decisions concerning their first or next career opportunity. It provides regular features and columns about specific aspects of the search process." Estab. 1991. Circ. 80,000 physicians. Pays 30 days after acceptance. Publishes ms an average of 2 months after acceptance. Byline given. Offers 15-33% kill fee. Buys first North American serial, electronic rights. Editorial lead time 3 months. Submit seasonal material 6 months in advance. Responds in 2 months to queries. Sample copy for 9×12 SAE and 6 first-class stamps. Writer's guidelines for #10 SASE.
Nonfiction: Practice options and information of interest to physicians in career transition. **Buys 14 mss/year.** Query with published clips. Length: 1,500-3,500 words. **Pays $750-2,000.** Sometimes pays expenses of writers on assignment.
Photos: State availability with submission. electronic rights. Negotiates payment individually. Identification of subjects, model releases required.
Columns/Departments: Remarks (opinion from physicians and industry experts on physician career issues), 500-1,000 words; Technology (technical articles relating to medicine or medical practice and business) 1,000-1,500 words. Query with published clips. **Payment negotiated individually.**

The online magazine carries original content not found in the print edition.

Tips: "Submit queries via letter or e-mail with ideas for articles that directly pertain to physician career issues, such as specific or unusual practice opportunities, relocation or practice establishment subjects, etc. Feature articles are most open to freelancers. Physician sources are most important, with tips and advice from both the physicians and business experts. Physicians like to know what other physicians think and do and appreciate suggestions from other business people."

MUSIC

Publications for musicians and for the recording industry are listed in this section. Other professional performing arts publications are classified under Entertainment & the Arts. Magazines featuring music industry news for the general public are listed in the Consumer Entertainment and Music sections. (Markets for songwriters can be found in *Songwriter's Market*, Writer's Digest Books.)

$ CLAVIER MAGAZINE, The Instrumentalist Publishing Co., 200 Northfield Rd., Northfield IL 60093. (847)446-5000. Fax: (847)446-6263. **Contact:** Judy Nelson, editor. **1% freelance written.** Magazine published 10 times/year. featuring practical information on teaching subjects that are of value to studio piano teachers and interviews with major artists. Estab. 1937. Circ. 16,000. Pays on publication. Publishes ms an average of 18 months after acceptance. Byline given. Buys all rights. Submit seasonal material 6 months in advance. Accepts queries by mail, fax, phone. Responds in 6 weeks to queries. Sample copy and writer's guidelines free.

Nonfiction: "Articles should be of interest and direct practical value to concert pianists, harpsichordists and organists who are teachers of piano, organ, harpsichord and electronic keyboards. Topics may include pedagogy, technique, performance, ensemble playing and accompanying." Historical/nostalgic, how-to, interview/profile, photo feature. Length: 10-12 double-spaced pages. **Pays small honorarium.**

Reprints: Occasionally we will reprint a chapter in a book.

Photos: Digital artwork should be sent in TIF, EPS, JPEG files for PhotoShop at 300 dpi. Send photos with submission. Reviews negatives, 2¼×2¼ transparencies, 3×5 prints. Buys all rights. Offers no additional payment for photos accepted with ms. Identification of subjects required.

MUSIC CONNECTION, The West Coast Music Trade Magazine, Music Connection, Inc., 4215 Coldwater Canyon Blvd., Studio City CA 91604. (818)755-0101. Fax: (818)755-0102. E-mail: markn@musicconnection.com. Website: www.musicconnection.com. **Contact:** Mark Nardone, senior editor. **40% freelance written.** Biweekly Magazine. "Biweekly magazine geared toward working musicians and/or other industry professionals, including producers/engineers/studio staff, managers, agents, publicists, music publishers, record company staff, concert promoters/bookers, etc." Estab. 1977. Circ. 75,000. Pays after publication. Publishes ms an average of 2 months after acceptance. Byline given. Kill fee varies. Buys all rights. Editorial lead time 2 months. Submit seasonal material 2 months in advance. Sample copy for $5.

Nonfiction: How-to (music industry related), interview/profile, new product, technical. Query with published clips. Length: 1,000-5,000 words. **Payment varies.** Sometimes pays expenses of writers on assignment.

Photos: State availability with submission. Reviews transparencies, Prints. Buys one-time rights. Negotiates payment individually. Identification of subjects required.

Tips: "Articles must be informative music/music industry-related pieces, geared toward a trade-reading audience comprised mainly of musicians. No fluff."

OFFICE ENVIRONMENT & EQUIPMENT

$ $ OFFICE DEALER, Updating the Office Products Industry, P.O. Box 1028, Mt. Airy NC 27030. (336)783-0000. Fax: (336)783-0045. E-mail: epowell@os-od.com. Website: www.os-od.com. **Contact:** Edwin T. Powell, managing editor. **80% freelance written.** Bimonthly magazine covering the office product industry. "*Office Dealer* is an industry publication serving subscribers involved in the reselling of office supplies, furniture and equipment." Estab. 1987. Circ. 17,000. Pays on publication. Byline given. Buys first North American serial rights. Editorial lead time 4 months. Submit seasonal material 6 months in advance. Accepts queries by mail, e-mail, fax. Accepts simultaneous submissions. Responds in 1 month to queries; 2 months to mss. Sample copy and writer's guidelines free.

Nonfiction: Book excerpts, interview/profile, new product, technical. "We do not publish a great deal of computer-related information—although that will continue to change as the digital age evolves." **Buys 30 mss/year.** Length: 1,500-2,200 words. **Pays $400-650.** Sometimes pays expenses of writers on assignment.

Photos: State availability with submission. Reviews contact sheets, prints. Buys one-time rights. Negotiates payment individually. Captions, identification of subjects, model releases required.

Columns/Departments: Selling Power (sales tips/techniques), 800-1,000 words. **Buys 6 mss/year.** Query. **Pays $150-300.**

Tips: "Feature articles for the year are outlined in an editorial calendar published each fall. Although changes can occur, we make every effort to adhere to the published calendar. Feature articles are written by our staff or by freelance writers. We do not accept corporate 'byline' articles. We seek publishable stories written to an agreed-upon length, with text for agreed-upon components—such as sidebars. Stories should be as generic as possible, free of jargon, vague statements, unconfirmed facts and figures, and corporate superlatives. Each query should include the primary focus of the proposed article, the main points of discussion, and a list of any sources to be described or interviewed in the story. Samples of a writer's past work and clips concerning the proposed story are helpful."

$ $ OFFICE SOLUTIONS, The Magazine for Office Professionals, Quality Publishing, P.O. Box 1028, Mt. Airy NC 27030. (336)783-0000. Fax: (336)783-0045. E-mail: epowell@os-od.com. Website: www.os-od.com. **Contact:** Edwin T. Powell, managing editor. **80% freelance written.** Magazine published 10 times/year covering the office environment. "*Office Solutions* subscribers are responsible for the management of their office environments." Estab. 1984. Circ. 107,000. Pays on publication. Publishes ms an average of 2 months after acceptance. Byline given. Buys first North American serial rights. Editorial lead time 3 months. Submit seasonal material 4 months in advance. Accepts queries by mail, e-mail, fax. Accepts simultaneous submissions. Responds in 3 weeks to queries; 2 months to mss. Sample copy and writer's guidelines free.

Nonfiction: "Our audience is responsible for general management of an office environment, so articles should be broad in scope and not too technical in nature." Book excerpts, interview/profile, new product, technical. **Buys 75 mss/year.** Query. Length: 1,500-2,200 words. **Pays $400-650.** Sometimes pays expenses of writers on assignment.

Photos: State availability with submission. Reviews contact sheets, prints..Buys one-time rights. Negotiates payment individually. Captions, identification of subjects, model releases required.

Columns/Departments: Cyberspeak (computer terminology), 800-1,000 words; Do It Yourself (how to run the office better), 1,000-2,000 words; Wireless World (wireless technology development), 1,000-1,200 words. **Buys 20 mss/year.** Query. **Pays $150-400.**

Fillers: Facts, short humor. **Buys 10-15 issue/year.** Length: 500-800 words. **Pays $150-250.**

Tips: "Feature articles for the year are outlined in an editorial calendar published each fall. Although changes can occur, we make every effort to adhere to the published calendar. Feature articles are written by our staff or by freelance writers. We seek publishable stories written to an agreed-upon length, with text for agreed-upon components—such as sidebars. Stories should be as generic as possible, free of jargon, vague statements, unconfirmed facts and figures, and corporate superlatives. Each query should include the primary focus of the proposed article, the main points of discussion, and a list of any sources to be described or interviewed in the story. Queries should be a single page or less and include a SASE for reply. Samples of a writer's past work and clips concerning the proposed story are helpful."

PAPER

$ $ THE PAPER STOCK REPORT, News and Trends of the Paper Recycling Markets, McEntee Media Corp., 9815 Hazelwood Ave., Cleveland OH 44149. (440)238-6603. Fax: (440)238-6712. E-mail: psr@recycle.cc. Website: www.recycle.cc. **Contact:** Ken McEntee, editor. Biweekly Newsletter covering market trends, news in the paper recycling industry. "Audience is interested in new innovative markets, applications for recovered scrap paper as well as new laws and regulations impacting recycling." Estab. 1990. Circ. 2,000. Pays on publication. Publishes ms an average of 1 month after acceptance. Byline given. Buys first, all rights. Editorial lead time 2 months. Submit seasonal material 2 months in advance. Accepts queries by mail, e-mail, fax, phone. Accepts simultaneous submissions. Responds in 1 month to queries. Sample copy for #10 SAE with 55¢ postage.

Nonfiction: Book excerpts, essays, exposé, general interest, historical/nostalgic, interview/profile, new product, opinion, photo feature, technical, All related to paper recycling. **Buys 0-13 mss/year.** Send complete ms. Length: 250-1,000 words. **Pays $50-250 for assigned articles; $25-250 for unsolicited articles.** Pays expenses of writers on assignment.

Photos: State availability with submission. Reviews contact sheets. Negotiates payment individually. Identification of subjects required.

The online magazine carries original content not found in the print edition. Contact: Ken McEntee, online editor.

Tips: "Article must be valuable to readers in terms of presenting new market opportunities or cost-saving measures."

N $ $ PULP & PAPER CANADA, 1 Holiday St., #705, East Tower, Pointe-Claire, Quebec H9R 5N3, Canada. (514)630-5955. Fax: (514)630-5980. E-mail: anyao@businessinformationgroup.ca. Publisher: Jim Bussiere. **Contact:** Anya Orzechowska, managing editor. **5% freelance written.** Monthly magazine. Prefers to work with published/established writers. Estab. 1903. Circ. 10,361. Pays on publication. Publishes ms an average of Publishes ms after acceptance. Byline given. Negotiates kill fee. Buys first North American serial rights. Accepts queries by mail, e-mail. Responds in 1 month to queries. Sample copy for free.

Break in with an article about a Canadian paper mill case study, e.g., problem/solution type or maintenance-related articles.

Nonfiction: Articles with photographs (b&w glossy) or other good quality illustrations will get priority review. How-to (related to processes and procedures in the industry), interview/profile (of Canadian leaders in pulp and paper industry), technical (relevant to modern pulp and/or paper industry). No fillers, short industry news items, or product news items. **Buys 5 mss/year.** Query with published clips or send complete ms. Length: 1,200 words maximum (with photos). **Pays $160 (Canadian)/published page including photos, graphics, charts, etc.**

Tips: "Any return postage must be in either Canadian stamps or International Reply Coupons *only*."

$ $ RECYCLED PAPER NEWS, Independent Coverage of Environmental Issues in the Paper Industry, McEntee Media Corporation, 9815 Hazelwood Ave., Cleveland OH 44149. (440)238-6603. Fax: (440)238-6712. E-mail: rpn@recycle.cc. Website: www.recycle.cc. **Contact:** Ken McEntee, president. **10% freelance written.** Monthly Newsletter. "We are interested in any news impacting the paper recycling industry as well as other environmental issues in the paper industry, i.e., water/air pollution, chlorine-free paper, forest conservation, etc., with special emphasis on new laws and regulations." Estab. 1990. Pays on publication. Publishes ms an average of 2 months after acceptance. Buys first, all rights. Editorial lead time 1 month. Submit seasonal material 1 month in advance. Accepts queries by mail, e-mail, fax, phone. Accepts simultaneous submissions. Responds in 2 months to queries. Sample copy for 9×12 SAE and 55¢ postage. Writer's guidelines for #10 SASE.

Nonfiction: Book excerpts, essays, how-to, interview/profile, new product, opinion, personal experience, photo feature, technical, new business; legislation; regulation; business expansion. **Buys 0-5 mss/year.** Query with published clips. **Pays $10-500.** Pays writers with contributor copies or other premiums by prior agreement.
Reprints: Accepts previously published submissions.
Columns/Departments: Query with published clips. **Pays $10-500.**
Tips: "We appreciate leads on local news regarding recycling or composting, i.e., new facilities or businesses, new laws and regulations, unique programs, situations that impact supply and demand for recyclables, etc. International developments are also of interest."

PETS

Listed here are publications for professionals in the pet industry—pet product wholesalers, manufacturers, suppliers, and retailers, and owners of pet specialty stores, grooming businesses, aquarium retailers, and those interested in the pet fish industry. Publications for pet owners are listed in the Consumer Animal section.

$ $ PET AGE, H.H. Backer Associates, Inc., 200 S. Michigan Ave., Suite 840, Chicago IL 60604-2383-2404. (312)663-4040. Fax: (312)663-5676. E-mail: petage@hhbacker.com. Editor Karen Long MacLeod. **Contact:** Cathy Foster. **90% freelance written.** Monthly magazine for pet/pet supplies retailers, covering the complete pet industry. Prefers to work with published/established writers. Will consider new writers. Estab. 1971. Circ. 23,022. **Pays on acceptance.** Publishes ms an average of 3 months after acceptance. Byline given. Buys first North American serial, one-time rights, exclusive industry rights. Sample copy available.
Nonfiction: How-to articles on marketing/merchandising companion animals and supplies; how-to articles on retail store management; industry trends and issues; animal health care and husbandry. How-to. No profiles of industry members and/or retail establishments or consumer-oriented pet articles. **Buys 80 mss/year.** Query with published clips. Length: 1,500-2,200 words. **Pays 15¢/word for assigned articles.** Pays documented telephone expenses.
Tips: "This is a business publication for busy people, and must be very informative in easy-to-read, concise style. Articles about animal care or business practices should have the pet-retail angle or cover issues specific to this industry."

$ $ PET PRODUCT NEWS, Fancy Publications, P.O. Box 6050, Mission Viejo CA 92690. (949)855-8822. Fax: (949)855-3045. **Contact:** Marilyn Iturri, editor. **70% freelance written.** Monthly magazine. "*Pet Product News* covers business/legal and economic issues of importance to pet product retailers, suppliers and distributors, as well as product information and animal care issues. We're looking for straightforward articles on the proper care of dogs, cats, birds, fish and exotics (reptiles, hamsters, etc.) as information the retailers can pass on to new pet owners." Estab. 1947. Circ. 26,000. Pays on publication. Byline given. Offers $50 kill fee. Buys first North American serial rights. Editorial lead time 3 months. Submit seasonal material 4 months in advance. Accepts queries by mail, fax. Responds in 2 weeks to queries. Sample copy for $5.50. Writer's guidelines for #10 SASE.
Nonfiction: General interest, interview/profile, new product, photo feature, technical. "No cute animal stories or those directed at the pet owner." **Buys 150 mss/year.** Query. Length: 500-1,500 words. **Pays $175-350.**
Columns/Departments: The Pet Dealer News™ (timely news stories about business issues affecting pet retailers), 800-1,000 words; Industry News (news articles representing coverage of pet product suppliers, manufacturers, distributors and associations), 800-1,000 words; Pet Health News™ (pet health and articles relevant to pet retailers); Dog & Cat (products and care of), 1,000-1,500 words; Fish & Bird (products and care of), 1,000-1,500 words; Small Mammals (products and care of), 1,000-1,500 words; Pond/Water Garden (products and care of), 1,000-1,500 words. **Buys 120 mss/year.** Query. **Pays $150-300.**
Tips: "Be more than just an animal lover. You have to know about health, nutrition and care. Product and business articles are told in both an informative and entertaining style. Talk to pet store owners and see what they need to know to be better business people in general, who have to deal with everything from balancing the books and free trade agreements to animal rights activists. All sections are open, but you have to be knowledgeable on the topic, be it taxes, management, profit building, products, nutrition, animal care or marketing."

PLUMBING, HEATING, AIR CONDITIONING & REFRIGERATION

$ $ HEATING PLUMBING AIR CONDITIONING, 777 Bay St., Toronto, Ontario M5W 1A7, Canada. (416)596-5000. Fax: (416)596-5536. **Contact:** Kerry Turner, editor. **20% freelance written.** Monthly magazine. For a prompt reply, "enclose a sheet on which is typed a statement either approving or rejecting the suggested article which can either be checked off, or a quick answer written in and signed and returned." Estab. 1923. Circ. 16,500. Pays on publication. Publishes ms an average of 3 months after acceptance. Accepts queries by mail, e-mail, fax, phone. Responds in 2 months to queries. Sample copy for free.

O→ Break in with technical, "how-to," Canadian-specific applications/stories.

Nonfiction: News, business management articles that will inform, educate, motivate and help readers to be more efficient and profitable who design, manufacture, install, sell, service maintain or supply all mechanical components and systems in residential, commercial, institutional and industrial installations across Canada. How-to, technical. Length: 1,000-1,500 words. **Pays 25¢/word.** Sometimes pays expenses of writers on assignment.

Reprints: Send tearsheet or photocopy with rights for sale noted and information about when and where the material previously appeared.
Photos: Prefers 4×5 or 5×7 glossies. Photos purchased with ms.
Tips: "Topics must relate directly to the day-to-day activities of *HPAC* readers in Canada. Must be detailed, with specific examples, quotes from specific people or authorities—show depth. We specifically want material from other parts of Canada besides southern Ontario. Not really interested in material from US unless specifically related to Canadian readers' concerns. We primarily want articles that show *HPAC* readers how they can increase their sales and business step-by-step based on specific examples of what others have done."

$ INDOOR COMFORT NEWS, Institute of Heating & Air Conditioning Industries, Inc., 454 W. Broadway, Glendale CA 91204. (818)551-1555. Fax: (818)551-1115. E-mail: s.fitzpatrick@ihaci.org. Website: www.ihaci.org. **Contact:** Shawn Fitzpatrick, editor. **25% freelance written.** Monthly tabloid. "We cover the heating, cooling, ventilating and refrigeration industries in Washington, Oregon, California, Nevada, Arizona and Texas. Our audience is made up of contractors, engineers and service technicians." Estab. 1955. Circ. 25,000. Pays on publication. Publishes ms an average of 3 months after acceptance. Byline given. Buys one-time rights. Editorial lead time 1 month. Submit seasonal material 3 months in advance. Accepts queries by mail, fax. Responds in 2 weeks to queries; 1 month to mss. Sample copy available.
Nonfiction: Book excerpts, essays, historical/nostalgic, how-to (equipment, sales, etc.), humor, interview/profile, new product, personal experience, technical. **Buys 10-15 mss/year.** Query with published clips. Length: 700-1,500 words. **Pays $75-150.** Sometimes pays expenses of writers on assignment.
Photos: Send photos with submission. Reviews Reviews 3×5 prints. Buys one-time rights. Offers no additional payment for photos accepted with ms. Captions, identification of subjects required.
Tips: "We're looking for specific coverage of industry events and people in the geographic areas we cover. Know the industry. Send a query rather than making original contact via phone."

$ SNIPS MAGAZINE, 755 W. Big Beaver Rd., Troy MI 48084-4900. (248)244-6467. Fax: (248)362-0317. E-mail: base@bnp.com. Website: www.snipsmag.com. **Contact:** Ed Bas, editor/publisher. **2% freelance written.** Monthly magazine for sheet metal, warm air heating, ventilating, air conditioning and roofing contractors. Estab. 1932. Publishes ms an average of 3 months after acceptance. Buys all rights. Accepts queries by mail, e-mail, fax, phone.

O-→ Break in with a "profile of a local contractor in our industries."

Nonfiction: Material should deal with information about contractors who do sheet metal, warm air heating, airconditioning, ventilation and metal roofing work; also about successful advertising and/or marketing campaigns conducted by these contractors and the results. Length: Under 1,000 words unless on special assignment. **Pays $200-300.**
Photos: Negotiable.

$ $ WESTERN HVACR NEWS, Trade, News International, 4444 Riverside Dr., #202, Burbank CA 91505-4048. Fax: (818)848-1306. E-mail: News@hvacrnews.com. Website: www.hvacrnews.com. **Contact:** Gary McCarty. Monthly tabloid covering heating, ventilation, air conditioning and refrigeration. "We are a trade publication writing about news and trends for those in the trade." Estab. 1981. Circ. 31,000. Pays on publication. Byline sometimes given. Buys first North American serial rights. Editorial lead time 2 months. Submit seasonal material 2 months in advance. Accepts queries by mail, e-mail. Responds in 1 month to queries. Sample copy online. Writer's guidelines by e-mail.
Nonfiction: General interest, how-to, interview/profile, photo feature, technical. **Buys 25 mss/year.** Query with published clips. Length: 250-1,000 words. **Pays 25¢/word.** Sometimes pays expenses of writers on assignment.
Photos: Send photos with submission. Buys one-time rights. Offers $10 minimum. Negotiates payment individually. Identification of subjects required.
Columns/Departments: Technical only. **Buys 24 mss/year. Pays 20¢/word.**
Tips: "Writers must be knowledgeable about the HVACR industry."

PRINTING

$ $ IN-PLANT GRAPHICS, North American Publishing Co., 401 N. Broad St., Philadelphia PA 19108. Fax: (215)238-5457. E-mail: editor.ipg@napco.com. Website: www.ipgonline.com. **Contact:** Bob Neubauer, editor. **10% freelance written.** "*In-Plant Graphics* features articles designed to help in-house printing departments increase productivity, save money and stay competitive. *IPG* features advances in graphic arts technology and shows in-plants how to put this technology to use. Our audience consists of print shop managers working for (non-print related) corporations (i.e., hospitals, insurance companies, publishers, non-profits), universities and government departments. They often oversee graphic design, prepress, printing, bindery and mailing departments." Estab. 1951. Circ. 24,000. Pays on publication. Publishes ms an average of 5 months after acceptance. Byline given. Buys first North American serial rights. Editorial lead time 2 months. Submit seasonal material 3 months in advance. Accepts queries by mail, e-mail, fax. Writer's guidelines online.
Nonfiction: "Stories include profiles of successful in-house printing operations (not commercial or quick printers); updates on graphic arts technology (new features, uses); reviews of major graphic arts and printing conferences (seminar and new equipment reviews)." New product (graphic arts), technical (graphic arts/printing/prepress). No articles on

desktop publishing software or design software. No Internet publishing articles. **Buys 5 mss/year.** Query with published clips. Length: 800-1,500 words. **Pays $300-450.** Pays writers with contributor copies or other premiums for consultants who agree to write just for exposure.

Photos: State availability with submission. Reviews transparencies, Prints. Buys one-time rights. Negotiates payment individually. Captions, identification of subjects required.

The online magazine carries original content not found in the print edition. Contact: Bob Neubauer.

Tips: "To get published in *IPG*, writers must contact the editor with an idea in the form of a query letter that includes published writing samples. Writers who have covered the graphic arts in the past may be assigned stories for an agreed-upon fee. We don't want stories that tout only one vendor's products and serve as glorified commercials. All profiles must be well-balanced, covering a variety of issues. If you can tell us about an in-house printing operation that is doing innovative things, we will be interested."

N $ $ **SCREEN PRINTING**, 407 Gilbert Ave., Cincinnati OH 45202-2285. (513)421-2050. Fax: (513)421-5144. E-mail: screen@stmediagroup.com. Website: www.screenweb.com. **Contact:** Tom Frecska. **30% freelance written.** Monthly magazine for the screen printing industry, including screen printers (commercial, industrial and captive shops), suppliers and manufacturers, ad agencies and allied professions. Works with a small number of new/unpublished writers each year. Estab. 1953. Circ. 17,000. Pays on publication. Publishes ms an average of 3 months after acceptance. Byline given. Buys all rights. Accepts queries by mail, e-mail, fax. Response time varies to queries. Sample copy available. Writer's guidelines for #10 SASE.

Nonfiction: "Because the screen printing industry is a specialized but diverse trade, we do not publish general interest articles with no pertinence to our readers. Subject matter is open, but should fall into one of four categories—technology, management, profile, or news. Features in all categories must identify the relevance of the subject matter to our readership. Technology articles must be informative, thorough, and objective—no promotional or 'advertorial' pieces accepted. Management articles may cover broader business or industry specific issues, but they must address the screen printer's unique needs. Profiles may cover serigraphers, outstanding shops, unique jobs and projects, or industry personalities; they should be in-depth features, not PR puff pieces, that clearly show the human interest or business relevance of the subject. News pieces should be timely (reprints from non-industry publications will be considered) and must cover an event or topic of industry concern." Unsolicited mss not returned. **Buys 10-15 mss/year.** Query. **Pays $400 minimum for major features.**

Photos: Cover photos negotiable; b&w or color. Published material becomes the property of the magazine.

The online magazine carries information from the print edition, as well as original content not found in the print edition. Contact: John Tymoski.

Tips: "Be an expert in the screen-printing industry with supreme or special knowledge of a particular screen-printing process, or have special knowledge of a field or issue of particular interest to screen-printers. If the author has a working knowledge of screen printing, assignments are more readily available. General management articles are rarely used."

PROFESSIONAL PHOTOGRAPHY

Journals for professional photographers are listed in this section. Magazines for the general public interested in photography techniques are in the Consumer Photography section. (For listings of markets for freelance photography use *Photographer's Market*, Writer's Digest Books.)

$ $ **NEWS PHOTOGRAPHER**, National Press Photographers, Inc., 1446 Conneaut Ave., Bowling Green OH 43402. (419)352-8175. Fax: (419)354-5435. E-mail: magazine@nppa.org. Website: www.nppa.org. **Contact:** James R. Gordon, editor. Published 12 times/year. "*News Photographer* magazine is dedicated to the advancement of still and television news photography. The magazine presents articles, interviews, profiles, history, new products, electronic imaging and news related to the practice of photojournalism." Estab. 1946. Circ. 11,000. **Pays on acceptance.** Publishes ms an average of 4 months after acceptance. Byline given. Offers 100% kill fee. Buys one-time, and archival electronic rights for the World Wide Web and searchable databases. Editorial lead time 2 months. Submit seasonal material 2 months in advance. Accepts queries by mail, e-mail, fax, phone. Accepts previously published material. Accepts simultaneous submissions. Responds in 1 month to queries. Sample copy for 9×12 SAE and 3 first-class stamps. Writer's guidelines free.

Nonfiction: Historical/nostalgic, how-to, interview/profile, new product, opinion, personal experience, photo feature, technical. **Buys 10 mss/year.** Query. Length: 1,500 words. **Pays $300.** Pays expenses of writers on assignment.

Photos: State availability with submission. Reviews negatives, 35mm transparencies, 8×10 prints. Buys one-time rights. Negotiates payment individually. Captions, identification of subjects required.

Columns/Departments: Query.

$ $ **THE PHOTO REVIEW**, 140 E. Richardson Ave., Suite 301, Langhorne PA 19047. (215)891-0214. Fax: (215)891-9358. E-mail: info@photoreview.org. Website: www.photoreview.org. Managing Editor: Nancy Brokaw. **Contact:** Stephen Perloff, chief editor. **50% freelance written.** Quarterly magazine covering art photography and criticism. "*The Photo Review* publishes critical reviews of photography exhibitions and books, critical essays, and interviews. We do not publish how-to or technical articles." Estab. 1976. Circ. 2,000. Pays on publication. Publishes ms an average of

9-12 months after acceptance. Byline given. Buys first rights. Editorial lead time 3 months. Submit seasonal material 6 months in advance. Accepts queries by mail. Accepts simultaneous submissions. Responds in 2 months to queries; 3 months to mss. Sample copy for $7. Writer's guidelines for #10 SASE.
Nonfiction: Interview/profile, photography essay; critical review. No how-to articles. **Buys 20 mss/year.** Send complete ms. Length: 2-20 typed pages. **Pays $10-250.**
Reprints: Send tearsheet, photocopy or typed ms with rights for sale noted and information about when and where the material previously appeared. Payment varies.
Photos: Send photos with submission. Reviews contact sheets, transparencies, prints. Buys all rights. Offers no additional payment for photos accepted with ms. Captions required.

$ $ PHOTOGRAPHIC PROCESSING, Cygnus Publishing, 445 Broad Hollow Rd., Melville NY 11747. Fax: (631)845-2797. E-mail: bill.schiffner@cygnuspub.com. Website: www.labsonline.com. **Contact:** Bill Schiffner, editor. **30% freelance written.** Monthly magazine covering photographic (commercial/minilab) and electronic processing markets. Estab. 1965. Circ. 23,000. Pays on publication. Publishes ms an average of 4 months after acceptance. Byline given. Offers $75 kill fee. Editorial lead time 3 months. Submit seasonal material 3 months in advance. Accepts simultaneous submissions. Sample copy and writer's guidelines free.
Nonfiction: How-to, interview/profile, new product, photo processing/digital imaging features. **Buys 20-30 mss/year.** Query with published clips. Length: 1,500-2,200 words. **Pays $275-350 for assigned articles; $250-275 for unsolicited articles.**
Photos: Looking for digitally manipulated covers. Send photos with submission. Reviews 4×5 transparencies, 4×6 prints. Buys one-time rights. Offers no additional payment for photos accepted with ms. Captions required.
Columns/Departments: Surviving in 2000 (business articles offering tips to labs on how to make their businesses run better), 1,500-1,800 words; Business Side (getting more productivity out of your lab). **Buys 10 mss/year.** Query with published clips. **Pays $150-250.**

$ $ TODAY'S PHOTOGRAPHER INTERNATIONAL, American Image Press Inc., P.O. Box 777, Lewisville NC 27023. (336)945-9867. Fax: (336)945-3711. Website: www.aipress.com. **Contact:** Vonda H. Blackburn, editor. **100% freelance written.** Bimonthly "The make money with your camera magazine." Estab. 1984. Circ. 93,000. Pays on publication. Publishes ms an average of 4 months after acceptance. Byline given. Buys simultaneous rights. Editorial lead time 4 months. Submit seasonal material 8 months in advance. Accepts simultaneous submissions. Responds in 1 month to queries; 2 months to mss. Sample copy for $3. Writer's guidelines free.
Nonfiction: How freelance photographers make money. How-to (make money with your camera). Nothing outside making money with a camera. Query. Length: 800-2,000 words. **Payment negotiable.**
Photos: State availability with submission. Reviews contact sheets, transparencies, prints. Buys one-time rights. Offers no additional payment for photos accepted with ms. Captions, identification of subjects, model releases required.
Columns/Departments: Query with published clips.

REAL ESTATE

$ $ AREA DEVELOPMENT MAGAZINE, Sites and Facility Planning, Halcyon Business Publications, Inc., 400 Post Ave., Westbury NY 11590. (516)338-0900, ext. 211. Fax: (516)338-0100. E-mail: gerri@areadevelopment.com. Website: www.areadevelopment.com. **Contact:** Geraldine Gambale, editor. **80% freelance written.** Prefers to work with published/established writers. Monthly magazine covering corporate facility planning and site selection for industrial chief executives worldwide. Estab. 1965. Circ. 45,000. Pays on publication. Publishes ms an average of 2 months after acceptance. Byline given. Buys all rights. Accepts queries by mail, e-mail, fax. Responds in 3 months to queries. Sample copy for free. Writer's guidelines for #10 SASE.
Nonfiction: Related areas of site selection and facility planning such as taxes, labor, government, energy, architecture and finance. Historical/nostalgic (if it deals with corporate facility planning), how-to (experiences in site selection and all other aspects of corporate facility planning), interview/profile (corporate executives and industrial developers). **Buys 75 mss/year.** Query. Length: 1,500-2,000 words. **Pays 30¢/word.** Sometimes pays expenses of writers on assignment.
Photos: State availability with submission. Reviews transparencies. Negotiates payment individually. Captions, identification of subjects required.

The online version of this publication contains material not found in the print edition. Contact: Geraldine Gambale, online editor.

$ $ CANADIAN PROPERTY MANAGEMENT, Mediaedge Communications Inc., 5255 Yonge St., Suite 1000, North York, Ontario M2N 6P4, Canada. (416)512-8186 or (866)216-0860. Fax: (416)512-8344. E-mail: kris@mediaedge.ca. Website: www.mediaedge.ca. **Contact:** Kris Scheuer, editor. **10% freelance written.** Magazine published 8 times/year covering Canadian commercial, industrial, institutional (medical and educational), residential properties. "*Canadian Property Management* magazine is a trade journal supplying building owners and property managers with Canadian industry news, case law reviews, technical updates for building operations and events listings. Feature building and professional profile articles are regular features." Estab. 1985. Circ. 14,500. Pays on publication. Publishes ms an average of 3 months after acceptance. Byline given. Buys all rights. Editorial lead time 2 months. Submit seasonal material 2 months in advance. Accepts queries by mail, e-mail, fax, phone. Accepts simultaneous submissions. Responds in 3 weeks to queries; 2 months to mss. Sample copy for $5, subject to availability. Writer's guidelines free.

Nonfiction: Interview/profile, technical. "No promotional articles (e.g., marketing a product or service geared to this industry)!" Query with published clips. Length: 700-1,200 words. **Pays 35¢/word.**
Photos: State availability with submission. Reviews transparencies, 3×5 prints. Offers no additional payment for photos accepted with ms. Captions, identification of subjects, model releases required.
Tips: "We do not accept promotional articles serving companies or their products. Freelance articles that are strong, information-based pieces that serve the interests and needs of property managers and building owners stand a better chance of being published. Proposals and inquiries with article ideas are appreciated the most. A good understanding of the real estate industry (management structure) is also helpful for the writer."

$ $ $ $ COMMERCIAL INVESTMENT REAL ESTATE, CCIM, 430 N. Michigan Ave., Suite 800, Chicago IL 60611-4092. (312)321-4460. Fax: (312)321-4530. E-mail: magazine@ccim.com. Website: www.ccim.com/magazine. **Contact:** Jennifer Norbut, editor. **10% freelance written.** Bimonthly magazine. "*CIRE* offers practical articles on current trends and business development ideas for commercial investment real estate practitioners." Estab. 1982. Circ. 12,500. **Pays on acceptance.** Publishes ms an average of 4 months after acceptance. Byline given. Buys all rights. Editorial lead time 4 months. Submit seasonal material 4 months in advance. Accepts queries by mail, e-mail, fax. Responds in 2 weeks to queries; 1 month to mss. Sample copy and writer's guidelines online.

Break in by sending résumé and feature-length clips, "including commercial real estate-related clips if available. We keep writers' materials on file for assigning articles."

Nonfiction: How-to, technical, Business strategies. **Buys 6-8 mss/year.** Query with published clips. Length: 2,000-3,500 words. **Pays $1,000-1,600.**
Photos: May ask writers to have sources. Send images to editors.
Tips: "Always query first with a detailed outline and published clips. Authors should have a background in writing on business or real estate subjects."

$ $ THE COOPERATOR, The Co-op and Condo Monthly, Yale Robbins, LLC, 31 E. 28th St., 12th Floor, New York NY 10016. (212)683-5700. Fax: (212)696-1268. E-mail: judy@cooperator.com. Website: www.cooperator.com. **Contact:** Judith C. Grover, managing editor. **70% freelance written.** Monthly tabloid covering New York City real estate. "*The Cooperator* covers condominium and cooperative issues in New York and beyond. It is read by condo unit owners and co-op shareholders, board members and managing agents." Estab. 1980. Circ. 60,000. Pays on publication. Publishes ms an average of 3 months after acceptance. Byline given. Buys all rights, makes work-for-hire assignments. Submit seasonal material 3 months in advance. Accepts queries by mail, e-mail, fax. Responds in 1 month to queries. Sample copy and writer's guidelines free.
Nonfiction: All articles related to co-op and condo ownership. Interview/profile, new product, personal experience. No submissions without queries. Query with published clips. Length: 1,500-2,000 words. **Pays $200-250.** Sometimes pays expenses of writers on assignment.
Photos: State availability with submission. Reviews contact sheets, negatives, transparencies, prints. Rights purchased vary. Negotiates payment individually. Captions, identification of subjects required.
Columns/Departments: Profiles of co-op/condo-related businesses with something unique; Building Finance (invesment and financing issues); Buying and Selling (market issues, etc.); management/board relations and interacting with professionals (issues dealing with board members and the professionals that help run the building); interior design; building maintenance, all 1,500 words. **Buys 55 mss/year.** Query with published clips. **Pays $200-250.**
Tips: "You must have experience doing journalistic reporting, especially real estate, business, legal or financial. Must have published clips to send in with résumé and query."

$ $ FLORIDA REALTOR MAGAZINE, Florida Association of Realtors, 7025 Augusta National Dr., Orlando FL 32822-5017. (407)438-1400. Fax: (407)438-1411. E-mail: flrealtor@fl.realtorusa.com. Website: floridarealtormagazine.com. Assistant Editor: Jeff Louderback. **Contact:** Tracey Lawton, editor-in-chief. **30% freelance written.** Journal published 11 times/year covering Florida real estate. "As the official publication of the Florida Association of Realtors, we provide helpful articles for our 67,000 members. We try to stay up on the trends and issues that affect business in Florida's real estate market." Estab. 1925. Circ. 67,000. Pays on publication. Publishes ms an average of 1 month after acceptance. Byline given. Editorial lead time 2 months. Accepts queries by mail, e-mail, fax, phone. Accepts simultaneous submissions. Sample copy online.
Nonfiction: Book excerpts, how-to, inspirational, interview/profile, new product, all with real estate angle—Florida-specific is good. "No fiction, poetry." **Buys varying number of mss/year.** Query with published clips. Length: 800-1,500 words. **Pays $300-700.** Sometimes pays expenses of writers on assignment. Accepts previously published submissions.
Photos: State availability with submission. Buys one-time rights. Negotiates payment individually. Captions, identification of subjects, model releases required.
Columns/Departments: "Rarely used." Occasionally publishes: Promotional Strategies, 900 words; Technology & You, 1,000 words; Realtor Advantage, 1,500 words. **Buys varying number of mss/year. Payment varies.**
Fillers: Short humor. **Buys varying number/year.**
Tips: "Build a solid reputation for specializing in real estate-specific writing in state/national publications."

N **$ $ JOURNAL OF PROPERTY MANAGEMENT**, Institute of Real Estate Management, P.O. Box 109025, Chicago IL 60610-9025. (312)329-6058. Fax: (312)661-7958. E-mail: adruckman@irem.org. Website: www.irem.org. **Contact:** Amanda Druckman, associate editor. **30% freelance written.** Bimonthly magazine covering real estate management. "The *Journal* has a feature/information slant designed to educate readers in the application of new techniques and to keep them abreast of current industry trends." Circ. 20,000. **Pays on acceptance.** Publishes ms an average of 3 months after acceptance. Byline given. Buys all rights. Accepts queries by mail, e-mail, fax. Responds in 6 weeks to queries; 1 month to mss. Sample copy for free. Writer's guidelines free.

Nonfiction: Demographic shifts in business employment and buying patterns, marketing. How-to, interview/profile, technical (building systems/computers). "No non-real estate subjects, personality or company, humor." **Buys 8-12 mss/year.** Query with published clips. Length: 1,200-1,500 words. Sometimes pays expenses of writers on assignment.

Reprints: Send tearsheet, photocopy or typed ms. Pays 35% of amount paid for an original article.

Photos: State availability with submission. Reviews contact sheets. Buys one-time rights. May offer additional payment for photos accepted with ms. Identification of subjects, model releases required.

Columns/Departments: Insurance Insights, Tax Issues, Technology, Maintentance, Personal Development, Legal Issues. Length: 500-750 words. **Buys 6-8 mss/year.** Query.

$ $ $ MULTIFAMILY EXECUTIVE, MGI Publications, 385 Oxford Valley Rd., Suite 420, Yardley PA 19067. (215)321-5112. Fax: (215)321-5122. E-mail: mlupkin@mgipublications.com. Website: www.multifamilyexecutive.com. President/Editor-in-Chief: Edward J. McNeill, Jr. **Contact:** Miriam Lupkin, editor. **10% freelance written.** Magazine published 12 times/year. "We target senior level executives in the multifamily housing industry—builders, developers, owners and managers." Circ. 25,000. Pays on publication. Publishes ms an average of 2 months after acceptance. Byline given. Buys first North American serial rights. Editorial lead time 3 months. Submit seasonal material 4 months in advance. Accepts queries by mail, e-mail, fax, phone. Responds in 2 months to queries. Sample copy for 9×12 SAE and 8 first-class stamps. Writer's guidelines free.

Nonfiction: Book excerpts, how-to, interview/profile, new product, opinion. **Buys 12 mss/year.** Length: 750-1,500 words. **Pays $100-1,000 for assigned articles; $100-500 for unsolicited articles.** Sometimes pays expenses of writers on assignment.

Photos: State availability with submission. Reviews transparencies. Buys all rights. Negotiates pay individually. Identification of subjects, model releases required.

Columns/Departments: Financial, Legal, Senior Housing, Affordable Housing (all written to an advanced level of multifamily executives); all 750-1,500 words. **Buys 12 mss/year.** Query with published clips. **Pays $100-400.**

$ $ $ NATIONAL RELOCATION & REAL ESTATE, RIS Media, 50 Water St., Norwalk CT 06854. (203)855-1234. Fax: (203)852-7208. E-mail: erin@rismedia.com. Website: rismedia.com. Editor: Frank Sziros. **Contact:** Erin Harrison, executive editor. **30-50% freelance written.** Monthly magazine covering residential real estate and corporate relocation. "Our readers are professionals within the relocation and real estate industries; therefore, we require our writers to have sufficient knowledge of the workings of these industries in order to ensure depth and accuracy in reporting." Estab. 1980. Circ. 45,000. Pays on publication. Byline sometimes given. Offers 20-50% kill fee. Buys all rights. Editorial lead time 4 months. Accepts queries by mail, e-mail. Responds in 2 weeks to queries. Sample copy for free.

Nonfiction: Exposé, how-to (use the Internet to sell real estate, etc.), interview/profile, new product, opinion, technical. Query with published clips. Length: 250-1,500 words. Pays unsolicited article writers with contributor copies upon use. Sometimes pays expenses of writers on assignment.

Photos: Send photos with submission. Reviews transparencies. Offers no additional payment for photos accepted with ms. Captions required.

Columns/Departments: Query with published clips.

The online magazine carries original content not found in the print edition. Website features daily news service, written submissions and other information on publication. Contact: Mike Patrick.

Tips: "All queries must be done in writing. Phone queries are unacceptable. Any clips or materials sent should indicate knowledge of the real estate and relocation industries. In general, we are open to all knowledgeable contributors."

N $ $ $ OFFICE BUILDINGS MAGAZINE, Yale Robbins, Inc., 31 E. 28th St., New York NY 10016. (212)683-5700. Fax: (212)545-0764. E-mail: debbie@yrinc.com. Website: www.yrinc.com or www.mrofficespace.com. **Contact:** Debbie Estock, managing editor. **15% freelance written.** Annual magazine. "Annual magazine covering market statistics, trends and thinking of area professionals on the current and future state of the real estate market." Estab. 1987. Circ. 10,500. Pays half on acceptance and half on publication. Byline sometimes given. Offers 25% kill fee. Buys all rights. Editorial lead time 2 months. Accepts queries by mail, e-mail, fax. Sample copy for free. Writer's guidelines free.

Nonfiction: Survey of specific markets. **Buys 15-20 mss/year.** Query with published clips. Length: 1,200-2,000 words. **Pays $500-1,200.** Sometimes pays expenses of writers on assignment.

RESOURCES & WASTE REDUCTION

$ $ COMPOSTING NEWS, The Latest News in Composting and Scrap Wood Management, McEntee Media Corporation, 9815 Hazelwood Ave., Cleveland OH 44149. (440)238-6603. Fax: (440)238-6712. E-mail: cn@recycle.cc. **Contact:** Ken McEntee, editor. **5% freelance written.** Monthly Newsletter. "We are interested in any news impacting the composting industry including new laws, regulations, new facilities/programs, end-uses, research, etc." Estab. 1992. Circ. 1,000. Pays on publication. Publishes ms an average of 1 month after acceptance. Buys first, all rights. Editorial lead time 1 month. Submit seasonal material 1 month in advance. Accepts queries by mail, e-mail, fax, phone. Accepts previously published material. Accepts simultaneous submissions. Responds in 2 months to queries. Sample copy for 9×12 SAE and 55¢ postage. Writer's guidelines for #10 SASE.

Nonfiction: Book excerpts, essays, general interest, how-to, interview/profile, new product, opinion, personal experience, photo feature, technical, new business, legislation, regulation, business expansion. **Buys 0-5 mss/year.** Query with published clips. Length: 100-5,000 words. **Pays $10-500.** Pays writers with contributor copies or other premiums by prior agreement.

Columns/Departments: Query with published clips. **Pays $10-500.**

The online magazine carries original content not found in the print edition. Contact: Ken McEntee.

Tips: "We appreciate leads on local news regarding composting, i.e., new facilities or business, new laws and regulations, unique programs, situations that impact supply and demand for composting. International developments are also of interest."

$ $ $ EROSION CONTROL, The Journal for Erosion and Sediment Control Professionals, Forester Communications, Inc., 5638 Hollister Ave., Suite 301, Santa Barbara CA 93117. (805)681-1300. Fax: (805)681-1311. E-mail: eceditor@forester.net. Website: www.erosioncontrol.com. **Contact:** Janice Kaspersen, editor. **60% freelance written.** Magazine published 7 times/year covering all aspects of erosion prevention and sediment control. "*Erosion Control* is a practical, hands-on, 'how-to' professional journal. Our readers are civil engineers, landscape architects, builders, developers, public works officials, road and highway construction officials and engineers, soils specialists, farmers, landscape contractors and others involved with any activity that disturbs significant areas of surface vegetation." Estab. 1994. Circ. 20,000. Pays 30 days after acceptance. Publishes ms an average of 3 months after acceptance. Byline given. Buys all rights. Editorial lead time 4 months. Submit seasonal material 4 months in advance. Accepts queries by mail, e-mail, fax, phone. Responds in 3 weeks to queries. Sample copy and writer's guidelines free.

Nonfiction: Photo feature, technical. **Buys 15 mss/year.** Query with published clips. Length: 3,000-4,000 words. **Pays $700-850.** Sometimes pays expenses of writers on assignment.

Photos: Send photos with submission. Reviews transparencies, Prints. Buys all rights. Offers no additional payment for photos accepted with ms. Captions, identification of subjects, model releases required.

Tips: "Writers should have a good grasp of technology involved, good writing and communication skills. Most of our freelanced articles include extensive interviews with engineers, contractors, developers, or project owners, and we often provide contact names for articles we assign."

$ $ MSW MANAGEMENT, The Journal for Municipal Solid Waste Professionals, Forester Communications, Inc., 5638 Hollister Ave., Suite 301, Santa Barbara CA 93117. (805)681-1300. Fax: (805)681-1311. E-mail: editor@forester.net. Website: www.mswmanagement.net. **Contact:** John Trotti, editor. **70% freelance written.** Bimonthly magazine. "*MSW Management* is written for *public sector* solid waste professionals—the people working for the local counties, cities, towns, boroughs and provinces. They run the landfills, recycling programs, composting, incineration. They are responsible for all aspects of garbage collection and disposal; buying and maintaining the associated equipment; and designing, engineering and building the waste processing facilities, transfer stations and landfills." Estab. 1991. Circ. 25,000. Pays on publication. Byline given. Buys all rights. Editorial lead time 4 months. Submit seasonal material 4 months in advance. Accepts queries by mail, e-mail, fax, phone. Accepts simultaneous submissions. Responds in 6 weeks to queries; 2 months to mss. Sample copy and writer's guidelines free.

Nonfiction: Photo feature, technical. "No rudimentary, basic articles written for the average person on the street. Our readers are experienced professionals with years of practical, in-the-field experience. Any material submitted that we judge as too fundamental will be rejected." **Buys 15 mss/year.** Query. Length: 3,000-4,000 words. **Pays $350-650.** Sometimes pays expenses of writers on assignment.

Photos: Send photos with submission. Reviews transparencies, Prints. Buys all rights. Offers no additional payment for photos accepted with ms. Captions, identification of subjects, model releases required.

The online version of *MSW Management* includes material not found in the print edition. Contact: John Trotti.

Tips: "We're a small company, easy to reach. We're open to any and all ideas as to possible editorial topics. We endeavor to provide the reader with usable material, and present it in full color with graphic embellishment whenever possible. Dry, highly technical material is edited to make it more palatable and concise. Most of our feature articles come from freelancers. Interviews and quotes should be from public sector solid waste managers and engineers—*not* PR people, *not* manufacturers. Strive to write material that is 'over the heads' of our readers. If anything, attempt to make them 'reach.' Anything submitted that is too basic, elementary, fundamental, rudimentary, etc. cannot be accepted for publication."

$ $ $ STORMWATER, The Journal for Surface Water Quality Professionals, Forester Communications, Inc., 5638 Hollister Ave., Suite 301, Santa Barbara CA 93117. (805)681-1300. Fax: (805)681-1311. E-mail: sweditor@forester.net. Website: www.stormh2o.com. **Contact:** Janice Kaspersen, editor. **10% freelance written.** "*Stormwater* is a practical business journal for professionals involved with surface water quality issues, protection, projects, and programs. Our readers are municipal employees, regulators, engineers, and consultants concerned with stormwater management." Estab. 2000. Circ. 20,000. Publishes ms an average of 3 months after acceptance. Byline given. Editorial lead time 4 months. Submit seasonal material 4 months in advance. Accepts queries by mail, e-mail. Responds in 3 weeks to queries. Writer's guidelines free.

Nonfiction: Technical. **Buys 8-10 mss/year.** Query with published clips. Length: 3,000-4,000 words. **Pays $700-850.** Sometimes pays expenses of writers on assignment.

Photos: Send photos with submission. Buys all rights. Offers no additional payment for photos accepted with ms. Captions, identification of subjects, model releases required.
Tips: "Writers should have a good grasp of the technology and regulations involved in stormwater management and good interviewing skills. Our freelanced articles include extensive interviews with engineers, stormwater managers, and project owners, and we often provide contact names for articles we assign. See past editorial content online."

N $ $ WASTE AGE MAGAZINE, The Business Magazine For Waste Industry Professionals, Intertec Publishing, 6151 Powers Ferry Rd. NW, Atlanta GA 30339-2941. (770)618-0112. Fax: (770)618-0349. E-mail: billuswolpin@intertec.com. Editorial Director: Bill Wolpin. **Contact:** Patti Tom, managing editor. **50% freelance written.** Monthly magazine. "*Waste Age* reaches individuals and firms engaged in the removal, collection, processing, transportation, and disposal of solid/hazardous liquid wastes. This includes: private refuse contractors; landfill operators; municipal, county and other government officials; recyclers and handlers of secondary materials; major generators of waste, such as plants and chain stores; engineers, architects and consultants; manufactures and distributors of equipment; universities, libraries and associations; and legal, insurance and financial firms allied to the field. Readers include: owners, presidents, vice-presidents, directors, superintendents, engineers, managers, supervisors, consultants, purchasing agents and commissioners." Estab. 1958. Circ. 43,000. Pays on publication. Publishes ms an average of 4 months after acceptance. Byline given. Editorial lead time 2 months. Responds in 1 week to queries; 1 month to mss. Sample copy for free. Writer's guidelines free.
Nonfiction: How-to (practical information on improving solid waste management, i.e., how to rehabilitate a transfer station, how to improve recyclable collection, how to manage a landfill, etc.), interview/profile (of prominent persons in the solid waste industry.). "No feel-good 'green' articles about recycling. Remember our readers are not the citizens but the governments and private contractors. No 'why you should recycle' articles." **Buys over 50 mss/year.** Query. Length: 700-2,500 words. **Pays Pays $75 flat rate to $175/printed page.** Pays expenses of writers on assignment.
Photos: Send photos with submission. Reviews contact sheets, negatives, transparencies, Prints. Negotiates payment individually. Identification of subjects required.
Tips: "Read the magazine and understand our audience. Write useful articles with sidebars that the readers can apply to their jobs. Use the Associated Press style book. Freelancers can send in queries or manuscripts or can fax a letter of interest (including qualifications/résumé) in possible assignments. Writers must be deadline-oriented."

$ $ WATER WELL JOURNAL, National Ground Water Association, 601 Dempsey Rd., Westerville OH 43081. Fax: (614)898-7786. E-mail: jross@ngwa.org. Website: www.ngwa.org. **Contact:** Jill Ross, director of publications. **25% freelance written.** Monthly magazine covering the ground water industry; well drilling. "Each month the *Water Well Journal* covers the topics of drilling, rigs and heavy equipment, pumping systems, water quality, business management, water supply, on-site waste water treatment, and diversification opportunities, including geoexchange installations, environmental remediation, irrigation, dewatering and foundation installation. It also offers updates on regulatory issues that impact the ground water industry." Estab. 1948. Circ. 30,000. Pays on publication. Publishes ms an average of 3 months after acceptance. Byline given. Buys all rights. Editorial lead time 2 months. Submit seasonal material 3 months in advance. Accepts queries by mail, e-mail, fax, phone. Responds in 2 weeks to queries; 1 month to mss. Sample copy for 9×12 SAE and 2 first-class stamps. Writer's guidelines free.
Nonfiction: Essays (sometimes), historical/nostalgic (sometimes), how-to (recent examples include how to chlorinate a well; how to buy a used rig; how to do bill collections), interview/profile, new product, personal experience, photo feature, technical, business managment. No company profiles; extended product releases. **Buys up to 20 mss/year.** Query with published clips. Length: 1,000-4,000 words. **Pays $100-600.**
Photos: State availability with submission. Offers $50-250/photo. Captions, identification of subjects required.
Tips: "Some previous experience or knowledge in groundwater/drilling/construction industry helpful. Published clips a must."

SELLING & MERCHANDISING

Sales personnel and merchandisers interested in how to sell and market products successfully consult these journals. Publications in nearly every category of Trade also buy sales-related materials if they are slanted to the product or industry with which they deal.

$ $ BALLOONS AND PARTIES MAGAZINE, Partilife Publications, 65 Sussex St., Hackensack NJ 07601. (201)441-4224. Fax: (201)342-8118. E-mail: mark@balloonsandparties.com. Website: www.balloonsandparties.com. **Contact:** Mark Zettler, publisher. **10% freelance written.** International trade journal for professional party decorators and for gift delivery businesses published 6 times/year. Estab. 1986. Circ. 7,000. Pays on publication. Publishes ms an average of 3 months after acceptance. Byline given. Buys all rights. Submit seasonal material 6 months in advance. Accepts queries by mail, e-mail, fax, phone. Responds in 6 weeks to queries. Sample copy for 9×12 SAE.
Nonfiction: Essays, how-to, interview/profile, new product, personal experience, photo feature, technical, craft. **Buys 12 mss/year.** Query with or without published clips or send complete ms. Length: 500-1,500 words. **Pays $100-300 for assigned articles; $50-200 for unsolicited articles.** Sometimes pays expenses of writers on assignment.
Reprints: Send ms with rights for sale noted and information about when and where the material previously appeared Length: up to 2,500 words. Pays 10¢/word.

Photos: Send photos with submission. Reviews 2×2 transparencies, 3×5 prints. Buys all rights. Captions, identification of subjects, model releases required.
Columns/Departments: Problem Solver (small business issues); Recipes That Cook (centerpiece ideas with detailed how-to), 400-1,000 words. Send complete ms with photos.
Tips: "Show unusual, lavish, and outstanding examples of balloon sculpture, design and decorating and other craft projects. Offer specific how-to information. Be positive and motivational in style."

N **$ $ $ CONSUMER GOODS TECHNOLOGY**, Edgell Communications, 4 Middlebury Blvd., Randolph NJ 07867. (973)252-0100. Fax: (973)252-9020. Website: www.consumergoods.com. **Contact:** John Hall, managing editor (jhall@edgellmail.com) or Kim Zimmerman, assistant managing editor (kzimmerman@edgellmail.com). **40% freelance written.** Monthly tabloid benchmarking business technology performance. Estab. 1987. Circ. 25,000. Pays on publication. Publishes ms an average of 2 months after acceptance. Byline given. Buys first North American serial, second serial (reprint), electronic, all rights. Editorial lead time 3 months. Accepts queries by e-mail. Sample copy online. Writer's guidelines by e-mail.
Nonfiction: "We create several supplements annually, often using freelance." Essays, exposé, interview/profile. **Buys 60 mss/year.** Query with published clips. Length: 700-1,900 words. **Pays $600-1,200.** Sometimes pays expenses of writers on assignment.
Photos: Review. Buys all rights. Negotiates payment individually. Identification of subjects, model releases required.
Columns/Departments: Columns 400-750 words—featured columnists. **Buys 4 mss/year.** Query with published clips. **Pays 75¢-$1/word.**
Tips: "All stories in *Consumer Goods Technology* are told through the voice of the consumer goods executive. We only quote VP-level or C-level CG executives. No vendor quotes. We're always on the lookout for freelance talent. We look in particular for writers with an in-depth understanding of the business issues faced by consumer goods firms and the technologies that are used by the industry to address those issues successfully. 'Bits and bytes' tech writing is not sought; our focus is on benchmarketing the business technology performance of CG firms, CG executives, CG vendors, and CG vendor products. Our target reader is tech-savvy, CG C-level decision maker. We write to, and about, our target reader."

$ $ CONVENIENCE STORE DECISIONS, Donohue-Meehan Publishing, Two Greenwood Square, #410, Bensalem PA 19020. Fax: (215)245-4060. E-mail: bdonahue@penton.com. Website: www.c-storedecisions.com. Editor-in-Chief: Jay Gordon. **Contact:** Bill Donahue, managing editor. **15-20% freelance written.** Monthly magazine covering convenience retail/petroleum marketing. "*CSD* is received by top-level executives in the convenience retail and petroleum marketing industry. Writers should have knowledge of the industry and the subjects it encompasses." Estab. 1990. Circ. 42,000. Pays on publication. Byline given. Buys all rights, makes work-for-hire assignments. Editorial lead time 3-5 months. Submit seasonal material 3 months in advance. Accepts queries by mail, e-mail, fax. Accepts simultaneous submissions. Responds in 3 weeks to queries. Sample copy for free. Writer's guidelines free.

O→ Break in with a "demonstrated knowledge of finance and business, with special emphasis on retail. Keen powers of observation and attention to detail are also prized."

Nonfiction: Interview/profile (retailers), photo feature, technical. No self-serving, vendor-based stories. "We need real-life, retailer-based work." **Buys 12 mss/year.** Query with published clips. Length: 1,000-2,000 words. **Pays $200-500 for assigned articles.** Sometimes pays expenses of writers on assignment.
Photos: State availability with submission. Buys all rights. Negotiates payment individually. Identification of subjects required.
Tips: Offer experience. "We get queries from freelancers daily. We are looking for writers with industry experience. Bring us a story."

$ EVENTS MEDIA NETWORK, INC., (formerly *Events Business News*), 523 Route 38, Suite 207, Cherry Hill NJ 08002. (856)488-5255. Fax: (856)488-8324. **Contact:** Norman Zelnick, assistant to the editor. **20% freelance written.** Bimonthly magazine covering special events across North America, including festivals, fairs, auto shows, home shows, trade shows, etc. Covers 15 categories of shows/events. Byline given. Buys first rights. Submit seasonal material 3 months in advance. Accepts queries by mail. Sample copy and writer's guidelines free.
Nonfiction: How-to, interview/profile, new product, event review. Special issues: Annual special event directory, covering over 38,000 events. No submissions unrelated to selling at events. Query. Length: 400-750 words. **Pays $2.50/column inch.**
Reprints: Send photocopy of article and information about when and where the article previously appeared.
Photos: Send photos with submission. Reviews contact sheets. Buys one-time rights. Offers $20/photo. Captions required.
Columns/Departments: Five columns monthly (dealing with background of event, vendors or unique facets of industry in North America). Length: 400-700 words. Query with published clips. **Pays $3/column inch.**

$ $ $ GIFTWARE BUSINESS, VNU Business Media, 770 Broadway, New York NY 10003. Fax: (646)654-4977. E-mail: mmorgenthal@giftwarebusiness.com. Website: www.giftwarebusiness.com. Editor: Chris Gigley. **Contact:** Michael Morgenthal, managing editor. **10% freelance written.** Monthly magazine, newsletter and online product. "The magazine is for the serious gift retailer." Estab. 1943. Circ. 30,000. Pays on publication. Publishes ms an average of 3 months after acceptance. Byline given. Buys all rights. Editorial lead time 2 months. Submit seasonal material 6 months in advance. Accepts queries by mail, e-mail, fax. Sample copy for free. Writer's guidelines not available.

Nonfiction: How-to, interview/profile, new product, personal experience. Query with published clips. Length: 400-2,000 words. **Pays 50-75¢/word.** Sometimes pays expenses of writers on assignment.
Photos: Send photos with submission. Reviews 4×6 transparencies, 5×7 prints, digital images. Buys all rights. Offers no additional payment for photos accepted with ms. Captions required.
Columns/Departments: Pays 50¢/word.

$ $ GIFTWARE NEWS, Talcott Corp., 20 N. Walker Dr., Suite 1865, Chicago IL 60606. (312)849-2220. Fax: (312)849-2174. **Contact:** John Saxtan, editor. **55% freelance written.** Monthly magazine covering gifts, collectibles, and tabletops for giftware retailers. Estab. 1976. Circ. 35,000. Pays on publication. Publishes ms an average of 2 months after acceptance. Byline given. Buys all rights. Submit seasonal material 4 months in advance. Responds in 2 months to mss. Sample copy for $5.
Nonfiction: How-to (sell, display), new product. **Buys 50 mss/year.** Query with published clips or send complete ms. Length: 1,500-2,500 words. **Pays $200-350 for assigned articles; $150-250 for unsolicited articles.**
Photos: Send photos with submission. Reviews 4×5 transparencies, 5×7 prints, electronic images. Offers no additional payment for photos accepted with ms. Identification of subjects required.
Columns/Departments: Stationery, giftbaskets, collectibles, holiday, merchandise, tabletop, wedding market and display—all for the gift retailer. Length: 1,500-2,500 words. **Buys 36 mss/year.** Send complete ms. **Pays $100-250.**
Tips: "We are not looking so much for general journalists but rather experts in particular fields who can also write."

$ $ NEW AGE RETAILER, Continuity Publishing, 1300 N. State St., #105, Bellingham WA 98225. (800)463-9243. Fax: (360)676-0932. E-mail: luanne@newageretailer.com. Website: www.newageretailer.com. **Contact:** Luanne Napoli, editor-in-chief. **90% freelance written.** Bimonthly magazine for retailers of New Age books, music and merchandise. "The goal of the articles in *New Age Retailer* is usefulness—we strive to give store owners and managers practical, in-depth information they can begin using immediately. We have three categories of articles: retail business methods that give solid information about the various aspects of running an independent store; inventory articles that discuss a particular New Age subject or trend and include lists of books, music, and products suitable for store inventory; and education articles that help storeowners and managers gain knowledge and stay current in New Age subjects." Estab. 1987. Circ. 6,000. Pays on publication. Publishes ms an average of 4 months after acceptance. Byline given. Offers 10% kill fee. Buys first North American serial, second serial (reprint), simultaneous, electronic rights. Editorial lead time 4 months. Submit seasonal material 4 months in advance. Accepts queries by mail, e-mail, fax, phone. Accepts simultaneous submissions. Responds in 1 month to queries; 2 months to mss. Sample copy for $5.
Nonfiction: Book excerpts, how-to, interview/profile, new product, opinion, personal experience, technical, business principles, spiritual. No self-promotion for writer's company or product. Writer must understand independent retailing and New Age subjects. **Buys 50 mss/year.** Query with published clips. Length: 1,500-5,000 words. **Pays $150-300 for assigned articles; $75-250 for unsolicited articles.** Sometimes pays with advertisement space in magazine. Sometimes pays expenses of writers on assignment.
Photos: State availability of or send photos with submission. Reviews 2x3 minimum size prints, digital images at 300 dpi. Buys one-time rights. Negotiates payment individually. Captions required.
Tips: "E-mail Luanne Napoli (luanne@newageretailer.com), or phone her at (800)463-9243, ext. 3014. Describe your expertise in the New Age market and independent retailing. Have an idea for an article ready to pitch. Promise only what you can deliver."

$ $ NICHE, The Magazine For Craft Gallery Retailers, The Rosen Group, 3000 Chestnut Ave., Suite 304, Baltimore MD 21211. (410)889-3093. Fax: (410)243-7089. E-mail: hoped@rosengrp.com. **Contact:** Hope Daniels, editor. **75% freelance written.** Quarterly business-to-business magazine for the progressive craft gallery retailer. Each issue includes retail gallery profiles, store design trends, management techniques, financial information and merchandising strategies for small business owners. Estab. 1988. Circ. 20,000. Pays on publication. Publishes ms an average of 6 months after acceptance. Byline given. Buys first North American serial rights. Editorial lead time 6 months. Submit seasonal material 9-12 months in advance. Accepts queries by mail, e-mail, fax. Responds in 6 weeks to queries; 6 weeks to mss. Sample copy for $3.
Nonfiction: *Niche* is looking for in-depth articles on store security, innovative merchandising/display, design trends or marketing and promotion. Stories of interest to independent retailers, such as gallery owners, may be submitted. Interview/profile, photo feature, articles targeted to independent retailers and small business owners. **Buys 20-28 mss/year.** Query with published clips. **Pays $300-700.** Sometimes pays expenses of writers on assignment.
Photos: Send photos with submission. Reviews 4×5 transparencies, slides. Negotiates payment individually. Captions required.
Columns/Departments: Retail Details (short items at the front of the book, general retail information); Artist Profiles (biographies of American Craft Artists); Resources (book/video/seminar reviews/educational opportunities pertaining to retailers). Query with published clips. **Pays $25-150.**

$ O&A MARKETING NEWS, KAL Publications Inc., 559 S. Harbor Blvd., Suite A, Anaheim CA 92805. (714)563-9300. Fax: (714)563-9310. E-mail: kathy@kalpub.com. Website: www.kalpub.com. **Contact:** Kathy Laderman, editor-in-chief. **3% freelance written.** Bimonthly tabloid. "*O&A Marketing News* is editorially directed to people engaged in the distribution, merchandising, installation and servicing of gasoline, oil, TBA, quick lube, carwash, convenience store, alternative fuel and automotive aftermarket products in the 13 Western states." Estab. 1966. Circ. 7,500. Pays on publication. Publishes ms an average of 2 months after acceptance. Byline sometimes given. Buys first, electronic rights.

Editorial lead time 1 month. Submit seasonal material 1 month in advance. Accepts queries by mail, e-mail, fax. Accepts simultaneous submissions. Responds in 2 months to queries; 2 months to mss. Sample copy for 9×13 SAE and 10 first-class stamps. Writer's guidelines not available.

Nonfiction: Interview/profile, photo feature, industry news. Nothing that doesn't pertain to the petroleum marketing industry in the 13 Western states. **Buys 35 mss/year.** Send complete ms. Length: 100-500 words. **Pays $1.25/column inch.**

Photos: State availability of or send photos with submission. Reviews contact sheets, 4×6 prints. electronic rights. Offers $5/photo. Captions, identification of subjects required.

Columns/Departments: Oregon News (petroleum marketing news in state of Oregon). **Buys 7 mss/year.** Send complete ms. **Pays $1.25/column inch.**

Fillers: Gags to be illustrated by cartoonist, short humor. **Buys 7/year.** Length: 1-200 words. **Pays per column inch.**

Tips: "Seeking Western industry news pertaining to the petroleum marketing industry. It can be something simple—like a new gas station or quick lube opening. News from "outlying" states such as Montana, Idaho, Wyoming, New Mexico and Hawaii is always needed—but any timely, topical *news*-oriented stories will be considered."

$ $ $ $ OPERATIONS & FULFILLMENT, Primedia Inc., 11 Riverbend Dr. S., P.O. Box 4949, Stamford CT 06907-2524. (203)358-4124, ext. 764. E-mail: dpluviose@primediabusiness.com. Website: www.opsandfulfillment.com. **Contact:** David Pluviose, assistant editor. **25% freelance written.** Monthly magazine covering catalog/direct mail operations. "*Operations & Fulfillment (O&F)* is a monthly publication that offers practical solutions for catalog online, and direct response operations management. The magazine covers such critical areas as material handling, bar coding, facility planning, transportation, call centers, warehouse management, information systems, online fulfillment and human resources." Estab. 1993. Circ. 17,600. Pays on publication. Publishes ms an average of 2 months after acceptance. Buys first North American serial rights. Editorial lead time 2 months. Accepts queries by mail, e-mail, phone. Responds in 1 week to queries. Sample copy and writer's guidelines free.

Nonfiction: Book excerpts, how-to, interview/profile, new product, technical. **Buys 4-6 mss/year.** Query with published clips. Length: 2,500-3,000 words. **Pays $1,000-1,800.**

Photos: "In addition to the main article, you must include at least one sidebar of about 400 words that contains a detailed example or case study of how a direct-to-customer catalog company implements or benefits from the process you're writing about; a check list or set of practical guidelines (e.g., "Twelve Ways to Ship Smarter") that describe how to implement what you suggest in the article; supporting materials such as flow charts, graphs, diagrams, illustrations and photographs (these must be clearly labeled and footnoted); and an author biography of no more than 75 words." Send photos with submission. Captions, identification of subjects required.

Tips: "Writers need some knowledge of the direct-to-customer industry. They should be able to deal clearly with highly technical material; provide attention to detail and painstaking research."

$ $ PARTY & PAPER RETAILER, 107 Mill Plain Rd., Suite 204, Danbury CT 06811-6100. (203)730-4090. Fax: (203)730-4094. E-mail: editor@partypaper.com. Website: www.partypaper.com. **Contact:** Jacqueline Shanley, editor-in-chief. **90% freelance written.** Monthly magazine covering "every aspect of how to do business better for owners of party and fine stationery shops. Tips and how-tos on display, marketing, success stories, merchandising, operating costs, e-commerce, retail technology, etc." Estab. 1986. Circ. 20,000. Pays on publication. Offers 15% kill fee. Buys first North American serial rights. Editorial lead time 6 months. Submit seasonal material 6 months in advance. Accepts queries by mail, e-mail, fax. Responds in 2 months to queries. Sample copy for $6.

O→ Especially interested in news items on party retail industry for our Press Pages. Also, new column on Internet retailing ("Cyberlink") which covers all www-related topics.

Nonfiction: Book excerpts, how-to (retailing related), new product. No articles written in first person. **Buys 100 mss/year.** Query with published clips. Length: 800-1,800 words. Pays phone expenses only of writers on assignment.

Reprints: Send tearsheet or photocopy of article and information about when and where the article previously appeared.

Photos: State availability with submission. Reviews transparencies. Buys one-time rights. Negotiates payment individually. Captions, identification of subjects required.

Columns/Departments: Shop Talk (successful party/stationery store profile), 1,800 words; Storekeeping (selling, employees, market, running store), 800 words; Cash Flow (anything finance related), 800 words. **Buys 30 mss/year.** Query with published clips. **Payment varies.**

[N] **$ $ SPECIALTY COFFEE RETAILER, The Coffee Business Monthly**, Adams Business Media, 250 S. Wacker Dr., Suite 1150, Chicago IL 60606-5827. (847)427-2003. Fax: (847)427-2041. E-mail: sgillerlain@mail.aip.com. Website: www.specialty-coffee.com. Sue Gillerlain, editor-in-chief. **Contact:** Managing Editor: Jenifer Everley. **60% freelance written.** Monthly magazine covering cofee—retail and roasting, tea. "*Specialty Coffee Retailer* is the business monthly for the specialty coffee industry. The magazine provides practical business information for the profitable operation of a coffeehouse, cart/kiosk/drive-through or tea house. Featured topics include business management and finance, marketing and promotion, site selection, store design, equipment selection and maintenance, drink preparation, tea trends, new products and more." Estab. 1994. Circ. 7,500. Pays on publication. Publishes ms an average of 2 months after acceptance. Byline given. Buys first North American serial, electronic rights. Editorial lead time 2 months. Submit seasonal material 5 months in advance. Accepts queries by mail, e-mail, fax. Accepts simultaneous submissions. Sample copy by e-mail.

Nonfiction: How-to (select a roaster, blend coffees, purchse tea, market chai). No opinion, essays, book reviews, humor, personal experience. **Buys 36 mss/year.** Query with published clips. Length: 1,800-2,500 words. **Pays $300-425.** Sometimes pays expenses of writers on assignment.
Photos: Send photos with submission. Reviews transparencies, 3×5 prints. Offers no additional payment for photos accepted with ms.
Tips: "Be willing to contact industry experts for inclusion in stories."

$ $ TRAVEL GOODS SHOWCASE, The source for luggage, business cases and accessories, Travel Goods Association, 5 Vaughn Dr., Suite 105, Princeton NJ 08540. (609)720-1200. Fax: (609)720-0620. E-mail: john@travel-goods.org. Website: www.travel-goods.org. Editor: Michele M. Pittenger. **Contact:** John Misiano, senior editor. **5-10% freelance written.** Bimonthly magazine covering travel goods, accessories, trends and new products. "*Travel Goods Showcase* contains articles for retailers, dealers, manufacturers and suppliers, about luggage, business cases, personal leather goods, handbags and accessories. Special articles report on trends in fashion, promotions, selling and marketing techniques, industry statistics and other educational and promotional improvements and advancements." Estab. 1975. Circ. 14,500. **Pays on acceptance.** Publishes ms an average of 2 months after acceptance. Byline given. Offers $50 kill fee. Editorial lead time 3 months. Submit seasonal material 2 months in advance. Accepts queries by mail, e-mail. Responds in 2 weeks to queries; 1 month to mss. Sample copy and writer's guidelines free.
Nonfiction: Interview/profile, new product, technical, travel, retailer profiles with photos. "No manufacturer profiles." **Buys 3 mss/year.** Query with published clips. Length: 1,200-1,600 words. **Pays $200-500.**

SPORT TRADE

Retailers and wholesalers of sports equipment and operators of recreation programs read these journals. Magazines about general and specific sports are classified in the Consumer Sports section.

N **$ $ AQUATICS INTERNATIONAL**, Hanley-Wood, LLC, 4160 Wilshire Blvd., Los Angeles CA 90010. Website: www.aquaticsintl.com. **Contact:** Len Hochberg, editor. published 10 times/year. Magazine covering public swimming pools and waterparks. Estab. 1989. Circ. 30,000. Pays on publication. Publishes ms an average of 3 months after acceptance. Byline given. Buys international rights in perpetuity and makes work-for-hire assignments. Editorial lead time 3 months. Responds in 1 month to queries. Sample copy for $10.50.
Nonfiction: How-to, interview/profile, technical. **Buys 6 mss/year.** Query with published clips. Length: 1,500-2,500 words. **Pays $525 for assigned articles.**
Columns/Departments: Pays $250.
Tips: "Query letter with samples."

N **$ $ BOATING INDUSTRY INTERNATIONAL, The Management Magazine for the Recreational Marine Industry, (formerly** *Boating Industry*), National Trade Publications, 13 Century Hill Dr., Latham NY 12110. (518)783-1281. Fax: (518)783-1386. E-mail: lwalz@boating-industry.com. Website: www.boating-industry.com. **Contact:** Liz Walz, executive editor. **10-20% freelance written.** Bimonthly magazine covering recreational marine industry management. "We write for those in the industry—not the consumer. Our subject is the business of boating. All of our articles must be analytical and predictive, telling our readers where the industry is going, rather than where it's been." Estab. 1929. Circ. 23,000. **Pays on acceptance.** Publishes ms an average of 2 months after acceptance. Byline given. Offers 50% kill fee. Buys first, electronic rights. Editorial lead time 2 months. Submit seasonal material 2 months in advance. Accepts queries by mail, e-mail, fax. Responds in 1 month to queries. Sample copy online. Writer's guidelines free.

O→ "We actively solicit items for our electronic news service. See the News Flash section of our website. This is an excellent way to break in, especially for writers based outside the U.S."

Nonfiction: Technical, business. **Buys 30 mss/year.** Query with published clips. Length: 250-2,500 words. **Pays $25-250.** Sometimes pays expenses of writers on assignment.
Photos: State availability with submission. Reviews 2x2 transparencies, 4×6 prints. Buys one-time rights. Negotiates payment individually. Captions, identification of subjects required.

$ $ FITNESS MANAGEMENT, Issues and Solutions in Fitness Services, Leisure Publications, Inc., 4160 Wilshire Blvd., Los Angeles CA 90010. (323)964-4800. Fax: (323)964-4835. E-mail: edit@fitnessmanagement.com. Website: www.fitnessmanagement.com. Publisher: Chris Ballard. **Contact:** Ronale Tucker, editor. **50% freelance written.** Monthly magazine. "Readers are owners, managers and program directors of physical fitness facilities. *FM* helps them run their enterprises safely, efficiently and profitably. Ethical and professional positions in health, nutrition, sports medicine, management, etc., are consistent with those of established national bodies." Estab. 1985. Circ. 26,000. Pays on publication. Publishes ms an average of 5 months after acceptance. Byline given. Offers 50% kill fee. all rights (all articles published in FM are also published and archived on its website). Submit seasonal material 6 months in advance. Accepts queries by mail, e-mail, fax. Responds in 3 months to queries. Sample copy for $5. Writer's guidelines for #10 SASE.

Nonfiction: Book excerpts (prepublication), how-to (manage fitness center and program), new product (no pay), photo feature (facilities/programs), technical, News of fitness research and major happenings in fitness industry. No exercise instructions or general ideas without examples of fitness businesses that have used them successfully. **Buys 50 mss/year.** Query. Length: 750-2,000 words. **Pays $60-300 for assigned articles.** Pays expenses of writers on assignment.

Photos: Send photos with submission. Reviews contact sheets, 2×2 and 4×5 transparencies, Prefers glossy prints, 5×7 to 8×10. Captions, model releases required.

The online magazine carries original content not found in the print edition. Includes sample articles. Contact: Ronale Tucker.

Tips: "We seek writers who are expert in a business or science field related to the fitness-service industry or who are experienced in the industry. Be current with the state of the art/science in business and fitness and communicate it in human terms (avoid intimidating academic language; tell the story of how this was learned and/or cite examples or quotes of people who have applied the knowledge successfully)."

$ $ GOLF COURSE NEWS, The Newspaper for the Golf Course Industry, United Publications Inc., P.O. Box 997, 106 Lafayette St., Yarmouth ME 04096. (207)846-0600. Fax: (207)846-0657. E-mail: aoverbeck@golfcoursenews.com. Website: www.golfcoursenews.com. Managing Editor: Derek Rice. **Contact:** Andrew Overbeck, editor. **15% freelance written.** Monthly tabloid "written with the golf course superintendent in mind. Our readers are superintendents, course architects and builders, owners and general managers." Estab. 1989. Circ. 25,000. **Pays on acceptance.** Publishes ms an average of 2 months after acceptance. Byline given. Buys first North American serial rights. Editorial lead time 1 month. Submit seasonal material 2 months in advance. Accepts queries by mail, e-mail, fax, phone. Responds in 2 months to queries; 2 months to mss. Sample copy and writer's guidelines free.

Nonfiction: Book excerpts, general interest, interview/profile, new product, opinion, photo feature. "No how-to articles." **Buys 24 mss/year.** Query with published clips. Length: 500-1,000 words. **Pays $200.** Sometimes pays expenses of writers on assignment.

Photos: Send photos with submission. Reviews negatives, transparencies, prints. Buys one-time rights. Offers no additional payment for photos accepted with ms. Identification of subjects required.

Columns/Departments: On the Green (innovative ideas on the golf course), 500-800 words; Shop Talk (in the maintenance facility). **Buys 4 mss/year.** Query with published clips. **Pays $200-500.**

The online magazine carries original content not found in the print edition. Contact: Andrew Overbeck, online editor.

Tips: "Keep your eye out for news affecting the golf industry. Then contact us with your story ideas. We are a national paper and accept both national and regional interest articles. We are interested in receiving features on development of golf projects."

N $ $ HOCKEY BUSINESS NEWS, Transcontinental Sports Publications, 25 Sheppard Ave. W., Suite 100, Toronto, Ontario M2N 6S7, Canada. (416)733-7600. Fax: (416)340-2786. E-mail: karlw@transcontinental.ca. Website: www.hockeynews.com. **Contact:** Wayne Karl, editor. **70% freelance written.** published 8 times/year. Journal covering the hockey industry. Estab. 1994. Circ. 6,000. Pays on publication. Publishes ms an average of 1 month after acceptance. Byline given. Kill fee negotiated. Buys first North American serial, electronic, all rights. Editorial lead time 2 months. Accepts queries by mail, e-mail, fax, phone. Accepts simultaneous submissions. Responds in 2 weeks to queries; 1 month to mss. Writer's guidelines by e-mail.

Nonfiction: Exposé, general interest, how-to, interview/profile, new product, opinion, technical. Query with published clips. **Pays 35¢/word.** Sometimes pays expenses of writers on assignment.

Photos: State availability with submission. Reviews transparencies, Prints. Buys all rights. Negotiates payment individually. Identification of subjects required.

Columns/Departments: Buys 8 mss/year. Query with published clips. **Pays 35¢/word "or terms discussed."**

IDEA HEALTH & FITNESS SOURCE, IDEA Inc., Dept. WM, 6190 Cornerstone Court E., Suite 204, San Diego CA 92121. (858)535-8979. Fax: (858)535-8234. E-mail: ryanp@ideafit.com. Website: www.ideafit.com. **Contact:** Pat Ryan, vice president of education. **70% freelance written.** Magazine published 10 times/year "for fitness professionals—aerobics instructors, one-to-one trainers and studio and health club owners—covering topics such as aerobics, nutrition, injury prevention, entrepreneurship in fitness, fitness-oriented research and exercise programs." Estab. 1984. Circ. 23,000. **Pays on acceptance.** Publishes ms an average of 4 months after acceptance. Byline given. Buys all rights. Accepts queries by mail, e-mail, fax. Accepts simultaneous submissions. Responds in 2 months to queries. Sample copy for $4.

Nonfiction: How-to, technical. No general information on fitness; our readers are pros who need detailed information. **Buys 15 mss/year.** Query. Length: 1,000-3,000 words. **Pay varies.**

Photos: State availability with submission. Buys all rights. Offers no additional payment for photos with ms. Model releases required.

Columns/Departments: Research (detailed, specific info; must be written by expert), 750-1,500 words; Industry News (short reports on research, programs and conferences), 150-300 words; Fitness Handout (exercise and nutrition info for participants), 750 words. **Buys 80 mss/year.** Query. **Pay varies.**

Tips: "We don't accept fitness information for the consumer audience on topics such as why exercise is good for you. Writers who have specific knowledge of, or experience working in, the fitness industry have an edge."

$ $ NSGA RETAIL FOCUS, National Sporting Goods Association, 1601 Feehanville Dr., Suite 300, Mt. Prospect IL 60056-6035. (847)296-6742. Fax: (847)391-9827. E-mail: info@nsga.org. Website: www.nsga.org. **Contact:** Larry N. Weindruch, editor/publisher. **25% freelance written.** Works with a small number of new/unpublished writers each year. Bimonthly magazine. "*NSGA Retail Focus* serves as a bimonthly trade journal for sporting goods retailers who are members of the association." Estab. 1948. Circ. 3,000. Pays on publication. Publishes ms an average of 1 month after acceptance. Byline given. Offers kill fee. Buys first, second serial (reprint), electronic rights. Submit seasonal material 6 months in advance. Accepts queries by mail, e-mail. Sample copy for 9×12 SAE and 5 first-class stamps.
Nonfiction: Interview/profile, photo feature. "No articles written without sporting goods retail businesspeople in mind as the audience. In other words, no generic articles sent to several industries." **Buys 12 mss/year.** Query with published clips. **Pays $75-300.** Sometimes pays expenses of writers on assignment.
Photos: State availability with submission. Reviews contact sheets, negatives, transparencies, 5×7 prints. Buys one-time rights. Payment negotiable.
Columns/Departments: Personnel Management (succinct tips on hiring, motivating, firing, etc.); Sales Management (in-depth tips to improve sales force performance); Retail Management (detailed explanation of merchandising/inventory control); Advertising (case histories of successful ad campaigns/ad critiques); Legal Advisor; Computers; Store Design; Visual Merchandising; all 1,500 words. **Buys 12 mss/year.** Query. **Pays $75-300.**

$ $ PADDLE DEALER, The Trade Magazine for Paddlesports, Paddlesport Publishing, Inc., P.O. Box 5450, Steamboat Springs CO 80477-5450. (970)879-1450. Fax: (970)870-1404. E-mail: rico@paddlermagazine.com. Website: www.paddlermagazine.com. Editor: Eugene Buchanan. **Contact:** Frederick Reivers, managing editor. **70% freelance written.** Quarterly magazine covering the canoeing, kayaking and rafting industry. Estab. 1993. Circ. 7,500. Pays on publication. Publishes ms an average of 6 months after acceptance. Byline given. first North American serial and one-time electronic rights. Editorial lead time 2 months. Submit seasonal material 6 months in advance. Accepts queries by mail, e-mail, fax. Accepts simultaneous submissions. Responds in 3 months to queries. Sample copy for 8½×11 SAE and $1.78. Writer's guidelines for #10 SASE.
Nonfiction: New product, technical, business advice. **Buys 8 mss/year.** Query or send complete ms. Length: 2,300 words. **Pays 20-25¢/word.** Sometimes pays expenses of writers on assignment.
Photos: State availability with submission. Reviews transparencies, 5×7 prints. Buys one-time rights.
Columns/Departments: Profiles, how-to, great ideas, computer corner. **Buys 12 mss/year.** Query or send complete ms. **Pays 10-20¢/word.**

$ $ POOL & SPA NEWS, Hanley-Wood, LLC, 4160 Wilshire Blvd., Los Angeles CA 90010. (323)964-4800. Fax: (323)964-4842. E-mail: psn@poolspanews.com. Website: poolspanews.com. **Contact:** Pervin Lakdawalla, editor. **15% freelance written.** Bimonthly magazine covering the swimming pool and spa industry for builders, retail stores and service firms. Estab. 1960. Circ. 16,300. Pays on publication. Publishes ms an average of 2 months after acceptance. Buys all rights. Accepts queries by mail. Responds in 2 weeks to queries. Sample copy for $5 and 9×12 SAE and 11 first-class stamps.
Nonfiction: Interview/profile, technical. Send résumé with published clips. Length: 500-2,000 words. **Pays $150-600.** Pays expenses of writers on assignment.
Reprints: Send ms with rights for sale noted and information about when and where the material previously appeared. Payment varies.
Photos: Payment varies.
Columns/Departments: Pay varies.

The online magazine carries original content not found in the print edition. Contact: Pervin Lakdawalla, online editor.

N $ $ REFEREE, Referee Enterprises, Inc., P.O. Box 161, Franksville WI 53126. Fax: (262)632-5460. E-mail: jarehart@referee.com. Website: www.referee.com. Editor: Bill Topp. **Contact:** Jim Arehart, associate editor. **75% freelance written.** Monthly magazine covering sports officiating. "Referee is a magazine for and read by sports officials of all kinds with a focus on baseball, basketball, football, softball and soccer officiating." Estab. 1976. Circ. 40,000. **Pays on acceptance.** Publishes ms an average of 6 months after acceptance. Byline given. Kill fee negotiable. Buys all rights. Editorial lead time 6 months. Accepts queries by mail, e-mail, fax. Responds in 2 weeks to queries; 1 month to mss. Sample copy for #10 SASE. Writer's guidelines free.
Nonfiction: Book excerpts, essays, historical/nostalgic, how-to (sports officiating related), humor, interview/profile, opinion, photo feature, technical (as it relates to sports officiating). "We don't want to see articles with themes not relating to sport officiating. General sports articles, although of interest to us, will not be published." **Buys 40 mss/year.** Query with published clips. Length: 500-2,500 words. **Pays $100-400.** Sometimes pays expenses of writers on assignment.
Photos: State availability with submission. Reviews contact sheets, negatives, transparencies, Prints. Purchase of rights negotiable. Offers $35-40 per photo. Identification of subjects required.
Tips: "Query first and be persistent. We may not like your idea but that doesn't mean we won't like your next one. Professionalism pays off."

$ $ SKI AREA MANAGEMENT, Beardsley Publications, P.O. Box 644, 45 Main St. N, Woodbury CT 06798. (203)263-0888. Fax: (203)266-0452. E-mail: sam@saminfo.com. Website: www.saminfo.com. Editor: Jennifer Rowan. **Contact:** Rick Kahl, managing editor. **85% freelance written.** Bimonthly magazine covering everything involving the management and development of ski resorts. "We are the publication of record for the North American ski industry. We report on new ideas, developments, marketing and regulations with regard to ski and snowboard resorts. Everyone from the CEO to the lift operator of winter resorts reads our magazine to stay informed about the people and procedures that make ski areas successful." Estab. 1962. Circ. 4,500. Pays on publication. Byline given. Offers kill fee. Buys all rights. Editorial lead time 2 months. Submit seasonal material 3 months in advance. Accepts queries by mail, e-mail. Responds in 2 weeks to queries. Sample copy for 9×12 SAE with $3 postage or online. Writer's guidelines for #10 SASE.

Nonfiction: Historical/nostalgic, how-to, interview/profile, new product, opinion, personal experience, technical. "We don't want anything that does not specifically pertain to resort operations, management or financing." **Buys 25-40 mss/year.** Query. Length: 500-2,500 words. **Pays $50-400.**

Reprints: Accepts previously published submissions.

Photos: Send photos with submission. Reviews transparencies, Prints. Buys one-time rights or all rights. Offers no additional payment for photos accepted with ms. Identification of subjects required.

The online magazine carries original content not found in the print edition. Contact: Olivia Rowan.

Tips: "Know what you are writing about. We are read by people dedicated to skiing and snowboarding and to making the resort experience the best possible for their customers."

$ $ THOROUGHBRED TIMES, Thoroughbred Times Company, Inc., 496 Southland Dr., P.O. Box 8237, Lexington KY 40533. (859)260-9800. **Contact:** Mark Simon, editor. **10% freelance written.** Weekly tabloid "written for professionals who breed and/or race thoroughbreds at tracks in the U.S. Articles must help owners and breeders understand racing to help them realize a profit." Estab. 1985. Circ. 23,000. Pays on publication. Publishes ms an average of 1 month after acceptance. Byline given. Offers 50% kill fee. Buys first publication rights. Submit seasonal material 2 months in advance. Responds in 2 weeks to mss. Sample copy not available.

Nonfiction: General interest, historical/nostalgic, interview/profile, technical. **Buys 52 mss/year.** Query. Length: 500-2,500 words. **Pays 10-20¢/word.** Sometimes pays expenses of writers on assignment.

Photos: State availability with submission. Reviews prints. Buys one-time rights. Offers $25/photo. Identification of subjects required.

Columns/Departments: Vet Topics; Business of Horses; Pedigree Profiles; Bloodstock Topics; Tax Matters; Viewpoints; Guest Commentary.

Tips: "We are looking for farm stories and profiles of owners, breeders, jockeys and trainers."

$ $ WHITETAIL BUSINESS, Krause Publications, Inc., 700 E. State St., Iola WI 54990. (715)445-2214 ext. 472. Fax: (715)445-4087. Website: www.whitetailbusiness.com. **Contact:** Dan Schmidt, editor. Annual magazine. "*Whitetail Business* targets the hunting industry's driving force, the white-tailed deer hunting market. Archery, modern firearm and muzzleloader retail dealers make their largest profit from whitetail hunters, and *Whitetail Business* devotes itself to this largest profit category." Estab. 1997. Circ. 11,000. **Pays on acceptance.** Byline given. Offers $50 kill fee. Buys first North American serial rights. Editorial lead time 1 year. Submit seasonal material 1 year in advance. Accepts queries by mail. Sample copy and writer's guidelines free.

Nonfiction: Personal experience, technical, retail management and topics relating to trade shows and the outdoor industry. No humor. Query with or without published clips. Length: 400-1,500 words. **Pays $200-350.**

Photos: State availability with submission. Reviews transparencies. Buys one-time rights. Offers $25-300/photo. Identification of subjects required.

Columns/Departments: Archery, Firearms/Muzzleloaders, Marketing (all dealing with white-tailed deer hunting); all 400 words. Query with published clips. **Pays $250 maximum.**

Fillers: Anecdotes. Length: 100 words maximum. **Pays $25 maximum.**

Tips: "Keep it short."

STONE, QUARRY & MINING

$ $ CANADIAN MINING JOURNAL, Southam Magazine Group Limited, 1450 Don Mills Rd., Don Mills, Ontario M3B 2X7, Canada. (416)510-6742. Fax: (416)442-2175. E-mail: jwerniuk@corporate.southam.ca. **Contact:** Jane Werniuk, editor. **5% freelance written.** Bimonthly magazine covering mining and mineral exploration by Canadian companies. "*Canadian Mining Journal* provides articles and information of practical use to those who work in the technical, administrative and supervisory aspects of exploration, mining and processing in the Canadian mineral exploration and mining industry." Estab. 1879. Circ. 10,000. Pays on publication. Publishes ms an average of 3 months after acceptance. Byline given. Buys one-time, electronic rights, makes work-for-hire assignments. Submit seasonal material 3 months in advance. Accepts queries by mail, e-mail, fax, phone. Responds in 1 week to queries; 1 month to mss.

Nonfiction: Opinion, technical, operation descriptions. **Buys 6 mss/year.** Query with published clips. Length: 500-1,400 words. **Pays $100-600.** Pays expenses of writers on assignment.

Photos: State availability with submission. Reviews 4×6 prints or high resolution files. Buys one-time rights. Negotiates payment individually. Captions, identification of subjects required.

Columns/Departments: Guest editorial (opinion on controversial subject related to mining industry), 600 words. **Buys 3 mss/year.** Query with published clips. **Pays $150.**

Tips: "I need articles about mine sites that it would be expensive/difficult for me to reach. I also need to know that the writer is competent to understand and describe the technology in an interesting way."

$ COAL PEOPLE MAGAZINE, Al Skinner Inc., Dept. WM, 629 Virginia St. W, P.O. Box 6247, Charleston WV 25362. (304)342-4129. Fax: (304)343-3124. Editor/Publisher: Al Skinner. **Contact:** Christina Karawan, president. **50% freelance written.** Monthly magazine. "Most stories are about people or historical—either narrative or biographical on all levels of coal people, past and present—from coal execs down to grass roots miners. Most stories are upbeat—showing warmth of family or success from underground up!" Estab. 1976. Circ. 11,000. Pays on publication. Publishes ms an average of 3 months after acceptance. Byline given. Buys first, second serial (reprint) rights, makes work-for-hire assignments. Submit seasonal material 2 months in advance. Responds in 3 months to mss. Sample copy for 9×12 SAE and 10 first-class stamps.

Nonfiction: Book excerpts (and film if related to coal), historical/nostalgic (coal towns, people, lifestyles), humor (including anecdotes and cartoons), interview/profile (for coal personalities), personal experience (as relates to coal mining), photo feature (on old coal towns, people, past and present). Special issues: calendar issue for more than 300 annual coal shows, association meetings, etc. (January); surface mining/reclamation award (July); Christmas in Coal Country (December). No poetry, fiction or environmental attacks on the coal industry. **Buys 32 mss/year.** Query with published clips. Length: 5,000 words. **Pays $90 for assigned articles.**

Reprints: Send tearsheet and information about when and where the material previously appeared. Pays 50% of amount paid for an original article.

Photos: Send photos with submission. Reviews contact sheets, transparencies, 5×7 prints. Buys one-time reprint rights. Captions, identification of subjects required.

Columns/Departments: Editorials—anything to do with current coal issues (non-paid); Mine'ing Our Business (bull pen column—gossip—humorous anecdotes); Coal Show Coverage (freelance photojournalist coverage of any coal function across the US). Length: 300-500 words. **Buys 10 mss/year.** Query. **Pays $50.**

Fillers: Anecdotes. Length: 300 words. **Pays $35.**

Tips: "We are looking for good feature articles on coal people, towns, companies—past and present, color slides (for possible cover use) and b&w photos to complement stories. Could also use a few news writers to take photos and do journalistic coverage on coal events across the country. Slant stories more toward people and less on historical. More faces and names than old town, company store photos. Include more quotes from people who lived these moments!" The following geographical areas are covered: Eastern Canada; Mexico; Europe; China; Russia; Poland; Australia; as well as U.S. states: Alabama, Tennessee, Virginia, Washington, Oregon, North and South Dakota, Arizona, Colorado, Alaska and Wyoming.

$ $ COLORED STONE, Lapidary Journal/Primedia Inc., 60 Chestnut Ave., Suite 201, Devon PA 19333-1312. (610)964-6300. Fax: (610)293-0977. E-mail: cs_editorial@primediamags.com. Website: www.colored-stone.com. **Contact:** Morgan Beard, editor-in-chief. **50% freelance written.** Bimonthly magazine covering the colored gemstone industry. "*Colored Stone* covers all aspects of the colored gemstone (i.e., no diamonds) trade. Our readers are manufacturing jewelers and jewelry designers, gemstone dealers, miners, retail jewelers and gemologists." Estab. 1987. Circ. 11,000. **Pays on acceptance.** Publishes ms an average of 2 months after acceptance. Byline given. Buys one-time, all rights. Editorial lead time 2 months. Submit seasonal material 4 months in advance. Accepts queries by mail, e-mail, fax. Accepts simultaneous submissions. Responds in 1 month to queries; 2 months to mss. Sample copy and writer's guidelines free.

Nonfiction: Exposé, interview/profile, new product, technical. "No articles intended for the general public." **Buys 35-45 mss/year.** Query with published clips. Length: 400-2,200 words. **Pays $200-600.**

Photos: State availability with submission. Reviews any size transparencies, 4×6 prints and up. Buys one-time rights. Offers $15-50/photo. Captions, identification of subjects, model releases required.

Tips: "A background in the industry is helpful but not necessary. Please, no recycled marketing/new technology/etc. pieces."

$ $ CONTEMPORARY STONE & TILE DESIGN, Business News Publishing Co., 210 Route 4 E., Suite 311, Paramus NJ 07652. (201)291-9001. Fax: (201)291-9002. E-mail: info@stoneworld.com. Website: www.stoneworld.com. Publisher: Alex Bachrach. **Contact:** Michael Reis, senior editor, or Jennifer Adams, editor. Quarterly magazine covering the full range of stone and tile design and architecture—from classic and historic spaces to current projects. Estab. 1995. Circ. 14,000. Pays on publication. Publishes ms an average of 3 months after acceptance. Byline given. Buys first rights. Submit seasonal material 6 months in advance. Responds in 3 weeks to queries. Sample copy for $10.

Nonfiction: Overall features on a certain aspect of stone design/tile work, or specific articles on individual architectural projects. Interview/profile (prominent architect/designer or firm), photo feature, technical, architectural design. **Buys 8 mss/year.** Query with published clips. Length: 1,500-3,000 words. **Pays $6/column inch.** Pays expenses of writers on assignment.

Photos: State availability with submission. Reviews transparencies, prints. Buys one-time rights. Pays $10/photo accepted with ms. Captions, identification of subjects required.

Columns/Departments: Upcoming Events (for the architecture and design community); Stone Classics (featuring historic architecture); question and answer session with a prominent architect or designer. Length: 1,500-2,000 words. **Pays $6/inch.**

Tips: "The visual aspect of the magazine is key, so architectural photography is a must for any story. Cover the entire project, but focus on the stonework or tile work and how it relates to the rest of the space. Architects are very helpful in describing their work and often provide excellent quotes. As a relatively new magazine, we are looking for freelance submissions and are open to new feature topics. This is a narrow subject, however, so it's a good idea to speak with an editor before submitting anything."

$ $ PIT & QUARRY, Advanstar Communications, 7500 Old Oak Blvd., Cleveland OH 44130. (440)891-2607. Fax: (440)891-2675. E-mail: mkuhar@advanstar.com. Website: www.pitandquarry.com. Managing Editor: Darren Constantino. **Contact:** Mark S. Kuhar, editor. **10-20% freelance written.** Monthly magazine covering nonmetallic minerals, mining and crushed stone. Audience has "knowledge of construction-related markets, mining, minerals processing, etc." Estab. 1916. Circ. 25,000. **Pays on acceptance.** Publishes ms an average of 6 months after acceptance. Byline given. Buys first North American serial rights. Editorial lead time 6 months. Accepts queries by mail, e-mail, fax, phone. Accepts simultaneous submissions. Responds in 1 month to queries; 4 months to mss. Sample copy for 9×12 SAE and 4 first-class stamps.

Nonfiction: How-to, interview/profile, new product, technical. No humor or inspirational articles. **Buys 12-15 mss/year.** Query. Length: 1,000-1,500 words. **Pays $250-700 for assigned articles; $250-500 for unsolicited articles.** Pays writers with contributor copies or other premiums for simple news items, etc. Sometimes pays expenses of writers on assignment.

Photos: State availability with submission. Buys one-time rights. Offers no additional payment for photos accepted with ms. Identification of subjects, model releases required.

Columns/Departments: Brand new, techwatch, e-business, software corner, equipment showcase. Length: 250-750 words. **Buys 5-6 mss/year.** Query. **Pays $250-300.**

The online magazine sometimes carries original content not found in the print edition.

Tips: "Be familiar with quarry operations (crushed stone or sand and gravel), as opposed to coal or metallic minerals mining. Know construction markets. We always need equipment-focused features on specific quarry operations."

$ $ STONE WORLD, Business News Publishing Company, 210 Route 4 E., Suite 311, Paramus NJ 07652. (201)291-9001. Fax: (201)291-9002. E-mail: info@stoneworld.com. Website: www.stoneworld.com. **Contact:** Michael Reis, editor, or Jennifer Adams, managing editor. Monthly magazine on natural building stone for producers and users of granite, marble, limestone, slate, sandstone, onyx and other natural stone products. Estab. 1984. Circ. 21,000. Pays on publication. Publishes ms an average of 4 months after acceptance. Byline given. Buys first North American serial, second serial (reprint) rights. Submit seasonal material 6 months in advance. Responds in 2 months to queries. Sample copy for $10.

Nonfiction: How-to (fabricate and/or install natural building stone), interview/profile, photo feature, technical, architectural design, artistic stone uses, statistics, factory profile, equipment profile, trade show review. **Buys 10 mss/year.** Query with or without published clips or send complete ms. Length: 600-3,000 words. **Pays $6/column inch.** Pays expenses of writers on assignment.

Reprints: Send photocopy with rights for sale noted and information about when and where the material previously appeared. Pays 50% of amount paid for an original article.

Photos: State availability with submission. Reviews transparencies, prints, slides, digital images. Buys one-time rights. Pays $10/photo accepted with ms. Captions, identification of subjects required.

Columns/Departments: News (pertaining to stone or design community); New Literature (brochures, catalogs, books, videos, etc., about stone); New Products (stone products); New Equipment (equipment and machinery for working with stone); Calendar (dates and locations of events in stone and design communities). Query or send complete ms. Length 300-600 words. **Pays $6/inch.**

Tips: "Articles about architectural stone design accompanied by professional color photographs and quotes from designing firms are often published, especially when one unique aspect of the stone selection or installation is highlighted. We are also interested in articles about new techniques of quarrying and/or fabricating natural building stone."

TOY, NOVELTY & HOBBY

$ $ MODEL RETAILER, Resources for Successful Hobby Retailing, Kalmbach Publishing Co., 21027 Crossroads Circle, Waukesha WI 53187-1612. (262)796-8776. Fax: (262)796-1383. E-mail: staff@modelretailer.com. Website: www.modelretailer.com. **Contact:** Mark Savage, editor. **10% freelance written.** Monthly magazine. "*Model Retailer* covers the business of hobbies, from financial and shop management issues to industry trends and the latest product releases. Our goal is to provide hobby shop entrepreneurs with the tools and information they need to be successful retailers." Estab. 1987. Circ. 6,000 (controlled circulation). **Pays on acceptance.** Publishes ms an average of 3 months after acceptance. Byline given. Buys first rights. Editorial lead time 3 months. Submit seasonal material 6 months in advance. Accepts queries by mail, e-mail, fax. Sample copy and writer's guidelines free.

Nonfiction: How-to (business), new product. "No articles that do not have a strong hobby or small retail component." **Buys 3-5 mss/year.** Query with published clips. Length: 750-2,000 words. **Pays $250-500 for assigned articles; $100-250 for unsolicited articles.** Sometimes pays expenses of writers on assignment.

Photos: State availability with submission. Reviews 4×6 prints. Buys one-time rights. Negotiates payment individually. Captions, identification of subjects required.

Columns/Departments: Shop Management, Sales Marketing, Technology Advice, 500-750 words; Industry Trends. **Buys 5-8 mss/year.** Query with published clips. **Pays $100-200.**

TRANSPORTATION

These publications are for professional movers and people involved in the transportation of goods. For magazines focusing on trucking see also Auto & Truck.

N $ BUS CONVERSIONS, The First and Foremost Bus Converters Magazine, MAK Publishing, 7246 Garden Grove Blvd., Westminster CA 92683. (714)799-0062. Fax: (714)799-0042. E-mail: editor@busconversions.com. Website: www.busconversions.com. **Contact:** Tiffany Christian, editorial assistant. **95% freelance written.** Monthly magazine covering the bus conversion industry. Estab. 1992. Circ. 20,000. Pays on publication. Buys first North American serial rights. Accepts queries by mail, e-mail.

Nonfiction: Each month, *Bus Conversions* publishes a minimum of 2 coach reviews, usually anecdotal stories told by those who have completed their own bus conversion. Publishes some travel/destination stories (all of which are related to bus/RV travel). Looking for articles on engine swaps, exterior painting and furniture. How-to (articles on the electrical, plumbing, mechanical, decorative and structural aspects of bus conversions; buses that are converted into RVs). **Pays $25-50.**

Photos: Include color photos (glossy) or slides with submission. Photos/slides not returned unless and SASE is included.

Columns/Departments: Industry Update; Products of Interest; Electrical Shorts; Building a Balanced Energy System; Ask the Experts; One For the Road; Road Fix.

Tips: "Most of our writers are our readers. Knowledge of bus conversions and the associate lifestyle is a prerequisite."

$ $ METRO MAGAZINE, Bobit Publishing Co., 21061 S. Western Ave., Torrance CA 90501. E-mail: info@metro-magazine.com. Website: www.metro-magazine.com. Editor: Steve Hirano. **Contact:** Leslie Davis, managing editor. **10% freelance written.** Magazine published 9 times/year covering public transportation. "*Metro Magazine* delivers business, government policy and technology developments that are *industry specific* to public transportation." Estab. 1904. Circ. 20,500. **Pays on acceptance.** Publishes ms an average of 2 months after acceptance. Byline given. Offers 10% kill fee. Buys all rights. Editorial lead time 3 months. Submit seasonal material 3 months in advance. Accepts queries by e-mail. Responds in 2 weeks to queries; 1 month to mss. Sample copy for $8. Writer's guidelines by e-mail.

Nonfiction: How-to, interview/profile (of industry figures), new product (related to transit—bus and rail—private bus), technical. **Buys 6-10 mss/year.** Query. Length: 400-1,500 words. **Pays $80-400.**

Photos: State availability with submission. Buys all rights. Negotiates payment individually. Captions, identification of subjects, model releases required.

Columns/Departments: Query. **Pays $20¢/word.**

The online magazine carries original content not found in the print edition. Contact: Leslie Davis.

N $ $ SCHOOL BUS FLEET, Bobit Publishing Co., 21061 S. Western Ave., Torrance CA 90501. (310)533-2400. Fax: (310)533-2502. E-mail: sbf@bobit.com. Website: www.schoolbusfleet.com. **Contact:** Steve Hirano, editor. **10% freelance written.** Magazine covering school transportation of K-12 population. "Most of our readers are school bus operators, public and private." Estab. 1965. Circ. 24,000. **Pays on acceptance.** Publishes ms an average of 3 months after acceptance. Byline given. Offers 25% kill fee or $50. Buys first North American serial rights. Editorial lead time 3 months. Submit seasonal material 3 months in advance. Accepts queries by mail, e-mail, fax. Responds in 1 month to queries. Sample copy for free. Writer's guidelines free.

Nonfiction: Interview/profile, new product, technical. **Buys 6 mss/year.** Query with published clips. Length: 600-1,800 words. **Pays 20-25¢/word.** Sometimes pays expenses of writers on assignment.

Photos: State availability with submission. Reviews transparencies, 4×6 prints. Buys one-time rights. Negotiates payment individually. Captions, identification of subjects required.

Columns/Departments: Shop Talk (maintenance information for school bus mechanics), 650 words. **Buys 2 mss/year.** Query with published clips. **Pays $100-150.**

Tips: "Freelancers should submit ideas about innovations in school bus safety and operations."

TRAVEL

Travel professionals read these publications to keep up with trends, tours, and changes in transportation. Magazines about vacations and travel for the general public are listed in the Consumer Travel section.

N $ $ $ CRUISE INDUSTRY NEWS, Cruise Industry News, 441 Lexington Ave., New York NY 10017. (212)986-1025. Fax: (212)986-1033. Website: www.cruiseindustrynews.com. **Contact:** Oivind Mathisen, editor. **20% freelance written.** Quarterly magazine covering cruise shipping. "We write about the *business* of cruise shipping for the industry. That is, cruise lines, shipyards, financial analysts, etc." Estab. 1991. Circ. 10,000. Pays on acceptance or on publication. Publishes ms an average of 4 months after acceptance. Byline given. Offers 25% kill fee. Buys first rights. Editorial lead time 3 months. Accepts queries by mail. Reponse time varies to queries. Sample copy for $15. Writer's guidelines for #10 SASE.

Nonfiction: Interview/profile, new product, photo feature, travel, Business. No travel stories. **Buys more than 20 mss/year.** Query with published clips. Length: 500-1,500 words. **Pays $500-1,000 for assigned articles.** Sometimes pays expenses of writers on assignment.

Photos: State availability with submission. Buys one-time rights. Pays $25-50/photo.

$ $ LEISURE GROUP TRAVEL, Premier Tourism Marketing, 4901 Forest Ave., Downers Grove IL 60515. (630)964-1431. Fax: (630)852-0515. E-mail: info@premiertourismmarketing.com. Website: www.leisuregrouptravel.com. **Contact:** Jeff Gayduk, editor. **15% freelance written.** Bimonthly magazine covering group travel. We cover destinations and editorial relevant to the group travel market. Estab. 1994. Circ. 15,012. Pays on publication. Byline given. Buys first rights. Editorial lead time 6 months. Submit seasonal material 6 months in advance. Accepts queries by mail, e-mail. Sample copy not available.

Nonfiction: Travel. **Buys 6-12 mss/year.** Query with published clips. Length: 1,200-3,000 words. **Pays $0-500.**

Tips: "Experience in writing for 50+ travel marketplace a bonus."

$ $ $ RV BUSINESS, Affinity Group, Inc., 2575 Vista del Mar Dr., Ventura CA 93001. (800)765-1912. Fax: (805)667-4484. E-mail: rvb@tl.com. **Contact:** John Sullaway, editor. **50% freelance written.** Monthly magazine. "*RV Business* caters to a specific audience of people who manufacture, sell, market, insure, finance, service and supply, components for recreational vehicles." Estab. 1972. Circ. 21,000. **Pays on acceptance.** Publishes ms an average of 2 months after acceptance. Byline given. Offers kill fee. Buys first North American serial rights. Editorial lead time 3 months. Accepts queries by mail, e-mail. Sample copy for free.

Nonfiction: New product, photo feature, industry news and features. "No general articles without specific application to our market." **Buys 300 mss/year.** Query with published clips. Length: 125-2,200 words. **Pays $35-1,500.** Sometimes pays expenses of writers on assignment.

Photos: Send photos with submission. Reviews 35mm transparencies. Buys one-time rights. Offers $25-400/photo. Captions, identification of subjects required.

Columns/Departments: Top of the News (RV industry news), 75-400 words; Business Profiles, 400-500 words; Features (indepth industry features), 800-2,000 words. **Buys 300 mss/year.** Query. **Pays $35-1,500.**

Tips: "Query. Send one or several ideas and a few lines letting us know how you plan to treat it/them. We are always looking for good authors knowledgeable in the RV industry or related industries. We need more articles that are brief, factual, hard hitting and business oriented. Review other publications in the field, including enthusiast magazines."

$ $ SPECIALTY TRAVEL INDEX, Alpine Hansen, 305 San Anselmo Ave., #313, San Anselmo CA 94960. (415)455-1643. Fax: (415)459-4974. E-mail: info@specialtytravel.com. Website: www.specialtytravel.com. Editor: C. Steen Hansen. **Contact:** Susan Kostrzewa, managing editor. **90% freelance written.** Semiannual magazine covering adventure and special interest travel. Estab. 1980. Circ. 45,000. Pays on receipt and acceptance of all materials. Byline given. Buys one-time rights. Editorial lead time 3 month. Submit seasonal material 3 months in advance. Accepts queries by mail, e-mail. Writer's guidelines on request.

Nonfiction: How-to, personal experience, photo feature, travel. **Buys 15 mss/year.** Query. Length: 1,250 words. **Pays $200 minimum.**

Reprints: Send tearsheet. Pays 100% of amount paid for an original article.

Photos: State availability with submission. Reviews 35mm transparencies, 5×7 prints. Negotiates payment individually. Captions, identification of subjects required.

Tips: "Write about group travel and be both creative and factual. The articles should relate to both the travel agent booking the tour and the client who is traveling."

$ STAR SERVICE, Northstar Travel Media, 500 Plaza Dr., Secaucus NJ 07094. (201)902-2000. Fax: (201)319-1797. E-mail: sgordon@ntmllc.com. Website: www.starserviceonline.com. **Contact:** Steven R. Gordon, editor-in-chief. "Eager to work with new/unpublished writers as well as those working from a home base abroad, planning trips that would allow time for hotel reporting, or living in major ports for cruise ships." Worldwide guide to accommodations and cruise ships sold to travel professionals on subscription basis. Estab. 1960. Pays 15 days after publication. Buys all rights. Accepts queries by mail, e-mail, fax. Responds in 1 month to queries. Writer's guidelines and list of available assignments for #10 SASE.

O→ Break in by "being willing to inspect hotels in remote parts of the world."

Nonfiction: Objective, critical evauations of hotels and cruise ships suitable for international travelers, based on personal inspections. Freelance correspondents ordinarily are assigned to update an entire state or country. "Assignment involves on-site inspections of all hotels and cruise ships we review; revising and updating published reports; and reviewing new properties. Qualities needed are thoroughness, precision, perserverance and keen judgment. Solid research skills and powers of observation are crucial. Travel writing experience is highly desirable. Reviews must be colorful, clear, and documented with hotel's brochure, rate sheet, etc. We accept no advertising or payment for listings, so reviews should dispense praise and criticism where deserved." Now accepting queries for destination assignments with deadlines through June 2003. Query should include details on writer's experience in travel and writing, clips, specific forthcoming travel plans, and how much time would be available for hotel or ship inspections. Sponsored trips are acceptable. **Buys 4,500 mss/year. Pays $25/report used.**

▣ The online magazine carries original content not found in the print edition. Contact: Steven R. Gordon.

Tips: "We may require sample hotel or cruise reports on facilities near freelancer's hometown before giving the first assignment. No byline because of sensitive nature of reviews."

$ $ VACATION INDUSTRY REVIEW, Interval International, 6262 Sunset Dr., Miami FL 33143. (305)666-1861 ext. 7238. Fax: (305)668-3408. E-mail: mmcdaniel@interval-intl.com. Website: www.resortdeveloper.com. **Contact:** Matthew McDaniel, editor-in-chief. **30% freelance written.** Quarterly magazine covering leisure lodgings (timeshare resorts, fractionals, and other types of vacation-ownership properties). "The international readership of *VIR* consists of people who develop, finance, market, sell, and manage timeshare resorts and mixed-use projects such as hotels, resorts, and second-home communities with a vacation-ownership component worldwide; and suppliers of products and services to the vacation-ownership industry." Prefers to work with published/established writers. Estab. 1982. Circ. 27,000. Pays on publication. Publishes ms an average of 6 months after acceptance. Byline given. all rights or makes work-for-hire assignments Submit seasonal material 6 months in advance. Accepts queries by mail, e-mail, fax. Responds in 1 month to queries. Sample copy for 9×12 SAE and 3 first-class stamps or online. Writer's guidelines for #10 SASE.

O→ Break in by writing a letter to tell us about yourself, and enclosing 2 or 3 (non-returnable) samples of published work that show you can meet our specialized needs.

Nonfiction: How-to, interview/profile, technical. No consumer travel, hotel, or non-vacation real-estate material. **Buys 6-8 mss/year.** Query with published clips. Length: 1,000-1,500 words. **Pays 30¢/word.**

Photos: Only send photos on assignment. Reviews 35mm transparencies, 5×7 or larger prints, electronic images. Buys one-time rights. Generally offers no additional payment for photos accepted with ms. Captions, identification of subjects required.

Tips: "We *do not* want consumer-oriented destination travel articles. We want articles about the business aspects of the vacation-ownership industry: entrepreneurship, project financing, design and construction, sales and marketing, operations, management—anything that will help our readers plan, build, sell and run a quality timeshare or vacation-ownership property that satisfies the owners/guests and earns a profit for the developer and marketer. We're also interested in owner associations at vacation-ownership resorts (not residential condos). Requires electronic submissions. Query for details."

VETERINARY

$ $ VETERINARY ECONOMICS, Business Solutions for Practicing Veterinarians, Veterinary Healthcare Communications, 8033 Flint, Lenexa KS 66214. (913)492-4300. Fax: (913)492-4157. E-mail: ve@vetmedpub.com. Website: www.vetmedpub.com. Managing Editor: Portia Stewart. **Contact:** Marnette Falley, editor. **20% freelance written.** Monthly magazine covering veterinary medicine. "We address the business concerns and management needs of practicing veterinarians." Estab. 1960. Circ. 52,000. Pays on publication. Publishes ms an average of 3 months after acceptance. Byline given. Buys first rights. Editorial lead time 3 months. Submit seasonal material 3 months in advance. Accepts queries by mail, e-mail, fax. Accepts simultaneous submissions. Responds in 3 months to queries. Sample copy and writer's guidelines free.

Nonfiction: How-to, interview/profile, new product, personal experience. **Buys 24 mss/year.** Query with or without published clips or send complete ms. Length: 1,000-2,000 words. **Pays $50-400.**

Photos: Send photos with submission. Reviews transparencies, prints. Buys one-time rights. Offers no additional payment for photos accepted with ms. Captions, identification of subjects required.

Columns/Departments: Practice Tips (easy, unique business tips), 200-300 words. Send complete ms. **Pays $35.**

Tips: "Among the topics we cover: Veterinary hospital design, client relations, contractual and legal matters, investments, day-to-day management, marketing, personal finances, practice finances, personnel, collections, and taxes. We also cover news and issues within the veterinary profession; for example, articles might cover the effectiveness of Yellow Pages advertising, the growing number of women veterinarians, restrictive-covenant cases, and so on. Freelance writers are encouraged to submit proposals or outlines for articles on these topics. Most articles involve interviews with a nationwide sampling of veterinarians; we will provide the names and phone numbers if necessary. We accept only a small number of unsolicited manuscripts each year; however, we do assign many articles to freelance writers. All material submitted by first-time contributors is read on speculation, and the review process usually takes 12 to 16 weeks. Our style is concise yet conversational, and all manuscripts go through a fairly rigorous editing process. We encourage writers to provide specific examples to illustrate points made throughout their articles."

Scriptwriting

Scriptwriting makes some particular demands, but one thing remains the same for authors of novels, nonfiction books, and scripts: You'll learn to write by rewriting. Draft after draft your skills improve until, hopefully, someone likes your work enough to hire you.

Whether you are writing a video to train doctors in a new surgical technique, alternative theater for an Off-Broadway company, or you want to see your name on the credits of the next Harrison Ford movie, you must perfect both writing and marketing skills. A successful scriptwriter is a talented artist and a savvy business person. But marketing must always be secondary to writing. A mediocre pitch for a great script will still get you farther than a brilliant pitch for a mediocre script. The art and craft of scriptwriting lies in successfully executing inspiration.

Writing a script is a private act. Polishing it may involve more people as you ask friends and fellow writers to take a look at it. The polishing (and rewriting) is completed based on the knowledge of the entire filmmaking team (producers, directors, actors, cinematographers, etc.). The team's experience helps shape the production of a script. Scripts, unlike other forms of writing, are not just meant to be read—they are meant to be produced.

Marketing takes your script public in an effort to find the person willing to give the most of what you want, whether it's money, exposure, or control, in return for your work. There are accepted ground rules to presenting and marketing scripts. Following those guidelines will maximize your chances of getting your work before an audience.

Presenting your script professionally earns a serious consideration of its content. Certain scripts have a definite format and structure. An educational video written in a one-column format, a feature film much longer than 120 pages, or an hour-long TV show that peaks during the first 20 minutes indicates an amateur.

Submission guidelines are similar to those for other types of writing. The initial contact is a one-page query letter, with a brief synopsis and a few lines as to your credits or experience relevant to the subject of your script. Never send a complete manuscript until it is requested. Almost every script sent to a producer, studio, or agent must be accompanied by a release form. Ask the producer or agent for this form when invited to submit the complete script. Always include a SASE if you want your work returned.

Most writers break in with spec scripts, written "for free," which serve as calling cards to show what they can do. These scripts plant the seeds of your professional reputation by making the rounds of influential people looking to hire writers, from advertising executives to movie moguls. Spec scripts are usually written for existing TV shows because people are most likely

For More Information

FORMATTING RESOURCES

- *Formatting & Submitting Your Manuscript*, by Jack and Glenda Neff and Don Prues (Writer's Digest Books).
- *The Complete Guide to Standard Script Formats*, by Hilis R. Cole and Judith H. Haag (CMC Publishing).

to be familiar with the characters and basic structure of an existing series. Also, new writers are rarely trusted with the launch of a new TV series. Most writers must earn their wings by writing for an existing series.

Good writing is more important than a specific plot. Have several spec scripts completed, as a producer will often decide that a story is not right for him, or a similar work is already in production, but will want to know what else you have. Be ready for that invitation.

Writing a script is a matter of learning how to refine your writing so that the work reads as a journey, not a technical manual. The best scripts have concise, visceral scenes that demand to be presented in a specific order and accomplish definite goals.

Educational videos have a message that must be expressed economically and directly, engaging the audience in an entertaining way while maintaining interest in the topic. Character and dialogue that expose a thematic core and engender enthusiasm or involvement in the conflict drive theatrical plays. Cinematic screenplays, while more visually-oriented, are a series of discontinuous scenes stacked to illuminate the characters, the obstacles confronting them, and the resolution they reach.

A script is a difficult medium—written words that sound natural when spoken, characters that are original yet resonate with the audience, believable conflicts and obstacles in tune with the end result.

BUSINESS & EDUCATIONAL WRITING

Scripts for corporate training, business management, and education videos have become as sophisticated as those designed for TV and film, and they carry the additional requirement of conveying specific content. With an audience that is increasingly media literate, anything that looks and feels like a "training film" will be dead in the water. The trick is to produce a script that engages, compels, *and* informs about the topic.

Larger companies often have in-house video production companies, but others rely on freelance writers. Your best bet would be to find work with companies that specialize in making educational and corporate videos while at the same time making yourself known to the creative directors of in-house video staffs in large corporations. Advertising agencies are also a good source of work, as they often are asked by their clients for help in creating films and use freelance writers and producers.

Business and educational videos are a market-driven industry, with material created either in response to a general need or a specific demand. The production company usually identifies a subject and finds the writer. As such, there is a perception that a spec script will not work in this media. While it is true that, as in TV and theatrical films, a writer's spec script is rarely produced, it is a good résumé of qualifications and sample of skills. Your spec script should demonstrate knowledge of this industry's specific format. For the most part, video scripts are written in two columns, video on the left, audio on the right.

Aside from the original script, another opportunity for the writer is the user's guide that often accompanies a video. If you are hired to create the auxiliary material you'll receive a copy of the finished video and write a concurrent text for the teacher or implementor to use.

Budgets are tighter for educational or corporate videos than for theatrical films. You'll want to work closely with the producer to make sure your ideas can be realized within the budget. Your fee will vary with each job, but generally a script written for a production house in a subject area with broad marketability will pay $5,000-7,000. A custom-produced video for a specific company will usually pay less. The pay does not increase exponentially with your experience; large increases come if you choose to direct and produce as well as write.

Information on business and educational script markets listed in the previous edition of *Writer's Market* but not included in this edition can be found in the General Index.

ABS ENTERPRISES, P.O. Box 5127, Evanston IL 60204-5127. (847)982-1414. Fax: (847)982-1418. E-mail: absenterprises@mindspring.com. **Contact:** Alan Soell, owner. "We produce material for all levels of corporate, medical, cable and educational institutions for the purposes of training and development, marketing and meeting presentations. We also are developing programming for the broadcast areas." **75% freelance written.** Buys all rights. Accepts previously produced material. Query with synopsis, résumé. Responds in 2 weeks to queries. **Pays by contractual agreement.**

Needs: Videotapes, multimedia kits, tapes and cassettes, Internet audio, television shows/series. Currently interested in "sports instructional series that could be produced for the consumer market on tennis, gymnastics, bowling, golf, aerobics, health and fitness, cross-country skiing and cycling. Also motivational and self-improvement type videos and film ideas to be produced. These could cover all ages '6-60' and from professional to blue collar jobs. These two areas should be 30 minutes and be timeless in approach for long shelf life. Sports audience, age 25-45; home improvement 25-65. Cable TV needs include the two groups of programming detailed here. We are also looking for documentary work on current isssues, nuclear power, solar power, urban development, senior citizens—but with a new approach."

Tips: "Send a listing of past experience, plus project ideas and expertise. I am looking for innovative approaches to old problems that just don't go away. The approach should be simple and direct so there is immediate audience identification with the presentation. I also like to see a sense of humor used. Trends in the media field include interactive video with disk—for training purposes."

A/V CONCEPTS CORP., 30 Montauk Blvd., Oakdale NY 11769-1399. (631)567-7227. Fax: (631)567-8745. E-mail: editor@edconpublishing.com. Website: www.edconpublishing.com. **Contact:** Laura Solimene, editor. Estab. 1971. Produces supplementary materials for elementary-high school students, either on grade level or in remedial situations. **100% freelance written.** "All scripts/titles are by assignment only. Do not send manscripts." Employs video, book and personal computer media. Buys all rights. Writing samples returned with 9×12 SAE with 5 first-class stamps. Responds in 1 month to outline, 6 weeks on final scripts. **Pays $300 and up.**

Needs: Main concentration in language arts, mathematics and reading. "Manuscripts must be written using our lists of vocabulary words and meet our readability formula requirements. Specific guidelines are devised for each level. Student activities required. Length of manuscript and subjects will vary according to grade level for which material is prepared. Basically, we want material that will motivate people to read."

Tips: "Writers must be highly creative and disciplined. We are interested in high interest/low readability materials. Send writing samples, published or unpublished."

SAM BLATE ASSOCIATES, LLC, 10331 Watkins Mill Dr., Montgomery Village MD 20886-3950. (301)840-2248. Fax: (301)990-0707. E-mail: info@writephotopro.com. Website: www.writephotopro.com. **Contact:** Sam Blate, manager. "Produces educational and multimedia for business, education, institutions and state and federal governments." **Works with 2 local writers/year on a per-project basis—it varies as to business conditions and demand.** Buys first rights when possible. Query with writing samples and SASE for return. Responds in 1 month to queries. **Payment depends on contact with client. Pays some expenses.**

Needs: Scripts on technical, business and outdoor subjects.

Tips: "Writers must have a strong track record of technical and aesthetic excellence."

HAYES SCHOOL PUBLISHING CO., INC., 321 Pennwood Ave., Wilkinsburg PA 15221-3398. (412)371-2373. Fax: (412)371-6408. E-mail: chayes@hayespub.com. Website: www.hayespub.com. **Contact:** Clair N. Hayes III, president. Estab. 1940. Produces material for school teachers and principals, elementary through high school. Also produces charts, workbooks, teacher's handbooks, posters, bulletin board material and reproducible blackline masters (grades K-12). **25% freelance written**. Prefers to work with published/established writers. **Buys 5-10 scripts/year from unpublished/unproduced writers. 100% of scripts produced are unagented submissions.** Buys all rights. Query. Responds in 3 months to scripts. **Pays $25 minimum.**

Needs: Educational materials only. Particularly interested in foreign language material and educational material for elementary school level.

JIST PUBLISHING, 8902 Otis Ave., Indianapolis IN 46216. (317)613-4200. Fax: (317)613-4309. E-mail: info@jist.com. Website: www.jist.com. **Contact:** Kelli Lawrence, video production manager. Estab. 1981. Produces career counseling, motivational materials (youth to adult) that encourage good planning and decision making for a successful future. **Buys 2-3 script(s)/year. Works with 3-4 writer(s)/year.** Buys all rights. Accepts previously produced material. Catalog for SAE with first-class stamps. Query with synopsis. Responds in 3 months to queries.

Needs: Videotapes, multimedia kits. 15-30 minute video VHS tapes on job search materials and related markets.

Tips: "We occasionally farm out scripts and instructor's guides. More important right now, though, is our wish to acquire more titles relevant to our subject matter and audience. We pay a royalty on finished video productions—repackaging, marketing, duplicating and taking care of all other expenses as we acquire the rights to them. Contact us, in writing, for details."

CHARLES RAPP ENTERPRISES, INC., 1650 Broadway, New York NY 10019. (212)247-6646. **Contact:** Howard Rapp, president. Estab. 1954. Produces materials for firms and buyers. **Works with 5 writers/year.** Accepts previously produced material. Submit résumé or sample of writing. Responds in 1 month to queries; 2 months to scripts. **Pays in accordance with WGA standards.**

Needs: Videotapes, treatments; scripts.

PETER SCHLEGER COMPANY, 200 Central Park S., 27-B, New York NY 10019-1415. (212)245-4973. E-mail: pschleger@yahoo.com; eBay name: PRS44. Website: www.schleger.com. **Contact:** Peter Schleger, president. Produces material primarily for employee populations in corporations and nonprofit organizations. "I am also now listing completed tapes on eBay that will be of interest to some segment of the population. Search by seller, PRS44, to get an idea. If you have something you think might work, contact me by mail. Day job: Typical programs are customized workshops or specific individual programs from subjects such as listening and presentation skills to medical benefits communication. No program is longer than 10 minutes. If they need to be, they become shorter modules." Buys all rights. Accepts previously produced material. Submit completed script, résumé, when requested. **Makes outright purchase.**
Needs: Video and printed materials, such as leader's guides, participants manuals, eBay fodder.
Tips: "We are looking to receive and keep on file a 1-page snail-mailed résumé with work experience for future reference. We want communications professionals with a training background or who have written training programs, modules and the like. We want to know of people who have written print material, as well. We do not want to see scripts that have been written and are looking for a producer/director. As we produce video and audio media, we will work with writers who have clients needing these services. We are able to provide programs worldwide and pay handsome commissions for clients you bring to us. See my website."

SPENCER PRODUCTIONS, INC., P.O. Box 2247, Westport CT 06880. (212)865-8829. **Contact:** Bruce Spencer, general manager; Alan Abel, creative director. Produces material for high school students, college students and adults. Occasionally uses freelance writers with considerable talent. Query. Responds in 1 month to queries. **Payment negotiable.**
Needs: Tapes and Cassettes. Satirical material only.
Tips: "For a comprehensive view of our humor requirements, we suggest viewing our feature film production, *Is There Sex After Death* (Rated R), starring Buck Henry. It is available at video stores. Or read *Don't Get Mad ... Get Even* and *How to Thrive on Rejection* by Alan Abel (published by W.W. Norton), both available from Barnes & Noble or Amazon." Also Books-on-Tape. "Send brief synopsis (one page) and outline (2-4 pages)."

TALCO PRODUCTIONS, 279 E. 44th St., New York NY 10017-4354. (212)697-4015. Fax: (212)697-4827. **Contact:** Alan Lawrence, president; Marty Holberton, vice president. Estab. 1968. Produces variety of material for TV, radio, business, trade associations, nonprofit organizations, public relations (chiefly political and current events), etc. Audiences range from young children to senior citizens. **20-40% freelance written. Buys scripts from published/produced writers only.** Buys all rights. No previously produced material. Submit résumé, production history. Responds in 3 weeks to queries. **Makes outright purchase. Pays in accordance with WGA standards. Sometimes pays the expenses of writers on assignment.**
Needs: Films, videotapes, tapes and cassettes, CDs. "We maintain a file of writers and call on those with experience in the same general category as the project in production. *We do not accept unsolicited manuscripts.* We prefer to receive a writer's résumé listing credits. If his/her background merits, we will be in touch when a project seems right." Talco reports that it is doing more public relations-oriented work: Print, videotape and radio.
Tips: "Concentration is now in TV productions. Production budgets will be tighter."

PLAYWRITING

TV and movies are visual media where the words are often less important than the images. Writing plays uses different muscles, different techniques. Plays are built on character and dialogue—words put together to explore and examine characters.

The written word is respected in the theater by producer, cast, director, and even audience, to a degree unparalleled in other formats. While any work involving so many people to reach its final form is in essence a collaboration, it is presided over by the playwright, and changes can be made only with her approval, a power many screenwriters can only envy. If a play is worth producing, it will be produced "as is."

Counterbalancing the greater freedom of expression are the physical limitations inherent in live performance: a single stage, smaller cast, limited sets and lighting, and, most importantly, a strict, smaller budget. These conditions affect not only what but also how you write.

Start writing your play by reading. Reading gives you a feel for how characters are built, layer by layer, word by word, how each interaction presents another facet of a character. Exposition must mean something to the character, and the story must be worth telling for a play to be successful.

Once your play is finished you begin marketing it, which can take as long (or longer) than writing it. Before you begin you must have your script bound (three brads and a cover are fine) and copyrighted at the Copyright Office of the Library of Congress (see Minding the Details for information on obtaining a copyright) or registered with the Writers Guild of America (www.wga.org).

Your first goal will be to get at least a reading of your play. You might be lucky and get a small production. Community theaters or smaller regional houses are good places to start. Volunteer at a local theater. As prop mistress or spotlight operator you will get a sense of how a theater operates, the various elements of presenting a play, and what can and cannot be done, physically as well as dramatically. Personal contacts are important. Get to know the literary manager or artistic director of local theaters, which is the best way to get your script considered for production. Find out about any playwrights' groups in your area through local theaters or the drama departments of nearby colleges and universities. Use your creativity to connect with people that might be able to push your work higher.

For More Information

RESOURCES

- *The Dramatists Sourcebook* (Theatre Communications Group).
- *Grants and Awards Available to American Writers* (PEN American Center).
- NEA Theater Program Fellowship for Playwrights (http://arts.endow.gov), 1100 Pennsylvania Ave. NW, Washington DC 20506. (202)682-5400.
- The Dramatists Guild (www.dramaguild.com), 1501 Broadway, Suite 701, New York NY 10036.
- The International Women's Writing Guild (www.iwwg.com), P.O. Box 810, Gracie Station, New York NY 10028-0082.
- Playwrights' Center (www.pwcenter.org), 2301 Franklin Ave. E., Minneapolis MN 55406-1099. (612)332-7481.
- Northwest Playwrights Guild (www.nwpg.org), 318 SW Palatine Hill Rd., Portland OR 97219.

Contests can be a good way to get noticed. Many playwriting contests offer a prize—at least a staged reading and often a full production. Once you've had a reading or workshop production, set your sights on a small production. Use this as a learning experience. Seeing your play on stage can help you view it more objectively and give you the chance to correct any flaws or inconsistencies. Incorporate any comments and ideas from the actors, director, or even audience, that you feel are on the mark, into revisions of your script.

You can also use a small production as a marketing tool. Keep track of all the press reviews, any interviews with you, members of the cast, or production, and put together a "press kit" for your play that can make the rounds with the script.

After you've been produced you have several directions to take your play. You can aim for a larger commercial production; you can try to get it published; you can seek artistic grants. After you have successfully pursued at least one of those avenues you can look for an agent. Choosing one direction does not rule out pursuing others at the same time.

Good reviews in a smaller production can get you noticed by larger theaters paying higher royalties and doing more ambitious productions. To submit your play to larger theaters you'll put together a submission package. This will include a one-page query letter to the literary manager or dramaturg briefly describing the play. Mention any reviews and give the number of cast members and sets. You will also send a two- to three-page synopsis, a ten-page sample of the most interesting section of your play, your résumé, and the press kit you've assembled. Do not send your complete manuscript until it is requested.

You can also explore publishing your play. *Writer's Market* lists many play publishers. When your script is published, your play will make money while someone else does the marketing. You'll be listed in a catalog that is sent to hundreds or thousands of potential performance spaces—high schools, experimental companies, regional and community theaters—for possible production. You'll receive royalty checks for both performance fees and book sales. In contacting publishers you'll want to send your query letter with the synopsis and reviews.

Once you have been produced on a commercial level, your play has been published, or you have won an important grant, you can start pursuing an agent. This is not always easy. Fewer agents represent playwrights alone—there's more money in movies and TV. No agent will represent an unknown playwright. Having an agent does *not* mean you can sit back and enjoy the ride. You will still need to get out and network, establishing ties with theaters, directors, literary managers, other writers, producers, state art agencies, and publishers, trying to get your work noticed.

There is always the possibility of moving from plays to TV and movies. There is a certain cachet in Hollywood surrounding successful playwrights. The writing style will be different—more visually oriented, less dependent on your words. The money is better, but you will have less command over the work once you've sold that copyright. It seems to be easier for a playwright to cross over to movies than for a screenwriter to cross over to plays.

Information on playwriting markets listed in the previous edition of *Writer's Market* but not included in this edition can be found in the General Index.

A.S.K. THEATER PROJECTS, 11845 W. Olympic Blvd., Suite 1250W, Los Angeles CA 90064. (310)478-3200. Fax: (310)478-5300. E-mail: info@askplay.org. Website: www.askplay.org. **Contact:** Matt Almos, literary manager. Estab. 1989. "A.S.K. offers an energetic, year-round slate of developmental programs, each one designed to address new work for the stage at a different level of its evolution. Please consult our website for more detailed information and submission deadlines." Query with synopsis and sample pages. Responds in 4 months. Obtains no rights. **Pays $150 for staged readings; $500 for writer's retreat.**

• A.S.K. publishes a biannual journal, *Parabasis*, which focuses on news and issues surrounding the art, business and craft of contemporary playwriting. Playwrights are asked to query about proposed articles.

Needs: "We are always looking for adventurous new work by highly original voices. Because our focus is on development opportunities rather than production, we favor works in progress that can still benefit from one of our developmental programs."

Tips: "We are a nonprofit organization dedicated to new plays and playwrights. We do not produce plays for commercial runs, nor do we request any future commitment from the playwright should their play find a production through our reading or workshop programs."

ABINGDON THEATRE CO., 432 W. 42nd St., 4th Floor, New York NY 10036. (212)736-6604. Fax: (212)736-6608. E-mail: alcnyc@aol.com. Website: www.abingdon-nyc.org. **Contact:** Pamela Paul, artistic director. Estab. 1993. **Produces 2 main stage and 3 workshop plays/year.** Professional productions for a general audience. Submit full-length script. No one-acts. Responds in 4 months. Buys variable rights. **Payment is negotiated.** Include SASE for return of manuscript.

Needs: All scripts should be suitable for small stages. No musicals where the story line is not very well-developed and the driving force of the piece.

ACT II PLAYHOUSE, P.O. Box 555, Ambler PA 19002. (215)654-0200. Fax: (215)654-5001. E-mail: act2playhouse@aol.com. Website: www.act2.org. **Contact:** Stephen Blumenthal, literary manager. Estab. 1998. **Produces 5 plays/year.** Query and synopsis. Responds in 1 month. **Payment negotiable.**

Needs: Contemporary comedy, drama, musicals. Full length. 6 character limitation; 1 set or unit set. Does not want period pieces. Limited number of scenes per act.

ACTORS & PLAYWRIGHTS' INITIATIVE, 359 S. Kalamazoo Mall, Suite 205, Kalamazoo MI 49007. (616)343-8090. Fax: (616)343-8450. E-mail: theaterapi@aol.com. **Contact:** Tucker Rafferty, literary manager. Estab. 1989. **Produces 7 main stage selections with 3 'Late Night' experimentals/year.** Professional theatre with resident company. Member of Theatre Communications Group. Season: September to July. Audience is primarily 25-45 liberal professionals and academics. Must write for submission guidelines. *No unsolicited scripts.*

Needs: Character driven, social/political and adaptations. *No musicals.* API is a 120-seat "black box" theatre with flexible staging in a new multi-purpose arts center in downtown Kalamazoo. Cast limit 10; emphasis on character and lighting, not sets.

Tips: "Study the greats—from Sophocles to Mamet."

ACTORS THEATRE OF LOUISVILLE, 316 W. Main St., Louisville KY 40202-4218. (502)584-1265. Fax: (502)561-3300. E-mail: tpalmer@actorstheatre.org. Website: www.actorstheatre.org. **Contact:** Tanya Palmer, literary manager. Estab. 1964. **Produces approximately 30 new plays of varying lengths/year.** Professional productions are

performed for subscription audience from diverse backgrounds. Agented submissions only for full-length plays; open submissions to National Ten-Minute Play Contest (plays 10 pages or less). Responds in 9 months to submissions, mostly in the fall. Buys variable rights. **Offers variable royalty.**
Needs: "We are interested in full-length, one-act and 10-minute plays and in plays of ideas, language, humor, experiment and passion."

ALLEYWAY THEATRE, 1 Curtain Up Alley, Buffalo NY 14202-1911. (716)852-2600. Fax: (716)852-2266. E-mail: email@alleyway.com. Website: alleyway.com. **Contact:** Literary Manager. Estab. 1990. **Produces 4 full-length, 10-15 short plays/year.** Submit complete script; include tape for musicals. Responds in 6 months. Buys first production, credit rights. **Pays 7% royalty plus travel and accommodations for opening.**

- Alleyway Theatre also sponsors the Maxim Mazumdar New Play Competition. See the Contest & Awards section for more information.

Needs: "Theatrical" work as opposed to mainstream TV.
Tips: Sees a trend toward social issue-oriented works. Also interested in "non-traditional" children's pieces. "Plays on social issues should put action of play ahead of political message. Not interested in adapted screen plays. Theatricality and setting are central."

ALLIANCE THEATRE COMPANY, 1280 Peachtree St. NE, Atlanta GA 30309. (404)733-4650. Fax: (404)733-4625. E-mail: ATCLiterary@woodruffcenter.org. Website: www.alliancetheatre.org. **Contact:** Freddie Ashley, literary associate. Estab. 1969. **Produces 11 plays/year.** Professional production for local audience. Query with synopsis or submit through agent. Enclose SASE. Responds in 9 months.
Needs: Full-length scripts and scripts for young audiences (max. length 60 minutes).
Tips: "The Alliance is committed to producing works that speak especially to a culturally diverse community; chief among these are plays with compelling stories or engaging characters told in adventurous or stylish ways. Please submit via mail, e-mail or fax."

ALLIED THEATRE GROUP, 3055 South University Dr., Fort Worth TX 76109-5608. (817)784-9378. Fax: (817)924-9454. E-mail: atg@flash.net. Website: www.alliedtheatre.org. Artistic Director: Jim Covault. **Contact:** Natalie Gaupp, literary associate. Estab. 1979. **Produces 8 plays/year.** "Six plays are performed in our 200-seat regional theatre, in Fort Worth's Stage West; 2 plays are performed as Shakespeare in the Park, in Fort Worth's Trinity Park." Audience varies. Query with synopsis; please submit sample pages in lieu of complete script. Responds in 6 months. Buys negotiable rights. **Payment is negotiated.**
Needs: A variety of plays, including new works as well as classics. No children's theatre contributions, please.
Tips: *Please* submit sample pages rather than the entire script.

AMERICAN CONSERVATORY THEATER, 30 Grant Ave., San Francisco CA 94108-5800. (415)439-2445. Website: www.act-sfbay.org. Artistic Director: Carey Perloff. **Contact:** Paul Walsh, dramaturg. Estab. 1965. **Produces 8 plays/year.** Plays are performed in Geary Theater, a 1,000-seat classic proscenium. No unsolicited scripts.

AMERICAN RENEGADE THEATRE CO., 11136 Magnolia Blvd., North Hollywood CA 91601. (818)763-1834. Fax: (818)763-8082. Website: www.americanrenegade.com. Artistic Director: David A. Cox. **Contact:** Barry Thompson, dramaturg. Estab. 1991. **Produces 6-8 plays/year.** Plays will be performed in an Equity 99 seat plan for adult audiences; 99 seat theater and 45 seat theater in the heart of thriving Noho Arts District. Query with synopsis and SASE. **Pays 6% royalty.**
Needs: "Predominantly naturalistic, contemporary full length, but also one-acts and more experimental material on smaller stage. Mostly American authors and subject matter." No one-person plays.

APPLE TREE THEATRE, 595 Elm Pl., Suite 210, Highland Park IL 60035. (847)432-8223. Fax: (847)432-5214. E-mail: appletreetheatre@yahoo.com. Website: www.appletreetheatre.com. Artistic Director: Eileen Boevers. **Contact:** Literary Assistant. Estab. 1983. **Produces 5 plays/year.** "Professional productions intended for an adult audience mix of subscriber base and single-ticket holders. Our subscriber base is extremely theater-savvy and intellectual." Submit query and synopsis, along with tapes for musicals. Rights obtained vary. **Pays variable royalty.** Return SASE submissions only if requested.
Needs: "We produce a mixture of musicals, dramas, classical, contemporary and comedies. Length: 90 minutes-2 ½ hours. Small space, unit set required. No fly space, 3¼ thrust stage. Maximum actors 15.
Tips: "No farces or large-scale musicals. Theater needs small shows with one-unit sets due to financial concerns. Also note the desire for non-linear pieces that break new ground. *Please do not submit unsolicited manuscripts—send letter and description*; if we want more, we will request it."

ARENA PLAYERS REPERTORY COMPANY, 296 Route 109, East Farmingdale NY 11735. (516)293-0674. Fax: (516)777-8688. E-mail: arena10@aol.com. Producer/Director: Frederic De Feis. **Contact:** Audrey Perry, production coordinator. Estab. 1954. **Produces 19 (at least 1 new) plays/year.** Professional production on either Arena Players' Main Stage or Second Stage Theatres. Intended for a conventional, middle-class audience. Query with synopsis or submit complete ms. Responds in 1 year. **Pays flat fee of $400-600.**
Needs: Main Stage season consists of Neil Simon-type comedies, Christie-esque mysteries and contemporary dramas. Prefers single set plays with a minimal cast (2 to 8 people). Only full-length plays will be considered.
Tips: No one-acts and musicals.

ARENA STAGE, 1101 Sixth St. SW, Washington DC 20024. (202)554-9066. Fax: (202)488-4056. E-mail: vworthington@arenastage.org. Website: www.arenastage.org. Artistic Director: Molly Smith. **Contact:** Cathy Madison, literary manager. Estab. 1950. **Plus various reading series in the Old Vat Room.** This is a professional theater. The Kreeger Theater seats 514 (modified thrust stage). The Fichandler Stage seats 827 (arena stage). The Old Vat Room seats 110 (cabaret stage). Accepts unsolicited scripts from Washington, DC, Maryland and Virginia writers only; all other writers should send synopsis, bio, 10-page diologue sample and letter of inquiry. Responds in 1 week to queries, 1 year to scripts.
Needs: Full length comedy, drama, satire, musicals, translations, adaptations, solo pieces. Special interests include unrpdocued works, plays for a multicultural company, plays by women, writers of color, physically disabled writers and other "non-mainstream" artists. We prefer cast sizes under 10, unless the play is a musical.
Tips: "Best for writer if he/she is agent-represented."

ARIZONA THEATRE COMPANY, P.O. Box 1631, Tucson AZ 85702. (520)884-8210. Fax: (520)628-9129. E-mail: swyer@aztheatreco.org. Website: www.aztheatreco.org. **Contact:** Samantha K. Wyer, associate artistic director. Estab. 1966. **Produces 6 plays/year.** Arizona Theatre Company is the State Theatre of Arizona and plans the season with the population of the state in mind. Agented submissions only, though Arizona writers may submit unsolicited scripts. Responds in 6 months. **Payment negotiated.**
Needs: Full length plays of a variety of genres and topics and full length musicals. No one-acts.
Tips: "Please include in the cover letter a bit about your current situation and goals. It helps in responding to plays."

ARKANSAS REPERTORY THEATRE, P.O. Box 110, Little Rock AR 72203-0110. (501)378-0445. Fax: (501)378-0012. E-mail: therep@alltel.net. Website: www.therep.org. Producing Director: Robert Hupp. **Contact:** Brady Mooy, literary manager. Estab. 1976. **Produces 8-10 plays/year.** "Professional productions for adult audiences. No kids' shows please." Query and synopsis. Responds in 6 months. Keeps 5% rights for 5 years. **Payment varies on the script, number of performances, if it was commissioned, which stage it's produced on.**
Needs: "We produce plays for a general adult audience. We do everything from intense dramas to farce. Only full-length plays." "We look for shows with less than 10 characters, but we have done epics as well. Smaller casts are preferred."
Tips: No one-acts or children's shows. Playwrights are invited to enter the Arkansas Repertory Theatre Competition for New American Comedy. See the Contests & Awards section for details.

ART STATION THEATRE, 5384 Manor Dr., P.O. Box 1998, Stone Mountain GA 30086. (770)469-1105. Fax: (770)469-0355. E-mail: info@artstation.org. Website: www.artstation.org. **Contact:** Jon Goldstein, literary manager. Estab. 1986. **Produces 5 plays/year.** "ART Station Theatre is a professional theater located in a contemporary arts center in Stone Mountain, which is part of Metro Atlanta." Audience consists of middle-aged to senior, suburban patrons. Query with synopsis or submit complete ms. Responds in 6 months. **Pays 5-7% royalty.**
Needs: Full length comedy, drama and musicals, preferably relating to the human condition in the contemporary South. Cast size no greater than 6.

ARTISTS REPERTORY THEATRE, 1516 S.W. Alder St., Portland OR 97205. E-mail: allen@artistsrep.org. Website: www.artistsrep.org. **Contact:** Allen Nause, artistic director. Estab. 1982. **Produces 6 plays/year.** Plays performed in professional theater with a subscriber-based audience. Send synopsis, sample and résumé. No unsolicited mss accepted. Responds in 6 months. **Pays royalty.**
Needs: "Full-length, hard-hitting, emotional, intimate, actor-oriented shows with small casts (rarely exceeds 10-13, usually 2-7). Language and subject matter are not a problem." No one-acts or children's scripts.

ATTIC THEATRE, 2245 W. 25th St., Los Angeles CA 90018. (323)734-8977. E-mail: atticthheatre@aol.com. Website: www.attictheatre.org. Artistic Director: James Carey. **Contact:** Literary Manager. Estab. 1987. **Produces 3 plays/year.** "We are considered semi-professional. We are based in Los Angeles and play to industry and regular joes. We use professional actors; however, our house is very small, and the salaries we pay, including the royalties are very small because of that." Send query and synopsis or check out website. Responds in 4 months. Buys first producer rights. **Payment is negotiated on a case by case basis.**
Needs: "We will consider any type of play except musicals and large cast historical pieces with multiple hard sets." "Plays featuring elderly casts cannot be done because of our acting ages."
Tips: "Please send an SASE and read our guidelines on the website. Follow all the directions."

BAILIWICK REPERTORY, Bailiwick Arts Center, 1229 W. Belmont Ave., Chicago IL 60657-3205. (773)883-1090. Fax: (773)883-2017. E-mail: bailiwickr@aol.com. Website: www.bailiwick.org. **Contact:** David Zak, artistic director. Estab. 1982. **Produces 5 mainstage plays (classic and newly commissioned) each year; 50 one-acts in annual Directors Festival.** Pride Performance Series (gay and lesbian), includes one-acts, poetry, workshops, and staged adaptations of prose. Submit year-round. One-act play fest runs July-August. Responds in 9 months for full-length only. **Pays 6% royalty.**
Needs: "We need daring scripts that break the mold. Large casts or musicals are OK. Creative staging solutions are a must."
Tips: "Know the rules, then break them creatively and *boldly*! Please send SASE for manuscript submission guidelines *before you submit* or get manuscript guidelines at our website."

BAKER'S PLAYS PUBLISHING CO., P.O. Box 699222, Quincy MA 02269-9222. (617)745-0805. Fax: (617)745-9891. E-mail: 411@bakersplays.com. Website: www.bakersplays.com. **Contact:** John B. Welch, chief editor. Estab. 1845. **Publishes 20-30 straight plays and musicals. Works with 2-3 unpublished/unproduced writers annually. 80% freelance written. 75% of scripts unagented submissions**. Plays performed by amateur groups, high schools, children's theater, churches and community theater groups. Submit complete script with news clippings, résumé. Submit complete cassette of music with musical submissions. Responds in 4 months. **Payment varies; negotiated royalty split of production fees; 10% book royalty.**

Needs: "We are finding strong support in our new division—plays from young authors featuring contemporary pieces for high school production."

Tips: "We are particularly interested in adaptation of lesser-known folk tales from around the world. Also of interest are plays which feature a multicultural cast and theme. Collections of one-act plays for children and young adults tend to do very well. Also, high school students: Write for guidelines for our High School Playwriting Contest."

BARTER THEATRE, P.O. Box 867, Abingdon VA 24212-0867. (276)628-2281. Fax: (276)628-4551. E-mail: barter@naxs.com. Website: www.bartertheatre.com. **Contact:** Debbie Addison, associate artistic director. Estab. 1933. **Produces 17 plays/year.** Plays performed in residency at 2 facilities, a 500-seat proscenium theater and a smaller 150-seat flexible theater. "Our plays are intended for diversified audiences of all ages." Submit synopsis and dialogue sample only with SASE. Responds in 9 months. **Pays negotiable royalty.**

- Barter Theatre often premieres new works.

Needs: "We are looking for good plays, comedies and dramas, that entertain and are relevant; plays that comment on the times and mankind; plays that are universal. We prefer casts of 4-12, single or unit set. Hard language can be a factor."

Tips: "Looking for material that can appeal to a diverse audience and have a strong family audience."

N BILINGUAL FOUNDATION OF THE ARTS, 421 North Ave. 19, Los Angeles CA 90031. (323)225-4044. Fax: (323)225-1250. E-mail: bfa2001@earthlink.net. Artistic Director: Margarita Galban. **Contact:** Estela Scarlata, associate producer/production manager. Estab. 1973. **Produces 4 plays plus 6-9 staged readings/year.** "Productions are presented at home theater in Los Angeles, California. Our audiences are largely Hispanic and all productions are performed in English and Spanish. The Bilingual Foundation of the Arts produces plays in order to promote the rich heritage of Hispanic history and culture. Though our plays must be Hispanic in theme, we reach out to the entire community." Send complete script. Responds in 6 months. Rights negotiable. **Pays royalty.**

Needs: "Plays must be Hispanic in theme. Comedy, drama, light music, children's theater, etc., are accepted for consideration. More plays in Spanish are needed. Theater is 99-seater, no flies."

BLOOMSBURG THEATRE ENSEMBLE, Box 66, Bloomsburg PA 17815. (570)784-5530. Fax: (570)784-4912. Ensemble Director: James Goode. **Contact:** Play Section Chair. Estab. 1979. **Produces 6 plays/year.** Professional productions for a non-urban audience. Query and synopsis. Responds in 9 months. Buys negotiable rights **Pays 6-9% royalty. Pays $50-70 per performance.** "Because of our non-urban location, we strive to expose our audience to a broad range of theatre—both classical and contemporary. We are drawn to language and ideas and to plays that resonate in our community. We are most in need of articulate comedies and cast sizes under 6."

Tips: "Because of our non-urban setting we are less interested in plays that focus on dilemmas of city life in particular. Most of the comedies we read are cynical. Many plays we read would make better film scripts; static/relationship-heavy scripts that do not use the 'theatricality' of the theatre to an advantage."

BOARSHEAD THEATER, 425 S. Grand Ave., Lansing MI 48933. Website: www.boarshead.org. **Contact:** John Peakes, founding art director. Estab. 1966. **Produces 8 plays/year (6 mainstage, 2 Young People's Theater productions inhouse), 4 or 5 staged readings.** Mainstage Actors' Equity Association company; also Youth Theater—touring to schools by our intern company. Query with one-page synopsis, cast list (with descriptions), 5-10 pages of representative dialogue, description of setting, special needs and self-addressed postcard for our response. Responds in 1 month to queries and synopsis. Full scripts (if requested) in 8 months. **Pays royalty for mainstage productions, transport/per diem for staged readings.**

Needs: Thrust stage. Cast usually 8 or less; occasionally up to 20; one-acts. Prefer staging which depends on theatricality rather than multiple sets. "No musicals considered. Send full length plays (only) to John Peakes, founding art director; no one-acts. For Young People's Theater, send one-act plays (only); 4-5 characters."

Tips: Plays should not have multiple realistic sets—too many scripts read like film scripts. Focus on intelligence, theatricality, crisp, engaging humorous dialogue. "Write a good play and prove it in a precise 10 pages of great dialogue. Also, don't tape your submission so it takes 3 minutes to open. Puts me in a negative mood."

N CALIFORNIA THEATER CENTER, P.O. Box 2007, Sunnyvale CA 94087. (408)245-2978. Fax: (408)245-0235. E-mail: ctc@ctcinc.org. Website: www.ctcing.org. **Contact:** Will Huddleston, literary manager/resident director. Estab. 1976. **Produces 15 plays/year.** "Plays are for young audiences in both our home theater and for tour." Query and synopsis. Responds in 6 months. **Negotiates set fee.**

Needs: All plays must be suitable for young audiences, must be around 1 hour in length. Cast sizes vary. Many shows require touring sets.

Tips: "Almost all new plays we do are for young audiences, one-acts with fairly broad appeal, not over an hour in length, with mixed casts of two to eight adult, professional actors. We read plays for all ages, though plays for kindergarten through fourth grade have the best chance of being chosen. Plays with memorable music are especially looked for, as well as plays based upon literary works or historical material young people know from school. Serious plays written in the style of psychological realism must be especially well written. Satires and parodies are difficult for our audiences unless they are based upon material familiar to children. Anything "cute" should be avoided. In the summer we seek large cast plays that can be performed entirely by children in our Summer Conservatory programs. We particularly look for plays that can do well in difficult venues, such as high school gymnasiums, multi-purpose rooms, etc."

N **CENTER STAGE**, 700 N. Calvert St., Baltimore MD 21202-3686. (410)685-3200. **Contact:** Charlotte Standt, resident dramaturg. Estab. 1963. **Produces 6-8 plays/year.** LORT 'C' and LORT 'D' theaters. Audience is both subscription and single-ticket. Wide-ranging audience profile. Query with synopsis, 10 sample pages and résumé, or submit through agent. Responds in 3 months. Rights negotiated. **Payment negotiated.**
Needs: Produces dramas, comedies, musical theater works. "Casts over 12 would give us pause. Be inventive, theatrical, not precious; we like plays with vigorous language and stage image. Domestic naturalism is discouraged; strong political or social interests are encouraged." No one-act plays. "Plays about bourgeois adultery, life in the suburbs, Amelia Earhart, Alzheimer's, mid-life crises, 'wacky southerners', fear of intimacy, Hemingway, Bible stories, backstage life, are unacceptable, as are spoofs and mysteries."
Tips: "We are interested in reading adaptations and translations as well as original work. Strong interest in plays about the African-American experience."

CENTRE STAGE—SOUTH CAROLINA!, P.O. Box 8451, Greenville SC 29604-8451. (864)233-6733. Fax: (864)233-3901. E-mail: information@centrestage.org. Website: www.centrestage.org. **Contact:** Terri Eisman, Play Reading Committee chair. Estab. 1983. **Produces 10 plays/year.** "We are a TCG professional theater. Our mainstage targets all ages." Query with synopsis or send complete ms. Reports in 2 months; written acknowledgement sent on receipt. **Pays negotiable royalty.**
Needs: "Our productions include all types—musicals, comedies, dramas. We produce for entertainment, education and issue themes." Seeking full-length plays that have not had prior production; can be one-act if the material is fully developed, i.e. "How I Learned to Drive" or "Wit." Cast size 1-25. Staging: Single set or revolve. Props: Some limitation, particularly with extra large prop requirements.
Tips: No restrictions on material. Sees "a shift in what attracts today's audiences, and what competes for their time. The more uplifting a production is, the larger the audience that is attracted to it."

CHILDREN'S STORY SCRIPTS, Baymax Productions, 2219 W. Olive Ave., PMB 130, Burbank CA 91506-2648. (818)787-5584. E-mail: baymax@earthlink.net. **Contact:** Deedra Bebout, editor. Estab. 1990. "Our audience consists of children, grades K-8 (5-13-year-olds)." Send complete script with SASE. Responds in 1 month. Licenses all rights to story; author retains copyright. **Pays graduated royalty based on sales.**
Needs: "We add new titles as we find appropriate stories. We look for stories which are fun for kids to read, involve a number of readers throughout, and dovetail with school subjects. This is a must! Not life lessons...school subjects."
Tips: "The scripts are not like theatrical scripts. They combine dialogue and prose narration, á la Readers Theatre. If a writer shows promise, we'll work with him. Our most important goal is to benefit children. We want stories that bring alive subjects studied in classrooms. Facts must be worked unobtrusively into the story—the story has to be fun for the kids to read. Send #10 SASE for guidelines with samples. We do not respond to submissions without SASE."

CHILDSPLAY, INC., P.O. Box 517, Tempe AZ 85280. (480)858-2127. Fax: (480)350-8584. E-mail: info@childsplayaz.org. Website: childsplayaz.org. **Contact:** Graham Whitehead, associate artistic director. Estab. 1978. **Produces 5-6 plays/year.** "Professional touring and in-house productions for youth and family audiences." Submit synopsis, character descriptions and 7- to 10-page dialogue sample. Responds in 6 months. **Pays royalty of $20-35/performance (touring) or pays $3,000-8,000 commission. Holds a small percentage of royalties on commissioned work for 3-5 years.**
Needs: Seeking *theatrical* plays on a wide range of contemporary topics. "Our biggest market is K-6. We need intelligent theatrical pieces for this age group that meet touring requirements and have the flexibility for in-house staging. The company has a reputation, built up over 25 years, of maintaining a strong aesthetic. We need scripts that respect the audience's intelligence and support their rights to dream and to have their concerns explored. Innovative, theatrical and *small* is a constant need." Touring shows limited to 5-6 actors; in-house shows limited to 6-10 actors.
Tips: No traditionally-handled fairy tales. "Theater for young people is growing up and is able to speak to youth and adults. The material *must* respect the artistry of the theater and the intelligence of our audience. Our most important goal is to benefit children. If you wish your materials returned send SASE."

N **CIRCLE THEATRE**, 2015 S. 60th St., Omaha NE 68106. (402)553-4715. E-mail: dmarr10523@aol.com. **Contact:** Doug Marr, artistic director. Estab. 1983. **Produces 5 plays/year.** Professional productions, general audience. Query and synopsis. Responds in 2 months. **Pays $15-30 per performance.**
Needs: Comedies, dramas, musicals—original unproduced works. Full length, all styles/topics. Small casts, simple sets.

CIRCUIT PLAYHOUSE/PLAYHOUSE ON THE SQUARE, 51 S. Cooper, Memphis TN 38104. (901)725-0776. **Contact:** Jackie Nichols, artistic director. **Produces 16 plays/year. 100% of scripts unagented submissions. Works with 1 unpublished/unproduced writer/year**. Professional plays performed for the Memphis/Mid-South area. Member of the Theatre Communications Group. Contest held each fall. Submit complete script. Responds in 6 months. Buys percentage of royalty rights for 2 years. **Pays $500.**
Needs: All types; limited to single or unit sets. Casts of 20 or fewer.

Tips: "Each play is read by three readers through the extended length of time a script is kept. Preference is given to scripts for the southeastern region of the U.S."

I.E. CLARK PUBLICATIONS, P.O. Box 246, Schulenburg TX 78956-0246. Website: www.ieclark.com. **Contact:** Donna Cozzaglio, general manager. Estab. 1956. Publishes 10-15 plays/year for educational theater, children's theater, religious theater, regional professional theater and community theater. Publishes unagented submissions. Catalog for $3. Writer's guidelines for #10 SASE. Submit complete script, 1 at a time with SASE. Responds in 6 months. Buys all available rights; "We serve as an agency as well as a publisher." **Pays standard book and performance royalty, amount and percentages dependent upon type and marketability of play.**

- "One of our specialties is "Young Adult Awareness Drama"—plays for ages 13 to 25 dealing with sex, drugs, popularity, juvenile, crime, and other problems of young adults. We also need plays for children's theatre, especially dramatizations of children's classic literature."

Needs: "We are interested in plays of all types—short or long. Audiotapes of music or videotapes of a performance are requested with submissions of musicals. We require that a play has been produced (directed by someone other than the author); photos, videos and reviews of the production are helpful. No limitations in cast, props, staging, etc. Plays with only one or two characters are difficult to sell. We insist on literary quality. We like plays that give new interpretations and understanding of human nature. Correct spelling, punctuation and grammar (befitting the characters, of course) impress our editors."

Tips: Publishes plays only. "Entertainment value and a sense of moral responsibility seem to be returning as essential qualities of a good play script. The era of glorifying the negative elements of society seems to be fading rapidly. Literary quality, entertainment value and good craftsmanship rank in that order as the characteristics of a good script in our opinion. 'Literary quality' means that the play must—in beautiful, distinctive, and un-trite language—say something; preferably something new and important concerning man's relations with his fellow man or God; and these 'lessons in living' must be presented in an intelligent, believable and creative manner. Plays for children's theater are tending more toward realism and childhood problems, but fantasy and dramatization of fairy tales are also needed."

CLEVELAND PLAY HOUSE, 8500 Euclid Ave., Cleveland OH 44106. E-mail: sgordon@clevelandplayhouse.com. Website: www.clevelandplayhouse.com. Artistic Director: Peter Hackett. **Contact:** Seth Gordon, director of new play development. Estab. 1915. **Produces 10 plays/year.** "We have five theatres, 100-550 seats." 10 page sample with synopsis is best introduction. Responds in 6 months. **Payment is negotiable.**

Needs: All styles and topics of new plays.

CLEVELAND PUBLIC THEATRE, 6415 Detroit Ave., Cleveland OH 44102. (216)631-2727. Fax: (216)631-2575. E-mail: cpt@en.com. Website: www.clevelandartists.net/cpt. **Contact:** Literary Manager. Estab. 1982. **Produces 6-8 full productions/year.** Also sponsors biennial Festival of New Plays. 150-seat "Main Stage" and 700-seat Gordon Square Theatre. "Our audience believes that art touches your heart and your nerve endings." Query with synopsis and dialogue sample for full season. Rights negotiable. **Pays $15-100 per performance.**

Needs: Poetic, experimental, avant-garde, political, multicultural works that need a stage (not a camera); interdisciplinary cutting-edge work (dance/performance art/music/visual); works that stretch the imagination and conventional boundaries. CPT presents performed work that addresses the issues and challenges of modern life. Particular focus is given to alternative, experimental, poetic, political works, with particular attention to those created by women, people of color, gays/lesbians.

Tips: "No conventional comedies, musicals, adaptations, children's plays—if you think Samuel French would love it, we probably won't. No TV sitcoms or soaps masquerading as theater. Theater is *not* TV or films. Learn the impact of what live bodies do to an audience in the same room. We are particularly interested in artists from our region who can grow with us on a longterm basis."

COLONY THEATRE COMPANY, (formerly Colony Studio Theatre), 555 N. Third St., Burbank CA 91502-1103. Website: www.colonytheatre.org. **Contact:** Wayne Liebman, literary manager. **Produces 6 plays/year.** Professional 276-seat theater with thrust stage. Casts from resident company of professional actors. Send SASE for query guidelines or check online. Responds only if interested. Negotiated rights. **Pays royalty for each performance.**

Needs: Full length (90-120 minutes) with a cast of 4-12. No musicals or experimental works.

Tips: "We seek works of theatrical imagination and emotional resonance on universal themes."

CONFRONTATION, A Literary Journal, C.W. Post of Long Island University, Brookville NY 11548-1300. (516)299-2720. Fax: (516)299-2735. E-mail: mtucker@liu.edu. **Contact:** Martin Tucker, editor. Estab. 1968. **Publishes 2 plays/year.** Submit complete script. Responds in 2 months. Obtains first serial and reprint rights. **Pays up to $50.**

Needs: "We have an annual one-act play contest, open to all forms and styles. Award is $200 and publication."

CONTEMPORARY DRAMA SERVICE, Meriwether Publishing Ltd., P.O. Box 7710, Colorado Springs CO 80933. Fax: (719)594-9916. E-mail: merpcds@aol.com. Website: www.contemporarydrama.com. Editor: Arthur Zapel. **Contact:** Theodore Zapel, associate editor. Estab. 1969. **Publishes 50-60 plays/year.** "We are specialists in theater arts books and plays for middle grades, high schools and colleges. We publish textbooks for drama courses of all types. We also publish for mainline liturgical churches—drama activities for church holidays, youth activities and fundraising entertainments. These may be plays, musicals or drama-related books." Query with synopsis or submit complete script. Responds in 6 weeks. Obtains either amateur or all rights. **Pays 10% royalty or negotiates purchase.**

• Contemporary Drama Service is now looking for play or musical adaptations of classic stories by famous authors and playwrights. Also looking for parodies of famous movies or historical and/or fictional characters, i.e. Robin Hood, Rip Van Winkle, Buffalo Bill, Huckleberry Finn.

Needs: "Most of the plays we publish are one-acts, 15-45 minutes in length. We also publish full-length two-act musicals or three-act plays 90 minutes in length. We prefer comedies. Musical plays must have name appeal either by prestige author or prestige title adaptation. Musical shows should have large casts for 20 to 25 performers. Comedy sketches, monologues and plays are welcomed. We prefer simple staging appropriate to middle school, high school, college or church performance. We like playwrights who see the world with a sense of humor. Offbeat themes and treatments are accepted if the playwright can sustain a light touch. In documentary or religious plays we look for good research and authenticity. We are publishing many scenebooks for actors (which can be anthologies of great works excerpts), scenebooks on special themes and speech and theatrical arts textbooks. We also publish many books of monologs for young performers. We are especially interested in authority-books on a variety of theater-related subjects."

Tips: Contemporary Drama Service is looking for creative books on comedy, monologs, staging amateur theatricals and Christian youth activities. "Our writers are usually highly experienced in theatre as teachers or performers. We welcome books that reflect their experience and special knowledge. Any good comedy writer of monologs and short scenes will find a home with us."

[A] **A CONTEMPORARY THEATRE**, 700 Union St., Seattle WA 98101. (206)292-7660. Fax: (206)292-7670. Website: www.acttheatre.org. **Contact:** Kurt Beattie, associate art director. Estab. 1965. **Produces 6-7 mainstage plays/year.** "Our plays are performed in our 2 mainstages and third smaller space for our local Seattle audience. Sometimes our world premieres move onto other cities to play at regional theatres across the country." *Agented submissions only* or through theatre professional's recommendation. Query and synopsis only for Northwest playwrights. Responds in 6 months. **Pays 5-10% royalty.**

Needs: "We produce full length plays of varying sizes and shapes: anywhere from a one person play in our smaller house to a much larger ensemble. We tend to produce contemporary work, as the title of our theatre suggests; stories with current concerns. We are open to casting concerns—we often try to produce a 'big play' (over 10 characters) in every season, though we do have budgetary restrictions, and cannot produce more than one a season."

Tips: "At times it feels that 'telling the story' becomes less of a concern and gets subsumed by how it's told. At ACT, we look for the compelling story, and want to be compelled and brought in. Often we find this gets lost in stylistic grandiosity."

[N] **CREEDE REPERTORY THEATRE**, P.O. Box 269, Creede CO 81130-0269. (719)658-2541. **Contact:** Maurice Lemee, director. Estab. 1966. **Produces 6 plays/year.** Plays performed for a smaller audience. Query and synopsis. Responds in 1 year. **Royalties negotiated with each author—paid on a per performance basis.**

Needs: One-act children's scripts. Special consideration given to plays focusing on the cultures and history of the American West and Southwest.

Tips: "We seek new adaptations of classical or older works as well as original scripts."

[N] **MICHAEL D. CUPP**, P.O. Box 256, Dept. SWV, Hazelhurst WI 54531-0256. (715)356-7173 ext. 958. Fax: (715)356-1851. E-mail: nlplays@newnorth.net. **Contact:** Ed Whitehead, artistic director. Estab. 1976. **Produces 6 plays/year.** Professional Summer Theatre & Professional Dinner Theatre. Audience mostly senior-family oriented. Query with synopsis, cast breakdown and set requirements. Responds in 6 months. **Pays royalty, per performance or makes outright purchase.**

Needs: Comedies (2 hours), children's theatre (1 hour). Prefers cost efficient productions.

Tips: No sexy, racy or lewd productions, no dramas. "Remember you are writing for the audience. Be commercial."

DETROIT REPERTORY THEATRE, 13103 Woodrow Wilson, Detroit MI 48238-3686. (313)868-1347. Fax: (313)868-1705. **Contact:** Barbara Busby, literary manager. Estab. 1957. **Produces 4 plays/year.** Professional theater, 194 seats operating on A.E.A. SPT contract Detroit metropolitan area. Submit complete ms in bound folder, cast list and description with SASE. Responds in 6 months. **Pays royalty.**

Needs: Wants issue-oriented works. Cast limited to no more than 7 characters. No musicals or one-act plays.

DIVERSIONARY THEATRE, 4545 Park Blvd., San Diego CA 92116. (619)220-6830. **Contact:** Chuck Zito, executive director. Estab. 1985. **Produces 5 plays/year.** Non-professional productions for primarily gay, lesbian, bisexual and transgender audiences. Not accepting unsolicited scripts at this time.

DIXON PLACE, 309 E. 26th St., New York NY 10010-1902. (212)532-1546. Fax: (212)532-1094. E-mail: contact@dixonplace.org. Website: www.dixonplace.org. **Contact:** Ellie Covan, executive director. Estab. 1986. **Produces 12 plays/year.** "We present play readings at our downtown, off-off Broadway performance venue." Audience is usually made up of supporters of the writer and other artists. Submit 10-page script sample with synopsis. Responds in 6 months. **Pays flat fee.**

Needs: Musicals, one-acts, full-length plays, not already read or workshopped in New York. Particularly interested in non-traditional, either in character, content, structure and/or themes. "We almost never produce kitchen sink, soap opera-style plays about AIDS, coming out, unhappy love affairs, getting sober or lesbian parenting. We regularly present new works, plays with innovative structure, multi-ethnic content, non-naturalistic dialogue, irreverent musicals and the elegantly bizarre. We are an established performance venue with a very diverse audience. We have a reputation for bringing our audience the unexpected."

🄰 **DORSET THEATRE FESTIVAL**, Box 510, Dorset VT 05251-0510. (802)867-2223. Fax: (802)867-0144. E-mail: theatre@sover.net. Website: www.theatredirectories.com. **Contact:** John Nassivera, producing artistic director. Estab. 1976. **Produces 5 plays/year (1 a new work).** "Our plays will be performed in our Equity summer stock theatre and are intended for a sophisticated community." Agented submissions only. Responds in 6 months. **Rights and compensation negotiated.**

Needs: "Looking for full-length contemporary American comedy or drama." Limited to a cast of 6.

Tips: "Language and subject matter appropriate to general audience."

DRAMATIC PUBLISHING, 311 Washington St., Woodstock IL 60098. (815)338-7170. Fax: (815)338-8981. E-mail: plays@dramaticpublishing.com. Website: www.dramaticpublishing.com. **Contact:** Linda Habjan, editor. **Publishes 40-50 titles/year.** Publishes paperback acting editions of original plays, musicals, adaptations and translations. **Receives 250-500 queries and 600 mss/year.** Catalog and script guidelines free. **Pays 10% royalty on scripts; performance royalty varies.**

Needs: Interested in playscripts appropriate for children, middle and high schools, colleges, community, stock and professional theaters. Send full ms.

Tips: "We publish all kinds of plays for the professional stock and amateur market: full lengths, one acts, children's plays, musicals, adaptations."

DRAMATICS MAGAZINE, 2343 Auburn Ave., Cincinnati OH 45219. (513)421-3900. Fax: (513)421-7077. E-mail: dcorathers@etassoc.org. Website: www.cdta.org. **Contact:** Don Corathers, editor. Estab. 1929. **Publishes 7 plays/year.** For high school theater students and teachers. Submit complete script. Responds in 3 months. Buys first North American serial rights only.

Needs: "We are seeking one-acts to full-lengths that can be produced in an educational theater setting." No musicals.

Tips: "No melodrama, farce, children's theater, or cheap knock-offs of TV sitcoms or movies. Fewer writers are taking the time to learn the conventions of theater—what makes a piece work on stage, as opposed to film and television—and their scripts show it. We're always looking for good interviews with working theatre professionals."

ELDRIDGE PUBLISHING CO., P.O. Box 1595, Venice FL 34284. (941)496-4679. Fax: (941)493-9680. E-mail: info@histage.com. Website: www.histage.com. Editor: Susan Shore. Estab. 1906. **Publishes 100-110 new plays/year for junior high, senior high, church and community audience.** Query with synopsis (acceptable) or submit complete ms (preferred). Please send cassette tapes with any musicals. Responds in 2 months. Buys All rights. **Pays 50% royalties and 10% copy sales in general market. Makes outright purchase of $200-600 in religious market.**

Needs: "We are most interested in full-length plays and musicals for our school and community theater market. Nothing lower than junior high level, please. We always love comedies but also look for serious, high caliber plays reflective of today's sophisticated students. We also need one-acts and plays for children's theater. In addition, in our religious market we're always searching for holiday or any time plays."

Tips: "Submissions are welcomed at any time. Authors are paid royalties twice a year. They receive complimentary copies of their published plays, the annual catalog and 50% discount if buying additional copies."

🄰 **THE EMPTY SPACE THEATRE**, 3509 Fremont Ave. N, Seattle WA 98103. (206)547-7633. Fax: (206)547-7635. E-mail: literary@emptyspace.org. Website: www.emptyspace.org. **Contact:** Adam Greenfield, literary manager (literary@emptyspace.org). Estab. 1970. **Produces 5 plays/year between October and July.** Professional productions. *Agented submissions only*, unless a writer is from the Northwest. Reponds to queries in 2 months, scripts in 4 months **Typically, we ask for something close to 5% of the author's royalties for 5 years. Pays 6-10% royalty or $2,500-10,000 playwright commission.**

Needs: Full-length plays, full-length musicals, solo pieces, translations, adaptations. "The Empty Space strives to make theatre an event—bold, provocative, celebratory—brings audience and artists to a common ground through an uncommon experience." Prefers small casts.

Tips: "The Empty Space produces work that specifically supports our artistic vision—generally rough and bold plays that seek to engage audiences on a visceral level; highly theatrical works."

ENCORE PERFORMANCE PUBLISHING, P.O. Box 692, Orem UT 84059-0692. (801)376-6199. Fax: (801)796-3965. E-mail: encoreplay@aol.com. Website: www.encoreplay.com. **Contact:** Michael C. Perry, editor. Estab. 1979. **Produces 30 plays/year.** "Our audience consists of all ages with emphasis on the family; educational institutions from elementary through college/university, community theaters and professional theaters." No unsolicited mss. Query with synopsis, production history and SASE. Responds in 1 month to queries; 3 months to scripts. Submit from May-August. **Pays 50% performance royalty; 10% book royalty.**

Needs: "We are looking for plays with strong message about or for families, plays with young actors among cast, any length, all genres. We prefer scripts with at least close or equal male/female roles, could lean to more female roles." Plays must have had at least 2 fully staged productions. Unproduced plays can be read with letter of recommendation accompanying the query. This letter must be written and signed by someone not related to the author.

Tips: "No performance art pieces or plays with overtly sexual themes or language. Looking for adaptations of Twain and other American authors."

THE ENSEMBLE STUDIO THEATRE, 549 W. 52nd St., New York NY 10019. (212)247-4982. Fax: (212)664-0041. Website: www.ensemblestudiotheatre.org. Artistic Director: Curt Dempster. **Contact:** Tom Rowan, literary manager. Estab. 1971. **Produces 250 projects/year for off-off Broadway developmental theater in a 100-seat house, 60-seat workshop space.** Do not fax mss or résumés. Submit complete ms. Responds in 6 months. **Standard production contract: mini contract with Actors' Equity Association or letter of agreement. Pays $80-1,000.**

Needs: Full-length plays with strong dramatic actions and situations and solid one-acts, humorous and dramatic, which can stand on their own. Musicals also accepted; send tape of music. Special programs include Going to the River Series, which workshops new plays by African-American women, and the Sloan Project, which commissions new works on the topics of science and technology. Seeks "original plays with strong dramatic action, believable characters and dynamic ideas. We are interested in writers who respect the power of language." No verse-dramas or elaborate costume dramas.

Tips: Deadline for one-act play marathon submissions is December 1. Full-length plays accepted year-round. "We are dedicated to developing new American plays."

ENSEMBLE THEATRE OF CINCINNATI, 1127 Vine St., Cincinnati OH 45248. (513)421-3555. Fax: (513)562-4103. Website: cincyetc.com. **Contact:** D. Lynn Meyers, producing artistic director. Estab. 1987. **Produces 9 plays/year.** Professional year-round theater. Query with synopsis, submit complete ms or submit through agent. Responds in 6 months. **Pays 5-10% royalty.**

Needs: Dedicated to good writing, any style for a contemporary, small cast. Small technical needs, big ideas.

FIRST STAGE, P.O. Box 38280, Los Angeles CA 90038. (323)850-6271. Fax: (323)850-6295. E-mail: firststagela@aol.com. Website: www.firststagela.org. **Contact:** Dennis Safren, literary manager. Estab. 1983. **Produces 50 plays/year; 130 short plays (under 15 minutes) for annual fundraiser.** First Stage is a non-profit organization dedicated to bringing together writers, actors and directors in the development of new material for stage and screen. Submit complete script. Responds in 6 months.

Needs: Original non-produced plays in any genre. Correct play format. No longer than two hours. Produces one-act play contest. Deadline August 1. The deadline for "Playwright's Express" is February 28.

Tips: No TV sitcoms. "We are a development organization."

[A] **FLORIDA STAGE**, 262 S. Ocean Blvd., Manalapan FL 33462. (561)585-3404. Fax: (561)588-4708. Website: www.floridastage.org. **Contact:** Des Gallant, literary manager. Estab. 1985. **Produces 5 plays/year.** Professional equity productions; 250 seat thrust; looking for edgy work that deals with issues and ideas; stylistically innovative. Agented submissions only. Responds in 1 year. Buys production rights only. **Pays royalty.**

Needs: "We need drama and comedy; issue-oriented plays, innovative in their use of language, structure and style." No more than 8 actors.

Tips: No kitchen sink; no Neil Simon type comedy; no TV sitcom type material. "We see a propensity for writing scripts that forget the art of the theater and that are overly influenced by TV and film. Theater's most important asset is language. It is truly refreshing to come across writers who understand this. Eric Overmyer is a great example.

FLORIDA STUDIO THEATRE, 1241 N. Palm Ave., Sarasota FL 34236. (941)366-9017. Fax: (941)955-4137. E-mail: james@fst2000.org. **Contact:** James Ashford, casting and literary coordinator. **Produces 7 established and 9 new plays/year.** FST is a professional, equity, not-for-profit theater. Plays are produced in 173-seat mainstage and 109-seat cabaret theater for subscription audiences. FST operates under a small professional theater contract of Actor's Equity. No unsolicited scripts. Send synopsis and 10 pages of dialogue. Responds in 1 month. **Pays $200 for workshop production of new script.**

Needs: Contemporary plays, musicals, musical revues. Prefers casts of no more than 8 and single sets on mainstage, 3-4 in cabaret.

Tips: "We are looking for material for our Cabaret Theatre—musical revues, one-two character musicals. All should be in two acts and run no longer than 70 minutes, including a 15 minute intermission. Also seeking dramas and comedies for the mainstage."

THE FOOTHILL THEATRE COMPANY, P.O. Box 1812, Nevada City CA 95959. (530)265-9320. Fax: (530)265-9325. E-mail: ftc@foothilltheatre.org. Website: www.foothilltheatre.org. **Contact:** Gary Wright, literary manager. Estab. 1977. **Produces 6-9 plays/year.** "We are a professional theater company operating under an Actors' Equity Association contract for part of the year, and performing in the historic 246-seat Nevada Theatre (built in 1865) and at an outdoor amphitheatre on the north shore of Lake Tahoe. We also produce a new play development program called New Voices of the Wild West that endeavors to tell the stories of the non-urban Western United States." The audience is a mix of locals and tourists. Query with synopsis or submit complete script. Responds in 6 months-1 year. Buys negotiable rights. **Payment varies.**

Needs: "We are most interested in plays which speak to the region and its history, as well as to its current concerns. No melodramas. Theatrical, above all."

Tips: "At present, we're especially interested in unproduced plays that speak to the rural and semi-rural American West for possible inclusion in our new play reading and development program, New Voices of the Wild West. History plays are okay, as long as they don't sound like you wrote them with an encyclopedia open in your lap. The best way to get our attention is to write something we haven't seen before, and write it well."

FOUNTAIN THEATRE, 5060 Fountain Ave., Los Angeles CA 90029. (323)663-2235. Fax: (323)663-1629. E-mail: ftheatre@aol.com. Website: fountaintheatre.com. Artistic Directors: Deborah Lawlor, Stephen Sachs. **Contact:** Simon

Levy, dramaturg. Estab. 1990. Produces both a theater and dance season. Produced at Fountain Theatre (99-seat equity plan). *Professional recommendation only.* Query with synopsis to Simon Levy, producing director/dramaturg. Responds in 6 months. Rights acquired vary. **Pays royalty.**

Needs: Original plays, adaptations of American literature, "material that incorporates dance or language into text with unique use and vision."

THE FREELANCE PRESS, P.O. Box 548, Dover MA 02030-2207. (508)785-8250. Fax: (508)785-8291. **Contact:** Narcissa Campion, managing director. Estab. 1984. **Publishes 4 plays/year.** Submit complete ms with SASE. Responds in 4 months. **Pays 70% of performance royalties to authors. Pays 10% script and score royalty.**

Needs: "We publish original musical theater to be performed by young people, dealing with issues of importance to them. Also adapt 'classics' into musicals for 8- to 16-year-old age groups to perform." Large cast, flexible.

SAMUEL FRENCH, INC., 45 W. 25th St., New York NY 10010. (212)206-8990. Fax: (212)206-1429. E-mail: samuelfrench@earthlink.net. Website: www.samuelfrench.com. **Contact:** Lawrence Harbison, senior editor. Estab. 1830. **Publishes 30-40 titles/year.** Publishes paperback acting editions of plays. Receives 1,500 submissions/year, mostly from unagented playwrights. 10% of publications are from first-time authors; 20% from unagented writers. **Pays 10% royalty on retail price, plus amateur and stock royalties on productions.**

Needs: Comedies, mysteries, children's plays, high school plays.

Tips: "Broadway and Off-Broadway hit plays, light comedies and mysteries have the best chance of selling to our firm. Our market is comprised of theater producers—both professional and amateur—actors and students. Read as many plays as possible of recent vintage to keep apprised of today's market; write plays with good female roles; and be one hundred percent professional in approaching publishers and producers. We recommend (not require) that submissions be in the format used by professional playwrights in the U.S., as illustrated in our playlet *Guidelines*, which sells for $4 post-paid. No plays with all-male casts, radio plays or verse plays."

N **WILL GEER THEATRICUM BOTANICUM**, P.O. Box 1222, Topanga CA 90290. (310)455-2322. Fax: (310)455-3724. E-mail: theatricum@earthlink.net. Website: www.theatricum.com. **Contact:** Ellen Geer, artistic director. Estab. 1973. **Produces 3 classical and 1 new play if selected/year.** Professional productions for summer theater. Send synopsis, sample dialogue and tape if musical. Responds in 6 months. **Pays 6% royalty or $150 per show.**

Needs: Socially relevant plays, musicals; all full-length. Cast size of 4-10 people. "We are a large outdoor theatre—small intimate works could be difficult."

Tips: "September submissions have best turn around."

THE GENESIUS GUILD INC., P.O. Box 2213, New York NY 10108-2213. (212)946-5625. Fax: (212)591-6503. E-mail: literary@genesiusguild.org. Website: www.genesiusguild.org. Artistic Director: Thomas Morrissey. **Contact:** Stephen Bishop Seely, literary liaison. Estab. 1993. **Produces 4-6 plays/year.** "We produce professional productions under Equity showcase, LOA, TYA, and staged reading guidelines depending upon project and venue." Query with synopsis, writing sample, résumé, production history and production requirements. Responds in 6 months. **Pays $500 option fee against box office royalties of usually 5% for first year.**

Needs: "We accept and are looking for all types of plays and musicals. Our goal is to develop and produce the next new groundbreaking or impactful theatre. We also provide a range of developmental programs for new musicals and plays; inhouse readings, staged readings, workshop and showcase productions."

Tips: "As a busy NYC non-profit theatre company please be patient and understanding of our limited resources and realize that we cannot always get back to each writer as quickly or with as much feedback as we'd like."

GEORGIA REPERTORY THEATRE, c/o Department of Drama, University of Georgia, Athens GA 30602-3154. (706)542-2836. Fax: (706)542-2080. E-mail: partridg@arches.uga.edu. **Contact:** Allen Partridge, dramaturg. Estab. 1991. **Produces 1-2 plays/year.** Professional productions on university campus. Query with sample scene. Responds in 6 weeks. Buys rights for initial (premiere) production. **Pays honorarium plus expenses for playwright.**

Needs: Full-length plays with moderate-sized casts.

GEVA THEATRE, 75 Woodbury Blvd., Rochester NY 14607. (585)232-1366. **Contact:** Marge Betley, literary manager. **Produces 7-10 plays/year.** Professional and regional theater, modified thrust, 552 seats; second stage, 180 seats. Subscription and single-ticket sales. Query with sample pages, synopsis and résumé. Responds in 2 months.

Needs: Full-length plays, translations and adaptations.

N **THE GOODMAN THEATRE**, 170 N. Dearborn St., Chicago IL 60601-3205. (312)443-3811. Fax: (312)443-3821. E-mail: staff@goodman-theatre.org. Website: www.goodman-theatre.org. **Contact:** Literary Manager. Estab. 1925. **Produces 9 plays/year.** "The Goodman is a professional, not-for-profit theater producing both a mainstage and studio series for its subscription-based audience. The Goodman does not accept unsolicited scripts from playwrights or agents, nor will it respond to synopsis of plays submitted by playwrights, unless accompanied by a stamped, self-addressed postcard. The Goodman may request plays to be submitted for production consideration after receiving a letter of inquiry or telephone call from recognized literary agents or producing organizations." Responds in 6 months. Buys variable rights. **Pays variable royalty.**

Needs: Full-length plays, translations, musicals; special interest in social or political themes.

THE HARBOR THEATRE, 160 W. 71st St., 20A, New York NY 10023. (212)787-1945. Website: www.harbortheatre.org. **Contact:** Stuart Warmflash, artistic director. Estab. 1993. **Produces 1-2 plays/year.** Off-off Broadway showcase. Query and synopsis. Responds in 10 weeks. **Makes outright purchase of $500.** Include SASE for return of submission.
Needs: Full-length and one-act festival. *"We only accept plays developed in our workshop."* .

HEUER PUBLISHING CO., 210 2nd St., Suite 301, Cedar Rapids IA 52406-0248. (319)364-6311. Fax: (319)364-1771. E-mail: editor@hitplays.com. Website: www.hitplays.com. Owner/Editor: C. Emmett McMullen. **Contact:** Geri Albrecht, associate editor. Estab. 1928. Publishes plays, musicals and theatre texts for junior and senior high schools and community theatres. Query with synopsis or submit complete script. Responds in 2 months. Purchases amateur rights only. **Pays royalty or makes outright purchase.**
Needs: "One-, two- and three-act plays and musicals suitable for middle, junior and senior high school productions. Preferably comedy or mystery/comedy with a large number of characters and minimal set requirements. Please avoid controversial or offensive subject matter."

HONOLULU THEATRE FOR YOUTH, 2846 Ualena St., Honolulu HI 96819-1910. (808)839-9885, ext. 17. Fax: (808)839-7018. E-mail: mark@htyweb.org. Website: www.htyweb.org. **Contact:** Mark Lutwak, artistic director. Estab. 1955. **Produces 8 plays/year.** Professional company performing for young people and families throughout the state of Hawaii. Query and synopsis. **Pays 6-7½% royalty.** Include SASE for return of submission.
Needs: Plays that will speak to the children of Hawaii about their culture(s), history, and the world. Plays are targeted to narrow age ranges: Lower and upper elementary, middle school, high school and preschool. Six actors maximum; 75 minutes maximum. No large cast musicals.
Tips: "Avoid omniscient narrators and talking down to children."

HORIZON THEATRE COMPANY, P.O. Box 5376, Atlanta GA 31107. (404)523-1477. E-mail: horizonco@mindspring.com. Website: www.horizontheatre.com. **Contact:** Lisa Adler, artistic director. Estab. 1983. **Produces 5 plays/year.** Professional productions. Query with synopsis and résumé. Responds in 6 months. Buys rights to produce in Atlanta area. **Pays 6-8% royalty or $50-75/performance.**
Needs: "We produce contemporary plays with realistic base, but which utilize heightened visual or language elements. Interested in comedy, satire, plays that are entertaining and topical, but also thought provoking. Also particular interest in plays by women or with Southern themes." No more than 10 in cast.
Tips: "No plays about being in theater or film; no plays without hope; no plays that include playwrights as leading characters; no all-male casts; no plays with all older (50 plus) characters. Southern theme plays considered for New South for the New Century new play festival."

ILLINOIS THEATRE CENTRE, 371 Artists' Walk, P.O. Box 397, Park Forest IL 60466. (708)481-3510. Fax: (708)481-3693. E-mail: ilthctr@bigplanet.com. Website: www.ilthctr.org. Artistic Director: Etel Billig. **Contact:** Alexandra Murdoch, literary manager. Estab. 1976. **Produces 8 plays/year.** Professional Resident Theatre Company in our own space for a subscription-based audience. Query with synopsis or agented submission. Responds in 2 months. Buys casting and directing and designer selection rights. **Pays 7-10% royalty.**
Needs: All types of 2-act plays, musicals, dramas. Prefers cast size of 6-10.
Tips: Always looking for mysteries and comedies. "Make sure your play arrives between November and January when play selections are made."

IMAGINATION STAGE, 7300 Whittier Blvd., Bethesda MD 20833. (301)320-2550. Fax: (301)320-1860. E-mail: info@imaginationstage.org. Website: www.imaginationstage.org. **Contact:** Janet Stanford, artistic director. Estab. 1979. **Produces 12 plays/year.** "We do 5 plays for children on our professional mainstage each season—small cast shows. We also produce shows with students in summer camps and during the year—large cast, often musical." Query and synopsis. Responds in 2 months. Buys performance rights only. **Payment negotiable.**
Needs: On main stage—sophisticated, literary, innovative material for ages 4-12; for student stage—large cast ensemble pieces with good acting roles for performers ages 7-18. Does not want spoofs of fairytales. "We are interested in technically challenging, multimedia material as well as more traditional works."

INDIANA REPERTORY THEATRE, 140 W. Washington St., Indianapolis IN 46204-3465. (317)635-5277. Fax: (317)236-0767. Artistic Director: Janet Allen. **Contact:** Literary Manager. Estab. 1972. **Produces 9 plays/year.** Plays are produced and performed at the Indiana Repertory Theatre, the state's only professional, nonprofit resident theatre. Audiences range from child to adult, depending on show. Query with synopsis. Responds in 2 months to synopsis; 6 months to ms. Rights and payment negotiated individually.
Needs: Full-length plays; adaptations of well-known literary works; plays about Indiana and the Midwest; African-American plays; Native American plays; contemporary comedies; plays with compelling characters, situations, language and theatrical appeal. Prefer casts of 8 or fewer.
Tips: No musicals or plays that would do as well in film and on TV.

INTERACT THEATRE COMPANY, The Adrienne, 2030 Sansom St., Philadelphia PA 19103. (215)568-8077. Fax: (215)568-8095. E-mail: interact@interacttheatre.org or loebell@interacttheatre.org. Website: www.interacttheatre.org. **Contact:** Larry Loebell, literary manager/dramaturg. Estab. 1988. **Produces 3 plays/year.** Produces professional productions for adult audience. Query with synopsis and bio. No unsolicited scripts. Responds in 4 months. **Pays 2-8% royalty or $25-100/performance.**

Needs: Contemporary dramas and comedies that explore issues of political, social, cultural or historical significance. "Virtually all of our productions have political content in the foregound of the drama." Prefer plays that raise interesting questions without giving easy, predictable answers. "We are interested in new plays." Limit cast to 10. No romantic comedies, family dramas, agit-prop.

[N] [A] **INTIMAN THEATRE**, P.O. Box 19760, Seattle WA 98119. (206)269-1901. Fax: (206)269-1928. E-mail: intiman@scn.org. Website: www.seattlesquare.com/Intiman. **Contact:** Literary Manager. Artistic Director: Bartlett Sher. Estab. 1972. **Produces 6 plays/year.** LORT C Regional Theater in Seattle. Best submission time is November through April. *Agented submissions only* or by professional recommendation.
Needs: Well-crafted dramas and comedies by playwrights who full utilize the power of language and character relationships to explore enduring themes. Prefers non-naturalistic plays and plays of dynamic theatricality.

JEWEL BOX THEATRE, 3700 N. Walker, Oklahoma City OK 73118-7099. (405)521-1786. Fax: (405)525-6562. **Contact:** Charles Tweed, production director. Estab. 1956. **Produces 6 plays/year.** Amateur productions. 3,000 season subscribers and general public. Submit complete script. Responds in 4 months. **Pays $500 contest prize.**
Needs: Send SASE for entry form during September-October. "We produce dramas and comedies. Only full-length plays can be accepted. Our theater is in-the-round, so we adapt plays accordingly." Deadline: mid-January.

JEWISH ENSEMBLE THEATRE, 6600 W. Maple Rd., West Bloomfield MI 48322. (248)788-2900. E-mail: jetplay@aol.com. **Contact:** Evelyn Orbach, artistic director. Estab. 1989. **Produces 5 plays/year.** Professional productions at the Aaron DeRoy theatre (season) and Masonic Temple(schools), as well as tours to schools. Submit complete script. Responds in 1 year. Obtains rights for our season productions and staged readings for festival. **Pays 6-10% royalty for full production or honorarium for staged reading—$100/full-length play.**
Needs: "We do few children's plays except original commissions; we rarely do musicals." Cast limited to a maximum of 8 actors.
Tips: "We are a theatre of social conscience with the following mission: to produce work on the highest possible professional level; to deal with issues of community & humanity from a Jewish perspective; to provide a platform for new voices and a bridge for understanding to the larger community."

KITCHEN DOG THEATER, 3120 McKinney Ave., Dallas TX 75204. (214)953-2258. Fax: (214)953-1873. **Contact:** Dan Day, artistic director. Estab. 1990. **Produces 8 plays/year.** Kitchen Dog has two performance spaces: a 100-seat black box and a 200-seat thrust. Submit complete manuscript with SASE. Each year the deadline for submissions is March 15. Writers are notified by May 15. Buys rights to full production. **Pays $40-75 per performance; $500-1,000 for winner of New Works Festival.**
Needs: "We are interested in experimental plays, literary adaptations, historical plays, political theater, gay and lesbian work, culturally diverse work, and small musicals. Ideally, cast size would be 1-5, or more if doubling roles is a possibility." No romantic/light comedies or material that is more suited for television than the theater.
Tips: "We are interested in plays that are theatrical and that challenge the imagination—plays that are for the theater, rather than T.V. or film."

KUMU KAHUA, 46 Merchant St., Honolulu HI 96813. (808)536-4222. Fax: (808)536-4226. **Contact:** Harry Wong, artistic director. Estab. 1971. **Produces 5 productions, 3-4 public readings/year.** "Plays performed at new Kumu Kahua Theatre, flexible 120-seat theater, for community audiences." Submit complete script. Responds in 4 months. **Pays royalty of $50/performance; usually 12 performances of each production.**
Needs: "Plays must have some interest for local Hawai'i audiences, preferably by being set in Hawai'i or dealing with some aspect of the Hawaiian experience." Prefer small cast, with simple staging demands.
Tips: "We need time to evaluate scripts (our response time is four months)."

LILLENAS PUBLISHING CO., P.O. Box 419527, Kansas City MO 64141-6527. (816)931-1900. Fax: (816)412-8390. E-mail: drama@lillenas.com. Website: www.lillenasdrama.com. **Contact:** Kim Messer, product manager. Estab. 1926. "We publish on two levels: (1) Program Builders—seasonal and topical collections of recitations, sketches, dialogues and short plays; (2) Drama Resources which assume more than one format: (a) full-length scripts, (b) one-acts, shorter plays and sketches all by one author, (c) collection short plays and sketches by various authors. All program and play resources are produced with local church and Christian school in mind. Therefore there are taboos." Queries are encouraged, but synopsis and complete scripts are read. Responds in 3 months. "First rights are purchased for Program Builder scripts. For Drama Resources, we purchase all print rights." **Drama Resources are paid on a 10% royalty, whether full-length scripts, one-acts, or sketches. No advance.**

- This publisher is more interested in one-act and full-length scripts—both religious and secular. Monologues are of lesser interest than previously. There is more interest in Readers' Theatre.

Needs: 98% of Program Builder materials are freelance written. Scripts selected for these publications are outright purchases; verse is minimum of 25¢/line, prose (play scripts) are minimum of $5/double-spaced page. "Lillenas Drama Resources is a line of play scripts that are, for the most part, written by professionals with experience in productions as well as writing. However, while we do read unsolicited scripts, more than half of what we publish is written by experienced authors whom we have already published."
Tips: "All plays need to be presented in standard play script format. We welcome a summary statement of each play. Purpose statements are always desirable. Approximate playing time, cast and prop lists, etc. are important to include. We are interested in fully scripted traditional plays, reader's theater scripts, choral speaking pieces. Contemporary

settings generally have it over Biblical settings. Christmas and Easter scripts must have a bit of a twist. Secular approaches to these seasons (Santas, Easter bunnies, and so on), are not considered. We sell our product in 10,000 Christian bookstores and by catalog. We are probably in the forefront as a publisher of religious drama resources." Request a copy of our newsletter and/or catalog.

LIVE BAIT THEATER, 3914 N. Clark St., Chicago IL 60613. (773)871-1212. Fax: (773)871-3191. **Contact:** Sharon Evans, artistic director. Estab. 1987. **Produces 2-4 plays/year.** "Professional, non-Equity productions here at our space in Chicago, for sophisticated local audiences." Query with synopsis or submit complete script. Responds in 6 months. Buys first production rights and residuals. **Pays 3-6% royalty.** Include SASE for return of submitted materials.
Needs: "We produce only new works by local playwrights (Chicago area). We produce both original plays and adaptations of literature to the stage. We seek properties that put a heavy emphasis on the visual element, use rich and compelling language, and explore unconventional subject matter." Prefers plays with smaller casts, suitable for an intimate 50-70 seat space.

[A] **LONG WHARF THEATRE**, 222 Sargent Dr., New Haven CT 06511. (203)787-4284. Fax: (203)776-2287. Website: www.longwharf.org. **Contact:** Kelly Miller, literary associate. Estab. 1965. **Produces 8 plays/year.** Professional regional theatre. Agented submissions only. Responds in 2 months to queries.
Needs: Full-length plays, translations, adaptations. Special interest: Dramatic plays and comedies about human relationships, social concerns, ethical and moral dilemmas.

MAGIC THEATRE, INC., Bldg. D, Fort Mason, San Francisco CA 94123. (415)441-8001. Fax: (415)771-5505. E-mail: magicthtre@aol.com. Website: www.magictheatre.org. Artistic Director: Larry Eilenberg. **Contact:** Laura Hope Owen, literary manager and festival director. Estab. 1967. **Produces 6 mainstage plays/year, plus monthly reading series and several festivals each year which contain both staged readings and workshop productions.** Regional theater. Query with synopsis, SASE, dialogue sample (10 pages). Responds in 6-8 months. **Pays royalty or per performance fee.**
Needs: "Plays that are innovative in theme and/or craft, cutting-edge political concerns, intelligent comedy. Full-length only, strong commitment to multicultural work."
Tips: "Not interested in classics, conventional approaches and cannot produce large-cast (over 10) plays. Send query to Laura Hope Owen, literary manager."

MANHATTAN THEATRE CLUB, 311 W. 43rd St., 8th Floor, New York NY 10036. (212)399-3000. Fax: (212)399-4329. E-mail: lit@mtc-nyc.org. Website: www.manhattantheatreclub.com. Director of Play Development: Paige Evans. **Contact:** Elizabeth Bennett, literary manager. **Produces 8 plays/year.** Two-theater performing arts complex classified as off-Broadway, using professional actors. Solicited and agent submissions only. No queries. Responds within 6 months.
Needs: "We present a wide range of new work, from this country and abroad, to a subscription audience. We want plays about contemporary concerns and people. All genres are welcome. Multiple set shows are discouraged. Average cast is eight. MTC also maintains an extensive play development program."

MERIWETHER PUBLISHING LTD., 885 Elkton Dr., Colorado Springs CO 80907-3557. Fax: (719)594-9916. E-mail: Merpcds@aol.com. Website: meriwetherPublishing.com. President: Mark Zapel. Editor: Arthur L. Zapel. **Contact:** Ted Zapel, associate editor. Estab. 1969. "We publish how-to materials in book and video formats. We are interested in materials for middle school, high school and college level students only." Query with synopsis/outline, résumé of credits, sample of style and SASE. Catalog available for $2 postage. Responds in 1 month to queries; 2 months to full-length mss. **Offers 10% royalty or makes outright purchase.**
Needs: Musicals for a large cast of performers. 1-act or 2-act comedy plays with large casts. Book mss on theatrical arts subjects, especially books of short scenes for amateur and professional actors. "We are now looking for scenebooks with special themes: 'scenes for young women,' 'comedy scenes for two actors,' etc. These need not be original, provided the compiler can get letters of permission from the original copyright owner. We are interested in all textbook candidates for theater arts subjects. Christian children's activity book mss also accepted. We will consider elementary level religious materials and plays, but no elementary level children's secular plays."
Tips: "We publish a wide variety of speech contest materials for high-school students. We are publishing more full length play scripts and musicals based on classic literature or popular TV shows, provided the writer includes letter of clearance from the copyright owner. Our educational books are sold to teachers and students at college and high-school levels. Our religious books are sold to youth activity directors, pastors and choir directors. Another group of buyers is the professional theater, radio and TV category. We will be especially interested in full length (two- or three-act) plays with name recognition, either the playwright or the adaptation source."

METROSTAGE, 1201 N. Royal St., Alexandria VA 22314. (703)548-9044. Fax: (703)548-9089. Website: www.metrostage.org. **Contact:** Carolyn Griffin, producing artistic director. Estab. 1984. **Produces 4-5 plays/year.** Professional productions for 150-seat theatre, general audience. Query with synopsis, 10 page dialogue sample, play production history. Responds in 3 months. **Payment negotiable, sometimes royalty percentage, sometimes per performance.**
Needs: Contemporary themes, small cast (up to 6 actors), unit set.
Tips: "Plays should have *already* had readings and workshops before being sent for our review. Do not send plays that have never had a staged reading."

MILL MOUNTAIN THEATRE, Market Square, Center in Square, Roanoke VA 24011-1437. (540)342-5749. Fax: (540)342-5745. E-mail: outreach@millmountain.org. Website: www.millmountain.org. Executive Director: Jere Lee

Hodgin. **Contact:** Maryke Huyding, literary coordinator. **Produces 8 established plays, 10 new one-acts and 2 new full-length plays/year.** Mill Mountain Theatre, 400 seats, flexible proscenium stage; Theatre B, 125 seats, flexible stage. "Some of the professional productions will be on the main stage and some in our smaller Waldron stage." Accepts unsolicited one-acts only. Send query, synopsis and 10-page dialogue sample for all other submissions. Include cassette for musicals. Responds to queries in 6 weeks; responds to scripts in 8 months.

Needs: Full-length plays, one-acts, musicals, solo pieces. Interested in plays with racially mixed casts. Accepts submissions for 'Centerpieces' (monthly lunchtime staged readings of unpublished 25-35 minute one-acts by emerging playwrights). Cast limit of 15 for plays, 24 for musicals. Prefers unit set.

Tips: "Subject matter and character variations are open, but gratuitous language and acts are not acceptable unless they are artistically supported. A play based on large amounts of topical reference or humor has a very short life. Be sure you have written a play and not a film script." Mill Mountain Theatre sponsors an annual new play competition. See the Contests & Awards section for details.

MOVING ARTS, 514 South Spring St., Los Angeles CA 90013-2304. (213)622-8906. Fax: (213)622-8946. E-mail: treynichols@movingarts.org. Website: www.movingarts.org. Artistic Directors: Lee Wochner and Julie Briggs. **Contact:** Trey Nichols, literary director. Estab. 1992. **Produces 10 plays/year.** Professional productions produced under Actors Equity Association 99-Seat Plan. "Our audiences are eclectic, literate, diverse adults." Query with synopsis, 10-20 page dialogue sample, bio, cover letter. Responds in 9 months. Obtains 5% of future income for 5-year period. **Pays 6% of box office gross.** Include SASE for return of submissions.

Needs: Full-length and one-act plays. (One-act plays accepted *only* for our Premiere One-Act Competition. $10 entry fee, $200 1st prize. Submission period is November 1-February 28. Send SASE or e-mail for full guidelines.) "Original drama or comedy that is bold, challenging, and edgy; plays that speak to the human condition in a fresh and startling way. We are not limited to any particular style or genre; we are confined only by the inherent truth of the material." Cast limit of 8. Theatre is a 60-seat black box. Limited backstage space, no fly space, limited wing space. "No plays that are like sitcoms or showcases, or too 'well-made.' We don't do plays for children (although we welcome young audiences) and tend to stay away from period pieces, heavy dramas, and performance art. Los Angeles has a very exciting theatre scene today. The most exhilarating work is in the smaller theatres (Circle X, Evidence Room, Zoo District, Theatre of NOTE, and Actors Gang, to name a few). The BCT (Big Cheap Theatre) ethic, its spirit and grace and sense of wonder, is the blood that pumps life into this recent shift in the American theatre aesthetic, and writers—*especially* writers—need to know what this is about."

Tips: "If you're a Southern California playwright, come see our play readings and shows. Party with us! Get to know us, our spirit and our work. If not, control the controllable. You can't control our reaction to your work, but you can keep your cover letter brief, polite and to the point. If you've been referred by a writer or director we've worked with, mention it. If you've seen prior productions, we appreciate it. When we read your work, we respond to the writing, but professionalism (or lack thereof) affects our evaluation in terms of potential artistic relationship, 3-hole punch script, 2-3 fasteners, SASE, clean copy, it all matters. Be patient with our process. Don't pester with follow-up queries. We love playwrights, so trust that your work will recieve as much time and attention as our limited but committed resources allow."

N **NEBRASKA THEATRE CARAVAN**, 6915 Cass St., Omaha NE 68132. Fax: (402)553-6288. E-mail: caravan@omahaplayhouse.com. Website: www.omahaplayhouse.com. **Contact:** Rick Scott, director of outreach and touring. Estab. 1976. **Produces 4-5 plays/year.** "Nebraska Theatre Caravan is a touring company which produces professional productions in schools, arts centers, and small and large theaters for elementary, middle, high school and family audiences." Query and synopsis. Responds in 3 weeks. Negotiates production rights "unless the work is commissioned by us." **Pays $20-50 per performance.**

Needs: "All genres are acceptable bearing in mind the student audiences. We are truly an ensemble and like to see that in our choice of shows; curriculum ties are very important for elementary and hich school shows; 75 minutes for middle/high school shows. No sexually explicit material."

Tips: "We tour eight months of the year to a variety of locations. Flexibility is important as we work in both beautiful performing arts facilities and school multipurpose rooms."

NEW AMERICAN THEATER, 118 N. Main St., Rockford IL 61101. (815)963-9454. Fax: (815)963-7215. Website: www.newamericantheater.com. **Contact:** Richard Raether, artistic director. Estab. 1972. The New American Theater is a professional equity theater company performing on two stages: A thrust stage with 280-seat house and a 90-seat second stage. Submit synopsis and sample dialog with SASE—send full scripts only when requested.

Needs: New works for "New Voices in the Heartland," an annual play festival of staged readings. The works may have been workshopped, but not previously produced. Event is in September. 2002 festival queries accepted until December 2001.

Tips: "We look for new work that addresses contemporary issues. More than 1 synopsis may be submitted; however, only 1 full script will be considered."

THE NEW GROUP, 154 Christopher St., Suite 2A-A, New York NY 10014. (212)691-6730. Fax: (212)691-6798. Artistic Director: Scott Elliott. **Contact:** Ian Morgan, literary manager. Estab. 1991. **Produces 3 plays/year.** Off-Broadway theater. Submit complete script. Responds in 9 months to submissions. **Pays royalty. Makes outright purchase.**

Needs: "We produce challenging, character-based scripts with a contemporary sensibility." Does not want to receive musicals, historical scripts or science fiction.

NEW JERSEY REPERTORY COMPANY, Lumia Theatre, 179 Broadway, Long Branch NJ 07740. (732)229-3166. Estab. 1997. **Produces 6 plays/year.** Professional productions year round. Submit complete script. Responds in 1 year. Rights negotiable. **Makes outright purchase.**
Needs: Prefers small cast and unit or simple set.

NEW PLAYS INCORPORATED, P.O. Box 5074, Charlottesville VA 22905. (434)979-2777. Fax: (434)984-2230. E-mail: patwhitton@aol.com. Website: www.newplaysforchildren.com. **Contact:** Patricia Whitton Forrest, publisher. Estab. 1964. **Publishes 3-6 plays/year.** Publishes for children's or youth theaters. Submit complete script. Attempts to respond in 2 months, sometimes longer. Buys all semi-professional and amateur rights in U.S. and Canada. **Pays 50% royalty on productions, 10% on sale of books.**
Needs: "I have eclectic taste—plays must have quality and originality in whatever genres, topics, styles or lengths the playwright chooses."
Tips: "No adaptations of stuff that has already been adapted a million times, e.g., *Tom Sawyer*, *A Christmas Carol*, or plays that sound like they've been written by the guidance counselor. There will be more interest in youth theater productions with moderate to large casts (15 people). Plays must have been produced, directed by someone other than the author or author's spouse. People keep sending us material suitable for adults—this is not our market. Read our online catalog."

NEW REPERTORY THEATRE, P.O. Box 610418, Newton Highlands MA 02161-0418. (617)332-7058. Fax: (617)527-5217. E-mail: info@newrep.org. Website: www.newrep.org. **Contact:** Rick Lombardo, producing artistic director. Estab. 1984. **Produces 5 plays/year.** Professional theater, general audience. Query with synopsis and dialogue sample. Buys production and subsidiary rights. **Pays 5-10% royalty.**
Needs: Idea laden, all styles, full-length only. Small cast, unit set.
Tips: No sit-coms like comedies. Incorporating and exploring styles other than naturalism.

NEW THEATRE, 4120 Laguna St., Coral Gables FL 33155. (305)443-5373. Fax: (305)443-1642. E-mail: rda@new-theatre.org. Website: www.new-theatre.org. **Contact:** Rafael De Acha, artistic director. Estab. 1986. **Produces 7 plays/year.** Professional productions. Query and synopsis. Responds in 2 months. Rights subject to negotiation. **Payment negotiable.**
Needs: Full-length. Interested in non-realistic, language plays. No musicals; no large casts.
Tips: "No kitchen sink realism. Send a simple query with synopsis. Be mindful of social issues."

NEW TUNERS THEATRE, 1225 W. Belmont Ave., Chicago IL 60657. (773)929-7367 ext. 22. Fax: (773)327-1404. E-mail: tbtuners@aol.com. Website: www.theatrebuilding.org. **Contact:** John Sparks, artistic director. **Produces mostly readings of new works, 4 skeletal productions, and the.** "Mostly developed in our New Tuners workshop. Some scripts produced are unagented submissions. Plays performed in 3 small off-Loop theaters are seating 148 for a general theater audience, urban/suburban mix." Submit synopsis, sample scene, CD or cassette tape and piano/vocal score of three songs, and author bios. Responds in 3 months.
Needs: Musicals *only*. "We're interested in all forms of musical theater including more innovative styles. Our production capabilities are limited by the lack of space, but we're very creative and authors should submit anyway. The smaller the cast, the better. We are especially interested in scripts using a younger (35 and under) ensemble of actors. We mostly look for authors who are interested in developing their scripts through workshops, readings and production." No casts over 12. No one-man shows or 'single author' pieces.
Tips: "We would like to see the musical theater articulating something about the world around us, as well as diverting an audience's attention from that world." Offers Script Consultancy—A new program designed to assist authors and composers in developing new musicals through private feedback sessions with professional dramaturgs and musical directors. For further info contact (773)929-7367, ext. 22.

NEW YORK STATE THEATRE INSTITUTE, 37 First St., Troy NY 12180. (518)274-3200. Fax: (518)274-3815. E-mail: nysti@capital.net. Website: www.nysti.org. **Contact:** Ed. Lange, associate artistic director. **Produces 5 plays/year.** Professional regional productions for adult and family audiences. Query and synopsis. Responds in 6 weeks. **Payment varies.**
Needs: "We are not interested in material for 'mature' audiences. Submissions must be scripts of substance and intelligence geared to family audiences."
Tips: Do not submit complete script unless invited after review of synopsis.

NEW YORK THEATRE WORKSHOP, 83 E. Fourth St., New York NY 10003. Fax: (212)460-8996. Artistic Director: James C. Nicola. **Contact:** Kate Spencer, artistic associate/literary. Estab. 1979. **Produces 6-7 full productions and approximately 50 readings/year.** Plays are performed off-Broadway, Equity off-Broadway contract. Audience is New York theater-going audience and theater professionals. Query with synopsis, 10-page sample scene and tape/CD/video (if appropriate). Responds in 5-7 months. Buys option to produce commercially; percentage of box office gross from commercial and percentage of author's net subsidiary rights within specified time limit from our original production. **Pays fee because of limited run, with additional royalty payments for extensions; $1,500-2,000 fee range.**

- The New York Theatre Workshop offers Van Lier Playwriting Fellowships for emerging writers of color based in New York City. Address inquiries to Chiori Miyagawa, artistic associate.

Needs: Full-length plays, translations/adaptions, music theater pieces; proposals for performance projects. Socially relevant issues, innovative form and language.
Tips: "No overtly commercial and conventional musicals or plays."

NORTH SHORE MUSIC THEATRE, 62 Dunham Rd., Beverly MA 01915. (978)232-7203. Fax: (978)921-0793. E-mail: jlarock@nsmt.org. Website: www.nsmt.org. **Contact:** John La Rock, associate producer. Estab. 1955. **Produces 8 plays/year.** Plays are performed at Arena theater for 24,000 subscribers. Submit letter of interest, synopsis, production details, music tape/CD, SASE. Responds in 2 months. Rights negotiable. **Payment negotiable.**
Needs: Musicals only (adult and children's), with cast size under 15.
Tips: No straight plays, opera.

NORTHERN WESTCHESTER CENTER FOR THE ARTS, 272 N. Bedford Rd., Mounr Kisco NY 10549. E-mail: paul@nwcaonline.org. Website: nwcaonline.org. **Contact:** Paul Andrew Perez, theater director. Estab. 1982. **Produces 6 plays/year.** Plays are amateur productions performed in a 300 seat black box. Send a synopsis and a writing sample. If a musical, send a CD or a cassette with at least 3 songs. Responds in 6 weeks. **Pays 5% royalty.** Submissions accompanied by a SASE will be returned.
Needs: "Up to this point, we have produced mainly children's musicals, but I am expanding into adult plays. I will be presenting a staged reading series in the fall with 6 readings as well as 2 full performances." There are no real production limitations.
Tips: "Keep costs down! Don't write too many characters."

NORTHLIGHT THEATRE, 9501 Skokie Blvd., Skokie IL 60077. (847)679-9501. Fax: (847)679-1879. Website: www.northlight.org. **Contact:** Gavin Witt, literary manager. Estab. 1975. **Produces 5 plays/year.** "We are a professional, Equity theater, LORT D. We have a subscription base of over 8,000 and have a significant number of single ticket buyers." Query with synopsis and SASE/SASP for response. No unsolicited mss accepted. Responds in 3 months. Buys production rights plus royalty on future mountings. **Pays royalty.**
Needs: "Full-length plays, translations, adaptations, musicals. Interested in plays of 'ideas'; plays that are passionate and/or hilarious; plays of occasional intelligence and complexity. Generally looking for cast size of 6 or fewer, but there are exceptions made for the right play."
Tips: "Please, do not try to do what television and film do better; preferably, we are looking for heightened realism. However, we are a mainstream regional rep theater, so unlikely to consider anything overtly experimental or absurdist."

[N] **EUGENE O'NEIL THEATER CENTER, NATIONAL MUSIC THEATER CONFERENCE**, 234 W. 44th St., New York NY 10036. Fax: (212)921-5538. Developmental process for new music theater works creative artists in residence with artistic staff and equity company of actors/singers public and private readings, script in hand, piano only. For guidelines and application deadlines, send SASE to address above. **Pays stipend, room and board.**

THE O'NEILL PLAYWRIGHTS CONFERENCE, (formerly The National Playwrights Conference/New Drama for Media Project at the Eugene O'Neill Theater Center), 534 W. 42 St., New York NY 10036. (212)244-7008. Fax: (212)967-2957. Artistic Director: James Houghton. **Contact:** Beth Whitaker, artistic associate. Estab. 1965. **Produces 12-15 plays/year.** The O'Neill Center theater is located in Waterford, Connecticut, and operates under an Equity LORT contract. There are three theaters: Barn—250 seats, Ampitheater—300 seats, Edith Oliver Theater—150 seats. "Please send #10 SASE for guidelines in the fall, or call to be added to our mailing list." *Do not send full scripts.* Decision by late April. We accept submissions September 15-November 1 of each year. Conference takes place during June/July each summer. Playwrights selected are in residence for one month and receive a four-day workshop and two script-in-hand readings with professional actors and directors. **Pays stipend plus room, board and transportation.**

[N] **ODYSSEY THEATRE ENSEMBLE**, 2055 S. Sepulveda Blvd., Los Angeles CA 90025. (310)477-2055. Fax: (310)444-0455. **Contact:** Sally Essex-Lopresti, director of literary programs. Estab. 1965. **Produces 9 plays/year.** Plays performed in a 3-theater facility. "All 3 theaters are Equity 99-seat theater plan. We have a subsciption audience of 4,000 for a nine-play main season, and they are offered a discount on our rentals and co-productions. Remaining seats are sold to the general public." Query with résumé, synopsis, sample dialogue, and cassette if musical. Responds in 1 month. Buys negotiable rights. **Pays 5-7% royalty.** Does not return scripts without SASE.
Needs: Scripts must be securely bound. "Full-length plays only with either an innovative form and/or provocative subject matter. We desire highly theatrical pieces that explore possibilities of the live theater experience. We are seeking full-length musicals and some plays with smaller casts (2-4). We are not reading one-act plays or light situation comedies."

OLDCASTLE THEATRE COMPANY, Box 1555, Bennington VT 05201-1555. (802)447-1267. Fax: (802)442-3704. E-mail: oldcastl@sover.net. Website: www.oldcastle.org. **Contact:** Eric Peterson, producing artistic director. **Produces 6 plays/year.** A not-for-profit theater company. Plays are performed in the new Bennington Center for the Arts, by a professional Equity theater company (in a May-October season) for general audiences, including residents of a three-state area and tourists during the vacation season. Submit complete script. Responds in 6 months. **Payment negotiable**
Needs: Produces classics, musicals, comedy, drama, most frequently American works. Usual performance time is 2 hours.

ONE ACT PLAY DEPOT, Box 335, Spiritwood Saskatchewan S0J 2M0, Canada. E-mail: balvenie@oneactplays.virtualave.net. Website: oneactplays.virtualave.net. Submit complete script by mail or via e-mail as a plaintxt file or pasted into the body of the message.
Needs: Interested only in one-act plays. Does not want musicals, farces. Do not mail originals. "Our main focus will be black comedy, along with well-written dramatic and comedic pieces."
Tips: "All non-.txt attachments will be destroyed unread."

THE OPEN EYE THEATER, P.O. Box 959, Margaretville NY 12455. (845)586-1660. Fax: (845)586-1660. E-mail: openeye@catskill.net. Website: www.theopeneye.org. **Contact:** Amie Brockway, producing artistic director. The Open Eye is a not-for-profit professional theater company working in New York City since 1972, in the rural villages of Delaware County, NY since 1991, and on tour. The theater specializes in the development of new plays for multi-generational audiences (children ages 8 and up, and adults of all ages). Ensemble plays with music and dance, culturally diverse and historical material, myth, folklore, and stories with universal themes are of interest. Program includes readings, developmental workshops, and fully staged productions.
Tips: Send one-page letter with one-paragraph plot synopsis, cast breakdown and setting, résumé and SAE. "We will provide the stamp and contact you *if we want to see the script*."

OREGON SHAKESPEARE FESTIVAL, P.O. Box 158, Ashland OR 97520. Website: www.osfashland.org. **Contact:** Stephany Smith-Pearson, literary assistant. Estab. 1935. **Produces 11 plays/year.** The Angus Bowmer Theater has a thrust stage and seats 600. The New Theatre is an experimental space that seats 260-350. The Elizabethan Outdoor Theatre seats 1,200 (stages almost exclusively Shakespearean productions there, mid-June-September). Agented submissions only. Responds in 6 months. Negotiates individually for rights with the playwright's agent. **Pays royalty.**
Needs: "A broad range of classic and contemporary scripts. One or two fairly new scripts/season. Also a play readings series which focuses on new work. Plays must fit into our ten-month rotating repertory season. New Theatre shows usually limited to seven actors." Small musicals OK. Submissions from women and minority writers are strongly encouraged. Specifically seeking work by women and minorities. Submissions should include a cast list that specifies gender, age and race, plot synopsis and 10-page dialogue sample. Best time to submit is September-December. No one-acts.
Tips: "We're always looking for a good comedy which has scope. We tend to prefer plays with a literary quality. We want plays to explore the human condition with language, metaphor and theatricality. We encourage translations of foreign plays as well as adaptations of non-dramatic material."

[N] **JOSEPH PAPP PUBLIC THEATER**, 425 Lafayette St., New York NY 10003. (212)539-8500. Website: www.publictheater.org. Producer: George C. Wolf. **Contact:** Rick Des Rochers, literary manager. Estab. 1964. **Produces 5 plays/year.** Professional productions. Query with synopsis and 10-page sample. Responds in 1 month.
Needs: All genres, no one-acts.

PEGASUS THEATRE, 3916 Main St., Dallas TX 75226-1228. (214)821-6005. Fax: (214)826-1671. E-mail: comedy@pegasustheatre.org. Website: www.pegasustheatre.com. **Contact:** Steve Erwin, new plays manager. Estab. 1985. **Produces 3 plays/year.** Produces plays under an Umbrella Agreement with AEA. "Our productions are presented for the general public to attend. Our audience is primarily in the 20-60 range with middle to high level income. We are exclusively focused on the presentation of new, original, contemporary comedies." Query with synopsis, 10 sample pages. Responds in 6 months. **Pays 5-8% royalty.**
Needs: New and original comedies with a satiric slant. Limit cast size to under 10, single set.
Tips: "No murder-mysteries, please. We'd rather not look at one-acts that don't have companion pieces or at plays that read and play like extended-length sitcoms. Neatness and proper formatting always make a better impression—even with the best of scripts."

[N] **PERSEVERANCE THEATRE**, 914 Third St., Douglas AK 99824. (907)364-2421. Fax: (907)364-2603. Peter DuBois. **Contact:** Peter DuBois, artistic/editorial director. Estab. 1979. **Produces 6 plays/year.** Semi-professional productions for the Juneau community audiences and, on tour, statewide. "We don't accept unsolicited submissions unless the writer is Alaskan." Responds in 6 months. Rights purchased varies. World-premiere credit most commonly. **Makes outright purchase of $2,000.**
Needs: "Great interest in Alaskana, Native Alaskan, and Alaska native work."

[A] **PHILADELPHIA THEATRE COMPANY**, 230 S. 15th St., 4th Floor, Philadelphia PA 19102. (215)985-1400. Fax: (215)985-5800. Website: www.phillytheatreco.com. **Contact:** Michele Volansky, dramaturg. Estab. 1974. **Produces 4 plays/year.** Agented submissions only.
Needs: Philadelphia Theatre Company produces contemporary American plays. No musicals or children's plays.
Tips: "Our work is challenging and risky—look to our history for guidance."

PIONEER DRAMA SERVICE, INC., P.O. Box 4267, Englewood CO 80155-4267. (303)779-4035. Fax: (303)779-4315. E-mail: playwrights@pioneerdrama.com. Website: www.pioneerdrama.com. Publisher: Steven Fendrich. **Contact:** Beth Somers, submissions editor. Estab. 1963. **Publishes 30 plays/year.** Plays are performed by schools, colleges, community theaters, recreation programs, churches and professional children's theaters for audiences of all ages. Query preferred. Responds in 2 weeks. Retains all rights. Buys All rights. **Pays royalty.**

- All submissions automatically entered in Shubert Fendrich Memorial Playwriting Contest.

Needs: "Musicals, comedies, mysteries, dramas, melodramas and children's theater. Two-acts up to 90 minutes; children's theater, 1 hour. Prefers many female roles, simple sets. Plays need to be appropriate for amateur groups." Prefers secular plays.
Tips: Interested in adaptations of classics of public domain works appropriate for children and teens. Also plays that deal with social issues for teens and preteens. "Check out the website to see what we carry and if your material would be appropriate. Make sure to include query letter, proof of productions and an SASE."

PITTSBURGH PUBLIC THEATER, 621 Penn Ave., Pittsburgh PA 15222. (412)316-8200. Fax: (412)316-8216. Website: www.ppt.org. Artistic Director: Ted Pappas. **Contact:** Becky Rickard, assistant to the artistic director. Estab. 1975. **Produces 7 plays/year.** O'Reilly Theater, 650 seats, thrust seating. Query with synopsis or agented submissions between February and April. Responds in 4 months.
Needs: Full-length plays, adaptations and musicals.
Tips: "We ask for a letter, character breakdown, synopsis and 10-page dialogue sample."

PLAYERS PRESS, INC., P.O. Box 1132, Studio City CA 91614-0132. **Contact:** Robert W. Gordon, editorial vice president. **Publishes 20-30 plays/year; 20 books/year.** "We deal in all entertainment areas and handle publishable works for film and television as well as theater. Performing arts books, plays and musicals. All plays must be in stage format for publication." Also produces scripts for video and material for cable television. Query with #10 SASE, reviews and proof of production. Responds in 1 month. Buys negotiable rights. "We prefer all rights." **Pays 10-75% royalty. Makes outright purchase of $100-25,000. Pays per performance royalties.**
Needs: "We prefer comedies, musicals and children's theater, but are open to all genres. We will rework the script after acceptance. We are interested in the quality, not the format. Performing Arts Books that deal with theater how-to are of strong interest."
Tips: "Send only material requested. Do not telephone."

N **PLAYS-IN-PROGRESS**, 615 4th St., Eureka CA 95501. (707)443-3724. **Contact:** Artistic Director: Susan Bigelow-Marsh. Estab. 1988. **Produces 5 plays/year.** Non-profit, with adult audiences. Submit complete script. Responds in 6 months. **Pays 10% royalty.**
Needs: Innovative, socially relevant, full-length drama and comedies. Simple scenes; cast limit 8.
Tips: Do not want to see musicals, children plays. "Bound scripts only. All must contain SASE."

PLAYSCRIPTS, INC., (formerly Playscripts.com), P.O. Box 237060, New York NY 10023. E-mail: info@playscripts.com. Website: www.playscripts.com. **Contact:** Douglas Rand, editor. Estab. 1999. Audience is professional, community, college, high school and children's theaters worldwide. Send complete ms, preferably via e-mail; see website for guidelines. Responds in 8 months. Buys exclusive publication and performance licensing rights. **Pays negotiated book and production royalties.**
Needs: "Playscripts, Inc. publishes one-act and full-length plays for professional, community, college, high school and children's theaters. We are open to a wide diversity of writing styles and content."
Tips: "Playscripts, Inc. is a play publishing company optimized for the Internet. We provide all of the same licensing and book production services as a traditional play publisher, along with unique online features that maximize the exposure of each dramatic work."

PLAYWRIGHTS HORIZONS, 630 Ninth Ave., #708, New York NY 10036. (212)564-1235. Fax: (212)594-0296. Website: www.playwrightshorizons.org. Artistic Director: Tim Sanford. **Contact:** Sonya Sobieski, literary manager (plays); send musicals Attn: Musical Theatre Program. Estab. 1971. **Produces 6 plays/year.** Plays performed off-Broadway for a literate, urban, subscription audience. Submit complete ms with author bio; include tape or CD for musicals. Responds in 6 months. Negotiates for future rights. **Pays royalty. Makes outright purchase.**
Needs: "We are looking for new, full-length plays and musicals by American authors."
Tips: "No adaptations, children's theater, biographical or historical plays. We look for plays with a strong sense of language and a clear dramatic action that truly use the resources of the theater."

PLAYWRIGHTS THEATRE OF NEW JERSEY, P.O. Box 1295, Madison NJ 07940-1295. (973)514-1787. Fax: (973)514-2060. E-mail: playNJ@aol.com. Website: www.PTNJ.org. Artistic Director: John Pietrowski. **Contact:** Peter Hays, literary manager. Estab. 1986. **Produces 3 plays/year.** "We operate under a Small Professional Theatre Contract (SPT), a development theatre contract with Actors Equity Association. Readings are held under a staged reading code." Submit synopsis, first 10 pages, short bio, and production history with SASE. Responds in 1 year. "For productions we ask the playwright to sign an agreement that gives us exclusive rights to the play for the production period and for 30 days following. After the 30 days we give the rights back with no strings attached, except for commercial productions. We ask that our developmental work be acknowledged in any other professional productions." **Makes outright purchase of $750.**

- Scripts are accepted September 1 through April 30 only. Write for guidelines before submitting.

Needs: Any style or length; full length, one acts, musicals.
Tips: "We are looking for American plays in the early stages of development—plays of substance, passion, and light (comedies and dramas) that raise challenging questions about ourselves and our communities. We prefer plays *that can work only on the stage* in the most theatrical way possible—plays that are not necessarily 'straight-on' realistic, but rather ones that use imagery, metaphor, poetry and musicality in new and interesting ways. Plays go through a three-step development process: A roundtable (inhouse reading), a public concert reading and then a workshop production."

N **THE PLAYWRIGHTS' CENTER'S PLAYLABS**, 2301 Franklin Ave. E., Minneapolis MN 55406. (612)332-7481. Fax: (612)332-6037. E-mail: pwcenter@mtn.org. Website: www.pwcenter.org. **Contact:** Kirsten Gandrow, playwrights' services director:. Estab. 1971. "Playlabs is a 2-week developmental workshop for new plays. The program is held in Minneapolis and is open by script competition. It is an intensive two-week workshop focusing on the development of a script and the playwright. 3-4 new plays are given rehearsed public readings at the site of the workshop." Announcements of playwrights by May 1. Playwrights receive honoraria, travel expenses, room and board.

Needs: "We are interested in playwrights with talent, ambitions for a sustained career in theater and scripts which could benefit from an intensive developmental process involving professional dramaturgs, directors and actors." US citizens or permanent residents, only. Participants must attend all of conference. Send SASE after October 15 for application. Submission deadline: December 1. Call for information on competitions. No previously produced materials.

Tips: "We do not buy scripts or produce them. We are a service organization that provides programs for developmental work on scripts for members."

PLAYWRIGHTS' PLATFORM, 164 Brayton Rd., Boston MA 02135. (617)630-9704. **Contact:** George Sauer, producing director. Estab. 1974. **Produces 50-80 readings/year.** Plays are read in staged readings at Massachusetts College of Art (Boston). Query and synopsis. Responds in 2 months. Include SASE for return of submission.

Needs: Any types of plays. "We will not accept scripts we think are sexist or racist." Massachusetts residents only.

A **PLOWSHARES THEATRE CO.**, 2870 E. Grand Blvd., Suite 600, Detroit MI 48202-3146. (313)872-0279. Fax: (313)872-0067. E-mail: plowshares@earthlink.net. Website: www.plowshares.org. **Contact:** Gary Anderson, producing artistic director. Estab. 1989. **Produces 5 plays/year.** Professional productions of plays by African-American writers for African-American audience and those who appreciate African-American culture. Agented submissions only. Responds in 8 months.

Tips: "You'll increase the chances of your submission if it is written by an African-American and with the willingness to be developed. It must also be very good, while the writer should be ready to make a commitment."

POLARIS NORTH, c/o Martella, 1265 Broadway #803, New York NY 10001. (212)684-1985. **Contact:** Diane Martella, treasurer. Estab. 1974. **Produces 15-20 plays/year.** "We have a studio workshop with professional actors and directors and mixed general-theater and professional audiences." Submit complete manuscript. Must include #10 SASE for response or ms SASE for script return. Responds in 2 months. **No payment.**

- "Workshops are to assist writers—no charge to audience."

Needs: "We workshop one-act plays only. (Less than 30 minutes, not previously produced or workshopped. No musicals; no monologues; no situational skits; good writing and characters more important than genre or topic)."

Tips: No sexually oriented plays, no stage nudity. "The mission of our One Acts in Performance Project is to encourage and develop new playwrights by giving them an opportunity to see their work done (and be involved in the creative process) and to get audience feedback on their work."

PRIMARY STAGES COMPANY, INC., 131 W. 45 St., 2nd fl., New York NY 10036. (212)840-9705. Fax: (212)840-9725. **Contact:** Tyler Marchant, associate artistic director. Estab. 1985. **Produces 4 plays/year.** All plays are produced professionally off-Broadway at Primary Stages Theatre, 99 seat proscenium stage; Phil Bosakowski Theatre, 45 seat proscenium stage. Agented submissions or synopsis, 10 sample pages, résumé, SASE; cassette or CD for musicals. Responds in 6 months. **Pays flat fee.** Guidelines for SASE.

Needs: Full-length plays, small cast (6 or fewer) musicals. New York City or American Premiers only, written by American playwrights. Small cast (1-6), unit set or simple changes, no fly or wing space.

Tips: Best submission time: September-June. Chances: Over 1,000 scripts read, 4-5 produced. Women and minorities encouraged to submit.

PRINCE MUSIC THEATER, (formerly American Music Theatre Festival), 100 S. Broad St., Suite 650, Philadelphia PA 19110. (215)972-1000. Fax: (215)972-1020. Website: www.princemusictheater.org. **Contact:** Majorie Samoff, producing director. Estab. 1984. **Produces 4 musicals/year.** Professional musical productions. Send synopsis and sample audio tape with no more than 4 songs. Responds in 6 months. **Pays royalty.**

Needs: Song-driven music theater/opera pieces, varied musical styles. Nine in orchestra, 10-14 cast, 36x60 stage.

Tips: Innovative topics and use of media, music, technology a plus. Sees trends of arts in technology (interactive theater, virtual reality, sound design); works are shorter in length (1-1½ hours with no intermissions or 2 hours with intermission).

PUERTO RICAN TRAVELING THEATRE, 141 W. 94th St., New York NY 10025. (212)354-1293. Fax: (212)307-6769. **Contact:** Miriam Colon Valle, founder/artistic director. Estab. 1967. **Produces 3 plays/year.** Two plays performed in our theater, one during the summer in the streets, parks, playgrounds. Professional Theatre, Actors Equity LOA contract. Query and synopsis. Retain some subsidiary rights. Fee negotiable, but we are a small theater. **Payment negotiable.**

Needs: Primarily plays by Latinos or Spaniards. Prefer strong story lines. Limit 8 characters. No fly space, little wing space. The stage is 21×19. No sitcoms or revues.

Tips: "Make certain the play is for the stage, not for TV or films. That means larger than life characters, heightened language."

PULSE ENSEMBLE THEATRE, 432 W. 42nd St., New York NY 10036. (212)695-1596. Fax: (212)736-1255. E-mail: pet@pulseensembletheatre.org. Website: www.pulseensembletheatre.org. Alexa Kelly. **Contact:** Nina Da Vinci

Nichols, literary manager. Estab. 1989. **Produces 6 plays/year.** Plays performed in our theatre in either our Studio or Man Atage Theatre (off-off-Broadway). Query and synopsis. Responds in 3 months. Buys variable rights. **Usually pays 2% of gross.**

Needs: Meaningful theatre. No production limitations. Does not want to see fluff, vanity theatre.

THE PURPLE ROSE THEATRE CO., P.O. Box 220, Chelsea MI 48118. (734)433-7782. Fax: (734)475-0802. E-mail: purplerose@earthlink.net. Website: www.purplerosetheatre.org. **Contact:** Anthony Caselli, associate artistic director. Estab. 1990. **Produces 4 plays/year.** PRTC is a regional theater with an S.P.T. Equity contract which produces plays intended for Midwest/Middle American audience. Query with synopsis, character breakdown, and 10-page dialogue sample. Responds in 9 months. **Pays 5-10% royalty.**

Needs: Modern, topical full length, 75-120 minutes. Prefers scripts that use comedy to deal with serious subjects. 10 cast maximum. No fly space, unit set preferable but not required. Intimate 168 seat ¾ thrust house.

ROUND HOUSE THEATRE, 12210 Bushey Dr. #101, Silver Spring MD 20902. (301)933-9530, ext. 26. Fax: (301)933-2321. E-mail: dcrosby@round-house.org. Website: www.Round-House.org. Artistic Director: Jerry Whiddon. **Contact:** Danisha Crosby, director of productions. **Produces 5-7 plays/year. Also produces New Voices, a play reading series of** *local* playwrights (6/year). Professional AEA Theatre. Query with synopsis; send complete scripts for New Voices. Responds in 2-12 months. **Pays negotiated percentage for productions; no payment for New Voices readings.** Include SASE for return of submission.

Needs: Full-length, multiple genres and styles. Casts of 12 and under preferred.

SALTWORKS THEATRE COMPANY, 2553 Brandt School Rd., Wexford PA 15090-7931. (724)934-2820. Fax: (724)934-2815. Website: www.saltworks.org. **Contact:** Scott Kirk, artistic director. Estab. 1981. **Produces 8-10 plays/year.** Educational tour: 200+ performances in PA, OH, WV, MD, NJ; mainstage; local professional productions. Query and synopsis. Responds in 2 months. Obtains regional performance rights for educational grants. **Pays $25 per performance.**

Needs: Social issues addressing violence prevention, sexual responsibility, peer pressures, tobacco use, bullying, racial issues/diversity, drug and alcohol abuse (grades 1-12). Limited to 5 member cast, 2 men/2 women/1 either.

Tips: "Check website for current play contest rules and deadlines."

N A **SEATTLE CHILDREN'S THEATRE**, 201 Thomas St., Seattle WA 98109. (206)443-0807. **Contact:** Madeline Oldham, literary manager/dramaturg. Estab. 1975. **Produces 6 plays/year.** Professional (adult actors) performing for young audiences, families and school groups. Resident company—not touring. Agented submissions only. Responds in 8 months. **Payment varies.**

Needs: Full-length plays for young and family audiences.

N **SEATTLE REPERTORY THEATRE**, 155 Mercer St., Seattle WA 98109. Website: www.seattlerep.org. Artistic Director: Sharon Ott. **Contact:** Mervin P. Antonio, director of new project development. Estab. 1963. **Produces 9 plays/year.** 5 in the 800 seat Bagley Wright Theatre, 4 in the 300 seat Leo K Theatre. Send query, résumé, synopsis and 10 sample pages. Responds in 6 months. Buys percentage of future royalties. **Pays royalty.**

Needs: "The Seattle Repertory Theatre produces eclectic programming. We welcome a wide variety of writing."

N **SECOND STAGE THEATRE**, 307 W. 43rd St., New York NY 10036. (212)787-8302. Fax: (212)397-7066. **Contact:** Christopher Burney, associate artistic director. Estab. 1979. **Produces 4 plays/year.** Professional off-Broadway productions. Adult and teen audiences. Query with synopsis and 10-page writing sample or agented submission. Responds in 6 months. **Payment varies.**

Needs: "We need socio-political plays, comedies, musicals, dramas—full lengths for full production, one-acts for workshops (comedies only)."

Tips: "No biographical or historical dramas. Writers are realizing that audiences can be entertained while being moved. Patience is a virtue but persistence is appreciated."

SHAW FESTIVAL THEATRE, P.O. Box 774, Niagara-on-the-Lake, Ontario L0S 1J0, Canada. (905)468-2153. Fax: (905)468-5438. Website: shawfest.sympatico.ca. **Contact:** Christopher Newton, artistic director. Estab. 1962. **Produces 10 plays/year.** "Professional summer festival operating three theaters (Festival: 861 seats; Court House: 324 seats; Royal George: 328 seats). We also host some music and some winter rentals. Shaw Festival presents the work of George Bernard Shaw and his contemporaries written during his lifetime (1856-1950) and in 2000 we expanded the mandate to include works written about the period of his lifetime." Query with SASE or SAE and IRC's, depending on country of origin. We prefer to hold rights for Canada and northestern US, also potential to tour. **Pays 5-10% royalty.**

Needs: "We operate an acting ensemble of up to 75 actors; this includes 14 actors/singers and we have sophisticated production facilities. During the summer season (April-October) the Academy of the Shaw Festival sometimes organizes workshops of new plays."

Tips: "We are a large acting company specializing in plays written between 1856-1950 (during Shaw's lifetime) and in plays about that period."

SOUTH COAST REPERTORY, P.O. Box 2197, Costa Mesa CA 92628-1197. (714)708-5500. Fax: (714)545-0391. E-mail: theatre@scr.org. Website: www.scr.org. Dramaturg: Jerry Patch. **Contact:** Jennifer Kiger, literary manager. Estab. 1964. **Produces 11 plays/year.** Professional nonprofit theater; a member of LORT and TCG. "We operate in our own facility which houses the 507-seat Segerstrom theater and 336-seat Julianne Argyros theater. We have a combined subscription audience of 21,000." Query with synopsis and 10 sample pages of dialogue. Scripts considered with agent. Responds in 4 months. Acquires negotiable rights. **Pays royalty.**

Needs: "We produce full lengths. We prefer plays that address contemporary concerns and are dramaturgically innovative. A play whose cast is larger than 15-20 will need to be extremely compelling, and its cast size must be justifiable."

Tips: "We don't look for a writer to write for us—he or she should write for him or herself. We look for honesty and a fresh voice. We're not likely to be interested in writers who are mindful of *any* trends. Originality and craftsmanship are the most important qualities we look for."

SOUTH COAST REPERTORY'S HISPANIC PLAYWRIGHT'S PROJECT, P.O. Box 2197, Costa Mesa CA 92628-2197. (714)708-5500, ext. 5405. Fax: (714)545-0391. E-mail: juliette@scr.org. Website: www.scr.org. **Contact:** Juliette Carrillo, director of HPP. Estab. 1985. **Produces at least 3 workshops/readings/year.** "The Hispanic Playwrights Project is a workshop for the development of new plays by Latina/Latino writers. While focusing on the developmental process, the Project also serves to increase the visibility of work by emerging and established Hispanic-American playwrights and to encourage production of that work in the nation's resident theatres. In the past 15 years, more than half of the plays developed have gone on to productions at theatres across the U.S. Playwrights chosen for HPP will be brought to Costa Mesa to participate in a workshop with a director, dramaturg, and cast of professional actors. Together, they will work on the script, preparing it for a presentation before a public audience." Submit complete script with a synopsis and biography by January 15, 2003. Early submissions are highly encouraged. Include SASE if script is to be returned. Responds in 2 months. Holds rights to do production for 30 days after reading. **Pays per diem, travel and lodging for workshop.**

Needs: Writers must be of Latino heritage. No plays entirely in Spanish (must be mostly English). No musicals or solo pieces. New and unproduced plays are preferred, but previously produced plays that would benefit from further development may also be considered. Selected playwrights will be notified by April 1, 2003.

SOUTHERN APPALACHIAN REPERTORY THEATRE (SART), Mars Hill College, P.O. Box 1720, Mars Hill NC 28754. (828)689-1384. E-mail: sart@mhc.edu. Artistic Director: William Gregg. Estab. 1975. **Produces 5-6 plays/year.** "Since 1975 the Southern Appalachian Repertory Theatre has produced 47 world premieres in the 175-seat Owen Theatre on the Mars Hill College campus. The theater's goals include producing quality theatre and seeking integrity, both in artistic form and in the treatment of various aspects of the human condition. SART is a professional summer theater company whose audiences range from students to senior citizens." SART also conducts an annual Southern Appalachian Playwrights Conference in which 4-5 playwrights are invited for a weekend of public readings of their new scripts in the Owen Theatre. The conference is held in late March/early April. Submissions must be postmarked by October 31. If a script read at the 2003 conference is selected for production, it will be given a fully-staged production in the 2004 summer season. Playwrights receive honorarium and housing. Enclose SASE for return of script.

Needs: Comedies, dramas and musicals. Since 1975, one of SART's goals has been to produce at least one original play each summer season. To date, 46 original scripts have been produced. Plays by Southern Appalachian playwrights or about the history, culture or human experience of the Southern Appalachian region are preferred, but by no means exclusively. Complete scripts of full-length plays and musicals (include recording of at least 4 songs) are welcomed; new plays are defined as those that are unpublished and have not received a first-class production. "Workshops and other readings do not constitute a first-class production."

STAGE ONE: The Louisville Children's Theatre, 501 W. Main St., Louisville KY 40202-3300. (502)589-5946. Fax: (502)588-5910. E-mail: stageone@stageone.org. Website: www.stageone.org. **Contact:** Moses Goldberg, producing director. Estab. 1946. **Produces 6-7 plays/year.** Plays performed by an Equity company for young audiences ages 4-18; usually does different plays for different age groups within that range. Submit complete script. Responds in 4 months. **Pays negotiable royalty.**

Needs: "Good plays for young audiences of all types: Adventure, fantasy, realism, serious problem plays about growing up or family entertainment. Ideally, cast at twelve or less. Honesty, visual potentiality, worthwhile story and characters are necessary. An awareness of children and their schooling is a plus. No campy material or anything condescending to children. Musicals accepted if they are fairly limited in orchestration."

STAGES REPERTORY THEATRE, 3201 Allen Parkway, Suite 101, Houston TX 77091. (713)527-0220. Fax: (713)527-8669. Website: www.stagestheatre.com. **Contact:** Rob Bundy, artistic director. Estab. 1975. **Produces 12-14 plays/year.** Query with synopsis and SASE. Responds in 8 months. **Pays 3-10% royalty.**

Needs: Full-length, theatrical, non-realistic work. 6-8 characters maximum. "Unit set with multiple locations is preferable." No "kitchen sink" dramas. Plays also accepted October 1-February 14 for submission into the Southwest Festival of New Plays, held every June. Categories include Women's Playwrights' Division, Texas Playwrights' Division, Children's Theatre Playwrights' Division and Latino Playwrights' Division. More information can be found on website.

A **STAMFORD THEATRE WORKS**, 95 Atlantic St., Stamford CT 06901. (203)359-4414. Fax: (203)356-1846. E-mail: STWCT@aol.com. Website: www.stamfordtheatreworks.org. **Contact:** Steve Karp, producing director. Estab. 1988. **Produces 4-6 plays/year.** Professional productions for an adult audience. Agented submissions or queries with a professional recommendation. Responds in 3 months. **Pays 5-8% royalty.** Include SASE for return of submission.

Needs: Plays of social relevance; contemporary work. Limited to unit sets; maximum cast of about 8.

STATE THEATER COMPANY, 719 Congress Ave., Austin TX 78701. (512)472-5143. Fax: (512)472-7199. E-mail: mpolyer@austintheateralliances.org. **Contact:** Michelle Polyer, associate artistic director. Estab. 1982. **Produces 5 plays/year.** "Strong commitment to and a history of producing new work." Responds in late summer. **Pays royalty.**

Needs: Full length, adaptations.

Tips: Also sponsors annual new play awards. Submit first 10 pages of plays, brief synopsis, and résumé.

[A] **STEPPENWOLF THEATRE COMPANY**, 758 W. North Ave., Chicago IL 60610. (312)335-1888. Fax: (312)335-0808. Website: www.steppenwolf.org. Artistic Director: Martha Lavey. **Contact:** Edward Sobel, literary manager. Estab. 1976. **Produces 9 plays/year.** 500 and 300 seat subscriber audience. Many plays produced at Steppenwolf have gone to Broadway. "We currently have 20,000 savvy subscribers." Agented submissions only with full scripts. "We do accept unsolicited 10-page samples, including bio/résumé, synopsis." Responds in 6 months. Buys commercial, film and television in addition to production rights. **Pays 6-8% royalty.**

Needs: "Actor-driven works are crucial to us, plays that explore the human condition in our time. We max at around ten characters."

Tips: No musicals or romantic/light comedies. Plays get produced at STC based on ensemble member interest.

[A] **STUDIO ARENA THEATRE**, 710 Main St., Buffalo NY 14202. (716)856-8025. Website: www.studioarena.org. **Contact:** Mark Hogan, assistant to the artistic director. Estab. 1965. **Produces 6-8 plays/year.** Professional productions. Agented submissions only.

Needs: Full-length plays. No fly space.

Tips: "Do not fax or send submissions via the Internet. Submissions should appeal to a diverse audience. We do not generally produce musicals. Please send a character breakdown and 1-page synopsis for a faster reply."

TADA!, 120 W. 28th St., New York NY 10001. (212)627-1732. Fax: (212)243-6736. E-mail: tada@tadatheater.com. Website: www.tadatheater.com. **Contact:** Janine Nina Trevens, artistic director. Estab. 1984. **Produces 2-4 plays/year.** "TADA! produces original musicals and plays performed by children at our 95-seat theater. Productions are for family audiences." Submit complete script and tape, if musical. Responds in 6 months. **Pays 5% royalty. Commission fee.**

- TADA! also sponsors a one-act play competition for their Spring Staged Reading Series. Works must be original, unproduced and unpublished one-acts. Plays may be geared toward teen audiences. Call for deadlines.

Needs: "Generally pieces run from 45-70 minutes. Must be enjoyed by children and adults and performed by a cast of children ages 8-17."

Tips: "No redone fairy tales or pieces where children are expected to play adults. Be careful not to condescend when writing for children's theater."

[N] **TEATRO VISION**, 1700 Alum Rock Ave., San Jose CA 95116. (408)272-9926. Fax: (408)928-5589. **Contact:** Elisa Marina Gonzalez, artistic director. Estab. 1984. **Produces 3 plays/year.** Professional productions for a Latino population. Query with synopsis or submit complete ms. Responds in 6 months. **Pays 5-10% royalty. Makes outright purchase of $500-1,000. Pays $50-60 per performance.**

Needs: "We produce plays by Latino playwrights. Plays that highlight the Chicano/Latino experience."

Tips: "No material written by non-Latino writers."

TENNESSEE STAGE COMPANY AND ACTOR'S CO-OP, P.O. Box 1186, Knoxville TN 37901. (865)546-4280. Fax: (865)546-9677. **Contact:** Tom Parkhill, artistic director. Estab. 1989 Tennessee Stage Company; 1997 Actor's Co-op. **Produces 13 plays/year.** "Venue is a 100 seat black box theater. They are professional productions (non-Equity) for a general audience in the Knoxville area." Submit complete script. Responds in 3 months. **Pays small royalty.**

Needs: The Tennessee Stage Company runs toward comedy and prefers a play with a subtle approach and feel as if there is a message intended. The Actor's Co-op is a broader based company producing mainstream work, off-beat material and experimental work. Any material will be considered. "Generally our productions run toward a simple staging. While heavily technical plays will be considered, a more simple piece will have a stronger chance of getting an opportunity here."

Tips: "Write a good light comedy with a smallish cast and a simple setting."

THEATER AT LIME KILN, 14 S. Randolph St., Lexington VA 24450. E-mail: JHlimekiln@aol.com. Website: www.theateratlimekiln.com. **Contact:** John Healey, artistic director. Estab. 1984. **Produces 3 (1 new) plays/year.** Outdoor summer theater. Query and synopsis. Responds in 3 months. Buys performance rights. **Pays $25-75 per performance.**

Needs: Plays that explore the history and heritage of the Appalachian region. Minimum set required.

Tips: "Searching for plays that can be performed in outdoor space. Prefer plays that explore the cultural and/or history of the Appalichian region."

THEATER BY THE BLIND, 306 W. 18th St., New York NY 10011. (212)243-4337. Fax: (212)243-4337. E-mail: ashiotis@panix.com. Website: www.tbtb.org. **Contact:** Ike Schambelan, artistic director. Estab. 1979. **Produces 2 plays/year.** "Off-off Broadway, Theater Row, general audiences, seniors, students, disabled. If play transfers, we'd like a piece." Submit complete script. Responds in 3 months. **Pays $250-500 per production.**

Needs: Genres about blindness.

THE THEATER OF NECESSITY, 11702 Webercrest, Houston TX 77048. (713)733-6042. Estab. 1981. **Produces 8 plays/year.** "We usually keep script on file unless we are certain we will never use it." Plays are produced in a small professional theater. Submit complete script. Responds in 2 years. Buys performance rights. **Pays standard royalties (average $500/run).**
Needs: "Any play in a recognizable genre must be superlative in form and intensity. Experimental plays are given an easier read. We move to larger venue if the play warrants the expense."

THEATER OF THE FIRST AMENDMENT, George Mason University, MS 3E6, Fairfax VA 22030. Website: www.gmu.edu/cfa. **Contact:** Kristin Johnsen-Neshati, artistic associate. Estab. 1990. **Produces 3 plays/year.** Professional productions performed in an Equity SPT 150-seat theater. Query and synopsis. Responds in 3 months. **Pays combination of percentage of box office gross against a guaranteed minimum royalty.**
Needs: "We are interested in cultural history made dramatic, as distinct from history dramatized; large battles joined; hard questions asked; word and image stretched."

THEATRE & COMPANY, 36 King St. W, P.O. Box 876, Kitchener, Ontario N2G 4C5, Canada. (519)571-7080, ext. 223. Fax: (519)571-9051. Website: www.theatreandcompany.org. Artistic Director: Stuart Scadron-Wattles. **Contact:** Lisa O'Connell, literary manager. Estab. 1988. **Produces 6 plays/year.** Professional productions for a general audience. Query with synopsis, 10 pages of sample dialogue and SAE with IRCs. Responds in 1 year. **Pays $50-100 per performance.**

- Theatre & Company is particularly interested in work by Canadians.

Needs: Full-length; comedy or drama. Looking for small cast (less than 8) ensemble comedies. "Our emphasis is on regional writers familiar with our work. There is no 'best bet.' We want good stage writing that hits hard on a number of levels: Heart, head, gut and funnybone." No cast above 10; prefers unit staging.
Tips: Looks for "innovative writing for an audience which loves the theater. Avoid current trends toward shorter scenes. Playwrights should be aware that they are writing for the stage, not television."

[N] **THEATRE DE LA JEUNE LUNE**, 105 N. First St., Minneapolis MN 55401-1411. (612)332-3968. Fax: (612)332-0048. **Contact:** Barbara Berlovitz, Vincent Garcieux, Robert Rosen, Dominique Serrand, artistic directors. Estab. 1979. **Produces 3-4 plays/year.** Professional nonprofit company producing September-June for general audience. Query and synopsis. Indefinite response time **Pays royalty or per performance**
Needs: "All subject matter considered, although plays with universal themes are desired; plays that concern people of today." No unsolicited scripts please. No psychological drama or plays that are written alone in a room without the input of outside vitality and life.
Tips: "We are an acting company that takes plays and makes them ours; this could mean cutting a script or not heeding a writer's stage directions. We are committed to the performance in front of the audience as the goal of all the contributing factors; therefore, the actor's voice is extremely important. Most of our plays are created by the company. We have never produced a play that was sent to us."

THEATRE IV, 114 W. Broad St., Richmond VA 23220. (804)783-1688. Fax: (804)775-2325. E-mail: bmiller@theatreiv.org. Website: www.theatreiv.org. **Contact:** Bruce Miller, artistic director. Estab. 1975. **Produces 40 plays/year.** National tour of plays for young audiences—maximum cast of 5, maximum length of an hour. Mainstage plays for young audiences in 600 or 350 seat venues. Studio season for cutting edge adult audiences in 82 seat venue. Query and synopsis. Responds in 1 year. Buys standard production rights. **Payment varies.**
Needs: Touring and mainstage plays for young audiences; cutting edge plays for adults. Touring—maximum cast of 5, length of 60 minutes. Adult—limited budgets in 82 seat theatre. Does not want cynical perspectives, major use of profanity or sexual content.

[N] **THEATRE RHINOCEROS**, 2926 16th St., San Francisco CA 94103. (415)552-4100. Website: www.therhino.org. **Contact:** Duca Knezevic, dramaturg. Estab. 1977. **Produces 5 plays/year.** Lesbian, gay, bisexual and transgendered audience, equity productions. Send unsolicited mss accompanied by bio, synopsis, production history, SASE. Responds in 6 months. **Pays negotiable royalty**
Needs: LBGT oriented works. Cast size no larger than 10.

THEATRE THREE, P.O. Box 512, 412 Main St., Port Jefferson NY 11777-0512. (631)928-9202. Fax: (631)928-9120. Website: www.theatrethree.org. **Contact:** Jeffrey Sanzel, artistic director. Estab. 1969. "We produce an Annual Festival of One-Act Plays on our Second Stage." Deadline for submission is September 30. Send SASE for festival guidelines. Responds in 6 months. "We ask for exclusive rights up to and through the festival." **Pays $70 for the run of the festival.**
Needs: One-act plays. Maximum length: 40 minutes. "Any style, topic, etc. We require simple, suggested sets and a maximum cast of six. No adaptations, musicals or children's works."
Tips: "Too many plays are monologue-dominant. Please—reveal your characters through action and dialogue."

[A] **THEATRE THREE**, 2800 Routh St., Dallas TX 75201. (214)871-3300. Fax: (214)871-3139. E-mail: theatre3@airmail.net. Website: www.theater3dallas.com. **Contact:** Jac Alder, executive producer-director. Estab. 1961. **Produces 7 plays/year.** Professional regional theatre, in-the-round. Audience is college age to senior citizens. Query with synopsis; agented submissions only. Responds in 6 months. **Contractual agreements vary.**
Needs: Musicals, dramas, comedies, bills of related one-acts. Modest production requirement; prefer casts no larger than 10.

Tips: No parodies or political commentary/comedy. Most produced playwrights at Theatre Three (to show "taste" of producer) are Moliere, Sondheim, Ayckbourne, Miller, Stoppard, Durong (moralists and irony-masters).

THEATRE WEST, 3333 Cahuenga W., Los Angeles CA 90068-1365. (323)851-4839. Fax: (323)851-5286. E-mail: theatrewest@theatrewest.org. Website: www.theatrewest.org. **Contact:** Chris DiGiovanni and Doug Haverty, moderators of the Writers Workshop. Estab. 1962. "99-seat waiver productions in our theater. Audiences are primarily young urban professionals." Residence in Southern California is vital as it's a weekly workshop. Submit script, résumé and letter requesting membership. Responds in 4 months. Contracts a percentage of writer's share to other media if produced on MainStage by Theatre West. **Pays royalty based on gross box office,**
Needs: Full-length plays only, no one-acts. Uses minimalistic scenery, no fly space.
Tips: "Theatre West is a dues-paying membership company. Only members can submit plays for production. So you must first seek membership to the Writers Workshop. We accept all styles of theater writing, but theater only—no screenplays, novels, short stories or poetry will be considered for membership."

THEATRE WEST VIRGINIA, P.O. Box 1205, Beckley WV 25802-1205. (304)256-6800. Fax: (304)256-6807. E-mail: twv@cwv.net. Website: wvweb.com/www/TWV. **Contact:** Marina Dolinger, artistic director. Estab. 1955. **Produces 6 plays/year.** Professional educational touring theatre—K-6 and 7-12 grade levels. Outdoor drama, musicals. Query and synopsis. Responds in 3 months. **Pays 3-6% royalty.**
Needs: Appropriate material for K through 12. Cast limited to 6 actors/van and truck tour.
Tips: Material needs to be educational, yet entertaining.

THEATREWORKS/USA, 151 W. 26th St., 7th Floor, New York NY 10001. (212)647-1100. Fax: (212)924-5377. E-mail: malltop@theatreworksusa.org. Website: www.theatreworksusa.org. **Contact:** Michael Alltop, assistant artistic director. Estab. 1961. **Produces 3-4 plays/year.** Professional Equity productions for young audiences. Weekend series at Equitable Towers, NYC. Also, national and regional tours of each show. Query and synopsis. Responds in 6 months. Obtains performing rights. **Pays 6% royalty.**
Needs: "One-hour musicals or plays with music written for K-3rd or 3rd-7th grade age groups. Subjects: Historical, biography, classic literature, fairy tales with specific point of view, contemporary literature. Also, adaptations of classic literature for high school, up to all actors." Limited to 5-6 actors (11 for high school show) and a portable set. Do not rely on lighting or special effects.
Tips: "No campy, 'fractured' fairy tales, shows specifically written to teach or preach, shows relying heavily on narrators or 'kiddy theater' filled with pratfalls, bad jokes and audience participation. Write smart. Kids see a lot these days, and they are sophisticated. Don't write down to them. They deserve a good, well-told story. Seeing one of our shows will provide the best description. We commission almost all of our own work, so most submissions will not have a chance of being produced by us. We read submissions to gauge a playwright's style and appropriateness for possible future projects."

TROUPE AMERICA INC., 528 Hennepin Ave., Suite 206, Minneapolis MN 55403. (612)333-3302. Fax: (612)333-4337. E-mail: cwollan@mninter.net. Website: www.troupeamerica.com. **Contact:** Curt Wollan, president/executive director. Estab. 1987. **Produces 10-12 plays/year.** Professional production in Minneapolis or on the road. Intended for general and family audiences as well as community arts series and University Arts Series audiences. Query with sample of script, synopsis and CD or cassette tape of music. Responds in 1 year. Buys the right to perform and license the production for 10 years. **Pays 2½-5% royalty.**
Needs: Family holiday musicals—2 hours with intermission and small cast musicals. Biographic musicals—2 hours with intermission. Musical adaptations of famous works—2 hours with intermission. Smaller contained musicals get attention and single set scripts do as well.
Tips: No heavy dramas, political plays (unless satirical) and any play dealing with sex, drugs or violence. The size of the cast is important. The smaller the size, the more likely it will get produced. Economics is a priority. If possible, send an invitation to other productions of the script.

N **TRUSTUS THEATRE**, P.O. BOX 11721, Columbia SC 29211-1721. (803)254-9732. Fax: (803)771-9153. **Contact:** Jon Tuttle, literary manager. Estab. 1984. **Produces 13-20 plays/year.** Trustus Mainstage Theatre—T.C.G. Professional Company. Query and synopsis. Responds in 3 months. All rights revert to author after production. **Pays standard royalty.**
Needs: Experimental, hard-hitting, off-the-wall one-act comedies or "dramadies" suitable for open-minded Late-Night series audiences; no topic taboo; no musicals or plays for young audiences. Small cast, modest production demands.

UNICORN THEATRE, 3828 Main St., Kansas City MO 64111. (816)531-7529 ext. 18. Fax: (816)531-0421. Website: www.unicorntheatre.org. Producing Artistic Director: Cynthia Levin. **Contact:** Herman Wilson, literary assistant. **Produces 6-8 plays/year.** "We are a professional Equity Theatre. Typically, we produce plays dealing with contemporary issues." Send complete script (to Herman Wilson) with brief synopsis, cover letter, bio, character breakdown and SASE if script is to be returned. Include SASE if acknowledgement of receipt is desired. Responds in 8 months.
Needs: Prefers contemporary (post-1950) scripts. Does not accept musicals, one-acts, or historical plays. A royalty/prize of $1,000 will be awarded the playwright of any play selected through this process, The New Play Development Award. This script receives production as part of the Unicorn's regular season.

URBAN STAGES, 17 E. 47th St., New York NY 10017. (212)421-1380. Fax: (212)421-1387. E-mail: UrbanStage@aol.com. Website: www.urbanstages.org. Artistic Director: Frances Hill. Literary Manager: David Sheppard. **Contact:** T.L.

Reilly, producing director. Estab. 1986. **Produces 2-4 plays/year.** Professional productions off or off off Broadway—throughout the year. General audience. Submit complete script. Responds in 4 months. If produced, option for 6 months. **Pays royalty.**

Needs: Full-length; generally 1 set or styled playing dual. Good imaginative, creative writing. Cast limited to 3-7.

Tips: "We tend to reject 'living-room' plays. We look for imaginative settings. Be creative and interesting with intellectual content. All submissions should be bound. Send SASE. We are looking for plays with ethnic backgrounds."

N **UTAH SHAKESPEAREAN FESTIVAL**, Plays in Progress, 351 W. Center St., Cedar City UT 84720-2498. (435)586-7884. Fax: (435)865-8003. Fred C. Adams. **Contact:** R. Scott Phillips, managing director. Estab. 1961. **Produces 9 plays/year.** Travelling audiences ranging in ages from 6-80. Programming includes classic plays, musicals, new works. Submit complete script. Responds in 3-4 months. Buys rights for produced work. **Pays small stipend in addition to travel and hotel expenses for staged readings only.**

Needs: The USF is only interested in material that explores characters and ideas that focus on the West and our Western experience, spirit and heritage. Preference is given to writers whose primary residence is in the Western United States. Cast size is a consideration due to the limited time of rehearsal and the actors available during the USF production period. Does not want plays that do not match criteria.

Tips: "We want previously unproduced plays with western themes by western playwrights."

WATERLOO COMMUNITY PLAYHOUSE, P.O. Box 433, Waterloo IA 50704-0433. (319)235-0367. Fax: (319)235-7489. E-mail: wcpbhct@cedarnet.org. **Contact:** Charles Stilwill, managing artistic director. Estab. 1917. **Produces 11 plays/year.** Plays performed by Waterloo Community Playhouse with a volunteer cast. "We are one of the few theaters with a committment to new scripts. We do at least one and have done as many as four a year. We have 4,300 season members. Average attendance is 330. We do a wide variety of plays. Our public isn't going to accept nudity, too much sex, too much strong language. We don't have enough Black actors to do all-Black shows. Theater has done plays with as few as 2 characters and as many as 98. We also produce children's theater. Please, no loose pages." Submit complete script. Responds in 1 year. **Makes outright purchase of $400-500.**

Needs: "For our Children's Theater and our Adult Annual Holiday (Christmas) show, we are looking for good adaptations of name stories. Most recently: *Miracle on 34th Street, Best Christmas Pageant Ever*, and *It's A Wonderful Life*."

WEST COAST ENSEMBLE, P.O. Box 38728, Los Angeles CA 90038. (323)876-9337. Fax: (323)876-8916. Website: wcensemble.org. **Contact:** Les Hanson, artistic director. Estab. 1982. **Produces 6 plays/year.** Plays performed at a theater in Hollywood. Submit complete script. Responds in 9 months. Obtains exclusive rights in southern California to present the play for the period specified. Ownership and rights remain with the playwright. **Pays $25-45 per performance.**

Needs: Prefers a cast of 6-12.

Tips: "Submit the script in acceptable dramatic script format."

WILLOWS THEATRE COMPANY, 1425 Gasoline Alley, Concord CA 94520. (925)798-1300. Fax: (925)676-5726. E-mail: willowsth@aol.com. Website: www.willowstheatre.org. Artistic Director: Richard Elliott. **Produces 6 plays/year.** "Professional productions for a suburban audience." Accepts new manuscripts in April and May only; accepts queries year-round. Responds in 6 months to scripts. **Pays standard royalty.**

Needs: "Commercially viable, small-medium size musicals or comedies that are popular, rarely produced or new. Certain stylized plays or musicals with a contemporary edge to them (e.g., *Les Liasons Dangereuses, La Bete, Candide*)." No more than 15 actors. Unit or simple sets with no fly space, no more than 7 pieces. "We are not interested in one-character pieces."

Tips: "Our audiences want light entertainment, comedies and musicals. Also, have an interest in plays and musicals with an historical angle." Submission guidelines are on website.

A **THE WILMA THEATER**, 265 S. Broad St., Philadelphia PA 19107. (215)893-9456. Fax: (215)893-0895. E-mail: info@wilmatheater.org. Website: www.wilmatheater.org. **Contact:** Nakissa Etemad, literary manager/dramaturg. Estab. 1980. **Produces 4 plays/year.** LORT-C 300 seat theater, 7,500 subscribers. *Agented submissions only* or full ms recommended by a literary manager, dramaturg or other theater professional. Responds in 6 months.

Needs: Full-length plays, translations, adaptations and musicals from an international repertoire with emphasis on innovative, bold staging; world premieres; ensemble works; works with poetric dimension; plays with music; multimedia works; social issues. Prefers maximum cast size of 12. Stage 44'x46'.

Tips: "Before submitting any material to The Wilma Theater, please research our production history. Considering the types of plays we have produced in the past, honestly assess whether or not your play would suit us. In general, I believe researching the various theaters to which you send your play is important in the long and short run. Different theaters have different missions and therefore seek out material corresponding with those goals. In other words, think through what is the true potential of your play and this theater, and if it is a compatible relationship."

WOMEN'S PROJECT AND PRODUCTIONS, 55 West End Ave., New York NY 10023. (212)765-1706. Fax: (212)765-2024. Website: www.womensproject.org. **Contact:** Karen Keagle, literary manager. Estab. 1978. **Produces 3 plays/year.** Professional Off-Broadway productions. Query with synopsis and 10 sample pages of dialogue. Responds in 8 months.

Needs: "We are looking for full-length plays, written by women."

SCREENWRITING

Practically everyone you meet in Los Angeles, from your airport cabbie on, is writing a script. It might be a feature film, movie of the week, TV series, or documentary, but the sheer amount of competition can seem overwhelming. Some will never make a sale, while others make a decent living on sales and options without ever having any of their work produced. But there are those writers who make a living doing what they love and seeing their names roll by on the credits. How do they get there? How do *you* get there? Work on your writing. You'll improve with each script, so there's no way of getting around the need to write and write some more. It's a good idea to read as many scripts as you can get your hands on.

Writing for TV

To break into TV you must have spec scripts—work written for free that serves as a calling card and gets you in the door. A spec script showcases your writing abilities and gets your name in front of influential people. Whether a network has invited you in to pitch some ideas, or a movie producer has contacted you to write a first draft for a feature film, the quality of writing in your spec script got their attention and that may get you the job.

It's a good idea to have several spec scripts, perhaps one each for three of the top five shows in the format you prefer to work in, whether it's sitcom (half-hour comedies), episodic (one-hour series), or movie of the week (two-hour dramatic movies). Perhaps you want to showcase the breadth of your writing ability; your portfolio could include a few prime time sitcoms (i.e., *Friends*, *Everybody Loves Raymond*, *Will & Grace*), and one or two episodics in a particular genre (i.e., *The Sopranos*, *Law and Order*, *NYPD Blue*). These are all "hot" shows for writers and can demonstrate your abilities to create believable dialogue for characters already familiar to your intended readers. For TV and cable movies you should have completed original scripts (not sequels to existing movies) and you might also have a few for episodic TV shows.

In choosing the shows you write spec scripts for, you must remember one thing: Don't write a script for a show you want to work on. If you want to write for *Will & Grace*, for example, you'll send a *Dharma & Greg* script and vice versa. It may seem contradictory, but it's standard practice. It reduces the chances of lawsuits, and writers and producers can feel very proprietary about their show and their stories. They may not be objective enough to fairly evaluate your writing. In submitting another similar type of show you'll avoid these problems while demonstrating comparable skills.

In writing your TV script you must get *inside* the show and understand the characters' internal motivations. You must immerse yourself in how the characters speak, think, and interact. Don't introduce new characters in a spec script for an existing show—write believable dialogue for the characters as they are portrayed. Be sure to choose a show that you like—you'll be better able to demonstrate your writing ability through characters you respond to.

You must also understand the external factors. How the show is filmed bears on how you write. Most sitcoms are shot on videotape with three cameras, on a sound stage with a studio audience. Episodics are often shot with one camera and include on-location shots. Another important external influence in writing for TV is the timing of commercials in conjunction with the act structure. Generally, a sitcom has a teaser (short opening scene), two acts, and a tag (short closing scene), and an episodic has a teaser, four acts, and a tag. Each act closes with a turning point. Watching TV analytically and keeping a log of events will reveal some elements of basic structure.

Writing for the movies

An original movie script contains characters you have created, with story lines you design, allowing you more freedom than you have in TV. However, your writing must still convey believable dialogue and realistic characters, with a plausible plot and high-quality writing carried through roughly 120 pages. The characters must have a problem that involves the audience. When you go to a movie you don't want to spend time watching the *second* worst night of a character's life. You're looking for the big issue that crystallizes a character, that portrays a journey with important consequences.

At the same time you are creating, you should also be constructing. Be aware of the basic three-act structure for feature films. Scenes can be of varying lengths, but are usually no longer than three- to three-and-a-half pages. Some writers list scenes that must occur, then flesh them out from beginning to end, writing with the structure of events in mind. The beginning and climactic scenes are the easiest; it's how they get there from here that's difficult.

Many novice screenwriters tend to write too many visual cues and camera directions into their scripts. Your goal should be to write something readable, like a "compressed novella." Write succinct resonant scenes and leave the camera technique to the director and producer.

It seems to be easier for TV writers to cross over to movies. Cable movies bridge the two, and are generally less derivative and more willing to take chances with a higher quality show designed to attract an audience not interested in network offerings. Cable is also less susceptible to advertiser pullout, which means it can tackle more controversial topics.

Feature films and TV are very different and writers occupy different positions. TV is a medium for writers and producers; directors work for them. Many TV writers are also producers. In feature films the writers and producers work for the director and often have little or no say about what happens to the work once the script has been sold. For TV the writer pitches the idea; for feature films generally the producer pitches the idea and then finds a writer.

Marketing your scripts

If you do intend to make writing your profession, you must act professionally. Accepted submission practices should become second nature.

- The initial pitch is made through a query letter, which is no longer than one page with a one-paragraph synopsis and brief summary of your credits if they are relevant to the subject of your script.
- Never send a complete manuscript until it is requested.
- Almost every script sent to a producer, studio, or agent must be accompanied by a release form. Ask for that company's release form when you receive an invitation to submit the whole script. Mark your envelope "release form enclosed" to prevent it being returned unread.
- Always include a SASE if you want your work returned; a disposable copy may be accompanied by a self-addressed postcard for reply.
- Allow four to six weeks from receipt of your manuscript before writing a follow-up letter.

When your script is requested, be sure it's written in the appropriate format. Unusual binding, fancy cover letters, or illustrations mark an amateur. Three brass brads with a plain or black cover indicate a pro.

There are a limited number of ideas in the world, so it's inevitable that similar ideas occur to more than one person. Hollywood is a buyer's market and a release form states that clearly. An idea is not copyrightable, so be careful about sharing premises. The written expression of that idea, however, can be protected and it's a good idea to do so. The Writers Guild of America (see the For More Information box under Playwriting in this section) can register scripts for TV and theatrical motion pictures, series formats, story lines, and step outlines.

Information on screenwriting markets listed in the previous edition of *Writer's Market* but not included in this edition can be found in the General Index.

ALEXANDER/ENRIGHT AND ASSOCIATES, 201 Wilshire Blvd., 3rd Floor, Santa Monica CA 90401. **Contact:** Sarah Schuster, development associate. Produces for a general television audience. **Buys 3 script(s)/year. Works with many writer(s)/year.** Buys TV and film rights only. Accepts previously produced material. Query with synopsis. Responds in 1 month to queries; 6 weeks to scripts.
Needs: Women-driven dramas, but will accept others. Also, reality-based stories as well as 1 hour documentary ideas. No unsolicited mss. No extreme violence, horror or stalkers.

□ **ALLIED ARTISTS, INC.**, P.O. Box 73033, Las Vegas NV 89170-3033. (702)991-9011. Fax: (248)282-0764. E-mail: alliedartistsinc@usa.net. Website: www.alliedartistsonline.com. **Contact:** John Nichols, vice president, development. Estab. 1990. Produces material for broadcast and cable television, home video and film. **Buys 3-5 script(s)/year. Works with 10-20 writer(s)/year.** Buys first or all rights. Accepts previously produced material. Submit synopsis, outline. Responds in 2 months to queries; 3 months to scripts. **Pays in accordance with WGA standards.**
Needs: Films, videotapes. Social issue TV special (30-60 minutes); special interest home video topics; positive values feature screenplays.
Tips: "We are looking for positive, up-lifting dramatic stories involving real people situations. Future trend is for more reality-based programming, as well as interactive television programs for viewer participation. Send or e-mail brief query. Do not send scripts or additional material until requested."

THE AMERICAN MOVING PICTURE COMPANY INC., 838 N. Doheny Dr., #904, Los Angeles CA 90069. (310)276-0750. E-mail: mm2k@earthlink.net. **Contact:** Isabel Casper, vice president/creative affairs. Estab. 1979. Theatrical motion picture audience. Produced 4 theatrical motion pictures. Buys screenplay rights and ancillaries. Does not return submissions. Query with synopsis. Responds in 1 month to queries. **Pays in accordance with WGA standards.**
Needs: Films (35mm), commercial. "We want commercial and unique material."

ANGEL FILMS, 967 Highway 40, New Franklin MO 65274-9778. (573)698-3900. Fax: (573)698-3900. E-mail: angelfilm@aol.com. **Contact:** Matthew Eastman, vice president of production. Estab. 1980. Produces material for feature films, television. **Buys 10 script(s)/year. Works with 20 writer(s)/year.** Buys all rights. Accepts previously produced material. Query with synopsis. Responds in 1 month to queries; 2 months to scripts. **Makes outright purchase.**
Needs: Films (35mm), videotapes. "We are looking for projects that can be used to produce feature film and television feature film and series work. These would be in the areas of action adventure, comedy, horror, thriller, science fiction, animation for children." Also looking for direct to video materials.
Tips: "Don't copy others. Try to be original. Don't overwork your idea. As far as trends are concerned, don't pay attention to what is 'in.' By the time it gets to us it will most likely be on the way 'out.' And if you can't let your own grandmother read it, don't send it. Slow down on western submissions. They are not selling. If you wish material returned, enclose proper postage with all submissions. Send SASE for response to queries and return of scripts."

ANGEL'S TOUCH PRODUCTIONS, 4872 Topanga Canyon Blvd., Suite 344, Woodland Hills CA 91364. **Contact:** Phil Nemy, director of development. Estab. 1986. Professional screenplays and teleplays. Rights negotiated. Submit synopsis. Responds in 8 months to queries. **Payment negotiated.**
Needs: Films. All types, all genres, only full-length teleplays and screenplays—no one-acts.
Tips: "We only seek feature film screenplays and television screenplays. No phone calls!"

AVALANCHE ENTERTAINMENT, 11041 Santa Monica Blvd., Suite 511, Los Angeles CA 90025. E-mail: info@avalanche-ent.com. **Contact:** Richard Hull. Estab. 1993. All audiences. **Buys 2 script(s)/year. Works with 10-15 writer(s)/year.** Buys all rights. Accepts previously produced material. Query with synopsis or résumé. Responds in 1 month to queries; 3 months to scripts.
Needs: Films (35 mm), videotapes. High concept, excellent dialogue, screenplays, especially youth-oriented (age 35 and under) "feel-good" movies, music-oriented movies. Big budget movie set in corporate America. Sports movie.

THE BADHAM COMPANY, 3344 Clerendon Rd., Beverly Hills CA 90210. (818)990-9495. Fax: (818)981-9163. Website: www.badhamcompany.com. **Contact:** Cammie Crier-Herbert, co-producer/head of development. Estab. 1991. Theatrical audience. **Buys 1 script(s)/year. Works with 2 writer(s)/year.** Buys first rights. Accepts previously produced material. Query with synopsis. Responds in 1 month to queries.
Needs: Films (35 mm).
Tips: "It's too easy to write action and ignore characters."

[N] **BARNSTORM FILMS**, 73 Market St., Venice CA 90291. (310)396-5937. Fax: (310)450-4988. E-mail: tbtb@medione.net. **Contact:** Tony Bill, president. Estab. 1969. Produces feature films. **Buys 2-3 script(s)/year. Works with 4-5 writer(s)/year.**
Tips: "Looking for strong, character-based commercial strips. Not interested in science fiction or fantasy. Must send SASE with synopsis. Query first, do not send script unless we request it!"

BAUMGARTEN-MERIMS ENTERTAINMENT, 1640 S. Sepulveda Blvd., Suite 218, Los Angeles CA 90025. (310)996-1885. Fax: (310)996-1892. E-mail: baumgartenmerims@yahoo.com. **Contact:** Adam Merims, producer, or Grant Stoner, creative executive. Estab. 2000. Audience is motion picture and television viewers. **Buys 35 script(s)/year. Works with 100 writer(s)/year.** Buys motion picture and television rights. Accepts previously produced material. Query with synopsis. Responds in 1 month to queries. **Pays in accordance with WGA standards.**

Needs: Films (35 mm), videotapes. "We have feature projects in development at all the studios. We have TV projects with all the cable networks. We are always looking for good material."
Tips: Interested in original motion picture, television and cable material, movies and dramatic series.

BIG EVENT PICTURES, 11288 Ventura Blvd., #909, Studio City CA 91604. E-mail: bigevent1@hotmail.com. **Contact:** Michael Cargile, president. Produces feature films for theaters, cable TV and home video. PG, R, and G-rated films. Query by e-mail. Producers will respond if interested.
Needs: Films. All genres. Looking for good material from writers who have taken the time to learn the unique and difficult craft of scriptwriting.
Tips: "Interesting query letters intrigue us—and tell us something about the writer. Query letter should include a short 'log line' or 'pitch' encapsulating 'what this story is about' and should be no more than 1 page in length. We look for unique stories with strong characters and would like to see more action and science fiction submissions. We make movies that we would want to see. Producers are known for encouraging new (e.g. unproduced) screenwriters and giving real consideration to their scripts."

BIG STAR ENTERTAINMENT GROUP, INC., (formerly Big Star Motion Pictures, Ltd.), 13025 Yonge St., #201, Richmond Hill Ontario L4E 1Z5, Canada. (416)720-9825. Fax: (905)773-3153. Website: www.bigstarentertainment.tv. **Contact:** Frank A. Deluca. Estab. 1991. **Buys 1-2 script(s)/year. Works with 1-3 writer(s)/year.** Query with synopsis. Script should be submitted by agent or lawyer. Responds in 3 months to queries; 3 months to scripts.
Needs: Films (35 mm). "We are active in all medias, but are primarily looking for television projects, cable, network, etc. Family films are of special interest as well as published works."

CLC PRODUCTIONS, 1223 Wilshire Blvd., Suite 404, Santa Monica CA 90403. (310)454-0664. Fax: (310)459-2889. E-mail: cathylee@cathylee.com. Website: www.cathylee.com. **Contact:** Alison Doyle. Estab. 1994. TV and film. Has own financing. Open to co-productions with established companies or producers. "We are interested in suspense, comedy, action/adventure with a strong female role age 35-45." **Buys 4-5 script(s)/year. Works with 5-10 writer(s)/year.** Buys all rights. Responds in 1 month to scripts.

COBBLESTONE FILMS, 1484 Reeves St., Suite 203, Los Angeles CA 90035. E-mail: cstonefilms@aol.com. **Contact:** Jacqui Adler and Ben Adler, producers. Estab. 1997. TV and film. Query with synopsis via e-mail only. Responds in 1 month to queries. **Pays in accordance with WGA standards.**
Needs: Films (35 mm). Looking for completed screenplays only for the following genres: suspense-thrillers, dramas, as well as strong concept driven material.
Tips: "Please send 1-page query letters."

CODIKOW FILMS, 8899 Beverly Blvd., 501, Los Angeles CA 90048. (310)246-9388. Fax: (310)246-9877. E-mail: codikowflm@aol.com. Website: www.codikowfilms.com. **Contact:** Stacy Codikow, producer. Estab. 1990. **Buys 6 script(s)/year. Works with 12 writer(s)/year.** Buys all rights. Query with synopsis, résumé. Responds in 2 months to scripts. **Pays in accordance with WGA standards.**
Needs: Films (35 mm). Commercial and independent screenplays; good writing—all subjects.
Tips: "Screenwriters should submit ideas for finished screenplays in the form of a one-page synopsis that clearly captures the essence of the story. We are open to developing ideas with writers; however, we prefer completed screenplays."

CPC ENTERTAINMENT, 840 N. Larrabee St., #2322, Los Angeles CA 90069. (310)652-8194. E-mail: chane@compuserve.com. Website: www.cpcentertainment.com. **Contact:** Peggy Chane, producer/director; Sylvie de la Riviere, vice president creative affairs; Steve Nemiroff, manager development. Feature and TV. **Buys 10 script(s)/year. Works with 15 writer(s)/year.** Buys all rights. Submit resumé, 1 sentence premise, and 3 sentence synopsis. Prefers e-mail queries. Responds in 2 weeks to queries; 3 months to scripts. **Makes outright purchase. Pays in accordance with WGA standards.**
Needs: Needs feature and TV movie screenplays: small independent, or any budget for thrillers, true stories, action/adventure, character driven stories of any genre.

LOUIS DIGIAIMO & ASSOCIATES, 214 Sullivan St., Suite 2C, New York NY 10012. (212)253-5510. E-mail: l.digiaimo@att.net. **Contact:** Lou DiGiaimo, Jr., producer. Estab. 1970. All audiences. **Buys 4-5 script(s)/year. Works with 3-4 writer(s)/year.** Buys all rights. Accepts previously produced material. Query with synopsis. Responds in 1 month to queries; 2 months to scripts. **"Prices differ depending on project. We don't have a studio deal, therefore we don't offer large option prices."**
Needs: Films.

ENTERTAINMENT PRODUCTIONS, INC., 2118 Wilshire Blvd., #744, Santa Monica CA 90403. (310)456-3143. Fax: (310)456-8950. **Contact:** M.E. Lee, story editor; Edward Coe, producer. Estab. 1971. Produces theatrical and television productions for worldwide distribution. Query with synopsis and a Writer Submission Release. Responds to queries in 1 month only if SASE is included. **Purchases rights by negotiations.**
Needs: Scripts having the power to attract audiences worldwide. Will consider participation, co-production.
Tips: "Submit your one strongest writing."

FAST CARRIER PICTURES INC., c/o Showtime, 10880 Wilshire Blvd., #1500, Los Angeles CA 90024. (310)234-5376. E-mail: steve.rubin@showtime.net. Website: www.Fastcarrier.com. **Contact:** Steve Rubin, president.

Estab. 2000. Mass market motion picture/TV audience. **Buys 8-10 script(s)/year. Works with 10-20 writer(s)/year.** Buys all rights. No previously produced material. Catalog Online At Website. Query with synopsis. Responds to queries immediately; 1-2 months to scripts.

Needs: Films (35mm). In addition to lower-budget theatrical, cable and TV movie and series projects, the company is actively developing larger, more ambitious films for the theatrical market. "We are more apt to jump at a little film with mass market appeal (okay, so I'll mention *Blair Witch Project*, so shoot me) than a huge epic sci-fi picture that I can't sell at this point. As I say on our website, we're a popcorn picture company, we like audience friendly pictures—no druggies, serial killers, gross violence or sickening humor. Some of the genres that work for us right now are true stories, which can include historical, contemporary military drama, romantic comedy, gothic horror." Does not want non-mainstream comedies, serial killers, the wild no-holds-barred life of contemporary musicians, obscure murder cases, child abuse, pornography, teen sex comedies, any movie that exploits women and minorities.

FEURY/GRANT ENTERTAINMENT, (formerly Joseph Feury Entertainment), 441 West End Ave. #10A, New York NY 10024-5328. (212)724-9290. Fax: (212)724-9233. **Contact:** Joseph Feury, executive producer. Estab. 1982. Buys all rights. Accepts previously produced material. Query with synopsis. **Pays negotiated option.**

Needs: Films.

FILMSAAVY ENTERTAINMENT, 16931 Dearborn St., Northridge CA 91343. E-mail: filmsaavy@aol.com. Website: www.FilmSaavy.Saavedra.com. **Contact:** Michael Eastin, story editor. Estab. 1995. **Buys 2-5 script(s)/year. Works with 5 writer(s)/year.** Buys all rights. Accepts previously produced material. Query with synopsis. Responds in 2 months to queries; 3 months to scripts. **Pays in accordance with WGA standards.**

Needs: Films (35 mm). Feature length motion-picture screenplays based on original ideas. Any genre accepted, but prefer comedies, dramas and historical biographies.

Tips: "Literate stories with strong, original characters, fresh ideas and life-affirming themes get our attention. We're a production company that primarily seeks product for director Craig Saavedra, and therefore material with a director already attached is less appealing to us."

[N] **JACK FREEDMAN PRODUCTIONS**, 14225 Ventura Blvd., #200, Sherman Oaks CA 91423. (818)789-9306. **Contact:** Story Department. Estab. 1988. Commercial films. **Buys 0-10 script(s)/year. Works with 10-15 writer(s)/year.** Buys all rights. No previously produced material. Query with synopsis. Provide SASE, e-mail address. Responds in 1 week to queries; 2 weeks to scripts. **Payment varies.**

Needs: Films (for theatrical).

[N] ☐ **THE GARY-PAUL AGENCY**, 84 Canaan Ct., Suite #17, Stratford CT 06614. (203)336-0257. E-mail: gcmaynard@aol.com. Website: www.thegarypaulagency.com. **Contact:** Garret C. Maynard, owner. Estab. 1992. Material intended for cinema/television. **Buys 10-15 script(s)/year. Works with 100-150 writer(s)/year.** Buys mostly film rights (first rights, all rights, etc.). Accepts previously produced material. Query with synopsis. Responds in 1-2 months to queries; 1-2 months to scripts. **Pays in accordance with WGA standards.** Films, videotapes. Need all genres of screenplays made for the cinema.

Tips: "Family relationship stories in which one replaces another; baby boomer having to deal with parents getting old or dying. It's a good idea that the writer take some iniative and invest in a DPK or digital press kit. It replaces the old EPKs which were on videotape. A DPK is on DVD and features: 1. an interview with the writer; 2. a professionally performed scene with visuals and music/fx track; 3. the writer's bio. Have a look at our website for details."

[N] **GINTY FILMS**, 16255 Ventura Blvd., Suite 625, Encino CA 91436. (310)277-1408. E-mail: rwginty@aol.com. Website: www.robertginty.com. **Contact:** Layla Bennett, assistant. Estab. 1989. Commercial audience. **Buys 12-15 script(s)/year. Works with 10-20 writer(s)/year.** Buys first rights, all rights. Accepts previously produced material. Query with synopsis, production history. Responds in 1 month to queries; 1 month to scripts. **Pays in accordance with WGA standards.**

Needs: Films.

GRADE A ENTERTAINMENT, 368 N. La Cienega Blvd., Los Angeles CA 90048-1925. E-mail: GradeAProd@aol.com. **Contact:** Andy Cohen. Estab. 1996. All audiences. **Buys 5-10 script(s)/year. Works with 25 writer(s)/year.** Buys all rights. Accepts previously produced material. Query with synopsis via e-mail only. Responds in 1 month to queries. **Pays in accordance with WGA standards.**

Needs: Films (35mm). Looking for well-written, well-developed, completed feature film scripts only.

STEPHAN GRAY, 205 S. Beverly Dr., Suite 212, Los Angeles CA 90212. (310)888-0090. E-mail: Bhlit@cs.com. Website: www.beverlyhillslit.com. **Contact:** Stephan Gray, CEO. **Works with 4-8 writer(s)/year.** Options scripts. Accepts previously produced material. Query with synopsis.

Needs: Films (35mm). "Most writers should review my website at www.beverlyhillslit.com."

GREEN GRASS BLUE SKY COMPANY, 10000 Riverside Dr., Suites 15-17, Toluca Lake CA 91602. E-mail: ggbscompany@hotmail.com. **Contact:** Frank Catalano, president. Estab. 1997. General audience. Buys all rights. Accepts previously produced material. Query only (no scripts). Responds in 2 months to queries. **Payment varies depending upon project.**

Needs: Films.

Tips: "Seeks projects with poetry and spirit. No shoot-em ups."

BETH GROSSBARD PRODUCTIONS, 5168 Otis Ave., Tarzana CA 91356. Fax: (818)705-7366 or (310)841-5934. **Contact:** K. Jacobs, development associate; Beth Grossbard, producer. Estab. 1994. **Buys 6 script(s)/year. Works with 20+ writer(s)/year.** Buys first rights and true-life story rights. Query with synopsis, treatment/outline. Responds in 2 months to queries; 3 months to scripts. **Pays in accordance with WGA standards.**
Needs: Films (35 mm).
Tips: "Develops material for television, cable and feature film markets. Areas of interest include: true stories, literary material, family dramas, social issues, young adult themed and children's stories, historical/biographical accounts. Will also consider plays, book proposals, small press books, or concept pages for film development."

[N] **A HAPPY PLACE**, 15 Brooks Ave., Venice CA 90266. E-mail: chris@happyplaceonline.com. **Contact:** Christopher Tipton, creative executive. Estab. 2001. Intended audience ages 13-35. **Buys 10 script(s)/year. Works with 10 writer(s)/year.** Buys all rights. Accepts previously produced material. Query with synopsis. Responds in 1 month to queries; 1 month to scripts. **Payment is negotiable for each circumstance.**
Needs: Films (35mm). "We are looking for high concept feature length scripts. Please no thrillers or science fiction."
Tips: "Keep writing. Don't spend all your time perfecting one script. Never become too attached to your work; you can always write another script. Stay clear of stories about Hollywood or about a struggling writer or actor trying to 'make it' in Hollywood."

[A] **HBO FILMS**, 2049 Century Park E., Suite 3600, Los Angeles CA 90067. Fax: (310)201-9552. Website: www.hbo.com. **Contact:** Caroline Rule, story editor HBO Films. Query with synopsis (1 page or shorter) **through agent or lawyer only**. No unrepresented writers. Do *not* email your query. Responds in 1 month to queries. **Payment varies.**
Needs: Features for TV. Looks at all genres except family films with children as main protagonists. Focus on socially relevant material and true stories. "HBO looks for true stories, known people, controversy, politics, etc." "*Not* looking for standard movie-of-the-week fare. HBO Films does not do family films, straight 'genre' movies, broad comedies or high-budget action movies."
Tips: "Make sure industry standards are adhered to. Not interested in looking at work that is unprofessionally presented. Only submit synopsis if you have a true story or fiction completed script or book. Not interested in partially completed projects. You should send a one-page synopsis only, through your agent or lawyer. Generally, HBO Films prefers nonfiction. Stories that have a political or social angle, are controversial, edgy or interesting above and beyond are the typical TV movie."

[N] **HINTERLAND ENTERTAINMENT**, 13547 Ventura Blvd., #294, Sherman Oaks CA 91423. E-mail: hinterent@aol.com. **Contact:** Karen Lee Arbeeny, producer/director. Estab. 1996. All audiences. Buys film, TV, novelization rights. Accepts previously produced material. Query via e-mail only. Responds in 2 months to queries. **Payment varies.**
Needs: Character-driven, large budget action or thriller, romantic comedy, female-driven, historical drama/epic. Screenplays for theatrical or MOW accepted; TV scripts for 1 hour drama or sitcom accepted.

□ **IFM FILM ASSOCIATES INC.**, 1328 E. Palmer Ave., Glendale CA 91205-3738. (818)243-4976. Fax: (818)550-9728. E-mail: ifmfilm@aol.com or ifmfilm@reelplay.com. **Contact:** Brad Benjamin, executive assistant. Estab. 1994. Film and television all media world wide. **Buys 10 script(s)/year. Works with 30 writer(s)/year.** Buys all rights. Catalog for SAE with $3. Query with synopsis. Responds in 1 month to queries; 3 months to scripts. **Pays in accordance with WGA standards.**
Needs: Films (35mm). Thrillers, family, action.

INTERNATIONAL HOME ENTERTAINMENT, 1440 Veteran Ave., Suite 650, Los Angeles CA 90024. (323)663-6940. **Contact:** Jed Leland, Jr., assistant to the president. Estab. 1976. Buys first rights. Query. Responds in 2 months to queries. **Pays in accordance with WGA standards.**

O→ Looking for material that is international in scope.

Tips: "Our response time is faster on average now (3-6 weeks), but no replies without a SASE. No unsolicited mss. We do not respond to unsolicited phone calls or e-mail."

JOADA PRODUCTIONS, INC., 1437 Rising Glen Rd., Los Angeles CA 90069. **Contact:** David Sheldon, producer. Estab. 1980. Produces feature films as well as movies and series for television. Buys all rights. Query with synopsis, writing samples, SASE. Responds in 2 months to queries. **Pays in accordance with WGA standards.**
Needs: "We look for all types of fresh and unique material, including comedy, family, suspense, drama, horror, sci-fi, thrillers, action-adventure." True stories should include news articles or other documentation.
Tips: "A synopsis should tell the entire story with the entire plot—including the beginning, the middle and the end. The producers have been in business with 20th Century Fox, Orion/MGM, Columbia Pictures and currently have contracts with Montel Williams, Baltimore Spring Creek Productions and Paramount Pictures."

MARTY KATZ PRODUCTIONS, 1250 6th St., Suite 205, Santa Monica CA 90401. (310)260-8501. Fax: (310)260-8502. Website: www.hollywood-101.com. **Contact:** Frederick Levy, vice president, development. Estab. 1992. Produces material for all audiences. Buys first, all and film rights. Accepts previously produced material. Query. Responds in 1 month to queries, if interested.
Needs: Films (35 mm).

THE KAUFMAN COMPANY, 2700 Colorado Ave., 2nd Floor, Santa Monica CA 90404. E-mail: submit@thekaufmancompany.com. Website: www.thekaufmancompany.com. **Contact:** Courtney Morrison, manager of development. Estab.

1990. Intended for all audiences. **Buys 5-10 script(s)/year. Works with 10 writer(s)/year.** Buys all rights. Query with synopsis. Responds in 3 weeks to queries; 3 months to scripts. **Pays in accordance with WGA standards.** Submit loglines to submit@thekaufmancompany.com.

Needs: We option screenplays and mss for television, cable and film. "Must be a truly engaging story—no personal slice-of-life melodramas."

N KN'K PRODUCTIONS INC., 5230 Shira Dr., Valley Village CA 91607-2300. (818)760-3106. Fax: (818)760-2478. E-mail: katharinekramer@hotmail.com. **Contact:** Katherine Kramer, creative director. Estab. 1992. "Looking for film material with strong roles for mature women (ages 40-55 etc.). Also roles for young women and potential movie musicals, message movies." **Buys 3 script(s)/year. Works with 5 writer(s)/year.** Buys all rights. No previously produced material. Catalog for #10 SASE. Query with synopsis, completed script, résumé. Responds in 3 months to queries. **Pays in accordance with WGA standards.**

Needs: Multimedia Kits. "Doing more partnerships with writers as opposed to just WGA minimum. Concentration on original vehicles for the mature actress to fill the gap that's missing from mainstream cinema."

Tips: "We are looking for young adult, teen, college age films. Character driven comedies or dramas with young male/female roles. If there is any material with roles 18-25 with a socially conscious message, that would be ideal."

LANCASTER GATE ENTERTAINMENT, 16001 Ventura Blvd., #110, Encino CA 91436. (818)995-6000. **Contact:** Brian K. Schlichter, vice president, development and production. Estab. 1989. Theatrical and television. **Works with dozens of writer(s)/year.** Rights purchased negotiable. Query. Responds in 1 month to queries. **Pays in accordance with WGA standards.**

Needs: Films (35-70 mm). Feature and television scripts, pitches.

DAVID LANCASTER PRODUCTIONS, 3356 Bennett Dr., Los Angeles CA 90068-1704. (323)874-1415. Fax: (323)874-7749. E-mail: dlasstkbiegel@yahoo.com. **Contact:** Kevin Biegel, director of development. Estab. 1985. **Buys 8-10 script(s)/year. Works with 18-25 writer(s)/year.** Buys film and TV rights. Query with synopsis and pitch.

Needs: Looking for strong character pieces in the thriller, noir, action and true to life genres. High-concept indedependent features with a budget of $2-4 million.

Tips: "Submissions must be solicited by the company. Open to pitches via fax or e-mail. Writer does not need to have representation. All submissions should be professional in nature (i.e., proper format, proper binding, free from mistakes, etc." Accepts pitches/synopses by e-mail or fax. No phone pitches.

N LAST MINUTE PRODUCTIONS, 2515 Astral Dr., Los Angeles CA 90046. **Contact:** Henry Bloomstein or Dick Kline. Last Minute Productions, the low budget/independent division of Red Hots Entertainment, favors horror, thrillers, urban culture dramas and comedies that can be filmed on a restricted economical budget, $500,000-1.5 million.

ARNOLD LEIBOVIT ENTERTAINMENT, P.O. Box 261, Cedar City UT 84721. E-mail: director@scifistation.com. Website: www.scifistation.com. **Contact:** Barbara Schimpf, vice president, production; Arnold Leibovit, director/producer. Estab. 1988. Produces material for motion pictures and television. **Works with 1 writer(s)/year.** Query with synopsis. A submission release must be included with all queries. Responds in 2 months to queries. **Pays in accordance with WGA standards.**

Needs: Films (35mm), videotapes. "Prefers high concept, mixed genres, comedy, adventure, sci-fi/fantasy, as well as unusual, visually rich, character-driven smaller works with unusual twists, comic sensibility, pathos and always the unexpected." Does not want novels, plays, poems, treatments; no submissions on disk.

Tips: "New policy: Submission of logline and synopsis for evaluation first. Do not send scripts until we ask for them. An Arnold Leibovit Entertainment release form must be completed and returned with material. Accepting loglines via e-mail at director@scifistation.com."

LEO FILMS, 6249 Langdon Ave., Van Nuys CA 91411. (323)666-7140. Fax: (323)666-7414. E-mail: steve eofilms.com. Website: www.leofilms.com. **Contact:** Steve Lustgarten, president. Estab. 1989. Feature/film. **Buys 2 script(s)/year. Works with 2 writer(s)/year.** Buys all rights. Accepts previously produced material. Query with synopsis. Responds in 1 month to queries; 2 months to scripts. **Payment varies—options and sales.**

Needs: Films (35 mm). "Looking for good stories-honor, urban, action."

Tips: E-mail first if available. "Will also consider novels, short stories and treatments that have true movie potential."

LICHT/MUELLER FILM CORP., 132-A S. Lasky Dr., Suite 200, Beverly Hills CA 90212. **Contact:** Attn: Queries. Estab. 1983. Produces material for all audiences. Accepts previously produced material. Query with synopsis to query department. Responds in 1 month to queries; 3 months to scripts.

Needs: Films (35 mm). "Scripts for feature films."

Tips: "We tend to focus on comedy, but are open to all genres."

LOCKWOOD FILMS (LONDON) INC., 12569 Boston Dr., RR #41, London Ontario N6H 5L2, Canada. (519)657-3994. Fax: (519)657-3994. E-mail: nancycjohnson@hotmail.com. **Contact:** Nancy Johnson, president. Estab. 1974. Entertainment and general broadcast for kids 9-12 and family viewing. **Works with 5-6 writer(s)/year.** Query with synopsis, résumé, writing samples. Submissions will not be considered without a signed proposal agreement; we will send one upon receiving submissions. **Pays negotiated fee.**

Needs: Family entertainment: series, seasonal specials, mini-series, and MOW. Also feature films, documentaries.

Tips: "Potential contributors should have a fax machine and should be prepared to sign a 'proposal submission agreement.' We are in development with national broadcaster on live-action family drama series. Looking for international co-production opportunities. Writers from the US sending proposals with a SASE with American postage should understand we can not mail those envelopes in Canada. If they send a Union Postale Universelle (International Response Coupon) we can respond."

MARSHAK/ZACHARY, (formerly Zachary Entertainment), 8840 Wilshire Blvd., 1st Floor, Beverly Hills CA 90211. Fax: (310)358-3192. E-mail: zacharyent@aol.com. **Contact:** Alan W. Mills, associate. Estab. 1981. Audience is film goers of all ages, television viewers. **Buys 3-5 script(s)/year. Works with 10 writer(s)/year.** Rights purchased vary. Query with synopsis. Responds in 2 weeks to queries; 3 months to scripts. **Payment varies.**
Needs: Films for theatrical, cable and network television release.
Tips: "Submit logline (one line description) and a short synopsis of storyline. Short biographical profile, focus on professional background. SASE required for all mailed inquiries. If submissions are sent via e-mail, subject must include specific information or else run the risk of being deleted as junk mail. All genres accepted but ideas must be commercially viable, high concept, original and marketable."

MEDIACOM DEVELOPMENT CORP., P.O. Box 73033, Las Vegas NV 89170-3033. (702)991-9011. Fax: (248)282-0764. E-mail: fgirard@mail.com. Website: www.mediacorp.org. **Contact:** Felix Girard, director/program development. Estab. 1978. **Buys 8-12 script(s)/year.** Buys all rights or first rights. Query with writing samples. Responds in 1 month to queries. **Negotiates payment depending on project.**
Needs: Films, videotapes, multimedia kits, tapes and cassettes. Publishes software ("programmed instruction training courses"). Looking for new ideas for CD-ROM and DVD titles.
Tips: "E-mail brief query before sending material. Especially interested in flexibility to meet clients' demands, creativity in treatment of precise subject matter. We are looking for good, fresh projects (both special and series) for cable and pay television markets. A trend in the audiovisual field that freelance writers should be aware of is the move toward more interactive video disc/computer CRT delivery of training materials for corporate markets."

MICHAEL MELTZER PRODUCTIONS, 12207 Riverside Dr., #208, Valley Village CA 91607. (310)289-0702. Fax: (818)766-5936. E-mail: melmax@aol.com. **Contact:** Michael Meltzer, producer. Query with synopsis. Responds in 1 month to queries; 2 months to scripts.
Needs: Films (35 mm).

MGP, INC., 16161 Ventura Blvd., #664, Encino CA 91436. **Contact:** Michael Gallant, president.
Tips: "We are not accepting any new submissions until after August 1, 2003."

MINDSTORM LLC, 1434 Sixth St., Suite 1, Santa Monica CA 91401. Fax: (310)393-6622. **Contact:** Karina Duffy, president. Estab. 1998. Audience is mid-20s-30s. **Buys 6 script(s)/year. Works with 8 writer(s)/year.** Buys all rights. Query with synopsis, résumé, writing samples, production history. Query by fax only. Responds in 1 month to queries. **Pays in accordance with WGA standards.**
Needs: Please send cover letter first.
Tips: "Create a script that is unique, has good character development and a solid point to it. Looking for talented young up and coming directors with shorts. Also looking for female-driven scripts, mostly drama or romantic comedy."

MONAREX HOLLYWOOD CORPORATION, 9421½ W. Pico Blvd., Los Angeles CA 90035. **Contact:** Chris D. Nebe, president. Estab. 1978. All audiences. **Buys 3-4 script(s)/year. Works with 5-10 writer(s)/year.** Buys all rights. Query with synopsis. Responds in 1 month to queries. **Pays in accordance with WGA standards.**
Needs: Films (35mm), videotapes. Needs dramatic material with strong visuals, action, horror, dance, romantic comedies, anything commercially viable. We are only interested in screenplays.

MWG PRODUCTIONS, 8075 West 3rd St., Suite 402, Los Angeles CA 90048. (323)937-8339. Fax: (323)937-5239. E-mail: wynne9@aol.com. Website: www.AlaskaDQ.com. **Contact:** Max Goldenson, executive producer. Estab. 1981. **Buys 3 script(s)/year. Works with 10 writer(s)/year.** Buys all rights. Accepts previously produced material. Query with synopsis, résumé. Responds in 1 month to queries; 3 months to scripts. **Pays in accordance with WGA standards.**
Needs: Films, videotapes, multimedia kits.

NHO ENTERTAINMENT, 11962 Darlington Ave., Los Angeles CA 90049. E-mail: submissions@nhoentertainment.com. Website: www.nhoentertainment.com. **Contact:** Mark Costa, partner. Estab. 1999. All audiences. **Buys 5 script(s)/year. Works with 10 writer(s)/year.** Buys all rights. Accepts previously produced material. Catalog for #10 SASE. Query with synopsis, résumé, writing samples, production history. Via e-mail. Responds in 1 month to queries. **Pays in accordance with WGA standards.**
Needs: Films, videotapes, multimedia kits, tapes and cassettes. "We are currently accepting all forms of submissions and encourage all writers with material to send query letters."

POP/ART FILM FACTORY, 513 Wilshire Blvd., #215, Santa Monica CA 90401. E-mail: dzpff@earthlink.net. Website: www.home.earthlink.net/~dzpff. **Contact:** Daniel Zirilli, CEO/director. Estab. 1990. Produces material for "all audiences/feature films." Query with synopsis. **Pays on per project basis.**
Needs: Films (35mm), multimedia kits, documentaries. "Looking for interesting productions of all kinds. We're producing 3 feature films/year, and 15-20 music-oriented projects. Also exercise and other special interest videos."

Tips: "Send a query/pitch letter and let me know if you are willing to write on spec (for the first job only; you will be paid if the project is produced). Be original. Do not play it safe. If you don't receive a response from anyone you have ever sent your ideas to, or you continually get rejected, don't give up if you believe in yourself. Good luck and keep writing!" Will look at "reels" (1 or VHS).

PROMARK ENTERTAINMENT GROUP, 3599 Cahuenga Blvd. W., Los Angeles CA 90026. (323)878-0404. Fax: (323)878-0486. E-mail: gwishnick@promarkgroup.com. **Contact:** Gil-Adrienne Wishnick, vice president development. Promark is a foreign sales company, producing theatrical films for the foreign market. **Buys 8-10 script(s)/year. Works with 8-10 writer(s)/year.** Buys all rights. Query with synopsis (shorter is better). Responds in 1 month to queries; 2 months to scripts. **Makes outright purchase.**

Promark is concentrating on action-thrillers in the vein of *The Fugitive*.

Needs: Films (35mm). "We are only looking for screenplays in the action thriller genre. Our aim is to produce lower budget films that have a solid, novel premise—a smart but smaller scale independent film. Our films are male-oriented, urban in setting with a strong male lead. We try to find projects with a clever hook and strong characters. We are not interested in comedies, dramas or horror films, ever. Among the recent films we've produced are: *Contaminated Man*, a medical thriller, starring William Hurt and Peter Weller; *Pilgrim* with Ray Liotta; *The Stick Up* with James Spader."

THE PUPPETOON STUDIOS, P.O. Box 261, Cedar City UT 84721. E-mail: director@scifistation.com. Website: www.scifistation.com. **Contact:** Arnold Leibovit, director/producer. Estab. 1987. "Broad audience." **Works with 1 writer(s)/year.** Query with synopsis. Submission release required with all queries. Do not send script unless requested. Responds in 2 month to queries. **Pays in accordance with WGA standards.**

Needs: Films (35mm). "We are seeking animation properties including presentation drawings and character designs. The more detailed drawings with animation scripts the better. Always looking for fresh broad audience material." No novels, plays, poems, treatments; no submissions on disk.

RANDWELL PRODUCTIONS, INC., 11111 Santa Monica Blvd., Suite 525, Los Angeles CA 90025-3339. E-mail: rrobinson@randwell.com. Website: www.randwell.com. **Contact:** Tom Kageff, vice president. Estab. 1997. TV and features audience. **Buys 3-4 script(s)/year. Works with 2-3 writer(s)/year.** Buys all rights. Query with synopsis. Responds in 2 weeks to queries; 3 months to scripts. **Pays in accordance with WGA standards.**

Needs: Films (35mm). Good character pieces with a strong plot and/or strong concepts. No sci-fi, no westerns.

Tips: "Please keep synopsis to no more than one page. We hardly if ever request a copy of unsolicited material so don't be surprised if we pass."

RED HOTS ENTERTAINMENT, 3105 Amigos Dr., Burbank CA 91504-1806. E-mail: chipdaniel2@excite.com. **Contact:** Kit Gleason, head story editor, Senior Vice President/Creative Director: Dan Pomeroy. Producer/Director: Chip Miller. Estab. 1990. **Buys 1 script(s)/year. Works with 1-2 writer(s)/year.** Buys first and all rights. No previously produced material. Query with synopsis, release form, personal bio, SASE. Responds in 5 months to queries; 6 months to scripts. **Pays in accordance with WGA standards. Negotiable on writer's previous credits, etc.**

Needs: Films (16 and 35mm), videotapes. "We are a feature film and television and music video production company and have no audiovisual material needs."

Tips: "Best advice possible: originality, uniqueness, write from your instincts and don't follow trends. Screenplays and T.V. scripts should be mailed to our Burbank, CA production office with a proper industry release form, a 1-page synopsis, and SASE, please. No hi-tech stories, fatal disease things. Looking for youth-driven material and solid literate material with unique premise and characters with substance. No period themes."

REEL LIFE WOMEN, 10158 Hollow Glen Circle, Bel Air CA 90077. (310)271-4722. Fax: (310)274-0503. E-mail: feigenparrentlit@aol.com. **Contact:** Joanne Parrent, co-president. Estab. 1996. Mass audiences. **Buys 3-4 script(s)/year.** Accepts previously produced material. Query with synopsis, résumé. SASE. Responds in 2 months to queries. **Pays in accordance with WGA standards.**

Needs: Films. Looking for full-length scripts for feature films or television movies only. Must be professionally formatted and under 130 pages. All genres considered particularly drama, comedy, action, suspense. No series or episode TV scripts.

Tips: "Must be professional screenwriters. We are not interested in writers who don't know their craft well. That said, we are looking for interesting, unique stories, which have good roles for actresses. We are not interested in women in stereotypical roles, as the male hero's sidekick, as passive helpmates, etc."

TIM REID PRODUCTIONS, One New Millennium Dr., Petersburg VA 23805. (804)957-4200. **Contact:** Jarene Fleming, development executive. Estab. 1996. MOW's for network TV. Query with synopsis. Responds in 1 month to queries.

Needs: Character driven feature scripts for modest budgets.Multicultural TV movies with positive black images, also series and documentary.

Tips: Does not want to see stereotypical urban dysfunctional premises.

N EDGAR J. SCHERICK ASSOCIATES, 1950 Sawtelle Blvd., Suite 282, Los Angeles CA 90025. (310)996-2376. E-mail: ejsa@msn.com. **Contact:** Stephen Abronson, director of development. Network and cable TV, theatrical audience. **Buys 3 script(s)/year. Works with 10 writer(s)/year.** Buys all rights. Accepts previously produced material. Query with synopsis.

Needs: Historical pieces and biopics. "We are looking for dramas, thrillers and mysteries."

SHORELINE ENTERTAINMENT, INC., (formerly Shoreline Pictures), 1875 Century Park E., Suite 600, Los Angeles CA 90067. (310)551-2060. Fax: (310)201-0729. E-mail: handerson@shorelineentertainment.com. Website: www.shorelineentertainment.com. **Contact:** Holly Anderson, director of development. Estab. 1993. Mass audience. **Buys 8 script(s)/year. Works with 8 writer(s)/year.** Buys all rights. Query. Responds in 2 weeks to queries.

Needs: Films (35, 70mm). Looking for commercial, exciting films. Thrillers (suspense/action) and big budget action fare. Completed screenplays only. Principal of our company co-produced *Glengarry Glen Ross; The Visit; Price of Glory;* and *Flight of Fancy.*"

Tips: "Looking for character driven films that are commercial as well as independent. Completed screenplays only. Especially looking for big-budget action, thrillers. We accept submissions by mail, e-mail or fax. No unsolicited screenplays, please."

SILVER LION FILMS, 701 Santa Monica Blvd., Suite 240, Santa Monica CA 90401. (310)393-9177. Fax: (310)458-9372. E-mail: dkzfilms@earthlink.net. **Contact:** David Kohner Zuckerman, director of development. Estab. 1988. General audience. Query. Responds in 3 months to queries; 6 months to scripts. **Pays percentage of budget.**

Needs: Films (35mm), TV/cable MOW's and TV series pitches.

□ **SKYLARK FILMS**, 1123 Pacific St., Santa Monica CA 90405. (310)396-5753. Fax: (310)396-5753. E-mail: skyfilm@aol.com. **Contact:** Brad Pollack, executive producer. Estab. 1990. **Buys 6 script(s)/year.** Buys first or all rights. Accepts previously produced material. Query with synopsis. Responds in 1 month to queries; 2 months to scripts. **Pays in accordance with WGA standards.**

O→ Skylark Films is now seeking action, suspense and thrillers.

Needs: Films (TV, cable, feature).

Tips: "True stories of romance or tragedy/redemption stories and contemporary issues for TV MOW's and cable. High concept, high stakes, action or romantic comedy for feature film."

SKYLINE PARTNERS, 10550 Wilshire Blvd., #304, Los Angeles CA 90024. (310)470-3363. Fax: (310)470-0060. E-mail: fkuehnert@earthlink.com. **Contact:** Fred Kuehnert. Estab. 1990. Produces material for theatrical, television, video audiences. **Buys 3 script(s)/year.** Buys all rights. Query with synopsis. Responds to query/synopsis within 2 weeks and if script is requested will respond within 1 month. **Payment negotiable.**

Needs: Films (35mm).

Tips: "First, send a treatment so a determination can be made if the genre or concept is something we're looking for. Secondly, we will contact writer if there is preliminary interest. Thirdly, send complete script plus release form."

SOUTH FORK PRODUCTIONS, P.O. Box 1935, Santa Monica CA 90406-1935. Fax: (310)829-5029. E-mail: sullivanprods@ireland.com. **Contact:** Jim Sullivan, producer. Estab. 1980. Produces material for TV and film. **Buys 2 script(s)/year. Works with 4 writer(s)/year.** Buys all rights. Query with synopsis, résumé, SASE. **Pays in accordance with WGA standards.**

O→ South Fork is currently looking for Irish-based scripts.

Needs: Films (16, 35mm), videotapes.

Tips: "Follow established formats for treatments. SASE for return."

SPIRIT DANCE ENTERTAINMENT, 1023 North Orange Dr., Los Angeles CA 90038-2317. (323)512-7988. E-mail: spiritdancemail@netscape.net. **Contact:** Robert Wheaton, story editor. Estab. 1997. A general film audience of all ages. Particularly interested in reaching young, college-educated adults. **Buys 1-5 script(s)/year. Works with 1-5 writer(s)/year.** Buys all rights. Accepts previously produced material. Query. Responds in 2 months to queries. **Pays in accordance with WGA standards.**

Needs: Films (35mm). "Well-crafted feature length (approximately 90-120 pages) scripts with a strong emotional core and well-developed characters. We will consider contemporary material of almost any genre which is broad in scope and appeal. With more intimate stories and period pieces, the writing must be exceptional. We are always interested in female driven stories and material that explores people of different cultures. Youth-oriented scripts (including children's stories) that are fresh and original are also of interest to us."

Tips: "Queries should be no longer than two pages. Material should demonstrate writer's passion for the material and not simply be written for the market. Due to the enormous volume of submissions, we are unable to respond to every query. If you have received no response after 2 months, assume that the company has passed on your submission. If there is interest in seeing the complete work, it must be submitted through a WGA signatory agent, entertainment attorney or a bona fide production company (i.e., has major production credits and/or studio deal). As a policy, we do not accept material by unrepresented writers (this includes writers who sign release forms). Under no circumstances should complete scripts be sent without first contacting us."

STARLIGHT PICTURES, 1725 S. Rainbow Blvd., #2-186, Las Vegas NV 89102. E-mail: ideamaster@aol.com. **Contact:** Brian McNeal, development executive. Estab. 1989. Audience is world-wide movie-going public. **Buys 3 script(s)/year. Works with 3 writer(s)/year.** Buys all rights. Accepts previously produced material. Query with synopsis. Responds in 3 months to queries; 4 months to scripts. **Pays in accordance with WGA standards or sometimes an option against larger purchase amounts.**

Needs: Films (35 mm). "Not necessarily looking at this time, but 'good' scripts will always get our attention. Prefer well-written dramatic scripts set in *any* genre."

Tips: "It is sad to say that Hollywood is inundated with scripts by writers that possess 7th grade writing skills. This makes it harder for the 'good' scripts by real writers to get noticed. Please learn your craft before submitting material."

STUDIO MERRYWOOD, a division of EduMedia, 125 Putnam Ave., Suite 232, Hamden CT 06517-2899. (203)407-8793. Fax: (203)407-8794. E-mail: rdsetc@att.net. Website: www.enaware.com/bardsworld/BARDSWB.html. **Contact:** Raúl daSilva, CEO/creative director. Estab. 1984. Produces feature films, TV series, documentaries. "We are not seeking any externally written screenplays for features but will engage produced screenwriters as consultants if they have been further recognized in the industry through leadership or international competitive festival prizes."
Needs: "Currently, no external material is sought. This may change. Thus, seasoned, professional writers may e-mail us for a status on needs. As in Tips, below, please lead your e-mail letter with a paragraph on your qualifications."
Tips: "This is not a market for novice writers. We are a small, creative shop and cannot train neophyte, unpublished or unproduced writers who would best try larger markets and media facilities. We cannot return or even acknowledge any unsolicited material and will discard such material. Those qualified please contact us first by e-mail with your qualifications and your offerings."

N TOO NUTS PRODUCTIONS, L.P., a division of Creative Hive, LLC, 1511 Sawtelle Blvd., Suite 113, Los Angeles CA 90025. (310)694-0499. E-mail: toonutsproductions@yahoo.com. Website: www.creativehivegroup.com. **Contact:** Ralph Scott, president/co-executive producer. Estab. 1994. Audience is children. **Buys 4-10 script(s)/year. Works with 4-6 writer(s)/year.** Buys both first and all rights. Query with synopsis, résumé, writing samples, production history. Responds in 3 months to queries; 6 months to scripts. **Pays royalty, makes outright purchase.**
Needs: Videotapes, multimedia kits, tapes and cassettes, CD-ROMs. Audio books and half-hour television education with a twist. Storylines for our current television and multimedia state, including "Toad Pizza," "The Salivating Salamander," "The Contest-Ants," "Anonymouse," etc.
Tips: "Suggestion: Use the words 'Too Nuts' at least twice in your query. If you don't know how to giggle all the way to the bank, don't contact us. If you've already exorcised your inner child, don't contact us either!"

VANGUARD PRODUCTIONS, 12111 Beatrice St., Culver City CA 90230. **Contact:** Terence M. O'Keefe, president. Estab. 1985. **Buys 1 script(s)/year.** Buys all rights. Accepts previously produced material. Query with synopsis, résumé. Responds in 3 months to queries; 6 months to scripts. **Pays in accordance with WGA standards. Negotiated option.**
Needs: Films (35mm), videotapes.

☐ WOODBERRY PRODUCTIONS, 3410 Descanso Dr., Suite 4, Los Angeles CA 90026. (323)668-9170. E-mail: lindagrae@aol.com. **Contact:** Linda Graeme, producer. Estab. 1994. Drama producer—film and TV. **Works with 2-3 writer(s)/year.** Options film & TV rights only. Query with synopsis, writing samples. Responds in 1 month to queries; 3 months to scripts. **Pays in accordance with WGA standards.**
Needs: Drama production for film and TV. Looking for character-driven dramatic material. Usual 2-hour. No big-budget, high-action studio fare.
Tips: Break in with a "letter/email with short and concise description of project, plus brief rundown of writing history."

THE WOOFENILL WORKS, INC., 516 E. 81st St., Suite #3, New York NY 10028-2530. (212)734-2578. Fax: (212)734-3186. E-mail: woofenill@earthlink.net. Website: home.earthlink.net/~woofenill/. **Contact:** Kathy Winthrop, creative executive. Estab. 1990. Theatrical motion pictures. **Buys 2-4 script(s)/year.** Buys all rights. Query with synopsis. Responds in 1 month to queries. **Acquires option, then payment on production.**
Needs: Films (35mm). Do not send e-mail or scripts unless requested.
Tips: "We suggest that interested writers first review the company's website and in particular, the section General Business Parameters."

Syndicates

Newspaper syndicates distribute columns, cartoons, and other written material to newspapers around the country—and sometimes around the world. Competition for syndication slots is stiff. Coveted spots in general interest, humor, and political commentary are held by big-name columnists such as Ellen Goodman, Bob Herbert, and Cal Thomas. Multitudes of aspiring writers wait in the wings, hoping one of these heavy hitters will move on to something else and leave the spotlight open.

Although this may seem discouraging, there are in fact many areas in which less-known writers are syndicated. Syndicates are not looking for general interest or essay columns. What they are looking for are fresh voices that will attract readers. As consumer interests and lifestyles change, new doors are being opened for innovative writers capable of covering emerging trends.

Most syndicates distribute a variety of columns, cartoons, and features. Although the larger ones are usually only interested in running ongoing material, smaller ones often accept short features and one-shots in addition to continuous columns. Specialized syndicates—those that deal with a single area such as business—often sell to magazines, trade journals, and other business publications as well as to newspapers.

THE WINNING COMBINATION

In presenting yourself and your work, note that most syndicated columnists start out writing for local newspapers. Many begin as staff writers, develop a following in a particular area, and are then picked up by a syndicate. Before approaching a syndicate, write for a paper in your area. Develop a good collection of clips that you feel is representative of your best writing.

New ideas are paramount to syndication. Sure, you'll want to study the popular columnists to see how their pieces are structured (most are short—from 500-750 words—and really pack a punch), but don't make the mistake of imitating a well-known columnist. Syndicates are looking for original material that is timely, saleable, and original. Do not submit a column to a syndicate on a subject it already covers. The more unique the topic, the greater your chances. Most importantly, be sure to choose a topic that interests you and one you know well.

APPROACHING MARKETS

Request a copy of a syndicate's writer's guidelines. It will give you information on current needs, submission standards, and response times. Most syndicates prefer a query letter and about six sample columns or writing samples and a SASE. You may also want to include a client list and business card if available. If you have a particular area of expertise pertinent to your submission, mention this in your letter and back it up by sending related material. For highly specialized or technical matter, provide credentials to show you are qualified to handle the topic.

In essence, syndicates act as agents or brokers for the material they handle. Writing material is usually sold as a package. The syndicate will promote and market the work to newspapers (and sometimes to magazines) and keep careful records of sales. Writers receive 40-60 percent of gross receipts. Some syndicates may also pay a small salary or flat fee for one-shot items.

Syndicates usually acquire all rights to accepted material, although a few are now offering writers and artists the option of retaining ownership. In selling all rights, writers give up ownership and future use of their creations. Consequently, sale of all rights is not the best deal for writers, and has been the reason many choose to work with syndicates that buy less restrictive rights. Before signing a contract with a syndicate, you may want to go over the terms with an

For More Information

SYNDICATE RESOURCES

- *Editor & Publisher Syndicate Directory*, 770 Broadway, New York NY 10003-9595. A complete list of syndicates with contact names and the features they represent.
- *Editor & Publisher*, 770 Broadway, New York NY 10003-9595. This weekly magazine contains news articles about syndicates and can provide you with information about changes and events in the industry.

attorney who has a background in law or with an agent. The best contracts will usually offer the writer a percentage of gross receipts (as opposed to net receipts) and will not bind the writer for longer than five years.

THE SELF-SYNDICATION OPTION

Many writers choose to self-syndicate. This route allows you to retain all rights, and gives you the freedom of a business owner. But as a self-syndicated writer, you must also act as your own manager, marketing team, and sales force. You must develop mailing lists and a pricing, billing, and collection structure.

Payment is usually negotiated on a case-by-case basis. Small newspapers may offer only $10-20 per column, but larger papers may pay much more. The number of papers you deal with is only limited by your marketing budget and your tenacity.

If you self-syndicate be aware that some newspapers are not copyrighted, so you should copyright your own material. It's less expensive to copyright columns as a collection than individually. For more information on copyright procedures, see the Copyright information in The Business of Writing section.

Information on syndicates listed in the previous edition of *Writer's Market* but not included in this edition can be found in the General Index.

[N] **AMERICAN PRESS SERVICE**, P.O. Box 917, Van Nuys CA 91408. (818)997-6497. E-mail: ISCS3ASSOC@aol.com. **Contact:** Israel Bick, senior editor. Estab. 1955. "We are just now considering using outside sources." Syndicates to newspapers. Send complete ms. Responds as soon as possible. Buys all rights. **Pays on acceptance.**
Needs: Newspaper columns, newspaper features, fillers. Buys single (one shot) features, articles series. **Additional payment for photos.** Arts and entertainment, business, women's issues, and advice to singles.

AMERICAS BEST AUTO, 6708 Auburn Ave. W., Bradenton FL 34207. (941)758-5039. E-mail: brucehubbard@earthlink.net. **Contact:** Bruce Hubbard. Estab. 1990. **50% freelance written on contract. Buys 50 feature(s)/year.** Syndicates to magazines, newspapers, Internet. Query with or without published clips. Responds in 1 week. Buys second serial (reprint) rights. **Pays often on acceptance.**
Needs: Newspaper columns. Buys single (one shot) features, articles series. **Pays $100 minimum. Pays $25-700 for photos.** *Americas Best Auto, 100 Best Hotels, One Tank Test Drive.*

ARTISTMARKET.COM, 35336 Spring Hill, Farmington Hills MI 48331-2044. (248)661-8585. Fax: (248)788-1022. E-mail: editor@artistmarket.com. Website: www.artistmarket.com. **Contact:** David Kahn, editor. Estab. 1996. Syndicates to magazines, newspapers, Internet. Submit written features in 250 words or less via e-mail, postal mail or disk (PC format).
Needs: Fillers, short humor features, all written works for publication in magazines, newspapers, etc. Send samples. **Pays 50% author's percentage.** Currently syndicates cartoonists, comic strips, puzzles, fillers, etc. Publishes "www.artistmarket.com" website directed to newspaper, magazine editors and website publishers.

- For writer's guidelines, see "Writers' Bloc" on website.

AUTO DIGEST SYNDICATE, P.O. Box 459, Prineville OR 97754-0459. (541)923-4688. Fax: (815)346-9002. E-mail: adigest@iname.com. **Contact:** Bill Schaffer, co-owner. Estab. 1992. **17% freelance written on contract. Buys 50 feature(s)/year. Works with 3-4 writer(s)/year.** Syndicates to newspapers, Internet. Query. Responds in 2 months. Buys first North American serial rights. **Pays when paid by publication.**

Needs: Newspaper columns, news items. **All writers equally split fee after expenses.** Currently syndicates *New Car Reviews*, by Bill and Barbara Schaffer (800-1,000 words plus photo); *Auto Update* and *Car Quiz*, by Bill and Barbara Schaffer (400-500 words); *Auto Forum*, by Chip Keen (400-500 words).

N **BUDDY BASCH FEATURE SYNDICATE**, 720 West End Ave., Suite 1612, New York NY 10025-6299. (212)666-2300. **Contact:** Buddy Basch, publisher. Estab. 1950. **6-10% freelance written on contract; 50-60% freelance written on one-time basis.** Syndicates to magazines, newspapers. Query. Responds in 2-3 weeks. Buys first North American serial rights. **Pays on acceptance.**
Needs: Magazine columns, magazine features, newspaper columns, newspaper features. Buys single (one shot) features. **Payment varies. Additional payment for photos.**

BLACK PRESS SERVICE, INC., 166 Madison Ave., New York NY 10016. (212)686-6850. Fax: (212)686-7308. **Contact:** Roy Thompson, editor. Estab. 1966. **10% freelance written on contract; 10% freelance written on one-time basis. Buys hundreds of feature(s)/year. Works with hundreds of writer(s)/year.** Syndicates to magazines, newspapers, Radio. Send complete ms. Responds in 2 months. Buys all rights.
Needs: Magazine columns, magazine features, newspaper columns, newspaper features, news items, radio broadcast material. Buys single (one shot) features, articles series, current events-oriented article series. **Pays variable flat rate.** Currently syndicates *Daily Report*, by staff (roundup of minority-oriented news).

N **THE CANADIAN PRESS**, 36 King St. E., Toronto Ontario M5C 2L9, Canada. (416)364-0321. **Contact:** Paul Loong. Estab. 1917. **80% freelance written on contract; 20% freelance written on one-time basis.** Query with published clips. Buys all rights. **Pays on acceptance.**
Needs: "We buy spot news stories of specific interest to Canada only that we cannot get from our usual news sources outside Canada—the AP." Buys single (one shot) features. **Pays flat rate. Additional payment for photos.**

N **CINEMAN SYNDICATE, LLC**, 16 School St., Suite 105, Rye NY 10580. (914)967-5353. E-mail: cineman@frontiernet.net. **Contact:** John P. McCarthy. Estab. 1978. **50% freelance written on contract; 50% freelance written on one-time basis. Buys 300 feature(s)/year. Works with 10 writer(s)/year. Works with 2 new previously unpublished writer(s)/year.** Syndicates to newspapers, Internet. Query with published clips. Responds in 3 weeks. Buys second serial (reprint) rights. **Pays on publication.** Free writer's guidelines.
Needs: Movie reviews, trivia questions. Buys single (one shot) features. **Payment negotiable/published review or trivia question. No additional payment for photos.** Currently syndicates *Mini Movie Reviews*; *Mini Music Reviews* by Stephen Israel; *Star Interviews* by Prairie Miller.
Tips: "We are seeking writers capable of delivering cogent, critical capsule reviews of movies on deadline. We are also seeking writers capable of devising entertaining trivia quizzes."

CONTINENTAL FEATURES/CONTINENTAL NEWS SERVICE, 501 W. Broadway, P.M.B #265 Plaza A, San Diego CA 92101-3802. (858)492-8696. E-mail: continentalnewstime@lycos.com. Website: pages.hotbot.com/current/newstime. **Contact:** Gary P. Salamone, editor-in-chief. Estab. 1981. **100% freelance written on contract.** "Writers who offer the kind and quality of writing we seek stand an equal chance regardless of experience." Syndicates to magazines, newspapers. Query. Responds in 1 month. Writer's guidelines for #10 SASE.
Needs: Magazine features, newspaper features. "Feature material should fit the equivalent of one-quarter to one-half standard newspaper page, and *Continental News* considers an ultra-liberal or ultra-conservative slant inappropriate." **Pays 70% author's percentage.** Currently syndicates *News and Comment*, by Charles Hampton Savage (general news commentary/analysis); *Portfolio*, (cartoon/caricature art); *Sports and Families*, by former American League Pitcher David Frost; *Traveler's Checks*, by Ann Hattes; and *OnVideo*, by Harley Lond; over 50 features in all.
Tips: "*CF/CNS* is working to develop a feature package of greater interest and value to an English-speaking international audience. That is, those writers who can accompany their economic-social-political analyses (of foreign countries) with photo(s) of the key public figure(s) involved are particularly in demand. Official photos (8×10 down to 3×5) of key government leaders available from the information ministry/press office/embassy will be acceptable. *CF/CNS* emphasizes analytical/explanatory articles, but muckraking articles (where official-photo requests are inopportune) are also encouraged."

COPLEY NEWS SERVICE, P.O. Box 120190, San Diego CA 92112. (619)293-1818. E-mail: infofax@copleynews.com. Website: www.copleynews.com. **Contact:** Glenda Winders, editorial director. Most stories produced by news bureaus or picked up from Copley newspapers. Columnists are experts in their fields. Uses freelancers for travel and occasional special features only. **Offers more than 100 features/week**. Syndicates to newspapers, Internet. Query with published clips. Responds in 6 months. Buys first rights.
Needs: Comic strips, travel stories, columns on technology, new ideas. **Pays negotiated monthly salary.**
Tips: "Writer needs to have a sense of competition for space in newspapers and offer features of broad, timely appeal. Competition is keen, but we are always on the lookout for good writers and fresh ideas."

CRICKET COMMUNICATIONS, INC., P.O. Box 527, Ardmore PA 19003-0527. (610)789-2480 or (610)924-9158. Fax: (610)924-9159. E-mail: crcktinc@aol.com. **Contact:** E. A. Stern, senior editor. Estab. 1975. **10% freelance written on contract; 10% freelance written on one-time basis. Works with 2-3 new previously unpublished writer(s)/year.** Syndicates to newspapers, trade magazines. Query with published clips. Responds in 1 month. Buys all rights.

Needs: Magazine columns, magazine features, newspaper columns, newspaper features, news items. All tax and financial-oriented (700-1,500 words); also newspaper columns, features and news items directed to small business. **Pays $50-500.** Currently syndicates *Hobby/Business*, by Mark E. Battersby (tax and financial); *Farm Taxes*, by various authors; and *Small Business Taxes*, by Mark E. Battersby.

CROSSWORD.ORG, P.O. Box 1503, New York NY 10021. (212)535-6811. **Contact:** Alfred Neumann, editor. Estab. 1998. **60% freelance written on contract; 40% freelance written on one-time basis.** Syndicates to magazines, newspapers. Responds in 1 month. Buys all rights.
Needs: Crossword puzzles. **Pays $350 for Sunday puzzle; $150 for daily puzzle.** Currently publishes online with PuzzleAmerica.com.

DEMKO'S AGEVENTURE SYNDICATED NEWS SERVICE, 21946 Pine Trace, Boca Raton FL 33428-3057. (561)482-6271. E-mail: ageventure@demko.com. Website: www.demko.com. Estab. 1983. **25% freelance written on contract; 25% freelance written on one-time basis. Buys 52 feature(s)/year. Works with 27 writer(s)/year.** Syndicates to magazines, radio, newspapers, Internet. Query via e-mail. Responds in 1 month. **Pays on acceptance.** Writer's guidelines by e-mail.
Needs: News items. Buys single (one shot) features, articles series. Currently syndicates *Senior Living* (lifestyle feature columns; 500-750 words) by staff writer; *Sonic Boomers* (personal profiles, ages 40-50; 150-200 words and photo); *Aging America* (mature market news items; 50-75 words).
Tips: "Stick with what you know in order to avoid superficial content. Query via e-mail with 2-3 work samples. Be assertive and upfront—specify your product and costs/prices in advance."

EDITORIAL CONSULTANT SERVICE, P.O. Box 524, West Hempstead NY 11552-1206. Fax: (516)481-5487. E-mail: Alongo42033@aol.com. **Contact:** Arthur A. Ingoglia, editorial director. Estab. 1964. **40% freelance written on contract; 25% freelance written on one-time basis.** Adds about 10 new columnists/year. **Works with 75 writer(s)/year.** Syndicates to magazines, radio, newspapers, Automotive trade and consumer publications. Query. Responds in 2 months. Buys all rights. Writer's guidelines for #10 SASE.
Needs: Magazine columns, magazine features, newspaper columns, newspaper features, news items, radio broadcast material. Prefers carefully documented material with automotive slant. Also considers automotive trade features. Will consider article series. Submit 2-3 columns. No horoscope, child care, lovelorn or pet care. **Payment varies, usually averages 50% author's percentage. Additional payment for 8×10 b&w and color photos accepted with ms.**
Tips: "Emphasis is placed on articles and columns with an automotive slant. We prefer consumer-oriented features, how to save money on your car, what every woman should know about her car, how to get more miles per gallon, etc."

ENVIRONMENT NEWS SERVICE (ENS), 4132 S. Rainbow Blvd., #389, Las Vegas NV 89103. (702)889-0247. E-mail: news@ens-news.com. Website: ens-news.com. **Contact:** Sunny Lewis. Estab. 1990. **20% freelance written on contract. Works with 125 writer(s)/year. Works with 10-15 new previously unpublished writer(s)/year.** Syndicates to Internet. Does not return submissions. Query only. Responds in 1-2 days. Buys worldwide rights. **Pays on publication.** Free writer's guidelines.
Needs: News items. Late-breaking news only. **Pays flat rate. No additional payment for photos.**
Tips: "Covers legislation, court rulings, demonstrations, conferences, air, land, water, climate, spills, species, protected areas."

HISPANIC LINK NEWS SERVICE, 1420 N St. NW, Washington DC 20005-2895. (202)234-0280. Fax: (202)234-4090. E-mail: editor@hispaniclink.org. **Contact:** Charles Ericksen, publisher; Cynthia L. Orosco, editor. Estab. 1980. **50% freelance written on contract; 50% freelance written on one-time basis.** Syndicates to 60 newspapers and magazines with circulations from 5,000 to 300,000. **Buys 156 feature(s)/year. Works with 50 writer(s)/year. Works with 5 new previously unpublished writer(s)/year.** Query or send complete ms. For reprints, send photocopy of article. Responds in 1 month. Buys second serial (reprint) rights, negotiable rights. Free writer's guidelines and sample of national newsweekly *Hispanic Link Weekly Report*.
Needs: Newspaper columns, newspaper features. "We prefer 650-700 word op/ed, analysis, or news features geared to a general national audience, but focus on issue or subject of particular interest to Hispanics. Some longer pieces accepted occasionally." **Pays $25-100. Pays $25 for guest columns.** Currently syndicates *Hispanic Link*, by various authors (opinion and/or feature columns). Syndicated through *Los Angeles Times Syndicate*, a division of Tribune Media Services.

O‑ "We're always looking for strong news features or personal stories relating to holidays—Christmas, Mother's/Father's Day, Valentines, Easter, etc."

Tips: "We especially like topical material and vignettes relating to Hispanic presence and progress in the U.S. and Puerto Rico. Provide insights on Hispanic experience geared to a general audience. Of the columns we accept, 85-90% are authored by Hispanics; the Link presents Hispanic viewpoints and showcases Hispanic writing talent through its subscribing newspapers and magazines. Copy can be submitted in English or Spanish. We syndicate both languages."

HOLLYWOOD INSIDE SYNDICATE, P.O. Box 49957, Los Angeles CA 90049-0957. (818)509-7840. Fax: (818)509-7840. E-mail: holywood@ez2.net. Website: www.ez2.net/hollywood. **Contact:** John Austin, editor. Estab. 1968. **10% freelance written on contract; 40% freelance written on one-time basis.** Purchases entertainment-oriented mss for syndication to newspapers in San Francisco, Philadelphia, Detroit, Montreal, London, Sydney, Manila, South Africa, etc. Accepts previously published submissions, only if published in the US or Canada. Responds in 3 months. Response time depends on timeliness of material.

Needs: News items (column items concerning entertainment—motion pictures—personalities and jet setters for syndicated column; 250-300 words). Also considers series of 1,500-word articles. "Query first. We also syndicate nonfiction book subjects—sex, travel, etc., to overseas markets. Also require 1,500-word celebrity profiles on internationally-recognized celebrities. We stress *internationally.*" Currently syndicates *Books of the Month* column and *Celebri-Quotes, Movie Trivia Quiz, Hollywood Inside*.

O→ Writing for the Hollywood Inside Syndicate should be geared for the World Wide Web and the international consumer, concise and to the point, without "flowery" sentences. "Anything on worldwide celebrities will be welcome but not in the first person. No: 'I asked him/her...' etc. We concentrate on film 'stars,' not TV."

Tips: "Study the entertainment pages of Sunday (and daily) newspapers to see the type of specialized material we deal in. Perhaps we are different from other syndicates, but we deal with celebrities. Many freelancers submit material from the 'dinner theater' and summer stock circuit of 'gossip type' items from what they have observed about the 'stars' or featured players in these productions—how they act off stage, who they romance, etc. We use this material."

INTERNATIONAL PUZZLE FEATURES, 4507 Panther Place, Charlotte NC 28269. Website: www.cleverpuzzles.com. **Contact:** Pat Battaglia, owner. Estab. 1990. **5-10% freelance written on one-time basis. Buys 10 feature(s)/year. Works with some new previously unpublished writer(s)/year.** Syndicates to newspapers. Send complete ms. Responds in 1 month. Writer's guidelines for #10 SASE.

Needs: Concisely written, entertaining word puzzles. **Pays $5/puzzle flat rate.** Currently syndicates *If You're So Smart...*, by Pat Battaglia (word puzzles).

Tips: "Puzzles that have the best chance of being chosen for publication will be concise, clever, appealing to readers of all ages, and have answers, that after becoming known, will seem surprisingly easy. We are not interested in crossword, word search, cryptogram, mathematical or trivia puzzles."

INTERPRESS OF LONDON AND NEW YORK, 90 Riverside Dr., New York NY 10026. (212)873-0772. **Contact:** Jeffrey Blyth, editor-in-chief. Estab. 1971. **10% freelance written on one-time basis. Buys 10-12 feature(s)/year.** Syndicates to radio, newspapers. Query. Responds in 1 week. Buys all rights. Writer's guidelines for #10 SASE.

Needs: Magazine features, newspaper features, off-beat feature stories. Buys single (one shot) features. **Pays 60% author's percentage. Additional payment for photos.** Currently syndicates *Destination America*, by various writers (travel series); *Book World*, by Myrna Grier (book news/reviews); *Dateline NY*, by various writers (show biz news/features); *Music World* (news about new CDs and recordings). Also columns on media and medical news.

[N] **MAIN STREET FEATURES**, 4725 Dorsey Hall Dr., PMB A500, Ellicott City MD 21043-7713. (410)442-1638. **Contact:** Larry E. Sturgill. Estab. 1991. **10% freelance written on contract; 10% freelance written on one-time basis. Buys 20-30 feature(s)/year. Works with 10-15 writer(s)/year. Works with 1-3 new previously unpublished writer(s)/year.** Syndicates to magazines, newspapers, Internet, trade publications. Query with published clips. Responds in 4-6 weeks. Buys first North American serial rights, all rights. **Payment depends on publication venue.**

Needs: Magazine columns, magazine features, newspaper columns, newspaper features, news items, fillers, occasional contract articles. Does not want political topics, cartoons. Buys single (one shot) features, articles series on various topics; length of articles vary with subject and venue. **Pays flat rate for contract writers only. There is an additional variable amount paid for photos.** Currently syndicates *Down on Main Street*, by Larry E. Sturgill (current topics); *December Rose*, by Cynthia Rose Sparrow (over 50 women's issues); *And, Elsewhere*, by J.D. Sparrow (interesting, often humorous stories from Small Town, USA).

MEGALO MEDIA, P.O. Box 1503, New York NY 10021. Website: www.puzzleamerica.com. **Contact:** J. Baxter Newgate, president. Estab. 1972. **50% freelance written on contract; 50% freelance written on one-time basis. Works with 5 new previously unpublished writer(s)/year.** Syndicates to magazines, newspapers. Query. Responds in 1 month. Buys all rights. Writer's guidelines for #10 SASE.

Needs: Crossword puzzles. Buys single (one shot) features. **Pays flat rate of $450 for Sunday puzzle.** Currently syndicates *National Challenge*, by J. Baxter Newgate (crossword puzzle); *Crossword Puzzle* by J. Baxter Newgate.

MOTOR NEWS MEDIA CORPORATION, 7177 Hickman Rd., Suite 11-D, Urbandale IA 50322. (515)270-6782. Fax: (515)270-8752. E-mail: mnmedia@uswest.net. Website: www.motornewsmedia.com. Estab. 1995. **90% freelance written on contract; 10% freelance written on one-time basis. Buys 132-150 feature(s)/year. Works with 10-12 writer(s)/year. Works with 2-4 new previously unpublished writer(s)/year.** Syndicates to newspapers, Internet. Query. Responds in 6 weeks. Buys first North American serial rights, second serial (reprint) rights. **Pays within 45 days of publication.**

Needs: Newspaper features. Buys single (one shot) features, articles series, automotive series. Currently syndicates *Roadworthy*, by Ken Chester, Jr.; *Credit & Coverage*, by Tom Brownell; *Hard Bargains*, by Neal White; *Dateline: Detroit!*, by Kailoni Yates; *Street Talk*, by Mike Fornataro; *Neal's Garage* by Neal White; *High & Mighty*, by Robin Bailey; *Ask Mr. Fix-It*, by Andy Mikonis; *Ask Dr. Gizmo*, by Phil Arendt; *Motocycling*, by Jim Kelly; *Timeless Nostalgia*, by Bill Vance; *Car Concerns*, by Susan Frissell; and *RV Traveling*, by Bill and Jan Moeller.

Tips: "We look for unique automotive content to round out our current offerings. Not interested in new vehicle reviews."

THE NATIONAL FINANCIAL NEWS SERVICES, 331 W. Boot Rd., West Chester PA 19380. (610)344-7380 or (800)939-NFNS. Fax: (610)696-1184. E-mail: brucenfns@aol.com. Website: www.nfns.com. **Contact:** Bruce Myers. Estab. 1985. **2% freelance written on contract. Buys 52 feature(s)/year. Works with 1 new previously unpublished writer(s)/year.** Syndicates to newspapers. Query. Buys all rights. **Pays on acceptance.**
Needs: Pays flat rate. Currently syndicates *Mortgages This Week*, by Al Bowman.

N NATIONAL GAY/LESBIAN TRAVEL DESK, 2790 Wrondel Way, PMB #444, Reno NV 89502. (775)348-7990. **Contact:** Sylvia Seltyer. Estab. 1995. **25% freelance written on contract; 80% freelance written on one-time basis. Buys 30 feature(s)/year. Works with 12-15 writer(s)/year.** Syndicates to magazines, newspapers, single magazines/newspapers, senior newspapers. Send complete ms. Responds in 1-2 months. Buys first North American serial rights. **Pays on publication.** Writer's guidelines for #10 SASE.
Needs: Magazine features, newspaper features. Buys single (one shot) features, articles series, 1,200 word stories on a city; can be done in 2 or 3 parts (maximum). **Pays $15/story, if published; $25/story, "If you get a local newspaper to become a member of the National Gay/Lesbian Travel Desk."** Currently syndicates *The Top 20 Attractions in Colorado Springs*, by Ira Gruber; *What's New in Kansas City*, by Ralph Ruben; *Fort Lauderdale—Casablanca of Gay America*, by Luis Rodriguez.
Tips: "Travel writing is vastly improved when gay/lesbian newspapers, senior and single newspapers decide to have a regular travel page."

NATIONAL NEWS BUREAU, P.O. Box 43039, Philadelphia PA 19129-0628. (215)849-9016. E-mail: nnbfeature@aol.com. Website: www.nationalnewsbureau.com. **Contact:** Harry Jay Katz, editor. **20% freelance written on contract; 35-40% freelance written on one-time basis. Buys 100 feature(s)/year. Works with 200 writer(s)/year. Works with 50% new previously unpublished writer(s)/year.** Syndicates to magazines, newspapers. Query with published clips. Responds in 2 weeks. Buys all rights. **Pays on publication.** Writer's guidelines for 9×12 SAE with 3 First-class Stamps.
Needs: Magazine features, newspaper columns, newspaper features. "We do many reviews and celebrity interviews. Only original, assigned material." Buys single (one shot) features, articles series, film reviews, etc. **Pays $5-200 flat rate or 50% author's percentage. Offers $5-200 additional payment for photos accompanying ms.**

NEW LIVING, P.O. Box 1519, Stony Brook NY 11790. (631)751-8819. Fax: (631)751-8910. E-mail: newliving@aol.com. Website: www.newliving.com. **Contact:** Christine Lynn Harvey, publisher. Estab. 1991. **20% freelance written on contract. Buys 20 feature(s)/year. Works with 20 writer(s)/year. Works with 5 new previously unpublished writer(s)/year.** Query with published clips. Buys all rights. Writer's guidelines for #10 SASE.
Needs: Magazine columns, magazine features, newspaper columns, newspaper features, news items, fillers, radio broadcast material. Seeks holistic health and fitness news on topics such as herbal medicine, clinical nutrition, mind/body medicine, fitness, healthy recipes, product reviews, energy healing (reiki, chakra, and sound), hypnosis, past life regression. Buys single (one shot) features, articles series. **Offers $25-100 for photos accepted with ms.**
- Nonpaid articles offers to list author's business affiliation, address, and phone number in article.

Tips: "Be highly qualified in the area that you are writing about. If you are going to write a medical column, you must be a doctor, or at least affiliated with a nationally recognized medical organization."

N NEW WAVE SYNDICATION, P.O. Box 232, North Quincy MA 02171. (617)471-8733. **Contact:** Dr. Tim Lynch, editor/publisher. Estab. 1991. Syndicates to newspapers. Query. Responds in 1 month. Buys first North American serial rights.
Needs: Newspaper columns, comics. **Pays 60% author's percentage.**

NEWS USA, 7777 Leesburg Pike, #307, Falls Church VA 22305. (703)734-6300. Website: www.newsusa.com. **Contact:** Diana Duvall, executive editor. Estab. 1988. **90% freelance written on contract. Buys 200 feature(s)/year. Works with 20 writer(s)/year.** Syndicates to radio, newspapers, Internet. Query. Responds in 2 months. Buys all rights. **Pays on acceptance.** Writer's guidelines for #10 SASE.
Needs: Newspaper features. "I only buy articles I commission from freelancers." **Pays $50 flat rate.**

N OASIS NEWSFEATURES, P.O. Box 2114, Middletown OH 45044. (800)582-4391. E-mail: KWilliams@OASISNewsfeatures.com. Website: www.OASISNewsfeatures.com. **Contact:** Kevin Williams. Estab. 1991. **95% freelance written on contract. Buys very few feature(s)/year. Works with 3-5 writer(s)/year. Works with 2-3 new previously unpublished writer(s)/year.** Syndicates to newspapers. Query with published clips. Responds in 2 months. Buys first North American serial rights. **Pays on publication.** Writer's guidelines for #10 SASE.
Needs: Magazine columns, comics. Buys single (one shot) features, articles series. **Authors are paid monthly, 40% first year under contract, 45% second year, 50% and up third year and beyond.** Currently syndicates *The Amish Cook*, *The Handwriting Dr.*, *Family Daze*, *The Kitchen Scientist*.
Tips: "This field is extremely competative. Please, no slice-of-life Erma Bombeck type stuff. We're looking for high quality comic strips or very original sports features. Come up with something specific and unique and please don't call me."

PRESS ASSOCIATES, INC., 1000 Vermont Ave. NW, Suite 101, Washington DC 20005. (202)898-4825. Fax: (202)898-9004. E-mail: unionnews@hotmail.com. Website: www.inetba.com/pressassociates. **Contact:** Mark Gruenberg, president/editor. Estab. 1957. **5% freelance written on contract. Buys 100 feature(s)/year. Works with 2 writer(s)/year.** Union newspapers and publications. Query. Responds in 2 months. Buys first North American serial rights. **Pays on publication.** Free writer's guidelines.

Needs: News items. "One-paragraph proposals with SASE only. Must be news—no opinion pieces—and pro-worker." Buys single (one shot) features. **Pays 25¢/published word; maximum of $25. Additional payment for photos.**

Tips: "We are *labor*-oriented. We do not syndicate outside of our subscribing readers."

N **RACING INFORMATION SYSTEMS**, 2314 Harriman Lane, Unit A, Redondo Beach CA 90278-4426. (310)374-3750. E-mail: racing@compuserve.com. **Contact:** Michael F. Hollander, editor. Estab. 1979. **25% freelance written on contract. Buys 45-50 feature(s)/year. Works with 100 writer(s)/year. Works with 1-5 new previously unpublished writer(s)/year.** Syndicates to newspapers. Query. Responds in 1 week. Buys first North American serial rights. **Pays on publication.** Writer's guidelines by e-mail.

Needs: Newspaper features, news items. Buys single (one shot) features; material must be timely and related to motor sport. **Pays 25% author's percentage. $5/outlet running the photo.** Features are stories about motor sports and those that are motor sports related. "Ron Fleshman, Ed Hollowell, Tom Beeler, Thad Byars and others have written stories for us."

Tips: "Writers should join the CompuServe Motor Sports Forum to get a feel for the type of material we want. Read the online stories and consider expansion to 500-600 words, plus 4 high-resolution photos."

SCRAMBL-GRAM INC., 41 Park Dr., Port Clinton OH 43452. (419)734-2600. Website: www.puzzlebuffs.com. **Contact:** S. Bowers, managing editor. Estab. 1978. **50% freelance written on one-time basis. Buys 300 feature(s)/year. Works with 20-30 writer(s)/year. Works with 3-5 new previously unpublished writer(s)/year.** Syndicates to magazines, newspapers, Internet. Responds in 1 month. Buys all rights. **Pays on acceptance.**

Needs: "We accept only crossword puzzles. Submit 1 or 2 examples of your work and if interested, we will send you information and materials to produce puzzles for us." **Rates are based on the size of the crossword.**

Tips: "Our crosswords appear weekly in *STAR Magazine*, *National Enquirer*, *Country Weekly*, and numerous other magazines and newspapers. Crosswords should be edited to remove obscure and archaic words. Foreign words should be kept to a minimum. The puzzle should be fun and challenging but achievable."

SENIOR WIRE, 2377 Elm St., Denver CO 80207. (303)355-3882. E-mail: clearmountain1@msn.com. Website: www.seniorwire.net. **Contact:** Allison St. Claire, editor/publisher. Estab. 1988. Monthly news, information, and feature syndication service to various senior publications, and companies interested in senior market. Circulation nationwide, in Canada and India, varies/article depending on which articles are bought for publication. Submit seasonal/holiday material 3 months in advance. Prefers mss; queries only with SASE. Responds in 3 months. **Pays 50% of fee for each use of ms ($15-50). Pays on publication.** Writer's guidelines for $1 with SASE.

Needs: Does not want "anything aimed at less than age 55-plus market; anything patronizing or condescending to seniors." Buys single (one shot) features, seasonal features, especially those with a nostalgic angle (750-800 words); personal travel experiences as a mature traveler (700-1,000 words); personal essays and commentary (500-750 words). The following topics currently are covered by assigned columnists and similar material has little chance of immediate acceptance: national legislation; financial and legal advice; golf; Internet; automotive; fitness; food; collectibles; Q&A on relationships. Accepts 12 mss in each category/year.

Tips: "That quintessential sweet little old lady in the rocking chair, Whistler's mother, was just 50 years old when she posed for that painting. Today, the average age of the Rolling Stones is 57. Most of our client papers like to emphasize active, thoughtful, concerned seniors and are currently picking up material that shows seniors living in the 'real,' i.e., contemporary, world. For example, do you have your own personal fax yet; how has a computer changed your life; what kind of new cars are you looking at? What adventures have you been involved in? What impact are you/seniors having on the world around them—and vice versa? Currently overloaded with humor. Seeking regular columnists in following: senior sexuality, sports fitness, and national trends."

THE SPORTS NETWORK, 2200 Byberry Rd., Suite 200, Hatboro PA 19040. (215)441-8444. Fax: (215)441-9019. E-mail: psokol@sportsnetwork.com. Website: www.sportsnetwork.com. Estab. 1980. **30% freelance written on contract; 10-15% freelance written on one-time basis. Buys 200-250 feature(s)/year. Works with 50-60 writer(s)/year. Works with 10-15 new previously unpublished writer(s)/year.** Syndicates to magazines, radio, newspapers, Has the added benefit of being an international sports wire service with established awareness globally furnishing exposure worldwide for its writers/clients. Query with published clips. Responds immediately. Buys all rights. Free writer's guidelines.

Needs: Magazine columns, magazine features, newspaper columns, newspaper features, news items, fillers, radio and broadcast material. Looking for single features (timely sports pieces, from 700-1,000 words). Seeking ongoing coverage pieces of teams (professional), leagues (professional), conferences (college), and sports, 1-2 times weekly. **Payments variable.** Currently syndicates *The Sandlot Shrink*, by Dennis LePore; *Infosport*, by Julie Lanzillo; *The Women's Basketball Journal, Bball Stats,* by Robert Chaikin.

Tips: "The competition for sports is fast and furious, so right time and place, with a pinch of luck, are ingredients that complement talent. Making inroads to 1 syndicate for even 1 feature is an amazing door opener. Focus on the needs of that syndicate or wire service (as in the case with TSN), and use that as a springboard to establish a proven track record with quality work that suits specific needs. Don't give up and don't abandon the day job. This takes commitment, desire, knowledge of the topic, and willingness to work at it while being able to handle rejection. No one who reads submissions really 'knows' and the history of great rejections would fill volumes, from *Gone with the Wind* to Snoopy and Garfield. We are different in that we are looking for specific items and not a magical cartoon (although sports cartoons will work), feature, or story. Give us your best in sports and make certain that is is in tune with what is happening right now or is able to stand the test of time, be an evergreen and everlasting if it is a special feature."

TEENAGE CORNER, INC., 70-540 Gardenia Ct., Rancho Mirage CA 92270. **Contact:** Mrs. David J. Lavin. **Buys 122 feature(s)/year.** Syndicates to newspapers. Send complete ms. Responds in 1 week.
Needs: Newspaper features (500 words). **Pays $25, material is not copyrighted.**

TV DATA, 333 Glen St., Glens Falls NY 12801. (518)792-9914. Fax: (800)660-7185. E-mail: mskotnicki@tvdata.com. Website: www.tvdata.com. **Contact:** Monique Skotnicki, features managing editor. **95% freelance written by staff or freelancers supplying weekly columns. 5% freelance written on one-time basis. Buys 20 feature(s)/year. Works with 10 writer(s)/year.** Syndicates to newspapers, Internet. Query with published clips. Responds in 1 month. Buys all rights. **Pays on publication.**
Needs: Newspaper columns, newspaper features, fillers.

O→ Submissions must be: TV-related; no more than 1,000 words; written according to AP style; sent as a Quark or Microsoft Word attachment.

Tips: "Submissions should be television-related features about trends, stars, sports, movies, the Internet, etc. They should be approximately 1,000 words and written according to AP style."

[N] UNITED FEATURE SYNDICATE/NEWSPAPER ENTERPRISE ASSOCIATION, 200 Madison Ave., New York NY 10016. (212)293-8500. Fax: (212)293-8760. Website: www.unitedfeatures.com. **Contact:** Liz Martinez DeFranco, managing editor. Estab. 1902. **100% freelance written on contract. Buys 4 feature(s)/year. Works with 4 writer(s)/year.** Syndicates to newspapers. Query with published clips. Responds in 3 months. Buys all rights. **Pays on publication.** Writer's guidelines online at website.
Needs: Newspaper columns, newspaper features. **Payment negotiable.** Currently syndicates *Miss Manners*, by Judith Martin (advice/etiquette); *Hardball*, by Chris Matthews (political commentary); Scripps Howard News Service, hundreds of stories each week, plus photos, graphics and special sections.
Tips: "Find a niche that isn't being filled in the newspaper market, and fit it with your work."

[N] WHITEGATE FEATURES SYNDICATE, 71 Faunce Dr., Providence RI 02906. (401)274-2149. E-mail: 102404.574@compuserve.com. **Contact:** Ene Green. Estab. 1988. **100% freelance written on contract. Buys 3-10 feature(s)/year.** Syndicates to magazines, radio, newspapers, Internet. "We contact you if we can do anything—also, we file things for the future." Query with published clips. Slow response time. Buys negotiable rights. **Pays on publication.**
Needs: Newspaper columns. "We do regular weekly columns." Buys article series, sometimes considers topical material. **Pays 50% author's percentage. Offers negotiable payment for photos.** Currently syndicates Jane Adler (gardening); Diane Abrams (health, beauty, fashion, travel).
Tips: "Come up with some fresh, new ideas."

Greeting Cards & Gift Ideas

How many greeting cards did you buy last year? Americans buy approximately seven billion cards annually. That's according to figures published by The Greeting Card Association, a national trade organization representing the multi-billion dollar greeting card industry.

Card manufacturers rely on writers to supply them with enough skillfully crafted sentiments to meet the annual demand for cards. The perfect greeting card verse is one that will appeal to a large audience, yet will make each buyer feel that the card was written exclusively for him or her.

Currently, there are more than 2,000 greeting card publishers in the U.S., some owned by major corporations and others by small, family-run businesses.

A PROFESSIONAL APPROACH TO MARKETS

As markets become more focused, it's important to stay current on specific company needs. Familiarize yourself with the differences among lines of cards by visiting card racks. Ask retailers which lines are selling best.

Once you find a card line that appeals to you, write to the company and request its market list, catalog, or submission guidelines (usually available for a SASE or a small fee). This information will help you determine whether or not your ideas are appropriate for that market.

Submission procedures vary among greeting card publishers, depending on the size and nature of the company. Keep in mind that many companies (especially the large ones) will not review your writing samples until you've signed and returned their disclosure contract or submission agreement, assuring them that your material is original and has not been submitted elsewhere.

Some editors prefer to see individual card ideas on 3×5 cards, while others prefer to receive a number of complete ideas on 8½×11 bond paper. Be sure to put your best pieces at the top of the stack. Most editors do not want to see artwork unless it's professional, but they do appreciate conceptual suggestions for design elements. If your verse depends on an illustration to make its point, or if you have an idea for a unique card shape or foldout, include a dummy card with your writing samples.

The usual submission includes from 5 to 15 card ideas and an accompanying cover letter, plus mechanical dummy cards, if necessary. Some editors also like to receive a résumé, client list, and business card. Some do not. Be sure to check the listings and the company's writer's guidelines for such specifications before submitting material.

Payment for greeting card verse varies, but most firms pay per card or per idea; a handful pay small royalties. Some companies prefer to test a card first and will pay a small fee for a test card idea. In some instances, a company may even purchase an idea and never use it.

Greeting card companies will also buy ideas for gift products and may use card material for a number of subsequent items. Licensing—the sale of rights to a particular character for a variety of products from mugs to T-shirts—is a growing part of the industry. Because of this, however, note that most card companies buy all rights. We include, in this section, markets for licensed product lines such as mugs, bumper stickers, buttons, posters, and the like.

MANAGING YOUR SUBMISSIONS

Because you will be sending out many samples, you may want to label each sample. Establish a master card for each verse idea and record where and when each was sent and whether it was rejected or purchased. Keep all cards sent to one company in a batch and give each batch a number. Write this number on the back of your return SASE to help you match up your verses as they are returned.

For More Information

GREETING CARDS & GIFT RESOURCES

- *Gifts and Decorative Accessories* (www.giftsanddec.com) and *Party and Paper Retailer* (www.p-artypaper.com). These magazines will keep you apprised of changes and events within the field, including seminars and trade shows.
- Greeting Card Association (www.greetingcard.org), 1156 15th Street NW, Suite 900, Washington DC 20005. Offers information of interest to writers wishing to know more about working in the greeting card industry.

Information on greeting card companies listed in the previous edition of *Writer's Market* but not included in this edition can be found in the General Index.

AMBERLEY GREETING CARD CO., 11510 Goldcoast Dr., Cincinnati OH 45249-1695. (513)489-2775. Fax: (513)489-2857. Website: www.amberleygreeting.com. **Acquisitions:** Editor. Estab. 1966. **90% freelance written. Bought 200 freelance ideas last year.** Responds in 1 month. Material copyrighted. Buys all rights. **Pays on acceptance.** Writer's guidelines/market list for #10 SASE.

● Amberley Greetings is now accepting alternative humor.

Needs: Humorous. "Original, easy to understand, belly-laugh or outrageous humor. We sell to the 'masses, not the classes,' so keep it simple and to the point. Humor accepted in all captions, including general birthday, family birthday, get well, anniversary, thank you, friendship, etc. No nonhumorous material needed or considered this year." Submit 10 ideas/batch. **Pays $150/card idea.**

Tips: "Send SASE for our writer's guidelines before submitting. Amberley publishes humorous specialty lines in addition to a complete conventional line that is accented with humor. Since humor is our specialty, we are highly selective. Be sure your SASE has correct U.S. postage. Otherwise it will not be returned."

AMERICAN GREETINGS, Dept. WM, One American Rd., Cleveland OH 44144-2398. (216)252-7300. Fax: (216) 252-6777. **Acquisitions:** Leia Madden, creative recruitment. No unsolicited material. Experienced, talented writers should submit a cover letter and résumé describing their education and content experience for contract-to-permanent staff writing positions.

Needs: Humorous.

Tips: "In this competitive arena, we're only looking for gifted humor writers and cartoonists who are interested in adapting their skillsets to the uniqueness of greeting card composition."

JOHN BARLOW, PUBLISHER, 2147 Windmill View Rd., El Cajon CA 92020. **Acquisitions:** John Barlow, president. Estab. 2002. For market list the company supplies photographs. The captions must be written to match them. New sets of photographs will be available every 6 months. "We publish greeting cards featuring reproductions of old photographs—presently 1880-1930, but soon expanding into 1940s, 1950s, 1960s, and 1970s. The photos depict children or adults in cute, funny, or interesting situations. We supply the photographs—the captions must be written to match them. We want clean humor, nostalgic messages, loving, or sweet sentiments, and for Christmas and Easter cards, traditional captions. We prefer 1- or 2-line captions. Our categories include birthday, get well, friends/thinking of you, congratulations, graduation, new baby, anniversary, marriage congratulations, thank you, Mother's Day, Father's Day, Valentine's Day, Christmas, and Easter." **50% freelance written. Receives 500 submissions/year; bought 30 (hoping to increase this number) freelance ideas last year.** Responds in 2 months. Material copyrighted. Buys worldwide exclusive rights in all commercial formats. **Pays on acceptance.** Writer's guidelines for 9X12 SAE with 3 First-class Stamps.

Needs: Conventional, humorous, informal, sensitivity, traditional for Christmas and Easter cards. Prefers unrhymed verse ideas.

BRILLIANT ENTERPRISES, 117 W. Valerio St., Santa Barbara CA 93101-2927. **Acquisitions:** Ashleigh Brilliant, president. Estab. 1967. Responds in 2 weeks. Buys all rights. Catalog and sample set for $2.

Needs: Postcards. "Messages should be of a highly original nature, emphasizing subtlety, simplicity, insight, wit, profundity, beauty and felicity of expression. Accompanying art should be in the nature of oblique commentary or decoration rather than direct illustration. Messages should be of universal appeal, capable of being appreciated by all types of people and of being easily translated into other languages. Because our line of cards is highly unconventional, it is essential that freelancers study it before submitting. No topical references or subjects limited to American culture or puns." Submit words and art in black on 3½ x 3½ horizontal, thin white paper in batches of no more than 15. Limit of 17 words/card. **Pays $60 for "complete, ready-to-print word and picture design."**

THE CALLIGRAPHY COLLECTION INC., 2604 NW 74th Place, Gainesville FL 32653. (352)375-8530. Fax: (352)374-9957. E-mail: artistkaty@aol.com. **Acquisitions:** Katy Fischer, owner. Responds in 6 months. Buys all rights. Pays on publication.
Needs: Conventional, humorous, inspirational, sensitivity, soft line. "A line of framed prints of watercolors with calligraphy." Prefers unrhymed verse, but will consider rhymed. Submit 3 ideas/batch. **Pays $75-200/framed print idea.**
Other Product Lines: Gift books, plaques, musical picture frames.
Tips: "We are looking for sentimental and inspirational sayings such as can be given to friends or family, or used as a wedding or graduation gift, but that do not mention specific occasions as such. For example, Mother saying that could be given all year as well as on Mother's Day. Our main markets are women 20 to 50 years of age. We are looking for verses that tell someone significant how much they mean to you, how important their friendship is or what is special about knowing them. All that in 35 words or less. We are looking for sayings to incorporate into items that caring people would like to give as lasting gifts."

CARDMAKERS, P.O. Box 236, 66 High Bridge Rd., Lyme NH 03768. (603)795-4422. Fax: (603)795-4222. E-mail: info@cardmakers.com. Website: www.cardmakers.com. **Acquisitions:** Peter D. Diebold, owner. Estab. 1978. **Receives hundreds of submissions/year.** Submit seasonal/holiday material 10 months in advance. Responds in 3 months. Buys greeting card rights. **Pays on acceptance.** Writer's guidelines/market list for #10 SASE.
Needs: Humorous, holiday (mostly) and everyday. "We like upbeat humor, skip sick or raunchy. Our customers use our cards to greet their customers. So a positive approach/result is desirable." Prefers unrhymed verse ideas.
Tips: "We are primarily a direct marketer of business-to-business greetings targeted to specific interest groups—i.e., stockbrokers, boaters, etc. We also publish everyday cards for those same specific interests. So far, all our ideas and captions have been generated internally. We work with many freelancers on design and have recently decided to solicit ideas from writers. Please don't call or e-mail. To get our attention, make a card that reflects your most clever idea. Mail it to us with a return postcard (postage paid of course) and give us check-off options with degree of interest from 0-10. We'll know if you have what we need and you'll hear from us quicker."

COMSTOCK CARDS, 600 S. Rock, Suite 15, Reno NV 89502-4115. (775)856-9400. Fax: (775)856-9406. E-mail: production@comstockcards.com. Website: www.comstockcards.com. **Acquisitions:** Cindy Thomas, production manager. Estab. 1986. **35% freelance written. Receives 2,000 submissions/year; bought 150 freelance ideas last year.** Submit seasonal/holiday material 12 months in advance. Responds in 5 weeks. Buys all rights. **Pays on acceptance.** Writer's guidelines for #10 SASE. Market list issued one time only.
Needs: Humorous, informal, invitations. "Puns, put-downs, put-ons, outrageous humor aimed at a sophisticated, adult female audience. Also risqué cartoon cards." No conventional, soft line or sensitivity hearts and flowers, etc. **Pays $50-75/card idea. Cartoons negotiable.**
Other Product Lines: Notepads, cartoon cards, invitations.
Tips: "Always keep holiday occasions in mind and personal me-to-you expressions that relate to today's occurrences. Ideas must be simple and concisely delivered. A combination of strong image and strong gag line make a successful greeting card. Consumers relate to themes of work, sex and friendship combined with current social, political and economic issues."

N **DUCK AND COVER PRODUCTIONS**, P.O. Box 21640, Oakland CA 94620. E-mail: Duckcover@aol.com. **Acquisitions:** Jim Buser, editor. Estab. 1990. **50% freelance written. Receives 1,000 submissions/year; bought 120 freelance ideas last year.** Responds in 3 weeks. Buys all rights. Pays on publication. Writer's guidelines/market list for #10 SASE.
Other Product Lines: "We do **not** make greeting cards." Buttons, magnets and bumper stickers only. **Pays $40/idea.**
Tips: "Duck and Cover holds the trump cards for intelligent, contemporary humor. We are a smorgasbord of existential angst, psychotic babble, dry wit and outrageous zingers. Our products appeal to anyone with an offbeat, irreverent sense of humor. We sell to novelty stores, head shops, record stores, bookstores, sex shops, comic stores, etc. There are no taboos for our writers; we encourage them to be as weird and/or rude as they like, as long as they are funny. Let your inner child thumb his nose at society. Cerebral material that makes use of contemporary pop vocabulary is a plus. We do not want to see old clichés or slogans already in the market. Drink a six pack, read the newspaper from beginning to end, and then try to make humorous reflections about what you've just read."

EPHEMERA, INC., P.O. Box 490, Phoenix OR 97535. E-mail: mail@ephemera-inc.com. Website: www.ephemera-inc.com. **Acquisitions:** Editor. Estab. 1979. **95% freelance written. Receives 1,050 submissions/year.** Bought 200 slogans for novelty buttons, stickers and magnets last year. Responds in 3 months. Buys all rights. **Pays on acceptance.** Writer's guidelines/market list for #10 SASE. Complete full-color catalog for $4.
Needs: Humorous. "Make us laugh out loud. We want provocative, irreverent and outrageously funny slogans. Topics include women's issues, the President, job attitudes, current events, pop culture, advertising satire, religion, pets, coffee, booze, pot, drugs, sexual come-ons and put-downs, aging, slacker angst, gays and lesbians, etc. We sell these high

impact gems of wit to trendy card and gift shops, bookstores, record shops, fashion boutiques, head shops, sex shops, gay, feminist and political stores, etc. For over 20 years we have been known as *the* place for intelligent, in-your-face humor." **Pays $40/slogan.**

GALLANT GREETINGS, P.O. Box 308, Franklin Park IL 60131. Website: www.gallantgreetings.com. **Acquisitions:** JL-PD. Publishers of everyday and seasonal greeting cards.

KATE HARPER DESIGNS,. E-mail: kateharp@aol.com. **Acquisitions:** Via e-mail. Estab. 1993. "We have different themes card lines. See specific web addresses for detailed guidelines on each theme. **Everyday Card Line** (all subjects and topics with humor, includes seasonal): http://hometown.aol.com/kateharp/myhomepage/poetry.html; **Cardz with an Attitude** (for a younger, 20-something crowd): http://hometown.aol.com/kha1781344//myhomepage/writing.html; and **Kids Card Line** (quotes by children): http://hometown.aol.com/kateharp/myhomepage/business.html." **100% freelance written.** Submit seasonal/holiday material 12 months in advance. Pays flat fee for usage, not exclusive, plus author's name credit. **Pays on acceptance.** Online at website or by e-mail.

- Ms. Harper notes she wants to see more quotes by children.

Needs: Humorous, intelligent, edgy, birthday, love, thanks. Unrhymed verse ideas *only.* Submit 10 ideas/batch.

Tips: "Quotes needed about work, life, career, technology and marriage with a twist of humor. Something you would laugh at, and tips on how to have it all and still live to tell about it. Be adventurous and say what you really think in first person. What is ironic about this world we live in? What is the message you want to put out in the world? Don't be afraid to take risks and push beyond greeting card stereotypes. Nothing cute or sweet, such as comparing love to rainbows. Eliminate 99% of all adjectives. Instead, write like people speak. Please avoid rhymes, similes, quotes about PMS, chocolate, sex, or anything that might be insulting to the recipient, such as being old or overweight. Test: Imagine how you would feel if someone sent you this quote. When submitting birthday themes, please avoid making fun of or insulting the card recipient. Do not send cliché themes of old age, forgetfulness, wrinkles, etc. Try to think outside of the traditional birthday card. Here are some quotes we've purchased in the past: 'Happy Birthday. With age comes wisdom, self-confidence and the ability to tell people to get lost'; 'Happy Birthday. You're not over the hill, you're on top of the world'; and 'If you are old enough to know better, you probably don't even care. Happy Birthday.' For other tips on 'How to write good card text,' see our webpage http://hometown.aol.com/kateharp/myhomepage/profile.html."

INSPIRATIONS UNLIMITED, P.O. Box 9097, Cedar Pines Park CA 92322. Estab. 1984. **Bought 50 freelance ideas last year.** Submit seasonal/holiday material 6 months in advance. Responds in 1 month. Pays on publication.

Needs: Conventional, informal, inspirational, sensitivity. Submit 10 ideas/batch on numbered 3×5 cards. Prefers unrhymed verse ideas.

Tips: "Send heart-to-heart messages—something that tugs at the heart."

KOEHLER COMPANIES, INC., 8758 Woodcliff Rd., Bloomington MN 55438. (952)830-9050. Fax: (952)830-9051. E-mail: bob@koehlercompanies.com. Website: www.koehlercompanies.com. **Acquisitions:** Bob Koehler. Estab. 1988. "We combine art and message to create a product that a consumer will like enough to want to look at for a year or longer." **65% freelance written. Receives 100 submissions/year; bought 25 freelance ideas last year.** Responds in 1 month. **Pays on acceptance.**

O-ᴛ "Verse that works best is: topics such as golf, fishing, pets, and other passions. Sisters, Mom, Family, words to inspire without getting preachy, verse that speaks to women. Also verse for men, usually humorous. See our website for examples of our work."

Needs: Humorous, inspirational, some religious. **"We pay $125/selected verse and limit the use to our products so that a writer may resell their work for other uses."**

Other Product Lines: Decorative wall plaques.

Tips: "We sell wholesale to the retail market and the mail order catalog industry as well. Lengthy verse is sometimes challenging. Usually under 12 lines is best. Would prefer to have work submitted by e-mail or mail."

LIFE GREETINGS, P.O. Box 468, Little Compton RI 02837. (401)635-8535. Fax: (401)635-4918. **Acquisitions:** Kathy Brennan. Estab. 1972. "We publish 'Christian' greetings." **100% freelance written.** Submit seasonal/holiday material 6 months in advance. Responds in 2 weeks. Buys all rights. **Pays on acceptance.** Writer's guidelines/market list for #10 SASE.

Needs: Conventional, inspirational, juvenile, sensitivity. Accepts rhymed or unrhymed verse.

NOVO CARD PUBLISHERS, INC., 3630 W. Pratt Ave., Lincolnwood IL 60712. (847)763-0077. Fax: (847)763-0020. E-mail: art@novocard.net. Website: www.novocard.net. Estab. 1926. **80% freelance written. Receives 500 submissions/year; bought 200 freelance ideas last year.** Submit seasonal/holiday material 8 months in advance. Responds in 2 months. Buys worldwide greeting card rights. **Pays on acceptance.** Writer's guidelines/market list for #10 SASE. Market list available to writer on mailing list basis.

Needs: Announcements, conventional, humorous, informal, inspirational, invitations, juvenile, sensitivity, soft line, studio.

OATMEAL STUDIOS, P.O. Box 138W3, Rochester VT 05767. (802)767-3171. **Acquisitions:** Helene Lehrer, creative director. Estab. 1979. **85% freelance written. Bought 200-300 freelance ideas last year.** Responds in 6 weeks. **Pays on acceptance.** Current market list for #10 SASE.

- "Humor, conversational in tone and format, sells best for us."

Needs: Humorous, birthday, friendship, anniversary, get well cards, etc. Also Christmas, Hanukkah, Mother's Day, Father's Day, Easter, Valentine's Day, etc. Will review concepts. Humorous material (clever and very funny) year-round. Prefers unrhymed verse ideas. **Current pay schedule available with guidelines.**
Other Product Lines: Notepads, stick-on notes.
Tips: "The greeting card market has become more competitive with a greater need for creative and original ideas. We are looking for writers who can communicate situations, thoughts, and relationships in a funny way and apply them to a birthday, get well, etc., greeting and we are willing to work with them in targeting our style. We will be looking for material that says something funny about life in a new way."

P.S. GREETINGS, 5730 N. Tripp Ave., Chicago IL 60646. Fax: (773)267-6150. Website: www.psgreetings.com. **Acquisitions:** Art Director. **100% freelance written. Bought 200-300 freelance ideas last year.** Submit seasonal/holiday material 6 months in advance. Responds in 1 month. **Pays on acceptance.** Writer's guidelines/market list for #10 SASE or check them out on the website.
Needs: Conventional, humorous, inspirational, invitations, juvenile, sensitivity, soft line, studio. Accepts rhymed or unrhymed verse. Submit 10 ideas/batch. **Pays one-time flat fee.**

THE PAPER MAGIC GROUP, INC., 401 Adams Ave., Scranton PA 18510. (800)278-4085. Fax: (717)348-8389. E-mail: stacey.harris@papermagic.com. Website: www.papermagic.com. **Acquisitions:** Stacey Harris, assistant product manager. Estab. 1907. **50% freelance written. Receives 500 submissions/year.** Submit seasonal/holiday material 6 months in advance. **Pays on acceptance.** No market list. Christmas boxed cards only. Submit Christmas sentiments only. No relative titles, juvenile. Submit 6-12 ideas/batch.

PORTAL PUBLICATIONS, 201 Almeda Del Prado, Novato CA 94949. (800)227-1720. Fax: (415) 382-3377. Website: www.portalpub.com. **Acquisitions:** Editorial Department. Estab. 1954. "Please no phone calls; written submissions only." **25% freelance written. Receives 400 submissions/year; bought 100 freelance ideas last year.** Responds in 3 months. **Pays on acceptance.**
Needs: Inspirational, general and alternative humor. Also copy for humorous and inspirational posters. "Please send 10-15 samples of your work so that we may keep it on file. If in the future, we have need for writers for our greeting cards or other products we will contact you."
Other Product Lines: Calendars, posters.
Tips: "Upscale, cute, alternative, humorous cards for bookstores, card stores, chain stores and college bookstores."

ROCKSHOTS, INC., 20 Vandam St., New York NY 10013. (212)243-9661. Fax: (212)604-9060. Website: www.rockshots.com. **Acquisitions:** Bob Vesce, editor. Estab. 1979. **Bought 75 greeting card verse (or gag) freelance ideas last year.** Responds in 1 month. Buys greeting card rights. Writer's guidelines/market list for #10 SASE.
Needs: Humorous, soft line. Looking for a combination of sexy and humorous come-on type greeting ("sentimental is not our style"); and insult cards ("looking for cute insults"). "Card gag can adopt a sentimental style, then take an ironic twist and end on an off-beat note." No sentimental or conventional material. Prefers gag lines on 8x11 paper with name, address, and phone and social security numbers in right corner, or individually on 3×5 cards. Submit 10 ideas/batch. **Pays $50/gag line.**
Tips: "Rockshots is an outrageous, witty, adult, and sometimes shocking card company. Our range of style starts at cute and whimsical and runs the gamut all the way to totally outrageous and unbelievable. Rockshot cards definitely stand out from all the 'mainstream' products on the market today. Some of the images we are famous for include 'sexy' photos of 500- to 600-pound female models, smart-talking grannies, copulating animals, and of course, incredibly sexy shots of nude and seminude men and women. Some of our best-selling cards are photos with captions that start out leading the reader in one direction, and then zings them with a punch line totally out of left field, but also hysterically apropos. As you can guess, we do not shy away from much. Be creative, be imaginative, be funny, but most of all, be different. Do not hold back because of society's imposed standards, but let it all pour out. It's always good to mix sex and humor, as sex always sells. Remember that 70% to 80% of our audience is women, so get in touch with your 'feminine' side, your bitchy feminine side. Your gag line will be illustrated by a Rockshots photograph or drawing, so try and think visually. It's always a good idea to preview our cards at your local store, if this is possible, to give you a feeling of our style."

SCHURMAN FINE PAPERS, 101 New Montgomery St., 6th Floor, San Francisco CA 94105. Fax: (707) 428-0641. **Acquisitions:** Text Editor. Estab. 1950. **10% freelance written. Receives 500 submissions/year; bought 25 freelance ideas last year.** Responds in 2 months. **Pays on acceptance.** Writer's guidelines/market list for #10 SASE.
Needs: Inspirational, sentimental, contemporary, romance, friendship, seasonal, and everyday categories. Send humor ideas to: Laffs by Marcel at address above. Prefers unrhymed verse, but on juvenile cards rhyme is OK. Submit 10-15 ideas/batch.
Tips: "Offer clever, sophisticated, fresh text concepts. Avoid 'bathroom humor' and other off-color text directions. Sentimental text works best if it is short and elegant (not long, maudlin, or syrupy). We do not use poetry as card text. Historically, our nostalgic and art museum cards sell best. However, we are moving toward more contemporary cards and humor. Target market: upscale, professional, well-educated, average age 40, more female. Be original."

SNAFU DESIGNS, Box 16643, St. Paul MN 55116. E-mail: guidelines@snafucards.com. **Acquisitions:** Scott F. Austin, editor. Estab. 1985. Responds in 6 weeks. Buys all rights. **Pays on acceptance.** Writer's guidelines/market list for #10 SASE.

Needs: Humorous, informal. Specifically seeking birthday, friendship, thank you, anniversary, congratulations, get well, new baby, Christmas, Valentine's Day. Submit no more than 10 ideas/batch. **Pays $100/idea.**
Tips: "We use clever ideas that are simple and concisely delivered and are aimed at a sophisticated adult audience. Off-the-wall humor that pokes fun at the human condition. Please do not submit anything cute."

SPS STUDIOS INC., Publishers of Blue Mountain Arts, Dept. WM, P.O. Box 1007, Boulder CO 80306-1007. Fax: (303)447-0939. E-mail: editorial@spsstudios.com. Website: www.sps.com. **Acquisitions:** Editorial Department. Estab. 1971. **Bought over 200 freelance ideas last year.** Submit seasonal/holiday material 4 months in advance. Responds in 4-6 months. Buys worldwide, exclusive rights, anthology rights. Pays on publication. Writer's guidelines online at website.

O→ "We like to receive original, sensitive poetry and prose on love, friendship, family, philosophies, and any other topic that one person might want to communicate or share with another person. Writings on special occasions (birthday, anniversary, graduation, etc.) as well as the challenges, difficulties, and aspirations of life are also considered. Important note: Because of the large volume of poetry we receive written to mothers, sons, and daughters, we are only accepting highly original and creative poetry that expresses new thoughts and sentiments on these themes."

Needs: Announcements, sensitivity. "We are interested in reviewing poetry and writings that would be appropriate for greeting cards, which means that they should reflect a message, feeling, or sentiment that one person would want to share with another. We'd like to receive sensitive, original submissions about love relationships, family members, friendships, philosophies, and any other aspect of life. Poems and writings for specific holidays (Christmas, Valentine's Day, etc.) and special occasions, such as graduation, birthdays, anniversary, and get well are also considered." **Pays $200/poem for each of first two works chosen for publication on a card (payment scale escalates after that); $25 for anthology rights.**
Other Product Lines: Calendars, gift books, prints, mugs.
Tips: "We strongly suggest that you familiarize yourself with our products before submitting material, although we caution you not to study them too hard. We do not need more poems that sound like something we've already published. We're looking for poetry that expresses real emotions and feelings, so we suggest that you have someone specific in mind (a friend, relative, etc.) as you write. The majority of the poetry we publish does not rhyme. We prefer that submissions be typewritten, one poem per page, with name and address on every page. Only a small portion of the freelance material we receive is selected each year, either for publication on a notecard or in a gift anthology, and the review process can also be lengthy, but please be assured that every manuscript is given serious consideration."

SUZY'S ZOO, 9401 Waples St., Suite 150, San Diego CA 92121. (858)452-9401. E-mail: jbush@suzyszoo.com. Website: www.suzyszoo.com. **Acquisitions:** Judi Bush, sales/marketing analyst. Estab. 1968. Submit seasonal/holiday material 18 months in advance. Responds in 4 months. Material copyrighted. Buys all rights. **Pays on acceptance.** Writer's guidelines/market list for #10 SASE.
Needs: Announcements, conventional, humorous, informal, inspirational, invitations. Prefers unrhymed verse ideas. Submit 15 ideas/batch.
Tips: "Cards that make people smile, touches their heart no matter what the occasion. Suzy's Zoo greeting cards are purchased primarily by women to give to their family and friends. We are looking for fresh, happy, witty verse that reflects the culture of today's family."

UNIQUE GREETINGS, INC., P.O. Box 5783, Manchester NH 03108. Estab. 1988. **10% freelance written. Receives 15 submissions/year.** Submit seasonal/holiday material 12 months in advance. Responds in 6 months. Buys all rights. Writer's guidelines/market list for SASE. Market list regularly revised.
Needs: Watercolors, cute animals, flower scenes, etc. Prefers unrhymed verse ideas. Submit 12 ideas/batch.
Tips: "General and Happy Birthday sell the best."

VAGABOND CREATIONS, INC., 2560 Lance Dr., Dayton OH 45409. (937)298-1124. E-mail: vagabond@siscom.net. Website: www.vagabondcreations.com. **Acquisitions:** George F. Stanley, Jr., editor. **10% freelance written. Bought 5 freelance ideas last year.** Submit seasonal/holiday material 6 months in advance. Responds in 1 week. Buys all rights. **Pays on acceptance.** Writer's guidelines/market list for #10 SASE. Market list issued one time only.
Needs: Cute, humorous greeting cards (illustrations and copy) often with animated animals or objects in people-situations with short, subtle tie-in message on inside page only. No poetry. Also theme ideas (and copy) for line of illustrated stationery each with 24 assorted inside pages—6 ideas repeated 4 times or 4 ideas repeated 6 times.
Other Product Lines: Stationery.

WARNER PRESS, PUBLISHERS, 1200 E. Fifth St., P.O. Box 2499, Anderson IN 46018-9988. E-mail: krhodes@warnerpress.org. **Acquisitions:** Karen Rhodes, product/marketing editor. **10% freelance written.** Responds in 2 months. Buys all rights for bulletin use only. **Pays on acceptance.**

O→ "Presentation is important. Image isn't everything but handwritten submissions do not make a positive impression. Neatly typed or computer-generated pieces are much easier to read. Your ability to communicate clearly and professionally will receive a more favorable response."

Needs: Inspirational. Religious themes; sensitive prose and inspirational verse for Sunday bulletins. Write for guidelines, then submit 10 pieces of writing appropriate to their needs, 1-5 poems, and 5 devotionals, or 10 of one category. Mss not returned without SASE.

Other Product Lines: Also accepts ideas for coloring and activity books. Warner Press is now accepting material for boxed cards.

Tips: "We receive large numbers of submissions for Christmas and Easter—writing for less popular holidays heightens the chance of your work being published. Communion may seem to be a less interesting topic, but we need more submissions for that topic because we design a variety of bulletins with the communion theme. Submit material that relates to a wide audience, not just material that is meaningful to you personally. We receive a number of submissions dealing with the death of family members and other personal experiences that are beautiful and touching, but that do not relate to a larger audience."

Contests & Awards

The contests and awards listed in this section are arranged by subject. Nonfiction writers can turn immediately to nonfiction awards listed alphabetically by the name of the contest or award. The same is true for fiction writers, poets, playwrights and screenwriters, journalists, children's writers, and translators. You'll also find general book awards, fellowships offered by arts councils and foundations, and multiple category contests.

New contests and awards are announced in various writer's publications nearly every day. However, many lose their funding or fold—and sponsoring magazines go out of business just as often. We have contacted the organizations whose contests and awards are listed here with the understanding that they are valid through 2003-2004. If you are using this section in 2005 or later, keep in mind that much of the contest information listed here will not be current. Requirements such as entry fees change, as do deadlines, addresses, and contact names.

To make sure you have all the information you need about a particular contest, always send a SASE to the contact person in the listing before entering a contest. The listings in this section are brief, and many contests have lengthy, specific rules and requirements that we could not include in our limited space. Often a specific entry form must accompany your submission. A response with rules and guidelines will not only provide specific instructions, it will also confirm that the award is still being offered.

When you receive a set of guidelines, you will see that some contests are not for some writers. The writer's age, previous publication, geographic location, and length of the work are common matters of eligibility. Read the requirements carefully to ensure you don't enter a contest for which you are not qualified. You should also be aware that every year, more and more contests, especially those sponsored by "little" literary magazines, are charging entry fees.

Contest and award competition is very strong. While a literary magazine may publish ten short stories in an issue, only one will win the prize in a contest. Give yourself the best chance of winning by sending only your best work. There is always a percentage of manuscripts cast off immediately as unpolished, amateurish, or wholly unsuitable for the competition.

To avoid first-round rejection, make certain that you and your work qualify in every way for the award. Some contests are more specific than others. There are many contests and awards for a "best poem," but some award only the best lyric poem, sonnet or haiku.

For More Information

The following resources provide additional listings of contests and awards:

- *Novel & Short Story Writer's Market* (Writer's Digest Books)—fiction.
- *Poet's Market* (Writer's Digest Books)—poetry.
- *Children's Writer's & Illustrator's Market* (Writer's Digest Books)—children's.
- Old Dominion University's *Associated Writing Programs Newsletter*—literary.
- *Editor & Publisher*'s annual Journalism Awards Issue (published in the last week of December)—journalism.
- The Dramatists Guild's newsletter—playwriting.

Winning a contest or award can launch a successful writing career. Take a professional approach by doing a little extra research. Find out who the previous winner of the award was by investing in a sample copy of the magazine in which the prize-winning article, poem, or short story appeared. Attend the staged reading of an award-winning play. Your extra effort will be to your advantage in competing with writers who simply submit blindly.

If a contest or award requires nomination by your publisher, ask your publisher to nominate you. Many welcome the opportunity to promote a work (beyond their own conventional means). Just be sure the publisher has plenty of time before the deadline to nominate your work.

Information on contests and awards listed in the previous edition of *Writer's Market* but not included in this edition can be found in the General Index.

General

ABSTRACTS-EZINE MONTHLY CONTEST, Abstracts-Ezine, P.O. Box 22744, Louisville KY 40252. (502)412-2012. Fax: (443)785-1283. E-mail: erpeake@abstracts-ezine.com. Website: www.abstracts-ezine.com. **Contact:** Nicole Thomas; Elizabeth Peake. Deadline: 1st day of contest month. Guidelines for SASE. Charges $3. Prize: 1st place consists of $35, published on Web and in print magazine, one print copy, and inclusion in yearly anthology; 2nd place consists of $25, published on Web and in print magazine, one print copy; 3rd place consists of $15, published on Web and in print magazine, one print copy. Judged by *Abstracts*' staff. Acquires one-time rights for e-zine, magazine, anthology, archives. Open to any writer.

THE ANISFIELD-WOLF BOOK AWARDS, The Cleveland Foundation, 1422 Euclid Ave., Suite 1300, Cleveland OH 44115. (216)861-3810. Fax: (216)861-1729. E-mail: contactus@clevefdn.org. Website: www.anisfield-wolf.org. **Contact:** Marcia Bryant. "The Anisfield-Wolf Book Award annually honors books which contribute to our understanding of racism or our appreciation of the diversity of human culture published during the year of the award." Judged by 5-member panel chaired by Dr. Henry Louis Gates of Harvard University and including Joyce Carol Oates, Rita Dove, Steven Pinker, and Simon Schama. Any work addressing issues of racial bias or human diversity may qualify. Deadline: January 31. Guidelines for SASE. Prize: $20,000 divided among the winners.

ARTSLINK PROJECTS AWARD, CEC International Partners, 12 W. 31st St., New York NY 10001. (212)643-1985, ext. 22. Fax: (212)643-1996. E-mail: artslink@cecip.org. Website: www.cecip.org. **Contact:** Jennifer Gullace, ArtsLink coordinator. Offered annually to enable artists of all media to work in Central and Eastern Europe with colleagues there on collaborative projects. Check website for deadline and other information. Prize: Up to $10,000.

BANTA AWARD, Wisconsin Library Association, c/o Literary Awards Comm., 5250 E. Terrace Dr., Suite A-1, Madison WI 53718-8345. (608)245-3640. Website: www.wla.lib.wi.us. **Contact:** Chair, Literary Award Committee. Offered annually for books published during the year preceding the award. The Literary Awards Committee reviews all works by Wisconsin authors that are not edited, revised editions, textbooks, or written in foreign languages. Review copies or notification of books, along with verification of the author's ties to Wisconsin, may be submitted to the Committee, by the publisher or author. Only open to writers born, raised, or currently living in Wisconsin. Deadline: March of calendar year following publication. Prize: $500, a trophy given by the Banta Corporation Foundation, and presentation at the Annual Conference of the Wisconsin Library Association between late October and early November.

N **THE BEST TRUE ADVENTURE AND EXPLORATIONS WRITING OF 2003**, The Narrative Press, P.O. Box 2487, Santa Barbara CA 93121. (805)884-0160. Fax: (805)884-6127. E-mail: editor@narrativepress.com. Website: www.narrativepress.com. **Contact:** Chris Parks. The Narrative Press, publisher of true, first-person adventure and exploration books, is calling for contest entries for its 2003 edition of *The Best True Adventure and Exploration Stories*. This upcoming book will be a collection of over 30 adventures, from jungle treks to mountain climbing, desert crossings to south seas sailings, from treasure hunts to espionage, from archeological digs to river running. The trade paperback (and the e-book edition) of *The Best True Adventure and Exploration Stories* will be included in The Narrative Press' regular 2003 book catalog, and will be made available through all major book distribution and retail outlets, including bookstores and online resellers. Submissions can be previously published or unpublished. "By submitting your story, you agree, that if chosen, The Narrative Press will have the right to edit your story at its sole discretion; The Narrative Press will have the nonexclusive right to publish your story in any format and media; The Narrative Press will pay you a royalty on all sales of the 2003 edition of *The Best True Adventure and Exploration Stories* equal to 15% of the net sales divided by the number of winning entries, paid annually; and The Narrative Press will pay you 50% of any other net sales through other media (i.e. magazines, films, etc.)." Net sales are defined as all money actually collected by The Narrative Press from the sale of the story, less any printing costs, shipping expenses, sales commissions, and returns of prior sales. Annually. Deadline: November 30, 2002. Guidelines for SASE. Charges $15 entry fee. Prize: All 30 winners will have their story published in the 2003 edition of *The Best True Adventure and Exploration Stories* (to be released in January 2003); will receive a portion of the royalties on the sale of the trade paperback and e-book editions; will receive 3 free copies of the printed trade paperback and an unlimited number of e-book copies; will have their story published individually in The Narrative Press newsletter; and will receive a certificate of their accomplishments. The first ($2,000)-, second ($1,000)- and third ($500)-place winners will also receive gift certificates to The Territory

Ahead clothing catalog ("Clothes for the Journey," www.territoryahead.com) and The Narrative Press Catalog. Everyone who submits a story gets a 20%-off coupon good toward all purchases from The Narrative Press for a year. Judged by The Narrative Press editors. Open to any writer.

THE BOARDMAN TASKER AWARD FOR MOUNTAIN LITERATURE, The Boardman Tasker Charitable Trust, Pound House, Cock St., Llangennith, Gower West Glamorgan SA3 1JE, Wales. 01792 386215. E-mail: margaretbody@lineone.net. **Contact:** Margaret Body. Offered annually for books published for the first time in the UK between November 1 of previous year and October 31 of year of the prize. This award recognizes "a book which has made an outstanding contribution to mountain literature in book format and not the format of a magazine or other periodical. It must be written or have been translated into the English language." Writers may obtain information but entry is by publishers only. "No restriction of nationality, but work must be published or distributed in the UK." Deadline: August 1. Guidelines for SASE. Prize: £2,000 and attendant publicity.

EDITORS' BOOK AWARD, Pushcart Press, P.O. Box 380, Wainscott NY 11975. (516)324-9300. **Contact:** Bill Henderson, president. Unpublished books. "All manuscripts must be nominated by an editor in a publishing house." Open to any writer. Deadline: October 15. Guidelines for SASE.

N **FRIENDS OF THE DALLAS PUBLIC LIBRARY AWARD**, The Texas Institute of Letters, Southwest Texas State University, San Marcos TX 78666. (512)245-2428. Fax: (512)245-7462. E-mail: mb13@swt.edu. **Contact:** Mark Busby. Offered annually for submissions published January 1-December 31 of previous year to recognize the writer of the book making the most important contribution to knowledge. Writer must have been born in Texas, have lived in the state at least 2 consecutive years at some time, or the subject matter of the book should be associated with the state. Deadline: January 3. Guidelines for SASE. Prize: $1,000.

HOLLYWOOD COLUMBUS BOOK DISCOVERY AWARD, (formerly Columbus Book Discovery Award), Hollywood Network, Inc., 433 N. Camden Dr. #600, Beverly Hills CA 90210. (310)288-1881. Fax: (310)475-0193. E-mail: awards@screenwriters.com. Website: www.screenwriters.com. **Contact:** Carlos de Abreu. Offered annually for unpublished material. Deadline: November 1. Guidelines for SASE. Charges $75 fee. Prize: 1st Place: $1,500; 2nd Place: $1,000; 3rd Place: $500.

JACK KAVANAGH MEMORIAL YOUTH BASEBALL RESEARCH AWARD, Society for American Baseball Research (SABR), 812 Huron Rd. E. #719, Cleveland OH 44115. (216)575-0500. Fax: (216)575-0502. E-mail: sabrrodney@aol.com. Website: www.sabr.org. **Contact:** Rodney Johnson, contest/award director. Offered annually for unpublished work. Purpose is to stimulate interest in baseball research by youth under age of 21. Deadline: June 1, 2001. Deadline is typically 4 weeks prior to our National Convention, usually held in late June or early July. Guidelines for SASE. Prize: Award is $200 cash prize, publication in *SABR Journal* and/or website, 3-year SABR membership, plaque honoring award. Up to 3 finalists also receive 1-year SABR membership. Judged by the Youth/Education Chairman, a chairman of one of SABR's Research Committees, and the SABR Publications Director. Acquires nonexclusive rights to SABR to publish the entrants' submissions in printed and/or electronic form.

CORETTA SCOTT KING AWARDS, American Library Association, 50 E. Huron St., Chicago IL 60611. (312)280-4294. Fax: (312)280-3256. E-mail: olos@ala.org. Website: www.ala.org/srrt/csking. **Contact:** Tanga Morris, administrative assistant. Offered annually to an African-American author and illustrator to promote understanding and appreciation of culture and contributions of all people. Guidelines for SASE. Prize: $1,000, and set of encyclopedias from World Book & Encyclopedia Britannica.

DOROTHEA LANGE—PAUL TAYLOR PRIZE, Center for Documentary Studies at Duke University, 1317 W. Pettigrew St., Durham NC 27705. (919)660-3663. Fax: (919)681-7600. E-mail: alexad@duke.edu. Website: cds.aas.duke/l-t/. **Contact:** Alexa Dilworth. Offered annually to "promote the collaboration between a writer and a photographer in the formative or fieldwork stages of a documentary project. Collaborative submissions on any subject are welcome." Guidelines for SASE or on website. Deadline: January 31. Submissions accepted during January only. Prize: $10,000.

FENIA AND YAAKOV LEVIANT MEMORIAL PRIZE, (formerly Fenia and Yaakov Leviant Memorial Prize in Yiddish Culture), Modern Language Association of America, 26 Broadway, 3rd Floor, New York NY 10004-1789. (646)576-5141. Fax: (646)458-0030. E-mail: awards@mla.org. Website: www.mla.org. **Contact:** Alicia Walker, coordinator of book prizes and special projects. This prize is to honor, in alternating years, an outstanding English translation of a Yiddish literary work or an outstanding scholarly work in any language in the field of Yiddish. Offered every two years. In 2004, it will be awarded to a scholarly work published between 1999 and 2003. In 2005 it will be awarded to a translation published between 2002 and 2005. Open to MLA members and nonmembers. Authors or publishers may submit titles. Guidelines for SASE or by e-mail. Deadline: May 1, 2004. Prize: $500 and a certificate, to be presented at the Modern Language Association's annual convention in December.

MATURE WOMAN GRANTS, The National League of American Pen Women, 1300 17th St. NW, Washington DC 20036. Website: members.aol.com/penwomen/pen.htm. **Contact:** Mary Jane Hillery, national scholarship chair, 66 Willow Rd., Sudbury MA 01776-2663. Offered every 2 years to further the 35+ age woman and her creative purposes in art, music, and letters. Open to US citizens. Award announced by March 1, even-numbered years. Send letter stating age, background, and purpose for the monetary award. No phone calls, please. Send SASE for information. Deadline: October 1, odd-numbered years. Charges $8 fee with entry. Prize: $1,000 each in art, letters, and music.

MEGA FOUNDATION ESSAY CONTEST, Mega Foundation, P.O. Box 894, Eastport NY 11941. E-mail: info@megafoundation.org. Website: www.megafoundation.org. **Contact:** Dr. Gina Lynne LoSasso, contest/award director. Offered annually for unpublished work. Deadline: August 31. Guidelines for SASE. Charges $15 and includes 1-year subscription to the Mega Foundation journal, *Ubiquity*. Prize: $250 and certificate. Winning entry and honorable mention will be printed in our private circulation e-zine. Judged by Board of Directors. Open to any writer.

MISSISSIPPI REVIEW PRIZE, Mississippi Review, U.S.M. Box 5144, Hattiesburg MS 39406. (601)266-4321. Fax: (601)266-5757. E-mail: rief@netdoor.com. Website: www.mississippireview.com. **Contact:** Rie Fortenberry, contest director. Offered annually for unpublished fiction and poetry. Guidelines available online or with SASE. Charges $15 fee. Prize: $1,000 each for fiction and poetry winners.

NATIONAL OUTDOOR BOOK AWARDS, (formerly National Book Award), Box 8128, Idaho State University, Pocatello ID 83209. (208)282-3912. E-mail: wattron@isu.edu. Website: www.isu.edu/outdoor/bookpol.htm. **Contact:** Ron Watters. Offered annually for books published June 1, 2001-September 1, 2002. Eight categories: History/biography, outdoor literature, instructional texts, outdoor adventure guides, nature guides, childrens' books, design/artistic merit, and nature and the environment. Additionally, a special award, the Outdoor Classic Award, is given annually to books which, over a period of time, have proven to be exceptionally valuable works in the outdoor field. Application forms and eligibilty requirements are available online. Deadline: September 1. Charges $55 fee. Prize: Winning books are promoted nationally and are entitled to display the National Outdoor Book Award (NOBA) medallion.

N **NEW CENTURY WRITER AWARDS (NOVELS/NOVELLAS)**, New Century Writer, 32 Alfred St., Suite B, New Haven CT 06512-3927. (203)469-8824. Fax: (203)468-0333. E-mail: newcenturywriter@yahoo.com. Website: www.newcenturywriter.org. **Contact:** Jason Marchi, executive director. Offered annually to discover and encourage emerging writers of novels and novellas. Guidelines/entry fee for the asking, no SASE required. All entrants receive a 1-year subscription to *The Anvil*, an educational newsletter for writers. Open to all writers, both nonpublished and those with a limited publication history. Call if in doubt about your eligibility. New Century Writer also provides the annual Ray Bradbury Short Story Fellowship for 1 or 2 short story writers to attend the *Zoetrope* Short Story Writers' Workshop at Francis Ford Coppola's Blancaneaux Lodge in Belize, Central America (see the Ray Bradbury Short Story Fellowship listing for complete details). Deadline: March 30. Charges $30 entry fee. Prize: 1st Place: $2,000; 2nd Place: $1,000; 3rd Place: $500; 4th-10th Place: $100.

OHIOANA WALTER RUMSEY MARVIN GRANT, Ohioana Library Association, 274 E. First Ave., Columbus OH 43201. (614)466-3831. Fax: (614)728-6974. E-mail: ohioana@sloma.state.oh.us. Website: www.oplin.lib.oh.us/OHIOANA. **Contact:** Linda Hengst. Offered annually to encourage young writers; open to writers under age 30 who have not published a book. Entrants must have been born in Ohio or have lived in Ohio for at least 5 years. Enter 6 pieces of prose totaling 10-60 pages. Deadline: January 31. Prize: $1,000.

PEN CENTER LITERARY AWARDS, (formerly PEN Center West Literary Awards), PEN Center USA, 672 S. Lafayette Park Place, #42, Los Angeles CA 90057. (213)365-8500. Fax: (213)365-9616. E-mail: pen@penusa.org. Website: www.penusa.org. **Contact:** Literary Awards Coordinator. Offered for work published or produced in the previous calendar year. Open to writers living west of the Mississippi River. Award categories: Drama, screenplay, teleplay, journalism. Deadline: 4 copies must be received by January 31. Prize: $1,000 cash award.

PULITZER PRIZES, The Pulitzer Prize Board, 709 Journalism, Columbia University, New York NY 10027. (212)854-3841. Website: www.pulitzer.org. **Contact:** Seymour Topping, administrator. Estab. 1917. Journalism in US newspapers (published daily or weekly), and in letters, drama, and music by Americans. Deadline: February 1 (journalism); March 1 (music and drama); July 1 and November 1 (letters).

DAVID RAFFELOCK AWARD FOR PUBLISHING EXCELLENCE, National Writers Association, 3140 S. Peoria, #295, Aurora CO 80014. (303)841-0246. Fax: (303)841-2607. E-mail: sandywrter@aol.com. Website: www.nationalwriters.com. **Contact:** Sandy Whelchel. Contest is offered annually for books published the previous year. The purpose of this contest is to assist published authors in marketing their works and to reward outstanding published works. Deadline: May 1. Guidelines for SASE. Charges $100 fee. Prize: Publicity tour, including airfare, valued at $5,000.

ROCKY MOUNTAIN ARTISTS' BOOK COMPETITION, Hemingway Western Studies Center, Boise State University, 1910 University Dr., Boise ID 83725. (208)426-1999. Fax: (208)426-4373. E-mail: ttrusky@boisestate.edu. Website: www.boisestate.edu/hemingway/. **Contact:** Tom Trusky. Offered annually "to publish multiple edition artists' books of special interest to Rocky Mountain readers. Topics must be public issues (race, gender, environment, etc.). Authors may hail from Topeka or Ulan Bator, but their books must initially have regional appeal." Acquires first rights. Open to any writer. Deadline: September 1-December 1. Guidelines for SASE. Prize: $500, publication, standard royalties.

WILLIAM SANDERS SCARBOROUGH PRIZE, Modern Language Association of America, 26 Broadway, 3rd Floor, New York NY 10004-1789. (646)576-5141. Fax: (646)458-0030. E-mail: awards@mla.org. Website: www.mla.org. **Contact:** Alicia Walker, coordinator of book prizes and special projects. Offered annually for work published in the previous year. "Given in honor of a distinguished man of letters and the first African-American member of the Modern Language Association, this prize will be awarded to an outstanding scholarly study of black American literature or culture." Open to MLA members and nonmembers. Authors or publishers may enter titles. Guidelines for SASE or by e-mail. Deadline: May 1. Prize: $1,000 and a certificate, to be presented at the Modern Language Association's annual convention in December.

BYRON CALDWELL SMITH AWARD, Hall Center for the Humanities, 1540 Sunflower Rd., Lawrence KS 66045-7618. (785)864-4798. Website: www.hallcenter.ku.edu. **Contact:** Janet Crow, executive director. Offered in odd years to an individual who lives or is employed in Kansas, and who has authored an outstanding book published in the previous 2 calendar years. Translations are eligible. Deadline: March 1. Guidelines for SASE. Prize: $2,000.

TORONTO MUNICIPAL CHAPTER IODE BOOK AWARD, Toronto Municipal Chapter IODE, 40 St. Clair Ave. E., Toronto, Ontario M4T 1M9, Canada. (416)925-5078. Fax: (416)925-5127. **Contact:** IODE Education Committee. Offered annually for childrens' books published by a Canadian publisher. Author and illustrator must be Canadian citizens residing in or around Toronto. Deadline: Late November. Prize: $1,000.

TOWSON UNIVERSITY PRIZE FOR LITERATURE, College of Liberal Arts, Towson University, Towson MD 21252. (410)704-2128. **Contact:** Dean, College of Liberal Arts. Estab. 1979. Book or book-length ms that has been accepted for publication, written by a Maryland author who must have resided within the state of Maryland at least 3 years at the time of nomination, and must be a resident of the state of Maryland at the time the prize is awarded. Deadline: June 15. Guidelines for SASE. Prize: $2,000.

FRED WHITEHEAD AWARD, Texas Institute of Letters, Southwest Texas State University, San Marcos TX 78666. (512)245-2428. Fax: (512)245-7462. E-mail: mb13@swt.edu. Website: www.English.swt.edu/css/TIL/rules.htm. **Contact:** Mark Busby. Offered annually for the best design for a trade book. Open to Texas residents or those who have lived in Texas for 2 consecutive years. Deadline: January 3. Guidelines for SASE. Prize: $750.

WHITING WRITERS' AWARDS, Mrs. Giles Whiting Foundation, 1133 Avenue of the Americas, 22nd Floor, New York NY 10036. Website: whitingfoundation.org. **Contact:** Kellye Rosenheim, associate director. "The Foundation gives annually $35,000 each to up to 10 writers of poetry, fiction, nonfiction, and plays. The awards place special emphasis on exceptionally promising emerging talent." Direct applications and informal nominations are not accepted by the Foundation.

WORLD FANTASY AWARDS ASSOCIATION, P.O. Box 43, Mukilteo WA 98275-0043. Website: www.worldfantasy.org. **Contact:** Peter Dennis Pautz, president. Estab. 1975. Offered annually for previously published work recommended by previous convention attendees in several categories, including life achievement, novel, novella, short story, anthology, collection, artist, special award-pro, and special award nonpro. Works are recommended by attendees of current and previous 2 years' conventions, and a panel of judges. Deadline: July 1.

WRITERS' LEAGUE OF TEXAS MANUSCRIPT CONTEST, Writers' League of Texas, 1501 W. Fifth St., #E-2, Austin TX 78703. (512)499-8914. Fax: (512)499-0441. E-mail: awl@writersleague.org. Website: www.writersleague.org. **Contact:** Stephanie Sheppard. Offered annually for unpublished work. "The contest is open to all writers in 4 categories: mainstream, mystery/suspense/action-adventure, romance, and science fiction/fantasy/horror." Deadline: May 1. Guidelines for SASE. Charges $20-35 fee. Prize: Recognition at Agents & Editors Conference and meeting with an agent or editor who selected winner.

Nonfiction

ANTHEM ESSAY CONTEST, The Ayn Rand Institute, P.O. Box 6099, Department DB, Inglewood CA 90312. (310)306-9232. Fax: (310)306-4925. E-mail: essay@aynrand.org. Website: www.aynrand.org/contests. **Contact:** Marilee Dahl. Estab. 1992. Offered annually to encourage analytical thinking and excellence in writing, and to expose students to the philosophic ideas of Ayn Rand. "For information contact your English teacher or guidance counselor or visit our website." Annually. Deadline: March 18. Prize: 1st Place: $2,000; 2nd Place (10): $500; 3rd Place (20): $200; Finalist (45): $50; Semifinalist (175): $30.

ATLAS SHRUGGED ESSAY COMPETITION, Ayn Rand Institute, 4640 Admiralty Way, Suite 406, Marina del Rey CA 90292. (310)306-9232. Fax: (310)306-4925. E-mail: seans@aynrand.org. Website: www.aynrand.org/contests. **Contact:** Marilee Dahl. Offered annually to encourage analytical thinking and excellence in writing, and to expose students to the philosophic ideas of Ayn Rand. Essays are judged both on style and content. Essay length: 1,000-1,200 words. Guidelines on website. Open to students enrolled full-time in an undergraduate program. Deadline: September 16. Prize: 1st Place: $5,000; 2nd Place(3 awards): $1,000; 3rd Place (5 awards): $400.

BANCROFT PRIZE, Columbia University-Office of University Ceremonies, 202A Low Library, New York NY 10027. (212)854-2825. Fax: (212)854-6466. E-mail: jrb60@columbia.edu. Website: www.columbia.edu/cu/lweb/eguides/amerihist/bancroft.html. **Contact:** Jennifer Brogan. Offered annually for work published previously. Winning submissions will be chosen in either or both of the following categories: American history (including biography) and diplomacy. Deadline: November 1. Guidelines for SASE. Prize: $4,000 for the winning entry in each category.

RAY ALLEN BILLINGTON PRIZE, Organization of American Historians, 112 N. Bryan Ave., Bloomington IN 47408-4199. (812)855-9852. Fax: (812)855-0696. E-mail: awards@oah.org. Website: www.oah.org. **Contact:** Kara

Hamm. Offered in even years for the best book in American frontier history, defined broadly so as to include the pioneer periods of all geographical areas and comparison between American frontiers and others. Guidelines available on website. Deadline: October 1. Prize: $1,000, a certificate, and a medal.

BIRKS FAMILY FOUNDATION AWARD FOR BIOGRAPHY, Canadian Authors Association, Box 419, 320 S. Shores Rd., Campbellford, Ontario K0L 1L0, Canada. (705)653-0323. Fax: (705)653-0593. E-mail: canauth@redden.on.ca. Website: www.canauthors.org. **Contact:** Alec McEachern. Offered annually for a previously published biography about a Canadian. Entry form required. Obtain entry form from contact name or download from website. Deadline: December 15. Guidelines for SASE. Charges $20 (Canadian) entry fee. Prize: $2,500 and a silver medal.

THE BROSS PRIZE, The Bross Foundation, Lake Forest College 555 N. Sheridan, Lake Forest IL 60045. (847)735-5175. Fax: (847)735-6192. E-mail: rmiller@lfc.edu. **Contact:** Professor Ron Miller. Offered every 10 years for unpublished work "to award the best book or treatise on the relation between any discipline or topic of investigation and the Christian religion." Next contest in 2010. Manuscripts awarded prizes become property of the college. Open to any writer. Deadline: September 1 of contest year. Guidelines for SASE. Prize: Award varies depending on interest earned.

JOHN BULLEN PRIZE, Canadian Historical Association, 395 Wellington, Ottawa, Ontario K1A 0N3, Canada. (613)233-7885. Fax: (613)567-3110. E-mail: cha-shc@archives.ca. Website: www.cha-shc.ca. **Contact:** Joanne Mineault. Offered annually for an outstanding historical dissertation for a doctoral degree at a Canadian university. Open only to Canadian citizens or landed immigrants. Deadline: November 30. Guidelines for SASE. Prize: $500.

CANADIAN AUTHORS ASSOCIATION LELA COMMON AWARD FOR CANADIAN HISTORY, Box 419, 320 S. Shores Rd., Campbellford, Ontario K0L 1L0, Canada. (705)653-0323. Fax: (705)653-0593. E-mail: canauth@redden.on.ca. Website: www.canauthors.org. **Contact:** Alec McEachern. Offered annually for a work of historical nonfiction on a Canadian topic by a Canadian author. Entry form required. Obtain entry form from contact name or download from website. Deadline: December 15. Guidelines for SASE. Charges $20 (Canadian) entry fee. Prize: $2,500 and a silver medal.

CANADIAN LIBRARY ASSOCIATION STUDENT ARTICLE CONTEST, Canadian Library Association, 328 Frank St., Ottawa, Ontario K2P 0X8, Canada. (613)232-9625, ext. 318. Fax: (613)563-9895. Website: www.cla.ca. **Contact:** Brenda Shields. Offered annually to "unpublished articles discussing, analyzing, or evaluating timely issues in librarianship or information science." Open to all students registered in or recently graduated from a Canadian library school, a library techniques program or faculty of education library program. Submissions may be in English or French. Deadline: April 1. Guidelines for SASE. Prize: 1st Place: $150, publication, and trip to CLA's annual conference; 1st runner-up: $150 and $75 in CLA publications; 3rd runner-up: $75 and $75 in CLA publications.

THE DOROTHY CHURCHILL CAPPON CREATIVE NONFICTION AWARD, *New Letters*, 5101 Rockhill Rd., Kansas City MO 64110. (816)235-1168. Fax: (816)235-2611. E-mail: newletters@umkc.edu. Website: www.umkc.edu/newletters. **Contact:** Aleatha Ezra or Mary Ellen Buck. Contest is offered annually for unpublished work to discover and reward new and upcoming authors. Acquires first North American serial rights. Open to any writer. Deadline: Third week of May. Guidelines for SASE. Charges $10 fee. Prize: 1st Place: $1,000, and publication in a volume of *New Letters*; 2 runners-up will receive a year's subscription and will be considered for publication.

MORTON N. COHEN AWARD, Modern Language Association, 26 Broadway, 3rd Floor, New York NY 10004-1789. (646)576-5141. Fax: (646)458-0030. E-mail: awards@mla.org. Website: www.mla.org. **Contact:** Coordinator of Book Prizes. Estab. 1989. Awarded in odd-numbered years for a distinguished edition of letters. At least 1 volume of the edition must have been published during the previous 2 years. Editors need not be members of the MLA. Deadline: May 1. Guidelines for SASE. Prize: $1,000 and a certificate.

CARR P. COLLINS AWARD, The Texas Institute of Letters, Southwest Texas State University, San Marcos TX 78666. (512)245-2428. Fax: (512)245-7462. E-mail: mb13@swt.edu. Website: www.English.swt.ecu/css/TIL/rules.htm. **Contact:** Mark Busby. Offered annually for work published January 1-December 31 of the previous year to recognize the best nonfiction book by a writer who was born in Texas or who has lived in the state for at least 2 consecutive years at one point or a writer whose work has some notable connection with Texas. Deadline: January 3. Guidelines for SASE. Prize: $5,000.

AVERY O. CRAVEN AWARD, Organization of American Historians, 112 N. Bryan Ave., Bloomington IN 47408-4199. (812)855-9852. Fax: (812)855-0696. E-mail: awards@oah.org. Website: www.oah.org. **Contact:** Kara Hamm. Offered annually for the most original book on the coming of the Civil War, the Civil War years, or the Era of Reconstruction, with the exception of works of purely military history. Guidelines on website. Deadline: October 1. Prize: $500, and a certificate.

THE CREATIVE NON-FICTION CONTEST, *subTERRAIN* magazine, P.O. Box 3008, MPO, Vancouver British Columbia V6B 3X5, Canada. (604)876-8710. Fax: (604)879-2667. E-mail: subter@portal.ca. **Contact:** Brian Kaufman. Offered annually for creative nonfiction, not limited to any specific topic or subject. Length: 2,000-4,000 words. Submissions to be accompanied by a SASE (include IRC if outside Canada) and typed 8½×11 paper, double spaced (no disks or e-mail submissions, please). Deadline: August 1. Charges $15/story. Prize: $250 cash prize, plus publication in the fall issue of *subTERRAIN* magazine. All entrants receive a 1-year subscription to *subTERRAIN*.

ANNIE DILLARD AWARD IN CREATIVE NONFICTION, Bellingham Review, Mail Stop 9053, Western Washington University, Bellingham WA 98225. (360)650-4863. E-mail: bhreview@cc.wwu.edu. Website: www.wwu.edu/~bhreview. **Contact:** Brenda Miller. Offered annually for unpublished essays on any subject and in any style. Deadline: December 1-March 15. Guidelines for SASE. Prize: 1st Place: $1,000; 2nd Place: $300; 3rd Place: $200, plus publication and copies.

GORDON W. DILLON/RICHARD C. PETERSON MEMORIAL ESSAY PRIZE, American Orchid Society, Inc., 16700 AOS Lane, Delray Beach FL 33446-4351. (561)404-2043. Fax: (561)404-2045. E-mail: jmengel@aos.org. Website: www.orchidweb.org. **Contact:** Jane Mengel. Estab. 1985. "An annual contest open to all writers. The theme is announced each May in the *Orchids* magazine. All themes deal with an aspect of orchids, such as repotting, growing, hybridizing, etc. Unpublished submissions only." Themes in past years have included Orchid Culture, Orchids in Nature, and Orchids in Use. Buys one-time rights. Deadline: November 30. Prize: Cash award and certificate. Winning entry usually published in the May issue of *Orchids* magazine.

THE DONNER PRIZE, The Award for Best Book on Canadian Public Policy, The Donner Canadian Foundation, c/o 112 Braemore Gardens, Toronto, Ontario M6G 2C8, Canada. (416)656-3722. Fax: (416)658-5205. E-mail: meisner@interlog.com. Website: www.donnerbookprize.com. **Contact:** Meisner Publicity, prize manager; Sherry Naylor or Susan Meisner. Offered annually for nonfiction published January 1-December 31, 2001, that highlights the importance of public policy and to reward excellent work in this field. Entries must be published in either English or French. Open to Canadian citizens. Deadline: November 30. Guidelines for SASE. Prize: 1st Place: $25,000; 2 runners-up: $10,000 each.

THE FREDERICK DOUGLASS BOOK PRIZE, Gilder Lehrman Center for the Study of Slavery, Resistance & Abolition of Yale University, P.O. Box 208206, New Haven CT 06520-8206. (203)432-3339. Fax: (203)432-6943. E-mail: gilder.lehrman.center@yale.edu. Website: www.yale.edu/glc. **Contact:** Robert P. Forbes, associate director. Write or fax, Attention: Douglass Prize. Offered annually for books published the previous year. "The annual prize of $25,000 is awarded for the most outstanding book published on the subject of slavery, resistance, and/or abolition. Works related to the American Civil War are eligble only if their primary focus is slavery, resistance, or abolition." Deadline: March 29, 2002. Guidelines for SASE. Prize: $25,000 and a bronze medallion.

EDUCATOR'S AWARD, The Delta Kappa Gamma Society International, P.O. Box 1589, Austin TX 78767-1589. (512)478-5748. Fax: (512)478-3961. E-mail: ebarron@deltakappagamma.org. Website: www.deltakappagamma.org. **Contact:** Evelyn Barron, executive coordinator. Offered annually for quality research and nonfiction published January-December of previous year. This award recognizes educational research and writings of women authors whose work may influence the direction of thought and action necessary to meet the needs of today's complex society. The book must be written by 1 or 2 women who are citizens of any country in which The Delta Kappa Gamma Society International is organized: Canada, Costa Rica, El Salvador, Finland, Germany, Great Britain, Guatemala, Iceland, Mexico, The Netherlands, Norway, Puerto Rico, Sweden, US. Guidelines (required) for SASE. Deadline: February 1. Prize: $1,500.

EVERETT E. EDWARDS MEMORIAL AWARD, Agricultural History Society, 618 Ross Hall, Iowa University, Ames IA 50011-1202. (515)294-5620. Fax: (515)294-6390. E-mail: aghist@iastate.edu. Website: www.iastate.edu/~history_info/ahahs/awards.htm. **Contact:** R. Douglas Hurt. Offered annually for best graduate paper written during the calendar year on any aspect of agricultural and rural studies, broadly interpreted, submitted by a graduate student. Open to submission by any graduate student. Send mss directly to R. Douglas Hurt. Deadline: December 31. Prize: $200 and publication of the paper in the scholarly journal, *Agricultural History*.

DAVID W. AND BEATRICE C. EVANS BIOGRAPHY & HANDCART AWARDS, Mountain West Center for Regional Studies, Utah State University, Logan UT 84322-0735. (435)797-3630. Fax: (435)797-3899. E-mail: mwc@usu.edu. Website: www.usu.edu/~pioneers/mwc.html. **Contact:** Glenda Nesbit, office manager. Estab. 1983. Offered to encourage the writing of biography about people who have played a role in Mormon Country. (Not the religion, the country: Intermountain West with parts of Southwestern Canada and Northwestern Mexico.) Publishers or authors may nominate books. Criteria for consideration: Work must be a biography or autobiography on "Mormon Country"; must be submitted for consideration for publication year's award; new editions or reprints are not eligible; manuscripts are not accepted. Submit 5 copies. Deadline: December 1. Guidelines for SASE. Prize: $10,000 and $1,000.

GILBERT C. FITE DISSERTATION AWARD, Agricultural History Society, 618 Ross Hall, Ames IA 50011-1202. (515)294-5620. Fax: (515)294-6390. E-mail: aghist@iastate.edu. Website: www.iastate.edu/~history_info/ahahs/awards.htm. **Contact:** R. Douglas Hart. Award is presented to the author of the best dissertation on agricultural history, broadly construed, completed during the calendar year. Deadline: December 31. Guidelines for SASE. Prize: $300 honorararium.

N DIXON RYAN FOX MANUSCRIPT PRIZE, New York State Historical Association, P.O. Box 800, Cooperstown NY 13326. (607)547-1491. Fax: (607)547-1405. E-mail: goodwind@nysha.org. Website: www.nysha.org. **Contact:** Daniel Goodwin, director of publications. Offered annually for the best unpublished book-length ms dealing with some aspect of the history of New York State. Open to any writer. Deadline: January 20. Guidelines for SASE. Prize: $3,000 and assistance in finding a publisher.

GEORGE FREEDLEY MEMORIAL AWARD, Theatre Library Association, Benjamin Rosenthal Library, Queens College, C.U.N.Y., 65-30 Kissena Blvd., Flushing NY 11367. (718)997-3672. Fax: (718)997-3753. E-mail: rlw$lib@qc1.

qc.edu. Website: tla.library.unt.edu. **Contact:** Richard Wall, book awards committee chair. Estab. 1968. Offered for a book published in the US within the previous calendar year on a subject related to live theatrical performance (including cabaret, circus, pantomime, puppetry, vaudeville, etc.). Eligible books may include biography, history, theory, criticism, reference, or related fields. Deadline: February 15 of year following eligibility. Prize: $250 and certificate to the winner; $100 and certificate for honorable mention.

GEILFUSS, HUNTER & SMITH FELLOWSHIPS, Wisconsin Historical Society, 816 State St., Madison WI 53706-1482. (608)264-6461. Fax: (608)264-6486. E-mail: jkcalder@whs.wisc.edu. Website: www.wisconsinhistory.org. **Contact:** Kent Calder. Offered quarterly for unpublished writing on Wisconsin history. Guidelines for SASE or on website at: www.wisconsinhistory.org/research/fellowships.html. Rights acquired if award is accepted. Prize: $500-3,000.

GOVERNOR GENERAL'S LITERARY AWARD FOR LITERARY NONFICTION, Canada Council for the Arts, 350 Albert St., P.O. Box 1047, Ottawa, Ontario K1P 5V8, Canada. (613)566-4414, ext. 5576. Fax: (613)566-4410. E-mail: joanne.larocque-poirier@canadacouncil.ca. Website: www.canadacouncil.ca. **Contact:** Joanne Larocque-Poirier. Offered for work published September 1, 2001-September 30, 2002. Given annually to the best English language and the best French language work of literary nonfiction by a Canadian. Publishers submit titles for consideration. Deadline: April 15 or August 7, 2002, depending on the book's publication date. Prize: $15,000.

JAMES T. GRADY—JAMES H. STACK AWARD FOR INTERPRETING CHEMISTRY FOR THE PUBLIC, American Chemical Society, 1155 16th St. NW, Washington DC 20036-4800. (202)452-2109. Fax: (202)776-8211. E-mail: awards@acs.org. Website: www.acs.org/awards/grady-stack.html. **Contact:** Alicia Harris. Offered annually for previously published work to recognize, encourage, and stimulate outstanding reporting directly to the public, which materially increases the public's knowledge and understanding of chemistry, chemical engineering, and related fields. Guidelines online at website. Rules of eligibility: A nominee must have made noteworthy presentations through a medium of public communication to increase the American public's understanding of chemistry and chemical progress. This information shall have been disseminated through the press, radio, television, films, the lecture platform, books, or pamphlets for the lay public. Deadline: February 1. Prize: $3,000, gold medallion with a presentation box and certificate, plus travel expenses to the meeting at which the award will be presented.

GUIDEPOSTS YOUNG WRITERS CONTEST, *Guideposts*, 16 E. 34th St., New York NY 10016. (212)251-8100. Website: gp4teens.com. **Contact:** Kathryn Slattery. Offered annually for unpublished high school juniors and seniors. Stories "needn't be about a highly dramatic situation, but it should record an experience that affected you and deeply changed you. Remember, Guideposts stories are true, not fiction, and they show how faith in God has made a specific difference in a person's life. We accept submissions after announcement is placed in the October issue each year. If the manuscript is placed, we require all rights to the story in that version." Open only to high school juniors or seniors. Deadline: November 25, 2002. Prize: 1st Place: $10,000; 2nd Place: $8,000; 3rd Place: $6,000; 4th Place: $4,000; 5th Place: $3,000; 6th-10th Place: $1,000; 11th-20th Place: $250 gift certificate for college supplies.

JOHN GUYON NONFICTION PRIZE, *Crab Orchard Review*, English Dept., Southern Illinois University Carbondale, Carbondale IL 62901-4503. Website: www.siu.edu/~crborchd. **Contact:** Jon C. Tribble, managing editor. Offered annually for unpublished work. This competition seeks to reward excellence in the writing of creative nonfiction. This is not a prize for academic essays. *Crab Orchard Review* acquires first North American serial rights to submitted works. Deadline: February 1-March 15. Guidelines for SASE. Charges $10/essay (limit of 3 essays of up to 6,500 words each, and indicate "literary nonfiction" on the outside of the entry's mailing envelope). U.S. citizens only. Prize: $1,000 and publication.

ALBERT J. HARRIS AWARD, International Reading Association, Division of Research and Policy, 800 Barksdale Rd., Newark DE 19714-8139. (302)731-1600, ext. 423. Fax: (302)731-1057. E-mail: research@reading.org. **Contact:** Marcella Moore. Offered annually to recognize outstanding published works on the topics of reading disabilities and the prevention, assessment, or instruction of learners experiencing difficulty learning to read. Open to any writer. Deadline: September 15. Guidelines for SASE. Prize: Monetary award and recognition at the International Reading Association's annual convention.

ELLIS W. HAWLEY PRIZE, Organization of American Historians, 112 N. Bryan Ave., Bloomington IN 47408-4199. (812)855-9852. Fax: (812)855-0696. E-mail: awards@oah.org. Website: www.oah.org. **Contact:** Kara Hamm. Offered annually for the best book-length historical study of the political economy, politics, or institutions of the US, in its domestic or international affairs, from the Civil War to the present. Books must be written in English. Guidelines available on website. Deadline: October 1. Prize: $500 and a certificate.

HENDRICKS MANUSCRIPT AWARD, New Netherland Project, New York State Library, Cultural Exchange Center, 8th Floor, Madison Ave., Empire State Plaza, Albany New York 12230. (518)474-6067. Fax: (518)473-0472. E-mail: cgehring@mail.nysed.gov. Website: www.nnp.org. **Contact:** Charles Gehring. Offered annually for the best published or unpublished ms focusing on any aspect of the Dutch colonial experience in North America. Deadline: February 15. Guidelines for SASE. Prize: $1,500.

HIGHSMITH LIBRARY LITERATURE AWARD, American Library Association, 50 E. Huron St., Chicago IL 60611. (312)280-3247. Fax: (312)280-3257. E-mail: awards@ala.org. Offered annually to previously published books that make an outstanding contribution to library literature. Guidelines for SASE or by e-mail. Deadline: December 1. Prize: $500, and framed citation.

THE KIRIYAMA PACIFIC RIM BOOK PRIZE, Kiriyama Pacific Rim Institute, 650 Delancey St., Suite 101, San Francisco CA 94107. (415)777-1628. Fax: (415)777-1646. E-mail: admin@pacificrimvoices.org. Website: www.pacificrimvoices.org. **Contact:** Jeannine Cuevas, prize manager. Offered for work published from October 1 of the previous year through October 31 of the current prize year to promote books that will contribute to greater mutual understanding and increased cooperation throughout all areas of the Pacific Rim and South Asia. Guidelines and entry form on request, or may be downloaded from the prize website. Books must be submitted for entry by the publisher. Proper entry forms must be submitted. Contact the administrators of the prize for complete rules and entry forms. Deadline: July 2, 2003. Prize: $30,000 to be divided equally between the author of 1 fiction and of 1 nonfiction book.

KATHERINE SINGER KOVACS PRIZE, Modern Language Association, 26 Broadway, 3rd Floor, New York NY 10004-1789. (646)576-5141. Fax: (646)458-0030. E-mail: awards@mla.org. Website: www.mla.org. **Contact:** Coordinator of Book Prizes. Estab. 1990. Offered annually for a book published during the previous year in English in the field of Latin American and Spanish literatures and cultures. Books should be broadly interpretive works that enhance understanding of the interrelations among literature, the other arts, and society. Author need not be a member of the MLA. Deadline: May 1. Guidelines for SASE. Prize: $1,000 and a certificate.

LINCOLN PRIZE AT GETTYSBURG COLLEGE, Gettysburg College and Lincoln & Soldiers Institute, 233 N. Washington St., Gettysburg PA 17325. (717)337-6590. Fax: (717)337-6596. E-mail: civilwar@gettysburg.edu. Website: www.gettysburg.edu/lincoln_prize. **Contact:** Diane Brennan. Offered annually for the finest scholarly work in English on the era of the American Civil War. The award will usually go to a book published in the previous year; however articles, essays, and works of fiction may be submitted. Guidelines for SASE or on website. Deadline: November 1. Prize: $50,000.

JAMES RUSSELL LOWELL PRIZE, Modern Language Association, 26 Broadway, 3rd Floor, New York NY 10004-1789. (646)576-5141. Fax: (646)458-0030. E-mail: awards@mla.org. Website: www.mla.org. **Contact:** Coordinator of Book Prizes. Offered annually for literary or linguistic study, or critical edition or biography published in previous year. Open to MLA members only. Deadline: March 1. Guidelines for SASE. Prize: $1,000 and a certificate.

SIR JOHN A. MACDONALD PRIZE, Canadian Historical Association, 395 Wellington, Ottawa, Ontario K1A 0N3, Canada. (613)233-7885. Fax: (613)567-3110. E-mail: cha-shc@archives.ca. Website: www.cha-shc.ca. **Contact:** Joanne Mineault. Offered annually to award a previously published nonfiction work of Canadian history "judged to have made the most significant contribution to an understanding of the Canadian past." Open to Canadian citizens only. Deadline: December 1. Guidelines for SASE. Prize: $1,000.

MACLEAN HUNTER ENDOWMENT LITERARY NON-FICTION PRIZE, PRISM international, Buch E462 - 1866 Main Mall, Vancouver, British Columbia V6T 1Z1, Canada. (604)822-2514. Fax: (604)822-3616. E-mail: prism@interchange.ubc.ca. Website: prism.arts.ubc.ca. **Contact:** Belinda Bruce, executive editor. Offered annually for published and unpublished writers to promote and reward excellence in literary nonfiction writing. PRISM buys North American serial rights upon publication. "We also buy limited Web rights for pieces selected for website." Open to anyone except students and faculty of the Creative Writing Program at UBC. All entrants receive a 1-year subscription to *Prism*. Deadline: September 30. Guidelines for SASE. Charges $25, plus $5 for each additional entry (outside Canada use US funds). Prize: $1,500 for the winning entry, plus $20/page for the publication of the winner in *PRISM*'s winter issue.

HOWARD R. MARRARO PRIZE, Modern Language Association, 26 Broadway, 3rd Floor, New York NY 10004-1789. (646)576-5141. Fax: (646)458-0030. E-mail: awards@mla.org. Website: www.mla.org. **Contact:** Coordinator of Book Prizes. Offered in even-numbered years for a scholarly book or essay on any phase of Italian literature or comparative literature involving Italian, published in previous 2 years. Authors must be members of the MLA. Deadline: May 1, 2004. Guidelines for SASE. Prize: $1,000 and a certificate.

MID-LIST PRESS FIRST SERIES AWARD FOR CREATIVE NONFICTION, Mid-List Press, 4324 12th Ave. S., Minneapolis MN 55407-3218. Fax: (612)823-8387. E-mail: guide@midlist.org. Website: www.midlist.org. **Contact:** Lane Stiles, publisher. Open to any writer who has never published a book of creative nonfiction. Submit either a collection of essays or a single book-length work; minimum length 50,000 words. Accepts simultaneous submissions. Guidelines and entry form for SASE or on website. Deadline: July 1. Charges $20 fee. Prize: Awards include publication and an advance against royalties.

KENNETH W. MILDENBERGER PRIZE, Modern Language Association, 26 Broadway, 3rd Floor, New York NY 10004-1789. (646)576-5141. Fax: (646)458-0030. E-mail: awards@mla.org. Website: www.mla.org. **Contact:** Coordinator of Book Prizes. Offered annually for a research publication (articles in odd-numbered years and books in even-numbered years) from the previous biennium in the field of teaching foreign languages and literatures. In 2003 the award will be given to an article published in 2001 or 2002. Author need not be a member. Deadline: May 1. Guidelines for SASE. Prize: $500 for articles and $1,000 for books, a certificate, and a year's membership in the MLA.

MLA PRIZE FOR A DISTINGUISHED BIBLIOGRAPHY, Modern Language Association, 26 Broadway, 3rd Floor, New York NY 10004-1789. (646)576-5141. Fax: (646)458-0030. E-mail: awards@mla.org. Website: www.mla.org. **Contact:** Coordinator of Book Prizes. Offered in even-numbered years for enumerative and descriptive bibliographies published in monographic, book, or electronic format in the 2 years prior to the competition. Open to any writer or publisher. Deadline: May 1, 2004. Guidelines for SASE. Prize: $1,000 and a certificate.

MLA PRIZE FOR A DISTINGUISHED SCHOLARLY EDITION, Modern Language Association, 26 Broadway, 3rd Floor, New York NY 10004-1789. (646)576-5141. Fax: (646)458-0030. E-mail: awards@mla.org. Website: www.mla.org. **Contact:** Coordinator of Book Prizes. Offered in odd-numbered years. Work published in 2001 or 2002 qualifies for the 2003 competition. To qualify for the award, an edition should be based on an examination of all available relevant textual sources; the source texts and the edited text's deviations from them should be fully described; the edition should employ editorial principles appropriate to the materials edited, and those principles should be clearly articulated in the volume; the text should be accompanied by appropriate textual and other historical contextual information; the edition should exhibit the highest standards of accuracy in the presentation of its text and apparatus; and the text and apparatus should be presented as accessibly and elegantly as possible. Editor need not be a member of the MLA. Deadline: May 1. Guidelines for SASE. Prize: $1,000 and a certificate.

MLA PRIZE FOR A FIRST BOOK, Modern Language Association, 26 Broadway, 3rd Floor, New York NY 10004-1789. (646)576-5141. Fax: (646)458-0030. E-mail: awards@mla.org. Website: www.mla.org. **Contact:** Coordinator of Book Prizes. Offered annually for the first book-length scholarly publication by a current member of the association. To qualify, a book must be a literary or linguistic study, a critical edition of an important work, or a critical biography. Studies dealing with literary theory, media, cultural history, and interdisciplinary topics are eligible; books that are primarily translations will not be considered. Deadline: April 1. Guidelines for SASE. Prize: $1,000 and a certificate.

MLA PRIZE FOR INDEPENDENT SCHOLARS, Modern Language Association, 26 Broadway, 3rd Floor, New York NY 10004-1789. (646)576-5141. Fax: (646)458-0030. E-mail: awards@mla.org. Website: www.mla.org. **Contact:** Coordinator of Book Prizes. Offered annually for a book in the field of English, or another modern language, or literature published in the previous year. Authors who are enrolled in a program leading to an academic degree or who hold tenured or tenure-track positions in higher education are not eligible. Authors need not be members of MLA. Guidelines and application form for SASE. Deadline: May 1. Prize: $1,000, a certificate, and a year's membership in the MLA.

NATIONAL BUSINESS BOOK AWARD, PricewaterhouseCoopers and Bank of Montreal, 77 King St. W., Toronto, Ontario M5K 1G8, Canada. (416)941-8344. Fax: (416)941-8345. E-mail: maf@idirect.com. Website: www.pwcglobal.com. **Contact:** Faye Mattachione. Offered annually for books published January 1-December 31 to recognize excellence in business writing in Canada. Publishers nominate books. Deadline: December 31. Prize: $10,000.

NATIONAL WRITERS ASSOCIATION NONFICTION CONTEST, The National Writers Association, 3140 S. Peoria, #295, Aurora CO 80014. (303)841-0246. Fax: (303)841-2607. E-mail: sandywrter@aol.com. **Contact:** Sandy Whelchel, director. Annual contest "to encourage writers in this creative form and to recognize those who excel in nonfiction writing." Deadline: December 31. Guidelines for SASE. Charges $18 fee. Prize: 1st Place: $200; 2nd Place: $100; 3rd Place: $50.

THE FREDERIC W. NESS BOOK AWARD, Association of American Colleges and Universities, 1818 R St. NW, Washington DC 20009. (202)387-3760. Fax: (202)265-9532. E-mail: info@aacu.nw.dc.us. Website: www.aacu-edu.org. **Contact:** Bethany Sutton. Offered annually for work published in the previous year. "Each year the Frederic W. Ness Book Award Committee of the Association of American Colleges and Universities recognizes books which contribute to the understanding and improvement of liberal education." Guidelines for SASE and on website. "Writers may nominate their own work; however, we send letters of invitation to publishers to nominate qualified books." Deadline: May 1. Prize: $2,000, and presentation at the association's annual meeting; transportation and 1 night hotel for meeting are also provided.

NORTH AMERICAN INDIAN PROSE AWARD, University of Nebraska Press, 233 N. Eighth St., Lincoln NE 68588-0255. Fax: (402)472-0308. E-mail: gdunham1@unl.edu. **Contact:** Gary H. Dunham, editor, Native American studies. Offered for the best new nonfiction work by an American-Indian writer. Deadline: July 1. Prize: Publication by the University of Nebraska Press with a $1,000 advance.

OUTSTANDING DISSERTATION OF THE YEAR AWARD, International Reading Association, 800 Barksdale Rd., P.O. Box 8139, Newark DE 19714-8139. (302)731-1600, ext. 423. Fax: (302)731-1057. E-mail: research@reading.org. **Contact:** Marcella Moore. Offered annually to recognize dissertations in the field of reading and literacy. Deadline: October 1. Guidelines for SASE. Prize: $1,000.

N **FRANK LAWRENCE AND HARRIET CHAPPELL OWSLEY AWARD**, Southern Historical Association, Department of History University of Georgia, Athens GA 30602-1602. (706)542-8848. Fax: (706)542-2455. Website: www.uga.edu/~sha. **Contact:** Secretary-Treasurer. Estab. 1934. Managing Editor: John B. Boles. Offered in odd-numbered years for recognition of a distinguished book in Southern history published in even-numbered years. Publishers usually submit the books. Deadline: March 1.

LOUIS PELZER MEMORIAL AWARD, Organization of American Historians, Journal of American History, 1215 E. Atwater, Indiana University, Bloomington IN 47401. (812)855-9852. Fax: (812)855-0696. E-mail: awards@oah.org. Website: www.oah.org. **Contact:** Kara Hamm. Offered annually for the best essay in American history by a graduate student. The essay may be about any period or topic in the history of the US, and the author must be enrolled in a graduate program at any level, in any field. Length: 7,000 words maximum. Guidelines available on website. Deadline: December 1. Prize: $500, a medal, a certificate, and publication of the essay in the *Journal of American History.*

PEN/MARTHA ALBRAND AWARD FOR FIRST NONFICTION, PEN American Center, 568 Broadway, New York NY 10012. (212)334-1660. Fax: (212)334-2181. E-mail: jm@pen.org. **Contact:** John Morrone, coordinator. Offered annually for a first published book of general nonfiction distinguished by qualities of literary and stylistic excellence. Eligible books must have been published in the calendar year under consideration. Authors must be American citizens or permanent residents. Although there are no restrictions on the subject matter of titles submitted, nonliterary books will not be considered. Books should be of adult nonfiction for the general or academic reader. Publishers, agents, and authors themselves must submit 3 copies of each eligible title. Deadline: December 15. Prize: $1,000.

PEN/MARTHA ALBRAND AWARD FOR THE ART OF THE MEMOIR, Pen American Center, 568 Broadway, New York NY 10012. (212)334-1660. Fax: (212)334-2181. E-mail: jm@pen.org. **Contact:** John Morrone. Offered annually to an American author for his/her memoir published in the current calendar year, distinguished by qualities of literary and stylistic excellence. Send 3 copies of each eligible book. Open to American writers. Deadline: December 15. Prize: $1,000.

PEN/JERARD FUND, PEN American Center, 568 Broadway, New York NY 10012. (212)334-1660. Fax: (212)334-2181. E-mail: jm@pen.org. **Contact:** John Morrone. Estab. 1986. Biennial grant offered in odd-numbered years for an American woman writer of nonfiction for a book-length work-in-progress. Deadline: January 2, 2003. Prize: $5,500 grant.

PEN/SPIELVOGEL-DIAMONSTEIN AWARD, PEN American Center, 568 Broadway, New York NY 10012. (212)334-1660. Fax: (212)334-2181. E-mail: jm@pen.org. **Contact:** John Morrone. Offered for the best previously unpublished collection of essays on any subject by an American writer. "The $5,000 prize is awarded to preserve the dignity and esteem that the essay form imparts to literature." The essays included in books submitted may have been previously published in magazines, journals, or anthologies, but must not have collectively appeared before in book form. Books will be judged on literary character and distinction of the writing. Publishers, agents, or the authors must submit 4 copies of each eligible title. Deadline: December 15. Prize: $5,000.

PHILLIP D. REED MEMORIAL AWARD FOR OUTSTANDING WRITING ON THE SOUTHERN ENVIRONMENT, Southern Environmental Law Center, 201 W. Main St., Charlottesville VA 22902. (434)977-4090. Fax: (434)977-1483. E-mail: selcva@selcva.org. Website: www.SouthernEnvironment.org. **Contact:** Cathryn McCue, award director. Offered annually for nonfiction pieces published in the previous calendar year "to encourage and promote writing about natural resources in the South." Minimum length: 3,000 words. Deadline: March 31. Guidelines for SASE. Prize: $1,000.

EVELYN RICHARDSON NONFICTION AWARD, (formerly Evelyn Richardson Memorial Literary Award), Writers' Federation of Nova Scotia, 1113 Marginal Rd., Halifax, Nova Scotia B3H 4P7, Canada. (902)423-8116. Fax: (902)422-0881. E-mail: talk@writers.ns.ca. Website: www.writers.ns.ca. **Contact:** Jane Buss, executive director. "Nova Scotia's highest award for a book of nonfiction written by a Nova Scotian, the Evelyn Richardson Nonfiction Award is presented annually by the Writers' Federation of Nova Scotia. The Award is named for Nova Scotia writer Evelyn Richardson, whose book *We Keep a Light* won the Governor General's Literary Award for nonfiction in 1945." There is no entry fee or form. Full-length books of nonfiction written by Nova Scotians, and published as a whole for the first time in the previous calendar year, are eligible. Publishers: Send 4 copies and a letter attesting to the author's status as a Nova Scotian, and the author's current mailing address and telephone number. Deadline: First Friday in December. Prize: $1,000.

THE CORNELIUS RYAN AWARD, The Overseas Press Club of America, 40 W. 45th St., New York NY 10036. (212)626-9220. Fax: (212)626-9210. **Contact:** Sonya Fry, executive director. Offered annually for excellence in a nonfiction book on foreign affairs. Generally publishers nominate the work, but writers may also submit in their own name. The work must be published and on the subject of foreign affairs. Deadline: End of January. Charges $125 fee. Prize: $1,000 and certificate.

THEODORE SALOUTOS AWARD, Agricultural History Society, Iowa State University, Ames IA 50011-1202. (515)294-1596. Fax: (515)294-6390. E-mail: rdhurt@iastate.edu. Website: www.iastate.edu/~istory-info/aghistry.htm. **Contact:** R. Douglas Hurt. Offered annually for best book on US agricultural history broadly interpreted. Open nominations. Deadline: December 31. Prize: $500.

SASKATCHEWAN NONFICTION AWARD, Saskatchewan Book Awards, Inc., Box 1921, Regina, Saskatchewan S4P 3E1, Canada. (306)569-1585. Fax: (306)569-4187. E-mail: director@bookawards.sk.ca. Website: www.bookawards.sk.ca. **Contact:** Joyce Wells, executive director. Offered annually for work published October to September of that year. This award is presented to a Saskatchewan author for the best book of nonfiction, judged on the quality of writing. Deadline: First deadline: July 31; Final deadline: September 14. Guidelines for SASE. Charges $15 (Canadian). Prize: $1,500.

SASKATCHEWAN SCHOLARLY WRITING AWARD, Saskatchewan Book Awards, Inc., Box 1921, Regina, Saskatchewan S4P 3E1, Canada. (306)569-1585. Fax: (306)569-4187. E-mail: director@bookawards.sk.ca. Website: www.bookawards.sk.ca. **Contact:** Joyce Wells, executive director. Offered annually for work published September 15 to September 14 annually. This award is presented to a Saskatchewan author for the best contribution to scholarship.

The work must recognize or draw on specific theoretical work within a community of scholars, and participate in the creation and transmission of knowledge. Deadline: First deadline: July 31; Final deadline: September 14. Guidelines for SASE. Charges $15 (Canadian). Prize: $1,500.

THE BARBARA SAVAGE 'MILES FROM NOWHERE' MEMORIAL AWARD, The Mountaineers Books, 1001 SW Klickitat Way, Suite 201, Seattle WA 98134. (206)223-6303. Fax: (206)223-6306. E-mail: mbooks@mountaineersbooks.org. Website: www.mountaineers.org. **Contact:** Mary Metz. Offered in even-numbered years for previously unpublished book-length nonfiction personal adventure narrative. Narrative must be based on an outdoor adventure involving hiking, mountain climbing, bicycling, paddle sports, skiing, snowshoeing, nature, conservation, ecology, or adventure travel not dependent upon motorized transport. Subjects *not* acceptable include hunting, fishing, or motorized or competitive sports. Deadline: May 1, 2004. Guidelines for SASE. Prize: $3,000 cash award, a $12,000 guaranteed advance against royalties, and publication by The Mountaineers.

ALDO AND JEANNE SCAGLIONE PRIZE FOR COMPARATIVE LITERARY STUDIES, (formerly Aldo and Jeanne Scaglione Prize in Comparative Literary Studies), Modern Language Association, 26 Broadway, 3rd Floor, New York NY 10004-1789. (646)576-5141. Fax: (646)458-0030. E-mail: awards@mla.org. Website: www.mla.org. **Contact:** Coordinator of Book Prizes. Offered annually for outstanding scholarly work published in the preceding year in the field of comparative literary studies involving at least 2 literatures. Author must be a member of the MLA. Works of scholarship, literary history, literary criticism, and literary theory are eligible; books that are primarily translations are not eligible. Deadline: May 1. Guidelines for SASE. Prize: $2,000 and a certificate.

ALDO AND JEANNE SCAGLIONE PRIZE FOR FRENCH AND FRANCOPHONE STUDIES, (formerly Aldo and Jeanne Scaglione Prize in French and Francophone Studies), Modern Language Association, 26 Broadway, 3rd Floor, New York NY 10004-1789. (646)576-5141. Fax: (646)458-0030. E-mail: awards@mla.org. Website: www.mla.org. **Contact:** Coordinator of Book Prizes. Offered annually for work published in the preceding year that is an outstanding scholarly work in the field of French or francophone linguistic or literary studies. Author must be a member of the MLA. Works of scholarship, literary history, literary criticism, and literary theory are eligible; books that are primarily translations are not eligible. Deadline: May 1. Guidelines for SASE. Prize: $2,000 and a certificate.

ALDO AND JEANNE SCAGLIONE PRIZE FOR ITALIAN STUDIES, Modern Language Association, 26 Broadway, 3rd Floor, New York NY 10004-1789. (646)576-5141. Fax: (646)458-0030. E-mail: awards@mla.org. Website: www.mla.org. **Contact:** Coordinator of Book Prizes. Offered in odd-numbered years for a scholarly book on any phase of Italian literature or culture, or comparative literature involving Italian, including works on literary or cultural theory, science, history, art, music, society, politics, cinema, and linguistics, preferably but not necessarily relating other disciplines to literature. Books must have been published in year prior to competition. Authors must be members of the MLA. Deadline: May 1. Guidelines for SASE. Prize: $2,000 and a certificate.

ALDO AND JEANNE SCAGLIONE PRIZE FOR STUDIES IN GERMANIC LANGUAGES & LITERATURE, (formerly Aldo and Jeanne Scaglione Prize for Studies in Germanic Languages), Modern Language Association, 26 Broadway, 3rd Floor, New York NY 10004-1789. (646)576-5141. Fax: (646)458-0030. E-mail: awards@mla.org. Website: www.mla.org. **Contact:** Coordinator of Book Prizes. Offered in even-numbered years for outstanding scholarly work appearing in print in the previous 2 years and written by a member of the MLA, on the linguistics or literatures of the Germanic languages. Works of literary history, literary criticism, and literary theory are eligible; books that are primarily translations are not eligible. Deadline: May 1. Guidelines for SASE. Prize: $2,000 and a certificate.

ALDO AND JEANNE SCAGLIONE PRIZE FOR STUDIES IN SLAVIC LANGUAGES AND LITERATURES, Modern Language Association, 26 Broadway, 3rd Floor, New York NY 10004-1789. (646)576-5141. Fax: (646)458-0030. E-mail: awards@mla.org. Website: www.mla.org. **Contact:** Coordinator of Book Prizes. Offered each odd-numbered year for books published in the previous 2 years. Books published in 2001 or 2002 are eligible for the 2003 award. Membership in the MLA is not required. Works of literary history, literary criticism, philology, and literary theory are eligible; books that are primarily translations are not eligible. Deadline: May 1. Guidelines for SASE. Prize: $2,000 and a certificate.

ALDO AND JEANNE SCAGLIONE PUBLICATION AWARD FOR A MANUSCRIPT IN ITALIAN LITERARY STUDIES, Modern Language Association, 26 Broadway, 3rd Floor, New York NY 10004-1789. (646)576-5141. Fax: (646)458-0030. E-mail: awards@mla.org. Website: www.mla.org. **Contact:** Coordinator of Book Prizes. Awarded annually to an author of a ms dealing with any aspect of the languages and literatures of Italy, including medieval Latin and comparative studies, or intellectual history if main thrust is clearly related to the humanities. Materials from ancient Rome are eligible if related to postclassical developments. Also translations of classical works of prose and poetry produced in Italy prior to 1900 in any language (e.g., neo-Latin, Greek) or in a dialect of Italian (e.g., Neapolitan, Roman, Sicilian). Work can be in English or Italian. Manuscript must have been favorably evaluated by a not-for-profit press that is a member of the Association of American University Presses. Authors must be members of the MLA and currently reside in the United States or Canada. Deadline: August 1. Guidelines for SASE. Prize: Subvention to press for publication of manuscript and a certificate to author.

SCIENCE WRITING AWARDS IN PHYSICS AND ASTRONOMY, American Institute of Physics, 1 Physics Ellipse, College Park MD 20740-3843. (301)209-3090. Fax: (301)209-0846. E-mail: pubinfo@aip.org. Website: www.aip.org/aip/writing. **Contact:** Flory Gonzalez. Offered for previously published articles, booklets, or books "that improves the general public's appreciation and understanding of physics and astronomy." Four categories: Articles or books intended for children, preschool-15 years old; broadcast media involving radio or television; journalism, written by a professional journalist; and science, written by physicists, astronomers, or members of AIP or affiliated societies. Guidelines by phone, e-mail, or website. Deadline: March 1. Prize: $3,000, engraved Windsor chair, and certificate awarded in each category.

MINA P. SHAUGHNESSY PRIZE, Modern Language Association, 26 Broadway, 3rd Floor, New York NY 10004-1789. (646)576-5141. Fax: (646)458-0030. E-mail: awards@mla.org. Website: www.mla.org. **Contact:** Coordinator of Book Prizes. Offered annually for research publication (book) in the field of teaching English language, literature, rhetoric, and composition published during preceding year. Authors need not be members of the MLA. Deadline: May 1. Guidelines for SASE. Prize: $1,000, a certificate, and a year's membership in the MLA.

N **FRANCIS B. SIMKINS AWARD**, Southern Historical Association, Department of History University of Georgia, Athens GA 30602-1602. (706)542-8848. Fax: (706)542-2455. Website: www.uga.edu/~sha. **Contact:** John C. Inscoe, secretary-treasurer. Estab. 1934. Managing Editor: John B. Boles. Offered in odd-numbered years for recognition of the best first book by an author in the field of Southern history over a 2-year period.

N **CHARLES S. SYDNOR AWARD**, Southern Historical Association, Department of History University of Georgia, Athens GA 30602. (706)542-8848. Fax: (706)542-2455. Website: www.uga.edu/~sha. **Contact:** Southern Historical Association. Offered in even-numbered years for recognition of a distinguished book in Southern history published in odd-numbered years. Publishers usually submit books.

AMAURY TALBOT PRIZE FUND FOR AFRICAN ANTHROPOLOGY, Barclays Bank Trust, Ltd., E&T Centre, P.O. Box 15, Osborne Court, Gadbrook Park, Rudheath Northwich Cheshire CW9 7UE, England. Annual award for previously published nonfiction on anthropological research relating to Africa. Only works published the previous calendar year are eligible. Preference given to those relating to Nigeria and then West Africa. All applications, together with 2 copies of the book, article, or work in question, should be sent by January 31 to: Amaury Talbot Prize coordinator, Royal Anthropological Institute, 50 Fitzroy St., London W1P 5HS England. Open to any writer. Guidelines for SASE. Prize: The Institute undertakes the administration of the Prize on behalf of the Trustees, Barclays Bank Trust Company, Ltd. Entries will *not* be returned.

THE THEATRE LIBRARY ASSOCIATION AWARD, Theatre Library Association, Benjamin Rosenthal Library, Queens College, C.U.N.Y., 65-30 Kissena Blvd., Flushing NY 11367. (718)997-3672. Fax: (718)997-3753. E-mail: rlw$lib@qc1.qc.edu. Website: tla.library.unt.edu. **Contact:** Richard Wall, book awards committee chair. Estab. 1973. Offered for a book published in the US within the previous calendar year on a subject related to recorded or broadcast performance (including motion pictures, television, and radio). Eligible books may include biography, history, theory, criticism, reference, or related fields. Deadline: February 15 of year following eligibility. Prize: $250 and certificate to the winner; $100 and certificate for honorable mention.

HARRY S. TRUMAN BOOK AWARD, Harry S. Truman Library Institute for National & International Affairs, 500 West U.S. Hwy. 24, Independence MO 64050-1798. (816)833-0425. Fax: (816)833-2715. E-mail: lisa.sullivan@nara.gov. Website: www.trumanlibrary.org. **Contact:** Book Award Administrator. Offered in even-numbered years for a book published January 1, 2002-December 31, 2003, dealing "primarily and substantially with some aspect of the history of the United States between April 12, 1945 and January 20, 1953, or with the public career of Harry S. Truman." Deadline: January 20, 2004. Guidelines for SASE. Prize: $1,000.

N **WESTERN HISTORY ASSOCIATION AWARDS**, Western History Association, Mesa Vista 1080 University of New Mexico, Albuquerque NM 87131-1181. (505)277-5234. Fax: (505)277-5275. E-mail: wha@unm.edu. Website: www.unm.edu/~wha. Director: Paul Hutton. Seventeen awards in various aspects of the American West. Guidelines for SASE.

L. KEMPER AND LEILA WILLIAMS PRIZE, The Historic New Orleans Collection and Louisiana Historical Association, 533 Royal St., New Orleans LA 70130-2179. Fax: (504)598-7108. E-mail: johnl@hnoc.org. Website: www.hnoc.org. **Contact:** Chair, Williams Prize Committee. Director: John H. Lawrence. Offered annually for the best published work on Louisiana history. Deadline: January 15. Prize: $1,500 and a plaque.

WRITERS' JOURNAL ANNUAL TRAVEL WRITING CONTEST, Val-Tech Media, P.O. Box 394, Perham MN 56573. (218)346-7921. Fax: (218)346-7924. E-mail: writersjournal@lakesplus.com. Website: www.writersjournal.com. **Contact:** Leon Ogroske. Offered annually for unpublished work. Buys one-time rights. Open to any writer. 2,000 word maximum. No e-mail submissions accepted. Deadline: November 30. Guidelines for SASE. Charges $5 fee. Prize: 1st Place: $50; 2nd Place: $25; 3rd Place: $15, plus honorable mentions. Prize-winning stories and selected honorable mentions will be published in *Writer's Journal* magazine.

LAMAR YORK PRIZE FOR NONFICTION CONTEST, *The Chattahoochee Review*, Georgia Perimeter College, 2101 Womack Rd., Dunwoody GA 30338-4497. (770)551-3019. Website: www.chattahoochee-review.org. **Contact:** JoAnn Adkins, managing editor. Offered annually for unpublished creative nonfiction and nonscholarly essays. *The Chattahoochee Review* buys first rights only for winning essay/manscript for the purpose of publication in the summer issue. Deadline: January 15. Guidelines for SASE. Charges $10 fee per entry. Prize: $1,000 and publication in the summer issue.

Fiction

AIM MAGAZINE SHORT STORY CONTEST, P.O. Box 1174, Maywood IL 60153-8174. (708)344-4414. E-mail: apiladoone@aol.com. Website: www.aimmagazine.org. **Contact:** Myron Apilado, editor. Estab. 1974. Offered for unpublished short stories (4,000 words maximum) "promoting brotherhood among people and cultures." Deadline: August 15.

SHERWOOD ANDERSON SHORT FICTION AWARD, *Mid-American Review*, Dept. of English, Bowling Green State University, Bowling Green OH 43403. (419)372-2725. Fax: (419)372-6805. E-mail: karenka@bgnet.bgsu.edu. Website: www.bgsu.edu/midamericanreview. **Contact:** Michael Czyzniejewski, fiction editor. Contest is open to all writers not associated with judge or *Mid-American Review*. Annually, must be unpublished. Deadline: October 1. Guidelines for SASE. Charges $10. Prize: Publication in the spring issue of *Mid-American Review*, plus $500. Judged by editors and a well-known writer, e.g. Peter Ho Davies or Melanie Rae Thon. Open to any writer.

SHERWOOD ANDERSON WRITER'S GRANT, Sherwood Anderson Foundation, 216 College Rd., Richmond VA 23229. (804)282-8008. Fax: (804)287-6052. E-mail: mspear@richmond.edu. Website: www.richmond.edu/~journalm/comp.html. **Contact:** Michael M. Spear, foundation co-president. Annually. Deadline: April 1. Prize: Award for the last 3 years has been $10,000. Judged by a committee established by the foundation. Open to any writer.

ANVIL PRESS INTERNATIONAL 3-DAY NOVEL WRITING CONTEST, Anvil Press, 204-A 175 E. Broadway, Vancouver, British Columbia V5T 1W2, Canada. (604)876-8710. Fax: (604)879-2667. E-mail: subter@portal.ca. Website: www.anvilpress.com. **Contact:** Brian Kaufman or Lisa Sweanor. Estab. 1988. Offered annually for the best novel written in 3 days (Labor Day weekend). Entrants return finished novels to Anvil Press for judging. To register, send SASE (IRC if from outside Canada) for details. Deadline: Friday before Labor Day weekend. Charges $35 fee.

ART COOP FICTION FELLOWSHIP, Cottonwood Art Co-operative, 1124 Columbia NE, Albuquerque NM 87106. E-mail: art_coop@yahoo.com. Website: www.geocities.com/art_coop. **Contact:** Editor-in-Chief. For most recent information, please visit website or write for guidelines with SASE. Submit with cover sheet, bio, and publications list. Open to any writer. Annually. Deadline: December 1 (annually). Charges $15 for 3-50 page portfolio. For additional flat fee of $15 and SASE, feedback provided on fiction. Prize: Cash award to be determined, not less than $250, and Internet-publication to support serious, aspiring authors. Open to any writer.

BARD FICTION PRIZE, Bard College, P.O. Box 5000, Annandale-on-Hudson NY 12504-5000. (845)758-7087. E-mail: bfp@bard.edu. Estab. 2001. Annually. Guidelines for SASE. Prize: $30,000 cash award and appointment as writer-in-residence at Bard College for 1 semester.

BEST PRIVATE EYE NOVEL CONTEST, Private Eye Writers of America and St. Martin's Press, 175 Fifth Ave., New York NY 11215. (212)674-5151. Fax: (212)254-4553. **Contact:** Julie Sullivan. Offered annually for unpublished, book-length mss in the "private-eye" genre. Open to authors who have not published a "private-eye" novel. Deadline: August 1. Guidelines for SASE. Prize: Advance against future royalties of $10,000, and publication by St. Martin's Press.

BONOMO MEMORIAL LITERATURE PRIZE, Italian Americana, URI/CCE, 80 Washington St., Providence RI 02903. (401)277-5306. Fax: (401)277-5100. E-mail: bonomoal@etal.uri.edu. Website: www.uri.edu/prov/italian/italian.html. **Contact:** Carol Bonomo Albright, editor. Offered annually for the best fiction, essay, or memoir that is published annually by an Italian-American. Acquires first North American serial rights. Guidelines for SASE. Prize: $250.

BOSTON REVIEW SHORT STORY CONTEST, *Boston Review*, E-53-407 MIT, Cambridge MA 02139. Website: bostonreview.mit.edu. Stories should not exceed 4,000 words and must be previously unpublished. Deadline: September 1. Charges $15 fee, payable to *Boston Review*, check or money order. Prize: $1,000 and publication in the December/January issue of *Boston Review*.

BOULEVARD SHORT FICTION CONTEST FOR EMERGING WRITERS, *Boulevard Magazine*, 6614 Clayton Rd., PMB #325, Richmond Heights MO 63117. (314)862-2643. Fax: (314)781-7250. Website: www.richardburgin.com. **Contact:** Richard Burgin, senior editor. Offered annually for unpublished short fiction to award a writer who has not yet published a book of fiction, poetry, or creation nonfiction with a nationally distributed press. "We hold first North American rights on anything not previously published." Open to any writer with no previous publication by a nationally known press. Deadline: December 15. Guidelines for SASE. Charges $15 fee/story; includes 1-year subscription to *Boulevard*. Prize: $1,500 and publication in one of the next year's issues.

RAY BRADBURY SHORT STORY FELLOWSHIP, New Century Writer Awards, 32 Alfred St., Suite B, New Haven CT 06512-3927. (203)469-8824. Fax: (203)468-0333. E-mail: newcenturywriter@yahoo.com. Website: www.newcenturywriter.org. **Contact:** Jason Marchi, executive director. Open to all writers, both nonpublished and those with limited publication history, who enter at least 1 short story into the annual New Century Writers Award Competition (see listing for complete details). Open to all genres, not just science fiction. The first-place winner (and possibly the second-place winner) of each annual Ray Bradbury Fellowship attends the highly touted week-long *Zoetrope* Short Story Writer's Workshop at Francis Ford Coppola's Blancaneaux Lodge in Belize, Central America, during the first week of July. Special note: The remaining Top 10 short-story winners who are not awarded a Bradbury Fellowship receive cash awards. In addition, the Top 10 short stories will be considered for publication in the print magazines

Verbidice and *Futures*, and are invited for inclusion in the annual *Top 10* short story and poetry anthology published by Scissor Press (www.scissorpress.com). See website for details on the *Zoetrope* Workshop and a list of past instructors. Guidelines/entry forms free. No SASE required. Deadline: February 15. Charges $15 for one short story; $10/story for 2 or more stories. Prize: The fellowship is worth approximately $4,500-5,000, and includes aifrare, workshop fees, a private (and beautiful) room, and all meals at Blancaneaux Lodge (excluding alcoholic beverages), and $500 spending money.

BRAZOS BOOKSTORE SHORT STORY AWARD, The Texas Institute of Letters, Southwest Texas State University, San Marcos TX 78666. (512)245-2428. Fax: (512)245-7462. E-mail: mb13@swt.edu. Website: www.English.swt.ecu/css/TIL/rules.htm. **Contact:** Mark Busby. Offered annually for work published January 1-December 31 of previous year to recognize the best short story. The story submitted must have appeared in print for the first time to be eligible. Writers must have been born in Texas, must have lived in Texas for at least two consecutive years or the subject matter of the work must be associated with Texas. Deadline: January 3. Guidelines for SASE. Prize: $750.

N **SANDRA BROWN AWARD FOR OUTSTANDING SHORT FICTION**, *descant*, Texas Christian University's literary journal, TCU Box 297270, Fort Worth TX 76129. (817)257-6537. Fax: (817)257-6239. E-mail: descant@tcu.edu. **Contact:** Dave Kuhne, editor. Offered annually for unpublished short stories. Publication retains copyright but will transfer it to the author upon request. Deadline: September-April. Guidelines for SASE. Prize: $250. Open to any writer.

CANADIAN AUTHORS ASSOCIATION AWARD FOR FICTION, Box 419, 320 South Shores Rd., Campbellford, Ontario K0L 1L0, Canada. (705)653-0323. Fax: (705)653-0593. E-mail: canauth@redden.on.ca. Website: www.canauthors.org. **Contact:** Alec McEachern. Offered annually for a full-length novel by a Canadian citizen. Entry form required. Obtain entry form from contact name or download from website. Deadline: December 15. Guidelines for SASE. Charges $20 fee (Canadian). Prize: $2,500 and a silver medal.

CANADIAN AUTHORS ASSOCIATION JUBILEE AWARD FOR SHORT STORIES, P.O. Box 419, 320 S. Shores Rd., Campbellford, Ontario K0L 1L0, Canada. (705)653-0323. Fax: (705)653-0593. E-mail: canauth@redden.on.ca. Website: www.canauthors.org. **Contact:** Alec McEachern. Offered annually for a collection of short stories by a Canadian author. Entry form required. Obtain entry form from contact name or download from website. Deadline: December 15. Guidelines for SASE. Charges $20 fee (Canadian). Prize: $2,500 and a medal.

THE ALEXANDER PATTERSON CAPPON FICTION AWARD, *New Letters*, 5101 Rockhill Rd., Kansas City MO 64110. (816)235-1168. Fax: (816)235-2611. E-mail: newletters@umkc.edu. Website: www.umkc.edu/newletters. **Contact:** Aleatha Ezra or Mary Ellen Buck. Offered annually for unpublished work to discover and reward new and upcoming writers. Buys first North American serial rights. Open to any writer. Deadline: Third week in May. Guidelines for SASE. Charges $10. Prize: 1st Place: $1,000, and publication in a volume of *New Letters*; 2 runners-up will receive a year's subscription and will be considered for publication.

G.S. SHARAT CHANDRA PRIZE FOR SHORT FICTION, BkMk Press, University of Missouri-Kansas City, 5101 Rockhill Rd., Kansas City MO 64110. (816)235-2558. Fax: (816)235-2611. E-mail: bkmk@umkc.edu. Website: www.umkc.edu/bkmk. **Contact:** Ben Furnish. Offered annually for the best book-length ms collection (unpublished) of short fiction in English by a living author. Translations are not eligible. Initial judging is done by a network of published writers. Final judging is done by a writer of national reputation. Guidelines for SASE, by e-mail, or on website. Deadline: December 1 (postmarked). Charges $25 fee. Prize: $1,000, plus book publication by BkMk Press.

DISCOVER GREAT NEW WRITERS AWARD, Barnes & Noble, Inc., 122 Fifth Ave., New York NY 10011. (212)633-3511. Fax: (212)352-3602. E-mail: jlamar@bn.com. Website: www.bn.com. **Contact:** Jill Lamar. Two prizes offered annually for the most promising writers of literary fiction and narrative nonfiction published each year. Publishers submit titles for consideration; self-published titles not accepted. Prize: 1st Place: $10,000 and a crystal award for each award winner; marketing support valued at over $75,000; 2nd Place: $2,500; 3rd Place: $1,000.

DAVID DORNSTEIN MEMORIAL CREATIVE WRITING CONTEST FOR YOUNG ADULT WRITERS, The Coalition for the Advancement of Jewish Education, 261 W. 35th St., Floor 12A, New York NY 10001. (212)268-4210. Fax: (212)268-4214. E-mail: cajeny@caje.org. Website: www.caje.org. **Contact:** Operations Manager. Contest offered annually for unpublished short story based on a Jewish theme or topic. Writer must prove age of 18-35 years old. Submit only 1 story each year. Guidelines on website or available on request from CAJE office. Deadline: December 31. Prize: 1st Place: $700; 2nd Place: $200; 3rd Place: $100, and publication in the *Jewish Education News*.

JACK DYER FICTION PRIZE, *Crab Orchard Review*, Deptartment of English, Southern Illinois University Carbondale, Carbondale IL 62901-4503. Website: www.siu.edu/~crborchd. **Contact:** Jon C. Tribble, managing editor. Offered annually for unpublished short fiction. *Crab Orchard Review* acquires first North American serial rights to all submitted work. Open to any writer. Deadline: February 1-March 15. Guidelines for SASE. Charges $10/story (limit of 3 stories of up to 6,000 words each, and indicate 'fiction' on outer envelope of entry), which includes a year's subscription to *Crab Orchard Review*. Prize: $1,000 and publication.

THE WILLIAM FAULKNER CREATIVE WRITING COMPETITION, The Pirate's Alley Faulkner Society, 624 Pirate's Alley, New Orleans LA 70116-3254. (504)586-1609. E-mail: faulkhouse@aol.com. Website: www.wordsandmusic.org. **Contact:** Rosemary James, director. Offered annually for unpublished mss to encourage publisher interest in a promising writer's novel, novella, novel-in-progress, short story, personal essay, poem, or short story by a high school student. The Society retains the right to publish excerpts of longer fiction, short stories, essays, poems in toto. Open to all authors working in English. Additional information on the competition and the festival is on the website. Deadline: April 30. Charges entry fee: Novel—$35; novella—$30; novel-in-progress—$30; short story, personal essay, and individual poem—$25; high school short story—$10 (paid by school). Prize: Novel: $7,500; novella: $2,500; novel-in-progress: $2,000; short story: $1,500; personal essay: $1,000; individual poem: $750; high school: $750 for student and $250 for sponsoring teacher. The Society also awards gold medals in William Faulkner's likeness; airfare and hotel expenses for winners to attend Words & Music: A Literary Feast in New Orleans, encompassing a major national writers' conference and Happy Birthday, Mr. Faulkner!, the Faulkner Society's gala annual meeting, at which winners are presented by their judges. Note: For foreign residents the Society pays airfare only from selected US points of entry.

THE $5000 SHORT STORY COMPETITION, Scribendi.com, 4 Sherman St., Thamesville, Ontario N0P 2K0, Canada. Fax: (801)469-6206. E-mail: contactus@scribendi.com. Website: www.scribendi.com. **Contact:** Chandra Clarke. Contest is offered every 6 months. "The contest is designed to give mainstream/literary short story authors a chance at 2 things they generally lack early in their careers—substantial financial reward and publication. We will have categories for genre fiction in the future." Must be unpublished. Deadline: March 15. September 15. Guidelines for SASE. Charges $10. Prize: 1st prize consists of up to $5,000, publication in the *Literati* short story anthology, and a certificate; 2nd prize consists of up to $500, free publication of a book-length work under the *Literati* imprint, publication in the *Literati* short story anthology, and a certificate; 3rd prize consists of up to $50, free sign-up for publication of a book-length work under the *Literati* imprint, publication in the *Literati* short story anthology, and a certificate; 4th-15th Place: Publication in the *Literati* short story anthology, and a certificate. Judged by the editorial staff at Scribendi.com and/or published short story authors, if they are available.

N **THE JOHN GARDNER FICTION BOOK AWARD**, Creative Writing Program, Binghamton University-State University of New York, P.O. Box 6000, Binghamton NY 13902-6000. (607)777-6134. Fax: (607)777-2408. E-mail: mgillan@binghamton.edu. Website: www.binghamton.edu/english. **Contact:** Maria Mazziotti Gillan, director, creative writing program. Annually. Must have appeared in print between January 1-December 31 of year preceding award. Deadline: April 1. Guidelines for SASE. Prize: $1,000. Judged by a professional writer not on the Binghamton University faculty. Open to any writer.

THE JOHN GARDNER MEMORIAL PRIZE FOR FICTION, *Harpur Palate at Binghamton University*, Department of English, Binghamton University, P.O. Box 6000, Binghamton NY 13902-6000. (607)355-4761. Website: go.to/hpjournal.com; harpurpalate.binghamton.edu. **Contact:** Managing Editor. Contest offered annually for previously published fiction in any genre, up to 8,000 words. Deadline: January 1-March 1. Guidelines for SASE. Charges $10/story. Prize: $500 and publication in summer issue of *Harpur Palate*. All entrants receive a copy of the issue in which the winning story appears. Name and contact information should appear in the cover letter only. Acquires first North American serial rights. Open to any writer.

DANUTA GLEED LITERARY AWARD FOR FIRST BOOK OF SHORT FICTION, The Writers' Union of Canada, 40 Wellington St. E., 3rd Floor, Toronto, Ontario M5E 1C7, Canada. (416)703-8982, ext. 223. Fax: (416)504-7656. E-mail: projects@writersunion.ca. Website: www.writersunion.ca. **Contact:** Caroline Sin. Offered annually to Canadian writers for the best first collection of published short stories in the English language. Must have been published in the previous calendar year. Submit 4 copies. Deadline: January 31. Guidelines for SASE. Prize: 1st Place: $5,000; $500 to each of 2 runners-up.

GOVERNOR GENERAL'S LITERARY AWARD FOR FICTION, Canada Council for the Arts, 350 Albert St., P.O. Box 1047, Ottawa, Ontario K1P 5V8, Canada. (613)566-4414, ext. 5576. Fax: (613)566-4410. E-mail: joanne.larocque-poirier@canadacouncil.ca. Website: www.canadacouncil.ca. **Contact:** Joanne Larocque-Poirier. Offered annually for the best English-language and the best French-language work of fiction by a Canadian published September 1, 2001-September 30, 2002. Publishers submit titles for consideration. Deadline: April 15 or August 7, 2002, depending on the book's publication date. Prize: $15,000.

DRUE HEINZ LITERATURE PRIZE, University of Pittsburgh Press, 3400 Forbes Ave., 5th Floor, Eureka Bldg., Pittsburgh PA 15260. (412)383-2492. Fax: (412)383-2466. E-mail: susief@pitt.edu. Website: www.pitt.edu/~press. **Contact:** Sue Borello, assistant to the director. Estab. 1981. Collection of short fiction. Offered annually to writers who have published a book-length collection of fiction or a minimum of 3 short stories or novellas in commercial magazines or literary journals of national distribution. Does not return mss. Deadline: Submit in May and June only. Guidelines for SASE. Prize: $10,000.

ERNEST HEMINGWAY FOUNDATION PEN AWARD FOR FIRST FICTION, PEN New England, P.O. Box 400725, North Cambridge MA 02140. (617)499-9550. Fax: (617)353-7134. E-mail: mary@pen-ne.org. Website: www.pen-ne.org. **Contact:** Mary Louise Sullivan. Offered for first-published novel or short story collection by an American author. Guidelines and entry form for SASE. Deadline: December 15.

LORIAN HEMINGWAY SHORT STORY COMPETITION, Hemingway Days Festival, P.O. Box 993, Key West FL 33041-0993. (305)294-0320. Fax: (305)292-3653. E-mail: calico2419@aol.com. Website: www.shortstorycompetition.com. **Contact:** Carol Shaughnessy, co-coordinator. Estab. 1981. Fax and e-mail for guideline requests only. Guidelines for SASE or by e-mail. Offered annually for unpublished short stories up to 3,000 words. Deadline: May 15. Charges $10/story postmarked by May 1, $15/story postmarked by May 15; no stories accepted after May 15. Prize: 1st Place: $1,000; 2nd and 3rd Place: $500; runner-up awards; honorable mentions will also be awarded.

L. RON HUBBARD'S WRITERS OF THE FUTURE CONTEST, P.O. Box 1630, Los Angeles CA 90078. (323)466-3310. Website: www.writersofthefuture.com. **Contact:** Contest Administrator. Offered for unpublished work "to find, reward, and publicize new speculative fiction writers so they may more easily attain to professonal writing careers." Open to new and amateur writers who have not professionally published a novel or short novel, more than 1 novelette, or more than 3 short stories. Eligible entries are short stories or novelettes (under 17,000 words) of science fiction or fantasy. Guidelines for SASE or on website. Deadline: December 31, March 31, June 30, September 30. Prize: Awards quarterly 1st Place: $1,000; 2nd Place: $750; and 3rd Place: $500. Annual Grand Prize: $4,000.

INDIANA REVIEW FICTION CONTEST, *Indiana Review*, BH 465/Indiana University, Bloomington IN 47405-7103. (812)855-3439. Fax: (812)855-4253. E-mail: inreview@indiana.edu. Website: www.indiana.edu/~inreview/ir.html. **Contact:** David Daniels. Maximum story length is 15,000 words (no minimum). Offered annually for unpublished work. Deadline: Late October. Guidelines for SASE. Charges $12 fee (includes prize issue). Prize: $1,000. Judged by guest judges. Jim Grimsley judged the 2001 contest. Open to any writer.

JAPANOPHILE ANNUAL SHORT STORY CONTEST, Japanophile, P.O. Box 7977, 415 N. Main St., Ann Arbor MI 48107-7977. (734)930-1553. Fax: (734)930-9968. E-mail: jpnhand@japanophile.com. Website: www.japanophile.com. **Contact:** Susan Aitken, editor; Madeleine Vala, associate editor. Offered annually for unpublished work to encourage good fiction writing that contributes to understanding of Japan and Japanese culture. Deadline: December 31. Guidelines for SASE. Charges $5 fee. Prize: $100, certificate, and publication.

JESSE H. JONES AWARD, The Texas Institute of Letters, Southwest Texas State University, San Marcos TX 78666. (512)245-2428. Fax: (512)245-7462. E-mail: mb13@swt.edu. Website: www.English.swt.ecu/css/TIL/rules.htm. **Contact:** Mark Busby. Offered annually for work published January 1-December 31 of year before award is given to recognize the writer of the best book of fiction entered in the competition. Writers must have been born in Texas, or have lived in the state for at least two consecutive years at some time, or the subject matter of the work should be associated with the state. Deadline: January 3. Guidelines for SASE. Prize: $6,000.

JAMES JONES FIRST NOVEL FELLOWSHIP, Wilkes University, English Department, Kirby Hall, Wilkes-Barre PA 18766. (570)408-4530. Fax: (570)408-7829. E-mail: english@wilkes.edu. Website: www.wilkes.edu/humanities/jones.html. **Contact:** Jacqueline Mosher, coordinator. Offered annually for unpublished novels, novellas, and closely-linked short stories (all works-in-progress). "The award is intended to honor the spirit of unblinking honesty, determination, and insight into modern culture exemplified by the late James Jones." The competition is open to all American writers who have not previously published novels. Deadline: March 1. Charges $20 fee. Prize: 1st Place: $6,000; $250 honorarium (runner-up).

N KLOPP ANTHOLOGIST'S ANNUAL SHORT STORY AWARD FOR NEW WRITERS, Klopp Anthologist Publications, 23 Pine Grove St., Woodstock NY 12498. E-mail: kloppanthologist@hotmail.com. Website: community.webtv.net/kloppanthologist/doc. **Contact:** Kenneth Bender. Offered annually for unpublished short fiction to showcase new and emerging writers. Guidelines available for SASE, by e-mail and on website. "We reserve first-time publishing rights, after which all rights revert back to the writer." Open to any writer; however, all submissions must be in English. Deadline: September 30, 2002 (postmark date). Charges $20 for each story submitted. Prize: 1st Place: $300; 2nd Place: $150; 3rd Place: $75. All applicants will receive a free copy of the publication. Judged by a panel of readers in the literary field.

LAURIE, Smoky Mountain Romance Writers, P.O. Box 70802, Knoxville TN 37938. (865)947-4595. E-mail: laurie_coordinator@yahoo.com. Website: www.smrw.org. **Contact:** Leanne Hinkle. Offered annually to honor excellence in unpublished romance fiction. Guidelines and entry forms for SASE or on website. Participants must furnish a valid Romance Writers of America membership number to enter. Deadline: February 7. Charges $25 fee. Prize: Finalists have their entry read by an acquiring editor or agent. 1st Place: A Laurie Pendant; finalist and winners receive certificates.

THE LAWRENCE FOUNDATION AWARD, *Prairie Schooner*, 201 Andrews Hall, P.O. Box 880334, Lincoln NE 68588-0334. (402)472-0911. Fax: (402)472-9771. E-mail: eflanagan2@unl.edu. Website: www.unl.edu/schooner/psmain.htm. **Contact:** Hilda Raz. Offered annually for the best short story published in *Prairie Schooner* in the previous year. Prize: $1,000.

URSULA K. LEGUIN PRIZE FOR IMAGINATIVE FICTION, *Rosebud*, P.O. Box 459, Cambridge WI 53523. E-mail: jrodclark@smallbytes.net. Website: www.rsbd.net. **Contact:** J. Roderick Clark, editor. Biennial (odd years) contest for unpublished stories. Next contest opens April 1, 2003. Acquires first rights. Open to any writer. Deadline: September 30. Charges $10/story fee. Prize: $1,000, plus publication in *Rosebud*.

MALICE DOMESTIC GRANTS FOR UNPUBLISHED WRITERS, Malice Domestic, P.O. Box 31137, Bethesda MD 20284-1137. Website: www.malicedomestic.org. **Contact:** Grants chair. Offered annually for unpublished work. Malice awards two grants to unpublished writers in the Malice Domestic genre at its annual convention in May. The competition is designed to help the next generation of Malice authors get their first work published and to foster quality Malice literature. Writers who have been published previously in the mystery field, including publication of a mystery novel, short story, or nonfiction work, are ineligible to apply. Members of the Malice Domestic Board of Directors and their families are ineligible to apply. Malice encourages applications from minority candidates. Guidelines on website. Deadline: December 15. Prize: $1,000.

MAYHAVEN AWARDS FOR FICTION, Mayhaven Publishing, 803 Buckthorn Circle, P.O. Box 557, Mahomet IL 61853. (217)586-4493. Fax: (217)586-6330. E-mail: ibfipone@aol.com. Website: www.mayhavenpublishing.com. **Contact:** Doris Replogle Wenzel. Offered annually for unpublished work "to provide additional opportunities for authors. We give awards in both adult and children's fiction." All entrants will be notified of the contest winners. Deadline: December 31. Guidelines for SASE. Charges $45 fee. Prize: 1st Place: Publication of work and royalties on sales.

MARY MCCARTHY PRIZE IN SHORT FICTION, Sarabande Books, P.O. Box 4456, Louisville KY 40204. (502)458-4028. Fax: (502)458-4065. E-mail: sarabandeb@aol.com. Website: www.SarabandeBooks.org. **Contact:** Kirby Gann, managing editor. Offered annually to publish an outstanding collection of stories, novellas, or short novel (less than 250 pages). All finalists considered for publication. Deadline: January 1-February 15. Guidelines for SASE. Charges $20 fee. Prize: $2,000 and publication, standard royalty contract.

MID-LIST PRESS FIRST SERIES AWARD FOR SHORT FICTION, Mid-List Press, 4324 12th Ave. S., Minneapolis MN 55407-3218. Fax: (612)823-8387. E-mail: guide@midlist.org. Website: www.midlist.org. **Contact:** Lane Stiles, publisher. Open to any writer who has never published a book-length collection of short fiction (short stories, novellas); minimum 50,000 words. Accepts simultaneous submissions. Guidelines and entry form for SASE or on website. Deadline: July 1. Charges $20 fee. Prize: Awards include publication and an advance against royalties.

MID-LIST PRESS FIRST SERIES AWARD FOR THE NOVEL, Mid-List Press, 4324-12th Ave. S., Minneapolis MN 55407-3218. (612)822-3733. Fax: (612)823-8387. E-mail: guide@midlist.org. Website: www.midlist.org. **Contact:** Lane Stiles, publisher. Offered annually for unpublished novels to locate and publish quality mss by first-time writers, particularly those mid-list titles that major publishers may be rejecting. Guidelines for SASE or on website. Open to any writer who has never published a novel. Deadline: February 1. Charges $20 fee. Prize: Advance against royalties, plus publication.

MILKWEED NATIONAL FICTION PRIZE, Milkweed Editions, 1011 Washington Ave. S., Suite 300, Minneapolis MN 55415. (612)332-3192. Fax: (612)215-2550. Website: www.milkweed.org. **Contact:** Elisabeth Fitz, first reader. Estab. 1986. Annual award for unpublished works. "Milkweed is looking for a novel, novella, or a collection of short stories. Manuscripts should be of high literary quality and must be double-spaced and between 150-400 pages in length. Due to new postal regulations, writers who need their work returned must include a check for $5 rather than a SAS book mailer. Manuscripts not accompanied by a check for postage will be recycled." Winner will be chosen from the mss Milkweed accepts for publication each year. All mss submitted to Milkweed will automatically be considered for the prize. Submission directly to the contest is no longer necessary. "Must be written in English. Writers should have previously published a book of fiction or three short stories (or novellas) in magazines/journals with national distribution." Catalog available on request for $1.50. Guidelines for SASE or online. Deadline: Open. Prize: Publication by Milkweed Editions and a cash advance of $5,000 against royalties agreed upon in the contractual arrangement negotiated at the time of acceptance.

C. WRIGHT MILLS AWARD, The Society for the Study of Social Problems, 901 McClung Tower, University of Tennessee, Knoxville TN 37996-0490. (865)974-3620. Fax: (865)974-7013. E-mail: mkoontz3@utk.edu. Website: www.it.utk.edu/sssp. **Contact:** Michele Smith Koontz, admistrative officer. Offered annually for a book published the previous year that most effectively critically addresses an issue of contemporary public importance; brings to the topic a fresh, imaginative perspective; advances social scientific understanding of the topic; displays a theoretically informed view and empirical orientation; evinces quality in style of writing; and explicitly or implicitly contains implications for courses of action. Deadline: January 15. Prize: $500 stipend.

MOONLIGHT & MAGNOLIA FICTION WRITING CONTEST, P.O. Box 180489, Richmond MS 39218-0489. (601)825-7263. E-mail: Hoover59@aol.com. **Contact:** K. Mark Hoover. Offered annually for unpublished work to recognize and encourage new and unpublished writers throughout the South while rewarding excellence in genre writing. "Southern writers are encouraged to participate, but the contest is worldwide. Regional contestants will not be given any preference during judging." Open to works of science fiction, fantasy, and horror. Length: 10,000 words maximum. Open to writers who have not published more than 2 stories in a nationally-distributed magazine with a circulation over 5,000. Judge changes annually and is always a professional genre writer/editor who knows what it takes to write/market/publish a good story. 2002 final judge is Richard Parks. Deadline: December 15, 2002. Guidelines for SASE. Charges $7.50, $2.50 each additional story; maximum 3 stories/contestant. Prize: 1st Place: $250; 2nd Place: $100; 3rd Place: $50. Top 10 finalists receive certificates suitable for framing. Winners announced January 31.

MOTA 2003, TripleTree Publishing, P.O. Box 5684, Eugene OR 97405. (541)338-3184. Fax: (541)484-5358. E-mail: Liz@TripleTreePub.com. Website: www.TripleTreePub.com. **Contact:** Liz Cratty, Publisher. Themed. Theme for 2003 is Courage—fiction only; theme for 2004 is Integrity. Submissions must be unpublished. Deadline: November 1. Guidelines for SASE. Charges $12 entry fee. Prize: 1st prize consists of $100 and publication in the *MOTA 2003* short story anthology; 2nd prize consists of $50 and possible publication; 3rd prize consists of $25 and possible publication. Judged by a panel of fiction writers, along with the year's guest editor. Acquires one-time nonexclusive publication rights.

MYSTERY NOVEL AWARD, Salvo Press, P.O. Box 9095, Bend OR 97708. E-mail: publisher@salvopress.com. Website: www.salvopress.com. **Contact:** Scott Schmidt, publisher. Offered annually for the best unpublished mystery, suspense, thriller or espionage novel. Guidelines for SASE or on website. Deadline: July 15. Charges $25 fee. Prize: Publication under a standard royalty contract by Salvo Press.

NATIONAL WRITERS ASSOCIATION NOVEL WRITING CONTEST, The National Writers Association, 3140 S. Peoria, #295, Aurora CO 80014. (303)841-0246. Fax: (303)841-2607. **Contact:** Sandy Whelchel, director. Annual contest "to help develop creative skills, to recognize and reward outstanding ability, and to increase the opportunity for the marketing and subsequent publication of novel manuscripts." Deadline: April 1. Charges $35 fee. Prize: 1st Place: $500; 2nd Place: $300; 3rd Place: $200.

NATIONAL WRITERS ASSOCIATION SHORT STORY CONTEST, The National Writers Association, 3140 S. Peoria, #295, Aurora CO 80014. (303)841-0246. Fax: (303)841-2607. **Contact:** Sandy Whelchel, director. Annual contest "to encourage writers in this creative form, and to recognize those who excel in fiction writing." Deadline: July 1. Guidelines for SASE. Charges $15 fee. Prize: 1st Place: $200; 2nd Place: $100; 3rd Place: $50.

NEW CENTURY WRITER AWARDS (FICTION), 32 Alfred St., Suite B, New Haven CT 06512-3927. (203)469-8824. Fax: (203)468-0333. E-mail: newcenturywriter@yahoo.com. Website: www.newcenturywriter.org. **Contact:** Jason J. Marchi, executive director. Offered annually to discover emerging writers of short stories and novels. Guidelines/entry forms free. All entrants receive 1-year subscription to *The Anvil*, an educational newsletter for writers. Open to all writers, both non-published and those with limited publication history. Call if you doubt your eligibility. Also provides the annual Ray Bradbury Short Story Fellowship for a short fiction writer to attend the Zoetrope Short Story Writers' Workshop at Francis Ford Coppola's Blancaneaux Lodge in Belize, Central America (see Ray Bradbury Short Story Fellowship listing for complete details). Deadline: January 31. Charges $15-30 entry fee. Prize: 1st Place: $3,000; 2nd Place: $1,000; 3rd Place: $500; 4th-10th Place: $100.

NEW MUSE AWARD, Broken Jaw Press, Box 596 Station A, Fredericton, New Brunswick E3B 5A6, Canada. E-mail: jblades@nbnet.nb.ca. Website: www.brokenjaw.com. **Contact:** Joe Blades. Offered annually for unpublished fiction mss of 80-120 pages to encourage development of book-length mss by Canadian writers without a first fiction book published. Guidelines for SASE or go to www.brokenjaw.com/newmuse.htm. Deadline: January 31. Charges $20 fee (all entrants receive copy of winning book upon publication). Prize: $500 cash and book publication on trade terms.

FRANK O'CONNOR AWARD FOR SHORT FICTION, *descant*, Texas Christian University's literary journal, TCU Box 297270, Fort Worth TX 76129. (817)257-6537. Fax: (817)257-6239. E-mail: descant@tcu.edu. **Contact:** Dave Kuhne, editor. Offered annually for unpublished short stories. Publication retains copyright but will transfer it to the author upon request. Deadline: September-April. Guidelines for SASE. Prize: $500.

THE FLANNERY O'CONNOR AWARD FOR SHORT FICTION, The University of Georgia Press, 330 Research Dr., Athens GA 30602-4901. (706)369-6135. Fax: (706)369-6131. E-mail: emontjoy@ugapress.uga.edu. Website: www.uga.edu/ugapress. **Contact:** Emily Montjoy, competition coordinator. Estab. 1981. Does not return mss. Manuscripts must be 200-275 pages long. Authors do not have to be previously published. Deadline: April 1-May 31. Guidelines for SASE. Charges $20 fee. Prize: $1,000 and publication under standard book contract.

THE OMAHA PRIZE, The Backwaters Press, 3502 N. 52nd St., Omaha NE 68104-3506. (402)451-4052. Fax: (402)421-4052. E-mail: gkosm62735@aol.com. Website: www.thebackwaterspress.homestead.com. **Contact:** Greg Kosmicki. Offered annually for unpublished novels, no collaborations, though parts of the submitted novels may have been previously published in magazines. Guidelines for SASE, by e-mail or on website. Deadline: December 4 (postmark). Charges $25. Prize: $1,000 and publication in an edition of at least 750 copies under standard book contract.

PATERSON FICTION PRIZE, One College Blvd., Paterson NJ 07505-1179. (973)684-6555. Fax: (973)684-5843. E-mail: mgillan@pccc.cc.nj.us. Website: www.pccc.cc.nj.us/poetry. **Contact:** Maria Mazziotti Gillan, director. Offered annually for a novel or collection of short fiction published the previous calendar year. Deadline: April 1. Guidelines for SASE. Prize: $1,000.

WILLIAM PEDEN PRIZE IN FICTION, *The Missouri Review*, 1507 Hillcrest Hall, Columbia MO 65211. (573)882-4474. Fax: (573)884-4671. Website: www.missourireview.org. **Contact:** Hoa Ngo, managing editor. Offered annually "for the best story published in the past volume year of the magazine. All stories published in *MR* are automatically considered." Prize: $1,000 and reading/reception.

PEN/FAULKNER AWARDS FOR FICTION, PEN/Faulkner Foundation, 201 E. Capitol St., Washington DC 20003. (202)675-0345. Fax: (202)608-1719. E-mail: delaney@folger.edu. Website: www.penfaulkner.org. **Contact:** Janice F. Delaney, executive director. Offered annually for best book-length work of fiction by an American citizen published in a calendar year. Deadline: October 31. Prize: $15,000 (one winner); $5,000 (4 nominees).

PHOEBE WINTER FICTION CONTEST, *Phoebe*, George Mason University, 4400 University Dr., Fairfax VA 22030-4444. (703)993-2915. E-mail: phoebe@gmu.edu. Website: www.gmu.edu. **Contact:** Emily Tuszynska. Offered annually for unpublished work. Deadline: December 1. Guidelines for SASE. Charges $10 entry fee. Prize: $1,000 and publication in Fall 2002 issue. All entrants receive a free issue. Judged by outside judge—recognized fiction writer hired by *Phoebe*— who changes each year. Acquires first serial rights, if work is accepted for publication. Open to any writer.

POCKETS FICTION-WRITING CONTEST, The Upper Room, 1908 Grand Ave., P.O. Box 340004, Nashville TN 37203-0004. (615)340-7333. E-mail: pockets@upperroom.org. Website: www.pockets.org. **Contact:** Lynn W. Gilliam. Offered annually for unpublished work to discover new writers. Deadline: March 1-August 15. Guidelines for SASE. Prize: $1,000 and publication in *Pockets*.

PRISM INTERNATIONAL ANNUAL SHORT FICTION CONTEST, Prism International, Creative Writing Program, UBC, Buch E462, 1866 Main Mall, Vancouver, British Columbia V6T 1Z1, Canada. (604)822-2514. Fax: (604)822-3616. E-mail: prism@interchange.ubc.ca. Website: prism.arts.ubc.ca. **Contact:** Fiction Contest Manager. Offered annually for unpublished work to award the best in contemporary fiction. Works of translation are eligible. Guidelines for SASE, by e-mail or on website. Acquires first North American serial rights upon publication, and limited Web rights for pieces selected for website. Open to any writer. Deadline: January 31, 2003. Charges $22/story, $5 each additional story (outside Canada pay US currency); includes subscription. Prize: 1st Place: $2,000; runners-up (5): $200 each; winner and runners-up published.

THOMAS H. RADDALL ATLANTIC FICTION PRIZE, Writers' Federation of Nova Scotia, 1113 Marginal Rd., Halifax, Nova Scotia B3H 4P7, Canada. (902)423-8116. Fax: (902)422-0881. E-mail: talk@writers.ns.ca. Website: www.writers.ns.ca. **Contact:** Jane Buss, executive director. "This award was established by the Writers' Federation of Nova Scotia and the Writers' Development Trust in 1990 to honor the achievement of Thomas H. Raddall, and to recognize the best Atlantic Canadian adult fiction. Thomas Head Raddall is probably best-known for *His Majesty's Yankees* (1942), *The Governor's Lady* (1960), *The Nymph and the Lamp* (1950), and *Halifax, Warden of the North* (1948)." There is no entry fee or form. Full-length books of fiction written by Atlantic Canadians, and published as a whole for the first time in the previous calendar year, are eligible. Entrants must be native or resident Atlantic Canadians who have either been born in Newfoundland, Prince Edward Island, Nova Scotia, or New Brunswick, and spent a substantial portion of their lives living there, or who have lived in 1 or a combination of these provinces for at least 24 consecutive months prior to entry deadline date. Publishers: Send 4 copies and a letter attesting to the author's status as an Atlantic Canadian, and the author's current mailing address and telephone number. Deadline: First Friday in December. Prize: $10,000.

HAROLD U. RIBALOW AWARD, Hadassah WZOA, 50 W. 58th St., New York NY 10019. (212)688-0227. Fax: (212)446-9521. E-mail: hadamag@aol.com or dsilfen@hadassah.org. **Contact:** Dorothy Silfen, coordinator. Editor: Alan Tigay. Offered annually for English-language books of fiction (novel or short stories) on a Jewish theme published the previous calendar year. Books should be submitted by the publisher. Deadline: April. Prize: $1,000.

RIVER CITY WRITING AWARDS IN FICTION, The University of Memphis/Hohenberg Foundation, Department of English, Memphis TN 38152. (901)678-4591. Fax: (901)678-2226. Website: www.people.memphis.edu/~rivercity. **Contact:** Mary Leader. Offered annually for unpublished short stories of 7,500 words maximum. Guidelines for SASE or on website. Deadline: March 15. Charges $10/story, which is put toward a 1-year subscription for *River City*. Prize: 1st Place: $2,000; 2nd Place: $500; 3rd Place: $300.

THE SANDSTONE PRIZE IN SHORT FICTION, The Ohio State University Press and the MFA Program in Creative Writing at The Ohio State University, 1070 Carmack Rd., Columbus OH 43210-1002. (614)292-1462. Fax: (614)292-2065. E-mail: ohiostatepress@osu.edu. Website: ohiostatepress.org. **Contact:** Lee Martin, fiction editor. Offered annually to published and unpublished writers. Submissions may include short stories, novellas, or a combination of both. Manuscripts must be 150-300 typed pages; novellas must not exceed 125 pages. No employee or student of The Ohio State University is eligible. Deadline: Accepts in January only. Charges $20 fee. Prize: $1,500, publication under a standard book contract, an invitation to The Ohio State University to give a public reading and give a master class in creative writing.

SASKATCHEWAN FICTION AWARD, Saskatchewan Book Awards, Inc., Box 1921, Regina, Saskatchewan S4P 3E1, Canada. (306)569-1585. Fax: (306)569-4187. E-mail: director@bookawards.sk.ca. Website: www.bookawards.sk.ca. **Contact:** Joyce Wells, executive director. Offered annually for work published September 15 to September 14 annually. This award is presented to a Saskatchewan author for the best book of fiction (novel or short fiction), judged on the quality of writing. Deadline: First deadline: July 31; Final deadline: September 14. Guidelines for SASE. Charges $15 (Canadian). Prize: $1,500.

MICHAEL SHAARA AWARD FOR EXCELLENCE IN CIVIL WAR FICTION, US Civil War Center, LSU, Raphael Semmes Dr., Baton Rouge LA 70803. (225)578-3151. Fax: (225)578-4876. E-mail: lwood@lsu.edu. Website: www.cwc.lsu.edu. **Contact:** Leah Jewett, director. Offered annually for fiction published January 1-December 31 "to encourage examination of the Civil War from unique perspectives or by taking an unusual approach." All Civil War fiction, except children's books, is eligible. Nominations should be made by publishers, but authors and critics can nominate as well. Deadline: December 31. Guidelines for SASE. Prize: $1,500 which includes travel stipend.

ELIZABETH SIMPSON SMITH AWARD, Charlotte Writers Club, P.O. Box 220954, Charlotte NC 28222-0954. E-mail: akalnik@carolina.rr.com. **Contact:** Andrew Kalnik, 2002 ESS award chairperson. Offered annually for unpublished short stories by North Carolina and South Carolina residents. Deadline: April 30. Guidelines for SASE. Charges $10 fee. Prize: $500 and a plaque.

SNAKE NATION PRESS ANNUAL AWARD FOR SHORT FICTION, Snake Nation Press, 110 W. Force St., Valdosta GA 31601. (229)244-0752. E-mail: jeana@snakenationpress.org. Website: www.snakenationpress.org.

Contact: Jean Arambula. Contest for a collection of unpublished short stories by a new or underpublished writer. Entries accepted year round. Must Be Unpublished. Deadline: June 15. Guidelines for SASE. Charges $20 reading fee. Prize: $1,000 and publication. Judged by an independent judge. Open to any writer.

KAY SNOW WRITING AWARDS, Willamette Writers, 9045 SW Barbur Blvd., Suite 5A, Portland OR 97219. (503)452-1592. Fax: (503)452-0372. E-mail: wilwrite@teleport.com. Website: www.willamettewriters.com. **Contact:** Elizabeth Shannon. Contest offered annually to "offer encouragement and recognition to writers with unpublished submissions." Acquires right to publish excerpts from winning pieces one time in their newsletter. Deadline: May 15. Guidelines for SASE. Charges $15 fee; no fee for student writers. Prize: 1st Place: $300; 2nd Place: $150; 3rd Place: $50; excerpts published in Willamette Writers newsletter, and winners acknowledged at banquet during writing conference. Student writers win $50 in categories for grades 1-5, 6-8, and 9-12. $500 Liam Callen Memorial Award goes to best overall entry.

N **SOUL OF THE WRITER AWARD**, Grammar Bytes, 3044 Shepherd of Hills PMB519, Branson MO 65616. E-mail: contest@grammarbytes.com. Website: www.grammarbytes.com. **Contact:** Shane Jeffries. Offered once a year to unpublished submissions. "Soul of the Writer Award was created to aid writers in their journey toward ultimate literary goals—whatever they may be. We look at fiction of any genre, any style." Deadline for entry postmarked by May 31, 2003. Guidelines for SASE. Limit of 15,000 words. Previous winners will select semi-finalists, then a committee of 3 prominent writers will make final decision. Writers retain all rights. Open to any writer. Deadline: May 31, 2003. Charges $15. Prize: 1st Place: $250; 2nd Place: $100; 3rd Place: $25, plus certificate.

SOUTH CAROLINA FICTION PROJECT, South Carolina Arts Commission, 1800 Gervais St., Columbia SC 29201. (803)734-8696. Fax: (803)734-8526. E-mail: goldstsa@arts.state.sc.us. Website: www.state.sc.us/arts. **Contact:** Sara June Goldstein, contest director. Offered annually for unpublished short stories of 2,500 words or less. *The Post and Courier* newspaper (Charleston SC) purchases first publication rights. Open to any writer who is a legal resident of South Carolina and 18 years of age or older. Twelve stories are selected for publication. Deadline: January 31. Guidelines for SASE. Prize: $500.

THE SOUTHERN REVIEW/LOUISIANA STATE UNIVERSITY SHORT FICTION AWARD, Louisiana State University, 43 Allen Hall, Baton Rouge LA 70803. (225)578-5108. Fax: (225)578-5098. E-mail: bmacon@LSU.edu or mgriffi@LSU.edu. Offered for first collections of short stories by Americans published in the US during the previous year. Publisher or author may enter by mailing 2 copies of the collection. Deadline: January 31.

subTERRAIN SHORT STORY CONTEST, (formerly *sub-TERRAIN* Short Story Contest), *subTERRAIN* Magazine, P.O. Box 3008 MPO, Vancouver, British Columbia V6B 3X5, Canada. (604)876-8710. Fax: (604)879-2667. E-mail: subter@portal.ca. **Contact:** Brian Kaufman. Offered annually to foster new and upcoming writers. 2,000 word limit. Deadline: January 1-May 15. Guidelines for SASE. Charges $15 fee for first story, $5 for additional entries. Prize: $500 (Canadian), publication in summer issue, and 1-year subscription to *subTERRAIN*.

THOROUGHBRED TIMES FICTION CONTEST, *Thoroughbred Times Magazine*, 496 Southland Dr., Lexington KY 40503. (859)260-9800. Fax: (859)260-9812. E-mail: copy@thoroughbredtimes.com. Website: www.thoroughbredtimes.com. **Contact:** Amy Owens. Offered every 2 years for unpublished work to recognize outstanding fiction written about the Thoroughbred racing industry. Maximum length: 5,000 words. *Thoroughbred Times* receives first North American serial rights and reserves the right to publish any and all entries in the magazine. Deadline: December 31, 2003. Prize: 1st Place: $800, and publication in *Thoroughbred Times* in March 2003; 2nd Place: $400, and publication; 3rd Place: $200, and publication.

THREE OAKS PRIZE FOR FICTION, Story Line Press, P.O. Box 1240, Ashland OR 97520-0055. (541)512-8792. Fax: (541)512-8793. E-mail: mail@storylinepress.com. Website: www.storylinepress.com. Offered annually to find and publish the best work of fiction. Open to any writer. Deadline: April 30. Guidelines for SASE. Charges $25. Prize: $1,500 advance, and book publication.

STEVEN TURNER AWARD, The Texas Institute of Letters, Southwest Texas State University, San Marcos TX 78666. (512)245-2428. Fax: (512)245-7462. E-mail: mb13@swt.edu. Website: www.English.swt.ecu/css/TIL/rules.htm. **Contact:** Mark Busby. Offered annually for work published January 1-December 31 for the best first book of fiction. Writers must have been born in Texas, or have lived in the state for at least two consecutive years at some time, or the subject matter of the work should be associated with the state. Deadline: January 3. Guidelines for SASE. Prize: $1,000.

WAASMODE FICTION CONTEST, *Passages North*, Dept. of English, Northern Michigan University, 1401 Presque Isle Ave., Marquette MI 49855. (906)227-1203. Fax: (906)227-1096. E-mail: passages@nmu.edu. Website: vm.nmu.edu/passages/http/home.html. **Contact:** Katie Hanson. Offered every 2 years to publish new voices in literary fiction. Deadline: Submit September 15-January 15. Guidelines for SASE. Charges $8 reading fee/story. Prize: $1,000 and publication for winner; 2 honorable mentions also published; all entrants receive a copy of *Passages North*.

PAUL A. WITTY SHORT STORY AWARD, Executive Office, International Reading Association, P.O. Box 8139, Newark DE 19714-8139. (302)731-1600 ext. 293. Fax: (302)731-1057. Website: www.reading.org. **Contact:** Janet Butler, public information associate. Offered to reward author of an original short story published in a children's periodical which serves as a literary standard that encourages young readers to read periodicals. Write for deadlines and guidelines. Prize: $1,000.

TOBIAS WOLFF AWARD IN FICTION, *Bellingham Review*, Mail Stop 9053, Western Washington University, Bellingham WA 98225. (360)650-4863. E-mail: bhreview@cc.wwu.edu. Website: www.wwu.edu/~bhreview/. **Contact:** Brenda Miller. Offered annually for unpublished work. Deadline: December 1-March 15. Guidelines for SASE. Prize: 1st Place: $1,000; 2nd Place: $300; 3rd Place: $200; plus publication and subscription.

WRITERS' JOURNAL ANNUAL FICTION CONTEST, Val-Tech Media, P.O. Box 394, Perham MN 56573. (218)346-7921. Fax: (218)346-7924. E-mail: writersjournal@lakesplus.com. Website: www.writersjournal.com. **Contact:** Leon Ogroske. Offered annually for previously unpublished fiction. Open to any writer. Deadline: January 30. Guidelines for SASE. Charges $5 reading fee. Prize: 1st Place: $50; 2nd Place: $25; 3rd Place: $15, plus honorable mentions. Prize-winning stories and selected honorable mentions published in *Writers' Journal* magazine.

WRITERS' JOURNAL ANNUAL HORROR/GHOST CONTEST, Val-Tech Media, P.O. Box 394, Perham MN 56573. (218)346-7921. Fax: (218)346-7924. E-mail: writersjournal@lakesplus.com. Website: www.writersjournal.com. **Contact:** Leon Ogroske. Offered annually for previously unpublished works. Open to any writer. Deadline: March 30. Guidelines for SASE. Charges $5 fee. Prize: 1st Place: $50; 2nd Place: $25; 3rd Place: $15, plus honorable mentions. Prize-winning stories and selected honorable mentions published in *Writers' Journal* magazine.

WRITERS' JOURNAL ANNUAL ROMANCE CONTEST, Val-Tech Media, P.O. Box 394, Perham MN 56573. (218)346-7921. Fax: (218)346-7924. E-mail: writersjournal@lakesplus.com. Website: www.writersjournal.com. **Contact:** Leon Ogroske. Offered annually for previously unpublished works. Open to any writer. Deadline: July 30. Guidelines for SASE. Charges $5 fee. Prize: 1st Place: $50; 2nd Place: $25; 3rd Place: $15, plus honorable mentions. Prize-winning stories and selected honorable mentions published in *Writers' Journal* magazine.

WRITERS' JOURNAL ANNUAL SHORT STORY CONTEST, Val-Tech Media, P.O. Box 394, Perham MN 56573. (218)346-7921. Fax: (218)346-7924. E-mail: writersjournal@lakesplus.com. Website: www.writersjournal.com. **Contact:** Leon Ogroske. Offered annually for previously unpublished short stories. Open to any writer. Deadline: May 30. Guidelines for SASE. Charges $7 reading fee. Prize: 1st Place: $300, 2nd Place: $100; 3rd Place: $50, plus honorable mentions. Prize-winning stories and selected honorable mentions published in *Writers' Journal* magazine.

ZOETROPE SHORT STORY CONTEST, *Zoetrope: All-Story*, 916 Kearny St., San Francisco CA 94133. (415)788-7500. Fax: (415)989-7910. Website: www.all-story.com. **Contact:** Francis Ford Coppola, publisher. Annual contest for unpublished short stories. Guidelines for SASE or on website. Open to any writer. Deadline: October 1. Charges $15 fee. Prize: 1st Place: $1,000; 2nd Place: $500, 3rd Place: $250; plus 10 honorable mentions.

Poetry

THE MILTON ACORN PRIZE FOR POETRY, Poetry Forever, P.O. Box 68018, Hamilton, Ontario L8M 3M7, Canada. (905)312-1779. The purpose of this contest is to fund the publication of full-size collections by the People's Poet, Milton Acorn (1923-1986). All profits from this contest will be used for this purpose. Offered annually for poems up to 30 lines. Poems should be typed or neatly printed. Photocopied submissions are OK. Make checks payable to Poetry Forever. Entries will not be returned. Please include a SASE if you wish to receive a list of winners. Deadline: May 15, 2002. Charges $3 fee. Prize: There are first-, second- and third-place prizes. The amount varies because 50% of the entry fees will be awarded as prizes each year. This will, however, be no less than $100. The top three poems will receive broadsheet publication. Judged by blind judging.

THE ACORN-RUKEYSER CHAPBOOK CONTEST, Mekler & Deahl, Publishers, 237 Prospect St. S., Hamilton, Ontario L8M 2Z6, Canada. (905)312-1779. Fax: (905)312-8285. E-mail: james@meklerdeahl.com. Website: www.meklerdeahl.com. Offered annually for published or unpublished poetry mss up to 30 pages. Deadline: September 30. Charges $10 fee (US). Prize: 1st Place: $100, and 50 copies of the chapbook; Runner-Up: $100.

ANHINGA PRIZE FOR POETRY, Anhinga Press, P.O. Box 10595, Tallahassee FL 32302. (850)521-9920. Fax: (850)442-6363. E-mail: info@anhinga.org. Website: www.anhinga.org. **Contact:** Rick Campbell. Offered annually for a book-length collection of poetry by an author who has not published more than one book of poetry. Guidelines for SASE or on website. Open to any writer writing in English. Deadline: February 15-May 1. Charges $20 fee. Prize: $2,000 and publication.

[N] **ANNUAL GIVAL PRESS OSCAR WILDE AWARD**, Gival Press, LLC, P.O. Box 3812, Arlington VA 22203. (703)351-0079. Fax: (703)351-0079. E-mail: givalpress@yahoo.com. Website: www.givalpress.com. **Contact:** Robert L. Giron. Award given to the best previously unpublished original poem written in English of any length, in any style, typed, double spaced on one side only, which best relates alternative lifestyles, often referred to as gay/lesbian/bisexual/transgendered, by a poet who is 18 or older. Entrants are asked to submit their poems in the following manner: (1) without any kind of identification, with the exception of titles, and (2) with a separate cover page with the following information: name, address (street, city, and state with zip code), telephone number, e-mail address, if available, and a list of poems by title. Checks drawn on American banks should be made out to Gival Press, LLC, and mailed to: Gival Press, P.O. Box 3812, Arlington VA, 22203. Deadline: June 27 (postmarked). Charges $5 reading fee (USD). Prize: $75 (USD), and the poem, along with information about the poet, will be published on the website of Gival Press. Open to any writer.

N ANNUAL GIVAL PRESS POETRY CONTEST, Gival Press, LLC, P.O. Box 3812, Arlington VA 22203. (703)351-0079. Fax: (703)351-0079. E-mail: givalpress@yahoo.com. Website: www.givalpress.com. **Contact:** Robert L. Giron. Offered annually for previously published or unpublished poems in a collection that has not been published as a book of poetry. The competition seeks to award well-written, original poetry in English on any topic, in any style. Guidelines for SASE or by e-mail. Entrants are asked to submit their poems in the following manner: (1) without any kind of identification, with the exception of the titles, and (2) with a separate cover page with the following information: name, address (street, city, state, and zip code), telephone number, e-mail address (if available), and a list of the poems by title. Checks drawn on American banks should be made out to Gival Press, LLC, and mailed to: Gival Press, P.O. Box 3812, Arlington VA 22203. Deadline: December 15 (postmarked). Charges $15. Prize: $500, plus publication in a limited run and 10 author copies. Open to any writer.

N ANNUAL GIVAL PRESS TRI-LANGUAGE POEM CONTEST, Gival Press, LLC, P.O. Box 3812, Arlington VA 22203. (703)351-0079. Fax: (703)351-0079. E-mail: givalpress@yahoo.com. Website: www.givalpress.com. **Contact:** Robert L. Giron. Previously unpublished original poems written in English, French, or Spanish, of 20 lines or less, typed and double-spaced, on any topic, in any style, are eligible. Poets may submit up to 3 poems. Entrants are asked to submit their poems in the following manner: (1) without any kind of identification, with the exception of the titles, and (2) with a separate cover page with the following information: name, address (street, city, state, and zip code), telephone number, e-mail address (if available), and a list of the poems by title. Checks drawn on American banks should be made out to Gival Press, LLC, and mailed to: Gival Press, P.O. Box 3812, Arlington VA 22203. Deadline: October 12 (postmarked). Charges $5 reading fee. Prize: The winning poems written in English, French, or Spanish, will receive $75 (USD), and the poems, along with the information about the poets, will be published on the website of Gival Press (www.givalpress.com). Open to any writer.

THE ANNUAL PRAIRIE SCHOONER STROUSSE AWARD, Prairie Schooner, 201 Andrews Hall, P.O. Box 880334, Lincoln NE 68588-0334. (402)472-0911. Fax: (402)472-9771. E-mail: eflanagan2@unl.edu. Website: www.unl.edu/schooner/psmain.htm. **Contact:** Hilda Raz. Offered annually for the best poem or group of poems published in *Prairie Schooner* in the previous year. Prize: $500.

ART COOP POETRY FELLOWSHIP, Cottonwood Art Co-operative, 1124 Columbia NE, Albuquerque NM 87106. E-mail: art_coop@yahoo.com. Website: www.geocities.com/art_coop. **Contact:** Editor-in-Chief. For most recent information, please visit website or write for guidelines with SASE. Submit with cover sheet, bio, and publications list. Open to any writer. Annually. Deadline: December 1 (annually). Charges $15 for up to 3 poems, $2 each thereafter. For additional flat $15 fee and SASE, feedback provided on poems. Prize: Cash award to be determined, not less than $250, and Internet-publication to support serious, aspiring poets. Open to any writer.

N ATLANTIC POETRY PRIZE, Writers' Federation of Nova Scotia, 1113 Marginal Rd., Halifax, Nova Scotia B3H 4P7, Canada. (902)423-8116. Fax: (902)422-0881. E-mail: talk@writers.ns.ca. Website: www.writers.ns.ca. **Contact:** Jane Buss, executive director. Full-length books of adult poetry written by Atlantic Canadians, and published as a whole for the first time in the previous calendar year, are eligible. Entrants must be native or resident Atlantic Canadians who have either been born in Newfoundland, Prince Edward Island, Nova Scotia, or New Brunswick, and spent a susbstantial portion of their lives living there, or who have lived in one or a combination of these provinces for at least 24 consecutive months prior to entry deadline date. Publishers: Send 4 copies and a letter attesting to the author's status as an Atlantic Canadian and the author's current mailing address and telephone number. Deadline: First Friday in December. Prize: $1,000.

THE BACKWATERS PRIZE, The Backwaters Press, 3502 N. 52nd St., Omaha NE 68104-3506. (402)451-4052. E-mail: gkosm62735@aol.com. Website: www.thebackwaterspress.homestead.com. **Contact:** Greg Kosmicki. Offered annually to find the best collection of poems, or single long poem, no collaborations, to publish and help further the poet's career. Collections must be unpublished, however parts of the ms may have been published as a chapbook, or individual poems may have been previously published in magazines. Deadline: June 4. Charges $25 fee. Prize: $1,000 and publication of the winning ms in an edition of at least 750 copies in perfect bound format.

THE HERB BARRETT AWARD, for Short Poetry in the Haiku Tradition, Mekler & Deahl, Publishers, 237 Prospect St. S., Hamilton, Ontario L8M 2Z6, Canada. (905)312-1779. Fax: (905)312-8285. E-mail: james@meklerdeahl.com. Website: www.meklerdeahl.com. Offered annually for short poems in the haiku tradition. Writers retain all rights. Open to any writer. Deadline: November 30. Charges $10 fee (US); maximum 10 entries. Prize: 1st Place: $200 (US); 2nd Place: $150 (US); 3rd Place: $100 (US); all entrants receive a copy of the published anthology, entrants with poetry in the anthology receive 2 copies.

BLUESTEM POETRY AWARD, Department of English, Emporia State University 1200, Emporia KS 66801. (620)341-5216. Fax: (620)341-5547. E-mail: bluestem@emporia.edu. Website: www.emporia.edu/bluestem/index.htm. **Contact:** Philip Heldrich, award director. Offered annually "to recognize outstanding poetry." Full-length, single-author collections, at least 48 pages long. Deadline: March 1. Charges $18 fee. Prize: $1,000, and a published book.

THE FREDERICK BOCK PRIZE, *Poetry*, 60 W. Walton St., Chicago IL 60610. (312)255-3703. E-mail: poetry@poetrymagazine.org. Website: www.poetrymagazine.org. **Contact:** Joseph Parisi, editor. Offered annually for poems published in *Poetry* during the preceding year (October through September). *Poetry* buys all rights to the poems published in the magazine. Copyrights are returned to the authors on request. Any writer may submit poems to *Poetry.* Guidelines for SASE. Prize: $300.

THE BORDIGHERA BILINGUAL ITALIAN-AMERICAN POETRY PRIZE, Sonia Raiziss-Giop Foundation, 57 Montague St. #8G, Brooklyn NY 11201-3356. E-mail: daniela@garden.net. Website: www.ItalianAmericanWriters.com. **Contact:** Daniela Gioseffi. Offered annually for an unpublished collection of poetry "to find the best manuscripts of poetry in English, by an American of Italian descent, to be translated into quality Italian and published bilingually." Deadline: May 31. Guidelines for SASE. Prize: $2,000 and bilingual book publication to be divided between poet and translator.

BOSTON REVIEW POETRY CONTEST, *Boston Review*, E-53-407 MIT, Cambridge MA 02139. Website: bostonreview.mit.edu. Submit up to 5 unpublished poems, no more than 10 pages total. Deadline: June 1. Charges $15 fee, payable to *Boston Review*, check or money order. Prize: $1,000 and publication in the October/November issue of *Boston Review.*

bp NICHOL CHAPBOOK AWARD, Phoenix Community Works Foundation, 316 Dupont St., Toronto, Ontario M5R 1V9, Canada. (416)964-7919. Fax: (416)964-6941. E-mail: info@pcwf.ca. Website: www.pcwf.ca. **Contact:** Philip McKenna, award director. Offered annually to a chapbook (10-48 pp) of poetry in English, published in Canada in the previous year. Deadline: March 30. Guidelines for SASE. Prize: $1,000 (Canadian).

BARBARA BRADLEY AWARD, New England Poetry Club, 11 Puritan Rd., Arlington MA 02476-7710. **Contact:** Virginia Thayer. Offered annually for a lyric poem under 21 lines, written by a woman. Deadline: June 30. Guidelines for SASE. Charges $10 entry fee for nonmembers (up to 3 poems). Prize: $200.

BRITTINGHAM PRIZE IN POETRY/FELIX POLLAK PRIZE IN POETRY, University of Wisconsin Press, Department of English, 600 N. Park St., University of Wisconsin, Madison WI 53706. Website: www.wisc.edu/wisconsinpress/poetryguide.html. **Contact:** Ronald Wallace, contest director. Estab. 1985. Offered for unpublished book-length mss of original poetry. Submissions must be *received* by the press *during* the month of September, accompanied by a SASE for contest results. Does *not* return mss. One entry fee covers both prizes. Guidelines for SASE or online. Charges $20 fee, payable to University of Wisconsin Press. Prize: $1,000, and publication of the 2 winning mss.

CAA JACK CHALMERS POETRY AWARD, (formerly Canadian Authors Association Award for Poetry), Box 419, 320 S. Shores Rd., Campbellford, Ontario K0L 1L0, Canada. (705)653-0323. Fax: (705)653-0593. E-mail: canauth@redden.on.ca. Website: www.canauthors.org. **Contact:** Alec McEachern. Offered annually for a volume of poetry by a Canadian citizen. Entry form required. Obtain form from contact name or download from website. Deadline: December 15. Guidelines for SASE. Charges $20 fee (Canadian). Prize: $2,500 and a silver medal.

HAYDEN CARRUTH AWARD, Copper Canyon Press, P.O. Box 271, Port Townsend WA 98368. (360)385-4925. Fax: (360)385-4985. E-mail: poetry@coppercanyonpress.org. Website: www.coppercanyonpress.org. **Contact:** Office Manager. Offered annually for unpublished work. Contest is for new and emerging poets who have published no more than 2 full-length books of poetry. Chapbooks of 32 pages or less are not considered to be full-length, and books published in other genres do not count toward the 2-book limit. Deadline: November 1-30 (reading period). Guidelines for SASE. Charges $20 fee. Prize: $1,000 advance, and book publication by Copper Canyon Press.

JOHN CIARDI POETRY AWARD FOR LIFETIME ACHIEVEMENT, Italian Americana, URI/CCE, 80 Washington St., Providence RI 02903-1803. Fax: (401)277-5100. E-mail: bonomoal@etal.uri.edu. Website: www.uri.edu/prov/italian/italian.html. **Contact:** Carol Bonomo Albright, editor. Offered annually for *lifetime* achievement in all aspects of poetry: Creative, critical, etc. Applicants should have at least 2 books published. Open to Italian-Americans only. Guidelines for SASE. Prize: $1,000.

JOHN CIARDI PRIZE FOR POETRY, BkMk Press, University of Missouri-Kansas City, 5101 Rockhill Rd., Kansas City MO 64110. (816)235-2558. Fax: (816)235-2611. E-mail: bkmk@umkc.edu. Website: www.umkc.edu/bkmk. **Contact:** Ben Furnish. Offered annually for the best book-length collection (unpublished) of poetry in English by a living author. Translations are not eligible. Initial judging is done by a network of published writers. Final judging is done by a writer of national reputation. Guidelines for SASE, by e-mail, or on website. Deadline: December 1 (postmarked). Charges $25 fee. Prize: $1,000, plus book publication by BkMk Press.

CLEVELAND STATE UNIVERSITY POETRY CENTER PRIZES, (formerly Cleveland State University Poetry Center Prize), Cleveland State University Poetry Center, 2121 Euclid Ave., Cleveland OH 44115-2214. (216)687-3986. Fax: (216)687-6943. E-mail: poetrycenter@csuohio.edu. Website: www.csuohio.edu/poetrycenter. **Contact:** Rita Grabowski, poetry center coordinator. Estab. 1962. Offered annually to identify, reward, and publish the best unpublished book-length poetry ms submitted (40 pages of poetry, maximum) in 2 categories: First Book and Open Competition (for poets who have published a collection at least 48 pages long, with a press run of 500). "Submission implies willingness to sign standard contract for publication if manuscript wins." One or more of the other finalist mss may also be published for standard contract (no prize). Does not return mss. Deadline: Submissions accepted November-January only (postmark deadline is February 1). Guidelines for SASE. Charges $20 fee. Prize: $1,000, and publication.

THE COLORADO PRIZE FOR POETRY, Colorado Review/Center for Literary Publishing, Department of English, Colorado State University, Ft. Collins CO 80523. (970)491-5449. E-mail: creview@colostate.edu. Website: www.coloradoreview.com. **Contact:** Stephanie G'Schwind, managing editor. Offered annually to an unpublished collection of poetry. Deadline: January 13, 2003. Charges $25 fee. Prize: $1,500 and publication of book.

BETSY COLQUITT AWARD FOR POETRY, *descant*, Texas Christian University's literary journal, TCU Box 297270, Fort Worth TX 76129. (817)257-6537. Fax: (817)257-6239. E-mail: descant@tcu.edu. **Contact:** Dave Kuhne, editor. Offered annually for unpublished poems or series of poems. Publication retains copyright but will transfer it to the author upon request. Deadline: September-April. Guidelines for SASE. Prize: $500.

CONTEMPORARY POETRY SERIES, University of Georgia Press, 330 Research Dr., Suite B100, Athens GA 30602-4901. (706)369-6135. Fax: (706)369-6131. E-mail: emontjoy@ugapress.uga.edu. Website: www.uga.edu/ugapress. **Contact:** Emily Montjoy. Offered 2 times/year. Two awards: One for poets who have not had a full-length book of poems published (deadline in September), and 1 for poets with at least 1 full-length publication (deadline in January). Guidelines for SASE. Charges $20 fee.

CRAB ORCHARD AWARD SERIES IN POETRY, *Crab Orchard Review* and Southern Illinois University Press, Department of English, Carbondale IL 62901-4503. Website: www.siu.edu/~crbor. **Contact:** Jon C. Tribble, series editor. Offered annually for collections of unpublished poetry. U.S. citizens only. Visit website for current deadlines. Charges $20 fee. Prize: 1st Place: $3,000 and publication; 2nd Place: $1,000 and publication.

ALICE FAY DI CASTAGNOLA AWARD, Poetry Society of America, 15 Gramercy Park S., New York NY 10003. (212)254-9628. Fax: (212)673-2352. Website: www.poetrysociety.org. **Contact:** Brett Lauer, programs associate. Offered annually for a manuscript-in-progress of poetry or verse-drama. Guidelines for SASE or on website. Deadline: December 21. Prize: $1,000.

EMILY DICKINSON AWARD IN POETRY, Universities West Press, P.O. Box 0788, Flagstaff AZ 86002-0788. (928)774-9574. Fax: (928)774-9574. E-mail: glenn@usa.net. Website: popularpicks.com. **Contact:** Glenn Reed. Offered annually for unpublished poetry in any form or style, and on any subject. Winner and finalists grants UWP rights to publish the winning poems on the popularpicks.com website and in its anthology. "A submission should include: no more than 3 poems, total entry not to exceed 6 pages, short biographical statement, reading fee of $12, and a SASE or e-mail address (preffered) for results. Awards are open to all writers except those who are currently students or employees of Northern Arizona University." Visit the website (popularpicks.com) or send a SASE for guidelines. Deadline: August 31. Charges $12 reading fee. Prize: First Award: $1,200; Second Award: $750; Third Award: $500. All award-winning poems, as well as finalists' poems will be featured in an anthology of poems annually published by Universities West Press. Award winners and finalists will each receive, without charge, a copy of the anthology. Final judging of submitted poems will be done by a poet of national/international reputation.

DISCOVERY/THE NATION, The Joan Leiman Jacobson Poetry Prizes, The Unterberg Poetry Center of the 92nd Street YM-YWHA, 1395 Lexington Ave., New York NY 10128. (212)415-5759. Website: www.92ndsty.org. Open to poets who have not published a book of poems (chapbooks, self-published books included). Must have guidelines; send SASE, call, or see website. Deadline: January. Charges $5 fee.

MILTON DORFMAN POETRY PRIZE, Rome Art & Community Center, 308 W. Bloomfield St., Rome NY 13440. (315)336-1040. Fax: (315)336-1090. Website: www.borg.com/~racc. **Contact:** Deborah O'Shea, executive director. Estab. 1990. "The purpose of the Milton Dorfman Poetry Prize is to offer poets an outlet for their craft. All submissions must be previously unpublished." Deadline: July 1-December 1. Guidelines for SASE. Charges $5 fee/poem. Prize: 1st Place: $500; 2nd Place: $200; 3rd Place: $100. Judged by a professional, published poet.

EDITORS' PRIZE, Spoon River Poetry Review, Campus Box 4241, English Deptartment, Illinois State University, Normal IL 61790-4241. (309)438-7906. Website: www.litline.org/spoon. **Contact:** Lucia Cordell Getsi, editor. Offered annually for unpublished poetry "to identify and reward excellence." Guidelines for SASE or on website. Open to all writers. Deadline: April 15. Charges fee of $16/3 poems (entitles entrant to a year's subscription valued at $15). Prize: 1st Place: $1,000; 2 $100 runner-up prizes; publication of first place, runners-up, and selected honorable mentions.

T.S. ELIOT PRIZE FOR POETRY, Truman State University Press, New Odyssey Series, 100 E. Normal St., Kirksville MO 63501-4221. (660)785-7336. Fax: (660)785-4480. E-mail: tsup@truman.edu. Website: tsup.truman.edu. **Contact:** Nancy Reschly. Annual competition for unpublished poetry collection. Guidelines for SASE, on website or by e-mail. Deadline: October 31 (postmarked). Charges $25 fee. Prize: $2,000 and publication.

MAURICE ENGLISH POETRY AWARD, 2222 Rittenhouse Square, Philadelphia PA 19103-5505. Fax: (215)732-1382. **Contact:** Helen W. Drutt English. Offered annually for a distinguished book of poems published in the previous calendar year. Poets must be over 50 years of age to enter the contest. "No entry forms; no telephone calls please." Deadline: April 1. Prize: $3,000, plus a public reading in Philadelphia. Judged by a sole judge.

ROBERT G. ENGLISH/POETRY IN PRINT, P.O. Box 30981, Albuquerque NM 87190-0981. (505)888-3937. Fax: (505)888-3937. Website: www.poets.com/RobertEnglish.html. **Contact:** Robert G. English, owner. Offered annually "to help a poetry writer accomplish their own personal endeavors. Hopefully the prize amount of the Poetry in Print award will grow to a higher significance. The contest is open to any writer of any age. Hopefully to prepare writers other than just journalists with a stronger desire to always tell the truth." No limit to number of entries; 30-line limit/poem. Deadline: August 1. Charges $5/poem. Prize: $500.

FIELD POETRY PRIZE, Oberlin College Press/FIELD, 10 N. Professor St., Oberlin OH 44074-1095. (440)775-8408. Fax: (440)775-8124. E-mail: oc.press@oberlin.edu. Website: www.oberlin.edu/~ocpress. **Contact:** Linda Slocum, managing editor. Offered annually for unpublished work. "The FIELD Poetry Prize contest seeks to encourage the finest in contemporary poetry writing." No simultaneous submissions. Open to any writer. Deadline: Submit in May only. Guidelines for SASE. Charges $22 fee, which includes a 1-year subscription. Prize: $1,000, and book published in Oberlin College Press's FIELD Poetry Series.

FIVE POINTS JAMES DICKEY PRIZE FOR POETRY, Five Points, Georgia State University University Plaza, Atlanta GA 30303-3083. (404)651-0071. Fax: (404)651-3167. E-mail: msexton@gsu.edu. Website: www.webdelsol.com/Five_Points. **Contact:** Megan Sexton. Offered annually for unpublished poetry. Deadline: November 30. Guidelines for SASE. Charges $15 fee (includes 1-year subscription). Prize: $1,000, plus publication.

FOLEY POETRY CONTEST, America Press, 106 W. 56th St., New York NY 10019. (212)581-4640. Fax: (212)399-3596. Website: www.americapress.org. **Contact:** Paul Mariani, poetry editor. Estab. 1909. Offered annually for unpublished works between January and April. Deadline: April. Guidelines for SASE. Prize: Prize consists of $1,000, usually awarded in June. Open to any writer.

THE 49th PARALLEL POETRY AWARD, *Bellingham Review*, Mail Stop 9053, Western Washington University, Bellingham WA 98225. (360)650-4863. E-mail: bhreview@cc.wwu.edu. Website: www.wwu.edu/~bhreview/. **Contact:** Brenda Miller. Estab. 1977. Offered annually for unpublished poetry. Deadline: December 1-March 15. Guidelines for SASE. Prize: 1st Place: $1,000 and publication; 2nd Place: $300; 3rd Place: $200; all finalists considered for publication, all entrants receive subscription.

FOUR WAY BOOKS POETRY PRIZES, Four Way Books, P.O. Box 535, Village Station, New York NY 10014. (212)619-1105. Fax: (212)406-1352. E-mail: four_way_editors@yahoo.com. Website: www.fourwaybooks.com. **Contact:** K. Clarke, contest coordinator. Four Way Books runs different prizes annually. For guidelines send a SASE or download from website. Deadline: March 31. Prize: Cash honorarium and book publication.

ROBERT FROST POETRY AWARD, The Robert Frost Foundation, Heritage Place, 439 S. Union, Lawrence MA 01843. (978)725-8828. Fax: (978)725-8828. E-mail: mejaneiro@aol.com. Website: www.frostfoundation.org. **Contact:** Mary Ellen Janeiro. Offered annually for unpublished work "to recognize poets writing today in the tradition of Frost and other American greats. Poems should be written in the spirit of Frost, as interpreted by the poet's knowledge of Frost's poetry, life, persona, etc." More than one poem may be entered. Open to any writer. Deadline: September 1. Guidelines for SASE. Charges $10 fee/poem. Prize: $1,000.

GIBBS SMITH POETRY COMPETITION, (formerly Peregrine Smith Poetry Contest), Gibbs Smith, Publisher, P.O. Box 667, Layton UT 84041. (801)544-9800. Fax: (801)544-5582. E-mail: info@gibbs-smith.com. Website: www.gibbs-smith.com. **Contact:** Monica Weeks, poetry editor; Suzanne Taylor, children's editor; Madge Baird, V.P. editorial. Offered annually to recognize and publish a previously unpublished work. Submissions accepted only during the month of April. Deadline: April 30. Guidelines for SASE. Charges $20 fee. Prize: $1,000, and publication.

ALLEN GINSBERG POETRY AWARDS, The Poetry Center at Passaic County Community College, One College Blvd., Paterson NJ 07505-1179. (973)684-6555. Fax: (973)684-5843. E-mail: mgillan@pccc.cc.nj.us. Website: www.pccc.cc.nj.us/poetry. **Contact:** Maria Mazziotti Gillan, executive director. Offered annually for unpublished poetry "to honor Allen Ginsberg's contribution to American literature." The college retains first publication rights. Open to any writer. Deadline: April 1. Guidelines for SASE. Charges $13, which covers the cost of a subscription to *The Paterson Literary Review*. Prize: $1,000.

GIVAL PRESS CHAPBOOK COMPETITION, Gival Press, LLC, P.O. Box 3812, Arlington VA 22203. (703)351-0079. Fax: (703)351-0079. E-mail: givalpress@yahoo.com. Website: www.givalpress.com. **Contact:** Robert L. Giron. Offered annually for previously published or unpublished poetry. The competition seeks to award well-written poetry in English. Guidelines for SASE or by e-mail. Deadline: December 15. Charges $15. Prize: $500, plus publication in a limited run.

GOVERNOR GENERAL'S LITERARY AWARD FOR POETRY, Canada Council for the Arts, 350 Albert St., P.O. Box 1047, Ottawa, Ontario K1P 5V8, Canada. (613)566-4414, ext. 5576. Fax: (613)566-4410. E-mail: joanne.larocque-poirier@canadacouncil.ca. Website: www.canadacouncil.ca. **Contact:** Joanne Larocque-Poirier. Offered for the best English-language and the best French-language work of poetry by a Canadian published September 1, 2001-September 30, 2002. Publishers submit titles for consideration. Deadline: April 15 or August 7, 2002, depending on the book's publication date. Prize: $15,000.

GREEN ROSE PRIZE IN POETRY, *New Issues Poetry & Prose*, Department of English, Western Michigan University, 1903 W. Michigan Ave., Kalamazoo MI 49008-5331. (616)387-8185. Fax: (616)387-2562. E-mail: herbert.scott@wmich.edu. Website: www.wmich.edu/newissues. **Contact:** Herbert Scott, editor. Offered annually for unpublished poetry. The university will publish a book of poems by a poet writing in English who has published one or more full-length books of poetry. Guidelines for SASE or on website. *New Issues Poetry & Prose* obtains rights for first publication. Book is copyrighted in author's name. Deadline: September 30. Charges $20 fee. Prize: $1,000 and publication of book. Author also receives 10% of the printed edition.

GROLIER POETRY PRIZE, Grolier Poetry Book Shop, Inc. & Ellen LaForge Memorial Poetry Foundation, Inc., 6 Plympton St., Cambridge MA 02138. (617)253-4452. E-mail: jjhildeb@mit.edu. **Contact:** John Hildebidle. Estab. 1973. When e-mailing, please put "Grolier Prize" in subject line. The prize, entering its 29th year, is intended to encourage and introduce developing poets, is open to all poets who have not published a previous volume (chapbook, small press, trade, or vanity) of poetry. Submissions (in duplicate) should include no more than 5 poems (none simultaneously submitted or previously published), running to 10 double-spaced pages or 5 single-spaced pages. Separate cover sheet should include information about author address and telephone number, titles of poems, and brief biography. The author's name and other identifying information should not appear on the same pages as the poems. Entries must be submitted in duplicate. Include a SASE to be informed about receipt of ms. Annually. Deadline: May 1. Charges $7 fee.

GREG GUMMER POETRY AWARD, *Phoebe*, George Mason University, 4400 University Dr., Fairfax VA 22030-4444. (703)993-2915. E-mail: phoebe@gmu.edu. Website: www.gmu.edu/pups/phoebe. **Contact:** Emily Tuszynska. Offered annually for unpublished work. Deadline: December 1. Guidelines for SASE. Charges $10 fee. Prize: $1,000, and publication in Fall 2002 issue. All entrants receive free Fall 2002 issue. Judged by outside judge—a recognized poet hired by *Phoebe* each year. Acquires first serial rights, if work is to be published. Open to any writer.

VIOLET REED HAAS POETRY CONTEST, Snake Nation Press, 110 W. Force St., Valdosta GA 31601. (229)244-0752. E-mail: jeana@snakenationpress.org. Website: www.snakenationpress.org. **Contact:** Jean Arambula. Offered annually for poetry mss of 50-75 pages. Deadline: June 15. Charges $10 reading fee. Prize: $500 and publication. Judged by an independent judge.

CECIL HEMLEY MEMORIAL AWARD, Poetry Society of America, 15 Gramercy Park S., New York NY 10003. (212)254-9628. Fax: (212)673-2352. E-mail: brett@poetrysociety.org. Website: www.poetrysociety.org. **Contact:** Brett Lauer, programs associate. Offered for unpublished lyric poems on a philosophical theme. Open to PSA members only. For guidelines send SASE. Deadline: December 21. Prize: $500.

THE BESS HOKIN PRIZE, *Poetry*, 60 W. Walton St., Chicago IL 60610. (312)255-3703. E-mail: poetry@poetrymagazine.org. Website: www.poetrymagazine.org. **Contact:** Joseph Parisi, editor. Offered annually for poems published in *Poetry* during the preceding year (October-September). *Poetry* buys all rights to the poems published in the magazine. Copyrights are returned to the authors on request. Any writer may submit poems to *Poetry*. Guidelines for SASE. Prize: $500.

HONICKMAN/APR FIRST BOOK PRIZE, The American Poetry Review, 1721 Walnut St., Philadelphia PA 19103. (215)496-0439. Fax: (215)569-0808. Website: www.aprweb.org. Offered annually for a poet's first unpublished book-length ms. Judging is by a different distinguished poet each year. Past judges include Adrienne Rich, Derek Walcott, Robert Creeley, and Louise Gluck. Open to any writer. Deadline: October 31. Guidelines for SASE. Charges $20 fee. Prize: Publication by APR (distrubution by Copper Canyon Press through Consortium), $3,000 cash prize, plus $1,000 to support a book tour.

FIRMAN HOUGHTON AWARD, New England Poetry Club, 11 Puritan Rd., Arlington MA 02476-7710. **Contact:** Virginia Thayer. Offered annually for a lyric poem worthy of the former NEPC president. Deadline: June 30. Guidelines for SASE. Charges nonmembers $10 for 3 poems. Prize: $250.

IOWA POETRY PRIZES, University of Iowa Press, 119 W. Park Rd., Iowa City IA 52242. (319)335-2000. Fax: (319)335-2055. E-mail: rhonda-wetjen@uiowa.edu. Website: www.uiowa.edu/~uipress. **Contact:** Rhonda Wetjen. Offered annually to encourage poets and their work. Submit mss in April; put name on title page only. Open to writers of English (US citizens or not). Manuscripts will not be returned. Previous winners are not eligible. Deadline: April. Charges $20 fee.

IRA LEE BENNETT HOPKINS PROMISING POET AWARD, International Reading Association, P.O. Box 8139, Newark DE 19714-8139. (302)731-1600. Fax: (302)731-1051. E-mail: exec@reading.org. Website: www.reading.org. Offered every 3 years to a promising new poet of children's poetry (for children and young adults up to grade 12) who has published no more than 2 books. Deadline: December 1. Guidelines for SASE. Prize: $500.

THE JUNIPER PRIZE, University of Massachusetts, Amherst MA 01003. (413)545-2217. Fax: (413)545-1226. E-mail: info@umpress.umass.edu. Website: www.umass.edu/umpress/juniper.html. **Contact:** Alice I. Maldonado, assistant editor/Web manager. Estab. 1964. Awarded annually for an original ms of poems. In alternating years, the program is open to poets either with or without previously published books. Deadline: September 30. Charges $15 fee. Prize: The University of Massachusetts Press publishes the winning ms, and a $1,000 prize is awarded in lieu of royalties on the first print run.

KALLIOPE'S ANNUAL SUE SANIEL ELKIND POETRY CONTEST, *Kalliope, a journal of women's literature and art*, 3939 Roosevelt Blvd., Jacksonville FL 32205. (904)381-3511. Website: www.fccj.org/kalliope. **Contact:** Mary Sue Koeppel, editor. Offered annually for unpublished work. "Poetry may be in any style and on any subject. Maximum poem length is 50 lines. Only unpublished poems are eligible." No limit on number of poems entered by any one poet. The winning poem is published as are the finalists' poems. Copyright then returns to the authors. Deadline: November 1. Guidelines for SASE. Charges $4/poem or $10 for 3 poems. Prize: $1,000, publication of poem in *Kalliope*.

BARBARA MANDIGO KELLY PEACE POETRY AWARDS, Nuclear Age Peace Foundation, PMB 121, 1187 Coast Village Rd., Suite 1, Santa Barbara CA 93108-2794. Fax: (805)568-0466. E-mail: wagingpeace@napf.org. Website: www.wagingpeace.org. **Contact:** Chris Pizzinat. Offered annually for unpublished poems "to encourage poets to explore and illuminate positive visions of peace and the human spirit." Guidelines for SASE or on website. The Nuclear Age Peace Foundation reserves the right to publish and distribute the award-winning poems. Deadline: July 1 (postmarked). Charges $10 for up to 3 poems; no fee for youth entries. Prize: Adult: $1,000; Youth (13-18): $200; Youth (12 and under): $200. Winners announced by October 31. Winners and honorable mentions will be notified by mail.

N THE MILT KESSLER POETRY BOOK AWARD, Creative Writing Program, Binghamton University-State University of New York, P.O. Box 6000, Binghamton NY 13902-6000. (607)777-6134. Fax: (607)777-2408. E-mail: mgillan@binghamton.edu. Website: www.binghamton.edu/english. **Contact:** Maria Mazziotti Gillan, director, creative writing program. Offered annually for previously published work. Open to any writer over 40. Book must be published, be 48 pages or more with a press run of 500 copies or more. "Please explain any special criteria (such as residency) or nominating process that must be met before a writer's entry will be considered." Must have appeared in print between January 1-December 31 of year preceding award. Deadline: April 1. Guidelines for SASE. Prize: $1,000. Judged by professional poet not on Binghamton University faculty.

THE MILTON KESSLER MEMORIAL PRIZE FOR POETRY, *Harpur Palate at Binghamton University*, Department of English, Binghamton University, P.O. Box 6000, Binghamton NY 13902-6000. (607)355-4761. Website: go.to/hpjournal.com; harpurpalate.binghamton.edu. **Contact:** Managing Editor. Contest offered annually for previously unpublished poems in any style, form, or genre of no more than 3 pages. Deadline: July 1-October 1. Guidelines for SASE. Charges $10/5 poems. Prize: $500 and publication in Winter issue of *Harpur Palate*. All entrants receive a copy of the issue in which the winning poem appears. Name and contact information should appear in the cover letter only. Acquires first North American serial rights. Open to any writer.

(HELEN AND LAURA KROUT MEMORIAL) OHIOANA POETRY AWARD, Ohioana Library Association, 274 E. First Ave., Columbus OH 45201. (614)466-3831. Fax: (614)728-6974. E-mail: ohioana@sloma.state.oh.us. Website: www.oplin.lib.oh.us/OHIOANA/. **Contact:** Linda R. Hengst. Offered annually "to an individual whose body of published work has made, and continues to make, a significant contribution to poetry and through whose work, interest in poetry has been developed." Recipient must have been born in Ohio or lived in Ohio at least 5 years. Deadline: December 31. Guidelines for SASE. Prize: $1,000.

THE LADY MACDUFF POETRY CONTEST, P.O. Box 563, Hackensack NJ 07602-0563. (201)342-4455. Fax: (201)342-7396. E-mail: rexdalepublishco@cs.com. Website: www.rexdalepublishing.com. **Contact:** Elaine Rexdale. Offered annually for poetry written in English. Open to any writer. Deadline: November 30. Guidelines for SASE. Charges $25 fee. Prize: Grand Prize: $500, publication, and 10 copies; 1st Place: $100.

GERALD LAMPERT MEMORIAL AWARD, The League of Canadian Poets, 54 Wolseley St., Suite 204, Toronto, Ontario M5T 1A5, Canada. (416)504-1657. Fax: (416)504-0096. E-mail: league@poets.ca. Website: www.poets.ca. **Contact:** Edita Page. Offered annually for a first book of poetry by a Canadian poet published in the preceding year. Guidelines for SASE and on website. Deadline: November 1. Charges $15 fee. Prize: $1,000.

THE JAMES LAUGHLIN AWARD, The Academy of American Poets, 588 Broadway, Suite 1203, New York NY 10012-3250. (212)274-0343. Fax: (212)274-9427. E-mail: academy@poets.org. Website: www.poets.org. **Contact:** Awards Director. Offered annually for a ms of original poetry, in English, by a poet who has already published 1 book of poems in a standard edition (40 pages or more in length and 500 or more copies). Only mss that have come under contract with a US publisher between May 1 of the preceding year and April 30 of the year of the deadline are eligible. Deadline: April 30. Guidelines for SASE. Prize: $5,000 and the Academy will purchase at least 9,000 hardcover copies for distribution.

THE LEDGE ANNUAL POETRY CHAPBOOK CONTEST, *The Ledge Magazine*, 78-44 80th St., Glendale NY 11385. **Contact:** Timothy Monaghan. Offered annually to publish an outstanding collection of poems. Open to any writer. Deadline: October 31. Guidelines for SASE. Charges $12 fee. Prize: $1,000, publication of chapbook and 50 copies; all entrants receive a copy of winning chapbook.

THE LEDGE POETRY AWARD, *The Ledge Magazine*, 78-44 80th St., Glendale NY 11385. **Contact:** Timothy Monaghan. Offered annually for an unpublished poem of exceptional quality and significance. All poems considered for publication in the magazine. Open to any writer. Deadline: April 30. Guidelines for SASE. Charges $10 for 3 poems; $3/additional poem ($13 subscription gains free entry for the first 3 poems). Prize: 1st Place: $1,000, and publication in *The Ledge Magazine*; 2nd Place: $500, and publication in *The Ledge Magazine*; 3rd Place: $100, and publication in *The Ledge Magazine*.

LENA-MILES WEVER TODD POETRY SERIES, Pleiades Press & Winthrop University, Department of English, Central Missouri State University, Warrensburg MO 64093. (660)543-8106. Fax: (660)543-8544. E-mail: kdp8106@cms u2.cmsu.edu. **Contact:** Kevin Prufer. Offered annually for an unpublished book of poetry by an American or Canadian poet. Guidelines for SASE or by e-mail. The winning book is copyrighted by the author and Pleiades Press. Deadline: Generally September 15; e-mail for firm deadline. Charges $15, which includes a copy of the winning book. Prize: $1,000 and publication of winning book in paperback edition. Distribution through Louisiana State University Press.

THE LEVINSON PRIZE, *Poetry*, 60 W. Walton St., Chicago IL 60610. (312)255-3703. E-mail: poetry@poetrymagazine.org. Website: www.poetrymagazine.org. **Contact:** Joseph Parisi, editor. Offered annually for poems published in *Poetry* during the preceding year (October-September). *Poetry* buys all rights to the poems published in the magazine. Copyrights are returned to the authors on request. Any writer may submit poems to *Poetry*. Guidelines for SASE. Prize: $500.

THE LARRY LEVIS PRIZE FOR POETRY, *Prairie Schooner*, 201 Andrews Hall, P.O. Box 880334, Lincoln NE 68588-0334. (402)472-0911. Fax: (402)472-9771. E-mail: eflanagan2@unl.edu. Website: www.unl.edu/schooner/psmain.htm. **Contact:** Hilda Raz. Offered annually for poetry published in *Prairie Schooner* in the previous year. Prize: $1,000.

THE RUTH LILLY POETRY PRIZE, The Modern Poetry Association, 60 W. Walton St., Chicago IL 60610-3305. E-mail: poetry@poetrymagazine.org. Website: www.poetrymagazine.org. **Contact:** Joseph Parisi. Estab. 1986. Offered annually to a poet whose accomplishments in the field of poetry warrant extraordinary recognition. No applicants or nominations are accepted. Deadline: Varies. Prize: $100,000.

FRANCES LOCKE MEMORIAL POETRY AWARD, The Bitter Oleander Press, 4983 Tall Oaks Dr., Fayetteville NY 13066-9776. (315)637-3047. Fax: (315)637-5056. E-mail: bones44@ix.netcom.com. Website: www.bitteroleander.com. **Contact:** Paul B. Roth. Offered annually for unpublished, imaginative poetry. Open to any writer. Deadline: June 15. Guidelines for SASE. Charges $10 for 5 poems, $2 for each additional poem. Prize: $1,000 and 5 copies of issue.

LOUISIANA LITERATURE PRIZE FOR POETRY, Louisiana Literature, SLU—Box 792, Southeastern Louisiana University, Hammond LA 70402. (504)549-5022. Fax: (504)549-5021. E-mail: lalit@selu.edu. Website: www.selu.edu/orgs/lalit/. **Contact:** Jack Bedell, contest director. Estab. 1984. Offered annually for unpublished poetry. All entries considered for publication. Deadline: April 1. Guidelines for SASE. Charges $12 fee. Prize: $400.

LOUISE LOUIS/EMILY F. BOURNE STUDENT POETRY AWARD, Poetry Society of America, 15 Gramercy Park S., New York NY 10003. (212)254-9628. Fax: (212)673-2352. Website: www.poetrysociety.org. **Contact:** Brett Lauer, programs associate. Offered annually for unpublished work to promote excellence in student poetry. Open to American high school or preparatory school students (grades 9 to 12). Guidelines for SASE and on website. Judged by prominent American poets. Deadline: December 21. Charges $1 for a student submitting a single entry; $20 for a high school submitting unlimited number of its students' poems. Prize: $250.

PAT LOWTHER MEMORIAL AWARD, 54 Wolseley St., Toronto, Ontario M5T 1A5, Canada. (416)504-1657. Fax: (416)504-0096. E-mail: league@poets.ca. Website: www.poets.ca. **Contact:** Edita Page. Estab. 1966. Offered annually to promote new Canadian poetry/poets and also to recognize exceptional work in each category. Submissions to be published in the preceding year (awards). Enquiries from publishers welcome. Open to Canadians living at home and abroad. The candidate must be a Canadian citizen or landed imigrant, though the publisher need not be Canadian. Call, write, fax, or e-mail for rules. Deadline: November 1. Charges $15 fee/title. Prize: $1,000.

N LULLWATER PRIZE FOR POETRY, *Lullwater Review*, Emory University, P.O. Box 22036, Atlanta GA 30322. (404)727-6184. **Contact:** Laurel DeCou; Gwyneth Driskill. Offered annually for unpublished submissions. Deadline: April 2002. Guidelines for SASE. Charges $8 entry fee. Prize: $500, plus publication in *The Lullwater Review*. Judged by Patricia Cahill, professor of Medieval drama and English at Emory University. Open to any writer.

LYRIC POETRY AWARD, Poetry Society of America, 15 Gramercy Park S., New York NY 10003. (212)254-9628. Fax: (212)673-2352. E-mail: brett@poetrysociety.org. Website: www.poetrysociety.org. **Contact:** Brett Lauer, programs associate. Offered annually for unpublished work to promote excellence in lyric poetry. Line limit 50. Open to PSA members only. For guidelines send SASE. Deadline: December 21. Prize: $500.

NAOMI LONG MADGETT POETRY AWARD, Lotus Press, Inc., P.O. Box 21607, Detroit MI 48221. (313)861-1280. Fax: (313)861-4740. E-mail: lotuspress@aol.com. **Contact:** Constance Withers. Offered annually to recognize an outstanding unpublished poetry ms by an African-American. Guidelines for SASE or by e-mail. Deadline: April 1-June 1. Prize: $500, and publication by Lotus Press.

THE MALAHAT REVIEW LONG POEM PRIZE, *The Malahat Review*, Box 1700 STNCSC, Victoria, British Columbia V8W 2Y2, Canada. E-mail: malahat@uvic.ca (queries only). Website: web.uvic.ca/malahat. **Contact:** Marlene Cookshaw. Offered every 2 years to unpublished long poems. Preliminary reading by editorial board; final judging by the editor and 2 recognized poets. Obtains first world rights. After publication rights revert to the author. Open to any writer. Deadline: March 1. Guidelines for SASE. Charges $30 fee (includes a 1-year subscription to the *Malahat*, published quarterly). Prize: $400, plus payment for publication ($30/page).

LUCILLE MEDWICK MEMORIAL AWARD, Poetry Society of America, 15 Gramercy Park S., New York NY 10003. (212)254-9628. Fax: (212)673-2352. E-mail: brett@poetrysociety.org. Website: www.poetrysociety.org. **Contact:** Brett Lauer, programs associate. Original poem in any form on a humanitarian theme. For guidelines send SASE. Guidelines subject to change. Open to PSA members only. Deadline: December 21. Prize: $500.

MID-LIST PRESS FIRST SERIES AWARD FOR POETRY, Mid-List Press, 4324 12th Ave. S., Minneapolis MN 55407-3218. Fax: (612)823-8387. E-mail: guide@midlist.org. Website: www.midlist.org. **Contact:** Lane Stiles, publisher. Estab. 1990. Offered annually for unpublished book of poetry to encourage new poets. Guidelines for SASE or on website. Contest is open to any writer who has never published a book of poetry. "We do not consider a chapbook to be a book of poetry." Deadline: February 1. Charges $20 fee. Prize: Publication and an advance against royalties.

N **THE MILTON CENTER AWARD FOR EXCELLENCE IN WRITING—POETRY**, The Milton Center at Newman University, 3100 McCormick Ave., Wichita KS 67213-2097. (316)942-4291, ext. 326. Fax: (316)942-4483. E-mail: miltonc@newmanu.edu. **Contact:** Essie Sappenfield. Offered annually for unpublished work. Translations are not eligible. "The award is given for a single poem in English that elevates the human spirit. Beyond this, there are no thematic restrictions. The Milton Center supports work by writers who seek to animate the Christian imagination, foster intellectual integrity, and explore the human condition with honesty and compassion. It seeks out and encourages new writers who will carry on and expand the tradition of Christian letters in our secular culture." Guidelines for SASE or by e-mail. Send your guideline request to miltonc@newmanu.edu. Deadline: November 15. Charges $15 for 3 poems; $5 for every poem thereafter. Prize: $1,000, and publication in national literary magazine (at the current time, this magazine is *American Literary Review*); 2nd Place: $500; 3rd Place: $250. Judged by Pulitzer-prize winner Henry Taylor. Acquires *American Literary Review* (or participating magazine) gets first North American serial rights on the first-place poem.

MISSISSIPPI VALLEY NON-PROFIT POETRY CONTEST, Midwest Writing Center, P.O. Box 3188, Rock Island IL 61204-3188. (309)359-1057. **Contact:** Max Molleston, chairman. Estab. 1972. Unpublished poetry: Adult general, student division, Mississippi Valley, senior citizen, religious, rhyming, jazz, humorous, haiku, history, and ethnic. Up to 5 poems may be submitted with a limit of 50 lines/poem. Annually. Deadline: April 1. Charges $5 fee, $3 for students.

MORSE POETRY PRIZE, Northeastern University English Department, 406 Holmes Hall, Boston MA 02115. (617)437-2512. E-mail: g.rotella@neu.edu. Website: www.casdn.neu.edu/~english. **Contact:** Guy Rotella. Offered annually for previously published poetry, book-length mss of first or second books. Deadline: September 15. Charges $15 fee. Prize: $1,000 and publication by Northeastern University Press.

KATHRYN A. MORTON PRIZE IN POETRY, Sarabande Books, P.O. Box 4456, Louisville KY 40204. (502)458-4028. Fax: (502)458-4065. E-mail: sarabandeb@aol.com. Website: www.SarabandeBooks.org. **Contact:** Kirby Gann, managing editor. Offered annually to publish an outstanding collection of poetry. All finalists considered for publication. Deadline: January 1-February 15. Guidelines for SASE. Charges $20 fee. Prize: $2,000 and publication under standard royalty contract.

SHEILA MOTTON AWARD, New England Poetry Club, 11 Puritan Rd., Arlington MA 02476-7710. **Contact:** Virginia Thayer. For a poetry book published in the last 2 years. Send 2 copies of the book and $10 entry fee. Prize: $500.

MOVING WORDS, Arlington County Cultural Affairs Division, Ellipse Arts Center, 4350 N. Fairfax Dr., Arlington VA 22203. (703)228-7710. E-mail: oblong@erols.com. Website: www.arlingtonarts.org. **Contact:** Kim Roberts. Offered annually for published and unpublished poetry. Open only to writers who live, work, or maintain a studio in Arlington, Virginia. Deadline: January 31. Guidelines for SASE. Prize: Publication on bus posters and website; $100 honorarium for 6 adult winners (a separate contest for students is also held); and public reading at the Ellipse Arts Center in Arlington, Virginia.

ERIKA MUMFORD PRIZE, New England Poetry Club, 11 Puritan Rd., Arlington MA 02476-7710. **Contact:** Virginia Thayer. Offered annually for a poem in any form about foreign culture or travel. Deadline: June 30. Guidelines for SASE. Charges $10 for up to 3 poems. Prize: $250.

NATIONAL WRITERS ASSOCIATION POETRY CONTEST, The National Writers Association, 3140 S. Peoria, #295, Aurora CO 80014. (303)841-0246. Fax: Fax:(303)841-2607. **Contact:** Sandy Whelchel, director. Annual contest "to encourage the writing of poetry, an important form of individual expression but with a limited commercial market." Guidelines for SASE. Charges $10 fee. Prize: 1st Place: $100; 2nd Place: $50; 3rd Place: $25.

HOWARD NEMEROV SONNET AWARD, *The Formalist: A Journal of Metrical Poetry*, 320 Hunter Dr., Evansville IN 47711. **Contact:** Mona Baer. Offered annually for an unpublished sonnet to encourage poetic craftsmanship, and to honor the memory of the late Howard Nemerov, third US Poet Laureate. Final judge for year 2002: Wyatt Prunty. Acquires first North American serial rights for those sonnets chosen for publication. Upon publication all rights revert to the author. Open to the international community of writers. Deadline: June 15. Guidelines for SASE. Charges $3/sonnet. Prize: $1,000, and publication in *The Formalist*; 11 other finalists also published.

N **NEW CENTURY WRITER AWARDS (POETRY)**, New Century Writer, 32 Alfred St., Suite B, New Haven CT 06512-3927. (203)469-8824. Fax: (203)468-0333. E-mail: newcenturywriter@yahoo.com. Website: www.newcentur

ywriter.org. **Contact:** Jason Marchi, executive director. Offered annually to discover and encourage emerging writers of poetry. All genres. Winners announced on website in September. Guidelines/entry fee for the asking, no SASE required. All entrants receive a 1-year susbcription to *The Anvil*, an educational newsletter for writers. Open to all poets, both unpublished and those with a limited history of publishing their poetry. Call if in doubt about your eligibility. New Century Writer also provides the annual Ray Bradbury Short Story Fellowship for 1 or 2 short story writers to attend the *Zoetrope* Short Story Writers' Workshop at Francis Ford Coppola's Blancaneaux Lodge in Belize, Central America (see the Ray Bradbury Short Story Fellowship listing for complete details). Deadline: May 31. Charges $3/poem. Prize: 1st Place: $500; 2nd Place: $250; 3rd Place: $100; 4th-10th Place: $25.

NEW ISSUES FIRST BOOK OF POETRY PRIZE, *New Issues Poetry & Prose*, Department of English, Western Michigan University, 1903 W. Michigan Ave., Kalamazoo MI 49008-5331. (616)387-8185. Fax: (616)387-2562. E-mail: herbert.scott@wmich.edu. Website: www.wmich.edu/newissues. **Contact:** Herbert Scott, editor. Offered annually for publication of a first book of poems by a poet writing in English who has not previously published a full-length collection of poems in an edition of 500 or more copies. *New Issues Poetry & Prose* obtains rights for first publication. Book is copyrighted in author's name. Guidelines for SASE or on website. Deadline: November 30. Charges $15. Prize: $1,000, and publication of book. Author also receives 10% of the printed edition.

THE NEW LETTERS POETRY AWARD, *New Letters*, 5101 Rockhill Rd., Kansas City MO 64110. (816)235-1168. Fax: (816)235-2611. E-mail: newletters@umkc.edu. Website: www.umkc.edu/newletters. **Contact:** Aleatha Ezra. Offered annually for unpublished work to discover and reward new and upcoming writers. Buys first North American serial rights. Open to any writer. Deadline: Third week of May. Guidelines for SASE. Charges $10 fee. Prize: 1st Place: $1,000, and publication in *New Letters*; 2 runners-up will receive a 1-year subscription and will be considered for publication.

NEW RIVER POETS QUARTERLY POETRY AWARDS, New River Poets, a chapter of Florida State Poets Association, Inc., 5545 Meadowbrook St., Zephyrhills FL 33541-2715. **Contact:** June Owens, awards coordinator. Offered quarterly (February, May, August, and November) for previously published and unpublished work to acknowledge and reward outstanding poetic efforts. Previous winners have been Joyce Odam (CA), Glenna Holloway (IL), Sandra Lake Lassen (NC), and Norma Jagendorf (NY). Deadline: February 15, May 15, August 15, and November 15. Guidelines for SASE. Charges $4 fee for 1-3 poems, $1 each additional poem (no limit). Prize: $60/$40/$30 each quarter. Judged by the first-place winning authors in each quarterly competition who judge the unscreened entries in a subsequent competition. Open to any writer.

THE JOHN FREDERICK NIMS MEMORIAL PRIZE, *Poetry*, 60 W. Walton St., Chicago IL 60610. (312)255-3703. E-mail: poetry@poetrymagazine.org. Website: www.poetrymagazine.org. **Contact:** Joseph Parisi, editor. Offered annually for poems published in *Poetry* during the preceding year (October-September). Judged by the editors of *Poetry*. *Poetry* buys all rights to the poems published in the magazine. Copyrights are returned to the authors on request. Any writer may submit poems to *Poetry*. Guidelines for SASE. Prize: $500.

NLAPW INTERNATIONAL POETRY CONTEST, The National League of American Pen Women (Palamar Branch), 11929 Caminito Corriente, San Diego CA 92128. **Contact:** Helen J. Sherry. Offered annually for unpublished work. All proceeds from this contest provide an annual scholarship for a student entering college in the fields of art, letters, or music. Categories: Haiku (any style) and Poety (any style, 30 line limit). Open to any writer. Please do not call. Send SASE for information. Deadline: First Friday in March. Charges $5/poem or $5 for 2 haiku. Prize: $50; $25; $10; and honorable mentions in each category. Winning poems will be published in a chapbook.

THE OHIO STATE UNIVERSITY PRESS/THE JOURNAL AWARD IN POETRY, The Ohio State University Press and The Journal, 1070 Carmack, Columbus OH 43210. (614)292-6930. Fax: (614)292-2065. E-mail: ohiostatepress@osu.edu. Website: www.ohiostatepress.org. **Contact:** David Citino, poetry editor. Offered annually for unpublished work, minimum of 48 pages of original poetry. Deadline: Entries accepted September 1-30. Charges $20 fee. Prize: $1,000, and publication.

ORION PRIZE FOR POETRY, *Poetry Forever*, P.O. Box 68018, Hamilton, Ontario L8M 3M7, Canada. (905)312-1779. Offered for poetry to fund the publication of a full-size collection by Ottawa poet Marty Flomen (1942-1997). All profits from the Orion contest will be used for this purpose. Open to any writer. Poems must be typed or neatly printed. Photocopied submissions are OK. Poems may be no longer than 30 lines. Make checks payable to Poetry Forever. Entries will not be returned. Please include a SASE if you wish to receive a list of winners. Deadline: June 15, 2002. Charges $3/poem fee. Prize: There are first-, second- and third-place prizes. The amount varies because 50% of the entry fees will be awarded as prizes each year. This will, however, be no less than $100. The top three poems will receive broadsheet publication. Judged by blind judging.

NATALIE ORNISH POETRY AWARD, The Texas Institute of Letters, Southwest Texas State University, San Marcos TX 78666. (512)245-2428. Fax: (512)245-7462. E-mail: mb13@swt.edu. Website: www.English.swt.edu/css/TIL/rules.htm. **Contact:** Mark Busby. Offered annually for the best book of poems published January 1-December 31 of previous year. Poet must have been born in Texas, have lived in the state at some time for at least two consecutive years, or subject matter is associated with the state. Deadline: January 3. Guidelines for SASE. Prize: $1,000.

THE PATERSON POETRY PRIZE, The Poetry Center at Passaic County Community College, One College Blvd., Paterson NJ 07505-6555. (973)684-6555. Fax: (973)684-5843. E-mail: mgillan@pccc.cc.nj.us. Website: www.pccc.cc.nj.us/poetry. **Contact:** Maria Mazziotti Gillan, director. Offered annually for a book of poetry published in the previous year. Deadline: February 1. Guidelines for SASE. Prize: $1,000.

PAUMANOK POETRY AWARD, Visiting Writers Program, SUNY Farmingdale, SUNY Farmingdale/Knapp Hall, Route 110, Farmingdale NY 11735. Fax: (516)420-2051. E-mail: brownml@farmingdale.edu. Website: www.farmingdale.edu/CampusPages/ArtsSciences/EnglishHumanities/paward.html. **Contact:** Margery L. Brown, director, Visiting Writers Program. Offered annually for published or unpublished poems. Send cover letter, 1-paragraph bio, 3-5 poems (name and address on each poem). Include SASE for notification of winners. (Send photocopies only; mss will *not* be returned.) Deadline: September 15. Charges $25 fee, payable to SUNY Farmingdale VWP. Prize: 1st Place: $1,000, plus expenses for a reading in 2002-2003 series; Runners-up (2): $500, plus expenses for a reading in series.

PEARL POETRY PRIZE, Pearl Editions, 3030 E. Second St., Long Beach CA 90803. (562)434-4523. Fax: (562)434-4523. E-mail: mjohn5150@aol.com. Website: www.pearlmag.com. **Contact:** Marilyn Johnson, editor/publisher. Offered annually "to provide poets with further opportunity to publish their poetry in book-form and find a larger audience for their work." Manuscripts must be original works written in English. Guidelines for SASE or on website. Deadline: July 15. Charges $20. Prize: $1,000, and publication by Pearl Editions.

PHILBRICK POETRY AWARD, Providence Athenaeum, 251 Benefit St., Providence RI 02903. (401)421-6970. Fax: (401)421-2860. E-mail: lee_teverow@hotmail.com. Website: providenceathenaeum.org. **Contact:** Lee Teverow. Offered annually for New England poets who have not yet published a book. Previous publication of individual poems in journals or anthologies is allowed. Judged by nationally-known poets. Mei-Mei Berssenbrugge is the 2003 judge. Guidelines for SASE or on website. Deadline: June 15-October 15. Charges $5 fee. Prize: $500, publication of winning manuscript as a chapbook, and a public reading at Providence Athenaeum with the final judge/award presenter.

POET'S CORNER AWARD, Broken Jaw Press, Box 596 Stn. A, Fredericton, New Brunswick E3B 5A6, Canada. (506)454-5127. Fax: (506)454-5127. E-mail: jblades@nbnet.nb.ca. Website: www.brokenjaw.com. Offered annually to recognize the best book-length ms by a Canadian poet. Guidelines for SASE or on website at www.brokenjaw.com/poetscorner.htm. Deadline: December 31. Charges $20 fee (which includes copy of winning book upon publication). Prize: $500, plus trade publication of poetry ms.

POETIC LICENCE CONTEST FOR CANADIAN YOUTH, League of Canadian Poets, 54 Wolseley St., Toronto, Ontario M5T 1A5, Canada. (416)504-1657. Fax: (416)504-0096. E-mail: league@poets.ca. Website: www.poets.ca or www.youngpoets.ca. Offered annually for unpublished work to seek and encourage new poetic talent in two categories: Grades 7-9 and 10-12. Open to Canadian citizens and landed immigrants only. Guidelines for SASE or on website. For more information about the contest see website. Deadline: March 1. Charges $5 fee/poem. Prize: 1st Place: $500; 2nd Place: $350; 3rd Place: $250.

THE POETRY CENTER BOOK AWARD, The Poetry Center, San Francisco State University, 1600 Holloway Ave., San Francisco CA 94132-9901. (415)338-2227. Fax: (415)338-0966. E-mail: newlit@sfsu.edu. Website: www.sfsu.edu/~newlit/welcome.htm. **Contact:** Steve Dickison, director. Estab. 1980. Offered annually for books of poetry and chapbooks, published in year of the prize. "Prize given for an extraordinary book of American poetry." Please include a cover letter noting author name, book title(s), name of person issuing check, and check number. Will not consider anthologies or translations. Deadline: December 31. Charges $10 reading fee/entry. Prize: $500 and an invitation to read in the Poetry Center Reading Series.

POETRY CHAPBOOK COMPETITION, The Center for Book Arts, 28 W. 27th St., 3rd Floor, New York NY 10001. (212)481-0295. Fax: (212)481-9853. E-mail: info@centerforbookarts.org. Website: www.centerforbookarts.org. **Contact:** Rory Golden. Offered annually for unpublished collections of poetry. Individual poems may have been previously published. Collection must not exceed 500 lines or 24 pages. Deadline: December 1. Guidelines for SASE. Charges $15 fee. Prize: $500 award, $500 honorarium for a reading, publication, and 10 copies of chapbook. Judged by Sharon Dolin and Lynn Emanuel (2001 judges). Open to any writer.

N POETRY SOCIETY OF VIRGINIA CONTESTS, Poetry Society of Virginia, P.O. Box 650962, Potomac Falls VA 20165. (703)904-9671. E-mail: poetryinva@aol.com. Website: www.poetrysocietyofvirginia.org. **Contact:** Lori C. Fraind, adult categories; Shann Palmer, student categories. Annual contest for unpublished poetry in several categories. Some categories are open to any writer, others are open only to members or students. Guidelines for SASE or on website. Deadline: January 19. Charges $2/poem for nonmembers, free for members, free for student categories. Prize: $25-100 in each category.

LEVIS READING PRIZE, Virginia Commonwealth University, Department of English, P.O. Box 842005, Richmond VA 23284-2005. (804)828-1329. Fax: (804)828-8684. E-mail: eng_grad@vcu.edu. Website: www.has.vcu.edu/eng/grad/Levis_Prize.htm. **Contact:** Jeff Lodge. Offered annually for books of poetry published in the previous year to encourage poets early in their careers. The entry must be the writer's first or second published book of poetry. Previously published books in other genres, or previously published chapbooks, do not count as books for this purpose. Deadline: January 15. Guidelines for SASE. Prize: $1,000 honorarium, and an expense-paid trip to Richmond to present a public reading.

RED ROCK POETRY AWARD, *Red Rock Review*, Community College of Southern Nevada, English Department, 3200 E. Cheyenne Ave., North Las Vegas NV 89030. (702)651-4094. Fax: (702)651-4639. E-mail: rich_logsdon@ccsn.nevada.edu. Website: www.ccsn.nevada.edu/english/redrockreview/contest.htm. **Contact:** Rich Logsdon. Offered annually for unpublished poetry. Open to any writer. Deadline: October 31. Guidelines for SASE. Charges $6 for 3 poems. Prize: $500.

RIVER CITY WRITING AWARDS IN POETRY, The University of Memphis/Hohenberg Foundation, Department of English, Memphis TN 38152. (901)678-4591. Fax: (901)678-2226. Website: www.people.memphis.edu/~rivercity. **Contact:** Mary Leader. Offered annually for unpublished poem of 2 pages maximum. Guidelines for SASE or on website. Deadline: March 15. Charges $5 fee/poem. Prize: 1st Place: $1,000; 2nd and 3rd Place: Publication and 1-year subscription.

NICHOLAS ROERICH POETRY PRIZE, Story Line Press, Three Oaks Farm, P.O. Box 1240, Ashland OR 97520-0055. (541)512-8792. Fax: (541)512-8793. E-mail: mail@storylinepress.com. Website: www.storylinepress.com. **Contact:** Roerich Prize Coordinator. Estab. 1988. Offered annually for full-length book of poetry. Any writer who has not previously published a full-length collection of poetry (48 pages or more) in English is eligible to apply. Guidelines for SASE or on website. Deadline: May 1-October 31. Charges $20 fee. Prize: $1,000 advance, publication, and reading at the Nicholas Roerich Museum in New York.

BENJAMIN SALTMAN POETRY AWARD, Red Hen Press, P.O. Box 3537, Granada Hills CA 91394. (818)831-0649. Fax: (818)831-6659. E-mail: editors@redhen.org. Website: www.redhen.org. **Contact:** Kate Gale. Offered annually for unpublished work "to publish a winning book of poetry." Open to any writer. Deadline: October 31. Guidelines for SASE. Charges $15 fee. Prize: $1,000 and publication.

THE SANDBURG-LIVESAY ANTHOLOGY CONTEST, Mekler & Deahl, Publishers, 237 Prospect St. S., Hamilton, Ontario L8M 2Z6, Canada. (905)312-1779. Fax: (905)312-8285. E-mail: james@meklerdeahl.com. Website: www.meklerdeahl.com. Offered annually for published or unpublished poetry (up to 70 lines). Writers retain all rights. Open to any writer. Deadline: October 31. Charges $12 fee (US); maximum 10 entries. Prize: 1st Place: $250 (US) and anthology publication; 2nd Place: $150 (US) and anthology publication; 3rd Place: $100 (US) and anthology publication. All entrants receive a copy of the published anthology, entrants with poetry in the anthology receive 2 copies.

SASKATCHEWAN POETRY AWARD, Saskatchewan Book Awards, Inc., Box 1921, Regina, Saskatchewan S4P 3E1, Canada. (306)569-1585. Fax: (306)569-4187. E-mail: director@bookawards.sk.ca. Website: www.bookawards.sk.ca. **Contact:** Joyce Wells, executive director. Offered annually for work published September 15 to September 14 annually. This award is presented to a Saskatchewan author for the best book of poetry, judged on the quality of writing. Deadline: First deadline: July 31. Final deadline: September 14. Guidelines for SASE. Charges $15 (Canadian). Prize: $1,500.

THE HELEN SCHAIBLE INTERNATIONAL SHAKESPEAREAN/PETRARCHAN SONNET CONTEST, Poets' Club of Chicago, 1212 S. Michigan Ave., Chicago IL 60605. E-mail: roby@sxu.edu. **Contact:** Tom Roby, president. Estab. 1954. Offered annually for original and unpublished Shakespearean or Petrarchan sonnets. One entry/author. Submit 2 copies, typed and doublespaced; 1 with name and address, 1 without. Send SASE for winners list. Deadline: September 1. Prize: 1st Place: $50; 2nd Place: $35; 3rd Place: $15; 3 honorable mentions.

SLAPERING HOL PRESS CHAPBOOK COMPETITION, The Hudson Valley Writers' Center, 300 Riverside Dr., Sleepy Hollow NY 10591. (914)332-5953. Fax: (914)332-4825. E-mail: info@writerscenter.org. Website: www.writerscenter.org. **Contact:** Stephanie Strickland or Margo Stever, co-editors. The annual competition is open to poets who have not published a book or chapbook, though individual poems may have already appeared. Limit: 16-20 pages. The press was created in 1990 to provide publishing opportunities for emerging poets. Judged by a nationally known poet. Deadline: May 15. Guidelines for SASE. Charges $10 fee. Prize: $500, publication of chapbook, and a reading at The Hudson Valley Writers' Center.

SLIPSTREAM ANNUAL POETRY CHAPBOOK COMPETITION, Slipstream, Box 2071, Niagara Falls NY 14301. (716)282-2616 after 5 P.M. EST. E-mail: editors@slipstreampress.org. Website: www.slipstreampress.org. **Contact:** Dan Sicoli, co-editor. Offered annually to help promote a poet whose work is often overlooked or ignored. Open to any writer. Deadline: December 1. Guidelines for SASE. Charges $15. Prize: $1,000, and 50 copies of published chapbook.

THE SOW'S EAR CHAPBOOK PRIZE, The Sow's Ear Poetry Review, 19535 Pleasant View Dr., Abingdon VA 24211-6827. (276)628-2651. E-mail: richman@preferred.com. **Contact:** Larry K. Richman, contest director. Estab. 1988. Offered for poetry mss of 22-26 pages. Guidelines for SASE or by e-mail. Deadline: Submit March-April. Charges $10 fee. Prize: 1st Place: $1,000, 25 copies, and distribution to subscribers; 2nd Place: $200; 3rd Place: $100.

THE SOW'S EAR POETRY PRIZE, The Sow's Ear Poetry Review, 19535 Pleasant View Dr., Abingdon VA 24211-6827. (276)628-2651. E-mail: richman@preferred.com. **Contact:** Larry K. Richman, contest director. Estab. 1988. Offered for previously unpublished poetry. Guidelines for SASE or by e-mail. All submissions considered for publication. Deadline: Submit September-October. Charges $2 fee/poem. Prize: $1,000, $250, $100, and publication, plus option of publication for 20-25 finalists.

ANN STANFORD POETRY PRIZE, The Southern California Anthology, c/o Master of Professional Writing Program, WPH 404, U.S.C., Los Angeles CA 90089-4034. (213)740-3252. Website: www.usc.edu/dept/LAS/mpw. **Contact:** James Ragan, contest director. Estab. 1988. Offered annually for previously unpublished poetry to honor excellence in poetry in memory of poet and teacher Ann Stanford. Submit cover sheet with name, address, phone number and titles of the 5 poems entered. Deadline: April 15. Guidelines for SASE. Charges $10 fee. Prize: 1st Place: $1,000; 2nd Place: $200; 3rd Place: $100. Winning poems are published in *The Southern California Anthology* and all entrants receive a free issue.

THE EDWARD STANLEY AWARD, *Prairie Schooner*, 201 Andrews Hall, P.O. Box 880334, Lincoln NE 68588-0334. (402)472-0911. Fax: (402)472-9771. E-mail: eflanagan2@unl.edu. Website: www.unl.edu/schooner/psmain.htm. **Contact:** Hilda Raz. Offered annually for poetry published in *Prairie Schooner* in the previous year. Prize: $1,000.

THE AGNES LYNCH STARRETT POETRY PRIZE, University of Pittsburgh Press, 3400 Forbes Ave., Pittsburgh PA 15261. Website: www.pitt.edu/~press. **Contact:** Susan Borello. Estab. 1980. Series Editor: Ed Ochester. Offered annually for first book of poetry for poets who have not had a full-length book published. Mandatory guidelines for SASE. Deadline: March and April only. Charges $20 fee. Prize: $5,000.

subTERRAIN POETRY CONTEST, (formerly *sub-TERRAIN* Poetry Contest), *subTERRAIN* Magazine, P.O. Box 3008 MPO, Vancouver, British Columbia V6B 3X5, Canada. (604)876-8710. Fax: (604)879-2667. E-mail: subter@portal.ca. Website: www.anvilpress.com. Offered annually for unpublished poetry; theme to be announced in summer issue. Deadline: August 1-January 31. Guidelines for SASE. Charges $15 fee, 4 poem limit. Prize: $250, publication in spring issue, and 1-year subscription to *subTERRAIN*.

HOLLIS SUMMERS POETRY PRIZE, Ohio University Press, Scott Quadrangle, Athens OH 45701. (740)593-1155. Fax: (740)593-4536. Website: www.ohio.edu/oupress. **Contact:** David Sanders. Offered annually for unpublished poetry books. Books will be eligible if individual poems or sections have been published previously. Open to any writer. Deadline: October 31. Guidelines for SASE. Charges $15. Prize: $500, and publication of the ms in book form.

MAY SWENSON POETRY AWARD, Utah State University Press, 7800 Old Main Hill, Logan UT 84322-7800. (435)797-1362. Fax: (435)797-0313. E-mail: MSpooner@upress.usu.edu. Website: www.usu.edu/usupress. **Contact:** Michael Spooner. Offered annually in honor of May Swenson, one of America's greatest poets. Contest for unpublished mss in English, 50-100 pages; not only a "first book" competition. Entries are screened by 6 professional writers and teachers. The finalists are judged by a nationally known poet. Former judges include: John Hollander, Mary Oliver, Richard Howard, and Mark Doty. Open to any writer. Deadline: September 30. Guidelines for SASE. Charges $25 fee. Prize: $1,000, publication of ms, and royalties.

TIDEPOOL PRIZE FOR POETRY, *Poetry Forever*, P.O. Box 68018, Hamilton, Ontario L8M 3M7, Canada. (905)312-1779. Offered for poetry to fund the publication of a full-size collection by Hamilton poet Herb Barrett (1912-1995). All profits from the Tidepool contest will be used for this purpose. Open to any writer. Poems should be typed or neatly printed. Photocopied submissions are OK. Poems may be no longer than 30 lines. Make checks payable to Poetry Forever. Entries will not be returned. Please include a SASE if you wish to receive a list of winners. Deadline: July 15, 2002. Charges $3/poem fee. Prize: There are first-, second- and third-place prizes. The amount varies because 50% of the entry fees will be awarded as prizes each year. This will, however, be no less than $100. The top three poems will receive broadsheet publication. Judged by blind judging.

TRANSCONTINENTAL POETRY AWARD, Pavement Saw Press, P.O. Box 6291, Columbus OH 43206. (614)263-7115. E-mail: info@pavementsaw.org. Website: pavementsaw.org. **Contact:** David Baratier, editor. Offered annually for a first book of poetry. Judged by Editor David Baratier and a guest judge (2001 judge David Bromige). Guidelines on website. Deadline: August 15. Charges $15 fee. Prize: $1,500, 25 copies for judge's choice, standard royalty contract for editor's choice. Open to any writer.

KATE TUFTS DISCOVERY AWARD, Claremont Graduate University, 160 E. 10th St., Harper B7, Claremont CA 91711-6165. (909)621-8974. Fax: (909)621-8438. Website: www.cgu.edu/tufts. **Contact:** Betty Terrell, awards coordinator. Estab. 1993. Offered annually for a first book by a poet of genuine promise. Entries must be a published book completed Sept. 15, 2001-Sept. 15, 2002. Open to US residents only. Guidelines for SASE or on website. Deadline: Sept. 15. Prize: $10,000.

KINGSLEY TUFTS POETRY AWARD, Claremont Graduate University, 160 E. 10th St., Harper B7, Claremont CA 91711-6165. (909)621-8974. Fax: (909)621-8438. Website: www.cgu.edu/tufts. **Contact:** Betty Terrell, awards coordinator. Estab. 1992. Offered annually "for a work by an emerging poet, one who is past the very beginning but who has not yet reached the acknowledged pinnacle of his or her career." Guidelines for SASE or on website. Deadline: Sept. 15. Prize: $100,000.

UNION LEAGUE CIVIC AND ARTS POETRY PRIZE, *Poetry*, 60 W. Walton St., Chicago IL 60610. (312)255-3703. E-mail: poetry@poetrymagazine.org. Website: www.poetrymagazine.org. **Contact:** Joseph Parisi, editor. Offered annually for poems published in *Poetry* during the preceding year (October-September). *Poetry* buys all rights to the poems published in the magazine. Copyrights are returned to the authors on request. Any writer may submit poems to *Poetry*. Guidelines for SASE. Prize: $1,500.

DANIEL VAROUJAN AWARD, New England Poetry Club, 11 Puritan Rd., Arlington MA 02476-7710. **Contact:** Virginia Thayer. Offered annually for "an unpublished poem worthy of Daniel Varoujan, a poet killed by the Turks at the onset of the first genocide of this century which decimated three-fourths of the Armenian population." Send poems in duplicate. Open to any writer. Deadline: June 30. Guidelines for SASE. Charges $10 for 3 entries. Prize: $1,000.

CHAD WALSH POETRY PRIZE, *Beloit Poetry Journal*, 24 Berry Cove Rd., Lamoine ME 04605-4617. (207)667-5598. Website: www.bpj.org. **Contact:** Marion K. Stocking, editor. Offered annually to honor the memory of poet Chad Walsh, a founder of the *Beloit Poetry Journal*. The editors select a strong poem or group of poems from the poems published in the journal that year. Prize: $3,000.

THE ROBERT PENN WARREN POETRY PRIZE COMPETITION, *Cumberland Poetry Review*, P.O. Box 120128, Acklen Station, Nashville TN 37212. **Contact:** Eva Touster, contest/award director. Offered annually for unpublished work. Deadline: March 1. Guidelines for SASE. Charges $18. Prize: 1st Place: $500; 2nd Place: $300; 3rd Place: $200. Publication of winners in the Fall issue of *Cumberland Poetry Review*. Judged by the editors of *CPR*. The judge who makes the final decision is an internationally-known poet selected each year. Open to any writer.

THE WASHINGTON PRIZE, The Word Works, Inc., P.O. Box 42164, Washington DC 20015. E-mail: editor@wordworksdc.com. Website: www.wordworksdc.com. **Contact:** Miles David Moore. Offered annually "for the best full-length poetry manuscript (48-64 pp.) submitted to The Word Works each year. The Washington Prize contest is the only forum in which we consider unsolicited manuscripts." Submissions accepted in the month of February. Acquires first publication rights. Open to any American writer. Deadline: March 1 (postmarked). Guidelines for SASE. Charges $20 fee. Prize: $1,500 and book publication; all entrants receive a copy of the winning book.

WHITE PINE PRESS POETRY PRIZE, White Pine Press, P.O. Box 236, Buffalo NY 14201. E-mail: wpine@whitepine.org. Website: www.whitepine.org. **Contact:** Elaine LaMattina, managing editor. Offered annually for previously published or unpublished poets. Manuscript: Up to 96 pages of original work; translations are not eligible. Poems may have appeared in magazines or limited-edition chapbooks. "We hold rights until the book is out of print; then rights revert to the author. With previously published work, the author is responsible for obtaining permission for publication by White Pine Press." Open to any US citizen. Additional information via e-mail or send a SASE. Deadline: December 31. Guidelines for SASE. Charges $20 fee. Prize: $1,000 and publication.

THE WALT WHITMAN AWARD, The Academy of American Poets, 588 Broadway, Suite 1203, New York NY 10012-3210. (212)274-0343. Fax: (212)274-9427. E-mail: academy@poets.org. Website: www.poets.org. **Contact:** Awards Director. Offered annually to publish and support a poet's first book. Submissions must be in English by a single poet. Translations are not eligible. Contestants must be living citizens of the US and have neither published nor committed to publish a volume of poetry 40 pages or more in length in an edition of 500 or more copies. Deadline: September 15-November 15. Guidelines for SASE. Charges $25 fee. Prize: $5,000, a residency for 1 month at the Vermont Studio Center, and publication by Louisiana State University Press.

WICK POETRY CHAPBOOK SERIES 'OPEN' COMPETITION, Wick Poetry Program, Department of English, Kent State University, P.O. Box 5190, Kent OH 44242-0001. (330)672-2067. Fax: (330)672-2567. E-mail: wickpoet@kent.edu. Website: www.kent.edu/wick. **Contact:** Maggie Anderson, director. Offered annually for a chapbook of poems by a poet currently living in Ohio. Deadline: October 31. Guidelines for SASE. Prize: Publication of the chapbook by the Kent State University Press.

WICK POETRY CHAPBOOK SERIES 'STUDENT' COMPETITION, Wick Poetry Program, Department of English, Kent State University, P.O. Box 5190, Kent OH 44242-0001. (330)672-2067. Fax: (330)672-2567. E-mail: wickpoet@kent.edu. Website: www.kent.edu/wick. **Contact:** Maggie Anderson, coordinator. Offered annually for publication of a chapbook of poems by a poet currently enrolled in an Ohio college or university. Deadline: October 31. Guidelines for SASE. Prize: Publication of the chapbook by the Kent State University Press.

STAN AND TOM WICK POETRY PRIZE, Wick Poetry Program, Department of English, Kent State University, P.O. Box 5190, Kent OH 44242-0001. (330)672-2067. Fax: (330)672-2567. E-mail: wickpoet@kent.edu. Website: www.kent.edu/wick. **Contact:** Maggie Anderson, coordinator. Open to anyone writing in English who has not previously published a full-length book of poems (a volume of 48 pages or more published in an edition of 500 or more copies). Deadline: May 1. Guidelines for SASE. Charges $20 fee. Prize: $2,000, and publication by the Kent State University Press.

THE RICHARD WILBUR AWARD, The University of Evansville Press, University of Evansville, Evansville IN 47722. **Contact:** The Editors. Offered in even-numbered years for an unpublished poetry collection. Deadline: December 1, 2002. Guidelines for SASE. Charges $25 fee. Prize: $1,000 and publication by the University of Evansville Press.

WILLIAM CARLOS WILLIAMS AWARD, Poetry Society of America, 15 Gramercy Park S., New York NY 10003. (212)254-9628. Fax: (212)673-2352. Website: www.poetrysociety.org. **Contact:** Brett Lauer, programs associate. Offered annually for a book of poetry published by a small press, nonprofit, or university press. Winning books are distributed to PSA members upon request and while supplies last. Deadline: December 21. Guidelines for SASE. Charges $10 fee. Prize: $500-1,000.

ROBERT H. WINNER MEMORIAL AWARD, Poetry Society of America, 15 Gramercy Park S., New York NY 10003. (212)254-9628. Fax: (212)673-2352. E-mail: brett@poetrysociety.org. Website: www.poetrysociety.org. **Con-**

tact: Brett Lauer, programs associate. Recognizing and rewarding the work of someone in midlife. Open to poets over 40, still unpublished or with 1 book. For guidelines send SASE. Deadline: December 21. Charges $15 fee for nonmembers; free to PSA members. Prize: $2,500.

THE J. HOWARD AND BARBARA M.J. WOOD PRIZE, *Poetry*, 60 W. Walton St., Chicago IL 60610. (312)255-3703. E-mail: poetry@poetrymagazine.org. Website: www.poetrymagazine.org. **Contact:** Joseph Parisi, editor. Offered annually for poems published in *Poetry* during the preceding year (October-September). *Poetry* buys all rights to the poems published in the magazine. Copyrights are returned to the authors on request. Any writer may submit poems to *Poetry*. Guidelines for SASE. Prize: $5,000.

THE WRITER MAGAZINE/EMILY DICKINSON AWARD, Poetry Society of America, 15 Gramercy Park S., New York NY 10003. (212)254-9628. Fax: (212)673-2352. E-mail: brett@poetrysociety.org. Website: www.poetrysociety.org. **Contact:** Brett Lauer, programs associate. Offered annually for a poem inspired by Emily Dickinson, though not necessarily in her style. For guidelines send SASE. Guidelines subject to change. Open to PSA members only. Deadline: December 21. Prize: $250.

WRITERS' JOURNAL POETRY CONTEST, Val-Tech Media, Inc., P.O. Box 394, Perham MN 56573. (218)346-7921. Fax: (218)346-7924. E-mail: writersjournal@lakesplus.com. Website: www.writersjournal.com. **Contact:** Esther M. Leiper. Offered for previously unpublished poetry. Deadline: April 30, August 30, December 30. Guidelines for SASE. Charges $2 fee first poem; $1 each thereafter. Prize: 1st Place: $25; 1st, 2nd, 3rd prize and selected honorable mention winners will be published in *Writers' Journal* magazine.

YALE SERIES OF YOUNGER POETS, Yale University Press, P.O. Box 209040, New Haven CT 06520-9040. E-mail: yyp@yalepress3.unipress.edu. Website: www.yale.edu/yup. **Contact:** Poetry Editor. Offered annually for a first book of poetry by poet under the age of 40. Deadline: Submit during January. Guidelines for SASE. Charges $15 fee. Prize: Winning ms is published by Yale University Press under royalty contract.

Playwriting & Scriptwriting

ALBERTA PLAYWRITING COMPETITION, Alberta Playwrights' Network, 1134 Eighth Ave. SW, 2nd Floor, Calgary, Alberta T2P 1J5, Canada. (403)269-8564; (800)268-8564. Fax: (403)265-6773. E-mail: apn@nucleus.com. Website: www.nucleus.com/~apn. Offered annually for unproduced plays with full-length and Discovery categories. Discovery is open only to previously unproduced playwrights. Open only to residents of Alberta. Deadline: January 15. Charges $40 fee (Canadian). Prize: Full length: $3,500 (Canadian); Discovery: $1,500 (Canadian).

N **THE ANNUAL BLANK THEATRE COMPANY YOUNG PLAYWRIGHTS FESTIVAL**, The Blank Theatre Co., 1301 Lucile Ave., Los Angeles CA 90026-1519. (323)662-7734. Fax: (323)661-3903. E-mail: steele@theblank.com. Website: www.youngplaywrights.com; www.theblank.com. **Contact:** Christopher Steele. Offered annually for unpublished work to encourage young writers to write for the theatre by presenting their work as well as through our mentoring programs. Open to all writers 19 or younger on the submission date. Deadline: March 15. Prize: Workshop of the winning plays by professional theatre artists.

ANNUAL INTERNATIONAL ONE PAGE PLAY COMPETITION, Lamia Ink!, P.O. Box 202, Prince Street Station, New York NY 10012. **Contact:** Cortland Jessup, founder/artistic director. Offered annually for previously published or unpublished 1-page plays. Acquires "the rights to publish in our magazine and to be read or performed at the prize awarding festival." Playwright retains copyright. Deadline: March 15. Guidelines for SASE. Charges $2/play or $5/3 plays. Prize: $200, staged reading, and publication of 12 finalists.

ANNUAL NATIONAL PLAYWRITING CONTEST, Wichita State University, School of Performing Arts, 1845 Fairmount, Wichita KS 67260-0153. (316)978-3368. Fax: (316)978-3951. E-mail: kiralyfa@twsuvm.uc.twsu.edu. **Contact:** Bela Kiralyfalvi, contest director. Offered annually for full-length plays (minimum of 90 minutes playing time) or 2-3 short plays on related themes (minimum 90 minutes playing time). Deadline: February 15. Guidelines for SASE. Prize: Production by the Wichita State University Theatre. Winner announced April 15.

BARBARA ANTON PLAYWRITING AWARD, Florida Studio Theatre, 1241 N. Palm Ave., Sarasota FL 34236. (941)366-9017. Fax: (941)955-4137. E-mail: james@fst2000.org. Website: www.fst2000.org. **Contact:** James Ashford. Offered annually to a playwright of proven promise. Prize: Residency at Florida Studio Theatre, and $1,000 stipend.

AUSTIN HEART OF FILM FESTIVAL FEATURE LENGTH SCREENPLAY COMPETITION, 1604 Nueces, Austin TX 78701. (512)478-4795. E-mail: austinfilm@aol.com. Website: www.austinfilmfestival.com. **Contact:** BJ Burrow, competition director. Offered annually for unpublished screenplays. The Austin Film Festival is looking for quality screenplays which will be read by industry professionals. Two competitions: Adult/Family Category and Comedy Category. Guidelines for SASE or call (800)310-3378. The writer must hold the rights when submitted; it must be original work. The screenplay must be between 90 and 120 pages. It must be in standard screenplay format (industry standard). Deadline: May 15. Charges $40 entry fee. Prize: $5,000 in each category.

BAKER'S PLAYS HIGH SCHOOL PLAYWRITING CONTEST, Baker's Plays, P.O. Box 699222, Quincy MA 02269-9222. (617)745-0805. Fax: (617)745-9891. E-mail: help@bakersplays.com. Website: www.bakersplays.com.

Contact: Kurt Gombar, general manager. Offered annually for unpublished work about the "high school experience," but can be about any subject, so long as the play can be reasonably produced on the high school stage. Plays may be of any length. Plays must be accompanied by the signature of a sponsoring high school drama or English teacher, and it is recommended that the play receive a production or a public reading prior to the submission. Multiple submissions and co-authored scripts are welcome. Teachers may not submit a student's work. The ms must be firmly bound, typed, and come with SASE that includes enough postage to cover the return of the ms. Plays that do not come with an SASE will not be returned. Do not send originals; copies only. Deadline: January 31. Guidelines for SASE. Prize: 1st Place: $500, and publication; 2nd Place: $250; 3rd Place: $100.

BAY AREA PLAYWRIGHTS FESTIVAL, Produced by The Playwrights Foundation, 1360 Mission St., 3rd Floor, San Francisco CA 94103. (415)263-3986. E-mail: info@playwrightsfoundation.org. Website: www.playwrightsfoundation.org. **Contact:** Amy Mueller, artistic director; Christine Young, literary manager. Offered annually for unpublished plays by established and emerging theatre writers nationally to support and encourage development of a new work. Unproduced full-length plays only. Open to all writers. Deadline: February 15. Guidelines for SASE. Prize: Small stipend and in-depth development process with dramaturg and director, and a professionally staged reading in San Francisco.

WALDO M. & GRACE C. BONDERMAN IUPUI/IRT NATIONAL YOUTH THEATRE PLAYWRITING COMPETITION AND DEVELOPMENT WORKSHOP, CA 309, 425 University Blvd., Indianapolis IN 46202. (317)709-3765. Fax: (317)278-1025. E-mail: Bonderman@msn.com. Website: w3liberalarts.iupui.edu/bonderman. **Contact:** Dorothy Webb. Offered every 2 years for unpublished plays to encourage writers to create artistic scripts for young audiences. "It provides a forum through which each playwright receives constructive criticism and the support of a development team consisting of a professional director and dramaturg. Plays will be cast from professional and experienced area actors." Guidelines for SASE or on website. "Plays should be intended for young audiences 1st grade through high school (no play is expected to appeal to all ages simultaneously). Playwrights must suggest the appropriate age category on official entry form." Deadline: September 1, 2002 (postmarked), received by Sept. 8, 2002. Prize: Awards will be presented to up to 10 finalists. In addition to the development work, 4 cash awards of $1,000 each will be presented to the 4 playwrights whose plays are selected for development.

RICHARD & BETTY BURDICK NEW PLAY FESTIVAL, *Florida Studio Theatre*, 1241 N. Palm Ave., Sarasota FL 34236. (941)366-9017. Fax: (941)955-4137. E-mail: james@fst2000.org. Website: www.fst2000.org. **Contact:** James Ashford. Offered annually for unpublished plays. "All submissions to *Florida Studio Theatre* are considered for this festival. It is a developmental process followed by workshop productions of 3 new plays by writers from around the country." Anyone wishing to submit a full-length play should first send a cover letter, synopsis, 5-10 pages of sample dialogue, and a SASE. *Florida Studio Theatre* reserves the right to produce the premiere full production. Open to any writer. Deadline: End of January. Guidelines for SASE. Prize: Development and workshop production, including housing and stipend while in Sarasota.

N **CAA CAROL BOLT AWARD FOR DRAMA**, Canadian Authors Association with the support of the Playwrights Union of Canada and Playwrights Canada Press, 320 S. Shores Rd., P.O. Box 419, Campbellford, Ontario K0L 1L0, Canada. (705)653-0323. Fax: (705)653-0593. E-mail: canauth@redden.on.ca. Website: www.CanAuthors.org. **Contact:** Alec McEachern. Contest for the best English-language play for adults by an author who is Canadian or landed immigrant. Submissions should be previously published or performed in the year prior to the giving of the award. For instance, in 2001 for this year's award to be given in July 2002. Open to Canadian citizens or landed immigrants. Annually. Deadline: December 15, except for plays published or performed in December, in which case the deadline is January 15. Guidelines for SASE. Charges $20 (Canadian funds) fee. Prize: $1,000 and a silver medal. Judged by a trustee for the award (appointed by the CAA). The trustee appoints up to three judges. The identities of the trustee and judges are confidential. Short lists are not made public. Decisions of the trustee and judges are final, and they may choose not to award a prize.

CALIFORNIA YOUNG PLAYWRIGHTS CONTEST, Playwrights Project, 450 B St., Suite 1020, San Diego CA 92101-8093. (619)239-8222. Fax: (619)239-8225. E-mail: write@playwrightsproject.com. Website: www.playwrightsproject.com. **Contact:** Cecelia Kouma, managing director. Offered annually for previously unpublished plays by young writers to stimulate young people to create dramatic works, and to nurture promising writers. Scripts must be a minimum of 10 standard typewritten pages; send 2 copies. Scripts will *not* be returned. All entrants receive detailed evaluation letter. Writers must be California residents under age 19 as of the deadline date. Deadline: April 1. Guidelines for SASE. Prize: Professional production of 3-5 winning plays at the Old Globe Theatre in San Diego, plus royalty.

COE COLLEGE PLAYWRITING FESTIVAL, Coe College, 1220 First Ave. NE, Cedar Rapids IA 52402-5092. (319)399-8624. Fax: (319)399-8557. E-mail: swolvert@coe.edu. Website: www.public.coe.edu/departments/theatre/. **Contact:** Susan Wolverton. Estab. 1993. Offered biennially for unpublished work to provide a venue for new works for the stage. "There is usually a theme for the festival. We are interested in full-length productions, *not* one acts or musicals. There are no specific criteria although a current résumé and synopsis is requested." Open to any writer. Deadline: Before June 1. Notified by September 1. Guidelines for SASE. Prize: $325, plus 1-week residency as guest artist with airfare, room and board provided.

THE COLUMBUS SCREENPLAY DISCOVERY AWARDS, 433 N. Camden Dr., #600, Beverly Hills CA 90210. (310)288-1882. Fax: (310)475-0193. E-mail: awards@hollywoodawards.com. Website: www.HollywoodAwards.com.

Contact: Carlos de Abreu. Monthly and annual contest "to discover new screenplay writers." Judged by reputable industry professionals (producers, development executives, story analysts). Writer must give option to purchase if selected. Open to any writer. Deadline: November 1. Guidelines for SASE. Charges $55 fee. Prize: Options up to $10,000, plus professional development guidance, software, and access to agents, producers, and studios.

THE CUNNINGHAM COMMISSION FOR YOUTH THEATRE, The Theatre School, DePaul University, 2135 N. Kenmore, Chicago IL 60614. (773)325-7938. Fax: (773)325-7920. E-mail: lgoetsch@depaul.edu. Website: theatreschool.depaul.edu/programs/prize.htm. **Contact:** Lara Goetsch. Chicago-area playwrights only. Commission will result in a play for younger audiences that "affirms the centrality of religion, broadly defined, and the human quest for meaning, truth, and community." Deadline: October 1, 2002 (Committee will offer the commission to the winner by February 1, 2003). Guidelines for SASE. Prize: $5,000 ($2,000 when commission is contracted, $1,000 if script moves to workshop, $2,000 as royalty if script is produced by the theatre school). Open to any writer.

DAYTON PLAYHOUSE FUTUREFEST, The Dayton Playhouse, 1301 E. Siebenthaler Ave., Dayton OH 45414-5357. (937)333-7469. Fax: (937)277-9539. **Contact:** Dave Seyer, theater manager. "Three plays selected for full productions, 3 for readings at July FutureFest weekend; the 6 authors will be given travel and lodging to attend the festival." Professionally adjudicated. Guidelines for SASE. Guidelines can also be faxed. Deadline: October 30. Prize: $1,000, and $100 to the other 5 playwrights.

DRURY UNIVERSITY ONE-ACT PLAY CONTEST, Drury University, 900 N. Benton Ave., Springfield MO 65802-3344. E-mail: sasher@drury.edu. **Contact:** Sandy Asher. Offered in even-numbered years for unpublished and professionally unproduced plays. One play/playwright. Guidelines for SASE or by e-mail. Deadline: December 1.

ESSENTIAL THEATRE PLAYWRITING AWARD, The Essential Theatre, 995 Greenwood Ave. #6, Atlanta GA 30306. (404)876-8471. E-mail: pmhardy@aol.com. **Contact:** Peter Hardy. Offered annually for unproduced, full-length plays by Georgia writers. No limitations as to style or subject matter. Deadline: April 15. Prize: $400 and full production.

SHUBERT FENDRICH MEMORIAL PLAYWRITING CONTEST, Pioneer Drama Service, Inc., P.O. Box 4267, Englewood CO 80155. (303)779-4035. Fax: (303)779-4315. E-mail: playwrights@pioneerdrama.com. Website: www.pioneerdrama.com. **Contact:** Beth Somers, assistant editor. Offered annually for unpublished, but previously produced, submissions to encourage the development of quality theatrical material for educational and community theater. Rights acquired only if published. People already published by Pioneer Drama are not eligible. Deadline: March 1. Guidelines for SASE. Prize: $1,000 royalty advance, publication.

FESTIVAL OF FIRSTS, City of Carmel-by-the-Sea Community and Cultural Department, P.O. Box 1950, Carmel CA 93921-1950. (831)624-3996. Fax: (831)624-0147. **Contact:** Brian Donoghue, award director. Offered annually for unpublished plays to recognize and foster the art of playwriting. Send SASE for guidelines. Deadline: June 15-August 31. Charges $15/script. Prize: Up to $1,000.

[N] **FIREHOUSE THEATRE PROJECT NEW PLAY COMPETITION**, The Firehouse Theatre Project, P.O. Box 5165, Richmond VA 23220. (804)355-2001. E-mail: newplays@firehousetheatre.org. Website: www.firehousetheatre.org. **Contact:** Jack Parrish, literary manager FTP. "The award is intended to encourage American playwrights to continue to produce new scripts for the theatre; thereby maintaining a fertile base for American voices in the dramatic literature of current times and the years to come. The scripts must be full-length theatrical scripts in English on any topic. All scripts must be submitted by an agent or accompanied by a professional letter of recommendation from a director, literary manager or dramaturg. Translations, adaptations, musicals, one-acts, film and television screenplays are ineligible and will not be considered." Open to US residents only. Submissions must be unpublished. Visit www.firehousetheatre.org for complete submission guidelines. Annually. Deadline: August 31, 2003. Prize: 1st Prize: $1,000 with a production or a fully produced staged reading at the 2004 FTP Festival of New American Plays (January 2004); 2nd Prize: $500 with a staged reading at the 2004 FTP Festival; 3rd Prize: $250 with a possible staged reading at the 2004 FTP Festival. Judged by a committee selected by the executive board of the Firehouse Theatre Project. Acquires the right to produce the winning scripts for the 2004 FTP Festival of New American Plays. Following the Festival production dates, all rights are relinquished to the author.

FLORIDA PLAYWRIGHTS FESTIVAL, Florida Studio Theatre, 1241 N. Palm Ave., Sarasota FL 34236. (941)366-9017. Fax: (941)955-4137. E-mail: james@fst2000.org. Website: www.fst2000.org. **Contact:** James Ashford. Offered annually (August) for full-length plays by Florida writers. Send complete script. Two plays are chosen for the festival; each play rehearses for 1 week before the festival and receives 1 public performance. Deadline: Submissions accepted year-round. Prize: Participation in rehearsal and rewrite process, public performance, travel, housing, small stipend.

FULL-LENGTH PLAY COMPETITION, West Coast Ensemble, P.O. Box 38728, Los Angeles CA 90038. (323)876-9337. Fax: (323)876-8916. Website: www.wcensemble.org. **Contact:** Les Hanson, artistic director. Offered annually "to nurture, support, and encourage" unpublished playwrights. Permission to present the play is granted if work is selected as finalist. Deadline: December 31. Guidelines for SASE. Prize: $500, and presentation of play.

JOHN GASSNER MEMORIAL PLAYWRITING COMPETITION, New England Theatre Conference, Northeastern University, 360 Huntington Ave., Boston MA 02115. E-mail: mail@netconline.org. Website: www.netconline.org.

Contact: Tara McCarthy, executive director. Offered annually to unpublished full-length plays and scripts. Open to New England residents and NETC members. Playwrights living outside New England may participate by joining NETC. Deadline: April 15. Guidelines for SASE. Charges $10 fee. Prize: 1st Place: $1,000; 2nd Place: $500.

GILMAN & GONZALEZ-FALLA THEATER FOUNDATION AWARD, 109 E. 64th St., New York NY 10021. (212)734-8011. Fax: (212)734-9606. E-mail: soncel@aol.com. Website: www.ggftheater.org. **Contact:** Jenny Buccos, foundation coordinator. Offered annually for body of work to encourage the creative elements in the American musical theater. The lyricist, book writer, or composer should have a work produced in the US in either a commercial theater or a professional not-for-profit theater. Two letters of recommendation from professionals involved in the theater are required. Open to US residents and American citizens. Deadline: December 31. Guidelines for SASE. Prize: $25,000.

GOVERNOR GENERAL'S LITERARY AWARD FOR DRAMA, Canada Council for the Arts, 350 Albert St., P.O. Box 1047, Ottawa, Ontario K1P 5V8, Canada. (613)566-4414, ext. 5576. Fax: (613)566-4410. E-mail: joanne.larocque-poirier@canadacouncil.ca. Website: www.canadacouncil.ca. **Contact:** Joanne Larocque-Poirier. Offered for the best English-language and the best French-language work of drama by a Canadian published September 1, 2001- September 30, 2002. Publishers submit titles for consideration. Deadline: April 15 or August 7, 2002, depending on the book's publication date. Prize: $15,000.

AURAND HARRIS MEMORIAL PLAYWRITING AWARD, The New England Theatre Conference, Inc., Northeastern University 360 Huntington Ave., Boston MA 02115. (617)424-9275. Fax: (617)424-1057. E-mail: imail@netconline.org. Website: www.netconline.org. Offered annually for an unpublished full-length play for young audiences. Guidelines for SASE. "No phone calls, please." Open to New England residents and/or members of the New England Theatre Conference. Deadline: May 1. Charges $20 fee. Prize: 1st-$1,000, 2nd-$500. Open to any writer.

HENRICO THEATRE COMPANY ONE-ACT PLAYWRITING COMPETITION, Henrico Recreation & Parks, P.O. Box 27032, Richmond VA 23273. (804)501-5138. Fax: (804)501-5284. E-mail: per22@co.henrico.va.us. Website: www.co.henrico.va.us/rec. **Contact:** Amy A. Perdue. Offered annually for previously unpublished or unproduced plays or musicals to produce new dramatic works in one-act form. "Scripts with small casts and simpler sets given preference. Controversial themes and excessive language should be avoided." Deadline: July 1. Guidelines for SASE. Prize: Winner: $300; Runner-up: $200. Winning entries may be produced; videotape sent to author.

HISPANIC PLAYWRIGHTS' DIVISION SOUTHWEST FESTIVAL OF NEW PLAYS,, Stages Repertory Theatre, 3201 Allen Pkwy., Suite 101, Houston TX 77019. (713)527-0220. Fax: (713)527-8669. Website: www.stagestheatre.com. **Contact:** Chris Jimmerson. Offered annually to provide an outlet for playwrights of Hispanic/Latino heritage. Open to full-length plays, musicals, and series of related shorts. Guidelines for SASE or on website. Winners notified in May. Deadline: October 1-February 15. Prize: 1st Place: reading by professional actors; Runners-up (2): Selected scenes read.

HISPANIC PLAYWRIGHTS' PROJECT, South Coast Repertory Theatre, P.O. Box 2197, Costa Mesa CA 92628-2197. (714)708-5500, ext. 5405. Fax: (714)545-0391. E-mail: juliette@scr.org. Website: www.scr.org. **Contact:** Juliette Carrillo. Offered annually for unpublished plays to develop work by Latino writers across the US. Guidelines for SASE or call for a brochure and leave address. Deadline: January 15. Prize: Workshop or reading of the play.

JEWEL BOX THEATRE PLAYWRIGHTING COMPETITION, Jewel Box Theatre, 3700 N. Walker, Oklahoma City OK 73118-7099. (405)521-1786. **Contact:** Charles Tweed, production director. Estab. 1982. Offered annually for full-length plays. Send SASE in October for guidelines. Deadline: January 15. Prize: $500.

THE KENNEDY CENTER FUND FOR NEW AMERICAN PLAYS, J.F. Kennedy Center for the Performing Arts, Washington DC 20566. (202)416-8024. Fax: (202)416-8205. E-mail: rsfoster@kennedy-center.org. Website: kennedy-center.org/fnap. **Contact:** Rebecca Foster, manager, theater programming. Estab. 1988. Offered for previously unproduced work. "Program objectives: To stimulate and foster the development of new plays; to nurture American playwrights and support the creation of new works; to provide nonprofit professional theatre organizations with additional resources to mount enhanced productions of new plays; to encourage playwrights to write, and nonprofit professional theaters to produce new American plays; to ease the financial burdens of nonprofit professional theater organizations producing new plays; to provide a playwright with a better production of the play than the producing theater would normally be able to accomplish." Nonprofit professional theater organizations can mail in name and address to be placed on the mailing list or check website. Submissions and funding proposals only through the producing theater. Production grants are given to theaters to underwrite specific or extraordinary expenses relating to: Creative support, actor support, and production support. Development grants are given to theaters to underwrite expenses for a reading and workshop of a new play in development. Deadline: Early May. Prize: Production grant: Playwright receives $10,000 (theatre receives an amount determined by budget submitted). Development grant: Playwright receives $2,500 (theatre receives an amount determined by budget submitted); a few encouragement grants of $2,500 may be given to promising playwrights chosen from the submitted proposals.

MARC A. KLEIN PLAYWRITING AWARD FOR STUDENTS, Department of Theater Arts, Case Western Reserve University, 10900 Euclid Ave., Cleveland OH 44106-7077. (216)368-4868. Fax: (216)368-5184. E-mail: ksg@po.cwru.edu. Website: www.cwru.edu/artsci/thtr. **Contact:** Ron Wilson, reading committee chair. Estab. 1975. Offered annually for an unpublished, professionally unproduced full-length play, or evening of related short plays, by a student at an American college or university. Deadline: May 15. Prize: $1,000, which includes $500 to cover residency expenses; production.

KUMU KAHUA/UHM THEATRE DEPARTMENT PLAYWRITING CONTEST, Kumu Kahua Theatre, Inc./ University of Hawaii at Manoa, Department of Theatre and Dance, 46 Merchant St., Honolulu HI 96813. (808)536-4222. Fax: (808)536-4226. E-mail: kkt@pixi.com. Website: www.kumukahua.com. **Contact:** Harry Wong III, artistic director. Offered annually for unpublished work to honor full-length and short plays. Guidelines available every September. First 2 categories open to residents and nonresidents. For Hawaii Prize, plays must be set in Hawaii or deal with some aspect of the Hawaiian experience. For Pacific Rim prize, plays must deal with the Pacific Islands, Pacific Rim, or Pacific/Asian/American experience—short plays only considered in 3rd category. Deadline: January 2. Prize: $500 (Hawaii Prize); $400 (Pacific Rim); $200 (Resident).

L.A. DESIGNERS' THEATRE-COMMISSIONS, L.A. Designers' Theatre, P.O. Box 1883, Studio City CA 91614-0883. (323)650-9600 or (323)654-2700 T.D.D. Fax: (323)654-3210. E-mail: ladesigners@juno.com. **Contact:** Richard Niederberg, artistic director. Quarterly contest "to promote new work and push it onto the conveyor belt to filmed or videotaped entertainment." All submissions must be registered with copyright office and be unpublished. Material will *not* be returned. "Do not submit anything that will not fit in a #10 envelope." "No rules, guidelines, fees, or entry forms. Just present an *idea* that can be commissioned into a full work." Proposals for uncompleted works are encouraged. Unpopular political, religious, social, or other themes are encouraged; 'street' language and nudity are acceptable. Open to any writer. Deadline: March 15, June 15, September 15, December 15. Prize: Production or publication of the work in the Los Angeles market. "We only want 'first refusal.'"

MAXIM MAZUMDAR NEW PLAY COMPETITION, Alleyway Theatre, One Curtain Up Alley, Buffalo NY 14202-1911. (716)852-2600. Fax: (716)852-2266. E-mail: email@alleyway.com. Website: alleyway.com. **Contact:** Dramaturg. Estab. 1990. Annual competition. Full Length: Not less than 90 minutes, no more than 10 performers. One-Act: Less than 40 minutes, no more than 6 performers. Children's plays. Musicals must be accompanied by audio tape. Finalists announced October 1. "Playwrights may submit work directly. There is no entry form. Annual playwright's fee $5; may submit 1 in each category, but pay only 1 fee. Please specify if submission is to be included in competition." "Alleyway Theatre must receive first production credit in subsequent printings and productions." Deadline: July 1. Prize: Full length: $400, travel, plus lodging, production and royalties; One act: $100, production, plus royalties.

N **McKNIGHT ADVANCEMENT GRANT**, The Playwrights' Center, 2301 Franklin Ave. E., Minneapolis MN 55406-1099. (612)332-7481. Fax: (612)332-6037. E-mail: info@pwcenter.org. Website: www.pwcenter.org. **Contact:** Kristen Gandrow, director of playwright services. Offered annually for either published or unpublished playwrights to recognize those whose work demonstrates exceptional artistic merit and potential and whose primary residence is in the state of Minnesota. The grants are intended to significantly advance recipients' art and careers, and can be used to support a wide variety of expenses. Applications available December 1. Guidelines for SASE. Additional funds of up to $1,500 are available for workshops and readings. The Playwrights' Center evaluates each application and forwards finalists to a panel of three judges from the national theater community. Applicant must have been a citizen or permanent resident of the US and a legal resident of the state of Minnesota for 6 months prior to the application deadline. (Residency must be maintained during fellowship year.) Applicant must have had a minimum of one work fully produced by a professional theater at the time of application. Deadline: February 1. Prize: $25,000 which can be used to support a wide variety of expenses, including writing time, artistic costs of residency at a theater or arts organization, travel and study, production or presentation.

McLAREN MEMORIAL COMEDY PLAYWRITING COMPETITION, Midland Community Theatre, 2000 W. Wadley, Midland TX 79705. (915)682-2544. Fax: (915)682-6136. E-mail: alatheajim@aol.com. Website: www.mctmidland.org. **Contact:** Alathea Blischke, McLaren co-chair. Estab. 1990. Offered annually for full-length and one-act comedies for adults, teens, or children. Work must not have received professional production. Deadline: December 1-January 31. Charges $10 fee/play. Prize: $300 for best full-length play; $100 for best one-act play; staged readings for 3 finalists.

MILL MOUNTAIN THEATRE NEW PLAY COMPETITION, Mill Mountain Theatre, Center in the Square, 1 Market Square, 2nd Floor, Roanoke VA 24011-1437. (540)342-5749. Fax: (540)342-5745. E-mail: outreach@millmountain.org. Website: www.millmountain.org. **Contact:** New Play Competition Coordinator. Estab. 1985. Offered annually for previously unpublished and unproduced plays by US residents, full-length for up to 10 cast members; musicals and solo pieces also accepted. Plays must be agent submitted—or have the recommendation of a director, literary manager, or dramaturg. Deadline: Submit between October 1, 2002, and January 1, 2003. Guidelines for SASE. Prize: $1,000, staged reading, and possible full production; travel stipend and housing for limited residency.

MOVING ARTS PREMIERE ONE-ACT COMPETITION, Moving Arts, 514 S. Spring St., Los Angeles CA 90013-2304. (213)622-8906. Fax: (213)622-8946. E-mail: treynichols@movingarts.org. Website: www.movingarts.org. **Contact:** Trey Nichols, literary director. Offered annually for unproduced one-act plays in the Los Angeles area and "is designed to foster the continued development of one-act plays." All playwrights are eligible except Moving Arts resident artists. Guidelines for SASE or by e-mail. Deadline: February 28 (postmark). Charges $10 fee/script. Prize: 1st Place: $200, plus a full production with a 4-8 week run. 2nd and 3rd Place: Program mention and possible production.

MUSICAL STAIRS, West Coast Ensemble, P.O. Box 38728, Los Angeles CA 90038. (323)876-9337. Fax: (323)876-8916. **Contact:** Les Hanson. Offered annually for unpublished writers "to nurture, support, and encourage musical creators." Permission to present the musical is granted if work is selected as finalist. Deadline: June 30. Prize: $500, and presentation of musical.

NANTUCKET SHORT PLAY COMPETITION AND FESTIVAL, Nantucket Theatrical Productions, Box 2177, Nantucket MA 02584. (508)228-5002. **Contact:** Jim Patrick, artistic director. Offered annually for unpublished plays to "seek the highest quality of playwriting distilled into a short-play format." Selected plays receive staged readings. Plays must be less than 40 pages. Deadline: January 1. Charges $10 fee. Prize: $200, plus staged readings.

NATIONAL AUDIO DRAMA SCRIPT COMPETITION, National Audio Theatre Festivals, 115 Dikeman St., Hempstead NY 11150. (516)483-8321. Fax: (516)538-7583. Website: www.natf.org. **Contact:** Sue Zizza. Offered annually for unpublished radio scripts. "NATF is particularly interested in stories that deserve to be told because they enlighten, intrigue, or simply make us laugh out loud. Contemporary scripts with strong female roles, multi-cultural casting, and diverse viewpoints will be favorably received." Preferred length is 25 minutes. Guidelines on website. Open to any writer. NATF will have the right to produce the scripts for the NATF Live Performance Workshop; however, NATF makes no commitment to produce any script. The authors will retain all other rights to their work. Deadline: November 15. Charges $25 fee (US currency only please). Prize: $800 split between 2-4 authors, and free workshop production participation.

NATIONAL CANADIAN ONE-ACT PLAYWRITING COMPETITION, Ottawa Little Theatre, 400 King Edward Ave., Ottawa, Ontario K1N 7M7, Canada. (613)233-8948. Fax: (613)233-8027. E-mail: olt@sympatico.ca. Website: www.o-l-t.com. **Contact:** Elizabeth Holden, office manager. Estab. 1913. Purpose is "to encourage literary and dramatic talent in Canada." Guidelines for #10 SASE with Canadian postage or #10 SAE with 1 IRC. Deadline: January-May. Prize: $1,000; $700; $500.

NATIONAL CHILDREN'S THEATRE FESTIVAL, Actors' Playhouse at the Miracle Theatre, 280 Miracle Mile, Coral Gables FL 33134. (305)444-9293. Fax: (305)444-4181. Website: www.actorsplayhouse.org. **Contact:** Earl Maulding. Offered annually for unpublished musicals for young audiences. Target age is between 5-12. Script length should be 45-60 minutes. Maximum of 8 actors to play any number of roles. Settings which lend themselves to simplified scenery. Bilingual (English/Spanish) scripts are welcomed. Call or visit website for guidelines. Open to any writer. Deadline: August 1. Charges $10 fee. Prize: 1st Place: Full production, $500.

NATIONAL LATINO PLAYWRITING AWARD, (formerly National Hispanic Playwriting Award), Arizona Theatre Co. in affiliation with Centro Cultural Mexicano, 40 E. 14th St., Tucson AZ 85701. (520)884-8210. Fax: (520)628-9129. E-mail: ERomero@aztheatreco.org. Website: www.aztheatreco.org. **Contact:** Elaine Romero, playwright-in-residence. Offered annually for unproduced (professionally), unpublished plays over 50 pages in length. "The plays may be in English, bilingual, or in Spanish (with English translation). The award recognizes exceptional full-length plays by Latino playwrights on any subject." Open to Latino playwrights currently residing in the US, its territories, and/or Mexico. Deadline: November 30. Guidelines for SASE. Prize: $1,000.

NATIONAL ONE-ACT PLAYWRITING COMPETITION, Little Theatre of Alexandria, 600 Wolfe St., Alexandria VA 22314. (703)683-5778. Fax: (703)683-1378. E-mail: ltlthtre@erols. **Contact:** Carolyn Winters, chairman. Estab. 1978. Offered annually to encourage original writing for theatre. Submissions must be original, unpublished, unproduced one-act stage plays. "We usually produce top 2 or 3 winners." Deadline: Submit scripts for year 2002 contest from January 1-May 31, 2002. Guidelines for SASE. Charges $20/play; 2 play limit. Prize: 1st Place: $350; 2nd Place: $250; 3rd Place: $150.

NATIONAL PLAYWRITING COMPETITION, (formerly Young Playwrights Festival), Young Playwrights, Inc., 306 W. 38th St., Suite 300, New York NY 10018. (212)307-1140. Fax: (212)307-1454. E-mail: writeaplay@aol.com. Website: youngplaywrights.org. **Contact:** Literary Department. Offered annually for stage plays of any length (no musicals, screenplays, or adaptations). Writers ages 18 or younger (as of deadline) are invited to send scripts. Annually. Deadline: December 1. Prize: Professional staged reading in off-Broadway theater.

NATIONAL TEN-MINUTE PLAY CONTEST, Actors Theatre of Louisville, 316 W. Main St., Louisville KY 40202-4218. (502)584-1265. E-mail: tpalmer@actorstheatre.org. Website: www.actorstheatre.org. **Contact:** Tanya Palmer, literary manager. Offered annually for previously (professionally) unproduced 10-minute plays (10 pages or less). "Entries must *not* have had an Equity or Equity-waiver production." One submission/playwright. Scripts are not returned. Please write or call for submission guidelines. Open to US residents. Deadline: December 1 (postmarked). Prize: $1,000.

NEW AMERICAN COMEDY WORKSHOP, Ukiah Players Theatre, 1041 Low Gap Rd., Ukiah CA 95482. (707)462-1210. Fax: (707)462-1790. E-mail: players@pacific.net. Website: ukiahplayerstheatre.org. **Contact:** Kate Magruder, community cultural development director. Offered every 2 years to playwrights seeking to develop their unproduced, full-length comedies into funnier, stronger scripts. Two scripts will be chosen for staged readings; 1 of these will be chosen for full production. Deadline: November 30 of odd-numbered years. Guidelines for SASE. Prize: Playwrights chosen for readings will receive a $25 royalty/performance. The playwright chosen for full production will receive a $50 royalty/performance, travel (up to $500) to Ukiah for a one-week workshop/rehearsal, lodging, and per diem.

[N] NEW CENTURY WRITER AWARDS (PLAYWRITING), New Century Writer, 32 Alfred St., Suite B, New Haven CT 06512-3927. (203)469-8824. Fax: (203)468-0333. E-mail: newcenturywriter@yahoo.com. Website: www.newcenturywriter.org. **Contact:** Jason Marchi, executive director. Offered annually to discover and encourage emerging writers of stage plays and musicals. All genres. Winners announced on website in December. Guidelines/entry free for the asking, no SASE required. All entrants receive a 1-year susbcription to *The Anvil*, an educational newsletter for writers. Open to all playwrights, both non-produced and those with a limited production history. Call if in doubt about your eligibility. New Century Writer also provides the annual Ray Bradbury Short Story Fellowship for 1 or 2 short story writers to attend the *Zoetrope* Short Story Writers' Workshop at Francis Ford Coppola's Blancaneaux Lodge in Belize, Central America (see the Ray Bradbury Short Story Fellowship listing for complete details). Deadline: July 31. Charges $30 entry fee. Prize: 1st Place: $2,000; 2nd Place: $1,000; 3rd Place: $500; 4th-10th Place: $200.

NEW CENTURY WRITER AWARDS (SCREENWRITING), 32 Alfred St., Suite B, New Haven CT 06512-3927. (203)469-8824. Fax: (203)468-0333. E-mail: newcenturywriter@yahoo.com. Website: www.newcenturywriter.org. **Contact:** Jason J. Marchi, executive director. Offered annually to discover and encourage emerging writers of screenplays, stage plays, TV scripts, TV movie scripts, and musicals. All genres. Winners announced on website in December. Guidelines/entry free for the asking. All entrants receive a 1-year subscription to *The Anvil*, an educational newsletter for writers. Open to all writers, both nonproduced and those with limited production history. Call if in doubt about your eligibility. New Century Writer also provides the annual Ray Bradbury Short Story Fellowship for 1 or 2 short story writers to attend the *Zoetrope* Short Story Writer's Workshop at Francis Ford Coppola's Blancaneaux Lodge in Belize, Central America (see the Ray Bradbury Short Story Fellowship listing for complete details). Deadline: July 31. Charges $30 entry fee. Prize: 1st Place: $3,000; 2nd Place: $1,500; 3rd Place: $500; 4th-10th Place: $200.

[N] NEW PLAYS STAGED READING CONTEST, TADA!, 120 W. 28th St., New York NY 10001. (212)627-1732. Fax: (212)243-6736. E-mail: tada@ziplink.net. Website: www.tadatheater.com. **Contact:** Janine Nina Trevens, contest director. Offered annually for unpublished and unproduced work to introduce the playwriting process to family audiences in a staged reading series featuring the winning entries. The cast must be predominantly children, the children are cast from the TADA! company, and adult actors will be hired. The plays must be appropriate for children and teenage audiences. Please send cover letter and play with SASE for return. If the play is a musical, include a tape of the music. No application form necessary. Deadline: Varies each year, usually in early spring/late winter. Guidelines for SASE. Prize: $100-500, and staged reading held in TADA!'s theater. Grand prize is a workshopped production. Open to any writer.

NEW VOICE SERIES, Remembrance Through the Performing Arts, P.O. Box 162446, Austin TX 78716. E-mail: RemPerArts@aol.com. **Contact:** Marla Dean Macdonald, director of new play development. Offered annually "to find talented Central Texas playwrights who are in the early stages of script development. We develop these scripts on the page through a Work-In-Progress production." Playwrights need to send script, bio, and a script-size SASE. Open to Central Texas playwrights only. Deadline: Ongoing. Prize: Free development of their play with our company and representation of their play to theaters nationally for world premieres.

NEW YORK CITY PUBLIC SCHOOL PLAYWRITING CONTEST, Young Playwrights, Inc., 306 W. 38th St., Suite 300, New York NY 10018. (212)307-1140. Fax: (212)307-1454. E-mail: writeaplay@aol.com. Website: youngplaywrights.org. **Contact:** Literary Department. Offered annually for plays by NYC public school students only. Deadline: April 1. Prize: Varies.

'THE NEXT STAGE' NEW PLAY READING FESTIVAL, The Cleveland Play House, P.O. Box 1989, Cleveland OH 44106-0189. Fax: (216)795-7005. E-mail: sgordon@clevelandplayhouse.com. Website: www.clevelandplayhouse.com. **Contact:** Seth Gordon, director of new play development. Offered annually for unpublished/unproduced submissions. " 'The Next Stage' is our annual new play reading series. Up to 6 writers are brought to our theater for 1 week of rehearsal/development. The plays are then given public staged readings, and at least 1 is chosen for a full production in the upcoming season." Deadline: Ongoing. Guidelines for SASE. Prize: Staged reading of play, fee, travel, and housing, consideration for full production. Writers sign a 3-month option for production of script.

DON AND GEE NICHOLL FELLOWSHIPS IN SCREENWRITING, Academy of Motion Picture Arts & Sciences, 8949 Wilshire Blvd., Beverly Hills CA 90211-1972. (310)247-3059. E-mail: nicholl@oscars.org. Website: www.oscars.org/nicholl. **Contact:** Greg Beal, program coordinator. Estab. 1985. Offered annually for unproduced screenplays to identify talented new screenwriters. Guidelines for SASE, available January 1-April 30. Recipients announced late October. Open to writers who have not earned more than $5,000 writing for films or TV. Deadline: May 1. Charges $30 fee. Prize: $30,000 in fellowships (up to 5/year).

OGLEBAY INSTITUTE TOWNGATE THEATRE PLAYWRITING CONTEST, Oglebay Institute, Stifel Fine Arts Center, 1330 National Rd., Wheeling WV 26003. (304)242-7700. Fax: (304)242-7747. Website: www.oionline.com. **Contact:** Kate H. Crosbie, director of performing arts. Estab. 1976. Offered annually for unpublished works. "All full-length *non-musical* plays that have never been professionally produced or published are eligible." Open to any writer. Deadline: January 1; winner announced May 31. Guidelines for SASE. Prize: Run of play and cash award.

ONE ACT MARATHON, Attic Theatre, 2245 W. 25th St., Los Angeles CA 90018. (323)734-8977. E-mail: AtticTheatre1@aol.com. Website: www.AtticTheatre.org. **Contact:** Literary Manager. Offered annually for unpublished work. Deadline: September 30. Guidelines for SASE. Charges $15. Prize: 1st Place: $200; 2nd Place: $100; 1st-3rd- place scripts will be produced. Acquires 6-month window for 1st-6th place entries for exclusive option.

OPUS MAGNUM DISCOVERY AWARD, Christopher Columbus Society, 433 N. Camden Dr., #600, Beverly Hills CA 90210. (310)288-1881. Fax: (310)288-0257. E-mail: awards@hollywoodawards.com. Website: screenwriters.com. **Contact:** Carlos de Abreu, president. Annual award to discover new authors with books/mss that can be optioned for features or TV movies. Judged by entertainment industry story analysts and producers. Deadline: December 1. Guidelines for SASE. Charges $75 fee. Prize: Option moneys to winner, up to $10,000.

MILDRED & ALBERT PANOWSKI PLAYWRITING AWARD, Forest A. Roberts Theatre, Northern Michigan University, Marquette MI 49855-5364. (906)227-2559. Fax: (906)227-2567. Website: www.nmu.edu/theatre. **Contact:** Lindsey Harman, award coordinator. Estab. 1977. Offered annually for unpublished, unproduced, full-length plays. Guidelines and application for SASE. Deadline: August 15-November 22 (due at office on the 22nd). Prize: $2,000, a fully-mounted production, and transportation to Marquette to serve as Artist-in-Residence the week of the show.

PEACE PLAYWRITING CONTEST, Goshen College, 1700 S. Main, Goshen IN 46526. (219)535-7393. Fax: (219)535-7660. E-mail: douglc@goshen.edu. **Contact:** Douglas L. Caskey, director of theater. Offered every 2 years for unpublished work dealing with social issues and other issues related to the broader theme of peace. Open to any writer. Deadline: December 31, 2003. Guidelines for SASE. Prize: 1st Place: $500, production, room and board to attend rehearsals, and/or production; 2nd Place: $100, possible production.

PERISHABLE THEATRE'S WOMEN'S PLAYWRITING FESTIVAL, P.O. Box 23132, Providence RI 02903. (401)331-2695. Fax: (401)331-7811. E-mail: info@perishable.org. Website: www.perishable.org. **Contact:** Vanessa Gilbert, associate artistic director. Offered annually for unproduced, one-act plays (up to 30 minutes in length when fully produced) to encourage women playwrights. Judged by reading committee, the festival director, and the artistic director of the theater. Open to women playwrights exclusively. Deadline: October 15. Guidelines for SASE. Charges $5 fee/playwright (limit 2 plays/playwright). Prize: $500 and travel to Providence.

PETERSON EMERGING PLAYWRIGHT COMPETITION, Catawba College Thearte Arts Department, 2300 W. Innes St., Salisbury NC 28144. (704)637-4440. Fax: (704)637-4207. E-mail: lfkessler@catawba.edu. Website: www.catawba.edu. **Contact:** Linda Kessler, theatre arts department administrative assistant. Offered annually for full-length unpublished work "to assist emerging playwrights in the development of new scripts, hopefully leading to professional production. Competition is open to all subject matter except children's plays. Playwrights may submit more than 1 entry." Open to any writer. Deadline: February 15. Guidelines for SASE. Prize: Production of the winning play at Catawba College; $2,000 cash award; transportation to and from Catawba College for workshop and performance; lodging and food while in residence; professional response to the performance of the play.

ROBERT J. PICKERING AWARD FOR PLAYWRIGHTING EXCELLENCE, Coldwater Community Theater, c/o 89 Division, Coldwater MI 49036. (517)279-7963. Fax: (517)279-8095. **Contact:** J. Richard Colbeck, committee chairperson. Estab. 1982. Previously unproduced monetarily. "To encourage playwrights to submit their work, to present a previously unproduced play in full production." Submit script with SASE. "We reserve the right to produce winning script." Deadline: End of year. Guidelines for SASE. Prize: 1st Place: $300; 2nd Place: $100; 3rd Place: $50.

PILGRIM PROJECT GRANTS, 156 Fifth, #400, New York NY 10010. (212)627-2288. Fax: (212)627-2184. E-mail: davida@firstthings.com. **Contact:** Davida Goldman. Grants for a reading, workshop production, or full production of plays that deal with questions of moral significance. Deadline: Ongoing. Guidelines for SASE. Prize: Grants of $1,000-7,000.

PLAYHOUSE ON THE SQUARE NEW PLAY COMPETITION, Playhouse on the Square, 51 S. Cooper, Memphis TN 38104. **Contact:** Jackie Nichols. Submissions required to be unproduced. Deadline: April 1. Guidelines for SASE. Prize: $500 and production.

PLAYWRIGHT DISCOVERY AWARD, (formerly Playwright Discovery Program), VSA Arts Connection, 1300 Connecticut Ave. NW, Suite 700, Washington DC 20036. (202)628-2800. Fax: (202)737-0725. E-mail: playwright@vsarts.org. Website: www.vsarts.org. **Contact:** Dani Fox, special events manager. Invites students with and without disabilities (grades 6-12) to submit a one-act play that documents the experience of living with a disability. Two plays will be selected for production at the John F. Kennedy Center for the Performing Arts. Deadline: April 15. Guidelines for SASE. Prize: Monetary award, and a trip to Washington D.C. to view the production or staged reading.

PRIME TIME TELEVISION COMPETITION, Austin Film Festival, 1604 Nueces, Austin TX 78701. (512)478-4795. E-mail: austinfilm@aol.com. Website: www.austinfilmfestival.com. **Contact:** BJ Burrow. Offered annually for unpublished work to discover talented television writers and introduce their work to production companies. Categories: Drama and Sitcom. Contest open to writers who do not earn a living writing for television or film. Deadline: June 15. Guidelines for SASE. Charges $25. Prize: $1,500 in each category.

PRINCESS GRACE AWARDS PLAYWRIGHT FELLOWSHIP, Princess Grace Foundation—USA, 150 E. 58th St., 21st Floor, New York NY 10155. (212)317-1470. Fax: (212)317-1473. E-mail: pgfusa@pgfusa.com. Website: www.pgfusa.com. **Contact:** Ms. Toby E. Boshak, executive director. Offered annually for unpublished, unproduced submissions to support playwright-through-residency program with New Dramatists, Inc., located in New York City. Entrants must be US citizens or have US status. Guidelines for SASE or on website. Deadline: March 31. Prize: $7,500, plus residency with New Dramatists, Inc., in New York City, and representation/publication by Samuel French, Inc.

PUTTIN' ON THE RITZ, ONE-ACT PLAY CONTEST, Puttin' On the Ritz, Inc., 915 White Horse Pike, Oaklyn NJ 08107. (856)858-5230. Fax: (856)858-0812. E-mail: srcoar@aol.com. Website: www.puttinontheritz.org. **Contact:** Stephen R. Coar, outreach director/new play festival director. Offered every other year "to encourage playwrights by the production of their new works. We especially encourage playwrights from the New Jersey/Philadelphia region." "We receive about 125 plays, and of those, produce 3 or 4." Plays that have been professionally produced will not be considered. "Plays that run 40 minutes or less preferred. Plays without a SASE will not be returned." Open to any writer. Now accepting plays for June of 2003. Deadline: January 31. Prize: Production of selected plays.

RICHARD RODGERS AWARDS IN MUSICAL THEATER, American Academy of Arts and Letters, 633 W. 155th St., New York NY 10032-7599. (212)368-5900. Fax: (212)491-4615. **Contact:** Lydia Kaim. Estab. 1978. The Richard Rodgers Awards subsidize full productions, studio productions, and staged readings by nonprofit theaters in New York City of works by composers and writers who are not already established in the field of musical theater. Authors must be citizens or permanent residents of the US. Guidelines and application for SASE. Deadline: November 1.

THE LOIS AND RICHARD ROSENTHAL NEW PLAY PRIZE, Cincinnati Playhouse in the Park, Box 6537, Cincinnati OH 45206-0537. (513)345-2242. Website: www.cincyplay.com. **Contact:** Literary Associate. Annual award for playwrights and musical playwrights. "The Lois and Richard Rosenthal New Play Prize was established in 1987 to encourage the development of new plays that are original, theatrical, strong in character and dialogue, and make a significant contribution to the literature of American theater. Residents of Cincinnati, the Rosenthals are committed to supporting arts organizations and social agencies that are innovative and that foster social change." Plays must be full-length in any style: comedy, drama, musical, etc. Translations, adaptations, individual one-acts, and any play previously submitted for the Rosenthal Prize, are not eligible. Collaborations are welcome, in which case prize benefits are shared. Plays must be unpublished prior to submission and may not have received a full-scale, professional production. Plays that have had a workshop, reading, or nonprofessional production are still eligible. Playwrights with past production experience are especially encouraged to submit new work. Submit a 2-page maximum abstract of the play including title, character breakdown, story synopsis, and playwright information (bio or résumé). Also include up to 5 pages of sample dialogue. If submitting a musical, please include a tape or CD of selections from the score. All abstracts and dialogue samples will be read. From these, selected mss will be solicited. Do not send a ms with, or instead of, the abstract. Unsolicited mss will not be read. Submitted materials, including tapes and CDs,will be returned only if a SASE, with adequate postage, is provided. Only 1 submission/playwright each year. Deadline: July 1-December 31. Prize: A full production at Cincinnati Playhouse in the Park as part of the annual season and regional and national promotion; and $10,000 award plus travel and residency expenses for the Cincinnati rehearsal period.

THE SCREENWRITER'S PROJECT, Cyclone Entertainment Group/Cyclone Productions, P.O. Box 148849, Chicago IL 60614-8849. (773)665-7600. Fax: (773)665-7660. E-mail: cycprod@aol.com or cyclone@cyclone-entertainment.com. Website: www.cyclone-entertainment.com. **Contact:** Lee Alan, director. Offered annually to give both experienced and first-time writers the opportunity to begin a career as a screenwriter. Cyclone Productions, Inc. intends to produce the finest of submissions to The Screenwriter's Project. Deadline: August 1. Guidelines for SASE. Charges $40 fee for July 1 deadline; $45 fee for August 1 deadline; $50 fee for September 1 deadline. Prize: Three $5,000 grants.

SIENA COLLEGE INTERNATIONAL PLAYWRIGHTS COMPETITION, Siena College Theatre Program, 515 Loudon Rd., Loudonville NY 12211-1462. (518)783-2381. Fax: (518)783-2381. E-mail: maciag@siena.edu. Website: www.siena.edu/theatre. **Contact:** Gary Maciag, director of theatre. Offered every 2 years for unpublished plays "to allow students to explore production collaboration with the playwright. In addition, it provides the playwright an important development opportunity. Plays should be previously unproduced, unpublished, full-length, nonmusicals and free of copyright and royalty restrictions. Plays should require unit set or minimal changes and be suitable for a college-age cast of 3-10. There is a required 4-6 week residency." Guidelines for SASE. Guidelines are available after November 1 in odd-numbered years. Winning playwright must agree that the Siena production will be the world premiere of the play. Deadline: February 1-June 30 in even-numbered years. Prize: $2,000 honorarium; up to $2,000 to cover expenses for required residency; full production of winning script.

DOROTHY SILVER PLAYWRITING COMPETITION, The Eugene S. & Blanche R. Halle Theatre of the Jewish Community Center, 3505 Mayfield Rd., Cleveland Heights OH 44118. (216)382-4000, ext. 274. Fax: (216)382-5401. E-mail: halletheatre@clevejcc.org. **Contact:** Amy Kenerup, administrative director. Estab. 1948. All entries must be original works, not previously produced, suitable for a full-length presentation; directly concerned with the Jewish experience. Deadline: June 15. Prize: Cash award, plus staged reading.

SOUTHEASTERN THEATRE CONFERENCE NEW PLAY PROJECT, P.O. Box 9868, Greensboro NC 27429. (336)272-3645. Fax: (336)272-8810. E-mail: setc@mindspring.com. Website: www.setc.org. **Contact:** Susan Sharp. Offered annually for the discovery, development, and publicizing of worthy new unproduced plays and playwrights. Eligibility limited to members of 10 state SETC Region: AL, FL, GA, KY, MS, NC, SC, TN, VA, or WV. Bound full-length or 2 related one-acts under single cover (one submission only). No musicals or children's plays. Deadline: March 1-June 1. Guidelines for SASE. Prize: $1,000, staged reading at SETC Convention, expenses paid trip to convention, and preferred consideration for National Playwrights Conference.

SOUTHERN APPALACHIAN PLAYWRIGHTS CONFERENCE, Southern Appalachian Repertory Theatre, P.O. Box 1720, Mars Hill NC 28754. (828)689-1384. Fax: (828)689-1272. E-mail: SART@mhc.edu. Website: www.sartheatre.com. **Contact:** Deborah Compton, managing director. Offered annually for unpublished, unproduced plays to promote the development of new plays. All plays are considered for later production with honorarium provided for the playwright. Deadline: October 31 (postmark). Guidelines for SASE. Prize: 4-5 playwrights are invited for staged readings in March or April, room and board provided.

SOUTHERN PLAYWRIGHTS COMPETITION, Jacksonville State University, 700 Pelham Rd. N., Jacksonville AL 36265-1602. (256)782-5414. Fax: (256)782-5441. E-mail: swhitton@jsucc.jsu.edu. Website: www.jsu.edu/depart/english/southpla.htm. **Contact:** Steven J. Whitton. Estab. 1988. Offered annually to identify and encourage the best of Southern playwriting. Playwrights must be a native or resident of AL, AR, FL, GA, KY, LA, MO, NC, SC, TN, TX, VA, or WV. Deadline: February 15. Guidelines for SASE. Prize: $1,000, and production of the play.

STANLEY DRAMA AWARD, Department of Theatre, Wagner College, One Campus Rd., Staten Island NY 10301. (718)390-3157. Fax: (718)390-3323. **Contact:** Tanya Sweet, director. Offered for original full-length stage plays, musicals, or one-act play sequences that have not been professionally produced or received trade book publication. Deadline: October 1. Guidelines for SASE. Prize: $2,000.

TCG/METLIFE FOUNDATION EXTENDED COLLABORATION GRANTS, (formerly TCG/Metropolitan Life Foundation Extended Collaboration Grants), Theatre Communications Group, Inc., 355 Lexington Ave., New York NY 10017-6603. (212)697-5230. Fax: (212)983-4847. E-mail: grants@tcg.org. Website: www.tcg.org. **Contact:** Emilya Cachapero, director of artistic programs. Program is "designed to allow writers to work collaboratively with other artists for a period beyond the sponsoring theatre's normal preproduction and rehearsal schedule. Grants of $5,500 will be awarded 2 times in 2002. Only artistic leaders of TCG constituent member theatres can apply on behalf of the writer. Applications will be mailed to TCG constituent theatres."

TEXAS PLAYWRIGHT'S DIVISION, Stages Repertory Theatre, 3201 Allen Pkwy., Suite 101, Houston TX 77019. (713)527-0220. Fax: (713)527-8669. Website: www.stagestheatre.com. **Contact:** Chris Jimmerson, artistic associate. Offered annually to provide an outlet for unpublished Texas playwrights. Guidelines for SASE or on website. Writer must be a current or previous resident of Texas, or the play must be set in Texas or have a Texas theme. Deadline: October 1-February 15. Prize: A reading by professional actors and prizes awarded.

THEATRE BC'S ANNUAL CANADIAN NATIONAL PLAYWRITING COMPETITION, Theatre BC, P.O. Box 2031, Nanaimo, British Columbia V9R 6X6, Canada. (250)714-0203. Fax: (250)714-0213. E-mail: pwc@theatrebc.org. Website: www.theatrebc.org. **Contact:** Robb Mowbray, executive director. Offered annually to unpublished plays "to promote the development and production of previously unproduced new plays (no musicals) at all levels of theater. Categories: Full-Length (2 acts or longer); One-Act (less than 60 minutes); and an open Special Merit (juror's discretion). Guidelines for SASE or on website. Winners are also invited to New Play Festival: 18 hours with a professional dramaturg, registrant actors, and a public reading in Kamloops (every spring). Production and publishing rights remain with the playwright. Open to Canadian residents. All submissions are made under pseudonyms. E-mail inquiries welcome. Deadline: Fourth Monday in July. Charges $35/entry, and optional $25 for written critique. Prize: Full-Length: $1,500; One-Act: $1,000; Special Merit: $750.

THEATRE CONSPIRACY ANNUAL NEW PLAY CONTEST, Theatre Conspiracy, 10091 McGregor Blvd., Ft. Myers FL 33919. (941)936-3239. Fax: (941)936-0510. E-mail: theatreconspiracy@prodigy.net. **Contact:** Bill Taylor, award director. Offered annually for unpublished full-length plays with 8 or less characters and simple production demands. Open to any writer. Deadline: November 30, 2002. Guidelines for SASE. Charges $5 fee. Prize: $600, and full production.

THEATREFEST REGIONAL PLAYWRITING CONTEST, Theatrefest, Montclair State University, Upper Montclair NJ 07043. (973)655-7071. Fax: (973)655-5335. E-mail: kellyl@mail.montclair.edu. Website: www.montclair.edu. **Contact:** John Wooten, artistic director. Offered annually for unpublished work to encourage and nurture the work of American dramatists. Open to any writer in the tri-state area (New Jersey, New York, Connecticut). Guidelines are available September through January, send a SASE. Deadline: January 7. Prize: 1st Place: $1,500 and equity production; Runners-up (2): $500. Theatrefest has option to re-option play after production at Theatrefest.

THUNDERBIRD FILMS SCREENPLAY COMPETITION, Thunderbird Films, 214 Riverside Dr. #112, New York NY 10025. (212)352-4498. Website: home.att.net/thunderbirdfilms. **Contact:** Eric Stannard. Offered annually for unpublished work to encourage, promote, and reward writers of original, well-crafted screenplays. Open to any writer. Deadline: Varies. Guidelines for SASE. Charges $40 fee. Prize: $1,000 and possible option by Thunderbird Films.

TRUSTUS PLAYWRIGHTS' FESTIVAL, Trustus Theatre, Box 11721, Columbia SC 29211-1721. (803)254-9732. Fax: (803)771-9153. E-mail: trustus@trustus.org. Website: www.trustus.org. **Contact:** Jon Tuttle, literary manager. Offered annually for professionally unproduced full-length plays; cast limit of 8; prefer challenging, innovative dramas and comedies; no musicals, plays for young audiences, or "hillbilly" southern shows. Guidelines and application for SASE. Deadline: March 1; no submissions before January 1. Prize: Public staged-reading and $250, followed after a 1-year development period by full production, $500, plus travel/accommodations to attend opening.

UBC'S CREATIVE WRITING RESIDENCY PRIZE IN STAGEPLAY, (formerly University of British Columbia's Creative Writing Residency in Stageplay), *PRISM International* and the Department of Theatre, Film, and Creative Writing at the University of British Columbia, c/o PRISM International, Creative Writing Program, UBC, Buch. E462-1866 Main Mall, Vancouver, British Columbia V6T 1Z1, Canada. Website: www.creativewriting.ubc.ca/resprize. UBC's Creative Writing Residency Prize in Stageplay is the result of a cooperative venture between the literary magazine *PRISM International* and the Department of Theatre, Film, and Creative Writing at the University of British Columbia. The prize will be awarded tri-annually. Plays should be original, previously unproduced, with 2 or more acts, and have a running time of at least 75, and no more than 120, minutes. Scripts should be in stageplay format and in English. Entries (with entry fee) will be accepted beginning October 1, 2002; the postmark deadline for entries is March 31, 2003. The winner will be announced October 1, 2003. For complete rules and entry guidelines, visit the official website: www.creativewriting.ubc.ca/resprize. Prize: $10,000 (Canadian), plus expenses for a 1-month residency at the University, during which time, the winning playwright will be available for consultation with students. The winning play will be published as part of *PRISM*'s regular volume year, and as a separate book publication. The theater program at UBC has an option to produce the winning play as part of their regular season at the Freddie Wood Theatre, The Chan Centre for the Performing Arts, or in co-production with a local theater company.

UNICORN THEATRE NEW PLAY DEVELOPMENT, Unicorn Theatre, 3828 Main St., Kansas City MO 64111. (816)531-7529, ext. 18. Fax: (816)531-0421. Website: www.unicorntheatre.org. **Contact:** Herman Wilson, literary assistant. Offered annually to encourage and assist the development of an unpublished and unproduced play. Acquires 2% subsidiary rights of future productions for a 5-year period. Deadline: Ongoing. Guidelines for SASE. Prize: $1,000 and production.

VERMONT PLAYWRIGHT'S AWARD, The Valley Players, P.O. Box 441, Waitsfield VT 05673. (802)496-3751. E-mail: valleyplayers@madriver.com. Website: www.valleyplayers.com. **Contact:** Jennifer Howard, chair. Offered annually for unpublished, nonmusical, full-length play suitable for production by a community theater group to encourage development of playwrights in Vermont, New Hampshire, and Maine. Deadline: February 1. Prize: $1,000.

VSA ARTS PLAYWRIGHT DISCOVERY AWARD, VSA arts, John F. Kennedy Center for the Performing Arts, 1300 Connecticut Ave. NW, Suite 700, Washington DC 20036. (202)628-2800. Fax: (202)737-0725. E-mail: playwright@vsarts.org. Website: www.vsarts.org. **Contact:** Dani Fox, events manager. Offered annually for unpublished work. "Students grades 6-12 are invited to submit an original one-act script that examines the experience of living with a disability. The award challenges student writers with and without disabilities to create a one-act script about their own life, or about experiences in the life of another person or fictional character." Authors must be US citizens or permanent residents of the US. Guidelines for SASE, by e-mail, or on website. Deadline: April 15. Prize: Monetary award along with an expense-paid trip to the Kennedy Center in Washington DC to see their scripts performed live.

WEST COAST ENSEMBLE FULL-PLAY COMPETITION, West Coast Ensemble, P.O. Box 38728, Los Angeles CA 90038. (323)876-9337. Fax: (323)876-8916. **Contact:** Les Hanson, artistic director. Estab. 1982. Offered annually for unpublished plays in Southern California. No musicals or children's plays for full-play competition. No restrictions on subject matter. Deadline: December 31.

JACKIE WHITE MEMORIAL NATIONAL CHILDREN'S PLAYWRITING CONTEST, Columbia Entertainment Co., 309 Parkade, Columbia MO 65202. (573)874-5628. **Contact:** Betsy Phillips, director. Offered annually for unpublished plays. "Searching for good scripts suitable for audiences of all ages to be performed by the 25-40 students, grade 6-9, in our theater school." Deadline: June 1. Guidelines for SASE. Charges $10 fee. Prize: $250, full production and travel expenses to see production; company reserves the right to grant prize money without production. All entrants receive written evaluation.

WICHITA STATE UNIVERSITY PLAYWRITING CONTEST, University Theatre, Wichita State University, Wichita KS 67260-0153. (316)978-3360. Fax: (316)978-3202. E-mail: bela.kiralytalri@wichita.edu. Website: www.finearts.twsu.edu/performing/theatre.asp. **Contact:** Bela Kiralyfalvi. Estab. 1974. Offered for unpublished, unproduced full-length or 2-3 short plays of at least 90 minutes playing time. No musicals or children's plays. Contestants must be graduate or undergraduate students in a US college or university. Deadline: February 15. Guidelines for SASE. Prize: Production of winning play (ACTF), and expenses-paid trip for playwright to see final rehearsals and/or performances.

YEAR END SERIES (YES) NEW PLAY FESTIVAL, Department of Theatre, Nunn Dr., Northern Kentucky University, Highland Heights KY 41099-1007. (859)572-6362. Fax: (859)572-6057. E-mail: forman@nku.edu. **Contact:** Sandra Forman, project director. Receives submissions from May 1-October 31 in even-numbered years for the Festivals which occur in April of odd-numbered years. Open to all writers. Deadline: October 31. Guidelines for SASE. Prize: $500, and an expense-paid visit to Northern Kentucky University to see the play produced.

ANNA ZORNIO MEMORIAL CHILDREN'S THEATRE PLAYWRIGHTING COMPETITION, University of New Hampshire, Dept. of Theatre and Dance, PCAC, 30 College Rd., Durham NH 03824-3538. (603)862-2919. Fax: (603)862-0298. E-mail: mike.wood@unh.edu. Website: www.unh.edu/theatre-dance. **Contact:** Michael Wood. Offered every 4 years for unpublished well-written plays or musicals appropriate for young audiences with a maximum length of 60 minutes. Guidelines and entry forms for SASE. May submit more than 1 play, but not more than 3. Open to all playwrights in US and Canada. All ages are invited to participate. Deadline: September 1, 2004. Prize: $1,000 and play produced and underwritten as part of the season by the UNH Department of Theatre and Dance. Winner will be notified in November 2004.

Journalism

N **AAAS SCIENCE JOURNALISM AWARDS**, American Association for the Advancement of Science, 1333 H St. NW, Washington DC 20005. (202)326-6440. Fax: (202)789-0455. E-mail: tayers@aaas.org. Website: www.aaas.org. Offered annually for previously published work July 1-June 30 to reward excellence in reporting on science and its applications in daily newspapers with circulation over 100,000; newspapers with circulation under 100,000; general circulation magazines; radio; television and online." Sponsored by the Whitaker Foundation. Deadline: August 1. Prize: $2,500, plaque, trip to AAAS Annual Meeting.

THE AMERICAN LEGION FOURTH ESTATE AWARD, The American Legion, 700 N. Pennsylvania, Indianapolis IN 46206. (317)630-1253. Fax: (317)630-1368. E-mail: PR@legion.org. Website: www.legion.org. Offered annually for journalistic works published the previous calendar year. "Subject matter must deal with a topic or issue of national interest or concern. Entry must include cover letter explaining entry, and any documention or evidence of the entry's impact on the community, state, or nation. No printed entry form." Guidelines for SASE or on website. Judged by a volunteer panel of 4 practicing print or broadcast journalists and/or educators. Judges submit their recommendation to the National Public Relations Commission for final approval. Deadline: January 31. Prize: $2,000 stipend to defray expenses of recipient accepting the award at The American Legion National Convention in September.

AMY WRITING AWARDS, The Amy Foundation, P.O. Box 16091, Lansing MI 48901. (517)323-6233. Fax: (517)323-7293. E-mail: amyfoundtn@aol.com. Website: www.amyfound.org. **Contact:** James Russell, president. Estab. 1985. Offered annually for nonfiction articles containing scripture published in the previous calendar year in the secular media. Deadline: January 31. Prize: $10,000; $5,000; $4,000; $3,000; $2,000; and 10 prizes of $1,000.

AVENTIS PASTEUR MEDAL FOR EXCELLENCE IN HEALTH RESEARCH JOURNALISM, Canadians for Health Research, P.O. Box 126, Westmount, Quebec H3Z 2T1, Canada. (514)398-7478. Fax: (514)398-8361. E-mail: info@chrcrm.org. Website: www.chrcrm.org. **Contact:** Linda Bazinet. Offered annually for work published the previous calendar year in Canadian newspapers or magazines. Applicants must have demonstrated an interest and effort in reporting health research issues within Canada. Guidelines for SASE or on website. Deadline: February. Prize: $2,500, and a medal. The winner's name also appears on a permanent plaque at the Canadian Medical Hall of Fame in London, Ontario.

ERIK BARNOUW AWARD, Organization of American Historians, 112 N. Bryan Ave., Bloomington IN 47408-4199. (812)855-9852. Fax: (812)855-0696. E-mail: awards@oah.org. Website: www.oah.org. **Contact:** Kara Hamm. One or 2 awards are given annually in recognition of outstanding reporting or programming on network or cable television, or in documentary film, concerned with American history, the study of American history, and/or the promotion of history. Entries must have been released the year of the contest. Guidelines available on website. Deadline: December 1. Prize: Certificate.

THE WHITMAN BASSOW AWARD, Overseas Press Club of America, 40 W. 45th St., New York NY 10036. (212)626-9220. Fax: (212)626-9210. Website: www.opcofamerica.org. **Contact:** Sonya Fry, executive director. Offered annually for best reporting in any medium on international environmental issues. Work must be published by US-based publications or broadcast. Deadline: End of January. Charges $125 fee. Prize: $1,000, and certificate.

MIKE BERGER AWARD, Columbia University Graduate School of Journalism, 2950 Broadway, New York NY 10027-7004. (212)854-5047. Fax: (212)854-3148. E-mail: ja5@columbia.edu. Website: www.jrn.columbia.edu. **Contact:** Jonnet S. Abeles, assistant dean for public affairs. Offered annually honoring "human interest reporting about the daily life of New York City in the traditions of the late Meyer 'Mike' Berger. All newspaper reporters whose beat is New York City, whether they report for dailies, weeklies, or monthlies, are eligible." Deadline: February 15. Guidelines for SASE. Prize: Cash prize.

THE WORTH BINGHAM PRIZE, The Worth Bingham Memorial Fund, 1616 H St. NW, 3rd Floor, Washington DC 20006. (202)737-3700. Fax: (202)737-0530. E-mail: susan@icfj.org. **Contact:** Susan Talaly, project director. Offered annually to articles published during the year of the award. "The Prize honors newspaper or magazine investigative reporting of stories of national significance where the public interest is being ill-served. Entries may include a single story, a related series of stories, or up to 3 unrelated stories. Please contact us for guidelines and entry form." Deadline: January 3. Guidelines for SASE. Prize: $10,000.

NICHOLAS BLAKE FOREIGN FREE-LANCE REPORTING GRANT, Family of Nicholas Blake, Nicholas Blake Grant Program, 1500A Lafayette Rd., Box 320, Portsmouth NH 03801. Estab. 2001. Contest offered annually for material published between January 1, 2001-December 31, 2002. The purpose of the grant program is to support current freelance print journalists who specialize in foreign reporting on national (or significant regional) political or armed conflicts within foreign countries. The grant program was created in honor of Nicholas C. Blake, an American freelance journalist who died in 1985 while pursuing a story on the Guatemalan civil war. The grant program seeks to recognize that freelance foreign reporting is an important but under-emphasized branch of print journalism and to reward high-quality, innovative foreign reporting by these journalists. The program is intended to recognize the difficult conditions under which many freelance foreign print reporters work, and to foster their important role in foreign reporting by providing them needed financial support. An additional goal is to assist in the career development of these individuals, whether it is freelance reporting or as foreign correspondents with news organizations. These guidelines are the sole basis for a journalist to determine their entry. Deadline: September 1-December 31, 2002. Prize: $5,000 grant.

HEYWOOD BROUN AWARD, The Newspaper Guild-CWA, 501 Third St. NW, Washington DC 20001-2797. (202)434-7173. Fax: (202)434-1472. E-mail: azipser@cwa-union.org. Website: www.newsguild.org. **Contact:** Andy Zipser. Offered annually for works published the previous year. "This annual competition is intended to encourage and recognize individual journalistic achievement by members of the working media, particularly if it helps right a wrong or correct an injustice. First consideration will be given to entries on behalf of individuals or teams of no more than 2." Deadline: Last Friday in January. Guidelines for SASE. Prize: $5,000, and plaque.

HARRY CHAPIN MEDIA AWARDS, World Hunger Year, 505 Eighth Ave., Suite 2100, New York NY 10018-6582. (212)629-8850 ext. 122. Fax: (212)465-9274. E-mail: media@worldhungeryear.org. Website: www.worldhungeryear.org. **Contact:** Lisa Ann Batitto. Estab. 1982. Open to works published the previous calendar year. Critical issues of domestic and world hunger, poverty and development (newspaper, periodical, TV, radio, photojournalism, books). Deadline: mid-January. Guidelines for SASE. Charges $25 for 1 entry, $40 for 2 entries or $50 for 3-5 entries. Prize: Several prizes from $1,000-2,500.

CONGRESSIONAL FELLOWSHIP PROGRAM, American Political Science Association, 1527 New Hampshire Ave. NW, Washington DC 20036-1206. (202)483-2512. Fax: (202)483-2657. E-mail: amdonald@apsanet.org. Website: www.apsanet.org/about/CFP/. **Contact:** Allison MacDonald. Offered annually for professional journalists who have 2-10 years of full-time professional experience in newspaper, magazine, radio, or television reporting at time of application to learn more about the legislative process through direct participation. Visit our website for deadlines. Open to journalists and scholars. Prize: $38,000 and travel allowance for 3 weeks' orientation and legislation aide assignments December-August.

FREEDOM OF THE PRESS AWARD, National Press Club, General Manager's Office, National Press Club, National Press Bldg., Washington DC 20045. (202)662-7532. Fax: (202)662-7512. E-mail: jbooze@npcpress.org. Website: npc.press.org. **Contact:** Joann Booze. Offered annually "to recognize members of the news media who have, through the publishing or broadcasting of news, promoted or helped to protect the freedom of the press" during the previous calendar year. Categories: A US journalist or team for work published or broadcast in the US; a foreign journalist or team for work published or broadcast in their home country. Guidelines on website. Open to professional journalists. Deadline: April 1. Prize: $1,000 in each category.

THE GREAT AMERICAN TENNIS WRITING AWARDS, Tennis Week, 15 Elm Place, Rye NY 10580. (914)967-4890. Fax: (914)967-8178. E-mail: tennisweek@tennisweek.com. Website: www.tennisweek.com. **Contact:** Heather Holland, managing editor. Estab. 1974. Category 1: Unpublished ms by an aspiring journalist with no previous national byline. Category 2: Unpublished ms by a non-tennis journalist. Category 3: Unpublished ms by a tennis journalist. Categories 4-6: Published tennis-related articles and book award. Deadline: December 15.

O. HENRY AWARD, The Texas Institute of Letters, Southwest Texas State University, San Marcos TX 78666. (512)245-2428. Fax: (512)245-7462. E-mail: mb13@swt.edu. Website: www.english.swt.edu/css/til/rules.htm. **Contact:** Mark Busby, secretary. Offered annually for work published January 1-December 31 of previous year to recognize the best-written work of journalism appearing in a magazine or weekly newspaper. Judged by a panel chosen by the TIL Council. Writer must have been born in Texas, have lived in Texas for at least two consecutive years at some time, or the subject matter of the work should be associated with Texas. Deadline: January 3. Guidelines for SASE. Prize: $1,000.

ICIJ AWARD FOR OUTSTANDING INTERNATIONAL INVESTIGATIVE REPORTING, International Consortium of Investigative Journalists, The Center for Public Integrity, 910 17th St. NW, 7th Floor, Washington DC 20006. (202)466-1300. Fax: (202)466-1101. E-mail: info@icij.org. Website: www.icij.org. **Contact:** Laura Peterson, reporter/researcher. Offered annually for stories published between June 1, 2001, and June 1, 2002. Works produced in print, broadcast, and online media are eligible; books are not eligible. Work must be on a transnational topic of world significance. Guidelines for SASE or on website. Deadline: July 15, 2002. Prize: 1st Place: $20,000; up to 5 finalist awards of $1,000 each.

THE IOWA AWARD/THE TIM McGINNIS AWARD, *The Iowa Review*, 308 EPB, University of Iowa, Iowa City IA 52242. (319)335-0462. E-mail: iowa-review@uiowa.edu. Website: www.uiowa.edu/~iareview. **Contact:** David Hamilton. Offered annually for work already published in our magazine, usually within the previous year. The Iowa Award is a judge's choice of the best work of the year. The McGinnis Award is the editors' choice of a work that usually expresses an off-beat and (we hope) sophisticated sense of humor. Guidelines for SASE or on website. No entry form. Prize: $1,000 for Iowa Award; $500 for McGinnis Award.

DONALD E. KEYHOE JOURNALISM AWARD, Fund for UFO Research, P.O. Box 20815, Alexandria VA 22320-1815. (703)684-6032. Fax: (703)684-6032. E-mail: fufor@fufor.org. Website: www.fufor.com. **Contact:** Don Berliner, chairman. Estab. 1979. Offered annually for the best article or story published or broadcast in a newspaper, magazine, TV, or radio news outlet during the previous calendar year. Prize: Separate awards for print and broadcast media; also makes unscheduled cash awards for published works on UFO phenomena research or public education.

LIVINGSTON AWARDS FOR YOUNG JOURNALISTS, Mollie Parnis Livingston Foundation, Wallace House, 620 Oxford, Ann Arbor MI 48104. (734)998-7575. Fax: (734)998-7979. E-mail: LivingstonAwards@umich.edu. Website: www.livawards.org. **Contact:** Charles Eisendrath. Offered annually for journalism published January 1-December 31 the previous year to recognize and further develop the abilities of young journalists. Includes print, online, and broadcast. Guidelines on website. Judges include Mike Wallace, Ellen Goodman, and Tom Brokaw. Open to journalists who are 34 years or younger as of December 31 of previous year and whose work appears in US-controlled print or broadcast media. Prize: (3)$10,000: 1 each for local reporting, national reporting, and international reporting.

FELIX MORLEY JOURNALISM COMPETITION, Institute for Humane Studies, 3301 N. Fairfax Dr., Suite 440, Arlington VA 22201-4432. (800)697-8799. Fax: (703)993-4890. E-mail: dalban@gmu.edu. Website: www.theihs.org/morley. **Contact:** Dan Alban. Offered annually for nonfiction published July 1, 2001-November 29, 2002, to reward young writers who effectively address individual rights and free markets in their work. Writers must be either full-time students or under age 25 as of the November 29 deadline. Prize: 1st Place: $2,500; 2nd Place: $1,000; 3rd Place: $750; and $250 to several runners-up.

FRANK LUTHER MOTT-KAPPA TAU ALPHA RESEARCH AWARD IN JOURNALISM, University of Missouri School of Journalism, 120 Neff Hall, Columbia MO 65211. (573)882-7685. E-mail: ktahq@showme.missouri.edu. Website: www.missouri.edu/~KTAHQ. **Contact:** Dr. Keith Sanders, executive director, Kappa Tau Alpha. Offered annually for best researched book in mass communication. Submit 6 copies; no forms required. Deadline: December 9. Prize: $1,000.

NATIONAL MAGAZINE AWARDS, National Magazine Awards Foundation, 109 Vanderhoof Ave., Suite 207, Toronto, Ontario M4G 2H7, Canada. (416)422-1358. Fax: (416)422-3762. E-mail: nmaf@interlog.com. Website: www.nmaf.net. **Contact:** Pat Kendall. Offered annually for work by Canadian citizens or landed immigrants published in a Canadian magazine during the previous calendar year. Awards presented for writers, art directors, illustrators and photographers in written and visual categories. Deadline: early January. Charges $50 per entry. Prize: Gold, Silver, Honorable Mention.

NATIONAL PRESS CLUB JOSEPH D. RYLE AWARD FOR EXCELLENCE IN WRITING ON THE PROBLEMS OF GERIATRICS, National Press Club, General Manager's Office, National Press Club, National Press Bldg., Washington DC 20045. (202)662-7532. Fax: (202)662-7512. Website: npc.press.org. **Contact:** Joann Booze. Offered annually for work published in the previous year. This award emphasizes excellence and objectivity in coverage of the problems faced by the elderly. Guidelines on website. Open to professional print journalists. Deadline: April 1. Prize: $2,000.

NATIONAL PRESS CLUB SANDY HUME MEMORIAL AWARD FOR EXCELLENCE IN POLITICAL JOURNALISM, National Press Club, General Manager's Office, National Press Club, National Press Bldg., Washington DC 20045. (202)662-7532. Fax: (202)662-7512. E-mail: jbooze@npcpress.org. Website: npc.press.org. **Contact:** Joann Booze. Offered annually for work published in the previous calendar year. "This award honors excellence and objectivity in political coverage by reporters 34 years old or younger. Named in memory of Sandy Hume, the reporter for *The Hill* who broke the story of the aborted 1997 coup against House Speaker Newt Gingrich, this prize can be awarded for a single story of great distinction or for continuing coverage of 1 political topic." Guidelines on website. Open to professional journalists 34 or younger. Deadline: April 1. Prize: $1,000.

ALICIA PATTERSON JOURNALISM FELLOWSHIP, Alicia Patterson Foundation, 1730 Pennsylvania Ave. NW, Suite 850, Washington DC 20006. (202)393-5995. Fax: (301)951-8512. E-mail: info@aliciapatterson.org. Website: www.aliciapatterson.org. **Contact:** Margaret Engel. Offered annually for previously published submissions to give 8-10 fulltime print journalists or photojournalists a year of in-depth research and reporting. Applicants must have 5 years of professional print journalism experience and be US citizens. Fellows write 4 magazine-length pieces for the *Alicia Patterson Reporter*, a quarterly magazine, during their fellowship year. Fellows must take a year's leave from their jobs, but may do other freelance articles during the year. Write, call, fax, or check website for applications. Deadline: October 1. Prize: $35,000 stipend for calendar year.

PRINT MEDIA AWARD, International Reading Association, P.O. Box 8139, Newark DE 19714-8139. (302)731-1600, ext. 293. Fax: (302)731-1057. E-mail: jbutler@reading.org. Website: www.reading.org. **Contact:** Janet Butler. Offered annually for journalism published January 1-December 31 to recognize outstanding reporting in newspapers, magazines, and wire services. Open to professional journalists. Deadline: January 15. Prize: Awards certificate, announced at annual convention.

THE MADELINE DANE ROSS AWARD, Overseas Press Club of America, 40 W. 45th St., New York NY 10036. (212)626-9220. Fax: (212)626-9210. E-mail: sonya@opcofamerica.org. Website: www.opcofamerica.org. **Contact:** Sonya Fry, executive director. Offered annually for best international reporting in any medium showing a concern for the human condition. Work must be published by US-based publications or broadcast. Deadline: Late January; date changes each year. Charges $100 fee. Prize: $1,000, and certificate.

SCIENCE IN SOCIETY AWARD, National Association of Science Writers, Inc., P.O. Box 294, Greenlawn NY 11740. (516)757-5564. E-mail: diane@nasw.org. Website: www.nasw.org. **Contact:** Diane McGurgan. Offered annually for investigative or interpretive reporting about the sciences and their impact for good and bad. Six categories: Newspaper, magazine, television, radio, book, and Internet. Material may be a single article or broadcast or a series. Works must have been first published or broadcast in North America between June 1, 2001, and May 31, 2002; books must have a 2001 copyright date and may have been published any time that year. Deadline: July 1. Guidelines for SASE. Prize: $1,000 and a certificate of recognition.

SOVEREIGN AWARD, OUTSTANDING NEWSPAPER STORY, OUTSTANDING FEATURE STORY, The Jockey Club of Canada, P.O. Box 156, Rexdale, Ontario M9W 5L2, Canada. (416)675-7756. Fax: (416)675-6378. E-mail: tjcc@ftn.net. **Contact:** Bridget Bimm, executive director. Estab. 1973. Offered annually to recognize outstanding achievement in the area of Canadian thoroughbred racing journalism published November 1-October 31 of the previous year. Newspaper Story: Appeared in a newspaper by a racing columnist on Canadian Racing subject matter. Outstanding Feature Story: Appeared in a magazine book or newspaper, written as feature story on Canadian Racing subject matter. There is no nominating process other than the writer submitting no more than 1 entry/category. A copy of the newspaper article or magazine story must be provided along with a 3.25" disk containing the story in an ASCII style format. Deadline: October 31.

THE TEN BEST 'CENSORED' STORIES OF 2001, Project Censored—Sonoma State University, Rohnert Park CA 94928. (707)664-2500. Fax: (707)664-2108. E-mail: censored@sonoma.edu. Website: www.sonoma.edu/projectcensored/. **Contact:** Peter Phillips, director. Offered for current published, nonfiction stories of national social significance that have been overlooked or under-reported by the news media. Peter Phillips and Project Censored choose 25 stories that have been underreported to make up *Censored: The News That Didn't Make the News and Why*, published by Seven Stories Press. Deadline: October 1.

STANLEY WALKER JOURNALISM AWARD, The Texas Institute of Letters, Southwest Texas State University, San Marcos TX 78666. (512)245-2428. Fax: (512)245-7462. E-mail: mb13@swt.edu. **Contact:** Mark Busby. Offered annually for work published January 1-December 31 of previous year to recognize the best writing appearing in a daily newspaper. Writer must have been born in Texas, or must have lived in the state for two consecutive years at some time, or the subject matter of the article must be associated with the state. Deadline: January 3. Guidelines for SASE. Prize: $1,000.

EDWARD WEINTAL PRIZE FOR DIPLOMATIC REPORTING, Georgetown University Institute for the Study of Diplomacy, 1316 36th St. NW, Washington DC 20007. (202)965-5735, ext. 3010. Fax: (202)965-5811. E-mail: dolgas@gunet.georgetown.edu. Website: data.georgetown.edu/sfs/programs/isd. **Contact:** Charles Dolgas, contest/award director. Offered annually to honor previously published journalists whose work reflects initiative, hard digging, and bold thinking in the coverage of American diplomacy and foreign policy. Writer should place name on award mailing list to receive notice of nominations being sought. "Nominations are made by the editor on the basis of a specific story or series, or on the basis of a journalist's overall news coverage." Deadline: Mid-January. Prize: $5,000.

Writing for Children & Young Adults

THE GEOFFREY BILSON AWARD FOR HISTORICAL FICTION FOR YOUNG PEOPLE, The Canadian Children's Book Centre, 101-40 Orchard View Blvd., Toronto, Ontario M4R 1B9, Canada. (416)975-0010. Fax: (416)975-8970. E-mail: brenda@bookcentre.ca. Website: www.bookcentre.ca. **Contact:** (Ms.) Brenda Halliday, librarian. Created in Geoffrey Bilson's memory in 1988. Offered annually for a previously published "outstanding work of historical fiction for young people by a Canadian author." Open to Canadian citizens and residents of Canada for at least 2 years. Deadline: December 31, 2002. Prize: $1,000. Judged by a jury selected by the Canadian Children's Book Centre.

IRMA S. AND JAMES H. BLACK AWARD, Bank Street College of Education, 610 W. 112th St., New York NY 10025. (212)875-4450. Fax: (212)875-4558. E-mail: lindag@bnkst.edu. Website: streetcat.bnkst.edu/html/isb.html. **Contact:** Linda Greengrass, director. Estab. 1972. Offered annually for a book for young children, for excellence of both text and illustrations. Entries must have been published during the previous calendar year. Deadline: January 1 after book is published.

MARGUERITE DE ANGELI PRIZE, Delacorte Press Books for Young Readers, Random House, Inc., 1540 Broadway, New York NY 10036. (212)782-9000. Fax: (212)782-9452. Website: www.randomhouse.com/kids. Estab. 1992. Offered annually for an unpublished fiction ms suitable for readers 7-10 years of age, set in North America, either contemporary or historical. Guidelines on website. Deadline: April 1-June 30. Prize: $1,500 in cash, publication, and $3,500 advance against royalties; world rights acquired.

DELACORTE PRESS PRIZE FOR A FIRST YOUNG ADULT NOVEL, Delacorte Press, 1540 Broadway, New York NY 10036. (212)782-9000. Fax: (212)782-9452. Website: www.randomhouse.com/kids. Offered annually "to encourage the writing of contemporary young adult fiction." Open to US and Canadian writers who have not previously published a young adult novel. Buys world rights to winning ms. Guidelines on website. Deadline: October 1-December 31 (postmarked). Prize: $1,500 cash, publication, and $6,000 advance against royalties.

THE NORMA FLECK AWARD FOR A CANADIAN CHILDREN'S NONFICTION BOOK, The Canadian Children's Book Centre, 101-40 Orchard View Blvd., Toronto, Ontario M4R 1B9, Canada. (416)975-0010. Fax: (416)975-8970. E-mail: info@bookcentre.ca. Website: www.bookcentre.ca. **Contact:** Charlotte Teeple, executive director. The Norma Fleck Award was established by the Fleck Family Foundation in May 1999 to honor the life of Norma

Marie Fleck, and to recognize exceptional Canadian nonfiction books for young people. Publishers are welcome to nominate books using the online form found at www.bookcentre.ca. Offered annually for books published between May 1, 2001 and April 30, 2002. Open to Canadian citizens or landed immigrants. Deadline: March 30, 2002. Schedule decided upon annually. Prize: $10,000 goes to the author (unless 40% or more of the text area is composed of original illustrations, in which case the award will be divided equally between the author and the artist). $5,000 in matching funding will be made available for promotional purposes to the publishers of the 5 books on the short list. Judged by a minimum of 3 jury members and the total number, if more, will be an even number. The jury will always include at least 3 of the following: a teacher, a librarian, a bookseller, and a reviewer. There should be at least 1 new jury member each year. A juror will have a deep understanding of, and some involvement with, Canadian children's books. The Canadian Children's Book Centre will select the jury members.

GOLDEN KITE AWARDS, Society of Children's Book Writers and Illustrators (SCBWI), 8271 Beverly Blvd., Los Angeles CA 90048. (323)782-1010. E-mail: scbwi@scbwi.org. Website: www.scbwi.org. **Contact:** Mercedes Coats, coordinator. Estab. 1973. Offered annually for children's fiction, nonfiction, and picture illustration books by SCBWI members published in the calendar year. Deadline: December 15.

GOVERNOR GENERAL'S LITERARY AWARD FOR CHILDREN'S LITERATURE, Canada Council for the Arts, 350 Albert St., P.O. Box 1047, Ottawa, Ontario K1P 5V8, Canada. (613)566-4414, ext. 5576. Fax: (613)566-4410. E-mail: joanne.larocque-poirier@canadacouncil.ca. Website: www.canadacouncil.ca. **Contact:** Joanne Larocque-Poirier. Offered for the best English-language and the best French-language works of children's literature by a Canadian in 2 categories: text and illustration. Books must have been published between September 1, 2001, and September 30, 2002. Publishers submit titles for consideration. Deadline: April 15 or August 7, 2002, depending on the book's publication date. Prize: $15,000.

HIGHLIGHTS FOR CHILDREN FICTION CONTEST, *Highlights for Children*, 803 Church St., Honesdale PA 18431-1824. (570)253-1080. Website: www.highlightsforchildren.com. **Contact:** Marileta Robinson, senior editor. Offered for stories for children ages 2-12; category varies each year. Stories should be limited to 900 words for older readers, 500 words for younger readers. No crime or violence, please. Specify that ms is a contest entry. Deadline: January 1-February 28 (postmarked). Guidelines for SASE. Prize: $1,000 to 3 winners.

INTERNATIONAL READING ASSOCIATION CHILDREN'S BOOK AWARDS, International Reading Association, P.O. Box 8139, Newark DE 19714-8139. (302)731-1600 ext. 293. Fax: (302)731-1057. Website: www.reading.o rg. **Contact:** Janet Butler. Offered annually for an author's first or second published book in fiction and nonfiction in 3 categories: Primary (preschool-age 8) intermediate (ages 9-13); and young adult (ages 14-17). To recognize newly published authors who show unusual promise in the children's book field. Guidelines and deadlines for SASE. Prize: $500 and a medal for each category.

CORETTA SCOTT KING BOOK AWARD, Coretta Scott King Task Force, American Library Association, 50 E. Huron St., Chicago IL 60611. (800)545-2433. Fax: (312)280-3256. E-mail: olos@ala.org. Website: www.ala.org/olos/awards.html. **Contact:** Tanga Morris. Offered annually for children's books by African-American authors and/or illustrators published the previous year. Three categories: Preschool-grade 4; grades 5-8; grades 9-12. Deadline: December 1. Guidelines for SASE.

N ANNE SPENCER LINDBERGH PRIZE IN CHILDREN'S LITERATURE, The Charles A. & Anne Morrow Lindbergh Foundation, 2150 Third Ave. N., Suite 310, Anoka MN 55303. (763)576-1596. Fax: (763)576-1664. E-mail: info@lindberghfoundation.org. Website: www.lindberghfoundation.org. **Contact:** Executive Director. Offered every 2 years in even years for a children's fantasy novel published in that or the preceding year. Entries must include 4 copies of the book and an application fee of $25, payable to the Lindbergh Foundation, for each title submitted. Open to any writer. Deadline: November 1.

MILKWEED PRIZE FOR CHILDREN'S LITERATURE, Milkweed Editions, 1011 Washington Ave. S., Suite 300, Minneapolis MN 55415. (612)332-3192. Fax: (612)215-2550. Website: www.milkweed.org. **Contact:** Elisabeth Fitz, first reader. Estab. 1993. Annual prize for unpublished works. "Milkweed is looking for a novel intended for readers aged 8-13. Manuscripts should be of high literary quality and must be double-spaced, 90-200 pages in length. The Milkweed Prize for Children's Literature will be awarded to the best manuscript for children ages 8-13 that Milkweed accepts for publication during each calendar year by a writer not previously published by Milkweed Editions." All mss submitted to Milkweed will automatically be considered for the prize. Submission directly to the contest is not necessary. Must review guidelines, available at website or for SASE. Catalog for $1.50 postage. Prize: $5,000 advance on royalties agreed upon at the time of acceptance.

THE NATIONAL CHAPTER OF CANADA IODE VIOLET DOWNEY BOOK AWARD, National Chapter of Canada IODE, 40 Orchard View Blvd., Suite 254, Toronto, Ontario M4R 1B9, Canada. (416)487-4416. Fax: (416)487-4417. E-mail: iodecanada@sympatico.ca. Website: www.iodecanada.ca. **Contact:** Sandra Connery, contest/award director. Offered annually for children's books of at least 500 words. Entries must have appeared in print January 1-December 31. Open to Canadian citizens only. Deadline: December 31. Guidelines for SASE. Prize: $3,000 (Canadian funds).

PATERSON PRIZE FOR BOOKS FOR YOUNG PEOPLE, The Poetry Center at Passaic County Community College, One College Blvd., Paterson NJ 07505-1179. (973)684-6555. Fax: (973)684-5843. E-mail: mgillan@pccc.cc.nj.

us. Website: www.pccc.cc.nj.us/poetry. **Contact:** Maria Mazziotti Gillan, director. Offered annually for books published the previous calendar year. Three categories: Pre-kindergarten-grade 3; grades 4-6; and grades 7-12. Open to any writer. Deadline: April 1. Guidelines for SASE. Prize: $500 in each category.

PEN/PHYLLIS NAYLOR WORKING WRITER FELLOWSHIP, PEN American Center, 568 Broadway, New York NY 10012. (212)334-1660. Fax: (212)334-2181. E-mail: jm@pen.org. **Contact:** John Morrone. Offered annually to a "writer of children's or young-adult fiction in financial need, who has published at least 2 books, and no more than 3, in the past 10 years, which may have been well reviewed and warmly received by literary critics, but which have not generated sufficient income to support the author." Writers must be nominated by an editor or fellow writer. Deadline: January 31. Prize: $5,000.

PRIX ALVINE-BELISLE, Association pour L'avancement des sciences et des techniques de la documentation, ASTED, Inc., 3414 av. Parc #202, Montreal, Quebec H2X 2H5, Canada. (514)281-5012. Fax: (514)281-8219. E-mail: lcabral@asted.org. Website: www.asted.org. **Contact:** Louis Cabral, executive director. Offered annually for work published the previous year before the award to promote authors of French youth literature in Canada. Deadline: April 1. Prize: $500.

SASKATCHEWAN CHILDREN'S LITERATURE AWARD, Saskatchewan Book Awards, Inc., Box 1921, Regina, Saskatchewan S4P 3E1, Canada. (306)569-1585. Fax: (306)569-4187. E-mail: director@bookawards.sk.ca. Website: www.bookawards.sk.ca. **Contact:** Joyce Wells, executive director. Offered annually for work published September 15, 2001-September 14, 2002. This award is presented to a Saskatchewan author for the best book of children's or young adult's literature, judged on the quality of writing. Deadline: First deadline: July 31; final deadline: September 14. Guidelines for SASE. Charges $15 (Canadian). Prize: $1,500.

SYDNEY TAYLOR BOOK AWARD, Association of Jewish Libraries, 20 Lamplighter Court, Baltimore MD 21208. (410)580-1812. E-mail: llibbylib@aol.com; white_libby@juno.com. Website: www.jewishlibraries.org. **Contact:** Libby White, chair. Offered annually for work published in the year of the award. "Given to distinguished contributions to Jewish literature for children. One award for older readers, 1 for younger." Publishers submit books. Deadline: December 31. Guidelines for SASE. Prize: Certificate, cash award, and gold seal for cover of winning book.

TEDDY AWARD FOR BEST CHILDREN'S BOOK, Writers' League of Texas (formerly the Austin Writers' League), 1501 W. Fifth St., Suite E-2, Austin TX 78703. (512)499-8914. Fax: (512)499-0441. E-mail: awl@writersleague.org. Website: www.writersleague.org. **Contact:** Stephanie Sheppard, director. Offered annually for work published June 1, 2002-May 31, 2003. Honors an outstanding book for children published by a member of the Writers' League of Texas. Writer's League of Texas dues may accompany entry fee. Deadline: May 31. Guidelines for SASE. Charges $10 fee. Prize: $1,000 and trophy.

(ALICE WOOD MEMORIAL) OHIOANA AWARD FOR CHILDREN'S LITERATURE, Ohioana Library Association, 274 E. First Ave., Columbus OH 43201. (614)466-3831. Fax: (614)728-6974. E-mail: ohioana@sloma.state.oh.us. Website: www.oplin.lib.oh.us/OHIOANA/. **Contact:** Linda R. Hengst. Offered to an author whose body of work has made, and continues to make, a significant contribution to literature for children or young adults and through their work as a writer, teacher, administrator, or through community service, interest in children's literature has been encouraged and children have become involved with reading. Nomination forms for SASE. Recipient must have been born in Ohio or lived in Ohio at least 5 years. Deadline: December 31. Prize: $1,000.

WORK-IN-PROGRESS GRANT, Society of Children's Book Writers and Illustrators (SCBWI) and Judy Blume, 8271 Beverly Blvd., Los Angeles CA 90048. (323)782-1010. E-mail: scbwi@scbwi.org. Website: www.scbwi.org. Two grants—1 designated specifically for a contemporary novel for young people—to assist SCBWI members in the completion of a specific project. Open to SCBWI members only. Deadline: March 1. Guidelines for SASE.

WRITING FOR CHILDREN COMPETITION, The Writers' Union of Canada, 40 Wellington St. E., 3rd Floor, Toronto, Ontario M5E 1C7. (416)703-8982, ext. 223. Fax: (416)504-7656. E-mail: projects@writersunion.ca. Website: www.writersunion.ca. **Contact:** Caroline Sin. Offered annually "to discover developing Canadian writers of unpublished children's/young adult fiction or nonfiction." Open to Canadian citizens or landed immigrants who have not been published in book format, and who do not currently have a contract with a publisher. Deadline: April 23. Charges $15 entry fee. Prize: $1,500; the winner and 11 finalists' pieces will be submitted to 3 Canadian publishers of children's books.

Translation

ASF TRANSLATION PRIZE, The American-Scandinavian Foundation, 58 Park Ave., New York NY 10016-3007. (212)879-9779. Fax: (212)249-3444. E-mail: ahenkin@amscan.org. Website: www.amscan.org. **Contact:** Andrey Henkin. Offered annually to a translation of Scandinavian literature into English of a Nordic author born within last 200 years. "The Prize is for an outstanding English translation of poetry, fiction, drama, or literary prose originally written in Danish, Finnish, Icelandic, Norwegian, or Swedish that has not been previously published in the English language." Deadline: June 1. Guidelines for SASE. Prize: $2,000, publication of an excerpt in an issue of *Scandinavian Review* , and a commemorative bronze medallion. Runner-up receives the Leif and Inger Sjöberg Prize: $1,000, publication of an excerpt in an issue of *Scandinavian Review*, and a commemorative bronze medallion.

SOEURETTE DIEHL FRASER TRANSLATION AWARD, The Texas Institute of Letters, Southwest Texas State University, San Marcos TX 78666. (512)245-2428. Fax: (512)245-7462. E-mail: mb13@swt.edu. Website: www.English.swt.edu/css/TIL/rules.htm. **Contact:** Mark Busby. Offered annually for work published January 1-December 31 of previous year to recognize the best translation of a literary book into English. Translator must have been born in Texas or have lived in the state for at least two consecutive years at some time. Deadline: January 3. Guidelines for SASE. Prize: $1,000.

GERMAN PRIZE FOR LITERARY TRANSLATION, American Translators Association, 225 Reinekers Lane, Suite 590, Alexandria VA 22314. (703)683-6100. Fax: (703)683-6122. E-mail: ata@atanet.org. Website: www.atanet.org. **Contact:** Jo Anne Englebert. Offered in odd-numbered years for a previously published book translated from German to English. In even-numbered years, the Lewis Galentiere Prize is awarded for translations other than German to English. Deadline: May 15. Prize: $1,000, a certificate of recognition, and up to $500 toward expenses for attending the ATA Annual Conference.

GOVERNOR GENERAL'S LITERARY AWARD FOR TRANSLATION, Canada Council for the Arts, 350 Albert St., P.O. Box 1047, Ottawa, Ontario K1P 5V8, Canada. (613)566-4414, ext. 5576. Fax: (613)566-4410. E-mail: joanne.larocque-poirier@canadacouncil.ca. Website: www.canadacouncil.ca. **Contact:** Joanne Larocque-Poirier. Offered for the best English-language and the best French-language work of translation by a Canadian published September 1, 2001-September 30, 2002. Publishers submit titles for consideration. Deadline: April 15 or August 7, 2002, depending on the book's publication date. Prize: $15,000.

LOCKERT LIBRARY OF POETRY IN TRANSLATION, Princeton University Press, 41 William St., Princeton NJ 08540. Fax: (609)258-6305. Website: www.pup.princeton.edu. **Contact:** Fred Appel, associate editor. Book-length poetry translation of a single poet. "We favor translations of poets who are prominent in their own culture, but have as yet little profile in the Anglo-American world; and translations of classics or canonical works that merit a fresh look."

PEN/BOOK-OF-THE-MONTH CLUB TRANSLATION PRIZE, PEN American Center, 568 Broadway, New York NY 10012. (212)334-1660. Fax: (212)334-2181. E-mail: jm@pen.org. **Contact:** John Morrone. Offered for a literary book-length translation into English published in the calendar year. No technical, scientific, or reference books. Publishers, agents, or translators may submit 3 copies of each eligible title. Deadline: December 15. Prize: $3,000.

THE RAIZISS/DE PALCHI TRANSLATION FELLOWSHIP, The Academy of American Poets, 584 Broadway, Suite 1208, New York NY 10012-3250. (212)274-0343. Fax: (212)274-9427. E-mail: academy@poets.org. Website: www.poets.org. **Contact:** Awards Director. Offered in even-numbered years to recognize outstanding unpublished translations of modern Italian poetry into English. Applicants must verify permission to translate the poems or that the poems are in the public domain. Open to any US citizen. Deadline: September 1-November 1, 2002. Guidelines for SASE. Prize: $20,000, and a 1-month residency at the American Academy in Rome.

96 INC BRUCE P. ROSSLEY LITERARY AWARD, (formerly Bruce P. Rossley Literary Award), P.O. Box 15558, Boston MA 02215. (617) 267-0543. Fax: (617)262-3568. **Contact:** Vera Gold, executive director. Offered in even years to give greater recognition to a writer of merit. In addition to writing, accomplishments in the fields of teaching and community service are considered. Nominations accepted August 1-September 30. "The 96 Inc Bruce P. Rossley Literary Awards will be presented next in 2004. We are revising guidelines with input from our 60-member committee (available in 2003)." Any writer may be nominated, but the focus is merit and those writers who have been under-recognized. Deadline: September 30. Charges $10 fee. Prize: $1,000.

LOIS ROTH AWARD FOR A TRANSLATION OF A LITERARY WORK, Modern Language Association, 26 Broadway, 3rd Floor, New York NY 10004-1789. (646)576-5141. Fax: (646)458-0030. E-mail: awards@mla.org. Website: www.mla.org. **Contact:** Coordinator of Book Prizes. Offered every 2 years (odd years) for an outstanding translation into English of a book-length literary work published the previous year. Translators need not be members of the MLA. Deadline: April 1. Guidelines for SASE. Prize: $1,000, and a certificate.

ALDO AND JEANNE SCAGLIONE PRIZE FOR A TRANSLATION OF A LITERARY WORK, Modern Language Association, 26 Broadway, 3rd Floor, New York NY 10004-1789. (646)576-5141. Fax: (646)458-0030. E-mail: awards@mla.org. Website: www.mla.org. **Contact:** Coordinator of Book Prizes. Offered in even-numbered years for the translation of a book-length literary work appearing in print during the previous year. Translators need not be members of the MLA. Deadline: April 1. Guidelines for SASE. Prize: $2,000, and a certificate.

ALDO AND JEANNE SCAGLIONE PRIZE FOR A TRANSLATION OF A SCHOLARLY STUDY OF LITERATURE, Modern Language Association, 26 Broadway, 3rd Floor, New York NY 10004-1789. (646)576-5141. Fax: (646)458-0030. E-mail: awards@mla.org. Website: www.mla.org. **Contact:** Coordinator of Book Prizes. Offered in odd-numbered years "for an outstanding translation into English of a book-length work of literary history, literary criticism, philology, or literary theory published during the previous biennium." Translators need not be members of the MLA. Deadline: May 1. Guidelines for SASE. Prize: $2,000, and a certificate.

Multiple Writing Areas

ALLIGATOR JUNIPER AWARD, *Alligator Juniper*/Prescott College, 220 Grove Ave., Prescott AZ 86301. (928)778-2090, ext. 2012. E-mail: aj@prescott.edu. Website: www.prescott.edu. **Contact:** Melanie Bishop. Offered annually for unpublished work. Guidelines on website. All entrants receive a copy of the next issue of *Alligator Juniper*, a $7.50 value. Deadline: October 1. Charges $10. Prize: $500, plus publication. Judged by the staff and occasional guest judges. Acquires First North American Rights. Open to any writer.

AMERICAN LITERARY REVIEW CONTEST, *American Literary Review*, P.O. Box 311307, University of North Texas, Denton TX 76203-1307. (940)565-2755. E-mail: americanliteraryreview@yahoo.com. Website: www.engl.unt.edu/alr. **Contact:** Managing Editor. Offered annually for unpublished work. This contest alternates annually between poetry and fiction. Open to any writer. Deadline: Varies each year. Guidelines for SASE. Charges $10 entry fee. Prize: $500, and publication.

ANNUAL U.S. MARITIME LITERATURE AWARDS, 222 Main St., Box 190, Annapolis MD 21401. E-mail: sailr@pyramid3.net. Website: www.usmaritimeawards.org. Offered annually for unpublished short stories (nonfiction), poetry, limericks, and environmental essays. All entries must include a US geographical maritime location and theme. The term "maritime" may include both freshwater and saltwater bodies such as lakes, creeks, coastlines, ports, oceans, etc. Themes may include fishing, tragedy, discovery, adventure, weather, romance, kayaking, environment, diving, etc. Three divisions: Adult (18 and older); students ages 13-17; and students under age 13. Guidelines on website at www.usmaritimeawards.com/aausm.html Deadline: December 31 (postmarked). Prize: Short story: $100; Poetry: $100; Essay: $100; Limerick: $25.

ARIZONA AUTHORS' ASSOCIATION ANNUAL NATIONAL LITERARY CONTEST, Arizona Authors' Association, P.O. Box 87857, Phoenix AZ 85080-7857. (623)780-0053. Fax: (623)780-0468. E-mail: info@azauthors.com. Website: www.azauthors.com. **Contact:** Toby Heathcotte, contest coordinator. Offered annually for previously unpublished poetry, short stories, essays, and articles. New awards for published books in fiction, anthology, nonfiction, and children's. Winners announced at an award banquet in Phoenix in November, and short pieces published in *Arizona Literary Magazine*. Deadline: July 1. Charges $10 fee for poetry; $15 for short stories and essays; and $30 for books. Prize: 1st Place: Unpublished novel wins publication in e-book and print-on-demand by 1stbooks.com. All winners interviewed on Book Crazy Radio Network.

ART COOP TRAVELING FELLOWSHIP, Cottonwood Art Co-operative, 1124 Columbia NE, Albuquerque NM 87106. E-mail: art_coop@yahoo.com. Website: www.geocities.com/art_coop. **Contact:** Editor-in-Chief. For most recent information, please visit website or write for guidelines with SASE. Submit cover letter explaining project and location, anticipated budget, bio, and publications list. Submit 3-50 page portfolio of fiction or creative nonfiction, 10-20 pages of poetry, or slides of visual artwork with SASE. Deadline: December 1 (annually). Charges $20. Prize: Cash award to be determined and Internet-publication to support serious, aspiring poets, essayists, fiction writers, and visual artists in completing a project that requires travel. Open to any writer/artist.

N **ATLANTIC WRITING COMPETITION FOR UNPUBLISHED MANUSCRIPTS**, Writers' Federation of Nova Scotia, 1113 Marginal Rd., Halifax, Nova Scotia B3H 4P7. (902)423-8116. Fax: (902)422-0881. E-mail: talk@writers.ns.ca. Website: www.writers.ns.ca. **Contact:** Jane Buss, executive director. "Established in 1975 under the auspices of the Nova Scotia Branch of the Canadian Authors' Association, the Atlantic Writing Competition has been sponsored by the Writers' Federation of Nova Scotia since 1976. We encouarge all writers in Atlantic Canada to explore and celebrate their talents by sending in their new, untried work. Manuscripts are read by a team of 2 or 3 judges. WFNS chooses judges carefully, trying to balance skills, points of view, and taste. Judges are professionals who work as writers, editors, booksellers, librarians, or teachers. Because our aim is to help Atlantic Canadian writers grow, judges return written comments when the competition is concluded. Anyone resident in the Atlantic Provinces for at least 6 months prior to August 2002 is eligible to enter. Only 1 entry/category is allowed. Writers whose work has been professionally published in book form, or frequently in periodical or media production, may not enter in the genre in which they have been published or produced. Entries must be the original, unpublished work of the writer, and must not have been accepted for publication or submitted elsewhere. The same work may not be submitted again. Entry forms will be available from the WFNS office by March 2002. For more information on the Atlantic Writing Competition, visit our website at www.writers.ns.ca/competitions." Deadline: First Friday in August. Charges $15 fee ($10 for WFNS members); $25 for novel ($20 for WFNS members). Prize: Novel: $200, $150, $100; Writing for Children: $150, $75, $50; Poetry: $100, $75, $50; Short Story: $100, $75, $50; Essay/Magazine Article: $150, $75, $50.

AWP AWARD SERIES, Associated Writing Programs, Tallwood House, Mail Stop 1E3, George Mason University, Fairfax VA 22030. (703)993-4301. Fax: (703)993-4302. E-mail: awp@gmu.edu. Website: http://awpwriter.org. **Contact:** Supriya Bhatnagar. Offered annually to foster new literary talent. Categories: poetry, short fiction, creative nonfiction, and novel. Guidelines for SASE and on website. Open to any writer. Deadline: Must be postmarked January 1-February 28. Charges $20 for nonmembers, $10 for members. Prize: Cash honorarium (novel: $10,000; other categories: $2,000), and publication by a participating press.

BAKELESS LITERARY PUBLICATION PRIZES, Bread Loaf Writers' Conference, Middlebury College, Middlebury VT 05753. (802)443-2018. Fax: (802)443-2087. E-mail: bakeless@middlebury.edu. Website: www.middlebury.edu/~blwc. **Contact:** Ian Pounds, contest director. Offered annually for unpublished authors of poetry, fiction, and creative nonfiction. Open to all writing in English who have not yet published a book in their entry's genre. Deadline: October 1-November 15. Guidelines for SASE. Charges $10 fee. Prize: Publication of book-length ms by Houghton Mifflin, and a fellowship to attend the Bread Loaf Writers' Conference.

EMILY CLARK BALCH AWARD, *Virginia Quarterly Review*, 1 West Range, P.O. Box 400223, Charlottesville VA 22904-4233. (434)924-3124. Fax: (434)924-1397. Website: www.virginia.edu/vqr. **Contact:** Staige D. Blackford, editor. Best short story/poetry accepted and published by the *Virginia Quarterly Review* during a calendar year. No deadline.

BERTELSMANN FOUNDATION'S WORLD OF EXPRESSION SCHOLARSHIP PROGRAM, Bertelsmann, 1540 Broadway, New York NY 10036. (212)930-4520. Fax: (212)782-0349. E-mail: bwoesp@bmge.com. Website: www.worldofexpression.org. **Contact:** Christina Carrothers. Offered annually for unpublished work to NYC public high school seniors. Three categories: Poetry, fiction/drama, and personal essay. Deadline: Feb. 1. Guidelines for SASE. Prize: 72 awards given in literary (3) and nonliterary (2) categories. Awards range from $500-10,000.

THE BOSTON AUTHORS CLUB BOOK AWARDS, The Boston Authors Club, 121 Follen Rd., Lexington MA 02421. **Contact:** Andrew McAleer. Offered annually for books published the previous year. Two awards are given, 1 for trade books of fiction, nonfiction, or poetry, and the second for children's books. Authors must live or have lived within 100 miles of Boston. Deadline: January 1. Prize: Certificate and honorarioum of $500 in each category.

BURNABY WRITERS' SOCIETY CONTEST, Burnaby Writers' Society, 6584 Deer Lake Ave., Burnaby, British Columbia V5G 3T7, Canada. E-mail: lonewolf@portal.ca. Website: www.bws.bc.ca. **Contact:** Eileen Kernaghan. Offered annually for unpublished work. Categories vary from year-to-year. Send SASE for current rules. Purpose is to encourage talented writers in all genres. Deadline: May 31. Guidelines for SASE. Charges $5 fee. Prize: $200; $100; $50; and public reading.

BYLINE MAGAZINE AWARDS, P.O. Box 5240, Edmond OK 73083-5240. (405)348-5591. E-mail: MPreston@bylinemag.com. Website: www.bylinemag.com. **Contact:** Marcia Preston, award director. Contest includes several monthly contests, open to anyone, in various categories that include fiction, nonfiction, poetry, and children's literature; an annual poetry chapbook award which is open to any poet; and an annual *ByLine* Short Fiction and Poetry Award open only to our subscribers. For chapbook award and subscriber awards, publication constitutes part of the prize, and winners grant first North American rights to *ByLine*. Deadline: Varies. Charges $3-5 for monthly contests and $15 for chapbook contest. Prize: Monthly contests: Cash and listing in magazine; Chapbook Award: Publication of chapbook, 50 copies and $200; *ByLine* Short Fiction and Poetry Award: $250 in each category, plus publication in the magazine.

CANADIAN AUTHORS ASSOCIATION AWARDS PROGRAM, P.O. Box 419, Campbellford, Ontario K0L 1L0, Canada. (705)653-0323. Fax: (705)653-0593. E-mail: canauth@redden.on.ca. Website: www.canauthors.org. **Contact:** Alec McEachern. Offered annually for short stories, fiction, poetry, history, drama, biography, short stories for children, and to promising writers under age 30. Entrants must be Canadians by birth, naturalized Canadians, or landed immigrants. Entry form required for most awards. Obtain entry form from contact name or download from website. Deadline: Varies. Guidelines for SASE. Prize: Prizes range from air travel for 2 to $10,000.

CELTIC VOICE WRITING CONTEST, Bardsong Press, P.O. Box 775396, Steamboat Springs CO 80477-5396. (970)870-1401. Fax: (970)879-2657. E-mail: celts@bardsongpress.com. Website: www.bardsongpress.com. Offered annually for unpublished work to encourage and celebrate Celtic heritage and culture through poetry, short stories, essays, and creative nonfiction. Guidelines for SASE or on website. Deadline: September 30. Charges $10 fee. Prize: Cash award for category winners. Publication for winners and honorable mentions.

CHICAGO LITERARY AWARD, Left Field Press/*Another Chicago Magazine*, P.O. Box 180017, Chicago IL 60618. E-mail: editors@anotherchicagomag.com. Website: www.anotherchicagomag.com. **Contact:** Editors. Offered annually for unpublished works to recognize excellence in poetry and fiction. Guidelines for SASE and on website. Buys first North American serial rights. Open to any writer. Deadline: December 15. Charges $10 fee. Prize: $1,000, and publication.

THE CITY OF VANCOUVER BOOK AWARD, Office of Cultural Affairs, 453 W. 12th Ave., Vancouver, British Columbia V5Y 1V4, Canada. (604)873-7487. Fax: (604)871-6048. E-mail: oca@city.vancouver.bc.ca. Website: www.city.vancouver.bc.ca/oca. Offered annually for books published the previous year which exhibit excellence in 1 or more of 4 categories: content, illustration, design, and format. The book must contribute significantly to the appreciation and understanding of the city of Vancouver and heighten awareness of 1 or more of the following: Vancouver's history, the city's unique character, or achievements of the city's residents. The book may be fiction, nonfiction, poetry, or drama written for adults or children and may deal with any aspects of the city: history, geography, current affairs, or the arts. Guidelines on website. Prize: $2,000.

CNW/FLORIDA STATE WRITING COMPETITION, Florida Freelance Writers Association, P.O. Box A, North Stratford NH 03590-0167. (603)922-8338. Fax: (603)922-8339. E-mail: contest@writers-editors.com. Website: www.writers-editors.com. **Contact:** Dana Cassell, executive director. Subject areas include: adult articles, adult short stories, writing for children, novels, poetry; categories within these areas vary from year-to-year. Entry fees vary from year-to-year; in 2001 were $3-20. Open to any writer. Deadline: March 15. Guidelines for SASE. Prize: Cash, certificates.

COLORADO BOOK AWARDS, Colorado Center for the Book, 2123 Downing, Denver CO 80205. (303)839-8320. Fax: (303)839-8319. E-mail: ccftb@compuserve.com. Website: www.ColoradoBook.org. **Contact:** Christiane H. Citron, executive director. Offered annually for work published by December of previous year or current calendar year. The purpose is to champion all Colorado authors and in particular to honor the award winners and a reputation for Colorado as a state whose people promote and support reading, writing, and literacy through books. The categories are children, young adult, fiction, nonfiction & poetry, and other categories as determined each year. Open to authors who reside or have resided in Colorado. Guidelines for SASE. Charges $45 fee. Prize: $250 in each category and an annual gala event where winners are honored.

COMMONWEALTH CLUB OF CALIFORNIA BOOK AWARDS, 595 Market St., San Francisco CA 94105. (415)597-4846. Fax: (415)597-6729. E-mail: blane@commonwealthclub.org. Website: www.commonwealthclub.org. **Contact:** Barbara Lane. Estab. 1931. Offered annually for published submissions appearing in print January 1-December 31 of the previous year. "Purpose of award is the encouragement and production of literature in California. Categories include: fiction, nonfiction, poetry, first work of fiction, juvenile ages up to 10, juvenile 11-16, works in translation, notable contribution to publishing and Californiana." Can be nominated by publisher as well. Open to California residents (or residents at time of publication). Deadline: December 31. Guidelines for SASE. Prize: Medals and cash prizes to be awarded at publicized event.

VIOLET CROWN BOOK AWARDS, Writers' League of Texas, 1501 W. Fifth St., Suite E-2, Austin TX 78703. (512)499-8914. Fax: (512)499-0441. E-mail: awl@writersleague.org. Website: www.writersleague.org. **Contact:** Stephanie Sheppard, director. Offered annually for work published June 1, 2002-May 31, 2003. Honors 3 outstanding books published in fiction, nonfiction and literary categories by Writers' League of Texas members. Membership dues may accompany entry fee. Deadline: May 31. Guidelines for SASE. Charges $10 fee. Prize: 3 $1,000 prizes and trophies.

N **CUNARD FIRST BOOK AWARD**, Writers' Federation of Nova Scotia, 1113 Marginal Rd., Halifax, Nova Scotia B3H 4P7. (902)423-8116. Fax: (902)422-0881. E-mail: talk@writers.ns.ca. Website: www.writers.ns.ca. **Contact:** Jane Buss, executive director. This award was established by the Atlantic Book Week Steering Committee to honor the first published book by an Atlantic-Canadian author. Full-length books of fiction, nonfiction, or poetry written by Atlantic Canadians, and published as a whole for the first time in the previous calendar year, are eligible. Entrants must be native or resident Atlantic Canadians who have either been born in Newfoundland, Prince Edward Island, Nova Scotia, or New Brunswick, and spent a susbstantial portion of their lives living there, or who have lived in 1 or a combination of these provinces for at least 24 consecutive months prior to entry deadline date. Entries submitted to the Atlantic Poetry Prize, Evelyn Richardson Nonfiction Award, Thomas Head Raddall Atlantic Fiction Award, Dartmouth Book Award, and/or Ann Connor Brimer Award are automatically entered in the competition. Publishers: Send 4 copies and a letter attesting to the author's status as an Atlantic Canadian and the author's current mailing address and telephone number. Deadline: First Friday in December. Prize: $500.

DANA AWARDS IN THE NOVEL, SHORT FICTION AND POETRY, 7207 Townsend Forest Court, Browns Summit NC 27214-9634. (336)656-7009. E-mail: danaawards@pipeline.com. Website: http://danaawards.home.pipeline.com. **Contact:** Mary Elizabeth Parker, chair. Offered annually for unpublished work written in English. Purpose is monetary award for work that has not been previously published or received monetary award, but we will accept work published simply for friends and family. Works previously published online are not eligible. No work accepted by or for persons under 16. Three awards: Novel: For the first 50 pages of a novel completed or in progress. Short fiction: Short fiction (no memoirs) up to 10,000 words. Poetry: For best group of 5 poems based on excellence of all 5 (no light verse, no single poem over 100 lines). "Contest is open to writers who are 16 or older and who write in English. Most submissions are from authors in their late 20s through 60s." Deadline: October 31 (postmarked). Charges $20 fee/novel entry, $10 fee/short fiction or poetry entry. Prize: $1,000 in each category.

EMERGING LESBIAN WRITERS FUND AWARD, ASTRAEA Lesbian Action Foundation, 116 E. 16th St., 7th Floor, New York NY 10003. (212)529-8021. Fax: (212)982-3321. E-mail: info@astraea.org. Website: www.astraea.org. **Contact:** Christine Lipat, senior program officer. Offered annually to encourage and support the work of new lesbian writers of fiction and poetry. Guidelines for SASE or on website. Entrants must be a lesbian writer of either fiction or poetry, a US resident, work includes some lesbian content, at least 1 piece of writing (in any genre) has been published in a newspaper, magazine, journal, anthology, or professional website, and not more than 1 book. (Published work may be in any discipline; self-published books are not included in the 1 book maximum.) Deadline: International Women's Day, March 8 (postmarked). Charges $5 fee. Prize: $10,000 grants.

EXPLORATIONS AWARDS FOR LITERATURE, (formerly Explorations Prizes for Literature), UAS Explorations, University of Alaska Southeast, 11120 Glacier Hwy., Juneau AK 99801. E-mail: art.petersen@uas.alaska.edu. Website: www.geocities.com/artpetersen. **Contact:** Art Petersen, editor. Offered annually for poets and writers across North America and Europe. Guidelines for SASE, by e-mail, and on website. Open to any writer. Deadline: May 15. Charges $6 for 1-2 poems, $3 for each additional poem (60 line maximum); $6/fiction (3,000 word maximum). No limit to submissions. Prize: 1st Place: $1,000; 2nd Place: $500; 3rd Place (2): $100. Judged by the editors and editorial board (blind judging).

THE VIRGINIA FAULKNER AWARD FOR EXCELLENCE IN WRITING, *Prairie Schooner*, 201 Andrews Hall, P.O. Box 880334, Lincoln NE 68588-0334. (402)472-0911. Fax: (402)472-9771. E-mail: eflanagan2@unl.edu. Website: www.unl.edu/schooner/psmain.htm. **Contact:** Hilda Raz. Offered annually for work published in *Prairie Schooner* in the previous year. Prize: $1,000.

N **FINELINE COMPETITION FOR PROSE POEMS, SHORT SHORTS, AND ANYTHING IN BETWEEN**, *Mid-American Review*, Department of English, Bowling Green State University, Bowling Green OH 43403. (419)372-2725. E-mail: karenka@bgnet.bgsu.edu. Website: www.bgsu.edu/midamericanreview. **Contact:** Michael

Czyzniejewski, editor-in-chief. Contest open to all writers not associated with current judge or *Mid-American Review*. Offered annually for unpublished works. Deadline: October 1. Guidelines for SASE. Charges $10/group of 3 pieces or $5 each. All $10-and-over participants receive prize-winning issue. Prize: First: $250 plus publication in spring issue of *Mid-American Review*; 10 finalists receive notation plus possible publication. Judged by Finalists judged by well-known writer, e.g., Michael Martone, Alberto Rios. Open to any writer.

THE GREENSBORO REVIEW LITERARY AWARD IN FICTION AND POETRY, *The Greensboro Review*, English Department, 134 McIver Bldg., P.O. Box 6170, Greensboro NC 27402-6170. (336)334-5459. E-mail: jlclark@uncg.edu. Website: www.uncg.edu/eng/mfa. **Contact:** Jim Clark, editor. Offered annually for fiction (7,500 word limit) and poetry recognizing the best work published in the spring issue of *The Greensboro Review*. Sample issue for $5. Deadline: September 15. Guidelines for SASE. Prize: $500 each for best short story and poem. Acquires Rights revert to author upon publication. Open to any writer.

GSU REVIEW WRITING CONTEST, (formerly Georgia State University Review Writing Contest), *GSU Review*, Attn: Annual Contest, Georgia State University Plaza, Campus Box 1894, Atlanta GA 30303-3083. (404)651-4804. E-mail: kchaple@emory.edu. **Contact:** Katie Chaple, editor. Offered annually "to publish the most promising work of up-and-coming writers of poetry (3-5 poems, none over 50 lines) and fiction (8,000 word limit)." Rights revert to writer upon publication. Deadline: January 31. Guidelines for SASE. Charges $10 fee. Prize: $1,000 to winner of each category, plus a copy of winning issue to each paid submission.

GULF COAST POETRY & SHORT FICTION PRIZE, *Gulf Coast*, English Department, University of Houston, Houston TX 77204-3012. (713)743-3223. E-mail: gulfcoast@www.gulfcoast.uh.edu. Website: www.gulfcoast.uh.edu. **Contact:** Pablo Peschiera, managing editor. Offered annually for poetry and short stories. Open to any writer. Deadline: February 15. Guidelines for SASE. Charges $15 fee, which includes subscription. Prize: $1,000, and publication in *Gulf Coast* each for best poem and short story.

HEART ANNUAL POETRY AND SHORT FICTION AWARD, HEArt—Human Equity Through Art, P.O. Box 81038, Pittsburgh PA 15217-0538. (412)244-0122. Fax: (412)244-0210. E-mail: lesanne@ix.netcom.com. Website: trfn.clpgh.org/heart/. **Contact:** Leslie Anne Mcilroy. Offered annually for unpublished work "to encourage poets and writers to use their work as a means of confronting discrimination and promoting social justice; and to give voice and recognition to quality contemporary activist literature." Open to any writer. Deadline: December 31. Guidelines for SASE. Charges $15 fee (includes winning issue) or $21 fee (includes 1-year subscription). Prize: $500, and publication in each category (poetry and short fiction).

LARRY LEVIS EDITORS' PRIZE IN POETRY/THE MISSOURI REVIEW EDITOR'S PRIZE IN FICTION & ESSAY, *The Missouri Review*, 1507 Hillcrest Hall, Columbia MO 65211. (573)882-4474. Fax: (573)884-4671. Website: www.missourireview.org. **Contact:** Hoa Ngo. Offered annually for unpublished work in 3 categories: fiction, essay, and poetry. Guidelines for SASE after June. Deadline: October 15. Charges $15 fee (includes a 1-year subscription). Prize: Winners receive $2,000 in each genre, plus publication; 3 finalists in each category receive a minimum of $100.

THE HUGH J. LUKE AWARD, *Prairie Schooner*, 201 Andrews Hall, P.O. Box 880334, Lincoln NE 68588-0334. (402)472-0911. Fax: (402)472-9771. E-mail: eflanagan2@unl.edu. Website: www.unl.edu/schooner/psmain.htm. **Contact:** Hilda Raz. Offered annually for work published in *Prairie Schooner* in the previous year. Prize: $250.

MANITOBA WRITING AND PUBLISHING AWARDS, c/o Manitoba Writers Guild, 206-100 Arthur St., Winnipeg, Manitoba R3B 1H3, Canada. (204)942-6134. Fax: (204)942-5754. E-mail: mbwriter@escape.ca. Website: www.mbwriter.mb.ca. **Contact:** Robyn Maharaj. Offered annually: The McNally Robinson Book of Year Award (adult); The McNally Robinson Book for Young People Awards (8 and under and 9 and older); The John Hirsch Award for Most Promising Manitoba Writer; The Mary Scorer Award for Best Book by a Manitoba Publisher; The Carol Shields Winnipeg Book Award; The Eileen Sykes McTavish Award for Best First Book; The Margaret Laurence Award for Fiction; The Alexander Kennedy Award for Non-Fiction; 2 Book Publishers Awards; and the biennial Les Prix Litteraires. Guidelines and submission forms available upon request. Open to Manitoba writers only. Deadline: December 1 (books published December 1-31 will be accepted until mid-January). Prize: Several prizes up to $3,000 (Canadian).

MID-LIST PRESS FIRST SERIES AWARDS, Mid-List Press, 4324 12th Ave. S., Minneapolis MN 55407-3218. (612)822-3733. Fax: (612)823-8387. E-mail: guide@midlist.org. Website: www.midlist.org. **Contact:** Lane Stiles. Offered annually for authors who have yet to publish books in any of 4 categories: creative nonfiction, short fiction, poetry, and novels. Guidelines for SASE or online at website. Deadline: Varies. Charges $20 fee. Prize: An advance against royalties and publication.

THE MILTON CENTER POSTGRADUATE FELLOWSHIP, The Milton Center, 3100 McCormick Ave., Wichita KS 67213. (316)942-4291, ext. 226. Fax: (316)942-4483. E-mail: miltonc@newmanu.edu. **Contact:** Essie Sappenfield, program director. Offered annually to new writers of Christian commitment to complete their first book-length ms of fiction, poetry, or creative nonfiction. The Milton Center exists to encourage work by writers who seek to animate the Christian imagination, foster intellectual integrity, and explore the human condition with honesty and compassion. "Write well and have mature work habits. Don't worry about doctrinal matters, counting Christian symbols, etc. What you believe will automatically show up in your writing." Deadline: March 15. Guidelines for SASE. Charges $15 fee. Prize: Stipend of $1,225/month, residency in Wichita September-May. Two fellowships awarded each year.

JENNY McKEAN/MOORE VISITING WRITER, English Department, George Washington University, Washington DC 20052. (202)994-6180. Fax: (202)994-7915. E-mail: dmca@gwu.edu. Website: www.gwu.edu/~english. **Contact:** David McAleavey. Offered annually to provide 1-year visiting writers to teach 1 G.W. course and 1 free community workshop each semester. Guidelines for SASE or on website. This contest seeks someone specializing in a different genre each year; for 2002-2003 we will seek someone in creative nonfiction; in 2003-2004, a poet; in 2004-2005, a fiction writer. Deadline: November 15. Prize: Annual stipend approximately $50,000, plus reduced-rent townhouse (not guaranteed).

NATIONAL LOOKING GLASS CHAPBOOK COMPETITION, Pudding House Publications, 60 N. Main St., Johnstown OH 43031. (740)967-6060. E-mail: pudding@johnstown.net. Website: www.puddinghouse.com. **Contact:** Jennifer Bosveld. Offered twice/year for "a collection of poems, short short stories, or other creative writing that represents our editorial slant: popular culture, social justice, psychological, sociological, travel, political, environmental. Submissions might be themed or not." Guidelines on website. Past winners include Roy Bentley, David Hernandez, Rebecca Baggett, Willie Abraham Howard Jr., Michael Day, Bill Noble, William Keener, Mark Taksa, Ron Moran, and many others. Deadline: June 30, September 30. Charges $10 fee. Prize: $100, publication of chapbook, 20 free books.

THE NEBRASKA REVIEW AWARDS IN FICTION, POETRY AND CREATIVE NONFICTION, *The Nebraska Review*, FAB 212, University of Nebraska-Omaha, Omaha NE 68182-0324. (402)554-3159. E-mail: jreed@unomaha.edu. **Contact:** Susan Aizenberg (poetry), James Reed (fiction), or John Price (creative nonfiction). Estab. 1973. Offered annually for previously unpublished fiction, creative nonfiction, and a poem or group of poems. Deadline: November 30. Charges $15 fee (includes a subscription to *The Nebraska Review*). Prize: $500 for each category.

[N] **NEW LETTERS LITERARY AWARDS**, *New Letters*, 5101 Rockhill Rd., Kansas City MO 64110-2499. (816)235-1168. Fax: (816)235-2611. E-mail: newletters@umkc.edu. Website: www.umkc.edu/newletters. **Contact:** Aleatha Ezra. Award has 3 categories (fiction, poetry, and creative nonfiction) with 1 winner in each. Offered annually for previously unpublished work. Deadline: May 17, 2002. Always the closest Friday to May 15. Guidelines for SASE. Charges $10 fee. Prize: 1st Place: $1,000, plus publication; Runners-Up: A year's subscription to *New Letters* and consideration for publication. Judged by 2 rounds of regional writers (preliminary judging). Winners picked by an anonymous judge of national repute. Acquires first North American serial rights. Open to any writer.

NEW WRITERS AWARDS, Great Lakes Colleges Association New Writers Awards, English Department, The College of Wooster, Wooster OH 44691. (330)263-2575. Fax: (330)263-2693. E-mail: dbourne@mail.wooster.edu. **Contact:** Prof. Daniel Bourne, award director. Offered annually to the best first book of poetry and the best first book of fiction among those submitted by publishers. An honorarium of at least $300 will be guaranteed the author by each of the colleges visited. Open to any first book of poetry or fiction submitted by a publisher. Deadline: February 28. Guidelines for SASE. Prize: Winning authors tour the GLCA colleges, where they will participate in whatever activities they and the college deem appropriate.

NIMROD, The University of Tulsa, 600 S. College, Tulsa OK 74104-3189. (918)631-3080. Fax: (918)631-3033. E-mail: nimrod@utulsa.edu. Website: www.utulsa.edu/nimrod. **Contact:** Francine Ringold, editor. Offered annually for unpublished fiction and poetry for Katherine Anne Porter Prize for Fiction and Pablo Neruda Prize for Poetry. Theme issue in the spring. *Nimrod*/Hardman Awards issue in the fall. For contest or theme issue guidelines send SASE. Open to any writer. Deadline: April 30. Charges $20 fee, includes 2 issues. Prize: 1st Place: $2,000 in each genre; 2nd Place: $1,000.

NLAPW VIRGINIA LIEBELER BIENNIAL GRANTS FOR MATURE WOMEN, National League of American Pen Women, Inc., 1300 17th St. NW, Washington DC 20036-1973. (202)785-1997. **Contact:** Mary Jane Hillery. Offered in even years for career enhancement in the creative arts. Three categories: art, letters, and music. Open to women 35 and over who are US citizens. No phone calls. Deadline: October 1, 2003. Guidelines for SASE. Charges $8. Prize: $1,000 grant in each category.

OHIOANA BOOK AWARDS, Ohioana Library Association, 274 E. First Ave., Columbus OH 43201-3673. (614)466-3831. Fax: (614)728-6974. E-mail: ohioana@sloma.state.oh.us. Website: www.oplin.lib.oh.us/OHIOANA. **Contact:** Linda Hengst, director. Offered annually to bring national attention to Ohio authors and their books (published in the last 2 years). Categories: Fiction, nonfiction, juvenile, poetry, and books about Ohio or an Ohioan. Books about Ohio or an Ohioan need not be written by an Ohioan. Writers must have been born in Ohio or lived in Ohio for at least 5 years. Deadline: December 31. Guidelines for SASE.

PEACE WRITING INTERNATIONAL WRITING AWARDS, Consortium of Peace Research, Education & Development, 2582 Jimmie, Fayettville AR 72703-3420. (501)442-4600. E-mail: jbennet@uark.edu. Website: comp.uark.edu/~jbennet. **Contact:** Dick Bennett. Offered annually for unpublished books. "PeaceWriting encourages writing about war and international nonviolent peacemaking and peacemakers. PeaceWriting seeks book manuscripts about the causes, consequences, and solutions to violence and war, and about the ideas and practices of nonviolent peacemaking and the lives of nonviolent peacemakers." Three categories: Nonfiction Prose (history, political science, memoirs); Imaginative Literature (novels, collections of short stories, collections of poetry, collections of short plays); and Works for Young People. Open to any writer. Enclose SASE for ms return. Deadline: December 1. Guidelines for SASE. Prize: $500 for best nonfiction; $500 for best imaginative work; and $500 for best work for young people.

PEN CENTER USA WEST ANNUAL LITERARY AWARDS, PEN Center USA West, 672 S. Lafayette Park Place, #42, Los Angeles CA 90057. (213)365-8500. Fax: (213)365-9616. E-mail: awards@penusa.org. Website: www.penusa.org. **Contact:** Gail Christian, executive director. Offered annually for fiction, nonfiction, poetry, children's literature, or translation published January 1-December 31 of the current year. Open to authors west of the Mississippi River. Deadline: December 31. Guidelines for SASE. Charges $25 fee. Prize: $1,000.

PEN WRITING AWARDS FOR PRISONERS, PEN American Center, 568 Broadway, New York NY 10012. (212)334-1660. Fax: (212)334-2181. E-mail: pen@echonyc.com. Website: www.pen.org. Offered annually to the authors of the best poetry, plays, short fiction, and nonfiction received from prison writers in the US. Deadline: Submit January 1-September 1. Guidelines for SASE. Prize: 1st Place: $100; 2nd Place: $50; 3rd Place: $25 (in each category).

POSTCARD STORY COMPETITION, The Writers' Union of Canada, 40 Wellington St. E., 3rd Floor, Toronto, Ontario M5E 1C7, Canada. (416)703-8982, ext. 223. Fax: (416)504-7656. E-mail: projects@writersunion.ca. Website: www.writersunion.ca. **Contact:** Caroline Sin. Offered annually for original and unpublished fiction, nonfiction, prose, verse, dialogue, etc. with a maximum 250 words in length. Open to Canadian citizens or landed immigrants only. Deadline: February 14. Guidelines for SASE. Charges $5 entry fee. Prize: $500.

THE PRESIDIO LA BAHIA AWARD, Sons of the Republic of Texas, 1717 Eighth St., Bay City TX 77414. (979)245-6644. Fax: (979)244-3819. E-mail: srttexas@srttexas.org. Website: www.srttexas.org. **Contact:** Janet Hick. Offered annually "to promote suitable preservation of relics, appropriate dissemination of data, and research into our Texas heritage, with particular attention to the Spanish Colonial period." Deadline: June 1-September 30. Guidelines for SASE. Prize: $2,000 total; 1st Place: Minimum of $1,200, 2nd and 3rd prizes at the discretion of the judges.

QUINCY WRITER'S GUILD ANNUAL CREATIVE WRITING CONTEST, Quincy Writer's Guild, P.O. Box 433, Quincy IL 62306-0433. E-mail: chillebr@adams.net. Website: www.quincylibrary.org/guild.htm. **Contact:** Carol Hillebrenner, contest coordinator. Categories include serious poetry, light poetry, nonfiction, fiction. "No identification should appear on manuscripts, but send a separate 3×5 card for each entry with name, address, phone number, e-mail address, word count, and title of work." Only for previously unpublished work: serious or light poetry (2 page/poem maximum), fiction (2,000 words maximum), nonfiction (2,000 words maximum). Guidelines for SASE or by e-mail. Period of Contest: January 1-April 1. Charges $2/poem; $4/fiction or nonfiction. Prize: Cash prizes.

QWF LITERARY AWARDS, Quebec Writers' Federation, 1200 Atwater Ave., Montreal, Quebec H3Z 1X4, Canada. (514)933-0878. Fax: (514)934-2485. E-mail: qspell@total.net. Website: www.qwf.org. **Contact:** Diana McNeill. Offered annually for a book published October 1-September 30 to honor excellence in English-language writing in Quebec. Categories: fiction, nonfiction, poetry and First Book, and translation. Author must have resided in Quebec for 3 of the past 5 years. Deadline: May 31 for books, and August 15 for books and finished proofs. Guidelines for SASE. Charges $10/title. Prize: $2,000 in each category; $1,000: First Book.

SUMMERFIELD G. ROBERTS AWARD, Sons of the Republic of Texas, 1717 Eighth St., Bay City TX 77414. (979)245-6644. Fax: (979)244-3819. E-mail: srttexas@srttexas.org. Website: www.srttexas.org. **Contact:** Janet Hicks. Offered annually for submissions published during the previous calendar year "to encourage literary effort and research about historical events and personalities during the days of the Republic of Texas, 1836-1846, and to stimulate interest in the period." Deadline: January 15. Prize: $2,500.

SASKATCHEWAN BOOK OF THE YEAR AWARD, Saskatchewan Book Awards, Inc., Box 1921, Regina, Saskatchewan S4P 3E1, Canada. (306)569-1585. Fax: (306)569-4187. E-mail: director@bookawards.sk.ca. Website: www.bookawards.sk.ca. **Contact:** Joyce Wells, executive director. Offered for work published September 15 to September 14 annually. This award is presented to a Saskatchewan author for the best book, judged on the quality of writing. Books from the following categories will be considered: children's; drama; fiction (short fiction by a single author, novellas, novels); nonfiction (all categories of nonfiction writing except cookbooks, directories, how-to books, or bibliographies of minimal critical content); poetry. Deadline: First deadline: July 31; Final deadline: September 14. Guidelines for SASE. Charges $15 (Canadian). Prize: $1,500.

SHORT GRAIN WRITING CONTEST, *Grain* Magazine, P.O. Box 1154, Regina, Saskatchewan S4P 3B4, Canada. (306)244-2828. Fax: (306)244-0255. E-mail: grain.mag@sk.sympatico.ca. Website: www.skwriter.com/grain. **Contact:** Jennifer Still. Contest Director: Elizabeth Philips. Offered annually for unpublished dramatic monologues, postcard stories (narrative fiction) and prose (lyric) poetry, and nonfiction creative prose. Maximum length for short entries, 500 words; Long Grain of Truth (nonfiction), 5,000 words or less. Guidelines for SAE and IRC or Canadian stamps. All entrants receive a 1-year subscription to *Grain*. *Grain* purchases first Canadian serial rights only; copyright remains with the author. Open to any writer. No fax or e-mail submissions. Deadline: January 31. Charges $22 fee for 2 entries, plus $5 for additional entries; US and international entries $22, plus $4 postage in US funds (nonCanadian). Prize: Three prizes of $500.

SHORT PROSE COMPETITION FOR DEVELOPING WRITERS, The Writers' Union of Canada, 40 Wellington St. E., 3rd Floor, Toronto, Ontario M5E 1C7, Canada. (416)703-8982, ext. 223. Fax: (416)504-7656. E-mail: projects@writersunion.ca. Website: www.writersunion.ca. **Contact:** Caroline Sin. Offered annually "to discover developing Canadian writers of unpublished prose fiction and nonfiction." Length: 2,500 words maximum. Open to Canadian citizens or landed immigrants who have not been published in book format, and who do not currently have a contract with a publisher. Deadline: November 3. Guidelines for SASE. Charges $25 entry fee. Prize: $2,500 and publication in a literary journal.

THE BERNICE SLOTE AWARD, *Prairie Schooner*, 201 Andrews Hall, PO Box 880334, Lincoln NE 68588-0334. (402)472-0911. Fax: (402)472-9771. E-mail: eflanagan2@unl.edu. Website: www.unl.edu/schooner/psmain.htm. **Contact:** Hilda Raz. Offered annually for the best work by a beginning writer published in *Prairie Schooner* in the previous year. Prize: $500.

SOUTHWEST REVIEW AWARDS, Southern Methodist University, 307 Fondren Library W., P.O. Box 750374, Dallas TX 75275-0374. (214)768-1036. Fax: (214)768-1408. E-mail: swr@mail.smu.edu. Website: www.southwestreview.org. **Contact:** Elizabeth Mills. "The $500 John H. McGinnis Memorial Award is given each year for fiction and nonfiction that has been published in the *Southwest Review* in the previous year. Stories or articles are not submitted directly for the award, but simply for publication in the magazine. The Elizabeth Matchett Stover Award, an annual prize of $250, is awarded to the author of the best poem or group of poems published in the magazine during the preceding year."

WALLACE STEGNER FELLOWSHIPS, Creative Writing Program, Stanford University, Department of English, Stanford CA 94305-2087. (650)723-2637. Fax: (650)723-3679. E-mail: gay.pierce@leland.stanford.edu. Website: www.stanford.edu/dept/english/cw/. **Contact:** Gay Pierce, program administrator. Offered annually for a 2-year residency at Stanford for emerging writers to attend the Stegner workshop to practice and perfect their craft under the guidance of the creative writing faculty. Guidelines available. Deadline: December 1. Charges $50 fee. Prize: Living stipend (currently $22,000/year) and required workshop tuition of $6,500/year.

subTERRAIN MAGAZINE AWARDS, (formerly *sub-TERRAIN* Magazine Awards), *subTERRAIN* Magazine, 175 E. Broadway, #204A, Vancouver, British Columbia V5T 1W2, Canada. (604)876-8710. Fax: (604)879-2667. E-mail: subter@portal.ca. Website: www.anvilpress.com. **Contact:** Brian Kaufman, managing editor. Offered annually for nonfiction, poems, short stories, and photography. Contests include the *subTERRAIN* Creative Nonfiction Writing Contest, Poetry Contest, and Annual Short Story Contest. The magazine acquires one-time rights only; after publication rights revert to the author. Deadline: Varies. Charges $15 fee, which includes a subscription to the magazine. Prize: Cash and publication.

TENNESSEE WRITERS ALLIANCE LITERARY COMPETITION, Tennessee Writers Alliance, P.O. Box 120396, Nashville TN 37212. (615)831-0072. Website: www.tn-writers.org. **Contact:** Dawn Pharris, executive director. Offered annually for unpublished short fiction and poetry. Membership open to all, regardless of residence, for $25/year; $15/year for students. " For more information and guidelines visit our website or send a SASE." Deadline: June 15. Charges $10 fee for members, $15 fee for nonmembers. Prize: 1st Place: $500; 2nd Place: $250; 3rd Place: $100.

THOUGHT MAGAZINE WRITER'S CONTEST, *Thought Magazine*, P.O. Box 117098, Burlingame CA 94011-7098. E-mail: ThoughtMagazine@yahoo.com. Website: www.thoughtmagazine.org. **Contact:** Kevin J. Feeney. Offered twice a year "to recognize and publish quality writing in the areas of short fiction, poetry, and short nonfiction, and to identify and give exposure to writers who have not yet been published." Fiction and nonfiction maximum of 3,000 words; poetry maximum of 100 lines. Include name, address, phone number, and/or e-mail. Buys one-time publication rights for winning entries. Deadline: August 15 and April 15. Guidelines for SASE. Charges $5/story or essay or 3 poems. Prize: 1st Place: $75, plus publication; 2nd Place: $50, plus publication; all submissions considered for publication.

TORONTO BOOK AWARD, City of Toronto c/o Toronto Protocol, 100 Queen St. W., 10th Floor, West Tower, City Hall, Toronto, Ontario M5H 2N2, Canada. (416)392-8191. Fax: (416)392-1247. Website: www.city.toronto.on.ca. **Contact:** Bev Kurmey, protocol consultant. Offered annually for previously published fiction, nonfiction, or juvenile books that are "evocative of Toronto." Deadline: February 28. Guidelines for SASE. Prize: Awards total $15,000.

MARK TWAIN AWARD FOR SHORT FICTION, *Red Rock Review*/Community College of Southern Nevada, English Department, 3200 E. Cheyenne Ave., N. Las Vegas NV 89030. (702)651-4094. Fax: (702)651-4639. E-mail: richard_logsdon@ccsn.nevada.edu. Website: www.ccsn.nevada.edu/english/redrockreview/contest.htm. **Contact:** Rich Logsdon, editor. Offered annually for unpublished fiction to emerging writers of fiction and poetry. Deadline: October 31. Charges $10 fee. Prize: $1,000.

WESTERN HERITAGE AWARDS, National Cowboy & Western Heritage Museum, 1700 NE 63rd, Oklahoma City OK 73111. (405)478-6404. Fax: (405)478-4714. E-mail: editor@nationalcowboymuseum.org. Website: www.nationalcowboymuseum.org. **Contact:** M.J. VanDeventer, publications director. Offered annually for excellence in representation of great stories of the American West published November 30-December 1. Competition includes 7 literary categories: nonfiction; western novel; juvenile book; art book; short story; poetry book; and magazine article.

WESTERN MAGAZINE AWARDS, Western Magazine Awards Foundation, Main Post Office, Box 2131, Vancouver, British Columbia V6B 3T8, Canada. (604)669-3717. Fax: (604)669-3701. E-mail: wma@direct.ca. Website: www.westernmagazineawards.com. **Contact:** Bryan Pike. Offered annually for magazine work published January 1-December 31 of previous calendar year. Entry categories include business, culture, science, technology and medicine, entertainment, fiction, political issues, and much more. Guidelines for SASE or on website. Applicant must be Canadian citizen, landed immigrant, or full-time resident. The work must have been published in a magazine whose main editorial office is in Western Canada, the Northwest Territories, and Yukon. Deadline: February 23. Charges $27 for work in magazines with circulation under 20,000; $35 for work in magazines with circulation over 20,000. Prize: $500.

WESTMORELAND SHORT STORY & POETRY CONTEST, Westmoreland Arts & Heritage Festival, RD2, Box 355A, Latrobe PA 15650-9415. (724)834-7474. Fax: (724)834-2717. E-mail: info@artsandheritage.com. Website: www.artsandheritage.com. **Contact:** Donnie A. Gutherie. Offered annually for unpublished work. Writers are encouraged to submit short stories from all genres. The purpose of the contest is to provide writers varied competition in 2 categories: short story and poetry. Entries must be 4,000 words or less. No erotica or pornography. Deadline: March 2. Guidelines for SASE. Charges $10 fee/story, $10 fee/2 poems. Prize: Publication on the festival website, a reading at the festival, and cash prizes from $75-200.

WIND MAGAZINE CONTESTS, *Wind Magazine*, P.O. Box 24548, Lexington KY 40524. (859)277-6849. Website: www.wind.wind.org. **Contact:** Chris Green, editor. Offered annually for unpublished poems, chapbooks, and short stories. Deadline: March 1 for poems; July 30 for short stories; October 31 for chapbooks. Guidelines for SASE. Charges $3/poem, $10/short story, and $15/chapbook. Prize: $500, and publication in *Wind Magazine* for winning poem and short story; $100 plus 25 copies of winning chapbook; chapbook is published as summer issue of *Wind*. All entries receive copy of chapbook. All finalists receive a 1-year subscription to the magazine. Enclose SASE for results.

Arts Councils & Foundations

ALASKA STATE COUNCIL ON THE ARTS CAREER OPPORTUNITY GRANT AWARD, Alaska State Council on the Arts, 411 W. 4th Ave., Suite 1E, Anchorage AK 99501-2343. (907)269-6610. Fax: (907)269-6601. E-mail: info@ecd.state.ak.us. Website: www.aksca.org. **Contact:** Director. Grants help artists take advantage of impending, concrete opportunities that will significantly advance their work or careers. Deadline: Applications must be received by the first of the month preceding the proposed activity. Prize: Up to $1,000.

AMERICAN REGIONAL HISTORY PUBLISHING AWARDS, Tamarack Books, Inc., P.O. Box 190313, Boise ID 83719. (208)922-2229. Fax: (208)922-5880. Offered in even-numbered years for a work of regional history published during the previous 2 years. At least 90% of the work must represent 1 of the following 5 geographic regions: Northeastern states, Southeastern states, Central/Midwest states, Western states, Pacific states. Deadline: February 1 of even years. Guidelines for SASE. Charges $30. Prize: Extensive publicity of award.

ARIZONA COMMISSION ON THE ARTS FELLOWSHIPS IN CREATIVE WRITING, Arizona Commission on the Arts, 417 W. Roosevelt, Phoenix AZ 85018. (602)255-5882. Fax: (602)256-0282. E-mail: general@ArizonaArts.org. Website: www.ArizonaArts.org. **Contact:** Paul Morris, literature director. Offered annually for previously published or unpublished fiction or poetry written within the last 3 years. Guidelines on website. Open to Arizona residents 18 years or older. Deadline: September 12, 2002 (poetry); mid-September 2003 (fiction). Prize: $5,000.

ARTIST ASSISTANCE FELLOWSHIP, Minnesota State Arts Board, Park Square Court, 400 Sibley St., Suite 200, St. Paul MN 55101-1928. (651)215-1600 or (800)866-2787. Fax: (651)215-1602. E-mail: amy.frimpong@arts.state.mn.us. Website: www.arts.state.mn.us. **Contact:** Amy Frimpong. Literary categories include prose, poetry, playwriting, and screenwriting. Open to Minnesota residents. Prize: Annual fellowships of $8,000 to be used for time, materials, living expenses.

ARTIST FELLOWSHIP, Japan Foundation, 39th Floor, 152 W. 57th St., New York NY 10019. (212)489-0299. Fax: (212)489-0409. E-mail: katherine_wearne@jfny.org. Website: www.jfny.org/. **Contact:** Katherine Wearne. Offered annually. "Contact us in September by mail or fax. Keep in mind that this is an international competition. Due to the breadth of the application pool only 4 artists are selected for awards in the U.S. Applicants need not submit a writing sample, but if one is submitted it must be brief. Three letters of recommendation must be submitted from peers. One letter will double as a letter of affiliation, which must be submitted by a *Japan-based* (not necessarily an ethnic Japanese) peer artist. The applicant must present a concise and cogent project objective, and must be a professional writer/artist with accessible qualifications, i.e., a list of major works or publications." Deadline: December 1.

ARTIST FELLOWSHIP AWARDS, Wisconsin Arts Board, 101 E. Wilson St. 1st Floor, Madison WI 53702. (608)266-0190. Fax: (608)267-0380. E-mail: artsboard@arts.state.wi.us. Website: www.arts.state.wi.us. **Contact:** Mark Fraire, grant programs and services specialist. Offered every 2 years (even years), rewarding outstanding, professionally active Wisconsin artists by supporting their continued development, enabling them to create new work, complete work in progress, or pursue activities which contribute to their artistic growth. If the deadline falls on a weekend, the deadline is extended to the following Monday. Application is found on the Wisconsin Arts Board website at www.arts.state.wi.us on August 2, 2002. The Arts Board requires permission to use the work sample, or a portion thereof, for publicity or educational purposes. Contest open to professionally active artists who have resided in Wisconsin 1 year prior to application. Artists who are full-time students pursuing a degree in the fine arts at the time of application are not eligible. Deadline: September 17, 2002. Prize: $8,000 fellowship awarded to 8 Wisconsin writers.

ARTISTS FELLOWSHIP PROGRAM IN POETRY & PROSE, Illinois Art Council, 100 W. Randolph, Suite 10-500, Chicago IL 60601. (312)814-6740. Fax: (312)814-1471. E-mail: susan@arts.state.il.us. Website: www.state.il.us/

agency/iac. **Contact:** Susan Eleuterio, director, literature. Offered annually for Illinois writers of exceptional talent to enable them to pursue their artistic goals. Applicant must have been a resident of Illinois for at least 1 year prior to the deadline. Guidlines for SASE. Deadline: December 1. Prize: Nonmatching award of $7,000; finalist award of $700.

ARTS RECOGNITION AND TALENT SEARCH, National Foundation for Advancement in the Arts, 800 Brickell Ave., Suite 500, Miami FL 33131. (305)377-1140 or (800)970-ARTS. Fax: (305)377-1149. E-mail: nfaa@nfaa.org. Website: www.ARTSawards.org. **Contact:** Lisanne Martin, programs manager. Estab. 1981. For achievements in dance, music, jazz, photography, theater, film & videos, visual art, voice, and writing. Applications available on website or by phone request. Deadline: Early-June 1 ($25 fee); regular-October 1 ($35 fee). Prize: Exceptionally talented young artists have access to an award package totaling up to $800,000—$3 million in scholarship opportunities and the chance to be named Presidential Scholars in the Arts.

GEORGE BENNETT FELLOWSHIP, Phillips Exeter Academy, 20 Main St., Exeter NH 03833-2460. Website: www.exeter.edu. **Contact:** Charles Pratt, coordinator, selection committee. Estab. 1968. Annual award for Fellow and family "to provide time and freedom from material considerations to a person seriously contemplating or pursuing a career as a writer. Applicants should have a manuscript in progress which they intend to complete during the fellowship period." Duties: To be in residency for the academic year; to make oneself available informally to students interested in writing. Guidelines for SASE or on website. The committee favors writers who have not yet published a book with a major publisher. Residence at the Academy during the Fellowship period required. Deadline: December 1. Prize: Annual award of $6,000 stipend, room and board.

BUSH ARTIST FELLOWS PROGRAM, The Bush Foundation, E-900 First National Bank Bldg., 332 Minnesota St., St. Paul MN 55101. (651)227-0891. Fax: (651)297-6485. Website: www.bushfoundation.org. **Contact:** Kathi Polley, program assistant. Estab. 1976. Award for Minnesota, North Dakota, South Dakota, and western Wisconsin residents 25 years or older (students are not eligible) "to buy 12-18 months of time for the applicant to further his/her own work." All application categories rotate on a 2-year cycle. Publishing, performance, and/or option requirements for eligibility. Applications available August 2002. Deadline: October. Prize: Up to 15 fellowships/year, $44,000 each.

N **ChLA RESEARCH FELLOWSHIPS & SCHOLARSHIPS**, Children's Literature Association, P.O. Box 138, Battle Creek MI 49016-0138. (616)965-8180. Fax: (616)965-3568. E-mail: kkiessling@childlitassn.org. Website: www.childlitassn.org. **Contact:** ChLA Scholarship Chair. Offered annually. "The fellowships are available for proposals dealing with criticism or original scholarship with the expectation that the undertaking will lead to publication and make a significant contribution to the field of children's literature in the area of scholarship or criticism." Funds are not intended for work leading to the completion of a professional degree. Deadline: February 1. Guidelines for SASE. Prize: $250-1,000.

CREATIVITY FELLOWSHIP, Northwood University, Alden B. Dow Creativity Center, 4000 Whiting Dr., Midland MI 48640-2398. (989)837-4478. Fax: (989)837-4468. E-mail: creativity@northwood.edu. Website: www.northwood.edu/abd. **Contact:** Award Director. Estab. 1979. Ten-week summer residency for individuals in any field who wish to pursue new and creative ideas that have potential impact in their fields. No accommodations for family/pets. Write for guidelines or check website. Authors must be US citizens. Deadline: December 31 (postmarked).

N **FELLOWSHIP PROGRAM**, New Jersey State Council on the Arts, 225 W. State St., P.O. Box 306, Trenton NJ 08625. (609)292-6130. Fax: (609)989-1440. E-mail: njsca@njartscouncil.org. Website: www.njartscouncil.org. **Contact:** Beth A. Vogel, program officer. Offered every other year. Writers may apply in either poetry, playwriting, or prose. Fellowship awards are intended to provide support for the artist during the year to enable him or her to continue producing new work. Send for guidelines and application, or visit website. Must be NJ residents; may *not* be undergraduate or graduate matriculating students. Deadline: July 15. Prize: $5,000-12,000.

FELLOWSHIP-LITERATURE, Alabama State Council on the Arts, 201 Monroe St., Montgomery AL 36130. (334)242-4076, ext. 224. Fax: (334)240-3269. E-mail: randy@arts.state.al.us. Website: www.arts.state.al.us. **Contact:** Randy Shoults. Literature Fellowship offered every year, for previously published or unpublished work to set aside time to create and to improve skills. Two-year Alabama residency required. Guidelines available. Deadline: March 1. Prize: $10,000 or $5,000.

FELLOWSHIPS (LITERATURE), RI State Council on the Arts, 83 Park St., 6th Floor, Providence RI 02903. (401)222-3880. Fax: (401)222-3018. E-mail: info@risca.state.ri.us. Website: www.risca.state.ri.us. **Contact:** Fellowship Coordinator. Offered every year for previously published or unpublished works in the categories of poetry, fiction, and playwriting/screenwriting. Open to Rhode Island residents only. Deadline: April 1, 2002. Guidelines for SASE. Prize: $5,000 fellowship; $1,000 runner-up.

FELLOWSHIPS TO ASSIST RESEARCH AND ARTISTIC CREATION, John Simon Guggenheim Memorial Foundation, 90 Park Ave., New York NY 10016. (212)687-4470. Fax: (212)697-3248. E-mail: fellowships@gf.org. Website: www.gf.org. Offered annually to assist scholars and artists to engage in research in any field of knowledge and creation in any of the arts, under the freest possible conditions and irrespective of race, color, or creed. Application form is required. Deadline: October 1.

FLORIDA INDIVIDUAL ARTIST FELLOWSHIPS, Florida Department of State, Division of Cultural Affairs, The Capitol, Tallahassee FL 32399-0250. (850)487-2980, ext. 117. Fax: (850)922-5259. E-mail: vohlsson@mail.dos.state.fl.us. Website: www.dos.state.fl.us. **Contact:** Valerie Ohlsson, arts administrator. Open to Florida writers only. Deadline: February. Prize: $5,000 each for fiction, poetry, and children's literature.

N **GIFT OF FREEDOM**, A Room of Her Own Foundation, P.O. Box 778, Placitas NM 87043. E-mail: info@aroomofherownfoundation.org. Website: www.aroomofherownfoundation.org. **Contact:** Darlene Chandler Bassett. Award to provide very practical help both materially and in professional guidance and moral support, to women who need assistance in making their creative contribution to the world. Annually. Deadline: May 30, 2002. The deadline is always sometime in the spring. Guidelines for SASE. Charges $15. Prize: Up to $50,000 over two years, also a mentor for advice and dialogue, and access to the Advisory Council for professional and business consultation. Judged by members of AROHO's Board of Directors, Advisory Council and volunteers from a wide variety of backgrounds.

THE HODDER FELLOWSHIP, The Council of the Humanities, Joseph Henry House, Princeton University, Princeton NJ 08544. (609)258-4717. Fax: (609)258-2783. E-mail: humcounc@princeton.edu. Website: www.princeton.edu/~humcounc/. **Contact:** Cass Garner. The Hodder Fellowship is awarded to a humanist in the early stages of a career for the pursuit of independent work at Princeton in the humanities. The recipient has usually written 1 book and is working on a second. Preference is given to applicants outside of academia. "The Fellowship is designed specifically to identify and nurture extraordinary potential rather than to honor distinguished achievement." Candidates for the Ph.D. are not eligible. Submit résumé, sample of work (up to 10 pages), proposal, and SASE. Deadline: November 1. Prize: Approximately $51,000 stipend.

INDIVIDUAL ARTIST FELLOWSHIPS/MINI-FELLOWSHIPS, Kansas Arts Commission, 700 SW Jackson St., Suite 1004, Topeka KS 66603-3761. (785)296-3335. Fax: (785)296-4989. E-mail: kac@arts.state.ks.us. Website: arts.state.ks.us. **Contact:** Karen Brady. Offered annually for Kansas artists, both published and unpublished. Fellowships are offered in 10 artistic disciplines, rotating 5 disciplines every other year, and are awarded based on artistic merit. The fellowship disciplines are music composition, choreography, film/video, interdisciplinary/performance art, playwriting, fiction, poetry, 2-dimensional visual art, 3-dimensional visual art, and crafts. Mini-fellowships (up to 12) are awarded annually to emerging artists in the same 10 disciplines. Guidelines on website. Deadline: Varies. Prize: Fellowship: $5,000. Mini-fellowship: $500.

INDIVIDUAL ARTISTS FELLOWSHIPS, Nebraska Arts Council, 3838 Davenport St., Omaha NE 68131-2329. (402)595-2122. Fax: (402)595-2334. E-mail: swise@nebraskaartscouncil.org. Website: www.nebraskaartscouncil.org. **Contact:** Suzanne Wise. Estab. 1991. Offered every 3 years (literature alternates with other disciplines) to recognize exemplary achievements by originating artists in their fields of endeavor and support the contributions made by Nebraska artists to the quality of life in this state. "Generally, distinguished achievement awards are $5,000 and merit awards are $1,000-2,000. Funds available are announced in September prior to the deadline." Must be a resident of Nebraska for at least 2 years prior to submission date; 18 years of age; not enrolled in an undergraduate, graduate, or certificate-granting program in English, creative writing, literature, or related field. Deadline: November 15, 2002. Prize: $5,000, and merit awards are $1,000-2,000.

N **CHRISTOPHER ISHERWOOD FELLOWSHIPS**, Christopher Isherwood Foundation, Box 650, Montrose AL 36559. E-mail: james@americanartists.org. Website: www.isherwoodfoundation.org. **Contact:** James P. White, contest director. Awards are given annually to selected novelists who have published a novel. Deadline: October 1, 2002. Prize: Fellowship consists of $3,000. Judges chosen by advisory board. Open to any writer.

JOSEPH HENRY JACKSON AWARD, The San Francisco Foundation, Administered by Intersection for the Arts, 446 Valencia St., San Francisco CA 94103. (415)626-2787. Fax: (415)626-1636. E-mail: info@theintersection.org. **Contact:** Kevin B. Chen, program director. Estab. 1965. Offered annually for unpublished, work-in-progress fiction (novel or short story), nonfiction, or poetry by an author age 20-35, with 3-year consecutive residency in northern California or Nevada prior to submission. Deadline: November 15-January 31. Guidelines for SASE.

EZRA JACK KEATS MEMORIAL FELLOWSHIP, Ezra Jack Keats Foundation (funding) awarded through Kerlan Collection, University of Minnesota, 113 Andersen Library, 222 21st Ave. S., Minneapolis MN 55455. (612)624-4576. Fax: (612)625-5525. E-mail: CLRC@tc.umn.edu. Website: special.lib.umn.edu/clrc/. **Contact:** Library Assistant. Purpose is "to award a talented writer and/or illustrator of children's books who wishes to use Kerlan Collection for the furtherance of his or her artistic development. Special consideration will be given to someone who would find it difficult to finance the visit to the Kerlan Collection." Open to any writer and illustrator. Deadline: May 1. Guidelines for SASE. Prize: $1,500 for travel to study at Kerlan Collection.

KENTUCKY ARTS COUNCILS FELLOWSHIPS IN WRITING, Kentucky Arts Council, Old Capitol Annex, 300 W. Broadway, Frankfort KY 40601. (502)564-3757 or (888)833-2787. Fax: (502)564-2839. E-mail: heather.lyons@mail.state.ky.us. Website: www.kyarts.org. **Contact:** Heather Lyons. Offered in even-numbered years for development/artist's work. Guidelines for SASE (3 months before deadline). Must be Kentucky resident. Deadline: September 15, 2002. Prize: $7,500.

MONEY FOR WOMEN, Barbara Deming Memorial Fund, Inc., P.O. Box 630125, The Bronx NY 10463. **Contact:** Susan Pliner. "Small grants to individual feminists in art, fiction, nonfiction, and poetry, whose work addresses women's concerns and/or speaks for peace and justice from a feminist perspective." Guidelines and required entry forms for

SASE. "The Fund does not give educational assistance, monies for personal study or loans, monies for dissertation, research projects, or self-publication, grants for group projects, business ventures, or emergency funds for hardships." Open to citizens of the US or Canada. The fund also offers 2 awards, the "Gertrude Stein Award" for outstanding works by a lesbian and the "Fannie Lou Hamer Award" for work which combats racism and celebrates women of color. No special application necessary for these 2 awards. Recipients will be chosen from all the proposals. Deadline: December 31 and June 30. Prize: Grants up to $1,500.

LARRY NEAL WRITERS' COMPETITION, DC Commission on the Arts and Humanities, 410 Eighth St., NW, 5th Floor, Washington DC 20004. (202)724-1475. Fax: (202)727-4135. E-mail: lionellt@hotmail.com. Website: www.capaccess.org/dccah. **Contact:** Lionell C. Thomas, grants and legislative officer. Offered annually for unpublished poetry, fiction, essay, and dramatic writing. Call or visit website for current deadlines. Open to Washington DC residents only. Prize: Cash awards.

PEW FELLOWSHIPS IN THE ARTS, The University of the Arts, 230 S. Broad St., Suite 1003, Philadelphia PA 19102. (215)875-2285. Fax: (215)875-2276. Website: www.pewarts.org. **Contact:** Melissa Franklin, director. Offered annually to provide financial support directly to artists so that they may have the opportunity to dedicate themselves wholly to the development of their artwork for up to 2 years. Areas of interest have included fiction, creative nonfiction, poetry, playwriting, and screenwriting. Call for guidelines or view from the website. Entrants must be 25 or older and have been Pennsylvania residents of Bucks, Chester, Delaware, Montgomery, or Philadelphia counties for 2 years or longer. Current students are not eligible. Deadline: December. Prize: $50,000 fellowship.

JAMES D. PHELAN LITERARY AWARD, The San Francisco Foundation, administered by Intersection for the Arts, 446 Valencia St., San Francisco CA 94103. (415)626-2787. Fax: (415)626-1636. E-mail: info@theintersection.org. **Contact:** Kevin B. Chen, program director. Estab. 1965. Offered annually for unpublished, work-in-progress fiction, nonfiction, short story, poetry, or drama by a California-born author age 20-35. Deadline: November 15-January 31. Guidelines for SASE.

STUDENT RESEARCH GRANT, the Society for the Scientific Study of Sexuality, P.O. Box 416, Allentown PA 18105-0416. (610)530-2483. Fax: (610)530-2485. E-mail: thesociety@inetmail.att.net. Website: www.sexscience.org. **Contact:** Ilsa Lottes. Offered twice a year for unpublished works. "The student research grant award is granted twice yearly to help support graduate student research on a variety of sexually related topics." Guidelines and entry forms for SASE. Open to students pursuing graduate study. Deadline: February 1 and September 1. Prize: $1,000.

STUDENT TRANSLATION PRIZE, American Translators Association, 225 Reinekers Lane, Suite 590, Alexandria VA 22314. (703)683-6100. Fax: (703)683-6122. E-mail: ata@atanet.org. Website: www.atanet.org. **Contact:** Jo Anne Englebert. Support is granted for a promising project to an unpublished student enrolled in a translation program at a US college or university. Must be sponsored by a faculty member. Deadline: April 15. Prize: $500, and up to $500 toward expenses for attending the ATA Annual Conference.

TRILLIUM BOOK AWARD/PRIX TRILLIUM, Ontario Ministry of Tourism, Culture and Recreation, 400 University Ave., 5th Floor, Toronto, Ontario M7A 2R9, Canada. (416)314-7786. Fax: (416)314-7460. E-mail: edward.yanofsky@MCZCR.gov.on.ca. Website: www.tourism.gov.on.ca. **Contact:** Edward Yanofsky, cultural industries officer. Offered annually for work previously published January 1-December 31. This is the Ontario government's annual literary award. There are 2 categories—an English-language category and a French-language category. Publishers submit books on behalf of authors. Authors must have been Ontario residents 3 of the last 5 years. Deadline: mid-December. Prize: The winning author in each category receives $12,000; the winning publisher in each category receives $2,500.

UCROSS FOUNDATION RESIDENCY, 30 Big Red Lane, Clearmont WY 82835. (307)737-2291. Fax: (307)737-2322. E-mail: ucross@wyoming.com. Website: www.ucrossfoundation.org. **Contact:** Sharon Dynak, executive director. Eight concurrent positions open for artists-in-residence in various disciplines (includes writers, visual artists, music, humanities, natural sciences) extending from 2 weeks-2 months. No charge for room, board, or studio space. Deadline: March 1 and October 1. Charges $20 application fee.

VERMONT ARTS COUNCIL, 136 State St., Drawer 33, Montpelier VT 05633-6001. (802)828-3291. Fax: (802)828-3363. E-mail: mbailey@arts.vca.state.vt.us. Website: www.vermontartscouncil.org. **Contact:** Michele Bailey. Offered quarterly for previously published or unpublished works. Opportunity Grants are for specific projects of writers (poetry, playwriters, fiction, nonfiction) as well as not-for-profit presses. Also available are Artist Development funds to provide technical assistance for Vermont writers. Write or call for entry information. Open to Vermont residents only. Prize: $250-5,000.

WRITERS FELLOWSHIPS, NC Arts Council, Department of Cultural Resources, Raleigh NC 27699-4632. (919)715-1519. E-mail: debbie.mcgill@ncmail.net. Website: www.ncarts.org. **Contact:** Deborah McGill, literature director. Offered every 2 years "to serve writers of fiction, poetry, literary nonfiction, and literary translation in North Carolina, and to recognize the contribution they make to this state's creative environment." Write for guidelines. Writer must have been a resident of NC for at least a year as of the application deadline and may not be enrolled in any degree-granting program at the time of application. Deadline: November 1, 2002. Prize: We offer 11 $8,000 grants every 2 years.

Resources

Publications

In addition to newsletters and publications from local and national organizations, there are trade publications, books, and directories which offer valuable information about writing and about marketing your manuscripts and understanding the business side of publishing. Some also list employment agencies that specialize in placing publishing professionals, and some announce actual freelance opportunities.

TRADE MAGAZINES

ADVERTISING AGE, Crain Communications, Inc., 711 Third Ave., New York NY 10017-4036. (212)210-0100. Website: www.adage.com. *Weekly magazine covering advertising in magazines, trade journals, and business.*

AMERICAN JOURNALISM REVIEW, 1117 Journalism Bldg. University of Maryland, College Park MD 20742-7111. (301)405-8803. Website: www.ajr.org. *10 issues/year magazine for journalists and communications professionals.*

DAILY VARIETY, Daily Variety Ltd./Reed Business Info, 5700 Wilshire Blvd., Suite 120, Los Angeles CA 90036. (323)857-6600. Website: www.variety.com. *Trade publication on the entertainment industry with helpful information for screenwriters.*

EDITOR & PUBLISHER, The Editor & Publisher Co., 770 Broadway, New York NY 10003-9595. (800)722-6658. Website: www.editorandpublisher.com. *Weekly magazine covering the newspaper publishing industry.*

FOLIO: The Magazine for Magazine Management, Cowles Business Media, 11 Riverbend Dr. S., P.O. Box 4272, Stamford CT 06907-0272. (203)358-9900. *Monthly magazine covering the magazine publishing industry.*

GIFTS & DECORATIVE ACCESSORIES, Reed Business Info, 345 Hudson St., 4th Floor, New York NY 10014. (212)519-7200. Website: www.giftsanddec.com. *Monthly magazine covering greeting cards among other subjects, with an annual buyer's directory in September.*

HORN BOOK MAGAZINE, 56 Roland St., Suite 200, Boston MA 02129. (617)628-0225. Website: www.hbook.com. *Bimonthly magazine covering children's literature.*

PARTY & PAPER RETAILER, 4 Ward Corp., 107 Mill Plain Rd., Suite 204, Danbury CT 06811. (203)730-4090. Website: www.partypaper.com. *Monthly magazine covering the greeting card and gift industry.*

PUBLISHERS WEEKLY, Bowker Magazine Group, Reed Business Info, 245 W. 17th St., 6th Floor, New York NY 10011. (212)645-0067. Website: www.publishersweekly.com. *Weekly magazine covering the book publishing industry.*

TRAVELWRITER MARKETLETTER, P.O. 1782, Springfield VA 22151-0782 (253)399-6270. Website: www.travelwriterml.com. *Monthly newsletter for travel writers with market listings as well as trip information.*

WRITER'S DIGEST, 4700 E. Galbraith Rd., Cincinnati OH 45236. (800)333-0133. Website: www.writersdigest.com. *Monthly writers' magazine.*

BOOKS AND DIRECTORIES

AV MARKET PLACE, R.R. Bowker, A Reed Reference Publishing Co., 630 Central Ave., New Providence NJ 07974. (888)269-5372. Website: www.bowker.com.

BACON'S NEWSPAPER & MAGAZINE DIRECTORIES, Bacon's Information, Inc., 332 S. Michigan Ave., Suite 900, Chicago IL 60604. (312)922-2400. Website: www.bacons.com.

THE COMPLETE BOOK OF SCRIPTWRITING, by J. Michael Straczynski, Writer's Digest Books, 4700 E. Galbraith Rd., Cincinnati OH 45236. (800)448-0915. Website: www.writersdigest.com.

THE COMPLETE GUIDE TO LITERARY CONTESTS, compiled by Literary Fountain, Prometheus Books, 59 John Glenn Dr., Amherst NY 14228-2197. (800)421-0351. Website: www.prometheusbooks.com.

THE COMPLETE GUIDE TO SELF-PUBLISHING, by Marilyn and Tom Ross, Writer's Digest Books, 4700 E. Galbraith Rd., Cincinnati OH 45236. (800)448-0915. Website: www.writersdigest.com.

DRAMATISTS SOURCEBOOK, edited by Kathy Sova, Theatre Communications Group, Inc., 355 Lexington Ave., 4th Floor, New York NY 10017. (212)697-5230. Website: www.tcg.org.

EDITORS ON EDITING: What Writers Need to Know About What Editors Do, edited by Gerald Gross, Grove/Atlantic Press, 841 Broadway, New York NY 10003. (212)614-7890.

FORMATTING & SUBMITTING YOUR MANUSCRIPT, by Jack and Glenda Neff, Don Prues and the editors of *Writer's Market*, Writer's Digest Books, 4700 E. Galbraith Rd., Cincinnati OH 45236. (800)448-0915. Website: www.writersdigest.com.

GRANTS AND AWARDS AVAILABLE TO AMERICAN WRITERS, PEN American Center, 568 Broadway, New York NY 10012. (212)334-1660. Website: www.pen.org.

GUERRILLA MARKETING FOR WRITERS, by Jay Conrad Levinson, Rick Frishman & Michael Larsen, Writer's Digest Books, 4700 E. Galbraith Rd., Cincinnati OH 45236. (800)448-0915. Website: www.writersdigest.com.

GUIDE TO LITERARY AGENTS, edited by Rachel Vater. Writer's Digest Books, 4700 E. Galbraith Rd., Cincinnati OH 45236. (800)448-0915. Website: www.writersdigest.com.

HOW TO WRITE IRRESISTIBLE QUERY LETTERS, by Lisa Collier Cool, Writer's Digest Books, 4700 E. Galbraith Rd., Cincinnati OH 45236. (800)448-0915. Website: www.writersdigest.com.

INTERNATIONAL DIRECTORY OF LITTLE MAGAZINES & SMALL PRESSES, edited by Len Fulton, Dustbooks, P.O. Box 100, Paradise CA 95967. (530)877-6110. Website: www.dustbooks.com.

JUMP START YOUR BOOK SALES, by Marilyn & Tom Ross, Writer's Digest Books, 4700 E. Galbraith Rd., Cincinnati OH 45236. (800)448-0915. Website: www.writersdigest.com.

LITERARY MARKET PLACE and INTERNATIONAL LITERARY MARKET PLACE, R.R. Bowker, A Reed Reference Publishing Co., 630 Central Ave., New Providence NJ 07974. (888)269-9372. Website: www.bowker.com.

MY BIG SOURCEBOOK, eei Communications, 66 Canal Center Plaza, Suite 200, Alexandria VA 22314-5507. (703)683-0683. Website: www.eeicommunications.com.

ONLINE MARKETS FOR WRITERS: How to Make Money By Selling Your Writing On the Internet, by Anthony Tedesco with Paul Tedesco, Owl Books/Henry Holt, 115 W. 18th St., New York NY 10011. (212)886-9200. E-mail: anthony@marketsforwriters.com.

STANDARD DIRECTORY OF ADVERTISING AGENCIES, National Register Publishing, A Reed Reference Publishing Co., 121 Chanlon Rd., New Providence NJ 07974. (800)473-7020. Website: www.nationalregisterpub.com.

SUCCESSFUL SCRIPTWRITING, by Jurgen Wolff and Kerry Cox, Writer's Digest Books, 4700 E. Galbraith Rd., Cincinnati OH 45236. (800)448-0915. Website: www.writersdigest.com.

WRITER'S ONLINE MARKETPLACE, by Debbie Ridpath Ohi, Writer's Digest Books, 4700 E. Galbraith Rd., Cincinnati OH 45236. (800)448-0915. Website: www.writersdigest.com.

WRITER'S MARKET COMPANION, by Joe Fiertag and Mary Carmen Cupito, Writer's Digest Books, 4700 E. Galbraith Rd., Cincinnati OH 45236. (800)448-0915. Website: www.writersdigest.com.

Websites

The Internet provides a wealth of information for writers. The number of websites devoted to writing and publishing is vast and continues to expand. Below is a short—and thus incomplete—list of websites that offer information and hypertext links to other pertinent sites relating to writing and publishing. Because the Internet is such an amorphous, evolving, mutable entity with website addresses launching, crashing, and changing daily, some of these addresses may be obsolete by the time this book goes to print. But this list does give you a few starting points for your online journey. If, in the course of your electronic ventures, you find additional websites of interest, please let us know by e-mailing us at writersmarket@fwpubs.com.

Link sites

Books A to Z: www.booksatoz.com

Information on publications, services, and leads to other useful websites, including areas for book research, production services, self-publishing, bookstores, organizations, and publishers.

Bookwire: www.bookwire.com

A gateway to finding information about publishers, booksellers, libraries, authors, reviews, and awards. Also offers information about frequently asked publishing questions and answers, a calendar of events, a mailing list, and other helpful resources.

Dictionary.com: www.dictionary.com

If you're not sure about what the word "meticulous" means, then use this searchable site. The site also provides links to Roget's Thesaurus, *international dictionaries, and translator tools.*

Encyclopedia.com: www.encyclopedia.com

This free encyclopedia offers more than 50,000 articles, plus links to more.

Freelance Writers: www.freelancewrite.about.com

Links to resources relating to jobs, business writing, contracts, and grantwriting.

Pilot-search: www.pilot-search.com

This search engine features more than 11,000 literary links. Writing advice is given, and information is posted on workshops, fellowships, and literary job openings.

Publishers' Catalogues Home Page: www.lights.com/publisher

A mammoth link collection of publishers around the world arranged geographically. This site is one of the most comprehensive directories of publishers on the Internet.

Thesaurus.com: www.thesaurus.com

Need to find another word for "super"? Then use this searchable thesaurus to find synonyms for words as well as links to Roget's Thesaurus, *international dictionaries, and translator tools.*

Writing for Dollars: www.awoc.com/AWOC-home.cfm

Besides the free newsletter, freelance writers will find money-making tips.

Zuzu's Petals Literary Resource: www.zuzu.com

Contains more than 10,000 organized links to helpful resources for writers, researchers, and others. Zuzu's Petals also publishes an electronic quarterly.

Miscellaneous

Delphi Forums: www.delphiforums.com

This site hosts forums on many topics including writing and publishing. Just type "writing" in the search bar, and you'll find 30 pages where you can talk about your craft.

Freelance Online: www.freelanceonline.com

A directory of and resource center for freelancers in the field of communications. Jobs, message boards, a searchable directory of over 700 freelancers, frequently asked questions, resources, and networking for beginning freelancers. The FAQ for freelancers has lots of useful information catalogued and linked especially for freelancing beginners.

Hollywood Network: http://hollywoodnetwork.com

This site covers everything in Hollywood whether it's dealmaking, music, screenwriting, or profiles of agents and Hollywood executives.

Mr. Magazine: www.mrmagazine.com

Find the latest information on consumer magazines. Look for the 30 Most Notable Launches of the previous year and the monthly titles page—a comprehensive list of every new magazine launched each month.

Novel Advice: www.noveladvice.com

A cyber-journal devoted to the craft of writing. This site offers advice, online courses on the craft of writing (for a fee), and an extensive list of research resources.

ShawGuides: www.shawguides.com

Searchable database of writers' conferences.

United States Postal Service: www.usps.com

Domestic and international postage rate calculator, stamp ordering, zip code look-up, express mail tracking, etc.

Multiple services

Authorlink: www.authorlink.com

An information and news service for editors, literary agents, and writers. Showcasing and matching quality manuscripts to publishers' needs, this site also contains interviews with editors and agents, publishing industry news, links, and writer's guidelines.

Book Zone: www.bookzone.com

A catalog source for books, audio books, and more, with links to other publishing opportunities, diversions and distractions such as news, classifieds, contests, magazines, and trade groups.

BookWeb: www.ambook.org

This site of the American Booksellers Association offers books news, markets, discussions groups, events, resources, and other book-related information.

Children's Writing Resource Center: www.write4kids.com

Presented by Children's Book Insider, The Newsletter for Children's Writers. *Offers information on numerous aspects of publishing and children's literature, such as an InfoCenter, a Research Center, results of various surveys, and secrets on getting published.*

Creative Freelancers: www.freelancers.com

A meeting spot for freelancers and employers. Writers post their résumés for free, and employers post job listings in writing, editing, proofreading, etc.

Editor & Publisher: www.editorandpublisher.com

The Internet source for Editor & Publisher*, this site provides up-to-date industry news, with other opportunities such as a research area and bookstore, a calendar of events, and classifieds.*

Online Markets for Writers: www.marketsforwriters.com

Site rooted in groundbreaking book, Online Markets for Writers: How to Make Money By Selling Your Writing on the Internet *(Owl Books/Henry Holt & Co.), offering online market information, interviews, extensive resources, and advice from expert contributors including the National Writers Union (NWU) and the American Society of Journalists and Authors (ASJA).*

RoseDog.com: www.rosedog.com

This site is for readers, writers, agents, and publishers. Post excerpts from your unpublished work at no cost, to be reviewed by agents and publishers.

Small Publisher Association of North America (SPAN): www.SPANnet.org

This site includes membership information, publishing events and calendar, links, book sales, and other services.

Writers Write: www.writerswrite.com

Offers current writing and publishing news, message boards, and job listings.

Research

AcqWeb: www.library.vanderbilt.edu/law/acqs/acqs.html

Although geared toward librarians and researchers, AcqWeb provides reference information useful to writers, such as library catalogs, bibliographic services, Books in Print, *and other Web reference resources.*

The Acronym Database: www.ucc.ie/acronyms/acro.html

Research to find the names behind the acronyms or the acronyms for the names.

CopyLaw: www.copylaw.com

Confused about copyrights? Many beginning writers may find the task of copyright searches daunting, but this site helps plan permission requests and locate copyrights.

The Currency Site Historical Tables, Current Rates and Forecasts for World Currencies: www.oanda.com

Find current names for the world's currencies and exchange rates.

The Electronic Newsstand: www.enews.com

One of the largest directories of magazines on the Web. The Electronic Newsstand not only provides links to their magazines, but also tracks the content of many major magazines on a continually updated basis. It also allows users to customize their own newsstands to view only the magazines of their choice.

FindLaw: www.findlaw.com

Contains information on landmark legal decisions, and includes legal publishers and state and local bar association information.

InfoNation: www.un.org/Pubs/CyberSchoolBus/infonation/e_infonation.htm

A two-step database that allows you to view and compare the most up-to-date statistical data for the Member States of the United Nations.

Information Please Almanac: www.infoplease.com

General reference.

International Trademark Association: www.inta.org

Check the correct spelling of nearly 4,000 trademarks and service marks, and get the correct generic term.

Library of Congress: http://lcweb.loc.gov/

Provides access to Library of Congress catalogues and other research vehicles, including full access to bills under consideration in the U.S. House of Representatives and Senate.

Literary Market Place: www.literarymarketplace.com

Provides contact information for U.S., Canadian, and international publishers (small and large), and agents. Focused searches available.

Media Resource Service: www.mediaresource.org

This service provided by the Scientific Research Society helps writers find reputable sources of scientific information at no charge.

Mediafinder: www.oxbridge.com

Contains basic facts about 100,000 publications.

Newswise: www.newswise.com

A comprehensive database of news releases from top institutions engaged in scientific, medical, liberal arts, and business research.

Painted Rock: www.paintedrock.com

Check out Painted Rock Research, a free research e-mail list. You can find articles, interviews, and other writing resources in the free newsletter.

The Polling Report: www.pollingreport.com

Includes recent public opinion poll results from leading U.S. polling firms on politics, business, social issues, news events, sports, and entertainment.

ProfNet: www.profnet.com

Contains names of 6,000 news and information officers at colleges and universities, corporations, think tanks, national labs, medical centers, nonprofits, and PR agencies courtesy of this PR Newswire service.

Publishing Law Center: www.publaw.com

Links and articles about intellectual property and other legal issues.

RefDesK: www.refdesk.com

Provides an easy-to-navigate, searchable index of websites that provide facts, figures, and interesting information.

SharpWriter.com: www.sharpwriter.com

Dictionaries, encyclopedic references, grammar tips.

U.S. Copyright Office: www.loc.gov/copyright/search

Locate the copyright status of millions of books, music recordings, movies, and software.

World Factbook: www.odci.gov/cia/publications/factbook/index.html

Includes facts on every country in the world, on subjects from population to exports.

Writer's Digest: www.writersdigest.com

This site includes information about writing books and magazine pieces from Writer's Digest.

Retail

Amazon.com: www.amazon.com

Calling itself "A bookstore too big for the physical world," Amazon.com has books available on their website at discounted prices, plus a personal notification service of new releases, reader reviews, bestseller, and suggested book information.

Barnes and Noble Online: www.barnesandnoble.com or www.bn.com
The world's largest bookstore chain's website contains in-stock titles at discount prices as well as personalized recommendations, online events with authors, and book forum access for members.

Master Freelancer: www.masterfreelancer.com
Products and services for freelance writers.

Writers' organizations

Academy of American Poets: www.poets.org/index.cfm
Offers poems, discussion groups, and articles for the poet in us all.

Artslynx: International Writing Resources: www.artslynx.org/writing
The site lists organizations for writers and poets and links to relevant writing-related sites.

Association of Authors' Representatives: www.aar-online.org
If you're looking for an agent who doesn't charge fees, check out the list of member agents and their area of specialty.

The Authors Guild: www.authorsguild.org
Organization of published authors that offers information on contracts, copyrights, contract negotiation, and more.

Children's Book Council: www.cbcbooks.org
A great resource for all facets of children's books. Has a beginner's guide to children's writing, a bimonthly theme-based showcase, and a monthly rundown of upcoming titles written by CBC members.

Freedom Forum Online: www.freedomforum.org
An excellent place to keep up on the state of journalism, nationally and internationally.

HTML Writers Guild: www.hwg.org
An international organization of Web authors. For nonmembers, there is access to information on Web writing-financial, marketing, and design aspects, as well as html and new technology resources.

International Journalists' Network: www.ijnet.org
This is the International Center for Journalists' online source for media assistance, journalism training opportunities, and media directories. You'll find a list of Codes of Ethics, as well as information on fellowships and awards.

The National Writers Union: www.nwu.org
A labor union for freelance writers of all genres that offers grievance assistance, contract advice, jobs, and more.

Society for Technical Communication: www.stc.org
Access to salary surveys, STC grants and loans information, and recommended books.

Organizations

Whether you write nonfiction or science fiction, self-help or short stories, there are national organizations representing your field as a whole or representing their members in court. Hundreds more smaller, local groups are providing assistance from paragraph to paragraph. There is an organization—probably several—to suit your needs.

ACADEMY OF AMERICAN POETS, 588 Broadway, Suite 1203, New York NY 10012-3210. (212)274-0343. Fax: (212)274-9427. E-mail: academy@poets.org. Website: www.poets.org. Chairman: Paul Gottleib.

AMERICAN BOOK PRODUCERS ASSOCIATION, 156 Fifth Ave., New York NY 10010. (212)645-2368. Fax: (212)989-7542. E-mail: office@ABPAonline.org. Website: www.abpaonline.org. President: Susan Knopf.

AMERICAN MEDICAL WRITERS ASSOCIATION, 40 W. Gude Dr., Suite 101, Rockville MD 20850-1199. (301)294-5303. Fax: (301)294-9006. E-mail: info@amwa.org. Website: www.amwa.org. Executive Director: Donn Munari.

AMERICAN SOCIETY OF JOURNALISTS AND AUTHORS (ASJA), 1501 Broadway, Suite 302, New York NY 10036. (212)997-0947. Fax: (212)768-7414. E-mail: execdir@asja.org. Website: www.asja.org. Executive Director: Brett Harvey.

AMERICAN TRANSLATORS ASSOCIATION, 225 Reinekers Lane, Suite 590, Alexandria VA 22314-0214. (703)683-6100. Fax: (703)683-6122. E-mail: ata@atanet.org. Website: www.atanet.org. President: Thomas L. West III.

ASIAN AMERICAN WRITERS' WORKSHOP, 16 W. 32nd St., Suite 10A, New York NY 10001. (212)494-0061. Fax: (212)494-0062. E-mail: desk@aaww.org. Website: www.aaww.org. Managing Director: Quang Bao.

ASSOCIATED WRITING PROGRAMS, Tallwood House MSN1E3, George Mason University, Fairfax VA 22030. (703)993-4301. Fax: (703)993-4302. E-mail: awp@gmu.edu. Website: www.awpwriter.org. Executive Director: D.W. Fenza.

ASSOCIATION OF AMERICAN PUBLISHERS, INC.,71 Fifth Ave., New York NY 10003-3004. (212)255-0200. Fax: (212)255-7007. Website: www.publishers.org. President and Chief Executive Officer: Patricia S. Schroeder.

ASSOCIATION OF AUTHORS' REPRESENTATIVES, P.O. Box 237201 Ansonia Station, New York NY 10003. Website: www.aar-online.org.

ASSOCIATION OF DESK-TOP PUBLISHERS, 3401-A800 Adams Ave., San Diego CA 92116-2490. (619)563-9714.

THE AUTHORS GUILD, 31 E. 28th St., 10th Floor, New York NY 10016. (212)563-5904. Fax: (212)564-5363. E-mail: staff@authorsguild.org. Website: www.authorsguild.org. President: Nick Taylor.

THE AUTHORS LEAGUE OF AMERICA, INC., 31 E. 28th St., 10th Floor, New York NY 10016. (212)564-8350. Executive Director: Paul Aiken.

CANADIAN AUTHORS ASSOCIATION, P.O. Box 419, Campbellford, Ontario K0L 1L0, Canada. (705)653-0323. Fax: (705)653-0593. E-mail: canauth@redden.on.ca. Website: www.canauthors.org. Contact: Alec McEachern.

THE DRAMATISTS GUILD OF AMERICA, 1501 Broadway, Suite 701, New York NY 10036-5601. (212)398-9366. Fax: (212)944-0420. E-mail: Igor@Dramaguild.com. Website: www.dramatistsguild.com. President: John Weidman.

EDITORIAL FREELANCERS ASSOCIATION, 71 W. 23rd St., Suite 1910, New York NY 10010. (212)929-5400. Fax: (212)929-5439. E-mail: info@the-efa.org. Website: www.the-efa.org.

EDUCATION WRITERS ASSOCIATION, 2122 P St. NW, Suite 201, Washington DC 20037. (202)452-9830. Fax: (202)452-9837. E-mail: ewa@ewa.org. Website: www.ewa.org.

INTERNATIONAL ASSOCIATION OF BUSINESS COMMUNICATORS, One Hallidie Plaza, Suite 600, San Francisco CA 94102. (415)544-4700 or (800)776-4222. E-mail: service_centre@iabc.com. Website: www.iabc.com. Chairman: John G. Clemons.

INTERNATIONAL WOMEN'S WRITING GUILD, Box 810, Gracie Station, New York NY 10028-0082. (212)737-7536. Website: www.iwwg.com. Executive Director: Hannelore Hahn.

MYSTERY WRITERS OF AMERICA, INC., 17 E. 47th St., 6th Floor, New York NY 10017. (212)888-8171. Fax: (212)888-8107. E-mail: mwa_org@earthlink.net. Website: www.mysterywriters.org. President: William Link.

NATIONAL ASSOCIATION OF SCIENCE WRITERS, INC., Box 294, Greenlawn NY 11740. (631)757-5664. E-mail: diane@nasw.org. Website: www.nasw.org. Executive Director: Diane McGurgan.

NATIONAL WRITERS ASSOCIATION, 3140 S. Peoria, #295PMB, Aurora CO 80014. (303)841-0246. Fax: (303)751-8593. Website: www.nationalwriters.com.

NATIONAL WRITERS UNION, 113 University Place, 6th Floor, New York NY 10003. (212) 254-0279. Fax: (212) 254-0673. E-mail: nwu@nwu.org. Website: www.nwu.org. President: Jonathan Tasini.

NEW DRAMATISTS, 424 W. 44th St., New York NY 10036. (212)757-6960. E-mail: newdramatists@newdramatists.org. Website: www.newdramatists.org. Executive Director: Joel K. Ruark.

NOVELISTS, INC., P.O. Box 1166, Mission KS 66222-0166. Website: www.ninc.com. President: Patricia Rice.

PEN AMERICAN CENTER, 568 Broadway, New York NY 10012. (212)334-1660. Fax: (212)334-2181. E-mail: pen@pen.org. Website: www.pen.org.

POETRY SOCIETY OF AMERICA, 15 Gramercy Park, New York NY 10003. (212)254-9628. Website: www.poetrysociety.org. Executive Director: Alice Quinn.

PUBLIC RELATIONS SOCIETY OF AMERICA, 33 Irving Place, New York NY 10003. (212)995-2230. Website: www.prsa.org. Executive Director: Catherine A. Bolton.

ROMANCE WRITERS OF AMERICA, 3707 FM 1960 W., Suite 55, Houston TX 77068. (281)440-6885. Fax: (281)440-7510. Website: www.rwanational.com. President: Harold Lowry.

SCIENCE FICTION AND FANTASY WRITERS OF AMERICA, INC., P.O. Box 877, Chestertown MD 21620. 352 La Guardia Place, #632, New York NY 10012-1428. New York NY 10012-1428. E-mail: execdir@sfwa.org. Website: www.sfwa.org. President: Sharon Lee.

SOCIETY OF AMERICAN BUSINESS EDITORS & WRITERS, INC., University of Missouri, School of Journalism, 76 Gannett Hall, Columbia MO 65211. (573)882-7862. Fax: (573)884-1372. E-mail: sabew@missouri.edu. Website: www.sabew.org. Contact: Carolyn Guniss, executive director.

SOCIETY OF AMERICAN TRAVEL WRITERS, 1500 Sunday Dr., Suite 102, Raleigh NC 27607. (919)787-5181. Fax: (919)787-4916. E-mail: satw@satw.org. Website: www.satw.org.

SOCIETY OF CHILDREN'S BOOK WRITERS AND ILLUSTRATORS, 8271 Beverly Blvd., Los Angeles CA 90048. (323)782-1010. Fax: (323)782-1892. E-mail: scbwi@scbwi.org. Website: www.scbwi.org. President: Stephen Mooser. Executive Director: Lin Oliver.

SOCIETY OF PROFESSIONAL JOURNALISTS, 3909 N. Meridian St., Indianapolis IN 46208. (317)927-8000. Fax: (317)920-4789. E-mail: questions@spj.org. Website: www.spj.org.

VOLUNTEER LAWYERS FOR THE ARTS, One E. 53rd St., 6th Floor, New York NY 10022. (212)319-2787. Fax: (212)752-6575.

WESTERN WRITERS OF AMERICA, % James Crutchfield, Secretary-Treasurer, 1012 Fair St., Franklin TN 37064. Website: www.westernwriters.org.

WOMEN WRITING THE WEST, 8547 E. Arapahoe Rd., J541, Greenwood CO 80112-1436. (303)674-5450. Website: www.womenwritingthewest.org. President: Paige Ramsey-Palmer.

WRITERS GUILD OF ALBERTA, 11759 Groat Rd., Edmonton, Alberta, T5M 3K6, Canada. (780)422-8174. E-mail: mail@writersguild.ab.ca. Website: www.writersguild.ab.ca. Executive Director: Norma Lock.

WRITERS GUILD OF AMERICA, East Chapter: 555 W. 57th St., New York NY 10019, (212)767-7800; West Chapter: 7000 W. Third St., Los Angeles CA 90048, (323)951-4000. Website: www.wga.org. President: Victoria Riskin.

Glossary

Key to symbols and abbreviations appears on the front and back inside covers.

Advance. A sum of money a publisher pays a writer prior to the publication of a book. It is usually paid in installments, such as one-half on signing the contract; one-half on delivery of a complete and satisfactory manuscript. The advance is paid against the royalty money that will be earned by the book.

Advertorial. Advertising presented in such a way as to resemble editorial material. Information may be the same as that contained in an editorial feature, but it is paid for or supplied by an advertiser and the word "advertisement" appears at the top of the page.

Agent. A liaison between a writer and editor or publisher. An agent shops a manuscript around, receiving a commission when the manuscript is accepted. Agents usually take a 10-15% fee from the advance and royalties, 10-20% if a co-agent is involved, such as in the sale of dramatic rights.

All rights. See Rights and the Writer in the Minding the Details article.

Anthology. A collection of selected writings by various authors or a gathering of works by one author.

Assignment. Editor asks a writer to produce a specific article for an agreed-upon fee.

Auction. Publishers sometimes bid for the acquisition of a book manuscript that has excellent sales prospects. The bids are for the amount of the author's advance, advertising and promotional expenses, royalty percentage, etc. Auctions are conducted by agents.

Avant-garde. Writing that is innovative in form, style, or subject, often considered difficult and challenging.

B&W. Abbreviation for black and white photographs.

Backlist. A publisher's list of its books that were not published during the current season, but that are still in print.

Belles lettres. A term used to describe fine or literary writing—writing more to entertain than to inform or instruct.

Bimonthly. Every two months. See also *semimonthly.*

Bio. A sentence or brief paragraph about the writer. It can appear at the bottom of the first or last page of a writer's article or short story or on a contributor's page.

Biweekly. Every two weeks.

Boilerplate. A standardized contract. When an editor says "our standard contract," he means the boilerplate with no changes. Writers should be aware that most authors and/or agents make many changes on the boilerplate.

Book packager. Draws all elements of a book together, from the initial concept to writing and marketing strategies, then sells the book package to a book publisher. Also known as book producer or book developer.

Business-size envelope. Also known as a #10 envelope, it is the standard size used in sending business correspondence.

Byline. Name of the author appearing with the published piece.

Category fiction. A term used to include all various labels attached to types of fiction. See also *genre.*

CD-ROM. Compact Disc-Read Only Memory. A computer information storage medium capable of holding enormous amounts of data. Information on a CD-ROM cannot be deleted. A computer user must have a CD-ROM drive to access a CD-ROM.

Chapbook. A small booklet, usually paperback, of poetry, ballads, or tales.

Circulation. The number of subscribers to a magazine.

Clean copy. A manuscript free of errors, cross-outs, wrinkles, or smudges.

Clips. Samples, usually from newspapers or magazines, of your *published* work.

Coffee-table book. An oversize book, heavily illustrated.

Column inch. The amount of space contained in one inch of a typeset column.

Commercial novels. Novels designed to appeal to a broad audience. These are often broken down into categories such as western, mystery, and romance. See also *genre.*

Commissioned work. See *assignment.*

Concept. A statement that summarizes a screenplay or teleplay—before the outline or treatment is written.

Confessional. Genre of fiction essay in which the author or first-person narrator confesses something shocking or embarassing.

Contact sheet. A sheet of photographic paper on which negatives are transferred so you can see the entire roll of shots placed together on one sheet of paper without making separate, individual prints.

Contributor's copies. Copies of the issues of magazines sent to the author in which the author's work appears.

Cooperative publishing. See *co-publishing.*

Co-publishing. Arrangement where author and publisher share publication costs and profits of a book. Also known as *cooperative publishing*. See also *subsidy publisher.*

Copyediting. Editing a manuscript for grammar, punctuation, and printing style, not subject content.

Copyright. A means to protect an author's work. See Copyright in the Minding the Details section.

Cover letter. A brief letter, accompanying a complete manuscript, especially useful if responding to an editor's request for a manuscript. A cover letter may also accompany a book proposal. A cover letter is *not* a query letter; see Targeting Your Ideas in the Getting Published section.

Creative nonfiction. Nonfictional writing that uses an innovative approach to the subject and creative language.

CV. Curriculum vita. A brief listing of qualifications and career accomplishments.

Derivative works. A work that has been translated, adapted, abridged, condensed, annotated, or otherwise produced by altering a previously created work. Before producing a derivative work, it is necessary to secure the written permission of the copyright owner of the original piece.

Desktop publishing. A publishing system designed for a personal computer. The system is capable of typesetting, some illustration, layout, design, and printing—so that the final piece can be distributed and/or sold.

Docudrama. A fictional film rendition of recent newsmaking events and people.

Eclectic. Publication features a variety of different writing styles of genres.

Electronic submission. A submission made by modem or on computer disk.

El-hi. Elementary to high school.

E-mail. Electronic mail. Mail generated on a computer and delivered over a computer network to a specific individual or group of individuals. To send or receive e-mail, a user must have an account with an online service, which provides an e-mail address and electronic mailbox.

Erotica. Fiction or art that is sexually oriented.

Experimental. See *avant-garde.*

Fair use. A provision of the copyright law that says short passages from copyrighted material may be used without infringing on the owner's rights.

Feature. An article giving the reader information of human interest rather than news. Also used by magazines to indicate a lead article or distinctive department.

Filler. A short item used by an editor to "fill" out a newspaper column or magazine page. It could be a timeless news item, a joke, an anecdote, some light verse or short humor, puzzle, etc.

First North American serial rights. See Rights and the Writer in the Minding the Details article.

First-person point of view. In nonfiction, the author reports from his or her own perspective; in fiction, the narrator tells the story from his or her point of view. This viewpoint makes frequent use of "I," or occasionally, "we."

Formula story. Familiar theme treated in a predictable plot structure—such as boy meets girl, boy loses girl, boy gets girl.

Frontlist. A publisher's list of its books that are new to the current season.

Galleys. The first typeset version of a manuscript that has not yet been divided into pages.

Genre. Refers either to a general classification of writing, such as the novel or the poem, or to the categories within those classifications, such as the problem novel or the sonnet. Genre fiction describes commercial novels, such as mysteries, romances, and science fiction. Also called category fiction.

Ghostwriter. A writer who puts into literary form an article, speech, story, or book based on another person's ideas or knowledge.

Gift book. A book designed as a gift item. Often small in size with few illustrations and placed close to a bookstore's checkout as an "impulse" buy, gift books tend to be written to a specific niche, such as golfers, mothers, etc.

Glossy. A black and white photograph with a shiny surface as opposed to one with a nonshiny matte finish.

Gothic novel. A fiction category or genre in which the central character is usually a beautiful young girl, the setting an old mansion or castle, and there is a handsome hero and a real menace, either natural or supernatural.

Graphic novel. An adaptation of a novel in graphic form, long comic strip, or heavily illustrated story, of 40 pages or more, produced in paperback form.

Hard copy. The printed copy of a computer's output.

Hardware. All the mechanically-integrated components of a computer that are not software. Circuit boards, transistors, and the machines that are the actual computer are the hardware.

High-lo. Material written for newer readers, generally adults, with a *high* interest level and *low* reading ability.

Home page. The first page of a World Wide Web document.

Honorarium. Token payment—small amount of money, or a byline and copies of the publication.

How-to. Books and magazine articles offering a combination of information and advice in describing how something can be accomplished. Subjects range widely from hobbies to psychology.

Hypertext. Words or groups of words in an electronic document that are linked to other text, such as a definition or a related document. Hypertext can also be linked to illustrations.

Illustrations. May be photographs, old engravings, artwork. Usually paid for separately from the manuscript. See also *package sale*.

Imprint. Name applied to a publisher's specific line or lines of books (e.g., Avon Eos is an imprint of HarperCollins).

Interactive. A type of computer interface that takes user input, such as answers to computer-generated questions, and then acts upon that input.

Interactive fiction. Works of fiction in book or computer software format in which the reader determines the path the story will take. The reader chooses from several alternatives at the end of a "chapter," and thus determines the structure of the story. Interactive fiction features multiple plots and endings.

Internet. A worldwide network of computers that offers access to a wide variety of electronic resources.

Invasion of privacy. Writing about persons (even though truthfully) without their consent.

Kill fee. Fee for a complete article that was assigned but which was subsequently cancelled.

Lead time. The time between the acquisition of a manuscript by an editor and its actual publication.

Libel. A false accusation or any published statement or presentation that tends to expose another to public contempt, ridicule, etc. Defenses are truth; fair comment on a matter of public interest; and privileged communication—such as a report of legal proceedings or client's communication to a lawyer.

List royalty. A royalty payment based on a percentage of a book's retail (or "list") price. Compare to *net royalty.*

Literary fiction. The general category of serious, nonformulaic, intelligent fiction.

Little magazine. Publications of limited circulation, usually on literary or political subject matter.

LORT. An acronym for League of Resident Theatres. Letters from A to D follow LORT and designate the size of the theater.

Magalog. Mail order catalog with how-to articles pertaining to the items for sale.

Mainstream fiction. Fiction that transcends popular novel categories such as mystery, romance, and science fiction. Using conventional methods, this kind of fiction tells stories about people and their conflicts with greater depth of characterization, background, etc., than the more narrowly focused genre novels.

Mass market. Nonspecialized books of wide appeal directed toward a large audience. Smaller and more cheaply produced than trade paperbacks, they are found in many nonbookstore outlets, such as drugstores or supermarkets.

Memoir. A narrative recounting a writer's (or fictional narrator's) personal or family history.

Microcomputer. A small computer system capable of performing various specific tasks with data it receives. Personal computers are microcomputers.

Midlist. Those titles on a publisher's list that are not expected to be big sellers, but are expected to have limited sales. Midlist books are mainstream, not literary, scholarly, or genre, and are usually written by new or unknown writers.

Model release. A paper signed by the subject of a photograph (or the subject's guardian, if a juvenile) giving the photographer permission to use the photograph editorially or for advertising purposes or for some specific purpose as stated.

Modem. A device used to transmit data from one computer to another via telephone lines.

Monograph. A detailed and documented scholarly study concerning a single subject.

Multimedia. Computers and software capable of integrating text, sound, photographic-quality images, animation, and video.

Multiple submissions. Sending more than one poem, gag, or greeting card idea at the same time. This term is often used synonymously with *simultaneous submission.*

Narrative nonfiction. A narrative presentation of actual events.

Narrative poem. Poetry that tells a story. One of the three main genres of poetry (the others being dramatic poetry and lyric poetry).

Net royalty. A royalty payment based on the amount of money a book publisher receives on the sale of a book after booksellers' discounts, special sales discounts, and returns. Compare *list royalty.*

Network. A group of computers electronically linked to share information and resources.

New Age. A "fringe" topic that has become increasingly mainstream. Formerly New Age included UFOs and occult phenomena. The term has evolved to include more general topics such as psychology, religion, and health, but emphasizing the mystical, spiritual, or alternative aspects.

Newsbreak. A brief, late-breaking news story added to the front page of a newspaper at press time or a magazine news item of importance to readers.

Nostalgia. A genre of reminiscence, recalling sentimental events or products of the past.

Novella. A short novel, or a long short story; 7,000 to 15,000 words approximately. Also known as a novelette.

Novelization. A novel created from the script of a popular movie, usually called a movie "tie-in" and published in paperback.

On spec. An editor expresses an interest in a proposed article idea and agrees to consider the finished piece for publication "on speculation." The editor is under no obligation to buy the finished manuscript.

One-shot feature. As applies to syndicates, single feature article for syndicate to sell; as contrasted with article series or regular columns syndicated.

One-time rights. See Rights and the Writer in the Minding the Details article.

Online Service. Computer networks accessed via modem. These services provide users with various resources, such as electronic mail, news, weather, special interest groups, and shopping. Examples of such providers include America Online and CompuServe.

Outline. A summary of a book's contents in five to 15 double-spaced pages; often in the form of chapter headings with a descriptive sentence or two under each one to show the scope of the book. A screenplay's or teleplay's outline is a scene-by-scene narrative description of the story (ten-15 pages for a ½-hour teleplay; 15-25 pages for a one-hour teleplay; 25-40 pages for a 90-minute teleplay; 40-60 pages for a two-hour feature film or teleplay).

Over-the-transom. Describes the submission of unsolicited material by a freelance writer.

Package sale. The editor buys manuscript and photos as a "package" and pays for them with one check.

Page rate. Some magazines pay for material at a fixed rate per published page, rather than per word.

Parallel submission. A strategy of developing several articles from one unit of research for submission to similar magazines. This strategy differs from simultaneous or multiple submission, where the same article is marketed to several magazines at the same time.

Parody. The conscious imitation of a work, usually with the intent to ridicule or make fun of the work.

Payment on acceptance. The editor sends you a check for your article, story, or poem as soon as he decides to publish it.

Payment on publication. The editor doesn't send you a check for your material until it is published.

Pen name. The use of a name other than your legal name on articles, stories, or books when you wish to remain anonymous. Simply notify your post office and bank that you are using the name so that you'll receive mail and/or checks in that name. Also called a *pseudonym.*

Photo feature. Feature in which the emphasis is on the photographs rather than on accompanying written material.

Plagiarism. Passing off as one's own the expression of ideas and words of another writer.

Potboiler. Refers to writing projects a freelance writer does to "keep the pot boiling" while working on major articles—quick projects to bring in money with little time or effort. These may be fillers such as anecdotes or how-to tips, but could be short articles or stories.

Proofreading. Close reading and correction of a manuscript's typographical errors.

Proposal. A summary of a proposed book submitted to a publisher, particularly used for nonfiction manuscripts. A proposal often contains an individualized cover letter, one-page overview of the book, marketing information, competitive books, author information, chapter-by-chapter outline, two to three sample chapters and attachments (if relevant) such as magazine articles about the topic and articles you have written (particularly on the proposed topic).

Proscenium. The area of the stage in front of the curtain.

Prospectus. A preliminary written description of a book or article, usually one page in length.

Pseudonym. See *pen name*.

Public domain. Material that was either never copyrighted or whose copyright term has expired.

Query. A letter to an editor intended to raise interest in an article you propose to write.

Release. A statement that your idea is original, has never been sold to anyone else, and that you are selling the negotiated rights to the idea upon payment.

Remainders. Copies of a book that are slow to sell and can be purchased from the publisher at a reduced price. Depending on the author's book contract, a reduced royalty or no royalty is paid on remainder books.

Reporting time. The time it takes for an editor to report to the author on his/her query or manuscript.

Reprint rights. See Rights and the Writer in the Minding the Details article.

Round-up article. Comments from, or interviews with, a number of celebrities or experts on a single theme.

Royalties, standard hardcover book. 10% of the retail price on the first 5,000 copies sold; 12½% on the next 5,000; 15% thereafter.

Royalties, standard mass paperback book. 4 to 8% of the retail price on the first 150,000 copies sold.

Royalties, standard trade paperback book. No less than 6% of list price on the first 20,000 copies; 7½% thereafter.

Scanning. A process through which letter-quality printed text or artwork is read by a computer scanner and converted into workable data.

Screenplay. Script for a film intended to be shown in theaters.

Self-publishing. In this arrangement, the author keeps all income derived from the book, but he pays for its manufacturing, production, and marketing.

Semimonthly. Twice per month.

Semiweekly. Twice per week.

Serial. Published periodically, such as a newspaper or magazine.

Serial fiction. Fiction published in a magazine in installments, often broken off at a suspenseful spot.

Series fiction. A sequence of novels featuring the same characters.

Short-short. A complete short story of 1,500 words maximum, and around 250 words minimum.

Sidebar. A feature presented as a companion to a straight news report (or main magazine article) giving sidelights on human-interest aspects or sometimes elucidating just one aspect of the story.

Similar submission. See *parallel submission*.

Simultaneous submissions. Sending the same article, story, or poem to several publishers at the same time. Some publishers refuse to consider such submissions.

Slant. The approach or style of a story or article that will appeal to readers of a specific magazine. For example, a magazine may always use stories with an upbeat ending.

Slice-of-life vignette. A short fiction piece intended to realistically depict an interesting moment of everyday living.

Slides. Usually called transparencies by editors looking for color photographs.

Slush pile. The stack of unsolicited or misdirected manuscripts received by an editor or book publisher.

Software. The computer programs that control computer hardware, usually run from a disk drive of some sort. Computers need software in order to run. These can be word processors, games, spreadsheets, etc.

Speculation. The editor agrees to look at the author's manuscript with no assurance that it will be bought.

Style. The way in which something is written—for example, short, punchy sentences or flowing narrative.

Subsidiary rights. All those rights, other than book publishing rights included in a book contract—such as paperback, book club, movie rights, etc.

Subsidy publisher. A book publisher who charges the author for the cost to typeset and print his book, the jacket, etc., as opposed to a royalty publisher who pays the author.

Synopsis. A brief summary of a story, novel, or play. As part of a book proposal, it is a comprehensive summary condensed in a page or page and a half, single-spaced. See also *outline*.

Tabloid. Newspaper format publication on about half the size of the regular newspaper page, such as *The Star.*

Tagline. A caption for a photo or a comment added to a filler.

Tearsheet. Page from a magazine or newspaper containing your printed story, article, poem, or ad.

Teleplay. A play written for or performed on television.

TOC. Table of Contents.

Trade. Either a hardcover or paperback book; subject matter frequently concerns a special interest. Books are directed toward the layperson rather than the professional.

Transparencies. Positive color slides; not color prints.

Treatment. Synopsis of a TV or film script (40-60 pages for a two-hour feature film or teleplay).

Unsolicited manuscript. A story, article, poem, or book that an editor did not specifically ask to see.

Vanity publisher. See *subsidy publisher.*

Word processor. A computer program that allows for easy, flexible manipulation and output of printed copy.

World Wide Web (WWW). An Internet resource that utilizes hypertext to access information. It also supports formatted text, illustrations, and sounds, depending on the user's computer capabilities.

Work-for-hire. See Copyright in the Minding the Details article.

YA. Young adult books.

Book Publisher Subject Index

This index will help you find publishers that consider books on specific subjects—the subjects you choose to write about. Remember that a publisher may be listed here only under a general subject category such as Art and Architecture, while the company publishes *only* art history or how-to books. Be sure to consult each company's detailed individual listing, its book catalog and several of its books before you send your query or proposal. The page number of the detailed listing is provided for your convenience.

FICTION

Adventure

Comic Books

Confession

Erotica

Ethnic

Experimental

Fantasy

Feminist

Gay/Lesbian

Gothic

Hi-Lo

Historical

Horror

Humor

Juvenile

Literary

Mainstream/Contemporary

Military/War

Multicultural

Multimedia

Mystery

Occult

Picture Books

Plays

Poetry (Including Chapbooks)

Poetry In Translation

Regional

Religious

Romance

Science Fiction

Short Story Collections

Spiritual (New Age, etc.)

Sports

Suspense

Translation

Western

Young Adult

NONFICTION

Agriculture/Horticulture

Americana

Animals

Anthropology/Archaeology

Art/Architecture

Astrology/Psychic/New Age

Biography

Business/Economics

Child Guidance/Parenting

Coffeetable Books

Computers/Electronic

Contemporary Culture

Cookbooks

Cooking/Foods/Nutrition

Creative Nonfiction

Educational

Ethnic

Fashion/Beauty

Film/Cinema/Stage

Gardening

Gay/Lesbian

General Nonfiction

Gift Books

Government/Politics

Health/Medicine

BOOK PUBLISHERS SUBJECT INDEX

History

Hobby

How-To

Humor

Illustrated Books

Juvenile Books

Language and Literature

BOOK PUBLISHERS SUBJECT INDEX

Memoirs

Military/War

Money/Finance

Multicultural

Multimedia

Music/Dance

Nature/Environment

Philosophy

Photography

Psychology

Recreation

Reference

BOOK PUBLISHERS SUBJECT INDEX

Regional

Religion

Science/Technology

Self-Help

Sex

Sociology

Software

Spiritual

Sports

Technical

Textbook

Translation

Travel

True Crime

Women's Issues/Studies

World Affairs

General Index

This index lists every market appearing in the book; use it to find specific companies you wish to approach. Markets that appeared in the 2002 edition of *Writer's Market*, but are not included in this edition are identified by a two-letter code explaining why the market was omitted: (**ED**)—Editorial Decision, (**NS**)—Not Accepting Submissions, (**NR**)—No or Late Response to Listing Request, (**OB**)—Out of Business, (**RR**)—Removed by Market's Request, (**UC**)—Unable to Contact, (**RP**)—Business Restructured or Purchased, (**NP**)—No Longer Pays or Pays in Copies Only, (**SR**)—Subsidy/Royalty Publisher, (**UF**)—Uncertain Future, (**Web**)—a listing that appears on our website at www.WritersMarket.com

B

C

E

F

G

M

N

O

P

S